The Jeffersonian

A comprehensive collection of the views of
Thomas Jefferson classified and arranged in alphabetical
order under nine thousand titles relating to government,
politics, law, education, political economy, finance,
science, art, literature, religious freedom, morals, etc

Thomas Jefferson

John P. Foley

Alpha Editions

This edition published in 2019

ISBN : 9789353804329

Design and Setting By
Alpha Editions
email - alphaedis@gmail.com

THE
Jeffersonian Cyclopedia

A COMPREHENSIVE COLLECTION OF THE
VIEWS OF

THOMAS JEFFERSON

Classified and Arranged in Alphabetical Order Under Nine Thousand Titles :: :: :: ::

RELATING TO GOVERNMENT, POLITICS, LAW,
EDUCATION, POLITICAL ECONOMY, FINANCE,
SCIENCE, ART, LITERATURE, RELIGIOUS FREE-
DOM, MORALS, ETC. :: :: :: :: :: :: :: :: :: ::

EDITED BY
JOHN P. FOLEY

"I have sworn upon the altar of God eternal hostility against
every form of tyranny over the mind of man."—*Thomas Jefferson*

FUNK & WAGNALLS COMPANY
NEW YORK AND LONDON
1900

PREFACE

THE JEFFERSONIAN CYCLOPEDIA is designed to be a complete classified arrangement of the Writings of Thomas Jefferson on Government, Politics, Law, Education, Commerce, Agriculture, Manufactures, Navigation, Finance, Morals, Religious Freedom, and many other topics of permanent human interest. It contains everything of importance that Jefferson wrote on these subjects.

Why and wherefore the publication of this volume now? The answer is this: More than three-quarters of a century ago, one of the earlier biographers of Jefferson wrote: " It would be a happy circumstance for America and for the mass of mankind if the works of Jefferson could obtain a circulation which would place them in the hands of every individual. Unfortunately, the form in which they have appeared is not the most advantageous to the accomplishment of this desirable purpose. The publication is too voluminous, and consequently too expensive, to admit of a general introduction among all classes, *nor is the mode of arrangement the best adapted to its reception into ordinary use as a work of reference.*"

From that distant day to the present time, no attempt has been made to arrange and classify the theories and principles of Jefferson, so as to make them available in ready reference form.

THE JEFFERSONIAN CYCLOPEDIA aims to do this—to be a Manual of Jeffersonian Doctrine, accurate, complete, impartial, giving Jefferson's views, theories, and ideas in his own words. No edition of Jefferson's Writings, printed at either public or private expense, contains so comprehensive a collection of Jefferson's opinions as this volume. This fact will be clearly seen by all who consult it.

Not alone to the American people, but to all peoples, are Jefferson's opinions on Government of deep and abiding interest. Among the Statesmen of all time, he is the foremost Expounder of the Rights of Man, of the unalienable right of every human being to life, liberty, and the pursuit of happiness. That is the object of all just Government, to preserve which Jeffersonian principles must be sacredly cherished.

J. P. F.

Brooklyn, July 31st, 1900.

LIST OF ILLUSTRATIONS

	PAGE
Portrait by Stuart	*Frontispiece*
Portrait by Peale	96
Portrait by Desnoyers	192
Portrait by Brumidi	288
Bronze Statue by d'Angers	384
Portrait by Stuart	480
Monticello, the Home of Thomas Jefferson	590
Portrait by Sully	714
Marble Statue by Powers	800
Portrait by Otis	896

CHRONOLOGY OF THOMAS JEFFERSON

Born at Shadwell, Albemarle Co., Va.	April 2 (O. S.), 13 (N. S.), 1743
Death of his Father, Peter Jefferson	August 17, 1757
Entered William and Mary College	March, 1760
Graduation	April 25, 1762
Entered Law Office of George Wythe	April, 1762
Admitted to Bar	1767
Elected to Virginia House of Burgesses	March, 1769
Marriage to Martha Wayles Skelton	January, 1772
Birth of his First Daughter, Martha	September 27, 1772
Appointed Surveyor of Albemarle County	October, 1773
Birth of Second Daughter, Jane Randolph	April 3, 1774
Elected Deputy to Continental Congress —	March, 1775
Attends Continental Congress —	June 21, 1775
Death of his Mother	March 31, 1776
Appointed on Committee to prepare Declaration of Independence —	June 11, 1776
Draft of Declaration Reported	June 28, 1776
Elected Commissioner to France	September 26, 1776
Attends Virginia Assembly	October, 1776
Appointed on Committee to Revise Virginia Laws	November 6, 1776
Birth of Son	May 28, 1777
Death of Son	June 14, 1777
Birth of Third Daughter, Mary	August 1, 1778
Elected Governor of Virginia	June 1, 1779
Reelected Governor of Virginia	June 1, 1780
Fourth Daughter Born	November 3, 1780
Resigns Governorship	June 1, 1781
Assembly Orders Investigation of his Administration	June 5, 1781
Appointed Peace Commissioner by Continental Congress	June 14, 1781
Appointment Declined	June 30, 1781
Attends Virginia Assembly	November 5, 1781
Committee Appointed to State Charges Against Him	November 26, 1781
Elected Delegate to Congress	November 30, 1781
Voted Thanks of Assembly	December 12, 1781
Daughter Lucy Elizabeth Born	May 8, 1782
Death of Mrs. Jefferson	September 6, 1782
Appointed Peace Commissioner to Europe	November 12, 1782
Appointment Withdrawn	April 1, 1783
Elected Delegate to Congress	June 6, 1783
Elected Chairman of Congress	March 12, 1784
Elected Minister to France	May 7, 1784
Arrived in Paris	August 6, 1784
Elected French Minister by Congress	March 10, 1785
Audience at French Court	May 17, 1785
Death of Youngest Daughter, Lucy	November, 1785
Presented to George III. at Windsor	March 22, 1786
Made an LL.D. by Yale	October, 1786
Made an LL.D. by Harvard	June, 1788
Prepares Charter for France	June 3, 1789

Nominated to be Secretary of State . . . . September 25, 1789
Confirmed by Senate . . . . September 26, 1789
Leaves France . . . . October, 1789
At Monticello . . . . December 24, 1789
Accepts Secretaryship of State . . . . February 14, 1790
Marriage of Daughter Martha to Thomas Mann Randolph . . . February 28, 1790
Writes to Washington of Intention to Resign from Cabinet . . . May 23, 1792
Reconsiders Resignation . . . . January, 1793
Offered French Mission . . . . February, 1793
Resigns Secretaryship of State . . . . December 31, 1793
Offered Foreign Mission . . . . September, 1794
Elected Vice-President . . . . November 4, 1796
Elected President of Philosophical Society . . . . . January, 1797
Takes Oath of Office as Vice-President . . . . . . March 4, 1797
Marriage of Mary Jefferson to John Wayles Eppes . . . . October 13, 1797
Writes Essay on Study of Anglo-Saxon . . . . . . October, 1798
Drafts Kentucky Resolutions . . . . October, 1798
Revises Madison's Virginia Resolutions . . . . . . November, 1798
Plans University of Virginia . . . . January 18, 1800
Prepares Parliamentary Manual . . . . February, 1800
Republican Caucus Nominates Jefferson and Burr . . . . May, 1800
Congress Begins to Ballot for President . . . . . . February 11, 1801
Elected President . . . . February 17, 1801
Farewell Address to Senate . . . . February 28, 1801
Inauguration as President . . . . March 4, 1801
Louisiana Treaty Signed at Paris . . . . May 2, 1803
Louisiana Treaty Ratified . . . . October 20, 1803
Message on Taking Possession of Louisiana . . . . . January 18, 1804
Reelected President of United States . . . . . . November, 1804
Elected President of American Philosophical Society . . . January, 1807
Signs Bill to End Slave Trade . . . . March 2, 1807
Proposes to Seize the Floridas . . . . September 1, 1807
Embargo Act Signed . . . . December 22, 1807
Repeal of Embargo Signed . . . . March 1, 1809
Retires from Presidency . . . . March 4, 1809
Arrives at Monticello . . . . March 17, 1809
Resigns Presidency of American Philosophical Society . . . November, 1814
Congress Passes Bill to Buy Library . . . . January, 1815
Drafts Virginia Protest . . . . December, 1825
Executes Will . . . . March 16, 1826
Declines Invitation to Fourth of July Celebration in Washington . June 24, 1826
Writes Last Letter . . . . June 25, 1826
Death . . . . July 4, 1826

LIST OF PATRONS

THIS CYCLOPEDIA HAS BEEN BROUGHT TO A SUCCESSFUL COMPLETION AND ITS PUBLI-
CATION MADE PRACTICABLE THROUGH THE CO-OPERATION OF A LARGE NUMBER OF
ADMIRERS OF THOMAS JEFFERSON, WHO RECOGNIZED IN ADVANCE THE DESIRABILITY
OF SUCH A WORK AND WHO SHARE IN THE HONOR OF ITS PRODUCTION. THE NAMES
OF THESE PATRONS OF THE JEFFERSONIAN CYCLOPEDIA ARE AS FOLLOWS:

Abbott, A. F....................Fredericktown, Mo.
Abbott, M. J...................Hayes Centre, Neb.
Abersol, Edward J..................Metamora, Ill.
Adams, Hon. Alva.....................Pueblo, Colo.
Adams, Charles B...............Kansas City, Mo.
Adams, Charles S.............Volga City, Iowa
Adams, C. M.....................Alexandria, Va.
Adams, Jed. C.....................Kaufman, Tex.
Adams, William R..............New York, N. Y.
Adkins, William H..................Easton, Md.
Agar, John G....................New York City
Aikens, Frank R...........Sioux Falls, So. Dak.
Ainslie, George...................Boise City, Idaho
Albert Barnes Memorial Library...Philadelphia, Pa.
Albright, Fontaine E............Fort Worth Tex.
Albright, J. G....................Milwaukee, Wis.
Alden, Charles A...................New York City
Aldrich, Charles H..................Evanston, Ill.
Alexander, Hope H................Thomasville, Ga.
Alexander, Hugh................Concordia, Kan.
Alison, J. Smyser, M.D..............Swartz, La.
Allee, W. S., M.D....................Olean, Mo.
Allen, G. R. C.................Wheeling, W. Va.
Allen, Harry K....................Gallatin, Mo.
Allen, H. Jerome, M.D.........Washington, D. C.
Allen, John L. M..................New York City
Allen, Richard E...................Augusta, Ga.
Alley, S. S.......................Wilber, Neb.
Allison, Hon. William B............Dubuque, Iowa
Alrich, Enrique..................El Paso Texas.
Alston, David M...................Pittsburg, Pa.
Altgelt, George C.............San Antonio, Tex.
Alvord, W. C.......................Peoria, Ill.
Anderbery, C. P...................Minden, Neb.
Anderson, E. B...........Harmony Grove, Ga.
Anderson, Henry W..............Richmond, Va.
Anderson, James T.............Stanberry, Mo.
Anderson, Jefferson Randolph.......Savannah, Ga.
Anderson, Joseph R..................Lee, Va.
Anderson, T. P..............Kansas City, Kan.
Andrews, Theodore E...........Minneapolis, Minn.
Andrus, John A....................Ashton, Ill.
Ansley, Hudson..................Salamanca, N. Y.
Archibald, J. W..............Jacksonville, Fla.
Armgardt, H., M.D..............Brooklyn, N. Y.
Armstrong, Hunter S.........St. Clairsville, Ohio
Armstrong, W. E.....................Waco, Tex.
Arner, Calvin E...................Allentown, Pa.
Arthur, John G.....................Omaha, Neb.
Asbury, D. F..................Newport News, Va.
Ash, Robert.................San Francisco, Cal.
Ashworth, J. S......................Bristol, Va.
Atkinson, J. A.....................Creede, Colo.
Atkinson, Louis E...............Mifflintown, Pa.
Autenrieth, Henry G..............New York City
Avritt, Samuel.................Louisville, Ky.
Aycock, William T...............Columbia, S. C.
Ayers, Harry J...............Big Stone Gap, Va.
Bacon, Rev. T. S., D.D........Buckeystown, Md.
Bader, D. M....................Cleveland, Ohio
Bagley, George C..............Minneapolis, Minn.
Bagley, W. D......................Rockdale, Tex.
Bailey, Mrs. James Stacey..........Waycross, Ga.
Baird, C. E....................Philadelphia, Pa.
Baird, William..................Marine City, Mich.
Baker, Rosa....................Rochester, N. Y.
Baker, William H..................Buffalo, N. Y.
Baker, William V................Columbus, Ohio
Baldwin, B. J., Jr...................Paris, Tex.
Baldwin, Frank A............Bowling Green, Ohio
Baldwin, W. H...................Rockport, Tex.
Ballance, William P., M.D.........Juneau, Alaska
Ballard, Guy, A.B..............Anderson, Ind.
Ballard, W. Harrison, M.D.......Los Angeles, Cal.

Banta, D. A....................Great Bend, Kan.
Barber, Theodore M...............Pittsburg, Pa.
Bard, H. Burton..................Lansing, Mich.
Barker, Joseph D................Petersburg, Ind.
Barnes, Carl L., M.D., LL.B........Chicago, Ill.
Barnes, Charles A...............Jacksonville, Ill.
Barnes, E. H....................Healdsburg, Cal.
Barnes, O. H...............Middlebourne, W. Va.
Barnett, DeWitt C............Harrisonville, Mo.
Barnett, M. S.......................Cuba, Mo.
Barney, J. A....................Mayville, Wis.
Barrett, James M..............Fort Wayne, Ind.
Barrick, Charles W........New Martinsville, W. Va.
Bartlett, C. L......................Macon, Ga.
Bartlett, George A..................Eureka, Nev.
Barton, Alexander J................Allegheny, Pa.
Batcheller, George Clinton............New York City
Batchelor, R. Horton...............New York City
Bates, Benjamin F...............Brooklyn, N. Y.
Bates, William S................Houston, Miss.
Bausman, Frederick..............Seattle, Wash.
Bayne, John.......................Salem, Ore.
Beach, M. W......................Carroll, Iowa
Beach, W. H.....................Holland, Mich.
Beach, William A..................Syracuse, N. Y.
Beale Memorial Library..........Bakersfield, Cal.
Beall & Kemp....................El Paso, Tex.
Beeber, William P..............Williamsport, Pa.
Beecher, Walter H...............Cincinnati, Ohio
Behrns, C. L....................Cherokee, Tex.
Beidelman, William...................Easton, Pa.
Belcher, Bart....................Dikeville, Ky.
Belford, James B...................Denver, Colo.
Bell, Hal.........................New York City
Bell, James D...................Brooklyn, N. Y.
Bell, R. R.....................Gainesville, Tex.
Bell, Theodore A....................Napa, Cal.
Bender, John S....................Plymouth, Ind.
Benedict, C. B.....................Attica, N. Y.
Bennett, Lewis J..................Buffalo, N. Y.
Bentley, A. C.....................Pittsfield, Ill.
Bentley, James H................Ridley Park, Pa.
Benton, J. M....................Winchester, Ky.
Berdrow, L. G...................David City, Neb.
Bernheim, Isaac W................Louisville, Ky.
Bernstein, Ernest R..............Shreveport, La.
Berrien, R. Noble, Jr............Waynesboro, Ga.
Bertram, G. Webb..................Oberlin, Kan.
Betts, Frederick..................New York City
Bettzhoover, F. E.................Carlisle, Pa.
Biddle, W. R..................Fort Scott, Kan.
Bidwell, H. G., M.D...........Jersey City, N. J.
Birnie, C., M.D................Taneytown, Md.
Bischoff, Henry, Jr...............New York City
Bittenbender, H. C...............Lincoln, Neb.
Bittiner, Edmund.................New York City
Black, Charles J..............Jersey City, N. J.
Black, Chauncey F...................York, Pa.
Black, Cyrenius P................Lansing, Mich.
Black, Howard C................Plain City, Ohio
Blackford, William M..........Lewistown, Mont.
Blackmore, James W..............Gallatin, Tenn.
Blackwell, Samuel.............New Decatur, Ala.
Blain, Alexander W................Detroit, Mich.
Blair, George....................New York City
Blake, W. H.....................Wetumpka, Ala.
Blakeley, W. A...................Pittsburg, Pa.
Blanchard, Nathan W..........Santa Paula, Cal.
Blanck, Joseph E., M.D...........Green Lane, Pa
Blee, John W.....................Sandwich, Ill.
Bloom, S. S.......................Shelby, Ohio
Blose, G. Ament..................Hamilton, Pa.
Bohannan, J. E..................Falmouth, Ky.
Bohannon, L. T., M.D.........Orphan Home, Tex.

Boles, Thomas......................Fort Smith, Ark.
Boller, J. F.........................Porterville, Cal.
Bomar, T. B....................Forth Worth Tex.
Boney, Richard K..................Duckport, La.
Bonsall, Charles......................Salem, Ohio
Booher, Charles F................Savannah, Mo.
Booker, A. G......................Wadena, Minn.
Boone, L. L.....................San Diego, Cal.
Boothe, J. B...........................Sardis, Miss.
Boren, George E.....................Bristol, Tenn.
Borkert, Rev. J. W............Grass Creek, Ind.
Bouck, Gabe.......................Oshkosh, Wis.
Bouldin, Virgil....................Scottsboro, Ala.
Bowers, F. E.....................Perrysburg, Ohio
Bowie, J. C.......................Talladega, Ala.
Bowie, Sydney J...................Anniston, Ala.
Bowser, O. P..........................Dallas, Tex.
Boyce, John J.................Santa Barbara, Cal.
Boyd, Henry A.................Warrenton, N. C.
Boyle, Wilbur F.....................St. Louis, Mo.
Brace, William.......................Chicago, Ill.
Bradford, Ernest W............Washington, D. C.
Bradford, Mary S.................Cleveland, Ohio
Bradley, Herbert E................Columbus, Ohio
Bradley, John H....................Senath, Mo.
Bradley, Washington...............Kinmundy, Ill.
Bradshaw, Homer S.............Ida Grove, Iowa
Branch, Oliver E..............Manchester, N. H.
Branch, W. W..............Charleston, W. Va.
Brandon, William R., M.D........Brandon, La.
Bransford, C. W..................Owensboro, Ky.
Brantley, W. G..................Brunswick, Ga.
Breckinridge, Hon. William C. P...Lexington, Ky.
Brenner, G..................San Francisco, Cal.
Briant, Paul H.................San Angelo, Tex.
Brice, J. S.........................Yorkville, S. C.
Bridenbaugh, W. H...................Altoona, Pa.
Bridges, W. A........................Center, Tex.
Brock, Cyrus C....................Pittsburg, Pa.
Bronson, Alice...................Wellsville, N. Y.
Brooks, W. P., M.D....................Cook Neb.
Brougher, E. E.....................Linden, Tex.
Brown, Irving..................Haverstraw, N. Y.
Brown, J. A....................Chadbourn, N. C.
Brown, James L............Oklahoma City, Okla.
Brown, James R....................New York City
Brown, James W................Falls Church, Va.
Brown, J. E.....................Scottsboro, Ala.
Brown, Dr. J. W....................Camden, Ark.
Brown, M. R..................Bellefontaine, Ohio
Brown, Ralph H......................Atlanta, Ga.
Browne, Jefferson B...............Key West, Fla.
Browne, Richard H...............New Orleans, La.
Browne, Dr. Walker G................Atlanta, Ga.
Brubaker, Joseph Stauffer............Vinton, Iowa
Bruce, George W................Pleasant Hill, Mo.
Brumback, Hon. O. S..................Toledo, Ohio
Bruyere, Dr. John...................Trenton, N. J.
Bryan, H. A......................Ruthven, Iowa
Bryan, John D......................El Paso, Tex.
Bryan, R. W. D........Albuquerque, New Mexico
Buchman, Edwin..................Valley Falls, N. Y.
Buckner, James H...................Cincinnati, Ohio
Budd, J. D., M.S., M.D........Two Harbors, Minn.
Budd, William N..................Bunker Hill, Ill.
Burbank, William F............Los Angeles, Cal.
Burckhalter, James B..................Vinita, I. T.
Burgess, Edward G.................Montclair, N. J.
Burke, Frank B..................Indianapolis, Ind.
Burke, John F....................Milwaukee, Wis.
Burke, Walter J...................New Iberia, La.
Burson, George......................Winamac, Ind.
Burtt, Henry A................Jeffersonville, Ind.
Bush, Matthew.....................Corunna, Mich.
Bushnell, A. R....................Madison, Wis.
Butler, Sarah.....................Cincinnati, Ohio
Butler, William J.................Springfield, Ill.
Butt, I. T......................Clarksdale, Miss.
Byrd, R. E......................Winchester, Va.
Byrne, E. J..........................Austin, Tex.
Cadwallader, A. D..................Springfield, Ill.
Cahill, John H....................New York City
Cain, William M..................David City, Neb.
Calhoon, Judge S. S..................Jackson, Miss.
Camp, E. T........................Gadsden, Ala.
Campbell, Daniel.......West New Brighton, N. Y.
Campbell, Edward, Jr.................Fairfield, Iowa
Carey, Henry W....................Eastlake, Mich.
Carmichael, D. W..................Sacramento, Cal.
Carr, John........................Lincoln, Neb.
Carr, Julian S.....................Durham, N. C.
Carson, J. A. G....................Savannah, Ga.
Carter, A. Edson...............Los Angeles, Cal.
Carter, F. M.......................Farmington, Mo.

Carton, James D.................Asbury Park, N. J.
Carver, Edwin O......................Fitzhugh, Fla.
Carver, M. H...................Natchitoches, La.
Case, Halbert B................Chattanooga, Tenn.
Cass, J. E........................Eau Claire, Wis.
Castle, Bryan J.....................Madison, Wis.
Caywood, John...................Miles City, Mont.
Cazier, M. H.........................Chicago, Ill.
Cease, D. L.......................Cleveland, Ohio
Chalkley, John W...............Big Stone Gap, Va.
Chambers, David W.............New Castle, Ind.
Chambers, Emmett.....................Dallas, Tex.
Champlin, John W............Grand Rapids, Mich.
Chapman, Oliver J.............Breckinridge, Mo.
Charters, W. A..................Dahlonega, Ga.
Chase, C. C.......................Covington, Ky.
Chidester, Arthur Mercer.....New Waterford, Ohio
Chidester, T. Edwin.............Philadelphia, Pa.
Child, James E.....................Waseca, Minn.
Chisholm, W. W............Salt Lake City, Utah
Cissel, W. W. L...................Highland, Md.
Clancy, William.....................Butte, Mont.
Clardy, Martin L...................St. Louis, Mo.
Clark, Ezra W.................League Island, Pa.
Clark, Frank...................Jacksonville, Fla.
Clark, Gibson....................Cheyenne, Wyo.
Clark, Orlando E....................Appleton, Wis.
Clark, R. S.....................Eau Claire, Wis.
Clark, William H....................Dallas, Tex.
Clarke, Enos......................Kirkwood, Mo.
Clarke, James T., M.D...........Mount Solon, Va.
Clarke, James W...............East Orange, N. J.
Clarke, Peyton Neale..............Louisville, Ky.
Clay, Rhodes........................Mexico, Mo.
Clay, William Lewis.............Huntsville, Ala.
Clement, Charles M..................Sunbury, Pa.
Clemson Agricultural College, Clemson College, S. C.
Cleveland Cider Co......Unionville, Lake Co., Ohio
Clinch, Edward S..................New York City
Closson, James Harwood, M.D.,
                        Germantown, Philadelphia, Pa.
Clute, Lemuel..........................Ionia, Mich.
Clute, S. R.....................Montezuma, Iowa
Clyne, Benjamin, M.D.................Yale, Mich.
Cochran, Rev. F. J..................Roxana, Del.
Cockrell, Joseph E...................Dallas, Tex.
Cohen, Ira......................New York City
Cohen, Lewis....................Bloomsburg, Pa.
Colby University Library............Waterville, Me.
Coleman, Henry, President Nat'l Business College,
                                Newark, N. J.
Collier, B. K....................Etna Mills, Cal.
Collier, F. S.......................Hampton, Va.
Collier, Thomas A..............Jamestown, Tenn.
Collins, Charles H.................Hillsboro, Ohio
Collins, John T..................Rutherford, N. J.
Collins, Winfield S...................Basin, Wyo.
Colton, William H..................Wapello, Iowa
Comstock, C. N......................Albany, Mo.
Condon, John T....................Seattle, Wash.
Condon, William H...................Chicago, Ill.
Coney, P. H.........................Topeka, Kan.
Conkling, Cook...................Rutherford, N. J.
Conkling, Newlan...................Norborne, Mo.
Connaughton, J. J...............Wapeconeta, Ohio
Connell, J. H................College Station, Tex.
Conover, William A..................Chicago Ill.
Conroy, E. M., M.D..................Ogden, Utah
Cook, Benjamin H., M.D...........Wilkinson, Ind.
Cook, John T.......................Albany, N. Y.
Cook, Samuel E....................Huntington, Ind.
Cooke, J. H.........................Moultrie, Ga.
Cookinham, D. A., M.D...............Holton, Kan.
Coolidge, T. Jefferson..............Boston, Mass.
Cooper, A. W........................Forest, Miss.
Cooper, H. P.......................Lebanon, Ky.
Cooper, J. M. F., M.D...........Waterville, Wash.
Copeland, Alfred M...............Springfield, Mass.
Corbett, William P...................Detroit, Mich.
Corbin, John..................New Harmony, Ind.
Cosgrave, George......................Fresno, Cal.
Coshocton Free School Library.....Coshocton, Ohio
Costello, S. V..................San Francisco, Cal.
Coulter, J. E..................Grand Rapids, Mich.
Courtney, Major A. R................Richmond, Va.
Courtright, Samuel W., LL.D.......Circleville, Ohio
Courts, Dr. W. J.................Reidsville, N. C.
Covell, A. G...................Sykeston, No. Dak.
Cowen, Gen. B. R.................Cincinnati, Ohio
Cowdery, J. F................San Francisco, Cal.
Cowles, George M..................Monroe, Iowa
Cowper, George....................Winston, N. C.
Cox, Henry C.....................La Grange, Ill.
Cox, Jefferson D.................Claremore, I. T.

Cox, Jennings S.	New York City
Cox, Stephen J.	New York City
Crain, Robert	Baltimore, Md.
Crane, Elvin W.	Newark, N. J.
Cranston, John A.	Alexandria, Minn.
Cravath, E. M.	Nashville, Tenn.
Cravath, Paul D.	New York City
Cravens, Robert O.	Sacramento, Cal.
Crawford, E. C.	Oakdale, Cal.
Crawford, Thomas Olin	Oakland, Cal.
Crocheron, David E.	New York City
Crossland, Samuel H.	Mayfield, Ky.
Crouch, B. W.	Saluda, S. C.
Crouch, David N.	Humphreys, Mo.
Crunden, Frederick M.	St. Louis, Mo.
Cullen, John J.	Jersey City, N. J.
Cumming, Robert	Peoria, Ill.
Cunningham, Oliver M.	South Bend, Ind.
Cunningham, W. J.	Abilene, Tex.
Curd, Thomas N.	Richmond, Va.
Curdy, Scott Eugene	Kingsley, Mich.
Curley, John J.	Rockaway Beach, N. Y.
Cussons, John	Glen Allen, Va.
Dabney, I. T.	Bloomfield, Iowa
Dagg, J. L.	Vidalia, La.
Dalton, James L.	Poplar Bluff, Mo.
Daly, Peter Francis	New Brunswick, N. J.
Dalzell, John	Washington, D. C.
Danforth, C. R.	Minonk, Ill.
Daniels, Josephus.	Raleigh, N. C.
Darden, W. M.	Speights Bridge, N. C.
Darlington, Barton	Los Angeles, Cal.
Darlington, J. J.	Washington, D. C.
Davidson, O. C.	Commonwealth, Wis.
Davies, William Gilbert	New York City
Davis, C. E.	Deadwood, S. Dak.
Davis, Charles E.	Madison, Fla.
Davis, Ernest M.	Camilla, Ga.
Davis, William L.	Canton, Ohio
Davison, Charles Stewart	New York City
Dawkins, Walter I.	Baltimore, Md.
Dayton, George D.	Worthington, Minn.
Dean, Claude M.	Richmond, Va.
Dean, Gerard Q.	New York City
Dean, J. A.	Owensboro, Ky.
Dean, J. R.	Broken Bow, Neb.
Dean, J. R.	Woodward, Okla.
Dean, S. W.	Centerville, Tex.
Dean, Walter E.	San Francisco, Cal.
Dechert, Henry M.	Philadelphia, Pa.
De Haven, John J.	San Francisco, Cal.
De Lacy, John F.	Eastman, Ga.
Delery, W. S.	Houston, Tex.
Denmark, Brantley A.	Savannah, Ga.
Dent, William Hamilton	Decorah, Iowa
Denton, John S.	Cookeville, Tenn.
Denver Athletic Club Library	Denver, Colo.
De Pue, E. L.	Olivia, Minn.
Dersheimer, C. O.	Tunkhannock, Pa.
de Steuben, T. J.	Jensen, Fla.
Deuel, Joseph M.	New York City
Devecmon, W. C.	Cumberland, Md.
Devine, Michael A.	Atlantic City, N. J.
Devine, Miles J.	Chicago, Ill
Deweese, B. C.	Lexington, Ky.
De Weese, K. McC.	Kansas City, Mo.
Dierking, John	St. Clair, Mo.
Diggs, Annie L.	Topeka, Kan.
Diggs, Rev. P. W.	Unity, Va.
Digney, John M.	White Plains, N. Y.
Diller, Peter	Bluffton, Ohio
Dillon, Thomas H.	Petersburg, Ind.
Dines, Tyson S.	Denver, Colo.
Dively, A. V.	Altoona, Pa.
Dixon, Warren	Jersey City, N. J.
Dixon, W. W.	Union, S. C.
Dobbins, W. P.	Corinth, Miss.
Dockstader, G. W.	Cawker City, Kan.
Dodd, Amzi	Newark, N. J.
Dodge, Frank L.	Lansing, Mich.
Dodge, Geo. E.	Little Rock, Ark.
Dodge, Samuel D.	Cleveland, Ohio
Dollard, Robert	Scotland, S. Dak.
Domer, S. P.	Spokane, Wash.
Donahoe, John T.	Joliet, Ill.
Doocy, Edward	Pittsfield, Ill.
Dooley, Edward J.	Brooklyn, N. Y.
Dorsey, J. S.	Columbia, Mo.
Dougherty, J. W.	Washington, Ill.
Douglas, John A.	New York City
Douglass, P. A.	Danville, Ark.
Douglass, Joshua	Meadville, Pa.
Dowd, Thomas H.	Salamanca, N. Y.
Dowling, James E.	Springfield, Ill.
Downing, H. H.	Front Royal, Va.
Downing, Thomas J.	New London, Mo.
Downs, S. A.	Mena, Ark.
Doyle, Michael J.	Green Bay, Wis.
Drake, Thomas	Pierre, S. Dak.
Draper, A. L.	Glenville, Ohio
Dressler, Rev. John M.	Boelus, Neb.
Dreys, Otto L.	Delray, Mich.
Drinkle, H. C.	Lancaster, Ohio
Dudley, James G.	Paris, Tex.
Duffy, Rodolph	Catharine Lake, N. C.
Dunbar, D. C.	Salt Lake City, Utah
Duncan, John F.	Lewisburg, Pa.
Duncan, John M.	Tyler, Tex.
Duncan, W. C.	Columbus, Ind.
Dunford, P. P.	Montague, Tex.
Dunn, Chauncey H.	Sacramento, Cal.
Durand, John S.	New York City
Durham, T. F.	Danville, Ky.
Durst, George M.	Thayer, Mo.
Dutcher, Frederick L.	Rochester, N. Y.
Dyer, Elihu B.	Saybrook, Ill.
Dygert, George B.	Butte, Mont.
Dykman, William N.	Brooklyn, N. Y.
Eagan, John J.	Hoboken, N. J.
Easly, James J.	Seattle, Wash.
Eastham, H. C.	Baker City, Ore.
Eastman, Charles H.	Nashville, Tenn.
Eaton, Willard L.	Osage, Iowa
Ebner, F. E.	Aitkin, Minn.
Echols, John Warnock	Washington, D. C.
Eckert, O. V.	Northwood, Iowa
Edmunds, Earl	Correctionville, Iowa
Edwards, Charles W.	Bordentown, N. J.
Edwards, S. B.	Pottsville, Pa.
Edwards, T. M., D.Ps.	Fortuna, Cal.
Egan, John F.	Sapulpa, I. T.
Eggen, J. A.	Milwaukee, Wis.
Eickhoff, Henry	San Francisco, Cal.
Einstein, Louis	Fresno, Cal.
Eldridge, E. R.	Chicago, Ill.
Eliel, Adolph	Dillon, Mont.
Ellegood, James E.	Salisbury, Md.
Elliott, Frank W.	Topeka, Kan.
Ellis, G. W.	Hattiesburg, Miss.
Ellis, Matt H.	Philadelphia, Pa.
Ellis, O.	Uvalde, Tex.
Ellis, Stephen D.	Amite City, La.
Ellison, T. E.	Fort Wayne, Ind.
Elver, Elmore Theodore	Madison, Wis.
Embry, James H.	Washington, D. C.
Emery, George D.	Minneapolis, Minn.
Emmert, J. M., M.D.	Atlantic, Iowa
English, John C.	Helena, Mont.
Ennes, John D.	Norfolk, Va.
Epes, T. Freeman	Blackstone, Va.
Eskridge, J. T., M.D.	Denver, Colo.
Evans, E. G.	Des Moines, Iowa
Evarts, H. P.	Grand Rapids, Mich.
Everett, Howard	Terril, Iowa
Ewing, Pressley K.	Houston, Tex.
F. & C. Co-operative Co.	Fort Gaines, Ga.
Falconer, John	San Francisco, Cal.
Falloon, Edwin	Falls City, Neb.
Fanner, Charles H.	Walterboro, S. C.
Fanning, William J.	New York City
Farmer, R. J.	Detroit, Mich.
Farnham, George R.	Evergreen, Ala.
Farnsworth, W. H.	Sioux City, Iowa
Farr, Mark C.	Chicago, Ill.
Farrar, J. H.	Groesbeeck, Tex.
Farrell, Clinton P.	New York City
Farrell, Rev. W. B.	Hempstead, L. I., N. Y.
Farrelly, Robert W.	Washington, D. C.
Faulkner, Charles J.	Martinsburg, W. Va.
Faxon, John W.	Chattanooga, Tenn.
Featherston, W. B.	Cleburne, Tex.
Feliz, F. P.	Monterey, Cal.
Ferguson, F. S.	Birmingham, Ala.
Ferguson, H. G.	St. Louis, Mo.
Ferris, M. J. H.	New York City
Ficke, C. A.	Davenport, Iowa
Field, Frank Harvey	Brooklyn, N. Y.
Field, J. H.	Dickinson, N. Dak.
Filson, Frank M.	Cameron, Mo.
Finch, A. T., M.D.	Blacksburg, Va.
Finley, D. C.	Kansas City, Mo.
Firehammer, J. H.	Alameda, Cal.
Fischer, Frederick	Brooklyn, N. Y.
Fishback, W. H.	Laramie, Wyo.
Fisher, William	Pensacola, Fla.
Fitzgerald, H. R.	Danville, Va.
Fitzgerald, John E.	New York City
Fitz-Randolph, Leslie	Nortonville, Kan.

Flagg, John H..............New York City
Fleming, Hon. William H...........Augusta, Ga.
Fletcher, A. S..............Huntsville, Ala.
Fletcher, James H., Jr......Accomack C. H., Va.
Fletcher, R. D..............Titusville, Pa.
Flournoy, George, Jr........Bakersfield, Cal.
Floyd, G. S.................Waterville, Wash.
Foley, Hamilton, U.S.A.
Foley, Paul, U.S.N.
Follett, A. D..............Marietta, Ohio
Ford, Charles M.............Denver, Colo.
Fordyce, John...............Weyauwega, Wis.
Foster, E. Agate, M.D......Patchogue, L. I., N. Y.
Foster, Samuel M............Fort Wayne, Ind.
Fox, Hon. A. F.............West Point, Miss.
Frank, Henry...............New York City
Frankenheimer, John........New York City
Franklin, David, M.D.......New York City
Freeman, W. R..............Denver, Colo.
French, D. E...............Keystone, W. Va.
French, E. L...............Lancaster, Mo.
Frick, J. E................Salt Lake City, Utah
Frost, A. C................Chicago, Ill.
Frost, E. Allen............Chicago, Ill.
Fuller, Judge Ceylon Canfield....Big Rapids Mich.
Fuller, Edward M., M.D.....Chicago, Ill.
Fuller, T. A...............San Antonio, Tex.
Funk, M. P.................Rantoul, Ill.
Furlong, Henry J...........New York City
Gaffney, F. O..............Lake City, Mich.
Gage, George W.............Chester, S. C.
Gail Borden Public Library.........Elgin, Ill.
Gaither, Charles A.........Erie, Pa.
Galloway, Charles V........Park Place, Ore.
Garcin, Ramon D., M.D......Richmond, Va.
Gardner, Lawrence..........Washington, D. C.
Gardner, Levi..............Atlanta, N. Y.
Garman, John M.............Nanticoke, Pa.
Garner, James W............Kansas City, Mo.
Garth, Col. William Willis.........Huntsville, Ala.
Gates, Theodore B..........Brooklyn, N. Y.
Gaylord, Samuel A..........St. Louis, Mo.
Gearhart, Cicero...........Stroudsburg, Pa.
Gehrz, Gustave G...........Milwaukee, Wis.
Genter, E. W...............Salt Lake City, Utah
George, James A............Deadwood, S. Dak.
Gibbes, Heyward M..........Jerome, Ariz.
Gibbes, Hunter A...........Columbia, S. C.
Gibbons, James E...........Purcell, I. T.
Gibson, T. B...............McColl, S. C.
Gibson, William F..........San Francisco, Cal.
Gillan, George C...........Lexington, Neb.
Gillespie, George W........Tazewell, Va.
Gillespie, John F..........Pine Bluff, Ark.
Ginter, H. E...............Du Bois, Pa.
Gleason, Orton W...........Detroit, Mich.
Gleason, P.................Le Roy, N. Y.
Godsman, P. B..............Burlington, Colo.
Goeke, J. H................Wapakoneka, Ohio
Goeschel, Louis............Bay City, Mich.
Goldberg, Abraham..........New Orleans, La.
Goodding, Roscoe E.........La Plata, Mo.
Goode, George W............Grangeville, Idaho
Goodnight, I. H............Franklin, Ky.
Gordon, Wellington.........Columbia, Mo.
Goss, D. F.................Seymour, Tex.
Gould, Will D..............Los Angeles, Cal.
Goulder, Holding & Masten........Cleveland, Ohio
Gourley, William B.........Paterson, N. J.
Gow, John R................Bellaire, Ohio
Graham, W. H...............Uniontown, Pa.
Grant, Bishop A............Philadelphia, Pa.
Grant, M. R................Meridian, Miss.
Grason, William............Towson, Md.
Graves, Alvin M............Cincinnati, Ohio
Graves, Ernest.............San Luis Obispo, Cal.
Graves, Hamilton...........Roanoke, Va.
Gray, Alfred W.............Niagara Falls, N. Y.
Graybill, Capt. George.....York, Pa.
Grayston, W. E.............Joplin, Mo.
Greaves, Charles D.........Hot Springs, Ark.
Greble, H. K...............Hamilton, Ohio
Green, Henry D.............Reading, Pa.
Greenburg, Rev. Dr. William H....Sacramento, Cal.
Greene, Thomas G...........Portland, Ore.
Greenfield, Leo............New York City
Greenway, J. Henry.........Havre de Grace, Md.
Greenwood, A. G............Palestine, Tex.
Greenwood, Frederick.......Norfolk, Va.
Greer, H. H................Mount Vernon, Ohio
Gregory, James P...........Louisville, Ky.
Griffiths, G. Charles......Chicago, Ill.
Grimes, H. H...............Lincoln, Neb.
Grosshans, Frank E.........East Liverpool, Ohio

Group, John W..............Rauchtown, Pa.
Grout, Edward M............Brooklyn, N. Y.
Guerin, Claude V...........Asbury Park, N. J.
Guerry, Du Pont............Macon, Ga.
Guerry, Homer..............Washington, D. C.
Guigon, A. B...............Richmond, Va.
Guilfoyle, Frank J.........Syracuse, N. Y.
Gunn, Julien...............Richmond, Va.
Gunnell, W. M..............Marlin, Tex.
Gustavus, C. D.............Oakwoods, Tex.
Guthrie, Ben Eli...........Macon, Mo.
Guthrie, William A.........Durham, N. C.
Hackney, Edward T..........Wellington, Kan.
Hager, John F..............Ashland, Ky.
Haggan, Rodney.............Winchester, Ky.
Haire, Col. R. J...........New York City
Halderman, Grant E.........Longmont, Colo.
Hale, Hon. Horace M........Denver, Colo.
Hale, Morris...............Hot Springs, Ala.
Hale, S. J.................Milner, Ga.
Hall, Anthony..............Paris, Ark.
Hall, Charles S............Binghamton, N. Y.
Hall, Dr. D. H.............Pikeville, Tenn.
Hall, R. W.................Vernon, Tex.
Hall, William Roland.......Houston, Miss.
Halligan, John J...........North Platte, Neb.
Ham, H. W. J...............Gainesville, Ga.
Hamby, C. C................Prescott, Ark.
Hamill, F. P...............Temple, Tex.
Hamilton, Gen. E. B........Quincy, Ill.
Hamlin, Byron D............Smethport, Pa.
Hammersley, H..............Cleveland, Ohio
Hammond, George T..........Brooklyn, N. Y.
Hammond, J. T..............Salt Lake City, Utah
Hammond, Dr. Robert L......Woodsboro, Md.
Hampson, J. K., M.D........Nodena, Ark.
Hampton, Charles D.........El Reno, Okla. T.
Hampton, Charles S.........Detroit, Mich.
Hampton, William Wade......Gainesville, Fla.
Hansbrough, Hon. Henry C...Washington, D. C.
Hanson, Dr. T. C...........Winnemucca, Nev.
Harden, Alfred D...........New York City
Harding, Gilbert N.........Lacona, N. Y.
Hardman, Rev. A. L.........Natchez, Miss.
Harmon, Gilbert............Toledo, Ohio
Harne, J. Lee..............New Martinsville, W. Va.
Harper, P. L...............Wallace, Neb.
Harrington, M. F...........O'Neill, Neb.
Harris, A. A...............Duluth, Minn.
Harris, James C............Sheffield, Ala.
Harris, John T.............Harrisonburg, Va.
Harrison & Long............Lynchburg, Va.
Hart, E. H.................San Francisco, Cal.
Hartigan, M. A.............Hastings, Neb.
Hartjen, John..............Brooklyn, N. Y.
Hartman, J. H..............Claflin, Kan.
Harvey, Edwin Clinton......New York City
Hatcher, E. H..............Columbia, Tenn.
Hatfield, Charles S........Clifton, Ohio
Hatton, Goodrich...........Portsmouth, Va.
Haviland, C. Augustus......Brooklyn, N. Y.
Hawkins, A. S..............Midland, Tex.
Hawkins, J. E..............Langlois, Ore.
Hawkins, John J............Prescott, Ariz.
Hawley, David..............Yonkers, N. Y.
Hayes, George B............New York City
Hayes, John E..............New York City
Hayman, L. H., M.D.........Boscobel, Wis.
Haynie, William Duff.......Chicago, Ill.
Head, J. C.................Richmond, Ark.
Heagany, Richard...........Hartford City, Ind.
Heath, Thomas T............Cincinnati, Ohio
Heatley, Thomas W..........Cleveland, Ohio
Heaton, Willis Edgar.......Hoosick Falls, N. Y.
Hebroy, J. L., Jr..........Leland, Miss.
Hedden, C. P...............Irvington, N. J.
Heffelfinger, Jacob........Hampton, Va.
Heinly, Harvey F...........Reading, Pa.
Heiskell, S. G.............Knoxville, Tenn.
Held, W. D. L..............Ukiah, Cal.
Hemmeter, John C...........Cleveland, Ohio
Hemphill, John J...........Washington, D. C.
Hendrick, C. C.............Jersey City, N. J.
Henkel, Vernon A...........Farmersville, Ohio
Henry, John N..............Champlin, Minn.
Hensler, Gus...............Anacortes, Wash.
Hermann, Dr. G. J..........Newport, Ky.
Hero, William S............New Orleans, La.
Hewitt, Hon. Abram S.......New York City
Hewitt, Robert A., Jr......Maysville, Mo.
Hibbard, Bertrand Lesly....Monroeville, Ala.
Hickey, W. H., M.D.........Leipsic, Ohio
Hickok, S. J...............Canton, Pa.
Higgins, W. E..............La Porte, Ind.

Higginson, O. F....Needles, Cal.
Hildebrand, Edward....New York City
Hildebrand, H. E....San Antonio, Tex.
Hildreth, Melvin A....Fargo, N. Dak.
Hill, Ex-Gov. David B....Albany, N. Y.
Hill, H. W., M.D....Mooresville, Ala.
Hill, James W....Peoria, Ill.
Hill, Joseph M....Fort Smith, Ark.
Hill, W. D....Defiance, Ohio
Hilton, Charles S....Clarksburg, Md.
Hilton, George....Oshkosh, Wis.
Himes, George W....Shippensburg, Pa.
Hinckley, J. F....Sapulpa, I. T.
Hine, Willis G....Savannah, Mo.
Hines, Fletcher S....Malatt Park, Ind.
Hines, James D....Bowling Green, Ky.
Hinson, William G....James Island, S. C.
Hite, W. W....Louisville, Ky.
Hitt, Orlando....Mexico, Mo.
Hobbs, J. W....Nineveh, N. Y.
Hobson, F. G....Norristown, Pa.
Hoffman, George W....Boonsboro, Md.
Hoffmann, L. O....Price, Utah
Holcomb, O. R....Ritzville, Wash.
Holcomb, Ex-Gov. Silas A....Lincoln, Neb.
Holding, S. H....Cleveland, Ohio
Holihan, John....Auburn, N. Y.
Holland, L. T., M.D....Los Angeles, Cal.
Holliday, W. H....Laramie, Wyo.
Hollister, W. R....Monticello, Mo.
Holman, J. H....Fayetteville, Tenn.
Holmes, D. A....Chicago, Ill.
Holmes, John T....Detroit, Mich.
Holmes, J. T....Columbus, Ohio
Hood, R. B....Weatherford, Tex.
Hooper, George J....Richmond, Va.
Hooper, P. O., M.D....Little Rock, Ark.
Hooper & Hooper....Oshkosh, Wis.
Hoos, Hon. Edward....Jersey City, N. J.
Hoover, S. S....Elkhart, Ind.
Hopkins, J. G......Hampstead, Albemarle Co., Va.
Hopper, P. L....Havre de Grace, Md.
Hopwood, R. F....Uniontown, Pa.
Horton, Hiler H....St. Paul, Minn.
Horton, H. M....Midland, Tex.
Hoskins, H. C....Madera, Cal.
Houser, Frederick W....Los Angeles, Cal.
Howard, Josiah....Emporium, Pa.
Howard, W. A., M.D....Waco, Tex.
Hoyt, Dr. Frank C....Mt. Pleasant, Iowa
Hubbert, George....Neosho, Mo.
Huber, A. H....Westminster, Md.
Hudson, F. M....Pine Bluff, Ark.
Hudson, Less. L....Fort Worth, Tex.
Hudson, T. J....Fredonia, Kan.
Hug, Edward V., M.D....Lorain, Ohio
Hughes, Adrian....Baltimore, Md.
Hughes, Charles J., Jr....Denver, Colo.
Hughes, C. W., M.D....Eleanor, Pa.
Hughes, L. C....Tucson, Ariz.
Hull, John M....Cleveland, Ohio
Humes, Milton....Huntsville, Ala.
Humphrey, J. O....Springfield, Ill.
Humphries, W. A....Portland, Ind.
Hunt, C. C....Montezuma, Iowa
Hunter, Henry B....Milwaukee, Wis.
Hunter, Peter....Eddystone, Pa.
Hunter, Sam J....Fort Worth, Tex.
Huntington, D. W. C....Lincoln, Neb.
Huntington, R. M....Hot Springs, Ark.
Hurley, Rev. John A....Emerald, Kan.
Hurst, Elmore W....Rock Island, Ill.
Hutchings, William T....Muscogee, I. T.
Hutter, C. S....Lynchburg, Va.
Hutton, A. W....Los Angeles, Cal.
Hyde, G. W., M.D....Clinton, Ill.
Hyde, W. L....Buchanan, Va.
Hyland, Judge M. H....San José, Cal.
Inches, Dr. James W....St. Clair, Mich.
Ingersoll, Henry H....Knoxville, Tenn.
Irwin, Charles....Kingston, N. Y.
Israel, G. C....Olympia, Wash.
Itell, Thomas J....Johnstown, Pa.
Jackson, E. G....Hoboken, N. J.
Jackson, George P. B....St. Louis, Mo.
Jackson, J. K. P....Margaretville, N. Y.
Jacobs, J. H....Reading, Pa.
James, C. F., D.D....Danville, Va.
James, H. Clay....Huntsville, Tenn.
Janes, F. P., M.D....Lake Creek, Tex.
Jarvis, George J....Faulkton, S. Dak.
Jelleff, A. C....Ripon, Wis.
Jenkins, C. H....Brownwood, Tex.
Jenkins, J. C....Marysville, Cal.

Jenkins, John J....Chippewa Falls, Wis.
Jennings, Hyde....Fort Worth, Tex.
Jennings, T. A....Tampa, Fla.
Jeter, W. M....Dumas, Tex.
Jewett, F. T....San Francisco, Cal.
Jewks, George A....Brookville, Pa.
Johanson, Fritz....Chinook, Wash.
John, Samuel Will....Birmingham, Ala.
Johns, John E....Massillon, Ohio
Johnson, Alvin J....Knoxville, Tenn.
Johnson, Clyde B....St. Mary's, W. Va.
Johnson, Ex-Gov. Charles P....St. Louis, Mo.
Johnson, David M., Jr....Chester, Pa.
Johnson, Francis....Little Rock, Ark.
Johnson, Greene F....Monticello, Ga.
Johnson, James....Pittsburg, Pa.
Johnson, Mrs. James V....Brooklyn, N. Y.
Johnson, J. B....Nevada, Mo.
Johnson, J. B....Des Moines, Iowa
Johnson, J. M....Hillsboro, Tex.
Johnson, John G....Peabody, Kan.
Johnson, L. H....Eureka, Kan.
Johnson, Owens....Brunswick, Ga.
Johnson, Col. R. M....Elkhart, Ind.
Johnson, Thomas M....Osceola, Mo.
Johnson, W. Carter....Louisville, Ky.
Johnston, H. M....Fresno, Cal.
Jolly, George W....Owensboro, Ky.
Jones, Benjamin O....Metropolis, Ill.
Jones, Daniel M....Anson, Tex.
Jones, Dr. H. C....Mt. Vernon, N. Y.
Jones, James C....St. Louis, Mo.
Jones, James H....Henderson, Tex.
Jones, J. Dunlop....Grayson, Ky.
Jones, L. A....Como, Miss.
Jones, Richard A....St. Louis, Mo.
Jones, Richmond L....Reading, Pa.
Jones, Ricy H....Brigham City, Utah
Jones, W. H....Riverside, Iowa
Jones, William H., M.D....Bethlehem, Pa.
Jones, William Jarvis....Chicago, Ill.
Jordan, Judge James H....Martinsville, Ind.
Jordan, J. Eugene....Seattle, Wash.
Jordan, Warren S....Peekskill, N. Y.
Jordin, J. F....Gallatin, Mo.
Judd, John W....Nashville, Tenn.
Kane, M. N....Warwick, N. Y.
Keast, Alderman J. W....St. John, N. B.
Keenan, S. A....Clark, S. Dak.
Keene, John Henry....Baltimore, Md.
Keffer, J. L....Dunbar, Pa.
Keiser, C. W....Hazleton, Pa.
Keizer, Lewis R....Baltimore, Md.
Keller, John W....New York City
Kelley, Marshall C....Muskegon, Mich.
Kellogg, A. C....Portage, Wis.
Kellogg, Frank E....Goleta, Cal.
Kelly, B. A....Benton, La.
Kelly, Frank P....San Francisco, Cal.
Kelly, James R....San Francisco, Cal.
Kelly, John T....Milwaukee, Wis.
Kelso, A. W....Grant City, Mo.
Kelton, W. H. S....Alvarado, Tex.
Kenfield, William F....Woonsocket, S. Dak.
Kennedy, Hon. A. M....Mexia, Tex.
Kennedy, Crammond....Alpine, N. J.
Kennedy, James L....Greensburg, Pa.
Kent, Henry T....St. Louis, Mo.
Kent, Volney....Marshalltown, Iowa
Kern, John W....Indianapolis, Ind.
Kern, R. H....St. Louis, Mo.
Kerr, Charles....Lexington, Ky.
Keyes, W. S....San Francisco, Cal.
Kidd, Gideon P., M.D....Roann, Ind.
Kilbourne, James....Columbus, Ohio
Killebrew, J. B....Nashville, Tenn.
Kimbrough, E. R. E....Danville, Ill.
King, Henry B....Augusta, Ga.
King, Col. H. M....Evergreen, Ala.
King, John C....Baltimore, Md.
King, J. W....Kittanning, Pa.
King, Wilbur E....Columbus, Ohio
Kingsbury, S. B....Boise, Idaho
Kinne, James E....Ft. Edward, N. Y.
Kirkpatrick, J. M....Dodge City, Kan.
Kissick, W. A....Brooklyn, N. Y.
Kitts, Charles W....Grass Valley, Cal.
Klaas, Albert R....Pittsburg, Pa.
Klar, A. Julian....Brooklyn, N. Y.
Klein, Alfred....Philadelphia, Pa.
Kleberg, Robert J....Corpus Christi, Tex.
Klinedinst, David P....York, Pa.
Klugh, James C....Abbeville, S. C.
Kluttz, Theodore F....Salisbury, N. C.

Knapp, F. M..................................Racine, Wis.
Knappe, W. Trevitt, M.D...........Vincennes, Ind.
Knight, George A.............................Brazil, Ind.
Knight, R. Huston.....................Los Angeles, Cal.
Knoebel, Thomas.......................East St. Louis, Ill.
Knox, Chris L...........................Corsicana, Tex.
Knox, J. W.....................................Merced, Cal.
Knudson, Charles O.................Canton, S. Dak.
Kocher, Charles F........................Newark, N. J.
Koepke, Charles A..........................Chicago, Ill.
Kontz, Ernest C................................Atlanta, Ga.
Koontz, J. B.................Washington C. H., Ohio
Koontz, J. R..............................Ansted, W. Va.
Krebs, David L..........................Clearfield, Pa.
Kroeer, Lewis.............................Sheffield, Pa.
Kruttschnitt, E. B...................New Orleans, La.
Krum, Chester.............................St. Louis, Mo.
Kryder, John F.............................Alliance, Ohio
La Buy, M. A.................................Chicago, Ill.
Lackland, H. C..........................St. Charles, Mo.
La Due, A......................................Mt. Dora, Fla.
La Force, William N........................Portland, Ore.
Lake, Lewis F..............................Rockford, Ill.
Lake, Luther E........................Huntington, Ark.
Lamar, J. R....................................Augusta, Ga.
Lamb, Edwin M................................Butte, Mont.
Lambert, Stenson, M.D..............Owensboro, Ky.
Lambeth, J. T...........................Lambethville, Ark.
Lamoreaux, Frank B..............Stevens Point, Wis.
Lamson, John D. R...........................Toledo, Ohio
Landes, S. Z.........................Mt. Carmel, Ill.
Landis, William P.....................Philadelphia, Pa.
Lansden, John M.................................Cairo, Ill.
Lapp, J. E..................................Cincinnati, Ohio
Larkins, Rev. S. C....................Long Creek, N. C.
Larner, John B.......................Washington, D. C.
Larrazolo, O. R.............Las Vegas, New Mexico
Latham, W. H....................................Curtis, Neb.
Laughlin, Randolph........................St. Louis, Mo.
Laurence, Howard E.....................Brooklyn, N. Y.
Lawson McGhee Library.............Knoxville, Tenn.
Lawther, Henry P.............................Dallas, Tex.
Lawyer, George............................Albany, N. Y.
Lay, W. P....................................Gadsden, Ala.
Leber, Henry..............................Oakland, Cal.
Lee, Prof. Duncan Campbell, Cornell University,
                                          Ithaca, N. Y.
Lee, Harry H................................Denver, Colo.
Lee, N. L.........................Junction City, Ore.
Leck, Rev. John D..............................Dixon, Ill.
Leeper, A. B., Ad'jt Gen'l., G.A.A.V., Owaneco, Ill.
Lees, Robert.....................................Alma, Wis.
Leffler, John. M.D..................San Francisco, Cal.
Lehmayer, Martin.........................Baltimore, Md.
Leigh, A., A.M., M.D., F.R.M.S...Hiawatha, Kan.
Lentz, Hon. John J.....................Columbus, Ohio
Leonard, Charles R..........................Butte, Mont.
Leonard, H. B.............................Yoakum, Tex.
Leslie, Preston H.........................Helena, Mont.
Lester, Rufus E...........................Savannah, Ga.
Letcher, Greenlee D......................Lexington, Va.
Levagood, M. H.................................Elyria, Ohio
Levis, G. W..................................Madison, Wis.
Lewis, Rev. Barney W...................Chunkey, Miss.
Lewis, H. Claude...............Salt Lake City, Utah
Lewis, Dr. John V..........................Alliance, Ohio
Lewis, Lyman W...............................Kewanee, Ill.
Lewis, Dr. Walter...........................Decatur, Neb.
Libby, M. D......................El Reno, Okla. T.
Liebig, G. M..........................Sparrow's Point, Md.
Lienesch, T. H..............................Dayton, Ohio
Lightfoot, Henry W..........................Paris, Tex.
Lindsey, S. A....................................Tyler, Tex.
Line, Benajah A., M.D...............Alexandria, Ind.
Lippmann, Leopold J...................New York City
Litz, A. W.................................Charleston, Ill.
Livingston, Alfred T., M.D.....Jamestown, N. Y.
Livingston, Hon. J. B................Lancaster, Pa.
Livingston, John Henry....Tivoli-on-Hudson, N. Y.
Locker, W. H.............................Waynesville, Mo.
Lockett, John W............................Henderson, Ky.
Lodge, J. C.................................Waverly, Wash.
Logan, D. B................................Pineville, Ky.
Logan, J. A................................Kingman, Ariz.
Lomax, Tennent.......................Montgomery, Ala.
Long, Eugene R...........................Batesville, Ark.
Long, George S..................................Troy, Ohio
Long, J. Grier..........................Spokane, Wash.
Long, Solomon L...........................Grenola, Kan.
Long, Theodore K..........................Chicago, Ill.
Longan, Edward Everett.................St. Louis, Mo.
Longfelder, David..........................Wabash, Ind.
Lonigo, E. V..................................Jackson, Cal.
Lookabaugh, I. H..................Watonga, Okla. T.

Looney, R. H................................Colorado, Tex.
Loucks, Zachariah Kepner............Philadelphia, Pa.
Love, J. King, M.D...........................Yardley, Pa.
Low, M. A....................................Topeka, Kan.
Lowden, Frank Orren......................Chicago, Ill.
Lowe, J. M.............................Kansas City, Mo.
Lowe, Robert J.........................Birmingham, Ala.
Lowenberg, Harry L.........................Norfolk, Va.
Lower, J. C................................Cleveland, Ohio
Lowry, T. C..............................Richmond, Ky.
Lozier, Ralph F............................Carrollton, Mo.
Lubers, H. L........................Las Animas, Colo.
Lucas, J. T...............................Moshannon, Pa.
Lucking, Alfred.............................Detroit, Mich.
Ludlow, James M., D.D., L.H.D..E. Orange, N. J.
Ludwig, Henry T. J...............Mt. Pleasant, N. C.
Ludwig, John H...........................New York City
Luf, Charles B..........................New York City
Lumbard, Samuel J........................Chicago, Ill.
Lykins, Joseph C...........................Campton, Ky.
Lyman, J. P................................Grinnell, Iowa
Lynch, Martin P., LL.B.................Brooklyn, N. Y.
Lynham, J. Arthur....................Washington, D. C.
Lyter, M. M.............................Great Falls, Mont.
McAtee, Judge John L............................Enid, Okla.
McCarren, P. H..........................Brooklyn, N. Y.
McCarthy, C. C.....................Grand Rapids, Minn.
McCarthy, John Henry...................New York City
McCarty, A. P.................................Bronte, Tex.
McCarty, Homer.............................Monroe, Utah
McCaskill, J. M..............................Rison, Ark.
McComas, George J.................Huntington, W. Va.
McCoy, Benjamin.........................Oskaloosa, Iowa
McCoy, D. W. F..........................New York City
McCoy John W......................Fairmont, W. Va.
McCravy, S. T......................Spartanburg, S. C.
McCullock, P. D............................Marianus, Ark.
McCully, H. G.........................Jersey City, N. J.
McDaniel, P. A............................Abbeville, Ala.
McDavitt, J. C.............................Memphis, Tenn.
McDermot, R. B......................Coshocton, Ohio
McDonald, James H........................Detroit, Mich.
McDonald, J. H.........................Cedar City, Utah
McDowell, John A......................Millersburg, Ohio
McElligott, Thomas G.......................Chicago, Ill.
McGoorty, John P............................Chicago, Ill.
McGowan, P. J..............................Astoria, Ore.
McGrath, Robert H....................Philadelphia, Pa.
McGraw, E. W.....................San Francisco, Cal.
McGraw, John T...........................Grafton, W. Va.
McGuffey, John G........................Columbus, Ohio
McGuire, John C..........................Brooklyn, N. Y.
McHolland (Miss) B....................Durango, Colo.
McIlwaine, C. R........................Knoxville, Tenn.
McIlwaine, William B...................Petersburg, Va.
McIntyre, John F..........................New York City
McIntyre, William J......................Riverside, Cal.
McKeighan, J. E.........................St. Louis, Mo.
McKinley, H. C.............................Gaylord, Mich.
McKnight, William F...........Grand Rapids, Mich.
McLaughlin, I. W...........................Macedon, N. Y.
McLaughlin, W. L...................Deadwood, S. Dak.
McLean, W. T., M.D., D.D.S.....Cincinnati, Ohio
McMahon, Charles C.........................Fulton, Ill.
McMahon, J. K..............................Chicago, Ill.
McMahon, Richard Randolph,
                                  Harper's Ferry, W. Va.
McMackin, John............................Albany, N. Y.
McMillan, F. H................................Atlanta, Ga.
McMorrow, M.................................Brazil, Ind.
McNair, A. C........................Brookhaven, Miss.
McNamara, James J.....................Baltimore, Md.
McNamara, John W.........................Albany, N. Y.
McNamee, F. R............................Delamar, Nev.
McNaughton, D. W.....................Boardman, N. C.
McNiel, Dr. W. N..........................Longfield, Va.
McPheeters, James............................Benton, Mo.
McRae, A. J......................West Superior, Wis.
McRae, Thomas C............................Prescott, Ark.
McMurray, J. L.............................Tacoma, Wash.
McSherry, James.........................Frederick, Md.
McWilliams, Howard.....................New York City
McWilliams, J. K...........................Sunbury, Pa.
MacDougall, R. S...................Los Angeles, Cal.
Mackenzie, John R., M.D........Weatherford, Tex.
Mackey, C. H............................Sigourney, Iowa
Mackey, Robert K.......................New York City
MacPhail, Donald T., M.D.......Purdy Sta., N. Y.
Macquarrie, Neil A..........................Jackson, Cal.
MacRae, Donald........................Wilmington, N. C.
Macomber, Charles S..................Ida Grove, Iowa
Madden, Charles J...........................Tennille, Ga.
Magee, Judge Christopher..............Pittsburg, Pa.
Maloney, Thomas...........................Ogden, Utah

Mann, Edgar P................Greenfield, Mo.
Mapes, Dorchester...............Chicago, Ill.
Markey, Edward J...............Brooklyn, N. Y.
Marsh, Craig A................Plainfield, N. J.
Marsh, E. J.................Big Rapids, Mich.
Marshall, Linus R...............Springfield, Ohio
Martin, I. L..................Uvalde, Tex.
Martin, John Burlington............Covington, Ind.
Martin, Lyman W................Seale, Ala.
Martine, Hon. Godfrey R., M.D..Glens Falls, N. Y.
Marvin, Charles................Elmira, N. Y.
Marvin, D. P.................Woodward, Okla.
Marvin, John L................Jacksonville, Fla.
Mason, F. O..................Geneva, N. Y.
Mason, James H................Brooklyn, N. Y.
Mason, P. G..................Le Roy, N. Y.
Masters, Edgar L...............Chicago, Ill.
Mathews, Thomas J...............Merrill, Wis.
Matoon, Charles M., M.D...........Brookville, Pa.
Mattes, John, Jr...............Nebraska City, Neb.
Matthews, W. B................Washington, D. C.
Maulsby, Israel T..............Tillamook City, Ore.
May, S. D...................Tazewell, Va.
Maybury, Hon. William C............Detroit, Mich.
Means, George W................Brookville, Pa.
Medill, Thomas J..............Rock Island, Ill.
Meek, J. F..................Coshocton, Ohio
Mercantile Library..............St. Louis, Mo.
Merchant, Edward L..............Horatio, Ark.
Meredith, Milo................Wabash, Ind.
Merrill, John B........Long Island City, N. Y.
Metcalf, Arthur A., M.D............Dunbar, Wis.
Millar, A. C.................Conway, Ark.
Miller, B. S.................Columbus, Ga.
Miller, Dewitt................Philadelphia, Pa.
Miller, George Knox.............Talladega, Ala.
Miller, Jacob F................New York City
Miller, James R................Watertown, N. Y.
Miller, John A., M.D............San Francisco, Cal.
Miller, John D................Susquehanna, Pa.
Miller, Mary E................Chicago, Ill.
Million, E. C................Mt. Vernon, Wash.
Mills, W. P..................Sidney, Neb.
Milner, J. Cooper..............Vernon, Ala.
Minor, F. D..................Galveston, Tex.
Mitchell, Edward P..............New York City
Mitchell, R. C................Duluth, Minn.
Momsen, John................Mt. Vernon, S. Dak.
Monahan, Patrick W..............Red Cliff, Colo.
Monjeau, C..................Middletown, Ohio
Monnette, O. E................Bucyrus, Ohio
Monroe, Chilton...............Dallas, Tex.
Monroe, Henry S...............Chicago, Ill.
Monroe, Robert W..............Kingwood, W. Va.
Montandon, A. F...............Boise City, Idaho
Moon, George C................New York City
Mooney, John H................New York City
Mooney, William...............Joliet, Ill.
Moore, A. C., M.D..............North Amherst, Ohio
Moore, Felix W................Union City, Tenn.
Moore, Frank N................Chicago, Ill.
Moore, M. Herndon..............Columbia, S. C.
Moran, Dr. James...............New York City
Moroney, John F...............Brooklyn, N. Y.
Morris, James E................Arthur, Ill.
Morrissey, Andrew M.............Valentine, Neb.
Morrow, Thomas R..............Kansas City, Mo.
Morse, S. F. B................Houston, Tex.
Moss, Nathanel P...............Lafayette, La.
Mott, John Sabert, M.D...........Kansas City, Mo.
Mountjoy, Wiley..............Twin Bridges, Mont.
Mounts, William L..............Carlinville, Ill.
Mouton, Homer................Lafayette, La.
Moyer, George W.............Salt Lake City, Utah
Muir, P. B..................Louisville, Ky.
Mullins, G. M.................Papillion, Neb.
Mumford, Beverley B.............Richmond, Va.
Murphy, D. E.................Milwaukee, Wis.
Murphy, John H................Denver, Colo.
Murphy, J. M. C................Lodi, Cal.
Murphy, T. J.................Mayfield, Ky.
Murphy, Rev. William............Seward, Neb.
Murray, Arthur................Pine Bluff, Ark.
Murray, William H..............Tishomingo, I. T.
Napton, Charles M..............St. Louis, Mo.
Nash, John A.................Audubon, Iowa
Nash, Wiley N................Starkville, Miss.
Neal, E. A..................Cuero, Tex.
Neff, George H................Sunbury, Pa.
Nelms, W. W.................Georgetown, Tex.
Neville, Richard L..............New York City
Newby, Nathan................Los Angeles, Cal.
Newson, John A................Buffalo, Tex.
Newton, Hon. C................Monroe, La.

New York University Library,
                University Heights, New York City
Nicholas, S. H................Coshocton, Ohio
Nichols, Joseph F..............Greenville, Tex.
Nicholson, B. H................Attala, Ala.
Nilsson, M. T................Laurens, Iowa
Noe, Noah S.................Kearny, N. J.
Norman, J. Felix...............Thayer, Mo.
Norman, Louis W...............Kandiyohi, Minn.
Norrell, A. G............Salt Lake City, Utah
Northern State Normal School....Marquette, Mich.
Norton, James................Garrettsville, Ohio
Norwood, G. A., Jr.............Goldsboro, N. C.
Nutt, George D., M.D............Williamsport, Pa.
Nye, Frederick A...............Kearney, Neb.
O'Brien, Quin................Chicago, Ill.
O'Brien, Thomas E..............New York City
O'Bryan, William H..............Altruria, Cal.
O'Callaghan, M. J..............Philadelphia, Pa.
O'Connell, J. B................Chicago, Ill.
O'Connor, Cornelius.............New York City
O'Donnell, Joseph A.............Chicago, Ill.
O'Gorman, Hon. James A...........New York City
O'Hara, R. A.................Hamilton, Mont.
O'Keeffe, P. J................Chicago, Ill.
O'Malley, John, M.D.............Scranton, Pa.
O'Sullivan, Michael.............New York City
O'Sullivan, W. J...............New York City
Oakes, Dr. I. N..........North Ridgeville, Ohio
Oakley, Horace S...............Chicago, Ill.
Ockford, George M., M.D..........Ridgewood, N. J.
Odell, Spurgeon...............Marshall, Minn.
Ogden, R. N.................Deadwood, S. Dak.
Oliver, George A...............Onawa, Iowa
Olney, Peter B................New York City
Oneonta Public Library...........Oneonta, N. Y.
Ornelas, Dr. P...............San Antonio, Tex.
Orr, J. S..................Steel City, Neb.
Orrick, William P., D.D...........Reading, Pa.
Osborne, H. E................Chicago, Ill.
Osborne, John E................Rawlins, Wyo.
Osborne, S. J.................Quanah, Tex.
Osthaus, Herman...............Scranton, Pa.
Otis, A. Walker...............New York City
Otts, J. Cornelius..............Gaffney, S. C.
Overmyer, John..............North Vernon, Ind.
Owsley, Alvin C................Denton, Tex.
Packwood, S. E................Magnolia, Miss.
Paden, George................Armona, Cal.
Paine, Bayard H.............Grand Island, Neb.
Paine, Karl.................Idaho City, Idaho
Palmer, Clarence S..............Kansas City, Mo.
Palmer, Irving H...............Cortland, N. Y.
Panabaker, P. F...............Hartington, Neb.
Parker, Silas C................Mansfield, Ohio
Parker, Dr. Thomas J............Detroit, Mich.
Parker, W. S.................Henderson, N. C.
Parker, W. W.................Baltimore, Md.
Parkhurst, Frank E..............Frankfort, N. Y.
Parrish, Robert L..............Covington, Va.
Parrott, James M...............Kinston, N. C.
Parrott, R. B...............Des Moines, Iowa
Paterson, Van R.............San Francisco, Cal.
Patrick, Albert T..............New York City
Patrick, John E................Jackson, Ky.
Patterson, Benjamin.............New York City
Patterson, Charles B.............El Paso, Tex.
Patterson, R. S................Safford, Ariz.
Patterson, Thomas M.............Denver, Colo.
Patton, D. H................Woodward, Okla.
Patton, George S...............San Gabriel, Cal.
Patty, C. N.................Pontiac, Ill.
Pauly, R. J., Sr...............St. Louis, Mo.
Payne, Gen. Walter S............Fostoria, Ohio
Pearson, L. W., M.D.............Brooklyn, N. Y.
Peck, John H.................Troy, N. Y.
Pendennis Club...............Louisville, Ky.
Penney, James E.............New Decatur, Ala.
Penwell, Lewis................Helena, Mont.
Peoria Public Library............Peoria, Ill.
Pereles, Thomas Jefferson.........Milwaukee, Wis.
Perkins, Hon. George C..........Washington, D. C.
Perkins, John C...............Sisseton, S. Dak.
Perky, K. I...............Mountain Home, Idaho
Perry, W. C.................Kansas City, Mo.
Peterkin, Dr. Guy S.............Seattle, Wash.
Peterkin, W. G.............Parkersburg, W. Va.
Pettit, William B...............Palmyra, Va.
Pettus & Lester...............Athens, Ala.
Pharr, Olin.................McRae, Ga.
Phelps, O. C.................Warren, Ohio
Philips, H. B................Jacksonville, Fla.
Phillips, George B..............Key West, Fla.
Phipps, J. M................Key West, Fla.

Pickens, Samuel O...............Indianapolis, Ind.
Pickering, A. O., M.D.........Chuckey City, Tenn.
Pickett, N. J., M.D......................Milford, Tex.
Pike, Vinton.......................St. Joseph, Mo.
Pile, J. M...............................Wayne, Neb.
Pinckney, John M...................Hempstead, Tex.
Pinney, William E.................Valparaiso, Ind.
Pitts, John A......................Nashville, Tenn.
Pitzer, U. S. G.................Martinsburg, W. Va.
Planten, J. R.....................New York City
Platt, George G......................Butte, Mont.
Plumer, Samuel.....................Franklin, Pa.
Plummer, Edwin L...............Indianapolis, Ind.
Pock, John H............................Troy, N. Y.
Poindexter, Joseph..................Cleburne, Tex.
Pool, Lawrence P..................Manchester, Va.
Porter, Charles H..................Baltimore, Md.
Porter, Dr. L. L....................Roslyn, Wash.
Porter, S. W.........................Sherman, Tex.
Porter, W. F........................Baltimore, Md.
Post, Charles A....................Cleveland, Ohio
Post, Duff...............................Tampa, Fla.
Post, Floyd L........................Midland, Mich.
Poston, R. C..........................Corydon, Iowa
Potter, C. C........................Gainesville, Tex.
Potter, C. L........................Gainesville, Tex.
Potts, H. Cameron..Germantown, Philadelphia, Pa.
Potts, W. S...........................Lisbon, Ohio
Pound, James T......................Newton, Iowa
Pounders, R. L...................Mt. Vernon, Tex.
Powell, Arthur Gray..................Blakely, Ga.
Powell, Joseph H...................Bridgeton, N. J.
Power, John.........................Escanaba, Mich.
Powers, J. N...............Salt Lake City, Utah
Prendergast, Joseph, M.D.............Chicago, Ill.
Prest, John E........................Cohoes, N. Y.
Preston, E. F...................San Francisco, Cal.
Preston, Joseph W., Jr..................Macon, Ga.
Price, Daniel T......................Yoakum, Tex.
Price, Sim T.........................St. Louis, Mo.
Price, William B......................Lincoln, Neb.
Price, William S.................Philadelphia, Pa.
Pritchett, H. C.....................Huntsville, Tex.
Public Library and Museum..........Dayton, Ohio
Quackenbush, A. W..................Stanberry, Mo.
Quick, W. H.....................Rockingham, N. C.
Quinn, Frank J........................Peoria, Ill.
Quinn, Lawrence R.................New York City
Rader, Perry S..................Jefferson City, Mo.
Ragland, H. Clay...................Logan, W. Va.
Rainey, Anson...........................Dallas, Tex.
Ralston, Jackson H.................Hyattsville, Md.
Ralston, Samuel M...................Lebanon, Ind.
Ralston, T. A.....................New York City
Ralston, Thomas E...................St. Louis, Mo.
Ramsland, O. T..................Sacred Heart, Minn.
Ranney, Henry C...................Cleveland, Ohio
Rathbun, W. A....................Springfield, Mo.
Ravenel, Rene..................Monks Corner, S. C.
Ray, Al.............................Charleston, Ill.
Read, Charles A......................Atlanta, Ga.
Rector, H. M., M.D.............Hot Springs, Ark.
Redd, Samuel C..........Beaver Dam P. O., Va.
Reid, James W.......................Lewiston, Idaho
Reid, Rev. J. L...................Bardstown, Ky.
Reid, Willard P.....................Babylon, N. Y.
Reifkogel, William................Plainview, Minn.
Reppy, Samuel A.....................De Soto, Mo.
Reuter, Dominic......................Trenton, N. J.
Reynolds, Walter D...............Philadelphia, Pa.
Rice, Charles E..................Wilkes-Barre, Pa.
Rich, Albert R........................Du Bois, Pa.
Richards, F. S..............Salt Lake City, Utah
Richardson, Edmund F...............Denver, Colo.
Rickards, Hon. J. E..................Butte, Mont.
Ricketts, A......................Wilkes-Barre, Pa.
Riddle, George D...................Pittsburg, Pa.
Riley, Harry I......................Pittsburg, Pa.
Riordan, T. J.........................Salinas, Cal.
Ritchie, Alfred G................Los Angeles, Cal.
Riviere, Georges Alphonse..............Mobile, Ala.
Roark, Joe Sam....................Valparaiso, Ind.
Roberts, John W....................Riverside, Cal.
Robertson, Andrew C................Pittsburg, Pa.
Robertson, George...................Mexico, Mo.
Robertson, James, Jr.................Washta, Iowa
Robertson, W. F..................Georgetown, Tex.
Robinson, C. W..................Newport News, Va.
Robinson, Edward M...................Mobile, Ala.
Robinson, George L. F.........Highmore, S. Dak.
Robinson, George R..............Minneapolis, Minn.
Robinson, H. R..................Minneapolis, Minn.
Robinson, Joe T........................Lonoke, Ark.
Robinson, M. L.......................Columbus, Ga.

Rochford, William E............Minneapolis, Minn.
Rodgers, James M................Watsonville, Cal.
Rogers, J. R......................Olympia, Wash.
Roote, Jesse B.......................Butte, Mont.
Rosenwald, David S.............Roswell, N. Mex.
Ross, P. A..............................Eustis, Fla.
Rubrecht, Franklin................Columbus, Ohio
Rush, J. S......................Des Moines, Iowa
Russel, Andrew...................Jacksonville, Ill.
Russell, William Hepburn..........New York City
Ryan, Joseph T....................New York City
Ryan, O'Neill......................St. Louis, Mo.
Ryan, T. C...........................Wausau, Wis.
Ryan, William J...................Menominee, Mich.
Rynearson, J. M..................La Fayette, Ind.
Sackett, Henry W.................New York City
Saffolds, W. S.........................Guyton, Ga.
Sale, Lee............................St. Louis, Mo.
Sample, A.........................Bloomington, Ill.
Sanders, George A................Springfield, Ill.
Sankey, R. A.........................Wichita, Kan.
Sargent, Brad V..................Salinas City, Cal.
Sargent, C. H......................Jefferson, Ohio
Savage, John H..................McMinnville, Tenn.
Savage, Michael...................Clarksville, Tenn.
Sawdey, D. A...........................Erie, Pa.
Sawyer, A. J..........................Lincoln, Neb.
Sawyer, A. L.....................Menominee, Mich.
Sawyer, John H.......................Auburn, N. Y.
Scales, S. S.........................Crawford, Miss.
Scarlett, James.......................Danville, Ill.
Scattergood, Caleb..............Philadelphia, Pa.
Schaefer, Charles..................Sedgwick, Kan.
Scharfer, E.............................Toccoa, Ga.
Schevers, A. J........................Chicago, Ill.
Schieck, Christian, Jr.............New York City
Schilling, A. J.......................Urbana, Ill.
Schilling, N....................Cedar Bayou, Tex.
Schlegel, Hon. Henry................Lapeer, Mich.
Schlichter, G. V..................Brooklyn, N. Y.
Schnell, L.......................St. Charles, Miss.
Schoenfeld, Rev. W...............New York City
Schroeder, James..................Guttenberg, Iowa
Schubert, C.......................Brooklyn, N. Y.
Schurnight, W. J.................Mishawaka, Ind.
Schultz, Irvine W...............Phillipsburg, N. J.
Scott, A. G..........................Chicago, Ill.
Scott, C. H..........................Elkins, W. Va.
Scott, George W...................Davenport, Iowa
Scott, Joseph.....................Los Angeles, Cal.
Scott, Tully..........................Oberlin, Kan.
Scott, W........................Clarksburg, W. Va.
Scott, Walter E., M.D..................Adel, Iowa
Scott, W. W., State Librarian.......Richmond, Va.
Seaberg, Hugo..................Springer, N. Mex.
Seabury, Samuel...................New York City
Searcy, Jefferson B.................Eminence, Mo.
Sebastian. James M.................Booneville, Ky.
Seiders, C. A.........................Toledo, Ohio
Seiss, Joseph A., D.D., LL.D.....Philadelphia, Pa.
Selby, T. J...........................Hardin, Ill.
Seney, Hon. Henry W................Toledo, Ohio
Sennott, John S., M.D.............Waterloo, Ill.
Sentinel of Liberty..................Chicago, Ill.
Sexton, H. A. J................Jefferson City, Mo.
Shabad, Henry M....................Chicago, Ill.
Shackleford, Thomas M...............Tampa, Fla.
Shaffer, C. W........................Emporium, Pa.
Shank, Corwin S....................Seattle, Wash.
Shannon, I. M.........................Clarion, Pa.
Shattuck, F. R...................Philadelphia, Pa.
Shaw, James H...................Bloomington, Ill.
Shaw, O. W............................Austin, Minn.
Sheard, Titus...................Little Falls, N. Y.
Shearman, Thomas G................Brooklyn, N. Y.
Sheean, David.........................Galena, Ill.
Sheeks, Ben.........................Tacoma, Wash.
Shelton, D. C............................Tulsa, I. T.
Shepherd, W. C.....................Hamilton, Ohio
Shepherd, William G............Seneca Falls, N. Y.
Sheppard, Howard R..............Philadelphia, Pa.
Shick, Robert P......................Reading, Pa.
Shields, Moses, Jr.................Nicholson, Pa.
Shime, Patrick C...................Spokane, Wash.
Shipp, C. J...........................Cordele, Ga.
Shirley, D. D.........................Allerton, Iowa
Shirley, Robert B.................Carlinville, Ill.
Short, John P......................Brooklyn, N. Y.
Shortz, Edwin....................Wilkes-Barre, Pa.
Sibley, Hiram S.....................Marietta, Ohio
Sidebottom, Earl E.............Santa Fe, N. Mex.
Silberman, Louis....................Albany, N. Y.
Silha, John A........................Chicago, Ill.
Sim, John R.......................New York City

Simms, A. H..........................Birmingham, Ala.
Simonds, C. H........................Conneaut, Ohio
Simonton, Dr. A. C....................Roslyn, Wash.
Simpson, William J., M.D..............Weston, Mo.
Sioux City Public Library............Sioux City, Iowa
Skelton, W. H........................Alvarado, Tex.
Skipworth, E. R......................Eugene, Ore.
Slack, Dr. Henry R...................La Grange, Ga.
Slater, W. T.........................Salem, Ore.
Slinkard, W. L.......................Bloomfield, Ind.
Sloan, J. R..........................Stanley, Kan.
Slocum, C. E., Jr....................Beatrice, Neb.
Slocum, Charles E., M.D., Ph.D.......Defiance, Ohio
Smith, Benjamin N....................Los Angeles, Cal.
Smith, Ephraim P.....................Yorkville, Tenn.
Smith, Gilbert D..................Middebourne, W. Va.
Smith, Harrison B....................Charleston, W. Va.
Smith, J. Alfred.....................Philadelphia, Pa.
Smith, J. P..........................Fort Worth, Tex.
Smith, Oscar B.......................Washington, Ga.
Smith, Quincy A......................Lansing, Mich.
Smith, W. Wickham....................Brooklyn, N. Y.
Smyth, David.........................Wichita, Kan.
Smythe, P. Henry.....................Burlington, Iowa
Snedeker, J. O.......................Marshall, Ill.
Snider, Millard F..................Clarksburg, W. Va.
Soliday, George W..................Carrington, N. Dak.
Solter, George A.....................Baltimore, Md.
Somermier, W. H......................Winfield, Kan.
Somers, James W......................San Diego, Cal.
Somerville, Robert...................Greenville, Miss.
Southall, E. W., M.D.................Geneseo, N. Y.
Spain, John A........................Sardis, Miss.
Spannhorst, Henry J..................St. Louis, Mo.
Sparr, R. W..........................Lawrence, Kan.
Spearman, Robert F...................Greenville, Tex.
Speer, D. R..........................Greenville, S. C.
Speer, James A.......................New York City
Spekker, Staas.......................Lewiston, Idaho
Spell, W. E..........................Hillsboro, Tex.
Spencer, H. N., M.D..................St. Louis, Mo.
Spencer, H. R........................Duluth, Minn.
Spencer, S. S........................Eugene, Ore.
Spencer, Thomas H....................Chicago, Ill.
Spencer, William W...............Indianapolis, Ind.
Spooner, Lewis C.....................Morris, Minn.
Sporer, Thomas D.....................Jacksboro, Tex.
Spratt, William E....................St. Joseph, Mo.
Sprigg, Joseph.......................Cumberland, Md.
Spriggs, J. P........................Woodfield, Ohio
Squire, William Russell..............New York City
Stahlman, E. C.......................Nashville, Tenn.
Standish, A. B.......................St. Ignace, Mich.
Stansel, M. L........................Carrollton, Ala.
Staples, John W......................Harriman, Tenn.
Starnes, P. M........................Des Moines, Iowa
Starrett, William R..................New York City
Steck, John M........................Winchester, Va.
Steckler, Louis......................New York City
Steele, Robert W.....................Denver, Colo.
Steenerson, H........................Crookston, Minn.
Stehle, Rev. Walter, O.S.B...........Allegheny, Pa.
Steinman, E. W.......................Belleville, Ill.
Stephens, H. A.......................Wallace, N. Y.
Stephenson, Albert G.................New York City
Stephenson, W. H.....................Hartington, Neb.
Sterrett, David......................Washington, Pa.
Stevens, B. J........................Madison, Wis.
Stewart, I. J........................Richfield, Utah
Stewart, William C...................Soapstone, Ala.
Stewart, W. E........................Clanton, Ala.
Stewart, Hon. William M..........Washington, D. C.
Stimpson, H. C. S....................New York City
Stites, O. W.........................Durham, N. C.
Stocker, R. M........................Honesdale, Pa.
Stoddart, George B...................Oyster Bay, N. Y.
Stokes, J. William...................Orangeburg, S. C.
Stone, Alfred Holt...................Greenville, Miss.
Stone, Russell J.....................Attica, N. Y.
Stone, William J.....................St. Louis, Mo.
Stonesipher, John R..................Zanesville, Ohio
Straka, Louis........................David City, Neb.
Stranahan, N. N......................Fulton, N. Y.
Strattan, Edward K...................Newcastle, Ind.
Strattan, Oliver H...................Louisville, Ky.
Street, Oliver Day...................Guntersville, Ala.
Street, Robert G.....................Galveston, Tex.
Strode, Aubrey E.....................Amherst, Va.
Strong, William J....................Chicago, Ill.
Stuart, Wesley A.....................Sturgis, S. Dak.
Sullivan, John J.....................New York City
Sulzer, Hon. William.................New York City
Summers, L. P........................Abingdon, Va.
Sumpter, Orlando H...................Hot Springs, Ark.

Sure, A. T. H........................Alameda, Cal.
Sutton, R. H., M.D...................Shenandoah, Iowa
Sutton, Robert L.....................Troy, Mo.
Sutton, W. Henry.....................Haverford, Pa.
Sweet, Silas C.......................Des Moines, Iowa
Swigart, Frank.......................Logansport, Ind.
Sydnor, Walker.......................Ashland, Va.
Sykes, M. L..........................New York City
Sypher, Gen. J. Hale.................Washington, D. C.
Syracuse Central Library.............Syracuse, N. Y.
Tadlock, J. M........................Phillipsburg, Kan.
Tait, A. O...........................Oakland, Cal.
Tartt, J. B..........................Terrell, Tex.
Tatum, I. R..........................Corsicana, Tex.
Tayloe, S. G.........................Sonora, Tex.
Taylor, Col. Charles H...............Boston, Mass.
Taylor, C. S.........................Keeseville, N. Y.
Taylor, Edward B.....................Pittsburg, Pa.
Taylor, G. F.........................Effingham, Ill.
Taylor, John H.......................Chillicothe, Mo.
Taylor, John L.......................Boonville, Ind.
Taylor, Hon. Thomas P................Bridgeport, Conn.
Taylor, Thomas T.....................Lake Charles, La.
Teall, Frank DeWitt..................Gettysburg, S. Dak.
Templer, James N.....................Muncie, Ind.
Ten Broeck, W. H.....................Paris, Ill.
Terrell, J. C., Jr...................Fort Worth, Tex.
Terrell, R. A........................Birmingham, Ala.
The Free Library of Philadelphia....Philadelphia, Pa.
Theobald, Thomas D...................Grayson, Ky.
The World............................New York City
Thiele, Theodore B...................Evanston, Ill.
Thomas, Alfred Jefferson.............Wooster, Ohio
Thompson, Cleveland C................Plattsburg, Mo.
Thompson, Col. J. K. P...............Rock Rapids, Iowa
Thompson, Oliver Silas, D.D..........Cherokee, Iowa
Thompson, Seymour D..................Brooklyn, N. Y.
Thompson, William D..................Racine, Wis.
Thompson, W. H.......................Grand Island, Neb.
Thorn, Samuel S., M.D................Toledo, Ohio
Thornburgh, A., M.D..................Chattanooga, Tenn.
Thorp, F. S..........................South Bend, Wash.
Thrift, J. E.........................Madison, Va.
Thurman, William J., M.D.............Lisbon, Ark.
Tileston, H. B., D.D.S...............Louisville, Ky.
Titus, Robert C......................Buffalo, N. Y.
Tobey, Walter L......................Hamilton, Ohio
Todd, Robert S.......................Owensboro, Ky.
Toler, Frank.........................Carbondale, Ill.
Tongue, Thomas H.....................Hillsboro, Ore.
Tompkins, Prof. Leslie J.............New York City
Toomer, John Sheldon.................Lake Charles, La.
Towne, Charles A.....................Duluth, Minn.
Trainor, P. F........................New York City
Trammell, John W.....................Oxford, Neb.
Travis, John W...................Traverse City. Mich.
Treacy, Daniel F.....................New York City
Trevvett, Herbert E..................Utica, N. Y.
Trewin, James H......................Lansing, Iowa
Trice, H. H..........................Norfolk, Va.
Trimble, James M.....................Montclair, N. J.
Tritch, Dr. J. C.....................Findlay, Ohio
Trueworthy, Dr. J. W.................Los Angeles, Cal.
Truitt, Warren.......................Moscow, Idaho
Tuchock, I. W........................Pueblo, Colo.
Tucker, C. H.........................Lawrence, Kan.
Tucker, Joseph T.....................Winchester, Ky.
Turley, Hon. Thomas B................Memphis, Tenn.
Turman, Solon T......................Tampa, Fla.
Turner. E. J.........................Washington, D. C.
Turner, I. Frank.....................Easton, Md.
Turner, Jesse........................Van Buren, Ark.
Turner, J. H.........................Henderson, Tex.
Turner, T. A.........................Jackson, Tenn.
Turney, Thomas E.....................Cameron, Mo
Tuttle, G. N.........................Painesville, Ohio
Tuttle, Dr. Jay......................Astoria, Ore.
Urlls, P. A......................So. Omaha, Neb.
Utopian Club Library.................Ballston Spa, N. Y.
Van Alstyne, P.......................New York City
Van Auken, M. W......................Utica, N. Y.
van Benschoten, H. L.................Belding, Mich.
Van Cott, Ray....................Salt Lake City, Utah
Van Deusen, Claudius.................Leeds, N. Y.
Van Etten, John E....................Kingston, N. Y.
Van Loo, C...........................Zeeland, Mich.
Van Sickle, W. L.....................Columbus, Ohio
Van Siclen, J. C.....................New York City
Van Vliet, Purdy.....................New York City
Van Wyck, Stephen....................New York City
Vaughan, Horace W....................Texarkana, Tex.
Vaughan, W. A., M.D..................Timberville, Va.
Veale, John W........................Amarillo, Tex.
Vernier, R. P........................Ansonia, Ohio

Vert, C. J...............Plattsburgh, N. Y.
Vickers, Carl B............New Comerstown, Ohio
Vincent, James U............Stephenville, Tex.
Virginia State Library............Richmond, Va.
Volger, Bernard G............Brooklyn, N. Y.
Volger, Theodore G............Park Ridge, N. J.
Vollmer, Henry............Davenport, Iowa
Vollrath, Edward............Bucyrus, Ohio
von Beust, Bernhard, M.D........New Albany, Ind.
Wakefield, Judge George W........Sioux City, Iowa
Wakeman, Prof. Thaddeus B., Liberal University,
............Silverton, Ore.
Walker, Frank............State Centre, Iowa
Walker, F. A., M.D............Norfolk, Va.
Walker, John F............Luverne, Ala.
Walker, Stuart W............Martinsburg, W. Va.
Wall, James A............Salinas, Cal.
Wallace, Richard T............New York City
Ward, A. D............New Bern, N. C.
Ward, C. A., Jr............Douglas, Ga.
Ward, Warren P............Douglas, Ga.
Warner, C. O............Beloit, Wis.
Warner, P. G............Red Bank, N. J.
Warren, George M............Swainsboro, Ga.
Wash, Frank H............San Antonio, Tex.
Wasson, J. E............Giltedge, Mont.
Waters, John H............Johnstown, Pa.
Watkins, Charles B............Clinton, Miss.
Watkins, O. W............Eureka Springs, Ark.
Watkins, R. A............Lancaster, Wis.
Watson, E. P............Bentonville, Ark.
Watson, John C............Nebraska City, Neb.
Watterson, Henry............Louisville, Ky.
Watts, Legh R............Portsmouth, Va.
Weadock, Thomas A. E............Detroit, Mich.
Weaver, William R............Philadelphia, Pa.
Webb, B. W............Fort Smith, Ark.
Webb, Dr. DeWitt............St. Augustine, Fla.
Weedon, L. W............Tampa, Fla.
Wehmeyer, Aug. H............Quincy, Ill.
Weinberg, Benjamin M............Newark, N. J.
Weinstock, H............Sacramento, Cal.
Weir, A. R............Au Sable, Mich.
Welborne, R. D............Chickasha, I. T.
Welbourn, E. L., M.D............Union City, Ind.
Welch, Aikman............St. Louis, Mo.
Welch, Judge Stanley............Corpus Christi, Tex.
Wellman, B. J............Fort Madison, Iowa
Wells, G. Wiley............Santa Monica, Cal.
Wells, R. H............Clarksville, Tex.
Welsh, John............New York City
Westbrook, M. H............Lyons, Iowa
Wester, J. K............Jacksboro, Tex.
Westerfield, William W............New Orleans, La.
Weston, Francis H............Columbia, S. C.
Wetmore, Hon. George Peabody....Newport, R. I.
Wetmore, J. Douglas............Jacksonville, Fla.
Wetmore, J. W............Erie, Pa.
Weygandt, C. N............Philadelphia, Pa.
Whalen, Frank............Ballston Spa, N. Y.
Whalen, Hon. John............New York City
Wheeler, B. A............Denver, Colo.
Wheeler, Charles H............Greeley, Colo.
Wheeler, W. C., M.D............Huntsville, Ala.
White, E. D............Livingston, Tenn.
White, Harry............Indiana, Pa.
White, Henry Kirk............Birmingham, Ala.
White, L. E............Columbus, Ga.

White, Lewis P............New Whatcom, Wash.
White, Robert E. L............Washington, D. C.
White, Samuel............Baker City, Ore.
White, W. H............Olympia, Wash.
White, Dr. William W............Cuero, Tex.
Whitecraft, John E............Macksville, Kan.
Whitehead, N. E............Greenwood, Miss.
Whitmore, John A............Acrora, Neb.
Whitney, Thomas H............Atlantic, Iowa
Wilcox, E. K............Cleveland, Ohio
Wilcox, H. D............Elmira, N. Y.
Wilcox, M. C............Oakland, Cal.
Wildermuth, P. A............Philadelphia, Pa.
Williams, James T............Greenville, S. C.
Williams, P. B............Rocky Comfort, Ark.
Willis, H. C............Norfolk, Va.
Willis, W. L............Houston, Tex.
Willits, J. Quincy............Lakeview, Ore.
Wilson, Edwin A............Springfield, Ill.
Wilson, N. V. F............Bridgeport, Ohio
Wilson, Stephen Eugene......Hot Springs, S. Dak.
Wilson, Sidney............Sherman, Tex.
Wilson, Thomas A............Jackson, Mich.
Wilson, Thomas E............Sylvan Lake, Fla.
Wilson, Thomas F............Tucson, Ariz.
Wilsson, M. T............Laurens, Iowa
Winborne, R. W............Buena Vista, Va.
Wing, John D............New York City
Wingo, Col. Charles E............Richmond, Va.
Winkler, F. C............Milwaukee, Wis.
Winne, Douglas T............Appleton, Wis.
Winship, John O............Cleveland, Ohio
Winslow, H. M............Carrollton, Ky.
Winter, Phil E............Omaha, Neb.
Witcover, H............Marion, S. C.
Withey, Charles A............Reed City, Mich.
Witmark, Isidore............New York City
Witter, William C............New York City
Wolverton, S. P............Sunbury, Pa.
Womack, Thomas B............Raleigh, N. C.
Wood, William P............Washington, D. C.
Wood, Will R............Lafayette, Ind.
Woodard, F. A............Wilson, N. C.
Woodard, John............Nashville, Tenn.
Woodring, James T............So. Bethlehem, Pa.
Woodward, C. S............Ballinger, Tex.
Woods, D. A............Kokomo, Ind.
Woolling, J. H............Indianapolis, Ind.
Worley, Joshua, M.D............Belle Plaine, Iowa
Wrenn, Rev. V............Amelia C. H., Va.
Wright, E. B............Boardman, N. C.
Wright, Eugene I............Chicago, Ill.
Wright, Lucius W............Chicago, Ill.
Wright, William B............Effingham, Ill.
Wyatt, W. F............Galena, Kan.
Yancey, John C............Batesville, Ark.
Yates, Benjamin............New York City
Yeaman, Caldwell............Denver, Colo.
Yerex, A. E............Chicago, Ill.
Yonge, Henry............Brooklyn, N. Y.
Young, Duncan F............Amite City, La.
Young, Hugh............Wellsboro, Pa.
Young, James R............Raleigh, N. C.
Zabel, John O............Petersburg, Mich.
Zallars, Allen............Fort Wayne, Ind.
Zang, William............Kewanee, Ill.
Zangerle, John A............Cleveland, Ohio
Zenk, Frederick G., M.D............Troy, Ill.

THE JEFFERSONIAN CYCLOPEDIA

PLAN OF THE WORK AND EXPLANATION
OF ABBREVIATIONS

Two editions of Jefferson's Writings have been utilized in the preparation of this volume. One of them is THE WRITINGS OF THOMAS JEFFERSON, edited by H. A. Washington and printed by the United States Congress in 1853–54. The other edition is THE WRITINGS OF THOMAS JEFFERSON, collected and edited by Paul Leicester Ford, and published by G. P. Putnam's Sons, 1892–99. The FORD EDITION contains a large number of valuable letters and papers which are not printed in the WASHINGTON EDITION, while the latter gives many letters that are not included by Mr. Ford in his volumes.

The quotations in THE JEFFERSONIAN CYCLOPEDIA are credited to both works if they contain them. Quotations with a single credit are printed only in the edition indicated.

There are, in addition, some quotations from the DOMESTIC LIFE OF JEFFERSON. These are marked D. L. J.

The name of the person written to is given after the extract as, under *Abuse*, "To EDWARD RUTLEDGE," then the volume and edition where found are given, as "iv, 151," refers to the WASHINGTON EDITION, while "FORD ED., viii, 93," is self-explanatory; next the place and date are given, as (M., Dec. 1796) = Monticello, Dec. 1796.

The names of places from which Jefferson wrote are abbreviated as follows:

Albemarle, Va.,	Alb.	Nice	Ne.
Annapolis,	A.	Nismes,	Ns.
Baltimore,	B.	Paris,	P.
Chesterfield, Va.,	Ches.	Philadelphia,	Pa.
Eppington, Va.,	Ep.	Popular Forest, Va.,	P.F.
Fairfield, Va.,	F.	Richmond,	R.
Germantown,	G.	Tuckahoe, Va.,	T.
London,	L.	Washington,	W.
Monticello,	M.	Williamsburg, Va.,	Wg.
New York,	N.Y.		

In the quotations the mark * * * indicates an omission in the text.

Words not in the text, but supplied by the Editor are, in all cases, enclosed within brackets.

THE

JEFFERSONIAN CYCLOPEDIA

1. ABILITIES, Appreciate.—I cannot help hoping that every friend of genius, when the other qualities of the competitor are equal, will give a preference to superior abilities.—To WILLIAM PRESTON. FORD ED., i, 368. (1768.)

2. ABILITIES, Attract.—Render the [State] executive a more desirable post to men of abilities by making it more independent of the legislature.—To ARCHIBALD STUART. iii, 315. FORD ED., v, 410. (Pa., 1791.)

3. ABILITIES, Education and.—It is often said there have been shining examples of men of great abilities, in all businesses of life, without any other science than what they had gathered from conversation and intercourse with the world. But, who can say what these men would not have been, had they started in the science on the shoulders of a Demosthenes or Cicero, of a Locke, or Bacon, or a Newton?—To JOHN BRAZIER. vii, 133. (1819.)

4. ABILITIES, Few Men of.—Men of high learning and abilities are few in every country: and by taking in [the judiciary] those who are not so, the able part of the body have their hands tied by the unable.—To ARCHIBALD STUART. iii, 315. FORD ED., v, 410. (Pa., 1791.) See ARISTOCRACY, TALENTS.

— ABLATIVE CASE IN GREEK.— See LANGUAGES.

— ABOLITION OF SLAVERY.—See SLAVERY.

5. ABORIGINES OF AMERICA, Derivation.—Whence came those aboriginals of America? Discoveries, long ago made, were sufficient to show that the passage from Europe to America was always practicable, even to the imperfect navigation of ancient times. In going from Norway to Iceland, from Iceland to Greenland, from Greenland to Labrador, the first traject is the widest; and this having been practised from the earliest times of which we have any account of that part of the earth, it is not difficult to suppose that the subsequent trajects may have been sometimes passed. Again, the late discoveries of Captain Cook, coasting from Kamchatka to California, have proved that if the two continents of Asia and America be separated at all, it is only by a narrow strait. So that from this side also, inhabitants may have passed into America; and the resemblance between the Indians of America and the eastern inhabitants of Asia, would induce us to conjecture, that the former are the descendants of the latter, or the latter of the former; excepting indeed the Esquimaux, who, from the same circumstance of resemblance, and from identity of language, must be derived from the Greenlanders, and these probably from some of the northern parts of the old continent.—NOTES ON VIRGINIA. viii, 344. FORD ED., iii, 205. (1782.)

6. ABORIGINES OF AMERICA, Languages.—A knowledge of their several languages would be the most certain evidence of their derivation which could be produced. In fact, it is the best proof of the affinity of nations which ever can be referred to. How many ages have elapsed since the English, the Dutch, the Germans, the Swiss, the Norwegians, Danes and Swedes have separated from their common stock? Yet how many more must elapse before the proofs of their common origin, which exist in their several languages will disappear? It is to be lamented, then, very much to be lamented, that we have suffered so many of the Indian tribes already to extinguish without our having previously collected and deposited in the records of literature, the general rudiments at most of the languages they spoke. Were vocabularies formed of all the languages spoken in North and South America, preserving their appellations of the most common objects in nature, of those which must be present to every nation barbarous or civilized, with the inflections of their nouns and verbs, their principles of regimen and concord, and these deposited in all the public libraries, it would furnish opportunities to those skilled in the languages of the old world to compare them with those, now, or at any future time, and hence to construct the best evidence of the derivation of their part of the human race.—NOTES ON VIRGINIA, viii, 344. FORD ED., iii, 206. (1782.)

7. —— —— The question whether the Indians of America have emigrated from another continent is still undecided. Their vague and imperfect traditions can satisfy no mind on that subject. I have long considered their languages as the only remaining monument of connection with other nations, or the want of it, to which we can now have access. They will likewise show their connection with one another.

Very early in life, therefore, I formed a vocabulary of such objects as, being present everywhere, would probably have a name in every language; and my course of life having given me opportunities of obtaining vocabularies of many Indian tribes, I have done so on my original plan, which, though far from being perfect, has the valuable advantage of identity, of thus bringing the languages to the same points of comparison. * * * The Indians west of the Mississippi and south of the Arkansas, present a much longer list of tribes than I had expected; and the relations in which you stand with them * * * induce me to hope you will avail us of your means of collecting their languages for this purpose.—To DR. SIBLEY. iv, 580. (W., 1805.)

8. —— —— I suppose the settlement of our continent is of the most remote antiquity. The similitude between its inhabitants and those of eastern parts of Asia renders it probable that ours are descended from them, or they from ours. The latter is my opinion, founded on this single fact: Among the red inhabitants of Asia, there are but a few languages radically different, but among our Indians, the number of languages is infinite, and they are so radically different as to exhibit at present no appearance of their having been derived from a common source. The time necessary for the generation of so many languages must be immense.—To EZRA STILES. FORD ED., iv, 298. (P., 1786.) See INDIANS.

— ABSENCE FROM THE CAPITAL.— See VACATION.

— ABSTINENCE.—See INTEMPERANCE.

9. ABUSE, Newspaper.—It is hardly necessary to caution you to let nothing of mine get before the public: a single sentence got hold of by the " Porcupines," * will suffice to abuse and persecute me in their papers for months.—To JOHN TAYLOR, iv, 248. FORD ED., vii, 266. (Pa., 1798.) See LIBELS, MINISTERS, NEWSPAPERS and SLANDER.

10. ABUSE, Personal.—You have seen my name lately tacked to so much of eulogy and of abuse that I dare say you hardly thought that it meant your old acquaintance of '76. In truth, I did not know myself under the pens either of my friends or foes. It is unfortunate for our peace that unmerited abuse wounds, while unmerited praise has not the power to heal. These are hard wages for the services of all the active and healthy years of one's life.—To EDWARD RUTLEDGE. iv, 151. FORD ED., vii, 93. (M., Dec. 1796.) See CALUMNY, LIBELS, MINISTERS, NEWSPAPERS and SLANDER.

11. —— —— If you had lent to your country the excellent talents you possess, on you would have fallen those torrents of abuse which have lately been poured forth on me. So far I praise the wisdom which has descried and steered clear of a waterspout ahead.—To EDWARD RUTLEDGE. iv, 152. FORD ED., vii, 94. (M., 1796.)

— ABUSE OF POWER.—See POWER.

— ABUSE OF THE PRESS.—See CALUMNY, LIBELS, NEWSPAPERS, and SLANDER.

*" Peter Porcupine " was the pen-name of William Cobbett.—EDITOR.

12. ABUSES, Arraignment of.—The arraignment of all abuses at the bar of public reason, I deem [one of the] essential principles of our government and consequently, [one] which ought to shape its administration. FIRST INAUGURAL ADDRESS. viii, 4. FORD ED., viii, 5. (1801.)

13. ABUSES, Barriers against.—We are to guard against ourselves; not against ourselves as we are, but as we may be; for who can now imagine what we may become under circumstances not now imaginable?—To JEDEDIAH MORSE. vii, 236. FORD ED., x, 206. (M., 1822.) .

14. ABUSES, The Constitution and.— In questions of power * * * let no more be heard of confidence in man, but bind him down from mischief by the chains of the Constitution.—KENTUCKY RESOLUTIONS. ix, 471. FORD ED., vii, 305. (1798.) See CONFIDENCE.

15. —— —— Aware of the tendency of power to degenerate into abuse, the worthies of our own country have secured its independence by the establishment of a Constitution and form of government for our nation, calculated to prevent as well as to correct abuse.—R. TO A WASHINGTON TAMMANY SOCIETY. viii, 156. (1809.)

16. ABUSES, Correction of.—My confidence is that there will for a long time be virtue and good sense enough in our countrymen to correct abuses.—To E. RUTLEDGE. ii, 435. FORD ED., v, 42. (P., 1788.)

17. ABUSES, Economy and.—The new government has now, for some time, been under way. Abuses under the old forms have led us to lay the basis of the new in a rigorous economy of the public contributions.— To M. DE PINTO. iii, 174. (N. Y., 1790.)

18. ABUSES, Education and.—Education is the true corrective of abuses of constitutional power.—To WILLIAM C. JARVIS. vii, 179. FORD ED., x, 161. (M.. 1820.)

19. ABUSES, Elections and.—A jealous care of the right of election by the people,— a mild and safe corrective of abuses which are lopped by the sword of revolution where peaceable remedies are unprovided, I deem [one of the] essential principles of our government and, consequently, [one] which ought to shape its administration.—FIRST INAUGURAL ADDRESS. viii, 4. FORD ED., viii, 4. (1801.)

20. ABUSES, Liability to.—What institution is insusceptible of abuse in wicked hands?—To L. H. GIRARDIN. vi, 440. FORD ED., ii, 151. (M., 1815.)

21. ABUSES, Monarchical.—Nor should we wonder at the pressure [for a fixed Constitution in France in 1788-9], when we consider the monstrous abuses of power under which this people were ground to powder, when we pass in review the weight of their taxes, and inequality of their distribution: the oppressions of the tithes, of the tailles,

the corvées, the gabelles, the farms and barriers: the shackles on commerce by monopolies: on industry by guilds and corporations: on the freedom of conscience, of thought, and of speech: on the press by the Censors and of person by *lettres de cachet;* the cruelty of the criminal code generally, the atrocities of the Rack, the venality of judges, and their partialities to the rich; the monopoly of military honors by the noblesse; the enormous expenses of the Queen, the princes and the court; the prodigalities of pensions: and the riches, luxury, indolence, and immorality of the clergy. Surely under such a mass of misrule and oppression, a people might justly press for a thorough reformation, and might even dismount their rough-shod riders, and leave them to walk on their own legs.—AUTOBIOGRAPHY. i, 86. FORD ED., i, 118. (1821.)

22. ABUSES, Patrimonies in.—Happy for us that abuses have not yet become patrimonies, and that every description of interest is in favor of rational and moderate government.—To RALPH IZARD. ii, 429. (P., 1788.)

— ABUSES OF POWER.—See POWER.

23. ABUSES, Revolution and.—When a long train of abuses and usurpations *begun at a distinguished period and* * pursuing invariably the same object, evinces a design to reduce them under absolute despotism, it is their right, it is their duty, to throw off such government, and to provide new guards for their future security.—DECLARATION OF INDEPENDENCE AS DRAWN BY JEFFERSON.

24. ABUSES, Temptations to.—Nor should our Assembly be deluded by the integrity of their own purposes, and conclude that these unlimited powers will never be abused, because themselves are not disposed to abuse them. They should look forward to a time, and that not a distant one, when corruption in this as in the country from which we derive our origin, will have seized the heads of government, and be spread by them through the body of the people; when they will purchase the voices of the people and make them pay the price. Human nature is the same on each side of the Atlantic, and will be alike influenced by the same causes. The time to guard against corruption and tyranny is before they shall have gotten hold of us. It is better keep the wolf out of the fold, than to trust to drawing his teeth and talons after he shall have entered. —NOTES ON VIRGINIA. viii, 362. FORD ED., iii, 224. (1782.)

25. ABUSES, Tendency to.—Mankind soon learns to make interested uses of every right and power which they possess, or may assume. The public money and public liberty * * * will soon be discovered to be sources of wealth and dominion to those who hold them; distinguished, too, by this tempting circumstance. that they are the instrument, as well as the object of acquisition. With money we will get men, said Cæsar, and with

* Congress struck out the words in italics.— EDITOR.

men we will get money.—NOTES ON VIRGINIA. viii, 362. FORD ED., iii, 224. (1782.)

26. ACADEMY (The Military), Beginning.—It was proposed [at a meeting of the cabinet] to recommend [in the President's speech to Congress] the establishment of a Military Academy. I objected that none of the specified powers given by the Constitution to Congress would authorize this. * * * The President [said], though it would be a good thing, he did not wish to bring on anything which might generate heat and ill humor. It was, therefore, referred for further consideration and inquiry. [At the next meeting] I opposed it as unauthorized by the Constitution. Hamilton and Knox approved it without discussion. Edmund Randolph was for it, saying that the words of the Constitution authorizing Congress to lay taxes &c., *for the common defence,* might comprehend it. The President said he would not choose to recommend anything against the Constitution; but if it was *doubtful,* he was so impressed with the necessity of this measure, that he would refer it to Congress, and let them decide for themselves whether the Constitution authorized it or not.—ANAS. ix, 182. FORD ED., i, 270. (Nov. 1793.)

27. ACADEMY (The Military), Enlargement.—The scale on which the Military Academy at West Point was originally established, is become too limited to furnish the number of well-instructed subjects in the different branches of artillery and engineering which the public service calls for. The want of such characters is already sensibly felt, and will be increased with the enlargement of our plans of military preparation. The chief engineer having been instructed to consider the subject, and to propose an augmentation which might render the establishment commensurate with the present circumstances of our country, has made the report I now transmit for the consideration of Congress.— SPECIAL MESSAGE. viii, 101. (March 1808.)

28. ACADEMY (The Military), Importance of.—I have ever considered that establishment as of major importance to our country, and in whatever I could do for it, I viewed myself as performing a duty only. * * * The real debt of the institution is to its able and zealous professors.—To JARED MANSFIELD. vii, 203. (M., 1821.)

29. ACADEMY (The Military), Removal.—The idea suggested by the chief engineer of removing the institution to this place [Washington], is worthy of attention. Beside the advantage of placing it under the immediate eye of the Government, it may render its benefits common to the naval department, and will furnish opportunities of selecting on better information. the characters most qualified to fulfil the duties which the public service may call for.—SPECIAL MESSAGE. viii, 101. (March 1808.)

30. ACADEMY, A National.—I have often wished we could have a Philosophical Society, or Academy, so organized as that while the central academy should be at the seat of government, its members dispersed over the States, should constitute filiated academies in each State, publish their communications, from which the Central Academy should select unpublished what should be most choice. In this way all the members, wheresoever dispersed, might be brought into action, and an useful emulation might arise between the filiated societies. Perhaps the great societies, now existing, might incorporate themselves in this way with the National one. To JOEL BARLOW. FORD ED., viii, 424. (Feb. 1806.)

31. ACADEMY, Need of a Naval.—I think * * * that there should be a school of instruction for our Navy as well as artillery; and I do not see why the same establishment might not suffice for both. Both require the same basis of general mathematics, adding projectiles and fortifications for the artillery exclusively, and astronomy and theory of navigation exclusively for the naval students. Berout conducted both schools in France, and has left us the best book extant for their joint and separate instruction. It ought not to require a separate professor.*—To JOHN ADAMS. vii, 218. (M., 1821.)

32. ACADEMY, Transfer of Geneva.—I * * * enclose for your perusal and consideration * * * the proposition of M. D'Ivernois, a Genevan of considerable distinction, to translate the Academy of Geneva in a body to this country. You know well that the colleges of Edinburgh and Geneva as seminaries of science, are considered as the two eyes of Europe. While Great Britain and America give the preference to the former, all other countries give it to the latter. I am fully sensible that two powerful obstacles are in the way of this proposition. First, the expense; secondly, the communication of science in foreign languages; that is to say, in French and Latin; but I have been so long absent from my own country as to be an incompetent judge either of the force of the objections, or of the disposition of those who are to decide on them. * * What I have to request of you is, that you will * * * consider his proposition, consult on its expediency and practicability with such gentlemen of the Assembly [of Virginia], as you think best, and take such other measures as you shall think best to ascertain what would be the sense of that body, were the proposition to be hazarded to them. If yourself and friends approve of it, and there is hope that the Assembly will do so, your zeal for the good of our country in general, and the promotion of science, as an instrument towards that, will, of course, induce you and them to bring it forward in such a way as you shall judge best. If, on the contrary, you disapprove of it yourselves, or think it would be desperate with the Assembly, be so good as to return it to me with such information as I may hand forward to M. D'Ivernois, to put the matter by all means out of the public papers, and particularly, * * * do not couple my name with the proposition if brought forward, because it is much my wish to be in nowise implicated in public affairs.—To WILSON NICHOLAS. iv, 109. FORD ED., vi, 513. (M., Nov. 1794.)

* The Naval Academy at Annapolis was opened in 1845. The credit of its foundation is due to George Bancroft, who was then Secretary of the Navy.— EDITOR.

33. ——. —— I have returned, with infinite appetite, to the enjoyment of my farm, my family and my books, and had determined to meddle in nothing beyond their limits. Your proposition, however, for transplanting the college of Geneva to my own country, was too analogous to all my attachments to science, and freedom, the first-born daughter of science, not to excite a lively interest in my mind, and the essays which were necessary to try its practicability. This depended altogether on the opinions and dispositions of our State Legislature, which was then in session. I immediately communicated your papers to a member of the Legislature, whose abilities and zeal pointed him out as proper for it, urging him to sound as many of the leading members of the Legislature as he could, and if he found their opinions favorable, to bring forward the proposition; but if he should find it desperate, not to hazard it; because I thought it best not to commit the honor either of our State or of your college, by an useless act of eclat. * * * The members were generally well-disposed to the proposition, and some of them warmly; however, there was no difference in the conclusion, that it could not be effected. The reasons which they thought would with certainty prevail against it, were 1, that our youth, not familiarized but with their mother tongue, were not prepared to receive instructions in any other; 2, that the expense of the institution would excite uneasiness in their constituents, and endanger its permanence; and 3, that its extent was disproportioned to the narrow state of the population with us. Whatever might be urged on these several subjects, yet as the decision rests with others, there remained to us only to regret that circumstances were such, or were thought to be such, as to disappoint your and our wishes.—To M. D'IVERNOIS. iv, 113. FORD ED., vii, 2. (M., Feb. 1795.)

34. ACADEMY, Wish for Geneva.—I should have seen with peculiar satisfaction the establishment of such a mass of science in my country, and should probably have been tempted to approach myself to it, by procuring a residence in its neighborhood, at those seasons of the year at least when the operations of agriculture are less active and interesting.—To M. D'IVERNOIS. iv, 114. FORD ED., vii, 4. (M., Feb. 1795.)

35. ACADEMIES, Architectural Reform.—I consider the common plan followed in this country, but not in others, of making one large and expensive building, as unfortunately erroneous. It is infinitely better to erect a small and separate lodge for each separate professorship, with only a hall below for his class, and two chambers above for himself; joining these lodges by barracks for a certain portion of the students, opening into a covered way to give a dry communication between all the schools. The whole of these arranged around an open square of grass and trees, would make it, what it should be in fact, an academical village, instead of a large and common den of noise, of filth and of fetid air. It would afford that quiet retirement so friendly to study, and lessen the dangers of fire, infection and tumult. Every professor would be the police officer of the students adjacent to his own lodge, which should include those of his own class of preference, if, as I suppose, it can be reconciled with the necessary economy to dine them in smaller and separate parties, rather than in a large and common mess. These separate buildings, too, might be erected successively and occasionally, as the number of professors and students should be increased, as the funds become competent.— To Hugh L. White. v, 521. (M., 1810.)

— ACCENT, The Greek.—See Languages.

36. ACCOUNTS, Complicated.—Alexander Hamilton * * * in order that he might have the entire government of his [Treasury] machine, determined so to complicate it as that neither the President nor Congress should be able to understand it, or to control him. He succeeded in doing this, not only beyond their reach, but so that he at length could not unravel it himself. He gave to the debt, in the first instance, in funding it, the most artificial and mysterious form he could devise. He then moulded up his appropriations of a number of scraps and remnants, many of which were nothing at all, and applied them to different objects in reversion and remainder, until the whole system was involved in impenetrable fog; and while he was giving himself the airs of providing for the payment of the debt, he left himself free to add to it continually, as he did in fact, instead of paying it.—To Albert Gallatin. iv, 428. Ford ed., viii, 140. (W., 1801.)

37. ACCOUNTS, Keeping.—All these articles are very foreign to my talents, and foreign also, as I conceive, to the nature of my duties. * * * I suppose it practicable for your board to direct the administration of your moneys here [Paris] in every circumstance.—To Samuel Osgood. i, 451. (P., 1785.)

38. ACCOUNTS, Neglected.—It is a fact, which we [Virginia] are to lament, that, in the earlier part of our struggles, we were so wholly occupied by the great object of establishing our rights, that we attended not at all to those little circumstances of taking receipts and vouchers, keeping regular accounts, and preparing subjects for future disputes with our friends. If we could have supported the whole Continent, I believe we should have done it, and never dishonored our nation by producing accounts; sincerely assured that, in no circumstances of future necessity or distress, a like free application of anything therein would have been thought hardly of, or would have rendered necessary an appeal to accounts. Hence, it has happened that, in the present case, the collection of vouchers of the arms furnished by this State has become tedious and difficult.—To the President of Congress. Ford ed., ii, 283. (W., 1779.)

39. ACCOUNTS, Simple.—The accounts of the United States ought to be, and may be made, as simple as those of a common farmer, and capable of being understood by common farmers.—To James Madison. iv, 131. Ford ed., vii, 61. (M., 1796.)

40. ———. If * * * [there] can be added a simplification of the form of accounts in the Treasury department, and in the organization of its officers, so as to bring everything to a single centre, we might hope to see the finances of the Union as clear and intelligible as a merchant's books, so that

every member of Congress, and every man of any mind in the Union, should be able to comprehend them, to investigate abuses, and consequently to control them. Our predecessors have endeavored by intricacies of system, and shuffling the investigation over from one officer to another, to cover everything from detection. I hope we shall go in the contrary direction. and that, by our honest and judicious reformations, we may be able in the limits of our time, to bring things back to that simple and intelligible system, on which they should have been organized at first.—To Albert Gallatin. iv, 429. Ford ed., viii, 141. (W., 1802.)

— ACQUISITION OF TERRITORY.— See Territory.

41. ACTIONS, Approved.—The very actions [on] which Mr. Pickering arraigns [me] have been such as the great majority of my fellow citizens have approved. The approbation of Mr. Pickering, and of those who thought with him [the Federalists], I had no right to expect.—To Martin Van Buren. vii, 363. Ford ed., x. 306. (M., 1824.)

42. ACTIONS, Disinterested.—I am conscious of having always intended to do what was best for my fellow citizens; and never, for a single moment, to have listened to any personal interest of my own.—To Richard M. Johnston. v, 256. (W., 1808.)

43. ——— ——— My public proceedings were always directed by a single view to the best interests of our country.—To Dr. E. Griffith. v, 450. (M., 1809.)

44. ——— ——— In the transaction of the [public] affairs I never felt one interested motive.—To W. Lambert. v, 450. (M., May 1809.)

45. ACTIONS, Government and.—The legislative powers of government reach actions only and not opinions.—R. to A. Danbury Baptist Address. viii, 113. (1802.)

46. ACTIONS, Honest Principles and.—Every honest man will suppose honest acts to flow from honest principles, and the rogues may rail without intermission.—To Dr. Benjamin Rush. iv, 426. Ford ed., viii, 128. (W., 1801.)

47. ACTIONS, Indulgent to.—I owe infinite acknowledgments to the republican portion of my fellow citizens for the indulgence with which they have viewed my proceedings generally.—To W. Lambert. v, 450. (M., May 1809.) See Disinterestedness.

48. ACTIONS, Judgment and.—Upwards of thirty years passed on the stage of public life and under the public eye. may surely enable them to judge whether my future course is likely to be marked with those departures from reason and moderation, which the passions of men have been willing to foresee.—To William Jackson. iv, 358. (M., 1801.)

49. ACTIONS, Lawful.—Every man should be protected in his lawful acts.—To ISAAC MCPHERSON. vi, 175. (M., 1813.)

50. ACTIONS, Present and future.—Our duty is to act upon things as they are, and to make a reasonable provision for whatever they may be.—SIXTH ANNUAL MESSAGE. viii, 69. FORD ED., viii, 405. (Dec. 1806.)

51. ACTIONS, Publicity and.—I fear no injury which any man can do me. I have never done a single act, or been concerned in any transaction, which I fear to have fully laid open, or which could do me any hurt if truly stated. I have never done a single thing with a view to my personal interest, or that of any friend, or with any other view than that of the greatest public good; therefore, no threat or fear on that head will ever be a motive of action with me. *—ANAS. ix, 209. FORD ED., i, 312. (1806.)

52. ACTIONS, Purity of.—I can conscientiously declare that as to myself, I wish that not only no act but no thought of mine should be unknown.—To JAMES MAIN. v. 373. (W., 1808.)

53. ACTIONS, Right.—The precept of Providence is, to do always what is right, and leave the issue to Him.—To MRS. COSWAY. ii, 41. FORD ED., iv. 320. (P., 1786.)

54. ACTIONS, Rule for.—Whenever you are to do a thing, though it can never be known but to yourself, ask yourself how you would act were all the world looking at you, and act accordingly.†—To PETER CARR. i, 396. (Ps., 1785.)

55. —— —— When tempted to do anything in secret, ask yourself if you would do it in public; if you would not, be sure it is wrong.‡—To FRANCIS EPPES. D. L. J. 365.

56. ACTIONS, Virtuous.—If no action is to be deemed virtuous for which malice can imagine a sinister motive, then there never was a virtuous action; no, not even in the life of our Saviour Himself. But He has taught us to judge the tree by its fruit, and to leave motives to Him who can alone see into them.—To MARTIN VAN BUREN. vii, 363. FORD ED., x, 307 (M., 1824.)

— ADAIR (James), Views on Indians.—See INDIANS.

57. ADAMS (John), Administration of.—If the understanding of the people could be rallied to the truth on the subject [of the French negotiations and the X. Y. Z. plot,]§ by exposing the deception practiced on them, there are so many other things about to bear on them favorably for the resurrection of their republican spirit, that a reduction of the administration to constitutional principles cannot fail to be the effect. There are the

* Aaron Burr, in asking Jefferson for office, intimated that he could do Jefferson "much harm." This was Jefferson's defiance.—EDITOR.
† Peter Carr was the young nephew of Jefferson.—EDITOR.
‡ Francis Eppes was a grandson, then at school.—EDITOR.
§ See X. Y. Z. plot *post*.—EDITOR.

Alien and Sedition laws, the vexations of the stamp act, the disgusting particularities of the direct tax, the additional army without an enemy, and recruiting officers lounging at every court house, a navy of fifty ships, five millions to be raised to build it, on the ruinous interest of eight per cent., the perseverance in war on our part, when the French government shows such an anxious desire to keep at peace with us, taxes of ten millions now paid by four millions of people, and yet a necessity, in a year or two, of raising five millions more for annual expenses. Those things will immediately be bearing on the public mind, and if it remain not still blinded by a supposed necessity, for the purpose of maintaining our independence and defending our country, they will set things to rights. I hope you will undertake this statement.—To EDMUND PENDLETON. iv, 275. FORD ED., vii, 337. (Pa., Jan. 1799.) See 1056.

58. —— —— We were far from considering you as the author of all the measures we blamed. They were placed under the protection of your name, but we were satisfied they wanted much of your approbation. We ascribed them to their real authors, the Pickerings, Wolcotts, the Tracys, the Sedgwicks, *et id genus omne*, with whom we supposed you in a state of duresse. I well remember in a conversation with you in the morning of the day on which you nominated to the Senate a substitute for Pickering, in which you expressed a just impatience under "the legacy of secretaries which General Washington had left you," and whom you seemed, therefore, to consider as under public protection. Many other incidents showed how differently you would have acted with less impassioned advisers; and subsequent events have proved that your minds were not together. You would do me great injustice, therefore, by taking to yourself what was intended for men who were then your secret, as they are now your open enemies.—To JOHN ADAMS. vi, 126. FORD ED., ix, 387. (M., June 1813.)

— ADAMS (John), Aristocracy and.—See ARISTOCRACY.

59. ADAMS (John), Attacks on.—With respect to the calumnies and falsehoods which writers and printers at large published against Mr. Adams, I was as far from stooping to any concern or approbation of them, as Mr. Adams was respecting those of "Porcupine," Fenno, or Russell, who published volumes against me for every sentence vended by their opponents against Mr. Adams. But I never supposed Mr. Adams had any participation in the atrocities of these editors, or their writers. I knew myself incapable of that base warfare, and believed him to be so. On the contrary, whatever I may have thought of the acts of the administration of that day, I have ever borne testimony to Mr. Adams's personal worth; nor was it ever impeached in my presence, without a just vindication of it on my part. I never supposed that any person who knew either of us, could believe that either of us meddled in that dirty work.—To Mrs. John Adams. iv, 555. Ford ed., viii, 309. (W., July 1804.)

60. —— —— Mr. Adams has been alienated from me, by belief in the lying suggestions contrived for electioneering purposes, that I perhaps mixed in the activity and intrigues of the occasion. My most intimate friends can testify that I was perfectly passive. They would sometimes, indeed, tell me what was going on; but no man ever heard me take part in such conversations; and none ever misrepresented Mr. Adams in my presence, without my asserting his just character. With very confidential persons I have doubtless disapproved of the principles and practices of his administration. This was unavoidable. But never with those with whom it could do him any injury. Decency would have required this conduct from me, if disposition had not, and I am satisfied Mr. Adams's conduct was equally honorable towards me. But I think it part of his character to suspect foul play in those of whom he is jealous, and not easily to relinquish his suspicions.—To Dr. Benjamin Rush. v, 563. Ford ed., ix, 299. (M., Jan. 1811.)

61. ADAMS (John), Character.—He is vain, irritable, and a bad calculator of the force and probable effect of the motives which govern men. This is all the ill which can possibly be said of him. He is as disinterested as the Being who made him. He is profound in his views, and accurate in his judgment, except where knowledge of the world is necessary to form a judgment. He is so amiable that I pronounce you will love him, if ever you become acquainted with him. He would be, as he was, a great man in Congress.—To James Madison. ii, 107. (P., 1787.)

62. —— —— His vanity is a lineament in his character which had entirely escaped me. His want of taste I had observed. Notwithstanding all this he has a sound head on substantial points, and I think he has integrity.—To James Madison. Ford ed., iii, 309. (B., Feb. 1783.)

63. —— —— The President's title, as proposed by the Senate, was the most superlatively ridiculous thing I ever heard of. It is a proof the more of the justice of the character given by Dr. Franklin of my friend. Always an honest man, often a great one, but sometimes absolutely mad.—To James Madison. Ford ed., v, 104. (P., July 1789.)

64. ADAMS (John), Declaration of Independence and.—John Adams was the pillar of its [Declaration of Independence] support on the floor of Congress; its ablest advocate and defender against the multifarious assaults it encountered. For many excellent persons opposed it on doubts whether we were provided sufficiently with the means of supporting it, whether the minds of our constituents were yet prepared to receive it &c., who, after it was decided, united zealously in the measures it called for.—To William P. Gardner. Ford ed., ix, 377. (M., 1813.)

65. —— —— He supported the Declaration with zeal and ability, fighting fearlessly for every word of it. No man's confident and fervent addresses, more than Mr. Adams's encouraged and supported us through the difficulties surrounding us, which, like the ceaseless action of gravity, weighed on us by night and by day. *—To James Madison. vii, 305. Ford ed., x, 268. (M., 1823.)

66. —— ——. His deep conceptions, nervous style, and undaunted firmness, made him truly our bulwark in debate.—To Samuel A. Wells. i, 121. Ford ed., x, 131. (M., 1819.) See Declaration of Independence.

67. ADAMS (John), Departure from Europe.—I learn with real pain the resolution you have taken of quitting Europe. Your presence on this side the Atlantic gave me a confidence that, if any difficulties should arise within my department, I should always have one to advise with on whose counsels I could rely. I shall now feel bewidowed. I do not wonder at your being tired out by the conduct of the court you are at.—To John Adams. ii, 127. (P., 1787.)

— ADAMS (John), France and.—See France.

68. ADAMS (John), Friendship of Jefferson for.—Mr. Adams's friendship and mine began at an early date. It accompanied us through long and important scenes. The different conclusions we had drawn from our political reading and reflections, were not permitted to lessen personal esteem; each party being conscious they were the result of an honest conviction in the other. Like differences of opinion existing among our fellow citizens, attached them to one or the other of us, and produced a rivalship in their minds which did not exist in ours. We never stood in one another's way; for if either had been withdrawn at any time, his favorers would not have gone over to the other, but would have sought for some one of homogeneous opinions. This consideration was sufficient to keep down all jealousy between us, and to guard our friendship from any disturbance by sentiments of rivalship.†—To Mrs. John Adams. iv, 545. Ford ed., viii, 306. (W., June 1804.)

69. —— ——. I write you this letter as due to a friendship coeval with our government, and now attempted to be poisoned, when too late in life to be replaced by new affections. I had for some time observed in the public papers, dark hints and mysterious innuendoes of a correspondence of yours with a friend, to whom you had opened your bosom without reserve, and which was to be made public by that friend or

* Daniel Webster visited Jefferson at Monticello toward the close of 1824. He quoted Jefferson as having then said in conversation: "John Adams was our Colossus on the floor. He was not graceful, nor elegant, nor remarkably fluent; but he came out, occasionally, with a power of thought and expression that moved us from our seats." Webster introduced the quotation in his speech on "Adams and Jefferson," August 2, 1826. The conversation entire is printed in the *Private Correspondence of Webster* (i, 364), and in the Ford ed. of Jefferson's Writings, x, 327.—Editor.
† A reference to the "Midnight Appointments"of Mr. Adams in this letter led Mrs. Adams to make a spirited attack on Jefferson's administration. Jefferson's reply, and also his correspondence with Dr. Rush, which led to a reconciliation with Mr. Adams will be found in the Appendix to this volume.—Editor.

his representative. And now it is said to be actually published. It has not yet reached us, but extracts have been given, and such as seemed most likely to draw a curtain of separation between you and myself. Were there no other motive than that of indignation against the author of this outrage on private confidence, whose shaft seems to have been aimed at yourself more particularly, this would make it the duty of every honorable mind to disappoint that aim, by opposing to its impression a sevenfold shield of apathy and insensibility. With me, however, no such armor is needed. The circumstances of the times in which we have happened to live, and the partiality of our friends at a particular period, placed us in a state of apparent opposition, which some might suppose to be personal also; and there might not be wanting those who wished to make it so, by filling our ears with malignant falsehoods, by dressing up hideous phantoms of their own creation, presenting them to you under my name, to me under yours, and endeavoring to instil into our minds things concerning each other the most destitute of truth. And if there had been, at any time, a moment when we were off our guard, and in a temper to let the whispers of these people make us forget what we had known of each other for so many years, and years of so much trial, yet all men who have attended to the workings of the human mind, who have seen the false colors under which passion sometimes dresses the actions and motives of others, have seen also those passions subsiding with time and reflection, dissipating like mists before the rising sun, and restoring to us the sight of all things in their true shape and colors. It would be strange, indeed, if, at our years, we were to go back an age to hunt up imaginary or forgotten facts, to disturb the repose of affections so sweetening to the evening of our lives. Be assured, my dear sir, that I am incapable of receiving the slightest impression from the effort now made to plant thorns on the pillow of age, worth and wisdom, and to sow tares between friends who have been such for near half a century. Beseeching you, then, not to suffer your mind to be disquieted by this wicked attempt to poison its peace, and praying you to throw it by among the things which have never happened, I add sincere assurances of my unabated and constant attachment, friendship and respect.— To JOHN ADAMS. vii, 314. FORD ED., x, 273. (M., 1823.)

70. —— ——. Fortune had disjointed our first affections, and placed us in opposition in every point. This separated us for awhile. But on the first intimation through a friend, we re-embraced with cordiality, recalled our ancient feelings and dispositions, and everything was forgotten but our first sympathies.— I bear ill-will to no human being.—To JAMES MONROE. FORD ED., x, 298. (M., 1824.)

71. ADAMS (John), George III. and.— The sentiments you expressed [in your address on presentation to the King] were such as were entertained in America till the commercial proclamation, and such as would again return were a rational conduct to be adopted by Great Britain. I think, therefore, you by no means compromised yourself, or our country, nor expressed more than it would be our interest to encourage, if they were disposed to meet us.—To JOHN ADAMS. i, 436. (P., September 1785.)

72. ADAMS (John), Honesty.—I have the same good opinion of Mr. Adams which I ever had. I know him to be an honest man, an able one with his pen, and he was a powerful advocate on the floor of Congress.—To DR. BENJAMIN RUSH. v, 562. FORD ED., ix, 298. (M., 1811.)

73. ADAMS (John), Integrity.—Though I saw that our ancient friendship was affected by a little leaven, produced partly by his constitution, partly by the contrivance of others, yet I never felt a diminution of confidence in his integrity, and retained a solid affection for him. His principles of government I knew to be changed, but conscientiously changed.— To JAMES MADISON. iv, 161. FORD ED., vii, 108. (M., Jan. 1797.)

74. ADAMS (John), Jefferson and Election of.—The public and the papers have been much occupied lately in placing us in a point of opposition to each other. I trust with confidence that less of it has been felt by ourselves personally. In the retired canton where I am, I learn little of what is passing; pamphlets I never see; papers but a few, and the fewer the happier. Our latest intelligence from Philadelphia at present is of the 16th inst., but though at that date your election to the first magistracy seems not to have been known as a fact, yet with me it has never been doubted. I knew it impossible you should lose a vote North of the Delaware, and even if that of Pennsylvania should be against you in the mass, yet that you would get enough South of that to place your succession out of danger. I have never one single moment expected a different issue; and though I know I shall not be believed, yet it is not the less true that I have never wished it. My neighbors as my compurgators could aver that fact, because they see my occupations and my attachment to them. Indeed it is impossible that you may be cheated of your succession by a trick worthy the subtlety of your arch-friend of New York [Alexander Hamilton] who has been able to make of your real friends tools to defeat their and your just wishes. Most probably he will be disappointed as to you; and my inclinations place me out of his reach. I leave to others the sublime delights of riding in the storm, better pleased with sound sleep and a warm berth below, with the society of neighbors, friends and fellow-laborers of the earth, than of spies and sycophants. No one then will congratulate you with purer disinterestedness than myself. The share, indeed, which I may have had in the late vote, I shall value highly as an evidence of the share I have in the esteem of my fellow citizens. But while in this point of view, a few votes less would be little sensible, the difference in the effect of a few more would be very sensible and oppressive to me. I have no ambition to govern men. It is a painful and thankless office. Since the day, too, on which you signed the treaty of Paris our horizon was never so overcast. I devoutly wish you may be able to shun for us this war by which our agriculture, commerce and credit will be destroyed. If you are, the glory will be all your own; and that your administration may be filled with glory, and happiness to yourself and advantage to us is the sincere wish of one

who, though in the course of our own voyage through life various little incidents have happened or been contrived to separate us, retains still for you the solid esteem of the moments when we were working for our independence, and sentiments of respect and affectionate attachment.*—To JOHN ADAMS. iv, 153. FORD ED., vii, 95. (Dec. 28, 1796.)

75. —— ——. Mr. Adams and myself were cordial friends from the beginning of the Revolution. Since our return from Europe, some little incidents have happened, which were capable of affecting a jealous mind like his. His deviation from that line of politics on which we had been united, has not made me less sensible of the rectitude of his heart; and I wished him to know this, and also another truth, that I am sincerely pleased at having escaped the late draft for the helm, and have not a wish which he stands in the way of. That he should be convinced of these truths, is important to our mutual satisfaction, and perhaps to the harmony and good of the public service. But there was a difficulty in conveying them to him, and a possibility that the attempt might do mischief there or somewhere else; and I would not have hazarded the attempt, if you had not been in place to decide upon its expediency.—To JAMES MADISON. iv, 166. FORD ED., vii, 115. (M., Jan. 1797.)

76. —— ——. You express apprehensions that stratagems will be used to produce a misunderstanding between the President and myself. Though not a word having this tendency has ever been hazarded to me by anyone, yet I consider as a certainty that nothing will be left untried to alienate him from me. These machinations will proceed from the Hamiltonians by whom he is surrounded, and who are only a little less hostile to him than to me. It cannot but damp the pleasure of cordiality when we suspect that it is suspected. I cannot help thinking that it is impossible for Mr. Adams to believe that the state of my mind is what it really is: that he may think I view him as an obstacle in my way. I have no supernatural power to impress truth on the mind of another, nor he any to discover that the estimate he may form, on a just view of the human mind as generally constituted, may not be just in its application to a special constitution. This may be a source of private uneasiness to us; I honestly confess that it is so to me at this time. But neither of us is capable of letting it have effect on our public duties. Those who may endeavor to separate us, are probably excited by the fear that I might have influence on the Executive councils; but when they shall know that I con-

* Jefferson sent this letter to Madison who decided that it would be inexpedient to forward it to Adams. "I am very thankful," Jefferson wrote to Madison in January, 1797 (iv, 166, FORD ED., vii, 115), "for the discretion you have exercised over the letter. That has happened to be the case, which I knew to be possible, that the honest expression of my feelings towards Mr. Adams might be rendered *malapropos* from circumstances existing, and known at the seat of government, but not known by me in my retired situation."—EDITOR.

sider my office as constitutionally confined to legislative functions, and that I could not take any part whatever in executive consultations, even were it proposed, their fears may perhaps subside, and their object be found not worth a machination.—To ELBRIDGE GERRY. iv, 171. FORD ED., vii, 120. (May 1797.)

77. ADAMS (John), Jefferson's Election and.—The nation passed condemnation on the political principles of the federalists, by refusing to continue Mr. Adams in the Presidency. On the day on which we learned in Philadelphia the vote of the city of New York, which it was well known would decide the vote of the State, and that, again, the vote of the Union, I called on Mr. Adams on some official business. He was very seriously affected, and accosted me with these words: "Well, I understand that you are to beat me in this contest, and I will only say that I will be as faithful a subject as any you will have." "Mr. Adams," said I, "this is no personal contest between you and me. Two systems of principles on the subject of government divide our citizens into two parties. With one of these you concur, and I with the other. As we have been longer on the public stage than most of those now living, our names happen to be more generally known. One of these parties, therefore, has put your name at its head, the other mine. Were we both to die to-day, to-morrow two other names would be in the place of ours, without any change in the motion of the machinery. Its motion is from its principle, and not from you or myself." "I believe you are right," said he, "that we are but passive instruments, and should not suffer this matter to affect our personal dispositions." But he did long retain this just view of the subject. I have always believed that the thousand calumnies which the federalists, in bitterness of heart, and mortification at their ejection, daily invented against me, were carried to him by their busy intriguers, and made some impression.—To DR. BENJAMIN RUSH. v, 560. FORD ED., ix, 296. (M., Jan. 1811.)

78. —— ——. When the election between Burr and myself was kept in suspense by the federalists, and they were meditating to place the President of the Senate at the head of the government, I called on Mr. Adams with a view to have this desperate measure prevented by his negative. He grew warm in an instant, and said with a vehemence he had not used towards me before: "Sir, the event of the election is within your own power. You have only to say you will do justice to the public creditors, maintain the navy, and not disturb those holding offices, and the government will instantly be put into your hands. We know it is the wish of the people it should be so." "Mr. Adams," said I, "I know not what part of my conduct, in either public or private life, can have authorized a doubt of my fidelity to the public engagements. I say, however, I will not come into the government by capitulation. I will not enter on it, but in

perfect freedom to follow the dictates of my own judgment." I had before given the same answer to the same intimation from Gouverneur Morris. "Then," said he, "things must take their course." I turned the conversation to something else, and soon took my leave. It was the first time in our lives we had ever parted with anything like dissatisfaction.—To DR. BENJAMIN RUSH. v, 561. FORD ED., ix, 297. (M., Jan. 1811.)

79. ADAMS (John), Jefferson, Paine and.—I am afraid the indiscretion of a printer has committed me with my friend Mr. Adams, for whom, as one of the most honest and disinterested men alive, I have a cordial esteem, increased by long habits of concurrence in opinion in the days of his republicanism: and even since his apostasy to hereditary monarchy and nobility, though we differ, we differ as friends should do. Beckley had the only copy of Paine's pamphlet [Rights of Man], and lent it to me, desiring when I should read it, that I would send it to a Mr. J. B. Smith, who had asked it for his brother to reprint it. Being an utter stranger to J. B. Smith, both by sight and character, I wrote a note to explain to him why I (a stranger to him) sent him a pamphlet, to wit, that Mr. Beckley had desired it; and to take off a little of the dryness of the note, I added that I was glad to find it was to be reprinted, that something would, at length, be publicly said against the political heresies which had lately sprung up among us, and that I did not doubt our citizens would rally again round the standard of "Common Sense." That I had in my view the "Discourses on Davila," which have filled Fenno's papers for a twelvemonth, without contradiction, is certain, but nothing was ever further from my thoughts than to become myself the contradictor before the public. To my great astonishment, however, when the pamphlet came out, the printer had prefixed my note to it, without having given me the most distant hint of it. Mr. Adams will unquestionably take to himself the charge of political heresy, as conscious of his own views of drawing the present government to the form of the English constitution, and, I fear, will consider me as meaning to injure him in the public eye. I learn that some Anglo-men have censured it in another point of view, as a sanction of Paine's principles tends to give offence to the British government. Their real fear, however, is that this popular and republican pamphlet, taking wonderfully, is likely at a single stroke, to wipe out all the unconstitutional doctrines which their bell-weather, "Davila," has been preaching for a twelvemonth. I certainly never made a secret of my being anti-monarchical, and anti-aristocratical; but I am sincerely mortified to be thus brought forward on the public stage, where to remain, to advance or to retire, will be equally against my love of silence and quiet, and my abhorrence of dispute.—To PRESIDENT WASHINGTON. iii, 257. FORD ED., v, 329. (Pa., 1791.)

80. ———— ————. I have a dozen times taken up my pen to write to you, and as often laid it down again, suspended between opposing considerations. I determine, however, to write from a conviction that truth, between candid minds, can never do harm. The first of Paine's pamphlets on the "Rights of Man," which come to hand here, belonged to Mr. Beckley. He lent it to Mr. Madison, who lent it to me; and while I was reading it, Mr. Beckley called on me for it, and, as I had not finished it,

he desired me, as soon as I should have done so, to send it to Mr. Jonathan B. Smith, whose brother meant to reprint it. I finished reading it, and, as I had no acquaintance with Mr. Jonathan B. Smith, propriety required that I should explain to him why I, a stranger to him, sent him the pamphlet. I accordingly wrote a note of compliment, informing him that I did it at the desire of Mr. Beckley, and, to take off a little of the dryness of the note, I added that I was glad it was to be reprinted here, and that something was to be publicly said against the political heresies which had sprung up among us, &c. I thought so little of this note, that I did not even keep a copy of it; nor ever heard a tittle more of it, till, the week following, I was thunderstruck with seeing it come out at the head of the pamphlet.* I hoped, however, it would not attract notice. But I found, on my return from a journey of a month, that a writer came forward, under the signature of "Publicola," attacking not only the author and principles of the pamphlet, but myself as its sponsor, by name. Soon after came hosts of other writers, defending the pamphlet, and attacking you, by name, as the writer of "Publicola." Thus were our names thrown on the public stage as public antagonists. That you and I differ in our ideas of the best forms of government, is well known to us both; but we have differed as friends should do, respecting the purity of each other's motives, and confining our difference of opinion to private conversation. And I can declare with truth, in the presence of the Almighty, that nothing was further from my intention or expectation than to have either my own or your name brought before the public on this occasion. The friendship and confidence which have so long existed between us, required this explanation from me, and I know you too well to fear any misconstruction of the motives of it. Some people here who would wish me to be, or to be thought, guilty of improprieties, have suggested that I was "Agricola," that I was "Brutus," &c., &c. I never did in my life, either by myself or by any other, have a sentence of mine inserted in a newspaper without putting my name to it; and I believe I never shall.—To JOHN ADAMS. iii, 270. FORD ED., v, 353. (Pa., 1791.)

81. ———— ————. I was happy to find that you saw in its true point of view the way in which I had been drawn into the scene, which must have been so disagreeable to you. The importance which you still seem to allow to my note, and the effect you suppose it to have had, though unintentional in me, induce me to show you that it really had no effect. Paine's pamphlet, with my note, was published here about the second week in May. Not a word ever appeared in the public papers here [Philadelphia] on the subject for more than a month; and I am certain not a word on the subject would ever have been said, had not a writer, under the name "Publicola" [John, Quincy Adams] at length undertaken to attack Mr. Paine's principles, which were the principles of the citizens of the United States. Instantly a host of writers attacked "Publicola" in support

* The note was as follows: "After some prefatory remarks, the Secretary of State, Mr. Jefferson, in a note to a Printer in Philadelphia, accompanying a copy of this Pamphlet for republication observes: 'I am extremely pleased to find it will be reprinted here, and that something is at length to be publicly said against the political heresies which have sprung up among us. I have no doubt our citizens will rally a second time round the standard of Common Sense.'"—EDITOR.

of those principles. He had thought proper to misconstrue a figurative expression in my note; and these writers so far noticed me as to place the expression in its true light. But this was only an incidental skirmish preliminary to the general engagement, and they would not have thought me worth naming, had he not thought proper to have brought me on the scene. His antagonists, very criminally, in my opinion, presumed you to be "Publicola," and on that presumption hazarded a personal attack on you. No person saw with more uneasiness than I did, this unjustifiable assault; and the more so, when I saw it continued after the printer had declared you were not the author. But you will perceive from all this, my dear sir, that my note contributed nothing to the production of these disagreeable pieces. As long as Paine's pamphlet stood on its own feet and on my note, it was unnoticed. As soon as "Publicola" attacked Paine, swarms appeared in his defence. To "Publicola," then, and not in the least degree to my note, this whole contest is to be ascribed and all its consequences. You speak of the execrable paragraph in the Connecticut papers. This, it is true, appeared before "Publicola"; but it has no more relation to Paine's pamphlet and my note than to the Alcoran. I am satisfied the writer of it had never seen either; for when I passed through Connecticut about the middle of June, not a copy had ever been seen by anybody, either in Hartford or New Haven, nor probably in that whole State: and that paragraph was so notoriously the reverse of the disinterestedness of character which you are known to possess by everybody who knows your name, that I never heard a person speak of the paragraph, but with an indignation in your behalf, which did you entire justice. This paragraph, then, certainly did not flow from my note, any more than the publications which "Publicola" produced. Indeed it was impossible that my note should occasion your name to be brought into question; for so far from meaning you, I had not even in view any writing which I might suppose to be yours, and the opinions I alluded to were principally those I had heard in common conversation from a sect aiming at the subversion of the present government to bring in their favorite form of a king, lords and commons. Thus I hope, my dear sir, that you will see me to have been as innocent in effect as I was in intention. I was brought before the public without my own consent, and from the first moment of seeing the effort of the real aggressors, in this business to keep me before the public, I determined that nothing should induce me to put pen to paper in the controversy. The business is now over, and I hope its effects are over, and that our friendship will never be suffered to be committed, whatever use others may think proper to make of our names.—To JOHN ADAMS. iii, 291. FORD ED., v, 380. (Pa., Aug. 1791.)

82. ADAMS (John), Midnight Appointments of.—One act of Mr. Adams's life, and one only, ever gave me a moment's personal displeasure. I did consider his last appointments to office as personally unkind. They were from among my most ardent political enemies, from whom no faithful cooperation could ever be expected; and laid me under the embarrassment of acting through men whose views were to defeat mine, or to encounter the odium of putting others in their places. It seemed but common justice to leave a successor free to act by instruments of his own choice. If my respect for him did not permit me to ascribe the whole blame to the influence of others, it left something for friendship to forgive, and after brooding over it for some little time, and not always resisting the expression of it, I forgave it cordially, and returned to the same state of esteem and respect for him which had so long existed. * * * I maintain for him, and shall carry into private life, an uniform and high measure of respect and good will, and for yourself a sincere attachment.—To MRS. JOHN ADAMS. iv, 546. FORD ED., viii, 307. (W., June 1804.) See COMMISSIONS.

83. ———— ————. Those scenes of midnight appointment, * * * have been condemned by all men. The last day of his political power, the last hours, and even beyond the midnight, were employed in filling all offices, and especially permanent ones, with the bitterest federalists, and providing for me the alternative, either to execute the government by my enemies, whose study it would be to thwart and defeat all my measures, or to incur the odium of such numerous removals from office, as might bear me down.—To DR. BENJAMIN RUSH. v, 561. FORD ED., ix, 297. (M., Jan. 1811.)

— ADAMS (John), Opinions on U. S. Senate.—See SENATE.

84. ADAMS (John), Peace Commission.—I am glad that he is of the [Peace] Commission, and expect he will be useful in it. His dislike of all parties and all men, by balancing his prejudices, may give them some fair play to his reason as would a general benevolence of temper. At any rate honesty may be extracted even from poisonous weeds.—To JAMES MADISON. FORD ED., iii, 309. (B., Feb. 1783.)

— ADAMS (John), Political Addresses of.—See 103, 105.

85. ADAMS (John), Political Principles of.—Mr. Adams had originally been a republican. The glare of royalty and nobility, during his mission to England, had made him believe their fascination a necessary ingredient in government; and Shays's rebellion, not sufficiently understood where he then was, seemed to prove that the absence of want and oppression, was not a sufficient guarantee of order. His book on the "American Constitutions" having made known his political bias, he was taken up by monarchical Federalists, in his absence, and on his return to the United States, he was by them made to believe that the general disposition of our citizens was favorable to monarchy. He then wrote his "Davila," as a supplement to the former work, and his election to the Presidency confirmed him in his errors. Innumerable addresses, too, artfully and industriously poured in upon him, deceived him into a confidence that he was on the pinnacle of popularity, when a gulf was yawning at his feet, which was to swallow up him and his deceivers. For, when General Washington was withdrawn, these *energumeni* of royalism, kept in check hitherto by the dread of his honesty, his firmness, his patriotism, and the authority of his name, now mounted on the car of state and free from control, like Phäeton on that of the sun, drove headlong and wild, looking neither to right nor left, nor regarding anything but the objects they were driving at; until, displaying these fully, the eyes of the nation were opened, and a general disbandment of them from the public councils took place. Mr. Adams, I am sure, has been long since convinced of the treacheries with which he was surrounded during his administration. He has since thoroughly seen that his constituents were devoted to republican government, and whether his judgment is resettled on its ancient basis, or not, he is conformed as a good citizen to the will of the majority, and would now, I am persuaded, maintain its republican structure with the zeal and fidelity belonging to his character. For even an enemy has said, " he is always an honest man, and often a great one." But in the fervor of the fever and follies of those who made him their stalking horse, no man who did not witness it, can form an idea of their unbridled madness, and the terrorism with which they surrounded themselves.—THE ANAS. ix, 97. FORD ED., i, 166. (1818.)

86. ———. Adams was for two hereditary [legislative] branches and an honest elective one.—THE ANAS. ix, 96. FORD ED., i, 166. (1818.)

87. ———. Can anyone read Mr. Adams's " Defence of the American Constitutions," without seeing that he was a monarchist? And J. Q. Adams, the son, was more explicit than the father in his answer to Paine's " Rights of Man."—TO WILLIAM SHORT. vii, 390. FORD ED., x, 332. (M., 1825.)

88. ADAMS (John), Proposed office for.—A little time and reflection effaced in my mind this temporary dissatisfaction [because of the midnight appointments, &c.] with Mr. Adams, and restored me to that just estimate of his virtues and passions, which a long acquaintance had enabled me to fix. And my first wish became that of making his retirement easy by any means in my power; for it was understood he was not rich. I suggested to some republican members of the delegation from his State, the giving him, either directly or indirectly, an office, the most lucrative in that State, and then offered to be resigned, if they thought he would not deem it affrontive. They were of opinion he would take great offence at the offer; and moreover, that the body of republicans would consider such a step in the outset as arguing very ill of the course I meant to pursue. I dropped the idea, therefore, but did not cease to wish for some opportunity of renewing our friendly understanding.—TO DR. BENJAMIN RUSH. v, 562. FORD ED., ix, 298. (M., Jan. 1811.)

— ADAMS (John), Saves Fisheries.—See FISHERIES.

89. ADAMS (John), Views on English Constitution.—While Mr. Adams was Vice-President, and I Secretary of State, I received a letter from President Washington, then at Mount Vernon, desiring me to call together the Heads of Departments, and to invite Mr. Adams to join us (which, by-the-bye, was the only instance of that being done) in order to determine on some measure which required despatch; and he desired me to act on it, as decided, without again recurring to him. I invited them to dine with me, and after dinner, sitting at our wine, having settled our question, other conversation came on, in which a collision of opinion arose between Mr. Adams and Colonel Hamilton, on the merits of the British Constitution. Mr. Adams giving it as his opinion, that, if some of its defects and abuses were corrected, it would be the most perfect constitution of government ever devised by man. Hamilton, on the contrary, asserted, that with its existing vices, it was the most perfect model of government that could be formed; and that the correction of its vices would render it an impracticable government. And this you may be assured was the real line of difference between the political principles of these two gentlemen. Another incident took place on the same occasion, which will further delineate Mr. Hamilton's political principles. The room being hung around with a collection of the portraits of remarkable men, among them were those of Bacon, Newton and Locke. Hamilton asked me who they were. I told him they were my trinity of the three greatest men the world had ever produced, naming them. He paused for some time: " The greatest man," said he, " that ever lived, was Julius Cæsar." Mr. Adams was honest as a politician as well as a man; Hamilton honest as a man, but, as a politician, believing in the necessity of either force or corruption to govern men. To DR. BENJAMIN RUSH. v, 559. FORD ED., ix, 295. (M., Jan. 1811.)

90. ADAMS (John), Washington and. —General Washington certainly did not love Mr. Adams.—To DR. BENJAMIN RUSH. iv, 508. FORD ED., viii, 265. (W., 1803.)

91. ADAMS (John), Writings of.—I have read your book with infinite satisfaction and improvement. It will do great good in America. Its learning and its good sense will, I hope, make it an institute for our politicians, old as well as young.—To JOHN ADAMS. ii, 128. (P., 1787.)

92. ———. I enclose you a Boston paper * * * . You will recognize Mr. A.—— under the signature of " Camillus." He writes in every week's paper now and generally under different signatures This is the first in which he has omitted some furious incartade against me.—To JAMES MADISON. iv, 53. FORD ED., vi, 402. (Pa., Sept. 1793.)

— ADAMS (Mrs. John), Correspondence with.—See APPENDIX.

93. ADAMS (John Quincy), Early Promise.—This young gentleman is I think very promising. To a vast thirst after useful knowledge he adds a facility in acquiring it. What his judgment may be I am not well enough acquainted with him to decide; but I expect it is good, and much hope it, as he may become a valuable and useful citizen.—To JAMES MONROE. FORD ED., iv, 42. (P., 1785.)

94. ADAMS (John Quincy), Foreign Minister.—The nomination of John Quincy Adams to Berlin, had been objected to as extending our diplomatic establishment. It was approved by eighteen to fourteen.—To JAMES MADISON. iv, 179. FORD ED., vii, 132. (Pa., June 1797.)

95. ADAMS (John Quincy), Respect for.—I have never entertained for Mr. Adams any but sentiments of esteem and respect; and if we have not thought alike on political subjects, I yet never doubted the honesty of his opinions.—To —————— ——————. vii, 432. (M., 1826.) See EMBARGO.

96. ADAMS (John Quincy), Secretary of State.—I have barely left myself room to express my satisfaction at your call to the important office * you hold, and to tender you the assurance of my great esteem and respect.— To JOHN QUINCY ADAMS. vii, 90. (1817.)

97. —————— ——————. I congratulate Mrs. Adams and yourself on the return of your excellent and distinguished son, and our country still more on such a minister of their foreign affairs.—To JOHN ADAMS. vii, 83. FORD ED. (1817.)

98. ADAMS (Samuel), Ability.—He was truly a great man, wise in council, fertile in resources, immovable in his purposes, and had, I think, a greater share than any other member, in advising and directing our measures in the northern war especially. * * * Although not of fluent elocution, he was so rigorously logical, so clear in his views, abundant in good sense, and master always of his subject, that he commanded the most profound attention whenever he rose in an assembly by which the froth of declamation was heard with the most sovereign contempt. —To S. A. WELLS. vii, 126. FORD ED., x, 131. (M., 1819.)

99. ADAMS (Samuel), Patriarch of Liberty.—I addressed a letter to you, my very dear and ancient friend, on the 4th of March; not indeed to you by name, but through the medium of some of my fellow citizens, whom occasion called on me to address. In meditating the matter of that address, I often asked myself, is this exactly in the spirit of the patriarch of liberty, Samuel Adams? Is it as he would express it? Will he approve of it? I have felt a great deal for our country in the times we have seen. But, individually, for no one so much as yourself. When I have been told that you were avoided, insulted, frowned on, I could not but ejaculate, " Father, forgive them, for they know what they do." I confess I felt an indignation for you, which for myself I have been able, under every trial, to keep entirely passive. * * * How much I lament that time has deprived me of your aid. It would have been a day of glory which should have called you to the first office of the Administration. But give us your counsel, and give us your blessing, and be assured that there exists not in the heart of man a more faithful esteem than mine to you.—To SAMUEL ADAMS. iv, 389. FORD ED., viii, 38 (W., 1801.)

* Secretary of State.—EDITOR.

100. ADAMS (Samuel), Principles of.— His principles, founded on the immovable basis of equal right and reason, have continued pure and unchanged. Permit me to place here my sincere veneration for him.—To JAMES SULLIVAN. iv, 169. FORD ED., vii, 118. (M., 1797.)

101. —————— ——————. Your principles have been tested in the crucible of time, and have come out pure. You have proved that it was monarchy, and not merely British monarchy, you opposed.—To SAMUEL ADAMS. iv, 321. FORD ED., vii, 425. (Pa., 1800.)

102. ADAMS (Samuel), Services of.— I always considered him as more than any other member [in Congress] the fountain of our important measures. And although he was neither an eloquent nor easy speaker, whatever he said was sound, and commanded the profound attention of the House. In the discussions on the floor of Congress he reposed himself on our main pillar in debate, Mr. John Adams. These two gentlemen were verily a host in our councils.—To DR. BENJAMIN WATERHOUSE. FORD ED., x, 124. (M., 1819.)

— ADDRESS, History of Washington's Farewell.—See WASHINGTON.

— ADDRESS, Jefferson to Inhabitants of Albemarle Co., Va.—See APPENDIX.

103. ADDRESSES, Indiscreet Political. —Indiscreet declarations and expressions of passion may be pardoned to a multitude acting from the impulse of the moment. But we cannot expect a foreign nation to show that apathy to the answers of the President [Adams] which are more thrasonic than the addresses. Whatever choice for peace might have been left us * * * is completely lost by these answers.—To JAMES MADISON. iv, 238. FORD ED., vii, 247. (Pa., May 1798.)

104. ADDRESSES, Self Respect and.— Though the expressions of good will from my fellow citizens cannot but be grateful to me, yet I would rather relinquish the gratification, and see republican self-respect prevail over movements of the heart too capable of misleading the person to whom they are addressed. However, their will, not mine, be done.—To SAMUEL SMITH. FORD ED., viii, 28. (W., March 1801.)

— ADDRESSES, Text of Jefferson's Inaugural Addresses.—See APPENDIX. *

105. ADDRESSES, Threatening Replies to.—Nor is it France alone, but his own fellow citizens, against whom President [Adams's] threats are uttered. In Fenno['s paper] * * * you will see one, wherein he says to the address from Newark, " the delusions and misrepresentations which have misled so many citizens, must be discountenanced by authority as well as by the citizens at large," evidently alluding to those letters from the Representatives to their constituents, which they have been so in the habit of seek-

* The principles in the Inaugural Addresses are classified in this work.—EDITOR.

ing after and publishing; while those sent by the tory part of the House to their constituents, are ten times more numerous, and replete with the most atrocious falsehoods and calumnies. What new law they will propose on this subject has not yet leaked out.*—To JAMES MADISON. iv, 239. FORD ED., vii, 247. (Pa., May 1798.)

106. ADDRESSES, Utilizing.—Averse to receive addresses, yet unable to prevent them, I have generally endeavored to turn them to some account, by making them the occasion, of sowing useful truths and principles among the people, which might germinate and become rooted among their political tenets.—To LEVI LINCOLN. iv, 427. FORD ED., viii, 129. (1802.)

107. ADJOURNMENT, Congress and.—A bill having passed both houses of Congress, and being now before the President, declaring that the seat of the Federal Government shall be transferred to the Potomac in the year 1790, that the sessions of Congress next ensuing the present shall be held in Philadelphia, to which place the offices shall be transferred before the 1st of December next, a writer in a public paper of July 13, has urged on the consideration of the President, that the Constitution has given to the two houses of Congress the exclusive right to adjourn themselves; that the will of the President mixed with theirs in a decision of this kind, would be an inoperative ingredient, repugnant to the Constitution, and that he ought not to permit them to part, in a single instance, with their constitutional rights; consequently, that he ought to negative the bill. That is now to be considered.

Every man, and every body of men on earth, possesses the right of self-government. They receive it with their being from the hand of nature. Individuals exercise it by their single will; collections of men by that of their majority; for the law of the *majority* is the natural law of every society of men. When a certain description of men are to transact together a particular business, the times and places of their meeting and separating, depend on their own will; they make a part of the natural right of self-government. This, like all other natural rights, may be abridged or modified in its exercise by their own consent, or by the law of those who depute them, if they meet in the right of others; but as far as it is not abridged or modified, they retain it as a natural right, and may exercise it in what form they please, either exclusively by themselves, or in association with others, or by others altogether, as they shall agree.

Each house of Congress possesses this natural right of governing itself, and, consequently, of fixing its own times and places of meeting, so far as it has not been abridged by the law of those who employ them, that is to say, by the Constitution. This act manifestly considers them as possessing this right

* Jefferson added a P. S. suggesting that Adams may have been looking to the sedition bill that had been spoken of. —EDITOR

of course, and, therefore, has nowhere given it to them. In the several different passages where it touches this right, it treats it as an existing thing, not as one called into existence by them. To evince this, every passage of the Constitution shall be quoted, where the right of adjournment is touched; and it will be seen that no one of them pretends to give that right; that, on the contrary, every one is evidently introduced either to enlarge the right where it would be too narrow, to restrain it where, in its natural and full exercise, it might be too large, and lead to inconvenience, to defend it from the latitude of its own phrases, where these were not meant to comprehend it, or to provide for its exercise by others, when they cannot exercise it themselves.

"A majority of each house shall constitute a quorum to do business; but a smaller number may adjourn from day to day, and may be authorized to compel the attendance of absent members." Art. 1. Sec. 5. A majority of every collection of men being naturally necessary to constitute its will, and it being frequently to happen that a majority is not assembled, it was necessary to enlarge the natural right by giving to "a smaller number than a majority" a right to compel the attendance of the absent members, and, in the meantime, to adjourn from day to day. This clause, then, does not pretend to give to a majority a right which it knew that majority would have of themselves, but to a number *less* than a *majority*, a right to which it knew that lesser number could not have of themselves.

"Neither house, during the session of Congress, shall, without the consent of the other, adjourn for more than three days, nor to any other place than that in which the two houses shall be sitting." *Ibid*. Each house exercising separately its natural right to meet when and where it should think best, it might happen that the two houses would separate either in time or place, which would be inconvenient. It was necessary, therefore, to keep them together by restraining their natural right of deciding on separate times and places, and by requiring a concurrence of will.

But, as it might happen that obstinacy, or a difference of object, might prevent this concurrence, it goes on to take from them, in that instance, the right of adjournment altogether, and to transfer it to another, by declaring, Art. 2. Sec. 3, that "in case of disagreement between the two houses, with respect to the time of adjournment, the President may adjourn them to such time as he shall think proper."

These clauses, then, do not import a gift, to the two houses, of a general right of adjournment, which it was known they would have without that gift, but to restrain or abrogate the right it was known they would have, in an instance where, exercised in its full extent, it might lead to inconvenience, and to give that right to another, who would not naturally have had it. It also gives to the President a right, which he otherwise would not have had, "to convene both houses.

or either of them, on extraordinary occasions." Thus substituting the will of another, where they are not in a situation to exercise their own.

" Every order, resolution, or vote, to which the concurrence of the Senate and House of Representatives may be necessary (except on a question of adjournment), shall be presented to the President for his approbation, &c., Art. I. Sec. 7. The latitude of the general words here used would have subjected the natural right of adjournment of the two houses to the will of the President, which was not intended. They, therefore, expressly " except questions of adjournment" out of their operation. They do not here give a right of adjournment, which it was known would exist without their gift, but they defend the existing right against the latitude of their own phrases, in a case where there was no good reason to abridge it. The exception admits they will have the right of adjournment, without pointing out the source from which they will derive it.

These are all the passages of the Constitution (one only excepted, which shall be presently cited,) where the right of adjournment is touched; and it is evident that none of these are introduced to give that right; but every one supposes it to be existing, and provides some specific modification for cases where either defeat in the natural right, or a too full use of it, would occasion inconvenience.

The right of adjournment, then, is not given by the Constitution, and consequently it may be modified by law without interfering with that instrument. It is a natural right, and, like all other natural rights, may be abridged or regulated in its exercise by law and the concurrence of the third branch in any law regulating its exercise is so efficient an ingredient in that law, that the right cannot be otherwise exercised but after a repeal by a new law. The express terms of the Constitution itself show that this right may be modified *by law*, when, in Art. I. Sec. 4. (the only remaining passage on the subject not yet quoted) it says, " The Congress shall assemble at least once in every year, and such meeting shall be the first Monday in December, unless they shall, *by law*, appoint a different day." Then another day may be appointed *by law;* and the President's assent is an efficient ingredient in that law. Nay, further, they cannot adjourn over the first Monday of December but by *a law*. This is another constitutional abridgment of their natural right of adjournment; and completing our review of all the clauses in the Constitution which touch that right, authorizes us to say no part of that instrument gives it; and that the houses hold it, not from the Constitution, but from nature.

A consequence of this is. that the houses may, by a joint resolution, remove themselves from place to place, because it is a part of their right of self-government; but that as the right of self-government does not comprehend the government of others, the two houses cannot, by a joint resolution of their

majorities only, remove the Executive and Judiciary from place to place. These branches possessing, also, the rights of self-government from nature, cannot be controlled in the exercise of them but by a law, passed in the forms of the Constitution The clause of the bill in question, therefore, was necessary to be put into the form of a law, and to be submitted to the President, so far as it proposes to effect the removal of the Executive and Judiciary to Philadelphia. So far as respects the removal of the present houses of legislation thither, it was not necessary to be submitted to the President; but such a submission is not repugnant to the Constitution. On the contrary, if he concurs, it will so far fix the next session of Congress at Philadelphia that it cannot be changed but by a regular law.

The sense of Congress itself is always respectable authority. It has been given very remarkably on the present subject. The address to the President in the paper of the 13th, is a complete digest of all the arguments urged on the floor of the Representatives against the constitutionality of the bill now before the President; and they were overruled by a majority of that house, comprehending the delegation of all the States south of the Hudson, except South Carolina. At the last session of Congress, when the bill for remaining a certain term at New York, and then removing to Susquehanna, or Germantown, was objected to on the same ground, the objection was overruled by a majority comprehending the delegations of the northern half of the Union with that of South Carolina. So that the sense of every State in the Union has been expressed, by its delegation, against this objection, South Carolina excepted, and excepting also Rhode Island, which has never yet had a delegation in place to vote on the question. In both these instances, the Senate concurred with the majority of the Representatives. The sense of the two houses is stronger authority in this case, as it is given against their own supposed privilege.

It would be as tedious, as it is unnecessary, to take up and discuss one by one, the objects proposed in the paper of July 13. Every one of them is founded on the supposition that the two houses hold their right of adjournment from the Constitution. This error being corrected, the objections founded on it fall of themselves.

It would also be work of mere supererogation to show that, granting what this writer takes for granted, (that the President's assent would be an inoperative ingredient, because excluded by the Constitution, as he says,) yet the particular views of the writer would be frustrated, for on every hypothesis of what the President may do, Congress must go to Philadelphia. 1. If he assents to the bill, that assent makes good law of the part relative to the Potomac; and the part for holding the next session at Philadelphia is good, either as an ordinance, or a vote of the two houses, containing a complete declaration of their will in a case where it is competent to the object; so that they must go to Philadelphia in that case. 2. If he dissents from the bill, it annuls the part relative to the Potomac; but as to the clause for adjourning to Philadelphia, his dissent being as inneficient as his assent, it remains a good ordinance, or vote, of the two houses for going thither, and consequently they must go in this case also. 3. If the President withholds his will out of the bill altogether, by a ten day's silence, then the part relative to the Potomac becomes a good law without his will, and that relative to Philadelphia is good also, either as a law, or an ordinance, or a vote of the two houses; and consequently in this case also they go to Philadelphia.—OPINION ON RESIDENCE BILL. vii, 495. FORD ED., v, 205. (July 1790.)

108. ADJOURNMENT, Executives and. —The Administrator shall not possess the prerogative * * * of dissolving, proroguing, or adjourning either House of Assembly.— PROPOSED VA. CONSTITUTION. FORD ED., ii, 18. (June 1776.)

109. ADMINISTRATION, Acceptable. —The House of Representatives having concluded their choice of a person for the chair of the United States, and willed me that office, it now becomes necessary to provide an administration composed of persons whose qualifications and standing have possessed them of the public confidence, and whose wisdom may ensure to our fellow citizens the advantage they sanguinely expect.—To HENRY DEARBORN. iv, 356. FORD ED., vii, 495. (W., Feb. 1801.) See CABINET.

— ADMINISTRATION, John Adams's. —See 57, 58, 142.

110. ADMINISTRATION, Antagonism to.—I have received many letters stating to me in the spirit of prophecy, caricatures which the writers, it seems, know are to be the principles of my administration. To these no answer has been given, because the prejudiced spirit in which they have been written proved the writers not in a state of mind to yield to truth or reason.—To WILLIAM JACKSON. iv, 357. (W., 1801.)

111. ADMINISTRATION, Arduous.— The helm of a free government is always arduous, and never was ours more so, than at a moment when two friendly peoples are likely to be committed in war by the ill temper of their administrations.—To JAMES SULLIVAN. iv, 168. FORD ED., vii, 117. (M., Feb. 1797.)

112. ADMINISTRATION, Confidence in.—In a government like ours it is necessary to embrace in its administration as great a mass of confidence as possible, by employing those who have a character with the public, of their own, and not merely a secondary one through the Executive.*—ANAS. ix, 208. FORD ED., i, 312. (April, 1806.)

113. —— ——. On the whole, I hope we shall make up an administration which will

* Answer to Aaron Burr's solicitations for an office. —EDITOR.

unite a great mass of confidence, and bid defiance to the plans of opposition meditated by leaders who are now almost destitute of followers.—To HORATIO GATES. FORD ED., viii, 11. (W., March 1801.)

114. ADMINISTRATION, Confident.— The important subjects of the government I meet with some degree of courage and confidence, because I do believe the talents to be associated with me, the honest line of conduct we will religiously pursue at home and abroad, and the confidence of my fellow citizens dawning on us, will be equal to these objects.—To WILLIAM B. GILES. iv, 380. FORD ED., viii, 25. (W., March 1801.)

115. ADMINISTRATION, Devoted.—If ever the earth has beheld a system of administration conducted with a single and steadfast eye to the general interest and happiness of those committed to it, one which, protected by truth, can never know reproach, it is that to which our lives have been devoted. —To JAMES MADISON. vii, 435. FORD ED., x, 378. (M., 1826.)

116. ADMINISTRATION, Difficult.— Our situation is difficult; and whatever we do is liable to the criticism of those who wish to represent it awry. If we recommend measures in a public message, it may be said that members are not sent here to obey the mandates of the President, or to register the edicts of a sovereign. If we express opinions in conversation, we have then our Charles Jenkinsons, and back-door counsellors. If we say nothing, "we have no opinions, no plans, no cabinet." In truth, it is the fable of the old man, his son and ass, over again.— To WILLIAM DUANE. iv, 592. FORD ED., viii, 433. (W., 1806.)

117. ADMINISTRATION, Disapproved. —There was but a single act of my whole administration of which the federal party approved. That was the proclamation on the attack of the Chesapeake. And when I found they approved of it, I confess I began strongly to apprehend I had done wrong, and to exclaim with the Psalmist, "Lord, what have I done that the wicked should praise me."— To ELBRIDGE GERRY. vi, 63. FORD ED., ix, 359. (M., 1812.)

118. ADMINISTRATION, Disinterested.—A disinterestedness administration of the public trusts is essential to perfect tranquillity of mind.—To SAMUEL HAWKINS. v, 392. (W., 1808.)

119. ADMINISTRATION, England and the.—All the troubles and difficulties in the government during our time proceeded from England; at least all others were trifling in comparison with them.—To HENRY DEARBORN. v, 455. (M., 1809.)

120. ADMINISTRATION, Errors in.— It is our consolation and encouragement that we are serving a just public, who will be indulgent to any error committed honestly, and relating merely to the means of carrying into effect what they have manifestly willed to be a law.—To W. H. Cabell. v, 162. Ford ed., ix, 96. (M., 1807.) See Error.

121. ADMINISTRATION, Foreign Policy.—In the transaction of your foreign affairs, we have endeavored to cultivate the friendship of all nations, and especially of those with which we have the most important relations. We have done them justice on all occasions, favored where favor was lawful, and cherished mutual interests and intercourse on fair and equal terms. We are firmly convinced, and we act on that conviction, that with nations, as with individuals, our interests soundly calculated, will ever be found inseparable from our moral duties; and history bears witness to the fact, that a just nation is taken on its word, when recourse is had to armaments and wars to bridle others.—Second Inaugural Address. viii, 40. Ford ed., viii, 343. (1805.)

122. ADMINISTRATION, Formalities and.—The necessity of these abridgments of formalities in our present. distant situations requires that I should particularly suggest to you the expediency of desiring General Knox to communicate to the foreign ministers *himself directly* any matters relative to the interpositions of his department through the governors. For him to send these to me from Boston to this place [Monticello] merely that I may send them back to the ministers at Philadelphia or New York, might be an injurious delay of business.—To President Washington. Ford ed., vi, 435. (M., Oct. 1793.) See Formalities.

123. ADMINISTRATION, Fundamental Principles.—To cultivate peace and maintain commerce and navigation in all their lawful enterprises; to foster our fisheries and nurseries of navigation and for the nurture of man, and protect the manufactures adapted to our circumstances; to preserve the faith of the nation by an exact discharge of its debts and contracts, expending the public money with the same care and economy we would practice with our own, and impose on our citizens no unnecessary burden; to keep in all things within the pale of our constitutional powers, and cherish the Federal Union as the only rock of our safety—these are the landmarks by which we are to guide ourselves in all our proceedings. By continuing to make these our rule of action, we shall endear to our countrymen the true principles of their Constitution, and promote a union of sentiment and of action equally auspicious to their happiness and safety.—Second Annual Message. viii, 21. Ford ed., viii, 186. (1802.) See Inaugural Addresses, Appendix.

124. —— ——. Our wish is * * * that the public efforts may be directed honestly to the public good, that peace be cultivated, civil and religious liberty unassailed, law and order preserved, equality of rights maintained, and that state of property, equal or unequal, which results to every man from his own industry or that of his fathers.—Second Inaugural Address. viii, 44. Ford ed., viii, 347. (1805.)

125. —— ——. That all should be satisfied with any one order of things is not to be expected, but I indulge the pleasing persuasion that the great body of our citizens will concur in honest and disinterested efforts, which have for their object to preserve the General and State governments in their constitutional form and equilibrium; to maintain peace abroad and order and obedience to the laws at home; to establish principles and practices of administration favorable to the security of liberty and prosperity, and to reduce expenses to what is necessary for the useful purposes of government.—First Annual Message. viii, 15. Ford ed., viii, 125. (Dec. 1801.)

126. —— ——. Believing that (excepting the ardent monarchists) all our citizens agreed in ancient whig principles, I thought it advisable to define and declare them, and let them see the ground on which we could rally. And the fact proving to be so, that they agree in these principles, I shall pursue them with more encouragement.—To General Henry Knox. iv, 386. Ford ed., viii, 36. (W., March 1801.)

127. ADMINISTRATION, Good Republican.—A good administration in a republican government, securing to us our dearest rights, and the practical enjoyment of all our liberties, can never fail to give consolation to the friends of free government, and mortification to its enemies.—R. to A. Rhode Island Republicans. viii, 162. (1809.)

128. ADMINISTRATION, Harmonious.—That there is only one minister who is not opposed to me, is totally unfounded. There never was a more harmonious, a more cordial administration. nor ever a moment when it has been otherwise. And while differences of opinion have been always rare among us, I can affirm, that as to present matters, there was not a single paragraph in my message to Congress, or those supplementary to it, in which there was not a unanimity of concurrence in the members of the administration.—To William Duane. iv, 591. Ford ed., viii, 432. (W., March 1806.)

129. ADMINISTRATION, Hesitancy and.—On every question the lawyers are about equally divided, and were we to act but in cases where no contrary opinion of a lawyer can be had, we should never act.—To Albert Gallatin. v, 369. (M., 1898.)

130. ADMINISTRATION, Honest.—The measures of my administration * * * have been pursued with honest intentions, unbiased by any personal or interested views.—R. to A. Wilmington Citizens. viii, 149. (1809.)

131. ADMINISTRATION, Indebted.—I do not mean, fellow citizens, to arrogate to myself the merit of the measures [of the administration]; that is due, in the first place, to the reflecting character of our citizens at large, who, by the weight of public opinion, influence and strengthen the public measures; it is due to the sound discretion with which they select from among themselves those to whom they confide the legislative duties; it is due to the zeal and wisdom of the characters selected, who lay the foundations of public happiness in wholesome laws, the execution of which alone remains for others; and it is due to the able and faithful auxiliaries, whose patriotism has associated with me in the executive functions.—SECOND INAUGURAL ADDRESS. viii, 43. FORD ED., viii, 345. (1805.)

132. ADMINISTRATION, Indulgence to.—There are no mysteries in the public administration. Difficulties indeed sometimes arise; but common sense and honest intentions will generally steer through them, and, where they cannot be surmounted, I have ever seen the well-intentioned part of our fellow citizens sufficiently disposed not to look for impossibilities.— To DR. J. B. STUART. vii, 64. (M., 1817.)

133. —— ——. A consciousness that I feel no desire but to do what is best, without passion or predilection, encourages me to hope for an indulgent construction of what I do.—To JOHN PAGE. iv, 377. (W., 1801.)

— ADMINISTRATION, Madison's.— See MADISON.

134. ADMINISTRATION, Meritorious. —I wish support from no quarter longer than my object, candidly scanned shall merit it; and especially, not longer than I shall vigorously adhere to the Constitution.—To BENJAMIN STODDERT. iv, 360. FORD ED., vii, 499. (W., Feb. 1801.)

135. ADMINISTRATION, Moderate.— I am very much in hopes we shall be able to restore union to our country. Not, indeed, that the federal leaders can be brought over. They are invincibles; but I really hope their followers may. The bulk of these last were real republicans, carried over from us by French excesses. This induced me to offer a political creed [in the inauguration address], and to invite to conciliation first; and I am pleased to hear, that these principles are recognized by them, and considered as no bar of separation. A moderate conduct throughout which may not revolt our new friends, and which may give them tenets with us, must be observed.—To JOHN PAGE. iv, 378. (W., March 1801.)

136. ADMINISTRATION, Public Opinion and.—It will always be interesting to me to know the impression made by any particular thing on the public mind. My idea is that where two measures are equally right, it is a duty to the people to adopt that one which is most agreeable to them; and where a measure not agreeable to them has been adopted, it is desirable to know it, because it is an admonition to a review of that measure to see if it has been really right, and to correct it if mistaken.—To WILLIAM FINDLEY. FORD ED., viii, 27. (W., March 1801.)

137. ADMINISTRATION, Reasonable. —Unequivocal in principle, reasonable in manner, we shall be able, I hope, to do a great deal of good to the cause of freedom and harmony.—To ELBRIDGE GERRY. iv, 392. FORD ED., viii, 43. (W., March 1801.)

138. ADMINISTRATION, Responsibility and.—We can only be answerable for the orders we give and not for the execution. If they are disobeyed from obstinacy of spirit, or want of coercion in the laws, it is not our fault.—To GENERAL STEUBEN. FORD ED., ii, 492. (R., 1781.)

139. ADMINISTRATION, Routine.— The ordinary affairs of a nation offer little difficulty to a person of any experience.—To JAMES SULLIVAN. v, 252. (W., 1808.)

140. ADMINISTRATION, Salutary.— I am sure the measures I mean to pursue are such as would in their nature be approved by every American who can emerge from preconceived prejudices; as for those who cannot, we must take care of them as of the sick in our hospitals. The medicine of time and fact may cure some of them.—To THEODORE FOSTER. FORD ED., viii, 50. (W., May 1801.)

141. ADMINISTRATION, Secrecy in.— The same secrecy and mystery are affected to be observed by the present, which marked the former administration.—To AARON BURR. iv, 185. FORD ED., vii, 147. (Pa., June 1797.)

142. ADMINISTRATION, Slip-shod.— The administration [of Mr. Adams] had no rule for anything.—To WILLIAM SHORT. iv, 413. FORD ED., viii, 96. (W., 1801.)

143. ADMINISTRATION, Successors in.—I have thought it right to take no part myself in proposing measures, the execution of which will devolve on my successor.—To DR. LOGAN. v, 404. (W., Dec. 1808.)

144. —— ——. I should not feel justified in directing measures which those who are to execute them would disapprove.—To LEVI LINCOLN. v, 387. FORD ED., ix, 227. (W., Nov. 1808.)

145. —— ——. I am now so near the moment of retiring, that I take no part in affairs beyond the expression of an opinion. I think it fair that my successor should now originate those measures of which he will be charged with the execution and responsibility, and that it is my duty to clothe them with the forms of authority.—To JAMES MONROE. v, 420. FORD ED., ix, 243. (W., Jan. 1809.)

146. —— ——. I hope that my successor will enter on a calmer sea than I did. He will at least find the vessel of State in the hands of his friends, and not of his foes.—To RICHARD M. JOHNSON. v, 257. (W., 1808.)

147. ADMINISTRATION, Summary of Jefferson's first.—To do without a land tax, excise, stamp tax and the other internal taxes, to supply their place by economies, so as still to support the government properly, and to apply $7,300,000 a year steadily to the payment of the public debt; to discontinue a great portion of the expenses on armies and navies, yet protect our country and its commerce with what remains; to purchase a country as large and more fertile than the one we possessed before, yet ask neither a new tax, nor another soldier to be added, but to provide that that country shall by its own income, pay for itself before the purchase money is due; to preserve peace with all nations, and particularly an equal friendship to the two great rival powers, France and England, and to maintain the credit and character of the nation in as high a degree as it has ever enjoyed, are measures which I think must reconcile the great body of those who thought themselves our enemies; but were in truth only the enemies of certain Jacobinical, atheistical, anarchical, imaginary caricatures, which existed only in the land of the raw head and bloody bones, beings created to frighten the credulous. By this time they see enough of us to judge our characters by what we do, and not by what we never did, nor thought of doing, but in the lying chronicles of the newspapers.—To TIMOTHY BLOODWORTH. iv, 523. (W., Jan. 1804.)

148. ADMINISTRATION, Temporizing.—Mild laws, a people not used to prompt obedience, a want of provisions of war, and means of procuring them render our orders often ineffectual, oblige us to temporize, and when we cannot accomplish an object in one way to attempt it in another. Your knowledge of these circumstances, with a temper to accommodate them, ensure me your co-operation in the best way we can, when we shall not be able to pursue the way we would wish.—To MAJOR GENERAL DE LAFAYETTE. FORD ED., ii, 493. (R., March 1781.)

149. ADMINISTRATION, Tranquil.—The path we have to pursue is so quiet that we have nothing scarcely to propose to our Legislature. A noiseless course, not meddling with the affairs of others, unattractive of notice, is a mark that society is going on in happiness.—To THOMAS COOPER. iv, 453. FORD ED., viii, 178. (W., Nov. 1802.)

150. ADMINISTRATION, Unmeddling.—The quiet track into which we are endeavoring to get, neither meddling with the affairs of other nations, nor with those of our fellow citizens, but letting them go on in their own way, will show itself in the statement of our affairs to Congress.—To DR. JOSEPH PRIESTLEY. FORD ED., viii, 180. (W., Dec. 1802.)

151. ADMINISTRATION, Unsuccessful.—Two measures have not been adopted, which I pressed on Congress repeatedly at their meetings. The one, to settle the whole ungranted territory of Orleans, by donations of land to able-bodied young men, to be engaged and carried there at the public expense, who would constitute a force always ready on the spot to defend New Orleans. The other was to class the militia according to the years of their birth, and make all those from twenty to twenty-five liable to be trained and called into service at a moment's warn-

ing. This would have given us a force of three hundred thousand young men, prepared by proper training, for service in any part of the United States; while those who had passed through that period would remain at home, liable to be used in their own or adjacent States. Those two measures would have completed what I deemed necessary for the entire security of our country. They would have given me, on my retirement from the government of the nation, the consolatory reflection, that having found, when I was called to it, not a single seaport town in a condition to repel a levy of contribution by a single privateer or pirate, I had left every harbor so prepared by works and gunboats, as to be in a reasonable state of security against any probable attack; the territory of Orleans acquired, and planted with an internal force sufficient for its protection; and the whole territory of the United States organized by such a classification of its male force, as would give it the benefit of all its young population for active service, and that of a middle and advanced age for stationary defence. But these measures will, I hope, be completed by my successor.—To GENERAL KOSCIUSKO. v, 507. (M., Feb. 1810.)

— ADMINISTRATION, Washington's. —See WASHINGTON.

152. ADMINISTRATIONS, British.—In general the [British] administrations are so changeable, and they are obliged to descend to such tricks to keep themselves in place, that nothing like honor or morality can ever be counted on in transactions with them.— To PRESIDENT MADISON. v, 465. (M., Aug. 1809.)

153. ADMINISTRATIONS, Ill-tempered.—We have received a report that the French Directory has proposed a declaration of war against the United States to the Council of Ancients, who have rejected it. Thus we see two nations, who love one another affectionately, brought by the ill temper of their executive administrations, to the very brink of necessity to imbrue their hands in the blood of each other.—To AARON BURR. iv, 187. FORD ED., vii, 148. (Pa., June 1797.)

154. ADMIRALTY COURTS, Decisions of British.—I thank you for the case of *Demsey vs.* the *Insurers,* which I have read with great pleasure, and entire conviction. Indeed it is high time to withdraw all respect from courts acting under the arbitrary orders of governments who avow a total disregard of those moral rules which have hitherto been acknowledged by nations, and have served to regulate and govern their intercourse. I should respect just as much the rules of conduct which governed Cartouche or Blackbeard, as those now acted on by France or England. If your argument is defective in anything, it is in having paid to the antecedent decisions of the British Courts of Admiralty the respect of examining them on grounds of reason; and not having rested the decision at once on the profligacy of those tribunals, and openly declared against permitting their sentences to be ever more quoted or listened to until those nations return to the practice of justice, to an acknowledgment that there is a moral law which ought to govern mankind, and by sufficient evidences of contrition for their present flagitiousness, make it safe to receive them, again into the society of civilized nations. I hope this will be done on a proper occasion. Yet knowing that religion does not furnish grosser bigots than law, I expect little from old judges. Those now at the bar may be bold enough to follow reason rather than precedent, and may bring that principle on the bench when promoted to it; but I fear this effort is not for my day. It has been said that when Harvey discovered the circulation of the blood, there was not a physician of Europe of forty years of age, who assented to it. I fear you will experience Harvey's fate; but it will become law when the present judges are dead.—To THOMAS COOPER. v, 531. (M., 1810.)

155. ADMIRALTY COURTS, Jurisdiction.—They [Parliament] have extended the jurisdiction of courts of admiralty beyond their ancient limits.—DECLARATION ON TAKING UP ARMS. FORD ED., i, 468. (July 1775.)

— ADMISSION OF NEW STATES.— See STATES.

156. ADVERTISEMENTS, Appreciated.—I read but one newspaper and that * * * more for its advertisements than its news.— To CHARLES PINCKNEY. vii, 180. FORD ED., x, 162. (M., 1820.)

157. ADVERTISEMENTS, Principle and.—I think it might be well to advertise my lands at Elkhill for sale, and therefore enclose you the form of an advertisement, in which, you will observe, I have omitted the name of the proprietor, which, as long as I am in public, I would wish to keep out of view in everything of a private nature.—To NICHOLAS LEWIS. FORD ED., v, 281. (Pa., 1791.)

158. ADVERTISEMENTS, Truth and.—Advertisements contain the only truths to be relied on in a newspaper.—To NATHANIEL MACON. vii, 111. FORD ED., x, 120. (M., 1819.)

159. ADVICE, A Duty.—Duty tells me that the public interest is so deeply concerned in your perfect knowledge of the characters employed in its high stations, that nothing should be withheld which can give you useful information.—To PRESIDENT MADISON. vi, 101. (M., 1813.)

160. ADVICE, Friendship in.—No apologies for writing or speaking to me freely are necessary. On the contrary, nothing my friends can do is so dear to me, and proves to me their friendship so clearly, as the information they give me of their sentiments and those of others on interesting points where I am to act, and where information and warning are so essential to excite in me that due reflection which ought to precede action.—To WILSON C. NICHOLAS. iv, 507. FORD ED., viii, 248. (M., 1803.)

161. ——— ———. I always consider it as the most friendly service which can be rendered me, to be informed of anything which is going amiss, and which I can remedy.— To WILSON C. NICHOLAS. v, 400. (W., 1808.)

162. ADVICE, A Legacy of.—Your affectionate mother requests that I would address to you, as a namesake, something which might have a favorable influence on the course of life you have to run. Few words are necessary, with good dispositions on your part. Adore God; reverence and cherish your parents; love your neighbor as yourself, and your country more than life. Be just; be true; murmur not at the ways of Providence—and the life into which you may have entered will be one of eternal and ineffable bliss. And if to the dead it is permitted to care for the things of this world, every action of your life will be under my regard. Farewell.—To THOMAS JEFFERSON GROTJAN. FORD ED., x, 287. (M., 1824.)

163. ADVICE, Proffering.—How easily we prescribe for others a cure for their difficulties, while we cannot cure our own.—To JOHN ADAMS. vii, 201. FORD ED., x, 187. (M., 1821.)

164. ADVICE, Ten Precepts of.—A Decalogue of Canons for Observation in Practical Life:—

1. Never put off till to-morrow what you can do to-day.

2. Never trouble another for what you can do yourself.

3. Never spend your money before you have it.

4. Never buy what you do not want, because it is cheap; it will be dear to you.

5. Pride costs us more than hunger, thirst and cold.

6. We never repent of having eaten too little.

7. Nothing is troublesome that we do willingly.

8. How much pain have cost us the evils which have never happened.

9. Take things always by their smooth handle.

10. When angry, count ten, before you speak: if very angry, an hundred.—To THOMAS JEFFERSON SMITH. vii, 401. FORD ED., x, 341. (M., 1825.)

165. ADVICE, Thankful for.—I am ever thankful for communications which may guide me in the duties which I wish to perform as well as I am able.—To JOHN DICKINSON. v, 29. FORD ED., ix, 8. (W., 1807.)

166. ——— ———. I have always received with thankfulness the ideas of judicious persons on subjects interesting to the public.— To BENJAMIN STODDERT. v, 426. FORD ED., ix, 246. (W., 1809.)

167. ——— ———. In all cases I invite and shall receive with great thankfulness your opinion and that of others on the course of things, and particularly in the suggestion of characters who may worthily be appointed.— To Pierrepont Edwards. Ford ed., viii, 45. (W., March 1801.)

168. —— ——. Far from arrogating the office of advice, no one will more passively acquiesce in it than myself.—To John H. Pleasants. vii, 346. Ford ed., x, 304. (M., 1824.)

169. ADVICE, Valued.—I value no act of friendship so highly as the communicating facts to me, which I am not in the way of knowing otherwise, and could not therefore otherwise guard against.—To W. C. Nicholas. v, 260. (W., 1808.)

170. —— ——. It is impossible for my friends ever to render me so acceptable a favor, as by communicating to me, without reserve, facts and opinions. I have none of that sort of self-love which winces at it; indeed, both self-love and the desire to do what is best strongly invite unreserved communication.—To Wilson C. Nicholas. v, 48. Ford ed., ix, 32. (W., 1807.)

171. ADVICE, Unbiased.—The greatest favor which can be done me is the communication of the opinions of judicious men, of men who do not suffer their judgments to be biased by either interests or passions.— To Chandler Price. v, 46. (W., 1807.)

— AERONAUTICS.—See Balloons.

172. AFFECTION, Early.—I find as I grow older, that I love those most whom I loved first.—To Mrs. John Bolling. Ford ed., iv, 412. (P., 1787.)

173. AFFECTION, Of friendship.—The happiest moments my heart knows are those in which it is pouring forth its affections to a few esteemed characters.—To Mrs. Trist. Ford ed., iv, 331. (P., 1786.) See Friendship.

174. AFFECTION, Parental.—Is not parental love the strongest affection known? Is it not greater than that of self-preservation?—Note. i, 149. Ford ed., ii, 206. (1778.)

175. —— ——. Although parental be yet stronger than filial affection. * * * Note. i, 150. Ford ed., ii, 207. (1778.)

176. AFFECTION, Patriotic.—My affections are first for my own country, and then, generally, for all mankind.—To Thomas Law. v, 556. Ford ed., ix, 293. (M., 1811.)

177. AFFECTION, Rewarded by.—The affection of my countrymen * * * was the only reward I ever asked or could have felt.—To James Monroe. i, 318. Ford ed., iii, 57. (M., 1782.) See Family, Home.

178. AFFLICTION, Consolation in.— Tried myself in the school of affliction, by the loss of every form of connection which can rive the human heart, I know well, and feel what you have lost, what you have suffered, are suffering, and have yet to endure. The same trials have taught me that for ills so immeasurable, time and silence are the only medicine. I will not, therefore, by useless condolences, open afresh the sluices of your

grief, nor, although mingling sincerely my tears with yours, will I say a word more where words are vain.—To John Adams. vii, 107. Ford ed., x, 114. (M., 1818.)

179. AFFLICTION, Schooled in.—There is no degree of affliction, produced by the loss of those dear to us, which experience has not taught me to estimate. I have ever found time and silence the only medicine, and these but assuage, they never can suppress, the deep drawn sigh which recollection forever brings up, until recollection and life are extinguished together.—To John Adams. vi, 221. (M., 1813.)

180. AFFLICTION, Sympathy in.—Long tried in the same school of affliction, no loss which can rend the human heart is unknown to mine; and a like one particularly, at about the same period in life, had taught me to feel the sympathies of yours. The same experience has proved that time, silence and occupation are its only medicines.—To Governor Claiborne. v, 520. (M., 1810.)

— AFRICAN SLAVE TRADE.—See Slavery.

181. AGE, Advancing.—Being very sensible of bodily decays from advancing years, I ought not to doubt their effect on the mental faculties. To do so would evince either great self-love or little observation of what passes under our eyes; and I shall be fortunate if I am the first to perceive and to obey this admonition of nature.—To Mr. Weaver. v, 88. (W., June 1807.)

182. AGE, Change and.—I am now of an age which does not easily accommodate itself to new manners and new modes of living.— To Baron Geismer. i, 427. (P., 1785.)

183. AGE, Deformity in.—Man, like the fruit he eats, has his period of ripeness. Like that, too, if he continues longer hanging to the stem, it is but an useless and unsightly appendage.—To Henry Dearborn. vii, 214. Ford ed., x. 191. (M., 1821.)

184. AGE, Desire in.—Tranquillity is the *summum bonum* of old age.—To Mark L. Hill. vii, 154. (M., 1820.)

185. AGE, Dread of old.—I have ever dreaded a doting old age; and my health has been generally so good, and is now so good, that I dread it still. The rapid decline of my strength during the last winter has made me hope sometimes that I see land. During the summer I enjoy its temperature, but I shudder at the approach of winter, and wish I could sleep through it with the dormouse, and only wake with him in the spring, if ever.—To John Adams. vii, 244. Ford ed., x, 216. (M., 1822.)

186. AGE, Duty in old.—Nothing is more incumbent on the old, than to know when they should get out of the way, and relinquish to younger successors the honors they can no longer earn, and the duties they can no longer perform.—To John Vaughan. vi, 417. (M., 1815.)

187. —— ——. I resign myself cheerfully to the managers of the ship, and the more

contentedly, as I am near the end of my voyage.—To EDWARD LIVINGSTON. vii, 342. FORD ED., x, 300. (M., 1824.)

188. AGE, Evils of protracted.—The solitude in which we are left by the death of our friends is one of the great evils of protracted life. When I look back to the days of my youth, it is like looking over a field of battle. All, all dead! and ourselves left alone midst a new generation whom we know not, and who know not us.—To FRANCIS A. VAN DER KEMP. FORD ED., x, 337. (M., 1825.)

189. AGE, Fear of old.—My only fear is that I may live too long. This would be a subject of dread to me.—To PHILIP MAZZEI. FORD ED., viii, 15. (M., March 1801.)

190. AGE, Insensible to.—It is wonderful to me that old men should not be sensible that their minds keep pace with their bodies in the progress of decay. Our old revolutionary friend Clinton, for example, who was a hero, but never a man of mind, is wonderfully jealous on this head. He tells eternally the stories of his younger days to prove his memory, as if memory and reason were the same faculty. Nothing betrays imbecility so much as the being insensible of it. Had not a conviction of the danger to which an unlimited occupation, of the Executive chair would expose the republican constitution of our government, made it conscientiously a duty to refuse when I did, the fear of becoming a dotard, and of being insensible of it, would of itself have resisted all solicitations to remain.—To DR. BENJAMIN RUSH. vi, 3. FORD ED., ix, 328. (P.F., 1816.)

191. AGE, Offerings of.—Good wishes are all an old man has to offer to his country or friends.—To THOMAS LAW. v, 557. FORD ED., ix, 293. (M., 1811.)

192. AGE, Oppressed by.—The hand of age is upon me. All my old friends are nearly gone. Of those in my neighborhood, Mr. Divers and Mr. Lindsay alone remain. If you could make it a *partie quarreé*, it would be a comfort indeed. We would beguile our lingering hours with talking over our youthful exploits, our hunts on Peter's mountain, with a long train of *et cetera*, in addition, and feel, by recollection at least, a momentary flash of youth. Reviewing the course of a long and sufficiently successful life, I find in no portion of it happier moments than these were.—To JAMES MAURY. vi, 54. FORD ED., ix, 351. (M., 1812.)

193. ——— ———. The hand of age is upon me. The decay of bodily faculties apprizes me that those of the mind cannot be unimpaired, had I not still better proofs. Every year counts my increased debility, and departing faculties keep the score. The last year it was the sight, this it is the hearing, the next something else will be going, until all is gone. Of all this I was sensible before I left Washington, and probably my fellow laborers saw it before I did. The decay of

memory was obvious; it is now become distressing. But the mind, too, is weakened. When I was young, mathematics was the passion of my life. The same passion has returned upon me, but with unequal powers. Processes which I then read off with the facility of common discourse, now cost me labor, and time, and slow investigation. When I offered this, therefore, as one of the reasons deciding my retirement from office, it was offered in sincerity and a consciousness of truth. And I think it a great blessing that I retain understanding enough to be sensible how much of it I have lost, and to avoid exposing myself as a spectacle for the pity of my friends; that I have surmounted the difficult point of knowing when to retire. As a compensation for faculties departed, nature gives me good health, and a perfect resignation to the laws of decay which she has prescribed to all the forms and combinations of matter.—To WILLIAM 'DUANE. vi, 80. FORD ED., ix, 367. (M., Oct. 1812.)

194. ——— ———. The epistolary industry * * * is gone from me. The aversion has been growing on me for a considerable time, and now, near the close of seventy-five, is become almost insuperable. I am much debilitated in body, and my memory sensibly on the wane. Still, however, I enjoy good health and spirits, and am as industrious a reader as when a student at college. Not of newspapers. These I have discarded. I relinquish, as I ought to do, all intermeddling with public affairs, committing myself cheerfully to the watch and care of those for whom, in my turn, I have watched and cared.—To BENJAMIN WATERHOUSE. vii, 100. FORD ED., x, 103. (M., 1818.)

195. AGE, Vigor in.—It is objected * * * that Mr. Goodrich is seventy-seven years of age; but at a much more advanced age, our Franklin was the ornament of human nature. —To THE NEW HAVEN COMMITTEE. iv, 403. FORD ED., viii, 68. (W., 1801.)

196. AGE, Warned by.—Time, which wears all things, does not spare the energies of body and mind of a *presque octogenaire*. While I could, I did what I could, and now acquiesce cheerfully in the law of nature which, by unfitting us for action, warns us to retire and leave to the generation of the day the direction of its own affairs. The prayers of an old man are the only contributions left in his power. To MRS. K. D. MORGAN. FORD ED., viii, 473. (M., 1822.)

197. ——— ———. A decline of health at the age of 76, was naturally to be expected, and is a warning of an event which cannot be distant, and whose approach I contemplate with little concern; for indeed, in no circumstance has nature been kinder to us, than in the soft gradations by which she prepares us to part willingly with what we are not destined always to retain. First one faculty is withdrawn and then another, sight, hearing, memory, affection and friends, filched one by one, till we are left among strangers, the mere monuments of times, facts, and specimens of antiquity for the observation of the curious.—To Mr. Spafford. vii, 118. (M., 1819.)

198. AGE, Yielding to.—I am not the champion called for by our present dangers. *"Non tali auxilio, nec defensoribus istis, tempus eget."* A waning body, a waning mind, and waning memory, with habitual ill health warn me to withdraw and relinquish the arena to younger and abler athletes. I am sensible myself, if others are not, that this is my duty. If my distant friends know it not, those around me can inform them that they should not, in friendship, wish to call me into conflicts, exposing only the decays which nature has inscribed among her unalterable laws, and injuring the common cause by a senile and puny defence.—To C. W. Glooch. vii, 430. (M., 1826.) See Life.

— AGENTS.—See Foreign Agents.

199. AGGRESSION, Condemned.—We did not invade their [the British peoples'] island, carrying death or slavery to its inhabitants.—Declaration on Taking up Arms. Ford ed., i, 475. (July 1775.)

200. AGGRESSION, Encouraging.—It is to be lamented that any of our citizens, not thinking with the mass of the nation as to the principles of our government, or of its administration, and seeing all its proceedings with a prejudiced eye, should so misconceive and misrepresent our situation as to encourage aggressions from foreign nations. Our expectation is, that their distempered views will be understood by others as they are by ourselves; but should wars be the consequence of these delusions, and the errors of our dissatisfied citizens find atonement only in the blood of their sounder brethren, we must meet it as an evil necessarily flowing from that liberty of speaking and writing which guards our other liberties.—R. to Philadelphia Democratic Republicans. viii, 128. (May 1808.)

— AGGRESSION, Equal Rights and.—See Rights.

201. AGGRESSION, Maritime.—The ocean, which, like the air, is the common birthright of mankind, is arbitrarily wrested from us, and maxims, consecrated by time, by usage, and by an universal sense of right, are trampled on by superior force.—R. to A. N. Y. Tammany Society. viii, 127. (1808.) See Ocean.

202. AGGRESSION, Military.—We did not embody a soldiery to commit aggression on them [the British people].—Declaration on Taking up Arms. Ford ed., i, 475. (July 1775.)

203. AGGRESSION, Prohibited.—We will not permit aggressions to be committed on our part, against which we remonstrated to Spain on her part.—To Robert Smith. v, 368. (M., Sep. 1808.)

204. AGGRESSION, Punishment for.—The interests of a nation, when well understood, will be found to coincide with their moral duties. Among these it is an important one to cultivate habits of peace and friendship with our neighbors. To do this we should make provisions for rendering the justice we must sometimes require from them. I recommend, therefore, to your consideration whether the laws of the Union should not be extended to restrain our citizens from committing acts of violence within the territories of other nations, which would be punished were they committed within our own.*—Paragraphs for President's Message. Ford ed., vi, 119. (1792.) See Filibusters.

205. AGITATION, Necessity for.—In peace as well as in war, the mind must be kept in motion.—To Marquis Lafayette. vii, 325. Ford ed., x, 280. (M., 1823.)

206. AGITATION, Submission.—The force of public opinion cannot be resisted, when permitted freely to be expressed. The agitation it produces must be submitted to. It is necessary to keep the waters pure.—To Marquis Layfayette vii, 325. Ford ed., x, 280. (M., 1823.)

207. AGRARIANISM, Laws of.—The tax on importations * * * falls exclusively on the rich, and with the equal partition of intestates' estates constitutes the best agrarian law.—To Dupont de Nemours. v, 584. Ford ed., ix, 321. (M., 1811.) See Entails, Primogeniture, Monopoly.

208. AGRICULTURE, Art of.—The first and most precious of all the arts.—To Robert R. Livingston. Ford ed., vii, 445. (Pa., 1800.)

209. AGRICULTURE, Atmosphere and.—The atmosphere is certainly the great workshop of nature for elaborating the fertilizing principles and insinuating them into the soil. It has been relied on as the sole means of regenerating our soil by most of the land-holders in the canton I inhabit, and where rest has been resorted to before a total exhaustion, the soil has never failed to recover. If, indeed, it be so run down as to be incapable of throwing weeds or herbage of any kind, to shade the soil from the sun, it either goes off in gullies, and is entirely lost, or remains exhausted till a growth springs up of such trees as will rise in the poorest soils. Under the shade of these and the cover soon formed of their deciduous leaves, and a commencing herbage, such fields sometimes recover in a long course of years; but this is too long to be taken into a course of hus-

* Jefferson subsequently recast these paragraphs as follows: "All observations are unnecessary on the value of peace with other nations. It would be wise however, by timely provisions, to guard against those acts of our own citizens, which might tend to disturb it, and to put ourselves in a condition to give satisfaction to foreign nations, which we may sometimes have occasion to require from them. I particularly recommend to your consideration the means of preventing those aggressions by our citizens on the territory of other nations, and other infractions of the law of nations, which, furnishing just subject of complaint, might endanger our peace with them."

bandry. Not so, however, is the term within which the atmosphere alone will reintegrate a soil rested in due season. A year of wheat will be balanced by one, two, or three years of rest and atmospheric influence, according to the quality of the soil.—To —— iv, 224. (Pa., 1798.)

210. AGRICULTURE, Commerce and. —With honesty and self-government for her portion, agriculture may abandon contentedly to others the fruits of commerce and corruption.—To HENRY MIDDLETON. vi, 91. (M., Jan. 1813.)

211. AGRICULTURE, Corn vs. pasturage.—In every country as fully peopled as France, it would seem good policy to encourage the employment of its lands in the cultivation of corn rather than in pasturage, and consequently to encourage the use of all kinds of salted provisions, because they can be imported from other countries.—To M. NECKAR. iii, 120. (P., 1789.)

212. AGRICULTURE, Devastated.—A very considerable portion of this country [France] has been desolated by a hail [storm] * * * Great contributions, public and private, are making for the sufferers. But they will be like the drop of water from the finger of Lazarus. There is no remedy for the present evil, but to bring the people to such a state of ease, as not to be ruined by the loss of a single crop. This hail may be considered as the *coup de grace* to an expiring victim.—To M. DE CREVECOEUR. ii, 458. (P., Aug. 1788.)

213. AGRICULTURE, Discrimination against.—Shall we permit the greatest part of the produce of our fields to rot on our hands, or lose half its value by subjecting it to high insurance, [in the event of war,] merely that our shipbuilders may have brisker employ? Shall the whole mass of our farmers be sacrificed to the class of shipwrights?—OFFICIAL OPINION. vii, 625. (1793.)

214. AGRICULTURE, Encouragement of.—[The] encouragement of agriculture, and of commerce as its handmaid, I deem [one of the] essential principles of our government and, consequently [one] which ought to shape its administration.—FIRST INAUGURAL ADDRESS. viii, 4. FORD ED., viii, 5. (1821.)

215. AGRICULTURE, Equilibrium of. —An equilibrium of agriculture, manufactures and commerce is certainly become essential to our independence.—To JAMES JAY. v, 440. (M., 1809.)

216. AGRICULTURE, Freedom of.— Agriculture, manufactures, commerce and navigation, the four pillars of our prosperity, are the most thriving when left most free to individual enterprise. Protection from casual embarrassments, however, may sometimes be seasonably interposed.—FIRST ANNUAL MESSAGE. viii, 13. FORD ED., viii, 123. (Dec. 1801.)

217. AGRICULTURE, French and English.—I traversed England much, and own both town and country fell short of my expectations. Comparing it with France, I found a much greater proportion of barrens, a soil, in other parts, not naturally so good as this, not better cultivated, but better manured, and therefore more productive. This proceeds from the practice of long leases there, and short ones here.—To JOHN PAGE. i, 549. FORD ED., iv, 213. (P., 1786.)

218. AGRICULTURE, Grasses.—I send some seeds of a grass, found very useful in the southern part of Europe, and particularly, and almost solely cultivated in Malta. It is called by the names of Sulla, and Spanish St. Foin, and is the Hedysarum coronarium of Linnæus. It is usually sown early in autumn.—To WILLIAM DRAYTON. i, 554. (P., 1786.)

219. ——— ———. I send a little Spanish San Foin, represented to me as a very precious grass in a hot country. I would have it sowed in one of the vacant lots of my grass ground.—To NICHOLAS LEWIS. FORD ED., iv, 344. (P., 1786.)

220. ——— ———. I am much obliged to you for your attention to my trees and grass. The latter is one of the principal pillars on which I shall rely for subsistence when I shall be at liberty to try projects without injury to anybody.—To NICHOLAS LEWIS. FORD ED., iv, 343. (P., 1786.)

221. AGRICULTURE, Happiness and. —The United States * * * will be more virtuous, more free and more happy, employed in agriculture, than as carriers or manufacturers. It is a truth, and a precious one for them, if they could be persuaded of it.— To M. DE WARVILLE. ii, 11. FORD ED., iv, 281. (P., 1786.)

222. ——— ———. How far it may lessen our happiness to be rendered merely agricultural; how far that state is more friendly to principles of virtue and liberty, are questions yet to be solved.—To HORATIO GATES. iv, 213. FORD ED., vii, 205. (Pa., 1798.)

223. ——— ———. In general, it is a truth that if every nation will employ itself in what it is fittest to produce, a greater quantity will be raised of the things contributing to human happiness, than if every nation attempts to raise everything it wants within itself.—To MR. LASTEYRIE. v, 315. (W., 1808.)

224. AGRICULTURE, Hunting and.— A little labor in the earth will produce more food than the best hunts you can now make, and the women will spin and weave more clothing than the men can procure by hunting. We shall very willingly assist you in this course by furnishing you with the necessary tools and implements, and with persons to instruct you in the use of them.—ADDRESS TO CHICKASAWS. viii, 199. (1805.)

225. AGRICULTURE, Income from.— The moderate and sure income of husbandry begets permanent improvement, quiet, life, and orderly conduct, both public and private.—To GENERAL WASHINGTON. ii, 252. (P., 1787.)

226. AGRICULTURE, Land, labor and.—The indifferent state of agriculture among us does not proceed from a want of knowledge merely; it is from our having such quantities of land to waste as we please. In Europe the object is to make the most of their land, labor being abundant; here it is to make the most of our labor, land being abundant.—NOTES ON VIRGINIA. viii, 332. FORD ED., iii, 190. (1782.)

227. AGRICULTURE, Manufactures, commerce and.—I trust the good sense of our country will see that its greatest prosperity depends on a due balance between agriculture, manufactures and commerce.—To THOMAS LEIPER. v, 417. FORD ED., ix, 239. (W., 1809.)

228. AGRICULTURE, Model plow.—I shall with great pleasure attend to the construction and transmission to the Society [Agricultural Society of Paris] of a plow with my mould board. This is the only part of that useful instrument to which I have paid any particular attention. But knowing how much the perfection of the plough must depend, 1st, on the line of traction; 2nd, on the direction of the share; 3rd, on the angle of the wing; 4th, on the form of the mould board; and persuaded that I shall find the three first advantages, eminently exemplified in that which the Society sends me, I am anxious to see combined with these a mould-board of my form, in the hope it will still advance the perfection of that machine.—To M. SYLVESTRE. v, 313. (W., 1808.)

229. ——— ———. I have received the medal of gold by which the Society of Agriculture at Paris have been pleased to mark their approbation of a form of the mould-board which I had proposed; also * * * the information that they had honored me with the title of foreign associate to their society. I receive with great thankfulness these testimonies of their favor, and should be happy to merit them by greater services.—To M. SYLVESTRE. v, 83. (W., 1807.)

230. AGRICULTURE, Morals and.—The pursuits of agriculture * * * are the best preservative of morals.—To J. BLAIR. ii, 248. (Pa., 1787.)

231. AGRICULTURE, New cultures.—The greatest service which can be rendered any country is to add an useful plant to its culture; especially a bread grain; next in value to bread is oil.—SERVICES OF JEFFERSON. i, 176. FORD ED., vii, 477. (1800?)

232. ——— ———. Perhaps I may render some service by forwarding to the [Agricultural] Society* [of South Carolina] such new objects of culture, as may be likely to succeed in the soil and climate of South Carolina. In an infant country, as ours is, these

* The Society had elected Jefferson a member.—EDITOR.

experiments are important. We are probably far from possessing, as yet, all the articles of culture for which nature has fitted our country. To find out these, will require abundance of unsuccessful experiments. But if, in a multitude of these, we make one useful acquisition, it repays our trouble. Perhaps it is the peculiar duty of associated bodies to undertake these experiments. Under this sense of the views of the society, * * * I shall be attentive to procure for them the seeds of such plants as they will be so good as to point out to me, or as shall occur to myself as worthy their notice.—To WILLIAM DRAYTON. i, 554. (P., 1786.)

233. ——— ———. I received the seeds of the bread-tree. * * * One service of this kind rendered to a nation, is worth more to them than all the victories of the most splendid pages of their history, and becomes a source of exalted pleasure to those who have been instrumental in it.—To M. GIRAUD. iv, 175. (1797.)

234. ——— ———. The introduction of new cultures, and especially of objects of leading importance to our comfort, is certainly worthy the attention of every government, and nothing short of the actual experiment should discourage an essay of which any hope can be entertained.—To M. LASTEYRIE. v, 315. (W., 1808.)

235. AGRICULTURE, Prosperity and.—A prosperity built on the basis of agriculture is that which is most desirable to us, because to the efforts of labor it adds the efforts of a greater proportion of soil.—CIRCULAR TO CONSULS. iii, 431. (Pa., 1792.) See 216.

236. AGRICULTURE, Prostration of.—The long succession of years of stunted crops, of reduced prices, the general prostration of the farming business, under levies for the support of manufacturers, &c., with the calamitous fluctuations of value in our paper medium, have kept agriculture in a state of abject depression, which has peopled the western States by silently breaking up those on the Atlantic, and glutted the land market, while it drew off its bidders. In such a state of things, property has lost its character of being a resource for debts. Highland in Belford, which, in the days of our plethory, sold readily for from fifty to one hundred dollars the acre, (and such sales were many then,) would not now sell for more than from ten to twenty dollars, or one-quarter or one-fifth of its former price.—To JAMES MADISON. vii, 434. FORD ED., x, 377. (M., February 1826.)

— AGRICULTURE, Rice.—See RICE.

237. AGRICULTURE, Riches and.—The pursuits of agriculture are the surest road to affluence.—To J. BLAIR. ii, 248. (P., 1787.)

238. AGRICULTURE, Rotation of crops.—By varying the articles of culture, we multiply the chances for making something and disarm the seasons in a proportionable degree, of their calamitous effect.—To WILLIAM DRAYTON. ii, 199. (P., 1787.)

239. —— ——. I find * * * that a ten years abandonment of my lands to the ravages of overseers, has brought on them a degree of degradation far beyond what I had expected. As this obliges me to adopt a milder course of cropping, * * * I have determined on a division of my farm into six fields, to be put under this rotation: first year, wheat; second, corn, potatoes, peas; third, rye or wheat, according to circumstances; fourth and fifth, clover where the fields will bring it, and buckwheat dressings where they will not; sixth, folding, and buckwheat dressings. But it will take me from three to six years to get this plan under way.—To PRESIDENT WASHINGTON. iv, 106. FORD ED., vi, 509. (M., May 1794.)

240. —— ——. I find the degradation of my lands by ill usage much beyond what I had expected, and at the same time much more open land than I had calculated on. One of these circumstances forces a milder course of cropping on me, and the other enables me to adopt it. I drop, therefore, two crops in my rotation, and instead of five crops in eight years, take three in six years, in the following order. 1. Wheat. 2. Corn and potatoes in the strongest moiety, potatoes alone or pease alone in the other moiety, according to its strength. 3. Wheat or rye. 4. Clover. 6. Folding and buckwheat dressing. In such of my fields as are too much worn for clover, I propose to try St. Foin, which I know will grow in the poorest land, bring plentiful crops, and is a great ameliorator.—To JOHN TAYLOR. FORD ED., vi, 506. (M., 1794.)

241. —— ——. It has been said that no rotation of crops will keep the earth in the same degree of fertility without the aid of manure. But it is well known here that a space of rest greater or less in spontaneous herbage, will restore the exhaustion of a single crop. This then is a rotation; and as it is not to be believed that spontaneous herbage is the only or best covering during rest, so may we expect that a substitute for it may be found which will yield profitable crops. Such perhaps are clover, peas, vetches, &c. A rotation then may be found, which by giving time for the slow influence of the atmosphere, will keep the soil in a constant and equal state of fertility. But the advantage of manuring is that it will do more in one than the atmosphere would require several years to do, and consequently enables you so much the oftener to take exhausting crops from the soil, a circumstance of importance where there is much more labor than land.—To ——. iv, 225. (Pa., 1798.)

242. —— ——. I have lately received the proceedings of the Agricultural Society of Paris. * * * I have been surprised to find that the rotation of crops and substitution of some profitable growth preparatory for grain, instead of the useless and expensive fallow,

is yet only dawning among them.—To ROBERT R. LIVINGSTON. v, 224. (W., 1808.)

243. AGRICULTURE, Societies.—I have on several occasions been led to think on some means of uniting the State agricultural societies into a central society; and lately it has been pressed from England with a view to a cooperation with their Board of Agriculture. You know some have proposed to Congress to incorporate such a society. I am against that, because I think Congress cannot find in all the enumerated powers any one which authorizes the act, much less the giving the public money to that use. I believe, too, if they had the power, it would soon be used for no other purpose than to buy with sinecures useful partisans. I believe it will thrive best if left to itself, as the Philosophical Societies are. There is certainly a much greater abundance of material for Agricultural Societies than Philosophical. But what should be the plan of union? Would it do for the State societies to agree to meet in a central society by a deputation of members? If this should present difficulties, might they not be lessened by their adopting into their society some one or more of their delegates in Congress, or of the members of the Executive residing here, who assembling necessarily for other purposes, could occasionally meet on the business of their societies? Your [New York] Agricultural Society, standing undoubtedly on the highest ground, might set the thing agoing by writing to such State societies as already exist, and these once meeting centrally might induce the other States to establish societies, and thus complete the institution. This is a mere idea of mine, not sufficiently considered or digested, and hazarded merely to set you to thinking on the subject, and propose something better or to improve this. Will you be so good as to consider it at your leisure, and give me your thoughts on the subject?—To ROBERT R. LIVINGSTON. FORD ED., vii, 492. (W., Feb. 1801.)

244. —— ——. Our Agricultural Society has at length formed itself. Like our American Philosophical Society, it is voluntary, and unconnected with the public, and is precisely an execution of the plan I formerly sketched to you. Some State societies have been formed heretofore; the other States will do the same. Each State society names two of its members of Congress to be their members in the Central Society, which is of course together during the sessions of Congress. They are to select matter from the proceedings of the State societies, and to publish it. * * * Mr. Madison, the Secretary of State, is their President.—To SIR JOHN SINCLAIR. iv, 491. (W., 1803.)

245. —— ——. Were practical and observing husbandmen in each county to form themselves into a society, commit to writing themselves, or state in conversations at their meetings to be written down by others, their practices, and observations, their experiences and ideas, selections from these might be made from time to time by every one for his own use, or by the society or a committee of it, for more general purposes. By an interchange of these selections among the societies of the different counties, each might thus become possessed of the useful ideas and processes of the whole; and every one adopt such of them as he should deem suitable to his own situation. Or to abridge the labor of such multiplied correspondences, a central society might be agreed on to which, as a common deposit, all the others should send their communications. The society thus honored by the general confidence would doubtless feel and fulfil the duty of selecting such papers as should be worthy of entire communication, of extracting and digesting from others whatever might be useful, and of condensing their matter within such compass as might reconcile it to the reading, as well as to the purchase of the great mass of practical men. Many circumstances would recommend, for the central society, that which should be established in the county of the seat of government.—PLAN FOR AGRICULTURAL SOCIETIES. ix, 480. (1811.)

246. AGRICULTURE, Strawberry.— There are two or three objects which you should endeavor to enrich our country with. One is the Alpine strawberry.—To JAMES MONROE. FORD ED., vii, 21. (M., 1795.)

247. AGRICULTURE, Support from.— Agriculture is the basis of the subsistence, the comforts and the happiness of man.—To BARON DE MOLL. vi, 363. (M., 1814.)

248. AGRICULTURE, Threshing machine.— I shall thank you most sincerely for the model of the threshing machine, besides replacing the expense of it. The threshing out our wheat immediately after harvest being the only preservative against the weavil in Virginia, the service you will thereby render that State will make you to them a second Triptolemus.—To THOMAS PINCKNEY. FORD ED., vi, 214. (Pa., 1793.)

249. AGRICULTURE, Tobacco.— Tobacco is a culture productive of infinite wretchedness. Those employed in it are in a continual state of exertion beyond the power of nature to support. Little food of any kind is raised by them; so that the men and animals on these farms are badly fed, and the earth is rapidly impoverished. The cultivation of wheat is the reverse in every circumstance. Besides clothing the earth with herbage, and preserving its fertility, it feeds the laborers plentifully, requires from them only a moderate toil, except in the season of harvest, raises great numbers of animals for food and service, and diffuses plenty and happiness among the whole. We find it easier to make an hundred bushels of wheat than a thousand weight of tobacco, and they are worth more when made.—NOTES ON VIRGINIA. viii, 407. FORD ED., iii, 271. (1782.)

250. AGRICULTURE, Utility.— Agriculture is the most useful of the occupations of man.—To M. SILVESTRE. v, 83. (W., 1807.)

251. AGRICULTURE, Virginia.— Good husbandry with us consists in abandoning Indian corn and tobacco; tending small grain, some red clover, fallowing, and endeavoring to have, while the lands are at rest, a spontaneous cover of white clover. I do not present this as a culture judicious in itself, but as good, in comparison with what most people there pursue. Mr. [Arthur] Young has never had an opportunity of seeing how slowly the fertility of the soil is exhausted, with moderate management of it. I can affirm that the James River low-grounds, with the cultivation of small grain, will never be exhausted; because we know, that, under that condition, we must now and then take them down with Indian corn, or they become, as they were originally, too rich to bring wheat. The highlands where I live, have been cultivated about sixty years. The culture was tobacco and Indian corn, as long as they would bring enough to pay the labor; then they were turned out. After four or five years rest, they would bring good corn again, and in double that time, perhaps, good tobacco. Then they would be exhausted by a second series of tobacco and corn.—To PRESIDENT WASHINGTON. iv, 4. FORD ED., vi, 83. (1793.)

— AGRICULTURE, Wheat.—See 249, and WHEAT.

252. AGRICULTURE, Wisest of pursuits.— Agriculture is the wisest pursuit of all.—To R. IZARD. i, 442. (P., 1785.)

253. ——— ———. Agriculture is our wisest pursuit, because it will in the end contribute most to real wealth, good morals and happiness.—To GENERAL WASHINGTON. ii, 252. (P., 1787.)

254. AGRICULTURE, Writings on.— Writings on agriculture are peculiarly pleasing to me, for, as they tell us, we are sprung from the earth, so to that we naturally return.*—To ROBERT R. LIVINGSTON. v., 224. (W., 1808.) See FARMERS and FARMING.

— AIR.—See 209.

— ALBEMARLE COUNTY.—See APPENDIX.

255. ALEXANDER OF RUSSIA, Character of.— A more virtuous man, I believe, does not exist, nor one who is more enthusiastically devoted to better the condition of mankind. He will probably, one day, fall a victim to it, as a monarch of that principle does not suit a Russian noblesse. He is not of the very first order of understanding, but

* Jefferson was always an enthusiast in agriculture. He was never too busy to find time to note the dates of the planting and the ripening of his vegetables and fruits. He left behind him a table enumerating thirty-seven esculents, and showing the earliest date of the appearance of each one of them in the Washington market in each of eight successive years. He had ever a quick observation and a keen intelligence ready for every fragment of new knowledge or hint of a useful invention in the way of field work. All through his busy official life, abroad and at home, he appears ceaselessly to have an eye on the soil and one ear open to its cultivators; he is always comparing varying methods and results, sending new seeds hither and thither, making suggestions, trying experiments, till, in the presence of his enterprise and activity, one begins to think that the stagnating character so commonly attributed to the Virginia planters must be fabulous.—JOHN T. MORSE, JR., *Life of Jefferson.*

he is of a high one. He has taken a peculiar affection to this country and its government, of which he has given me public as well as personal proofs. Our nation being, like his, habitually neutral, our interests as to neutral rights, and our sentiments agree. And whenever conferences for peace shall take place, we are assured of a friend in him. In fact, although in questions of restitution he will be with England, in those of neutral rights he will be with Bonaparte, and with every other power in the world except England; and I do presume that England will never have peace until she subscribes to a just code of marine law. I am confident that Russia (while her present monarch lives) is the most cordially friendly to us of any power on earth, will go furthest to serve us, and is most worthy of conciliation.—To WILLIAM DUANE. v, 140. FORD ED., ix, 120. (W., June 1807.)

256. —— ——. I owe an acknowledgment to your Imperial Majesty for the great satisfaction I have received from your letter of Aug. 20th, 1895, and embrace the opportunity it affords of giving expression to the sincere respect and veneration I entertain for your character. It will be among the latest and most soothing comforts of my life, to have seen advanced to the government of so extensive a portion of the earth, and at so early a period of his life, a sovereign whose ruling passion is the advancement of the happiness and prosperity of his people; and not of his own people only, but who can extend his eye and his good will to a distant and infant nation, unoffending in its course, unambitious in its views.—To THE EMPEROR OF RUSSIA. v, 7. FORD ED., viii, 430. (W., April 1806.)

257. ALEXANDER OF RUSSIA, France and.—I have no doubt that the firmness of Alexander in favor of France, after the disposition of Bonaparte, has saved that country from evils still more severe than she is suffering, and perhaps even from partition.— To GEORGE LOGAN. vii, 20. (M., 1816.)

258. ALEXANDER OF RUSSIA, Friendliness to U. S.—Of Alexander's sense of the merits of our form of government, of its wholesome operation on the condition of the people, and of the interest he takes in the success of our experiment, we possess the most unquestionable proofs; and to him we shall be indebted if the rights of neutrals, to be settled whenever peace is made, shall be extended beyond the present belligerents; that is to say, European neutrals, as George and Napoleon, of mutual consent and common hatred against us, would concur in excluding us. I thought it a salutary measure to engage the powerful patronage of Alexander at conferences for peace, at a time when Bonaparte was courting him; and although circumstances have lessened its weight, yet it is prudent for us to cherish his good dispositions, as those alone which will be exerted in our favor when that occasion shall occur. He, like ourselves, sees and feels the atrociousness of both the belligerents.—To WILLIAM DUANE. v, 553. FORD ED., ix, 287. (M., Nov. 1810.)

259. —— ——. He is the only sovereign who cordially loves us.—To WILLIAM DUANE. v, 553. FORD ED., ix, 287. (M., 1810.)

260. ALEXANDER OF RUSSIA, Gift of Books to.—A little before Dr. Priestley's death, he informed me that he had received intimations, through a channel he confided in, that the Emperor entertained a wish to know something of our Constitution. I have, therefore, selected the two best works we have on that subject, for which I pray you to ask a place in his library.—To MR. HARRIS. v, 6. (W., 1806.)

261. ALEXANDER OF RUSSIA, Mission to.—Desirous of promoting useful intercourse and good understanding between your Majesty's subjects and the citizens of the United States and especially to cultivate the friendship of your Majesty, I have appointed William Short,* one of our distinguished citizens, to be in quality of Minister Plenipotentiary of the United States, the bearer to you of assurances of their sincere friendship, and of their desire to maintain with your Majesty and your subjects the strictest relations of amity and commerce; he will explain to your Majesty the peculiar position of these States, separated by a wide ocean from the powers of Europe, with interests and pursuits distinct from theirs, and consequently without the motives or the appetites for taking part in the associations or oppositions which a different system of interests produces among them: he is charged to assure your Majesty more particularly of our purpose to observe a faithful neutrality towards the contending powers, in the war to which your Majesty is a party, rendering to all the services and courtesies of friendship, and praying for the reestablishment of peace and right among them; and we entertain an entire confidence that this just and faithful conduct on the part of the United States will strengthen the friendly dispositions you have manifested towards them, and be a fresh motive with so just and magnanimous a sovereign to enforce, by the high influence of your example, the respect due to the character and the rights of a peaceable nation.—To THE EMPEROR OF RUSSIA. v, 358. FORD ED., ix, 206. (W., Aug. 1808.)

262. ALEXANDER OF RUSSIA, Neutral Rights and.—The northern nations of Europe, at the head of which your Majesty is distinguished, are habitually peaceable. The United States of America, like them, are attached to peace. We have then with them a common interest in the neutral rights. Every nation indeed, on the continent of Europe, belligerent as well as neutral, is interested in maintaining these rights, liberalizing them progressively with the progress of science and refinement of morality, and in relieving them from restrictions which the extension of the arts has long since rendered unreasonable and vexatious.—To THE EMPEROR OF RUSSIA. v, 8. FORD ED., viii, 440. (W., April 1806.)

263. —— ——. The events of Europe come to us so late, and so suspiciously, that observations on them would certainly be stale, and possibly wide of their actual state. From their general aspect, however, I collect that your Majesty's interposition in them has been disinterested and generous, and having in view only the general good of the great European family. When you shall proceed to the pacification which is to reestablish peace and commerce, the same dispositions of mind will lead you to think of the general intercourse of nations, and to make that provision for its

* Mr. Short's appointment was negatived by the senate partly on personal grounds, but more especially because of an unwillingness to increase the diplomatic establishment.—EDITOR.

future maintenance which, in times past, it has so much needed.—To THE EMPEROR OF RUSSIA. v, 8. FORD ED., viii, 439. (W., April 1806.)

264. —— ——. Having taken no part in the past or existing troubles of Europe, we have no part to act in its pacification. But as principles may then be settled in which we have a deep interest, it is a great happiness for us that we are placed under the protection of an umpire, who, looking beyond the narrow bounds of an individual nation, will take under the cover of his equity the rights of the absent and unrepresented. It is only by a happy concurrence of good characters and good occasions, that a step can now and then be taken to advance the well-being of nations. If the present occasion be good, I am sure your Majesty's character will not be wanting to avail the world of it. By monuments of such good offices, may your life become an epoch in the history of the condition of man; and may He who called it into being, for the good of the human family, give it length of days and success, and have it always in His holy keeping.—To THE EMPEROR OF RUSSIA. v, 8. FORD ED., viii, 440. (W., April 1806.)

265. —— ——. Two personages in Europe, of which your Majesty is one, have it in their power, at the approaching pacification, to render eminent service to nations in general, by incorporating into the act of pacification a correct definition of the rights of neutrals on the high seas. Such a definition declared by all the powers lately or still belligerent, would give to those rights a precision and notoriety, and cover them with an authority, which would protect them in an important degree against future violation; and should any further sanction be necessary, that of an exclusion of the violating nation from commercial intercourse with all the others, would be preferred to war, as more analogous to the offence, more easily and likely to be executed with good faith. The essential articles of these rights, too, are so few and simple as to be easily defined.—To THE EMPEROR OF RUSSIA. v, 8. FORD ED., viii, 440. (W., April 1806.)

266. —— ——. That the Emperor may be able, whenever a pacification takes place, to show himself the father and friend of the human race, to restore to nations the moral laws which have governed their intercourse, and to prevent, forever, a repetition of those ravages by sea and land, which will distinguish the present as an age of Vandalism, I sincerely pray.—To COUNT PAHLEN. v, 527. (M., 1810.)

267. ALEXANDER OF RUSSIA, Reform and.—The apparition of such a man [as Alexander] on a throne is one of the phenomena which will distinguish the present epoch so remarkable in the history of man. But he must have an herculean task to devise and establish the means of securing freedom and happiness to those who are not capable of taking care of themselves. Some preparation seems necessary to qualify the body of a nation for self-government. Who could have thought the French nation incapable of it? Alexander will doubtless begin at the right end, by taking means for diffusing instruction and a sense of their natural rights through the mass of his people, and for relieving them in the meantime from actual oppression.—To DR. JOSEPH PRIESTLEY. FORD ED., viii, 179. (W., Nov. 1802.)

268. —— ——. The information * * * as to Alexander kindles a great deal of interest in his existence, and strong spasms of the heart in his favor. Though his means of doing good are great, yet the materials on which he is to work are refractory. Whether he engages in private correspondences abroad, as the King of Prussia did much, his grandfather sometimes, I know not; but certainly such a correspondence would be very interesting to those who are sincerely anxious to see mankind raised from their present abject condition.—To THOMAS COOPER. iv, 452. FORD ED., viii, 177. (W., Nov. 1802.)

269. ALEXANDER OF RUSSIA, Tribute to.—I am much flattered by the kind notice of the Emperor, which you have been so obliging as to communicate to me. The approbation of the good is always consoling; but that of a sovereign whose station and endowments are so pre-eminent, is received with a sensibility which the veneration for his character inspires. Among other motives of commiseration which the calamities of Europe cannot fail to excite in every virtuous mind, the interruption which these have given to the benevolent views of the Emperor, is prominent. The accession of a sovereign, with the dispositions and qualifications to improve the condition of a great nation, and to place its happiness on a permanent basis, is a phenomenon so rare in the annals of mankind that when the blessing occurs, it is lamentable that any portion of it should be usurped by occurrences of the character we have seen. If separated from these scenes by an ocean of a thousand leagues breadth, they have required all our cares to keep aloof from their desolating effects, I can readily conceive how much more they must occupy those to whose territories they are contiguous.—To COUNT PAHLEN. v, 526. (M., 1810.)

270. ALEXANDER OF RUSSIA, Triumphs of.—To the wonders of Bonaparte's rise and fall, we may add that of a Czar of Muscovy, dictating, in Paris, laws and limits to all the successors of the Cæsars, and holding even the balance in which the fortunes of this new world are suspended.—To JOHN ADAMS. vi, 353. FORD ED., ix, 461. (M., 1814.)

271. ALEXANDER OF RUSSIA, Vienna Congress and.—The magnanimity of Alexander's conduct on the first capture of Paris still magnified everything we had believed of him; but how he will come out of his present trial remains to be seen. That the sufferings which France had inflicted on other countries justified severe reprisals, cannot be questioned; but I have not yet learned what crimes of Poland, Saxony, Belgium, Venice, Lombardy and Genoa, had merited for them, not merely a temporary punishment, but that of permanent subjugation and a destitution of independence and self-government. The fable of Æsop of the lion dividing the spoils, is, I fear, becoming true history, and the moral code of Napoleon and the English government a substitute for that of Grotius, of Puffendorf, and even of the pure doctrine of the great author of our holy religion.—To DR. GEORGE LOGAN. vi, 497. (M., Oct. 1815.)

272. —— ——. His character is undoubtedly good, and the world, I think, may expect good effects from it. * * * I sincerely wish that the history of the secret proceedings at Vienna may become known, and may reconcile to our good opinion of him his participation in the demolition of ancient and independent States, transferring them and their

inhabitants as farms and stocks of cattle at a market to other owners, and even taking a part of the spoil himself. It is possible to suppose a case excusing this, and my partiality for his character encourages me to expect it, and to impute to others, known to have no moral scruples, the crimes, of that conclave, who under pretence of punishing the atrocities of Bonaparte, reached them themselves, and proved that with equal power they were equally flagitious.—To DR. LOGAN. vii, 20. (M., 1816.)

273. ALEXANDER OF RUSSIA, Virtues of.—I had * * * formed the most favorable opinion of the virtues of Alexander, and considered his partiality to this country as a prominent proof of them.—To DR. GEORGE LOGAN. vi, 497. (M., 1815.)

274. ALEXANDRIA, Baltimore and.—It is not amiss to encourage Alexandria, because it is a rival in the very bosom of Baltimore.—To JAMES MONROE. FORD ED., iv, 19. (P., 1784.)

275. ALEXANDRIA, Future of.—Alexandria on the Potomac will undoubtedly become a very great place, but Norfolk would be best for cotton manufactures.—To M. DE LA VALEE. i, 430. (P., 1785.)

— ALGIERS.—See BARBARY POWERS and 1137.

276. ALIENAGE, Law of Violated.—The bill for establishing a National Bank undertakes * * * to form the subscribers into a corporation, [and] to enable them, in their corporate capacities, to make alien subscribers capable of holding lands; and so far is against the laws of *Alienage.*—OPINION ON THE BANK BILL. vii, 555. FORD ED., v, 284. (February 1791.)

— ALIENATION OF TERRITORY.—See TERRITORY.

277. ALIEN AND SEDITION LAWS, Hatching.—One of the war party, in a fit of unguarded passion, declared some time ago they would pass a citizen bill, an alien bill, and a sedition bill; accordingly, some days ago, Coit laid a motion on the table of the House of Representatives for modifying the citizen law. Their threats point at Gallatin, and it is believed they will endeavor to reach him by this bill. Yesterday Mr. Hillhouse laid on the table of the Senate a motion for giving power to send away suspected aliens. This understood to be meant for Volney and Collot. But it will not stop there when it gets into a course of execution. There is now only wanting, to accomplish the whole declaration before mentioned, a sedition bill, which we shall certainly soon see proposed.—To JAMES MADISON. iv, 237. FORD ED., vii, 244. (Pa., April 26 1798.)

278. ALIEN AND SEDITION LAWS, Introduction of.—They have brought into the lower House a sedition bill, which, among other enormities, undertakes to make printing certain matters criminal, though one of the amendments to the Constitution has so expressly taken religion, printing presses, &c. out of their coercion. Indeed this bill, and the

alien bill are both so palpably in the teeth of the Constitution as to show they mean to pay no respect to it.—To JAMES MADISON. FORD ED., vii, 266. (Pa., June 1798.)

279. ALIEN AND SEDITION LAWS, Petitions against.—Petitions and remonstrances against the Alien and Sedition laws are coming from various parts of New York, Jersey and Pennsylvania. * * * I am in hopes Virginia will stand so countenanced by those States as to repress the wishes of the Government to coerce her, which they might venture on if they supposed she would be left alone. Firmness on our part, but a passive firmness, is the true course. Anything rash or threatening might check the favorable dispositions of these middle States, and rally them again around the measures which are ruining us.—To JAMES MADISON. iv, 279. FORD ED., vii, 341. (Pa., Jan. 1799.)

280. ALIEN AND SEDITION LAWS, Planning Insurrection against.—In Pennsylvania, we fear that the ill-designing may produce insurrection [against the Alien and Sedition laws]. Nothing could be so fatal. Anything like force would check the progress of the public opinion, and rally them around the government. This is not the kind of opposition the American people will permit. But keep away all show of force, and they will bear down the evil propensities of the government, by the constitutional means of election and petition.—To EDWARD PENDLETON. iv, 287. FORD ED., vii, 356. (Pa., Feb. 1799.)

281. ———— ————. Several parts of this State [Pennsylvania] are so violent that we fear an insurrection. This will be brought about by some if they can. It is the only thing we have to fear. The appearance of an attack of force against the government would check the present current of the middle States, and rally them around the government; whereas if suffered to go on, it will pass on to a reformation of abuses.—To ARCHIBALD STUART. iv, 286. FORD ED., vii, 354. (Pa., Feb. 1799.)

282. ALIEN AND SEDITION LAWS, Report on.—Yesterday witnessed a scandalous scene in the House of Representatives. It was the day for taking up the report of their committee against the Alien and Sedition laws, &c. They [the Federalists] held a caucus and determined that not a word should be spoken on their side, in answer to anything which should be said on the other. Gallatin took up the Alien, and Nicholas the Sedition law; but after a little while of common silence, they began to enter into loud conversations, laugh, cough, &c., so that for the last hour of these gentlemen's speaking, they must have had the lungs of a vendue master to have been heard. Livingston, however, attempted to speak. But after a few sentences, the Speaker called him to order, and told him what he was saying was not to the question. It was impossible to proceed. The question was carried in favor of the report, 52 to 48:

the real strength of the two parties is 56 to 50.—To JAMES MADISON. iv, 298. FORD ED., vii, 371. (Pa., Feb. 1799.)

283. ALIEN AND SEDITION LAWS, Scheme of.—I consider these laws as merely an experiment on the American mind, to see how far it will bear an avowed violation of the Constitution. If this goes down, we shall immediately see attempted another act of Congress, declaring that the President shall continue in office during life, reserving to another occasion the transfer of the succession to the heirs, and the establishment of the Senate for life. At least, this may be the aim of the Oliverians, while Monk and the Cavaliers, (who are perhaps the strongest,) may be playing their game for the restoration of his most gracious Majesty, George III. That these things are in contemplation, I have no doubt; nor can I be confident of their failure, after the dupery of which our countrymen have shown themselves susceptible.—To S. T. MASON. iv, 258. FORD ED., vii, 283. (M., 1798.)

284. ALIEN AND SEDITION LAWS, Suits under.—I discharged every person under punishment or prosecution under the Sedition law, because I considered, and now consider, that law to be a nullity, as absolute and as palpable as if Congress had ordered us to fall down and worship a golden image; and that it was as much my duty to arrest its execution in every stage, as it would have been to have rescued from the fiery furnace those who should have been cast into it for refusing to worship the image. It was accordingly done in every instance, without asking what the offenders had done, or against whom they had offended, but whether the pains they were suffering were inflicted under the pretended Sedition law.—To MRS. JOHN ADAMS. iv, 536. FORD ED., viii, 309. (W., July 1804.)

285. ———— ————. With respect to the dismission of the prosecutions for sedition in Connecticut, it is well known to have been a tenet of the republican portion of our fellow citizens, that the Sedition law was contrary to the Constitution and, therefore, void. On this ground I considered it as a nullity whenever I met it in the course of my duties; and on this ground I directed *nolle prosequis* in all the prosecutions which had been instituted under it; and, as far as the public sentiment can be inferred from the occurrences of the day, we must say that this opinion had the sanction of the nation. The prosecutions, therefore, which were afterwards instituted in Connecticut, of which two were against printers, two against preachers, and one against a judge, were too inconsistent with this principle to be permitted to go on. We were bound to administer to others the same measure of law, not which they had meted to us, but we to ourselves, and to extend to all equally the protection of the same constitutional principles. These prosecutions, too. were chiefly for charges against myself, and I had from the beginning laid it down as a

rule to notice nothing of the kind. I believed that the long course of services in which I had acted on the public stage, and under the eye of my fellow citizens, furnished better evidence to them of my character and principles, than the angry invectives of adverse partisans in whose eyes the very acts most approved by the majority were subjects of the greatest demerit and censure. These prosecutions against them, therefore, were to be dismissed as a matter of duty—To GIDEON GRANGER. vi, 332. FORD ED., ix, 456. (M., 1814.)

286. ALIEN AND SEDITION LAWS, Tyrannical.—If the Alien and Sedition Acts should stand, these conclusions would flow from them: that the General Government may place any act they may think proper on the list of crimes, and punish it themselves whether enumerated or not enumerated by the Constitution as cognizable by them: that they may transfer its cognizance to the President, or any other person, who may himself be the accuser. counsel, judge and jury, whose *suspicion* may be the evidence, his *order* the sentence, his *officer* the executioner, and his breast the sole record of the transaction: that a very numerous and valuable description of the inhabitants of these states being, by this precedent, reduced, as outlaws, to the absolute dominion of one man, and the barrier of the Constitution thus swept away from us all, no rampart now remains against the passions and the powers of a majority in Congress to protect from a like exportation, or other more grievous punishment, the minority of the same body, the legislatures, judges, governors, and counsellors of the States, nor their other peaceable inhabitants, who may venture to reclaim the constitutional rights and liberties of the States and people, or who for other causes, good or bad, may be obnoxious to the views, or marked by the suspicions of the President. or be thought dangerous to his or their election, or other interests, public or personal: that the friendless alien has indeed been selected as the safest subject of a first experiment; but the citizen will soon follow, or rather, has already followed. for already has a Sedition Act marked him as its prey: that these and successive acts of the same character, unless arrested at the threshold, necessarily drive these States into revolution and blood, and will furnish new calumnies against republican government. and new pretexts for those who wish it to be believed that man cannot be governed but by a rod of iron.—KENTUCKY RESOLUTIONS. ix, 469. FORD ED., vii, 302. (1798.)

287. ALIEN AND SEDITION LAWS, Unconstitutional.—For the present, I should be for resolving the Alien and Sedition laws to be against the Constitution and merely void, and for addressing the other States to obtain similar declarations; and I would not do anything at this moment which should commit us further, but reserve ourselves to shape our future measures, or no measures, by the events which may happen.—To JOHN TAYLOR. iv, 260. FORD ED., vii, 311. (M., Nov. 1798.)

288. —— ——. Alien friends are under the jurisdiction and protection of the laws of the State wherein they are: no power over them has been delegated to the United States, nor prohibited to the individual States, distinct from their power over citizens. And it being true as a general principle, and one of the amendments to the Constitution having also declared that "the powers not delegated to the United States by the Constitution, nor prohibited by it to the States, are reserved to the States respectively, or to the people," the act of the Congress of the United States, passed on the —— day of July, 1798, intituled "An Act concerning Aliens," which assumes powers over alien friends, not delegated by the Constitution, is not law, but is altogether void, and of no force.—KENTUCKY RESOLUTIONS. ix, 466. FORD ED., vii, 296. (1798.)

289. **ALIEN AND SEDITION LAWS, Viciousness of.**—The Alien bill * * * is a most detestable thing.—To JAMES MADISON. iv, 244. FORD ED., vii, 260. (Pa., May 1798.)

290. —— ——. That libel on legislation. —To DR. JOSEPH PRIESTLEY. iv, 374. FORD ED., viii, 22. (W., March 1801.) See SEDITION LAW.

291. **ALIENS, Forcible Removal of.**—In addition to the general principle, as well as the express declaration, that powers not delegated are reserved, another and more special provision, inserted in the Constitution from abundant caution, has declared that "the migration or importation of such persons as any of the States now existing shall think proper to admit, shall not be prohibited by the Congress prior to the year 1808." * * * This Commonwealth [Kentucky] does admit the migration of alien friends, described as the subject of the said act concerning aliens. * * * A provision against prohibiting their migration is a provision against all acts equivalent thereto, or it would be nugatory. * * * To remove them when migrated, is equivalent to a prohibition of their migration, and is, therefore, contrary to the said provision of the Constitution, and void.—KENTUCKY RESOLUTIONS. ix, 466. FORD ED., vii, 296. (1798.)

292. **ALIENS, The Revolution and.**—I do not know that there has been any American determination on the question whether American citizens and British subjects, born before the Revolution, can be aliens to one another? I know there is an opinion of Lord Coke's, in Colvin's case, that if England and Scotland should, in the course of descent, pass to separate kings, those born under the same sovereign during the union, would remain natural subjects and not aliens. Common sense urges some considerations against this. Natural subjects owe allegiance; but we owe none. Aliens are the subjects of a foreign power; we are not subjects of a for-

eign power. The King, by the treaty, acknowledges our independence; how, then, can we remain natural subjects? The King's power is, by the Constitution, competent to the making peace, war and treaties. He had, therefore, authority to relinquish our allegiance by treaty. But if an act of parliament had been necessary, the parliament passed an act to confirm the treaty. So that it appears to me that, in this question, fictions of law alone are opposed to sound sense.—To JOHN ADAMS. i, 530. (P., 1786.)

293. **ALLEGIANCE, Renounced.**—We, therefore, the representatives of the United States of America in General Congress assembled, do in the name and by the authority of the good people of these *States reject and renounce all allegiance and subjection to the kings of Great Britain and all others who may hereafter claim by, through, or under them; we utterly dissolve all political connection which may heretofore have subsisted between us and the people or parliament of Great Britain.** — DECLARATION OF INDEPENDENCE AS DRAWN BY JEFFERSON.

294. **ALLEGIANCE, Repudiated.**—He has abdicated government here, *withdrawing his governors, and declaring us out of his allegiance and protection.*†—DECLARATION OF INDEPENDENCE AS DRAWN BY JEFFERSON.

295. **ALLEN, Protection of Ethan.**—It is with pain we fear that Mr. [Ethan] Allen and others, taken with him while fighting bravely in their country's cause, are sent to Britain in irons, to be punished for pretended treason; treasons, too, created by one of those very laws whose obligation we deny, and mean to contest by the sword. This question will not be decided by seeking vengeance on a few helpless captives but by achieving success in the fields of war, and gathering there those laurels which grow for the warrior brave. * * * We have ordered Brigadier General Prescot to be bound in irons, and to be confined in close jail, there to experience corresponding miseries to those which shall be inflicted on Mr. Allen. His life shall answer for that of Mr. Allen.‡—CONGRESS RESOLUTION. FORD ED., i, 494 (Dec. 1775.)

296. **ALLIANCE, Abjure.**—I sincerely join you in abjuring all political connection with every foreign power; and though I cordially wish well to the progress of liberty in all nations, and would forever give it the weight of our countenance, yet they are not

* Congress struck out the italicized words and inserted: "Colonies, solemnly publish and declare, that these United Colonies are, and of right ought to be, Free and Independent States; that they are absolved from all allegiance to the British crown, and that all political connection between them and the State of Great Britain, is, and ought to be, totally dissolved." Congress also inserted after the word "assembled," the words, "appealing to the Supreme Judge of the World for the rectitude of our intentions."—EDITOR.

† Congress struck out the words in italics and inserted "by declaring us out of, his protection, and waging war against us."—EDITOR.

‡ Not adopted by Congress.—EDITOR.

to be touched without contamination from their other bad principles.—To T. LOMAX. iv, 301. FORD ED., vii, 374. (M., March 1799.)

297. ALLIANCE, Coercion and.—The British ministers equivocate on every proposal of a treaty of commerce * * * unless, indeed, we would agree to make it a treaty of *alliance* as well as *commerce*, so as to undermine our obligations with France. This method of stripping that rival nation of its alliances, they tried successfully with Holland, endeavored at it with Spain, and have plainly and repeatedly suggested to us. For this they would probably relax some of the rigors they exercise against our commerce.—OFFICIAL REPORT. vii, 518. (December 1790.)

298. ALLIANCE, Dangerous.—An alliance [with Great Britain] with a view to partition of the Floridas and Louisiana, is not what we would wish, because it may eventually lead us into embarrassing situations with our best friend, and put the power of two neighbors into the hands of one. Lord Lansdowne has declared he gave the Floridas to Spain rather than the United States as a bone of discord with the House of Bourbon, and of reunion with Great Britain.—INSTRUCTIONS TO WILLIAM CARMICHAEL. ix, 413. FORD ED., v, 227. (1790.)

299. ALLIANCE, Deprecated.—I sincerely deplore the situation of our affairs with France. War with them, and consequent alliance with Great Britain, will completely compass the object of the Executive council, from the commencement of the war between France and England; taken up by some of them from that moment, by others, more latterly. I still, however, hope it will be avoided. —To JAMES MADISON. iv, 162. FORD ED., vii, 108. (M., Jan. 1797.)

300. ALLIANCE, Destructive.—To take part in European conflicts would be to divert our energies from creation to destruction.— To GEORGE LOGAN. FORD ED., viii, 23. (W., March 1801.)

301. ALLIANCE, Divorce from all.—As to everything except commerce, we ought to divorce ourselves from them all. But this system would require time, temper, wisdom, and occasional sacrifice of interest; and how far all of these will be ours, our children may see, but we shall not. The passions are too high at present, to be cooled in our day.—To EDWARD RUTLEDGE. iv, 191. FORD ED., vii, 154. (Pa., 1797.)

302. ———. Better keep together as we are, haul off from Europe as soon as we can and from all attachments to any portions of it.—To JOHN TAYLOR. iv, 247. FORD ED., vii, 265. (Pa., 1798.)

303. ———. Commerce with all nations, alliance with none, should be our motto. —To T. LOMAX. iv, 301. FORD ED., vii, 374. (M., March 1799.)

304. ———. It ought to be the very first object of our pursuits to have nothing to do with the European interests and politics. Let them be free or slaves, at will, navigators or agriculturists, swallowed into one government or divided into a thousand, we have nothing to fear from them in any form.— To GEORGE LOGAN. FORD ED., viii, 23. (W., March 1801.)

305. ALLIANCES, Entangling.—I know that it is a maxim with us, and I think it a wise one, not to entangle ourselves with the affairs of Europe.—To E. CARRINGTON. ii, 334. FORD ED., iv, 483. (P., 1787.)

306. ———. I am for free commerce with all nations; political connection with none; and little or no diplomatic establishment. And I am not for linking ourselves by new treaties with the quarrels of Europe; entering that field of slaughter to preserve their balance, or joining in the confederacy of Kings to war against the principles of liberty.—To ELBRIDGE GERRY. iv, 268. FORD ED., vii, 328. (Pa., 1799.)

307. ———. Let our affairs be disentangled from those of all other nations, except as to commerce.—To GIDEON GRANGER. iv, 331. FORD ED., vii, 452. (M., 1800.)

308. ———. The Constitution thought it wise to restrain the Executive and Senate from entangling and embroiling our affairs with those of Europe.—PARLIAMENTARY MANUAL. ix, 81. (1800.)

309. ———. Honest friendship with all nations, entangling alliances with none, I deem [one of the] essential principles of our government and, consequently, [one] which ought to shape its administration.—FIRST INAUGURAL ADDRESS. viii, 4. FORD ED., viii, 4. (1801.)

310. ———. Determined as we are to avoid, if possible, wasting the energies of our people in war and destruction, we shall avoid implicating ourselves with the powers of Europe, even in support of principles which we mean to pursue. They have so many other interests different from ours, that we must avoid being entangled in them. We believe we can enforce these principles, as to ourselves, by peaceable means, now that we are likely to have our public councils detached from foreign views.—To THOMAS PAINE. iv, 370. FORD ED., viii, 18. (W., March 1801.)

311. ———. Peace, and abstinence from European interferences, are our objects. —To M. DUPONT DE NEMOURS. iv, 436. (W., April 1802.)

312. ———. It is against our system * * * to entangle ourselves at all with the affairs of Europe.—To PHILIP MAZZEI. iv, 553. (W., July 1864.)

313. ———. Our nation has wisely avoided entangling itself in the system of European interests, has taken no side between its rival powers, attached itself to none of its ever-changing confederacies.— R. TO A. OF BALTIMORE BAPTISTS. viii, 137. (1808.)

314. —— ——. The less we have to do with the amities or enmities of Europe the better.—To THOMAS LEIPER. vi, 465. FORD ED., ix, 520. (M., 1815.)

315. —— ——. All entanglements with that quarter of the globe [Europe] should be avoided if we mean that peace and justice shall be the polar stars of the American Societies.—To J. CORREA. vii, 184. FORD ED., x, 164. (M., 1820.)

316. —— ——. The fundamental principle of our government,—never to entangle us with the broils of Europe.—To M. CORAY. vii, 318. (M., 1823.)

317. —— ——. I have ever deemed it fundamental for the United States never to take active part in the quarrels of Europe. Their political interests are entirely distinct from ours. Their mutual jealousies, their balance of power, their complicated alliances, their forms and principles of government, are all foreign to us. They are nations of eternal war.—To PRESIDENT MONROE. vii, 288. FORD ED., x, 257. (M., 1823.)

318. ALLIANCE, A generous.—If there could have been a doubt before as to the event of the war, it is now totally removed by the interposition of France, and the generous alliance she has entered into with us.—To ——. i, 208. FORD ED., ii, 157. (W., 1778.)

— **ALLIANCE. The Holy.**—See HOLY ALLIANCE.

319. ALLIANCE, Horror of.—We have a perfect horror at everything like connecting ourselves with the politics of Europe.—To WILLIAM SHORT. iv, 414. FORD ED., viii, 98. (W., 1801.)

320. ALLIANCE, Inadmissible.—The British talk of * * * a treaty of commerce and alliance. If the object of the latter be honorable, it is useless; if dishonorable, inadmissible.—To GOUVERNEUR MORRIS. iii, 182. FORD ED., v, 224. (N. Y., 1790.)

321. ALLIANCE, Inevitable.—The day that France takes possession of New Orleans * * * seals the union of two nations, who, in conjunction, can maintain exclusive possession of the ocean. From that moment, we must marry ourselves to the British fleet and nation. We must turn all our attention to a maritime force * * *.—To ROBERT R. LIVINGSTON. iv, 432. FORD ED., viii, 145. (W., April 1802.)

322. ALLIANCE, A lost.—Were the British court to return to their senses in time to seize the little advantage which still remains within their reach, from this quarter, I judge, that, on acknowledging our absolute independence and sovereignty, a commercial treaty beneficial to them, and perhaps even a league of mutual offence and defence might, not seeing the expense or consequences of such a measure, be approved by our people, if nothing, in the meantime, done on your part should prevent it. But they will continue to grasp at their desperate sovereignty, till every

benefit short of that is forever out of their reach.—To BENJAMIN FRANKLIN. i, 205. FORD ED., ii, 132. (August 1777.)

323. ALLIANCE, Suggested French.—If we can obtain from Great Britain reasonable conditions of commerce, (which, in my idea, must forever include an admission into her [West India] islands,) the first ground between these two nations would seem to be the best. But if we can obtain no equal terms from her, perhaps Congress might think it prudent, as Holland has done, to connect us unequivocally with France. Holland has purchased the protection of France. The price she pays is *aid in time of war*. It is interesting for us to purchase a free commerce with the French islands. But whether it is best to pay for it, by *aids in war, or by privileges in commerce, or not to purchase it at all*, is the question.—REPORT TO CONGRESS. ix, 244. FORD ED., iv, 130. (P., 1785.)

324. ALLIANCE, Unwise.—I join you * * * in a sense of the necessity of restoring freedom to the ocean. But I doubt, with you, whether the United States ought to join in an armed confederacy for that purpose; or rather I am satisfied they ought not.—To GEORGE LOGAN. FORD ED., viii, 23. (W., March 1801.)

325. ALLIANCES, Insufficiency of.—Treaties of alliance are generally insufficient to enforce compliance with their mutual stipulations.— THE ANAS. ix, 88. FORD ED., i, 157. (1818.)

326. ALLIANCES, International Marriage.—What a crowd of lessons do the present miseries of Holland teach us! * * * Never to let a citizen ally himself with Kings * * *.—To JOHN ADAMS. ii, 283. FORD ED., iv, 455. (P., 1787.)

— **ALLODIAL TENURE.**—See LAND.

— **ALLOY IN MONEY.**—See DOLLAR.

327. ALLSTON, Burr and Washington.—I send you Allston's letter for perusal. He thinks to get over this matter by putting a bold face on it. I have the names of three persons whose evidence, *taken together*, can fix on him the actual endeavor to engage men in Burr's enterprise.—To ALBERT GALLATIN. FORD ED., ix, 13. (W., 1807.)

328. —— ——. The enclosed copy of an affidavit from General Wilkinson authenticates the copy of a letter from Colonel Burr to the General, affirming that Mr. Allston his son-in-law, is engaged in the unlawful enterprises he is carrying on, and is to be an actor in them. * * * It is further well known in Washington that Mr. Allston is an endorser to a considerable amount, of the bills which have enabled Colonel Burr to prepare his treasons. Nobody is a better judge than yourself whether any and what measures can be taken on this information.—To CHARLES PINCKNEY. v, 34. FORD ED., ix, 13. (W., Jan. 1807.)

— **ALLUVIUM.**—See BATTURE.

329. ALMANACS, Improvements in.—I received your letter on the publication of an ephemeris. I have long thought it desirable that something of that kind should be published in the United States, holding a middle station between the nautical and the common popular almanacs. * * * What you propose to insert is very well so far; but I think you might give it more of the character desired by the addition of some other articles which would not enlarge it more than a leaf or two. For instance, the equation of time is essential to the regulation of our clocks and watches, and would only add a narrow column to your second page. The sun's declination is often desirable and would only add another narrow column. This last would be the more useful as an element for obtaining the rising and setting of the sun in every part of the United States * * * if you would add a formula for that calculation.—To MELATIAH NASH. vi, 29. (M., 1811.)

330. ALMANACS, Value of Old.—But why, you will ask, do I send you old almanacs, which are proverbially useless? Because, in these publications have appeared from time to time, some of the most precious things in astronomy. I have searched out those particular volumes which might be valuable to you on his account. That of 1781, contains De la Caille's catalogue of fixed stars reduced to the commencement of that year, and a table of the aberrations and mutations of the principal stars. 1784 contains the same catalogue with the nebuleuses of Messier. 1785 contains the famous catalogue of Hamsteed, with the positions of the stars reduced to the beginning of the year 1784, and which supersedes the use of that immense book. 1786 gives von Euler's lunar tables corrected; and 1787 the tables for the planet Herschel. The two last needed not an apology, as not being within the description of old almanacs. * * * The volume of 1787 gives you Mayer's catalogue of the zodiacal stars. To DR. STILES. i, 363. (P., 1785.)

— **ALMIGHTY, The.**—See DEITY.

— **ALMS.**—See CHARITY.

331. ALTERCATIONS, Injurious.—An instance of acquiescence on our part under a wrong, rather than disturb our friendship by altercations, may have its value in some future case.—To JOHN JAY. i, 603. (P., 1786.)

332. ALTERCATIONS, Nursing.—If the British troops should pass [through our territory] without having asked leave, I should be for expressing our dissatisfaction to the British Court, and keeping alive an altercation on the subject, till events should decide whether it is most expedient to accept their apologies, or profit of the aggression as a cause of war.—To GENERAL WASHINGTON. ii, 510. FORD ED., v, 239. (1790.)

— **AMALGAMATION OF PARTIES.**—See PARTIES.

— **AMBASSADORS.**—See MINISTERS.

333. AMBITION, Defeating.—The minds of the people at large should be illuminated, as far as practicable, * * * that they may be enabled to know ambition under all its shapes, and prompt to exert their natural powers to defeat its purposes.—DIFFUSION OF KNOWLEDGE BILL. FORD ED., ii, 221. (1779.)

334. AMBITION, Eradicated.—Before I ventured to declare to my countrymen my determination to retire from public employment, I examined well my heart to know whether it were thoroughly cured of every principle of political ambition, whether no lurking particle remained which might leave me uneasy, when reduced within the limits of mere private life. I became satisfied that every fibre of that passion was thoroughly eradicated.—To JAMES MONROE. i, 317. FORD ED., iii, 56. (M., 1782.)

335. AMBITION, Family.—I feel no impulse from personal ambition to the office now proposed to me, but on account of yourself and your sister and those dear to you.—To MARY JEFFERSON EPPES. D. L. J. 274. (W., Feb. 1801.)

336. AMBITION, Government and.—I have no ambition to govern men; no passion which would lead me to delight to ride in a storm.—To EDWARD RUTLEDGE. iv, 152. FORD ED., vii, 94. (M., 1796.)

337. ———. I have no ambition to govern men. It is a painful and thankless office.—To JOHN ADAMS. iv, 154. FORD ED., vii, 98. (M., 1796.)

338. ———. I have no inclination to govern men. I should have no views of my own in doing it; and as to those of the governed, I had rather that their disappointment (which must always happen) should be pointed to any other cause, real or supposed, than to myself.—To MR. VOLNEY. iv, 158. (M., 1797.)

339. AMBITION, Lost.—The little spice of ambition which I had in my younger days has long since evaporated, and I set still less store by a posthumous than present name.—To JAMES MADISON. iv, 117. FORD ED., vii, 10. (M., April 1795.)

340. AMENDMENTS TO CONSTITUTION, First.—Congress were to proceed about the 1st of June to propose amendments to the new Constitution. The principal would be, the annexing a declaration of rights to satisfy the mind of all on the subject of their liberties.—To WILLIAM CARMICHAEL. iii, 89. (P., Aug. 1789.) See CONSTITUTION (FEDERAL.)

341. AMERICA, Europe and.—The European nations constitute a separate division of the globe; their treaties make them part of a distinct system; they have a set of interests of their own in which it is our business never to engage ourselves. America has a hemisphere to itself. It must have its separate system of interests, which must not be subordinated to those of Europe. The insulated state in which nature has placed the American continent, should so far avail it that no spark of war kindled in the other quarters of the globe should be wafted across the wide oceans which separate us from them. And it will be so.—To BARON VON HUMBOLDT. vi, 268. FORD ED., ix, 431. (Dec. 1813.) See CANADA, COLONIES, SOUTH AMERICA, UNITED STATES.

342. —— ——. Nothing is so important as that America shall separate herself from the systems of Europe, and establish one of her own. Our circumstances, our pursuits, our interests, are distinct; the principles of our policy should be so also. All entanglements with that quarter of the globe should be avoided if we mean that peace and justice shall be the polar stars of the American societies. * * * It would be a leading principle with me had I longer to live.—To J. CORREA DE SERRA. vii, 184. FORD ED., x, 164. (M., Oct. 1820.) See POLICY.

343. AMERICA, No Kings nor Emperors for.—I rejoice to learn that Iturbide is a mere usurper, and slenderly supported. Although we have no right to intermeddle with the form of government of other nations, yet it is lawful to wish to see no emperors nor kings in our hemisphere, and that Brazil as well as Mexico will homologize with us.—To JAMES MONROE. FORD ED., x, 244.

— AMERICA, South.—See SOUTH AMERICA.

— AMERICA, A Summary View of the Rights of British America.—See APPENDIX.

— AMERICAN REVOLUTION.—See REVOLUTION.

344. AMERICUS VESPUCCIUS, Picture of.—I have sent to Florence for pictures of Columbus (if it exists), of Americus Vespuccius, Magellan, &c.—To WILLIAM S. SMITH. FORD ED., v, 2. (P., 1788.)

345. ANARCHY, Averted.—Much has been gained by the new [Federal] Constitution, for the former was terminating in anarchy, as necessarily consequent to inefficiency.—To GEORGE MASON. iii, 148. FORD ED., v, 183. (N. Y., 1790.)

346. ANARCHY, Fatal.—Our falling into anarchy would decide forever the destinies of mankind, and seal the political heresy that man is incapable of self-government.—To JOHN HOLLINS. v, 597. (M., 1811.)

347. ANARCHY, Imputed.—From the London gazettes and the papers copying them, you are led to suppose that all in America is anarchy, discontent and civil war. Nothing, however, is less true. There are not on the face of the earth more tranquil governments than ours, nor a happier and more contented people.—To BARON GEISMER. i, 427. (P., 1785.)

348. —— ——. Wonderful is the effect of impudent and persevering lying. The British ministry have so long hired their gazetteers to repeat, and model into every form, lies about our being in anarchy, that the world has at length believed them, * * * and what is more wonderful, we have believed them ourselves. Yet where does this anarchy exist? Where did it ever exist, except in the single instance of Massachusetts? And can history produce one instance of rebellion so honorably conducted?—To W. S. SMITH. ii, 318. FORD ED., iv, 466. (P., 1787.)

349. ANARCHY, Suppress.—Let this b the distinctive mark of an American that, i cases of commotion, he enlists himself unde no man's banner, inquires for no man's name but repairs to the standard of the laws. D this and you need never fear anarchy o tyranny. Your government will be perpet ual.—FROM JEFFERSON'S MSS. FORD ED., vii I. (1801?)

350. ANATOMY, Knowledge of.—N knowledge can be more satisfactory to a ma than that of his own frame, its parts, thei functions and actions.—To THOMAS COOPER vi, 390. (M., 1814.)

351. —— ——. I have just received * * two volumes of Comparative Anatomy b Cuvier, probably the greatest work in that lin that has ever appeared. His comparisons em brace every organ of the animal carcass; an from man to the rotifer.—To DR. BENJAMIN RUSH. iv, 385. FORD ED., viii, 33. (W., 1801.

352. ANCESTORS, Practices of.—I am not bigotted to the practices of our fore fathers. It is that bigotry which keeps th Indians in a state of barbarism in the mids of the arts, would have kept us in the sam state even now, and still keeps Connecticu where their ancestors were when they landed on these shores.—To ROBERT FULTON. v, 516 (M., 1810.)

353. ANCESTORS, Regimen of.—W might as well require a man to wear still th coat which fitted him when a boy, as civil ized society to remain ever under the regimer of their barbarous ancestors.—To SAMUEL KERCHIVAL. vii, 15. FORD ED., x, 43. (M. 1816.)

354. ANCESTRY, Equality vs.—Th foundation on which all [our constitutions] are built, is the natural equality of man, the denial of every pre-eminence but that annexed to legal office and, particularly, the de nial of a pre-eminence by birth.—To GENERAL WASHINGTON. i, 334. FORD ED., iii, 466. (A. 1784.)

355. ANCESTRY, Thomas Jefferson's. —The tradition in my father's family was that their ancestor came to this country from Wales and from near the mountain of Snowdon, the highest in Great Britain. I noted once a case from Wales, in the law reports, where a person of our name was either plaintiff or defendant; and one of the same name was secretary to the Virginia Company.* These are the only instances in which I have met with the name in that country. I have found it in our early records; but the first particular information I have of any ancestor was of my grandfather, who lived at the place in Chesterfield called Ozborne's, and owned the lands afterwards the glebe of the parish. He had three sons: Thomas who died young, Field who settled on the waters of Roanoke and left numerous descendants, and Peter, my father, who settled on the lands I still own, called Shadwell, adjoining my present residence. He was born February

* No Jefferson was ever Secretary of the Virginia Company, but John Jefferson was a member of the Company. He came to Virginia in the Bona Nova in 1619.—NOTE IN FORD'S EDITION OF JEFFERSON'S WRITINGS.

29, 1707-8, and intermarried 1739, with Jane Randolph, of the age of 19, daughter of Isham Randolph, one of the seven sons of that name and family, settled at Dungeoness in Goochland. They trace their pedigree far back in England and Scotland, to which let every one ascribe the faith and merit he chooses.—AUTOBIOGRAPHY, i, 1. FORD ED., i, 1. (1831.)

356. ANGELS, Kings as.—Have we found angels in the form of kings to govern him?—FIRST INAUGURAL ADDRESS. viii, 3. FORD ED., viii, 3. (1801.)

357. ANGER, Control over.—When angry, count ten before you speak; if very angry, an hundred.—To THOMAS JEFFERSON SMITH. vii, 402. FORD ED., x, 341. (M., 1825.)

358. ANGLOMANIA, Danger in.—I fear nothing for our liberty from the assaults of force; but I have seen and felt much, and fear more from English books, English prejudices, English manners, and the apes, the dupes, and designs among our professional crafts. When I look around me for security against these seductions, I find it in the wide spread of our agricultural citizens, in their unsophisticated minds, their independence and their power, if called on, to crush the Humists [Tories] of our cities, and to maintain the principles which severed us from England.—To HORATIO G. SPAFFORD. vi, 335. (M., 1814.)

359. ANGLOMANIA, Eradicate.—The eradication of English partialities is one of the most consoling expectations from the war. —To WILLIAM DUANE. vi, 76. FORD ED., ix, 366. (M., Aug. 1812.)

360. ANGLOMANIA, Politics and.—The Anglicism of 1808, against which we are now struggling, is but the same thing [as the Toryism of 1777 and the Federalism of 1799] in still another form. It is a longing for a king, and an English King rather than any other.—To JOHN LANGDON. v, 512. (M., 1810.)

361. ———— ————. Anglomany, monarchy, and separation are the principles of the Essex federalists. Anglomany and monarchy, those of the Hamiltonians, and Anglomany alone, that of the portion of the *people* who call themselves federalists.—To JOHN MELISH. vi, 96. FORD ED., ix, 375. (M., 1813.)

362. ANGLOMANIA, Servile.—I wish any events could induce us to cease to copy such a model, [the British government,] and to assume the dignity of being original. They had their paper system, stockjobbing, speculations, public debt, moneyed interest, &c., and all this was contrived for us. They raised their cry against jacobinism and revolutionists, we against democratic societies and anti-federalists; their alarmists sounded insurrection, ours marched an army to look for one, but they could not find it. I wish the parallel may stop here, and that we may avoid, instead of imitating, a general bankruptcy and disastrous war.—To HORATIO GATES. iv, 178. FORD ED., vii, 130. (Pa., 1797.)

363. ANGLOPHOBIA, Washington's Cabinet and.—The Anglophobia has seized violently on three members of our council. This sets almost every day on questions of neutrality. * * * Everything hangs upon the opinion of a single person [Edmund Randolph], and that the most indecisive one I ever had to do business with. He always contrives to agree in principle with one but in conclusion with the other. Anglophobia, secret Anti-Gallomany, a *federalisme outrée* and a present ease in his circumstances not usual, have decided the complexion of our dispositions, and our proceedings towards the conspirators against human liberty, and the asserters of it, which is unjustifiable in principle, in interest, and in respect to the wishes of our constituents.—To JAMES MADISON. iii, 556. FORD ED., vi, 250. (May 1793.)

ANGLO-SAXON LANGUAGE.—See LANGUAGES.

— ANIMALS, Do they Degenerate in America?—See BUFFON.

364. ANIMOSITIES, Individual.—The great cause which divides our countries is not to be decided by individual animosities. The harmony of private societies cannot weaken national efforts. To contribute by neighborly intercourse and attention to make others happy, is the shortest and surest way of being happy ourselves. As these sentiments seem to have directed your conduct, we should be as unwise as illiberal, were we not to preserve the same temper of mind.—To GEN. WILLIAM PHILLIPS. D. L. J., 53. (1779.)

365. ANIMOSITIES, National.—The animosities of sovereigns are temporary, and may be allayed; but those which seize the whole body of a people, and of a people, too, who dictate their own measures, produce calamities of long duration.*—To C. W. F. DUMAS. i, 553. (P., 1786.)

366. ANIMOSITIES, Political.—Party animosities here have raised a wall of separation between those who differ in political sentiments. They must love misery indeed who would rather, at the sight of an honest man, feel the torment of hatred and aversion than the benign spasms of benevolence and esteem. —To MRS. CHURCH. FORD ED., vi, 116. (Pa., Oct. 1792.)

367. ———— ————. While I cherish with feeling the recollections of my friends, I banish from my mind all political animosities which might disturb its tranquillity, or the happiness I derive from my present pursuits.—To WILLIAM DUANE. v. 532. (M., 1810.)

368. ANIMOSITIES, Rekindling.—Peace with all the world, and a quiet descent through the remainder of my time, are now so necessary to my happiness that I am unwilling, by the expression of any opinion before the public, to rekindle ancient animosi-

* Jefferson was describing the "hatred" of America by the English people.—EDITOR.

ties, covered under their ashes indeed, but not extinguished.—To GEORGE HAY. FORD ED., x, 265. (M., 1823.)

— **ANNAPOLIS (FEDERAL) CONVENTION.**—See CONVENTION.

— **ANNEXATION OF TERRITORY.** —See TERRITORY.

369. ANNUITIES, Government Loans and.—Annuities for single lives are also beyond our powers, because the single life may pass the term of a generation. This last practice is objectionable too, as encouraging celibacy, and the disinherison of heirs.—To J. W. EPPES. vi, 198. FORD ED., ix, 397. (P. F., 1813.) See GENERATIONS.

370. ANONYMOUS WRITING, Newspaper.—I never did in my life, either by myself or by any other, have a sentence of mine inserted in a newspaper without putting my name to it; and I believe I never shall.—To JOHN ADAMS. iii, 272. FORD ED., v, 355. (Pa., 1791.)

371. ANTI-FEDERALISTS, Jefferson and.—You say that I have been dished up to you as an anti-federalist, and ask me if it be just. My opinion was never worthy enough of notice to merit citing; but since you ask it, I will tell it to you. I am not a federalist, because I never submitted the whole system of my opinions to the creed of any party of men whatever, in religion, in philosophy, in politics, or in anything else, where I was capable of thinking for myself. Such an addiction is the last degradation of a free and moral agent. If I could not go to heaven but with a party, I would not go there at all. Therefore, I am not of the party of federalists. But I am much farther from that of the anti-federalists. I approved from the first moment of the great mass of what is in the new Constitution; the consolidation of the government; the organization into executive, legislative and judiciary; the subdivision of the legislative; the happy compromise of interests between the great and little States, by the different manner of voting in the different Houses; the voting by persons instead of States; the qualified negative on laws given to the Executive, which, however, I should have liked better if associated with the judiciary also, as in New York; and the power of taxation. I thought at first that the latter might have been limited. A little reflection soon convinced me it ought not to be. What I disapproved from the first moment also, was the want of a bill of rights, to guard liberty against the legislative as well as the executive branches of the government; that is to say, to secure freedom in religion, freedom of the press, freedom from monopolies, freedom from unlawful imprisonment, freedom from a permanent military, and a trial by jury in all cases determinable by the laws of the land. I disapproved also the perpetual re-eligibility of the President. To these points of disapprobation I adhere. My first wish was that the nine first conventions might accept the Constitution, as the means of securing to us

the great mass of good it contained, and that the four last might reject it, as the means of obtaining amendments. But I was corrected in this wish the moment I saw the much better plan of Massachusetts, and which had never occurred to me. With respect to the declaration of rights, I suppose the majority of the United States are of my opinion; for I apprehend all the anti-federalists and a very respectable proportion of the federalists think that such a declaration should now be annexed. The enlightened part of Europe have given us the greatest credit for inventing this instrument of security for the rights of the people, and have been not a little surprised to see us so soon give it up. With respect to the re-eligibility of the President, I find myself differing from the majority of my countrymen; for I think there are but three States out of the eleven which have desired an alteration of this. And, indeed, since the thing is established, I would wish it not to be altered during the life of our great leader, whose executive talents are superior to those, I believe, of any man in the world, and who, alone, by the authority of his name and the confidence reposed in his perfect integrity, is fully qualified to put the new government so under way, as to secure it against the efforts of opposition. But, having derived from our error all the good there was in it, I hope we shall correct it, the moment we can no longer have the same name at the helm. These are my sentiments, by which you will see I was right in saying I am neither federalist nor anti-federalist; that I am of neither party, nor yet a trimmer between parties. These, my opinions, I wrote within a few hours after I had read the Constitution, to one or two friends in America. I had not then read one single word printed on the subject. I never had an opinion in politics or religion which I was afraid to own. A costive reserve on these subjects might have procured me more esteem from some people, but less from myself. My great wish is to go on in a strict but silent performance of my duty; to avoid attracting notice, and to keep my name out of newspapers, because I find the pain of a little censure, even when it is unfounded, is more acute than the pleasure of much praise. The attaching circumstance of my present office [Minister] is that I can do its duties unseen by those for whom they are done.—To F. HOPKINSON. ii, 585. FORD ED., v, 75. (P., March 13, 1789.)

372. ANTI-FEDERALISTS, Malevolence of.—Anti-federalism is not yet dead in this country. The gentlemen who opposed the new Constitution retain a good deal of malevolence towards the new government. Henry is its avowed foe.—To WILLIAM SHORT. FORD ED., v, 136. (Ep., Dec. 1789.)

373. ANTI-FEDERALISTS, Overthrown.—The opposition to our new Constitution has almost totally disappeared. Some few indeed had gone such lengths in their declarations of hostility that they feel it awkward perhaps to come over; but the amendments proposed by Congress have brought over almost all their followers. * * * The little *vautrien*, Rhode Island, will come over with a little more time.—To MARQUIS LAFAYETTE. iii, 132. FORD ED., v, 152. (N. Y., April 1790.)

374. ANTIQUITIES, American.—I thank you for the extract of the letter * * * on the antiquities found in the western country. I wish that the persons who go thither would make very exact descriptions of what they see of that kind, without forming any theories. The moment a person forms a theory, his imagination sees, in every object, only the traits which favor that theory. But it is too early to form theories on those antiquities. We must wait with patience till more facts are collected. I wish your Philosophical Society would collect exact descriptions of the several monuments as yet known, and insert them naked in their Transactions. Patience and observation may enable us in time, to solve the problem, whether those who formed the scattering monuments in our western country, were colonies sent off from Mexico, or the founders of Mexico itself? Whether both were the descendants or the progenitors of the Asiatic red men.—To CHARLES THOMSON. ii, 276. (Pa., 1787.)

375. ANTIQUITIES, Roman.—From Lyons to Nismes I have been nourished with the remains of Roman grandeur. * * * At Vienne, the Prætorian Palace, as it is called, comparable, for its fine proportions, to the Maison quarrée, defaced by the barbarians who have converted it to its present purpose, its beautiful fluted Corinthian columns cut out, in part, to make space for Gothic windows, and hewed down, in the residue, to the plane of the building, was enough * * * to disturb my composure. At Orange, I thought of you. I was sure you had seen with pleasure the sublime triumphal arch of Marius at the entrance of the city. I went then to the Arenæ. Would you believe that in this eighteenth century, in France, under the reign of Louis XVI., they are at this moment pulling down the circular wall of this superb remain, to pave a road? And that, too, from a hill which is itself an entire mass of stone, just as fit, and more accessible. * * * I thought of you again * * * at the Pont du Gard, a sublime antiquity, and well-preserved; but most of all here [Nismes], whose Roman taste, genius and magnificence excite ideas analogous to yours at every step. * * * You will not expect news. Were I to attempt to give it, I should tell you stories one thousand years old. I should detail to you the intrigues of the courts of the Cæsars, how they affect us here, the oppressions of their prætors, prefects, &c. I am immersed in antiquities from morning to night. For me, the city of Rome is actually existing in all the splendor of its empire. I am filled with alarms for the event of the irruptions daily mak'ng on us, by the Goths, the Visigoths, Ostrogoths, and Vandals, lest they should reconquer us to our original barbarism.—To LA COMTESSE DE TESSE. ii, 132. (N., 1787.)

— ANTOINETTE, MARIE.—See MARIE ANTOINETTE.

376. APOSTASY, Defined.—It is to be considered as apostasy only when they [schismatizing republicans] purchase the votes of federalists with a participation in honor and power.—To THOMAS COOPER. v, 121. FORD ED., ix, 102. (W., 1807.)

377. APOSTASY, Punished.—As to the effect of Mr. [Patrick] Henry's name among the people, I have found it crumble like a dried leaf, the moment they became satisfied of his apostasy.—To TENCH COXE. FORD ED., vii, 381. (M., 1799.)

378. APPLAUSE, Courting.—I am not reconciled to the idea of a Chief Magistrate parading himself through the several States, as an object of public gaze, and in quest of applause which, to be valuable, should be purely voluntary. I had rather acquire silent good will by a faithful discharge of my duties, than owe expressions of it to my putting myself in the way of receiving them.—To JAMES SULLIVAN. v, 102. FORD ED., ix, 77. (W., 1807.)

379. APPLAUSE, Deserve.—Go on deserving applause, and you will be sure to meet with it; and the way to deserve it is to be good, and to be industrious.—To J. W. EPPES. ii, 192. (P., 1787.)

380. APPOINTMENT, The Power of.—The Constitution, having declared that the President shall *nominate* and, by and with the advice and consent of the Senate, shall *appoint* ambassadors, other public ministers, and consuls * * * has taken care to circumscribe this [power] within very strict limits: for it gives the *nomination* of the foreign agents to the President, the *appointments* to him and the Senate jointly, and the *commissioning* to the President. This analysis calls our attention to the strict import of each term. To *nominate* must be to *propose*. *Appointment* seems that act of the will which constitutes or makes the agent, and the *commission* is the public evidence of it.—OPINION ON POWERS OF SENATE. vii, 465. FORD ED., v, 161. (1790.)

— APPOINTMENTS TO OFFICE.—See OFFICE.

381. APPORTIONMENT, Basis of.—The number of Representatives for each county, or borough, shall be so proportioned to the number of its qualified electors, that the whole number of representatives shall not exceed 300, nor be less than 125. For the present there shall be one representative for every—qualified electors in each county or borough; but whenever this, or any future proportion, shall be likely to exceed or fall short of the limits before mentioned, it shall be again adjusted by the House of Representatives.—PROPOSED VA. CONSTITUTION. FORD ED., ii, 15. (June 1776.)

382. APPORTIONMENT RATIO, Arbitrary.—If the [ratio of] representation [is] obtained by any process not prescribed in the Constitution, it becomes arbitrary and inadmissible.—OPINION ON APPORTIONMENT BILL. vii, 595. FORD ED., v, 494. (1792.)

383. APPORTIONMENT RATIO, Common.—The Constitution has declared that representatives and direct taxes shall be apportioned among the several States according to their respective numbers. * * * That is to say, they shall be apportioned by some common ratio—for proportion and ratio are equivalent words; and in the definition of *proportion among numbers,* that they have a ratio common to all, or in other words, a common divisor.—OPINION ON APPORTIONMENT BILL. vii, 594. FORD ED., v, 493. (April 1792.)

384. APPORTIONMENT RATIO, Fractions and.—It will be said that, though, for taxes there may always be found a divisor which will apportion them among the States according to numbers exactly, without leaving any remainder, yet, for *representatives,* there can be no such common ratio, or divisor, which, applied to the several numbers, will divide them exactly, without a remainder or fraction. I answer, then, that taxes must be divided *exactly,* and representatives *as nearly* as the *nearest ratio* will admit; and the fractions must be neglected, because the Constitution calls absolutely that there be an *apportionment or common ratio,* and if any fractions result from the operation, it has left them unprovided for. In fact it could not but foresee that such fractions would result, and it meant to submit to them. It knew they would be in favor of one part of the Union at one time, and of another at another, so as, in the end, to balance occasional irregularities. —OPINION ON APPORTIONMENT BILL. vii, 596. FORD ED., v, 495. (1792.)

385. APPORTIONMENT RATIO, Nearest Common.—The phrase [of the Constitution] that "the number of representatives shall not exceed one for every 30,000," is violated by this bill which has given to eight States a number exceeding one for every 30,000, to wit, one for every 27,770. In answer to this, it is said that this phrase may mean either the 30,000 *in each State,* or the 30,000 *in the whole Union,* and that in the latter case it serves only to find the amount of the whole representation; which, in the present state of population, is 120 members. Suppose the phrase might bear both meanings, which will common sense apply to it? Which did the universal understanding of our country apply to it? Which did the Senate and Representatives apply to it during the pendency of the first bill, and even till an advanced stage of this second bill, when an ingenious gentleman found out the doctrine of fractions, a doctrine so difficult and inobvious, as to be rejected at first sight by the very persons who afterwards became its most zealous advocates? The phrase stands in the midst of a number of others, every one of which relates to States in their separate capacity. Will not plain common sense, then, understand it, like the rest of its context, to relate to States in their separate capacities? But if the phrase of one for 30,000 is only meant to give the aggregate of representatives, and not at all to influence their apportionment among the States, then the 120 being once found, in order to apportion them, we must recur to the former rule which does it according to the numbers of *the respective States;* and we must take the

nearest common divisor, as the ratio of distribution, that is to say, that divisor which, applied to every State, gives to them such numbers as, added together, come nearest to 120. This nearest common ratio will be found to be 28,058, and will distribute 119 of the 120 members leaving only a single residuary one. It will be found, too, to place 96,648 fractional numbers in the eight northernmost States, and 105,582 in the seven southernmost. * * * Whatever may have been the intention, the effect of neglecting the nearest divisor (which leaves but one residuary member), and adopting a distant one (which leaves eight), is merely to take a member from New York and Pennsylvania, each, and give them to Vermont and New Hampshire. But,it will be said, this is giving more than one for 30,000. True, but has it not been just said that the one for 30,000 is prescribed only to fix the aggregate number, and that we are not to mind it when we come to apportion them among the States? That for this we must recur to the former rule which distributes them according to the numbers in each State? Besides does not the bill itself apportion among seven of the States by the ratio of 27,770? which is much more than one for 30,000.—OPINION ON APPORTIONMENT BILL. vii, 597. FORD ED., v, 496. (1792.)

386. APPORTIONMENT RATIO, Two Divisors.—Instead of such a *single* common ratio, or uniform divisor, as prescribed by the Constitution, the bill has applied *two ratios,* at least, to the different States, to wit, that of 30,026 to the seven following: Rhode Island, New York, Pennsylvania, Maryland, Virginia, Kentucky, and Georgia; and that of 27,770 to the eight others, namely: Vermont, New Hampshire, Massachusetts, Connecticut, New Jersey, Delaware, North Carolina, and South Carolina. * * * And if *two* ratios be applied, then *fifteen* may, and the distribution become arbitrary, instead of being apportioned to numbers. Another member of the clause of the Constitution * * * says "The number of representatives shall not exceed one for every 30,000, but each State shall have at least one representative." This last phrase proves that it had no contemplation that all fractions, or *numbers below the common ratio* were to be unrepresented: and it provides especially that in the case of a State whose whole number shall be below the common ratio, one representative shall be given to it. This is the single instance where it allows representation to any smaller number than the common ratio, and by providing especially for it in this, shows it was understood that, without special provision, the smaller number would in this case, be involved in the general principle.—OPINION ON APPORTIONMENT BILL. vii, 596. FORD ED., v, 495. (1792.)

387. APPORTIONMENT RATIO, Surplus Members.—Where a phrase is susceptible of two meanings, we ought certainly to adopt that which will bring upon us the fewest inconveniences. Let us weigh those resulting from both constructions. From that giving to each State a member for every 30,000 in that State results the single inconvenience that there may be large portions unrepresented, but it being a mere hazard on which State this will fall, hazard will equalize it in the long run. From the others result exactly the same inconvenience. A thousand cases may be imagined to prove it. Take one. Suppose eight of the States had 45,000 inhabitants each, and the other seven 44,999 each, that is to say, each one less than each of the others. The aggregate would be 674,993, and the number of representatives at one for 30,000 of the aggregate, would be 22. Then, after giving one member to each State, distribute the seven residuary members among the seven highest fractions, and though the difference of population be only an unit, the representation would be double. * * * Here a single inhabitant the more would count as 30,000. Nor is this case imaginable only, it will resemble the real one whenever the fractions happen to be pretty equal through the whole States. The numbers of our census happen by accident to give the fractions all very small, or very great, so as to produce the strongest case of inequality that could possibly have occurred, and which may never occur again. The probability is that the fractions will descend gradually from 29,999 to 1. The inconvenience, then, of large unrepresented fractions attends both constructions; and while the most obvious construction is liable to no other, that of the bill incurs many and grievous ones. 1. If you permit the large fraction in one State to choose a representative for one of the small fractions in another State, you take from the latter its election, which constitutes real representation, and substitute a virtual representation of the disfranchised fractions. * * * 2. The bill does not say that it has given the residuary representatives *to the greatest fraction:* though in fact it has done so. It seems to have avoided establishing that into a rule, lest it might not suit on another occasion. Perhaps it may be found the next time more convenient to distribute them *among the smaller States;* at another time *among the larger States;* at other times according to any other crotchet which ingenuity may invent, and the combinations of the day give strength to carry; or they may do it arbitrarily by open bargains and cabal. In short, this construction introduces into Congress a scramble, or a vendue for the surplus members. It generates waste of time, hot blood, and may at some time, when the passions are high, extend a disagreement between the two Houses, to the perpetual loss of the thing, as happens now in the Pennsylvania Assembly; whereas the other construction reduces the apportionment always to an arithmetical operation, about which no two men can ever possibly differ. 3. It leaves in full force the violation of the precept which declares that representatives shall be *apportioned* among the States according to their numbers *i. e.,* by some common ratio.—OPINION ON APPORTIONMENT BILL. vii, 599. FORD ED., v, 498. (1792.)

388. APPORTIONMENT   RATIO, Tricks in.—No invasions of the Constitution are fundamentally so dangerous as the tricks played on their own numbers, apportionment, and other circumstances respecting themselves, and affecting their legal qualifications to legislate for the Union.—OPINION ON APPORTIONMENT BILL. vii, 601. FORD ED., v, 500. (1792.)

389. APPORTIONMENT BILL, Opposition to.—The ground of the opposition to the apportionment bill has been founded on the discovery that the ratio of 30,000 gave smaller fractions to the southern than to the eastern States, and to prevent this a variety of propositions have been made, among which is the following: To apply the ratio of 30,000 to the aggregate population of the Union (not that of the individual States) which will give 120 members, and then apportion those members among the several States by as many different ratios as there are States; or to the population of each State, giving them one for every 30,000 as far as it will go, making 112, and then distribute the remaining eight members among those States having the highest fractions of which 5 will be given to the States east of this [Pennsylvania]. * * * The effect of this principle must be deemed a very pernicious one, and in my opinion [is a] subversion of that contained in the Constitution, which in the 3d paragraph of the 2d Section, first Article, founds the representation on the population of each State, in terms as explicit as it could well have been done. Besides it takes the fractions of some States to supply the deficiency of others, and thus makes the people of Georgia the instrument of giving a member to New Hampshire. * * * On our part, the principle will never be yielded, for when such obvious encroachments are made on the plain meaning of the Constitution, the bond of Union ceases to be the equal measure of justice to all its parts. On theirs, a very persevering firmness is likewise observed. They appear to me to play a hazardous game. The government secures them many important blessings, all those which it gives to us and many more, and yet with these they seem not to be satisfied.—To ARCHIBALD STUART. FORD ED., v, 453. (Pa., March 1792.)

390. APPORTIONMENT BILL, Veto of Advised.—Viewing this bill either as a *violation* of the Constitution, or as giving an *inconvenient exposition of its words,* is it a case wherein the President ought to interpose his negative? I think it is. * * * The majorities by which this bill has been carried (to wit: of one in the Senate and two in the Representatives) show how divided the opinions were there. The whole of both Houses admit the Constitution will bear the other exposition, whereas the minorities in both deny it will bear that of the bill. The application of any one ratio is intelligible to the people and will, therefore, be approved, whereas the complex operations of this bill will never be comprehended by them, and though they may acquiesce, they cannot approve what they do not understand.—OPINION ON APPORTIONMENT BILL. vii, 601. FORD ED., v, 500. (1792.)

391. APPORTIONMENT BILL, Veto Message.—The Constitution has prescribed that representatives shall be apportioned among the several States according to their respective numbers; and there is no one proportion or division which, applied to the respective numbers of the States, will yield the number and allotment of representatives proposed by the bill. The Constitution has also provided that the number of representatives shall not exceed one for every thirty thousand, which restriction is by the contract, and by fair and obvious construction, to be applied to the separate and respective numbers of the States; and the bill has allotted to eight of the States more than one for thirty thousand.—DRAFT FOR VETO MESSAGE. FORD ED., v, 501. (April 1792.)

392. APPORTIONMENT BILL, History of Veto.—The President [Washington] * * * [referred] to the representation bill, which he had now in his possession for the tenth day. I had before given him my opinion in writing, that the method of apportionment was contrary to the Constitution. He agreed that it was contrary to the common understanding of that instrument, and to what was understood at the time by the makers of it; that yet it would bear the construction which the bill put, and he observed that the vote for and against the bill was perfectly geographical, a northern against a southern vote, and he feared he should be thought to be taking side with a southern party. I admitted this motive of delicacy, but that it should not induce him to do wrong; urged the dangers to which the scramble for the fractionary members would always lead. He here expressed his fear that there would, ere long, be a separation of the Union; that the public mind seemed dissatisfied and tending to this. He went home, sent for Randolph, the Attorney General, desired him to get Mr. Madison immediately and come to me, and if we three concurred in opinion that he should negative the bill, he desired to hear nothing more about it, but that we would draw the instrument for him to sign. They came. Our minds had been before made up. We drew the instrument. Randolph carried it to him, and told him we all concurred in it. He walked with him to the door, and as if he still wished to get off, he said, "and you say you approve of this yourself." "Yes, Sir," says Randolph, "I do upon my honor." He sent it to the House of Representatives instantly. A few of the hottest friends of the bill expressed passion, but the majority were satisfied, and both in and out of doors, it gave pleasure to have, at length, an instance of the negative being exercised.—THE ANAS. ix, 115. FORD ED., i, 192. April 1792.)

393. APPROBATION, Consolation in.—Though I have made up my mind not to suffer calumny to disturb my tranquillity, yet I retain all my sensibilities for the approbation of the good and just. That is, indeed, the chief consolation for the hatred of so many, who, without the least personal knowledge, and on the sacred evidence of "Porcupine" and Fenno alone, cover me with their implacable hatred. The only return I will ever make to them will be to do them all the good I can, in spite of their teeth.—To SAMUEL SMITH. iv, 256. FORD ED., vii, 279. (M., 1798.)

394. ——— ———. I thank God for an opportunity of retiring without censure, and carrying with me the most consoling proofs of public approbation.—To DUPONT DE NEMOURS. v, 432. (W., 1809.)

395. APPROBATION OF THE DISCRIMINATING.—With those who wish to think amiss of me, I have learned to be perfectly indifferent; but where I know a mind to be ingenuous, and to need only truth to set it to rights, I cannot be as passive.—To MRS. JOHN ADAMS. iv, 560. FORD ED., viii, 311. (M., 1804.)

396. APPROBATION BY THE GOOD. —To be praised by those who themselves deserve all praise, is a gratification of high order. Their approbation who, having been high in office themselves, have information and talents to guide their judgment, is a consolation deeply felt. A conscientious devotion to republican government, like charity in religion, has obtained for me much indulgence from my fellow citizens, and the aid of able counsellors has guided me through many difficulties.—To LARKIN SMITH. v, 441. (M., April 1809.)

397. APPROBATION, Intelligent.—It has been a great happiness to me, to have received the approbation of so great a portion of my fellow citizens, and particularly of those who have opportunities of inquiring, reading and deciding for themselves.—To C. F. WELLES. v, 484. (M., 1809.)

398. APPROBATION, Legislative.—I learn with pleasure the approbation, by the General Assembly of Rhode Island, of the principles declared by me [in the inaugural address]; principles which flowed sincerely from the heart and judgment, and which, with sincerity, will be pursued. While acting on them, I ask only to be judged with truth and candor.—To THE RHODE ISLAND ASSEMBLY. iv, 397. (W., May 1801.)

399. ——— ———. For the approbation which the Legislature of Vermont has been pleased to express of the principles and measures pursued in the management of their affairs, I am sincerely thankful; and should I be so fortunate as to carry into retirement the equal approbation and good will of my fellow citizens generally, it will be the comfort of my future days, and will close a service of forty years with the only reward it ever wished.*— R. To A. VERMONT LEGISLATURE. viii, 121. (1807.)

400. ——— ———. The assurances of your approbation, and that my conduct has given satisfaction to my fellow citizens generally, will be an important ingredient in my future happiness.—R. To A. VIRGINIA ASSEMBLY. viii, 148. (1809.)

401. APPROBATION OF NEIGHBORS. —It is a sufficient happiness to me to know that my fellow citizens of the country generally entertain for me the kind sentiments which have prompted this proposition [to

* To addresses from Georgia, New York, Maryland, Pennsylvania and Rhode Island, received about the same time, similar replies were sent.— EDITOR.

meet him on his way home] without giving to so many the trouble of leaving their homes to meet a single individual. I shall have opportunities of taking them individually by the hand at our court house and other public places, and of exchanging assurances of mutual esteem. Certainly it is the greatest consolation to me to know, that in returning to the bosom of my native country, I shall be again in the midst of their kind affections: and I can say with truth that my return to them will make me happier than I have been since I left them.—To T. M. RANDOLPH. v, 431. FORD ED., ix, 247. (W., Feb. 1809.)

402. APPROBATION, Old friends and.—The approbation of my ancient friends is, above all things, the most grateful to my heart. They know for what objects we relinquished the delights of domestic society, tranquillity and science, and committed ourselves to the ocean of revolution, to wear out the only life God has given us here in scenes the benefits of which will accrue only to those who follow us.—To JOHN DICKINSON. iv, 424. (W., 1801.)

403. APPROBATION, Popular.—The approbation of my constituents is truly the most valued reward for any services it has fallen to my lot to render them—their confidence and esteem the greatest consolation of my life.—R. To A. MASSACHUSETTS LEGISLATURE. viii, 116. (Feb. 1807.)

404. ———— ————. In a virtuous and free State, no rewards can be so pleasing to sensible minds, as those which include the approbation of our fellow citizens.—INAUGURATION SPEECH AS GOVERNOR. FORD ED., ii, 187. (1779.)

405. APPROBATION, Principle and.—Our part is to pursue with steadiness what is right, turning neither to right nor left for the intrigues or popular delusions of the day, assured that the public approbation will in the end be with us.—To GENERAL BRECKENRIDGE. vii, 238. (M., 1822.)

406. APPROBATION, Rewarded by.—The approbation of my fellow citizens is the richest reward I can receive.—To RICHARD M. JOHNSON. v, 256. (W., 1808.)

407. ———— ————. The approving voice of our fellow citizens, for endeavors to be useful, is the greatest of all earthly rewards.*—R. To A. NEW LONDON METHODISTS. viii, 147. (1809.)

408. ———— ————. If, in my retirement to the humble station of a private citizen, I am accompanied with the esteem and approbation of my fellow citizens, trophies obtained by the blood-stained steel, or the tattered flags of the tented field, will never be envied.—R. To A. MARYLAND REPUBLICANS. viii, 165. (1809.)

409. APPROBATION, Right and.—I have ever found in my progress through life,

* Jefferson retired with a reputation and popularity hardly inferior to that of Washington.—John T. Morse, Jr., *Life of Jefferson.* 318.

that, acting for the public, if we do always what is right, the approbation denied in the beginning will surely follow us in the end. It is from posterity we are to expect remuneration for the sacrifices we are making for their service, of time, quiet and good will.—To JOSEPH C. CABELL. vii, 394. (M., 1825.)

410. APPROBATION, Undeserved.—I have never claimed any other merit than of good intentions, sensible that in the choice of measures, error of judgment has too often had its influence; and that with whatever indulgence my countrymen * * * have been so kind as to view my course, yet they would certainly not know me in the picture here drawn, and would, I fear, say in the words of the poet, " praise undeserved is satire in disguise." Were, therefore, the piece to be prepared for the press, I should certainly entreat you to revise that part with a severe eye.—To AMELOT DE LA CROIX. v, 422. (W., 1809.)

411. APPROBATION BY THE VIRTUOUS.—Sentiments of esteem from men of worth, of reflection, and of pure attachment to republican government, are my consolation against the calumnies of which it has suited certain writers to make me the object. Under these I hope I shall never bend.—To HARRY INNES. FORD ED., vii, 383. (M., 1799.)

412. APPROPRIATIONS, Borrowing from.—There are funds sufficient and regularly appropriated to the fitting out [ships], but for manning the proper funds are exhausted, consequently we must borrow from other funds, and state the matter to Congress.—ANAS. FORD ED., i, 308. (1805.)

413. APPROPRIATIONS, The Constitution and.—In the answer to Turreau, I think it would be better to lay more stress on the constitutional bar to our furnishing the money, because it would apply in an occasion of peace as well as war. I submit to you, therefore, * * * the inserting, " but, in indulging these dispositions, the President is bound to stop at the limits prescribed by our Constitution and law to the authorities in his hands. One of the limits is that ' no money shall be drawn from the Treasury but in consequence of appropriations made by law.' and no law having made any appropriation of money for any purpose similar to that expressed in your letter, it lies, of course, beyond his constitutional powers."—To JAMES MADISON. FORD ED., viii, 474. (M., Sep. 1806.)

414. APPROPRIATIONS, Discretion over.—The question whether the Berceau was to be delivered up under the treaty was of Executive cognizance entirely, and without appeal. So was the question as to the condition in which she should be delivered. And it is as much an invasion of its independence for a coordinate branch to call for the reasons of the decision, as it would be to call on the Supreme Court for its reasons on any judiciary decision. If an appropriation were asked, the Legislature would have a right to ask reasons. But in this case they had confided an appropriation (for naval contingencies) to the discretion of the Executive. Under this appropriation our predecessors *bought* the vessel (for there was no order of Congress authorizing them to buy) and began her repairs; we completed them. I will not say that a very gross abuse of discretion in a past appropriation would not furnish ground to the Legislature to take notice of it. In what form is not now necessary to decide. But so far from a gross abuse, the decision in this case was correct, honorable and advantageous to the nation. I cannot see to what legitimate objects any resolution of the House on the subject can lead; and if one is passed on ground not legitimate, our duty will be to resist it.—To WILLIAM B. GILES. FORD ED., viii, 142. (April 1802.)

415. APPROPRIATIONS, Diverting.— The diversion of the [French] money from its legal appropriation offers a flaw against the Executive which may place them in the wrong.—To PRESIDENT WASHINGTON. FORD ED., vi, 179. (1793.)

416. —— ——. If it should appear that the Legislature has done their part in furnishing the money for the French nation, and that the Executive departments have applied it to other purposes, then it will certainly be desirable that we get back on legal ground as soon as possible, by pressing on the domestic funds and availing ourselves of any proper opportunity which may be furnished of replacing the money to the foreign creditors.—To PRESIDENT WASHINGTON. FORD ED., vi, 177. (1793.)

417. APPROPRIATIONS, Estimates and.— I like your idea of kneading all Hamilton's little scraps and fragments into one batch, and adding to it a complementary sum, which, while it forms it into a single mass from which everything is to be paid, will enable us, should a breach of appropriation ever be charged on us, to prove that the sum appropriated, and more, has been applied to its specific object.—To ALBERT GALLATIN. iv, 428. FORD ED., viii, 140. (W., 1802.)

418. —— ——. Congress, aware that too minute a specification has its evil as well as a too general one, does not make the estimate a part of their law, but gives a sum in gross, trusting the Executive discretion for that year, and that sum only; so in other departments, as of War, for instance, the estimate of the Secretary specifies all the items of clothing, subsistence, pay, &c., of the army. And Congress throws this into such masses as they think best, to wit, a sum in gross for clothing, another for subsistence, a third for pay, &c., binding up the Executive discretion only by the sum, and the object generalized to a certain degree. The minute details of the estimate are thus dispensed with in point of obligation, and the discretion of the officer is enlarged to the limits of the classification which Congress thinks it best for the public interest to make.—To ALBERT GALLATIN. iv, 529. (1804.)

419. APPROPRIATIONS, Executive power over.— The Executive * * * has the power, though not the right, to apply money contrary to its legal appropriations. Cases may be imagined, however, where it would be their duty to do this. But they must be cases of *extreme necessity. The payment of interest to the domestic creditors* has been mentioned as one of the causes of diverting the foreign fund. But this is not an object of greater necessity than that to which it was legally appropriated. It is taking the money from our *foreign creditors* to pay it to the *domestic ones;* a preference which neither justice, gratitude, nor the estimation in which these two descriptions of creditors are held in this country will justify. *The payment of the Army and the daily expenses of the government* have been also mentioned as objects of withdrawing this money. These indeed are pressing objects, and might produce that degree of distressing necessity which would be a justification.— To PRESIDENT WASHINGTON. FORD ED., vi, 176. (Pa., 1793.)

420. APPROPRIATIONS, Expenditures and.— A violation of a law making appropriations of money, is a violation of that section of the Constitution of the United States which requires that no money shall be drawn from the Treasury but in consequences of appropriations made by law.—GILES TREASURY RESOLUTIONS. FORD ED., vi, 168. (1793.)

421. APPROPRIATIONS, Specific.— It is essential to the due administration of the government of the United States, that laws making specific appropriations of money should be strictly observed by the Secretary of the Treasury thereof.—GILES TREASURY RESOLUTIONS. FORD ED., vi, 168. (1793.)

422. —— ——. In our care of the public contributions intrusted to our direction, it would be prudent to multiply barriers against their dissipation, by appropriating specific sums to every specific purpose susceptible of definition; by disallowing applications of money varying from the appropriation in object, or transcending it in amount; by reducing the undefined field of contingencies, and thereby circumscribing discretionary powers over money; and by bringing back to a single department all accountabilities for money where the examination may be prompt, efficacious, and uniform.—FIRST ANNUAL MESSAGE. viii, 10. FORD ED., viii, 120. (Dec. 1801.) See MONEY BILLS.

423. ARBITRATION, Offer of.— As to our dispute with Schweighauser and Dobrée, in the conversation I had with Dobrée at Nantes, he appeared to think so rationally on the subject, that I thought there would be no difficulty in accommodating it with him, and I wished rather to settle it by accommodation, than to apply to the minister. I afterwards had it intimated to him * * *, that I had it in idea to propose a reference to arbitrators. He expressed a cheerful concurrence in it. I thereupon made the proposition to him formally, by letter, mentioning particularly, that we would choose our arbitrators of some neutral nation, and, of preference, from among the Dutch refugees in Paris. I was surprised to receive an answer from him, wherein, after expressing his own readiness to accede to this proposition, he added, that on consulting with Mr. Puchilberg, he had declined it.—To JOHN JAY. ii, 496. (P., 1788.)

424. —— ——. I began by offering to Schweighauser and Dobrée an arbitration before honest and judicious men of a neutral nation. They declined this, and had the modesty to propose an arbitration before *merchants of their own town*. I gave them warning then, that as the offer on the part of a sovereign nation to submit to a private arbitration was an unusual condescendence, if they did not accept them, it would not be repeated, and that the United States would judge the case for themselves hereafter. They continued to decline it.—To WILLIAM SHORT. FORD ED., v, 365.. (Pa., 1791.)

425. ARBORICULTURE, Coffee tree.— Bartram is extremely anxious to get a large supply of seeds of the Kentucky coffee tree. I told him I would use all my interest with you to obtain it, as I think I heard you say that some neighbors of yours had a large number of trees. Be so good as to take measures for bringing a good quantity, if possible, to Bartram when you come to Congress.—To JAMES MADISON. iii, 569. FORD ED., vi, 279. (1793.)

426. ARBORICULTURE, Cork Oak.—I expect from the South of France some acorns of the cork oak, which I propose for your society [Agricultural], as I am persuaded they will succeed with you. I observed it to grow in England without shelter, not well, indeed, but so as to give hopes that it would do well with you.—To WILLIAM DRAYTON. i, 555. (P., 1786.)

427. —— ——. I sent you a parcel of acorns of the cork oak by Colonel Franks. To WILLIAM DRAYTON. ii, 202. (Pa., 1787.)

428. —— ——. I have been long endeavoring to procure the cork tree from Europe, but without success. A plant which I brought with me from Paris died after languishing some time, and of several parcels of acorns received from a correspondent at Marseilles, not one has ever vegetated. I shall continue my endeavors, although disheartened by the nonchalance of our southern fellow citizens, with whom alone they can thrive.—To JAMES RONALDSON. vi, 92. FORD ED., ix, 370. (M., Jan. 1813.)

429. ARBORICULTURE, Fruit trees.— Should you be able to send me any plants of good fruit, and especially of peaches and eating grapes, they will be thankfully received.—To PHILLIP MAZZEI. FORD ED., viii, 16. (W., March 1801.)

—— ARBORICULTURE, the Olive.—See OLIVE.

430. ARBORICULTURE, Pecan.—The pecan nut is, as you conjecture, the Illinois nut. The former is the vulgar name south of the Potomac, as also with the Indians and Spaniards, and enters also into the botanical name which is *Juglano Pacan*.—To FRANCIS HOPKINSON. ii, 74. (P., 1786.)

431. —— ——. Procure me two or three hundred pecan nuts from the western country. —To F. HOPKINSON. i, 506. (P., 1786.)

432. —— ——. I thank you for the pecan nuts.—To JAMES MADISON. ii, 156. FORD ED., iv, 396. (P., 1787.)

433. ARBORICULTURE, Sensitive Plant.—Your attention to one burthen I laid on you, encourages me to remind you of another, which is the sending me some of the seeds of the *Dionæa Muscipula*, or Venus flytrap, called also with you, I believe, the Sensitive Plant.—To MR. HAWKINS. ii, 3. (P., 1786.)

434. ARBORICULTURE, Trees.—I send a packet of the seeds of trees which I would wish Anthony to sow in a large nursery, noting well their names.—To NICHOLAS LEWIS. FORD ED., iv, 344. (P., 1786.)

435. ARBORICULTURE, Vines.—I am making a collection of vines for wine and for the table.—To A. CAREY. i, 508. (P., 1786.)

436. ARCHITECTURE, Bad.—The genius of architecture seems to have shed its maledictions over this land [Virginia].— NOTES ON VIRGINIA. viii, 394. FORD ED., iii, 258. (1782.)

437. ARCHITECTURE, Beauty in.— How is a taste in this beautiful art to be formed in our countrymen unless we avail ourselves of every occasion when public buildings are to be erected, of presenting to them models for their study and imitation?—To JAMES MADISON. i, 433. (P., 1785.)

438. ARCHITECTURE, Brick, Stone, Wood.—All we shall do in the way of reformation will produce no permanent improvement to our country, while the unhappy prejudice prevails that houses of brick or stone are less wholesome than those of wood. A dew is often observed on the walls of the former in rainy weather, and the most obvious solution is, that the rain has penetrated through these walls. The following facts, however, are sufficient to prove the error of this solution: 1. This dew on the walls appears when there is no rain, if the state of the atmosphere be moist. 2. It appears on the partition as well as the exterior walls. 3. So, also on pavements of brick or stone. 4. It is more copious in proportion as the walls are thicker; the reverse of which ought to be the case, if this hypothesis were just. If cold water be poured into a vessel of stone, or glass, a dew forms instantly on the outside; but if it be poured into a vessel of wood, there is no such appearance. It is not supposed, in the first case. that the water has exuded through the glass, but that it is precipitated from the circumambient air; as the humid particles of vapor, passing from the boiler of an alembic through its refrigerant, are precipitated from the air, in which they are suspended, on the internal surface of the refrigerant. Walls of brick or stone act as the refrigerant in this instance. They are sufficiently cold to condense and precipitate the moisture suspended in the air of the room, when it is heavily charged therewith. But walls of wood are not so. The question then is, whether the air in which this moisture is left floating, or that which is deprived of it, be most wholesome? In both cases, the remedy is easy. A little fire kindled in the room, whenever the air is damp, prevents the precipitation on the walls; and this practice, found healthy in the warmest as well as coldest seasons, is as necessary in a wooden as in a stone or brick house. I do not mean to say, that the rain never penetrates through walls of brick. On the contrary, I have seen instances of it. But with us it is only through the northern and eastern walls of the house, after a north-easterly storm, these being the only ones which continue long enough to force through the walls. This, however, happens too rarely to give a just character of unwholesomeness to such houses. In a house, the walls of which are of well-burnt brick and good mortar, I have seen the rain penetrate through but twice in a dozen or fifteen years. The inhabitants of Europe, who dwell chiefly in houses of stone or brick, are surely as healthy as those of Virginia. These houses have the advantage, too, of being warmer in winter and cooler in summer than those of wood; of being cheaper in their first construction, where lime is convenient, and infinitely more durable. The latter consideration renders it of great importance to eradicate this prejudice from the minds of our countrymen. A country whose buildings are of wood, can never increase in its improvements to any considerable degree. Their duration is highly estimated at fifty years. Every half century then our country becomes a *tabula rasa*, whereon we have to set out anew, as in the first moment of seating it. Whereas when buildings are of durable materials, every new edifice is an actual and permanent acquisition to the State, adding to its value as well as to its ornament.—NOTES ON VIRGINIA. viii, 395. FORD ED., iii, 258. (1782.)

439. ARCHITECTURE, Delight in.—Architecture is my delight, and putting up and pulling down, one of my favorite amusements.—RAYNER'S LIFE OF JEFFERSON. 524.

440. ARCHITECTURE, Economy in.—I have scribbled some general notes on the plan of a house you enclosed. I have done more. I have endeavored to throw the same area, the same extent of walls, the same number of rooms, and of the same sizes, into another form so as to offer a choice to the builder. Indeed. I varied my plan by showing what it would be with alcove bed rooms, to which I am so much attached.—To JAMES MADISON. FORD ED., vi, 259. (Pa., 1793.)

441. ARCHITECTURE, English.—English architecture is in the most wretched style I ever saw, not meaning to except America, where it is bad, nor even Virginia, where it is worse than in any other part of America, which I have seen.—To JOHN PAGE. i, 550. FORD ED., iv, 214. (P., 1786.)

442. ARCHITECTURE, Fascination of.—Here I am gazing whole hours at the Maison quarrée, like a lover at his mistress. The stocking weavers and silk spinners around it consider me a hypochondriac Englishman, about to write with a pistol the last chapter of his history. This is the second time I have been in love since I left Paris. The first was with a Diana at the Chateau de Laye-Epinaye in Beaujolois, a delicious morsel of sculpture, by M. A. Slodtz. This, you will say, was in rule, to fall in love with a female beauty; but with a house! it is out of all precedent. No, madame, it is not without a precedent in my own history. While in Paris I was violently smitten with the Hotel de Salm, and used to go to the Tuileries almost daily. to look at it.—To MADAME LA COMTESSE DE TESSE. ii, 131. (N., 1787.)

443. ARCHITECTURE, Faulty.—Buildings are often erected, by individuals, of considerable expense. To give these symmetry and taste, would not increase their cost. It would only change the arrangement of the materials, the form and combination of the members. This would often cost less than the burden of barbarous ornaments with which these buildings are sometimes charged. But the first principles of the art are unknown, and there exists scarcely a model among us sufficiently chaste to give an idea of them.—NOTES ON VIRGINIA. viii, 394. FORD ED., iii, 258. (1782.)

444. ARCHITECTURE, French.—Were I to proceed to tell you how much I enjoy French architecture * * * I should want words.—To MR. BELLINI. i, 445. (P., 1785.)

445. ARCHITECTURE, Importance of.—Architecture is worth great attention. As we double our number every twenty years we must double our houses. * * * It is, then, among the most important arts; and it is desirable to introduce taste into an art which shows so much.—TRAVELLING HINTS. ix, 404. (1788.)

446. ARCHITECTURE, Plan of Prison.—With respect to the plan of a Prison, requested [by the Virginia authorities] in 1785. (being then in Paris), I had heard of a benevolent society. in England, which had been indulged by the government, in an experiment of the effect of labor, in *solitary confinement*, on some of their criminals: which experiment had succeeded beyond expectation. The same idea had been suggested in France, and an architect of Lyons had proposed a plan of a well-contrived edifice, on the principle of solitary confinement. I procured a copy, and as it was too large for our purposes, I drew one on a scale less extensive. but susceptible of additions as they should be wanting. This I sent to the directors, instead of a plan of a common prison, in the hope that it would suggest the idea of labor in solitary confinement, instead of that on the public works, which we had adopted in our Revised Code. Its principle, accordingly, but not its exact form, was adopted by Latrobe in carrying the plan into execution, by the erection of what is now called the Penitentiary, built under his direction.—AUTOBIOGRAPHY. i, 46. FORD ED., 64. (1821.)

447. ARCHITECTURE, Porticos.—A portico may be from five to ten diameters of the column deep, or projected from the building. If of more than five diameters, there must be a column in the middle of each flank, since it must never be more than five diameters from center to center of column. The portico of the Maison quarrée is three intercolonnations deep. I never saw as much to a private house.—To JAMES MADISON. FORD ED., vi, 327. (1793.)

— ARCHITECTURE, Roman.—See ANTIQUITIES.

448. ARCHITECTURE, Ugly.—The private buildings [in Virginia] are very rarely constructed of stone or brick, much the greater portion being of scantling and boards, plastered with lime. It is impossible to devise things more ugly, uncomfortable, and happily more perishable.—NOTES ON VIRGINIA. viii, 393. FORD ED., iii, 257. (1782.)

449. ARCHITECTURE, Virginia Capitol.—I was written to in 1785 (being then in Paris) by directors appointed to superintend the building of a Capitol in Richmond, to advise them as to a plan, and to add to it one of a Prison. Thinking it a favorable opportunity of introducing into the State an example of architecture, in the classic style of antiquity, and the Maison qarrée of Nismes, an ancient Roman temple, being considered as the most perfect model existing of what may be called Cubic architecture, I applied to M. Clerissault, who had published drawings of the Antiquities of Nismes, to have me a model of the building made in stucco, only changing the order from Corinthinan to Ionic, on account of the difficulty of the Corinthian capitals. I yielded, with reluctance, to the taste of Clerissault, in his preference of the modern capital of Scamozzi to the more noble capital of antiquity. This was executed by the artist whom Choiseul Gouffier had carried with him to Constantinople, and employed, while ambassador there, in making those beautiful models of the remains of Grecian architecture which are to be seen at Paris. To adapt the exterior to our use, I drew a plan for the interior, with the apartments necessary for legislative, executive, and judiciary purposes; and accommodated in their size and distribution to the form and dimensions of the building. These were forwarded to the directors, in 1786, and were carried into execution, with some variations, not for the better, the most important of which, however, admit of future correction.—AUTOBIOGRAPHY. i, 45. FORD ED., i, 63. (1821.)

450. —— ——. We took for our model what is called the Maison quarrée of Nismes, one of the most beautiful, if not the most beautiful and precious morsel of architecture left us by antiquity. It was built by Caius and Lucius Cæsar, and repaired by Louis XIV., and has the suffrage of all the judges of architecture who have seen it, as yielding to no one of the beautiful monuments of Greece, Rome, Palmyra and Balbec, which late travellers have communicated to us. It is very simple, but it is noble beyond expression, and would have done honor to our country, as presenting to travellers a specimen of taste in our infancy, promising much for our maturer age.—To JAMES MADISON. i, 432. (P., 1785.)

451. —— ——. I shall send them a plan taken from the best morsel of ancient architecture now remaining. It has obtained the approbation of fifteen or sixteen centuries, and is, therefore, preferable to any design which might be newly contrived. It will give more room, be more convenient and cost less than the plan they sent me. Pray encourage them to wait for it, and to execute it. It will be superior in beauty to anything in America, and not inferior to anything in the world. It is very simple.—To JAMES MADISON. i, 415. (P., 1785.)

452. —— ——. The designs for the Capitol are simple and sublime. More cannot be said. They are not the brat of a whimsical conception never before brought to light, but copied from the most precious, the most perfect model, of ancient architecture remaining on earth; one which has received the approbation of near 2000 years, and which is sufficiently remarkable to have been visited by all travellers. —To DR. JAMES CURRIE. FORD ED., iv, 133. (P., 1786.)

453. —— ——. I have been much mortified with information I received * * * from Virginia, that the first brick of the Capitol would be laid within a few days. But surely, the delay of this piece of a summer would have been repaired by the savings in the plan preparing here, were we to value its other superiorities as nothing.—To JAMES MADISON. i, 432. (P., 1785.)

454. —— ——. Do * * * exert yourself to get the plan [of the Capitol] begun on, set aside and that adopted which was drawn here. It was taken from a model which has been the admiration of sixteen centuries; which has been the object of as many pilgrimages as the tomb of Mahomet; which will give unrivalled honor to our State, and furnish a model whereon to form the taste of our young men. It will cost much less, too, than the one begun because it does not cover one-half the area.—To JAMES MADISON. i, 534. FORD ED., iv, 196. (P., 1785.)

455. —— ——. Pray try if you can effect the stopping of this work. * * * The loss will be only of the laying the bricks already laid, or a part of them. The bricks themselves will do again for the interior walls, and one side wall and one end wall may remain, as they will answer equally well for our plan. This loss is not to be weighed against the saving of money which will arise, against the comfort of laying out the public money for something honorable, the satisfaction of seeing an object and proof of national good taste, and the regret and mortification of erecting a monument of our barbarism, which will be loaded with execrations as long as it shall endure.—To JAMES MADISON. i, 433. (P., 1785.)

456. —— ——. Our new Capitol, when the corrections are made, of which it is susceptible, will be an edifice of first rate dignity. Whenever it shall be finished with the proper ornaments belonging to it (which will not be in this age), it will be worthy of being exhibited alongside the most celebrated remains of antiquity. Its extreme convenience has acquired it universal approbation.—To WILLIAM SHORT. FORD ED., v, 136. (1789.)

457. —— ——. The capitol in the city of Richmond, in Virginia, is the model of the Temples of Erectheus at Athens, of Balbec, and of the Maison quarrée of Nismes. All of which are nearly of the same form and proportions, and are considered as the most perfect examples of cubic architecture, as the

Pantheon of Rome is of the spherical. Their dimensions not being sufficient for the purposes of the Capitol, they were enlarged, but their proportions rigorously observed. The Capitol is of brick, one hundred and thirty four feet long, seventy feet wide, and forty-five feet high, exclusive of the basement. Twenty-eight feet of its length is occupied by a portico of the whole breadth of the house, showing six columns in front, and two intercolonnations in flank. It is of a single order, which is Ionic; its columns four feet two inches diameter, and their entablature running round the whole building. The portico is crowned by a pediment, the height of which is two-ninths of its span.—JEFFERSON MANUSCRIPTS. ix, 446.

458. ARCHITECTURE, Washington Capitol.—I have had under consideration Mr. Hallet's plans for the Capitol, which undoubtedly have a great deal of merit. Dr. Thornton has also given me a view of his. * * * The grandeur, simplicity and beauty of the exterior, the propriety with which the apartments are distributed, and economy in the mass of the whole structure, will, I doubt not, give it a preference in your eyes, as it has done in mine and those of several others whom I have consulted. * * * Some difficulty arises with respect to Mr. Hallet, who you know was in some degree led into his plan by ideas we all expressed to him. This ought not to induce us to prefer it to a better; but while he is liberally rewarded for the time and labor he has expended on it, his feelings should be saved and soothed as much as possible.—To THE WASHINGTON COMMISSIONERS. iii, 507. (1793.)

459. —— ——. Dr. Thornton's plan of a Capitol has * * * so captivated the eyes and judgment of all as to leave no doubt you will prefer it. * * * Among its admirers none is more decided than he [Washington] whose decision is most important. It is simple, noble, beautiful, excellently distributed, and moderate in size. * * * A just respect for the right of approbation in the commissioners will prevent any formal decision in the President till the plan shall be laid before you and be approved by you.—To MR. CARROLL. iii, 508. (Pa., 1793.)

460. —— ——. The Representative's chamber will remain a durable monument of your talents as an architect. * * * The Senate room I have never seen.—To MR. LATROBE. vi, 75. (M., 1812.)

461. —— ——. I shall live in the hope that the day will come when an opportunity will be given you of finishing the middle building in a style worthy of the two wings, and worthy of the first temple dedicated to the sovereignty of the people, embellishing with Athenian taste the course of a nation looking far beyond the range of Athenian destinies.—To MR. LATROBE. vi, 75. (M., 1812.) See CAPITOL (U. S.) and WASHINGTON CITY.

462. ARCHITECTURE, Williamsburg Capitol.—The only public buildings worthy mention [in Virginia] are the Capitol, the Palace, the College, and the Hospital for Lunatics, all of them in Williamsburg, heretofore the seat of our government. The Capitol is a light and airy structure, with a portico in front of two orders, the lower of which, being Doric, is tolerably just in its proportions and ornaments, save only that the intercolonnations are too large. The upper is Ionic, much too small for that on which it is mounted, its ornaments not proper to the order, nor proportioned within themselves. It is crowned with a pediment, which is too large for its span. Yet, on the whole, it is the most pleasing piece of architecture we have. The Palace is not handsome without, but it is spacious and commodious within, is prettily situated, and with the grounds annexed to it, is capable of being made an elegant seat. The College and Hospital are rude, misshapen piles, which, but that they have roofs, would be taken for brick-kilns. There are no other public buildings but churches and court-houses, in which no attempts are made at elegance. Indeed, it would not be easy to execute such an attempt, as a workman could scarcely be found here capable of drawing an order.—NOTES ON VIRGINIA. viii, 394. FORD ED., iii, 257. (1782.)

463. ARISTOCRACY, Artificial vs. Natural.—There is a natural aristocracy among men. The grounds of this are virtue and talents. Formerly, bodily powers gave place among the aristoi. But since the invention of gunpowder has armed the weak as well as the strong with missile death, bodily strength, like beauty, good humor, politeness and other accomplishments, has become but an auxiliary ground of distinction. There is, also, an artificial aristocracy, founded on wealth and birth, without either virtue or talents: for with these it would belong to the first class. The natural aristocracy I consider as the most precious gift of nature for the instruction, the trusts, and government of society. And indeed, it would have been inconsistent in creation to have formed man for the social state, and not to have provided virtue and wisdom enough to manage the concerns of the society. May we not even say, that that form of government is the best, which provides the most effectually for a pure selection of these natural aristoi into the offices of government? The artificial aristocracy is a mischievous ingredient in government, and provision should be made to prevent its ascendency. On the question, what is the best provision, you and I differ; but we differ as rational friends, using the free exercise of our own reason, and mutually indulging its errors. You think it best to put the pseudo-aristoi into a separate chamber of legislation, where they may be hindered from doing mischief by their coordinate branches and where, also, they may be a protection to wealth against the agrarian and plundering enterprises of the majority of the people. I think that to give them power in order to prevent them from doing mischief, is arming them for it, and increasing instead of remedying the evil. For, if the coordinate branches can arrest their action, so may they that of the coordinates. Mischief may be done negatively as well as positively. Of this, a cabal in the Senate of the United States has furnished many proofs. Nor do I believe them necessary to protect the wealthy; because enough of these will find their way into every branch of the legislature to protect themselves. From fifteen to twenty legislatures of our own, in action for thirty years past, have proved that no fears of an equalization of property are to be apprehended from them. I think the best remedy is exactly that provided by all our constitutions, to leave to the citizens the free election and separation of the aristoi from the pseudo-aristoi. of the wheat from the chaff. In general they will elect the really good and wise. In some instances, wealth may corrupt, and birth blind them, but not in sufficient degree to endanger the society.—To JOHN ADAMS. vi, 223. FORD ED., ix, 425. (M., 1813.)

464. ARISTOCRACY,   Banking.—I hope we shall * * * crush in its birth the aristocracy of our moneyed corporations, which dare already to challenge our government to a trial of strength and bid defiance to the laws of our country.—To GEORGE LOGAN. FORD ED., x, 69. (P. F., Nov. 1816.)

— ARISTOCRACY, Cincinnati Society and.—See CINCINNATI..

465. ARISTOCRACY, Despised.—An industrious farmer occupies a more dignified place in the scale of beings, whether moral or political, than a lazy lounger, valuing himself on his family, too proud to work, and drawing out a miserable existence by eating on that surplus of other men's labor, which is the sacred fund of the helpless poor.—To M. DE MEUNIER. ix, 271. FORD ED., iv, 176. (P., 1786.)

466. ARISTOCRACY, Education and.—The bill [of the Revised Code of Virginia] for the more general diffusion of learning proposed to divide every county into wards of five or six miles square, like the [New England] townships; to establish in each ward a free school for reading, writing and common arithmetic; to provide for the annual selection of the best subjects from these schools, who might receive, at the public expense, a higher degree of education at a district school; and from these district schools to select a certain number of the most promising subjects, to be completed at an University, where all the useful sciences should be taught. Worth and genius would thus have been sought out from every condition of life. and completely prepared by education for defeating the competition of wealth and birth for public trusts.—To JOHN ADAMS. vi, 225. FORD ED., ix, 427. (P., 1813.)

467. ———. This bill on education would have raised the mass of the people to the high ground of moral respectability necessary to their own safety, and to orderly government; and would have completed the great object of qualifying them to secure the veritable aristoi for the trusts of government to the exclusion of the pseudalists. * * * Although this law has not yet been acted on but in a small and inefficient degree, it is still considered as before the Legislature, * * * and I have great hope that some patriotic spirit will, at a favorable moment, call it up, and make it the key stone of the arch of our government.—To JOHN ADAMS. vi, 226. FORD ED., ix, 428. (M., 1813.)

468. ARISTOCRACY, Evils of.—To detail the real evils of aristocracy, they must be seen in Europe.—To M. DE MEUNIER. ix, 267. FORD ED.. iv, 172. (P., 1786.)

469. ———. A due horror of the evils which flow from these distinctions could be excited in Europe only, where the dignity of man is lost in arbitrary distinctions, where the human species is classed into several stages of degradation, where the many are crushed under the weight of the few, and where the order established can present to the contemplation of a thinking being no other picture than that of God Almighty and his angels trampling under foot the host of the damned.—To M. DE MEUNIER. ix, 270. FORD ED., iv, 175. (P.. 1786.)

470. ———. To know the mass of evil which flows from this fatal source, a person must be in France. He must see the finest soil, the finest climate. the most compact state, the most benevolent character of people, and every earthly advantage combined, insufficient to prevent this scourge from rendering existence a curse to twenty-four out of twenty-five parts of the inhabitants of this country.—To GENERAL WASHINGTON. ii, 62. FORD ED., iv, 329. (P., 1786.)

471. ARISTOCRACY,   Insurrection against.—But even in Europe a change has sensibly taken place in the mind of man. Science has liberated the ideas of those who read and reflect, and the American example has kindled feelings of right in the people. An insurrection has consequently begun of science, talents, and courage, against rank and birth, which have fallen into contempt. It has failed in its first effort, because the mobs of the cities, the instrument used for its accomplishment, debased by ignorance, poverty and vice, could not be restrained to rational action. But the world will soon recover from the panic of this first catastrophe. Science is progressive. and talents and enterprise are on the alert. Resort may be had to the people of the country, a more governable power from their principles and subordination; and rank. and birth, and tinsel-aristocracy will finally shrink into insignificance, even there. This, however, we have no right to meddle with. It suffices for us, if the moral and physical condition of our own citizens qualifies them to select the able and good for the direction of their government, with a recurrence of elections at such short periods as will enable them to displace an unfaithful servant, before the mischief he meditates may be irremediable.—To JOHN ADAMS. vi, 227. FORD ED., ix, 429. (M., 1813.)

— ARISTOCRACY, Kings, Priests and.—See 472.

472. ARISTOCRACY, Liberty and.—The complicated organization of kings, nobles, and priests, is not the wisest or best to effect the happiness of associated man. * * * The trappings of such a machinery consume by their expense those earnings of industry they were meant to protect, and, by the inequalities they produce, expose liberty to sufferance.—To WILLIAM JOHNSON. vii, 291. FORD ED., x, 227. (M., 1823.)

473. ARISTOCRACY, Religious.—The law for religious freedom, * * * put down the aristocracy of the clergy [in Virginia] and restored to the citizen the freedom of the mind.—To JOHN ADAMS. vi, 226. FORD ED., ix, 428. (M., 1813.)

474. ARISTOCRACY, Repressed by.—A heavy aristocracy and corruption are two bridles in the mouths of the Irish which will prevent them from making any effectual efforts against their masters.—To JAMES MADISON. FORD ED., iv, 38. (P., 1785.)

475. ARISTOCRACY, Reverence for.—From what I have seen of Massachusetts and Connecticut myself, and still more from what I have heard, and the character given of the former by yourself, who know them so much better, there seems to be in those two States a traditionary reverence for certain families, which has rendered the offices of the government nearly hereditary in those families. I presume that from an early period of your history, members of those families happening to possess virtue and talents, have honestly exercised them for the good of the people, and by their services have endeared their names to them. In coupling Connecticut with you, I mean it politically only, not morally. For having made the Bible the common law of their land, they seem to have modeled their morality on the story of Jacob and Laban. But although this hereditary succession to office with you, may, in some degree, be founded in real family merit, yet in a much higher degree, it has proceeded from your strict alliance of Church and State. Those families are canonized in the eyes of the people on common principles, " you tickle me, and I will tickle you."—To JOHN ADAMS. vi, 224. FORD ED., ix, 426. (M., 1813.)

476. ARISTOCRACY, Royalty and.—The [French] aristocracy [in 1788-9] was cemented by a common principle of preserving the ancient régime, or whatever should be nearest to it. Making this their Polar star, they moved in phalanx, gave preponderance on every question to the minorities of the Patriots, and always to those who advocated the least change.—AUTOBIOGRAPHY. i, 104. FORD ED., i, 144. (1821.)

— **ARISTOCRACY, Trappings of.**—See 472.

477. ARISTOCRACY, Unpopular.—In Virginia, we have no traditional reverence for certain families. Our clergy, before the Revolution, having been secured against rivalship by fixed salaries, did not give themselves the trouble of acquiring influence over the people. Of wealth, there were great accumulations in particular families, handed down from generation to generation, under the English law of entails. But the only object of ambition for the wealthy was a seat in the King's council. All their court was paid to the crown and its creatures; and they Philipised in all collisions between the King and the people. Hence they were unpopular; and that unpopularity continues attached to their names. A Randolph, a Carter, or a Burwell must have great personal superiority over a common competitor to be elected by the people even at this day.—To JOHN ADAMS. vi 224. FORD ED., ix, 426. (M., 1813.)

478. ARISTOCRACY, Uprooting.—At the first session of our Legislature after the Declaration of Independence, we passed a law abolishing entails. And this was followed by one abolishing the privilege of primogeniture, and dividing the lands of intestates equally among all the children, or other representatives. These laws, drawn by myself laid the axe to the root of pseudo-aristocracy. And had another which I had prepared been adopted by the Legislature, our work would have been complete. It was a bill for the more general diffusion of learning.—To JOHN ADAMS. vi, 225. FORD ED., ix, 427. (M., 1813.)

479. ——— ———. I considered four of these bills [of the Revised Code of Virginia] * * * as forming a system by which every fibre would be eradicated of ancient or future aristocracy; and a foundation laid for a government truly republican. The repeal of the laws of entail would prevent the accumulation and perpetuation of wealth, in select families, and preserve the soil of the country from being daily more and more absorbed in mortmain. The abolition of primogeniture, and equal partition of inheritances removed the feudal and unnatural distinctions which made one member of every family rich, and all the rest poor, substituting equal partition, the best of all Agrarian laws. The restoration of the rights of conscience relieved the people from taxation for the support of a religion not theirs; for the Establishment was truly of the religion of the rich, the dissenting sects being entirely composed of the less wealthy people; and these, by the bill for a general education, would be qualified to understand their rights, to maintain them, and to exercise with intelligence their parts in self-government; and all this would be effected without the violation of a single natural right of any one individual citizen.—AUTOBIOGRAPHY. i, 49. FORD ED., i, 68. (1821.)

480. ARISTOCRACY IN VIRGINIA.—To state the difference between the classes of society and the lines of demarcation which separated them [in Virginia] would be difficult. The law admitted none except as to our twelve counsellors. Yet in a country insulated from the European world, insulated from its sister colonies, with whom there was scarcely any intercourse, little visited by foreigners, and having little matter to act upon within itself, certain families had risen to splendor by wealth and the preservation of it from generation to generation under the law of entails; some had produced a series of men of talents; families in general had remained stationary on the grounds of their forefathers, for there was no emigration to the westward in those days; the wild Irish, who had gotten possession of the valley between the Blue Ridge and North Mountain, forming a barrier over which none ventured to leap, and would still less venture to settle among. In such a state of things, scarcely admitting any change of station, society would settle itself down into several strata, separated by no marked lines, but shading off imperceptibly from top to bottom, nothing disturbing the order of their repose. There were there aristocrats, half-breeds, pretenders, a solid yeomanry, looking askance at those above yet venturing to jostle them, and last and lowest, a *feculum* of beings called overseers, the most abject, degraded and unprincipled race, always cap in hand to the Dons who employed them, and furnishing materials for the exercise of their pride, insolence and spirit of domination.—To WILLIAM WIRT. vi, 484. FORD ED., ix, 473. (M., 1815.)

481. —— ——. You surprise me with the account you give of the strength of family distinction still existing in Massachusetts. With us it is so totally extinguished, that not a spark of it is to be found but working in the hearts of some of our old tories; but all bigotries hang to one another, and this in the Eastern States hangs, as I suspect, to that of the priesthood. Here youth, beauty, mind and manners, are more valued than a pedigree.— To JOHN ADAMS. vi, 305. (M., 1814.)

482. ARISTOCRACY, Virtuous.—Nature has wisely provided an aristocracy of virtue and talent for the direction of the interests of society, and scattered it with equal hand through all its conditions.—AUTOBIOGRAPHY. i, 36. FORD ED., i, 49. (1821.)

483. ARISTOCRACY OF WEALTH.—An aristocracy of wealth [is] of more harm and danger than benefit to society.—AUTOBIOGRAPHY. i, 36. FORD ED., i, 49. (1821.)

484. ARISTOCRATS, Impotent.—We, too, have our aristocrats and monocrats, and as they float on the surface, they show much though they weigh little.—To J. P. BRISSOT DE WARVILLE. FORD ED., vi, 249. (Pa., 1793.)

485. ARISTOCRATS, The People and.—Aristocrats fear the people, and wish to transfer all power to the higher classes of society. —To WILLIAM SHORT. vii, 391. FORD ED., x, 335. (M., 1825.)

486. ARISTOTLE, Writings of.—So different was the style of society then, and with those people, from what it is now and with us, that I think little edification can be obtained from their writings on the subject of government. They had just ideas of the value of personal liberty, but none at all of the structure of government best calculated to preserve it. They knew no medium between a democracy (the only pure republic, but impracticable beyond the limits of a town) and an abandonment of themselves to an aristocracy, or a tyranny independent of the people. It seems not to have occurred that where the citizens can not meet to transact their business in person, they alone have the right to choose the agents who shall transact it; and that in this way a republican, or popular government, of the second grade of purity, may be exer-

cised over any extent of country. The full experiment of a government, democratical, but representative, was and is still reserved for us. * * * The introduction of this new principle of representative democracy has rendered useless almost everything written before on the structure of government; and, in a great measure, relieves our regret, if the political writings of Aristotle, or of any other ancient, have been lost, or are unfaithfully rendered or explained to us.—To ISAAC H. TIFFANY. vii, 32. (M., 1816.)

— ARITHMETIC.—See MATHEMATICS.

487. ARMS, Loan of.—I am in hopes that your State [New York] will provide by the loan of arms for your immediate safety.—To JACOB J. BROWN. v, 240. (W. 1808.)

488. —— ——. I enclose you * * * an application from * * * citizens of New York, residing on the St. Lawrence and Lake Ontario, setting forth their defenceless situation for the want of arms, and praying to be furnished from the magazines of the United States. Similar applications from other parts of our frontier in every direction have sufficiently shown that did the laws permit such a disposition of the arms of the United States, their magazines would be completely exhausted, and nothing would remain for actual war. But it is only when troops take the field, that the arms of the United States can be delivered to them. For the ordinary safety of the citizens of the several States, whether against dangers within or without, their reliance must be on the means to be provided by their respective States. Under the circumstances I have thought it my duty to transmit to you the representation received, not doubting that you will have done for the safety of our fellow citizens, on a part of our frontier so interesting and so much exposed, what their situation requires, and the means under your control may permit. —To GOVERNOR TOMPKINS. v, 238. (W., 1808.)

489. ARMS, Right to bear.—No freeman shall be debarred the use of arms [within his own lands].*—PROPOSED VA. CONSTITUTION. FORD ED., ii, 27. (June, 1776.)

—ARMS OF CABOT FAMILY.—See BIRDS.

490. ARMS, Device for the American States.—A proper device (instead of arms) for the American states united would be the Father presenting the bundle of rods to his sons. The motto "*Insuperabiles si Inseparabiles*", an answer given in part to the H. of Lds & Comm. 4. Inst. 35. He cites 4. H. 6. ru. 12. parl. rolls, which I suppose was the time it happd. †—FORD ED., i, 420.

* Brackets by Jefferson.—EDITOR.
† This is a note written in Jefferson's copy of the *Virginia Almanack* for—1774. All his other entries in this volume are contemporary with the date of the almanac, and if, as all the internal evidence indicates, this was also written at that time, it is not merely interesting as a proposed emblem, but even more so as the earliest reference to the "American States." In a letter of John Adams (*Familiar Letters*, 211), Aug. 4, 1776, on the subject of the national arms, is the following: "Mr. Jefferson proposed the children of Israel in the wilderness, led by a cloud by day and a pillar of fire by night; and on the other side, Hengist and Horsa, the Saxon chiefs from whom we claim the honor of being descended, and whose political principles and forms of government we have assumed." —NOTE IN FORD'S ED.

491. ARMS, Device for Virginia State.
—I like the device of the first side of the seal
[for Virginia] much. The second I think, is
too much crowded, nor is the design so striking. But for God's sake what is the "*Deus
nobis hæc otia facit*"! It puzzles everybody
here. If my country really enjoys that otium
it is singular, as every other Colony seems
to be hard struggling. I think it was agreed
on before Dunmore's flight from Gwyn's
Island, so that it can hardly be referred to the
temporary *holiday* that was given you. This
device is too enigmatical. Since it puzzles
now, it will be absolutely insoluble fifty years
hence.—To JOHN PAGE. FORD ED., ii, 70. (Pa.,
1776.)

492. ARMS OF JEFFERSON FAMILY.
—Search the Herald's office for the arms of
my family. I have what I have been told were
the family arms, but on what authority I know
not. It is possible there may be none. If so,
I would with your assistance become a purchaser, having Sterne's word for it that a coat
of arms may be purchased as cheap as any other
coat.—To THOMAS ADAMS. FORD ED., i, 388.
(M., 1771.)

**493. ARMSTRONG (John), Hostility
against.**—An unjust hostility against General Armstrong will, I am afraid, show itself
whenever any treaty [with Spain] made by
him shall be offered for ratification.—To
WILSON C. NICHOLAS. v, 4. FORD ED., viii,
435. (W., April 1806.)

**494. ARMSTRONG (John), Secretary
of War.**—I have long ago in my heart congratulated my country on your call to the
place you now occupy. * * * Whatever you
do in office, I know will be honestly and ably
done, and although we who do not see the
whole ground may sometimes impute error,
it will be because we, not you, are in the
wrong ; or because your views are defeated by
the wickedness or incompetence of those you
are obliged to trust with their execution.—To
GENERAL JOHN ARMSTRONG. vi, 103. (M., Feb.
1813.)

495. ———— ————. Armstrong is presumptuous, obstinate and injudicious.—To J. W.
EPPES. FORD ED., ix, 484. (M., 1814.)

496. ARMY, Adverse to large.—The
spirit of this country is totally adverse to a
large military force.—To CHANDLER PRICE.
v, 47. (W., 1807.)

497. ARMY, Control over.—I like the
declaration of rights as far as it goes, but I
should have been for going further. For instance, the following alterations and additions
would have pleased me: * * * Article 10.
All troops of the United States shall stand
ipso facto disbanded, at the expiration of the
term for which their pay and subsistence shall
have been last voted by Congress, and all officers and soldiers, not natives of the United
States, shall be incapable of serving in their
armies by land except during a foreign war.—
To JAMES MADISON. iii, 101. FORD ED., v,
113. (P., Aug. 1789.)

498. ARMY, Deserters.—Deserters [Brit-
ish] ought never to be enlisted [by us].—To
JAMES MADISON. FORD ED., ix, 128. (M., 1807.)

499. ARMY, Deserters from Enemy's.
—American citizens, * * * whether impressed or enlisted into the British service,
* * * [are] equally right in returning to
the duties they owe their own country.—To
JAMES MADISON. v, 173. FORD ED., ix, 128.
(M., Aug. 1807.)

500. ———— ————. Resolved, that [Con-
gress] will give all such of the * * * foreign
[Hessian] officers as shall leave the armies of
his Britannic Majesty in America, and choose
to become citizens of these States, unappropriated lands in the following quantities and
proportions to them and their heirs in absolute dominion.*—CONGRESS RESOLUTION. FORD
ED., ii, 89. (August 1776.)

501. ARMY, Discipline of.—The British
consider our army * * * a rude, undisci-
plined rabble. I hope they will find it a
Bunker's Hill rabble.—To FRANCIS EPPES.
FORD ED., ii, 77. (Pa., Aug. 1776.)

502. ARMY, Enlistments in.—Tardy
enlistments proceed from the happiness of our
people at home.—To JAMES MONROE. vi, 130.
(M., June 1813.)

503. ———— ————. Our men are so happy at
home that they will not hire themselves to
be shot at for a shilling a day. Hence we can
have no standing armies for defence, because
we have no paupers to furnish the materials.
—To THOMAS COOPER. vi, 379. (M., 1814.)

504. ARMY, Fear of.—How happy that
our army had been disbanded [before the
Presidential crisis of 1801]! What might
have happened otherwise seems rather a subject of reflection than explanation.—To
NATHANIEL NILES. iv, 377. FORD ED., viii,
24. (W., March 1801.)

505. ARMY, Increase of.—An act has
passed for raising upon the regular establishment for the war 3000 additional troops and a
corps of 300 more, making in the whole about
5000 men. To this I was opposed from a conviction they were useless and that 1200 or
1500 woodsmen would soon end the [Indian]
war, and at a trifling expense.—To ARCHI-
BALD STUART. FORD ED., v, 454. (Pa., March
1792.)

506. ———— ————. It is agreed [in cabinet]
that about 15000 regular troops will be requisite for garrisons, and about as many more
as a disposable force, making in the whole
30,000 regulars.—ANAS. FORD ED., i, 329.
(July 1807.)

507. ———— ————. We are raising some
regulars in addition to our present force, for
garrisoning our seaports, and forming a nu-
cleus for the militia to gather to.—To GEN-
ERAL KOSCIUSKO. v, 282. (W., May 1808.)

508. ARMY, Inefficiency in.—I thank
you for the military manuals. * * * This is
the sort of book most needed in our country,
where even the elements of tactics are unknown. The young have never seen service,
the old are past it, and of those among them
who are not superannuated themselves, their

* Jefferson, Franklin and Adams reported this resolution which was adopted.—EDITOR.

science is become so.—To WILLIAM DUANE. vi, 75. FORD ED., ix, 365. (M., 1812.)

509. ARMY, A mercenary.—He [George III.] has endeavored to pervert the exercise of the kingly office in Virginia into a detestable and insupportable tyranny * * * by transporting at this time a large army of foreign mercenaries [to complete] the works of death, desolation, and tyranny, already begun with circumstances of cruelty and perfidy so unworthy the head of a civilized nation.—PROPOSED VA. CONSTITUTION. FORD ED., ii, 11. (June 1776.)

510. —— ——. He is at this time, transporting large armies of foreign mercenaries to complete the works of death, desolation, and tyranny, already begun, with circumstances of cruelty and perfidy* unworthy the head of a civilized nation.—DECLARATION OF INDEPENDENCE AS DRAWN BY JEFFERSON.

511. —— ——. At this very time, too, they [British people] are permitting their chief magistrate to send over not only soldiers of our common blood, but Scotch and foreign mercenaries to invade and destroy us. —DECLARATION OF INDEPENDENCE AS DRAWN BY JEFFERSON.

512. ARMY, Morality in.—It is more a subject of joy [than of regret] that we have so few of the desperate characters which compose modern regular armies. But it proves more forcibly the necessity of obliging every citizen to be a soldier; this was the case with the Greeks and Romans, and must be that of every free State. Where there is no oppression there can be no pauper hirelings.—To JAMES MONROE. vi, 130. (M., June 1813.)

513. ARMY, An obedient.—Some think the [French] army could not be depended on by the government; but the breaking men to military discipline, is breaking their spirits to principles of passive obedience.—To JOHN JAY. ii, 392. (P., 1788.)

514. ARMY, Obligations to the.—We feel with you our obligations to the army in general, and will particularly charge ourselves with the interests of those confidential officers, who have attended your person to this affecting moment.—CONGRESS TO WASHINGTON SURRENDERING HIS COMMISSION. (Dec. 1783.)

515. ARMY, Overpowering.—There is neither head nor body in the [French] nation to promise a successful opposition to two hundred thousand regular troops.—To JOHN JAY. ii, 392. (P., 1788.)

516. ARMY, The People as an.—I am satisfied the good sense of the people is the strongest army our government can ever have, and that it will not fail them.—To WILLIAM CARMICHAEL. ii, 81. FORD ED., iv, 346. (P., 1786.)

* Congress inserted after "perfidy" the words " scarcely paralleled in the most barbarous ages and totally."—EDITOR.
† Congress struck out this passage.—EDITOR.

517. —— ——. I am persuaded myself that the good sense of the people will always be found to be the best Army.—To EDWARD CARRINGTON. ii, 99. FORD ED., iv, 359. (P., 1787.)

518. ARMY, Reduction of.—A statement has been formed by the Secretary of War * * * of all the posts and stations where garrisons will be expedient, and of the number of men requisite for each garrison. The whole amount is considerably short of the present military establishment. For the surplus no particular use can be pointed out. For defence against invasion, their number is as nothing; nor is it conceived needful or safe that a standing army should be kept up in time of peace for that purpose.—FIRST ANNUAL MESSAGE. viii, 11. FORD ED., viii, 121. (Dec. 1801.)

519. —— ——. The army is undergoing a chaste reformation.—To NATHANIEL MACON. iv, 397. (W., May 1801.)

520. —— ——. The session of the first Congress convened since republicanism has recovered its ascendency * * * will probably completely fulfil all the desires of the people. They have reduced the army * * * to what is barely necessary.—To GENERAL KOSCIUSKO. iv, 430. (W., April 1802.)

521. —— ——. We are now actually engaged in reducing our military establishment one-third, and discharging one-third of our officers. We keep in service no more than men enough to garrison the small posts dispersed at great distances on our frontiers, which garrisons will generally consist of a captain's company only, and in no cases of more than two or three, in not one, of a sufficient number to require a field officer.*—To GENERAL KOSCIUSKO. iv, 430. (W., April 1802.)

522. ARMY, Regulation of.—The wise proposition of the Secretary of War for filling our ranks with regulars, and putting our militia into an effective form, seems to be laid aside.—To M. CORREA. vi, 406. (M., Dec. 1814.)

523. —— ——. To supply the want of men, nothing more wise or efficient could have been imagined than what you proposed. It would have filled our ranks with regulars, and that, too, by throwing a just share of the burthen on the purses of those whose persons are exempt either by age or office; and it would have rendered our militia, like those of the Greeks and Romans, a nation of warriors.—To JAMES MONROE. vi, 408. FORD ED., ix, 497. (M., Jan. 1815.)

524. —— ——. Nothing wiser can be devised than what the Secretary of War (Monroe) proposed in his report at the commencement of Congress. It would have kept our regular army always of necessity full, and by classing our militia according to ages, would have put them into a form ready for

* Kosciusko had written to Jefferson, recommending Polish officers for employment.—EDITOR.

whatever service, distant or at home, should require them.—To W. H. CRAWFORD. vi, 418. FORD ED., ix, 502. (M., Feb. 1815.)

525. ARMY, Seniority in.—We received from Colonel R. H. Lee a resolution of Convention, recommending us to endeavor that the promotions of the officers be according to seniority without regard to regiments or companies. In one instance, indeed, the Congress reserved to themselves a right of departing from seniority; that is where a person either out of the line of command, or in an inferior part of it, has displayed eminent talents. Most of the general officers have been promoted in this way. Without this reservation, the whole continent must have been supplied with general officers from the Eastern Colonies, where a large army was formed and officered before any other colony had occasion to raise troops at all, and a number of experienced, able and valuable officers must have been lost to the public merely from the locality of their situation.—To GOVERNOR PATRICK HENRY. FORD ED., ii, 67. (Pa., 1776.)

526. —— ——. We [Congress] wait your recommendation for the two vacant majorities. Pray regard militaryment alone.—To JOHN PAGE. FORD ED., ii, 88. (Pa., 1776.)

527. —— ——. Several vacancies having happened in our battalions, we [Congress] are unable to have them filled for want of a list of the officers, stating their seniority. We must beg the favor of you to furnish us with one.—To GOVERNOR HENRY. FORD ED., ii, 67. (Pa., 1776.)

528. —— ——. The unfortunate obstinacy of the Senate in preferring the greatest blockhead to the greatest military genius, if one day longer in commission, renders it doubly important to sift well the candidates for command in new corps, and to marshal them at first, towards the head, in proportion to their qualifications.—To GENERAL ARMSTRONG. FORD ED., ix, 380. (M., Feb. 1813.)

529. —— ——. There is not, I believe, a service on earth where seniority is permitted to give a right to advance beyond the grade of captain.—To GENERAL ARMSTRONG. FORD ED., ix, 380. (M., Feb. 1813.)

530. —— ——. We are doomed. * * * to sacrifice the lives of our citizens by thousands to this blind principle, for fear the peculiar interest and responsibility of our Executive should not be sufficient to guard his selection of officers against favoritism.—To GENERAL ARMSTRONG. FORD ED., ix, 380. (M., 1813.)

531. —— ——. When you have new corps to raise you are free to prefer merit: and our mechanical law of promotion, when once men have been set in their places, makes it most interesting indeed to place them originally according to their capacities. It is not for me even to ask whether in the raw regiments now to be raised, it would not be advisable to draw from the former the few officers who may already have discovered military talent, and to bring them forward

in the new corps to those higher grades, t which, in the old, the blocks in their way d not permit you to advance them?—To GENERAL ARMSTRONG. FORD ED., ix, 380. (M Feb. 1813.) See GENERALS.

532. ARMY, A standing.—Standing armies [are] inconsistent with the freedom [c the Colonies], and subversive of their quiet.—REPLY TO LORD NORTH'S PROPOSITION. FORD ED., i, 477. (July 1775.)

533. —— ——. There shall be no standing army but in time of actual war.—PROPOSED VA. CONSTITUTION. FORD ED., ii, 27 (June 1776.)

534. —— ——. He [George III.] has endeavored to pervert the exercise of the kingly office in Virginia into a detestable and insupportable tyranny * * * by [keeping among us], in time of peace, standing armies and ships of war.—PROPOSED VA. CONSTITUTION. FORD ED., ii, 10. (June 1776.)

535. —— ——. He has kept among us, in times of peace, standing armies and ships o war * without the consent of our legislatures—DECLARATION OF INDEPENDENCE AS DRAWN BY JEFFERSON.

536. —— ——. I do not like [in the new Federal Constitution] the omission of a bill o rights, providing clearly and without the aid of sophisms for * * * protection against standing armies.—To JAMES MADISON. ii, 329. FORD ED., iv, 476. (P., Dec 1787.)

537. —— ——. I sincerely rejoice at the acceptance of our new Constitution by nin States. It is a good canvas, on which some strokes only want retouching. What these are, I think are sufficiently manifested by the general voice from north to south, which calls for a bill of rights. It seems pretty generally understood that this should go to * * * standing armies. * * * If no check can be found to keep the number o standing troops within safe bounds, while they are tolerated as far as necessary, abandon them altogether, discipline well the militia, and guard the magazines with them More than magazine guards will be useless if few, and dangerous if many. No European nation can ever send against us such a regular army as we need fear, and it is hard if our militia are not equal to those of Canada or Florida.—To JAMES MADISON. ii, 445 FORD ED., v, 45. (P., July 1788.)

538. —— ——. By declaration of rights, I mean one which shall stipulate * * * no standing armies.—To A. DONALD. ii, 355. (P. 1788.)

539. —— ——. There are instruments so dangerous to the rights of the nation, and which place them so totally at the mercy of their governors, whether legislative or executive, should be restrained from keeping such instruments on foot, but in well-defined cases. Such an in-

*Congress struck out "and ships of war."—EDITOR.

strument is a standing army.—To DAVID HUMPHREYS. iii, 13. FORD ED., v, 90. (P., 1789.)

540. ——. I hope a militia bill will be passed. Anything is preferable to nothing, as it takes away one of the arguments for a standing army.—To ARCHIBALD STUART. FORD ED., v, 454. (Pa., 1792.)

541. ——. I am not for a standing army in time of peace, which may overawe the public sentiment.—To ELBRIDGE GERRY. iv, 268. FORD ED., vii, 328. (Pa., 1799.)

542. ——. Bonaparte has transferred the destinies of the republic from the civil to the military arm. Some will use this as a lesson against the practicability of republican government. I read it as a lesson against the danger of standing armies.—To SAMUEL ADAMS. iv, 322. FORD ED., vii, 425. (Pa., Feb. 1800.)

543. ——. It is not conceived needful or safe that a standing army should be kept up in time of peace for defence against invasion.—FIRST ANNUAL MESSAGE. viii, 11. FORD ED., 121. (1801.)

544. ——. I hope Kentucky will * * * finish the matter [Burr's enterprise] for the honor of popular government, and the discouragement of all arguments for standing armies.—To REV. CHARLES CLAY. v, 28. FORD ED., ix, 7. (W., 1807.)

545. ——. We propose to raise seven regiments only for the present year, depending always on our militia for the operations of the first year of war. On any other plan, we should be obliged always to keep a large standing army.—To CHARLES PINCKNEY. v, 266. (W., March 1808.)

546. ——. The Greeks and Romans had no standing armies, yet they defended themselves. The Greeks by their laws, and the Romans by the spirit of their people, took care to put into the hands of their rulers no such engine of oppression as a standing army. Their system was to make every man a soldier, and oblige him to repair to the standard of his country whenever that was reared. This made them invincible; and the same remedy will make us so.—To THOMAS COOPER. vi, 379. (M., 1814.)

547. ARMY, Threatened by an.—We cannot, my lord, close with the terms of that Resolution, [Lord North's conciliatory propositions] * * * because at the very time of requiring from us grants, they are making disposition to invade us with large armaments by sea and land, which is a style of asking gifts not reconcilable to our freedom.—ADDRESS TO LORD DUNMORE. FORD ED., i, 457. (1775.)

548. ARMY, An unnecessary.—One of my favorite ideas is, never to keep an unnecessary soldier.—THE ANAS. ix, 431. FORD ED., i, 198. (1792.)

549. ——. Were armies to be raised whenever a speck of war is visible in our horizon, we never should have been without them. Our resources would have been exhausted on dangers which have never happened, instead of being reserved for what is really to take place.—SIXTH ANNUAL MESSAGE. viii, 69. FORD ED., viii, 495. (Dec. 1806.)

550. ARMY, An unauthorized.—When, in the course of the late war, it became expedient that a body of Hanoverian troops should be brought over for the defence of Great Britain, his Majesty's grandfather, our late sovereign, did not pretend to introduce them under any authority he possessed. Such a measure would have given just alarm to his subjects in Great Britain, whose liberties would not be safe if armed men of another country, and of another spirit, might be brought into the realm at any time without the consent of their legislature. He, therefore, applied to Parliament, who passed an act for that purpose, limiting the number to be brought in, and the time they were to continue. In like manner is his Majesty restrained in every part of the empire.—RIGHTS OF BRITISH AMERICA. i, 140. FORD ED., i, 445. (1774.)

551. ——. He has combined with others to subject us to a jurisdiction foreign to our constitutions, and unacknowledged by our laws; giving his assent to their acts of pretended legislation for quartering large bodies of armed troops among us; for protecting them by a mock trial from punishment for any murders which they should commit on the inhabitants of these States.—DECLARATION OF INDEPENDENCE AS DRAWN BY JEFFERSON.

552. ——. He [George III.] has endeavored to pervert the exercise of the kingly office in Virginia into a detestable and insupportable tyranny * * * by combining with others to subject us to a foreign jurisdiction, giving his assent to their pretended acts of legislation for quartering large bodies of armed troops among us.—PROPOSED VA. CONSTITUTION. FORD ED., ii, 10. (June 1776.)

553. ——. In order to enforce [his] arbitrary measures * * * his Majesty has, from time to time, sent among us large bodies of armed forces, not made up of the people here, nor raised by authority of our laws. Did his Majesty possess such a right as this, it might swallow up all our other rights whenever he should think proper. But his Majesty has no right to land a single armed man on our shores, and those whom he sends here are liable to our laws made for the suppression and punishment of riots, and unlawful assemblies; or are hostile bodies, invading us in defiance of the law.—RIGHTS OF BRITISH AMERICA. i, 140. FORD ED., i, 445. (1774.)

554. ——. The proposition [of Lord North] is altogether unsatisfactory * * * because it does not propose to repeal the acts of Parliament * * * for quartering sol-

diers on us in times of profound peace.—RE-
PLY TO LORD NORTH S PROPOSITION. FORD ED.,
i, 480. (July 1775.)

555. ARMY, A volunteer.—[With respect to] the proposition for substituting
32.000 twelve-month volunteers instead of
15,000 regulars as a disposable force, I like
the idea much. It will, of course, be a subject
of consideration when we all meet again, but
I repeat that I like it greatly.—To GENERAL
DEARBORN. v, 155. FORD ED., ix, 123. (M.,
Aug. 1807.)

556. —— ——. General Dearborn has
sent me a plan of a war establishment
for 15,000 regulars for garrisons, and instead of 15,000 others, as a disposable
force, to substitute 32,000 twelve-month
volunteers, to be exercised and paid three
months in the year, and consequently costing no more than 8,000 permanent, giving
us the benefit of 32.000 for any expedition,
who would be themselves nearly equal to
regulars, but could on occasion be put into
the garrisons, and the regulars employed in
the expedition *primâ facie*. I like it well.—
To JAMES MADISON. v. 154. FORD ED., ix,
123. (M., Aug. 1807.) See WAR.

**557. ARMY, (French), Dangerous
standing.**—The French flatter themselves
they shall form a better Constitution than the
English one. I think it will be better in some
points—worse in others. * * * It will
be worse, as their situation obliges them to
keep up the dangerous machine of a standing
army.—To DR. PRICE. ii, 557. (P., Jan.
1789.)

558. ARMY (French), Decision by the.
—If the appeal to arms is made [in France]
it will depend entirely on the disposition of
the army whether it issue in liberty or despotism.—To E. RUTLEDGE. ii, 435. FORD ED.,
v, 42. (P., 1788.)

**559. ARMY OFFICERS, Accountabil-
ity of.**—Whereas it is apprehended that
sufficient care and attention hath not been
always had by officers to the cleanliness, to
the health and to the comfort of the soldiers
entrusted to their command. Be it therefore
enacted, that so long as any troops from this
Commonwealth [Virginia] shall be in any service to the northward thereof, it shall and may
be lawful for our delegates in Congress, and
they are hereby required from time to time
to enquire into the state and condition of the
troops, and the conduct of the officers commanding; and where any troops, raised in this
Commonwealth, are upon duty within the same,
or anywhere to the southward, there the
Governor and Council are required to make
similar enquiry by such ways or means as shall
be in their power: and whensoever it shall be
found that any officer, appointed by this Commonwealth, shall have been guilty of negligence, or want of fatherly care, of the soldiers under his command, they are hereby respectively required to report to this Assembly
the whole truth of the case, who hereby reserve to themselves a power of removing such
officer; and whenever they shall find that such
troops shall have suffered through the negligence or inattention of any officer of Conti-

nental appointment, they are, in like manner,
to make report thereof to this Assembly, whose
duty it will be to represent the same to Congress: and they are further respectively required, from time to time, to procure and lay
before this Assembly exact returns of the
numbers and conditions of such of their troops.
—ARMY BILL. FORD ED., ii, 115. (1776.)

560. ARMY OFFICERS, Foreign.—I
believe I mentioned to you, on a former occasion, that the last act of Congress for raising
additional troops required that the officers,
should all be citizens of the United States.
Should there be war, however, I am persuaded
this policy must be abandoned, and that we
must avail ourselves of the experience of other
nations, in certain lines of service at least.—
To AMELOT DE LA CROIX. v, 422. (W., Feb.
1809.)

**561. ARMY OFFICERS, Prosecutions
of.**—Many officers of the army being involved in the offence of intending a military
enterprise [Burr's] against a nation at peace
with the United States, to remove the whole
without trial, by the paramount authority of the
executive, would be a proceeding of unusual
gravity. Some line must, therefore, be drawn
to separate the more from the less guilty. The
only sound one which occurs to me is between
those who believed the enterprise was with the
approbation of the government, open or secret,
and those who meant to proceed in defiance of
the government. Concealment would be no line
at all, because all concealed it. Applying the
line of *defiance* to the case of Lieutenant Mead,
it does not appear by any testimony I have seen,
that he meant to proceed in defiance of the government, but, on the contrary, that he was made
to believe the government approved of the expedition. If it be objected that he concealed a
part of what had taken place in his communications to the Secretary of War, yet if a concealment of the whole would not furnish a proper
line of distinction, still less would the concealment of a part. This too would be a removal
for *prevarication*, not for *unauthorized* enterprise, and could not be a proper ground for exercising the extraordinary power of removal
by the President.—To GENERAL DEARBORN. v,
60. FORD ED., ix, 38. (W., March 1807.)

**562. ARMY OFFICERS, Undesirable
French.**—I would not advise that the French
gentlemen should come here. [Philadelphia.]
We have so many of that country, and have
been so much imposed on that the Congress
begins to be sore on that head. * * * If
you approve of the Chevalier de St. Aubin, why
not appoint him yourselves, as your troops of
horse are colonial, not continental?--To JOHN
PAGE. FORD ED., ii, 70. (Pa., 1776.)

**563. ARNOLD (Benedict), Expedition
to Quebec.**—The march of Arnold [to Que-
bec] is equal to Xenophon's retreat.—To JOHN
PAGE. FORD ED., i, 496. (1775.)

564. —— ——. I never understood that
Arnold formed this enterprise, nor do I believe
he did. I heard and saw all General Washington's letters on this subject. I do not think
he mentioned Arnold as author of the proposition; yet he was always just in ascribing to
every officer the merit of his own works; and
he was disposed particularly in favor of
Arnold. This officer is entitled to great merit
in the execution, but to ascribe to him that of
having formed the enterprise, is probably to
ascribe to him what belongs to General Wash-

ington or some other person.—Answers to M. Soules. ix, 301. Ford ed., iv, 300. (P., 1786.)

565. ———— ————. General Arnold, (a fine sailor) has undertaken to command our fleet on the Lakes.—To Francis Eppes. Ford ed., ii, 77. (Pa., 1776.)

566. ARNOLD (Benedict), Reward for capture of.—It is above all things desirable to drag Arnold from those under whose wing he is now sheltered. On his march to and from this place [Richmond], I am certain it might have been done with facility by men of enterprise and firmness. I think it may still be done. * * * Having peculiar confidence in the men from the western side of the mountains, I meant, as soon as they should come down, to get the enterprise proposed to a chosen number of them; such whose courage and whose fidelity would be above all doubt. Your perfect knowledge of those men personally, and my confidence in your discretion, induce me to ask you to pick from among them proper characters, in such number as you think best, to reveal to them our desire, and engage them to undertake to seize and bring off this greatest of all traitors. Whether this may be best effected by their going in (within the British lines) as friends and awaiting their opportunity, or otherwise, is left to themselves. The smaller the number the better, so that they be sufficient to manage him. Every necessary caution must be used on their part, to prevent a discovery of their design by the enemy; as, should they be taken, the laws of war will justify against them the most rigorous sentence. I will undertake, if they are successful in bringing him off alive, that they shall receive five thousand guineas reward among them. And to men, formed for such an enterprise, it must be a great incitement to know that their names will be recorded with glory in history, with those of Van Wart, Paulding and Williams.*—To ————. i, 289. Ford ed., ii, 441. (R., 1781.)

567. ARNOLD (Benedict), Treason of.—The parricide Arnold.—To General Washington. i, 284. Ford ed., ii, 408. (R., 1781.)

568. ART, Selecting works of.—With respect to the figures. I could only find three of those you named, matched in size. Those were Minerva, Diana and Apollo. I was obliged to add a fourth, unguided by your choice. They offered me a fine Venus; but I thought it out of taste to have two at table at the same time. Paris and Helen were represented. I conceived it would be cruel to remove them from their peculiar shrine. When they shall pass the Atlantic, it will be to sing a requiem over our freedom and happiness. At length a fine Mars was offered, calm, bold, his falchion not drawn but ready to be drawn. This will do, thinks I, for the table of the American Minister in London, where those whom it may concern may look and learn that though Wisdom is our guide, and the Song and Chase our supreme delight, yet we offer adoration to that tutelar God also who rocked the cradle of our birth, who has accepted our infant offerings, and has shown himself the patron of our rights and avenger of our wrongs. The group then was closed and your party formed. Envy and malice will never be quiet. I hear it already whis-

* This letter is without an address, but, it is thought was written to General George Rogers Clark or to General Muhlenberg. Jefferson was Governor of Virginia.—Editor.

pered to you that in admitting Minerva to your table, I have departed from the principle which made me reject Venus; in plain English that I have paid a just respect to the daughter but failed to the mother. No, Madam, my respect to both is sincere. Wisdom, I know, is social. She seeks her fellows, but Beauty is jealous, and illy bears the presence of a rival.—To Mrs. John Adams. Ford ed., iv, 99. (P., 1785.)

569. ARTISANS, Americans as.—While we have land to labor, let us never wish to see our citizens occupied at a work-bench, or twirling a distaff. Carpenters, masons, and smiths, are wanting in husbandry; but for the general operations of manufacture, let our workshops remain in Europe.—Notes on Virginia. viii, 405. Ford ed., iii, 269. (1782.)

570. ARTISANS, Condemnation of.—I consider the class of artificers as the panders of vice, and the instruments by which the liberties of a country are generally overturned.—To John Jay. i, 404. Ford ed., iv, 88. (P., 1785.)

571. ARTISANS, Explanation of views on.—Mr. Duane informed me that he meant to publish a new edition of the Notes on Virginia, and I had in contemplation some particular alterations which would require little time to make. My occupations by no means permit me at this time to revise the text, and make those changes in it which I should now do. I should in that case certainly qualify several expressions * * * which have been construed differently from what they were intended. I had under my eye, when writing, the manufacturers of the great cities in the old countries, at the time present, with whom the want of food and clothing necessary to sustain life, has begotten a depravity of morals, a dependence and corruption, which render them an undesirable accession to a country whose morals are sound. My expressions looked forward to the time when our great cities would get into the same state. But they have been quoted as if meant for the present time here. As yet our manufacturers are as much at their ease, as independent and moral as our agricultural inhabitants, and they will continue so as long as there are vacant lands for them to resort to; because whenever it shall be attempted by the other classes to reduce them to the minimum of subsistence, they will quit their trades and go to laboring the earth. A first question is, whether it is desirable for us to receive at present the dissolute and demoralized handicraftsmen of the old cities of Europe? A second and more difficult one is, when even good handicraftsmen arrive here, is it better for them to set up their trade, or go to the culture of the earth? Whether their labor in their trade is worth more than their labor on the soil, increased by the creative energies of the earth? Had I time to revise that chapter, this question should be discussed, and other views of the subject taken, which are presented by the wonderful changes which have taken place here since 1781, when the Notes on Virginia were written.—To Mr. Lithgow. iv, 563. Ford ed., iii, 269. (W., Jan. 1805.)

572. ARTISANS, French and English.—The English mechanics certainly exceed all others in some lines. But be just to your own nation. They have not patience, it is true, to sit rubbing a piece of steel from morning to night, as a lethargic Englishman will do, full charged with porter. But do not their benevolence, their cheerfulness, their amiability, when compared with the growling temper and manners of the people among whom you are, compensate their want of patience?—To MADAME DE CARNY. ii, 161. (P., 1787.)

573. ARTISANS, Science and.—The mechanic needs ethics, mathematics, chemistry and natural philosophy. To them the languages are but ornament and comfort.—To JOHN BRAZIER. vii, 133. (P. F., 1819.)

574. ARTISTS, Member of Society of. —I am very justly sensible of the honor the Society of Artists of the United States has done me in making me an honorary member of their Society. * * * I fear that I can be but a very useless associate. Time which withers the fancy, as the other faculties of the mind and body presses on me with a heavy hand, and distance intercepts all personal intercourse. I can offer, therefore, but my zealous good wishes for the success of the institution, and that, embellishing with taste a country already overflowing with the useful productions, it may be able to give an innocent and pleasing direction to accumulations of wealth, which would otherwise be employed in the nourishment of coarse and vicious habits.—To THOMAS SULLY. vi, 34. (M., Jan. 1812.)

575. ARTS, Enthusiasm for the.—I am an enthusiast on the subject of the arts. But it is an enthusiasm of which I am not ashamed, as its object is to improve the taste of my countrymen, to increase their reputation, to reconcile to them the respect of the world, and procure them its praise.—To JAMES MADISON. i, 433. (P., 1785.)

576. ARTS, French Excellence in.— Were I to proceed to tell you how much I enjoy the architecture, sculpture, painting, music [of the French], I should want words. It is in these arts they shine.—To MR. BELLINI. i, 445. (P., 1785.)

577. ARTS, Mechanical.—The mechanical arts in London are carried to a wonderful perfection. But of these I need not speak, because of them my countrymen have unfortunately* too many samples before their eyes.— To JOHN PAGE. i, 550. FORD ED., iv, 214. (P., 1786.)

578. ASSASSINATION, Government and.—Assassination, poison, perjury * * * were legitimate principles [of government] in the dark ages which intervened between ancient and modern civilization, but exploded and held in just horror in the eighteenth century.—To JAMES MADISON. iii, 99. FORD ED., v, 111. (P., 1789.)

— ASSEMBLIES.—See LEGISLATURES.

— ASSENISIPIA, Proposed State of.— See WESTERN TERRITORY.

579. ASSIGNATS, Payments in.—I have communicated to the President what passed between us * * * on the subject of the payments made to France by the United States in the *assignats* of that country, since they have lost their par with gold and silver; and after conferences, by his instruction, with the Secretary of the Treasury, I am authorized to assure you, that the

* The allusion is to the extravagance of the period. —EDITOR.

government of the United States have no idea of paying their debt in a depreciated medium, and that in the final liquidation of the payments * * * due regard will be had to an equitable allowance for the circumstance of depreciation.*—To JEAN BAPTISTE TERNANT. FORD ED., v, 383. (Pa., Nov. 1791.)

580. ASSUMPTION OF STATE DEBTS, Acrimony over.—The assumption of State debts has appeared as revolting to several States as their non-assumption to others. It is proposed to strip the proposition of the injustice it would have done by leaving the States who have redeemed much of their debts on no better footing than those who have redeemed none; on the contrary, it is recommended to assume a fixed sum, allotting a portion of it to every State in proportion to its census. Consequently, every State will receive exactly what they will have to pay, or they will be exonerated so far by the General Government's taking their creditors off their hands. There will be no injustice then. But there will be the objection still, that Congress must then lay taxes for those debts which would have been much better laid and collected by the State governments. And this is the objection on which the accommodation now hangs with the non-assumptioners, many of whom committed themselves in their advocation of the new Constitution by arguments drawn from the improbability that Congress would ever lay taxes where the States could do it separately. These gentlemen feel the reproaches which will be levelled at them personally. I have been, and still am of their opinion that Congress should always prefer letting the States raise money in their own way, where it can be done. But, in the present instance, I see the necessity of yielding for this time to the cries of the creditors in certain parts of the Union; for the sake of Union, and to save us from the greatest of all calamities, the total extinction of our credit in Europe.—To JAMES MONROE. iii, 153. FORD ED., v, 188. (N. Y., June 1790.)

581. ASSUMPTION OF STATE DEBTS, Compromise plans.—The question for assuming the State debts has created greater animosities than I ever yet saw take place on any occasion. There are three ways in which it may terminate. 1. A rejection of the measure, which will prevent their funding any part of the public debt, and will be something very like a dissolution of the government. 2. A bargain between the Eastern members, who have had it so much at heart, and the middle members, who are indifferent about it, to adopt those debts without any modification on condition of removing the seat of government to Philadelphia or Baltimore. 3. An adoption of them with this modification, that the whole sum to be assumed shall be divided among the States in proportion to their census; so that each shall receive as much as they are to pay; and perhaps this might bring about so much good humor as to induce them to give the temporary seat of government to Philadelphia, and then to Georgetown permanently. It is evident that this last is the least bad of all the turns the thing can take. The only objection to it will be

* Jefferson's first draft of this letter ended as follows: " And that they will take measures for making these payments in their just value, avoiding all benefit from depreciation, and desiring on their part to be guarded against any unjust loss from the circumstances of mere exchange." It was changed to meet Hamilton's views.—EDITOR.

that Congress will then have to lay and collect taxes to pay these debts, which could much better have been laid and collected by the State governments. This, though an evil, is a less one than any of the others in which it may issue, and will probably give us the seat of government at a day not very distant, which will vivify our agriculture and commerce by circulating through our State an additional sum every year of half a million of dollars.—To DR. GEORGE GILMER. iii, 150. FORD ED., v, 192. (N. Y., June 1790.)

582. ASSUMPTION OF STATE DEBTS, Credit, Union and.—Congress has been long embarrassed by two of the most irritating questions that can ever be raised among them: 1. The funding of the public debt; and 2. the fixing on a more central residence. After exhausting their arguments and patience on these subjects, they have for some time been resting on their oars, unable to get along as to these businesses, and indisposed to attend to anything else till they are settled. And, in fine, it has become probable that unless they can be reconciled by some plan of compromise, there will be no funding bill agreed to; our credit (raised by late prospects to be the first on the exchange at Amsterdam, where our money is above par), will burst and vanish, and the States separate, to take care every one of itself. This prospect appears probable to some well-informed and well-disposed minds. Endeavors are, therefore, using to bring about a disposition to some mutual sacrifices.—To JAMES MONROE. iii, 153. FORD ED., v, 187. (N. Y., June 1790.)

583. ASSUMPTION OF STATE DEBTS, Federal capital and.—It is proposed to pass an act fixing the temporary residence of twelve or fifteen years at Philadelphia, and that at the end of that time, it shall stand *ipso facto*, and without further declaration transferred to Georgetown. In this way, there will be something to displease and something to soothe every part of the Union but New York, which must be contented with what she has had. If this plan of compromise does not take place, I fear one infinitely worse, an unqualified assumption, and the perpetual residence on the Delaware. The Pennsylvania and Virginia delegates have conducted themselves honorably and unexceptionably on the question of residence. Without descending to talk about bargains, they have seen that their true interests lay in not listening to insidious propositions, made to divide and defect them, and we have seen them at times voting against their respective wishes rather than separate.—To JAMES MONROE. iii, 153. FORD ED., v, 189. (N. Y., June 1790.)

584. ASSUMPTION OF STATE DEBTS, Justice and.—The assumption must be admitted, but in so qualified a form as to divest it of its injustice. This may be done by assuring to the creditors of every State, a sum exactly proportioned to the contribution of the State; so that the State will on the whole neither gain nor lose. There will remain against the measure only the objection that Congress must lay taxes for these debts which might be better laid and collected by the States.—To T. M. RANDOLPH. FORD ED., v, 185. (N. Y., 1790.)

585. ———— ————. I am in hopes the assumption will be put into a just form, by assuming to the creditors of each State in proportion to the census of each State, so that the State will be exonerated towards its creditors just as much as it will have to contribute to the as-

sumption, and consequently no injustice done. —To FRANCIS EPPES. FORD ED., v, 194. (N. Y., July 1790.)

586. ASSUMPTION OF STATE DEBTS, Mutual sacrifices.—The impossibility that certain States could ever pay the debts they had contracted, the acknowledgment that nine-tenths of these debts were contracted for the general defence as much as those contracted by Congress directly, the clamors of the creditors within those States, and the possibility that they might defeat the funding of any part of the public debt, if theirs also were not assumed, were motives not to be neglected. I saw the first proposition for their assumption with as much aversion as any man, but the development of circumstances have convinced me that if it is obdurately rejected, something much worse will happen. Considering it, therefore, as one of the cases in which mutual sacrifice and accommodation are necessary, I shall see it pass with acquiescence.—To JOHN HARVIE. FORD ED., v, 214. (N. Y., July 1790.)

587. ASSUMPTION OF STATE DEBTS, Opposition engendered.—It is not to be expected that our system of finance has met your approbation in all its parts. It has excited even here great opposition; and more especially that part of it which transferred the State debts to the General Government. The States of Virginia and North Carolina are peculiarly dissatisfied with this measure. I believe, however, that it is harped on by many to mask their disaffection to the government on other grounds.—To GOUVERNEUR MORRIS. iii, 198. FORD ED., v, 250. (Pa., Nov. 1790.)

588. ASSUMPTION OF STATE DEBTS, Payment by States.—With respect to the increase of the debt by the Assumption, I observed to him [Washington] that what was meant and objected to was, that it increased the debt of the General Government, and carried it beyond the possibility of payment; that if the balances had been settled, and the debtor States directed to pay their deficiencies to the creditor States, they would have done it easily, and by resources of taxation in their power, and acceptable to the people; by a direct tax in the South, and an excise in the North.—THE ANAS. ix, 118. FORD ED., i, 200. (July 1792.)

589. ASSUMPTION OF STATE DEBTS, Review of.—The game [Funding the debt] was over, and another was on the carpet at the moment of my arrival* [in New York in 1790], and to this I was most ignorantly and innocently made to hold the candle. This fiscal maneuvre is well known by the name of the Assumption. Independently of the debts of Congress, the States had, during the war, contracted separate and heavy debts; and Massachusetts particularly in an absurd attempt, absurdly conducted, on the British post of Penobscott; and the more debt Hamilton could rake up the more plunder for his mercenaries. This money, whether wisely or foolishly spent, was pretended to have been spent for general purposes, and ought, therefore, to be paid from

* Jefferson has here made the curious errors of separating the funding and assumption act, and of supposing the latter "was over" before he reached New York. Hamilton's report was debated in the House of Representatives from February to April, and it was not till May 6th that the funding bill was presented, the section relating to assumption having been negatived in committee. This bill passed the House on June 2d, and in the Senate had the assumption section restored. Not till August 4th did the bill so altered become a law.—NOTE IN FORD'S ED.

the general purse. But it was objected that nobody knew what these debts were, what their amount, or what their proofs. No matter; we will guess them to be twenty millions. But of these twenty millions, we do not know how much should be reimbursed to one State, nor how much to another. No matter; we will guess. And so another scramble was set on foot among the several States, and some got much, some little, some nothing. But the main object was attained, the phalanx of the treasury was reinforced by additional recruits. This measure produced the most bitter and angry contests ever known in Congress, before or since the Union of the States. I arrived in the midst of it. But a stranger to the ground, a stranger to the actors on it, so long absent [in France] as to have lost all familiarity with the subject, and as yet unaware of its object, I took no concern in it.. The great and trying question, however, was lost in the House of Representatives. So high were the feuds excited by this subject, that on its rejection business was suspended. Congress met and adjourned from day to day without doing anything, the parties being too much out of temper to do business together. The Eastern members particularly, who, with Smith from South Carolina, were the principal gamblers in these scenes, threatened a secession and dissolution. Hamilton was in despair. As I was going to the President's one day, I met him in the street. He walked me backwards and forwards before the President's door for half an hour. He painted pathetically the temper into which the Legislature had been wrought; the disgust of those who were called the creditor States; the danger of the secession of their members, and the separation of the States. He observed that the members of the administration ought to act in concert; that though this question was not one of my department, yet a common duty should make it a common concern; that the President was the centre on which all administrative questions ultimately rested, and that all of us should rally around him, and support, with joint efforts, measures approved by him; and that the question having been lost by a small majority only, it was probable that an appeal from me to the judgment and discretion of some of my friends might effect a change in the vote, and the machine of government, now suspended, might be again set into motion. I told him that I was really a stranger to the whole subject; that not having yet informed myself of the system of finance adopted, I knew not how far this was a necessary sequence; that undoubtedly, if its rejection endangered a dissolution of our Union at this incipient stage, I should deem it the most unfortunate of all consequences, to avert which all partial and temporary evils should be yielded. I proposed to him, however, to dine with me the next day, and I would invite another friend or two, to bring them into conference together, and I thought it impossible that reasonable men, consulting together coolly, could fail, by some mutual sacrifices of opinion, to form a compromise which was to save the Union. The discussion took place. I could take no part in it, but an exhortatory one, because I was a stranger to the circumstances which should govern it. But it was finally agreed that, whatever importance had been attached to the rejection of this proposition, the preservation of the Union, and of concord among the States was more important, and that therefore, it would be better that the vote of rejection should be rescinded, to effect which some members should change their votes. But it was observed that this bill would be

peculiarly bitter to the Southern States, and that some concomitant measure should be adopted, to sweeten it a little to them. There had before been proposals to fix the seat of government either at Philadelphia, or at Georgetown on the Potomac ; and it was thought that by giving it to Philadelphia for ten years, and to Georgetown permanently afterwards, this might, as an anodyne, calm in some degree the ferment which might be excited by the other measure alone. So two of the Potomac members ([Alexander] White and [Richard Bland] Lee but White with a revulsion of stomach almost convulsive), agreed to change their votes, and Hamilton undertook to carry the other point. In doing this the influence he had established over the Eastern members, with the agency of Robert Morris with those of the middle States effected his side of the engagement, and so the Assumption was passed, and twenty millions of stock divided among the favored States, and thrown in as pabulum to the stock-jobbing herd. This added to the number of votaries to the Treasury, and made its Chief the master of every vote in the Legislature which might give to the government the directions suited to his political views.—THE ANAS. ix, 92. FORD ED., i, 161. (1818.)

590. ASSUMPTION OF STATE DEBTS, Jefferson's agency in.—The Assumption of the State debts in 1790, was a supplementary measure in Hamilton's fiscal system. When attempted in the House of Representatives it failed. This threw Hamilton himself, and a number of members into deep dismay. Going to the President's one day I met Hamilton, as I approached the door. His look was sombre, haggard, and dejected beyond description; even his dress uncouth and neglected. He asked to speak with me. He stood in the street near the door; he opened the subject of the Assumption of the State debts, the necessity of it in the general fiscal arrangement, and its indispensable necessity towards a preservation of the Union; and particularly of the New England States, who had made great expenditures during the war on expeditions which, though of their own undertaking, were for the common cause: that they considered the Assumption of these by the Union so just, and its denial so probably injurious that they would make it a *sine qua non* of a continuance of the Union. That as to his own part, if he had not credit enough to carry such a measure as that, he could be of no use and was determined to resign. He observed at the same time, that though our particular business lay in separate departments, yet the administration and its success was a common concern, and that we should make common cause in supporting one another. He added his wish that I would interest my friends from the South, who were those most opposed to it. I answered that I had been so long absent from my country [in France] that I had lost a familiarity with its affairs, and being but lately returned had not yet got into the train of them; that the fiscal system being out of my department I had not yet undertaken to consider and understand it; that the Assumption had struck me in an unfavorable light, but still, not having considered it sufficiently, I had not concerned [myself] in it, but that I would revolve what he had urged in my mind. It was a real fact that the Eastern and Southern members (South Carolina however was with the former) had got into the most extreme ill humor with one another. This broke out on every question with the most alarming heat; the bitterest animosity seemed to be engendered, and though they met every day, little or nothing could be done from mutual distrust and antipathy. On considering the situation of things, I thought the first step towards some conciliation of views would be to bring Mr. Madison and Colonel Hamilton to a friendly discussion of the subject. I immediately wrote to each to come and dine with me the next day, mentioning that we should be alone, that the object was to find some temperament for the present fever, and that I was persuaded that men of sound heads and honest views needed nothing more than explanation and mutual understanding to enable them to unite in some measures which might enable us to get along. They came; I opened the subject to them, acknowledged that my situation had not permitted me to understand it sufficiently but encouraged them to consider the thing together. They did so. It ended in Mr. Madison's acquiescence in a proposition that the question should be again brought before the House by way of amendment from the Senate: that though he would not vote for it, nor entirely withdraw his opposition, yet he should not be strenuous but leave it to its fate. It was observed, I forget by which of them, that as the pill would be a bitter one to the Southern States, something should be done to soothe them; that the removal of the seat of government to the Potomac was a just measure, and would probably be a popular one with them, and would be a proper one to follow the Assumption. It was agreed to speak to Mr. [Hugh] White and Mr. [Richard Bland] Lee whose districts lay on the Potomac, and to refer to them to consider how far the interests of their particular districts might be a sufficient inducement in them to yield to the Assumption. This was done. Lee came into it without hesitation: Mr. White had some qualms but finally agreed. The measure came down by way of amendment from the Senate and was finally carried by the change of White and Lee's votes. But the removal to the Potomac could not be carried unless Pennsylvania could be engaged in it. This Hamilton took on himself, and chiefly, as I understood, through the agency of Robert Morris, obtained a vote of that State, on agreeing to an intermediate residence at Philadelphia. This is the real history of the Assumption, about which many erroneous conjectures have been published. It was unjust in itself, oppressive to the States, and was acquiesced in merely from a fear of discussion. While our government was still in its most infant state, it enabled Hamilton so to strengthen himself by corrupt services to many that he could afterwards carry his bank scheme, and every measure he proposed in defiance of all opposition. In fact, it was a principal ground whereon was reared up that speculating phalanx, in and out of Congress, which has since been able to give laws to change the political complexion of the government of the United States.—To —— ——. FORD ED., vi, 172. (1793.)

591. ASTOR'S SETTLEMENT, Protection of.—I learn with great pleasure the progress you have made towards an establishment on Columbia river. I view it as the germ of a great, free, and independent empire on that side of our continent, and that liberty and self-government spreading from that as well as from this side, will insure their complete establishment over the whole. It must be still more gratifying to yourself to foresee that your name will be handed down with that of Columbus and Raleigh, as the father of the establishment and

founder of such an empire. It would be an afflicting thing, indeed, should the English be able to break up the settlement. Their bigotry to the bastard liberty of their own country, and habitual hostility to every degree of freedom in any other, will induce the attempt; they would not lose the sale of a bale of furs for the empire of the whole world. But I hope your party will be able to maintain themselves * * * and have no doubt our government will do for its success whatever they have power to do and especially that at the negotiations for peace, they will provide, by convention with the English, for the safety and independence of that country, and an acknowledgment of our right of patronizing the Indians in all cases of injury from foreign nations.—To JOHN JACOB ASTOR. vi, 247. (M., 1813.) See FUR TRADE.

592. ASTOR'S SETTLEMENT, Territory and.—On the waters of the Pacific, we can found no claim in right of Louisiana. If we claim that country at all, it must be on Astor's settlement near the mouth of the Columbia, and the principle of the *jus gentium* of America, that when a civilized nation takes possession of the mouth of a river in a new country, that possession is considered as including all its waters.—To JOHN MELISH. vii, 51. (M., 1816.)

593. ASTRONOMY, Apparatus for.—This letter [is] to remind you of your kind promise of making me an accurate clock; which, being intended for astronomical purposes only, I would have divested of all apparatus for striking, or for any other purpose, which, by increasing its complication, might disturb its accuracy.. A companion to it, for keeping seconds, and which might be moved easily, would greatly add to its value.—To DAVID RITTENHOUSE. i, 210. FORD ED., ii, 162. (M., 1778.)

594. ASTRONOMY, Bowditch's papers.—I am indebted to you for Mr. Bowditch's very learned mathematical papers, the calculations of which are not for every reader, although their results are readily enough understood.. One of these impairs the confidence I had reposed in Laplace's demonstration, that the eccentricities of the planets of our system could oscillate only within narrow limits, and therefore could authorize no inference that the system must, by its own laws, come one day to an end. This would have left the question one of infinitude, at both ends of the line of time, clear of physical authority.—To JOHN ADAMS. vii, 112. (M., 1819.)

595. ASTRONOMY, Discoveries in.—Herschel has pushed his discoveries of double stars, now, to upwards of nine hundred, being twice the number of those communicated in the Philosophical Transactions. You have probably seen, that a Mr. Pigott had discovered periodical variations of light in the star Algol. He has observed the same in the η of Antinous, and makes the period of variation seven days, four hours, and thirty minutes, the duration of the increase sixty-three hours, and of the decrease thirty-six hours. What are we to conclude from this? That there are suns which have their orbits of revolution too? But this would suppose a wonderful harmony in their planets, and present a new scene, where the attracting powers should be without, and not within the orbit. The motion of our sun would be a miniature of this. But this must be left to you astronomers.—To PROFESSOR JAMES MADISON. i, 447. (P., 1785.)

596. ASTRONOMY, Planet Herschel.—I shall send you * * * the "Connoissance de Tems" for the years 1786 and 1787, being all as yet published. You will find in these the tables for the planet Herschel, as far as the observations hitherto made, admit them to be calculated. You will see, also, that Herschel was only the first astronomer who discovered it to be a planet, and not the first who saw it. Meyer saw it in the year 1756, and placed it in the catalogue of his zodiacal stars, supposing it to be such. A Prussian astronomer, in the year 1781, observed that the 964th star of Meyer's catalogue was missing; and the calculations now prove that at the time Meyer saw his 964th star, the planet Herschel should have been precisely in the place where he noted that star.—To John Page. i, 402. (P., 1785.)

597. —— ——. It is fixed on grounds which scarcely admit a doubt that the planet Herschel was seen by Meyer in the year 1756, and was considered by him as one of the zodiacal stars, and, as such, arranged in his catalogue, being the 964th which he describes. This 964th of Meyer has been since missing, and the calculations for the planet Herschel show that it should have been, at the time of Meyer's observation, where he places his 964th star.—To Dr. Stiles. i, 363. (P., 1785.)

598. ASTRONOMY, Solar eclipse.—We were much disappointed in Virginia generally on the day of the great eclipse, which proved to be cloudy. In Williamsburg, where it was total, I understand only the beginning was seen. At this place, (Monticello,) which is latitude 38° 8' and longitude west from Williamsburg, about 1° 45', as is conjectured, 11 digits only were supposed to be covered. It was not seen at all until the moon had advanced nearly one-third over the sun's disc. Afterwards it was seen at intervals through the whole. The egress particularly was visible. It proved, however, of little use to me, for want of a time piece that could be depended on.—To David Rittenhouse. i, 210. Ford ed., ii, 162. (M., July, 1778.)

599. ASTRONOMY, Variations of light.—I think your conjecture that the periodical variation of light in certain fixed stars proceeds from maculæ, is more probable than that of Maupertius, who supposes those bodies may be flat, and more probable also than that which supposes the star to have an orbit of revolution so large as to vary sensibly its degree of light. The latter is rendered more difficult of belief from the shortness of the period of variation.—To Professor J. Madison. ii, 247. (P., 1787.)

600. ASYLUM, America as an.—America is now, I think, the only country of tranquillity, and should be the asylum of all those who wish to avoid the scenes which have crushed our friends in Paris.—To Mrs. Church. Ford ed., vi, 289. (Pa., 1793.)

601. —— ——. I think it fortunate for the United States to have become the asylum for so many virtuous patriots of different denominations; but their circumstances, with which you were so well acquainted before, enabled them to be but a bare asylum, and to offer nothing for them but an entire freedom to use their own means and faculties as they please.—To M. de Meunier. Ford ed., vii, 13. (M., 1795.)

602. —— ——. Small means of being useful to you are left to me, but they shall be freely exercised for your advantage, and that, not on the selfish principle of increasing our own population at the expense of other nations, * * * but to consecrate a sanctuary for those whom the misrule of Europe may compel to seek happiness in other climes. This refuge, once known, will produce reaction on the happiness even of those who remain there, by warning their task-masters that when the evils of Egyptian oppression become heavier than those of the abandonment of country, another Canaan is open where their subjects will be received as brothers, and secured against like oppressions by a participation in the right of self government.—To George Flower. vii, 84. (P.F., 1817.)

603. ASYLUM, Consuls and.—The clause in the Consular convention with France of 1784 giving the right of sanctuary to consuls' houses, was reduced to a protection of their chancery room and its papers.—Notes on Consular Convention. ix, 463. (1803.)

604. ASYLUM, Public vessels and.—Article 12 [of the French treaty], giving asylum in the ports of either to the armed vessels of the other, with the prizes taken from the enemies of that other, must be qualified as it is in the 19th article of the Prussian treaty; as the stipulation in the latter part of the article, "that no shelter or refuge shall be given in the ports of the one, to such as shall have made prize on the subjects of the other of the parties," would forbid us in case of a war between France and Spain, to give shelter in our ports to prizes made by the latter on the former, while the first part of the article would oblige us to shelter those made by the former on the latter—a very dangerous covenant, and which ought never to be repeated in any other instance.—Mississippi River Instructions. vii, 588. Ford ed., v, 478. (March 1792.)

605. —— ——. The Executive has never denied the right of asylum in our ports to the public armed vessels of [the British] nation. They, as well as the French, are free to come to them, in all cases of weather, piracies, enemies, or other urgent necessity, and to refresh, victual and repair, &c.—To George Hammond. iv, 65. Ford ed., vi, 423. (Pa., 1793.) See Expatriation, Fugitives, Impressment.

606. ATHEISM, Calumnious charges of.—As to the calumny of Atheism, I am so broken to calumnies of every kind, from every department of government, Executive, Legislative, and Judiciary, and from every minion of theirs holding office or seeking it, that I entirely disregard it, and from Chace it will have less effect than from any other man in the United States.—To James Monroe. Ford ed., vii, 447. (Ep., May 1800.)

607. ATHEIST, Not an.—An atheist * * * I can never be.—To John Adams. vii, 281. (M., 1823.)

608. ATHENS, Government of.—The government of Athens was that of the people of one city making laws for the whole country subjected to them. That of Lacedæmon was the rule of military monks over the laboring class of the people, reduced to abject slavery. These are not the doctrines of the present age. The equal rights of man, and the happiness of every individual, are now acknowledged to be the only legitimate objects of government.—To M. Coray. vii, 319. (M., 1823.)

— **ATMOSPHERE.**—See 209.

— **ATTACHMENTS, Foreign.**—See For-eign Influence.

609. ATTAINDER, Bills of.—The occasion and proper office of a bill of attainder is this: When a person charged with a crime withdraws from justice, or resists it by force, either in his own or a foreign country, no other recourse of bringing him to trial or punishment being practicable, a special act is passed by the legislature adapted to the particular case. This prescribes to him a sufficient time to appear and submit to a trial by his peers; declares that his refusal to appear shall be taken as a confession of guilt, as in the ordinary case of an offender at the bar refusing to plead, and pronounces the sentence which would have been rendered on his confession or conviction in a court of law. No doubt that these acts of attainder have been abused in England as instruments of vengeance by a successful over a defeated party. But what institution is insusceptible of abuse in wicked hands?—To L. H. Girardin. vi, 440. Ford ed., ii, 151. (M., 1815.)

— **ATTIRE.**—See Dress.

610. ATTORNEY GENERAL, Appointment of.—An Attorney General shall be appointed by the House of Representatives. Proposed Va. Constitution. Ford ed., ii, 20. (June 1776.)

611. ATTORNEYS, Federal District.—The only shield for our republican citizens against the federalism of the courts is to have the attorneys and marshals republicans. —To A. Stuart. iv, 394. Ford ed., viii. 47. (M., April 1801.)

612. —— ——. Republican attorneys and marshals, being the doors of entrance into the courts, are indispensably necessary as a shield to the republican part of our fellow citizens, which, I believe, is the main body of the people.—To William B. Giles. iv, 381. Ford ed., viii, 25. (W., 1801.)

613. AUBAINE, Droit d'.—The expression in the eleventh article of our treaty of commerce and amity with France, "that the subjects of the United States shall not be reputed Aubaines in France, and consequently shall be exempted from the Droit d'Aubaine, or other similar duty, under what name soever," has been construed so rigorously to the letter, as to consider us as Aubaines in the colonies of France. Our intercourse with those colonies is so great, that frequent and important losses will accrue to individuals, if this construction be continued. * * * I presume that the enlightened Assembly now engaged in reforming the remains of feudal

abuse among them, will not leave so inhospitable an one as the Droit d'Aubaine existing in France, or any of its dominions. If this may be hoped it will be better that you should not trouble the minister with any application for its abolition in the colonies as to us. This would be creating into a special favor to us the extinction of a general abuse, which will, I presume, extinguish of itself. Only be so good as to see, that in abolishing this odious law in France, its abolition in the colonies, also, be not omitted by mere oversight; but if, contrary to expectation, this fragment of barbarism be suffered to remain, then it will become necessary to bring forward the enclosed case, and press a liberal and just exposition of our treaty, so as to relieve our citizens from this species of risk and ruin hereafter.—To William Short. iii, 189. Ford ed., v, 234. (N.Y., 1790.)

— **AURORA NEWSPAPER.**—See Duane.

— **AUSTRIA, Emperor of.**—See Joseph II.

614. AUTHORITY, Civil and Military.—Instead of subjecting the military to the civil power, his Majesty has expressly made the civil subordinate to the military. But can his Majesty thus put down all law under his feet? Can he erect a power superior to that which erected himself? He has done it indeed by force, but let him remember that force cannot give right.—Rights of British America. i, 140. Ford ed., i, 445. (1774.)

615. —— ——. He [George III.], has endeavored to pervert the exercises of the Kingly office in Virginia into a detestable and insupportable tyranny, * * * by [affecting] to render the military independent of and superior to the civil power.—Proposed Va. Constitution. Ford ed., ii, 19. (June 1776.)

616. —— ——. He has affected to render the military independent of, and superior to, the civil power.—Declaration of Independence as Drawn by Jefferson.

617. —— ——. The military shall be subordinate to the civil power.—Proposed Va. Constitution. viii, 452. Ford ed., iii, 322. (1783.)

618. —— ——. A distinction is kept up between the civil and military which it is for the happiness of both to obliterate.—To General Washington. i, 335. Ford ed., iii. 467. (A., 1784.)

619. —— ——. A distinction [will be continued] between the civil and military which it would be for the good of the whole to obliterate as soon as possible.—To M. de Meunier. ix, 270. Ford ed., iv, 175. (P., 1786.)

620. —— ——. I do not see how they [the framers of the French constitution] can prohibit altogether the aid of the military in cases of riot, and yet I doubt whether they can descend from the sublimity of ancient military pride, to let a Marechal of France with his troops, be commanded by a magistrate. They cannot conceive that General Washington, at the head of his army, during the late war, could have been commanded by a common constable to go as his *posse comitatus* to suppress a mob, and that Count Rochambeau, when he was arrested at the head of his army by a sheriff, must have gone to jail if he had not given bail to appear in court. Though they have gone astonishing lengths, they are not yet thus far. It is probable, therefore, that not knowing how to use the military as a civil weapon, they will do too much or too little with it.—To WILLIAM CARMICHAEL. iii, 90. (P., Aug. 1789.)

621. —— ——. The military shall be subordinate to the civil authority.—FRENCH CHARTER OF RIGHTS. iii. 47. FORD ED., v, 102. (P., 1789.)

622. —— ——. Bonaparte has transferred the destinies of the republic from the civil to the military arm. Some will use this as a lesson against the practicability of republican government. I read it as a lesson against the danger of standing armies.—To SAMUEL ADAMS. iv, 322. FORD ED., vii. 425. (Pa., Feb. 1800.)

623. —— ——. The supremacy of the civil over the military authority. I deem [one of the] essential principles of our government and, consequently [one] which ought to shape its administration.—FIRST INAUGURAL ADDRESS. viii, 4. FORD ED., viii, 5. (1801.)

624. —— ——. I sincerely wish General Wilkinson could be appointed as you propose. But besides the objection from principle, that no military commander should be so placed as to have no civil superior, his residence at Natchez is entirely inconsistent with his superintendence of the military posts. —To SAMUEL SMITH. FORD ED., viii, 29. (W., March 1801.)

625. —— ——. Not a single fact has appeared, which occasions me to doubt that I could have made a fitter appointment than General Wilkinson. One qualm of principle I acknowledge I do feel, I mean the union of the civil and military authority. You remember that when I went into office * * * he was pressed on me to be made Governor of the Mississippi Territory, and that I refused it on that very principle. When, therefore, the House of Representatives took that ground, I was not insensible to its having some weight. But in the appointment to Louisiana, I did not think myself departing from my own principle, because I consider it not as a civil government, but merely a military station. The Legislature had sanctioned that idea by the establishment of the office of the Commandant, in which were completely blended the civil and military powers. It seemed therefore, that the Governor should be in suit with them. I observed, too, that the House of Representatives, on the very day they passed the stricture on this union of authorities, passed a bill making the Governor of Michigan com-

mander of the regular troops which should at any time be within his government.—To SAMUEL SMITH. v, 13. FORD ED., viii, 450. (W., May 1806.)

626. AUTHORITY, Civil and Military united.—From a belief that, under the pressure of the [British] invasion under which we [Virginia] were then [1781] laboring, the public would have more confidence in a military chief, and that the military commander, being invested with the civil power also, both might be wielded with more energy, promptitude and effect for the defence of the State, I resigned the administration [the Governorship] at the end of my second year, [1781] and General Nelson was appointed to succeed me.—AUTOBIOGRAPHY. i, 50. FORD ED., i, 70. (1821.)

627. AUTHORITY, Conflict of.—Congress having * * * directed that they [British prisoners in Virginia] should not be removed, and our Assembly that they should, the Executive [of Virginia] are placed in a very disagreeable situation. We can order them to the banks of the Potomac, but our authority will not land them on the opposite shore.— To BENJAMIN HARRISON. FORD ED., ii. 439. (R., 1781.)

628. AUTHORITY, Constitution and. —The authority of the people is a necessary foundation for a constitution.—To JOHN H. PLEASANTS. vii. 345. FORD ED., x, 302. (M., 1824.)

629. AUTHORITY, Custom as.—General example is weighty authority.—NOTES ON COINAGE. vii, 164. (1790.)

630. AUTHORITY, Enforcing.—We would do anything in our power to support and manifest your authority, were anything wanting. But nothing can be added to the provision which the military institutions have made to enforce obedience, and it would be presumption in us to say what is that provision to you.—To MAJOR-GENERAL STEUBEN. FORD ED., ii, 491. (R., 1781.)

631. —— ——. We cannot be respected by France as a neutral nation, nor by the world ourselves as an independent one, if we do not take effectual measures to support, at every risk, our authority in our own harbors. —To JAMES MADISON. iv, 558. FORD ED., viii, 315. (M., Aug. 1804.)

632. AUTHORITY, Habits of.—If the President can be preserved a few years till habits of authority and obedience [to the new government] can be established generally, we have nothing to fear.—To M. DE LAFAYETTE. iii, 132. FORD ED., v, 152. (N.Y., April 1790.)

633. AUTHORITY, Obligation and.—It is not the name, but the authority that renders an act obligatory.—NOTES ON VIRGINIA. viii, 365. FORD ED., iii, 228. (1782.)

634. AUTHORITY, Opposition to.—My long and intimate knowledge of my countrymen satisfies me, that let there ever be occasion to display the banners of the law, and

the world will see how few and pitiful are those who will array themselves in opposition.—To DR. JAMES BROWN. v, 379. FORD ED., ix, 211. (W., 1808.)

635. AUTHORITY, The People and.— Leave no authority not responsible to the people.—To ISAAC H. TIFFANY. vii, 32. (M., 1816.)

636. —— ——. All authority belongs to the people.—To SPENCER ROANE. vii, 213. FORD ED., x, 190. (M., 1821.)

637. AUTHORITY, Religion and Federal.—Civil powers alone have been given to the President of the United States, and no authority to direct the religious exercises of his constituents.—To REV. SAMUEL MILLER. v, 237. FORD ED., ix, 175. (W., 1808.)

638. —— ——. No power to prescribe any religious exercise, or to assume authority in religious discipline, has been delegated to the General Government. It must then rest with States, so far as it can be in any human authority.—To REV. SAMUEL MILLER. v, 237. FORD ED., ix, 174. (W., 1808.)

639. AUTHORITY, Repudiated.—The British Parliament has no right to exercise authority over us.—RIGHTS OF BRITISH AMERICA. i, 130. FORD ED., i, 434. ((1774.)

640. AUTHORITY, Resistance to usurped.—It is a dangerous lesson to say to the people "whenever your functionaries exercise unlawful authority over you, if you do not go into actual resistance, it will be deemed acquiescence and confirmation." How long had we acquiesced under usurpations of the British parliament? Had that confirmed them in right, and made our Revolution a wrong? Besides no authority has yet decided whether this resistance must be instantaneous: when the right to resist ceases, or whether it has yet ceased?—To JOHN HAMBDEN PLEASANTS. vii, 345. FORD ED., x, 302. (M., 1824.)

641. AUTHORITY, Self-constituted.—I deem no government safe which is under the vassalage of any self-constituted authorities, or any other authority than that of the nation, or its regular functionaries.—To ALBERT GALLATIN. iv, 519. FORD ED., viii, 285. (W., Dec. 1803.)

642. AUTHORITY, Source of.—I consider the source of authority with us to be the Nation. Their will, declared through its proper organ, is valid, till revoked by their will declared through its proper organ again also. Between 1776 and 1789, the proper organ for pronouncing their will, whether legislative or executive, was a Congress formed in a particular manner. Since 1789, it is a Congress formed in a different manner, for laws, and a President, elected in a particular way, for making appointments and doing other executive acts. The laws and appointments of the ancient Congress were as valid and permanent in their nature, as the laws of the new Congress, or appointments of the new Executive; these laws and appointments, in both cases, deriving equally their source from the will of the Nation.—To PRESIDENT WASHINGTON. iii, 332. FORD ED., v, 437. (Pa., 1792.)

643. —— ——. I consider the people who constitute a society or nation as the source of all authority in that nation; as free to transact their common concerns by any agents they think proper; to change these agents individually, or the organization of them in form or function whenever they please; that all the acts done by these agents under the authority of the nation are the acts of the nation, are obligatory to them and inure to their use, and can in no wise be annulled or affected by any change in the form of the government, or of the persons administering it.—OPINION ON FRENCH TREATIES. vii, 612. FORD ED., vi, 220. (1793.)

644. AUTHORITY, Upholding.—In no country on earth is it [forcible opposition to the law] so impracticable as in one where every man feels a vital interest in maintaining the authority of the laws, and instantly engages in it as in his own personal cause.—To BENJAMIN SMITH. v, 293. FORD ED., ix, 195. (M., 1808.)

645. —— ——. Forcible opposition [to the embargo] will rally the whole body of republicans of every shade to a single point.—that of supporting the public authority.—To ALBERT GALLATIN. v, 347. (M., Aug. 1808.)

646. AUTHORITY, Usurpation of.—Necessities which dissolve a government do not convey its authority to an oligarchy or a monarchy. They throw back into the hands of the people the powers they had delegated, and leave them as individuals to shift for themselves.—NOTES ON VIRGINIA. viii, 369. FORD ED., iii, 233. (1782.)

647. AUTHORITY, Washington and Civil.—You [General Washington] have conducted the great military contest with wisdom and fortitude, invariably regarding the rights of the civil power through all disasters and changes.*—CONGRESS TO GEN. WASHINGTON. (Dec. 23, 1783.)

— AUTHORS.—See LITERATURE.

648. AVARICE, Commercial.—It seems to me that in proportion as commercial avarice and corruption advance on us from the North and East, the principles of free government are to retire to the agricultural States of the South and West, as their last asylum and bulwark.—To HENRY MIDDLETON. vi, 91. (M., 1813.)

— BACON'S REBELLION.—See REBELLION.

649. BADGES, Utilizing.—Let them [Cincinnati society] melt up their eagles and add the mass to the distributable fund, that

* Jefferson wrote the address to Washington on surrendering his commission. It is not included in either of the two leading editions of Jefferson's writings.—EDITOR.

their descendants may have no temptation to hang them in their button holes.—To M. DE MEUNIER. ix, 271. FORD ED., iv., 176. (P., 1786.) See BIRTHDAY.

650. BAINBRIDGE (William), Victory of.—After the loss of the Philadelphia, Captain Bainbridge had a character to redeem. He has done it most honorably, and no one is more gratified by it than myself.—To MATTHEW CARR. vi, 132. (M., 1813.)

651. BALLOONS, Experiments with.—There seems a possibility that the great desideratum in the use of the balloon may be obtained. There are two persons at Javel (opposite to Auteuil), who are pushing this matter. They are able to rise and fall at will, without expending their gas, and they can deflect forty-five degrees from the course of the wind.—To R. IZARD. i, 443. (P., 1785.)

652. BALLOONS, Fall from.—An accident has happened here [France] which will probably damp the ardor with which aërial navigation has been pursued. Monsieur Pilatre de Rozier had been waiting for many months at Boulogne a fair wind to cross the channel in a balloon which was compounded of one of inflammable air, and another called a Mont-golfier with rarefied air only. He at length thought the wind fair and with a companion, Romain, ascended. After proceeding in a proper direction about two leagues, the wind changed and brought them again over the French coast. Being at the height of about six thousand feet, some accident, unknown, burst the balloon of inflammable air, and the Mont-golfier, being unequal alone to sustain their weight, they precipitated from that height to the earth and were crushed to atoms.—To JOSEPH JONES. i, 353. (P., June 1785.)

653. ——— ———. The arts, instead of advancing, have lately received a check which will probably render stationary for awhile, that branch of them which had promised to elevate us to the skies. Pilatre de Roziere, who had first ventured into that region, has fallen a sacrifice to it. In an attempt to pass from Boulogne over to England, a change in the wind having brought him on the coast of France, some accident happened to his balloon of inflammable air, which occasioned it to burst, and that of rarefied air combined with it being then unequal to the weight, they fell to the earth from a height, which the first reports made six thousand feet, but later ones have reduced to sixteen hundred. Pilatre de Roziere was dead when a peasant distant one hundred yards away, ran to him; but Romain, his companion, lived about ten minutes, though speechless, and without his senses.—To CHARLES THOMSON. i, 355. (P., 1785.)

654. BALLOONS, Peril of.—Though navigation by water is attended with frequent accidents, and in its infancy must have been attended with more, yet these are now so familiar that we think little of them, while that which has signalized the two first martyrs to the aëronautical art will probably deter very many from the experiments they would have been disposed to make.—To CHARLES THOMSON. i, 354. (P., 1785.)

— **BALLOT.**—See SUFFRAGE.

— **BANISHMENT.**—See EXILE.

655. BANK (National 1813), Charter of.—The scheme is for Congress to establish a national bank, suppose of thirty millions capital, of which they shall contribute ten millions in six per cent. stock, the States ten millions, and individuals ten millions, one half of the two last contributions to be of a similar stock, for which the parties are to give cash to Congress; the whole, however, to be under the exclusive management of the individual subscribers. who are to name all the directors; neither Congress nor the States having any power of interference in its administration. Discounts are to be at five per cent., but the profits are expected to be at seven per cent. Congress then will be paying six per cent. on twenty millions, and receiving seven per cent. on ten millions, being its third of the institution; so that on the ten millions cash which they receive from the States and individuals, they will, in fact, have to pay but five per cent. interest. This is the bait. The charter is proposed to be for forty or fifty years, and if any future augmentations should take place, the individual proprietors are to have the privilege of being the sole subscribers for that. Congress are further allowed to issue to the amount of three millions of notes. bearing interest, which they are to receive back in payment for lands at a premium of five or ten per cent., or as subscriptions for canals, roads, and bridges, in which undertakings they are. of course, to be engaged. This is a summary of the case as I understand it; but it is very possible I may not understand it in all its parts, these schemes being always made unintelligible for the gulls who are to enter into them.—To J. W. EPPES. vi. 228. FORD ED., ix, 403. (M. Nov. 1813.)

656. BANK (National 1813), Considerations on.—The advantages and disadvantages shall be noted promiscuously as they occur; leaving out the speculation of canals &c., which, being an episode only in the scheme. may be omitted, to disentangle it as much as we can. 1. Congress are to receive five millions from the States (if they will enter into this partnership, which few probably will), and five millions from the individual subscribers, in exchange for ten millions of six per cent. stock, one per cent. of which, however, they will make on their ten millions of stock remaining in bank, and so reduce it in effect, to a loan of ten millions at five per cent. interest. This is good; but, 2. They authorize this bank to throw into circulation ninety millions of dollars (three times the capital), which increases our circulating medium fifty per cent.; depreciates proportionably the present value of a dollar, and raises the price of all future purchases in the same proportion. 3. This loan of ten millions at five per cent., is to be once for all, only. Neither the terms of the scheme, nor their own prudence could ever permit them to add to the circulation in the same, or any other way, for the supplies of the succeeding years of the war. These succeeding years then are to be left unprovided for, and the means of doing it in a great measure precluded. 4. The individual subscribers, on paying their own five millions of cash to Congress, become the depositors of ten millions of stock belonging to Congress, five millions belonging to the States, and five millions to themselves, say twenty millions, with which, as no one has a right ever to see their books, or to ask a question, they may choose their time for running away, after adding to their booty the proceeds of as much of their own notes as they shall be able to throw into circulation. 5. The subscribers may be one, two, or three, or more individuals (many single individuals being able to pay in the five millions), whereupon this bank oligarchy or monarchy enters the field with ninety millions of dollars, to direct and control the politics of the nation; and of the influence of these institutions on our politics, and into what scale it will be thrown, we have had abundant experience. Indeed, England herself may be the real, while her friend and trustee here shall be the nominal and sole subscriber. 6. This state of things is to be fastened on us, without the power of relief, for forty or fifty years. That is to say, the eight millions of people now existing, for the sake of receiving one dollar and twenty-five cents apiece, at five per cent. interest, are to subject the fifty millions of people who are to succeed them within that term, to the payment of forty-five millions of dollars, principal and interest, which will be payable in the course of the fifty years. 7. But the great and national advantage is to be the relief of the present *scarcity of money*, which is produced and proved by, 1. The additional industry created to supply a variety of articles for the troops, ammunition, &c. 2. By the cash sent to the frontiers, and the vacuum occasioned in the trading towns by that. 3. By the late loans. 4. By the necessity of recurring to *shavers* with *good* paper, which the existing banks are not able to take up; and 5. By the numerous applications of bank charters showing that an increase of circulating medium is wanting.—To J. W. EPPES. vi, 229. FORD ED., ix, 403. (M., Nov. 1813.)

657. BANK (National 1813), Increased Medium and.—Let us examine these causes and proofs of the want of our increase of medium, one by one. 1. The additional industry created to supply a variety of articles for troops, ammunition, &c. Now, I had always supposed that war produced a diminution of industry, by the number of hands it withdraws from industrious pursuits for employment in arms, &c., which are totally unproductive. And if it calls for new industry in the articles of ammunition and other military supplies, the hands are borrowed from other branches on which the demand is slackened by the war; so that it is but a shifting of these hands from one pursuit to another. 2. The cash sent to the frontiers occasions a vacuum in the trading towns, which requires a new supply. Let us examine what are the calls for money to the frontiers. Not for clothing, tents, ammunition, arms, which are all bought in the trading towns. Not for provisions; for although these are bought partly in the immediate country, bank bills are more acceptable there than even in the trading towns. The pay of the army calls for some cash, but not a great deal, as bank notes are as acceptable with the military men, perhaps more so; and what cash is sent must find its way back again in exchange for the wants of the upper from the lower country. For we are not to suppose that cash stays accumulating there forever. 3. This scarcity has been occasioned by the late loans. But does the government borrow money to keep it in their coffers? Is it not instantly restored to circulation by payment for its necessary supplies? And are we to restore a vacuum of twenty millions of dollars by an emission of ninety millions? 4. The want of medium is proved by the recurrence of individuals with *good* paper to brokers at exorbitant interest; and 5. By the numerous applications to the State governments for additional banks; New York wanting eighteen millions, Pennsylvania ten millions, &c. But say more correctly, the speculators and spendthrifts of New York and Pennsylvania, but never consider them as being the States of New York and Pennsylvania. These two items shall be considered together.—To J. W. EPPES. vi, 231. FORD ED., ix, 405. (M., Nov. 1813.)

658. BANK (National 1813), Paper, Specie and.—It is a litigated question, whether the circulation of paper, rather than of specie, is a good or an evil. In the opinion of England and of English writers it is a good; in that of all other nations it is an evil; and excepting England and her copyist, the United States, there is not a nation existing, I believe, which tolerates a paper circulation. The experiment is going on, however, desperately in England, pretty boldly with us, and at the end of the chapter, we shall see which opinion experience approves: for I believe it to be one of those cases where mercantile clamor will bear down reason, until it is corrected by ruin.—To J. W. EPPES. vi, 232. FORD ED., ix, 405. (M., Nov. 1813.)

659. BANK (National 1813), Unconstitutional.—After the solemn decision of Congress against the renewal of the charter of the Bank of the United States, and the grounds of that decision (the want of constitutional power), I had imagined that question at rest, and that no more applications would be made to them for the incorporation of banks. The opposition on that ground to its first establishment, the small majority by which it was overborne, and the means practiced for obtaining it, cannot be already forgotten. The law having passed, however, by a majority, its opponents, true to the sacred principle of submission to a majority, suffered the law to flow through its term without obstruction. During this, the nation had time to consider the constitutional question, and when the renewal was proposed, they condemned it, not by their representatives in Congress only, but by express instructions from different organs of their will. Here then we might stop, and consider the memorial as answered. But, setting authority apart, we will examine whether the Legislature ought to comply with it, even if they had the power.— To J. W. EPPES. vi, 232. FORD ED., ix, 406. (M., Nov. 1813.)

660. ——— ———. The idea of creating a national bank, I do not concur in, because it seems now decided that Congress has not that power (although I sincerely wish they had it exclusively), and because I think there is already a vast redundancy, rather than a scarcity of paper medium. The rapid rise in the nominal price of land and labor (while war and blockade should produce a fall) proves the progressive state of the depreciation of our medium.—To THOMAS LAW. FORD ED., ix, 433. (M., 1813.)

661. BANK OF NORTH AMERICA, Incorporation of.—The Philadelphia Bank was incorporated by Congress. This is, perhaps, the only instance of their having done that which they had no power to do. Necessity obliged them to give this institution the appearance of their countenance, because in that moment they were without any other resource for money.—COUNT VAN HOGENDORP. ii, 24. FORD ED., iv, 286. (P., 1786.)

662. BANK OF NORTH AMERICA, Pennsylvania and.—The Legislature of Pennsylvania passed an act of incorporation for the bank, and declared that the holders of stock should be responsible only to the amount of their stock. Lately that Legislature has repealed their act. The consequence is, that the bank is now altogether a private institution, and every holder is liable for its engagements in his whole property. This has had a curious effect. It has given those who deposit money in the bank a greater faith in it, while it has rendered the holders very discontented, as being more exposed to risk, and it has induced many to sell it, so that I have heard (I know not how truly) the bank stock sells somewhat below par.— To COUNT VAN HOGENDORP. ii, 24. FORD ED., iv, 286. (P., 1786.)

663. BANK (U. S.), Beginning of. —A division, not very unequal, had * * * taken place in the honest part of * * * [Congress in 1791] between the parties styled republican and federal. The latter, being monarchists in principle, adhered to [Alexander] Hamilton of course, as their leader in that principle, and this mercenary phalanx,* added to them, ensured him always a majority in both Houses; so that the whole action of the Legislature was now under the direction of the Treasury. Still the machine was not complete. The effect of the Funding system, and of the Assumption [of the State debts], would be temporary. It would be lost with the loss of the individual members whom it had enriched, and some engine of influence more permanent must be

* Those members of Congress who, Jefferson believed and charged, voted for the Assumption of the State debts from corrupt motives. See ASSUMPTION. —EDITOR.

contrived while these myrmidons were yet in place to carry it through all opposition. This engine was the Bank of the United States.— THE ANAS. ix, 95. FORD ED., i, 164. (1818.)

664. BANK (U. S.), Constitutionality of.—The bill for establishing a National Bank undertakes among other things :—1. To form the subscribers into a corporation. 2. To enable them in their corporate capacities to receive grants of land; and so far is against the laws of *Mortmain.** 3. To make alien subscribers capable of holding lands; and so far is against the laws of *Alienage.* 4. To transmit these lands, on the death of a proprietor, to a certain line of successors; and so far changes the course of Descents. 5. To put the lands out of the reach of forfeiture or escheat; and so far is against the laws of *Forfeiture and Escheat.* 6. To transmit personal chattels to successors in a certain line; and so far is against the laws of *Distribution.* 7. To give them the sole and exclusive right of banking under the national authority; and so far is against the laws of *Monopoly.* 8. To communicate to them a power to make laws paramount to the laws of the States; for so they must be construed, to protect the institution from the control of the State Legislatures; and so, probably, they will be construed.

I consider the foundation of the Constitution as laid on this ground :† That " all powers not delegated to the United States by the Constitution, nor prohibited by it to the States, are reserved to the States or to the people." (XIIth amendment.) To take a single step beyond the boundaries thus specially drawn around the powers of Congress is to take possession of a boundless field of power, no longer susceptible of any definition The incorporators of a bank, and the powers assumed by this bill, have not, in my opinion been delegated to the United States, by the Constitution. I. They are not among the powers specially enumerated: for these are: 1st. A power to lay taxes for the purpose of paying the debts of the United States; but no debt is paid by this bill, nor any tax laid Were it a bill to raise money, its origination in the Senate would condemn it by the Constitution. 2nd " To borrow money." But this bill neither borrows money nor ensures the borrowing it. The proprietors of the bank will be just as free as any other money holders, to lend or not to lend their money to the public. The operation proposed in the bill, first, to lend them two millions, and then to borrow them back again, cannot

* Though the Constitution controls the laws of Mortmain so far as to permit Congress itself to hold land for certain purposes, yet not so far as to permit them to communicate a similar right to other corporate bodies.—NOTE BY JEFFERSON.
† Washington requested the written opinions of the Cabinet on the constitutionality of the bill Those of the Secretaries of the Treasury, and of War, were in favor of the constitutionality of the act Those of the Secretary of State, and Attorney General, were against it. The opinion of Jefferson is an unanswerable argument against the doctrine of implied powers, and is justly considered the text of the true republican faith, on the subject of constitutional interpretation.—RAYNER'S *Life of Jefferson*, p. 304.

change the nature of the latter act, which will still be in a payment, and not a loan, call it by what name you please. 3rd To " regulate commerce with foreign nations, and among the States, and with the Indian tribes." To erect a bank, and to regulate commerce, are very different acts. He who erects a bank, creates a subject of commerce in its bills; so does he who makes a bushel of wheat, or digs a dollar out of the mines: yet neither of these persons regulates commerce thereby. To make a thing which may be bought and sold, is not to prescribe regulations for buying and selling. Besides, if this was an exercise of the power of regulating commerce, it would be void, as extending as much to the internal commerce of every State as to its external. For the power given to Congress by the Constitution does not extend to the internal regulation of the commerce of a State (that is to say of the commerce between citizen and citizen), which remains exclusively with its own legislature; but to its external commerce only, that is to say, its commerce with another State, or with foreign nations, or with the Indian tribes. Accordingly the bill does not propose the measure as a regulation of trade. but as, " productive of considerable advantages to trade." Still less are these powers covered by any other of the special enumerations.

II. Nor are they within either of the general phrases, which are the two following:— 1. To lay taxes to provide for the general welfare of the United States, that is to say, " to lay taxes for *the purpose* of providing for the general welfare." For the laying of taxes is the *power,* and the general welfare the *purpose* for which the power is to be exercised. They are not to lay taxes *ad libitum for any purpose they please;* but only *to pay the debts or provide for the welfare of the Union.* In like manner, they are not *to do anything they please* to provide for the general welfare. but only to *lay taxes* for that purpose. To consider the latter phrase, not as describing the purpose of the first, but as giving a distinct and independent power to do any act they please, which might be for the good of the Union, would render all the preceding and subsequent enumerations of power completely useless. It would reduce the whole instrument to a single phrase, that of instituting a Congress with power to do whatever would be for the good of the United States; and, as they would be the sole judges of 'the good or evil, it would be also a power to do whatever evil they please. It is an established rule of construction where a phrase will bear either of two meanings, to give to it that which will allow some meaning to the other parts of the instrument and not that which would render all the others useless. Certainly no such universal power was meant to be given them. It was intended to lace them up straitly within the enumerated powers, and those without which, as means, these powers could not be carried into effect. It is known that the very power now proposed *as a means* was rejected as *an end* by the Convention

which formed the Constitution. A proposition was made to them to authorize Congress to open canals, and an amendatory one to empower them to incorporate. But the whole was rejected, and one of the reasons for rejection urged in debate was, that then they would have power to erect a bank, which would render the great cities, where there were prejudices and jealousies on the subject. adverse to the reception of the Constitution. 2. The second general phrase is, " to make all laws *necessary* and proper for carrying into execution the enumerated powers." But they can all be carried into execution without a bank. A bank therefore is not *necessary,* and consequently not authorized by this phrase.

It has been urged that a bank will give great facility or convenience in the collection of taxes. Suppose this were true: yet the Constitution allows only the means which are "*necessary,*" not those which are merely " convenient " for effecting the enumerated powers. If such a latitude of construction be allowed to this phrase as to give any non-enumerated power, it will go to every one, for there is not one which ingenuity may not torture into a *convenience* in some instance or other, to *some one* of so long a list of enumerated powers. It would swallow up all the delegated powers, and reduce the whole to one power, as before observed. Therefore it was that the Constitution restrained them to the *necessary* means, that is to say, to those means without which the grant of power would be nugatory. But let us examine this convenience and see what it is. The report on this subject, page 3, states the only *general* convenience to be, the preventing the transportation and retransportation of money between the States and the treasury (for I pass over the increase of circulating medium, ascribed to it as a want, and which, according to my ideas of paper money, is clearly a demerit). Every State will have to pay a sum of tax money into the treasury; and the treasury will have to pay, in every State, a part of the interest on the public debt, and salaries to the officers of government resident in that State. In most of the States there will still be a surplus of tax money to come up to the seat of government for the officers residing there. The payments of interest and salary in each State may be made by treasury orders on the State collector. This will take up the great export of the money he has collected in his State, and consequently prevent the great mass of it from being drawn out of the State. If there be a balance of commerce in favor of that State against the one in which the government resides, the surplus of taxes will be remitted by the bills of exchange drawn for that commercial balance. And so it must be if there was a bank. But if there be no balance of commerce, either direct or circuitous, all the banks in the world could not bring up the surplus of taxes, but in the form of money. Treasury orders then, and bills of exchange may prevent the displacement of the main mass of the money collected, without the aid of any bank; and where these fail, it cannot be prevented even with that aid. Perhaps, indeed, bank bills may be a more *convenient* vehicle than treasury orders. But a little *difference* in the degree of *conveniences,* cannot constitute the necessity which the Constitution makes the ground for assuming any non-enumerated power.

Besides; the existing banks will, without a doubt, enter into arrangements for lending their agency, and the more favorable, as there will be a competition among them for it; whereas the bill delivers us up bound to the national bank, who are free to refuse all arrangement, but on their own terms, and the public not free, on such refusal, to employ any other bank. That of Philadelphia, I believe, now does this business, by their postnotes, which, by an arrangement with the treasury, are paid by any State collector to whom they are presented. This expedient alone suffices to prevent the existence of that *necessity* which may justify the assumption of a non-enumerated power as a means for carrying into effect an enumerated one. The thing may be done, and has been done, and well done, without this assumption: therefore, it does not stand on that degree of *necessity* which can honestly justify it. It may be said that a bank whose bills would have a currency all over the States, would be more convenient than one whose currency is limited to a single State. So it would be still more convenient that there should be a bank, whose bills should have a currency all over the world. But it does not follow from this superior conveniency, that there exists anywhere a power to establish such a bank; or that the world may not go on very well without it. Can it be thought that the Constitution intended that for a shade or two of *convenience,* more or less, Congress should be authorized to break down the most ancient and fundamental laws of the several States; such as those against Mortmain, the laws of Alienage, the rules of Descent, the acts of Distribution, the laws of Escheat and Forfeiture, the laws of Monopoly? Nothing but a necessity invincible by any other means, can justify such a prostitution of laws, which constitute the pillars of our whole system of jurisprudence. Will Congress be too straight-laced to carry the Constitution into honest effect, unless they may pass over the foundation laws of the State government for the slightest convenience of theirs?

The negative of the President is the shield provided by the Constitution to protect against the invasions of the Legislature: 1. The right of the Executive. 2. Of the Judiciary. 3. Of the States and State Legislatures. The present is the case of a right remaining exclusively with the States, and consequently one of those intended by the Constitution to be placed under its protection. It must be added, however, that unless the President's mind on a view of everything which is urged for and against this bill, is tolerably clear that it is unauthorized by the Constitution; if the pro and the con hang so

even as to balance his judgment, a just respect for the wisdom of the Legislature would naturally decide the balance in favor of their opinion. It is chiefly for cases where they are clearly misled by error, ambition, or interest, that the Constitution has placed a check in the negative of the President.—NATIONAL BANK OPINION. vii, 555. FORD ED., v, 284. (February 1791.)

665. BANK (U. S.), Directors of.— While the Government remained at Philadelphia, a selection of members of both Houses were constantly kept as directors, who, on every question interesting to that institution, or to the views of the federal head, voted at the will of that head; and, together with the stockholding members, could always make the federal vote that of the majority. By this combination, legislative expositions were given to the Constitution, and all the administrative laws were shaped on the model of England, and so passed. And from this influence we were not relieved, until the removal from the precincts of the Bank, to Washington.—THE ANAS. ix, 95. FORD ED., i, 164. (1818.)

666. BANK (U. S.), Dividends of.— The bank has just notified its proprietors that they may call for a dividend of ten per cent. on their capital for the last six months. This makes a profit of twenty-six per cent. per annum. Agriculture, commerce, and everything useful must be neglected, when the useless employment of money is so much more lucrative.—To PLUMARD DE RIEUX. FORD ED., v. 420. (Pa., 1792.)

667. BANK (U. S.), Fall in stock.— The failure of some stock gamblers and some other circumstances, have brought the public paper low. The 6 per cents have fallen from 26 to 211-4, and bank paper stock from 115 or 120 to 73 or 74, within two or three weeks. This nefarious business is becoming more and more the public detestation, and cannot fail, when the knowledge of it shall be sufficiently extended, to tumble its authors headlong from their heights.—To WILLIAM SHORT. iii, 342. FORD ED., v, 459. (Pa., March 1792.)

668. BANK (U. S.), Hostility to U. S. Government.— This institution is one of the most deadly hostility existing, against the principles and form of our Constitution. The nation is, at this time, so strong and united in its sentiments, that it cannot be shaken at this moment. But suppose a series of untoward events should occur, sufficient to bring into doubt the competency of a republican government to meet a crisis of great danger, or to unhinge the confidence of the people in the public functionaries: an institution like this, penetrating by its branches every part of the Union, acting by command and in phalanx, may, in a critical moment, upset the government.. I deem no government safe which is under the vassalage of any self-constituted authorities, or any other authority than that of the nation, or its regular functionaries. What an obstruction could not this Bank of the United States, with all its branch banks, be in time of war? It might dictate to us the peace we should accept, or withdraw its aids. Ought we then to give further growth to an institution so powerful, so hostile? That it is so hostile we know: 1, from a knowledge of the principles of the persons composing the body of directors in every bank, principal or branch; and those of most of the stockholders; 2, from their opposition to the measures and principles of the government, and to the election of those friendly to them; and 3, from the sentiments of the newspapers they support. Now, while we are strong, it is the greatest debt we owe to the safety of our Constitution, to bring its powerful enemy to a perfect subordination under its authorities. The first measure would be to reduce them to an equal footing only with other banks, as to the favors of the government. But, in order to be able to meet a general combination of the banks against us, in a critical emergency, could we not make a beginning towards an independent use of our own money, towards holding our own bank in all the deposits where it is received, and letting the treasurer give his draft or note, for payment at any particular place, which, in a well-conducted government, ought to have as much credit as any private draft, or bank note, or bill, and would give us the same facilities which we derive from the banks?—To ALBERT GALLATIN. iv, 519. FORD ED., viii, 284. (W., Dec. 1803.)

669. BANK (U. S.), Inflation projects. —The Bank is so firmly mounted on us that we must go where they will guide. They openly publish a resolution, that the national property being increased in value, they must by an increase of circulating medium furnish an adequate representation of it, and by further additions of active capital promote the enterprises of our merchants. It is supposed that the paper in circulation in and around Philadelphia, amounts to twenty millions of dollars, and that in the whole Union, to one hundred millions.—To JAMES MONROE. iv, 140. FORD ED., vii, 80. (M., June 1796.)

670. BANK (U. S.), Regulation of.— The Attorney General having considered and decided that the prescription in the law for establishing a bank, that the officers in the subordinate offices of discount and deposit, shall be appointed "on the same terms and in the same manner practiced in the principal bank," does not extend to them the principle of rotation, established by the Legislature in the body of directors in the principal bank, it follows that the extension of that principle has been merely a voluntary and prudential act of the principal bank, from which they are free to depart. I think the extension was wise and proper on their part, because the Legislature having deemed rotation useful in the principal bank constituted by them, there would be the same reason for it in the subordinate banks to be established by the principal. It breaks in upon the *esprit de corps*

so apt to prevail in permanent bodies: it gives a chance for the public eye penetrating into the sanctuary of those proceedings and practices, which the avarice of the directors may introduce for their personal emolument, and which the resentments of excluded directors, or the honesty of those duly admitted, might betray to the public; and it gives an opportunity at the end of the year, or at other periods, of correcting a choice, which, on trial, proves to have been unfortunate: an evil of which themselves complain in their distant institutions. Whether, however, they have a power to alter this, or not, the Executive has no right to decide: and their consultation with you has been merely an act of complaisance, or a desire to shield so important an innovation under the cover of executive sanction. But ought we to volunteer our sanction in such a case? Ought we to disarm ourselves of any fair right of animadversion, whenever that institution shall be a legitimate subject of consideration? I own, I think the most proper answer would be that we do not think ourselves authorized to give an opinion on the question.—To ALBERT GALLATIN. iv, 518. FORD ED., viii, 284. (W., 1803.)

671. BANK (U. S.), Richmond Branch. —It seems nearly settled with the Treasurobankites that a branch shall be established at Richmond. Could not a counter-bank be set up to befriend the agricultural man by letting him have money on a deposit of tobacco notes, or even wheat, for *a short time*, and would not such a bank enlist the legislature in its favor, and against the Treasury bank?— To JAMES MADISON. FORD ED., vi, 98. (Pa., 1792.)

672. BANK (U. S.), Ruin by.—It was impossible the Bank and paper mania should not produce great and extensive ruin. The President is fortunate to get off just as the bubble is bursting, leaving others to hold the bag. Yet, as his departure will mark the moment when the difficulties begin to work, you will see, that they will be ascribed to the new administration, and that he will have his usual good fortune of reaping credit from the good acts of others, and leaving to them that of his errors.—To JAMES MADISON. FORD ED., vii, 104. (Jan. 1797.)

673. BANK (U. S.), Saddled by.—We are completely saddled and bridled, and the bank is so firmly mounted on us that we must go where they will guide.—To JAMES MONROE. iv, 140. FORD ED., vii, 80. (M., June 1796.)

674. BANK (U. S.), Subscriptions to.— You will have seen the rapidity with which the subscriptions to the bank were filled. As yet the delirium of speculation is too strong to admit sober reflection. It remains to be seen whether in a country whose capital is too small to carry on its own commerce, to establish manufactures, erect buildings, &c., such sums should have been withdrawn from these useful pursuits to be employed in gambling? Whether it was well judged to force on the public a paper circulation of so many millions for which they will be paying about 7 per cent. per ann. and thereby banish as many millions of gold and silver for which they would have paid no interest? I am afraid it is the intention to nourish this spirit of gambling by throwing in from time to time new aliment.—To EDMUND PENDLETON. FORD ED., v, 357. (Pa., 1791.)

675. —— ——. The subscriptions to the Bank from Virginia were almost none. * * * This gives so much uneasiness to Colonel Hamilton that he thinks to propose to the President to sell some of the public shares to subscribers from Virginia and North Carolina, if any more should offer. This partiality would offend the other States without pleasing those two: for I presume they would rather the capitals of their citizens should be employed in commerce than be locked up in a strong box here [Philadelphia]: nor can sober thinkers prefer a paper medium at 13 per cent. interest to gold and silver for nothing.—To JAMES MADISON. FORD ED., v, 350. (Pa., 1791.)

676. —— ——. The bank filled and overflowed in the moment it was opened. Instead of twenty thousand shares, twenty-four thousand were offered, and a great many were presented, who had not suspected that so much haste was necessary. Thus it is that we shall be paying 13 per cent. per ann. for eight millions of paper money, instead of having that circulation of gold and silver for nothing. Experience has proved to us that a dollar of silver disappears for every dollar of paper emitted; and, for the paper emitted from the bank, seven per cent. profits will be received by the subscribers for it as bank paper (according to the last division of profits by the Philadelphia bank), and six per cent. on the public paper of which it is the representative. Nor is there any reason to believe, that either the six millions of public paper, or the two millions of specie deposited, will not be suffered to be withdrawn, and the paper thrown into circulation. The cash deposited by strangers for safe keeping will probably suffice for cash demands.—To JAMES MONROE. iii, 268. FORD ED., v, 352. (Pa., 1791.)

677. BANKRUPTCY, Agriculture, Commerce and.—I find you are to be harassed again with a bankrupt law. Could you not compromise between agriculture and commerce by passing such a law which like the by-laws of incorporate towns, should be binding on the inhabitants of such towns only, being the residence of commerce, leaving the agriculturists, inhabitants of the country, in undisturbed possession of the rights and modes of proceedings to which their habits, their interests and their partialities attach them? This would be as *uniform* as other laws of local obligation.—To JAMES PLEASANTS. FORD ED., x, 198. (M., 1821.)

678. BANKRUPTCY, Agriculturists and.—A bankrupt bill is brought in in such a form as to render almost all the landholders south of Pennsylvania liable to be declared bankrupts. Hitherto we had imagined that the General Government could not meddle with the title to lands.—To T. M. RANDOLPH. FORD ED., vi. 149. (Pa., 1792.)

679. —— ——. The bankrupt bill is brought on with some very threatening features to landed and farming men, who are in danger of being drawn into its vortex. It assumes the right of seizing and selling lands, and so cuts the knotty question of the Constitution, whether the General Government may direct the transmission of land by descent or otherwise.—To JOHN FRANCIS MERCER. iii, 495. FORD ED., vi, 148. (Pa., 1792.)

680. BANKRUPTCY, English Law of.—The British statute excepts expressly *farmers, graziers, drovers,* as such though they buy to sell again. This bill has no such exception. The British adjudications exempt the buyers and sellers of bank stock, government paper, &c. What feelings guided the draughtsman [of this bill] in adhering to his original in this case and then departing from it in the other? The British courts adjudge that any artists may be bankrupts if the materials of their art are bought, such as shoemakers, blacksmiths, carpenters, &c. Will the body of our artists desire to be brought within the vortex of this law? It will follow as a consequence that the master who has an artist of this kind in his family, whether hired, indentured, or a slave, to serve the purposes of his farm or family, but who may at leisure time do something for his neighbors also, may be a bankrupt. The British law makes a departure from the *realm, i. e.* out of the mediation of British law, an act of bankruptcy. This bill makes a departure from the *State wherein he resides* (though into a neighboring one where the laws of the United States run equally), an act of bankruptcy. The commissioners may enter houses, break open doors, chests &c. Are we really ripe for this? Is that spirit of independence and sovereignty, which a man feels in his own house, and which Englishmen felt when they denominated their houses their castles, to be absolutely subdued, and is it expedient that it should be subdued? The lands of the bankrupt are to be taken, sold. Is not this a predominant question between the General and State legislatures? Is commerce so much the basis of the existence of the United States as to call for a bankrupt law? On the contrary, are we not almost agricultural? Should not all laws be made with a view essentially to the poor husbandman? When laws are wanting for particular descriptions of other callings, should not the husbandman be carefully excused from their operation, and preserved under that of the general system only, which general system is fitted to the condition of the husbandman?*—NOTES ON THE BANKRUPT BILL. ix, 431. FORD ED., vi, 145. (Dec. 1792.)

---

* This paper is without date. Jefferson gave it this caption: "Extempore thoughts and doubts on very superficially running over the bankrupt bill." A bankrupt bill, introduced in the House in December, 1792, by W. L. Smith, is probably the one referred to. —EDITOR.

681. BANKS, Abuses of.—The crisis of the abuses of banking is arrived. The banks have pronounced their own sentence of death. Between two and three hundred millions of dollars of their promissory notes are in the hands of the people, for solid produce and property sold, and they formally declare they will not pay them. This is an act of bankruptcy, of course, and will be so pronounced by any court before which it shall be brought. But *cui bono?* The laws can only uncover their insolvency, by opening to its suitors their empty vaults. Thus by the dupery of our citizens, and tame acquiescence of our legislators, the nation is plundered of two or three hundred millions of dollars, treble the amount of debt contracted in the Revolutionary war, and which, instead of redeeming our liberty, has been expended on sumptuous houses, carriages, and dinners. A fearful tax! if equalized on all; but overwhelming and convulsive by its partial fall.—To THOMAS COOPER. vi, 381. (M., Sep. 1814.)

682. —— ——. Everything predicted by the enemies of banks, in the beginning, is now coming to pass. We are to be ruined now by the deluge of bank paper, as we were formerly by the old Continental paper. It is cruel that such revolutions in private fortunes should be at the mercy of avaricious adventurers, who, instead of employing their capital, if any they have, in manufactures, commerce, and other useful pursuits, make it an instrument to burthen all the interchanges of property with their swindling profits, profits which are the price of no useful industry of theirs. Prudent men must be on their guard in this game of *Robin's alive*, and take care that the spark does not extinguish in their hands. I am an enemy to all banks discounting bills or notes for anything but coin. But our whole country is so fascinated by this Jack-lantern wealth, that they will not stop short of its total and fatal explosion.*—To DR. THOMAS COOPER. vi, 295. (M., Jan. 1814.)

683. —— ——. The enormous abuses of the banking system are not only prostrating our commerce, but producing revolution of property, which without more wisdom than we possess, will be much greater than were produced by the Revolutionary paper. That, too, had the merit of purchasing our liberties, while the present trash has only furnished aliment to usurers and swindlers.—To RICHARD RUSH. FORD ED., x, 133. (M., June 1819.)

684. BANKS, Aristocracy.—I hope we shall * * * crush in its birth the aristocracy of our moneyed corporations, which dare already to challenge our government to a trial of strength, and bid defiance to the laws of our country.—To GEORGE LOGAN. FORD ED., x. 69. (P.F., Nov. 1816.)

685. —— ——. The bank mania * * * is raising up a moneyed aristocracy in our country which has already set the government at defiance, and although forced at

* This accordingly took place four years later.— NOTE, WASHINGTON EDITION.

length to yield a little on this first essay of their strength, their principles are unyielded and unyielding. These have taken deep root in the hearts of that class from which our legislators are drawn, and the sop to Cerberus from fable has become history. Their principles lay hold of the good, their pelf of the bad, and thus those whom the Constitution had placed as guards to its portals, are sophisticated or suborned from their duties.—To DR. J. B. STUART. vii, 64. (M., 1817.)

686. BANKS, Capital and.—At the time we were funding our national debt, we heard much about "a public debt being a public blessing"; that the stock representing it was a creation of active capital for the aliment of commerce, manufactures and agriculture. This paradox was well adapted to the minds of believers in dreams, and the gulls of that size entered *bonâ fide* into it. But the art and mystery of banks is a wonderful improvement on that. It is established on the principle that "*private* debts are a public blessing." That the evidences of those private debts, called bank notes, become active capital, and aliment the whole commerce, manufactures, and agriculture of the United States. Here are a set of people, for instance, who have bestowed on us the great blessing of running in our debt about two hundred millions of dollars, without our knowing who they are, where they are, or what property they have to pay this debt when called on; nay, who have made us so sensible of the blessings of letting them run in our debt, that we have exempted them by law from the repayment of these debts beyond a given proportion (generally estimated at one-third). And to fill up the measure of blessing, instead of paying, they receive an interest on what they owe from those to whom they owe; for all the notes, or evidences of what they owe, which we see in circulation, have been lent to somebody on an interest which is levied again on us through the medium of commerce. And they are so ready still to deal out their liberalities to us, that they are now willing to let themselves run in our debt ninety millions more, on our paying them the same premium of six or eight per cent. interest, and on the same legal exemption from the repayment of more than thirty millions of the debt, when it shall be called for. But let us look at this principle in its original form, and its copy will then be equally understood. "A public debt is a public blessing." That our debt was juggled from forty-three up to eighty millions, and funded at that amount, according to this opinion was a great public blessing, because the evidences of it could be vested in commerce, and thus converted into active capital, and then the more the debt was made to be, the more active capital was created. That is to say, the creditors could now employ in commerce the money due them from the public, and make from it an annual profit of five per cent., or four millions of dollars. But observe, that the public were at the same time paying on it an interest of exactly the same amount of four millions of dollars. Where, then, is the gain to either party, which makes it a public blessing? There is no change in the state of things, but of persons only. A has a debt due to him from the public, of which he holds their certificate as evidence, and on which he is receiving an annual interest. He wishes, however, to have the money itself, and to go into business with it. B has an equal sum of money in business, but wishes now to retire, and live on the interest. He therefore gives it to A in exchange for A's certificates of public stock. Now, then, A has the money to employ in business, which B so employed before. B has the money on interest to live on, which A lived on before; and the public pays the interest to B which they paid to A before. Here is no new creation of capital, no additional money employed, nor even a change in the employment of a single dollar. The only change is of place between A and B in which we discover no creation of capital, nor public blessing. Suppose, again, the public to owe nothing. Then A not having lent his money to the public, would be in possession of it himself, and would go into business without the previous operation of selling stock. Here again, the same quantity of capital is employed as in the former case, though no public debt exists. In neither case is there any creation of active capital, nor other difference than that there is a public debt in the first case, and none in the last; and we safely ask which of the two situations is most truly a public blessing? If, then, a *public* debt be no public blessing, we may pronounce, *à fortiori*, that a private one cannot be so. If the debt which the banking companies owe be a blessing to anybody, it is to themselves alone, who are realizing a solid interest of eight or ten per cent. on it. As to the public, these companies have banished all our gold and silver medium, which, before their institution, we had without interest, which never could have perished in our hands, and would have been our salvation now in the hour of war; instead of which they have given us two hundred millions of froth and bubble, on which we are to pay them heavy interest, until it shall vanish into air, as Morris's notes did. We are warranted, then, in affirming that this parody on the principle of "a public debt being a public blessing," and its mutation into the blessing of private instead of public debts, is as ridiculous as the original principle itself.—To J. W. Eppes. vi, 239. Ford ed., ix, 411. (M., Nov. 1813.)

687. —— ——. Capital may be produced by industry, and accumulated by economy; but jugglers only will propose to create it by legerdemain tricks with paper.—To J. W. Eppes. vi, 241. Ford ed., ix, 413. (M., Nov. 1813.)

688. BANKS, Criticism of.—I am too desirous of tranquillity to bring such a nest of hornets on me as the fraternity of banking companies.—To Joseph C. Cabell. vi, 300. (M., 1814.)

689. BANKS, Dangerous.—Banking establishments are more dangerous than standing armies.—To John Taylor. vi, 608. Ford ed., x, 31. (M., 1816.)

690. BANKS, Deposit.—Banks of *deposit*, where cash should be lodged, and a paper acknowledgment taken out as its representative, entitled to a return of the cash on demand, would be convenient for remittances, traveling persons, &c. But, liable as its cash would be to be pilfered and robbed, and its paper to be fraudulently reissued, or issued without deposit, it would require skilful and strict regulation. This would differ from the bank of Amsterdam, in the circumstance that the cash could be redeemed on returning the note.—To J. W. Eppes. vi, 247. Ford ed., ix, 417. (M., Nov. 1813.)

691. BANKS, Depreciated Paper of.—Everything predicted by the enemies of banks, in the beginning, is now coming to pass. We are to be ruined now by the deluge of bank paper, as we were formerly by the old Continental paper. It is cruel that such revolutions in private fortunes should be at the mercy of avaricious adventurers, who, instead of employing their capital, if they have any, in manufactures, commerce, and other useful pursuits, make it an instrument to burden all the interchanges of property with their swindling profits, profits which are the price of no useful industry of theirs. Prudent men must be on their guard in this game of *Robin's alive*, and take care that the spark does not extinguish in their hands. I am an enemy to all banks discounting bills or notes for anything but coin. But our whole country is so fascinated by this Jack-lantern wealth, that they will not stop short of its total and fatal explosion.—To Thomas Cooper. vi, 295. (M., Jan. 1814.)

692. —— ——. Already there is so much of their trash afloat that the great holders of it show vast anxiety to get rid of it. They perceive that now, as in the Revolutionary war, we are engaged in the old game of *Robin's alive*. They are ravenous after lands and stick at no price. In the neighborhood of Richmond, the seat of that sort of sensibility, they offer twice as much now as they would give a year ago.—To President Madison. Ford ed., ix, 453. (M., Feb. 1814.)

693. —— ——. The depreciation of bank paper swells nominal prices, without furnishing any stable index of value. I will endeavor briefly to give you an idea of this state of things by an outline of its history.

In 1781 we had 1 bank, its capital $1,000,000.

In 1791 we had 6 banks, their capital $13,135,000.

In 1794 we had 17 banks, their capital $18,642,000.

In 1796 we had 24 banks, their capital $20,472,000.

In 1803 we had 34 banks, their capital $29,112,000.

In 1804 we had 66 banks, their amount of capital not known.

And at this time we have probably one hundred banks, with capital amounting to one hundred millions of dollars, on which they are authorized by law to issue notes to three times that amount, so that our circulating medium may now be estimated at from two to three hundred millions of dollars, on a population of eight and a half millions. The banks were able for awhile, to keep this trash at par with metallic money, or rather to depreciate the metals to a par with their paper, by keeping deposits of cash sufficient to exchange for such of their notes as they were called on to pay in cash. But the circumstances of the war draining away all our specie, all these banks have stopped payment, but with a promise to resume specie exchanges whenever circumstances shall produce a return of the metals. Some of the most prudent and honest will possibly do this: but the mass of them never will nor can. Yet, having no other medium, we take their paper, of necessity, for purposes of the instant, but never to lay by us. The government is now issuing treasury notes for circulation, bottomed on solid funds, and bearing interest. The banking confederacy (and the merchants bound to them by their debts) will endeavor to crush the credit of these notes; but the country is eager for them, as something they can trust to, and so soon as a convenient quantity of them can get into circulation, the bank notes die.—To JEAN BAPTISTE SAY. vi, 434. (M., March 1815.)

694. BANKS, Difficulties caused by.— For the emolument of a small proportion of our society, who prefer those demoralizing pursuits [banking and commerce] to labors useful to the whole, the peace of the whole is endangered. and all our present difficulties produced.—To ABBE SALIMANKIS. v, 516. (M., 1810.)

695. —— ——. The fatal possession of the whole circulating medium by our banks, the excess of those institutions, and their present discredit, cause all our difficulties.— To W. H. CRAWFORD. vi, 419. FORD ED., ix, 503. (M., Feb. 1815.)

696. BANKS, Dominion of.— The dominion of the banks must be broken, or it will break us.—To JAMES MONROE. vi, 409. FORD ED., ix, 498. (M., Jan. 1815.)

697. BANKS, Dropsical.— I wish I could see Congress get into a better train of finance. Their banking projects are like dosing dropsy with more water. * * * Their new bank. if not abortive at its birth, will not last through one campaign; and the taxes proposed cannot be paid.—To WILLIAM SHORT. vi, 400. (M., Nov. 1814.)

698. BANKS, Evils of.— The evils they [the banks] have engendered are now upon us, and the question is how we are to get out of them? Shall we build an altar to the old paper money of the Revolution, which ruined individuals but saved the republic, and burn on that all the bank charters, present and future, and their notes with them? For these are to ruin both republic and individuals. This cannot be done. The mania is too strong. It has seized by its delusions and corruptions, all the members of our governments, general, special and individual.—To JOHN ADAMS. vi, 305. (M., Jan. 1814.)

699. —— ——. I think it impossible but that the whole system must blow up before the year is out; and thus a tax of three or four hundred millions will be levied on our citizens who had found it a work of so much time and labor to pay off a debt of eighty millions which had redeemed them from bondage.—To PRESIDENT MADISON. FORD ED., ix, 453. (M., Feb. 1814.)

700. —— ——. I see that this infatuation of banks must take its course, until actual ruin shall awaken us from its delusions. Until the gigantic banking propositions of this winter had made their appearance in the different Legislatures, I had hoped that the evil might still be checked; but I see now that it is desperate, and that we must fold our arms and go to the bottom with the ship.—To JOSEPH C. CABELL. vi, 300. (M., Jan. 1814.)

701. —— ——. The evils of this deluge of paper money are not to be removed until our citizens are generally and radically instructed in their cause and consequences, and silence by their authority the interested clamors and sophistry of speculating. shaving, and banking institutions. Till then we must be content to return, *quoad hòc*, to the savage state. to recur to barter in the exchange of our property, for want of a stable, common measure of value, that now in use being less fixed than the beads and wampum of the Indian, and to deliver up our citizens. their property and their labor, passive victims to the swindling tricks of bankers and mountebankers.—To JOHN ADAMS. vii, 115. (M., 1819.)

702. BANKS, Excess of.— That we are overdone with banking institutions, which have banished the precious metals, and substituted a more fluctuating and unsafe medium, that these have withdrawn capital from useful improvements and employments to nourish idleness * * * are evils more easily to be deplored than remedied.—To ABBE SALIMANKIS. v, 516. (M., 1810.)

703. —— ——. A parcel of mushroom banks have set up in every State. have filled the country with their notes, and have thereby banished all our specie. A twelvemonth ago they all declared they could not pay cash for their own notes, and notwithstanding this act of bankruptcy, this trash has of necessity been passing among us, because we have no other medium of exchange, and is still taken and passed from hand to hand, as you remember the old Continental money to have been in the Revolutionary war: every one getting rid of it as quickly as he can, by laying it out in property of any sort at double, treble and manifold higher prices. * * * A general crush is daily expected when this trash will be lost in the hands of the holders. This will take place the moment some specie returns among us, or so soon as the government will issue bills of circulation. The little they have issued is greatly sought after, and a premium given for them which is rising fast.—To PHILLIP MAZZEI. FORD ED., ix, 524. (M., Aug. 1815.)

704. BANKS, Failures of.—The failure of our banks will occasion embarrassment for awhile, although it restores to us a fund which ought never to have been surrendered by the nation, and which now, prudently used, will carry us through all the fiscal difficulties of the war.—To PRESIDENT MADISON. vi, 386. (M., Sep. 1814.)

705. ——— ———. The banks have discontinued themselves. We are now without any medium; and necessity, as well as patriotism, and confidence, will make us all eager to receive treasury notes, if founded on specific taxes. Congress may now borrow of the public, and without interest, all the money they may want, to the amount of a competent circulation, by merely issuing their own promissory notes, of proper denominations for the larger purposes of circulation. but not for the small. Leave that door open for the entrance of metallic money.—To THOMAS COOPER. vi, 382. (M., Sep. 1814.)

706. ——— ———. Providence seems, indeed, by a special dispensation, to have put down for us, without a struggle, that very paper enemy which the interest of our citizens long since required ourselves to put down, at whatever risk. The work is done. The moment is pregnant with futurity, and if not seized at once by Congress, I know not on what shoal our bark is next to be stranded. —To THOMAS COOPER. vi, 382. (M.. Sep. 1814.)

707. ——— ———. The crush will be tremendous; very different from that brought on by our paper money. That rose and fell so gradually that it kept all on their guard, and affected severely only early or long-winded contracts. Here the contract of yesterday crushes in an instant the one or the other party. The banks stopping payment suddenly, all their mercantile and city debtors do the same; and all, in short, except those in the country, who, possessing property, will be good in the end. But this resource will not enable them to pay a cent on the dollar.— To THOMAS COOPER. vi, 381. (M., Sep. 1814.)

708. ——— ———. The paper interest is now defunct. Their gossamer castles are dissolved, and they can no longer impede and overawe the salutary measures of the government. Their paper was received on a belief that it was cash on demand. Themselves have declared it was nothing, and such scenes are now to take place as will open the eyes of credulity and of insanity itself to the dangers of a paper medium, abandoned to the discretion of avarice and of swindlers. It is impossible not to deplore our past follies, and their present consequences, but let them at least be warnings against like follies in future.—To THOMAS COOPER. vi, 382. (M., Sep. 1814.)

709. BANKS, Fictitious Capital.—The banks themselves were doing business on capitals, three-fourths of which were fictitious; and to extend their profit they furnished fictitious capital to every man, who having nothing and disliking the labors of the plow, chose rather to call himself a merchant, to set up a house of $5,000 a year expense, to dash into every species of mercantile gambling, and if that ended as gambling generally does, a fraudulent bankruptcy was an ultimate resource of retirement and competence. This fictitious capital, probably of one hundred millions of dollars, is now to be lost, and to fall on somebody; it must take on those who have property to meet it, and probably on the less cautious part, who, not aware of the impending catastrophe have suffered themselves to contract, or to be in debt, and must now sacrifice their property of a value many times the amount of their debt. We have been truly sowing the wind, and are now reaping the whirlwind. If the present crisis should end in the annihilation of these pennyless and ephemeral interlopers only, and reduce our commerce to the measure of our own wants and surplus productions, it will be a benefit in the end. But how to effect this, and give time to real capital, and the holders of real property, to back out of their entanglements by degrees requires more knowledge of political economy than we possess. I believe it might be done, but I despair of its being done. The eyes of our citizens are not sufficiently open to the true cause of our distress. They ascribe them to everything but their true cause, the banking system; a system, which, if it could do good in any form, is yet so certain of leading to abuse, as to be utterly incompatible with the public safety and prosperity. At present, all is confusion, uncertainty and panic.—To RICHARD RUSH. FORD ED., x, 133. (M., June 1819.)

710. BANKS, Government Deposits and.—The application of the Bank of Baltimore is of great importance. The consideration is very weighty that it is held by citizens, while the stock of the United States bank is held in so great a proportion by foreigners. Were the Bank of the United States to swallow up the others and monopolize the whole banking business of the United States, which the demands we furnish them with tend shortly to favor. we might, on a misunderstanding with a foreign power, be immensely embarrassed by any disaffection in that bank. It is certainly for the public good to keep all the banks competitors for our favors by a judicious distribution of them. and thus to engage the individuals who belong to them in the support of the reformed order of things, or at least in an acquiescence under it. I suppose that. on the condition of participating in the deposits, the banks would be willing to make such communications of their operations and the state of their affairs as might satisfy the Secretary of the Treasury of their stability. It is recommended to Mr. Gallatin to leave such an opening in his answer to this letter, as to leave us free to do hereafter what

shall be advisable on a broad view of all the banks in the different parts of the Union.—To ALBERT GALLATIN. FORD ED., viii, 172. (Oct. 1802.)

711. —— ——. As to the patronage of the Republican Bank at Providence, I am decidedly in favor of making all the banks republican, by sharing deposits with them in proportion to the dispositions they show. If the law now forbids it, we should not permit another session of Congress to pass without amending it. It is material to the safety of republicanism to detach the mercantile interest from its enemies and incorporate them into the body of its friends.—To ALBERT GALLATIN. FORD ED., viii, 252. (July 1803.)

712. BANKS, Jefferson's disapprobation of Paper.—My original disapprobation of banks circulating paper is not unknown, nor have I since observed any effects either on the morals or fortunes of our citizens, which are any counter balance for the public evils produced.—To J. W. EPPES. vi, 203. FORD ED., ix, 402. (P.F., Sep. 1813.)

713. —— ——. The toleration of banks of paper-discount costs the United States one half their war taxes; or, in other words, doubles the expense of every war.—To J. W. EPPES. vi, 201. FORD ED., ix, 400. (P.F., Sep. 1813.)

714. —— ——. From the establishment of the United States Bank to this day, I have preached against this system, and have been sensible no cure could be hoped, but in the catastrophe now happening.—To THOMAS COOPER. vi, 381. (M., 1814.)

715. —— ——. I have ever been the enemy of banks, not of those discounting for cash, but of those foisting their own paper into circulation, and thus banishing our cash. My zeal against those institutions was so warm and open at the establishment of the Bank of the United States, that I was derided as a maniac by the tribe of bank-mongers, who were seeking to filch from the public their swindling and barren gains.—To JOHN ADAMS. vi, 305. (M., Jan. 1814.)

716. —— ——. I am an enemy to all banks discounting bills or notes for anything but coin.—To DR. THOMAS COOPER. vi, 295. (M., Jan. 1814.)

717. —— ——. The system of banking we have both equally and ever reprobated. I contemplate it as a blot left in all our constitutions, which, if not covered, will end in their destruction, which is already hit by the gamblers in corruption, and is sweeping away in its progress the fortunes and morals of our citizens.—To JOHN TAYLOR. vi, 605. FORD ED., x, 28. (M., May 1816.)

718. —— ——. I do not know whether you may recollect how loudly my voice was raised against the establishment of banks in the beginning; but like that of Cassandra it was not listened to. I was set down as a madman by those who have since been victims to them. I little thought then how much

I was to suffer by them myself; for I, too, am taken in by endorsements for a friend to the amount of $20,000, for the payment of which I shall have to make sale of that much of my property. And yet the general revolution of fortunes, which these instruments have produced, seems not at all to have cured our country of this mania.—To THOMAS LEIPER. FORD ED., x, 254. (May 1823.)

719. BANKS, Mania for.—We are undone if this banking mania be not suppressed. *Aut Carthago, aut Roma delenda est.*—To ALBERT GALLATIN. vi, 498. (M., Oct. 1815.)

720. —— ——. The mania * * * has seized, by its delusions and corruptions, all the members of our governments, general, special, and individual.—To JOHN ADAMS. vi, 306. (M., Jan. 1814.)

721. —— ——. Knowing well that the Bank mania still possessed the great body of our countrymen, it was not expected that any radical cure of that could be at once effected. We must go further wrong, probably to a *ne plus ultra* before we shall be forced into what is right. Something will be obtained however, if we can excite, in those who think, doubt first, reflection next, and conviction at last.—To JOSEPH C. CABELL. FORD ED., ix, 499. (M., 1815.)

722. —— ——. Like a dropsical man calling out for water, water, our deluded citizens are clamoring for more banks, more banks. The American mind is now in that state of fever which the world has so often seen in the history of other nations. We are under the bank bubble, as England was under the South Sea bubble, France under the Mississippi bubble, and as every nation is liable to be, under whatever bubble, design or delusion may puff up in moments when off their guard. —To CHARLES YANCEY. vi, 515. FORD ED., x, 2. (M., Jan. 1816.)

723. —— ——. This infatuation of banks is a torrent which it would be a folly for me to get in the way of. I see that it must take its course, until actual ruin shall awaken us from its delusions.—To JOSEPH C. CABELL. vi, 300. (M., Jan. 1814.)

724. BANKS, Monopoly.—The monopoly of a single bank is certainly an evil. The multiplication of them was intended to cure it; but it multiplied an influence of the same character with the first, and completed the supplanting of the precious metals by a paper circulation. Between such parties the less we meddle the better.—To ALBERT GALLATIN. iv, 446. FORD ED., viii, 158. (W., 1802.)

725. BANKS, Paper.—Interdict forever, to both the State and National governments the power of establishing any paper bank; for without this interdiction we shall have the same ebbs and flows of medium, and the same revolutions of property to go through every twenty or thirty years.—To W. C. RIVES. vii, 147. FORD ED., x, 151. (M., 1819.)

726. BANKS, Power to establish.—The States should be applied to, to transfer the right of issuing circulating paper to Congress exclusively, *in perpetuum,* if possible, but during the war at least, with a saving of charter rights.—To J. W. EPPES. vi, 140. FORD ED., ix, 393. (M., June 1813.)

727. —— ——. The States should be urged to concede to the General Government, with a saving of chartered rights, the exclusive power of establishing banks of discount for paper.—To J. W. EPPES. vi, 427. FORD ED., ix, 417. (M., Nov. 1813.)

728. —— ——. I still believe that on proper representations of the subject, a great proportion of the Legislatures would cede to Congress their power of establishing banks, saving the charter rights already granted. And this should be asked, not by way of amendment to the Constitution, because until three-fourths should consent, nothing could be done; but accepted from them one by one, singly, as their consent might be obtained. Any single State, even if no other should come into the measure, would find its interest in arresting foreign bank paper immediately, and its own by degrees. Specie would flow in on them as paper disappeared. Their own banks would call in and pay off their notes gradually, and their constituents would thus be saved from the general wreck. Should the greater part of the States concede, as is expected, their power over banks to Congress, besides insuring their own safety, the paper of the non-conceding States might be so checked and circumscribed, by prohibiting its receipt in any of the conceding States, and even in the non-conceding as to duties, taxes, judgments, or other demands of the United States, or of the citizens of other States, that it would soon die of itself, and the medium of gold and silver be universally restored. This is what ought to be done. But it will not be done. *Carthago non delibitur.* The overbearing clamor of merchants, speculators, and projectors, will drive us before them with our eyes open, until, as in France, under the Mississippi bubble, our citizens will be overtaken by the crash of this baseless fabric, without other satisfaction than that of execrations on the heads of those functionaries, who, from ignorance, pusillanimity or corruption, have betrayed the fruits of their industry into the hands of projectors and swindlers.—To J. W. EPPES. vi, 245. FORD ED., ix, 415. (M., Nov. 1813.)

729. —— ——. The State Legislature should be immediately urged to relinquish the right of establishing banks of discount. Most of them will comply, on patriotic principles, under the convictions of the moment and the non-complying may be crowded into concurrence by legitimate devices.—To THOMAS COOPER. vi, 382. (M., Sep. 1814.)

730. —— ——. I do not remember the conversation between us which you mention * * * on your proposition to vest in Congress the exclusive power of establishing banks. My opposition to it must have been grounded, not on taking the power from the States, but on leaving any vestige of it in existence, even in the hands of Congress, because it would only have been a change of the organ of abuse.—To JOHN ADAMS. vi, 305. (M., Jan. 1814.)

731. BANKS, Precautions against.—In order to be able to meet a general combination of the banks against us, in a critical emergency, could we not make a beginning towards an independent use of our own money, towards holding our own bank in all the deposits where it is received, and letting the treasurer give his draft or note, for payment at any particular place, which, in a well-conducted government, ought to have as much credit as any private draft, or bank note, or bill, and would give us the same facilities which we derive from the banks.—To ALBERT GALLATIN. v, 520. FORD ED., viii, 285. (W., Dec. 1803.)

732. BANKS, Private Fortunes and.—Private fortunes, in the present state of our circulation, are at the mercy of those self-created money-lenders, and are prostrated by the floods of nominal money with which their avarice deluges us. He who lent his money to the public or to an individual, before the institution of the United States Bank, twenty years ago, when wheat was well sold at a dollar the bushel, and receives now his nominal sum when it sells at two dollars, is cheated of half his fortune; and by whom ? By the banks, which, since that, have thrown into circulation ten dollars of their nominal money where there was one at that time.—To JOHN W. EPPES. vi, 142. FORD ED., ix, 394. (M., June 1813.)

733. —— ——. It is cruel that such revolutions in private fortunes should be at the mercy of avaricious adventurers, who instead of employing their capital, if any they have, in manufactures, commerce, and other useful pursuits, make it an instrument to burden all the interchanges of property with their swindling profits, profits which are the price of no useful industry of theirs.—To DR. THOMAS COOPER. vi, 295. (M., 1814.)

734. —— ——. The flood of paper money had produced an exaggeration of nominal prices, and at the same time a facility of obtaining money, which not only encouraged speculations on fictitious capital, but seduced those of real capital, even in private life, to contract debts too freely. Had things continued in the same course, these might have been manageable; but the operations of the United States bank for the demolition of the State banks obliged these suddenly to call in more than half their paper, crushed all fictitious and doubtful capital, and reduced the prices of property and produce suddenly to one-third of what they had been.—To ALBERT GALLATIN. FORD ED., x, 176. (M., Dec. 1820.)

735. BANKS, Scarcity of Medium and.—Instead of yielding to the cries of scarcity of medium set up by speculators, projectors and commercial gamblers, no endeavors should be spared to begin the work of reducing it by such gradual means as may give time to private fortunes to preserve their poise, and settle down with the subsiding medium.—To J. W. EPPES. vi, 246. FORD ED., ix, 417. (M., Nov. 1813.)

736. —— ——. We are called on to add ninety millions more to the circulation. Proceeding in this career, it is infallible, that we must end where the Revolutionary paper ended. Two hundred millions was the whole amount of all the emissions of the old Congress, at which point their bills ceased to circulate. We are now at that sum, but with treble the population, and of course a longer tether. Our depreciation is, as yet, but about two for one. Owing to the support its credit receives from the small reservoirs of specie in the vaults of the banks, it is impossible to say at what point their notes will stop. Nothing is necessary to effect it but a general alarm; and that may take place whenever the public shall begin to reflect on, and perceive the impossibility that the banks should repay this sum. At present, caution is inspired no farther than to keep prudent men from selling property on long payments. Let us suppose the panic to arise at three hundred millions, a point to which every session of the Legislature hastens us by long strides. Nobody dreams that they would have three hundred millions of specie to satisfy the holders of their notes. Were they even to stop now, no one supposes they have two hundred millions in cash, or even the sixty-six and two-third millions, to which amount alone the law compels them to repay. One hundred and thirty-three and one-third millions of loss, then, is thrown on the public by law; and as to the sixty-six and two-thirds, which they are legally bound to pay, and ought to have in their vaults, every one knows there is no such amount of cash in the United States, and what would be the course with what they really have there? Their notes are refused. Cash is called for. The inhabitants of the banking towns will get what is in the vaults, until a few banks declare their insolvency; when, the general crush becoming evident, the others will withdraw even the cash they have, declare their bankruptcy at once, and have an empty house and empty coffers for the holders of their notes. In this scramble of creditors, the country gets nothing, the towns but little. What are they to do? Bring suits? A million of creditors bring a million of suits against John Nokes and Robert Styles, wheresoever to be found? All nonsense. The loss is total. And a sum is thus swindled from our citizens, of seven times the amount of the real debt, and four times that of the fictitious one of the United States, at the close of the war. All this they will justly charge on their Legislatures; but this will be poor satisfaction for the two or three hundred millions they will have lost. It is time, then, for the public functionaries to look to this. Perhaps it may not be too late. Perhaps, by giving time to the banks, they may call in and pay off their paper by degrees. But no remedy is ever to be expected while it rests with the State Legislatures. Personal

motive can be excited through so many avenues to their will, that, in their hands, it will continue to go on from bad to worse, until the catastrophe overwhelms us.—To J. W. EPPES. vi, 243. FORD ED., ix, 414. (M., Nov. 1813.)

737. —— —— Our circulating paper of the last year was estimated at two hundred millions of dollars. The new banks now petitioned for, to the several Legislatures, are for about sixty millions additional capital, and of course one hundred and eighty millions of additional circulation, nearly doubling that of the last year, and raising the whole mass to near four hundred millions, or forty for one, of the wholesome amount of circulation for a population of eight millions circumstanced as we are, and you remember how rapidly our money went down after our forty for one establishment in the Revolution. I doubt if the present trash can hold as long. I think the three hundred and eighty millions must blow all up in the course of the present year, or certainly it will be consummated by the reduplication to take place of course at the legislative meetings of the next winter. Should not prudent men, who possess stock in any moneyed institution, either draw and hoard the cash now while they can, or exchange it for canal stock, or such other as being bottomed on immovable property will remain unhurt by the crush?—To JOHN ADAMS. vi, 306. (M., Jan. 1814.)

738. —— ——. Two hundred millions in actual circulation and two hundred millions more likely to be legitimated by the legislative sessions of this winter, will give us about forty times the wholesome circulation for eight millions of people. When the new emissions get out, our legislatures will see, what they otherwise cannot believe, that it is possible to have too much money.—To PRESIDENT MADISON. FORD ED., ix, 453. (M., Feb. 1814.)

739. —— ——. The evils of this deluge of paper money are not to be removed, until our citizens are generally and radically instructed in their course and consequences, and silence by their authority the interested clamors and sophistry of speculating, shaving, and banking institutions. Till then we must be content to return, *quoad hoc*, to the savage state, to recur to barter in the exchange of our property, for the want of a stable, common measure of value, that now in use being less fixed than the beads and wampum of the Indian, and to deliver up our citizens, their property and their labor, passive victims to the swindling tricks of bankers and mountebankers.—To JOHN ADAMS. vii, 115. (M., 1819.)

740. BANKS, Sound Money.—But, it will be asked, are we to have no banks? Are merchants and others to be deprived of the resource of short accommodations, found so convenient? I answer, let us have banks; but let them be such as are alone to be found in any country on earth, except Great Britain. There is not a bank of discount on the continent of Europe (at least there was not one when I was there), which offers anything but cash in exchange for discounted bills. No one has a natural right to the trade of a money lender, but he who has the money to lend. Let those then among us, who have a moneyed capital, and who prefer employing it in loans rather than otherwise, set up banks, and give cash or national bills for the notes they discount. Perhaps, to encourage them, a larger interest than is legal in the other cases might be allowed them, on the condition of their lending for short periods only. It is from Great Britain we copy the idea of giving paper in exchange for discounted bills; and while we have derived from that country some good principles of government and legislation, we unfortunately run into the most servile imitations of all her practices, ruinous as they prove to her, and with the gulf yawning before us into which these very practices are precipitating her.—To JOHN W. EPPES. vi, 141. FORD ED., ix, 394. (M., June 1813.)

741. ———. Let banks continue if they please, but let them discount for cash alone or for treasury notes. They discount for cash alone in every other country on earth except Great Britain, and her too often unfortunate copyist, the United States. If taken in time they may be rectified by degrees, but if let alone till the alternative forces itself on us, of submitting to the enemy for want of funds, or the suppression of bank paper, either by law or by convulsion, we cannot foresee how it will end.—To J. W. EPPES. vi, 199. FORD ED., ix, 399. (P. F., Sept. 1813.)

742. ———. To the existence of banks of *discount for cash*, as on the continent of Europe, there can be no objection, because there can be no danger of abuse, and they are a convenience both to merchants and individuals. I think they should even be encouraged, by allowing them a larger than legal interest on short discounts, and tapering thence in proportion as the term of discount is lengthened, down to legal interest on those of a year or more.—To J. W. EPPES. vi, 247. FORD ED., ix, 417. (M., Nov. 1813.)

743. BANKS, Suspend Specie Payments.—The paper bubble is burst. This is what you and I, and every reasoning man, seduced by no obliquity of mind or interest, have long foreseen. We were laboring under a dropsical fulness of circulating medium. Nearly all of it is now called in by the banks, who have the regulation of the safety-valves of our fortunes, and who condense and explode them at their will. Lands in this State [Virginia] cannot now be sold for a year's rent; and unless our Legislature have wisdom enough to effect a remedy by a gradual diminution only of the medium, there will be a general revolution of property in this State. Over our own paper and that of other States coming among us, they have competent powers: over that of the Bank of the United States there is doubt, not here, but elsewhere.

That bank will probably conform voluntarily to such regulations as the Legislature may prescribe for the others. If they do not, we must shut their doors, and join the other States which deny the right of Congress to establish banks, and solicit them to agree to some mode of settling this constitutional question. They have themselves twice decided against their right, and twice for it. Many of the States have been uniform in denying it, and between such parties the Constitution has provided no umpire.—To JOHN ADAMS. vii, 142. FORD ED., x, 147. (M. Nov. 1819.) See MONEY and PAPER MONEY

744. BANNEKER (Benjamin), Talents of.—We have now in the United States a negro, the son of a black man born in Africa and a black woman born in the United States who is a very respectable mathematician. I procured him to be employed under one of our chief directors in laying out the new Federal city on the Potomac, and in the intervals of his leisure, while on that work, he made an almanac for the next year, which he sent me in his own handwriting, and which I enclose to you. I have seen very elegant solutions of geometrical problems by him. Add to this that he is a very worthy and respectable member of society. He is a free man. I shall be delighted to see these instances of moral eminence so multiplied as to prove that the want of talents observed in them, is merely the effect of their degraded condition, and not proceeding from any difference in the structure of the parts on which intellect depends.—To MARQUIS DE CONDORCET. FORD ED., v, 379. (Pa., 1791.)

745. BARBARISM, America and.—We are destined to be a barrier against the return of ignorance and barbarism.—To JOHN ADAMS. vii, 27. (M., 1816.)

746. BARBARISM, End to.—Barbarism * * * will in time, I trust, disappear from the earth.—To WILLIAM LUDLOW. vii, 377. (M. 1824.)

— BARBARY STATES, Algerine Captives.—See CAPTIVES.

747. BARBARY STATES, A Confederation against.—I was very unwilling that we should acquiesce in the European humiliation of paying a tribute to those * * * pirates, and endeavored to form an association of the powers subject to habitual depredations from them. I accordingly prepared, and proposed to their ministers at Paris, for consultation with their governments, articles of a special confederation.—AUTOBIOGRAPHY. i, 65. FORD ED., i, 91. (1821.)

748. BARBARY STATES, Confederation Articles.—Proposals for concerted operation among the powers at war with the piratical States of Barbary: 1. It is proposed, that the several powers at war with the piratical States of Barbary, or any two or more of them who shall be willing, shall enter into a convention to carry on their operations against those States, in concert, beginning with the Algerines. 2. This convention shall remain open to any other power who shall at any future time wish to accede to it; the parties reserving the right to prescribe the conditions of such accession, according to the circumstances existing at the time it shall be proposed. 3.

The object of the convention shall be to compel the piratical States to perpetual peace, without price, and to guarantee that peace to each other. 4. The operations for obtaining this peace shall be constant cruisers on their coast, with a naval force now to be agreed on. It is not proposed that this force shall be so considerable as to be inconvenient to any party. It is believed that half a dozen frigates, with as many tenders or Xebecs, one half of which shall be in cruise, while the other half is at rest, will suffice. 5. The force agreed to be necessary shall be furnished by the parties in certain quotas now to be fixed; it being expected that each will be willing to contribute in such proportion as circumstances may render reasonable. 6. The miscarriages often proceed from the want of harmony among officers of different nations, the parties shall now consider and decide whether it will not be better to contribute their quotas in money to be employed in fitting out, and keeping on duty, a single fleet of the force agreed on. 7. The difficulties and delays too which will attend the management of these operations, if conducted by the parties themselves separately, distant as their Courts may be from one another, and incapable of meeting in consultation, suggest a question whether it will not be better for them to give full powers for that purpose to their Ambassadors or other Ministers Resident at some one Court of Europe, who shall form a Committee or Council for carrying this convention into effect; wherein the vote of each member shall be computed in proportion to the quota of his sovereign, and the majority so computed shall prevail in all questions within the view of this convention. The Court of Versailles is proposed, on account of its neighborhood to the Mediterranean, and because all those powers are represented there, who are likely to become parties to this convention. 8. To save to that council the embarrassment of personal solicitations for office, and to assure the parties that their contributions will be applied solely to the object for which they are destined, there shall be no establishment of officers for the said Council, such as Commissioners, Secretaries, or any other kind, with either salaries or perquisites, nor any other lucrative appointments but such whose functions are to be exercised on board the said vessels. 9. Should war arise between any two of the parties to this convention it shall not extend to this enterprise, nor interrupt it; but as to this they shall be reputed at peace. 10. When Algiers shall be reduced to peace, the other piratical States, if they refuse to discontinue their piracies, shall become the objects of this convention, either successively or together, as shall seem best. 11. Where this convention would interfere with treaties actually existing between any two of the parties and the said States of Barbary, the treaty shall prevail, and such party shall be allowed to withdraw from the operations against that State.—AUTOBIOGRAPHY. i, 65. FORD ED., i, 91.

749. BARBARY STATES, Congress and.—Nothing was now wanting to bring it into direct and formal consideration but the assent of our government, and their authority to make the formal proposition. I communicated to them the favorable prospect of protecting our commerce from the Barbary depredations, and for such a continuance of time as, by an exclusion of them from the sea, to change their habits and characters from a predatory to an agricultural people: towards which however it was expected they

would contribute a frigate, and its expenses to be in constant cruise. But they were in no condition to make any such engagement. Their recommendatory powers for obtaining contributions were so openly neglected by the several States that they declined an engagement which they were conscious they could not fulfil with punctuality; and so it fell through.—AUTOBIOGRAPHY. i, 67. FORD ED., i, 93. (1821.)

750. BARBARY STATES, Europe and.—Spain had just concluded a treaty with Algiers, at the expense of three millions of dollars, and did not like to relinquish the benefit of that until the other party should fail in their observance of it. Portugal, Naples, the two Sicilies, Venice, Malta, Denmark and Sweden were favorably disposed to such an association; but their representatives at Paris expressed apprehensions that France would interfere, and, either openly or secretly support the Barbary powers; and they required that I should ascertain the dispositions of the Count de Vergennes on the subject. I had before taken occasion to inform him of what we were proposing, and therefore did not think it proper to insinuate any doubt of the fair conduct of his government; but stating our propositions, I mentioned the apprehensions entertained by us that England would interfere in behalf of those piratical governments. "She dares not do it," said he. I pressed it no further. The other Agents were satisfied with this indication of his sentiments.—AUTOBIOGRAPHY. i, 67. FORD ED., i, 93. (1821.)

751. BARBARY STATES, Great Britain and.—I hinted to the Count de Vergennes that I thought the English capable of administering aid to the Algerines. He seemed to think it impossible on account of the scandal it would bring on them.—To JOHN JAY. i, 575. FORD ED., iv, 228. (P., 1786.)

752. BARBARY STATES, Jefferson's Views on.—Our instructions relative to the Barbary States having required us to proceed by way of negotiation to obtain their peace, it became our duty to do this to the best of our power. Whatever might be our private opinions, they were to be suppressed, and the line marked out to us was to be followed. It has been so, honestly and zealously. It was, therefore, never material for us to consult together, on the best plan of conduct toward these States. I acknowledge, I very early thought it would be best to effect a peace through the medium of war. Though it is a question with which we have nothing to do, yet as you propose some discussion of it, I shall trouble you with my reasons. Of the four positions laid down by you, I agree to the three first, which are, in substance, that the good offices of our friends cannot procure us a peace without paying its price; that they cannot materially lessen that price; and that paying it, we can have the peace in spite of the intrigues of our enemies. As to the fourth, that the longer the negotiation is delayed, the larger will be the demand; this will depend on the intermediate captures: if they are many and rich, the price may be raised; if few and poor, it will be lessened. However, if it is decided that we shall buy a peace, I know no reason for delaying the operation, but should rather think it ought to be hastened; but I should prefer the obtaining it by war. 1. Justice is in favor of this opinion. 2. Honor favors it. 3. It will procure us respect in Europe; and respect is a safeguard to interest. 4. It will arm the Federal head with the safest of all the instruments of coercion over its delinquent members, and prevent it from using what would be less safe. I think that so far, you go with me. But in the next steps, we shall differ. 5. I think it least expensive. I ask a fleet of one hundred and fifty guns, the one-half of which shall be in constant cruise. This fleet, built, manned and victualled for six months will cost four hundred and fifty thousand pounds sterling. Its annual expense will be three hundred pounds sterling a gun, including everything; this will be forty-five thousand pounds sterling a year. I take the British experience for the basis of my calculation; though we know, from our own experience, that we can do it in this way, for pounds lawful, what costs them pounds sterling. Were we to charge all this to the Algerine war, it would amount to little more than we must pay, if we buy peace. But as it is proper and necessary that we should establish a small marine force (even were we to buy a peace from the Algerines), and as that force, laid up in our dockyards, would cost us half as much annually, as if kept in order for service, we have a right to say that only twenty-two thousand and five hundred pounds sterling, per annum, should be charged to the Algerine war. 6. It will be as effectual. To all the mismanagements of Spain and Portugal, urged to show that war against these people is ineffectual, I urge a single fact to prove the contrary, where there is any management. About forty years ago, the Algerines having broken their treaty with France, that court sent Monsieur de Massiac, with one large and two small frigates; he blockaded the harbor of Algiers three months, and they subscribed to the terms he proposed. If it be admitted, however, that war, on the fairest prospects, is still exposed to uncertainties, I weigh against this the greater uncertainty of the duration of a peace bought with money, from such a people, from a Dey eighty years old, and by a nation who, on the hypothesis of buying peace, is to have no power on the sea to enforce an observance of it. So far, I have gone on the supposition that the whole weight of this war would rest on us. But, 1. Naples will join us. The character of their naval minister (Acton), his known sentiments with respect to the peace Spain is officiously trying to make for them, and his dispositions against the Algerines, give the best grounds to believe it. 2. Every principle of reason assures us that Portugal will join us. I state this as taking for granted, what all seem to believe, that they will not be at peace with Algiers. I suppose, then, that a convention might be formed between Portugal, Naples and the United States, by which the burthen of the war might be quotaed on them, according to their respective wealth; and the term of it should be, when Algiers should subscribe to a peace with all three, on equal terms. This might be left open for other nations to accede to, and many, if not most, of the powers of Europe (except France, England, Holland, and Spain, if her peace be made), would sooner or later enter into the confederacy, for the sake of having their peace with the piratical States guaranteed by the whole. I suppose, that, in this case, our proportion of force would not be the half of what I first calculated on.—To JOHN ADAMS. i, 591. (P., July 1786.)

753. ——— ———. Were the honor and advantage of establishing such a confederacy [against the piratical powers] out of the question, yet the necessity that the United States should have some marine force, and the happiness of this, as the ostensible cause for beginning it, would decide on its propriety. It will be said, there is no money in the treasury. There never will be money in the treasury, till the confederacy shows its teeth. The States must see the rod; perhaps it must be felt by some one of them. I am persuaded, all of them would rejoice to see every one obliged to furnish its contributions. It is not the difficulty of furnishing them, which beggars the treasury, but the fear that others will not furnish as much. Every rational citizen must wish to see an effective instrument of coercion, and should fear to see it on any other element than the water.—To JAMES MONROE. i, 606. FORD ED., iv, 264. (P., 1786.)

754. BARBARY STATES, The Mediterranean and.—Algiers, Tunis and Tripoli, remaining hostile, will shut up the Mediterranean to us.—To GOVERNOR HENRY. i, 601. (P., 1786.)

755. ——— ———. The Algerines form an obstacle; but the object of our commerce in the Mediterranean is so immense that we ought to surmount that obstacle, and I believe it can be done by means in our power, and which, instead of fouling us with the dishonorable and criminal baseness of France and England, will place us in the road to respect with all the world.—To E. RUTLEDGE. iii, 110. (P., 1789.)

—— BARBARY STATES, Morocco.—See MOROCCO.

756. BARBARY STATES, Purchasing Peace with.—What will you do with the piratical States? Buy a peace at their enormous price; force one; or abandon the carriage into the Mediterranean to other powers? All these measures are disagreeable.—To ELBRIDGE GERRY. i, 557. (P., 1786.)

757. ——— ———. The States of Algiers, Tunis and Tripoli hold their peace at a price which would be felt by every man in his settlement with the taxgatherer.—To PATRICK HENRY. i, 601. (P., 1786.)

758. ——— ———. It is not in the choice of the States, whether they will pay money to cover their trade against the Algerines. If they obtain a peace by negotiation, they must pay a great sum of money for it; if they do nothing, they must pay a great sum of money in the form of insurance; and in either way, as great a one as in the way of force, and probably less effectual.—To JAMES MONROE. i, 607. FORD ED., iv, 265. (P., 1786.)

759. ——— ———. Congress must begin by getting money. When they have this, it is a matter of calculation whether they will buy a peace, or force one, or do nothing.—To JOHN ADAMS. i, 585. (P., 1786.)

760. ——— ———. The continuance of [a purchased] peace with the Barbary States will depend on their idea of our power to enforce it, and on the life of the particular Dey, or other head of the government, with whom it is contracted. Congress will, no doubt, weigh these circumstances against the expense and probable success of compelling a peace by arms. —To JAMES MONROE. i, 565. FORD ED., iv, 221. (P., 1786.)

761. ——— ———. In London Mr. Adams and I had conferences with a Tripoline ambassador, named Abdrahaman. He asked us thirty thousand guineas for a peace with his court, and as much for Tunis, for which he said he could answer. What we were authorized to offer, being to this but as a drop to a bucket, our conferences were repeated only for the purpose of obtaining information. If the demands of Algiers and Morocco should be in proportion to this, according to their superior power, it is easy to foresee that the United States will not buy a peace with money.—To WILLIAM CARMICHAEL. i, 551. (P., 1786.)

762. —— ——. The Tripoline ambassador offered peace for 30,000 guineas for Tripoli, and as many for Tunis. Calculating on this scale, Morocco should ask 60,000, and Algiers 120,000.—To DAVID HUMPHREYS. i, 559. (P., 1786.)

763. —— ——. A second plan might be to obtain peace by purchasing it. For this we have the example of rich and powerful nations, in this instance counting their interest more than their honor.—REPORT ON MEDITERRANEAN TRADE. vii, 522. (1790.)

764. —— ——. As the duration of this peace cannot be counted on with certainty, and we look forward to the necessity of coercion by cruises on their coast, to be kept up during the whole of their cruising season, you will be pleased to inform yourself * * * of every circumstance which may influence or guide us in undertaking and conducting such an operation.—To JOHN PAUL JONES. iii, 438. (Pa., 1792.)

765. BARBARY STATES, Suppression of.—The attempts heretofore made to suppress the [Barbary] powers have been to exterminate them at one blow. They are too numerous and powerful by land for that. A small effort, but long continued, seems to be the only method. By suppressing their marine and trade totally, and continuing this till the present race of seamen should be pretty well out of the way, and the younger people betake themselves to husbandry for which their soil and climate are well fitted, these nests of banditti might be reformed.—To JAMES MONROE. FORD ED., iv, 33. (P., 1785.)

766. BARBARY STATES, Tribute to. —It is impossible I fear to find out what [tribute] is given by other countries [to the piratical States]. Either shame or jealousy makes them wish to keep it secret.—To JAMES MONROE. FORD ED., iv, 31. (P., 1785.)

767. —— ——. The Algerines, I fear, will ask such a tribute for the forbearance of their piracies as the United States would be unwilling to pay. When this idea comes across my mind my faculties are absolutely suspended between indignation and impotence. I think whatever sums we are obliged to pay for freedom of navigation in the European seas, should be levied on European commerce with us, by a separate impost; that these powers may see that they protect these enormities for their own loss. To NATHANIEL GREENE. FORD ED., iv, 25. (P., 1785.)

768. —— ——. Such [European] powers as should refuse [to join a confederation to suppress the Barbary piracies] would give us a just right to turn pirates also on their West India trade, and to require an annual tribute which might reimburse what we may be obliged to pay to obtain a safe navigation in their seas. —To JAMES MONROE. FORD ED., iv, 33. (P., 1785.)

769. BARBARY STATES, War with. —From what I learn from the temper of my countrymen and their tenaciousness of money, it will be more easy to raise ships to fight these pirates into reason than money to bribe them.— To EZRA STILES. ii, 78. (P., 1786.)

770. —— ——. The motives pleading for war rather than tribute [to the piratical States] are numerous and honorable; those opposing them are mean and short-sighted.—To JAMES MONROE. FORD ED., iv, 32. (P., 1785.)

— BARBARY STATES, War with Tripoli.—See TRIPOLI.

771. BARBARY STATES, Weakness of.—These pirates are contemptibly weak. Morocco, who has just dared to commit an outrage on us, owns only four or five frigates of 18 or 20 guns. There is not a port in their country which has more than 13 feet of water. Tunis is not quite so strong (having three or four frigates only, small and worthless); is more mercantile than predatory, and would easily be led to treat either by money or fear. Tripoli has one frigate only. Algiers alone possesses any power, and they are brave. As far as I have been able to discover, she possesses about sixteen vessels, from 22 up to 52 guns; but the vessels of all these powers are wretched in the last degree, being mostly built of the discordant pieces of other vessels which they take and pull asunder; their cordage and sails are of the same kind, taken from vessels of different sizes and powers, seldom any two guns of the same bore and all of them light.—To JAMES MONROE. FORD ED., iv, 31. (P., 1785.) See MOROCCO, TRIPOLI and TUNIS.

772. BARCLAY (Thomas), Missions to Morocco.—Though we are not authorized to delegate to Mr. Barclay the power of ultimately signing the treaty, yet such is our reliance on his wisdom, his integrity, and his attention to the instructions with which he is charged, that we assure his Majesty, the conditions which he shall arrange and send to us, shall be returned with our signature.*—To THE EMPEROR OF MOROCCO. i, 419. (P., 1785.)

773. —— ——. Mr. Barclay's mission has been attended with complete success. For this we are indebted, unquestionably, to the influence and good offices of the court of Madrid.—To JOHN JAY. ii, 85. (P., 1786.)

774. —— ——. You have my full and hearty approbation of the treaty you obtained from Morocco, which is better and on better terms than I expected.—To THOMAS BARCLAY. ii, 125. (P., 1787.)

775. —— ——. You are appointed by the President * * * to go to the court of Morocco, for the purpose of obtaining from the new Emperor, a recognition of our treaty with his father. As it is thought best that you should go in some definite character, that of consul has been adopted.—To THOMAS BARCLAY. iii, 261. (P., 1791.)

776. —— ——. As you have acted since my arrival in France, in the characters of Consul General for that country, and Minister to the Court of Morocco, and also as agent in some particular transactions for the State of Virginia, I think it is a duty to yourself, to truth, and to justice, on your departure for America, to declare that in all these characters,

* Mr. Barclay was U. S. Consul-General at Paris. Jefferson and Adams appointed him to negotiate a treaty with the Emperor of Morocco.—EDITOR.

as far as has come within my notice, you have acted with judgment, with attention, with integrity and honor.*—To THOMAS BARCLAY. ii, 211. (P., 1787.)

777. BARLOW (Joel), Proposed History by.—Mr. Madison and myself have cut out a piece of work for you, which is to write the history of the United States, from the close of the war downwards. We are rich ourselves in materials, and can open all the public archives to you; but your residence here [Washington] is essential, because a great deal of the knowledge of things is not on paper, but only within ourselves, for verbal communication. John Marshall is writing the life of General Washington from his papers. It is intended to come out just in time to influence the next Presidential election. It is written, therefore, principally with a view to electioneering purposes. But it will consequently be out in time to aid you with information, as well as to point out the perversions of truth necessary to be rectified.—To JOEL BARLOW. iv, 438. FORD ED., viii, 151. (W., May 1802.)

778. —— ——. You owe to republicanism, and indeed to the future hopes of man, a faithful record of the *march* of this government, which may encourage the oppressed to go and do likewise. Your talents, your principles, and your means of access to public and private sources of information, with the leisure which is at your command, point you out as the person who is to do this act of justice to those who believe in the improvability of the condition of man, and who have acted on that behalf, in opposition to those who consider man as a beast of burthen made to be ridden by him who has genius enough to get a bridle into his mouth.—To JOEL BARLOW. v, 496. FORD ED., ix, 269. (M., 1810.)

779. —— ——. I felicitate you on your destination to Paris [as minister]. * * * Yet it is not unmixed with regret. What is to become of our post-revolutionary history? Of the antidotes of truth to the misrepresentations of Marshall? This example proves the wisdom of the maxim, never put off till to-morrow what can be done to-day.—To JOEL BARLOW. v, 587. FORD ED., ix, 322. (M., April 1811.)

780. BARLOW (Joel), Works of.—I thank you for your "Conspiracy of Kings" and advice to the privileged orders. Be assured that your endeavors to bring the trans-Atlantic world into the road of reason, are not without their effect in America. Some here are disposed to move retrograde, and to take their stand in the rear of Europe, now advancing to the high ground of natural right.—To JOEL BARLOW. iii, 451. FORD ED., vi, 88. (P., 1792.)

781. —— ——. Thomas Jefferson returns thanks to Mr. Barlow for the copy of the "Columbiad" he has been so kind as to send him; the eye discovers at once the excellence of the mechanical execution of the work, and he is persuaded that the mental part will be found to have merited it. He will not do it the injustice of giving it such a reading as his situation here [Washington] would admit,

* Mr. Barclay, while acting for the United States in Europe, was engaged in commercial transactions on his own account. His arrest for debt by creditors led to some discussion with the French government which is embodied in Jefferson's Writings. —EDITOR.

of a few minutes at a time, and at intervals of many days. He will reserve it for that retirement after which he is panting, and not now very distant, where he may enjoy it in full concert with its kindred scenes, amidst those rural delights which join in chorus with the poet and give to his song all its magic effect.—To JOEL BARLOW. v, 238. (W., 1808.)

—— **BARRUEL (Abbe), Book by.**—See ILLUMINATI.

—— **BARRY, Commodore J.**—See MOURNING.

782. BASTILE, Fall of the.—The mob now openly joined by the French guards forced the prison of St. Lazare, released all the prisoners, and took a great store of corn which they carried to the corn market. Here they got some arms, and the French guards began to form and train them. The committee determined to raise forty-eight thousand Bourgeoise, or rather to restrain their numbers to forty-eight thousand. On the 14th [July], they sent one of their members (Monsieur de Corny, whom we knew in America) to the Hotel des Invalides, to ask arms for their Garde Bourgeoise. He was followed by, or by found there, a great mob. The Governor of the Invalides came out, and represented the impossibility of delivering his arms, without the orders of those from whom he received them. De Corny advised the people then to retire and retired himself; and the people took possession of the arms. It was remarkable, that not only the Invalides themselves made no opposition, but that a body of five thousand foreign troops, encamped within four hundred yards, never stirred. Monsieur de Corny and five others were then sent to ask arms of Monsieur de Launey, Governor of the Bastile. They found a great collection of people already before the place, and they immediately planted a flag of truce, which was answered by a like flag hoisted on the parapet. The deputation prevailed on the people to fall back a little, advanced themselves to make their demand of the Governor, and in that instant a discharge from the Bastile killed four of those nearest to the deputies. The deputies retired; the people rushed against the place, and almost in an instant were in possession of a fortification, defended by one hundred men, of infinite strength, which in other times had stood several regular sieges, and had never been taken. How they got in, has, as yet, been impossible to discover. Those who pretend to have been of the party tell so many different stories, as to destroy the credit of them all. They took all the arms, discharged the prisoners, and such of the garrison as were not killed in the first moment of fury; carried the Governor and Lieutenant Governor to the Gréve (the place of public execution), cut off their heads, and sent them through the city in triumph to the Palais Royal.—To JOHN JAY. iii, 76. (P., July 1, 1789.)

783. BASTROP'S CASE, Account of.—I find Bastrop's case less difficult than I had expected. My view of it is this: The Governor of Louisiana being desirous of introducing the culture of wheat into that province engages Bastrop as an agent for carrying that object into effect. He agrees to lay off twelve leagues square on the Washita and Bayou liard as a settlement for the culture of wheat to which Bastrop is to bring five hundred families, each of which families is to have four hundred arpens of the land; the residue of the twelve leagues square, we may understand, was to be Bastrop's premium. The government was to bear the expense of bringing these emigrants from New Madrid, and was to allow them rations for six months,—Bastrop undertaking to provide the rations, and the government paying a seal and a half for each. Bastrop binds himself to settle the five hundred families in three years, and the Governor especially declares that if within that time the major part of the establishment shall not have been made good, the *twelve leagues square*, destined for Bastrop's settlers, shall be occupied by the families first presenting themselves for that purpose. Bastrop brings on some settlers,—how many does not appear, and the intendant, from a want of funds, suspends further proceeding in the settlement until the King's decision. (His decision of what? Doubtless whether the settlement shall proceed on these terms, and the funds be furnished by the King? or shall be abandoned?) He promises Bastrop, at the same time, that the former limitation of three years shall be extended to two years, after the course of the contract shall have again commenced to be executed, and the determination of the King shall be made known to Bastrop. Here, then, is a complete suspension of the undertaking until the King's decision, and his silence from that time till, and when, he ceded the province, must be considered as an abandonment of the project. There are several circumstances in this case offering ground for question, whether Bastrop is entitled to any surplus of the lands. But this will be an investigation for the Attorney General. But the uttermost he can claim is a surplus proportioned to the number of families to be settled, that is to say, a quota of land bearing such a proportion to the number of families he settled (deducting four hundred arpens for each of them) as one hundred and forty-four square leagues bear to the whole number of five hundred families. The important fact, therefore, to be settled, is the number of families he established there before the suspension.—To ALBERT GALLATIN. v, 231. (Jan. 1808.)

784. BATTURE, Authority over.—Mr. Livingston, * * * finding that we considered the Batture as now resting with Congress,* and that it is our duty to keep it clear of all adversary possession till their decision is obtained [has written] a letter to the Secretary of State, which, if we understand it, amounts to a declaration that he will * * * bring the authority of the court into array against that of the Executive, and endeavor to obtain a forcible possession. But I presume that the court knows too well that the title of the United States to land is subject to the jurisdiction of no court, it having never been deemed safe to submit the major interests of the nation to an ordinary tribunal, or to any one but such as the Legislature establishes for the special occasion; and the marshal will find his duty too plainly marked out in the act of March 3, 1807, to be at a loss to determine what authority he is to obey.—To GOVERNOR CLAIBORNE. v, 319. (W., July 1808.)

785. BATTURE, Jefferson's action in.—The interposition noticed by the Legislature of Orleans was an act of duty of the office I then occupied. Charged with the care of the general interests of the nation, and among these with the preservation of their lands from intrusion, I exercised, on their behalf, a right

* Jefferson in a special message, March 7, 1808, laid the case before Congress for its action.—EDITOR.

given by nature to all men, individual or associated, that of rescuing their own property wrongfully taken. In cases of forcible entry on individual possessions, special provisions, both of the common and civil law, have restrained the right of rescue by private force, and substituted the aid of the civil power. But no law has restrained the right of the nation itself from removing by its own arm, intruders on its possessions. On the contrary, a statute recently passed, had required that such removals should be diligently made. The Batture of New Orleans, being a part of the bed contained between the two banks of the river, a naked shoal indeed at low water, but covered through the whole season of its regular full tides, and then forming the ground of the port and harbor for the upper navigation, over which vessels ride of necessity when moored to the bank, I deemed it public property, in which all had a common use. The removal, too, of the force which had possessed itself of it, was the more urgent from the interruption it might give to the commerce, and other lawful uses, of the inhabitants of the city and of the Western waters generally.—To GOVERNOR CLAIBORNE. v, 518. (M., 1810.)

786. BATTURE, Livingston's suit.—Livingston has served a writ on me, stating damages at $100,000.—To PRESIDENT MADISON. FORD ED., ix, 275. (M., 1810.)

787. BATTURE, Marshall's bias and.—In speaking of Livingston's suit, I omitted to observe that it is a little doubted that his knowledge of Marshall's character has induced him to bring this action. His twistifications in the case of Marbury, in that of Burr, and the Yazoo case show how dexterously he can reconcile law to his own personal biasses; and nobody seems to doubt that he is ready prepared to decide that Livingston's right to the batture is unquestionable, and that I am bound to pay for it with my private fortune.—To PRESIDENT MADISON. FORD ED., ix, 276. (M., 1810.)

788. ——. What the issue of the case ought to be, no unbiased man can doubt. What it will be, no one can tell. The judge's [Marshall's] inveteracy is profound, and his mind of that gloomy malignity which will never let him forego the opportunity of satiating it on a victim. His decisions, his instructions to a jury, his allowances and disallowances and garblings of evidence, must all be subjects of appeal. I consider that as my only chance of saving my fortune from entire wreck. And to whom is my appeal? From the judge in Burr's case to himself and his associate judges in the case of Marbury v. Madison. Not exactly, however. I observe old Cushing is dead. At length, then, we have a chance of getting a republican majority in the Supreme judiciary.—To ALBERT GALLATIN. FORD ED., ix, 284. (M., Sep. 1810.)

789. BATTURE, Title to.—I have no concern at all in maintaining the title to the batture. It would be totally unnecessary for me to employ counsel to go into the question at all for my own defence. That is solidly built on the simple fact, that if I were in error, it was honest, and not imputable to that gross and palpable corruption or injustice which makes a public magistrate responsible to a private party.—To ALBERT GALLATIN. v, 537. (M., 1810.)

790. BATTURE, True course in.—If human reason is not mere illusion, and law a labyrinth without a clew, no error has been committed [in the Batture case].—BATTURE CASE. viii, 604. (1812.)

791. BAYARD (James A.), Aaron Burr and.—Edward Livingston tells me that Bayard applied to-day or last night to General Samuel Smith, and represented to him the expediency of his coming over to the States who vote for Burr [for President], that there was nothing in the way of appointment which he might not command, and particularly mentioned the Secretaryship of the Navy. Smith asked him if he was authorized to make the offer. He said he was authorized. Smith told this to Livingston, and to W. C. Nicholas who confirms it to me. Bayard, in like manner, tempted Livingston, not by offering any particular office, but by representing to him his (Livingston's) intimacy and connection with Burr; that from him he had everything to expect, if he would come over to him. To Doctor Linn of New Jersey, they have offered the government of New Jersey.—THE ANAS. ix, 202. FORD ED., i, 291. (Feb. 1808.) See ELECTIONS, PRESIDENTIAL, 1800.

792. BEAUMARCHAIS (M.), Claim of.—I hear that Mr. Beaumarchais means to make himself heard, if the memorial which he sends by an agent in the present packet is not attended to as he thinks it ought to be. He called on me with it and desired me to recommend his case to a decision, and to note in my dispatch that it was the first time he had spoken to me on the subject. This is true, it being the first time I ever saw him; but my recommendations would be as displaced as unnecessary. I assured him Congress would do in that business what justice should require, and their means enabled them.—To JOHN JAY. ii, 232. (P., 1787.)

793. ———— ————. A final decision of some sort should be made on Beaumarchais's affairs. —To JAMES MADISON. ii, 209. FORD ED., iv, 423. (P., 1787.)

794. BEE, The Honey.—The honey-bee is not a native of our continent. Marcgrove, indeed, mentions a species of honey-bee in Brazil. But this has no sting, and is therefore different from the one we have, which resembles perfectly that of Europe. The Indians concur with us in the tradition that it was brought from Europe; but when, and by whom, we know not. The bees have generally extended themselves into the country, a little in advance of the white settlers. The Indians, therefore, call them the white man's fly, and consider their approach as indicating the approach of the settlements of the whites.— NOTES ON VIRGINIA. viii, 319. FORD ED., iii, 175. (1782.)

795. ———— ————. How far northwardly have these insects been found? That they are unknown in Lapland. I infer from Scheffer's information, that the Laplanders eat the pine bark, prepared in a certain way, instead of those things sweetened with sugar. * * * Certainly if they had honey, it would be a better substitute for sugar than any preparation of the pine bark. Kalm tells us the honey-bee cannot live through the winter in Canada. They furnish then an additional remarkable fact, first observed by the Count de Buffon, and which has thrown such a blaze of light on the field of natural history, that no animals are found in both continents, but those which are able to bear the cold of those regions where they prob-

ably join.—NOTES ON VIRGINIA. viii, 320. FORD ED., iii, 176. (1782.)

796. BEER vs. WHISKY.—There is before the Assembly [of Virginia] a petition of a Captain Miller, which I have at heart, because I have great esteem for the petitioner as an honest and useful man. He is about to settle in our country, and to establish a brewery, in which art I think him as skilful a man as has ever come to America. I wish to see this beverage become common instead of the whisky which kills one-third of our citizens, and ruins their families. He is staying with me until he can fix himself, and I should be thankful for information from time to time of the progress of his petition.—To CHARLES YANCEY. vi, 515. FORD ED., x, 2. (M., 1815.)

797. BELLIGERENTS, Code of Rules for.—First. The original arming and equipping of vessels in the ports of the United States by any of the belligerent powers for military service, offensive or defensive, is deemed unlawful. Second. Equipment of merchant vessels by either of the belligerent parties in the ports of the United States, purely for the accommodation of them as such, is deemed lawful. Third. Equipments in the ports of the United States of vessels of war in the immediate service of the government of any of the belligerent parties, which, if done to other vessels, would be of a doubtful nature, as being applicable either to commerce or war, are deemed lawful, except those which shall have made prize of the subjects, people or property of France, coming with their prizes into the ports of the United States, pursuant to the seventeenth article of our treaty of amity and commerce with France. Fourth. Equipments in the ports of the United States by any of the parties at war with France, of vessels fitted for merchandise and war, whether with or without commissions, which are doubtful in their nature, as being applicable either to commerce or war, are deemed lawful, except those which shall have made prize, &c. Fifth. Equipments of any of the vessels of France in the ports of the United States, which are doubtful in their nature, as being applicable to commerce or war, are deemed lawful. Sixth. Equipments of every kind in the ports of the United States of privateers of the powers at war with France, are deemed unlawful. Seventh. Equipments of vessels in the ports of the United States which are of a nature solely adapted to war, are deemed unlawful; except those stranded or wrecked, as mentioned in the eighteenth article of our treaty with France, the sixteenth of our treaty with the United Netherlands, the ninth of our treaty with Prussia, and except those mentioned in the nineteenth article of our treaty with France, the seventeenth of our treaty with the United Netherlands, the eighteenth of our treaty with Prussia. Eighth. Vessels of either of the parties not armed, or armed previous to their coming into the ports of the United States, which shall not have infringed any of the foregoing rules may lawfully engage or enlist therein their own subjects, or aliens not being inhabitants of the United

States, except privateers of the powers at war with France, and except those vessels which shall have made prize, &c. The foregoing rules, having been considered by us [the Cabinet] at several meetings, and being now unanimously approved, they are submitted to the President of the United States.—CABINET DECISION. ix, 440. FORD ED., vi, 358. (Aug. 3, 1793.)

798. BELLIGERENTS, History of Rules.—At a cabinet meeting on account of the British letter-of-marque ship Jane, said to have put up waste boards, to have pierced two port-holes, and mounted two cannon (which she brought in) on new carriages which she did not bring in, and consequently having sixteen, instead of fourteen, guns mounted, it was agreed that a letter-of-marque, or vessel *armé en guerre*, and *en marchandise*, is not a privateer, and, therefore, not to be ordered out of our ports. It was agreed by Hamilton, Knox, and myself, that the case of such a vessel does not depend on the treaties, but on the law of nations. Edmund Randolph thought, as she had a mixed character of merchant vessel and privateer, she might be considered under the treaty; but this being overruled, the following paper was written: Rules proposed by Attorney General: 1. That all equipments purely for the accommodation of vessels, as merchantmen, be admitted. (Agreed.) 2d. That all equipments, doubtful in their nature, and applicable equally to commerce or war, be admitted, as producing too many minutiæ. (Agreed.) 3. That all equipments, solely adapted to military objects, be prohibited. (Agreed.) Rules proposed by the Secretary of the Treasury: 1st. That the original arming and equipping of vessels for military service, offensive or defensive, in the ports of the United States, be considered as prohibited to all. (Agreed.) 2d. That vessels which were armed before their coming into our ports, shall not be permitted to augment these equipments in the ports of the United States, but may repair or replace any military equipments which they had when they began their voyage for the United States; that this, however, shall be with the exception of privateers of the parties opposed to France, who shall not fit or repair (Negatived, the Secretary of the Treasury only holding this opinion). 3d. That for convenience. vessels armed and commissioned before they come into our ports, may engage their own citizens, not being inhabitants of the United States. (Agreed.) I subjoined the following: I concur in the rules proposed by the Attorney-General, as far as respects materials or means of annoyance furnished by us; and I should be for an additional rule, that as to means or materials brought into this country, and belonging to themselves, they are free to use them.—THE ANAS. ix, 161. FORD ED., i, 250. (July 1793.)

799. BELLIGERENTS, Policy toward.—Far from a disposition to avail ourselves of the peculiar situation of any belligerent nation to ask concessions incompatible with their rights, with justice, or reciprocity, we have never proposed to any the sacrifice of a single right: and in consideration of existing circumstances, we have ever been willing, where our duty to other nations permitted us, to relax for a time, and in some cases, that strictness of right which the laws of nature, the acknowledgments of the civilized world, and the equality and independence of nations entitle us to.—R. To A. ORLEANS LEGISLATURE. viii, 129. (June 1808.)

800. BELLIGERENTS, Recruiting by.—May an armed vessel, arriving here, be prohibited to employ their own citizens found here, as seamen or mariners? They cannot be prohibited to recruit their own citizens.—THE ANAS. ix, 158. FORD ED., i, 242. (1793.)

801. BELLIGERENTS, Sale of Arms to.—Our citizens have been always free to make, vend and export arms. It is the constant occupation and livelihood of some of them. To suppress their callings, the only means perhaps of their subsistence, because a war exists in foreign and distant countries, in which we have no concern, would scarcely be expected. It would be hard in principle, and impossible in practice. The law of nations, therefore. respecting the rights ot those at peace, does not require from them such an internal derangement in their occupations. It is satisfied with the external penalty pronounced in the President's proclamation. that of confiscation of such portion of these arms as shall fall into the hands of any of the belligerent powers on their way to the ports of their enemies. To this penalty our citizens are warned that they will be abandoned; and that even private contraventions may work no inequality between the parties at war. the benefits of them will be left equally free and open to all.—To GEORGE HAMMOND. iii, 558. FORD ED., vi, 253. (May 1793.)

802. BELLIGERENTS, Sale of Ships to.—The United States, being a ship-building nation. may they sell ships, prepared for war, to both parties? They may sell such ships in their ports to both parties, or carry them for sale to the dominions of both parties.—ANAS. ix, 158. FORD ED., i, 242. (1793.)

803. BELLIGERENTS, Transit Privileges.—It is well enough agreed, in the law of nations, that for a neutral power to give or refuse permission to the troops of either belligerent party to pass through their territory, is no breach of neutrality, provided the same refusal or permission be extended to the other party.—OFFICIAL OPINION. vii. 500. (Aug. 1790.) See NEUTRALITY.

804. BENEFICENCE, Humanity and.—I believe * * * that every human mind feels pleasure in doing good to another.—To JOHN ADAMS. vii, 39. (M., 1816.)

805. BERLIN DECREES, Piratical Meaning of.—These decrees and orders [of council]. taken together. want little of amounting to a declaration that every neutral vessel found on the high seas, whatsoever be her cargo, and whatsoever foreign port be that of her departure or destination, shall be deemed lawful prize; and they prove, more and more, the expediency of retaining our vessels, our seamen, and property, within our own harbors, until the dangers to which they are exposed can be removed or lessened.— SPECIAL MESSAGE. viii, 100. FORD ED., ix, 185. (March 17 1808.) See EMBARGO.

806. BIBLE, Circulation of the.—I had not supposed there was a family in this State [Virginia] not possessing a Bible, and wishing without having the means to procure one. When, in earlier life, I was intimate with every class, I think I never was in a house where that was the case. However, circumstances may have changed, and the [Bible] Society, I presume, have evidence of the fact. I, therefore, enclose you cheerfully, an order * * * for fifty dollars, for the purposes of the Society.—To SAMUEL GREENHOW. vi, 308. (M., 1814.)

807. BIBLE, Morality in the.—There never was a more pure and sublime system of morality delivered to man than is to be found in the four Evangelists.—To SAMUEL GREENHOW. vi, 309. (M., 1814.)

808. BIBLE, Protestants and the.—As to tradition, if we are Protestants we reject all tradition, and rely on the Scripture alone, for that is the essence and common principle of all the Protestant churches.—NOTES ON RELIGION. FORD ED., ii, 96. (1776?.)

809. BIBLE, Translation of the.—I propose [after retirement], among my first employments, to give to the Septuagint an attentive perusal.*—To CHARLES THOMSON. v. 403. FORD ED., ii, 234. (W., 1808.)

810. BIGOTRY, A Disease.—Bigotry is the disease of ignorance, of morbid minds; enthusiasm of the free and buoyant. Education and free discussion are the antidotes of both.—To JOHN ADAMS. vii, 27. (M., 1816.)

811. BIGOTRY, Political and Religious.—What an effort of bigotry in politics and religion have we gone through! The barbarians really flattered themselves they should be able to bring back the times of Vandalism, when ignorance put everything into the hands of power and priestcraft. All advances in science were proscribed as innovations. They pretended to praise and encourage education, but it was to be the education of our ancestors. We were to look backwards, not forwards for improvement; the President himself [John Adams] declaring * * * that we were never to expect to go beyond them in real science.—To DR. JOSEPH PRIESTLEY. iv, 373. FORD ED., viii, 21. (W., March 1801.)

812. BIGOTRY, Self-government and. —Ignorance and bigotry, like other insanities, are incapable of self-government.—To MARQUIS LAFAYETTE. vii, 67. FORD ED., x, 84. (M., 1817.)

* Thomson's translation of the Septuagint.—EDITOR.

813. BIGOTRIES, Union of.—All bigotries hang to one another.—To JOHN ADAMS. vi, 305. (M., 1814.)

814. BILL OF RIGHTS, An American Idea.—The enlightened part of Europe have given us the greatest credit for inventing this instrument of security for the rights of the people, and have been not a little surprised to see us so soon give it up [not having incorporated one in the new Constitution].—To F. HOPKINSON. ii, 586. FORD ED., v, 77. (P., March 1789.)

815. BILL OF RIGHTS, The Constitution and.—I do not like [in the Federal Constitution] first, the omission of a bill of rights, providing clearly and without the aid of sophisms for freedom of religion, freedom of the press, protection against standing armies, restriction against monopolies, the eternal and unremitting force of the *habeas corpus* laws, and trials by jury in all matters of fact triable by the laws of the land, and not by the law of nations. To say, as Mr. Wilson does, that a bill of rights was not necessary, because all is reserved in the case of the General Government which is not given, while in the particular ones, all is given which is not reserved, might do for the audience to whom it was addressed; but it is surely a *gratis dictum*, opposed by strong inferences from the body of the instrument, as well as from the omission of the clause of our present confederation, which had declared that in express terms. It was a hard conclusion to say, because there has been no uniformity among the States as to the cases triable by jury, because some have been so incautious as to abandon this mode of trial, therefore the more prudent States shall be reduced to the same level of calamity. It would have been much more just and wise to have concluded the other way, that as most of the States had judiciously preserved this palladium, those who had wandered should be brought back to it, and to have established general right instead of general wrong.* Let me add that a bill of rights is what the people are entitled to against every government on earth, general or particular; and what no just government should refuse or rest on inferences.—To JAMES MADISON. ii, 329. FORD ED., iv, 476. (P., Dec. 1787.)

816. —— ——. I am in hopes that the annexation of a bill of rights to the Constitution will alone draw over so great a proportion of the minorities, as to leave little danger in the opposition of the residue; and that this annexation may be made by Congress and the Assemblies, without calling a convention which might endanger the most valuable parts of the system.—To GENERAL WASHINGTON. ii, 533. FORD ED., v, 56. (P., Dec. 1788.)

* The Congress edition contains the following passage: "For I consider all the ill as established, which may be established. I have a right to nothing, which another has a right to take away; and Congress will have a right to take away trials by jury in all civil cases."—EDITOR.

817. BILL OF RIGHTS, Demand for.—
I sincerely rejoice at the acceptance of our new Constitution by nine States. It is a good canvas on which some strokes only want retouching. What these are, I think are sufficiently manifested by the general voice from north to south, which calls for a bill of rights. It seems pretty generally understood that this should go to juries, *habeas corpus*, standing armies, printing, religion, and monopolies. I conceive there may be difficulty in finding general modifications of these, suited to the habits of all the States. But if such cannot be found, then it is better to establish trials by jury, the right of *habeas corpus*, freedom of the press, and freedom of religion, in all cases, and to abolish standing armies in time of peace, and monopolies in all cases, than not to do it in any. The few cases wherein these things may do evil, cannot be weighed against the multitude wherein the want of them will do evil. In disputes between a foreigner and a native, a trial by jury may be improper. But if this exception cannot be agreed to, the remedy will be to model the jury by giving the *mediatas linguæ* in civil as well as criminal cases. Why suspend the *habeas corpus* in insurrections and rebellions? The parties who may be arrested, may be charged instantly with a well-defined crime; of course, the judge will remand them. If the public safety requires that the government should have a man imprisoned on less probable testimony in this than in other emergencies, let him be taken and tried, and retaken and retried, while the necessity continues, only giving them redress against the government, for damages. Examine the history of England. See how few of the cases of the suspension of the *habeas corpus* law have been worthy of that suspension. They have been either real treason, wherein the parties might as well have been charged at once, or sham plots, where it was shameful they should ever have been suspected. Yet for the few cases wherein the suspension of the *habeas corpus* has done real good, that operation is now become habitual, and the mass of the nation almost prepared to live under its constant suspension. A declaration, that the Federal government will never restrain the presses from printing anything they please, will not take away the liability of the printers for false facts printed. The declaration, that religious faith shall be unpunished, does not give impunity to criminal acts, dictated by religious error. The saying there shall be no monopolies, lessens the incitements to ingenuity, which is spurred on by the hope of a monopoly for a limited time, as of fourteen years; but the benefit of even limited monopolies is too doubtful to be opposed to that of their general suppression. If no check can be found to keep the number of standing troops within safe bounds, while they are tolerated as far as necessary, abandon them altogether; discipline well the militia, and guard the magazines with them. More than magazine guards will be useless if few, and dangerous if many. No European nation can ever send against us such a regular army as

we need fear; and it is hard if our militia are not equal to those of Canada or Florida. My idea then, is that though proper exceptions to these general rules are desirable, and probably practicable, yet if the exceptions cannot be agreed on, the establishment of the rules in all cases will do ill in very few. I hope, therefore, a bill of rights will be formed, to guard the people against the Federal Government, as they are already guarded against their State governments in most instances.—To JAMES MADISON. ii, 445. FORD ED., v, 45. (P., July 1788.)

818. BILL OF RIGHTS, Fetters against Evil.—By a declaration of rights I mean one which shall stipulate freedom of religion, freedom of the press, freedom of commerce against monopolies, trial by juries in all cases, no suspensions of the *habeas corpus*, no standing armies. These are fetters against doing evil which no honest government should decline.—To A. DONALD. ii, 355. (P., Feb. 1788.)

819. BILL OF RIGHTS, A Guard to Liberty.—I disapproved from the first moment [in the new Constitution] the want of a bill of rights, to guard liberty against the legislative as well as the executive branches of the government; that is to say, to secure freedom in religion, freedom of the press, freedom from monopolies, freedom from unlawful imprisonment, freedom from a permanent military, and a trial by jury, in all cases determinable by the laws of the land.—To F. HOPKINSON. ii, 586. FORD ED., v, 76. (P., March 1789.)

820. BILL OF RIGHTS, An Insufficient.—I like the declaration of rights as far as it goes, but I should have been for going further. For instance, the following alterations and additions would have pleased me. "Article IV. The people shall not be deprived or abridged of their right to speak, to write, or *otherwise* to publish anything but false facts affecting injuriously the life, liberty, or reputation of others, or affecting the peace of the Confederacy with foreign nations. Article VII. All facts put in issue before any judicature shall be tried by jury except, 1, in cases of admiralty jurisdiction wherein a foreigner shall be interested; 2, in cases cognizable before a court martial, concerning only the regular officers and soldiers of the United States, or members of the militia in actual service in time of war or insurrection; and, 3, in impeachments allowed by the Constitution. Article VIII. No person shall be held in confinement more than —— days after he shall have demanded and been refused a writ of *habeas corpus* by the judge appointed by law, nor more than —— days after such a writ shall have been served on the person holding him in confinement, and no order given on due examination for his remandment or discharge, nor more than —— hours in any place of a greater distance than —— miles from the usual residence of some judge authorized to issue the writ of *habeas corpus*: nor shall that writ be suspended for any term exceeding one year, nor in any place more than —— miles distant from the station or encampment of enemies, or of insurgents. Article IX. Monopolies may be allowed to persons for their own productions in literature, and their own inventions in the arts, for a term not exceeding —— years, but for no longer term, and for no other purpose. Article X. All troops of the United States shall stand *ipso facto* disbanded, at the expiration of the term for which their pay and subsistence shall have been last voted by Congress, and all officers and soldiers, not natives of the United States, shall be incapable of serving in their armies by land, except during a foreign war." These restrictions, I think, are so guarded as to hinder evil only. However, if we do not have them now. I have so much confidence in my countrymen, as to be satisfied that we shall have them as soon as the degeneracy of our government shall render them necessary.—To JAMES MADISON. iii, 100. FORD ED., v, 112. (P., Aug. 1789.)

821. BILL OF RIGHTS, The Judiciary and.—In the arguments in favor of the declaration of rights, you omit one which has great weight with me: the legal check which it puts into the hands of the judiciary. This is a body which, if rendered independent and kept strictly to their own department, merits great confidence for their learning and integrity. In fact, what degree of confidence would be too much for a body composed of such men as Wythe, Blair and Pendleton? On characters like these, the *" civium ardor prava jubentium "* would make no impression. I am happy to find that, on the whole, you are a friend to this amendment. The declaration of rights is, like all other human blessings, alloyed with some inconveniences, and not accomplishing fully its object. But the good in this instance vastly outweighs the evil.—To JAMES MADISON. iii, 3. FORD ED., v. 80. (P., March 1789.)

822. BILL OF RIGHTS, The People and.—A bill of rights is what the people are entitled to against every government on earth, general or particular; and what no just government should refuse, or rest on inferences. —To JAMES MADISON. ii, 330. FORD ED., iv, 477. (P., Dec. 1787.)

823. BILL OF RIGHTS, Security in.— A general concurrence of opinion seems to authorize us to say the Constitution has some defects. I am one of those who think it a defect that the important rights, not placed in security by the frame of the Constitution itself, were not explicitly secured by a supplementary declaration. There are rights which it is useless to surrender to the government, and which governments have yet always been found to invade. These are the rights of thinking, and publishing our thoughts by speaking or writing; the right of free commerce: the right of personal freedom. There are instruments for administering the government so particularly trustworthy, that we should never leave the legis-

lature at liberty to change them. The new Constitution has secured these in the Executive and Legislative departments: but not in the Judiciary. It should have established trials by the people themselves, that is to say by jury. There are instruments so dangerous to the rights of the nation, and which place them so totally at the mercy of their governors, that those governors, whether legislative or executive, should be restrained from keeping such instruments on foot, but in well defined cases. Such an instrument is a standing army. We are now allowed to say such a declaration of rights, as a supplement to the Constitution where that is silent, is wanting, to secure us in these points. The general voice has legitimated this objection.— To DAVID HUMPHREYS. iii, 12. FORD ED., v 89. (P., March 1789.)

824. ——— ———. I am one of those who think it a defect [in the new Constitution] that the important rights, not placed in security by the frame of the Constitution it self. were not explicitly secured by a sup plementary declaration [of rights].—To DA VID HUMPHREYS. iii, 12. FORD ED., v, 89 (P., March 1789.)

825. BILL OF RIGHTS, Where Nec essary.—I cannot refrain from making shor answers to the objections which your lette states to have been raised. 1. That th rights in question are reserved by the man ner in which the Federal powers are granted Answer. A constitutive act may, certainly be so formed as to need no declaration o rights. The act itself has the force of a dec laration as far as it goes; and if it goes t all material points, nothing more is wanting In the draft of a Constitution which I ha once a thought of proposing in Virginia, endeavored to reach all the great objects o public liberty. and did not mean to add declaration of rights. Probably the objec was imperfectly executed; but the deficien cies would have been supplied by others, i the course of discussion. But in a constitu tive act which leaves some precious article unnoticed. and raises implications agains others, a declaration of rights becomes nec essary by way of supplement. This is th case of our new Federal Constitution. Thi instrument forms us into one State, as t certain objects, and gives us a legislative an executive body for these objects. It shoul therefore. guard against their abuses of powe within the field submitted to them. 2. positive declaration of some essential right could not be obtained in the requisite lati tude. Answer. Half a loaf is better tha no bread. If we cannot secure all our right let us secure what we can. 3. The limite powers of the Federal Government. and jeal ousy of the subordinate governments. af ford a security which exists in no other in stance. Answer. The first member of thi seems resolvable into the first objection be fore stated. The jealousy of the subordi nate governments is a precious reliance. Bu observe that these governments are onl agents. They must have principles furnishe them whereon to found their opposition. The declaration of rights will be the text, whereby they will try all the acts of the Federal Government. In this view, it is necessary to the Federal Government also, as by the same text, they may try the opposition of the subordinate governments. 4. Experience proves the inefficacy of a Bill of Rights. Answer. True. But though it is not absolutely efficacious under all circumstances, it is of great potency always and rarely inefficacious. A brace the more will often keep up the building which would have fallen with that brace the less. There is a remarkable difference between the characters of the inconveniences which attend a declaration of rights, and those which attend the want of it. The inconveniences of the declaration are that it may cramp government in its useful exertions. But the evil of this is short-lived, moderate and reparable. The inconveniences of the want of a declaration are permanent, afflicting and irreparable. They are in constant progression from bad to worse. The executive, in our governments. is not the sole, it is scarcely the principal, object of my jealousy. The tyranny of the legislatures is the most formidable dread at present, and will be for many years. That of the executive will come in its turn; but it will be at a remote period. I know there are some among us who would now establish a monarchy. But they are inconsiderable in number and weight of character. The rising race are all republicans. We were educated in royalism; no wonder if some of us retain that idolatry still. Our young people are educated in republicanism; an apostasy from that to royalism is unprecedented and impossible. I am much pleased with the prospect that a declaration of rights will be added; and I hope it will be done in that way which will not endanger the whole frame of government, or any essential part of it.—To JAMES MADISON. iii. 4. FORD ED., v, 81. (P., March 1789.)

826. BILL OF RIGHTS (French), Draft of.—1. The States General shall assemble, uncalled, on the first day of November. annually, and shall remain together so long as they shall see cause. They shall regulate their own elections and proceedings, and until they shall ordain otherwise, their elections shall be in the forms observed in the present year, and shall be triennial. 2. The States General alone shall levy money on the nation. and shall appropriate it. 3. Laws shall be made by the States General only, with the consent of the King. 4. No person shall be restrained of his liberty. but by regular process from a court of justice, authorized by a general law. (Except that a Noble may be imprisoned by order of a court of justice, on the prayer of twelve of his nearest relations.) On complaint of an unlawful imprisonment, to any judge whatever, he shall have the prisoner immediately brought before him. and shall discharge him, if his imprisonment be unlawful. The officer in whose custody the prisoner is. shall obey the orders of the judge; and both judge and officer shall be

responsible, civilly and criminally, for a failure of duty herein. 5. The military shall be subordinate to the civil authority. 6. Printers shall be liable to legal prosecution for printing and publishing false facts, injurious to the party prosecuting; but they shall be under no other restraint. 7. All pecuniary privileges and exemptions, enjoyed by any description of persons, are abolished. 8. All debts already contracted by the King, are hereby made the debts of the nation; and the faith thereof is pledged for their payment in due time. 9. Eighty million of livres are now granted to the King. to be raised by loan, and reimbursed by the nation; and the taxes heretofore paid, shall continue to be paid to the end of the present year, and no longer. 10. The States General shall now separate, and meet again on the 1st day of November next. Done, on behalf of the whole nation, by the King and their representatives in the States General, at Versailles, this —— day of June, 1789. Signed by the King. and by every member individually, and in his presence.*—FRENCH CHARTER OF RIGHTS. iii. 47. FORD ED., v. 101. (P., June 1789.)

827. BILL OF RIGHTS (French), History of.—After you [M. de St. Etienne] quitted us yesterday evening, we continued our conversation (Monsr de Lafayette, Mr. Short and myself) on the subject of the difficulties which environ you. The desirable object being to secure the good which the King has offered and to avoid the ill which seems to threaten, an idea was suggested, which appearing to make an impression on Mons de Lafayette. I was encouraged to pursue it on my return to Paris, to put it into form, and now to send it to you and him. It is this. that the King, in a *seance royale* should come forward with a Charter of Rights in his hand, to be signed by himself. and by every member of the three orders. This Charter to contain the five great points which the Resultat of December offered on the part of the King, the abolition of pecuniary privileges offered by the privileged orders. and the adoption of the national debt, and a grant of the sum of money asked from the nation. This last will be a cheap price for the preceding articles. and let the same act declare your immediate separation till the next anniversary meeting. You will carry back to your constituents more good than ever was effected before without violence, and you will stop exactly at the point where violence would otherwise begin. Time will be gained, the public mind will continue to ripen and to be informed. a basis of support may be prepared with the people themselves, and expedients occur for gaining still something further at your next meeting. and for stopping again at the point of force. I have ventured to send to yourself and Monsieur de Lafayette a sketch of my ideas of what this act might contain without endangering any dispute. But it is offered merely as a canvas

*This paper is entitled "A Charter of Rights, Solemnly established by the King and Nation".—EDITOR.

for you to work on, if it be fit to work on at all. I know too little of the subject, and you know too much of it to justify me in offering anything but a hint. I have done it too in a hurry; insomuch that since committing it to writing it occurs to me that the 5th article may give alarm, that it is in a good degree included in the 4th, and is, therefore, useless. But, after all, what excuse can I make, Sir, for this presumption? I have none but an unmeasurable love for your nation, and a painful anxiety lest despotism, after an unaccepted offer to bind its own hands, should seize you again with tenfold fury.—To M. DE ST. ÉTIENNE. FORD ED., v, 99. (P., June 1789) See RIGHTS.

— BIMETALISM.—See DOLLAR and MONEY.

828. BINGHAM (William), Character of.—Though Bingham is not in diplomatic office, yet as he wishes to be so, I will mention such circumstances of him, as you might otherwise be deceived in. He will make you believe he was on the most intimate footing with the first characters in Europe, and versed in the secrets of every cabinet. Not a word of this is true. He had a rage for being presented to great men, and had no modesty in the methods by which he could if he attained acquaintance.—To JAMES MADISON. ii, 108. FORD ED., iv, 366. (P., 1787.)

829. BIRDS, Mocking-bird.—Teach all the children to venerate the mocking-bird as a superior being in the form of a bird, or as a being which will haunt them if any harm is done to itself or its eggs. I shall hope that the multiplication of the cedar in the neighborhood, and of the trees and shrubs round the house [Monticello] will attract more of them; for they like to be in the neighborhood of our habitations if they furnish cover.—To MARTHA JEFFERSON RANDOLPH. D. L. J., 221. (Pa., 1793.)

830. BIRDS, Nightingale.—I have heard the nightingale in all its perfection, and I do not hesitate to pronounce that in America it would be deemed a bird of the third rank only, our mocking-bird, and fox-colored thrush being unquestionably superior to it.—To MRS. JOHN ADAMS. FORD ED., iv, 63. (P., 1785.)

831. ———— ————. I have been for a week past sailing on the canal of Languedoc, cloudless skies above, limpid waters below, and on each hand a row of nightingales in full chorus. This delightful bird had given me a rich treat before, at the fountain of Vaucluse. After visiting the tomb of Laura at Avignon, I went to see this fountain—a noble one of itself, and rendered famous forever by the songs of Petrarch, who lived near it. I arrived there somewhat fatigued, and sat down by the fountain to repose myself. It gushes, of the size of a river, from a secluded valley of the mountains, the ruins of Petrarch's chateau being perched on a rock two hundred feet perpendicular above. To add to the enchantment of the scene, every tree and bush was filled with nightingales in full song. I think you told me that you had not yet noticed this bird. As you have trees in the garden of the convent, there might be nightingales in them, and this is the season of their song. Endeavor to make yourself acquainted with the music of this bird, that when you return to your own country, you may be able to estimate its merit in comparison with that of the mocking-bird. The latter has the advantage of singing through a

great part of the year, whereas the nightingale sings about five or six weeks in the spring, and a still shorter term, and with a more feeble voice, in the fall.—To MARTHA JEFFERSON. FORD ED., iv, 388. (1787.)

832. BIRDS, Skylark.—There are two or three objects which you should endeavor to enrich our country with,—the skylark, the red-legged partridge. I despair too much of the nightingale to add that.—To JAMES MONROE. FORD ED., vii, 21. (M., 1795.)

833. BIRDS, Turkey.—I suppose the opinion to be universal that the turkey is a native of America. Nobody, as far as I know, has ever contradicted it but Daines Barrington; and the arguments he produces are such as none but a head, entangled and kinked as his is, would ever have urged. Before the discovery of America, no such bird is mentioned in a single author, all those quoted by Barrington, by description referring to the crane, hen, pheasant, or peacock; but the book of every traveller, who came to America soon after its discovery, is full of accounts of the turkey and its abundance; and immediately after that discovery we find the turkey served up at the feasts of Europe, as their most extraordinary rarity.—To DR. HUGH WILLIAMSON. iv, 346. FORD ED., vii, 480. (W., Jan. 1801.)

834. BIRDS, The Crested Turkey.—I have taken measures to obtain the crested turkey, and will endeavor to perpetuate that beautiful and singular characteristic, and shall be not less earnest in endeavors to raise the Moronnier.—To M. CORREA. vii, 95. (P. F., 1817.)

835. BIRDS, The Turkey in Heraldry.—Mr. William Strickland, the eldest son of St. George Strickland, of York, in England, told me this anecdote: Some ancestor of his commanded a vessel in the navigations of Cabot. Having occasion to consult the Herald's office concerning his family, he found a petition from that ancestor to the Crown, stating that Cabot's circumstances being slender, he had been rewarded by the bounties, he needed from the Crown; that as to himself, he asked nothing in that way, but that as a consideration for his services in the same way, he might be permitted to assume for the crest of his family arms, the turkey, an American bird; and Mr. Strickland observed that their crest is actually a turkey.—To DR. HUGH WILLIAMSON. iv, 346. FORD ED., vii, 480. (W., Jan. 1801.)

836. BIRTH, Public Office and.—For promoting the public happiness, those persons, whom nature has endowed with genius and virtue, should be rendered by liberal education worthy to receive, and able to guard the sacred deposit of the rights and liberties of their fellow citizens; and they should be called to that charge without regard to * * * birth, or other accidental condition or circumstance.—DIFFUSION OF KNOWLEDGE BILL. FORD ED., ii, 221. (1779.)

837. BIRTHDAY, Jefferson's.—Disapproving myself of transferring the honors and veneration for the great birthday of our Republic to any individual, or of dividing them with individuals, I have declined letting my own birthday be known, and have engaged my family not to communicate it. This has been the uniform answer to every application of the kind.—To LEVI LINCOLN. iv, 504. FORD ED., viii, 246. (M., Aug. 1803.)

838. —— ——. The only birthday which I recognize is that of my country's liberties.*—RAYNER'S LIFE OF JEFFERSON, p. 18.

839. BIRTHDAY, Celebration of Washington's.—A great ball is to be given here [Philadelphia] on the 22d, and in other great towns of the Union. This is, at least, very indelicate, and probably excites uneasy sensations in some. I see in it, however, this useful deduction, that the birthdays, which have been kept, have been, not those of the President, but of the General.—To JAMES MADISON. iv, 212. FORD ED., vii, 203. (Pa., Feb. 1798.)

840. —— ——. The late birth-night has certainly sown tares among the exclusive federalists. It has winnowed the grain from the chaff. The sincerely Adamites did not go. The Washingtonians went religiously, and took the secession of the others in high dudgeon. The one sect threaten to desert the levees, the other the parties. The whigs went in number, to encourage the idea that the birth-nights hitherto kept had been for the General and not the President, and of course that time would bring an end to them.—To JAMES MADISON. iv, 218. FORD ED., vii, 211. (Pa., Feb. 1798.)

841. BISHOP (Samuel), Appointment as Collector.—I have received the remonstrance you were pleased to address to me, on the appointment of Samuel Bishop to the office of Collector of New Haven, lately vacated by the death of Daniel Austin. The right of our fellow citizens to represent to the public functionaries their opinion on proceedings interesting to them, is unquestionably a constitutional right, often useful, sometimes necessary, and will always be respectfully acknowledged by me. Of the various executive duties, no one excites more anxious concern than that of placing the interests of our fellow citizens in the hands of honest men, with understandings sufficient for their stations. No duty, at the same time, is more difficult to fulfil. The knowledge of characters possessed by a single individual is, of necessity, limited. To seek out the best through the whole Union, we must resort to other information, which, from the best of men, acting disinterestedly and with the purest motives, is sometimes incorrect. In the case of Samuel Bishop, however, the subject of your remonstrance, time was taken, information was sought, and such obtained as could leave no room for doubt of his fitness. From private sources it was learned that his understanding was sound, his integrity pure, his character unstained. And the offices confided to him within his own State, are public evidences of the estimation in which he is held by the State in general, and the city and township particularly in which he lives. He is said to be the town clerk, a justice of the peace, mayor of the city of New Haven, an office held at the will of the legislature, chief judge of the court of common pleas for New Haven County, a court of high criminal and

civil jurisdiction wherein most causes are decided without the right of appeal or review, and sole judge of the court of Probates. wherein he singly decides all questions of wills, settlement of estates, testate and intestate, appoints guardians, settles their accounts, and in fact has under his jurisdiction and 'care all the property, real and personal, of persons dying. The two last offices, in the annual gift of the legislature, were given to him in May last. Is it possible that the man to whom the legislature of Connecticut has so recently committed trusts of such difficulty and magnitude, is "unfit to be the collector of the district of New Haven," though acknowledged in the same writing, to have obtained all this confidence "by a long life of usefulness"? It is objected, indeed, in the remonstrance, that he is seventy-seven years of age; but at a much more advanced age, our Franklin was the ornament of human nature. He may not be able to perform in person all the details of his office; but if he gives us the benefit of his understanding, his integrity, his watchfulness and takes care that all the details are well performed by himself or his necessary assistants, all public purposes will be answered. The remonstrance, indeed, does not allege that the office *has been* illy conducted, but only apprehends that it *will be* so. Should this happen in event, be assured I will do in it what shall be just and necessary for the public service. In the meantime, he should be tried without being prejudged.—To THE NEW HAVEN COMMITTEE. iv, 402. FORD ED, viii, 67. (W., July 1801.)

842. BISHOP (Samuel), Goodrich's removal and.—The removal, as it is called, of Mr. [Elizur] Goodrich. promises another subject of complaint. Declarations by myself in favor of *political* tolerance, exhortations to *harmony* and affection in social intercourse, and to respect for the *equal rights* of the minority, have, on certain occasions, been quoted and misconstrued into assurances that the tenure of offices was to be undisturbed. But could candor apply such a construction? It is not, indeed, in the remonstrance that we find it; but it leads to the explanations which that calls for. When it is considered, that during the late administration, those who were not of a particular sect of politics were excluded from all office: when, by a steady pursuit of this measure, nearly the whole officers of the United States were monopolized by that sect; when the public sentiment at length declared itself, and burst open the doors of honor and confidence to those whose opinions they more approved, was it to be imagined that this monopoly of office was still to be continued in the hands of the minority? Does it violate their *equal rights*, to assert some rights in the majority also? Is it *political intolerance* to claim a proportionate share in the direction of the public affairs? Can they not *harmonize* in society unless they have everything in their own hands? If the will of the nation, manifested by their various

---

* Jefferson thought he discovered in the birthday celebrations of particular persons, a germ of aristocratical distinction, which it was incumbent upon all such persons, by a timely concert of example, to crush in the bud.—RAYNER'S *Life of Jefferson*, p. 17.

elections, calls for an administration of government according with the opinions of those elected; if, for the fulfilment of that will, displacements are necessary, with whom can they so justly begin as with persons appointed in the last moments of an administration, not for its own aid, but to begin a career at the same time with their successors, by whom they had never been approved, and who could scarcely expect from them a cordial coöperation? Mr. Goodrich was one of these. Was it proper for him to place himself in office, without knowing whether those whose agent he was to be would have confidence in his agency? Can the preference of another, as the successor to Mr. Austin, be candidly called a removal of Mr. Goodrich? If a due participation of office is a matter of right, how are vacancies to be obtained? Those by death are few; by resignation, none. Can any other mode than that of removal be proposed? This is a painful office; but it is made my duty, and I meet it as such. I proceed in the operation with deliberation and inquiry, that it may injure the best men least, and effect the purposes of justice and public utility with the least private distress; that it may be thrown, as much as possible, on delinquency, on oppression, on intolerance, on incompetence, on ante-revolutionary adherence to our enemies. The remonstrance laments " that a change in the administration must produce a change in the subordinate officers," in other words, that it should be deemed necessary for all officers to think with their principal? But on whom does this imputation bear? On those who have excluded from office every shade of opinion which was not theirs? Or on those who have been so excluded? I lament sincerely that unessential differences of political opinion should ever have been deemed sufficient to interdict half the society from the rights and blessings of self-government, to proscribe them as characters unworthy of every trust. It would have been to me a circumstance of great relief, had I found a moderate participation of office in the hands of the majority. I would gladly have left to time and accident to raise them to their just share. But their total exclusion calls for prompter correctives. I shall correct the procedure; but that done, disdain to follow it, shall return with joy to that state of things, when the only questions concerning a candidate shall be: Is he honest? Is he capable? Is he faithful to the Constitution?—To THE NEW HAVEN COMMITTEE. iv, 403. FORD ED., viii, 69. (W., July 1801.)

843. BISHOP (Samuel), New Haven Remonstrance and.—Mr. Goodrich's removal has produced a bitter *remonstrance*, with much personality against the two Bishops. I am sincerely sorry to see the inflexibility of the *federal* spirit there, for I cannot believe they are all *monarchists.*—To LEVI LINCOLN. iv, 399. FORD ED., viii, 67. (W., July 1801.)

844. ———— ————. Some occasion of public explanation was eagerly desired, when the New Haven remonstrance offered us that occasion. The answer was meant as an explanation to our friends. It has had on them, everywhere, the most wholesome effect. Appearances of schismatizing from us have been entirely done away. I own I expected it would check the current with which the republican federalists were returning to their brethren, the republicans. I extremely lamented this effect; for the moment which should convince me that a healing of the nation into one is impracticable, would be the last moment of my wishing to remain where I am.—To LEVI LINCOLN. iv, 406. FORD ED., viii, 84. (M., Aug. 1801.) See GOODRICH.

845. BLACKSTONE (Sir William), Commentaries.—The exclusion from the courts of the malign influence of all authorities after the *Georgium Sidus* became ascendant, would uncanonize Blackstone, whose book, although the most elegant and best digested of our law catalogue, has been perverted, more than all others, to the degeneracy of legal science. A student finds there a smattering of everything, and his indolence easily persuades him that if he understands that book, he is master of the whole body of the law. The distinction between these, and those who have drawn their stores from the deep and rich mines of Coke on Littleton, seems well understood even by the unlettered common people, who apply the appellation of Blackstone lawyers to these ephemeral insects of the law.—To JUDGE TYLER. vi, 66. (M., 1812.)

846. BLACKSTONE (Sir William), Toryism of.—Blackstone and Hume have made tories of all England, and are making tories of those young Americans whose native feelings of independence do not place them above the wily sophistries of a Hume or a Blackstone. These two books, but especially the former, have done more towards the suppression of the liberties of man, than all the million of men in arms of Bonaparte, and the millions of human lives with the sacrifice of which he will stand loaded before the judgment seat of his Maker.—To HORATIO G. SPAFFORD. vi, 335. (M., 1814.)

847. BLAND (Richard), Character of.—Colonel Richard Bland was the most learned and logical man of those who took prominent lead in public affairs, profound in constitutional lore, a most ungraceful speaker (as were Peyton Randolph and Robinson, in a remarkable degree.) He wrote the first pamphlet on the nature of the connection with Great Britain which had any pretension to accuracy of view on that subject, but it was a singular one. He would set out on sound principles, pursue them logically till he found them leading to the precipice which he had to leap, start back alarmed, then resume his ground, go over it in another direction, be led again by the correctness of his reasoning to the same place, and again back out, and try other processes to reconcile right and wrong, but finally left his reader and himself bewildered between the steady index of the compass in their hand, and the phantasm to which it seemed to point. Still there was more sound matter in his pamphlet than in the celebrated " Farmer's Letters," which were really but an *ignis fatuus,* mislead-ing us from true principles.—To WILLIAM WIRT. vi, 485. FORD ED., ix, 474. (M., 1815.)

848. BLOCKADES, Law of.—When the fleet of any nation actually beleaguers the port of its enemy, no other has a right to enter their line any more than their line of battle in the open sea, or their lines of cir-cumvallation, or of encampment, or of battle array on land. The space included within their lines in any of those cases, is either the property of their enemy, or it is common property, assumed and possessed for a mo-ment, which cannot be intruded on, even by a neutral, without committing the very tres-pass we are now considering, that of intrud-ing into the lawful possession of a friend.—To ROBERT R. LIVINGSTON. iv, 410. FORD ED., viii, 91. (M., 1801.)

849. BLOCKADES, Neutrals and.—When two nations go to war, it does not abridge the rights of neutral nations but in the two articles of blockade and contraband of war.—To BENJAMIN STODDERT. v, 425. FORD ED., ix, 245. (W., 1809.)

850. BLOCKADES, Seizure of Ships.—The instruction [to commanders of British war ships] which allows the armed vessels of Great Britain to seize, for condemnation, all vessels, on their first attempt to enter a blockaded port, except those of Denmark and Sweden, which are to be prevented only, but not seized, on their first attempt. Of the nations inhabiting the shores of the Atlantic ocean, and practising its navigation, Den-mark, Sweden and the United States, alone are neutral. To declare, then, all *neutral* vessels (for as to the vessels of the *belliger-ent* powers no order was necessary) to be legal prize, which shall attempt to enter a blockaded port, except those of *Denmark and Sweden,* is exactly to declare *that the vessels of the United States* shall be lawful prize, and those of Denmark and Sweden shall not. It is of little consequence that the article has avoided naming the United States, since it has used a description ap-plicable to them, and to them alone, while it exempts the others from its operation, by name. You will be pleased to ask an ex-planation of this distinction; and you will be able to say in discussing its justice, that in every circumstance, we treat Great Brit-ain on the footing of the most favored na-tion, where our treaties do not preclude us, and that even these are just as favorable to her as hers are to us. Possibly she may be bound by treaty to admit this exception in favor of Denmark and Sweden, but she can-not be bound by treaty to withhold it from us; and if it be withheld merely because not established with us by treaty, what might not we, on the same ground, have with-held from Great Britain, during the short course of the present war, as well as the peace which has preceded it?—To THOMAS PINCKNEY. iv, 62. FORD ED., vi, 416. (Pa., Sept. 1793.)

851. —— ——. You express your appre-hension that some of the belligerent powers may stop our vessels going with grain to the ports of their enemies, and ask instructions which may meet the question in various points of view, intending, however, in the meantime to contend for the amplest freedom of neutral nations. Your intention in this is perfectly proper, and coincides with the ideas of our own government in the particu-lar case you put, as in general cases. Such a stoppage to an unblockaded port would be so unequivocal an infringement of the neu-tral rights, that we cannot conceive it will be attempted.—To THOMAS PINCKNEY. iii, 551. FORD ED., vi. 242. (Pa., May 1793.)

852. BLOUNT (William), Impeach-ment of.—It is most evident, that the anti-republicans wish to get rid of Blount's impeach-ment. Many metaphysical niceties are handing about in conversation, to show that it cannot be sustained. To show the contrary, it is evident must be the task of the republicans, or of no-body.—To JAMES MADISON. iv, 206. FORD ED., vii, 190. (Pa., Jan. 1798.) See IMPEACH-MENT.

853. BOLINGBROKE, Writings of Lord.—Lord Bolingbroke and Thomas Paine were alike in making bitter enemies of the priests and pharisees of their day. Both were honest men; both advocates for human liberty. Paine wrote for a country which per-mitted him to push his reasoning to whatever length it would go. Lord Bolingbroke in one restrained by a constitution, and by public opin-ion. He was called indeed a tory; but his writings prove him a stronger advocate for lib-erty than any of his countrymen, the whigs of the present day. Irritated by his exile, he com-mitted one act unworthy of him, in connecting himself momentarily with a prince rejected by his country. But he redeemed that single act by his establishment of the principles which proved it to be wrong. These two persons dif-fered remarkably in the style of their writing, each leaving a model of what is most perfect in both extremes of the simple and sublime. No writer has exceeded Paine in ease and fa-miliarity of style, in perspicuity of expression, happiness of elucidation, and in simple and un-assuming language. In this he may be com-pared with Dr. Franklin; and indeed his Com-mon Sense was, for awhile, believed to have been written by Dr. Franklin, and published under the borrowed name of Paine, who had come over with him from England. Lord Bolingbroke's, on the other hand, is a style of the highest order. The lofty, rythmical, full-flowing eloquence of Cicero; periods of just measure, their members proportioned, their close full and round. His conceptions, too, are bold and strong, his diction copious, polished and commanding as his subject. His writings are certainly the finest samples in the English language of the eloquence proper for the sen-ate. His political tracts are safe reading for the most timid religionist, his philosophical, for those who are not afraid to trust their reason with discussions of right and wrong.—To FRANCIS EPPES. vii, 197. FORD ED., x, 183. (M., 1821.)

854. BOLLMAN (Eric), Burr and.—I am sorry to tell you that Bollman was Burr's right hand man in all his guilty schemes. On being brought to prison here [Washington], he communicated to Mr. Madison and myself the whole of the plans, always, however, apolo-getically for Burr, as far as they would bear. But his subsequent tergiversations have proved him conspicuously base. I gave him a pardon, however, which covers him from everything but infamy. I was the more astonished at his engaging in this business, from the peculiar motives he should have felt for fidelity. When I came into the government, I sought him out on account of the services he had rendered you, cherished him, offered him two different appointments of value, which, after keeping them long under consideration, he declined for commercial views, and would have given him anything for which he was fit. Be assured he is unworthy of ever occupying again the care of any honest man.—To MARQUIS DE LAFAYETTE. v, 130. FORD ED., ix, 114. (W., July 1807.)

855. BOLLMAN (Eric), Pardon of.— Dr. Bollman, on his arrival in Washington in custody in January, voluntarily offered to make communications to me, which he accordingly did, Mr. Madison also being present. I previously and subsequently assured him (without, however, his having requested it), that they should never be used *against himself*. Mr. Madison on the same evening committed to writing, by memory, what he had said; and I moreover asked of Bollman to do it himself, which he did, and I now enclose it to you. The object is, as he is to be a witness, that you may know how to examine him, and draw everything from him. I wish the paper to be seen and known only to yourself and the gentlemen who aid you, and to be returned to me. If he should prevaricate, I should be willing you should go so far as to ask him whether he did not say so and so to Mr. Madison and myself, in order to let him see that his prevarications will be marked. Mr. Madison will forward you a pardon for him, which we mean should be delivered previously. It is suspected by some he does not intend to appear. If he does not, I hope you will take effectual measures to have him immediately taken into custody. Some other blank pardons are sent on to be filled up at your discretion, if you should find a defect of evidence, and believe that this would supply it, * * * avoiding to give them to the gross offenders, unless it be visible that the principal will otherwise escape.— To GEORGE HAY. FORD ED., ix, 52. (W., May 1807.)

856. BONAPARTE (Jerome), Marriage of.—A report reaches us from Baltimore, * * * that Mr. Jerome Bonaparte, brother of the First Consul, is married to Miss Patterson, of that city. The effect of this measure on the mind of the First Consul, is not for me to suppose; but as it might occur to him, *prima facie*, that the Executive of the United States ought to have prevented it, I have thought it advisable to mention the subject to you, that, if necessary, you may by explanation set that idea to rights. You know that by our laws, all persons are free to enter into marriage, if of twenty-one years of age, no one having a power to restrain it, not even their parents; and that under that age, no one can prevent it but the parent or guardian. The lady is under age, and the parents, placed between her affections, which were strongly fixed, and the considerations opposing the measure, yielded with pain and anxiety to the former. Mr. Patterson is the President of the Bank of Baltimore, the wealthiest man in Maryland, perhaps in the United States, except Mr. Carroll; a man of great virtue and respectability; the mother was the sister of the lady of General Samuel Smith; and, consequently, the station of the family in society is with the first of the United States. These circumstances fix

rank in a country where there are no hereditary titles.—To ROBERT R. LIVINGSTON. iv, 510. FORD ED., viii, 277. (W., Nov. 1803.)

857. BONAPARTE (N.), Brutuses for. —If Bonaparte declares for royalty, either in his own person, or for Louis XVIII., he has but a few days to live. In a nation of so much enthusiasm, there must be a million of Brutuses who will devote themselves to destroy him.—To HENRY INNES. iv, 315. FORD ED., vii, 412. (Pa., Jan. 1800.)

858. ——— ———. Had the consuls been put to death in the first tumult, and before the nation had time to take sides, the Directory and Councils might have reestablished themselves on the spot. But that not being done, perhaps it is now to be wished that Bonaparte may be spared, as, according to his protestations, he is for liberty, equality and representative government, and he is more able to keep the nation together, and to ride out the storm than any other. Perhaps it may end in their establishing a single representative, and that in his person. I hope it will not be for life, for fear of the influence of the example on our countrymen. It is very material for the latter to be made sensible that their own character and situation are materially different from the French; and that whatever may be the fate of republicanism there, we are able to preserve it inviolate here.—To JOHN BRECKENRIDGE. FORD ED., vii, 418. (Pa., Jan. 1800.)

859. BONAPARTE (N.), Cromwell, Washington and.—My confidence has been placed in the head, not in the heart of Bonaparte. I hoped he would calculate truly the difference between the fame of a Washington and a Cromwell.—To SAMUEL ADAMS. iv, 321. FORD ED., vii, 425. (Pa., Feb. 1800.)

860. BONAPARTE (N.), Detested.—No man on earth has stronger detestation than myself of the unprincipled tyrant who is deluging the continent of Europe with blood. No one was more gratified by his disasters of the last compaign.*—To DR. GEORGE LOGAN. vi, 216. FORD ED., ix, 423. (M., Oct. 1813.)

861. BONAPARTE (N.), Embargo and. —The explanation of his principles given you by the French Emperor, in conversation, is correct as far as it goes. He does not wish us to go to war with England, knowing we have no ships to carry on that war. To submit to pay to England the tribute on our commerce which she demands by her orders of council, would be to aid her in the war against him, and would give her just ground to declare war with us. He, concludes, there-

* This extract got into the newspapers contrary to Jefferson's wishes, and led to a long interruption of the correspondence between him and Dr. Logan. At length, in 1816, he wrote to Logan, complaining of the publication, and said: "this [extract] produced to me more complaints from my best friends and called for more explanations than any transaction of my life had ever done. They inferred from this partial extract an approbation of the conduct of England, which yet the same letter censured with equal rigor. It produced, too, from the minister of Bonaparte a complaint, not indeed formal, for I was but a private citizen, but serious, of my volunteering with England in the abuse of his sovereign."—EDITOR.

fore, as every rational man must, that the Embargo, the only remaining alternative, was a wise measure. These are acknowledged principles, and should circumstances arise which may offer advantage to our country in making them public, we shall avail ourselves of them. But as it is not usual nor agreeable to governments to bring their conversations before the public, I think it would be well to consider this on your part as confidential, leaving to the government to retain or make it public, as the general good may require. Had the Emperor gone further, and said that he condemned our vessels going voluntarily into his ports in breach of his municipal laws, we might have admitted it rigorously legal, though not friendly. But his condemnation of vessels taken on high seas, by his privateers and carried involuntarily into his ports, is justifiable by no law; is piracy, and this is the wrong we complain of against him.—To ROBERT R. LIVINGSTON. v, 370. FORD ED., ix, 209. (W., Oct. 1808.)

862. BONAPARTE (N.), England and. —To complete and universalize the desolation of the globe, it has been the will of Providence to raise up, at the same time, a tyrant as unprincipled and as overwhelming, for the ocean. Not in the poor maniac George, but in his government and nation. Bonaparte will die, and his tyrannies with him. But a nation never dies. The English government, and its piratical principles and practices, have no fixed term of duration. Europe feels, and is writhing under the scorpion whips of Bonaparte. We are assailed by those of England. The one continent thus placed under the gripe of England, and the other of Bonaparte, each has to grapple with the enemy immediately pressing on itself. We must extinguish the fire kindled in our own house, and leave to our friends beyond the water that which is consuming theirs.—To MADAME DE STAEL. vi, 115. (M., May 1813.)

863. BONAPARTE (N.), Execrated.—I know nothing which can so severely try the heart and spirit of man, and especially of the man of science, as the necessity of a passive acquiescence under the abominations of an unprincipled tyrant who is deluging the earth with blood to acquire for himself the reputation of a Cartouche or a Robin Hood. The petty larcenies of the Blackbeards and Buccaneers of the ocean, the more immediately exercised on us, are dirty and grovelling things addressed to our contempt, while the horrors excited by the Scelerat of France are beyond all human execrations.—To DR. MORRELL. vi, 100. (M., Feb. 1813.)

864. BONAPARTE (N.), A Great Scoundrel.—Bonaparte was a lion in the field only. In civil life, a cold-blooded, calculating, unprincipled usurper, without a virtue; no statesman, knowing nothing of commerce, political economy, or civil government, and supplying ignorance by bold presumption. I had supposed him a great man until his entrance into the Assembly *des cinq cens*,

eighteen Brumaire (an. 8.) From that date, however, I set him down as a great scoundrel only.—To JOHN ADAMS. vi, 352. FORD ED., ix, 461. (M., July 1814.)

865. BONAPARTE (N.), Hatred of United States.—Bonaparte hates our government because it is a living libel on his — To WILLIAM DUANE. v, 553. FORD ED., ix, 287. (M., 1810.)

866.—— ——. Bonaparte's hatred of us is only a little less than that he bears to England, and England to us. Our form of government is odious to him, as a standing contrast between republican and despotic rule; and as much from that hatred, as from ignorance in political economy, he had excluded intercourse between us and his people, by prohibiting the only articles they wanted from us, cotton and tobacco.—To THOMAS LEIPER. vi, 464. FORD ED., ix, 520. (M., June 1815.)

867.—— ——. It is not possible Bonaparte should love us; and of that our commerce had sufficient proof during his power. Our military achievements, indeed, which he is capable of estimating, may in some degree, moderate the effect of his aversions; and he may, perhaps, fancy that we are to become the natural enemies of England, as England herself has so steadily endeavored to make us, and as some of our own over-zealous patriots would be willing to proclaim; and in this view, he may admit a cold toleration of some intercourse and commerce between the two nations. He has certainly had time to see the folly of turning the industry of France from the cultures for which nature has so highly endowed her, to those of sugar, cotton, tobacco, and others, which the same creative power has given to other climates; and, on the whole, if he can conquer the passions of his tyrannical soul, if he has understanding enough to pursue from motives of interest, what no moral motives lead him to, the tranquil happiness and prosperity of his country, rather than a ravenous thirst for human blood, his return may become of more advantage than injury to us.—To JOHN ADAMS. vi, 458 (M., June 1815.)

868. BONAPARTE (N.), Havoc by.— A conqueror roaming over the earth with havoc and destruction.—To DR. WALTER JONES. v, 511. FORD ED., ix, 274. (M., 1810.)

869. BONAPARTE (N.), His Ideas on Government.—Should it be really true that Bonaparte has usurped the government with an intention of making it a free one, whatever his talents may be for war, we have no proofs that he is skilled in forming governments friendly to the people. Wherever he has meddled, we have seen nothing but fragments of the old Roman government stuck into materials with which they can form no cohesion. We see the bigotry of an Italian to the ancient splendor of his country, but nothing which bespeaks a luminous view of the organization of rational government. Perhaps, however, this may end better than we augur: and it certainly will, if his head is equal to true and

solid calculations of glory.—To T. M. RAN-
DOLPH. iv, 319. FORD ED., vii, 422. (Pa.,
Feb. 1800.)

**870. BONAPARTE (N.), Human Mis-
ery and.**—Bonaparte has been the author of
more misery and suffering to the world, than
any being who ever lived before him. After
destroying the liberties of his country, he has
exhausted all its resources, physical and moral, to indulge his own maniac ambition, his
own tyrannical and overbearing spirit. His
sufferings cannot be too great.—To ALBERT
GALLATIN. vi, 499. (M., Oct. 1815.)

**871. BONAPARTE (N.), Ignorance of
Commerce.**—Of the principles and advantages of commerce, Bonaparte appears to be
ignorant.—To JOEL BARLOW. v, 601. (M.,
1812.)

**872. BONAPARTE (N.), Imprison-
ment of.**—The Attila of the age dethroned,
the ruthless destroyer of ten millions of the
human race, whose thirst for blood appeared
unquenchable, the great oppressor of the
rights and liberties of the world, shut up
within the circle of a little island of the Mediterranean, and dwindled to the condition of
an humble and degraded pensioner on the
bounty of those he had most injured. How
miserable, how meanly, has he closed his
inflated career! What a sample of the bathos
will his history present! He should have perished on the swords of his enemies, under the
walls of Paris.—To JOHN ADAMS. vi, 352.
FORD ED., ix, 461. (M., July 1814.)

**873. BONAPARTE (N.), Invasion of
U. S. by.**—The fear that Bonaparte will
come over and conquer us also, is too chimerical to be genuine. Supposing him to have
finished Spain and Portugal, he has yet England and Russia to subdue. The maxim of
war was never sounder than in this case, not
to leave an enemy in the rear; and especially
where an insurrectionary flame is known to
be under the embers, merely smothered, and
ready to burst at every point. These two
subdued (and surely the Anglomen will not
think the conquest of England alone a short
work), ancient Greece and Macedonia, the
cradle of Alexander, his prototype, and Constantinople, the seat of empire for him, would
would glitter more in his eye than our bleak
mountains and rugged forests. Egypt, too,
and the golden apples of Mauritania, have for
more than half a century fixed the longing
eyes of France; and with Syria, you know,
he has an old affront to wipe out. Then come
"Pontus and Galatia, Cappadocia, Aeolia and
Bithynia," the fine countries on the Eu-
phrates and Tigris, the Oxus and Indus, and
all beyond the Hypasis, which bounded the
glories of his Macedonian rival; with the invitations of his new British subjects on the
banks of the Ganges, whom, after receiving
under his protection the mother country, he
cannot refuse to visit. When all this is done
and settled, and nothing of the old world remains unsubdued, he may turn to the new
one. But will he attack us first, from whom
he will get but hard knocks and no money?

Or will he first lay hold of the gold and silver
of Mexico and Peru, and the diamonds of
Brazil? A *republican* emperor, from his affection to republics, independent of motives
of expediency, must grant to ourselves the
Cyclop's boon of being the last devoured.
While all this is doing, are we to suppose the
chapter of accidents read out, and that nothing can happen to cut short or disturb his
enterprises?—To JOHN LANGDON. v, 512.
(M., March 1810.)

**874. BONAPARTE (N.), Louisiana
and.**—I assured M. Pichon [French Minis-
ter] that I had more confidence in the word
of the First Consul than in all the parchment
we could sign.—To ROBERT R. LIVINGSTON.
iv, 511. FORD ED., viii, 278. (W., Nov. 1803.)

875. ——— ———. Your emperor has done
more splendid things, but he has never done
one which will give happiness to so great a
number of human beings as the ceding of
Louisiana to the United States.*—To MAR-
QUIS DE LAFAYETTE. FORD ED., ix, 67. (W.,
May 1807.) See LOUISIANA.

**876. BONAPARTE (N.), No Moral
Sense.**—O'Meara's book proves that nature
had denied Bonaparte the moral sense, the first
excellence of well organized man. If he could
seriously and repeatedly affirm that he had
raised himself to power without ever having
committed a crime, it proves that he wanted
totally the sense of right and wrong. If he
could consider the millions of human lives
which he had destroyed, or caused to be destroyed, the desolations of countries by plun-
derings, burnings and famine, the destitutions
of lawful rulers of the world without the
consent of their constituents, to place his
brothers and sisters on their thrones, the cutting up of established societies of men and
jumbling them discordantly together again at
his caprice, the demolition of the fairest hopes
of mankind for the recovery of their rights
and amelioration of their condition, and all
the numberless train of his other enormities;
the man I say, who could consider all these
as no crimes, must have been a moral monster, against whom every hand should have
been lifted to slay him.—To JOHN ADAMS.
vii, 275. (M., 1823.)

877. BONAPARTE (N.), Peace and.—
Bonaparte's restless spirit leaves no hope of
peace to the world.—To THOMAS LEIPER.
vi, 464. FORD ED., ix, 520. (M., 1815.)

**878. BONAPARTE (N.), Policy to-
ward United States.**—As to Bonaparte, I
should not doubt the revocation of his edicts,
were his government by reason. But his policy
is so crooked that it eludes conjecture.
I fear his first object now is to dry up
the sources of British prosperity by excluding her manufactures from the continent. He may fear that opening the
ports of Europe to our vessels will open them
to an inundation of British wares. He ought

* This accession of territory strengthens forever
the power of the United States, and I have just given
to England a maritime rival that will sooner or later
humble her pride.—NAPOLEON.

to be satisfied with having forced her to re-voke the orders [in council] on which he pretended to retaliate, and to be particularly satisfied with us, by whose unyielding ad-herence to principle she has been forced into the revocation. He ought the more to con-ciliate our good will, as we can be such an obstacle to the new career opening on him in the Spanish Colonies. That he would give us the Floridas to withhold intercourse with the residue of those colonies, cannot be doubted. But that is no price; because they are ours in the first moment of the first war; and until a war they are of no particular ne-cessity to us. But, although with difficulty, he will consent to our receiving Cuba into our Union, to prevent our aid to Mexico and the other provinces. That would be a price, and I would immediately erect a column on the southernmost limit of Cuba, and inscribe on it a *ne plus ultra* as to us in that direction. We should then only have to include the North in our Confederacy, which would be of course in the first war, and we should have such an empire for liberty as she has never surveyed since the creation; and I am per-suaded no Constitution was ever before so well calculated as ours for extensive empire and self-government.—To PRESIDENT MAD-ISON. v, 444. (M., April 1809.)

879. BONAPARTE (N.), Political Wick-edness of.—I view Bonaparte as a political engine only, and a very wicked one; you, I believe, as both political and religious, and obeying, as an instrument, an Unseen Hand. I still deprecate his becoming sole lord of the continent of Europe, which he would have been, had he reached in triumph the gates of St. Petersburg. The establishment in our day of another Roman Empire, spread-ing vassalage and depravity over the face of the globe, is not, I hope, within the purposes of Heaven.—To THOMAS LEIPER. vi, 463. FORD ED., ix, 519. (M., June 1815.)

880. BONAPARTE (N.), Promises of.—Promises cost him nothing when they could serve his purpose. On his return from Elba, what did he not promise? But those who had credited them a little, soon saw their total in-significance, and, satisfied that they could not fall under worse hands, refused every ef-fort after the defeat of Waterloo.—To BEN-JAMIN AUSTIN. vi, 554. FORD ED., x, 11. (M., 1816.)

881. BONAPARTE (N.), Republicans and.—Here you will find rejoicings on the [restoration] of Bonaparte, and by a strange *quid pro quo*, not by the party hostile to lib-erty, but by its zealous friends. In this they see nothing but the scourge reproduced for the back of England. They do not permit themselves to see in it the blast of all the hopes of mankind, and that however it may jeopardize England, it gives to her self-de-fence the lying countenance again of being the sole champion of the rights of man, to which in all other nations she is most ad-verse.— To M. DUPONT DE NEMOURS. vi, 457. (M., May 1815.)

882. ———— ————. I have grieved to see even good republicans so infatuated as to this man, as to consider his downfall as calamitous to the cause of liberty. In their indignation against England which is just, they seem to consider all *her* enemies as *our* friends, when it is well known there was not a being on earth who bore us so deadly a hatred. * * * To whine after this exorcised demon is a disgrace to republicans, and must have arisen either from want of reflection, or the indul-gence of passion against principle.—To BEN-JAMIN AUSTIN. vi, 553. FORD ED., x, 11. (M., Feb. 1816.)

883. BONAPARTE (N.), Restoration of.—You despair of your country, and so do I. A military despotism is now fixed upon it permanently, especially if the son of the ty-rant should have virtues and talents. What a treat it would be to me, to be with you, and to learn from you all the intrigues, apostacies and treacheries which have produced this last death's blow to the hopes of France. For, al-though not in the will, there was in the im-becility of the Bourbons a foundation of hope that the patriots of France might obtain a moderate representative government.—To M. DUPONT DE NEMOURS. vi, 457. (M., May 1815.)

884. BONAPARTE (N.), Rights of Na-tions and.—The new treaty of the allied powers declares that the French nation shall not have Bonaparte, and shall have Louis XVIII. for their ruler. They are all then as great rascals as Bonaparte himself. While he was in the wrong, I wished him exactly as much success as would answer our purposes, and no more. Now that they are in the wrong and he in the right, he shall have all my prayers for success, and that he may de-throne every man of them.—To THOMAS LEIPER. vi, 467. FORD ED., ix, 522. (M., June 1815.)

885. ———— ————. As far as we can judge from appearances, Bonaparte, from being a mere military usurper, seems to have become the choice of his nation; and the allies in their turn, the usurpers and spoliators of the European world. The rights of nations to self-government being my polar star, my par-tialities are steered by it, without asking whether it is a Bonaparte or an Alexander towards whom the helm is directed.—To M. CORREA. vi, 480. (M., June 1815.)

886. ———— ————. No man more severely condemned Bonaparte than myself during his former career, for his unprincipled enterprises on the liberty of his own country, and the independence of others. But the allies hav-ing now taken up his pursuits, and he ar-rayed himself on the legitimate side, I also am changed as to him. He is now fighting for the independence of nations, of which his whole life hitherto had been a continued viola-tion, and he has now my prayers as sincerely for success as I had before for his over-throw. He has promised a free government to his own country, and to respect the rights of others; and although his former conduct does not inspire entire faith in his promises; yet we had better take the chance of his word for doing right than the certainty of the wrong which his adversaries avow.—To PHILLIP MAZZEI. FORD ED., ix, 525. (M., Aug. 1815.)

887. —— ——. At length Bonaparte has got on the right side of a question. From the time of his entering the legislative hall to his retreat to Elba, no man has execrated him more than myself. I will not except even the members of the Essex Junto; although for very different reasons; I, because he was warring against the liberty of his own country, and independence of others; they, because he was the enemy of England, the Pope and the Inquisition. But at length, and as far as we can judge, he seems to have become the choice of his nation. At least, he is defending the cause of his nation, and that of all mankind, the rights of every people to independence and self-government. He and the allies have now changed sides. They are parcelling out among themselves, Poland, Belgium, Saxony, Italy, dictating a ruler and government to France, and looking askance at our republic, the splendid libel on their governments, and he is fighting for the principles of national independence of which his whole life hitherto has been a continued violation. He has promised a free government to his own country, and to respect the rights of others; and although his former conduct inspires little confidence in his promises, yet we had better take the chance of his word for doing right, than the certainty of the wrong which his adversaries are doing and avowing. If they succeed ours is only the boon of the Cyclops to Ulysses, of being the last devoured.*—To JOHN ADAMS. vi, 490. FORD ED., ix, 529. (M., Aug. 1815.)

888. BONAPARTE (N.), Robespierre and.—Robespierre met the fate, and his memory the execration, he so justly merited. The rich were his victims, and perished by thousands. It is by millions that Bonaparte destroys the poor, and he is eulogized and deified by the sycophants even of science. These merit more than the mere oblivion to which they will be consigned; and the day will come when a just posterity will give to their hero the only preeminence he has earned, that of having been the greatest of the destroyers of the human race. What year of his military life has not consigned a million of human beings to death, to poverty and wretchedness! What field in Europe may not raise a monument of the murders, the burnings, the desolations, the famines, and miseries it has witnessed from him? And all

* To the letter from which this extract is taken Jefferson appended a postscript as follows: "I had finished my letter yesterday and this morning (Aug. 11), received the news of Bonaparte's second abdication. Very well. For him, personally, I have no feeling but reprobation. The representatives of the nations have deposed him. They have taken the allies at their word, that they had no object in the war but his removal. The nation is now free to give itself a good government, either with or without a Bourbon; and France, unsubdued, will still be a bridle on the enterprises of the combined powers, and a bulwark to others."—EDITOR.

this to acquire a reputation, which Cartouche attained with less injury to mankind, of being fearless of God or man.—To MADAME D STAEL. vi. 114. (M., May 1813.)

889. BONAPARTE (N.), Self-government and.—I see in Bonaparte's expulsion of the Bourbons, a valuable lesson to the world, as showing that its ancient dynastie may be changed for their misrule. Should the allied powers presume to dictate a rule and government to France, and follow the example he had set of parcelling and usurping to themselves their neighbor nations, I hope he will give them another lesson in vindication of the rights of independence and self government. which himself had hitherto so much abused, and that in this contest he will wear down the maritime power of England to limitable and safe dimensions. So far good. It cannot be denied, on the other hand that his successful perversion of the force (committed to him for vindicating the right and liberties of his country) to usurp its government, and to enchain it under an hereditary despotism, is of baneful effect in encouraging future usurpations, and deterring those under oppression from rising to redress themselves.—To THOMAS LEIPER. vi, 464 FORD ED., ix, 519. (M., 1815.)

890. —— ——. If adversity should have taught him wisdom, of which I have little expectation, he may yet render some service to mankind, by teaching the ancient dynastie that they can be changed for misrule, and by wearing down the maritime power of England to limitable and safe dimensions.—To JOHN ADAMS. vi, 458. (M., June 1815.)

891. BONAPARTE (N.), Selfishness of.—Bonaparte saw nothing in this world but himself, and looked on the people under him as his cattle, beasts for burthen and slaughter —To BENJAMIN AUSTIN. vi, 553. FORD ED. x, 11. (M., 1816.)

892. BONAPARTE (N.), Statesmanship of.—I have just finished reading O'Meara's Bonaparte. It places him in a higher scale of understanding than I had allotted him. I had thought him the greatest of all military captains, but an indifferent statesman, and misled by unworthy passions. The flashes, however, which escaped from him in these conversations with O'Meara, prove a mind of great expansion, although not of distinct development and reasoning. He seizes results with rapidity and penetration, but never explains logically the processes of reasoning by which he arrives at them.—To JOHN ADAMS. vii, 275. (M., 1823.)

893. BONAPARTE (N.), Sufferings of.—O'Meara's Bonaparte makes us forget his atrocities for a moment, in commiseration of his sufferings. I will not say that the authorities of the world, charged with the care of their country and people, had not a right to confine him for life, as a lion or a tiger, on the principle of self-preservation. There was no safety to nations while he was permitted to roam at large. But the putting him to death in cold blood, by lingering tortures of mind, by vexations, insults, and deprivations, was a degree of inhumanity to which the poisonings and assassinations of the school of Borgia and the den of Marat never attained.—To JOHN ADAMS. vii, 275. (M., 1823.)

894. BONAPARTE (N.), Temper of.—Bonaparte's domineering temper deafens him to the dictates of interest, of honor, and of morality.—To JOEL BARLOW. v, 601. (M., 1811.)

895. BONAPARTE (N.), Tyranny of.—A ruthless tyrant, drenching Europe in blood to obtain through future time the character of the destroyer of mankind.—To HENRY MIDDLETON. vi, 91. (M., Jan. 1813.)

896. —— ——. That Bonaparte is an unprincipled tyrant, who is deluging the continent of Europe with blood, there is not a human being, not even the wife of his bosom who does not see.—To THOMAS LEIPER. vi, 283. FORD ED., ix, 445. (M., Jan. 1814.)

897. BONAPARTE (N.), United States and.—Considering the character of Bonaparte, I think it material at once to let him see that we are not of the powers who will receive his orders.—To JAMES MADISON. iv, 585. FORD ED., viii, 377. (M., Aug. 1805.)

898. —— ——. I never expected to be under the necessity of wishing success to Bonaparte. But the English being equally tyrannical at sea as he is on land, and that tyranny bearing on us in every point of either honor or interest, I say, "down with England," and as for what Bonaparte is then to do to us, let us trust to the chapter of accidents. I cannot, with the Anglomen, prefer a certain present evil to a future hypothetical one.—To THOMAS LEIPER. FORD ED., ix, 130. (M., Aug. 1807.)

899. —— ——. Although we neither expected, nor wished any act of friendship from Bonaparte, and always detested him as a tyrant, yet he gave employment to much of the force of the nation who was our common enemy. So far, his downfall was illy timed for us; it gave to England an opportunity to turn full-handed on us, when we were unprepared. No matter, we can beat her on our own soil, leaving the laws of the ocean to be settled by the maritime powers of Europe, who are equally oppressed and insulted by the usurpations of England on that element.—To W. H. CRAWFORD. vi, 418. FORD ED., ix, 502. (M., Feb. 1815.)

900. BONAPARTE (N.), United States, Russia and.—There cannot, I think, be a doubt as to the line we wish drawn between Bonaparte's successes and those of Alexander. Surely none of us wish to see Bonaparte conquer Russia, and lay thus at his feet the whole continent of Europe. This done, England would be but a breakfast; and although I am free from the visionary fears which the votaries of England have affected to entertain, because I believe he cannot effect the conquest of Europe; yet put all Europe into his hands,

and he might spare such a force, to be sent in British ships, as I would as lief not have to encounter, when I see how much trouble a handful of soldiers in Canada has given us. No. It cannot be to our interest that all Europe should be reduced to a single monarchy. The true line of interest for us, is, that Bonaparte should be able to effect the complete exclusion of England from the whole continent of Europe, in order, by this peaceable engine of constraint to make her renounce her views of dominion over the ocean, of permitting no other nation to navigate it but with her license, and on tribute to her, and her aggressions on the persons of our citizens who may choose to exercise their right of passing over that element. And this would be effected by Bonaparte succeeding so far as to close the Baltic against her. This success I wished him the last year, this I wish him this year; but were he again advanced to Moscow, I should again wish him such disasters as would prevent his reaching St. Petersburg. And were the consequences even to be the longer continuance of our war, I would rather meet them than see the whole force of Europe wielded by a single hand.—To THOMAS LEIPER. vi, 283. FORD ED., ix, 445. (M., Jan. 1814.)

901. —— ——. I have gone into this explanation * * * because I am willing to trust to your discretion the explaining me to our honest fellow laborers, and the bringing them to pause and reflect, if any of them have not sufficiently reflected on the extent of the success we ought to wish to Bonaparte, with a view to our own interests only; and even were we not men, to whom nothing human should be indifferent. But is our particular interest to make us insensible to all sentiments of morality? Is it then become criminal, the moral wish that the torrents of blood this man is shedding in Europe, the sufferings of so many human beings, good as ourselves, on whose necks he is trampling, the burnings of ancient cities, devastations of great countries, the destruction of law and order, and demoralization of the world, should be arrested, even if it should place our peace a little further distant? No. You and I cannot differ in wishing that Russia, and Sweden, and Denmark, and Germany, and Spain, and Portugal, and Italy, and even England, may retain their independence.—To THOMAS LEIPER. vi, 283. FORD ED., ix, 446. (M., Jan. 1814.)

902. —— ——. It is cruel that we should have been forced to wish any success to such a destroyer of the human race. Yet while it was our interest and that of humanity that he should not subdue Russia, and thus lay all Europe at his feet, it was desirable to us that he should so far succeed as to close the Baltic to our enemy, and force him, by the pressure of internal distress, into a disposition to return to the paths of justice towards us.—To JOHN CLARKE. vi, 308. (M., Jan. 1814.)

903. BONAPARTE (N.), Vanquished.—The unprincipled tyrant of the land is fallen, his power reduced to its original nothingness, his person only not yet in the madhouse, where it ought always to have been.—To CÆSAR A. RODNEY. vi, 448. (M., 1815.)

904. —— ——. On the general scale of nations, the greatest wonder is Napoleon at St. Helena; and yet it would have been well for the lives and happiness of millions and millions, had he been deposited there twenty years ago. France would now have a free government, unstained by the enormities she has enabled him to commit on the rest of the world, and unprostrated by the vindictive hand, human or divine, now so heavily bearing upon her.—To MRS. TRIST. D. L. J. 363. (P. F., April 1816.)

905. —— ——. What is infinitely interesting [in the letters you enclosed to me], is the scene of the exchange of Louis XVIII. for Bonaparte. What lessons of wisdom Mr. [John Quincy] Adams must have read in that short space of time! More than fall to the lot of others in the course of a long life. Man, and the man of Paris, under those circumstances, must have been a subject of profound speculation! It would be a singular addition to that spectacle to see the same beast in the cage at St. Helena, like a lion in the tower. That is probably the closing verse of the chapter of his crimes.—To MRS. JOHN ADAMS. vii, 52. FORD ED., x, 69. (M., 1817.)

906. —— ——. Had Bonaparte reflected that such is the moral construction of the world, that no national crime passes unpunished in the long run, he would not now be in the cage of St. Helena.—M. DE MARBOIS. vii, 76. (M., 1817.) See FRANCE.

907. BOOKS AS CAPITAL.—Some few years ago when the tariff was before Congress. I engaged some of our members of Congress to endeavor to get the duty repealed, and wrote on the subject to some other acquaintances in Congress, and pressingly to the Secretary of the Treasury. The effort * * * failed. * * * There is a consideration going to the injustice of the tax * * *. Books constitute capital. A library book lasts as long as a house, for hundreds of years. It is not, then, an article of mere consumption but fairly of capital, and often in the case of professional men, setting out in life, it is their only capital. Now there is no other form of capital which is first taxed 18 per cent. on the gross, and the proprietor then left to pay the same taxes in detail with others whose capital has paid no tax on the gross. Nor is there a description of men less proper to be singled out for extra taxation.—To JAMES MADISON. FORD ED., x, 194. (M., Sep. 1821.)

908. BOOKS, Censorship of.—I am mortified to be told that, in the United States of America, the sale of a book * can become a subject of inquiry, and of criminal inquiry too, as an offence against religion; that a

* A work in French by M. De Becourt entitled "Sur la Création du Monde, un Système d'Organisation Primitive".—EDITOR.

question like this can be carried before the civil magistrate. Is this then our freedom of religion? And are we to have a censor whose imprimatur shall say what books may be sold, and what we may buy? And who is thus to dogmatize religious opinions for our citizens? Whose foot is to be the measure to which ours are all to be cut or stretched? Is a priest to be our inquisitor, or shall a layman, simple as ourselves, set up his reason as the rule for what we are to read, and what we must believe? It is an insult to our citizens to question whether they are rational beings or not, and blasphemy against religion to suppose it cannot stand the test of truth and reason. If M. de Becourt's book be false in its facts, disprove them; if false in its reasoning, refute it. But, for God's sake, let us freely hear both sides, if we choose. I know little of its contents, having barely glanced over here and there a passage, and over the table of contents. From this, the Newtonian philosophy seemed the chief object of attack, the issue of which might be trusted to the strength of the two combatants; Newton certainly not needing the auxiliary arm of the government, and still less the Holy Author of our religion, as to what in it concerns Him. I thought the work would be very innocent, and one which might be confided to the reason of any man; not likely to be much read if let alone, but, if persecuted, it will be generally read. Every man in the United States will think it a duty to buy a copy, in vindication of his right to buy, and to read what he pleases.—To M. DUFIEF. vi, 340. (M., 1814.)

909. —— ——. I have been just reading the new constitution of Spain. One of its fundamental bases is expressed in these words: "The Roman Catholic religion, the only true one, is, and always shall be, that of the Spanish nation. The government protects it by wise and just laws, and prohibits the exercise of any other whatever." Now I wish this presented to those who question what you may sell,* or we may buy with a request to strike out the words, "Roman Catholic." and to insert the denomination of their own religion. This would ascertain the code of dogmas which each wishes should domineer over the opinions of all others, and be taken, like the Spanish religion, under the "protection of wise and just laws." It would show to what they wish to reduce the liberty for which one generation has sacrificed life and happiness. It would present our boasted freedom of religion as a thing of theory only, and not of practice, as what would be a poor exchange for the theoretic thraldom, but practical freedom of Europe.—To M. DUFIEF. vi, 340. (M., 1814.)

910. BOOKS, Duty on.—To prohibit us from the benefit of foreign light, is to consign us to a long darkness.—To —— ——. vii, 221. (M., 1821.)

911. —— ——. I hope a crusade will be kept up against the duty on books until those

* M. Dufief was a Philadelphia bookseller.—EDITOR.

in power shall become sensible of this stain on our legislation, and shall wipe it from their code, and from the remembrance of man, if possible.—To JARED SPARKS. vii, 335. FORD ED., x. 293. (M., 1824.)

912. —— ——. I hear nothing definitive of the three thousand dollars duty [on books for the University of Virginia] of which we are asking the remission from Congress.—To JAMES MADISON. vii, 433. FORD ED., x, 376. (M., 1826.)

913. —— ——. The government of the United States, at a very early period, when establishing its tariff on foreign importations, were very much guided in their selection of objects by a desire to encourage manufactures within ourselves. Among other articles then selected were books, on the importation of which a duty of fifteen per cent. was imposed, which, by ordinary custom house charges, amounts to about eighteen per cent., and adding the importing booksellers' profit on this, becomes about twenty-seven per cent. This was useful at first, perhaps, towards exciting our printers to make a beginning in that business here. But it is found in experience that the home demand is not sufficient to justify the reprinting any but the most popular English works, and cheap editions of a few of the classics for schools. For the editions of value, enriched by notes, commentaries, &c., and for books in foreign living languages, the demand here is too small and sparse to re-imburse the expense of reprinting them. None of these, therefore, are printed here, and the duty on them becomes consequently not a protecting, but really a prohibitory one. It makes a very serious addition to the price of the book and falls chiefly on a description of persons little able to meet it. Students who are destined for professional callings, as most of our scholars are, are barely able for the most part to meet the expenses of tuition. The addition of eighteen or twenty-seven per cent. on the books necessary for their instruction, amounts often to a prohibition as to them. For want of these aids, which are open to the students of all other nations but our own, they enter on their course on a very unequal footing with those of the same professions in foreign countries, and our citizens at large, too, who employ them, do not derive from that employment all the benefit which higher qualifications would give them. It is true that no duty is required on books imported for seminaries of learning, but these, locked up in libraries, can be of no avail to the practical man when he wishes a recurrence to them for the uses of life. Of many important books of reference there is not perhaps a single copy in the United States: of others but a few, and these too distant often to be accessible to scholars generally. It is believed, therefore, that if the attention of Congress could be drawn to this article, they would, in their wisdom, see its impolicy. Science is more important in a republican than in any other government. And in an infant country like ours, we must much depend for improvement

on the science of other countries, longer established, possessing better means, and more advanced than we are. To prohibit us from the benefit of foreign light, is to consign us to long darkness. The northern seminaries following with parental solicitude the interest of their *elevès* in the course for which they have prepared them, propose to petition Congress on this subject, and wish for the cooperation of those of the south and west, and I have been requested, as more convenient in position than they are, to solicit that cooperation. Having no personal acquaintance with those who are charged with the direction of the college of —— ——, I do not know how more effectually to communicate these views to them, than by availing myself of the knowledge I have of your zeal for the happiness and improvement of our country. I take the liberty, therefore, of requesting you to place the subject before the proper authorities of that institution, and if they approve the measure, to solicit a concurrent proceeding on their part to carry it into effect. Besides petitioning Congress, I would propose that they address, in their corporate capacity, a letter to their delegates and senators in Congress, soliciting their best endeavors to obtain the repeal of the duty on imported books. I cannot but suppose that such an application will be respected by them, and will engage their votes and endeavors to effect an object so reasonable. A conviction that science is important to the preservation of our republican government, and that it is also essential to its protection against foreign power, induces me, on this occasion, to step beyond the limits of that retirement to which age and inclination equally dispose me.— To —— —— vii, 220. (M., 1821.)

914. BOOKS, Lending.—The losses I have sustained by lending my books will be my apology to you for asking your particular attention to the replacing them in the presses as fast as you finish them, and not to lend them to anybody else, nor suffer anybody to have a book out of the study under cover of your name.—To JOHN GARLAND JEFFERSON. FORD ED., v, 182. (N. Y., 1790.)

915. BOOKS, Love of.—I cannot live without books.—To JOHN ADAMS. vi, 460. (M., 1815.)

916. BOOKS, Prices of.—French books are to be bought here [Paris] for two-thirds of what they can in England. English and Greek and Latin authors cost from twenty-five to fifty per cent. more here than in England.—To EDMUND RANDOLPH. i, 434. (P., 1785.)

917. —— ——. Greek and Roman authors are dearer here [France] than I believe anywhere in the world. Nobody here reads them, wherefore they are not printed.—To JAMES MADISON. i, 414. (P., 1785.)

918. BOOKS, Recommending.—It is with extreme reluctance that I permit myself to usurp the office of an adviser of the public, what books they should read, and what not. I yield, however, on this occasion to your wish and that of Colonel Taylor, and do

what (with a single exception only) I never did before, on the many similar applications made to me.—To SPENCER ROANE. vii, 212. FORD ED., x, 189. (M., 1821.)

919. —— ——. This book [" Constructions Construed "] is the most effectual retraction of our government to its original principles which has ever yet been sent by heaven to our aid. Every State in the Union should give a copy to every member they elect, as a standing instruction, and ours should set the example.—To ARCHIBALD THWEAT. vii, 199. FORD ED., x, 184. (M., 1821.)

920. —— ——. You ask for my opinion of the work you send me, and to let it go out to the public. This I have ever made a point of declining (one or two instances only excepted). Complimentary thanks to writers who have sent me their works, have betrayed me sometimes before the public, without my consent having been asked. But I am far from presuming to direct the reading of my fellow citizens, who are good enough judges themselves of what is worthy their reading.—To THOMAS RITCHIE. vii, 192. FORD ED., xvi, 171. (M., 1820.)

921. BOOKS, Time and.—The [French] literati are half a dozen years before us. Books, really good, acquire just reputation in that time, and so become known to us, and communicate to us all their advances in knowledge. Is not this delay compensated, by our being placed out of the reach of that swarm of nonsensical publications which issues daily from a thousand presses, and perishes almost in issuing?—To MR. BELLINI. i, 445. (P., 1785.)

922. BOOKS, Translations of.—I make it a rule never to read translations when I can read the original.—To EDMUND RANDOLPH. iv, 101. (M., 1794.)

923. BOOKS, Warfare by.—After the severe chastisement given by Mr. Walsh in his American Register to English scribblers, which they well deserved, and I was delighted to see, I hoped there would be an end of this intercrimination, and that both parties would prefer the course of courtesy and conciliation, and I think their considerate writers have since shown their disposition, and that it would prevail if equally cultivated by us. Europe is doing us full justice; why then detract from her?—To CHARLES JARED INGERSOLL. FORD ED., x, 325. (M., 1824.)

924. BOSTON PORT BILL, Denounced.—All such assumptions of unlawful power [as the Boston Port act] are dangerous to the right of the *British* empire in general, and should be considered as its common cause; and we will ever be ready to join with our fellow-subjects in every part of the same, in executing all those rightful powers which God has given us, for the reestablishment and guaranteeing * * * their constitutional rights, when, where, and by whomsoever invaded.*—RESOLUTION OF ALBEMARLE COUNTY. FORD ED., i, 419. (July 26, 1774.)

925. BOSTON PORT BILL, A Fast Proclaimed.—The Legislature of Virginia happened to be in session, in Williamsburg, when news was received of the passage by the British Parliament of the Boston Port Bill, which was to take effect on the first day of June [1774] then ensuing. The House of Burgesses thereupon passed a resolution, recommending to their fellow citizens, that that day should be set apart for fasting and prayer to the Supreme Being, imploring Him to avert the calamities then threatening us, and to give us one heart and one mind to oppose every invasion of our liberties. The next day, May 20, 1774, the Governor dissolved us.—JEFFERSON PAPERS. i, 122. (1821.) See FAST DAYS.

926. BOSTON PORT BILL, Ruin by.—By an act (7. G. 3) to discontinue in such manner, and for such time as they are therein mentioned, the landing and discharging, lading or shipping of goods, wares and merchandize, at the town and within the harbor of Boston, * * * a large and populous town, whose trade was their sole subsistence, was deprived of that trade, and involved in utter ruin. Let us for a while, suppose the question of right suspended, in order to examine this act on principles of justice: An act of Parliament had been passed imposing duties on teas, to be paid in America, against which act the Americans had protested as inauthoritative. The East India Company, who till that time had never sent a pound of tea to America on their own account, step forth on that occasion the asserters of Parliamentary right, and send hither many ship loads of that obnoxious commodity. The masters of their several vessels, however, on their arrival in America, wisely attended to admonition, and returned with their cargoes. In the province of Massachusetts alone, the remonstrances of the people were disregarded, and a compliance, after being many days waited for, was flatly refused. Whether in this the master of the vessel was governed by his obstinacy, or his instructions, let those who know say. There are extraordinary situations which require extraordinary interposition. An exasperated people, who feel that they possess power, are not easily restrained within limits strictly regular. A number of them assembled in the town of Boston, threw the tea into the ocean, and dispersed without doing any other act of violence. If in this they did wrong, they were known and were amenable to the laws of the land, against which it could not be objected that they had ever, in any instance, been obstructed or diverted from their regular course in favor of popular offenders. They should, therefore, not have been distrusted on this occasion. But that ill-fated colony had formerly been bold in their enmities against the house of Stuart, and were now devoted to ruin by that unseen hand which governs the momentous affairs of this great empire. On the partial representations of a few worthless ministerial dependents, whose constant office it has been to keep that government embroiled, and who, by their treacheries, hope to obtain the dignity of British Knighthood,* without calling for the party accused, with-

---

* Jefferson's own county.—EDITOR.

* Alluding to the Knighting of Sir Francis Bernard.—NOTE BY JEFFERSON.

out asking a proof, without attempting a distinction between the guilty and the innocent, the whole of that ancient and wealthy town, is in a moment reduced from opulence to beggary. Men who had spent their lives in extending the British commerce, who had invested in that place the wealth their honest endeavors had merited, found themselves and their families thrown at once on the world for subsistence by its charities. Not the hundredth part of the inhabitants of that town had been concerned in the act complained of; many of them were in Great Britain and in other parts beyond the sea; yet all were involved in one indiscriminate ruin by a new executive power, unheard of till then, that of a British Parliament. A property of the value of many millions of money was sacrificed to revenge, not repay, the loss of a few thousands. This is administering justice with a heavy hand indeed! And when is this tempest to be arrested in its course? Two wharves are to be opened again when his Majesty shall think proper. The residue, which lined the extensive shores of the Bay of Boston, are forever interdicted the exercise of commerce. This little exception seems to have been thrown in for no other purpose than that of setting a precedent for investing his Majesty with legislative powers. If the pulse of his people shall beat calmly under this experiment, another and another shall be tried, till the measure of despotism be filled up. It would be an insult on common sense to pretend that this exception was made in order to restore its commerce to that great town. The trade which cannot be received at two wharves alone must of necessity be transferred to some other place; to which it will soon be followed by that of the two wharves. Considered in this light, it would be insolent and cruel mockery at the annihilation of the town of Boston.—RIGHTS OF BRITISH AMERICA. i, 131. FORD ED., i, 436. (1734.) See DEPORTATION, TEA.

927. BOTANY, Attractiveness of.—You will find botany offering its charms to you, at every step during summer.—To T. M. RANDOLPH, JR. FORD ED., iv, 290. (P., 1786.)

928. BOTANY, New York.—We were * * * pleased with the botanical objects which continually presented themselves. Those either unknown or rare in Virginia were the sugar maple in vast abundance, the silver fir, white pine, pitch pine, spruce pine, a shrub with decumbent stems which they call juniper, an azalea, very different from the nudiflora, with very large clusters of flowers, more thickly set on the branches, of a deeper red, and high pink-fragrance. It is the richest shrub I have seen. The honeysuckle of the gardens growing wild on the banks of Lake George, the paper birch, an aspen with a velvet leaf, a shrub willow with downy catkins, a wild gooseberry, the wild cherry with single fruit (not the bunch cherry), strawberries in abundance.—To T. M. RANDOLPH. FORD ED., v, 340. (June 1791.)

929. BOTANY, School of.—It is time to think of the introduction of the school of Botany into our institution. (University of Virginia). * * * 1. Our first operation must be the se-

lection of a piece of ground of proper soil and site, suppose of about six acres, as M. Correa proposes. In choosing this we are to regard the circumstances of soil, water, and distance. I have diligently examined all our grounds with this view, and think that on the public road, at the upper corner of our possessions, where the stream issues from them, has more of the requisite qualities than any other spot we possess. One hundred and seventy yards square, taken at that angle, would make the six acres we want. * * * 2. Enclose the ground with a serpentine brick wall seven feet high. This would take about 80,000 bricks and cost $800, and it must depend on our finances whether they will afford that immediately, or allow us, for awhile, but enclosure of posts and rails. 3. Form all the hill sides into level terraces of convenient breadth, curving with the hill, and the level ground into beds and alleys. 4. Make out a list of the plants thought necessary and sufficient for botanical purposes, and of the trees we propose to introduce, and take measures in time for procuring them. As to the seeds of plants, much may be obtained from the gardeners of our own country. I have, moreover, a special resource. For three and twenty years of the last twenty-five, my good old friend Thonin, superintendent of the Jardin des Plantes at Paris, has regularly sent me a box of seeds of such exotics, as to us, as would suit our climate, and containing nothing indigenous to our country. These I regularly sent to the public and private gardens of the other States, having as yet no employment for them here. * * * The trees I should propose would be exotics of distinguished usefulness, and accommodated to our climate; such as the Larch, Cedar of Libanus, Cork, Oak, the Maronnier, Mahogany? the Catachu or Indian rubber tree of Napul (30°), Teak tree, or Indian oak of Burmah (23°), the various woods of Brazil, &c. The seed of the Larch can be obtained from a tree at Monticello. Cones of the Cedar of Libanus are in most of our seed shops, but may be had fresh from the trees in the English gardens. The Maronnier and Cork tree I can obtain from France. There is a Maronnier at Mount Vernon, but it is a seedling and not, therefore, select. The others may be got through the means of our ministers and consuls in the countries where they grow, or from the seed shops of England, where they may very possibly be found. Lastly, a gardener of sufficient skill must be found.*—To DR. EMMETT. vii, 438. (M., 1826.)

930. BOTANY, Value of.—Botany I rank with the most valuable sciences, whether we consider its subjects as furnishing the principal subsistence of life to man and beast, delicious varieties for our tables, refreshments from our orchards, the adornments of our flower borders, shade and perfume of our groves, materials for our buildings, or medicaments for our bodies. To the gentleman it is certainly more interesting than mineralogy (which I by no means, however, undervalue), and is more at hand for his amusement; and to a country family it constitutes a great portion of their social entertainment. No country gentleman should be without what amuses every step he takes into his fields.—To THOMAS COOPER. vi, 390. (M., 1814.)

—BOTTA'S (C.), History.—See HISTORY.

931. BOTTETOURT (Lord), Character of.—Lord Bottetourt was an honourable man.

* Dr. Emmett was Professor of Natural History in the University of Virginia.—EDITOR.

His government had authorized him to make certain assurances to the people here [Virginia], which he made accordingly. He wrote to the minister that he had made these assurances, and that, unless he should be enabled to fulfil them, he must retire from his situation. This letter he sent unsealed to Peyton Randolph for his inspection. Lord Bottetourt's great respectability, his character for integrity, and his general popularity, would have enabled him to embarrass the measures of the patriots exceedingly. His death was, therefore, a fortunate event for the cause of the Revolution. He was the first governor in chief that had ever come over to Virginia. Before his time, we had received only deputies, the governor residing in England, with a salary of five thousand pounds, and paying his deputy one thousand pounds.—CONVERSATION WITH DANIEL WEBSTER. FORD ED., x, 330. (1824.)

932. BOUNDARIES, Louisiana.—The boundaries of Louisiana, which I deem not admitting question, are the highlands on the western side of the Mississippi enclosing all its waters, the Missouri of course, and terminating in the line drawn from the northwestern point of the Lake of the Woods to the nearest source of the Mississippi, as lately settled between Great Britain and the United States. We have some claims, to extend on the seacoast westwardly to the Rio Norte or Bravo, and better, to go eastwardly to the Rio Perdido, between Mobile and Pensacola, the ancient boundary of Louisiana. Those claims will be a subject of negotiation with Spain, and if, as soon as she is at war, we push them strongly with one hand, holding out a price in the other, we shall certainly obtain the Floridas, and, all in good time. In the meanwhile, without waiting for permission, we shall enter into the exercise of the natural right we have always insisted on with Spain, to wit, that of a nation holding the upper part of streams, having a right of innocent passage through them to the ocean. We shall prepare her to see us practice on this, and she will not oppose it by force.—To JOHN C. BRECKENRIDGE. iv, 498. FORD ED., viii, 242. (M., Aug. 1803.)

933. —— ——. We are attached to the retaining of the Bay of St. Bernard, because it was the first establishment of the unfortunate La Salle, was the cradle of Louisiana, and more incontestibly covered and conveyed to us by France, under that name, than any other spot in the country.—To JAMES BOWDOIN. v, 19. (W., 1806.)

934. —— ——. You know the French considered themselves entitled to the Rio Bravo, and that Laussat declared his orders to be to receive possession to that limit, but not to Perdido; and that France has to us been always silent as to the western boundary, while she spoke decisively as to the eastern. You know Turreau agreed with us that neither party should strengthen themselves in the disputed country during negotiation; and [General] Armstrong, who says Monroe concurs with him, is of opinion, from the character of the Emperor, that were we to restrict ourselves to taking posts on the west side of the Mississippi, and threaten a cessation of intercourse with Spain, Bonaparte would interpose efficiently to prevent the quarrel going further. Add to these things the fact that Spain has sent five hundred colonists to San Antonio, and one hundred troops to Nacogdoches, and probably has fixed or prepared a post at the Bay of St. Bernard, at Matagordo. Supposing,

then, a previous alliance with England to guard us in the worst event, I should propose that Congress should pass acts, 1, authorizing the Executive to suspend intercourse with Spain at discretion; 2, to dislodge the new establishments of Spain between the Mississippi and Bravo; and, 3, to appoint commissioners to examine and ascertain all claims for spoliation that they might be preserved for future indemnification.—To JAMES MADISON. iv, 587. FORD ED., viii, 379. (M., Sept. 1805.)

935. —— ——. By the charter of Louis XIV. all the country comprehending the waters which flow into the Mississippi, was made a part of Louisiana. Consequently its northern boundary was the summit of the highlands in which its northern waters rise. But by the Xth Art. of the Treaty of Utrecht, France and England agreed to appoint commissioners to settle the boundary between their possessions in that quarter, and those commissioners settled it at the 49th degree of latitude. (See Hutchinson's Topographical Description of Louisiana, p. 7.) This it was which induced the British Commissioners, in settling the boundary with us, to follow the northern water line to the Lake of the Woods, at the latitude of 49°, and then go off on that parallel. This, then, is the true northern boundary of Louisiana. The western boundary of Louisiana is, rightfully, the Rio Bravo (its main stream), from its mouth to its source, and thence along the highlands and mountains dividing the waters of the Mississippi from those of the Pacific. The usurpations of Spain on the east side of that river, have induced geographers to suppose the Puerco or Salado to be the boundary. The line along the highlands stands on the charter of Louis XIV., that of the Rio Bravo on the circumstance that, when La Salle took possession of the Bay of St. Bernard, Panuco was the nearest possession of Spain, and the Rio Bravo the natural half-way boundary between them. On the waters of the Pacific, we can found no claims in right of Louisiana.—To JOHN MELLISH. vii, 51. (M., 1816.)

936. BOUNDARIES, Massachusetts and New York.—I enclose you a Massachusetts paper, whereby you will see that some acts of force have taken place on our eastern boundary. * * * The want of an accurate map of the Bay of Passamaquoddy renders it difficult to form a satisfactory opinion in the point in contest. * * * There is a report that some acts of force have taken place on the northern boundary of New York, and are now under the consideration of the government of that State. The impossibility of bringing the court of London to an adjustment of any difference whatever, renders our situation perplexing. Should any applications from the States or their citizens be so urgent as to require something to be said before your return, my opinion would be that they should be desired to make no new settlements on our part, nor suffer any to be made on the part of the British, within the disputed territory; and if any attempt should be made to remove them from the settlements already made, that they are to repel force by force, and ask aid of the neighboring militia to do this and no more. I see no other way of forcing the British government to come forward themselves and demand an amicable settlement.—To PRESIDENT WASHINGTON. iii, 230. (Pa., March 1791.)

937. BOUNDARIES, Northwest.—[In a conversation with George Hammond, the

British minister], he observed that the treaty [of peace] was of itself so vague and inconsistent in many of its parts as to require an explanatory convention. He instanced the two articles, one of which gave them the navigation of the Mississippi, and the other bounded them by a due west line from the Lake of the Woods, which being now understood to pass beyond the most northern sources of the Mississippi, intercepted all access to that river; that to reconcile these articles, that line should be so run as to give them access to the navigable waters of the Mississippi, and that it would even be for our interest to introduce a third power between us and the Spaniards. He asked my idea of the line from the Lake of the Woods, and of now settling it. I told him I knew of no objection to the settlement of it; that my idea of it was, that if it was an impassable line, as proposed in the treaty, it should be rendered passable by as small and unimportant an alteration as might be, which I thought would be to throw in a line running due north from the northernmost source of the Mississippi till it should strike the western line from the Lake of the Woods: that the article giving them a navigation in the Mississippi did not relate at all to this northern boundary, but to the southern one, and to the secret article respecting that; that he knew that our Provisional Treaty was made seven weeks before that with Spain; that at the date of ours, their ministers had still a hope of retaining Florida, in which case they were to come up to the 32d degree, and in which case also the navigation of the Mississippi would have been important; but that they had not been able, in event, to retain the country to which the navigation was to be an appendage. (It was evident to me that they had it in view to claim a slice on our northwestern quarter, that they may get into the Mississippi; indeed, I thought it presented as a sort of make-weight with the Posts to compensate the great losses their citizens had sustained by the infractions charged on us).—THE ANAS. ix, 428. FORD ED., i, 195. (June 1792.)

938. BOUNDARIES, Pennsylvania and Virginia.—The principle on which the boundary between Pennsylvania and this State is to be run having been fixed, it is now proposed by President Reed that commissioners proceed to execute the work from the termination of Mason and Dixon's line to the completion of five degrees of longitude, and thence on a meridian to the Ohio. We propose that the extent of the five degrees of longitude shall be determined by celestial observation. Of course it will require one set of astronomers to be at Philadelphia, and another at Fort Pitt. We ask the favor of yourselves to undertake this business, the one to go to the one place, the other to the other, meaning to add a coadjutor to each of you.—TO REV. JAMES MADISON AND ROBERT ANDREWS. FORD ED., ii, 513. (R., 1781.)

939. ——— ———. No mode of determining the extent of the five degrees of longitude of Delaware river, in the latitude of Mason and Dixon's Line having been pointed out by your Excellency [Joseph Reed], I shall venture to propose that this be determined by astronomical observations, to be made at or near the two extremities of the line, as being in our opinion the most certain and unexceptionable mode of determining that point which, being fixed, everything else will be easy.—TO PRESIDENT REED. FORD ED., iii, 15. (R., 1781.)

940. BOUNDARIES, United States and Great Britain.—A further knowledge of the ground in the north-eastern and north-western angles of the United States has evinced that the boundaries established by the treaty of Paris, between the British territories and ours in those parts, were too imperfectly described to be susceptible of execution. It has, therefore, been thought worthy of attention, for preserving and cherishing the harmony and useful intercourse subsisting between the two nations, to remove by timely arrangements what unfavorable incidents might otherwise render a ground of future misunderstanding. A convention has, therefore, been entered into, which provides for a practical demarcation of those limits to the satisfaction of both parties. —THIRD ANNUAL MESSAGE. viii, 26. FORD ED., viii, 270. (Oct. 1803.)

941. BOUNDARIES, United States and Spain.—The southern limits of Georgia depend chiefly on, 1. The charter of Carolina to the Lords Proprietors, in 1663, extending southwardly to the river Matheo, now called St. John's, supposed in the charter to be in latitude 31°, and 50° west in a direct line as far as the South Sea. See the charter in 4th Manoires de l'Amerique, 554. 2. On the proclamation of the British King, in 1763, establishing the boundary between Georgia and the two Floridas, to begin in the Mississippi, in thirty-one degrees of latitude north of the equator, and running eastwardly to the Apalachicola; thence, along the said river to the mouth cf the Flint; thence, in a direct line, to the source of the St Mary's River, and down the same to the ocean. 3. On the treaties between the United States and Great Britain, of November 30, 1782, and September 3, 1783, repeating and confirming these ancient boundaries. There was an intermediate transaction, to wit: a convention concluded at the Pardo, in 1739, whereby it was agreed that Ministers Plenipotentiary should be immediately appointed by Spain and Great Britain for settling the limits of Florida and Carolina. The convention is to be found in the collections of treaties. But the proceedings of the Plenipotentiaries are unknown here. * * * —MISSISSIPPI RIVER INSTRUCTIONS. vii, 573. FORD ED., v, 464. (1792.)

942. ——— ———. To this demonstration of our rights may be added the explicit declaration of the court of Spain, that she would accede to them. This took place in conversations and correspondence thereon between Mr. Jay, Minister Plenipotentiary for the United States at the court of Madrid, the Marquis de Lafayette, and the Count de Florida Blanca. Monsieur de Lafayette, in his letter of February 19, 1783, to the Count de Florida Blanca, states the result of their conversations on limits in these words: "With respect to limits, his Catholic Majesty has adopted those that are determined by the preliminaries of the 30th of November, between the United States and the court of London." The Count de Florida Blanca, in his answer of February 22d, to M. de Lafayette, says, "although it is his Majesty's intention to abide for the present by the limits established by the treaty of the 30th of November, 1782, between the English and the Americans, the King intends to inform himself particularly whether it can be in any ways inconvenient or prejudicial to settle that affair amicably with the United States;" and M. de Lafayette, in his letter of the same day to Mr. Jay, wherein he had inserted the preceding, says, "On receiving the answer of the

Count de Florida Blanca (to wit: his answer, before mentioned, to M. de Lafayette), I desired an explanation respecting the addition that relates to the limits. I was answered that it was a fixed principle to abide by the limits established by the treaty between the English and the Americans: that his remark related only to mere unimportant details, which he wished to receive from the Spanish commandants, which would be amicably regulated, and *would by no means oppose the general principle.* I asked him, before the Ambassador of France (M. de Montmorin), whether he would give me his word of honor for it; he assured me he would, and that I might engage it to the United States."—MISSISSIPPI RIVER INSTRUCTIONS. vii, 574. FORD ED., v, 465. (1792.)

943. —— ——. To conclude the subject of boundary, the following condition is to be considered by the commissioners as a *sine quâ non:* That our southern boundary remain established at the completion of thirty-one degrees of latitude on the Mississippi, and so on to the ocean, * * * and our western line along the middle of the channel of the Mississippi, however that channel may vary, as it is constantly varying, and that Spain cease to occupy, or to exercise jurisdiction in any part northward or eastward of these boundaries.—MISSISSIPPI RIVER INSTRUCTIONS. vii, 585. FORD ED., v, 475. (1792.)

944. —— ——. It is not true that our ministers, in agreeing to establish the Colorado as our western boundary, had been obliged to exceed the authority of their instructions. Although we considered our title good as far as the Rio Bravo, yet in proportion to what they could obtain east of the Mississippi, they were to relinquish to the westward, and successive sacrifices were marked out, of which even the Colorado was not the last.*—To W. A. BURWELL. v, 20. FORD ED., viii, 469. (M., Sep. 1806.)

945. BOUNDARIES, Virginia and Maryland.—I suppose you are informed of the proceeding commenced by the Legislature of Maryland, to claim the south branch of the Potomac as their boundary, and thus of Albemarle, now the central county of the State, to make a frontier. As it is impossible upon any consistent principles, and after such a length of undisturbed possession, that they can expect to establish their claim, it can be ascribed to no other than intention to irritate and divide; and there can be no doubt from what bow the shaft is shot. However, let us cultivate Pennsylvania, and we need not fear the universe. The Assembly have named me among those who are to manage this controversy. But I am so averse to motion and contest, and the other members are so fully equal to the business, that I cannot undertake to act in it. I wish you were added to them.—To JAMES MADISON. iv, 162. FORD ED., vii, 109. (M., Jan. 1797.)

946. BOUNTIES, Policy regarding.—It is not the policy of the government in America to give aid to works of any kind. They let things take their natural course without help or impediment, which is generally the best policy.—To THOMAS DIGGES. ii, 413. FORD ED., v, 29. (P., 1788.)

947. BOUNTIES, Recommended.—Among the purposes to which the Constitution

permits Congress to apply money, the granting premiums or bounties is not enumerated, and there has never been a single instance of their doing it, although there has been a multiplicity of applications. The Constitution has left these encouragements to the separate States. I have in two or three messages to Congress recommended an amendment to the Constitution, which shall extend their power to these objects. But nothing is yet done in it. I fear, therefore, that the institution you propose must rest on the patronage of the State in which it is to be. I wish I could have answered you more to my own mind, as well as yours; but truth is the first object.—To DR. MAESE. v, 412. (W., Jan. 1809.)

948. BOURBONS, Incompetent.—A new trial of the Bourbons has proved to the world their incompetence to the functions of the stations they have occupied; and the recall of the usurper has clothed him with the semblance of a legitimate autocrat.—To JOHN ADAMS. vi, 458. (M., June 1815.)

949. BOWLES (W. A.), Incites Creek Indians.—I * * * enclose you [the British Minister] an extract of a letter * * * giving information of a Mr. Bowles,* lately come from England into the Creek country, endeavoring to excite that nation of Indians to war against the United States, and pretending to be employed by the government of England. We have other testimony of these pretensions, and that he carries them much farther than there stated. We have too much confidence in the justice and wisdom of the British government to believe they can approve of the proceedings of this incendiary and impostor, or countenance for a moment a person who takes the liberty of using their name for such a purpose.—To GEORGE HAMMOND. FORD ED., v. (Pa., 1791.)

950. —— ——. Of this adventurer the Spanish government rid us.—To CARMICHAEL AND SHORT. iv, 11. FORD ED., vi, 332. (Pa., 1793.)

951. BOYS, Sound Principles and.—The boys of the rising generation are to be the men of the next, and the sole guardians of the principles we deliver over to them.—To REV. MR. KNOX. v, 502. (M., 1810.) See CHILDREN.

952. BRAZIL, Condition of.—Procure for us all the information possible as to the strength, riches. resources, lights and dispositions of Brazil. The jealousy of the court of Lisbon on this subject will, of course, inspire you with due caution in making and communicating these inquiries.—To DAVID HUMPHREYS. FORD ED., v, 317. (Pa., 1791.)

953. BRAZIL, Empire of.—Having learned the safe arrival of your Royal Highness at the city of Rio Janeiro I perform with pleasure the duty of offering you my sincere congratulations * * *. I trust that this event will be as propitious to the prosperity of your faithful subjects as to the happiness of your Royal Highness in which the United

---

* This was one of the newspaper charges made by John Randolph against the administration of Jefferson.—EDITOR.

* A Maryland Loyalist, who later styled himself a chief of the Creek Indians. See FORD's *Writings of Washington*, xii. 159, and *Maryland Loyalist*, 33.—NOTE in FORD ED.

States of America have ever taken a lively
interest. Inhabitants now of the same land,
of that great continent which the genius of
Columbus has given to the world, the United
States feel sensibly that they stand in new
and closer relations with your Royal Highness, and that the motives which heretofore
nourished the friendly relations which have so
happily prevailed, have acquired increased
strength on the transfer of your residence to
their shores. They see in prospect, a system
of intercourse between the different regions
of this hemisphere of which the peace and
happiness of mankind may be the essential
principle. To this principle your long tried
adherence, for the benefit of those you governed, in the midst of warring powers, is a
pledge to the new world that its peace, its
free and friendly intercourse, will be your
chief concern. On the part of the United
States I assure you, that these which have
hitherto been their ruling objects, will be most
particularly cultivated with your Royal Highness and your subjects at Brazil, and they
hope that that country so favored by the gifts
of nature, now advanced to a station under
your immediate auspices, will find, in the interchange of mutual wants and supplies, the
true aliment of an unchanging friendship with the United States of America.—
To the Emperor of Brazil. v, 285. (May
1808.)

954. BRAZIL, Republicanism in.—I
shall not wonder if Brazil should revolt in
mass, and send their royal family back to Portugal. Brazil is more populous, more wealthy,
more energetic, and as wise as Portugal.—To
Marquis Lafayette. vii, 68. Ford ed., x,
85. (M., 1817.)

955. ———— ————. Although we have no
right to intermeddle with the form of government of other nations, yet it is lawful to
wish to see no emperors nor kings in our
hemisphere, and that Brazil as well as Mexico will homologize with us.—To President
Monroe. Ford ed., x, 244. (M., Dec. 1822.)

956. BRIBERY, Electoral.—No person
shall be capable of acting in any office, civil,
military, or ecclesiastical, who shall have
given any bribe to obtain such office.—Proposed Va. Constitution. Ford ed., ii, 28.
(June 1776.)

957. ———— ————. Every person * * *
qualified to elect [to the House of Representatives of Virginia], shall be capable of being
elected [to the House of Representatives];
provided he shall have given no bribe, either
directly or indirectly, to any elector.—Proposed Va. Constitution. Ford ed., ii, 14.
(June 1776.)

958. ———— ————. The Senators' qualifications shall be * * * the having given no
bribe, directly or indirectly, to obtain their appointment.—Proposed Va. Constitution.
Ford ed., ii, 16. (June 1776.)

959. BRIBERY, Great Britain and.—
The known practice [of the British Govern-
ment] is to bribe whom they can, and whom

they cannot to calumniate. They have found
scoundrels in America, and either judging
from that, or their own principles, they would
pretend to believe all are so. If pride of
character be of worth at any time, it is when
it disarms the efforts of malice. What a miserable refuge is individual slander to so glorious a nation as Great Britain has been.—To
General Nelson. Ford ed., ii, 464. (R.,
1781.)

960. BRIBERY, Jefferson and.—Of
you, my neighbors, I may ask, in the face of
the world, " whose ox have I taken, or whom
have I defrauded? Whom have I oppressed,
or of whose hand have I received a bribe to
blind mine eyes therewith? On your verdict I rest with conscious security.—To the
Inhabitants of Albemarle County. v, 439.
Ford ed., ix, 251. (M., April 1809.)

961. BRIBERY OF OFFICIALS.—In
general, I am confident that you will receive
notice of the [trade] regulations of this country [France] respecting their islands. by the
way of those islands before you will from
hence [Paris]. Nor can this be remedied but
by a system of bribery which would end in the
corruption of your own ministers, and produce no good adequate to the expense.—To
James Monroe. i, 590. Ford ed., iv, 250. (P.,
1786.) See Corruption.

**962. BRIGGS (Isaac), Scientific At-
tainments of.**—I have appointed Isaac
Briggs, of Maryland, surveyor of the lands
south of Tennessee. He is a Quaker, a sound
republican, and of a pure and unspotted character. In point of science, in astronomy,
geometry and mathematics, he stands in a line
with Mr. Ellicott, and second to no man in the
United States. I recommend him to your
particular patronage; the candor, modesty and
simplicity of his manners cannot fail to gain
your esteem. For the office of surveyor, men of
the first order of science in astronomy and
mathematics are essentially necessary.—To Governor Claiborne. iv, 489. (W., 1803.)

**963. BROGLIO (Marshal de), Charac-
ter of.**—The Marshal de Broglio, is a high
flying aristocrat, cool and capable of everything.—To John Jay. iii, 74. (P., 1789.)

964. BROWN (James), Loyalty of.—
That you ever participated in any plan for a
division of the Union, I never for a moment
believed. I knew your Americanism too well.
But as the enterprise against Mexico was of a
very different character, I had supposed what I
heard on that subject to be possible. You disavow it; that is enough for me, and I forever
dismiss the idea.—To Dr. James Brown. v,
378. Ford ed., ix, 210. (W., 1808.)

965. BUBBLES, Speculative.—The American mind is now in that state of fever
which the world has so often seen in the history of other nations. We are under the bank
bubble, as England was under the South Sea
bubble, France under the Mississippi bubble,
and as every nation is liable to be, under whatever bubble, design, or delusion may puff up
in moments when off their guard.—To
Charles Yancey. vi, 515. Ford ed., x, 2.
(M., Jan. 1816.) See Speculation.

966. BUCHAN (Earl of), Character.—
He is an honorable, patriotic, and virtuous character [and], was in correspondence with Dr. Franklin and General Washington.—To JAMES MONROE. FORD ED., viii, 287. (W., 1804.)

967. BUCHANAN (George), Works of.
—The title of the tract of Buchanan which you propose to translate was familiar to me, and I possessed the tract; but no circumstance had ever led me to look into it. Yet I think nothing more likely than that, in the free spirit of that age and state of society, principles should be avowed, which were felt and followed, although unwritten in the Scottish constitution. Undefined powers had been intrusted to the crown, undefined rights retained by the people, and these depended for their maintenance on the spirit of the people, which, in that day was dependence sufficient.*—To REV. MR. KNOX. v, 502. (M., 1810.)

968. ——— ———. His latinity is so pure as to claim a place in school reading.—To REV. MR. KNOX. v, 502. (M., 1810.)

969. BUFFON (Count de), Animal theories refuted.—The opinion advanced by the Count de Buffon, is, 1. That the animals common both to the old and new world are smaller in the latter. 2. That those peculiar to the new are on a smaller scale. 3. That those which have been domesticated in both have degenerated in America; and 4. That on the whole it exhibits fewer species. And the reason he thinks is, that the heats of America are less; that more waters are spread over its surface by nature, and fewer of these drained off by the hand of man. In other words, that *heat* is friendly, and *moisture* adverse to the production and development of large quadrupeds. I will not meet this hypothesis on its first doubtful ground, whether the climate of America is comparatively more humid, because we are not furnished with observations sufficient to decide this question. And though, till it be decided, we are as free to deny as others are to affirm the fact, yet for a moment let it be supposed. The hypothesis after this supposition, proceeds to another: that *moisture* is unfriendly to animal growth. The truth of this is inscrutable to us by reasonings *à priori*. Nature has hidden from us her *modus agendi*. Our only appeal on such questions is to experience; and I think that experience is against the supposition. It is by the assistance of heat and moisture that vegetables are elaborated from the elements of earth, air, water, and fire. We accordingly see the more humid climates produce the greater quantity of vegetables. Vegetables are mediately or immediately the food of every animal; and in proportion to the quantity of food, we see animals not only multiplied in their numbers, but improved in their bulk, as far as the laws of their nature will admit. Of this opinion is the Count de Buffon himself in another part of his work: "En general il paroit que les pays un peu *froids* conviennent mieux á nos boeufs que les pays chauds et qu'ils sont d'autant plus gros et plus grands que le climat est plus

* Buchanan's works were publicly burned at Oxford. See Macaulay's *History of England*, Chap. II.—EDITOR.

humide et plus abondans en paturages. Les boeufs de Danemarck, de la Podolie, de l'Ukraine et de la Tartarie qu'habitent les Calmouques sont les plus grands de tous." Here then a race of animals, and one of the largest too, has been increased in its dimensions by *cold* and *moisture*, in direct opposition to the hypothesis, which supposes that these two circumstances diminish animal bulk, and that it is their contraries, *heat* and *dryness* which enlarge it.—NOTES ON VIRGINIA. viii, 290. FORD ED., iii, 135. (1782.)

970. ——— ———. The mammoth should have sufficed to have rescued the earth it inhabited, and the atmosphere it breathed, from the imputation of impotence in the conception and nourishment of animal life on a large scale; to have stifled, in its birth, the opinion of a writer, the most learned, too, of all others in the science of animal history, that in the new world. "La nature vivante est beaucoup moins agissante, beaucoup moins forte"; that nature is less active, less energetic on one side of the globe than she is on the other. As if both sides were not warmed by the same genial sun; as if a soil of the same chemical composition was less capable of elaboration into animal nutriment; as if the fruits and grains from that soil and sun yielded a less rich chyle, gave less extension to the solids and fluids of the body, or produced sooner in the cartilages, membranes, and fibres, that rigidity which restrains all further extension, and terminates animal growth. The truth is that a pigmy and a Patagonian, a mouse and a mammoth, derive their dimensions from the same nutritive juices. The difference of increment depends on circumstances unsearchable to beings with our capacities. Every race of animals seems to have received from their Maker certain laws of extension at the time of their formation. Their elaborate organs were formed to produce this, while proper obstacles were opposed to its further progress. Below these limits they cannot fall, nor rise above them. What intermediate station they shall take may depend on soil, on climate, on food, on a careful choice of breeders. But all the manna of heaven would never raise the mouse to the bulk of the mammoth.—NOTES ON VIRGINIA. viii, 289. FORD ED., iii, 134. (1782.) See MAMMOTH.

971. BUFFON (Count de), Gifts to.—
I wrote to some of my friends in America desiring they would send me such of the spoils of the moose, caribou, elk and deer, as might throw light on that class of animals. * * * I am happy to be able to present to you * * * the bones and skin of a moose, the horns of the caribou, the elk, the deer, the spiked horned buck, and the roebuck of America. They all come from New Hampshire and Massachusetts. —To COMTE DE BUFFON. ii, 285. FORD ED., iv, 457. (P., 1787.)

972. BUNKER HILL, Battle of.—Bunker's Hill, or rather Breed's Hill, whereon the action was, is a peninsula joined to the mainland by a neck of land almost level with the water, a few paces wide, and about one or two hundred *toises* long. On one side of this neck lay a vessel of war, and on the other several gunboats. The body of our army was on the mainland; and only a detachment had been sent into the peninsula. When the enemy determined to make the attack, they sent the vessel of war and gunboats to take the position, before mentioned, to cut off all reinforcements, which they effectually did. Not so much as a company could venture to the relief of the men engaged, who therefore fought through the whole action, and at length were obliged to retire across the neck through the cross fire of the vessels before mentioned. Single persons passed along the neck during the engagement, particularly General Putnam.—To M. SOULES. ix, 293. FORD ED., iv, 301. (P., 1786.)

973. BURKE (Edmund), Toryism of.— The Revolution of France does not astonish me so much as the revolution of Mr. Burke. I wish I could believe the latter proceeded from as pure motives as the former. But what demonstration could scarcely have established before, less than the hints of Dr. Priestley and Mr. Paine establish firmly now. How mortifying that this evidence of the rottenness of his mind must oblige us now to ascribe to wicked motives those actions of his life which wore the mark of virtue and patriotism.—To BENJAMIN VAUGHAN. FORD ED., v, 333. (1791.)

974. BUSINESS, Visionary Principles in.— Men come into business at first with visionary principles. It is practice alone which can correct and conform them to the actual current of affairs. In the meantime, those to whom their errors were first applied have been their victims.—To JAMES MADISON. FORD ED., v, 16. (P., 1788.)

975. BURR (Aaron), Characteristics of. —I never thought him an honest, frank-dealing man, but considered him as a crooked gun, or other perverted machine, whose aim or shot you could never be sure of. Still, while he possessed the confidence of the nation, I thought it my duty to respect in him their confidence, and to treat him as if he deserved it.—To WILLIAM B. GILES. v, 68. FORD ED., ix, 46. (M., April 1807.)

976. BURR (Aaron), Distrust of.— I had never seen Colonel Burr till he came here as a member of the Senate. His conduct very soon inspired me with distrust. I habitually cautioned Mr. Madison against trusting him too much. I saw afterwards that under General Washington's and Mr. Adams's administrations, whenever a great military appointment or a diplomatic one was to be made, he came post to Philadelphia to show himself and in fact that he was always at market, if they had wanted him. He was indeed told by Dayton in 1800 he might be Secretary of War; but this bid was too late. His election as V. P. was then foreseen. With these impressions of Colonel Burr there never had been any intimacy between us, and but little association. When I destined him for a high appointment, it was out of respect for the favor he had obtained with the republican party by his extraordinary exertions and successes in the New York election in 1800.—ANAS. ix, 207. FORD ED., i, 304. (1804.)

977. BURR (Aaron), Feeling toward.— Against Burr, personally, I never had one

hostile sentiment.—To WILLIAM B. GILES. v, 68. FORD ED., ix, 46. (M., April 1807.)

978. BURR (Aaron), Honesty and.— No man's history proves better the value of honesty. With that, what might he not have been!—To LEVI LINCOLN. v, 55. (W., 1807.)

979. BURR (Aaron), Overrated Talents.— Burr has indeed made a most inglorious exhibition of his much overrated talents.—To ROBERT R. LIVINGSTON. v, 55. FORD ED., ix, 38. (W., 1807.)

980. ——— ———. A great man in little things, he is really small in great ones.—To GEORGE HAY. v, 88. FORD ED., ix, 55. (W., 1807.)

981. BURR (Aaron), Political Services. —He has certainly greatly merited of his country, and the republicans in particular, to whose efforts his have given a chance of success.—To PIERCE BUTLER. FORD ED., vii, 449. (Aug. 1800.)

982. ——— ———. While I must congratulate you on the issue of this contest [the Presidential], because it is more honorable, and, doubtless, more grateful to you than any station within the competence of the Chief Magistrate, yet for myself, and for the substantial service of the public, I feel most sensibly the loss we sustain of your aid in our new administration. It leaves a chasm in my arrangements, which cannot be adequately filled up. I had endeavored to compose an administration whose talents, integrity, names, and dispositions, should at once inspire unbounded confidence in the public mind, and insure a perfect harmony in the conduct of the public business. I lose you from the list, and am not sure of all the others. Should the gentlemen, who possess the public confidence, decline taking a part in their affairs, and force us to take persons unknown to the people, the evil genius of this country may realize his avowal that " he will beat down the administration."—To AARON BURR. iv, 341. FORD ED., vii, 467. (W., Dec. 1800.)

983. BURR (Aaron), Presidential Contest.— It was to be expected that the enemy would endeavor to sow tares between us, that they might divide us and our friends. Every consideration satisfies me you will be on your guard against this, as I assure you I am strongly. I hear of one stratagem so imposing and so base that it is proper I should notice it to you. Mr. Munford says he saw at New York an original letter of mine to Judge Breckenridge, in which are sentiments highly injurious to you. He knows my handwriting, and did not doubt that to be genuine. I enclose you a copy taken from the press copy of the only letter I ever wrote to Judge Breckenridge in my life. * * * Of consequence, the letter seen by Mr. Munford must be a forgery, and if it contains a sentiment unfriendly or disrespectful to you, I affirm it solemnly to be a forgery; as also if it varies from the copy enclosed. With the common trash of slander I should not think of troubling you; but the forgery of one's handwriting is too imposing to be neglected.— To AARON BURR. iv, 349. FORD ED., vii, 485. (W., Feb. 1801.) See ELECTIONS—PRESIDENTIAL, 1800.

984. BURR (Aaron), Relations with Jefferson.— Colonel Burr, the Vice President, called on me in the evening [January 26th, 1804], having previously asked an opportunity of conversing with me. He began by recapitulating summarily, that he had come to New York a stranger, some years ago; that he found the country in possession of two rich families (the Livingstons and Clintons); that his pursuits were not political, and he meddled not. When the crisis, however, of 1800 came on, they found their influence worn out, and solicited his aid with the people. He lent it without any views of promotion. That his being named as a candidate for Vice-President was unexpected by him. He acceded to it with a view to promote my fame and advancement, and from a desire to be with me, whose company and conversation had always been fascinating to him. That since, those great families had become hostile to him, and had excited the calumnies which I had seen published. That in this Hamilton had joined, and had even written some of the pieces against him. That his attachment to me had been sincere, and was still unchanged, although many little stories had been carried to him, and he supposed to me also, which he despised: but that attachment must be reciprocal or cease to exist, and, therefore, he asked if any change had taken place in mine towards him; that he had chosen to have this conversation with myself directly and not through any intermediate agent. He reminded me of a letter written to him about the time of counting the votes (say February, 1801), mentioning that his election had left a chasm in my arrangements; that I had lost him from my list in the Administration, &c. He observed, he believed it would be for the interest of the republican cause for him to retire; that a disadvantageous schism would otherwise take place; but that were he to retire, it would be said he shrunk from the public sentence, which he never would do; that his enemies were using my name to destroy him, and something was necessary from me to prevent and deprive them of that weapon, some mark of favor from me which would declare to the world that he retired with my confidence.

I answered by recapitulating to him what had been my conduct previous to the election of 1800. That I had never interfered directly or indirectly with my friends or any others, to influence the election either for him or myself; that I considered it as my duty to be merely passive, except that in Virginia, I had taken some measures to procure for him the unanimous vote of that State, because I thought any failure there might be imputed to me. That in the election now coming on, I was observing the same conduct, held no councils with anybody respecting it, nor suffered any one to speak to me on the subject, believing it my duty to leave myself to the free discussion of the public; that I do not at this moment know, nor have ever heard, who were to be proposed as candidates for the public choice, except so far as could be gathered from the newspapers. That as to the attack excited against him in the newspapers, I had noticed it but as the passing wind; that I had seen complaints that Cheetham, employed in publishing the laws, should be permitted to eat the public bread and abuse its second officer; that as to this, the publishers of the laws were appointed by the Secretary of State, without any reference to me; that to make the notice general, it was often given to one republican and one federal printer of the same place; that these federal printers did not in the least intermit their abuse of me, though receiving emoluments from the government, and that I never thought it

proper to interfere for myself, and consequentl not in the case of the Vice-President. That a to the letter he referred to, I remembered i and believed he had only mistaken the date a which it was written; that I thought it mus have been on the first notice of the event o the election of South Carolina; and that I ha taken that occasion to mention to him, that had intended to have proposed to him one o the great offices, if he had not been elected but that his election in giving him a higher sta tion had deprived me of his aid in the Admin istration. The letter alluded to was, in fact mine to him of December the 15th, 1800. now went on to explain to him verbally, what meant by saying I had lost him from my list That in General Washington's time, it had bee signified to him that Mr. Adams, the Vice-Presi dent, would be glad of a foreign embassy; tha General Washington mentioned it to me, ex pressed his doubts whether Mr. Adams was fit character for such an office, and his stil greater doubts, indeed his conviction, that i would not be justifiable to send away the person who, in case of his death, was provided by the Constitution to take his place; that i would moreover appear indecent for him to he disposing of the public trusts, in apparently buying off a competitor for the public favor. concurred with him in the opinion, and, if recollect rightly, Hamilton, Knox, and Randolph were consulted and gave the same opinions. That when Mr. Adams came to the Administration, in his first interview with me, he mentioned the necessity of a mission to France and how desirable it would have been to him i he could have got me to undertake it; but that he conceived it would be wrong in him to send me away, and assigned the same reasons Genera Washington had done; and, therefore, he should appoint Mr. Madison, &c. That I had mysel contemplated his (Colonel Burr's) appointment to one of the great offices, in case he was no elected Vice-President; but that as soon as that election was known, I saw it could not be done, for the good reasons which had led Genera Washington and Mr. Adams to the same conclusion; and therefore, in my first letter to Colonel Burr, after the issue was known, I had mentioned to him that a chasm in my arrangements had been produced by this event. I was thus particular in rectifying the date of this letter, because it gave me an opportunity of explaining the grounds on which it was written, which were, indirectly an answer to his present hints. He left the matter with me for consideration, and the conversation was turned to indifferent subjects. I should here notice, that Colonel Burr must have thought that I could swallow strong things in my own favor, when he founded his acquiescence in the nomination as Vice-President, to his desire of promoting my honor, the being with me, whose company and conversation had always been fascinating with him, &c.—THE ANAS. ix, 204. FORD ED., i, 301. (Jan. 1804.)

985. BURR (Aaron), Threatens Jefferson.—About a month ago [March 1806] Colonel Burr called on me, and entered into a conversation, in which he mentioned that a little before my coming into office, I had written to him a letter intimating that I had destined him for high employ, had he not been placed by the people in a different one; that he had signified his willingness to resign as Vice-President, to give aid to the Administration in any other place, that he had never asked an office, however; he asked aid of nobody, but could walk on his own legs and take care of himself; that

I had always used him with politeness, but nothing more; that he aided in bringing on the present order of things; that he had supported the Administration; and that he could do me much harm; he wished, however, to be on different ground; he was now disengaged from all particular business—willing to engage in something—should be in town some days, if I should have anything to propose to him. I observed to him, that I had always been sensible that he possessed talents which might be employed greatly to the advantage of the public, and that as to myself, I had a confidence that if he were employed, he would use his talents for the public good; but that he must be sensible the public had withdrawn their confidence from him, and that in a government like ours it was necessary to embrace in its administration as great a mass of public confidence as possible, by employing those who had a character with the public, and not merely a secondary one through the Executive. He observed, that if we believed a few newspapers, it might be supposed he had lost the public confidence, but that I knew how easy it was to engage newspapers in anything. I observed, that I did not refer to that kind of evidence of his having lost the public confidence, but to the late Presidential election, when, though in possession of the office of Vice-President, there was not a single voice heard for his retaining it. That as to any harm he could do me, I knew no cause why I should desire it, but, at the same time, I feared no injury which any man could do me; that I never had done a single act, or been concerned in any transaction, which I feared to have fully laid open, or which could do me any hurt, if truly stated; that I had never done a single thing with a view to my personal interest, or that of any friend, or with any other view than that of the greatest public good; that, therefore, no threat or fear on that head would ever be a motive of action with me. I did not commit these things to writing at the time, but I do it now, because in a suit between him and Cheetham, he has had a deposition of Mr. Bayard, which seems to have no relation to the suit, nor to any other object than to calumniate me. Bayard pretends to have addressed to me, during the pending of the Presidential election in February, 1801, through General Samuel Smith, certain conditions on which my election might be obtained, and that General Smith, after conversing with me, gave answers from me. This is absolutely false. No proposition of any kind was ever made to me on that occasion by General Smith, nor any answer authorized by me. And this fact General Smith affirms at this moment.— THE ANAS. ix, 208. FORD ED., i, 311. (April 1806.)

986. BURR'S (A.) TREASON, Counteracted.

—During the last session of Congress, Colonel Burr who was here [Washington], finding no hope of being employed in any department of the government, opened himself confidentially to some persons on whom he thought he could rely, on a scheme of separating the Western from the Atlantic States, and erecting the former into an independent confederacy. He had before made a tour of those States which had excited suspicions, as every nation does of such a Catalinian character. * * * We [the cabinet] are of opinion unanimously, that confidential letters be written to the Governors of Ohio, Indiana, Mississippi and Orleans * * * to have him strictly watched and on his committing any overt act unequivocally, to have him arrested and tried for treason,

misdemeanor, or whatever other offence the act may amount to. And in like manner to arrest and try any of his followers committing acts against the laws.—ANAS. FORD ED., i, 318. (July 1806.)

987. BURR'S (A.) TREASON, Decoys.

—Burr has been able to decoy a great proportion of his people by making them believe the government secretly approves of this expedition against the Spanish territories. We are looking with anxiety to see what exertions the Western country will make in the first instance for their own defence; and I confess that my confidence in them is entire.—To GOVERNOR CLAIBORNE. FORD ED., viii, 502. (W., Dec. 1806.)

988. ————.

It is understood that wherever Burr met with subjects who did not choose to embark in his projects, unless approved by their government, he asserted that he had that approbation. Most of them took his word for it, but it is said that with those who would not, the following stratagem was practiced. A forged letter, purporting to be from General Dearborn, was made to express his approbation, and to say that I was absent at Monticello, but that there was no doubt that, on my return, my approbation of his enterprises would be given. This letter was spread open on his table, so as to invite the eye of whoever entered his room, and he contrived occasions of sending up into his room those whom he wished to become witnesses of his acting under sanction. By this means he avoided committing himself to any liability to prosecution for forgery, and gave another proof of being a great man in little things, while he is really small in great ones. I must add General Dearborn's declaration, that he never wrote a letter to Burr in his life, except that when here, once in a winter, he usually wrote him a billet of invitation to dine.—To GEORGE HAY. v, 87. FORD ED., ix, 54. (W., June 1807.)

989. BURR'S (A.) TREASON, Designs of.

—The designs of our Cataline are as real as they are romantic, but the parallel he has selected from history for the model of his own course corresponds but by halves. It is true in its principal character, but the materials to be employed are totally different from the scourings of Rome. I am confident he will be completely deserted on the appearance of the proclamation, because his strength was to consist of people who had been persuaded that the government connived at the enterprise.—To CAESAR A. RODNEY. FORD ED., viii, 497. (W., Dec. 1806.)

990. ————.

Burr's object is to take possession of New Orleans, as a station whence to make an expedition against Vera Cruz and Mexico. His party began their formation at the mouth of the Beaver, whence they started the 1st or 2d of this month, and would collect all the way down the Ohio. We trust that the opposition we have provided at Marietta, Cincinnati. Louisville, and Massac will be sufficient to stop him; but we are not certain because we do not know his strength. It is, therefore, possible he may escape, and then his great rendezvous is to be at Natchez. * * * We expect you will collect all your force of militia, act in conjunction with Colonel Freeman, and take such a stand as shall be concluded best.— To GOVERNOR CLAIBORNE. FORD ED., viii, 501. (W., Dec. 1806.)

991. ————.

His first enterprise was to have been to seize New Orleans, which he supposed would powerfully bridle the upper country, and place him at the door of Mexico.—To MARQUIS DE LAFAYETTE. v, 131. FORD ED., x, 144. (W., July 1807.)

992. —— ——. Burr's enterprise is the most extrarodinary since the days of Don Quixote. It is so extravagant that those who know his understanding, would not believe it if the proofs admitted doubt. He has meant to place himself on the throne of Montezuma, and extend his empire to the Alleghany, seizing on New Orleans as the instrument of compulsion for western States.—To REV. CHAS. CLAY. v, 28. FORD ED., ix, 7. (W., Jan. 1807.)

993. BURR'S (A.) TREASON, Fearless of.—For myself, even in Burr's most flattering periods of the conspiracy, I never entertained one moment's fear. My long and intimate knowledge of my countrymen, satisfied and satisfies me, that let there ever be occasion to display the banners of the law, and the world will see how few and pitiful are those who shall array themselves in opposition.—To DR. JAMES BROWN. v, 379. FORD ED., ix, 211. (W., Oct. 1808.)

994. BURR'S (A.) TREASON, Flagitious.—His conspiracy has been one of the most flagitious of which history will ever furnish an example. He meant to separate the Western States from us, to add Mexico to them, place himself at their head, establish what he would deem an energetic government, and thus provide an example and an instrument for the subversion of our freedom. The man who could expect to effect this, with American materials, must be a fit subject for Bedlam.—To MARQUIS DE LAFAYETTE. v, 129. FORD ED., ix, 113. (W., July 1807.)

995. —— ——. Burr's conspiracy has been one of the most flagitious of which history will ever furnish an example. He had combined the objects of separating the Western States from us, of adding Mexico to them, and of placing himself at their head. But he who could expect to effect such objects by the aid of American citizens, must be perfectly ripe for Bedlam.—To DUPONT DE NEMOURS. v, 128. FORD ED., ix, 111. (W., July 1807.)

996. BURR'S (A.) TREASON, Louisiana and.—It has given me infinite satisfaction that not a single native Creole of Louisiana, and but one American, settled there before the delivery of the country to us, were in his interest. His partisans there were made up of fugitives from justice, or from their debts, who had flocked there from other parts of the United States, after the delivery of the country, and of adventurers and speculators of all descriptions.—To DUPONT DE NEMOURS. v, 128. FORD ED., ix, 113. (W., July 1807.)

997. —— ——. The native inhabitants were unshaken in their fidelity. But there was a small band of American adventurers who had fled from their debts, and who were longing to dip their hands into the mines of Mexico, enlisted in Burr's double project of attacking that country, and severing our Union. Had Burr had a little success in the upper country, these parricides would have joined him.—To MARQUIS DE LAFAYETTE. FORD ED., ix, 65. (W., May 1807.)

998. BURR'S (A.) TREASON, The People and.—The hand of the people has given the mortal blow to a conspiracy which, in other countries, would have called for an appeal to armies, and has proved that government to be the strongest of which every man feels himself a part. It is a happy illustration, too, of the importance of preserving to the State authorities all that vigor which the Constitution foresaw would be necessary, not only for their own safety, but for that of the whole.—To GOVERNOR H. D. TIFFIN. v, 38. FORD ED., ix, 21. (W., Feb. 1807.)

999. —— ——. The whole business has shown that neither Burr nor his [associates] knew anything of the people of this country. A simple proclamation informing the people of these combinations, and calling on them to suppress them, produced an instantaneous *levee en masse* of our citizens wherever there appeared anything to lay hold of, and the whole was crushed in one instant.—To MARQUIS DE LAFAYETTE. FORD ED., ix, 66. (W., May 1807.)

1000. BURR'S (A.) TREASON, Punishment of.—Their crimes are defeated, and whether they shall be punished or not belongs to another department, and is not the subject of even a wish on my part.—To J. H. NICHOLSON. v, 45. FORD ED., ix, 31. (W., Feb. 1807.)

1001. BURR'S (A.) TREASON, Self-government and.—The suppression of the late conspiracy by the hand of the people, uplifted to destroy it wherever it reared its head, manifests their fitness for self-government, and the power of a nation, of which every individual feels that his own will is part of the public authority.—R. TO A. NEW JERSEY LEGISLATURE viii, 122. (Dec. 1807.)

1002. BURR'S (A.) TREASON, Strength of Government and.—The proof we have lately seen of the innate strength of our government, is one of the most remarkable which history has recorded, and shows that we are a people capable of self-government, and worthy of it. The moment that a proclamation apprised our citizens that there were traitors among them, and what was the object, they rose upon them wherever they lurked, and crushed by their own strength what would have produced the march of armies and civil war in any other country. The government which can wield the arm of the people must be the strongest possible.—To MR. WEAVER. v, 89. (W., June 1807.)

1003. —— ——. Nothing has ever so strongly proved the innate force of our form of government, as this conspiracy. Burr had probably engaged one thousand men to follow his fortunes, without letting them know his projects, otherwise than by assuring them that the government approved them. The moment a proclamation was issued, undeceiving them, he found himself left with about thirty desperadoes only. The people rose in mass wherever he was, or was suspected to be, and by their own energy the thing was crushed in one instant, without its having been necessary to employ a man of the military but to take care of their respective stations.—To MARQUIS DE LAFAYETTE. v, 130. FORD ED., ix, 114. (W., July 1807.)

1004. —— ——. This affair has been a great confirmation in my mind of the innate strength of the form of our government. He had probably induced near a thousand men to engage with him, by making them believe the government connived at it. A proclamation alone, by undeceiving them, so completely disarmed him, that he had not above thirty men left, ready to go all lengths with him.—To DUPONT DE NEMOURS. v, 128. FORD ED., ix, 111. (W., July 1807.)

1005. BURR'S (A.) TREASON, Suppressed.—I informed Congress at their last session * of the enterprises against the public peace which were believed to be in preparation by Aaron Burr and his associates, of the measures taken to defeat them, and to bring the offenders to justice. Their enterprises were happily defeated by the patriotic exertions of the militia wherever called into action, by the fidelity of the army, and energy of the commander-in-chief in promptly arranging the difficulties presenting themselves on the Sabine, repairing to meet those arising on the Mississippi, and dissipating, before their explosion, plots engendering them.—SEVENTH ANNUAL MESSAGE. viii, 87. FORD ED., ix, 162. (Oct. 1807.)

1006. BURR'S (A.) TREASON, Western Loyalty.—The enterprise has done good by proving that the attachment of the people in the West is as firm as that in the East to the union of our country, and by establishing a mutual and universal confidence.—To MARQUIS DE LAFAYETTE. FORD ED., ix, 66. (W., May 1807.)

1007. BURR'S (A.) TRIAL, Arrest.—Your sending here [Washington] Swartwout and Ballman and adding to them Burr, Blennerhassett and Tyler, should they fall into your hands, will be supported by the public opinion. * * * I hope, however, you will not extend this deportation to persons against whom there is only suspicion, or shades of offence not strongly marked. In that case, I fear the public sentiment would desert you: because seeing no danger here, violations of law are felt with strength.—To GENERAL WILKINSON. v, 39. FORD ED., ix, 4. (W., Feb. 1807.)

1008. —— ——. That the arrest of Colonel Burr was military has been disproved; but had it been so, every honest man and good citizen is bound, by any means in his power, to arrest the author of projects so daring and dangerous.—To EDMUND PENDLETON GAINES. v, 141. FORD ED., ix, 122. (W., July 1807.)

— BURR'S (A.) TRIAL, Bollman's confession.—See BOLLMAN.

1009. BURR'S (A.) TRIAL, Charges.—I do suppose the following overt acts will be proved. 1. The enlistment of men in a regular way. 2. The regular mounting of guard round Blennerhassett's Island * * *. 3. The rendezvous of Burr with his men at the mouth of the Cumberland. 4. His letter to the acting Governor of Mississippi, holding up the prospect of civil war. 5. His capitulation regularly signed with the aids of the Governor, as between two independent and hostile commanders.—To WILLIAM B. GILES. v, 66. FORD ED., ix, 43. (M., April 1807.)

1010. BURR'S (A.) TRIAL, Conviction doubtful.—That there should be anxiety and doubt in the public mind, in the present defective state of the proof, is not wonderful; and this has been sedulously encouraged by the tricks of the judges to force trials before it is possible to collect the evidence, dispersed through a line of two thousand miles from Maine to Orleans.—To WILLIAM B. GILES. v, 65. FORD ED., ix, 42. (M., April 1807.)

1011. —— ——. Although there is not a man in the United States who doubts his guilt, such are the jealous provisions of our laws in

* Jefferson sent a message to Congress, January 22, 1807, giving a record of the facts in Burr's conspiracy.—EDITOR.

favor of the accused against the accuser, that I question if he is convicted.—To MARQUIS DE LAFAYETTE. v, 130. FORD ED., ix, 113. (W., July 1807.)

1012. BURR'S (A.) TRIAL, Court rulings.—Hitherto we have believed our law to be, that suspicion on probable grounds was sufficient cause to commit a person for trial, allowing time to collect witnesses till the trial. But the judges have decided, that conclusive evidence of guilt must be ready in the moment of arrest, or they will discharge the malefactor. If this is still insisted on, Burr will be discharged; because his crimes having been sown from Maine through the whole line of the western waters to New Orleans, we cannot bring the witnesses here under four months.—To JAMES BOWDOIN. v, 65. FORD ED., ix, 41. (W., April 1807.)

1013. BURR'S (A.) TRIAL, Evidence required.—A moment's calculation will show that the evidence cannot be collected under four months, probably five, from the moment of deciding when and where the trial shall be. I desired Mr. Rodney [Attorney General] expressly to inform the Chief Justice of this, inofficially. But Mr. Marshall says: "More than five weeks have elapsed since the opinion of the Supreme Court has declared the necessity of proving the overt acts, if they exist. Why are they not proved?" In what terms of decency can we speak of this? As if an express could go to Natchez, or the mouth of the Cumberland, and return in five weeks, to do what has never taken less than twelve. Again: "If, in November or December last, a body of troops had been assembled on the Ohio, it is impossible to suppose the affidavits establishing the fact could not have been obtained by the last of March." But I ask the judge where they should have been lodged? At Frankfort? at Cincinnati? at Nashville? St. Louis? Natchez? New Orleans? These were the probable places of apprehension and examination. It was not known at *Washington* till the 26th of March that Burr would escape from the Western tribunals, be retaken and brought to an Eastern one; and in five days after (neither five months nor five weeks, as the judge calculated), he says, "it is impossible to suppose the affidavits could not have been obtained". Where? At Richmond he certainly meant, or meant only to throw dust in the eyes of his audience. But all the principles of law are to be perverted which would bear on the favorite offenders who endeavor to overturn this odious Republic. "I understand", says the judge, "*probable* cause of guilt to be a case made out by *proof* furnishing good reason to believe", &c. Speaking as a lawyer, he must mean legal proof, i. e., proof on oath, at least. But this is confounding *probability and proof*. We had always before understood that where there was reasonable ground to believe guilt, the offender must be put on his trial. That guilty intentions were probable, the judge believed. And as to the overt acts, were not the bundle of letters of information in Mr. Rodney's hands, the letters and facts published in the local newspapers, Burr's flight, and the universal belief or rumor of his guilt, probable ground for presuming the facts of enlistment, military guard, rendezvous, threats of civil war, or capitulation, so as to put him on trial? Is there a candid man in the United States who does not believe some one, if not all, of these overt acts to have taken place?—To WILLIAM B. GILES. v, 67. FORD ED., ix, 44. (M., April 1807.)

— BURR'S (A.) TRIAL, Executive Papers demanded.—See PAPERS (EXECUTIVE).

1014. BURR'S (A.) TRIAL, Federalist support.—The federalists appear to make Burr's cause their own, and to spare no efforts to screen his adherents. Their great mortification is at the failure of his plans. Had a little success dawned on him, their openly joining him might have produced some danger.—To COLONEL G. MORGAN. v, 57. (W., March 1807.)

1015. ———. The federalists, too, give all their aid, making Burr's cause their own, mortified only that he did not separate the Union or overturn the government, and proving, that had he had a little dawn of success, they would have joined him to introduce his object, their favorite monarchy, as they would any other enemy, foreign or domestic, who could rid them of this hateful Republic for any other government in exchange.—To WILLIAM B. GILES. v, 66. FORD ED., ix, 42. (M., April 1807.)

1016. ———. The fact is that the federalists make Burr's case their own, and exert their whole influence to shield him from punishment, as they did the adherents of Miranda. And it is unfortunate that federalism is still predominant in our Judiciary department, which is in opposition to the Legislative and Executive branches, and is able to baffle their measures often.—To JAMES BOWDOIN. v, 65. FORD ED., ix, 41. (W., April 1807.)

1017. ———. The first ground of complaint [by the federalists] was the supine inattention of the Administration to a treason stalking through the land in open day. The present one, that they have crushed it before it was ripe for execution, so that no overt acts can be produced. This last may be true; though I believe it is not. Our information having been chiefly by way of letter, we do not know of a certainty yet what will be proved. We have set on foot an inquiry through the whole of the country which has been the scene of these transactions, to be able to prove to the courts, if they will give time, or to the public by way of communication to Congress, what the real facts have been. For obtaining this, we are obliged to appeal to the patriotism of particular persons in different places, of whom we have requested to make the inquiry in their neighborhood, and on such information as shall be voluntarily offered. Aided by no process or facilities from the *federal* courts, but frowned on by their new born zeal for the liberty of those men whom we would not permit to overthrow the liberties of their country, we can expect no revealments from the accomplices of the chief offender. Of treasonable intentions the judges have been obliged to confess there is probable appearance. What loophole they will find in the case, when it comes to trial, we cannot foresee. Eaton, Stoddart, Wilkinson, and two others whom I must not name, will satisfy the world, if not the judges, of Burr's guilt.—To WILLIAM B. GILES. v, 66. FORD ED., ix, 42. (M., April 1807.)

1018. BURR'S (A.) TRIAL, Grand Jury and.—The favor of the marshal and the judge promises Burr all which can depend on them. A grand jury of two "feds", four "quids" and ten republicans, does not seem to be a fair representation of the State of Virginia. I have always entertained a high opinion of the marshal's integrity and political correctness. But in a State where there are not more than eight "quids", how five of them should have

been summoned to one jury, is difficult to explain from accident. But all this will show the original error of establishing a judiciary independent of the nation, and which, from the citadel of the law, can turn its guns on those they were meant to defend, and control and fashion their proceedings to its own will.—To JOHN W. EPPES. FORD ED., ix, 68. (W., May 1807.)

1019. BURR'S (A.) TRIAL, Guilt clear.—Before an impartial jury, Burr's conduct would convict himself, were not one word of testimony to be offered against him. But to what a state will our law be reduced by party feelings in those who administer it? *—To GEORGE HAY. v, 174. FORD ED., ix, 62. (M., Aug. 1807.)

— BURR'S (A.) TRIAL, Jefferson Subpœnaed.—See PRESIDENT.

1020. BURR'S (A.) TRIAL, Judiciary Partisanship.—If there ever had been an instance in this or the preceding administrations, of federal judges so applying principles of law as to condemn a federal or acquit a republican offender, I should have judged them in the present case with more charity. All this, however, will work well. The nation will judge both the offender and judges for themselves. If a member of the Executive or Legislature does wrong, the day is never far distant when the people will remove him. They will see then and amend the error in our Constitution, which makes any branch independent of the nation. They will see that one of the great coordinate branches of the government, setting itself in opposition to the other two, and to the common sense of the nation, proclaims impunity to that class of offenders which endeavors to overturn the Constitution, and are themselves protected in it by the Constitution itself; for impeachment is a farce which will not be tried again. If their protection of Burr produces this amendment, it will do more good than his condemnation would have done. * * * If his punishment can be commuted now for an useful amendment of the Constitution, I shall rejoice in it.—To WILLIAM B. GILES. v, 68. FORD ED., ix, 45. (M., April 1807.)

1021. ——— ———. Burr's trial goes on to the astonishment of all, as to the manner of conducting it.—To ALBERT GALLATIN. v, 172. (M., Aug. 1807.)

1022. ——— ———. The scenes which have been acted at Richmond are such as have never before been exhibited in any country where all regard to public character has not yet been thrown off. They are equivalent to a proclamation of impunity to every traitorous combination which may be formed to destroy the Union; and they preserve a head for all such combinations as may be formed within, and a centre for all the intrigues and machinations which foreign governments may nourish to disturb us. However, they will produce an amendment to the Constitution which, keeping the judges independent of the Executive, will not leave them so, of the nation.—To GENERAL WILKINSON. v, 198. FORD ED., ix, 142. (M., Sep. 1807.)

1023. ——— ———. The scenes which have been acting at Richmond are sufficient to fill us with alarm. We had supposed we possessed fixed laws to guard us equally against treason and oppression. But it now appears we have no law but the will of the judge. Never will chicanery have a more difficult task than has been

* Hay was the U. S. District Attorney.—EDITOR.

now accomplished to warp the text of the law to the will of him who is to construe it. Our case, too, is the more desperate, as the attempt to make the law plainer by amendment is only throwing out new amendments for sophistry.—To WILLIAM THOMPSON. FORD ED., ix, 143. (M., Sep. 1807.)

— BURR'S (A.) TRIAL, Judge Marshall and.—See MARBURY vs. MADISON, MARSHALL.

1024. BURR'S (A.) TRIAL, Release.— The event has been—(blank in the original) not only to clear Burr, but to prevent the evidence from ever going before the world. But this latter case must not take place. It is now, therefore, more than ever indispensable, that not a single witness be paid or permitted to depart until his testimony has been committed to writing, either as delivered in court, or taken by yourself in the presence of any of Burr's counsel, who may choose to attend to cross-examine. These whole proceedings will be laid before Congress, that they may decide whether the defect has been in the evidence of guilt, or in the law, or in the application of the law, and that they may provide the proper remedy for the past and the future.—To GEORGE HAY. v, 188. (M., Sep. 1807.)

1025. —— ——. The criminal is preserved to become the rallying point of all the disaffected and the worthless of the United States, and to be the pivot on which all the intrigues and the conspiracies which foreign governments may wish to disturb us with, are to turn. If he is convicted of the misdemeanor, the judge must in decency give us a respite by some short confinement of him; but we must expect it to be very short.—To GEORGE HAY. v, 187. (M., Sept. 1807.)

1026. BURR'S (A.) TRIAL, Relegated to Congress.—Be * * * the result before the formal tribunal fair or false, it becomes our duty to provide that full testimony shall be laid before the Legislature, and through them the public. For this purpose, it is necessary that we be furnished with the testimony of every person who shall be with you as a witness. * * * Go into any expense necessary for this purpose * * * .—To GEORGE HAY. v, 81. FORD ED., ix, 52. (W., May 1807.)

1027. —— ——. I shall think it my duty to lay before you the proceedings and the evidence publicly exhibited on the arraignment of the principal offenders before the Circuit Court of Virginia. You will be enabled to judge whether the defeat was in the testimony, in the law, or in the administration of the law; and wherever it shall be found, the Legislature alone can apply or originate the remedy. The framers of our Constitution certainly supposed they had guarded, as well their government against destruction by treason, as their citizens against oppression, under pretence of it; and if these ends are not attained, it is of importance to inquire by what means, more effectual, they may be secured.*—SEVENTH ANNUAL MESSAGE. viii, 87. FORD ED., viii, 163. (Oct. 1807.)

1028. CABELL (J. C.), University of Va. and.—We always counted on you as the main pillar of their [University of Virginia measures] support.—To JOSEPH C. CABELL. FORD ED., ix, 500. (M., 1815.)

1029. CABINET, Confidence in.—The Cabinet Council of the President should be of

* As a result Congress enacted additional rigorous legislation respecting treason.—EDITOR.

his bosom confidence. Our geographical position has been an impediment to that.—To SAMUEL DEXTER. iv, 359. FORD ED., vii, 498. (W., Feb. 1801.)

1030. CABINET, Contentions.—In the discussions [on the affairs of France and England], Hamilton and myself were daily pitted in the cabinet like two cocks. We were then but four in number, and, according to the majority, which of course was three to one, the President decided. The pain was for Hamilton and myself, but the public experienced no inconvenience.—To DR. WALTER JONES. v, 510. FORD ED., ix, 273. (M., 1810.)

1031. —— ——. The method of separate consultation, practiced sometimes in the Cabinet, prevents disagreeable collisions.—To JOEL BARLOW. v, 496. FORD ED., ix, 269. (M., 1810.)

1032. CABINET, Enmity in.—I have learned, with real sorrow, that circumstances have arisen among our executive counsellors, which have rendered foes those who once were friends. To themselves it will be a source of infinite pain and vexation, and therefore chiefly I lament it, for I have a sincere esteem for both parties. To the President, it will be really inconvenient; but to the nation I do not know that it can do serious injury, unless we were to believe the newspapers, which pretend that Mr. Gallatin will go out. That, indeed, would be a day of mourning for the United States; but I hope that the position of both gentlemen may be made so easy as to give no cause for either to withdraw.—To DR. WALTER JONES. v, 509. FORD ED., ix, 273. (M., March 1810.)

1033. —— ——. The dissensions between two members of the Cabinet are to be lamented. But why should these force Mr. Gallatin to withdraw? They cannot be greater than between Hamilton and myself, and yet we served together four years in that way. We had indeed no personal dissensions. Each of us, perhaps, thought well of the other as a man, but as politicians it was impossible for two men to be of more opposite principles.—To JOEL BARLOW. v, 496. FORD ED., ix, 269. (M., 1810.)

1034. CABINET, Equipoise of Opinion in.—President Washington [said to me] that he thought it important to preserve the check of my opinions in the Administration, in order to keep things in their proper channel, and prevent them from going too far.—THE ANAS. ix, 121. FORD ED., i, 204. (Oct. 1792.)

1035. CABINET, Harmonious.—Our Administration now drawing towards a close, I have a sublime pleasure in believing it will be distinguished as much by having placed itself above all the passions which could disturb its harmony, as by the great operations by which it will have advanced the well-being of the nation.—To ALBERT GALLATIN. v, 23. FORD ED., viii, 476. (W., 1806.)

1036. —— ——. I have so much reliance on the superior good sense and candor of all those associated with me, as to be satisfied that they will not suffer either friend or foe to sow tares among us.—To ALBERT GALLATIN. v, 23. FORD ED., viii, 476. (W., 1806.)

1037. ——— ———. Among the felicities which have attended my administration, I am most thankful for having been able to procure coadjutors so able, so disinterested, and so harmonious. Scarcely ever has a difference of opinion appeared among us which has not, by candid consultation, been amalgamated into something which all approved; and never one which in the slightest degree affected our personal attachments.—To MR. WEAVER. v, 89. (W., 1807.)

1038. ——— ———. I look back with peculiar satisfaction on the harmony and cordial good will which, to ourselves and to our brethren of the Cabinet, so much sweetened our toils.—To ROBERT SMITH. v, 451. (M., June 1809.)

1039. ——— ———. I have thought it among the most fortunate circumstances of my late Administration that, through its eight years' continuance, it was conducted with a cordiality and harmony among all its members, which never were ruffled on any, the greatest or smallest occasion.—To WILLIAM DUANE. v, 533. (M., 1810.)

1040. ——— ———. The harmony among us was so perfect, that whatever instrument appeared most likely to effect the object, was always used without jealousy.—To WILLIAM WIRT. v, 594. FORD ED., ix, 318. (M., 1811.)

1041. ——— ———. The affectionate harmony of our Cabinet is among the sweetest of my recollections.—To CÆSAR RODNEY. vi, 448. (M., 1815.)

1042. CABINET, Indebtedness to.—Far from assuming to myself the merit of the measures you note, they belong first, to a wise and patriotic Legislature, which has given them the form and sanction of law, and next to my faithful and able fellow laborers in the Executive administration.—R. To A. MASSACHUSETTS LEGISLATURE. viii, 116. (1807.)

1043. ——— ———. For the advantages flowing from the measures of the government, you are indebted principally to a wise and patriotic Legislature, and to the able and inestimable coadjutors with whom it has been my good fortune to be associated in the direction of affairs.—R. To A. PHILADELPHIA CITIZENS. viii, 145. (1809.)

1044. ——— ———. Whatever may be the merit or demerit of the acquisition of Louisiana, I divide it with my colleagues, to whose counsels I was indebted for a course of administration which, notwithstanding this late coalition of clay and brass,, will, I hope, continue to receive the approbation of our country.—To HENRY DEARBORN. vii, 215. FORD ED., x, 192. (M., August 1821.)

1045. CABINET, Intrigue in.—It is impossible for you to conceive what is passing in our conclave; and it is evident that one or

two at least, under pretence of avoiding war on the one side, have no great antipathy to run foul of it on the other, and to make a part in the confederacy of princes against human liberty.—To JAMES MADISON. iii, 563. FORD ED., vi, 261. (Pa., May 1793.)

1046. CABINET, A Kitchen.—That there is an ostensible Cabinet and a concealed one, a public profession and concealed counteraction, is false.—To WILLIAM DUANE. iv 592. FORD ED., viii, 433. (W., 1806.)

1047. CABINET, Rules of Jefferson's.— Coming all of us into executive office, new and unfamiliar with the course of business previously practiced, it was not to be expected we should in the outset, adopt in every part a line of proceeding so perfect as to admit no amendment. The mode and degrees of communication, particularly between the President and heads of departments, have not been practiced exactly on the same scale in all of them. Yet it would certainly be more safe and satisfactory for ourselves as well as the public, that not only the best, but also an uniform course of proceeding as to manner and degree, should be observed. Having been a member of the first Administration under General Washington, I can state with exactness what our course then was. Letters of business came addressed sometimes to the President, but most frequently to the heads of departments. If addressed to himself, he referred them to the proper department to be acted on; if to one of the Secretaries, the letter, if it required no answer, was communicated to the President, simply for his information. If an answer was requisite, the Secretary of the department communicated the letter and his proposed answer to the President. Generally they were simply sent back after perusal, which signified his approbation. Sometimes he returned them with an informal note, suggesting an alteration or a query. If a doubt of any importance arose, he reserved it for conference. By this means, he was always in accurate possession of all facts and proceedings in every part of the Union, and to whatsoever department they related; he formed a central point for the different branches; preserved an unity of object and action among them; exercised that participation in the suggestion of affairs which his office made incumbent on him; and met himself the due responsibility for whatever was done. During Mr. Adam's Administration, his long and habitual absences from the seat of government, rendered this kind of communication impracticable, removed him from any share in the transaction of affairs, and parcelled out the government, in fact, among four independent heads, drawing sometimes in opposite directions. That the former is preferable to the latter course, cannot be doubted. It gave, indeed, to the heads of departments the trouble of making up, once a day, a packet of all their communications for the perusal of the President; it commonly also retarded one day their despatches by mail. But in pressing cases, this injury was prevented by presenting that case singly for immediate attention; and it produced us in return the benefit of his sanction for every act we did. Whether any change in circumstances may render a change in this procedure necessary, a little experience will show us. But I cannot withhold recommending to heads of departments, that we should adopt this course for the present, leaving any necessary modifications of it to time and trial. I am sure my conduct must have proved, better than a thousand declarations would, that my confidence in those whom I am so happy as to have associated with me, is unlimited, unqualified, and unabated. I am well satisfied that everything goes on with a wisdom and rectitude which I could not improve. If I had the universe to choose from, I could not change one of my associates to my better satisfaction. My sole motives are those before expressed, as governing the first Administration in chalking out the rules of their proceeding; adding to them only a sense of obligation imposed on me by the public will, to meet personally the duties to which they have appointed me.—To THE HEADS OF THE DEPARTMENTS. iv, 415. FORD ED., viii, 99. (W., Nov. 1801.)

1048. —— ——. In ordinary affairs every head of a department consults me on those of his department, and where anything arises too difficult or important to be decided between us, the consultation becomes general.— To WILLIAM DUANE. iv, 592. FORD ED., viii, 432. (W., 1806.)

1049. —— ——. Something now occurs almost every day on which it is desirable to have the opinions of the heads of departments, yet to have a formal meeting every day would consume so much of their time as to seriously obstruct their regular business. I have proposed to them, as most convenient for them, and wasting less of their time, to call on me at any moment of the day which suits their separate convenience, when, besides any other business they may have to do, I can learn their opinions separately on any matter which has occurred, and also communicate the information received daily.—To ALBERT GALLATIN. v, 122. FORD ED., ix, 104. (W., July 1807.)

1050. CABINET, Theory and the.—Our Government, although in theory subject to be directed by the unadvised will of the President, is, and from its origin has been, a very different thing in practice. The minor business in each department is done by the head of the department, on consultation with the President alone. But all matters of importance or difficulty are submitted to all the heads of departments composing the Cabinet: sometimes by the President consulting them separately and successively, as they happen to call on him; but in the gravest cases, by calling them together, discussing the subject maturely, and finally taking the vote, in which the President counts himself but as one. So that in all important cases the Executive is, in fact, a directory, which certainly the President might control; but of this there was never an

example, either in the first or the present administration. I have heard, indeed, that my predecessor sometimes decided things against his council by dashing and trampling his wig on the floor. This only proves what you and I know, that he had a better heart than head. —To WILLIAM SHORT. v, 94. FORD ED., ix, 69. (W., 1807.)

1051. CABINET, An Unbroken.—It would have been to me the greatest of consolations to have gone through my term with the same coadjutors, and to have shared with them the merit, or demerit, of whatever good or evil we may have done.—To HENRY DEARBORN. v, 229. FORD ED., ix, 171. (W., Jan. 1808.)

1052. CABINET, Verbal and Written Opinions.—I practiced the method [of assembling the Cabinet members and taking their opinions verbally], because the harmony was so cordial among us all, that we never failed, by a contribution of mutual views on a subject, to form an opinion acceptable to the whole. I think there never was one instance to the contrary, in any case of consequence.— To DR. WALTER JONES. v, 510. FORD ED., ix, 273. (M., 1810.)

1053. —— ——. The [method of taking the opinions of the Cabinet verbally] does, in fact, transform the Executive into a directory, and I hold the other method [opinions in writing,] to be more constitutional. It is better calculated, too, to prevent collision and irritation, and to cure it, or at least suppress its effects when it has already taken place.—To DR. WALTER JONES. v, 510. FORD ED., ix, 273. (M., 1810.)

1054. —— ——. The ordinary business of every day is done by consultation between the President and the head of the department alone to which it belongs. For measures of importance or difficulty, a consultation is held with the heads of departments, either assembled, or by taking their opinions separately in conversation or in writing. The latter is most strictly in the spirit of the Constitution: because the President, on weighing the advice of all, is left free to make up an opinion for himself. In this way they are not brought together, and it is not necessarily known to any what opinion the others have given. This was General Washington's practice for the first two or three years of his Administration, till the affairs of France and England threatened to embroil us, and rendered consideration and discussion desirable.—To DR. WALTER JONES. v, 510. FORD ED., ix, 273. (M., 1810.)

1055. CABINET, Vice-President and.— The Vice-President, Secretaries of the Treasury and War, and myself, met. * * * We unanimously advised an immediate order*

---

* Before the President set out on his Southern tour in April, 1791, he addressed a letter of the 4th of that month, from Mt. Vernon to the Secretaries of State, Treasury and War, desiring that if any serious and important cases should arise during his absence, they would consult and act on them, and he requested that the Vice-President should also be consulted. This

* * * .—To President Washington. iii,
247. Ford ed., v, 320. (Pa., April 1791.)

1056. —— ——. My letters inform me
that Mr. Adams speaks of me with great
friendship and with satisfaction in the prospect of administering the government in concurrence with me. * * * If by that he
means the Executive Cabinet, both duty and
inclination will shut that door to me. I cannot have a wish to see the scenes of 1793 revived as to myself, and to descend daily into
the arena like a gladiator, to suffer martyrdom in every conflict.—To James Madison.
iv, 161. Ford ed., vii, 107. (M., Jan. 1797.)

1057. CABINET OFFICERS, Congress
and.—An attempt has been made to give further extent to the influence of the Executive
over the Legislature, by permitting the heads
of departments to attend the House, and explain their measures vivâ voce. But it was
negatived by a majority of 35 to 11, which
gives us some hope of the increase of the republican vote.—To T. M. Randolph. iii, 491.
Ford ed., vi, 134. (Pa., Nov. 1792.)

1058. CABINET OFFICERS, Courtesy
between.—It is but common decency to leave
to my successor [in the State Department] the
moulding of his own business.—To William
Short, iii, 504. Ford ed., vi, 156. (1793.)

1059. CABINET OFFICERS, Newspapers and.—Is not the dignity, and even decency of government committed, when one of
its principal ministers enlists himself as an
anonymous writer or paragraphist for either
the one or the other paper? *—To President
Washington. iii, 467. Ford ed., vi, 108.
(M., 1792.)

1060. CABINET OFFICERS, Public
Confidence in.—It is essential to assemble in
the outset persons to compose our Administration, whose talents, integrity and revolutionary name and principles may inspire the
nation at once, with unbounded confidence,
and impose an awful silence on all the maligners of republicanism; as may suppress in embryo the purpose avowed by one of their most
daring and effective chiefs, of beating down
the Administration. These names do not
abound at this day. So few are they, that
yours cannot be spared among them without
leaving a blank which cannot be filled. If I
can obtain for the public the aid of those I
have contemplated, I fear nothing. If this
cannot be done, then we are unfortunate indeed! We shall be unable to realize the prospects which have been held out to the people,
and we must fall back into monarchism, for
want of heads, not hands to help us out of it.
This is a common cause, common to all republicans. Though I have been too honorably
placed in front of those who are to enter the
breach so happily made, yet the energies of
every individual are necessary, and in the very
place where his energies can most serve the

was the only occasion on which that officer was ever
requested to take part in a Cabinet question.—The
Anas. ix, 96. Ford ed., i, 165. (1818.)
* Refering to Alexander Hamilton's newspaper
articles.—Editor.

enterprise. * * * The part which circumstances constrain us to propose to you is the
Secretaryship of the Navy. * * * Come
forward, then, and give us the aid of your
talents, and the weight of your character towards the new establishment of republicanism: I say, for its new establishment, for
hitherto we have only seen its travesty.—To
Robert R. Livingston. iv, 338. Ford ed., vii,
464. (M., Dec. 1800.)

1061. CABINET OFFICERS, Society
and.—The gentlemen who composed General
Washington's first Administration took up,
too universally, a practice of general entertainment, which was unnecessary, obstructive of
business, and so oppressive to themselves, that
it was among the motives for their retirement.
Their successors profited by the experiment,
and lived altogether as private individuals,
and so have ever continued to do. Here,
[Washington] indeed, it cannot be otherwise,
our situation being so rural, that during the
vacations of the Legislature we shall have no
society but of the officers of the government,
and in time of sessions the Legislature is become and becoming so numerous, that for the
last half dozen years nobody but the President
has pretended to entertain them.—To Robert
R. Livingston. iv, 339. Ford ed., vii, 465.
(W., Dec. 1800.)

— CABOT FAMILY, Arms of.—See
Birds, Turkey.

— CÆSAR.—See Cicero.

1062. CALLENDER (J. T.), Defence of.
—I think it essentially just and necessary that
Callender should be substantially defended.
Whether in the first stages by public interference, or private contributors, may be a question,
Perhaps it might be as well that it should be
left to the Legislature, who will meet in time,
and before whom you can lay the matter so
as to bring it before them. It is become peculiarly their cause, and may furnish them a
fine opportunity of showing their respect to the
Union, and at the same time of doing justice in
another way to those whom they cannot protect
without committing the public tranquillity.—To
James Monroe. Ford ed., vii, 448. (Ep., May
1800.)

1063. CALLENDER (J. T.), Federalists
and.—I enclose you a paper which shows the
tories mean to pervert these charities to Callender as much as they can. They will probably
first represent me as the patron and support of
the "Prospect Before Us," and other things of
Callender's; and then picking out all the scurrilities of the author against General Washington,
Mr. Adams, and others, impute them to me. I,
as well as most other republicans who were in
the way of doing it, contributed what I could
afford to the support of the republican papers
and printers, paid sums of money for The Bee,
the Albany Register, &c., when they were stag-
gering under the Sedition law; contributed to
the fines of Callender himself, of Holt, Brown
and others, suffering under that law. I discharged, when I came into office, such as were
under the persecution of our enemies, without
instituting any prosecutions in retaliation.
They may, therefore, with the same justice,
impute to me, or to every republican contribu-
tor, everything which was ever published in

those papers, or by those persons.—To JAMES MONROE. iv, 447. FORD ED., viii, 167. (W., 1802.)

1064. CALLENDER (J. T.), Fine paid. —To take from Callender all room for complaint, I think, with you, we had better refund his fine by private contributions. I enclose you an order * * * for fifty dollars, which, I believe, is one-fourth of the whole sum.—To JAMES MONROE. FORD ED., viii, 58. (W., May 1801.)

1065. CALLENDER (J. T.), Persecution of.—The violence which was meditated against you lately has excited a very general indignation in this part of the country. Our State, from its first plantation, has been remarkable for its order and submission to the laws. But three instances are recollected in its history of an organized opposition to the laws. The first was Bacon's rebellion; the second, our Revolution; the third, the Richmond association, who, by their committee, have in the public papers avowed their purpose of taking out of the hands of the law the function of declaring who may or may not have free residence among us. But these gentlemen miscalculate the temper and force of this country extremely if they supposed there would have been a want of either to support the authority of the laws; and equally mistake their own interests in setting the example of club-law. Whether their self-organized election of a committee, and publication of their manifesto, be such overt acts as bring them within the pale of the law; the law, I presume is to decide; and there it is our duty to leave it.—To J. T. CALLENDER. FORD ED., vii, 392. (M., Sep. 1799.)

1066. CALLENDER (J. T.), Relations with Jefferson.—I am really mortified at the base ingratitude of Callender. It presents human nature in a hideous form. It gives me concern, because I perceive that relief, which was afforded him on mere motives of charity, may be viewed under the aspect of employing him as a writer. When the "*Political Progress of Britain*" first appeared in this country, it was in a periodical publication called *The Bee*, where I saw it. I was speaking of it in terms of strong approbation to a friend in Philadelphia, when he asked me if I knew that the author was then in the city, a fugitive from prosecution on account of that work, and in want of employ for his subsistence. This was the first of my learning that Callender was author of the work. I considered him as a man of science fled from persecution, and assured my friend of my readiness to do whatever could serve him. It was long after this before I saw him; probably not till 1798. He had, in the meantime, written a second part of the *Political Progress*, much inferior to the first, and his *History of the United States*. In 1798, I think, I was applied to by Mr. Leiper to contribute to his relief. I did so. In 1799, I think, S. T. Mason applied for him. I contributed again. He had, by this time, paid me two or three personal visits. When he fled in a panic from Philadelphia to General Mason's, he wrote to me that he was a fugitive, in want of employ, wished to know if he could get into a counting-house or a school, in my neighborhood or in that of Richmond; that he had materials for a volume, and if he could get as much money as would buy the paper, the profit of the sale would be all his own. I availed myself of this pretext to cover a mere charity, by desiring him to consider me a subscriber for as many copies of his book as the money enclosed (fifty dollars)

amounted to; but to send me two copies only, as the others might lie till called for. But I discouraged his coming into my neighborhood. His first writings here had fallen far short of his original *Political Progress*, and the scurrilities of his subsequent ones began evidently to do mischief. As to myself, no man wished more to see his pen stopped; but I considered him still as a proper object of benevolence. The succeeding year, he again wanted money to buy paper for another volume. I made his letter, as before, the occasion of giving him another fifty dollars. He considers these as proofs of my approbation of his writings, when they were mere charities, yielded under a strong conviction that he was injuring us by his writings. It is known to many that the sums given to him were such, and even smaller than I was in the habit of giving to others in distress, of the federal as well as the republican party, without attention to political principles. Soon after I was elected to the government, Callender came on here [Washington] wishing to be made postmaster at Richmond. I knew him to be totally unfit for it; and however ready I was to aid him with my own charities (and I then gave him fifty dollars). I did not think the public offices confided to me to give away as charities. He took it in mortal offence, and from that moment has been hauling off to his former enemies, the federalists. Besides the letters I wrote him in answer to the one from General Mason, I wrote him another, containing answers to two questions he addressed to me. 1. Whether Mr. Jay received salary as Chief Justice and Envoy at the same time; and 2. something relative to the expenses of an embassy to Constantinople. I think these were the only letters I ever wrote him in answer to volumes he was perpetually writing to me. This is the true state of what has passed between him and me. I do not know that it can be used without committing me in controversy, as it were, with one too little respected by the public to merit that notice. I leave to your judgment what use can be made of these facts. Perhaps it will be better judged of, when we see what use the tories will endeavor to make of their new friend.—To JAMES MONROE. iv. 444. FORD ED., viii, 164. (W., July 1802.)

1067. CALLENDER (J. T.), Threats of. —Callender is arrived here [Washington]. He did not call on me; but understanding he was in distress I sent Captain Lewis to him with fifty dollars, to inform him we were making some enquiries as to his fine which would take a little time, and lest he should suffer in the meantime, I had sent him, &c. His language to Captain Lewis was very high-toned. He intimated that he was in possession of things which he could and would make use of in a certain case; that he received the fifty dollars, not as a charity but a due, in fact as hush money; that I knew what he expected, viz., a certain office, and more to this effect. Such a misconstruction of my charities puts an end to them forever. You will, therefore, be so good as to make no use of the order* I enclosed you. He knows nothing of me which I am not willing to declare to the world myself. I knew him first as the author of the *Political Progress* of Britain, a work I had read with great satisfaction, and as a fugitive from persecution for this very work. I gave to him from time to time such aids as I could afford, merely as a man of genius suffering under persecution, and not

* An order for fifty dollars towards payment of Callender's fine.—EDITOR.

as a writer in our politics. It is long since I wished he would cease writing on them, as doing more harm than good.—To JAMES MONROE. FORD ED., viii, 61. (W., May 1801.)

1068. CALONNE (C. A. de), Character of.—The memoir of M. de Calonne, though it does not prove him to be more innocent than his predecessors, shows him not to have been that exaggerated scoundrel which the calculations and the clamors of the public have supposed.—To MADAME DE CARNY. D. L. J., 132. (P., 1787.)

1069. CALUMNY, Character and.—I laid it down as a law to myself, to take no notice of the thousand calumnies issued against me, but to trust my character to my own conduct, and the good sense and candor of my fellow citizens.—To WILSON C. NICHOLAS. v, 452. FORD ED., ix, 253. (M., 1809.)

1070. CALUMNY, Contradiction of.—I have never even contradicted the thousands of calumnies so industriously propagated against myself.—To THOMAS SEYMOUR. v, 43. FORD ED., ix, 30. (W., 1807.)

1071. CALUMNY, Foolish.—Of all the charges brought against me by my political adversaries, that of possessing some science has probably done them the least credit. Our countrymen are too enlightened themselves to believe that ignorance is the best qualification for their service.—To C. F. WELLS. v, 483. (M., 1809.)

1072. CALUMNY, Forgotten.—The expression respecting myself, stated in your letter to have been imputed to you by your calumniators, had either never been heard by me, or, if heard, had been unheeded and forgotten. I have been too much the butt of such falsehoods myself to do others the injustice of permitting them to make the least impression on me. My consciousness that no man on earth has me under his thumb is evidence enough that you never used the expression.—To GENERAL WILKINSON. v, 573. (M., 1811.)

1073. CALUMNY, Newspaper.—Were I to undertake to answer the calumnies of the newspapers, it would be more than all my own time, and that of twenty aids could effect. For while I should be answering one, twenty new ones would be invented. I have thought it better to trust to the justice of my countrymen, that they would judge me by what they see of my conduct on the stage where they have placed me, and what they knew of me before the epoch since which a particular party has supposed it might answer some view of theirs to villify me in the public eye. Some, I know, will not reflect how apocryphal is the testimony of enemies so palpably betraying the views with which they give it. But this is an injury to which duty requires every one to submit whom the public think proper to call into its councils.—To SAMUEL SMITH. iv, 255. FORD ED., vii, 279. (M., 1798.)

1074. CALUMNY, Political.—With the aid of lying renegado from republicanism [Callender], the federalists have opened all

their sluices of calumny. They say we lied them out of power, and, openly avow they will do the same by us. But it was not lies or arguments on our part which dethroned them, but their own foolish acts, Sedition laws, Alien laws, taxes, extravagance and heresies. "Porcupine," their friend wrote them down. Callender, their new recruit, will do the same. Every decent man among them revolts at his filth.—To ROBERT R. LIVINGSTON. iv, 448. FORD ED., viii, 173. (W., Oct. 1802.)

1075. ———. It has been a source of great pain to me, to have met with so many among our opponents, who had not the liberality to distinguish between political and social opposition; who transferred at once to the person, the hatred they bore to his political opinions. I suppose, indeed, that in public life, a man whose political principles have any decided character, and who has energy enough to give them effect, must always expect to encounter political hostility from those of adverse principles. But I came to the government under circumstances calculated to generate peculiar acrimony. I found all its offices in the possession of a political sect, who wished to transform it ultimately into the shape of their darling model, the English government; and in the meantime, to familiarize the public mind to the change, by administering it on English principles, and in English forms. The elective interposition of the people had blown all their designs, and they found themselves and their fortresses of power and profit put in a moment into the hands of other trustees. Lamentations and invective were all that remained to them. This last was naturally directed against the agent selected to execute the multiplied reformations, which their heresies had rendered necessary. I became, of course, the butt of everything which reason, ridicule, malice and falsehood could supply. They have concentrated all their hatred on me, till they have really persuaded themselves, that I am the sole source of all their imaginary evils.—To RICHARD M. JOHNSON. v, 256. (W., 1808.)

1076. ———. The large share I have enjoyed, and still enjoy of anti-republican hatred and calumny, gives me the satisfaction of supposing that I have been some obstacle to anti-republican designs; and if truth should find its way into history, the object of these falsehoods and calumnies will render them honorable to me.—To W. LAMBERT. v, 450. (M., May 1809.)

1077. ———. If, brooding over past calamities, the adherents of federalism can, by abusing me, be diverted from disturbing the course of government, they will make me useful longer than I had expected to be so. Having served them faithfully for a term of twelve or fourteen years, in the terrific station of Rawhead and Bloodybones, it was supposed that, retired from power, I should have been *functus officio*, of course, for them also. If, nevertheless, they wish my continuance in that awful office, I yield, and the rather as it may be exercised at home, without interfering with the tranquil enjoyment of my farm, my family, my friends and books. In truth, having never felt a pain from their abuse, I bear them no malice.—To W. D. G. WORTHINGTON. v, 504. (M., 1810.)

1078. CALUMNY, Posterity and.—It is fortunate for those in public trust that posterity will judge them by their works and not by the malignant vituperations and invectives of the Pickerings and Gardiners of their age. —To JOHN ADAMS. vii, 62. (M., 1817.)

1079. CALUMNY, Public Service and. —Calumny would not weigh an atom with me on any occasion where my avowal of either facts or opinions would be of public use; but whenever it will not, I then think it useful to keep myself out of the way of calumny.—To J. T. CALLENDER. FORD ED., vii, 394. (M., 1799.)

1080. CALUMNY, Religion and.—From the moment that a portion of my fellow citizens looked towards me with a view to one of their highest offices, the flood-gates of calumny have been opened upon me; not where I am personally known, and where their slanders would be instantly judged and suppressed from the general sense of their falsehood; but in the remote parts of the Union, where the means of detection are not at hand, and the trouble in an enquiry is greater than would suit the hearers to undertake. I know that I might have filled the courts of the United States with actions for these slanders, and have ruined, perhaps, many persons who are not innocent. But this would be no equivalent to the loss of character. I leave them, therefore, to the reproof of their own consciences. If these do not condemn them, there will yet come a day when the false witness will meet a Judge who has not slept over his slanders. If the Rev. Cotton Mather Smith, of Shena, believed this as firmly as I do, he would surely never have affirmed that " I had obtained my property by fraud and robbery; that in one instance, I had defrauded and robbed a widow and fatherless children of an estate and to which I was executor, of ten thousand pounds sterling by keeping the property and paying then in money at the nominal rate, when it was worth no more than forty for one; and that all this could be proved." Every tittle of it is fable; there not having existed a single circumstance of my life to which any part of it can hang. I never was executor but in two instances, both of which having taken place about the beginning of the Revolution, which withdrew me immediately from all private pursuits, I never meddled in either executorship. In one of the cases only, were there a widow and children. She was my sister. She retained and managed the estate in her own hands, and no part of it was ever in mine. In the other, I was a co-partner, and only received on a division the equal portion allotted to me. To neither of these executorships, therefore, could Mr. Smith refer. Again, my property is all patrimonial, except about seven or eight hundred

pounds worth of lands, purchased by myself and paid for not, to widows and orphans, but to the very gentleman from whom I purchased. If Mr. Smith, therefore, thinks the precepts of the gospel intended for those who preach them as well for others, he will doubtless some day feel the duties of repentance, and of acknowledgment in such forms as to correct the wrong he has done. Perhaps he will have to wait till the passions of the moment have passed away. All this is left to his own conscience.—To URIAH McGREGORY. iv, 333. (M., Aug. 1800.)

1081. CALUMNY, Silence under.— Though I see the pen of the Secretary of the Treasury [Alexander Hamilton] plainly in the attack on me, yet, since he has not chosen to put his name to it, I am not free to notice it as his. I have preserved through life a resolution, set in a very early part of it, never to write in a public paper without subscribing my name, and to engage openly an adversary who does not let himself be seen, is staking all against nothing. The indecency, too, of newspaper squabbling between two public ministers, besides my own sense of it, has drawn something like an injunction from another quarter [President Washington]. Every fact alleged under the signature of " An American " as to myself, is false, and can be proved so * * *. But for the present, lying and scribbling must be free to those mean enough to deal in them, and in the dark.—To EDMUND RANDOLPH. iii, 470. FORD ED., vi, 112. (M., 1792.)

1082. CALUMNY, Unnoticed.—My rule of life has been never to harass the public with fendings and provings of personal slanders. * * * I have ever trusted to the justice and consideration of my fellow citizens, and have no reason to repent it, or to change my course.—To MARTIN VAN BUREN. vii, 372. FORD ED., x, 315. (M., 1824.)

1083. CAMDEN, Battle of.—I sincerely condole with you on our late misfortune [the battle of Camden], which sits the heavier on my mind as being produced by my own countrymen. Instead of considering what is past, however, we are to look forward and prepare for the future.—To GENERAL EDWARD STEVENS. i, 250. FORD ED., ii, 333. (R., 1780.)

1084. ——— ———. I am extremely mortified at the misfortune [the battle of Camden] incurred in the South, and the more so as the militia of our State concurred so eminently in producing it.—To GENERAL GATES. FORD ED., ii, 332. (R., 1780.)

1085. CAMPBELL (Col.), Battle of King's Mountain.—Your favor * * * gives me the first information * * * that the laurels which Colonel Campbell so honorably won in the battle of King's Mountain had ever been brought into question by any one. To him has been ever ascribed so much of the success of that brilliant action as the valor and conduct of an able commander might justly claim. * * * It was the joyful annunciation of that turn of the tide of success which terminated the Revolutionary war with the seal of our Independence. * * * The descendants of Colonel Campbell may rest their heads quietly on the pillow of his renown. History has consecrated, and will forever preserve it in the faithful annals of a grateful country.—To JOHN CAMPBELL. vii, 268. (M., 1822.)

1086. CANADA, The Colonies and.— They [Parliament] have erected in a neighboring province [Quebec], acquired by the joint arms of Great Britain and America, a tyranny dangerous to the very existence of all these Colonies.—DECLARATION ON TAKING UP ARMS. FORD ED., i, 468. (July 1775.)

1087. —— ——. The proposition [of Lord North] is altogether unsatisfactory * * * because it does not propose to repeal the several acts of Parliament * * * extending the boundaries and changing the government and religion of Quebec.—REPLY TO LORD NORTH'S PROPOSITION. i, 480. (July 1775.)

1088. —— ——. The cooperation of the Canadians is taken for granted in all the ministerial schemes. We hope, therefore, they will be dislocated by the events in that quarter.—To FRANCIS EPPES. FORD ED., i, 487. (Pa., Oct. 1775.)

1089. —— ——. In a short time, we have reason to hope, the delegates of Canada will join us in Congress and complete the American union, as far as we wish to have it completed.—To JOHN RANDOLPH. i, 202. FORD ED., i, 492. (Pa., Nov. 1775.)

1090. CANADA, Conquest of.— The British [by forcing us into war] will oblige us to take from them Canada and Nova Scotia which it is not our interest to possess.—To WILLIAM CARMICHAEL. FORD ED., iv, 453. (P., Sep. 1787.)

1091. —— ——. One of our first [Cabinet] consultations must be on the question whether we shall not order all the militia and volunteers destined for the Canadas to be embodied on the 26th of October, and to march immediately to such points on the way to their destination as shall be pointed out, there to await the decision of Congress?—To JAMES MADISON. v, 197. FORD ED., ix, 141. (M., Sep. 1807.)

1092. —— ——. [It was agreed in Cabinet to] prepare all necessaries for an attack of Upper Canada, and the upper part of Lower Canada, as far as the mouth of Richelieu river; also to take possession of the islands of Campobello, &c., in the bay of Passamaquoddy.—ANAS. FORD ED., i, 326. (July 1807.)

1093. —— ——. The acquisition of Canada this year, as far as the neighborhood of Quebec, will be a mere matter of marching, and will give us experience for the attack of Halifax the next, and the final expulsion of England from the American continent.—To WILLIAM DUANE. vi, 75. FORD ED., ix, 366. (M., Aug. 1812.)

1094. —— ——. Our present enemy will have the sea to herself, while we shall be equally predominant at land, and shall strip her of all her possessions on this continent.—To GENERAL KOSCIUSKO. vi, 68. FORD ED. ix, 361. (M., June 1812.)

1095. —— ——. To continue the war popular, * * * it is necessary to stop Indian barbarities. The conquest of Canada will do this.—To PRESIDENT MADISON. vi, 70. FORD ED., ix, 364. (M., June 1812.)

1096. —— ——. The declaration of war is entirely popular here [Virginia], the only opinion being that it should have been issued the moment the season admitted the militia to enter Canada.—To PRESIDENT MADISON. vi, 70. FORD ED., ix, 364. (M., June 1812.)

1097. —— ——. I know your feelings on the present state of the world, and hope they will be cheered by the successful course of our war, and the addition of Canada to our confederacy. The infamous intrigues of Great Britain to destroy our government (of which Henry's is but one sample), and with the Indians to tomahawk our women and children, prove that the cession of Canada, their fulcrum for these Machiavelian levers, must be a *sine qua non* at a treaty of peace.—To GENERAL KOSCIUSKO. vi, 70. FORD ED., ix, 363. (M., June 1812.)

1098. —— ——. We have taken Upper Canada, * * * and hope to remove the British fully and finally from our continent.—To MADAME DE TESSE. vi, 273. FORD ED., ix, 440. (Dec. 1813.)

1099. CANADA, Indemnification and. —With Canada in hand we can go to treaty with an off-set for spoliation before the war. —To PRESIDENT MADISON. vi, 78. (M., Aug. 1812.)

1100. —— ——. For one thousand ships taken, and six thousand seamen impressed, give us Canada for indemnification, and the only security they can give us against their Henrys and the savages.—To MR. WRIGHT. vi, 78. (M., Aug. 1812.)

1101. —— ——. If we could but get Canada to Trois Rivières in our hands we should have a set-off against spoliations to be treated of, and in the meantime separate the Indians from them, and set the friendly to attack the hostile part with our aid.—To PRESIDENT MADISON. FORD ED., ix, 370. (M., Nov. 1812.)

1102. —— ——. We have a great and a just claim of indemnifications against the British for the thousand ships they have taken piratically, and six thousand seamen impressed. Whether we can, on this score, successfully insist on curtailing their American possessions, by the meridian of Lake Huron so as to cut them off from the Indians bordering on us, would be matter for conversation and experiment at the treaty of pacification.— To WILLIAM SHORT. vi, 129. (M., June 1813.)

1103. —— ——. Could we acquire that country, we might perhaps insist successfully at St. Petersburg on retaining all westward of the meridian of Lake Huron, or of Ontario or of Montreal, according to the pulse of the place, as an indemnification for the past and security for the future. To cut them off from the Indians even west of the Huron would be a great future security.—To James Monroe. vi, 131. (M., June 1813.)

1104. —— ——. A thousand ships taken unjustifiably in time of peace, and thousands of our citizens impressed, warrant expectations of indemnification; such a Western frontier, perhaps, given to Canada, as may put it out of their power to employ the tomahawk and scalping knife of the Indians on our women and children; or, what would be nearly equivalent, the exclusive right to the Lakes.— To Dr. George Logan. vi, 216. Ford ed., ix, 422. (M., Oct. 1813.)

1105. —— ——. The conduct of the British during the war in exciting the Indian hordes to murder and scalp the women and children on our frontier, renders peace forever impossible but on the establishment of such a meridian boundary to their possessions, as that they never more can have such influence with the savages as to excite again the same barbarities. The thousand ships, too, they took from us in peace, and the six thousand seamen impressed call for this indemnification.—To Don. V. Toronda Coruna. vi, 275. (M., Dec. 1813.)

1106. CANADA, Value of.—If the war is lengthened we shall take Canada, which will relieve us from Indians, and Halifax, which will put an end to their occupation of the American Seas, because every vessel must then go to England to repair every accident. To retain these would become objects of first importance to us, and of great importance to Europe, as the means of curtailing the British marine. But at present, being merely *in posse,* they should not be an impediment to peace.—To William Short. vi, 129. (M., June 1813.)

1107. CANAL, Big Beaver.—I remember having written to you, while Congress sat at Annapolis, on the water communication between ours and the western country, and to have mentioned particularly the information I had received of the plain face of the country between the sources of Big Beaver and Cayohoga, which made me hope that a canal of no great expense might unite the navigation of Lake Erie and the Ohio. You must since have had occasion of getting better information on this subject, and if you have, you would oblige me by a communication of it. I consider this canal, if practicable, as a very important work. —To General Washington. ii, 250. (P. 1787.)

1108. —— ——. I thank you for the information * * * on the communication between the Cayohoga and Big Beaver. I have ever considered the opening of a canal between those two water courses as the most important work in that line which the State of Virginia could undertake. It will infallibly turn through the Potomac all the commerce of Lake Erie, and the country west of that, except what may pass down the Mississippi; and it is important that it be soon done, lest that commerce should, in the meantime, get established in another channel. * * * I take the liberty of sending you the notes I made when I examined the canal of Languedoc, through its whole course, last year. You may find in them some-

thing, perhaps, which may be turned to account, some time or other, in the prosecution of the Potomac canal.—To General Washington. ii, 370. Ford ed., v, 7. (P., 1788.)

1109. —— ——. Another vast object, and of much less difficulty, is to, add, also, all the country on the Lakes and their waters. This would enlarge our [Virginia's] field immensely, and would certainly be effected by an union of the Ohio and Lake Erie. The Big Beaver and Cayohoga offer the most direct line. * * * The States of Maryland and Virginia should make a common object of it. The navigation, again, between Elizabeth River and the Sound, is of vast importance, and in my opinion, it is much better that these should be done at public than private expense.—To General Washington. iii, 30. Ford ed., v, 93. (P., 1789.)

1110. CANAL, Erie.—The most gigantic undertaking yet proposed is that of New York, for drawing the waters of Lake Erie into the Hudson. The expense will be great, but its effect incalculably powerful in future to the Atlantic States.—To F. H. Alexander Von Humboldt. vii, 75. Ford ed., x, 89. (M., 1817.)

1111. CANAL, James River.—The opinion I have ever expressed of the advantages of a western communication through the James River, I still entertain: and that the Cayuga is the most promising of the links of communication. To William Short. vii, 156. (M., 1820.)

1112. CANAL, Languedoc.—I am now about setting out on a journey to the South of France. * * * I shall carefully examine the canal of Languedoc.—To Colonel Monroe. ii, 70. (P., 1786.)

1113. CANAL, New Orleans.—The United States feel a strong interest in the New Orleans canal, * * * and in some conversations * * * on the subject the winter before last, there was a mutual understanding that the company would complete the canal, and the United States would make the locks. This we are still disposed to do; and so anxious are we to get this means of defence completed, that to hasten it we would contribute any other encouragement within the limits of our authority which might produce this effect.—To Governor Claiborne. v, 306. (W., July 1808.)

1114. —— ——. The first interests of the company will be to bring a practicable navigation from the Lake Pontchartrain through the Bayou St. Jean and Canal de Carondelet to the city, because that entitles them to a toll on the profitable part of the enterprise. But this would answer no object of the government unless it was carried through to the Mississippi, so that our armed vessels drawing five feet of water might pass through. Instead therefore of the ground I suggested in my last letter, I would propose to lend them a sum of money on the condition of their applying it entirely to that part of the canal which, beginning at the Mississippi, goes round the city to a junction with the canal of Carondelet; and we may moreover at our own expense erect the locks. —To Governor Claiborne. v, 319. (W., July 1808.)

1115. —— ——. The Canal Company ask specifically that we should either lend them fifty thousand dollars, or buy the remaining part of their shares now on hand. On consultation with Mr. Madison, Mr. Gallatin and Mr.

Rodney, we concluded it best to say we would lend them a sum of money if they would agree to lay out the whole of it in making the canal from the Mississippi round the town to its junction with the canal of Carondelet.—To HENRY DEARBORN. v, 321. (W., 1808.)

1116. CANAL, Panama.—The Spaniards are, at this time, desirous of trading to the Philippine Islands, by the way of the Cape of Good Hope; but opposed in it by the Dutch, under authority of the treaty of Munster, they are examining the practicability of a common passage through the Straits of Magellan or round Cape Horn. Were they to make an opening through the Isthmus of Panama, a work much less difficult than some even of the inferior canals of France, however small this opening should be in the beginning, the tropical current, entering it with all its force, would soon widen it sufficiently for its own passage. —To M. LE ROY DE L'ACADEMIE DES SCIENCES. ii, 59. (P., 1786.) *See GULF STREAM.

1117. —— ——. I have been told that the cutting through the Isthmus of Panama, which the world has so often wished, and supposed practicable, has at times been thought of by the government of Spain, and that they once proceeded so far as to have a survey and examination made of the ground; but that the result was either impracticable or of too great difficulty. Probably the Count de Campornanes, or Don Ulloa, can give you information on this head. I should be exceedingly pleased to get as minute details as possible on it, and even copies of the survey, report, &c., if they could be obtained at a moderate expense. I take the liberty of asking your assistance in this.—To WILLIAM CARMICHAEL. ii, 325. FORD ED., iv, 473. (P., 1787.)

1118. —— ——. With respect to the Isthmus of Panama, I am assured by Burgoyne * * * that a survey was made, that a canal appeared very practicable, and that the idea was suppressed for political reasons altogether. He has seen and minutely examined the report. This report is to me a vast desideratum, for reasons political and philosophical.—To WILLIAM CARMICHAEL. ii, 397. FORD ED., v, 22. (P., 1788.)

1119. CANAL, Potomac and Ohio.—I consider the union of the Potomac and the Ohio rivers as among the strongest links of communication between the eastern and western sides of our confederacy. It will, moreover, add to the commerce of Virginia, in particular, all the upper parts of the Ohio and its waters. * * * With respect to the doubts which you say are entertained by some, whether the upper waters of the Potomac can be rendered capable of navigation on account of the falls and rugged banks, they are answered, by observing that it is reduced to a maxim that whenever there is water enough to float a batteau, there may be navigation for a batteau. Canals and locks may be necessary, and they are expensive; but I hardly know what expense would be too great for the object in question.—To GENERAL WASHINGTON. iii, 29. FORD ED., v, 93. (P., 1789.)

1120. CANAL, Santee and Cooper Rivers.—As to the Santee and Cooper rivers canal, I shall be glad to do anything I can to promote it. But I confess I have small expectations for the following reason: General Washington sent me a copy of the Virginia act for opening the Potomac. * * * It was pushed here [Paris] among the moneyed men

to obtain subscriptions, but not a single one could be obtained. The stockjobbing in this city offered greater advantages than to buy shares in the canal.—To M. TERRASSON. ii, 383. (P., 1788.)

1121. CANDOR, Appeal to.—I ask only to be judged with truth and candor.—To THE RHODE ISLAND ASSEMBLY. iv, 397. (W., May 1801.)

1122. CANDOR, Appreciating.—If those, who thought I might have been remiss, would have written to me on the subject, I would have admired them for their candor, and thanked them for it; for I have no jealousies nor resentments at things of this kind, where I have no reason to believe they have been excited by a hostile spirit.—To JAMES MONROE. i, 589. FORD ED., iv, 248. (P., 1786.)

1123. CANNIBALS, Rulers as.—Cannibals are not to be found in the wilds of America only, but are revelling on the blood of every living people.—To CHARLES CLAS. vi, 413. (M., 1815.)

1124. CANNING (George), Policy of.—Canning's equivocations degrade his government as well as himself.—To PRESIDENT MADISON. v, 468. (M., Sep. 1809.)

1125. CANOVA (A.), Washington's Statue and.—Who should make the Washington statue? There can be but one answer to this. Old Canova, of Rome. No artist in Europe would place himself in a line with him; and for thirty years, within my own knowledge, he has been considered by all Europe as without a rival.—To NATHANIEL MACON. vi, 534. (M., 1816.)

1126. CAPITAL, Corruption through.—The capital employed in paper speculation * * * has furnished effectual means of corrupting such a portion of the Legislature, as turns the balance between the honest voters, whichever way it is directed. This corrupt squadron, deciding the voice of the Legislature, have manifested their dispositions to get rid of the limitations imposed by the Constitution on the General Legislature, limitations, on the faith of which, the States acceded to that instrument.—To PRESIDENT WASHINGTON. iii, 361. FORD ED., vi, 3. (Pa., May 1792.)

1127. CAPITAL, Creation of.—Capital may be produced by industry, and accumulated by economy; but jugglers only will propose to create it by legerdemain tricks with paper.—To J. W. EPPES. vi, 241. FORD ED., ix, 413. (M., Nov. 1813.)

1128. CAPITAL, Opportunities for.—The citizens of a country like ours will never have unemployed capital. Too many enterprises are open, offering high profits, to permit them to lend their capitals on a regular and moderate interest. They are too enterprising and sanguine themselves not to believe they can do better with it.—To PRESIDENT MADISON. vi, 393. FORD ED., ix, 491. (M., 1815.)

1129. CAPITAL, Stock-jobbing and.—The capital employed in paper speculation

* * * nourishes in our citizens habits of vice and idleness, instead of industry and morality.—To PRESIDENT WASHINGTON. iii, 361. FORD ED., vi, 3. (Pa., 1792.)

1130. —— ——. The capital employed in paper speculation is barren and useless, producing, like that on a gaming table, no accession to itself, and is withdrawn from commerce and agriculture, where it would have produced addition to the common mass.—To PRESIDENT WASHINGTON. iii, 361. FORD ED., vi, 3. (Pa., 1792.)

— **CAPITAL LAWS.**—See DEATH PENALTY.

— **CAPITAL, National.**—See WASHINGTON CITY.

1131. CAPITALS (State), Location of. —The equal rights of all the inhabitants require that the seat of government should be as nearly central to all as may be.*—BILL TO REMOVE VA. CAPITAL. FORD ED., ii, 106. (1776.)

1132. —— ——. The seat of government [in Virginia] had been originally fixed in the peninsula of Jamestown, the first settlement of the colonists; and had been afterwards removed a few miles inland to Williamsburg. But this was at a time when our settlements had not extended beyond the tide waters. Now they had crossed the Alleghany; and the centre of population was very far removed from what it had been. Yet Williamsburg was still the depository of our archives, the habitual residence of the Governor and many other of the public functionaries, the established place for the sessions of the legislature, and the magazine of our military stores; and its situation was so exposed that it might be taken at any time in war, and, at this time particularly, an enemy might in the night run up either of the rivers, between which it lies, land a force above, and take possession of the place, without the possibility of saving either persons or things. I had proposed its removal so early as October, '76; but it did not prevail until the session of May, '79.—AUTOBIOGRAPHY. i, 40. FORD ED., i, 55. (1821.)

1133. CAPITOL (United States), Burning of.—The Vandalism of our enemy has triumphed at Washington over science as well as the arts, by the destruction of the public library with the noble edifice in which it was deposited. Of this transaction, as of that of Copenhagen, the world will entertain but one sentiment. They will see a nation suddenly withdrawn from a great war, full armed and full handed, taking advantage of another whom they had recently forced into it, unarmed, and unprepared, to indulge themselves in acts of barbarism which do not belong to a civilized age. When Van Ghent destroyed their shipping at Chatham, and De Ruyter rode triumphantly up the Thames, he might in like manner, by the acknowledgment of their own historians, have forced all their

* This principle has governed the selection of nearly every State capital from 1776 to the present time.—EDITOR.

ships up to London Bridge, and there have burned them, the Tower, and city, had these examples been then set. London, when thus menaced, was near a thousand years old, Washington is but in its teens.—To S. H. SMITH. vi, 383. FORD ED., ix, 485. (M., Sep. 1814.)

1134. CAPITOL (United States), Inscription for.—If it be proposed to place an inscription on the Capitol, the lapidary style requires that essential facts only should be stated, and these with a brevity admitting no superfluous word. The essential facts in the two inscriptions proposed are these: "FOUNDED 1791.—BURNT BY A BRITISH ARMY 1814.—RESTORED BY CONGRESS 1817." The reasons for this brevity are that the letters must be of extraordinary magnitude to be read from below; that little space is allowed them, being usually put into a pediment or in a frieze, or on a small tablet on the wall; and in our case, a third reason may be added, that no passion can be imputed to this inscription, every word being justifiable from the most classical examples. But a question of more importance is whether there should be one at all? The barbarism of the conflagration will immortalize that of the nation. It will place them forever in degraded comparison with the execrated Bonaparte, who, in possession of almost every capitol in Europe, injured no one. Of this, history will take care, which all will read, while our inscription will be seen by few.—To JAMES MONROE. vii, 41. FORD ED., x, 65. (M., 1816.)

1135. CAPITOL (United States), Wisdom of Inscription.—But a question of more importance is whether there should be one at all? The barbarism of the conflagration will immortalize that of the nation. It will place them forever in degraded comparison with the execrated Bonaparte, who, in possession of almost every capitol in Europe, injured no one. Of this, history will take care, which all will read, while our inscription will be seen by few. Great Britain, in her pride and ascendancy, has certainly hated and despised us beyond every earthly object. Her hatred may remain, but the hour of her contempt is passed and is succeeded by dread; not a present, but a deep and distant one. It is the greater as she feels herself plunged into an abyss of ruin from which no human means point out an issue. We have also more reason to hate her than any nation on earth. But she is not now an object for hatred. She is falling from her transcendant sphere, which all men ought to have wished, but not that she should lose all place among nations. It is for the interest of all that she should be maintained *nearly* on a par with other members of the republic of nations. Her power absorbed into that of any other, would be an object of dread to all, and to us more than all, because we are accessible to her alone and through her alone. The armies of Bonaparte with the fleets of Britain would change the aspect of our destinies. Under these circumstances should we perpetuate hatred against her? Should we not, on the contrary, begin to open ourselves to other and more rational dispositions? It is not improbable that the circumstances of the war [1812] and her own circumstances may have brought her wise men to begin to view us with other and even with kindred eyes. Should not our wise men, then, lifted above the passions of the ordinary citizen, begin to contemplate what *will be* the interests of our country on so important a change among the elements which influence it? I think it would be better to give her time to show her present temper, and to prepare the minds of our citizens for a corresponding change of disposition, by acts of comity towards England rather than by commemoration of hatred. These views might be greatly extended. Perhaps, however, they are premature, and that I may see the ruin of England nearer than it really is. This will be matter of consideration with those to whose councils we have committed ourselves, and whose wisdom, I am sure, will conclude on what is best. Perhaps they may let it go off on the single and short consideration that the thing can do no good, and may do harm.—To JAMES MONROE. vii, 42. FORD ED., x, 66. (M., 1816.) See ARCHITECTURE.

1136. CAPTIVES, American in Algiers. —The Algerines have taken two of our vessels, and I fear they will ask such a tribute for a forbearance of their piracies as the United States would be unwilling to pay. When this idea comes across my mind, my faculties are absolutely suspended between indignation and impatience.—To GENERAL GREENE. i, 509. (P., 1786.)

1137. CAPTIVES, Attempts at Ransom.—If Congress decide to redeem our captives, * * * it is of great importance that the first redemption be made at as low a price as possible, because it will form the future tariff. If these pirates find that they can have a very great price for Americans, they will abandon proportionally their pursuits against other nations to direct them towards ours.—To JOHN JAY. ii, 113. (P., 1787.)

1138. CAPTIVES, Failure to Release.— The demands of Algiers for the ransom of our prisoners, and also for peace, are so infinitely beyond our instructions that we must refer the matter back to Congress.*—To WM. CARMICHAEL. i, 580. (P., 1786.)

1139. CAPTIVES, Intercession of the Mathurins.—That the choice of Congress may be enlarged as to the instruments they may use for effecting the redemption [of our captives], I think it my duty to inform them that there is an order of priests called the Mathurins, the object of whose institution is to beg alms for the redemption of captives. They keep members always in Barbary, searching out the captives of their country, and redeem, I believe, on better terms than any other

* Congress sent a Mr. Lambe to Europe with instructions respecting Algiers. Jefferson and Adams made him their agent to visit Algiers, but his mission resulted in failure. Referring to it, Jefferson wrote to Monroe (i, 606 [1786]. FORD ED., iv, 264) that, "an angel sent on this business, and so much limited in his terms, could have done nothing".— EDITOR.

body, public or private. It occurred to me, that their agency might be obtained for the redemption of our prisoners at Algiers. I obtained conference with the General, and with some members of the order. The General, with all the benevolence and cordiality possible, undertook to act for us, if we should desire it. He told me that their last considerable redemption was of about three hundred prisoners, who cost them somewhat upwards of fifteen hundred livres apiece; but that they should not be able to redeem ours as cheap as they do their own, and that it must be absolutely unknown that the public concern themselves in the operation, or the price would be greatly enhanced. The difference of religion was not once mentioned, nor did it appear to me to be thought of. It was a silent reclamation and acknowledgment of fraternity between two religions of the same family which historical events of ancient date had rendered more hostile to one another than to their common adversaries.*—To JOHN JAY. ii, 113. (P., 1787.)

1140. CAPTIVES, Jefferson and.—I do not wonder that Captain O'Bryan has lost patience under his long continued captivity, and that he may suppose some of the public servants have neglected him and his brethren. He may possibly have imputed neglect to me, because a forbearance to correspond with him would have that appearance, though it was dictated by the single apprehension, that if he received letters from me as Minister Plenipotentiary of the United States at Paris, or as Secretary of State, it would increase the expectations of his captors, and raise the ransom beyond what his countrymen would be disposed to give, and so end in their perpetual captivity. But, in truth, I have labored for them constantly and zealously in every situation in which I have been placed. In the first moment of their captivity, I first proposed to Mr. Adams to take upon ourselves their ransom, though unauthorized by Congress. I proposed to Congress and obtained their permission to employ the Order of Mercy in France for their ransom, but never could obtain orders for the money till just as I was leaving France, and was obliged to turn the matter over to Mr. Short. As soon as I came here, I laid the matter before the President and Congress in two long reports, but Congress could not decide until the beginning of 1792, and then clogged their ransom by a previous requisition of peace. The unfortunate death of two successive commissioners [Paul Jones and Mr. Barclay] have still retarded their relief, and even should they be now relieved, will probably deprive me of the gratification of seeing my endeavors for them crowned at length with success by their arrival when I am here. It would, indeed, be grating to me if, after all, I should be supposed by them to have been indifferent to their situation. I will ask of your friendship to do me justice in their eyes, that to the pain I have already felt for them, may not be added that of their dissatisfaction.—To COLONEL DAVID. iii, 531. (Pa., 1793.)

1141. CARMICHAEL (William), Character.—Mr. Carmichael is, I think, very little known in America. I never saw him, and while I was in Congress I formed rather a disadvantageous idea of him. His letters * * * showed him vain, and more attentive to ceremony and etiquette, than we suppose men

* The Mathurins were employed, but the negotiations were fruitless, and the captives remained in prison. In December, 1790, Jefferson made an exhaustive report on the subject to Congress.—EDITOR.

of sense should be. I have now a constant correspondence with him, and find him a little hypochondriac and discontented. He possesses a very good understanding, though not of the first order. I have had great opportunities of searching into his character, and have availed myself of them. Many persons of different nations, coming from Madrid to Paris, all speak of him as in high esteem, and I think it certain that he has more of the Count de Blanca's friendship, than any diplomatic character at that court. As long as that minister is in office, Carmichael can do more than any other person, who could be sent there.—To JAMES MADISON. ii, 107. FORD ED., iv, 365. (P., 1787.)

1142. ———— ————. Neither Mr. J. nor Mr. ———— ever mentioned one word of any want of decorum in Mr. Carmichael.—To EDMUND RANDOLPH. iv, 108. FORD ED., vi, 513. (M., 1794.)

1143. CARMICHAEL (William), Spanish Mission and.—I think it probable that Mr. Carmichael will impute to me an event which must take place this year. In truth, it is so extraordinary a circumstance, that a public agent placed in a foreign court for the purpose of correspondence, should, in three years, have found means to get but one letter to us, that he must himself be sensible that if he could have sent us letters, he ought to be recalled as negligent, and if he could not, he ought to be recalled as useless. I have, nevertheless, procured his continuance, in order to give him an opportunity which occurred of his rendering a sensible service to his country, and thereby drawing some degree of favor on his return.— To COLONEL DAVID. iii, 532. (Pa., 1793.)

1144. CARMICHAEL (William), Standing in Spain.—With Mr. Carmichael I am unacquainted personally, but he stands on advantageous grounds in the opinion of Europe, and most especially in Spain. Every person, whom I see from there, speaks of him with great esteem. I mention this for your private satisfaction, as he seemed to be little known in Congress. Mr. Jay, however, knows him well. —To COL. MONROE. i, 526. (P., 1786.)

— CAROLINA (North).—See NORTH CAROLINA.

— CAROLINA (South).—See SOUTH CAROLINA.

1145. CARONDELET (Baron), Animosity of.—We are quite disposed to believe that the late wicked excitements [among the Indians] to war have proceeded from the Baron de Carondelet himself, without authority from his court. If so, have we not reason to expect the removal of such an officer from our neighborhood, as an evidence of the disavowal of his proceedings?—To CARMICHAEL AND SHORT. iii, 481. FORD ED., vi, 130. (Pa., 1792.)

1146. CARR (Dabney), Character.— His character was of a high order. A spotless integrity, sound judgment, handsome imagination, enriched by education and reading, quick and clear in his conceptions, of correct and ready elocution, impressing every hearer with the sincerity of the heart from which it flowed. His firmness was inflexible in whatever he thought was right; but when no moral principle stood in the way, never had man more of the milk of human kindness, of indulgence, of softness, of pleasantry of conversation and conduct. The number of his friends and the warmth of their affection, were proofs of his worth, and of their estimate of it. To give to

those now living, an idea of the affliction produced by his death in the minds of all who knew him, I liken it to that lately felt by themselves on the death of his eldest son, Peter Carr, so like in all his endowments and moral qualities, and whose recollection can never recur without a deep-drawn sigh from the bosom of any one who knew him.—To DABNEY CARR, JR. vi, 528. FORD ED., x, 17. (M., 1816.)

1147. ———— ————. Dabney Carr, * * * mover of the proposition of March, 1773, for Committees of Correspondence, the first fruit of which was the call of an American Congress, merits honorable mention in your history, if any proper occasion offers.—To MR. GIRARDIN. vi, 411. (M., 1815.)

1148. ———— ————. This friend of ours, Page, in a very small house, with a table, half a dozen chairs, and one or two servants, is the happiest man in the universe. Every incident in life he so takes as to render it a source of pleasure. With as much benevolence as the heart of man will hold, but with an utter neglect of the costly apparatus of life, he exhibits to the world a new phenomenon in philosophy—the Samian sage in the tub of the cynic.*—To JOHN PAGE. i, 195. FORD ED., i, 373. (1770.)

1149. CARRIAGES, Tax on.—Almost every carriage owner has been taken in for a double-tax; information through the newspapers not being actual, though legal, in a country where they are little read. This circumstance has made almost every man, so taken in, a personal enemy to the tax. I escaped the penalty only by sending an express over the country to search out the officer the day before the forfeiture would have been incurred.—To JAMES MADISON. FORD ED., vii, 2. (M., Feb. 1795.)

1150. CARRYING TRADE, Preservation of the.—Admitting their right of keeping their markets to themselves, ours cannot be denied of keeping our carrying trade to ourselves.—REPORT ON THE FISHERIES. vii, 554. (1791.) See NAVIGATION.

1151. CARRYING TRADE, Protection of.—We find in some parts of Europe monopolizing discriminations, which, in the form of duties, tend effectually to prohibit the carrying thither our own produce in our own vessels. From existing amities, and a spirit of justice, it is hoped that friendly discussion will produce a fair and adequate reciprocity. But should false calculations of interest defeat our hope, it rests with the Legislature to decide whether they will meet inequalities abroad with countervailing inequalities at home, or provide for the evil in any other way.—SECOND ANNUAL MESSAGE. viii, 16. FORD ED., viii, 182. (Dec. 1802.)

1152. CARTER (Landon), Speeches of. —Landon Carter's speeches, like his writings, were dull, vapid, verbose, egotistical, smooth as the lullaby of the nurse, and commanding, like that, the repose only of the hearer.—To WILLIAM WIRT. vi, 486. FORD ED., ix, 474. (M., 1815.)

1153. CARTHAGE, History of.—It has often been a subject of regret, that Carthage

* Dabney Carr married Jefferson's sister.—EDITOR.

had no writer to give her side of her own history, while her wealth, power and splendor prove she must have had a very distinguished policy and government.—To JOHN ADAMS. vii. 63. (M., 1817.)

1154. CENSORS, Government and.—No government ought to be without censors; and where the press is free, no one ever will.—To PRESIDENT WASHINGTON. iii, 467. FORD ED., vi, 108. (M., 1792.)

1155. CENSURE, Pain of.—I find the pain of a little censure, even when it is unfounded, is more acute than the pleasure of much praise.—To F. HOPKINSON. ii, 587. FORD ED., v. 78. (P., 1789.)

1156. CENSUS, First U. S.—I enclose you a copy of the census which I have made out for you.—To JAMES MADISON. FORD ED., v, 371. (Pa., 1791.)

1157. ——— ———. Nearly the whole of the States have now returned their census. I send you the result. * * * Making a very small allowance for omissions, we are upwards of four millions; and we know in fact that the omissions have been very great.—To DAVID HUMPHREYS. FORD ED., v, 372. (Pa., Aug. 1791.)

1158. CENSUS, Perfecting the.—For the articles of a statistical table, I think the last census of Congress presented what was proper, as far as it went, but did not go far enough. It required detailed accounts of our manufactures, and an enumeration of our people, according to ages, sexes and colors. But to this should be added an enumeration according to their occupations. We should know what proportion of our people are employed in agriculture, what proportion are carpenters, smiths, shoemakers, tailors, bricklayers, merchants, seamen, &c. No question is more curious than that of the distribution of society into occupations, and none more wanting. I have never heard of such tables being effected but in the instance of Spain, where it was first done under the administration, I believe, of Count D'Aranda, and a second time under the Count de Florida Blanca, and these have been considered as the most curious and valuable tables in the world. The combination of callings with us would occasion some difficulty, many of our tradesmen being, for instance, agriculturists also; but they might be classed under their principal occupation.—To THOMAS W. MAURY. vi, 548. (M., 1816.)

1159. CENTRALIZATION, Advancing toward.—I told the President [Washington] that they [the Hamilton party] had now brought forward a proposition, far beyond every one ever yet advanced, and to which the eyes of many were turned, as the decision which was to let us know, whether we live under a limited or an unlimited government. * * * [to wit], that in the Report on Manufactures which, under color of giving *bounties* for the encouragement of particular manufactures, meant to establish the doctrine, that the power given by the Constitution to

collect taxes to provide for the *general welfare* of the United States, permitted Congress to take everything under their management which *they* should deem for the *public welfare*, and which is susceptible of the application of money; consequently, that the subsequent enumeration of their powers was not the description to which resort must be had, and did not at all constitute the limits of their authority; that this was a very different question from that of the Bank [of the United States], which was thought an incident to an enumerated power.—THE ANAS. ix, 104. FORD ED., i, 177. (Feb. 1792.)

1160. ——— ———. I wish to see maintained that wholesome distribution of powers established by the Constitution for the limitation of both; and never to see all offices transferred to Washington, where, further withdrawn from the eyes of the people, they may more secretly be bought and sold as at market.—To WILLIAM JOHNSON. vii, 297. FORD ED., x, 232. (M., 1823.)

1161. CENTRALIZATION, Balance of Power and.—I said to [President Washington] that if the equilibrium of the three great bodies, Legislative, Executive, and Judiciary, could be preserved, if the Legislature could be kept independent, I should never fear the result of such a government; but that I could not but be uneasy when I saw that the Executive had swallowed up the Legislative branch.—ANAS. ix, 122. FORD ED., i, 204. (1792.)

1162. CENTRALIZATION, Corruption and.—Our government is now taking so steady a course as to show by what road it will pass to destruction, to wit: by consolidation first, and then corruption, its necessary consequence. The engine of consolidation will be the Federal judiciary; the two other branches the corrupting and corrupted instruments.—To NATHANIEL MACON. vii, 223. (M., 1821.)

1163. ——— ———. I do verily believe that * * * a single consolidated government would become the most corrupt government on the earth.—To GIDEON GRANGER. iv, 331. FORD ED., vii, 451. (M., Aug. 1800.)—

1164. CENTRALIZATION, Disguised Toryism.—Consolidation is but toryism in disguise.—To NATHANIEL MACON. FORD ED., x, 379. (M., 1826.)

1165. ——— ———. The consolidationists may call themselves republicans if they please, but the school of Venice, and all of this principle, I call at once tories.—To NATHANIEL MACON. FORD ED., x, 378. (M., 1826.)

1166. CENTRALIZATION, Eastern States and.—I fear our eastern associates wish for consolidation, in which they would be joined by the smaller States generally.—To NATHANIEL MACON. vii, 223. FORD ED., x, 194. (M., 1821.)

1167. CENTRALIZATION, Enumerated Powers and.—To take from the States all the powers of self-government and transfer them to a general and consolidated government, without regard to the special delegations and reservations solemnly agreed to in [the Federal] compact, is not for the peace, happiness or prosperity of these States.—KENTUCKY RESOLUTIONS. ix, 468. FORD ED., vii, 300. (1798.)

1168. CENTRALIZATION, Jobbery and. —You hvve seen the practices by which the public servants have been able to cover their conduct, or, where that could not be done, delusions by which they have varnished it for the eye of their constituents. What an augmentation of the field for jobbing, speculating, plundering, office-building and office-hunting would be produced by an assumption of all the State powers into the hands of the General Government.—To GIDEON GRANGER. iv, 331. FORD ED., vii, 451. (M., Aug. 1800.)

1169. CENTRALIZATION, Judiciary drives on to.—After twenty years' confirmation of the federal system by the voice of the nation, declared through the medium of elections, we find the judiciary on every occasion, still driving us into consolidation.—To SPENCER ROANE. vii, 134. FORD ED., x, 140. (P.F., 1819.)

1170. ———— ————. It has long been my opinion, and I have never shrunk from its expression (although I do not choose to put it into a newspaper, nor like a Priam in armor to offer myself as its champion), that the germ of dissolution of our Federal Government is in the constitution of the Federal Judiciary; an irresponsible body (for impeachment is scarcely a scare-crow), working like gravity by night and by day, gaining a little to-day and a little to-morrow, and advancing its noiseless step like a thief, over the field of jurisdiction, until all shall be usurped from the States, and the government of all be consolidated into one. To this I am opposed; because, when all government, domestic and foreign, in little as in great things, shall be drawn to Washington as the centre of all power, it will render powerless the checks provided of one government on another, and will become as venal and oppressive as the government from which we separated. It will be, as in Europe, where every man must be either pike or gudgeon, hammer or anvil. Our functionaries and theirs are wares from the same workshop; made of the same materials and by the same hand. If the States look with apathy on this silent descent of their government into the gulf which is to swallow all, we have only to weep over the human character formed uncontrollable but by a rod of iron, and the blasphemers of man, as incapable of self-government, become his true historians.—To C. HAMMOND. vii, 216. (M., 1821.)

1171. ———— ————. We already see the power, installed for life, responsible to no authority (for impeachment is not even a scare-crow), advancing with a noiseless and steady pace to the great object of consolidation. The foundations are already deeply laid by their decisions for the annihilation of constitutional State rights, and the removal of every check, every counterpoise to the ingulfing power of which themselves are to make a

sovereign part. If ever this vast country is brought under a single government, it will be one of the most extensive corruption, indifferent and incapable of a wholesome care over so wide a spread of surface. This will not be borne, and you will have to choose between reformation and revolution. If I know the spirit of this country, the one or the other is inevitable. Before the canker is become inveterate, before its venom has reached so much of the body politic as to get beyond control, remedy should be applied.—To WILLIAM T. BARRY. vii, 256. (M., 1822.)

1172. ———— ————. There is no danger I apprehend so much as the consolidation of our government by the noiseless, and, therefore, unalarming instrumentality of the Supreme Court. This is the form in which federalism now arrays itself, and consolidation is the present principle of distinction between republicans and the pseudo-republicans but real federalists.— To WILLIAM JOHNSON. vii, 278. FORD ED., x, 248. (M., 1823.)

1173. CENTRALIZATION, Liberty and. —It is a singular phenomenon, that while our State governments are the very *best in the world*, without exception or comparison, our General Government has, in the rapid course of nine or ten years, become more arbitrary, and has swallowed more of the public liberty than even that of England.—To JOHN TAYLOR. iv, 260. FORD ED., vii, 311. (M., 1798.)

1174. ———— ————. What has destroyed the liberty and the rights of man in every government which has ever existed under the sun? The generalizing and concentrating all cares and powers into one body, no matter whether of the autocrats of Russia or France, or of the aristocrats of a Venetian Senate.—To JOSEPH C. CABELL. vi, 543. (M., 1816.)

1175. CENTRALIZATION, Limitless.— It is but too evident that the branches of our foreign department of government, Executive, Judiciary and Legislative, are in combination to usurp the powers of the domestic branch, all so reserved to the States, and consolidate themselves into a single government without limitation of powers. I will not trouble you with details of the instances which are threadbare and unheeded. The only question is, what is to be done? Shall we give up the ship? No, by heavens, while a hand remains able to keep the deck. Shall we, with the hot-headed Georgian, stand at once to our arms? Not yet, nor until the evil, the only greater one than separation, shall be all upon us, that of living under a government of discretion. Between these alternatives there can be no hesitation. But, again, what are we to do? * * * We had better, at present, rest awhile on our oars and see which way the tide will set in Congress and in the State Legislatures. —To WILLIAM F. GORDON. FORD ED., x, 358. (M., Jan. 1826.)

1176. CENTRALIZATION, Local Government vs.—It is not by the consolidation, or concentration of powers, but by their distribution, that good government is effected.

Were not this great country already divided into States, that division must be made, that each might do for itself what concerns itself directly, and what it can so much better do than a distant authority. Every State again is divided into counties, each to take care of what lies within its local bounds; each county again into townships or wards, to manage minuter details; and every ward into farms, to be governed each by its individual proprietor. * * * It is by this partition of cares, descending in gradation from general to particular, that the mass of human affairs may be best managed, for the good and prosperity of all.—AUTOBIOGRAPHY. i, 82. FORD ED., i, 113. (1821.)

1177. CENTRALIZATION, Local Interest and.—Of the two questions of the tariff and public improvements, the former, perhaps, is not yet at rest, and the latter will excite boisterous discussions. It happens that both these measures fall in with the western interests, and it is their secession from the agricultural States which gives such strength to the manufacturing and consolidating parties, on these two questions. The latter is the most dreaded, because thought to amount to a determination in the Federal government to assume all powers non-enumerated as well as enumerated in the Constitution, and by giving a loose to construction, make the text say whatever will relieve them from the bridle of the States. These are difficulties for your day; I shall give them the slip.—To RICHARD RUSH. vii, 380. FORD ED., x, 322. (M., 1824.)

1178. CENTRALIZATION, Opposition to.—I fear an explosion in our State Legislature. I wish they may restrain themselves to a strong but temperate protestation. Virginia is not at present in favor with her co-States. An opposition headed by her would determine all the anti-Missouri States to take the contrary side. She had better lie by, therefore, till the shoe shall pinch an eastern State.—To NATHANIEL MACON. vii, 223. FORD ED., x, 194. (M., Oct. 1821.)

1179. CENTRALIZATION, Plunder and.—Our country is too large to have all its affairs directed by a single government. Public servants at such a distance, and from under the eye of their constituents, must, from the circumstance of distance, be unable to administer and overlook all the details necessary for the good government of the citizens; and the same circumstance, by rendering detection impossible to their constituents, will invite the public agents to corruption, plunder and waste.—To GIDEON GRANGER. iv, 331. FORD ED., vii, 451. (M., Aug. 1800.)

— CENTRALIZATION, Plundered Yeomanry and.—See YEOMANRY.

1180. CENTRALIZATION, Poverty and.—Were we directed from Washington when to sow, and when to reap, we should soon want bread.—AUTOBIOGRAPHY. i, 82. FORD ED., i, 113. (1821.)

1181. CENTRALIZATION, Resistance to.—Although I have little hope that the tor-rent of consolidation can be withstood, I should not be for giving up the ship without efforts to save her. She lived well through the first squall, and may weather the present one.—To C. W. GOOCH. vii, 430. (M., January 1826.)

1182. CENTRALIZATION, Revolution and.—I have been blamed for saying, that a prevalence of the doctrines of consolidation would one day call for reformation or *revolution*. I answer by asking if a single State of the Union would have agreed to the Constitution had it given all powers to the General Government? If the whole opposition to it did not proceed from the jealousy and fear of every State, of being subjected to the other States in matters merely its own? And if there is any reason to believe the States more disposed now than then, to acquiesce in this general surrender of all their rights and powers to a consolidated government, one and undivided?—To SAMUEL JOHNSON. vii, 293. FORD ED., x, 228. (M., 1823.)

1183. CENTRALIZATION, States' Rights and.—I see with the deepest affliction, the rapid strides with which the Federal branch of our government is advancing towards the usurpation of all the rights reserved to the States, and the consolidation in itself of all powers, foreign and domestic; and that too, by constructions which, if legitimate, leave no limits to their power. Take together the decisions of the Federal Court, the doctrines of the President [John Quincy Adams], and the misconstructions of the constitutional compact acted on by the legislature of the Federal branch, and it is but too evident, that the three ruling branches of that department are in combination to strip their colleagues, the State authorities, of the powers reserved by them, and to exercise themselves all functions foreign and domestic. Under the power to regulate commerce, they assume indefinitely that also over agriculture and manufactures, and call it regulation to take the earnings of one of these branches of industry, and that, too, the most depressed, and put them into the pockets of the other, the most flourishing of all. Under the authority to establish post roads, they claim that of cutting down mountains for the construction of roads, of digging canals, and aided by a little sophistry on the words " general welfare," a right to do, not only the acts to effect that, which are specifically enumerated and permitted, but whatsoever they shall think, or pretend will be for the general welfare. And what is our resource for the preservation of the Constitution? Reason and argument? You might as well reason and argue with the marble columns encircling them. The representatives chosen by ourselves? They are joined in the combination, some from incorrect views of government, some from corrupt ones, sufficient voting together to outnumber the sound parts; and with majorities only of one, two, or three, bold enough to go forward in defiance. Are we then *to stand to our arms*, with the hot-headed Georgian? No. That must be the last resource, not to be thought of until much longer and greater sufferings. If every infraction of a compact of so many parties is to be resisted at once, as a dissolution of it, none can ever be formed which would last one year. We must have patience and longer endurance then with our brethren while under delusion; give them time for reflection and experience of consequences; keep ourselves in a situation to profit by the chapter of accidents; and separate from our companions only when the sole alternatives left, are the dissolution of our Union with them, or submission to a government without limitation of powers. Between these two evils, when we must make a choice, there can be no hesitation. But, in the meanwhile, the States should be watchful to note every material usurpation on their rights; denounce them as they occur in the most peremptory terms; to protest against them as wrongs to which our present submission shall be considered, not as acknowledgments or precedents of right, but as a temporary yielding to the lesser evil, until their accumulation shall overweigh that of separation. I would go still further, and give to the Federal member, by a regular amendment of the Constitution, a right to make roads and canals of intercommunication between the States, providing sufficiently against corrupt practices in Congress (log-rolling, &c.) by declaring that the Federal proportion of each State of the moneys so employed, shall be in works within the State, or elsewhere with its consent, and with a due *salvo* of jurisdiction. This is the course which I think safest and best as yet.—To WILLIAM B. GILES. vii, 426. FORD ED., x, 354. (M., Dec. 1825.)

1184. CENTRALIZATION, Venality and.—When all government, domestic and foreign, in little as in great things, shall be drawn to Washington as the centre of all power, it will render powerless the checks provided of one government on another, and will become as venal and oppressive as the government from which we separated.—To C. HAMMOND. vii, 216. (M., 1821.)

1185. CEREMONY, Suppression of monarchical.—We have suppressed all those public forms and ceremonies which tended to familiarize the public eye to the harbingers of another form of government.—To GENERAL KOSCIUSKO. iv, 430. (W., April 1802.)

1186. CEREMONY, Unnecessary.—Mr. Adams, your predecessor, seemed to understand, on his being presented to the Court [of St. James's] that a letter was expected for the Queen also. You will be pleased to inform yourself whether the custom of that court requires this from us; and to enable you to comply with it, if it should, I enclose a letter sealed for the Queen, and a copy of it open for your own information. Should its delivery not be a requisite, you will be so good as to return it, as we do not wish to set a precedent which may bind us hereafter to a single unnecessary ceremony.—To THOMAS PINCKNEY. iii, 441. FORD ED., vi, 74. (Pa., 1792.)

1187. CEREMONY, Yellow fever and.—Those [in Philadelphia] who caught the yellow fever seemed to consider every man as their personal enemy who would not catch their disorder, and many suffered themselves to think it was a sufficient cause for breaking off society with them. I became sensible of this on my next arrival in town, on perceiving that many declined visiting me with whom I had been on terms of the greatest friendship and intimacy. I determined, for the first time in my life, to stand on the ceremony of the first visit, even with my friends; because it served to sift out those who chose a separation.—To WILLIAM HAMILTON. FORD ED., vii, 441. (Pa., 1800.)

1188. CHANCELLORS, Inconsistencies of English.—The English Chancellors have gone on from one thing to another without any comprehensive or systematic view of the whole field of equity, and therefore they have sometimes run into inconsistencies and contradictions.—To PETER CARR. iii, 452. FORD ED., vi, 92. (Pa., 1792.)

— CHANCERY COURTS.—See COURTS.

1189. CHAPLAINS, Appointment of.—These small preferments [chaplains to legislative bodies] should be reserved to reward and encourage genius, and not be strowed with an indiscriminating hand among the common herd of competitors.—To COLONEL W. PRESTON. FORD ED., i, 368. (1768.)

1190. CHARACTER, Evidence of.—The uniform tenor of a man's life furnishes better evidence of what he has said or done on any particular occasion than the word of any enemy, and of an enemy, too, who shows that he prefers the use of falsehoods which suit him to truths which do not.—To DE WITT CLINTON. iv, 520. (W., 1803.)

1191. CHARACTER, Public Service and.—There is sometimes an eminence of character on which society have such peculiar claims as to control the predilections of the individual for a particular walk of happiness, and restrain him to that alone arising from the present and future benedictions of mankind.—To PRESIDENT WASHINGTON. iii, 364. FORD ED., vi, 5. (Pa., 1792.)

1192. CHARACTER, Rational.—Like the rest of mankind, General Washington was disgusted with atrocities of the French Revolution, and was not sufficiently aware of the difference between the rabble who were used as instruments of their perpetration, and the steady and rational character of the American people, in which he had not sufficient confidence.—INTRODUCTION TO ANAS. ix, 99. FORD ED., i, 168. (1818.)

1193. CHARACTER, Steady American.—The steady character of our countrymen is a rock to which we may safely moor.—To ELBRIDGE GERRY. iv, 392. FORD ED., viii, 43. (W., March 1801.)

1194. CHARACTER, Strong American.—The order and good sense displayed in this recovery from delusion, and in the momentous crisis [Presidential election] which lately arose, really bespeak a strength of character in our nation which augurs well for the duration of our Republic; and I am much better satisfied now of its stability than I was before it was tried.—To Dr. Joseph Priestley, iv, 374. Ford ed., viii, 22. (W., March 1801.)

1195. CHARITY, A duty. — Private charities, as well as contributions to public purposes in proportion to every one's circumstances, are certainly among the duties we owe to society.—To Charles Christian. vi, 44. (M., 1812.)

1196. CHARITY, Principles of Distributing.—We are all doubtless bound to contribute a certain portion of our income to the support of charitable and other useful public institutions. But it is a part of our duty also to apply our contributions in the most effectual way we can to secure their object. The question, then, is whether this will not be better done by each of us appropriating our whole contributions to the institutions within our reach, under our own eye; and over which we can exercise some useful control? Or, would it be better that each should divide the sum he can spare among all the institutions of his State, or of the United States? Reason, and the interest of these institutions themselves, certainly decide in favor of the former practice. This question has been forced on me, heretofore, by the multitude of applications which have come to me from every quarter of the Union on behalf of academies, churches, missions, hospitals, charitable establishments, &c. Had I parcelled among them all the contributions which I could spare, it would have been for each too feeble a sum to be worthy of being either given or received. If each portion of the State, on the contrary, will apply its aids and its attentions exclusively to those nearest around them, all will be better taken care of. Their support, their conduct, and the best administration of their funds, will be under the inspection and control of those most convenient to take cognizance of them, and most interested in their prosperity.—To Samuel Kerchival. v, 489. (M., 1810.)

1197. ——— ———. It is a duty certainly to give our sparings to those who want; but to see also that they are faithfully distributed, and duly apportioned to the respective wants of those receivers. And why give through agents whom we know not, to persons whom we know not, and in countries from which we get no account, when we can do it at short hand, to objects under our eye, through agents we know, and to supply wants we see?—To Mr. Megear. vii, 286. (M., 1823.)

1198. CHARITY, Rules in bestowing. —I deem it the duty of every man to devote a certain portion of his income for charitable purposes; and that it is his further duty to see it so applied as to do the most good of which it is capable. This I believe to be best insured, by keeping within the circle of his own inquiry and information the subjects of distress to whose relief his contributions shall be applied. If this rule be reasonable in private life, it becomes so necessary in my situation, that to relinquish it would leave me without rule or compass. The applications of this kind from different parts of our own, and foreign countries, are far beyond any resources within my command. The mission of Serampore, in the East Indies, the object of the present application, is but one of many items. However disposed the mind may feel to unlimited good, our means having limits, we are necessarily circumscribed by them. They are too narrow to relieve even the distresses under my own eye; and to desert these for others which we neither see nor know, is to omit doing a certain good for one which is uncertain. I know, indeed, there have been splendid associations for effecting benevolent purposes in remote regions of the earth. But no experience of their effect has proved that more good would not have been done by the same means employed nearer home. In explaining, however, my own motives of action, I must not be understood as impeaching those of others. Their views are those of an expanded liberality. Mine may be too much restrained by the law of usefulness. But it is a law to me, and with minds like yours, will be felt as a justification.—To Dr. Rogers. iv, 589. (W., 1806.)

1199. ——— ———. The general relation in which I, some time since, stood to the citizens of all our States, drew on me such multitudes of applications as exceeded all resource. Nor have they abated since my retirement to the limited duties of a private citizen, and the more limited resources of a private fortune. They have obliged me to lay down as a law of conduct for myself, to restrain my contributions for public institutions to the circle of my own State, and for private charities to that which is under my own observation; and these calls I find more than sufficient for everything I can spare.—To Charles Christian. vi, 44. (M., 1812.)

1200. CHARTERS, Abolishing. — He has combined with others * * * for taking away our charters.—Declaration of Independence as Drawn by Jefferson.

1201. CHARTERS, Altering.—But, what is of more importance [than the loss of property], and what they keep in this proposal [of Lord North] out of sight, as if no such point was in contest, they claim a right of altering all our charters and established laws, which leaves us without the least security for our lives or liberties.—Reply to Lord North's Proposition. Ford ed., i, 481. (July 1775.)

1202. CHARTERS, Violation of.—They [Parliament] have attempted fundamentally to alter the form of government in one of these Colonies, a form secured by charters on the part of the crown and confirmed by acts of its own legislature.—Declaration on Taking up Arms. Ford ed., i, 468. (July 1775.)

1203. CHASE (Samuel), Independence and.—A Fourth of July oration, delivered in the town of Milford, in your State, gives to Samuel Chase the credit of having "first started the cry of Independence in the ears of his countrymen". Do you remember anything of this? I do not. I have no doubt it was uttered in Massachusetts even before it was by Thomas Paine. But, certainly, I never considered Samuel Chase as foremost, or even forward in that hallowed cry. I know that Maryland hung heavily on our backs, and that Chase, although first named, was not most in unison with us of that delegation.—To JOHN ADAMS. vii, 218. (1821.)

1204. CHASE (Samuel), Partisan charge of.—You must have heard of the extraordinary charge of Chase to the grand jury at Baltimore. Ought this seditious and official attack on the principles of our Constitution, and on the proceedings of a State, to go unpunished? And to whom so pointedly as yourself will the public look for the necessary measures? I ask these questions for your consideration; for myself it is better that I should not interfere.—To MR. NICHOLSON. iv, 486. (W., May 1803.)

1205. CHATHAM (Lord), Colonies and.—When I saw Lord Chatham's bill, I entertained high hope that a reconciliation could have been brought about. The difference between his terms and those offered by our Congress might have been accommodated, if entered on by both parties with a disposition to accommodate.—To DR. WILLIAM SMALL. i, 199. FORD ED., i, 454. (1775.)

1206. CHATHAM (Lord), Gratitude to.—I hope Lord Chatham may live till the fortune of war puts his son into our hands, and enables us by returning him safe to his father, to pay a debt of gratitude.—To JOHN PAGE. FORD ED., 496. (1775.)

1207. CHEMISTRY, Application of.—I have wished to see chemistry applied to domestic objects, to malting, for instance, brewing, making cider, to fermentation and distillation generally, to the making of bread, butter, cheese, soap, to the incubation of eggs, &c.—To THOMAS COOPER. vi, 73. (M., 1812.)

1208. CHEMISTRY, Experiments in.—The contradictory experiments of chemists leave us at liberty to conclude what we please. My conclusion is, that art has not yet invented sufficient aids to enable such subtle bodies [air, light, &c.] to make a well-defined impression on organs as blunt as ours; that it is laudable to encourage investigation but to hold back conclusion.—To REV. JAMES MADISON. ii, 431. (P., 1788.)

1209. CHEMISTRY, Merits attention.—I do not know whether you are fond of chemical reading. There are some things in this science worth reading.—To MR. RITTENHOUSE. i, 517. (P., 1786.)

1210. CHEMISTRY, Nomenclature.—The attempt of Lavoisier to reform the chemical nomenclature is premature. One single experiment may destroy the whole filiation of his terms; and his string of sulphates, sulphites, and sulphures, may have served no other end than to have retarded the progress of the science by a jargon, from the confusion of which time will be requisite to extricate us.—To REV. JAMES MADISON. ii, 432. (P., 1788.)

1211. ——— ———. You have heard of the new chemical nomenclature endeavored to be introduced by Lavoisier, Fourcroy, &c. Other chemists of this country, of equal note, reject it, and prove in my opinion that it is premature, insufficient and false. These latter are joined by the British chemists; and upon the whole, I think the new nomenclature will be rejected, after doing more harm than good. There are some good publications in it, which must be translated into the ordinary chemical language before they will be useful.—To DR. CURRIE. ii, 544. (P., 1788.)

1212. ——— ———. A schism has taken place among the chemists. A particular set of them in France have undertaken to remodel all the terms of the science, and to give to every substance a new name, the composition, and especially the termination of which, shall define the relation in which it stands to other substances of the same family. But the science seems too much in its infancy as yet, for this reformation; because in fact, the reformation of this year must be reformed again the next year, and so on, changing the names of substances as often as new experiments develop properties in them undiscovered before. The new nomenclature has, accordingly, been already proved to need numerous and important reformations. * * * It is espoused by the minority only here, and by very few, indeed, of the foreign chemists. It is particularly rejected in England.—To DR. WILLARD. iii, 15. (P., 1789.)

1213. CHEMISTRY, System of.—Chemistry is yet, indeed, a mere embryo. Its principles are contested; experiments seem contradictory; their subjects are so minute as to escape our senses; and their result too fallacious to satisfy the mind. It is probably an age too soon to propose the establishment of a system.—To REV. JAMES MADISON. ii, 431. (P., 1788.)

1214. CHEMISTRY, Utility of.—Speaking one day with Monsieur de Buffon, on the present ardor of chemical inquiry, he affected to consider chemistry but as cookery, and to place the toils of the laboratory on a footing with those of the kitchen. I think it, on the contrary, among the most useful of sciences, and big with future discoveries for the utility and safety of the human race.—To REV. JAMES MADISON. ii, 431. (P., 1788.)

1215. CHERBOURG, Expense of.—That work will be steadily pursued, and, in all probability, be finally successful. They calculate on half a million of livres, say twenty thousand pounds sterling, for every cone, and that there will be from seventy to eighty cones. Probably they must make more cones. Suppose one hundred; this will be two millions of pounds sterling. Versailles has cost fifty millions of pounds sterling. Ought we to doubt then that they will persevere to the end in a work, small and useful in proportion as the other was great and foolish?—To MR. CUTTING. ii, 438. (P., 1788.)

1216. CHERBOURG, Harbor of.—The King's visit to Cherbourg has made a great sensation in England and here [France]. It proves to the world, that it is a serious object to this country, and that the King commits himself for the accomplishment of it. Indeed, so many cones have been sunk, that no doubt remains of the practicability of it. It will contain, as is said, eighty ships of the line, be one of the best harbors in the world, and by means of two entrances, on different sides, will admit vessels to come in and go out with every wind. The effect of this, in another war with England, defies calculation.—To JAMES MONROE. i, 587. FORD ED., iv, 245. (P., 1786.)

1217. CHERBOURG, Invasion of England from.—An event seems to be preparing, in the order of things, which will probably decide the fate of that country [England]. It is no longer doubtful that the harbor of Cherbourg will be completed, that it will be a most excellent one, and capacious enough to hold the whole navy of France. Nothing has ever been wanting to enable France to invade that but a naval force conveniently stationed to protect the transports. This change of situation must oblige the English to keep up a great standing army, and there is no king, who, with sufficient force, is not always ready to make himself absolute.—To GEORGE WYTHE.* ii, 8. FORD ED., iv, 269. (P., 1786.)

1218. ———. This port will enable them in case of a war with England, to invade that country, or to annihilate its commerce, and of course its marine. Probably, too, it will oblige them to keep a standing army of considerable magnitude.—To MR. HAWKINS. ii, 3. (P., 1786.)

1219. ———. The harbor of Cherbourg will .* * * hold the whole [French] navy. This is putting a bridle into the mouth of England.—To DAVID HUMPHREYS. ii, 11. (P., 1786.)

1220. CHEROKEE INDIANS, Hopewell Treaty and.—Were the treaty of Hopewell, and the act of acceptance of Congress to stand in any point in direct opposition to each other, I should consider the act of acceptance as void in that point; because the treaty is a law made by two parties, and not revocable by one of the parties either acting alone or in conjunction with a third party. If we consider the acceptance as a legislative act of Congress, it is the act of one party only; if we consider it as a treaty between Congress and North Carolina, it is but a subsequent treaty with another power, and cannot make void a preceding one, with a different power. But I see no such opposition between these two instruments. The Cherokees were entitled to the sole occupation of the lands within the limits guaranteed to them. The State of North Carolina, according to the *jus gentium* established for America by universal usage, had only a right of preemption of these lands against all other

nations. It could convey, then, to its citizens only this right of preemption, and the right of occupation could not be united to it until obtained by the United States from the Cherokees. The act of cession of North Carolina only preserves the rights of its citizens in the same state as they would have been, *had that act never been passed.* It does not make imperfect titles perfect; but only prevents their being made worse. Congress, by their act, accept on these conditions. The claimants of North Carolina, then, and also the Cherokees, are exactly where they would have been, had neither the act of cession, nor that of acceptance, been ever made; that is, the latter possess the right of occupation, and the former the right of preemption. Though these deductions seem clear enough, yet the question would be a disagreeable one between the General Government, a particular government, and individuals, and it would seem very desirable to draw all the claims of preemption within a certain limit, by commuting for those out of it, and then to purchase of the Cherokees the right of occupation.—To HENRY KNOX. iii, 192. FORD ED., v, 237. (N.Y., 1790.)

— CHERRONESUS, Proposed State of. —See WESTERN TERRITORY.

1221. CHESAPEAKE, Attack on Frigate.—On the 22nd day of June last [1807], by a formal order from the British admiral, the frigate Chesapeake. leaving her port for distant service, was attacked by one of those vessels which had been lying in our harbors under the indulgences of hospitality, was disabled from proceeding, had several of her crew killed, and four taken away. On this outrage no commentaries are necessary. Its character has been pronounced by the indignant voice of our citizens with an emphasis and unanimity never exceeded. I immediately, by proclamation, interdicted our harbors and waters to all British armed vessels, forbade intercourse with them, and uncertain how far hostilities were intended, and the town of Norfolk, indeed, being threatened with immediate attack, a sufficient force was ordered for the protection of that place, and such other preparations commenced and pursued as the prospect rendered proper. An armed vessel of the United States was dispatched with instructions to our ministers at London to call on that government for the satisfaction and security required by the outrage. A very short interval ought now to bring the answer. * * * The aggression thus begun has been continued on the part of the British commanders by remaining within our waters, in defiance of the authority of the country, by habitual violations of its jurisdiction, and at length by putting to death one of the persons whom they had forcibly taken from on board the Chesapeake. These aggravations necessarily lead to the policy, either of never admitting an armed vessel into our harbors, or of maintaining in every harbor such an armed force as may constrain obedience to the laws, and protect the lives and property of our citizens, against their armed guests. But the expense of such a standing force, and its inconsistence with our principles, dispense with those obligations of hospitality which would necessarily call for it, and leave us equally free to exclude the navy, as we are the army of a foreign power, from entering our limits.—SEVENTH ANNUAL MESSAGE. viii, 83. FORD ED., viii, 152. (Oct. 27, 1807.)

1222. CHESAPEAKE, Demand for reparation.—We now send a vessel to call upon the British government for reparation for the past outrage, and security for the future, nor will anything be deemed security but a renunciation of the practice of taking persons out of our vessels, under the pretence of their being English.—To JOHN ARMSTRONG. v, 134. FORD ED., ix, 116. (W., July 1807.)

1223. —— ——. You will have seen by the proclamation the measures adopted. We act on these principles, 1. That the usage of nations requires that we shall give the offender an opportunity of making reparation and avoiding war.* 2. That we should give time to our merchants to get in their property and vessels and our seamen now afloat. And, 3. That the power of declaring war being with the Legislature, the Executive should do nothing, necessarily committing them to decide for war in preference to non-intercourse, which will be preferred by a great many.—To VICE-PRESIDENT CLINTON. v, 116. FORD ED., ix, 100. (W., July 1807.)

1224. —— ——. We have acted on these principles; 1, to give that government an opportunity to disavow and make reparation; 2, to give ourselves time to get in the vessels, property and seamen, now spread over the ocean; 3, to do no act which might compromit Congress in their choice between war, non-intercourse, or any other measure.— To BARNABAS BIDWELL. v, 126. FORD ED., ix, 106. (W., 1807.)

1225. —— ——. Whether the outrage is a proper cause of war, belonging exclusively to Congress, it is our duty not to commit them by doing anything which would have to be retracted. We may, however, exercise the powers entrusted to us for preventing future insults within our harbors, and claim firmly satisfaction for the past. This will leave Congress free to decide whether war is the most efficacious mode of redress in our case, or whether, having taught so many other useful lessons to Europe, we may not add that of showing them that there are peaceable means of repressing injustice, by making it the interest of the aggressor to do what is just, and abstain from future wrong. —To W. H. CABELL. v, 114. FORD ED., ix, 87. (W., June 1807.)

1226. CHESAPEAKE, Excitement Over. —This country has never been in such a state

* The action of the commander of the Leopard was disavowed by the British government, and it also disclaimed the right of search in the case of ships of war.—EDITOR.

of excitement since the battle of Lexington.—To JAMES BOWDOIN. v, 124. FORD ED., ix, 105. (July 1807.)

1227. —— ——. Never since the battle of Lexington have I seen this country in such a state of exasperation as at present, and even that did not produce such unanimity. The federalists themselves coalesce with us as to the object, though they will return to their trade of censuring every measure taken to obtain it.—To DUPONT DE NEMOURS. v, 127. FORD ED., ix, 110. (W., July 1807.)

1228. CHESAPEAKE,   Hostilities Threatened.—You will perceive by the enclosed copies of letters from Captain Decatur that the British commanders have their foot on the threshold of war. They have begun the blockade of Norfolk; have sounded the passage to the town, which appears practicable for three of their vessels, and menace an attack on the Chesapeake and Cybele. These, with four gunboats, form the present defence, and there are four more gunboats in Norfolk nearly ready. The four gunboats at Hampton are hauled up, and in danger, four in Mopjack bay are on the stocks. Blows may be hourly possible.—To GENERAL DEARBORN. v, 117. FORD ED., ix, 101. (W., July 1807.)

1229. CHESAPEAKE, Interdiction of British ships.—The *interdicted* ships are *enemies*. Should they be forced, by stress of weather, to run up into safer harbors, we are to act towards them as we would towards enemies in regular war, in a like case. Permit no intercourse, no supplies; and if they land, kill or capture them as enemies. If they lie still, Decatur has orders not to attack them without stating the case to me, and awaiting instructions. But if they attempt to enter the Elizabeth River, he is to attack them without awaiting for instructions. Other armed vessels, putting in from sea in distress, are *friends*. They must report themselves to the collector, he assigns them their station, and regulates their repairs, supplies, intercourse and stay. Not needing flags, they are under the direction of the collector alone, who should be reasonably liberal as to their repairs and supplies, furnishing them for a voyage to any of their American ports.—To JAMES MADISON. v, 173. FORD ED., ix, 130. (M., Aug. 1807.)

1230. —— ——. The intention of the [British] squadron in the bay is so manifestly pacific, that your instructions are perfectly proper, not to molest their boats merely for approaching the shore. While they are giving up slaves and citizen seamen, and attempting nothing ashore, it would not be well to stop this by any new restriction.—To W. H. CABELL. v, 191. (M., Sep. 1807.)

1231. —— ——. If they come ashore, they must be captured, or destroyed if they cannot be captured, because we mean to enforce the proclamation rigorously in preventing supplies.—To W. H. CABELL. v, 191. (M., Sep. 1807.)

1232. —— ——. The authority of the proclamation is to be maintained, no supplies to be permitted to be carried to the British vessels, nor their vessels permitted to land. For these purposes force, and to any extent, is to be applied, if necessary, but not unless necessary; nor, considering how short a time the present state of things has to continue, would I recommend any extraordinary vigilance or great industry in seeking even just occasions for collision. It will suffice to do what is right when the occasion comes into their way.—To Albert Gallatin. v, 202. (Oct. 1807.)

1233. CHESAPEAKE, New injuries.— Should the British government give us reparation of the past, and security for the future, yet the continuance of their vessels in our harbors in defiance constitutes a new injury, which will not be included in any settlement with our ministers, and will furnish good ground for declaring their future exclusion from our waters, in addition with the reasonable ground before existing.—To James Madison. v, 195. Ford ed., ix, 139. (M., Sep. 1807.)

1234. CHESAPEAKE, Premeditation suspected.— Though in the first moments of the outrage on the Chesapeake I did not suppose it was by authority from their government, I now more and more suspect it, and of course, that they will not give the reparation for the past and security for the future, which alone may prevent war. The new depredations committing on us, with this attack on the Chesapeake, and their calling on Portugal to declare on the one side or the other, if true, prove they have coolly calculated it will be to their benefit to have everything on the ocean fair prize, and to support their navy by plundering all mankind. * * * It is really mortifying that we should be forced to wish success to Bonaparte, and to look to his victories as our salvation.—To Colonel John Taylor. v, 149. (W., Aug. 1807.)

1235. CHESAPEAKE, Preparations at New York.— The spirit of the orders to Decatur should be applied to New York. So long as the British vessels merely enter the Hook, or remain quiet there, I would not precipitate hostilities. I do not sufficiently know the geography of the harbor to draw the line which they should not pass. * * * But a line should be drawn which if they attempt to pass, Commodore Rogers should attack them with all his force.—To Robert Smith. v, 196. Ford ed., ix, 140. (M., Sep. 1807.)

1236. CHESAPEAKE, Status of British captives.— The relation in which we stand with the British naval force within our waters is so new, that differences of opinion are not to be wondered at respecting the captives, who are the subject of your letter. Are they insurgents against the authority of the laws? Are they public enemies, acting under the orders of their sovereign? Or will it be more correct to take their character from the act of Congress for the preservation of peace in our harbors, which authorizes a qualified war

against persons of their demeanor, defining its objects, and limiting its extent? Considering this act as constituting the state of things between us and them, the captives may certainly be held as prisoners of war. If we restore them it will be an act of favor, and not of any right they can urge. Whether Great Britain will give us that reparation for the past and security for the future, which we have categorically demanded, cannot as yet be foreseen; but we have believed we should afford an opportunity of doing it, as well from justice and the usage of nations, as a respect to the opinion of an impartial world, whose approbation and esteem are always of value. This measure was requisite, also, to produce unanimity among ourselves. * * * It was necessary, too, for our own interests, afloat on the ocean. * * * These considerations render it still useful that we should avoid every act which may precipitate immediate and general war, or in any way shorten the interval so necessary for our own purposes; and they render it advisable that the captives, in the present instance, should be permitted to return, with their boat, arms, &c., to their ships. * * * And we wish the military to understand that while, for special reasons, we restore the captives in this first instance, we applaud the vigilance and activity which, by taking them, have frustrated the object of their enterprise, and urge a continuance of them, to intercept all intercourse with the vessels, their officers and crews, and to prevent them from taking or receiving supplies of any kind; and for this purpose, should the use of force be necessary, they are unequivocally to understand that force is to be employed without reserve or hesitation.—To W. H. Cabell. v, 141. Ford ed., ix, 89. (W., July 1807.)

1237. CHESAPEAKE, Tergiversation of Great Britain.— The communications made to Congress at their last session explained the posture in which the close of the discussion, relating to the attack by a British ship of war on the frigate Chesapeake, left a subject on which the nation had manifested so honorable a sensibility. Every view of what had passed authorized a belief that immediate steps would be taken by the British government for redressing a wrong, which, the more it was investigated, appeared the more clearly to require what had not been provided for in the special mission. It is found that no steps have been taken for the purpose. On the contrary, it will be seen, in the documents laid before you, that the inadmissible preliminary which obstructed the adjustment is still adhered to; and moreover, that it is now brought into connection with the distinct and irrelative case of the orders in council.—Eighth Annual Message. viii, 105. Ford ed., ix, 220. (Nov., 1808.)

1238. CHILDREN, Affection for.— No considerations in this world would compensate to me a separation from yourself and your sister.—To Mary Jefferson Eppes. Ford ed., vii, 478. (W., Jan. 1801.)

1239. —— ——. Francis will ever be to me one of the dearest objects in life.—To JOHN W. EPPES. FORD ED., ix, 107. (W., 1807.)

1240. CHILDREN, A blessing.—I sincerely congratulate you on the addition to your family. The good old Book, speaking of children says, " happy is the man who hath his quiver full of them ".—To CÆSAR A. RODNEY. FORD ED., ix, 144. (W., 1807.)

1241. CHILDREN, Good humor in.—In the ensuing autumn, I shall be sending on to Philadelphia a grandson of about fifteen years of age, to whom I shall ask your friendly attentions. Without that bright fancy which captivates, I am in hopes he possesses sound judgment and much observation; and, what I value more than all things, good humor.—To DR. BENJAMIN RUSH. v, 225. (W., 1808.)

1242. CHILDREN, Happiness and.—An only daughter and numerous family of grandchildren, will furnish me great resources of happiness.—To CHARLES THOMSON. v, 403. FORD ED., ix, 234. (W., 1808.)

1243. —— ——. My expectations from you are high, yet not higher than you may attain. Industry and resolution are all that are wanting. Nobody in this world can make me so happy, or so miserable, as you. Retirement from public life will ere long become necessary for me. To your sister and yourself I look to render the evening of my life serene and contented. Its morning has been clouded by loss after loss, till I have nothing left but you. I do not doubt either your affections or your dispositions. But great exertions are necessary, and you have little time left to make them. Be industrious, then, my child. Think nothing insurmountable by resolution and application, and you will be all that I wish you to be.—To MARTHA JEFFERSON. FORD ED., iv, 374. (1787.)

1244. CHILDREN, Moral training of.—When your sister arrives [in France] she will become a precious charge on your hands. The difference of your age and your common loss of a mother, will put that office on you. Teach her above all things to be good, because without that we can neither be valued by others nor set any value on ourselves. Teach her always to be true; no vice is so mean as the want of truth, and at the same time so useless. Teach her never to be angry; anger only serves to torment ourselves; and divert others, and alienate their esteem. And teach her industry, and application to useful pursuits. I will venture to assure you that if you inculcate this in her mind, you will make her a happy being herself, a most interesting friend to you, and precious to all the world.—To MARTHA JEFFERSON. FORD ED., iv, 375.

1245. CHILDREN, Prattle of.—You were never more mistaken than in supposing you were too long on the prattle, &c., of little Anne [his granddaughter], I read it with quite as much pleasure as you write it.—To MARTHA JEFFERSON RANDOLPH. FORD ED., vi, 163. (Pa., 1793.)

1246. CHINA, Conciliation of.—Punqua Winchung the Chinese Mandarin, has, I believe, his headquarters at New York, and therefore his case is probably known to you. He came to Washington just as I had left it [for Monticello], and therefore wrote to me, praying for permission to depart to his own country with his property, in a vessel to be engaged by himself. * * * I consider it as a case of national comity, and coming within the views of the first section of the first embargo act. The departure of this individual with good dispositions, may be the means of making our nation known advantageously at the source of power in China, to which it is otherwise difficult to convey information. It may be of sensible advantage to our merchants in that country. I cannot, therefore, but consider that a chance of obtaining a permanent national good will should overweigh the effect of a single case taken out of the great field of the embargo. The case, too, is so singular, that it can lead to no embarrassment as a precedent.—To ALBERT GALLATIN. v, 325. (M., July 1808.)

1247. —— ——. In the case of the Chinese Mandarin, * * * the opportunity hoped from that, of making known through one of its own characters of note, our nation, our circumstances and character, and of letting that government understand at length the difference between us and the English, and separate us in its policy, rendered that measure a diplomatic one in my view, and likely to bring lasting advantage to our merchants and commerce with that country.—To ALBERT GALLATIN. v, 344. (M., Aug. 1808.)

1248. CHOCOLATE, Tea, coffee and.—The superiority of chocolate, both for health and nourishment, will soon give it the same preference over tea and coffee in America, which it has in Spain.—To JOHN ADAMS. i, 494. (P., 1785.)

— **CHRISTIANITY, The Common Law and.**—See COMMON LAW.

1249. CHURCH, Definition of a.—A church is " a *voluntary* society of men, joining themselves together of their own accord, in order to the public worshipping of God in such a manner as they judge acceptable to Him and effectual to the salvation of their souls ". It is *voluntary*, because no man is by *nature* bound to any church. The hope of salvation is the cause of his entering into it. If he find anything wrong in it, he should be as free to go out as he was to come in.—NOTES ON RELIGION. FORD ED., ii, 101. (1776?)

1250. CHURCH, Jurisdiction. — Each church being free, no one can have jurisdiction over another one, not even when the civil magistrate joins it. It neither acquires the right of the sword by the magistrate's coming to it, nor does it lose the rights of instruction or excommunication by his going from it. It cannot by the accession of any new member acquire jurisdiction over those who do not accede. He brings only himself, having no power to bring others. Suppose, for instance, two churches, one of Arminians, another of Calvinists in Constantinople, has either any right over the other? Will it be said the orthodox one has? Every church is to itself orthodox; to others erroneous or heretical.—NOTES ON RELIGION. FORD ED., ii, 99. (1776?)

1251. CHURCH, Law of.—What is the power of that church? As it is a society, it must have some laws for its regulation. Time and place of meeting; admitting and excluding members, &c., must be regulated. But as it was a spontaneous joining of members, it follows that its laws extend to its own members only, not to those of any other voluntary society; for then, by the same rule, some other voluntary society might usurp power over them.—NOTES ON RELIGION. FORD ED., ii, 101. (1776?)

1252. CHURCH, Regulation of.—If anything pass in a religious meeting seditiously and contrary to the public peace, let it be punished in the same manner and no otherwise than as if it had happened in a fair or market. These meetings ought not to be sanctuaries for faction and flagitiousness.—NOTES ON RELIGION. FORD ED., ii, 102. (1776?)

1253. CHURCH (Anglican in Virginia), Disestablishment of.—The first settlers of Virginia were Englishmen, loyal subjects to their king and church, and the grant to Sir Walter Raleigh contained an express proviso that their laws " should not be against the true Christian faith, now professed in the Church of England ". As soon as the state of the colony admitted, it was divided into parishes, in each of which was established a minister of the Anglican church, endowed with a fixed salary, in tobacco, a glebe house and land with the other necessary appendages. To meet these expenses, all the inhabitants of the parishes were assessed, whether they were or not, members of the established church. Towards Quakers who came here, they were most cruelly intolerant, driving them from the colony by the severest penalties. In process of time, however, other sectarisms were introduced, chiefly of the Presbyterian family; and the established clergy, secure for life in their glebes and salaries, adding to these, generally, the emoluments of a classical school, found employment enough, in their farms and school-rooms, for the rest of the week, and devoted Sunday only to the edification of their flock, by service, and a sermon at their parish church. Their other pastoral functions were little attended to. Against this inactivity, the zeal and industry of sectarian preachers had an open and undisputed field; and by the time of the Revolution, a majority of the inhabitants had become dissenters from the established church, but were still obliged to pay contributions to support the pastors of the minority. This unrighteous compulsion, to maintain teachers of what they deemed religious errors, was grievously felt during the regal government, and without a hope of relief. But the first republican legislature, which met in '76, was crowded with petitions to abolish this spiritual tyranny.

These brought on the severest contests in which I have ever been engaged. Our great opponents were Mr. Pendleton and Robert Carter Nicholas; honest men, but zealous churchmen. The petitions were referred to the " committee of the Whole House on the State of the Country ";* and, after desperate contests in that committee, almost daily from the 11th of October to the 5th of December, we prevailed so far only, as to repeal the laws which rendered criminal the maintenance of any religious opinions, the forbearance of repairing to church, or the exercise of any mode of worship; and further, to exempt dissenters from contributions to the support of the established church; and to suspend, only until the next session, levies on the members of that church for the salaries of their own incumbents. For although the majority of our citizens were dissenters, as has been observed, a majority of the legislature were churchmen. Among these, however, were some reasonable and liberal men, who enabled us, on some points, to obtain feeble majorities. But our opponents carried, in the general resolutions of the committee of Nov. 19, a declaration that religious assemblies ought to be regulated, and that provision ought to be made for continuing the succession of the clergy, and superintending their conduct. And, in the bill, now passed,† was inserted an express reservation of the question, whether a general assessment should not be established by law, on every one, to the support of the pastor of his choice; or whether all should be left to voluntary contributions; and on this question, debated at every session, from '76 to '79 (some of our dissenting allies, having now secured their particular object, going over to the advocates of a general assessment), we could only obtain a suspension from session to session until '79, when the question against a general assessment was finally carried, and the establishment of the Anglican church entirely put down. In justice to the two honest but zealous opponents, who have been named, I must add, that although, from their natural temperaments, they were more disposed generally to acquiesce in things as they are, than to risk innovations, yet whenever the public will had once decided, none were more faithful or exact in their obedience to it.—AUTOBIOGRAPHY. i, 38. FORD ED., i, 52. (1821.)

1254. ———— ————. The restoration of the rights of conscience relieved the people from taxation for the support of a religion not theirs; for the [Church of England] Estab-

---

* A note in the FORD edition says these petitions were referred to the "Committee of Religion" of which Jefferson was a member. This committee was subsequently discharged of this question, and it was referred to the "Committee of the Whole House upon the State of the Country".—EDITOR.

† Entitled: "An Act for exempting the different societies of dissenters from contributing to the support and maintenance of the church as by law established, and its ministers, and for other purposes therein mentioned." Passed by the House of Delegates, December 5th. Concurred in by the Senate, December 9th. Re-enacted January 1, 1778. It is printed in *A Collection of Public Acts of Virginia*, Richmond, 1785, p. 39.—NOTE, FORD ED.

lishment was truly of the religion of the rich, the dissenting sects being entirely composed of the less wealthy people.*—AUTOBIOGRAPHY. i, 49. FORD ED., i, 69. (1821.)

— **CHURCH (Anglican in Virginia), Persecution by.**—See QUAKERS.

1255. CHURCH AND STATE, Constitutional provisions against.—No person shall be compelled to frequent or maintain any religious institution.—PROPOSED VA. CONSTITUTION. FORD ED., ii, 27. (June 1776.)

1256. —— ——. The General Assembly shall not have power * * * to abridge the civil rights of any person on account of his religious belief; to restrain him from professing and supporting that belief, or compel him to contributions, other than those he shall have personally stipulated for the support of that or any other.—PROPOSED VA. CONSTITUTION. viii, 445. FORD ED., iii, 325. (1783.)

1257. —— ——. No man shall be compelled to frequent, or support, any religious worship, place, or ministry, whatsoever; nor shall be enforced, restrained, molested, or burthened in his body or goods, or shall otherwise suffer, on account of his religious opinions or belief; but * * * all men shall be free to profess, and by argument to maintain, their opinion in matters of religion, and * * * the same shall in no wise diminish, enlarge, or affect their civil capacities.—STATUTE OF RELIGIOUS FREEDOM. viii, 455. FORD ED., ii, 239. (1779.)

1258. CHURCH AND STATE, Evils of union.—If the magistracy had vouchsafed to interpose in other sciences, we should have as bad logic, mathematics, and philosophy as we have divinity in countries where the law settles orthodoxy.—NOTES ON RELIGION. FORD ED., ii, 95. (1776?)

1259. —— ——. To suffer the civil magistrate to intrude his powers into the field of opinion, and to restrain the profession or propagation of principles on supposition of their ill tendency, is a dangerous fallacy, which at once destroys all religious liberty, because he being, of course, judge of that tendency will make his opinions the rule of judgment, and approve or condemn the sentiments of others only as they shall square with or suffer from his own.—STATUTE OF RELIGIOUS FREEDOM. viii, 455. FORD ED., ii, 239. (1779.)

1260. CHURCH AND STATE, False Religions.—The impious presumption of legislators and rulers, civil as well as ecclesiastical, who, being themselves but fallible and uninspired men, have assumed dominion over the faith of others, setting up their own opinions and modes of thinking as the only true and infallible, and as such endeavoring to impose them on others, hath established and maintained false religions over the greatest part of the world and through all time.—STATUTE OF RELIGIOUS FREEDOM. viii, 454. FORD ED., ii, 38. (1779.)

* See Note to ENTAIL.—EDITOR.

1261. CHURCH AND STATE, Guidance by.—I cannot give up my guidance to the magistrate, because he knows no more of the way to heaven than I do, and is less concerned to direct me right than I am to go right.—NOTES ON RELIGION. FORD ED., ii, 100. (1776?)

1262. —— ——. If it be said the magistrate may make use of arguments and so draw the heterodox to truth, I answer, every man has a commission to admonish, exhort, convince another of error.—NOTES ON RELIGION. FORD ED., ii, 101. (1776?)

1263. —— ——. If the magistrate command me to bring my commodity to a public store-house, I bring it because he can indemnify me if he erred, and I thereby lose it; but what indemnification can he give one for the kingdom of heaven?—NOTES ON RELIGION. FORD ED., ii, 100. (1776?)

1264. CHURCH AND STATE, New York, Pennsylvania and.—Our sister States of Pennsylvania and New York have long subsisted without any establishment at all. The experiment was new and doubtful when they made it. It has answered beyond conception. They flourish infinitely. Religion is well supported; of various kinds, indeed, but all good enough; all sufficient to preserve peace and order; or if a sect arises, whose tenets would subvert morals, good sense has fair play, and reasons and laughs it out of doors, without suffering the State to be troubled with it. They do not hang more malefactors than we do. They are not more disturbed with religious dissensions. On the contrary, their harmony is unparalleled, and can be ascribed to nothing but their unbounded tolerance, because there is no other circumstance in which they differ from every nation on earth. They have made the happy discovery, that the way to silence religious disputes, is to take no notice of them.—NOTES ON VIRGINIA. viii, 402. FORD ED., iii, 265. (1782.)

1265. CHURCH AND STATE, People and.—The people have not given the magistrate the care of souls because they could not. They could not, because no man has the right to abandon the care of his salvation to another.—NOTES ON RELIGION. FORD ED., ii, 101. (1776?)

1266. CHURCH AND STATE, Right of opinion and.—The opinions of men are not the object of civil government, nor under its jurisdiction.*—STATUTE OF RELIGIOUS FREEDOM. FORD ED., ii, 238. (1779.)

1267. CHURCH AND STATE, Support of.—To compel a man to furnish contribu-

* Parton in his *Life of Jefferson*, p. 211, says: "This vigorous utterance of Thomas Jefferson was the arsenal from which the opponents of the forced support of religion drew their weapons, during the whole period of about fifty years that elapsed between its publication and the repeal of the last State law which taxed a community for the support of the clergy; nor will it cease to have a certain value as long as any man, in any land, is distrusted, or undervalued, or abridged of his natural rights, on account of any opinion whatever." This extract is not in the Statute as printed in the Congress Edition.—EDITOR.

tions of money for the propagation of opinions which he disbelieves and abhors, is sinful and tyrannical.—STATUTE OF RELIGIOUS FREEDOM. viii, 454. FORD ED., ii, 238. (1779.)

1268. ———— ————. The forcing a man to support this or that teacher even of his own religious persuasion, is depriving him of the comfortable liberty of giving his contributions to the particular pastor whose morals he would make his pattern, and whose powers he feels most persuasive to righteousness; and is withdrawing from the ministry those temporary rewards, which, proceeding from an approbation of their personal conduct, are an additional incitement to earnest and unremitting labors for the instruction of mankind.—STATUTE OF RELIGIOUS FREEDOM. viii, 454. FORD ED., ii, 238. (1779.)

1269. CHURCH AND STATE, Wall of separation.—Believing that religion is a matter which lies solely between man and his God, that he owes account to none other for his faith or his worship, that the legislative powers of government reach actions only, and not opinions, I contemplate with sovereign reverence that act of the whole American people which declared that their Legislature should " make no law respecting an establishment of religion, or prohibiting the free exercise thereof ", thus building a wall of separation between Church and State.*—R. TO A. DANBURY BAPTISTS. viii, 113. (1802.)

1270. CICERO, Letters of.—The letters of Cicero breathe the purest effusions of an exalted patriot, while the parricide Cæsar is lost in odious contrast.—To JOHN ADAMS. vii, 148. FORD ED., x, 152. (M., 1819.)

1271. CINCINNATI SOCIETY, Foundation.—When the army was about to be disbanded, and the officers to take final leave, perhaps never again to meet, it was natural for men who had accompanied each other through so many scenes of hardship, of difficulty, and danger, who, in a variety of instances, must have been rendered mutually dear by those aids and good offices to which their situations had given occasion; it was natural, I say, for these to seize with fondness any proposition which promised to bring them together again at certain and regular periods. And this, I take for granted, was the origin and object of this institution; and I have no suspicion that they foresaw, much less intended, those mischiefs which exist perhaps in the forebodings of politicians only. I doubt, however, whether, in its execution, it would be found to answer the wishes of those who framed it, and to foster those friendships it was intended to preserve. The members would be brought together at their annual assemblies, no longer to encounter a common enemy, but to encounter one another in debate and sentiment. For something, I suppose, is to be done at these meetings, and, however unimportant, it will suffice to produce difference of opinion, contradiction and irritation. The way to make friends quarrel is to put them in disputation under the public eye. An experience of near twenty years has taught me that few friendships stand this test, and that public assemblies, where every one is free to act and speak, are the most powerful looseners of the bands of private friendship. I think, therefore, that this institution would fail in its principal object, the perpetuation of the personal friendships contracted through the war.*—To GENERAL WASHINGTON. i, 333. FORD ED., iii, 465. (A., April 1784.)

1272. CINCINNATI SOCIETY, Objections to.—The objections of those who are opposed to the institution shall be briefly sketched. They urge that it is against the Confederation—against the letter of some of our constitutions, against the spirit of all of them—that the foundation on which all these are built is the natural equality of man, the denial of every preeminence but that annexed to legal office, and, particularly, the denial of preeminence by birth; that, however, in their present dispositions, citizens might decline accepting honorary instalments into the order, a time may come, when a change of dispositions would render these flattering, when a well-directed distribution of them might draw into the order all the men of talents, of office and wealth, and, in this case, would probably procure an ingraftment into the government; that in this, they will be supported by their foreign members, and the wishes and influence of foreign courts; that experience has shown that the hereditary branches of modern governments are the patrons of privilege and prerogative, and not of the natural rights of the people, whose oppressors they generally are; that, besides these evils, which are remote, others may take place more immediately; that a distinction is kept up between the civil and military, which it is for the happiness of both to obliterate; that when the members assemble they will be proposing to do something, and what that something may be, will depend on actual circumstances; that being an organized body under habits of subordination, the first obstructions to enterprise will be already surmounted; that the moderation and virtue of a single character have probably prevented this Revolution from being closed, as most others have been, by a subversion of that liberty it was intended to establish; that he is not immortal, and his successor, or some of his successors, may be led

---

* Before sending this reply to the Danbury Baptists, Jefferson enclosed a copy of it to Levi Lincoln, his Attorney General, with a note (FORD ED., viii. 129) in which he said: " The Baptist address admits of a condemnation of the alliance between Church and State, under the authority of the Constitution. It furnishes an occasion, too, which I have long wished to find, of saying why I do not proclaim fastings and thanksgivings, as my predecessors did. * * * I know it will give great offence to the New England clergy; but the advocate of religious freedom is to expect neither peace nor forgiveness from them. Will you be so good as to examine the answer, and suggest any alterations which might prevent an ill effect, or promote a good one among the people? You understand the temper of those in the North, and can weaken it, therefore, to their stomachs; it is at present seasoned to the Southern taste only."—EDITOR.

* Washington asked Jefferson's opinions on the subject.—EDITOR.

by false calculation into a less certain road to glory. — To GENERAL WASHINGTON. i, 334. FORD ED., iii, 466. (A., April 1784.)

1273. CINCINNATI SOCIETY, Opposition in Congress.—What are the sentiments of Congress on this subject, and what line they will pursue, can only be stated conjecturally. Congress, as a body, if left to themselves, will, in my opinion, say nothing on the subject. They may, however, be forced into a declaration by instructions from some of the States, or by other incidents. Their sentiments, if forced from them, will be unfriendly to the institution. If permitted to pursue their own path, they will check it by side-blows whenever it comes in their way, and in competitions for office, on equal or nearly equal ground, will give silent preference to those who are not of the fraternity. My reasons for thinking this are, 1. The grounds on which they lately declined the foreign order proposed to be conferred on some of our citizens. 2. The fourth of the fundamental articles of constitution for the new States. * * * 3. Private conversations on this subject with the members. * * * I have taken occasion to extend these, not, indeed, to the military members, because, being of the order, delicacy forbade it, but to the others pretty generally; and among these, I have as yet found but one who is not opposed to the institution.— To GENERAL WASHINGTON. i, 335. FORD ED., iii, 467. (A., April 1784.)

1274. CINCINNATI SOCIETY, Sentiment in France. — What has heretofore passed between us on this institution, makes it my duty to mention to you that I have never heard a person in Europe, learned or unlearned, express his thoughts on this institution, who did not consider it as dishonorable and destructive to our governments; and that every writing which has come out since my arrival here [Paris] in which it is mentioned, considers it, even as now reformed, as the germ whose development is one day to destroy the fabric we have reared. I did not apprehend this while I had American ideas only. But I confess that what I have seen in Europe has brought me over to that opinion; and that though the day may be at some distance, beyond the reach of our lives, perhaps, yet it will certainly come, when a single fibre left of this institution will produce an hereditary aristocracy, which will change the form of our governments from the best to the worst in the world. To know the mass of evil which flows from this fatal source, a person must be in France. He must see the finest soil, the finest climate, the most compact State, the most benevolent character of people, and every earthly advantage combined, insufficient to prevent this scourge from rendering existence a curse to twenty-four out of twenty-five parts of the inhabitants of this country. With us, the branches of this institution cover all the States. The southern ones at this time are aristocratical in their disposition; and that that spirit should grow and extend itself, is within the natural order of things. I do not flatter myself with the im-

mortality of our governments; but I shall think little also of their longevity, unless this germ of destruction be taken out. When the society themselves shall weigh the possibility of evil against the impossibility of any good to proceed from this institution, I cannot help hoping they will eradicate it. I know they wish the permanence of our governments as much as any individuals composing them.—To GENERAL WASHINGTON. ii, 61. FORD ED., iv, 328. (P., Nov. 1786.)

1275. CIPHER, Jefferson's.—A favorable and confidential opportunity offering by M. Dupont de Nemours, who is revisiting his native country * * * I send you a cipher to be used between us, which will give you some trouble to understand, but, once understood, is the easiest to use, the most undecipherable, and varied by a new key with the greatest facility of any I have ever known. I am in hopes the explanation enclosed will be sufficient. Let our key of letters be [some figures which are illegible] and the key of lines be [figures illegible], and lest we should lose our key or be absent from it, it is so formed as to be kept in the memory and put upon paper at pleasure; being produced by writing our names and residences at full length, each of which containing twenty-seven letters is divided into three parts of nine letters each; and each of the nine letters is then numbered according to the place it would hold if the nine were arranged alphabetically thus [so blotted as to be illegible]. The numbers over the letters being then arranged as the letters to which they belong stand in our names, we can always construct our key. But why a cipher between us, when official things go naturally to the Secretary of State, and things not political need no cipher? 1. Matters of a public nature, and proper to go on our records, should go to the Secretary of State. 2. Matters of a public nature, not proper to be placed on our records, may still go to the Secretary of State, headed by the word "private." But, 3, there may be matters merely personal to ourselves, and which require the cover of a cipher more than those of any other character. This last purpose and others, which we cannot foresee, may render it convenient and advantageous to have at hand a mask for whatever may need it.—To ROBERT R. LIVINGSTON. iv, 431. FORD ED., viii, 143. (W., 1802.)

1276. CIRACCHI, Genius of.—Ciracchi was second to no sculptor living except Canova; and, if he had lived, he would have rivalled him. His style had been formed on the fine models of antiquity in Italy, and he had caught their ineffable majesty of expression. On his return to Rome, he made the bust of General Washington in marble, from that in plaster; it was sent over here, was universally considered as the best effigy of him ever executed, was bought by the Spanish minister for the King of Spain, and sent to Madrid.—To NATHANIEL MACON. vi, 535. (M., 1816.)

1277. CITIES, Corruption and.—When we get piled upon one another in large cities, as in Europe, we shall become as corrupt as in Europe.*—To JAMES MADISON. FORD ED., iv, 479. (P., Dec. 1787.)

* In the Congress edition (ii, 332) this extract has been *edited* so as to read : " When we get piled upon one another in large cities, as in Europe, we shall become corrupt as in Europe, and go to eating one another as they do there."—EDITOR.

1278. CITIES, Evils of.—I view great cities as pestilential to the morals, the health, and the liberties of man. True, they nourish some of the elegant arts, but the useful ones can thrive elsewhere, and less perfection in the others, with more health, virtue and freedom, would be my choice.—To DR. BENJAMIN RUSH. iv, 335. FORD ED., vii, 459. (M., 1800.)

1279. CITIES, Federalist strongholds. —The cities [were] the strongholds of federalism.—To WILLIAM JOHNSON. vii, 292. FORD ED., x, 227. (M., 1823.)

1280. —— ——. The inhabitants of the commercial cities are as different in sentiment and character from the country people as any two distinct nations, and are clamorous against the order of things [republicanism] established by the agricultural interest.—To M. PICTET. iv, 463. (W., 1803.)

1281. CITIES, Foreign Character of.— In our cities your son will find distant imitations of the cities of Europe. But if he wishes to know the nation, its occupations, manners, and principles, they reside not in the cities. He must travel through the country, accept the hospitalities of the country gentlemen, and visit with them the school of the people.—To MADAME DE STAEL. v, 133. (W., 1807.)

1282. —— ——. Our cities exhibit specimens of London only; our country is a different nation.—To M. DASHKOFF. v, 463. (M., 1809.)

1283. CITIES, Founding. — There are places [in Virginia] at which * * * the laws have said there shall be towns; but nature has said there shall not. * * * Accidental circumstances, however, may control the indications of nature, and in no instance do they do it more frequently than in the rise and fall of towns.—NOTES ON VIRGINIA. viii, 351. FORD ED., iii, 213. (1782.)

1284. CITIES, Life in.—A city life offers indeed more means of dissipating time, but more frequent, also, and more painful objects of vice and wretchedness.—To WILLIAM SHORT. vii, 310. (M., 1823.)

1285. CITIES, Misery in.—Even here we find too strong a current from the country to the towns; and instances are beginning to appear of that species of misery, which you are so humanely endeavoring to relieve with you. Although we have in the old countries of Europe the lesson of their experience to warn us, yet I am not satisfied we shall have the firmness and wisdom to profit by it.— To DAVID WILLIAMS, v, 514. (W., 1803.)

1286. —— ——. The general desire of men to live by their heads rather than their hands, and the strong allurements of great cities to those who have any turn for dissipation threaten to make them here, as in Europe, the sinks of voluntary misery.—To DAVID WILLIAMS. iv, 514. (W., 1803.)

1287. CITIES, Political influence of.— The commercial cities, though, by the command of newspapers, they make a great deal of noise, have little effect in the direction of the government.—To M. PICTET. iv, 463. (W., 1803.)

1288. CITIZENS, Adopted.—Born in other countries, yet believing you could be happy in this, our laws acknowledge, as they should do, your right to join us in society, conforming * * * to our established rules. That these rules shall be as equal as prudential considerations will admit, will certainly be the aim of our legislatures, general and particular.—REPLY TO ADDRESS. iv, 394. (W., May 1801.)

1289. —— ——. If the unexampled state of the world has, in any instance, occasioned among us temporary departures from the system of equal rule, the restoration of tranquility will doubtless produce reconsideration; and your knowledge of the liberal conduct heretofore observed towards strangers settling among us will warrant the belief that what is right will be done.—REPLY TO ADDRESS. iv, 394. (May 1801.)

1290. CITIZENS, Dangerous.—Every society has a right to fix the fundamental principles of its association, and to say to all individuals, that, if they contemplate pursuits beyond the limits of these principles, and involving dangers which the society chooses to avoid, they must go somewhere else for their exercise; that we want no citizens, and still less ephemeral and pseudo-citizens, on such terms. We may exclude them from our territory, as we do persons infected with disease. We have most abundant resources of happiness within ourselves, which we may enjoy in peace and safety without permitting a few citizens, infected with the mania of rambling and gambling, to bring danger on the great mass engaged in innocent and safe pursuits at home.—To WILLIAM H. CRAWFORD. i, 6. FORD ED., x, 34. (M., 1816.)

1291. CITIZENS, Fraudulent and real. —[As to citizens] there is a distinction which we ought to make ourselves, and with which the belligerent powers [France and England] ought to be content. Where, after the commencement of a war, a merchant of either comes here and is naturalized, the purpose is probably fraudulent against the other, and intended to cloak their commerce under our flag. This we should honestly discountenance, and never reclaim their property when captured. But merchants from either, settled and made citizens before a war, are citizens to every purpose of commerce, and not to be distinguished in our proceedings from natives. Every attempt of Great Britain to enforce her principle of " once a subject, always a subject " beyond the case of *her own subjects,* ought to be repelled.—To ALBERT GALLATIN. FORD ED., viii, 251. (July 1803.) See EXPATRIATION.

1292. CITIZENS, Government and.— Give to every citizen, personally, a part in the administration of the public affairs.—To SAMUEL KERCHIVAL. vii, 13. FORD ED., x, 41. (M., 1816.)

1293. CITIZENS, Military service and. —Every citizen [should] be a soldier. This was the case with the Greeks and Romans, and must be that of every free State.—To James Monroe. vi, 131. (M., 1813.)

1294. CITIZENS, Protection of.—It is an obligation of every government to yield protection to its citizens as the consideration of their obedience.—To John Jay. i, 458. (P., 1785.)

1295. —— ——. The first foundations of the social compact would be broken up, were we definitely to refuse to its members the protection of their persons and property, while in their lawful pursuits.—To James Maury. vi, 52. Ford ed., ix, 348. (M., 1812.)

1296. —— ——. The persons and property of our citizens are entitled to the protection of our government in all places where they may lawfully go.—Official Opinion. vii, 624. (1793.)

1297. CITIZENS, Relief of imprisoned. —There are in the prison of St. Pol de Leon six or seven citizens of the United States of America, charged with having attempted a contraband of tobacco, but, as they say themselves, forced into that port by stress of weather. I believe that they are innocent. Their situation is described to me as deplorable as should be that of men found guilty of the worst of crimes. They are in close jail, allowed three sous a day only, and unable to speak a word of the language of the country. I hope their distress, which it is my duty to relieve, * * * will apologize for the liberty I take of asking you to advise them what to do for their defence, to engage some good lawyer for them, and to pass them the pecuniary reliefs necessary. I write to Mr. Lister Asquith, the owner of the vessel, that he may draw bills on me from time to time, for a livre a day for every person of them, and what may be necessary to engage a lawyer for him.—To M. Desbordes. i, 402. (P., 1785.)

1298. —— ——. I take the liberty of troubling your excellency on behalf of six citizens of the United States who have been for some time confined in the prison of St. Pol de Leon, and of referring for particulars to the enclosed state of their case. * * * I have thus long avoided troubling your Excellency with this case, in hopes it would receive its decision in the ordinary course of law, and I relied that that would indemnify the sufferers, if they had been used unjustly; but though they have been in close confinement, now near three months, it has yet no appearance of approaching to decision. In the meantime, the cold of the winter is coming on, and, to men in their situation, may produce events which would render all indemnification too late. I must, therefore, pray the assistance of your Excellency, for the liberation of their persons, if the established order of things may possibly admit of it.—To Count de Vergennes. i, 479. (P., 1785.)

1299. CITIZENS, Rights of distressed. —Citizens [in a foreign country] under un-expected calamity have a right to call for the patronage of the public servants.—To John Jay. i, 583. (P., 1786.) See Alien and Sedition Laws, Expatriation, Naturalization.

1300. CITIZENSHIP, Government and. —No Englishman will pretend that a right to participate in government can be derived from any other source than a *personal* right, or a right of property. The conclusion is inevitable that he, who had neither his *person* nor property in America, could rightfully assume a participation in its government.—To M. Soulés. ix, 299. Ford ed., iv, 306. (P., 1786.)

— CIVIL SERVICE.—See Office.

1301. CIVILIZATION, Letters and.— Our experience with the Indians has proved that letters are not the first, but the last step in the progression from barbarism to civilization.—To James Pemberton. v, 303. (W., 1808.)

1302. CIVILIZATION, Progress of.— The idea which you present of the progress of society from its rudest state to that it has now attained, seems conformable to what may be probably conjectured. Indeed, we have under our eyes tolerable proofs of it. Let a philosophic observer commence a journey from the savages of the Rocky Mountains, eastwardly to our seacoast. These he would observe in the earliest stages of association living under no law but that of nature, subsisting and covering themselves with the flesh and skins of wild beasts. He would next find those on our frontiers in the pastoral state, raising domestic animals to supply the defects of hunting. Then succeed our semi-barbarous citizens, the pioneers of the advance of civilization, and so in his progress he would meet the gradual shades of improving man until he would reach his, as yet, most improved state in our seaport towns. This, in fact, is equivalent to a survey, in time, of the progress of man from the infancy of creation to the present day. I am eighty-one years of age, born where I now live, in the first range of mountains in the interior of our country. And I have observed this march of civilization advancing from the sea coast, passing over us like a cloud of light, increasing our knowledge and improving our condition, insomuch as that we are at this time more advanced in civilization here than the seaports were when I was a boy. And where this progress will stop no one can say. Barbarism has, in the meantime, been receding before the steady step of amelioration; and will in time, I trust, disappear from the earth. You seem to think that this advance has brought on us too complicated a state of society, and that we should gain in happiness by treading back our steps a little way. I think, myself, that we have more machinery of government than is necessary, too many parasites living on the labor of the industrious. I believe it might be much simplified to the relief of those who maintain it. Your experiment seems to have this in view. A society of seventy families, the number you name, may very possibly be governed as a single family, subsisting on their common industry, and holding all things in common. Some regulators of the family you still must have, and it remains to be seen at what period of your increasing population your simple regulations will cease to be sufficient to preserve order, peace, and justice.—To WILLIAM LUDLOW. vii, 377. (M., 1824.)

1303. CLAIBORNE (W. C. C.), Appointed Governor.—Among the enclosed commissions is one for yourself as Governor of the Territory of Orleans. With respect to this I will enter into frank explanations. This office was originally destined for a person* whose great services and established fame would have rendered him peculiarly acceptable to the nation at large. Circumstances, however, exist, which do not now permit his nomination, and perhaps may not at any time hereafter. That, therefore, being suspended and entirely contingent, your services have been so much approved as to leave no desire to look elsewhere to fill the office. Should the doubts you have sometimes expressed, whether it would be eligible for you to continue, still exist in your mind, the acceptance of the commission gives you time to satisfy yourself by further experience, and to make the time and manner of withdrawing, should you ultimately determine on that, agreeable to yourself.—To GOVERNOR CLAIBORNE. iv, 558. (M., Aug. 1804.)

1304. CLAIBORNE (W. C. C.), Federalists and.—The federalists have been long endeavoring to batter down the Governor, who has always been a firm republican. There were characters superior to him whom I wished to appoint, but they refused the office. I know no better man who would accept of it, and it would not be right to turn him out for one not better. —To JOHN DICKINSON. v, 30. FORD ED., ix, 8. (W., 1807.)

1305. CLAIMANTS, Assistance to.—It is impossible for me to give any authority for the advance of moneys to Mr. Wilson. Were we to do it in his case, we should, on the same principles, be obliged to do it in several others, wherein foreign nations decline or delay doing justice to our citizens. No law of the United States would cover such an act of the executive; and all we can do legally is to give him all the aid which our patronage of his claims with the British court can effect. —To THOMAS PINCKNEY. iii, 526. (Pa., 1793.)

1306. CLAIMS, Settle just.—Mr. Cutting has a claim against the government. * * * I have only to desire that you will satisfy yourself as to the facts * * * and communicate the same to me, that justice may be done between the public and the claimant.—To THOMAS PINCKNEY. iii, 445. (Pa., 1792.)

1307. CLARK (George Rogers), Greatness of.—I know the greatness of General Clark's mind and am the more mortified at the cause which obscures it. Had not this unhappily taken place, there was nothing he might not have hoped; could it be surmounted, his lost ground might yet be recovered. No man alive rated him higher than I did, and would

* In the margin is written by Jefferson, "Lafayette".—EDITOR.

again, were he to become what I knew him. We are made to hope he is writing an account of his expeditions north of Ohio. They will be valuable morsels of history, and will justify to the world those who have told them how great he was.—To HARRY INNES. iii, 217. FORD ED., v, 295. (Pa., 1791.)

1308. CLARKE (Daniel), Consul at New Orleans.—I have appointed Mr. Daniel Clarke, at New Orleans, our consul there. His worth and influence will aid you powerfully in the interfering interests of those who go, and who reside there.—To WILLIAM C. CLAIBORNE. FORD ED., viii, 72. (W., July 1801.)

— CLASSICS, Study of the.—See LANGUAGES.

1309. CLAY (Henry), Opposition to Jefferson.—It is true, as you have heard, that a distance has taken place between Mr. Clay and myself. The cause I never could learn, nor imagine. I had always known him to be an able man, and I believe him an honest one. I had looked to his coming into Congress with an entire belief that he would be cordial with the administration, and, even before that, I had always had him in my mind for a high and important vacancy which had been, from time to time, expected, but is only now about to take place. I feel his loss, therefore, with real concern, but it is irremediable from the necessity of harmony and cordiality between those who are to manage the public concerns. Not only his withdrawing from the usual civilities of intercourse with me (which even the federalists with two or three exceptions keep up), but his open hostility in Congress to the administration, leave no doubt of the state of his mind as a fact, although the cause be unknown.—To THOMAS COOPER. v, 183. (M., Sep. 1807.)

1310. CLERGY, Benefit of.—This privilege, originally allowed to the clergy, is now extended to every man, and even to women. It is a right of exemption from capital punishment, for the first offence, in most cases. It is, then, a pardon by the law. In other cases, the Executive gives the pardon. But when laws are made as mild as they should be both these pardons are absurd. The principle of Beccaria is sound. Let the legislators be merciful, but the executors of the law inexorable.—To M. DE MEUNIER. ix, 263. FORD ED., iv, 168. (P., 1786.)

1311. CLERGY, Public office and.—In the scheme of constitution for Virginia which I prepared in 1783, I observe an abridgment of the right of being elected, which after seventeen years more of experience and reflection, I do not approve. It is the incapacitation of a clergyman from being elected. The clergy, by getting themselves established by law, and ingrafted into the machine of government, have been a very formidable engine against the civil and religious rights of man. They are still so in many countries, and even in some of these United States. Even in 1783 we doubted the stability of our recent measures for reducing them to the footing of other useful callings. It now appears that our means were effectual. The clergy here seem to have relinquished all pretension to privilege, and to stand on a footing with lawyers, physicians, &c. They ought, therefore, to possess the same rights.—To Jeremiah Moor. Ford ed., vii, 454. (M., Aug. 1800.)

1312. CLERGY, Support of.—In the ancient feudal times of our good old forefathers, when the seigneur married his daughter, or knighted his son, it was the usage for his vassals to give him a year's rent extra in the name of an *aid.* I think it as reasonable when our pastor builds a house, that each of his flock should give him an *aid* of a year's contribution. I enclose mine as a tribute of justice, which of itself indeed is nothing, but as an example, if followed, may become something. In any event, be pleased to accept it as an offering of duty.—To The Rev. Mr. Hatch. Ford ed., x, 197. (M., 1821.) See Church, Church and State, Ministers, Religion.

1313. CLIMATE, American and European.—The comparison of climate between Europe and North America, taking together its corresponding parts, hangs chiefly on three great points. 1. The changes between heat and cold in America are greater and more frequent, and the extremes comprehend a greater scale on the thermometer in America than in Europe. Habit, however, prevents these from affecting us more than the smaller changes of Europe affect the European. But he is greatly affected by ours. 2. Our sky is always clear; that of Europe always cloudy. Hence a greater accumulation of heat here than there, in the same parallel. 3. The changes between wet and dry are much more frequent and sudden in Europe than in America. Though we have double the rain, it falls in half the time. Taking all these together, I prefer much the climate of the United States to that of Europe. I think it a more cheerful one. It is our cloudless sky which has eradicated from our constitutions all disposition to hang ourselves, which we might otherwise have inherited from our English ancestors. During a residence of between six and seven years in Paris, I never, but once, saw the sun shine through a whole day, without being obscured by a cloud in any part of it; and I never saw the moment, in which, viewing the sky through its whole hemisphere, I could say there was not the smallest speck of a cloud in it. I arrived at Monticello, on my return from France, in January; and during only two months' stay there, I observed to my daughters, who had been with me to France, that, twenty odd times within that term, there was not a speck of cloud in the whole atmosphere. Still, I do not wonder that an European should prefer his gray to our azure sky. Habit decides our taste in this, as in most other cases.—To C. F. Volney. iv, 570. (W., 1805.)

1314. CLIMATE, Enjoyment and.—Certainly it is a truth that climate is one of the sources of the greatest sensual enjoyment.—To Dr Joseph Priestley. iv, 441. Ford ed., viii, 160. (W., 1802.)

1315. CLIMATE, Habit and.—In no case, perhaps, does habit attach our choice or judgment more than in climate. The Canadian glows with delight in his sleigh and snow; the very idea of which gives me the shivers.—To C. F. Volney. iv, 569. (W., 1805.)

1316. CLIMATE, Humidity.—It has been an opinion pretty generally received among philosophers, that the atmosphere of America is more humid than that of Europe. Monsieur de Buffon makes this hypothesis one of the two pillars whereon he builds his system of the degeneracy of animals in America. Having had occasion to controvert this opinion of his, as to the degeneracy of animals there, I expressed a doubt of the fact assumed that our climates are more moist. I did not know of any experiments which might authorize a denial of it. Speaking afterwards on the subject with Dr. Franklin, he mentioned to me the observations he had made on a case of magnets, made for him by Mr. Nairne in London. Of these you will see a detail, in the second volume of the American Philosophical Transactions, in a letter from Dr. Franklin to Mr. Nairne, wherein he recommends to him to take up the principle therein explained, and endeavor to make an hygrometer, which, taking slowly the temperature of the atmosphere, shall give its mean degree of moisture, and enable us to make with more certainty, a comparison between the humidities of different climates. May I presume to trouble you with an inquiry of Mr. Nairne, whether he has executed the Doctor's idea? and if he has, to get him to make for me a couple of the instruments he may have contrived. They should be made of the same piece, and under like circumstances, that sending one to America, I may rely on its indications there, compared with those of the one I shall retain here [Paris]. Being in want of a set of magnets also, I would be glad if he would at the same time send me a set, the case of which should be made as Dr. Franklin describes his to have been, so that I may repeat his experiment.—To Mr. Vaughan. ii, 82. (P., 1786.)

1317. CLIMATE, Humidity gauge.—I think Mr. Rittenhouse never published an invention of his in this way, which was a very good one. It was of an hygrometer which, like the common ones, was to give the actual moisture of the air. He has two slips of mahogany about five inches long, three-fourths of an inch broad, and one-tenth of an inch thick, the one having the grain running lengthwise, and the other crosswise. These are glued together by their faces, so as to form a piece five inches long, three-fourths of an inch broad, and one-third of an inch thick, which is stuck by its lower end into a little plinth of wood, presenting their edge to the view. The fibres of the wood, you know, are dilated, but not lengthened by moisture. The slip, therefore, whose grain is lengthwise, becomes a standard, retaining always the same precise length. That which has its grain crosswise, dilates with moisture, and contracts for the want of it. If the right hand piece be the cross-grained one, when the air is very moist, it lengthens, and forces its companion to form a kind of interior annulus of a circle on the left. When the air is dry, it contracts, draws its companion to the right, and becomes itself the interior annulus. In order to show this dilation and contraction, an index is fixed on the upper end of two of the slips; a plate of metal or wood is fixed on the upper end of two of the slips; a plate of metal or wood is fastened to the front of the plinth, so as to cover the two slips from the eye. A slit, being nearly the portion of a circle, is cut in this plate, so that the shank of the index may play freely through its whole range. On the edge of the slit is a graduation. The objection to this instrument is, that it is not fit for comparative observations, because no. two pieces of wood being of the same texture exactly, no two will yield exactly alike to the same agent. However, it is less objectionable on this account than are most of the substances used. Mr. Rittenhouse had a thought of trying ivory; but I do not know whether he executed it. All these substances not only vary from one another at the same time, but from themselves at different times. All of them, however, have some peculiar advantages, and I think this, on the whole, appeared preferable to any other I had ever seen.—To Mr. Vaughan. ii, 83. (P., 1786.)

1318. CLIMATE, Madeira.—[I am] told that the temperature of Madeira is generally from 55° to 65°, its extreme about 50° and 70° If I ever change my climate for health, it should be for that Island.—To Dr. Hugh Williamson. iv, 346. Ford ed., vii, 479. (W., 1801.)

1319. CLIMATE, Old persons and.—I have a great opinion of the favorable influence of genial climates in winter, and especially on old persons.—To Dr. Joseph Priestley. Ford ed., viii, 180. (W., 1802.)

1320. CLIMATE, Preference for warm. —I wonder that any human being should remain in a cold country who could find room in a warm one.—To Dr. Hugh Williamson. iv, 346. Ford ed., vii, 479. (W., 1801.)

1321. ——— ———. I have often wondered that any human being should live in a cold country who can find room in a warm one.—To William Dunbar. iv, 347. Ford ed., vii, 482. (W., Jan. 1801.)

1322. CLIMATE, Sufferings from cold. —I have no doubt but that cold is the source of more suffering to all animal nature than hunger, thirst, sickness, and all the other pains of life and of death itself put together. I live in a temperate climate, and under circumstances which do not expose me often to cold. Yet when I recollect, on one hand, all the sufferings I have had from cold, and, on the other, all my other pains, the former preponderate greatly. What, then, must be the sum of that evil if we take in the vast proportion of men who are obliged to be out in all weather, by land and by sea; all the families of beasts, birds, reptiles, and even the vegetable kingdom! for that, too, has life, and where there is life there may be sensation.—To William Dunbar. iv, 347. Ford ed., vii, 482. (W., Jan. 1801.)

1323. CLIMATE, Theories concerning. —I thank you for your pamphlet on the climate of the west, and have read it with great satisfaction. Although it does not yet establish a satisfactory theory, it is an additional step towards it. Mine was perhaps the first attempt, not to form a theory, but to bring together the few facts then known, and suggest them to public attention. They were written between forty and fifty years ago, before the close of the Revolutionary war, when the western country was a wilderness, untrodden but by the foot of the savage or the hunter. It is now flourishing in population and science, and after a few years more of observation and collection of facts, they will doubtless furnish a theory of solid foundation. Years are requisite for this, steady attention to the thermometer, to the plants growing there, the times of their leafing and flowering, its animal inhabitants, beasts, birds, reptiles, and insects; its prevalent winds, quantities or rain and snow, temperature of fountains, and other indexes of climate. We want this indeed for all the States, and the work should be repeated once or twice in a century, to show the effect of clearing and culture towards changes of climate. My Notes give a very imperfect idea of what our climate was, half a century ago, at this place [Monticello], which being nearly central to the State may be taken for its medium. Latterly, after seven years of close and exact observation, I have prepared an estimate of what it is now, which may some day be added to the former work; and I hope something like this is doing in the other States, which, when all shall be brought together, may produce theories meriting confidence.—To Lewis M. Beck. vii, 375. (1824.)

1324. CLIMATE OF VIRGINIA.—A change in our [Virginia] climate is taking place very sensibly. Both heats and colds are becoming much more moderate within the memory even of the middle-aged. Snows are less frequent and less deep. They do not often lie, below the mountains, more than, one, two, or three days, and very rarely a week. They are remembered to have been formerly frequent, deep, and of long continuance. The elderly inform me, the earth used to be covered with snow about three months in every year. The rivers, which then seldom failed to freeze over in the course of the winter, scarcely ever do so now.—Notes on Virginia. viii, 327. Ford ed., iii, 185. (1782.)

1325. ——— ———. The change which has taken place in our [Virginia] climate, is one of those facts which all men of years are sensible of, and yet none can prove by regular evidence; they can only appeal to each other's general observation for the fact. I remember when I was a small boy (say sixty years ago), snows were frequent and deep in every winter—to my knee very often, to my waist sometimes—and that they covered the earth long. And I remember while yet young, to have heard from very old men, that in their youth, the winters had been still colder, with deeper and longer snows. In the year 1772, we had a snow two feet deep in the champaign parts of Virginia, and three feet in the counties next below the mountains. That year is still marked in conversation by the designation of "the year of the deep snow." But I know of no regular diaries of the weather very far back. In latter times, they might perhaps be found. While I lived at Washington, I kept a diary, and by recurring to that, I observe that from the winter of 1802-3, to that of 1808-9, inclusive, the average fall of snow of the seven winters was only fourteen and a half inches, and that the ground was covered but sixteen days in each winter on an average of the whole. The maximum in any one winter, during that period, was twenty-one inches fall, and thirty-four days on the ground.—To Dr. Chapman. v, 487. (M., 1809.)

1326. ——— ———. I find nothing anywhere else, in point of climate, which Virginia need envy to any part of the world. Here [northern New York] they are locked up in snow and ice for six months. Spring and autumn, which make a paradise of our country, are rigorous winter with them; and a tropical summer breaks on them all at once. When we consider how much climate contributes to the happiness of our condition, by the fine sensations it excites, and the productions it is the parent of, we have reason to value highly the accident of birth in such a one as that of Virginia.—To Martha Jefferson Randolph. Ford ed., v, 338. (1791.) See Weather.

1327. CLINTON (De Witt), Defends Jefferson.—Thomas Jefferson presents his compliments to Mr. Clinton, and his thanks for the pamphlet sent him.* He recollects the having read it at the time with a due sense of his obligation to the author, whose name was surmised, though not absolutely known, and a conviction that he had made the most of his matter. The ground of defence might have been solidly aided by the assurance (which is the absolute fact) that the whole story fathered on Mazzei, was an unfounded falsehood. Dr. Linn, as aware of that, takes care to quote it from a dead man, who is made to quote from one residing in the remotest part of Europe. Equally false was Dr. Linn's other story about Bishop Madison's lawn sleeves, as the Bishop can testify, for certainly Th: J. never saw him in lawn sleeves. Had the Doctor ventured to name time, place, and person, for his third lie (the government without religion), it is probable he might have been convicted on that also. But these are slander and slanderers, whom Th: J. has thought it best to leave to the scourge of public opinion.—To De Witt Clinton. v, 80. Ford ed., ix, 59. (W., 1807.)

1328. CLINTON (George), Election as Governor.—It seems probable that Mr. Jay had a majority of the qualified voters, and I think not only that Clinton would have honored himself by declining to accept, and agreeing to take another fair start, but that probably such a conduct would have ensured him a majority on a new election. To retain the office, when it is probable the majority was against him, is dishonorable.—To James Monroe. Ford ed., vi, 94. (Pa., June 1792.)

1329. ———. It does not seem possible to defend Clinton as a just or disinterested man, if he does not decline the office [of Governor], of which there is no symptom; and I really apprehend that the cause of republicanism will suffer if its votaries be thrown into schism by embarking in support of this man, and for what? To draw over the anti-federalists who are not numerous enough to be worth drawing over.—To James Madison. Ford ed., vi, 89. (Pa., 1792.)

1330. CLINTON (George), English war ships and.—I congratulate you on your safe arrival with Miss Clinton at New York, and especially on your escape from British violence. This aggression is of a character so distinct from that on the Chesapeake, and of so aggravated a nature, that I consider it as a very material one to be presented with that to the British government. I pray you, therefore, to write me a letter, stating the transaction, and in such form as that it may go to that government.—To Vice-President Clinton. v, 115. Ford ed., ix, 100. (W., July 1807.)

1331. CLINTON (George), Estrangement from Jefferson.—I already perceive my old friend Clinton, estranging himself from me. No doubt lies are carried to him, as they will be to the two other candidates [for the Presidency], under forms which, however false, he can scarcely question. Yet, I have been equally careful as to him also, never to say a word on this subject.—To James Monroe. v, 247. Ford ed., ix, 177. (W., Feb. 1808.)

1332. CLINTON (George), Mental decay.—It is wonderful to me that old men

should not be sensible that their minds keep pace with their bodies in the progress of decay. Our old revolutionary friend Clinton, for example, who was a hero, but never a man of mind, is wonderfully jealous on this head. He tells eternally the stories of his younger days to prove his memory, as if memory and reason were the same faculty. Nothing betrays imbecility so much as the being insensible of it.—To Benjamin Rush. vi, 3. Ford ed., ix, 328. (P.F., 1811.)

— **COAST DEFENCE.**—See Defence.

1333. COAST LINE, Jurisdiction and.—Governments and jurisconsults have been much divided in opinion as to the distance from their sea coasts to which they might reasonably claim a right of prohibiting the commitment of hostilities. The greatest distance, to which any respectable assent among nations has been at any time given, has been the extent of the human sight, estimated at upwards of twenty miles; and the smallest distance, I believe, claimed by any nation whatever, is the utmost range of a cannon ball, usually stated at one sea league. Some intermediate distances have also been insisted on, and that of three sea-leagues has some authority in its favor. The character of our coast, remarkable in considerable parts of it for admitting no vessels of size to pass the shores, would entitle us in reason to as broad a margin of protected navigation as any nation whatever. Not proposing, however, at this time, and without a respectful and friendly communication with the powers interested in this navigation, to fix on the distance to which we may ultimately insist on the right of protection, the President gives instructions to the officers acting under his authority, to consider those heretofore given them as restrained, for the present, to the distance of one sea-league, or three geographical miles, from the sea shore. This distance can admit of no opposition, as it is recognized by treaties between some of the powers with whom we are connected in commerce and navigation, and is as little or less than is claimed by any one of them on their own coasts.*—To E. C. Genet. iv, 75. Ford ed., vi, 440. (G., Nov. 1793.)

1334. ———. I think myself that the limits of our [marine] protection are of great consequence, and would not hesitate the sacrifice of money to obtain them large. I would say, for instance, to Great Britain, "we will pay you for such of these vessels [taken by France] as you choose; only requiring in return that the distance of their capture from shore shall, as between us, be ever considered as within our limits; now say for yourself, which of these vessels you will accept payment for". With France it might not be so easy to purchase distance by pecuniary sacrifices; but if by giving up all further reclamation of the vessels in their hands, they could be led to fix the same limits (say three leagues) I should think it an advantageous purchase.—To President Washington. Ford ed., vi, 434. (M., Oct. 1793.)

* "A vindication of Thomas Jefferson, against the charges contained in a pamphlet entitled 'Serious Considerations'. By Grotius, N. Y., 1800".—Editor.

* Jefferson wrote to the same effect to Mr. Hammond, the British Minister.—Editor.

1335. COAST LINE, Limits of.—The rule of the common law is that wherever you can see from land to land, all the water within the line of sight is in the body of the adjacent country, and within common law jurisdiction. Thus, if in this curvature 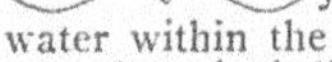

you can see from a to b, all the water within the line of sight is within common law jurisdiction, and a murder committed at c is to be tried as at common law. Our coast is generally visible, I believe, by the time you get within about twenty-five miles. I suppose that at New York you must be some miles out of the Hook before the opposite shores recede twenty-five miles from each other. The three miles of marine jurisdiction is always to be counted from this line of sight.—To ALBERT GALLATIN. iv, 559. FORD ED., viii, 319. (M., 1804.)

1336. COAST LINE, Rivers, Bays and.—For the jurisdiction of the rivers and bays of the United States, the laws of the several States * * * have made provision, and they are, moreover, as being land-locked, within the body of the United States.—To GEORGE HAMMOND. iv, 76. FORD ED., vi, 442. (G., 1793.)

1337. COCKADES, Politics and.—Some of the young men, who addressed the President [John Adams] on Monday, mounted the black (or English) cockade. The next day, numbers of the people appeared with the tricolored (or French) cockade. Yesterday being the fast day, the black cockade again appeared, on which the tricolor also showed itself. A fray ensued, the light horse were called in, and the city [Philadelphia] was so filled with confusion, from about 6 to 10 o'clock last night, that it was dangerous going out.—To JAMES MADISON. FORD ED., vii, 251. (Pa., May 10, 1798.)

1338. ——— ———. In the first moments of the tumult in Philadelphia, the cockade assumed by one party was mistaken to be the tricolor. It was the old blue and red, adopted in some places in an early part of the Revolutionary war. It is laid aside, but the black is still frequent.—To JAMES MADISON. FORD ED., vii, 253. (Pa., May 1798.)

1339. COERCION OF A STATE, The Confederation and.—It has been often said that the decisions of Congress are impotent because the Confederation provides no compulsory power. But when two or more nations enter into compact, it is not usual for them to say what shall be done to the party who infringes it. Decency forbids this, and it is as unnecessary as indecent, because the right of compulsion naturally results to the party injured by the breach. When any one State in the American Union refuses obedience to the Confederation by which they have bound themselves, the rest have a natural right to compel them to obedience. Congress would probably exercise long patience before they would recur to force; but if the case ultimately required it, they would use that recurrence. Should this case ever arise, they will probably coerce by a naval force, as being more easy, less dangerous to liberty, and less likely to produce much bloodshed.—To M. DE MEUNIER. ix, 291. FORD ED., iv, 147. (P., 1786.)

1340. COERCION OF A STATE, Law o[f] Nature and.—The coercive powers suppose[d] to be wanting in the federal head, I am o[f] opinion they possess by the law of nature which authorizes one party to an agreemen[t] to compel the other to performance. A delinquent State makes itself a party against th[e] rest of the confederacy.—To EDWARD RANDOLPH. ii, 211. (P., 1787.)

1341. ——— ———. It has been so often said as to be generally believed, that Congress hav[e] no power by the Confederation to enforc[e] anything, for example, contributions o[f] money. It was not necessary to give the[m] that power expressly, for they have it by th[e] law of nature. When two parties make a compact, there results to each a power o[f] compelling the other to execute it.—To E. CARRINGTON. ii, 217. FORD ED., iv, 424. (P. Aug. 1787.)

1342. COERCION OF A STATE, Methods of.—Peaceable means should be contrived for the Federal head to enforce complianc[e] on the part of the States.—To GEORGE WYTHE. ii, 267. FORD ED., iv, 445. (P., Sept. 1787.)

1343. COERCION OF A STATE, A navy and.—Compulsion was never so easy as in our case, where a single frigate would soon levy on the commerce of any State the deficiency of its contributions; nor more safe than in the hands of Congress which has always shown that it would wait, as it ought to do, to the last extremities before it would execute any of its powers which are disagreeable.—To E. CARRINGTON. ii, 218. FORD ED., iv, 424. (P., August 1787.)

1344. COERCION OF A STATE, Necessity of.—There never will be money in the treasury till the confederacy shows its teeth. The States must see the rod; perhaps it must be felt by some of them. I am persuaded all of them would rejoice to see every one obliged to furnish its contributions. It is not the difficulty of furnishing them, which beggars the treasury, but the fear that others will not furnish as much. Every rational citizen must wish to see an effective instrument of coercion, and should fear to see it on any other element than the water. A naval force can never endanger our liberties, nor occasion bloodshed: a land force would do both.—To JAMES MONROE. i, 606. FORD ED., iv, 265. (P., 1786.)

— COINAGE OF UNITED STATES.—See DOLLAR.

1345. COKE (Lord), Opinions of.—Lord Cokes opinion it is ever dangerous to neglect.—NOTE TO CRIMES BILL. i, 150. FORD ED., ii, 208. (1779.)

— COLD, Suffering caused by.—See CLIMATE.

1346. COLES (Edward), Jefferson's secretary.—Mr. Coles, the bearer of public despatches, by an *aviso*, has lived with me as Secretary, is my wealthy neighbor at Monticello, and worthy of all confidence. His intimate knowledge of our situation has induced us to send him, because he will be a full supplement as to all those things which cannot be detailed in writing.—To JOHN ARMSTRONG. v, 433. (W., March 1809.)

1347. ———. To give you a true description of the state of things here, I must refer you to Mr. Coles, the bearer of this [letter], my Secretary, a most worthy, intelligent and well-informed young man, whom I recommend to your notice. * * * His discretion and fidelity may be relied on.—To DUPONT DE NEMOURS. v, 432. (W., 1809.)

— COLLEGES Arrangement, of buildings for.—See ACADEMIES.

1348. COLONIES (The American), Beginning of the.—America was conquered, and her settlements made, and firmly established, at the expense of individuals, and not of the British public. Their own blood was spilt in acquiring lands for their settlement, their own fortunes expended in making that settlement effectual; for themselves they fought, for themselves they conquered, and for themselves alone they have right to hold. No shilling was ever issued from the public treasuries of his Majesty, or his ancestors, for their assistance, till of very late times, after the colonies had become established on a firm and permanent footing.—RIGHTS OF BRITISH AMERICA. i, 126. FORD ED., i, 430. (1774.) See RIGHTS OF BRITISH AMERICA, APPENDIX.

1349. COLONIES (The American), The Crown and.—Our forefathers, inhabitants of the island of Great Britain, left their native land to seek on these shores a residence for civil and religious freedom. At the expense of their blood, to the ruin of their fortunes. with the relinquishment of everything quiet and comfortable in life, they effected settlements in the inhospitable wilds of America; and there established civil societies with various forms of constitution. To continue their connection with the friends whom they had left, they arranged themselves by charters of compact under the same common King, who thus completed their powers of full and perfect legislation and became the link of union between the several parts of the empire.—DECLARATION ON TAKING UP ARMS. FORD ED., i, 464. (July 1775.)

1350. ——— ———. That settlement having been thus effected in the wilds of America, the emigrants thought proper to adopt that system of laws under which they had hitherto lived in the mother country, and to continue their union with her, by submitting themselves to the same common sovereign, who was thereby made the central link, connecting the several parts of the empire thus newly multiplied.—RIGHTS OF BRITISH AMERICA. i, 126. FORD ED., i, 431. (1774.)

— COLONIES (The American), George III. and.—See GEORGE III.

1351. COLONIES (The American), Harassed by the Stuarts.—But not long were the Colonies permitted, however far they thought themselves removed from the hand of oppression, to hold undisturbed the rights acquired at the hazard of their lives and loss of their fortunes. A family of princes was then on the British throne. whose treasonable crimes against their people brought on them, afterwards, the exertion of those sacred and sovereign rights of punishment, reserved in the hands of the people for cases of extreme necessity, and judged by the constitution unsafe to be delegated to any other judicature. While every day brought forth some new and unjustifiable exertion of power over their subjects on that side of the water, it was not to be expected that those here, much less able at the time to oppose the designs of despotism, should be exempted from injury. Accordingly, this country which had been acquired by the lives, the labors, and fortunes of individual adventurers, was by these Princes, several times, parted* out and distributed among the favorites and followers of their fortunes; and, by an assumed right of the Crown alone, was erected into distinct and independent governments; a measure which, it is believed, his Majesty's prudence and understanding would prevent him from imitating at this day; as no exercise of such power of dividing and dismembering a country has ever occurred in his Majesty's realm of England, though now of very ancient standing; nor could it be justified or acquiesced under there, or in any other part of his Majesty's empire.—RIGHTS OF BRITISH AMERICA. i, 127. FORD ED., i, 431. (1774.)

1352. COLONIES (The American), Parliamentary encroachments.—In 1650, the parliament, considering itself as standing in the place of their deposed king, and as having succeeded to all his powers, without as well as within the realm, began to assume a right over the Colonies, passing an act for inhibiting their trade with foreign nations. This succession to the exercise of kingly authority gave the first color for parliamentary interference with the Colonies, and produced that fatal precedent which they continued to follow, after they had retired, in other respects, within their proper functions.—NOTES ON VIRGINIA. viii, 355. FORD ED., iii, 217. (1782.)

1353. ——— ———. What powers the Parliament might rightfully exercise over us. and whether any, had never been declared either by them or us. They had very early taken the gigantic step of passing the Navigation Act. The Colonies remonstrated violently against it, and one of them, Virginia. when she capitulated to the Commonwealth of England, expressly stipulated for a free

* In 1621, Nova Scotia was granted by James I. to Sir William Alexander. In 1632, Maryland was granted by Charles I. to Lord Baltimore. In 1664, New York was granted by Charles II. to the Duke of York; as also New Jersey, which the Duke of York conveyed again to Lord Berkely and Sir George Carteret. So also were the Delaware counties, which the same Duke conveyed to Wm. Penn. In 1665, the country including North and South Carolina, Georgia and the Floridas was granted by Charles II. to the Earl of Clarendon, Duke of Albemarle, Earl of Craven, Lord Berkely, Lord Ashley, Sir George Carteret, Sir John Coleton, and Sir Wm. Berkely. In 1681, Pennsylvania was granted by Charles II. to Wm. Penn.—NOTE BY JEFFERSON.

trade. This capitulation, however, was as little regarded as the original right, restored by it, had been. The Navigation Act was reenacted by Charles II., and was enforced. And we had been so long in the habit of seeing them consider us merely as objects for the extension of their *commerce*, and of submitting to every duty or regulation imposed with that view, that we had ceased to complain of them.—NOTES ON M. SOULÉS'S BOOK. ix, 294. FORD ED., iv, 302. (P., 1786.)

1354. COLONIES (The American), Political relations of.—The settlement of the Colonies was not made by public authority, or at the public expense of England; but by the exertions, and at the expense of individuals. Hence it happened that their constitutions were not formed systematically, but according to the circumstances which happened to exist in each. Hence, too, the principles of the political connection between the old and new countries were never settled. That it would have been advantageous to have settled them, is certain; and, particularly to have provided a body which should decide. in the last resort, all cases wherein both parties were interested. But it is not certain that that right would have been given, or ought to have been given to the Parliament; much less, that it resulted to the Parliament. without having been given to it expressly. Why was it necessary that there should have been a body to decide in the last resort? Because it would have been for the good of both parties. But this reason shows it ought not to have been the Parliament, because that would have exercised it for the good of one party only.—To M. DE MEUNIER. ix, 255. FORD ED., iv, 160. (P., 1786.)

1355. COLONIES (The American), Reconciliation of.—There was * * * a plan of accommodation offered in Parliament, which, though not entirely equal to the terms we had a right to ask, yet differed but in few points from what the General Congress had held out. Had Parliament been disposed sincerely, as we are, to bring about a reconciliation, reasonable men had hoped. that by meeting us on this ground something might have been done. Lord Chatham's Bill, on the one part, and the terms of Congress on the other, would have formed a basis for negotiations, which a spirit of accommodation on both sides might, perhaps, have reconciled. It came recommended. too, from one whose successful experience in the art of government should have insured it some attention from those to whom it was intended. He had shown to the world. that Great Britain with her Colonies united firmly under a just and honest Government formed a power which might bid defiance to the most potent enemies. With a change of Ministers, however. a total change of measures took place. The component parts of the Empire have from that moment been falling asunder. and a total annihilation of its weight in the political scale of the world seems justly to be apprehended.—ADDRESS OF VA. HOUSE OF BURGESSES TO LORD DUNMORE. FORD ED., i, 458. (1775.)

1356. ——— ———. Though desirous and determined to consider, in the most dispassionate view, every advance towards reconciliation made by the British Parliament, let our brethren of Britain reflect what would have been the sacrifice to men of free spirits, had even fair terms been proffered, * * * as these were, with circumstances of insult and defiance.—REPLY TO LORD NORTH'S PROPOSITION. FORD ED., i, 478. (July 1775.)

1357. ——— ———. With what patience could Britain have received articles of treaty from any power on earth, when borne on the point of the bayonet by military plenipotentiaries?—REPLY TO LORD NORTH'S PROPOSITION. FORD ED., i, 479. (July 1775.)

1358. ——— ———. If * * * Great Britain, disjoined from her Colonies, be a match for the most potent nations of Europe, with the Colonies thrown into their scale, they may go on securely. But if they are not assured of this, it would be certainly unwise. by trying the event of another campaign, to risk our accepting a foreign aid, which, perhaps, may not be obtainable, but on condition of everlasting avulsion from Great Britain. This would be thought a hard condition to those who still wish for reunion with their parent country. I am sincerely one of those, and would rather be in dependence on Great Britain. properly limited, than on any nation on earth, or than on no nation. But I am one of those. too, who, rather than submit to the rights of legislating for us, assumed by the British Parliament, and which late experience has shown they will so cruelly exercise, would lend my hand to sink the whole Island in the ocean.—To JOHN RANDOLPH. i, 201. FORD ED., i, 484. (M., August 1775.)

1359. COLONIES (The American), Resistance to Unjust Taxation.—When Parliament proposed to consider us as objects of *taxation*, all the States took the alarm. Yet so little had we attended to this subject. that our advocates did not know at first on what ground to take their stand. Mr. Dickinson, a lawyer of more ingenuity than sound judgment, and still more timid than ingenious, not daring to question the authority to regulate commerce so as best to answer their own purpose. to which we had long submitted, admitted that authority in its utmost extent. He acknowledged * * * that they could levy duties. internal or external, payable in Great Britain or in the States. He only required that these duties should be *bonâ fide* for the *regulation* of commerce, and not to raise a solid *revenue*. He admitted, therefore, that they might control our commerce. but not tax us. This mysterious system took for a moment in America as well as in Europe. But sounder heads saw in the first moment that he who could put down the loom. could stop the spinning wheel. and he who could stop the spinning wheel could tie the hands which turned it. They saw that this flimsy fabric could not be supported. Who were to be the judges whether duties were imposed with a view to burden and suppress a branch of manufacture or to raise a revenue? If either party, exclusively of the other, it was plain where that would end. If both parties, it was plain where that would end also. They saw, therefore, no sure clew to lead them out of their difficulties but reason and right. They dared to follow them, assured that they alone could lead them to defensible ground. The first elements of our reason showed that the members of Parliament could have no power which the people of the several counties had not; that these had naturally a power over their own farms, and collectively over all England. But if they had any power over counties out of England, it must be founded on compact or force. No compact could be shown, and neither party chose to bottom their pretensions on force. It was objected that this annihilated the Navigation Act. True, it does. The Navigation Act, therefore, becomes a proper subject of treaty between the two nations. Or, if Great Britain does not choose to have its basis questioned, let us go on as we have done. Let no new shackles be imposed, and we will continue to submit to the old. We will consider the restrictions on our commerce now actually existing as compensations yielded by us for the protection and privileges we actually enjoy, only trusting that if Great Britain on a revisal of these restrictions, is sensible that some of them are useless to her and oppressive to us, she will repeal them. But on this she shall be free. Place us in the condition we were when the King came to the throne, let us rest so, and we will be satisfied. This was the ground on which all the States very soon found themselves rallied, and that there was no other which could be defended.—NOTES ON M. SOULÉS'S BOOK. ix, 295. FORD ED., iv, 302. (P., 1786.) See TAXATION.

— **COLONIES (The American), Restrictions on trade of.**—See TRADE.

1360. COLONIES (The American), Separation from England.—It is neither our wish nor our interest to separate from Great Britain. We are willing, on our part, to sacrifice everything which reason can ask to the restoration of that tranquillity for which all must wish. On their part, let them be ready to establish union on a generous plan. Let them name their terms, but let them be just. Accept of every commercial privilege which it is in our power to give, for such things as we can raise for their use, or they make for ours. But let them not think to exclude us from going to other markets to dispose of those commodities which they cannot use, or to supply those wants which they cannot supply. Still less, let it be proposed, that our properties within our own territories shall be taxed or regulated by any power on earth but our own. The God who gave us life, gave us liberty at the same time: the hand of force may destroy, but cannot disjoin them. This, Sire, is our last, our determined resolution. And that you will be pleased to interpose with that efficacy which your earnest

endeavors may insure to procure redress of these our great grievances, to quiet the minds of your subjects in British America against any apprehensions of future encroachment, to establish fraternal love and harmony and love through the whole empire, and that that may continue to the latest ages of time, is the fervent prayer of all British America.—RIGHTS OF BRITISH AMERICA. i, 141. FORD ED., i, 446. (1774.)

1361. ——. Before the commencement of hostilities I never had heard a whisper of disposition to separate from Great Britain. And after that, its possibility was contemplated with affliction by all.—To GEORGE A. OTIS. FORD ED., x, 188. (M., 1821.)

1362. COLONIES (The American), Toryism of George III. and.—The tory education of the King was the first preparation for that change in the British government which that party never ceases to wish. This naturally ensured tory administration during his life. At the moment he came to the throne and cleared his hands of his enemies by the peace of Paris, the assumptions of unwarrantable right over America commenced. They were so signal, and followed one another so close, as to prove they were part of a system, either to reduce it under absolute subjection, and thereby make it an instrument for attempts on Great Britain itself, or to sever it from Britain, so that it might not be a weight in the Whig scale. This latter alternative, however, was not considered as the one which would take place. They knew so little of America, that they thought it unable to encounter the little finger of Great Britain.—NOTES ON M. SOULÉS'S WORK. ix, 299. FORD ED., iv, 307. (P., 1786.) See GEORGE III.

— **COLONIES (The American), Tyranny of George III. and.**—See TYRANNY.

1363. COLONIES (The American), Union of.—We cannot, my Lord, close with the terms of that Resolution [Lord North's Conciliatory Proposition] because * * * [it] involves the interests of all the other Colonies. We are now represented in General Congress by members approved by this House, where the former union, it is hoped, will be so strongly cemented, that no partial applications can produce the slightest departure from the common cause. We consider ourselves as bound in honor, as well as interest, to share one general fate with our sister Colonies; and should hold ourselves base deserters of that union to which we have acceded, were we to agree on any measures distinct and apart from them.—ADDRESS TO LORD DUNMORE FROM VA. HOUSE OF BURGESSES. FORD ED., i, 457. (1775.)

1364. ——. [Lord North's] proposition * * * is unreasonable and insidious: unreasonable because if we declare we accede to it, we declare, without reservation, we will purchase the favor of Parliament, not knowing at the same time at what price they will please to estimate their favor; it is insidious because any individual Colonies, having bid and bidden again till they find the avidity of the seller too great for all their powers, are then to return into opposition, divided from their sister Colonies, whom the minister will have previously detached by a grant of easier terms, or by an artful procrastination of a definitive answer.—REPLY OF CONGRESS TO LORD NORTH'S PROPOSITION. FORD ED., i, 478. (July 1775.)

1365. ———— ————. We will ever be ready to join with our fellow-subjects in every part of the *British* empire, in executing all those rightful powers which God has given us, for the reestablishment and guaranteeing * * .* their constitutional rights, when, where, and by whomsoever invaded.*—RESOLUTION OF ALBEMARLE COUNTY. FORD ED., i, 419. (July 26, 1774.) See COMMITTEES OF CORRESPONDENCE.

—COLONIES (The American), Violations of Charters.—See CHARTERS.

1366. COLONIES, Ancient and Modern. —Ancient nations considered colonies principally as receptacles for a too numerous population, and as natural and useful allies in time of war; but modern nations, viewing commerce as an object of first importance, value colonies chiefly as instruments for the increase of that. This is principally effected by their taking commodities from the mother State, whether raised within herself, or obtained elsewhere in the course of her trade, and furnishing in return colonial productions necessary for her consumption or for her commerce of exchange with other nations. In this way the colonies of Spain, Portugal, France and England, have been chiefly subservient to the advantages of their mother country. In this way, too, in a smaller degree has Denmark derived utility from her American colonies, and so, also, has Holland, except as to the island of St. Eustatius.—To BARON STAHEL. FORD ED., iv, 238. (P., 1786.)

1367. COLONIES, European nations and their.—The habitual violation of the equal rights of the colonist by the dominant (for I will not call them the mother) countries of Europe, the invariable sacrifice of their highest interests to the minor advantages of any individual trade or calling at home, are as immoral in principle as the continuance of them is unwise in practice, after the lessons they have received.—To CLEMENT CAINE. vi, 13. FORD ED., ix, 329. (M., 1811.)

1368. COLONIZATION (Negro), Africa and.—In the disposition of these unfortunate people, there are two rational objects to be distinctly kept in view. First. The establishment of a colony on the coast of Africa, which may introduce among the aborigines the arts of cultivated life and the blessings of civilization and science. By doing this, we may make to them some retribution for

* Jefferson's own county.—EDITOR.

the long course of injuries we have been committing on their population. And considering that these blessings will descend to the "*nati natorum et qui nascentur ab illis*", we shall in the long run have rendered them perhaps more good than evil. To fulfil this object, the colony of Sierra Leone promises well, and that of Mesurado adds to our prospect of success. Under this view the Colonization Society is to be considered as a missionary society, having in view, however, objects more humane, more justifiable, and less aggressive on the peace of other nations than the others of that appellation. The second object, and the most interesting to us, as coming home to our physical and moral characters, to our happiness and safety, is to provide an asylum to which we can, by degrees, send the whole of that population from among us, and establish them under our patronage and protection, as a separate, free and independent people, in some country and climate friendly to human life and happiness. That any place on the coast of Africa should answer the latter purpose, I have ever deemed entirely impossible. And without repeating the other arguments which have been urged by others, I will appeal to figures only, which admit no controversy.*—To JARED SPARKS. vii, 332. FORD ED., x, 290. (M., 1824.)

1369. COLONIZATION (Negro), Emancipation and.—There is, I think, a way in which [the removal of the slaves to another country] can be done; that is by emancipating the after-born, leaving them, on due compensation, with their mothers, until their services are worth their maintenance, and then putting them to industrious occupations until a proper age for deportation. This was the result of my reflections on the subject five and forty years ago, and I have never yet been able to conceive any other practicable plan. It was sketched in the "Notes on Virginia". The estimated value of the new-born infant is so low (say twelve dollars and fifty cents) that it would probably be yielded by the owner gratis, and would thus reduce the six hundred millions of dollars, the first head of expense, to thirty-seven millions and a half; leaving only the expenses of nourishment while with the mother, and of transportation.—To JARED SPARKS. vii, 333. FORD ED., x, 291. (M., 1824.)

1370. COLONIZATION (Negro), Expenses of.—From what fund are these expenses to be furnished? Why not from that of the lands which have been ceded by the very States now needing this relief? And ceded on no consideration, for the most part, but that of the general good of the whole. These cessions already constitute one-fourth of the States of the Union. It may be said

* Jefferson then made a calculation showing that it would require six hundred millions of dollars to purchase the slaves, while the cost of transportation, provisions, support in the settlement, &c., would take three hundred million dollars additional,—an amount which made it "impossible to look at the question a second time".—EDITOR.

that these lands have been sold; are now the property of the citizens composing those States; and the money long ago received and expended. But an equivalent of lands in the territories since acquired may be appropriated to that object, or so much, at least, as may be sufficient; and the object, although more important to the slave States, is highly so to the others also, if they were serious in their arguments on the Missouri question. The slave States, too, if more interested, would also contribute more by their gratuitous liberation, thus taking on themselves alone the first and heaviest item of expense.— To JARED SPARKS. vii, 334. FORD ED., x, 291. (M., 1824.)

1371. COLONIZATION (Negro), San Domingo and.—In the plan sketched in the "Notes on Virginia", no particular place of asylum was specified; because it was thought possible that in the revolutionary state of America, then commenced, events might open to us some one within practicable distance. This has now happened. Santo Domingo has become independent, and with a population of that color only; and if the public papers are to be credited, their Chief offers to pay their passage, to receive them as free citizens, and to provide them employment. This leaves, then, for the general confederacy, no expense but that of nurture with the mother for a few years, and would call, of course, for a very moderate appropriation of the vacant lands. * * * In this way no violation of private right is proposed.—To JARED SPARKS. vii, 334. FORD ED., x, 292. (M., 1824.) See COLONY, SLAVES.

1372. COLONY (Penal), Establishment of.—Questions would arise whether the establishment of a [negro penal] colony* within our limits, and to become a part of our Union, would be desirable to the State of Virginia itself, or to other States—especially those who would be in its vicinity. Could we procure lands beyond the limits of the United States to form a receptacle for these people? On our northern boundary, the country not occupied by British subjects, is the property of Indian nations, whose title would have to be extinguished, with the consent of Great Britain; and the new settlers would be British subjects. It is hardly to be believed that either Great Britain or the Indian proprietors have so disinterested a regard for us, as to be willing to relieve us, by receiving such a colony themselves. * * * On our western and southern frontiers, Spain holds an immense country, the occupancy of which, however, is in the Indian natives, except a few insulated spots possessed by Spanish subjects. It is very questionable, indeed, whether the Indians would sell? whether Spain would be willing to receive these people? and nearly certain that she would not alienate the sovereignty. The same question

to ourselves would recur here also, as did in the first case: should we be willing to have such a colony in contact with us? However our present interests may restrain us within our own limits, it is impossible not to look forward to distant times, when our rapid multiplication will expand itself beyond those limits, and cover the whole northern, if not the southern continent, with a people speaking the same language, governed in similar forms, and by similar laws; nor can we contemplate with satisfaction either blot or mixture on that surface. Spain, France, and Portugal hold possessions on the southern continent, as to which I am not well enough informed to say how far they might meet our views. But either there or in the northern continent, should the constituted authorities of Virginia fix their attention, of preference, I will have the dispositions of those powers sounded in the first instance.—To JAMES MONROE. iv, 420. FORD ED., viii, 104. (W., 1801.)

1373. COLONY (Penal), Sierra Leone and.—The course of things in the * * * West Indies appears to have given a considerable impulse to the minds of the slaves in * * * the United States. A great disposition to insurgency has manifested itself among them, which, in one instance, in the State of Virginia, broke out into actual insurrection. This was easily suppressed; but many of those concerned (between twenty and thirty, I believe) fell victims to the law. So extensive an execution could not but excite sensibility in the public mind, and beget a regret that the laws had not provided for such cases, some alternative, combining more mildness with equal efficacy. The Legislature of the State * * * took the subject into consideration, and have communicated to me through the Governor of the State, their wish that some place could be provided, out of the limits of the United States, to which slaves guilty of insurgency might be transported; and they have particularly looked to Africa as offering the most desirable receptacle. We might, for this purpose, enter into negotiations with the natives, on some part of the coast, to obtain a settlement; and, by establishing an African company, combine with it commercial operations, which might not only reimburse expenses, but procure profit also. But there being already such an establishment on that coast by the English Sierra Leone Company, made for the express purpose of colonizing civilized blacks to that country, it would seem better, by incorporating our emigrants with theirs, to make one strong, rather than two weak colonies. This would be the more desirable because the blacks settled at Sierra Leone, having chiefly gone from the States, would often receive among those whom we should send, their acquaintances and relatives. The object of this letter is to ask * * * you to enter into conference with such persons, private and public, as would be necessary to give us permission to send thither the persons under contemplation. * * * They are not felons, or common malefactors, but per-

---

* James Monroe, then Governor of Virginia, wrote to Jefferson asking his good offices towards the establishment of a penal colony in America. A short time before, there had been a negro insurrection in Virginia and the House of Representatives of the State had passed a resolution on the subject.—EDITOR.

sons guilty of what the safety of society, under actual circumstances, obliges us to treat as a crime, but which their feelings may represent in a far different shape. They will be a valuable acquisition to the settlement, * * * and well calculated to cooperate in the plan of civilization.—To RUFUS KING. iv, 442. FORD ED., viii, 161. (W., 1802.)

1374. —— ——. The consequences of permitting emancipations to become extensive, unless a condition of emigration be annexed to them, furnish matter of solicitude to the Legislature of Virginia. Although provision for the settlement of emancipated negroes might perhaps be obtained nearer home than Africa, yet it is desirable that we should be free to expatriate this description of people also to the colony of Sierra Leone. if considerations respecting either themselves or us should render it more expedient. I pray you, therefore, to get the same permission extended to the reception of these as well as the [insurgents]. Nor will there be a selection of bad subjects; the emancipations, for the most part, being either of the whole slaves of the master, or of such individuals as have particularly deserved well. The latter are most frequent.—To RUFUS KING. iv, 443. FORD ED., viii, 163. (W., 1802.)

1375. COLONY (Penal), Transportation to.—As the expense of so distant a transportation would be very heavy, and might weigh unfavorably in deciding between the modes of punishment, it is very desirable that it should be lessened as much as is practicable. If the regulations of the place would permit these emigrants to dispose of themselves, as the Germans and others do who come to this country poor, by giving their labor for a certain time to some one who will pay their passage; and if the master of the vessel could be permitted to carry articles of commerce from this country and take back others from that, which might yield him a mercantile profit sufficient to cover the expenses of the voyage, a serious difficulty would be removed.—To RUFUS KING. iv, 443. FORD ED., viii, 162. (W., 1802.)

1376. COLONY (Penal), West Indies and.—The West Indies offer a more probable and practicable retreat for them. Inhabited already by a people of their own race and color; climates congenial with their natural constitution; insulated from the other descriptions of men; nature seems to have formed these islands to become the receptacle of the blacks transplanted into this hemisphere. Whether we could obtain from the European sovereigns of those islands leave to send thither the persons under consideration, I cannot say; but I think it more probable than the former propositions, because of their being already inhabited more or less by the same race. The most promising portion of them is the island of St. Domingo, where the blacks are established into a sovereignty de facto, and have organized themselves under regular laws and government. I should conjecture that their present ruler might be willing * * *

to receive over that description which would be exiled for acts deemed criminal by us, but meritorious, perhaps, by him. The possibility that these exiles might stimulate and conduct vindictive or predatory descents on our coasts, and facilitate concert with their brethren remaining here, looks to a state of things between that island and us not probable on a contemplation of our relative strength. * * * Africa would offer a last and undoubted resort, if all others more desirable should fail us. Whenever the Legislature of Virginia shall have brought its mind to a point, so that I may know exactly what to propose to foreign authorities, I will execute their wishes with fidelity and zeal.—To JAMES MONROE. iv, 421. FORD ED., viii, 105. (W., 1801.)

— COLUMBIA RIVER, Fur trading posts on.—See ASTOR'S SETTLEMENT and FUR TRADE.

1377. COLUMBUS, Portrait of.—While I resided at Paris, knowing that the portraits of Columbus and Americus Vespucius were in the gallery of Medici at Florence, I took measures for engaging a good artist to take and send me copies of them. I considered it as even of some public concern that our country should not be without the portraits of its first discoverers.—To MR. DELAPLAINE. vi, 343. (M., 1814.)

1378. COMMERCE, Agriculture and.— The exercise, by our own citizens. of so much commerce as may suffice to exchange our superfluities for our wants. may be advantageous for the whole. But it does not follow, that with a territory so boundless, it is the interest of the whole to become a mere city of London, to carry on the business of one half the world at the expense of eternal war with the other half. The agricultural capacities of our country constitute its distinguishing feature; and the adapting our policy and pursuits to that. is more likely to make us a numerous and happy people, than the mimicry of an Amsterdam, a Hamburg. or a city of London.—To WILLIAM H. CRAWFORD. vii. 6. FORD ED., x, 34. (M., 1816.)

1379. —— ——. I am sensible of the great interest which Rhode Island justly feels in the prosperity of commerce. It is of vital interest also to States more agricultural, whose produce, without commerce, could not be exchanged.—To THE RHODE ISLAND ASSEMBLY. iv, 398. (W., May 1801.)

1380. COMMERCE, Agriculture, manufactures and.—I trust the good sense of our country will see that its greatest prosperity depends on a due balance between agriculture, manufactures and commerce. — To THOMAS LEIPER. v, 417. FORD ED., ix, 239. (W., 1809.) See MANUFACTURES.

1381. COMMERCE, But no alliance.— Commerce with all nations. alliance with none, should be our motto.—To T. LOMAX. iv, 301. FORD ED., vii, 374. (M., March 1799.)

1382. COMMERCE, Cherish.—As the handmaid of agriculture, commerce will be cherished by me both from principle and duty. —To THE RHODE ISLAND ASSEMBLY. iv, 398. (W., May 1801.)

1383. —— ——. Unconscious of partiality between the different callings of my fellow citizens, I trust that a fair review of my attention to the interests of commerce in particular, in every station of my political life, will afford sufficient proofs of my just estimation of its importance in the social system. What has produced our present difficulties, and what will have produced the impending war, if that is to be our lot? Our efforts to save the rights of commerce and navigation. From these, solely and exclusively, the whole of our present dangers flow.—R. TO A. LEESBURG CITIZENS. viii, 161. (1809.)

1384. —— ——. One imputation in particular has been remarked till it seems as if some at least believe it: that I am an enemy to commerce. They admit me as a friend to agriculture, and suppose me an enemy to the only means of disposing of its produce.—To MAJOR WILLIAM JACKSON. iv, 358. (M., Feb. 1801.)

1385. COMMERCE, Coercion of Europe by.—War is not the best engine for us to resort to; nature has given us one *in our commerce,* which, if properly managed, will be a better instrument for obliging the interested nations of Europe to treat us with justice. If the commercial regulations had been adopted which our Legislature were at one time proposing, we should at this moment have been standing on such an eminence of safety and respect as ages can never recover. But having wandered from that, our object should now be to get back, with as little loss as possible, and when peace shall be restored to the world, endeavor so to form our *commercial* regulations as that justice from other nations shall be their mechanical result.—To THOMAS PINCKNEY. iv, 177. FORD ED., vii, 129. (Pa., May 1797.)

—— **COMMERCE, The Confederation and.** —See CONFEDERATION.

1386. COMMERCE, Control by Congress.—A general disposition is taking place to commit the whole management of our commerce to Congress.* This has been much promoted by the interested policy of England which, it was apparent, could not be counterworked by the States separately.—To W. CARMICHAEL. i, 393. (P., 1785.)

1387. —— ——. I am much pleased with the proposition to the States to invest Congress with the regulation of their trade, reserving its revenue to the States. I think it a happy idea, removing the only objection which could have been justly made to the proposition. The time, too, is the present, before the admission of the Western States.— To JAMES MONROE. i, 347. FORD ED., iv, 52. (P., 1785.)

* The Congress of the Confederation. This movement finally resulted in the adoption of the Federal Constitution.—EDITOR.

1388. —— ——. The late proceedings in America have produced a wonderful sensation in England in our favor. I mean the disposition which seems to be becoming general, to invest Congress with the regulation of our commerce, and, in the meantime, the measures taken to defeat the avidity of the British government grasping at our carrying business. I can add with truth, that it was not till these symptoms appeared in America that I have been able to discover the smallest token of respect towards the United States in any part of Europe.—To JAMES MADISON. i, 413. (P., Sep. 1785.)

1389. —— ——. Congress have desired to be invested with the whole regulation of their trade, and forever; and to prevent all temptations to abuse the power, and all fears of it, they propose that whatever moneys shall be levied on commerce, either for the purpose of revenue, or by way of forfeitures or penalty, shall go directly into the coffers of the State wherein it is levied, without being touched by Congress. From the present temper of the States, and the conviction which your country [England] has carried home to their minds, that there is no other method of defeating the greedy attempts of other countries to trade with them on equal terms, I think they will add an article for this purpose to their Confederation.—To DAVID HARTLEY. i, 425. FORD ED., iv, 94. (P., 1785.)

1390. —— ——. The British * * * attempt without disguise to possess themselves of the carriage of our produce, and to prohibit our own vessels from participating of it. This has raised a general indignation in America. The States see, however, that their constitutions have provided no means of counteracting it. They are, therefore, beginning to invest Congress with the absolute power of regulating their commerce, only reserving all revenue arising from it to the State in which it is levied. This will consolidate our Federal building very much, and for this we shall be indebted to the British.—To COUNT VAN HOGENDORP. i, 465. FORD ED., iv, 104. (P., Oct. 1785.)

1391. —— ——. The determination of the British cabinet to make no equal treaty [of commerce] with us, confirms me in the opinion * * * that the United States must pass a navigation act against Great Britain, and load her manufactures with duties, so as to give a preference to those of other countries; and I hope our Assemblies will wait no longer, but transfer such a power to Congress, at the sessions of this fall.—To JOHN ADAMS. ii, 486. (P., Nov. 1785.)

1392. —— ——. I have heard with great pleasure that the [Virginia] Assembly have come to the resolution of giving the regulation of their commerce to the federal head. I will venture to assert, that there is not one of its opposers who, placed on this ground [Europe] would not see the wisdom of this measure. The politics of Europe render it indispensably necessary that with respect to everything external, we be one nation only, firmly hooped together. * * * If it were seen in Europe that all our States could be brought to concur in what the Virginia Assembly has done, it would produce a total revolution in their opinion of us, and respect for us.—To JAMES MADISON. i, 531. FORD ED., iv, 192. (P., February 1786.)

1393. —— ——. All the States have agreed to the impost. But New York has annexed such conditions that it cannot be accepted. It is thought, therefore, they will grant it unconditionally. But a new difficulty has started up. Three or four States had coupled the grant of the impost with the grant of the supplementary funds, asked by Congress at the same time, declaring that they should come into force only when all the States had granted both. One of these, Pennsylvania, refuses to let the impost come into being alone. We are still to see whether they will persist in this.—To WILLIAM CARMICHAEL. ii, 19. (P., 1786.)

1394. COMMERCE, Cultivate.—All the world is becoming commercial. Were it practicable to keep our new empire separated from them, we might indulge ourselves in speculating whether commerce contributes to the happiness of mankind. But we cannot separate ourselves from them. Our citizens have had too full a taste of the comforts furnished by the arts and manufactures to be debarred the use of them. We must, then, in our defence endeavor to share as large a portion as we can of this modern source of wealth and power.—To GENERAL WASHINGTON. FORD ED., iii, 422. (A., 1784.)

1395. —— ——. I am decidedly of opinion we should take no part in European quarrels, but cultivate peace and commerce with all.—To GENERAL WASHINGTON. ii, 533. FORD ED., v, 57. (P., 1788.)

1396. COMMERCE, Debt and.—No earthly consideration could induce my consent to contract such a debt as England has by her wars for commerce, to reduce our citizens by taxes to such wretchedness, as that laboring sixteen of the twenty-four hours, they are still unable to afford themselves bread, or barely to earn as much oatmeal or potatoes as will keep soul and body together. And all this to feed the avidity of a few millionary merchants, and to keep up one thousand ships of war for the protection of their commercial speculations.—To WILLIAM H. CRAWFORD. vii, 7. FORD ED., x, 35. (M., 1816.)

1397. COMMERCE, Discriminating Duties.—It is true we must expect some inconvenience in practice from the establishment of discriminating duties. But in this, as in so many other cases, we are left to choose between two evils. These inconveniences are nothing when weighed against the loss of wealth and loss of force, which will follow our perseverance in the plan of indiscrimination. When once it shall be perceived that we are either in the system or in the habit of

giving equal advantages to those who extinguish our commerce and navigation by duties and prohibitions, as to those who treat both with liberality and justice, liberality and justice will be converted by all into duties and prohibitions. It is not to the moderation and justice of others we are to trust for fair and equal access to market with our productions, or for our due share in the transportation of them; but to our own means of independence, and the firm will to use them. Nor do the inconveniences of discrimination merit consideration. Not one of the nations before mentioned, perhaps not a commercial nation on earth, is without them. In our case, one distinction alone will suffice: that is to say, between nations who favor our productions and navigation, and those who do not favor them. One set of moderate duties, say the present duties, for the first, and a fixed advance on these as to some articles, and prohibitions as to others, for the last.—REPORT ON FOREIGN COMMERCE AND NAVIGATION. vii, 650. FORD ED., vi, 483. (Dec. 1793.)

— COMMERCE, Drawbacks and.—See DRAWBACKS.

— COMMERCE, The Embargo and.— See EMBARGO.

1398. COMMERCE, Encouragement of. —[The] encouragement of agriculture, and of commerce as its handmaid, I deem [one of the] essential principles of our government and, consequently [one] which ought to shape its administration.—FIRST INAUGURAL ADDRESS. viii, 4. FORD ED., viii, 5. (1801.)

1399. COMMERCE, Exchange of productions.—A commerce carried on by exchange of productions is the most likely to be lasting and to meet mutual encouragement.— To DR. RAMSAY. ii, 50. (P., 1786.)

1400. —— ——. I hope that the policy of our country will settle down with as much navigation and commerce only as our own exchanges will require, and that the disadvantage will be seen of our undertaking to carry on that of other nations. This, indeed, may bring gain to a few individuals, and enable them to call off from our farms more laborers to be converted into lackeys and grooms for them, but it will bring nothing to our country but wars, debt, and dilapidation.—To J. B. STUART. vii, 64. (M., 1817.)

— COMMERCE, Drawbacks and.—See FRANCE.

1401. COMMERCE, Freedom of.—If we are to contribute equally with the other parts of the empire, let us equally with them enjoy free commerce with the whole world.—REPLY TO LORD NORTH'S PROPOSITION. FORD ED., i, 479. (July 1775.)

1402. —— ——. Our interest will be to throw open the doors of commerce, and to knock off all its shackles, giving perfect freedom to all persons for the vent of whatever they may choose to bring into our ports, and asking the same in theirs.—NOTES ON VIRGINIA. viii, 412. FORD ED., iii, 279. (1782.)

1403. —— ——. By a declaration of rights, I mean one which shall stipulate * * * freedom of commerce against monopolies * * *.—To A. Donald. ii, 355. (P., 1788.)

1404. —— ——. One of my favorite ideas is to leave commerce free.—The Anas. ix, 431. Ford ed., i, 198. (1792.)

1405. —— ——. Instead of embarrassing commerce under piles of regulating laws, duties and prohibitions, could it be relieved from all its shackles in all parts of the world, could every country be employed in producing that which nature has best fitted it to produce, and each be free to exchange with others mutual surpluses for mutual wants the greatest mass possible would then be produced of those things which contribute to human life and human happiness; the numbers of mankind would be increased, and their condition bettered. Would even a single nation begin with the United States this system of free commerce, it would be advisable to begin it with that nation; since it is one by one only that it can be extended to all. Where the circumstances of either party render it expedient to levy a revenue, by way of impost, on commerce, its freedom might be modified, in that particular, by mutual and equivalent measures, preserving it entire in all others.—Report on Foreign Commerce and Navigation. vii, 646. Ford ed., vi, 479. (Dec. 1793.)

1406. —— ——. I am for free commerce with all nations.—To Elbridge Gerry. iv, 268. Ford ed., vii, 328. (Pa., 1799.)

— COMMERCE WITH GREAT BRITAIN.—See England.

1407. COMMERCE, Independence and. —To have submitted our rightful commerce to prohibitions and tributary exactions from others, would have been to surrender our independence.—Reply to a Boston Request. viii, 133. (Aug. 1808.)

1408. COMMERCE, Individual enterprise and.—Agriculture, manufactures, commerce, and navigation, the four pillars of our prosperity, are the most thriving when left most free to individual enterprise. Protection from casual embarrassments, however, may sometimes be seasonably interposed.—First Annual Message. viii, 13. Ford ed., viii, 123. (Dec. 1801.)

1409. COMMERCE, Interdicted.—By several acts of parliament * * * they [the British ministers] have interdicted all commerce to one of our principal towns.—Declaration on Taking up Arms. Ford ed., i, 468. (July 1775.)

1410. COMMERCE, Laws governing.—George Mason's proposition in the [Federal] Convention was wise, that on laws regulating commerce, two-thirds of the votes should be required to pass them.—To James Madison. iv, 323. Ford ed., vii, 432. (Pa., March 1800.)

1411. COMMERCE, Madness for.—We are running commerce mad.—To Joseph Priestley. iv, 311. Ford ed., vii, 406. (Pa., Jan. 1800.)

1412. COMMERCE, Maintain.—To maintain commerce and navigation in all their lawful enterprises * * * [is one of] the landmarks by which we are to guide ourselves in all our proceedings.—Second Annual Message. viii, 21. Ford ed., viii, 186. (Dec. 1802.)

1413. COMMERCE, Merchants and.—Where a nation refuses permission to our merchants and factors to reside within certain parts of their dominions, we may, if it should be thought expedient. refuse residence to theirs in any and every part of ours, or modify their transactions.—Report on Foreign Commerce and Navigation. vii, 649. Ford ed., vi, 482. (Dec. 1793.)

1414. —— ——. The merchants will manage commerce the better, the more they are left free to manage for themselves.—To Gideon Granger. iv, 331. Ford ed., vii, 452. (M., 1800.)

— COMMERCE, Navigation and.—See Navigation, Ocean.

1415. COMMERCE, Neutrality and.—If the new government wears the front which I hope it will, I see no impossibility in availing ourselves of the wars of others to open the other parts * of America to our commerce, as the price of our neutrality.—To General Washington. ii, 533. Ford ed., v, 57. (P., 1788.)

— COMMERCE, The Ocean and.—See Ocean.

1416. COMMERCE, Oppressing.—I am principally afraid that commerce will be overloaded by the assumption [of the State debts]. believing that it would be better that property should be duly taxed.—To Mr. Randolph. iii, 185. (N.Y., 1790.)

1417. COMMERCE, Power of Congress over.—The power given to Congress by the Constitution does not extend to the internal regulation of the commerce of a State (that is to say of the commerce between citizen and citizen), which remains exclusively with its own Legislature; but to its external commerce only, that is to say, its commerce with another State, or with foreign nations, or with the Indian tribes.—National Bank Opinion. vii, 557. Ford ed., v, 286. (1791.)

1418. COMMERCE, Protection of.—If we wish our commerce to be free and uninsulted, we must let [the European] nations see that we have an energy which at present they disbelieve. The low opinion they entertain of our powers, cannot fail to involve us soon in a naval war.—To John Page. i, 401. (P., 1785.)

1419. —— ——. Should any nation, contrary to our wishes, suppose it may better find its advantage by continuing its system of prohibitions, duties and regulations, it behooves us to protect our citizens, their commerce and navigation, by counter prohibitions, duties and regulations, also. Free

* The Colonies of the European powers.—Editor.

commerce and navigation are not to be given in exchange for restrictions and vexations; nor are they likely to produce a relaxation of them.—REPORT ON COMMERCE AND NAVIGATION. vii. 647. FORD ED., vi, 480. (Dec. 1793.)

— COMMERCE WITH PRUSSIA.—See FREDERICK THE GREAT.

1420. COMMERCE, Pursuit of.—You ask what I think on the expediency of encouraging our States to be commercial? Were I to indulge my own theory, I should wish them to practice neither commerce nor navigation, but to stand, with respect to Europe, precisely on the footing of China. We should thus avoid wars, and all our citizens would be husbandmen. Whenever, indeed, our numbers should so increase as that our produce would overstock the markets of those nations who should come to seek it, the farmers must either employ the surplus of their time in manufactures, or the surplus of our hands must be employed in manufactures, or in navigation. But that day would, I think, be distant, and we should long keep our workmen in Europe, while Europe should be drawing rough materials, and even subsistence from America. But this is theory only, and a theory which the servants of America are not at liberty to follow. Our people have a decided taste for navigation and commerce. They take this from their mother country; and their servants are in duty bound to calculate all their measures on this datum: we wish to do it by throwing open all the doors of commerce, and knocking off its shackles. But as this cannot be done for others, unless they will do it for us, and there is no probability that Europe will do this, I suppose we shall be obliged to adopt a system which may shackle them in our ports, as they do us in theirs.—To COUNT VAN HOGENDORP. i, 465. FORD ED., iv, 104. (P., 1785.)

1421. COMMERCE, Reciprocity.—Some nations, not yet ripe for free commerce in all its extent, might still be willing to mollify its restrictions and regulations for us, in proportion to the advantages which an intercourse with us might offer. Particularly they may concur with us in reciprocating the duties to be levied on each side, or in compensating any excess of duty by equivalent advantages of another nature. Our commerce is certainly of a character to entitle it to favor in most countries. The commodities we offer are either necessaries of life, or materials for manufacture, or convenient subjects of revenue; and we take in exchange, either manufactures, when they have received the last finish of art and industry, or mere luxuries. Such customers may reasonably expect welcome and friendly treatment at every market. Customers, too, whose demands, increasing with their wealth and population, must very shortly give full employment to the whole industry of any nation whatever, in any line of supply they may get into the habit of calling for from it.—REPORT ON FOREIGN COMMERCE AND NAVIGATION. vii. 646. FORD ED., vi. 479. (Dec. 1793.)

1422. COMMERCE, Regulation of.—The interests of commerce require steady regulations.—To COMTE DE MONTMORIN. ii, 531. (P., 1788.)

1423. COMMERCE, Restrictions on.—The question is, in what way may best be removed, modified or counteracted, the restrictions on the commerce and navigation of the United States? As to commerce, two methods occur. 1. By friendly arrangements with the several nations with whom these restrictions exist: Or, 2. by the separate act of our own legislatures for countervailing their effects. There can be no doubt but that of these two, friendly arrangement is the most eligible. * * * Friendly arrangements are preferable with all who will come into them; and we should carry into such arrangements all the liberality and spirit of accommodation which the nature of the case will admit.—REPORT ON FOREIGN COMMERCE AND NAVIGATION. vii, 645-650. FORD ED., vi, 479-483. (Dec. 1793.)

1424. COMMERCE, Routes of.—Commerce is slow in changing its channel.—To COMTE DE MONTMORIN. ii, 300. (P., 1787.)

1425. COMMERCE, Selfish.—The selfish spirit of commerce knows no country, and feels no passion or principle but that of gain. —To LARKIN SMITH. v, 441. (M., 1809.)

1426. COMMERCE, The States and.—As long as the States exercise, separately, those acts of power which respect foreign nations, so long will there continue to be irregularities committed by some one or other of them, which will constantly keep us on an ill footing with foreign nations.—To JAMES MADISON. i, 531. FORD ED., iv, 192. (P., February 1786.)

1427. COMMERCE, Suppression of.—They [Parliament] have cut off the commercial intercourse of whole Colonies with foreign countries.—DECLARATION ON TAKING UP ARMS. FORD ED., i, 468. (July 1775.)

1428. COMMERCE, Swollen.—That the wars of the world have swollen our commerce beyond the wholesome limits of exchanging our own productions for our own wants, and that, for the emolument of a small proportion of our society, who prefer these demoralizing pursuits to labors useful to the whole, the peace of the whole is endangered, * * * are evils more easily to be deplored than remedied.—To ABBÉ SALIMANKIS. v, 516. (M., 1810.)

1429. — —. You have fairly stated the alternatives between which we are to choose: 1, licentious commerce and gambling speculations for a few, with eternal war for the many; or, 2, restricted commerce, peace, and steady occupations for all. If any State in the Union will declare that it prefers separation with the first alternative, to a continuance in union without it, I have no hesitation in saying "let us separate." I would rather the States should withdraw which are for unlimited commerce and war, and confederate with those alone which are for peace and agriculture. I know that every nation in Europe would join in sincere amity with the latter, and hold the former at arm's length, by jealousies, prohibitions, restrictions, vexations and war.—To WILLIAM H. CRAWFORD. vii, 7. FORD ED., x, 35. (M., 1816.)

— COMMERCE, Treaties of.—See TREATIES.

1430. COMMERCE, Vices of. — Our greediness for wealth, and fantastical expense, have degraded, and will degrade, the minds of our maritime citizens. These are the peculiar vices of commerce.—To JOHN ADAMS. vii, 104. FORD ED., x, 107. (M., 1818.)

1431. COMMERCE, War and.—The actual habits of our countrymen attach them to commerce. They will exercise it for themselves. Wars, then, must sometimes be our lot; and all the wise can do, will be to avoid that half of them which would be produced by our own follies, and our own acts of injustice; and to make for the other half the best preparations we can. Of what nature should these be? A land army would be useless for offence, and not the best nor safest instrument of defence. For either of these purposes, the sea is the field on which we should meet an European enemy. On that element it is necessary we should possess some power. —NOTES ON VIRGINIA. viii, 413. FORD ED., iii, 279. (1782.)

1432. ——— ———. My principle has ever been that war should not suspend either exports or imports.—To WILLIAM SHORT. vi, 128. (M., 1813.)

1433. ——— ———. Whether we shall engage in every war of Europe, to protect the mere agency of our merchants and shipowners in carrying on the commerce of other nations, even were these merchants and shipowners to take the side of their country in the contest, instead of that of the enemy, is a question of deep and serious consideration. —To JOHN ADAMS. vi, 460. (M., June 1815.)

— COMMERCE, West Indies and.—See WEST INDIES.

— COMMERCE, Western Routes of.— See CANALS.

1434. COMMISSIONS, Adams's Midnight.—Among the midnight appointments of Mr. Adams were commissions to some federal justices of the peace for Alexandria. These were signed and sealed by him but not delivered. I found them on the table of the department of State, on my entrance into office, and I forbade their delivery. Marbury, named in one of them, applied to the Supreme Court for a mandamus to the Secretary of State (Mr. Madison) to deliver the commission intended for him. The Court determined at once that, being an original process, they had no cognizance of it; and, therefore, the question before them was ended. But the Chief Justice went on to lay down what the law would be, had they jurisdiction of the case, to wit: that they should command the delivery. The object was clearly to instruct any other court, having the jurisdiction, what they should do if Marbury should apply to them.—To WILLIAM JOHNSON. vii, 295. FORD ED., x, 230. (M., 1823.)

1435. COMMISSIONS, Blank.—In matters of government, there can be no question but that a commission sealed and signed with a blank for the name, date, place, &c., is good; because government can in no country be carried on without it. The most vital proceedings of our own government would soon become null were such a construction to prevail, and the *argumentum ab inconvenienti*, which is one of the great foundations of the law, will undoubtedly sustain the practice, and sanction it by the maxim " *qui facit per alium, facit per se.*" I would not, therefore, give the countenance of the government to so impracticable a construction by issuing a new commission.—To ALBERT GALLATIN. v, 371. (W., 1808.)

1436. COMMISSIONS, Delivery of.— In the case of Marbury and Madison, the Federal judges declared that commissions, signed and sealed by the President, were valid, although not delivered. I deemed delivery essential to complete a deed, which, as long as it remains in the hands of the party, is yet no deed; it is in *posse* only, but not in *esse*, and I withheld delivery of the commissions.— To SPENCER ROANE. vii, 135. FORD ED., x, 142. (P.F., 1819.)

1437. ——— ———. The Constitution, having given to the Judiciary branch no means of compelling the Executive either to *deliver* a commission, or to make a record of it, shows that it did not intend to give the Judiciary that control over the Executive, but that it should remain in the power of the latter to do it or not.—To GEORGE HAY. v, 84. FORD ED., ix, 53. (W., 1807.)

1438. COMMISSIONS, Signing of.—The delivery of a commission is immaterial. As it may be sent by letter to any one, so it may be delivered by hand to him anywhere. The place of *signature by the sovereign* is the material thing. Were that to be done in any other jurisdiction than his own, it might draw the validity of the act into question.—To THOMAS PINCKNEY. iii, 583. FORD ED., vi, 302. (Pa., June 1793.)

1439. COMMISSIONERS, Executive.— To the list may be added the appointment of Gouverneur Morris to negotiate with the court of London, by letter written and signed by General Washington, and David Humphreys to negotiate with Liston by letter. Commissions were not given in form because no ministers had been sent here by those courts. But all the powers were given them, and half the salary (as they were not to display the diplomatic ranks, half-salary was thought sufficient) but they were completely officers on salaries, and no notice given the Senate till afterwards.—To WILSON C. NICHOLAS. FORD ED., viii, 131. (W., Jan. 1802.)

— **COMMITTEE OF THE STATES.**— See CONFEDERATION.

1440. COMMON LAW, Christianity and.—I was glad to find in your book a formal contradiction of the judiciary usurpation of legislative powers; for such the judges have usurped in their repeated decisions, that Christianity is a part of the common law. The proof of the contrary, which you have adduced, is incontrovertible; to wit, that the common law existed while the Anglo-Saxons were yet Pagans, at a time when they had never heard the name of Christ pronounced, or knew that such a character had ever existed. But it may amuse you, to show when, and by what means, they stole this law in upon us. In a case of *quare impedit* in the Year Book 34, H. 6, folio 38 (anno 1458.) a question was made, how far the ecclesiastical law was to be respected in a common law court? And Prisot, Chief Justice, gives his opinion in these words: " A tiel leis qu'ils de seint eglise ont en *ancien scripture,* covient à nous à donner credence; car ceo common ley sur quels touts manners leis sont fondés. Et auxy, Sir, nous sumus oblègés de conustre lour ley de saint eglise; et semblablement its sont obligés de consustre nostre ley. Et, Sir, si poit apperer or à nous que l'evesque ad fait come un ordinary fera en tiel cas, adong nous devons cee adjuger bon, ou auterment nemy," æc. See S. C. Fitzh. Abr. Qu. imp. 89, Bro. Abr. Qu. imp. 12. Finch in his first book c. 3, is the first afterwards who quotes this case and mistakes it thus: " To such laws of the church as have warrant in *holy scripture,* our law giveth credence." And cites Prisot; mistranslating *" ancien scripture,"* into *" holy scripture."* Whereas Prisot palpably says, " to such laws as those of holy church have in *ancient writing,* it is proper for us to give credence," to wit, to their *ancient written* laws. This was in 1613, a century and a half after the dictum of Prisot. Wingate, in 1658, erects this false translation into a maxim of the common law, copying the words of Finch, but citing Prisot, Wing. Max. 3. And Sheppard, title, " Religion," in 1675, copies the same mistranslation. quoting the Y. B. Finch and Wingate. Hale expresses it in these words: " Christianity is parcel of the laws of England." 1 Ventr. 293, 3 Keb. 607. But he quotes no authority. By these echoings and re-echoings from one to another, it had become so established in 1728, that in the case of the King *vs.* Woolston, 2 Stra. 834, the court would not suffer it to be debated, whether to write against Christianity was punishable in the temporal court at common law? Wood, therefore, 409, ventures still to vary the phrase, and say, that all blasphemy and profaneness are offences by the common law; and cites 2 Stra. Then Blackstone, in 1763, iv. 59, repeats the words of Hale, that " Christianity is part of the laws of England," citing Ventris and Strange. And finally, Lord Mansfield, with a little qualification, in Evans' case, in 1767. says. that " the essential principles of revealed religion are part of the common law." Thus ingulphing Bible, Testament and all into the common law, without citing any authority. And thus we find this chain of authorities, hanging link by link, one

upon another, and all ultimately on one and the same hook, and that a mistranslation of the words *" ancien scripture,"* used by Prisot. Finch quotes Prisot; Wingate does the same. Sheppard quotes Prisot, Finch and Wingate. Hale cites nobody. The court in Woolston's case, cites Hale. Wood cites Woolston's case. Blackstone quotes Woolston's case and Hale. And Lord Mansfield, like Hale, ventures it on his own authority. Here I might defy the best-read lawyer to produce another scrip of authority for this judiciary forgery; and I might go on further to show, how some of the Anglo-Saxon priests interpolated into the text of Alfred's laws, the 20th, 21st, 22d, and 23d chapters of Exodus, and the 15th, of the Acts of the Apostles, from the 23d to the 29th verses. But this would lead my pen and your patience too far. What a conspiracy this between Church and State!—To JOHN CARTWRIGHT. vii, 359. (M., 1824.)

1441. ——— ———. Those who read Prisot's opinion with a candid view to understand and not to chicane it, cannot mistake its meaning. The reports in the Year-Books were taken very short. The opinions of the judges were written down sententiously, as notes or memoranda. and not with all the development which they probably used in developing them. Prisot's opinion, to be fully expressed, should be thus paraphrased: " To such laws as those holy church have recorded. and preserved in their ancient books and writings, it is proper for us to give credence; for so is, or so says the Common Law, or law of the land, on which all manner of other laws rest for their authority, or are founded; that is to say, the Common Law, or the law of the land common to us all, and established by the authority of us all, is that from which is derived the authority of all other special and subordinate branches of law, such as the canon law, law merchant, law maritime, law of gavelkind, Borough English, corporation laws, local customs and usages, to all of which the common law requires its judges to permit authority in the special or local cases belonging to them. The evidence of these laws is preserved in their ancient treatises, books and writings, in like manner as our common law itself is known, the text of its original enactments having been long lost, and its substance only preserved in ancient and traditionary writings. And if it appears, from their ancient books, writings and records, that the bishop, in this case. according to the rules prescribed by these authorities, has done what an ordinary would have done in such case, then we should adjudge it good, otherwise not." To decide this question, they would have to turn to the ancient writings and records of the canon law, in which they would find evidence of the laws of advowsons, *quare impedit.* the duties of bishops and ordinaries, for which terms Prisot could never have meant to refer them to the Old or New Testament. *les saincts scriptures,* where surely they would not be found. A license which should permit *" ancien scrip-*

ture," to be translated "holy scripture," annihilates at once all the evidence of language. With such a license, we might reverse the sixth commandment into "Thou shalt not omit murder." It would be the more extraordinary in this case, where the mistranslation was to effect the adoption of the whole code of the Jewish and Christian laws into the text of our statutes, to convert religious offenses into temporal crimes, to make the breach of every religious precept a subject of indictment; to submit the question of idolatry, for example, to the trial of a jury, and to a court, its judgment, to the third and fourth generation of the offender. Do we allow our judges this lumping legislation?—To EDWARD EVERETT. vii, 381. (M., 1824.)

1442. COMMON LAW, Codification of. —Whether we should undertake to reduce the common law, our own, and so much of the English statutes as we have adopted, to a text, is a question of transcendent difficulty. It was discussed at the first meeting of the committee of the Revised Code [of Virginia] in 1776, and decided in the negative, by the opinions of Wythe, Mason and myself, against Pendleton and Thomas Lee. Pendleton proposed to take Blackstone for that text, only purging him of what was inapplicable or unsuitable to us. In that case, the meaning of every word of Blackstone would have become a source of litigation, until it had been settled by repeated legal decisions. And to come at that meaning, we should have had produced, on all occasions, that very pile of authorities from which it would be said he drew his conclusion, and which, of course, would explain it, and the terms in which it is couched. Thus we should have retained the same chaos of law lore from which we wished to be emancipated, added to the evils of the uncertainty which a new text and new phrases would have generated. An example of this may be found in the old statutes, and commentaries on them, in Coke's Second Institute, but more remarkably in the Institute of Justinian, and the vast masses explanatory or supplementary of that which fill the libraries of the civilians. We were deterred from the attempt by these considerations, added to which, the bustle of the times did not admit leisure for such an undertaking.—To JOHN TYLER. vi, 66. (M., 1812.)

1443. COMMON LAW, The Colonists and.—I deride with you the ordinary doctrine, that we brought with us from England *the common law rights.* This narrow notion was a favorite in the first moment of rallying to our rights against Great Britain. But it was that of men who felt their rights before they had thought of their explanation. The truth is, that we brought with us the *rights of men;* of expatriated men. On our arrival here, the question would at once arise, by what law will we govern ourselves? The resolution seems to have been, by that system with which we are familiar, to be altered by ourselves occasionally, and adapted to our new situation. The proofs of this resolution

are to be found in the form of the oaths of the judges, 1. Henings Stat. 169. 187: of the Governor, *ib.* 504; in the act for a provisional government, *ib,* 372; in the preamble to the laws of 1661-2; the uniform current of opinions and decisions, and in the general recognition of all our statutes, framed on that basis. But the state of the English law at the date of our emigration, constituted the system adopted here. We may doubt, therefore, the propriety of quoting in our courts English authorities subsequent to that adoption; still more the admission of authorities posterior to the Declaration of Independence, or rather to the accession of that King, whose reign, *ab initio,* was the very tissue of wrongs which rendered the Declaration at length necessary. The reason for it had inception at least as far back as the commencement of his reign. This relation to the beginning of his reign, would add the advantage of getting us rid of all Mansfield's innovations, or civilizations of the Common Law. For, however, I admit the superiority of the civil over the common law code, as a system of perfect justice, yet an incorporation of the two would be like Nebuchadnezzar's image of metals and clay, a thing without cohesion of parts. The only natural improvement of the common law, is through its homogeneous ally, the Chancery, in which new principles are to be examined, concocted and digested. But when, by repeated decisions and modifications, they are rendered pure and certain, they should be transferred by statute to the courts of common law and placed within the pale of juries. The exclusion from the courts of the malign influence of all authorities after the *Georgium Sidus* became ascendant, would uncanonize Blackstone, whose book, although the most elegant and best digested of our law catalogue, has been perverted more than all others, to the degeneracy of legal science. A student finds there a smattering of everything, and his indolence easily persuades him that if he understands that book, he is master of the whole body of the law. The distinction between these, and those who have drawn their stores from the deep and rich mines of Coke on Littleton, seems well understood even by the unlettered common people who apply the appellation of Blackstone lawyers to these ephemeral insects of the law.*—To JOHN TYLER. vi, 65. (1812.)

1444. COMMON LAW, The Constitution and.—I consider all the encroachments made on the Constitution, heretofore, as nothing, as mere retail stuff compared with the wholesale doctrine, that there is a Common Law in force in the United States of which, and of all the cases within its provi-

* W. G. Hammond, in his edition of *Blackstone's Commentaries,* (i. 276) says: "Jefferson and the party he represented were always disposed to disown the Common Law and claim their freedom as one of the 'rights of man', but the majority of the 'rebels' insisted only on what they considered their common-law rights, and maintained that the English Colonists had brought these with them over the sea. The Declaration of Independence unites both positions in the most skilful manner."—EDITOR.

sions, their courts have cognizance.* It is complete consolidation. [Judges] Ellsworth and Iredell have openly recognized it. [Bushrod] Washington has squinted at it, and I have no doubt it has been decided to cram it down our throats.—To CHARLES PINCKNEY. FORD ED., vii, 398. (M., Oct. 1799.)

1445. COMMON LAW, Corruption and.

—I do verily believe, that if the principle were to prevail, of a Common Law being in force in the United States (which principle possesses the General Government at once of all the powers of the State governments, and reduces us to a single consolidated government), it would become the most corrupt

* The subjoined extracts from Jefferson's ANAS, bear on the assertion of this doctrine in the United States Senate:

1—Mr. Dexter, Mr. Hillhouse and Mr. Read insisted [in the Senate] in the fullest and most explicit terms, that the Common Law of England is in force in these States, and may be the rule of adjudication in all cases where the laws of the United States have made no provision. Mr. Livermore seemed to urge the same, though he seemed to think that in *criminal* cases it might be necessary to adopt by an express law. Mr. Tracy was more reserved on this occasion. He only said that Congress might by a law adopt the provisions of the Common Law on any subjects by a reference to that, without detailing the particulars; as in this bill it was proposed that the marshals should summon juries "according to the practice of the Common Law". THE ANAS. FORD ED., i, 288. (April 1800.)

2—Dexter maintained that the Common Law as to crimes is in force in the courts of the United States. Chipman says that the principles of common right are Common Law. And he says the Common Law of England is in force here. There being no law in Vermont for appointing juries which the marshal can follow, he says he may appoint them as provided by the Common Law of England, though that part of the Common Law was never adopted in Vermont. THE ANAS. FORD ED., i, 286. (March 19, 1800.)

3—Heretical doctrines maintained in Senate on the motion against the *Aurora* * * * that the Common Law authorizes the proceeding proposed against the *Aurora*, and is in force here. By Read. * * * Tracy says he would not exactly say that the Common Law of England in all its extent is in force here; but common sense, reason and morality, which are the foundations of the Common Law, are in force here and establish a Common Law. He held himself so nearly half way between the Common Law of England and what everybody else has called natural law, and not Common Law, that he could hold to either the one or the other, as he should find expedient. Dexter maintained that the Common Law, as to crimes, is in force in the United States. Chipman says that the principles of common right are Common Law.—THE ANAS. ix, 198. FORD ED., i, 285. (1800.)

4—The jury bill before the Senate. Mr. Read says that, if from any circumstances of inaptitude the marshal cannot appoint a jury analogously with the State juries, the Common Law steps in, and he may name them according to that. And March 12, same bill, Mr. Chipman speaking of the case of Vermont, where a particular mode of naming jurors was in force under a former law of that State, when the law of the United States passed declaring that juries shall be appointed in their courts in the several States in the mode "now" in use in the same State. Vermont has since altered their mode of naming them. Mr. Chipman admits the Federal courts cannot adopt the new mode, but in that case he says their marshal may name them according to the rules of the Common Law. Now observe that that is a part of the Common Law which Vermont had never adopted, but, on the contrary, had made a law of their own, better suited to their circumstances.—THE ANAS. FORD ED., i, 286. (March 11, 1800.)

5—See in the *Wilmington Mirror* of Feb. 14th, Mr. Bayard's elaborate argument to prove that the Common Law, as modified by the laws of the respective States at the epoch of the ratification of the Constitution, attached to the courts of the United States.—THE ANAS. ix, 203. FORD ED., i, 291. (Feb. 1801.)

government on the earth.—To GIDEON GRANGER. iv, 331. FORD ED., vii, 451. (M., Aug. 1800.)

1446. COMMON LAW, Origin of.

—The term "common law," although it has more than one meaning, is perfectly definite, *secundum subjectam materiem.* Its most probable origin was on the conquest of the Heptarchy by Alfred, and the amalgamation of their several codes of law into one, which became *common* to them all. The authentic text of these enactments has not been preserved; but their substance has been committed to many ancient books and writings, so faithfully as to have been deemed genuine from generation to generation, and obeyed as such by all. We have some fragments of them collected by Lambard, Wilkins and others, but abounding with proofs of their spurious authenticity. Magna Charta is the earliest statute, the text of which has come down to us in an authentic form, and thence downward we have them entire. We do not know exactly when the *common* law and *statute* law, the *lex scripta et non scripta,* began to be contra-distinguished, so as to give a second acceptation to the former term; whether before, or after Prisot's day, at which time we know that nearly two centuries and a half of statutes were in preservation. In later times, on the introduction of the chancery branch of law, the term *common* law began to be used in a third sense, as the correlative of *chancery* law.—To EDWARD EVERETT. vii, 382. (M., 1824.)

1447. COMMON LAW, State Laws and.

—On the settlement of the colonies now composing the United States, and the settlement of a legislature in each of them, that legislature, in some cases, finding that the enacting a complete code of laws which should reach every transaction needing legislation, would be far beyond their time and abilities, adopted, by an express act of their own, the laws of England as they stood at that date, comprehending the common law, statutes to that period, and the chancery law. In other cases, instead of adopting them by an express statute of their own, they considered themselves as having brought with them, and been, even on their passage, under the constant obligation of the laws of the mother country, and on their arrival they continued to practice them without any act of adoption, which practice or usage is evidence that there was an adoption by general consent. In the case of Connecticut, they did not adopt the common law of England at all as their basis, but declared by an act of their own, that the law of God, as it stood revealed in the Old and New Testaments, should be the basis of their laws, to be subject to such alterations as they should make. In all the cases where the common law, or laws of England, were adopted either expressly or tacitly, the legislatures held of course, and exercised the power of making additions and alterations. As the different States were settled at very different periods, and the adoption for each State was the laws of England as they stood at the moment of the adoption by the State, it is evident that the system as adopted in 1607 by Virginia, was one thing, as by Pennsylvania was another thing, as by Georgia, in 1759, was still a different one. And when to this is added the very diversified modifications of the adopted code, produced by the subsequent laws passed by the legislatures of the different States, the system of common law in force in any one State on the 24th of September, 1789, when Congress assumed the jurisdiction given them by the Constitution, was very different from the systems in force at the same moment in the several other States: that in all of these the common law was in force by virtue of the adoption of the State, express or tacit, and that it was not in force in Connecticut, because they had never adopted it.—OBSERVATIONS ON HARDIN'S CASE. ix, 485. (Nov. 1812.)

1448. COMMON LAW, United States Law and.—Having settled by way of preliminary, to what extent, and by what authority, the common law of England is the law of each of the States, we will proceed to consider how far, and by what authority, it is the law of the United States as a national government. By the Constitution, the General Government has jurisdiction in all cases arising under the Constitution, under the (constitutional) laws of the United States, and under treaties; in all cases, too, of ambassadors, of admiralty jurisdiction, where the United States is a party, between a State or its citizens, or another State or its citizens, or foreign State or its citizens. The General Government, then, had a right to take under their cognizance all these cases, and no others. This might have been done by Congress, by passing a complete code, assuming the whole field of their jurisdiction, and by applying uniformly to every State, without any respect to the laws of that State. But, like the State legislatures, who had been placed before in a similar situation, they felt that it was a work of too much time and difficulty to be undertaken. Observing, therefore, that (except cases of piracy and murder on the high seas) all the cases within the jurisdiction must arise in some of the States, they declared by the act of September, 24, 1789. C. 20 § 34, "that the laws of the several States, except where the Constitution, treaties, or statutes of the United States shall otherwise provide, shall be regarded as rules of decision in trials at *common law* in the courts of the United States in cases where they apply." Here, then, Congress adopted for each State the laws of that State; and among the laws so adopted were portions of the common law, greater or less in different States, and in force, not by any innate authority of its own, but by the adoption or enacting of it by the State authority. Now what was the opinion to which this was opposed? Several judges of the General Government declared that "the common law of England is the unwritten law of the United States in their national and federal capacity." A State judge, in a printed work, lays it down as "certainly wrong to say that the judiciary power of the nation can

exercise no authority but what depends for its principle on acts of the national legislature." And then, quoting the preamble to the Constitution of the United States, which says that its object is, "to insure domestic tranquillity, promote the general welfare" &c., he adds, that "what is here expressed is the *common law* of the whole country," and that "whatever is in opposition to it, whether treason, insurrection, sedition, murder, riot, assaults, batteries, thefts or robberies, may be punished as crimes, independent of any act of Congress." And opinions equivalent to these were declared by one party on the floor of Congress. This is the doctrine which the republicans declared heretical. They deny that Congress can pass any law not authorized by the Constitution, and that the judges can act on any law not authorized by Congress, or by the Constitution in very direct terms. If the true doctrine then be, that certain portions of the common and statute law of England be in force in the different States by virtue of the adoption in that State, and in the Federal courts of the same State by virtue of the adoption by Congress of the laws of that State within its limits, then whenever a case is presented to a Federal court, they are to ask themselves the following questions: 1. Is this case within any of the definitions of jurisdiction given by the Constitution to the General Government? If it be decided that it is, then, 2. Has Congress by any positive statute assumed cognizance of this case as permitted them by the Constitution? To determine this question, the judge must first look into the statutes of Congress generally; if he finds it not there, he must look into the laws of the State, as well as that portion of the English code which the State may have adopted, as the acts passed specially by the legislature. If the case be actually found provided for in these laws, another question still remains, viz.: 3. Is the law of the State applicable to the analogous case of the General Government? for it may happen that a law of the State, adapted perfectly to its own organization and local circumstances, may not tally with the different organizations or circumstances of the Federal government. If the difference be such as to defeat the application, it must be considered as a case unprovided for by Congress, and not cognizable in their courts. Just so parts of the common or statute law of England are found by the State judges inapplicable to their State from a difference of circumstances. These differences of circumstances will be shaded off from nothing to direct inconsistence, and it will be only by many decisions on a great variety of cases that the line will at length be drawn. Let us apply these questions to Hardin's case, which is simply this: Congress by an express statute, 1802, c. 13, § 6, have made the murder of an Indian within the territory of the United States, punishable by death. A murder is committed on an Indian in that territory. The murderers fly to Kentucky. They are demanded by the Governor of Indiana of the Governor of Kentucky; under whose authority our officer attempting to take them, they were protected by Hardin and others in arms. 1. Is this case within the jurisdiction of Congress? *Answer.* Congress having a right " to make all rules and regulations respecting the territory of the United States," have declared this to be a case of murder. As they can " make all laws necessary and proper for carrying their power into execution," they can make the protecting a murderer criminal in any part of the United States. 2. Has Congress assumed cognizance of the offence of Hardin? We must first examine whether the act of Congress, 1799. c. 9, § 22, takes in this offence. Then whether the laws of Kentucky, common, statute, or State law, as adopted by Congress comprehend this offence. 3. Whether any difference of organization or other circumstance renders the law of Kentucky inapplicable to this offence, can be decided by those only who are particularly acquainted with that law.—OBSERVATIONS ON HARDIN'S CASE. ix, 486. (Nov. 1812.)

1449. —— ——. I read the sixth chapter of your book with interest and satisfaction, on the question whether the common law (of England) makes a part of the laws of our General Government. That it makes more or less a part of the laws of the States is, I suppose, an unquestionable fact. Not by *birthright,* * * * but by adoption. But, as to the General Government, the Virginia Report on the Alien and Sedition laws, has so completely pulverized this pretension that nothing new can be said on it. Still, seeing the judges of the Supreme Court (I recollect, for example, Ellsworth and Story) had been found capable of such paralogism, I was glad to see that the Supreme Court had given it up. In the case of Libel in the United States District Court of Connecticut, the rejection of it was certainly sound ; because no law of the General Government had made it an offence. But such a case might, I suppose, be sustained in the State courts which have State laws against libels. Because as to the portions of power within each State assigned to the General Government, the President is as much the Executive of the State, as their particular governor is in relation to State powers.—To MR. GOODENOW. vii, 251. (M., 1822.)

1450. COMMON SENSE, Authority and.—Common sense is the foundation of all authorities, of the laws themselves, and of their construction.—BATTURE CASE. viii, 575. (1812.)

1451. COMMON SENSE, Confidence in. —I have great confidence in the common sense of mankind in general.—To JEREMIAH MOOR. FORD ED., vii, 455. (M., 1800.)

1452. COMMON SENSE, Kings and.— No race of kings has ever presented above one man of common sense in twenty generations. To BENJAMIN HAWKINS. ii, 221. FORD ED., iv, 426. (P., 1787.)

1453. COMMON SENSE, Safety in.—I can never fear that things will go far wrong where common sense has fair play.—To JOHN ADAMS. ii, 73. (P., 1786.)

1454. —— ——. Let common sense and common honesty have fair play and they will soon set things to rights.—To EZRA STILES ii, 77. (P., 1786.)

1455. COMMON SENSE, Stock-jobbing and.—Happy if the victims of the stock-jobbers now * * * get back into the tract o' plain, unsophisticated common sense which they ought never to have been decoyed from.— To NICHOLAS LEWIS. FORD ED., v, 508. (Pa. 1792.) See SENSE.

1456. COMPACT, The Federal.—The States in North America which confederated to establish their independence of the Government of Great Britain, of which Virginia was one, became, on that acquisition free and independent States, and as such, authorized to constitute governments, each for itself, in such form as it thought best. They entered into a compact (which is called the Constitution of the United States of America) by which they agreed to unite in a single government as to their relations with each other and with foreign nations, and as to certain other articles particularly specified. They retained at the same time, each to itself the other rights of independent government, comprehending mainly their domestic interests. For the administration of their Federal branch, they agreed to appoint, in conjunction a distinct set of functionaries, legislative, executive and judiciary, in the manner settled in that compact: while to each, severally, and of course remained· its original right of appointing, each for itself, a separate set of functionaries. legislative, executive and judiciary, also for administering the domestic branch of their respective governments. These two sets of officers, each independent of the other, constitute thus a *whole* of government, for each State separately ; the powers ascribed to the one, as specifically made federal, exercisable over the whole. the residuary powers, retained to the other, exercisable exclusively over its particular State, foreign herein. each to the others, as they were before the original compact.— DECLARATION AND PROTEST OF VIRGINIA. ix, 496. FORD ED., x, 349. (Dec. 1825.)

1457. COMPACTS, Enforcing.—The coercive powers supposed to be wanting in the federal head I am of opinion they possess by the law of nature, which authorizes one party to an agreement to compel the other to performance. A delinquent State makes itself a party against the rest of the confederacy.— To EDWARD RANDOLPH. ii, 211. (P., 1787.) See COERCION.

1458. COMPACTS, Infractions of.—As in all other cases of compact among powers having no common judge, each party has an equal right to judge for itself, as well of infractions as of the mode and measure of redress.—KENTUCKY RESOLUTIONS. ix, 465. FORD ED., vii, 292. (1798.)

1459. —— ——. Where a party from necessity or danger withholds compliance with part of a treaty, it is bound to make compensation where the nature of the case admits and does not dispense with it.—OPINION ON FRENCH TREATIES. vii, 617. FORD ED., vi, 224. (1793.)

1460. COMPACTS, Self-preservation and.—Obligation is [to observe compacts] not suspended till the danger [of self-preservation] is become real, and the moment of it so imminent, that we can no longer avoid decision without forever losing the opportunity to do it.—OPINION ON FRENCH TREATIES. vii, 615. FORD ED., vi, 222. (1793.)

1461. COMPACTS, Straining.—However strong the cord of compact may be, there is a point of tension at which it will break.—To EDWARD LIVINGSTON. vii, 404. (M., 1825.) See TREATIES.

1462. COMPROMISE, Necessity of.—It is necessary to give as well as take in a government like ours.—To GEORGE MASON. iii, 147. FORD ED., v, 184. (N.Y., 1790.)

1463. COMPROMISE OF OPINION.—I see the necessity of sacrificing our opinions sometimes to the opinions of others for the sake of harmony.—To FRANCIS EPPES. FORD ED., v, 194. (N.Y., 1790.)

1464. ———. A government held together by the bands of reason only, requires much compromise of opinion; that things even salutary should not be crammed down the throats of dissenting brethren, especially when they may be put into a form to be willingly swallowed, and that a great deal of indulgence is necessary to strengthen habits of harmony and fraternity.—To EDWARD LIVINGSTON. vii, 343. FORD ED., x, 301. (M., 1824.)

— CONCHOLOGY.—See SHELLS.

1465. CONCILIATION, Coalition and. —If we can hit on the true line of conduct which may conciliate the honest part of those who were called federalists, and do justice to those who have so long been excluded from it, I shall hope to be able to obliterate, or rather to unite the names of federalists and republicans.—To HORATIO GATES. FORD ED., viii, 11. (W., March 1801.)

1466. CONCILIATION, Principle and. —My inaugural address * * * will present the leading objects to be conciliation and adherence to sound principle. This, I know, is impracticable with the leaders of the late faction, whom I abandon as incurables, and will never turn an inch out of my way to reconcile them. But with the main body of the federalists, I believe it very practicable.—To JAMES MONROE. iv, 367. FORD ED., viii, 8. (W., March 1801.)

1467. ———. After the first unfavorable impressions of doing too much* in the opinion of some, and too little in that of others, shall be got over. I should hope a steady line of conciliation very practicable, and that without yielding a single republican prin-

* With respect to appointments and removals.— EDITOR.

ciple. A certainty that these principles prevailed in the breasts of the main body of federalists, was my motive for stating them as the ground of reunion.—To DR. BENJAMIN RUSH. iv, 384. FORD ED., viii, 32. (W., March 1801.)

— CONDOLENCE.—See SYMPATHY.

1468. CONDORCET (M. J. A. N. C. de), Genius of.—I am glad the bust of Condorcet has been saved. His genius should be before us; while the lamentable, but singular act of ingratitude which tarnished his latter days, may be thrown behind us.—To WILLIAM SHORT. vii, 141. FORD ED., x, 145. (M., 1819.)

1469. CONDUCT, Advice as to.—Be very select in the society you attach yourself to; avoid taverns, drinkers, smokers, idlers, and dissipated persons generally * * * and you will find your path more easy and tranquil.—To THOMAS JEFFERSON RANDOLPH. v, 391. FORD ED., ix, 233. (W., 1808.)

1470. ———. A determination never to do what is wrong, prudence and good humor, will go far towards securing to you the estimation of the world. When I recollect that at fourteen years of age, the whole care and direction of myself was thrown on myself entirely, without a relation or friend qualified to advise or guide me, and recollect the various sorts of bad company with which I associated from time to time, I am astonished I did not turn off with some of them, and become as worthless to society as they were. I had the good fortune to become acquainted very early with some characters of very high standing, and to feel the incessant wish that I could ever become what they were. Under temptations and difficulties, I would ask myself what would Dr. Small, Mr. Wythe, Peyton Randolph do in this situation? What course in it will insure me their approbation? I am certain that this mode of deciding on my conduct, tended more to its correctness than any reasoning powers I possessed. Knowing the even and dignified line they pursued, I could never doubt for a moment which of two courses would be in character for them. Whereas, seeking the same object through a process of moral reasoning, and with the jaundiced eye of youth, I should often have erred. From the circumstances of my position, I was often thrown into the society of horse racers, card players, fox hunters, scientific and professional men, and of dignified men; and many a time have I asked myself, in the enthusiastic moment of the death of a fox, the victory of a favorite horse, the issue of a question eloquently argued at the bar, or in the great council of the nation, well, which of these kinds of reputation should I prefer? That of a horse jockey? a fox hunter? an orator? or the honest advocate of my country's rights? Be assured, my dear Jefferson, that these little returns into ourselves, this self-catechising habit, is not trifling nor useless, but leads to the prudent selection and steady pursuit of what is right.—To THOMAS JEFFERSON RANDOLPH. v, 388. FORD ED., ix, 231. (W., 1808.)

1471. CONFEDERATION, The Articles of.—On Friday, July 12 [1776], the committee appointed to draw the Articles of Confederation reported them, and, on the 22d, the House resolved themselves into a committee to take them into consideration. On the 30th and 31st of that month, and 1st of the ensuing, those Articles were debated which determined the proportion, or quota, of money which each State should furnish to the common treasury, and the manner of voting in Congress. The first of these Articles was expressed in the original draft in these words. "Art. XI. All charges of war and all other expenses that shall be incurred for the common defence, or general welfare, and allowed by the United States assembled, shall be defrayed out of a common treasury, which shall be supplied by the several colonies in proportion to the number of inhabitants of every age, sex, and quality, except Indians not paying taxes, in each Colony, a true account of which, distinguishing the white inhabitants, shall be triennially taken and transmitted to the Assembly of the United States." * * * [Here follows Jefferson's report of the debates, printed in the Appendix to this volume.] These Articles, reported July 12, '76, were debated from day to day, and time to time, for two years, were ratified July 9, '78, by ten States, by New Jersey on the 26th of November of the same year, and by Delaware on the 23d of February following. Maryland alone held off two years more, acceding to them March 1, '81, and thus closing the obligation.—AUTOBIOGRAPHY. i, 26. FORD ED., i, 38. (1821.)

1472. CONFEDERATION, Commerce and.—Congress, by the Confederation, have no original and inherent power over the commerce of the States. But, by the 9th article, we are authorized to enter into treaties of commerce. The moment these treaties are concluded, the jurisdiction of Congress over the commerce of the States springs into existence, and that of the particular States is superseded so far as the articles of the treaty may have taken up the subject. There are two restrictions only, on the exercise of the power of treaty by Congress. 1st. That they shall not, by such treaty, restrain the legislatures of the States from imposing such duties on foreigners as their own people are subject to; nor, 2ndly, from prohibiting the exportation or importation of any particular species of goods. Leaving these two points free, Congress may, by treaty, establish any system of commerce they please; but, as I before observed, it is by treaty alone they can do it. Though they may exercise their other powers by resolution or ordinance, those over commerce can only be exercised by forming a treaty, and this probably by an accidental wording of our Confederation.—To JAMES MONROE. i, 349. FORD ED., iv, 54. (P., 1785.) See TREATIES.

1473. CONFEDERATION, Congress under the.—Our body [the Confederation Congress] was little numerous, but very contentious. Day after day was wasted on the most unimportant questions. My colleague [John F.] Mercer, was one of those afflicted with the morbid rage of debate, of an ardent mind, prompt imagination, and copious flow of words, who heard with impatience any logic which was not his own. Sitting near me on some occasion of a trifling but wordy debate,

he asked how I could sit in silence, hearing so much false reasoning, which a word should refute? I observed to him, that to refute was easy, but to silence was impossible; that in measures brought forward by myself, I took the laboring oar, as was incumbent on me; but that in general, I was willing to listen; that if every sound argument or objection was used by some one or other of the numerous debaters, it was enough; if not, I thought it sufficient to suggest the omission, without going into a repetition of what had been already said by others; that this was a waste and abuse of the time and patience of the House, which could not be justified. And I believe, that if the members of deliberative bodies were to observe this course generally, they would do in a day what takes them a week; and it is really more questionable, than may at first be thought, whether Bonaparte's dumb legislature which said nothing and did much, may not be preferable to one which talks much and does nothing.—AUTOBIOGRAPHY. i, 58. FORD ED., i, 81. (1821.) See CONGRESS.

— CONFEDERATION, Consuls and.— See CONSULS.

— CONFEDERATION, Debates on Articles.—See APPENDIX.

1474. CONFEDERATION, Defects of.— There are some alterations which experience proves to be wanting. Those are principally three. 1. To establish a general rule for the admission of new States into the Union. * * * 2. The Confederation, in its eighth article, decides that the quota of money, to be contributed by the several States, shall be in proportion to the value of the landed property in the State. Experience has shown it impracticable to come at this value. Congress have, therefore, recommended to the States to agree that their quotas shall be in proportion to the number of their inhabitants, counting five slaves, however, but as equal to three free inhabitants. 3. The Confederation forbids the States individually to enter into treaties of commerce, or of any other nature, with foreign nations; and it authorizes Congress to establish such treaties, with two reservations however, viz., that they shall agree to no treaty which would, 1, restrain the legislatures from imposing such duties on foreigners as matters are subject to; or 2, from prohibiting the exportation or importation of any species of commodities. Congress may, therefore, be said to have a power to regulate commerce, so far as it can be effected by conventions with other nations, and by conventions which do not infringe the two fundamental reservations before mentioned. But this is too imperfect. Because till a convention be made with any particular nation, the commerce of any one of our States with that nation may be regulated by the State itself, and even when a convention is made, the regulation of commerce is taken out of the hands of the several States only so far as it is covered or provided for by that convention or treaty. But treaties are made in such general terms, that the greater part of the regulations would still result to the legislatures. * * * The commerce of the States cannot be regulated to the best advantage but by a single body, and no body so proper as Congress. * * * —Answers to M. de Meunier. ix, 285. Ford ed., iv, 141. (P., 1786.)

1475. ——— ———. Its greatest defect is the imperfect manner in which matters of commerce have been provided for.—To E. Carrington. ii, 217. Ford ed., iv, 424. (P., 1787.)

1476. ——— ———. The fundamental defect of the Confederation was that Congress was not authorized to act immediately on the people, and by its own officers. Their power was only requisitory, and these requisitions were addressed to the several Legislatures, to be by them carried into execution, without other coercion than the moral principle of duty. This allowed in fact a negative to every Legislature, on every measure proposed by Congress; a negative so frequently exercised in practice as to benumb the action of the Federal Government, and to render it inefficient in its general objects, and more especially in pecuniary and foreign concerns. The want, too, of a separation of the Legislative, Executive, and Judiciary functions, worked disadvantageously in practice. Yet this state of things afforded a happy augury of the future march of our confederacy, when it was seen that the good sense and good dispositions of the people, as soon as they perceived the incompetence of their first compact, instead of leaving its correction to insurrection and civil war, agreed with one voice to elect deputies to a general Convention, who should peaceably meet and agree on such a Constitution as " would ensure peace, justice, liberty, the common defence and general welfare."—Autobiography. i, 78. Ford ed., i, 108. (1821.)

1477. CONFEDERATION, Distribution of Powers.—To make us one nation as to foreign concerns, and keep us distinct in domestic ones, gives the outline of the proper division of power between the general and particular governments. But, to enable the Federal head to exercise the power given it, to best advantage, it should be organized, as the particular ones are, into Legislative, Executive and Judiciary. The first and last are already separated. The second should also be. When last with Congress, I often proposed to members to do this, by making of the Committees of the States, an Executive Committee during the recess of Congress, and, during its sessions, to appoint a Committee to receive and despatch all executive business, so that Congress itself should meddle only with what should be legislative. But I question if any Congress (much less all successively) can have self-denial enough to go through with this distribution. The distribution, then, should be imposed on them.—To James Madison. ii, 66. Ford ed., iv, 333. (P., Dec. 1786.)

— CONFEDERATION, Executive Committee for.—See 1477.

1478. CONFEDERATION, Failure of.—Our first essay, in America, to establish a federative government had fallen, on trial, very short of its object. During the war of Independence, while the pressure of an external enemy hooped us together, and their enterprises kept us necessarily on the alert, the spirit of the people, excited by danger, was a supplement to the Confederation, and urged them to zealous exertions, whether claimed by that instrument, or not; but, when peace and safety were restored, and every man became engaged in useful and profitable occupation, less attention was paid to the calls of Congress.—Autobiography. i, 78. Ford ed., i, 107. (1821.)

1479. CONFEDERATION, Financial Embarrassments under.—Mr. Adams, while residing at the Hague, had a general authority to borrow what sums might be requisite for ordinary and necessary expenses. Interest on the public debt, and the maintenance of the diplomatic establishment in Europe, had been habitually provided in this way. He was now elected Vice-President of the United States, was soon to return to America, and had referred our bankers to me for future counsel on our affairs in their hands. But I had no powers, no instructions, no means, and no familiarity with the subject. It had always been exclusively under his management, except as to occasional and partial deposits in the hands of Mr. Grand, banker in Paris, for special and local purposes. These last had been exhausted for some time, and I had frequently pressed the Treasury Board to replenish this particular deposit, as Mr. Grand now refused to make further advances. They answered candidly that no funds could be obtained until the new government should get into action, and have time to make its arrangements. Mr. Adams had received his appointment to the court of London while engaged at Paris, with Dr. Franklin and myself, in the negotiations under our joint commissions. He had repaired thence to London, without returning to the Hague to take leave of that government. He thought it necessary, however, to do so now, before he should leave Europe, and accordingly went there. I learned of his departure from London by a letter from Mrs. Adams received on the very day on which he would arrive at the Hague. A consultation with him, and some provision for the future was indispensable, while we could yet avail ourselves of his powers; for when they would be gone, we should be without resource. I was daily dunned by a Company who had formerly made a small loan to the United States, the principal of which was now become due; and our bankers in Amsterdam had notified me that the interest on our general debt would be expected in June; that if we failed to pay it, it would be deemed an act of bankruptcy and would effectually destroy the credit of the United States and all future prospect of obtaining money there; that the loan they had been authorized to open, of which a third only was filled, had now ceased to get forward and rendered desperate that hope of resource. I saw that there was not a moment to lose, and set out for the Hague on the second morning after receiving the information of Mr. Adams's journey. * * * Mr. Adams concurred with me at once in opinion that something must be done, and that we ought to risk ourselves on doing it without instructions, to save the credit of the United States. We foresaw that before the new government could be adopted, assembled, establish its financial system, get the money into the Treasury and place it in Europe, considerable time would elapse; that, therefore, we had better provide at once for the years 1788, 1789 and 1790 in order to place our government at its ease, and our credit in security, during that trying interval. We set out * * * for Amsterdam.

I had prepared an estimate showing that:

There would be necessary for the year '88	531.937-10	Florins
There would be necessary for the year '89	538.540	"
There would be necessary for the year '90	473.540	"
Total	1.544.017-10	"
To meet this the bankers had in hand	79.268-2-8	florins
And the unsold bonds would yield	542.800	florins
	622.068-2-8	florins
Leaving a deficit of	921.949-7-4	florins
We proposed then to borrow a million, yielding	920.000	florins
Which would leave a small deficiency of	1.949-7-4	florins

Mr. Adams accordingly executed 1000 bonds, for 1000 florins each and deposited them in the hands of our bankers, with instructions, however, not to issue them until Congress should ratify the measure. * * * I had the satisfaction to reflect that by this journey our credit was secured, the new government was placed at ease for two years to come and that, as well as myself, relieved from the torment of incessant duns, whose just complaints could not be silenced by any means within our power.—AUTOBIOGRAPHY. i, 83. FORD ED., i, 114. (1821.)

1480. CONFEDERATION, Franklin's plan for.—I was absent from Congress from the beginning of January, 1776, to the middle of May. Either just before I left Congress, or immediately on my return to it (I rather think it was the former), Dr. Franklin put into my hands the draft of a plan of Confederation, desiring me to read it, and tell him what I thought of it. I approved it highly. He showed it to others. Some thought as I did; others were revolted at it. We found it could not be passed, and the proposing it to Congress as the subject for any vote whatever would startle many members so much, that they would suspect we had lost sight of reconciliation with Great Britain, and that we should lose much more ground than we should gain by the proposition. Yet, that the idea of a more firm bond of union than the undefined one under which we then acted might be suggested and

permitted to grow, Dr. Franklin inform Congress that he had sketched the outlines an instrument which might become necessa at a future day, if the ministry continued pe tinacious, and would ask leave for it to l on the table of Congress, that the membe might in the meantime be turning the subje in their minds, and have something mo perfect prepared by the time it should becon necessary. This was agreed to by the mo timid members, only on condition that entry whatever should be made in the jou nals of Congress relative to this instrumen This was to continue in force only till reconciliation with Great Britain. This is a that ever was done or proposed in Congre on the subject of a Confederation before Jun 1776, when the proposition was regularl made to Congress, a committee appointed draw an instrument of Confederation, wh accordingly drew one, very considerably di fering from the sketch of Dr. Franklin.— NOTES ON M. SOULÉS'S WORK. ix, 303. FOR ED., iv, 310. (P., 1786.)

1481. CONFEDERATION, Jealousy o government under.—Our first federal con stitution, or Confederation, as it was callee was framed in the first moments of our sepa ration from England, in the highest point o our jealousies of independence as to her, an as to each other. It formed, therefore, to weak a bond to produce an union of actio as to foreign nations. This appeared at onc on the establishment of peace, when the pres sure of a common enemy which had hoope us together during the war, was taken away Congress was found to be quite unable t point the action of the several States to common object. A general desire, therefore took place of amending the federal constitu tion.—To C. D. EBELING. FORD ED., vii, 4: (1795.)

1482. CONFEDERATION, Money req uisitions and.—Among the debilities of the government of the Confederation, no one wa more distinguished or more distressing than the utter impossibility of obtaining, from the States, the moneys necessary for the pay ment of debts, or even for the ordinary ex penses of the government. Some contributed a little, some less, and some nothing, and the last furnished at length an excuse for the first to do nothing also.—AUTOBIOGRAPHY. i, 82. FORD ED., i, 4. (1821.)

1483. CONFEDERATION, Perfection of.—The confederation is a wonderfully perfect instrument considering the circumstances under which it was formed.—To M. DE MEUNIER. ix, 285. FORD ED., iv, 141. (P., 1786.)

1484. ———. With all the imperfections of our present government, it is without comparison the best existing, or that ever did exist.—To E. CARRINGTON. ii, 217. FORD ED., iv, 424. (P., 1787.)

1485. CONFEDERATION, Representation under.—I learn from our delegates that the Confederation is again on the carpet, a great and a necessary work, but I fear almost desperate. The point of representation is what most alarms me, and I fear the great and small colonies are bitterly determined not to cede. Will you be so good as to collect the proposition I formerly made you in private, and try if you can work it into some good to save our union? It was, that any proposition might be negatived by the representatives of a majority of the people of America, or of a majority of the Colonies of America. The former secures the larger; the latter, the smaller Colonies. I have mentioned it to many here [Williamsburg]. The good Whigs, I think, will so far cede their opinions for the sake of the union, and others we care little for.—To John Adams. Ford ed., ii, 130. (Wg., May 1777.)

1486. CONFEDERATION, State Coercion and.—It has often been said that the decisions of Congress are impotent because the Confederation provides no compulsory power. But when two or more nations enter into compact, it is not usual for them to say what shall be done to the party who infringes it. Decency forbids this, and it is as unnecessary as indecent, because the right of compulsion naturally results to the party injured by the breach. When any one State in the American Union refuses obedience to the confederation by which they have bound themselves, the rest have a natural right to compel them to obedience. Congress would probably exercise long patience before they would recur to force; but if the case ultimately required it, they would use that recurrence. Should this case ever arise, they will probably coerce by a naval force, as being more easy, less dangerous to liberty, and less likely to produce much bloodshed.—To M. de Meunier, ix, 291. Ford ed., iv, 147. (P., 1786.) See Coercion.

1487. CONFEDERATION, The States' Committee.—The Committee of the States, which shall be appointed pursuant to the 9th article of Confederation and perpetual union, to sit in the recess of Congress for transacting the business of the United States, shall possess all the powers which may be exercised by seven States in Congress assembled, except that of sending ambassadors, ministers, envoys, resident-consuls or agents to foreign countries or courts: Establishing rules for deciding what captures on land or water shall be legal, and ᐧ what manner prizes, taken by land or naval forces in the service of the United States, shall be divided or appropriated: Establishing courts for receiving and determining finally appeals in cases of capture, constituting courts for deciding disputes and differences arising between two or more States: Fixing the standard of weights and measures for the United States: Changing the rate of postage on the papers passing through the post-offices established by Congress, and of repealing or contravening any ordinance or act passed by Congress. No question except for adjourning from day to day shall be determined without the concurrence of nine votes. A chairman to be chosen by the Committee shall preside. The

officers of Congress, when required, shall attend on the Committee. The Committee shall keep a journal of their proceedings, to be laid before Congress, and in these journals, which shall be published monthly, and transmitted to the Executives of the several States, shall be entered the yeas and nays of the members, when any one of them shall have desired it before the question be put.—Report on Com. of the States. Ford ed., iii, 392. (Jan. 1784.)

1488. ———. As the Confederation had made no provision for a visible head of the government during the vacations of Congress, and such a one was necessary to superintend the executive business, to receive and communicate with foreign ministers and nations, and to assemble Congress on sudden and extraordinary emergencies, I proposed early in April [April 14, 1784] the appointment of a committee, to be called the Committee of the States, to consist of a member from each State, who should remain in session during the recess of Congress: that the functions of Congress should be divided into executive and legislative, the latter to be reserved, and the former by a general resolution to be delegated to that Committee. This proposition was afterwards agreed to.—Autobiography. i, 54. Ford ed., i, 75. (1821.)

1489. ———. A Committee [of the States] was appointed who entered on duty on the subsequent adjournment of Congress [in 1784], quarrelled very soon, split into two parties, abandoned their post, and left the government without any visible head until the next meeting in Congress.* We have since seen the same thing take place in the Directory of France; and I believe it will forever take place in any Executive consisting of a plurality. Our plan best, I believe, combines wisdom and practicability, by providing a plurality of Counsellors, but a single Arbiter for ultimate decision.—Autobiography. i, 54. Ford ed., i, 75. (1821.)

— CONFIDENCE, Public.—See Public Confidence.

1490. CONFISCATION, George III. and.—He has incited treasonable insurrections of our fellow citizens, with the allurements of forfeiture and confiscation of our property.†—Declaration of Independence as Drawn by Jefferson.

1491. CONFISCATION, Loyalist Refugees and.—The British court had it extremely at heart to procure a restitution of the estates of the refugees who had gone over to their side [in the Revolution]; they proposed it in the first conferences [on the treaty of peace], and insisted on it to the last. Our commissioners, on the other hand, refused it from first to last, urging, 1st, that it was unreasonable to restore the confiscated property of the refugees unless they would reim-

* Jefferson adds that in speaking of this disruption of the Committee with Franklin in Paris, the latter told the famous story of the Eddystone lighthouse keepers.—Editor.
† Struck out by Congress.—Editor.

burse the destruction of the property of our citizens, committed on their part; and 2dly, that it was beyond the powers of the commissioners to stipulate, or of Congress to enforce. On this point, the treaty hung long. It was the subject of a special mission of a confidential agent of the British negotiator from Paris to London. It was still insisted on, on his return, and still protested against, by our commissioners; and when they were urged to agree only, that Congress should *recommend* to the State Legislatures to restore the estates, &c., of the refugees, they were expressly told that the Legislatures would not regard the recommendation. In proof of this, I subjoin extracts from the letters and journals of Mr. Adams and Dr. Franklin, two of our commissioners, the originals of which are among the records of the Department of State. * * * These prove, beyond all question, that the difference between an express agreement to do a thing, and to recommend it to be done, was well understood by both parties, and that the British negotiators were put on their guard by those on our part, not only that the Legislatures will be free to refuse, but that they probably would refuse. And it is evident from all circumstances, that Mr. Oswald accepted the *recommendation* merely to have something to oppose to the clamors of the *refugees*—to keep alive a hope in them that they might yet get their property from the State Legislatures; and that if they should fail in this, they would have ground to demand indemnification from their own government; and he might think it a circumstance of present relief at least, that the question of indemnification by them should be kept out of sight, till time and events should open it upon the nation insensibly. The same was perfectly understood by the British ministry, and by the members of both Houses in Parliament, as well those who advocated, as those who opposed the treaty; the latter of whom, being out of the secrets of the negotiation, must have formed their judgment on the mere import of the terms. *—To GEORGE HAMMOND. iii, 372. FORD ED., vi, 18. (Pa., May 1792.)

1492. CONFISCATION, Principles Underlying.—It cannot be denied that the state of war strictly permits a nation to seize the property of its enemies found within its own limits, or taken in war, and in whatever form it exists whether in action or possession. This is so perspicuously laid down by one of the most respectable writers on subjects of this kind, that I shall use his words. " Since it is a condition of war, that enemies may be deprived of all their rights, it is reasonable that everything of an enemy's, found among his enemies, should change its owner, and go to the treasury. It is, moreover, usually directed, in all declarations of war, that the goods of enemies, as well *those found among us*, as those taken in war, shall be confiscated. If we follow the mere right of war, even *im-*

movable property may be sold, and its price carried into the treasury, as is the custom with movable property. But in almost all Europe, it is only notified that their profits during the war, shall be received by the treasury; and the war being ended, the immovable property itself is restored, by agreement, to the former owner." Bynkersh. Quest. Jur Pub. L. 1 c. 7. Every nation, indeed, would wish to pursue the latter practice, if under circumstances leaving them their usual resources.—To GEORGE HAMMOND. iii, 369. FORD ED., vi, 15. (Pa., May 1792.)

1493. CONFISCATION, The Revolution and.—The circumstances of our war were without example; excluded from all commerce, even with neutral nations, without arms, money, or the means of getting them abroad we were obliged to avail ourselves of such resources as we found at home. Great Britain, too, did not consider it as an ordinary war but a rebellion; she did not conduct it according to the rules of war, established by the law of nations, but according to her acts of parliament, made from time to time, to suit circumstances. She would not admit our title even to the *strict rights* of ordinary war; she cannot then claim from us its *liberalities;* yet the confiscations of property were by no means universal, and that of debts still less so.—To GEORGE HAMMOND. iii, 369. FORD ED., vi, 16. (Pa., May 1792.)

1494. CONGRESS, Adjournment.—The Houses of Congress hold [the right of adjournment], not from the Constitution, but from nature.*—OFFICIAL OPINION. vii, 499. FORD ED., v, 209. (1790.) See ADJOURNMENT.

1495. ———— ————. The right of adjournment is not given by the Constitution, and consequently, it may be modified by law without interfering with that instrument.—OFFICIAL OPINION. vii, 498. FORD ED., v, 208. (1790.)

1496. CONGRESS, The Administration and.—I do not mean that any gentleman, relinquishing his own judgment, should implicitly support all the measures of the administration; but that, where he does not disapprove of them, he should not suffer them to go off in sleep, but bring them to the attention of the House, and give them a fair chance. Where he disapproves, he will of course leave them to be brought forward by those who concur in the sentiment. Shall I explain my idea by an example? The classification of the militia was communicated to General Varnum and yourself merely as a proposition which, if you approved, it was trusted you would support. I knew, indeed, that General Varnum was opposed to anything which might break up the present organization of the militia; but when so modified as to avoid this, I thought he might, perhaps, be reconciled to it. As soon as I

---

* The extract is from Jefferson's reply to Mr. Hammond, the British minister, on the infraction of the treaty of peace A summary of the confiscation laws of the different colonies is given in this masterly State paper.—EDITOR.

* In all the extracts respecting the National Legislature, the date sufficiently indicates the particular Congress—Continental, Federal, or Confederation, and United States,—to which Jefferson referred.— EDITOR.

found it did not coincide with your sentiments, I could not wish you to support it; but using the same freedom of opinion, I procured it to be brought forward elsewhere.—To Mr. BIDWELL. v, 15. (W., 1806.)

1497. —— ——. If members of Congress are to know nothing but what is important enough to be put into a public message, and indifferent enough to be made known to all the world; if the Executive is to keep all other information to himself and the House to plunge on in the dark, it becomes a government of chance and not of design.—To Mr. BIDWELL. v, 16. (W., 1806.)

1498. —— ——. When a gentleman, through zeal for the public service, undertakes to do the public business, we know that we shall hear the cant of backstairs councillors. But we never heard this while the declaimer [John Randolph] was himself a backstairs man, as he calls it, but in the confidence and views of the administration, as may more properly and respectfully be said.—To Mr. BIDWELL. v, 16. (W., 1806.)

1499. —— ——. The imputation [backstairs councillors] was one of those artifices used to despoil an adversary of his most effectual arms; and men of mind will place themselves above a gabble of this order.—To Mr. BIDWELL. v, 16. (W., 1806.)

1500. —— ——. All we have to wish is, that at the ensuing session, every one may take the part openly which he secretly befriends.—To Mr. BIDWELL. v, 17. (W., 1806.)

1501. CONGRESS, Appointment of Members.—Delegates to represent this colony [Va.] in the American Congress shall be appointed, when necessary, by the House of Representatives. After serving one year in that office, they shall not be capable of being reappointed to the same during an interval of one year. — PROPOSED VA. CONSTITUTION. FORD ED., ii, 20. (June 1776.)

1502. —— ——. The delegates to Congress shall be five in number; any three of whom, and no fewer, may be a representation. They shall be appointed by joint ballot of both houses of Assembly for any term not exceeding one year, subject to be recalled, within the term, by joint vote of both the said houses. They may, at the same time, be members of the legislative or judiciary departments, but not of the executive.—PROPOSED CONSTITUTION FOR VIRGINIA. viii, 452. FORD ED., iii, 331. (1783.)

1503. CONGRESS, Apportionment and. —No invasions of the Constitution are fundamentally so dangerous as the tricks played on their own numbers, apportionment, and other circumstances respecting themselves, and affecting their legal qualifications to legislate for the Union.—OPINION ON APPORTIONMENT BILL. vii, 601. FORD ED., v, 500. (1792.) See APPORTIONMENT.

— CONGRESS, Arrest of Members.— See 1572.

1504. CONGRESS, Attendance. — That every State should be represented in the great council of the nation, is not only the interest of each, but of the whole united, who have a right to be aided by the collective wisdom and information of the whole, in questions which are to decide on their future wellbeing. I trust that your Excellency will deem it incumbent on you to call an immediate meeting of your [Tennessee's] Legislature, in order to put it in their power to fulfil this high duty, by making special and timely provision for the representation of their State at the ensuing meeting of Congress; to which measures I am bound earnestly to exhort yourself and them. I am not insensible of the personal inconvenience of this special call to the members composing the Legislature of so extensive a State; but neither will I do them the injustice to doubt their being ready to make much greater sacrifices for the common safety, should the course of events still lead to a call for them.—To GOVERNOR SEVIER. v, 421. (W., Jan. 1809.)

1505. CONGRESS, Authority.—The authority of Congress can never be wounded without injury to the present Union.—To THE PRESIDENT OF CONGRESS. FORD ED., ii, 286. (Wg., 1779.)

1506. —— ——. The sense of Congress itself is always respectable authority.—OFFICIAL OPINION. vii, 499. FORD ED., v, 209. (1790.)

— CONGRESS, Bribery of Members.— See 1573.

1507. CONGRESS, Buildings for.—The United States should be made capable of acquiring and holding *in perpetuum* such grounds and buildings in and about the place of the session of [the Continental] Congress as may be necessary for the transaction of business by their own body, their committees and officers; each State should be made capable of acquiring and holding *in perpetuum* such grounds and buildings as they may at any time think proper to acquire and erect for the personal accommodation of their delegates; and all the grounds and buildings * * * should be exempt from taxation.—RESOLVE ON CONTINENTAL CONGRESS. FORD ED., iii, 463. (April 1784?)

1508. CONGRESS, Business Men in.— We want men of business [in Congress].* * * I am convinced it is in the power of any man who understands business, and who will undertake to keep a file of the business before Congress and press it, as he would his own docket in a court, to shorten the sessions a month one year with another, and to save in that way $30,000 a year. An ill-judged modesty prevents those from undertaking it who are equal to it. I really wish you were here.— To CÆSAR A. RODNEY. FORD ED., viii, 187. (W., Dec. 1802.)

1509. CONGRESS, Cabinet Officers in. —An attempt has been made to give further extent to the influence of the executive over the Legislature, by permitting the heads of departments to attend the House and explain their measures *vivâ voce.* But it was negatived by a majority of 35 to 11, which gives us some hope of the increase of the republican vote.—To T. M. RANDOLPH. iii, 491. FORD ED., vi. 134. (Pa., Nov. 1792.)

1510. CONGRESS, Call for Continental. —We (Patrick Henry, R. H. Lee, Francis R. Lee, Thomas Jefferson, and three or four other members of the Virginia House of Burgesses) * * * agreed to an association, and instructed the committee of correspondence to propose to the corresponding committees of the other Colonies, to appoint deputies to meet in Congress at such place, *annually,* as should be convenient, to direct from time to time, the measures required by the general interest: and we declared that an attack on any one Colony, should be considered as an attack on the whole. This was in May, 1774. We further recommended to the several counties to elect deputies to meet at Williamsburg, the 1st of August ensuing, to consider the state of the Colony, and particularly to appoint delegates to a general Congress, should that measure be acceded to by the committees of correspondence generally. It was acceded to: Philadelphia was appointed for the place, and the 5th of September for the time of meeting. —AUTOBIOGRAPHY. i, 7. FORD ED., i, 11. (1820.)

1511. CONGRESS, Compensation of Members.—You say you did not understand to what proceeding of Congress I alluded as likely to produce a removal of most of the members, and that by a spontaneous movement of the people, unsuggested by the newspapers, which had been silent on it. I alluded to the law giving themselves $1500 a year. There has never been an instant before of so unanimous an opinion of the people, and that through every State in the Union. A very few members of the first order of merit in the House will be reelected; Clay, of Kentucky, by a small majority, and a few others. But the almost entire mass will go out, not only those who supported the law or voted for it, or skulked from the vote, but those who voted against it or opposed it actively, if they took the money; and the examples of refusals to take it were very few.— To ALBERT GALLATIN. FORD ED., x, 63. (M., Sep. 1816.)

1512. —— ——. According to the opinion I hazarded to you, we have had almost an entire change in the body of Congress. The unpopularity of the compensation law was completed, by the manner of repealing it as to all the world except themselves. In some States, it is said, every member is changed: in all, many. What opposition there was to the original law, was chiefly from Southern members. Yet many of those have been left out, because they received the advanced wages. I have never known so unanimous a sentiment of disapprobation; and what is more remarkable is, that it was spontaneous. The newspapers were almost entirely silent, and the people not only unled by their leaders,

but in opposition to them. I confess I was highly pleased with this proof of the innate good sense, the vigilance, and the determination of the people to act for themselves.—To ALBERT GALLATIN. vii, 78. FORD ED., x, 90. (M., 1817.)

— **CONGRESS, Under the Confederation.**—See 1473.

1513. CONGRESS, The Constitution and.—Congress * * * [is] not a party but merely the creature of the [Federal] compact, and [is] subject, as to its assumptions of power, to the final judgment of those by whom, and for whose use, itself and its powers were all created and modified.—KENTUCKY RESOLUTIONS. ix, 469. FORD ED., vii, 302. (1798.)

1514. CONGRESS, Constitutional view of Continental.—There is one opinion in your book which I will ask you to reconsider, because it appears to me not entirely accurate, and not likely to do good. Page 362, "Congress [Continental] is not a legislative, but a diplomatic body." Separating into parts the whole sovereignty of our States, some of these parts are yielded to Congress. Upon these I should think them both legislative and executive, and that would have been judiciary also, had not the Confederation required them for certain purposes to appoint a judiciary. It has accordingly been the decision of our courts that the Confederation is a part of the law of the land, and superior in authority to the ordinary laws, because it cannot be altered by the legislature of any one State. I doubt whether they are at all a diplomatic assembly. —To JOHN ADAMS. ii, 128. (P., 1787.)

— **CONGRESS, Contempt of.**—See 1573.

1515. CONGRESS, Contracts to Members.—I am averse to giving contracts of any kind to members of the Legislature.—To ALBERT GALLATIN. v, 50. (W., 1807.)

1516. CONGRESS, Control over.—It is not from this branch of government [Congress] we have most to fear. Taxes and short elections will keep them right.—To THOMAS RITCHIE. vii, 192. FORD ED., x, 170. (M., 1820.)

1517. CONGRESS, Convening.—I have carefully considered the question whether the President may call Congress to any other place than that to which they have adjourned themselves, and think he cannot have such a right unless it has been given him by the Constitution, or the laws, and that neither of these has given it. The only circumstance which he can alter, as to their meeting is that of *time,* by calling them at an *earlier day* than that to which they stand adjourned, but no power to change the place is given. * * * I think * * * Congress must meet in Philadelphia, even if it be in the open fields, to adjourn themselves to some other place.— To PRESIDENT WASHINGTON. iv, 73. FORD ED., vi, 436. (M., Oct. 1793.)

1518. CONGRESS, Corruption and.—I told President [Washington] that it was a fact, as certainly known as that he and I were then conversing, that particular members of the Legislature, while those laws [Assumption, Funding, &c.] were on the carpet, had feathered their nests with paper, had then voted for the laws, and constantly since lent all the energy of their talents, and instrumentality of their offices, to the establishment and enlargement of the [Treasury] system.—THE ANAS. ix, 104. FORD ED., i, 177. (Feb. 1792.)

1519. —— ——. It [is] a cause of just uneasiness, when we [see] a legislature legislating for their own interests, in opposition to those of the people.—THE ANAS. ix, 118. FORD ED., i, 200. (1792.)

1520. —— ——. The capital employed in paper speculation * * * has furnished effectual means of corrupting such a portion of the Legislature, as turns the balance between the honest voters, which ever way it is directed. This corrupt squadron, deciding the voice of the Legislature, have manifested their dispositions to get rid of the limitations imposed by the Constitution on the general Legislature, limitations, on the faith of which, the States acceded to that instrument.—To PRESIDENT WASHINGTON. iii, 361. FORD ED., vi, 3. (Pa., May 1792.)

1521. —— ——. Of all the mischiefs objected to the system of measures [public debt, paper money] none is so afflicting as the corruption of the Legislature. As it was the earliest of these measures, it became the instrument for producing the rest, and will be the instrument for producing in future a king, lords and commons, or whatever else those who direct it may choose.—To PRESIDENT WASHINGTON. iii, 362. FORD ED., vi, 4. (Pa., May 1792.)

1522. ——. ——. Withdrawn such a distance from the eye of their constituents, and these so dispersed as to be inaccessible to public information, and particularly to that of the conduct of their own representatives, they will form the most corrupt government on earth, if the means of their corruption be not prevented.—To PRESIDENT WASHINGTON. iii, 362. FORD ED., vi, 4. (Pa., 1792.)

1523. —— ——. I told President Washington there was great difference between the little accidental schemes of self-interest, which would take place in every body of men, and influence their votes, and a regular system for forming a corps of interested persons, who should be steadily at the orders of the Treasury.—THE ANAS. ix, 122. FORD ED., i, 205. (1792.)

1524. —— ——. I indulge myself on one political topic only, that is, in declaring to my countrymen the shameless corruption of a portion of the representatives to the first and second Congresses, and their implicit devotion to the Treasury. I think I do good in this, because it may produce exertions to reform the evil, on the success of which the form of the government is to depend.—To EDMUND RANDOLPH. iv, 101. FORD ED., vi, 498. (M., Feb. 1794.)

1525. —— ——. Alexander Hamilton avowed the opinion that man could be governed by one of two motives only, force or interest. Force, he observed, in this country was out of the question; and the interests, therefore, of the members must be laid hold of to keep the Legislature in unison with the Executive. And with grief and shame it must be acknowledged that his machine was not without effect; that even in this, the birth of our government, some members were found sordid enough to bend their duty to their interests, and to look after personal rather than public good.—THE ANAS. ix, 91. FORD ED., i, 160. (1818.)

1526. CONGRESS, Credentials of Members.—We have had hopes till to-day of receiving an authentication of the next year's delegation [to the Continental Congress], but are disappointed. I know not who should have sent it,—the Governor, or President of the convention; but certainly somebody should have done it. What will be the consequence, I know not. We cannot be admitted to take our seat on any precedent, or the spirit of any precedent yet set. According to the standing rules, not only an authentic copy will be required, but it must be entered in the journals verbatim, that it may there appear we have right to sit.—To JOHN PAGE. FORD ED., ii, 74. (Pa., 1776.)

1527. —— ——. Some of the newspapers indeed mention that on such a day, such and such gentlemen were appointed to serve for the next year, but could newspaper evidence be received? They could not furnish the form of the appointment.—To JOHN PAGE. FORD ED., ii, 75. (Pa., 1776.)

— CONGRESS, Debate in.—See 1571.

1528. CONGRESS, Delegates.—Until their admission by their delegates into Congress, any of the said States, after the establishment of their temporary Government, shall have authority to keep a sitting member in Congress, with a right of debating, but not of voting.—WESTERN TERRITORY REPORT. FORD ED., iii, 409. (1784.)

1529. CONGRESS, Election of Members. —An election [of members of Congress] by districts would be best, if it could be general; but while ten States choose either by their legislatures or by a general ticket, it is folly and worse than folly for the other six not to do it. In these ten States the minority is entirely unrepresented; and their majorities not only have the weight of their whole State in their scale, but have the benefit of so much of our minorities as can succeed at a district election. This is, in fact, ensuring to our minorities the appointment of the Government. To state it in another form, it is merely a question whether we will divide the United States into sixteen or one hundred and thirty-seven districts. The latter being more chequered, and representing the people in smaller sections, would be more likely to be an exact representation of their diversified sentiments. But a representation of a part by great, and a part by small sections, would give a result very different from what would be the sentiment of the whole people of the United States, were they assembled together. —To JAMES MONROE. iv, 308. FORD ED., vii, 401. (Pa., 1800.)

1530. CONGRESS, Executive influence. —The republicans complain that the influence and patronage of the Executive are to become so great as to govern the Legislature. They endeavored a few days ago to take away one means of influence by condemning references to the heads of departments. They failed by a majority of five votes. They were more successful in their endeavor to prevent the introduction of a new means of influence, that of admitting the heads of departments to deliberate occasionally in the House in explanation of their measures.—To THOMAS PINCKNEY. iii, 493. FORD ED., vi, 143. (Pa., 1792.)

1531. CONGRESS, Executive information.—The Secretary of the Treasury [Alexander Hamilton] has been guilty of indecorum to this House, in undertaking to judge of its motives in calling for information which was demandable of him, from the constitution of his office; and in failing to give all the necessary information within his knowledge, relatively to the subjects of the reference made to him of the 19th, January, 1792, and of the 22d November, 1792, during the present session.—GILES TREASURY RESOLUTIONS. FORD ED., VI, 170. (1793.)

1532. CONGRESS, Expenditures and.— The subject of the debates was, whether the representatives of the people were to have no check on the expenditure of the public money, and the Executive to squander it at their will, leaving to the Legislature only the drudgery of furnishing the money. They begin to open their eyes on this to the Eastward, and to suspect they have been hoodwinked.— To EDMUND PENDLETON. iv, 229. FORD ED., vii, 228. (Pa., April 1798.)

1533. CONGRESS, Farmers in.—The only corrective of what is corrupt in our present form of government will be the augmentation of the members in the lower House so as to get a more agricultural representation, which may put that interest above that of the stock-jobbers.—To GEORGE MASON. iii, 209. FORD ED., v, 275. (Pa., 1791.)

1534. CONGRESS, Foreign Powers and. —The Legislature should never show itself in a matter with a foreign nation, but where the case is very serious, and they mean to commit the nation on its issue.—To JAMES MADISON. iii, 296. FORD ED., v, 391. (1791.)

1535. CONGRESS, Influencing.—As I never had the desire to influence the members, so neither had I any other means than my friendships, which I valued too highly to risk by usurpation on their freedom of judgment, and the conscientious pursuit of their own sense of duty.—To PRESIDENT WASHINGTON. iii, 460. FORD ED., vi, 102. (M., 1792.)

1536. —— ——. If it has been supposed that I have ever intrigued among the members of the Legislature to defeat the plans of the Secretary of the Treasury, it is contrary to all truth. * * * That I have utterly, in my private conversations, disapproved of the system of the Secretary of the Treasury, I acknowledge and avow; and this was not merely a speculative difference.—To PRESIDENT WASHINGTON. iii, 460. FORD ED., vi, 102. (M., 1792.)

— CONGRESS, Instructing Members.— See INSTRUCTIONS.

— CONGRESS, Insult to Members.—See 1572, 1575.

1537. CONGRESS, Intermeddling with. —With the affairs of the Legislature, I never did intermeddle.—To PRESIDENT WASHINGTON. iii, 467. FORD ED., vi, 108. (M., 1792.)

1538. —— ——. When I embarked in the government, it was with a determination to intermeddle not at all with the Legislature.— To PRESIDENT WASHINGTON. iii, 460. FORD ED., vi, 102. (M., 1792.)

1539. CONGRESS, Jobbery in.—I have always observed that in questions of expense, where members may hope either for offices or jobs for themselves or their friends, some few will be debauched, and that is sufficient to turn the decision where a majority is, at most, but small.—To JAMES MADISON. iv, 103. FORD ED., vi, 503. (M., April 1794.)

1540. CONGRESS, The Judiciary vs.— Were I called upon to decide whether the people had best be omitted in the Legislative or Judiciary department, I would say it is better to leave them out of the Legislative. The execution of the laws is more important than the making them.—To M. L'ABBÉ ARNOND. iii, 82. FORD ED., v, 104. (P., 1789.)

1541. CONGRESS, Lawyers in.—I have much doubted whether, in case of a war, Congress would find it practicable to do their part of the business. That a body containing one hundred lawyers in it, should direct the measures of a war, is, I fear, impossible; and that thus that member of our Constitution, which is its bulwark, will prove to be an impracticable one from its cacoethes loquendi. It may be doubted how far it has the power, but I am sure it has not the resolution to reduce the right of talking to practicable limits.—To PRESIDENT MADISON. FORD ED., ix, 337. (M., Feb. 1812.)

1542. —— ——. How can expedition be expected from a body which we have saddled with an hundred lawyers, whose trade is talking.—To THOMAS LEIPER. vi, 466. FORD ED., ix, 521. (M., 1815.) See DEBATE, LAWYERS.

1543. CONGRESS, Leadership in.—I wish sincerely you were back in the Senate; and that you would take the necessary measures to get yourself there. Perhaps, as a preliminary, you should go to our [Virginia] Legislature. * * * A majority of the Senate means well. But Tracy and Bayard are too dexterous for them, and have very much influenced their proceedings. Tracy has been of nearly every committee during the session, and for the most part the chairman, and of course drawer of the reports. Seven federalists voting always in phalanx, and joined by some discontented republicans, some oblique ones, some capricious, have so often made a majority, as to produce very serious embarrassment to the public operations; and very much do I dread the submitting to them, at the next session, any treaty which can be made with either England or Spain, when I consider that five joining the federalists, can defeat a friendly settlement of our affairs.—To WILSON C. NICHOLAS. v, 4. FORD ED., viii, 435. (W., April 1806.)

1544. —— ——. The House of Representatives is as well disposed as I ever saw one. The defection of so prominent a leader [John Randolph], threw them into dismay and confusion for a moment; but they soon rallied to their own principles, and let him go off with five or six followers only. One half of these are from Virginia. His late declaration of perpetual opposition to this administration, drew off a few others who at first had joined him, supposing his opposition occasional only, and not systematic. The alarm the House has had from this schism, has produced a rallying together and a harmony, which carelessness and security had begun to endanger. On the whole, this little trial of the firmness of our representatives in their principles, and that of the people also, which is declaring itself in support of their public functionaries, has added much to my confidence in the stability of our government; and to my conviction, that, should things go wrong at any time, the people will set them to rights by the peaceable exercise of their elective rights.—To WILSON C. NICHOLAS. v, 5. FORD ED., viii, 435. (W., April 1806.)

1545. —— ——. There never was a time when the services of those who possess talents, integrity, firmness, and sound judgment, were more wanted in Congress. Some one of that description is particularly wanted to take the lead in the House of Representatives, to consider the business of the nation as his own business, to take it up as if he were singly charged with it, and carry it through. I do not mean that any gentleman, relinquishing his own judgment, should implicitly support all the measures of the administration; but that, where he does not disapprove of them, he should not suffer them to go off in sleep, but bring them to the attention of the House, and give them a fair chance. Where he disapproves, he will of course leave them to be brought forward by those who concur in the sentiment.—To MR. BIDWELL. v, 15. (W., 1806.)

1546. —— ——. Mr. T. M. Randolph is, I believe, determined to retire from Congress, and it is strongly his wish, and that of all here, that you should take his place. Never did the calls of patriotism more loudly assail you than at this moment. After excepting

the Federalists who will be twenty-seven, and the little band of schismatics, who will be three or four (all tongue), is as well-disposed House of Representatives is as well-disposed a body of men as I ever saw collected. But there is no one whose talents and standing, taken together, have weight enough to give him the lead. The consequence is, that there is no one who will undertake to do the public business, and it remains undone. Were you here, the whole would rally round you in an instant, and willingly cooperate in whatever is for the public good. Nor would it require you to undertake drudgery in the House. There are enough, able and willing to do that. A rallying point is all that is wanting. Let me beseech you, then, to offer yourself.—To WILSON C. NICHOLAS. v, 48. FORD ED., ix, 32. (W., 1807.)

1547. CONGRESS, Legislation and.— Whatever of the enumerated objects [in the Constitution] is proper for a law, Congress may make the law.—To WILSON C. NICHOLAS. iv, 506. FORD ED., viii, 248. (M., 1803.)

— CONGRESS, Long speeches in.—See 1571 and 1579.

1548. CONGRESS, Majority.—What [you ask] has led Congress to determine that the concurrence of seven votes is requisite in questions which, by the Confederation, are submitted to the decision of a majority of the United States, in Congress assembled? The ninth article of Confederation, section six, evidently establishes three orders of questions in Congress. 1. The greater ones, which relate to making peace or war, alliances, coinage, requisitions for money, raising military force, or appointing its commander-in-chief. 2. The lesser ones, which comprehend all other matters submitted by the Confederation to the federal head. 3. The single question of adjourning from day to day. This gradation of questions is distinctly characterized by the article. In proportion to the magnitude of these questions, a greater concurrence of the voices composing the Union was thought necessary. Three degrees of concurrence, well distinguished by substantial circumstances, offered themselves to notice. 1. A concurrence of a *majority of the people* of the Union. It was thought that this would be ensured by requiring the voices of nine States; because according to the loose estimates which had been made of the inhabitants, and the proportion of them which were free, it was believed that even the nine smallest would include a majority of the free citizens of the Union. The voices, therefore, of nine States were required in the greater questions. 2. A concurrence of the *majority of the States.* Seven constitute that majority. This number, therefore, was required in the lesser questions. 3. A concurrence of the *majority of Congress*, that is to say, of the States actually present in it. As there is no Congress, when there are not seven States present, this concurrence could never be of less than four States. But these might happen to be the four smallest, which would not include one-ninth part of the free citizens of the Union. This kind of majority, therefore, was entrusted with nothing but the power of adjourning themselves from day to day. Here, then, are three kinds of majorities. 1. Of the people. 2. Of the States. 3. Of the Congress; each of which is entrusted to a certain length.—To M. DE MEUNIER. ix, 244. FORD ED., iv, 148. (P., 1786.)

1549. CONGRESS, Messages to.—The first communication to the next Congress will be, like all subsequent ones, by me sage, to which no answer will be expected.—To NATHANIEL MACON. iv, 39⁶. FORD ED., viii, 52. (W., May 1801.)

1550. —— ——. The circumstances under which we find ourselves placed rendering inconvenient the mode heretofore practiced of making, by personal address, the first communications between the Legislative and Executive branches, I have adopted that by message, as used on all subsequent occasions through the session. In doing this, I have had principal regard to the convenience of the Legislature, to the economy of their time, to their relief from the embarrassment of immediate answers on subjects not yet fully before them, and to the benefits thence resulting to the public affairs. Trusting that a procedure founded on these motives will meet their approbation, I beg leave through you, Sir, to communicate the enclosed message, with the documents accompanying it, to the honorable the Senate, * * * .—To THE PRESIDENT OF THE SENATE. iv, 423. FORD ED., viii, 108. (W., Dec. 1801.)

1551. —— ——. By sending a message, instead of making a speech, * * * I have prevented the bloody conflict to which the making an answer would have committed them. They consequently were able to set into real business at once, without losing ten or twelve days in combating an answer.—To DR. BENJAMIN RUSH. iv, 426. FORD ED., viii, 127. (W., 1801.)

1552. CONGRESS, Mutiny against.—The conduct of [the Federation] Congress was marked with indignation and firmness. They received no propositions from the mutineers. They came to the resolutions which may be seen in the journals of June the 21st, 1783, then adjourned regularly, and went through the body of the mutineers to their respective lodgings. The measures taken by Dickinson, the President of Pennsylvania, for punishing this insult, not being satisfactory to Congress, they assembled, nine days after, at Princeton, in Jersey. The people of Pennsylvania sent petitions declaring their indignation at what passed, their devotion to the federal head, and their dispositions to protect it, and praying them to return; the Legislature, as soon as assembled, did the same thing; the Executive, whose irresolution had been so exceptionable, made apologies. But Congress was now removed; and, to the opinion that this example was proper, other causes were now added, sufficient to *prevent* their return to

Philadelphia.—To M. DE MEUNIER. ix, 258. FORD ED., iv, 163. (Pa., 1786.)

1553. CONGRESS, Non-attendance.—It is now above a fortnight since Congress should have met, and six States only appear. We have some hopes of Rhode Island coming in to-day, but when two more will be added seems as insusceptible of calculation as when the next earthquake will happen.—To JAMES MADISON. FORD ED., iii, 347. (A., Dec. 1783.)

1554. —— ——. I am sorry to say that I see no immediate prospect of making up nine States [requisite to ratify the definitive treaty of peace with Great Britain], so careless are either the States or their delegates to their particular interests, as well as the general good which would require that they be all constantly and fully represented in Congress.—To GOVERNOR BENJ. HARRISON. FORD ED., iii, 350. (A., Dec. 1783.)

1555. —— ——. We have never yet had more than seven States [in attendance], and very seldom that, a Maryland is scarcely ever present, and we are now without a hope of its attending till February. Consequently, having six States only we do nothing. Expresses and letters are gone forth to hasten on the absent States, that we may have nine for a ratification of the definitive treaty. Jersey perhaps may come in, and if Beresford will not come to Congress, Congress must go to him to do this one act.—To JAMES MADISON. FORD ED., iii, 371. (A., Jan. 1, 1784.)

1556. —— ——. We have but nine States present, seven of which are represented by only two members each. There are fourteen gentlemen, then, any one of whom differing from the rest, stops our proceeding on questions requiring the concurrence of nine States. * * * It is my expectation that after having tried several of these questions successively, and finding it impossible to obtain a single determination, Congress will find it necessary to adjourn till the Spring, first informing the States that they adjourn because from the inattendance of members their business cannot be done, recommending to them to instruct and *enable* their members to come on at the day appointed, and that they constantly keep three at least with Congress while it shall be sitting. I believe if we had thirteen States present represented by three members each, we could clear off our business in two or three months, and hereafter a session of two or three months in the year could suffice.—To GOVERNOR BENJ. HARRISON. FORD ED., iii, 379. (A., Jan. 1784.)

1557. —— ——. We cannot make up a Congress at all. There are eight States in town, six of which are represented by two members only. Of these, two members of different States are confined by the gout, so that we cannot make a House. We have not sat above three days, I believe, in as many weeks. Admonition after admonition has been sent to the States, to no effect. We have sent one to-day. If it fails, it seems as well we should all retire. There have never been nine States on the floor but for the ratification of the treaty [of peace with England] and a day or two after.—To JAMES MADISON. FORD ED., iii, 399. (A., Feb. 20, 1784.)

1558. —— ——. We have only nine States present, eight of which are represented by two members each and, of course, on all great questions not only an unanimity of States but of members is necessary, an unanimity which can never be obtained on a matter of any importance. The consequence is that we are wasting our time and labor in vain efforts to do business. Nothing less than the presence of thirteen States, represented by an odd number of delegates, will enable us to get forward a single capital point.—To GEORGE WASHINGTON. FORD ED., iii, 420. (A., 1784.)

1559. —— ——. Delaware and South Carolina, we lost within these two days by the expiration of their powers. The other absent States are New York, Maryland and Georgia. We have done nothing, and can do nothing in this condition, but waste our time, temper, and spirits, in debating things for days and weeks and then losing them by the negative of one or two individuals.—To JAMES MADISON. FORD ED., iii, 426. (A., 1784.)

1560. CONGRESS, Opportunity and.— Congress is the great commanding theatre of this nation, and the threshold to whatever department of office a man is qualified to enter.—To WILLIAM WIRT. v, 233. (W., 1808.)

1561. CONGRESS, Opposition in.—You now see the composition of our public bodies, and how essential system and plan are for conducting our affairs wisely with so bitter a party in opposition to us, who look not at all to what is best for the public, but how they may thwart whatever we may propose, though they should thereby sink their country.—To CÆSAR A. RODNEY. FORD ED., viii, 296. (W., 1804.)

1562. CONGRESS, Parliament and.— There is a difference between the British Parliament and our Congress. The former is a legislature, an inquest and a council for the king. The latter is, by the Constitution, a legislature and an inquest, but not a council. —THE ANAS. ix, 113. FORD ED., i, 190. (1792.)

1563. CONGRESS, Partisan.— I had hoped that the proceedings of this session of Congress would have rallied the great body of our citizens at once to one opinion. But the inveteracy of their quondam leaders has been able by intermingling the grossest lies and misrepresentations to check the effect in some small degree until they shall be exposed. The great sources and authors of these are in Congress. Besides the slanders in their speeches, such letters have been written to their constituents as I shall forbear to qualify by the proper terms.—To CÆSAR A. RODNEY. FORD ED., viii, 147. (W., April 1802.)

1564. —— ——. And what is our resource for the preservation of the Constitution? Reason and argument? You might as well reason and argue with the marble columns encircling them. The representatives chosen by ourselves? They are joined in the combination, some from incorrect views of government, some from corrupt ones, sufficient voting together to outnumber the sound parts; and with majorities only of one, two, or three, bold enough to go forward in defiance.—To W. B. GILES. vii, 427. FORD ED., x, 355. (M., 1825.)

1565. CONGRESS, The People and.—I look for our safety to the broad representation of the people [in Congress]. It will be more difficult for corrupt views to lay hold of so large a mass.—To T. M. RANDOLPH. FORD ED., v, 455. (Pa., 1792.)

1566. —— ——. The only hope of safety hangs now on the numerous representation which is to come forward the ensuing year. Some of the new members will be, probably, either in principle or interest, with the present majority, but it is expected that the great mass will form an accession to the republican party. They will not be able to undo all which the two preceding Legislatures, and especially the first, have done. Public faith and right will oppose this. But some parts of the system may be rightfully reformed, a liberation from the rest unremittingly pursued as fast as right will permit, and the door shut in future against similar commitments of the nation.—To PRESIDENT WASHINGTON. iii, 362. FORD ED., vi, 4. (Pa., May 1792.)

1567. CONGRESS, Power over papers. —At a meeting of the cabinet the subject [of discussion] was the resolution of the House of Representatives of March 27, to appoint a committee to inquire into the causes of the failure of the late expedition under Major General St. Clair, with power to call for such persons, papers and records as may be necessary to assist their inquiries. The President [Washington] said he had called us to consult, merely because it was the first example, and he wished that so far as it should become a precedent, it should be rightly conducted. He neither acknowledged nor denied, nor even doubted the propriety of what the House were doing, for he had not thought upon it, nor was acquainted with subjects of this kind. He could readily conceive there might be papers of so secret a nature as that they ought not to be given up. [The cabinet was not then ready to give their opinions, but another meeting was held two days later when] we had all considered and were of one mind: 1. That the House was an inquest, and, therefore, might institute inquiries. 2. That it might call for papers generally. 3. That the Executive ought to communicate such papers as the public good would permit, and ought to refuse those, the disclosure of which would injure the public. Consequently, [they] were to exercise discretion. 4. That neither the Committee nor the House had a right to call on the head of a Department, who and whose papers were under the President alone; but that the Committee should instruct their Chairman to move the House to address the President. * * * Hamilton agreed with us in all these points except as to the power of the House to call on the heads of Departments. He observed, that as to his Department, the act constituting it had made it subject to Congress in some points, but he thought himself not so far subject, as to be obliged to produce all papers they might call for. They might demand secrets of a very mischievous nature. * * * I observed here a difference between the British Parliament and our Congress, that the former was a legislature, an inquest, and a council for the King. The latter was, by the Constitution, a legislature and an inquest but not a council. [It was] finally agreed, to speak [separately] to the members of the Committee, and bring them by persuasion into the right channel. It was agreed in this case, that there was not a paper which might not be properly produced, that copies only should be sent, with an assurance, that if they should desire it, a clerk should attend with the originals to be verified by themselves.—THE ANAS. ix, 112. FORD ED., i, 189. (April 1792.)

1568. CONGRESS, Prayer in.—I enclose you (to amuse your curiosity) the form of the prayer substituted in the room of the prayer for the King by Mr. Duché, chaplain to the Congress. I think by making it so general as to take in conventions, assemblies, &c., it might be used instead of that for the Parliament.—To JOHN PAGE. FORD ED., ii, 75. (Pa., 1776.)

1569. CONGRESS, Precedence.—As the United States in Congress assembled, represent the sovereignty of the whole Union, their body collectively, and their President individually, should on all occasions have precedence of all other bodies and persons.—CONGRESS RESOLUTION. FORD ED., iii, 464. (1784?)

1570. ———— ————. During the recess of Congress the Committee of the States, being left to pursue the same objects and under the same circumstances, their body, their members and their President, should respectively be placed on the same footing with the body, the members, and the President of Congress.— CONGRESS RESOLUTION. FORD ED., iii, 464. (April 1784?)

1571. CONGRESS, Previous question in.—I observe the House is endeavoring to remedy the eternal protraction of debate by sitting up all night, or by the use of the previous question. Both will subject them to the most serious inconvenience. The latter may be turned upon themselves by a trick of their adversaries. I have thought that such a rule as the following would be more effectual and less inconvenient: "Resolved, that at [VIII.] o'clock in the evening (whenever the House shall be in session at that hour) it shall be the duty of the Speaker to declare that hour arrived, whereupon all debate shall cease. If there be then before the House a main question for the reading or passing of a bill,

resolution or order, such main question shall immediately be put by the Speaker, and decided by yeas and nays. If the question before the House be secondary, as for amendment, commitment, postponement, adjournment of the debate or question, laying on the table, reading papers, or a previous question, such secondary (or any other which may delay the main question) shall stand *ipso facto* discharged, and the main question shall then be before the House, and shall be immediately put and decided by yeas and nays. But a motion for adjournment of the House, may once and once only, take place of the main question, and if decided in the negative, the main question shall then be put as before. Should any question of order arise, it shall be decided by the Speaker instanter, and without debate or appeal; and questions of privilege arising, shall be postponed till the main question be decided. Messages from the President or Senate may be received but not acted on till after the decision of the main question. But this rule shall be suspended during the [three] last days of the session of Congress." No doubt this, on investigation, will be found to need amendment; but I think the principle of it better adapted to meet the evil than any other which has occurred to me.—To J. W. EPPES. v, 491. FORD ED., ix, 268. (M., 1810.)

1572. CONGRESS, Privilege.—Delegates to Congress ought to be invested in the place where they may be sitting with such privileges and immunities as will cover them from molestation and disturbance, and leave them in freedom and tranquillity to apply their whole time and attention to the objects of their delegation. * * * Long experience has led the civilized nations of Europe to an ascertainment of those principles and immunities, which may enable the representatives of an independent nation, exercising high functions within another, to do the same unawed and undisturbed, and, therefore, the privileges and immunities annexed by the law and usage of nations to such characters should be allowed to the Congress of the United States collectively, and to their members individually, by the laws of the States in and adjacent to which they may be sitting, and should be secured in their continuance by sufficient sanctions.—RESOLVE ON CONTINENTAL CONGRESS. FORD ED., iii, 463. (April 1784?)

1573. ———— ————. In December, 1795, the House of Representatives committed two persons of the names of Randall and Whitney, for attempting to corrupt the integrity of certain members, which they considered as a contempt and breach of the privileges of the House; and the facts being proved, Whitney was detained in confinement a fortnight, and Randall three weeks, and was reprimanded by the Speaker. In March, 1796, the House of Representatives voted a challenge given to a member of their House, to be a breach of the privileges of the House; but satisfactory apologies and acknowledgments being made, no further proceedings were had. The editor of the *Aurora* having in his paper of February 19, 1800, inserted some paragraphs defamatory to the Senate, and failed in his appearance, he was ordered to be committed. In debating the legality of this order, it was insisted in support of it, that every man, by the law of nature, and every body of men, possesses the right of self-defence; that all public functionaries are essentially invested with the powers of self-preservation; that they have an inherent right to do all acts necessary to keep themselves in a condition to discharge the trusts confided to them; that whenever authorities are given, the means of carrying them into execution are given by necessary implication; that thus we see the British Parliament exercise the right of punishing contempts; all the State Legislatures exercise the same power; and every Court does the same; that if we have it not, we sit at the mercy of every intruder who may enter our doors or gallery, and by noise and tumult render proceeding in business impracticable; that if our tranquillity is to be perpetually disturbed by newspaper defamation, it will not be possible to exercise our functions with the requisite coolness and deliberation; and that we must, therefore, have a power to punish these disturbers of our peace and proceedings. To this it was answered, that the Parliament and Courts of England have cognizance of contempts by the express provisions of their law; that the State Legislatures have equal authority, because their powers are plenary; they represent their constituents completely, and possess all their powers, except such as their Constitutions have expressly denied them; that the Courts of the several States have the same powers by the laws of their States, and those of the Federal Government by the same State laws, adopted in each State by a law of Congress; that none of these bodies, therefore, derive those powers from natural or necessary right, but from express law; that Congress have no such natural or necessary power, nor any powers but such as are given them by the Constitution; that that has given them directly exemption from personal arrest; exemption from question elsewhere for what is said in the House, and power over their own members and proceedings; for these, no further law is necessary, the Constitution being the law; that, moreover, by that article of the Constitution which authorizes them " to make all laws necessary and proper for carrying into execution the powers vested by the Constitution in them," they may provide by law for an undisturbed exercise of their functions, c. g. for the punishment of contempts, of affrays, or tumults in their presence, &c.; but, till the law be made, it does not exist; and does not exist, from their own neglect; that in the meantime, however, they are not unprotected, the ordinary magistrates and courts of law being open and competent to punish all unjustifiable disturbances or defamations, and even their own sergeant, who may appoint deputies *ad libitum* to aid him (3 *Grey*, 59. 147, 255), is equal to the smallest disturbances; that, in requiring a previous law, the Constitution has regard to the inviolability of the citizen as well as of the member; as, should one House, in the regular form of a bill, aim at too broad privileges, it may be checked by the other, and both by the President; and also as, the law being promulgated, the citizen will know how to avoid offence. But, if one branch may assume its own privileges without control; if it may do it on the spur of the occasion, conceal the law in its own breast, and after the fact committed make its sentence both the law and the judgment on that fact; if the offence is to be kept undefined, and to be declared only *ex re nata*, and according to the passions of the moment, and there be no limitation either in the manner or measure of the punishment, the condition of the citizen will be perilous indeed. Which of these doctrines is to prevail, time will decide. Where there is no fixed law, the judgment on any particular case is the law of that single case only, and dies with it. When a new and even similar case arises, the judgment which is to make, and, at the same time, apply, the law, is open to question and consideration, as are all new laws. Perhaps Congress, in the meantime, in their care for the safety of the citizen, as well as that for their own protection, may declare by law what is necessary and proper to enable them to carry into execution the powers vested in them, and thereby hang up a rule for the inspection of all, which may direct the conduct of the citizen, and, at the same time, test the judgments they shall themselves pronounce in their own case.—PARLIAMENTARY MANUAL. ix, 9.

1574. —— ——. It was probably from this view* of the encroaching character of privilege, that the framers of our Constitution, in their care to provide that the laws shall bind equally on all, and especially that those who make them shall not be exempt themselves from their operation, have only privileged " Senators and Representatives " themselves from the single act of arrest in all cases except treason, felony, and breach of the peace, during their attendance at the session of their respective Houses, and in going to and returning from the same, and from being questioned in any other place for any speech or debate in either House.—PARLIAMENTARY MANUAL. ix, 8.

1575. —— ——. J. Randolph * * * used an unguarded word in his first speech [on the bill suspending intercourse with France], applying the word " ragamuffin " to the common soldiery. He took it back of his own accord, and very handsomely, the next day, when he had occasion to reply. Still, in the evening of the second day, he was jostled, and his coat pulled at the theatre by two officers of the

* "The maxims upon which they[Parliament] proceed, together with the method of proceeding, rest entirely in their own breast, and are not defined and ascertained by any particular stated laws." — 1 BLACKSTONE, 163, 164.

Navy, who repeated the word "ragamuffin." His friends present supported him spiritedly, so that nothing further followed. Conceiving, and. as I think justly, that the House of Representatives (not having passed a law on the subject) could not punish the offenders, he wrote a letter to the President, who laid it before the House. * * * He has conducted himself with great propriety, and I have no doubt will come out with increase of reputation, being determined himself to oppose the interposition of the House when they have no law for it.—To MARY JEFFERSON EPPES. FORD ED., vii, 404. (Pa., Jan. 1800.)

1576. CONGRESS, Public Opinion and. —I think it a duty in those entrusted with the administration of their affairs to conform themselves to the decided choice of their constituents.—To JOHN JAY. i, 404. FORD ED., iv, 89. (P., 1785.)

1577. CONGRESS, Qualifications of Members.—You ask my opinion on the question, whether the States can add any qualifications to those which the Constitution has prescribed for their members of Congress? It is a question I had never before reflected on; yet had taken up an off-hand opinion, agreeing with your first, that they could not; that to add new qualifications to those of the Constitution, would be as much an alteration as to detract from them. And so I think the House of Representatives decided in some case; I believe that of a member from Baltimore. But your letter having induced me to look into the Constitution, and to consider the question a little, I am again in your predicament, of doubting the correctness of my first opinion. Had the Constitution been silent, nobody can doubt but that the right to prescribe all the qualifications and disqualifications of those they would send to represent them, would have belonged to the State. So also the Constitution might have prescribed the whole, and excluded all others. It seems to have preferred the middle way. It has exercised the power in part, by declaring some disqualifications, to wit, those of not being twenty-five years of age, of not having been a citizen seven years, and of not being an inhabitant of the State at the time of election. But it does not declare, itself, that the member shall not be a lunatic, a pauper, a convict of treason, of murder, of felony, or other infamous crime, or a non-resident of his district; nor does it prohibit to the State the power of declaring these, or any other disqualifications which its particular circumstances may call for: and these may be different in different States. Of course, then, by the tenth amendment, the power is reserved to the State. If, wherever the Constitution assumes a single power out of many which belong to the same subject, we should consider it as assuming the whole, it would vest the General Government with a mass of power never contemplated. On the contrary, the assumption of particular powers seems an exclusion of all not assumed. This reasoning appears to me to be sound; but, on so recent a

change of view, caution requires us not to be too confident, and that we admit this to be one of the doubtful questions on which honest men may differ with the purest motives; and the more readily, as we find we have differed from ourselves on it.—To JOSEPH C. CABELL. vi, 309. FORD ED., ix, 451. (M., 1814.)

1578. ———— ————. I have always thought that where the line of demarcation between the powers of the General and the State governments was doubtfully or indistinctly drawn, it would be prudent and praiseworthy in both parties, never to approach it but under the most urgent necessity. Is the necessity now urgent, to declare that no non-resident of his district shall be eligible as a member of Congress? It seems to me that, in practice, the partialities of the people are a sufficient security against such an election; and that if, in any instance, they should ever choose a non-resident, it must be one of such eminent merit and qualifications, as would make it a good, rather than an evil; and that, in any event, the examples will be so rare, as never to amount to a serious evil. If the case then be neither clear nor urgent, would it not be better to let it lie undisturbed? Perhaps its decision may never be called for. But if it be indispensable to establish this disqualification now, would it not be better to declare such others, at the same time, as may be proper?—To JOSEPH C. CABELL. vi, 310. FORD ED., ix, 452. (M., Jan. 1814.)

1579. CONGRESS, Reconsideration.— "How far" [you ask] "is it permitted to bring on the reconsideration of a question which Congress has once determined?" The first Congress which met, being composed mostly of persons who had been members of the legislatures of their respective States, it was natural for them to adopt those rules in their proceedings to which they had been accustomed in their legislative houses; and the more so, as there happened to be nearly the same, as having been copied from the same original, those of the British Parliament. One of these rules of proceeding was, that "a question, once determined, cannot be proposed a second time in the same session." Congress, during the first session, in the autumn of 1774, observed this rule strictly. But before their meeting in the spring of the following year, the war had broken out. They found themselves at the head of that war, in an Executive as well as Legislative capacity. They found that a rule, wise and necessary for a legislative body, did not suit an executive one, which, being governed by events, must change their purposes, as those change. Besides, their session was likely then to become of equal duration with the war; and a rule, which should render their legislation immutable during all that period could not be submitted to. They, therefore, renounced it in practice, and have ever since continued to reconsider their questions freely. The only restraint as yet provided against the abuse of this permission to reconsider, is that when a question has been decided, it cannot be proposed for reconsideration but by some one who voted in favor of the former decision, and declares that he has since changed his opinion.—Answers to M. de Meunier. ix, 246. Ford ed., iv, 149. (P., 1786.)

1580. CONGRESS, Reform and.—They [new Congress] will not be able to undo all which the two preceding Legislatures, and especially the first, have done. Public faith and. right will oppose this. But some parts of the system may be rightfully reformed, a liberation from the rest unremittingly pursued as fast as right will permit, and the door shut in future against similar commitments of the nation.—To President Washington. iii, 362. Ford ed., vi, 4. (Pa., 1792.)

1581. —— ——. The representatives of the people in Congress are alone competent to judge of the general disposition of the people, and to what precise point of reformation they are ready to go.—To Mr. Rutherford. iii, 499. (Pa., 1792.)

1582. —— ——. The session of the first Congress, convened since republicanism has recovered its ascendancy, * * * will pretty completely fulfil all the desires of the people. They have reduced the army and navy to what is barely necessary. .They are disarming executive patronage and preponderance, by putting down one-half the offices of the United States, which are no longer necessary. These economies have enabled them to suppress all the internal taxes, and still to make such provision for the payment of their public debt as to discharge that in eighteen years. They have lopped off a parasite limb, planted by their predecessors on their judiciary for party purposes, and they are opening the doors of hospitality to the fugitives from the oppressions of other countries.—To General Kosciusko. iv, 430. (W., April 1802.)

1583. CONGRESS, Republicanism and. —In the General Government, the House of Representatives is mainly republican; * * * as elected by the people directly.—To John Taylor. vi, 607. Ford ed., x, 30. (M., 1816.)

— CONGRESS, Residence of Members.— See 1577, 1578.

1584. CONGRESS, Rules for.—No person to read printed papers. Every Colony present, unless divided, to be counted. No person to vote unless present when the question is put. No person to walk while the question is putting. Every person to sit while not speaking. Orders of day at 12 o'clock. Amendments first proposed to be first put. Committees or officers to be named before ballot. Call of the House every morning; absentees to be noted and returned to Convention. No members to be absent without leave of the House, or written order of Convention on pain of being returned to Convention.*—Notes of Rules for Congress. Ford ed., ii, 60. (1776.)

* Jefferson was member of a committee to frame rules for the Congress.—Editor.

1585. CONGRESS, Salaries of Members.—Our [financial] distresses ask notice [by the Virginia Legislature]. I had been from home four months, and had expended $1200 before I received one farthing. By the last post we received about seven weeks' allowance. In the meantime, some of us had had the mortification to have our horses turned out of the livery stable for want of money. There is really no standing this. The supply gives us no relief because it was mortgaged. We are trying to get something more effectual from the treasury, having sent on express to inform them of our predicament.—To James Madison. Ford ed., iii, 404. (A., Feb. 1784.) See 1511.

1586. CONGRESS, Sessions of.—Each house of Congress possesses the natural right of governing itself, and, consequently, of fixing its own times and places of meeting, so far as it has not been abridged by the law of those who employ them, that is to say, by the Constitution.—Official Opinion. vii, 496. Ford ed., v, 206. (1790.)

1587. —— ——. To shorten the sessions, is to lessen the evils and burthens of the government on our country.—To James Monroe. iv, 243. Ford ed., vii, 259. (Pa., 1798.)

1588. —— ——. I was in hopes that all efforts to render the sessions of Congress permanent were abandoned. But a clear profit of three or four dollars a day is sufficient to reconcile some to their absence from home.—To James Madison. Ford ed., vii, 254. (1798.)

1589. —— ——. Congress separate in two ways only, to wit, by adjournment or dissolution by the efflux of their time. What then constitutes a session with them? A dissolution certainly closes one session, and the meeting of the new Congress begins another. The Constitution authorizes the President, "on extraordinary occasions, to convene both Houses, or either of them." If convened by the President's proclamation, this must begin a new session, and of course determine the preceding one to have been a session. So, if it meets under the clause of the Constitution, which says, "the Congress shall assemble, at least once in every year, and such meeting shall be on the first Monday in December, unless they shall by law appoint a different day," this must begin a new session. For even if the last adjournment was to this day, the act of adjournment is merged in the higher authority of the Constitution, and the meeting will be under that, and not under their adjournment. So far we have fixed landmarks for determining sessions. In other cases, it is declared by the joint vote authorizing the President of the Senate and the Speaker to close the session on a fixed day.—Parliamentary Manual. ix, 79.

1590. CONGRESS, Size of.—Our present federal limits are not too large for good government, nor will the increase of votes in Congress produce any ill effect. On the contrary, it will drown the little divisions ·at

present existing there.—To Archibald Stuart. i, 518. Ford ed., iv, 188. (P., Jan.
1786.)

**1591. CONGRESS, State representa-
tion in.**—I am captivated by the compromise
[in the Federal Constitution] of the opposite
claims of the great and little States, of the
latter to equal, and the former to proportional
influence.—To James Madison. ii, 329.
Ford ed., iv, 475. (P., 1787.)

1592. CONGRESS, Stock-jobbers in.—
Too many stock-jobbers and King-jobbers
have come into our Legislature, or rather too
many of our Legislature have become stock-
jobbers and King-jobbers.—To General Lafayette. iii, 450. Ford ed., vi, 78. (Pa.,
1792.)

1593. ———. I told President Washington that my wish was to see both Houses
of Congress cleansed of all persons interested in the bank or public stocks; and that
a pure Legislature being given us. I should
always be ready to acquiesce under their determinations, even if contrary to my own
opinions; for that I subscribe to the principle, that the will of the majority, honestly
expressed, should give law.—Anas. ix, 131.
Ford ed., i, 215. (Feb. 1793.)

1594. CONGRESS, Taxation and.—I
like the power given the Legislature [in the
Federal Constitution] to levy taxes, and for
that reason solely approve of the greater
House being chosen by the people directly.
For though I think a House chosen by them
will be very illy qualified to legislate for the
Union, for foreign nations, &c., yet this evil
does not weigh against the good of preserving
inviolate the fundamental principle that the
people are not to be taxed but by representatives chosen immediately by themselves.—To
James Madison. ii, 328. Ford ed., iv, 475.
(P., 1787.)

1595. CONGRESS, Term of Members.—
To prevent every danger which might arise to
American freedom by continuing too long
in office the members of the Continental Congress, to preserve to that body the confidence
of their friends, and to disarm the malignant
imputation of their enemies: It is earnestly
recommended to the several Provinces, Assemblies or Conventions of the United Colonies, that in their future elections of delegates to the Continental Congress, one half,
at least, of the persons chosen be such as were
not of the delegation next preceding, and the
residue be of such as shall not have served in
that office longer than two years. *—Ford ed.,
ii, 61. (1776?)

1596. ———. No person who shall
have served two years in Congress, shall be
capable of serving therein again, till he shall
have been out of the same one whole year. †—
Congress Bill. Ford ed., ii, 128. (1777)

* This resolution * * * was probably offered in
July, 1776, when Congress was establishing rules for
its own guidance, and rejected.—Note in Ford ed.
† From a bill drafted by Jefferson and passed by
the Virginia House of Delegates. The representation of the Colony in the Continental Congress ex-

1597. CONGRESS, Verbosity in.—Her
[Delaware's] long speeches and wicked workings at this session have added at least thirty
days to its length, cost us $30,000, and filled
the Union with falsehoods and misrepresentations.—To Cæsar A. Rodney. Ford ed., viii,
148. (W., April 1802.)

1598. ———. I observe that the House
of Representatives are sensible of the ill effects of the long speeches in their house on
their proceedings. But they have a worse
effect in the disgust they excite among the
people, and the disposition they are producing
to transfer their confidence from the Legislature to the Executive branch, which would
soon sap our Constitution. These speeches,
therefore, are less and less read, and if continued will soon cease to be read at all.—To
John Wayles Eppes. v, 490. Ford ed., ix,
267. (M., 1810.) See Debate.

1599. CONGRESS, Voting in.—I am
much pleased with the substitution [in the
Federal Constitution] of the method of voting
by persons, instead of that of voting by
States.—To James Madison. ii, 329. Ford
ed., iv, 475. (P., 1787.)

1600. CONGRESS, Wisdom of.—Their
decisions are almost always wise; they are
like pure metal.—To James Madison. ii, 152.
Ford ed., iv, 391. (P., 1787.)

1601. CONGRESS, Young men and.—
Congress is a good school for our young
statesmen. It gives them impressions friendly
to the Federal Government instead of those
adverse, which too often take place in persons
confined to the politics of their State.—To
James Madison. Ford ed., iii, 472. (A.,
1784.)

1602. ———. I see the best effects
produced by sending our young statesmen [to
Congress]. They see the affairs of the Confederacy from a high ground: they learn the
importance of the Union, and befriend federal
measures when they return. Those who never
come here, see our affairs insulated, pursue
a system of jealousy and self-interest, and distract the Union as much as they can.—To
James Madison. Ford ed., iii, 403. (A.,
Feb. 1784.)

1603. CONNECTICUT, Bigotry of.—In
Connecticut, they are so priest-ridden that
nothing is expected from them but the most
bigoted, passive obedience.—To James Madison. iv, 219. Ford ed., vii, 213. (Pa., 1789.)

1604. ———. Connecticut remains riv-
eted in her political and religious bigotry.—
To James Madison. Ford ed., vii, 344. (Pa.,
Feb. 1799.)

— CONNECTICUT, Federal offices in.
—See Bishop.

1605. CONNECTICUT, Government in.
—The nature of your government being a
cited bitter factional animosity. Richard Henry
Lee, being the leader of one party, and Benjamin
Harrison, with whom Jefferson acted, of the other.—
Editor.

subordination of the civil to the ecclesiastical power, I consider it as desperate for long years to come. Their steady habits exclude the advances of information, and they seem exactly where they were when they separated from the saints of Oliver Cromwell. And there your clergy will always keep them if they can. You will follow the bark of liberty only by the help of a tow-rope.—To PIERREPONT EDWARDS. FORD ED., viii, 74. (W., July 1801.)

1606. CONNECTICUT, Politics of.— Connecticut is still federal by a small majority. She will be with us in a short time.—To C. F. VOLNEY. iv, 573. (W., 1805.)

1607. CONNECTICUT, Republicanism and.— I rejoice that in some forms, though not in all, republicanism shows progress in Connecticut. A clerical bondage is the root of the evil. * * * The lawyers, the other pillar of federalism, are from the nature of their calling so ready to take either side, that as soon as they see as much, or perhaps more money to be got on one side than the other, they will tack over. The clergy are unwilling to exchange the certain resource of legal compulsion for the uncertain one of their own merit and industry.—To GIDEON GRANGER. FORD ED., viii, 232. (W., May 1803.)

1608. CONNECTICUT, Resurrection of. —What need we despair of after the resurrection of Connecticut to light and liberty? I had believed that the last retreat of monkish darkness, bigotry, and abhorrence of those advances of the mind which had carried the other States a century ahead of them. They seemed still to be exactly where their forefathers were when they schismatized from the covenant of works, and to consider as dangerous heresies all innovations, good or bad. I join you, therefore, in sincere congratulations that this den of the priesthood is at length broken up, and that a Protestant Popedom is no longer to disgrace the American history and character. *—To JOHN ADAMS. vii, 62. (M., 1817.)

1609. ——. Even Connecticut, as a State, and the last one expected to yield its steady habits (which were essentially bigoted in politics as well as religion), has chosen a republican governor, and republican legislature.—To MARQUIS DE LAFAYETTE. vii, 66. FORD ED., x, 83. (M., 1817.)

1610. CONQUEST, Avoid.— If there be one principle more deeply rooted than any other in the mind of every American, it is that we should have nothing to do with conquest.—To WILLIAM SHORT. iii, 275. FORD ED., v, 364. (Pa., 1791.)

1611. CONQUEST, Compact and equality vs.— I have much confidence that we shall

* Mr. Adams replied : "Do you think that Protestant Popedom is annihilated in America? Do you recollect, or have you ever attended to the ecclesiastical strifes in Maryland, Pennsylvania, New York, and every part of New England? What a mercy it is that these people cannot whip, and crop and pillory, and roast, *as yet* in the United States! If they could, they would."—EDITOR.

proceed successfully for ages to come, and that, contrary to the principle of Montesquieu it will be seen that the larger the extent of country, the more firm its republican structure, if founded, not on conquest, but in principles of compact and equality.—To M. DE MARBOIS. vii, 77. (M., 1817.)

1612. CONQUEST, Disavowed.— We did not raise armies for glory or for conquest.— DECLARATION ON TAKING UP ARMS. FORD ED., i. 475. (July 1775.)

1613. CONQUEST, Submission to.— The government of a nation may be usurped by the forcible intrusion of an individual into the throne. But to conquer its will, so as to rest the right on that, the only legitimate basis, requires long acquiescence and cessation of all opposition.—To —— ——. vii, 413. (M., 1825.)

1614. CONQUEST, Title by.— It is an established principle that conquest gives only an inchoate right, which does not become perfect till confirmed by the treaty of peace, and by a renunciation or abandonment by the former proprietor.—MISSISSIPPI RIVER INSTRUCTIONS. vii, 572. FORD ED., v, 463. (1792.)

1615. CONQUEST, Un-American.— Conquest is not in our principles. It is inconsistent with our government.—INSTRUCTIONS TO WILLIAM CARMICHAEL. ix, 414. FORD ED., v, 230. (1790.)

1616. CONSCIENCE, Coercing.— It is inconsistent with the spirit of our laws and Constitution to force tender consciences.— PROCLAMATION CONCERNING PAROLES. FORD ED., ii, 430. (P., 1781.)

1617. CONSCIENCE, Elections and.— Every officer of the government may vote at elections according to his conscience; but we should betray the cause committed to our care, were we to permit the influence of official patronage to be used to overthrow that cause.—To LEVI LINCOLN. iv, 451. FORD ED., viii, 176. (W., Oct. 1802.)

1618. ——. Our principles render federalists in office safe, if they do not employ their influence in opposing the government, and only give their own vote according to their conscience. And this principle we act on as well with those put in office by others, as by ourselves.—To LEVI LINCOLN. v, 264. (W., March 1808.)

1619. CONSCIENCE, Freedom of.— We are bound, you, I, and every one, to make common cause, even with error itself, to maintain the common right of freedom of conscience.—To EDWARD DOWSE. iv, 478. (W., 1803.)

1620. ——. Nor should we wonder at * * * [the] pressure [for a fixed constitution in 1788-9] when we consider the monstrous abuses of power under which * * * the [French] people were ground to powder; when we pass in review * * * the shackles on the freedom of conscience.— AUTOBIOGRAPHY. i, 86. FORD ED., i, 118. (1821.)

1621. CONSCIENCE, A guide.—Conscience is the only sure clew which will eternally guide a man clear of all doubts and inconsistencies.—To General Washington. iii, 31. Ford ed., v, 96. (P., 1789.)

1622. CONSCIENCE, Inquisition over.—I am averse to the communication of my religious tenets to the public: because it would countenance the presumption of those who have endeavored to draw them before that tribunal, and to seduce public opinion to erect itself into that inquisition over the rights of conscience. which the laws have so justly proscribed.—To Dr. Benjamin Rush. iv, 480. Ford ed., viii, 224. (W., April 1803.)

1623. CONSCIENCE, Liberty of.—It behooves every man who values liberty of conscience for himself, to resist invasions of it in the case of others; or their case may, by change of circumstances, become his own. It behooves him. too, in his own case, to give no example of concession, betraying the common right of independent opinion, by answering questions of faith, which the laws have left between God and himself.—To Dr. Benjamin Rush. iv, 480. Ford ed., viii, 224. April 1803.)

1624. —— ——. This blessed country of free inquiry and belief has surrendered its creed and conscience to neither kings nor priests.—To Dr. Benjamin Waterhouse. vii, 253. Ford ed., x, 220. (M., 1822.)

1625. CONSCIENCE, Moral laws and.—The true fountains of evidence [are] the head and heart of every rational and honest man, It is there nature has written her moral laws, and where every man may read them for himself.—French Treaties Opinion. vii, 613. Ford ed., vi, 221. (1793.)

1626. CONSCIENCE, Office and.—If their conscience urges them [federalists] to take an active and zealous part in opposition, it ought also to urge them to retire from a post which they could not conscientiously conduct with fidelity to the trust reposed in them.—To John Page. v, 136. Ford ed., ix, 119. (W., 1807.)

1627. CONSCIENCE, Rights of.—The error seems not sufficiently eradicated, that the operations of the mind, as well as the acts of the body, are subject to the coercion of the laws. But our rulers can have no authority over such natural rights, only as we have submitted to them. The rights of conscience we never submitted, we could not submit. We are answerable for them to our God.—Notes on Virginia. viii, 400. Ford ed., iii, 263. (1782.)

1628. —— ——. A right to take the side which every man's conscience approves in a civil contest is too precious a right, and too favorable to the preservation of liberty, not to be protected by all its well informed friends. The Assembly of Virginia have given sanction to this right in several of their laws, discriminating honorably those who took

side against us, before the Declaration of Independence, from those who remained among us, and strove to injure us by their treacheries.—To Mrs. Sprowle. Ford ed., iv, 66. (P., 1785.)

1629. —— ——. No provision in our Constitution ought to be dearer to man than that which protects the rights of conscience against the enterprises of the civil authority. It has not left the religion of its citizens under the power of its public functionaries, were it possible that any of these should consider a conquest over the conscience of men either attainable or applicable to any desirable purpose.—R. To A. New London Methodists. viii, 147. (1809.)

1630. —— ——. The restoration of the rights of conscience [in the Revised Code of Virginia] relieved the people from taxation for the support of a religion not theirs: for the [Church of England] Establishment was truly of the religion of the rich, the dissenting sects being entirely composed of the less wealthy people.—Autobiography. i, 49. Ford ed., i, 69. (1821.)

— CONSENT OF THE GOVERNED.— See Government.

— CONSOLIDATION.—See Centralization.

1631. CONSTANTINOPLE, The Key of Asia.—Constantinople is the Key of Asia. Who shall have it? is the question.—To George Wythe. ii, 267. Ford ed., iv, 444. (P., 1787.) See Turks.

1632. CONSTITUTION, Definition of a.—A constitution, *ex vi termini*, means " an act above the powers of the ordinary legislature." *Constitutio, constitutum, statutum, lex,* are convertible terms. " *Constitutio dicitur jus quod a principe conditur.*" *Constitutum quod ab imperatoribus rescriptum statutumve est.*" " *Statutum,* idem quod lex." (Calvini Lexicon juridicum.) *Constitution* and *statute* were originally terms of the* civil law, and from thence introduced by ecclesiastics into the English law. Thus in the statute 25 Hen. viii, c. 19, § 1, " *Constitutions* and *ordinances* " are used as synonymous. The term *constitution* has many other significations in physics and politics; but in jurisprudence, whenever it is applied to any act of the legislature, it invariably means a statute, law, or ordinance.—Notes on Virginia. viii, 365. Ford ed., iii, 227. (1782.)

1633. CONSTITUTION (The Federal), Acceptance of.—I am glad to hear that the new Constitution is received with favor. I sincerely wish that the nine first conventions may receive, and the four last reject it. The former will receive it finally, while the latter will oblige them to offer a declaration of rights in order to complete the Union. We

* To bid, to set, was the ancient legislative word of the English. Ll. Hlotharri and Eadrici. Ll. Inæ. Ll. Eadwerdi, Ll. Æthelstani.—Note by Jefferson.

shall thus have all its good, and cure its principal defect.—To James Madison. Ford ed., v, 5. (P., Feb. 1788.)

1634. ———. I wish with all my soul that the nine first conventions may accept the new Constitution, because this will secure to us the good it contains which I think great and important. But I equally wish that the four latest conventions, whichever they may be, may refuse to accede to it till a declaration of rights be annexed. This would probably command the offer of such a declaration, and thus give to the whole fabric, perhaps, as much perfection as any one of that kind ever had.—To A. Donald. ii, 355. (P., Feb. 1788.)

1635. ———. I am glad to hear that our new Constitution is pretty sure of being accepted by States enough to secure the good it contains, and to meet such opposition in some others as to give us hopes it will be accommodated to them by the amendment of its most glaring faults, particularly the want of a declaration of rights.—To William Rutledge. ii, 350. Ford ed., v, 4. (P., Feb. 1788.)

1636. ———. I learn with great pleasure the progress of the new Constitution. Indeed I have presumed it would gain on the public mind, as I confess it has on my own. At first, though I saw that the great mass and groundwork were good, I disliked many appendages. Reflection and discussion have cleared off most of these.—To E. Carrington. ii, 404. Ford ed., v, 19. (P., May 1788.)

1637. ———. My first wish was that nine States would adopt it in order to ensure what was good in it, and that the others might, by holding off, produce the necessary amendments. But the plan of Massachusetts is far preferable, and will, I hope, be followed by those who are yet to decide.—To E. Carrington. ii, 404. Ford ed., v, 20. (P., May 1788.)

1638. ———. It will be easier to get the assent of nine States to correct what is wrong in the way pointed out by the Constitution itself, than to get thirteen to concur in a new convention and another plan of confederation. I therefore sincerely pray that the remaining States may accept it, as Massachusetts has done, with standing instructions to their delegates to press for amendments till they are obtained. They cannot fail of being obtained when the delegates of eight States shall be under such perpetual instructions.—To T. Lee Shippen. ii, 415. (P., June 1788.)

1639. ———. I sincerely rejoice at the acceptance of our new Constitution by nine States. It is a good canvas, on which some strokes only want retouching. What these are, I think are sufficiently manifested by the general voice from north to south, which calls for a bill of rights. It seems pretty generally understood, that this should go to juries, *habeas corpus*, standing armies, print-

ing, religion and monopolies.—To James Madison. ii, 445. Ford ed., v, 45. (P., July 1788.)

1640. CONSTITUTION (The Federal), Action by the States.—With respect to the new government, nine or ten States will probably have accepted by the end of this month. The others may oppose it. Virginia, I think, will be of this number. Besides other objections of less moment, she will insist on annexing a bill of rights to the new Constitution, *i. e.* a bill wherein the government shall declare that, 1. Religion shall be free. 2. Printing presses free. 3. Trials by jury preserved in all cases. 4. No monopolies in commerce. 5. No standing army. Upon receiving this bill of rights, she will probably depart from her other objections, and the bill is so much to the interest of all the States, that I presume they will offer it, and thus our Constitution be amended, and our Union closed by the end of the present year. In this way, there will have been opposition enough to do good, and not enough to do harm.—To C. W. F. Dumas. ii, 356. (P., Feb. 1788.)

1641. ———. At first, I wished that when nine States should have accepted the Constitution, so as to ensure us what is good in it, the other four might hold off till the want of the bill of rights, at least, might be supplied. But I am now convinced that the plan of Massachusetts is the better, that is, to accept, and to amend afterwards. If the States which were to decide after her, should all do the same, it is impossible but they must obtain the essential amendments. It will be more difficult if we lose this instrument, to recover what is good in it, than to correct what is bad, after we shall have adopted it. It has, therefore, my hearty prayers.—To William Carmichael. ii, 399. Ford ed., v, 25. (P., May 1788.)

1642. ———. The conduct of Massachusetts has been noble. She accepted the Constitution, but voted that it should stand as a perpetual instruction to her delegates, to endeavor to obtain such and such reformations; and the minority, though very strong both in numbers and abilities, declared *viritim* and *scriatim*, that acknowledging the principle that the majority must give the law, they would now support the new Constitution with their tongues, and with their blood, if necessary.—To William Carmichael. ii, 398. Ford ed., v, 24. (P., 1788.)

1643. ———. I congratulate you on the accession of your State [South Carolina] to the new Federal Constitution. I expect to hear daily that my own has followed the good example. Our government needed bracing. Still, we must take care not to run from one extreme to another; not to brace too high.—To E. Rutledge. ii, 435. Ford ed., v, 41. (P., July 1788.)

1644. ———. In New York, two-thirds of the State were against it [the new Constitution], and certainly, if they had been called to the decision in any other stage of the business, they would have rejected it; but before they put it to the vote, they would certainly have heard that eleven States had joined in it, and they would find it safer to go with those eleven, than put themselves into opposition, with Rhode Island only.—To WILLIAM CARMICHAEL. ii, 465. (P., Aug. 1788.)

1645. —— ——. No news from North Carolina; but in such a case no news is good news, as an unfavorable decision of the 12th State would have flown like an electrical shock through America and Europe.—To MR. SHIPPEN. ii, 484. (P., Sep. 1788.)

1646. —— ——. I have seen with infinite pleasure our new Constitution accepted by eleven States, not rejected by the twelfth; and that the thirteenth happens to be a State of the least importance. It is true, that the minorities in most of the accepting States have been very respectable; so much so as to render it prudent, were it not otherwise reasonable, to make some sacrifice to them. I am in hopes that the annexation of a bill of rights to the Constitution will alone draw over so great a proportion of the minorities, as to leave little danger in the opposition of the residue; and that this annexation may be made by Congress and the Assemblies, without calling a convention which might endanger the most valuable parts of the system.—To GENERAL WASHINGTON. ii, 533. FORD ED., v, 56. (P., Dec. 1788.)

1647. —— ——. The Virginia Assembly, furiously anti-federal, have passed a bill rendering every person holding any Federal office incapable of holding at the same time any State office. This is a declaration of war against the new Constitution.—To WILLIAM SHORT. ii, 576. (P., Feb. 1789.)

1648. CONSTITUTION (The Federal), Adopt and amend.—Were I in America, I would advocate it warmly till nine [States] should have adopted and then as warmly take the other side to convince the remaining four that they ought not to come into it till the declaration of rights is annexed to it. By this means we should secure all the good of it, and procure so respectable an opposition as would induce the accepting States to offer a bill of rights. This would be the happiest turn the thing could take.—To WILLIAM STEPHENS SMITH. FORD ED., v, 2. (P., Feb. 1788.)

1649. —— ——. Under this hope [that the necessary amendments will be made] I look forward to the general adoption of the new Constitution with anxiety, as necessary for us under our present circumstances.—To GENERAL WASHINGTON. ii, 375. FORD ED., v, 8. (P., May 1788.)

1650. —— ——. I see in this instrument a great deal of good. The consolidation of our government, a just representation, an administration of some permanence, and other features of great value will be gained by it. There are, indeed, some faults which revolted me a good deal in the first moment; but we must be contented to travel on towards per-

fection, step by step. We must be contented with the ground which this Constitution will gain for us, and hope that a favorable moment will come for correcting what is amiss in it.— To COMTE DE MOUSTIER. ii, 388. FORD ED., v, 11. (P., May 1788.)

1651. —— ——. I should deprecate with you, indeed, the meeting of a new convention. I hope they will adopt the mode of amendment by Congress and the Assemblies, in which case I should not fear any dangerous innovation in the plan. But the minorities are too respectable not to be entitled to some sacrifice of opinion in the majority; especially, when a great proportion of them would be contented with a bill of rights.—To JAMES MADISON. ii, 506. FORD ED., v, 53. (P., Nov. 1788.)

1652. CONSTITUTION (The Federal), Amendments to.—We must be contented to accept of its good, and to cure what is evil in it hereafter. It seems necessary for our happiness at home; I am sure it is so for our respectability abroad.—To JOHN BROWN. ii, 397. FORD ED., v, 19. (P., May 1788.)

1653. —— ——. There are two amendments only which I am anxious for: 1. A bill of rights, which it is so much the interest of all to have, that I conceive it must be yielded. The first amendment proposed by Massachusetts * will in some degree answer this end, but not so well. It will do too much in some instances, and too little in others. It will cripple the Federal Government in some cases where it ought to be free, and not restrain it in some others where restraint would be right. The 2d amendment which appears to me essential is the restoring the principle of necessary rotation, particularly to the Senate and Presidency, but most of all to the last. * * * Of the correction of this article, however, I entertain no present hope, because I find it has scarcely excited an objection in America. And if it does not take place ere long, it assuredly never will.—To E. CARRINGTON. ii, 404. FORD ED., v, 20. (P., May 1788.)

1654. —— ——. Though I approve of the mass, I would wish to see some amendments, further than those which have been proposed, fixing it more surely on a republican basis. * * * To secure the ground we gain, and gain what more we can, is the wisest course. —To GEORGE MASON. iii, 147. FORD ED., v, 183. (N.Y., 1790.)

1655. —— ——. It is too early to think of a declaratory act as yet, but the time is approaching and not distant. Two elections more will give us a solid majority in the House of Representatives, and a sufficient one in the Senate. As soon as it can be depended on, we must have " A Declaration of the Principles of the Constitution," in nature of a Declaration of Rights, in all the points in

* The 1st amendment of Massachusetts was: " That it explicitly declare that all powers, not expressly delegated by the aforesaid Constitution, are reserved to the several States, to be by them exercised."—EDITOR.

which it has been violated.—To P. N. NICH-OLAS. iv, 327. FORD ED., vii, 439. (Pa., April 1800.)

1656. —— ——. How the good [in the new Constitution] should be secured and the ill brought to right was the difficulty. To refer it back to a new Convention might endanger the loss of the whole. My first idea was that the nine States, first acting, should accept it unconditionally, and thus secure what in it was good and that the four last should accept on the previous condition, that certain amendments should be agreed to; but a better course was devised of accepting the whole and trusting that the good sense and honest intentions of our citizens would make the alterations which should be deemed necessary. Accordingly, all accepted, six without objection and seven with recommendations of specified amendments.—AUTOBIOGRAPHY. i, 79. FORD ED., i, 109. (1821.)

1657. —— ——. Let us go on perfecting the Constitution by adding, by way of amendment, those forms which time and trial show are still wanting.—To WILSON C. NICHOLAS. iv, 506. FORD ED., viii, 248. (M., 1803.)

1658. —— ——. The States are now so numerous that I despair of ever seeing another amendment to the Constitution, although the innovations of time will certainly call, and now already call, for some.—To GEORGE HAY. FORD ED., x, 265. (M., 1823.)

1659. —— ——. Those who formerly usurped the *name* of federalists, which *in fact,* they never were, have now openly abandoned it, and are as openly marching by the road of construction, in a direct line to that consolidation which was always their real object. They, almost to a man, are in possession of one branch of the government, and appear to be very strong in yours. The three great questions of amendment now before you, will give the measure of their strength. I mean, 1st, the limitation of the term of the Presidential service; 2nd, the placing the choice of President effectually in the hands of the people; 3rd, the giving to Congress the power of internal improvement, on condition that each State's federal proportion of the moneys so expended shall be employed within the State. The friends of consolidation would rather take these powers by construction than accept them by direct investiture of the States. Yet, as to internal improvement particularly, there is probably not a State in the Union which would not grant the power on the condition proposed, or which would grant it without that. * * * If I can see these three great amendments prevail, I shall consider it as a renewed extension of the term of our lease, shall live in more confidence and die in more hope.—To ROBERT J. GARNETT. vii, 336. FORD ED., x, 294. (M., Feb. 1824.)

1660. —— ——. The real friends of the Constitution in its federal form, if they wish it to be immortal, should be attentive, by amendments, to make it keep pace with the advance of the age in science and experience. Instead of this, the European governments

have resisted reformation, until the people, seeing no other resource, undertake it themselves by force, their only weapon, and work it out through blood, desolation and long-continued anarchy. Here it will be by large fragments breaking off, and refusing reunion, but on condition of amendment, or perhaps permanently.—To ROBERT J. GARNETT. vii, 336. FORD ED., x, 295. (M., 1824.)

1661. —— ——. I have read with pleasure and satisfaction the very able and eloquent speech you have been so kind as to send me on the amendment of the Constitution, proposed by Mr. McDuffie, and concur with much of its contents.—To EDWARD EVERETT. vii, 437. FORD ED., x, 385. (M., April 1826.)

1662. CONSTITUTION (The Federal), Approval of.—I like much the general idea of framing a government which should go on of itself, peaceably, without needing continual recurrence to the State Legislatures. I like the organization of the government into Legislative, Judiciary and Executive. I like the power given the Legislature to levy taxes, and for that reason solely, I approve of the greater House being chosen by the people directly. For though I think a House chosen by them will be very illy qualified to legislate for the Union, for foreign nations, &c., yet this evil does not weigh against the good of preserving inviolate the fundamental principle that the people are not to be taxed but by representatives chosen immediately by themselves. I am captivated by the compromise of the opposite claims of the great and little States, of the latter to equal, and the former to proportional influence. I am much pleased, too, with the substitution of the method of voting by persons instead of that of voting by States: and I like the negative given to the Executive, conjointly with a third of either House; although I should have liked it better, had the Judiciary been associated for that purpose, or invested separately with a similar power. There are other good things of less moment.—To JAMES MADISON. ii, 328. FORD ED., iv, 475. (P., Dec. 20, 1787.)

1663. —— ——. It is a good canvas, on which some strokes only want retouching.—To JAMES MADISON. ii, 445. FORD ED., v, 45. (P., July 1788.)

1664. —— ——. I approved, from the first moment, of the great mass of what is in the new Constitution; the consolidation of the government; the organization into Executive, Legislative, and Judiciary; the subdivision of the Legislative; the happy compromise of interests between the great and little States, by the different manner of voting in the different Houses; the voting by persons instead of States; the qualified negative on laws given to the Executive, which, however, I should have liked better if associated with the Judiciary also as in New York; and the power of taxation. I thought at first that the latter might have been limited. A little reflection soon convinced me it ought not to be.—To F. HOPKINSON. ii, 586. FORD ED., v, 76. (P., March 1789.)

— **CONSTITUTION (The Federal), Bill of Rights and.**—See BILL OF RIGHTS.

1665. CONSTITUTION (The Federal), Compromises of.—The Constitution was a matter of compromise; a capitulation between conflicting interests and opinions.—To SAMUEL KERCHIVAL. vii, 37. FORD ED., x, 46. (M., 1816.)

— **CONSTITUTION (The Federal), Consolidation and.**—See CENTRALIZATION.

1666. CONSTITUTION (The Federal), Construction of.—I told the President [Washington] * * * that they [the Hamilton members of the Legislature] had chained it [the Treasury system] about our necks for a great length of time, and, in order to keep the game in their hands had, from time to time, aided in making such legislative constructions of the Constitution, as made it a very different thing from what the people thought they had submitted to.—THE ANAS. ix, 104. FORD ED., i, 177. (Feb. 1792.)

1667. —— ——. Our peculiar security is in the possession of a written Constitution. Let us not make it a blank paper by construction. I say the same as to the opinion of those who consider the grant of the treaty-making power as boundless. If it is, then we have no Constitution. If it has bounds, they can be no others than the definitions of the powers which that instrument gives. It specifies and delineates the operations permitted to the Federal Government, and gives all the powers necessary to carry these into execution. Whatever of these enumerated objects is proper for a law, Congress may make the law; whatever is proper to be executed by way of a treaty, the President and Senate may enter into the treaty; whatever is to be done by a judicial sentence, the Judges may pass the sentence. Nothing is more likely than that their enumeration of powers is defective. This is the ordinary case of all human works. Let us then go on perfecting it, by adding, by way of amendment to the Constitution those powers which time and trial show are still wanting.—To WILSON C. NICHOLAS. iv, 505. FORD ED., viii. 247. (M., Sep. 1803.)

1668. —— ——. When an instrument admits two constructions, the one safe the other dangerous; the one precise, the other indefinite, I prefer that which is safe and precise. I had rather ask an enlargement of power from the nation, where it is found necessary, than to assume it by a construction which would make our powers boundless.—To WILSON C. NICHOLAS. iv, 506. FORD ED., viii, 247. (M., 1803.)

1669. —— ——. Strained constructions * * * loosen all the bands of the Constitution.—To GEORGE TICKNOR. FORD ED., x, 81. (1817.)

1670. —— ——. In denying the right they [the Supreme Court] usurp of exclusively explaining the Constitution, I go further than you do, if I understand rightly your quotation from the *Federalist*, of an opinion that ' the judiciary is the last resort in relation *to the other departments* of the government, but not in relation to the rights of the parties to the compact under which the judiciary is derived." If this opinion be sound, then indeed is our Constitution a complete *felo de se.* For intending to establish three departments, co-ordinate and independent, that they might check and balance one another, it has given, according to this opinion, to one of them alone, the right to prescribe rules for the government of the others, and to that one, too, which is unelected by and independent of the nation. For experience has already shown that the impeachment it has provided is not even a scare-crow; that such opinions as the one you combat, sent cautiously out, as you observe also, by detachment, not belonging to the case often, but sought for out of it, as if to rally the public opinion beforehand to their views, and to indicate the line they are to walk in, have been so quietly 'passed over as never to have excited animadversion, even in a speech of any one of the body entrusted with impeachment. The Constitution, on this hypothesis, is a mere thing of wax in the hands of the judiciary, which they may twist and shape into any form they please. * * * My construction of the Constitution is very different from that you quote. It is that each department is truly independent of the others, and has an equal right to decide for itself what is the meaning of the Constitution in the cases submitted to its action; and especially, where it is to act ultimately and without appeal.—To SPENCER ROANE. vii, 134. FORD ED., x, 140. (P.F., 1819.)

1671. —— ——. Each of the three departments has equally the right to decide for itself what is its duty under the Constitution, without any regard to what the others may have decided for themselves under a similar question.—To SPENCER ROANE. vii, 136. FORD ED., x, 142. (P.F., 1819.)

1672. —— ——. My construction of the Constitution is * * * that each department is truly independent of the others, and has an equal right to decide for itself what is the meaning of the Constitution in the cases submitted to its action; and especially, where it is to act ultimately and without appeal. I will explain myself by examples, which, having occurred while I was in office, are better known to me, and the principles which governed them. A Legislature had passed the Sedition law. The Federal courts had subjected certain individuals to its penalties of fine and imprisonment. On coming into office, I released these individuals by the power of pardon committed to executive discretion, which could never be more properly exercised than where citizens were suffering without the authority of law, or, which was equivalent, under a law unauthorized by the Constitution, and therefore null. In the case of Marbury *vs.* Madison, the Federal judges declared that commissions, signed and sealed by the President, were valid, although not delivered. I deemed delivery essential to complete a deed, which, as long as it remains in the hands of the party, is as yet no deed, it is in *posse* only, but not in *esse*, and I withheld delivery of the commissions. They cannot issue a *mandamus* to the President or Legislature, or to any of their officers.* When the British treaty of —— arrived, without any provision against the impressment of our seamen, I determined not to ratify it. The Senate thought I should ask their advice. I thought that would be a mockery of them, when I was predetermined against following it, should they advise its ratification. The Constitution had made their advice necessary to confirm a treaty, but not to reject it. This has been blamed by some; but I have never doubted its soundness. In the cases of two persons, *antenati*, under exactly similar circumstances, the Federal court had determined that one of them (Duane) was not a citizen; the House of Representatives nevertheless determined that the other (Smith, of South Carolina) was a citizen, and admitted him to his seat in their body. Duane was a republican, and Smith a federalist, and these decisions were made during the federal ascendency. These are examples of my position, that each of the three departments has equally the right to decide for itself what is its duty under the Constitution, without any regard to what the others may have decided for themselves under a similar question.—To SPENCER ROANE. vii, 135. FORD ED., x, 141. (P.F., 1819.)

1673. —— ——. The judges are practicing on the Constitution by inferences, analogies, and sophisms, as they would on an ordinary law. They do not seem aware that it is not even a *constitution,* formed by a single authority, and subject to a single superintendence and control; but that it is a compact of many independent powers, every single one of which claims an equal right to understand it, and to require its observance. However strong the cord of compact may be, there is a point of tension at which it will break. A few such doctrinal decisions, as barefaced as that of the Cohens, happening to bear immediately on two or three of the large States, may induce them to join in arresting the march of government, and in arousing the co-States to pay some attention to what is passing, to bring back the compact to its original principles, or to modify it legitimately by the express consent of the parties themselves, and not by the usurpation of their created agents. They imagine they can lead us into a consolidate government, while their road leads directly to its dissolution.—To EDWARD LIVINGSTON. vii, 403. (M., 1825.) See 1684.

— CONSTITUTION (The Federal), Corporations and.—See INCORPORATION.

1674. CONSTITUTION (The Federal), Disapproval of.—How do you like our new Constitution? I confess there are things in it which stagger all my dispositions to subscribe to what such an assembly has proposed.

* Jefferson adds this note: "The Constitution controlling the common law in this particular."—EDITOR.

The House of Federal representatives will not be adequate to the management of affairs, either foreign or federal. Their President seems a bad edition of a Polish king. He may be elected from four years to four years for life. Reason and experience prove to us that a chief magistrate, so continuable, is an officer for life. When one or two generations shall have proved that this is an office for life, it becomes on every occasion worthy of intrigue, of bribery, of force, and even of foreign interference. It will be of great consequence to France and England to have America governed by a Galloman, or an Angloman. Once in office, and possessing the military force of the Union, without the aid or check of a council, he would not be easily dethroned even if the people could be induced to withdraw their votes from him. I wish that at the end of four years they had made him forever ineligible a second time. Indeed, I think all the good of this new Constitution might have been couched in three or four new articles, to be added to the good, old and venerable fabric, which should have been preserved even as a religious relique.—To JOHN ADAMS. ii, 316. (P., Nov. 13, 1787.)

1675. —— ——. There are very good articles in it, and very bad. I do not know which preponderate.—To W. S. SMITH. ii, 318. FORD ED., iv, 466. (P., Nov. 1787.)

1676. —— ——. I dislike, and greatly dislike, the abandonment in every instance, of the necessity of rotation in office, and most particularly in the case of the President. Experience concurs with reason in concluding that the first magistrate will always be re-elected, if the Constitution permits it. He is then an officer for life. This once observed, it becomes of so much consequence to certain nations to have a friend or a foe at the head of our affairs, that they will interfere with money and with arms. A Galloman, or an Angloman will be supported by the nation he befriends. If once elected, and at a second or third election outvoted by one or two votes, he will pretend false votes, foul play, hold possession of the reins of government, be supported by the States voting for him, especially if they are the central ones, lying in a compact body themselves, and separating their opponents; and they will be aided by one nation of Europe, while the majority are aided by another. The election of a President of America, some years hence will be much more interesting to certain nations of Europe than ever the election of a King of Poland was. Reflect on all the instances in history, ancient and modern, of elective monarchies, and say if they do not give foundation for my fears. The Roman Emperors, the Popes, while they were of any importance; the German Emperors, till they became hereditary in practice; the Kings of Poland; the Deys of the Ottoman Dependencies. It may be said that if elections are to be attended with these disorders, the seldomer they are renewed the better. But experience shows that the only way to prevent disorder is to render them uninteresting by frequent changes. An incapacity to be elected a second time would have been the only effectual preventive. The power of removing him every fourth year by the vote of the people, is a power which will not be exercised. The King of Poland is removable every day by the Diet, yet he is never removed. Smaller objections are, the appeal in fact as well as law, and the binding all persons, legislative, executive, and judiciary by oath to maintain that Constitution. I do not pretend to decide what would be the best method of procuring the establishment of the manifold good things in this Constitution, and of getting rid of the bad. Whether by adopting it, in hopes of future amendment; or after it has been duly weighed and canvassed by the people, after seeing the parts they generally dislike, and those they generally approve, to say to them: "We see now what you wish. Send together your deputies again, let them frame a constitution for you, omitting what you have condemned, and establishing the powers you approve. Even these will be a great addition to the energy of your government." At all events, I hope you will not be discouraged from other trials, if the present one should fail of its full effect. I have thus told you freely what I like and dislike; merely as a matter of curiosity, for I know your own judgment has been formed on all these points after having heard everything which could be urged on them. * * * After all, it is my principle that the will of the majority should always prevail. If they approve the proposed convention in all its parts, I shall concur in it cheerfully, in·hopes that they will amend it whenever they shall find it works wrong.—To JAMES MADISON. ii, 330. FORD ED., iv, 477. (P., December 20, 1787.)

1677. ———. As to the new Constitution, I find myself nearly a neutral. There is a great mass of good in it, in a very desirable form; but there is also to me a bitter pill or two.—To E. CARRINGTON. ii, 334. FORD ED., iv, 481. (P., Dec. 1787.)

1678. ———. I was much pleased with many and essential parts of this instrument from the beginning. But I thought I saw in it many faults, great and small. What I have read and reflected has brought me over from several of my objections of the first moment, and to acquiesce under some others. Two only remain of essential consideration, to wit, the want of a bill of rights, and the expunging the principle of necessary rotation in the offices of President and Senator.—To WILLIAM CARMICHAEL. ii, 398. FORD ED., v, 25. (P., May 1788.)

1679. ———. What I disapproved from the first moment was the want of a bill of rights, to guard liberty against the Legislative as well as the Executive branches of the government; that is to say, to secure freedom in religion, freedom of the press, freedom from monopolies, freedom from unlawful imprisonment, freedom from a permanent military, and a trial by jury, in all cases determinable by the laws of the land. I disapproved, also, the perpetual re-eligibility of the President. To these points of disapprobation I adhere. My first wish was that the nine first conventions might accept the Constitution, as the means of securing to us the great mass of good it contained; and that the four last might reject it, as the means of obtaining amendments. But I was corrected in this wish the moment I saw the much better plan of Massachusetts, and which had never occurred to me. With respect to the declaration of rights, I suppose the majority of the United States are of my opinion; for, I apprehend, all the anti-federalists, and a very respectable proportion of the federalists, think that such a declaration should now be annexed. The enlightened part of Europe have given us the greatest credit for inventing this instrument of security for the rights of the people, and have not been a little surprised to see us so soon give it up. With respect to the re-eligibility of the President, I find myself differing from the majority of my countrymen; for I think there are but three States out of the eleven which have desired an alteration of this. And, indeed, since the thing is established, I would wish it not to be altered during the life of our great leader, whose executive talents are superior to those I believe, of any man in the world, and who, alone, by the authority of his name, and the confidence reposed in his perfect integrity, is fully qualified to put the new government so under way, as to secure it against the efforts of opposition. But, having derived from our error all the good there was in it, I hope we shall correct it, the moment we can no longer have the same name at the helm. * * * These, my opinions, I wrote within a few hours after I had read the Constitution, to one or two friends in America.—To F. HOPKINSON. ii, 586. FORD ED., v, 76. (P., March 1789.)

1680. ———. I received a copy [of the new Federal Constitution] early in November [1787] and read and contemplated its provisions with great satisfaction. As not a member of the Convention, however, nor probably a single citizen of the Union had approved it in all its parts, so I, too, found articles which I thought objectionable. The absence of express declarations ensuring freedom of religion, freedom of the press, freedom of the person under the uninterrupted protection of the *habeas corpus*, and trial by jury in civil as well as in criminal cases excited my jealousy; and the re-eligibility of the President for life I quite disapproved. I expressed freely in letters to my friends and most particularly to Mr. Madison and General Washington my approbations and objections.—AUTOBIOGRAPHY. i, 79. FORD ED., i, 108. (1821.)

— CONSTITUTION (The Federal), Federal Convention and.—See CONVENTION.

1681. CONSTITUTION (The Federal), Foundation of.—I consider the foundation of the Constitution as laid on this ground:

That "all powers not delegated to the United States, by the Constitution, nor pro-hibited by it to the States, are reserved to the States or to the people." [XIIth Amendment.] To take a single step beyond the boundaries thus specifically drawn around the powers of Congress, is to take possession of a boundless field of power, no longer susceptible of any definition.—NATIONAL BANK OPINION. vii, 556. FORD ED., v, 285. (1791.)

— CONSTITUTION (The Federal), General Welfare clause of.—See GENERAL WEL-FARE CLAUSE.

1682. CONSTITUTION (The Federal), Infractions of.—If on [one] infraction [of the Constitution] we build a second, on that second a third. &c.. any one of the powers in the Constitution may be made to comprehend every power of government.—To ALBERT GALLATIN. iv, 450. FORD ED., viii. 175. (1802.)

1683. CONSTITUTION (The Federal), Intention of.—We ought always to presume that the real intention [of the Constitution] which is alone consistent with the Constitution.—To ALBERT GALLATIN. iv, 449. FORD ED., viii, 174. ((1802.)

— CONSTITUTION (The Federal), Internal Improvements and.—See INTERNAL IMPROVEMENTS.

1684. CONSTITUTION (The Federal), Interpretation of.—Where a phrase is susceptible of two meanings, we ought certainly to adopt that which will bring upon us the fewest inconveniences.—OPINION ON APPORTIONMENT BILL. vii, 599. FORD ED., v, 498. (1792.)

1685. —— ——. The Constitution * * * was meant to be republican, and we believe it to be republican according to every candid interpretation. Yet we have seen it so interpreted and administered, as to be truly what the French have called, a *monarchie masquée*.—To ROBERT R. LIVINGSTON. iv, 338. FORD ED., vii, 464. (W., Dec. 1800.)

1686. —— ——. The Constitution on which our Union rests, shall be administered by me according to the safe and honest meaning contemplated by the plain understanding of the people of the United States. at the time of its adoption,—a meaning to be found in the explanations of those who advocated, not those who opposed it, and who opposed it merely lest the construction should be applied which they denounced as possible.—REPLY TO ADDRESS. iv, 387. (W., March 1801.)

1687. —— ——. The Constitution is a compact of many independent powers. every single one of which claims an equal right to understand it, and to require its observance.—To EDWARD LIVINGSTON. vii, 404. (M., 1825.)

1688. —— ——. The Constitution of the United States is a compact of independent nations, subject to the rules acknowledged in similar cases, as well that of amendment provided within itself, as. in case of abuse, the justly dreaded but unavoidable *ultima ratio gentium.*—To EDWARD EVERETT. vii, 437. FORD ED., x, 385. (M.. 1826.)

1689. CONSTITUTION (The Federal), Jefferson and.—One passage in the paper you enclosed me must be corrected. It is the following: "And all say it was yourself more than any other individual that planned and established the Constitution." I was in Europe when the Constitution was planned, and never saw it till after it was established. On receiving it. I wrote strongly to Mr. Madison, urging the want of provision for the freedom of religion. freedom of the press, trial by jury, *habeas corpus,* and substitution of militia for a standing army, and an express reservation to the State of all rights not specifically granted to the Union. He accordingly moved in the first session of Congress for these amendments, which were agreed to and ratified by the States as they now stand. This is all the hand I had in what related to the Constitution.—To DR. JOSEPH PRIESTLEY. iv, 441. FORD ED., viii, 159. (W.. 1802.)

1690. CONSTITUTION (The Federal), Jurisdiction of.—It may be impracticable to lay down any general formula of words which shall decide at once and with precision in every case. this limit of jurisdiction. But there are two canons which will guide us safely in most of the cases. 1st. The capital and leading object of the Constitution was to leave with the States all authorities which respected their own citizens only, and to transfer to the United States those which respected citizens of foreign or other States; to make us several as to ourselves, but one as to all others. In the latter case, then, constructions should lean to the general jurisdiction, if the words will bear it, and in favor of the States in the former, if possible to be so construed. And, indeed, between citizens and citizens of the same State and under their own laws, I know but a single case in which a jurisdiction is given to the General Government. That is where anything but gold or silver is made a lawful tender, or the obligation of contracts is any otherwise impaired. The separate legislatures had so often abused that power that the citizens themselves chose to trust it to the general rather than to their own special authorities. 2d. On every question of construction. carry ourselves back to the time when the Constitution was adopted, recollect the spirit manifested in the debates, and instead of trying what meaning may be squeezed out of the text, or invented against it. conform to the probable one in which it was passed.—To WILLIAM JOHNSON. vii, 296. FORD ED.. x, 230. (M., 1823.)

1691. CONSTITUTION (The Federal), Model for France.—Ours [Constitution] has been professedly their model, in which such changes are made as a difference of circumstances rendered necessary, and some others neither necessary nor advantageous, but into which men will ever run, when versed in theory and new in the practice of the government, when acquainted with man only as they see him in their books, and not in the world.—To JAMES MADISON. iii, 98. FORD ED., v. 109. (P., Aug. 1789.)

1692. CONSTITUTION (The Federal), Monarchizing.—I am opposed to the monarchizing its features by the forms of its administration, with a view to conciliate a first transition to a President and Senate for life, and from that to an hereditary tenure of these offices. and thus to worm out the elective principle.—To ELBRIDGE GERRY. iv, 268. FORD ED., vii, 327. (Pa., 1799.)

1693. CONSTITUTION (The Federal), Necessity for.—Our new Constitution has succeeded beyond what I apprehended it would have done. I did not at first believe that eleven States out of thirteen would have consented to a plan consolidating themselves as much into one. A change in their dispositions, which had taken place since I left them, had rendered this consolidation necessary, that is to say, had called for a federal government which could walk upon its own legs, without leaning for support on the State Legislatures. A sense of necessity, and a submission to it, is to me a new and consolatory proof that whenever the people are well-informed, they can be trusted with their own government; that whenever things get so far wrong as to attract their notice, they may be relied on to set them to rights.—To DR. PRICE. ii, 553. (P., 1789.) See 1648.

1694. CONSTITUTION (The Federal), Preservation of.—The preservation of the Federal Constitution is all we need contend for.—To ARCHIBALD STUART. iii, 314. FORD ED., v, 409. (Pa., 1791.)

1695. ——— ———. The preservation of the General Government in its whole constitutional vigor, as the sheet anchor of our peace at home and safety abroad, I deem [one of] the essential principles of our government, and consequently [one of] those which ought to shape its administration.—FIRST INAUGURAL ADDRESS. viii, 4. FORD ED., viii, 4. (1801.)

1696. ——— ———. I do, with sincere zeal, wish an inviolable preservation of our present Federal Constitution according to the true sense in which it was adopted by the States; that in which it was advocated by its friends, and not that which its enemies apprehended, who therefore became its enemies.—To ELBRIDGE GERRY. iv, 268. FORD ED., vii, 327. (Pa., 1799.)

1697. ——— ———. May you and your cotemporaries meet them [attacks on the Constitution] with the same determination and effect, as your father and his did the Alien and Sedition laws, and preserve inviolate a constitution, which, cherished in all its chastity and purity, will prove in the end a blessing to all the nations of the earth.—To MR. NICHOLAS. vii, 230. (M., 1821.)

1698. ——— ———. To preserve the republican forms and principles of our Constitution, and cleave to the salutary distribution of powers which that has established, * * * are the two sheet anchors of our Union. If driven from either we shall be in danger of foundering.—To WILLIAM JOHNSON. vii, 298. FORD ED., x, 232. (M., 1823.)

1699. CONSTITUTION (The Federal), Principles of.—The principle of the Constitution is that of a separation of Legislative, Executive and Judiciary functions, except in cases specified. If this principle be not expressed in direct terms, it is clearly the spirit of the Constitution, and it ought to be so commented and acted on by every friend of free government.—To JAMES MADISON. iv, 161. FORD ED., vii, 108. (M., Jan. 1797.)

1700. ——— ———. The leading principle of our Constitution is the independence of the Legislative, Executive and Judiciary of one another.—To GEORGE HAY. v, 103. FORD ED., ix, 60. (W., 1807.)

1701. ——— ———. The adored principles of our Constitution.—To JEDEDIAH MORSE. vii, 235. FORD ED., x, 205. (M., 1822.)

1702. CONSTITUTION (The Federal), Republican opposition to.—Our first federal constitution, or Confederation, as it was called, was framed in the first moments of our separation from England, in the highest point of our jealousies of independence as to her, and as to each other. It formed, therefore, too weak a bond to produce a union of action as to foreign nations. This appeared at once on the establishment of peace, when the pressure of a common enemy which had hooped us together during the war, was taken away. Congress was found to be quite unable to point the action of the several States to a common object. A general desire, therefore. took place of amending the federal constitution. This was opposed by some of those who wished for monarchy, to wit, the refugees, now returned; the old tories, and the timid whigs who prefer tranquillity to freedom, hoping monarchy might be the remedy if a state of complete anarchy could be brought on. A convention, however, being decided on, some of the monocrats got elected, with a hope of introducing an English constitution, when they found that the great body of the delegates were strongly for adhering to republicanism, and for giving due strength to their government under that form, they then directed their efforts to the assimilation of all the parts of the new government to the English constitution as nearly as was attainable. In this they were not altogether without success; insomuch that the monarchical features of the new Constitution produced a violent opposition to it from the most zealous republicans in the several States. For this reason, and because they also thought it carried the principle of a consolidation of the States farther than was requisite for the purpose of producing a union of action as to foreign powers, it is still doubted by some whether a majority of the people of the United States were not against adopting it. However it was carried through all the assemblies of the States, though by very small majorities in the larger States.— To C. D. EBELING. FORD ED., vii, 45. (1795.)

1703. CONSTITUTION (The Federal), Reverence for.—With the House of Representatives of Vermont I join cordially in admiring and revering the Constitution of the United States,—the result of the collected wisdom of our country.—REPLY TO ADDRESS. iv, 418. (W., 1801.)

1704. CONSTITUTION (The Federal), Safety in.—Our national Constitution, the ark of our safety, and grand palladium of our peace and happiness.—R. TO A MASSACHUSETTS CITIZENS. viii. 160. (1800.)

1705. CONSTITUTION (The Federal), Security in.—A constitution has been acquired, which, though neither of us thinks perfect, yet both consider as competent to render our fellow citizens the happiest and the securest on whom the sun has ever shone.—To JOHN ADAMS. vi, 227. FORD ED., ix, 429. (M., 1813.)

1706. CONSTITUTION (The Federal), Self-government and.—No constitution was ever before so well calculated as ours for extensive empire and self-government.—To PRESIDENT MADISON. v, 444. (M., April 1809.)

1707. CONSTITUTION (The Federal), Theory of.—The true theory of our Constitution is surely the wisest and best, that the States are independent as to everything within themselves, and united as to everything respecting foreign affairs. Let the General Government be reduced to foreign concerns only, and let our affairs be disentangled from those of all other nations, except as to commerce, which the merchants will manage the better. the more they are left free to manage for themselves, and our General Government may be reduced to a very simple organization, and a very inexpensive one; a few plain duties to be performed by a few servants.—To GIDEON GRANGER. iv, 331. FORD ED., vii, 451. (M., 1800.)

1708. CONSTITUTION (The Federal), Value of.—Much has been gained by the new Constitution; for the former was terminating in anarchy, as necessarily consequent to inefficiency.—To GEORGE MASON. iii, 148. FORD ED., v, 183. (N.Y., 1790.)

1709. CONSTITUTION (The Federal), Wisdom of.—The Constitution * * * is unquestionably the wisest ever yet presented to men, and some of the accommodations of interest which it has adopted are greatly pleasing to me, who have had occasions of seeing how difficult those interests were to accommodate.—To DAVID HUMPHREYS. iii, 12. FORD ED., v, 80. (P., March 1789.)

1710. CONSTITUTION (French), Advice of Jefferson on.—I wish you success in your meeting [of the Notables]. I should form

better hopes of it, if it were divided into two houses instead of seven. Keeping the good model of your neighboring country [England] before your eyes, you may get on, step by step, towards a good constitution. Though that model is not perfect, yet, as it would unite more suffrages than any new one which could be proposed. it is better to make that the object. If every advance is to be purchased by filling the royal coffers with gold, it will be gold well employed.—To MARQUIS LAFAYETTE. ii, 131. (P., 1787.)

1711. CONSTITUTION (French), Amelioration of.—If the *Etats Genereux*, when they assemble, do not aim at too much, they may begin a good constitution. There are three articles which they may easily obtain; 1. their own meeting, periodically; 2. the exclusive right of taxation; 3. the right of registering laws, and proposing amendments to them, as exercised now by the parliaments. This last would be readily approved by the court, on account of their hostility against the parliaments, and would lead immediately to the origination of laws. The second has been already solemnly avowed by the King; and it is well understood there would be no opposition to the first. If they push at much more, all may fail.—To JAMES MADISON. ii, 506. FORD ED., v, 54. (P., Nov. 1788.)

1712. CONSTITUTION (French), Amendments contemplated.—No plan [of a constitution] is yet reported; but the leading members [of the National Assembly] (with some small differences of opinion) have in contemplation the following: The Executive power in a hereditary King, with a negative on laws, and power to dissolve the legislature; to be considerably restrained in the making of treaties, and limited in his expenses. The Legislative is a House of Representatives. They propose a Senate also, chosen on the plan of our Federal Senate by the Provincial Assemblies, but to be for life, of a certain age (they talk of forty years), and certain wealth (four or five hundred guineas a year), but to have no other power against the laws but to remonstrate against them to the Representatives, who will then determine their fate by a simple majority. This, you will readily perceive, is a mere council of revision, like that of New York, which, in order to be something, must form an alliance with the King, to avail themselves of his veto. The alliance will be useful to both, and to the nation. The Representatives to be chosen every two or three years. The Judiciary system is here prepared than any other part of the plan; however, they will abolish the parliaments, and establish an order of judges and justices, general and provincial, a good deal like ours, with trial by jury in criminal cases certainly, perhaps also in civil. The provinces will have Assemblies for their provincial government, and the cities a municipal body for municipal government, all founded on the basis of popular election. These subordinate governments, though completely dependent on the general one, will be entrusted with almost the whole of the details which our State governments exercise. They will have their own judiciary, final in all but great cases; the Executive business will principally pass through their hands, and a certain local legislature will be allowed them. In short, ours has been professedly their model, in which such changes are made as a difference of circumstances rendered necessary, and some others, neither necessary nor advantageous, but into which men will ever run, when versed in theory and new in the practice of government, when acquainted with man only as they see him in their books, and not in the world.—To JAMES MADISON. iii, 97. FORD ED., v, 108. (P., Aug. 1789.)

1713. CONSTITUTION (French), Amendments demanded.—The [National] Assembly * * * proceeded to arrange the order in which they would take up the heads of their constitution as follows: First, and as preliminary to the whole, a general Declaration of the Rights of Man. Then, specifically, the Principles of the Monarchy; Rights of the Nation; Rights of the King; Rights of the Citizens; organization and rights of the National Assembly; forms necessary for the enactment of Laws; organization and functions of the Provincial and Municipal Assemblies; duties and limits of the Judiciary power; functions and duties of the Military power. A Declaration of the Rights of Man, as the preliminary of their work, was accordingly prepared and proposed by the Marquis de Lafayette.—AUTOBIOGRAPHY. i, 96. FORD ED., i, 132. (1821.)

1714. CONSTITUTION (French), Cooperation of Jefferson invited.—The Assembly appointed a committee for the "reduction of a project" of a constitution, at the head of which was the Archbishop of Bordeaux. I received from him, as chairman of the committee, a letter of July 20th [1789], requesting me to attend and assist at their deliberations; but I excused myself, on the obvious considerations that my mission was to the King as Chief Magistrate of the nation, that my duties were limited to the concerns of my own country, and forbade me to intermeddle with the internal transactions of that in which I had been received under a specific character only.—AUTOBIOGRAPHY. i, 103. FORD ED., i, 143. (1821.)

1715. CONSTITUTION (French), Divergent views on.—The plan of a constitution was discussed in sections, and so reported from time to time, as agreed to by the committee. The first respected the general frame of the government; and that this should be formed into three departments, Executive, Legislative and Judiciary, was generally agreed. But when they proceeded to subordinate developments, many and various shades of opinion came into conflict, and schism, strongly marked, broke the Patriots into fragments of very discordant principles. The first question: Whether there should be a King? met with no open opposition; and it was readily agreed that the government of France should be monarchical and hereditary. Shall the King have a negative on the laws? Shall that negative be absolute or suspensive only? Shall there be two Chambers of Legislation, or one only? If two, shall one of them be hereditary? or for life? or for a fixed term? and named by the King? or elected by the people? These questions found strong differences of opinion, and produced repulsive combinations among the Patriots. The Aristocracy was cemented by a common principle of preserving the ancient *régime*, or whatever should be nearest to it. Making this their polar star, they moved in phalanx, gave preponderance on every question to the minorities of the Patriots, and always to those who advocated the least change. The features of the new constitution were thus assuming a fearful aspect, and great alarm was produced among the honest Patriots by these dissensions in their ranks.—AUTOBIOGRAPHY. i, 103. FORD ED., i, 144. (1821.)

— CONSTITUTION (French), Jefferson's Bill of Rights for.—See BILL OF RIGHTS.

1716. CONSTITUTION (French), Jefferson, Patriots and.—The features of the new Constitution were thus assuming a fearful aspect, and great alarm was produced among the honest Patriots in their ranks. In this uneasy state of things, I received one day a note from the Marquis de Lafayette, informing me that he should bring a party of six or eight friends to ask a dinner of me the next day. * * * When they arrived, they were Lafayette himself, Duport, Barnave, Alexander La Meth, Blacon, Mounier, Maubourg and Dagout. These were leading Patriots, of honest but differing opinions, sensible of the necessity of effecting a coalition by mutual sacrifices, knowing each other, and not afraid, therefore, to unbosom themselves mutually. This last was a material principle in the selection. With this view, the Marquis had invited the conference, and had fixed the time and place inadvertently as to the embarrassment under which it might place me. The cloth being removed, wine set on the table, after the American manner, the Marquis introduced the objects of the conference, by summarily reminding them of the state of things in the Assembly, the course which the principles of the Constitution were taking, and the inevitable result unless checked by more concord among the Patriots themselves. He observed, that although he also had his opinion, he was ready to sacrifice it to that of his brethren of the same cause; but that a common opinion must now be formed, or the Aristocracy would carry everything and that, whatever they should now agree on, he, at the head of the National force, would maintain. The discussions began at the hour of four and were continued till ten o'clock in the evening; during which time I was a silent witness to a coolness and candor of argument, unusual in the conflicts of political opinion; to a logical reasoning and chaste eloquence, disfigured by no gaudy tinsel of rhetoric or declamation, and truly worthy of being placed in parallel with the finest dialogues of antiquity, as handed to us by Xenophon, by Plato and Cicero. The result was an agreement that the King should have a suspensive veto on the laws, that the legislature should be composed of a single body only, and that to be chosen by the people. This Concordat decided the fate of the Constitution. The Patriots all rallied to the principles thus settled, carried every question agreeably to them, and reduced the Aristocracy to insignificance and impotence.—AUTOBIOGRAPHY. i, 104. FORD ED., i, 144. (1821.)

1717. CONSTITUTION (French), Montmorin, Jefferson and.—But duties of exculpation were now incumbent on me. I waited on Count Montmorin the next morning, and explained to him with truth and candor how it had happened that my house had been made the scene of conferences of such a character. He told me he already knew everything which had passed, that so far from taking umbrage at the use of my house on that occasion, he earnestly wished I would habitually assist at such conferences, being sure that I should be useful in moderating the warmer spirits, and promoting a wholesome and practicable reformation only. I told him I knew too well the duties I owed to the King, to the nation and to my own country, to take any part in councils concerning their internal government, and that I should persevere, with care, in the character of a neutral and passive spectator, with wishes only and very sincere ones, that those measures might prevail which would be for the greatest good of the nation. I have no doubts, indeed, that this conference was previously known and approved by this honest minister, who was in confidence and communication with the Patriots, and wished for a reasonable reform of the Constitution.—AUTOBIOGRAPHY. i, 105. FORD ED., i, 146. (1821.)

1718. CONSTITUTION (French), Necessity for.—Nor should we wonder at the pressure, [for a fixed constitution] when we consider the monstrous abuses of power under which * * * the [French] people were ground to powder; when we pass in review the weight of their taxes, and the inequality of their distribution; the oppressions of the tithes, the tailles, the corvées, the gabelles, the farms and barriers; the shackles on commerce by monopolies; on industry by guilds and corporations; on the freedom of conscience, of thought, and of speech; on the freedom of the press by the Censure; and of the person by *Lettres de Cachet*; the cruelty of the Criminal code generally; the atrocities of the Rack; the venality of the judges, and their partialities to the rich; the monopoly of Military honors by the Noblesse; the enormous expenses of the Queen, the Princes and the Court; the prodigalities of pensions; and the riches, luxury, indolence and immorality of the Clergy. Surely under such a mass of misrule and oppression, a people might justly press for a thorough reformation, and might even dismount their rough-shod riders, and leave them to walk on their own legs.—AUTOBIOGRAPHY. i, 86. FORD ED., i, 118. (1821.)

1719. CONSTITUTION (Great Britain's), Root of.—I think your book has deduced the constitution of the English nation from its rightful root, the Anglo-Saxon. It is really wonderful that so many able and learned men should have failed in their attempts to define it with correctness. No wonder, then, that [Thomas] Paine, who thought more than he read, should have credited the great authorities who have declared, that the will of parliament is the constitution of England. So Marbois, before the French Revolution, observed to me, that the Almanac Royal was the constitution of France. Your derivation of it from the Anglo-Saxons, seems to be made on legitimate principles. Having driven out the former inhabitants of that part of the island called England, they become aborigines as to you, and your lineal ancestors. They, doubtless, had a constitution; and although they have not left it in a written formula, to the precise text of which you may always appeal, yet they have left fragments of their history and laws, from which it may be inferred with considerable certainty. What ever their history and laws show to have been practiced with approbation, we may presume was permitted by their constitution; whatever was not so practiced, was not permitted. And, although this constitution was violated and set at naught by Norman force, yet force cannot change right. A perpetual claim was kept up by the nation, by their perpetual demand of a restoration of their Saxon laws; which shows they were never relinquished by the will of the nation. In the pullings and haulings for these ancient rights, between the nation, and its kings of the races of Plantagenets, Tudors and Stuarts, there was sometimes gain, and sometimes loss, until the final re-conquest of their rights from the Stuarts. The destitution and expulsion of this race broke the thread

of pretended inheritance, extinguished all regal usurpations, and the nation reentered into all its rights; and although in their Bill of Rights they specifically reclaimed some only, yet the omission of the others was no renunciation of the right to assume their exercise also, whenever occasion should occur. The new King received no rights or powers, but those expressly granted to him. It has ever appeared to me, that the difference between the whig and the tory of England is, that the whig deduces his rights from the Anglo-Saxon source and the tory from the Norman. And Hume, the great apostle of toryism, says, in so many words (note AA to chapter 42), that, in the reign of the Stuarts, "it was the people who encroached upon the sovereign, not the sovereign who attempted, as is pretended, to usurp upon the people." This supposes the Norman usurpations to be rights in his successors. And again (C. 159), "the commons established a principle, which is noble in itself, and seems specious, but is belied by all history and experience, *that the people are the origin of all just power*." And where else will this degenerate son of science, this traitor to his fellow men, find the origin of *just* powers, if not in the majority of the society? Will it be in the minority? Or in an individual of that minority? Our Revolution commenced on more favorable ground. It presented us an album on which we were to write what we pleased. We had no occasion to search into musty records, to hunt up royal parchments, or to investigate the laws and institutions of a semi-barbarous ancestry. We appealed to those of nature, and found them engraved on our hearts. Yet, we did not avail ourselves of all the advantages of our position. We had never been permitted to exercise self-government. When forced to assume it, we were novices in its science. Its principles and forms had entered little into our former education. We established some, although not all its important principles.—To JOHN CARTWRIGHT. vii, 355. (M., 1824.)

1720. CONSTITUTION (Spanish), Proposed.—The Constitution proposed has one feature which I like much; that which provides that when the three coordinate branches differ in their construction of the Constitution, the opinion of two branches shall overrule the third. Our Constitution has not sufficiently solved this difficulty.—To VALENTINE DE FORONDA. v, 473. (M., 1809.)

1721. CONSTITUTION (Spanish), State Church.—There are parts of the new Constitution of Spain in which you would expect, of course, that we should not concur. One of these is the intolerance of all but the Catholic religion; and no security provided against the reestablishment of an Inquisition, the exclusive judge of Catholic opinions, and authorized to proscribe and punish those it shall deem anti-Catholic.—To CHEVALIER DE ONIS. vi, 342. (M., 1814.)

1722. CONSTITUTION (Spanish), Suffrage.—There is one provision [in the new Constitution of Spain] which will immortalize its inventors. It is that which, after a certain epoch, disfranchises every citizen who cannot read and write. This is new, and is the fruitful germ of the improvement of everything good, and the correction of everything imperfect in the present Constitution. This will give you an enlightened people, and an energetic public opinion which will control and enchain the aristocratic spirit of the government.—To CHEVALIER DE ONIS. vi, 342. (M., 1814.)

1723. —— ——. In the Constitution of Spain, as proposed by the late Cortes, there was a principle entirely new to me, * * * that no person, born after that day, should ever acquire the rights of citizenship until he could read and write. It is impossible sufficiently to estimate the wisdom of this provision. Of all those which have been thought of for securing fidelity in the administration of the government, constant ralliance to the principles of the Constitution, and progressive amendments with the progressive advances of the human mind, or changes in human affairs, it is the most effectual. Enlighten the people generally, and tyranny and oppressions of body and mind will vanish like evil spirits at the dawn of day. Although I do not, with some enthusiasts, believe that the human condition will ever advance to such a state of perfection as that there shall no longer be pain or vice in the world, yet I believe it susceptible of much improvement, and most of all, in matters of government and religion; and that the diffusion of knowledge among the people is to be the instrument by which it is to be effected. The Constitution of the Cortes had defects enough; but when I saw in it this amendatory provision, I was satisfied all would come right in time, under its salutary operation.—To Dupont de Nemours. vi, 592. Ford ed., x, 24. (M., 1816.)

— **CONSTITUTION** (Spanish-American).—See Spanish America.

— **CONSTITUTION OF VIRGINIA.**— See Virginia.

1724. CONSTITUTIONS (American), **Amending.**—Happily for us, that when we find our constitutions defective and insufficient to secure the happiness of our people, we can assemble with all the coolness of philosophers, and set them to rights, while every other nation on earth must have recourse to arms to amend or to restore their constitutions.—To C. W. F. Dumas. ii, 264. (P., Sep. 1787.)

1725. —— ——. Had our former Constitution been unalterable (pardon the absurdity of the hypothesis), we must have gone to ruin with our eyes open.—To Benjamin Vaughan. v, 334. (P., 1791.)

1726. —— ——. Whatever be the Constitution, great care must be taken to provide a mode of amendment, when experience or change of circumstances shall have manifested that any part of it is unadapted to the good of the nation. In some of our States it requires a new authority from the whole people, acting by their representatives, chosen for this express purpose, and assembled in convention. This is found too difficult for remedying the imperfections which experience develops from time to time in an organization of the first impression. A greater facility of amendment is certainly requisite to maintain it in a course of action accommodated to the times and changes through which we are ever passing.—To A. Coray. vii, 323. (M., 1823.)

1727. CONSTITUTIONS (American), **Best of all Constitutions.**—The worst of the American constitutions is better than the best which ever existed before in any other country, and they are wonderfully perfect for a first essay. Yet, every human essay must have defects.—To T. M. Randolph. ii, 175. Ford ed., iv, 403. (P., 1787.)

1728. CONSTITUTIONS (American), **Characteristics of.**—Our Revolution * * * presented us an album on which we were free to write what we pleased. * * * Yet we did not avail ourselves of all the advantages of our position. We had never been permitted to exercise self-government. When forced to assume it, we were novices in its science. Its principles and forms had entered little into our former education. We established, however, some although not all its important principles. The constitutions of most of our States assert that all power is inherent in the people; that they may exercise it by themselves, in all cases to which they think themselves competent (as in electing their functionaries executive and legislative, and deciding by a jury of themselves, in all judiciary cases in which any fact is involved), or they may act by representatives, freely and equally chosen; that it is their right and duty to be at all times armed; that they are entitled to freedom of person, freedom of religion, freedom of property, and freedom of the press. In the structure of our legislatures, we think experience has proved the benefit of subjecting questions to two separate bodies of deliberants; but in constituting these, natural right has been mistaken, some making one of these bodies, and some both, the representatives of property instead of persons; whereas the double deliberation might be as well obtained without any violation of true principle, either by requiring a greater age in one of the bodies, or by electing a proper number of representatives of persons, dividing them by lots into two chambers, and renewing the division at frequent intervals, in order to break up all cabals.—To John Cartwright. vii, 356. (M., 1824.)

1729. CONSTITUTIONS (American), **English Constitution and.**—The first principle of a good government is, certainly, a distribution of its powers into executive, judiciary and legislative, and a subdivision of the latter into two or three branches. It is a good step gained, when it is proved that the English Constitution, acknowledged to be better than all which have preceded it, is only better in proportion as it has approached nearer to this distribution of powers. From this, the last step is easy, to show by a comparison of our constitutions with that of England, how much more perfect they are.—To John Adams. ii, 282. Ford ed., iv, 454. (P., 1787.)

1730. CONSTITUTIONS (American), **Happiness under.**—It is a misfortune that our countrymen do not sufficiently know the value of their constitutions, and how much happier they are rendered by them than any other people on earth by the governments under which they live.—To John Adams. ii, 282. Ford ed., iv, 455. (P., 1787.)

1731. CONSTITUTIONS (American), Permanent.—A permanent constitution must be the work of quiet, leisure, much inquiry, and great deliberation.—To A. Coray. vii, 320. (M., 1823.)

1732. CONSTITUTIONS (American), Principles of.—There are certain principles in which our constitutions all agree, and which all cherish as vitally essential to the protection of the life, liberty, property, and safety of the citizen. 1. Freedom of religion, restricted only from *acts* of trespass on that of others. 2. Freedom of person, securing every one from imprisonment, or other bodily restraint, but by the laws of the land. This is effected by the law of *habeas corpus*. 3. Trial by jury, the best of all safe-guards for the person, the property, and the fame of every individual. 4. The exclusive right of legislation and taxation in the representatives of the people. 5. Freedom of the press, subject only to liability for personal injuries.—To A. Coray. vii, 323. (M., 1823.)

1733. CONSTITUTIONS (American), Revision of.—Some men look at constitutions with sanctimonious reverence, and deem them like the ark of the covenant, too sacred to be touched. They ascribe to the men of the preceding age a wisdom more than human, and suppose what they did to be beyond amendment. I knew that age well: I belonged to it, and labored with it. It deserved well of its country. It was very like the present, but without the experience of the present; and forty years of experience in government is worth a century of book-reading; and this they would say themselves, were they to rise from the dead. I am certainly not an advocate for frequent and untried changes in laws and constitutions. I think moderate imperfections had better be borne with; because, when once known, we accommodate ourselves to them and find practical means of correcting their ill effects. But I know, also, that laws and institutions must go hand in hand with the progress of the human mind. As that becomes more developed, more enlightened, as new discoveries are made, new truths disclosed, and manners and opinions change with the change of circumstances, institutions must advance also, and keep pace with the times. We might as well require a man to wear still the coat which fitted him when a boy, as civilized society to remain ever under the regimen of their barbarous ancestors. It is this preposterous idea which has lately deluged Europe in blood. Their monarchs, instead of wisely yielding to the gradual change of circumstances, of favoring progressive accommodation to progressive improvement, have clung to old abuses, entrenched themselves behind steady habits, and obliged their subjects to seek through blood and violence rash and ruinous innovations, which, had they been referred to the peaceful deliberations and collected wisdom of the nation, would have been put into acceptable and salutary forms. Let us follow no such examples, nor weakly believe that one generation is not as capable as another of taking care of itself, and of ordering its own affairs. Let us [Virginia], as our sister States have done, avail ourselves of our reason and experience, to correct the crude essays of our first and unexperienced, although wise, virtuous, and well meaning councils. And lastly, let us provide in our Constitution for its revision at stated periods. What these periods should be, nature herself indicates. By the European tables of mortality, of the adults living at any one moment of time, a majority will be dead in about nineteen years. At the end of that period then, a new majority is come into place; or, in other words, a new generation. Each generation is as independent of the one preceding as that was of all which has gone before. It has, then, like them, a right to choose for itself the form of government it believes most promotive of its own happiness; consequently, to accommodate to the circumstances in which it finds itself, that received from its predecessors; and it is for the peace and good of mankind, that a solemn opportunity of doing this every nineteen or twenty years, should be provided by the Constitution; so that it may be handed on, with periodical repairs, from generation to generation, to the end of time, if anything human can so long endure. It is now forty years since the Constitution of Virginia was formed. The same tables inform us, that, within that period, two-thirds of the adults then living are now dead. Have, then, the remaining third, even if they had the wish, the right to hold in obedience to their will, and to laws heretofore made by them, the other two-thirds, who, with themselves, compose the present mass of adults? If they have not, who has? The dead? But the dead have no rights. They are nothing; and nothing can not own something. Where there is no substance, there can be no accident. This corporeal globe, and everything upon it, belong to its present corporeal inhabitants, during their generation. They alone have a right to direct what is the concern of themselves alone, and to declare the law of that direction; and this declaration can only be made by their majority. That majority, then, has a right to depute representatives to a convention, and to make the constitution what they think will be the best for themselves. . . . If this avenue be shut to the call of sufferance, it will make itself heard through that of force, and we shall go on, as other nations are doing, in the endless circle of oppression, rebellion, reformation; and oppression, rebellion, reformation, again; and so on forever.—To Samuel Kerchival, vii, 14. Ford ed., x, 42. (M., 1816.)

1734. CONSTITUTIONS (American), Written.—Though written constitutions may be violated in moments of passion or delusion, yet they furnish a text to which those who are watchful may again rally and recall the people. They fix, too, for the people the principles of their political creed.—To Dr. Joseph Priestley. iv, 441. Ford ed., viii, 159. (W., 1802.)

1735. ———. Virginia was not only the first of the American States, but the first nation in the world, at least within the records of history, which, peaceably by its wise men, formed on free deliberation a constitution of government for itself, and deposited it in writing among their archives, always ready and open to the appeal of every citizen.—To John Hambden Pleasants. vii. 344. Ford ed., x. 302. (M., 1824.)

1736. ———— ————. Virginia was not only the first of the States, but, I believe I may say, the first of the nations of the earth, which assembled its wise men peaceably together to form a fundamental constitution, to commit it to writing and place it among their archives, where everyone should be free to appeal to its text. But this act was very imperfect. The other States, as they proceeded successively to the same work, made successive improvements: and several of them, still further corrected by experience, have, by conventions, still further amended their first forms. Virginia has gone on so far with its *premiere ebauche;* but is now proposing a convention for amendment.—To John Cartwright. vii, 357. (M., 1824.)

1737. CONSTRUCTION OF THE CONSTITUTION.—Our peculiar security is in the possession of a written Constitution. Let us not make it a blank paper by construction.— To Wilson C. Nicholas. iv, 506. Ford ed., viii, 247. (M., 1803.) See 1666.

1738. CONSTRUCTION OF INSTRUMENTS.—When an instrument admits two constructions, the one safe, the other dangerous, the one precise, the other indefinite, I prefer that which is safe and precise.—To Wilson C. Nicholas. iv. 506. Ford ed., viii. 247. (M., 1803.)

1739. CONSULAR CONVENTION, History of French.—In 1784 a convention was entered into between Dr. Franklin and the Count de Vergennes concerning consuls. It contained many things absolutely inadmissible by the laws of the several States, and inconsistent with their genius and character. Dr. Franklin not being a lawyer, and the project offered by the Count de Vergennes being a copy of the conventions which were established between France and the despotic States on the continent (for with England they never had one), he seems to have supposed it a formula established by universal experience, and not to have suspected that it might contain matters, inconsistent with the principles of a free people. He returned to America soon after the signature of it. Congress received it with the deepest concern. They honored Dr. Franklin, they were attached to the French nation; but they could not relinquish fundamental principles. They declined ratifying it, and sent it back with new powers and instructions to Mr. Jefferson, who succeeded Dr. Franklin at Paris. The most objectionable matters were the privileges and exemptions given to the consuls, and their powers over persons of the nation, establishing a jurisdiction independent of that of the nation in which it was exercised, and uncon-

trollable by it. The French government valued these because they then apprehended a very extensive emigration from France to the United States, which this convention enabled them to control. It was, therefore, with the utmost reluctance, and inch by inch, that they could be induced to relinquish those conditions. The following changes, however, were effected by the convention of 1788: The clauses of the convention of 1784, clothing consuls with the privileges of the laws of nations, were struck out, and they were expressly subjected in their persons and property, to the laws of the land. The giving the right of sanctuary to their houses was reduced to a protection of their chancery room and its papers. Their coercive power over passengers were taken away; and those whom they might have termed deserters of their nation, were restrained to deserted seamen only. The clause allowing them to arrest and send back vessels was struck out, and instead of it they were allowed to exercise a police over the ships of their nation generally. So was that which declared the indelibility of the character of subject, and the explanation and extension of the eleventh article of the treaty of amity. The innovations in the laws of evidence were done away; and the convention, from being perpetual, was limited to twelve years. Although strong endeavors were made to do away some other disagreeable articles, yet it was found that more could not be done without disturbing the good humor, which Congress wished so much to preserve, and the limitation obtained for the continuance of the convention insured our getting finally rid of the whole. Congress, therefore, satisfied with having so far amended their situation, ratified the convention of 1788 without hesitation.*— To Mr. Wingate. ix, 462. (1803.)

1740. ———— ————. A consular convention had been agreed on in 1784, between Dr. Franklin and the French government, containing several articles, so entirely inconsistent with the laws of the several States, and the general spirit of our citizens, that Congress withheld their ratification, and sent it back to me with instructions to get those articles expunged, or modified, so as to render them compatible with our laws. The Minister unwillingly released us from these concessions, which, indeed, authorized the exercise of powers very offensive in a free State. After much discussion, the convention was reformed in a considerable degree, and was signed by the Count Montmorin and myself, on the 14th of November, 1788; not, indeed, such as I would have wished, but such as could be obtained with good humor and friendship.—Autobiography. i, 85. Ford ed., i, 117. (1821.)

1741. CONSULS, The Confederation and.—As the States have renounced the separate power of making treaties with foreign nations, they cannot separately receive a consul; and as Congress have, by the confederation, no immediate jurisdiction over com-

* This convention is the basis of our consular system, which is practically the same as Jefferson arranged it.—Editor.

merce, as they have only a power of bringing that jurisdiction into existence by entering into a treaty, till such treaty be entered into, Congress themselves cannot receive a consul. Till a treaty, then, there exists no power in any part of our government, federal or particular, to admit a consul among us. * * * Nothing less than a new article, to be agreed to by all the States, would enable Congress, or the particular States, to receive him.—To DAVID HARTLEY. i, 426. FORD ED., iv, 96. (P., 1785.)

1742. CONSULS, Creation of.—A consul is the creature of a treaty. No nation without an agreement, can place an officer in another country, with any powers or jurisdiction whatever.—To DAVID HARTLEY. i, 426. FORD ED., iv, 96. (P., 1785.)

1743. ——— ———. A consul is the creature of a convention altogether: without this he must be unknown. and his jurisdiction unacknowledged by the laws of the country in which he is placed. The will of the sovereign in most countries can give a jurisdiction by a simple order. With us, the Confederation admitting Congress to make treaties with foreign powers, they can by treaty or convention. provide for the admission and jurisdiction of consuls and the Confederation, and whatever is done under it, being paramount to the laws of the States, this establishes the power of the consuls. But without a convention, the laws of the States cannot take any notice of a consul. nor permit him to exercise any jurisdiction.—To WILLIAM CARMICHAEL. ii, 17. (P., 1786.)

1744. CONSULS, Excluded.—With respect to the placing consuls in the British [West India] Islands, we are so far from being permitted that a common mercantile factor is not permitted by their laws.—To MR. COXE. iv, 69. (1793.)

1745. CONSULS, Inutility of.—As to ourselves, we do not find the institution of consuls very necessary. Its history commences in times of barbarism, and might well have ended with them. During these, they were perhaps useful, and may still be so in countries not yet emerged from that condition. But all civilized nations at this day. understand so well the advantages of commerce, that they provide protection and encouragement for merchant strangers and vessels coming among them. So extensive. too, have commercial connections now become, that every mercantile house has correspondents in almost every port. They address their vessels to these correspondents, who are found to take better care of their interests, and to obtain more effectually the protection of the laws of the country for them, than the consul of their nation can. He is generally a foreigner. unpossessed of the little details of knowledge of greatest use to them. He makes national questions of all the difficulties which arise; the correspondent prevents them. We carry on commerce with good success in all parts of the world: yet we have not a consul in a single port, nor a complaint for the want of

one, except from the persons who wish to be consuls themselves. Though these considerations may not be strong enough to establish the absolute inutility of consuls, they may make us less anxious to extend their privileges and jurisdictions, so as to render them objects of jealousy and irritation in the places of their residence. That the government [of France] thinks them useful, is sufficient reason for us to give them all the functions and facilities which our circumstances will admit. Instead, therefore, of declining, every article [in the consular convention] which will be useless to us, we accede to everyone which will not be inconvenient. Had this nation alone been concerned, our desire to gratify them, might have tempted us to press still harder on the laws and opinions of our country. But your Excellency knows, that we stand engaged in treaties with some nations, which will give them occasion to claim whatever privileges we yield to any other. This renders circumspection more necessary.—To COUNT DE MONTMORIN. ii, 420. (P., 1788.)

1746. CONSULS, Law of Nations and. —The law of nations does not of itself extend to consuls at all. They are not of the diplomatic class of characters, to which alone that law extends of right. Convention. indeed, may give it to them. and sometimes has done so; but in that case, the convention can be produced. In ours with France, it is expressly declared that consuls shall not have the privileges of that law, and we have no convention with any other nation. * * * Independently of law, consuls are to be considered as distinguished foreigners, dignified by a commission from their sovereign, and specially recommended by him to the respect of the nation with whom they reside. They are subject to the laws of the land, indeed, precisely as other foreigners are, a convention, where there is one, making a part of the laws of the land; but if at any time, their conduct should render it necessary to assert the authority of the laws over them. the rigor of those laws should be tempered by our respect for their sovereign, as far as the case will admit. This moderate and respectful treatment towards foreign consuls, it is my duty to recommend and press on our citizens, because I ask it for their good towards our own consuls, from the people with whom they reside.—To T. NEWTON. iii, 295. (1791.)

1747. CONSULS, Market Reports and. —It would be useful if the consuls could forward directly to me, from time to time, the prices current of their place, and any other circumstance which it might be interesting to make known to our merchants without delay.—CIRCULAR TO CONSULS. iii, 430. (Pa., 1792.)

1748. CONSULS, Native Citizens for.— With respect to the consular appointments it is a duty on me to add some observations, which my situation here has enabled me to make. I think it was in the spring of 1784, that Congress (harassed by multiplied applications of foreigners, of whom nothing was known but on their own information, or on that of others as unknown as themselves) came to a resolution, that the interest of America would not permit the naming any person, not a citizen, to the office of consul, vice-consul, agent or commissary. This was intended as a general answer to that swarm of foreign pretenders. It appears to me, that it will be best still to preserve a part of this regulation. *Native* citizens, on several valuable accounts, are preferable to aliens, and to citizens alien-born. They possess our language, know our laws, customs, and commerce; have, generally, acquaintance in the United States; give better satisfaction, and are more to be relied on in point of fidelity. Their disadvantages are an imperfect acquaintance with the language of this country, and an ignorance of the organization of its judicial and executive powers, and consequent awkwardness, whenever application to either of these is necessary, as it frequently is. But it happens that in some of the principal ports of France, there is not a single American (as in Marseilles, L'Orient, and Havre), in others but one (as in Nantes and Rouen), and in Bordeaux only, are there two or three. Fortunately for the present moment, most of these are worthy of appointments. But we should look forward to future times, when there may happen to be no native citizens in a port, but such as, being bankrupt, have taken asylum in France from their creditors, or young ephemeral adventurers in commerce, without substance or conduct, or other descriptions, which might disgrace the consular office, without protecting our commerce. To avail ourselves of our good *native citizens,* when we have one in a port, and when there are none, to have yet some person to attend to our affairs, it appears to me advisable, to declare by a standing law that no person but a native citizen shall be capable of the office of consul, and that the consul's presence in his port shall suspend, for the time, the functions of the vice-consul. This is the rule of 1784, restrained to the office of consul, and to *native* citizens. The establishing this, by a standing law, will guard against the effect of particular applications, and will shut the door against such appplications.—To JOHN JAY. ii, 494. (P., 1788.)

1749. —— ——. The office of vice-consul may be given to the best subject in the port, whether citizen or alien; and that of consul be kept open for any native citizen of superior qualifications, who might come afterwards to establish himself in the port. The functions of the vice-consul would become dormant during the presence of his principal, come into activity again on his departure, and thus spare us and them the painful operation of revoking and reviving their commissions perpetually. Add to this that during the presence of the consul, the vice-consul would not be merely useless, but would be a valuable counsellor to his principal, new in the office, the language, laws and customs of the country. Every consul and vice-consul should be restrained in his jurisdiction to the port for which he is named, and the territory nearer to that than to any other consular or vice-consular port, and no idea be permitted to arise that the grade of consul gives a right to any authority whatever over a vice-consul, or draws on any dependence.—To JOHN JAY. ii, 496. (P., 1788.)

1750. —— ——. The determination to appoint natives only is generally proper, but not always. These places are for the most part of little consequence to the public; and if they can be made resources of profit to our ex-military worthies, they are so far advantageous. You and I, however, know that one of these novices, knowing nothing of the laws, or authorities of his port, nor speaking a word of its language, is of no more account than the fifth wheel of a coach.—To JAMES MONROE. vi, 552. (M., 1816.)

1751. CONSULS, Punished.—One of Genet's consuls* has committed a pretty serious deed at Boston, by going with an armed force taken from a French frigate in the harbor, and rescuing a vessel out of the hands of the marshal who had arrested her by process from a court of justice; in another instance, he kept off the marshal by an armed force from serving a process on a vessel. He is ordered, consequently, to be arrested himself, prosecuted and punished for the rescue, and his exequatur will be revoked.—To JAMES MADISON. iv, 52. FORD ED., vi, 401. (Pa., Sep. 1793.)

1752. —— ——. The President is informed * * * that M. Duplaine, consul of France at Boston, has * * * rescued a vessel from the officer of the court of justice, by process from which she was under arrest in his custody; and that he has in like manner, with an armed force, opposed and prevented the officer, charged with process from a court against another vessel, from serving that process. This daring violation of the laws requires the more attention, as it is by a foreigner clothed with a public character, arrogating an unfounded right to Admiralty jurisdiction, and probably meaning to assert it by this act of force. By the law of nations, consuls are not diplomatic characters, and have no immunities whatever against the laws of the land. To put this altogether out of dispute, a clause was inserted in our consular convention with France, making them amenable to the laws of the land, as other inhabitants. Consequently, M. Duplaine is liable to arrest, imprisonment, and other punishments, even capital, as other foreign subjects resident here. * * * You will immediately institute such a prosecution against him as the laws will warrant.—To CHRISTOPHER GORE. iv, 55. FORD ED., vi, 404. (Pa., Sep. 1793.)

1753. —— ——. If there be any doubt as to the character of his offence, whether of a higher or a lower grade, it will be best to prosecute for that which will admit the least doubt, because an acquittal, though it might

* The consuls appointed by Genet when he came here as Minister of the French Republic.—EDITOR.

be founded on the opinion that the grade of offence with which he is *charged* is higher than his *act* would support, yet it might be construed by the uninformed to be a judiciary decision against his amenability to the law, or perhaps in favor of the jurisdictions these consuls [Genet's appointments] are assuming. The process, therefore, should be of the surest kind, and all the proceedings well grounded.—To CHRISTOPHER GORE. iv, 55. FORD ED., vi, 405. (Pa., Sep. 1793.)

1754. —— ——. If an arrest * * * be the first step, it should be so managed as to leave room neither for escape nor rescue. It should be attended with every mark of respect, consistent with safe custody, and his confinement as mild and comfortable also, as that would permit. These are the distinctions to which a consul is entitled, that is to say, of a particular decorum of deportment towards him, indicative of respect to the sovereign whose officer he is.—To CHRISTOPHER GORE. iv, 55. FORD ED., vi, 405. (Pa., Sep. 1793.)

1755. CONSULS, Reception of.—We are very far from admitting your principle, that the government on their side has no other right, on the presentation of a consular commission, than to certify that, having examined it, they find it according to rule. The governments of both nations have a right, and that of yours has exercised it as to us, of considering the character of the person appointed; the place for which he is appointed, and other material circumstances; and of taking precautions as to his conduct, if necessary; and this does not defeat the general object of the convention, which, in stipulating that consuls shall be promoted on both sides, could not mean to supersede reasonable objections to particular persons, who might at the moment be obnoxious to the nation to which they were sent, or whose conduct might render them so at any time hereafter. In fact, every foreign agent depends on the double will of the two governments, of that which sends him, and of that which is to permit the exercise of his functions within their territory; and when either of these wills is refused or withdrawn, his authority to act within that territory becomes incomplete.—To E. C. GENET. iv, 90. FORD ED., vi, 463. (Pa., Dec. 1793.)

1756. —— ——. By what member of the government the right of giving or withdrawing permission is to be exercised here, is a question on which no foreign agent can be permitted to make himself the umpire. It is sufficient for him, under our government, that he is informed of it by the Executive.—To E. C. GENET. iv, 90. FORD ED., vi, 463. (Pa., Dec. 1793.)

1757. CONSULS, Uniform for.—The consuls and vice-consuls of the United States are free to wear the uniform of their navy, if they choose to do so. This is a deep blue coat with red facings, lining and cuffs, the cuffs slashed and a standing collar; a red waistcoat (laced or not at the election of the wearer) and blue breeches; yellow buttons with a foul anchor, and black cockades and small swords.—To THE CONSULS OF THE U. S. iii, 187. (1790.)

1758. CONSULS, Usurpation of Jurisdiction by.—I have it in charge, from the President of the United States, to give notice to all the consuls and vice-consuls of France, that if any of them * * * shall assume any jurisdiction not expressly given by the convention between France and the United States, the exequatur of the consul so transgressing will be immediately revoked, and his person submitted to such prosecutions and punishments as the laws may prescribe for the case.—CIRCULAR TO FRENCH CONSULS. FORD ED., vi, 417. (Sep. 1793.)

1759. —— ——. We learn * * * that the [French] consul of New York, in the first instance, and yourself in a subsequent one, forbade an officer of justice to serve the process with which he was charged from his court, on the British brig William Tell, taken by a French armed vessel, within a mile of our shores, * * * and that you had even given orders to the French squadron there to protect the vessel against any person who should attempt to take her from their custody. If this opposition were founded, * * * on the indulgence of the letters before cited [with respect to the William Tell], it was extending that to a case not within their purview; and even had it been precisely the case to which they were to be applied, is it possible to imagine you might assert it, within the body of the country, by force of arms? I forbear to make the observations which such a measure must suggest, and cannot but believe that a moment's reflection will evince to you the depth of the error committed in this opposition to an officer of justice, and in the means proposed to be resorted to in support of it. I am, therefore, charged to declare to you expressly, that the President expects and requires, that the officer of justice be not obstructed, in freely and peaceably serving the process of his court; and that, in the meantime, the vessel and her cargo be not suffered to depart, till the judiciary, if it will undertake it, or himself, if not, shall decide whether the seizure has been within the limits of our protection.—To E. C. GENET. iv, 68. FORD ED., vi, 421. (Pa., Sep. 1793.)

1760. —— ——. With respect to the usurpation of admiralty jurisdiction by the consuls of France, within these States, the honor and rights of the States themselves were sufficient motives for the Executive to take measures to prevent its continuance, as soon as they were apprised of it. They have been led, by particular considerations, to await the effect of these measures, believing they would be sufficient; but finding at length they were not, such others have been lately taken, as can no longer fail to suppress this irregularity completely.—To GEORGE HAMMOND. iv, 66. FORD ED., vi, 424. (Pa., Sep. 1793.)

1761. CONTENTION, Horror of.—There may be people to whose tempers and dispositions contention is pleasing and who, therefore, wish a continuance of confusion, but to me it is of all states but one the most horrid.—To JOHN RANDOLPH. i, 200. FORD ED., i, 482. (M., 1775.)

1762. CONTENTMENT, Wisdom of.—It is wise and well to be contented with the good things which the Master of the feast places before us, and to be thankful for what we have, rather than thoughtful about what we have not.—To MRS. JOHN ADAMS. vii, 53. FORD ED., x, 71. (M., 1817.)

— CONTINENTAL CONGRESS.—See CONGRESS.

1763. CONTRABAND OF WAR, Abusive Seizures.—We believe the practice of seizing what is called contraband of war, is an abusive practice, not founded in natural right. War between two nations cannot diminish the rights of the rest of the world remaining at peace. The doctrine that the rights of nations remaining quietly under the exercise of moral and social duties, are to give way to the convenience of those who prefer plundering and murdering one another, is a monstrous doctrine; and ought to yield to the more rational law, that "the wrongs which two nations endeavor to inflict on each other, must not infringe on the rights or conveniences of those remaining at peace".—To ROBERT R. LIVINGSTON. iv, 410. FORD ED., viii, 90. (M., 1801.)

1764. CONTRABAND OF WAR, National Law and.—What is contraband by the law of nature? Either everything which may aid or comfort an enemy or nothing. Either all commerce which would accommodate him is unlawful, or none is. The difference between articles of one or another description, is a difference in degree only. No line between them can be drawn. Either all intercourse must cease between neutrals and belligerents, or all be permitted. Can the world hesitate to say which shall be the rule? Shall two nations turning tigers, break up in one instant the peaceable relations of the whole world? Reason and nature clearly pronounce that the neutral is to go on in the enjoyment of all its rights, that its commerce remains free, not subject to the jurisdiction of another, nor consequently its vessels to search, or to inquiries whether their contents are the property of an enemy, or are of those which have been called contraband of war.—To ROBERT R. LIVINGSTON. iv, 410. FORD ED., viii, 90. (M., 1801.)

1765. CONTRABAND OF WAR, Naval Stores and.—I have had a consultation with Mr. Madison on the application of the British vessel of war for *stores*. We are both of opinion that if by this term he meant *sea stores* only, or even *munitions de bouche*, or provisions generally, there can be no objection to their taking them, or indeed anything except *contraband of war*. But what should be deemed contraband of war in this case we are not agreed. He thinks that as the English deem *naval stores* to be contraband, and as such take them from our vessels at sea,

we ought to retaliate their own definition on them. I think we ought to act on the opinion that they are not contraband; because by treaties between all the nations (I think) having treaties with another they are agreed not to be contraband; even England herself, with every nation but ours, makes them non-contraband, and the only treaty making them contraband (Jay's) is now expired. We ought, then, at once to rally with all the other nations on the ground that they are non-contraband; and if England treats them as contraband in our ships, instead of admitting it by retaliation, let us contest it on its true ground. Mr. Madison thinks France might complain of this; but I think not, as we shall permit both nations equally to take naval stores; or at least such articles of them as may be used for peaceable as well as warlike purposes; this being the true line.—To ALBERT GALLATIN. FORD ED., viii, 455. (June 1806.)

1766. CONTRABAND OF WAR, Provisions and.—Certainly *provisions* are not allowed by the consent of nations, to be contraband but where everything is so, as in the case of a blockaded town, with which all intercourse is forbidden.—To EDWARD EVERETT. vii, 270. (M., 1823.)

1767. CONTRACTS, Abiding by.—To preserve the faith of the nation by an exact discharge of its debts and contracts * * * [is one of] the landmarks by which we are to guide ourselves in all our proceedings.—SECOND ANNUAL MESSAGE. viii, 21. FORD ED., viii, 187. (Dec. 1802.)

1768. CONTRACTS, Congressmen and.—I am averse to giving contracts of any kind to members of the Legislature.—To ALBERT GALLATIN. v, 50. (W., 1807.)

1769. CONTRACTS, Impairment of.—Between citizens and citizens of the same State, and under their own laws, I know but a single case in which a jurisdiction is given to the General Government. That is, where anything but gold or silver is made a lawful tender, or the obligation of contracts is any otherwise impaired. The separate legislatures had so often abused that power, that the citizens themselves chose to trust it to the general rather than to their own special authorities.—To WILLIAM JOHNSON. vii, 296. FORD ED., x, 231. (M., 1823.)

1770. CONTRACTS, Liberation from.—There are circumstances which sometimes excuse the non-performance of contracts between man and man; so are there also between nation and nation. When performance, for instance, *becomes impossible*, non-performance is not immoral; so if performance becomes *self-destructive* to the party, the law of self-preservation overrules the laws of obligation in others.—FRENCH TREATIES OPINION. vii, 613. FORD ED., vi, 220. (1793.)

1771. —— ——. Reason, which gives the right of self-liberation from a contract in certain cases, has subjected it to certain just limitations. The danger which absolves us

must be great, inevitable and imminent.—
FRENCH TREATIES OPINION. vii, 614. FORD
ED., vi, 221. (1793.)

1772. —— ——. Obligation is not suspended till the danger is become real, and the moment of it so imminent, that we can no longer avoid decision without forever losing the opportunity to do it.—FRENCH TREATIES OPINION. vii, 615. FORD ED., vi, 222. (1793.)

1773. CONTRACTS, Possibilities and.—
If possibilities would void contracts, there never could be a valid contract, for possibilities hang over everything.—FRENCH TREATIES OPINION. vii, 614. FORD ED., vi, 222. (1793.)

1774. CONTROVERSY, Aversion to.—
Having an insuperable aversion to be drawn into controversy in the public papers, I must request not to be quoted.—To JOSEPH DELAPLAINE. vii, 21. FORD ED., x, 56. (M., 1816.)

1775. CONTROVERSY, Avoiding.—So many persons have of late found an interest or a passion gratified by imputing to me sayings and writings which I never said or wrote, or by endeavoring to draw me into newspapers to harass me personally, that I have found it necessary for my quiet and my other pursuits to leave them in full possession of the field, and not to take the trouble of contradicting them even in private conversation.—To ALEXANDER WHITE. iv, 201. FORD ED., vii, 174. (M., 1797.)

1776. CONTROVERSY, Declining.—As to myself, I shall take no part in any discussions. I leave others to judge of what I have done, and to give me exactly the place which they shall think I have occupied. Marshall has written libels on one side; others, I suppose, will be written on the other side; and the world will sift both and separate the truth as well as they can.—To JOHN ADAMS. vi, 127. FORD ED., ix, 388. (M., 1813.)

1777. CONVENT, Entering a.—And Madame Cosway in a convent! I knew that to much goodness of heart she joined enthusiasm and religion; but I thought that very enthusiasm would have prevented her from shutting up her adoration of the God of the universe within the walls of a cloister; that she would rather have sought the mountain top.—To MRS. CHURCH. FORD ED., vi, 455. (G., 1793.)

1778. CONVENTION (Federal), Call for.—The want of some authority which should procure justice to the public creditors, and an observance of treaties with foreign nations, produced the call of a convention of the States at Annapolis.*—THE ANAS. ix, 89. FORD ED., i, 158. (1818.)

1779. —— ——. All the States have come into the Virginia proposition for a commercial convention, the deputies of which are to agree on the form of an article giving to Congress the regulation of their commerce. Maryland alone has not named deputies, con-

* For quotation purposes the Annapolis Commercial Convention, and the Philadelphia Federal Convention are treated as one body.—EDITOR.

ceiving that Congress might as well propose the article. They are, however, for giving the power, and will, therefore, either nominate deputies to the convention, or accede to their measures.—To M. DE LAFAYETTE. ii, 21. (P., 1786.)

1780. CONVENTION (Federal), Character of.—It is really an assembly of demi-gods.*—To JOHN ADAMS. ii, 260. (P., 1787.)

1781. —— ——. The convention holding at Philadelphia consists of the ablest men in America.—To C. W. F. DUMAS. ii, 149. (P., 1787.)

1782. —— ——. A more able assembly never sat in America.—To C. W. F. DUMAS. ii, 264. (P., 1787.)

1783. CONVENTION (Federal), Publicity and.—I am sorry the Federal Convention began their deliberations by so abominable a precedent as that of tying up the tongues of their members. Nothing can justify this example but the innocence of their intentions; and ignorance of the value of public discussions.—To JOHN ADAMS. ii, 260. (P., 1787.)

1784. CONVENTION (Federal), Reform and.—I remain in hopes of great and good effects from the decision of the Assembly over which you are presiding.—To GENERAL WASHINGTON. ii, 250. (P., Aug. 1787.)

1785. —— ——. I look to the Federal Convention for an amendment of our Federal affairs.—To BENJAMIN HAWKINS. ii, 220. FORD ED., iv, 426. (P., 1787.)

1786. CONVENTION (Federal), Representation in.—I find by the public papers that your commercial convention [at Annapolis] failed in point of representation. If it should produce a full meeting in May, and a broader reformation, it will still be well.—To JAMES MADISON. ii, 65. FORD ED., iv, 332. (P., Dec. 1786.)

1787. CONVENTION, National Republican.—If * * * the [Federal] government should expire on the 3d of March by the loss of its head, there is no regular provision for reorganizing it, nor any authority but in the people themselves. They may authorize a convention to reorganize, and even amend the machine.—To BENJAMIN SMITH BARTON. iv, 353. FORD ED., vii, 490. (W., Feb. 14, 1801.)

1788. —— ——. The Federalists in Congress were completely alarmed at the resource for which we declared, to wit, a convention to reorganize the government, and to amend it. The very word convention gives them the horrors, as in the present democratical spirit of America, they fear they should lose some of the favorite morsels of the Constitution.—To JAMES MONROE. iv, 354. FORD ED., vii, 491. (W., Feb. 15, 1801.)

1789. —— ——. I have been, above all things, solaced by the prospect which opened on us [in the Presidential contest in 1801] in the event of a non-election of a President;

* Philadelphia Convention.—EDITOR.

in which case, the Federal Government would have been in the situation of a clock or watch run down. There was no idea of force, nor of any occasion for it. A convention, invited by the Republican members of Congress, with the virtual President and Vice-President, would have been on the ground in eight weeks, would have repaired the Constitution where it was defective, and wound it up again. This peaceable and legitimate resource, to which we are in the habit of implicit obedience, superseding all appeal to force, and being always within our reach, shows a precious principle of self-preservation in our composition, till a change of circumstances shall take place, which is not within prospect at any definite period.—To JOSEPH PRIESTLEY. vii, 374. FORD ED., viii, 22. (W., March 21, 1801.)

1790. CONVENTION (Virginia), First. —On the discontinuance of Assemblies [in Virginia], it became necessary to substitute in their place some other body, competent to the ordinary business of government, and to the calling forth the powers of the state for the maintenance of our opposition to Great Britain. Conventions were, therefore, introduced, consisting of two delegates from each county, meeting together and forming one House, on the plan of the former House of Burgesses, to whose places they succeeded. These were at first chosen anew for every particular session. But in March, 1775, they recommended to the people to choose a convention, which should continue in office a year.—NOTES ON VIRGINIA. viii, 363. FORD ED., iii, 225. (1782.)

1791. CONVENTION (Virginia), Powers of.—The convention of Virginia, which organized their new government, had been chosen before a separation from Great Britain had been thought of in their State. They had, therefore, none but the ordinary powers of legislation. This leaves their act for organizing the government subject to be altered by every legislative assembly, and though no general change in it has been made, yet its effect has been controlled in several special cases.—To M. DE MEUNIER. viii, 283. FORD ED., iv, 139. (P., 1786.)

1792. ———— ————. To our convention no special authority had been delegated by the people to form a permanent Constitution, over which their successors in legislation should have no powers of alteration. They had been elected for the ordinary purposes of legislation only, and at a time when the establishment of a new government had not been proposed or contemplated. Although, therefore, they gave to this act the title of a constitution, yet it could be no more than an act of legislation, subject, as their other acts were, to alteration by their successors.—To JOHN HAMBDEN PLEASANTS. vii, 344. FORD ED., x, 302. (M., 1824.)

1793. CONVENTIONS, Constitutional. —The * * * States in the Union have been of opinion that to render a form of government unalterable by ordinary acts of As-

sembly, the people must delegate persons with special powers. They have accordingly chosen special conventions to form and fix their governments.—NOTES ON VIRGINIA. viii, 367. FORD ED., iii, 229. (1782.)

1794. ———— ————. Happy for us that we are yet able to send our wise and good men together to talk over our form of government, discuss its weaknesses, and establish its remedies with the same *sang froid* as they would a subject of agriculture.—To RALPH IZARD. ii, 429. (P., 1788.)

1795. ———— ————. The example of changing a constitution by assembling the wise men of the State, instead of assembling armies, will be worth as much to the world as the former examples we had given them.—To DAVID HUMPHREYS. iii, 12. FORD ED., v, 89. (P., 1789.)

1796. ———— ————. This corporeal globe, and everything upon it, belong to its present corporeal inhabitants, during their generation. They alone have a right to direct what is the concern of themselves alone, and to declare the law of that direction; and this declaration can only be made by their majority. That majority, then, has a right to depute representatives to a convention, and to make the constitution what they think will be the best for themselves. * * * If this avenue be shut to the call of sufferance it will make itself through that of force, and we shall go on, as other nations are doing, in the endless circle of oppression, rebellion, reformation; and oppression, rebellion, reformation, again; and so on forever.—To SAMUEL KERCHIVAL. vii, 16. FORD ED., x, 44. (M., 1816.)

1797. CONVICTS, Transported.—The malefactors sent to America were not sufficient in number to merit enumeration, as one class out of three which peopled America. It was at a late period of their history that this practice began. * * * I do not think the whole number sent would amount to two thousand, and being principally men, eaten up with disease, they married seldom and propagated little. I do not suppose that themselves and their descendants are at present four thousand, which is little more than one-thousandth part of the whole inhabitants.—To M. DE MEUNIER. ix, 254. FORD ED., iv, 158. (P., 1786.)

— COOKERY.—See GASTRONOMY.

1798. COOPER (Thomas), University of Va. and.—I do sincerely lament that untoward circumstances have brought on us the irreparable loss of this professor, whom I have looked to as the corner stone of our edifice [University of Virginia]. I know no one who could have aided us so much in forming the future regulations of our infant institution; and although we may perhaps obtain from Europe equivalents in science, they can never replace the advantages of his experience, his knowledge of the character, habits and manners of our country, his identification with its sentiments and principles, and high reputation he has obtained in it generally.*—To GENERAL TAYLOR. vii, 164. (M., 1820.)

* Dr. Cooper was an Englishman, and the son-in-law of Dr. Priestley, with whom he came to America in 1792. Cooper edited Priestley's writings and wa—

1799. —— ——. You may have heard of the hue and cry raised from the different pulpits on our appointment [to be professor in the University of Virginia] of Dr. Cooper, whom they charge with Unitarianism as boldly as if they knew the fact, and as presumptuously as if it were a crime, and one for which, like Servetus, he should be burned * * *. For myself, I was not disposed to regard the denunciations of these satellites of religious inquisition; but our colleagues, better judges of popular feeling, thought that they were not to be altogether neglected; and that it might be better to relieve Dr. Cooper, ourselves and the institution from this crusade.—To GENERAL TAYLOR. vii, 162. (M., 1820.)

1800. COPYING PRESS, Appreciated.— Have you a copying press? If you have not, you should get one. Mine (exclusive of paper, which costs a guinea a ream) has cost me about fourteen guineas. I would give ten times that sum to have had it from the date of the Stamp Act.—To JAMES MADISON. i, 415. (P., 1785.)

1801. —— ——. I shall be able to have a small copying press completed for you here [Paris] in about three weeks.—To M. DE LAFAYETTE. ii, 22. (P., 1786.)

1802. COPYING PRESS, Jefferson's portable.—Having a great desire to have a portable copying machine, and being satisfied from some experiments that the principle of the large machines might be applied in a small one, I planned one when in England, and had it made. It answers perfectly. I have since set a workman to making them here, and they are in such demand that he has his hands full. * * * I send you one. The machine costs 96 livres, the appendages 24 livres. * * * You must expect to make many essays before you succeed perfectly. A soft brush, like a shaving brush, is more convenient than the sponge.—To JAMES MADISON. ii, 110. FORD ED., iv, 369. (P., 1787.)

— COPYRIGHT.—See BOOKS, GENERATIONS and MONOPOLY.

1803. CORAY (A.), Works of.—I recollect with pleasure the short opportunity of acquaintance with you afforded me in Paris * * * and the fine editions of the classical writers of Greece, which have been announced by you from time to time, have never permitted me to lose the recollection. Until those of Aristotle's Ethics and the Strategicos of Onesander, with which you have now favored me * * * I had seen only your Lives of Plutarch. * * * I profited much by your valuable *scholia*. * * * You have certainly begun at the right end towards preparing [your countrymen] for the great object they are now contending for, by improving their minds and qualifying them for self-government. For this they will owe you lasting honors. Nothing is more likely to forward this object than a study of the fine models of science left by their ancestors, to whom *we* also are all indebted for the

regarded as a Unitarian. He was well-versed in chemistry, physics and physiology; was one of the earliest writers in this country on political economy, and the first to introduce the study of Roman law by his edition of Justinian. He was a professor in Dickinson College, a lecturer in the University of Pennsylvania and became a Judge. His liberal views on religion aroused the antagonism of the orthodox clergy of Virginia and their attacks led to his retirement from the University of Virginia. In 1820, he became President of the College of South Carolina. He died in 1839.—EDITOR.

lights which originally led ourselves out of Gothic darkness.—To A. CORAY. vii, 318. (M., 1823.)

— CORK TREE.—See TREES.

1804. CORNWALLIS (Lord), Ravages of in Virginia.—Lord Cornwallis remained in this position [from Point of Fork along the main James River] ten days, his own headquarters being in my house [Elk-hill] at that place. I had time to remove most of the effects out of the house. He destroyed all my growing crops of corn and tobacco; he burned all my barns, containing the same articles of the last year, having first taken what corn he wanted; he used, as was to be expected, all my stock of cattle, sheep and hogs, for the sustenance of his army, and carried off all the horses capable of service; of those too young for service, he cut the throats; and he burned all the fences on the plantation, so as to leave it an absolute waste. He carried off also about thirty slaves. Had this been to give them freedom, he would have done right; but it was to consign them to inevitable death from the small-pox and putrid fever, then raging in his camp. This I knew afterwards to be the fate of twenty-seven of them. I never had news of the remaining three, but presume they shared the same fate. When I say that Lord Cornwallis did all this, I do not mean that he carried about the torch in his own hands, but that it was all done under his eye; the situation of the house in which he was, commanding a view of every part of the plantation, so that he must have seen every fire. I relate these things on my own knowledge in a great degree, as I was on the ground soon after he left it. He treated the rest of the neighborhood somewhat in the same style, but not with that spirit of total extermination with which he seemed to rage over my possessions. Wherever he went, the dwelling houses were plundered of everything that could be carried off. Lord Cornwallis's character in England would forbid the belief that he shared in the plunder; but that his table was served with the plate thus pillaged from private houses, can be proved by many hundred eyewitnesses. From an estimate I made at that time, on the best information I could collect, I supposed the State of Virginia lost under Lord Cornwallis's hands, that year, about thirty thousand slaves; and that of these, about twenty-seven thousand died of the small pox and camp fever, and the rest were partly sent to the West Indies, and exchanged for rum, sugar, coffee and fruit, and partly sent to New York, whence they went, at the peace, either to Nova Scotia or England. From this last place, I believe they have been lately sent to Africa. History will never relate the horrors committed by the British army in the Southern States of America. They raged in Virginia six months only, from the middle of April to the middle of October, 1781, when they were all taken prisoners; and I give you a faithful specimen of their transactions for ten days of that time, and on one spot only. *Ex pede Herculem.* I suppose their whole devastations during those six months amounted to about three millions sterling.—To DR. WILLIAM GORDON. ii, 426. FORD ED., v, 39. (P., 1788.)

1805. —— ——. Lord Cornwallis encamped ten days on an estate of mine at Elk Island, having his headquarters in my house. He burned all the tobacco houses and barns on the farm with the produce of the former year in them. He burned all the enclosures, and wasted the fields in which the crop of that year (it was in the month of June) was growing. He killed or carried off every living animal, cutting the throats of those which were too young for service. Of the slaves he carried away thirty.—To WILLIAM JONES. FORD ED., iv, 354. (P., 1787.)

1806. CORNWALLIS (Lord), Trumbull's picture of.—The painting lately executed by Colonel Trumbull, I have never seen, but as far back as the days of Horace at least, we are told that *"pictoribus atque poetis; Quidlibet audendi semper fuit æqua potestas."* He has exercised this *licentia pictoris* in like manner in the surrender of Yorktown, where he has placed Lord Cornwallis at the head of the surrender although it is well known that he was excused by General Washington from appearing.—To SAMUEL A. WELLS. FORD ED., x, 133. (M., 1819.)

1807. CORONERS, Election of.—Coroners of Counties shall be annually elected by those qualified to vote for Representatives.— PROPOSED VA. CONSTITUTION. FORD ED., ii, 20. (June 1776.)

— CORPORATION.—See INCORPORATION.

1808. CORREA DE SERRA (J.), Learned.—I found him one of the most learned and amiable of men.—To BARON VON HUMBOLDT. vi, 267. FORD ED., ix, 430. (1813.)

1809. CORREA DE SERRA (J.), Minister at Washington.—We have to join in mutual congratulations on the appointment of our friend Correa, to be minister or envoy of Portugal, here (Washington). This, I hope, will give him to us for life.—To F. W. GILMER. vii, 5. FORD ED., x, 33. (M., 1816.)

1810. CORREA DE SERRA (J.), Regrets for.—No foreigner, I believe, has ever carried with him more friendly regrets.—To JAMES MADISON. vii, 190. FORD ED., x, 169. (P.F., 1820.)

1811. CORREA DE SERRA (J.), University of Va. and.—M. Correa is here (Monticello) on his farewell visit to us. He has been much pleased with the plan and progress of our University, and has given some valuable hints to its botanical branch. He goes to do, I hope, much good in his new country (Brazil); the public instruction there, as I understand, being within the department destined for him.—To WILLIAM SHORT. vii, 168. (M., 1820.)

1812. CORRESPONDENCE, Between Citizens.—A right of free correspondence between citizen and citizen, on their joint interests, whether public or private, and under whatsoever laws these interests arise (to wit, of the State, of Congress, of France, Spain, or Turkey), is a natural right; it is not the gift of any municipal law, either of England, or of Virginia, or of Congress; but in common with all our other natural rights, is one of the objects for the protection of which society is formed, and municipal laws established.—To JAMES MONROE. iv, 199. FORD ED., vii, 172. (M., 1797.)

1813. —— ——. The right of free correspondence between citizen and citizen on their joint interests, public or private, and under whatsoever laws these interests arise, is a natural right of every individual citizen, not

the gift of municipal law, but among the objects for the protection of which municipal laws are instituted.—JURY PETITION. ix, 451. FORD ED., vii, 161. (1797.)

— CORRESPONDENCE, Revolutionary Committees of.—See APPENDIX.

1814. CORRESPONDENCE, Constituents and representatives.—By the Constitution of Virginia, established from its earliest settlement, the people thereof have professed the right of being governed by laws to which they have consented by representatives chosen by themselves immediately. In order to give to the will of the people the influence it ought to have, and the information which may enable them to exercise it usefully, it was a part of the common law, adopted as the law of this land, that their representatives, in the discharge of their functions, should be free from the cognizance or coercion of the coordinate branches, Judiciary and Executive; and that their communications with their constituents should of right, as of duty also, be free, full, and unawed by any. So necessary has this intercourse been deemed in the country from which they derive principally their descent and laws, that the correspondence between the representative and constituent is privileged there to pass free of expense through the channel of the public post, and that the proceedings of the legislature have been known to be arrested and suspended at times until the Representatives could go home to their several counties and confer with their constituents.—JURY PETITION. ix, 448. FORD ED., vii, 158. (1797.)

1815. CORRESPONDENCE, Judiciary and.—For the Judiciary to interpose in the Legislative department between the constituent and his representative, to control them in the exercise of their functions or duties towards each other, to overawe the free correspondence which exists and ought to exist between them, to dictate what may pass between them, and to punish all others, to put the representative into jeopardy of criminal prosecution, of vexation, expense, and punishment before the Judiciary, if his communications, public or private, do not exactly square with their ideas of fact or right, or with their designs of wrong, is to put the Legislative department under the feet of the Judiciary, is to leave us, indeed, the shadow, but to take away the substance of representation, which requires essentially that the representative be as free as his constituents would be, that the same interchange of sentiment be lawful between him and them as would be lawful among themselves were they in the personal transaction of their own business; is to do away the influence of the people over the proceedings of their representatives by excluding from their knowledge, by the terror of punishment, all but such information or misinformation as may suit their own views.*—JURY PETITION. ix, 450. FORD ED., vii, 160. (1797.)

* In 1797, a Federal Grand Jury in Virginia made a presentment of the act of Samuel J. Cabell, a mem-

1816. CORRESPONDENCE, Literary.—
I set the more value on literary correspondence, inasmuch as I can make private friendships instrumental to the public good, by inspiring a confidence which is denied to public and official communications.—To JAMES MONROE. FORD ED., viii, 287. (W., 1804.)

1817. CORRESPONDENCE, Longing for.—But why has nobody else written to me? Is it that one is forgotten as soon as their back is turned? I have a better opinion of men.—To JAMES MONROE. FORD ED., iv, 45. (P., 1785.)

1818. CORRESPONDENCE, Men of Worth and.—I cannot relinquish the right of correspondence with those whom I have learned to esteem. If the extension of common acquaintance in public life be an inconvenience, that with select worth is more than a counterpoise.—To LEVI LINCOLN. vi, 7. (M., 1811.)

1819. CORRESPONDENCE, Natural Right and.—The right of free correspondence is not claimed under the Constitution of the United States, nor the laws or treaties derived from it, but as a natural right, placed originally under the protection of our municipal laws, and retained under the cognizance of our own courts.—JURY PETITION. ix, 452. FORD ED., vii, 162. (1797.)

1820. CORRESPONDENCE, Punctuality and.—I never was a punctual correspondent to any person, as I must own to my shame.—To RICHARD HENRY LEE. FORD ED., ii, 193. (Wg., 1779.)

1821. CORRESPONDENCE, Rank and.
—If it be possible to be certainly conscious of anything, I am conscious of feeling no difference between writing to the highest or lowest being on earth.—To JAMES MONROE. iv, 401. FORD ED., viii, 59. (W., 1801.) See LETTERS.

1822. CORRESPONDENCE, State courts and.—The Federal Constitution alienates from [the State courts] all cases arising, 1st, under the Constitution; 2d, under the laws of Congress; 3d, under treaties, &c. But the right of free correspondence, whether with a public representative in General Assembly, in Congress, in France, in Spain, or with a private one charged with a pecuniary trust, or with a private friend, the object of our esteem, or any other, has not been given to us under, 1st, the Federal Constitution; 2dly, any law of Congress; or 3dly, any treaty; but * * * by nature. It is, therefore, not alienated, but remains under the protection of our courts.—To JAMES MONROE. iv, 200. FORD ED., vii, 172. (M., 1797.) See LETTERS.

1823. CORRUPTION, Agriculturists and.—Corruption of morals in the mass of cultivators is a phenomenon of which no age nor nation has furnished an example. It is the mark set on those, who, not looking up to ber of Congress from Virginia, in writing political circular-letters to his constituents.—EDITOR.

heaven, to their own soil and industry, as does the husbandman, for their subsistence, depend for it on casualties and caprice of customers.—NOTES ON VIRGINIA. viii, 405. FORD ED., iii, 268. (1782.)

1824. CORRUPTION, British.—I have been among those who have feared the design to introduce the corruptions of the English government here, and it has been a strong reason with me for wishing there was an ocean of fire between that island and us.—To JOHN ADAMS. FORD ED., vii, 57. (M., 1796.)

1825. CORRUPTION, Centralization.—
Our country is too large to have all its affairs directed by a single government. Public servants at such a distance, and from under the eye of their constituents, must, from the circumstance of distance, be unable to administer and overlook all the details necessary for the good government of the citizens, and the same circumstance, by rendering detection impossible to their constituents, will invite the public agents to corruption, plunder, and waste. And I do verily believe, that if the principle were to prevail, of a common law being in force in the United States (which principle possesses the general government at once of all the powers of the State governments, and reduces us to a single consolidated government), it would become the most corrupt government on the earth.—To GIDEON GRANGER. iv, 331. FORD ED., vii, 451. (M., 1800.)

1826. ———— ————. Consolidation first, and then corruption, its necessary consequence.—To NATHANIEL MACON. vii, 223. FORD ED., x, 193. (M., 1821.)

1827. ———— ————. If ever this vast country is brought under a single government, it will be one of the most extensive corruption, indifferent and incapable of a wholesome care over so wide a spread of surface.—To WILLIAM T. BARRY. vii, 256. (M., 1822.)

1828. CORRUPTION, Cities and.—When they [the people] get piled upon one another in large cities, as in Europe, they will become corrupt as in Europe.*—To JAMES MADISON. FORD ED., iv, 479. (P., Dec. 1787.)

1829. CORRUPTION, Congress.—I said that he [President Washington] must know, and everybody knew, there was a considerable squadron in both [Houses] whose votes were devoted to the paper and stock-jobbing interest, that the names of a weighty number were known, and several others suspected on good grounds. That on examining the votes of these men, they would be found uniformly for every Treasury measure, and that as most of these measures had been carried by small majorities, they were carried by these very votes: that, therefore, it was a cause of just uneasiness, when we saw a legislature legislating for their own interests, in opposition to those of the people.—THE ANAS. ix, 117. FORD ED., i, 200. (July 1792.)

* In the Congress edition (ii, 332), the reading is: "When we get piled upon one another in large cities, as in Europe, we shall become corrupt as in Europe, and go to eating one another as they do there." The FORD version is the correct one.—EDITOR.

1830. —— ——. With grief and shame it must be acknowledged that his [Alexander Hamilton's] [financial] machine was not without effect; that even in this, the birth of our government, some members were found sordid enough to bend their duty to their interests and to look after personal rather than public good.—THE ANAS. ix, 91. FORD ED., i, 160. (1818.)

1831. —— ——. I indulge myself on one political topic only, that is, the shameless corruption of a portion of the Representatives in the first and second Congresses, and their implicit devotion to the treasury. I think I do good in this, because it may produce exertions to reform the evil, on the success of which the form of the government is to depend.—To E. RANDOLPH. iv, 101. FORD ED., vi, 498. (M., Feb. 1794.)

1832. CORRUPTION, Extirpating.—I would prefer a native Frenchman [for the office of surveyor and inspector for the port of Bayou St. John], if you can find one proper and disposed to cooperate with us in extirpating that corruption which has prevailed in those offices under the former government, and had so familiarized itself as that men, otherwise honest, could look on it without horror. I pray you to be alive to the suppression of this odious practice, and that you bring to punishment and brand with eternal disgrace every man guilty of it, whatever be his station.—To GOVERNOR CLAIBORNE. iv, 551. (W., 1804.)

1833. CORRUPTION, Government and. —In every government on earth is some trace of human weakness, some germ of corruption and degeneracy, which cunning will discover, and wickedness insensibly open, cultivate and improve. Every government degenerates when trusted.to the rulers of the people alone. The people themselves, therefore, are its only safe depositories. And to render even them safe, their minds must be improved to a certain degree. This, indeed, is not all that is necessary, though it be essentially necessary. An amendment to our Constitution [Virginia] must here come in aid of the public education. The influence over government must be shared among all the people. If every individual which composes their mass, participates of the ultimate authority, the government will be safe; because the corrupting the whole mass will exceed any private resources of wealth; and public ones cannot be provided but by levies on the people. In this case, every man would have to pay his own price. The government of Great Britain has been corrupted, because but one man in ten has a right to vote for members of Parliament. The sellers of the government, therefore, get nine-tenths of their price clear. It has been thought that corruption is restrained by confining 'he right of suffrage to a few of the wealthier of the people; but it would be more effectually restrained, by an extension of that right, to such members as would bid defiance to the means of corruption.—NOTES ON VIRGINIA. viii, 390. FORD ED., iii, 254. (1782.)

1834. —— ——. [We] should look forward to a time, and that not a distant one, when a corruption in this, as in the country from which we derive our origin, will have seized the heads of government, and be spread by them through the body of the people; when they will purchase the voices of the people, and make them pay the price. Human nature is the same on every side of the Atlantic, and will be alike influenced by the same causes.—NOTES ON VIRGINIA. viii, 362. FORD ED., iii, 225. (1782.)

1835. —— ——. Mankind soon learn to make interested uses of every right and power which they possess, or may assume. The public money and public liberty, intended [in the Virginia constitution] to have been deposited with three branches of magistracy, but found inadvertently to be in the hands of one only, will soon be discovered to be sources of wealth and dominion to those who hold them; distinguished, too, by this tempting circumstance, that they are the instrument, as well as the object, of acquisition. With money we will get men, said Cæsar, and with men we will get money.—NOTES ON VIRGINIA. viii, 362. FORD ED., iii, 224. (1782.)

1836. CORRUPTION, Guarding against. The time to guard against corruption and tyranny is before they shall have gotten hold of us. It is better to keep the wolf out of the fold, than to trust to drawing his teeth and talons after he shall have entered.—NOTES ON VIRGINIA. viii, 363. FORD ED., iii, 225. (1782.)

1837. CORRUPTION, Influence through.—I wonder to see such an arrearage from the Department of State to our bankers in Holland. Our predecessors seem to have levied immense sums from their constituents merely to feed favorites by large advances, and thus to purchase by corruption an extension of their influence and power.—To JAMES MADISON. FORD ED., viii, 93. (M., Sep. 1801.)

1838. CORRUPTION, Innocent of.— Recurring to the tenor of a long life of public service, against the charge of malice and corruption (in the New Orleans Batture case) I stand conscious and erect.—THE BATTURE CASE. viii, 604. (1812.)

1839. CORRUPTION, Monarchical.— A germ of corruption indeed has been transferred from our dear mother country, and has already borne fruit, but its blight is begun from the breath of the people.—To J. P. BRISSOT DE WARVILLE. FORD ED., vi, 249. (Pa., 1793.)

1840. CORRUPTION, Principles and.— Time indeed changes manners and notions, and so far we must expect institutions to bend to them. But time produces also corruption of principles, and against this it is the duty of good citizens to be ever on the watch, and if the gangrene is to prevail at last, let the day be kept off as long as possible.—To SPENCER ROANE. vii, 211. FORD ED., x, 188. (M., 1821.)

1841. CORRUPTION, Refuge from.—It seems to me that in proportion as commercial avarice and corruption advance on us from the North and East, the principles of free government are to retire to the agricultural States of the South and West as their last asylum and bulwark.—To HENRY MIDDLETON. vi, 91. (M., 1813.)

1842. COTTON, Early Conditions.—The four southernmost States make a great deal of cotton. Their poor are almost entirely clothed in it in winter and summer. In winter they wear shirts of it, and outer clothing of cotton and wool mixed. In summer their shirts are linen, but the outer clothing cotton. The dress of the women is almost entirely of cotton manufactured by themselves, except the richer class, and even many of these wear a good deal of home-spun cotton. It is as well manufactured as the calicoes of Europe. These four States furnish a great deal of cotton to the States north of them, who cannot make it, as being too cold.—To J. P. BRISSOT DE WARVILLE. ii, 12. FORD ED., iv, 281. (P., 1786.)

1843. COTTON, Plans to raise.—Much enquiry is made of me here [Paris] about the cultivation of cotton, and I would thank you to give me your opinion how much a hand would make cultivating that as his principal crop instead of tobacco.—To NICHOLAS LEWIS. FORD ED., v, 36. (P., 1788.)

1844. COTTON GIN, Invention.—Your favor of Oct. 15 [1793] inclosing a drawing of your cotton gin, was received on the 6th inst. The only requisite of the law now uncomplied with is the forwarding a model, which being received your patent may be made out and delivered to your order immediately.—To ELI WHITNEY. FORD ED., vi, 448. (G., Nov. 16, 1793.)

1845. COTTON GIN, Practicability of. —As the State of Virginia * * * carries on household manufactures of cotton to a great extent, as I also do myself, and one of our great embarrassments is the clearing the cotton of the seed, I feel a considerable interest in the success of your invention, for family use. Permit me, therefore, to ask information from you on these points. Has the machine been thoroughly tried in the ginning of cotton, or is it yet but a machine of theory? What quantity of cotton has it cleared on an average of several days, and worked by hand, and by how many hands? What will be the cost of one of them, made to be worked by hand? Favorable answers to these questions would induce me to engage one of them.—To ELI WHITNEY. FORD ED., vi, 448. (G., Nov. 1793.)

1846. COUNCIL, Appointment of.—A Privy Council shall be annually appointed by the House of Representatives, whose duties it shall be to give advice to the Administrator, when called on by him. With them the Deputy Administrator shall have session and suffrage.—PROPOSED VA. CONSTITUTION. FORD ED., ii, 20. (June 1776.)

1847. COUNCIL, Duties.—A *Council of State* shall be chosen by joint ballot of both houses of Assembly, who shall hold their of-

fices seven years and be ineligible a second time, and who, * * * shall hold no other office or emolument under this State, or any other State or power whatsoever. Their duty shall be to * * * advise the Governor when called on by him, and their advice in any case shall be a sanction to him. They shall also have power, and it shall be their duty, to meet at their own will, and to give their advice, though not required by the governor, in cases where they shall think the public good calls for it. * * * They shall annually choose a *President*, who shall preside in council in the absence of the Governor, and who, in case of his office becoming vacant by death or otherwise, shall have authority to exercise all his functions, till a new appointment be made, as he shall also in any interval during which the Governor shall declare himself unable to attend to the duties of his office.—PROPOSED CONSTITUTION FOR VIRGINIA. viii, 447. FORD ED., iii, 327. (1783.)

1848. COUNCIL, Expensive.—What will you do with the Council? They are expensive, and not constantly nor often necessary; yet to drop them would be wrong. I think you had better require their attendance twice a year to examine the executive department, and see that it be going on rightly, advise on that subject the Governor, or inform the Legislature, as they shall see occasion. Give them fifty guineas for each trip, fill up only five of the places, and let them be always subject to summons on great emergencies by the Governor, on which occasions their expenses only should be paid. At an expense of five hundred guineas you will then preserve this member of the Constitution always fit for use. Young and ambitious men will leave it to go into the Assembly; but the elderly and able, who have retired from the legislative field as too turbulent, will accept of the offices.—To JAMES MADISON. FORD ED., iii, 404. (A., Feb. 1784.)

— COUNCIL, Orders in.—See ORDERS IN COUNCIL.

1849. COUNCIL, Shelter of a.—Responsibility is a tremendous engine in a free government. Let the Executive [of Virginia] feel the whole weight of it then, by taking away the shelter of his Executive Council. Experience both ways has already established the superiority of this measure.—To ARCHIBALD STUART. iii, 315. FORD ED., v, 315. (Pa., 1791.)

1850. ——— ———. Leave no screen of a council behind which to skulk from responsibility.—To SAMUEL KERCHIVAL. vii, 12. FORD ED., x, 39. (M., 1816.)

1851. COUNCIL, Useless.—[The Governor's] Council * * * is at best but a fifth wheel to a wagon.—To SAMUEL KERCHIVAL. vii, 10. FORD ED., x, 38. (M., 1816.)

1852. COUNCIL, Votes in.—In answer to your inquiry whether, in the early times of our [Virginia] government, the practice was for the Governor to give the deciding vote? I must observe that, correctly speaking, the Governor not being a counsellor, his vote could make no part of an advice of Council. That would be to place an advice on their journals which they did not give, and could not give because of their equal division. But he did what was equivalent in effect. While I was in the administration, no doubt was ever suggested that where the Council, divided in opinion, could give no advice, the Governor was free and bound to act on his own opinion and his own responsibility. Had this been a change of the practice of my predecessor, Mr. Henry, the first Governor, it would have produced some discussion, which it never did. Hence, I conclude it was the opinion and practice from the first institution of the government. During Arnold's and Cornwallis's invasion, the Council dispersed to their several homes, to take care of their families. Before their separation, I obtained from them a capitulary of standing advices for my government in such cases as ordinarily occur: such as the appointment of militia officers, justices, inspectors, &c., on the recommendations of the courts; but in the numerous and extraordinary occurrences of an invasion, which could not be foreseen, I had to act on my own judgment and my own responsibility. The vote of general approbation, at the session of the succeeding winter, manifested the opinion of the Legislature, that my proceedings had been correct. General Nelson, my successor, staid mostly, I think, with the army; and I do not believe his Council followed his camp, although my memory does not enable me to affirm the fact. Some petitions against him for impressment of property without authority of law, brought his proceedings before the next Legislature; the questions necessarily involved were whether necessity, without express law, could justify the impressment, if it could, whether he could order it without the advice of Council. The approbation of the Legislature amounted to a decision of both questions. I remember this case the more especially, because I was then a member of the Legislature, and was one of those who supported the Governor's proceedings, and I think there was no division of the House on the question. I believe the doubt was first suggested in Governor Harrison's time, by some member of the Council, on an equal division. Harrison, in his dry way, observed that instead of one governor and eight counsellors, there would then be eight governors and one counsellor, and continued, as I understood, the practice of his predecessors. Indeed, it is difficult to suppose it could be the intention of those who framed the Constitution. that when the Council should be divided, the government should stand still; and the more difficult as to a constitution formed during a war, and for the purpose of carrying on that war, that so high an officer as their Governor should be created and salaried, merely to act as the clerk and authenticator of the votes of the Council. No doubt it was intended that the advice of the Council should control the Governor. But the action of the controlling power being withdrawn, his would be left free to proceed on its own responsibility. Where from division, absence, sickness, or other obstacle, no advice could be given, they could not mean that their Governor, the person of their peculiar choice and confidence, should stand by, an inactive spectator, and let their government tumble to pieces for want of a will to direct it. In executive cases, where promptitude and decision are all important, an adherence to the letter of a law against its probable intentions (for every law must intend that itself shall be executed), would be fraught with incalculable

danger. Judges may await further legislative explanations, but a delay of executive action might produce irretrievable ruin. The State is invaded, militia to be called out, an army marched, arms and provisions to be issued from the public magazines, the Legislature to be convened, and the Council is divided. Can it be believed to have been the intention of the framers of the Constitution, that the Constitution itself and their constituents with it should be destroyed for want of a will to direct the resources they had provided for its preservation? Before such possible consequences all verbal excuses must vanish; construction must be made *secundum arbitrium boni viri*, and the constitution be rendered a practicable thing. That exposition of it must be vicious, which would leave the nation under the most dangerous emergencies without a directing will. The cautious maxims of the bench, to seek the will of the legislator and his words only, are proper and safe for judicial government. They act ever on an individual case only, the evil of which is partial, and gives time for correction. But an instant of delay in executive proceedings may be fatal to the whole nation. They must not, therefore, be laced up in the rules of the judiciary department. They must seek the intention of the legislator in all the circumstances which may indicate it in the history of the day, in the public discussions, in the general opinion and understanding, in reason and in practice. The three great departments having distinct functions to perform, must have distinct rules adapted to them. Each must act under its own rules, those of no one having any obligation on either of the others. Where the opinion first began that a governor could not act when his council could not or would not advise, I am uninformed. Probably not till after the war; for, had it prevailed then, no militia could have been opposed to Cornwallis, nor necessaries furnished to the opposing army of Lafayette.—To JAMES BARBOUR. vi, 38. FORD ED., ix, 335. (M., 1812.)

1853. COUNTIES, Administration of.—
I have two great measures at heart, without which no republic can maintain itself in strength. 1. That of general education, to enable every man to judge for himself what will secure or endanger his freedom. 2. To divide every county into hundreds, of such size that all the children of each will be within reach of a central school in it. But this division looks to many other fundamental provisions. Every hundred, besides a school, should have a justice of the peace, a constable, and a captain of militia. These officers, or some others within the hundred, should be a corporation to manage all its concerns, to take care of its roads, its poor, and its police by patrols, &c. (as the selectmen of the Eastern townships). Every hundred should elect one or two jurors to serve where requisite, and all other elections should be made in the hundreds separately, and the votes of all the hundreds be brought together. Our present captaincies might be declared hundreds for the present, with a power to the courts to alter them occasionally. These little republics would be the main strength of the great one. We owe to them the vigor given to our Revolution in its commencement in the Eastern States, and by them the Eastern States were enabled to repeal the Embargo in oppo-

sition to the Middle, Southern, and Western States, and their large and lubberly division into counties which can never be assembled. General orders are given out from a centre to the foreman of every hundred, as to the sergeants of an army, and the whole nation is thrown into energetic action, in the same direction in one instant and as one man, and becomes absolutely irresistible. Could I once see this I should consider it as the dawn of the salvation of the republic, and say with old Simeon, " nunc dimittas, Domine." But our children will be as wise as we are, and will establish in the fulness of time those things not yet ripe for establishment.—To John Tyler. v, 525. Ford ed., ix, 277. (M., 1810.)

1854. —— ——. The organization of our [Virginia] county administration may be thought * * * difficult; but follow principle and the knot unties itself. Divide the counties into wards of such size as that every citizen can attend, when called on, and act in person. Ascribe to them the government of their wards in all things relating to themselves exclusively. A justice, chosen by themselves, in each, a constable, a military company, a patrol, a school, the care of their own poor, their own portion of the public roads, the choice of one or more jurors to serve in some court, and the delivery, within their own wards, of their own votes for all elective officers of higher sphere, will relieve the county administration of nearly all its business, will have it better done, and by making every citizen an acting member of the government, and in the offices nearest and most interesting to him, will attach him by his strongest feelings to the independence of his country, and its republican constitution.—To Samuel Kerchival. vii, 12. Ford ed., x, 40. (M., 1816.)

1855. COUNTIES, Division of.—In what terms reconcilable to Majesty, and at the same time to truth, shall we speak of a late instruction to the Governor of the Colony of Virginia, by which he is forbidden to assent to any law for the division of a county, unless the new county will consent to have no representative in Assembly? That Colony has as yet fixed no boundary to the westward. Their westward counties, therefore, are of indefinite extent. Some of them are actually seated many hundreds of miles from their eastern limits. Is it possible, then, that his Majesty can have bestowed a single thought on the situation of those people, who, in order to obtain justice for injuries, however great or small, must, by the laws of that Colony, attend their County Court, at such a distance, with all their witnesses, monthly, till their litigation be determined.—Rights of British America. i, 136. Ford ed., i, 441. (1774.)

1856. —— ——. The article, nearest my heart, is the division of counties into wards. These will be pure and elementary republics, the sum of all which, taken together, composes the State, and will make of the whole a true democracy as to the business of the wards, which is that of nearest and daily concern. The affairs of the larger sections, of counties, of States, and of the Union, not admitting personal transactions by the people, will be delegated to agents elected by themselves; and representation will thus be substituted, where personal action becomes impracticable. Yet, even over these representative organs, should they become corrupt and perverted, the division into wards constituting the people, in their wards, a regularly organized power, enables them by that organization to crush, regularly and peaceably, the usurpations of their unfaithful agents, and rescues them from the dreadful necessity of doing it insurrectionally. In this way we shall be as republican as a large society can be; and secure the continuance of purity in our government, by the salutary, peaceable, and regular control of the people.—To Samuel Kerchival. vii, 35. Ford ed., x, 45. (M., 1816.)

1857. —— ——. As Cato concluded every speech with the words " Carthago delenda est," so do I every opinion, with the injunction, " divide the counties into wards."—To Joseph C. Cabell. vi, 544. (M., 1816.)

1858. —— ——. These wards, called townships in New England, are the vital principle of their governments, and have proved themselves the wisest invention ever devised by the wit of man for the perfect exercise of self-government, and for its preservation.—To Samuel Kerchival. vii, 13. Ford ed., x, 41. (M., 1816.)

1859. COUNTIES, The State and.—A county of a State * * * cannot be governed by its own laws, but must be subject to those of the State of which it is a part.—To William Lee. vii, 57. (M., 1817.)

1860. —— ——. Every State is divided into counties, each to take care of what lies within its local bounds; each county again into townships or wards, to manage minuter details.—Autobiography. i, 82. Ford ed., i, 113. (1821.)

1861. COURTESY, Diplomatic.—Whenever Mr. Hammond [the British Minister] applies to our government on any matter whatever, be it ever so new or difficult, if he does not receive his answer in two or three days or a week, we are goaded with new letters on the subject. Sometimes it is the sailing of the packet, which is made the pretext for forcing us into premature and undigested determinations. You know best how far your applications meet such early attentions, and whether you may with propriety claim a return of them : you can best judge, too, of the expediency of an imitation, that where dispatch is not reciprocal it may be expedient and justifiable that delay should be so.—To Thomas Pinckney. iii, 583. Ford ed., vi, 302. (Pa., June 1793.)

1862. COURTIERS, Unprincipled.—Courtiers had rather give up power than pleasures; they will barter, therefore, the usurped prerogatives of the King, for the

money of the people.—To COUNT DE MOUS-
TIER. ii, 389. (P., May 1788.)

— COURTS, Admiralty.—See ADMIRALTY.

1863. COURTS, Erection of.—The Administrator* shall not possess the prerogative * * * of erecting courts.—PROPOSED VA. CONSTITUTION. FORD ED., ii, 19. (June 1776.)

1864. COURTS, Organization of Virginia.—The Judiciary powers shall be exercised: First, by County Courts, and other inferior jurisdictions. Secondly, by a General Court and a High Court of Chancery. Thirdly, by a Court of Appeals.—PROPOSED VA. CONSTITUTION. FORD ED., ii, 22. (June 1776.)

1865. COURTS, Jurisdiction of.—The courts of this commonwealth [Virginia] (and among them the General Court, as a court of impeachment), are originally competent to the cognizance of all infractions of the rights of one citizen by another citizen; and they still retain all their judiciary cognizances not expressly alienated by the Federal Constitution.—To JAMES MONROE. iv, 199. FORD ED., vii, 172. (M., 1797.)

1866. COURTS (Appeals), Judges of.—The Court of Appeals shall consist of not less than seven nor more than eleven members, to be appointed by the House of Representatives.—PROPOSED VA. CONSTITUTION. FORD ED., ii, 23. (June 1776.)

1867. —— ——. The members of the Court of Appeals * * * shall hold their offices during good behavior, for breach of which they shall be removable by an act of the Legislature only.—PROPOSED VA. CONSTITUTION. FORD ED., ii, 23. (June 1776.)

1868. —— ——. The jurisdiction [of the Court of Appeals] shall be to determine finally all causes removed before them from the General Court, or High Court of Chancery, or of the County Court, or other inferior jurisdictions, for misbehavior; to try impeachments.—PROPOSED VA. CONSTITUTION. FORD ED., ii, 23. (June 1776.)

1869. —— ——. In the Court of Appeals, the judges of the General Court and High Court of Chancery shall have session and deliberative voice, but no suffrage.—PROPOSED VA. CONSTITUTION. FORD ED., ii, 23. (June 1776.)

1870. COURTS OF CHANCERY, Beginning of.—In ancient times, when contracts and transfers of property were more rare, and their objects more simple, the imperfections of the administration of justice according to the letter of the law were less felt. But when commerce began to make progress, when the transfer of property came into daily use, when the modifications of these transfers were infinitely diversified, when with the improvement of other faculties that of the moral sense became also improved. and learnt to re-

* The Governor.—EDITOR.

spect justice in a variety of cases which it had not formerly discriminated, the instances of injustice left without remedy by courts adhering to the letter of the law, would be so numerous as to produce a general desire that a power should be found somewhere which would redress them. History renders it probable that appeals were made to the king himself in these cases, and that he exercised this power sometimes in person, but more generally by his chancellor to whom he referred the case. This was most commonly an Ecclesiastic, learning being rare in any other class at that time. Roman learning, and a prejudice in favor of Roman institutions are known to have been a leading feature in the ecclesiastical character. Hence it happened that the forms of proceeding in the Court of Chancery, and the rules of its decisions were assimilated to those of the Roman law. The distinction in that system between the *jus prætorium,* or discretion of the Prætor, and the general law is well known. Among the Romans, and in most modern nations. these were and are exercised by the same person. But the Chancellors of England, finding the ordinary courts in possession of the administration of general law, and confined to that. assumed to themselves by degrees that of the *jus prætorium,* and made theirs be considered as a court of conscience, or of equity. The history of the struggles between the ordinary. or common law courts, and the Court of Equity or Chancery, would be beyond our purpose. It is sufficient to say that the interpositions of the Chancellor were at first very rare, that they increased insensibly, and were rather tolerated from their necessity, than authorized by the laws in the earlier periods of history. Lord Bacon first introduced regularity into their proceedings, and Finch, Earl of Nottingham, in the reign of Charles II. opened to view that system which has been improving from that time to this.—To PHILLIP MAZZEI. FORD ED., iv, 110. (P., 1785.)

1871. COURTS OF CHANCERY, Common Law and.—One practice only is wanting to render the Court of Chancery completely valuable. That is that when a class of cases has been formed, and has been the subject of so many decisions in the Court of Chancery as to have been seen there under all circumstances, and in all its combinations, and the rules for its decision are modified accordingly and thoroughly digested, the Legislature should reduce these rules to a text and transplant them into the department of the Common Law, which is competent then to the application of them, and is a safer depository for the general administration of justice. This would be to make the Chancery a nursery only for the forming new plants for the department of the Common Law. Much of the business of Chancery is now actually in a state of perfect preparation for removal into the Common Law.—To PHILLIP MAZZEI. FORD ED., iv, 113. (P., 1785.)

1872. —— ——. It has often been predicted in England that the Chancery would swallow up the Common Law. During many centuries, however, that these two courts have gone on together, the jurisdiction of the Common Law has not been narrowed in a single article; on the contrary, it has been enlarged from time to time by act of the Legislature; but jealousy, uncorrected by reason or experience, sees certainty wherever there is a possibility, and sensible men still think that the danger from this court overweighs its utility.—To PHILLIP MAZZEI. FORD ED., iv, 113. (P., 1785.)

1873. COURTS OF CHANCERY, Judges of.—The Judges of the General Court and of the High Court of Chancery, * * * if kept united, shall be five in number; if separate, there shall be five for the General Court, and three for the High Court of Chancery.—PROPOSED VA. CONSTITUTION. FORD ED., ii, 22. (June 1776.)

1874. —— ——. The Judges of the General Court and of the High Court of Chancery shall be appointed by the Administrator and Privy Council.—PROPOSED VA. CONSTITUTION. FORD ED., ii, 22. (June 1776.)

1875. —— ——. The appointment of the Judges of the General Court and of the High Court of Chancery shall be made from the faculty of the law, and of such persons of that faculty as shall have actually exercised the same at the bar of some court, or courts of record within this Colony, for seven years.—PROPOSED VA. CONSTITUTION. FORD ED., ii, 22. (June 1776.)

1876. —— ——. The Judges of the General Court and of the High Court of Chancery * * * shall hold their commissions during good behavior, for breach of which they shall be removable by the Court of Appeals.—PROPOSED VA. CONSTITUTION. FORD ED., ii, 23. (June 1776.)

1877. —— ——. The judges of the high court of chancery, general court, and court of admiralty shall * * * be appointed by joint ballot of both houses of Assembly, and hold their offices during good behavior.—PROPOSED CONSTITUTION FOR VIRGINIA. viii, 448. FORD ED., iii, 328. (1783.)

1878. COURTS OF CHANCERY, Juries in.—All facts in causes whether of Chancery, Common, Ecclesiastical, or Marine law, shall be tried by a jury upon evidence given *vivâ voce*, in open court; but where witnesses are out of the Colony, or unable to attend through sickness, or other invincible necessity, their deposition may be submitted to the credit of the jury.—PROPOSED VA. CONSTITUTION. FORD ED., ii, 24. (June 1776.)

1879. —— ——. To guard still more effectually against the dangers apprehended from a Court of Chancery, the Legislature of Virginia have very wisely introduced into it the trial by jury for all matters of fact.—To PHILIP MAZZEI. FORD ED., iv, 116. (P., 1785.)

1880. —— ——. In your new station [Legislature of Va.] let me recommend to you the jury system; as also the restoration of juries in the Court of Chancery, which a law not long since repealed, because "the trial by jury is troublesome and expensive." If the reason be good, they should abolish it at common law also.—To JAMES MADISON. iv, 307. FORD ED., vii, 400. (M., Nov. 1799.)

1881. —— ——. I was once a great advocate for introducing into chancery *vivâ voce* testimony, and trial by jury. I am still so as to the latter, but have retired from the former opinion on the information received from both your State [Kentucky] and ours, that it worked inconveniently. I introduced it into the Virginia law, but did not return to the bar, so as to see how it answered.—To JOHN BRECKENRIDGE. iv, 318. FORD ED., vii, 416. (Pa., Jan. 1800.)

1882. —— ——. In that one of the bills for organizing our [Va.] judiciary system, which proposed a court of Chancery, I had provided for a trial by jury of all matters of fact, in that as well as in the courts of law. Edmund Pendleton defeated it by the introduction of four words only, "*if either party choose.*" The consequence has been, that as no suitor will say to his judge, "Sir, I distrust you, give me a jury," juries are rarely, I might say, perhaps, never seen in that court, but when called for by the Chancellor of his own accord.—AUTOBIOGRAPHY. i, 37. FORD ED., i, 50. (1821.)

1883. COURTS OF CHANCERY, Jurisdiction of.—The Court of Chancery, whilst developing and systematizing its powers, has found, in the jealousy of the nation and its attachment to certain and impartial law, an obstacle insuperable beyond that line. It has been obliged therefore to establish for itself certain barriers as the limitation of its power, which, whenever it transcends the general jurisdiction which superintends all the Courts, and receives appeals from them, corrects its encroachments, and reverses its decisions. This is the House of Lords in England, and the Court of Appeals in Virginia. These limitations are: 1. That it cannot take cognizance of any case wherein the Common Law can give complete remedy. 2. That it cannot interpose in any case against the express letter and intention of the Legislature. If the Legislature means to enact an injustice, however palpable, the Court of Chancery is not the body with whom a correcting power is lodged. 3. That it shall not interpose in any case which does not come within a general description, and admit of redress by a general and practicable rule. This is to prevent partiality. When a Chancellor pretends that a case is distinguished from all others, it is thought better that that singular case should go without remedy, than that he should be at liberty to cover partial decisions under pretence of singular circumstances, which ingenious men can always invent. Hence all the cases remediable in Chancery are reduced to certain classes. When a new case presents itself, not found in any of these classes, it is dismissed as irremediable. If in the progress of commerce, and of the developments of moral duties, the same case is presented so often that the Chancellor can seize certain leading features which submit to a general description, and show that it is a proper object for the application of some moral rule,—here is a new class of cases formed and brought within the regular relief of the Court of Chancery, which thus continues the administration of justice progressive almost in equal pace with the progress of commerce and refinement of morality.—To PHILLIP MAZZEI. FORD ED., iv, 112. (P., 1785.)

1884. COURTS OF CHANCERY, Lord Mansfield and.—Unhappily for England a very unexpected revolution is working in their laws of late years. Lord Mansfield, a man of the clearest head and most seducing eloquence, coming from a country where the powers of the common law and chancery are united in the same court, has been able since his admission to the bench of judges in England, to persuade the courts of common law to revise the practice of construing their text equitably. The object of former judges has been to render the law more and more certain; that of this person to render it more uncertain under pretence of rendering it more reasonable. No period of the English law, of whatever length it be taken, can be produced wherein so many of its settled rules have been reversed as during the time of this judge. His decisions will be precious in those States where no chancery is established; but his accession to the bench should form the epoch, after which all recurrence to English decisions should be proscribed in those States which have separated the two courts. His plan of rendering the Chancery useless by administering justice in the same way in the courts of common law has been admirably seconded by the celebrated Doctor Blackstone, a judge in the same department, who has endeavored seriously to prove that the jurisdiction of the Chancery is a chaos, irreducible to system, insusceptible of fixed rules, and incapable of definition or explanation. Were this true, it would be a monster whose existence should not be suffered one moment in a free country wherein every power is dangerous which is not bound up by general rules.—To PHILLIP MAZZEI. FORD ED., iv, 115. (P., 1785.)

1885. COURTS OF CHANCERY, Utility of.—Even some of the States in our Union have chosen to do without this court; and it has been proposed to others to follow their example in this case. One of two consequences must follow. Either, 1—the cases now remediable in Chancery must be left without remedy, in which event the clamorers for justice which originally begat this court, would produce its re-institution; or 2—the courts of common law must be permitted to perform the discretionary functions of the Chancery. This will be either by adopting at once all the rules of the Chancery, with the consent of the Legislature, or if that is withheld, these courts will be led, by the desire of doing justice, to extend the text of the law

according to its equity as was done in England before the Chancery took a regular form. This will be worse than running on Scylla to avoid Charybdis, for at present nine-tenths of our legal contestations are perfectly remedied by the common law, and can be carried before that judicature only. This proportion then of our rights is placed on sure ground. Relieve the judges from the rigor of text law, and permit them, with prætorian discretion, to wander into its equity, and the whole legal system becomes uncertain. This has been its fate in every country where the fixed and the discretionary law have been committed into the same hands. It is probable that the singular certainty, with which justice has been administered in England, has been the consequence of their distribution into two distinct departments.—To PHILLIP MAZZEI. FORD ED., iv, 114. (P., 1785.)

1886. COURTS (County), Appointment of Judges.—The judges of the County Courts, and other inferior jurisdictions, shall be appointed by the Administrator, subject to the negative of the Privy Council. They shall not be fewer than five in number.—PROPOSED VA. CONSTITUTION FOR VIRGINIA. FORD ED., ii, 22. (June 1776.)

1887. COURTS (County), Election of Judges.—I acknowledge the value of this institution [County Courts]; that it is in truth our principal executive and judiciary, and that it does much for little *pecuniary* reward. It is their self-appointment I wish to correct; to find some means of breaking up a cabal, when such a one gets possession of the bench. When this takes place, it becomes the most afflicting of tyrannies, because its powers are so various, and exercised on everything most immediately around us.—To JOHN TAYLOR. vii, 18. FORD ED., x, 52. (M., 1816.)

1888. ————. It has been thought that the people are not competent electors of judges *learned in the law*. But I do not know that this is true, and, if doubtful, we should follow principle. In this, as in many other elections, they would be guided by reputation, which would not err oftener, perhaps, than the present mode of appointment. In one State of the Union, at least, it has long been tried, and with the most satisfactory success. The judges of Connecticut have been chosen by the people every six months, for nearly two centuries, and I believe there has hardly ever been an instance of change; so powerful is the curb of incessant responsibility. If prejudice, however, derived from a monarchical institution, is still to prevail against the vital elective principle of our own, and if the existing example among ourselves of periodical election of judges by the people be still mistrusted, let us at least not adopt the evil, and reject the good, of the English precedent; let us [Virginia] retain amovability on the concurrence of the executive and legislative branches, and nomination by the executive alone.—To SAMUEL KERCHIVAL. vii, 12. FORD ED., x, 39. (M., 1816.)

1889. COURTS (County), Jurisdiction.—The jurisdictions of the judges of the County Courts * * * shall be defined from time to time by the Legislature.—Proposed Va. Constitution. Ford ed., ii, 22. (June 1776.)

1890. COURTS (County), Removal of Judges.—The judges of the County Courts * * * shall be removable for misbehavior by the Court of Appeals.—Proposed Va. Constitution. Ford ed., ii, 22. (June 1776.)

— **COURTS (Federal).**—See Judiciary.

1891. COURTS (Inferior), Judges.—The justices or judges of the inferior court * * * shall be appointed by the governor, on advice of the Council of State.—Proposed Constitution for Virginia. viii, 450. Ford ed., iii, 329. (1783.)

1892. —— ——. The justices or judges of the inferior courts may be members of the Legislature.—Proposed Constitution for Virginia. viii, 450. Ford ed., iii, 330. (1783.)

1893. COURTS (French Plenary), Composition of.—The composition of the Plenary Court is, indeed, vicious in the extreme; but the basis of that court may be retained, and its composition changed. Make of it a representative of the people, by composing it of members sent from the Provincial Assemblies, and it becomes a valuable member of the constitution.—To Count de Moustier. ii, 388. (P., May 1788.)

1894. —— ——. Two innovations must be fundamentally condemned: the abolishing, in so great a degree, of the parliaments, and the substitution of so ill-composed a body as the *Cour Pleniere.* If the King has power to do this, the government of this country is a pure despotism.—To Mr. Cutting. ii, 438. (P., July 1788.)

1895. —— ——. The right of registering the laws is taken from the parliaments and transferred to a Plenary court, created by the King. This last is the measure most obnoxious to all persons. Though the members are to be for life, yet a great proportion of them are from descriptions of men always candidates for the royal favor in other lines.—To John Jay. ii, 391. (P., May 1788.)

1896. COURTS (Monarchical), Character of.—Courts are to be seen as you would see the tower of London, or menagerie of Versailles with their lions, tigers, hyenas and other beasts of prey, standing in the same relation to their fellows. A slight acquaintance with them will suffice to show you that, under the most imposing exterior, they are the weakest and worst part of mankind. Their manners, could you ape them, would not make you beloved in your own country, nor would they improve it could you introduce them there to the exclusion of that honest simplicity now prevailing in America, and worthy of being cherished.—Travelling Hints. ix, 405. (1788.)

1897. COURTS (Monarchical), Inscrutable.—The designs of these [European] courts are unsearchable.—To James Monroe. i, 346. Ford ed., iv, 51. (P., 1785.)

1898. COURTS (Monarchical), The People and.—Courts love the people always, as wolves do the sheep.—To John Jay. ii, 561. (P., 1789.)

1899. COURTS (Monarchical), Unaffectionate.—A court has no affections; but those of the people whom they govern influence their decisions, even in the most arbitrary governments.—To James Monroe. i, 346. Ford ed., iv, 51. (P., 1785.)

— **COURTS (State).**—See Judiciary.

1900. CRAWFORD (William H.), Presidency and.—A baseless and malicious attack on Mr. Crawford has produced from him so clear, so incontrovertible, and so temperate a justification of himself as to have added much to the strength of his interest. The question will ultimately be, as I suggested in a former letter to you, between Crawford and Adams, with this in favor of Crawford that, although many States have a different first favorite, he is the second with nearly all, and that if it goes into the Legislature he will surely be elected.—To Richard Rush. Ford ed., x, 305. (M., June 1824.)

— **CREATION, Jefferson's Views on.**—See Earth.

1901. CREDIT, American.—The real credit of the United States depends on the ability, and the immutability of their will, to pay their debts.—To C. W. F. Dumas. Ford ed., vi, 70. (Pa., 1792.)

1902. —— ——. We beg * * * to assure the French nation, that among the important reasons which lead us to economize and foster our public credit, a strong one is the desire of preserving to ourselves the means of discharging our debts to them with punctuality and good faith in the terms and sums which have been stipulated between us. —To Edmond Charles Genet. Ford ed., vi, 295. (Pa., 1793.)

1903. CREDIT, Destroyed.—They [attacks in English newspapers] have destroyed our credit, and thus checked our disposition to luxury; and, forcing our merchants to buy no more than they have ready money to pay for, they force them to go to those markets where that ready money will buy most. Thus * * * they check our luxury, they force us to connect ourselves with all the world, and they prevent foreign emigrations to our country, all of which I consider as advantageous to us.—To Count Van Hogendorp. i, 464. Ford ed., iv, 104. (P., 1785.)

1904. —— ——. I heartily wish the States may, by their contributions, enable you to re-establish a credit, which cannot be lower than at present, to exist at all. This is partly owing to their real deficiencies, and partly to the lies propagated by the London papers, which are probably paid for by the minister, to reconcile the people to the loss of us. * * * Should this produce the amendment of our federal constitution * * * we shall receive a permanent indemnification for a temporary loss.—To Samuel Osgood. i, 450. (P., 1785.)

1905. —— ——. Desperate of finding relief from a free course of justice, I look forward to the abolition of all credit as the only other remedy which can take place. I have seen, therefore, with pleasure, the exaggerations of our want of faith with which the London papers teem. It is, indeed, a strong medicine for sensible minds, but it is a medicine. It will prevent their crediting us abroad, in which case we cannot be credited at home.—To A. Donald. ii, 194. Ford ed., iv, 414. (P., 1787.)

1906. CREDIT, Establishing.—I told the President [Washington] all that was ever necessary to establish our credit, was an efficient government, and an honest one, declaring it would sacredly pay our debts, laying taxes for this purpose and applying them to it.—The Anas. ix, 123. Ford ed., i, 205. (Oct. 1792.)

1907. CREDIT, Faith in American.—I had rather trust money in the hands of the United States than in those of any government on earth.—To C. W. F. Dumas. ii, 121. (P., 1787.)

1908. CREDIT, Funding and.—The funding the public debt will secure to us the credit we now hold at Amsterdam, where our European paper is above par, which is the case of no other nation. Our business is to have great credit and to use it little.—To James Monroe. Ford ed., v, 198. (N.Y., 1790.)

1909. —— ——. The consolidation and funding their debts will give the French government a credit which then will enable them to do what they please.—To David Humphreys. iii, 12. Ford ed., v, 88. (P., 1789.)

1910. CREDIT, High.—Our loan in Amsterdam for two and a half millions of florins was filled in two hours and a half after it was opened.—To President Washington. iii, 255. Ford ed., v, 327. (Pa., May 1791.)

1911. CREDIT, Interest and.—The bankers of Holland consider us as the surest nation on earth for the repayment of the capital, but as the punctual payment of interest is of absolute necessity in their arrangements, we cannot borrow but with difficulty and disadvantage.—To General Washington. ii, 374. (P., 1788.)

1912. —— ——. If the first money operations of the government under the new Constitution are injudiciously begun, correction, whenever they shall be corrected, will come too late. Our borrowings will always be difficult and disadvantageous. If they begin well, our credit will immediately take the first station. Equal provision for the interest, adding to it a certain prospect for the principal, will give us [in Holland] a preference to all nations, the English not excepted.—To James Madison. ii, 376. (P., 1788.)

1913. CREDIT, Low.—American reputation in Europe is not such as to be flattering to its citizens. Two circumstances are particularly objected to us; the non-payment of our debts, and the want of energy in our government. These discourage a connection with us. I own it to be my opinion, that good will arise from the destruction of our credit. I see nothing else which can restrain our disposition to luxury, and to the loss* of those manners which alone can preserve republican government. As it is impossible to prevent credit, the best way would be to cure its ill effects, by giving an instantaneous recovery to the creditor. This would be reducing purchases on credit to purchases for ready money. A man would then see a prison painted on everything he wished, but had not ready money to pay for.—To Archibald Stuart. i, 518. Ford ed., iv, 188. (P., 1786.)

1914. CREDIT, Manufactures and.—If credit alone can be obtained for the manufactures of the country, it will still help to clothe our armies, or to increase at market the necessaries our people want.—To John Adams. i, 206. Ford ed., ii, 134. (Alb., 1777.)

1915. CREDIT, National Existence and.—The existence of a nation having no credit is always precarious.—To James Madison. ii, 376. (P., 1788.)

1916. CREDIT, Necessity of.—The sense of the necessity of public credit is so universal and so deeply rooted, that no other necessity will ever prevail against it.—To William Short. vi, 401. (M., Nov. 1814.)

1917. CREDIT, Paper, Prices and.—Though the price of public paper is considered as the barometer of the public credit, it is truly so only as to the general average of prices.—To C. W. F. Dumas. vi, 70. (Pa., 1792.)

1918. CREDIT, Sustaining.—I think nothing can bring the security of our continent and its cause into danger, if we can support the credit of our paper. To do that, I apprehend, one of two steps must be taken. Either to procure free trade by alliance with some naval power able to protect it; or, if we find there is no prospect of that, to shut our ports totally, to all the world, and turn our colonies into manufactories. The former would be most eligible, because most conformable to the habits and wishes of our people.—To Benj. Franklin. i, 205. Ford ed., ii, 132. (Aug. 1777.)

1919. CREDIT, Taxation and.—It is a wise rule, and should be a fundamental in a government disposed to cherish its credit, and at the same time to restrain the use of it within the limits of its faculties, "never to borrow a dollar without laying a tax in the same instant for paying the interest annually, and the principal within a given term; and to

* "Change" of those manners in the Congress edition.—Editor.

consider that tax as pledged to the creditors on the public faith." On such a pledge as this, sacredly observed, a government may always command, on a *reasonable interest*, all the lendable money of their citizens, while the necessity of an equivalent tax is a salutary warning to them and their constituents against oppressions, bankruptcy, and its inevitable consequence, revolution. But the term of redemption must be moderate, and at any rate within the limit of their rightful powers. But what limits, it will be asked, does this prescribe to their powers? What is to hinder them from creating a perpetual debt? The laws of nature, I answer. The earth belongs to the living, not to the dead. The will and the power of man expire with his life, by nature's law.—To JOHN W. EPPES. vi, 136. FORD ED., ix, 389. (M., June 1813.)

1920. CREDIT, Using.—I am anxious about everything which may affect our credit. My wish would be to possess it in the highest degree, but to use it little. Were we without credit, we might be crushed by a nation of much inferior resources, but possessing higher credit.—To GENERAL WASHINGTON. ii, 374. (P., 1788.)

1921. —— ——. Though I am an enemy to the using our credit but under absolute necessity, yet the possessing a good credit I consider as indispensable, in the present system of carrying on war.—To JAMES MADISON. ii, 376. (P., 1788.)

1922. —— ——. We consider it as of the first importance to possess the first credit at Amsterdam, and to use it little.—To C. W. F. DUMAS. iii, 155. FORD ED., v, 190.. (N. Y., 1790.)

1923. CREDIT, War and.—War requires every resource of taxation and credit.—To GENERAL WASHINGTON. ii, 533. FORD ED., v, 57. (P., 1788.)

1924. —— ——. The present system of war renders it necessary to make exertions far beyond the annual resources of the State, and to consume in one year the efforts of many. And this system we cannot change. It remains, then, that we cultivate our credit with the utmost attention.—To GENERAL WASHINGTON. ii, 374. (P., 1788.) See DEBT.

1925. CREDIT (Private), Evils of.—As it is impossible to prevent credit, the best way would be to cure its ill effects by giving an instantaneous recovery to the creditor. This would be reducing purchases on credit to purchases for ready money. A man would then see a prison painted on everything he wished but had not the ready money to pay for.—To ARCHIBALD STUART. i, 518. FORD ED., iv, 188. (P., 1786.)

1926. CREDULITY, Mankind and.— What is it men cannot be made to believe!— To RICHARD H. LEE. i, 541. FORD ED., iv, 207. (L., 1786.)

1927. CREEK INDIANS, Carthaginians and.—I shall be very glad to receive the conjectures of your philosopher on the descent of the Creek Indians from the Carthaginians, supposed to have been separated from Hanno's fleet, during his periplus. I see nothing impossible in his conjecture. I am glad he means to appeal to similarity of language, which I consider as the strongest kind of proof it is possible to adduce. I have somewhere read that the language of the ancient Carthaginians is still spoken by their descendants, inhabiting the mountainous interior parts of Barbary, to which they were obliged to retire by the conquering Arabs. If so, a vocabulary of their tongue can still be got, and if your friend will get one of the Creek languages, the comparison will decide. * * * My wish, like his, is to ascertain the history of the American aborigines.—To E. RUTLEDGE. ii, 434. FORD ED., v, 41. (P., 1788.)

1928. CREEK INDIANS, Civilization of.—The Cherokee nation, consisting now of about 2,000 warriors, and the Creeks of about 3,000 are far advanced in civilization. They have good cabins, enclosed fields, large herds of cattle and hogs, spin and weave their own clothes of cotton, have smiths and other of the most necessary tradesmen, write and read, are on the increase in numbers, and a branch of Cherokees is now instituting a regular representative government. Some other tribes are advancing in the same line.—To JOHN ADAMS. vi, 62. FORD ED., ix, 358. (M., 1812.) See INDIANS.

—— CREEK INDIANS, Commerce with. —See MONOPOLY.

—— CRESAP (Captain), Logan and.—See LOGAN.

1929. CRIME, Adequate punishment.— Whereas, it frequently happens that wicked and dissolute men, resigning themselves to the dominion of inordinate passions, commit violations on the lives, liberties and property of others, and the secure enjoyment of these having principally induced men to enter into society, government would be defective in its principal purpose, were it not to restrain such criminal acts, by inflicting due punishments on those who perpetrate them.—CRIMES BILL. i. 147. FORD ED., ii, 203. (1779.)

1930. —— ——. The punishment of all real crimes is certainly desirable, as a security to society; the security is greater in proportion as the chances of avoiding punishment are less.—REPORT ON SPANISH CONVENTION. iii, 353. FORD ED., v, 482. (1792.)

1931. CRIME, Breach of Prison.—The law of nature impels every one to escape from confinement; it should not, therefore, be subjected to punishment. Let the legislator restrain his criminal by walls, not parchment. As to strangers breaking prison to enlarge an offender, they should, and may be fairly considered as accessories after the fact.—NOTE TO CRIMES BILL. i, 159. FORD ED., ii, 218. (1779.)

—— CRIME, Death Penalty.—See DEATH PENALTY.

1932. CRIME, Disproportionate punishment.—The punishment of crimes against property is, in most countries, immensely disproportionate to the crime. In England, and probably in Canada, to steal a hare, is death the first offence. To steal above the value of twelve pence is death the second offence.—REPORT ON SPANISH CONVENTION. iii, 353. FORD ED., v, 483. (1792.)

1933. CRIME, Flight from debts.—The carrying away of the property of another may be reasonably made to found a civil action. A convention, then, may include forgery and the carrying away the property of others under the head of "Flight from Debts." To remit the fugitive in this case, would be to remit him in every case; for in the present state of things, it is next to impossible not to owe something. But I see neither injustice nor inconvenience in permitting the fugitive to be sued in our courts. The laws of some countries punishing the unfortunate debtor by perpetual imprisonment, he is right to liberate himself by flight, and it would be wrong to reimprison him in the country to which he flies. Let all process, therefore, be confined to his property.—REPORT ON SPANISH CONVENTION. iii, 354. FORD ED., v, 484. (1792.)

1934. CRIME, Forgery.—There is one crime against property, pressed by its consequences into more particular notice, to wit, forgery, whether of coin, or paper; and whether paper, of public, or private obligation. But the fugitive for forgery, is punished by exile and confiscation of the property he leaves. To which, add by Convention a civil action against the property he carries or acquires, to the amount of the special damage done by his forgery.—REPORT ON SPANISH CONVENTION. iii, 354. FORD ED., v, 484. (1792.)

1935. CRIME, Horse-stealing.—The offence of horse-stealing seems properly distinguishable from other larcenies, here, where these animals generally run at large, the temptation being so great and frequent, and the facility of commission so remarkable.*—NOTE ON CRIMES BILL. i, 157. FORD ED., ii, 215. (1779.)

1936. CRIME, Jurisdiction over.—The Constitution of the United States, * * * having delegated to Congress a power to punish treason, counterfeiting the securities and current coin of the United States, piracies and felonies committed on the high seas, and offences against the law of nations, and no other crimes whatsoever; and it being true, as a general principle, and one of the amendments to the Constitution having also declared, that "the powers not delegated to the United States by the Constitution, nor prohibited by it to the States, are reserved to the States respectively, or to the people," therefore the act of Congress, passed on the 14th day of July, 1798, and intituled, "An Act in addition to the act intituled An Act for the punishment of certain crimes against the United States," as also the act passed by them on the —— day of June, 1798, intituled,

---

* For horse-stealing, the bill provided a punishment of three years hard labor in the public works and reparation to the person injured.—EDITOR.

"An Act to punish frauds committed on the Bank of the United States" (and all other acts which assume to create, define, or punish crimes, other than those so enumerated in the Constitution), are altogether void, and of no force; and that the power to create, define, and punish such other crimes is reserved, and, of right, appertains solely and exclusively to the respective States, each within its own territory.—KENTUCKY RESOLUTIONS. ix, 465. FORD ED., vii, 292. (1798.)

1937. CRIME, Lex Talionis and.—They [the members of the Revision Committee of the Virginia Code] were agreed * * * that for other felonies [than treason and murder] hard labor in the public works should be substituted, and in some cases, the *lex talionis*. How this last revolting principle came to obtain our* approbation, I do not remember. There remained, indeed, in our laws, a vestige of it in a single case of a slave; it was the English law, in the time of the Anglo-Saxons, copied probably from the Hebrew Law of "an eye for an eye, a tooth for a tooth," and it was the law of several ancient people; but the modern mind had left it far in the rear of its advances.—AUTOBIOGRAPHY. i, 43. FORD ED., i, 60. (1821.)

1938. CRIME, National.—No national crime passes unpunished in the long run.—To M. DE MARBOIS. vii, 76. (M., 1817.)

1939. CRIME, Natural Laws and.—It is not only vain, but wicked, in a legislator to frame laws in opposition to the laws of nature, and to arm them with the terrors of death. This is truly creating crimes in order to punish them.—NOTE ON CRIMES BILL. i, 159. FORD ED., ii, 218. (1779.)

1940. CRIME, Principles of Punishing.—In forming a scale of crimes and punishments, two considerations have principal weight. 1. The atrocity of the crime. 2. The peculiar circumstances of a country which furnish greater temptations to commit it, or greater facilities for escaping detection. The punishment must be heavier to counterbalance this. Were the first the only consideration, all nations would form the same scale. But, as the circumstances of a country have influence on the punishment, and no two countries exist precisely under the same circumstances, no two countries will form the same scale of crimes and punishments. For example in America, the inhabitants let their horses go at large in the uninclosed lands, which are so extensive as to maintain them altogether. It is easy, therefore, to steal them, and easy to escape. Therefore, the laws are obliged to oppose these temptations with a heavier degree of punishment. For this reason, the stealing of a horse in America is punished more severely than stealing the same value in any other form. In Europe, where horses are confined so securely that it is impossible to steal them, that species of theft need not be punished

---

* Jefferson was a member of the Committee.—EDITOR.

more severely than any other. In some countries of Europe, stealing fruit from trees is punished capitally. The reason is, that it being impossible to lock fruit trees up in coffers, as we do our money, it is impossible to oppose physical bars to this species of theft. Moral ones are, therefore, opposed by the laws. This, to an unreflecting American, appears the most enormous of all the abuses of power; because he has been used to see fruits hanging in such quantities that if not taken by men, they would rot. He has been used to consider them therefore, as of no value, and as not furnishing materials for the commission of a crime.—To M. DE MEUNIER. ix, 264. FORD ED., iv, 169. (P., 1786.)

1941. CRIMINALS, Reformation of.—A member of society, committing an inferior injury, does not wholly forfeit the protection of his fellow citizens, but after suffering a punishment in proportion to his offence, is entitled to their protection from all greater pain, so that it becomes a duty in the Legislature to arrange, in a proper scale. the crimes which it may be necessary for them to repress, and to adjust thereto a corresponding gradation of punishments.—CRIMES BILL. i, 147. FORD ED., ii, 204. (1779.)

1942. CRITICISM, Canons of.—I have always very much despised the artificial canons of criticism. When I have read a work in prose or poetry, or seen a painting, a statue, &c., I have only asked myself whether it gives me pleasure, whether it is animating, interesting, attaching? If it is, it is good for these reasons.—To WILLIAM WIRT. FORD ED., x, 61. (P.F., 1816.)

1943. CRITICISM, Freedom of.—In mentioning me in your Essays, and canvassing my opinions, you have done what every man has a right to do, and it is for the good of society that that right should be freely exercised. No republic is more real than that of letters, and I am the last in principles, as I am the least in pretensions, to any dictatorship in it. Had I other dispositions, the philosophical and dispassionate spirit with which you have expressed your own opinions in opposition to mine, would still have commanded my approbation.—To NOAH WEBSTER. iii, 201. FORD ED., v, 254. (P., 1790.)

— CROAKINGS OF WEALTH.—See WEALTH.

1944. CRUELTY, British in America.—If M. de Meunier proposes to mention the facts of cruelty of which he * * * spoke yesterday, these facts are: 1. The death of upwards of eleven thousand American prisoners in one prison ship (the Jersey), and in the space of three years. 2. General Howe's permitting our prisoners, taken at the battle of Germantown, and placed under a guard in the yard of the State-house of Philadelphia, to be so long without any food furnished them that many perished with hunger. Where the bodies lay, it was seen that they had eaten all the grass around them within their reach, after they had lost the power of rising, or moving from their place. 3. The second fact was the act of a commanding officer; the first

of several commanding officers, and for so long a time as must suppose the approbation of government, itself. But the following was the act of the government itself. During the periods that our affairs seemed unfavorable, and theirs successful, that is to say, after the evacuation of New York, and again, after the taking of Charleston, in South Carolina, they regularly sent our prisoners, taken on the seas and carried to England, to the East Indies. This is so certain, that in the month of November or December, 1785, Mr. Adams having officially demanded a delivery of the American prisoners sent to the East Indies. Lord Carmarthen answered, officially, that orders were immediately issued for their discharge. M. de Meunier i at liberty to quote this fact. 4. A fact to be ascribed not only to the government, but to the parliament, who passed an act for that purpose in the beginning of the war, was the obliging our prisoners taken at sea to join them, and fight against their countrymen. This they effected by starving and whipping them. * * * The fact is referred to in that paragraph of the Declaration of Independence, which says, " He has constrained our fellow-citizens, taken captive on the high seas, to bear arms against their country, to become the executioners of their friends and brethren, or to fall themselves by their hands." This was the most afflicting to our prisoners of all the cruelties exercised on them. The others affected the body only, but this the mind; they were haunted by the horror of having, perhaps, themselves shot the ball by which a father or a brother fell. Some of them had constancy enough to hold out against half allowance of food and repeated whippings. These were generally sent to England, and from thence to the East Indies. One of them escaped from the East Indies, and got back to Paris, where he gave an account of his sufferings to Mr. Adams.—To M. DE MEUNIER. ix, 277. FORD ED., iv, 183. (P., 1786.)

1945. ——— ———. I doubt whether humanity is the character of the British nation in general. But [your] history, and every one which is impartial, must in its relation of the [American] war show, in such repeated instances, that they conducted it, both in theory and practice, on the most barbarous principles, that the expression here cited* will stand in contradiction to the rest of the work. As examples of their theory, recollect the act of Parliament for constraining our prisoners, taken on the sea, to bear arms against their fathers, brothers, &c. For their practice, recollect the exciting the savages against us, insurrections of our slaves, sending our prisoners to the East Indies, killing them in prison ships, keeping them on half rations, and of the most unwholesome quality, cruel murders of unarmed individuals of every sex, massacres of those in arms after they had asked quarter, &c., &c.—NOTES ON M. SOULES WORK. ix, 300. FORD ED., iv, 308. (P., 1786.)

1946. ——— ———. I confess that when I heard of the atrocities committed by the English troops at Hampton, I did not believe them, but subsequent evidence has placed them beyond doubt. To this has been added information from another quarter which proves the violation of women to be their habitual practice in war. Mr. Hamilton, a son of Alexander Hamilton, of course, a federalist and Angloman, and who was with the British army in Spain, declares it is their constant practice, and that at the taking of Badajoz, he was himself eye-

* "L'humanité des Britons."—EDITOR.

witness to it in the streets, and that the officers did not attempt to restrain it. The information contained in your letter proves it is not merely a recent practice. This is a trait of barbarism, in addition to their encouragement of the savage cruelties, and their brutal treatment of prisoners of war, which I had not attached to their character.—To JOSIAH MEIGS. FORD ED., ix, 419. (M., 1813.) See CORNWALLIS and RETALIATION.

1947. CUBA, Acquisition by United States.—I candidly confess, that I have ever looked on Cuba as the most interesting addition which could ever be made to our system of States. The control which, with Florida Point, this island would give us over the Gulf of Mexico, and the countries an isthmus bordering on it, as well as all those whose waters flow into it, would fill up the measure of our political well-being.—To PRESIDENT MONROE. vii. 316. FORD ED., x, 278. (M., 1823.)

1948. ——— ———. Certainly, her addition to our confederacy is exactly what is wanting to round our power as a nation to the point of its utmost interest.—To PRESIDENT MONROE. vii, 300. FORD ED., x, 261. (M., June 23, 1823.)

1949. ——— ———. It is better to lie still in readiness to receive that interesting incorporation when solicited by herself.—To PRESIDENT MONROE. vii, 300. FORD ED., x, 261. (M., June 1823.)

1950. ——— ———. It will be objected to our receiving Cuba, that no limit can then be drawn to our future acquisitions. Cuba can be defended by us without a navy, and this develops the principle which ought to limit our views. Nothing should ever be accepted which would require a navy to defend it.—To PRESIDENT MADISON. v, 445. (M., 1809.)

1951. ——— ———. Bonaparte, although with difficulty, will consent to our receiving Cuba into our Union, to prevent our aid to Mexico and the other [Spanish] provinces. That would be a price, and I would immediately erect a column on the southernmost limit of Cuba, and inscribe on it a *ne plus ultra* as to us in that direction.—To PRESIDENT MADISON. v, 444. FORD ED., ix, 25. (M., April 1809.)

1952. CUBA, England, France and.—Patriots of Spain have no warmer friends than the administration of the United States, but it is our duty to say nothing and to do nothing for or against either. If they succeed, we shall be well satisfied to see Cuba and Mexico remain in their present dependence; but very unwilling to see them in that of either France or England, politically or commercially. We consider their interests and ours as the same, and that the object of both must be to exclude all European influence from this hemisphere. * * * These are sentiments which I would wish you to express to any proper characters of either of these two countries, and particularly that we have nothing more at heart than their friendship.—To GOVERNOR CLAIBORNE. v, 381. FORD ED., ix, 212. (W., Oct. 1808.)

1953. CUBA, Possession by England.—Cuba alone seems at present to hold up a speck of war to us. Its possession by Great Britain would indeed be a great calamity to us. Could we induce her to join us in guaranteeing its independence against all the world, *except* Spain, it would be nearly as valuable to us as if it were our own.* But should she take it, I would not immediately go to war for it; because the first war on other accounts will give it to us; or the island will give itself to us, when able to do so.—To PRESIDENT MONROE. vii, 288. FORD ED., x, 257. (M., 1823.)

1954. CUBA, Spain, Bonaparte and.—I suppose the conquest of Spain will soon force a delicate question on you as to the Floridas and Cuba, which will offer themselves to you. Napoleon will certainly give his consent without difficulty to our receiving the Floridas, and with some difficulty possibly Cuba. And though he will disregard the obligation whenever he thinks he can break it with success, yet it has a great effect on the opinion of our people and the world to have the moral right on our side, of his agreement as well as that of the people of those countries.—To PRESIDENT MADISON. v, 442. FORD ED., ix, 251. (M., April 1809.)

1955. CUBA, Spanish Retention of.—I shall sincerely lament Cuba's falling into any hands but those of its present owners. Spanish-America is at present in the best hands for us, and "*Chi sta bene, non si muove*" should be our motto.—To ALBERT GALLATIN. v, 290. (M., 1808.)

1956. ——— ———. [The Cabinet was] unanimously agreed in the sentiments which should be unauthoritatively expressed by our agents to influential persons in Cuba and Mexico, to wit: "If you remain under the dominion of the Kingdom and family of Spain, we are contented; but we should be extremely unwilling to see you pass under the dominion or ascendency of France or England. In the latter cases should you choose to declare independence, we cannot now commit ourselves by saying we would make common cause with you, but must reserve ourselves to act according to the then existing circumstances; but in our proceedings we shall be influenced by friendship to you, by a firm belief that our interests are intimately connected, and by the strongest repugnance to see you under subordination to either France or England, either politically or commercially."—ANAS. FORD ED., i, 334. (Oct. 1808.)

— CURRENCY.—See BANKS, DOLLAR, NATIONAL CURRENCY, and MONEY.

* Jefferson wrote, two weeks later, to President Monroe, withdrawing this opinion, it having been "founded on an error of fact," with regard to the existence of an English interest in Cuba, and the possibility of its falling into the possession of Great Britain. "We are surely," said Jefferson, "under no obligation to give her, gratis, an interest which she has not; and the whole inhabitants being averse to her, and the climate mortal to strangers, its continued military occupation by her would be impracticable. It is better, then, to lie still in readiness to receive that interesting incorporation when solicited by herself."—EDITOR.

1957. "CURTIUS," Letters of.—I send you * * * one of the pieces, "Curtius" * * * . It is evidently written by [Alexander] Hamilton, giving a first and general view of the subject, that the public mind might be kept a little in check, till he could resume the subject more at large from the beginning, under his second signature of "Camillus." The piece called "The Features of the Treaty," I do not send, because you have seen it in the newspapers. It is said to be written by Coxe, but I should rather suspect, by Beckley. The antidote is certainly not strong enough for the poison of "Curtius." If I had not been informed the present came from Beckley, I should have suspected it from Jay or Hamilton. I gave a copy or two, by way of experiment, to honest, sound-hearted men of common understanding, and they were not able to parry the sophistry of "Curtius." * * * For God's sake take up your pen, and give a fundamental reply to "Curtius" and "Camillus." *—To JAMES MADISON. iv, 121. FORD ED., vii, 31. (M., Sep. 1795.)

—— **CUSHING (William), Death of.**—See SUPREME COURT.

1958. DALRYMPLE (—), Republicanism of.—Mr. Dalrymple, secretary to the legation of Mr. Crawford * * * is a young man of learning and candor, and exhibits a phenomenon I never before met with, that is, a republican born on the north side of the Tweed.—To JOHN ADAMS. i, 501. (P., 1785.)

1959. DANCING, Women and.—Dancing is a necessary accomplishment, although of short use; for the French rule is wise, that no lady dances after marriage. This is founded in solid physical reasons.—To N. BURWELL. vii, 102. FORD ED., x, 105. (M., 1818.)

1960. DASHKOFF (M.), Welcome to.—I hail you with particular pleasure, as the first harbinger of those friendly relations with your country [Russia], so desirable to ours.—To M. DASHKOFF. v, 463. (M., Aug. 1809.)

1961. DAVID (Jacques Louis), Paintings of.—We have nothing new and excellent in your charming art of painting. In fact, I do not feel an interest in any pencil but that of David.—To MADAME DE BREHAN. ii, 591. FORD ED., v, 80. (P., 1789.)

1962. DAYTON (Jonathan), Becomes a Federalist.—You will have perceived that Dayton has gone over completely. He expects to be appointed Secretary of War, in the room of M'Henry, who, it is said, will retire. He has been told, as report goes, that they would not have confidence enough in him to appoint him. The desire of inspiring them with more, seems the only way to account for the *eclat* which he chooses to give to his conversion.†—To JAMES MADISON. iv, 211. FORD ED., vii, 202. (P., Feb. 1798.)

1963. DEAD, Binding power of the.—Rights and powers can only belong to per-

* The letters of "Curtius" were written by Noah Webster, except numbers 6-7, which were from the pen of James Kent.—NOTE IN FORD EDITION.

† Dayton became implicated with Aaron Burr in his treasonable enterprise, and in August, 1807, applied to Jefferson to be admitted to bail. Jefferson declined on the ground that, "when a person, charged with an offence, is placed in the possession of the Judiciary authority, the laws commit to that solely the whole direction of the case; and any interference with it on the part of the Executive would be an encroachment on their independence, and open to just censure."—FORD ED., ix, 126.

sons, not to things, not to mere matter, unendowed with will. The dead are not even things. The particles of matter which composed their bodies make part now of the bodies of other animals, vegetables, or minerals, of a thousand forms. To what, then, are attached the rights and powers they held while in the form of men? A generation may bind itself as long as its majority continues in life; when that has disappeared, another majority is in place, holds all the rights and powers their predecessors once held, and may change their laws and institutions to suit themselves.—To JOHN CARTWRIGHT. vii, 359. (M., 1824.) See EARTH.

1964. DEAD, No Rights attached to.—The dead have no rights. They are nothing; and nothing cannot own something. Where there is no substance, there can be no accident.—To SAMUEL KERCHIVAL. vii, 16. FORD ED., x, 44. (M., 1816.) See GENERATIONS.

1965. DEANE (Silas), Official books of.—About three weeks ago, a person called on me and informed me that Silas Deane had taken him in for a sum of one hundred and twenty guineas, and that being unable to obtain any other satisfaction, he had laid hands on his account book and letter book, and had brought them off to Paris, to offer them first to the United States, if they would repay him his money, and if not, that he should return to London, and offer them to the British minister. I desired him to leave them with me four and twenty hours, that I might judge whether they were worth our notice. He did so. They were two volumes. One contained all his accounts with the United States, from his first coming to Europe, to January the 10th, 1781. * * * The other volume contained all his correspondence from March the 30th to August the 23d, 1777. * * * On perusal of many of them, I thought it desirable that they should not come to the hands of the British minister, and from an expression dropped by the possessor of them, I believe he would have fallen to fifty or sixty guineas. I did not think them important enough, however, to justify my purchasing them without authority; though, with authority, I should have done it. Indeed, I would have given that sum to cut out a single sentence, which contained evidence of a fact, not proper to be committed to the hands of enemies. I told him I would state his proposition to you, and await orders.—To JOHN JAY. ii, 454. (P., Aug. 1788.)

1966. —— ——. A Monsieur Foulloy, who has been connected with Deane, lately offered me for sale two volumes of Deane's letter books and account books, that he had taken instead of money which Deane owed him. I have purchased them on public account. He tells me Deane has still six or eight volumes more, and being to return soon to London, he will try to get them also, in order to make us pay high for them. You are sensible of the impropriety of letting such books get into hands which might make an unfriendly use of them. You are sensible of the immorality of an ex-minister's selling his secrets for money; and consequently that there can be no immorality in tempting him with money to part with them; so that they may be restored to that government to whom they properly belong. Your former acquaintance with Deane may, perhaps, put it in your power to render our country the service of recovering those books. It would not do to propose it to him as for Congress. * * * I suppose his distresses and his crapulous habits will not render him difficult on this head. On the supposition that there are six or eight volumes, I think you might venture as far as fifty guineas, and proportionably for fewer.—To DR. EDWARD BANCROFT. ii, 578. (P., 1789.)

1967. DEANE (Silas), Poverty of.—Silas Deane is coming over to finish his days in America, not having one sou to subsist on elsewhere. He is a wretched monument of the consequences of a departure from right.—To JAMES MADISON. iii, 101. FORD ED., v, 114. (P., 1789.)

1968. DEARBORN (Henry), Appointment to Cabinet.—On a review of the characters in the different States proper for the different departments, I have had no hesitation in considering you as the person to whom it would be most advantageous to the public to confide the Department of War. May I hope that you will give your country the aid of your talents?—To HENRY DEARBORN. iv, 356. FORD ED., vii, 496. (W., 1801.)

1969. DEARBORN (Henry), Esteem for.—In public or in private, and in all situations, I shall retain for you the most cordial esteem, and satisfactory recollections of the harmony and friendship with which we have run our race together.—To HENRY DEARBORN. v, 230. FORD ED., ix, 172. (W., Jan. 1808.)

1970. DEARBORN (Henry), Political Attacks on.—That you as well as myself, and all our brethren, have maligners, who from ill-temper, or disappointment, seek opportunities of venting their angry passions against us, is well known, and too well understood by our constituents to be regarded. No man who can succeed you will have fewer, nor will any one enjoy a more extensive confidence through the nation.—To HENRY DEARBORN. v, 229. FORD ED., ix, 171. (W., Jan. 1808.)

1971. DEARBORN (Henry), Services of.—The integrity, attention, skill, and economy with which you have conducted your department (War) have given me the most complete and unqualified satisfaction, and this testimony I bear to it with all the sincerity of truth and friendship; and should a war come on, there is no person in the United States to whose management and care I could commit it with equal confidence.—To HENRY DEARBORN. v, 229. FORD ED., ix, 171. (W., 1808.)

1972. —— ——. Nor among the incidents of the war, will we forget your services. * * * Your capture of York and Fort George first turned the tide of success in our favor; and the subsequent campaigns sufficiently wiped away the disgrace of the first.—To GENERAL DEARBORN. vi, 450. (M., 1815.)

1973. DEARBORN (Henry), Retirement of.—If it were justifiable to look to your own happiness only, your resolution to retire from all public business could not but be approved. But you are too young to ask a discharge as yet, and the public councils too much needing the wisdom of our ablest citizens, to relinquish their claim on you. And surely none needs your aid more than your own State.—To GENERAL DEARBORN. vi, 451. (M., March 1815.)

1974. DEATH, Blighted by.—The part you take in my loss makes an affectionate concern for the greatness of it. It is great indeed. Others may lose of their abundance, but I, of my want, have lost even the half of all I had. My evening prospects now hang on the slender thread of a single life. Perhaps I may be destined to see even this last cord of parental affection broken. The hope with which I had looked forward to the moment, when, resigning public cares to younger hands, I was to retire to that domestic comfort from which the last step is to be taken, is fearfully blighted.—To JOHN PAGE. iv, 547. (W., 1804.)

1975. DEATH, A Conqueror.—When you and I look back on the country over which we have passed, what a field of slaughter does it exhibit! Where are all the friends who entered it with us, under all the inspiring energies of health and hope? As if pursued by the havoc of war, they are strewed by the way, some earlier, some later, and scarce a few stragglers remain to count the numbers fallen, and to mark yet, by their own fall, the last footsteps of their party. Is it a desirable thing to bear up through the heat of the action, to witness the death of all our companions, and merely to be the last victim? I doubt it. We have, however, the traveller's consolation. Every step shortens the distance we have to go; the end of our journey is in sight, the bed wherein we are to rest, and to rise in the midst of the friends we have lost.—To JOHN PAGE. iv, 547. (W., 1804.)

1976. DEATH, Decay and.—To me every mail, in the departure of some contemporary, brings warning to be in readiness myself also, and to cease from new engagements. It is a warning of no alarm. When faculty after faculty is retiring from us, and all the avenues to cheerful sensation closing, sight failing now, hearing next, then memory, debility of body, torpitude of mind, nothing remaining but a sickly vegetation, with scarcely the relief of a little locomotion, the last cannot be but a *coup de grace.*—To MR. JOHN MELISH. vi, 403. (M., 1814.)

1977. DEATH, Generations and.—When we have lived our generation out, we should not wish to encroach on another. I enjoy good health: I am happy in what is around me, yet I assure you I am ripe for leaving all, this year, this day, this hour.—To JOHN ADAMS. vii, 26. (M., 1816.)

1978. —— ——. There is a ripeness of time for death, regarding others as well as ourselves, when it is reasonable we should drop off, and make room for another growth. When we have lived our generation out, we should not wish to encroach on another.—To JOHN ADAMS. vii, 26. (M., 1816.)

1979. DEATH, Life and.—When all our faculties have left, or are leaving us, one by one, sight, hearing, memory, every avenue of pleasing sensation is closed, and athymy, debility, and malaise left in their places; when friends of our youth are all gone, and a new generation is risen around us whom we know not, is death an evil? * * * I think not. I have ever dreaded a doting old age; and my health has been generally so good, and is now so good, that I dread it still.—To JOHN ADAMS. vii, 243. FORD ED., x, 216. (M., 1822.)

1980. DEATH, Meeting after.—Our next meeting must be in the country to which [those years] have flown,—a country for us not now very distant. For this journey we shall need neither gold nor silver in our purse, nor scrip, nor coats, nor staves. Nor is the provision for it more easy than the preparation has been kind. Nothing proves more than this, that the Being who presides over the world is essentially benevolent. Stealing from us, one by one, the faculties of enjoyment, searing our sensibilities, leading us, like the horse in his mill, round and round the same beaten circle,

—— To see what we have seen,
To taste the tasted, and at each return
Less tasteful; o'er our palates to decant
Another vintage—

Until satiated and fatigued with this leaden iteration, we ask our own *congé*. I heard once a very old friend, who had troubled himself with neither poets nor philosophers, say the same thing in plain prose, that he was tired of pulling off his shoes and stockings at night and putting them on again in the morning.—To MRS. JOHN ADAMS. vii, 53. FORD ED., x, 70. (M., 1817.)

1981. DEATH, Prepared for.—Mine is the next turn, and I shall meet it with good will; for after one's friends are all gone before him, and our faculties leaving us, too, one by one, why wish to linger in mere vegetation, as a solitary trunk in a desolate field, from which all its former companions have disappeared.—To MRS. COSWAY. D. L. J., 374. (M., 1820.)

1982. DEATH, Problem of.—The great problem, untried by the living, unreported by the dead.—To M. CORREA. vii, 95. (P.F., 1817.)

1983. DEATH, A Time for.—There is a fulness of time when men should go, and not occupy too long the ground to which others have a right to advance.—To DR. BENJAMIN RUSH. vi, 4. FORD ED., ix, 329. (P.F., 1811.)

1984. DEATH PENALTY, Crimes Punishable by.—The General Assembly [of Virginia] shall have no power to pass any law inflicting death for any crime, excepting murder; and those offences in the military service for which they shall think punishment by death absolutely necessary: and all capital punishments in other cases are hereby abolished.—PROPOSED VA. CONSTITUTION. FORD ED., ii, 17. (June 1776.)

1985. —— ——. No crime shall be henceforth punished by the deprivation of life or limb, except those hereinafter ordained to be so punished.*—CRIMES BILL. i, 148. FORD ED., ii, 205. (1779.)

* Those crimes, so ordained, were treason and murder. When Jefferson made this humane propo-

1986. DEATH PENALTY, Criminal Reform and.—The reformation of offenders, though an object worthy the attention of the laws, is not effected at all by capital punishments, which exterminate instead of reforming, and should be the last melancholy resource against those whose existence is become inconsistent with the safety of their fellow citizens; which also weaken the State, by cutting off so many who, if reformed, might be restored sound members to society, who, even under a course of correction, might be rendered useful in various labors for the public, and would be living and long continued spectacles to deter others from committing the like offences.—CRIMES BILL. i, 147. FORD ED., ii, 204. (1779.)

1987. —— ——. Beccaria, and other writers on crimes and punishments, had satisfied the reasonable world of the unrightfulness and inefficacy of the punishment of crimes by death; and hard labor on roads, canals and other public works, had been suggested as a proper substitute. The Revisors [of the Virginia laws] had adopted these opinions; but the general idea of our country had not yet advanced to that point. The bill, therefore, for proportioning crimes and punishments, was lost in the House of Delegates by a majority of a single vote. I learned afterwards, that the substitute of hard labor in public, was tried (I believe it was in Pennsylvania) without success. Exhibited as a public spectacle, with shaved heads and mean clothing, working on the high roads, produced in the criminals such a prostration of character, such an abandonment of self-respect, as instead of reforming, plunged them into the most desperate and hardened depravity of morals and character.—AUTOBIOGRAPHY. i, 45. FORD ED., i, 62. (1821.)

1988. DEATH PENALTY, Indians and. —It will be worthy the consideration of the Legislature, whether the provisions of the law inflicting on Indians, in certain cases, the punishment of death by hanging, might not permit its commutation into death by military execution, the form of the punishment in the former way being peculiarly repugnant to their ideas, and increasing the obstacles to the surrender of the criminal.—SPECIAL MESSAGE. viii, 22. (Jan. 1802.)

1989. DEATH PENALTY, Pardons and.—If all these people are convicted, there will be too many to be punished with death. My hope is that they will send me full statements of every man's case, that the most guilty may be marked as examples, and the less so suffer long imprisonment under reprieves from time to time.—To ALBERT GALLATIN. vii, 363. (M., 1808.)

1990. DEBATE, In Congress.—Was there ever a proposition so plain as to pass Congress without a debate?—To JAMES MADISON. ii, 152. FORD ED., iv, 391. (P., 1787.) See 1473, 1571.

sition, the penal code of England comprehended more than two hundred offences, besides treason and murder, punishable by hanging.—EDITOR.

1991. DEBATE, Lawyers and.—If the present Congress errs in too much talking, how can it be otherwise in a body to which the people send one hundred and fifty lawyers, whose trade it is to question everything, yield nothing, and talk by the hour? That one hundred and fifty lawyers should do business together ought not to be expected.—Autobiography. i, 58. Ford ed., i, 82. (1821.)

1992. DEBATE, Secrecy and.—I am sorry the Federal convention began their deliberations by so abominable a precedent as that of tying up the tongues of their members. Nothing could justify this example but the innocence of their intentions and ignorance of the value of public discussions.—To John Adams. ii, 260. (P., 1787.)

1993. DEBATE, Washington and Franklin in.—I served with General Washington in the Legislature of Virginia before the Revolution and, during it, with Dr. Franklin in Congress. I never heard either of them speak ten minutes at a time, nor to any but the main point which was to decide the question. They laid their shoulders to the great points, knowing that the little ones would follow of themselves.—Autobiography. i, 58. Ford ed., i, 82. (1821.)

1994. DEBT, Avoiding.—The maxim of buying nothing but what we have money in our pockets to pay for lays, of all others, the broadest foundation for happiness.—To Mr. Skipwith. ii, 191. (P., 1787.)

1995. ———. The maxim of buying nothing without the money in our pockets to pay for it, would make of our country one of the happiest on earth. Experience during the war proved this; and I think every man will remember, that under all the privations it obliged him to submit to during that period, he slept sounder, and awoke happier than he can do now.—To A. Donald. ii, 193. Ford ed., iv, 414. (P., 1787.)

1996. ———. [We should] put off buying anything until we have the money to pay for it.—To Dr. Currie. ii, 219. (P., 1787.)

1997. DEBT, Blessing of a public.—As the doctrine is that a public debt is a public blessing, so they [the supporters of State debt assumption] think a perpetual one is a perpetual blessing and, therefore, wish to make it so large that we can never pay it off.—To Nicholas Lewis. iii, 348. Ford ed., v, 505. (Pa., 1792.)

1998. DEBT, Contracts and.—If there was ever any agreement between Mr. Ross and me to pay him any part of the account in tobacco, it must be paid in tobacco. But neither justice nor generosity can call for referring anything to any other scale than that of hard money. Paper money was a cheat. Tobacco was the counter-cheat. Every one is justifiable in rejecting both except so far as his contracts bind him.—To Francis Eppes. Ford ed., v, 211. (N.Y., 1790.)

1999. DEBT, Fashion, Folly and.—Everything I hear from my own country fills me with despair as to their recovery from their vassalage to Great Britain. Fashio[n] and folly are plunging them deeper an[d] deeper into distress; and the legislators of th[e] country becoming debtors also, there seems n[o] hope of applying the only possible remed[y] that of an immediate judgment and executio[n.] We should try whether the prodigal migh[t] not be restrained from taking on credit th[e] gewgaw held out to him in one hand, by see[ing] the keys of a prison in the other.—To T[.] Pleasants. i, 564. (P., 1786.)

2000. DEBT, Generations and.—That w[e] are bound to defray the expenses of the wa[r] within our own time, and unauthorized t[o] burthen posterity with them, I suppose t[o] have been proved in my former letter. I wi[ll] place the question nevertheless in one addi[-] tional point of view. The former regarde[d] their independent right over the earth; thi[s] over their own persons. There have existe[d] nations, and civilized and learned nations, who have thought that a father had a right t[o] sell his child as a slave, in perpetuity; tha[t] he could alienate his body and industry conjointly, and à fortiari his industry separately, and consume its fruits himself. A nation asserting this fratricide right might well suppose they could burthen with public as well as private debt their *nati natorum, et qui nascentur ab illis*. But we, this age, and in this country especially, are advanced beyond those notions of natural law. We acknowledge that our children are born free; that that freedom is the gift of nature, and not o[f] him who begot them; that though under ou[r] care during infancy, and therefore of necessity, under a duly tempered authority, that care is confided to us to be exercised for the good of the child only; and his labors during youth are given as a retribution for the charges of infancy. As he was never the property of his father, so when adult he is *sui juris*, entitled himself to the use of his own limbs and the fruits of his own exertions: so far we are advanced, without mind enough, it seems, to take the whole step. We believe, or we act as if we believed, that although an individual father cannot alienate the labor of his son, the aggregate body of fathers may alienate the labor of all their sons, or of their posterity in the aggregate, and oblige them to pay for all the enterprises, just or unjust, profitable or ruinous, into which our vices, our passions, or our personal interests may lead us. But I trust that this proposition needs only to be looked at by an American to be seen in its true point of view, and that we shall all consider ourselves unauthorized to saddle posterity with our debts, and morally bound to pay them ourselves; and consequently within what may be deemed the period of a generation, or the life of the majority. * * * We must raise, then, ourselves the money for this war, either by taxes within the year, or by loans; and if by loans, we must repay them ourselves, proscribing forever the English practice of perpetual funding; the ruinous consequences of which, putting right out of the question,

should be a sufficient warning to a consider-
ate nation to avoid the example.—To J. W.
EPPES. vi, 196. FORD ED., ix, 396. (P.F.,
Sep. 1813.) See GENERATIONS.

2001. —— ——. The public expenses of
England during the present reign have
amounted to the fee simple value of the
whole island. If its whole soil could be sold,
farm by farm, for its present market price,
it would not defray the cost of governing it
during the reign of the present King, as managed by him. Ought not then the right of
each successive generation to be guaranteed
against the dissipations and corruptions of
those preceding, by a fundamental provision
in our Constitution? And, if that has not
been made, does it exist the less; there being
between generation and generation, as between nation and nation, no other law than
that of nature? And is it the less dishonest
to do what is wrong, because not expressly
prohibited by written law? Let us hope our
moral principles are not yet in that stage of
degeneracy, and that in instituting the system of finance to be hereafter pursued, we
shall adopt the only safe, the only lawful and
honest one, of borrowing on such short terms
of reimbursement of interest and principal
as will fall within the accomplishment of our
own lives.—To J. W. EPPES. vi, 199. FORD
ED., ix, 398. (P.F., Sep. 1813.)

2002. —— ——. It is incumbent on every
generation to pay its own debts as it goes.
A principle which, if acted on, would save
one-half the wars of the world.—To DESTUTT
TRACY. FORD ED., x, 175. (M., 1820.) See
GENERATIONS.

2003. DEBT, Imprisonment for.—It may
be safely affirmed that neither natural right
nor reason subjects the body of a man to
restraint for debt. It is one of the abuses
introduced by commerce and credit, and
which even the most commercial nations have
been obliged to relax, in certain cases. The
Roman law, the principles of which are the
nearest to natural reason of those of any
municipal code hitherto known, allowed imprisonment of the body in criminal cases only,
or those wherein the party had expressly submitted himself to it. The French laws allow
it only in criminal or commercial cases. The
laws of England, in certain descriptions of
cases (as bankruptcy) release the body. Many
of the United States do the same in all cases,
on a cession of property by the debtor.—To
GEORGE HAMMOND. iii, 306. FORD ED., vi, 38.
(Pa., May 1792.)

2004. —— ——. The laws of some countries punishing the unfortunate debtor by
perpetual imprisonment, he is right to liberate
himself by flight, and it would be wrong to
re-imprison him in the country to which he
flies. Let all process, therefore, be confined
to his property.—REPORT ON SPANISH CON-
VENTION. iii, 354. FORD ED., v, 484. (1792.)

— **DEBT, Interest on.**—See INTEREST and
DEBTS DUE BRITISH.

2005. DEBT, Jefferson's personal.—You
will have seen in the newspapers some proceedings in the Legislature, which have cost
me much mortification.* My own debts had
become considerable, but not beyond the effect of some lopping of property, which would
have been but little felt, when our friend —†
gave me the *coup de grace.* Ever since that I
have been paying twelve hundred dollars a
year interest on his debt, which, with my own,
was absorbing so much of my annual income
as that the maintenance of my family
was making deep and rapid inroads on my
capital, and had already done it. Still, sales
at a fair price would leave me competently
provided. Had crops and prices for several
years been such as to maintain a steady competition of substantial bidders at market, all
would have been safe. But th. long succession of years of stunted crops, of reduced
prices, the general prostration of the farming
business, under levies for the support of
manufacturers, &c., with the calamitous fluctuations of value in our paper medium, have
kept agriculture in a state of abject depression, which has peopled the western States
by silently breaking up those on the Atlantic,
and glutted the land market, while it drew off
its bidders. In such a state of things, property has lost its character of being a resource
for debts. Highland in Bedford, which, in
the days of our plethory, sold readily for from
fifty to one hundred dollars the acre (and
such sales were many then), would not now
sell for more than from ten to twenty dollars,
or one-quarter or one-fifth of its former price.
Reflecting on these things, the practice occurred to me, of selling, on fair valuation,
and by way of lottery, often resorted to before the Revolution to effect large sales, and
still in constant usage in every State for individual as well as corporation purposes. If
it is permitted in my case, my lands here
alone, with the mills, &c., will pay everything
and leave me Monticello and a farm free. If
refused, I must sell everything here, perhaps
considerably in Bedford, move thither with
my family, where I have not even a log hut
to put my head into, and whether ground for
burial, will depend on the depredations which,
under the form of sales, shall have been committed on my property. The question then
with me was *ultrum horum?*—To JAMES
MADISON. vii, 433. FORD ED., x, 376. (M.,
February 1826.)

2006. —— ——. Had our land market remained in a healthy state everything might
have been paid, and have left me competently
provided. But the agricultural branch of industry with us had been so many years in a
state of abject prostration, that, combined
with the calamitous fluctuations in the value
of our circulating medium, those concerned
in it, instead of being in a condition to purchase, were abandoning farms no longer
yielding profit, and moving off to the western

---

* Application for authority to dispose of his property by lottery.—EDITOR.
† W. C. Nicholas.—EDITOR.

country.—To George Loyall. Ford ed., x, 380. (M., 1826.)

2007. ———. ———. A long succession of unfruitful years, long-continued low prices, oppressive tariffs levied on other branches to maintain that of manufactures, for the most flourishing of all, calamitous fluctuations in the value of our circulating medium, and, in my case, a want of skill in the management of our land and labor, these circumstances had been long undermining the state of agriculture, had been breaking up the landholders, and glutting the land market here, while drawing off its bidders to people the western country. Under such circumstances agricultural property had become no resource for the payment of debts.—To Thomas Ritchie. Ford ed., x, 381. (M., 1826.) See 2091.

2008. DEBT, Just Payment of.—What the laws of Virginia are, or may be, will in no wise influence my conduct. Substantial justice is my object, as decided by reason, and not by authority or compulsion.—To William Jones. Ford ed., iv, 352. (P., 1787.)

2009. DEBT, Misery of.—I am miserable till I shall owe not a shilling.—To Nicholas Lewis. Ford ed., iv, 343. (P., 1786.)

— DEBT, National.—See Debt, U. S.

2010. DEBT, Oppressive English.—George III. in execution of the trust confided to him, has, within his own day, loaded the inhabitants of Great Britain with debts equal to the whole fee-simple value of their island, and under pretext of governing it, has alienated its whole soil to creditors who could lend money to be lavished on priests, pensions, plunder and perpetual war. This would not have been so, had the people retained organized means of acting on their agents. In this example, then, let us read a lesson for ourselves, and not " go and do likewise."—To Samuel Kerchival vii, 36. Ford ed., x, 45. (M., 1816.)

2011. ———. ———. The interest of the [English] national debt is now equal to such a portion of the profits of all the land and the labor of the island, as not to leave enough for the subsistence of those who labor. Hence the owners of the land abandon it and retire to other countries, and the laborer has not enough of his earnings left to him to cover his back and to fill his belly. The local insurrections, now almost general, are of the hungry and the naked, who cannot be quieted but by food and raiment. But where are the means of feeding and clothing them? The landholder has nothing of his own to give; he is but the fiduciary of those who have lent him money; the lender is so taxed in his meat, drink and clothing, that he has but a bare subsistence left. The landholder, then, must give up his land, or the lender his debt, or they must compromise by giving up each one-half. But will either consent *peaceably*, to such an abandonment of property? Or must it not be settled by civil conflict? If peaceably compromised, will they agree to risk another ruin under the same government unreformed? I think not, but I would rather know what you think; because you have lived with John Bull, and know better than I do the character of his herd.—To John Adams. vii, 40. (M. 1816.)

2012. DEBT, Perpetual.—What is to hinder [the government] from creating a perpetual debt? The laws of nature, I answer. The earth belongs to the living not to the dead. The will and the power of man expire with his life, by nature's law. Some societies give it an artificial continuance, for the encouragement of industry; some refuse it, as our aboriginal neighbors, whom we call barbarians. The generations of men may be considered as bodies or corporations. Each generation has the usufruct of the earth during the period of its continuance. When it ceases to exist the usufruct passes on to the succeeding generation, free and unincumbered, and so on, successively, from one generation to another forever. We may consider each generation as a distinct nation, with a right, by the will of its majority, to bind themselves, but none to bind the succeeding generation, more than the inhabitants of another country. Or the case may be likened to the ordinary one of a tenant for life, who may hypothecate the land for his debts, during the continuance of his usufruct; but at his death, the reversioner (who is also for life only) receives it exonerated from all burden. The period of a generation, or the term of its life, is determined by the laws of mortality, which, varying a little only in different climates, offer a general average to be found by observation. I turn, for instance, to Buffon's tables, of twenty-three thousand nine hundred and ninety-four deaths, and the ages at which they happened, and I find that of the numbers of all ages living at one moment, half will be dead in twenty-four years and eight months. But (leaving out minors, who have not the power of self-government) of the adults (of twenty-one years of age) living at one moment, a majority of whom act for the society, one-half will be dead in eighteen years and eight months. At nineteen years, then, from the date of a contract, the majority of the contractors are dead, and their contract with them. Let this general theory be applied to a particular case. Suppose the annual births of the Stat- of New York to be twenty-three thousand nine hundred and ninety-four, the whole number of its inhabitants, according to Buffon, will be six hundred and seventeen thousand, seven hundred and three, of all ages. Of these there would constantly be two hundred and sixty-nine thousand two hundred and eighty-six minors, and three hundred and forty-eight thousand four hundred and seventeen adults, of which last, one hundred and seventy-four thousand two hundred and nine will be a majority. Suppose that majority, on the first day of the year 1794, had borrowed a sum of money equal to the fee-simple value of the State, and to have consumed it in eating, drinking and making merry in their day; or, if you please, in quarrelling and fighting with their unoffending neighbors. Within eighteen years and eight months, one-half of the adult citizens were dead. Till then, being the majority, they might rightfully levy the interest of their debt annually on themselves and their fellow-revellers, or fellow-champions. But at that period, say at this moment, a new majority have come into place, in their own right, and not under the rights, the conditions, or laws of their predecessors. Are they bound to acknowledge the debt, to consider the preceding generation as having had a right to eat up the whole soil of their country, in the course of a life, to alienate it from them (for it would be an alienation to the creditors), and would they think themselves either legally or morally bound to give up their country and emigrate to another for subsistence? Every one will say no; that the soil is the gift of God to the living, as much as it had been to the deceased generation; and that the laws of nature impose no obligation on them to pay this debt. And although, like some other natural rights, this has not yet entered into any declaration of rights, it is no less a law, and ought to be acted on by honest governments. It is, at the same time, a salutary curb on the spirit of war and indebtment, which, since the modern theory of the perpetuation of debt, has drenched the earth with blood, and crushed its inhabitants under burthens ever accumulating. Had this principle been declared in the British bill of rights, England would have been placed under the happy disability of waging eternal war, and of contracting her thousand millions of public debt. In seeking then, for an ultimate term for the redemption of our debts, let us rally to this principle, and provide for their payment within the term of nineteen years at the farthest.—To John Wayles Eppes. vi, 136. Ford ed., ix, 389. (M., June 1813.) See Generations.

2013. DEBT, Public.—At the time we were funding our national debt, we heard much about "a public debt being a public blessing"; that the stock representing it was a creation of active capital for the aliment of commerce, manufactures and agriculture. This paradox was well adapted to the minds of believers in dreams, and the gulls of that size entered *bonâ fide* into it. But the art and mystery of banks is a wonderful improvement on that. It is established on the principle that "*private* debts are a public blessing"; that the evidences of those private debts, called bank notes, become active capital, and aliment the whole commerce, manufactures, and agriculture of the United States. Here are a set of people, for instance, who have bestowed on us the great blessing of running in our debt about two hundred millions of dollars, without our knowing who they are, where they are, or want property they have to pay this debt when called on; nay, who have made us so sensible of the blessings of letting them run in our debt, that we have exempted them by law from the repayment of these debts beyond a given proportion (generally estimated at one-third). And to fill up the measure of blessing, instead of paying, they receive an interest on what they owe from those to whom they owe; for all the notes, or evidences of what they owe, which we see in circulation, have been lent to somebody on an interest which is levied again on us through the medium of commerce. And they are so ready still to deal out their liberalities to us, that they are now willing to let themselves run in our debt ninety millions more, on our paying them the same premium of six or eight per cent. interest, and on the same legal exemption from the repayment of more than thirty millions of the debt when it shall be called for. But let us look at this principle in its original form, and its copy will then be equally understood. "A public debt is a public blessing." That our debt was juggled from forty-three to eighty millions, and funded at that amount, according to this opinion a great public blessing, because the evidences of it could be vested in commerce, and thus converted into active capital, and then the more the debt was made to be, the more the active capital was created. That is to say, the creditors could now employ in commerce the money due them from the public, and make from it an annual profit of five per cent., or four millions of dollars. But observe, that the public were at the same time paying on it an interest of exactly the same amount of four millions of dollars. Where, then, is the gain to either party, which makes it a public blessing? There is no change in the state of things, but of persons only. A has a debt due to him from the public, of which he holds their certificate as evidence, and on which he is receiving an annual interest. He wishes, however, to have the money itself, and to go into business with it. B has an equal sum of money in business, but wishes now to retire, and live on the interest. He therefore gives it to A in exchange for A's certificates of public stock. Now, then, A has the money to employ in business, which B so employed before. B has the money on interest to live on, which A lived on before; and the public pays the interest to B which they paid to A before. Here is no new creation of capital, no additional money employed, nor even a change in the employment of a single dollar. The only change is of place between A and B in which we discover no creation of capital, nor public blessing. Suppose, again, the public to owe nothing. Then A not having lent his money to the public, would be in possession of it himself, and would go into business without the previous operation of selling stock. Here, again, the same quantity of capital is employed as in the former case, though no public debt exists. In neither case is there any creation of active capital, nor other difference than that there is a public debt in the first case, and none in the last; and we may safely ask which of the two situations is most truly a public blessing? If, then, a public debt be no public blessing, we may pronounce, *à fortiori*, that a private one cannot be so. If the debt which the banking companies owe be a blessing to anybody, it is to themselves alone, who are realizing a solid interest of eight or ten per cent. on it. As to the public, these companies have banished all our gold and silver medium, which, before their institution, we had without interest, which never could have perished in our hands, and would have been our salvation now in the hour of war; instead of which they have given us two hundred million of froth and bubble, on which we are to pay them heavy interest, until it shall vanish into air as the Morris notes did. We are warranted, then, in affirming that this parody on the principle of "a public debt being a public blessing," and its mutation into the blessing of private instead of public debts, is as ridiculous as the original principle itself. In both cases, the truth is, that capital may be produced by industry, and accumulated by economy; but jugglers only will propose to create it by legerdemain tricks with paper.—To J. W. EPPES. vi, 239. FORD ED., ix, 411. (M., Nov. 1813.)

2014. DEBT, Running in.—It is a miserable arithmetic which makes any single privation whatever so painful as a total privation of everything which must necessarily follow the living so far beyond our income. What is to extricate us I know not, whether law, or loss of credit. If the sources of the former are corrupted, so as to prevent justice, the latter must supply its place, leave us possessed of our infamous gains, but prevent all future ones of the same character.—To WILLIAM HAY. ii, 215. (P., 1787.)

2015. ———— ————. How happy a people were we during the war from the single circumstance that we could not run in debt.—To DR. CURRIE. ii, 219. (P., 1787.)

— DEBT, Of the States.—See ASSUMPTION.

2016. DEBT, Thraldom of.—Instead of the unalloyed happiness of retiring unembarrassed and independent, to the enjoyment of my estate, which is ample for my limited views, I have to pass such a length of time in a thraldom of mind never before known to me. Except for this, my happiness would have been perfect.—To GENERAL KOSCIUSKO. v, 509. (M., 1810.)

2017. DEBT, Tormented by.—The torment of mind I endure till the moment shall arrive when I shall not owe a shilling on earth is such really as to render life of little value. I cannot decide to sell my lands. I have sold too much of them already, and they are the only sure provision for my children; nor would I willingly sell the slaves as long as there remains any prospect of paying my debts with their labor. In this I am governed solely by views to their happiness, which will render it worth their while to use extraordinary exertions for some time to enable me to put them ultimately on an easier footing, which I will do the moment they

have paid the debts due from the estate, two-thirds of which have been contracted by purchasing them.—To NICHOLAS LEWIS. FORD ED., iv, 416. (P., 1787.)

2018. DEBT (French), Assignats and.—I have communicated to the President what passed between us * * * on the subject of the payments made to France by the United States in the assignats of that country, since they have lost their par with gold and silver; and after conferences, by his instruction, with the Secretary of the Treasury, I am authorized to assure you, that the government of the United States have no idea of paying their debt in a depreciated medium, and that in the final liquidation of the payments, which shall have been made, due regard will be had to an equitable allowance for the circumstance of depreciation.*—To JEAN BAPTISTE TERNANT. iii, 294. FORD ED., v, 383. (Pa., Sep. 1791.)

2019. DEBT (French), Complaints of officers.—A second year's interest is become due [to the French officers]. They have presented their demands. There is not money here [Paris] to pay them; the pittance remaining in Mr. Grand's hands being only sufficient to pay current expenses three months longer. The dissatisfaction of these officers is extreme, and their complaints will produce the worst effect. The Treasury Board has not ordered their payment, probably because they knew there would not be money. The amount of their demand is about forty-two thousand livres, and Mr. Grand has in his hands but twelve thousand. I have thought it my duty, under this emergency, to ask you whether you could order that sum for their relief from the funds in Holland? If you can, I am persuaded it will have the best of effects.—To JOHN ADAMS. i, 510. (P., 1786.)

2020. ———— ————. The payment of French officers, the last year, had the happiest effect imaginable. It procured so many advocates for the credit and honor of the United States, who were heard in all companies. I corrected the idea that we were unwilling to pay our debts. I fear that our present failure towards them will give new birth to new imputations, and a relapse of credit.—To THE TREASURY COMMISSIONERS. i, 521. (P., 1786.)

2021. ———— ————. The debt to the officers of France carries an interest of about two thousand guineas, so we may suppose its principal is between thirty and forty thousand. This makes more noise against us than all our other debts put together.—To JOHN ADAMS. ii, 164. FORD ED., iv, 399. (P., 1787.)

2022. ———— ————. Mr. Adams informs me he has borrowed money in Holland, which, if confirmed by Congress, will enable them to pay not only the interest due here to the foreign officers, but the principal. Let me beseech you to reflect on the expediency of transferring this debt to Holland. All our other debts in Europe do not injure our reputation so much as this. These gentlemen have connections both in and out of office, and these again their connections, so that our default on this article is further known, more blamed, and excites worse

* As written by Jefferson, the letter, after the words "depreciated medium" closed as follows "and that they will take measures for making these payments in their just value, avoiding all benefit from depreciation, and desiring on their part to be guarded against any unjust loss from the circumstances of mere exchange." It was changed to meet the views of Hamilton.—EDITOR.

dispositions against us, than you can conceive.
—To JAMES MADISON. ii, 209. FORD ED., iv,
422. (P., 1787.)

2023. DEBT (French), Desire to pay.—
We desire strongly to pay off our debt to
France, and for this purpose we will use our
credit as far as it will hold good. * * * Under
these dispositions and prospects, it would grieve
us extremely to see our debt pass into the hands
of speculators, and be subjected ourselves to the
chicaneries and vexations of private avarice.
We desire you, therefore, to dissuade the government * * * from listening to any overtures of that kind, and as to the speculators
themselves, whether native or foreign, to inform them without reserve that our government condemns their projects, and reserves to
itself the right of paying nowhere but into
the Treasury of France.—To WILLIAM SHORT.
iii, 253. (Pa., 1791.)

**2024. DEBT (French), Payments discon-
tinued.—**We are informed by the public papers that the late constitution of France, formally notified to us, is suspended, and a new
convention called. During the time of this suspension, and while no legitimate government
exists, we apprehend we cannot continue the
payments of our debt to France, because there is
no person authorized to receive it, and to give
us an unobjectionable acquittal. You are, therefore, desired to consider the payment as suspended, until further orders. Should circumstances oblige you to mention this (which it
is better to avoid if you can), do it with such
solid reasons as will occur to yourself, and accompany it with the most friendly declarations
that the suspension does not proceed from any
wish in us to delay the payment, the contrary
being our wish, nor from any desire to embarrass or oppose the settlement of their government in that way in which their nation shall
desire it; but from our anxiety to pay this debt
justly and honorably, and to the persons really
authorized by the nation (to whom we owe it)
to receive it for their use. Nor shall this suspension be continued one moment after we can
see our way clear out of the difficulty into which
their situation has thrown us.—To GOUVER-
NEUR MORRIS. iii, 476. FORD ED., vi, 121. (Pa.,
Oct. 1792.)

**2025. DEBT (French), Payments Re-
sumed.—**On the dissolution of the late constitution in France, by removing so integral a
part of it as the King, the National Assembly,
to whom a part only of the public authority had
been delegated, appear to have considered themselves as incompetent to transact the affairs
of the nation legitimately. They invited their
fellow-citizens, therefore, to appoint a National
Convention. In conformity with this their
idea of the defective state of the national authority, you were desired from hence to suspend
further payments of our debt to France till new
orders, with an assurance, however, to the acting power, that the suspension should not be
continued a moment longer than should be necessary for us to see the reestablishment of
some person or body of persons authorized to
receive payment and give us a good acquittal;
(if you should find it necessary to give any
assurance or explanation at all). In the meantime, we went on paying up the four million
of livres which had been destined by the last
constituted authorities to the relief of St. Domingo. Before this was completed, we received
information that a National Assembly had met,
with full powers to transact the affairs of the
nation, and soon afterwards, the minister of

France here presented an application for three
millions of livres, to be laid out in provisions
to be sent to France. Urged by the strongest
attachment to that country, and thinking it
even providential that moneys lent to us in distress could be repaid under like circumstances,
we had no hesitation to comply with the application, and arrangements are accordingly
taken, for furnishing this sum at epochs accommodated to the demand and our means of paying it. * * * We shall certainly use our utmost
endeavors to make punctual payments of the
instalments and interest hereafter becoming exigible, and to omit no opportunity of convincing
that nation how cordially we wish to serve them.
—To GOUVERNEUR MORRIS. iii, 521. FORD ED.,
vi, 199. (Pa., March 1793.)

**2026. DEBT (French), Proposition of
Genet.—**I cannot but think that to decline the
propositions* of M. Genet on the subject of
our debt, without assigning any reason at all,
would have a very dry and unpleasant aspect indeed. We are then to examine what are our
good reasons for the refusal, which of them
may be spoken out, and which may not. 1.
Want of confidence in the continuance of the
present form of government, and consequently
that *advances* to them might commit us with
their successors. This cannot be spoken out.
2. Since they propose to take the debt in produce, it would be better for us that it should
be done in moderate masses yearly, than all
in one year. This cannot be professed. 3.
When M. de Calonne was Minister of Finance,
a Dutch company proposed to buy up the whole
of our debt, by dividing it into actions or shares.
I think M. Claviere, now Minister of Finance,
was their agent. It was observed to M. de
Calonne, that to create such a mass of American
paper, divide it into shares, and let them deluge
the market, would depreciate the rest of our
paper, and our credit in general; that the credit
of a nation was a delicate and important thing,
and should not be risked on such an operation.
M. de Calonne, sensible of the injury of the operation to us, declined it. In May, 1791, there
came, through Mr. Otto, a similar proposition
from Schweizer, Jeanneret & Co. We had a
communication on the subject from Mr. Short,
urging this same reason strongly. It was referred to the Secretary of the Treasury, who,
in a letter to yourself, assigned the reasons
against it, and these were communicated to
Mr. Otto, who acquiesced in them. This objection, then, having been sufficient to decline
the proposition twice before, and having been
urged to the two preceding forms of government (the ancient and that of 1791), will not be
considered by them as founded in objections to
the present form. 4. The law allows the whole
debt to be paid only on condition it can be done
on terms *advantageous* to the United States.
The minister foresees this objection, and thinks
he answers it by observing the *advantage* which
the payment in *produce* will occasion. It would
be easy to show that this was not the sort of advantage the Legislature meant, but a *lower rate
of interest.* 5. I cannot but suppose that the
Secretary of the Treasury * * * would, on
examination, be able to derive practical objections from them. We pay to France but five
per cent. The people of this country would
never subscribe their money for less than six.
If, to remedy this, obligations at less than five
per cent. were offered, and accepted by M.
Genet, he must part with them immediately,
at a considerable discount, to indemnify the loss

* That the remainder of the debt be paid at once,
provided the sum be invested in produce.—EDITOR.

of the one per cent., and at still greater discount to bring them down to par with our present six per cent., so that the operation would be equally disgraceful to us and to losing to them, &c., &c. I think it very material myself to keep alive the friendly sentiments of that country, so far as can be done without risking war or double payment. If the instalments falling due this year can be advanced, without incurring those dangers, I should be for doing it. We now see by the declaration of the Prince of Saxe Coburg, on the part of Austria and Prusia, that the ultimate point they desire is to restore the constitution of 1791. Were this even to be done before the pay days of this year, there is no doubt in my mind but that that government (as republican as the present, except in the form of its Executive) would confirm an advance so moderate in sum and time. I am sure the *nation* of France would never suffer their government to go to war *with us* for such a *bagatelle*, and the more surely if that bagatelle shall have been granted by us so as to *please* and not *displease the nation;* so as to keep their affections engaged on our side. So that I should have no fear in advancing the instalments of this year at epochs convenient to the Treasury. But at any rate I should be for assigning reasons for not changing the form of the debt.—To PRESIDENT WASHINGTON. iii, 575. FORD ED., vi, 287. (June 1793.)

2027. DEBT (French), Reply to Genet.— The instalments as they are settled by convention between the two nations far exceed the ordinary resources of the United States. To accomplish them completely and punctually, we are obliged to anticipate the revenues of future terms by loans to as great an extent as we can prudently attempt. As they are arranged however by the convention, they give us time for successive and gradual efforts. But to crowd these anticipations all into a single one, and that to be executed, in the present instant, would more than hazard that state of credit, the preservation of which can alone enable us to meet the different payments at the time agreed on. To do even this hitherto, has required in the operations of borrowing, time, prudence and patience; and these operations are still going on in all the extent they will bear. To press them beyond this, would be to defeat them both now and hereafter.—To EDMOND CHARLES GENET. FORD ED., vi, 294. (Pa., June 1793.)

2028. DEBT (French), Speculators and. —I am of opinion, as I always have been, that the purchase of our debt to France by private speculators, would have been an operation extremely injurious to our credit; and that the consequence foreseen by our banker, that the purchasers would have been obliged, in order to make good their payments, to deluge the markets of Amsterdam with American paper of all sorts, and to sell it at any price, was a probable one. And the more so, as we know that the particular individuals who were engaged in that speculation, possess no means of their own adequate to the payments they would have had to make. While we must not doubt that these motives, together with a proper regard for the credit of the United States, had real and full weight with our bankers towards inducing them to counterwork these private speculations; yet, to ascribe their industry in this business wholly to these motives, might lead to a too great and dangerous confidence in them. It was obviously their interest to defeat all such speculations, because they tended to take out of their hands, or at least to divide

with them, the profits of the great operation of transferring the French debt to Amsterdam, an object of first rate magnitude to them, and on the undivided enjoyments of which they might count, if private speculators could be baffled. It has been a contest of dexterity and cunning, in which our champions have obtained the victory. The manœuvre of opening a loan of three millions of florins, has, on the whole, been useful to the United States, and though unauthorized, I think should be confirmed. The measure proposed by the Secretary of the Treasury, of sending a superintendent of their future operations, will effectually prevent their doing the like again, and the funding laws leave no danger that such an expedient might at any future time be useful to us.—OPINION ON FOREIGN DEBT. vii, 506. FORD ED., vi, 231. (August 1790.)

2029. DEBT (French), Transfer to Holland.— It being known that M. de Calonne, the Minister of Finance, is at his wit's ends to raise supplies for the ensuing year, a proposition has been made him by a Dutch company to purchase the debt of the United States to this country [France] for seventy millions of livres in hand. His necessities dispose him to accede to the proposition; but a hesitation is produced by the apprehension that it might lessen our credit in Europe, and perhaps be disagreeable to Congress. I have been consulted here only by the agent for that company. I informed him that I could not judge what effect it might have on our credit, and was not authorized either to approve or disapprove of the transaction. I have since reflected on this subject. If there be a danger that our payments may not be punctual, it might be better that the discontents which would thence arise should be transferred from a court, of whose goodwill we have so much need, to the breasts of a private company. But it has occurred to me, that we might find occasion to do what would be grateful to this court, and establish with them a confidence in our honor. I am informed that our credit in Holland is sound. Might it not be possible, then, to borrow the four and twenty millions due to this country and thus pay them their whole debt at once? This would save them from any loss on our account. Is it liable to the objection of impropriety in creating new debts before we have more certain means of paying them? It is only transferring from one creditor to another, and removing the causes of discontent to persons with whom they would do us less injury.—To JOHN JAY. ii, 28. (P., September 1786.)

2030. ——— ———. I think it would be advisable to have our debt transferred to individuals of your country [Holland]. There could, and would be no objection to the guarantee remaining as you propose; and a postponement of the first payments of capital would surely be a convenience to us. For though the resources of the United States are great and growing, and their dispositions good, yet their machine is new, and they have not got it to go well. It is the object of their general wish at present, and they are all in movement, to set it in a good train; but their movements are necessarily slow. They will surely effect it in the end, because all have the same end in view; the difficulty being only to get all the thirteen States to agree on the same means.—To C. W. F. DUMAS. ii, 120. (P., 1787.)

2031. ——— ———. Would to heaven Congress would authorize you to transfer the debt of France to Holland before you leave Europe.

Most especially is it necessary to get rid of the debt to the officers. Their connections at Court are such as to excite very unfavorable feelings there against us, and some very hard things have been said (particularly in the Assemblée des Notables) on the prospect relative to our debts. The payment of the interest to the officers would have kept them quiet; but there are two years now due to them. I dare not draw for it without instructions.—To JOHN ADAMS. ii, 181. (P., 1787.)

2032. DEBT (Revolutionary), Divisions of.—The first and great division of our federal debt, is, into 1, foreign; and 2, domestic. The foreign debt comprehends, 1, the loan from the government of Spain; 2, the loans from the government of France, and from the Farmers General; 3, the loans negotiated in Holland by order of Congress. This branch of our debt stands absolutely singular: no man in the United States having ever supposed that Congress, or their legislatures, can, in any wise, modify or alter it. They justly view the United States as the one party, and the lenders as the other, and that the consent of both would be requisite, were any modification to be proposed. But with respect to the domestic debt, they consider Congress as representing both the borrowers and lenders, and that the modifications which have taken place in this have been necessary to do justice between the two parties, and that they flowed properly from Congress as their mutual umpire. The domestic debt comprehends, 1, the army debt; 2, the loan office debt; 3, the liquidated debt; and 4, the unliquidated debt. The first term includes debts to the officers and soldiers for pay, bounty and subsistence. The second term means moneys put into the loan office of the United States. The third comprehends all debts contracted by quarter-masters, commissaries, and others duly authorized to procure supplies for the army, and which have been liquidated (that is, settled) by commissioners appointed under the resolution of Congress, of June 12, 1780, or by the officers who made the contract. The fourth comprehends the whole mass of debts, described in the preceding article, which have not yet been liquidated. These are in a course of liquidation and are passing over daily into the third class. * * * No time is fixed for the payment of the debts of this third class, that is the liquidated debt; no fund is yet determined, nor any firm provision for the interest in the meantime. The consequence is that the certificates of these debts sell greatly below par. When I left America, they could be bought for from two shillings and sixpence to fifteen shillings in the pound; this difference proceeding from the circumstance of some States having provided for paying the interest on those due in their own State, which others had not. Hence, an opinion had arisen with some, and propositions had even been made in the legislatures, for paying off the principal of these debts with what they had cost the holder, and interest on that. This opinion is far from being general, and I think will not prevail. But it is among possible events.—To MESSRS. VAN STAPHORST. i, 471. FORD ED., iv, 106. (P., 1785.)

2033. DEBT (Revolutionary), Foreign.—As to the foreign debt, Congress is considered as the representative of one party only, and I think I can say with truth, that there is not one single individual in the United States, either in or out of office, who supposes they can ever do anything which might impair their foreign contracts.—To C. W. F. DUMAS. iii, 155. FORD ED., v, 190. (N.Y., 1790.)

— DEBT (Revolutionary), Funding of. —See ASSUMPTION.

2034. DEBT (Revolutionary), Payment of.—I am in hopes you will persuade the States to commit their commercial arrangements to Congress and to enable them to pay their debts, interest and capital.—To EDWARD RANDOLPH. ii, 211. (P., 1787.)

2035. DEBT (Revolutionary), Payments on.—The public effects of the United States, such as their paper bills of credit, loan office bills, &c., were a commodity which varied its value from time to time. A scale of their value for every month has been settled according to what they sold for at market, in silver or gold. This value in gold or silver, with an interest of six per cent. annually til payment, is what the United States pay. This they are able to pay; but were they to propose to pay off all their paper, not according to what it cost the holder, in gold or silver, but according to the sum named in it, their whole country, if sold, and all their persons into the bargain, might not suffice. They would, in this case, make a bankruptcy where none exists, as an individual would, who being very able to pay the real debts he has contracted, would undertake to give to every man fifty times as much as he had received from him.—To M. TROUCHIN. ii, 360. (P., 1788.)

2036. DEBT (Revolutionary), Principle of Payment.—The principle on which it [the *paper money* debt] shall be paid I take to be settled, though not directly, yet virtually, by the resolution of Congress of June 3d, 1784; that is, that they will pay the holder, or his representative, what the money was worth at the time he received it, with an interest from that time of six per cent. per annum.—To H. S. CREVECOEUR. i, 595. FORD ED., iv, 253. (P., July 1786.)

2037. ———. It is not our desire to pay off those bills [of exchange] according to the present depreciation, but according to their actual value in hard money, at the time they were drawn with interest. The State having received value, so far as it is just it should be substantially paid.—To VA. DEL. IN CONGRESS. FORD ED., ii, 500. (R., 1781.)

2038. ———. The loan office certificates will be settled by the table of depreciation at their true worth in gold or silver at the time the paper dollars were lent. On that true value the interest has been paid, and continues to be paid to the creditors annually in America. That the principal will also be paid is as sure as any future fact can be.—To MESSRS. DELAP. ii, 102. (P., 1787.)

2039. DEBT (Revolutionary), Redemption of Domestic.—No man in America ever entertained a doubt that our foreign debt is to be paid fully; but some people in America have seriously contended, that the certificates and other evidences of our domestic debt, ought to be redeemed only at what they have cost the holder. * * * But this is very far from being a general opinion; a very great majority being firmly decided that they shall be paid fully. Were I the holder of any of them, I should not have the least fear of their full payment.—To MESSRS. VAN STAPHORST. i, 369. FORD ED., iv, 78. (P., 1785.)

2040. DEBT (Revolutionary), Settlement of Foreign.—The first act of the new government [under the Constitution] should be some operation whereby they may assume to themselves the [first] station [in point of credit]. Their European debts form a proper subject for this. Digest the whole, public and private, Dutch, French and Spanish, into a table, showing the sum of interest due every year, and the portions of principal payable the same year. Take the most certain branch of revenue, and one which shall suffice to pay the interest, and leave such a surplus as may accomplish all the payments of the capital, at terms somewhat short of those at which they will become due. Let the surpluses of those years, in which no reimbursement of principal falls, be applied to buy up our paper on the exchange of Amsterdam, and thus anticipate the demands of principal. In this way, our paper will be kept up at par; and this alone will enable us to command in four and twenty hours, at any time, on the exchange of Amsterdam, as many millions as that capital can produce. The same act, which makes this provision for the existing debts, should go on to open a loan to their whole amount; the produce of that loan to be applied, as fast as received, to the payment of such parts of the existing debts as admit of payment. The rate of interest to be as the government should privately instruct their agent, because it must depend on the effect these measures would have on the exchange. Probably it could be lowered from time to time.—To JAMES MADISON. ii, 377. (P., 1788.)

2041. DEBT (Revolutionary), Soundness of.—As a private individual and citizen of America, I can with propriety and truth deliver it to you as my firm belief, that the loan office certificate you showed me, and all others of the same kind, will be paid, principal and interest, as soon as the circumstances of the United States will permit; that I do not consider this as a distant epoch, nor suppose there is a public debt on earth less doubtful.— TO M. DIRIEKS. ii, 422. (P., 1788.)

2042. DEBT (Revolutionary), Speculation and.—In consequence of [the acceptance by nine States of the new Constitution] speculations are already begun here [Paris], to purchase up our domestic liquidated debt. Indeed, I suspect that orders may have been previously lodged in America to do this, as soon as the new Constitution was accepted effectually. If it is thought that this debt should be retained at home, there is not a moment to lose; and I know of no means of retaining it but those I suggested to the Treasury Board. The transfer of these debts to Europe, will exclusively embarrass, and perhaps totally prevent the borrowing any money in Europe, till these shall be paid off. This is a momentous object, and in my opinion should receive instantaneous attention.—To JOHN JAY. ii, 455. (P., Aug. 1788.)

2043. DEBT (Revolutionary), Transfer of Domestic.—If the transfer of the [domestic] debts to Europe meet with any encouragement from us, we can no more borrow money here, let our necessities be what they will. For who will give ninety-six per cent. for the foreign obligations of the same nation, whose domestic ones can be bought at the same market for fifty-five per cent.; the former, too, bearing an interest of only five per cent., while the latter yields six? If any discouragements can be honestly thrown on this transfer, it would seem advisable, in order to keep the domestic debt at home. It would be a very effectual one, if, instead of the title existing in

the Treasury books alone, it was made to exist in loose papers, as our loan office debts do. The European holder would then be obliged to risk the title paper of his capital, as well as his interest, in the hands of his agents in America, whenever the interest was to be demanded; whereas, at present, he trusts him with the interest only. This single circumstance would put a total stop to all future sales of domestic debt at this market. [Amsterdam.]—To THE TREASURY BOARD. ii, 368. (A., 1788.)

2044. DEBT (Revolutionary), Western Lands and.—It is made a fundamental that the proceeds [of the sale of our lands] shall be solely and sacredly applied as a sinking fund to discharge the capital only of the [national] debt.—To COUNT VAN HAGENDORP. i, 466. (P., 1785.)

2045. ———— . It will be yet a twelvemonth before we shall be able to judge of the efficacy of our Land office to sink our national debt. It is made a fundamental, that the proceeds shall be solely and sacredly applied as a sinking fund to discharge the capital only of the debt.—To COUNT VAN HOGENDORP. i, 466. FORD ED., iv, 106. (P., 1785.)

2046. ———— . I am uneasy at seeing that the sale of our western lands is not yet commenced. That precious fund for the immediate extinction of our debt will, I fear, be suffered to slip through our fingers. Every delay exposes it to events which no human foresight can guard against.—To JAMES MADISON. ii, 153. FORD ED., iv, 391. (P., 1787.)

2047. ———— . I am very much pleased to hear that our western lands sell so successfully. I turn to this precious resource as that which will in every event liberate us from our domestic debt, and perhaps too from our foreign one; and this much sooner than I had expected. —To E. CARRINGTON. ii, 333. FORD ED., iv, 481. (P., 1787.)

2048. ———— . I am much pleased that the sale of western lands is so successful. I hope they will absorb all the certificates of our domestic debt speedily, in the first place, and that then, offered for cash, they will do the same by our foreign one.—To JAMES MADISON. ii, 328. FORD ED., iv, 475. (P., 1787.)

2049. DEBT (United States), Dangers of.—I place economy among the first and most important of republican virtues, and public debt as the greatest of the dangers to be feared.—To GOVERNOR PLUMER. vii, 19. (M., 1816.)

2050. DEBT (United States), Economy and.—I am for applying all the possible savings of the public revenue to the discharge of the national debt.—To ELBRIDGE GERRY. iv, 268. FORD ED., vii, 327. (Pa., 1799.)

2051. DEBT (United States), Evils of.— If we run into such debts, as that we must be taxed in our meat and in our drink, in our necessaries and our comforts, in our labors and our amusements, for our callings and our creeds, as the people of England are, our people, like them, must come to labor sixteen hours in the twenty-four, give the earnings of fifteen of these to the government for their debts and daily expenses; and the sixteenth being insufficient to afford us bread, we must

live, as they now do, on oatmeal and potatoes; have no time to think, no means of calling the mismanagers to account; but be glad
to obtain subsistence by hiring ourselves out
to rivet their chains on the necks of our fellow-sufferers.—To SAMUEL KERCHIVAL. vii,
14. FORD ED., x, 41. (M., 1816.)

**2052. DEBT (United States), Increas-
ing.**—A further assumption of State debt has
been proposed by the Secretary of the Treasury [in order to raise money]. It has been rejected by a small majority; but the chickens
of the treasury have so many contrivances,
and are so indefatigable within doors and
without, that we all fear they will get it in
yet some way or other.—To NICHOLAS LEWIS.
iii, 348. FORD ED., 505. (Pa., 1792.)

2053. —— ——. I am not for increasing,
by every device, the public debt, on the principle of its being a public blessing.—To EL-
BRIDGE GERRY. iv, 268. FORD ED., vii, 327.
(Pa., 1799.)

2054. —— ——. A debt of an hundred
millions, growing by usurious interest, and an
artificial paper phalanx, overruling the agricultural mass of our country, * * * have a
portentous aspect.—To SAMUEL ADAMS. iv,
321. FORD ED., vii, 425. (Pa., Feb. 1800.)

2055. —— ——. The growth and entailment of a public debt is an indication soliciting the employment of the pruning knife.—
To SPENCER ROANE. vii, 212. FORD ED., x,
188. (M., 1821.)

**2056. DEBT (United States), Independ-
ence and.**—To preserve our independence, we
must not let our rulers load us with perpetual
debt. We must make our election between
*economy and liberty, or profusion and serv-
itude.*—To SAMUEL KERCHIVAL. vii, 14. FORD
ED., x, 41. (M., 1816.)

2057. DEBT (United States), Interest.—
I once thought that in the event of a war
we should be obliged to suspend paying the
interest of the public debt. But a dozen years
more of experience and observation on our
people and government, have satisfied me
it will never be done. The sense of the necessity of public credit is so universal and so
deeply rooted, that no other necessity will prevail against it.—To WILLIAM SHORT. vi, 401.
(M., Nov. 1814.)

**2058. DEBT (United States), Louisiana
and.**—Should the acquisition of Louisiana be
constitutionally confirmed and carried into effect, a sum of nearly thirteen millions of dollars will then be added to our public debt,
most of which is payable after fifteen years;
before which term the present existing debts
will all be discharged by the established operation of the sinking fund.—THIRD ANNUAL
MESSAGE. viii, 27. FORD ED., viii, 271. (Oct.
1803.)

**2059. DEBT (United States), Manufac-
tures and.**—The British war has left us in
debt; but that is a cheap price for the good it
has done us. The establishment of the neces-

sary manufactures among ourselves, the proof
that our government is solid, can stand the
shock of war, and is superior even to civil
schism, are precious facts for us; and of these
the strongest proofs were furnished, when,
with four eastern States tied to us, as dead to
living bodies, all doubt was removed as to the
achievements of the war, had it continued.
But its best effect has been the complete suppression of party. The federalists who were
truly American (and their great mass was
so), have separated from their brethren who
were mere Anglomen, and are received with
cordiality into the republican ranks.—To
MARQUIS DE LAFAYETTE. vii, 66. FORD ED.,
x, 83. (M., 1817.)

**2060. DEBT (United States), Payment
of.**—It is proposed to provide additional
funds, to meet the additional debt [assump-
tion], by a tax on spirituous liquors, foreign
and home-made, so that the whole interest
will be paid by taxes on consumption. If
a sufficiency can now be raised in this way
to pay the interest at present, its increase by
the increase of population (suppose five per
cent. per annum), will alone sink the principal
within a few years, operating as it will in the
way of compound interest. Add to this what
may be done by throwing in the aid of western
lands and other articles as a sinking fund,
and our prospect is really a bright one.—To
GOUVERNEUR MORRIS. iii, 198. FORD ED., v,
250. (Pa., 1790.)

2061. —— ——. No man is more ardently intent to see the public debt soon and
sacredly paid off than I am. This exactly
marks the difference between Colonel Hamilton's views and mine, that I would wish the
debt paid to-morrow; he wishes it never to
be paid, but always to be a thing wherewith
to corrupt and manage the Legislature.—To
PRESIDENT WASHINGTON. iii, 464. FORD ED.,
vi, 105. (M., 1792.)

2062. —— ——. The simple question appears to me to be what did the public owe,
principal and interest, when the Secretary's
[Hamilton's] taxes began to run? If less,
it must have been paid; but if he was paying
old debts with one hand and creating new
ones with the other, it is such a game as Mr.
Pitt is playing.—To JAMES MADISON. vi, 113.
(M., Sep. 1792.)

2063. —— ——. The honest payment of
our debts, I deem [one of the] essential principles of our government and, consequently,
[one] which ought to shape its administration.—FIRST INAUGURAL ADDRESS. viii, 4.
FORD ED., viii, 5. (1801.)

2064. —— ——. The economies [of the
first republican Congress] have enabled us to
suppress all the internal taxes, and still to
make such provision for the payment of the
public debt as to discharge that in eighteen
years.—To GENERAL KOSCIUSKO. iv, 430.
(W., April 1802.)

2065. —— ——. I consider the fortunes
of our republic as depending, in an eminent

degree, on the extinguishment of the public debt before we engage in any war; because that done, we shall have revenue enough to improve our country in peace and defend it in war, without recurring either to new taxes or loans. But if the debt should once more be swelled to a formidable size, its entire discharge will be despaired of, and we shall be committed to the English career of debt, corruption and rottenness, closing with revolution. The discharge of the public debt, therefore, is vital to the destinies of our government, and it hangs on Mr. Madison and yourself alone. We shall never see another President and Secretary of the Treasury making all their objects subordinate to this. Were either of you to be lost to the public, that great hope is lost.—To ALBERT GALLATIN. v, 477. FORD ED., ix, 264. (M., 1809.)

2066. ―― ――. There are two measures which if not taken we are undone. * * * [The second* is] to cease borrowing money, and to pay off the national debt. If this cannot be done without dismissing the army, and putting the ships out of commission, haul them up high and dry, and reduce the army to the lowest point at which it was ever established. There does not exist an engine so corruptive of the government and so demoralizing of the nation as a public debt. It will bring on us more ruin at home than all the enemies from abroad against whom this army and navy are to protect us. What interest have we in keeping ships in service in the Pacific Ocean? To protect a few speculative adventurers in a commerce dealing in nothing in which we have an interest. As if the Atlantic and Mediterranean were not large enough for American capital! As if commerce and not agriculture was the principle of our association.—To NATHANIEL MACON. FORD ED., x, 193. (M., Aug. 1821.)

2067. DEBT (United States), Perpetuation of.—As the doctrine is that a public debt is a public blessing, so they think a perpetual one is a perpetual blessing, and therefore wish to make it so large that we can never pay it off.—To NICHOLAS LEWIS. iii, 348. FORD ED., v, 505. (Pa., April 1792.)

2068. DEBT (United States), Prosperity and.—We are ruined if we do not overrule the principles that " the more we owe, the more prosperous we shall be "; " that a public debt furnishes the means of enterprise "; " that if ours should be once paid off, we should incur another by any means however extravagant."—To JAMES MONROE. FORD ED., v, 320. (Pa., 1791.)

2069. DEBT (United States), Public Faith and.—The payments made in discharge of the principal and interest of the national debt, will show that the public faith has been exactly maintained.—FIRST ANNUAL MESSAGE. viii, 11. FORD ED., viii, 121. (Dec. 1801.)

2070. ―― ――. To preserve the faith of the nation by an exact discharge of its debts and contracts * * * [is one of]the landmarks by which we are to guide ourselves in all our proceedings.—SECOND ANNUAL MESSAGE. viii, 21. FORD ED., viii, 187. (Dec. 1802.)

2071. DEBT (United States), Purchasing.—The saving of interest on the sum so to be bought [of the national debt] may be applied in buying up more principal, and thereby keep this salutary operation going.—OPINION ON FOREIGN DEBT. vii, 507. FORD ED., v, 233. (1790.)

2072. DEBT (United States), Reduction of.—The receipts of external duties for the last twelve months have exceeded those of any former year, and the ratio of increase has been also greater than usual. This has enabled us to answer all the regular exigencies of government, to pay from the treasury in one year upwards of eight millions of dollars, principal and interest, of the public debt, exclusive of upwards of one million paid by the sale of bank stock, and making in the whole a reduction of nearly five millions and a half of principal; and to have now in the treasury four millions and a half of dollars, which are in a course of application to a further discharge of debt and current demands. —SECOND ANNUAL MESSAGE. viii, 18. FORD ED., viii, 184. (Dec. 1802.)

2073. ―― ――. The amount of debt paid for the year ending September 30, 1803, is about three millions one hundred thousand dollars, exclusive of interest, and making, with the payment of the preceding year, a discharge of more than eight millions and a half of dollars of the principal of that debt, besides the accruing interest; and there remain in the treasury nearly six millions of dollars.*—THIRD ANNUAL MESSAGE. viii, 26. FORD ED., viii, 271. (Oct. 1803.)

2074. ―― ――. Eleven millions and a half of dollars, received in the course of the year ending on the 30th of September last, have enabled us, after meeting all the ordinary expenses of the year, to pay upwards of $3.600,000 of the public debt, exclusive of interest. This payment, with those of the two preceding years, has extinguished upwards of twelve millions of the principal, and a greater sum of interest, within that period.—FOURTH ANNUAL MESSAGE. viii, 38. FORD ED., viii, 331. (Nov. 1804.)

2075. ―― ――. The receipts * * * during the year * * * have exceeded the sum of thirteen millions of dollars, which with not quite five millions in the treasury at the beginning of the year, have enabled us, after meeting other demands, to pay nearly two millions of the debt contracted under the British treaty and convention, upwards of four millions of principal of the public debt,

---

* The first was to arrest the progress of centralization under the decisions of the Supreme Court.—EDITOR.

* In the six millions are to be included two millions of dollars which had been appropriated with a view of purchasing New Orleans and other territory. This fact is set forth in the message.—EDITOR.

and four millions of interest. These payments, with those which had been made in three years and a half preceding, have extinguished of the funded debt nearly eighteen millions of principal.—FIFTH ANNUAL MESSAGE. viii, 52. FORD ED., viii, 395. (Dec. 1805.)

2076. —— ——. The receipts * * * during the year * * * have amounted to near fifteen millions of dollars, which have enabled us, after meeting the current demands, to pay two millions seven hundred thousand dollars of the American claims, in part of the price of Louisiana; to pay of the funded debt upward of three millions of principal, and nearly four of interest; and in addition, to reimburse, * * * nearly two millions of five and a half per cent. stock. These payments and reimbursements of the funded debt, with those which have been made in four years and a half preceding, will, at the close of the present year, have extinguished upward of twenty-three millions of principal.— SIXTH ANNUAL MESSAGE. viii, 67. FORD ED., viii, 493. (Dec. 1806.)

2077. —— ——. The receipts have amounted to near sixteen millions of dollars, which, with the five millions and a half in the treasury at the beginning of the year, have enabled us * * * to pay more than four millions of the principal of our funded debt. These payments, with those of the preceding five and a half years, have extinguished of the funded debt twenty-five millions and a half of dollars, being the whole which could be paid or purchased within the limits of law, and of our contracts, and have left us in the treasury eight millions and a half of dollars. —SEVENTH ANNUAL MESSAGE. viii, 88. FORD ED., ix. 164. (Oct. 1807.)

2078. —— ——. The receipts have amounted to near eighteen millions of dollars, which with the eight millions and a half in the treasury at the beginning of the year, have enabled us * * * to pay two millions three hundred thousand dollars of the principal of our funded debt, and left us in the treasury, on that day, near fourteen millions of dollars. * * * These payments, with those made in the six years and a half preceding, will have extinguished thirty-three millions five hundred and eighty thousand dollars of the principal of the funded debt, being the whole which could be paid or purchased within the limits of the law and our contracts; and the amount of principal thus discharged will have liberated the revenue from about two millions of dollars of interest, and added that sum annually to the disposable surplus.—EIGHTH ANNUAL MESSAGE. viii, 109. FORD ED., ix. 224. (Nov. 1808.)

2079. DEBT (United States), Republicans and.—An alarm has been endeavored to be sounded as if the republican interest was indisposed to the payment of the public debt. Besides the general object of the calumny, it was meant to answer the special one of electioneering. Its falsehood was so notorious that it produced little effect.—To THOMAS PINCKNEY. iii, 493. FORD ED., vi, 143. (Pa., Dec. 1792.)

2080. DEBT (United States), Sacredness of.—The evidences of the public debt are solid and sacred. I presume there is not a man in the United States who would not part with his last shilling to pay them.—To FRANCIS EPPES. FORD ED., v, 507. (Pa., April 1792.)

2081. —— ——. There can never be a fear but that the paper which represents the public debt will be ever sacredly good. The public faith is bound for this, and no change of system will ever be permitted to touch this; but no other paper stands on ground equally sure.—To WILLIAM SHORT. iii, 343. FORD ED., v, 460. (Pa., March 1792.)

2082. DEBT (United States), Statements of.—An accurate statement of the original amount and subsequent augmentations or diminutions of the public debt, to be continued annually [in the message to Congress], is an article on which we have conferred before. A similar statement of the annual expenses of the government for a certain period back, and to be repeated annually, is another wholesome necessity we should impose on ourselves and our successors.—To ALBERT GALLATIN. FORD ED., viii, 181. (W., Dec. 1802.)

2083. DEBT (United States), Time and. —No nation can make a declaration against the validity of long-contracted debts, so disinterestedly as we, since we do not owe a shilling which will not be paid with ease, principal and interest, by the measures you [the new government] have taken, within the time of our own lives.—To JAMES MADISON. iii, 108. FORD ED., v, 123. (P., 1789.) See GENERATIONS.

2084. DEBT (United States), Wars and. —Our distance from the wars of Europe, and our disposition to take no part in them, will, we hope. enable us to keep clear of the debts which they may occasion to other powers.— To C. W. F. DUMAS. iii, 155. FORD ED., v, 190. (N.Y., 1790.)

2085. DEBT (United States), Wars for Commerce and.—No earthly consideration could induce my consent to contract such a debt as England has by her wars for commerce, to reduce our citizens by taxes to such wretchedness, as that laboring sixteen of the twenty-four hours, they are still unable to afford themselves bread, or barely to earn as much oatmeal or potatoes as will keep soul and body together. And all this to feed the avidity of a few millionary merchants, and to keep up one thousand ships of war for the protection of their commercial speculations. —To WILLIAM H. CRAWFORD. vii, 7. FORD ED., x, 35. (M., 1816.)

— DEBTORS, Fugitives.—See FUGITIVES.

2086. DEBTS DUE BRITISH, British government and.—It is uncertain how far we should have been able to accommodate our opinions [in the settlement of the debts]. But the absolute aversion of the [British] government to enter into any arrangement [with Mr. Adams and myself] prevented the object from being pursued. Each country is left to do justice to itself and to the other, according to its own ideas, as to what is past; and to scramble for the future as well as they can; to regulate their commerce by duties and prohibitions and, perhaps, by cannons and mortars; in which event, we must abandon the ocean, where we are weak, leaving to neutral nations the carriage of our commodities; and measure with them on land, where they alone can lose.*—To JAMES ROSS. i, 562. FORD ED., iv, 218. (P., 1786.)

2087. ———— ————. I wish it were in my power to inform you that arrangements were at length taken between the two nations for carrying into complete execution the late treaty of peace, and for settling those conditions which are essential to the continuance of a commerce between them. I suppose all arrangement is thought unnecessary here [London], as the subject has not been deemed worthy of a conference [with Mr. Adams and myself]. Both nations are left to pursue their own measures, and it is not easy to foresee what these will be.—To ALEXANDER MCCAUL. FORD ED., iv, 202. (L., April 1786.)

2088. DEBTS DUE BRITISH, Executions for.—The immensity of the [Virginia] debt [to British creditors] was another reason for forbidding such a mass of property to be offered for sale under execution at once, as, from the small quantity of circulating money, it must have been sold for little or nothing, whereby the creditor would have failed to receive his money, and the debtor would have lost his whole estate without being discharged of his debt.†—REPORT TO CONGRESS. ix, 241. FORD ED., iv, 127. (1785.)

2089. DEBTS DUE BRITISH, Interest on.—It is a general sentiment in America that the principal of these debts should be paid, and that that alone is stipulated by the treaty. But they [the British] think the interest also which arose before and since the war, is justly due. They think it would be as unjust to demand interest during the war. They urge that during that time they could not pay the debt, for that of the remittances attempted, two-thirds on an average were taken by the nation to whom they were due; that during that period they had no use of the money, as from the same circumstances of capturing their produce on the sea, tobacco sold at 5s. the hundred, which was not sufficient to bear the expenses of the estate; that they paid taxes and other charges on the property during that period, and stood its insurers in the ultimate event of the war. They admit, indeed, that such individual creditors, as were not engaged in privateering against them, have lost this interest; but that it was the fault of their own nation, and that this is the case where both parties having lost, each may justifiably endeavor to save himself. Setting aside this portion of the interest, I am persuaded the debts in America are generally good, and that there is an honest intention to pay them.—To ALEXANDER MCCAUL. FORD ED., iv, 203. (L., 1786.)

* These were debts due by Americans to British merchants and others previous to the war of the Revolution.—EDITOR.
† Report to Congress of a conference with Count de Vergennes, respecting commercial arrangements. —EDITOR.

2090. ———— ————. While the principal, and interest preceding and subsequent to the war, seem justly due from us [to the British], that which accrued during the war does not. Interest is a compensation for the use of money. Their money, in our hands, was in the form of lands and negroes. Tobacco, the produce of these lands and negroes (or as I may call it, the interest of them), being almost impossible of conveyance to the markets of consumption, because taken by themselves in its way there, sold during the war, at five or six shillings the hundred. This did not pay taxes, and for tools and other plantation charges. A man who should have attempted to remit to his creditor tobacco, for either principal or interest, must have remitted it three times before one cargo would have arrived safe; and this from the depredations of their own nation, and often of the creditor himself; for some of the merchants entered deeply into the privateering business. The individuals, who did not, say they have lost this interest; the debtor replies that he has not gained it, and that it is a case, where a loss having been incurred, every one tries to shift it from himself. The known bias of the human mind from motives of interest should lessen the confidence of each party in the justice of their reasoning; but it is difficult to say which of them should make the sacrifice, both of reason and interest.—To JAMES ROSS. i, 562. FORD ED., iv, 218. (P., 1786.) See INTEREST ON MONEY.

2091. DEBTS DUE BRITISH, Jefferson's Personal.—With respect to myself, I acknowledge to you that I do not think an interest justly demandable during the war. Whatever I owed, with interest previous and subsequent to the war, I have taken measures for paying as speedily as possible. My chief debts are to yourself, and to Mr. Jones, of Bristol. In the year 1776, before there was a shilling of paper money issued, I sold land for £4200 to pay these two debts. I did not receive the money till it was not worth oak leaves. I have lost the principal and interest of these debts once then in attempting to pay them. Besides this, Lord Cornwallis's army took off thirty of my slaves, burned one year's crop of tobacco in my houses, and destroyed another in the fields, with other damages to the amount of three or four thousand pounds. Still, I am renewing my efforts to pay what I justly ought; and I hope these will be more successful. My whole estate is left in the hands of Mr. Lewis, of Albemarle, and Mr. Eppes, of Chesterfield, to apply its whole profits to the payment of my debts. * * * Till payment is effected, I shall not draw one shilling from the estate, nor resume its possession. * * * I think it very possible that you will not concur with me in opinion as to the intermediate interest; and that so far I shall meet your censure. Both parties are liable to feel too strongly the arguments which tend to justify their endeavors to avoid this loss. Yet after making allowances for this prejudice, it seems to me impossible but that the hardships are infinitely greater on our side than on yours. You have lost the interest but it is not we who have gained it. We deem your nation the aggressors. They took those profits which arose from your property in our hands, and inflicted on us immeasurable losses besides. I urge these considerations because, while they decide my own opinion, I wish them to weigh so much as to preserve me yours, which I highly esteem, and should be afflicted were I to lose it.—To ALEXANDER MCCAUL. FORD ED., iv, 204. (L., 1786.)

2092. ———— ————. I am desirous of arranging with you such just and practicable conditions as will ascertain to you the terms at which you will receive my part of your debt, and give me the satisfaction of knowing that you are contented. * * * The first question which arises is as to the article of interest. For all the time preceding the war, and all subsequent to it, I think it reasonable that interest should be paid; but equally unreasonable during the war. Interest is a compensation for the use of money. Your money in my hands is in the form of lands and negroes. From these, during the war, no use, no profits could be derived. Tobacco is the article they produce. That can only be turned into money at a foreign market. But the moment it went out of our ports for that purpose, it was captured either by the King's ships, or by those of individuals. The consequence was that tobacco, worth from twenty to thirty shillings the hundred, sold generally in Virginia during the war for five shillings. This price, it is known, will not maintain the laborer and pay taxes. There was no surplus of profit then to pay an interest. In the meanwhile we stood insurers of the lives of the laborers, and of the ultimate issue of the war. He who attempted during the war to remit either his principal or interest, must have expected to remit three times to make one payment; because it is supposed that two out of three parts of the shipments were taken. It was not possible, then, for the debtor to derive any profit from the money which might enable him to pay an interest, nor yet to get rid of the principal by remitting it to his creditor.—To WILLIAM JONES. FORD ED., iv, 352. (P., 1787.)

2093. ———— ————. Besides these reasons in favor of the general mass of debtors, I have some peculiar to my own case. In the year 1776, before a shilling of paper money was issued, I sold lands to the amount of four thousand two hundred pounds sterling. In order to pay these two debts I offered the bonds of the purchasers to your agent, Mr. Evans, if he would acquit me, and accept of the purchasers as debtors in my place. They were as sure as myself had he done it. These debts, being turned over to you, would have been saved to you by the treaty of peace, but he declined it. Great sums of paper money were afterwards issued. This depreciated, and payment was made me in this money when it was but a shadow. Our laws do not entitle their own citizens to require repayment in these cases, though the treaty authorizes the British creditor to do it. Here, then, I lost the principal and interest once. Again Lord Cornwallis encamped ten days on an estate of mine at Elk island, having his headquarters in my house. He burned all the tobacco houses and barns on the farm, with the produce of the former year in them. He burned all the enclosures, and wasted the fields in which the crop of that year (it was the month of June), was growing. He killed or carried off every living animal, cutting the throats of those which were too young for service. Of the slaves, he carried away thirty. The useless and barbarous injury he did me, in that instance, was more than would have repaid your debt, principal and interest. Thus I lost it a second time. Still I lay my shoulder assiduously to the payment of it a third time. In doing this, however, I think yourself will be of opinion that I am authorized in justice to clear it of every article not demandable in strict right. Of this nature I consider interest during the war.—To WILLIAM JONES. FORD ED., iv, 353. (1787.)

2094. ———— ————. Another question is as to the paper money I deposited in the treasury of Virginia towards the discharge of this debt. I before observed that I had sold lands to the amount of four thousand two hundred pounds sterling before a shilling of paper money was emitted, with a view to pay this debt. I received this money in depreciated paper. The State was then calling on those who owed money to British subjects to bring it into the treasury, engaging to pay a like sum to the creditor at the end of the war. I carried the identical money therefore to the Treasury, where it was applied, as all the money of the same description was, to the support of the war. Subsequent events have been such that the State cannot, and ought not to pay the same nominal sum in gold or silver which they received in paper, nor is it certain what they will do. * * * Whatever the State decides you shall receive * * * the debt fully. I am ready to remove all difficulty arising from this deposit, to take back to myself the demand against the State, and to consider the deposit as originally made for myself and not for you.—To WILLIAM JONES. FORD ED., iv, 355. (P., 1787.) See 2005 to 2010.

2095. DEBTS DUE BRITISH, Liquidation of.—There are two circumstances of difficulty in the payment of these debts. To speak of [Virginia], the particular State with which you and I are best acquainted, we know that its debt is ten times the amount of its circulating cash. To pay that debt at once then is a physical impossibility. Time is requisite. Were all the creditors to rush to judgment together, a mass of two millions of property would be brought to market, where there is but the tenth of that sum of money in circulation to purchase it. Both debtor and creditor would be ruined, as debts would be thus rendered desperate which are in themselves good. Of this truth I find the merchants here [London] sufficiently sensible, and I have no doubt we should have arranged the article of time to mutual satisfaction, allowing judgment to pass immediately, and dividing the execution into instalments.—To ALEXANDER MCCAUL. FORD ED., iv, 202. (1786.)

2096. DEBTS DUE BRITISH, Plan to pay.—They [British merchants whom I met in London] were certainly disposed to consent to accommodation as to the article of debts. I was not certain, when I left England, that they would relinquish the interest during the war. A letter received since, from the first character among the American merchants in Scotland, satisfies me they would have relinquished it to insure the capital and residue of interest. Would to heaven all the States, therefore, would settle a uniform plan. To open the courts to them, so that they might obtain judgments; to divide the executions into so many equal annual instalments, as that the last might be paid in the year 1790; to have the payments in actual money; and, to include the capital, and interest preceding and subsequent to the war, would give satisfaction to the world, and to the merchants in general. Since it is left for each nation to pursue their own measures in the execution of the late treaty, may not Congress with propriety recommend a mode of executing that article respecting the debts, and send it to each State to be passed into law. Whether England gives up the [Western] posts or not, these debts must be paid, or our character stained with infamy among all nations and through all time.

As to the satisfaction for slaves carried off, it is a bagatelle, which, if not made good before the last instalment becomes due, may be secured out of that.—To JAMES MONROE. i, 565. FORD ED., iv, 221. (P., 1786.)

2097. DEBTS DUE BRITISH, Privateering and.—With respect to the creditors in Great Britain, they mostly turned their attention to privateering; and arming the vessels they had before employed in trading with us, they captured on the seas, not only the produce of the farms of their debtors, but of those of the whole State. They thus paid themselves by capture more than their annual interest, and we lost more. Some merchants, indeed, did not engage in privateering. These lost their interest. But we did not gain it. It fell into the hands of their countrymen. It cannot, therefore, be demanded of us. As between these merchants and their debtors, it is the case where, a loss being incurred, each party may justifiably endeavor to shift it from himself. Each has an equal right to avoid it. One party can never expect the other to yield a thing to which he has as good a right as the demander; we even think he has a better right than the demander in the present instance. This loss has been occasioned by the fault of the nation which was creditor. Our right to avoid it, then, stands on less exceptionable ground than theirs. But it will be said, that each party thought the other the aggressor. In these disputes there is but one umpire, and that has decided the question where the world in general thought the right lay.—To WILLIAM JONES. FORD ED., iv, 353. (1787.)

2098. DEBTS DUE BRITISH, Slaves and.—The British army, after ravaging the State of Virginia, had sent off a very great number of slaves to New York. By the seventh article of the treaty of peace, they stipulated not to carry away any of these. Notwithstanding this, it was known, when they were evacuating New York, that they were carrying away the slaves. General Washington made an official demand of Sir Guy Carleton, that he should cease to send them away. He answered, that these people had come to them under promise of the King's protection, and that that promise should be fulfilled in preference to the stipulation in the treaty. The State of Virginia, to which nearly the whole of these slaves belonged, passed a law to forbid the recovery of debts due to British subjects. They declared, at the same time, they would repeal the law, if Congress were of opinion they ought to do it. But, desirous that their citizens should be discharging their debts, they afterwards permitted British creditors to prosecute their suits, and to receive their debts in seven equal and annual payments; relying that the demand for the slaves would be either admitted or denied in time to lay their hands on some of the latter payments for reimbursement.—REPORT TO CONGRESS. ix, 240. FORD ED., iv, 127. (1785.)

2099. DEBTS DUE BRITISH, Virginia Loan and.—A citizen of the Commonwealth [of Virginia], who is debtor to a British subject, may lodge the money due, or any part thereof, in the * * * loan office, accounting sixteen pence of the lawful money of the Commonwealth, or two-thirds of a dollar in bills of credit there current, equal to twelve pence of any such debt payable in the debtor's name, signed by the commissioner of the loan office and delivering the same to the Governor whose receipt shall discharge the debt.*—BRITISH PROPERTY BILL. FORD ED., ii, 200. (1779.)

2100. DEBTS DUE BRITISH, Sum of Virginia's.—Virginia certainly owed two millions sterling to Great Britain at the conclusion of the war. Some have conjectured the debt as high as three millions. I think that State owed near as much as all the rest put together. This is to be ascribed to peculiarities in the tobacco trade. The advantages made by the British merchants, on the tobaccos consigned to them, were so enormous, that they spared no means of increasing those consignments. A powerful engine for this purpose was the giving good prices and credit to the planter, till they got him more immersed in debt than he could pay, without selling his lands or slaves. They then reduced the prices given for his tobaccos, so that, let his shipments be ever so great, and his demand of necessaries ever so economical, they never permitted him to clear off his debt. These debts had become hereditary from father to son, for many generations, so that the planters were a species of property, annexed to certain mercantile houses in London.—ANSWER TO M. DE MEUNIER. ix, 250. FORD ED., iv, 155. (P., 1786.)

2101. DECIMAL SYSTEM, Advantages of.—The most *easy ratio* of multiplication and division, is that by ten. Everyone knows the facility of Decimal Arithmetic. Every one remembers, that when learning Money-Arithmetic, he used to be puzzled with adding the farthings, taking out the fours and carrying them on; adding the pence, taking out the twelves and carrying them on; adding the shillings, taking out the twenties and carrying them on; but when he came to the pounds, where he had only tens to carry forward, it was easy and free from error. The bulk of mankind are schoolboys through life. These little perplexities are always great to them. And even mathematical heads feel the relief of an easier, substituted for a more difficult process. Foreigners, too, who trade and travel among us, will find a great facility in understanding our coins and accounts from this ratio of subdivision. Those who have had occasion to convert the livres, sols and deniers of the French: the gilders, stivers and pfennigs of the Dutch; the pounds, shillings, pence, and farthings of these several States, into each other, can judge how much they would have been aided, had their several subdivisions been in a decimal ratio. Certainly, in all cases, where we are free to choose between easy and difficult modes of operation, it is most rational to choose the easy. The Financier [Robert Morris], therefore, in his report. well proposes that our coins should be in decimal proportion to one another.—NOTES ON A MONEY UNIT. i, 163. FORD ED.. iii, 447. (1784.)

2102. DECIMAL SYSTEM, Approbation of.—The experiment made by Congress in the year one thousand seven hundred and eighty-six, by declaring that there should be

* The courts held that payments under [this law] did not liquidate the debts. * * * Among those to suffer the most was Jefferson, who had paid into the loan-office moneys due by him to John Randolph, Kippent & Co., and William Jones.—NOTE FORD EDITION.

one money of account and payment through the United States, and that its parts and multiples should be in a decimal ratio, has obtained such general approbation, both at home and abroad, that nothing seems wanting but the actual coinage, to banish the discordant pounds, shillings, pence and farthings of the different States, and to establish in their stead the new denominations.—COINAGE, WEIGHTS AND MEASURES REPORT. vii. 477. (July 1790.)

2103. DECIMAL SYSTEM, France and. —The convenience of [the decimal system] in our moneyed system has been approved by all, and France has followed the example.—To JOHN QUINCY ADAMS. vii, 89. (M., 1817.)

2104. DECIMAL SYSTEM, Weights, Measures and.—The divisions into dimes, cents and mills is now so well understood that it would be easy of introduction into the kindred branches of weights and measures. I use, when I travel, an odometer of Clarke's invention, which divides the mile into cents, and I find every one comprehends a distance readily, when stated to him in miles and cents; so he would in feet and cents, pounds and cents, &c.—AUTOBIOGRAPHY. i, 53. FORD ED., i, 75. (1821.)

— DECIUS, Charges of.—See RANDOLPH, JOHN.

— DECLARATION OF INDEPENDENCE.—See APPENDIX.*

2105. DECLARATION OF INDEPENDENCE, Action in Congress.—On the 15th of May, 1776, the Convention of Virginia instructed their delegates in Congress, to propose to that body to declare the Colonies independent of Great Britain, and appointed a committee to prepare a declaration of rights, and plan of government.

"In Congress, Friday, June 7, 1776. The delegates† from Virginia moved, in obedience to instructions from their constituents that the Congress should declare, that these United Colonies are, and of right ought to be, free and independent States, that they are absolved from all allegiance to the British crown, and that all political connection between them and the State of Great Britain is, and ought to be, totally dissolved; that measures should be immediately taken for procuring the assistance of foreign powers, and a Confederation be formed to bind the Colonies more closely together. The House being obliged to attend at that time to some other business, the proposition was referred to the next day, when the members were ordered to attend punctually at ten o'clock.

Saturday, June 8. They proceeded to take it into consideration, and referred it to a committee of the whole, into which they immediately resolved themselves, and passed that day and Monday, the 10th, in debating on the subject."‡—AUTOBIOGRAPHY. i, 12. FORD ED., i, 18. (1821.)

* The principles asserted in the Declaration are classified in this work. The text of the Declaration, as drawn by Jefferson, with the alterations made by Congress, is given in the APPENDIX.—EDITOR.
† Richard H. Lee, being the oldest member of the Virginia delegation, was selected to make the motion.—EDITOR.
‡ The quoted paragraphs are from notes made by Jefferson in the Congress.—EDITOR.

2106. ——— ———. It appearing in the course of these debates [on Independence], that the Colonies of New York, New Jersey, Pennsylvania, Delaware, Maryland, and South Carolina were not yet matured for falling from the parent stem, but that they were fast advancing to that state, it was thought most prudent to wait a while for them, and to postpone the final decision to July 1st; but, that this might occasion as little delay as possible, a committee was appointed to prepare a Declaration of Independence.—AUTOBIOGRAPHY. i, 17. FORD ED., i, 24. (1821.)

2107. ——— ———. On Monday, the 1st of July, the House resolved itself into a committee of the whole, and resumed the consideration of the original motion [to declare the Colonies independent States] made by the delegates of Virginia, which, being again debated through the day, was carried in the affirmative by the votes of New Hampshire, Connecticut, Massachusetts, Rhode Island, New Jersey, Maryland, Virginia, North Carolina, and Georgia. South Carolina and Pennsylvania voted against it. Delaware had but two members present and they were divided. The delegates from New York declared they were for it themselves, and were assured their constituents were for it; but that their instructions having been drawn near a twelvemonth before, when reconciliation was still the general object, they were enjoined by them to do nothing which should impede that object. They, therefore, thought themselves not justifiable in voting on either side, and asked leave to withdraw from the question, which was given them. The committee rose and reported their resolution to the House. Mr. Edward Rutledge, of South Carolina, then requested the determination might be put off to the next day, as he believed his colleagues, though they disapproved of the resolution, would then join in it for the sake of unanimity. The ultimate question, whether the House would agree to the resolution of the committee, was accordingly postponed to the next day, when it was again moved, and South Carolina concurred in voting for it. In the meantime, a third member had come post from the Delaware counties, and turned the vote of that Colony in favor of the resolution. Members of a different sentiment attending that morning from Pennsylvania also, her vote was changed, so that the whole twelve Colonies, who were authorized to vote at all, gave their voices for it; and within a few days (July 9) the convention of New York approved of it, and thus supplied the void occasioned by the withdrawing of her delegates from the vote.—AUTOBIOGRAPHY. i, 18. FORD ED., i, 24. (1821.)

2108. DECLARATION OF INDEPENDENCE, Committee on.—The committee were John Adams, Dr. Franklin, Roger Sherman, Robert R. Livingston and myself. * * *. The committee * * * desired me to do it.* It was accordingly done, and being approved by them, I reported

* To write the Declaration.—EDITOR.

it to the House on Friday, the 28th of June, when it was read, and ordered to lie on the table.—AUTOBIOGRAPHY. i, 17. FORD ED., i, 24. (1821.) See 2119.

2109. DECLARATION OF INDEPENDENCE, Consideration of.—Congress proceeded * * * on July 1st to consider the Declaration of Independence, which had been reported and laid on the table the Friday preceding, and on Monday referred to a committee of the whole. * * * The debates, having taken up the greater parts of the 2d. 3d and 4th days of July, were, on the evening of the last, closed; the Declaration was reported by the committee, agreed to by the House, and signed by every member present, except Mr. [John] Dickinson.*—AUTOBIOGRAPHY. i, 19. FORD ED., i, 28. (1821.) See 2122.

2110. DECLARATION OF INDEPENDENCE, Copies of.—I enclose [you] a copy of the Declaration of Independence, as agreed to by the House, and also as originally framed. You will judge whether it is the better or worse for the critics.—To RICHARD HENRY LEE. i, 204. FORD ED., ii, 59. (Pa., July 8, 1776.)

2111. —— ——. I am not able to give you any particular account of the paper handed you by Mr. Lee, as being either the original or a copy of the Declaration of Independence, sent by myself to his grandfather. The draft, when completed by myself, with a few verbal amendments by Dr. Franklin and Mr. Adams, two members of the Committee, in their own handwriting, is now in my possession, and a fair copy of this was reported to the Committee, passed by them without amendment, and then reported to Congress. This latter should be among the records of the old Congress; and whether this or the one from which it was copied and now in my hands, is to be called the original, is a question of definition. To that in my hands, if worth preserving, my relations with our University [of Virginia] give irresistible claims. Whenever, in the course of the composition, a copy became overcharged, and difficult to be read with amendments, I copied it fair, and when that also was crowded with other amendments, another fair copy was made, &c. These rough drafts I sent to distant friends who were anxious to know what was passing. But how many and to whom I do not recollect. One sent to Mazzei was given by him to the Countess de Tesse (aunt of Madame de Lafayette) *as the original*, and is probably now in the hands of her family. Whether the paper sent to R. H. Lee was one of these, or whether, after the passage of the instrument, I made a copy for him, with the amendments of Congress, may, I think, be known from the face of the paper.—To JOHN VAUGHAN. vii, 409. FORD ED., x, 345. (M., 1825.)

* "Thus," says Knight, in his History of England, "on the 4th of July, was completed what has been not unjustly termed the most memorable public document which history records."—EDITOR.

— DECLARATION OF INDEPENDENCE, Franklin and.—See 2115.

2112. DECLARATION OF INDEPENDENCE, History of.—On the 7th of June, 1776, the delegates from Virginia moved, in obedience to instructions from their constituents, that Congress should declare the Thirteen United Colonies to be independent of Great Britain, that a Confederation should be formed to bind them together, and measures be taken for procuring the assistance of foreign powers. The House ordered a punctual attendance of all their members the next day at ten o'clock, and then resolved themselves into a committee of the whole, and entered on the discussion. It appeared in the course of the debates that seven States, viz., New Hampshire, Massachusetts, Rhode Island, Connecticut, Virginia, North Carolina, and Georgia, were decided for a separation; but that six others still hesitated, to wit. New York, New Jersey, Pennsylvania Delaware, Maryland, and South Carolina Congress, desirous of unanimity, and seeing that the public mind was advancing rapidly to it, referred the further discussion to the 1st of July, appointing in the meantime a Committee to prepare a Declaration of Independence, a second to form Articles for the Confederation of the States, and a third to propose measures for obtaining foreign aid On the 28th of June, the Declaration of Independence was reported to the House, and was laid on the table for the consideration of the members. On the 1st day of July, they resolved themselves into a committee of the whole, and resumed the consideration of the motion of June 7 [declaring independence] It was debated through the day, and at length was decided in the affirmative by the vote of nine States, viz., New Hampshire, Massachusetts, Rhode Island. New Jersey, Maryland, Virginia, North Carolina and Georgia Pennsylvania and South Carolina voted against it. Delaware, having but two members present, was divided. The delegates from New York declared they were for it, and their constituents also; but that the instructions against it which had been given them a twelvemonth before, were still unrepealed that their convention was to meet in a few days, and they asked leave to suspend their vote till they could obtain a repeal of their instructions. Observe that all this was in committee of the whole Congress, and that according to the mode of their proceedings the resolution of that committee to declare themselves independent was to be put to the same persons reassuming their forms as a Congress. It was now evening, the members exhausted by a debate of nine hours, during which all the powers of the soul had been distended with the magnitude of the object, and the delegates of South Carolina desired that the final decision might be put off to the next morning that they might still weigh in their own minds their ultimate vote. It was put off, and in the morning of the 2d of July they joined the other nine States in voting for it. The members of the Pennsylvania delega tion, too, who had been absent the day before came in and turned the vote of their State in favor of independence, and a third member of the State of Delaware, who, hearing of the division in the sentiment of his two colleagues, had travelled post to arrive in time, now came in and decided the vote of that State also for the resolution. Thus twelve States voted for it at the time of its passage, and the delegates of New York, the thirteenth State, received instructions within a few days to add theirs to the general vote; so that * * * there was not a dissenting voice. Congress proceeded immediately to consider the Declaration of Independence which had been reported by their Committee on the 28th of June. The several paragraphs of that were debated for three days, viz., the 2d, 3d, and 4th of July. In the evening of the 4th, they were finally closed, and the instrument approved by an unanimous vote, and signed by every member, except Mr. Dickinson.— To THE EDITOR OF THE JOURNAL DE PARIS. ix, 300. FORD ED., iv, 440. (P., Aug. 1787.)

2113. DECLARATION OF INDEPENDENCE, Objects of.—With respect to our rights, and the acts of the British government contravening those rights, there was but one opinion on this side of the water. All American whigs thought alike on these subjects. When forced, therefore, to resort to arms for redress, an appeal to the tribunal of the world was deemed proper for our justification. This was the object of the Declaration of Independence. Not to find out new principles, or new arguments, never before thought of, not merely to say things which had never been said before; but to place before mankind the common sense of the subject, in terms so plain and firm as to command their assent, and to justify ourselves in the independent stand we were compelled to take. Neither aiming at originality of principle or sentiment, nor yet copied from any particular and previous writing, it was intended to be an expression of the American mind, and to give to that expression the proper tone and spirit called for by the occasion. All its authority rests, then, on the harmonizing sentiments of the day, whether expressed in conversation, in letters, printed essays, or in the elementary books of public right, as Aristotle, Cicero, Locke, Sidney, &c.—To HENRY LEE. vii, 407. FORD ED., x, 343. (M., 1825.)

2114. DECLARATION OF INDEPENDENCE, Opposition to.—Many excellent persons opposed it on doubts whether we were provided sufficiently with the means of supporting it, whether the minds of our constituents were yet prepared to receive, &c., who, after it was decided, united zealously in the measures it called for.—To WILLIAM P. GARDNER. FORD ED., ix, 377. (M., 1813.)

2115. ——— ———. When the Declaration of Independence was under the consideration of Congress, there were two or three unlucky expressions in it which gave offence to some members. The words "Scotch and other foreign auxiliaries," excited the ire of a gentleman or

two of that country. Severe strictures on the conduct of the British King, in negativing our repeated repeals of the law which permitted the importation of slaves, were disapproved by some Southern gentlemen whose reflections were not yet matured to the full abhorrence of that traffic. Although the offensive expressions were immediately yielded, these gentlemen continued their depredations on other parts of the instrument. I was sitting by Dr. Franklin who perceived that I was not insensible to these mutilations. "I have made it a rule," said he, "whenever in my power, to avoid becoming the draftsman of papers to be reviewed by a public body. I took my lesson from an incident which I will relate to you. When I was a journeyman printer, one of my companions, an apprentice hatter, having served out his time, was about to open shop for himself. His first concern was to have a handsome signboard, with a proper inscription. He composed it in these words: John Thompson, Hatter, makes and sells hats for ready money," with a figure of a hat subjoined. But he thought he would submit to his friends for their amendments. The first he showed it to thought the word "hatter" tautologous, because followed by the words, "makes hats," which show he was a hatter. It was struck out. The next observed that the word "makes" might as well be omitted, because his customers would not care who made the hats. If good and to their mind, they would buy by whomsoever made. He struck it out. A third said he thought the words "for ready money," were useless as it was not the custom of the place to sell on credit. Everyone who purchased expected to pay. They were parted with, and the inscription now stood, "John Thompson sells hats." "Sells hats," says his next friend? Why nobody will expect you to give them away. What, then, is the use of that word? It was stricken out, and "hats" followed it,—the rather as there was one painted on the board. So his inscription was reduced ultimately to "John Thompson" with the figure of a hat subjoined.—ANECDOTES OF DR. FRANKLIN. viii, 500. FORD ED., x, 119. (M., 1818.)

— DECLARATION OF INDEPENDENCE, Original ideas in.—See 2119.

2116. DECLARATION OF INDEPENDENCE, People of England and.—The pusillanimous idea that we had any friends in England worth keeping terms with, still haunted the minds of many. For this reason, those passages which conveyed censure on the people of England were struck out, lest they should give them offence.— AUTOBIOGRAPHY. i, 19. FORD ED., i, 28. (1821.)

2117. DECLARATION OF INDEPENDENCE, Pictures of.—Mr. Barralet's sketch of the ornaments proposed to accompany the publication of the Declaration of Independence, contemplated by Mr. Murray and yourself, has been received. I am too little versed in the art of design to be able to offer any suggestions to the artist. As far as I am a judge, the composition appears to be judicious and well-imagined. Were I to hazard a suggestion, it should be that Mr. Hancock, as President of Congress, should occupy the middle and principal place. No man better merited than did Mr. John Adams to hold a most conspicuous place in the design.—To WILLIAM P. GARDNER. FORD ED., ix, 377. (M., Feb. 1813.)

2118. ——— ———. The painting lately executed by Col. Trumbull, I have never seen, but as far back as the days of Horace, at least, we are told that *" pictoribus atque poetis; Quidlibet audendi semper fuit æqua potestas."* He has exercised this *licentia pictoris* in like manner in the surrender at Yorktown, where he has placed Lord Cornwallis at the head of the surrender, although it is well known that he was excused by General Washington from appearing.—To S. A. WELLS. FORD ED., x, 133. (M., 1819.)

2119. DECLARATION OF INDEPENDENCE, Recollections of by Adams.—You have doubtless seen Timothy Pickering's Fourth of July observations on the Declaration of Independence. If his principles and prejudices, personal and political, gave us no reason to doubt whether he had truly quoted the information he alleges to have received from Mr. Adams, I should then say, that in some of the particulars, Mr. Adams's memory has led him into unquestionable error. At the age of eighty-eight, and forty-seven years after the transactions of Independence, this is not wonderful. Nor should I, at the age of eighty, on the small advantage of that difference only, venture to oppose my memory to his, were it not supported by written notes, taken by myself at the moment, and on the spot. He says, " the Committee of five, to wit, Dr. Franklin, Sherman, Livingston, and ourselves, met, discussed the subject, and then appointed him and myself to make the draft; that we, as a sub-committee, met, and after the urgencies of each on the other, I consented to undertake the task; that the draft being made, we, the sub-committee, met, and conned the paper over, and he does not remember that he made, or suggested a single alteration." Now these details are quite incorrect. The Committee of five met; no such thing as a sub-committee was proposed, but they unanimously pressed on myself alone to undertake the draft. I consented; I drew it; but before I reported it to the Committee, I communicated it *separately* to Dr. Franklin and Mr. Adams, requesting their correction, because they were the two members of whose judgments and amendments I wished most to have the benefit, before presenting it to the Committee; and you have seen the original paper now in my hands, with the corrections of Dr. Franklin and Mr. Adams interlined in their own handwritings. Their alterations were two or three only, and merely verbal. I then wrote a fair copy, reported it to the Committee, and from them, unaltered, to Congress. This personal communication and consultation with Mr. Adams, he has misremembered into the actings of a sub-committee, Pickering's observations, and Mr. Adams's in addition, " that it contained no new ideas, that it is a common-place compilation, its sentiments hackneyed in Congress for two years before, and its essence contained in Otis's pamphlet," may all be true. Of that I am not to be the judge. Richard Henry Lee charged it as copied from Locke's Treatise on Civil Government. Otis's pamphlet I never saw, and whether I had gathered my ideas from reading or reflection, I do not know. I know only that I turned to neither book nor pamphlet while writing it. I did not consider it as any part of my charge to invent new ideas altogether, and to offer no sentiment which had ever been expressed before. Had Mr. Adams been so restrained, Congress would have lost the benefit of his bold and impressive advocacy of the rights of the Revolution. For no man's confident and fervid addresses, more than Mr. Adams's, encouraged and supported us through the difficulties surrounding us, which, like the ceaseless action of gravity, weighed on us by night and by day. Yet, on the same ground, we may ask what of these elevated thoughts was new, or can be affirmed never before to have entered the conceptions of man? Whether, also, the sentiments of Independence and the reasons for declaring it, which make so great a portion of the instrument, had been hackneyed in Congress for two years before the 4th of July, '76, or this dictum also of Mr. Adams be another slip of memory, let history say. This, however, I will say for Mr. Adams, that he supported the Declaration with zeal and ability, fighting fearlessly for every word of it. As for myself, I thought it a duty to be, on that occasion, a passive auditor of the opinions of others, more impartial judges than I could be, of its merits or demerits. During the debate I was sitting by Dr. Franklin, and he observed that I was writhing a little under the acrimonious criticisms on some of its parts; and it was on that occasion, that by way of comfort, he told me the story of John Thompson, the hatter, and his new sign. Timothy thinks the instrument the better for having a fourth of it expunged. He would have thought it still better, had the other three-fourths gone out also, all but the single sentiment (the only one he approves), which recommends friendship to his dear England, whenever she is willing to be at peace with us. His insinuations are, that although " the high tone of the instrument was in unison with the warm feelings of the times, this sentiment of habitual friendship to England should never be forgotten, and that the duties it enjoins should *especially* be borne in mind on every celebration of this anniversary." In other words, that the Declaration, as being a libel on the government of England, composed in times of passion, should now be buried in utter oblivion, to spare the feelings of our English friends and Angloman fellow-citizens. But it is not to wound them that we wish to keep it in mind; but to cherish the principles of the instrument in the bosoms of our fellow-citizens; and it is a heavenly comfort to see that these principles are yet so strongly felt as to render a circumstance so trifling as this lapse of memory of Mr. Adams, worthy of being solemnly announced and supported at an anniversary assemblage of the nation on its birthday. In opposition, however, to Mr. Pickering, I pray God that these principles may be eternal.—To JAMES MADISON. vii 304. FORD ED., x, 267. (M., Aug. 1823) See 64.

— DECLARATION OF INDEPEND-ENCE, Rights of Man and.—See 2120.

2120. DECLARATION OF INDE-PENDENCE, Semi-centennial of.—The kind invitation I received from you, on the part of the citizens of the city of Washington, to be present with them at their celebration on the fiftieth anniversary of American Independence, as one of the surviving signers of an instrument pregnant with our own and the fate of the world, is most flattering to myself, and heightened by the honorable accompaniment proposed for the comfort of such a journey. It adds sensibly to the sufferings of sickness, to be deprived by it of a personal participation in the rejoicings of that day. But acquiescence is a duty, under circumstances not placed among those we are permitted to control. I should, indeed, with peculiar delight, have met and exchanged there congratulations personally with the small band, the remnant of that host of worthies, who joined with us on that day, in the bold and doubtful election we were to make for our country, between submission or the sword; and to have enjoyed with them the consolatory fact, that our fellow-citizens, after half a century of experience and prosperity, continue to approve the choice we made. May it be to the world, what I believe it will be (to some parts sooner, to others later, but finally to all), the signal of arousing men to burst the chains under which monkish ignorance and superstition had persuaded them to bind themselves, and to assume the blessings and security of self-government. That form which we have substituted, restores the free right to the unbounded exercise of reason and freedom of opinion. All eyes are opened, or opening, to the rights of man. The general spread of the light of science has already laid open to every view the palpable truth, that the mass of mankind has not been born with saddles on their backs, nor a favored few, booted and spurred, ready to ride them legitimately, by the grace of God. These are grounds of hope for others. For ourselves, let the annual return of this day forever refresh our recollections of these rights, and an undiminished devotion to them. I will ask permission here to express the pleasure with which I should have met my ancient neighbors of the city of Washington and its vicinity, with whom I passed so many years of a pleasing social intercourse; an intercourse which so much relieved the anxieties of the public cares, and left impressions so deeply engraved in my affections, as never to be forgotten. With my regret that ill health forbids me the gratification of an acceptance, be pleased to receive for yourself, and those for whom you write, the assurance of my highest respect and friendly attachments.*—To ROGER C. WEIGHTMAN. vii, 450. FORD ED., x. 390. (M., June 24, 1826.)

2121. DECLARATION OF INDE-PENDENCE, Signers of.—Governor Mc-Kean, in his letter to McCorkle of July 16th,

* This was the last letter written by Jefferson. He died on the following Fourth of July.—EDITOR.

1817, has thrown some lights on the transactions of that day; but, trusting to his memory chiefly, at an age when our memories are not to be trusted, he has confounded two questions, and ascribed proceedings to one which belonged to the other. These two questions were, 1st, the Virginia motion of June the 7th, to declare Independence; and 2d, the actual Declaration, its matter and form. Thus he states the question on the Declaration itself as decided on the 1st of July; but it was the Virginia motion which was voted on that day in Committee of the Whole; South Carolina, as well as Pennsylvania, then voting against it. But the ultimate decision in *the House*, on the report of the Committee, being, by request, postponed to the next morning; all the States voted for it except New York, whose vote was delayed for the reason before stated. It was not till the 2d of July, that the Declaration itself was taken up; nor till the 4th, that it was decided, and it was signed by every member present, except Mr. Dickinson.—To SAMUEL A. WELLS. i, 120. FORD ED., x, 130. (M., 1819.)

2122. ——. The subsequent signatures of members who were not then present, and some of them not yet in office, is easily explained, if we observe who they were; to wit, that they were of New York and Pennsylvania. New York did not sign till the 15th, because it was not till the 9th (five days after the general signature), that their convention authorized them to do so. The Convention of Pennsylvania, learning that it had been signed by a minority only of their delegates, named a new delegation on the 20th, leaving out Mr. Dickinson, who had refused to sign, Willing and Humphreys who had withdrawn, reappointing the three members who had signed, Morris, who had not been present, and five new ones, to wit, Rush, Clymer, Smith, Taylor and Ross; and Morris, and the five new members were permitted to sign, because it manifested the assent of their full delegation and the express will of their Convention, which might have been doubted on the former signature of a minority only. Why the signature of Thornton, of New Hampshire, was permitted so late as the 4th of November, I cannot now say; but undoubtedly for some particular reason which we should find to have been good, had it been expressed. These were the only post-signers, and you see that there were solid reasons for receiving those of New York and Pennsylvania, and that this circumstance in no wise affects the faith of this Declaratory Charter of our rights, and of the rights of man.—To SAMUEL A. WELLS. i, 120. FORD ED., x, 130. (M., 1819.)

2123. —— ——. I have received the new publication of the Secret Journals of Congress, wherein is stated a resolution of July 19th, 1776, that the Declaration passed on the 4th, be fairly engrossed on parchment, and when engrossed, be signed by every member; and another of August 2d, that being engrossed and compared at the table, it was signed by the members; that is to say, the copy engrossed on parchment (for durability) was signed by the members, after being compared at the table, with the original one signed on paper as before stated.—MEMORANDUM BY JEFFERSON. i, 122. FORD ED., x, 132. (Aug. 1822.)

2124. —— ——. I observe your toast of Mr. [John] Jay on the 4th of July [1823] wherein you say that the omission of his signature to the Declaration of Independence was by *accident.* Our impressions as to this fact being different, I shall be glad to have mine corrected, if wrong. Jay, you know, had been in constant opposition to our laboring majority. Our estimate at the time was, that he, Dickinson and Johnson of Maryland, by their ingenuity, perseverance and partiality to our English connection, had constantly kept us a year behind where we ought to have been in our preparations and proceedings. From about the date of the Virginia instructions of May 15th, 1776, to declare Independence, Mr. Jay absented himself from Congress, and never came there again until December, 1778. Of course, he had no part in the discussions or decision of that question. The instructions to their Delegates by the Convention of New York, then sitting, to sign the Declaration, were presented to Congress on the 15th of July only, and on that day the journals show the absence of Mr. Jay, by a letter received from him, as they had done as early as the 29th of May by another letter. And I think he had been omitted by the convention on a new election of Delegates, when they changed their instructions. Of this last fact, however, having no evidence but an ancient impression, I shall not affirm it. But whether so or not, no agency of *accident* appears in the case. This error of fact, however, whether yours or mine, is of little consequence to the public. But truth being as cheap as error, it is as well to rectify it for our own satisfaction.—To JOHN ADAMS. vii, 308. FORD ED., x, 271. (M., 1823.)

2125. —— ——. Of the signers of the Declaration of Independence, I see now living not more than half a dozen on your side of the Potomac, and on this side, myself alone.—To JOHN ADAMS. vi, 37. FORD ED., ix, 334. (M., Jan. 1812.)

2126. —— ——. I think Mr. Adams will outlive us all, I mean the Declaration-men, although our senior since the death of Colonel Floyd. It is a race in which I have no ambition to win.—To HENRY DEARBORN. vii, 214. FORD ED., x, 191. (M., Aug. 1821.)

2127. DECLARATION OF INDEPENDENCE, Slavery clause.—The clause [in the draft] reprobating the enslaving the inhabitants of Africa, was struck out in complaisance to South Carolina and Georgia, who had never attempted to restrain the importation of slaves, and who, on the contrary, still wished to continue it. Our northern brethren also, I believe, felt a little tender under those censures, for though their people had very

few slaves themselves, yet they had been pretty considerable carriers of them to others.—AUTOBIOGRAPHY. i, 19. FORD ED., i, 28. (1821.)

2128. DECLARATION OF INDEPENDENCE, Spirit of.—The genuine effusion of the soul of our country at that time.* —To DR. JAMES MEASE. vii, 410. FORD ED., x, 346. (M., 1825.) See FOURTH OF JULY.

2129. DECLARATION OF INDEPENDENCE, The Union and.—This holy bond of our Union.—To DR. JAMES MEASE. vii, 410. FORD ED., x, 346. (M., 1825.)

2130. DECLARATION OF INDEPENDENCE, Virginia Constitution and. —The [Virginia] Constitution, with the Preamble, was passed on the 29th of June [1776], and the Committee of Congress had only the day before that reported to that body the draft of the Declaration of Independence. The fact is, that that Preamble was prior in composition to the Declaration; and both having the same object, of justifying our separation from Great Britain, they used necessarily the same materials of justification, and hence their similitude.†—To AUGUSTUS B. WOODWARD. vii, 406. FORD ED., x, 342. (M., 1825.)

2131. DECLARATION OF INDEPENDENCE, Where written.—The Declaration of Independence was written in a house on the north side of Chestnut Street, Philadelphia, between Third and Fourth, not a corner house. Heiskell's tavern, which has been pointed out as the house, is not the true one.—FROM DANIEL WEBSTER'S CONVERSATION WITH JEFFERSON. FORD ED., x, 327. (1824.)

2132. —— ——. At the time of writing the Declaration, I lodged in the house of a Mr. Graaf, a new brick house, three stories high, of which I rented the second floor, consisting of a parlor and bedroom, ready furnished. In that parlor I wrote habitually, and in it wrote this paper, particularly. So far I state from written proofs in my possession. The proprietor, Graaf, was a young man, son of a German, and then newly married. I think he was a bricklayer, and that his house was on the south side of Market street, probably between Seventh and Eighth streets, and if not the only house on that part of the street, I am sure there were few others near it. I have some idea that it was a corner house, but no other recollections throwing light on the question, or worth communication.‡—To DR. JAMES MEASE. vii, 410. FORD ED., x, 346. (M., 1825.)

* Bancroft in volume 8, chapter 70, of the History of the United States, says, "this immortal State paper which, for its composer, was the aurora of enduring fame, was 'the genuine effusion of the soul of the country at that time', the revelation of its mind, when in its youth, its enthusiasm, its sublime confronting of danger, it rose to the highest creative powers of which man is capable".—EDITOR.

† Jefferson wrote the Preamble of the Virginia Constitution. The phraseology of the indictment in it of George III. is nearly the same as that in the Declaration.—EDITOR.

‡ Jefferson had been asked to supply this information. In the letter, from which the quotation is made, he wrote: "It is not for me to estimate the importance of the circumstances concerning which your letter makes inquiry. They prove, even in their minuteness, the sacred attachments of our fellow citizens to the event of which the paper of July

2133. DECLARATION OF INDE-PENDENCE, The Mecklenburg.—You seem to think the Mecklenburg Declaration genuine. I believe it spurious. I deem it to be a very unjustifiable quiz, like that of the volcano, so minutely related to us as having broken out in North Carolina, some half a dozen years ago, in that part of the country, and perhaps in that very county of Mecklenburg, for I do not remember its precise locality. If this paper be really taken from the Raleigh Register, as quoted, I wonder it should have escaped Ritchie, who culls what is good from every paper, as the bee from every flower; and the National Intelligencer, too, which is edited by a North Carolinian; and that the fire should blaze out all at once in Essex,* one thousand miles from where the spark is said to have fallen. But if really taken from the Raleigh Register, who is the narrator, and is the name subscribed real, or is it as fictitious as the paper itself? It appeals, too, to an original book, which is burned, to Mr. Alexander, who is dead, to a joint letter from Caswell, Hughes and Hooper, all dead, to a copy sent to the dead Caswell, and another sent to Dr. Williamson, now probably dead, whose memory did not recollect, in the history he has written of North Carolina, this gigantic step of its county of Mecklenburg. Horry, too, is silent in his history of Marion, whose scene of action was the county bordering on Mecklenburg. Ramsay, Marshall, Jones, Girardin, Wirt, historians of the adjacent States, all silent. When Mr. Henry's resolutions, far short of Independence, flew like lightning through every paper, and kindled both sides of the Atlantic, this flaming declaration of the same date, of the independence of Mecklenburg county, of North Carolina, absolving it from the British allegiance, and abjuring all political connection with that nation, although sent to Congress too, is never heard of. It is not known even a twelve-month after, when a similar proposition is first made in that body. Armed with this bold example, would not you have addressed our timid brethren in peals of thunder on their tardy fears? Would not every advocate of Independence have rung the glories of Mecklenburg county in North Carolina, in the ears of the doubting Dickinson and others, who hung so heavily on us? Yet the example of independent Mecklenburg county, in North Carolina, was never once quoted. The paper speaks, too, of the continued exertions of their delegation (Caswell, Hooper, Hughes) " in the cause of liberty and independence." Now, you remember as well as I do, that we had not a greater tory in Congress than Hooper; that Hughes was very wavering, sometimes firm, sometimes feeble, according as the day was clear or cloudy; that Caswell, indeed, was a good whig, and kept these gentlemen to the notch, while he was present; but that he left us soon, and their line of conduct became then uncertain until Penn came, who fixed Hughes and the vote of the State. I must not be understood as suggesting any doubtfulness in the State of North Carolina. No State was more fixed or forward. Nor do I affirm, positively, that this paper is a fabrication; because the proof of a negative can only

4th, 1776, was but the declaration the genuine effusion of the soul of our country at that time. Small things may, perhaps, like the relics of saints, help to nourish our devotion to this holy bond of our Union, and keep it longer alive and warm in our affections. This effect may give importance to circumstances, however small." EDITOR.
* Adams had sent Jefferson a paper clipping about it from the Essex (Mass.) Register.—EDITOR.

be presumptive. But I shall believe it such until positive and solemn proof of its authenticity be produced. And if the name of Mc-Knitt be real, and not a part of the fabrication, it needs a vindication by the production of such proof. For the present, I must be an unbeliever in the apocryphal gospel.—To JOHN ADAMS. vii, 128. FORD ED., x, 136. (M., July 1819.)

2134. DEFENCE, Coast.—A steady, perhaps, a quickened pace in preparations for the defence of our seaport towns and waters; an early settlement of the most exposed and vulnerable parts of our country; a militia so organized that its effective portions can be called to any point in the Union, or volunteers instead of them to serve a sufficient time, are means which may always be ready yet never preying on our resources until actually called into use. They will maintain the public interests while a more permanent force shall be in course of preparation.—SIXTH ANNUAL MESSAGE. viii, 69. FORD ED., viii, 495. (Dec. 1806.) See MILITIA.

2135. ———, ———. For the purposes of defence, it has been concluded to combine—1st, land batteries, furnished with heavy cannon and mortars, and established on all the points around the place favorable for preventing vessels from lying before it; 2d, movable artillery which may be carried * * * to points unprovided with fixed batteries; 3d, floating batteries; and 4th, gunboats, which may oppose an enemy at its entrance and co-operate with the batteries for his expulsion.—SPECIAL MESSAGE. viii, 79. FORD ED., ix, 23. (Feb. 1807.)

— DEFENCE, Gunboats and.—See GUN-BOATS.

2136. DEFENCE, National.—To draw around the whole nation the strength of the General Government, as a barrier against foreign foes * * * is [one of the] functions of the General Government on which you have a right to call.—REPLY TO VERMONT ADDRESS. iv, 418. (W., 1801.)

2137. DEFENCE, Naval.—I am for such a naval force only * * * as may protect our coasts and harbors * * * .—To EL-BRIDGE GERRY. iv, 268. FORD ED., vii, 328. (Pa., 1799.) See NAVY.

2138. DEFENCE, Personal.—One loves to possess arms, though they hope never to have occasion for them.—To PRESIDENT WASHINGTON. iv, 143. FORD ED., vii, 84. (M., 1796.)

2139. DEFENCE, Preparations for.—The moment our peace was threatened [by the attack on the Chesapeake], I deemed it indispensable to secure a greater provision of those articles of military stores with which our magazines were not sufficiently furnished. To have awaited a previous and special sanction by law would have lost occasions which might not be retrieved. I did not hesitate, therefore, to authorize engagements for such supplements to our existing stock as would render it adequate to the emergencies threatening us; and I trust that the Legislature, feeling the same anxiety for the safety of our country, so materially advanced by this protection, will approve, when done, what they would have seen so important to be done, if then assembled.—SEVENTH ANNUAL MESSAGE. viii, 87. FORD ED., ix, 161. (Oct. 1807.) See LAW, TRANSCENDING.

2140. DEFENCE, Readiness for.—While we are endeavoring * * * to obtain by friendly negotiation a peaceable redress of the injury [suspension of deposit at New Orleans], and effectual provision against its repetition, let us array the strength of the nation, and be ready to do with promptitude and effect whatever a regard to justice and our future security may require.—To ——. iv, 469. (W., Feb. 1803.)

2141. —— ——. Although our prospect is peace, our policy and purpose are to provide for defence by all those means to which our resources are competent.—To JAMES BOWDOIN. v, 19. (W., 1806.)

2142. DEFENCE, The States and.—For the ordinary safety of the citizens of the several States, whether against dangers from within or without, reliance has been placed either on the domestic means of the individuals, or on those provided by the respective States.—To JACOB J. BROWN. v, 240. (W., 1808.) See FORTIFICATIONS.

— DEFENCE, Torpedoes.—See TORPEDOES.

2143. DEITY, Assistance Implored.—We commit our injuries to the even-handed justice of that Being, Who doth no wrong, earnestly beseeching Him to illuminate the councils, and prosper the endeavors of those to whom America hath confided her hopes, that through their wise direction we may again see reunited the blessings of liberty, property, and harmony with Great Britain.—ADDRESS VIRGINIA HOUSE OF BURGESSES TO LORD DUNMORE. FORD ED., i, 459. (June 1775.)

2144. —— ——. We devoutly implore assistance of Almighty God to conduct us happily through this great conflict.—DECLARATION ON TAKING UP ARMS. FORD ED., i, 476. (July 1775.)

2145. DEITY, Beneficence of.—It hath pleased the Sovereign Disposer of all human events to give to this [Revolution] appeal an issue favorable to the rights of the States.—PROPOSED CONSTITUTION FOR VIRGINIA. viii, 441. FORD ED., iii, 321. (1783.)

2146. DEITY, Deliverer of the Distressed.—When the measure of their [the Slaves] tears shall be full, when their groans shall have involved heaven itself in darkness, doubtless, a God of justice will awaken to their distress, and by diffusing light and liberality among their oppressors, or, at length, by His exterminating thunder, manifest His attention to the things of this world, and that they are not left to the guidance of a blind fatality.—To M. DE MEUNIER. ix, 279. FORD ED., iv, 185. (P., 1786.)

2147. DEITY, Existence of.—I think that every Christian sect gives a great handle to atheism by their general dogma, that, without a revelation, there would not be sufficient proof of the being of a God. Now, one-sixth of mankind only are supposed to be Christians; the other five-sixths, then, who do not believe in the Jewish and Christian revelation, are without a knowledge of the existence of a God! This gives completely a *gain de cause* to the disciples of Ocellus, Timœus, Spinosa, Diderot and D'Holbach. The argument which they rest on as triumphant and unanswerable is, that in every hypothesis of cosmogony, you must admit an eternal preexistence of something; and according to the rule of sound philosophy, you are never to employ two principles to solve a difficulty when one will suffice. They say, then, that it is more simple to believe at once in the eternal pre-existence of the world, as it is now going on, and may forever go on by the principle of reproduction which we see and witness, than to believe in the eternal pre-existence of an ulterior cause, or Creator of the world, a Being whom we see not and know not, of whose form, substance, and mode, or place of existence, or of action, no sense informs us, no power of the mind enables us to delineate or comprehend. On the contrary, I hold (without appeal to revelation) that when we take a view of the universe, in all its parts, general or particular, it is impossible for the human mind not to perceive and feel a conviction of design, consummate skill, and indefinite power in every atom of its composition. The movements of the heavenly bodies, so exactly held in their course by the balance of centrifugal and centripetal forces; the structure of our earth itself, with its distribution of lands, waters and atmosphere; animal and vegetable bodies, examined in all their minutest particles; insects, mere atoms of life, yet as perfectly organized as man or mammoth; the mineral substances, their generation and uses; it is impossible, I say, for the human mind not to believe, that there is in all this, design, cause, and effect, up to an ultimate cause, a fabricator of all things from matter and motion, their preserver and regulator while permitted to exist in their present forms, and their regeneration into new and other forms. We see, too, evident proofs of the necessity of a superintending power, to maintain the universe in its course and order. Stars, well known, have disappeared, new ones have come into view; comets in their incalculable courses, may run foul of suns and planets, and require renovation under other laws; certain races of animals are become extinct; and were there no restoring power, all existences might extinguish successively, one by one, until all should be reduced to a shapeless chaos. So irresistible are these evidences of an intelligent and powerful agent, that, of the infinite numbers of men who have existed through all time, they have believed, in the proportion of a million at least to a unit, in the hypothesis of an eternal pre-existence of a

Creator, rather than in that of a self-existent universe. Surely this unanimous sentiment renders this more probable, than that of the few in the other hypothesis. Some early Christians, indeed, have believed in the co-eternal pre-existence of both the Creator and the world, without changing their relation of cause and effect. That this was the opinion of St. Thomas, we are informed by Cardinal Toleta.—To JOHN ADAMS. vii, 281. (M., 1823.)

2148. DEITY, Favor Invoked.—May that Infinite Power which rules the destinies of the universe, lead our councils to what is best, and give them a favorable issue for your peace and prosperity.—FIRST INAUGURAL ADDRESS. viii, 5. FORD ED., viii, 6. (1801.)

2149. DEITY, Goodness of.—When we assemble together to consider the state of our beloved country, our just attentions are first drawn to those pleasing circumstances which mark the goodness of that Being from whose favor they flow, and the large measure of thankfulness we owe for His bounty.—SECOND ANNUAL MESSAGE. viii, 15. FORD ED., viii, 181. (Dec. 1802.)

2150. DEITY, Gratitude to the.—While we devoutly return thanks to the Beneficent Being who has been pleased to breath into our sister nations the spirit of conciliation and forgiveness, we are bound with peculiar gratitude to be thankful to Him that our own peace has been preserved.—FIRST ANNUAL MESSAGE. viii, 6. FORD ED., viii, 109. (Dec. 1801.)

2151. DEITY, Inalienable Rights and.—All men are * * * endowed by their Creator with inalienable rights.—DECLARATION OF INDEPENDENCE AS DRAWN BY JEFFERSON.

2152. DEITY, Liberty and the.—We * * * most solemnly, before God and the world declare that, * * * the arms we have been compelled to assume we will use with perseverance, exerting to their utmost energies all those powers which our Creator hath given us, to preserve that liberty which He committed to us in sacred deposit * * *.—DECLARATION ON TAKING UP ARMS. FORD ED., i, 476. (July 1775.)

2153. DEITY, National Equality and the.—When * * * it becomes necessary for one people * * * to assume among the powers of the earth the * * * equal station to which the laws of nature and of nature's God entitle them * * * .—DECLARATION OF INDEPENDENCE AS DRAWN BY JEFFERSON.

2154. DEITY, An Overruling.—We are not in a world ungoverned by the laws and the power of a Superior Agent. Our efforts are in His hand, and directed by it; and He will give them their effect in His own time.*—To DAVID BARROW. vi, 456. FORD ED., ix, 516. (M., 1815.)

* Jefferson was writing on the subject of negro emancipation.—EDITOR.

2155. DEITY, Prayers to.—I offer my sincere prayers to the Supreme Ruler of the Universe, that He may long preserve our country in freedom and prosperity.—To BENJAMIN WARING. iv, 379. (W., March 1801.)

2156. ———. I join in addressing Him whose Kingdom ruleth over all, to direct the administration of their affairs to their own greatest good.—REPLY TO VERMONT ADDRESS. iv, 419. (W., 1801.)

2157. ———. That the Supreme Ruler of the universe may have our country under His special care, will be among the latest of my prayers.—R. TO A. VIRGINIA ASSEMBLY. viii, 149. (1809.)

2158. DEITY, Protection of.—We join you [Washington] in commending the interests of our dearest country to the protection of Almighty God, beseeching Him to dispose the hearts and minds of its citizens to improve the opportunity afforded them of becoming a happy and respectable nation. And for you we address to Him our earnest prayers, that a life so beloved may be fostered with all His care; that your days may be happy as they have been illustrious; and that He will finally give you that reward which this world cannot give.*—ADDRESS OF CONGRESS TO GENERAL WASHINGTON. RAYNER'S LIFE OF JEFFERSON, 226.

2159. ———. I reciprocate your kind prayers for the protection and blessing of the Common Father and Creator of man.—R. TO A. DANBURY BAPTISTS. viii, 114. (1802.)

2160. DEITY, Submission to.—Whatever is to be our destiny, wisdom as well as duty, dictates that we should acquiesce in the will of Him whose it is to give and take away, and be contented in the enjoyment of those who are still permitted to be with us.—To JOHN PAGE. iv, 547. (1804.)

2161. DEITY, Supplications to.—I shall need the favor of that Being in whose hands we are, Who led our forefathers, as Israel of old. from their native land, and planted them in a country flowing with all the necessaries and comforts of life; Who has covered our infancy with His providence, and our riper years with His wisdom and power; and to whose goodness I ask you to join with me in supplications, that He will so enlighten the minds of your servants, guide their councils, and prosper their measures, that whatsoever they do shall result in your good, and shall secure to you the peace, friendship, and approbation of all nations.—SECOND INAUGURAL ADDRESS. viii, 45. FORD ED., viii, 347. (1805.)

2162. ———. I return your kind prayers with supplications to the same Almighty Being for your future welfare and that of our beloved country.—R. TO A. OF BALTIMORE BAPTISTS. viii, 138. (1808.)

* The quotation is from the Reply of Congress to General Washington on surrendering his commission Dec., 1783. The paper was written by Jefferson, but is not in either of the two principal editions of his writings.—EDITOR.

2163. —— ——. I supplicate the Being in whose hands we all are, to preserve our country in freedom and independence, and to bestow on yourselves the blessings of His favor.—R. TO A. NORTH CAROLINA LEGISLATURE. viii, 126. (1808.)

2164. —— ——. I join in supplications to that Almighty Being, Who has heretofore guarded our councils, still to continue His gracious benedictions towards our country.—R. TO A. NEW LONDON REPUBLICANS. viii, 152. (1809.)

2165. DELAWARE, Anglomany in.— Delaware is on a poise, as she has been since 1775, and will be till Anglomany with her yields to Americanism.—To C. F. VOLNEY. iv, 573. (W., 1805.)

2166. DELAWARE, An English County.—Delaware will probably remain what it ever has been, a mere county of England, conquered indeed, and held under by force, but always disposed to counter-revolution. I speak of its majority only. To MR. BIDWELL. v, 14. (W., 1806.)

2167. DELAY, Danger in.—An instant of delay in executive proceedings may be fatal to the whole nation.—To JAMES BARBOUR. vi, 40. FORD ED., ix, 337. (M., 1812.)

2168. DELUGE, Arguments against the.—Near the eastern foot of the North-Mountain [of Virginia] are immense bodies of *Schist*, containing impressions of shells in a variety of forms. I have received petrified shells of very different kinds from the first sources of Kentucky, which bear no resemblance to any I have ever seen on the tide-waters. It is said that shells are found in the Andes, in South America, fifteen thousand feet above the level of the ocean. This is considered by many, both of the learned and unlearned, as a proof of an universal deluge. To the many considerations opposing this opinion, the following may be added: The atmosphere, and all its contents, whether of water, air, or other matter, gravitate to the earth; that is to say, they have weight. Experience tells us, that the weight of all these together never exceeds that of a column of mercury of 31 inches height, which is equal to one of rain water of 35 feet high. If the whole contents of the atmosphere, then, were water, instead of what they are, it would cover the globe but 35 feet deep; but as these waters, as they fell, would run into the seas, the superficial measure of which is to that of the dry parts of the globe, as two to one, the seas would be raised only 52½ feet above their present level, and of course would overflow the lands to that height only. In Virginia this would be a very small proportion even of the champaign country, the banks of our tide waters being frequently, if not generally, of a greater height. Deluges beyond this extent, then, as for instance to the North mountain or to Kentucky, seem out of the laws of nature. But within it they may have taken place to a greater or less degree, in proportion to the combination of natural causes which may be supposed to have produced them.—NOTES ON VIRGINIA. viii, 275. FORD ED., iii, 116. (1782.)

2169. DELUGE, Cases of a Partial.— History renders probably some instances of a partial deluge in the country lying around the Mediterranean Sea. It has been often supposed, (2 Buffon Epoques, 96) and it is not unlikely that that sea was once a lake. While such, let us admit an extraordinary collection of the waters of the atmosphere from the other parts of the globe to have been discharged over that and the countries whose waters run into it. Or without supposing it a lake, admit such an extraordinary collection of the waters of the atmosphere, and an influx from the Atlantic ocean, forced by long-continued Western winds. That lake, or that sea, may thus have been so raised as to overflow the low lands adjacent to it, as those of Egypt and Armenia, which, according to a tradition of the Egyptians and Hebrews, were overflowed about 2300 years before the Christian era; those of Attica, said to have been overflowed in the time of Ogyges, about 500 years later; and those of Thessaly, in the time of Deucalion, still 300 years posterior.—NOTES ON VIRGINIA. vii, 275. FORD ED., iii, 117. (1782.)

2170. DELUGE, Mountain Shells and the.—But such deluges as those will not account for the shells found in the higher lands. A second opinion has been entertained; which is that, in times anterior to the records either of history or tradition, the bed of the ocean, the principal residence of the shelled tribe, has, by some great convulsion of nature, been heaved to the heights at which we now find shells and other remains of marine animals. The favorers of this opinion do well to suppose the great events on which it rests to have taken place beyond all the eras of history; for within these, certainly, none such are to be found; and we may venture to say farther, that no fact has taken place, either in our own days, or in the thousands of years recorded in history, which proves the existence of any natural agents, within or without the bowels of the earth, of force sufficient to heave, to the height of 15,000 feet, such masses as the Andes. The difference between the power necessary to produce such an effect, and that which shuffled together the different parts of Calabria in our days, is so immense, that, from the existence of the latter we are not authorized to infer that of the former.—NOTES ON VIRGINIA. viii, 276. FORD ED., iii, 118. (1782.)

2171. DELUGE, Voltaire's Shell theory and.—M. de Voltaire has suggested a third solution of this difficulty (Quest Encycl. Coquilles). He cites an instance in Touraine, where, in the space of 80 years a particular spot of earth had been twice metamorphosed into soft stone, which had become hard when employed in building. In this stone, shells of various kinds were produced, discoverable at first only with the microscope, but afterwards growing with the stone. From this fact, I suppose, he would have us infer that, besides the usual process for generating shells by the elaboration of earth and water in animal vessels, nature may have provided an equivalent operation, by passing the same materials through the pores of calcareous earths and stones; as we see calcareous drop-stones generating every day by percolation of water through limestone and new marble forming in the quarries from which the old has been taken out; and it might be asked, whether it is more difficult for nature to shoot the calcareous juice into the form of a shell, than other juices into the form of crystals, plants, animals, according to the construction of the vessels through which they pass? There is a wonder somewhere. Is it greatest on this branch of the dilemma; on that which supposes the existence of a power of which we have no evidence in any other case; or on the first, which requires us to believe the creation of a body of water, and its subsequent annihilation? The establishment of the instance, cited by M. de Voltaire, of the growth of shells unattached to animal bodies, would have been that of his theory. But he has not established it. He has not even left it on ground so respectable as to have rendered it an object of inquiry to the *literati* of his own country. Abandoning this fact, therefore, the three hypotheses are equally unsatisfactory; and we must be contented to acknowledge that this great phenomenon is as yet unsolved. Ignorance is preferable to error; and he is less remote from truth who believes nothing, than he who believes what is wrong.—Notes on Virginia. viii, 276. Ford ed., iii, 118. (1782.)

2172. DELUSION, A policy of.—Warring against the principles of the great body of the American people, the delusion of the people is necessary to the dominant party. I see the extent to which that delusion has been already carried, and I see there is no length to which it may not be pushed by a party in possession of the revenues and the legal authorities of the United States, for a short time, indeed, but yet long enough to admit much particular mischief. There is no event, therefore, however atrocious, which may not be expected.—To Samuel Smith. iv, 254. Ford ed., vii, 277. (M., 1798.) See X. Y. Z. Plot.

2173. DELUSION, Recovery from.—Our fellow citizens have been led hood-winked from their principles, by a most extraordinary combination of circumstances. But the band is removed, and they now see for themselves.—To John Dickinson. iv, 366. Ford ed., viii, 7. (W., March 1801.)

2174. ———. The late chapter of our history * * * furnishes a new proof of the falsehood of Montesquieu's doctrine that a republic can be preserved only in a small territory. The reverse is the truth. Had our territory been a third only of what it is, we were gone. But while frenzy and delusion like an epidemic, gained certain parts, the residue remained sound and untouched, and held on till their brethren could recover from the temporary delusion.—To Nathaniel Niles. iv, 376. Ford ed., viii, 24. (W., March 1801.)

2175. ———. The return of our citizens from the frenzy into which they had been wrought, partly by ill conduct in France, partly by artifices practiced on them, is almost entire, and will, I believe, become quite so.—To Thomas Paine. iv, 370. Ford ed., viii. 18. (W., March 1801.)

— DEMOCRACY.—See Parties, People, Representation, Republicans and Self-government.

2176. DEMOCRATIC SOCIETIES, Federalist condemnation of.—The denunciation of the Democratic Societies is one of the extraordinary acts of boldness of which we have seen so many from the faction of monocrats. It is wonderful, indeed, that the President [Washington] should have permitted himself to be the organ of such an attack on the freedom of discussion, the freedom of writing, printing and publishing. It must be a matter of rare curiosity to get at the modifications of these rights proposed by them, and to see what line their ingenuity would draw between democratical societies, whose avowed object is the nourishment of the republican principles of our Constitution, and the Society of the Cincinnati, *a self-created* one, carving out for itself hereditary distinctions, lowering over our Constitution eternally, meeting together in all parts of the Union, periodically, with closed doors, accumulating a capital in their separate treasury, corresponding secretly and regularly, and of which society the very persons denouncing the democrats are themselves the fathers, founders and high officers. Their sight must be perfectly dazzled by the glittering of crowns and coronets, not to see the extravagance of the proposition to suppress the friends of general freedom, while those who wish to confine that freedom to the few are permitted to go on in their principles and practices. I here put out of sight the persons whose misbehavior has been taken advantage of to slander the friends of popular rights; and I am happy to observe that as far as the circle of my observation and information extends, everybody has lost sight of them, and views the abstract attempt on their natural and constitutional rights in all its nakedness. I have never heard, or heard of, a single expression or opinion which did not condemn it as an inexcusable aggression.—To James Madison. iv, 111. Ford ed., vi, 516. (M., Dec. 1794.)

2177. DEMOCRATIC SOCIETIES, Freedom of Speech and.—The attempt which has been made to restrain the liberty of our citizens meeting together, interchanging sentiments on what subjects they please, and stating their sentiments in the public papers, has come upon us a full century earlier than I expected. To demand the censors of public measures to be given up for punishment, is to renew the demand of the wolves in the fable that the sheep should give up their dogs as hostages of the peace and confidence established between them.—To William Branch Giles. Ford ed., vi, 515. (M., Dec. 1794.)

2178. DEMOCRATIC SOCIETIES, Hamilton's Hostility to.—The servile copyist of Mr. Pitt thought he, too, must have his alarms, his insurrections, and plots against the Constitution. Hence the incredible fact that the freedom of association, of conversation, and of the press, should in the fifth year of our government, have been attacked under the form of a denunciation of the Democratic Societies, a measure which even England, as boldly as she is advancing to the establishment of an absolute monarchy, has not yet been bold enough to attempt.—To James Monroe. Ford ed., vii, 16. (M., May 1795.)

2179. DEMOCRATIC SOCIETIES, Proposed bill against.—We are in suspense in Virginia to see the fate and effect of Mr. Pitt's bill against democratic societies. I wish extremely to get at the true history of this effort to suppress freedom of meeting, speaking, writing and printing. * * * Pray get the outlines of the bill Sedgwick intended to have brought in for this purpose. This will enable us to judge whether we have the merit of the invention; whether we were really beforehand with the British minister on this subject. whether he took his hint from our proposition, or whether the concurrence in the sentiment is merely the result of the general truth that great men will think alike and act alike, though without intercommunication.—To WILLIAM B. GILES. iv, 132. FORD ED., vii, 65. (M., March 1796.)

2180. DEMOCRATS, Americans as.— We of the United States are constitutionally and conscientiously Democrats.—To DUPONT DE NEMOURS. vi, 589. FORD ED., x, 22. (P. F., 1816.)

2181. DEMOCRATS AND ARISTO-CRATS.—The appellation of aristocrats and democrats is the true one expressing the essence of all [political parties].—To H. LEE. vii, 376. FORD ED., x, 318. (M., 1824.)

2182. DEMOCRATS, The People and.— Democrats consider the people as the safest depository of power in the last resort; they cherish them, therefore, and wish to leave in them all the powers to the exercise of which they are competent.—To WILLIAM SHORT. vii, 391. FORD ED., x, 335. (M., 1825.)

2183. DENMARK, Commerce with.— The Baron de Blome, minister plenipotentiary at this court (France) from Denmark, informed me in February that he was instructed by his court to give notice to the ministers from the United States, appointed to negotiate a treaty of commerce with them, that the Baron de Waltersdorff, formerly commissioned by them for the same purpose, had received another destination which called him to the West Indies; that they were sensible of the advantages which would arise to the two countries from a commercial intercourse; that their ports accordingly were placed on a very free footing as they supposed ours to be also; that they supposed the commerce on each port might be well conducted under the actual arrangements, but that whenever any circumstances should arise which would render particular stipulations more eligible, they would be ready to concur with the United States in establishing them, being desirous of continuing on the terms of the strictest harmony and friendship with them.—To JOHN JAY. i, 571. (P., 1786.)

2184. DENMARK, Prize Claims against.—Dr. Franklin, during his residence at this court [Versailles] was instructed by Congress to apply to the court of Denmark for a compensation for certain vessels and cargoes, taken from the English during the late war, by the American squadron under the command of Commodore Paul Jones, carried into a port of Denmark, and by order of the court of Denmark, redelivered to the English. Dr. Franklin made the application through Baron de Waltersdorff, at that time charged with other matters relative to the two countries of Denmark and the United States of America. Baron de Waltersdorff, after having written to his

court, informed Dr. Franklin that he was authorized to offer a compensation of ten thousand guineas. This was declined, because it was thought that the value of the prizes was the true measure of compensation, and that that ought to be inquired into. Baron de Waltersdorff left this court sometime after, on a visit only, as he expected, to Copenhagen, and the matter was suffered to rest till his return. This was constantly expected till you did me the honor of informing me that he had received another destination. It being now, therefore, necessary to renew our application, it is thought better that Commodore Paul Jones should repair in person to Copenhagen. His knowledge of the whole transaction will best enable him to represent it to that court, and the world has had too many proofs of the justice and magnanimity of his Danish Majesty to leave a doubt that he will order full justice to be done to those brave men who saw themselves deprived of the spoils, won by their gallantry, and at the hazard of their lives, and on whose behalf the justice and generosity of His Majesty is now reclaimed.—To BARON BLOME. ii, 13. (P., 1786.)

2185. ———— ————. I am instructed * * * to bring again under the consideration of * * * the King of Denmark the case of the three prizes taken from the English during the late war, by an American squadron under the command of Commodore Paul Jones, put into Bergen in distress, there rescued from our possession by orders from the court of Denmark, and delivered back to the English. * * * The United States continue to be very sensibly affected by this delivery of their prizes to Great Britain, and the more so, as no part of their conduct had forfeited their claim to those rights of hospitality which civilized nations extend to each other.*—To LE COMTE BERNSTORFF. ii, 347. (P., Jan. 1788.)

2186. DENNIE (Joseph), A Monarchist.—Among the [Federalist] writers, Dennie, the editor of the Portfolio, who was a kind of oracle with them, and styled "the Addison of America," openly avowed his preference of monarchy over all other forms of government. prided himself on the avowal, and maintained it by argument freely and without reserve in his publications.—To WILLIAM SHORT. vii, 390. FORD ED., x, 334. (M., 1825.)

— DEPARTMENTS, Government.—See CABINET.

2187. DEPENDENCE, Evils of.—Dependence begets subservience and venality, suffocates the germ of virtue. and prepares fit tools for the designs of ambition.—NOTES ON VIRGINIA. viii, 405. FORD ED., iii, 269. (1782.)

2188. DEPORTATION ACT, Denounced.—By the act for the suppression of riots and tumults in the town of Boston (14. G. 3), passed also in the last session of Parliament, a murder committed there is. if the Governor pleases, to be tried in the court of King's Bench, in the island of Great Britain, by a jury of Middlesex. The witnesses, too, on receipt of such a sum as the Governor shall think it reasonable for them to expend, are to enter into recognizance to appear at

* Congress directed Jefferson to appoint a special agent to Copenhagen to present the claim. He selected Paul Jones. The claims were paid.—EDITOR.

the trial. This is, in other words, taxing them to the amount of their recognizance; and that amount may be whatever a Governor pleases. For who does his Majesty think can be prevailed on to cross the Atlantic for the sole purpose of bearing evidence to a fact? His expenses are to be borne, indeed, as they shall be estimated by a Governor; but who are to feed the wife and children whom he leaves behind, and who have had no other subsistence but his daily labor? Those epidemical disorders, too, so terrible in a foreign climate, is the cure of them to be estimated among the articles of expense, and their danger to be warded off by the almighty power of a Parliament? And the wretched criminal, if he happen to have offended on the American side, stripped of his privilege of trial by peers of his vicinage. removed from the place where alone full evidence could be obtained, without money, without counsel, without friends. without exculpatory proof, is tried before judges predetermined to condemn. The cowards who would suffer a countryman to be torn from the bowels of their society, in order to be thus offered a sacrifice to Parliamentary tyranny, would merit that everlasting infamy now fixed on the authors of the act!—RIGHTS OF BRITISH AMERICA. i, 133. FORD ED., i, 438. (1774.)

2189. —— ——.They [Parliament] have declared that American subjects, charged with certain offences, shall be transported beyond sea to be tried before the very persons against whose pretended sovereignty the offence is supposed to be committed.—DECLARATION ON TAKING UP ARMS. FORD ED., i, 468. (July 1775.)

2190. —— ——. The proposition [of Lord North] is altogether unsatisfactory * * * because it does not propose to repeal the * * * acts of Parliament transporting us into other countries, to be tried for criminal offences.—REPLY TO LORD NORTH'S PROPOSITION. FORD ED., i, 480. (July 1775.)

2191. DEPORTATION ACT, George III. and.—He [George III.] has endeavored to pervert the exercise of the kingly office in Virginia into a detestable and insupportable tyranny * * * by combining with others to subject us to a foreign jurisdiction, giving his assent to their pretended acts of legislation * * * for transporting us beyond the seas to be tried for pretended offences.—PROPOSED VA. CONSTITUTION. FORD ED., ii, 11. (June 1776.)

2192. —— ——. He has combined, with others. * * * for transporting us beyond seas to be tried for pretended offences.—DECLARATION OF INDEPENDENCE AS DRAWN BY JEFFERSON.

2193. DEPORTATION ACT, Unexecuted.—Notwithstanding the laws the English made, I think they never ventured to carry a single person to be tried in England. They knew that reprisals would be made, and probably on the person of the governor who ventured on the measure.—NOTES ON M. SOULE'S WORK. ix, 300. FORD ED., iv, 307. (P., 1786.)

2194. DEPORTATION OF ALIENS, Sedition laws and.—The imprisonment of a person under the protection of the laws of this Commonwealth [Kentucky]. on his failure to obey the simple *order* of the President to depart out of the United States, as is undertaken by * * * [the] act, intituled "An Act concerning Aliens," is contrary to the Constitution, one amendment to which has provided that "no person shall be deprived of liberty without due process of law"; and that another having provided, that "in all criminal prosecutions, the accused shall enjoy the right to public trial, by an impartial jury, to be informed of the nature and cause of the accusation, to be confronted with the witnesses against him, to have compulsory process for obtaining witnesses in his favor, and to have the assistance of counsel for his defence," the same act, undertaking to authorize the President to remove a person out of the United States, who is under the protection of the law, on his own suspicion, without accusation, without jury, without public trial. without confrontation of the witnesses against him. without hearing witnesses in his favor, without defence, without counsel, is contrary to the provision also of the Constitution, is therefore not law, but utterly void, and of no force; that transferring the power of judging any person, who is under the protection of the laws, from the courts to the President of the United States, as is undertaken by the same act concerning aliens, is against the article of the Constitution which provides that "the judicial power of the United States shall be vested in courts, the judges of which shall hold their offices during good behavior;" and * * * the said act is void for that reason also. And it is further to be noted, that this transfer of judiciary power is to that magistrate of the General Government who already possesses all the Executive, and a negative on all Legislative powers.—KENTUCKY RESOLUTIONS. ix. 467. FORD ED., vii, 297. (1798.)

2195. —— ——. The war hawks talk of septembrizing, deportation, and the examples for quelling sedition set by the French Executive. All the firmness of the human mind is now in a state of requisition.—TO JAMES MADISON. iv, 238. FORD ED., vii, 246. (Pa., April 1798.)

2196. DESCENTS, Law of.—Descents shall go according to the laws of Gavelkind, save only that females shall have equal rights with males.—PROPOSED VA. CONSTITUTION. FORD ED., ii, 26. (June 1776.)

2197. —— ——. The bill for establishing a National Bank undertakes * * * to form the subscribers into a corporation [and] to enable them, in their corporate capacities, to transmit these* lands, on the death of a proprietor,

* Lands held by aliens in their capacity as stockholders of the bank.—EDITOR.

to a certain line of successors; and so far changes the course of *Descents.*—NATIONAL BANK OPINION. vii, 555. FORD ED., v, 284. (1791.)

2198. DESERTERS, British, in Virginia.—The number of deserters from the British army who have taken refuge in this State [Virginia] is now considerably augmenting. These people, notwithstanding their coming over to us, being deemed in law alien enemies, and as such not admissible to be citizens, are not within the scope of the Militia and Invasion laws, under which citizens alone can be embodied.—To THE COUNTY LIEUTENANTS. FORD ED., ii, 513. (R., 1781.)

2199. DESERTERS, Political.—In all countries where parties are strongly marked, as the monocrats and republicans here, there will always be deserters from the one side to the other.—To JAMES MONROE. FORD ED., vii, 27. (M., Sep. 1795.)

2200. DESERTERS, Punishment of.—The desertions of your militia have taken away the necessity of answering the question how they shall be armed. * * * I have sent expresses into all the counties from which those militia went, requiring the County Lieutenants to exert themselves in taking them; and such is the detestation with which they have been received, that I have heard from many counties they were going back of themselves. You will, of course, hold courts martial on them, and make them soldiers for eight months. —To GENERAL STEVENS. i, 252. FORD ED., ii, 338. (R., 1780.) See HESSIANS.

2201. DESPAIR, The Republic and. —We are never permitted to despair of the commonwealth.—To JAMES MADISON. ii, 331. (P., 1787.)

2202. DESPOTISM, Revolution and.— When a long train of abuses and usurpations, *begun at a distinguished period and* pursuing invariably the same object, evinces a design to reduce them under absolute despotism, it is their right, it is their duty, to throw off such government, and to provide new guards for their future security.*—DECLARATION OF INDEPENDENCE AS DRAWN BY JEFFERSON.

2203. DESPOTISM, Single and Divided. —The question * * * whether a pure despotism in a single head, or one which is divided among a king, nobles, priesthood, and numerous magistracy, is the least bad, I should be puzzled to decide; but I hope [the French people] will have neither, and that they are advancing to a limited, moderate government, in which [they] * * * will have a good share.—To JAMES MADISON. ii, 445. FORD ED., v, 45. (P., 1788.)

2204. DESPOTISM, Submission to.—If the pulse of his [George the Third's] people shall beat calmly under this experiment,† another and another will be tried, till the measure of despotism be filled up.—RIGHTS OF BRITISH AMERICA. i, 133. FORD ED., i, 438. (1774.)

2205. DESPOTISM, Unlimited.—It delights me to find that there are persons who

* Congress struck out the words in italics.—EDITOR.
† Boston Port Bill.—EDITOR.

still think that all is not lost in France: that their retrogradation from a limited to an unlimited despotism is but to give themselves a new impulse. But I see not how or when. The press, the only tocsin of a nation, is completely silenced there, and all means of a general effort taken away. However, I am willing to hope, as long as anybody will hope with me; and I am entirely persuaded that the agitations of the public mind advance its powers, and that at every vibration between the points of liberty and despotism, something will be gained for the former. As men become better informed, their rulers must respect them the more.—To THOMAS COOPER. iv, 452. FORD ED., viii, 177. (W., Nov. 1802.)

2206. DESPOTS, Methods of.—It is the old practice of despots, to use a part of the people to keep the rest in order.—To JOHN TAYLOR. iv, 246. FORD ED., vii, 263. (Pa., 1798.)

— D'ESTAING, Count.—See ESTAING.

2207. DETAIL, Importance of.—In government, as well as in every other business of life, it is by division and sub-division of duties alone, that all matters, great and small, can be managed to perfection.—To SAMUEL KERCHIVAL. vii, 13. FORD ED., x. 41. (M., 1816.)

2208. DETROIT, Contemplated Capture.—The exposed and weak state of our western settlements and the danger to which they are subject from the northern Indians, acting under the influence of the British post at Detroit, render it necessary for us to keep from five to eight hundred men on duty for their defence. This is a great and perpetual expense. Could that post be reduced and retained, it would cover all the States to the southeast of it. We have long meditated the attempt under the direction of Colonel Clark but the expense would be so great that whenever we have wished to take it up, the circumstance has obliged us to decline it. Two different estimates make it amount to two millions of pounds present money. We could furnish the men, provisions and every necessary, except powder, had we the money, or could the demands from us be so far supplied from other quarters as to leave it in our power to apply such a sum to that purpose; and, when once done, it would save annual expenditures to a great amount. When I speak of furnishing the men, I mean they should be militia; such being the popularity of Colonel [George Rogers] Clark and the confidence of the Western people in him, that he could raise the requisite number at any time. We, therefore, beg leave to refer this matter to yourself to determine whether such an enterprise would not be for the general good and if you think it would, to authorize it at the general expense. This is become the more reasonable if, as I understand, the ratification of the Confederation has been rested on our cession of a part of our Western claim; a cession which (speaking my private opinion) I verily believe will be agreed to if the quantity demanded is not unreasonably great. Should this proposition be approved of, it should be immediately made known to us, as the season is now coming on at which some of the preparations must be made.—To GENERAL WASHINGTON i, 259. FORD ED., ii, 346. (R., 1780.)

2209. DETROIT, Expedition against.— The face of things has so far changed as to leave it no longer optional in us to attempt or decline the expedition [against Detroit], but compels us to decide in the affirmative, and to begin our preparations immediately. The army the enemy at present have in the South, the reinforcements still expected there, and their determination to direct their future exertions to that quarter, are not unknown to you. The regular force, proposed on our part to counteract those exertions, is such, either from the real or supposed inability of this State, as by no means to allow a hope that it may be effectual. It is, therefore, to be expected that the scene of war will either be within our country, or very nearly advanced to it; and that our principal dependence is to be on militia, for which reason it becomes incumbent to keep as great a proportion of our people as possible free to act in that quarter. In the meantime, a combination is forming in the westward, which, if not diverted, will call thither a principal and most valuable part of our militia. From intelligence received, we have reason to expect that a confederacy of British and Indians, to the amount of two thousand men, is formed for the purpose of spreading destruction and dismay through the whole extent of our frontier in the Spring. * * * There seems to me but one method of preventing this, which is, to give the western enemy employment in their own country. The regular force Colonel Clark already has, with a proper draft from the militia beyond the Alleghany, and that of three or four of our most northern counties, will be adequate to the reduction of Fort Detroit, in the opinion of Colonel Clark. * * * We have, therefore, determined to undertake it, and commit it to his direction. Whether the expense of the enterprise shall be defrayed by the Continental or State expense, we will leave to be decided hereafter by Congress. * * * In the meantime, we only ask the loan of such necessaries as, being already at Fort Pitt, will save time and an immense expense of transportation. * * * I hope your Excellency will think yourself justified in lending us this aid, without awaiting the effect of an application elsewhere, as such a delay would render the undertaking abortive. * * * Independent of the favorable effects which a successful enterprise against Detroit must produce to the United States in general, by keeping in quiet the frontier of the northern ones, and leaving our western militia at liberty to aid those of the South, we think the like friendly office performed by us to the States, whenever desired, and almost to the absolute exhausture of our own magazines, gives well-founded hopes that we may be accommodated on this occasion.—To GENERAL WASHINGTON. i, 279. FORD ED., ii, 375. (R., Dec. 1780.)

2210 DETROIT, Importance of.— If the post at Detroit be reduced we shall be quiet in future on our frontier, and thereby immense treasures of blood and money be saved; we shall be at leisure to turn our whole force to the rescue of our eastern country from subjugation; we shall divert through our own country a branch of commerce which the European States have thought worthy of the most important struggles and sacrifices, and in the event of peace on terms which have been contemplated by some powers, we shall form to the American Union a barrier against the dangerous extension of the British Province of Canada, and add to the Empire of liberty an extensive and fertile country, thereby converting dangerous enemies into valuable friends.—To GENERAL GEORGE R. CLARK. FORD ED., ii, 390. (R., Dec. 1780.)

2211. DETROIT, Instructions to Gen. Clark.— A powerful army forming by our enemies in the south renders it necessary for us to reserve as much of our militia as possible, free to act in that quarter. At the same time, we have reason to believe that a very extensive combination of British and Indian savages is preparing to invest our western frontier. To prevent the cruel murders and devastations which attend the latter species of war, and at the same time to prevent its producing a powerful diversion of our force from the southern quarter, in which they mean to make their principal effort, and where alone success can be decisive of their ultimate object, it becomes necessary that we aim the first stroke in the western country, and throw the enemy under the embarrassments of a defensive war rather than labor under them ourselves. We have, therefore, determined that an expedition shall be undertaken, under your command, at a very early season of the approaching year, into the hostile country beyond the Ohio, the principal object of which is to be the reduction of the British post at Detroit, and, incidental to it, the acquiring possession of Lake Erie.—To GENERAL GEORGE ROGERS CLARK. FORD ED., ii, 383. (R., Dec. 25, 1780.)

2212. ——— ———. Should you succeed in the reduction of the Post, you are to promise protection to the persons and property of the French and American inhabitants, or of such at least as shall not, on tender, refuse to take the oath of fidelity to the Commonwealth. You are to permit them to continue under the laws and form of government under which they at present live, only substituting the authority of this Commonwealth in all instances in lieu of that of his British Majesty, and exercising yourself under that authority, till further order. those powers which the British Commandant of the Post, or his principal in Canada, hath used regularly to exercise. To the Indian neighbors you will hold out either fear or friendship, as their disposition and your actual situation may render most expedient.—To GENERAL GEORGE ROGERS CLARK. FORD ED., ii, 389. (R., Dec. 1780.)

2213. DETROIT, Territory acquired. —The posts of Detroit and Mackinac, having been originally intended by the governments which established and held them, as mere depots for the commerce with the Indians, very small cessions of land around were obtained or asked from the native proprietors, and these posts depended for protection on the strength of their garrisons. The principle of our government leading us to the employment of such moderate garrisons in time of peace, as may merely take care of the post, and to a reliance on the neighboring militia for its support in the first moments of war, I have thought it would be important to obtain from the Indians such a cession of the neighborhood of these posts as might maintain a militia proportioned to this object; and I have particularly contemplated, with this view, the acquisition of the eastern moiety of the peninsula between the Lakes Huron, Michigan, and Erie, extending it to the Connecticut reserve, as soon as it could be effected with the perfect good will of the natives. By a treaty concluded at Detroit, on the 17th of November last, with the Ottawas, Chippewas, Wyandotts, and Pottawatomies, so much of this country has been obtained as ex-

tends from about Saginaw bay southwardly to
the Miami of the lakes, supposed to contain
upwards of five millions of acres, with a prospect of obtaining, for the present, a breadth
of two miles for a communication from the
Miami to the Connecticut reserve. The Senate
having advised and consented to this treaty, I
now lay it before both Houses of Congress as to
the exercise of their constitutional powers as to
the means of fulfilling it.—SPECIAL MESSAGE.
viii, 94. (Jan. 1808.)

2214. DETROIT, War of 1812.—With
respect to the unfortunate loss of Detroit and
our army, I with pleasure see the animation it
has inspired through our whole country, but
especially through the Western States, and the
determination to retrieve our loss and our honor
by increased exertions.—To THOMAS C. F.
TOURNOY. vi, 83. (M., Oct. 1812.)

— **DIAL.**—See SUN-DIAL.

2215. DICKINSON (John), Character.—
A more estimable man, or truer patriot, could
not have left us. Among the first of the advocates for the rights of his country when assailed
by Great Britain, he continued to the last the
orthodox advocate of the true principles of our
new government, and his name will be consecrated in history as one of the great worthies
of the Revolution. We ought to be grateful for having been permitted to retain the
benefit of his counsel to so good an old age.—
To JOSEPH BRINGHURST. v, 249. (W., 1808.)
See DECLARATION OF INDEPENDENCE.

2216. —— ——. He was so honest a man,
and so able a one that he was greatly indulged
even by those who could not feel his scruples.*
—AUTOBIOGRAPHY. i, 11. FORD ED., i, 17.
(1821.)

**2217. DICKINSON (John), Congress
and.**—Congress gave a signal proof of their
indulgence to Mr. Dickinson, and of their great
desire not to go too fast for any respectable
part of our body, in permitting him to draw
their second petition to the King according to
his own ideas, and passing it with scarcely
any amendment. The disgust against this humility was general; and Mr. Dickinson's delight at its passage was the only circumstance
which reconciled them to it. The vote being
passed, although further observation on it was
out of order, he could not refrain from rising
and expressing his satisfaction, and concluded
by saying, " there is but one word, Mr. President, in the paper which I disapprove, and that
is the word *Congress*"; on which Ben. Harrison
rose and said, " there is but one word in the
paper, Mr. President, of which I approve, and
that is the word *Congress*."—AUTOBIOGRAPHY.
i, 11. FORD ED., i, 17. (1821.)

2218. DICKINSON (John), Writings of.
—Of the papers of July, 1775, I recollect well
that Mr. Dickinson drew the petition to the
King.—To JOHN ADAMS. vi, 194. FORD ED.,
ix, 419. (M., 1813.)

**2219. DICTATOR, Attempt in Virginia
to appoint a.**—In December, 1776, our [Vir-
ginia] circumstances being much distressed, it
was proposed in the House of Delegates to
create a *dictator*, invested with every power

---

*John Dickinson was one of the delegates from
Delaware in the Continental Congress and in the
proceedings leading up to the Declaration of Independence, he, to quote Jefferson (i, 11), "retained
the hope of reconciliation with the mother country,
and was unwilling it should be lessened by offensive
statements".—EDITOR.

legislative, executive, and judiciary, civil and
military of life, and of death, over our persons
and over our properties; and in June, 1781,
again under calamity, the same proposition
was repeated, and wanted a few votes only
of being passed. One who entered into this
contest from a pure love of liberty, and a
sense of injured rights, who determined to
make every sacrifice, and to meet every
danger for the reestablishment of those rights
on a firm basis, who did not mean to expend
his blood and substance for the wretched purpose of changing this master for that, but to
place the powers of governing him in a plurality of hands of his own choice, so that the
corrupt will of no one man might in future
oppress him, must stand confounded and dis-
mayed when he is told, that a considerable
portion of that plurality had meditated the
surrender of them into a single hand, and, in
lieu of a limited monarch, to deliver him over
to a despotic one! How must he find his
efforts and sacrifices abused and baffled, if
he may still, by a single vote, be laid prostrate
at the feet of one man! In God's name, from
whence have they derived this power? Is
it from our ancient laws? None such can be
produced. Is it from any principle in our new
Constitution, expressed or implied? Every
lineament expressed or implied, is in full opposition to it. Its fundamental principle is,
that the State shall be governed as a Commonwealth. It provides a republican organization, proscribes under the name of *prerogative* the exercise of all powers undefined by
the laws; places on this basis the whole system of our laws; and by consolidating them
together, chooses that they should be left to
stand or fall together, never providing for any
circumstances, nor admitting that such could
arise, wherein either should be suspended; no,
not for a moment. Our ancient laws expressly declare, that those who are but delegates themselves, shall not delegate to others
powers which require judgment and integrity
in their exercise. Or was this proposition
moved on a supposed right in the movers, of
abandoning their posts in a moment of distress? The same laws forbid the abandonment of that post, even on ordinary occasions;
and much more a transfer of their powers
into other hands and other forms, without
consulting the people. They never admit the
idea that these, like sheep or cattle, may be
given from hand to hand without an appeal
to their own will. Was it from the necessity
of the case? Necessities which dissolve a
government, do not convey its authority to
an oligarchy, or a monarchy. They throw
back, into the hands of the people, the powers
they had delegated, and leave them as individuals to shift for themselves. A leader may
offer, but not impose himself, nor be imposed
on them. Much less can their necks be submitted to his sword, their breath be held at
his will or caprice. The necessity which
should operate these tremendous effects
should at least be palpable and irresistible.
Yet in both instances, where it was feared, or
pretended with us, it was belied by the event.

t was belied, too, by the preceding experience of our sister States, several of whom had grappled through greater difficulties without abandoning their forms of government. When the proposition was first made, Massachusetts had found even the government of committees sufficient to carry them through an invasion. But we at the time of that proposition, were under no invasion. When the second was made, there had been added to this example those of Rhode Island, New York, New Jersey, and Pennsylvania, in all of which the republican form had been found equal to the task of carrying them through the severest trials. In this State alone did there exist so little virtue, that fear was to be fixed in the hearts of the people, and to become the motive of their exertions, and the principle of their government? The very thought alone was treason against the people; was treason against mankind in general; as riveting forever the chains which bow down their necks, by giving to their oppressors a proof, which they would have trumpeted through the universe, of the imbecility of republican government, in times of pressing danger, to shield them from harm. Those who assume the right of giving away the reins of government in any case, must be sure that the herd, whom they hand on to the rods and hatchet of the dictator, will lay their heads on the block, when he shall nod to them. But if our Assemblies supposed such a resignation in the people, I hope they mistook their character. I am of opinion, that the government, instead of being braced and invigorated for greater exertions under their difficulties, would have been thrown back upon the bungling machinery of county committees for administration, till a convention could have been called, and its wheels again set into regular motion. What a cruel moment was this for creating such an embarrassment, for putting to the proof, the attachment of our countrymen to republican government?—Notes on Virginia. viii, 368. Ford ed., iii, 231. (1782.)

2220. DICTATOR, Misapplied Precedent for.—Those who meant well, of the advocates of this measure (and most of them meant well, for I knew them personally, had been their fellow-laborer in the common cause, and had often proved the purity of their principles), had been seduced in their judgment by the example of an ancient republic, whose constitution and circumstances were fundamentally different. They had sought this precedent in the history of Rome, where alone it was to be found, and where at length, too, it had proved fatal. They had taken it from a republic rent by the most bitter factions and tumults, where the government was of a heavy-handed unfeeling aristocracy, over a people ferocious and rendered desperate by poverty and wretchedness; tumults which could not be allayed under the most trying circumstances, but by the omnipotent hand of a single despot. Their constitution, therefore, allowed a temporary tyrant to be erected, under the name of a dic-

tator; and that temporary tyrant, after a few examples, became perpetual. They misapplied this precedent to a people mild in their dispositions, patient under their trial, united for the public liberty, and affectionate to their leaders. But if from the constitution of the Roman government there resulted to their senate a power of submitting all their rights to the will of one man, does it follow that the Assembly of Virginia have the same authority? What clause in our Constitution has substituted that of Rome, by way of residuary provision, for all cases not otherwise provided for? Or if they may step *ad libitum* into any other form of government for precedents to rule us by, for what oppression may not a precedent be found in this world of the *bellum omnium in omnia?* Searching for the foundations of this proposition, I can find none which may pretend a color of right or reason, but the defect * * * that there being no barrier between the legislative, executive, and judiciary departments. the Legislature may seize the whole; that having seized it and possessing a right to fix their own quorum, they may reduce that quorum to one. whom they may call a chairman, speaker, dictator, or any other name they please.—Notes on Virginia. viii, 370. Ford ed., iii, 234. (1782.)

2221. DICTIONARY, An Anglo-Saxon.—There are several things wanting to promote this improvement. [The recovery of the lost Anglo-Saxon and other words.] To reprint the Saxon books in modern type; reform their orthography; publish in the same way the treasures still existing in manuscript. And more than all things we want a dictionary on the plan of Stephens or Scapula, in which the Saxon root, placed alphabetically, shall be followed by all its cognate modifications of nouns, verbs, &c., whether Anglo-Saxon, or found in the dialects of subsequent ages.—To J. Evelyn Denison. vii, 418. (M., 1825.) See Languages.

2222. DICTIONARIES, Neology and.—Dictionaries are but the depositories of words already legitimated by usage. Society is the workshop in which new ones are elaborated. When an individual uses a new word, if ill-formed, it is rejected in society; if well formed, adopted, and after due time, laid up in the depository of dictionaries.—To John Adams. vii, 175. (M., 1820.) See Languages.

2223. DIFFICULTIES, True way out of.—If you ever find yourself environed with difficulties and perplexing circumstances, out of which you are at a loss how to extricate yourself, do what is right, and be assured that that will extricate you the best out of the worst situations. Though you cannot see, when you take one step, what will be the next, yet follow truth, justice, and plain dealing, and never fear their leading you out of the labyrinth, in the easiest manner possible. The knot which you thought a Gordian one, will untie itself before you. Nothing is so mistaken as the supposition that a person is to extricate himself from a difficulty by intrigue, by chicanery, by dissimulation, by trimming, by an untruth, by an injustice. This increases the difficulties tenfold; and those, who pursue these methods. get themselves so involved at length, that they can turn no way but their infamy becomes more exposed.—To Peter Carr. i, 396. (P., 1785.)

2224. DIGNITY, Maintain.—With the British who respect their own dignity so much, ours must not be counted at naught.—To Gouverneur Morris. iii, 182. Ford ed., v, 224. (N.Y., 1790.)

2225. DIPLOMACY, Demeanor.—Let what will be said or done, preserve your *sang froid* immovably, and to every obstacle, oppose patience, perseverance, and soothing language.—To William Short. iii, 342. Ford ed., v, 459. (Pa., 1792.)

2226. DIPLOMATIC ESTABLISH-MENT, Economy in.—The new government has now for some time been under way. * * * Abuses under the old forms have led us to lay the basis of the new in a rigorous economy of the public contributions. This principle will show itself in our diplomatic establishments; and the rather, as at such a distance from Europe, and with such an ocean between us, we hope to meddle little in its quarrels or combinations. Its peace and its commerce are what we shall court; and to cultivate these, we propose to place at the courts of Europe most interesting to us diplomatic characters of economical grade, and shall be glad to receive like ones in exchange.—To M. de Pinto. iii, 174. (N.Y., 1790.)

2227. DIPLOMATIC ESTABLISH-MENT, Extent of.—I am for * * * little or no diplomatic establishment.—To Elbridge Gerry. iv, 268. Ford ed., vii, 328. (Pa., 1799.)

2228. DIPLOMATIC ESTABLISH-MENT, Reduction of.—The diplomatic establishment in Europe will be reduced to three ministers.—To Nathaniel Macon. iv, 396. Ford ed., viii, 52. (W., May 1801.)

2229. —— ——. We call in our diplomatic missions, barely keeping up those to the most important nations. There is a strong disposition in our countrymen to discontinue even these; and very possibly it may be done.—To William Short. iv, 415. Ford ed., viii, 98. (W., 1801.) See Ministers.

— DIRECT TAX.—See Apportionment and Taxation.

— DIRECTORY.—See Executives.

2230. DISCIPLINE, Education and.—The article of discipline is the most difficult in American education. Premature ideas of independence, too little repressed by parents, beget a spirit of insubordination, which is the great obstacle to science with us, and a principal cause of its decay since the Revolution. I look to it with dismay in our institution [the Virginia University] as a breaker ahead, which I am far from being confident we shall be able to weather.—To Thomas Cooper. vii, 268. Ford ed., x, 244. (M., 1822.)

2231. —— ——. The rock which I most dread is the discipline of the institution [the University of Virginia], and it is that on which most of our public schools labor. The

insubordination of our youth is now the greatest obstacle to their education. We may lessen the difficulty, perhaps, by avoiding too much government, by requiring no useless observances, none which shall merely multiply occasion for dissatisfaction, disobedience and revolt by referring to the more discreet of themselves the minor discipline, the graver to the civil magistrates, as in Edinburgh.*—To George Ticknor. vii, 301. (M., 1823.)

2232. DISCIPLINE, Military.—Good dispositions and arrangements will not do without a certain degree of bravery and discipline in those who are to carry them into execution.—To General Gates. i, 314. Ford ed., iii, 52. (R., 1781.)

2233. —— ——. The breaking men to military discipline is breaking their spirits to principles of passive obedience.—To John Jay. ii, 392. (P., 1788.)

— DISCOUNT, Banks of.—See Banks.

2234. DISCRETION, Exercise of.—In operations at such a distance [case of Naval Agent Eaton in Tripoli], it becomes necessary to leave much to the discretion of the agents employed, but events may still turn up beyond the limits of that discretion. Unable in such case to consult his government, a zealous citizen will act as he believes that would direct him were it apprised of the circumstances, and will take on himself the responsibility. In all these cases, the purity and patriotism of the motives should shield the agent from blame, and even secure the sanction where the error is not too injurious.†—Special Message. viii, 56. (P., 1806.)

2235. DISCRETION, Law and.—A full representation at the ensuing session [of Congress] will doubtless * * * take measures for ensuring the authority of the laws over the corrupt maneuvers of the heads of departments under the pretext of exercising discretion in opposition to law.—To T. M. Randolph. Ford ed., vi, 195. (Pa., 1793.)

— DISCRIMINATING DUTIES.—See Duties.

2236. DISINTERESTEDNESS, Losses through.—I retired much poorer than when I entered the public service.‡—To Edward Rutledge. iv, 151. Ford ed., vii, 93. (M., 1796.)

2237. DISINTERESTEDNESS, Practice of.—I prefer public benefit to all personal considerations.—To J. W. Eppes. vi, 203. Ford ed., ix, 402. (P.F., Sep. 1813.)

2238. DISINTERESTEDNESS, Private fortune and.—When I first entered on

* The introduction of the "honor system", in collegiate education, is one of Jefferson's great reforms —Editor.

† In this message, Jefferson laid before Congress the case of Hamet Caramalli, with whom Eaton, a the agent of the U. S. Government, had cooperated in the attempt to recover his throne from the usurping Bashaw of Tripoli.—Editor.

‡ "Few persons," says Parton in his *Life of Jefferson* (p. 147) "have ever performed public duty at such a sacrifice of personal feeling and private interest as did Thomas Jefferson."—Editor.

the stage of public life (now twenty-four years ago), I came to a resolution never to engage while in public office in any kind of enterprise for the improvement of my fortune * * * . I have never departed from it in a single instance; and I have in multiplied instances found myself happy in being able to decide and to act as a public servant, clear of all interest, in the multiform questions that have arisen, wherein I have seen others embarrassed and biased by having got themselves into a more interested situation. Thus I have thought myself richer in contentment than I should have been with any increase of fortune. * * * My public career is now closing, and I will go through on the principle on which I have hitherto acted.—To —— ——. iii, 527. (Pa., 1793.)

2239. —— ——. I do not wish to make a shilling [as Minister to France], but only my expenses to be defrayed, and in a moderate style.—To SAMUEL OSGOOD. i, 452. (P., 1785.)

2240. —— ——. I have the consolation of having added nothing to my private fortune, during my public service, and of retiring with hands as clean as they are empty.—To COUNT DIODATI. v, 62. (W., 1807.)

2241. DISINTERESTEDNESS, Ruin and.—I had been thirteen years engaged in public service and, during that time, I had so totally abandoned all attention to my private affairs as to permit them to run into great disorder and ruin.—To JAMES MONROE. i, 318. FORD ED., iii, 56. (M., 1782.)

2242. DISPUTATION, Avoid.—In stating prudential rules for our government in society, I must not omit the important one of never entering into dispute or argument with another. I never saw an instance of one of two disputants convincing the other by argument. I have seen many, on their getting warm, becoming rude, and shooting one another. Conviction is the effect of our own dispassionate reasoning, either in solitude, or weighing within ourselves, dispassionately, what we hear from others, standing uncommitted in argument ourselves. It was one of the rules which, above all others, made Dr. Franklin the most amiable of men in society, "never to contradict anybody." If he was urged to announce an opinion, he did it rather by asking questions, as if for information, or by suggesting doubts. When I hear another express an opinion which is not mine, I say to myself, he has a right to his opinion, as I to mine; why should I question it? His error does me no injury, and shall I become a Don Quixote, to bring all men by force of argument to one opinion? If a fact be misstated, it is probable he is gratified by a belief of it, and I have no right to deprive him of the gratification. If he wants information, he will ask it, and then I will give it in measured terms; but if he still believes his own story, and shows a desire to dispute the fact with me, I hear him and say nothing. It

is his affair, not mine, if he prefers error.—To THOMAS JEFFERSON RANDOLPH. v, 390. FORD ED., ix, 232. (W., 1808.)

2243. DISPUTATION, Political.—There are two classes of disputants most frequently to be met with among us. The first is of young students, just entered the threshold of science, with a first view of its outlines, not yet filled up with the details and modifications which a further progress would bring to their knowledge. The other consists of the ill-tempered and rude men in society, who have taken up a passion for politics. From both of these classes of disputants, * * * keep aloof, as you would from the infected subjects of yellow fever or pestilence. Consider yourself, when with them, as among the patients of Bedlam, needing medical more than moral counsel. Be a listener only, keep within yourself, and endeavor to establish with yourself the habit of silence, especially on politics. In the fevered state of our country, no good can ever result from any attempt to set one of these fiery zealots to rights, either in fact or principle. They are determined as to the facts they will believe, and the opinions on which they will act. Get by them, therefore, as you would by an angry bull; it is not for a man of sense to dispute the road with such an animal. You will be more exposed than others to have these animals shaking their horns at you, because of the relation in which you stand with me. Full of political venom, and willing to see me and to hate me as a chief in the antagonistic party, your presence will be to them what the vomit grass is to the sick dog, a nostrum for producing ejaculation. Look upon them exactly with that eye, and pity them as objects to whom you can administer only occasional ease. My character is not within their power. It is in the hands of my fellow citizens at large, and will be consigned to honor or infamy by the verdict of the republican mass of our country, according to what themselves will have seen, not what their enemies and mine shall have said. Never, therefore, consider these puppies in politics as requiring any notice from you, and always show that you are not afraid to leave my character to the umpirage of public opinion.—To THOMAS JEFFERSON RANDOLPH. v, 391. FORD ED., ix, 232. (W., 1808.)

2244. DISPUTES, Children and.—In little disputes with your companions, give way rather than insist on trifles, for their love and the approbation of others will be worth more to you than the trifle in dispute.*—To FRANCIS EPPES. D. L. J. 365.

2245. DISSENSION, Evils of Political.—Political dissension is doubtless a less evil than the lethargy of despotism, but still it is a great evil, and it would be as worthy the efforts of the patriot as of the philosopher, to exclude its influence, if possible, from social life. The good are rare enough at best. There is no reason to subdivide them by

* Eppes was a little grandson.—EDITOR.

artificial lines. But whether we shall ever. be able so far to perfect the principles of society, as that political opinions shall, in its intercourse, be as inoffensive as those of philosophy, mechanics, or any other, may well be doubted.—To THOMAS PINCKNEY. iv, 176. FORD ED., vii, 128. (Pa., 1797.) See SOCIAL INTERCOURSE.

2246. DISTRIBUTION, Laws of.—The bill for establishing a National Bank undertakes * * * to form the subscribers into a corporation [and] to enable them, in their corporate capacities, * * * to transmit personal chattels to successors in a certain line; and, so far, is against the laws of *Distribution.*—NATIONAL BANK OPINION. vii. 555. FORD ED., v, 285. (1791.)

2247. DISUNION, New England and. —The fog which arose in the east in the last moments of my service, will doubtless clear away and expose under a stronger light the rocks and shoals which have threatened us with danger. It is impossible the good citizens of the east should not see the agency of England, the tools she employs among them, and the criminal arts and falsehoods of which they have been the dupes.—To GOVERNOR WRIGHT. viii, 167. (1809.) See HARTFORD CONVENTION and SECESSION.

— DIVINITY.—See DEITY.

— DOCKYARDS.—See NAVY.

2248. DOLLAR, Adaptedness for Unit. —In fixing the Unit of Money, these circumstances are of principal importance. 1. That it be of *convenient size* to be applied as a measure to the common money transactions of life. 2. That its parts and multiples be in an *easy proportion* to each other, so as to facilitate the money arithmetic. 3. That the unit and its parts, or divisions, be *so nearly of the value of some of the known coins,* as that they may be of easy adoption for the people. The Spanish dollar seems to fulfil all these conditions. Taking into our view all money transactions, great and small, I question if a common measure of more *convenient size* than the Dollar could be proposed. The value of 100, 1,000, 10,000 dollars is well estimated by the mind; so is that of the tenth or the hundredth of a dollar. Few transactions are above or below these limits. The expediency of attending to the size of the money Unit will be evident to anyone who will consider how inconvenient it would be to a manufacturer or merchant, if, instead of the yard for measuring cloth, either the inch or the mile had been made the Unit of Measure.*—NOTES ON A MONEY UNIT. i, 162. FORD ED., iii, 446. (1784.) See DECIMAL SYSTEM.

* Parton in his *Life of Jefferson* says: "Two years before, Gouverneur Morris, a clerk in the office of his uncle Robert Morris, had conceived the most happy idea of applying the decimal system to the notation of money. But it always requires several men to complete one great thing. The details of the system devised by Gouverneur Morris were so cumbrous and awkward as almost to neutralize the simplicity of the leading idea. Jefferson rescued the fine original conception by proposing our present system of dollars and cents; the dollar to be the Unit and the largest silver coin."—EDITOR.

2249. ——— ———. The Unit, or Dollar, is a known coin, and the most familiar of all, to the minds of the people. It is already adopted from South to North; has identified our currency, and therefore happily offers itself as a Unit already introduced. Our public debt, our requisitions, and their appointments, have given it actual and long possession of the place of Unit. The course of our commerce, too, will bring us more of this than of any other foreign coin. and, therefore, renders it more worthy of attention. I know of no Unit which can be proposed in competition with the dollar, but the Pound. But what is the Pound? 1547 grains of fine silver in Georgia; 1289 grains in Virginia, Connecticut, Rhode Island, Massachusetts and New Hampshire; 1031 1-4 grains in Maryland, Delaware, Pennsylvania and New Jersey; 966 3-4 grains in North Carolina and New York. Which of these shall we adopt? To which State give that preeminence of which all are so jealous? And on which impose the difficulties of a new estimate of their corn, their cattle and other commodities? Or shall we hang the pound sterling, as a common badge, about all their necks? This contains 1718 3-4 grains of pure silver. It is difficult to familiarize a new coin to the people; it is more difficult to familiarize them to a new coin with an old name. Happily, the dollar is familiar to them all, and is already as much referred to for a measure of value, as are their respective provincial pounds.—NOTES ON A MONEY UNIT. i, 165. FORD ED., iii, 448. (1784.)

2250. DOLLAR, Advantages as Unit.— The Financier [Robert Morris] * * * seems to concur with me in thinking his smallest fractional division too minute for a Unit and, therefore, proposes to transfer that denomination to his largest silver coin, containing 1000 of the units first proposed, (1440) and worth about 4s. 2d. lawful, or 25-36 of a Dollar. The only question then remaining between us is, whether the Dollar, or this coin, be best for the Unit. We both agree that *the case of adoption with the people,* is the thing to be aimed at. As to the Dollar. events have overtaken and superseded the question. It is no longer a doubt whether the people can adopt it with ease; they have adopted it. and will have to be turned out of that into another tract of calculation, if another Unit be assumed. They have now two Units. which they use with equal facility, viz., the Pound of their respective State, and the Dollar. The first of these is peculiar to each State; the second, happily, common to all. In each State, the people have an easy rule of converting the pound of their State into dollars, or dollars into pounds; and this is enough for them, without knowing how this may be done in every State of the Union. Such of them as live near enough the borders of their State to have dealings with their neighbors, learn also the rule of their neighbors; thus, in Virginia and the Eastern States. where the dollar is 6s. or 3-10 of a pound, to turn pounds into dollars, they multiply by 10 and divide by three. To turn dollars into pounds, they multiply by 3 and divide by 10. Those in Virginia who live near to Carolina, where the dollar is 8s. or 4-10 of a pound, learn the operation of that State, which is a multiplication by 4, and division by 10, *et e converso*. Those who live near Maryland, where the dollar is 7s. 6d. or 3-8 of a pound, multiply by 3, and divide by 8, *et e converso*. All these operations are easy, and have been found, by experience, not too much for the arithmetic of the people, when they have occasion to convert their old Unit into dollars, or the reverse.—SUPPLEMENTARY EXPLANATIONS. i, 171. FORD ED., iii, 455. (1784.) See MONEY, UNIT.

2251. ——— ———. In the States where the dollar is 3-10 of a pound, this Unit [of the Financier] will be 5-24. Its conversion into the pound, then, will be by a multiplication of 5 and a division by 24. In the States where the dollar is 3-8 of a pound, this Unit will be 25-96 of a pound, and the operation must be to multiply by 25, and divide by 96, *et e converso*. Where the dollar is 4-10 of a pound, this Unit will be 5-18. The simplicity of the fraction and, of course, the facility of conversion and reconversion is, therefore, against this Unit, and in favor of the dollar, in every instance. The only advantage it has over the dollar, is, that it will in every case, express our farthing without a remainder; whereas, though the dollar and its decimals will do this in many cases, it will not in all. But, even in these, by extending your notation one figure further, to wit, to thousands, you approximate to perfect accuracy within less than the two-thousandth part of a dollar; an atom in money which every one would neglect. Against this single inconvenience, the other advantages of the dollar are more than sufficient to preponderate. This Unit will present to the people a new coin, and whenever they endeavor to estimate its value by comparing it with a Pound, or with a Dollar, the Units they now possess, they will find the fraction very compound, and, of course, less accommodated to their comprehension and habits than the dollar. Indeed, the probability is, that they could never be led to compute in it generally.—SUPPLEMENTARY EXPLANATIONS. i, 171. FORD ED., iii, 455. (1784.)

2252. DOLLAR, Coinage.—If we adopt the Dollar for our Unit, we should strike four coins, one of gold, two of silver, and one of copper, viz.: 1. A golden piece, equal in value to ten dollars:[*] 2. The Unit or Dollar itself, of silver: 3. The tenth of a Dollar, of silver also: 4. The hundredth of a Dollar, of copper.—NOTES ON A MONEY UNIT. i, 163. FORD ED., iii, 447. (1784.)

2253. ——— ———. Perhaps it would not be amiss to coin three more pieces of silver, one of the value of five-tenths, or half a dollar, one of the value of two-tenths, which would

[*] Jefferson subsequently added the five-dollar gold coin to the list.—EDITOR.

be equal to the Spanish pistereen, and one of the value of five coppers, which would be equal to the Spanish half-bit. We should then have five silver coins, viz.:

1. The Unit or Dollar;
2. The half dollar or five-tenths:
3. The double-tenth, equal to 2, or one-fifth of a dollar, or to the pistereen;
4. The tenth, equal to a Spanish bit:
5. The five copper piece, equal to .5, or one-twentieth of a dollar, or the half bit.—NOTES ON A MONEY UNIT. i, 166. FORD ED., iii, 450. (1784.)

2254. DOLLAR, Copper coinage and.—The hundredth [of a dollar], or copper, will differ little from the copper of the four Eastern States, which is 1-108 of a dollar; still less from the penny of New York and North Carolina, which is 1-96 of a dollar; and somewhat more from the penny or copper of Jersey, Pennsylvania, Delaware and Maryland, which is 1-90 of a dollar. It will be about the medium between the old and the new coppers of these States, and will, therefore, soon be substituted for them both. In Virginia, coppers have never been in use. It will be as easy, therefore, to introduce them there of one value as of another. The copper coin proposed will be nearly equal to three-fourths of their penny, which is the same with the penny lawful of the Eastern States.—NOTES ON A MONEY UNIT. i, 165. FORD ED., iii, 449. (1784.)

2255. ——— ———. The Financier [Robert Morris] supposes that the 1-100 part of a dollar is not sufficiently small, where the poor are purchasers or vendors. If it is not, make a smaller coin. But I suspect that it is small enough. Let us examine facts, in countries where we are acquainted with them. In Virginia, where our towns are few, small, and, of course, their demand for necessaries very limited, we have never yet been able to introduce a copper coin at all. The smallest coin which anybody will receive there is the half-bit, or the 1-20 of a dollar. In those States where the towns are larger and more populous, a more habitual barter of small wants has called for a copper coin of 1-90, 1-96, or 1-108 of a dollar. In England, where the towns are many and populous, and where ages of experience have matured the conveniences of intercourse, they have found that some wants may be supplied for a farthing, or 1-208 of a dollar, and they have accommodated a coin to this want. This business is evidently progressive. In Virginia, we are far behind. In some other States, they are further advanced, to wit, to the appreciation of 1-90, 1-96, 1-108 of a dollar. To this most advanced state, then, I accommodated my smallest coin in the decimal arrangement, as *a money of payment*, corresponding with the *money of account*. I have no doubt the time will come when a smaller coin will be called for. When that comes, let it be made. It will probably be the half of the copper I suppose, that is to say, 5-1000 or .005 of a dollar, this being very nearly the farthing of England. But it will be time enough to make it, when the people shall be ready to receive it.—SUPPLEMENTARY EXPLANATIONS. i, 173. FORD ED., iii, 456. (1784.)

2256. ——. ——. The Secretary of State is * * * uncertain whether, instead of the larger copper coin, the Legislature might not prefer a lighter one of billon, or mixed metal, as is practiced with convenience, by several other nations.—COINAGE REPORT. vii, 463. (April 1790.)

2257. DOLLAR, Grains of Silver in.—If we determine that a Dollar shall be our Unit, we must then say with precision what a Dollar is. This coin, struck at different times, of different weights and fineness, is of different values. Sir Isaac Newton's assay and representation to the Lords of the Treasury, in 1717, of those which he examined, make their values as follows:

The Seville piece   dwt. grs.
  of eight...............17—12 containing 387 grains
                         of pure silver
The Mexico piece
  of eight...............17—10 5-9 containing 385 1-2
                      grains of pure silver.
The Pillar piece of eight..17—9 containing 385 3-4
                      grains of pure silver.
The new Seville piece
  of eight...............14— containing 308 7-10
                      grains of pure silver.

The Financier states the old Dollar as containing 376 grains of fine silver, and the new 365 grains. If the Dollars circulating among us be of every date equally, we should examine the quantity of pure metal in each, and from them form an average for our Unit. This is a work proper to be committed to mathematicians as well as merchants, and which should be decided on actual and accurate experiment.—NOTES ON A MONEY UNIT. i, 167. FORD ED., iii, 451. (1784.) See GOLD AND SILVER.

2258. ——. ——. Congress, in 1786, established the Money Unit at 375.64 Troy grains of pure silver. It is proposed to enlarge this by about the third of a grain in weight, or a mill in value; that it is to say, to establish it at 376 (or, more exactly, 375.989343) instead of 375.64 grains; because it will be shown that this, as the unit of coin, will link in system with the units of length, surface, capacity, and weight, whenever it shall be thought proper to extend the decimal ratio through all these branches. It is to preserve the possibility of doing this, that this very minute alteration is proposed. * * * Let it be declared, therefore, that the money unit or dollar of the United States, shall contain 371.262 American grains of pure silver.—COINAGE, WEIGHTS AND MEASURES REPORT. vii, 487. (July 1790.)

2259. ——. ——. Let the Money Unit, or dollar, contain eleven-twelfths of an ounce of pure silver. This will be 376 Troy grains (or more exactly, 375.989343 Troy grains), which will be about a third of a grain (or more exactly, .349343 of a grain) more than the present unit. This, with the twelfth of alloy already established, will make the dollar or unit, of the weight of an ounce, or of a cubic

inch of rain water, exactly. The series of mills, cents, dimes, dollars, and eagles, to remain as already established.—COINAGE, WEIGHTS AND MEASURES REPORT. vii, 490. (July 1790.)

2260. ——. ——. The pure silver in a dollar * * * [is] fixed by law at 347¼ grains, and all debts and contracts * * * [are] bottomed on that value * * * .—To DR. ROBERT PATTERSON. vi, 22. (M., Nov. 1811.)

2261. DOLLAR, Proportion of Alloy.—Some alloy is necessary to prevent the coin from wearing too fast; too much, fills our pockets with copper, instead of silver. The silver coin assayed by Sir Isaac Newton, varied from 1 1-2 to 76 pennyweights alloy, in the pound Troy of mixed metal. The British standard has 18 dwt.; the Spanish coins assayed by Sir Isaac Newton, have from 18 to 19 1-2 dwt.; the new French crown has in fact 19 1-2, though by edict, it should have 20 dwt., that is 1-12. The taste of our countrymen will require that their furniture plate should be as good as the British standard. Taste cannot be controlled by law. Let it then give the law, in a point which is indifferent to a certain degree. Let the Legislature fix the alloy of furniture plate at 18 dwt., the British standard, and Congress that of their coin at one ounce in the pound, the French standard. This proportion has been found convenient for the alloy of gold coin, and it will simplify the system of our mint to alloy both metals in the same degree. The coin, too, being the least pure, will be the less easily melted into plate. These reasons are light, indeed, and, of course, will only weigh if no heavier ones can be opposed to them.—NOTES ON A MONEY UNIT. i, 167. FORD ED., iii, 451. (1784.)

2262. ——. ——. As to the alloy for gold coin, the British is an ounce in the pound; the French, Spanish and Portuguese differ from that, only from a quarter of a grain, to a grain and a half. I should, therefore, prefer the British, merely because its fraction stands in a more simple form, and facilitates the calculations into which it enters.—NOTES ON A MONEY UNIT. i, 168. FORD ED., iii, 452. (1784.)

2263. ——. ——. I concur with you in thinking that * * * the alloy should be the same in both metals.—To ALEXANDER HAMILTON. iii, 330. (Feb. 1792.)

2264. DOLLAR, Reducing Value of.—With respect to the dollar, it must be admitted by all the world, that there is great uncertainty in the meaning of the term, and therefore all the world will have justified Congress for their first act of removing the uncertainty by declaring what they understand by the term; but the uncertainty once removed, exists no longer, and I very much doubt now a right to change the value, and especially to lessen it. It would lead to so easy a mode of paying off their debts. Besides, the parties injured by this reduction of the value would have so much matter to urge in support of the first point of fixation.—To ALEXANDER HAMILTON. iii, 330. (1792.)

2265. ———— ————. Should it be thought that Congress may reduce the value of the dollar, I should be for adopting for our unit, instead of the dollar, either one ounce of pure silver, or one ounce of standard silver, so as to keep the unit of money a part of the system of measures, weights and coins.—To ALEXANDER HAMILTON. iii, 330. (1792.)

2266. DOLLAR, Stopping Coinage.—I should approve of your employing the Mint on small silver coins, rather than on dollars and gold coins, so far as the consent of those who employ it can be obtained. It would be much more valuable to the public to be supplied with abundance of dimes and half dimes, which would stay among us, than with dollars and eagles which leave us immediately. Indeed I wish the law authorized the making two-cent and three-cent pieces of silver, and golden dollars, which would all be large enough to handle, and would be a great convenience to our own citizens.—To ROBERT PATTERSON. v, 61. (W., March 1807.)

2267. DOLLAR, Summary Review of measures.—Congress as early as January 7, 1782, had turned their attention to the moneys current in the several States, and had directed the Financier, Robert Morris, to report to them a table of rates at which the foreign coins should be received at the treasury. That officer, or rather his assistant, Gouverneur Morris, answered them on the 15th, in an able and elaborate statement of the denominations of money current in the several States, and of the comparative value of the foreign coins chiefly in circulation with us, He went into the consideration of the necessity of establishing a standard of value with us, and of the adoption of a money Unit. He proposed for that Unit, such a fraction of pure silver as would be a common measure of the penny of every State, without leaving a fraction. This common divisor he found to be the 1-1440 of a dollar, or 1-1600 of the crown sterling. The value of a dollar was, therefore, to be expressed by 1440 units, and of a crown by 1600; each Unit containing a quarter of a grain of fine silver. Congress turning again their attention to this subject the following year, the Financier, by a letter of April 30, 1783, further explained and urged the Unit he had proposed; but nothing more was done on it until the ensuing year, when it was again taken up, and referred to a committee, of which I was a member. The general views of the Financier were sound, and the principle was ingenious on which he proposed to found his Unit; but it was too minute for ordinary use, too laborious for computation, either by the head or in figures. The price of a loaf of bread, 1-20 of a dollar, would be 72 units. A pound of butter 1-5 of a dollar, 288 units. A horse or bullock of eighty dollars value would require a notation of six figures, to wit, 115,200, and the public debt, suppose of eighty millions, would require

twelve figures, to wit, 115,200,000,000 units. Such a system of money-arithmetic would be entirely unmanageable for the common purposes of Society. I propose, therefore, instead of this, to adopt the Dollar as our Unit of account and payment, and that its divisions and sub-divisions should be in the decimal ratio. I wrote some Notes on the subject, which I submitted to the consideration of the Financier. I received his answer and adherence to his general system, only agreeing to take for his Unit one hundred of those he first proposed, so that a Dollar should be 14 40-100, and a crown 16 units. I replied to this, and printed my notes and reply on a flying sheet, which I put into the hands of the members of Congress for consideration, and the Committee agreed to report on my principle. This was adopted the ensuing year, and is the system which now prevails.—AUTOBIOGRAPHY. i, 52. FORD ED., i, 73. (1820.) See MONEY, UNIT.

— **DOUBLE STANDARD.**—See MONEY.

2268. DOUBT, Caution in.—In case of doubt, it is better to say too little than too much.—To PRESIDENT WASHINGTON. FORD ED., v, 369. (Pa., 1791.)

2269. DRAFT, Unpopularity of.—In Virginia a draft was ever the most unpopular and impracticable thing that could be attempted. Our people, even under the monarchical government, had learned to consider it as the last of all oppressions.—To JOHN ADAMS. FORD ED., ii, 129. (Wg., 1777.)

2270. DRAWBACKS, Evils of.—With respect to the interests of the United States in this exuberant commerce which is now bringing war on us, we concur perfectly. It brings us into collision with other powers in every sea, and will force us into every war of the European powers. The converting this great agricultural country into a city of Amsterdam,—a mere headquarters for carrying on the commerce of all nations with one another, is too absurd. Yet this is the real object of the drawback system,—it enriches a few individuals, but lessens the stock of native productions, by withdrawing from them all the hands thus employed. It is essentially interesting to us to have shipping and seamen enough to carry our surplus produce to market; but beyond that, I do not think we are bound to give it encouragement by drawbacks or premiums. I wish you may be right in supposing that the trading States would now be willing to give up the drawbacks, and to denationalize all ships taking foreign articles on board for any other destination than the United States, on being secured by discriminating duties, or otherwise in the exclusive carryage of the produce of the United States. I should doubt it. Were such a proposition to come *from them*, I presume it would meet with little difficulty. Otherwise, I suppose it must wait till peace, when the right of drawback will be less valued than the exclusive carryage of our own produce.—To BENJAMIN STODDERT. v, 426. FORD ED., ix, 245. (W., Feb. 1809.)

2271. DRAWBACKS, Introduction of.—This most heterogeneous principle was transplanted into ours from the British system by a man [Alexander Hamilton] whose mind was really powerful, but chained by native partialities to everything English; who had formed exaggerated ideas of the superior perfection of the English constitution, the superior wisdom of their government, and sincerely believed it for the good of this country to make them their model in everything; without considering that what might be wise and good for a nation essentially commercial, and entangled in complicated intercourse with numerous and powerful neighbors, might not be so for one essentially agricultural, and insulated by nature from the abusive governments of the old world.—To WILLIAM H. CRAWFORD. vii, 6. FORD ED., x, 34. (M., 1816.)

2272. DRAWBACKS, Repeal of.—The inordinate extent given to commerce among us by our becoming the factors of the whole world, has enabled it to control the agricultural and manufacturing interests. When a change of circumstances shall reduce it to an equilibrium with these, to the carrying *our* produce only, to be exchanged for *our* wants, it will return to a wholesome condition for the body politic, and that beyond which it should never be encouraged to go. The repeal of the drawback system will either effect this, or bring sufficient sums into the treasury to meet the wars we shall bring on by our covering every sea with our vessels. But this must be the work of peace. The correction will be after my day, as the error originated before it.—To LARKIN SMITH. v, 441. (M., April 1809.)

2273. DRAWBACKS, Wars and.—I returned from Europe after our government had got under way, and had adopted from the British code the law of drawbacks. I early saw its effects in the jealousies and vexations of Britain; and that, retaining it, we must become, like her, an essentially warring nation, and meet, in the end, the catastrophe impending over her. No one can doubt that this alone produced the Orders of Council, the depredations which preceded, and the war which followed them. Had we carried but our own produce, and brought back but our own wants, no nation would have troubled us. * * * When war was declared, and especially after Massachusetts, who had produced it, took side with the enemy waging it, I pressed on some confidential friends in Congress to avail us of the happy opportunity of repealing the drawbacks and I do rejoice to find that you are in that sentiment. * * * It is one of three great measures necessary to insure us permanent prosperity. It preserves our peace. —To WILLIAM H. CRAWFORD. vii, 7. FORD ED., x, 35. (M., 1816.)

2274. DREAMS, Hints from.—We sometimes from dreams pick up some hint worth improving by * * * reflection.—To JAMES MONROE. FORD ED., x, 249. (M., 1823.)

2275. DREAMS, Utopian.—Mine, after all, may be an Utopian dream, but being inno-

cent, I have thought I might indulge in it till I go to the land of dreams, and sleep there with the dreamers of all past and future times.*— To M. CORREA. vii, 95. (P.F., 1817.)

2276. DRESS, Economy and.—The article of dress is perhaps that in which economy is the least to be recommended. It is so important [in married life] to each to continue to please the other, that the happiness of both requires the most pointed attention to whatever may contribute to it—and the more as time makes greater inroads on our person. Yet, generally, we become slovenly in proportion as personal decay requires the contrary.— To MARY JEFFERSON EPPES. D. L. J. 247. (Pa., 1798.)

2277. DRESS, Women's.—Some ladies think they may, under the privileges of the *déshabille*, be loose and negligent of their dress in the morning. But be you, from the moment you rise till you go to bed, as cleanly and properly dressed as at the hours of dinner or tea.—To MARTHA JEFFERSON. D. L. J. 71. (1783.)

— **DRUNKARDS.**—See INTEMPERANCE.

2278. DUANE (William), Assistance to. —The zeal, the disinterestedness, and the abilities with which you have supported the great principles of our [political] revolution, the persecutions you have suffered, and the firmness and independence with which you have suffered them, constitute too strong a claim on the good wishes of every friend of elective government to be effaced by a solitary case of difference in opinion. Thus I think, and thus I believed my much-esteemed friend Lieper would have thought; and I am the more concerned he does not, as it is so much more in his power to be useful to you than in mine. His residence, and his standing at the great seat of the moneyed institutions, command a credit with them, which no inhabitant of the country, and of agricultural pursuits only, can have. The two or three banks in our uncommercial State are too distant to have any relations with the farmers of Albemarle. We are persuaded you have not overrated the dispositions of this State to support yourself and your paper. They have felt its services too often to be indifferent in the hour of trial. They are well aware that the days of danger are not yet over. And I am sensible that if there were any means of bringing into concert the good will of the friends of the "Aurora" scattered over this State, they would not deceive your expectations. One month sooner might have found such an opportunity in the assemblage of our Legislature in Richmond. But that is now dispersed not to meet again under a twelvemonth. We, here, are but one of a hundred counties, and on consultation with friends of the neighborhood, it is their opinion that if we can find an endorser resident in Richmond, ten (for that is indispensable) or twelve persons of this county would readily engage, as you suggest, for their $100 each, and some of them for more. It is believed that the republicans in that city can and will do a great deal more; and perhaps their central position may enable them to communicate with other counties. We have written to a distinguished friend to the cause of liberty there to take the lead in the business, as far as

* Jefferson was discussing his popular and higher education plans for Virginia.—EDITOR.

concerns that place; and for our own, we are taking measures for obtaining the aid of the bank of the same place. In all this I am merely a cipher. Forty years of almost constant absence from the State have made me a stranger in it, have left me a solitary tree, from around which the axe of time has felled all the companions of its youth and growth. I have, however, engaged some active and zealous friends to do what I could not. * * * But our support can be but partial, and far short, both in time and measure, of your difficulties. They will be little more than evidences of our friendship.—To WILLIAM DUANE. v, 575. FORD ED., ix, 311. (M., 1811.)

2279. DUANE (William), Character of.—I believe Duane to be a very honest man and sincerely republican; but his passions are stronger than his prudence, and his personal as well as general antipathies render him very intolerant. These traits lead him astray, and require his readers, even those who value him for his steady support of the republican cause, to be on their guard against his occasional aberrations.—To WILLIAM WIRT. v, 595. FORD ED., ix, 319. (M., 1811.)

2280. DUANE (William), Defection of.—After so long a course of steady adherence to the general sentiments of the republicans, it would afflict me sincerely to see you separate from the body, become auxiliary to the enemies of our government, who have to you been the bitterest enemies, who are now chuckling at the prospect of division among us, and, as I am told, are subscribing for your paper.—To WILLIAM DUANE. v, 592. FORD ED., ix, 316. (M., April 1811.)

2281. DUANE (William), Office for.—Duane's defection from the republican ranks, his transition to the federalists, and giving triumph, in an important State, to wrong over right, have dissolved, of his own seeking, his connection with us. Yet the energy of his press when our cause was laboring, and all but lost under the overwhelming weight of its powerful adversaries, its unquestionable effect in the revolution produced in the public mind, which arrested the rapid march of our government towards monarchy, overweigh in fact the demerit of his desertion, when we had become too strong to suffer from it sensibly. He is, in truth, the victim of passions which his principles were not strong enough to control. Although, therefore, we are not bound to clothe him with the best robe, to put a ring on his finger, and to kill the fatted calf for him, yet neither should we leave him to eat husks with the swine.*—To JAMES MONROE. FORD ED., x, 275. (M. 1823.)

2282. ——— ———. I received a letter from some friend of yours who chose to be anonymous, suggesting that your situation might be bettered, and the government advantaged by availing itself of your services in some line. I immediately wrote to a friend whose situation enabled him to attend to this. I have received no answer but hope it is kept in view. I am long since withdrawn from the political world, think little, read less, and know all but nothing of what is going on; but I have not forgotten the past, nor those who were fellow laborers in the gloomy hours of federal ascendency when the spirit of republicanism was beaten down, its votaries arraigned as criminals, and such threats denounced as posterity would never believe.

* From a letter recommending Duane for office.—EDITOR.

My means of service are slender; but such as they are, if you can make them useful to you in any solicitation, they shall be sincerely employed.—To WILLIAM DUANE. FORD ED., x, 276. (M., 1824.)

2283. DUEL, Murder by.—Whosoever committeth murder by way of duel shall suffer death by hanging; and if he were the challenger, his body, after death, shall be gibbetted. He, who removeth it from the gibbet, shall be guilty of a misdemeanor, and the officer shall see that it be replaced.—CRIMES BILL. i, 150. FORD ED., ii, 207. (1779.)

2284. DUER (William), Failure of.—The stock-jobbing speculations have occupied some of our countrymen to such a degree as to give sincere uneasiness to those who would rather see their capitals employed in commerce, manufactures, buildings and agriculture. The failure of Mr. Duer, the chief of that description of people, has already produced some other bankruptcies, and more are apprehended. He had obtained money from great numbers of small tradesmen and farmers, tempting them by usurious interest, which has made the distress very extensive.—To DAVID HUMPHREYS. FORD ED., v, 502. (Pa., April 1792.)

2285. ——— ———. Duer, the King of the alley, is under a sort of check. The stocksellers say he will rise again. The stockbuyers count him out, and the credit and fate of the nation seem to hang on the desperate throws and plunges of gambling scoundrels.—To T. M. RANDOLPH. FORD ED., v, 455. (Pa., 1792.)

2286. DUER (William), Outbreak against.—It was reported here [Philadelphia] last night, that there had been a collection of people round the place of Duer's confinement, of so threatening an appearance, as to call out the Governor and militia, and to be fired on by them, and that several of them were killed. I hope it is not true. Nothing was wanting to fill up the criminality of this paper system, but to shed the blood of those whom it had cheated of their substance.—To FRANCIS EPPES. FORD ED., v, 508. (April 1792.)

2287. DUER (William), Threats of.—Duer now threatens that, if he is not relieved by certain persons, he will lay open to the world such a scene of villainy as will strike it with astonishment.—To JAMES MADISON. FORD ED., vi, 213. (Pa., 1793.)

2288. DUMAS (C. W. F.), Agency of.—Would it not be worth while to continue the agency of Dumas? * * * He is undoubtedly in the confidence of some one who has a part in the Dutch government, and who seems to allow him to communicate to us.—To JAMES MONROE. FORD ED., iv, 8. (P., 1784.)

2289. ——— ———. Mr. Dumas, very early in the [Revolutionary] war, was employed first by Dr. Franklin, afterwards by Mr. Adams, to transact the affairs of the United States in Holland. Congress never passed any express vote of confirmation, but they opened a direct correspondence with Mr. Dumas, sent him orders to be executed, confirmed and augmented his salary, made that augmentation retrospective, directed him to take up his residence in their hotel at the Hague, and passed such other votes from time to time as established him *de facto* their agent at the Hague. On the change in the organization of our government in 1789, no commission nor new appointment took place with respect to him, though it did in most other cases; yet the correspondence with him from the office of Foreign Affairs has been continued, and he has regularly received his salary.—To President Washington. iii, 331. Ford ed., v, 437. (Pa., 1792.)

2290. DUMAS (C. W. F.), Congress and.—On the 18th of this month, I received a letter from his Excellency, the Count de Vergennes, expressing the interest which he takes in your welfare, and recommending you to Congress.—To C. W. F. Dumas. i, 528. Ford ed., iv, 190. (P., 1786.)

2291. —— ——. I am pressed on so many hands to recommend Dumas to the patronage of Congress, that I cannot avoid it. Everybody speaks well of him, and his zeal in our cause. Anything done for him will gratify this court [France], and the patriotic party in Holland, as well as some distinguished individuals. —To Elbridge Gerry. i, 557. (P., 1786.)

2292. —— ——. I enclose you a letter from the Count de Vergennes in favor of Mr. Dumas. With the services of this gentleman to the United States, yourself and Dr. Franklin are better acquainted than I am. Those he has been able to render towards effecting the late alliance between France and the United Netherlands are the probable ground of the present application.—To John Jay. i, 524. (P., 1786.)

2293. —— ——. I was gratified with the receipt of your favor * * * containing a copy of the resolution of Congress of October 24th, 1785, in your favor, and which I wish had been more so.—To C. W. F. Dumas. i, 528. (P., 1786.)

2294. DUMAS (C. W. F.), Holland and. —Besides former applications to me in favor of Dumas, the Rhingrave of Salm (the effective minister of the government of Holland, while their two embassadors here are ostensible, and) who is conducting secret arrangements for them with this court, presses his interests on us. It is evident the two governments make a point of it. You ask why they do not provide for him themselves? I am not able to answer the question, but by a conjecture that Dumas's particular ambition prefers an appointment from us. I know all the difficulty about this application which Congress has to encounter. I see the reasons against giving him the primary appointment at that court, and the difficulty of his accommodating himself to a subordinate one. Yet I think something must be done in it to gratify this court [France], of which we must be always asking favors. In these countries, personal favors weigh more than public interest. The minister who has asked a gratification for Dumas, has embarked his own feelings and reputation in that demand. I do not think it was discreet by any means. But this reflection might, perhaps, aggravate a disappointment. I know not really what you can do; but yet hope something will be done.—To James Monroe. i, 568. Ford ed., iv, 226. (P., 1786.)

2295. —— ——. Dumas is a great favorite both of Holland and France.—To James Monroe. i, 526. (P., 1786.)

2296. DUMOURIEZ (C. F.), Apostacy of.—From the steadiness of the French people on the defection of so popular and capital a commander as Dumouriez, we have a proof that nothing can shake their republicanism.—To James Madison. iv, 8. Ford ed., vi, 325. (1793.)

2297. DUMOURIEZ (C. F.), A scoundrel.—Dumouriez was known to be a scoundrel in grain. I mentioned this from the beginning of his being placed at the head of the armies; but his victories at length silenced me. His apostasy has now proved that an unprincipled man, let his other fitnesses be what they will, ought never to be employed. It has proved, too, that the French army, as well as nation, cannot be shaken in their republicanism. Dumouriez's popularity put it to as severe a proof as could be offered.—To Dr. George Gilmer. iv, 5. Ford ed., vi, 324. (Pa., 1793.)

2298. DUMOURIEZ (C. F.), Without Virtue.—No confidence in Dumouriez's virtue opposes the story that he has gone over to the Austrians; for he has none.—To Martha Jefferson Randolph. Ford ed., vi, 267. (Pa., 1793.)

2299. DUNBAR (William), Esteem for. —I recommend to your particular civilities and respect Mr. William Dunbar, a person of great worth and wealth in New Orleans, and one of the most distinguished citizens of the United States in point of science. He is a correspondent of mine in that line in whom I set great store. As a native of Britain, he must have a predilection towards her; but as to every other nation he is purely American.—To William C. Claiborne. Ford ed., viii, 72. (W., 1801.)

2300. DUNMORE (Lord), Defeated.— Lord Dunmore has commenced hostilities in Virginia. That people bore with everything, till he attempted to burn the town of Hampton. They opposed and repelled him, with considerable loss on his side, and none on ours. It has raised our countrymen into a perfect phrenzy.— To John Randolph. i, 203. Ford ed., i, 492. (Pa., November 1775.)

2301. DUPLICITY, Disdained.—I disdain everything like duplicity.—To James Madison. iv, 194. Ford ed., vii, 166. (M., 1797.)

2302. DUPONT DE NEMOURS, America and.—I pray you to cherish Dupont. He has the best disposition for the continuance of friendship between the two nations, and perhaps you may be able to make a good use of him.—To Robert R. Livingston. iv, 434. Ford ed., viii, 147. (W., 1802.)

2303. DUPONT DE NEMOURS, Confidence in.—You will perceive the unlimited confidence I repose in your good faith, and in your cordial dispositions to serve both countries, when you observe that I leave the letters for Chancellor Livingston open for your perusal. The first page respects a cipher, as do the loose sheets folded with the letter. These are interesting to him and myself only, and therefore are not for your perusal. It is the second, third, and fourth pages which I wish you to read, to possess yourself of completely, and then seal the letter with wafers stuck under the flying seal, that it may be seen by nobody else if any accident should happen to you. I wish you to be possessed of the subject, because you may be able to impress on the government of France the inevitable consequences of their taking possession of Louisiana; and though, as I here mention, the cession of New Orleans and the Floridas to us would be a palliation, yet I believe it would be no more, and that this measure will cost France, and perhaps not very long hence, a war which will annihilate her on the ocean, and place that element under the despotism of two nations, which I am not reconciled to the more because my own would be one of them.—To M. DUPONT DE NEMOURS. iv, 435. (W., April 1802.)

2304. DUPONT DE NEMOURS, Louisiana Purchase and.—The confidence which the government of France reposes in you, will undoubtedly give great weight to your information [with respect to Louisiana]. An equal confidence on our part, founded on your knowledge of the subject, your just views of it, your good dispositions towards this country, and my long experience of your personal faith and friendship, assure me that you will render between us all the good offices in your power. The interests of the two countries being absolutely the same as to this matter, your aid may be conscientiously given. It will often, perhaps, be possible for you, having a freedom of communication, *omnibus horis*, which diplomatic gentlemen will be excluded from by forms, to smooth difficulties by representations and reasonings, which would be received with more suspicion from them. You will thereby render great good to both countries.—To P. S. DUPONT DE NEMOURS. iv, 457. FORD ED., viii, 205. (W., Feb. 1803.)

2305. DUPUIS (C. F.), Works of.—Your undertaking [to read] the twelve volumes of Dupuis, is a degree of heroism to which I could not have aspired even in my younger days. I have been contented with the humble achievement of reading the analysis of his work by Destutt Tracy, in two hundred pages octavo. I believe I should have ventured on his own abridgment of the work, in one octavo volume, had it ever come to my hands; but the marrow of it in Tracy has satisfied my appetite; and even in that, the preliminary discourse of the analyser himself, and his conclusion, are worth more in my eye than the body of the work. For the object of that seems to be to smother all history under the mantle of allegory. If histories so unlike as that of Hercules and Jesus, can, by a fertile imagination and allegorical interpretations, be brought to the same tally, no line of distinction remains between fact and fancy.—To JOHN ADAMS. vii, 38. (M., 1816.)

2306. DUTIES, Discriminating.—It is true we must expect some inconvenience in practice from the establishment of discriminating duties. But in this, as in so many other cases, we are left to choose between two evils. These inconveniences are nothing when weighed against the loss of wealth and loss of force, which will follow our perseverance in the plan of indiscrimination. When once it shall be perceived that we are either i.. the system, or in the habit, of giving equal advantages to those who extinguish our commerce and navigation by duties and prohibitions, as to those who treat both with liberality and justice, liberality and justice will be converted by all into duties and prohibitions. It is not to the moderation and justice of others we are to trust for fair and equal access to market with our productions, or for our due share in the transportation of them; but to our means of independence, and the firm will to use them. Nor do the incon-

veniences of discrimination merit consideration. * * * Perhaps not a commercial nation on earth is without them.—FOREIGN COMMERCE REPORT. vii, 650. FORD ED., vi, 483. (Dec. 1793.)

2307. ———— ————. Between nations who favor our productions and navigation and those who do not favor them, one distinction alone will suffice; one set of moderate duties for the first, and a fixed advance on these as to some articles; and prohibitions as to others, for the last.—FOREIGN COMMERCE REPORT. vii, 650. FORD ED., vi, 483. (Dec. 1793.)

2308. ———— ————. If the commercial regulations had been adopted which our Legislature were at one time proposing, we should at this moment have been standing on such an eminence of safety and respect as ages can never recover. But having wandered from that, our object should now be to get back, with as little loss as possible, and, when peace shall be restored to the world, endeavor so to form our *commercial* regulations as that justice from other nations shall be their mechanical result.—To THOMAS PINCKNEY. iv, 177. FORD ED., vii, 129. (Pa., May 1797.)

2309. ———— ————. To those [nations] who refuse the admission [to the West Indies] we must refuse our commerce, or load theirs by odious discriminations in our ports.—To JAMES MONROE. i, 351. FORD ED., iv, 58. (P,. 1785.)

2310. DUTIES, Prohibitory.—Should any nation, contrary to our wishes, suppose it may better find its advantage by continuing its system of prohibitions, duties and regulations, it behooves us to protect our citizens, their commerce and navigation, by counter prohibitions, duties and regulations, also. Free commerce and navigation are not to be given in exchange for restrictions and vexations; nor are they likely to produce a relaxation of them.—FOREIGN COMMERCE REPORT. vii, 647. FORD ED., vi, 480. (Dec. 1793.)

2311. DUTIES, Reciprocal.—Some nations not yet ripe for free commerce in all its extent, might still be willing to mollify its restrictions and regulations for us, in proportion to the advantages which an intercourse with us might offer. Particularly they may concur with us in reciprocating the duties to be levied on each side, or in compensating any excess of duty by equivalent advantages of another nature.—FOREIGN COMMERCE REPORT. vii, 646. FORD ED., vi, 479. (Dec. 1793.)

2312. DUTIES, Retaliatory.—Massachusetts has passed an act, the first object of which seemed to be, to retaliate on the British commercial measures, but in the close of it, they impose double duties on all goods imported in bottoms not wholly owned by citizens of our States. New Hampshire has followed the example. This is much complained of here [France], and will probably draw retaliating measures from the States of Europe, if generally adopted in America, or not corrected by the States which have adopted it. It must be our endeavor to keep them quiet on this side the water, under the hope that our countrymen will correct this step; as I trust they will do. It is no ways akin to their general system.—To WILLIAM CARMICHAEL. i, 475. (P., 1785.) See TARIFF.

2313. DUTIES (Governmental), Division of.—In government, as well as in every other business of life, it is by division and subdivision of duties alone, that all matters, great and small, can be managed to perfection. And the whole is cemented by giving to every citizen, personally, a part in the administration of the public affairs.—To SAMUEL KERCHIVAL. vii, 13. FORD ED., x, 41. (M., 1816.)

— DUTIES, Natural.—See DUTY and NATURAL RIGHTS.

2314. DUTY, Ability and.— A debt of service is due from every man to his country proportioned to the bounties which nature and fortune have measured to him.—To EDWARD RUTLEDGE. iv, 152. FORD ED., vii, 94. (M., 1796.) See OFFICE.

2315. DUTY, Administrative.—On taking this station [Presidency] on a former occasion, I declared the principles on which I believed it my duty to administer the affairs of our commonwealth. My conscience tells me that I have, on every occasion, acted up to that declaration, according to its obvious import, and to the understanding of every candid mind.—SECOND INAUGURAL ADDRESS. viii, 40. FORD ED., viii, 342. (1805.)

2316. —— ——. It was my lot to be placed at the head of the column which made the first breach in the ramparts of federalism, and to be charged on that event, with the duty of changing the course of the government from what we deemed a monarchical to its republican tack. This made me the mark for every shaft which calumny and falsehood could point against me. I bore them with resignation, as one of the duties imposed on me by my post. But * * * it was among the most painful duties from which I hoped to find relief in retirement.—To MARK LANGDON HILL. vii, 154. (M., 1820.)

2317. DUTY, Age and.—I should not shrink from the post of duty, had not the decays of nature withdrawn me from the list of combatants.—To SPENCER ROANE. vii, 211. FORD ED., x, 188. (M., 1821.)

2318. DUTY vs. COMFORT.—Renounce your domestic comforts for a few months, and reflect that to be a good husband and good father at this moment, you must be also a good citizen.—To ELBRIDGE GERRY. iv, 189. FORD ED., vii, 151. (Pa., 1797.)

2319. DUTY, Danger and.—I would really go away [from Philadelphia] because I think there is rational danger [from the yellow fever], but that I had before announced that I should not go till the begin-

ning of October, and I do not like to exhibit the appearance of panic. Besides that, I think there might serious ills proceed from there being not a single member of the administration in place.—To JAMES MADISON. FORD ED., vi, 419. (Sep. 1793.)

2320. DUTY, Filial.—A lively and lasting sense of filial duty is more effectually impressed on the mind of a son or daughter by reading King Lear, than by all the dry volumes of ethics and divinity that ever were written.—To ROBERT SKIPWITH. FORD ED., i, 398. (1771.)

2321. DUTY, Fulfilled.—I determined to set out for Virginia as soon as I could clear my own letter files. I have now got through it so as to leave not a single letter unanswered, or anything undone, which is in a state to be done.—To PRESIDENT WASHINGTON. FORD ED., vi, 428. (1793.)

2322. DUTY, Honest discharge of.—He who has done his duty honestly, and according to his best skill and judgment, stands acquitted before God and man.—THE BATTURE CASE. viii, 602. (1812.)

2323. DUTY, Imperial.—Only aim to do your duty, and mankind will give you credit where you fail.*—RIGHTS OF BRITISH AMERICA. i, 141. FORD ED., i, 446. (1774.)

2324. DUTY TO MANKIND.—We have, willingly, done injury to no man; and have done for our country the good which has fallen in our way, so far as commensurate with the faculties given us. That we have not done more than we could, cannot be imputed to us as a crime before any tribunal. I look, therefore, to the crisis as one *"qui summum nec metuit diem nec optat."*—To JOHN ADAMS. vii, 154. (1820.)

2325. —— ——. I have done for my country, and for all mankind, all that I could do, and I now resign my soul, without fear, to my God; my daughter, to my country.†—RAYNER'S LIFE OF JEFFERSON. 554. (1826.)

2326. DUTY, Men of eminence and.—Some men are born for the public. Nature by fitting them for the service of the human race on a broad scale, has stamped them with the evidences of her destination and their duty.—To JAMES MONROE. iv, 455. FORD ED., viii, 190. (W., 1803.)

2327. DUTY, Merit and.—If it be found that I have done my duty as other faithful citizens have done, it is all the merit I claim.—R. To A GEORGETOWN REPUBLICANS. viii, 159. (1809.)

2328. —— ——. One of those who entered into public life at the commencement of an era the most extraordinary which the

---

* To George III.—EDITOR.

† B. L. Rayner, in his *Life of Jefferson*, says: "These were the last words Jefferson articulated. * * * All that was heard from him afterwards, was a hurried repetition, in indistinct and scarcely audible accents, of his favorite ejaculation, *Nunc Dimittis, Domine—Nunc Dimittis, Domine.*"—EDITOR.

history of man has ever yet presented to his contemplation, I claim nothing more, for the part I have acted in it, than a common merit of having, with others, faithfully endeavored to do my duty in the several stations allotted to me.—R. To A. VIRGINIA ASSEMBLY. viii. 148. (1809.)

2329. DUTY, Natural.—Every man is under the natural duty of contributing to the necessities of the society; and this is all the laws should enforce on him.—To F. W. GILMER. vii, 3. FORD ED., x, 32. (M., 1816.)

2330. —— ——. No man having a natural right to be the judge between himself and another, it is his natural duty to submit to the umpirage of an impartial third.—To F. W. GILMER. vii, 3. FORD ED., x, 32. (M., 1816.) See NATURAL RIGHTS.

2331. DUTY, Obstacles and.—The zealous citizen, unable to do his duty so soon as was prescribed, will do it as soon as he can.—LETTER TO MEMBERS OF VA. ASSEMBLY. FORD ED., ii, 434. (R., 1781.)

2332. DUTY, Office and.—Could I have persuaded myself that public offices were made for private convenience, I should undoubtedly have preferred a continuance in the French mission, which placed me nearer to you; but believing, on the contrary, that a good citizen should take his stand where the public authority marshals him, I have acquiesced.—To MADAME LA DUCHESSE D'AUVILLE. iii, 134. FORD ED., v, 153. (N. Y., 1790.)

2333. DUTY, Rank and.—I think with the Romans of old, that the general of to-day should be a common soldier to-morrow, if necessary.—To JAMES MADISON. iv, 155. FORD ED., vii, 99. (1797.)

2334. DUTY, Rewards for.—The first of all our consolations is that of having faithfully fulfilled our duties; the next, the approbation and good will of those who have witnessed it.—To JAMES FISBACK. v, 471. (M., 1809.)

2335. DUTY, Right and.—Our part is to pursue with steadiness what is right, turning neither to right nor left for the intrigues or popular delusions of the day, assured that the public approbation will in the end be with us.—To GENERAL BRECKENRIDGE. vii, 238. (M., 1822.)

2336. DUTY, Silent performance of.—The attaching circumstance of my present office [Minister to France] is that I can do its duties unseen by those for whom they are done.—To F. HOPKINSON. ii, 587. FORD ED., v, 78. (P., 1789.)

2337. —— ——. My great wish is to go on in a strict but silent performance of my duty; to avoid attracting notice, and to keep my name out of newspapers.—To F. HOPKINSON. ii, 587. FORD ED., v, 78. (P., 1789.)

2338. DUTY, Suborned from.—Those whom the Constitution had placed as guards to its portals are sophisticated or suborned from their duties.—To DR. J. B. STUART. vii, 65. (M., 1817.)

—— DUTY, Tours of Official.—See OFFICE.

2339. EARTH, Belongs to the Living. —The ground * * * I suppose to be self-evident, "that *the earth belongs in usufruct to the living*"; that the dead have neither powers nor rights over it. The portion occupied by any individual ceases to be his when himself ceases to be, and reverts to the society.—To JAMES MADISON. iii, 103. FORD ED., v, 116. (P., 1789.)

2340. —— ——. The earth belongs always to the living generation. They may manage it, and what proceeds from it, as they please, during their usufruct.—To JAMES MADISON. iii, 106. FORD ED., v, 121. (P., 1789.)

2341. —— ——. The principle that the earth belongs to the living and not to the dead, is of very extensive application and consequences in every country, and most especially in France. It enters into the resolution of the questions, whether the nation may change the descent of lands holden in tail? Whether they may change the appropriation of lands given anciently to the Church, to hospitals, colleges, orders of chivalry, and otherwise in perpetuity? whether they may abolish the charges and privileges attached on lands, including the whole catalogue, ecclesiastical and feudal; it goes to hereditary offices, authorities and jurisdictions; to hereditary orders, distinctions and appellations; to perpetual monopolies in commerce, the arts or sciences; with a long train of *et ceteras;* and it renders the question of reimbursement a question of generosity and not of right. In all these cases the legislature of the day could authorize such appropriations and establishments for their own time, but no longer; and the present holders, even where they or their ancestors have purchased, are in the case of *bona fide* purchasers of what the seller had no right to convey.— To JAMES MADISON. iii, 107. FORD ED., v, 122. (P., 1789.)

2342. —— ——. The earth belongs to the living, not to the dead. The will and the power of man expire with his life, by nature's law. Some societies give it an artificial continuance, for the encouragement of industry; some refuse it, as our aboriginal neighbors, whom we call barbarians. The generations of men may be considered as bodies or corporations. Each generation has the usufruct of the earth during the period of its continuance. When it ceases to exist the usufruct passes on to the succeeding generation, free and unencumbered, and so on, successively, from one generation to another forever.—To JOHN WAYLES EPPES. vi, 136. FORD ED., ix, 389. (M., June 1813.)

2343. —— ——. This corporeal globe, and everything upon it, belong to its present cor-

poreal inhabitants, during their generation.—
To SAMUEL KERCHIVAL. vii, 16. FORD ED.,
x. 44. (M., 1816.)

2344. —— ——. Our Creator made the
earth for the use of the living and not of
the dead. Those who exist not have no use,
or right in it, no authority or power over it.—
To THOMAS EARLE. vii, 310. (M., 1823.)

2345. EARTH, Equal Rights in.—The
earth is given as a common stock for man to
labor and live on.—To REV. JAMES MADISON.
FORD ED., vii, 36. (Pa., 1785.)

2346. —— ——. If, for the encouragement of industry, we allow the earth to be
appropriated, we must take care that other
employment be provided to those excluded
from the appropriation. If we do not, the
fundamental right to labor the earth returns
to the employed.—To REV. JAMES MADISON.
FORD ED., vii, 36. (P., 1785.)

2347. EARTH, God's Gift.—The soil is
the gift of God to the living.—To JOHN W.
EPPES. vi, 138. FORD ED., ix, 391. M.,
1813.) See GENERATIONS.

2348. EARTH, Internal Heat of.—The
term "central heat" does of itself give us a
false idea of Buffon's hypothesis. If it means
a heat lodged in the centre of the earth, and diffusing its warmth from thence to the extremities, then certainly it would be less in proportion to the distance from that centre, and, of
course, less under the equator than the poles,
on high mountains than in deep valleys. But
Buffon's theory is that this earth was once in
a state of hot fusion, and that it has been, and
still continues to be cooling. What is the
course of this process? A heated body being
surrounded by a colder one, whether solid or
fluid, the heat, which is itself a fluid, flows into
the colder body equally from every point of the
hotter. Hence if a heated spheroid of iron cools
to a given degree, in a given space of time, an
inch deep from its surface in one point, it
has in the same time done the same in any and
every other point. In a given time more, it will
be cooled all around to double that depth. So
that it will always be equally cooled at equal
depths from the surface. This would be the
case with Buffon's earth, if it were a smooth
figure without unevennesses. But it has mountains and valleys. The tops of mountains will
cool to greater depths in the same time than
the sides of mountains, and than plains in

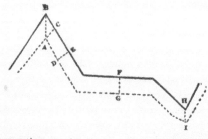

proportion as the line A. B. is longer than
A. C. or D. E. or F. G. In the valley line
H. I., on depth of the same temperature, will
be the same as on a plain. This, however, is
very different from Buffon's opinion. He says

that the earth, being thinnest at the poles, will
cool sooner there than under the equator, where
it is thicker. If my idea of the process of
cooling be right, his is wrong, and his whole
theory in the Epochs of Nature, is overset.—To
JAMES MADISON. FORD ED., iii. 369. (A., 1784.)

2349. EARTH, Theory of Creation.—I
give one answer to all theorists. That is as
follows: They all suppose the earth a created
existence. They must suppose a Creator then;
and that He possessed power and wisdom to a
great degree. As He intended the earth for
the habitation of animals and vegetables, is it
reasonable to suppose He made two jobs of His
creation, that He first made a chaotic lump and
set it into motion, and then, waiting the ages
necessary to form itself—that when it had done
this, He stepped in a second time, to create the
animals and plants which were to inhabit it?
As a hand of a Creator is to be called in, it
may as well be called in at one stage of the
process as another. We may as well suppose He
created the earth at once, nearly in the state
in which we see it, fit for the preservation of
the beings He placed on it. But, it is said, we
have a proof that He did not create it in its
present solid form, but in a state of fluidity;
because its present shape of an oblate spheroid
is precisely that which a fluid mass, revolving
on its axis, would assume; but I suppose the
same equilibrium between gravity and centrifugal force, which would determine a fluid
mass into the form of an oblate spheroid,
would determine the wise Creator of that mass,
if he made it in a solid state, to give it the
same spheroidical form. A revolving fluid
will continue to change its shape, till it attains
that in which its principles of contrary motion
are balanced; for if you suppose them not balanced, it will change its form. Now, the balanced form is necessary for the preservation of
a revolving solid. The Creator, therefore, of a
revolving solid, would make it an oblate
spheroid, that figure alone admitting a perfect
equilibrium. He would make it in that form
for another reason; that is, to prevent a shifting
of the axis of rotation. Had He created the
earth perfectly spherical, its axis might have
been perpetually shifting, by the influence of the
other bodies of the system, and by placing the
inhabitants of the earth successively under its
poles, it might have been depopulated; whereas,
being spheroidal, it has but one axis on which
it can revolve in *equilibrio*. Suppose the axis
of the earth to shift forty-five degrees; then
cut it into one hundred and eighty slices, making every section in the plane of a circle of
latitude perpendicular to the axis: every one
of these slices, except the equatorial one, would
be unbalanced, as there would be more matter
on one side of its axis than on the other.
There could be but one diameter drawn through
such a slice which would divide it into two
equal parts; on every other possible diameter,
the parts would hang unequal. This would produce an irregularity in the diurnal motion. We
may, therefore, conclude it impossible for the
poles of the earth to shift, if it was made
spheroidically, and that it would be made
spheroidal, though solid, to obtain this end.
I use this reasoning only on the supposition that
the earth has had a beginning. I am sure I
shall read your conjectures on this subject with
great pleasure. though I bespeak, beforehand,
a right to indulge my natural incredulity and
scepticism.—To CHARLES THOMSON. ii, 68.
FORD ED., iv, 338. (P., 1786.)

2350. EAST INDIES, Trade to.—Philadelphia and New York have begun trade to the

East Indies. Perhaps Boston may follow their example. But their importations will be sold only to the country adjacent to them. For a long time to come, the States south of the Delaware will not engage in a direct commerce with the East Indies. They neither have, nor will have ships or seamen for their other commerce; nor will they buy East India goods of the northern States. Experience shows that the States never bought foreign goods of one another. The reasons are that they would, in so doing, pay double freight and charges; and again that they would have to pay mostly in cash what they could obtain for commodities in Europe. I know that the American merchants have looked with some anxiety to the arrangements to be taken with Portugal, in expectation that they could, through her, get their East India articles on better and more convenient terms; and I am of opinion, Portugal will come in for a good share of this traffic with the southern States, if they facilitate our payments.—To JOHN ADAMS. i, 493. (P., 1785.)

2351. EAST AND WEST LINE, Meaning of.—On the question what is an east and west line? which, you say, has been a subject of discussion in the papers, I presume * * * that the parties have differed only in applying the same appellation to different things. The one defines an east and west line to be on a great circle of the earth, passing through the point of departure, its nadir point, and the centre of the earth, its plane rectangular, to that of the meridian of departure. The other considers an east and west line to be a line on the surface of the earth, bounding a plane at right angles with its axis, or a circle of latitude passing through the point of departure, or in other words, a line which, from the point of departure, passes every meridian at a right angle. Each party, therefore, defining the line he means, may be permitted to call it an east and west one, or at least it becomes no longer a mathematical but a philological question of the meaning of the words east and west. The last is what was meant probably by the east and west line in the treaty of Ghent. The same has been the understanding in running the numerous east and west lines which divide our different States. They have been run by observations of latitude at very short intervals, uniting the points of observation by short direct lines, and thus constituting in fact part of a polygon of very short sides.—To CHILES TERRIL. vii, 260. (M., 1822.)

2352. ECONOMY, Domestic.—Domestic economy * * * [is] of more solid value than anything else.—To MRS. EPPES. D. L. J. 127. (P., 1787.)

2353. ——— ———. In household economy, the mothers of our country are generally skilled, and generally careful to instruct their daughters. We all know its value, and that diligence and dexterity in all its processes are inestimable treasures. The order and economy of a house are as honorable to the mistress as those of the farm to the master. and if either be neglected, ruin follows, and children destitute of the means of living.— To N. BURWELL. vii, 103. FORD ED., x, 106. (M., 1818.)

2354. ECONOMY, An Essential Principle.—Economy in the public expense, that labor may be lightly burdened, I deem [one of the] essential principles of our government and, consequently [one] which ought to shape its administration.—FIRST INAUGURAL ADDRESS. viii, 4. FORD ED., viii, 5. (1801.)

2355. ——— ———. To expend the public money with the same care and economy [that] we would practice with our own, * * * [is one of] the land marks by which we are to guide ourselves in all our proceedings.—SECOND ANNUAL MESSAGE. viii, 21. FORD ED., viii, 187. (Dec. 1802.)

2356. ——— ———. The same prudence, which, in private life. would forbid our paying our money for unexplained projects, forbids it in the disposition of the public moneys. —To SHELTON GILLIAM. v, 301. (W., 1808.)

2357. ECONOMY, Evil of want of.—We see in England the consequences of the want of economy; their laborers reduced to live on a penny in the shilling of their earnings, to give up bread, and resort to oatmeal and potatoes for food; and their landholders exiling themselves to live in penury and obscurity abroad, because at home the government must have all the clear profits of their land. In fact, they see the fee simple of the island transferred to the public creditors, all its profits going to them for the interest of their debts. Our laborers and landholders must come to this also, unless they severely adhere to the economy you recommend.—To GOVERNOR PLUMER. vii, 19. (M., 1816.)

2358. ECONOMY, Happiness and.—If we can prevent the government from wasting the labors of the people, under the pretence of taking care of them, they must become happy. —To THOMAS COOPER. iv, 453. FORD ED., viii, 178. (W., 1802.)

2359. ECONOMY, Honesty and.—A rigid economy of the public contributions, and absolute interdiction of all useless expenses, will go far towards keeping the government honest and unoppressive.—To MARQUIS LAFAYETTE. vii, 325. FORD ED., x, 280. (M., 1823.)

2360. ECONOMY, Ignorance of Political.—I transmit for M. Tracy * * * a translation of his *Economie Politique*, which we have made and published here in the hope of advancing our countrymen somewhat in that science; the most profound ignorance of which threatened irreparable disaster during the late war, and by the parasite institutions of banks is now consuming the public industry.—To ALBERT GALLATIN. FORD ED., x, 116. (M., 1818.)

2361. ECONOMY, Insisting on.—We shall push Congress to the uttermost in economizing.—To NATHANIEL MACON. iv, 397. (W., May 1801.)

2362. ECONOMY, Liberty and.—We must make our election between *economy and liberty*, or *profusion* and *servitude*.—To SAMUEL KERCHIVAL. vii, 14. FORD ED., x, 41. (M., 1816.)

2363. ECONOMY, Necessity for.—[We are] conscious that our endeavors to reconcile economy and the public wants must meet with the approbation of every person, who attends at all to the dangers impending over us from circumscribed finances.—To THE PRESIDENT OF CONGRESS. FORD ED., ii, 337. (R., 1780.)

2364. ECONOMY vs. NEW LOANS.—I learn with great satisfaction that wholesome economies have been found, sufficient to relieve us from the ruinous necessity of adding annually to our debt by new loans. The deviser of so salutary a relief deserves truly well of his country.—To SAMUEL SMITH. vii, 284. FORD ED., x, 251. (M., 1823.) See LOANS.

2365. ECONOMY, Political.—In so complicated a science as political economy, no one axiom can be laid down as wise and expedient for all times and circumstances, and for their contraries.—To BENJAMIN AUSTIN. vi, 523. FORD ED., x, 10. (M., Jan. 1816.)

2366. —— ——. Political economy in modern times assumed the form of a regular science first in the hands of the political sect in France, called the Economists. They made it a branch only of a comprehensive system on the natural order of societies. Quesnay first, Gournay, Le Frosne, Turgot, and Dupont de Nemours, the enlightened, philanthropic, and venerable citizen, now of the United States, led the way in these developments, and gave to our inquiries the direction they have since observed. Many sound and valuable principles established by them have received the sanction of general approbation. Some, as in the infancy of a science might be expected, have been brought into question, and have furnished occasion for much discussion. Their opinions on production, and on the proper subjects of taxation, have been particularly controverted; and whatever may be the merit of their principles of taxation, it is not wonderful they have not prevailed; not on the questioned score of correctness, but because not acceptable to the people, whose will must be the supreme law. Taxation is, in fact, the most difficult function of government, and that against which their citizens are most apt to be refractory. The general aim is, therefore, to adopt the mode most consonant with the circumstances and sentiments of the country. Adam Smith, first in England, published a rational and systematic work on Political Economy, adopting generally the ground of the Economists, but differing on the subjects before specified. The system being novel, much argument and detail seemed then necessary to establish principles which now are assented to as soon as proposed. Hence his book, admitted to be able, and of the first degree of merit, has yet been considered as prolix and tedious. In France, John Baptisté Say has the merit of producing a very superior work on the subject of Political Economy. His arrangement is luminous, ideas clear, style perspicuous,

and the whole subject brought within half the volume of Smith's work. Add to this considerable advances in correctness and extension of principles. The work of Senator [Destutt] Tracy, now announced, comes forward with all the lights of his predecessors in the science, and with the advantages of further experience, more discussion, and greater maturity of subjects. It is certainly distinguished by important traits: a cogency of logic which has never been exceeded in any work, a rigorous enchainment of ideas, and constant recurrence to it to keep it in the reader's view, a fearless pursuit of truth whithersoever it leads, and a diction so correct that not a word can be changed but for the worse * * * —INTRODUCTION TO DESTUTT TRACY'S POLITICAL ECONOMY. vi, 570. (1816.) See TRACY.

2367. ECONOMY, Prodigality vs.—To reform the prodigalities of our predecessors is * * * peculiarly our duty, and to bring the government to a simple and economical course.—To JAMES MONROE. iv, 455. FORD ED., viii, 191. (W., 1803.)

2368. ECONOMY, A Republican virtue.—I place economy among the first and most important of republican virtues.—To GOVERNOR PLUMER. vii, 19. (M. 1816.)

2369. —— ——. I am for a government rigorously frugal and simple, applying all the possible savings of the public revenue to the discharge of the national debt.—To ELBRIDGE GERRY. iv, 268. FORD ED., vii, 327. (Pa., 1799.)

2370. ECONOMY, Rigorous.—The new government has now, for some time, been under way. * * * Abuses under the old forms have led us to lay the basis of the new in a rigorous economy of the public contributions.—To M. DE PINTO. iii, 174. (N. Y., 1790.)

2371. —— ——. We are endeavoring to reduce the government to the practice of a rigorous economy, to avoid burthening the people, and arming the magistrate with a patronage of money, which might be used to corrupt and undermine the principles of our government.—To M. PICTET. iv, 463. (W., 1803.)

2372. —— ——. I may err in my measures, but never shall deflect from the intention to fortify the public liberty by every possible means, and to put it out of the power of the few to riot on the labors of the many. —To JUDGE TYLER. iv, 548. (W., 1804.)

2373. ECONOMY vs. TAXATION.—When, merely by avoiding false objects of expense, we are able, without a direct tax, without internal taxes, and without borrowing, to make large and effectual payments toward the discharge of our public debt and the emancipation of our posterity from that moral canker, it is an encouragement of the highest order, to proceed as we have begun, in substituting economy for taxation, and in pursuing what is useful for a nation placed as we are, rather than what is practiced by others under different circumstances.—SECOND ANNUAL MESSAGE, viii, 19. FORD ED., viii, 185. (Dec. 1802.)

2374. ECONOMY, Wisdom of.—Our public economy is such as to offer drudgery and subsistence only to those entrusted with its administration,—a wise and necessary precaution against the degeneracy of the public servants.—To M. DE MEUNIER. FORD ED., vii, 14. (M., 1795.)

2375. EDEN (William), Hatred of the United States.—Mr. Eden is appointed ambassador from England to Madrid. To the hatred borne us by his court and country is added a recollection of the circumstances of the unsuccessful embassy to America, of which he made a part. I think he will carry to Madrid dispositions to do us all the ill he can.—To JOHN JAY. ii, 158. (P., 1787.)

2376. —— ——. We had often * * * occasions of knowing each other. His peculiar bitterness towards us had sufficiently appeared, and I had never concealed from him that I considered the British as our natural enemies, and as the only nation on earth who wished us ill from the bottom of their souls. And I am satisfied that were our continent to be swallowed up by the ocean, Great Britain would be in a bonfire from one end to the other.—To WILLIAM CARMICHAEL. ii, 323. FORD ED., iv, 469. (P., 1787.)

2377. —— ——. Mr. Eden sets out in a few days for Madrid. You will have to oppose in him the most bitter enemy against our country that exists. His late and sudden elevation makes the remembrance of the contempt we showed to his mission in America rankle the more in his breast.—To WILLIAM CARMICHAEL. FORD ED., iv, 453. (P., 1787.)

2378. EDITORS, Contention and.—The printers can never leave us in a state of perfect rest and union of opinion. They would be no longer useful and would have to go to the plow.—To ELBRIDGE GERRY. iv, 392. FORD ED., viii, 43. (W., March 1801.)

2379. —— ——. A coalition of sentiments is not for the interest of the printers. They, * * *, live by the zeal they can kindle, and the schisms they can create. It is contest of opinion in politics * * * which makes us take great interest in them, and bestow our money liberally on those who furnish aliment to our appetite.—To ELBRIDGE GERRY. iv, 391. FORD ED., viii, 42. (W., March 1801.)

2380. EDITORS, Ferocity of.—Our printers raven on the agonies of their victims, as wolves do on the blood of the lamb.—To JAMES MONROE. v, 598. FORD ED., ix, 324. (M., 1811.)

2381. EDITORS, Government, People and.—The printers and the public are very different personages. The former may lead the latter a little out of their track, while the deviation is insensible; but the moment they usurp their direction and that of their government, they will be reduced to their true places.—To JAMES MONROE. v, 598. FORD ED., ix, 324. (M., May 1811.)

2382. EDITORS, Independence of.—I think an editor should be independent, that is, of personal influence, and not be moved from his opinions on the mere authority of any individual. But with respect to the general opinion of the political section with which he habitually accords, his duty seems very like that of a member of Congress.—To WILLIAM DUANE. v, 591. FORD ED., ix, 315. (M., 1811.)

2383. EDITORS, Jefferson's Relations with.—In your letter it is said that, *for certain services performed* by Mr. James Lyon and Mr. Samuel Morse, formerly editors of the Savannah Republican. I promised them the sum of one thousand dollars. This is totally unfounded. I never promised to any printer on earth the sum of one thousand dollars, nor any other sum, for certain services performed, or for any services which that expression would imply. I have had no accounts with printers but for their newspapers, for which I have paid always the ordinary price and no more. I have occasionally joined in moderate contributions to printers, as I have done to other descriptions of persons, distressed or persecuted, not by promise, but the actual payment of what I contributed.—To JAMES L. EDWARDS. vi, 8. (M., 1811.)

2384. —— ——. I take the liberty of requesting a letter from you bearing testimony to the truth of my never having made to you, or within your knowledge or information, any such promise to yourself, your partner Morse, or any other. My confidence in your character leaves me without a doubt of your honest aid in repelling this base and bold attempt to fix on me practices to which no honors or powers in this world would ever have induced me to stoop. I have solicited none, intrigued for none. Those which my country has thought proper to confide to me have been of their own mere motion, unasked by me. Such practices as this letter-writer imputes to me, would have proved me unworthy of their confidence.—To JAMES LYON. vi, 10. (M., 1811.) See NEWSPAPERS.

2385. EDUCATION, Abuses of power and.—Education is the true corrective of abuses of constitutional power.—To WILLIAM C. JARVIS. vii, 179. FORD ED, x, 161. (M., 1820.)

2386. EDUCATION, Amelioration of mankind.—If the condition of man is to be progressively ameliorated, as we fondly hope and believe, education is to be the chief instrument in effecting it.—To M. JULLIEN. vii, 106. (M., 1818.)

2387. EDUCATION, Course of.—I have never thought a boy should undertake abstruse or difficult sciences, such as mathematics in general, till fifteen years of age at soonest. Before that time, they are best employed in learning the languages, which is merely a matter of memory.—To RALPH IZARD. ii, 428. (P. 1788.)

2388. EDUCATION, Devotion to.—A system of general instruction, which shall reach every description of our citizens from the richest to the poorest, as it was the earliest, so will it be the latest of all the public concerns in which I shall permit myself to take an interest. Nor am I tenacious of the form in which it shall be introduced. Be that what it may, our descendants will be as wise as we are, and w'll know how to amend and amend it, until it shall suit their circumstances. Give it to us then in any shape, and receive for the inestimable boon the thanks of the young and the blessings of the old, who are past all other services but prayers for the prosperity of their country, and blessings for those who promote it.—To Joseph C. Cabell. Ford ed.. x. 102. (M., 1818.)

— **EDUCATION, Discipline and.**—See Discipline and University of Virginia.

2389. EDUCATION, Drawing.—I have been quite anxious to get a good drawing master in the military or landscape line for the University [of Virginia]. It is a branch of male education most highly and justly valued on the continent of Europe.—To James Madison. Ford ed., x, 360. (M.. 1826.)

— **EDUCATION, Elective Studies.**—See University of Virginia.

— **EDUCATION, European.**—See Schools.

2390. EDUCATION, Female.—A plan of female education has never been a subject of systematic contemplation with me. It has occupied my attention so far only as the education of my own daughters occasionally required. Considering that they would be placed in a country situation, where little aid could be obtained from abroad, I thought it essential to give them a solid education, which might enable them, when become mothers, to educate their own daughters, and even to direct the course for sons, should their fathers be lost, or incapable, or inattentive. * * * A great obstacle to good education is the ordinate passion prevalent for novels, and the time lost in that reading which should be instructively employed. When this poison infects the mind it destroys its tone and revolts it against wholesome reading. Reason and fact, plain and unadorned, are rejected. Nothing can engage attention unless dressed in all the figments of fancy, and nothing so bedecked comes amiss. The result is a bloated imagination, sickly judgment, and disgust towards all the real businesses of life. This mass of trash, however, is not without some distinction; some few modelling their narratives, although fictitious. on the incidents of real life, have been able to make them interesting and useful vehicles of a sound morality. Such, I think, are Marmontel's new Moral Tales. but not his old ones, which are really immoral. Such are the writings of Miss Edgeworth, and some of those of Madame Genlis. For a like reason, too,

much poetry should not be indulged.' Some is useful for forming style and taste. Pope Dryden, Thomson, Shakespeare, and of the French Molière, Racine, the Corneilles, may be read with pleasure and improvement. The French language. become that of the general intercourse of nations, and from their extraordinary advances, now the depository of all science, is an indispensable part of education for both sexes. * * * The ornaments, too, and the amusements of life. are entitled to their portion of attention. ✓These. for a female, are dancing, drawing, and music. The first is a healthy exercise, elegant and very attractive for young people. Every affectionate parent would be pleased to see his daughter qualified to participate with her companions, and without awkwardness at least, in the circles of festivity, of which she occasionally becomes a part. It is a necessary accomplishment, therefore, although of short use; for the French rule is wise, that no lady dances after marriage. This is founded in solid physical reasons, gestation and nursing leaving little time to a married lady when this exercise can be either safe or innocent. Drawing is thought less of in this country than in Europe. It is an innocent and engaging amusement, often useful, and a qualification not to be neglected in one who is to become a mother and an instructor. Music is invaluable where a person has an ear. Where they have not, it should not be attempted. It furnishes a delightful recreation for the hours of respite from the cares of the day, and lasts us through life. The taste of this country, too, calls for this accomplishment more strongly than for either of the others. ✓I need say nothing of household economy, in which the mothers of our country are generally skilled, and generally careful to instruct their daughters. We all know its value. and that diligence and dexterity in all its processes are inestimable treasures. The order and economy of a house are as honorable to the mistress as those of the farm to the master, and if either be neglected. ruin follows, and children destitute of the means of living.—To N. Burwell. vii, 101. Ford ed., x, 104. (M., 1818.)

— **EDUCATION, Fostering Genius.**—See 2398, 2399, 2400.

2391. EDUCATION, Freedom and.—If a nation expects to be ignorant and free, in a state of civilization, it expects what never was and never will be.—To Charles Yancey. vi, 517. Ford ed., x, 4. (M.,1816.)

2392. EDUCATION, Freedom, Happiness and.—No other sure foundation can be devised for the preservation of freedom and happiness. * * * Preach a crusade against ignorance; establish and improve the law for educating the common people. Let our countrymen know that the people alone can protect us against the evils [of misgovernment].—To George Wythe ii, 7. Ford ed., iv, 268. (P., 1786.)

2393. EDUCATION, Friends of.—A wise direction of [the force friendly to education] will insure to our country its future prosperity and safety.—To Joseph C. Cabell. vii, 189. Ford ed., x, 167. (P.F., 1820.)

2394. EDUCATION, Good Government and.—No one more sincerely wishes the spread of information among mankind than I do, and none has greater confidence in its effect towards supporting free and good government.—To Hugh L. White. v, 521. (M., 1810.)

2395. EDUCATION, Higher.—I do most anxiously wish to see the highest degrees of education given to the higher degrees of genius, and to all degrees of it, so much as may enable them to read and understand what is going on in the world, and to keep their part of it going on right; for nothing can keep it right but their own vigilant and distrustful superintendence.—To Mann Page. iv, 119. Ford ed., vii. 24. (M., 1795.)

2396. —— ——. The greatest good [of the people] requires, that while they are instructed in general, competently to the common business of life, others should employ their genius with necessary information to the useful arts, to inventions for saving labor and increasing our comforts. to nourishing our health, to civil government, military science, &c.—To Joseph C. Cabell. vii. 187. Ford ed., x, 166. (P. F., 1820.)

2397. —— ——. When sobered by experience, I hope our successors will turn their attention to the advantages of education. I mean of education on the broad scale, and not that of the petty *academies*, as they call themselves, which are started up in every neighborhood, and where one or two men, possessing Latin and sometimes Greek, a knowledge of the globes, and the first six books of Euclid, imagine and communicate this as the sum of science. They commit their pupils to the theatre of the world, with just taste enough of learning to be alienated from industrious pursuits, and not enough to do service in the ranks of science. * * * I hope the necessity will at length be seen of establishing institutions here. as in Europe. where every branch of science useful at this day, may be taught in its highest degree.—To John Adams. vi. 356. Ford ed., ix. 464. (M., July 1814.)

2398. EDUCATION, Jefferson's Bills on.—The bill [on Education in the Revised Code of Virginia] proposes to lay off every county into small districts of five or six miles square, called hundreds, and in each of them to establish a school for teaching reading, writing, and arithmetic. The tutor to be supported by the hundred, and every person in it entitled to send their children three years gratis, and as much longer as they please, paying for it. These schools to be under a visitor who is annually to choose the boy of best genius in the school, of those whose parents are too poor to give them further education, and to send him forward to one of the grammar schools, of which twenty are proposed to be erected in different parts of the

country, for teaching Greek, Latin, geography, and the higher branches of numerical arithmetic. Of the boys thus sent in any one year, trial is to be made at the grammar schools one or two years, and the best genius of the whole selected, and continued six years, and the residue dismissed. By this means twenty of the best geniuses will be raked from the rubbish annually, and be instructed at the public expense, so far as the grammar schools go. At the end of six years instruction, one-half are to be discontinued (from among whom the grammar schools will probably be supplied with future masters); and the other half, who are to be chosen for the superiority of their parts and disposition, are to be sent and continued three years in the study of such sciences as they shall choose, at William and Mary College. * * * The ultimate result of the whole scheme of education would be the teaching all the children of the State reading, writing, and common arithmetic; turning out ten annually of superior genius, well taught in Greek, Latin, geography, and the higher branches of arithmetic; turning out ten others annually, of still superior parts, who, to those branches of learning, shall have added such branches of the sciences as their genius shall have led them to; the further furnishing to the wealthier part of the people convenient schools at which their children may be educated at their own expense.—Notes on Virginia. viii, 388. Ford ed., iii, 251. (1782.)

2399. —— ——. I have sketched and put into the hands of a member a bill, delineating a practicable plan, entirely within the means they [the Virginia Legislature] already have on hand, destined to this object. My bill proposes: 1. Elementary schools in every county, which shall place every householder within three miles of a school. 2. District colleges, which shall place every father within a day's ride of a college where he may dispose of his son. 3. An university in a healthy and central situation, with the offer of the lands, buildings, and funds of the Central College, if they will accept that place for their establishment. In the first will be taught reading, writing, common arithmetic, and general notions of geography. In the second, ancient and modern languages, geography fully, a higher degree of numerical arithmetic, mensuration, and the elementary principles of navigation. In the third, all the useful sciences in their highest degree. To all of which is added a selection from the elementary schools of subjects of the most promising genius, whose parents are too poor to give them further education, to be carried at the public expense through the colleges and university. The object is to bring into action that mass of talents which lies buried in poverty in every country, for want of the means of development, and thus give activity to a mass of mind, which, in proportion to our population, shall be the double or treble of what it is in most countries. The expense of the elementary schools for every county, is proposed to be levied on the wealth of the county, and all children rich and poor, to be educated at these three years gratis. * * * This is, in fact and substance, the plan I proposed in a bill forty years ago, but accommodated to the circumstances of this, instead of that day.—To M. CORREA. vii. 94. (P. F., 1817.)

2400. EDUCATION, Jefferson's Explanation of.—The general objects of this law are to provide an education adapted to the years, to the capacity, and the condition of every one, and directed to their freedom and happiness. Specific details were not proper for the law. These must be the business of the visitors entrusted with its execution. The first stage of this education being the schools of the hundreds, wherein the great mass of the people will receive their instruction, the principal foundations of future order will be laid here. Instead, therefore, of putting the Bible and the Testament into the hands of the children at an age when their judgments are not sufficiently matured for religious inquiries, their memories may here be stored with the most useful facts from Grecian, Roman, European and American history. The first elements of morality, too, may be instilled into their minds; such as, when further developed as their judgments advance in strength, may teach them how to work out their own greatest happiness, by showing them that it does not depend on the condition of life in which chance has placed them, but is always the result of a good conscience, good health, occupation, and freedom in all just pursuits. Those whom either the wealth of their parents or the adoption of the State shall destine to higher degrees of learning will go on to the grammar schools, which constitute the next stage, there to be instructed in the languages. The learning Greek and Latin, I am told, is going into disuse in Europe. I know not what their manners and occupations may call for; but it would be very ill-judged in us to follow their example in this instance. There is a certain period of life, say from eight to fifteen or sixteen years of age, when the mind, like the body is not yet firm enough for laborious and close operations. If applied to such, it falls an early victim to premature exertion; exhibiting, indeed, at first, in these young and tender subjects, the flattering appearance of their being men while they are yet children, but ending in reducing them to be children when they should be men. The memory is then most susceptible and tenacious of impressions; and the learning of languages being chiefly a work of memory, it seems precisely fitted to the powers of this period, which is long enough, too, for acquiring the most useful languages, ancient and modern. I do not pretend that language is science. It is only an instrument for the attainment of science. But that time is not lost which is employed in providing tools for future operation; more especially, as in this case, the books put into the hands of the youth for this purpose may be such as will, at the same time, impress their minds with useful facts and good principles. If this period be suffered to pass in idleness, the mind becomes lethargic and impotent, as would the body it inhabits, if unexercised during the same time. The sympathy between body and mind during their rise, progress, and decline, is too strict and obvious to endanger our being misled, while we reason from the one to the other.

As soon as they are of sufficient age, it is supposed they will be sent from the grammar schools to the university, which constitutes our third and last stage, there to study those sciences which may be adapted to their views. By that part of our plan which prescribes the selection of the youths of genius from among the classes of the poor, we hope to avail the State of those talents which nature has sown as liberally among the poor as the rich, but which perish without use, if not sought for and cultivated. But of all the views of this law none is more important, none more legitimate, than that of rendering the people the safe, as they are the ultimate, guardians of their own liberty. For this purpose the reading in the first stage, where *they* will receive their whole education, is proposed, as has been said, to be chiefly historical. History, by apprising them of the past, will enable them to judge of the future; it will avail them of the experience of other times and other nations; it will qualify them as judges of the actions and designs of men; it will enable them to know ambition under every disguise it may assume; and knowing it, to defeat its views. In every government on earth is some trace of human weakness, some germ of corruption and degeneracy, which cunning will discover, and wickedness insensibly open, cultivate and improve. ✓Every government degenerates when trusted to the rulers of the people alone. The people themselves, therefore, are its only safe depositories. And to render even them safe, their minds must be improved to a certain degree. This indeed is not all that is necessary, though it be essentially necessary. An amendment of our Constitution must have come in aid of the public education. The influence over government must be shared among all the people. If every individual which composes their mass participates of the ultimate authority, the government will be safe; because the corrupting the whole mass will exceed any private resources of wealth; and public ones cannot be provided but by levies on the people. In this case every man would have to pay his own price. The government of Great Britain has been corrupted, because but one man in ten has a right to vote for members of parliament. The sellers of the government, therefore, get nine-tenths of their price clear. ✓ It has been thought that corruption is restrained by confining the right of suffrage to a few of the wealthier of the people; but it would be more effectually restrained, by an extension of that right, to such members as would bid defiance to the means of corruption.—NOTES ON VIRGINIA. viii, 388. FORD ED., iii, 252. (1782.)

— **EDUCATION, Languages and.**—See LANGUAGES.

2401. EDUCATION, Large Cities and.—I am not a friend to placing young men in populous cities, because they acquire their habits and partialities which do not contribute to the happiness of their after life.—To DOCTOR WISTAR. v, 104. FORD ED., ix, 70. (W., 1807.)

2402. EDUCATION, Law and.—Laws will be wisely formed, and honestly administered, in proportion as those who form and administer them are wise and honest: whence it becomes expedient for promoting the public happiness that those persons, whom nature has endowed with genius and virtue, should be rendered by liberal education worthy to receive, and able to guard the sacred deposit of the rights and liberties of their fellow citizens; and that they should be called to that charge without regard to wealth, birth or other accidental condition or circumstance; but the indigence of the greater number disabling them from so educating, at their own expense, those of their children whom nature has fitly formed and disposed to become useful instruments for the public, it is better that such should be sought for and educated at the common expense of all, than that the happiness of all should be confined to the weak or wicked.—DIFFUSION OF KNOWLEDGE BILL. FORD ED., ii, 221. (1779.)

2403. EDUCATION, Material progress vs.—People generally have more feeling for canals and roads than education. However, I hope we can advance them with equal pace.— To JOEL BARLOW. v, 217. FORD ED., ix, 169. (W., 1807.)

2404. EDUCATION, Military instruction.—We must make military instruction a regular part of collegiate education. We can never be safe till this is done.*—To JAMES MONROE. vi, 131. (M., 1813.)

2405. EDUCATION, Municipal government and.—Education is not a branch of municipal government, but, like the other arts and sciences, an accident only.—To JOHN TAYLOR. vii, 17. FORD ED., x, 51. (M., 1816.)

— **EDUCATION, National University.** —See UNIVERSITY.

2406. EDUCATION, Neglect of.—If the children * * * are untaught, their ignorance and vices will, in future life cost us much dearer in their consequences, than it would have done, in their correction, by a good education.—To JOSEPH C. CABELL. FORD ED., x, 99. (1818.)

2407. EDUCATION, New York vs. Virginia.—Surely Governor Clinton's display of the gigantic efforts of New York towards the education of her citizens will stimulate the pride as well as the patriotism of our Legislature, to look to the reputation and safety

* Jefferson was the first to suggest military training in the schools.—EDITOR.

of their own country, to rescue it from the degradation of becoming the Barbary of the Union, and of falling into the ranks of our own negroes. To that condition it is fast sinking. We shall be in the hands of the other States, what our indigenous predecessors were when invaded by the science and arts of Europe. The mass of education in Virginia, before the Revolution, placed her with the foremost of her Sister Colonies. What is her education now? Where is it? The little we have we import, like beggars, from other States; or import their beggars to bestow on us their miserable crumbs. And what is wanting to restore us to our station among our confederates? Not more money from the people. Enough has been raised by them, and appropriated to this very object. It is that it should be employed understandingly, and for their greatest good.—To JOSEPH C. CABELL. vii, 186. FORD ED., x, 165. (P.F., 1820.)

2408. ——. Six thousand common schools in New York, fifty pupils in each, three hundred thousand in all; one hundred and sixty thousand dollars annually paid to the masters; forty established academies, with two thousand two hundred and eighteen pupils; and five colleges with seven hundred and eighteen students; to which last classes of institutions seven hundred and twenty thousand dollars have been given; and the whole appropriations for education estimated at two and a half millions of dollars! What a pigmy to this is Virginia become, with a population almost equal to that of New York! And whence this difference? From the difference their rulers set on the value of knowledge, and the prosperity it produces. But still, if a pigmy, let her do what a pigmy may do.—To JOSEPH C. CABELL. vii, 188. FORD ED., x, 167. (P.F., 1820.)

2409. EDUCATION, The People and.—Above all things, I hope the education of the common people will be attended to; convinced that on their good senses we may rely with the most security for the preservation of a due degree of liberty.*—To JAMES MADISON. FORD ED., iv, 480. (P., 1787.)

2410. ——. [To give] information to the people * * * is the most certain, and the most legitimate engine of government.— To JAMES MADISON. ii, 332. (1787.)

2411. ——. The diffusion of information, I deem [one] of the essential principles of our government and, consequently, [one] which ought to shape its administration.—FIRST INAUGURAL ADDRESS. viii, 4. FORD ED., viii, 5. (1801.)

2412. ——. Enlighten the people generally, and tyranny and oppressions of body and mind will vanish like spirits at the

* In Congress edition: (ii, 332.) "Educate and inform the whole mass of the people. Enable them to see that it is their interest to preserve peace and order and they will preserve them. And it requires no very high degree of education to convince them of this. They are the only sure reliance for the preservation of our liberty."—EDITOR.

dawn of day.—To Dupont De Nemours. vi, 592. Ford ed., x, 25. (P. F., 1816.)

2413. ———— ————. Nobody can doubt my zeal for the general instruction of the people. Who first started that idea? I may surely say, myself. Turn to the bill in the Revised Code, which I drew more than forty years ago, and before which the idea of a plan for the education of the people, generally, had never been suggested in this State. There you will see developed the first rudiments of the whole system of general education we are now urging and acting on: and it is well known to those with whom I have acted on this subject, that I never have proposed a sacrifice of the primary to the ultimate grade of instruction. Let us keep our eye steadily on the whole system.—To General Breckenridge. vii, 205. (M., 1821.) See People.

2414. EDUCATION, Perversion of power and.—The most effectual means of preventing the perversion of power into tyranny are to illuminate, as far as practicable, the minds of the people.—Diffusion of Knowledge Bill. Ford ed, ii, 221. (1799.)

2415. EDUCATION, Power and.—All the States but our own are sensible that knowledge is power. The Missouri question is for power. The efforts now generally making in all the States to advance their science is for power, while we are sinking into the barbarism of our Indian aborigines, and expect like them to oppose by ignorance the overwhelming mass of light and science by which we shall be surrounded. It is a comfort that I am not to live to see this. —To Joseph C. Cabell. Ford ed., x, 155. (M., 1820.)

2416. EDUCATION, Progress through. —I look to the diffusion of light and education as the resource most to be relied on for ameliorating the condition, promoting the virtue, and advancing the happiness of man.— To C. C. Blatchly. vii, 263. (M., 1822.) See 2386.

2417. EDUCATION, The Republic and. —I have two great measures at heart, without which no republic can maintain itself in strength. 1. That of general education, to enable every man to judge for himself what will secure or endanger his freedom. 2. To divide every county into hundreds, of such size that all the children of each will be within reach of a central school in it.—To John Tyler v, 525. Ford ed., ix, 277. (M., 1810.)

2418. EDUCATION, Safety in.—The information of the people at large can alone make them the safe, as they are the sole depository of our political and religious freedom.—To William Duane. v, 541. (M., 1810.)

2419. EDUCATION, Self-sufficiency and.—Our post-revolutionary youth are born under happier stars than you and I were. They acquire all learning in their mother's womb, and bring it into the world ready made. The information of books is no longer necessary; and all knowledge which is not innate, is in contempt, or neglect at least. Every folly must run its round; and so, I suppose, must that of self-learning and self-sufficiency; of rejecting the knowledge acquired in past ages, and starting on the new ground of intuition.—To John Adams. vi, 355. Ford ed., ix, 464. (M., 1814.)

2420. EDUCATION, Suffrage and.— There is one provision [in the new constitution of Spain] which will immortalize its inventors. It is that which, after a certain epoch, disfranchises every citizen who cannot read and write. This is new, and is the fruitful germ of the improvement of everything good, and the correction of everything imperfect in the present constitution. This will give you an enlightened people, and an energetic public opinion which will control and enchain the aristocratic spirit of the government.—To Chevalier de Ouis. vi, 342. (M., 1814.)

2421. EDUCATION, Suitable.—Promote in every order of men the degree of instruction proportioned to their condition, and to their views in life.—To Joseph C. Cabell. vii, 189. Ford ed., x, 167. (P. F., 1820.)

2422. EDUCATION, System and.—The truth is that the want of common education with us is not from our poverty, but from the want of an orderly system. More money is now paid for the education of a part than would be paid for that of the whole, if systematically arranged.—To Joseph C. Cabell. vii, 188. Ford ed., x, 167. (P.F., 1820.)

2423. EDUCATION, Taxes for.—The tax which will be paid for the purpose of education is not more than the thousandth part of what will be paid to kings, priests and nobles who will rise up among us if we leave the people in ignorance.—To George Wythe. ii, 7. Ford ed., iv, 269. (P., 1786.)

2424. ———— ————. If the Legislature would add to the literary fund a perpetual tax of a cent a head on the population of the State, it would set agoing at once, and forever maintain, a system of primary or ward schools, and an university where might be taught, in its highest degree, every branch of science useful in our time and country; and it would rescue us from the tax of toryism, fanaticism, and indifferentism to their own State, which we now send our youth to bring from those of New England.—To Charles Yancey. vi, 517. Ford ed., x, 4. (M., 1816.)

— EDUCATION, Technical.—See 2396.

2425. EDUCATION, Tyranny and.— Enlighten the people generally, and tyranny and oppressions of body and mind will vanish like evil spirits at the dawn of day.—To Dupont de Nemours. vi, 592. Ford ed., x, 25. (P. F., 1816.)

— EDUCATION vs. VICE.—See 2406.

2426. EDUCATION, The Wealthy and. —What will be the retribution of the wealthy individual [for his support of general education]? 1. The peopling of his neighborhood with honest, useful and enlightened citizens, understanding their own rights and firm in their perpetuation. 2. When his own descendants become poor, which they generally do within three generations (no law of primogeniture now perpetuating wealth in the same families), their children will be educated by the then rich, and the little advance he now makes to poverty, while rich himself, will be repaid by the then rich, to his descendants when become poor, and thus give them a chance of rising again. This is a solid consideration, and should go home to the bosom of every parent. This will be seed sowed in fertile ground. It is a provision for his family looking to distant times, and far in duration beyond what he has now in hand for them. Let every man count backward in his own family, and see how many generations he can go, before he comes to the ancestor who made the fortune he now holds. Most will be stopped at the first generation, many at the second, few will reach the third, and not one in the State [of Virginia] go beyond the fifth.—To JOSEPH C. CABELL. FORD ED., x, 100. (M., 1818.)

— EDUCATION, Zeal for.—See 2388.

2427. ELECTION, Abuses and.—Should things go wrong at any time, the people will set them to rights by the peaceable exercise of their elective rights.—To WILSON C. NICHOLAS. v, 5. FORD ED., viii, 435. (W., 1806.)

2428. ELECTION, Care of.—A jealous care of the right of election by the people,— a mild and safe corrective of abuses which are lopped by the sword of revolution where peaceable remedies are unprovided, I deem [one of the] essential principles of our government and, consequently [one] which ought to shape its administration. FIRST INAUGURAL ADDRESS. viii, 4. FORD ED., viii, 4. (1801.)

2429. ELECTION, Contested.—To retain the office, when it is probable the majority was against him [George Clinton] is dishonorable.*—To JAMES MONROE. FORD ED., vi, 94. (Pa., 1792.)

2430. ELECTION, Expenditures and.— The frequent recurrence of this chastening operation can alone restrain the propensity of governments to enlarge expense beyond income.—To ALBERT GALLATIN. FORD ED., x, 176. (M., 1820.)

2431. ELECTION vs. FORCE.—Keep away all show of force, and the people will bear down the evil propensities of the government by the constitutional means of election and petition.—To EDMUND PENDLETON. iv, 287. FORD ED., vii, 356. (Pa., 1799.)

2432. ELECTION, Government and.— Election * * * [is] a fundamental member in the structure of government.—To JOHN TAYLOR. vii, 18. FORD ED., x, 52. (M., 1816.)

* Jefferson was discussing the Clinton-Jay contest for the governorship in New York.—EDITOR.

— **ELECTION OF PRESIDENT.**—See ELECTIONS, PRESIDENTIAL and PRESIDENT.

2433. ELECTION, Republican Government and.—Governments are more or less republican as they have more or less of the element of popular election and control in their composition.—To JOHN TAYLOR. vi, 608. FORD ED., x, 31. (M. 1816.)

2434. ELECTION, Short Periods of.—A government by representatives, elected by the people at *short* periods, was our object; and our maxim at that day was, "where annual election ends, tyranny begins"; nor have our departures from it been sanctioned by the happiness of their effects.—To SAMUEL ADAMS. iv, 321. FORD ED., vii, 425. (Pa., Feb. 1800.)

2435. ——— ———. A representative government, responsible at short periods of election, * * * produces the greatest sum of happiness to mankind.—R. To A. VERMONT LEGISLATURE. viii, 121. (1807.)

2436. ——— ———. The rights [of the people] to the exercise and fruits of their own industry, can never be protected against the selfishness of rulers not subject to their control at short periods.—To ISAAC H. TIFFANY. vii, 32. (M., 1816.)

2437. ——— ———. Submit the members of the Legislature to approbation or rejection at short intervals.—To SAMUEL KERCHIVAL. vii, 11. FORD ED., x, 39. (M., 1816.)

2438. ELECTION, Congress and.— Short elections will keep Congress right.— To THOMAS RITCHIE. vii, 102. FORD ED., x, 170. (M., 1820.)

2439. ——— ———. The Legislative and executive branches may sometimes err, but elections and dependence will bring them to rights.—To ARCHIBALD THWEAT. vii, 199. FORD ED., x, 184. (M., 1821.)

2440. ELECTIONS, Federal Interference with.—Till the event of the [Presidential] election is known, it is too soon for me to say what should be done in such atrocious cases as those you mention of Federal officers obstructing the operation of the State governments. One thing I will say, that as to the future, interferences with elections, whether of the State or General Government, by officers of the latter, should be deemed cause of removal; because the constitutional remedy by the elective principle becomes nothing, if it may be smothered by the enormous patronage of the General Government.—To GOVERNOR THOMAS M'KEAN. iv, 350. FORD ED., vii, 486. (W., Feb. 1801.)

2441. ——— ———. I proposed soon after coming into office to enjoin the executive officers from intermeddling with elections, as inconsistent with the true principles of our Constitution. It was laid over for consideration; but late occurrences prove the propriety of it, and it is now under consideration. —To DE WITT CLINTON. FORD ED., viii, 322. (W., Oct. 1804.)

2442. —— ——. I think the officers of the Federal Government are meddling too much with the public elections. Will it be best to admonish them privately or by proclamation?—To ALBERT GALLATIN. iv, 559. FORD ED., viii, 320. (M., Sep. 1804.)

2443. —— ——. You mention that "Dr. Logan had informed the person that he had just received a letter from you [me], exhorting him to use all his influence to procure the reelection of Governor McKean, for that to displace him would be extremely injurious to the republican cause." Whatever may be the personal esteem I entertain for Governor McKean, and the harmony with which we acted when members of the same body, I never conceived that that would justify my taking sides against Mr. Snyder, or endeavoring in any way to influence the free choice of the State. I, therefore, have never written any such letter, nor a letter of such import to any mortal. And further. my long and intimate acquaintance with Dr. Logan, and my knowledge of his strict honor, leave the fullest conviction in my mind that there has been some mistake in the hearing, understanding, or quoting his words.—To THOMAS LIET. FORD ED., viii, 354. (M., Aug. 1805.)

2444. ELECTIONS, Intermeddling with.—From a very early period of my life I determined never to intermeddle with elections of the people, and have invariably adhered to this determination. In my own country, where there have been so many elections in which my inclinations were enlisted, I yet never interfered. I could the less do it in the present instance, your people so very distant from me, utterly unknown to me, and to whom I also am unknown; and above all, I a stranger, to presume to recommend one who is well known to them. The people could not but put this question to me, "who are you, pray"?—To CHARLES CLAY. iii, 469. FORD ED., vi, 111. (M., 1792.)

2445. ELECTIONS, Patronage and.—Every officer of the government may vote at elections according to his conscience; but we should betray the cause committed to our care, were we to permit the influence of official patronage to be used to overthrow that cause.—To LEVI LINCOLN. iv, 451. FORD ED., viii, 176. (W., October 1802.) See PATRONAGE.

2446. ELECTIONS (Presidential, 1796), Candidature of Jefferson.—My name was brought forward, without concert or expectation on my part, on my salvation I declare it.—To EDWARD RUTLEDGE. iv, 151. FORD ED., vii, 93. (M., Dec. 1796.)

2447. —— ——. I had neither claims nor wishes on the subject, though I know it will be difficult to obtain belief of this. When I retired from the office of Secretary of State, it was in the firmest contemplation of never more returning to Philadelphia. There had indeed been suggestions in the public papers, that I was looking towards a succession to the President's chair, but feeling a consciousness of their falsehood, and observing that the suggestions came from hostile quarters, I considered

them as intended merely to excite public odium against me. I never in my life exchanged a word with any person on the subject, till I found my name brought forward generally, in competition with that of Mr. Adams. Those with whom I then communicated could say, if it were necessary, whether I met the call with desire, or even with a ready acquiescence, and whether from the moment of my first acquiescence, I did not devoutly pray that the very thing might happen which has happened.—To ELBRIDGE GERRY. iv, 170. FORD ED., vii, 119. (Pa., May 1797.)

2448. —— ——. The first wish of my heart was that you should have been proposed for the administration of the government. On your declining it, I wish anybody rather than myself.—To JAMES MADISON. iv, 150. FORD ED., vii, 91. (M., Dec. 17, 1796.)

2449. ELECTIONS (Presidential, 1796), Dispute over.—It seems possible, that the Representatives may be divided. This is a difficulty from which the Constitution has provided no issue. It is both my duty and inclination, therefore, to relieve the embarrassment, should it happen: and in that case, I pray you, and authorize you fully, to solicit on my behalf that Mr. Adams may be preferred. He has always been my senior, from the commencement of my public life, and the expression of the public will being equal, this circumstance ought to give him the preference. And when so many motives will be operating to induce some of the members to change their vote, the addition of my wish may have some effect to preponderate the scale.—To JAMES MADISON. iv, 150. FORD ED., vii, 91. (M., Dec. 17, 1796.)

2450. ELECTIONS (Presidential, 1796), Eastern States and.—I have no expectation that the Eastern States will suffer themselves to be so much outwitted, as to be made the tools for bringing in Pinckney instead of Adams. I presume they will throw away their Second Vote. In this case, it begins to appear possible, that there may be an equal division where I had supposed the republican vote would have been considerably minor.—To JAMES MADISON. iv, 150. FORD ED., vii, 91. (M., Dec. 17, 1796.)

2451. ELECTIONS (Presidential, 1796), Jefferson's Vote.—I shall highly value, indeed, the share which I may have had in the late vote, as an evidence of the share I hold in the esteem of my countrymen. But in this point of view, a few votes more or less will be little sensible, and in every other, the minor will be preferred by me to the major vote.—To EDWARD RUTLEDGE. iv, 152. FORD ED., vii, 94. (M., Dec. 1796.)

2452. —— ——. I value highly, indeed, the part my fellow-citizens gave me in their late vote, as an evidence of their esteem, and I am happy in the information you are so kind as to give, that many in the Eastern quarter entertain the same sentiment.—To JAMES SULLIVAN. iv, 168. FORD ED., vii, 117. (M., Feb. 1797.)

2453. —— ——. I value the late vote highly; but it is only as the index of the place I hold in the esteem of my fellow citizens. In this point of view, the difference between sixty-eight and seventy-one votes is little sensible, and still less that between the real vote, which was sixty-nine and seventy; because one real elector in Pennsylvania was excluded from voting by the miscarriage of the votes, and one who was not an elector was admitted to vote.—To C. F. VOLNEY. iv, 158. (M., 1797.)

2454. ELECTIONS (Presidential, 1796), A Pseudo-President and.—I observe doubts are still expressed as to the validity of the Vermont election. Surely, in so great a case, substance, and not form, should prevail. I cannot suppose that the Vermont constitution has been strict in requiring particular forms of expressing the legislative will. As far as my disclaimer may have any effect, I pray you to declare it on every occasion, foreseen or not foreseen by me, in favor of the choice of the people substantially expressed, and to prevent the phenomenon of a Pseudo-President at so early a day.—To JAMES MADISON. FORD ED., vii, 105. (M., January 16, 1797.)

2455. ELECTIONS (Presidential, 1796), Result of.—I have never one moment doubted the result. I knew it was impossible Mr. Adams should lose a vote north of the Delaware, and that the free and moral agency of the South would furnish him an abundant supplement.—To EDWARD RUTLEDGE. iv, 151. FORD ED., vii, 93. (M., Dec. 27, 1796.)

2456. —— ——. The event of the election has never been a matter of doubt in my mind. I knew that the Eastern States were disciplined in the schools of their town meetings to sacrifice differences of opinion to the great object of operating in phalanx, and that the more free and moral agency practiced in the other States would always make up the supplement of their weight. Indeed the vote comes much nearer to an equality than I had expected.—To JAMES MADISON. iv, 154. FORD ED., vii, 98. (M., Jan. 1797.)

2457. ELECTIONS (Presidential, 1796), Vice-Presidency.—On principles of public respect I should not have refused [the Presidency]; but I protest before my God, that I shall, from the bottom of my heart, rejoice at escaping.—To EDWARD RUTLEDGE. iv, 151. FORD ED., vii, 93. (M., Dec. 1796.) See VICE-PRESIDENCY.

2458. —— ——. There is nothing I so anxiously hope as that my name may come out either second or third. These would be indifferent to me; as the last would leave me at home the whole year, and the other two-thirds of it.—To JAMES MADISON. iv, 150. FORD ED., vii, 91. (M., Dec. 1796.)

2459. —— ——. I have no ambition to govern men; no passion which would lead me to delight to ride in a storm. *Flumina amo, sylvasque, inglorius.* My attachment to my home has enabled me to make the calculation with rigor, perhaps with partiality, to the issue which keeps me there. The newspapers will permit me to plant my corn, peas, &c., in hills or drills as I please (and my oranges, by-the-bye, when you send them), while our eastern friend will be struggling with the storm which is gathering over us; perhaps be shipwrecked in it. This is certainly not a moment to covet the helm.—To EDWARD RUTLEDGE. iv, 152. FORD ED., vii, 94. (M., Dec. 1796.)

2460. —— ——. It is difficult to obtain full credit to declarations of disinclination to honors, and most so with those who still remain in the world. But never was there a more solid unwillingness, founded on rigorous calculation, formed in the mind of any man, short of peremptory refusal. No arguments,

therefore, were necessary to reconcile me to a relinquishment of the first office, or acceptance of the second. No motive could have induced me to undertake the first, but that of putting our vessel upon her republican tack, and preventing her being driven too far to leeward of her true principles. And the second is the only office in the world about which I cannot decide in my own mind, whether I had rather have it or not have it. Pride does not enter into the estimate. For I think with the Romans of old, that the General of to-day should be a common soldier to-morrow, if necessary. But as to Mr. Adams, particularly, I would have no feelings which would revolt at being placed in a secondary station to him. I am his junior in life, I was his junior in Congress, his junior in the diplomatic line, and lately his junior in our civil government.—To JAMES MADISON. iv, 154. FORD ED., vii, 98. (M., Jan. 1797.) See 74.

2461. ELECTIONS (Presidential, 1800), Action of Adams.—Mr. Adams embarrasses us. He keeps the offices of State and War vacant, but has named Bayard, Minister Plenipotentiary to France, and has called an unorganized Senate to meet the fourth of March.—To JAMES MADISON. iv, 356. FORD ED., vii, 495. (W., Feb. 18, 1801.)

2462. ELECTIONS (Presidential, 1800), Appointments and.—If the [choice] falls on me, I shall be embarrassed by finding the offices vacant, which cannot be even temporarily filled but with the advice of the Senate, and that body is called on the fourth of March, when it is impossible for the new members of Kentucky, Georgia, and South Carolina to receive notice in time to be here. * * * If the difficulties of the election, therefore, are got over, there are more and more behind, until new elections shall have regenerated the constituted authorities.—To TENCH COXE. iv, 352. FORD ED., vii, 488. (W., Feb. 1801.)

2463. —— ——. Should [the federalists] yield the election, I have reason to expect, in the outset, the greatest difficulties as to nominations. The late incumbents, running away from their offices and leaving them vacant, will prevent my filling them without the *previous* advice of the Senate. How this difficulty is to be got over I know not.—To JAMES MONROE. iv, 355. FORD ED., vii, 491. (W., Feb. 1801.)

2464. ELECTIONS (Presidential, 1800), Balloting in House.—This is the morning of the election by the House of Representatives. For some time past, a single individual had declared he would, by his vote, make up the ninth State. On Saturday last he changed, and it stands at present eight one way, six the other, and two divided. Which of the two will be elected, and whether either, I deem perfectly problematical; and my mind has long been equally made up for any one of the three events. * * * The defects of our Constitution under circumstances like the present, appear very great.—To TENCH COXE. iv, 352. FORD ED., vii, 488. (W., Feb. 11, 1801.)

2465. —— ——. This is the fourth day of the ballot, and nothing done; nor do I see any reason to suppose the six and a half States here will be less firm, as they call it, than your thirteen Senators; if so, and the Government should expire on the 3d of March, by the loss of its head, there is no regular provision for reorganizing it, nor any authority but in the people themselves. They may authorize a convention to reorganize and even amend the machine. There are ten individuals in the House of Representatives, any one of whom, changing his vote, could save us this troublesome operation.—To Dr. B. S. Barton. iv, 353. Ford ed., vii, 490. (W., Feb. 1801.)

2466. —— ——. Four days of balloting have produced not a single change of a vote. Yet it is confidently believed by most that to-morrow there is to be a coalition. I know of no foundation for this belief. To James Monroe. iv, 354. Ford ed., vii, 490. (W., Feb. 15, 1801.)

2467. —— ——. After exactly a week's balloting there at length appeared ten States for me, four for Burr, and two voted blanks. This was done without a single vote coming over. Morris, of Vermont, withdrew, so that Lyon's vote became that of the State. The four Maryland federalists put in blanks, so that the vote of the four republicans became that of their State. Mr. Hager, of South Carolina (who had constantly voted for me) withdrew by agreement, his colleagues agreeing in that case to put in blanks. Bayard, the sole member of Delaware, voted blank. They had before deliberated whether they would come over in a body, when they saw they could not force Burr on the republicans, or keep their body entire and unbroken to act in phalanx on such ground of opposition as they shall hereafter be able to conjure up. Their vote showed what they had decided on, and is considered as a declaration of perpetual war; but their conduct has completely left them without support.—To T. M. Randolph. iv, 358. Ford ed., vii, 497. (W., Feb. 19, 1801.)

2468. ELECTIONS (Presidential, 1800), Burr and.—The federalists were confident, at first, they could debauch Colonel Burr from his good faith by offering him their vote to be President, and having seriously proposed it to him. His conduct has been honorable and decisive, and greatly embarrasses them.—To Mary Jefferson Eppes. Ford ed., vii, 478. (W., Jan. 1801.)

2469. —— ——. Had the election terminated in the elevation of Mr. Burr, every republican would, I am sure, have acquiesced in a moment; because, however it might have been variant from the intentions of the voters, yet it would have been agreeable to the Constitution. No man would more cheerfully have submitted than myself, because I am sure the administration would have been republican, and the chair of the Senate permitting me to be at home eight months in the year, would, on that account, have been much more consonant to my real satisfaction.—To Thomas McKean. iv, 368. Ford ed., viii, 12. (W., March 1801.)

2470. ELECTIONS (Presidential, 1800), Demanding Terms.—Many attempts have been made to obtain terms and promises from me. I have declared to them unequivocally, that I would not receive the government on capitulation, that I would not go into it with my hands tied.—To James Monroe. iv, 354. Ford ed., vii, 491. (W., Feb. 1801.) See 78.

2471. —— ——. Aaron Burr, in a suit between him and Cheetham, has had a deposition of Mr. Bayard taken which seems to have no relation to the suit nor to any other object but to calumniate me. Bayard pretends to have addressed to me during the pending of the Presidential election in Feb. 1801. through General Samuel Smith, certain conditions on which my election might be obtained, and that General Smith after conversing with me gave answers from me. This is absolutely false. No proposition of any kind was ever made to me on that occasion by General Smith, nor any answer authorized by me. And this fact General Smith affirms at this moment. * * * But the following transactions took place about the same time, that is to say, while the Presidential election was in suspense in Congress, which, though I did not enter at the time [in the Anas], made such an impression on my mind that they are now as fresh as to their principal circumstances as if they had happened yesterday. Coming out of the Senate chamber one day I found Gouverneur Morris on the steps. He stopped me and began a conversation on the strange and portentous state of things then existing, and went on to observe that the reasons why the minority of States were so opposed to my being elected were that they apprehended that, 1. I should turn all federalists out of office. 2. Put down the Navy. 3. Wipe off the public debt and 4.* * * * . That I need only to declare, or authorize my friends to declare, that I would not take these steps, and instantly the event of the election would be fixed. I told him that I should leave the world to judge of the course I meant to pursue by that which I had pursued hitherto; believing it to be my duty to be passive and silent during the present scene; that I should certainly make no terms, should never go into the office of President by capitulation, nor with my hands tied by any conditions which should hinder me from pursuing the measures which I should deem for the public good. It was understood that Gouverneur Morris had entirely the direction of the vote of Lewis Morris of Vermont, who by coming over to Matthew Lyon would have added another vote and decided the election. About the same time, I called on Mr. Adams. We conversed on the state of things. I observed to him, that a very dangerous experiment was then in contemplation, to defeat the Presidential election by an act of Congress declaring the right of the Senate to name a President of the Senate, to devolve on him the government during any interregnum; that such a measure would probably produce resistance by force, and incalculable consequences, which it would be in his power to prevent by negativing such an act. He seemed to think such an act justifiable, and observed it was in my power to fix the election by a word in an instant, by declaring I would not turn out the federal officers, nor put down the Navy, nor spunge the national debt. Finding his mind made up as to the usurpation of the government by the President of the Senate, I urged it no further, observed the world must judge as to myself of the future by the past, and turned the conversation to something else. About the same time, Dwight Foster of Massachusetts called on me in my room one night, and went into a very long conversation on the state of affairs, the drift of which was to let me understand that the fears above-mentioned were the only obstacle to my election, to all of which I avoided giving any answer the one way or the other. From this moment he became most bitterly and personally opposed to me, and so has ever continued. I do not recollect that I ever had any particular conversation with General Samuel Smith on this subject. Very possibly I had, however, as the general subject and all its parts were the constant themes of conversation in the private *tête à têtes* with our friends.

* MS. cut out.—Ford Edition Note.

But certain I am, that neither he, nor any other republican, ever uttered the most distant hint to me about submitting to any conditions, or giving any assurance to anybody; and still more certainly, was neither he nor any other person ever authorized by me to say what I would or would not do.—ANAS. ix, 209. FORD ED., i, 312. (April 1806.)

2472. ELECTIONS (Presidential, 1800), Doubt Concerning.—South Carolina (the only State about which there was uncertainty), has given a republican vote, and saved us from the consequences of the annihilation of Pennsylvania.—To JOHN BRECKENRIDGE. iv, 342. FORD ED., vii, 469. (W., Dec. 1800.)

2473. —— ——. The election in South Carolina has in some measure decided the great contest. Though as yet we do not know the actual votes of Tennessee, Kentucky and Vermont, yet we believe the votes to be on the whole, J. 73, B. 73, A. 65, P. 64. Rhode Island withdrew one from P. There is a possibility that Tennessee may withdraw one from B., and Burr writes that there may be one vote in Vermont for J. But I told the latter impossible. and the former not probable; and that there will be an absolute parity between the two Republican candidates.—To JAMES MADISON. iv, 342. FORD ED., vii, 470. (W., Dec. 19, 1800.)

2474. ELECTIONS (Presidential, 1800), Efforts to Defeat.—A strong portion in the House of Representatives will prevent an election if they can. I rather believe they will not be able to do it, as there are six individuals of moderate character, any one of whom coming over to the republican vote will make a ninth State.—To THOMAS M'KEAN. iv, 350. FORD ED., vii, 486. (W., Feb. 1801.)

2475. ELECTIONS (Presidential, 1800), Federalists yield.—The minority in the House of Representatives, after seeing the impossibility of electing Burr, the certainty that a legislative usurpation would be resisted by arms, and a recourse to a convention to re-organize and amend the government, held a consultation on this dilemma, whether it would be better for them to come over in a body and go with the tide of the times, or by a negative conduct suffer the election to be made by a bare majority, keeping their body entire and unbroken, to act in phalanx on such ground of opposition as circumstances shall offer; and I know their determination on this question only by their vote of yesterday. [Feb. 17.] Morris, of Vermont, withdrew, which made Lyon's vote that of his State. The Maryland federalists put in four blanks, which made the positive ticket of their colleagues the vote of the State. South Carolina and Delaware put in six blanks. So there were ten States for one candidate, four for another, and two blanks. We consider this, therefore, as a declaration of war, on the part of this band. But their conduct appears to have brought over to us the whole body of federalists, who, being alarmed with the danger of a dissolution of the government, had been made most anxiously to wish the very administration they had opposed, and to view it, when obtained, as a child of their own. They [illegible] too their quondam leaders separated fairly from them, and themselves relegated under other banners. Even Hamilton and Higginson have been partisans for us. This circumstance, with the unbounded confidence which will at-

tach to the new ministry, as soon as known, will start us on right ground.*—To JAMES MADISON. iv, 355. FORD ED., vii, 494. (W., Feb. 18, 1801.)

2476. ELECTIONS (Presidential, 1800), Military Force and.—How happy that our army had been disbanded! What might have happened otherwise seems rather a subject of reflection than explanation.—To NATHANIEL NILES REGISTER. iv, 377. FORD ED., viii, 24. (W., March 1801.)

2477. ELECTIONS (Presidential, 1800), National Convention and.—I have been above all things, solaced by the prospect which opened on us, in the event of a non-election of a President; in which case, the Federal Government would have been in the situation of a clock or watch run down. There was no idea of force, nor of any occasion for it. A convention, invited by the republican members of Congress, with the virtual President and Vice-President, would have been on the ground in eight weeks, would have repaired the Constitution where it was defective, and wound it up again. This peaceable and legitimate resource, to which we are in the habit of implicit obedience, superseding all appeal to force, and being always within our reach, shows a precious principle of self-preservation in our composition, till a change of circumstances shall take place, which is not within prospect at any definite period.—To DR. JOSEPH PRIESTLEY. iv, 374. FORD ED., viii, 22. (W., March 1801.)

2478. —— ——. There was general alarm during the pending of the election in Congress, lest no President should be chosen, the government be dissolved, and anarchy ensue. But the cool determination of the really patriotic to call a convention in that case, which might be on the ground in eight weeks, and wind up the machine again which had only run down, pointed out to my mind a perpetual and peaceable resource against —— [force?] ——† in whatever extremity might befall us; and I am certain a convention would have commanded immediate and universal obedience.—To NATHANIEL NILES. iv, 377. FORD ED., viii, 24. (W., March 1801.)

2479. ELECTIONS (Presidential, 1800), Parity of Vote.—[The prospect of a parity between the two republican candidates] has produced great dismay and gloom on the republican gentlemen here, and exultation in the federalists, who openly declare they will prevent an election, and will name a President of the Senate *pro tem.* by what they say would only be a *stretch* of the Constitution.—To JAMES MADISON. iv, 343. FORD ED., vii, 470. (W., Dec. 19, 1800.)

2480. —— ——. We are brought into dilemma by the probable equality of the two Republican candidates. The federalists in Congress mean to take advantage of this, either to prevent an election altogether, or reverse what has been understood to have been the wishes of the people as to the President and Vice-President; wishes which the Constitution did not permit them specially to designate. The latter alternative still gives us a Republican administration. The former, a suspension of the Federal Government, for want of a head. This opens to us an abyss, at which every sincere patriot

* The last two sentences are omitted in the Congress edition.—EDITOR.
† Writing faded in MS.—EDITOR.

must shudder.—To John Breckenridge. iv, 342. Ford ed., vii, 469. (W., Dec. 1800.)

2481. ——— ———. Although we have not official information of the votes for President, and cannot have until the first week in February, yet the state of the votes is given on such evidence, as satisfies both parties that the two republican candidates stand highest. From South Carolina we have not even heard of the actual vote; but we have learned who were appointed electors, and with sufficient certainty how they would vote. It is said they would withdraw from yourself one vote. It has also been said that a General Smith, of Tennessee, had declared that he would give his second vote to Mr. Gallatin, not from any indisposition towards you, but extreme reverence to the character of Mr. Gallatin. It is also surmised that the vote of Georgia will not be entire. Yet nobody pretends to know these things of a certainty, and we know enough to be certain that what it is surmised will be withheld, will still leave you four or five votes at least above Mr. Adams. However, it was badly managed not to have arranged with certainty what seems to have been left to hazard. It was the more material, because I understand several of the high-flying federalists have expressed their hope that the two republican tickets may be equal, and their determination, in that case, to prevent a choice by the House of Representatives (which they are strong enough to do), and let the government devolve on a President of the Senate. Decency required that I should be so entirely passive during the late contest that I never once asked whether arrangements had been made to prevent so many from dropping votes intentionally, as might frustrate half the republican wish; nor did I doubt, till lately, that such had been made.—To Aaron Burr. iv, 340. Ford ed., vii, 466. (W., Dec. 1800.)

2482. ——— ———. It seems tolerably well ascertained (though not officially) that the two republican candidates * * * have a decided majority; probably of 73 to 65, but equally probable that they are even between themselves, and that the federalists are disposed to make the most of the embarrassment this occasions, by preventing any election by the House of Representatives. It is far from certain that nine representatives in that House can be got to vote for any candidate. What the issue of such a dilemma may be cannot be estimated.—To Caesar Rodney. Ford ed., vii, 472. (W., Dec. 1800.)

2483. ELECTIONS (Presidential, 1800), Party Amalgamation and.—The suspension of public opinion [pending the election in the House of Representatives], the alarm into which it threw all the patriotic part of the federalists, the danger of the dissolution of our Union, and unknown consequences of that, brought over the great body of them to wish with anxiety and solicitude for a choice to which they had before been strenuously opposed. In this state of mind, they separated from their congressional leaders, and came over to us; and the manner in which the last ballot was given has drawn a fixed line of separation between them and their leaders. When the election took effect, it was the most desirable of events to them. This made it a thing of their choice, and finding themselves aggregated with us accordingly, they are in a state of mind to be consolidated with us, if no intemperate measures on our part revolt them again. I am

persuaded that weeks of ill-judged conduct here, has strengthened us more than years of prudent and conciliatory administration could have done.—To Thomas Lomax. iv, 361. Ford ed., vii, 500. (W., Feb. 1801.)

2484. ——— ———. Our information from all quarters is that the whole body of federalists concurred with the republicans in the last elections, and with equal anxiety. They had been made to interest themselves so warmly for the very choice, which while before the people they opposed, that when obtained it came as a thing of their own wishes, and they find themselves embodied with the republicans, and their quondam leaders separated from them; and I verily believe they will remain embodied with us, so that this conduct of the minority has done in one week what very probably could hardly have been effected by years of mild and impartial administration.—To T. M. Randolph. iv, 359. Ford ed., vii, 359. (W., Feb. 1801.)

2485. ELECTIONS (Presidential, 1800), The People and.—The order and good sense displayed * * * in the momentous crisis which lately arose, really bespeak a strength of character in our nation which augurs well for the duration of our Republic; and I am much better satisfied now of its stability than I was before it was tried.—To Dr. Joseph Priestley. iv, 374. Ford ed., viii, 22. (W., March 1801.)

2486. ——— ———. The character which our fellow citizens have displayed on this occasion, gives us everything to hope for the permanence of our government.—To General Warren. iv, 376. (W., 1801.)

2487. ELECTIONS (Presidential, 1800), A President pro tem.—The federalists appear determined to prevent an election, and to pass a bill giving the government to Mr. Jay, appointed Chief Justice, or to Marshall as Secretary of State. Yet I am rather of opinion that Maryland and Jersey will give the seven republican majorities.—To James Madison. iv, 344. Ford ed., vii, 473. (W., Dec. 1800.)

2488. ——— ———. The prospect of preventing [the Senate from naming a President pro tem.] is as follows: Georgia, North Carolina, Tennessee, Kentucky, Vermont, Pennsylvania, and New York can be counted on for their vote in the House of Representatives, and it is thought by some that Baer of Maryland, and Linn, of New Jersey, will come over. Some even count on Morris, of Vermont. But you must know the uncertainty of such a dependence under the operation of caucuses and other federal engines. The month of February, therefore, will present us storms of a new character. Should they have a particular issue, I hope you will be here a day or two, at least, before the 4th of March. I know that your appearance on the scene before the departure of Congress, would assuage the minority, and inspire in the majority confidence and joy unbounded, which they would spread far and wide on their journey home. Let me beseech you, then, to come with a view of staying perhaps a couple of weeks, within which time things might be put into such a train, as would permit us both to go home for a short time, for removal.—To James Madison. iv, 343. Ford ed., vii, 470. (W., Dec. 1800.)

2489. ——— ———. We do not see what is to be the issue of the present difficulty. The federalists, among whom those of the republican section are not the strongest, propose to prevent an election in Congress, and to transfer the government by an act to the C. J. (Jay) or Secretary of State, or to let it devolve on the President *pro tem.* of the Senate, till next December, which gives them another year's predominance, and the chances of future events.—To Tench Coxe. iv, 345. Ford ed., vii, 475. (W., Dec. 1800.)

2490. ———. If the federalists could have been permitted to pass a law for putting the government into the hands of an officer, they would certainly have prevented an election. But we thought it best to declare openly and firmly, one and all, that the day such an act passed, the middle States would arm, and that no such usurpation, even for a single day, should be submitted to. This first shook them; and they were completely alarmed at the resource for which we declared, to wit, a convention to reorganize the Government and to amend it. The very word "convention" gives them the horrors, as in the present democratical spirit of America. they fear they should lose some of the favorite morsels of the Constitution.—To James Monroe. iv, 354. Ford ed., vii, 490. (W., Feb. 1801.)

2491. ELECTIONS (Presidential, 1800), The Republic and.—The storm [Presidential election] we have passed through proves our vessel indestructible.—To M. de Lafayette. iv, 363. (W., March 1801.)

2492. ———. We have passed through an awful scene in this country. * * * A few hardy spirits stood firm to their posts, and the ship has breasted the storm.—To M. de Lafayette. iv, 363. (W., March 1801.)

2493. ———. The late chapter of our history furnishes a lesson to man perfectly new. The times have been awful, but they have proved an useful truth, that the good citizen must never despair of the commonwealth. How many good men abandoned the deck, and gave up the vessel as lost.—To Nathaniel Niles. iv, 376. Ford ed., viii, 24. (W., March 1801.)

2494. ELECTIONS (Presidential, 1800), Republicans and.—The republicans propose to press forward to an election. If they fail in this, a concert between the two higher candidates may prevent the dissolution of the government and danger of anarchy, by an operation, bungling indeed and imperfect, but better than letting the Legislature take the nomination of the Executive entirely from the people.—To Tench Coxe. iv, 345. Ford ed., vii, 475. (W., Dec. 1800.)

2495. ELECTIONS (Presidential, 1800), Usurpation and.—In the event of an usurpation, I was decidedly with those who were determined not to permit it. Because that precedent once set, would be artificially reproduced, and end soon in a dictator. Virginia was bristling up, I believe. I shall know the particulars from Governor Monroe, whom I expect to meet in a short visit I must make home. —To Thomas McKean. iv, 369. Ford ed., viii, 12. (W., March 1801.)

2496. ELECTIONS (Presidential, 1804), Appeal to country.—The abominable slanders of my political enemies have obliged me to call for that verdict [on my conduct] from my country in the only way it can be obtained, and if obtained, it will be my sufficient voucher to the rest of the world and to posterity, and leave me free to seek, at a definite time,

the repose I sincerely wished to have retired to now. I suffer myself to make no inquiries as to the persons who are to be placed on the rolls of competition for the public favor. Respect for myself, as well as for the public, requires that I should be the silent and passive subject of their consideration.—To Thomas McKean. Ford ed., viii, 293. (W., Jan. 1804.)

2497. ELECTIONS (Presidential, 1804), Non-Interference with.—[I said to Colonel Burr] that in the election now coming on, I was observing the same conduct [as in 1800]; held no councils with anybody respecting it. nor suffered anyone to speak to me on the subject, believing it my duty to leave myself to the free discussion of the public; that I do not at this moment know, nor have ever heard, who were to be proposed as candidates for the public choice, except so far as could be gathered from the newspapers.—The Anas. ix, 205. Ford ed., i, 302. (January 1804.)

2498. ———. I never interfered directly or indirectly, with my friends or any others, to influence the election either for him [Aaron Burr] or myself. I considered it as my duty to be merely passive, except that in Virginia I had taken some measures to procure for him the unanimous vote of that State, because I thought any failure there might be imputed to me.—The Anas. ix, 205. Ford ed., i, 302. (1804.)

2499. ELECTIONS (Presidential, 1808), Neutrality of Jefferson.—I see with infinite grief a contest arising between yourself and another, who have been very dear to each other, and equally so to me. I sincerely pray that these dispositions may not be affected between you; with me I confidently trust they will not. For independently of the dictates of public duty, which prescribe neutrality to me, my sincere friendship for you both will ensure its sacred observance. I suffer no one to converse with me on the subject. I already perceive my old friend Clinton, estranging himself from me. No doubt lies are carried to him, as they will be to the other two candidates, under forms which, however false, he can scarcely question. Yet, I have been equally careful as to him also, never to say a word on this subject. The object of the contest is a fair and honorable one, equally open to you all: and I have no doubt the personal conduct of all will be so chaste, as to offer no ground of dissatisfaction with each other. But your friends will not be as delicate. I know too well from experience the progress of political controversy, and the exacerbation of spirit into which it degenerates, not to fear the continuance of your mutual esteem. One piquing thing said draws on another, that a third, and always with increasing acrimony, until all restraint is thrown off, and it becomes difficult for yourselves to keep clear of the toils in which your friends will endeavor to interlace you, and to avoid the participation in their passions which they will endeavor to produce. A candid recollection of what you know of each other will be the true corrective. With respect to myself, I hope they will spare me. My longings for retirement are so strong, that I with difficulty encounter the daily drudgeries of my duty. But my wish for retirement itself is not stronger than that of carrying into it the affections of all my friends. I have ever viewed Mr. Madison and yourself as two principal pillars of my happiness. Were either to be withdrawn, I should consider it as among the greatest calamities which could assail my future peace of mind. I have great confidence that the candor and high understanding of both will guard me against this misfortune, the bare possibility of which has so far weighed on my mind, that I could not be easy without unburthening it.—To JAMES MONROE. v, 247. FORD ED., ix, 177. (W., Feb. 1808.)

2500. ———. ———. In the present contest in which you are concerned I feel no passion, I take no part, I express no sentiment. Whichever of my friends is called to the supreme cares of the nation, I know that they will be wisely and faithfully administered, and as far as my individual conduct can influence, they shall be cordially supported.—To JAMES MONROE. v, 255. (March 1808.)

2501. ———. ———. The Presidential question is clearly up daily, and the opposition subsiding. It is very possible that the suffrage of the nation may be undivided. But with this question it is my duty not to intermeddle.—To MERIWETHER LEWIS. v, 321. FORD ED., ix, 200. (W., July 1808.)

2502. ELECTIONS (Presidential, 1816), Good Feeling in.—I have been charmed to see that a Presidential election now produces scarcely any agitation. On Mr. Madison's election there was little, on Monroe's all but none. In Mr. Adams's time and mine, parties were so nearly balanced as to make the struggle fearful for our peace. But since the decided ascendency of the republican body, federalism has looked on with silent but unresisting anguish. In the middle, southern and western States, it is as low as it ever can be; for nature has made some men monarchists and tories by their constitution, and some, of course, there always will be.—To ALBERT GALLATIN. vii, 80. FORD ED., x, 92. (M., 1817.)

2503. ELECTIONS (Presidential, 1824), Constitutional Construction and.—I hope the choice [of the next. President] will fall on some real republican, who will continue the administration on the express principles of the Constitution, unadulterated by constructions reducing it to a blank to be filled with what everyone pleases, and what never was intended.—To SAMUEL H. SMITH. FORD ED., x, 264. (M., Dec. 1823.)

2504. ———. ———. On the question of the next Presidential election, I am a mere looker-on. I never permit myself to express an opinion, or to feel a wish on the subject. I indulge a single hope only, that the choice may fall on one who will be a friend of peace, of economy, of the republican principles of our Constitution, and of the salutary distribution of powers made by that between the general and the local governments.—To SAMUEL SMITH. vii, 286. FORD ED., x, 253. (M., 1823.)

2505. ELECTIONS (Presidential, 1824), Lafayette's visit and.—The eclat of Lafayette's visit has almost merged the Presidential question on which nothing scarcely is said in our papers. That question will lie ultimately between Crawford and Adams; but, at the same time, the vote of the people will be so distracted by subordinate candidates, that possibly they may make no election, and let it go to the House of Representatives. There, it is thought, Crawford's chance is best.—To RICHARD RUSH. vii, 380. FORD ED., x, 322. (M., October 1824.)

2506. ELECTIONS (Presidential, 1824), Militarism and.—This Presidential election has given me few anxieties. With you this must have been impossible, independently of the question, whether we are at last to end our days under a civil or a military government.—To JOHN ADAMS. vii, 387. (M., 1825.)

2507. ELECTIONS (Presidential, 1824), Passiveness of Jefferson.—In the Presidential election I am entirely passive. * * * Both favorites are republican, both will administer the government honestly.—To THOMAS LEIPER. FORD ED., x, 299. (M., 1824.)

2508. ELECTIONS (Presidential, 1824), Sectionalism in.—Who is to be the next President? * * * The question will be ultimately reduced to the northernmost and southernmost candidate. The former will get every federal vote in the Union, and many republicans; the latter, all of those denominated of the old school; for you are not to believe that these two parties are amalgamated, that the lion and the lamb are lying down together.—To MARQUIS LAFAYETTE. vii, 325. FORD ED., x, 280. (M., 1823.)

— ELECTORAL COLLEGE.—See PRESIDENCY.

— ELECTRICITY.—See VEGETATION.

2509. ELLSWORTH (Oliver), Resignation.—Ellsworth remains in France for the benefit of his health. He has resigned his office of Chief Justice. Putting these two things together, we cannot misconstrue his views. He must have had great confidence in Mr. Adams's continuance to risk such a certainty as he held.—To JAMES MADISON. iv, 343. FORD ED., vii, 471. (W., Dec. 1800.)

2510. ELOQUENCE, Models of.—In a country and government like ours, eloquence is a powerful instrument, well worthy of the special pursuit of our youth. Models, indeed, of chaste and classical oratory are truly too rare with us; nor do I recollect any remarkable in England. Among the ancients the most perfect specimens are perhaps to be found in Livy, Sallust and Tacitus. Their pith and brevity constitute perfection itself for an audience of sages, on whom froth and fancy would be lost in air. But in ordinary cases, and with us particularly, more development is necessary. For senatorial eloquence, Demosthenes is the finest model; for the bar, Cicero. The former had more logic, the latter more imagination. Of the eloquence of the pen, we have fine samples in English. Robertson, Sterne, Addison, are of the first merit in the different characters of composition. Hume, in the circumstance of style, is equal to any; but his tory principles spread a cloud over his many and great excellences. The charms of his style and matter have made tories of all England, and doubtful republicans here.—To G. W. SUMMERS. vii, 231. (M., 1822.)

— EMANCIPATION.—See COLONIES, SLAVERY.

2511. EMBARGO, Action advised.—The communications * now made [to Congress] showing the great and increasing dangers with which our vessels, our seamen, and merchandise, are threatened on the high seas, and elsewhere, from the belligerent powers of Europe, and it being of great importance to keep in

* The decrees of the French government of November 21, 1806, and of Spain, February 19, 1807, with the orders of the British government of January and November, 1807.—EDITOR.

safety these essential resources, I deem it my duty to recommend the subject to the consideration of Congress, who will doubtless perceive all the advantages which may be expected from an inhibition of the departure of our vessels from the ports of the United States. Their wisdom will also see the necessity of making every preparation for whatever events may grow out of the present crisis.—SPECIAL MESSAGE. viii, 89. FORD ED., ix, 169. (Dec. 18, 1807.)

2512. ——— ———. Although the decree of the French government of November 21 [1807] comprehended, in its literal terms. the commerce of the United States, yet the prompt explanation by one of the ministers of that government that it was not so understood, and that our treaty would be respected, the practice which took place in the French ports conformably with that explanation, and the recent interference of that government to procure in Spain a similar construction of a similar decree there, had given well-founded expectation that it would not be extended to us; and this was much strengthened by the consideration of their obvious interests. But the information from our minister at Paris * * * is, that it is determined to extend the effect of that decree to us; and it is probable that Spain and the other Atlantic and Mediterranean States of Europe will cooperate in the same measure. The British regulations had before reduced us to a direct voyage to a single port of their enemies, and it is now believed they will interdict all commerce whatever with them. A proclamation, too, of that government (not officially, indeed, communicated to us, yet so given out to the public as to become a rule of action with them) seems to have shut the door on all negotiation with us, except as to the single aggression on the Chesapeake. The sum of these mutual enterprises on our national rights is that France, and her allies, reserving for further consideration the prohibiting our carrying anything to the British territories, have virtually done it, by restraining our bringing a return cargo from them; and Great Britain, after prohibiting a great proportion of our commerce with France and her allies, is now believed to have prohibited the whole. The whole world is thus laid under interdict by these two nations, and our vessels, their cargoes and crews, are to be taken by the one or the other, for whatever place they may be destined, out of our own limits. If, therefore, on leaving our harbors we are certainly to lose them. is it not better, as to vessels, cargoes, and seamen, to keep them at home? This is submitted to the wisdom of Congress, who alone are competent to provide a remedy.—To JOHN MASON. v, 217. (Dec. 1807.)

2513. ——— ———. These decrees and orders,* taken together, want little of amounting to a declaration that every neutral vessel found on the high seas. whatsoever be her cargo, and whatsoever foreign port be that of her departure or destination, shall be deemed lawful prize; and they prove, more and more, the expediency of retaining our vessels, our seamen, and property, within our own harbors, until the dangers to which they are exposed can be removed or lessened.—SPECIAL MESSAGE. viii, 100. FORD ED., ix, 185. (March 1808.)

* Jefferson sent with this message an additional decree of Bonaparte. dated December 17, 1807, and a similar decree of the King of Spain, dated January 3, 1808.—EDITOR.

— EMBARGO, Adams (J. Q.) and.—See 2587.

2514. EMBARGO, Alternative of war. —The alternative was between that and war, and, in fact, it is the last card we have to play, short of war.*—To LEVI LINCOLN. v, 265. (W., March 1808.)

2515. ——— ———. Could the alternative of war, or the Embargo, have been presented to the whole nation, as it occurred to their representatives, there could have been but the one opinion that it was better to take the chance of one year by the Embargo, within which the orders and decrees producing it may be repealed, or peace take place in Europe, which may secure peace to us.—To BENJAMIN SMITH. v, 293. FORD ED., ix, 194. (M., May 1808.)

2516. ——— ———. All regard to the rights of others having been thrown aside, the belligerent powers have beset the highway of commercial intercourse with edicts which, taken together, expose our commerce and mariners, under almost every destination, a prey to their fleets and armies. Each party. indeed, would admit our commerce with themselves, with a view of associating us in their war against the other. But we have wished war with neither. Under these circumstances were passed the laws of which you complain, by those delegated to exercise the powers of legislation for you, with every sympathy of a common interest in exercising them faithfully. In reviewing these measures, therefore, we should advert to the difficulties out of which a choice was of necessity to be made. To have submitted our rightful commerce to prohibitions and tributary exactions from others, would have been to surrender our independence. To resist them by armies was war, without consulting the state of things or the choice of the nation. The alternative preferred by the Legislature of suspending a commerce placed under such unexampled difficulties, besides saving to our citizens their property, and our mariners to their country, has the peculiar advantage of giving time to the belligerent nations to revise a conduct as contrary to their interests as it is to our rights.—REPLY TO A BOSTON REPEAL REQUEST. viii, 134. (Aug. 1808.)

2517. ——— ———. We have to choose between the alternatives of Embargo and war. There is indeed one and only one other, that is submission and tribute. For all the federal propositions for trading to the places permitted by the edicts of the belligerents, result in fact in submission, although they do not choose to pronounce the naked word.—To MR. LETUE. v, 384. (W., Nov. 1808.)

2518. ——— ———. The measures respecting our intercourse with foreign nations were the result of a choice between two evils, either to call and keep at home our seamen and property, or suffer them to be taken under the edicts of the belligerent powers. How a difference of opinion could arise between these alternatives is still difficult to explain on any acknowledged ground; and I am persuaded that when the storm and agitation characterizing the present

* "The Embargo," says Morse in his *Life of Jefferson*, "was a civilized policy, worthy of respect. Moreover, it was a sensible policy. Jefferson alone understood in that time the truth, which is now more generally appreciated, that by sheer growth in population, wealth and industry, a nation gains the highest degree of substantial power and authority. —EDITOR.

prejudice shall have yielded to reason its usurped place, and especially when posterity shall pass its sentence on the present times, justice will be rendered to the course which has been pursued. To the advantages derived from the choice which was made will be added the improvements and discoveries made and making in the arts, and the establishments in domestic manufacture, the effects whereof will be permanent and diffused through our wide-extended continent.—R. TO A. MARYLAND CITIZENS. viii, 164. (1809.)

2519. EMBARGO, Amendments to law. —If, on considering the doubts I shall suggest, you shall still think your draft of a supplementary Embargo law sufficient, in its present form, I shall be satisfied. 1. Is not the first paragraph against the Constitution, which says no preference shall be given to the ports of one State over those of another? You might put down those ports as ports of entry, if that could be made to do. 2. Could not your second paragraph be made to answer by making it say, that no clearance shall be furnished to any vessel laden with *provisions* or *lumber*, to go from one port to another of the United States, without special permission, &c. In that case, we might lay down rules for the necessary removal of provisions and lumber, inland, which should give no trouble to the citizens, but refuse licenses for all coasting transportation of those articles but on such applications from a Governor as may ensure us against any exportation but for the consumption of his State. Portsmouth, Boston, Charleston, and Savannah, are the only ports which cannot be supplied inland. I should like to prohibit *collections*, also, made evidently for clandestine importation. 3. I would rather strike out the words, "in conformity with treaty," in order to avoid any express recognition at this day of that article of the British treaty. It has been so flagrantly abused as to excite the Indians to war against us, that I should have no hesitation in declaring it null, as soon as we see means of supplying the Indians ourselves. I should have no objections to extend the exception to the Indian furs purchased by our traders and sent into Canada.—To ALBERT GALLATIN. v, 267. FORD ED., ix, 189. (W., March 1808.)

2520. EMBARGO, Approval of.—It is a circumstance of great satisfaction that the proceedings of the government are approved by the respectable Legislature of Massachusetts, and especially the late important measure of the Embargo. The hearty concurrence of the States in that measure, will have a great effect in Europe.—To JAMES SULLIVAN. v, 252. (W., March 1808.)

2521. —— ——. Through the body of our country generally our citizens appear heartily to approve and support the Embargo. —To BENJ. SMITH. v, 294. FORD ED., ix, 195. (M., May 1808.)

2522. —— ——. I see with satisfaction that this measure of self-denial is approved and supported by the great body of our real citizens, that they meet with cheerfulness the temporary privations it occasions.—R. TO A. NEW HAMPSHIRE LEGISLATURE. viii, 131. (1808.)

2523. —— ——. The Embargo appears to be approved, even by the federalists of every quarter except yours. [Massachusetts.] To LEVI LINCOLN. v, 265. (W., March 1808.)

2524. —— ——. That the Embargo is approved by the body of republicans through the Union, cannot be doubted. It is equally known that a great proportion of the federalists approve of it; but as they think it an engine which may be used advantageously against the republican system, they countenance the clamors against it.—To D. C. BRENT. v, 305. (W., June 1808.)

2525. —— ——. While the opposition to the late laws of Embargo has in one quarter amounted almost to rebellion and treason, it is pleasing to know that all the rest of the nation has approved of the proceedings of the constituted authorities. The steady union * * * of our fellow citizens of South Carolina, is entirely in their character. They have never failed in fidelity to their country and the republican spirit of the Constitution. Never before was that union more needed or more salutary than under our present crisis.— To MR. LETUE. v, 384. (W., Nov. 1808.)

2526. EMBARGO, Authority to suspend.—The decrees and orders of the belligerent nations having amounted nearly to declarations that they would take our vessels wherever found, Congress thought it best, in the first instance, to break off all intercourse with them. They * * * passed an act authorizing me to suspend the Embargo whenever the belligerents should revoke their decrees or orders as to us. The Embargo must continue, therefore, till they meet again in November, unless the measures of the belligerents should change. When they meet again, if these decrees and orders still continue, the question which they will have to decide will be, whether a continuance of the Embargo or war will be preferable.—To WILLIAM LYMAN. v, 279. (W., April 1808.)

2527. —— ——. If they repeal their orders, we must repeal our Embargo. If they make satisfaction for the Chesapeake, we must revoke our proclamation and generalize its operation by a law. If they keep up impressments, we must adhere to non-intercourse, manufacturer's and a navigation act.—To JAMES MADISON. v, 361. FORD ED., ix, 208. (M., Sep. 1808.)

2528. EMBARGO, Averts war.—The immediate danger * * * of a rupture with England, is postponed for this year. This is effected by the Embargo, as the question was simply between that and war.—To CHARLES PINCKNEY. v, 266. (W., March 1808.)

2529. —— ——. The Embargo, keeping at home our vessels, cargoes and seamen, saves us the necessity of making their capture the cause of immediate war; for, if going to England, France had determined to take them, if to any other place, England was to take them. Till they return to some sense of moral duty, therefore, we keep within ourselves. This gives time. Time may produce peace in Europe; peace in Europe removes all causes of difference, till another European war; and by that time our debt may be paid, our revenues clear, and our strength increased.—To JOHN TAYLOR. v, 227. (W., Jan. 1808.)

2530. EMBARGO, Belligerent Powers and.—I take it to be an universal opinion that war will become preferable to a continuance

of the Embargo after a certain time. Should we not, then, avail ourselves of the intervening period to procure a retraction of the obnoxious decrees peaceably, if possible? An opening is given us by both parties, sufficient to form a basis for such a proposition. I wish you, therefore, to consider the following course of proceeding, to wit: To instruct our ministers at Paris and London to propose immediately to both those powers a declaration on both sides that these decrees and orders shall no longer be extended to vessels of the United States, in which case we shall remain faithfully neutral; but, without assuming the air of menace, to let them both perceive that if they do not both withdraw these orders and decrees, there will arrive a time when our interests will render war preferable to a continuance of the Embargo; that when that time arrives, if one has withdrawn and the other not, we must declare war against that other; if neither shall have withdrawn, we must take our choice of enemies between them. This, it will certainly be our duty to have ascertained by the time Congress shall meet in the fall or beginning of winter; so that taking off the Embargo, they may decide whether war must be declared, and against whom.—To JAMES MADISON. v, 257. FORD ED., ix, 179. (W., March 1808.) See 2558.

2531. EMBARGO, Benefits of.—It has rescued from capture an important capital, and our seamen from the jails of Europe. It has given time to prepare for defence, and has shown to the aggressors of Europe that evil, as well as good actions, recoil on the doers.—R. TO A. PITTSBURG REPUBLICANS. viii, 141. (1808.)

2532. ————. I have been highly gratified with the late general expressions of public sentiment in favor of a measure which alone could have saved us from immediate war, and give time to call home eighty millions of property, twenty or thirty thousand seamen, and two thousand vessels. These are now nearly at home, and furnish a great capital, much of which will go into manufactures, and seamen to man a fleet of privateers, whenever our citizens shall prefer war to a longer continuance of the Embargo. Perhaps, however, the whole of the ocean may be tired of the solitude it has made on that element, and return to honest principles; and his brother robber on the land may see that, as to us, the grapes are sour.— To JOHN LANGDON. FORD ED., ix, 201. (M., Aug. 1808.)

2533. ————. It alone could have saved us from immediate war, and give time to call home eighty millions of property, twenty or thirty thousand seamen, and two thousand vessels. These are now nearly at home, and furnish a great capital, much of which will go into manufactures and remain to man a fleet of privateers, whenever our citizens shall prefer war to a longer continuance of the Embargo. Perhaps, however, the whole of the ocean may be tired of the solitude it has made on that element, and return to honest principles, and that his brother robber on the land may see that, as to us, the grapes are sour.— To GOVERNOR JOHN LANGDON. viii, 132. FORD ED., ix, 201. (M., Aug. 1808.)

2534. ————. We have the satisfaction, to reflect that in return for the privations by the measure, and which our fellow citizens in general have borne with patriotism, it has had the important effects of saving our mariners and our vast mercantile property, as well as of affording

time for prosecuting the defensive and provisional measures called for by the occasion. It has demonstrated to foreign nations the moderation and firmness which govern our councils, and to our citizens the necessity of uniting in support of the laws and the rights of their country, and has thus long frustrated those usurpations and spoliations which, if resisted, involve war; if submitted to, sacrificed a vital principle of our national independence.— EIGHTH ANNUAL MESSAGE. viii, 105. FORD ED., ix, 219. (1808.)

2535. ————. By withdrawing a while from the ocean we have suffered some loss; but we have gathered home our immense capital, exposed to foreign depredation, we have saved our seamen from the jails of Europe, and gained time to prepare for the defence of our country.—R. TO A. CONNECTICUT REPUBLICANS. viii, 140. (Nov. 1808.)

2536. ————. The edicts of the two belligerents, forbidding us to be seen on the ocean, we met by an Embargo. This gave us time to call home our seamen, ships and property, to levy men and put our seaports into a certain state of defence.—To DUPONT DE NEMOURS. v, 432. (W., March 1809.)

— EMBARGO, Bonaparte's views on.— See 861.

2537. EMBARGO, Coasting trade and. —With respect to the coasting trade, my wish is only to carry into full effect the intentions of the Embargo laws. I do not wish a single citizen in any of the States to be deprived of a meal of bread, but I set down the exercise of commerce, merely for profit, as nothing when it carries with it the danger of defeating the objects of the Embargo.—To ALBERT GALLATIN. v, 297. (M., May 1808.)

2538. EMBARGO, Coercion of Europe.— The resolutions of the republican citizens of Boston are worthy of the ancient character of the sons of Massachusetts, and of the spirit of concord with her sister States, which, and which alone, carried us successfully through the Revolutionary war, and finally placed us under that national government, which constitutes the safety of every part, by uniting for its protection the powers of the whole. The moment for exerting these united powers, to repel the injuries of the belligerents of Europe, seems likely to be pressed upon us.—To WILLIAM EUSTIS. v, 410. FORD ED., ix, 235. (W., Jan. 1809.)

2539. EMBARGO, Congress and.—The House of Representatives passed last night a bill for the meeting of Congress on the 22d of May. This substantially decides the course they mean to pursue; that is, to let the Embargo continue till then, when it will cease, and letters of marque and reprisal be issued against such nations as shall not then have repealed their obnoxious edicts. The great majority seem to have made up their minds on this, while there is considerable diversity of opinion on the details of preparation; to wit, naval force, volunteers, army, non-intercourse. —To THOMAS LIEPER. v, 417. FORD ED., ix, 238. (W., January 21, 1809.)

2540. EMBARGO, Duration of.—The embargo may go on a certain time, perhaps through the year, without the loss of property to our citizens, but only its remaining unemployed on their hands. A time would come, however, when war would be preferable to a continuance of the Embargo.—To CHARLES PINCKNEY. v, 266. (W., March 1808.)

2541. —— ——. The absurd opinion has been propagated, that this temporary and necessary arrangement was to be a permanent system, and was intended for the destruction of commerce. The sentiments expressed in the paper you were so kind as to enclose to me, [address of Boston republicans] show that those who have concurred in them have judged with more candor the intentions of their government, and are sufficiently aware of the tendency of the excitements and misrepresentations which have been practiced on this occasion.— To DR. WILLIAM EUSTIS. v, 410. FORD ED., ix, 235. (W., January 1809.)

2542. EMBARGO, Effect on industry.— Of the several interests composing those of the United States, that of manufactures would, of course, prefer to war a state of non-intercourse, so favorable to their rapid growth and prosperity. Agriculture, although sensibly feeling the loss of market for its produce, would find many aggravations in a state of war. Commerce and navigation, or that portion which is foreign, in the inactivity to which they are reduced by the present state of things, certainly experience their full share in the general inconvenience; but whether war would to them be a preferable alternative, is a question their patriotism would never hastily propose. It is to be regretted, however, that overlooking the real sources of the sufferings, the British and French edicts which constitute the actual blockade of our foreign commerce and navigation, they have, with too little reflection, imputed them to laws which have saved them from greater, and have preserved for our own use our vessels, property and seamen, instead of adding them to the strength of those with whom we might eventually have to contend. The Embargo, giving time to the belligerent powers to revise their unjust proceedings, and to listen to the dictates of justice, of interest and reputation, which equally urge the correction of their wrongs, has availed our country of the only honorable expedient for avoiding war; and should a repeal of these edicts supersede the cause for it, our commercial brethren will become sensible that it has consulted their interests, however against their own will. It will be unfortunate for their country if, in the meantime, these their expressions of impatience, should have the effect of prolonging the very sufferings which have produced them, by exciting a fallacious hope that we may, under any pressure, relinquish our equal right of navigating the ocean, go to such ports only as others may prescribe, and there pay the tributary exactions they may impose; an abandonment of national independence and of essential rights, revolting to every manly sentiment. While these edicts are in force, no American can ever consent to a return of peaceable intercourse with those who maintain them.— To THE CITIZENS OF BOSTON. viii, 136. (Aug. 1808.)

2543. EMBARGO, Enforcing.— I am for going substantially to the object of the law, and no further; perhaps a little more earnestly because it is the first expedient, and it is of great importance to know its full effect.—To ALBERT GALLATIN. v, 292. (M., May 1808.)

2544. —— ——. We have such complaints of the breach of Embargo by fraud and force on our northern water line, that I must pray your cooperation with the Secretary of the Treasury by rendezvousing as many new recruits as you can in that quarter.—To HENRY DEARBORN. v, 322. (W., July 1808.)

2545. —— ——. I am clearly of opinion this law ought to be enforced at any expense, *which may not exceed our appropriation.*—To ALBERT GALLATIN. v, 336. (M., Aug. 1808.)

2546. —— ——. In the support of the Embargo laws, our only limit should be that of the appropriations of the department.—To ROBERT SMITH. v, 337. (M., Aug. 1808.)

2547. —— ——. The great leading object of the Legislature was, and ours in execution of it ought to be, to give complete effect to the Embargo laws. They have bidden agriculture, commerce, navigation, to bow before that object, to be nothing when in competition with it. Finding all their endeavors at general rules to be evaded, they finally gave us the power of detention as the panacea, and I am clear we ought to use it freely that we may, by a fair experiment, know the power of this great weapon, the Embargo.—To ALBERT GALLATIN. v, 287. (May 1808.)

2548. —— ——. It is important to crush every example of forcible opposition to the law. —To ALBERT GALLATIN. v, 271. (1808.)

2549. —— ——. The pressure of the Embargo, although sensibly felt by every description of our fellow citizens, has yet been cheerfully borne by most of them, under the conviction that it was a temporary evil, and a necessary one to save us from greater and more permanent evils,—the loss of property and surrender of rights. But it would have been more cheerfully borne, but for the knowledge that, while honest men were religiously observing it, the unprincipled along our sea-coast and frontiers were fraudulently evading it; and that in some parts they had even dared to break through it openly, by an armed force too powerful to be opposed by the collector and his assistants. To put an end to this scandalous insubordination to the laws, the Legislature has authorized the President to empower proper persons to employ militia, for preventing or suppressing armed or riotous assemblages of persons resisting the custom-house officers in the exercise of their duties, or opposing or violating the Embargo laws. He sincerely hopes that, during the short time which these restrictions are expected to continue, no other instances will take place of a crime of so deep a dye. But it is made his duty to take the measures necessary to meet it. He, therefore, requests you, as commanding officer of the militia of your State, to appoint some officer of the militia, of known respect for the laws, in or near to each port of entry within your State, with orders, when applied to by the collector of the district, to assemble immediately a sufficient force of his militia, and to employ them efficaciously to maintain the authority of the laws respecting the Embargo. * * * He has referred this appointment to your Excellency because your knowledge of characters, or means of obtaining it, will enable you to select one who can be most confided in to exercise so serious a power, with all the discretion, the forbearance, the kindness even, which the enforcement of the law will possibly admit, —ever to bear in mind that the life of a citizen, is never to be endangered, but as the last melancholy effort for the maintenance of order and obedience to the laws.—To THE GOVERNORS OF THE STATES. v, 413. FORD ED., ix, 237. (W., Jan. 1809.)

2550. EMBARGO, Evasions of.—The evasions of the preceding Embargo laws went so far towards defeating their objects, and chiefly by vessels clearing out coast-wise, that Congress, by their act of April 25th, authorized the absolute detention of all vessels bound coast-wise with cargoes exciting suspicions of an intention to evade those laws. There being few towns on our sea-coast which cannot be supplied with flour from their interior country, shipments of flour become generally suspicious and proper subjects of detention. Charleston is one of the few places on our seaboard which need supplies of flour by sea for its own consumption. That it may not suffer by the cautions we are obliged to use, I request of your Excellency, whenever you deem it necessary that your present or any future stock should be enlarged, to take the trouble of giving your certificate in favor of any merchant in whom you have confidence, directed to the collector of any port, usually exporting flour, from which he may choose to bring it, for any quantity which you may deem necessary for consumption beyond your interior supplies, enclosing to the Secretary of the Treasury at the same time a duplicate of the certificate as a check on the falsification of your signature. In this way we may secure a supply of the real wants of our citizens, and at the same time prevent those wants from being made a cover for the crimes against their country which unprincipled adventurers are in the habit of committing.*—To THE GOVERNOR OF SOUTH CAROLINA. v, 286. (W., May 1808.)

2551. —— ——. Should these reasonable precautions [to insure adequate supplies of flour] be followed, as is surmised in your letter, by an artificial scarcity, with a view to promote turbulence of any sort or on any pretext, I trust for an ample security against this danger to the character of my fellow citizens of Massachusetts, which has, I think, been emphatically marked by obedience to law, and a love of order. And I have no doubt that whilst we do our duty, they will support us in it. The laws enacted by the General Government, have made it our duty to have the Embargo strictly enforced, for the general good; and we are sworn to execute the laws. If clamor ensue, it will be from the few only, who will clamor whatever we do.—To JAMES SULLIVAN. v, 341. FORD ED., ix, 206. (M., Aug. 1808.)

2552. —— ——. The belligerent edicts rendered our Embargo necessary to call home our ships, our seamen and property. We expected some effect too from the coercion of interest. Some it has had; but much less on account of evasions, and domestic opposition to it.—To GENERAL ARMSTRONG. v, 433. (W., March 1809.)

2553. EMBARGO, Exports and.—After fifteen months' continuance it is now discontinued, because, losing $50,000,000 of exports annually by it, it costs more than war, which might be carried on for a third of that, besides what might be got by reprisal. War, therefore, must follow if the edicts are not repealed before the meeting of Congress in May.—To GENERAL ARMSTRONG. v, 433. (W., March 1809.)

* A similar notification was sent to the Governors of New Orleans, Georgia, Massachusetts and New Hampshire.—EDITOR.

2554. EMBARGO, Fair trial of.—My principle is that the convenience of our citizens shall yield reasonably, and their taste greatly to the importance of giving the present experiment so fair a trial that on future occasions our legislators may know with certainty how far they may count on it as an engine for national purposes.—To ALBERT GALLATIN. v, 309. (W., July 1808.)

2555. EMBARGO, Federalists and.—The federalists during their short-lived ascendency have, by forcing us from the Embargo, inflicted a wound on our interests which can never be cured, and on our affections which will require time to cicatrize. I ascribe all this to one pseudo-republican, Story. He came on (in place of Crowningshield, I believe) and stayed only a few days; long enough, however, to get complete hold of Bacon, who, giving in to his representations, became panic-struck, and communicated his panic to his colleagues, and they to a majority of the sound members of Congress. They believed in the alternative of repeal or civil war, and produced the fatal measure of repeal.—To HENRY DEARBORN. v, 529. FORD ED., ix, 277. (M., July 1810.) See 2568, 2587.

2556. EMBARGO, Foreign subjects and.—The principle of our indulgence of vessels to foreign ministers was, that it was fair to let them send away all their subjects caught here by the Embargo, and who had no other means of getting away.—To ALBERT GALLATIN. v, 347. (M., Aug. 1808.)

2557. EMBARGO, Foreign trade and.—The Embargo laws will have hastened the day when an equilibrium between the occupations of agriculture, manufactures and commerce, shall simplify our foreign concerns to the exchange only of that surplus which we cannot consume for those articles of reasonable comfort, or convenience, which we cannot produce.—R. TO A. PENNSYLVANIA CITIZENS. viii, 163. (1809.)

2558. EMBARGO, France, England and.—Our ministers at London and Paris were instructed to explain to the respective governments there, our disposition to exercise the authority in such manner as would withdraw the pretext on which the aggressions were originally founded, and open a way for a renewal of that commercial intercourse which it was alleged on all sides had been reluctantly obstructed. As each of those governments had pledged its readiness to concur in renouncing a measure which reached its adversary through the incontestable rights of neutrals only, and as the measure had been assumed by each as a retaliation for an asserted acquiescence in the aggressions of the other, it was reasonably expected that an occasion would have been seized by both for evincing the sincerity of their profession, and for restoring to the commerce of the United States its legitimate freedom. The instructions to our ministers with respect to the different belligerents were necessarily modified with reference to their different circumstances, and to the condition annexed by law to the Executive power of suspension, requiring a degree of security to our commerce which would not result from a repeal of the decrees of France. Instead of a pledge, therefore, of a suspension of the Embargo as to her in case of such a repeal, it was presumed that a sufficient inducement might be found in other considerations, and particularly in the change produced by a compliance with our just demands by one belligerent, and a refusal by the other, in the relations between the other and the United States. To Great Britain, whose power on the ocean is so ascendant, it was deemed not inconsistent with that condition to state explicitly, that on her rescinding her orders in relation to the United States their trade would be opened with her, and remain shut to her enemy, in case of his failure to rescind his decrees also. From France no answer has been received, nor any indication that the requested change in her decrees is contemplated. The favorable reception of the proposition to Great Britain was the less to be doubted, as her orders of council had not only been referred for their vindication to an acquiescence on the part of the United States no longer to be pretended, but as the arrangement proposed, while it resisted the illegal decrees of France, involved, moreover, substantially, the precise advantages professedly aimed at by the British orders. The arrangement has, nevertheless, been rejected. This candid and liberal experiment having thus failed, and no other event having occurred on which a suspension of the Embargo by the Executive was authorized, it necessarily remains in the extent originally given to it.—EIGHTH ANNUAL MESSAGE. viii, 103. FORD ED., ix, 214. (Nov. 1808.)

2559. EMBARGO, Frauds under.—The Embargo law is certainly the most embarrassing one we have ever had to execute. I did not expect a crop of so sudden and rank growth of fraud, and open opposition by force could have grown up in the United States.—To ALBERT GALLATIN. v, 336. (M., Aug. 1808.)

2560. —— ——. If the whole quantity of [flour and corn] had been *bonâ fide* landed and retained in Massachusetts, I deemed it certain there could not be a real want for a considerable time, and, therefore, desired the issues of certificates might be discontinued. If, on the other hand, a part has been carried to foreign markets, it proves the necessity of restricting reasonably this avenue to abuse. This is my sole object, and not that a real want of a single individual should be one day unsupplied. In this I am certain we shall have the concurrence of all the good citizens of Massachusetts, who are too patriotic and too just to desire, by calling for what is superfluous, to open a door for the frauds of unprincipled individuals who are trampling on the laws, and forcing a commerce shut to all others, are enriching themselves on the sacrifices of their honester fellow citizens:—sacrifices to which these are generally submitting, as equally necessary whether to avoid or prepare for war.—To JAMES SULLIVAN. v, 340. FORD ED., ix, 205. (M., Aug. 1808.)

2561. EMBARGO, Manufactures and.—The Embargo laws will * * * produce the inestimable advantage of turning the attention and enterprise of our fellow citizens, and the patronage of our State Legislatures, to the establishment of useful manufacture in our country.—R. TO A. PENNSYLVANIA CITIZENS. viii, 163. (M., March 1809.)

2562. EMBARGO, Mitigation of.—I shall be ready to consider any propositions you may make for mitigating the Embargo law of April 25th, but so only as not to defeat the object of the law.—To ALBERT GALLATIN. v, 292. (M., May 1808.)

2563. EMBARGO, Necessity for.—We live in an age of affliction, to which the history of nations presents no parallel. We have for years been looking on Europe covered with blood and violence, and seen rapine spreading itself over the ocean. On this element it ha reached us, and at length in so serious a degree, that the Legislature of the nation ha thought it necessary to withdraw our citizen and property from it, either to avoid, or to pre pare for engaging in the general contest.—To CAPTAIN McGREGOR. v, 356. (M., 1808.)

2564. —— ——. During the delirium o the warring powers, the ocean having become a field of lawless violence, a suspension of our navigation for a time was equally necessary to avoid contest, or to enter it with advantage.—R. TO A. viii, 128. (May 1808.)

2565. —— ——. Those moral principle: and conventional usages which have heretofor been the bond of civilized nations, which have so often preserved their peace by furnishing common rules for the measure of their rights have now given way to force, the law of barbarians, and the nineteenth century dawns with the vandalism of the fifth. Nothing has been spared on our part to preserve the peace of our country during this distempered state of the world.—R. TO A. KETOCTON BAPTISTS. viii, 138. (1808.)

2566. —— ——. Assailed in our essentia rights by two of the most powerful nations on the globe, we have remonstrated, negotiated, and at length retired to the last stand, in the hope of peaceably preserving our rights. In this extremity I have entire confidence that no part of the *people* in any section of the Union, will desert the banners of their country, and co-operate with the enemies who are threatening its existence.—R. TO A. MASSACHUSETTS MILITIA. viii, 151. (1809.)

2567. —— ——. The belligerent power: of Europe [France and England] have interdicted our commerce with nearly the whole world. They have declared it shall be carried on with such places, in such articles, and in such measure only, as they shall dictate: thus prostrating all the principles of right which have hitherto protected it. After exhausting the cup of forbearance and of conciliation to its dregs, we found it necessary, on behalf of that commerce, to take time to call it home into a state of safety, to put the towns and harbors which carry it on into a condition of defence, and to make further preparation for enforcing the redress of its wrongs, and restoring it to its rightful freedom. This required a certain measure of time, which, although not admitting specific limitation, must, from its avowed objects, have been obvious to all; and the progress actually made towards the accomplishment of these objects, proves it now to be near its term.—To DR. WILLIAM EUSTIS. v, 410. FORD ED., ix, 235. (W., January 1809.)

—— EMBARGO, New England and.—See 2587.

2568. EMBARGO, Opposition to.—I am sorry that in some places, chiefly on our northern frontier, a disposition even to oppose the law by force has been manifested. In no country on earth is this so impracticable as in one where every man feels a vital interest in maintaining the authority of the laws, and instantly engages in it as in his own personal cause. Accordingly, we have experienced this spontaneous aid of our good citizens in the neighborhoods where there has been occasion, as I am persuaded we ever shall on such occasions. Through the body of our country generally our citizens appear heartily to approve and support the Embargo.—To Benjamin Smith. v, 293. Ford ed., ix, 195. (M., May 1808.)

2569. —— ——. That the federalists [of Massachusetts] may attempt insurrection is possible, and also that the Governor would sink before it. But the republican part of the State, and that portion of the federalists who approve the Embargo in their judgments, and at any rate would not court mob-law, would crush it in embryo. I have some time ago written to General Dearborn to be on the alert on such an occasion, and to take direction of the public authority on the spot. Such an incident will rally the whole body of republicans of every shade to a single point,—that of supporting the public authority.—To Albert Gallatin. v, 347. (M., Aug. 1808.)

2570. —— ——. The case of opposition to the Embargo laws on the Canada line, I take it to be that of distinct combinations of a number of individuals to oppose by force and arms the execution of those laws, for which purpose they go armed, fire upon the public guards, in one instance at least have wounded one dangerously, and rescue property held under these laws. This may not be an insurrection in the popular sense of the word, but being arrayed in warlike manner, actually committing acts of war, and persevering systematically in defiance of the public authority, brings it so fully within the legal definition of an insurrection, that I should not hesitate to issue a proclamation were I not restrained by motives of which your Excellency seems to be apprized. But as by the laws of New York an insurrection can be acted on without a previous proclamation, I should conceive it perfectly correct to act on it as such, and I cannot doubt it would be approved by every good citizen. Should you think proper to do so, I will undertake that the necessary detachments of militia, called out in support of the laws, shall be considered as in the service of the United States, and at their expense. * * * I think it so important in example to crush these audacious proceedings, and to make the offenders feel the consequences of individuals daring to oppose a law by force, that no effort should be spared to compass this object. —To Governor Tompkins. v, 343. (M., Aug. 1808.)

2571. —— ——. The tories of Boston openly threaten insurrection if their importation of flour is stopped. The next post will stop it. I fear your Governor is not up to the tone of these parricides, and I hope, on the first symptom of an open opposition to the law by force, you will fly to the scene, and aid in suppressing any commotion.—To Henry Dearborn. v, 334. Ford ed., ix, 201. (M., Aug. 1808.)

2572. —— ——. I have some apprehension the tories of Boston, &c., with so poor a head of a Governor, may attempt to give us trouble. I have requested General Dearborn to be on the alert, and fly to the spot where any open and forcible opposition shall be commenced, and to crush it in embryo. I am not afraid but that there is sound matter enough in Massachusetts to prevent an opposition of the laws by force.—To Robert Smith. v, 335. (M., Aug. 1808.)

2573. EMBARGO, Peace and.—An Embargo had, by the course of events, become the only peaceable card we had to play.—To James Bowdoin. v, 299. (M., May 1808.)

2574. —— ——. There never has been a situation of the world before, in which such endeavors as we have made would not have secured our peace. It is probable there never will be such another. If we go to war now, I fear we may renounce forever the hope of seeing an end of our national debt. If we can keep at peace eight years longer, our income, liberated from debt, will be adequate to any war, without new taxes or loans, and our position and increasing strength put us *hors d'insulte* from any nation.—To James Monroe. v, 420. Ford ed., ix, 243. (W., Jan. 1809.)

2575. EMBARGO, Political effects.— Our Embargo has worked hard. It has in fact federalized three of the New England States.— To William Short. v, 436. Ford ed., ix, 249. (W., March 1809.)

2576. EMBARGO, Proclamation suspending.—I never doubted the chicanery of the Anglomen on whatever measures you should take in consequence of the disavowal of Erskine; yet I am satisfied that both the proclamations have been sound. The first has been sanctioned by universal approbation; and although it was not literally the case foreseen by the Legislature, yet it was a proper extension of their provision to a case similar, though not the same. It proved to the whole world our desire of accommodation, and must have satisfied every candid federalist on that head. It was not only proper on the well-grounded confidence that the arrangement would be honestly executed, but ought to have taken place even had the perfidy of England been foreseen. Their dirty gain is richly remunerated to us by our placing them so shamefully in the wrong, and by the union it must produce among ourselves. The last proclamation admits of quibbles, of which advantage will doubtless be endeavored to be taken, by those for whom gain is their God, and their country nothing. But it is soundly defensible. The British minister assured us, that the orders of council would be revoked before the 10th of June. The Executive, trusting in that assurance, declared by proclamation that the revocation was to take place, and on that event the law was to be suspended. But the event did not take place, and the consequence, of course, could not follow. This view is derived from the former non-intercourse law only, having never read the latter one. I had doubted whether Congress must not be called; but that arose from another doubt, whether their second law had not changed the ground, so as to require their agency to give operation to the law.—To President Madison. v, 463. (M., Aug. 1809.)

2577. EMBARGO, Repeal.—I thought Congress had taken their ground firmly for continuing their Embargo until June and then war. But a sudden and unaccountable revolution of opinion took place the last week, chiefly among the New England and New York members, and in a kind of panic they voted the 4th of March for removing the Embargo, and by such a majority as gave all reason to believe they would not agree either to war or non-intercourse. This, too, after we had become satisfied that the Essex Junto had found their expectation desperate, of inducing the people there to either separation or forcible opposition. The majority of Congress, however, has now rallied to the removing the Embargo on the 4th of March, non-intercourse with France and Great Britain, trade everywhere else, and continued war preparations.—To T. M. Randolph. v, 424. Ford ed., ix, 244. (W., Feb. 7, 1809.)

2578. ———— ————. The House of Representatives passed yesterday, by a vote of 81 to 40, the bill from the Senate repealing the Embargo the 4th of March, except against Great Britain and France and their dependencies, establishing a non-intercourse with them, and having struck out the clause for letters of marque and reprisal, which it is thought the Senate will still endeavor to reinstate.—To T. M. Randolph. v, 430. Ford ed., ix, 248. (W., Feb. 28, 1809.)

2579. ———— ————. We have taken off the Embargo, except as to France and England and their territories, because fifty millions of exports, annually sacrificed, are the treble of what war would cost us: besides, that by war we should take something, and lose less than at present.—To Dupont de Nemours. v, 432. (W., March 2, 1809.)

2580. ———— ————. The repeal of the Embargo is the immediate parent of all our present evils, and has reduced us to a low standing in the eyes of the world. I should think that even the federalists themselves must now be made, by their feelings, sensible of their error. The wealth which the Embargo brought home safely, has now been thrown back into the laps of our enemies, and our navigation completely crushed, and by the unwise and unpatriotic conduct of those engaged in it.—To Henry Dearborn. v, 529. Ford ed., ix, 277. (M., July 1810.)

2581. ———— ————. Our business certainly was to be still. But a part of our nation chose to declare against this, in such a way as to control the wisdom of the government. I yielded with others, to avoid a greater evil. But from that moment, I have seen no system which could keep us entirely aloof from these agents of destruction. [France and England.]—To Dr. Walter Jones. v, 511. Ford ed., ix, 274. (M., 1810.)

2582. EMBARGO, Salutary.—That the Embargo laws were salutary and indispensably necessary to meet the obstructions [of our commerce], are truths as evident to every candid man, as it is worthy of every good citizen to declare his reprobation of that system of opposition which goes to an avowed and practical resistance of these laws.—R. to A. Annapolis Citizens. viii, 150. (1809.)

2583. EMBARGO, Seamen and.—The difficulties of the crisis will certainly fall with greater pressure on some descriptions of citizens than on others; and on none perhaps with greater than our seafaring brethren. Should any means of alleviation occur within the range of my duties, I shall with certainty advert to the situation of the petitioners, and, in availing the nation of their services, aid them with a substitute for their former occupations.—To Captain McGregor. v, 357. (M., 1808.)

2584. EMBARGO, Submission, or War?—The questions of submission, of war, or Embargo, are now before our country as unembarrassed as at first. Submission and tribute, if they be our choice, will be no baser now than at the date of the Embargo. But if, as I trust, that idea be spurned, we may now decide on the other alternatives of war and Embargo, with the advantage of possessing all the means which have been rescued from the grasp of capture.—R. to A. Connecticut Republicans. viii, 141. (Nov. 1808.)

2585. ———— ————. The congressional campaign is just opening. Three alternatives alone are to be chosen from. 1. Embargo. 2. War 3. Submission and tribute. And, wonderful to tell, the last will not want advocates. The real question, however, will lie between the two first, on which there is considerable division. As yet, the first seems most to prevail; but opinions are by no means yet settled down. Perhaps the advocates of the second may, to a formal declaration of war, prefer *general* letters of marque and reprisal, because, on a repeal of their edicts by the belligerent, a revocation of the letters of marque restores peace without the delay, difficulties, and ceremonies of a treaty. On this occasion, I think it is fair to leave to those who are to act on them, the decisions they prefer, being to be myself but a spectator. I should not feel justified in directing measures which those who are to execute them would disapprove. Our situation is truly difficult. We have been pressed by the belligerents to the very wall, and all further retreat is impracticable.—To Levi Lincoln. v, 387. Ford ed., ix, 227. (W., Nov. 1808.)

2586. ———— ————. Under a continuance of the belligerent measures which, in defiance of laws which consecrate the rights of neutrals, overspread the ocean with danger, it will rest with the wisdom of Congress to decide on the course best adapted to such a state of things; and bringing with them, as they do, from every part of the Union, the sentiments of our constituents, my confidence is strengthened, that in forming this decision they will, with an unerring regard to the essential rights and interests of the nation, weigh and compare the painful alternatives out of which a choice is to be made. Nor should I do justice to the virtues which on other occasions have marked the character of our fellow citizens, if I did not cherish an equal confidence that the alternative chosen, whatever it may be, will be maintained with all the fortitude and patriotism which the crisis ought to inspire.—Eighth Annual Message. viii, 105. Ford ed., ix, 220. (Nov. 1808.)

2587. EMBARGO, The Union and.—Mr. John Quincy Adams called on me pending the Embargo, and while endeavors were making to obtain its repeal. He made some apologies for the call, on the ground of our not being then in the habit of confidential communications, but that that which he had then to make, involved too seriously the interest of our country not to overrule all other considerations with him, and make it his duty to reveal it to myself particularly. I assured him there was no occasion for any apology for his visit; that, on the contrary, his communications would be thankfully received, and would add a confirmation the more to my entire confidence in the rectitude and patriotism of his conduct and principles. He spoke then of the dissatisfaction of the Eastern portion of our confederacy with the restraints of the Embargo then existing, and their restlessness under it; that there was nothing which might not be attempted, to rid themselves of it. That he had information of the most unquestionable certainty, that certain citizens of the Eastern States (I think he named Massachusetts particularly) were in negotiation with agents of the British government, the object of which was an agreement that the New England States should take no further part in the war then going on; that, without formally declaring their separation from the Union of the States, they should withdraw from all aid and obedience to them; that their navigation and commerce should be free from restraint and interruption by the British; that they should be considered and treated by them as neutrals, and as such might conduct themselves towards both parties; and, at the close of the war, be at liberty to rejoin the confederacy. He assured me that there was imminent danger that the convention would take place; that the temptations were such as might debauch many from their fidelity to the Union; and that, to enable its friends to make head against it, the repeal of the Embargo was absolutely necessary. I expressed a just sense of the merit of this information, and of the importance of the disclosure to the safety and even the salvation of our country; and however reluctant I was to abandon the measure (a measure which persevered in a little longer, we had subsequent and satisfactory assurance would have effected its object completely), from that moment, and influenced by that information, I saw the necessity of abandoning it, and instead of effecting our purpose by this peaceable weapon, we must fight it out, or break the Union. I then recommended to yield to the necessity of a repeal of the Embargo, and to endeavor to supply its place by the best substitute, in which they could procure a general concurrence.—To WILLIAM B. GILES. vii, 424. FORD ED., x, 353. (M., Dec. 1825.)

2588. —— ——. Far advanced in my eighty-third year, worn down with infirmities which have confined me almost entirely to the house for seven or eight months past, it afflicts me much to receive appeals to my memory for transactions so far back as that which is the subject of your letter. My memory is, indeed, become almost a blank, of which no better proof can probably be given you than by my solemn protestation, that I have not the least recollection of your intervention between Mr. John Q. Adams and myself, in what passed on the subject of the Embargo. Not the slightest trace of it remains in my mind. Yet I have no doubt of the exactitude of the statement in your letter. And the less, as I recollect the interview with Mr. Adams, to which the previous communications which had passed between him and yourself were probably and naturally the preliminary. That interview I remember well; not, indeed, in the very words which passed between us, but in their substance, which was of a character too awful, too deeply engraved in my mind, and influencing too materially the course I had to pursue, ever to be forgotten. * * * I cannot too often repeat that this statement is not pretended to be in the very words which passed; that it only gives faithfully the impression remaining on my mind. The very words of a conversation are too transient and fugitive to be so long retained in remembrance. But the substance was too important to be forgotten, not only from the revolution of measures it obliged me to adopt, but also from the renewals of it in my memory on the frequent occasions I have had of doing justice to Mr. Adams, by repeating this proof of his fidelity to his country, and of his superiority over all ordinary considerations when the safety of that was brought into question.—To WILLIAM B. GILES. vii, 424. FORD ED., x, 351. (M., 1825.)

2589. —— ——. You ask my opinion of the propriety of giving publicity to what is stated in your letter, as having passed between Mr. John Quincy Adams and yourself. Of this no one can judge but yourself. It is one of those questions which belong to the forum of feeling. This alone can decide on the degree of confidence implied in the disclosure; whether under no circumstances it was to be communicated to others? It does not seem to be of that character, or at all to wear that aspect. They are historical facts which belong

to the present, as well as future times. I doubt whether a single fact, known to the world, will carry as clear conviction to it, of the correctness of our knowledge of the treasonable views of the federal party of that day, as that disclosed by this, the most nefarious and daring attempt to dissever the Union, of which the Hartford Convention was a subsequent chapter; and both of these having failed, consolidation becomes the fourth chapter of the next book of their history. But this opens with a vast accession of strength from their younger recruits, who, having nothing in them of the feelings or principles of '76, now look to a single and splendid government of an aristocracy, founded on banking institutions, and moneyed incorporations under the guise and cloak of their favored branches of manufactures, commerce and navigation, riding and ruling over the plundered ploughman and beggared yeomanry. This will be to them a next best blessing to the monarchy of their first aim, and perhaps the surest stepping-stone to it.—To WILLIAM B. GILES. vii, 428. FORD ED., x, 356. (M., 1825.)

2590. —— ——. During the continuance of the Embargo Mr. John Quincy Adams informed me of a combination (without naming any one concerned in it), which had for its object a severance of the Union, for a time at least. Mr. Adams and myself not being then in the habit of mutual consultation and confidence, I considered it as the stronger proof of the purity of his patriotism, which was able to lift him above all party passions when the safety of his country was endangered.—To —— ——. vii, 431. (M., 1826.)

2591. EMBARGO, War preferable.—If peace does not take place in Europe, and if France and England will not consent to withdraw the operation of their decrees and orders from us, when Congress shall meet in December, they will have to consider at what point of time the Embargo, continued, becomes a greater evil than war.—LEVI LINCOLN. v, 265. (W., March 1808.)

2592. —— ——. Should neither peace, nor a revocation of the decrees and orders in Europe take place, the day cannot be distant when the Embargo will cease to be preferable to open hostility. Nothing just or temperate has been omitted on our part, to retard or avoid this unprofitable alternative.—To JAMES BOWDOIN. v, 299. (M., May 1808.)

2593. —— ——. How long the continuance of the Embargo may be preferable to war, is a question we shall have to meet, if the decrees and orders and war continue.—To BENJAMIN SMITH. vii, 293. FORD ED., ix, 195. (M., May 1808.)

2594. EMBARGO, War of 1812 and.—That a continuance of the Embargo for two months longer would have prevented our war, * * * I have constantly maintained.—To THOMAS LEIPER. vi, 465. FORD ED., ix, 521. (M., 1815.)

2595. EMBARGO (Virginian), Power to lay.—The Administrator [of Virginia] shall not possess the prerogative * * * of laying embargoes, or prohibiting the exportation of any commodity for a longer space than forty days.—PROPOSED VA. CONSTITUTION. FORD ED., ii, 19. (June 1776.)

2596. EMBARGO (Virginian), Proclamation of.—Whereas, the exportation of provisions from the State [of Virginia] will be attended with manifest injury to the United States, by supplying the enemy, and by rendering it difficult for the public agents and contractors to procure supplies for the American troops, and will. moreover, give encouragement to engrossers and monopolizers to prosecute their baneful practices, I have thought fit by and with the advice and consent of the Council of State, to issue this, my proclamation, for laying an embargo on provisions * * * to continue until the first of May next.—EMBARGO PROCLAMATION. FORD ED., ii, 281. (Nov. 1779.)

2597. EMIGRATION, The Colonies and. —These [emigration and settlement] were effected at the expense of our own blood and treasure, unassisted by the wealth or the strength of Great Britain.*—DECLARATION OF INDEPENDENCE AS DRAWN BY JEFFERSON.

2598. ———. Our emigration from England to this country gave her no more rights over us, than the emigrations of the Danes and Saxons gave to the present authorities of the mother country over England.—AUTOBIOGRAPHY. i, 8. FORD ED., i. 12. (1774.) See EXPATRIATION.

2599. EMIGRATION, Eastern.—The emigrations from the Eastern States are what I have long counted on. The religious and political tyranny of those in power with you, cannot fail to drive the oppressed to milder associations of men, where freedom of mind is allowed in fact as well as in pretense.—To DR. B. WATERHOUSE. FORD ED., ix, 533. (M., 1815.)

— EMIGRATION (European).—See IMMIGRATION.

2600. ENEMIES, Bias of.—An enemy generally says and believes what he wishes.—To C. W. F. DUMAS. ii, 367. (A., 1788.)

2601. ENEMIES, Distinction and.—That you have enemies, you must not doubt, when you reflect that you have made yourself eminent.—To JAMES STEPTOE. i, 324. FORD ED., iii, 63. (1782.)

2602. ENEMIES, Injured friends as.—An injured friend is the bitterest of foes.—FRENCH TREATIES OPINION. vii, 618. FORD ED., vi, 225. (1793.)

2603. ENEMIES, National.—We must endeavor to forget our former love for them, [the English people], and hold them as we hold the rest of mankind, enemies in war, in peace friends.—DECLARATION OF INDEPENDENCE AS DRAWN BY JEFFERSON.

2604. ENEMIES, Official and private. —I hail the day which is to relieve me from being viewed as an official enemy. In private life, I never had above one or two.—To WILLIAM SHORT. FORD ED., ix, 51. (W., May 1807.)

2605. ENEMIES, Patronage and.—We do not mean to leave arms in the hands of active enemies.—To ALBERT GALLATIN. iv, 544. (FORD ED., viii, 304. (1804.)

*Congress struck it out.—EDITOR.

2606. ENEMIES, Political.—Men of energy of character must have enemies; because there are two sides to every question, and taking one with decision, and acting on it with effect, those who take the other will of course be hostile in proportion as they feel that effect.—To JOHN ADAMS. vii, 62. (M., 1817.)

2607. ———. Dr. Franklin had many political enemies, as every character must, which, with decision enough to have opinions, has energy and talent to give them effect on the feelings of the adversary opinion.—To ROBERT WALSH. vii, 108. FORD ED., x, 116. (M., 1818.)

2608. ———. In public life, a man whose political principles have any decided character, and who has energy enough to give them effect, must always expect to encounter political hostility from those of adverse principles.—To RICHARD M. JOHNSON. v, 256. (W., 1808.)

2609. ENEMY GOODS, Right to seize. —I believe it cannot be doubted, but that by the general laws of nations, the goods of a friend found in the vessel of an enemy are free, and the goods of an enemy found in the vessel of a friend are lawful prize. Upon this principle, I presume, the British armed vessels have taken the property of French citizens found in our vessels, in the cases mentioned,* and I confess I should be at a loss on what principle to reclaim it. It is true that sundry nations, desirous of avoiding the inconveniences of having their vessels stopped at sea, ransacked, carried into port, and detained, under pretense of having enemy goods aboard, have, in many instances, introduced by their special treaties another principle between them, that enemy bottoms shall make enemy goods, and friendly bottoms friendly goods; a principle much less embarrassing to commerce, and equal to all parties in point of gain and loss. But this is altogether the effect of particular treaty, controlling in special cases the general principle of the law of nations, and therefore taking effect between such nations only as have so agreed to control it. England has generally determined to adhere to the rigorous principle, having, in no instance, as far as I can recollect, agreed to the modification of letting the property of the goods follow that of the vessel, except in the single one of her treaty with France. We have adopted this modification in our treaties with France, the United Netherlands and Russia; and therefore, as to them, our vessels cover the goods of their enemies, and we lose our goods when in the vessels of their enemies. * * * With England, Spain, Portugal, and Austria, we have no treaties; therefore, we have nothing to oppose to their acting according to the general law of nations, that enemy goods are lawful prize though found in the bottom of

*The capture of French citizens, with their slaves and merchandise, while on their way, in merchant vessels of the United States, from the French West Indies to the United States.—EDITOR.

a friend.—To E. C. Genet. iv, 24. Ford ed., vi, 356. (Pa., July 1793.)

2610. —— ——. I believe I may safely affirm * * * that France is the gainer, and we the loser by the principle of our treaty. Indeed, we are the losers in every direction of that principle; for when it works in our favor, it is to save the goods of our friends; when it works against us, it is to lose our own; and we shall continue to lose while the rule is only partially established. When we shall have established it with all nations, we shall be in a condition neither to gain nor lose, but shall be less exposed to vexatious searches at sea. To this condition we are endeavoring to advance; but as it depends on the will of other nations as well as our own, we can only obtain it when they shall be ready to concur.—To E. C. Genet. iv, 25. Ford ed., vi, 357. (Pa., July 1793.) See Free Ships, Free Goods.

— **ENERGY OF GOVERNMENT.**—See Government.

— **ENGINE, The Steam.**—See Steam.

2611. **ENGLAND, American antagonism.**—The war between France and England seems to be producing an effect not contemplated. All the old spirit of 1776, rekindling the newspapers from Boston to Charleston, proves this; and even the monocrat papers are obliged to publish the most furious philippics against England. A French frigate took a British prize off the capes of Delaware the other day, and sent her up here [Philadelphia]. Upon her coming into sight, thousands and thousands of the *yeomanry* of the city crowded and covered the wharves. Never before was such a crowd seen there; and when the British colors were seen *reversed*, and the French flying above them, they burst into peals of exultation. To James Monroe. iii, 548. Ford ed., vi, 238. (Pa., May 1793.)

— **ENGLAND, American colonies and.** —See Colonies.

2612. **ENGLAND, Amity with.**—No two nations on earth can be so helpful to each other as friends, nor so hurtful as enemies. And in spite of their insolence, I have ever wished for an honorable and cordial amity with them as a nation.—To Robert Walsh. Ford ed., x, 155. (M., 1820.)

— **ENGLAND, Anglo-Saxon language.** —See Languages.

2613. **ENGLAND, Aristocratic Government.**—The English government never dies because their King is no part of it; he is a mere formality and the real government is the aristocracy of the country, for the House of Commons is of that class.—To Doctor Samuel Brown. vi, 165. (M., 1813.)

2614. **ENGLAND, Bonaparte and.**—The events which have taken place in France have lessened in the American mind the motives of interest which it felt in that Revolution, and its amity towards that country now rests

on its love of peace and commerce. We see, at the same time, with great concern, the position in which Great Britain is placed, and should be sincerely afflicted were any disaster to deprive mankind of the benefit of such a bulwark against the torrent which has for some time been bearing down all before it. But her power and powers at sea seem to render everything safe in the end.—To Sir John Sinclair. iv, 491. (W., June 1803.) See Bonaparte.

— **ENGLAND, Burning of U. S. Capitol by.**—See Capitol.

— **ENGLAND, Canada and.**—See Canada.

2615. **ENGLAND, Commerce with.**—Our people and merchants must consider their business as not yet settled with England. After exercising the self denial which was requisite to carry us through the war, they must push it a little further to obtain proper peace arrangements with them. They can do it the better as all the world is open to them; and it is very extraordinary if the whole world besides cannot supply them with what they may want.—To James Monroe. Ford ed., iv, 40. (P., 1785.)

2616. —— ——. If we can obtain from Great Britain reasonable conditions of commerce (which, in my idea, must forever include an admission into her [West India] islands), the freest ground between these two nations would seem to be the best. But if we can obtain no equal terms from her, perhaps Congress might think it prudent, as Holland has done, to connect us unequivocally with France. Holland has purchased the protection of France. The price she pays, is *aid in time of war*. It is interesting for us to purchase a free commerce with the French islands. But whether it is best to pay for it by *aids in war, or by privileges in commerce, or not to purchase it at all*, is the question.— Report to Congress. ix, 244. Ford ed., iv, 130. (P., 1785.)

2617. —— ——. Nothing will bring the British to reason but physical obstruction, applied to their bodily senses. We must show that we are capable of foregoing commerce with them, before they will be capable of consenting to an equal commerce. We have all the world besides open to supply us with gewgaws, and all the world to buy our tobacco.— To James Madison. Ford ed., iv, 36. (P., 1785.)

2618. —— ——. I know nothing which would act more powerfully as a sumptuary law with our people than an inhibition of commerce with England. They are habituated to the luxuries of that country and will have them while they can get them. They are unacquainted with those of other countries; and therefore will not very soon bring them so far into fashion as that it shall be thought disreputable not to have them in one's house, or on their table.—To James Madison. Ford ed., iv, 37. (P., 1785.)

2619. —— ——. England declines all arrangements with us. They say their commerce is so necessary to us, that we shall not deny it to ourselves for the sake of the carrying business, as the only trade they leave us is that with Great Britain immediately, and that is a losing one. I hope we shall show them we have sense and spirit enough to suppress that, or at least to exclude them from any share in the carriage of our commodities. Their spirit towards us is deeply hostile and they seem as if they did not fear a war with us.—To David Humphreys. i, 559. (P., 1786.)

2620. —— ——. With respect to a commercial treaty with this country, be assured that the government not only has it not in contemplation at present to make any, but that they do not conceive that any circumstances will arise which shall render it expedient for them to have any political connection with us. They think we shall be glad of their commerce on their own terms.—To Richard Henry Lee. i, 541. Ford ed., iv, 206. (L., April 1786.)

2621. —— ——. The English think we cannot prevent our countrymen from bringing our trade into their laps. A conviction of this determines them to make no terms of commerce with us. They say they will pocket our carrying trade as well as their own. Our overtures of commercial arrangements have been treated with a derision, which shows their firm persuasion that we shall never unite to suppress their commerce, or even to impede it.—To John Page. i, 550. Ford ed., iv, 214. (P., 1786.)

2622. —— ——. That no commercial arrangements between Great Britain and the United States have taken place, cannot be imputed to us. The proposition has surely been often enough made, perhaps too often.—To Sir John Sinclair. iii, 283. (Pa., 1791.)

2623. —— ——. The bill lately passed in England, prohibiting the business of this country with France from passing through the medium of England, is a temporary embarrassment to our commerce, from the unhappy predicament of its all hanging on the pivot of London. It will be happy for us, should it be continued till our merchants may establish connections in the countries in which our produce is consumed, and to which it should go directly.—To Gouverneur Morris. iii, 580. Ford ed., vi, 300. (Pa., June 1793.)

2624. —— ——. My opinion of the British government is, that nothing will force them to do us justice but the loud voice of their people, and that this can never be excited but by distressing their commerce.—To President Washington. iv, 106. Ford ed., vi, 510. (M., 1794.) See Duties, Embargo, Navigation and Treaties.

2625. ENGLAND, Conciliation with.— I look upon all cordial conciliation with England as desperate during the life of the present King.—To President Madison. v, 465. (M., Aug. 1809.)

2626. ENGLAND, Corruption of government.—We know that the government of England, maintaining itself by corruption at home, uses the same means in other countries of which she has any jealousy, by subsidizing agitators and traitors among themselves to distract and paralyze them. She sufficiently manifests that she has no disposition to spare ours.—To Governor Plumer. vi, 415. (1815.) See Hartford Convention.

2627. ENGLAND, Crisis in.—I believe with you that the crisis of England is come. What will be its issue it is vain to prophesy; so many thousand contingencies may turn up to affect its direction. Were I to hazard a guess, it would be that they will become a military despotism. Their recollections of the portion of liberty they have enjoyed will render force necessary to retain them under pure monarchy. Their pressure upon us has been so severe and so unprincipled, that we cannot deprecate their fate, though we might wish to see their naval power kept up to the level of that of the other principal powers separately taken.—To William Duane. v, 552. Ford ed., ix, 286. (M., 1810.)

2628. —— ——. What England is to become on the crush of her internal structure, now seeming to be begun, I cannot foresee. Her moneyed interests, created by her paper system, and now constituting a baseless mass of wealth equal to that of the owners of the soil, must disappear with that system, and the medium for paying great taxes thus failing, her navy must be without support. That it shall be supported by permitting her to claim dominion of the ocean, and to levy tribute on every flag traversing that, as lately attempted and not yet relinquished, every nation must contest, even *ad internecionem*. And yet, that retiring from this enormity, she should continue able to take a fair share in the necessary equilibrium of power on that element, would be the desire of every nation.—To Thomas Law. v, 557. Ford ed., ix, 293. (M., 1811.)

2629. —— ——. The approach of this crisis is, I think, visible, in the departure of her precious metals, and depreciation of her paper medium. We, who have gone through that operation, know its symptoms, its course, and consequences. In England, they will be more serious than elsewhere, because half the wealth of her people is now in that medium, the private revenue of her money-holders, or rather of her paper-holders, being, I believe, greater than that of her land-holders. Such a proportion of property, imaginary and baseless as it is, cannot be reduced to vapor but with great explosion. She will rise out of its ruins. however, because her lands, her houses, her arts will remain, and the greater part of her men. And these will give her again that place among nations which is proportioned to her natural means, and which we all wish her to hold.—To James Maury. vi, 52. Ford ed., ix, 349. (M., April 1812.)

—— ENGLAND, Debts to citizens of.— See Debts Due British.

2630. ENGLAND, Detested.—The Count de Moustier [French Minister] will find the affections of the Americans with France. but their habits with England. Chained to that country by circumstances, embracing what they loathe, they realize the fable of the living and the dead bound together.—To COMTE DE MOUSTIER. ii, 295. (P., 1787.)

2631. ENGLAND, Dread of United States.—Great Britain, in her pride and ascendency, has certainly hated and despised us beyond every earthly object. Her hatred may remain, but the hour of her contempt is passed and is succeeded by dread; not a present, but a distant and deep one. It is the greater as she feels herself plunged into an abyss of ruin from which no human means point out an issue. We also have more reason to hate her than any nation on earth.—To JAMES MONROE. vii, 41. FORD ED., x, 66. (M., 1816.) See HARTFORD CONVENTION.

— **ENGLAND, Embargo and.**—See EMBARGO.

2632. ENGLAND, Flagitious government.—The regeneration of the British government will take a longer time than I have to live. * * * I shall make my exit with a bow to it, as the most flagitious of governments I leave among men.—To WILLIAM DUANE. vi, 77. FORD ED., ix, 367. (M., Aug. 1812.)

2633. —— ——. I consider [the British] government as the most flagitious which has existed since the days of Philip of Macedon, whom they make their model. It is not only founded in corruption itself, but insinuates the same poison into the bowels of every other, corrupts its councils, nourishes factions, stirs up revolutions, and places its own happiness in fomenting commotions and civil wars among others, thus rendering itself truly the *hostis humani generis*.—To JOHN ADAMS. vii, 46. (P. F., 1816.)

2634. ENGLAND AND FRANCE, Banditti.—Our lot happens to have been cast in an age when two nations to whom circumstances have given a temporary superiority over others, the one by land, the other by sea, throwing off all restraints of morality, all pride of national character, forgetting the mutability of fortune, and the inevitable doom which the laws of nature pronounce against departure from justice, individual or national, have declared to treat her reclamations with derision, and to set up force instead of reason as the umpire of nations. Degrading themselves thus from the character of lawful societies into lawless bands of robbers and pirates, they are abusing their brief ascendency by desolating the world with blood and rapine. Against such a banditti, war had become less ruinous than peace. for then peace was a war on one side only.—To J. W. EPPES. vi, 195. FORD ED., ix, 396. (P.F., Sep. 1813.)

2635. —— ——. How much to be lamented that the world cannot unite and destroy these two land and sea monsters. The one drenching the earth with human gore, the other ravaging the ocean with lawless piracies and plunder.—To DR. SAMUEL BROWN. vi, 165. (M., July 1813.)

2636. ENGLAND, Friendly advances of.—Our successors have deserved well of their country in meeting so readily the first friendly advance ever made to us by England. I hope it is the harbinger of a return to the exercise of common sense and common good humor, with a country with which mutual interests would urge a mutual and affectionate intercourse. But her conduct hitherto has been towards us so insulting. so tyrannical and so malicious, as to indicate a contempt for our opinions or dispositions respecting her. I hope she is now coming over to a wiser conduct, and becoming sensible how much better it is to cultivate the good will of the government itself, than of a faction hostile to it; to obtain its friendship gratis than to purchase its enmity by nourishing at great expense a faction to embarrass it, to receive the reward of an honest policy rather than of a corrupt and vexatious one. I trust she has at length opened her eyes to federal falsehood and misinformation, and learned, in the issue of the Presidential election, the folly of believing them. Such a reconciliation to the government, if real and permanent, will secure the tranquillity of our country, and render the management of our affairs easy and delightful to our successors, for whom I feel as much interest as if I were still in their place. Certainly all the troubles and difficulties in the government during our time proceeded from England; at least all others were trifling in comparison with them. —To HENRY DEARBORN. v, 455. (M., June 1809.)

— **ENGLAND, Friendship with United States.**—See FRIENDSHIP.

— **ENGLAND, George III.**—See GEORGE III.

2637. ENGLAND, Governing principles.—Great Britain's governing principles are conquest, colonization, commerce, monopoly.—To WILLIAM CARMICHAEL. ix, 414. FORD ED., v, 229. (1790.)

2638. ENGLAND, Growth of United States and.—Have you no statesmen who can look forward two or three score years? It is but forty years since the battle of Lexington. One-third of those now living saw that day, when we were about two millions of people. and have lived to see this, when we are ten millions. One-third of those now living who see us at ten millions, will live another forty years, and see us forty millions; and looking forward only through such a portion of time as has passed since you and I were scanning Virgil together (which I believe is near three score years), we shall be seen to have a population of eighty millions, and of not more than double the average density of the present. What may not such a people be worth to England as customers and friends? And what might she not apprehend from such a nation as enemies?—To JAMES MAURY. vi, 467. (M., 1815.)

2639. —— ——. Our growth is now so well established * * * that we may safely call ourselves * * * forty millions in forty years. * * * Of what importance then to Great Britain must such a nation be, whether as friends or foes? To SIR JOHN SINCLAIR. vii, 22. (M., 1816.)

2640. ENGLAND, Hatred of United States.—In spite of treaties, England is still our enemy. Her hatred is deep rooted and cordial, and nothing is wanting with her but the power, to wipe us and the land we live in out of existence. Her interest, however. is her ruling passion; and the late American measures have struck at that so vitally, and with an energy, too, of which she had thought us quite incapable, that a possibility seems to open of forming some arrangement with her. When they shall see decidedly, that, without it, we shall suppress their commerce with us, they will be agitated by their avarice on the one hand, and their hatred and their fear of us. on the other. The result of this conflict of dirty passions is yet to be awaited.—To JOHN LANGDON. i, 429. (P., 1785.)

2641. —— ——. That nation [England] hates us, their ministers hate us, and their King, more than all other men, hates us. They have the impudence to avow this; though they acknowledge our trade important to them * * * I think their hostility towards us is much more deeply rooted at present, than during the war.—To JOHN PAGE. i, 550. FORD ED., iv, 214. (P., 1786.)

2642. —— ——. The English hate us because they think our prosperity filched from theirs.—To WILLIAM DUANE. v, 553. FORD ED., ix, 287. (M., 1810.)

2643. —— ——. England would prefer losing an advantage over her enemy to giving one to us It is an unhappy state of mind for her, but I am afraid it is the true one.—To JAMES RONALDSON. v, 553. (M., 1810.)

2644. —— ——. A friendly, a just. and a reasonable conduct on the part of the British might make us the main pillar of their prosperity and existence. But their deep-rooted hatred to us seems to be the means which Providence permits to lead them to their final catastrophe. " Nullum enim in terris gentem esse, nullum infestiorem populum, nomini Romani," said the General who erased Capua from the list of powers. What nourishment and support would not England receive from an hundred millions of industrious descendants, whom some of her people now born will live to see here? What their energies are, she has lately tried. And what has she not to fear from an hundred millions of such men. if she continues her maniac course of hatred and hostility to them? I hope in God she will change.—To CÆSAR A. RODNEY. vi, 448. (M., March 1815.)

2645. ENGLAND, Hostility of.—I think the King, ministers, and nation are more bitterly hostile to us at present, than at any period of the late war. A like disposition on our part has been rising for some time. In what events these things will end, we cannot foresee. Our countrymen are eager in their passions and enterprises, and not disposed to calculate their interests against these. Our enemies (for such they are, in fact), have for twelve years past followed but one uniform rule, that of doing exactly the contrary of what reason points out. Having, early during our contest, observed this in the British conduct, I governed myself by it in all prognostications of their measures; and I can say, with truth, it never failed me but in the circumstance of their making peace with us.*—To WILLIAM CARMICHAEL. i, 552. (P., May 1786.) See TREATIES.

2646. —— ——. The spirit of hostility to us has always existed in the mind of the King, but it has now extended itself through the whole mass of the people, and the majority in the public councils. In a country, where the voice of the people influences so much the measures of administration, and where it coincides with the private temper of the King, there is no pronouncing on future events. It is true they have nothing to gain, and much to lose by a war with us. But interest is not the strongest passion in the human breast.—To JAMES ROSS. i, 561. FORD ED., iv, 217. (P., 1786.)

2647. —— ——. The Marquis of Lansdowne is thoroughly sensible of the folly of the present measures of this country, as are a few other characters about him. Dr. Price is among these, and is particularly disturbed at the present prospect. He acknowledges, however, that all change is desperate; which weighs more, as he is intimate with Mr. Pitt. This small band of friends, favorable as it is, does not pretend to say one word in public on our subject.—To JOHN JAY. i, 544. (L., 1786.)

2648. —— ——. There is no party in our favor here [London] either in power or out of power. Even the opposition concur with the ministry and the nation in this. I can scarcely consider as a party the Marquis of Landsdowne, and a half dozen characters about him, such as Dr. Price, &c., who are impressed with the utility of a friendly connection with us. The former does not venture this sentiment in parliament, and the latter are not in situations to be heard. * * * Were the Marquis to come into the ministry (of which there is not the most distant prospect), he must adopt the King's system, or go out again, as he did before, for daring to depart from it.—To RICHARD HENRY LEE. i, 541. FORD ED., iv, 206. (L., 1786.)

2649. —— ——. The English are still our enemies. The spirit existing there, and rising in America. has a very lowering aspect. To what events it may give birth. I cannot foresee. We are young and can survive them; but their rotten machine must crush under the trial.—To C. W. F. DUMAS. i, 553. (P., 1786.)

*This was written immediately after Adams and Jefferson had reported to Congress their failure to negotiate a commercial treaty with England.—EDITOR.

— ENGLAND, Impressment of American sailors.—See IMPRESSMENT.

2650. ENGLAND, Influence in United States.—The English can do us, as enemies, more harm than any other nation; and in peace and in war, they have more means of disturbing us internally. Their merchants established among us, the bonds by which our own are chained to their feet, and the banking combinations interwoven with the whole, have shown the extent of their control, even during a war with her. They are the workers of all the embarrassments our finances have experienced during the war. Declaring themselves bankrupt, they have been able still to chain the government to a dependence on them, and had the war continued, they would have reduced us to the inability to command a single dollar. They dared to proclaim that they would not pay their obligations, yet our government could not venture to avail themselves of this opportunity of sweeping their paper from the circulation, and substituting their own notes bottomed on specific taxes for redemption, which every one would have eagerly taken and trusted, rather than the baseless trash of bankrupt companies; our government, I say, have still been overawed from a contest with them, and has even countenanced and strengthened their influence, by proposing new establishments, with authority to swindle yet greater sums from our citizens. This is the British influence to which I am an enemy, and which we must subject to our government, or it will subject us to that of Britain.—To CÆSAR A. RODNEY. vi, 449. (M., March 1815.)

2651. ENGLAND, Insolence.—Of all nations on earth, the British require to be treated with the most *hauteur*. They require to be kicked into common good manners.—To COLONEL W. S. SMITH. ii, 284. (P., 1787.)

— ENGLAND, Intrigues to destroy U. S. Government.—See 1097.

— ENGLAND, Jay's treaty.—See JAY TREATY.

2652. ENGLAND, Jefferson and.—As a political man, the English shall never find any passion in me either for or against them. Whenever their avarice of commerce will let them meet us fairly half way, I should meet them with satisfaction, because it would be for our benefit.—To FRANCIS KINLOCH. iii, 197. FORD ED., v, 248. (Pa., 1790.)

2653. ———. I told [Mr. Erskine] I was going out of the Administration and, therefore, might say to him things which I would not do were I to remain in. I wished to correct an error which I, at first, thought his Government above being led into from newspapers, but I apprehend they had adopted it. This was the supposed partiality of the Administration and particularly myself in favor of France and against England. I observed that when I came into the Administration, there was nothing I so much desired as to be on a footing of intimate friendship with England; that I knew as long as she was our friend no enemy could hurt; that I would have sacrificed much to have effected it, and, therefore, wished Mr. King to have continued there as a favorable instrument; that if there had been an equal disposition on their part, I thought it might have been effected: for although the question of impressments was difficult on their side and insuperable with us, yet had that been the sole question, we might have shoved along in the hope of some compromise; that indeed there was a ground of accommodation which his ministry had on two occasions yielded to for a short time, but retracted; that during the administration of Mr. Addington and the short one of Mr. Fox, I had hoped such a friendship practicable, but that during all other administrations, I had seen a spirit so adverse to us that I now despaired of any change. That he might judge from the communications now before Congress whether there had been any partiality to France to whom, he would see, we had never made the proposition to revoke the Embargo immediately, which we did to England, and, again, that we had remonstrated strongly to them on the style of Mr. Champagny's letter, but had not to England on that of Canning, equally offensive; that the letter of Canning, now reading to Congress, was written in the high ropes and would be stinging to every American breast. —ANAS. FORD ED., i, 336. (Nov. 1808.)

2654. ——— ———. With respect to myself I saw great reason to believe their ministers were weak enough to credit the newspaper trash about a supposed personal enmity in myself towards England. This wretched party imputation was beneath the notice of wise men. England never did me a personal injury, other than in open war; and for numerous individuals there, I have great esteem and friendship. And I must have had a mind far below the duties of my station, to have felt either national partialities or antipathies in conducting the affairs confided to me. My affections were first for my own country, and then, generally, for all mankind; and nothing but minds placing themselves above the passions, in the functionaries of this country, could have preserved us from the war to which their provocations have been constantly urging us.—To THOMAS LAW. v, 556. FORD ED., ix, 292. (M., 1811.)

2655. ——— ———. The English newspapers suppose me the personal enemy of their nation. I am not so. I am the enemy to its injuries, as I am to those of France. If I could permit myself to have national partialities, and if the conduct of England would have permitted them to be directed towards her, they would have been so. * * * Had I been personally hostile to England, and biased in favor of either the character or views of her great antagonist, the affair of the Chesapeake put war into my hand. I had only to open it and let havoc loose. But if ever I was gratified with the possession of power, and of the confidence of those who had entrusted me with it, it was on that occasion when I was enabled to use both for the prevention of war, towards which the torrent of passion here was directed almost irresistibly, and when not another person in the United States, less supported by authority and favor, could have resisted it. And now that a definitive adherence to her impressments and Orders of Council renders war no longer unavoidable, my earnest prayer is that our government may enter into no compact of common cause with the other belligerent, but keep us free to make a separate peace, whenever England will separately give us peace and future security. But Lord Liverpool is our witness that this can never be but by her removal from our neighborhood.—To JAMES MAURY. vi, 53. FORD ED., ix, 349. (M., April, 1812.)

2656. ENGLAND, Kindred ties.—Were the English people under a government which should treat us with justice and equity, I should myself feel with great strength the ties which bind us together, of origin, language, laws, and manners; and I am persuaded the two people would become in future, as it was with the ancient Greeks, among whom it was reproachful for Greek to be found fighting against Greek in a foreign army.*—To JOHN ADAMS. vii, 45. (M., 1816.)

2657. ENGLAND, Loss of America.—The object of the present ministry is to buoy up the nation with flattering calculations of their present prosperity, and to make them believe they are better without us than with us. This they seriously believe· for what is it men cannot be made to believe! * * * The other day * * * a General Clark, a Scotchman and ministerialist * * * introduced the subject of American affairs, and in the course of the conversation told me that were America to petition Parliament to be again received on their former footing, the petition would be very generally rejected. He was serious in this, and I think it * * * is the sentiment perhaps of the nation. In this they are wise, but for a foolish reason. They think they lost more by suffering us to participate of their commercial privileges, at home and abroad, than they lose by our political severance. The true reason, however, why such an application should be rejected is that in a very short time, we should oblige them to add another hundred millions to their debt in unsuccessful attempts to retain the subjection offered to them. They are at present in a frenzy, and will not be recovered from it till they shall have leaped the precipice they are now so boldly advancing to.—To RICHARD HENRY LEE. i, 541. FORD ED., iv, 207. (L., 1786.)

2658. ENGLAND, Madison, Jefferson and.—Her ministers have been weak enough to believe from the newspapers that Mr. Madison and myself are personally her enemies. Such an idea is unworthy a man of sense; as we should have been unworthy our

*Adams wrote in reply: "Britain will never be our friend until we are her master. This will happen in less time than you and I have been struggling with her power. provided we remain united."—EDITOR.

trusts could we have felt such a motive of public action. No two men in the United States have more sincerely wished for cordial friendship with her; not as her vassals or dirty partisans, but as members of coequal States, respecting each other, and sensible of the good as well as the harm each is capable of doing the other. On this ground, there was never a moment we did not wish to embrace her. But repelled by their aversions, feeling their hatred at every point of contact, and justly indignant at its supercilious manifestations, that happened which has happened, that will follow which must follow, in progressive ratio, while such dispositions continue to be indulged. I hope they will see this, and do their part towards healing the minds and cooling the temper of both nations.—To MR. MAURY. vi, 468. (M., 1815.) See FRIENDSHIP WITH ENGLAND.

2659. ENGLAND, Maritime rivalry.—The only rivalry that can arise is on the ocean. England may, by petty larceny, thwartings, check us on that element a little, but nothing she can do will retard us one year's growth. We shall be supported there by other nations, and thrown into their scale to make a part of the great counterpoise to her navy. If, on the other hand, she is just to us, conciliatory, and encourages the sentiment of family feelings and conduct, it cannot fail to befriend the security of both. We have the seamen and materials for fifty ships of the line, and half that number of frigates; and were France to give us the money and England the dispositions to equip them, they would give to England serious proofs of the stock from which they are sprung, and the school in which they have been taught: and added to the efforts of the immensity of seacoast lately united under one power, would leave the state of the ocean no longer problematical. Were, on the other hand, England to give the money, and France the dispositions to place us on the sea in all our force, the whole world, out of the continent of Europe, might be our joint monopoly. We wish for neither of these scenes. We ask for peace and justice from all nations; and we will remain uprightly neutral in fact, though leaning in belief to the opinion that an English ascendency on the ocean is safer for us than that of France.—To JAMES MONROE. v, 12. FORD ED., viii, 449. (W., May 1806.)

2660. ENGLAND, Mendacity of Press.—The British government * * * have it much at heart to reconcile their nation to the loss of America. This is essential to the repose, perhaps even to the safety of the King and his ministers. The most effectual engines for this purpose are the public papers. You know well that that government always kept a kind of standing army of news-writers, who, without any regard to truth, or to what should be like truth, invented and put into the papers whatever might serve the ministers. This suffices with the mass of the people, who have no means of distinguishing the false from the true paragraphs of a newspaper.

When forced to acknowledge our independence, they were forced to redouble their efforts to keep the nation quiet. Instead of a few of the papers formerly engaged, they now engage every one. No paper, therefore, comes out without a dose of paragraphs against America. These are calculated for a secondary purpose also, that of preventing the emigrations of their people to America.—To COUNT VAN HOGENDORP. i, 464. FORD ED., iv, 103. (P., 1785.)

2661. ENGLAND, Morality of government.—It may be asked, what, in the nature of her government, unfits England for the observation of moral duties? In the first place, her King is a cipher; his only function being to name the oligarchy which is to govern her. The parliament is, by corruption, the mere instrument of the will of the administration. The real power and property in the government is in the great aristocratical families of the nation. The nest of office being too small for all of them to cuddle into at once, the contest is eternal, which shall crowd the other out. For this purpose, they are divided into two parties, the "Ins" and the "Outs," so equal in weight that a small matter turns the balance. To keep themselves in, when they are in, every stratagem must be practiced, every artifice used which may flatter the pride, the passions or power of the nation. Justice, honor, faith, must yield to the necessity of keeping themselves in place. The question whether a measure is moral, is never asked; but whether it will nourish the avarice of their merchants, or the piratical spirit of their navy, or produce any other effect which may strengthen them in their places. As to engagements, however positive, entered by the predecessors of the "Ins," why, they were their enemies: they did everything which was wrong; and to reverse everything which they did, must, therefore, be right. This is the true character of the English government in practice, however different its theory; and it presents the singular phenomenon of a nation, the individuals of which are as faithful to their private engagements and duties, as honorable, as worthy, as those of any nation on earth, and whose government is yet the most unprincipled at this day known. In an absolute government there can be no such equiponderant parties. The despot is the government. His power suppressing all opposition, maintains his ministers firm in their places. What he has contracted, therefore, through them, he has the power to observe with good faith; and he identifies his own honor and faith with that of his nation.—To JOHN LANGDON. v, 513. (M., March 1810.)

2662. ———. England presents a singular phenomenon of an honest people whose constitution, from its nature, must render their government forever dishonest; and accordingly, from the time that Sir Robert Walpole gave the constitution that direction which its defects permitted, morality has been expunged from their political code.—To JAMES RONALDSON. v, 554. (M., 1810.)

2663. ———. I consider the government of England as totally without morality, insolent beyond bearing, inflated with vanity and ambition, aiming at the exclusive dominion of the sea, lost in corruption, of deep-rooted hatred towards us, hostile to liberty wherever it endeavors to show its head, and the eternal disturber of the peace of the world.—To THOMAS LEIPER. vi, 463. FORD ED., ix, 510. (M., June 1815.)

2664. ENGLAND, National debt.—George the Third and his minister, Pitt, and successors, have spent the fee simple of the kingdom under pretense of governing it; their sinecures, salaries, pensions, priests, prelates, princes and eternal wars, have mortgaged to its full value the last foot of their soil. They are reduced to the dilemma of a bankrupt spendthrift, who, having run through his whole fortune, now asks himself what he is to do? It is in vain he dismisses his coaches and horses, his grooms, liveries, cooks and butlers. This done, he still finds he has nothing to eat. What was his property is now that of his creditors; if still in his hands, it is only as their trustee. To them it belongs, and to them every farthing of its profits must go. The reformation of extravagance comes too late. All is gone. Nothing is left for retrenchment or frugality to go on. The debts of England, however, being due from the whole nation to one-half of it, being as much the debt of the creditor as debtor, if it could be referred to a court of equity, principles might be devised to adjust it peaceably. Dismiss their parasites, ship off their paupers to this country, let the landholders give half their lands to the money lenders, and these last relinquish one-half of their debts. They would still have a fertile island, a sound and effective population to labor it, and would hold that station among political powers, to which their natural resources and faculties entitle them. They would no longer, indeed, be the lords of the ocean and paymasters of all the princes of the earth. They would no longer enjoy the luxuries of pirating and plundering everything by sea, and of bribing and corrupting everything by land; but they might enjoy the more safe and lasting luxury of living on terms of equality, justice and good neighborhood with all nations. As it is, their first efforts will probably be to quiet things awhile by the palliatives of reformation; to nibble a little at pensions and sinecures, to bite off a bit here, and a bit there to amuse the people; and to keep the government agoing by encroachments on the interest of the public debt, one per cent. of which, for instance, withheld, gives them a spare revenue of ten millions for present subsistence, and spunges, in fact, two hundred millions of the debt. This remedy they may endeavor to administer in broken doses of a small pill at a time. The first may not occasion more than a strong nausea in the money lenders; but the second will probably produce a revulsion of the stomach, barbarisms, and spasmodic calls for fair settlement and compromise. But it is not in the character of man to come to any peaceable compromise of such a state of things. The princes and priests will hold to the flesh-pots, the empty bellies will seize on them, and these being the multitude, the issue is obvious, civil war, massacre, exile as in France, until the stage is cleared of everything but the multitude, and the lands get into their hands by such processes as the revolution will engender.*—To JOHN ADAMS. vii, 43. (M., 1816.)

2665. —— ——. I have long considered the present crises of England, and the origin of the evils which are lowering over her, as produced by enormous excess of her expenditures beyond her income. To pay even the interest of the debt contracted, she is obliged to take from the industrious so much of their earnings as not to leave them enough for their backs and bellies. They are daily, therefore, passing over to the pauper-list, to subsist on the declining means of those still holding up, and when these shall also be exhausted, what next? Reformation cannot remedy this. It could only prevent its recurrence when once relieved from the debt. To effect that relief I see but one possible and just course. Considering the funded and real property as equal, and the debt as much of the one as the other, for the holder of property to give up one-half to those of the funds, and the latter to the nation the whole of what it owes them. But this the nature of man forbids us to expect without blows, and blows will decide it by a promiscuous sacrifice of life and property. The debt thus, or otherwise extinguished, a *real* representation introduced into the government of either property or people, or of both, renouncing eternal war, restraining future expenses to future income, and breaking up forever the consuming circle of extravagance, debt, insolvency, and revolution, the island would then again be in the degree of force which nature has measured out to it in the scale of nations, but not at their head. I sincerely wish she could peaceably get into this state of being, as the present prospects of southern Europe seem to need the acquisition of new weights in their balance, rather than the loss of old ones.—To EDWARD EVERETT. vii, 232. (M., 1822.)

2666. ENGLAND, Natural enemies of United States.—I consider the British as our natural enemies, and as the only nation on earth who wish us ill from the bottom of their souls. And I am satisfied that, were our continent to be swallowed up by the ocean, Great Britain would be in a bonfire from one end to the other.—To WILLIAM CARMICHAEL. ii, 323. FORD ED., iv, 469. (P., 1787.)

— ENGLAND, Neutral rights and.— See NEUTRALITY.

— ENGLAND, Parliament of.—See PARLIAMENT.

*The debt of Great Britain amounted at this period to eight hundred millions of pounds sterling. "It was in truth," says Macaulay (Hist. of England, c. 19) "a gigantic, a fabulous, debt; and we can hardly wonder that the cry of despair should have been louder than ever."—EDITOR.

2667. ENGLAND, People of.—The individuals of the [British] nation I have ever honored and esteemed, the basis of their character being essentially worthy.—To JOHN ADAMS. vii, 46. (P.F., 1816.)

2668. ENGLAND, Perversity of Court.—The British conduct, hitherto, has been most successfully prognosticated by reversing the conclusions of right reason.—To GENERAL WASHINGTON. i, 237. (1779.)

2669. —— ——. Ever since the accession of the present King of England, that court has unerringly done what common sense would have dictated not to do.—To WILLIAM CARMICHAEL. FORD ED., iv, 453. (P., 1787.)

2670. —— ——. I never yet found any other general rule for foretelling what the British will do, but that of examining what they ought not to do.—To JOHN ADAMS. ii, 283. FORD ED., iv, 456. (P., 1787.)

2671. —— ——. We, I hope, shall be left free to avail ourselves of the advantages of neutrality; and yet, much I fear the English, or rather their stupid King, will force us out of it. For thus I reason. By forcing us into the war against them, they will be engaged in an expensive land war, as well as a sea war. Common sense dictates, therefore, that they should let us remain neuter; *ergo*, they will not let us remain neuter.—To JOHN ADAMS. ii, 283. FORD ED., iv, 456. (P., 1787.)

2672. ENGLAND, Piratical policy of.—A pirate spreading misery and ruin over the face of the ocean.—To DR. WALTER JONES. v, 511. FORD ED., ix, 274. (M., 1810.)

2673. —— ——. As for France and England, with all their preëminence in science, the one is a den of robbers, and the other of pirates.—To JOHN ADAMS. vi, 37. FORD ED., ix, 333. (M., 1812.)

2674. —— ——. A nation of buccaneers, urged by sordid avarice, and embarked in the flagitious enterprise of seizing to itself the maritime resources and rights of all other nations.—To HENRY MIDDLETON. vi, 91. (M., Jan. 1813.)

2675. —— ——. The principle that force is right, is become the principle of the nation itself. They would not permit an honest minister, were accident to bring such an one into power, to relax their system of lawless piracy.—To CÆSAR A. RODNEY. v, 501. FORD ED., ix, 272. (M., 1810.)

2676. ENGLAND, Policy towards United States.—England has steadily endeavored to make us her natural enemies.—To JOHN ADAMS. vi, 459. (M., 1815.)

2677. ENGLAND, Prototype of.—The modern Carthage.—To WILLIAM DUANE. v, 552. FORD ED., ix, 287. (M., 1810.)

2678. ENGLAND, Punic faith of.—What is to be our security, that when embarked for her [Great Britain] in the war [with Bonaparte], she will not make a separate peace, and leave us in the lurch? Her good faith! The faith of a nation of merchants! The *Punica fides* of modern Carthage! Of the friend and protectress of Copenhagen! Of the nation who never admitted a chapter of morality into her political code! And is now boldly avowing that whatever power can make hers, is her's of right. Money, and not morality, is the principle of commerce and commercial nations.—To JOHN LANGDON. v, 513. (M., March 1810.)

2679. ENGLAND, Punished.—England is now a living example that no nation however powerful, any more than an individual, can be unjust with impunity. Sooner or later public opinion, an instrument merely moral in the beginning, will find occasion physically to inflict its sentences on the unjust. Nothing else could have kept the other nations of Europe from relieving her under her present crisis. The lesson is useful to the weak as well as the strong.—To JAMES MADISON. FORD ED., viii, 300. (M., April 1804.)

2680. ENGLAND, Reconquest of United States.—Monroe's letter is of an awful complexion, and I do not wonder the communication it contains made some impression on him. To a person placed in Europe, surrounded by the immense resources of the nations there, and the greater wickedness of their courts, even the limits which nature imposes on their enterprises are scarcely sensible. It is impossible that France and England should combine for any purpose: their mutual distrust and deadly hatred of each other admit no cooperation. It is impossible that England should be willing to see France repossess Louisiana, or get a footing on our continent, and that France should willingly see the United States reannexed to the British dominions. That the Bourbons should be replaced on their throne and agree to any terms of restitution, is possible; but that they and England joined, could recover us to British dominion, is impossible. If these things are not so, then human reason is of no aid in conjecturing the conduct of nations. Still, however, it is our unquestionable interest and duty to conduct ourselves with such sincere friendship and impartiality towards both nations, as that each may see unequivocally, what is unquestionably true, that we may be very possibly driven into her scale by unjust conduct in the other.—To JAMES MADISON. iv, 557. FORD ED., viii, 314. (M., Aug. 1804.)

2681. ENGLAND, Reduction of.—If, indeed, Europe has matters to settle which may reduce this *hostis humani generis* to a state of peace and moral order, I shall see that with pleasure, and then sing, with old Simeon, *nunc dimittas Domine.*—To M. CORREA. vi, 407. (M., 1814.)

2682. —— ——. While it is much our interest to see this power reduced from its towering and borrowed height, to within the limits of its natural resources, it is by no means our interest that she should be brought

below that, or lose her competent place among the nations of Europe.—To JOHN ADAMS. vii, 45. (P.F., 1816.)

2683. ENGLAND, Reform.—I am in hopes a purer nation will result, and a purer government be instituted, one which, instead of endeavoring to make us their natural enemies, will see in us, what we really are, their natural friends and brethren, and more interested in a fraternal connection with them than with any other nation on earth.—To JOHN ADAMS. vii, 46. (P.F., 1816.)

2684. ENGLAND, As a republic.—Probably the old hive will be broken up by a revolution, and a regeneration of its principles render intercourse with it no longer contaminating. A republic there like ours, and a reduction of their naval power within the limits of their annual facilities of payment, might render their existence even interesting to us. It is the construction of their government, and its principles and means of corruption, which make its continuance inconsistent with the safety of other nations. A change in its form might make it an honest one, and justify a confidence in its faith and friendship.—To WILLIAM DUANE. vi, 76. FORD ED., ix, 366. (M., Aug. 1812.)

2685. ENGLAND, Reunion with.—I am sincerely one of those who still wish for reunion with their parent country, and would rather be in dependence on Great Britain, properly limited, than on any nation on earth, or than on no nation.—To JOHN RANDOLPH. i, 201. FORD ED., i, 484. (M., August 1775.)

2686. ENGLAND, Self-interest and.—England is a nation which nothing but views of interest can govern.—To JAMES MADISON. i, 414. (P., 1785.)

2687. —— ——. Her interest is her ruling passion; and the late American measures have struck at that so vitally, and with an energy, too, of which she had thought us quite incapable, that a possibility seems to open of forming some arrangement with her. When they shall see decidedly, that without it, we shall suppress their commerce with us, they will be agitated by their avarice, on the one hand, and their hatred and their fear of us on the other. The result of this conflict of dirty passions is yet to be awaited.—To JOHN LANGDON. i, 429. (P., 1785.)

2688. —— ——. The administration of Great Britain are governed by the people, and the people by their own interested wishes without calculating whether they are just or capable of being effected.—To JAMES MADISON. FORD ED., iv, 36. (P., 1785.)

2689. ENGLAND, Selfishness of.—England's selfish principles render her incapable of honorable patronage or disinterested cooperation.—To MARQUIS LAFAYETTE. vii, 68. FORD ED., x, 85. (M., 1817.)

2690. ENGLAND, Subjugation of.—The subjugation of England would, indeed, be a general calamity. But happily it is impossible. Should it end in her being only republicanized, I know not on what principle a true republican of our country could lament it, whether he considers it as extending the blessings of a purer government to other portions of mankind, or strengthening the cause of liberty in our own country by the influence of that example. I do not, indeed, wish to see any nation have a form of government forced on them; but if it is to be done, I should rejoice at its being a freer one.*—To PEREGRINE FITZHUGH. iv, 217. FORD ED., vii, 211. (Pa., Feb. 1798.)

2691. ENGLAND, Tory principles of.— To judge from what we see published [in England], we must believe that the spirit of toryism has gained nearly the whole of the nation; that the whig principles are utterly extinguished except in the breasts of certain descriptions of dissenters. This sudden change in the principles of a nation would be a curious morsel in the history of man.—To BENJAMIN VAUGHAN. FORD ED., v, 333. (Pa., 1791.)

2692. ENGLAND, Tyrant of ocean.— Great Britain has certainly * * * declared to our government by an official paper, that the conduct of France towards her during this war has obliged her to take possession of the ocean, and to determine that no commerce shall be carried on with the nations connected with France; that, however, she is disposed to relax in this determination so far as to permit the commerce which may be carried on through the British ports. I have, for three or four years been confident that, knowing that her own resources were not adequate to the maintenance of her present navy, she meant with it to claim the conquest of the ocean, and to permit no nation to navigate it, but on payment of a tribute for the maintenance of the fleet necessary to secure that dominion. A thousand circumstances brought together left me without a doubt that that policy directed all her conduct, although not avowed. This is the first time she has thrown off the mask.— To ARCHIBALD STUART. v, 606. FORD ED., ix, 326. (M., Aug. 1811.)

2693. ———. I own, that while I rejoice, for the good of mankind, in the deliverance of Europe from the havoc which would never have ceased while Bonaparte should have lived in power, I see with anxiety the tyrant of the ocean remaining in vigor, and even participating in the merit of crushing his brother tyrant.—To JOHN ADAMS. vi, 353. FORD ED., ix, 461. (M., July 1814.) See OCEAN.

2694. ENGLAND, Unfaithful to alliances.— The nature of the English government forbids, of itself, reliance on her engagements; and it is well known she has been the least faithful to her alliances of any nation of Europe, since the period of her history wherein she has been distinguished for

*Jefferson was writing on the meditated invasion of England by France.—EDITOR.

her commerce and corruption, that is to sa under the houses of Stuart and Brunswic To Portugal alone she has steadily adhere because, by her Methuin treaty, she had mad it a colony, and one of the most valuable t her.—To JOHN LANGDON. v, 313. (M., 1810.)

2695. ENGLAND, United States and.— These two nations [the United States an Great Britain], holding cordially togethe have nothing to fear from the united worl They will be the models for regenerating th condition of man, the sources from whic representative government is to flow over th whole earth.—To J. EVELYN DENISON. vi 415. (M., 1825.)

2696. ENGLAND, United States an Colonies of.— It is the policy of Great Britai to give aliment to that bitter enmity betwee her States [in America] and ours, which ma secure her against their ever joining us. Bu would not the existence of a cordial friend ship between us and them, be the best bridl we could possibly put into the mouth of Eng land?—To JOHN ADAMS. i, 489. (P., 1785.

2697. ENGLAND, United States, Franc and.— We learn that Thornton thinks we ar not as friendly now to Great Britain as be fore our acquisition of Louisiana. This i totally without foundation. Our friendshi to that nation is cordial and sincere. So i that with France. We are anxious to se England maintain her standing, only wish ing she would use her power on the ocea with justice. If she had done this hereto fore, other nations would not have stoo by and looked on with unconcern on a con flict which endangers her existence. We ar not indifferent to its issue, nor should w be so on a conflict on which the existence o France should be in danger. We consider eac as a necessary instrument to hold in check the disposition of the other to tyrannize ove other nations.—To JAMES MONROE. FOR ED., viii, 291. (W., Jan. 1804.)

— **ENGLAND, War of 1812.**—See WAR

2698. ENGLAND, War with.— Englan is not likely to offer war to any nation, un less perhaps to ours. This would cost us ou whole shipping, but in every other respect w might flatter ourselves with success.—T EDMUND RANDOLPH. i, 435. (P., 1785.)

2699. ———. I judge that a war with America would be a popular war in England Perhaps the situation of Ireland may dete the ministry from hastening it on.—To R IZARD. i, 442. (P., 1785.)

2700. ———. I observed to Mr. Erskine [British Minister] that if we wished war with England, as the federalists charged us, and I feared his government might believe, nothing would have been so easy when the Chesapeake was attacked, and when even the federalists themselves would have concurred; but, on the contrary, that our endeavors had been to cool down our countrymen, and carry it before their government.— ANAS. FORD ED., i, 337. (Nov. 1808.)

2701. ———— ————. During the eight years of my administration. there was not a year that England did not give us such cause as would have provoked a war from any European government. But I always hoped that time and friendly remonstrances would bring her to a sounder view of her own interests, and convince her that these would be promoted by a return to justice and friendship towards us.—To DR. GEORGE LOGAN. vi, 215. FORD ED., ix, 421. (M., Oct. 1813.)

— ENGLAND, Western Posts.—See POSTS.

2702. ENGRAVING, New method.— One new invention in the arts is worth mentioning. It is a mixture of the arts of engraving and printing, rendering both cheaper. Write or draw anything on a plate of brass with the ink of the inventor, and in half an hour he gives you engraved copies of it, so perfectly like the original that they could not be suspected to be copies. His types for printing a whole page are all in one solid piece. An author, therefore, only prints a few copies of his work, from time to time, as they are called for. This saves the loss of printing more copies than may possibly be sold, and prevents an edition from being ever exhausted.—To JAMES MADISON. i, 534. FORD ED., iv, 197. (P., 1786.)

2703. ———— ————. There is a person here [Paris] who has hit on a new method of engraving. He gives you an ink of his own composition. Write on copper plates anything of which you would wish to take several copies, and, in an hour. the plate will be ready to strike them off; so of plans, engravings, &c. This art will be amusing to individuals, if he should make it known.—To DAVID RITTENHOUSE. i, 516. (P., 1786.)

2704. ENTAIL IN VIRGINIA, Abolition.—On the 12th of October, 1776, I obtained leave (in the Virginia Legislature) to bring in a bill declaring tenants in tail to hold their lands in fee-simple. In the earlier times of the colony, when lands were to be obtained for little or nothing, some provident individuals procured large grants; and, desirous of founding great families for themselves. settled them on their descendants in fee-tail. The transmission of this property from generation to generation, in the same name, raised up a distinct set of families, who, being privileged by law in the perpetuation of their wealth, were thus formed into a Patrician order, distinguished by the splendor and luxury of their establishments. From this order, too. the King habitually selected his Counsellors of State; the hope of which distinction devoted the whole corps to the interests and will of the crown. To annul this privilege, and instead of an aristocracy of wealth, of more harm and danger, than benefit, to society, to make an opening for the aristocracy of virtue and talent, which nature has wisely provided for the direction of the interests of Society, and scattered with equal hand through all its conditions, was deemed essential to a well-ordered republic. To effect it, no violence was necessary, no deprivation of natural right, but rather an enlarge-

ment of it by a repeal of the law. For this would authorize the present holder to divide the property among his children equally, as his affections were divided; and would place them, by natural generation on the level of their fellow citizens. But this repeal was strongly opposed by Mr. Pendleton, who was zealously attached to ancient establishments. * * * Finding that the general principle of entails could not be maintained, he took his stand on an amendment which he proposed, instead of an absolute abolition, to permit the tenant in tail to convey in fee-simple, if he chose it; and he was within a few votes of saving so much of the old law. But the bill passed finally for entire abolition. —AUTOBIOGRAPHY. i, 36. FORD ED., i, 49. (1821.)

2705. ———— ————. The repeal of the laws of entail would prevent the accumulation and perpetuation of wealth, in select families, and preserve the soil of the country from being daily, more and more absorbed in mortmain.* —AUTOBIOGRAPHY. i, 49. FORD ED., i, 69. (1821.)

2706. ENTAIL IN VIRGINIA, Preamble to Bill.—Whereas the perpetuation of property in certain families by means of gifts made to them in fee-simple is contrary to good policy, tends to deceive fair traders who give credit on the visible possession of such estates, discourages the holder thereof from taking care and improving the same, and sometimes does injury to the morals of youth by rendering them independent of, and disobedient to, their parents; and whereas the former method of docking such estates tail by special act of assembly, formed for every particular case, employed very much the time of the legislature, was burthensome to the public, and also to the individual who made application for such acts, Be it enacted &c.†—BILL TO ABOLISH ENTAILS. FORD ED., ii, 103. (1776.) See 477, 478, 479, 480.

— ENTANGLING ALLIANCES.—See ALLIANCES.

2707. ENTHUSIASM vs. MONEY.— The glow of one warm thought is to me worth more than money.—To CHARLES MCPHERSON. i, 196. FORD ED., i, 414. (A., 1773.)

2708. EPICURUS, Doctrines of.—The doctrines of Epicurus, notwithstanding the calumnies of the Stoics and caricatures of Cicero, is the most rational system remaining of the

---

* The bill for the abolition of entails was one of the measures of which Jefferson wrote in his Autobiography (i, 49,) as follows : "I considered four of these bills [of the Revised Code of Va.], passed or reported, as forming a system by which every fibre would be eradicated of ancient or future aristocracy; and a foundation laid for a government truly republican; and all this would be effected without the violation of a single natural right of any one individual citizen." The other three bills were those abrogating the right of Primogeniture, establishing Religious Freedom, and providing a system of general education.—EDITOR.

† In his *Life of Jefferson*, Parton, (210) says : "It was the earliest and quickest of Jefferson's triumphs, though he did not live long enough to outlast the enmity his victory engendered. Some of the old Tories found it in their hearts to exult that he, who had disappointed so many fathers, lost his only son before it was a month old."—EDITOR.

philosophy of the ancients, as frugal of vicious indulgence, and fruitful of virtue as the hyperbolical extravagances of his rival sects.—To CHARLES THOMPSON. vi, 518. FORD ED., x, 6. (M., 1816.)

2709. —— ——. I am an Epicurean. I consider the genuine (not the imputed) doctrines of Epicurus as containing everything rational in moral philosophy which Greece and Rome have left us. Epictetus indeed, has given us what was good of the Stoics; all beyond, of their dogmas, being hypocrisy and grimace. Their great crime was in their calumnies of Epicurus and misrepresentations of his doctrines; in which we lament to see the candid character of Cicero engaging as an accomplice.—To WILLIAM SHORT. vii, 138. FORD ED., x, 143. (M., 1819.)

2710. EPICURUS, Syllabus of Doctrines.—[I send you] a syllabus of the doctrines of Epicurus:

Physical.—The Universe eternal.
Its parts, great and small, interchangeable.
Matter and Void alone.
Motion inherent in matter which is weighty and declining.
Eternal circulation of the elements of bodies.
Gods, an order of beings next superior to man, enjoying in their sphere, their own felicities; but not meddling with the concerns of the scale of beings below them.
Moral.—Happiness the aim of life.
Virtue the foundation of happiness.
Utility the test of virtue.
Pleasure active and In-do-lent.
In-do-lence is the absence of pain, the true felicity.
Active, consists in agreeable motion; it is not happiness, but the means to produce it.
Thus the absence of hunger is an article of felicity; eating the means to obtain it.
The *summum bonum* is to be not pained in body, nor troubled in mind.—*i. e.* In-do-lence of body, tranquillity of mind.
To procure tranquillity of mind we must avoid desire and fear, the two principal diseases of the mind.
Man is a free agent.
Virtue consists in, 1. Prudence. 2. Temperance. 3. Fortitude. 4. Justice.
To which are opposed, 1. Folly. 2. Desire. 3. Fear. 4. Deceit.—To WILLIAM SHORT. vii, 141. FORD ED., x, 146. (M., 1819.) See SHORT.

2711. EPITAPH, Written by Jefferson.—

HERE WAS BURIED
THOMAS JEFFERSON
AUTHOR
OF THE DECLARATION OF
AMERICAN INDEPENDENCE,
OF
THE STATUTE OF VIRGINIA
FOR RELIGIOUS FREEDOM, AND
FATHER OF THE UNIVERSITY
OF VIRGINIA.
BORN APRIL 2d
1743. O. S.
DIED [JULY 4]
[1826]

FORD ED., x, 396.

2712. EQUALITY, America and.—In America no other distinction between man and man had ever been known but that of persons in office, exercising powers by authority of the laws, and private individuals. Among these last, the poorest laborer stood on equal ground with the wealthiest millionaire, and generally on a more favored one whenever their rights seemed to jar. It has been seen that a shoemaker, or other artisan, removed by the voice of his country from his work bench into a chair of office, has instantly commanded all the respect and obedience which the laws ascribe to his office. But of distinction by birth or badge, they had no more idea than they had of the mode of existence in the moon or planets. They had heard only that there were such, and knew that they must be wrong.—To M. DE MEUNIER. ix, 270. FORD ED., iv, 174. (P., 1786.) See ARISTOCRACY.

2713. EQUALITY, Constitutions and.—The foundation on which all [our constitutions] are built is the natural equality of man, the denial of every preeminence but that annexed to legal office, and particularly the denial of a preeminence by birth.—To GENERAL WASHINGTON. i, 334. FORD ED., iii, 466. (A., 1784.) See GOVERNMENT.

2714. EQUALITY, Law and.—An equal application of law to every condition of man is fundamental.—To GEORGE HAY. vii, 175. FORD ED., ix, 62. (M., 1807.)

2715. EQUALITY, Political.—All men are created equal.—DECLARATION OF INDEPENDENCE AS DRAWN BY JEFFERSON. See EQUAL RIGHTS and RIGHTS OF MAN.

2716. EQUALITY, Privileges.—To unequal privileges among members of the same society the spirit of our nation is, with one accord, adverse.—REPLY TO ADDRESS.—— iv, 394. (W., May 1801.) See PRIVILEGES.

2717. EQUAL RIGHTS, Aggression on. —No man has a natural right to commit aggression on the equal rights of another; and this is all from which the laws ought to restrain him.—To F. W. GILMER. vii, 3. FORD ED., x, 32. (M., 1816.)

2718. EQUAL RIGHTS, Government and.—The true foundation of republican government is in the equal right of every citizen, in his person and property, and in their management.—To SAMUEL KERCHIVAL. vii, 11. FORD ED., x, 39. (M., 1816.)

2719. —— ——. The equal rights of man, and the happiness of every individual, are now acknowledged to be the only legitimate objects of government.—To M. CORAY. vii, 319. (M., 1823.)

2720. EQUAL RIGHTS, Immovable.—The immovable basis of equal rights and reason.—To JAMES SULLIVAN. iv, 169. FORD ED., vii, 118. (M., 1797.)

2721. EQUAL RIGHTS, Perversion of. —To special legislation we are generally averse, lest a principle of favoritism should creep in and pervert that of equal rights.—To GEORGE FLOWER. vii, 83. (P.F., 1817.)

2722. EQUAL RIGHTS, Political.—The basis of our [Virginia] Constitution is in opposition to the principle of equal political rights, refusing to all but freeholders any participation in the natural right of self-government. * * * However nature may by mental or physical disqualifications have marked infants and the weaker sex for the protection rather than the direction of government, yet among the men who either pay or fight for their country, no line of right can be drawn.—To JOHN HAMBDEN PLEASANTS. vii, 345. FORD ED., x, 303. (M., 1824.)

2723. —— ——. Even among our citizens who participate in the representative privilege, the equality of political rights is entirely prostrated by our [Virginia] Constitution. Upon which principle of right or reason can any one justify the giving to every citizen of Warwick as much weight in the government as to twenty-two equal citizens in London, and similar inequalities among the other counties? If these fundamental principles are of no importance in actual government, then no principles are important, and it is as well to rely on the dispositions of administration, good or evil, as on the provisions of a constitution.—To JOHN HAMBDEN PLEASANTS. vii, 344. FORD ED., x, 303. (M., 1821.) See RIGHTS.

— **EQUITY.**—See CHANCELLORS.

2724. ERROR, Correcting.—There is more honor and magnanimity in correcting than persevering in an error.—BATTURE CASE. viii, 598. (1812.)

2725. —— ——. We have always a right to correct ancient errors, and to establish what is more conformable to reason and convenience. This is the ground we must take.—To JAMES MADISON. FORD ED., viii, 82. (M., 1801.)

2726. —— ——. It is better to correct error while new, and before it becomes inveterate by habit and custom.—CONGRESS REPORT. FORD ED., ii, 136. (1777.)

2727. ERROR, Deplored.—When I embarked in the government, it was with a determination to intermeddle not at all with the Legislature, and as little as possible with my co-departments. The first and only instance of variance from the former part of my resolution, I was duped into by the Secretary of the Treasury [Hamilton] and made a tool for forwarding his schemes, not then sufficiently understood by me; and of all the errors of my political life, this has occasioned me the deepest regret.*—To PRESIDENT WASHINGTON. iii, 460. FORD ED., vi, 102. (M., 1792.) See ASSUMPTION.

2728. ERROR, Evils of.—Error bewilders us in one false consequence after another in endless succession.—To JOHN ADAMS. vii, 149. FORD ED., x, 153. (M., 1819.)

2729. ERROR, Human Nature and.—The weakness of human nature, and the

* The assumption of the State debts.—EDITOR.

limits of my own understanding, will produce errors of judgment sometimes injurious to your interests.—SECOND INAUGURAL ADDRESS. viii, 45. FORD ED., viii, 347. (1805.)

2730. —— ——. I have no pretensions to exemption from error. In a long course of public duties, I must have committed many. And I have reason to be thankful that, passing over these, an act of duty has been selected as a subject of complaint, which the delusions of self interest alone could have classed among them, and in which, were there error, it has been hallowed by the benedictions of an entire province, an interesting member of our national family, threatened with destruction by the bold enterprise of one individual.*—THE BATTURE CASE. viii, 601. (1812.)

2731. —— ——. I cannot have escaped error. It is incident to our imperfect nature. But I may say with truth, my errors have been of the understanding, not of intention; and that the advancement of [the people's] rights and interests has been the constant motive of every measure.—EIGHTH ANNUAL MESSAGE. viii, 110. FORD ED., ix, 225. (1808.)

2732. —— ——. I may have erred at times. No doubt I have erred. This is the law of human nature.†—SPEECH TO THE U. S. SENATE. iv, 362. FORD ED., vii, 501. (1801.)

2733. ERROR, Ignorance and.—Ignorance is preferable to error; and he is less remote from the truth who believes nothing, than he who believes what is wrong.—NOTES ON VIRGINIA. viii, 277. FORD ED., iii, 119. (1782.)

2734. ERROR, Indulgence to honest.—For honest errors, indulgence may be hoped.—SPEECH TO THE U. S. SENATE. iv, 362. FORD ED., vii, 501. (1801.)

2735. —— ——. I shall often go wrong, through defect of judgment. When right, I shall often be thought wrong by those whose positions will not command a view of the whole ground. I ask your indulgence for my own errors, which will never be intentional; and your support against the errors of others, who may condemn what they would not if seen in all its parts.—FIRST INAUGURAL ADDRESS. viii, 5. FORD ED., viii, 5. (1801.)

2736. ERROR, Judges and.—If, indeed, a judge goes against law so grossly, so palpably, as no imputable degree of folly can account for, and nothing but corruption, malice or wilful wrong can explain, and especially if circumstances prove such motives, he may be punished for the corruption, the malice, the wilful wrong; but not for the error.—THE BATTURE CASE. viii, 602. (1812.)

* Edward Livingston in the New Orleans Batture suit against Jefferson.—EDITOR.
† From a short speech read to the Senate on retiring from the Vice-Presidency.—EDITOR.

2737. —— ——. I repeat that I do not charge the judges with wilful and ill-intentioned error, but honest error must be arrested where its toleration leads to public ruin.—AUTOBIOGRAPHY. i, 82. FORD ED., i, 113. (1821.)

2738. ERROR, Officials and.—Our Constitution has wisely distributed the administration of the Government into three distinct and independent departments. To each of these it belongs to administer law within its separate jurisdiction. The judiciary in cases of *meum* and *tuum,* and of public crimes; the Executive, as to laws executive in their nature; the Legislature in various cases which belong to itself, and in the important function of amending and adding to the system. Perfection in wisdom, as well as in integrity, is neither required, nor expected in these agents. It belongs not to man. Were the judge who, deluded by sophistry, takes the life of an innocent man, to repay it with his own; were he to replace, with his own fortune, that which his judgment has taken from another, under the beguilement of false deductions; were the Executive, in the vast mass of concerns of first magnitude, which he must direct, to place his whole fortune on the hazard of every opinion; were the members of the Legislature to make good from their private substance every law productive of public or private injury; in short, were every man engaged in rendering service to the public bound in his body and goods to indemnification for all his errors, we must commit our public affairs to the paupers of the nation, to the sweepings of hospitals and poor houses, who, having nothing to lose, would have nothing to risk. The wise know their weakness too well to assume infallibility; and he who knows most, knows how little he knows. The vine and the fig tree must withdraw, and the brier and bramble assume their places. But this is not the spirit of our law. It expects not impossibilities. It has consecrated the principle that its servants are not answerable for honest error of judgment.—BATTURE CASE. viii, 602. (1812.)

2739. —— ——. If a functionary of the highest trust, acting under every sanction which the Constitution has provided for his aid and guide, and with the approbation, expressed or implied, of its highest councils, still acts on his own peril, the honors and offices of his country would be but snares to ruin him.*—BATTURE CASE. viii, 603. (1812.)

2740. ERROR, The people and.—The people will err sometimes and accidentally, but never designedly and with a systematic and persevering purpose of overthrowing the free principles of the government.—To M. CORAY. vii, 319. (M., 1823.)

2741. —— ——. Do not be too severe upon the errors of the people, but reclaim

* Jefferson for his action in the New Orleans Batture Case, while President, was sued by Edward Livingston, who asked damages in the sum of $100,-000.—EDITOR.

them by enlightening them.—To EDWARD CARRINGTON. ii, 100. FORD ED., iv, 360. (P., 1787.)

2742. ERROR, Pointing out.—I would be glad to know when any individual member [of Congress] thinks I have gone wrong in any instance. If I know myself, it would not excite ill blood in me, while it would assist to guide my conduct, perhaps to justify it, and to keep me to my duty, alert.—To JAMES MADISON. ii, 327. FORD ED., iv, 474. (P., 1787.)

2743. ERROR, Political enemies and.—The best indication of error which my experience has tested, is the approbation of the federalists. Their conclusions necessarily follow the false bias of their principles.—To WILLIAM DUANE. v, 592. FORD ED., ix, 316. (M., 1811.)

2744. ERROR, Reason and.—The same facts impress us differently. This is enough to make me suspect an error in my process of reasoning, though I am not able to detect it.—To JOHN ADAMS. i, 593. (P., 1786.)

2745. ERROR, Reason vs.—Error of opinion may be tolerated where reason is left free to combat it.—FIRST INAUGURAL ADDRESS. viii, 3. FORD ED., viii, 3. (1801.)

2746. ERROR, Suppression of.—It is safer to suppress an error in its first conception than to trust to any after-correction.—CIRCULAR TO FOREIGN MINISTERS. iii, 509. FORD ED., vi, 180. (Pa., 1793.)

2747. ERROR, Time, truth and.—Time and truth will at length correct error.—To C. F. VOLNEY. iv, 572. (W., 1805.)

2748. ERROR, Toleration of.—Here, [the University of Virginia] we are not afraid to follow truth wherever it may lead, nor to tolerate any error so long as reason is left free to combat it.—To MR. ROSCOE. vii, 196. (M., 1820.)

2749. ERROR, Triumphant.—Error has often prevailed by the assistance of power or force. Truth is the proper and sufficent antagonist to error.—NOTES ON RELIGION. FORD ED., ii, 102. (1776?)

2750. ERROR, Truth vs.—Truth is the proper and sufficient antagonist to error, and has nothing to fear from the conflict, unless, by human interposition, disarmed of her natural weapons, free argument and debate, errors ceasing to be dangerous when it is permitted freely to contradict them.—STATUTE OF RELIGIOUS FREEDOM. viii, 455. FORD ED., ii, 239. (1779.)

2751. —— ——. It is error alone which needs the support of government. Truth can stand by itself.—NOTES ON VIRGINIA. viii, 401. FORD ED., iii, 264. (1782.)

2752. ERSKINE (William), Character.—I hope and doubt not that Erskine will justify himself. My confidence is founded in a belief of his integrity, and in the —— of Canning.—To PRESIDENT MADISON. v, 465. (M., Aug. 1809.)

2753. ESCHEAT, Bank charter and.—
The bill for establishing a National Bank
undertakes * * * to form the subscribers into a corporation [and] to enable them
in their corporate capacities, to put the lands
[they are authorized to hold] out of the
reach of forfeiture or escheat; and so far is
against the laws of *Forfeiture* and *Escheat.*
—NATIONAL BANK OPINION. vii, 555. FORD
ED., v, 284. (1791.)

2754. —— ——. All the property, real
and personal, within the Commonwealth [of
Virginia], belonging * * *, to any British
subject, * * * shall be deemed to be
vested in the Commonwealth, the real estate
by way of escheat, and the personal estate by
forfeiture.—ESCHEATS AND FORFEITURES BILL.
FORD ED., ii, 184. (May 1779.)

2755. ESCHEAT, Bill concerning.—
During the connection which subsisted between the now United States of America and
the other parts of the British empire, and their
subjection to one common Prince the inhabitants of either part had all the rights of natural born subjects in the other, and so might
lawfully take and hold real property, and transmit the same by descent to their heirs in fee-
simple, which could not be done by mere
aliens; * * * and, in like manner, had acquired personal property which, by their common laws, might be possessed by any other
than an alien enemy, and transmitted to executors and administrators; but when, by the
tyrannies of that Prince, and the open hostilities committed by his armies and subjects, inhabitants of the other parts of his dominions,
on the good people of the United States, they
are obliged to wage war in defence of their
rights, and finally to separate themselves from
the rest of the British empire, to renounce all
subjection to their common Prince, and to
become sovereign and independent States, the
said inhabitants of the other parts of the
British empire become aliens and enemies to
the said States, and as such incapable of holding the property, real or personal, so acquired
therein, and so much thereof as was within
this Commonwealth became by the laws vested
in the Commonwealth.—ESCHEATS AND FOR-
FEITURES BILL. FORD ED., ii, 182. (May
1779.)

2756. —— ——. The General Assembly
[of Virginia], though provoked by the example
of their enemies to a departure from that generosity which so honorably distinguishes the
civilized nations of the present age, yet desirous
to conduct themselves with moderation and temper, by an act passed * * * in 1777, took
measures for preventing * * * the property
of British subjects in this Commonwealth from
waste and destruction, by putting * * * [it]
into the hands and under the management of
commissioners, * * * so that it might be
in their power, if reasonable at some future day,
to restore to the former proprietors * * *
[its] full value.—ESCHEATS AND FORFEITURES
BILL. FORD ED., ii, 183. (May 1779.)

— ESQUIRE.—See TITLES.

**2757. ESTAING (Count d'), Land-grant
to.—**The State of Georgia has given twenty
thousand acres of land to the Count d'Estaing.
This gift is considered here [France] as very
honorable to him, and it has gratified him much.
—To JAMES MADISON. i, 533. FORD ED., iv,
195. (P., 1786.)

2758. ESTEEM, Basis of.—Integrity of
views more than their soundness, is the basis
of esteem.—To ELBRIDGE GERRY. iv, 273.
FORD ED., vii, 335. (Pa., 1799.)

2759. ETHICS, Law and.—I consider
ethics, as well as religion, as supplements
to law in the government of man.—To MR.
WOODWARD. vii, 339. (M., 1824.)

2760. ETHICS, System of.—I have but
one system of ethics for men and for nations,—to be grateful, to be faithful to all engagements and under all circumstances, to
be open and generous, promoting in the long
run even the interests of both; and I am
sure it promotes their happiness.—To LA
DUCHESSE D'AUVILLE. iii, 135. FORD ED.,
v, 153. (N.Y., 1790.)

**— ETHNOLOGY.—See ABORIGINES and
INDIANS.**

2761. ETIQUETTE, Disputed points.—
I am sorry that your first impressions [of the
United States] have been disturbed by matters of
etiquette. * * * These disputes are the most
insusceptible of determination, because they have
no foundation in reason. Arbitrary and sense-
less in their nature, they are arbitrarily decided
by every nation for itself. These decisions are
meant to prevent disputes, but they produce ten
where they prevent one. It would have been
better, therefore, in a new country to have excluded etiquette altogether; or if it must be
admitted in some form or other, to have it
depend on some circumstance founded in nature,
such as the age or stature of the parties.—To
COMTE DE MOUSTIER. ii, 388. FORD ED., v, 10.
(P., 1788.)

2762. ETIQUETTE, Liberation from.—
The distance of our nation [from Europe] and
difference of circumstances liberate [it], in some
degree, from an etiquette, to which it is a
stranger at home as well as abroad.—To M. DE
PINTO. iii, 175. (N.Y., 1790.)

2763. ETIQUETTE, Rules of.—I. In order to bring the members of society together in
the first instance, the custom of the country has
established that residents shall pay the first visit
to strangers, and, among strangers, first comers
to later comers, foreign and domestic; the character of stranger ceasing after the first visits.
To this rule there is a single exception. Foreign ministers, from the necessity of making
themselves known, pay the first visit to the
ministers of the nation, which is returned. II.
When brought together in society, all are perfectly equal, whether foreign or domestic, titled
or untitled, in or out of office. All other observances are but exemplifications of these two
principles. I. 1st. The families of foreign ministers, arriving at the seat of government, receive the first visit from those of the national
ministers, as from all other residents. 2d.
Members of the Legislature and of the Judiciary, independent of their offices, have a right
as strangers to receive the first visit. II. 1st.
No title being admitted here, those of foreigners
give no precedence. 2d. Differences of grade
among diplomatic members, give no precedence.
3d. At public ceremonies, to which the Government invites the presence of foreign ministers
and their families, a convenient seat or station
will be provided for them, with any other
strangers invited and the families of the national ministers, each taking place as they arrive, and without any precedence. 4th. To

maintain the principle of equality, or of *pêle mêle*, and prevent the growth of precedence out of courtesy, the members of the Executive will practice at their own houses, and recommend an adherence to the ancient usage of the country, of gentlemen in mass giving precedence to the ladies in mass, in passing from one apartment * * * into another.*—JEFFERSON PAPERS. ix, 454. FORD ED., viii, 276. (1803.)

2764. EUROPE, America and.—With all the defects of our constitutions, whether general or particular, the comparison of our governments with those of Europe, are like a comparison of heaven and hell. England, like the earth, may be allowed to take the intermediate station.—To JOSEPH JONES. ii, 249. FORD ED., iv, 438. (P., 1787.)

2765. EUROPE, Antagonism to America.—What is the whole system of Europe towards America but an atrocious and insulting tyranny? One hemisphere of the earth, separated from the other by wide seas on both sides, having a different system of interests flowing from different climates, different soils, different productions, different modes of existence, and its own local relations and duties, is made subservient to all the petty interests of the other, to *their* laws. *their* regulations, *their* passions and wars, and interdicted from social intercourse, from the interchange of mutual duties and comforts with their neighbors, enjoined on all men by the laws of nature. Happily these abuses of human rights are drawing to a close on both our continents, and are not likely to survive the present mad contest of the lions and tigers of the other.—To CLEMENT CAINE. vi, 13. FORD ED., ix, 329. (M., 1811.)

2766. EUROPE, Balance of power in.— We especially ought to pray that the powers of Europe may be so poised and counterpoised among themselves, that their own safety may require the presence of all their force at home, leaving the other quarters of the globe in undisturbed tranquillity.—To DR. CRAWFORD. vi, 33. (M., Jan. 1812.)

2767. EUROPE, Estimate of.—Behold me at length on the vaunted scene of Europe! * * * You are curious perhaps to know how this new scene has struck a savage of the mountains of America. Not advantageously, I assure you. I find the general fate of humanity here most deplorable. The truth of Voltaire's observation offers itself perpetually, that every man here must be either the hammer· or the anvil. It is a true picture of that country to which they say we shall pass hereafter. and where we are to see God and his angels in splendor, and crowds of the damned trampled under their feet. While the great mass of the people are thus suffering under physical and moral oppression. I have endeavored to examine more nearly the condition of the great, to appreciate the true value of the circumstances in their situation, which dazzle the bulk of spectators, and, especially, to compare it with

*Jefferson indorsed this paper as follows: "This rough paper contains what was agreed upon." That is by the cabinet.—EDITOR.

that degree of happiness which is enjoyed in America by every class of people. Intrigues of love occupy the younger, and those of ambition, the elder part of the great. Conjugal love having no existence among them. domestic happiness, of which that is the basis. is utterly unknown. In lieu of this, are substituted pursuits which nourish and invigorate all our bad passions, and which offer only moments of ecstacy amidst days and months of restlessness and torment. Much, very much inferior, this, to the tranquil, permanent felicity with which domestic society in America blesses most of its inhabitants; leaving them to follow steadily those pursuits which health and reason approve, and rendering truly delicious the intervals of those pursuits. In Science, the mass of the people are two centuries behind ours; their literati, half a dozen years before us. Books, really good, acquire just reputation in that time, and so become known to us, and communicate to us all their advances in knowledge. Is not this delay compensated by our being placed out of the reach of that swarm of nonsensical publications which issue daily from a thousand presses, and perish almost in issuing? With respect to what are termed polite manners, without sacrificing too much the sincerity of language, I would wish my countrymen to adopt just so much of European politeness, as to be ready to make all those little sacrifices of self, which really render European manners amiable, and relieve society from the disagreeable scenes to which rudeness often subjects it. Here, it seems that a man might pass a life without encountering a single rudeness. In the pleasures of the table, they are far before us, because, with good taste they unite temperance. They do not terminate the most sociable meals by transforming themselves into brutes. I have never yet seen a man drunk in France. even among the lowest of the people. Were I to proceed to tell you how much I enjoy their architecture, sculpture, painting, music. I should want words. It is in these arts they shine. The last of them, particularly, is an enjoyment, the deprivation of which with us, cannot be calculated.—To MR. BELLINI. i, 444. (P., 1785.)

2768. EUROPE, Exclusion from America.—We consider the interests of Cuba, Mexico and ours as the same, and that the object of both must be to exclude all European influence from this hemisphere.—To GOVERNOR CLAIBORNE. v, 381. (W., Oct. 1808.) See MONROE DOCTRINE.

2769. EUROPE, Governments of.—Experience declares that man is the only animal which devours his own kind, for I can apply no milder term to the governments of Europe, and to the general prey of the rich on the poor.—To EDWARD CARRINGTON. ii, 100. FORD ED., iv, 360. (P., 1787.)

2770. EUROPE, Ignorance in.—Ignorance, superstition, poverty, and oppression of body and mind, in every form, are so firmly settled on the mass of the people, that their redemption from them can never be hoped. If all the sovereigns of Europe were to set themselves to work to emancipate the minds of their subjects from their present ignorance and prejudices, and that. as zealously as they now endeavor the contrary, a thousand years would not place them on that high ground, on which our common people are now setting out. Ours could not have been so fairly placed under the control of the common sense of the people had they not been separated from their parent stock, and kept from contamination, either from them, or the other people of the old world, by the intervention of so wide an ocean. To know the worth of this, one must see the want of it here.—To GEORGE WYTHE. ii, 7. (P., 1786.)

2771. EUROPE, Intercourse with.— During the present paroxysm of the insanity of Europe. we have thought it wisest to break off all the intercourse with her.—To GENERAL ARMSTRONG. v, 280. FORD ED., ix, 194. (W., 1808.)

— EUROPE, Kings of.—See KINGS.

2772. EUROPE, Pretensions of.—In Europe, nothing but Europe is seen, or supposed to have any right in the affairs of nations.—To M. DUPONT DE NEMOURS. iv, 436. (W., April 1802.)

2773. EUROPE, Republican Government in.—Whether the state of society in Europe can bear a republican government, I doubted, you know, when with you, and I do now. A hereditary chief, strictly limited, the right of war vested in the legislative body, a rigid economy of the public contributions, and absolute interdiction of all useless expenses, will go far towards keeping the government honest and unoppressive.—To MARQUIS LAFAYETTE. vii, 325. FORD ED., x, 280. (M., 1823.)

2774. EUROPE, A world apart.—I consider Europe, at present, as a world apart from us, about which it is improper for us even to form opinions, or to indulge any wishes but the general one. that whatever is to take place in it, may be for its happiness.*—To JULIAN V. NIEMCEWIEZ. v, 69. (M., April 1807.)

2775. EUSTIS (William), Character.— Whether the head of the War Department is equal to his charge, I am not qualified to decide. I knew him only as a pleasant gentlemanly man in Society; and the indecision of his character added to the amenity of his conversation.—To WILLIAM DUANE. vi, 81. FORD ED., ix, 368. (M., Oct. 1812.)

2776. EVILS, Choice of.—It is the melancholy law of human societies to be compelled sometimes to choose a great evil in order to ward off a greater.—To WILLIAM SHORT. vi, 399. (M., 1814.)

2777. EVILS, Cure of.—It is a happy circumstance in human affairs that evils which are not cured in one way will cure themselves

* Niemcewiez was the assumed name of Kosciusko when he left the United States for Europe in 1807.— EDITOR.

in some other.—To SIR JOHN SINCLAIR. iii. 283. (Pa., 1791.)

2778. EVILS, Good from.—When great evils happen, I am in the habit of looking out for what good may arise from them as consolations to us.and Providence has in fact so established the order of things, as that most evils are the means of producing some good.— To DR. BENJAMIN RUSH. iv, 335. FORD ED., vii, 458. (M., 1800.)

2779. EXAMPLE, Good and bad.—I have ever deemed it more honorable and more profitable, too, to set a good example than to follow a bad one.—To M. CORREA. vi, 405. (M., 1814.)

2780. EXCISE, Defined.—Impost is a duty paid on an imported article, in the moment of its importation, and of course it is collected in the seaports only. Excise is a duty on an article, whether imported or raised at home, and paid in the hands of the consumer or retailer. * * * These are the true definitions of these words as used in England, and in the greater part of the United States. But in Massachusetts, they have perverted the word excise to mean a tax on all liquors, whether paid in the moment of importation or at a later moment, and on nothing else. So that on reading the debates of the Massachusetts convention. you must give this last meaning to the word excise.— To J. SARSFIELD. iii, 17. (P., 1798.)

2781. EXCISE LAW, Enactment.—It is proposed to provide additional funds, to meet the additional debt [created by the Assumption], by a tax on spirituous liquors. foreign and home-made, so that the whole interest will be paid by taxes on consumption.—To GOUVERNEUR MORRIS. v, 198. FORD ED., v, 250. (Pa., Nov. 1790.)

2782. EXCISE LAW, Infernal.—The excise law is an infernal one. The first error was to admit it by the Constitution; the second, to act on that admission; the third and last will be, to make it the instrument of dismembering the Union, and setting us all afloat to choose which part of it we will adhere to.—To JAMES MADISON. iv, 112. FORD ED., vi, 518. (M., Dec. 1794.)

2783. EXCISE LAW, Objectionable.— Congress * * * have passed an excise bill. which, considering the present circumstances of the Union, is not without objection.—To NICHOLAS LEWIS. FORD ED., v, 282. (Feb. 1791.)

2784. ———— ————. The excise law I have condemned uniformly from its first conception.—To JAMES MADISON. iii, 563. FORD ED., vi, 261. (Pa., May 1793.)

2785. EXCISE LAW, Odious.—The accumulation of debt * * * [created by the Assumption] has obliged [us] * * * to resort to an excise law. of odious character with the people, partial in its operation. unproductive unless enforced by arbitrary and vexatious means, and committing the authority of the government in parts where resistance is most probable, and coercion least practicable.—To President Washington. iii, 361. Ford ed., vi, 2. (Pa., May 1702.)

2786. EXCISE LAW, Resisted.—The people in the western parts of this State [Pennsylvania] have been to the excise officer, and threatened to burn his house, &c. They were blackened and otherwise disguised, so as to be unknown. He has resigned, and H [amilton] says there is no possibility of getting the law executed there, and that probably the evil will spread. A proclamation is to be issued, and another instance of my being forced to appear to approve what I have condemned uniformly from its first conception.—To James Madison. iii, 563. Ford ed., vi, 261. (Pa., May 1793.)

2787. EXCISE LAW, Riots and.—With respect to the transactions against the excise law, it appears to me that you are all swept away in the torrent of governmental opinions, or that we do not know what these transactions have been. We know of none which, according to the definitions of the law, have been anything more than riotous. There was indeed a meeting to consult about a separation. But to consult on a question does not amount to a determination of that question in the affirmative, still less to the acting on such a determination; but we shall see, I suppose, what the court lawyers, and courtly judges and would-be ambassadors will make of it.—To James Madison. iv, 111. Ford ed., vi, 517. (M., Dec. 1794.)

2788. EXCISE LAW Tea-act and.—Make friends with the trans-Alleganians. They are gone if you do not. Do not let false pride make a tea-act of your excise law.—To W. B. Giles. Ford ed., vi, 516. (Dec. 1794.)

2789. EXCISE LAW, Unnecessary.—The excise system, which I considered as prematurely and unnecessarily introduced, I was * * * glad to see fall. It was evident that our existing taxes were *then* equal to our existing debts. It was clearly foreseen also that the surplus from excise would only become aliment for useless offices, and would be swallowed in idleness by those whom it would withdraw from useful industry.—To Samuel Smith. vii, 284. Ford ed., x, 251. (M., 1823.)

2790. EXCISE LAW, Unpopular.—The excessive unpopularity of the excise and bank bills in the South I apprehend will produce a stand against the Federal Government.—To William Short. Ford ed., v, 296. (May 1791.)

2791. EXECUTIVE, Appointment of.—The Executive powers shall be exercised in manner following: One person, to be called the [Administrator], shall be annually appointed by the House of Representatives, on the second day of their first session, who, after having acted [one] year, shall be incapable of being again appointed to that office until he shall have been out of the same

[three] years.*—Proposed Va. Constitution. Ford ed., ii, 17. (June 1776.)

2792. —— ——. The Executive powers shall be exercised by a *Governor*, who shall be chosen by joint ballot of both houses of Assembly, and * * * shall remain in office five years, and be ineligible a second time.—Proposed Va. Constitution. viii, 446. Ford ed., iii, 325. (1783.)

2793. —— ——. Render the Executive [of Virginia] a more desirable post to men of abilities by making it more independent of the Legislature. To wit, let him be chosen by other electors, for a longer time, and ineligible forever after. Responsibility is a tremendous engine in a free government. Let him feel the whole weight of it then, by taking away the shelter of his Executive Council. Experience both ways has already established the superiority of this measure.—To Archibald Stuart. iii, 315. Ford ed., v, 410. (Pa., 1791.)

2794. —— ——. Submit the members of the Legislature to approbation or rejection at short intervals. Let the Executive be chosen in the same way, and for the same term, by those whose agent he is to be; and leave no screen of a Council behind which to skulk from responsibility.—To Samuel Kerchival. vii, 11. Ford ed., x, 39. (M., 1816.)

2795. —— ——. Under the Administrator shall be appointed by the same House [Representatives] and at the same time, a Deputy-Administrator, to assist his principal in the discharge of his office, and to succeed, in case of his death before the year shall have expired, to the whole powers thereof during the residue of the year.—Proposed Va. Constitution. Ford ed., ii, 18. (June 1776.)

2796. —— ——. The Deputy-Administrator shall have session and suffrage with the Privy Council.—Proposed Va. Constitution. Ford ed., ii, 20. (June 1776.)

2797. EXECUTIVE, Authority of.—The Administrator shall possess the power formerly held by the King; save only that he shall be bound by acts of the legislature, though not expressly named.—Proposed Va. Constitution. Ford ed., ii, 18. (June 1776.)

2798. —— ——. The Administrator shall not possess the prerogative * * * of raising or introducing armed forces, building armed vessels, forts or strongholds.—Proposed Va. Constitution. Ford ed., ii, 19. (June 1776.)

2799. —— ——. The Administrator [of Virginia] shall not possess the prerogative * * * of retaining or recalling a member of the State, but by legal process *pro delicto vel contractu.*—Proposed Va. Constitution. Ford ed., ii, 19. (June 1776.)

* The brackets are in the text of the instrument as drawn by Jefferson. The quotation, with those that immediately follow it, marks the development of Jefferson's ideas on the subject of State executive power.—Editor.

2800. —— ——. All other* officers, civil and military, shall be appointed by the Administrator; but such appointment shall be subject to the negative of the Privy Council, saving, however, to the Legislature a power of transferring to any other persons the appointment of such officers, or any of them.—Proposed Va. Constitution. Ford ed., ii, 21. June 1776.)

2801. EXECUTIVE, Authority over.— The Administrator shall be liable to action, though not to personal restraint, for private duties or wrongs.—Proposed Va. Constitution. Ford ed., ii, 18. (June 1776.)

2802. EXECUTIVE, The Confederation and.—As the Confederation had made no provision for a visible head of the government during vacations of Congress, and such a one was necessary to superintend the executive business, to receive and communicate with foreign ministers and nations, and to assemble Congress on sudden and extraordinary emergencies, I proposed early in April, 1784, the appointment of a committee to be called the "Committee of the States," to consist of a member from each State, who should remain in session during the recess of Congress: that the functions of Congress should be divided into Executive and Legislative. the latter to be reserved, and the former, by a general resolution, to be delegated to that Committee. This proposition was afterwards agreed to; a Committee appointed, who entered on duty on the subsequent adjournment of Congress, quarrelled very soon, split into two parties, abandoned their post, and left the government without any visible head until the next meeting in Congress. We have since seen the same thing take place in the Directory of France; and I believe it will forever take place in any Executive consisting of a plurality. Our plan, best, I believe, combines wisdom and practicability, by providing a plurality of counsellors, but a single Arbiter for ultimate decision.—Autobiography. i, 54. Ford ed., i, 75. (1820.)

2803. —— ——. I was in France when we heard of this schism and separation of our Committee, and, speaking with Dr. Franklin of this singular disposition of men to quarrel and divide into parties, he gave his sentiments, as usual, by way of apologue. He mentioned the Eddystone lighthouse in the British channel, as being built on a rock in the mid-channel, totally inaccessible in winter from the boisterous character of that sea, in that season; that, therefore, for the two keepers, employed to keep up the lights, all provisions for the winter were necessarily carried to them in autumn, as they could never be visited again till the return of the milder season; that, on the first practicable day in the spring a boat put off to them with fresh supplies. The boatmen met at the door one of the keepers and accosted him with a "How goes it, friend"? "Very well". "How is your companion"? "I do not know". "Don't know? Is he not here"? "I can't tell". "Have not you seen him to-day"? "No". "When did you see him"? "Not since last fall".

*Except members of the Privy Council, delegates to Congress, treasurer of the Colony. attorney-general, high sheriffs and coroners.—EDITOR.

"You have killed him"? "Not I, indeed". They were about to lay hold of him, as having certainly murdered his companion: but he desired them to go upstairs and examine for themselves. They went up, and there found the other keeper. They had quarrelled, it seems, soon after being left there, had divided into two parties, assigned the cares below to one, and those above to the other, and had never spoken to, or seen one another since.—Autobiography. i, 54. Ford ed., i, 76. (1820.)

2804. —— ——. The idea of separating the executive business of the Confederacy from Congress, as the Judiciary is already in some degree, is just and necessary. I had frequently pressed on the members individually, while in Congress, the doing this by a resolution of Congress for appointing an Executive committee to act during the sessions of Congress, as the Committee of the States was to act during their vacations. But the referring to this Committee all executive business, as it should present itself, would require a more persevering self-denial than I suppose Congress to possess. It will be much better to make that separation by a Federal act.—To James Madison. ii, 152. Ford ed., iv, 390. (P., June 1787.)

2805. EXECUTIVE, Control over.—The Executive [branch of the government], possessing the rights of self-government from nature, cannot be controlled in the exercise of them but by a law, passed in the forms of the Constitution.—Official Opinion. vii. 499. Ford ed., v, 209. (1790.)

2806. EXECUTIVE, Corruption of a plural.—All executive directories become mere sinks of corruption and faction.—To James Madison. vii, 190. Ford ed., x, 169. (P.F., 1820.)

2807. EXECUTIVE, French Consulate. —Without much faith in Bonaparte's heart, I have so much in his head, as to indulge another train of reflection. The republican world has been long looking with anxiety on the two experiments going on of a *single* elective Executive here, and a plurality there. Opinions have been considerably divided on the event in both countries. The greater opinion there has seemed to be heretofore in favor of a plurality; here it has been very generally, though not universally, in favor of a single elective Executive. After eight or nine years' experience of perpetual broils and factions in their Directory, a standing division (under all changes) of three against two, which results in a government by a single opinion, it is possible they may think the experiment decided in favor of our form, and that Bonaparte may be for a single executive, limited in time and power, and flatter himself with the election to that office; and that to this change the nation may rally itself; perhaps it is the only one to which all parties could be rallied. In every case it is to be feared and deplored that that nation has yet to wade through half a century of disorder and convulsions.—To Henry Innes. iv, 315. Ford ed., vii, 412. (Pa., Jan. 1800.)

2808. EXECUTIVE, French Directory. —I fear the oligarchical Executive of the French will not do. We have always seen a small council get into cabals and quarrels, the more bitter and relentless the fewer they are. We saw this in our Committee of the States; and that they were from their bad passions, incapable of doing the business of their country. I think that for the prompt, clear and consistent action so necessary in an Executive, unity of person is necessary as with us. I am aware of the objection to this, that the office becoming more important may bring on serious discord in elections. In our country, I think it will be long first; not within our day, and we may safely trust to the wisdom of our successors the remedies of the evils to arise in theirs.—To JOHN ADAMS. FORD ED., vii, 56. (M., Feb. 1796.)

2809. —— ——. I had formerly looked with great interest to the experiment which was going on in France of an Executive Directory, while that of a single elective Executive was under trial here. I thought the issue of them might fairly decide the question between the two modes. But the untimely fate of that establishment cut short the experiment. I have not, however, been satisfied whether the dissensions of that Directory (and which I fear are incident to a plurality) were not the most effective cause of the successful usurpations which overthrew them. It is certainly one of the most interesting questions to a republican, and worthy of great consideration.—To JUDGE WOODWARD. v. 449. (M., May 1809.)

2810. EXECUTIVE, Jealousy of the.— The Executive in our governments is not the sole, it is scarcely the principal object of my jealousy. The tyranny of the legislatures is the most formidable dread at present and will be for many years. That of the Executive will come in its turn, but it will be at a remote period.—To JAMES MADISON. iii, 5. FORD ED., v, 83. (P., 1789.)

2811. EXECUTIVE, The people and.— The people are not qualified to exercise themselves the Executive department; but they are qualified to name the person who shall exercise it. With us, therefore, they choose this officer every four years.—To M. L'ABBÉ ARNOND. iii, 81. FORD ED., v, 103. (P., 1789.)

2812. —— ——. In times of peace the people look most to their representatives; but in war, to the Executive solely.—To CÆSAR A. RODNEY. v, 501. FORD ED., ix, 272. (M., 1810.)

2813. EXECUTIVE, Republican and monarchical.— A monarchical head should confide the execution of its will to departments consisting each of a plurality of hands, who would warp that will as much as possible towards wisdom and moderation, the two qualities it generally wants. But a republican head, founding its decrees, originally, in these two qualities, should commit them to a single hand for execution, giving them, thereby, a

promptitude which republican proceedings generally want.—ANSWERS TO M. DE MEUNIER. ix, 247. FORD ED., iv, 151. (P., 1786.)

2814. EXECUTIVE, Single and plural. —When our present government was first established, we had many doubts on this question, and many leanings towards a supreme executive council. It happened that at that time the experiment of such an one was commenced in France, while a single Executive was under trial here. We watched the motions and effects of these two rival plans, with an interest and anxiety proportioned to the importance of a choice between them. The experiment in France failed after a short course, and not from any circumstances peculiar to the times or nation, but from those internal jealousies and dissensions in the Directory, which will ever arise among men equal in power, without a principal to decide and control their differences. We had tried a similar experiment in 1784, by establishing a Committee of the States, composed of a member from every State, then thirteen, to exercise the executive functions during the recess of Congress. They fell immediately into schisms and dissensions, which became at length so inveterate as to render all cooperation among them impracticable; they dissolved themselves, abandoning the helm of government, and it continued without a head, until Congress met the ensuing winter. This was then imputed to the temper of two or three individuals; but the wise ascribed it to the nature of man. The failure of the French Directory, and from the same cause, seems to have authorized a belief that the form of a plurality, however promising in theory, is impracticable with men constituted with the ordinary passions. While the tranquil and steady tenor of our single Executive, during a course of twenty-two years of the most tempestuous times the history of the world has ever presented, gives a rational hope that this important problem is at length solved. Aided by the counsels of a cabinet of heads of departments, originally four, but now five, with whom the President consults, either singly or altogether, he has the benefit of their wisdom and information, brings their views to one centre, and produces an unity of action and direction in all the branches of the government. The excellence of this construction of the executive power has already manifested itself here under very opposite circumstances. During the administration of our first President, his cabinet of four members was equally divided by as marked an opposition of principle as monarchism and republicanism could bring into conflict. Had that cabinet been a Directory, like positive and negative quantities in algebra, the opposing wills would have balanced each other and produced a state of absolute inaction. But the President heard with calmness the opinions and reasons of each, decided the course to be pursued, and kept the government steadily in it, unaffected by the agitation. The public knew well the dissensions of the cabinet, but never had an uneasy thought on their account, because they knew also they had provided a regulating power which would keep the machine in steady movement. I speak with an intimate knowledge of these scenes, *quorum pars fui;* as I may of others of a character entirely opposite. The third administration, which was of eight years, presented an example of harmony in a cabinet of six persons, to which perhaps history has furnished no parallel. There never arose, during the whole time, an instance of an unpleasant thought or word between the members. We sometimes met under differences of opinion, but scarcely ever failed, by conversing and reasoning, so to modify each other's ideas, as to produce an unanimous result. Yet, able and amicable as' these members were, I am not certain this would have been the case, had each possessed equal and independent powers. Ill-defined limits of their respective departments, jealousies, triffling at first, but nourished and strengthened by repetition of occasions, intrigues without doors of designing persons to build an importance to themselves on the divisions of others, might, from small beginnings, have produced persevering oppositions. But the power of decision in the President left no object for internal dissension, and external intrigue was stifled in embryo by the knowledge which incendiaries possessed, that no division they could foment would change the course of the executive power. I am not conscious that my participations in executive authority have produced any bias in favor of the single Executive; because the parts I have acted have been in the subordinate, as well as superior stations, and because, if I know myself, what I have felt, and what I have wished, I know that I have never been so well pleased, as when I could shift power from my own, on the shoulders of others; nor have I ever been able to conceive how any rational being could propose happiness to himself from the exercise of power over others. I am still, however, sensible of the solidity of your principle, that, to insure the safety of the public liberty, its depository should be subject to be changed with the greatest ease possible, and without suspending or disturbing for a moment the movements of the machine of government. You apprehend that a single Executive, with eminence of talent, and destitution of principle, equal to the object, might, by usurpation, render his powers hereditary. Yet I think history furnishes as many examples of a single usurper arising out of a government by a plurality, as of temporary trusts of power in a single hand rendered permanent by usurpation. I do not believe, therefore, that this danger is lessened in the hands of a plural Executive. Perhaps it is greatly increased, by the state of inefficiency to which they are liable from feuds and divisions among themselves. The conservative body you propose might be, so constituted, as, while it would be an admirable sedative in a variety of smaller cases, might also be a valuable sentinel and check on the liberticide views of an ambitious individual. I am friendly to this idea. But

the true barriers of our liberty in this country are our State governments; and the wisest conservative power ever contrived by man, is that of which our Revolution and present government found us possessed. Seventeen distinct States, amalgamated into one as to their foreign concerns, but single and independent as to their internal administration, regularly organized with a legislature and governor resting on the choice of the people, and enlightened by a free press, can never be so fascinated by the arts of one man, as to submit voluntarily to his usurpation. Nor can they be constrained to it by any force he can possess. While that may paralyze the single State in which it happens to be encamped, sixteen others, spread over a country of two thousand miles diameter, rise up on every side, ready organized for deliberation by a constitutional legislature, and for action by their governor, constitutionally the commander of the militia of the State, that is to say, of every man in it able to bear arms; and that militia, too, regularly formed into regiments and battalions, into infantry, cavalry and artillery, trained under officers general and subordinate, legally appointed, always in readiness, and to whom they are already in habits of obedience. The republican government of France was lost without a struggle because the party of *"un et indivisible"* had prevailed; no provisional organization existed to which the people might rally under authority of the laws, the seats of the Directory were virtually vacant, and a small force sufficed to turn the legislature out of their chamber, and to salute its leader chief of the nation. But with us, sixteen out of seventeen States rising in mass, under regular organization, and legal commanders, united in object and action by their Congress, or, if that be in *duresse,* by a Special Convention, present such obstacles to an usurper as forever to stifle ambition in the first conception of that object. Dangers of another kind might more reasonably be apprehended from this perfect and distinct organization, civil and military, of the States; to wit, that certain States from local and occasional discontents, might attempt to secede from the Union. This is certainly possible; and would be befriended by this regular organization. But it is not probable that local discontents can spread to such an extent, as to be able to face the sound parts of so extensive an Union; and if ever they should reach the majority, they would then become the regular government, acquire the ascendency in Congress, and be able to redress their own grievances by laws peaceably and constitutionally passed. And even the States in which local discontents might engender a commencement of fermentation, would be paralyzed and self-checked by that very division into parties into which we have fallen, into which all States must fall wherein men are at liberty to think, speak, and act freely, according to the diversities of their individual conformations, and which are, perhaps, essential to preserve the purity of the government, by the censorship which these parties habitually exercise over each other.— To M. Destutt Tracy. v, 567. Ford ed., ix, 306. (M., Jan. 1811.)

2815. ———. If experience has ever taught a truth, it is that a plurality in the Supreme Executive will forever split in the discordant factions, distract the nation, annihilate its energies, and force the nation, to rally under a single head, generally an usurper. We have, I think, fallen on the happiest of all modes of constituting the Executive, that of easing and aiding our President, by permitting him to choose Secretaries of State, of Finance, of War, and of the Navy, with whom he may advise, either separately or all together, and remedy their divisions by adopting or controlling their opinions at his discretion; this saves the nation from the evils of a divided will, and secures to it a steady march in the systematic course which the President may have adopted for that of his administration.—To M. Coray. vii, 321. (M., 1823.) See President.

2816. EXERCISE, Amount of.—Not less than two hours a day should be devoted to exercise.—To T. M. Randolph, Jr. Ford ed., iv, 294. (P., 1786.)

2817. ——— ———. Give about two hours every day, to exercise; for health must not be sacrificed to learning. A strong body makes the mind strong.*—To Peter Carr. i, 397. (P., 1785.)

2818. ——— ———. I give more time to exercise of the body than of the mind, believing it wholesome to both.—To David Howell. v, 555. (M., 1810.)

2819. EXERCISE, Carriage.—A carriage is no better than a cradle.—To T. M. Randolph, Jr. Ford ed., iv, 293. (P., 1786.)

2820. EXERCISE, The gun and.—As to the species of exercise, I advise the gun. While this gives a moderate exercise to the body, it gives boldness, enterprise, and independence to the mind. Games played with ball, and others of that nature, are too violent for the body, and stamp no character on the mind. Let your gun, therefore, be the constant companion of your walks.—To Peter Carr. i, 397. (P., 1785.)

2821. EXERCISE, Health and.—You are not to consider yourself as unemployed while taking exercise. That is necessary for your health, and health is the first of all objects.—To Martha Jefferson. Ford ed., iv, 372. (1787.)

2822. ——— ———. Exercise and recreation are as necessary as reading: I will say rather more necessary, because health is worth more than learning.—To John Garland Jefferson. Ford ed., v, 180. (N.Y., 1790.)

2823. EXERCISE, Horseback.—A horse gives but a kind of half exercise.—To T. M. Randolph, Jr. Ford ed., iv, 293. (P., 1786.) See Horses.

2824. EXERCISE, Invigoration by.—The sovereign invigorator of the body is exercise.—To T. M. Randolph, Jr. Ford ed., iv, 293. (P., 1786.)

*Peter Carr was Jefferson's nephew.—Editor.

2825. EXERCISE, Love of.—The loss of the power of taking exercise would be a sore affliction to me. It has been the delight of my retirement to be in constant bodily activity, looking after my affairs. It was never damped as the pleasures of reading are, by the question *cui bono?* * * * Your works show that of your mind. The habits of exercise which your calling has given to both, will tend long to preserve them. The sedentary character of my occupations sapped a constitution naturally strong and vigorous, and draws it to an earlier close.—To Dr. Benjamin Rush. vi, 4. Ford ed., ix, 328. (P.F., 1811.)

2826. EXERCISE, Reading and.—Never think of taking a book with you. The object of walking is to relax the mind. You should, therefore, not permit yourself even to think while you walk; but divert yourself by the objects surrounding you.—To Peter Carr. i, 398. (P., 1785.)

2827. EXERCISE, Time for.—I would advise you to take your exercise in the afternoon; not because it is the best time for exercise, for certainly it is not, but because it is the best time to spare from your studies; and habit will soon reconcile it to health, and render it nearly as useful as if you gave to that the more precious hours of the day.—To Peter Carr. i, 398. (P., 1785.)

2828. ——— ———. When you shall find yourself strong,* you may venture to take your walks in the evening, after the digestion of the dinner is pretty well over. This is making a compromise between health and study. The latter would be too much interrupted were you to take from it the early hours of the day, and habit will soon render the evening's exercise as salutary as that of the morning. I speak this from my own experience, having, from an early attachment to study, very early in life, made this arrangement of my time, having ever observed it, and still observing it, and always with perfect success.—To T. M. Randolph, Jr. Ford ed., iv, 294. (P., 1786.)

2829. EXERCISE, Walking.—Of all exercises walking is the best. * * * No one knows, till he tries, how easily a habit of walking is acquired. A person who never walked three miles will in the course of a month become able to walk fifteen or twenty without fatigue. I have known some great walkers, and had particular accounts of many more; and I never knew or heard of one who was not healthy and long lived.—To T. M. Randolph, Jr. Ford ed., iv, 293. (P., 1786.)

2830. ——— ———. Walking is the best possible exercise. Habituate yourself to walk very far. The Europeans value themselves on having subdued the horse to the uses of man; but I doubt whether we have not lost more than we have gained, by the use of this animal. No one has occasioned so much the degeneracy of the human body. An Indian goes on foot nearly as far in a day, for a long journey, as an enfeebled white does on his horse: and he will tire the best horses. There is no habit you will value so much as that of walking far without fatigue.—To Peter Carr. i, 398. (P., 1785.)

2831. ——— ———. Take a great deal of exercise and on foot.—To Peter Carr. ii, 241. Ford ed., iv, 433. (P., 1787.)

*Randolph was in feeble health, and while in that condition Jefferson recommended the middle of the day for walking.—Editor.

2832. EXERCISE, Weather and.—The weather should be little regarded. A person not sick will not be injured by getting wet. It is but taking a cold bath which never gives a cold to any one. Brute animals are the most healthy, and they are exposed to all weather and, of men, those are healthiest who are the most exposed. The recipe of these two descriptions of beings is simple diet, exercise and the open air, be its state what it will: and we may venture to say that this recipe will give health and vigor to every other description.—To T. M. RANDOLPH, JR. FORD ED., iv, 294. (P., 1786.)

2833. EXILE, Punishment by.—Exile [is] the most rational of all punishments for meditated treason.—To LEVI LINCOLN. vi, 8. (M., 1811.)

2834. EXPANSION, Safety in.—I know that the acquisition of Louisiana has been disapproved by some, from a candid apprehension that the enlargement of territory would endanger its Union. But who can limit the extent to which the federative principle may operate effectively? The larger our association, the less will it be shaken by local passions.—SECOND INAUGURAL ADDRESS. viii, 41. FORD ED., viii, 344. (1805.) See TERRITORY.

2835. EXPATRIATION, Assertion of the right.—Our ancestors, before their emigration to America, were the free inhabitants of the British dominions in Europe, and possessed a right, which nature has given to all men, of departing from the country in which chance, not choice, has placed them, of going in quest of new habitations, and of there establishing new societies, under such laws and regulations as, to them, shall seem most likely to promote public happiness. Their Saxon ancestors had, under this universal law, in like manner, left their native wilds and woods in the North of Europe, had possessed themselves of the Island of Britain, then less charged with inhabitants, and had established there that system of laws which has so long been the glory and protection of that country. Nor was ever any claim of superiority or dependence asserted over them by that mother country from which they had migrated; and were such a claim made, it is believed his Majesty's subjects in Great Britain have too firm a feeling of the rights derived to them from their ancestors, to bow down the sovereignty of their State before such visionary pretensions. And it is thought that no circumstance has occurred to distinguish, materially, the British from the Saxon emigration.*—RIGHTS OF BRITISH AMERICA. i, 125. FORD ED., i, 429. (1774.)

* Rayner in his *Life of Jefferson* (c. 3) says : "The correct definition and answer of the great question which formed the hinge of the American Revolution, to wit, of the right of taxation without representation, were original with Mr. Jefferson. He, following out the right of expatriation into all its legitimate consequences, advanced at once, to the necessary conclusion, and the only one which he deemed orthodox or tenable—that there was no political connection whatever between the Parliament of Great Britain and the Colonies : and consequently, that it had no right to tax them in *any* case —not even for the regulation of commerce. The other patriots, either not admitting the right of expatriation, or, which is most likely, not having pur-

2836. EXPATRIATION, Great Britain and.—Every attempt of Great Britain to enforce her principle of "Once a subject, always a subject", beyond the case of *her own subjects* ought to be repelled.—To ALBERT GALLATIN. FORD ED., viii, 251. (1803.)

2837. EXPATRIATION, A natural right.—I hold the right of expatriation to be inherent in every man by the laws of nature, and incapable of being rightfully taken from him even by the united will of every other person in the nation. If the laws have provided no particular mode by which the right of expatriation may be exercised, the individual may do it by any effectual and unequivocal act or declaration. The laws of Virginia have provided a mode; Mr. Cooper is said to have exercised his right solemnly and exactly according to that mode, and to have departed from the commonwealth; whereupon the law declares that "he shall henceforth be deemed no citizen". Returning afterwards he returns an alien, and must proceed to make himself a citizen if he desires it, as every other alien does. At present, he can hold no lands, receive nor transmit any inheritance, nor enjoy any other right peculiar to a citizen. The General Government has nothing to do with this question. Congress may, by the Constitution, "establish an uniform rule of naturalization", that is, by what rule an alien may become a citizen; but they cannot take from a citizen his natural right of divesting himself of the character of a citizen by expatriation.—To ALBERT GALLATIN. FORD ED., viii, 458. (W., June 1806.)

2838. ———— ————. My opinion on the right of expatriation has been, so long ago as the year 1776, consigned to record in the act of the Virginia code, drawn by myself, recognizing the right expressly, and prescribing the mode of exercising it. The evidence of this natural right, like that of our right to life, liberty, the use of our faculties, the pursuit of happiness, is not left to the feeble and sophistical investigations of reason, but is impressed on the sense of every man. We do not claim these under the charters of kings or legislators, but under the King of kings. If he has made it a law in the nature of man to pursue his own happiness, he has left him free in the choice of place as well as mode; and we may safely call on the whole body of English jurists to produce the map on which nature has traced, for each individual, the geographical line which she forbids him to cross in pursuit of happiness. It certainly does not exist in his mind. Where, then, is it? I believe, too, I might safely affirm, that there is not another nation, civilized or savage, which has ever denied this natural right. I doubt if there is another which refuses its exercise. I know it is allowed in some of the most respectable countries of continental Europe, nor have I

sued to the same extent, its necessary results. conceded the authority of Parliament over the Colonies, for the purposes of commercial regulation, though not of raising revenue."—EDITOR.

ever heard of one in which it was not. How it is among our savage neighbors, who have no law but that of Nature, we all know.—To Dr. John Manners. vii, 73. Ford ed., x, 87. (M., 1817.)

2839. —— ——. Expatriation [is] a natural right,* * * acted on as such by all nations, in all ages.—Autobiography. i, 8. Ford ed., i, 13. (1821.)

2840. —— ——. Early in the session [of the Virginia Assembly] of May, 1799, I prepared and obtained leave to bring in a bill declaring who should be deemed citizens, asserting the natural right of expatriation, and prescribing the mode of exercising it. This, when I withdrew from the House, on the 1st of June following, I left in the hands of George Mason, and it was passed on the 26th of that month.*—Autobiography. i, 40. Ford ed., i, 55. *(1821.)

2841. EXPERIENCE, Governmental.—Forty years of experience in government is worth a century of book-reading.—To Samuel Kerchival. vii, 15. Ford ed., x, 42. (M., 1816.)

2842. EXPERIMENT, Trying.—The precept is wise which directs us to try all things, and hold fast that which is good.—To William Drayton. ii, 347. (P., 1788.)

— EXPLORATION, Lewis and Clark.—See Lewis and Clark, and Ledyard.

2843. EXPORTS, Taxation of.—Your pamphlet is replete with sound views, some of which will doubtless be adopted. Some may be checked by difficulties. None more likely to be so than the proposition to amend the Constitution, so as to authorize Congress to tax exports. The provision against this in the framing of that instrument, was a *sine qua non* with the States of peculiar productions, as rice, indigo, cotton and tobacco, to which may now be added sugar. A jealousy prevailing that to the few States producing these articles, the justice of the others might not be a sufficient protection in opposition to their interest, they moored themselves to this anchor. Since the hostile dispositions lately manifested by the Eastern States, they would be less willing than before to place themselves at their mercy; and the rather, as the Eastern States have no exports which can be taxed equivalently. It is possible, however, that this difficulty might be got over: but the subject looking forward beyond my time, I leave it to those to whom its burdens and benefits will belong, adding only my prayers for whatever may be best for our country.—To Andrew G. Mitchell. vi, 483. (M., 1815.)

2844. EXTRAVAGANCE, Deplored.—All my letters [from America] are filled with details of our extravagance. From these accounts, I look back to the time of the war as a time of happiness and enjoyment, when

*This act is of constitutional and historical importance as the first enactment placing the doctrine of expatriation on a legal basis.—Editor.

amidst the privation of many things not essential to happiness, we could not run in debt, because nobody would trust us; when we practiced by necessity the maxim of buying nothing but what we had money in our pockets to pay for; a maxim which, of all others, lays the broadest foundation for happiness.—To Mr. Shipwith. ii, 191. (P., 1787.)

2845. EXTRAVAGANCE, Discontent and.—A continuation of inconsiderate expense seems to have raised the [French] nation to the highest pitch of discontent.—To M. de Crevecœur. ii, 234. (P., 1787.)

2846. EXTRAVAGANCE, Evil of.—I consider the extravagance which has seized [my countrymen] as a more baneful evil than toryism was during the war. It is the more so, as the example is set by the best and most amiable characters among us.—To John Page. i, 550. Ford ed., iv, 214. (P., 1786.)

2847. EXTRAVAGANCE, Governmental.—If we can prevent the government from wasting the labors of the people, under the pretence of taking care of them, they must become happy.—To Thomas Cooper. iv, 453. Ford ed., viii, 178. (W., 1802.)

2848. —— ——. Private fortunes are destroyed by public as well as by private extravagance.—To Samuel Kerchival. vii, 14. Ford ed., x, 42. (M., 1816.)

2849. —— ——. The increase of expense beyond income is an indication soliciting the employment of the pruning knife.—To Spencer Roane. vii, 212. Ford ed., x, 188. (M., 1821.)

2850. EXTRAVAGANCE, Wanton.—Our predecessors, in order to increase expense, debt, taxation, and patronage, tried always how much they could give.—To James Monroe. iv, 445. Ford ed., viii, 191. (W., 1803.)

2851. FACTION, Baleful.—In the present factions division of your State [Pennsylvania] an angel from heaven could do no good.—To W. T. Franklin. i, 555. (P., 1786.)

2852. FACTION, Government and.—With respect to the schism among the republicans of your State [Pennsylvania] I have ever declared to both parties that I consider the General Government as bound to take no part in it, and I have carefully kept both my judgment, my affections, and my conduct, clear of all bias to either.—To Thomas Cooper. v, 182. (M., 1807.)

2853. FACTION, Violent.—I have seen with regret the violence of the dissensions in your quarter [Mississippi]. We have the same in the Territories of Louisiana and Michigan. It seems that the smaller the society the bitterer the dissensions into which it breaks. Perhaps this observation answers all the objections drawn by Mr. [John] Adams from the small republics of Italy. I believe ours is to owe its permanence to its great extent, and the smaller portion comparatively, which can ever be convulsed at one time by local passions.—To Governor Robert Williams. v, 209. Ford ed., ix, 166. (Nov. 1807.)

2854. FAITH (Good), Adherence to.—It is a great consolation to me that our government, as it cherishes most its duties to its own citizens, so is it the most exact in its moral conduct towards other nations. I do not believe that in the four Administrations which have taken place, there has been a single instance of departure from good faith towards other nations. We may sometimes have mistaken our rights, or made an erroneous estimate of the actions of others, but no voluntary wrong can be imputed to us.—To George Logan. Ford ed., x, 68. (P.F., Nov. 1816.)

2855. FAITH (Good), Rule of.—Good faith ought ever to be the rule of action in public as well as in private transactions.—Sixth Annual Message. viii, 64. Ford ed., viii, 489. (1806.)

2856. FAITH (Good), The surest guide.—Good faith is every man's surest guide.*—Peace Proclamation. Ford ed., iii, 377. (1784.)

2857. FAITH (Public), Breach of impossible.—The separation of these troops (British prisoners in Virginia) would be a breach of public faith, therefore, I suppose it is impossible.—To Governor Henry. i, 221. Ford ed., ii, 179. (1779.)

2858. FAITH (Public), Cherishing.—I think it very certain that a decided majority of the next Congress will be actuated by a very different spirit from that which governed the two preceding Congresses. Public faith will be cherished equally, I would say more, because it will be on purer principles; and the tone and proceedings of the government will be brought back to the true spirit of the Constitution, without disorganizing the machine in its essential parts.—To Thomas Pinckney. Ford ed., vi, 214. (Pa., April 1793.)

2859. FAITH (Public), Preservation of.—[The] sacred preservation of the public faith, I deem [one of the] essential principles of our government and, consequently [one] which ought to shape its administration.—First Inaugural Address. viii, 4. Ford ed., viii, 5. (1801.)

2860. ———— ————. To preserve the faith of the nation by an exact discharge of its debts and contracts * * * [is one of] the landmarks by which we are to guide ourselves in all our proceedings.—Second Annual Message. viii, 21. Ford ed., viii, 187. (Dec. 1802.)

2861. ———— ————. There can never be a fear but that the paper which represents the

public debt will be ever sacredly good. The public faith is bound for this, and no change of system will ever be permitted to touch this; but no other paper stands on ground equally sure.—To William Short. iii, 343. Ford ed., v, 460. (Pa., March 1792.)

2862. FAITH (Public), Respect for.—A respect for public faith, though it was engaged by false brethren, must protect the funding phalanx.—To C. D. Ebeling. Ford ed., vii, 47. (1795.)

2863. FALSEHOOD, Truth and.—He who knows nothing is nearer the truth than he whose mind is filled with falsehoods and errors.—To John Norvell. v, 92. Ford ed., ix, 73. (W., 1807.)

2864. FAMILY, Affection.—The circle of our nearest connections is the only one in which a faithful and lasting affection can be found, one which will adhere to us under all changes and chances. It is, therefore, only soil on which it is worth while to bestow much culture. Of this truth you will become more convinced every day you ¿ lvance into life.—To Mary Jefferson Eppes. D. L. J. 255. (Pa., 1799.)

2865. FAMILY, Complications in.—If the lady has anything difficult in her disposition, avoid what is rough, and attach her good qualities to you.* Consider what are otherwise as a bad stop in your harpsichord, and do not touch on it, but make yourself happy with the good ones. Every human being must thus be viewed, according to what it is good for; for none of us, no not one, is perfect; and were we to love none who had imperfections, this world would be a desert for our love. All we can do is to make the best of our friends, love and cherish what is good in them, and keep out of the way of what is bad; but no more think of rejecting them for it, than of throwing away a piece of music for a flat passage or two. Your situation will require peculiar attentions and respect to both parties. Let no proof be too much for either your patience or acquiescence. Be you the link of love, union, and peace for the whole family. The world will give you the more credit for it, in proportion to the difficulty of the task, and your own happiness will be the greater as you perceive that you promote that of others.—To Martha Jefferson Randolph. D. L. J. 187. (N.Y., 1790.)

2866. FAMILY, A happy.—I now see our fireside formed into a group no one member of which has a fibre in their composition which can ever produce any jarring or jealousies among us. No irregular passions, no dangerous bias, which may render problematical the future fortunes and happiness of our descendants. We are quieted as to their condition for at least one generation more.—To Martha Jefferson Randolph. D. L. J. 245. (Pa., 1797.)

---

* The proclamation announcing the ratification of the definitive treaty of peace with Great Britain.—Editor.

* Jefferson was advising his daughter respecting her demeanor towards a young wife whom her father-in-law had married.—Editor.

2867. FAMILY, Love of.—It is in the love of one's family only that heartfelt happiness is known.—To Mary Jefferson Eppes. D. L. J. 281. (W., 1801.)

2868. FAMILY, Society.—When I look to the ineffable pleasure of my family society. I become more and more disgusted with the jealousies, the hatred, and the rancorous and malignant passions of this scene [the Capital], and lament my having ever again been drawn into public view. Tranquillity is now my object.—To Martha Jefferson Randolph. D. L. J. 245. (Pa., 1797.)

2869. FAMILY, Thoughts of.—Environed here in scenes of constant torment, malice, and obloquy, worn down in a station where no effort to render service can avail anything, I feel not that existence is a blessing, but when something recalls my mind to my family or farm.—To Mary Jefferson Eppes. D. L. J. 256. (Feb. 1799.)

2870. FAMILY TIES.—I find myself detaching very fast, perhaps too fast, from everything but yourself, your sister, and those who are identified with you. These form the last hold the world will have on me, the cords which will be cut only when I am loosened from this state of being.—To Martha Jefferson Randolph. D. L. J. 248. (Pa., 1798.)

2871. ———— ————. My attachments to the world, and whatever it can offer, are daily wearing off; but you are one of the links which hold to my existence, and can only break off with that.—To Mary Jefferson Eppes. D. L. J. 263. (Pa., 1800.)

2872. FAMILY, Unhappiness without.—By a law of our nature, we cannot be happy without the endearing connections of a family.—To W. Clarke. v, 468. (M., 1809.)

2873. FAMINE, Anarchy and.—The first thing to be feared for the French Republic is famine. This will infallibly produce anarchy. Indeed, that joined to a draft of soldiers, has already produced some serious insurrections.—To T. M. Randolph. iii, 570. (Pa., June 1793.)

2874. FAMINE, Insurrection and.—We are in danger of hourly insurrection [in Paris] for want of bread; and an insurrection once begun for that cause, may associate itself with those discontented for other causes, and produce incalculable events.—To E. Rutledge. iii, 111. (P., Sep. 1789.)

2875. FANATICISM, Education and.—The atmosphere of our country is unquestionably charged with a threatening cloud of fanaticism, lighter in some parts, denser in others, but too heavy in all. * * * The diffusion of instruction * * * will be the * * * remedy for this fever of fanaticism.—To Thomas Cooper. vii, 266. Ford ed., x, 242. (M., 1822.)

2876. FANATICISM, Growth and decline.—I hope and believe you are mistaken in supposing the reign of fanaticism to be on the advance. I think it certainly declining. It was first excited artificially by the sovereigns of Europe as an engine of opposition to Bonaparte and to France. It rose to a great height there, and became, indeed, a powerful engine of loyalism, and of support to their governments. But that loyalism is giving way to very different dispositions, and its prompter, fanaticism, is vanishing with it. In the meantime, it had been waf'ed across the Atlantic, and chiefly from England, with their other fashions, but it is here also on the wane.—To Thomas Cooper. vii, 170. (M., 1820.)

2877. FANEUIL HALL, Sedition and.—What mischief is this which is brewing anew between Faneuil Hall and the nation of God-dem-mees? Will that focus of sedition be never extinguished?—To Mrs. John Adams. Ford ed., iv, 68. (P., July 1785.)

2878. FARMER, Jefferson as a.—When I first entered on the stage of public life (now twenty-four years ago). I came to a resolution never * * * to wear any other character than that of a farmer.—To ———— ———— iii, 527. (Pa., 1793.)

2879. ———— ————. To keep a Virginia estate together requires in the owner both skill and attention. Skill, I never had, and attention I could not have; and, really, when I reflect on all circumstances, my wonder is that I should have been so long as sixty years in reaching the result to which I am now reduced.—To James Monroe. Ford ed., x, 383. (M., 1826.)

2880. FARMERS, Americanism of.—Farmers, whose interests are entirely agricultural, are the true representatives of the great American interests, and are alone to be relied on for expressing the proper American sentiments.—To Arthur Campbell. iv, 198. Ford ed., vii, 170. (M., 1797.)

2881. FARMERS, Barter and.—The truth is that farmers, as we all are, have no command of money. Our necessaries are all supplied, either from our farms, or a neighboring store. Our produce, at the end of the year, is delivered to the merchant, and thus the business of the year is done by barter, without the intervention of scarcely a dollar; and thus, also, we live with a plenty of everything except money.—To William Duane. v, 576. Ford ed., ix, 312. (M., 1811.)

2882. FARMERS, As citizens.—Cultivators of the earth are the most valuable citizens. They are the most vigorous, the most independent, the most virtuous, and they are tied to their country, and wedded to its liberty and interests, by the most lasting bonds. As long, therefore, as they can find employment in this line, I would not convert them into mariners, artisans, or anything else.—To John Jay. i, 403. Ford ed., iv, 88. (P., 1785.)

2883. ———— ————. Cultivators of the earth are the most virtuous citizens and possess most of the *amor patriæ*.—To M. de Meunier. ix, 288. Ford ed., iv, 143. (P., 1786.)

2884. —— ——. The proportion which the aggregate of the other classes of citizens bears in any State to that of its husbandmen, is, generally speaking. the proportion of its unsound to its healthy parts, and is a good enough barometer whereby to measure its degree of corruption.—Notes on Virginia. viii, 405. Ford ed., iii, 269. (1782.)

2885. —— ——. Cultivators of the earth are the most virtuous and independent citizens.—Notes on Virginia. viii, 413. Ford ed., iii, 279. (1782.)

2886. FARMERS, Education of.—The agriculturist needs ethics, mathematics, chemistry and natural philosophy. To them the languages are but ornament and comfort.—To John Brazier. vii. 133. (P.F., 1819.)

2887. FARMERS, Happiness of Virginia.—I know no condition happier than that of a Virginia farmer might be, conducting himself as he did during the war [of the Revolution]. His estate supplies a good table, clothes himself and his family with their ordinary apparel, furnishes a small surplus to buy salt, sugar, coffee, and a little finery for his wife and daughters. enables him to receive and to visit his friends and furnishes him pleasing and healthy occupation. To secure all this, he needs the one act of self-denial, to put off buying anything till he has the money to pay for it.—To Dr. Currie. ii, 219. (P., 1787.)

2888. FARMERS, Morals of.—Corruption of morals in the mass of cultivators is a phenomenon of which no age nor nation has furnished an example. It is the mark set on those, who, not looking up to heaven, to their own soil and industry, as does the husbandman, for their subsistence, depend for it on casualties and caprice of customers.—Notes on Virginia. viii, 405. Ford ed., iii, 268. (1782.)

2889. FARMERS, Neglected.—Here [Philadelphia, the seat of government], the *unmoneyed* farmer, as he is termed, his cattle and crops, are no more thought of than if they did not feed us. Scrip and stock are food and raiment here.—To T. M. Randolph. Ford ed., v, 455. (Pa., 1792.)

— FARMERS, Plundered.—See 2589.

2890. FARMERS, Prices and.—Our farmers are cheerful in the expectation of a good price for wheat in autumn. Their pulse will be regulated by this, and not by the successes or disasters of the war.—To President Madison. vi, 78. (M., Aug. 1812.)

2891. FARMERS, Sacrificing.—Shall the whole mass of our farmers be sacrificed to the class of shipwrights?—Opinion on Ship Passports. vii, 625. (May, 1793.)

2892. FARMERS, Virtues of.—Those who labor in the earth are the chosen people of God, if He ever had a chosen people, whose breasts He has made His peculiar deposit for substantial and genuine virtue. It is the focus in which he keeps alive that sa-

cred fire, which otherwise might escape from the face of the earth.—Notes on Virginia. viii, 405. Ford ed., iii, 268. (1782.)

— FARMERS GENERAL OF FRANCE. —See Monopoly.

2893. FARMING, Absorbed in.—If you visit me as a farmer, it must be as a co-disciple; for I am but a learner; an eager one indeed, but yet desperate, being too old now to learn a new art. However, I am as much delighted and occupied with it, as if I was the greatest adept. I shall talk with you about it from morning till night, and put you on very short allowance as to political aliment. Now and then a pious ejaculation for the French and Dutch republicans, returning with due dispatch to clover, potatoes, wheat, &c.—To W. B. Giles, iv, 118. Ford ed., vii, 12. (M., 1795.)

2894. FARMING, Ardor for.—I return to farming with an ardor which I scarcely knew in my youth, and which has got the better entirely of my love of study.—To John Adams. iv, 103. Ford ed., vi, 505. (M., April 1794.)

2895. FARMING, Beauty and.—In Virginia we are all farmers, but not in a pleasing style. We have so little labor in proportion to our land that, although perhaps we make more profit from the same labor, we cannot give to our grounds that style of beauty which satisfies the eye of the amateur.—To C. W. Peale. vi, 6. (P.F., 1811.)

2896. FARMING, Delight in.—No occupation is so delightful to me as the culture of the earth.—To C. W. Peale. vi. 6. (P.F., 1811.)

2897. FARMING, Management.—A farm, however large, is not more difficult to direct than a garden, and does not call for more attention or skill.—To J. B. Stuart. vii, 64. (M., 1817.)

2898. FARMING, Theory and practice. —Attached to agriculture by inclination, as well as by a conviction that it is the most useful of the occupations of man, my course of life has not permitted me to add to its theories the lessons of practice.—To M. Silvestre. v, 83. (W., 1807.)

2899. FASHION, Revolution and.—I have hopes that the majority of the nobles are already disposed to join the *Tiers Etat* in deciding that the vote [in the States General] shall be by persons. This is the opinion *a la mode* at present, and mode has acted a wonderful part in the present instance. All the handsome young women, for example, are for the *Tiers Etat*, and this is an army more powerful in France, than the 200,000 men of the King.—To David Humphreys. iii, 11. Ford ed., v, 87. (1789.)

2900. FAST-DAY, Appointment of a.— [After the promulgation of the Boston Port-bill in 1774] we [the young leaders in the Virginia House of Burgesses] were under the conviction of the necessity of arousing our people from the lethargy into which they had fallen as to passing events; and thought that the appointment of a day of general fasting and prayer would be most likely to call up and alarm their attention. No example of such a solemnity had existed since the days of our distresses in the war of 1755, since which a new generation had grown up. With the help, therefore, of Rushworth, whom we rummaged over for the revolutionary precedents and forms of the Puritans of that day, preserved by him, we cooked up a resolution, somewhat modernizing their phrases, for appointing the 1st day of June, on which the Port-bill was to commence, for a day of fasting, humiliation and prayer, to implore Heaven to avert from us the evils of civil war, to inspire us with firmness in support of our rights, and to turn the hearts of the King and Parliament to moderation and justice. To give greater emphasis to our proposition, we agreed to wait the next morning on Mr. [Robert Carter] Nicholas, whose grave and religious character was more in unison with the tone of our resolution, and to solicit him to move it. We accordingly went to him in the morning. He moved it the same day; the 1st of June was proposed; and it passed without opposition. The Governor dissolved us as usual. * * * We returned home, and in our several counties invited the clergy to meet assemblies of the people on the 1st of June, to perform the ceremonies of the day, and to address to them discourses suited to the occasion. The people met generally, with anxiety and alarm in their countenances, and the effect of the day through the whole Colony, was like a shock of electricity, arousing every man, and placing him erect and solidly on his centre.—AUTOBIOGRAPHY. i, 6. FORD ED., i, 9. (1820.)

2901. FAST-DAYS, Federal Government and.—I consider the government of the United States as interdicted by the Constitution from intermeddling in religious institutions, their doctrines, discipline, or exercises. This results not only from the provision that no law shall be made respecting the establishment or free exercise of religion, but from that also which reserves to the States the powers not delegated to the United States. Certainly, no power to prescribe any religious exercise, or to assume authority in religious discipline, has been delegated to the General Government. It must, then, rest with the States, so far as it can be in any human authority. But it is only proposed that I should *recommend*, not prescribe, a day of fasting and prayer. That is, that I should *indirectly* assume to the United States an authority over religious exercises, which the Constitution has directly precluded them from. It must be meant, too, that this recommendation is to carry some authority, and to be sanctioned by some penalty on those who disregard it; not indeed of fine and imprisonment, but of some degree of proscription perhaps in public opinion. And does the change in the nature of the penalty make the recommendation less a *law* or conduct for those to whom it is directed? I do not believe it is for the interest of religion to invite the civil magistrate to direct its exercises, its discipline, or its doctrines; nor of the religious societies, that the General Government should be invested with the power of effecting any uniformity of time

or matter among them. Fasting and prayer are religious exercises: the enjoining them an act of discipline. Every religious society has a right to determine for itself the times for these exercises, and the objects proper for them, according to their own particular tenets; and this right can never be safer than in their own hands, where the Constitution has deposited it. I am aware that the practice of my predecessors may be quoted. But I have ever believed that the example of State executives led to the assumption of that authority by the General Government, without due examination, which would have discovered that what might be a right in a State government, was a violation of that right when assumed by another. Be this as it may, every one must act according to the dictates of his own reason, and mine tells me that civil powers alone have been given to the President of the United States, and no authority to direct the religious exercises of his constituents.—To REV. SAMUEL MILLER. v, 236. FORD ED., ix, 174. (W., 1808.)

2902. ———— ————. In matters of religion, I have considered that its free exercise is placed by the Constitution independent of the power of the General Government. I have, therefore, undertaken on no occasion to prescribe the religious exercises suited to it; but have left them as the Constitution found them, under the direction and discipline of State or Church authorities acknowledged by the several religious societies.—SECOND INAUGURAL ADDRESS. viii, 42. FORD ED., VIII., 344. (1805.)

2903. FAUQUIER (Francis), Ability.—The ablest man who had ever filled that office [Governor of Virginia].*—AUTOBIOGRAPHY. i, 3. FORD ED., i, 4. (1821.)

2904. FAVORITISM, Equal rights vs.—To special legislation we are generally averse, lest a principle of favoritism should creep in and pervert that of equal rights.—To GEORGE FLOWER. vii, 83. (1817.)

2905. FAVORITISM, Justice and.—Deal out justice without partiality or favoritism.—To HUGH WILLIAMSON. FORD ED., v, 492. (Pa., 1792.)

2906. FAVORITISM, Regal.—The single interposition of an interested individual against a law was scarcely ever known to fail of success, though in the opposite scale were placed the interests of a whole country.—RIGHTS OF BRITISH AMERICA. i, 135. FORD ED., i, 440. (1774.)

2907. FAVORS, Personal.—In these countries [France and Holland] personal favors weigh more than public interest.—To JAMES MONROE. i, 569. FORD ED., iv, 226. (P., 1786.)

2908. FAVORS, Solicitation of.—Those who have had, and who may yet have, occa-

---

* Jefferson, while a student at William and Mary College, was introduced to Governor Fauquier "With him, and at his table," says Jefferson (Autobiography, i, 3), "Dr. Small and Mr. Wythe, his *amici omnium horarum*, and myself, formed a *partie quarrée*, and to the habitual conversations on these occasions I owed much instruction."—EDITOR.

sion to ask great favors, should never ask small ones.—To M. DE LAFAYETTE. i, 579. (P., 1786.)

— **FEDERAL CITY.**—See WASHINGTON CITY.

— **FEDERAL COURTS.**—See JUDICIARY and SUPREME COURT.

2909. FEDERAL GOVERNMENT, Birth of.—The new government has ushered itself to the world, as honest, masculine and dignified.—To JAMES MADISON. iii, 100. FORD ED., v, 112. (P., 1789.)

— **FEDERAL GOVERNMENT, Centralization.**—See CENTRALIZATION.

2910. FEDERAL GOVERNMENT, Expansion and.—Who can limit the extent to which the federative principle may operate effectively? The larger our association, the less will it be shaken by local passions.—SECOND INAUGURAL ADDRESS. viii, 41. FORD ED., viii, 344. (1805.)

2911. —— ——. I still believe that the Western extension of our confederacy will ensure its duration, by overruling local factions, which might shake a smaller association.—To HENRY DEARBORN. vii, 215. FORD ED., x. 192. (M., 1821.) See TERRITORY.

2912. FEDERAL GOVERNMENT, Formation of.—I find by the public papers, that your commercial convention [at Annapolis] failed in point of representation. If it should produce a full meeting in May, and a broader reformation, it will still be well. To make us one nation, as to foreign concerns, and keep us distinct in domestic ones, gives the outline of the proper division of powers between the general and particular governments. But, to enable the federal head to exercise the powers given it to best advantage, it should be organized, as the particular ones are, into legislative, executive and judiciary. The first and last are already separated. The second should also be. When last with Congress, I often proposed to members to do this, by making of the Committee of the States, an Executive Committee during the recess, of Congress, and, during its sessions, to appoint a committee to receive and despatch all executive business, so that Congress itself should meddle only with what should be legislative. But I question if any Congress (much less all successively) can have self-denial enough to go through with this distribution. The distribution, then, should be imposed on them.*—To JAMES MADISON. ii, 65. FORD ED., iv, 332. (P., Dec. 16, 1786.)

2913. —— ——. I think it very material to separate in the hands of Congress the ex-

* Alexander H. Stephens, in commenting on this passage in his *History of the United States*, page 278, says: "This, as far as the author has been able to discover, after no inconsiderable research, is the first embodied conception of the general outline of those proper changes of the old Constitution, or Articles of Confederation, which were subsequently actually and in fact ingrafted on the old system of confederations; and which make the most marked difference between ours, and all other like systems."—EDITOR.

ecutive and legislative powers, as the judiciary already are in some degree. * * * The want of it has been the source of more evil than we have experienced from any other cause. Nothing is so embarrassing nor so mischievous in a great assembly as the details of execution. The smallest trifle of that kind occupies as long as the most important act of legislation, and takes place of everything else. Let any man recollect, or look over the files of [the Confederation] Congress; he will observe the most important propositions hanging over, from week to week, and month to month, till the occasions have passed them, and the thing never done. I have ever viewed the executive details as the greatest cause of evil to us, because they, in fact, place us as if we had no federal head, by diverting the attention of that head from great to small objects; and should this division of power not be recommended by the convention, it is my opinion Congress should make it itself, by establishing an Executive Committee.—To E. CARRINGTON. ii, 218. FORD ED., iv, 424. (P., Aug. 1787.)

2914. —— ——. To give the Federal head some peaceable mode of enforcing its just authority, [and] to organize that head into legislative, executive and judiciary departments, are great desiderata in our Federal constitution.—To GENERAL WASHINGTON. ii, 250. (P., Aug. 1787.)

2915. —— ——. To make our States one as to all foreign concerns, [and] preserve them several as to all merely domestic * * * are great desiderata in our Federal constitution.—To GENERAL WASHINGTON. ii, 250. (P., Aug. 1787.)

2916. —— ——. You ask me what amelioration I think necessary in our Federal constitution. * * * My own general idea is that the States should severally preserve their sovereignty in whatever concerns themselves alone, and that whatever may concern another State, or any foreign nation, should be made a part of the Federal sovereignty; that the exercise of the Federal sovereignty should be divided among three several bodies, legislative, executive and judiciary, as the State sovereignties are; and that peaceable means should be contrived for the Federal head to enforce compliance on the part of the State.—To GEORGE WYTHE. ii, 267. FORD ED., iv, 445. (P., Sep. 1787.)

2917. —— ——. My idea is that we should be made one nation in every case concerning foreign affairs, and separate ones in whatever is merely domestic.—To J. BLAIR. ii, 249. (P., 1787.)

2918. —— ——. My idea is that the Federal government should be organized into legislative, executive, and judiciary, as are the State governments, and some peaceable means of enforcement devised for the Federal head over the States.—To J. BLAIR. ii, 249. (P., 1787.)

2919. —— ——. My general plan would be to make the States one as to everything connected with foreign nations, and several as to everything purely domestic.—To E. Carrington. ii, 217. Ford ed., iv, 424. (P., 1787.)

2920. FEDERAL GOVERNMENT, A frugal.—I am for a government rigorously frugal.—To Elbridge Gerry. iv, 268. Ford ed., vii, 327. (Pa., 1799.)

2921. ——— ———. Kindly separated by nature and a wide ocean from the exterminating havoc of one quarter of the globe; too high-minded to endure the degradations of the others; possessing a chosen country, with room enough for our descendants to the hundredth and thousandth generation; entertaining a due sense of our equal right to the use of our own faculties, to the acquisitions of our industry, to honor and confidence from our fellow citizens, resulting, not from birth, but from our actions, and their sense of them; enlightened by a benign religion, professed, indeed, and practiced in various forms, yet all of them inculcating honesty, truth, temperance, gratitude, and the love of man; acknowledging and adoring an overruling Providence, which, by all its dispensations, proves that it delights in the happiness of man here and his greater happiness hereafter,—with all these blessings, what more is necessary to make us a happy and prosperous people? Still one thing more, fellow-citizens—a wise and frugal government, which shall restrain men from injuring one another, which shall leave them otherwise free to regulate their own pursuits of industry and improvement, and shall not take from the mouth of labor the bread it has earned. This is the sum of good government, and this is necessary to close the circle of our felicities.—First Inaugural Address. viii, 3. Ford ed., viii, 3. (1801.)

2922. FEDERAL GOVERNMENT, Functions.—To draw around the whole nation the strength of the General Government, as a barrier against foreign foes, to watch the borders of every State, that no external hand may intrude, or disturb the exercise of self-government reserved to itself, to equalize and moderate the public contributions, that while the requisite services are invited by due remuneration, nothing beyond this may exist to attract the attention of our citizens from the pursuits of useful industry, nor unjustly to burthen those who continue in those pursuits—these are functions of the General Government on which you have a right to call * * * These shall be faithfully pursued according to the plain and candid import of the expressions in which they were announced [in the first inaugural address].—Reply to Vermont Address. iv, 418. (W., 1801.)

2923. FEDERAL GOVERNMENT, Happiness under.—That the [Federal] Government is calculated to produce general happiness, when administered in its true republican spirit, I am thoroughly persuaded.—To David Campbell. Ford ed., v, 489. (Pa., 1792.)

— FEDERAL GOVERNMENT, Judiciary.—See Judiciary and Supreme Court.

— FEDERAL GOVERNMENT, Offices.—See Offices.

2924. FEDERAL GOVERNMENT, Powers of.—If the three powers [of our government] maintain their mutual independence on each other it may last long, but not so if either can assume the authorities of the other.—To William C. Jarvis. vii, 179. Ford ed., x, 161. (M., 1820.) See Power.

2925. FEDERAL GOVERNMENT, Preservation of.—The fate of this country, whether it shall be irretrievably plunged into a form of government rejected by the makers of the Constitution, or shall get back to the true principles of that instrument, depends on the turn which things may take within a short period of time ensuing the present moment.—To Edmund Pendleton. iv, 287. Ford ed., vii, 355. (Pa., Feb. 1799.)

2926. ——— ———. The preservation of the General Government in its whole constitutional vigor, as the sheet anchor of our peace at home and safety abroad, I deem [one of the] essential principles of our government, consequently [one] which ought to shape its administration.—First Inaugural Address. viii, 4. Ford ed., viii, 4. (1801.)

2927. FEDERAL GOVERNMENT, Principles of.—About to enter, fellow citizens, on the exercise of duties which comprehend everything dear and valuable to you, it is proper that you should understand what I deem the essential principles of our government, and consequently those which ought to shape its administration. I will compress them within the narrowest compass they will bear, stating the general principle, but not all its limitations.—Equal and exact justice to all men, of whatever state or persuasion, religious or political; peace, commerce and honest friendship with all nations, entangling alliances with none; the support of the State governments in all their rights, as the most competent administrations for our domestic concerns, and the surest bulwark against antirepublican tendencies; the preservation of the General Government in its whole constitutional vigor, as the sheet anchor of our peace at home and safety abroad; a jealous care of the right of election by the people—a mild and safe corrective of abuses, which are lopped by the sword of revolution, where peaceable remedies are unprovided; absolute acquiescence in the decisions of the majority—the vital principle of republics, from which there is no appeal but to force, the vital principle and immediate parent of despotism; a well-disciplined militia—our best reliance in peace and for the first moments of war, till regulars may relieve them; the supremacy of the civil over the military authority; economy in the public expense, that labor may be lightly burdened; the honest payment of our debts and sacred preservation of the public faith; encouragement of agriculture, and of commerce as its handmaid; the diffusion of information, and the arraignment of all abuses at the bar of public reason; freedom of religion; freedom of the press: freedom of person, under the protection of the *habeas corpus;* and trial by juries impartially selected. These principles form the bright constellation which has gone before us, and guided our steps through an age of revolution and reformation. The wisdom of our sages and the blood of our heroes have been devoted to their attainment. They should be the creed of our political faith; the text of civil instruction; the touchstone by which to try the services of those we trust; and should we wander from them in moments of error or alarm, let us hasten to retrace our steps, and to regain the road which alone leads to peace, liberty, and safety.—First Inaugural Address. viii, 4. Ford ed., viii, 4. (1801.)

2928. ——— ———. The fundamental principle of the government is that the will of the majority is to prevail.—To William Eustis. v, 411. Ford ed., ix, 236. (W., Jan. 1809.)

2929. FEDERAL GOVERNMENT, Safety under.—The national government constitutes the safety of every part, by uniting for its protection the powers of the whole.—To Dr. William Eustis. v, 410. Ford ed., ix, 235. (W., 1809.)

2930. FEDERAL GOVERNMENT, Shield of.—Although under the pressure of serious evils at this moment, the governments of the other hemisphere cannot boast a more favorable situation. We certainly do not wish to exchange our difficulties for the sanguinary distresses of our fellow men beyond the water. In a state of the world unparalleled in times past, and never again to be expected, according to human probabilities, no form of government has, so far, better shielded its citizens from the prevailing afflictions.—R. To A. Connecticut Republicans. viii, 140. (Nov. 1808.)

2931. FEDERAL GOVERNMENT, Simplicity.—I am for a government rigorously * * * simple.—To Elbridge Gerry. iv, 268. Ford ed., vii, 327. (Pa., 1799.)

2932. FEDERAL GOVERNMENT, Strength of.—I know, indeed, that some honest men fear that a republican government cannot be strong; that this government is not strong enough. But would the honest patriot, in the full tide of successful experiment, abandon a government which has so far kept us free and firm, on the theoretic and visionary fear that this government, the world's best hope, may by possibility want energy to preserve itself? I trust not. I believe this, on the contrary, the strongest government on earth. I believe it is the only one where every man, at the call of the laws, would fly to the standard of the law, and would meet invasions of the public order as his own personal concern.—First Inaugural Address. viii, 3. Ford ed., viii. 3. (1801.)

2933. FEDERAL GOVERNMENT, State Governments and.—It is the duty of the General Government to guard its subor-dinate members from the encroachments of each other, even when they are made through error or inadvertence, and to cover its citizens from the exercise of powers not authorized by the law.—Official Opinion. vii, 515. Ford ed., v, 260. (1790.)

2934. ——— ———. The several States composing the United States of America, are not united on the principle of unlimited submission to their General Government; but * * * by a compact under the style and title of a Constitution for the United States, and of Amendments thereto, they constituted a General Government for special purposes,—delegated to that government certain definite powers, reserving, each State to itself, the residuary mass of right to their own self-government; and * * * whensoever the General Government assumes undelegated powers, its acts are unauthoritative, void, and of no force. * * * To this compact each State acceded as a State and is an integral party, its co-States forming, as to itself, the other party. * * * The Government created by this compact was not made the exclusive or final judge of the extent of the powers delegated to itself; since that would have made its discretion, and not the Constitution the measure of its powers, but * * * as in all cases of compact among powers having no common judge, each party has an equal right to judge for itself, as well of infractions as of the mode and measure of redress.—Kentucky Resolutions. ix, 464. Ford ed., vii, 289. (1798.)

2935. ——— ———. Foreign relations are our province; domestic regulations and institutions belong in every State, to itself.—To Cæsar Rodney. Ford ed., vii, 473. (W., Dec. 1800.)

2936. ——— ———. Our citizens have wisely formed themselves into one nation as to others, and several States as among themselves. To the united nation belong our external and mutual relations; to each State, severally, the care of our persons, our property, our reputation and religious freedom. This wise distribution, if carefully preserved, will prove, I trust from example, that while smaller governments are better adapted to the ordinary objects of society, larger confederations more effectually secure independence, and the preservation of republican government.—To the Rhode Island Assembly. iv, 398. (W., May 1801.)

2937. ——— ———. It is a fatal heresy to suppose that either our State governments are superior to the Federal, or the Federal to the States. The people, to whom all authority belongs, have divided the powers of government into two distinct departments, the leading characters of which are *foreign* and *domestic;* and they have appointed for each a distinct set of functionaries. These they have made coordinate, checking and balancing each other, like the three cardinal departments in the individual States; each equally supreme as to the powers delegated to itself, and neither authorized ultimately to decide what belongs to itself, or to its coparcener in government.

As independent, in fact, as different nations, a spirit of forbearance and compromise, therefore, and not of encroachment and usurpation, is the healing balm of such a Constitution; and each party should prudently shrink from all approach to the line of demarcation, instead of rashly overleaping it, or throwing grapples ahead to haul to hereafter. But, finally, the peculiar happiness of our blessed system is, that in differences of opinion between these different sets of servants, the appeal is to neither, but to their employers peaceably assembled by their representatives in convention. This is more rational than the *jus fortioris*, or the cannon's mouth, the *ultima et sola ratio regum.*—To Spencer Roane. vii, 213. Ford ed., x, 190. (M., 1821.)

2938. —— —— Maintain the line of power marked by the Constitution between the two coordinate governments, each sovereign and independent in its department; the States as to everything relating to themselves and their State; the General Government as to everything relating to things or persons out of a particular State. The one may be strictly called the domestic branch of government, which is sectional but sovereign; the other, the foreign branch of government, coordinate with the other domestic, and equally sovereign on its own side of the line.—To Samuel H. Smith. Ford ed., x. 263. (M., 1823.)

2939. —— —— The best general key for the solution of questions of power between our governments, is the fact that "every foreign and federal power is given to the Federal Government, and to the States every power purely domestic." I recollect but one instance of control vested in the Federal, over the State authorities, in a matter purely domestic, which is that of metallic tenders. The Federal is, in truth, our foreign government, which department alone is taken from the sovereignty of the separate States.—To Robert J. Garnett. vii, 336. Ford ed., x, 295. (M., 1824.)

2940. —— —— The radical idea of the character of the Constitution of our government, which I have adopted as a key in cases of doubtful construction, is, that the whole field of government is divided into two departments, domestic and foreign (the States in their mutual relations being of the latter); that the former department is reserved exclusively to the respective States within their own limits, and the latter assigned to a separate set of functionaries, constituting what may be called the foreign branch, which, instead of a federal basis, is established as a distinct government *quoad hoc*, acting as the domestic branch does on the citizens directly and coercively; that these departments have distinct directories, coordinate and equally independent and supreme, each in its own sphere of action. Whenever a doubt arises to which of these branches a power belongs, I try it by this test. I recollect no case where a question simply between citizens of the same State, has been transferred to the foreign

department, except that of inhibiting tenders but of metallic money, and *ex post facto* legislation.—To Edward Livingston. vii, 342. Ford ed., x, 300. (M., 1824.)

2941. —— —— With respect to our State and Federal governments, I do not think their relations correctly understood by foreigners.* They generally suppose the former subordinate to the latter. But this is not the case. They are coordinate departments of one simple and integral whole. To the State governments are reserved all legislation and administration, in affairs which concern their own citizens only, and to the Federal Government is given whatever concerns foreigners, or the citizens of other States; these functions alone being made Federal. The one is the domestic, the other the foreign branch of the same government; neither having control over the other, but within its own department. There are one or two exceptions only to this partition of power.—To John Cartwright. vii, 358. (M., 1824.)

2942. FEDERAL GOVERNMENT, Success of.—Our experience so far, has satisfactorily manifested the competence of a republican government to maintain and promote the best interests of its citizens; and every future year, I doubt not, will contribute to settle a question on which reason, and a knowledge of the character and circumstances of our fellow citizens, could never admit a doubt, and much less condemn them as fit subjects to be consigned to the dominion of wealth and force.—R. To A. Connecticut Republicans. viii, 140. (1808.)

2943. FEDERAL GOVERNMENT, Watchfulness over.—Our political machine is now pretty well wound up, but are the spirits of our people sufficiently wound down to let it work glibly. I trust it is too soon for that, and that we have many centuries to come yet before my countrymen cease to bear their government hard in hand.—To W. S. Smith. ii, 448. (P., 1788.)

2944. —— ——We, I hope, shall adhere to our republican government, and keep it to its original principles by narrowly watching it.—To —— ——. iii, 527. (Pa., 1793.)

2945. FEDERALISM, Consolidation.—Consolidation is the form in which federalism now arrays itself, and is the present principle of distinction between republicans and the pseudo-republicans but real federalists.—To William Johnson. vii, 278. Ford ed., x, 248. (M., 1823.) See Centralization.

2946. FEDERALISM, Dead.—Excepting in the north-eastern and your south-western corner of the Union, monarchism, which has been so falsely miscalled federalism, is dead and buried, and no day of resurrection will ever dawn upon it. It has retired to the two extreme and opposite angles of our land, whence it will have ultimately and shortly to take its final flight.—To Governor Claiborne. iv, 488. (W., 1803.)

* Cartwright was an Englishman.—Editor.

2947. —— —— Federalism is dead, without even the hope of a day of resurrection. The quondam leaders, indeed, retain their rancor and principles; but their followers are amalgamated with us in sentiment, if not in name.—To RICHARD M. JOHNSON. v, 257. (W., March 1808.)

2948. FEDERALISM, Judiciary and.— It is unfortunate that federalism is still predominant in our Judiciary department, which is consequently in opposition to the Legislative and Executive branches, and is able to baffle their measures often.—To JAMES BOWDOIN. v, 65. FORD ED., ix, 41. (W., 1807.)

2949. FEDERALISM, Monarchism and, —Federalism, stripped as it now nearly is, of its landed and laboring support, is monarchism and Anglicism, and whenever our own dissensions shall let these in upon us, the last ray of free government closes on the horizon of the world.—To WILLIAM DUANE. v, 602. (M., 1811.) See MONARCHY.

2950. FEDERALISM, Odious.—The name of federalism is become so odious that no party can rise under it.—To JOEL BARLOW. iv, 438. FORD ED., viii, 150. (W., May 1802.)

2951. FEDERALISM, Prostrated.—The Hartford Convention, the victory of Orleans, the peace of Ghent, prostrated the name of federalism. Its votaries abandoned it through shame and mortification and now call themselves republicans. But the name alone is changed, the principles are the same. * * * The line of division now, is the preservation of State rights as reserved in the Constitution, or by strained constructions of that instrument, to merge all into a consolidated government.—To MARQUIS LAFAYETTE. vii, 325. FORD ED., x, 281. (M., 1823.)

2952. FEDERALISM, Virginia and.— There is so little federalism in Virginia that it is not feared, nor attended to, nor a principle of voting. What little we have is in the string of Presbyterian counties in the valley between the Blue Ridge and North Mountain, where the clergy are as bitter as they are in Connecticut.—To GIDEON GRANGER. FORD ED., viii, 233. (W., May 1803.)

2953. FEDERALISTS, Anglomaniacs. —A party has risen among us, or rather has come among us, which is endeavoring to separate us from all friendly connection with France, to unite our destinies with those of Great Britain, and to assimilate our government to theirs. Our lenity in permitting the return of the old tories, gave the first body to this party; they have increased by large importations of British merchants and factors, by American merchants dealing on British capital, and by stock dealers and banking companies, who, by the aid of a paper system, are enriching themselves to the ruin of the country, and swaying the government by their possession of the printing presses, which their wealth commands, and by other means, not always honorable to the character of our countrymen. Hitherto, their influence and their system have been irresistible, and they have raised up an Executive power which is too strong for the Legislature. But I flatter myself they have passed their zenith. The people, while these things were doing, were lulled into rest and security from a cause which no longer exists. No prepossessions now will shut their ears to truth. They begin to see to what part their leaders were steering during their slumbers, and there is yet time to haul in, if we can avoid a war with France. —To ARTHUR CAMPBELL. iv, 197. FORD ED., vii, 169. (M., Sep. 1797.)

—— **FEDERALISTS, Callender and.—**See 1063.

2954. FEDERALISTS, Centralization and.—Consolidation becomes the fourth chapter of the next book of their history. But this opens with a vast accession of strength from their younger recruits, who, having nothing in them of the feelings or principles of '76, now look to a single and splendid government of an aristocracy, founded on banking institutions, and moneyed incorporations under the guise and cloak of their favored branches of manufactures, commerce and navigation, riding and ruling over the plundered ploughman and beggared yeomanry. This will be to them a next best blessing to the monarchy of their first aim, and perhaps the surest stepping stone to it.—To WILLIAM B. GILES. vii, 428. FORD ED., x, 356. (M., Dec. 1825.) See CENTRALIZATION.

2955. FEDERALISTS, Defeated.—Tell my old friend, Governor Gerry, that I give him glory for the rasping with which he rubbed down his herd of traitors. Let them have justice and protection against personal violence, but no favor. Powers and preeminences conferred on them are daggers put into the hands of assassins, to be plunged into our own bosoms in the moment the thrust can go home to the heart. Moderation can never reclaim them. They deem it timidity, and despise without fearing the tameness from which it flows. Backed by England, they never lose the hope that their day is to come, when the terrorism of their earlier power is to be merged in the more gratifying system of deportation and the guillotine.—To HENRY DEARBORN. v, 608. (P.F., Aug. 1811.)

2956. FEDERALISTS, Divisions among. —Among that section of our citizens called federalists, there are three shades of opinion. Distinguishing between the *leaders* and *people* who compose it, the *leaders* consider the English constitution as a model of perfection, some, with a correction of its vices, others, with all its corruptions and abuses. This last was Alexander Hamilton's opinion, which others, as well as myself, have often heard him declare, and that a correction of what are called its vices, would render the English an impracticable government. This government they wished to have established here, and only accepted and held fast *at first*, to the present Constitution, as a stepping stone to the final establishment of their favorite model. This party has, therefore, always clung to England as their prototype, and great auxiliary in promoting and effecting this change. A weighty MINORITY, however, of these *leaders*, considering the voluntary conversion of our government into a monarchy as too distant, if not desperate, wish to break off from our Union its eastern fragment, as being, in truth, the hotbed of American monarchism, with a view to a commencement of their favorite government, from whence the other States, may gangrene by degrees, and the whole be thus brought finally to the desired point. For Massachusetts, the prime mover in this enterprise, is the last State in the Union to mean a *final* separation, as being of all the most dependent on the others. Not raising bread for the sustenance of her own inhabitants, not having a stick of timber for the construction of vessels, her principal occupation, nor an article to export in them, where would she be, excluded from the ports of the other States, and thrown into dependence on England, her direct, and natural, but now insidious rival? At the head of this MINORITY is what is called the Essex Junto of Massachusetts. But the MAJORITY of these *leaders* do not aim at separation. In this, they adhere to the known principle of General Hamilton, never, under any views, to break the Union. Anglomany, monarchy and separation, then, are the principles of the Essex federalists. Anglomany and monarchy, those of the Hamiltonians, and Anglomany alone, that of the portion among the *people* who call themselves federalists. These last are as good republicans as the brethren whom they oppose, and differ from them only in their devotion to England and hatred of France, which they have imbibed from their leaders. The moment that these leaders should avowedly propose a separation of the Union, or the establishment of regal government, their popular adherents would quit them to a man, and join the republican standard; and the partisans of this change, even in Masschusetts, would thus find themselves an army of officers without a soldier. The party called republican is steadily for the support of the present Constitution. They obtained at its commencement, all the amendments to it they desired. These reconciled them to it perfectly, and if they have any ulterior view, it is only, perhaps, to popularize it further, by shortening the senatorial term, and devising a process for the responsibility of judges, more practicable than that of impeachment. They esteem the people of England and France equally, and equally detest the governing powers of both. This I verily believe, after an intimacy of forty years with the public councils and characters, is a true statement of the grounds on which they are at present divided, and that it is not merely an ambition for power.—To JOHN MELLISH. vi, 95. FORD ED., ix, 374. (M., Jan. 1813.)

— FEDERALISTS, Embargo and.—See EMBARGO.

2957. FEDERALISTS, Extinguishment of.—The Hartford Convention and the battle of New Orleans extinguished the name of federalists.—To HENRY DEARBORN. FORD ED., x, 237. (M., Oct. 1822.)

2958. ——— ———. The name of federalist was extinguished in the battle of New Orleans; and those who wear it now [1822] call themselves republicans. Like the fox pursued by the dogs, they take shelter in the midst of the sheep. They see that monarchism is a hopeless wish in this country, and are rallying anew to the next best point, a consolidated government. They are, therefore, endeavoring to break down the barriers of the State rights, provided by the Constitution against a consolidation.—To MARQUIS LAFAYETTE. FORD ED., x, 233. (M., 1822.)

2959. FEDERALISTS, Impotent.—The federalists have not been able to carry a single strong measure in the lower House the whole session [of Congress]. When they met, it was believed they had a majority of twenty; but many of these were new and moderate men, and soon saw the true character of the party to which they had been well disposed while at a distance. The tide, too, of public opinion sets so strongly against the federal proceedings, that this melted off their majority, and discouraged the heroes of the party.—To JAMES MADISON. iv, 329. FORD ED., vii, 446. (Pa., May 1800.)

2960. FEDERALISTS, Jay's Treaty and.—Though the Anglomen have in the end got their treaty through, and so far triumphed over the cause of republicanism, yet it has been to them a dear-bought victory. It has given the most radical shock to their party it has ever received; and there is no doubt, they would be glad to be replaced on the ground they possessed the instant before Jay's nomination extraordinary. They see that nothing can support them but the colossus of the President's merits with the people, and the moment he retires, that his successor, if a monocrat, will be overborne by the republican sense of his constituents; if a republican, he will, of course, give fair play to that sense, and lead things into the channel of harmony between the governors and governed. In the meantime, patience.—To JAMES MONROE. iv, 148. FORD ED., vii, 89. (M., July 1796.) See JAY TREATY.

2961. FEDERALISTS, Judiciary and.—They have retired into the judiciary as a stronghold. There the remains of federalism are to be preserved and fed from the treasury, and from that battery all the works of republicanism are to be beaten down and erased. By a fraudulent use of the Constitution, which has made judges irremovable, they have multiplied useless judges merely to strengthen their phalanx.—To JOHN DICKINSON. iv, 424. (W., 1801.) See JUDICIARY.

2962. FEDERALISTS, Justice to.—I never did them an act of injustice, nor failed in any duty to them imposed by my office.— To WILLIAM SHORT. FORD ED., ix, 51. (W., May 1807.)

2963. FEDERALISTS. Leaders of.— The quondam leaders of the people infuriated with the sense of their impotence, will soon be seen or heard only in the newspapers, which serve as chimneys to carry off noxious vapors and smoke.—To GENERAL KOSCIUSCO. iv, 430. (W., April 1802.)

2964. —— ——. There are some characters who have been too prominent to retract, too proud and impassioned to relent, too greedy after office and profit to relinquish their longings, and who have covered their devotion to monarchism under the mantle of federalism, who never can be cured of their enmities. These are incurable maniacs, for whom the hospitable doors of Bedlam are ready to open, but they are permitted to walk abroad while they refrain from personal assault.—To TIMOTHY BLOODWORTHY. iv, 524. (W., Jan. 1804.)

2965. —— ——. Though the people in mass have joined us, their leaders had committed themselves too far to retract. Pride keeps them hostile; they brood over their angry passions. and give them vent in the newspapers which they maintain. They still make as much noise as if they were the whole nation. Unfortunately, these being the mercantile papers, published chiefly in the seaports, are the only ones which find their way to Europe, and make very false impressions there.—To C. F. VOLNEY. iv, 573. (W., 1805.)

2966. —— ——. I hope that my retirement will abate some of their [federalists'] disaffection to the government of their country.—To RICHARD M. JOHNSON. v, 257. (W., 1808.)

2967. —— ——. Contented with our government, elective as it is in three of its principal branches, I wish not, on Hamilton's plan, to see two of them for life; and still less, hereditary, as others desire. I believe that the yeomanry of the federalists think on this subject with me. They are substantially republican. But some of their leaders. who get into the public councils, would prefer Hamilton's government, and still more the hereditary one. *Hinc illæ lachrymæ.* I wish them no harm, but that they may never get into power, not *for their harm,* but for the good of our country.—To W. D. G. WORTHINGTON. v, 504. (M., 1810.)

2968. FEDERALISTS, Madness of.—I am entirely confident that ultimately the great body of the people are passing over from the federalists. * * * The madness and extravagance of their career are what ensure it. —To E. LIVINGSTON. iv, 328. FORD ED., vii, 443. (Pa., April 1800.)

2969. —— ——. A little more prudence and moderation in those [federal leaders] who had mounted themselves on the fears [of the people], and it would have been long and

difficult to unhorse them. Their madness had done in three years what reason alone, acting against them, would not have effected in many; and the more, as they might have gone on forming new entrenchments for themselves from year to year.—To JOHN DICKINSON. iv, 424. (W.. 1801.)

2970. FEDERALISTS, Objects of.—I have been ever opposed to the party so falsely called federalists, because I believe them desirous of introducing into our government authorities, hereditary or otherwise, independent of the national will.—To DAVID HOWELL. v, 554. (M., 1810.)

2971. —— ——. The original objects of the federalists were, 1st, to warp our government more to the form and principles of monarchy; and 2d, to weaken the barriers of the State governments as coordinate powers. In the first they have been so completely foiled by the universal spirit of the nation that they have abandoned the enterprise, shrunk from the odium of their old appellation, taken to themselves a participation of ours, and under the pseudo-republican mask, are now aiming at their second object, and strengthened by unsuspecting or apostate recruits from our ranks, are advancing fast towards an ascendency.—To WILLIAM JOHNSON. vii, 293. FORD ED., x, 228. (M., 1823.) See MONARCHY.

2972. FEDERALISTS, Opposition of.— Though we may obtain, and I believe shall obtain, a majority in the Legislature of the United States, attached to the preservation of the Federal Constitution according to its obvious principles, and those on which it was known to be received; attached equally to the preservation to the States of those rights unquestionably remaining with them; friends to the freedom of religion, freedom of the press, trial by jury, and to economical government; opposed to standing armies, paper systems, war. and all connection, other than commerce. with any foreign nation; in short, a majority firm in all those principles which we have espoused and the federalists have opposed uniformly; still, should the whole body of New England continue in opposition to these principles of government, either knowingly or through delusion, our government will be a very uneasy one. It can never be harmonious and solid, while so respectable a portion of its citizens support principles which go directly to a change of the Federal Constitution, to sink the State governments, consolidate them into one and monarchize that.—To GIDEON GRANGER. iv, 330. FORD ED., vii, 450. (M.. Aug. 1800.)

2973. FEDERALISTS, Proposed coalition.—In our last conversation you mentioned a federal scheme afloat, of forming a coalition between the federalists and republicans, of what they called the seven eastern States. The idea was new to me, and after time for reflection I had no opportunity of conversing with you again. The federalists know, that, *eo nomine,* they are gone forever. Their object, therefore, is, how to return into power under some other form. Undoubtedly they have but one means, which is to divide the republicans, join the minority, and barter with them for the cloak of their name. I say, *join the minority;* because the majority of the republicans not needing them, will not buy them. The minority, having no other means of ruling the majority, will give a price for auxiliaries, and that price must be principle. It is true that the federalists, needing their numbers also, must also give a price, and principle is the coin they must pay in. Thus a bastard system of federo-republicanism will rise on the ruins of the true principles of our revolution. And when this party is formed, who will constitute the majority of it, which majority is then to dictate? Certainly the federalists. Thus their proposition of putting themselves into gear with the republican minority, is exactly like Roger Sherman's proposition to add Connecticut to Rhode Island. The idea of forming seven eastern States is moreover clearly to form the basis of a separation of the Union. Is it possible that real republicans can be gulled by such a bait? And for what? What do they wish that they have not? Federal measures? That is impossible. Republican measures? Have they them not? Can any one deny, that in all important questions of principle, republicanism prevails? But do they want that their individual will shall govern the majority? They may purchase the gratification of this unjust wish, for a little time, at a great price; but the federalists must not have the passions of other men, if, after getting thus into the seat of power, they suffer themselves to be governed by their minority. This minority may say, that whenever they relapse into their own principles, they will quit them, and draw the seat from under them. They may quit them, indeed, but, in the meantime, all the venal will have become associated with them, and will give them a majority sufficient to keep them in place, and to enable them to eject the heterogeneous friends by whose aid they get again into power. I cannot believe any portion of real republicans will enter into this trap; and if they do, I do not believe they can carry with them the mass of their States, advancing so steadily as we see them, to an union of principle with their brethren. It will be found in this, as in all other similar cases, that crooked schemes will end by overwhelming their authors and coadjutors in disgrace, and that he alone who walks strict and upright, and who, in matters of opinion, will be contented that others should be as free as himself, and acquiesce when his opinion is freely overruled, will attain his object in the end.—To Gideon Granger. iv, 542. Ford ed., viii, 298. (M., April 1804.)

2974. FEDERALISTS, Pusillanimous. —The federalists * * * wish to rub through this fragment of a year as they have through the four preceding ones, opposing patience to insult, and interest to honor. * * * This is, indeed, a most humiliating state of things, but it commenced in 1793. Causes have been adding to causes, and effects accumulating on

effects, from that time to this. We had, in 1793, the most respectable character in the universe. What the neutral nations think of us now, I know not; but we are low indeed with the belligerents. Their kicks and cuffs prove their contempt.—To Edward Rutledge. iv, 191. Ford ed., vii, 154. (Pa., June 1797.)

2975. FEDERALISTS, Republicans and.—My hope is that the distinction between republican and federalist will be soon lost, or at most that it will be only of republican and monarchist; that the body of the nation, even that part which French excesses forced over to the federal side, will rejoin the republicans, leaving only those who were pure monarchists, and who will be too few to form a sect.—To Dr. B. S. Barton. iv, 353. Ford ed., vii, 489. (W., Feb. 1801.)

2976. ——. I entertain real hope that the whole body of our citizens (many of whom had been carried away by the X. Y. Z. business), will shortly be consolidated * * *. When they examine the real principles of both parties, I think they will find little to differ about. I know, indeed, that there are some of their leaders who have so committed themselves, that pride, if no other passion, will prevent their coalescing. We must be easy with them.—To Moses Robinson. iv, 379. (March 1801.)

2977. ——. The manœuvres of the year X. Y. Z. carried over from us a great body of the people, real republicans, and honest men under virtuous motives. The delusion lasted a while. At length the poor arts of tub plots, &c., were repeated till the designs of the party became suspected. From that moment those who had left us began to come back. It was by their return to us that we gained the victory in November, 1800, which we should not have gained in November, 1799. But during the suspension of the public mind, from the 11th to the 17th of February [last], and the anxiety and alarm lest there should be no election, and anarchy ensue, a wonderful effect was produced on the mass of federalists who had not before come over. Those who had before become sensible of their error in the former change, and only wanted a decent excuse for coming back, seized that occasion for doing so. Another body, and a large one it is, who from timidity of constitution had gone with those who wished for a strong executive, were induced by the same timidity to come over to us rather than risk anarchy: so that, according to the evidence we receive from every direction, we may say that the whole of that portion of the people which were called federalists, were made to desire anxiously the very event they had just before opposed with all their energies, and to receive the election which was made, as an object of their earnest wishes, a child of their own. These people (I always exclude their leaders) are now aggregated with us. They look with a certain degree of affection and confidence to the administration, ready to become attached to it, if it avoids in the outset acts which might revolt and throw them off. To give time for a perfect consolidation seems prudent.—To JAMES MONROE. iv, 367. FORD ED., viii, 9. (W., March 1801.)

2978. —— ——. The revolutionary movements in Europe had, by industry and artifice, been wrought into objects of terror even to this country, and had really involved a great portion of our well-meaning citizens in a panic which was perfectly unaccountable, and during the prevalence of which they were led to support measures the most insane. They are now pretty thoroughly recovered from it, and sensible of the mischief which was done, and preparing to be done, had their minds continued a little longer under that derangement. The recovery bids fair to be complete, and to obliterate entirely the line of party division which had been so strongly drawn. Not that their late leaders have come over, or even can come over. But they stand, at present, almost without followers. The principal of them have retreated into the judiciary as a stronghold, the tenure of which renders it difficult to dislodge them. To JOEL BARLOW. iv, 369. (W., March 1801.)

2979. —— ——. I was always satisfied that the great body of those called federalists were real republicans as well as federalists.— To GENERAL HENRY KNOX. iv, 386. FORD ED., viii, 36. (W., March 1801.)

2980. —— ——. The federal sect of republicans * * * differ from us only in the shades of power to be given to the Executive, being, with us attached to republican government. The Essex junto and their associate monocrats in every part of the Union, wish to sap the Republic by fraud, if they cannot destroy it by force, and to erect an English monarchy in its place; some of them (as Mr. Adams) thinking its corrupt parts should be cleansed away, others (as Hamilton) thinking that it would make it an impracticable machine.—To LEVI LINCOLN. iv, 398. FORD ED., viii, 67. (W., July 1801.)

2981. —— ——. My idea is that the mass of our countrymen, even of those who call them federalists, are republicans. They differ from us but in a shade of more or less of power to be given to the Executive or Legislative organ. They were decoyed into the net of monarchists by the X. Y. Z. contrivance, but they are come or are coming back. So much moderation in our proceedings as not to revolt them, while doubting or newly joined with us, and they will coalesce and grow to us as one flesh. But any violence against their quondam leaders before they are thoroughly weaned from them, would carry them back again.—To THOMAS MCKEAN. FORD ED., viii, 78. (W., July 1801.)

2982. —— ——. I consider the pure federalist as a republican who would prefer a somewhat stronger Executive; and the republican as one more willing to trust the legislature as a broader representation of the people, and a safer deposit of power for many reasons. But both sects are republican, en-

titled to the confidence of their fellow citizens. Not so their quondam leaders, covering under the mask of federalism hearts devoted to monarchy. The Hamiltonians, the Essexmen, the Revolutionary tories, &c. They have a right to tolerance, but neither to confidence nor power.—To JOHN DICKINSON. FORD ED., viii, 76. (W., July 1801.)

2983. FEDERALISTS, Republican schisms and.—I consider the federalists as completely vanquished, and never more to take the field under their own banners. They will now reserve themselves to profit by the schisms among republicans, and to earn favors from minorities, whom they will enable to triumph over their more numerous antagonists. So long as republican minorities barely accept their votes, no great harm will be done; because it will only place in power one shade of republicanism, instead of another. But when they purchase the votes of the federalists, by giving them a participation of office, trust and power, it is a proof that anti-monarchism is not their strongest passion.—To JAMES SULLIVAN. v, 101. FORD ED., ix, 77. (W., June 1807.)

2984. FEDERALISTS, Self-government and.—The leaders of federalism say that man cannot be trusted with his own government. We must do no act which shall replace them in the direction of the experiment. —To GOVERNOR HALL. FORD ED., viii, 157. (W., 1802.)

2985. FEDERALISTS, States' rights and.—The federalists, baffled in their schemes to monarchize us, have given up their name, which the Hartford Convention had made odious, and have taken shelter among us and under our name. But they have only changed the point of attack. On every question of the usurpation of State powers by the Foreign or General Government, the same men rally together, force the line of demarcation and consolidate the government. The judges are at their head as heretofore, and are their entering wedge. The true old republicans stand to the line, and will I hope die on it if necessary.—To SAMUEL H. SMITH. FORD ED., x, 263. (M., Aug. 1823.)

2986. FEDERALISTS, Terrorism and treason.—When General Washington was withdrawn, these *energumeni* of royalism, [the federal leaders], kept in check hitherto by the dread of his honesty, his firmness, his patriotism, and the authority of his name, now mounted on the car of State and free from control, like Phäeton on that of the sun, drove headlong and wild, looking neither to right nor left, nor regarding anything but the objects they were driving at; until, displaying these fully, the eyes of the nation were opened, and a general disbandment of them from the public councils took place. * * * But no man who did not witness it can form an idea of their unbridled madness, and the terrorism with which they surrounded themselves. The horrors of the French Revolution, then raging, aided them mainly, and using that as a rawhead and bloody-bones, they were enabled by their stratagems of X. Y. Z. in which this historian [Judge Marshall] was a leading mountebank, their tales of tub-plots, ocean massacres, bloody buoys, and pulpit lyings, and slanderings, and maniacal ravings of their Gardiners, their Osgoods and Parishes, to spread alarm into all but the firmest breasts. Their Attorney-General had the impudence to say to a republican member, that deportation must be resorted to, of which, said he, " you republicans have set the example," thus daring to identify us with the murderous Jacobins of France. These transactions. now [1818] recollected, but as dreams of the night, were then sad realities; and nothing rescued us from their liberticide effect, but the unyielding opposition of those firm spirits who sternly maintained their post, in defiance of terror, until their fellow citizens could be aroused to their own danger, and rally, and rescue us standard of the Constitution. This has been happily done. Federalism and monarchism have languished from that moment until their treasonable combinations with the enemies of their country during the late war, their plots of dismembering the Union, and their Hartford Convention, have consigned them to the tomb of the dead; and I fondly hope we may now truly say, " we are all republicans, all federalists." and that the motto of the standard to which our country will forever rally, will be " Federal Union and Republican Government "; and sure I am we may say that, we are indebted for the preservation of this point of ralliance, to that opposition of which so injurious an idea is so artfully insinuated and excited in this history [MARSHALL'S LIFE OF WASHINGTON].—THE ANAS. ix, 97. FORD ED., i, 166. (1818.)

2987. FEDERALISTS, Unprogressive.— What a satisfaction have we in the contemplation of the benevolent effects of our efforts, compared with those of the leaders on the other side, who have discountenanced all advances in science as dangerous innovations, have endeavored to render philosophy and republicanism terms of reproach. to persuade us that man cannot be governed but by the rod. I shall have the happiness of living and dying in the contrary hope.—To JOHN DICKINSON. iv, 366. FORD ED., viii, 8. (W., March 1801.)

2988. FEDERALISTS, Violations of Constitution.—Their usurpations and violations of the Constitution at that period [the administration of John Adams] and their majority in both Houses of Congress, were so great. so decided, and so daring, that after combating their aggressions, inch by inch, without being able in the least to check their career, the republican leaders thought it would be best for them to give up their useless efforts there, go home, get into their respective Legislatures, embody whatever of resistance they could be formed into, and if ineffectual, to perish there as in the last ditch. All, therefore, retired, leaving Mr. Gallatin alone in the House of Representatives, and myself in the

Senate, where I then presided as Vice-President. Remaining at our posts, and bidding defiance to the brow-beatings and insults by which they endeavored to drive us off also. we kept the mass of republicans in phalanx together, until the Legislature could be brought up to the charge; and nothing on earth is more certain, than that if myself particularly, placed by my office of Vice-President at the head of the republicans, had given way and withdrawn from my post, the republicans throughout the Union would have given up in despair, and the cause would have been lost forever. By holding on. we obtained time for the Legislatures to come up with their weight; and those of Virginia and Kentucky particularly, but more especially the former, by their celebrated resolutions, saved the Constitution at its last gasp. No person who was not a witness of the scenes of that gloomy period, can form any idea of the afflicting persecutions and personal indignities we had to brook. They saved our country however. The spirits of the people were so much subdued and reduced to despair by the X. Y. Z. imposture, and other stratagems and machinations, that they would have sunk into apathy and monarchy, as the only form of government which could maintain itself.[*]— MISCELLANEOUS PAPERS. ix, 507. FORD ED., x, 368. (1826.)

2989. FEDERALISTS, Worthy and unworthy.—With respect to the federalists, I believe we think alike; for when speaking of them, we never mean to include a worthy portion of our fellow citizens, who consider themselves as in duty bound to support the constituted authorities of every branch, and to reserve their opposition to the period of election. Those having acquired the appellation of federalists, while a federal administration was in place, have not cared about throwing off their name, but adhering to their principle, are the supporters of the present order of things. The other branch of the federalists. those who are so in principle as well as in name, disapprove of the republican principles and features of our Constitution, and would, I believe. welcome any public calamity (war with England excepted) which might lessen the confidence of our country in those principles and forms. I have generally considered them rather as subjects for a madhouse. But they are now playing a game of the most mischievous tendency, without perhaps being themselves aware of it. They are endeavoring to convince England that we suffer more by the Embargo than they do, and that if they will but hold out awhile, we must abandon it. It is true, the time will come when we must abandon it. But if this is before the repeal of the orders of council. we must abandon it only for a state of war. The day is not distant, when that will be preferable to a longer continuance of the Embargo. But we can never remove that, and let our vessels

[*] Jefferson said, in the same paper, that he considered this action on his part " the most important, in its consequences. of any transaction in any portion of his life ".—EDITOR.

go out and be taken under these orders, without making reprisal. Yet this is the very state of things which these federal monarchists are endeavoring to bring about; and in this it is but too possible they may succeed. But the fact is, that if we have war with England it will be solely produced by their manœuvres.—To Dr. Thomas Leib. v, 304. Ford ed., ix, 196. (W., June 1808.) See Parties, Republicanism and Republicans.

2990. FENNER (James), Character of.— No one was more sensible than myself, while Governor Fenner was in the senate, of the soundness of his political principles, and rectitude of h's conduct. Among those of my fellow laborers of whom I had a distinguished opinion, he was one.—To David Howell. v, 554. (M., 1810.)

2991. FENNO (John), Gazette of.— [Fenno's Gazette] is a paper of pure toryism, disseminating the doctrines of monarchy, aristocracy, and the exclusion of the influence of the people.—To T. M. Randolph. Ford ed., v, 334. (Pa., 1791.)

2992. —— ——. The tory paper of Fenno rarely admits anything which defends the present form of government in opposition to his desire of subverting it to make way for a king, lords and commons.—To William Short. Ford ed., v, 361. (1791.)

— FEVER.—See Yellow Fever.

2993. FICTION, Education and.— A great obstacle to good education is the inordinate passion prevalent for novels, and the time lost in that reading which should be instructively employed. When this poison infects the mind, it destroys its tone and revolts it against wholesome reading. Reason and fact, plain and unadorned, are rejected. Nothing can engage attention unless dressed in all the figments of fancy, and nothing so bedecked comes amiss. The result is a bloated imagination, sickly judgment, and disgust towards all the real businesses of life.*—To N. Burwell. vii, 102. Ford ed., x, 104. (M., 1818.)

2994. FICTION, Value of sound.— A little attention to the nature of the human mind evinces that the entertainments of fiction are useful as well as pleasant. That they are pleasant when well written, every person feels who reads. But wherein is its utility, asks the reverend sage, big with the notion that nothing can be useful but the learned lumber of Greek and Roman reading with which his head is stored? I answer everything is useful which contributes to fix in the principles and practices of virtue. When any original act of charity or of gratitude, for instance, is presented either to our sight or imagination, we are deeply impressed with its beauty and feel a strong desire in ourselves of doing charitable and grateful acts also. On the contrary, when we see or read of any atrocious deed, we are disgusted with its deformity, and conceive an abhorrence of vice. Now every emotion of this kind is

* Jefferson made an exception in favor of Maria Edgeworth and others whose works inculcated a sound morality.—Editor.

an exercise of our virtuous dispositions, and dispositions of the mind, like limbs of the body, acquire strength by practice. But exercise produces habit, and in the instance of which we speak, the exercise being of the moral feelings, produces a habit of thinking and acting virtuously. We never reflect whether the story we read be truth or fiction. If the painting be lively, and a tolerable picture of nature, we are thrown into a reverie, from which if we awaken it is the fault of the writer. I appeal to every reader of feeling and sentiment whether the fictitious murder of Duncan by Macbeth, in Shakespeare, does not excite in him as great a horror of villainy, as the real one of Henry IV. by Ravaillac, as related by Davila? And whether the fidelity of Nelson and generosity of Blandford, in Marmontel, do not dilate his breast and elevate his sentiments as much as any similar incident which real history can furnish? Does he not in fact feel himself a better man while reading them, and privately covenant to copy the fair example? We neither know nor care whether Laurence Sterne really went to France, whether he was there accosted by the Franciscan, at first rebuked him unkindly, and then gave him a peace offering; or whether the whole be not fiction. In either case, we equally are sorrowful at the rebuke, and secretly resolve we will never do so: we are pleased with the subsequent atonement, and view with emulation a soul candidly acknowledging its fault and making a just reparation. Considering history as a moral exercise, her lessons would be too infrequent if confined to real life. Of those recorded by historians few incidents have been attended with such circumstances as to excite in any high degree this sympathetic emotion of virtue. We are, therefore, wisely framed to be as warmly interested for a fictitious as for a real personage. The field of imagination is thus laid open to our use and lessons may be formed to illustrate and carry home to the heart every moral rule of life. Thus a lively and lasting sense of filial duty is more effectually impressed on the mind of a son or daughter by reading King Lear, than by all the dry volumes of ethics and divinity that ever were written. This is my idea of well written Romance, of Tragedy, Comedy and Epic poetry.—To Robert Skipwith. Ford ed., i, 396. (M., 1771.)

2995. FILIBUSTERISM, Prevention.— If you will * * * give me such information as to persons and places as may indicate to what points the vigilance of the officers is to be directed, proper measures will be immediately taken for preventing every attempt to make any hostile expedition from these States against any of the dominions of France. The stronger the proofs you can produce, and the more pointed as to persons, the stronger will be the means of coercion which the laws will allow to be used.—To E. C. Genet. Ford ed., vi, 426. (Pa., Sep. 1793.)

2996. FILIBUSTERISM, Punishment of.— Let it be our endeavor * * * to restrain our citizens from embarking individually in a war* in which their country takes no part; to punish severely those persons, citizen or alien, who shall usurp the cover of our flag for vessels not entitled to it, infecting thereby with suspicion those of real Americans, and committing us into controversies for the redress of wrongs not our own.—THIRD ANNUAL MESSAGE. viii, 28. FORD ED., viii, 272. (1803.)

2997. —— ——. I am sorry to learn that a banditti from our country are taking part in the domestic contests of the country adjoining you; and the more so as from the known laxity of execution in our laws, they cannot be punished. It will give a wrongful hue to a rightful act of taking possession of Mobile, and will be imputed to the national authority, as Miranda's enterprise was, because not punished by it.—To DR. SAMUEL BROWN. vi, 165. (M., 1813.)

2998. FILIBUSTERISM, Restraining.— That individuals should undertake to wage private war, independently of the authority of their country, cannot be permitted in a well ordered society. Its tendency to produce aggression on the laws and rights of other nations, and to endanger the peace of our own is so obvious, that I doubt not you will adopt measures for restraining it effectually in future.—FOURTH ANNUAL MESSAGE. viii, 34. FORD ED., viii, 326. (1804.)

2999. FILIBUSTERISM, Suppression.— Having received information that a great number of private individuals were combining together, arming and organizing themselves contrary to law, to carry on military expeditions against the territories of Spain. I thought it necessary, by proclamations, as well as by special orders, to take measures for preventing and suppressing this enterprise, for seizing the vessels, arms, and other means provided for it, and for arresting and bringing to justice its authors and abettors. It was due to that good faith which ought ever to be the rule of action in public as well as in private transactions; it was due to good order and regular government, that while the public force was strictly on the defensive and merely to protect our citizens from aggression, the criminal attempts of private individuals to decide for their country the question of peace or war, by commencing active and unauthorized hostilities, should be promptly and efficaciously suppressed.—SIXTH ANNUAL MESSAGE. viii, 63. FORD ED., viii, 489. (Dec. 1806.)

3000. —— ——. The late piratical depredations which your commerce has suffered as well as ours, and that of other nations. seem to have been committed by renegade rovers of several nations, French, English, American, which they as well as we have not been careful enough to suppress. I hope our Congress * * * .will strengthen the measures of suppression. Of their disposition to do it there can be no doubt; for all men of moral principle must be shocked at these atrocities. I

*Between England and France.—EDITOR.

had repeated conversations on this subject with the President * * * . No man can abhor these enormities more deeply. I trust it will not have been in the power of abandoned rovers, nor yet of negligent functionaries, to disturb the harmony of two nations so much disposed to mutual friendship, and interested in it.—To J. CORREA. vii, 184. FORD ED., x, 164. (M., 1820.)

3001. FINANCES, Disordered.— I do not at all wonder at the condition in which the finances of the United States are found. Hamilton's object from the beginning, was to throw them into forms which should be utterly undecipherable. I ever said he did not understand their condition himself, nor was able to give a clear view of the excess of our debts beyond our credits, nor whether we were diminishing or increasing the debt. My own opinion was, that from the commencement of this government to the time I ceased to attend to the subject, we had been increasing our debt about a million of dollars annually. If Mr. Gallatin would undertake to reduce this chaos to order, present us with a clear view of our finances, and put them into a form as simple as they will admit, he will merit immortal honor. The accounts of the United States ought to be, and may be made as simple as those of a common farmer, and capable of being understood by common farmers.—To JAMES MADISON. iv, 131. FORD ED., vii, 61. (M., March 1796.)

3002. —— ——. The finances are said to have been left by the late financier in the utmost derangement, and his tools are urging the funding the new debts they have contracted. Thus posterity is to be left to pay the ordinary expenses of our government in time of peace.—To JAMES MONROE. FORD ED. vii, 60. (M., March 1796.)

3003. —— ——. I had always conjectured, from such facts as I could get hold of, that our public debt was increasing about a million of dollars a year. You will see by Gallatin's speeches that the thing is proved.—To JAMES MONROE. iv, 140. FORD ED., vii 80. (M., June 1796.)

3004. FINANCES, Misapplied.— The finances are now under such a course of application as nothing could derange but war or federalism. The gripe of the latter has shown itself as deadly as have the jaws of the former. Our adversaries say we are indebted to their providence for the means of paying the public debt. We never charged them with the want of foresight in providing money, but with the misapplication of it after they had levied it. We say they raised not only enough, but too much; and that, after giving back the surplus, we do more with a part than they did with the whole.—To THOMAS COOPER. iv, 453. FORD ED., viii, 178. (W., 1802.)

3005. FINANCES, Simplification of.— I think it an object of great importance. * * * to simplify our system of finance, and bring it within the comprehension of every member of Congress.—To ALBERT GALLATIN. iv, 428. FORD ED., viii, 139. (W., April 1802.) See 39.

3006. FINANCES, Sound system of.— The other great and indispensable object [in prosecuting the war] is to enter on such a system of finance, as can be permanently pursued to any length of time whatever. Let us be allured by no projects of banks, public or private, or ephemeral expedients, which, enabling us to gasp and flounder a little longer, only increase, by protracting the agonies of death.—To JAMES MONROE. vi, 395. FORD ED., ix, 492. (M., Oct. 1814.)

3007. ———. The British ministers found some hopes [of success in the war] on the state of our finances. It is true that the excess of our banking institutions, and their present discredit, have shut us out from the best source of credit we could ever command with certainty. But the foundations of credit still remain to us, and need but skill which experience will soon produce, to marshal them into an order which may carry us through any length of war.—To MARQUIS DE LAFAYETTE. vi, 425. FORD ED., ix, 508. (M., 1815.) See BANKS and DEBT.

3008. FISHERIES, British acts against. —To show they [Parliament] mean no discontinuance of injury, they pass acts, at the very time of holding out this proposition, for restraining * * * the fisheries of the province of New England.—REPLY TO LORD NORTH'S PROPOSITION. FORD ED., i, 480. (July 1775.)

3009. FISHERIES, British rivalry in. —England fears no rivals in the whale fishery but America; or rather, it is the whale fishery of America, of which she is endeavoring to possess herself. It is for this object she is making the present extraordinary efforts, by bounties and other encouragements; and her success, so far, is very flattering. Before the war, she had not one hundred vessels in the whale trade, while America employed three hundred and nine. In 1786, Great Britain employed one hundred and fifty-one vessels; in 1787, two hundred and eighty-six; in 1788, three hundred and fourteen, nearly the ancient American number; while the latter has fallen to about eighty. They have just changed places then; England having gained exactly what America lost. France, by her ports and markets, holds the balance between the two contending parties, and gives the victory, by opening and shutting them, to which she pleases.—To COMTE MONTMORIN. ii 523. (P., 1788.)

3010. FISHERIES, Competition in. — There is no other nation in present condition to maintain a competition with Great Britain in the whale fishery. The expense at which it is supported on her part seems enormous. Two hundred and fifty-five vessels, of seventy-five thousand four hundred and thirty-six tons, employed by her this year in the northern fishery, at forty-two men each; and fifty-nine in the southern at eighteen men each,

make eleven thousand seven hundred and seventy-two men. These are known to have cost the government fifteen pounds each, or one hundred and seventy-six thousand five hundred and eighty pounds, in the whole; and that, to employ the principal part of them, from three to four months only. The northern ships have brought home twenty, and the southern sixty tons of oil, on an average; making eighty-six hundred and forty tons. Every ton of oil, then, has cost the government twenty pounds in bounty. Still, if they can beat us out of the field and have it to themselves, they will think their money well employed.—To COMTE DE MONTMORIN. ii, 524. (P., 1788.)

3011. FISHERIES, Distresses of.—Of the disadvantages opposed to us [in the Fisheries] those which depend on ourselves, are: Tonnage and naval duties on the vessels employed in the fishery; impost duties on salt; on tea, rum, sugar, molasses, hooks, lines and leads, duck, cordage and cables, iron, hemp and twine, used in the fishery; coarse woollens, worn by the fishermen, and the poll tax levied by the State on their persons. * * * The amount of these, exclusive of the State tax and drawback on the fish exported * * * [is] $5.25 per man, or $57.75 per vessel of sixty-five tons. When a business is so nearly in equilibrio that one can hardly discern whether the profit be sufficient to continue it or not, smaller sums than these suffice to turn the scale against it. To these disadvantages, add ineffectual duties on the importation of foreign fish. In justification of these last, it is urged that the foreign fish received, is in exchange for the produce of agriculture. To which it may be answered, that the thing given, is more merchantable than that received in exchange, and agriculture has too many markets to be allowed to take away those of the fisheries.—REPORT ON THE FISHERIES. vii, 543. (1791.)

3012. FISHERIES, Encouragement of. —The encouragement of our fishery abridges that of a rival nation, whose power on the ocean has long threatened the loss of all balance on that element.—REPORT ON THE FISHERIES. vii, 541. (1791.)

3013. FISHERIES, Fostering.—To foster our fisheries and nurseries of navigation and for the nurture of man * * * [is one of] the landmarks by which we are to guide ourselves in all our proceedings.—SECOND ANNUAL MESSAGE. viii, 21. FORD ED., viii, 187. (Dec. 1802.)

3014. FISHERIES, Massachussetts and. —I fear there is foundation for the design intimated in the public papers, of demanding a cession of our rights in the fisheries. What will Massachusetts say to this? I mean her majority, which must be considered as speaking through the organs it has appointed itself, as the index of its will. She chose to sacrifice the liberties of our sea-faring citizens, in which we were all interested, and with them her obligations to the co-States, rather than war with England. Will she now sacrifice the fisheries to the same partialities? This question is interesting to her alone; for to the middle, the southern and western States, they are of no direct concern; of no more than the culture of tobacco, rice and cotton, to Massachusetts. I am really at a loss to conjecture what our refractory sister will say on this occasion. I know what, as a citizen of the Union, I would say to her. " Take this question *ad referendum.* It concerns you alone. If you would rather give up the fisheries than war with England, we give them up. If you had rather fight for them, we will defend your interests to the last drop of our blood, choosing rather to set a good example than follow a bad one." And I hope she will determine to fight for them.—To JOHN ADAMS. vi, 353. FORD ED., ix, 462. (M., July 1814.)

3015. FISHERIES, Preservation of.— As to the fisheries, England was urgent to retain them exclusively, France neutral, and I believe, that had they been ultimately made a *sine quâ non,* our commissioners (Mr. Adams excepted) would have relinquished them, rather than have broken off the treaty. [Of peace with Great Britain.] To Mr. Adams's perseverance alone, on that point, I have always understood we were indebted for their reservation.—To ROBERT WALSH. vii, 108. FORD ED., x, 117. (M., 1818.)

3016. FISHERIES, Prostrated.— The fisheries of the United States, annihilated during the war [of the Revolution], their vessels, utensils, and fishermen destroyed; their markets in the Mediterranean and British America lost, and their produce dutied in those of France; their competitors enabled by bounties to meet and undersell them at the few markets remaining open, without any public aid, and, indeed paying aids to the public;—such were the hopeless auspices under which this important business was to be resumed.—REPORT ON THE FISHERIES. vii, 542. (1791.)

3017. FISHERIES, Protection of.— It will rest with the wisdom of the Legislature to decide, whether prohibition should not be opposed to prohibition, and high duty to high duty, on the fish of other nations; whether any, and which, of the naval and other duties may be remitted, or an equivalent given to the fisherman, in the form of a drawback, or bounty; and whether the loss of markets abroad, may not, in some degree, be compensated, by creating markets at home; to which might contribute the constituting fish a part of the military ration, in stations not too distant from navigation, a part of the necessary sea stores of vessels, and the encouraging private individuals to let the fishermen share with the cultivator, in furnishing the supplies of the table. A habit introduced from motives of patriotism, would soon be followed from motives of taste; and who will undertake to fix the limits to this demand, if it can be once excited, with a nation which doubles, and will continue to double, at very short

periods.—REPORT ON FISHERIES. vii, 544. (1791.)

3018. ——— ———. The *ex parte* regulations which the English have begun for mounting their navigation on the ruins of ours, can only be opposed by counter regulations on our part. And the loss of seamen, the natural consequence of lost and obstructed markets for our fish and oil, calls in the first place, for serious and timely attention. It will be too late when the seaman shall have changed his vocation, or gone over to another interest. If we cannot recover and secure for him these important branches of employment, it behooves us to replace them by others equivalent.—REPORT ON FISHERIES. vii, 552. (1791.)

3019. FISHERIES, Relief of.— What relief does the condition of the whale fishery require? 1. A remission of duties on the articles used for their calling. 2. A retaliating duty on foreign oils, coming to seek a competition with them in or from our ports. 3. Free markets abroad. * * * The only nation whose oil is brought hither for competition with our own, makes ours pay a duty of about eighty-two dollars the ton, in their ports. Theirs is brought here, too, to be reshipped fraudulently, under our flag, and ought not to be covered by ours, if we mean to preserve our own admission into them.—REPORT ON THE FISHERIES. vii, 551. (1791.)

3020. ——— ———. The historical view we have taken of these fisheries, proves they are so poor in themselves, as to come to nothing with distant nations, who do not support them from their own treasury. We have seen that the advantages of our position place our fisheries on a ground somewhat higher, such as to relieve our treasury from giving them support; but not to permit it to draw support from them, nor to dispense the government from the obligation of effectuating free markets for them; that, from the great proportion of our salted fish, for our common oil, and a part of our spermaceti oil, markets may perhaps be preserved, by friendly arrangements towards those nations whose arrangements are friendly to us, and the residue be compensated by giving to the seamen, thrown out of business, the certainty of employment in another branch, of which we have the sole disposal (the carrying trade).—REPORT ON THE FISHERIES. vii, 538. (1791.)

3021. FISHERIES, Whale.— In 1715, the Americans began their whale fishery. They were led to it at first by the whales which presented themselves on their coasts. They attacked them there in small vessels of forty tons. As the whale, being infested, retired from the coast, they followed him farther and farther into the ocean, still enlarging their vessels with their adventures, to sixty, one hundred, and two hundred tons. Having extended their pursuit to the Western Islands, they fell in, accidentally, with the spermaceti whale, of a different species from that of

Greenland, which alone had hitherto been known in commerce; more fierce and active, and whose oil and head matter were found to be more valuable, as it might be used in the interior of houses without offending the smell. The distinction now first arose between the Northern and Southern fisheries; the object of the former being the Greenland whale, which frequents the Northern coasts and seas of Europe and America; that of the latter being the spermaceti whale, which was found in the Southern seas, from the Western Islands and coast of Africa, to that of Brazil, and still on to the Falkland Islands. Here, again, within soundings, on the coast of Brazil, they found a third species of whale, which they called the black or Brazil whale, smaller than the Greenland, yielding a still less valuable oil, fit only for summer use, as it becomes opaque at 50 degrees of Fahrenheit's thermometer, while that of the spermaceti whale is limpid to 41, and of the Greenland whale to 36, of the same thermometer. It is only worth taking, therefore, when it falls in the way of the fishermen, but not worth seeking, except when they have failed of success against the spermaceti whale, in which case, this kind, easily found and taken, serves to moderate their loss.—REPORT ON FISHERIES. vii, 545. (1791.)

3022. FLAG, Neutrality of.—The neutrality of our flag would render the carriage for belligerents an incalculable source of profit.—REPORT ON FISHERIES. vii, 554. (1791.) See NAVIGATION and NEUTRALITY.

3023. FLAG, Usurpation of.—It will be necessary for all our public agents to exert themselves with vigilance * * * to prevent the vessels of other nations from usurping our flag. This usurpation tends to commit us with the belligerent powers, to draw on those vessels truly ours, vigorous visitations to distinguish them from the counterfeits, and to take business from us.—To C. W. F. DUMAS. iii, 535. (Pa., 1793.)

3024. ———— ————. Present appearances in Europe render a general war there probable. * * * In the * * * event * * * give no countenance to the usurpation of our flag by foreign vessels, but * * * aid in detecting it, as without bringing to us any advantage, the usurpation will tend to commit us with the belligerent powers, and to subject those vessels, which are truly ours, to harassing scrutinies in order to distinguish them from the counterfeits.—To SAMUEL SHAW. iii, 530. (Pa., March 1793.)

3025. ———— ————. It is impossible to detest more than I do the fraudulent and injurious practice of covering foreign vessels and cargoes under the American flag; and I sincerely wish a systematic and severe course of punishment could be established.—To MR. GALLATIN. v, 223. FORD ED., x, 170. (W., 1807.)

3026. FLAG, Reception of.—If British officers set the example of refusing to receive a flag, let ours then follow it by never sending or receiving another.—To W. H. CABELL. v, 201. (W., Oct. 1807.)

3027. ———— ————. In answering [Minister Erskine's] last [letter], should he not be reminded how strange it is he should consider as a hostility our refusing to receive but under a flag, persons from vessels remaining and acting in our waters in defiance of the authority of the country?—To JAMES MADISON. v, 197. FORD ED., ix, 141. (M., Sep. 1807.)

3028. FLATTERY, Un-American.—Let those flatter who fear: it is not an American art.—RIGHTS OF BRITISH AMERICA. i, 141. FORD ED., i, 446. (1774.)

3029. ———— ————. According to the ideas of our country, we do not permit ourselves to speak even truths, when they may have the air of flattery.—To MARQUIS DE LAFAYETTE. ii, 136. (1787.)

3030. FLETCHER OF SALTOUN, Principles of.—The political principles of that patriot were worthy of the purest periods of the British constitution; They are those which were in vigor at the epoch of the American emigration. Our ancestors brought them here, and they needed little strengthening to make us what we are. But in the weakened condition of English whigism at this day, it requires more firmness to publish and advocate them than it then did to act on them. This merit is peculiarly your Lordships; and no one honors it more than myself.—To EARL OF BUCHAN. iv, 493. (W., 1803.)

3031. FLORIDA, Acquisition of.—Governor Quesada, by order of his court, is inviting foreigners to go and settle in Florida. This is meant for our people. * * * I wish a hundred thousand of our inhabitants would accept the invitation. It will be the means of delivering to us peaceably what may otherwise cost us a war. In the meantime, we may complain of this seduction of our inhabitants just enough to make them believe we think it very wise policy for them, and confirm them in it.—To PRESIDENT WASHINGTON. iii, 235. FORD ED., v, 316. (Pa., 1791.)

3032. FLORIDA, Buying.—It was agreed at a cabinet meeting that] Monroe be instructed to endeavor to purchase both Floridas if he can; West [Florida] if he cannot East, at the prices before agreed on; but if neither can be procured, then to stipulate a plenary right to use all the rivers rising within our limits and passing through theirs. * * * We are more indifferent about pressing the purchase of the Floridas, because of the money we have to provide for Louisiana, and because we think they cannot fail to fall into our hands. —THE ANAS. FORD ED., i, 300. (Oct. 1803.)

3033. ———— ————. The extension of the war in Europe leaving us without danger of a sudden peace, depriving us of the chance of an ally, I proposed [in cabinet] that we should address ourselves to France, informing her it was a last effort at amicable settlement with Spain, and offer to her or through her, 1. a sum of money for the rights of Spain east of Iberville, say the Floridas. 2. To cede the part of Louisiana from the Rio Bravo to the Guadaloupe. 3. Spain to pay within a certain time spoliations under her own flag, agreed to by the convention (which we guess to be one hundred vessels worth two million dollars); and those subsequent (worth as much more), and to hypothecate to us for those payments the country from Guadaloupe to Rio Bravo. Armstrong was to be employed. The 1st was to be the exciting motive with France to whom Spain is in arrears for subsidies, and who will be glad also to secure us from going into the scale of England. The 2d. the soothing motive with Spain, which France would press *bona fide*, because she claimed to the Rio Bravo. The 3d. to quiet our merchants. It was agreed to unanimously, and the sum to be offered fixed not to exceed five million dollars. Mr. Gallatin did not like purchasing Florida under an apprehension of war, lest we should be thought, in fact, to purchase peace. We thought this over-weighed by taking advantage of an opportunity, which might not occur again, of getting a country essential to our peace, and to the security of the commerce of the Mississippi.—ANAS. FORD ED., i, 308. (Nov. 12, 1805.)

3034. —— ——. Since our [the Cabinet's] last meeting, we have received a letter from General Armstrong, containing Talleyrand's propositions, which are equivalent to ours nearly, except as to the sum, he requiring seven million dollars. He advises that we alarm the fears of Spain by a vigorous language and conduct, in order to induce her to join us in appealing to the interference of the Emperor. We now agree to modify our propositions, so as to accommodate them to his as much as possible. We agree to pay five million dollars for the Floridas as soon as the treaty is ratified by Spain, a vote of credit obtained from Congress, and orders delivered us for the surrender of the country. We agree to his proposition that the Colorado shall be our Western boundary, and a belt of thirty leagues on each side of it be kept unsettled. We agree that joint commissioners shall settle all spoliations, and to take payment from Spain by bills on her colonies. We agree to say nothing about the French spoliators in Spanish ports which broke off the former convention. We propose to pay the five millions, after a simple vote of credit, by stock redeemable in three years, within which time we can pay it.—ANAS. FORD ED., i, 300. (Nov. 19, 1805.)

3035. —— ——. If you can succeed in procuring us Florida, and a good Western boundary, it will fill the American mind with joy. It will secure to our fellow citizens one of their most ardent wishes, a long peace with Spain and France. For be assured, the object of war with them and alliance with England, which, at the last session of Congress, drew off from the republican band about half a dozen of its members, is universally reprobated by our *native* citizens from north to south. I have never seen the nation stand more firmly to its principles, or rally so firmly to its constituted authorities, and in reprobation of the opposition to them.—TO JAMES BOWDOIN. v, 18. (W., 1806.)

3036. FLORIDA, England and.—England will immediately seize on the Floridas as a *point d'appui* to annoy us. What are we to do in that case? I think she will find that there is no nation on the globe which can gall her so much as we can.—TO JOHN ARMSTRONG. v, 135. FORD ED., ix, 117. (W., July 1807.) See 298.

3037. FLORIDA, France and.—That Bonaparte would give us the Floridas to withhold intercourse with the residue of the [Spanish] colonies cannot be doubted. But that is no price; because they are ours in the first moment of the first war; and until a war they are of no particular necessity to us.—TO PRESIDENT MADISON. v, 444. (M., April 1809.)

3038. FLORIDA, Reprisal and.—As soon as we have all the proofs of the Western intrigues [of Spain], let us make a remonstrance and demand of satisfaction, and, if Congress approves, we may in the same instant make reprisals on the Floridas, until satisfaction for that and for spoliations, and until a settlement of boundary.—TO JAMES MADISON. v, 164. FORD ED., ix, 124. (M., Aug. 1807.)

3039. —— ——. If England should be disposed to continue peace with us, and Spain gives to Bonaparte the occupation she promises, will not the interval be favorable for our reprisals on the Floridas for the indemnifications withheld?—TO HENRY DEARBORN. v, 335. (M., Aug. 1808.)

3040. —— ——. The situation of affairs in Spain * * * may produce a favorable occasion of doing ourselves justice in the South. We must certainly so dispose of our southern recruits and armed vessels as to be ready for the occasion.—TO ALBERT GALLATIN. v, 336. (M., Aug. 1808.)

3041. —— ——. Should England get to rights with us, while Bonaparte is at war with Spain, the moment may be favorable to take possession of our own territory held by Spain, and so much more as may make a proper reprisal for her spoliations. We ought, therefore, to direct the rendezvous of our southern recruits and gunboats so as to be in proper position for striking * * * in an instant, when Congress shall will it.—TO ROBERT SMITH. v, 337. (M., Aug. 1808.)

3042. —— ——. Should England make up with us, while Bonaparte continues at war with Spain, a moment may occur when we may without danger of commitment with either France or England seize to our own limits of Louisiana as of right, and the residue of the Floridas as reprisal for spoliations. It is our duty to have an eye to this in rendezvousing and stationing our new recruits and our armed vessels, so as to be ready, if Congress authorizes it, to strike in a moment.—TO HENRY DEARBORN. v, 338. (M., Aug. 1808.)

3043. —— ——. Should the conference [with Canning] announced in Mr. Pinckney's letter of June 5th, settle friendship between England and us, and Bonaparte continue at war with Spain, a moment may occur favorable, without compromitting us with either France or England, for seizing our own from the Rio Bravo to Perdido, as of right, and the residue of Florida, as a reprisal for spoliations. I have thought it proper to suggest this possibility to General Dearborn and Mr. Smith, and to recommend an eye to it in their rendezvousing and stationing the new southern recruits and gunboats, so that we may strike in a moment when Congress says so.—TO JAMES MADISON. v, 339. FORD ED., ix, 204. (M., Aug. 1808.)

3044. FLORIDA, Right to.—Florida, moreover, is ours. Every nation in Europe considers it such a right. We need not care for its occupation in time of peace and, in war, the first cannon makes it ours without offence to anybody. * * * The cession of the Floridas in exchange for Techas imports an acknowledgment of our right to it. This province, moreover, the Floridas and possibly Cuba, will join us on the acknowledgment of their independence, a measure to which their new government will probably accede voluntarily.—To PRESIDENT MONROE. vii, 160. FORD ED., x, 159. (M., 1820.)

3045. FLORIDA, Seizure of.—I wish you [Congress] would authorize the President to take possession of East Florida immediately. The seizing West Florida will be a signal to England to take Pensacola and St. Augustine; and be assured it will be done as soon as the order can return after they hear of our taking Baton Rouge, and we shall never get it from them but by a war, which may be prevented by anticipation. There never was a case where the adage was more true, " in for a penny, in for a pound "; and no more offence will be taken by France and Spain at our seizure of both than of one.—To J. W. EPPES. FORD ED., ix, 290. (M., Jan. 1811.)

3046. ——. The English will take East Florida, pretendedly for Spain. We should take it with a declaration; 1, that it is a reprisal for indemnities Spain has acknowledged due to us; 2, to keep it from falling into hands in which it would essentially endanger our safety; 3, that in our hands it will still be held as a subject of negotiation. The leading republican members should come to an understanding, close the doors, and determine not to separate till the vote is carried, and all the secrecy you can enjoin should be aimed at until the measure is executed.—To J. W. EPPES. FORD ED.,·ix, 291. (M., Jan. 1811.)

3047. ——. We are in a state of semi-warfare with your adjoining colonies, the Floridas. We do not consider this as affecting our peace with Spain, or any other of her former possessions. We wish her and them well; and under her present difficulties at home, and her doubtful future relations with her colonies, both wisdom and interest will, I presume, induce her to leave them to settle themselves the quarrels they draw on themselves from their neighbors. The commanding officers in the Floridas have excited and armed the neighboring savages to war against us, and to murder and scalp many of our women and children as well as men, taken by surprise—poor creatures! They have paid for it with the loss of the flower of their strength, and have given us the right, as we possess the power, to exterminate or to expatriate them beyond the Mississippi. This conduct of the Spanish officers will probably oblige us to take possession of the Floridas, and the rather as we believe the English will otherwise seize them, and use them as stations to distract and annoy us. But should we possess ourselves of them, and Spain retain her other colonies in this hemisphere, I presume we shall consider them in our hands as subjects of negotiation.—To DON V. TORANDA CORUNA. vi, 274. (M., Dec. 1813.)

3048. FLORIDA, Spain and.—Some fear our envelopment in the wars engendering from the unsettled state of our affairs with Spain, and therefore are anxious for a ratification of our treaty with her. I fear no such thing, and hope that if ratified by Spain it will be rejected here. We may justly say to Spain, " when this negotiation commenced, twenty years ago, your authority was acknowledged by those you are selling to us. That authority is now renounced, and their right of self-disposal asserted. In buying them from you, then, we buy but a war-title, a right to subdue them, which you can neither convey nor we acquire. This is a family quarrel in which we have no right to meddle. Settle it between yourselves, and we will then treat with the party whose right is acknowledged.'' With whom that will be, no doubt can be entertained. And why should we revolt them by purchasing them as cattle, rather than receiving them as fellow-men? Spain has held off until she sees they are lost to her, and now thinks it better to get something than nothing for them. When she shall see South America equally desperate, she will be wise to sell that also.—To M. DE LAFAYETTE. vii, 194. FORD ED., x, 179. (M., 1820.)

3049. ——. I am not sorry for the non-ratification of the Spanish treaty. Our assent to it has proved our desire to be on friendly terms with Spain; their dissent, the imbecility and malignity of their government towards us, have placed them in the wrong in the eyes of the world, and that is well; but to us the province of Techas will be the richest State of our Union, without any exception. Its southern part will make more sugar than we can consume, and the Red River, on its North, is the most luxuriant country on earth. Florida, moreover, is ours. Every nation in Europe considers it such a right. We need not care for its occupation in time of peace, and, in war, the first cannon makes it ours without offence to anybody. The friendly advisements, too, of Russia and France, as well as the change of government in Spain, now ensured, require a further and respectful forbearance. While their request will rebut the plea of proscriptive possession, it will give us a right to their approbation when taken in the maturity of circumstances. I really think, too, that neither the state of our finances, the condition of our country, nor the public opinion, urges us to precipitation into war. The treaty has had the valuable effect of strengthening our title to the Techas, because the cession of the Floridas in exchange for Techas imports an acknowledgment of our right to it. This province moreover, the Floridas and possibly Cuba, will join us on the acknowledgment of their independence, a measure to which their new government will probably accede voluntarily.—To PRESIDENT MONROE. vii, 160. FORD ED., x, 158. (M., May 1820.) See LOUISIANA, MONROE DOCTRINE, and SPAIN.

3050. FOLLY, National.—We, too. shall encounter follies; but if great, they will be short; if long, they will be light, and the vigor of our country will get the better of them.—To MR. DIGGES. v, 14. (W., 1806.)

3051. ——. We shall have our follies without doubt. Some one or more of them will always be afloat. But ours will be the follies of enthusiasm. not of bigotry * * * .—To JOHN ADAMS. vii, 27. (M., 1816.)

3052. FONTAINBLEAU, Description.—This is a village of about 5000 inhabitants when the Court is not here, and 20.000 inhabitants when they are; occupying a valley through which runs a brook, and on each side of it a ridge of small mountains most of which are naked rock. The King comes here, in the fall always, to hunt. His court attend him, as do also the foreign diplomatic corps. But as this is not indispensably required, and my finances do not admit the expense of a continued residence here. I propose to come occasionally to attend the King's levees, returning again to Paris, distant forty miles.—To REV. JAMES MADISON. FORD ED., vii, 33. (P., 1785.)

3053. FOPPERY, Admiration of.—As for admiration, I am sure the man who powders most, perfumes most, embroiders most, and talks most nonsense, is most admired. Though to be candid, there are some who have too much good sense to esteem such monkey-like animals as these, in whose formation, as the saying is, the tailors and barbers go halves with God Almighty.*—To JOHN PAGE. i, 183. FORD ED., i, 344. (1762.)

3054. FORCE, Despotism and.—Force [is] the vital principle and immediate parent of despotism.—FIRST INAUGURAL ADDRESS. viii, 4. FORD ED., viii. 4. (1801.)

3055. FORCE, Government and.—That nature has formed man insusceptible of any other government than that of force. is a conclusion not founded in truth nor experience.—To JAMES MADISON. ii, 104. FORD ED., iv, 362. (P., 1787.)

3056. FORCE, Money and.—The want of money cramps every effort. This will be supplied by the most unpalatable of all substitutes, force.—To GENERAL WASHINGTON. i, 242. FORD ED., ii, 309. (Wg., 1780.)

.3057. FORCE, Politics and.—Force is not the kind of opposition the American people will permit.—To EDMUND PENDLETON. iv, 287. FORD ED., vii, 356. (Pa., 1799.)

3058. FORCE, Reason vs.—The friends of reform, while they remain firm, [should] avoid every act and threat against the peace of the Union. That would check the favorable sentiments of the middle States, and rally them again around the measures which are ruining us. Reason, not rashness, is the only means of bringing our fellow citizens to their true minds.—To N. LEWIS. iv, 278. (1799.)

3059. FORCE, Right and.—Force cannot give right.—RIGHTS OF BRITISH AMERICA. i, 141. FORD ED., i, 445. (1774.)

3060. —— ——. With respect to America. Europeans in general, have been too long in the habit of confounding force with right. —To WILLIAM SHORT. iii, 276. FORD ED., v, 364. (Pa., 1791.)

3061. —— ——. Force cannot change right.—To JOHN CARTWRIGHT. vii, 355. (M., 1824.)

3062. FORCE, Wisdom and.—It is the multitude which possesses force, and wisdom must yield to that.—To DUPONT DE NEMOURS. vi, 592. FORD ED., x, 25. (P.F., 1816.)

3063. FOREIGN AGENTS, Authorization.—The sending an agent within our limits. we presume has been done without the authority or knowledge of the Spanish government. It has certainly been the usage, where one nation has wished to employ agents of any kind within the limits of another, to obtain the permission of that other, and even to regulate by convention, and on principles of reciprocity, the functions to be exercised by such agents.†—To THE SPANISH COMMISSIONERS. FORD ED., vi, 99. (Pa., 1792.)

* Jefferson was 19 years of age in 1762.—EDITOR.
† The Government of West Florida had established an agent within the Creek territory.—EDITOR.

3064. —— ——. I consider the keeping by Spain of an agent in the Indian Country as a circumstance which requires serious interference on our part; and I submit to your decision whether it does not furnish a proper occasion to us to * * * insist on a mutual and formal stipulation to forbear employing agents, or pensioning any persons, within each other's limits; and if this be refused, to propose the contrary stipulation, to wit, that each party may freely keep agents within the Indian territories of the other. in which case we might soon sicken them of the license.—To PRESIDENT WASHINGTON. FORD ED., vi, 101. (M., 1792.)

3065. —— ——. It is a general rule, that no nation has a right to keep an agent within the limits of another, without the consent of that other, and we are satisfied it would be best for both Spain and us, to abstain from having agents or other persons in our employ, or pay. among the savages inhabiting our respective territories, whether as subjects or independent. You are. therefore, desired to propose and press a stipulation to that effect. Should they absolutely decline it, it may be proper to let them perceive, that as the right of keeping agents exists on both sides, or on neither, it will rest with us to reciprocate their own measures.—To CARMICHAEL AND SHORT. iii, 475. FORD ED., vi, 119. (Pa., 1792.)

3066. FOREIGN AGENTS, Conciliation of.—I think it of real value to produce favorable dispositions in the agents of foreign nations here. Cordiality among nations depends very much on the representations of their agents mutually, and cordiality once established, is of immense value, even counted in money, from the favors it produces in commerce, and the good understanding it preserves in matters merely political.—To PRESIDENT WASHINGTON. FORD ED., vi, 152. (Pa., 1793.)

3067. FOREIGN AGENTS, Duty of.—The President of the United States being the only channel of communication between this country and foreign nations. it is from him alone that foreign nations or their agents are to learn what is or has been the will of the nation. and whatever he communicates as such, they have a right and are bound to consider as the expression of the nation, and no foreign agent can be allowed to question it, to interpose between him and any other branch of government, under the pretext of either's transgressing their functions. nor to make himself the umpire and final judge between them. I am, therefore, not authorized to enter into any discussions with you on the meaning of our Constitution in any part of it, or to prove to you that it has ascribed to him alone the admission or interdiction of foreign agents. I inform you of the fact by authority from the President.—To EDMOND CHARLES GENET. iv, 84. FORD ED., vi, 451. (G., Nov. 1793.)

3068. FOREIGN AGENTS, Intermeddling.—For a foreign agent, addressed to the Executive, to embody himself with the lawyers of a faction whose sole object is to embarrass and defeat all the measures of the country, and by their opinions, known to be always in opposition, to endeavor to influence our proceedings, is a conduct not to be permitted.—To ALBERT GALLATIN. v, 368. (M., 1808.)

3069. FOREIGN AGENTS, Secret.—We want an intelligent, prudent native, who will go to reside at New Orleans, as a secret correspondent, for $1000 a year. He might do a little business, merely to cover his real office. Do point out such a one. Virginia ought to offer more loungers equal to this, and ready for it, than any other State.—To JAMES MADISON. FORD ED., vi, 269. (Pa., 1793.)

3070. FOREIGN INFLUENCE, Deplored.—I do sincerely wish that we could take our stand on a ground perfectly neutral and independent towards all nations. It has been my constant object through my public life; and with respect to the English and French, particularly, I have too often expressed to the former my wishes, and made to them propositions, verbally and in writing, officially and privately, to official and private characters, for them to doubt of my views, if they would be content with equality. Of this they are in possession of several written and formal proofs, in my own hand-writing. But they have wished a monopoly of commerce and influence with us; and they have in fact obtained it. When we take notice that theirs is the workshop to which we go for all we want; that with them centre either immediately or ultimately all the labors of our hands and lands; that to them belongs, either openly or secretly, the great mass of our navigation; that even the factorage of their affairs here, is kept to themselves by factitious citizenships; that these foreign and false citizens now constitute the great body of what are called our merchants, fill our seaports, are planted in every little town and district of the interior country, sway everything in the former places, by their own votes, and those of their dependents, in the latter, by their insinuations and the influence of their ledgers; that they are advancing rapidly to a monopoly of our banks and public funds, and thereby placing our public finances under their control; that they have in their alliance the most influential characters in and out of office; when they have shown that by all these bearings on the different branches of the government, they can force it to proceed in whatever direction they dictate, and bend the interests of this country entirely to the will of another; when all this, I say, is attended to, it is impossible for us to say we stand on independent ground, impossible for a free mind not to see and to groan under the bondage in which it is bound. If anything after this could excite surprise, it would be that they have been able so far to throw dust in the eyes of our own citizens, as to fix on those who wish merely to recover self-government the charge of observing one foreign influence because they resist submission to another. But they possess our printing presses, a

powerful engine in their government of us. At this very moment they would have drawn us into a war on the side of England, had it not been for the failure of her bank. Such was their open and loud cry, and that of their gazettes, till this event. After plunging us in all the broils of the European nations, there would remain but one act to close our tragedy, that is, to break up our Union; and even this they have ventured seriously and solemnly to propose and maintain by arguments in a Connecticut paper. I have been happy, however, in believing from the stifling of this effort, that that dose was found too strong, and excited as much repugnance there as it did horror in other parts of our country, and that whatever follies we may be led into as to foreign nations, we shall never give up our Union, the last anchor of our hope, and that alone which is to prevent this heavenly country from becoming an arena of gladiators. Much as I abhor war, and view it as the greatest scourge of mankind, and anxiously as I wish to keep out of the broils of Europe, I would yet go with my brethren into these, rather than separate from them. But I hope we may still keep clear of them, notwithstanding our present thraldom, and that time may be given us to reflect on the awful crisis we have passed through, and to find some means of shielding ourselves in future from foreign influence, political, commercial, or in whatever other form it may be attempted. I can scarcely withhold myself from joining in the wish of Silas Deane, that there were an ocean of fire between us and the old world.*—To ELBRIDGE GERRY. iv, 172. FORD ED., vii, 121. (Pa., May 1797.)

3071. FOREIGN INFLUENCE, English.—The proof England exhibited on that occasion [the repeal of the Embargo] that she can exercise such an influence in this country as to control the will of its government and three-fourths of its people, and oblige the three-fourths to submit to one-fourth, is to me the most mortifying circumstance which has occurred since the establishment of our government. The only prospect I see of lessening that influence, is in her own conduct, and not from anything in our power. —To HENRY DEARBORN. v, 530. FORD ED., ix, 278. (M., July 1810.)

3072. FOREIGN INFLUENCE, Exclusion.—Our countrymen have divided themselves by such strong affections, to the French and the English, that nothing will secure us

* In the draft of the letter this paragraph was changed to the form above printed. Before the alteration it read: "I shall never forget the prediction of the Count de Vergennes, that we shall exhibit the singular phenomenon of a fruit rotten before it is ripe, nor cease to join in the wish of Silas Deane, that there were an ocean of fire between us and the old world. Indeed, my dear friend, I am so disgusted with this entire subjection to a foreign power, that if it were in the end to appear to be the wish of the body of my countrymen to remain in that vassalage, I should feel my unfitness to be an agent in their affairs, and seek in retirement that personal independence without which this world has nothing I value. I am confident you set the same store by it which I do; but perhaps your situation may not give you the same conviction of its existence."—FORD ED., vii, 123.

internally but a divorce from both nations.—
To ELBRIDGE GERRY. iv, 188. FORD ED., vii,
149. (Pa., 1797.)

3073. ———— ————. We consider their [Cuba's
and Mexico's] interests and ours as the same,
and that the object of both must be to exclude
all European influence from this hemisphere.
—To GOVERNOR CLAIBORNE. v, 381. FORD
ED., ix, 213. (W., October 1808.)

3074. FOREIGN INFLUENCE, French.
—Foreign influence is the present and just
object of public hue and cry, and, as often
happens, the most guilty are foremost and
loudest in the cry. If those who are truly
independent can so trim our vessel as to
beat through the waves now agitating us, they
will merit a glory the greater as it seems less
possible.—To THOMAS PINCKNEY. iv, 176.
FORD ED., vii, 128. (Pa., May 1797.)

3075. ———— ————. Those [members of Con-
gress] who have no wish but for the peace of
their country, and its independence of all foreign influence, have a hard struggle indeed.
overwhelmed by a cry as loud and imposing
as if it were true, of being under French
influence, and this raised by a faction composed of English subjects residing among us,
or such as are English in all their relations
and sentiments. However, patience will bring
all to rights, and we shall both live to see the
mask taken from their faces, and our citizens
sensible on which side true liberty and independence are sought.—To HORATIO GATES.
iv, 178. FORD ED., vii, 131. (Pa., May 1797.)

3076. FOREIGN INFLUENCE, Mercantile.—The commerce of England has
spread its roots over the whole face of our
country. This is the real source of all the
obliquities of the public mind.—To A. H.
ROWAN. iv, 257. FORD ED., vii, 280. (M.,
1798.)

3077. FOREIGN INTERVENTION,
Evils of.—Wretched, indeed, is the nation in
whose affairs foreign powers are once permitted to intermeddle.—To B. VAUGHAN. ii,
167. (P., 1787.)

3078. FOREIGN INTERVENTION,
Exclude.—What a crowd of lessons do the
present miseries of Holland teach us? * * *
Never to call in foreign nations to settle do-
mestic differences; * * * .—To JOHN
ADAMS. ii, 283. FORD ED., iv, 455. (P.,
1787.) See ALLIANCES, HEREDITARY BODIES,
WAR.

3079. ———— ————. Our young Republic
* * * should never call on foreign powers
to settle their differences.—To COLONEL
HUMPHREYS. ii, 253. (P., 1787.)

3080. FOREIGN INTERVENTION,
United States and.—We wish not to meddle
with the internal affairs of any country, nor
with the general affairs of Europe.—To C.
W. F. DUMAS. iii, 535. (Pa., 1793.)

— FOREIGNERS.—See ALIEN AND SE-
DITION LAWS, ALIENS, ASYLUM, CITIZENS and
EXPATRIATION.

3081. FORMALITIES, Business and.—
I have ever thought that forms should yield
to whatever should facilitate business.—To
JAMES MONROE. iv, 401. FORD ED., viii, 59.
(W., 1801.)

3082. FORMALITIES, Dispensing
with.—There are situations when form must
be dispensed with. A man attacked by assassins will call for help to those nearest him,
and will not think himself bound to silence
till a magistrate may come to his aid.—To
WILLIAM SHORT. iii, 305. FORD ED., v, 306.
(Pa., 1791.)

3083. FORMALITIES, Insisting upon.
—I noticed to you * * * that the commission of consul to M. Dannery ought to
have been addressed to the President of the
United States. * * * [As] we were persuaded * * * that the error in the address
had proceeded from no intention in the Executive Council of France to question the functions of the President, * * * no difficulty
was made in issuing the commission. We are
still under the same persuasion. But in your
letter of the 14th instant. you *personally* question the authority of the President, and, in
consequence of that, have not addressed to
him the commission of Messrs. Pennevert and
Chervi. Making a point of this formality on
your part, it becomes necessary to make a
point of it on ours also; and I am therefore
charged to return you those commissions, and
to inform you, that bound to enforce respect
to the order of things established by our
Constitution, the President will issue no
exequatur to any consul or vice-consul, not
directed to him in the usual form, after the
party from whom it comes, has been apprised
that such should be the address.—To E. C.
GENET. iv, 84. FORD ED., vi, 451. (G., Nov.
1793.)

3084. FORMALITIES, International.
—I am of opinion that all communications
between nations should pass through the
channels of their Executives. However, in
the instance of condolence on the death of
Dr. Franklin, the letter from our General
Government was addressed to the President
of the National Assembly; so was a letter
from the Legislature of Pennsylvania, containing congratulations on the achievement
of liberty to the French nation. I have not
heard that, in either instance, their Executive
took it amiss that they were not made the
channel of communication.—To GOVERNOR
LEE. iii, 456. (M., 1792.)

3085. FORMALITIES, Jefferson and.
—General Phillips * * * having * * *
taken great offence at a [recent] threat of
retaliation in the treatment of prisoners, enclosed his answer to my letter [with respect
to a passport for a supply vessel] under this
address, "To Thomas Jefferson, Esq., American Governor of Virginia". I paused on receiving the letter, and for some time would not
open it; however, when the miserable condition of our brethren in Charleston occurred
to me. I could not determine that they should
be left without the necessaries of life, while
a punctilio should be discussing between the

British General and myself; and, knowing that I had an opportunity of returning the compliment to Mr. Phillips in a case perfectly corresponding, I opened the letter. Very shortly after, I received, as I expected, the permission of the Board of War for the British vessel, then in Hampton Roads with clothing and refreshments, to proceed to Alexandria, I enclosed and addressed it, " To William Phillips, Esq., commanding the British forces in the Commonwealth of Virginia ". Personally knowing Phillips to be the proudest man of the proudest nation on earth, I well know he will not open this letter; but having occasion at the same time, to write to Captain Gerbach, the flag-master, I informed him that the Convention troops in this State should perish for want of necessaries, before any should be carried to them through this State, till General Phillips either swallowed this pill of retaliation, or made an apology for his rudeness. And in this, should the matter come ultimately to Congress, we hope for their support.*—To THE VIRGINIA DELEGATION IN CONGRESS. i, 308. (R., 1781.)

3086. FORMALITIES, Principles and. —No government can disregard formalities more than ours. But when formalities are attacked with a view to change princip'es, * * * it becomes material to defend formalities. They would be no longer trifles, if they could, in defiance of the national will, continue a foreign agent among us whatever might be his course of action.—To E. C. GENET. iv. 92. FORD ED., vi, 464. (Pa., 1793.)

3087. FORTIFICATIONS, The Administration of Washington and.—[Among] the heads of the [President's] speech [considered in cabinet] was a proposition to Congress to fortify the principal harbors. I opposed the expediency of the General Government's undertaking it. and the expediency of the President's proposing it. It was amended, by substituting a proposition to adopt means for enforcing respect to the jurisdiction of the United States within its waters. * * * The President acknowledged he had doubted the expediency of undertaking it. * * * The clause recommending the fortifications was left out of the speech.—ANAS. ix, 182. FORD ED., i, 269. (Nov. 1793.)

3088. —— ——. The putting the several harbors of the United States into a state of defence, having never yet been the subject of deliberation and decision with the Legislature, and consequently, the necessary moneys not having been appropriated or levied, the President does not find himself

*General Howe, in June 1776, sent a letter under a flag of truce to General Washington addressed to "George Washington, Esq." It was returned, unopened. Howe sent a second letter, and it also was sent back. A third one addressed to "George Washington, Esq.,&c., &c., &c.," was also refused. The fourth one was addressed to General George Washington and accepted. General Washington, in writing to Congress on the subject said : "I would not, on any occasion, sacrifice essentials to punctilio ; but, in this instance, I deemed it my duty to my country, and to my appointment, to insist upon that respect, which, in any other than a public view, I would willingly have waived." General Howe said that he had adopted this style of address to save himself from censure by his own government.— EDITOR.

in a situation competent to comply with the proposition on the subject of Norfolk.—To THE GOVERNOR OF VIRGINIA. iii, 564. (Pa., May 1793.)

3089. FORTIFICATIONS, Adequate.— Some of [the injuries of the belligerent powers] are of a nature to be met by force only, and all of them may lead to it. I cannot, therefore, but recommend such preparations as circumstances call for. The first object is to place our seaport towns out of the danger of insult. Measures have been already taken for furnishing them with heavy cannon for the service of such land batteries as may make a part of their defence against armed vessels approaching them. In aid of these it is desirable that we should have a competent number of gun-boats; and the number, to be competent, must be considerable.—FIFTH ANNUAL MESSAGE. viii, 49. FORD ED., viii, 391. (1805.)

3090. ——. I think it would make an honorable close of your term as well as mine. to leave our country in a state of substantial defence, which we found quite unprepared for it. Indeed, it would for me be a joyful annunciation to the next meeting of Congress, that the operations of defence are all complete. —To HENRY DEARBORN. v, 295. FORD ED., ix, 171. (M., May 1808.)

3091. FORTIFICATIONS, New York. —I wish you would stay long enough at New York to settle * * * the plan of defence for that place; and I am in hopes you will also see Fulton's [torpedo] experiments tried, and see how far his means may enter into your plan.—To GENERAL DEARBORN. v, 117. FORD ED., ix, 101. (W., July 1807.)

3092. —— —— Among the objects of our care, New York stands foremost in the points of importance and exposure; and if permitted we shall provide such defences for it as, in our opinion, will render it secure against attacks by sea.—To GOVERNOR TOMPKINS. v, 283. (W., 1808.)

3093. —— ——. The Legislature of New York may be assured that every exertion will be used to put the United States in the best condition of defence, that we may be fully prepared to meet the dangers which menace the peace of our country.—To GOVERNOR TOMPKINS. viii, 154. (1800.)

3094. FORTIFICATIONS, St. Lawrence.—Should our present differences [with England] be amicably settled, it will be a question for consideration whether we should not establish a strong post on the St. Lawrence, as near our northern boundary as a good position can be found. To do this at present would only produce a greater accumulation of hostile force in that quarter. —To GOVERNOR TOMPKINS. v, 239. (W., Jan. 1808.)

3095. —— ——. It appears to me that it would be well to have a post on the St. Lawrence, as near our line as a commanding position could be found, that it might afford some cover for our most advanced inhabitants.—To GOVERNOR TOMPKINS. v, 284. (W., 1808.)

3096. FORTIFICATIONS, Sites for.— I do not see that we can avoid agreeing to estimates made by worthy men of our own choice for the sites of fortifications, or that we could leave an important place undefended because too much is asked for the site. And, therefore, we must pay what the sites at Boston have been valued at. At the same time, I do not know on what principles of reasoning it is that good men think the public ought to pay more for a thing than they would themselves if they wanted it.—To HENRY DEARBORN. v, 293. (M., 1808.)

3097. —— —— In proceeding to carry into execution the act [providing for the public defence], it is found that the sites most advantageous for the defence of our harbors and rivers, and sometimes the only sites competent to that defence, are in some cases the property of minors, incapable of giving a valid assent to their alienation; in others belong to persons who on no terms will alienate; and in others the proprietors demand such exaggerated compensation as, however liberally the public ought to compensate in such cases, would exceed all bounds of justice or liberality. From this cause the defence of our seaboard, so necessary to be pressed during the present session will in various parts be defeated, unless the national Legislature can apply a constitutional remedy. The power of repelling invasions, and making laws necessary for carrying that power into execution, seem to include that of occupying those sites which are necessary to repel an enemy; observing only the amendment to the Constitution which provides that private property shall not be taken for public use without just compensation. I submit, therefore, to the consideration of Congress, where the necessary sites cannot be obtained by the joint and valid consent of parties, whether provision should be made by a process of *ad quod damnum*, or any other eligible means for authorizing the sites which are necessary for the public defence to be appropriated to that purpose. I am aware that as the consent of the Legislature of the State to the purchase of the site may not, in some instances have been previously obtained, exclusive legislation cannot be exercised therein by Congress until that consent is given. But, in the meantime, it will be held under the same laws which protect the property of individuals in that State, and other property of the United States, and the Legislatures at their next meetings will have opportunities of doing what will be so evidently called for by the interest of their own State.—MESSAGE ON PUBLIC DEFENCE. FORD ED., ix, 187. (March 1808.)

3098. FORTIFICATIONS, System of.— Whether we have peace or war, I think the present Legislature will authorize a complete system of defensive works, on such a scale as they think they ought to adopt. The state

of our finances now permits this.—To W. H. CABELL. v, 208. FORD ED., ix, 97. (W., Nov. 1807.)

3099. —— —— The surplus may partly, indeed, be applied towards completing the defence of the exposed points of our country, on such a scale as shall be adapted to our principles and circumstances. This object is doubtless among the first entitled to attention, in such a state of our finances, and it is one which, whether we have peace or war, will provide security where it is due.—SEVENTH ANNUAL MESSAGE. viii, 88. FORD ED., ix, 165. (1807.)

3100. —— ——. I hope, that this summer we shall get our whole seaports put into that state of defence, which Congress has thought proportioned to our circumstances and situation; that is to say, put *hors d'insulte* from a maritime attack, by a moderate squadron.—To CHARLES PINCKNEY. v, 266. (W., March 1808.) See DEFENCE.

3101. FORTITUDE, Virtue of.—Fortitude teaches us to meet and surmount difficulties; not to fly from them, like cowards; and to fly, too, in vain. for they will meet and arrest us at every turn of our road. Fortitude is one of the four cardinal virtues of Epicurus.—To WILLIAM SHORT. vii, 140. FORD ED., x, 145. (M., 1819.)

3102. FORTUNE, Injured.—I should have been much wealthier had I remained in that private condition which renders it lawful and even laudable to use proper efforts to better it.—To ——. iii, 527. (Pa., 1793.)

3103. FORTUNE, Public Service and. —When I first entered on the stage of public life (now twenty-four years ago), I came to a resolution never to engage while in public office in any kind of enterprise for the improvement of my fortune, [and] I have never departed from it in a single instance.—To —— —— iii, 527. (Pa., 1793.)

3104. —— —— I have the consolation of having added nothing to my private fortune, during my public service, and of retiring with hands as clean as they are empty.—To COMTE DIODATI. v, 62. (W., 1807.) See DISINTERESTEDNESS.

3105. FORTUNES, Imperilled.—Private fortunes, in the present state of our circulation, are at the mercy of those self-created money-lenders, and are prostrated by the floods of nominal money with which their avarice deluges us.—To J. W. EPPES. vi, 142. FORD ED., ix, 394. (M., 1813.)

3106. FORTUNES, Pledge of.—For the support of this Declaration,* we, mutually pledge to each other our lives, our fortunes, and our sacred honor.—DECLARATION OF INDEPENDENCE AS DRAWN BY JEFFERSON.

3107. FOURTH OF JULY, Despotism and.—The flames kindled on the Fourth of

* Congress inserted after Declaration, " with a firm reliance on the protection of Divine Providence."—EDITOR.

July, 1776, have spread over too much of the globe to be extinguished by the feeble engines of despotism; on the contrary, they will consume these engines and all who work them.—To JOHN ADAMS. vii, 218. (M., Sep. 1821.)

3108. FOURTH OF JULY, Europe and.
—The Fourth of July * * * divorced us from the follies and crimes of Europe.—To MR. DIGGES. v. 14. (W., 1806.) See BIRTHDAY and DECLARATION OF INDEPENDENCE.

3109. —— ——. The light which has been shed on the mind of man through the civilized world, has given it a new direction from which no human power can divert it. The sovereigns of Europe who are wise, or have wise counsellors, see this, and bend to the breeze which blows; the unwise alone stiffen and meet its inevitable crush.—To MARQUIS LAFAYETTE. vii, 193. FORD ED., x, 179. (1820.)

3110. FOX (Charles James), Character.
—In Mr. Fox, personally, I have more confidence than in any man in England, and it is founded in what, through unquestionable channels, I have had opportunities of knowing of his honesty and his good sense. While he shall be in the administration, my reliance on that government will be solid.—To JAMES MONROE. v, 11. FORD ED., viii, 449. (W., May 1806.)

3111. FOX (Charles James), Statesmanship.—His sound judgment saw that political interest could never be separated in the long run from moral right, and his frank and great mind would have made a short business of a just treaty with you.—To JAMES MONROE. FORD ED., viii, 477. (W., Oct. 1806.)

3112. FRANCE, Affection for.—It is very much our interest to keep up the affection of this country [France] for us, which is considerable.—To JAMES MONROE. i, 346. FORD ED., iv, 50. (P., 1785.)

3113. —— ——. A sincere affection between the two peoples is the broadest basis on which their peace can be built.—To COMTE DE VERGENNES. i, 456. (P., 1785.)

3114. —— ——. Nobody [is] more sensible than you are of the motives, both moral and political, which should induce us to bind the two countries together by as many ties as possible of interest and affection.—To DR. RAMSAY. ii, 49. (P., 1786.)

3115. —— ——. I am happy in concurring with you * * * in the sentiment, that as the principles of our governments become more congenial, the links of affection are multiplied between us. It is impossible, that they should multiply beyond our wishes.—To J. B. TERNANT. iii, 516. FORD ED., vi, 189. (Pa., 1793.)

3116. —— ——. Mutual good offices, mutual affection, and similar principles of government seem to destine the two nations for the most intimate communion.—To GOUVERNEUR MORRIS. iii. 522. FORD ED., vi, 200. (Pa., 1793.) See PEOPLE (FRENCH).

3117. FRANCE, Affronted by Adams.
—Mr. Adams's speech to Congress in May [1798] is deemed such a national affront, that no explanation on other topics can be entered on till that, as a preliminary, is wiped away by humiliating disavowals or acknowledgments. This working hard with our Envoys, and indeed seeming impracticable for want of that sort of authority, submission to a heavy amercement (upwards of a million sterling) was, * * * , suggested as an alternative, which might be admitted if proposed by us. These overtures had been through informal agents; and both the alternatives bringing the Envoys to their *ne plus*, they resolve to have no more communication through inofficial characters, but to address a letter directly to the government, to bring forward their pretensions.—To JAMES MADISON. iv, 232. FORD ED., vii, 234. (Pa., April 1798.) See X. Y. Z. PLOT.

3118. FRANCE, The Allied Powers and.—The sufferings of France. I sincerely deplore, and what is to be their term? The will of the Allies. There is no more moderation, forbearance, or even honesty in theirs, than in that of Bonaparte. They have proved that their object, like his, is plunder. They, like him, are shuffling nations together, or into their own hands, as if all were right which they feel a power to do. In the exhausted state in which Bonaparte has left France, I see no period to her sufferings, until this combination of robbers fall together by the ears. The French may then rise up and choose their side. And I trust they will finally establish for themselves a government of rational and well-tempered liberty. So much science cannot be lost; so much light shed over them can never fail to produce to them some good, in the end.—To ALBERT GALLATIN. vi, 500. (M., Oct. 1815.)

3119. FRANCE, American politics and.
—It is still a comfort to see by the address of Dumouriez * * * , that the constitution of 1791 is the worst thing which is to be forced on the French. But even the falling back to that would give wonderful vigor to our monocrats, and unquestionably affect the tone of administering our government. Indeed, I fear that if this summer should prove disastrous to the French, it will damp that energy of republicanism in our new Congress, from which I had hoped so much reformation.—To T. M. RANDOLPH. iii. 571. (Pa., June 1793.)

3120. FRANCE, Attraction of.—France, freed from that monster, Bonaparte, must again become the most agreeable country on earth. It would be the second choice of all whose ties of family and fortune give a preference to some other one, and the first choice of all not under those ties.—To WILLIAM SHORT. vi, 402. (M., 1814.)

— FRANCE, Bill of Rights for.—See BILL OF RIGHTS (FRENCH).

— FRANCE, Bonaparte and.—See BONAPARTE.

3121. FRANCE, Cabinet of Washington and.—The doubts I entertained that the offers of the French republic would be declined, will pretty certainly be realized. One person [Hamilton] represents them as a snare into which he hopes we shall not fall. His second [Knox] is of the same sentiment of course. He [Randolph] whose vote for the most part, or say always, is casting, has by two or three private conversations or rather disputes with me, shown his opinion to be against doing what would be a mark of predilection to one of the parties, though not a breach of neutrality in form. And an opinion of still more importance is still in the same way. I do not know what line will be adopted, but probably a procrastination, which will be immediately seen through.—To JAMES MADISON. FORD ED., vi, 268. (Pa., May 1793.) See NEUTRALITY.

— FRANCE, Cherbourg.—See CHERBOURG.

3122. FRANCE, Commerce with.—The mutual extension of their commerce was among the fairest advantages to be derived to France and the United States, from the independence of the latter. An exportation of eighty millions, chiefly in raw materials, is supposed to constitute the present limits of the commerce of the United States with the nations of Europe; limits, however, which extend as their population increases. To draw the best proportion of this into the ports of France, rather than of any other nation, is believed to be the wish and interest of both. —To COUNT DE MONTMORIN. ii, 186. (P., 1787.)

3123. —— ——. The French [in their recent treaty with England] have clearly reserved a right of favoring, specially, any nation not European; and there is no nation out of Europe, who could so probably have been in their eve at that time, as ours. They are wise. They must see it probable at least, that any concert with England, will be but of short duration; and they could hardly propose to sacrifice for that, a connection with us, which may be perpetual.—To JOHN JAY. ii, 112. (P., 1787.)

3124. —— ——. The system of the United States is to use neither prohibitions nor premiums. Where a government finds itself under the necessity of undertaking that regulation, it would seem that it should conduct it as an intelligent merchant would; that is to say, invite customers to purchase by facilitating their means of payment, and by adapting goods to their taste. If this idea be just, government here [France] has two operations to attend to with respect to the commerce of the United States: 1. to do away, or to moderate, as much as possible, the prohibitions and monopolies of their materials for payment; 2. to encourage the institution of the principal manufactures, which the necessities or the habits of their new customers call for.—To COUNT DE MONTMORIN. ii, 529. (P., 1788.)

3125. —— ——. I am happy to learn that the [people of Alexandria, Va.] have felt a benefit from the encouragements to our commerce, which have been given by an allied nation. But truth and candor oblige me, at the same time, to declare you are indebted for these encouragements solely to the friendly dispositions of that nation, which has shown itself ready on every occasion to adopt all arrangements which might strengthen our ties of mutual interest and friendship. —REPLY TO ADDRESS. iii, 127. FORD ED., v, 146. (1790.)

3126. —— ——. With respect to the reformation of the unfriendly restrictions on our commerce and navigation, we cannot be too pressing for its attainment, as every day's continuance gives it additional firmness, and endangers its taking root in their habits and constitution. Indeed, I think the French government should be told, that as soon as they are in a condition to act, if they do not revoke the late innovations, we must lay additional and equivalent burthens on *French Ships*, by name.—To GOUVERNEUR MORRIS. iii, 489. FORD ED., vi, 131. (Nov. 1792.)

3127. —— ——. I cannot too much press it on you, to improve every opportunity * * * for placing our commerce with France and its dependencies, on the freest and most encouraging footing possible.—To GOUVERNEUR MORRIS. iii, 522. FORD ED., vi, 200. (Pa., 1793.)

3128. —— ——. I was a sincere wellwisher to the success of the French Revolution, * * * but I have not been insensible under the atrocious depredations they have committed on our commerce.—To ELBRIDGE GERRY. iv, 269. FORD ED., vii, 329. (Pa., 1799.)

3129. —— ——. [In the negotiation of commercial treaties with France] I must say, in justice, that I found the government entirely disposed to befriend us on all occasions, and to yield us every indulgence not absolutely injurious to themselves.—AUTOBIOGRAPHY. i, 64. FORD ED., i, 90. (1821.) See TREATIES.

3130. FRANCE, The Consulate.—They have established Bonaparte, Sieyès, and Ducós into an executive, or rather Dictatorial Consulate, [and] given them a committee of between twenty and thirty from each council. Thus the Constitution of the Third year, which was getting consistency and firmness from time, is demolished in an instant, and nothing is said about a new one. How the nation will bear it is yet unknown.—To JOHN BRECKENRIDGE. FORD ED., vii, 417. (Pa., Jan. 1800.)

— FRANCE, Consuls of.—See CONSULS.

3131. FRANCE, Debt to.—Besides endeavoring on all occasions to multiply the points of contact and connection with France, * * * I have had it much at heart to remove from between us every subject of misunderstanding or irritation. Our debts to the King, to the Officers, to the Farmers, are of this description. The having complied with no part of our engagements in these. draws on us a great deal of censure. and occasioned a language in the Assemblée des Notables very likely to produce dissatisfaction between us.—To JOHN ADAMS. ii, 163. FORD ED., iv, 398. (P., 1787.)

3132. —— ——. I told [President Washington] I had meant on that day to take his orders for removing the suspension of payments to France, which had been imposed by my last letter to Gouverneur Morris, but was meant, as I supposed. only for the interval between the abolition of the late constitution by the dethronement of the King, and the meeting of some other body, invested by the will of the nation with powers to transact their affairs; that I considered the National Convention, then assembled. as such a body; and that, therefore. we ought to go on with the payments to them, or to any government they should establish.*—THE ANAS. ix, 128. FORD ED., i, 213. (Dec. 27, 1792.) See DEBTS (FRENCH).

3133. FRANCE, Den of Robbers.—As for France and England, with all their preeminence in science. the one is a den of robbers, and the other of pirates.—To JOHN ADAMS. vi, 37. FORD ED., ix, 333. (M., 1812.)

— FRANCE, Directory.—See EXECUTIVES.

3134. FRANCE, Errors of.—The French have been guilty of great errors in their conduct towards other nations, not only in insulting uselessly all crowned heads. but in endeavoring to force liberty on their neighbors in their own form.—To T. M. RANDOLPH. FORD ED., vi, 318. (Pa., June 1793.)

3135. FRANCE, Federalist Hostility to.—Nothing less than the miraculous string of events which have taken place, to wit, the victories of the Rhine and Italy, peace with Austria, bankruptcy of England, mutiny in her fleet, and King's writing letters recommending peace, could have cooled the fury of the British faction. Even that will not

* There had been a consultation at the President's (about the first week in November) on the expediency of suspending payments to France under her present situation. I had admitted that the late constitution was dissolved by the dethronement of the King; and the management of affairs surviving to the National Assembly only, this was not an integral legislature, and, therefore, not competent to give a legitimate discharge for our payments: that I thought, consequently. that none should be made till some legitimate body came into place. and that I should consider the National Convention called, but not met as we had yet heard, to be a legitimate body. Hamilton doubted whether it would be a legitimate body, and whether, if the King should be reestablished, he might not disallow such payments on good grounds. Knox, for once, dared to differ from Hamilton, and to express, very submissively, an opinion that a convention named by the whole body of the nation, would be competent to do anything. It ended by agreeing that I should write to Gouverneur Morris, to suspend payment generally, till further orders.—NOTE BY JEFFERSON. ix, 125. FORD ED., i, 208. (1792.)

prevent considerable efforts still in both Houses to show our teeth to France.—To JAMES MADISON. FORD ED., vii, 143. (Pa., June 1797.)

3136. —— ——. The inflammatory composition of the [President's] speech* excited [in Congress] sensations of resentment which had slept under British injuries, threw the wavering into the war scale, and produced the war address. Bonaparte's victories and those on the Rhine. the Austrian peace, British bankruptcy, mutiny of the [British] seamen, and Mr. King's exhortations to pacific measures [towards France], have cooled them down again, and the scale of peace preponderates.—To AARON BURR. iv, 185. FORD ED., vii, 146. (Pa., June 1797.)

3137. —— ——. The threatening propositions founded in the address [of Congress to the President], are abandoned one by one, and the cry begins now to be that we have been called together to do nothing. The truth is, there is nothing to do, the idea of war being scouted by the events of Europe; but this only proves that war was the object for which we were called. It proves that the Executive temper was for war; and that the convocation of the Representatives was an experiment of the temper of the nation, to see if it was in unison. Efforts at negotiation indeed were promised; but such a promise was as difficult to withhold, as easy to render nugatory. If negotiation alone had been meant, that might have been pursued without so much delay, and without calling the Representatives; and if strong and earnest negotiation had been meant, the additional nomination would have been of persons strongly and earnestly attached to the alliance of 1778. War then was intended.—To AARON BURR. iv, 185. FORD ED., vii, 146. (Pa., June 1797.)

3138. —— ——. President [Adams] has appointed, and the Senate approved Rufus King. to enter into a treaty of commerce with the Russians, at London, and William Smith (Phocian) Envoy Extraordinary and Minister Plenipotentiary, to go to Constantinople to make one with the Turks. So that as soon as there is a coalition of Turks, Russians and English, against France, we seize that moment to countenance it as openly as we dare by treaties, which we never had with them before. All this helps to fill up the measure of provocation towards France, and to get from them a declaration of war, which we are afraid to be the first in making.—To EDMUND PENDLETON. iv, 289. FORD ED., vii, 358. (Pa., Feb. 1799.)

— FRANCE, Free Ports.—See FREE PORTS.

3139. FRANCE, Friendship.—I cannot pretend to affirm that this country will stand by us on every just occasion, but I am sure, if this will not, there is no other that will.— To DR. RAMSAY. ii, 49. (P., 1786.)

* President Adams's message to Congress at the special session in May 1797.—EDITOR.

3140. —— ——. Nothing should be spared on our part to attach this country to us. It is the only one on which we can rely for support under every event. Its inhabitants love us more. I think, than they do any other nation on earth. This is very much the effect of the good dispositions with which the French officers returned.—To JAMES MADISON. ii, 109. FORD ED., iv, 367. (P., 1787.)

3141. —— ——. I consider France as our surest mainstay under every event.—To JOHN ADAMS. ii, 163. FORD ED., iv, 398. (P., 1787.)

3142. —— ——. Among the circumstances which will reconcile me to my new position [Secretary of State] the most powerful are the opportunities it will give me of cementing the friendship between our two nations.—To LA DUCHESSE D'AUVILLE. iii, 135. FORD ED., iii, 153. (N.Y., 1790.)

3143. —— ——. May this union of interests forever be the patriot's creed in both countries.—To COUNT DE MONTMORIN. iii, 137. (M., 1790.)

3144. —— ——. There is a fund of friendship and attachment between the mass of the two nations * * *. The present administration of this country have these feelings of their constituents, and will be true to them. We shall act steadily on the desire of cementing our interests and affections; and of this you cannot go too far in assuring them.—To ROBERT R. LIVINGSTON. FORD ED., viii, 138. (W., March 1802.)

— FRANCE, Genet.—See GENET.

3145. FRANCE, Government.—France is the wealthiest but worst governed country on earth.—To JOSEPH JONES. i, 353. (P., 1785.) See GOVERNMENT (FRENCH) and GOVERNMENT (RECOGNITION).

3146. FRANCE, Gratitude to.—Every American owes her gratitude, as our sole ally during the war of Independence.—To M. DE NEUVILLE. vii, 110. (M., 1818.)

3147. FRANCE, Honesty of.—A wise man, if nature has not formed him honest. will yet act as if he were honest; because he will find it the most advantageous and wise part in the long run. I have believed that this Court possesses this high species of wisdom even if its new faith be ostensible only. If they trip on any occasion it will be warning to us. I do not expect they will, but it is our business to be on the watch.—To JAMES MONROE. FORD ED., iv, 40. (P., 1785.)

3148. —— ——. There are great numbers of well enlightened men in this nation. The ministry is such. The King has an honest heart. The line of policy hitherto pursued by them has been such as virtue would dictate and wisdom approve. Relying on their wisdom only, I think they would not accept the bribe suppose it would be to relinquish that honorable character of disinterestedness and new faith which they have acquired by

many sacrifices and which has put in their hands the government, as it were, of Europe. —To JAMES MONROE. FORD ED., iv, 39. (P., 1785.)

3149. FRANCE, Influence of.—This summer is of immense importance to the future condition of mankind all over the earth, and not a little so to ours. For though its issue should not be marked by any direct change in our Constitution, it will influence the tone and principles of its administration so as to lead it to something very different in the one event from what it would be in the other.—To H. INNES. FORD ED., vi, 266. (Pa., May 1793.)

3150. FRANCE, Injuries by.—Nobody denies but that France has given just cause of war, but so has Great Britain, and she is now capturing our vessels as much as France, but the question was one merely of prudence, whether seeing that both powers in order to injure one another, bear down everything in their way, without regard to the rights of others, spoliating equally Danes, Swedes and Americans, it would not be more prudent in us to bear with it as the Danes and Swedes do, curtailing our commerce, and waiting for the moment of peace, when it is probable both nations would for their own interest and honor retribute for their wrongs.—To ARCHIBALD STUART. FORD ED., vii, 270. (Pa., June 1798.)

— FRANCE, Jacobins.—See JACOBINS.

— FRANCE, Louisiana Purchase.—See LOUISIANA.

3151. FRANCE, Manufactures of.—It is the interest of France as well as our interest to multiply the means of payment [for her manufactures]. These must be found in the catalogue of our exports, and among these will be seen neither gold nor silver. We have no mines of either of these metals. Produce, therefore, is all we can offer. Some articles of our produce will be found very convenient to France for her own consumption. Others will be convenient, as being more commerciable in her hands than those she will give in exchange for them.—To MARQUIS LAFAYETTE. i, 596. FORD ED., iv, 256. (P., 1786.)

3152. —— ——. A century's experience has shown that we double our numbers every twenty or twenty-five years. No circumstance can be foreseen at this moment, which will lessen our rate of multiplication for centuries to come. For every article of the productions and manufactures of France, then, which can be introduced into the habit there, the demand will double every twenty or twenty-five years. And to introduce the habit, we have only to let the merchants alone. —To COUNT DE MONTMORIN. ii, 190. (1787.) See MANUFACTURES.

— FRANCE, Monarchy.—See LOUIS XVI. and MARIE ANTOINETTE.

— FRANCE, Monopoly of Tobacco.—See MONOPOLY.

3153. FRANCE, Murray's Mission.— The President [John Adams] nominated to the Senate yesterday William Vans Murray, Minister Plenipotentiary to the French Republic, and added, that he shall be instructed not to go to France, without direct and unequivocal assurances from the French government that he shall be received in character, enjoy the due privileges, and a minister of equal rank, title and power, be appointed to discuss and conclude our controversy by a new treaty. This had evidently been kept secret from the federalists of both Houses, as appeared by their dismay. The Senate have passed over this day without taking it up. It is said they are gravelled and divided; some are for opposing, others do not know what to do. But, in the meantime, they have been permitted to go on with all the measures of war and patronage. and when the close of the session is at hand, it is made known. However, it silences all arguments against the sincerity of France, and renders desperate every further effort towards war.—To JAMES MADISON. iv, 292. FORD ED., vii, 362. (Pa., Feb. 19, 1799.)

3154. —— ——. We were for a moment flattered with the hope of a friendly accommodation of our differences with France, by the President's nomination of Mr. Murray, our Minister at the Hague, to proceed to Paris for that purpose. But our hopes have been entirely dashed by his revoking that, and naming Mr. Ellsworth, Mr. Patrick Henry and Murray. * * * The effect of the new nomination is completely to parry the advances made by France towards a reconciliation.—To BISHOP JAMES MADISON. iv, 299. FORD ED., vii, 372. (Pa., Feb. 1799.)

3155. —— ——. The face the federalists will put on this business is that they have frightened France into a respectful treatment. Whereas, in truth, France has been sensible that her measures to prevent the scandalous spectacle of war between the two republics, from the known impossibility of our injuring her, would not be imputed to her as a humiliation.—To EDMUND PENDLETON. iv, 294. FORD ED., vii, 365. (Pa., Feb. 1799.)

— FRANCE, Navigation and.—See NAVIGATION.

3156. FRANCE, Neutral rights and.— The French have behaved atrociously towards neutral nations. and us particularly; and though we might be disposed not to charge them with all the enormities committed in their name in the West Indies, yet they are to be blamed for not doing more to prevent them. A just and rational censure ought to be expressed on them, while we disapprove the constant billingsgate poured on them *officially.*—To EDMUND PENDLETON. iv, 289. FORD ED., vii, 358. (Pa., Feb. 1799.) See NEUTRALITY.

3157. —— ——. You have seen that the French Directory had published an *arret* declaring they would treat as pirates any neutrals they should take in the ships of their enemies. The President [Adams] communicated this to Congress as soon as he received it. A bill was brought into the Senate reciting that *arret*, and authorizing retaliation. The President received information almost the same instant that the Directory had suspended the *arret* (which fact was privately declared by the Secretary of State to two of the Senate), and, though it was known we were passing an act founded on that *arret*, yet the President has never communicated the suspension.—To ARCHIBALD STUART. iv, 286. FORD ED., vii, 353. (Pa., Feb. 1799.)

3158. FRANCE, Peace with.—It was with infinite joy to me, that you [Elbridge Gerry] were yesterday announced to the Senate, as Envoy Extraordinary, jointly with General [Charles Cotesworth] Pinckney and Mr. [John] Marshall, to the French Republic. It gave me certain assurance that there would be a preponderance in the mission, sincerely disposed to be at peace with the French government and nation. Peace is undoubtedly at present the first object of our nation. Interest and honor are also national considerations. But interest, duly weighed, is in favor of peace even at the expense of spoliations past and future; and honor cannot now be an object. The insults and injuries committed on us by both the belligerent parties, from the beginning of 1793 to this day. and still continuing. cannot now be wiped off by engaging in war with one of them. As there is great reason to expect this is the last campaign in Europe, it would certainly be better for us to rub through this year, as we have done through the four preceding ones, and hope that on the restoration of peace, we may be able to establish some plan for our foreign connections more likely to secure our peace, interest and honor in future. Our countrymen have divided themselves by such strong affections, to the French and the English, that nothing will secure us internally but a divorce from both nations; and this must be the object of every real American, and its attainment is practicable without much self-denial. But for this, peace is necessary. Be assured of this that if we engage in a war during our present passions, and our present weakness in some quarters, our Union runs the greatest risk of not coming out of that war in the shape in which it enters it. My reliance for our preservation is in your acceptance of this mission. I know the tender circumstances which will oppose themselves to it. But its duration will be short, and its reward long. You have it in your power, by accepting and determining the character of the mission, to secure the present peace and eternal union of your country. If you decline, on motives of private pain, a substitute may be named who has enlisted his passions in the present contest, and by the preponderance of his vote in the mission may entail on us calamities, your share in which, and your feelings. will far outweigh whatever pain a temporary absence from your family could give you. The sacrifice will be short, the remorse would be never-ending. Let me, then. conjure your acceptance, and that you will, by this act, seal the mission with the confidence of all parties. Your nomination has given a spring to hope, which was dead before.—To ELBRIDGE GERRY. iv, 187. FORD ED., vii, 149. (Pa., June 21, 1797.)

3159. —— ——. I know that both France and England have given, and are daily giving, sufficient cause of war; that in defiance of the laws of nations, they are every day trampling on the rights of the neutral powers, whenever they can thereby do the least injury, either to the other. But. as I view a peace between France and England the ensuing winter to be certain, I have thought it would have been better for us to continue to bear from France through the present summer. what we have been bearing both from her and England these four years, and still continue to bear from England, and to have required indemnification in the hour of peace. when I verily believe it would have been yielded by both. This seems to have been the plan of the other neutral nations; and whether this, or the commencing war on one of them. as we have done, would have been wiser, time and events must decide.—To SAMUEL SMITH. iv, 254. FORD ED., vii, 277. (M., Aug. 1798.)

3160. —— ——. All which the advocates of peace can now attempt. is to prevent war measures *externally,* consenting to every rational measure of *internal* defence and preparation. Great expenses will be incurred: and it will be left to those whose measures render them necessary, to provide to meet them.— To JAMES MADISON. iv, 234. FORD ED., vii, 237. (Pa., April 1798.)

3161. —— ——. I have not been insensible under the atrocious depredations they [the French] have committed on our commerce. * * * But though deeply feeling the injuries of France. I did not think war the surest means of redressing them. I did believe, that a mission sincerely disposed to preserve peace, would obtain for us a peaceable and honorable settlement and restitution; and I appeal to you to say. whether this might not have been obtained, if either of your colleagues had been of the same sentiment with yourself.—To ELBRIDGE GERRY. iv, 269. FORD ED., vii. 329. (P., 1799.)

3162. —— ——. The people now see that France has sincerely wished peace, and their seducers [federalists] have wished war, as well for the loaves and fishes which arise out of war expenses, as for the chance of changing the Constitution, while the people should have time to contemplate nothing but the levies of men and money.—To T. LOMAX. iv, 300. FORD ED., vii, 374. (M., 1799.)

— FRANCE, People of.—See PEOPLE.

3163. FRANCE, Policy towards.—We stand completely corrected of the error. that either the government or the nation of France has any remains of friendship for us. The portion of that country which forms an exception, though respectable in weight, is weak in numbers. On the contrary, it appears evident, that an unfriendly spirit prevails in the most important individuals of the government, towards us. In this state of things. we shall so take our distance between the two rival nations, as, remaining disengaged till necessity compels us, we may haul finally to the enemy of that which shall make it necessary. We see all the disadvantageous consequences of taking a side, and shall be forced into it only by a more disagreeable alternative; in which event, we must countervail the disadvantages by measures which will give us splendor and power, but not as much happiness as our present system. We wish, therefore, to remain well with France. But we see that no consequences, however ruinous to them, can secure us with certainty against the extravagance of her present rulers. I think. therefore, that while we do nothing which the first nation on earth would deem crouching. we had better give to all our communications with them a very mild, complaisant, and even friendly complexion. but always independent. Ask no favors, leave small and irritating things to be conducted by the individuals interested in them, interfere ourselves but in the greatest cases. and then not push them to irritation. No matter at present existing between them and us is important enough to risk a breach of peace; peace being indeed the most important of all things for us, except the preserving an erect and independent attitude.—To ROBERT R. LIVINGSTON. iv, 448. FORD ED., viii, 173. (W., Oct. 1802.)

— FRANCE, Privateers of.—See PRIVATEERS.

3164. FRANCE, Punishment of.—She deserves much punishment. and her successes and reverses will be a wholesome lesson to the world hereafter; but she has now had enough, and we may lawfully pray for her resurrection, and I am confident the day is not distant. No one who knows that people, and the elasticity of their character, can believe they will long remain crouched on the earth as at present. They will rise by acclamation, and woe to their riders. What havoc are we not yet to see!—To MRS. TRIST. D. L. J. 363. (P.F., April 1816.)

3165. FRANCE, Reconciliation overtures.—The event of events was announced in the Senate yesterday. It is this: It seems that soon after Gerry's departure, overtures must have been made by Pichon. French Chargé d'Affaires at the Hague, to Murray. They were so soon matured. that on the 28th of September, 1798, Talleyrand writes to Pichon, approving what had been done, and particularly of his having assured Murray that *whatever* Plenipotentiary the government of the United States should send to France to end our differences would undoubtedly be received with the respect due to the representative of a *free, independent and powerful nation;* declaring that the President's instructions to his envoys at Paris, if they contain the whole of the American government's intentions, announce dispositions which have been always entertained by the Directory; and desiring him to communicate these expressions to Murray, in order to convince him of the sincerity of the French government, and to prevail on him to transmit them to his government. This is dated September the 28th. and may have been received by Pichon October 1st: and nearly five months elapse before it is communicated.—To JAMES MADISON. iv, 292. FORD ED., vii, 362. (Pa., Feb. 19 1799.)

3166. —— ——. Mr. Gerry's communications, with other information, prove * * * that France is sincere in her wishes for reconciliation; and a recent proposition from that country, through Mr. Murray, puts the matter out of doubt.—To GENERAL KOSCIUSKO. iv, 294. (Pa., Feb. 1799.)

3167. FRANCE, Reformation of.— France is advancing to a change of constitution. The young desire it, the middle-aged are not averse. the old alone oppose it. They will die. The provincial assemblies will chalk out the plan; and the nation, ripening fast, will execute it.—To M. DE CREVECŒUR. ii, 234. (P., 1787.)

3168. FRANCE, Reliance on.—President Washington observed [that] there was no nation on whom we could rely. at all times, but France; and that, if we did not prepare in time some support. in the event of rupture with Spain and England, we might be charged with a criminal negligence. I was much pleased with the tone of these observations. It was the very doctrine which had been my polar star, and I did not need the successes of the republican arms in France, lately announced to us. to bring me to these sentiments * * * I, therefore, expressed to the President my cordial approbation of these ideas.— ANAS. ix, 128. FORD ED., i, 212. (December 1792.)

3169. FRANCE, Republican Government.—I look with great anxiety for the firm establishment of the new government in France. being perfectly convinced that if it takes place there, it will spread sooner or later all over Europe. On the contrary, a check there would retard the revival of liberty in other countries.—To GEORGE MASON. iii, 209. FORD ED., v, 274. (Pa., 1791.)

·**3170.** —— ——. With respect to the French government. we are under no call to express opinions which might please or offend any party, and, therefore, it will be best to avoid them on all occasions. public or private. Could any circumstances require unavoidably such expressions, they would naturally be in conformity with the great mass of our countrymen, who, having first in modern times. taken the ground of government founded on the will of the people, cannot but be delighted on seeing so distinguished and so esteemed a nation arrive on the same ground, and plant their standard by our side.—To GOUVERNEUR MORRIS. iii, 325. FORD ED., v, 428. (Pa., Jan. 1792.)

3171. —— ——. It accords with our principles to acknowledge any government to be rightful, which is formed by the will of the nation substantially declared. The late government was of this kind, and was accordingly acknowledged in like manner. With such a government *every kind* of business may be done.—To GOUVERNEUR MORRIS. iii, 489. FORD ED., vi, 131. (Pa., Nov. 1792.)

3172. —— ——. You express a wish in your letter to be generally advised as to the tenor of your conduct, in consequence of the late revolution in France, the questions relative to which, you observe, incidentally present themselves to you. It is impossible to foresee the particular circumstances which may require you to decide and act on that question. But. principles being understood, their application will be less embarrassing. We certainly cannot deny to other nations that principle whereon our government is founded, that every nation has a right to govern itself internally under what form it pleases, and to change these forms at its own will; and, externally, to transact business with other nations through whatever organ it chooses. whether that be a King, Convention, Assembly, Committee, President, or whatever it be. The only thing essential is the will of the nation. Taking this as your polar star, you can hardly err.—To THOMAS PINCKNEY. iii, 500. (Pa., Dec. 1792.)

3173. FRANCE, Republic recognized.— I have laid before the President of the United States your notification of the 17th instant. in the name of the Provisory Executive Council, charged with the administration of your Government, that the French nation has constituted itself into a Republic. The President receives. with great satisfaction, this attention of the Executive Council and the desire they have manifested of making known to us the resolution entered into by the National Convention, even before a definitive regulation of their new establishment could take place. Be assured, Sir, that the Government and the citizens of the United States view with the most sincere pleasure every advance of your nation towards its happiness, an object essentially connected with its liberty, and they consider the union of principles and pursuits between our two countries as a link which binds still closer their interests and affections. The genuine and general effusions of joy which you saw overspread our country on their seeing the liberties of yours rise superior to foreign invasion and domestic trouble. have proved to you that our sympathies are great and sincere, and we earnestly wish on our part that these, our mutual dispositions, may be improved to mutual good, by establishing our commercial intercourse on principles as friendly to natural right and freedom as are those of our Government.—To J. B. TERNANT. iii, 518. FORD ED., vi, 189. (Pa., Feb. 23, 1793.)

3174. FRANCE, Restoration of.—It is impossible that France should rest under her present oppressions and humiliations. She will rise in that gigantic strength which cannot be annihilated, and will fatten her fields with the blood of her enemies. I only wish she may exercise patience and forbearance until divisions among [the Allies] may give her a choice of sides.—To M. Dupont de Nemours. vi, 508. (M., 1815.)

3175. ———. France is too highminded, has too much innate force, intelligence and elasticity, to remain under its present compression. Samson will arise in his strength, as of old, and as of old, will burst asunder the withes and the cords, and the webs of the Philistines. But what are to be the scenes of havoc and horror, and how widely they may spread between brethren of the same house, our ignorance of the interior feuds and antipathies of the country places beyond our ken. It will end, nevertheless, in a representative government, in a government in which the will of the people will be an effective ingredient.—To Benjamin Austin. vi, 520. Ford ed., x, 8. (M., 1816.)

3176. ———. In the desolation of Europe, to gratify the atrocious caprices of Bonaparte, France sinned much; but she has suffered more than retaliation. Once relieved from the incubus of her late oppression, she will rise like a giant from her slumbers. Her soil and climate, her arts and eminent sciences, her central position and free constitution, will soon make her greater than she ever was.—To M. de Neuville. vii, 109. (M., 1818.)

— FRANCE, Revolution.—See Revolution (French).

3177. FRANCE, Self-Government in.— What government France can bear, depends not on the state of science, however exalted, in a select band of enlightened men, but on the condition of the general mind. * * * The last change of government was fortunate, inasmuch as the new will be less obstructive to the effects of that advancement.—To Marquis Lafayette. vii, 66. Ford ed., x, 82. (M., 1817.)

3178. ———. Whether the state of society in Europe can bear a republican government, I doubted, you know, when with you, and I do now. A hereditary chief, strictly limited, the right of war vested in the legislative body, a rigid economy of the public contributions, and absolute interdiction of all useless expenses, will go far towards keeping the government honest and unoppressive.—To Marquis Lafayette. vii, 325. Ford ed., x, 280. (M., 1823.)

3179. FRANCE, Strength.—As long as the French can be tolerably unanimous internally, they can resist the whole world. The laws of nature render a large country unconquerable if they adhere firmly together, and to their purpose.—To H. Innes. Ford ed., vi, 266. (Pa., 1793.)

3180. FRANCE, Sufferings of.—I grieve for France; although it cannot be denied that by the afflictions with which she wantonly

and wickedly overwhelmed other nations, she has merited severe reprisals. For it is no excuse to lay the enormities to the wretch who led to them.—To Albert Gallatin. vi, 499. (M., Oct. 1815.)

3181. FRANCE, Supplies to St. Domingo.—[Alexander] Hamilton called on me to speak about our furnishing supplies to the French colony of St. Domingo. He expressed his opinion, that we ought to be cautious, and not to go too far in our application of money to their use, lest it should not be recognized by the mother country. He did not even think that some kinds of government they might establish could give a sufficient sanction. I observed that the National Convention was now met, and would certainly establish a form of government; that as we had recognized the former government because established by the authority of the *nation*, so we must recognize any other which should be established by the authority of the nation. He said   had recognized the former, because it contained an important member of the ancient, to wit; the King, and wore the appearance of his consent; but if, in any future form, they should omit the King, he did not know that we could with safety recognize it, or pay money to its order. —The Anas. ix, 125. Ford ed., i, 208. (Nov. 1792.)

3182. FRANCE, Sympathy with.—The yeomanry of the city (not the fashionable people nor paper men), showed prodigious joy when, flocking to the wharves, they saw the British colors reversed, and the French flying above them.—To T. M. Randolph. Ford ed., vi, 241. (Pa., 1793.)

3183. ———. The [French forces] have lately sustained some severe checks. * * * Their defeats are as sensibly felt at Philadelphia as at Paris, and I foresee we are to have a trying campaign of it.—To James Monroe. iii, 549. Ford ed., vi, 240. (Pa., May 1793.)

— FRANCE, Talleyrand's Propositions. —See X. Y. Z. Plot.

— FRANCE, Treaties with.—See Treaties.

3184. FRANCE, Union with.—We wish to omit no opportunity of convincing [the French nation] how cordially we desire the closest union with them. Mutual good offices, mutual affection, and similar principles of government seem to have destined the two peoples for the most intimate communion, and even for a complete exchange of citizenship among the individuals composing them. —To Gouverneur Morris. Ford ed., vi, 151. (Pa., Dec. 1792.)

3185. FRANCE, United States, England and.—Our interest calls for a perfect equality in our conduct towards these two nations [France and England]; but no preference anywhere. If, however, circumstances should ever oblige us to show a preference, a respect for our character, if we had no better motive, would decide to which it should be given.—To JOHN ADAMS. i, 436. (P., 1785.)

3186. —— ——. When of two nations, the one has engaged herself in a ruinous war for us, has spent her blood and money to save us, has opened her bosom to us in peace, and received us almost on the footing of her own citizens, while the other has moved heaven. earth, and hell to exterminate us in war, has insulted us in all her councils in peace, shut her doors to us in every port where her interests would admit it, libelled us in foreign nations. endeavored to poison them against the reception of our most precious commodities; to place these two nations on a footing, is to give a great deal more to one than to the other, if the maxim be true, that to make unequal quantities equal, you must add more to one than the other. To say. in excuse, that gratitude is never to enter into the motives of national conduct, is to revive a principle which has been buried for centuries with its kindred principles of the lawfulness of assassination, poison, perjury, &c. All of these were legitimate principles in the dark ages, which intervened between ancient and modern civilization, but exploded and held in just horror in the eighteenth century. I know but one code of morality for men. whether acting singly or collectively. He who says I will be a rogue when I act in company with a hundred others, but an honest man when I act alone, will be believed in the former assertion, but not in the latter. I would say with the poet " *hic niger est, hunc tu Romane caveto.*" If the morality of one man produces a just line of conduct in him, acting individually, why should not the morality of one hundred men produce a just line of conduct in them, acting together? But I indulge myself in these reflections. because my own feelings run me into them; with you they were always acknowledged. Let us hope that our new government will take some other occasions to show that they mean to proscribe no virtue from the canons of their conduct with other nations. In every other instance, the new government has ushered itself to the world as honest, masculine, and dignified.—To JAMES MADISON. iii, 99. FORD ED., v, 111. (P., Aug. 1789.)

3187. FRANCE, War with England.—How the mighty duel is to end between Great Britain and France, is a momentous question. The sea which divides them makes it a game of chance; but it is narrow, and all the chances are not on one side. Should they make peace, still our fate is problematical.—To HORATIO GATES. iv, 213. (Pa., Feb. 1798.)

— FRANCE, West Indies.—See WEST INDIES.

— FRANCE, X. Y. Z. Plot.—See X. Y. Z. PLOT.

3188. FRANKING PRIVILEGE, Jefferson and.—The law making my letters post free goes to those *to* me only, not those *from*

me. The bill had got to its passage before this war was observed. * * * As the privilege of freedom was given to the letters *from* as well *as* to both my predecessors, I suppose no reason exists for making a distinction. And in so extensive a correspondence as I am subject to, and still considerably on public matters, it would be a sensible convenience to myself, as well as to those who have occasion to receive letters from me. * * * I state this matter to you as being my representative, which must apologize for the trouble of it.—To W. C. NICHOLAS. v, 454. FORD ED., ix, 254. (M., 1809.)

3189. FRANKLIN (Benjamin), America's Ornament.—The ornament of our country and, I may say, of the world.—To M. GRAND. iii, 140. (N.Y., 1790.)

3190. —— ——. The greatest man and ornament of the age and country in which he lived.—To SAMUEL SMITH. iv, 253. FORD ED., vii, 276. (M., 1798.)

3191. —— ——. America's Reception of.—At a large. table where I dined the other day, a gentleman from Switzerland expressed his apprehensions for the fate of Dr. Franklin, as he said he had been informed that he would be received with stones by the people, who were generally dissatisfied with the Revolution, and incensed against all those who had assisted in bringing it about. I told him nis apprehensions were just, and that the people of America would probably salute Dr. Franklin with the same stones they had thrown at the Marquis Lafayette. The reception of the Doctor is an object of very general attention, and will weigh in Europe as an evidence of the satisfaction or dissatisfaction of America with their Revolution. To JAMES MONROE. i, 407. FORD ED., iv, 87. (P., 1785.)

3192. —— ——. Europe fixes an attentive eye on your reception of Doctor Franklin. He is infinitely esteemed. Do not neglect any mark of your approbation which you think * * * proper. It will honor you here.—To JAMES MONROE. FORD ED., iv, 65. (P., 1785.)

3193. FRANKLIN (Benjamin), Argand's lamp.—A little before my arrival in France, Argand had invented his celebrated lamp, in which the flame is spread into a hollow cylinder, and thus brought into contact with the air within as well as without. Dr. Franklin had been on the point of the same discovery. The idea had occurred to him; but he had tried a bulrush as a wick, which did not succeed. His occupations did not permit him to repeat and extend his trials to the introduction of a larger column of air than could pass through the stem of a bulrush.—To REV. WILLIAM SMITH. iii, 213. FORD ED., v, 291. (Pa., 1791.)

3194. FRANKLIN (Benjamin), Beloved.—The venerable and beloved Franklin. —i, 108. FORD ED., i, 150. (1821.)

3195. FRANKLIN (Benjamin), Defence of.—I have seen, with extreme indignation, the blasphemies lately vended against the memory of the father of American philosophy.—To JONATHAN WILLIAMS. iv, 147. FORD ED., vii, 87. (M., 1796.)

3196. —— ——. As to the charge of subservience to France, besides the evidence of his friendly colleagues [Silas Deane and Mr. Laurens], two years of my own service with him at Paris, daily visits, and the most friendly and confidential conversation convince me it had not a shadow of foundation.—To ROBERT WALSH. vii, 109. FORD ED., x, 117. (M., 1818.)

3197. FRANKLIN (Benjamin), Diplomatic methods.—He possessed the confidence of the French government in the highest degree, insomuch, that it may truly be said, that they were more under his influence, than he under theirs. The fact is, that his temper was so amiable and conciliatory, his conduct so rational, never urging impossibilities, or even things unreasonably inconvenient to them, in short, so moderate and attentive to their difficulties, as well as our own, that what his enemies called subserviency, I saw was only that reasonable disposition, which, sensible that advantages are not all to be on one side, yielding what is just and liberal, is the more certain of obtaining liberality and justice. Mutual confidence produces, of course, mutual influence, and this was all which subsisted between Dr. Franklin and the government of France.—To ROBERT WALSH. vii, 109. FORD ED., x, 117. (M., 1818.)

3198. FRANKLIN (Benjamin), Discoveries of.—In physics we have produced a Franklin, than whom no one of the present age has made more important discoveries, nor has enriched philosophy with more, or more ingenious solutions of the phenomena of nature.—NOTES ON VIRGINIA. viii, 313. FORD ED., iii, 168. (1782.)

3199. FRANKLIN (Benjamin), Enduring fame.—Time will be making him greater while it is spunging us from its records.—To REV. WILLIAM SMITH. iii, 214. FORD ED., v, 293. (Pa., 1791.)

3200. ——— ———. His memory will be preserved and venerated as long as the thunder of heaven shall be heard or feared.—To JONATHAN EDWARDS. iv, 148. FORD ED., vii, 87. (M., 1796.)

3201. FRANKLIN (Benjamin), French admiration.—No greater proof of his estimation in France can be given than the late letters of condolence on his death, from the National Assembly of that country, and the community of Paris, to the President of the United States and to Congress, and their public mourning on that event. It is, I believe, the first instance of that homage having been paid by a public body of one nation to a private citizen of another.—To REV. WILLIAM SMITH. iii, 213. FORD ED., v, 292. (Pa., 1791.)

3202. ——— ———. I have it in charge from the President * * * to communicate to the National Assembly * * * the peculiar sensibility of Congress to the tribute paid to the memory of Benjamin Franklin. * * * That the loss of such a citizen should be lamented by us, among whom he lived, whom he so long and eminently served, and who feel their country advanced and honored by his birth, life and labors, was to be expected. But it remained for the National Assembly of France, to set the first example of the representative of one nation, doing homage, by a public act, to the private citizen of another, and by withdrawing arbitrary lines of separation, to reduce into one fraternity the good and the great, wherever they have lived or died. That these separations may disappear between us in all times and circumstances, and that the union of sentiment which mingles our sorrows on this occasion may continue long to cement the friendships of our two nations, is our constant prayer.—To THE PRESIDENT OF THE NATIONAL ASSEMBLY. iii, 218. (Pa., 1791.)

3203. ——— ———. When he left Passy* [for America], it seemed as if the village had lost its patriarch. On taking leave of the court, which he did by letter, the King ordered him to be handsomely complimented, and furnished him with a litter and mules of his own, the only kind of conveyance the state of his health could bear.—To REV. WILLIAM SMITH. iii, 213. FORD ED., v, 292. (Pa., 1791.)

3204. ——— ———. There appeared to me more respect and veneration attached to the character of Dr. Franklin in France, than to that of any other person in the same country, foreign or native.—To REV. WILLIAM SMITH. iii, 213. FORD ED., v, 213. (Pa., 1791.)

3205. FRANKLIN (Benjamin), Greatness of.—The succession to Doctor Franklin, at the court of France, was an excellent school of humility. On being presented to any one as the minister of America, the commonplace question used in such cases was " c'est vous, Monsieur, qui remplace le Docteur Franklin " ? " It is you, sir, who replace Doctor Franklin " ? I generally answered, " no one can replace him, sir; I am only his successor ".—To REV. WILLIAM SMITH. iii, 213. FORD ED., v, 293. (Pa., 1791.)

3206. FRANKLIN (Benjamin), Longevity.—His death was an affliction which was to happen to us at some time or other. We have reason to be thankful he was so long spared; that the most useful life should be the longest also; that it was protracted so far beyond the ordinary span allotted to man, as to avail us of his wisdom in the establishment of our own freedom, and to bless him with a view of its dawn in the East, where they seemed, till now, to have learned everything, but how to be free.—To REV. WILLIAM SMITH. iii, 213. FORD ED., v, 292. (Pa., 1791.)

3207. FRANKLIN (Benjamin), Loyalty.—That Dr. Franklin would have waived the formal recognition of our Independence, I never heard on any authority worthy notice.—To ROBERT WALSH. vii, 108. FORD ED., x, 117. (M., 1818.)

3208. FRANKLIN (Benjamin), Mesmerism unveiled.—The animal magnetism of the maniac Mesmer, * * * received its death wound from his hand in conjunction with his brethren of the learned committee appointed to unveil that compound of fraud and folly.—To REV. WILLIAM SMITH. iii, 212. FORD ED., v, 291. (Pa., 1791.)

3209. FRANKLIN (Benjamin), Philosophy's loss.—[In his death] Philosophy has to deplore one of its principal luminaries extinguished.—To REV. WILLIAM SMITH. iii, 212. FORD ED., v, 290. (Pa., 1791.)

3210. FRANKLIN (Benjamin), Presidency and.—Had I had a vote for the Presidentship, I doubt whether I should not have withheld it from you, that you might have leisure to collect and digest the papers you have written from time to time, and which the world will expect to be given them.—To DR. FRANKLIN. i, 525. (P., Jan. 1786.)

* Franklin lived in Passy, a suburb of Paris.—EDITOR.

3211. FRANKLIN (Benjamin), Respected.—Mr. Jay, Silas Deane, Mr. Laurens, his colleagues also, ever maintained towards him unlimited confidence and respect.—To ROBERT WALSH. vii, 108. FORD ED., x, 117. (M., 1818.)

3212. FRANKLIN (William Temple), Diplomatic Desires.—I wish with all my heart Congress may call you into the diplomatic line, as that seems to have attracted your own desires. It is not one in which you can do anything more than pass the present hour agreeably, without any prospect of future provision.—To W. T. FRANKLIN. i, 555. (P., 1786.)

3213. FRANKLIN (William Temple), Office-seeking.—Can nothing be done for young Franklin? He is sensible, discreet, polite, and good-humored, had fully qualified as a *Secretaire d' Ambassade*. His grandfather has none annexed to his legation at this Court [Versailles]. He is most sensibly wounded at his grandson's being superseded.—To JAMES MONROE. FORD ED., iv, 8. (P., 1784.)

3214. FRANKLIN (William Temple), Estimate of.—I have never been with Master Franklin enough to unravel his character with certainty. He seems to be good in the main. I see sometimes an attempt to keep himself unpenetrated, which perhaps is the effect of the old lesson of his grandfather. His understanding is good enough for common use, but not great enough for uncommon ones. * * * The Doctor is extremely wounded by the inattention of Congress to his application for him. He expects something to be done as a reward for his service. He will present * * * a determined silence on this subject in future.—To JAMES MONROE. FORD ED., iv, 65. (P., 1785.)

3215. FRANKLIN, State of.—North Carolina, by an act of their Assembly, ceded to Congress all their lands westward of the Alleghany. The people inhabiting that territory, thereon declared themselves independent, called their State by the name of Franklin, and solicited Congress to be received into the Union. But before Congress met, North Carolina (for what reasons I could never learn) resumed their Session. The people, however, persist; Congress recommended the State to desist from their opposition, and I have no doubt they will do it.—To DAVID HARTLEY. i, 424. FORD ED., iv, 93. (P., 1785.)

3216. FRANKNESS, Complete.—My dispositions are * * * against mysteries, innuendos and half-confidences.—To JOHN TAYLOR. iv, 259. FORD ED., vii, 309. (M., 1798.)

3217. ——— ———. Half-confidences are not in my character.—To ELBRIDGE GERRY. iv, 273. FORD ED., vii, 335. (Pa., 1799.)

3218. ——— ———. I cannot say things by halves.—To SAMUEL KERCHIVAL. vii, 17. FORD ED., x, 44. (M., 1816.)

3219. FRANKS (David), Office for.—Franks will doubtless be asking some appointment. I wish there may be one for which he is fit. He is light, indiscreet, active, honest, affectionate.—To JAMES MADISON. ii, 108. FORD ED., iv, 365. (P., 1787.)

3220. FREDERICK THE GREAT, Posthumous influence.—His kingdom, like a

machine, will go on for some time with the winding up he has given it.—To JAMES MONROE. i, 587. FORD ED., iv, 245. (P., July 1786.)

3221. ——— ———. The death of the King of Prussia will employ the pens, if not the swords, of politicians.—To EZRA STILES. FORD ED., iv, 300. (P., 1786.)

3222. FREDERICK THE GREAT, Treaty with.—Without urging, we* sounded the ministers of the several European nations at the Court of Versailles, on their dispositions towards mutual commerce, and the expediency of encouraging it by the protection of a treaty. Old Frederick, of Prussia, met us cordially and without hesitation, and appointing the Baron de Thulemeyer, his minister at the Hague, to negotiate with us, we communicated to him our *projêt*, which, with little alteration by the King was soon concluded.—AUTOBIOGRAPHY. i, 62. FORD ED., i, 87. (1820.) See TREATIES.

3223. FREDERICK WILLIAM II., Bulldog of tyranny.—If foreign troops should be furnished, it would be most probably by the King of Prussia, who seems to offer himself as the bulldog of tyranny to all his neighbors.—To JOHN JAY. iii, 118. (P., Sep. 1789.)

3224. FREDERICK WILLIAM II., Weakness of.—The King of Prussia does not seem to take into account the difference between his head and the late King's. This may be equal, perhaps, to half his army.—To C. W. F. DUMAS. ii, 492. (P., 1788.)

3225. FREEDOM, Birth.—Freedom,—the first-born daughter of science.—To M. D'IVERNOIS. iv, 113. FORD ED., vii, 3. (M., Feb. 1795.)

3226. FREEDOM, Gaining.—It is unfortunate, that the efforts of mankind to recover the freedom of which they have been so long deprived, will be accompanied with violence, with errors, and even with crimes. But while we weep over the means, we must pray for the end.—To M. D'IVERNOIS. iv, 115. FORD ED., vii, 5. (M., Feb. 1795.)

3227. FREEDOM, Solicitude for.—My future solicitude will be * * * to be instrumental to the happiness and freedom of all.—FIRST INAUGURAL ADDRESS. viii, 5. FORD ED., viii, 6. (1801.) See GOVERNMENT, LIBERTY and TYRANNY.

— FREEDOM OF OPINION.—See OPINION.

3228. FREEDOM OF PERSON, Federal Constitution and.—The imprisonment of a person under the laws of * * * [Kentucky], on his failure to obey the simple *order* of the President to depart out of the United States, as is undertaken by the act entitled "An Act concerning Aliens", is contrary to the Constitution, one amendment to which has provided that "no person shall be deprived of liberty without due process of law"; and that another having provided that "in all criminal prosecutions the accused shall en-

* Franklin, Adams and Jefferson, appointed by Congress to negotiate commercial treaties.—EDITOR.

joy the right to be tried by an impartial jury, to be informed of the nature and cause of the accusation, to be confronted with the witnesses against him. to have compulsory process for obtaining witnesses in his favor, and to have the assistance of counsel for his defense", the same act, undertaking to authorize the President to remove a person out of the United States, who is under the protection of the law, on his own suspicion. without accusation, without jury, without public trial, without confrontation of the witnesses against him, without hearing witnesses in his favor, without defence, without counsel. is contrary to the provision also of the Constitution, is therefore not law, but utterly void. and of no force; * * * [and the] transferring the power of judging any person, who is under the protection of the laws, from the courts to the President of the United States, as is undertaken by the same act concerning aliens. is against the article of the Constitution which provides that " the judicial power of the United States shall be vested in courts, the judges of which shall hold their offices during good behavior"; and * * * the said act is void for that reason also. And it is further to be noted, that this transfer of judiciary power is to that magistrate of the General Government who already possesses all the executive, and a negative on all legislative powers.—KENTUCKY RESOLUTIONS. ix, 467. FORD ED., vii. 297. (1798.)

3229. FREEDOM OF PERSON, Federal Government and.—Freedom of the person under the protection of the *habeas corpus*, I deem [one of the] essential principles of our government and, consequently, [one] which ought to shape its administration.—FIRST INAUGURAL ADDRESS. viii, 4. FORD ED., viii, 5. (1801.)

3230. FREEDOM OF PERSON, State Constitutions and.—There are certain principles in which the constitutions of our several States all agree, and which all cherish as vitally essential to the protection of the life, liberty, property and safety of the citizen. [One is] Freedom of Person. securing every one from imprisonment, or other bodily restraint, but by the laws of the land. This is effected by the well-known law of *habeas corpus.*—To M. CORAY. vii, 323. (M., 1823.) See HABEAS CORPUS.

— FREEDOM OF THE PRESS.—See PRESS.

— FREEDOM OF RELIGION.—See RELIGION.

3231. FREEDOM OF SPEECH, The Constitution and.—One of the amendments to the Constitution * * * expressly declares, that " Congress shall make no law respecting an establishment of religion, or prohibiting the free exercise thereof, or abridging the freedom of speech, or of the press "; thereby guarding in the same sentence, and under the same words, the freedom of religion, of speech. and of the press; insomuch, that whatever violates either, throws down

the sanctuary which covers the others.—KENTUCKY RESOLUTIONS. ix, 466. FORD ED., vii, 295. (1798.) See 820.

3232. FREEDOM OF SPEECH, Error and.—Truth is the proper and sufficient antagonist to error, and has nothing to fear from the conflict, unless, by human interposition, disarmed of her natural weapons, free argument and debate.—STATUTE OF RELIGIOUS FREEDOM. FORD ED., ii, 239. (1779.)

3233. FREEDOM OF SPEECH, Government invasion of.—There are rights which it is useless to surrender to the government, and which governments have yet always been found to invade. [Among] these are the rights of thinking, and publishing our thoughts by speaking or writing.—To DAVID HUMPHREYS. iii, 13. FORD ED., v, 89. (P., 1789.)

3234. FREEDOM OF SPEECH, Guard to liberty.—The liberty of speaking and writing guards our other liberties.—REPLY TO ADDRESS. viii, 129. (1808.)

3235. FREEDOM OF SPEECH, Opinion and.—Differences of opinion, when permitted * * * to purify themselves by free discussion, are but as * * * clouds overspreading our land transiently, and leaving our horizon more bright and serene.—To BENJAMIN WARING.—iv, 378. (W., March 1801.)

3236. FREEDOM OF SPEECH, Shackled.—Nor should we wonder at * * * [the] pressure [for a fixed constitution in 1788-9] when we consider the monstrous abuses of power under which * * * [the French] people were ground to powder; when we pass in review the shackles on * * * the freedom of thought and of speech.—AUTOBIOGRAPHY. i, 86. FORD ED., i, 118. (1821.)

3237. FREE PORTS, Honfleur.—Monsieur Famin called on me on the subject of making Honfleur a free port, and wished me to solicit it. I told him it was for our interest, as for that also of all the world, that every port of France, and of every other country, should be free; * * * but that I could not solicit it, as I had no instructions to do so.—To M. DE LAFAYETTE. i, 579. (P., 1786.)

3238. ——— ———. Some late regulations of the King and Council in favor of the commerce of the United States having given us room to hope that our endeavors may be successful to remove a good part of it from Great Britain to France, Honfleur presents itself as a more important instrument for this purpose than it had heretofore appeared. We are. therefore, now pressing more earnestly its establishment as a free port, and such other regulations in its favor as may invite the commerce to it.—To M. FAMIN. ii, 53. (P., 1786.)

3239. ——— ———. The enfranchising the port of Honfleur at the mouth of the Seine for multiplying the connections with us, is at present an object. It meets with opposition in the ministry but I am in hopes that it will prevail. If natural causes operate uninfluenced by accidental circumstances, Bourdeaux and Honfleur or Havre, must ultimately take the greatest part of our commerce. The former by the Garonne and canal of Languedoc opens the Southern provinces to us; the latter, the northern ones and Paris. Honfleur will be peculiarly advantageous for our rice and whale oil, of which the principal consumption is at Paris. Being free, they can be reexported when the market here shall happen to be overstocked.—To JOHN JAY. ii, 92. (P., 1787.)

3240. FREE PORTS, St. Bartholomew. —The island of St. Bartholomew, lately ceded to Sweden, is, if I am rightly informed, capable of furnishing little of its own productions to that country. It remains, then, to make it the instrument for obtaining through its intermediation such American productions as Sweden can consume or dispose of, and for finding in return a vent for the native productions of Sweden. Let us suppose it, then, made a free port without a single restriction. These consequences will follow: 1. It will draw to itself that tide of commerce which at present sets towards the Dutch and Danish islands, because vessels going to these are often obliged to negotiate a part of their cargoes at St. Eustatius, and to go to St. Thomas to negotiate the residue; whereas when they shall know that there is a port where all articles are free for both importation and exportation, they will go to that port which enables them to perform by one voyage the exchanges which hitherto they could only effect by two. 2. Every species of American produce, whether of the precious metals or commodities, which Sweden may want for its own consumption, or as aliment for its own commerce with other nations, will be collected either fairly or by contraband into the magazines of St. Bartholomew. 3. All the productions which Sweden can furnish from within itself, or obtain to advantage from other nations, will in like manner be deposited in the magazines of St. Bartholomew, and will be carried to the several ports of America in payment for what shall be taken from them.—To BARON STAHE. FORD ED., iv. 240. (P., 1786.)

3241. ——— ———. The interest of the United States is that St. Bartholomew be made a port of unlimited freedom, and such, too, is evidently the interest of Sweden. If it be freed by halves, the free ports of other nations, at present in possession of the commerce, will retain it against any new port offering no superior advantages. The situation of St. Bartholomew is very favorable to these views, as it is among the most windward, and therefore the most accessible of the West Indian Islands. —To BARON STAHE. FORD ED., iv, 242. (P., 1786.)

3242. FREE PORTS, St. Eustatius.—St. Eustatius is by nature a rock, barren and unproductive in itself, but its owners became sensible that what nature had denied it, policy could more than supply. It was conveniently situated for carrying on contraband trade with both the continents, and with the islands of America. They made it, therefore, an *entrepot* for all nations. Hither are brought the productions of every other port of America, and the Dutch give in exchange such articles as, in the course of their commerce, they can most advantageously gather up. And it is a question, on which they will not enable us to decide, whether by furnishing American productions to the commerce of Holland, and by finding vent for such productions of the old world as the Dutch merchants obtain to advantage, the barren rock of St. Eustatius does not give more activity to their commerce, and leave with them greater profits, than their more fer-

tile possessions on the continent of South America.—To BARON STAHE. FORD ED., iv, 239. (P., 1786.)

3243. FREE PORTS, San Juan.—Free ports in the Spanish possessions in America, and particularly at the Havana, San Domingo, in the island of that name, and St. John of Porto Rico, are more to be desired than expected. It can, therefore, only be recommended to the best endeavors of the commissioners to obtain them.—MISSISSIPPI RIVER INSTRUCTIONS. vii, 589. FORD ED., v, 478. (March 1792.)

3244. FREE SHIPS, Free goods, history of principle.—When Europe assumed the general form in which it is occupied by the nations now composing it, and turned its attention to maritime commerce, we found among its earliest practices, that of taking the goods of an enemy from the ship of a friend; and that into this practice every maritime State went sooner or later, as it appeared on the theatre of the ocean. If, therefore, we are to consider the practice of nations as the sole and sufficient evidence of the law of nature among nations, we should unquestionably place this principle among those of natural laws. But its inconveniences, as they affected neutral nations peaceably pursuing their commerce, and its tendency to embroil them with the powers happening to be at war, and thus to extend the flames of war, induced nations to introduce by special compacts, from time to time, a more convenient rule: "that free ships should make free goods"; and this latter principle has by every maritime nation of Europe been established, to a greater or less degree, in its treaties with other nations; insomuch, that all of them have, more or less frequently, assented to it, as a rule of action in particular cases. Indeed, it is now urged, and I think with great appearance of reason, that this is the genuine principle dictated by national morality; and that the first practice arose from accident, and the particular convenience of the States (Venice and Genoa) which first figured on the water, rather than from well digested reflections of the relations of friend and enemy, on the rights of territorial jurisdiction, and on the dictates of moral law applied to these. Thus it had never been supposed lawful, in the territory of a friend, to seize the goods of an enemy. On an element which nature has not subjected to the jurisdiction of any particular nation, but has made common to all for the purposes to which it is filled, it would seem that the particular portion of it which happens to be occupied by the vessel of any nation, in the course of its voyage, is for the moment, the exclusive property of that nation, and, with the vessel, is exempt from intrusion by any other, and from its jurisdiction, as much as if it were lying in the harbor of its sovereign. In no country, we believe, is the rule otherwise, as to the subjects of property common to all. Thus the place occupied by an individual in a highway, a church, a theatre, or other public assembly, cannot be intruded on, while its occupant holds it for the purposes of its institution. The persons on board a vessel traversing the ocean, carrying with them the laws of their nation, have among themselves a jurisdiction, a police, not established by their individual will, but by the authority of their nation, of whose territory their vessel still seems to compose a part, so long as it does not enter the exclusive territory of another. No nation ever pretended a right to govern by their laws the ship of another nation navigating the ocean. By what

law, then, can it enter that ship while in peaceable and orderly use of the common element?
We recognize no natural precept for submission to such a right; and perceive no distinction between the movable and immovable jurisdiction of a friend, which would authorize the
entering the one and not the other, to seize the
property of an enemy. It may be objected that
this proves too much, as it proves you cannot
enter the ship of a friend to search for contraband of war. But this is not proving too
much. We believe the practice of seizing what
is called contraband of war, is an abusive
practice, not founded in natural right. War
between two nations cannot diminish the rights
of the rest of the world remaining at peace.
The doctrine that the rights of nations remaining quietly in the exercise of moral and social
duties, are to give way to the convenience of
those who prefer plundering and murdering
one another, is a monstrous doctrine; and
ought to yield to the more rational law, that
"the wrong which two nations endeavor to
inflict on each other, must not infringe on the
rights or conveniences of those remaining at
peace". And what is *contraband*, by the law
of nature? Either everything which may aid
or comfort an enemy, or nothing. Either all
commerce which would accommodate him is unlawful, or none is. The difference between
articles of one or another description, is a difference in degree only. No line between them
can be drawn. Either all intercourse must
cease between neutrals and belligerents, or
all be permitted. Can the world hesitate to
say which shall be the rule? Shall two nations
turning tigers, break up in one instant the
peaceable relations of the whole world? Reason and nature clearly pronounce that the
neutral is to go on in the enjoyment of all its
rights, that its commerce remains free, not
subject to the jurisdiction of another, nor
consequently its vessels to search, or to enquiries whether their contents are the property
of an enemy, or are of those which have been
called contraband of war. Nor does this doctrine contravene the right of preventing vessels from entering a blockaded port. This
right stands on other ground. When the fleet
of any nation actually beleaguers the port of its
enemy, no other has a right to enter their line,
any more than their line of battle in the open
sea, or their lines of circumvallation, or of encampment, or of battle array on land. The
space included within their lines in any of those
cases, is either the property of their enemy,
or it is common property assumed and possessed for the moment, which cannot be intruded on, even by a neutral, without committing the very trespass we are now considering, that of intruding into the lawful possession
of a friend.*—To Robert R. Livingston. iv,
408. Ford ed., viii, 88. (M., Sep. 1801.)

**3245. FREE SHIPS, Free goods, Inter-
national Law and.**—On the question whether
the principle of "free bottoms making free
goods, and enemy bottoms enemy goods", is
now to be considered as established in the law
of nations, I will state to you a fact within my
own knowledge, which may lessen the weight
of our authority as having acted in the war of
France and England on the ancient principle
"that the goods of an enemy in the bottom of
a friend are lawful prize; while those of a
friend in an enemy bottom are not so". Eng-

*These principles were set forth by Jefferson in an
opinion on "Neutral Trade" in 1793. (ix, 443. Ford
ed., 485.)—Editor.

land became a party in the general war against
France on the 1st of February, 1793. We took
immediately the stand of neutrality. We were
aware that our great intercourse with these two
maritime nations would subject us to harassment by multiplied questions on the duties of
neutrality, and that an important and early one
would be which of the two principles above
stated should be the law of action with us.
We wished to act on the new one of "free bottoms, free goods"; and we had established it
in our treaties with other nations, but not with
England. We determined, therefore, to avoid,
if possible, committing ourselves on this question until we could negotiate with England her
acquiescence in the new principle. Although
the cases occurring were numerous, and the
ministers. Genet and Hammond, eagerly on the
watch, we were able to avoid any declaration
until the massacre of St. Domingo. The
whites, on that occasion, took refuge on board
our ships, then in their harbor, with all the
property they could find room for; and on their
passage to the United States, many of them
were taken by British cruisers, and their cargoes seized as lawful prize. The inflammable
temper of Genet kindled at once, and he wrote,
with his usual passion, a letter reclaiming an
observance of the principle of "free bottoms,
free goods", as if already an acknowledged law
of neutrality. I pressed him in conversation
not to urge this point; that although it had
been acted on by convention, by the armed
neutrality, it was not yet become a principle of
universal admission; that we wished indeed to
strengthen it by our adoption, and were negotiating an acquiescence on the part of Great
Britain; but if forced to decide prematurely,
we must justify ourselves by a declaration of
the ancient principle, and that no general consent of nations had as yet changed it. He was
immovable, and on the 25th of July wrote a
letter, so insulting, that nothing but a determined system of justice and moderation would
have prevented his being shipped home in the
first vessel. I had the day before answered his
of the 9th, in which I . ad been obliged in our
own justification, to declare that the ancient
was the established principle, still existing and
authoritative. Our denial, therefore, of the
new principle, and action on the old one, were
forced upon us by the precipitation and intemperance of Genet, against our wishes, and
against our aim; and our involuntary practice,
therefore, is of less authority against the new
rule.—To Edward Everett. vii, 271. (M.,
Feb. 1823.)

**3246. FREE SHIPS, Free goods, trea-
ties and.**—By the former usage of nations,
the goods of a friend were safe though taken
in an enemy bottom, and those of an enemy
were lawful prize though found in a free bottom. But in our treaties with France, &c., we
have established the simpler rule, that a free
bottom makes free goods, and an enemy bottom, enemy goods. The same rule has been
adopted by the treaty of armed neutrality between Russia, Sweden, Denmark, Holland and
Portugal, and assented to by France and Spain.
Contraband goods, however, are always excepted, so that they may still be seized; but
the same powers have established that naval
stores are not contraband goods; and this may
be considered now as the law of nations.
Though England acquiesced under this during
the late war, rather than draw on herself the
neutral powers, yet she never acceded to the
new principle.—To Mr. Cairnes. ii, 280. (P.,
1787.)

3247. —— ——. In our treaties with France, the United Netherlands, Sweden 'and Prussia, the principle of free bottoms, free goods, was uniformly maintained. In the instructions of 1784, given by Congress to their ministers appointed to treat with the nations of Europe generally, the same principle, and the doing away contraband of war, were enjoined, and were acceded to in the treaty signed with Portugal. In the late treaty with England, indeed, that power perseveringly refused the principle of free bottoms, free goods; and it was avoided in the late treaty with Prussia, at the instance of our then administration, lest it should seem to take side in a question then threatening decision by the sword. At the commencement of the war between France and England, the representative of the French Republic then residing in the United States [Genet], complaining that the British armed ships captured French property in American bottoms, insisted that the principle of " free bottoms, free goods ", was of the acknowledged law of nations; that the violation of that principle by the British was a wrong committed on us, and such an one as we ought to repel by joining in the war against that country. We denied his position, and appealed to the universal practice of Europe, in proof that the principle of " free bottoms, free goods ", was not acknowledged as of the natural law of nations, but only of its conventional law. And I believe we may safely affirm, that not a single instance can be produced where any nation of Europe, acting professedly under the law of nations alone, unrestrained by treaty, has, either by its executive or judiciary organs, decided on the principle of " free bottoms, free goods ". Judging of the law of nations by what has been *practiced* among nations, we were authorized to say that the contrary principle was their rule, and that but an exception to it, introduced by special treaties in special cases only; that having no treaty with England substituting this instead of the ordinary rule, we had neither the right nor the disposition to go to war for its establishment. But though we would not then, nor will we now, engage in war to establish this principle, we are nevertheless sincerely friendly to it. We think that the nations of Europe have originally set out in error; that experience has proved the error oppressive to the rights and interests of the peaceable part of mankind; that every nation but one has acknowledged this, by consenting to the change, and that one has consented in particular cases; that nations have a right to correct an erroneous principle, and to establish that which is right as their rule of action; and if they should adopt measures for effecting this in a peaceable way, we shall wish them success and not stand in the way to it. But should it become, at any time, expedient for us to co-operate in the establishment of this principle, the opinion of the executive on the advice of its constitutional counsellors, must then be given; and that of the Legislature, an independent and essential organ in the operation, must also be expressed; in forming which, they will be governed, every man by his own judgment, and may, very possibly, judge differently from the Executive. With the same honest views, the most honest men often form different conclusions. As far, however, as we can judge, the principle of " free bottoms, free goods ", is that which would carry the wishes of our nation.—To ROBERT R. LIVINGSTON. iv, 411. FORD ED., viii, 91. (M., Sep. 1801.)

3248. FREE TRADE, Alliance for.—I think nothing can bring the security of our continent and its cause into danger, if we can support the credit of our paper. To do that, I apprehend, one of two steps must be taken. Either to procure free trade by alliance with some naval power able to protect it; or, if we find there is no prospect of that, to shut our ports totally, to all the world, and turn our Colonies into manufactories. The former would be most eligible, because most conformable to the habits and wishes of our people.—To BENJAMIN FRANKLIN. i, 205. FORD ED., ii, 132. (1777.)

3249. FREE TRADE, Appeal for.—Our interest will be to throw open the doors of commerce, and to knock off all its shackles, giving perfect freedom to all persons for the vent of whatever they may choose to bring into our ports, and asking the same in theirs.—NOTES ON VIRGINIA. viii, 412. FORD ED., iii, 279. (1782.)

3250. FREE TRADE, Benefit of.—I think all the world would gain by setting commerce at perfect liberty.—To JOHN ADAMS, i, 371. FORD ED., iv, 81. (July 1785.)

3251. FREE TRADE, Confederation Congress and.—Congress had, in the year 1784, made up their minds as to the system of commercial principles they wished to pursue. These were very free. They proposed them to all the powers of Europe. All declined except Prussia. To this general opposition they may now find it necessary to present a very different general system to which their treaties will form cases of exception.—To C. W. F. DUMAS. ii, 321. (P., 1787.)

3252. FREE TRADE, Desire for.—I take for granted. that the commercial system, wished for by Congress, was such a one as should leave commerce on the freest footing possible. This was the plan on which we prepared our general draft for treating with all nations.—To JOHN ADAMS. i, 487. (P., 1785.)

3253. —— ——. Would even a single nation begin with the United States this system of free commerce, it would be advisable to begin it with that nation; since it is one by one only that it can be extended to all.—FOREIGN COMMERCE REPORT. vii, 646. FORD ED., vi, 479. (1793.)

3254. —— ——. I am for free commerce with all nations.—To ELBRIDGE GERRY. iv, 268. FORD ED., vii, 328. (Pa., 1799.)

3255. FREE TRADE, Encouragement.—The permitting an exchange of industries with other nations is a direct encouragement of your own, which without that. would bring you nothing for your comfort, and would of course cease to be produced.—To SAMUEL SMITH. vii, 286. FORD ED., x, 253. (M., 1823.)

3256. FREE TRADE, France and.—Merchandise received [in France] from the other nations of Europe takes employment from the poor of France; ours gives it. Their's is brought in the last stage of manu-

facture; ours in the first. We bring our tobaccos to be manufactured into snuff, our flax
and hemp into linen and cordage, our furs
into hats, skins into saddlery, shoes and
clothing. We take nothing till it has received
the last hand.*—To COUNT DE MONTMORIN. ii,
173. FORD ED., iv, 400. (P., 1787.)

3257. FREE TRADE, Great Britain and.
—The system into which the United States
wished to go, was that of freeing commerce
from every shackle. A contrary conduct in
Great Britain will occasion them to adopt
the contrary system, at least as to that island.—To W. W. SEWARD. i. 479. (P.,
1785.)

3258. ——— ———. I had persuaded myself
[in 1804] that a nation, distant as we are
from the contentions of Europe, avoiding all
offences to other powers, and not over-hasty
in resenting offence from them, doing justice to all, faithfully fulfilling the duties of
neutrality performing all offices of amity, and
administering to their interests by the benefits of our commerce, that such a nation, I
say, might expect to live in peace, and consider itself merely as a member of the great
family of mankind; that in such case it
might devote itself to whatever it could best
produce, secure of a peaceable exchange of
surplus for what could be more advantageously furnished by others, as takes place
between one country and another of France.
But experience has shown that continued
peace depends not merely on our own justice and prudence, but on that of others also;
that when forced into war, the interception of
exchanges which must be made across a wide
ocean, becomes a powerful weapon in the
hands of an enemy domineering over that element, and to the other distresses of war adds
the want of all those necessaries for which
we have permitted ourselves to be dependent
on others, even arms and clothing. This
fact, therefore. solves the question by reducing it to its ultimate form, whether profit or
preservation is the first interest of a State?
We are consequently become manufacturers
to a degree incredible to those who do not
see it. and who only consider the short period
of time during which we have been driven to
them by the suicidal policy of England.—To
J. B. SAY. vi, 430. (M., March 1815.)

**3259. FREE TRADE, Human happi-
ness and.**—Could each [country] be free to
exchange with others mutual surpluses for
mutual wants, the greatest mass possible
would then be produced of those things
which contribute to human life and human
happiness; the numbers of mankind would be
increased, and their condition bettered.—
FOREIGN COMMERCE REPORT. vii, 646. FORD
ED., vi 479. (Dec. 1793.)

3260. FREE TRADE, Natural right of.
—The exercise of a free trade with all parts of
the world, possessed by the American Colonists, as of natural right, and which no law

* Jefferson was arguing in favor of the free importation of American productions into France.—EDI-
TOR.

of their own had taken away or abridged,
was next the object of unjust encroachment.—RIGHTS OF BRITISH AMERICA. i. 127.
FORD ED., i, 432. (1774.)

**3261. FREE TRADE, Neighbor nations
and.**—An exchange of surpluses and wants
between neighbor nations, is both a right
and a duty under the moral law.—To WILL-
IAM SHORT. iii, 275. FORD ED., v, 364. (Pa.,
1791.) See AGRICULTURE, COMMERCE, MANU-
FACTURES, NAVIGATION, PROTECTION and TAR-
IFF.

3262. FRENEAU (Philip), Clerkship.—
The clerkship for foreign languages in my
office is vacant. The salary, indeed, is very
low, being but two hundred and fifty dollars a
year; but also, it gives so little to do as not to
interfere with any other calling the person may
choose, which would not absent him from the
seat of government. I was told a few days
ago, that it might perhaps be convenient to
you to accept it. If so, it is at your service.
It requires no other qualification than a moderate knowledge of the French.—To PHILIP
FRENEAU. iii, 215. (Pa., 1791.)

3263. FRENEAU (Philip), Gazette of.—
Freneau has come here [Philadelphia] to set up
a national gazette, to be published twice a
week, and on whig principles.—To DAVID
HUMPHREYS. FORD ED., v, 373. (Pa., 1791.)

3264. ——— ———. Freneau's paper is getting
into Massachusetts under the patronage of
Hancock and Sam Adams; and Mr. Ames, the
Colossus of the monocrats and paper men, will
either be left out or hard run. The people of
that State are republican; but hitherto they have
heard nothing but the hymns and lauds chanted
by Fenno.—To T. M. RANDOLPH. iii, 491.
FORD ED., vi, 134. (Pa., 1792.)

3265. ——— ———. As to the merits or demerits of his paper, they certainly concern me
not. He and Fenno are rivals for the public
favor. The one courts them by flattery, the
other by censure; and I believe it will be admitted that the one has been as servile, as the
other severe.—To PRESIDENT WASHINGTON.
iii, 466. FORD ED., vi, 108. (M., 1792.)

**3266. FRENEAU (Philip), Jefferson's
relations to.**—While the government was at
New York I was applied to in behalf of Freneau to know if there was any place within my
Department to which he could be appointed.
I answered there were but four clerkships, all
of which I found full, and continued without
any change. When we removed to Philadelphia, Mr. Pintard, the translating clerk, did not
choose to remove with us. His office then became vacant. I was again applied to there for
Freneau, and had no hesitation to promise the
clerkship for him. I cannot recollect whether
it was at the same time, or afterwards, that I
was told he had a thought of setting up a
newspaper there. But whether then, or afterwards, I considered it a circumstance of some
value, as it might enable me to do, what I had
long wished to have done, that is, to have the
material parts of the Leyden Gazette brought
under your eye, and that of the public, in order
to possess yourself and them of a juster view
of the affairs of Europe than could be obtained
from any other public source. This I had in-
effectually attempted through the press of Mr.
Fenno, while in New York, selecting and translating passages myself at first, then having it

done through Mr. Pintard, the translating clerk, but they found their way too slowly into Mr. Fenno's papers. Mr. Bache essayed it for me in Philadelphia, but his being a daily paper, did not circulate sufficiently in the other States. He even tried, at my request, the plan of a weekly paper of recapitulation from his daily paper, in hopes that that might go into the other States, but in this, too. we failed. Freneau, as translating clerk, and the printer of a periodical paper likely to circulate through the States (uniting in one person the parts of Pintard and Fenno), revived my hopes that the thing could at length be effected. On the establishment of his paper, therefore. I furnished him with the Leyden gazettes, with an expression of my wish that he could always translate and publish the material intelligence they contained, and have continued to furnish them from time to time, as regularly as I received them. But as to any further direction or indication of my wish how his press should be conducted, what sort of intelligence he should give, what essays encourage, I can protest, in the presence of Heaven, that I never did by myself, or any other, or indirectly, say a syllable, nor attempt any kind of influence. I can further protest, in the same awful presence, that I never did, by myself, or any other, directly or indirectly. write, dictate. or procure any one sentence or sentiment to be inserted *in his, or any other gazette*, to which my name was not affixed or that of my office. * * * Freneau's proposition to publish a paper, having been about the time that the writings of "Publicola", and the discourses on Davila, had a good deal excited the public attention. I took for granted from Freneau's character, which had been marked as that of a good whig, that he would give free place to pieces written against the aristocratical and monarchical principles these papers had inculcated. This having been in my mind, it is likely enough I may have expressed it in conversation with others; though I do not recollect that I did. To Freneau I think I could not, because I had still seen him but once. and that was at a public table, * * * as I passed through New York the last year. And I can safely declare that my expectations looked only to the chastisement of the aristocratical and monarchical writers, and not to any criticisms on the proceedings of government.—To PRESIDENT WASHINGTON. iii, 464. FORD ED., vi, 106. (M., 1792.)

3267. FRIENDS, College.—Friends we have, if we have merited them. Those of our earliest years stand nearest in our affections. Our college friends are the dearest.—To JOHN PAGE. iv, 547. (W., 1804.)

3268. FRIENDS, Inconstant.—During the whole of the Revolutionary war, which was trying enough I never deserted a friend because he had taken an opposite side; and those of my own State, who joined the British government, can attest my unremitting zeal in saving their property, and can point out the laws in our statute book which I drew. and carried through in their favor. However, I have seen during the late political paroxysm here [Philadelphia] numbers whom I had highly esteemed. draw off from me insomuch as to cross the street to avoid meeting me. The fever is abating, and doubtless some of them will correct the momentary wanderings of their heart, and return again. If they do, they will meet the constancy of

my esteem, and the same oblivion of this as of any other delirium which might happen to them.—To WILLIAM HAMILTON. FORD ED., vii, 441. (Pa., 1800.)

3269. FRIENDS, Political.—Of one thing I am certain. that they will not suffer personal dissatisfactions to endanger the republican cause. Their principles, I know, are far above all private considerations. And when we reflect that the eyes of the virtuous all over the earth are turned with anxiety on us, as the only depositories of the sacred fire of liberty, and that our falling into anarchy would decide forever the destinies of mankind, and seal the political heresy that man is incapable of self-government, the only contest between divided friends should be who will dare farthest into the ranks of the common enemy.—To JOHN HOLLINS. v. 596. (M., 1811.)

3270. FRIENDS, Separation of.—No one feels more painfully than I do, the separation of friends, and especially when their sensibilities are to be daily harrowed up by cannibal newspapers. In these cases, however, I claim from all parties the privilege of neutrality. and to be permitted to esteem all as I ever did. The harmony which made me happy while at Washington, is as dear to me now as then, and I should be equally afflicted, were it, by any circumstance. to be impaired as to myself.—To ALBERT GALLATIN. v, 588. (M., April 1811.)

3271. ——— ———. Near friends, falling out, never reunite cordially.—To A. DONALD. ii, 356. (P., 1788.)

3272. FRIENDS, Wounded.—Sincerely the friend of all the parties, I ask of none why they have fallen out by the way, and would gladly infuse the oil and wine of the Samaritan into all their wounds. I hope that time, the assuager of all evils, will heal these also; and I pray for them all a continuance of their affection, and to be permitted to bear to all the same unqualified esteem.—To JOHN HOLLINS. v. 596. (M., 1811.)

3273. FRIENDSHIP, Affectionate.—The happiest moments my heart knows are those in which it is pouring forth its affections to a few esteemed characters.—To MRS. TRIST. D. L. J., 84. (1786.)

3274. FRIENDSHIP, Ambition and.—I had rather be shut up in a very modest cottage, with my books, my family and a few old friends, dining on simple bacon, and letting the world roll on as it liked than to occupy the most splendid post which any human power can give.—To A. DONALD. ii, 356. (P., 1788.)

3275. FRIENDSHIP, Ancient.—I enjoy. in recollection, my ancient friendships, and suffer no new circumstances to mix alloy with them.—To DAVID HOWELL. v, 555. (M., 1810.)

3276. FRIENDSHIP, Broken.—The late misunderstandings at Washington have been a subject of real concern to me. I know that the dissolutions of personal friendship are among the most painful occurrences in human life. I have sincere esteem for all who have been affected by them, having passed with them eight years of great harmony and affection. These incidents are rendered more distressing in our country than elsewhere, because our printers ravin on the agonies of their victims, as wolves do on the blood of the lamb.—To JAMES MONROE. v. 598. FORD ED., ix, 323. (M., May 1811.)

3277. FRIENDSHIP, Comforts of.—What an ocean is life! And how our barks get separated in beating through it! One of the greatest comforts of the retirement to which I shall soon withdraw will be its rejoining me to my earliest and best friends, and acquaintances.—To ST. GEORGE TUCKER. FORD ED., vi. 425. (Pa., 1793.)

3278. ———. The only thing wanting to make me completely happy, is the more frequent society of my friends. It is the more wanting, as I am become more firmly fixed to the glebe.—To W. B. GILES. iv, 118. FORD ED., vii. 12. (M., 1795.)

3279. ———. So long a time has elapsed since we have been separated by events, that your favor was like a letter from the dead, and recalled to my memory very dear recollections. My subsequent journey through life has offered nothing which, in comparison with those, is not cheerless and dreary. It is a rich comfort sometimes to look back on them.—To T. LOMAX. iv, 300. FORD ED., vii, 373. (M., 1799.)

3280. FRIENDSHIP, Early.—As I grow older, I set a higher value on the intimacies of my youth, and am more afflicted by whatever loses one of them to me.—To A. DONALD. ii, 193. FORD ED., iv, 413. (P., 1787.)

3281. ———. I find as I grow older, that I love those most whom I loved first.—To MRS. BOWLING. FORD ED., iv, 412. (1787.)

3282. ———. The fond recollections of ancient times are much dearer to me than anything I have known since. * * * No attachments soothe the mind so much as those contracted in early life.—To A. DONALD. ii, 356. (P., 1788.)

3283. FRIENDSHIP, Enduring.—I never considered a difference of opinion in politics, in religion, in philosophy, as cause for withdrawing from a friend.—To WILLIAM HAMILTON. FORD ED., vii, 441. (Pa., 1800.)

3284. ———. Difference of opinion was never, with me, a motive of separation from a friend. In the trying times of Federalism, I never left a friend. Many left me, have since returned and been received with open arms.—To PRESIDENT MONROE. FORD ED., x, 298. (M., 1824.)

3285. FRIENDSHIP, False national.—No circumstances of morality, honor, in-

terest, or engagement are sufficient to authorize a secure reliance on any nation, at all times, and in all positions. A moment of difficulty, or a moment of error, may render forever useless the most friendly dispositions in the King, in the major part of his ministers, and the whole of his nation.—To JOHN JAY. ii, 304. (P., 1787.)

3286. FRIENDSHIP, Honest national.—Honest friendship with all nations, entangling alliances with none, I deem [one of the] essential principles of our government and, consequently, [one] which ought to shape its administration.—FIRST INAUGURAL ADDRESS. viii, 4. FORD ED., viii, 4. (1801.)

3287. ———. We have endeavored to cultivate the friendship of all nations.—SECOND INAUGURAL ADDRESS. viii, 40. FORD ED., viii, 343. (1805.)

3288. FRIENDSHIP, Precious.—Friendship is precious, not only in the shade, but in the sunshine of life; and thanks to a benevolent arrangement of things, the greater part of life is sunshine.—To MRS. COSWAY. ii, 39. FORD ED., iv, 319. (P.)

3289. FRIENDSHIP, Private.—I declare to you that I have never suffered political opinion to enter into the estimate of my private friendships; nor did I ever abdicate the society of a friend on that account till he had first withdrawn from mine. Many have left me on that account, but with many I still preserve affectionate intercourse, only avoiding to speak on politics, as with a Quaker or Catholic I would avoid speaking on religion.—To J. F. MERCER. iv. 563. (W., 1804.)

3290. FRIENDSHIP, Qualities of.—Wealth, title, office are no recommendations to my friendship. On the contrary, great good qualities are requisite to make amends for their having wealth, title and office.—To MRS. COSWAY. ii, 41. FORD ED., iv, 321. (P.. 1786.)

3291. FRIENDSHIP, Value of.—That is a miserable arithmetic which could estimate friendship at nothing, or at less than nothing. —To MRS. COSWAY. ii, 39. FORD ED., iv, 319. (P., 1786.)

3292. FRIENDSHIP, Like wine.—I find friendship to be like wine, raw when new, ripened with age, the true old man's milk and restorative cordial.—To DR. BENJAMIN RUSH. vi, 4. FORD ED., ix, 329. (P.F., 1811.)

3293. FRIENDSHIP, Youthful.—The friendships of my youth are those which adhere closest to me, and in which I most confide.—To JOHN PAGE. i, 399. (P.. 1785.)

3294. ———. I find in old age that the impressions of youth are the deepest and most indelible. Some friends, indeed, have left me by the way, seeking by a different political path. the same object, their country's good, which I pursued with the crowd along the common highway. It is a satisfaction to me that I was not the first to leave them. I have never thought that a difference in political, any more than in religious opinions, should disturb the friendly intercourse of society. There are so many other topics on which friends may converse and be happy, that it is wonderful they would select, of preference, the only one on which they cannot agree.—To DAVID CAMPBELL. v, 499. (M., 1810.)

3295. FRIENDSHIP WITH ENGLAND, Advantages.—Both the United States and England ought to wish for peace and cordial friendship; we, because you can do us more harm than any other nation; and you, because we can do you more good than any other. Our growth is now so well established by regular enumerations through a course of forty years, and the same grounds of continuance so likely to endure for a much longer period, that, speaking in round numbers, we may safely call ourselves twenty millions in twenty years, and forty millions in forty years. Many of the statesmen now living saw the commencement of the first term, and many now living will see the end of the second. It is not then a mere concern of posterity; a third of those now in life will see that day. Of what importance, then, to you must such a nation be, whether as friends or foes.—To SIR JOHN SINCLAIR. vii, 22. (M., 1816.)

3296. FRIENDSHIP WITH ENGLAND, Advocates and antagonists.—That [friendly] dispositions [towards Great Britain] have been strong on our part in every administration from the first to the present one, that we would at any time have gone our full half way to meet them, if a single step in advance had been taken by the other party, I can affirm of my own intimate knowledge of the fact. During the first year of my own administration, I thought I discovered in the conduct of Mr. Addington some marks of comity towards us, and a willingness to extend to us the decencies and duties observed towards other nations. My desire to catch at this, and to improve it for the benefit of my own country, induced me, in addition to the official declarations from the Secretary of State, to write with my own hand to Mr. King, then our Minister Plenipotentiary at London, in the following words: [See 3299.] My expectation was that Mr. King would show this letter to Mr. Addington, and that it would be received by him as an overture towards a cordial understanding between the two countries. He left the ministry, however, and I never heard more of it, and certainly never perceived any good effect from it. I know that in the present temper, the boastful, the insolent, and the mendacious newspapers, on both sides, will present serious impediments. Ours will be insulting your public authorities, and boasting of victories; and yours will not be sparing of provocations and abuse of us. But if those at our helms could not place themselves above these pitiful notices, and throwing aside all personal feelings, look only to the interest of their nations, they would be unequal to the trusts confided to them. I am equally confident, on our part, in the administration now in place, as in that which will succeed it; and that if friendship is not hereafter sincerely cultivated, it will not be their fault. * * * Although what I write is from no personal privity with the views or wishes of our government, yet believing them to be what they ought to be, and confident in their wisdom and integrity, I am sure I hazard no deception in what I have said of them, and I shall be happy indeed if some good shall result to both our countries.—To SIR JOHN SINCLAIR. vii, 23. (M., 1816.)

3297. FRIENDSHIP WITH ENGLAND, Common interest.—No two countries upon earth have so many points of common interest and friendship; and the rulers must be great bunglers indeed, if, with such dispositions, they break them asunder.—To JAMES MONROE. v, 12. FORD ED., viii, 449. (W., May 1806.)

3298. FRIENDSHIP WITH ENGLAND, Cultivation of.—As to the duties of your office [Minister to England], I shall only express a desire that they be constantly exercised in that spirit of sincere friendship which we bear to the English nation, and that in all transactions with the minister, his good dispositions be conciliated by whatever in language or attentions may tend to that effect.—To THOMAS PINCKNEY. iii, 441. FORD ED., vi, 75. (Pa., 1792.)

3299. ———— ————. I hope that through your agency we may be able to remove everything inauspicious to a cordial friendship between this country and the one in which you are stationed; a friendship dictated by too many considerations not to be felt by the wise and the dispassionate of both nations. It is, therefore, with the sincerest pleasure I have observed on the part of the British government various manifestations of just and friendly disposition towards us.* We wish to cultivate peace and friendship with all nations, believing that course most conducive to the welfare of our own. It is natural that these friendships should bear some proportion to the common interests of the parties. The interesting relations between Great Britain and the United States are certainly of the first order; and as such are estimated, and will be faithfully cultivated by us. These sentiments have been communicated to you from time to time in the official correspondence of the Secretary of State; but I have thought it might not be unacceptable to

* In the Ford edition, it is noted that in the draft of the letter to Mr. King, the following paragraph is stricken out: "These seeds are not sown in barren ground. I have too high an opinion of the understanding of those at the helm of British affairs to suppose they judge of the dispositions of this administration from the miserable trash of the public papers; and I trust they have more respect for our understandings than to suppose we are Gallomen or Anglomen, or anything but Americans and the friends of our friends. Peace and friendship are essential with all other nations."—EDITOR.

be assured that they perfectly concur with my own personal convictions, both in relation to yourself and the country in which you are.—To RUFUS KING. iv, 444. FORD ED., viii, 163. (W., July 1802.)

3300. FRIENDSHIP WITH ENGLAND, Desired.—Would to God that nation [England] would so far be just in her conduct as that we might with honor give her that friendship it is so much our interest to bear her.—To JAMES MADISON. FORD ED., viii, 300. (M., April 1804.)

3301. ———. Instead of fearing and endeavoring to crush our prosperity, had the British cultivated it in friendship, it might have become a bulwark instead of a breaker to them. There has never been an administration in this country which would not gladly have met them more than half way on the road to an equal, a just and solid connection of friendship and intercourse. And as to repressing our growth, they might as well attempt to repress the waves of the ocean.—To JOHN MELISH. vi, 403. (M., 1814.)

3302. ———. No one feels more indignation than myself when reflecting on the insults and injuries of that country to this. But the interests of both require that these should be left to history, and in the meantime be smothered in the living mind. I have, indeed, little personal concern in it. Time is drawing her curtain on me. But I should make my bow with more satisfaction, if I had more hope of seeing our countries shake hands together cordially.—To JAMES MAURY. vi, 469. (M., June 1815.)

3303. FRIENDSHIP WITH ENGLAND, Her advantage.—If the British adopt a course of friendship with us, the commerce of one hundred millions of people, which some now born will live to see will maintain them forever as a great unit of the European family. But if they go on checking, irritating, injuring, and hostilizing us, they will force on us the motto *"Carthago delenda est"*. And some Scipio Americanus will leave to posterity the problem of conjecturing where stood once the ancient and splendid city of London. * * * I hope the good sense of both parties will concur in travelling rather the paths of peace, of affection, and reciprocations of interests.—To C. F. GRAY. vi 439. (M., 1815.)

3304. FRIENDSHIP WITH ENGLAND, How obtained.—But is their friendship to be obtained by the irritating policy of fomenting among us party discord, and a teasing opposition; by bribing traitors, whose sale of themselves proves they would sell their purchasers also, if their treacheries were worth a price? How much cheaper would it be, how much easier, more honorable more magnanimous and secure, to gain the government itself by a moral, a friendly and respectful course of conduct, which is all they would ask for a cordial and faithful return.—To SIR JOHN SINCLAIR. vii, 22. (M., 1816.)

3305. FRIENDSHIP WITH ENGLAND, Influence of George III.—Circumstances have nourished between our kindred countries angry dispositions which both ought long since to have banished from their bosoms. I have ever considered a cordial affection as the first interest of both. No nation on earth can hurt us so much as yours, none be more useful to you than ours. The obstacle, we have believed, was in the obstinate and unforgiving temper of your late King, and a continuance of his prejudices kept up from habit, after he was withdrawn from power. I hope I now see symptoms of sounder views in your government; in which I know it will be cordially met by ours, as it would have been by every administration which has existed under our present Constitution. None desired it more cordially than myself, whatever different opinions were impressed on your government by a party who wishes to have its weight in their scale as its exclusive friends.—To MR. ROSCOE. vii, 196. (M., 1820.)

3306. FRIENDSHIP WITH ENGLAND, Mr. Merry and.—I thought that in the administration of Mr. Addington, I discovered some dispositions towards justice, and even friendship and respect for us, and began to pave the way for cherishing these dispositions, and improving them into ties of mutual good-will. But we had then a Federal minister there, whose dispositions to believe himself, and to inspire others with a belief in our sincerity, his subsequent conduct has brought into doubt; and poor Merry, the English minister here, had learned nothing of diplomacy but its suspicions, without head enough to distinguish when they were misplaced. Mr. Addington and Mr. Fox passed away too soon to avail the two countries of their dispositions.—To JAMES MAURY. vi, 53. FORD ED., ix, 350. (M., April 1812.)

3307. FRIENDSHIP WITH ENGLAND, Mutual interest.—Time and prudence on the part of the two governments may get over these [irritations, produced by the war of 1812]. Manifestations of cordiality between them, friendly and kind offices made visible to the people on both sides, will mollify their feelings, and second the wishes of their functionaries to cultivate peace and promote mutual interest.—To SIR JOHN SINCLAIR. vii, 23. (M., 1816.)

3308. FRIENDSHIP WITH ENGLAND, Obstacles to.—The war interests in England include a numerous and wealthy part of their population; and their influence is deemed worth courting by ministers wishing to keep their places. Continually endangered by a powerful opposition, they find it convenient to humor the popular passions at the expense of the public good. The shipping interest, commercial interest, and their janizaries of the navy, all fattening on war, will not be neglected by ministers of ordinary minds. Their tenure of office is so infirm that they dare not follow the dictates of wisdom, justice, and the well-calculated interests of their country. This vice in the English constitution, renders a dependence on that government very unsafe. The feelings of their King, too, fundamentally adverse to us, have added another motive for unfriendliness in his ministers. This obstacle to friendship, however, seems likely to be soon removed; and I verily believe the successor will come in with fairer and wiser dispositions towards us; perhaps on that event their conduct may be changed.—To THOMAS LAW. v. 556. FORD ED., ix, 293. (M., 1811.)

3309. ———— ————. Instead of cultivating the government itself, whose principles are those of the great mass of the nation, they [the British Ministry] have adopted the miserable policy of teasing and embarrassing it, by allying themselves with a faction here [the monarchical Federalists], not a tenth of the people, noisy and unprincipled, and which can never come into power while republicanism is the spirit of the nation, and that must continue to be so, until such a condensation of population shall have taken place as will require centuries. Whereas, the good will of the government itself would give them. and immediately, every benefit which reason or justice would permit it to give.—To THOMAS LAW. v, 556. FORD ED., ix, 292. (M., 1811.)

3310. FRIENDSHIP WITH ENGLAND, Price of.—What is the price we ask for our friendship? Justice, and the comity usually observed between nation and nation. Would there not be more of dignity in this, more character and satisfaction, than in her teasings and harrassings, her briberies and intrigues, to sow party discord among us, which can never have more effect here than the opposition within herself has there; which can never obstruct the begetting children, the efficient source of growth; and by nourishing a deadly hatred, will only produce and hasten events which both of us, in moments of sober reflection, should deplore and deprecate? One half of the attention employed in decent observances towards our Government, would be worth more to her than all the Yankee duperies played off upon her, at a great expense on her part of money and meanness, and of nourishment to the vices and treacheries of the Henrys and Hulls of both nations.—To JAMES MAURY. vi, 468. (M., 1815.)

3311. FRIENDSHIP WITH ENGLAND, Sacrifices for.—There is not a nation on the globe with whom I have more earnestly wished a friendly intercourse on equal conditions. On no other would I hold out the hand of friendship to any. I know that their creatures represent me as personally an enemy to England. But fools only can believe this, or those who think me a fool. I am an enemy to her insults and injuries. I am an enemy to the flagitious principles of her administration, and to those which govern her conduct towards other nations. But would she give to morality some place in her political code, and especially should she exercise decency, and at least neutral passions towards us, there is not, I repeat

it, a people on earth with whom I would sacrifice so much to be in friendship.—To CÆSAR A. RODNEY. vi, 449. (M., March 1815.)

3312. FRIENDSHIP WITH ENGLAND, Value of.—No man was more sensible than myself of the just value of the friendship of Great Britain. There are between us so many of those circumstances which naturally produce and cement kind dispositions, that if they could have forgiven our resistance to their usurpations. our connections might have been durable, and have insured duration to both our governments. I wished, therefore, a cordial friendship with them, and I spared no occasion of manifesting this in our correspondence and intercourse with them; not disguising, however. my desire of friendship with their enemy also. During the administration of Mr. Addington, I thought I discovered some friendly symptoms on the part of that government; at least, we received some marks of respect from the administration, and some of regret at the wrongs we were suffering from their country. So, also. during the short interval of Mr. Fox's power. But every other administration since our Revolution has been equally wanton in their injuries and insults, and have manifested equal hatred and aversion.—To THOMAS LAW. v, 555. FORD ED., ix, 292. (M., 1811.)

3313. ———— ————. I reciprocate congratulations with you sincerely on the restoration of peace between our two nations. * * * Let both parties now count soberly the value of mutual friendship. I am satisfied both will find that no advantage either can derive from any act of injustice whatever will be of equal value with those flowing from friendly intercourse.—To SIR JOHN SINCLAIR. vii, 22. (M., 1816.)

3314. FRUGALITY, Advocated.—Would a missionary appear, who would make frugality the basis of his religious system. and go through the land preaching it up as the only road to salvation, I would join his school, though not generally disposed to seek my religion out of the dictates of my own reason, and feelings of my own heart.—To JOHN PAGE. i, 550. FORD ED., iv, 214. (P., 1786.)

3315. FRUGALITY, Government and.—What more is necessary to make us a happy and prosperous people? Still one thing more: a wise and frugal Government, which shall restrain men from injuring one another, which shall leave them otherwise free to regulate their own pursuits of industry and improvement, and shall not take from the mouth of labor the bread it has earned. This is the sum of good government. and this is necessary to close the circle of our felicities. —FIRST INAUGURAL ADDRESS. viii, 3. FORD ED., viii, 4. (1801.)

3316. FUGITIVES, Debtors.—In the case of fugitive debtors and criminals, it is always well that coterminous States should understand one another, as far as their ideas on the rightful powers of government can be made to go together. When they separate, the cases may be left unprovided for.—To MESSRS. CARMICHAEL AND SHORT. iii, 349. (Pa., 1792.)

3317. FUGITIVES, England and.—England has no such convention with any nation, and their laws have given no power to their Executive to surrender fugitives of any description; they are accordingly constantly refused, and hence England has been the asylum of the Paolis, the La Mottes, the Calonnes, in short, of the most atrocious offenders as well as the most innocent victims, who have been able to get there.—To PRESIDENT WASHINGTON. iii, 299. FORD ED., v, 386. (Pa., 1791.)

3318. FUGITIVES, Exile and.—Does the fugitive from his country avoid punishment? He incurs exile, not voluntary, but under a moral necessity, as strong as physical. Exile, in some countries, has been the highest punishment allowed by the laws. To most minds it is next to death; to many beyond it. The fugitive, indeed, is not of the latter: he must estimate it somewhat less than death. It may be said that to some, as foreigners, it is no punishment.—REPORT ON SPANISH CONVENTION. iii, 353. FORD ED., v, 483. (1792.)

3319. FUGITIVES, Mariners.—When the consular convention with France was under consideration, this subject was attended to; but we could agree to go no further than is done in the ninth article of that instrument, when we agree mutually to deliver up "captains, officers, mariners, sailors, and all other persons being part of the crews of vessels", &c. Unless, therefore, the persons before named* be part of the crew of some vessel of the French nation, no person in this country is authorized to deliver them up; but, on the contrary, they are under the protection of the laws.—To E. C. GENET. FORD ED., vi, 426. (Pa., Sep. 1793.)

3320. FUGITIVES, Murderers.—Any person having committed murder of *malice prepense*, not of the nature of treason, within the United States or the Spanish provinces adjoining thereto, and fleeing from the justice of the country, shall be delivered up by the government where he shall be found, to that from which he fled, whenever demanded by the same.—PROJECT OF A SPANISH CONVENTION. iii, 350. FORD ED., v, 485. (1792.)

3321. ——— ———. Murder is one of the extreme crimes justifying a denial of habitation, arrest and redelivery. It should be carefully restrained by definition to homicide of *malice prepense, and not of the nature of treason.* * * * The only *rightful* subject then of arrest and delivery, for which we have *need* [to provide by convention], is murder.—REPORT ON SPANISH CONVENTION. iii, 352. FORD ED., v, 482. (1792.)

*M. Genet had requested the delivery of several persons "escaped from the ship Jupiter, and from the punishment of crime committed against the Republic of France".—EDITOR.

3322. FUGITIVES, Political.—However desirable it be that the perpetrators of crimes, acknowledged to be such by all mankind, should be delivered up to punishment, yet it is extremely difficult to draw the line between those and acts rendered criminal by tyrannical laws only; hence the first step always, is a convention defining the cases where a surrender shall take place.—To PRESIDENT WASHINGTON. iii, 300. FORD ED., v, 386. (Pa., 1791.)

3323. FUGITIVES, Protection of.—The laws of this country take no notice of crimes committed out of their jurisdiction. The most atrocious offender coming within their pale, is received by them as an innocent man, and they have authorized no one to seize or deliver him. The evil of protecting malefactors of every dye is sensibly felt here, as in other countries; but until a reformation of the criminal codes of most nations, to deliver fugitives from them, would be to become their accomplices; the former, therefore, is viewed as the lesser evil.—To EDMOND CHARLES GENET. FORD ED., vi, 426. (Pa., Sep. 1793.)

3324. FUGITIVES, Punishment of.—All excess of punishment is a crime. To remit a fugitive to excessive punishment, is to be accessory to the crime. Ought we to wish for the obligation, or the right to do it? Better on the whole, to consider these crimes as sufficiently punished by the exile.—REPORT ON SPANISH CONVENTION. iii, 354. FORD ED., v, 484. (1792.)

3325. FUGITIVES, Rights of.—Has a nation a right to punish a person who has not offended itself? Writers on the law of nature agree that it has not; that on the contrary, exiles and fugitives are to them as other strangers, and have a right of residence, unless their presence would be noxious; *e. g.*, infectious persons. One writer, (Vattel, L. I. 5, 233.) extends the exception to atrocious criminals, too imminently dangerous to society; namely, to pirates, murderers, and incendiaries.—REPORT ON SPANISH CONVENTION. iii, 352. FORD ED., v, 481. (1792.)

3326. FUGITIVES, Slaves.—Complaint has been made by the representatives of Spain that certain individuals of Georgia entered the State of Florida, and without any application to the Government, seized and carried into Georgia, certain persons, whom they claimed to be their slaves. This aggression was thought the more of, as there exists a convention between that government and the United States against receiving fugitive slaves. The minister of France has complained that the master of an American vessel, while lying within a harbor of St. Domingo, having enticed some negroes on board his vessel, under pretext of employment, brought them off, and sold them in Georgia as slaves. 1. Has the General Government cognizance of these offences? 2. If it has, is any law already provided for trying and punishing them? 1. The Constitution says " Congress shall have power to lay and collect taxes, duties, imposts and excises, to pay the debts. &c., provide for the common defence and *general welfare* of the United States". I do not consider this clause as reaching the point. * * * The Constitution says further, that Congress shall have power to " define and punish piracies and felonies committed on the high seas, and offences against the law of nations". These offences were not committed on the high seas, and consequently not within that branch of the clause. Are they against the law of nations, taken as it may be in its whole extent, as founded, 1st, in nature; 2d, usage; 3d, convention. So much may be said in the affirmative, that the legislators ought to send the case before the judiciary for discussion; and the rather, when it is considered that unless the offenders can be punished under this clause, there is no other which goes directly to their case, and consequently our peace with foreign nations will be constantly at the discretion of individuals. 2. Have the legislators sent this question before the Courts by any law already provided? The act of 1789, chapter 20, section 9, says the district courts shall have cognizance concurrent with the courts of the several States, or the circuit courts, of all causes, where an *alien sues for* a *tort only*, in violation of the law of nations; but what if there be no alien whose interest is such as to support an action for the tort? —which is precisely the case of the aggression on Florida. If the act in describing the jurisdiction of the Courts, had given them cognizance of proceedings by way of indictment or information against offenders under the law of nations, for the public wrong, and on the public behalf, as well as to an individual for the special tort, it would have been the thing desired. The same act, section 13, says, the " Supreme Court shall have exclusively all such jurisdiction of suits or proceedings against ambassadors, or other public ministers, or their domestics or domestic servants, as a court of law can have or exercise consistently, with the law of nations". Still this is not the case. no ambassador, &c., being concerned here. I find nothing else in the law applicable to this question, and therefore presume the case is still to be provided for, and that this may be done by enlarging the jurisdiction of the courts, so that they may sustain indictments and informations on the public behalf, for offences against the law of nations.*—OPINION ON FUGITIVE SLAVES. vii, 601. FORD ED., vi, 141. (1792.)

3327. FUGITIVES, Treaties Respecting.—Two neighboring and free governments. with laws equally mild and just, would find

*Jefferson added at a later period: "On further examination it does appear that the 11th section of the Judiciary Act, above cited, gives to the circuit courts exclusively, cognizance of all crimes and offences cognizable under the authority of the United States, and not otherwise provided for. This removes the difficulty, however, but one step further; for questions then arise, 1st: What is the peculiar character of the offence in question; to wit, treason, felony,

no difficulty in forming a convention for the interchange of fugitive criminals. Nor would two neighboring despotic governments, with laws of equal severity. The latter wish that no door should be opened to their subjects flying from the oppression of their laws. The fact is, that most of the governments on the continent of Europe have such conventions; but England, the only free one till lately, has never yet consented to enter into a convention for this purpose, or to give up a fugitive. The difficulty between a free government and a despotic one, is indeed great.—To GOVERNOR PINCKNEY. iii, 346. FORD ED., v, 492. (1792.)

3328. FUNDING, Posterity and.—The principle of spending money to be paid by posterity, under the name of funding, is but swindling futurity on a large scale.—To JOHN TAYLOR. vi, 608. FORD ED., x, 31. (M., 1816.)

3329. FUNDING, Redemption and.—Funding I consider as limited, rightfully, to a redemption of the debt within the lives of a majority of the generation contracting it; every generation coming equally. by the laws of the Creator of the world, to the free possession of the earth He made for their subsistence, unincumbered by their predecessors, who, like them, were but tenants for life.—To JOHN TAYLOR. vi. 605. FORD ED., x, 28. (M., May 1816.) See ASSUMPTION OF STATE DEBTS, DEBT, GENERATIONS, and HAMILTON.

3330. FUR TRADE, Aid to Astor.—I learn with great satisfaction the disposition of our merchants to form into companies for undertaking the Indian trade within our own territories. I have been taught to believe it an advantageous one for the individual adventurers, and I consider it as highly desirable to have that trade centered in the hands of our own citizens. * * * All beyond the Mississippi is ours exclusively, and it will be in our own power to give our own traders great advantages over their foreign competitors on this side the Mississippi. You may be assured that in order to get the whole of this business passed into the hands of our own citizens, and to oust foreign traders, who so much abuse their privilege by endeavoring to excite the Indians to war on us, every reasonable patronage and facility in the power of the Executive will be afforded.—To JOHN JACOB ASTOR. v, 269. (W., 1808.)

3331. —— ——. A powerful company is at length forming for taking up the Indian commerce on a large scale. They will employ a capital the first year of $300,000, and raise it afterwards to a million. The English Mackinac company will probably withdraw from the competition. It will be under the direction of a most excellent man, a Mr. Astor. merchant of New York, long engaged in the business, and perfectly master of it. He has some hope of seeing you at St. Louis, in which case I recommend him to your particular attention. Nothing but the exclusive possession of the Indian commerce can secure us their peace.—To MERIWETHER LEWIS. v, 321. FORD ED., ix, 199. (W., July 1808.)

misdemeanor, or trespass? 2d. What is its specific punishment, capital or what? 3d. Whence is the venue to come?"—EDITOR.

3332. FUR TRADE, Difficulties in.—I am sorry your enterprise for establishing a factory on the Columbia river, and a commerce through the line of that river and the Missouri, should meet with the difficulties stated in your letter. I remember well having invited your proposition on that subject, and encouraged it with the assurance of every facility and protection which the government could properly afford. I considered as a great public acquisition the commencement of a settlement on that point of the Western coast of America, and looked forward with gratification to the time when its descendants should have spread themselves through the whole length of that coast, covering it with free and independent Americans, unconnected with us but by the ties of blood and interest, and employing like us the rights of self-government. I hope the obstacles you state are not insurmountable; that they will not endanger, or even delay the accomplishment of so great a public purpose.—To John Jacob Astor. vi, 55. Ford ed., ix, 351. (M., May 1812.)

3333. FUR TRADE, Great Britain and.—In the present state of affairs between Great Britain and us, the government is justly jealous of the contraventions of those commercial restrictions which have been deemed necessary to exclude the use of British manufactures in these States, and to promote the establishment of similar ones among ourselves. The interests, too, of the revenue require particular watchfulness. But in the non-importation of British manufactures, and the revenue raised on foreign goods, the Legislature could only have in view the consumption of our own citizens, and the revenue to be levied on that. We certainly did not mean to interfere with the consumption of nations foreign to us, as the Indians of the Columbia and Missouri are, or to assume a right of levying an impost on that consumption; and if the words of the laws take in their supplies in either view, it was probably unintentional, and because their case not being under the contemplation of the Legislature, has been inadvertently embraced by it. The question with them would be not what manufactures these nations should use, or what taxes they should pay us on them, but whether we would give a transit for them through our country. We have a right to say we will not let the British exercise that transit. But it is our interest, as well as a neighborly duty, to allow it when exercised by our own citizens only. To guard against any surreptitious introduction of British influence among those nations, we may justifiably require that no Englishman be permitted to go with the trading parties, and necessary precautions should also be taken to prevent this covering the contravention of our own laws and views. But these once securely guarded, our interest would permit the transit free of duty.—To John Jacob Astor. vi, 55. Ford ed., ix, 351. (M., May 1812.)

3334. FUTURE, Dreams of.—I like the dreams of the future better than the history of the past.—To John Adams. vii, 27. (M., 1816.)

3335. FUTURE LIFE, Belief in.—Your son found me in a retirement I doat on, living like an antediluvian patriarch among my children and grandchildren, and tilling my soil. As he had lately come from Philadelphia, Boston, &c., he was able to give me a great deal of information of what is passing in the world, and I pestered him with questions pretty much

as our friends Lynch, Nelson, &c., will [pester] us, when we step across the Styx, for they will wish to know what has been passing above ground since they left us.—To Edward Rutledge. iv, 124. Ford ed., vii, 39. (M., Nov. 1795.)

3336. ——— ———. Your letter was like the joy we expect in the mansions of the blessed, when received with the embraces of our fathers, we shall be welcomed with their blessing as having done our part not unworthily of them.—To John Dickinson. iv, 365. Ford ed., viii, 7. (W., March 1801.)

3337. FUTURE LIFE, Felicity of.—Perhaps one of the elements of future felicity is to be a constant and unimpassioned view of what is passing here.—To Mrs. John Adams. vii, 53. Ford ed., x, 71. (M., 1817.)

3338. ——— ———. But these are speculations which we may as will deliver over to those who are to see their development. We shall only be lookers on, from the clouds above, as now we look down on the laborers, the hurry and bustle of the ants and bees. Perhaps in that super-mundane region, we may be amused with seeing the fallacy of our own guesses, and even the nothingness of those labors, which have filled and agitated our own time here.—To John Adams. vii, 105. Ford ed., x, 109. (M., 1818.)

3339. FUTURE LIFE, Reunion.—Your age of eighty-four and mine of eighty-one years insure us a speedy meeting. We may then commune at leisure, and more fully, on the good and evil which, in the course of our long lives, we have both witnessed.—To John Cartwright. vii, 361. (M., 1824.)

3340. GAGE (General Thomas), Appointment.—The substitution of Gage for Hutchinson was not intended as a favor, but, by putting the civil government into military hands, was meant to show they would enforce their measures by arms.—Notes on M. Soulés's Work. ix, 300. Ford ed., iv, 307. (P., 1786.)

3341. GAGE (General Thomas), Oppressor.—General Gage, by proclamation bearing date the 12th day of June, after reciting the grossest falsehoods and calumnies against the good people of these Colonies, proceeds to declare them all, either by name or description, to be rebels and traitors, to supersede the exercise of the common law of the said province [Massachusetts], and to proclaim and order instead thereof the use and exercise of the law martial. This bloody edict issued, he has proceeded to commit further ravages and murders in the same province, burning the town of Charlestown, attacking and killing great numbers of the people residing or assembled therein; and is now going on in an avowed course of murder and devastation, taking every occasion to destroy the lives and properties of the inhabitants. To oppose his arms we also have taken up arms. We should be wanting to ourselves, we should be perfidious to posterity, we should be unworthy that free ancestry from which we derive our descent, should we submit with folded arms to military butchery and depredation, to gratify the lordly ambition, or sate the avarice of a British ministry. We do, then, most solemnly, before God and the world declare that, regardless of every consequence, at the risk of every distress, the arms we have been compelled to assume we will use with perseverance, exerting to their utmost energies all those powers which our Creator hath given us, to preserve that liberty which he committed to us in sacred deposit and to protect from every hostile hand our lives and our properties.—DECLARATION ON TAKING UP ARMS. FORD ED., i, 473. (July 1775.)

3342. GALLATIN (Albert), Ability.— The ablest man except the President [Madison] who was ever in the administration.—To WILLIAM WIRT. v, 595. FORD ED., ix, 319. (M., May 1811.)

3343. ——— ———. Our worthy, our able, and excellent minister [to France].—To F. H. ALEXANDER VON HUMBOLDT. vii, 75. FORD ED., x, 89. (M., 1817.)

3344. GALLATIN (Albert), Advertising for.—The minister for Geneva has desired me to have enquiries made after the Mr. Gallatin named in the within paper. I will pray you to have the necessary advertisements inserted in the papers, and to be so good as to favor me with the result.—To JOHN JAY. i, 525. (P., 1786.)

3345. ——— ———. I am to thank you on the part of the minister of Geneva for the intelligence it contained on the subject of Gallatin, whose relations will be relieved by the receipt of it.—To JOHN JAY. i, 602. (P., 1786.)

3346. GALLATIN (Albert), Ark of safety.—There is no truer man than Mr. Gallatin, and after the President he is the ark of our safety.—To DABNEY CARR. FORD ED., ix, 317. (M., '1811.)

3347. GALLATIN (Albert), Cabinet dissensions.—In the earlier part of the administration, you witnessed the malignant and long continued efforts which the Federalists exerted in their newspapers, to produce misunderstanding between Mr. Madison and myself. Those failed completely. A like attempt was afterwards made, through other channels, to effect a similar purpose between General Dearborn and myself, but with no more success. The machinations of the last session to put you at cross purposes with us all, were so obvious as to be seen at the first glance of every eye. In order to destroy one member of the administration, the whole were to be set to loggerheads to destroy one another. I observe in the papers lately, new attempts to revive this stale artifice, and that they squint more directly towards you and myself. I cannot, therefore, be satisfied, till I declare to you explicitly, that my affections and confidence in you are nothing impaired, and that they cannot be impaired by means so unworthy the notice of candid and honorable minds. I make the declaration, that no doubts or jealousies. which often beget the facts they fear, may find a moment's harbor in either of our minds.—To ALBERT GALLATIN. v, 23. FORD ED., viii. 475. (W., Oct. 1806.)

3348. ——— ———. I have reflected much and painfully on the change of dispositions which has taken place among the members of the cabinet * * * . It would be, indeed, a great public calamity were it to fix you in the purpose you seemed to think possible [resignation]. I consider the fortunes of our republic as depending, in an eminent degree, on the

extinguishment of the public debt before we engage in any war: because, that done, we shall have revenue enough to improve our country in peace and defend it in war, without recurring either to new taxes or loans. But if the debt should once more be swelled to a formidable size, its entire discharge will be despaired of, and we shall be committed to the English career of debt, corruption and rottenness, closing with revolution. The discharge of the debt, therefore, is vital to the destinies of our government, and it hangs on Mr. Madison and yourself alone. We shall never see another President and Secretary of the Treasury making all other objects subordinate to this. Were either of you to be lost to the public, that great hope is lost. I had always cherished the idea that you would fix on that object the measure of your fame, and of the gratitude which our country will owe you. Nor can I yield up this prospect to the secondary considerations which assail your tranquillity. For, sure I am, they never can produce any other serious effect. Your value is too justly estimated by our fellow citizens at large, as well as their functionaries, to admit any remissness in their support of you. My opinion always was, that none of us ever occupied stronger ground in the esteem of Congress than yourself, and I am satisfied there is no one who does not feel your aid to be still as important for the future as it has been for the past. You have nothing, therefore, to apprehend in the dispositions of Congress, and still less of the President, who, above all men, is the most interested and affectionately disposed to support you. I hope, then, you will abandon entirely the idea you expressed to me, and that you will consider the eight years to come as essential to your political career. I should certainly consider any earlier day of your retirement, as the most inauspicious day our new government has ever seen. In addition to the common interest in this question, I feel particularly for myself the considerations of gratitude which I personally owe you for your valuable aid during my administration of public affairs, a just sense of the large portion of the public approbation which was earned by your labors and belongs to you, and the sincere friendship and attachment which grew out of our joint exertions to promote the common good.—To ALBERT GALLATIN. v, 477. FORD ED., ix, 264. (M. Oct. 1809.)

3349. ——— ———. The newspapers pretend that Mr. Gallatin will go out [of the cabinet]. That indeed would be a day of mourning for the United States.—To DR. WALTER JONES. v, 510. FORD ED., ix, 273. (M., 1810.)

3350. GALLATIN (Albert), Courage.—I believe Mr. Gallatin to be of a pure integrity, and as zealously devoted to the liberties and interests of our country as its most affectionate native citizen. Of this his courage in Congress in the days of terror, gave proofs which nothing can obliterate from the recollection of those who were witnesses of it. * * * An intercourse, almost daily, of eight years with him, has given me opportunities of knowing his character more thoroughly than perhaps any other man living.—To WILLIAM DUANE. v, 574. FORD ED., ix, 311. (M., 1811.)

3351. GALLATIN (Albert), Newspaper attacks.—I have seen with infinite grief the set which is made at you in the public papers, and with the more as my name has been so much used in it. I hope we both know one another too well to receive impression from circumstances of this kind. A twelve years' intimate and friendly intercourse must be better evidence to each of the dispositions of the other than the letters of foreign ministers to their courts, or tortured inferences from facts true or false. I have too thorough a conviction of your cordial good will towards me, and too strong a sense of the faithful and able assistance I received from you, to relinquish them on any evidence but of my own senses.—To ALBERT GALLATIN. v, 538. (M., 1810.)

3352. GALLATIN (Albert), Support of the bank.—Mr. Gallatin's support of the bank has, I believe, been disapproved by many. He was not in Congress when that was established, and therefore had never committed himself, publicly, on the constitutionality of that institution, nor do I recollect ever to have heard him declare himself on it. I know he derived immense convenience from it, because they gave the effect of ubiquity to his money wherever deposited. * * * He was, therefore, cordial to the bank. I often pressed him to divide the public deposits among all the respectable banks, being indignant myself at the open hostility of that institution to a government on whose treasuries they were fattening. But his repugnance to it prevented my persisting. And if he was in favor of the bank, what is the amount of that crime or error in which he had a majority, save one, in each House of Congress as participators?—To WILLIAM WIRT. v, 595. FORD ED., ix, 318. (M., May 1811.)

3353. GALLATIN (Albert), Tribute to. —They say Mr. Gallatin was hostile to me. This is false. I was indebted to nobody for more cordial aid [during my administration] than to Mr. Gallatin, nor could any man more solicitously interest himself in behalf of another than he did of myself.—To WILLIAM WIRT. v, 594. FORD ED., ix, 318. (M., 1811.)

3354. GALLATIN (Albert), Usefulness. —I congratulate you sincerely on your safe return to your own country, and without knowing your own wishes, mine are that you would never leave it again. I know you would be useful to us at Paris, and so you would anywhere; but nowhere so useful as here.—To ALBERT GALLATIN. vi, 498. (M., 1815.)

3355. GAMBLING, Evils of.—Gaming corrupts our dispositions, and teaches us a habit of hostility against all mankind.—To MARTHA JEFFERSON. FORD ED., iv, 389. (1787.)

— GARDENING.—See HORTICULTURE.

3356. GASTRONOMY, English.—I fancy it must be the quantity of animal food eaten by the English which renders their character insusceptible of civilization. I suspect it is in their kitchens, and not in their churches that their reformation must be worked, and that missionaries of that description from hence [Paris] would avail more than those who should endeavor to tame them by precepts of religion or philosophy.—To MRS. JOHN ADAMS. FORD ED., iv, 100. (P., 1785.)

3357. GASTRONOMY, French.—In the pleasures of the table they [the French] are far before us, because, with good taste they unite temperance. They do not terminate the most sociable meals by transforming themselves into brutes.—To MR. BELLINI. i, 445. (P., 1785.)

3358. GATES (General Horatio), Battle of Camden.—Good dispositions and ar-

rangements will not do without a certain degree of bravery and discipline in those who are to carry them into execution. This, the men whom you commanded, or the greater part of them at least, unfortunately wanted on that particular occasion. * I have not a doubt but that, on a fair enquiry, the returning justice of your countrymen will remind them of Saratoga, and induce them to recognize your merits. —To GENERAL GATES. i, 314. FORD ED., iii, 52. (M., 1781.)

3359. GATES (General Horatio), Civil office for.—General Gates would supply Short's place in the Council very well, and would act.—To JAMES MADISON. FORD ED., iii, 403. (A., Feb. 1784.)

3360. GEISMER (Baron), Friendship for.—From a knowledge of the man I am become interested in his happiness.†—To RICHARD HENRY LEE. FORD ED., ii, 181. (M., 1779.)

3361. ———. Whether fortune means to allow or deny me the pleasure of ever seeing you again, be assured that the worth which gave birth to my attachment, and which still animates it, will continue to keep it up while we both live.—To BARON GEISMER. i, 428. (P., 1785.)

3362. GEM (Doctor), Solicitude for.—I must ask you to see for me * * * and present my affectionate remembrances to him, Dr. Gem, an old English physician in the Faubourg St. Germains, who practiced only for his friends, and would take nothing, one of the most sensible and worthy men I have ever known.—To JAMES MONROE. FORD ED., vii. 19. (M., 1795.)

3363. GENERALS, Brave.—Our militia are heroes when they have heroes to lead them.—To W. H. CRAWFORD. vi, 420. (FORD ED., ix, 504. (M., 1815.)

3364. GENERALS, Costly.—The seeing whether our untried generals will stand proof is a very dear operation. Two of them have cost us a great many men.—To PRESIDENT MADISON. FORD ED., ix, 370. (M., Nov. 1812.)

3365. ———. The Creator has not thought proper to mark those in the forehead who are of stuff to make good generals. We are first, therefore, to seek them blindfold, and let them learn the trade at the expense of great losses.—To GENERAL BAILEY. vi, 100. (M., Feb. 1813.)

3366. ———. Our only hope is that these misfortunes will at length elicit by trial the characters qualified by nature from those unqualified, to be entrusted with the destinies of their fellow citizens.—To GENERAL ARMSTRONG. FORD ED., ix, 380. (M., Feb. 1813.)

3367. GENERALS, Discipline and.—Good dispositions and arrangements will not do without a certain degree of bravery and discipline in those who are to carry them into execution.—To GENERAL GATES. i, 314. FORD ED., iii, 52. (1781.)

* Battle of Camden.—EDITOR.
† From a letter recommending Geismer's exchange as a prisoner of war. He was one of the Hessian generals.—EDITOR.

3368. GENERALS, Discovering.—Our war on the land has commenced most inauspiciously. I fear we are to expect reverses until we can find out who are qualified for command, and until these can learn their profession.—To WILLIAM DUANE. vi, 99. (M., Jan. 1813.)

3369. —— ——. It is unfortunate that heaven has not set its stamp on the foreheads of those whom it has qualified for military achievement; that it has left us to draw for them in a lottery of so many blanks to a prize, and where the blank is to be manifested only by the public misfortunes. If nature had planted the *fœnum in cornu* on the front of treachery, of cowardice, of imbecility, the unfortunate *début* we have made on the theatre of war would not have sunk our spirits at home, and our character abroad.—To GENERAL JOHN ARMSTRONG. vi, 103. (M., Feb. 1813.)

3370. —— ——. These experiments will at least have the good effect of bringing forward those whom nature has qualified for military trust.—To PRESIDENT MADISON. FORD ED., ix, 380. (M., Feb. 1813.)

3371. GENERALS, Good.—Whenever we have good commanders, we shall have good soldiers, and good successes.—To PRESIDENT MADISON. FORD ED., ix, 380. (1813.)

3372. GENERALS, Incompetent.—On the land, indeed, we have been most unfortunate; so wretched a succession of generals never before destroyed the fairest expectations of a nation, counting on the bravery of its citizens, which has proved itself on all these trials.—To DR. BENJAMIN RUSH. vi, 106. (M., March 1813.)

3373. —— ——. I am happy to observe the public mind not discouraged, and that it does not associate its government with these unfortunate agents.—To PRESIDENT MADISON. FORD ED., ix, 380. (M., Feb. 1813.)

3374. —— ——. Will not [General] Van Rensselaer be broke for cowardice and incapacity? To advance such a body of men across a river without securing boats to bring them off in case of disaster, has cost 700 men; and to have taken no part himself in such an action, and against such a general would be nothing but cowardice.—To PRESIDENT MADISON. FORD ED., ix, 370. (M., Nov. 1812.)

3375. —— ——. No campaign is as yet opened. No generals have yet an interest in shifting their own incompetence on you.*— To JAMES MONROE. vi, 410. FORD ED., ix, 499. (M., 1815.)

3376. GENERALS, Lack of.—During the first campaign [in the war of 1812] we suffered several checks, from the want of capable and tried officers; all the higher ones of the Revolution having died off during an

* Monroe had been recently appointed Secretary of War.—EDITOR.

interval of thirty years of peace.—To DON V. T. CORUNA. vi, 275. (M., 1813.)

3377. —— ——. Perhaps we ought to expect such trials after deperdition of all military science consequent on so long a peace.—To PRESIDENT MADISON. FORD ED., ix, 380. (M., Feb. 1813.)

3378. GENERALS, Losses through.—Three frigates taken by our gallant navy, do not balance in my mind three armies lost by the treachery, cowardice, or incapacity of those to whom they were intrusted. I see that our men are good, and only want generals.—To WILLIAM DUANE. vi, 110. (M., April 1813.)

3379. GENERALS, Plumage of.—We can tell by his plumage whether a cock is dunghill or game. But with us cowardice and courage wear the same plume.—To PRESIDENT MADISON. FORD ED., ix, 370. (M., Nov. 1812.)

3380. GENERALS, Proving.—The proof of a general, to know whether he will stand fire, costs a more serious price than that of a cannon; these proofs have already cost us thousands of good men, and deplorable degradation of reputation, and as yet have elicited but a few negative and a few positive characters. But we must persevere till we recover the rank we are entitled to.—To WILLIAM DUANE. vi, 99. (M., 1813.)

3381. GENERALS, Self-sacrificing.—I think with the Romans of old, that the general of to-day should be a common soldier to-morrow, if necessary.—To JAMES MADISON. iv, 155. FORD ED., vii, 99. (1797.)

3382. GENERALS, Seniority and.—We are doomed * * * to sacrifice the lives of our citizens by thousands to this blind principle [seniority], for fear the peculiar interest and responsibility of our Executive should not be sufficient to guard his selection of officers against favoritism.—To GENERAL ARMSTRONG. FORD ED., ix, 380. (M., 1813.)

3383. GENERALS, Talents and.—We may yet hope that the talents which always exist among men will show themselves with opportunity, and that it will be found that this age also can produce able and honest defenders of their country, at what further expense, however, of blood and treasure is yet to be seen.—To WILLIAM DUANE. vi, 110. (M., April 1813.)

3384. —— ——. Experience had just begun to elicit those among our officers who had talents for war, and under the guidance of these one campaign would have planted our standard on the walls of Quebec, and another on those of Halifax.—To F. C. GRAY. vi, 438. (M., 1815.)

3385. —— ——. Our second and third campaigns * * * more than redeemed the disgraces of the first, and proved that although a republican government is slow to move, yet, when once in motion, its momentum becomes irresistible.—To F. C. GRAY. vi, 438. (M., 1815.)

3386. GENERALS, Unqualified.— Another general, it seems, has given proof of his military qualifications by the loss of another thousand men; for there cannot be a surprise but through the fault of the commanders, and especially by an enemy who has given us heretofore so many of these lessons. —To PRESIDENT MADISON. FORD ED., ix, 379. (M., Feb. 1813.)

3387. —— ——. Our men are good, but our generals unqualified. Every failure we have incurred has been the fault of the general, the men evincing courage in every instance.—To DR. SAMUEL BROWN. vi, 165. (M., July 1813.)

3388. —— ——. Our men are good, but force without conduct is easily baffled.—To GENERAL BAILEY. vi, 100. (M., 1813.)

3389. GENERALS, Usages of war and. —I would use any powers I have [as Governor of Virginia] for the punishment of any officer of our own, who should be guilty of excesses unjustifiable under the usages of civilized nations.—To COLONEL MATTHEWS. i, 234. FORD ED., ii, 263. (1779.)

3390. —— ——. The confinement and treatment of our officers, soldiers and seamen, have been so rigorous and cruel, that a very great portion of the whole of those captured in the course of this war. and carried to Philadelphia while in possession of the British army, and to New York, have perished miserably from that cause alone.—To SIR GUY CARLETON. FORD ED., ii, 249. (Wg., 1779.)

3391. GENERAL WELFARE CLAUSE, Interpretation.—To lay taxes to provide for the general welfare of the United States, that is to say, "to lay taxes for *the purpose* of providing for the general welfare". For the laying of taxes is the *power,* and the general welfare the *purpose* for which the power is to be exercised. They are not to lay taxes *ad libitum for any purpose they please;* but only *to pay the debts or provide for the welfare of the Union.* In like manner, they are not *to do anything they please* to provide for the general welfare, but only to *lay taxes* for that purpose. To consider the latter phrase, not as describing the purpose of the first, but as giving a distinct and independent power to do any act they please, which might be for the good of the Union, would render all the preceding and subsequent enumerations of power completely useless. It would reduce the whole instrument to a single phrase, that of instituting a Congress with power to do whatever would be for the good of the United States; and as they would be the sole judges of the good or evil, it would be also a power to do whatever evil they please. It is an established rule of construction where a phrase will bear either of two meanings, to give it that which will allow some meaning to the other parts of the instrument, and not that which would render all the others useless. Certainly no such universal power was meant to be given them.

It was intended to lace them up strictly within the enumerated powers, and those without which, as means, these powers could not be carried into effect.—NATIONAL BANK OPINION. vii, 557. FORD ED., v, 286. (1791.)

3392. —— ——. The Constitution says, "Congress shall have power to lay and collect taxes, duties, imposts, and excises, to pay the debts, &c., provide for the common defence and *general welfare* of the United States". I suppose the meaning of this clause to be, that Congress may collect taxes for the purpose of providing for the *general welfare,* in those cases wherein the Constitution empowers them to act for the general welfare. To suppose that it was meant to give them a distinct substantive power, to do *any act* which might tend to the *general welfare,* is to render all the enumerations useless, and to make their powers unlimited. —OPINION ON FUGITIVE SLAVES. vii, 602. FORD ED., vi, 141. (Dec. 1792.)

3393. —— ——. The construction applied by the General Government (as is evidenced by sundry of their proceedings) to those parts of the Constitution of the United States which delegate to Congress a power "to lay and collect taxes, duties, imposts, and excises, to pay the debts and provide for the common defence and general welfare of the United States", and "to make all laws which shall be necessary and proper for carrying into execution the powers vested by the Constitution in the government of the United States, or in any department or officer thereof", goes to the destruction of all limits prescribed to their power by the Constitution. * * * Words meant by the instrument to be subsidiary only to the execution of limited powers, ought not to be so construed as themselves to give unlimited powers, nor a part to be so taken as to destroy the whole residue of that instrument.—KENTUCKY RESOLUTIONS. ix, 468. FORD ED., vii, 299. (1798.)

3394. GENERAL WELFARE CLAUSE, Manufactures.—I told the President [Washington] that they [the Hamilton party in Congress] had now brought forward a proposition, far beyond every one ever yet advanced, and to which the eyes of many were turned as the decision which was to let us know, whether we live under a limited or an unlimited government. * * * [to wit] that in the Report on Manufactures which, under color of giving *bounties* for the encouragement of particular manufactures. meant to establish the doctrine, that the power given by the Constitution to collect taxes to provide for the *general welfare* of the United States, permitted Congress to take everything under their management which they should deem for the *public welfare,* and which is susceptible of the application of money; consequently, that the subsequent enumeration of their powers was not the description to which resort must be had. and did not at all constitute the limits of their authority; that this was a very different question from that of the Bank [of the United

States], which was thought an incident to an enumerated power; that, therefore, this decision was expected with great anxiety; that, indeed, I hoped the proposition would be rejected, believing there was a majority in both Houses against it, and that if it should be, it would be considered as a proof that things were returning into their true channel.—THE ANAS. ix, 104. FORD ED., i, 177. (Feb. 1792.)

3395. —— ——. In a Report on the subject of manufactures, it was expressly assumed that the General Government has a right to exercise all powers which may be for the *general welfare*, that is to say, all the legitimate powers of government; since no government has a legitimate right to do what is not for the welfare of the governed. There was, indeed, a sham limitation of the universality of this power *to cases where money is to be employed*. But about what is it that money cannot be employed?—To PRESIDENT WASHINGTON. iii, 461. FORD ED., vi, 103. (M., 1792.)

3396. **GENERAL WELFARE CLAUSE, Universal power.**—An act for internal improvement, after passing both houses, was negatived by the President. The act was founded, avowedly, on the principle that the phrase in the Constitution which authorizes Congress " to lay taxes, to pay the debts and provide for the general welfare ", was an extension of the powers specifically enumerated to whatever would promote the general welfare; and this, you know, was the federal doctrine. Whereas, our tenet ever was, and, indeed, it is almost the only landmark which now divides the federalists from the republicans, that Congress had not unlimited powers to provide for the general welfare, but were restrained to those specifically enumerated; and that, as it was never meant they should provide for that welfare but by the exercise of the enumerated powers, so it could not have been meant they should raise money for purposes which the enumeration did not place under their action; consequently, that the specification of powers is a limitation of the purposes for which they may raise money. * * * This phrase * * * by a mere grammatical quibble, has countenanced the General Government in a claim of universal power. For in the phrase, " to lay taxes, to pay the debts and provide for the general welfare ", it is a mere question of syntax, whether the two last infiritives are governed by the first or are distinct and coordinate powers; a question unequivocally decided by the exact definition of powers immediately following.—To ALBERT GALLATIN. vii, 78. FORD ED., x, 91. (M., June 1817.)

3397. —— ——. I hope our courts will never countenance the sweeping pretensions which have been set up under the words " general defence and public welfare ". These words only express the motives which induced the Convention to give to the ordinary legislature certain specified powers which they enumerate, and which they thought

might be trusted to the ordinary legislature, and not to give them the unspecified also; or why any specification? They could not be so awkward in language as to mean, as we say, " all and some ". And should this construction prevail, all limits to the Federal Government are done away. This opinion, formed on the first rise of the question, I have never seen reason to change, whether in or out of power; but, on the contrary, find it strengthened and confirmed by five and twenty years of additional reflection and experience: and any countenance given to it by any regular organ of the government, I should consider more ominous than anything which has yet occurred.—To SPENCER ROANE. vi, 494. FORD ED., ix, 531. (M., 1815.)

3398. **GENERATIONS, Binding power.** —The question whether one generation of men has a right to bind another, seems never to have been started either on this or our side of the water. Yet it is a question of such consequences as not only to merit decision, but place also, among the fundamental principles of every government. The course of reflection in which we are immersed here [Paris], on the elementary principles of society, has presented this question to my mind; and that no such obligation can be transmitted, I think very capable of proof. I set out on this ground, which I suppose to be self-evident, that the *earth belongs in usufruct to the living;* that the dead have neither powers nor rights over it. The portion occupied by an individual ceases to be his when himself ceases to be, and reverts to the society. If the society has formed no rules for the appropriation of its lands in severalty, it will be taken by the first occupants, and these will generally be the wife and children of the decedent. If they have formed rules of appropriation, those rules may give it to the wife and children, or to some one of them, or to the legatee of the deceased. So they may give it to its creditor. But the child, the legatee or creditor, takes it, not by natural right, but by a law of the society of which he is a member, and to which he is subject. Then, no man can, by *natural right*, oblige the lands he occupied, or the persons who succeed him in that occupation, to the payment of debts contracted by him. For if he could, he might during his own life, eat vp the usufruct of the lands for several generations to come; and then the lands would belong to the dead, and not to the living, which is the reverse of our principle. What is true of every member of the society, individually, is true of them all collectively; since the rights of the whole can be no more than the sum of the rights of the individuals. To keep our ideas clear when applying them to a multitude, let us suppose a whole generation of men to be born on the same day, to attain mature age on the same day, and to die on the same day, leaving a succeeding generation in the moment of attaining their mature age, all together. Let the ripe age be supposed of twenty-one years, and their period of life thirty-four years more, that being the average term given by the bills of mortality to persons of twenty-one years of age. Each successive generation would, in this way, come and go off the stage at a fixed moment, as individuals do now. Then I say, the earth belongs to each of these generations during its course, fully, and in its own right. The second generation receives it clear of the debts and incumbrances of the first, the third of the second, and so on. For if the first could charge it with a debt, then the earth would belong to the dead and not to the living generation. Then, no generation can contract debts greater than may be paid during the course of its own existence. At twenty-one years of age, they may bind themselves and their lands for thirty-four years to come; at twenty-two, for thirty-three; at twenty-three, for thirty-two; and at fifty-four, for one year only; because these are the terms of life which remain to them at the respective epochs. But a material difference must be noted between the succession of an individual and that of a whole generation. Individuals are parts only of a society, subject to the laws of a whole. These laws may appropriate the portion of land occupied by a decedent to his creditor rather than to any other, or to his child, on condition he satisfies the creditor. But when a whole generation, that is, the whole society dies, as in the case we have supposed, and another generation or society succeeds. this forms a whole, and there is no superior who can give their territory to a third society, who may have lent money to their predecessors beyond their faculties of paying.

What is true of a generation all arriving to self-government on the same day, and dying all on the same day, is true of those on a constant course of decay and renewal, with this only difference. A generation coming in and going out entire, as in the first case, would have a right in the first year of their self-dominion to contract a debt for thirty-three years; in the tenth, for twenty-four; in the twentieth, for fourteen; in the thirtieth, for four; whereas generations changing daily, by daily deaths and births, have one constant term beginning at the date of their contract, and ending when a majority of those of full age at that date shall be dead. The length of that term may be estimated from the tables of mortality, corrected by the circumstances of climate, occupation, &c., peculiar to the country of the contractors. Take, for instance, the table of M. de Buffon wherein he states that 23,994 deaths, and the ages at which they happened. Suppose a society in which 23,994 persons are born every year, and live to the ages stated in this table. The conditions of that society will be as follows. First, it will consist constantly of 617,703 persons of all ages; secondly, of those living at any one instant of time, one-half will be dead in twenty-four years, eight months; thirdly, 10,675 will arrive every year at the age of twenty-one years complete; fourthly, it will constantly have 348,417 persons of all ages above twenty-one years; fifthly, and the half of those of twenty-one years and upwards, living at any one instant of time, will be dead in eighteen years, eight months, or say nineteen years as the nearest integral number. Then nineteen years is the term beyond which neither the representatives of a nation, nor even the whole nation itself assembled, can validly extend a debt.

To render this conclusion palpable by example, suppose that Louis XIV. and XV. had contracted debts in the name of the French nation to the amount of ten thousand milliards of livres, and that the whole had been contracted in Genoa. The interest of this sum would be five hundred milliards, which is said to be the whole rent-roll, or net proceeds of the territory of France. Must the present generation of men have retired from the territory in which nature produced them, and ceded it to the Dutch creditors? No; they have the same rights over the soil on which they were

produced, as the preceding generations had. They derive these rights not from their predecessors, but from nature. They, then, and their soil, are by nature clear of the debts of their predecessors. Again, suppose Louis XV. and his contemporary generation had said to the money lenders of Holland, give us money that we may eat, drink, and be merry in our day; and on condition you will demand no interest till the end of nineteen years, you shall then forever after receive an annual interest of 12.5 per cent. The money is lent on these conditions, is divided among the living, eaten, drunk, and squandered. Would the present generation be obliged to apply the produce of the earth, and of their labor to replace their dissipations? Not at all.

I suppose that the received opinion, that the public debts of one generation devolve on the next, has been suggested by our seeing habitually in private life that he who succeeds to lands is required to pay the debts of his ancestor or testator, without considering that this requisition is municipal only, not moral, flowing from the will of the society, which has found it convenient to appropriate the lands become vacant by the death of their occupant on the condition of a payment of his debts; but that between society and society, or generation and generation, there is no municipal obligation, no umpire but the law of nature. We seem not to have perceived that, by the law of nature, one generation is to another as one independent nation to another.

The interest of the national debt of France being in fact but a two thousandth part of its rent-roll, the payment of it is practicable enough; and so becomes a question merely of honor or of expediency. But with respect to future debts, would it not be wise and just for that nation to declare in the constitution they are forming that neither the legislature, nor the nation itself can validly contract more debt than they may pay within their own age, or within the term of nineteen years. And that all future contracts shall be deemed void as to what shall remain unpaid at the end of nineteen years from their date? This would put the lenders, and the borrowers also, on their guard. By reducing, too. the faculty of borrowing within its natural limits, it would bridle the spirit of war, to which too free a course has been procured by the inattention of money lenders to this law of nature, that succeeding generations are not responsible for the preceding.

On similar ground, it may be proved that no society can make a perpetual constitution, or even a perpetual law. The earth belongs always to the living generation. They may manage it, then, and what proceeds from it, as they please, during their usufruct. They are masters, too, of their own persons, and consequently may govern them as they please. But persons and property make the sum of the object of government. The constitution and the laws of their predecessors are extinguished, then, in their natural course, with those whose will gave them being. This could preserve that being till it ceased to be itself, and no longer. Every constitution, then, and every law, naturally expire at the end of nineteen years. If it be enforced longer, it is an act of force and not of right.

It may be said that the succeeding generation exercising in fact the power of repeal, this leaves them as free as if the constitution or law had been expressly limited to nineteen years only. In the first place, this objection admits the right, in proposing an equivalent. But the power of repeal is not an equivalent. It might be, indeed, if every form of government were so perfectly contrived that the will of the majority could always be obtained fairly and without impediment. But this is true of no form. The people cannot assemble themselves; their representation is unequal and vicious. Various checks are opposed to every legislative proposition. Factions get possession of the public councils. Bribery corrupts them. Personal interests lead them astray from the general interests of their constituents; and other impediments arise so as to prove to every practical man that a law of limited duration is much more manageable than one which needs a repeal.

This principle that the earth belongs to the living and not to the dead, is of very extensive application and consequences in every country, and most especially in France. It enters into the resolution of the questions, whether the nation may change the descent of lands holden in tail; whether they may change the appropriation of lands given anciently to the church, to hospitals, colleges, orders of chivalry, and otherwise in perpetuity; whether they may abolish the charges and privileges attached on lands, including the whole catalogue, ecclesiastical and feudal; it goes to hereditary orders, distinctions and appellations, to perpetual monopolies in commerce, the arts or sciences, with a long train of *et ceteras*; and it renders the question of reimbursement a question of generosity and not of right. In all these cases, the legislature of the day could authorize such appropriations and establishments for their own time, but no longer, and the present holders, even where they or their ancestors have purchased, are in the case of *bona fide* purchasers of what the seller had no right to convey.

Turn this subject in your mind, and particularly as to the power of contracting debts, and develop it with that perspicuity and cogent logic which is so peculiarly yours. Your station in the public councils of our country gives you an opportunity of forcing it into discussion. At first blush it may be rallied as a theoretical speculation; but examination will prove it to be solid and salutary. It would furnish matter for a fine preamble to our first law for appropriating the public revenue; and it will exclude, at the threshold of our new government, the contagious and ruinous errors of this quarter of the globe, which have armed despots with means not sanctioned by nature for binding in chains their fellow men. We have already given, in example, one effectual check to the dog of war, by transferring the power of letting him loose from the Executive to the Legislative body, from those who are to spend to those who are to pay. I should be pleased to see this second obstacle held out also in the first instance. No nation can make a declaration against the validity of long-contracted debts so disinterestedly as we, since we do not owe a shilling which will not be paid with ease, principal and interest, within the time of our own lives. Establish the principle also in the new law to be passed for protecting copyrights and new inventions, by securing the exclusive right for nineteen instead of fourteen years [*a line entirely faded*], an instance the more of our taking reason for our guide instead of English precedents, the habit of which fetters us with all the political heresies of a nation, equally remarkable for its excitement from some errors, as long slumbering under others.*—To

* The hurry in which I wrote * * * to Mr. Madison * * *, occasioned an inattention to the difference between generations succeeding each other at fixed

James Madison. iii, 103. Ford ed., v, 115. (P., Sep. 1789.)

3399. —— ——. Can one generation of men, by any act of theirs, bind those which are to follow them? I say, by the laws of nature, there being between generation and generation, as between nation and nation, no other obligatory law.—To Joseph W. Cabell. vi, 299. (M., 1814.)

3400. GENERATIONS, The Earth and. —Every generation comes equally, by the laws of the Creator of the world, to the free possession of the earth which He made for their subsistence, unincumbered by their predecessors, who, like them, were but tenants for life.—To John Taylor. vi, 605. Ford ed., x, 28. (M., May 1816.)

3401. —— ——. That our Creator made the earth for the use of the living and not of t.. dead; that those who exist not can have no use nor right in it, no authority or power over it; that one generation of men cannot foreclose or burthen its use to another, which comes to it in its own right and by the same divine beneficence; that a preceding generation cannot bind a succeeding o— by its laws or contracts; these deriving their obligation from the will of the existing majority, and that majority being removed by death, another comes in its place with a will equally free to make its own laws and contracts; these are axioms so self-evident that no explanation can make them plainer: for he is not to be reasoned with who says that non-existence can control existence, or that nothing can move something. They are axioms also pregnant with salutary consequences. The laws of civil society, indeed, for the encouragement of industry, give the property of the parent to his family on his death, and in most civilized countries permit him even to give it, by testament, to whom he pleases. And it is also found more convenient to suffer the laws of our predecessors to stand on our implied assent, as if positively reenacted, until the existing majority positively repeals them. But this does not lessen the right of that majority to repeal whenever a change of circumstances or of will calls for it. Habit alone confounds what is civil practice with natural right.—To Thomas Earle. vii, 310. (M., 1823.)

3402. —— ——. Can one generation bind another, and all others, in succession forever? I think not. The Creator has made the earth for the living, not the dead. Rights and epochs and generations renewed daily and hourly. It is true that in the former case the generation, when at 21 years of age, may contract a debt for 34 years, because a majority of them will live so long. But a generation consisting of all ages, and which legislates by all its members above the age of 21 years, cannot contract for so long a time, because their majority will be dead much sooner. Buffon gives us a table of 23,994 deaths, stating the ages at which they happened. To draw from these the result I have occasion for, I suppose a society in which 23,994 persons are born every year and live to the ages stated in Buffon's table. Then the following inferences may be drawn. Such a society will consist constantly of 617,703 persons of all ages. Of those living at one instant of time, one-half will be dead in 24 years 8 months. In such a society, 10,675 will arrive every year at the age of 21 years complete. We will constantly have 348,417 persons of all ages above 21 years, and the half of those of 21 years and upwards living at any one instant of time will be dead in 18 years, 8 months, or say 19 years. "Then, the contracts, constitutions and laws of every such society become void in 19 years from their date."—To Dr. Gem. iii, 108.. Ford ed., v, 124. (P., 1789.)

powers can only belong to persons, not to things, not to mere matter, unendowed with will. The dead are not even things. The particles of matter which composed their bodies, make part now of the bodies of other animals, vegetables, or minerals, of a thousand forms. To what, then, are attached the rights and powers they held while in the form of men? A generation may bind itself as long as its majority continues in life; when that has disappeared, another majority is in place, holds all the rights and powers their predecessors once held, and may change their laws and institutions to suit themselves. Nothing, then, is unchangeable but the inherent and unalienable rights of man.—To JOHN CARTWRIGHT. vii, 359. (M., 1824.)

3403. GENERATIONS, Government and.—Let us * * * not weakly believe that one generation is not as capable as another of taking care of itself, and of ordering its own affairs. Let us, as our sisters have done, avail ourselves of our reason and experience, to correct the crude essays of our first and unexperienced, although wise, virtuous, and well-meaning councils. And lastly, let us provide in our constitution for its revision at stated periods. What these periods should be, nature herself indicates. By the European tables of mortality, of the adults living at any one moment of time, a majority will be dead in about nineteen years. At the end of that period, then, a new majority is come into place; or, in other words, a new generation. Each generation is as independent of the one preceding as that was of all which had gone before. It has, then, like them, a right to choose for itself the form of government it believes most promotive of its own happiness; consequently, to accommodate to the circumstances in which it finds itself, that received from its predecessors; and it is for the peace and good of mankind, that a solemn opportunity of doing this every nineteen or twenty years, should be provided by the constitution; so that it may be handed on, with periodical repairs, from generation to generation, to the end of time, if anything human can so long endure. It is now forty years since the constitution of Virginia was formed. The same tables inform us that, within that period, two-thirds of the adults then living are now dead. Have, then, the remaining third, even if they had the wish, the right to hold in obedience to their will, and to the laws heretofore made by them, the other two-thirds, who, with themselves, compose the present mass of adults? If they have not, who has? The dead? But the dead have no rights. They are nothing and nothing cannot own something. Where there is no substance, there can be no accident. This corporeal globe, and everything upon it, belong to its present corporeal inhabitants, during their generation. They alone have a right to direct what is the concern of themselves alone, and to declare the law of that direction; and this declaration can only be made by their majority.—To SAMUEL KERCHIVAL. vii, 15. FORD ED., x, 43. (M., 1816.)

3404. ———— ————. My wish is * * * to leave to those who are to live under it the settlement of their own constitution, and to pass in peace the remainder of my time.—To SAMUEL KERCHIVAL. vii, 35. FORD ED., x, 45. (M., 1816.)

3405. ———— ————. I willingly acquiesce in the institutions of my country, perfect or imperfect; and think it a duty to leave their

modifications to those who are to live under them, and are to participate of the good or evil they may produce. The present generation has the same right of self-government which the past one has exercised for itself.—To JOHN H. PLEASANTS. vii, 346. FORD ED., x, 303. (M., 1824.)

3406. ———— ————. I willingly leave to the present generation to conduct their affairs as they please.—To WILLIAM SHORT. vii, 392. FORD ED., x, 335. (M., 1825.)

3407. GENERATIONS, Succession of.—It is a law of nature that the generations of men should give way, one to another, and I hope that the one now on the stage will preserve for their sons the political blessings delivered into their hands by their fathers.—To SPENCER ROANE. vii, 211. FORD ED., x, 188. (M., 1821.)

3408. ———— ————. I yield the concerns of the world with cheerfulness to those who are appointed in the order of nature to succeed to them.—To GENERAL BRECKENRIDGE. vii, 206. (M., 1821.)

3409. GENERATIONS, Wisdom and.—Those who will come after us will be as wise as we are, and as able to take care of themselves as we have been.—To DUPONT DE NEMOURS. v, 584. FORD ED., ix, 322. (M., 1811.)

3410. ———— ————. I withdraw from all contests of opinion, and resign everything cheerfully to the generation now in place. They are wiser than we were, and their successors will be wiser than they, from the progressive advance of science.—To SPENCER ROANE. vii, 136. FORD ED., x, 142. (P.F., 1819.)

3411. ———— ————. The daily advance of science will enable the existing generation to administer the commonwealth with increased wisdom.—To MARQUIS LAFAYETTE. vii, 327. FORD ED., x, 283. (M., 1823.)

3412. GENEROSITY, Pleasures of.—Take more pleasure in giving what is best to another than in having it yourself, and then all the world will love you, and I more than all the world.—To MARY JEFFERSON. D. L. J., 181. (N.Y., 1790.)

3413. GENET (E. C.), Arrival.—We expect M. Genet in Philadelphia within a few days. It seems as if his arrival would furnish occasion for the *people* to testify their affections without respect to the cold caution of their government.—To JAMES MADISON. FORD ED., vi, 232. (Pa., April 1793.)

3414. GENET (E. C.), Calamitous appointment.—Never, in my opinion was so calamitous an appointment made as that of the present minister of France here. Hot-headed, all imagination, no judgment, passionate, disrespectful, and even indecent towards the President, in his written as well as verbal communications, talking of appeals from him to Congress, from them to the people, urging the most unreasonable and groundless propositions, and in the most dictatorial style, &c., &c., &c. If ever it should be necessary to lay his communications before Congress or the public, they will excite universal indignation. He renders my position immensely difficult. He does me justice personally, and, giving him time to vent himself, and then cool, I am on a footing to advise him freely, and he respects it; but he breaks out again on the very first occasion, so as to show that he is incapable of correcting himself. To complete our misfortune, we have no channel of our own through which we can correct the irritating representations he may make.—To JAMES MADISON. FORD ED., vi, 338. (July 1793.)

3415. ———— ————. Mr. Genet had been then but a little time with us; and but a little more was necessary to develop in him a character and conduct so unexpected, and so extraordinary, as to place us in the most distressing dilemma, between our regard for his nation, which is constant and sincere, and a regard for our laws, the authority of which must be maintained, which the Executive Magistrate is charged to preserve; for its honor, offended in the person of that Magistrate; and for its character grossly traduced in the conversations and letters of this gentleman.—To GOUVERNEUR MORRIS. iv, 31. FORD ED., vi, 372. (Pa., Aug. 1793.)

3416. GENET, Correspondence with.— We have kept the correspondence with Genet merely personal, convinced his nation will disapprove him. To them we have with the utmost assiduity given every proof of inviolate attachment.*—To THOMAS PINCKNEY. iv, 86. (G., Nov. 1793.)

3417. GENET, Functions.—Your functions as the missionary of a foreign nation here, are confined to the transactions of the affairs of your nation with the Executive of the United States; and the communications which are to pass between the Executive and Legislative branches, cannot be a subject for your interference. The President must be left to judge for himself what matters his duty or the public good may require him to propose to the deliberations of Congress.†—To E. C. GENET. iv, 100. FORD ED., vi, 496. (Pa., Dec. 1793.)

3418. GENET, Ignorance of.—Genet has been fully heard on his most unfounded pretensions under *the treaty*. His ignorance of everything written on the subject is astonishing. I think he has never read a book of any sort in that branch of science.—To JAMES MADISON. FORD ED., vi, 362. (Aug. 1793.)

3419. GENET (E. C.), Impetuosity.—I do not augur well of the mode of conduct of the new French minister; I fear he will enlarge the circle of those disaffected to his country. I am doing everything in my power to moderate the impetuosity of his movements, and to destroy the dangerous opinion which has been excited in him, that the people of the United States will disavow the acts of their Government, and that he has an appeal from the Executive to Congress, and from both to the people.—To JAMES MONROE. iv, 7. FORD ED., vi, 323. (Pa., June 1793.)

* Marshall, in his *Life of Washington* says: "The partiality for France that was conspicuous through the whole of the correspondence, detracted nothing from its merit in the opinion of the friends of the Administration, because, however decided their determination to support their own Government in any controversy with any nation whatever, they felt all the partialities for that Republic which the correspondence expressed. The hostility of his [Jefferson's] enemies, therefore, was, for a time considerably lessened, without a corresponding diminution of the attachment of his friends."—EDITOR.

† Genet had sent to Jefferson translations of the instructions given him by the Executive Council of France with a request that they should be laid before Congress by the President. Jefferson returned the papers to Genet.—EDITOR.

3420. GENET (E. C.), Indefensible conduct.—His conduct is indefensible by the most furious Jacobin.—To JAMES MONROE. iv, 20. FORD ED., vi, 348. (ṛa., July 1793.)

3421. ———— ————. His conduct has given room for the enemies of liberty and of France, to come forward in a style of acrimony against that nation, which they never would have dared to have done. The disapprobation of the agent mingles with the reprehension of his nation, and gives a toleration to that which it never had before. He has still some defenders in Freneau, and Greenleaf's paper, who they are I know not; for even Hutcheson and Dallas give him up. * * * Hutcheson says that Genet has totally overturned the republican interest in Philadelphia. However, the people going right themselves, if they always see their republican advocates with them, an accidental meeting with the monocrats will not be a coalescence.—To JAMES MADISON. iv, 53. FORD ED., vi, 402. (Pa., Sep. 1793.)

3422. GENET (E. C.), Instructions.—It is impossible for anything to be more affectionate, more magnanimous than the purport of [M. Genet's] mission. "We know that under present circumstances we have a right to call upon you for the guarantee of our Islands. But we do not desire it. We wish you to do nothing but what is for your own good, and we will do all in our power to promote it. Cherish your own peace and prosperity. You have expressed a willingness to enter into a more liberal treaty of commerce with us; I bring full powers (and he produced them) to form such a treaty, and a preliminary decree of the National Convention to lay open our country and its Colonies to you for every purpose of utility, without your participating the burthens of maintaining and defending them. We see in you the only person on earth who can love you sincerely, and merit to be so loved." In short, he offers everything, and asks nothing. Yet I know the offers will be opposed, and suspect they will not be accepted. In short, it is impossible for you to conceive what is passing in our conclave; and it is evident that one or two at least, under pretence of avoiding war on the one side have no great antipathy to run foul of it on the other, and to make a part in the confederacy of princes against human liberty.—To JAMES MADISON. iii, 563. FORD ED., vi. 260. (Pa., May 1793.)

3423. GENET, Libelous attack on.— The Minister Plenipotentiary of France has enclosed to me the copy of a letter * * * which he addressed to you, stating that some libelous publications had been made against him by Mr. Jay. Chief-Justice of the United States, and Mr. King, one of the Senators for the State of New York, and desiring that they might be prosecuted. This letter has been laid before the President, according to the request of the Minister; and the President, never doubting your readiness on all occasions to perform the functions of your office, yet thinks it incumbent on him to recommend it specially on the present occasion, as it concerns a public character peculiarly entitled to the protection of the laws. On the other hand, as our citizens ought not to be vexed with groundless prosecutions, duty to them requires it to be added, that if you judge the prosecution in question to be of that nature, you consider this recommendation as not extending to it; its only object being to engage you to proceed in this case according to the duties of your office

[Attorney General], the laws of the land, and the privileges of the parties concerned.—To EDMUND RANDOLPH. iv, 97. FORD ED., vi, 484. (Pa., Dec. 1793.)

3424. GENET (E. C.), Opposition to Law.—Genet has, at New York, forbidden a marshal to arrest a vessel, and given orders to the French squadron to protect her by force. Was there ever an instance before of a diplomatic man overawing and obstructing the course of the law in a country by an armed force?—To JAMES MADISON. iv, 64. FORD ED., vi, 418. (Sep. 1793.)

3425. GENET, Recall of.—[At a cabinet meeting] to consider what was to be done with Mr. Genet, * * * the following propositions were made: 1. That a full statement of Mr. Genet's conduct be made in a letter to G. Morris, and be sent with his correspondence, to be communicated to the Executive Council of France; the letter to be so prepared, as to serve for the form of communication to the Council. Agreed unanimously. 2. That in that letter his recall be required. Agreed by all, although I expressed a preference of expressing that desire with great delicacy; the others were for peremptory terms. 3. To send him off. This was proposed by Knox; but rejected by every other. 4. To write a letter to Mr. Genet, the same in substance with that written to G. Morris, and let him know we had applied for his recall. I was against this, because I thought it would render him extremely active in his plans, and endanger confusion. But I was overruled by the other three gentlemen and the President. 5. That a publication of the whole correspondence, and statement of the proceedings, should be made by way of appeal to the people. Hamilton made a jury speech of three-quarters of an hour, as inflammatory and declamatory as if he had been speaking to a jury. E. Randolph opposed it. I chose to leave the contest between them.—THE ANAS. ix, 162. FORD ED., i, 252. (Aug. 1793.)

3426. ———— ————. The *renvoi* of Genet was proposed [in cabinet] by the President. I opposed it on these topics. France, the only nation on earth sincerely our friend. The measure so harsh a one, that no precedent is produced where it has not been followed by war. Our messenger has now been gone eighty-four days; consequently, we may hourly expect the return, and to be relieved by their revocation of him. Were it now resolved on, it would be eight or ten days before the matter on which the order should be founded, could be selected, arranged, discussed, and forwarded. This would bring us within four or five days of the meeting of Congress. Would it not be better to wait and see how the pulse of that body, new as it is, would beat? They are with us now, probably, but such a step as this may carry many over to Genet's side. Genet will not obey the order, &c., &c. The President asked me what I would do if Genet sent the accusation to us to be communicated to Congress, as he threatened in a letter to Moultrie? I said I would not send it to Congress; but either put it in the newspapers, or send it back to him to be published if he pleased.*—THE ANAS. ix, 179. FORD ED., i, 267. (Nov. 1793.)

3427. ———— ————. We have decided unanimously to require the recall of Genet. He

* Hamilton and Knox were for dismissal. Randolph thought Genet was dead in public opinion, and the measure might restore his popularity. No determination was arrived at.—MEMORANDUM BY JEFFERSON.

will sink the republican interest if they do not abandon him.—To JAMES MADISON. FORD ED., vi, 361. (Aug. 1793.)

3428. ———— ————. Lay the case * * * immediately before his government. Accompany it with assurances, which cannot be stronger than true, that our friendship for the nation is constant and unabating; that, faithful to our treaties, we have fulfilled them in every point to the best of our understanding; that if in anything, however, we have construed them amiss, we are ready to enter into candid explanations, and to do whatever we can be convinced is right; that in opposing the extravagances of an agent, whose character they seem not sufficiently to have known, we have been urged by motives of duty to ourselves and justice to others, which cannot but be approved by those who are just themselves; and finally, that after independence and self-government, there is nothing we more sincerely wish than perpetual friendship with them.*—To GOUVERNEUR MORRIS. iv, 50. FORD ED., vi, 393. (P., Aug. 16, 1793.)

3429. ———— ————. It is with extreme concern I have to inform you that the proceedings of the person, whom the [French government] have unfortunately appointed their Minister Plenipotentiary here, have breathed nothing of the friendly spirit of the nation which sent him. Their tendency, on the contrary, has been to involve us in a war abroad, and discord and anarchy at home. So far as his acts, or those of his agents, have threatened our immediate commitment in the war, or flagrant insult to the authority of the laws, their effect has been counteracted by the ordinary cognizance of the laws, and by an exertion of the powers confided to me. Where their danger was not imminent, they have been borne with, from sentiments of regard to his nation, and from a sense of their friendship towards us, from a conviction that they would not suffer us to remain long exposed to the action of a person who has so little respected our mutual dispositions, and, I will add, from a firm reliance on the firmness of my fellow citizens in their principles of peace and order.—DRAFT OF PRESIDENT'S MESSAGE. FORD ED., vi, 457. (Nov. 1793.)

3430. GENET (E. C.), Reception of.—It was suspected that there was not a clear mind in the President's counsellors to receive Genet. The citizens, however, determined to receive him. Arrangements were taken for meeting him at Gray's Ferry in a great body. He escaped that by arriving in town with the letters which brought information that he was on the road. * * * The citizens determined to address Genet. Rittenhouse, Hutcheson, Dallas, Sargent, &c., were at the head of it. Though a select body of only thirty was appointed to present it, yet a vast concourse of people attended them. I have not seen it; but it is understood to be the counter address to the one presented to the President on the neutrality proclaimed, by the merchants, *i. e.*, Fitzsimmons & Co. It contained much wisdom but no affection.—To JAMES MADISON. iii, 562. FORD ED., vi, 260. (Pa., May 1793.)

3431. GENET (E. C.), Treachery.—I sometimes cannot help seriously believing Genet to be a Dumouriez, endeavoring to draw us into the war against France as Dumouriez,

* This quotation is the closing paragraph of the instructions to Gouverneur Morris, respecting the recall of Genet.—EDITOR.

while a minister, drew on her the war of the empire.—To JAMES MADISON. FORD ED., vi, 419. (1793.)

3432. GENET (E. C.), Washington and. —His inveteracy against the President leads him to meditate the embroiling him with Congress.—To JAMES MADISON. iv, 75. FORD ED., vi, 439. (Nov. 1793.)

3433. —— ——. Genet, by more and more denials of powers to the President and ascribing them to Congress, is evidently endeavoring to sow tares between them, and at any event to curry favor with the latter, to whom he means to turn his appeal, finding it was not likely to be well received by the people.—To JAMES MADISON. iv, 83. FORD ED., vi, 450. (G., Nov. 1793.)

3434. —— ——. Genet has thrown down the gauntlet to the President by the publication of his letter and my answer, and is himself forcing that appeal to the people, and risking that disgust which I had so much wished should have been avoided. The indications from different parts of the continent are already sufficient to show that the mass of the republican interest has no hesitation to disapprove of this intermeddling by a foreigner, and the more readily as his object was evidently, contrary to his professions, to force us into the war. I am not certain whether some of the more furious republicans may not schismatize with him.—To JAMES MADISON. iv, 52. FORD ED., vi, 397. (Pa., Aug. 1793.)

3435. GENIUS, Encouraging.—For promoting the public happiness, those persons whom nature has endowed with genius and virtue, should be rendered by liberal education worthy to receive, and able to guard the sacred deposit of the rights and liberties of their fellow citizens; and they should be called to that charge without regard to wealth, birth, or other accidental condition or circumstance.—DIFFUSION OF KNOWLEDGE BILL. FORD ED., ii, 221. (1779.)

3436. GENIUS, Higher.—Though * * * I am duly impressed with a sense of the arduousness of government, and the obligation those are under who are able to conduct it, yet I am also satisfied there is an order of geniuses above that obligation, and, therefore, exempted from it. Nobody can conceive that nature ever intended to throw away a Newton upon the occupations of a crown. * * * Cooperating with nature in her ordinary economy, we should dispose of and employ the geniuses of men according to their several orders and degrees.—To DAVID RITTENHOUSE. FORD ED., ii, 163. (M., 1778.)

3437. GEOGRAPHICAL LINES, Divisions on.—A geographical division * * * is a most fatal of all divisions, as no authority will submit to be governed by a majority acting merely on a geographical principle.—To SAMUEL H. SMITH. FORD ED., x, 191. (M., 1821.) See MISSOURI.

3438. GEORGE III., Appeal to.—No longer persevere in sacrificing the rights of one part of the empire to the inordinate desires of the other; but deal out to all equal and impartial right. Let no act be passed by any one legislature, which may infringe on the rights and liberties of another. This is the important post in which fortune has placed you, holding the balance of a great, if a well-poised empire. This, Sire, is the advice of your great American council, on the observance of which may perhaps depend your felicity and future fame, and the preservation of that harmony which alone can continue, both to Great Britain and America, the reciprocal advantages of their connection. It is neither our wish nor our interest to separate from her. We are willing, on our part, to sacrifice everything which reason can ask to the restoration of that tranquillity for which all most wish. On their part, let them be ready to establish union on a generous plan. Let them name their terms, but let them be just. * * * The God who gave us life, gave us liberty at the same time: the hand of force may destroy but cannot disjoin them. This, Sire, is our last, our determined resolution. And that you will be pleased to interpose with that efficacy which your earnest endeavors may insure to procure redress of these our great grievances, to quiet the minds of your subjects in British America against any apprehensions of future encroachment, to establish fraternal love and harmony through the whole empire, and that that may continue to the latest ages of time, is the fervent prayer of all British America.—RIGHTS OF BRITISH AMERICA. i, 141. FORD ED., i, 446. (1774.)

3439. GEORGE III., Bitterness of.—His obstinacy of character we know; his hostility we have known, and it is embittered by ill success. If ever this nation, during his life, enter into arrangements with us, it must be in consequence of events of which they do not at present see a possibility.—To RICHARD HENRY LEE. i, 541. FORD ED., iv, 207. (L., 1786.)

3440. GEORGE III., Control of.—His [George III.] minister is able, and that satisfies me that ignorance or wickedness, somewhere, controls him [the King].*—To JOHN RANDOLPH. i, 203. FORD ED., i, 493. (Pa., 1775.)

3441. GEORGE III., Deposed.—Be it enacted by the authority of the people that George —— Guelf be, and he hereby is, deposed from the kingly office within this government [of Virginia], and absolutely divested of all its rights, powers, and prerogatives: and that he and his descendants and all persons acting by or through him, and all other persons whatsoever shall be, and forever remain, incapable of the same: and that the said office shall henceforth cease and never more, either in name or substance, be reestablished within this Colony.—PROPOSED VIRGINIA CONSTITUTION. FORD ED., ii, 12. (June 1776.)

3442. —— ——. George Guelf has forfeited the kingly office, and has rendered it necessary for the preservation of the people that he should be immediately deposed from the same, and divested of all its privileges, powers and prerogatives.—PROPOSED VIRGINIA CONSTITUTION. FORD ED., ii, 12. (June 1776.)

3443. GEORGE III., Early reign of.— The following is an epitome of the first sixteen years of his reign: The Colonies were taxed internally and externally; their essential interests sacrificed to individuals in Great Britain: their legislatures suspended; charters annulled;

* Parton in his *Life of Jefferson*, p. 180, says: "This remark is interesting, as showing that Jefferson, at a time when the fact was not generally known, felt that a man of the calibre of Lord North was out of place in the cabinet of George III., and did not in his heart approve the King's policy."—EDITOR.

trials by jury taken away; their persons subjected to transportation across the Atlantic, and to trial before foreign judicatories; their supplications for redress thought beneath answer; themselves published as cowards in the councils of their mother country and courts of Europe; armed troops sent among them to enforce submission to these violences; and actual hostilities commenced against them. No alternative was presented but resistance, or unconditional submission. Between these could be no hesitation. They closed in the appeal to arms. They declared themselves independent States. They confederated together into one great republic; thus securing to every State the benefit of an union of their whole force.—NOTES ON VIRGINIA. viii, 358. FORD ED., iii, 221. (1782.)

3444. GEORGE III., History and.—
Open your breast, Sire, to liberal and expanded thought. Let not the name of George the Third be a blot on the page of history.—RIGHTS OF BRITISH AMERICA. i, 141. FORD ED., i, 446. (1774.)

3445. GEORGE III., Injuries and usurpations.—The history of the present King of Great Britain is a history of [unremitting]* injuries and usurpations [among which appears no solitary fact to contradict the uniform tenor of the rest, but all have] in direct object the establishment of an absolute tyranny over these States. To prove this, let facts be submitted to a candid world [for the truth of which we pledge a faith yet unsullied by falsehood].—DECLARATION OF INDEPENDENCE AS DRAWN BY JEFFERSON.

3446. GEORGE III., Lunacy.—The lunacy of the King of England is a decided fact, notwithstanding all the stuff the English papers publish about his fevers, delirium, &c. The truth is that the lunacy declared itself almost at once, and with as few concomitant complaints as usually attend the first development of that disorder.—To GENERAL WASHINGTON. ii, 534. (P., Dec. 1788.)

3447. GEORGE III., Ministers of.—You are surrounded by British counsellors, but remember that they are parties. You have no ministers for American affairs, because you have none taken from among us, nor amenable to the laws on which they are to give you advice. It behooves you, therefore, to think and to act for yourself and your people.—RIGHTS OF BRITISH AMERICA. i, 141. FORD ED., i, 446. (1774.)

3448. GEORGE III., Our bitterest enemy.—It is an immense misfortune to the whole empire, to have a King of such a disposition at such a time. We are told, and everything proves it true, that he is the bitterest enemy we have. His minister is able, and that satisfies me that ignorance or wickedness, somewhere, controls him. In an earlier part of this contest, our petitions told him, that from our King there was but one appeal. The admonition was despised, and that appeal forced on us. To undo his empire, he has but one truth more to learn; that, after the Colonies have drawn the sword, there is but one step more they can take. That step is now pressed upon us, by the measures adopted, as if they were afraid we would not take it.—To JOHN RANDOLPH. i, 203. FORD ED., i, 492. (Pa., November 1775.)

* Congress struck out the words in brackets and substituted " repeated " for " unremitting", and "having " for " have".—EDITOR.

3449. GEORGE III., Perversity of.—Our friend George is rather remarkable for doing exactly what he ought not to do.—To DR. RAMSAY. ii, 217. (P., 1787.)

3450. ——— ———. Has there been a better rule of prognosticating what he would do than to examine what he ought not to do?—To JOHN JAY. ii, 291. (P., 1787.)

3451. GEORGE III., Policy of.—I am pleased to see the answer of the King. It bears the marks of suddenness and surprise, and as he seems not to have had time for reflection, we may suppose he was obliged to find his answer in the real sentiments of his heart, if that heart has any sentiment. I have no doubt, however, that it contains the real creed of an Englishman, and that the word which he has let escape, is the true word of the enigma. " The moment I see such sentiments as yours prevail, and a disposition to give this country the *preference,* I will, &c." All this I steadily believe. But the condition is impossible. Our interest calls for a perfect equality in our conduct towards these two nations; but no preference anywhere. If, however, circumstances should ever oblige us to show a preference, a respect for our character, if we had no better motive, would decide to which it should be given.—To JOHN ADAMS. i, 436. (P., September 1785.)

3452. GEORGE III., Ruinous rule of.—It is a subject of deep regret to see a great nation reduced from an unexampled height of prosperity to an abyss of ruin, by the long-continued rule of a single chief.—To MR. RODMAN. vi, 54. (M., April 1812.)

3453. GEORGE III., Rumored death of.—We have a rumor that the King of England is dead. As this would ensure a general peace, I do not know that it would be any misfortune to humanity.—To HARRY INNES. iv, 315. FORD ED., vii, 412. (Pa., Jan. 1800.)

3454. GEORGE III., Services to America.—We have a blind story here [Paris] of somebody attempting to assassinate your* King. No man upon earth has my prayers for his continuance in life more sincerely than he. He is truly the American Messias, the most precious life that ever God gave. And may God continue it. Twenty long years has he been laboring to drive us to our good, and he labors and will labor still for it, if he can be spared. We shall have need of him for twenty more. The Prince of Wales on the throne. Lansdowne and Fox in the ministry and we are undone! We become chained by our habits to the tails of those who hate and despise us. I repeat it, then, that my anxieties are all alive for the health and long life of the King. He has not a friend on earth who would lament his loss as much and so long as I should.—To MRS. JOHN ADAMS. FORD ED., iv, 261. (P., 1786.)

3455. GEORGE III., Tyranny of.—He [George III.] has endeavored to pervert the exercise of the Kingly office in Virginia into a detestable and insupportable tyranny * * * by abandoning the helm of government and declaring us out of his allegiance and protection.—PROPOSED VIRGINIA CONSTITUTION. FORD ED., ii, 12. (June 1776.)

3456. GEORGE III., Unfit to rule.—A prince whose character is thus marked by every act which may define a tyrant, is unfit to be the ruler of a people who mean to be

* Mrs. Adams was then living in London.—EDITOR.

free. Future ages will scarcely believe that the hardiness of one man adventured within the short compass of twelve years only, to lay a foundation, so broad and undisguised for tyranny over a people fostered and fixed in principles of freedom.*—DECLARATION OF INDEPENDENCE AS DRAWN BY JEFFERSON.

3457. GEORGE IV., Character of.—As the character of the Prince of Wales is becoming interesting, I have endeavored to learn what it truly is. This is less difficult in his case than in that of other persons of rank, because he has taken no pains to hide himself from the world. * * * The total of his education was the learning a little Latin, but he speaks French without the slightest foreign accent, from the circumstance that, when very young, his father had put only French servants about him. He has not a single element of mathematics, of natural or moral philosophy, or of any other science on earth, nor has the society he has kept been such as to supply the void of education. It has been of the lowest, the most illiterate and profligate persons of the Kingdom, without choice of rank or mind, and with whom the subjects of conversation are only horses, drinking-matches, bawdy houses, and in terms the most vulgar. The young nobility, who begin by associating with him, soon leave him, disgusted with the insupportable profligacy of his society; and Mr. Fox, who has been supposed his favorite, and not over-nice in the choice of company, would never keep him company habitually. In fact, he never associated with a man of sense. He has not a single idea of justice, morality, religion, or of the rights of men, or any anxiety for the opinion of the world. He carries that indifference for fame so far, that he would probably be hurt were he to lose his throne, provided he could be assured of having always meat, drink, horses and women. * * * He had a fine person, but it is becoming coarse. He possesses good native common sense, is affable, polite and very good-humored. * * * The Duke of York, who was for some time cried up as the prodigy of the family, is as profligate, and of less understanding.—To JOHN JAY. ii, 559. FORD ED., v, 60. (P., 1789.)

3458. GEOLOGY, Imperfect knowledge of.—I have not much indulged myself in geological inquiries, from a belief that the skin-deep scratches which we can make or find on the surface of the earth, do not repay our time with as certain and useful deductions as our pursuits in some other branches.—To C. F. VOLNEY. iv, 569. (W., 1805.)

3459. ——— ———. I could not offer myself as geological correspondent in this State, because of all the branches of science it was the one I had the least cultivated. Our researches into the texture of our globe could be but so superficial, compared with its vast interior construction, that I saw no safety of conclusion from the one, as to the other; and therefore have pointed my own attentions to other objects in preference, as far as a heavy load of business would permit me to attend to anything else.—To THOMAS COOPER. v, 531. (M., 1810.)

3460. GEOLOGY, Limited usefulness.—To learn * * * the ordinary arrangement of the different strata of minerals in the earth,

* The first sentence was changed so as to read, "A prince whose character is thus marked by every act which may define a tyrant, is unfit to be the ruler of a free people", and the second one was struck out.—EDITOR.

to know from their habitual collocations and proximities where we find one mineral; whether another, for which we are seeking, may be expected to be in its neighborhood, is useful. But the dreams about the modes of creation, inquiries whether our globe has been formed by the agency of fire or water, how many millions of years it has cost Vulcan or Neptune to produce what the fiat of the Creator would effect by a single act of will, is too idle to be worth a single hour of any man's life.—To DR. JOHN P. EMMETT. vii, 443. (M., 1826.)

3461. GEOLOGY, Man's reason defied.—The several instances of trees, &c., found far below the surface of the earth * * * seem to set the reason of man at defiance.—To JAMES MADISON. ii, 67. FORD ED., iv, 335. (P., 1786.)

3462. GEOLOGY, Theories of.—With respect to the inclination of the strata of rocks, I had observed them between the Blue Ridge and North Mountains in Virginia, to be parallel with the pole of the earth. I observed the same thing in most instances in the Alps, between Cette and Turin; but in returning along the precipices of the Apennines, where they hang over the Mediterranean, their direction was totally different and various. You mention that in our Western country they are horizontal. This variety proves they have not been formed by subsidence, as some writers of the theories of the earth have pretended; for then they should always have been in circular strata, and concentric. It proves, too, that they have not been formed by the rotation of the earth on its axis, as it might have been suspected, had all these strata been parallel with that axis. They may, indeed, have been thrown up by explosions, as Whitehurst supposes, or have been the effect of convulsions. But there can be no proof of the explosion, nor is it probable that convulsions have deformed every spot of the earth. It is now generally agreed that rock grows, and it seems that it grows in layers in every direction, as the branches of trees grow in all directions. Why seek further the solution of this phenomenon? Everything in nature decays. If it were not reproduced then by growth there should be a chasm.—To CHARLES THOMSON. ii, 276. FORD ED., iv, 448. (P., 1787.)

3463. GERRY (Elbridge), Federalist hatred of.—As soon as it was known that you had consented to stay in Paris, there was no measure observed in the execrations of the war party. They openly wished you might be guillotined, or sent to Cayenne, or anything else.—To ELBRIDGE GERRY. iv, 273. FORD ED., vii, 335. (Pa., Jan. 1799.)

3464. ——— ———. The people will support you, notwithstanding the howlings of the ravenous crew from whose jaws they are escaping. —To ELBRIDGE GERRY. iv, 390. FORD ED., viii, 41. (W., March 1801.)

3465. GERRY (Elbridge), French negotiations.—You suppose that you have been abused by both parties. As far as has come to my knowledge, you are misinformed. I have never seen or heard a sentence of blame uttered against you by the republicans; unless we were so to construe their wishes that you had more boldly cooperated in a project of a treaty, and would more explicitly state, whether there was in your colleagues [Marshall and Pinckney] that flexibility, which persons earnest after peace would have practiced? Whether, on the contrary, their demeanor was not cold, reserved, and distant, at least, if not backward? And whether, if they had yielded to those informal conferences which Talleyrand seems to have courted, the liberal accommodation you suppose might not have been effected, even with their agency? Your fellow citizens think they have a right to full information in a case of such great concernment to them. It is their sweat which is to earn all the expenses of the war, and their blood which is to flow in expiation of the causes of it. It may be in your power to save them from these miseries by full communications and unrestrained details, postponing motives of delicacy to those of duty. It rests with you to come forward independently; to make your stand on the high ground of your own character; to disregard calumny, and to be borne above it on the shoulders of your grateful fellow citizens; or to sink into the humble oblivion, to which the federalists (self-called) have secretly condemned you; and even to be happy if they will indulge your oblivion, while they have beamed on your colleagues meridian splendor.—To ELBRIDGE GERRY. iv, 272. FORD ED., vii, 333. (Pa., Jan. 1799.)

3466. GERRY (Elbridge), Vice-Presidency.—The resolution of the republicans of Connecticut to propose you as Vice-President, * * * is a stamp of double proof. It is an indication to the factionaries that their nay is the yea of truth and its best test.—To ELBRIDGE GERRY. vi, 64. FORD ED., ix, 361. (M., 1812.)

3467. GILES (William B.), Hamilton resolutions.—Mr. Giles and one or two others were sanguine enough to believe that the palpableness of these resolutions rendered it impossible the House could reject them. Those who knew the composition of the House, 1, of bank directors; 2, holders of bank stock; 3, stock jobbers; 4, blind devotees; 5, ignorant persons who did not comprehend them; 6, lazy and good-humored persons, who comprehended and acknowledged them, yet were too lazy to examine, or unwilling to pronounce censure. The persons who knew these characters, foresaw that the three first descriptions making one-third of the House, the three latter would make one-half of the residue; and, of course, that they would be rejected by a majority of two to one. But they thought that even this rejection would do good, by showing the public the desperate and abandoned dispositions with which their affairs were conducted. The resolutions were proposed, and nothing spared to present them in the fulness of demonstration. There were not more than three or four who voted otherwise than had been expected.*—THE ANAS. ix, 139. FORD ED., i, 222. (March 1793.)

3468. GLORY, Undying.—The road to that glory which never dies is to use power for the support of the laws and liberties of our country, not for their destruction.—To EARL OF BUCHAN. iv, 494. (W., 1803.)

3469. GOD, Gifts of.—The God who gave us life gave us liberty at the same time.—RIGHTS OF BRITISH AMERICA. i, 142. FORD ED., i, 447. (1774.) See DEITY and PROVIDENCE.

— GOLD.—See DOLLAR and MONEY.

* The resolutions, moved in the House of Representatives on February 28th, against Hamilton. They were negatived by a majority ranging between 40 to 33, to a minority varying from 15 to 7.—NOTE IN FORD EDITION.

3470. GOODRICH (Elizur), Removal of.—There is one [case] in your State [Connecticut] which calls for decision, and on which Judge Lincoln will ask yourself and some others to consult and advise us. It is the case of Mr. Goodrich, whose being a recent appointment, made a few days only before Mr. Adams went out of office, is liable to the general nullification I affix to them. Yet, there might be reason for continuing him; or if that would do more harm than good, we should enquire who is the person in the State who, superseding Mr. Goodrich, would from his character and standing in society, most effectually silence clamor, and justify the Executive in a comparison of the two characters. For though I consider Mr. Goodrich's appointment as a nullity in effect, yet others may view it as a possession and removal, and ask if that removal has been made to put in a better man? I pray you to take a broad view of this subject, consider it in all its bearings, local and general, and communicate to me your opinion.—To GIDEON GRANGER. FORD ED., viii, 44. (W., March 1801.) See BISHOP.

3471. GOVERNMENT, Abdication.—He has abdicated government here, *withdrawing his governors, and declaring us out of his allegiance and* protection.*—DECLARATION OF INDEPENDENCE AS DRAWN BY JEFFERSON.

3472. GOVERNMENT, Abolition of destructive.—We hold these truths to be self evident: that all men are created equal; that they are endowed by their Creator with inherent and† inalienable rights; that among these are life, liberty, and the pursuit of happiness; that to secure these rights, governments are instituted among men, deriving their just powers from the consent of the governed; that whenever any form of government becomes destructive of these ends, it is the right of the people to alter or to abolish it, and to institute new government, laying its foundation on such principles, and organizing its powers in such form, as to them shall seem most likely to effect their safety and happiness.—DECLARATION OF INDEPENDENCE AS DRAWN BY JEFFERSON.

3473. GOVERNMENT, Altering.—The proposition [of Lord North] is altogether unsatisfactory * * * because it does not propose to repeal the * * * acts of Parliament altering the form of government of the Eastern Colonies.—REPLY TO LORD NORTH'S PROPOSITION. FORD ED., i, 480. (July 1775.)

3474. ———. He has combined, with others, * * * for altering, fundamentally, the forms of our governments.—DECLARATION OF INDEPENDENCE AS DRAWN BY JEFFERSON.

— GOVERNMENT, Ancient.—See ARISTOTLE.

3475. GOVERNMENT, Arbitrary.—He has combined, with others, * * * for abolishing the free system of English laws in a neighboring Province, establishing therein an arbitrary government, and enlarging its

* Congress struck out the words in italics, and inserted " by declaring us out of his protection, and waging war against us."—EDITOR.
† The words " inherent and " were struck out by Congress and the word " certain " was inserted—EDITOR.

boundaries, so as to render it at once an example and fit instrument for introducing the same absolute rule into these States.*— DECLARATION OF INDEPENDENCE AS DRAWN BY JEFFERSON.

3476. GOVERNMENT, Art of.—The whole art of government consists in the art of being honest.—RIGHTS OF BRITISH AMERICA. i, 141. FORD ED., i, 446. (1774.)

3477. GOVERNMENT, Censors.—No government ought to be without censors; and where the press is free, no one ever will.— To PRESIDENT WASHINGTON. iii, 467. FORD ED., vi, 108. (M., 1792.)

3478. —— ——. If virtuous, the government need not fear the fair operation of attack and defence. Nature has given to man no other means of sifting out the truth, either in religion, law, or politics.—To PRESIDENT WASHINGTON. iii, 467. FORD ED., vi, 108. (M., 1792.)

3479. —— ——. I think it is as honorable to the government neither to know, nor notice, its sycophants or censors, as it would be undignified and criminal to pamper the former and persecute the latter.—To PRESIDENT WASHINGTON. iii, 467. FORD ED., vi, 108. (M., 1792.)

— GOVERNMENT, Centralization.—See CENTRALIZATION.

3480. GOVERNMENT, Changing.—Prudence, indeed, will dictate that governments long established, should not be changed for light and transient causes; and, accordingly, all experience hath shown, that mankind are more disposed to suffer, while evils are sufferable, than to right themselves by abolishing the forms to which they are accustomed.— DECLARATION OF INDEPENDENCE AS DRAWN BY JEFFERSON.

3481. GOVERNMENT, Consent of governed.—Governments derive† their just powers from the consent of the governed.—DECLARATION OF INDEPENDENCE AS DRAWN BY JEFFERSON.

3482. —— ——. He has kept among us in times of peace standing armies and ships of war without the consent of our Legislatures.—DECLARATION OF INDEPENDENCE AS DRAWN BY JEFFERSON.

3483. —— ——. Civil government being the sole object of forming societies, its administration must be conducted by common consent.—NOTES ON VIRGINIA. viii, 331. FORD ED., iii, 189. (1782.)

3484. —— ——. The General Assembly of Virginia, at their session in 1785, passed an act declaring that the district, called Kentucky shall be a separate and independent State, on these conditions. 1. That the people of that district shall consent to it.—To M. DE MEUNIER. ix, 258. FORD ED., iv, 162. (P., 1786.)

* Congress inserted "Colonies" instead of "States".—EDITOR.
† "Deriving" in the Declaration.—EDITOR

3485. —— ——. [We] first in modern times [took] the ground of government founded on the will of the people.—To GOUVERNEUR MORRIS. iii, 325. FORD ED., v, 428. (Pa., 1792.)

3486. —— ——. I do not indeed wish to see any nation have a form of government forced on them; but if it is to be done, I should rejoice at its being a freer one.—To PEREGRINE FITZHUGH. iv, 218. FORD ED., vii, 211. (Pa., 1798.)

3487. —— ——. The will of the people is the only legitimate foundation of any government.—To BENJAMIN WARING. iv, 379. (W., March 1801.)

3488. —— ——. There is only one passage in President Monroe's message which I disapprove, and which I trust will not be approved by our Legislature. It is that which proposes to subject the Indians to our laws without their consent. A little patience and a little money are so rapidly producing their voluntary removal across the Mississippi, that I hope this immorality will not be permitted to stain our history. He has certainly been surprised into this proposition, so little in concord with our principles of government.— To ALBERT GALLATIN. FORD ED., x, 115. (M., Nov. 1818.)

3489. —— ——. The will [of the nation is] the only legitimate basis [of government]. —To ——. vii, 414. (M., 1825.)

3490. GOVERNMENT, Control of.— Unless the mass retains sufficient control over those entrusted with the powers of their government, these will be perverted to their own oppression, and to the perpetuation of wealth and power in the individuals and their families selected for the trust. Whether our Constitution has hit on the exact degree of control necessary, is yet under experiment; and it is a most encouraging reflection that distance and other difficulties securing us against the brigand governments of Europe, in the safe enjoyment of our farms and firesides, the experiment stands a better chance of being satisfactorily made here than on any occasion yet presented by history.—To M. VAN DER KEMP. vi, 45. (M., 1812.)

3491. GOVERNMENT, Corruption and. —In every government on earth is some trace of human weakness, some germ of corruption and degeneracy, which cunning will discover, and wickedness insensibly open, cultivate and improve.—NOTES ON VIRGINIA. viii, 390. FORD ED., iii, 254. (1782.)

3492. GOVERNMENT, De Facto.—There are *some matters* which, I conceive, might be transacted with a government *de facto;* such, for instance, as the reforming the unfriendly restrictions on our commerce and navigation. —To GOUVERNEUR MORRIS. iii, 489. FORD ED., vi, 131. (Pa., Nov. 1792.)

3493. GOVERNMENT, Despotic.—All the powers of government, legislative, executive and judiciary, result to the legislative body [under the first Virginia Constitution]. The concentrating these in the same hands is precisely the definition of despotic government. It will be no alleviation that these powers will be exercised by a plurality of hands, and not by a single one. One hundred and seventy-three despots would surely be as oppressive as one. Let those who doubt it turn their eyes on the Republic of Venice.—NOTES ON VIRGINIA. viii, 361. FORD ED., iii, 223. (1782.)

3494. ——— ———. I think the government in France is a pure despotism in theory, but moderated in practice by the respect which the public opinion commands. But the nation repeats, after Montesquieu, that the different bodies of magistracy, of priests and nobles, are barriers between the King and the people. It would be easy to prove that these barriers can only appeal to public opinion, and that neither these bodies, nor the people, can oppose any legal check to the will of the monarch.—To MR. CUTTING. ii, 438. (P., 1788.)

3495. GOVERNMENT, Elective.—Elective government is * * * the best permanent corrective of the errors or abuses of those entrusted with power.—REPLY TO ADDRESS. iv, 387. (W., March 1801.)

3496. GOVERNMENT, Energetic.—American reputation in Europe is not such as to be flattering to its citizens. Two circumstances are particularly objected to us,—the non-payment of our debts and the want of energy in our government. These discourage a connection with us.—To ARCHIBALD STUART. i, 518. FORD ED., iv, 188. (P., 1786.)

3497. ——— ———. I am not a friend to a very energetic government. It is always oppressive.—To JAMES MADISON. ii, 331. FORD ED., iv, 479. (P., 1787.)

3498. ——— ———. A free government is of all others the most energetic.—To JOHN DICKINSON. iv, 366. FORD ED., viii, 8. (W., March 1801.)

3499. ——— ———. The energy of the government depends mainly on the confidence of the people in the Chief Magistrate.—To DR. HORATIO TURPIN. v, 90. (W., 1807.)

— GOVERNMENT, English.—See ENGLAND.

3500. GOVERNMENT, Experiments in.—This I hope will be the age of experiments in government, and that their basis will be founded in principles of honesty, not of mere force. We have seen no instance of this since the days of the Roman Republic, nor do we read of any before that.—To JOHN ADAMS. FORD ED., vii, 56. (M., 1796.)

— GOVERNMENT, Extensive territory and.—See TERRITORY.

3501. GOVERNMENT, Extremes of.—We are now vibrating between too much and too little government, and the pendulum will rest finally in the middle.—To WILLIAM STEPHENS SMITH. FORD ED., v, 3. (P., 1788.)

3502. GOVERNMENT, Fallibility.—Was the government to prescribe to us our medicine and diet, our bodies would be in such keeping as our souls are now. Thus in France the emetic was once forbidden as a medicine, and the potato as an article of food. Government is just as infallible, too, when it fixes systems in physics. Galileo was sent to the Inquisition for affirming that the earth was a sphere; the government had declared it to be as flat as a trencher, and Galileo was obliged to abjure his error. This error, however, at length prevailed, the earth became a globe, and Descartes declared it was whirled round its axes by a vortex. The government in which he lived was wise enough to see that this was no question of civil jurisdiction, or we should all have been involved by authority in vortices. In fact, vortices have been exploded, and the Newtonian principle of gravitation is now more firmly established, on the basis of reason, than it would be were the government to step in, and to make it an article of necessary faith. Reason and experiment have been indulged, and error has fled before them. It is error alone which needs the support of government. Truth can stand by itself.—NOTES ON VIRGINIA. viii, 400. FORD ED., iii, 264. (1782.)

3503. GOVERNMENT, Fear and.—No government can be maintained without the principle of fear as well as of duty. Good men will obey the last, but bad ones the former only. If our government ever fails it will be from this weakness.—To J. W. EPPES. FORD ED., ix, 484. (M., 1814.)

— GOVERNMENT, The federal.—See FEDERAL GOVERNMENT.

3504. GOVERNMENT, Field for.—Never was a finer canvas presented to work on than our countrymen. All of them engaged in agriculture, or in the pursuits of honest industry, independent in their circumstances, enlightened as to their rights, and firm in their habits of order and obedience to the laws.—To JOHN ADAMS. FORD ED., vii, 56. (M., 1796.)

3505. GOVERNMENT, Forms of.—Societies exist under three forms, sufficiently distinguishable. 1. Without government, as among our Indians. 2. Under governments, wherein the will of every one has a just influence; as is the case in England, in a slight degree, and in our States, in a great one. 3. Under governments of force; as is the case in all other monarchies, and in most of the other republics. To have an idea of the curse of existence under these last, they must be seen. It is a government of wolves over sheep. It is a problem, not clear in my mind, that the first condition is not the best. But I believe it to be inconsistent with any great degree of population. The second state has a great deal of good in it. The mass of mankind under that, enjoys a precious degree of liberty and happiness. It has its evils, too; the principle of which is the turbulence to which it is subject. But weigh this against the oppressions of monarchy, and it becomes nothing. *Malo periculosam libertatem quam quietem servitutem.* Even this evil is productive of good. It prevents the degeneracy of government, and nourishes a general attention to the public affairs. I hold it that a little rebellion, now and then, is a good thing, and as necessary in the political world as storms are in the physical. Unsuccessful rebellions, indeed, generally establish the encroachments on the rights of the people, which have produced them. An observation of this truth should render honest republican governors so mild in their punishment of rebellions, as not to discourage them too much. It is a medicine necessary for the sound health of government.—To JAMES MADISON. ii, 105. FORD ED., iv, 362. (P., 1787.)

3506. GOVERNMENT, Foundation of. —The will of the people is the only legitimate foundation of any government, and to protect its free expression should be our first object.—To BENJAMIN WARING. iv, 379. (W., March 1801.)

3507. —— ——. The true foundation of republican government is the equal right of every citizen, in his person and property, and in their management.—To SAMUEL KERCHIVAL. vii, 11. FORD ED., x, 39. (M., 1816.)

3508. GOVERNMENT, Frugality.—I am for a government rigorously frugal.—To ELBRIDGE GERRY. iv, 268. FORD ED., vii, 327. (Pa., 1799.)

3509. GOVERNMENT, Good.—The first principle of a good government is certainly a distribution of its powers into executive, judiciary and legislative, and a subdivision of the latter into two or three branches.—To JOHN ADAMS. ii, 282. FORD ED., iv, 454. (P., 1787.)

3510. —— ——. A single good government is a blessing to the whole earth.—To GEORGE FLOWER. vii, 84. (P.F., 1817.)

3511. —— ——. No government can continue good, but under the control of the people.—To JOHN ADAMS. vii, 149. FORD ED., x, 153. (M., 1819.)

3512. GOVERNMENT, Harmony and.— It is for the happiness of those united in society to harmonize as much as possible in matters which they must of necessity transact together.—NOTES ON VIRGINIA. viii, 331. FORD ED., iii, 189. (1782.)

3513. GOVERNMENT, Hereditary branches of.—Experience has shown that the hereditary branches of modern governments are the patrons of privilege and prerogative, and not of the natural rights of the people. whose oppressors they generally are.—To GENERAL WASHINGTON. i, 335. FORD ED., iii, 467. (A., 1784.)

3514. —— ——. What a crowd of lessons do the present miseries of Holland teach us! Never to have an hereditary officer of any sort * * * .—To JOHN ADAMS. ii, 283. FORD ED., iv, 455. (P., 1787.)

3515. —— ——. Our young Republic * * * should guard against hereditary magistrates.—To DAVID HUMPHREYS. ii, 253. (P., 1787.)

3516. —— ——. We have chanced to live in an age which will probably be distinguished in history for its experiments in government on a larger scale than has yet taken place. But we shall not live to see the result. The grosser absurdities, such as hereditary magistracies, we shall see exploded in our day, long experience having already pronounced condemnation against them. But what is to be the substitute? This our children or grandchildren will answer. We may be satisfied with the certain knowledge that none can ever be tried, so stupid, so unrighteous, so oppressive, so destructive of every end for which honest men enter into government, as that which their forefathers had established. and their fathers alone venture to tumble headlong from the stations they have so long abused.—To M. D'IVERNOIS. iv, 115. FORD ED., vii, 5. (M., Feb. 1795.)

3517. —— ——. The principles of our Constitution are wisely opposed * * * to every practice which may lead to hereditary establishments.—REPLY TO ADDRESS. v, 473. (M., 1809.)

3518. —— ——. Hereditary authorities always consume the public contributions, and oppress the people with labor and poverty.— To DAVID HOWELL. v, 554. (M., 1810.)

3519. —— ——. Hereditary bodies, always existing, always on the watch for their own aggrandizement, profit of every opportunity of advancing the privileges of their order, and encroaching on the rights of the people.—To M. CORAY. vii, 319. (M., 1823.)

3520. GOVERNMENT, Inattention to. —If once the people become inattentive to the public affairs, you and I, and Congress and Assemblies, Judges and Governors. shall all become wolves. It seems to be the law of our general nature. in spite of individual exceptions; and experience declares that man is the only animal which devours his own kind; for I can apply no milder term to the governments of Europe, and to the general prey of the rich on the poor.—To EDWARD CARRINGTON. ii, 100. FORD ED., iv, 360. (P., 1787.)

3521. GOVERNMENT, Liberty and.— The natural progress of things is for liberty to yield and government to gain ground.—To E. CARRINGTON. ii, 404. FORD ED., v, 20. (P., 1788.)

3522. GOVERNMENT, Monarchical.— Blessed effect of a kingly government, where a pretended insult to the sister of a king, is to produce the wanton sacrifice of a hundred or two thousand of the people who have entrusted themselves to his government, and as many of his enemies! And we think ours a bad government.—To Governor Rutledge. ii, 234. (P., 1787.)

3523. —— ——. It is a government of wolves over sheep.—To James Madison. ii, 105. Ford ed., iv, 362. (P., 1787.)

3524. GOVERNMENT, Moral principles.—If ever the morals of a people could be made the basis of their own government, it is our case; and who could propose to govern such a people by the corruption of a Legislature, before he could have one night of quiet sleep, must convince himself that the human soul, as well as body, is mortal.—To John Adams. Ford ed., vii, 57. (M., 1796.)

3525. —— ——. When we come to the moral principles on which the government is to be administered, we come to what is proper for all conditions of society. I meet you there in all the benevolence and rectitude of your native character; and I love myself always most where I concur most with you. Liberty, truth, probity, honor, are declared to be the four cardinal principles of your Society. I believe with you that morality, compassion, generosity, are innate elements of the human constitution; that there exists a right independent of force; that a right to property is founded in our natural wants, in the means with which we are endowed to satisfy these wants, and the right to what we acquire by those means without violating the similar rights of other sensible beings; that no one has a right to obstruct another, exercising his faculties innocently for the relief of sensibilities made a part of his nature; that justice is the fundamental law of society; that the majority, oppressing an individual, is guilty of a crime, abuses its strength, and by acting on the law of the strongest breaks up the foundations of society; that [action by the citizens in person, in affairs within their reach and competence, and in all others by representatives, chosen immediately, and removable by themselves, constitutes the essence of a republic;] that all governments are more or less republican in proportion as this principle enters more or less into their composition; and that a government by representation is capable of extension over a greater surface of country than one of any other form. These are the essentials in which you and I agree; however in our zeal for their maintenance, we may be perplexed and divaricate, as to the structure of society most likely to secure them. —To Dupont de Nemours. vi, 591. Ford ed., x, 24. (P.F., 1816.)

3526. GOVERNMENT, Objects of.—Persons and property make the sum of the objects of government.—To James Madison. iii, 106. Ford ed., v, 121. (P., 1789.) See Generations.

3527. —— ——. The care of human life and happiness, and not their destruction, is the first and only legitimate object of good government.—R. to A. Maryland Republicans. viii, 165. (1809.)

3528. —— ——. The freedom and happiness of man * * * are the sole objects of all legitimate government.—To General Kosciusko. v, 509. (M., 1810.)

3529. —— ——. The only orthodox object of the institution of government is to secure the greatest degree of happiness possible to the general mass of those associated under it.—To M. Van Der Kemp. vi, 45. (M., 1812.)

3530. —— ——. The equal rights of man, and the happiness of every individual are now acknowledged to be the only legitimate objects of government. Modern times have the signal advantage, too, of having discovered the only device by which these rights can be secured, to wit: government by the people, acting not in person, but by representatives chosen by themselves, that is to say, by every man of ripe years and sane mind, who either contributes by his purse or person to the support of his country.—To M. Coray. vii, 319. (M., 1823.)

3531. GOVERNMENT, Origin of.—There is an error into which most of the speculators on government have fallen, and which the well-known state of society of our Indians ought, before now, to have corrected. In their hypothesis of the origin of government they suppose it to have commenced in the patriarchal or monarchical form. Our Indians are evidently in that state of nature which has passed the association of a single family; and not yet submitted to the authority of positive laws, or of any acknowledged magistrate. Every man, with them, is perfectly free to follow his own inclinations. But if, in doing this, he violates the rights of another, if the case be slight, he is punished by the disesteem of his society, or, as we say, by public opinion; if serious, he is tomahawked as a dangerous enemy. Their leaders conduct them by the influence of their character only; and they follow, or not, as they please, him of whose character for wisdom or war they have the highest opinion. Hence the origin of the parties among them, adhering to different leaders, and governed by their advice, not by their command. The Cherokees, the only tribe I know to be contemplating the establishment of regular laws, magistrates, and government, propose a government of representatives, elected from every town. But, of all things, they least think of subjecting themselves to the will of one man. This, the only instance of actual fact within our knowledge, will be then a beginning by republican, and not by patriarchal or monarchical government, as speculative writers have generally conjectured.— To F. W. Gilmer. vii, 4. Ford ed., x, 32. (M., 1816.)

3532. GOVERNMENT, Participation in. —Those who bear equally the burdens of government should equally participate of its benefits.—Address to Lord Dunmore. Ford ed., i, 457. (1775.)

3533. —— ——. No Englishman will pretend that a right to participate in government can be derived from any other source than a personal right, or a right of property. The conclusion is inevitable that he, who had neither his *person* nor *property* in America, could rightfully assume a participation in its government.—NOTES ON M. SOULÉS'S WORK. ix, 299. FORD ED., iv, 306. (P., 1786.)

3534. GOVERNMENT, The people and. —Every government degenerates when trusted to the rulers of the people alone. The people themselves, therefore, are its only safe depositories. And to render even them safe, their minds must be improved to a certain degree.—NOTES ON VIRGINIA. viii, 390. FORD ED., iii, 254. (1782.)

3535. —— ——. The influence over government must be shared among all the people. If every individual which composes their mass participates of the ultimate authority, the government will be safe; because the corrupting the whole mass will exceed any private resources of wealth; and public ones cannot be provided but by levies on the people. In this case, every man would have to pay his own price. The government of Great Britain has been corrupted, because but one man in ten has a right to vote for members of Parliament. The sellers of the government, therefore, get nine-tenths of their price clear.—NOTES ON VIRGINIA. viii, 390. FORD ED., iii, 254. (1782.)

3536. —— ——. Were I called upon to decide whether the people had best be omitted in the Legislative or Judiciary department, I would say it is better to leave them out of the Legislative. The execution of the laws is more important than the making them. However, it is best to have the people in all the three departments, where that is possible.—TO M. L'ABBÉ ARNOND. iii, 82. FORD ED., v, 104. (P., 1789.)

3537. GOVERNMENT, Perversion.— [While] certain forms of government are better calculated than others to protect individuals in the free exercise of their natural rights, and are at the same time themselves better guarded against degeneracy, yet experience hath shown that, even under the best forms, those entrusted with power have, in time, and by slow operations, perverted it into tyranny.—DIFFUSION OF KNOWLEDGE BILL. FORD ED., ii, 220. (1779.)

3538. GOVERNMENT, Powers of.—The Legislative, Executive and Judiciary offices shall be kept forever separate; no person exercising the one shall be capable of appointment to the others, or to either of them.— PROPOSED VA. CONSTITUTION. FORD ED., ii, 13. (June 1776.)

3539. —— ——. The legitimate powers of government extend to such acts only as are injurious to others.—NOTES ON VIRGINIA. viii, 400. FORD ED., iii, 263. (1782.)

3540. —— ——. The powers of government shall be divided into three distinct departments, each of them to be confided to a separate body of magistracy; to wit, those which are legislative to one, those which are judiciary to another, and those which are executive to another. No person, or collection of persons, being of one of these departments, shall exercise any power properly belonging to either of the others, except in the instances hereinafter expressly permitted. —PROPOSED CONSTITUTION FOR VIRGINIA. viii, 442. FORD ED., iii, 322. (1783.)

3541. GOVERNMENT, Principles of modern.—Either force or corruption has been the principle of every modern government, unless the Dutch perhaps be excepted, and I am not well enough informed to accept them absolutely.—TO JOHN ADAMS. FORD ED., vii, 57. (1796.)

3542. GOVERNMENT, Public welfare and.—No government has a legitimate right to do what is not for the welfare of the governed.—TO PRESIDENT WASHINGTON. iii, 461. FORD ED., vi, 103. (M., 1792.)

3543. GOVERNMENT, Purchases by.— I do not know on what principles of reasoning it is that good men think the public ought to pay more for a thing than they would themselves if they wanted it.—TO HENRY DEARBORN. v, 293. (M., 1808.)

3544. GOVERNMENT, Purity.—A government regulating itself by what is wise and just for the many, uninfluenced by the local and selfish views of the few who direct their affairs, has not been seen, perhaps, on earth. Or if it existed, for a moment, at the birth of ours, it would not be easy to fix the term of its continuance. Still, I believe it does exist here in a greater degree than anywhere else; and for its growth and continuance, * * * I offer sincere prayers.—TO WILLIAM CRAWFORD. vii, 8. FORD ED., x, 36. (M., 1816.)

3545. GOVERNMENT, Recognition of. —With what kind of government [in France] may you do business? It accords with our principles to acknowledge any government to be rightful, which is formed by the will of the nation substantially declared. The late government was of this kind, and was accordingly acknowledged by all the branches of ours. So, any alteration of it which shall be made by the will of the nation substantially declared, will doubtless be acknowledged in like manner. With such a government *every kind* of business may be done.—TO GOUVERNEUR MORRIS. iii, 489. FORD ED., vi, 131. (Pa., Nov. 1792.)

3546. —— ——. You express a wish * * * to be generally advised as to the tenor of your conduct in consequence of the late revolution in France. * * * We certainly cannot deny to other nations that principle whereon our government is founded, that every nation has a right to govern itself internally under what forms it pleases, and to change these forms at its own will; and externally to transact business with other nations through whatever organ it chooses, whether that be a king, convention, assembly, committee, president, or whatever it be. The only thing essential is, the will of the nation. Taking this as your polar star, you can hardly err.—To THOMAS PINCKNEY. iii, 500. (Pa., Dec. 1792.)

3547. —— ——. I am apprehensive that your situation must have been difficult during the transition from the late form of government to the reestablishment of some other legitimate authority, and that you may have been at a loss to determine with whom business might be done. Nevertheless when principles are well understood their application is less embarrassing. We surely cannot deny to any nation that right whereon our own government is founded, that every one may govern itself under whatever forms it pleases, and change these forms at its own will; and that it may transact its business with foreign nations through whatever organ it thinks proper, whether king, convention, assembly, committee, president, or whatever else it may choose. The will of the nation is the only thing essential to be regarded.— To GOUVERNEUR MORRIS. FORD ED., vi, 149. (Pa., Dec. 1792.)

3548. —— ——. On the dissolution of the late constitution in France, by the removal of so integral a part of it as the King, the National Assembly, to whom a part only of the public authority had been delegated, sensible of the incompetence of their powers to transact the affairs of the nation legitimately, incited their fellow citizens to appoint a national convention during this defective state of the national authority. Duty to our constituents required that we should suspend payment of the moneys yet unpaid of our debt to that country, because there was no person, or persons, substantially authorized by the nation of France to receive the moneys and give us a good acquittal. On this ground my last letter desired you to suspend payments till further orders, with an assurance, if necessary, that the suspension should not be continued a moment longer than should be necessary for us to see the reestablishment of some person, or body of persons, with authority to receive and give us a good acquittal. Since that we learn that a convention is assembled, invested with full powers by the nation to transact its affairs. Though we know that from the public papers only, instead of waiting for a formal annunciation of it, we hasten to act upon it by authorizing you, if the fact be true, to consider the suspension of payment, * * * as now taken off, and to proceed as if it had never been imposed; considering the convention, or the government they shall have established, as the lawful representative of the nation, and authorized to act for them. Neither the honor nor inclination of our country would justify our withholding our payment under a scrupulous attention to forms. On the contrary, they lent us that money when we were under their circumstances, and it seems providential that we can

not only repay them the same sum, but under the same circumstances.—To GOUVERNEUR MORRIS. FORD ED., vi, 150. (Pa., Dec. 1792.)

3549. —— ——. I am sensible that your situation must have been difficult during the transition from the late form of government [in France] to the reestablishment of some other legitimate authority, and that you may have been at a loss to determine with whom business might be done. Nevertheless, when principles are well understood, their application is less embarrassing. We surely cannot deny to any nation that right whereon our own government is founded, that every one may govern itself according to whatever form it pleases, and change these forms at its own will; and that it may transact its business with foreign nations through whatever organ it thinks proper, whether king, convention, assembly, committee, president, or anything else it may choose. The will of the nation is the only thing essential to be regarded.—To GOUVERNEUR MORRIS. iii, 521. FORD ED., vi, 199. (Pa., Mar. 1793.)

3550. —— ——. If the nation of France shall ever reestablish such an officer as Regent (of which there is no appearance at present), I should be for receiving a minister from him; but I am not for doing it from any Regent, so christened, and set up by any other authority.—To PRESIDENT WASHINGTON. FORD ED., vi, 219. (Pa., April 1793.)

3551. GOVERNMENT, Representative. —A representative government, responsible at short periods of election, * * * produces the greatest sum of happiness to mankind.— R. TO A. VERMONT LEGISLATURE. viii, 121. (1807.)

3552. —— ——. A government by representation is capable of extension over a greater surface of country than one of any other form.—To DUPONT DE NEMOURS. vi, 591. FORD ED., x, 24. (P.F., 1816.)

3553. —— ——. The advantages of representative government exhibited in England and America, and recently in other countries will procure its establishment everywhere in a more or less perfect form; and this will insure the amelioration of the condition of the world. It will cost years of blood, and be well worth them.—To ALBERT GALLATIN. FORD ED., x, 262. (M., 1823.)

3554. GOVERNMENT, Republican.— The republican is the only form of government which is not eternally at open or secret war with the rights of mankind.—REPLY TO ADDRESS. iii, 128. FORD ED., v, 147. (1790.)

3555. —— ——. A just and solid republican government maintained here, will be a standing monument and example for the aim and imitation of the people of other countries.—To JOHN DICKINSON. iv, 366. FORD ED., viii, 8. (W., March 1801.)

3556. —— ——. Governments are more or less republican as they have more or less of the element of popular election and con trol in their composition.—To JOHN TAYLOR. vi, 608. FORD ED., x, 31. (M., 1816.)

3557. —— ——. Governments are republican only in proportion as they embody the will of the people and execute it.—To SAMUEL KERCHIVAL. vii, 9. FORD ED., x, 37. (M., 1816.)

3558. —— ——. A government is republican in proportion as every member composing it has his equal voice in the direction of its concerns (not indeed in person, which would be impracticable beyond the limits of a city, or small township, but) by representatives chosen by himself, and responsib'e to him at short periods.—To SAMUEL KERCHIVAL. vii, 10. FORD ED., x, 38. (M., 1816.)

3559. —— ——. It is a misnomer to call a government republican, in which a branch of the supreme power is independent of the nation.—To JAMES PLEASANTS. FORD ED., x, 199. (M., 1821.)

3560. GOVERNMENT, Rights and.— To secure these rights (life, liberty, and the pursuit of happiness), governments are instituted among men, deriving their just powers from the consent of the governed.— DECLARATION OF INDEPENDENCE AS DRAWN BY JEFFERSON.

3561. —— ——. It is to secure our rights that we resort to government at all.—To M. D'IVERNOIS. iv, 114. FORD ED., vii, 4. (M., Feb. 1795.)

3562. GOVERNMENT, Safety of.— I deem no government safe which is under the vassalage of any self-constituted authorities, or any other authority than that of the nation, or its regular functionaries.—To ALBERT GALLATIN. iv, 519. FORD ED., viii, 285. (W., 1803.)

3563. GOVERNMENT, Scandalizing.— Few think there is any immorality in scandalizing governments or ministers.—To MADAME NECKER. ii, 570. (P., 1789.)

3564. GOVERNMENT, Simplicity.— I am for a government rigorously frugal and simple.—To ELBRIDGE GERRY. iv, 268. FORD ED., vii, 327. (Pa., 1799.) See SIMPLICITY.

3565. GOVERNMENT, Strongest.— The government which can wield the arm of the people must be the strongest possible.—To MR. WEAVER. v, 89. (W., 1807.)

3566. —— ——. That government is the strongest of which every man feels himself a part.—To GOVERNOR H. D. TIFFIN. v, 38. FORD ED., ix, 21. (W., 1807.)

3567. GOVERNMENT, Suitability of.— The excellence of every government is its adaptation to the state of those to be governed by it.—To DUPONT DE NEMOURS. vi, 589. FORD ED., x, 22. (P.F., 1816.)

3568. —— ——. The laws which must effect [their happiness] must flow from their own habits, their own feelings, and the resources of their own minds. No stranger to these could possibly propose regulations adapted to them. Every people have their own particular habits, ways of thinking, manners, &c., which have grown up with them from their infancy, are become a part of their nature, and to which the regulations which are to make them happy must be accommodated. No member of a foreign country can have a sufficient sympathy with these. The institutions of Lycurgus, for example, would not have suited Athens, nor those of So'on, Lacedæmon. The organizations of Locke were impracticable for Carolina, and those of Rousseau and Mably for Poland. Turning inwardly on myself from these eminent illustrations of the truth of my observation, I feel all the presumption it would manifest, should I undertake to do what this respectable society is alone qualified to do suitably for itself.*—To WILLIAM LEE. vii, 56. (M., 1817.)

3569. —— ——. The forms of government adapted to the age [of the classical writers of Greece] and [their] country are [not] practicable or to be imitated in our day. * * * The circumstances of the world are too much changed for that. The government of Athens, for example, was that of the people of one city, making laws for the whole country subjected to them. That of Lacedæmon was the rule of military monks over the laboring class of the people, reduced to abject slavery. These are not the doctrines of the present age. The equal rights of man, and the happiness of every individual, are now acknowledged to be the only legitimate objects of government. Modern times have the signal advantage, too, of having discovered the only device by which these rights can be secured, to wit: government by the people, acting not in person, but by representatives chosen by themselves, that is to say, by every man of ripe years and sane mind, who either contributes by his purse or person to the support of his country.—To M. CORAY. vii, 318. (M., 1823.)

— GOVERNMENT, Territory and.— See TERRITORY.

3570. GOVERNMENT, Too much.— The only condition on earth to be compared with ours, in my opinion, is that of the Indian, where they have still less law than we.—To GOVERNOR RUTLEDGE. ii, 234. (P., 1787.)

3571. —— ——. I think, myself, that we have more machinery of government than is necessary, too many parasites living on the labor of the industrious. I believe it might be much simplified to the relief of those who maintain it.—To WILLIAM LUDLOW. vii, 378. (M., 1824.)

3572. GOVERNMENT, Usurpation of. —The government of a nation may be usurped by the forcible intrusion of an individual into

* In 1817, a French society, organized for the purpose of applying to Congress for a grant of two hundred and fifty thousand acres of land on the Tombigbee River, requested Jefferson " to trace for them the basis of a social pact for their local regulations ". He declined on the grounds set forth in the quotation.—EDITOR.

the throne. But to conquer its will, so as to rest the right on that, the only legitimate basis, requires long acquiescence and cessation of all opposition.—To ——. vii, 413. (M., 1825.)

3573. GOVERNMENT, Works on.—In political economy, I think SMITH's *Wealth of Nations* the best book extant.—To T. M. RANDOLPH. iii, 145. FORD ED., v, 173. (N.Y., 1790.)

3574. —— ——. Locke's little book on government is perfect as far as it goes.—To T. M. RANDOLPH. iii, 145. FORD ED., v, 173. (N. Y., 1790.)

3575. —— ——. Descending from theory to practice, there is no better book than the *Federalist.*—To T. M. RANDOLPH. iii, 145. FORD ED., v, 173. (N.Y., 1790.)

3576. —— ——. In the science of government, MONTESQUIEU's *Spirit of Laws* is generally recommended. It contains, indeed, a great number of political truths; but also an equal number of heresies; so that the reader must be constantly on his guard.—To T. M. RANDOLPH. iii, 145. FORD ED., v, 173. (N. Y., 1790.)

3577. —— ——. I think there does not exist a good elementary work on the organization of society into civil government; I mean a work which presents in one full and comprehensive view the system of principles on which such an organization should be founded, according to the rights of nature. For want of a single work of that character, I should recommend LOCKE on *Government,* SIDNEY, PRIESTLEY's *Essay on the First Principles of Government,* CHIPMAN's *Principles of Government,* and the *Federalist;* adding, perhaps, BECCARIA on *Crimes and Punishments,* because of the demonstrative manner in which he has treated that branch of the subject. If your views of political inquiry go further, to the subjects of money and commerce, SMITH's *Wealth of Nations* is the best book to be read, unless SAY's *Political Economy* can be had, which treats the same subjects on the same principles, but in a shorter compass and more lucid manner.—To JOHN NORVELL. v, 90. FORD ED., ix, 71. (W., 1807.) See ARISTOTLE.

3578. GOVERNMENTS (American), Blessed.—My God! how little do my countrymen know what precious blessings they are in possession of, and which no other people on earth enjoy.—To JAMES MONROE. i, 352. FORD ED., iv, 59. (1785.)

3579. GOVERNMENTS (American), Contented.—There are not, on the face of the earth, more tranquil governments than ours, nor a happier and more contented people.—To BARON GEISMER. i, 427. (P., 1785.)

3580. GOVERNMENTS (American), Energy of.—It has been said that our governments, both Federal and particular, want energy; that it is difficult to restrain both individuals and States from committing wrong. This is true, and it is an inconvenience. On the other hand, that energy which absolute governments derive from an armed force, which is the effect of the bayonet constantly held at the breast of every citizen, and which resembles very much the stillness of

the grave, must be admitted also to have its inconveniences. We weigh the two together, and like best to submit to the former. Compare the number of wrongs committed with impunity by citizens among us with those committed by the sovereign in other countries, and the last will be found most numerous, most oppressive on the mind, and most degrading of the dignity of man.—To M. DE MEUNIER. ix, 292. FORD ED., iv, 147. (P., 1786.)

3581. GOVERNMENTS (American), Happy.—With all its defects, and with all those of our particular governments, the inconveniences resulting from them are so slight in comparison with those existing in every other government on earth, that our citizens may certainly be considered as in the happiest political situation which exists.—To GENERAL WASHINGTON. ii, 250. (P., Aug. 1787.)

3582. —— ——. With all the defects of our constitutions, whether general or particular, the comparison of our governments with those of Europe, is like a comparison of heaven and hell. England, like the earth, may be allowed to take an intermediate station.—To JOSEPH JONES. ii, 249. FORD ED., iv, 438. (P., 1787.)

3583. GOVERNMENTS (American), People and.—We think in America that it is necessary to introduce the people into every department of government, as far as they are capable of exercising it; and that this is the only way to ensure a long-continued and honest administration of its powers. To M. L'ABBÉ ARNOND. iii, 81. FORD ED., v, 103. (P., 1789.)

3584. GOVERNMENTS (American), Powers.—An *elective despotism* was not the government we fought for, but one which should not only be founded on true free principles, but in which the powers of government should be so divided and balanced among general bodies of magistracy, as that no one could transcend their legal limits without being effectually checked and restrained by the others.—NOTES ON VIRGINIA. viii, 361. FORD ED., iii, 224. (1782.)

3585. GOVERNMENTS (American), Principles.—Every species of government has its specific principles. Ours perhaps are more peculiar than those of any in the universe. It is a composition of the freest principles of the English constitution, with others derived from natural right and natural reason. To these nothing can be more opposed than the maxims of absolute monarchies.—NOTES ON VIRGINIA. viii, 331. FORD ED., iii, 189. (1782.)

3586. —— ——. We, of the United States, are constitutionally and conscientiously democrats. We consider society as one of the natural wants with which man has been created; that he has been endowed with faculties and qualities to effect its satisfaction by concurrence of others having the same want; that when, b·· the exercise of these faculties, he has procur·

a state of society, it is one of his acquisitions which he has a right to regulate and control, jointly, indeed, with all those who have concurred in the procurement, whom he cannot exclude from its use or direction more than they him. We think experience has proved it safer, for the mass of individuals composing the society, to reserve to themselves personally the exercise of all rightful powers to which they are competent, and to delegate those to which they are not competent to deputies named, and removable for unfaithful conduct, by themselves immediately. Hence, with us, the people (by which is meant the mass of individuals composing the society), being competent to judge of the facts occurring in ordinary life, they have retained the functions of judges of facts, under the name of jurors; but being unqualified for the management of affairs requiring intelligence above the common level, yet competent judges of human character, they choose, for their management, representatives, some by themselves immediately, others by electors chosen by themselves. Thus our President is chosen by ourselves directly in *practice*, for we vote for A as elector only on the condition he will vote for B; our representatives by ourselves immediately; our Senate and judges of law through electors chosen by ourselves. And we believe that this proximate choice and power of removal is the best security which experience has sanctioned for ensuring an honest conduct in the functionaries of society. Your three or four alembications have indeed a seducing appearance. We should conceive, *primâ facie*, that the last extract would be the pure alcohol of the substance, three or four times rectified. But in proportion as they are more and more sublimated, they are also farther and farther removed from the control of the society; and the human character, we believe, requires in general constant and immediate control, to prevent its being biased from right by the seductions of self-love. Your process produces, therefore, a structure of government from which the fundamental principle of ours is excluded. You first set down as zeros all individuals not having lands, which are the greater number in every society of long standing. Those holding lands are permitted to manage in person the small affairs of their commune or corporation, and to elect a deputy for the canton; in which election, too, every one's vote is to be an unit, a plurality, or a fraction, in proportion to his landed possessions. The assemblies of cantons, then, elect for the districts; those of districts for circles; and those of circles for the national assemblies. Some of these highest councils, too, are in a considerable degree self-elected, the regency partially, the judiciary entirely, and some are for life. Whenever, therefore, an *esprit de corps*, or of party, gets possession of them, which experience shows to be inevitable, there are no means of breaking it up, for they will never elect but those of their own spirit. Juries are allowed in criminal cases only. I acknowledge myself strong in affection to our own form, yet both of us act and think from the same motive; we both consider the people as our children, and love them with parental affection. But you love them as infants whom you are afraid to trust without nurses; and I as adults whom I freely leave to self-government. And you are right in the case referred to you; my criticism being built on a state of society not under your contemplation. It is, in fact, like a critic on Homer by the laws of the Drama.—To Dupont de Nemours. vi, 89. Ford ed., x, 22. (P.F., 1816.)

3587. GOVERNMENTS (American), Reforming.—We can surely boast of having set the world a beautiful example of a government reformed by reason, alone without bloodshed. But the world is too far oppressed to profit by the example.—To E. Rutledge. ii, 435. Ford ed., v, 42. (P., 1788.)

3588. ———. The example we have given to the world is single, that of changing our form of government under the authority of reason only, without bloodshed.—To Ralph Izard. ii, 429. (P., 1785.)

3589. GOVERNMENTS (American), Republican.—The governments [of the proposed new States] shall be in republican forms.—Western Territory Report. Ford ed., iii, 409. (1784.)

3590. ———. From the moment that to preserve our rights a change of government became necessary, no doubt could be entertained that a republican form was most consonant with reason, with right, with the freedom of man, and with the character and situation of our fellow citizens. To the sincere spirit of republicanism are naturally associated the love of country, devotion to its liberty, its rights and its honor. Our preference to that form of government has been so far justified by its success, and the prosperity with which it has blessed us.—R. to A. Virginia Legislature. viii. 148. (1809.)

3591. GOVERNMENTS (American), Virtuous.—I think our governments will remain virtuous for many centuries; as long as * * * [the people] are chiefly agricultural, and this will be as long as there shall be vacant lands in any part of America. When they get piled upon one another in large cities, as in Europe, they will become corrupt as in Europe.*—To James Madison. ii, 332. Ford ed., iv, 479. (P., 1787.)

3592. GOVERNMENTS (American), Ward administration.—The elementary republics of the wards, the county republics, the State republics, and the Republic of the Union, would form a gradation of authorities, standing each on the basis of law, holding every one its delegated share of powers, and constituting truly a system of fundamental balances and checks for the government. Where every man is a sharer in the direction of his ward-republic, or of some of the higher ones, and feels that he is a participator in the government of affairs, not merely at an election one day in the year, but every day; when there shall not be a man in the State who will not be a member of some one of its councils, great or small, he will let the heart be torn out of his body sooner than his power be wrested from him by a Cæsar or a Bonaparte.—To Joseph C. Cabell. vi, 543. (M., 1816.)

* The text of the Congress edition is: "When we get piled upon one another in large cities, as in Europe, we shall become corrupt as in Europe, and go to eating one another as they do there."—Editor.

3593. —— ——. How powerfully did we feel the energy of this organization in the case of the Embargo? I felt the foundations of the Government shaken under my feet by the New England townships. There was not an individual in their States whose body was not thrown with all its momentum into action; and although the whole of the other States were known to be in favor of the measure, yet the organization of this little selfish minority enabled it to overrule the Union. What would the unwieldy counties of the middle, the south and the west do? Call a county meeting, and the drunken loungers at and about the court houses would have collected, the distances being too great for the good people and the industrious generally to attend. The character of those who really met would have been the measure of the weight they would have had in the scale of public opinion.—To JOSEPH C. CA-BELL. vi, 544. (M., 1816.)

3594. GOVERNMENTS (European), Oppressive.—The European are governments of kites over pigeons.—To GOVERNOR RUTLEDGE. ii, 234. (P., 1787.)

3595. GRAMMAR, Rigor of.—Where strictness of grammar does not weaken expression, it should be attended to * * * . But where, by small grammatical negligences, the energy of an idea is condensed, or a word stands for a sentence, I hold grammatical rigor in contempt.*—To JAMES MADISON. FORD ED., viii, 108. (W., 1801.) See LANGUAGES.

3596. GRANGER (Gideon), Burr's enemy.—In the winter of 1803-4, another train of events took place which, * * * I think it but justice to yourself that I should state. I mean the intrigues which were in agitation, and at the bottom of which we believed Colonel Burr to be; to form a coalition of the five Eastern States, with New York and New Jersey, under the appellation of the seven Eastern States; either to overawe the Union by the combination of their power and their will, or by threats of separating themselves from it. Your intimacy with some of those in the secret gave you opportunities of searching into their proceedings, of which you made me daily and confidential reports. This intimacy to which I had such useful recourse, at the time, rendered you an object of suspicion with many as being yourself a partisan of Colonel Burr, and engaged in the very combination which you were faithfully employed in defeating. I never failed to justify you to all those who brought their suspicions to me, and to assure them of my knowledge of your fidelity. Many were the individuals, then members of the Legislature, who received these assurances from me, and whose apprehensions were thereby quieted. This first project of Burr having vanished in smoke, he directed his views to the Western country.—To GIDEON GRANGER. vi, 330. FORD ED., ix, 455. (M., 1814.)

3597. GRANGER (Gideon), Supreme Court.—I shall be perfectly happy if either you or [Levi] Lincoln is named, as I consider the substituting, in the place of [Judge] Cushing, a firm unequivocating republican, whose principles are born with him, and not an occasional ingraftment, as necessary to complete

——————
* From a note enclosing draft of first annual message and requesting suggestions thereon.—EDITOR.

that great reformation in our Government to which the nation gave its fiat ten years ago.—To GIDEON GRANGER. FORD ED., ix, 286. (M., 1810.)

3598. GRATITUDE, Happiness and.—I have but one system of ethics for men and for nations—to be grateful, to be faithful to all engagements, under all circumstances, to be open and generous, promoting in the long run the interests of both, and I am sure it promotes their happiness.—To LA DUCHESSE D'AUVILLE. iii, 135. FORD ED., v, 153. (N. Y. 1790.)

3599. GRATITUDE, National.—I think * * * that nations are to be governed with regard to their own interest, but I am convinced that it is their interest, in the long run, to be grateful, faithful to their engagements even in the worst of circumstances, and honorable and generous always.—To M. DE LAFAYETTE. iii, 132. FORD ED., v, 152. (N.Y., 1790.)

3600. GRATITUDE, Principles of.—To say that gratitude is never to enter into the motives of national conduct is to revive a principle which has been buried for centuries with its kindred principles of the lawfulness of assassination, poison, perjury, &c. All of these were legitimate principles in the dark ages, which intervened between ancient and modern civilization, but exploded and held in just horror in the eighteenth century.—To JAMES MADISON. iii, 99. FORD ED., v, 111. (P., 1789.)

— GREEK LANGUAGE.—See LANGUAGES.

3601. GREEKS, Ancient.—Should these thoughts * on the subject of national government furnish a single idea which may be useful to them [the Greeks], I shall fancy it a tribute rendered to the manes of your Homer, your Demosthenes, and the splendid constellation of sages and heroes, whose blood is still flowing in your veins, and whose merits are still resting, as a heavy debt, on the shoulders of the living, and the future races of men.—To M. CORAY. vii, 324. (M., 1823.)

3602. GREEKS, Government of.—Greece was the first of civilized nations which presented examples [in government] of what man should be.—To M. CORAY. vii, 318. (M., 1823.)

3603. GREEKS, Sympathy for.—No people sympathize more feelingly than ours with the sufferings of your countrymen, none offer more sincere and ardent prayers to heaven for their success. And nothing indeed but the fundamental principle of our government, never to entangle us with the broils of Europe, could restrain our generous youth from taking some part in this holy cause. Possessing ourselves the combined blessing of liberty and order, we wish the same to other countries, and to none more than yours. which, the first of civilized nations, presented examples of what man should be.—To M. CORAY. vii, 318. (M., 1823.)

3604. GREENE (Nathaniel), Estimate of.—Greene was truly a great man. He had not, perhaps, all the qualities which so peculiarly rendered General Washington the fittest man

——————
* Jefferson, at the request of M. Coray, wrote a paper outlining a system of government for Greece. —EDITOR.

on earth for directing so great a contest under so great difficulties. * * * But Greene was second to no one in enterprise, in resource, in sound judgment, promptitude of decision, and in every other military talent.—To WILLIAM JOHNSON. FORD ED., x, 222. (M., 1822.)

3605. GRIEF, Stupefying.—Your letter found me a little emerging from the stupor of mind which had rendered me as dead to the world as was she whose loss occasioned it.*— TO THE CHEVALIER DE CHATTELLUX. i, 322. FORD ED., iii, 64. (Am., 1782.)

3606. GRIEF, Value of.—When we put into the same scale the abuses [of grief] with the afflictions of soul which even the uses of grief cost us, we may consider its value in the economy of the human being, as equivocal at least. Those afflictions cloud too great a portion of life to find a counterpoise in any benefits derived from its uses. For setting aside its paroxysms on the occasions of special bereavements, all the latter years of aged men are overshadowed with its gloom. Whither, for instance, can you and I look without seeing the graves of those we have known? And whom can we call up, of our early companions, who has not left us to regret his loss? This, indeed, may be one of the salutary effects of grief.—To JOHN ADAMS. vii, 37. (M., 1816.)

3607. GRIMM (Baron de), Genius.—A man of genius, of taste, of point, an acquaintance, the measure and traverses of whose mind I know.—To JOHN ADAMS. vii, 27. (M., 1816.)

— GULF STREAM.—See CANAL, 1116.

3608. GUNBOATS, Naval views.—On this subject professional men were consulted as far as we had opportunity. General Wilkinson, and the late General Gates, gave their opinions in writing, in favor of the system, as will be seen by their letters now communicated. The higher officers of the navy gave the same opinions in separate conferences, as their appearance at the seat of government offered occasions of consulting them, and no difference of judgment appeared on the subjects. Those of Commodore Baron and Captain Tingley, * * * are * * * transmitted herewith to the Legislature.—SPECIAL MESSAGE. viii, 80. FORD ED., ix, 23. (Feb. 1807.)

3609. HABEAS CORPUS, Bill of Rights and.—I like the declaration of rights as far as it goes, but I should have been for going further. For instance, the following alterations and additions would have pleased me: * * * Article 8. "No person shall be held in confinement more than — days after he shall have demanded and been refused a writ of habeas corpus by the judge appointed by law, nor more than — days after such a writ shall have been served on the person holding him in confinement; and no order given on due examination for his remandment or discharge; nor more than — hours in any place at a greater di 'ance than — miles from the usual residence of some judge authorized to issue the writ of habeas corpus; nor shall such writ be suspended for any term exceeding one year, nor in any place more than — miles distant from the station or encampment of enemies or of insurgents."—To JAMES MADISON. iii, 100. FORD ED., v, 112. (P., Aug. 1789.)

* The death of Mrs. Jefferson.—EDITOR.

3610. HABEAS CORPUS IN ENGLAND.—Examine the history of England. See how few of the cases of the suspension of the habeas corpus law have been worthy of that suspension. They have been either real treason, wherein the parties might as well have been charged at once, or sham plots, where it was shameful they should ever have been suspected. Yet for the few cases wherein the suspension of the habeas corpus has done real good, that operation is now become habitual, and the minds of the nation almost prepared to live under its constant suspension.—To JAMES MADISON. ii, 446. FORD ED., v, 46. (P., July 1788.)

3611. HABEAS CORPUS, Force of.—I do not like [in the new Federal Constitution] the omission of a bill of rights, providing clearly and without the aid of sophisms for * * * the eternal and unremitting force of the habeas corpus laws.—To JAMES MADISON. ii, 329. FORD ED., iv, 476. (P., Dec. 1787.)

3612. HABEAS CORPUS, Suspension.—By a declaration of rights, I mean one which shall stipulate * * * no suspensions of the habeas corpus * * * .—To A. DONALD. ii, 355. (P., 1788.) See 818.

3613. ———— ————. I sincerely rejoice at the acceptance of our new Constitution by nine States. It is a good canvas, on which some strokes only want retouching. What these are, I think, are sufficiently manifested by the general voice from north to south, which calls for a bill of rights. It seems pretty generally understood that this should go to * * * habeas corpus. * * * Why suspend the habeas corpus in insurrections and rebellions? The parties who may be arrested may be charged instantly with a well defined crime; of course, the judge will remand them. If the public safety requires that the Government should have a man imprisoned on less probable testimony in those than in other emergencies, let him be taken and tried, retaken and retried, while the necessity continues, only giving him redress against the Government for damages.—To JAMES MADISON. ii, 445. FORD ED., v, 45. (P., 1788.)

— HAMILTON (Alexander), Accounts of.—See 36.

3614. HAMILTON (Alexander), Alliance with England.—Hamilton [at a meeting of the cabinet] thought that if we were unequal to the contest [with Spain] ourselves, it behooved us to provide allies for our aid. That in this view, two nations could be named, France and England. France was too intimately connected with Spain in other points, and of too great mutual value, ever to separate for us. * * * England alone, then, remained. It would not be easy to effect it with her; however, he was for trying it, and for sounding them on the proposition of a defensive treaty of alliance. * The President said the remedy would be worse than the disease.—THE ANAS. ix, 124. FORD ED., i, 206. (Oct. 1792.)

* The difficulty arose out of the execution of the treaty between the United States and the Creek Indians, and the contention as to boundaries between the United States and Spain.—EDITOR.

3615. HAMILTON (Alexander), Anglomaniac.—His mind was really powerful, but chained by native partialities to everything English. He had formed exaggerated ideas of the superior perfection of the English constitution, the superior wisdom of their government, and sincerely believed it for the good of this country to make them its model in everything; without considering that what might be wise and good for a nation essentially commercial, and entangled in complicated intercourse with numerous and powerful neighbors, might not be so for one essentially agricultural, and insulated by nature from the abusive governments of the old world.—To WILLIAM H. CRAWFORD. vii, 6. FORD ED., x, 34. (M., 1816.)

3616. HAMILTON (Alexander), Anti-Republican Colossus.—Hamilton is really a Colossus to the anti-republican party. Without numbers, he is an host within himself. They have got themselves into a defile where they might be finished; but too much security on the republican part will give time to his talents and indefatigableness to extricate them. We have had only middling performances to oppose to him. In truth, when he comes forward, there is nobody but yourself who can meet him. His adversaries having begun the attack, he has the advantage of answering them, and remains unanswered himself. * * * For God's sake take up your pen, and give a fundamental reply to " Curtius " and " Camillus."—To JAMES MADISON. iv, 121. FORD ED., vii, 32. (M., Sept. 1795.)

3617. HAMILTON (Alexander), Coalescence with Jefferson.—He [President Washington] proceeded to express his earnest wish that Hamilton and myself could coalesce in the measures of the government, and urged the general reasons for it which he had done to me in two former conversations. He said he had proposed the same thing to Hamilton, who expressed his readiness, and he thought our coalition would secure the general acquiescence of the public. I told him my concurrence was of much less importance than he seemed to imagine; that I kept myself aloof from all cabal and correspondence on the subject of the government, and saw and spoke with as few as I could. That as to a coalition with Mr. Hamilton, if by that was meant that either was to sacrifice his general system to the other, it was impossible. We had both, no doubt, formed our conclusions after the most mature consideration; and principles conscientiously adopted, could not be given up on either side.—THE ANAS. ix, 131. FORD ED., i, 215. (Feb. 1793.)

3618. HAMILTON (Alexander), Corruption and.—Hamilton was indeed a singular character. Of acute understanding, disinterested, honest, and honorable in all private transactions, amiable in society, and duly valuing virtue in private life, yet so bewitched and perverted by the British example, as to be under thorough conviction that corruption was essential to the government of a nation.—THE ANAS. ix, 97. FORD ED., i, 166. (1818.)

3619. HAMILTON (Alexander), Defence of bank.—In Fenno's newspaper you will discover Hamilton's pen in defence of the bank, and daring to call the republican party a faction.—To JAMES MADISON. FORD ED., vi, 95. (Pa., 1792.)

3620. HAMILTON (Alexander), English mission and.—I learn by your letters and Mr. Madison's that a special mission to England is meditated, and Hamilton the missionary. A more degrading measure could not have been proposed. And why is Pinckney to be recalled? For it is impossible he should remain after such a testimony that he is not confided in? I suppose they think him not thorough fraud enough. I suspect too the mission, besides the object of placing the aristocracy of this country under the patronage of that government, has in view that of withdrawing Hamilton from the disgrace, and the public execrations which sooner or later must fall on the man who, partly by erecting fictitious debt, partly by volunteering in the payment of the debts of others, who could have paid them so much more conveniently themselves, has alienated forever all our ordinary and easy resources, and will oblige us hereafter to extraordinary ones for every little contingency out of the common line; and who has lately brought the President forward with manifestations that the business of the Treasury had got beyond the limits of his comprehension.—To JAMES MONROE. FORD ED., vi, 504. (M., April 1794.)

3621. HAMILTON (Alexander), Funding jobbery.—It is well known that, during the [Revolutionary] war, the greatest difficulty we encountered was the want of money or means to pay our soldiers who fought, or our farmers, manufacturers and merchants, who furnished the necessary supplies of food and clothing for them. After the expedient of paper money had exhausted itself, certificates of debt were given to the individual creditors, with assurance of payment, so soon as the United States should be able. But the distresses of the people often obliged them to part with these for the half, the fifth, and even a tenth of their value; and speculators had made a trade of cozening them from the holders by the most fraudulent practices, and persuasions that they would never be paid. In the bill for funding and paying these, Hamilton made no difference between the original holders and the fraudulent purchasers of this paper. Great and just repugnance arose at putting these two classes of creditors on the same footing, and great exertions were used to pay the former the full value, and to the latter, the price only which they had paid, with interest. But this would have prevented the game which was to be played, and for which the minds of greedy members were already tutored and prepared. When the trial of strength on these several efforts had indicated the form in which the bill would finally pass, this being known within doors sooner than without, and especially, than to those who were in distant parts of the Union, the base scramble began. Couriers and relay horses by land, and swift-sailing pilot boats by sea, were flying in all directions. Active partners and agents were associated and employed in every State, town and country neighborhood, and this paper was bought up at five shillings, and often as low as two shillings in the pound, before the holder knew that Congress had already provided for its redemption at par. Immense sums were thus filched from the poor and ignorant, and fortunes accumulated by those who had themselves been poor enough before. Men thus enriched by the dexterity of a leader, would follow of course the chief who was leading them to fortune, and become the zealous instruments of all his enterprises.—THE ANAS. ix, 91. FORD ED., i, 160. (1818.)

3622. HAMILTON (Alexander), Giles resolutions and.—You have for some time past seen a number of reports from the Secretary of the Treasury on enquiries instituted by the House of Representatives. When these were all come in, a number of resolutions were prepared by Mr. Giles, expressing the truths resulting from the reports. Mr. Giles and one or two others were sanguine enough to believe that the palpableness of the truths rendered a negative of them impossible, and forced them on. Others contemplating the character of the present House, one-third of which is understood to be made up of bank directors and stock jobbers who would be voting on the case of their chief; and another third of persons blindly devoted to that party, of persons not comprehending the papers, or persons comprehending them, but too indulgent to pass a vote of censure, foresaw that the resolutions would be negatived by a majority of two to one. Still they thought that the negative of palpable truth would be of service, as it would let the public see how desperate and abandoned were the hands in which their interests were placed. The vote turned out to be what was expected, not more than three or four varying from what had been conceived of them. The public will see from this the extent of their danger, and a full representation at the ensuing session will doubtless find occasion to revise the decision, and take measures for ensuring the authority of the laws over the corrupt maneuvers of the heads of departments under the pretext of exercising discretion in opposition to law.—To T. M. RANDOLPH. FORD ED., vi, 194. (Pa., 1793.)

3623. HAMILTON (Alexander), Honesty.—Hamilton was honest as a man, but, as a politician, believing in the necessity of either force or corruption to govern men.— To DR. BENJAMIN RUSH. v, 560. FORD ED., ix, 296. (M., 1811.)

— HAMILTON (Alexander), A Monarchist.—See MONARCHY.

3624. HAMILTON (Alexander), The Republic and.—I mentioned to [Alexander] Hamilton a letter received from John Adams, disavowing " *Publicola**", and denying that he ever entertained a wish to bring this country under a hereditary Executive, or introduce an hereditary branch of legislature, &c. Hamilton, condemning Mr. Adams's writings and most particularly " *Davila†* ", as having a tendency to weaken the present government, declared in substance as follows: " I own it is my opinion, though I do not publish it in Dan or Beersheba, that the present government is not that which will answer the ends of society, by giving stability and protection to its rights, and that it will probably be found expedient to go into the British form. However, since we have undertaken the experiment, I am for giving it a fair course, whatever my expectations may be. The success, indeed, so far, is greater than I had expected, and therefore, at present, success seems more possible than it had done heretofore, and there are still other and other stages of improvement which, if the present does not succeed, may be tried, and ought to be tried before we give up the republican form altogether; for that mind must be really depraved, which would not prefer the equality of political rights, which is the foundation of pure republicanism,

* Over the signature " *Publicola*," John Quincy Adams wrote a series of articles against Thomas Paine in the *Massachusetts Centinel*. It was believed at first that his father was the author of them.—EDITOR.

† John Adams used this signature in a series of articles in the *Gazette of the United States.*—EDITOR.

if it can be obtained consistently with order. Therefore, whoever by his writings disturbs the present order of things, is really blamable, however pure his intentions may be, and he was sure Mr. Adams's were pure." This is the substance of a declaration made in much more lengthy terms, and which seemed to be more formal than usual for a private conversation between two, and as if intended to qualify some less guarded expressions which had been dropped on former occasions.—THE ANAS. ix, 99. FORD ED., i, 169. (Aug. 1791.)

3625. HAMILTON (Alexander), Subservient to England.—Hamilton is panic-struck, if we refuse our breach to every kick which Great Britain may choose to give it. He is for proclaiming at once the most abject principles, such as would invite and merit habitual insults; and indeed every inch of ground must be fought in our councils to desperation, in order to hold up the face of even a sneaking neutrality, for our votes are generally two and a half against one and a half. Some propositions have come from him which would astonish Mr. Pitt himself with their boldness. If we preserve even a sneaking neutrality, we shall be indebted for it to the President, and not to his counsellors.—To JAMES MONROE. iii, 548. FORD ED., vi. 238. (Pa., May 1793.)

3626. HAMILTON (Alexander), Treasury management.—Alexander Hamilton's [Treasury] system flowed from principles adverse to liberty, and was calculated to undermine and demolish the Republic, by creating an influence of his Department over the members of the Legislature. I saw this influence actually produced, and its first fruits to be the establishment of the great outlines of his project by the votes of the very persons who, having swallowed his bait, were laying themselves out to profit by his plans; and that had these persons withdrawn, as those interested in a question ever should, the vote of the disinterested majority was clearly the reverse of what they had made it. These were no longer the votes then of the representatives of the people, but of deserters from the rights and interests of the people; and it was impossible to consider their decisions, which had nothing in view but to enrich themselves, as the measures of the fair majority, which ought always to be respected.—To PRESIDENT WASHINGTON. iii, 461. FORD ED., vi, 102. (M., 1792.)

3627. —— ——. The most prominent suspicion excited by the Report of the Secretary of the Treasury of January 3. 1793, is that the funds raised in Europe, and which ought to have been applied to the payment of our debts there, in order to stop interest, have been drawn over to this country, and lodged in the Bank, to extend the speculations and increase the profits of that institution.*—No ADDRESS. FORD ED., vi, 165. (Feb. 1793.)

3628. —— ——. I do not at all wonder at the condition in which the finances of the United States are found. Hamilton's object from the beginning, was to throw them into forms which should be utterly undecipherable. I ever said he did not understand their condition himself, nor was able to give a clear view of the excess of our debts beyond our credits, nor whether we were diminishing or increasing the debt.—To JAMES MADISON. iv, 131. FORD ED., vii, 61. (M., 1796.)

* This paper contains an analysis of the receipts and disbursements of the Treasury in Europe.—EDITOR.

3629. —— ——. Hamilton's financial system * * * had two objects: first, as a puzzle, to exclude popular understanding and inquiry; secondly, as a machine for the corruption of the Legislature.—THE ANAS. ix, 91. FORD ED., i, 160. (1818.) See ASSUMPTION OF STATE DEBTS and BANK.

3630. HAMILTON (Henry), Cruelties.—The indiscriminate murder of men, women and children, with the horrid circumstances of barbarity practiced by the Indian savages, was the particular task of Governor Hamilton's employment; and if anything could have aggravated the acceptance of such an office, and have made him personally answerable in a high degree, it was that eager spirit with which he is said to have executed it; and which, if the representations before the [Virginia] Council are to be credited, seems to have shown that his own feelings and disposition were in unison with his employment.*—To THEODORICK BLAND, JR. FORD ED., ii, 191. (W., 1779.)

✗ 3631. HAPPINESS, Attainment.—Be assiduous in learning, take much exercise for your health, and practice much virtue. Health, learning and virtue will insure your happiness; they will give you a quiet conscience, private esteem and public honor. Beyond these, we want nothing but physical necessaries, and they are easily obtained.—To PETER CARR. ii, 409. (P., 1788.)

✗ 3632. HAPPINESS, Conditions of.—Our greatest happiness * * * does not depend on the condition of life in which chance has placed us, but is always the result of a good conscience, good health, occupation, and freedom in all just pursuits.—NOTES ON VIRGINIA. viii, 389. FORD ED., iii, 253. (1782.)

3633. HAPPINESS, Conjugal love and.—Conjugal love is the basis of domestic happiness.—To MR. BELLINI. i, 444. (1785.)

3634. HAPPINESS, Conservators of.—If anybody thinks that kings, nobles, or priests are good conservators of the public happiness, send him here [France]. It is the best school in the world to cure him of that folly.—To GEORGE WYTHE. ii, 7. FORD ED., iv, 268. (P., 1786.)

3635. HAPPINESS, Domestic.—The happiest moments of my life have been the few which I have passed at home in the bosom of my family.—To FRANCIS WILLIS. FORD ED., v, 157. (N.Y., 1790.)

3636. HAPPINESS, Education and.—In the present spirit of extending to the great mass of mankind the blessings of instruction, I see a prospect of great advancement in the happiness of the human race.—To C. C. BLATCHLY. vii, 263. (M., 1822.)

3637. HAPPINESS, Freedom and.—My future solicitude will be * * * to be instrumental to the happiness and freedom of all.—FIRST INAUGURAL ADDRESS. (1801.)

3638. —— ——. The freedom and happiness of man * * * are the sole objects of

* Lieutenant Governor Hamilton was a British official who had been forced to surrender to the Virginia troops while Jefferson was Governor of Virginia.—EDITOR.

all legitimate government.—To GENERAL KOSCIUSKO. v, 509. (M., 1810.)

3639. HAPPINESS, God and.—The Giver of life * * * gave it for happiness and not for wretchedness.—To JAMES MONROE. i, 319. FORD ED., iii, 59. (M., 1782.)

3640. HAPPINESS, Government and.—The only orthodox object of the institution of government is to secure the greatest degree of happiness possible to the general mass of those associated under it.—To M. VAN DER KEMP. vi, 45. (M., 1812.)

3641. HAPPINESS, Guardians of.—For promoting the public happiness, those persons, whom nature has endowed with genius and virtue, should be rendered by liberal education worthy to receive, and able to guard the sacred deposit of the rights and liberties of their fellow citizens; and they should be called to that charge without regard to wealth, birth, or other accidental condition or circumstance.—DIFFUSION OF KNOWLEDGE BILL. FORD ED., ii, 221. (1779.)

3642. HAPPINESS, High office and.—No slave is so remote from happiness as the minister of a commonwealth.—To MARQUIS DE LAFAYETTE. i, 312. FORD ED., iii, 49. (M., 1781.)

3643. HAPPINESS, Laws and.—The laws which must affect the happiness of every people must flow from their own habits, their own feelings, and the resources of their own minds. No stranger to these could possibly propose regulations adapted to them. Every people have their own particular habits, ways of thinking, manners, &c., which have grown up with them from their infancy, are become a part of their nature, and to which the regulations which are to make them happy must be accommodated.—To WILLIAM LEE. vii, 56. (M., 1817.)

3644. HAPPINESS, Mature.—The motion of my blood no longer keeps time with the tumult of the world. It leads me to seek for happiness in the lap and love of my family, in the society of my neighbors and my books, in the wholesome occupations of my farm and my affairs, in an interest or affection in every bud that opens, in every breath that blows around me, in an entire freedom of rest, of motion, of thought, owing account to myself alone of my hours and actions.—To JAMES MADISON. iii, 578. FORD ED., vi, 291. (June 1793.)

3645. HAPPINESS, No perfect.—Perfect happiness, I believe, was never intended by the Deity to be the lot of one of His creatures in this world; but that He has very much put in our power the nearness of our approaches to it, is what I have steadfastly believed.—To JOHN PAGE. i, 187. FORD ED., i, 349. (1763.)

3646. HAPPINESS, Peace and.—The happiness of mankind is best promoted by the useful pursuits of peace.—R. TO A. viii, 142. (1808.)

✕ **3647. HAPPINESS, Primitive.**—I am convinced that those societies (as the Indians) which live without government, enjoy in their general mass an infinitely greater degree of happiness than those who live under the European governments.—To EDWARD CARRINGTON. ii, 100. FORD ED., iv, 360. (P., 1787.)

3648. HAPPINESS, Public.—That people will be happiest whose laws are best, and are best administered.—DIFFUSION OF KNOWLEDGE BILL. FORD ED., ii, 221. (1779.)

3649. HAPPINESS, Public approbation and.—The anxieties you express to administer to my happiness, do, of themselves, confer that happiness, and the measure will be complete, if my endeavors to fulfil my duties in the several public stations to which I have been called, have obtained for me the approbation of my country.—TO THE INHABITANTS OF ALBEMARLE COUNTY, VA. v, 439. FORD ED., ix, 250. (M., April 1809.)

3650. HAPPINESS, Public servants and.—To the sacrifice of time, labor, fortune, a public servant must count upon adding that of peace of mind, and even reputation.—To DR. JAMES CURRIE. iv, 132. (P., 1786.)

3651. HAPPINESS, Purchased by bloodshed.—If the happiness of the mass of mankind can be secured at the expense of a little tempest* now and then, or even of a little blood it will be a precious purchase.—To EZRA STILES. ii, 77. (P., 1786.)

3652. HAPPINESS, Retrospective.—My principal happiness is now in the retrospect of life.—To JOHN PAGE. i, 399. (P., 1785.)

3653. HAPPINESS, Right to.—We hold these truths to be self-evident; that all men are created equal; that they are endowed by their Creator with inherent† and inalienable rights; that among these, are life, liberty, and the pursuit of happiness.—DECLARATION OF INDEPENDENCE AS DRAWN BY JEFFERSON.

3654. HAPPINESS, Simple.—This friend [Dabney Carr] of ours, in a very small house, with a table, half a dozen chairs, and one or two servants, is the happiest man in the universe. * * * He speaks, thinks and dreams of nothing but his young son. Every incident in life he so takes as to render it a source of pleasure. With as much benevolence as the heart of man will hold, but with an utter neglect of the costly apparatus of life, he exhibits to the world a new phenomenon in philosophy—the Samian sage in the tub of the cynic.—To JOHN PAGE. i, 195. FORD ED., i, 373. (1770.)

3655. HAPPINESS, Tranquillity and.—It is neither wealth nor splendor, but tranquillity and occupation, which give happiness. —To MRS. A. S. MARKS. D. L. J., 135. (P., 1788.)

* Jefferson was referring to Shays's rebellion.—EDITOR.
† Congress struck out "inherent and" and inserted "certain".—EDITOR.

3656. HAPPINESS, Virtue and.—Without virtue, happiness cannot be.—To AMOS J. COOK. vi, 532. (M., 1816.)

3657. HARMONY, Affection and.—Let us restore to social intercourse that harmony and affection without which liberty and even life itself are but dreary things.—FIRST INAUGURAL ADDRESS. viii, 2. FORD ED., viii, 2. (1801.)

3658. HARMONY, Blessings of.—The evanition of party discussions has harmonized intercourse, and sweetened society beyond imagination.—To MARQUIS DE LAFAYETTE. vii, 67. FORD ED., x, 84. (M., 1817.)

3659. HARMONY vs. DISSENSION.—I hope * * * the good sense and patriotism of the friends of free government of every shade will spare us the painful, the deplorable spectacle of brethren sacrificing to small passions the great, the immortal and immutable rights of men.—To JOHN DICKINSON. FORD ED., viii, 77. (W., July 1801.)

3660. HARMONY, Inaugural address and.—I am made very happy by learning that the sentiments expressed in my inaugural address gave general satisfaction, and holds out a ground on which our fellow citizens can once more unite. I am the more pleased, because these sentiments have been, long and radically mine, and therefore will be pursued honestly and conscientiously.—To DR. BENJAMIN RUSH. iv, 382. FORD ED., viii, 30. (W., March 1801.)

3661. ———— ————. It is with the greatest satisfaction I learn from all quarters that my inaugural address is considered as holding out a ground for conciliation and union. I am the more pleased with this, because the opinion therein stated as to the real ground of difference among us (to wit: the measures rendered most expedient by the French enormities), is that which I have long entertained.—To GENERAL HENRY KNOX. iv, 385. FORD ED., viii, 35. (W., March 1801.)

3662. HARMONY, Incumbent on all. —The times do certainly render it incumbent on all good citizens, attached to the rights and honor of their country, to bury in oblivion all internal differences, and rally around the standard of their country in opposition to the outrages of foreign nations. All attempts to enfeeble and destroy the exertions of the General Government, in vindication of our national rights, or to loosen the bands of union by alienating the affections of the people, or opposing the authority of the laws at so eventful a period, merit the discountenance of all.—To GOVERNOR TOMPKINS. viii, 153. (1809.)

3663. HARMONY, Love of country and.—My earnest prayers to all my friends [are] to cherish mutual good will, to promote harmony and conciliation, and above all things to let the love of our country soar above all minor passions.—To JOHN HOLLINS. v, 597. (M., 1811.)

3664. HARMONY, Measures for.—The measures we shall pursue, and propose for the amelioration of the public affairs, will be so confessedly salutary as to unite all men not monarchists in principle.—To LEVI LINCOLN. iv, 407. FORD ED., viii, 85. (M., 1801.)

3665. HARMONY, Monarchists and.—Of the monarchical federalists I have no expectations. They are incurables, to be taken care of in a mad-house, if necessary, and on motives of charity.—To LEVI LINCOLN. iv, 406. FORD ED., viii, 84. (M., Aug. 1801.)

3666. HARMONY, National.—The moment which should convince me that a healing of the nation into one is impracticable, would be the last moment of my wishing to remain where I am.—To LEVI LINCOLN. iv, 406. FORD ED., viii, 84. (M., Aug. 1801.)

3667. —— ——. Every wish of my heart will be completely gratified when that portion of my fellow citizens which has been misled as to the character of our measures and principles, shall, by their salutary effects, be corrected in their opinions, and joining with good will the great mass of their fellow citizens, consolidate an Union, which cannot be too much cherished.—REPLY TO ADDRESS. viii, 114. (1802.) See SECOND INAUGURAL ADDRESS in Appendix.

3668. HARMONY, In New England.—In the New England States union will be slower than elsewhere * * *. But we will go on attending with the utmost solicitude to their interests, doing them impartial justice, and I have no doubt they will in time do justice to us.—To HENRY KNOX. iv, 387. FORD ED., viii, 37. (W., March 1801.)

3669. HARMONY, Obstacles to.—[The federalists] now find themselves with us, and separated from their quondam leaders. If we can * * * avoid shocking their feelings by unnecessary acts of severity against their late friends, they will in a little time cement and form one mass with us, and by these means harmony and union be restored to our country, which would be the greatest good we could effect. It was a conviction that these people did not differ from us in principle, which induced me to define the principles which I deemed orthodox, and to urge a reunion on those principles; and I am induced to hope it has conciliated many. I do not speak of the desperadoes of the quondam faction in and out of Congress. These I consider as incurables, on whom all attentions would be lost, and therefore will not be wasted. But my wish is to keep their flock from returning to them.—To WILLIAM B. GILES. iv, 381. FORD ED., viii, 26. (W., March 1801.)

3670. —— ——. I know there is an obstacle which very possibly may check the confidence which would otherwise have been more generally reposed in my observance of these principles. This obstacle does not arise from the measures to be pursued, as to which I am in no fear of giving satisfaction, but from appointments and disappointments as to office.—To DR. BENJAMIN RUSH. iv, 382. FORD ED., viii, 30. (W., March 1801.) See OFFICE.

3671. HARMONY, Political and personal.—I never suffered a political to become a personal difference. I have been left on this ground by some friends whom I dearly loved, but I was never the first to separate. With some others, of politics different from mine, I have continued in the warmest friendship to this day, and to all, and to yourself particularly, I have ever done moral justice.—To TIMOTHY PICKERING. vii, 210. (M., 1821.)

3672. —— ——. I feel extraordinary gratification in addressing this letter to you, with whom shades of difference in political sentiment have not prevented the interchange of good opinion, nor cut off the friendly offices of society and good correspondence. This political tolerance is the more valued by me, who considers social harmony as the first of human felicities, and the happiest moments those which are given to the effusions of the heart.—To —— ——. (1798.) RAYNER, p. 545.

3673. HARMONY, Principles and.—I hope to see shortly a perfect consolidation, to effect which, nothing shall be spared on my part, short of the abandonment of the principles of our Revolution.—To JOHN DICKINSON. iv, 366. FORD ED., viii, 7. (W., March 1801.)

3674. —— ——. I hope we shall once more see harmony restored among our citizens, and an entire oblivion of past feuds. Some of the leaders who have most committed themselves cannot come into this. But I hope the great body of our fellow citizens will do it. I will sacrifice everything but principle to procure it.—To SAMUEL ADAMS. iv, 389. FORD ED., viii, 39. (W., March 1801.)

3675. HARMONY, Public good.—The greatest good we can do our country is to heal its party divisions, and make them one people.—To JOHN DICKINSON. FORD ED., viii, 76. (W., July 1801.)

3676. HARMONY, Restoration of.—To restore that harmony which our predecessors so wickedly made it their object to break up, to render us again one people, acting as one nation, should be the object of every man really a patriot. I am satisfied it can be done, and I own that the day which should convince me of the contrary would be the bitterest of my life.—To THOMAS MCKEAN. FORD ED., viii, 78. (W., July 1801.)

3677. HARMONY, Sacrifices for.—I see the necessity of sacrificing our opinions sometimes to the opinions of others for the sake of harmony.—To FRANCIS EPPES. FORD ED., v, 194. (N.Y., 1790.)

3678. HARTFORD CONVENTION, American maratists.—I do not say that all who met at Hartford were under the same motive of money, nor were those of France,

Some of them are "Outs" and wish to be "Ins"; some were mere dupes of the agitators, or of their own party passions, while the Maratists alone are in the real secret; but they have very different materials to work on. The yeomanry of the United States are not the *canaille* of Paris. We might safely give them leave to go through the United States recruiting their ranks, and I am satisfied they could not raise one single regiment (gambling merchants and silk-stocking clerks excepted) who would support them in any effort to separate from the Union. The cement of this Union is in the heart-blood of every American. I do not believe there is on earth a government established on so immovable a basis. Let them, in any State, even in Massachusetts itself, raise the standard of separation, and its citizens will rise in mass, and do justice themselves on their own incendiaries.—To MARQUIS LAFAYETTE. vi, 425. FORD ED., ix, 509. (M., 1815.)

3679. HARTFORD CONVENTION, Anarchy and.—The paradox with me is how any friend to the union of our country can, in conscience, contribute a cent to the maintenance of any one who perverts the sanctity of his desk to the open inculcation of rebellion, civil war, dissolution of the government, and the miseries of anarchy.—To GOVERNOR PLUMER. vi, 414. (M., 1815.)

3680. HARTFORD CONVENTION, British agitators.—The troubles in the East have been produced by English agitators, operating on the selfish spirit of commerce, which knows no country, and feels no passion or principle but that of gain.—To LARKIN SMITH. v, 441. (M., April 1809.)

3681. HARTFORD CONVENTION, Contempt for.—If they could have induced the government to some effort of suppression, or even to enter into discussion with them, it would have given them some importance, have brought them into some notice. But they have not been able to make themselves even a subject of conversation, either of public or private societies. A silent contempt has been the sole notice they excite; consoled, indeed, some of them, by the *palpable* favors of Philip [England].—To MARQUIS LAFAYETTE. vi, 426. FORD ED., ix, 509. (M., 1815.)

3682. HARTFORD CONVENTION, Crime of.—When England took alarm lest France, become republican, should recover energies dangerous to her, she employed emissaries with means to engage incendiaries and anarchists in the disorganization of all government here. These, assuming exaggerated zeal for republican government and the rights of the people, crowded their inscriptions into the Jacobin societies, and overwhelming by their majorities the honest and enlightened patriots of the original institution, distorted its objects, pursued its genuine founders under the name of Brissotines and Girondists unto death, intrigued themselves into the municipality of Paris, controlled by terrorism the proceedings of the legislature, in which they were faithfully aided by their costipendaries there, the Dantons and Marats of the Mountain, murdered their King, septembrized the nation, and thus accomplished their stipulated task of demolishing liberty and government with it. England now fears the rising force of this republican nation, and by the same means is endeavoring to effect the same course of miseries and destruction here; it is impossible where one sees like courses of events commence, not to ascribe them to like causes. We know that the government of England, maintaining itself by corruption at home, uses the same means in other countries of which she has any jealousy, by subsidizing agitators and traitors among ourselves to distract and paralyze them. She sufficiently manifests that she has no disposition to spare ours. We see in the proceedings of Massachusetts, symptoms which plainly indicate such a course, and we know as far as such practices can ever be dragged into light, that she has practiced, and with success, on leading individuals of that State. Nay, further, we see those individuals acting on the very plan which our information had warned us was settled between the parties. These elements of explanation history cannot stantly subject to his own will. The crime, of combining with the oppressors of the earth to extinguish the last spark of human hope, that here, at length, will be preserved a model government, securing to man his rights and the fruits of his labor, by an organization constantly subject to his own will. The crime indeed, if accomplished, would immortalize its perpetrators, and their names would descend in history with those of Robespierre and his associates, as the guardian genii of despotism, and demons of human liberty.—To GOVERNOR PLUMER. vi, 414. (M., 1815.)

3683. HARTFORD CONVENTION, English bribery.—But the British ministers hoped more in their Hartford convention [than in the disordered condition of our finances]. Their fears of republican France being now done away, they are directed to republican America, and they are playing the same game for disorganization here, which they played in your country. The Marats, the Dantons and Robespierres of Massachusetts are in the same pay, under the same orders, and making the same efforts to anarchise us, that their prototypes in France did there.—To MARQUIS DE LAFAYETTE. vi, 425. FORD ED., ix, 508. (M., 1815.)

3684. HARTFORD CONVENTION, Laughing stock.—No event, more than this, has shown the placid character of our Constitution. Under any other, their treasons would have been punished by the halter. We let them live as laughing stocks for the world, and punish them by the torment of eternal contempt.—To DR. B. WATERHOUSE. FORD ED., ix, 532. (M., 1815.)

3685. HARTFORD CONVENTION, Unpopular.—I do not mean to say that all who are acting with these men are under the same motives. I know some of them personally to be incapable of it. Nor was that the case with the disorganizers and assassins of Paris. Delusions there, and party perversions here, furnish unconscious assistants to the hired actors in these atrocious scenes. But I have never entertained one moment's fear on this subject. The people of this country enjoy too much happiness to risk it for nothing; and I have never doubted that whenever the incendiaries of Massachusetts should venture openly to raise the standard of separation, its citizens would rise in mass and do justice themselves to their own parricides.—To GOVERNOR PLUMER. vi, 415. (M., 1815.)

3686. HASTINGS (Warren), Trial of.—I presume you will remain at London to see the trial of Hastings. Without suffering yourself to be imposed on by the pomp in which it will be enveloped, I would recommend to you to consider and decide for yourself these questions. If his offense is to be decided by the law of the land, why is he not tried in that court in which his fellow-citizens are tried, that is, the King's Bench? If he is cited before another court that he may be judged, not according to the law of the land, but by the discretion of his judges, is he not disfranchised of his most precious right, the benefit of the laws of his country in common with his other fellow-citizens? I think you will find on investigating this subject that every solid argument is against the extraordinary court, and that every one in its favor is specious only. It is a transfer from a judicature of learning and integrity to one, the greatness of which is both illiterate and unprincipled. Yet such is the force of prejudice with some, and of the want of reflection in others, that many of our constitutions have copied this absurdity, without suspecting it to be one.—To WILLIAM RUT-LEDGE. ii, 349. FORD ED., v, 4. (P., 1788.)

3687. HAWKINS (Benjamin), Influence with Indians.—Towards the attainment of our two objects of peace and lands, it is essential that our agent acquire that sort of influence over the Indians which rests on confidence. In this respect, I suppose, that no man has ever obtained more influence than Colonel Hawkins. Towards the preservation of peace, he is omnipotent; in the encouragement he is indefatigable and successful.—To GENERAL ANDREW JACKSON. iv, 464. (W., 1803.)

3688. HEALTH vs. LEARNING.—Health must not be sacrificed to learning. A strong body makes the mind strong.—To PETER CARR. i, 397. (P., 1785.)

3689. ———— ————. Knowledge indeed is a desirable possession, * * * but health is more so.—To T. M. RANDOLPH, JR. FORD ED., iv, 293. (P., 1786.)

3690. ———— ————. Health is worth more than learning.—To JOHN GARLAND JEFFERSON. FORD ED., v, 181. (N.Y., 1790.)

3691. HEALTH, Morality and.—Health is the first requisite after morality.—To PETER CARR. ii, 241. FORD ED., iv, 433. (P., 1787.)

3692. HEALTH, Unhappiness without.—Without health there is no happiness. An attention to health, then, should take place of every other object. The time necessary to secure this by active exercises, should be devoted to it in preference to every other pursuit. I know the difficulty with which a studious man tears himself from his studies, at any given moment of the day; but his happiness, and that of his family depend on it. The most uninformed mind, with a healthy body, is happier than the wisest valetudinarian.—To T. M. RANDOLPH, JR. ii, 177. FORD ED., iv, 406. (P., 1787.)

3693. HEAVEN, Blessings of.—Retiring from the charge of their affairs, I carry with me the consolation of a firm persuasion that Heaven has in store for our beloved country long ages to come of prosperity and happiness.—EIGHTH ANNUAL MESSAGE. viii, 111. FORD ED., ix, 225. (Nov. 1808.)

3694. HENRY (Patrick), Ambitious.—Your character of Patrick Henry is precisely agreeable to the idea I had formed of him. I take him to be of unmeasured ambition.—To JAMES MADISON. FORD ED., iv, 35. (P., 1785.)

3695. HENRY (Patrick), Apostate.—His apostasy must be unaccountable to those who do not know all the recesses of his heart.—To ARCHIBALD STUART. FORD ED., vii, 378. (M., May 1799.)

3696. HENRY (Patrick), Avaricious.—Mr. Henry's ravenous avarice was the only passion paramount to his love of popularity.—To WILLIAM WIRT. FORD ED., ix, 339. (M., 1812.)

3697. HENRY (Patrick), Brilliant but illogical.—In ordinary business [in the House of Burgesses] he was a very inefficient member. He could not draw a bill on the most simple subject which would bear legal criticism, or even the ordinary criticism which looks to correctness of style and ideas, for indeed there was no accuracy of idea in his head. His imagination was copious, poetical, sublime, but vague also. He said the strongest things in the finest language, but without logic, without arrangement, desultorily.—To WILLIAM WIRT. FORD ED., ix, 341. (M., 1812.)

3698. HENRY (Patrick), Declined office.—The office of Secretary of State was offered to P. H. [Patrick Henry] in order to draw him over, and gain some popularity; but not till there was a moral certainty that he would not accept it.—To JAMES MONROE. FORD ED., vii, 59. (M., March 1796.)

3699. ———— ————. Most assiduous court is paid to Patrick Henry. He has been offered everything which they knew he would not accept. Some impression is thought to be made, but we do not believe it is radical. If they thought they could count upon him, they would run him for their Vice-President; their first object being to produce a schism in this State.—To JAMES MONROE. iv, 148. FORD ED., vii, 89. (M., July 1796.)

3700. HENRY (Patrick), Early manhood.—You ask some account of Mr. Henry's mind, information and manners in 1759-60, when I first became acquainted with him. We met at Nathan Dandridges, in Hanover, about the Christmas of that winter, and passed perhaps a fortnight together at the revelries of the neighborhood and season. His manners had something of the coarseness of the society he had frequented; his passion was fiddling, dancing and pleasantry. He excelled in the last and it attached every one to him. The occasion perhaps, as much as his idle disposition, prevented his engaging in any conversation which might give the measure either of his mind or information. Opportunity was not wanting, because Mr. John Campbell was there, who had married Mrs. Spotswood, the sister of Colonel Dandridge. He was a man of science, and often introduced conversations on scientific subjects. Mr. Henry had a little before broke up his store, or rather it had broken him up, and within three months after he came to Williamsburg for his license, and told me, I think, he had read law not more than six weeks.—To WILLIAM WIRT. vi, 487. FORD ED., ix, 475. (M., 1815.)

3701. HENRY (Patrick), Eloquence.—When the famous resolutions of 1765, against the Stamp Act, were proposed, I was yet a student of law in Williamsburg. I attended the debate, however, at the door of the lobby of the House of Burgesses and heard the splendid display of Mr. Henry's talents as a popular orator. They were great, indeed; such as I have never heard from any other man. He appeared to me to speak as Homer wrote.*—AUTOBIOGRAPHY. i, 4. FORD ED., i, 6. (1821.)

3702. ——— ———. Another of the great occasions on which he exhibited examples of eloquence such as probably had never been exceeded, was on the question of adopting the new Constitution in 1788. To this he was most violently opposed. To WILLIAM WIRT. FORD ED., ix, 344. (M., 1811?)

3703. HENRY (Patrick), Foe of Constitution.—Henry is the avowed foe of the new Constitution. He stands higher in public estimation [in Virginia] than he ever did, yet he was so often in the minority in the present assembly that he has quitted it, never more to return, unless an opportunity offers to overturn the new Constitution.—To WILLIAM SHORT. FORD ED., v, 136. (Dec. 1789.)

3704. HENRY (Patrick), Force of oratory.—Mr. Henry's first remarkable exhibition [in the House of Burgesses] was on the motion for the establishment of an office for lending money on mortgages of real property. * * * I can never forget a particular exclamation of his in the debate in which he electrified his hearers. It had been urged that from certain unhappy circumstances of the Colony, men of substantial property had contracted debts, which, if exacted suddenly, must ruin them and their families, but, with a little indulgence of time, might be paid with ease. "What, Sir!" exclaimed Mr. Henry in animadverting on this, "is it proposed then to reclaim the spendthrift from his dissipation and extravagance, by filling his pockets with money?" * * * He laid open with so much energy the spirit of favoritism on which the proposition was founded, and the abuses to which it would lead, that it was crushed in its birth.—To WILLIAM WIRT. vi, 364. FORD ED., ix, 466. (M., 1814.)

3705. HENRY (Patrick), Gerrymandering.—Mr. Henry is omnipotent in Virginia. Mr. Madison was left out as a Senator by eight or nine votes; and Henry has so modelled the districts for Representatives, as to tack Orange to counties where himself has great influence, that Madison may not be elected into the lower Federal House, which was the place he had wished to serve in, and not the Senate.—To WILLIAM SHORT. ii, 574. FORD ED., v, 70. (P., 1789.)

3706. HENRY (Patrick), Influence.—I have understood that Mr. Henry has always been opposed [to a new constitution for Virginia]: and I confess that I consider his talents and influence such as that, were it decided that we should call a convention for the purpose of amending, I should fear he might induce that convention either to fix the thing as at present, or change it for the worse. Would it not, therefore, be well that means should be adopted for coming at his ideas of the changes he would agree to, and for communicating to him those which we should propose? Perhaps he might find ours not so distant from his, but that some mutual sacrifices might bring them together.—To ARCHIBALD STUART. iii, 314. FORD ED., v, 408. (Pa., 1791.)

3707. HENRY (Patrick), Innate love of liberty.—No man ever more undervalued chartered titles than himself. He drew all natural rights from a purer source—the feelings of his own breast.—To WILLIAM WIRT. FORD ED., x, 60. (M., 1816.)

3708. HENRY (Patrick), Intrigue.—Our Legislature is filled with too great a mass of talents and principle to be now swayed by Mr. Henry. He will experience mortifications to which he has been hitherto a stranger. Still, I fear something from his intriguing and cajoling talents, for which he is still more remarkable than for his eloquence. As to the effect of his name among the people, I have found it crumble like a dried leaf, the moment they become satisfied of his apostasy.—To TENCH COXE. FORD ED., vii, 381. (M., May 1799.)

3709. HENRY (Patrick), Literary indolence.—He was the laziest man in reading I ever knew.—AUTOBIOGRAPHY. i, 8. FORD ED., i, 13. (1821.)

3710. HENRY (Patrick), Mysterious.—Henry, as usual, is involved in mystery. Should the popular tide run strongly in either direction he will fall in with it. Should it not, he will have a struggle between his enmity to the Lees, and his enmity to everything which may give influence to Congress.—To JAMES MADISON. FORD ED., iii, 318. (T., May 1783.)

3711. HENRY (Patrick), Philips case.—The censure of Mr. E. Randolph on Mr. Henry in the case of Philips, was without foundation. I remember the case, and took my part in it. Philips was a mere robber, who availing himself of the troubles of the times, collected a banditti, retired to the Dismal Swamp, and from thence sallied forth, plundering and maltreating the neighboring inhabitants, and covering himself, without authority, under the name of a British subject. Mr. Henry, then Governor, communicated the case to me. We both thought the best proceeding would be by bill of attainder, unless he delivered himself up for trial within a given time. Philips was afterwards taken; and Mr. Randolph being Attorney General, and apprehending he would plead that he was a British subject, taken in arms, in support of his lawful sovereign, and as a prisoner of war entitled to the protection of the law of nations, he thought the safest proceeding would be to indict him at common law as a felon and robber. Against this I believe Philips urged the same plea; he was overruled and found guilty.—To WILLIAM WIRT. vi, 369. FORD ED., ix, 470. (M., 1814.)

3712. HENRY (Patrick), Political alertness.—The people of Virginia are beginning to call for a new constitution for their State. This symptom of their wishes will probably bring over Mr. Henry to the proposition. He has been the great obstacle to it hitherto; but you know he is always alive to catch the first sensation of the popular breeze, that he may take the lead of that which in truth leads him.—To WILLIAM SHORT. FORD ED., vi, 122. (Pa., 1792.)

3713. HENRY (Patrick), Political fall.—[Alexander] Hamilton * * * became his idol; and, abandoning the republican advocates of the Constitution, the Federal Government on federal principles became his political creed. * * * His apostasy sunk him to nothing in the estimation of his country. He lost at once all that influence which federalism had hoped, by cajoling him, to transfer with him to itself, and a man who through a long and active life had been the idol of his country beyond any one that ever lived, descended to the grave with less than its indifference, and verified the saying of the philosopher, that no man must be called happy till he is dead.—To WILLIAM WIRT. FORD ED., ix, 344. (M., 1811?)

3714. HENRY (Patrick), Speculator.— The States of Virginia and North Carolina are peculiarly dissatisfied with the assumption of the State debts by the General Government. I believe, however, that it is harped on by many to mask their disaffection to the Government on other grounds. Its great foe in Virginia is an implacable one. He avows it himself, but does not avow all his motives for it. The measures and tone of the Government threaten abortion to some of his speculations; most particularly to that of the Yazoo territory. But it is too well nerved to be overawed by individual opposition.—To GOUVERNEUR MORRIS. iii, 198. FORD ED., v, 250. (Pa., 1790.)

3715. HENRY (Patrick), Virginia Constitution.— While Mr. Henry lives another bad constitution would be formed and forever on us.—To JAMES MADISON. FORD ED., iv, 16. (P., Dec. 1784.)

— HEREDITARY OFFICERS.— See GOVERNMENT.

3716. HERESY, False religion and.— Heresy and false religion are withheld from the cognizance of Federal tribunals.—KENTUCKY RESOLUTIONS. ix, 466. FORD ED., vii, 295. (1798.)

3717. HERESY, Political.— Establish principles and examples which * * * [shall] fence us against future heresies, preached now, to be practiced hereafter.—To COLONEL INNES. iii, 224. FORD ED., v, 300. (1791.)

3718. HERSCHEL (Sir William), Theories of.— Herschel's volcano in the moon you have doubtless heard of, and placed among the other vagaries of a head, which seems not organized for sound induction. The wildness of the theories hitherto proposed by him, on his own discoveries, seems to authorize us to consider his merit as that of a good optician only. —To REV. JAMES MADISON. ii, 429. (P., 1788.)

3719. HESSIANS, Employment of.— His Britannic Majesty, in order to destroy our freedom and happiness, * * * commenced against us a cruel and unprovoked war, and unable to engage Britons sufficient to execute his sanguinary measures, * * * applied for aid to foreign princes who were in the habit of selling the blood of their people for money, and from them * * * procured and transported hither, a considerable number of foreigners.— PROCLAMATION. FORD ED., ii, 445. (1781.) See ARMY (DESERTERS), and IMMIGRATION.

3720. HISTORY, Ancient vs. Modern.— I feel a much greater interest in knowing what passed two or three thousand years ago than in what is passing now. I read nothing, therefore, but of the heroes of Troy, of the wars of Lacedæmon and Athens, of Pompey and Cæsar, and of Augustus, too, the Bonaparte and parricide scoundrel of that day.—To NATHANIEL MACON. vii, 111. FORD ED., x, 120. (M., 1819.)

3721. ———— ————. I am happier while reading the history of ancient than of modern times. The total banishment of all moral principle from the code which governs the intercourse of nations, the melancholy reflection that after the mean, wicked and cowardly cunning of the cabinets of the age of Machiavelli had given place to the integrity and good faith which dignified the succeeding one of a Chatham and Turgot, that this is to be swept away again by the daring profligacy and avowed destitution of all moral principle of a Cartouche and a Blackbeard, sicken my soul unto death. I turn from the contemplation with loathing, and take refuge in the histories of other times, where, if they also furnished their Tarquins, their Catalines and Caligulas, their stories are handed to us under the brand of a Livy, a Sallust and a Tacitus, and we are comforted with the reflection that the condemnation of all succeeding generations has confirmed the sentence of the historian, and consigned their memories to everlasting infamy, a solace we cannot have with the Georges and Napoleons but by anticipation.—To WILLIAM DUANE. vi, 109. (M., April 1813.)

3722. HISTORY, Authors and compilers.— In all cases, I prefer original authors to compilers. For a course of ancient history, therefore [in the University of Virginia], of Greece and Rome especially, I should advise the usual suite of Herodotus, Thucydides, Xenophon, Diodorus, Livy, Cæsar, Suetonius, Tacitus and Dion, in their originals if understood, and in translations, if not. For its continuation to the final destruction of the Empire we must then be content with Gibbon, a compiler, and with Segur, for a judicious recapitulation of the whole. After this general course, there are a number of particular histories filling up the chasms, which may be read at leisure in the progress of life. Such is Arrian, Q. Curtius, Polybius, Sallust, Plutarch, Dionysius, Halicarnassus, Micasi, &c. The ancient Universal History should be on our shelves as a book of general reference, the most learned and most faithful perhaps that ever was written. Its style is very plain but perspicuous.—To ————— ————. vii, 411. (M., 1825.)

3723. HISTORY, Bad government and. —History, in general, only informs us what bad government is.—To JOHN NARVELL. v, 91. FORD ED., ix, 72. (W., 1807.)

3724. HISTORY, Genuine.— A morsel of genuine history is a thing so rare as to be always valuable.—To JOHN ADAMS. vii, 82. (P.F., 1817.)

3725. HISTORY, False.— Man is fed with fables through life, leaves it in the belief he knows something of what has been passing, when in truth he has known nothing but what has passed under his own eye.—To THOMAS COOPER. FORD ED., x, 286. (M., 1823.)

3726. HISTORY, Lawyers and.— History, especially, is necessary to form a lawyer. —To JOHN GARLAND JEFFERSON. FORD ED., v, 180. (N. Y., 1790.)

3727. HISTORY, Neglected Material.— It is truly unfortunate that those engaged in public affairs so rarely make notes of transactions passing within their knowledge. Hence history becomes fable instead of fact. The great outlines may be true, but the incidents and coloring are according to the faith or fancy of the writer. Had Judge Marsha'l taken half your pains in sifting and scrutinizing facts, he would not have given to the world, as true history a false copy of a record under his eye. Burke again has copied him, and being a second writer, doubles the credit of the copy. When writers are so indifferent as to the correctness of facts, the verification of which lies at their elbow, by what measure shall we estimate their relation of things distant, or of those given to us through the obliquities of their own vision? Our records it is true in the case under contemplation, were destroyed by the malice and Vandalism of the British military, perhaps of their government, under whose orders they committed so much useless mischief. But printed copies remained, as your examination has proved. Those which were apocryphal, then, ought not to have been hazarded without examination.—To WILLIAM WIRT. vi, 370. FORD ED., ix, 471. (M., 1814.)

3728. HISTORY, Panegyric and.—You have certainly practiced vigorously [in the Life of Patrick Henry] the precept of "*de mortuis nil nisi bonum.*" This presents a very difficult question,—whether one only or both sides of the medal shall be presented. It constitutes, perhaps, the distinction between panegyric and history.—To WILLIAM WIRT. FORD ED., x, 61. (P. F., 1816.)

3729. HISTORY, Peace and.—Wars and contentions, indeed, fill the pages of history with more matter. But more blessed is that nation whose silent course of happiness furnishes nothing for history to say.—To COUNT DIODATI. v, 62. (W., 1807.)

3730. HISTORY, Private letters and.—History may distort truth, and will distort it for a time, by the superior efforts at justification of those who are conscious of needing it most. The opening scenes of our present government will not be seen in their true aspect until the letters of the day, now held in private hoards, shall be broken up and laid open to public view.—To WILLIAM JOHNSON. vii, 292. FORD ED., x, 228. (M., 1823.)

3731. ――― ―――. Although I decline all newspaper controversy, yet when falsehoods have been advanced, within the knowledge of no one so much as myself, I have sometimes deposited a contradiction in the hands of a friend, which, if worth preservation, may, when I am no more, nor those whom I might offend, throw light on history, and recall that into the path of truth.—To MARTIN VAN BUREN. vii, 372. FORD ED., x, 315. (M., 1824.)

3732. HISTORY, Records of.—Time and accident are committing daily havoc on the originals of the valuable historical and State papers deposited in our public offices. The late war has done the work of centuries in this business. The last cannot be recovered, but let us save what remains; not by vaults and locks which fence them from the public eye and use in consigning them to the waste of time, but by such a multiplication of copies, as shall place them beyond the reach of accident.—To MR. HAZARD. iii, 211. (Pa., 1791.)

3733. HISTORY, Truthful.—We who are retired from the business of the world, are glad to catch a glimpse of truth, here and there as we can, to guide our path through the boundless field of fable in which we are bewildered by public prints, and even by those calling themselves histories. A word of truth to us is like the drop of water supplicated from the tip of Lazarus's finger. It is as an observation of latitude and longitude to the mariner long enveloped in clouds, for correcting the ship's way.—To JOHN QUINCY ADAMS. vii, 87. (M., 1817.)

3734. ――― ―――. True history, in which all will be believed, is preferable to unqualified panegyric, in which nothing is believed.—To JOSEPH DELAPLAINE. vii, 21. FORD ED., x, 56. (M., 1816.)

3735. HISTORY, Value of.—The most effectual means of preventing the perversion of power into tyranny are to illuminate, as far as practicable, the minds of the people at large, and more especially to give them knowledge of those facts, which history exhibits, that possessed thereby of the experience of other ages and countries, they may be enabled to know ambition under all its shapes, and prompt to exert their natural powers to defeat its purposes.—DIFFUSION OF KNOWLEDGE BILL. FORD ED., ii, 221. (1779.)

3736. ――― ―――. History, by apprising the people of the past, will enable them to judge of the future; it will avail them of the experience of other times and other nations; it will qualify them as judges of the actions and designs of men; it will enable them to know ambition under every disguise it may assume; and knowing it, to defeat its views.—NOTES ON VIRGINIA. viii, 390. FORD ED., iii, 254. (1782.)

3737. HISTORY, Writing.—You say I must go to writing history. While in public life I had not time, and now that I am retired, I am past the time. To write history requires a whole life of observation, of inquiry, of labor and correction. Its materials are not to be found among the ruins of a decayed memory.—To J. B. STUART. vii, 65. (M., 1817.)

3738. HISTORY (American), Collecting.—While I was in Europe, I purchased everything I could lay my hands on which related to any part of America, and particularly had a pretty full collection of the English, French, and Spanish authors on the subject of Louisiana.—To WILLIAM DUNBAR. iv, 539. (W., 1804.)

3739. HISTORY (American), Criticisms on.—It is impossible to read thoroughly such writings as those of Harper and Otis, who take a page to say what requires but a sentence, or rather, who give you whole pages of what is nothing to the purpose. A cursory race over the ground is as much as they can claim. It is easy for them, at this day, to endeavour to whitewash their party, when the greater part are dead of those who witnessed what passed, others old and become indifferent to the subject, and others indisposed to take the trouble of answering them. As to Otis, his attempt is to prove that the sun does not shine at midday; that that is not a fact which every one saw. He merits no notice. It is well known that Harper had little scruple about facts where detection was not obvious. By placing in false lights whatever admits it, and passing over in silence what does not, a plausible aspect may be presented of anything.—To WILLIAM SHORT. vii, 389. FORD ED., x, 328. (M., 1825.)

3740. HISTORY (American), Inaccuracies.—Botta * * * has put his own speculations and reasonings into the mouths of persons whom he names, but who, you and I know, never made such speeches. In this he has followed the example of the ancients, who made their great men deliver long speeches, all of them in the same style, and in that of the author himself. The work is nevertheless a good one, more judicious, more chaste, more classical, and more true than the party diatribe of Marshall. Its greatest fault is in having taken too much from him. To JOHN ADAMS. vi, 489. FORD ED., ix, 527. (M., 1815.)

3741. HISTORY (American), Naval.— Why omit all mention of the scandalous campaigns of Commodore Morris? A two years' command of an effective squadron, with discretionary instructions, wasted in sailing from port to port of the Mediterranean, and a single half day before the port of the enemy against which he was sent. All this can be seen in the proceedings of the court on which he was dismissed; and it is due to the honorable truths with which the book abounds, to publish those which are not so.—To MATTHEW CARR. vi, 132. (M., 1813.)

3742. HISTORY (American), Preservation of.—It is the duty of every good citizen to use all the opportunities which occur to him, for preserving documents relating to the history of our country.—To HUGH P. TAYLOR. vii, 313. (M., 1823.)

3743. HISTORY (American), Revolutionary.—On the subject of the history of the American Revolution, you ask who shall write it? Who can write it? And who will ever be able to write it? Nobody; except merely its external facts; all its councils, designs, and discussions having been conducted by Congress with closed doors, and with no members, as far as I know, having even made notes of them. These, which are the life and soul of history, must forever be unknown.—To JOHN ADAMS. vii, 489. FORD ED., ix, 527. (M., 1815.)

3744. —— ——. I am now reading Botta's History of our own Revolution. Bating the ancient practice which he has adopted of putting speeches into mouths which never made them, and fancying motives of action which we never felt, he has given that history with more detail, precision and candor, than any writer I have yet met with. It is, to be sure, compiled from those writers; but it is a good secretion of their matter, the pure from the impure, and presented in a just sense of right in opposition to usurpation.—To JOHN ADAMS. vii, 63. (M., 1817.)

3745. HISTORY (English), Distorted.— Hume's [History], were it faithful, would be the finest piece of history which has ever been written by man. Its unfortunate bias may be partly ascribed to the accident of his having written it backwards. His maiden work was the History of the Stuarts. It was a first essay to try his strength before the public. And whether as a Scotchman he had really a partiality for that family, or thought that the lower their degradation, the more fame he should acquire by raising them up to some favor, the object of his work was an apology for them. He spared nothing, therefore, to wash them white, and to palliate their misgovernment. For this purpose he suppressed truths, advanced falsehoods, forged authorities and falsified records. All this is proved on him unanswerably by Brodie. But so bewitching was his style and manner, that his readers were unwilling to doubt anything, swallowed everything, and all England became tories by the magic of his art. His pen revolutionized the public sentiment of that country more completely than

the standing armies could ever have done, which were so much dreaded and deprecated by the patriots of that day. Having succeeded so eminently in the acquisition of fortune and fame by this work, he undertook the history of the two preceding dynasties, the Plantagenets and Tudors. It was all important in this second work, to maintain the thesis of the first, that " it was the people who encroached on the sovereign, not the sovereign who usurped on the rights of the people ". And, again, chapter 53d, " the grievances under which the English labored [to wit: whipping, pillorying, cropping, imprisoning, fining, &c.], when considered in themselves, without regard to the constitution, scarcely deserve the name, nor were they either burthensome on the people's properties, or anywise shocking to the natural humanity of mankind ". During the constant wars, civil and foreign, which prevailed while those two families occupied the throne, it was not difficult to find abundant instances of practices the most despotic, as are wont to occur in times of violence. To make this second epoch support the third, therefore, required but a little garbling of authorities. And it then remained, by a third work, to make of the whole a complete history of England on the principles on which he had advocated that of the Stuarts. This would comprehend the Saxon and Norman Conquests, the former exhibiting the genuine form and political principles of the people constituting the nation, and founded in the rights of man; the latter built on conquest and physical force, not at all affecting moral rights, nor even assented to by the free will of the vanquished. The battle of Hastings, indeed, was lost, but the natural rights of the nation were not staked on the event of a single battle. Their will to recover the Saxon constitution continued unabated, and was at the bottom of all the unsuccessful insurrections which succeeded in subsequent times. The victors and vanquished continued in a state of living hostility, and the nation may still say, after losing the battle of Hastings,

> " What though the field be lost?
> All is not lost; the unconquerable will
> And study of revenge, immortal hate
> And courage never to submit or yield."

The government of a nation may be usurped by the forcible intrusion of an individual into the throne. But to conquer its will, so as to rest the right on that, the only legitimate basis, requires long acquiescence and cessation of all opposition. The whig historians of England, therefore, have always gone back to the Saxon period for the true principles of their constitution, while the tories and Hume, their Coryphæus, date it from the Norman Conquest, and hence conclude that the continual claim by the nation of the good old Saxon laws, and the struggles to recover them, were " encroachments of the people on the crown, and not usurpations of the crown on the people ".—To —— ——. vii, 412. (M., 1825.)

3746. HISTORY (English), Faithful authors.—Of England there is as yet no general history so faithful as Rapin's. He may be followed by Ludlow, Fox, Belsham, Hume and Brodie.—To —— ——. vii, 412. (M., 1825.)

3747. HISTORY (English), Hume's.— There is no general history of Great Britain which can be recommended. The elegant one of Hume seems intended to disguise and discredit the good principles of the government, and is so plausible and pleasing in its style and manner, as to instil its errors and heresies insensibly into the minds of unwary readers. Baxter has performed a good operation on it. He has taken the text of Hume as his ground work, abridging it by the omission of some details of little interest, and wherever he has found him endeavoring to mislead, by either the suppression of a truth, or by giving it a false coloring, he has changed the text to what it should be, so that we may properly call it Hume's history republicanized. He has moreover continued the history (but indifferently) from where Hume left it, to the year 1800. The work is not popular in England, because it is republican. * * * Adding to this Ludlow's Memoirs, Mrs. McCauley's and Belknap's histories, a sufficient view will be presented of the free principles of the English constitution. —To JOHN NORVELL. v, 91. FORD ED., ix, 72. (W., 1807.)

3748. ———— ————. Every one knows that judicious matter and charms of style have rendered Hume's History the manual of every student. I remember well the enthusiasm with which I devoured it when young, and the length of time, the research and reflection which were necessary to eradicate the poison it had instilled into my mind. It was unfortunate that he first took up the history of the Stuarts, became their apologist, and advocated all their enormities. To support his work, when done, he went back to the Tudors, and so selected and arranged the materials of their history as to present their arbitrary acts only, as the genuine samples of the const'tutional power of the crown, and, still writing backwards, he then reverted to the early history, and wrote the Saxon and Norman periods with the same perverted view. Although all this is known, he still continues to be put into the hands of all our young people, and to infect them with the poison of his own principles of government. It is this book which has undermined the free principles of the English government, has persuaded readers of all classes that there were usurpations on the legitimate and salutary rights of the crown, and has spread universal toryism over the land.—To WILLIAM DUANE. v, 533. (M., 1810.)

3749. ———— ————. This single book [Hume's History of England] has done more to sap the free principles of the English constitution than the largest standing army of which their patriots have been so jealous. It is like the portraits of our countryman Wright, whose eye was so unhappy as to seize all the ugly features of his subject, and to present them faithfully, while it was entirely insensible to every lineament of beauty. So Hume has concentrated, in his fascinating style, all the arbitrary proceedings of the English Kings, as true evidences of the constitution, and glided over its Whig principles as the unfounded pretensions of factious demagogues. He even boasts, in his life written by himself, that of the numerous alterations suggested by the readers of his work, he had never adopted one proposed by a Whig. —To JOHN ADAMS. v'i, 46. (P.F., 1816.)

3750. HISTORY (English), Part of American.—Our laws, language, religion, politics and manners are so deeply laid in English foundations, that we shall never cease to consider their history as a part of ours, and to study ours in that as its origin.—To WILLIAM DUANE. v, 533. (M., 1810.)

3751. HISTORY (English), Value of.— As we have employed some of the best materials of the British constitution in the construction of our own government, a knowledge of British history becomes useful to the American politician.—To JOHN NORVELL. v, 91. FORD ED., ix, 72. (W., 1807.)

3752. HISTORY, Roman.—I have been * * * delighted with reading a work, the title of which did not promise much useful information or amusement—L'Italia Avanti il Dominis dei Romani dal Micali." * * * Micali has given the counterpart of the Roman history for the nations over which they extended their dominion. For this he has gleaned up matter from every quarter, and furnished materials for reflection and digestion to those who, thinking as they read, have perceived that there was a great deal of matter behind the curtain, could that be fully withdrawn. He certainly gives new ideas of a nation whose splendor has masked and palliated their barbarous ambition.—To JOHN ADAMS. vii, 63. (M., 1817.)

3753. HOGENDORP (Count Van), Ability.—A very particular acquaintance with M. de Hogendorp * * * has led me to consider him as the best informed man of his age I have ever seen.—To GEORGE WASHINGTON. FORD ED., iii, 445. (A., 1784.)

3754. HOLLAND, America and.—Connected with Holland by the earliest ties of friendship, and maintaining with them uninterrupted relations of peace and commerce, no event which interests their welfare can be indifferent to us. It is, therefore, with great pleasure, I receive the assurances of your Majesty that you will continue to cherish these ancient relations; and we shall, on our part, endeavor to strengthen your good will by a faithful observance of justice, and by all the good offices which occasion shall permit.—To THE KING OF HOLLAND. v, 47. (W., 1807.)

3755. HOLLAND, Prince of Orange and. —The treasonable perfidy of the Prince of Orange, Stadtholder and Captain General of the United Netherlands, in the war which England waged against them, for entering into a treaty of commerce with the United States, is known to all. As their executive officer, charged with the conduct of the war, he contrived to baffle all the measures of the States General, to dislocate all their military plans, and played false into the hands of England against his own country on every possible occasion, confident in her protection, and in that of the King of Prussia, brother to his Princess. The States General, indignant at this patricidal conduct, applied to France for aid, according to the stipulations of the treaty concluded with her in 1785. It was assured to them readily and in cordial terms. * * * The object of the Patriots was to establish a representative and republican government. The majority of the States General were with them, but the majority of the populace of the towns was with the Prince of Orange; and that populace was played off with great effect by the triumvirate of [Sir James] Harris, the English ambassador, afterwards Lord Malmesbury, the Prince of Orange, a stupid man, and the Princess as much a man as either of her colleagues, in audaciousness, in enterprise and in the thirst of domination. By these the mobs of the Hague were excited against the members of the States General; their persons were insulted and endangered in the streets; the sanctuary of their houses was violated and the Prince, whose function and duty it was to repress and punish these violations of order, took no steps for that purpose. The States General for their own protection were, therefore, obliged to place their militia under the command of a committee. The Prince filled the courts of London and Berlin with complaints at this usurpation of his prerogatives and, forgetting that he was but the first servant of a republic, marched his regular troops against the city of Utrecht, where the States were in session. They were repulsed by the militia. His interests now became marshalled with those of the public enemy and against his own country. The States, therefore, exercising their rights of sovereignty, deprived him of all his powers. The great Frederic had died in August, 1786. He had never intended to break with France in support of the Prince of Orange. During the illness of which he died, he had, through the Duke of Brunswick, declared to the Marquis de Lafayette, * * * that he meant not to support the English interest in Holland; that he might assure the government of France his only wish was that some honorable place in the Constitution should be reserved for the Stadtholder and his children, and that he would take no part in the quarrel unless an entire abolition of the Stadtholderate should be attempted. But his place was now occupied by Frederic William, his great nephew, a man of little understanding, much caprice and very inconsiderate; and the Princess, his sister, although her husband was in arms against the legitimate authorities of the country, attempting to go to Amsterdam for the purpose of exciting the mobs of that place, and being refused permission to pass a military post on the way, he put the Duke of Brunswick at the head of twenty thousand men. and made demonstrations of marching on Holland. The King of France hereupon declared, by his Chargé des Affaires in Holland, that if the Prussian troops continued to menace Holland with an invasion, his Majesty, in quality of Ally, was determined to succor that province. In answer to this Eden gave official information to Count Montmorin, that England must consider as at an end, its convention with France relative to giving notice of its naval armaments and that she was arming generally. War being now imminent, Eden, since Lord Auckland, questioned me on the effect of our treaty with France in the case of a war, and what might be our dispositions. I told him frankly and without hesitation that our dispositions would be neutral, and that I thought it would be the interest of both these powers that we should be so; because it would relieve both from all anxiety as to feeding their West India islands; that England, too, by suffering us to remain so, would avoid a heavy land war on our continent, which might very much cripple her proceedings elsewhere; that our treaty, indeed, obliged us to receive into our ports the armed vessels of France, with their prizes, and to refuse admission to the prizes made on her by her enemies; that there was a clause also by which we guaranteed to France her American possessions, which might perhaps force us into the war, if these were attacked. "Then it will be war," said he, "for they will assuredly be attacked." Liston, at Madrid, about the same time, made the same inquiries of Carmichael. The government of France then declared a determination to form a camp of observation at Givet. commenced arming her marine, and named the Bailli de Suffrein their generalissimo on the ocean. She secretly engaged also in negotiations with Russia, Austria and Spain to form a quadruple alliance. The Duke of Brunswick, having advanced to the confines of Holland, sent some of his officers to Givet to reconnoitre the state of things there, and report them to him. * * *

Finding that there was not a single company there, he boldly entered the country, took their towns as fast as he presented himself before them, and advanced on Utrecht. The States had appointed the Rhingrave of Salm their Commander-in-Chief, a Prince without talents, without courage and without principle. He might have held out in Utrecht for a considerable time, but he surrendered the place without firing a gun, literally ran away and hid himself, so that for months it was not known what had become of him. Amsterdam was then attacked and capitulated. In the meantime the negotiations for the quadruple alliance were proceeding favorably, but the secrecy with which they were attempted to be conducted was penetrated by Fraser, Chargé des Affaires of England at St. Petersburg, who instantly notified his court, and gave the alarm to Prussia. The King saw at once what would be his situation between the jaws of France, Austria and Russia. In great dismay he besought the court of London not to abandon him, sent Alvensleben to Paris to explain and soothe, and England, through the Duke of Dorset and Eden, renewed her conferences for accommodation. The Archbishop, who shuddered at the idea of war, and preferred a peaceful surrender of right to an armed vindication of it, received them with open arms, entered into cordial conferences and a declaration and counter-declaration were cooked up at Versailles and sent to London for approbation. They were approved there, reached Paris at one o'clock of the 27th, and were signed that night at Versailles. It was said and believed at Paris that M. de Montmorin literally "pleurait comme un enfant" when obliged to sign this counter-declaration, so distressed was he by the dishonor of sacrificing the Patriots after assurances so solemn of protection and absolute encouragement to proceed. The Prince of Orange was reinstated in all his powers, now become regal. A great emigration of the Patriots took place; all were deprived of office, many exiled, and their property confiscated. They were received in France and subsisted for some time on her bounty. Thus fell Holland, by the treachery of her Chief, from her honorable independence to become a province of England; and so, also, her Stadtholder from the high station of the first citizen of a free Republic, to be the servile Viceroy of a foreign sovereign. And this was effected by a mere scene of bullying and demonstration; not one of the parties, France, England or Prussia having ever really meant to encounter actual war for the interest of the Prince of Orange. But it had all the effect of a real and decisive war.—AUTOBIOGRAPHY. i, 73. FORD ED., i, 101. (1821.)

3756. HOLY ALLIANCE, Despotism.— What are we to think of this northern triumvirate, arming their nations to dictate despotisms to the rest of the world?—To JOHN ADAMS. vii, 217. (M., 1821.)

3757. ———. With respect to the European combinations against the rights of man, I join an honest Irishman of my neighborhood in his Fourth of July toast: "The Holy Alliance,—to Hell the whole of them." —To THOMAS LEIPER. FORD ED., x, 298. (M., 1824.)

3758. HOLY ALLIANCE, Napoleon and. —Had Bonaparte reflected that such is the moral construction of the world that no national crime passes unpunished in the long run, he would not now be in the cage of St. Helena; and were your present oppressors to reflect on the same truth, they would spare to their own countries the penalties on their present wrongs which will be inflicted on them in future times. The seeds of hatred and revenge which they are now sowing with a large hand will not fail to produce their fruits in time. Like their brother robbers on the highway, they suppose the escape of the moment a final escape, and deem infamy and future risk countervailed by present gain.—To M. DE MARBOIS. vii, 76. (M., 1817.)

3759. HOLY ALLIANCE, Policy of.— During the ascendency of Bonaparte, the word among the herd of kings, was *sauve qui peut.* Each shifted for himself, and left his brethren to squander and do the same as they could. After the battle of Waterloo and the military possession of France, they rallied and combined in common cause, to maintain each other against any similar and future danger. And in this alliance, Louis, now avowedly, and George, secretly but solidly, were of the contracting parties; and there can be no doubt that the allies are bound by treaty to aid England with their armies, should insurrection take place among her people. The coquetry she is now playing off between her people and her allies is perfectly understood by the latter, and accordingly gives no apprehensions to France, to whom it is all explained. The diplomatic correspondence she is now displaying, these double papers fabricated merely for exhibition, in which she makes herself talk of morals and principle, as if her qualms of conscience would not permit her to go all lengths with her Holy Allies, are all to gull her own people. It is a theatrical farce, in which the five powers are the actors, England the Tartuffe, and her people the dupes.—To PRESIDENT MONROE. vii, 289. FORD ED., x, 258. (M., June 1823.) See ALLIANCES and MONROE DOCTRINE.

3760. HOME, Better than honors.— In truth, I wish for neither honors nor offices. I am happier at home than I can be elsewhere.— To JOHN LANGDON. iv, 164. FORD ED., vii, 112. (M., 1797.)

3761. HOME, Companions.— Monroe is buying land almost adjoining me. Short will do the same. What would I not give [if] you could fall into the circle. With such a society, I could once more venture home, and lay myself up for the residue of life, quitting all its contentions which grow daily more and more insupportable. Think of it. To render it practicable only requires you to think it so. Life is of no value but as it brings us gratifications. Among the most valuable of these is rational society. It informs the mind, sweetens the temper, cheers our spirits, and promotes health. There is a little farm of 140 acres adjoining mine, and within two miles, all of good land, though old, with a small indifferent house on it, the whole not worth more than £250. Such a one might be a farm of experiment, and support a little table and household. It is on the road to Orange, and so much nearer than I am. * * * Once more think of it.— To JAMES MADISON. FORD ED., iii, 406. (A., 1784.)

3762. ———. I once hinted to you the project of seating yourself in the neighborhood of Monticello, and my sanguine wishes made me look on your answer as not absolutely excluding the hope. Monroe is decided in settling there, and is actually engaged in the endeavor to purchase. Short is the same. Would you but make it a "*partie quarrée*" I should believe that life had still some happiness in store for me. Agreeable society is the first essential in constituting the happiness, and, of course, the value of our existence. And it is a circumstance worthy great attention when we are making first our choice of a residence. Weigh well the value of this against the difference in pecuniary interest, and ask yourself which will add most to the sum of your felicity through life. I think that, weighing them in this balance, your decision will be favorable to all our prayers. Looking back with fondness to the moment when I am again to be fixed in my own country, I view the prospect of this society as inestimable.—To JAMES MADISON. FORD ED., iv, 17. (P., Dec. 1784.)

3763. HOME, in France.— The domestic bonds here [France] are absolutely done away, and where can their compensation be found? Perhaps they may catch some moments of transport above the level of the ordinary tranquil joy we experience, but they are separated by long intervals, during which all the passions are at sea without rudder or compass. Yet, fallacious as the pursuits of happiness are, they seem on the whole to furnish the most effectual abstraction from a contemplation of the hardness of their government.—To MRS. TRIST. i, 394. (P., 1785.)

3764. HOME, Happy.— I employ my leisure moments in repassing often in my mind our happy domestic society when together at Monticello, and looking forward to the renewal of it. No other society gives me now any satisfaction, as no other is founded in sincere affection.— To MARY JEFFERSON EPPES. FORD ED., vii, 405. (1800.)

3765. ———. I look forward with hope to the moment when we are all to be reunited again.—To MARTHA JEFFERSON RANDOLPH. FORD ED., vii, 416. (Pa., 1800.)

3766. ———. My habits are formed to those of my own country. I am past the time of changing them, and am, therefore, less happy anywhere else than there.—To DR. CURRIE. ii, 220. (P., 1787.)

3767. HOME, No happiness elsewhere. —Abstracted from home, I know no happiness in this world.—To LIEUT. DE UNGER. i, 279. FORD ED., ii, 374. (R., 1780.)

3768. HOME, Independence.— I am savage enough to prefer the woods, the wilds, and the independence of Monticello, to all the brilliant pleasures of this gay capital [Paris].— To BARON GEISMER. i, 427. (P., 1785.)

3769. HOME, Longing for.— I am never a day without wishing to be with you, and more and more as the fine sunshine comes on, which was made for all the world but me.—To NICHOLAS LEWIS. iii, 348. FORD ED., v, 504. (Pa., 1792.)

3770. ———. When I indulge myself in these [agricultural] speculations, I feel with redoubled ardor my desire to return home to the pursuit of them, and to the bosom of my family, in whose love alone I live or wish to live, and in that of my neighbors. To T. M. RANDOLPH. FORD ED., v, 417. (Pa., Jan. 1792.)

3771. HOME, Pleasures of.—Having no particular subject for a letter, I find none more soothing to my mind than to indulge itself in expressions of the love I bear you, and the delight with which I recall the various scenes through which we have passed together in our wanderings over the world. These reveries alleviate the toils and inquietudes of my present situation [Secretary of State] and leave me always impressed with the desire of being at home once more, and of exchanging labor, envy, and malice for ease, domestic occupation, and domestic love and society; where I may once more be happy with you, with Mr. Randolph, and dear little Anne, with whom even Socrates might ride on a stick without being ridiculous. —To MARTHA JEFFERSON RANDOLPH. FORD ED., v, 422. (P., 1792.)

3772. HONESTY, Common sense and.— Let common sense and common honesty have fair play and they will soon set things to rights.—To EZRA STILES. ii, 77. (P., 1786.)

3773. HONESTY, Consciousness of.—Of you, my neighbors, I may ask, in the face of the world. " whose ox have I taken, or whom have I defrauded? Whom have I oppressed, or of whose hand have I received a bribe to blind mine eyes therewith "? On your verdict I rest with conscious security.—To THE INHABITANTS OF ALBEMARLE COUNTY, VA. v, 439. FORD ED., ix, 251. (M., April 1809.)

3774. HONESTY, Examples of.—It can give no great claims to any one to manage honestly and disinterestedly the concerns of others trusted to him. Abundant examples of this are always under our eye.—To MR. WEAVER. v, 88. (W., 1807.)

3775. HONESTY, Government and.— The whole art of government consists in the art of being honest.—RIGHTS OF BRITISH AMERICA. i, 141. FORD ED., i, 446. (1774.)

3776. HONESTY, Individual.—I know but one code of morality for men, whether acting singly or collectively. He who says I will be a rogue when I act in company with a hundred others, but an honest man when I act alone, will be believed in the former assertion, but not in the latter. I would say with the poet, " *hic niger est, hunc tu Romane cavato*". If the morality of one man produces a just line of conduct in him, acting individually, why should not the morality of one hundred men produce a just line of conduct in them, acting together?—To JAMES MADISON. iii, 99. FORD ED., v, 111. (P., 1789.)

3777. HONESTY, Interest and.—Honesty and interest are as intimately connected in the public as in the private code of morality.—To MR. MAURY. vi, 468. (M., 1815.)

3778. HONESTY, Opportunity and.— Men are disposed to live honestly, if the means of doing so are open to them.—To M. DE MARBOIS. vii, 77. (M., 1817.)

3779. HONESTY, Riches and.—I have not observed men's honesty to increase with

their riches.—To JEREMIAH MOOR. FORD ED., vii, 454. (M., 1800.)

3780. HONESTY, Roguery and.—Every country is divided between the parties of honest men and rogues.— To WILLIAM B. GILES. iv, 126. (1795.)

3781. HONESTY, Statesmen and.—The man who is dishonest as a statesman, would be a dishonest man in any station.—To GEORGE LOGAN. FORD ED., x, 68. (P.F., 1816.)

3782. HONESTY, Wisdom and.—A wise man, even if nature has not formed him honest, will yet act as if he were honest; because he will find it the most advantageous and wise part in the long run.—To JAMES MONROE. FORD ED., iv, 40. (P., 1785.)

3783. ———. An honest heart being the first blessing, a knowing head is the second.—To PETER CARR. i, 397. (P., 1785.)

3784. ———. Honesty is the first chapter in the book of wisdom.—To NATHANIEL MACON. vii, 112. FORD ED., x, 122. (M., 1819.)

3785. HONOR, False.—Peace and happiness are preferable to that false honor which, by eternal wars, keeps the [European] people in eternal labor, want and wretchedness. —To PRESIDENT MADISON. vi, 452. FORD ED., ix, 511. (M., 1815.)

3786. HONOR, Infraction.—As an American, I cannot help feeling a thorough mortification, that our Congress should have permitted an infraction of our public honor; as a citizen of Virginia, I cannot help hoping and confiding, that our Supreme Executive, whose acts will be considered as the acts of the Commonwealth, estimate that honor too highly to make its infraction their own act.*— To GOVERNOR PATRICK HENRY. i, 214. FORD ED., ii, 169. (Alb., 1779.)

3787. HONOR, Integrity and.—When your mind shall be well improved with science, nothing will be necessary to place you in the highest points of view, but to pursue the interests of your country, the interests of your friends, and your own interests also, with the purest integrity, the most chaste honor. The defect of these virtues can never be made up by all the other acquirements of body and mind. Make these, then, your first object.†—To PETER CARR. i, 395. (P., 1785.)

3788. HONOR, Pledge of.—And for the support of this Declaration, we mutually pledge to each other our * * * sacred honor.‡—DECLARATION OF INDEPENDENCE AS DRAWN BY JEFFERSON.

3789. HONOR, Wounded.—It seems much the general opinion here [Virginia] that our honor has been too much wounded not to

* Refers to separation of British prisoners in Virginia.—EDITOR.
† Peter Carr was the young nephew of Jefferson.—EDITOR.
‡ Congress inserted after Declaration, " with a firm reliance on the protection of Divine Providence ".—EDITOR.

equire reparation, and to seek it even in war, if that be necessary.—To TENCH COXE. iv, 05. FORD ED., vi, 508. (M., May 1794.)

3790. HONORS, Hostile to happiness.— There are minds which can be pleased by honors and preferments; but I see nothing in them but envy and enmity. It is only necessary to possess them, to know how little they contribute to happiness, or rather how hostile they are to it.—To A. DONALD. ii, 356. (P., 788.)

3791. HONORS, Political.—I have seen enough of political honors to know that they are but splendid torments.—To MARTHA JEFFERSON RANDOLPH. D. L. J., 245. (Pa., 1797.) See HOME.

3792. HONORS, Public approbation.— It is our happiness that honorable distinctions flow only from public approbation; and that finds no object in titled dignitaries and pageants.—REPLY TO ADDRESS. viii, 163. 1809.)

3793. HONORS, Undeserved.—I have never ceased, nor can I cease to feel that I am holding honors without yielding requital, and justly belonging to others.—To DR. ROBERT M. PATTERSON. vi, 397. (M., 1814.)

3794. ——— ———. I cannot be easy in holding, as a sinecure, an honor* so justly due to the talents and services of others.—To DR. ROBERT M. PATTERSON. vi, 396. (M., 1814.)

3795. HOPE vs. DESPAIR.—My theory has always been, that if we are to dream, the flatteries of hope are as cheap, and pleasanter than the gloom of despair.—To M. DE MARBOIS. vii, 77. (M., 1817.)

3796. ——— ———. Hope is sweeter than despair.—To MRS. COSWAY. ii, 41. FORD ED., v, 321. (P., 1786.)

3797. HOPKINSON (Francis), Genius of.—He is a man of genius, gentility, and great merit * * * and as capable of [filling] the office [of Director, or Master of the Mint], as any man I know. The appointment would give general pleasure, because he is generally esteemed.—To JAMES MONROE. FORD ED., iii, 496. (Pa., 1784.)

3798. HORSES, Arabian.—The culture of wheat by enlarging our [Virginia's] pasture, will render the Arabian horse an article of very considerable profit. Experience has shown that ours is the particular climate of America where he may be raised without degeneracy. Southwardly the heat of the sun occasions a deficiency of pasture, and northwardly the winters are too cold for the short and fine hair, the particular sensibility and constitution of that race. Animals transplanted into unfriendly climates, either change their nature and acquire new senses against the new difficulties in which they are placed, or they multiply poorly and become extinct. * * * Their patience of heat without injury, their superior wind, fit them better in this and the more southern climate even for the drudgeries of the plough and wagon. Northwardly they will become an object only to persons of taste and fortune, for the saddle and light carriages.—NOTES ON VIRGINIA. viii, 408. FORD ED., iii, 272. (1782.)

* Presidency of Philosophical Society.—EDITOR.

3799. HORSES, Effect on man.—The Europeans value themselves on having subdued the horse to the uses of man; but I doubt whether we have not lost more than we have gained by the use of this animal. No one has occasioned so much the degeneracy of the human body. An Indian goes on foot nearly as far in a day, for a long journey, as an enfeebled white does on his horse; and he will tire the best horses.—To PETER CARR. i, 398. (P., 1785.)

3800. HORSES, Tax on.—The proposed tax on horses, besides its partiality, is infinitely objectionable as foisting in a direct tax under the name of an indirect one.—To T. M. RANDOLPH. FORD ED., vi, 149. (1792.)

3801. HORTICULTURE, American.— Gardens [are] peculiarly worth the attention of an American [when travelling], because it is the country of all others where the noblest gardens may be made without expense. We have only to cut out the superabundant plants. —TRAVELLING HINTS. ix, 404. (1788.)

3802. HORTICULTURE, English.—The pleasure gardening in England is the article in which it surpasses all the earth.—To JOHN PAGE. i, 549. FORD ED., iv, 214. (P., 1786.)

3803. HORTICULTURE, Love of.—I have often thought that if Heaven had given me choice of my position and calling, it should have been on a rich spot of earth, well watered, and near a good market for the productions of the garden. No occupation is so delightful to me as the culture of the earth, and no culture comparable to that of the garden. * * * Under a total want of demand except for our family table, I am still devoted to the garden. But though an old man, I am but a young gardener.—To C. W. PEALE. vi, 6. (P.F., 1811.)

3804. HOSPITALITY, Natural laws of.—Among the first of the laws of nature is that which bids us to succor those in distress. For an obedience to this law, Don Blas Gonzalez* appears to have suffered; and we are satisfied, it is because his case has not been able to penetrate to his Majesty's ministers, at least in its true colors. We would not choose to be committed by a formal solicitation, but we would wish you to avail yourself of any good opportunity of introducing the truth to the ear of the minister, and of satisfying him, that a redress of this hardship on the governor would be received here with pleasure, as a proof of respect to those laws of hospitality which we would certainly observe in a like case, as a mark of attention towards us, and of justice to an individual for whose sufferings we cannot but feel.—To WILLIAM CARMICHAEL. ii, 139. FORD ED., iii, 155. (N.Y., 1790.)

3805. HOSPITALITY, Practice of.—You know our practice of placing our guests at their ease, by showing them we are so ourselves, and that we follow our necessary vocations, instead of fatiguing them by hanging unremittingly on their shoulders.—To F. W. GILMER. vii, 5. FORD ED., x, 33. (M., 1816.)

3806. HOSPITALITY, Social.—Call on me * * * whenever you come to town, and if it should be about the hour of three, I shall rejoice the more. You will find a bad dinner, a good glass of wine, and a host thankful for your favor, and desirous of encouraging repe-

*A Spanish governor who had been punished by his government for having succored an American ship in the island of Juan Fernandez.—EDITOR.

titions of it without number, form or ceremony.
—To RICHARD PETERS. FORD ED., v, 347.
(Pa., 1791.)

3807. HOUDON (Jean Antoine), Ability.—He is among the foremost, or, perhaps,
the foremost artist in the world.—To F. HOP-
KINSON. i, 504. (P., 1786.)

3808. HOUDON (Jean Antoine), Life
insurance.—Monsieur Houdon has agreed
to go to America to take the figure of General
Washington. In case of his death, between his
departure from Paris and his return to it, we
may lose twenty thousand livres. I ask the
favor of you to enquire what it will cost to
insure that sum on his life, in London, and
to give me as early an answer as possible, that
I may order the insurance if I think the terms
easy enough. He is, I believe, between thirty
and thirty-five years of age, healthy enough,
and will be absent about six months.—To JOHN
ADAMS. i, 361. (P., 1785.)

3809. HOUDON (Jean Antoine), Statue
of Washington.—M. Houdon is returned [to
Paris] with the necessary moulds and measures
for General Washington's statue. I fear the
expenses of his journey have been considerably
increased by the unlucky accident of his tools,
materials, clothes, &c., not arriving at Havre in
time to go with him to America, so that he
had to supply himself there.—To GOVERNOR
HENRY. i, 513. FORD ED., iv, 134. (P., 1786.)

3810. HOWE (Lord William), Friendly
to America.—Lord Howe seems to have been
friendly to America, and exceedingly anxious
to prevent a rupture.*—AUTOBIOGRAPHY. i, 110.
(1821.)

3811. HOWE (Lord William), Invasion
of Virginia.—What upon earth can Howe
mean by the manœuvre he is now practicing?
There seems to me no object in this country
which can be either of utility or reputation to
his cause. I hope it will prove of a piece with
all the other follies they have committed. The
forming a junction with the northern army up
the Hudson River, or taking possession of
Philadelphia might have been a feather in his
cap, and given them a little reputation in Europe—the former as being the design with
which they came, the latter as being a place of
the first reputation abroad, and the residence of
Congress. Here, he may destroy the little
hamlet of Williamsburg, steal a few slaves, and
lose half his army among the fens and marshes
of our lower country, or by the heat of the
climate.—To JOHN ADAMS. i, 207. FORD ED.,
ii, 134. (Alb., 1777.)

3812. HULL (William), Bravery.—The
detestable treason of Hull, has excited a deep
anxiety in all breasts. * * * His treachery, like
that of Arnold, cannot be a matter of blame on
our government. His character, as an officer of
skill and bravery, was established on the trials
of the last war, and no previous act of his life
had led to doubt his fidelity.—To WILLIAM
DUANE. vi, 80. FORD ED., ix, 368. (M., Oct.
1812.)

3813. HULL (William), Suspected treason.—Hull will of course be shot for cowardice and treachery.†—To PRESIDENT MAD-
ISON. FORD ED., ix, 370. (M., Nov. 1812.)

* Mr. Jefferson formed this opinion from a paper
which Benjamin Franklin, a short time before his
death, had given him to read.—EDITOR.

† General Hull's character is now free from all
stain.—EDITOR.

3814. HUMBOLDT (Baron von), Esteemed.—The receipt of your Distributi
Geographica Plantarum, with the duty of thank
ing you for a work which sheds so much ne-
and valuable light on botanical science, excite
the desire, also, of presenting myself to you
recollection, and of expressing to you thos
sentiments of high admiration and esteem
which, although long silent, have never slept.—
To F. H. ALEXANDER VON HUMBOLDT. vii, 7
FORD ED., x, 88. (M., 1817.)

3815. HUMBOLDT (Baron von), Trib
ute to.—We shall bear to you the honorabl
testimony that you have deserved well of th
republic of letters. * * * You have wisely lo
cated yourself in the focus of the science o
Europe. I am held by the cords of love to m
family and country, or I should certainly joi
you.—To BARON VON HUMBOLDT. v, 435. (W
1809.)

3816. HUMPHREYS (David), Attack
on.—Colonel Humphreys is attacked in th
[American] papers for his French airs, fo
bad poetry, bad prose, vanity, &c. It is said h
dress, in so gay a style, gives general disgu
against him. * * * He seems fixed with Ge
eral Washington.*—To WILLIAM SHORT. i
574. FORD ED., v, 71. (P., 1789.)

3817. HUMPHREYS (David), Minis
ter.—The President has nominated you Mi
ister Resident * * * at the Court of Lisbo
which was approved by the Senate. You wi
consequently receive herewith your commissio
—To DAVID HUMPHREYS. FORD ED., v, 30
(Pa., 1791.)

3818. HUMPHREYS (David), Talent
—Colonel Humphreys is sensible, prudent, an
honest, and may be firmly relied on, in ar
office which requires these talents.—To E
BRIDGE GERRY. i, 557. (P., 1786.)

3819. ———— ————. He is an excellent ma
an able one, and in need of some provision.—
To JAMES MONROE. i, 568. FORD ED., iv, 22
(P., 1786.)

3820. IDEAS, Erroneous.—It is alway
better to have no ideas than false ones; t
believe nothing than to believe what is wron
—To REV. JAMES MADISON. ii, 430. (P
1788.)

— IDEAS, Property in.—See INVENTION
and PATENTS.

3821. IDLENESS, Evils of.—Nothin
can contribute more to your future happine
(moral rectitude always excepted), than th
contracting a habit of industry and activit
Of all the cankers of human happiness nor
corrodes with so silent, yet so baneful an i
fluence as indolence. Body and mind bot
unemployed, our being becomes a burden, an
every object about us loathsome, even th
dearest. Idleness begets ennui, ennui th
hypochondriac, and that a diseased body.—T
MARTHA JEFFERSON. FORD ED., iv, 37
(1787.)

3822. IDLENESS, Needless.—In a wor
which furnishes so many employments whic
are so useful, so many which are amusin
it is our own fault if we ever know wha

* Washington made him his private secretary.
EDITOR.

ennui is, or if we are driven to the miserable resources of gaming, which corrupts our dispositions, and teaches us a habit of hostility against all mankind.—To MARTHA JEFFERSON. FORD ED., iv, 389. (1787.)

3823. IDLENESS, Time-destroyer.— Determine never to be idle. No person will have occasion to complain of the want of time who never loses any. It is wonderful how much may be done if we are always doing.— To MARTHA JEFFERSON. FORD ED., iv, 387. (M., 1787.)

3824. IDLENESS, Wretchedness and.— A mind always employed is always happy. This is the true secret, the grand recipe for felicity. The idle are * * * the wretched. —To MARTHA JEFFERSON. FORD ED., iv, 389. (Mar. 1787.)

3825. IGNORANCE, Barrier against.— We are destined to be a barrier against the return of ignorance and barbarism.—To JOHN ADAMS. vii, 27. (M., 1816.)

3826. IGNORANCE, Bigotry and.—Ignorance and bigotry, like other insanities, are incapable of self-government.—To MARQUIS LAFAYETTE. vii, 67. FORD ED., x, 84. (M., 1817.)

3827. IGNORANCE, Honest.—If science produces no better fruits than tyranny, murder, rapine and destitution of national morality, I would rather wish our country to be ignorant, honest and estimable, as our neighboring savages are.—To JOHN ADAMS. vi, 37. FORD ED., ix, 334. (M., 1812.)

3828. IGNORANCE, Misgovernment and.—Preach a crusade against ignorance. Establish and improve the law for educating the common people. Let our countrymen know that the people alone can protect us against these evils, and that the tax which will be paid for this purpose, is not more than the thousandth part of what will be paid to kings, priests and nobles, who will rise up among us, if we leave the people in ignorance. —To GEORGE WYTHE. ii, 8. FORD ED., iv, 269. (P., 1786.)

— ILLINOIA, Proposed State.—See WESTERN TERRITORY.

3829. ILLUMINATI, Order of.—I have lately by accident got a sight of a single volume (the 3d) of the Abbé Barruel's *Antisocial Conspiracy*", which gives me the first idea I have ever had of what is meant by the Illuminatism against which "Illuminate Morse", as he is now called, and his ecclesiastical and monarchical associates have been making such a hue and cry. Barruel's own parts of the book are perfectly the ravings of a Bedlamite. But he quotes largely from Wishaupt whom he considers as the founder of what he calls the order. As you may not have had an opportunity of forming a judgment of this cry of "mad dog", which has been raised against his doctrines, I will give you the idea I have formed from only an hour's reading of Barruel's quotations from him, which, you may be sure, are not the most favorable. Wishaupt seems to be an enthusiastic philanthropist. He is among those (as you know the excellent Price and

Priestley also are) who believe in the infinite perfectability of man. He thinks he may in time be rendered so perfect that he will be able to govern himself in every circumstance, so as to injure none, to do all the good he can, to leave government no occasion to exercise their powers over him, and, of course, to render political government useless. This, you know, is Godwin's doctrine, and this is what Robinson, Barruel, and Morse had called a conspiracy against all government. Wishaupt believes that to promote this perfection of the human character was the object of Jesus Christ. That his intention was simply to reinstate natural religion, and by diffusing the light of his morality, to teach us to govern ourselves. His precepts are the love of God, and love of our neighbor. And by teaching innocence of conduct, he expected to place men in their natural state of liberty and equality. He says, no one ever laid a surer foundation for liberty than our grand master, Jesus of Nazareth. He believes the Free Masons were originally possessed of the true principles and objects of Christianity, and have still preserved some of them by tradition, but much disfigured. The means he proposes to effect this improvement of human nature are "to enlighten men, to correct their morals and inspire them with benevolence". As Wishaupt lived under the tyranny of a despot and priests, he knew that caution was necessary even in spreading information, and the principles of pure morality. He proposed, therefore, to lead the Free Masons to adopt this object, and to make the objects of their institution the diffusion of science and virtue. He proposed to initiate new members into his body by gradations proportioned to his fears of the thunderbolts of tyranny. This has given an air of mystery to his views, was the foundation of his banishment, the subversion of the Masonic Order, and is the color for the ravings against him of Robinson, Barruel, and Morse, whose real fears are that the craft would be endangered by the spreading of information, reason, and natural morality among men. This subject being new to me, I imagine that if it be so to you also, you may receive the same satisfaction in seeing, which I have had in forming the analysis of it; and I believe you will think with me that if Wishaupt had written here, where no secrecy is necessary in our endeavours to render men wise and virtuous, he would not have thought of any secret machinery for that purpose; as Godwin, if he had written in Germany, might probably also have thought secrecy and mysticism prudent.—To BISHOP JAMES MADISON. FORD ED., vii, 419. (Pa., Jan. 1800.)

3830. IMBECILITY, Insensibility to. —Nothing betrays imbecility so much as the being insensible of it.—To DR. BENJAMIN RUSH. vi, 4. FORD ED., ix, 328. (P.F., 1811.)

3831. IMMIGRANTS, Aged.—That it may be for the benefit of your children and their descendants to remove to a country where, for enterprise and talents, so many avenues are open to fortune and fame, I have little doubt. But I should be afraid to affirm that, at your time of life, and with habits formed on the state of society in France, a change for one so entirely different would be for your personal happiness. —To JEAN BAPTISTE SAY. vi, 436. (M., 1815.)

3832. IMMIGRANTS, Assisted.—With respect to the German redemptioners, I can do nothing unless authorized by law. It would be made a question in Congress, whether any of the enumerated objects to which the Constitution authorizes the money of the Union to be applied, would cover an expenditure for importing settlers to Orleans.—To THOMAS PAINE. iv, 582. FORD ED., viii, 360. (W., 1805.)

3833. IMMIGRANTS, Colonized.—As to other [than English] foreigners, it is thought better to discourage their settling together in large masses, wherein, as in our German settlements, they preserve for a long time their own languages, habits and principles of government, and that they should distribute themselves sparsely among the natives for quicker amalgamation. English emigrants are without this inconvenience. They differ from us little but in their principles of government, and most of those (merchants excepted) who come here, are sufficiently disposed to adopt ours.—To GEORGE FLOWER. vii, 84. (P.F., 1817.)

3834. IMMIGRANTS, Indentured.—Indentured servants formed a considerable supply. These were poor Europeans, who went to America to settle themselves. If they could pay their passage, it was well. If not, they must find means of paying it. They were at liberty, therefore, to make an agreement with any person they chose, to serve him such a length of time as they agreed on, upon condition that he would repay to the master of the vessel the expenses of their passage. If, being foreigners, unable to speak the language, they did not know how to make a bargain for themselves, the captain of the vessel contracted for them with such persons as he could. This contract was by deed indented, which occasioned them to be called indented servants. * * * with the master of the vessel, they could *redeem* themselves from his power by paying their passage, which they frequently effected by hiring themselves on their arrival. In some States I know that these people had a right of marrying themselves without their masters' leave, and I did suppose they had that right everywhere. I did not know that in any of the States they demanded so much as a week for every day's absence without leave. I suspect this must have been at a very early period, while the governments were in the hands of the first emigrants, who, being mostly laborers, were narrow-minded and severe. I know that in Virginia the laws allowed their servitude to be protracted only two days for every one they were absent without leave. So mild was this kind of servitude, that it was very frequent for foreigners, who carried to America money enough, not only to pay their passage, but to buy themselves a farm, it was common I say for them to indent themselves to a master for three years, for a certain sum of money with a view to learn the husbandry of the country. I will here make a general observation. So desirous are the poor of Europe to get to America, where they may better their condition, that being unable to pay their passage, they will agree to serve two or three years on their arrival there, rather than not go.—To M. DE MEUNIER. ix, 254. FORD ED., iv, 159. (P., 1786.)

3835. IMMIGRANTS, Irish and German.—By the close of 1785, there had probably passed over 50,000 emigrants. Most of these were Irish. The greatest number of the residue were Germans. Philadelphia received most of them, and next to that Baltimore and New York.—To M. DE MEUNIER. ix, 284. FORD ED., iv, 140. (P., 1786.)

3836. ——— ———. The best tenants are foreigners, who do not speak the language. Unable to communicate with the people of the country, they confine themselves to their farms and families, compare their present state to what it was in Europe, and find great reason to be contented. Of all foreigners, I should prefer Germans. They are the easiest got, the best for their landlords, and do best for themselves.—To COLONEL R. CLAIBORNE. ii, 235. (P., 1787.)

3837. IMMIGRANTS, Protection of.—It has been the wise policy of these States to extend the protection of their laws to all those who should settle among them of whatsoever nation or religion, they might be, and to admit them to a participation of the benefits of civil and religious freedom; and the benevolence of this practice, as well as its salutary effects renders it worthy of being continued in future times.—PROCLAMATION CONCERNING FOREIGNERS. FORD ED., ii, 445. (R., 1781.)

3838. IMMIGRATION, Free.—Our country is open to all men, to come and go peaceably, when they choose.—To E. C. GENET. iv, 87. FORD ED., vi, 459. (Pa., Nov. 1793.)

3839. ——— ———. The session of the first Congress, convened since republicanism has recovered its ascendency, * * * are opening the doors of hospitality to fugitives from the oppressions of other countries.—To GENERAL KOSCIUSKO. iv, 430. (W., April 1802.)

3840. IMMIGRATION, Negro.—The papers from the free people of color in Grenada * * * I apprehend it will be best to take no notice of. They are parties in a domestic quarrel, which, I think, we should leave to be settled among themselves. Nor should I think it desirable, were it justifiable, to draw a body of sixty thousand free blacks and mulattoes into our country.—To PRESIDENT WASHINGTON. FORD ED., v, 342. (Pa., 1791.)

3841. IMMIGRATION, Obstructions to. —He has endeavored to prevent the population of these States; for that purpose obstructing the laws for naturalization of foreigners, refusing to pass others to encourage their migrations hither; and raising the conditions of new appropriations of lands.— DECLARATION OF INDEPENDENCE AS DRAWN BY JEFFERSON.

3842. IMMIGRATION, Regulation of. —The American governments are censured for permitting this species of servitude [Indenture], which lays the foundation of the happiness of these people. But what should these governments do? Pay the passage of all who choose to go into their country? They are not able; nor, were they able, do they think the purchase worth the price? Should they exclude these people from their shores? Those who know their situations in Europe and America would not say that this is the alternative which humanity dictates. It is said that these people are deceived by those who carry them over. But this is done in Europe. How can the American governments prevent it? * * * The individuals are generally satisfied in America with their adventure, and very few of them wish not to have made it. I must add that the Congress have nothing to do with this matter. It belongs to the legislatures of the several States.—To M. DE MEUNIER. ix, 255. FORD ED., iv, 160. (P., 1786.)

3843. —— ——. I had often thought on the subject you propose as to the mode of procuring German emigrants to take the place of our blacks. To this, however, the State Legislatures are alone competent, the General Government possessing no powers but those enumerated in the Constitution, and that of obtaining emigrants at the general expense not being one of the enumerated powers. With respect to the State governments, I not only doubt, but despair, of their taking up this operation, till some strong pressure of circumstance shall force it on them.—To J. P. REIBELT. FORD ED., viii, 402. (W., Dec. 1805.)

3844. IMMIGRATION, Revolution and.—My means of being useful to you [in founding a colony of English farmers] are small, [but] they shall be freely exercised for your advantage, and that, not on the selfish principle of increasing our own population at the expense of other nations, * * * but to consecrate a sanctuary for those whom the misrule of Europe may compel to seek happiness in other climes. This refuge once known will produce reaction on the happiness even of those who remain there, by warning their task-masters that when the evils of Egyptian opposition become heavier than those of the abandonment of country, another Canaan is open where their subjects will be received as brothers, and secured against like oppressions by a participation in the right of self-government. If additional motives could be wanting with us to the maintenance of this right, they would be found in the animating consideration that a single good government becomes thus a blessing to the whole earth, its welcome to the oppressed restraining within certain limits the measure of their oppressions. But should even this be counteracted by violence on the right of expatriation, the other branch of our example then presents itself for imitation, to rise on their rulers and do as we have done. You have set to your own country a good example, by showing them a peaceable mode of reducing their rulers to the necessity of becoming more wise, more moderate, and more honest, and I sincerely pray that the example may work for the benefit of those who cannot follow it, as it will for your own.—To GEORGE FLOWER. vii, 84. (P.F., 1817.)

3845. IMMIGRATION, Too rapid.— The present desire of America is to produce rapid population by as great importations of foreigners as possible. But is this founded in good policy? The advantage proposed is the multiplication of numbers. Now let us suppose (for example only) that, in this State, [Virginia] we could double our numbers in one year by the importation of foreigners; and this is a greater accession than the most sanguine advocate for immigration has a right to expect. Then I say, beginning with a double stock, we shall attain any given degree of population only twenty-seven years and three months sooner than if we proceed on our single stock. If we propose four millions and a half as a competent population for this State, we should be fifty-four and a half years attaining it, could we at once double our numbers; and eighty-one and three-quarter years, if we rely on natural propagation, as may be seen by the following table:

	Proceeding on our present stock.	Proceeding on a double stock.
1781..................	567,614	1,135,228
1808¼..................	1,135,228	2,270,456
1835½..................	2,270,456	4,540,912
1862¾..................	4,540,912	

In the first column are stated periods of twenty-seven and a quarter years; in the second are our numbers at each period, as they will be if we proceed on our actual stock; and in the third are what they would be, at the same periods, were we to set out from the double of our present stock. I have taken the term of four million and a half of inhabitants for example's sake only. Yet I am persuaded it is a greater number than the country spoken of. considering how much inarable land it contains. can clothe and feed without a material change in the quality of their diet. But are there no inconveniences to be thrown into the scale against the advantage expected from a multiplication of numbers by the importation of foreigners? It is for the happiness of those united in society to harmonize as much as possible in matters which they must of necessity transact together. Civil government being the sole object of forming societies, its administration must be conducted by common consent. Every species of government has its specific principles. Ours perhaps are more peculiar than those of any other in the universe. It is a composition of the freest principles of the English constitution, with others derived from natural right and natural reason. To these nothing can be more opposed than the maxims of absolute monarchies. Yet from such we are to expect the greatest number of emigrants. They will bring with them the principles of the governments they leave, imbibed in their early youth; or, if able to throw them off, it will be in exchange for an unbounded licentiousness, passing, as is usual, from one extreme to another. It would be a miracle were they to stop precisely at the point of temperate liberty. These principles, with their language, they will transmit to their children. In proportion to their numbers, they will share with us the legislation. They will infuse into it their spirit, warp and bias its directions, and render it a heterogeneous, incoherent, distracted mass. I may appeal to experience, during the present contest. for a verification of these conjectures. But, if they be not certain in event, are they not possible, are they not probable? Is it not safer to wait with patience twenty-seven years and three months longer, for the attainment of any degree of population desired or expected? May not our government be more homogeneous, more peaceable, more durable? Suppose twenty millions of republican Americans thrown all of a sudden into France, what would be the condition of that kingdom? If it would be more turbulent, less happy, less strong, we may believe that the addition of half a million of foreigners to our present numbers would produce a similar effect here. If they come of themselves they are entitled to all the rights of citizenship; but I doubt the expediency of inviting them by extraordinary encouragements. I mean not that these doubts should be extended to the importation of useful artificers. The policy of that measure depends on very different considerations. Spare no expense in obtaining them. They will after a while go to the plough and the hoe; but, in the meantime, they will teach us something we do not know. It is not so in agriculture. The indifferent state of that among us does not proceed from a want of knowledge merely; it is from our having such quantities of land to waste as we please. In Europe the object is to make the most of their land, labor being abundant; here it is to make the most of our labor, land being abundant.—NOTES ON VIRGINIA. viii, 330. FORD ED., iii, 188. (1782.)

3846. IMMORTALITY, Belief in.—The term is not very distant, at which we are to deposit in the same cerement, our sorrows and suffering bodies, and to ascend in essence to an ecstatic meeting with the friends we have loved and lost, and whom we shall still love and never lose again.—To JOHN ADAMS. vii, 108. FORD ED., x, 114. (M., 1818.)

3847. IMPEACHMENT, Abuse of.—History shows that in England impeachment has been an engine more of passion than justice.*—To JAMES MADISON. iv, 212. FORD ED., vii, 203. (Pa., 1798.)

3848. IMPEACHMENT, Contempt for.—Impeachment is scarcely a scarecrow.—To C. HAMMOND. vii, 216. (M., 1821.)

3849. ———. Impeachment is a bugbear which they [Judiciary] fear not at all.—To JAMES PLEASANTS. FORD ED., x, 199. (M., 1821.)

3850. ———. Experience has already shown that the impeachment the Constitution has provided is not even a scarecrow.—To SPENCER ROANE. vii, 134. FORD ED., x, 141. (P.F., 1819.)

3851. IMPEACHMENT, Courts of.—For misbehavior, the grand inquest of the Colony, the House of Representatives, should impeach them before the Governor and Council, when they should have time and opportunity to make their defence; and if convicted, should be removed from their offices, and subjected to such other punishment as shall be thought proper.—To GEORGE WYTHE. FORD ED., ii, 60. (1776.)

3852. ———. There shall be a *Court of Impeachments*, to consist of three members of the Council of State, one of each of the superior courts of Chancery, Common Law, and Admiralty, two members of the House of Delegates and one of the Senate, to be chosen by the body respectively of which they are. Before this Court any member of the three branches of government, that is to say,

* A sketch of some of the principles and practices of England with respect to impeachments is given in the Parliamentary Manual, ix, 82.—EDITOR.

the governor, any member of the Council, of the two houses of legislature, or of the superior courts, may be impeached by the governor, the Council, or either of the said houses or courts, and by no other, for such misbehavior in office as would be sufficient to remove him therefrom; and the only sentence they shall have authority to pass shall be that of deprivation and future incapacity of office. Seven members shall be requisite to make a court, and two-thirds of those present must concur in the sentence. The offences cognizable by this court shall be cognizable by no other, and they shall be triers of the fact as well as judges of the law.—PROPOSED CONSTITUTION FOR VIRGINIA. viii, 449. FORD ED., iii, 329. (1783.)

3853. IMPEACHMENT, Faction and.—I see nothing in the mode of proceeding by impeachment but the most formidable weapon for the purposes of dominant faction that ever was contrived. It would be the most effectual one for getting rid of any man whom they consider as dangerous to their views.—To JAMES MADISON. iv, 211. FORD ED., vii, 202. (Pa., Feb. 1798.)

3854. IMPEACHMENT, A farce.—Impeachment is a farce which will not be tried again.—To W. B. GILES. v, 68. FORD ED., ix, 46. (M., 1807.)

3855. IMPEACHMENT, Inefficient.—Experience has proved that impeachment in our forms is completely inefficient.—To EDWARD LIVINGSTON. vii, 404. (M., 1825.)

3856. IMPEACHMENT, The judiciary and.—Having found from experience that impeachment is an impracticable thing, a mere scarecrow, they [the Judiciary] consider themselves secure for life.—To THOMAS RITCHIE. vii, 192. FORD ED., x, 170. (M., 1820.)

3857. ———. In the General Government in this instance, we have gone even beyond the English caution, by requiring a vote of two-thirds, in one of the Houses, for removing a Judge; a vote so impossible, where any defence is made, before men of ordinary prejudices and passions, that our Judges are effectually independent of the nation. But this ought not to be.—AUTOBIOGRAPHY. i, 81. FORD ED., i, 112. (1821.)

3858. ———. Our different States have differently modified their several judiciaries as to the tenure of office. Some appoint their judges for a given term of time; some continue them during good behavior, and that to be determined on by the concurring vote of *two-thirds* of each legislative house. In England they are removable by a *majority* only of each house. The last is a practicable remedy; the second is not. The combination of the friends and associates of the accused, the action of personal and party passions, and the sympathies of the human heart, will forever find means of influencing one-third of either the one or the other house, will thus secure their impunity, and establish them in fact for life. The first remedy is the better, that of appointing for a term of years only, with a capacity of reappointment if their conduct has been approved.—To M. Coray. vii, 321. (M., 1823.)

3859. IMPEACHMENT, Juries and.— The Senate have before them a bill for regulating proceedings in impeachment. This will be made the occasion of offering a clause for the introduction of juries into these trials. (Compare the paragraph in the Constitution which says, that all crimes, *except in cases of impeachment,* shall be by jury. with the eighth amendment, which says, that in *all* criminal prosecutions the trial shall be by jury.) There is no expectation of carrying this; because the division in the Senate is of two to one, but it will draw forth the principles of the parties, and concur in accumulating proofs on which side all the sound principles are to be found.—To James Madison. iv, 208. Ford ed., vii, 192. (Pa., Jan. 1798.)

3860. —— ——. You mentioned that some of your Committee admitted that the introduction of juries into trials by impeachment under the VIIIth amendment depended on the question whether an impeachment for a misdemeanor be a criminal prosecution? I devoted yesterday evening to the extracting passages from the law authors, showing that in lawlanguage, the term crime is in common use applied to *misdemeanors,* and that *impeachments,* even when for *misdemeanors* only are *criminal prosecutions.* Those proofs were so numerous that my patience could go no further than two authors, Blackstone and Woodeson. They show that you may meet that question without the danger of being contradicted. The Constitution closes the proofs by explaining its own meaning when speaking of *impeachments, crimes,* and *misdemeanors.*— To Henry Tazewell. Ford ed., vii, 194. (Pa., Jan. 1798.)

3861. —— ——. The object in supporting this engraftment into impeachments is to lessen the dangers of the court of impeachment under its present form, and to induce dispositions in all parties in favor of a better constituted court of impeachment, which I own I consider as an useful thing, if so composed as to be clear of the spirit of faction.— To Henry Tazewell. Ford ed., vii, 195. (Pa., 1798.)

3862. IMPEACHMENT, Law Courts vs.— I know of no solid purpose of punishment which the courts of law are not equal to.—To James Madison. iv, 212. Ford ed., vii, 203. (Pa., 1798.)

3863. IMPEACHMENT, Power of.— An opinion [has been] declared, that not only officers of the State governments, but every private citizen of the United States, are impeachable. Whether they think this the time to make the declaration, I know not; but if they bring it on, I think there will not be more than two votes north of the Potomac against the universality of the impeaching power.—To James Madison. iv, 215. Ford ed., vii, 207. (Pa., Feb. 1798.)

3864. IMPEACHMENT, The Senate and.— The articles of impeachment against Blount have been received by the Senate. Some great questions will immediately arise. 1. Can they prescribe their own oath, the forms of pleadings, issue process against person or goods by their own orders, without the formality of a law authorizing it? Has not the 8th amendment of the Constitution rendered a trial by jury necessary? Is a Senator impeachable?—To James Monroe. Ford ed., vii, 198. (Pa., Feb. 1798.)

— IMPOST.—See Excise.

3865. IMPRESSMENT, Certificates and.— From the debates on the subject of our seamen. I am afraid as much harm as good will be done by our endeavors to arm our seamen against impressments. It is proposed to register them and give them certificates of citizenship to protect them. But these certificates will be lost in a thousand ways; a sailor will neglect to take his certificate; he is wet twenty times in a voyage; if he goes ashore without it, he is impressed; if with it, he gets drunk.; it is lost, stolen from him, taken from him, and then the want of it gives authority to impress. which does not exist now.—To William B. Giles. iv, 133. Ford ed., vii, 65. (M., March 1796.)

3866. IMPRESSMENT, Embargo and.— The stand which has been made on behalf of our seamen enslaved and incarcerated in foreign ships, and against the prostration of our rights on the ocean under laws of nature acknowledged by all civilized nations. was an effort due to the protection of our commerce, and to that portion of our fellow citizens engaged in the pursuits of navigation. The opposition of the same portion to the vindication of their peculiar rights, has been as wonderful as the loyalty of their agricultural brethren in the assertion of them has been disinterested and meritorious.—R. to A. Massachusetts Citizens. viii, 160. (1809.)

3867. —— ——. Enough of the non-importation law should be reserved to pinch the English into a relinquishment of impressments.—To President Madison. v, 442. Ford ed., ix, 251. (M., April 1809.)

3868. IMPRESSMENT, George III. and. —He has constrained our fellow citizens, taken captive on the high seas, to bear arms against their country, to become the executioners of their friends and brethren, or to fall themselves by their hands.—Declaration of Independence as Drawn by Jefferson.

3869. IMPRESSMENT, Pretexts for.— You are desired to persevere till you obtain a regulation to guard our vessels from having their hands impressed, and to inhibit the British navy-officers from taking them under the pretext of their being British subjects.— To Thomas Pinckney. iii, 552. Ford ed., vi, 243. (Pa., May 1793.)

3870. IMPRESSMENT, Protection against.— We entirely reject the mode [of protecting our seamen from impressment] which was the subject of conversation between Mr. [Gouverneur] Morris and the British minister, which was, that our seamen should always carry about them certificates of their citizenship. This is a condition never yet submitted to by any nation, one with which seamen would never have the precaution to comply. The casualties of their calling would expose them to the constant destruction or loss of this paper evidence, and thus, the British government would be armed with *legal authority* to impress the whole of our seamen. The simplest rule will be, that the vessel being American, shall be evidence that the seamen on board her are such. If they apprehend that our vessels might thus become asylums for the fugitives of their own nation from impress-gangs, the number of men to be protected by a vessel may be limited by her tonnage, and one or two officers only be permitted to enter the vessel in order to examine the numbers on board; but no press-gang should be allowed ever to go on board an American vessel, till after it shall be found that there are more than their stipulated number on board, nor till after the master shall have refused to deliver the supernumeraries (to be named by himself) to the press-officer who has come on board for that purpose; and even then, the American consul should be called in.—To Thomas Pinckney. iii, 443. Ford ed., vi, 76. (Pa., June 1792.)

3871. IMPRESSMENT, Remonstrances against.—On the impressment of our seamen, our remonstrances have never been intermitted. A hope existed at one moment of an arrangement which might have been submitted to, but it soon passed away, and the practice, though relaxed at times in the distant seas, has been constantly pursued in those in our neighborhood.—Special Message. viii, 58. Ford ed., viii, 417. (Jan. 1806.)

3872. IMPRESSMENT, Renunciation of.—Nothing will be deemed security but a renunciation of the practice of taking persons out of our vessels, under the pretence of their being English.—To John Armstrong. v, 134. Ford ed., ix, 116. (W., 1807.)

3873. IMPRESSMENT, Resistance to.—Our particular and separate grievance is only the impressment of our citizens. We must sacrifice the last dollar and drop of blood to rid us of that badge of slavery.—To W. H. Crawford. vi, 418. Ford ed., ix, 502. (M., Feb. 1815.)

3874. IMPRESSMENT, Treaty of Peace and.—No provision being made [in the treaty of peace] against the impressment of our seamen, it is in fact but an armistice, to be terminated by the first act of impressment committed on an American citizen.—To W. H. Crawford. vi, 420. Ford ed., ix, 504. (M., 1815.)

3875. ———. I presume that, having spared to the pride of England her formal acknowledgment of the atrocity of impress-

ment in an article of the treaty, she will concur in a convention for relinquishing it. Without this, she must understand that the present is but a truce, determinable on the first act of impressment of an American citizen, committed by an officer of hers.—To President Madison. vi, 453. Ford ed., ix, 512. (M., March 1815.)

3876. IMPRESSMENT, War against.—Continued impressments of our seamen by her naval commanders, whose interest it was to mistake them for theirs, her innovations on the law of nations to cover real piracies, could illy be borne; and perhaps would not have been borne, had not contraventions of the same law by France, fewer in number but equally illegal, rendered it difficult to single the object of war. England, at length, singled herself, and took up the gauntlet, when the unlawful decrees of France being revoked as to us, she, by the proclamation of her Prince Regent, protested to the world that she would never revoke hers until those of France should be removed as to all nations. Her minister, too, about the same time, in an official conversation with our *Chargé*, rejected our substitute for her practice of impressment; proposed no other; and declared explicitly that no admissible one for this abuse could be proposed. Negotiation being thus cut short, no alternative remained but war, or the abandonment of the persons and property of our citizens on the ocean. The last one, I presume, no American would have preferred. War was therefore declared, and justly declared; but accompanied with immediate offers of peace on simply doing us justice.—To Dr. George Logan. vi, 215. Ford ed., ix, 422. (M., Oct. 1813.)

3877. ———. On that point [impressment] we have thrown away the scabbard, and the moment an European war brings England back to this practice, adds us again to her enemies.—To Mr. Maury. vi, 467. (M., 1815.)

— INAUGURAL ADDRESSES, Text of. —See Appendix.

— INCOME TAX.—See Taxation.

3878. INCORPORATION, Enumerated powers and.—[It has been] proposed to Congress to incorporate an Agricultural Society. I am against that, because I think Congress cannot find in all the enumerated powers any one which authorizes the act, much less the giving the public money to that use. I believe, too, if they had the power, it would soon be used for no other purpose than to buy with sinecures useful partisans.—To Robert R. Livingston. Ford ed., vii, 493. (W., Feb. 1801.)

3879. INCORPORATION, Executive and.—The Administrator shall not possess the prerogative * * * of erecting corporations.—Proposed Va. Constitution. Ford ed., ii, 19. (June 1776.)

3880. INCORPORATION, Federal Convention and.—Baldwin of Kentucky, men-

tions at table the following fact: When the
Bank bill was under discussion in the House
of Representatives, Judge Wilson came in,
and was standing by Baldwin. Baldwin reminded him of the following fact which
passed in the grand Convention. Among the
enumerated powers given to Congress was one
to erect corporations. It was on debate struck
out. Several particular powers were then proposed. Among others, Robert Morris proposed to give Congress a power to establish
a National Bank. Gouverneur Morris opposed it, observing that it was extremely
doubtful whether the Constitution they were
framing could ever be passed at all by the
people of America; that to give it its best
chance, however, they should make it as
palatable as possible, and put nothing into it
not very essential which might raise up
enemies; that his colleague, Robert Morris,
well knew that "a bank" was in their
State (Pennsylvania) the very watchword of
party; that a bank had been the great bone of
contention between the two parties of the
State from the establishment of their constitution, having been erected, put down and
erected again as either party preponderated;
that, therefore, to insert this power would instantly enlist against the whole instrument the
whole of the anti-bank party in Pennsylvania;
whereupon, it was rejected, as was every
other special power except that of giving
copyrights to authors and patents to inventors, the general power of incorporation being
whittled down to this shred. Wilson agreed
to the fact.—THE ANAS. ix, 191. FORD ED., i,
278. (1798.)

3881. —— ——. A proposition was made
to the Convention which formed the [Federal]
Constitution to open canals, and an amendatory one to empower them to incorporate.
But the whole was rejected, and one of the
reasons for rejection urged in debate was,
that then they would have power to erect
a bank, which would render the great cities,
where there were prejudices and jealousies on
the subject, adverse to the reception of the
Constitution.—NATIONAL BANK OPINION. vii,
558. FORD ED., v, 287. (1791.)

3882. INCORPORATION, General welfare clause and.—We are here [Philadel-
phia] engaged in improving our Constitution
by construction, so as to make it what the
[federal] majority think it should have been.
The Senate received yesterday a bill from
the Representatives incorporating a company
for Roosevelt's copper mines in Jersey. This
is under the *sweeping clause* of the Constitution, and supported by the following pedigree
of necessities: Congress are authorized to defend the country; ships are necessary for that
defence; copper is necessary for ships; mines
are necessary to produce copper; companies
are necessary to work mines; and "this is
the house that Jack built".—To ROBERT R.
LIVINGSTON. FORD ED., vii, 445. (Pa., April
1800.)

3883. —— ——. The House of Representatives sent [to the Senate] yesterday a bill

for incorporating a company to work Roosevelt's copper mines in New Jersey. I do not
know whether it is understood that the Legislature of Jersey was incompetent to this, or
merely that we have concurrent legislation
under the sweeping clause. Congress are
authorized to defend the nation. Ships are
necessary for defence; copper is necessary for
ships; mines necessary for copper; a company
necessary to work mines; and who can doubt
this reasoning who has ever played at " This
is the House that Jack built". Under such
a process of filiation of necessities the sweeping
clause makes clea work.—To E. LIVINGSTON.
iv, 329. FORD ED., vii, 444. (Pa., April 1800.)

3884. INCORPORATION, Republican
party and.—It has always been denied by the
republican party in this country, that the Constitution had given the power of incorporation
to Congress. On the establishment of the
Bank of the United States, this was the great
ground on which that establishment was combatted; and the party prevailing supported it
only on the argument of its being an incident
to the power given them for raising money.
On this ground it has been acquiesced in, and
will probably be acquiesced in, as subsequently
confirmed by public opinion. But in no other
instance have they ever exercised this power
of incorporation out of this District, of which
they are the ordinary Legislature.—To DR.
MAESE. v, 412. (W., Jan. 1809.) See BANK
(U. S.), CONSTITUTIONALITY OF, GENERAL
WELFARE and MONOPOLY.

3885. INDEMNIFICATION, Adequate.
—To demand satisfaction *beyond* what is adequate is a wrong.—OFFICIAL OPINION. vii,
628. FORD ED., vi, 258. (1793.)

3886. INDEMNIFICATION, Effectual.
—One thousand ships taken, six thousand
seamen impressed, savage butcheries of our
citizens, and incendiary machinations against
our Union, declare that they and their allies,
the Spaniards, must retire from the Atlantic
side of our continent as the only security or
indemnification which will be effectual.—To
THOMAS LETRE. vi, 79. (M., Aug. 1812.)

3887. INDEMNIFICATION, Frigate
Chesapeake and.—We now send a vessel to
call upon the British government for repa-
ration for the past outrage [attack on the
Chesapeake] and security for the future.—To
JOHN ARMSTRONG. v, 134. FORD ED., ix, 116.
(W., 1807.)

3888. —— ——. Reparation for the past
and security for the future is our motto.—To
DUPONT DE NEMOURS. v, 127. FORD ED., ix,
111. (W., July 1807.)

3889. —— ——. An armed vessel of the
United States was dispatched with instructions to our ministers at London to call on
that government for the satisfaction and security required by the outrage. [Attack on
the Chesapeake.]—SEVENTH ANNUAL MES-
SAGE. viii, 84. FORD ED., ix, 153. (1807.)

3890. INDEMNIFICATION, National retribution.—That retribution which the laws of every country mean to extend to those who suffer unjustly.—To Count de Vergennes. i, 486. (P., 1785.)

3891. INDEMNIFICATION, National usage.—The usage of nations requires that we shall give the offender an opportunity of making reparation and avoiding war.—To Vice-President Clinton. v, 116. Ford ed., ix, 100. (W., 1807.)

3892. INDEMNIFICATION, Principle of.—I take the true principle to be, that "for violations of jurisdiction, with the consent of the sovereign, or his voluntary sufferance, indemnification is due; but that for others he is bound only to use all *reasonable* means to obtain indemnification from the aggressor, which must be calculated on his circumstances, and these endeavors *bonâ fide* made; and failing, he is no further responsible". It would be extraordinary, indeed, if we were to be answerable for the conduct of belligerents through our whole coasts, whether inhabited or not.—To James Madison. v, 69. Ford ed., ix, 47. (M., April 1807.)

3893. INDEMNIFICATION, Security and.—The sword once drawn, full justice must be done. "Indemnification for the past and security for the future" should be painted on our banners.—To Mr. Wright. vi, 78. (M., Aug. 1812.)

3894. INDEMNIFICATION, For slaves.—The President * * * authorized Mr. Gouverneur Morris to enter into conference with the British ministers in order to discover their sentiments on the * * * indemnification for the negroes carried off against the stipulations of the treaty of peace. The letters of Mr. Morris * * * [to the President] state the communications, oral and written, which have passed between him and the ministers; and from these the Secretary of State draws the following inference: That as to indemnification for the negroes, their measures for concealing them were in the first instance so efficacious, as to reduce our demand for them, so far as we can support it by direct proof, to be very small indeed. Its smallness seems to have kept it out of discussion. Were other difficulties removed, they would probably make none of this article. * * * The Secretary of State is of opinion * * * that the demands * * * of indemnification should not be again made till we are in readiness to do ourselves the justice which may be refused.—Report on British Negotiations. vii, 517. Ford ed., v, 261. (1790.)

3895. INDEPENDENCE, First idea of American.—In July 1775, a separation from Great Britain and establishment of republican government had never yet entered into any person's mind. * * * Independence, and the establishment of a new form of government, were not even the objects of the people at large. One extract from the pamphlet called "Common Sense" had appeared in the Virginia papers in February, and copies of the pamphlet itself had got in a few hands. But the idea had not been opened to the mass of the people in April, much less can it be said that they had made up their minds in its

favor.*—Notes on Virginia. viii, 363. Ford ed., iii, 225. (1782.) See Colonies, Declaration of Independence, Parliament and Revolution (American).

3896. INDIANS, Agriculture and.—The decrease of game rendering their subsistence by hunting insufficient, we wish to draw them to agriculture, to spinning and weaving. The latter branches they take up with great readiness, because they fall to the women, who gain by quitting the labors of the field for those which are exercised within doors.—To Governor Harrison. iv, 472. (W., 1803.)

3897. —— ——. I consider the business of hunting as already become insufficient to furnish clothing and subsistence to the Indians. The promotion of agriculture, therefore, and household manufacture, are essential in their preservation, and I am disposed to aid and encourage it liberally.—To Benjamin Hawkins. iv, 467. Ford ed., viii, 213. (1803.)

3898. INDIANS AS ALLIES.—They are a useless, expensive, ungovernable ally.—To John Page. Ford ed., ii, 88. (Pa., 1776.)

3899. INDIANS, Amalgamation.—The ultimate point of rest and happiness for them is to let our settlements and theirs meet and blend together, to intermix, and become one people. Incorporating themselves with us as citizens of the United States, this is what the natural progress of things will of course bring on, and it will be better to promote than to retard it.—To Benjamin Hawkins. iv, 467. Ford ed., viii, 214. (1803.)

3900. —— ——. Our settlements will gradually circumscribe and approach the Indians, and they will in time either incorporate with us as citizens of the United States, or remove beyond the Mississippi. The former is certainly the determination of their history most happy for themselves; but, in the whole course of this it is essential to cultivate their love.—To Governor Harrison. iv, 472. (W., 1803.)

3901. —— ——. I shall rejoice to see the day when the red men, our neighbors, become truly one people with us, enjoying all the rights and privileges we do, and living in peace and plenty as we do, without any one to make them afraid, to injure their persons, or to take their property without being punished for it according to fixed laws.—To the Cherokee Chiefs. viii, 214. (1808.)

3902. INDIANS, American Nations and.—[It is] an established principle of public law among the white nations of America, that while the Indians included within their limits retain all other natural rights, no other white nations can become their patrons, protectors or mediators, nor in any shape intermeddle between them and those within whose limits they are.—Anas. ix, 433. Ford ed., i, 210. (1792.)

3903. —— ——. We consider it as established by the usage of different nations into a

* In the Ford edition (iii, 226) attention is called to a letter written by Jefferson from Philadelphia, May, 16, 1776, to Thomas Nelson, in which he said: "I wish much to see you here, yet hope you will contrive to bring on as early as you can in convention the great questions of the session. I suppose they will tell us what to say on the subject of Independence, but hope respect will be expressed to the right opinion in other Colonies who may happen to differ from them. When at home I took great pains to enquire into the sentiments of the people on that head, in the upper counties I think I may safely say nine out of ten are for it."—Editor.

kind of *Jus gentium* for America, that a white nation settling down and declaring that such and such are their limits, makes an invasion of those limits by any other white nation an act of war, but gives no right of soil against the native possessors.—THE ANAS. ix, 429. FORD ED., i, 197. (1792.)

3904. INDIANS, Brotherhood of.—Made by the same Great Spirit, and living in the same land with our brothers, the red men, we consider ourselves as of the same family; we wish to live with them as one people, and to cherish their interests as our own.—ADDRESS TO INDIANS. viii, 184. (1802.)

3905. INDIANS, Catherine of Russia and.—What Professor Adelung mentions of the Empress Catherine's having procured many vocabularies of our Indians, is correct. She applied to M. de Lafayette, who, through the aid of General Washington, obtained several; but I never learnt of what particular tribes.— To MR. DUPONCEAU. vii, 96. (M., 1817.)

3906. INDIANS, Citizenship and.—We have already had an application from a settlement of Indians to become citizens of the United States. It is possible, perhaps probable, that this idea may be so novel as that it might shock the Indians, were it even hinted to them. Of course, you will keep it for your own reflection; but, convinced of its soundness, I feel it consistent with pure morality to lead them towards it, to familiarize them to the idea that it is for their interest to cede lands at times to the United States, and for us to procure gratifications to our citizens, from time to time, by new acquisitions of land.—To BENJAMIN HAWKINS. iv, 468. FORD ED., viii, 215, (W., 1803.)

3907. INDIANS, Civilizing.—It is evident that your society has begun at the right end for civilizing the Indians. Habits of industry, easy subsistence, attachment to property, are necessary to prepare their minds for the first elements of science, and afterwards for moral and religious instruction. To begin with the last has ever ended either in effecting nothing, or ingrafting bigotry on ignorance, and setting them to tomahawking and burning old women and others as witches, of which we have seen a commencement among them.—To JAMES PEMBERTON. v, 212. (W., 1807.)

3908. ———. They are our brethren, our neighbors; they may be valuable friends, and troublesome enemies. Both duty and interest enjoin, that we should extend to them the blessings of civilized life, and prepare their minds for becoming useful members of the American family.—R. TO A. viii, 118. (1807.)

3909. ———. The plan of civilizing the Indians is undoubtedly a great improvement on the ancient and totally ineffectual one of beginning with religious missionaries. Our experience has shown that this must be the last step of the process. The following is what has been successful: 1st, to raise cattle, &c., and thereby acquire a knowledge of the value of property; 2d, arithmetic, to calculate that value; 3d, writing, to keep accounts, and here they begin to enclose farms, and the men to labor, the women to spin and weave; 4th, to read "Aesop's Fables" and "Robinson Crusoe" are their first delight. The Creeks and Cherokees are advanced thus far, and the Cherokees are now instituting a regular government.—To JAMES JAY. v, 440. (M., April 1809.)

3910. ———. The civilization and improvement of the Indian tribes * * * I have ever had much at heart, and never omitted an occasion of promoting while I have been in situations to do it with effect; and nothing, even now, in the calm of age and retirement, would excite in me a more lively interest than an approvable plan of raising that respectable and unfortunate people from the state of physical and moral abjection, to which they have been reduced by circumstances foreign to them.—To JEDEDIAH MORSE. vii, 233. FORD ED., x, 203. (M., 1822.) See CIVILIZATION.

3911. INDIANS, Coercing.—Nothing ought more to be avoided than the embarking ourselves in a system of military coercion on the Indians. If we do this, we shall have general and perpetual war.—To MERIWETHER LEWIS. v, 350. (M., 1808.)

3912. INDIANS, Commiseration.—In the early part of my life, I was very familiar with the Indians, and acquired impressions of attachment and commiseration for them which have never been obliterated.—To JOHN ADAMS. vi, 61. FORD ED., ix, 358. (M., 1812.)

3913. INDIANS, Controlling.— The Indians can be kept in order only by commerce or war. The former is the cheaper.—To ALBERT GALLATIN. v, 227. (W., 1808.)

3914. INDIANS, Descent of.—Moreton's deduction of the origin of our Indians from the fugitive Trojans, * * * and his manner of accounting for the sprinkling of their Latin with Greek, is really amusing. Adair makes them talk Hebrew. Reinold Foster derives them from the soldiers sent by Kouli Khan to conquer Japan. Brerewood, from the Tartars, as well as our bears, wolves, foxes, &c., which, he says, " must of necessity fetch their beginning from Noah's ark, which rested, after the deluge in Asia, seeing they could not proceed by the course of nature, as the imperfect sort of living creatures do, from putrefaction". Bernard Romans is of opinion that God created an original man and woman in this part of the globe. Doctor Barton thinks they are not specifically different from the Persians; but, taking afterwards a broader range, he thinks, " that in all the vast countries of America, there is but one language, nay, that it may be proven, or rendered highly probable, that all the languages of the earth bear some affinity together". This reduces it to a question of definition, in which every one is free to use his own; to wit, what constitutes identity, or difference in two things, in the common acceptation of *sameness*. All languages may be called the same, as being all made up of the same primitive sounds. expressed by the letters of the different alphabets. But, in this sense, all things on earth are the same as consisting of matter. This gives up the useful distribution into genera and species, which we form, arbitrarily indeed, for the relief of our imperfect memories. To aid the question, from whence our Indian tribes are descended, some have gone into their religion, their morals, their manners, customs, habits, and physical forms. By such helps it may be learnedly proved, that our trees and plants of every kind are descended from those of Europe; because, like them, they have no locomotion, they draw nourishment from the earth, they clothe themselves with leaves in spring, of which they divest themselves in autumn for the sleep of winter, &c. Our animals, too, must be descended from those of Europe, because our wolves eat lambs, our deer are gregarious, our ants hoard, &c. But, when for convenience we distribute languages, according to common understanding, into classes originally different, as we choose to consider them, as the Hebrew, the Greek, the Celtic, the Gothic; and these again into genera, or families, as the Icelandic, German, Swedish, Danish, English; and these last into species, or dialects, as English, Scotch, Irish, we then ascribe other meanings to the terms "same" and "different". In some of these senses, Barton, and Adair, and Foster, and Brerewood, and Morton, may be right, every one according to his own definition of what constitutes "identity". Romans, indeed, takes a higher stand, and supposes a separate creation. On the same unscriptural ground, he had but to mount one step higher, to suppose no creation at all, but that all things have existed without beginning in time, as they now exist, and may forever exist, producing and reproducing in a circle, without end. This would very summarily dispose of Mr. Moreton's learning, and show that the question of Indian origin, like many others, pushed to a certain height, must receive the same answer, "Ignoro".—To John Adams. vi, 121. (M., May 1813.) See Aborigines.

3915. INDIANS, Driven westward.—I am sorry to hear that the Indians have commenced war, but greatly pleased you have been so decisive on that head. Nothing will reduce those wretches so soon as pushing the war into the heart of their country. But I would not stop there. I would never cease pursuing them while one of them remained on this side the Mississippi.—To John Page. Ford ed., ii, 73. (Pa., 1776.)

3916. ——— ———. The Indians backward [in civilization] will yield, and be thrown further back. They will relapse into barbarism and misery, lose numbers by war and want, and we shall be obliged to drive them with the beasts of the forest into the stony mountains.—To John Adams. vi, 62. Ford ed., ix, 358. (M., 1812.)

3917. INDIANS, Fire-hunting by.—You ask if the usage of hunting in circles has ever been known among any of our tribes of Indians? It has been practiced by them all; and is to this day, by those still remote from the settlements of the whites. But their numbers and enabling them like Genghis Khan's seven hundred thousand, to form themselves into circles of one hundred miles diameter, they make their circle by firing the leaves fallen on the ground, which gradually forcing the animals to a centre, they there slaughter them with arrows, darts and other missiles.—To John Adams. vi. 122. (M., 1813.)

3918. INDIANS, Fortifications.—I believe entirely with you that the remains of fortifications, found in the western country, have been the works of the natives.—To Harry Innes. iii, 217. Ford ed., v, 294. (Pa., 1791.)

3919. INDIANS, Friendship.—It is on their interests we must rely for their friendship, and not on their fears.—To Henry Dearborn. v, 349. (M., 1808.)

3920. INDIANS, Genius.—It is in North America we are to seek their [the Indians'] original character. And I am safe in affirming, that the proofs of genius given by the Indians of North America place them on a level with whites in the same uncultivated state. The North of Europe furnishes subjects enough for comparison with them, and for a proof of their equality, I have seen some thousands myself, and conversed much with them, and have found in them a masculine, sound understanding. * * * I believe the Indian to be in body and

mind equal to the white man.—To General Chastellux. i, 341. Ford ed., iii, 137. (P., 1785.)

3921. INDIANS, Government.—The practice [of dividing themselves into small societies] results from the circumstance of their having never submitted themselves to any laws, any coercive power, any shadow of government. Their only controls are their manners, and that moral sense of right and wrong, which, like the sense of tasting and feeling in every man, makes a part of his nature. An offence against these is punished by contempt, by exclusion from society, or, where the case is serious, as that of murder, by the individuals whom it concerns. Imperfect as this species of coercion may seem, crimes are very rare among them; insomuch that were it made a question, whether no law, as among the savage Americans, or too much law, as among the civilized Europeans, submits man to the greatest evil, one who has seen both conditions of existence would pronounce it to be the last; and that the sheep are happier of themselves, than under the care of the wolves. It will be said that great societies cannot exist without government. The savages, therefore, break them into small ones.—Notes on Virginia. viii, 338. Ford ed., iii, 195. (1782.)

3922. INDIANS, Great Britain and.—You know the benevolent plan we were pursuing here for the happiness of the aboriginal inhabitants in our vicinities. We spared nothing to keep them at peace with one another. To teach them agriculture and the rudiments of the most necessary arts, and to encourage industry by establishing among them separate property. In this way they would have been enabled to subsist and multiply on a moderate scale of landed possession. They would have mixed their blood with ours, and been amalgamated and identified with us within no distant period of time. On the commencement of the present war [with Great Britain], we pressed on them the observance of peace and neutrality, but the interested and unprincipled policy of England has defeated all our labors for the salvation of these unfortunate people. They have seduced the greater part of the tribes within our neighborhood, to take up the hatchet against us, and the cruel massacres they have committed on the women and children of our frontiers taken by surprise will oblige us now to pursue them to extermination, or drive them to new seats beyond our reach. * * * The confirmed brutalization, if not the extermination of this race in our America, is therefore to form an additional chapter in the English history of the same colored man in Asia, and of the brethren of their own color in Ireland, and wherever else Anglo-mercantile cupidity can find a two-penny interest in deluging the earth with human blood.—To Baron de Humboldt. vi, 269. Ford ed., ix, 431. (Dec. 1813.)

3923. INDIANS, Justice to.—The two principles on which our conduct towards the Indians should be founded are justice and fear. After the injuries we have done them, they cannot love us, which leaves us no alternative but that of fear to keep them from attacking us. But justice is what we should never lose sight of and, in time, it may recover their esteem.—To Mr. Hawkins. ii, 3. (P., 1786.)

3924. ——— ———. Nothing must be spared to convince the Indians of the justice and liberality we are determined to use towards them, and to attach them to us indissolubly.—To Dr. Sibley. iv, 581. (W., 1805.)

3925. INDIANS, Lands of.—It may be regarded as certain, that not a foot of land will ever be taken from the Indians, without their own consent. The sacredness of their rights is felt by all thinking persons in America as much as in Europe.—To M. DE MEUNIER. ix, 260. FORD ED., iv, 166. (P., 1786.)

3926. ——— ———. When they withdraw themselves to the culture of a small piece of land, they will perceive how useless to them are their extensive forests, and will be willing to pare them off from time to time in exchange for necessaries for their farms and families.—To GOVERNOR HARRISON. iv, 472. (W., 1803.)

3927. ——— ———. To promote the disposition to exchange lands, which they have to spare and we want, for necessaries, which we have to spare and they want, we shall push our trading uses, and be glad to see the good and influential individuals among them run in debt, because we observe that when these debts get beyond what the individuals can pay, they become willing to lop them off by a cession of lands. At our trading houses, too, we mean to sell so low as merely to repay us cost and charges, so as neither to lessen nor enlarge our capital.—To GOVERNOR HARRISON. iv, 472. (W., 1803.)

3928. ——— ———. I am myself alive to the obtaining lands from the Indians by all *honest* and *peaceable means*, and I believe that the honest and peaceable means adopted by us will obtain them as fast as the expansion of our settlements with due regard to compactness, will require.—To ANDREW JACKSON. iv, 464. (W., 1803.)

— INDIANS, Languages of.—See ABORIGINES.

3929. INDIANS, Outacite.—Before the Revolution, the Indians were in the habit of coming often and in great numbers to the seat of government [in Virginia], where I was very much with them. I knew much the great Outacité, the warrior and orator of the Cherokees; he was always the guest of my father on his journeys to and from Williamsburg. I was in his camp when he made his great farewell oration to his people the evening before his departure for England. The moon was in full splendor, and to her he seemed to address himself in his prayers for his own safety on the voyage, and that of his people during his absence; his sounding voice, distinct articulation, animated action, and the solemn silence of his people at their several fires, filled me with awe and veneration, although I did not understand a word he uttered.—To JOHN ADAMS. vi, 61. FORD ED., ix, 358. (M., 1812.)

3930. INDIANS, Peace with.—Our system is to live in perpetual peace with the Indians, to cultivate an affectionate attachment from them, by everything just and liberal which we can do for them within the bounds of reason, and by giving them effectual protection against wrongs from our own people.—To GOVERNOR HARRISON. iv, 472. (W., 1803.)

— INDIANS, Policy respecting.—See SECOND INAUGURAL ADDRESS, in APPENDIX.

3931. INDIANS, Priesthood.—You ask if the Indians have any order of priesthood among them, like the Druids, Bards or Minstrels of the Celtic nations? Adair alone, determined to see what he wished to see in every object, metamorphoses their conjurers into an order of priests, and describes their sorceries as if they were the great religious ceremonies of the nation. Lafitau called them by their proper names, Jongleurs, Devins, Sortileges; De Bry, præstigiatores; Adair himself sometimes Magi, Archimagi, cunning men, Seers, rain-makers; and the modern Indian interpreters call them conjurers and witches. They are persons pretending to have communications with the devil and other evil spirits, to foretell future events, bring down rain, find stolen goods, raise the dead, destroy some and heal others by enchantment, lay spells, &c. And Adair, without departing from his parallel of the Jews and Indians, might have found their counterpart much more aptly among the soothsayers, sorcerers and wizards of the Jews, their Gannes and Gambres, their Simon Magus, Witch of Endor, and the young damsel whose sorceries disturbed Paul so much; instead of placing them in a line with their high-priest, their chief-priests, and their magnificent hierarchy generally. In the solemn ceremonies of the Indians, the persons who direct or officiate, are their chiefs, elders and warriors, in civil ceremonies or in those of war; it is the head of the cabin in their private or particular feasts or ceremonies; and sometimes the matrons, as in their corn feasts. And even here, Adair might have kept up his parallel, without ennobling his conjurers. For the ancient patriarchs, the Noahs, the Abrahams, Isaacs and Jacobs, and even after the consecration of Aaron, the Samuels and Elijahs, and we may say further, every one for himself offered sacrifices on the altars. The true line of distinction seems to be, that solemn ceremonies, whether public or private, addressed to the Great Spirit, are conducted by the worthies of the nation, men or matrons, while conjurers are resorted to only for the invocation of evil spirits. The present state of the Indian tribes, without any public order of priests, is proof sufficient that they never had such an order. Their steady habits permit no innovations, not even those which the progress of science offers to increase the comforts, enlarge the understanding, and improve the morality of mankind. Indeed, so little idea have they of a regular order of priests, that they mistake ours for their conjurers, and call them by that name.—To JOHN ADAMS. vi, 60. FORD ED., ix, 357. (M., 1812.)

3932. INDIANS, Protection of.—It is a leading object of our present government to guarantee the Indians in their present possessions, and to protect their persons with the same fidelity which is extended to its own citizens.—To C. W. F. DUMAS. iii, 260. (Pa., 1791.)

3933. INDIANS, The Revolution and.—At the commencement of the war [of the Revolution], the United States laid it down as a rule of their conduct, to engage the Indian tribes within their neighborhood to remain strictly neutral. They accordingly strongly pressed it on them, urging that it was a family quarrel with which they had nothing to do, and in which we wished them to take no part; and we strengthened these recommendations by doing them every act of friendship and good neighborhood, which circumstances left in our power. With some, these solicitations prevailed; but the greater part of them suffered themselves to be drawn into the war against us. They waged it in their usual cruel manner, murdering and scalping men, women and children, indiscriminately, burning their houses, and desolating the country. They put us to vast expense, as well by the constant force we were obliged to keep up in that quarter, as by the expeditions of considerable magnitude which we were under the necessity of sending into their country from time to time.—To Carmichael and Short. iv, 9. Ford ed., vi, 331. (Pa., 1793.)

3934. —— ——. Peace being at length concluded with England, we had it also to conclude with them. They had made war on us without the least provocation or pretence of injury. They had added greatly to the cost of that war. They had insulted our feelings by their savage cruelties. They were by our arms completely subdued and humbled. Under all these circumstances, we had a right to demand substantial satisfaction and indemnification. We used that right, however, with real moderation. Their limits with us under the former government were generally ill defined, questionable, and the frequent cause of war. Sincerely desirous of living in their peace, of cultivating it by every act of justice and friendship, and of rendering them better neighbors by introducing among them some of the most useful arts, it was necessary to begin by a precise definition of boundary. Accordingly, at the treaties held with them, our mutual boundaries were settled; and notwithstanding our just right to concessions adequate to the circumstances of the case, we required such only as were inconsiderable; and for even these, in order that we might place them in a state of perfect conciliation, we paid them a valuable consideration, and granted them annuities in money which have been regularly paid, and were equal to the prices for which they have usually sold their lands.—To Carmichael and Short. iv, 10. Ford ed., vi, 331. (Pa., 1793.)

3935. INDIANS, Rights of.—The want of attention to their rights is a principal source of dishonor to the American character.—To Mr. Hawkins. ii, 3. (P., 1786.)

3936. INDIANS, Schools for.—The teaching of the Indian boys and girls to read and write, agriculture and mechanic trades to the former, spinning and weaving to the latter, may perhaps be acceded to by us advantageously for the Indians.—To Henry Dearborn. vii, 278. (1808.)

3937. INDIANS, Sioux.—On the Sioux nation we wish most particularly to make a friendly impression, because of their immense power, and because we learn that they are very desirous of being on the most friendly terms with us.—To Captain Meriwether Lewis. iv, 522. (W., 1804.)

3938. INDIANS, Temperance.—Our endeavors are to impress on them all profoundly, temperance, peace and agriculture; and I am persuaded they begin to feel profoundly the soundness of the advice.—To Dr. Logan. v, 404. (W., 1808.)

3939. INDIANS, Trade vs. Armies.— As soon as our factories on the Missouri and Mississippi can be in activity, they will have more powerful effects than so many armies.— To Meriwether Lewis. v, 351. (M., 1808.)

3940. —— ——. Have you thought of the Indian drawback? The Indians can be kept in order only by commerce or war. The former is the cheaper. Unless we can induce individuals to employ their capital in that trade, it will require an enormous sum of capital from the public treasury, and it will be badly managed. A drawback for four or five years is the cheapest way of getting that business off our hands.—To Albert Gallatin. v, 227. (W., 1808.)

3941. INDIANS, Traditions.—Some scanty accounts of the traditions of the Indians, but fuller of their customs and characters, are given us by most of the early travelers among them; these you know were mostly French. Lafitau, among them, and Adair an Englishman, have written on this subject. * * * But unluckily Lafitau had in his head a preconceived theory on the mythology, manners, institutions, and government of the ancient nations of Europe, Asia, and Africa, and seems to have entered on those of America only to fit them into the same frame, and to draw from them a confirmation of his general theory. He keeps up a perpetual parallel, in all those articles, between the Indians of America and the ancients of the other quarters of the globe. He selects, therefore, all the facts and adopts all the falsehoods which favor his theory, and very gravely retails such absurdities as zeal for a theory could alone swallow. He was a man of much classical and scriptural reading, and has rendered his book not unentertaining. He resided five years among the northern Indians as a missionary, but collects his matter much more from the writings of others, than from his own observation. Adair, too, had his kink. He believed all the Indians of America to be descended from the Jews; the same laws, usages, rites and ceremonies, the same sacrifices, priests, prophets, fasts and festivals, almost the same religion, and that they all spoke Hebrew. For, although he writes particularly of the southern Indians only, the Catawbas, Creeks, Cherokees, Chickasaws and Choctaws, with whom alone he was personally acquainted, yet he generalizes whatever he found among them, and brings himself to believe that the hundred languages of America, differing fundamentally every one from every other, as much as Greek from Gothic, yet have all one common prototype. He was a trader, a man of learning, a self-taught Hebraist, a strong religionist, and of as sound a mind as Don Quixote in whatever did not touch his religious chivalry. His book contains a great deal of real instruction on its subject, only requiring the reader to be constantly on his guard against the wonderful obliquities of his theory. —To John Adams. vi, 59. Ford ed., ix, 355 (M., 1812.)

3942. INDUSTRY, Fruits of.—Our wish is that * * * [there be] maintained that state of property, equal or unequal, which results to every man from his own industry, or that of his fathers.—Second Inaugural Address. viii, 44. Ford ed., viii, 347. (1805.)

3943. —— ——. The rights of the people to the exercise and fruits of their own industry, can never be protected against the selfishness of rulers not subject to their control at short periods.—To Isaac H. Tiffany. vii, 32. (M., 1816.)

3944. —— ——. To take from one, because it is thought that his own industry and that of his father's has acquired too much, in order to spare to others, who, or whose fathers have not exercised equal industry and skill, is to violate arbitrarily the first principle of association—the guarantee to every one of a free exercise of his industry, and the fruits acquired by it.—Note in Destutt Tracy's Political Economy. vi, 574. (1816.)

3945. —— ——. The Republican party believed that men, enjoying in ease and security the full fruits of their own industry, enlisted by all their interests on the side of law and order, habituated to think for themselves, and to follow their reason as their guide, would be more easily and safely governed, than with minds nourished in error, and vitiated and debased, as in Europe, by ignorance, indigence and oppression.—To WILLIAM JOHNSON. vii, 292. FORD ED., x, 227. (M., 1823.)

3946. INDUSTRY, Gambling and.—I told the President [Washington] that a system had there [in the Treasury Department] been contrived for deluging the States with paper money instead of gold and silver, for withdrawing our citizens from the pursuits of commerce, manufactures, buildings, and other branches of useful industry, to occupy themselves and their capitals in a species of gambling, destructive of morality, and which had introduced its poison into the government itself.—THE ANAS. ix, 104. FORD ED., i, 177. (Feb. 1792.)

3947. INDUSTRY, Goodness and.—Be good and be industrious and you will be what I most love in the world.—To MARTHA JEFFERSON. FORD ED., iv, 389. (1787.)

3948. INDUSTRY, Improvement and.—Restrain men from injuring one another, * * * [but] leave them otherwise free to regulate their own pursuits of industry and improvement.—FIRST INAUGURAL ADDRESS. viii, 3. FORD ED., viii, 4. (1801.)

3949. INDUSTRY, Shackles on.—Nor should we wonder at * * * [the] pressure [for a fixed constitution in 1788-9] when we consider the monstrous abuses of power under which * * * [the French] people were ground to powder; when we pass in review the * * * shackles on industry by guilds and corporations.—AUTOBIOGRAPHY. i, 86. FORD ED., i, 118. (1821.)

3950. INDUSTRY, Taxing.—Sound principles will not justify our taxing the industry of our fellow citizens to accumulate treasure for wars to happen we know not when, and which might not perhaps happen but from the temptations offered by that treasure.—FIRST INAUGURAL MESSAGE. viii, 9. FORD ED., viii, 119. (1801.)

— **INFLATION.**—See BANKS, and PAPER MONEY.

3951. INFORMATION, Essential to Executive.—It is essential for the public interest that I should receive all the information possible respecting either matters or persons connected with the public. To induce people to give this information, they must feel assured that when deposited with me it is secret and sacred. Honest men might justifiably withhold information, if they expected the communication would be made public, and commit them to war with their neighbors and friends. This imposes the duty on me of considering such information as mere suggestions for inquiry, and to put me on my guard; and to injure no man by forming any opinion until the suggestion be verified. Long ex-

perience in this school has by no means strengthened the disposition to believe too easily. On the contrary, it has begotten an incredulity which leaves no one's character in danger from any hasty conclusion.—To JOHN SMITH. v, 77. (M., 1807.) See PUBLICITY.

3952. INJURY, Accumulated.—The Indian chief said he did not go to war for every petty injury by itself, but put it into his pouch, and when that was full, he then made war. Thank Heaven, we have provided a more peaceable and rational mode of redress.—To WILLIAM JOHNSON. vii, 295. FORD ED., x, 230. (M., 1823.)

3953. INJURY, The Colonies and.—[During] the reigns which preceded his Majesty's [George III.], the violations of our rights were less alarming, because repeated at more distant intervals than that rapid and bold succession of injuries which is likely to distinguish the present from all other periods of American history. Scarcely have our minds been able to emerge from the astonishment into which one stroke of parliamentary thunder had involved us, before another more heavy, and more alarming, is fallen on us.—RIGHTS OF BRITISH AMERICA. i, 130. FORD ED., i, 435. (1774.) See COLONIES.

3954. ———. Our complaints were either not heard at all, or were answered with new and accumulated injuries.—REPLY TO LORD NORTH'S PROPOSITION. FORD ED., i, 481. (July 1775.)

3955. ———. The rapid and bold succession of injuries, which, during a course of eleven years, have been aimed at the Colonies.—REPLY TO LORD NORTH'S PROPOSITION. FORD ED., i, 481. (July 1775.)

3956. INJURY, By George III.—He, [George III.], has endeavored to pervert the exercise of the kingly office in Virginia into a detestable and insupportable tyranny * * * by answering our repeated petitions for redress with a repetition of injuries.—PROPOSED VA. CONSTITUTION. FORD ED., ii, 12. (June 1776.)

3957. INJURY, Peaceable Remedy.—Some of these injuries may perhaps admit a peaceable remedy. Where that is competent, it is always the most desirable.—FIFTH ANNUAL MESSAGE. viii, 49. FORD ED., viii, 391. (1805.)

3958. INJURY, Private.—An individual, thinking himself injured, makes more noise than a state.—To GEORGIA DELEGATES IN CONGRESS. i, 501. (1785.)

3959. INJURY, Redressed by war.—I did not think war the surest means of redressing the French injuries.—To ELBRIDGE GERRY. iv, 269. FORD ED., vii, 329. (Pa., 1799.)

3960. ———. If nations go to war for every degree of injury, there would never be peace on earth.—To MADAME DE STAEL. v, 133. (W., 1807.)

3961. INJURY, Unceasing.—To show they [Parliament] mean no discontinuance of injury, they pass acts, at the very time of holding out this proposition, for restraining the commerce and fisheries of the province of New England, and for interdicting the trade of the other colonies with all foreign nations.—REPLY TO LORD NORTH'S PROPOSITION. FORD ED., i, 480. (July 1775.)

3962. —— ——. The history of the present King of Great Britain is a history of unremitting* injuries * * * .—DECLARATION OF INDEPENDENCE AS DRAWN BY JEFFERSON.

3963. INHERITANCES, Equal.—If the overgrown wealth of an individual be deemed dangerous to the State, the best corrective is the law of equal inheritance to all in equal degree; and the better, as this enforces a law of nature, while extra taxation violates it.—NOTE TO TRACY'S POLITICAL ECONOMY. vi, 575. (1816.)

3964. —— ——. Equal partition of inheritances [is] the best of all agrarian laws.—AUTOBIOGRAPHY. i, 49. FORD ED., i, 69. (1821.)

3965. INHERITANCES, Legislation.—The General Government is incompetent to legislate on the subject of inheritances.—To PRESIDENT WASHINGTON. FORD ED., vi, 133. (1792.) See ENTAIL IN VIRGINIA.

3966. INNES (Henry), Ability.—I wish you would come forward to the Federal Legislature, and give your assistance on a larger scale than that on which you are acting at present. I am satisfied you could render essential service, and I have such confidence in the purity of your republicanism, that I know your efforts would go in a right direction. Zeal and talents added to the republican scale will do no harm in Congress.—To HENRY INNES. iii, 224. FORD ED., v, 300. (Pa., 1791.)

3967. INNOVATION, Forced.—Great innovations should not be forced on slender majorities.—To GENERAL KOSCIUSKO. v, 282. (1808.)

3968. INNOVATION, Opposition to.—Innovation in England is heresy and treason.—To JOHN QUINCY ADAMS. vii, 89. (M., 1817.)

3969. INNOVATION, Reasonable.—I am not myself apt to be alarmed at innovations recommended by reason. That dread belongs to those whose interests or prejudices shrink from the advance of truth and science.—To DR. JOHN MANNERS. vi, 323. (M., 1814.)

3970. INSTITUTIONS, Flexibility.—Time indeed changes manners and notions and so far we must expect institutions to bend to them.—To SPENCER ROANE. vii, 211. FORD ED., x, 188. (M., 1821.)

3971. INSTRUCTIONS, Congress and.—Congress, as a body, if left to themselves, will in my opinion say nothing on the subject

* Congress struck out " unremitting " and inserted " repeated ".—EDITOR.

[Society of the Cincinnati]. They may, however, be forced into a declaration by instructions from some of the States.—To GENERAL WASHINGTON. i, 335. FORD ED., iii, 467. (A., 1784.)

3972. INSTRUCTIONS, Principles and.—I am in great pain for the Marquis de Lafayette. His principles * * * are clearly with the people; but having been elected for the Noblesse of Auvergne, they have laid him under express instructions to vote for the decision by orders and not persons. This would ruin him with the Tiers Etat, and it is not possible he could continue long to give satisfaction to the noblesse. I have not hesitated to press on him to burn his instructions, and follow his conscience as the one sure clew, which will eternally guide a man clear of all doubts and inconsistencies.—To GENERAL WASHINGTON. iii, 31. FORD ED., v, 96. (1789.)

3973. INSTRUCTIONS, Representatives and.—[Your book*] settles unanswerably the right of instructing representatives, and their duty to obey.—To JOHN TAYLOR. vi, 605. FORD ED., x, 28. (M., 1816.)

3974. INSULT, Acquiescence under.—It is an eternal truth that acquiescence under insult is not the way to escape war.—To H. TAZEWELL. iv, 121. FORD ED., vii, 31. (M., 1795.)

3975. INSULT, National character and.—It should ever be held in mind, that insult and war are the consequences of a want of respectability in the national character.—To JAMES MADISON. i, 531. FORD ED., iv, 192. (P., 1786.)

3976. INSULT, Pocketing.—One insult pocketed soon produces another.—To PRESIDENT WASHINGTON. vii, 510. FORD ED., v, 239. (1790.)

3977. INSULT, Punishing.—I think it to our interest to punish the first insult; because an insult unpunished is the parent of many others.—To JOHN JAY. i, 405. FORD ED., iv, 89. (P., 1785.)

3978. INSULT, Reparation for.—Both reason and the usage of nations required we should give Great Britain an opportunity of disavowing and repairing the insult of their officers. It gives us at the same time an opportunity of getting home our vessels, our property and our seamen,—the only means of carrying on the kind of war we should attempt.—To THOMAS COOPER. v, 121. FORD ED., ix, 102. (W., July 1807.)

3979. INSULT, Resenting.—It is inconsistent for a nation which has been patiently bearing for ten years the grossest insults and injuries from their late enemies [the British] to rise at a feather against their friends and benefactors [the French].—OPINION ON LITTLE SARAH. ix, 154. FORD ED., vi, 342. (1793.)

3980. INSULT, War and.—Let it be our endeavor to * * * maintain the character

* " Enquiry into the Principles of our Government." —EDITOR.

of an independent nation, preferring every consequence to insult and habitual wrong.— THIRD ANNUAL MESSAGE. viii, 28. FORD ED., viii, 272. (1803.)

3981. INSURRECTION, American people and.—My long and intimate knowledge of my countrymen satisfies me, that let there be occasion to display the banners of the law, and the world will see how few and pitiful are those who shall array themselves in opposition.—To JAMES BROWN. v, 379. FORD ED., ix, 211. (W., 1808.)

3982. ———— ————. In no country on earth is [forcible opposition to the law] so impracticable as in one where every man feels a vital interest in maintaining the authority of the laws, and instantly engages in it as in his own personal cause.—To BENJAMIN SMITH. v, 293. FORD ED., ix, 195. (M., 1808.)

3983. INSURRECTION, George III. and.—He [George III.] has endeavored to pervert the exercise of the Kingly office in Virginia into a detestable and insupportable tyranny * * * by inciting insurrections of our fellow subjects with the allurements of forfeiture and confiscation.—PROPOSED VA. CONSTITUTION. FORD ED., ii, 11. (June 1776.)

3984. ———— ————. He has incited treasonable insurrections of our fellow citizens, with the allurements of forfeiture and confiscation of our property.*—DECLARATION OF INDEPENDENCE AS DRAWN BY JEFFERSON.

3985. ———— ————. He has [excited domestic insurrection among us and has] endeavoured to bring on the inhabitants of our frontiers the merciless Indian savages, whose known rule of warfare is an undistinguished destruction of all ages, sexes and conditions of existence.†—DECLARATION OF INDEPENDENCE AS DRAWN BY JEFFERSON.

3986. INSURRECTION, Precautions against.—In a country whose Constitution is derived from the will of the people, directly expressed by their free suffrages; where the principal executive functionaries, and those of the legislature, are renewed by them at short periods; where under the character of jurors, they exercise in person the greatest portion of the judiciary powers; where the laws are consequently so framed and administered as to bear with equal weight and favor on all, restraining no man in the pursuits of honest industry, and securing to every one the property which that acquires, it would not be supposed that any safeguards could be needed against insurrection or enterprise on the public peace or authority. The laws, however, aware that these should not be trusted to moral restraints only, have wisely provided punishments for these crimes when committed. But would it not be salutary to give also the means of preventing their commission? Where an enterprise is meditated by private individuals against a foreign nation in

* Struck out by Congress.—EDITOR.
† Congress inserted the words in brackets and struck out the words "of existence".—EDITOR.

amity with the United States, powers of prevention to a certain extent are given by the laws; would they not be as reasonable and useful were the enterprise preparing against the United States? While adverting to this branch of the law, it is proper to observe, that in enterprises meditated against foreign nations, the ordinary process of binding to the observance of the peace and good behavior, could it be extended to acts to be done out of the jurisdiction of the United States, would be effectual in some cases where the offender is able to keep out of sight every indication of his purpose which could draw on him the exercise of the powers now given by law.—SIXTH ANNUAL MESSAGE. viii, 65. FORD ED., viii, 490. (Dec. 1806.)

3987. INSURRECTION, Provoking.—An exasperated people, who feel that they possess power, are not easily restrained within limits strictly regular.—RIGHTS OF BRITISH AMERICA. i, 132. FORD ED., i, 437. (1774.)

3988. INSURRECTION, Punishing.—Where to stay the hand of the executioner is an important question. Those who have escaped from the immediate danger, must have feelings which would dispose them to extend the executions. Even here, where everything has been perfectly tranquil, but where a familiarity with slavery, and a possibility of danger from that quarter prepare the general mind for some severities, there is a strong sentiment that there has been hanging enough. The other States, and the world at large will forever condemn us if we indulge a principle of revenge, or go one step beyond absolute necessity. They cannot lose sight of the rights of the two parties, and the object of the unsuccessful one. Our situation is, indeed, a difficult one; for I doubt whether these people can ever be permitted to go at large among us with safety. To reprieve them and keep them in prison till the meeting of the Legislature will encourage efforts for their release. Is there no fort or garrison of the State or of the Union, where they could be confined, and where the presence of the garrison would preclude all ideas of attempting a rescue? Surely the Legislature would pass a law for their exportation, the proper measure on this and all similar occasions.— To JAMES MONROE. FORD ED., vii, 457. (M., Sep. 1800.)

3989. INSURRECTION, Suppressing.—I hope, on the first symptom of an open opposition to the law [Embargo] by force, you will fly to the scene and aid in suppressing any commotion.—To HENRY DEARBORN. v, 334. (M., Aug. 1808.) See REBELLION.

3990. INTEMPERANCE, Greatest calamity.—Of all calamities this is the greatest. —To MARY JEFFERSON EPPES. D. L. J., 246. (Pa., 1798.)

3991. INTEMPERANCE, Havoc by.—Spirituous liquors, the small pox, war, and an abridgment of territory to a people who lived principally on the spontaneous productions of nature, committed terrible havoc among the Virginia Indians.—NOTES ON VIRGINIA. viii, 339. FORD ED., iii, 196. (1782.)

3992. INTEMPERANCE, Restriction.—
The drunkard, as much as the maniac, requires restrictive measures to save him from the fatal infatuation under which he is destroying his health, his morals, his family, and his usefulness to society. One powerful obstacle to his ruinous self-indulgence would be a price beyond his competence.—To SAMUEL SMITH. vii, 285. FORD ED., x, 252. (M., 1823.)

3993. INTEREST, Government and.—
Alexander Hamilton avowed the opinion that man could be governed by one of two motives only,—force or interest. Force, he observed, in this country was out of the question; and the interests, therefore, of the members must be laid hold of to keep the Legislature in unison with the Executive. And with grief and shame it must be acknowledged that his machine was not without effect; that even in this, the birth of our government, some members were found sordid enough to bend their duty to their interests, and to look after personal rather than public good.—THE ANAS. ix, 91. FORD ED., i, 160. (1818.)

3994. INTEREST, Judgment and.—It is not enough that honest men are appointed judges. All know the influence of interest on the mind of man, and how unconsciously his judgment is warped by that influence.—AUTOBIOGRAPHY. i, 81. FORD ED., i, 112. (1821.)

3995. INTEREST, Motives of.—The known bias of the human mind from motives of interest should lessen the confidence of each party in the justice of their reasoning.—To JAMES ROSS. i, 562. FORD ED., iv, 218. (P., 1786.)

3996. INTEREST, The passions and.—
Interest is not the strongest passion in the human breast.—To JAMES ROSS. i, 561. FORD ED., iv, 217. (P., 1786.)

3997. INTEREST, Private.—In selecting persons for the management of affairs, I am influenced by neither personal nor family interests.—To DR. HORATIO TURPIN. v, 90. (W., 1807.)

3998. ———— ————. Bringing into office no desires of making it subservient to the advancement of my own private interests, it has been no sacrifice, by postponing them, to strengthen the confidence of my fellow citizens.—To DR. HORATIO TURPIN. v, 90. (W., 1807.)

3999. INTEREST, Virtue and.—Virtue and interest are inseparable.—To GEORGE LOGAN. FORD ED., x, 69. (P.F., 1816.)

4000. INTEREST (Money), Forfeited.—
There is one rule of your [the English] and our law, which, while it proves that every title of debt is liable to a disallowance of interest under special circumstances, is so applicable to our case, that I shall cite it as a text, and apply it to the circumstances of our case. It is laid down in Vin. Abr. Interest. c. 7, and 2 Abr. Eq. 5293, and elsewhere in these words: "Where, by a *general and national calamity*, nothing is made out of lands which are assigned for payment of interest, it ought not to run on *during the time of such calamity.*" This is exactly the case in question. Can a more *general national calamity* be conceived than that universal devastation which took place in many of these States during the war? Was it ever more exactly the case anywhere, *that nothing was made out of the lands which were to pay the interest?* The produce of those lands, for want of the opportunity of exporting it safely, was down to almost nothing in real money. For example, tobacco was less than a dollar the hundred weight. Imported articles of clothing or consumption were from four to eight times their usual price. A bushel of salt was usually sold for 100 lbs. of tobacco. At the same time, these lands, and other property, in which the money of the British creditor was vested, were paying high taxes for their own protection, and the debtor, as nominal holder, stood ultimate insurer of their value to the creditor, who was the real proprietor, because they were bought with his money. And who will estimate the value of this insurance, or say what would have been the forfeit, in a contrary event of the war? Who will say that the risk of the property was not worth the interest of its price? *General calamity*, then, prevented profit, and, consequently, stopped interest, which is in lieu of profit. The creditor says, indeed, he has laid out of his money; he has, therefore, lost the use of it. The debtor replies, that, if the creditor has lost, he has not gained it; that this may be a question between two parties, both of whom have lost. In that case, the courts will not double the loss of the one, to save all loss from the other. That is a rule of natural as well as municipal law, that in questions " *de damno evitando melior est conditio possidentis*". If this maxim be just, where each party is equally innocent, how much more so, where the loss has been produced by the act of the creditor? For, a nation, as a society, forms a moral person, and every member of it is personally responsible for his society. It was the act of the lender, or of his nation, which annihilated the profits of the money lent; he cannot then demand profits which he either prevented from coming into existence, or burned, or otherwise destroyed, after they were produced. If, then, there be no instrument, or title of debt so formal and sacred as to give right to interest under all possible circumstances, and if circumstances of exemption, stronger than in the present case, cannot possibly be found, then no instrument or title of debt, however formal or sacred, can give right to interest under the circumstances of our case. Let us present the question in another point of view. Your own law forbade the payment of in-

terest, when it forbade the receipt of American produce into Great Britain, and made that produce fair prize on its way from the debtor to the creditor, or to any other, for his use of reimbursement. All personal access between creditor and debtor was made illegal; and the debtor who endeavored to make a remitment of his debt, or interest, must have done it three times, to ensure its getting once to hand; for two out of three vessels were generally taken by the creditor nation, and, sometimes, by the creditor himself, as many of them turned their trading vessels into privateers.—To GEORGE HAMMOND. iii, 418. FORD ED., vi, 58. (Pa., 1792.)

4001. INTEREST (Money), Law and custom.—Nothing is said [in the treaty of peace] of *interest* on these debts; and the sole question is, whether, where a *debt* is given, interest thereon flows from the general principles of the law? Interest is not a part of the debt. but something added to the debt by way of damage for the detention of it. This is the definition of the English lawyers themselves, who say, " Interest is recovered by way of *damages ratione detentionis debiti*". 2 Salk. 622, 623. Formerly, all interest was considered as unlawful, in every country of Europe. It is still so in Roman Catholic countries, and countries little commercial. From this, as a general rule, a few special cases are excepted. In France, particularly, the exceptions are those of minors, marriage portions, and money, the price of lands. So thoroughly do their laws condemn the allowance of interest, that a party who has paid it voluntarily may recover it back again whenever he pleases. Yet this has never been taken up as a gross and flagrant denial of justice, authorizing national complaint against· those governments. In England, also, all interest was against law, till the stat. 37, H. 8, c. 9. The growing spirit of commerce, no longer restrained by the principles of the Roman Church, then first began to tolerate it. The same causes produced the same effect in Holland. and, perhaps, in some other commercial and Catholic countries. But, even in England, the allowance of interest is not given by *express law*, but rests on the *discretion of judges and juries*, as the arbiters of damages.—To GEORGE HAMMOND. iii, 416. FORD ED., vi, 57. (Pa., 1792.)

4002. INTEREST (Money), Right to.—There is not a single title to debt so formal and sacred as to give a right to interest under all possible circumstances either in England or America.—To MR. HAMMOND. iii, 426. (1792.)

4003. INTEREST (Money), Sacred obligation.—A sacred payment of interest is the only way to make the most of our resources, and a sense of that renders your income from our funds more certain than mine from lands.—To WILLIAM SHORT. vi, 402. (M., 1814.)

4004. INTEREST (Money), Tax for.—The new government should by no means be left by the old, to the necessity of borrowing a stiver, before it can tax for its interest. This will be to destroy the credit of the new government in its birth.—To JAMES MADISON. ii, 378. (P., 1788.)

4005. INTERNAL IMPROVEMENTS, Advocated.—I experience great satisfaction at seeing my country proceed to facilitate the intercommunications of its several parts, by opening rivers. canals and roads. How much more rational is this disposal of public money, than that of waging war.—To JAMES ROSS. i, 560. FORD ED., iv, 216. (P., 1786.)

4006. INTERNAL IMPROVEMENTS, Constitutional Amendment.—For authority to apply the surplus [taxes imposed for the support of the government and the payment of the Revolutionary debt] to objects of [internal] improvement, an amendment of the Constitution would have been necessary.—To J. W. EPPES. vi, 195. FORD ED., ix, 395. (P.F., Sep. 1813.)

4007. —— ——. Supposing that it might be for the good of the whole, as some of its co-States seem to think, that this power of making roads and canals should be added to those directly given to the Federal branch, as more likely to be systematically and beneficially directed, than by the independent action of the several States, this Commonwealth [Virginia], from respect to these opinions, and a desire of conciliation with its co-States, will consent, in concurrence with them, to make this addition, provided it be done regularly by an amendment of the compact, in the way established by that instrument. and provided, also, it be sufficiently guarded against abuses, compromises, and corrupt practices. not only of possible, but of probable occurrence.—VIRGINIA PROTEST. ix 499. FORD ED., x, 352. (1825.)

4008. INTERNAL IMPROVEMENTS, Demand for.—I have for some time considered the question of internal improvement as desperate. The torrent of general opinion sets so strongly in favor of it as to be irresistible.—To JAMES MADISON. vii, 422. FORD ED., x, 348. (M., 1825.)

4009. INTERNAL IMPROVEMENTS, Provision for.—I am a great friend to the improvement of roads, canals, and schools. But I wish I could see some provision for the former as solid as that of the latter,—something better than fog.—To CHARLES YANCEY. vi, 517. FORD ED., x, 4. (M., 1816.)

4010. INTERNAL IMPROVEMENTS, Reserved Powers.—[The Federal authorties] claim and have commencel the exercise of the right to construct roads, open canals. and effect other internal improvements within the territories and jurisdictions exclusively belonging to the several States, which this Assembly [Virginia] does declare has not been given to that branch by the constitutional compact, but remains to each State among its domestic and unalienated powers, exercisable within itself and by its domestic authorities alone.—VIRGINIA PROTEST. ix, 497. FORD ED., x, 350. (1825.)

4011. INTERNAL IMPROVEMENTS, State rights and.—When we consider the extensive and deep-seated opposition to this assumption [power of Internal Improvements], the conviction entertained by so many, that this deduction of powers by elaborate construction prostrates the rights reserved to the States, the difficulties with which it will rub along in the course of its exercise; that changes of majorities will be changing the system backwards and forwards, so that no undertaking under it will be safe; that there is not a State in the Union which would not give the power willingly, by way of amendment, with some little guard, perhaps, against abuse; I cannot but think it would be the wisest course to ask an express grant of the powers. * * * This would render its exercise smooth and acceptable to all and insure to it all the facilities which the States could contribute, to prevent that kind of abuse which all will fear, because all know it is so much practiced in public bodies, I mean the bartering of votes. It would reconcile everyone, if limited by the proviso, that the federal proportion of each State should be expended within the State. With this single security against partiality and corrupt bargaining, I suppose there is not a State, perhaps not a man in the Union, who would not consent to add this to the powers of the General Government.—To EDWARD LIVINGSTON. vii, 343. FORD ED., x, 300. (M., 1824.)

4012. INTERNAL IMPROVEMENTS, Surplus taxes and.—The fondest wish of my heart ever was that the surplus portion of these taxes, destined for the payment of that [Revolutionary] debt, should, when that object was accomplished, be continued by annual or biennial reenactments, and applied, in time of peace, to the improvement of our country by canals, roads and useful institutions, literary or others; and in time of war to the maintenance of the war.—To J. W. EPPES. vi, 195. FORD ED., ix, 395. (P.F., 1813.)

4013. ——— ———. We consider the employment [in public improvements] of the contributions which our citizens can spare, after feeding, and clothing, and lodging themselves comfortably, as more useful, more moral, and even more splendid, than that preferred by Europe, of destroying human life, labor, and happiness.—To BARON VON HUMBOLDT. vii, 75. FORD ED., x, 89. (M., 1817.)

4014. INTERNAL IMPROVEMENTS, Veto of Bill for.—An act for internal improvement, after passing both Houses, was negatived by the President. The act was founded, avowedly, on the principle that the phrase in the Constitution which authorizes Congress " to lay taxes, to pay the debts and provide for the general welfare ", was an extension of the powers specifically enumerated

to whatever would promote the general welfare and this, you know, was the federal doctrine. Whereas, our tenet ever was, and, indeed, it is almost the only landmark which now divides the federalists from the republicans, that Congress had not unlimited powers to provide for the general welfare, but were restrained to those specifically enumerated; and that, as it was never meant they should provide for that welfare but by the exercise of the enumerated powers, so it could not have been meant they should raise money for purposes which the enumeration did not place under their action; consequently, that the specification of powers is a limitation of the purposes for which they may raise money. I think the passage and rejection of this bill a fortunate incident. Every State will certainly concede the power; and this will be a national confirmation of the grounds of appeal to them, and will settle forever the meaning of this phrase, which, by a mere grammatical quibble, has countenanced the General Government in a claim of universal power. For in the phrase, " to lay taxes, to pay the debts and provide for the general welfare ", it is a mere question of syntax, whether the two last infinitives are governed by the first or are distinct and coordinate powers; a question unequivocally decided by the exact definition of powers immediately following. It is fortunate for another reason, as the States in conceding the power, will modify it, either by requiring the Federal ratio of expense in each State, or otherwise, so as to secure us against its partial exercise. Without this caution, intrigue, negotiation, and the barter of votes might become as habitual in Congress, as they are in those Legislatures which have the appointment of officers, and which, with us, is called " logging ", the term of the farmers for their exchanges of aid in rolling together the logs of their newly-cleared grounds.—To ALBERT GALLATIN. vii, 78. FORD ED., x, 91. (M., 1817.)

4015. INTERNAL IMPROVEMENTS, War and.—Farewell, then [should war with England take place], all our useful improvements of canals and roads, reformation of laws, and other rational employments.—To JAMES ROSS. i, 563. FORD ED., iv, 219. (P. 1786.)

4016. ——— ———. Give us peace till our revenues are liberated from debt, and then if war be necessary, it can be carried on without a new tax or loan, and during peace we may chequer our whole country with canals roads, &c. This is the object to which all our endeavors should be directed.—To MR LIEPER. v, 296. (M., May 1808.)

4017. ——— ———. The late pacification with England gives us a hope of eight years of peaceable and wise administration, within which time our revenue will be liberated from debt, and be free to commence that splendid course of public improvement and wise application of the public contributions, of which it remains for us to set the first example.—To DR. E. GRIFFITH. v, 451. (M., May 1809.)

4018. INTERNAL IMPROVEMENTS, Western people and.—A majority of the people are against us on this question. The Western States have especially been bribed by local considerations to abandon their ancient brethren, and enlist under banners alien to them in principles and interest.—To WILLIAM F. GORDON. FORD ED., x, 338. (M., Jan. 1826.)

4019. INTOLERANCE, Defiance of.—I never will, by any word or act, bow to the shrine of intolerance, or admit a right of inquiry into the religious opinions of others.— To EDWARD DOWSE. iv, 478. (1803.)

4020. INTOLERANCE, Delusion through.—Your part of the Union, though as absolutely republican as ours, had drunk deeper of the delusion, and is, therefore, slower in recovering from it. The ægis of government, and the temples of religion and of justice, have all been prostrated there to toll us back to the times when we burned witches. But your people will rise again. They will awake like Samson from his sleep, and carry away the gates and posts of the city.—To ELBRIDGE GERRY. iv, 390. FORD ED., viii, 41. (W., March 1801.)

4021. INTOLERANCE, Religious and political.—Having banished from our land that religious intolerance under which mankind so long bled and suffered, we have yet gained little if we countenance a political intolerance as despotic, as wicked, and capable of as bitter and bloody persecutions.—FIRST INAUGURAL ADDRESS. viii, 2. FORD ED., viii, 2. (1801.)

4022. INTOLERANCE, Victims.—I have seen with great grief yourself and so many other venerable patriots, retired and weeping in silence over the rapid subversion of those principles for the attachment of which you had sacrificed the ease and comforts of life; but I rejoice that you have lived to see us revindicate our rights, and regain manfully the ground from which fraud, not force, had for a moment driven us.—To GENERAL WARREN. iv, 375. (W., 1801.)

4023. INTRIGUE, Abhorrence of.—I meddled in no intrigues, pursued no concealed object.—AUTOBIOGRAPHY. i, 65. FORD ED., i, 91. (1821.)

4024. INTRODUCTION (Letters of), Apology for.—Solicitations, which cannot be directly refused, oblige me to trouble you often, with letters recommending and introducing to you persons who go hence from America. I will beg the favor of you to distinguish the letters wherein I appeal to recommendations from other persons, from those which I write on my own knowledge. In the former, it is never my intention to compromit myself, nor you. In both instances, I must beg you to ascribe the trouble I give you to circumstances which do not leave me at liberty to decline it.—To JAMES MADISON. ii, 447. FORD ED., v, 48. (P., 1788.)

4025. INTRODUCTION (Letters of), Refused.—I have been obliged to make it a rule to give no letters of introduction while in my present office.—To JAMES MONROE. FORD ED., viii, 286. (W., 1804.)

4026. INTRODUCTION (Letters of), Value of.—It is rendering mutual service to men of virtue and understanding to make them acquainted with one another.—To DR. PRICE. ii, 354. (P., 1788.)

4027. INVASION, Not feared.—I as little fear foreign invasion [as domestic insurrection]. I have indeed thought it a duty to be prepared to meet even the most powerful, that of a Bonaparte, for instance, by the only means competent, that of a classification of the militia, and placing the junior classes at the public disposal; but the lesson he receives in Spain extirpates all apprehensions from my mind. If, in a peninsula, the neck of which is adjacent to him and at his command, where he can march any army without the possibility of interception or obstruction from any foreign power, he finds it necessary to begin with an army of three hundred thousand men, to subdue a nation of five millions, brutalized by ignorance, and enervated by long peace, and should find constant reinforcements of thousands after thousands, necessary to effect at last a conquest as doubtful as deprecated, what numbers would be necessary against eight millions of free Americans, spread over such an extent of country as would wear him down by mere marching, by want of food, autumnal diseases, &c.? How would they be brought, and how reinforced across an ocean of three thousand miles, in possession of a bitter enemy, whose peace, like the repose of a dog, is never more than momentary? And for what? For nothing but hard blows. If the Orleanese Creoles would but contemplate these truths, they would cling to the American Union, soul and body, as their first affection, and we would be as safe there as we are everywhere else.—To DR. JAMES BROWN. v, 379. FORD ED., ix, 211. (W., 1808.)

4028. INVENTIONS, Air screw propeller.—I went some time ago to see a machine which offers something new. A man had applied to a light boat a very large screw, the thread of which was a thin plate, two feet broad, applied by its edge spirally around a small axis. It somewhat resembled a bottle brush, if you will suppose the hairs of the bottle brush joining together, and forming a spiral plane. This, turned on its axis in the air, carried the vessel across the Seine. It is, in fact, a screw which takes hold of the air and draws itself along by it; losing, indeed, much of its effort by the yielding nature of the body it lays hold of to pull itself on by. I think it may be applied in the water with much greater effect and to very useful purposes. Perhaps it may be used also for the balloon.—To PROFESSOR JAMES MADISON. i, 447. (P., 1785.)

4029. INVENTIONS, Copying press.—When I was in England, I formed a portable copying press on the principle of the large one they make here [Paris] for copying letters. I had a model made there, and it has answered perfectly. A workman here has made several from that model. * * * You must do me the favor to accept of one.—To WILLIAM CARMICHAEL. ii, 81. FORD ED., iv, 347. (P., 1786.)

4030. INVENTIONS, Essence d'Orient.—The manner of curing the Essence d'Orient is. as you are apprised, kept secret here [Paris]. There is no getting at it, therefore, openly. A friend has undertaken to try whether it can be obtained either by proposing the partnership you mention, or by finding out the process.—To FRANCIS HOPKINSON. FORD ED., iv, 270. (P., 1786.)

4031. —— ——. Your two phials of Essence d'Orient * * * got separated from the letters which accompanied them. * * * The pearl merchant * * * said you had a very considerable knowledge in the manner of preparing, but that there was still one thing wanting which made the secret of the art; that this is not only a secret of the art, but of every individual workman who will not communicate to his fellows, believing his own method best; that of ten different workmen, all will practice different operations, and only one of the ten be the right one; that the secret consists only in preparing the fish, all the other parts of the process in the pearl manufactory being known. That experience has provide it to be absólutely impossible for the matter to cross the sea without being spoiled; but that if you will send some in the best state you can, he will make pearls of it, and send to you that you may judge of them yourself.—To FRANCIS HOPKINSON. ii, 202. (P., 1787.)

4032. INVENTIONS, Felier Hydraulique.—I am thankful to you for the trouble you have taken in thinking of the felier hydraulique. To be put in motion by the same power which was to continue the motion was certainly wanting to that machine, as a better name still is. I would not give you the trouble of having a model made, as I have workmen who can execute from the drawing.—To ROBERT FULTON. v, 517. (M., 1810.)

4033. INVENTIONS, Government interposition.—Though the interposition of government in matters of invention has its use, yet it is in practice so inseparable from abuse that the government of my country think it better not to meddle with it.—To M. HOMMANDE. ii, 236. (P., 1787.)

4034. INVENTIONS, Hemp-brake.—The braking and beating hemp, which has been always done by hand, is so slow, so laborious, and so much complained of by our laborers, that I had given it up and purchased and manufactured cotton for their shirting. The advanced price of this, however, makes it a serious item of expense; and, in the meantime, a method of removing the difficulty of preparing hemp occurred to me, so simple and so cheap, that I return to its culture and manufacture. To a person having a threshing machine, the addition of a hemp-brake will not cost more than twelve or fifteen dollars. You know that the first mover in that machine is a horizontal horse-wheel with cogs on its upper face. On these is placed a wallower and shaft, which give motion to the threshing apparatus. On the opposite side of this same wheel I place another wallower and shaft, through which, and near its outer end, I pass a cross-arm of sufficient strength, projecting on each side fifteen inches in this form:

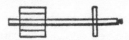

Nearly under the cross-arm is placed a very strong hemp-brake, much stronger and heavier than those for the hand. Its head block particu-

larly is massive, and four feet high, and near its upper end in front, is fixed a strong pin (which we may call its horn); by this the cross-arm lifts and lets fall the brake twice in every revolution of the wallower. * * * Something of this kind has been so long wanted by the cultivators of hemp, that as soon as I can speak of its effect with certainty I shall probably describe it anonymously in the public papers, in order to forestall the prevention of its use by some interloping patentee.—To GEORGE FLEMING. vi, 506. (M., 1815.)

— INVENTIONS, Patents for.—See PATENTS.

4035. INVENTIONS, Pedometer.—I send your pedometer. To the loop at the bottom of it, you must sew a tape, and at the other end of the tape, a small hook. * * * Cut a little hole in the bottom of your left watch pocket, pass the hook and tape through it, and down between the breeches and drawers, and fix the hook on the edge of your knee band, an inch from the knee buckle; then hook the instrument itself by its swivel hook, on the upper edge of the watch pocket. Your tape being well adjusted in length. Your double steps will be exactly counted by the instrument.—To JAMES MADISON. ii, 379. (P., 1788.)

4036. INVENTIONS, Polygraph.—A Mr. Hawkins, of Frankford, near Philadelphia, has invented a machine which he calls a polygraph, and which carries two, three, or four pens. That of two pens, is best; and is so perfect that I have laid aside the copying press, for a twelve-month past. and write always with the polygraph. I have directed one to be made, of which I ask your acceptance.—To C. F. VOLNEY. iv, 572. (W., 1805.)

4037. —— ——. It is for copying with one pen while you write with the other, and without the least additional embarrassment or exertion to the writer. I think it the finest invention of the present age. * * * As a secretary which copies for us what we write without the power of revealing it, I find it a most precious possession to a man in public business.—To JAMES BOWDOIN. vi, 17. (W., 1806.)

4038. INVENTIONS, Preserving flour. —Every discovery which multiplies the subsistence of man must be a matter of joy to every friend of humanity. As such, I learn with great satisfaction, that you have found the means of preserving flour more perfectly than has been done hitherto. But I am not authorized to avail my country of it, by making any offer to its communication. Their policy is to leave their citizens free, neither restraining nor aiding them in their pursuits.—To MONSIEUR L'HOMMANDE. ii, 236. (P., 1787.)

4039. INVENTIONS, Seed box.—The seed-box described in the agricultural transactions of New York, reduces the expense of seeding from six shillings to two shillings and three pence the acre, and does the business better than is possible to be done by the human hand. —To JAMES MADISON. iv, 117. FORD ED., vii, 11. (M., 1795.)

4040. INVENTIONS, Stylograph.—The apparatus for stylographic writing * * * is certainly very ingenious. * * * I had never heard of the invention till your letter announced it, for these novelties reach us very late.—To WILLIAM LYMAN. v, 279. (W., 1808.)

4041. INVENTIONS, Threshing machine.—My threshing machine has arrived at

New York. Mr. Pinckney writes me word that the original from which this is copied threshes one hundred and fifty bushels of wheat in eight hours, with six horses and five men. It may be moved either by water or horses. Fortunately the workman who made it (a millwright) is come in the same vessel to America. I have written to persuade him to go on immediately to Richmond, offering him the use of my model to exhibit, and to give him letters to get him into immediate employ in making them.—To JAMES MADISON. iv, 54. FORD ED., vi, 403. (Pa., 1793.)

4042. INVENTIONS, Useful.—I am not afraid of new inventions or improvements, nor bigoted to the practices of our forefathers. * * * Where a new invention is supported by well known principles, and promises to be useful, it ought to be tried.—To ROBERT FULTON. v, 516. (M., 1810.) See TORPEDO.

4043. INVENTIONS, Wooden wheels.—I was in Philadelphia when the first set of wheels arrived from London, and were spoken of by the gentleman (an Englishman) who brought them as a wonderful discovery. The idea of its being a new discovery was laughed at by the Philadelphians, who, in their Sunday parties across the Delaware, had seen every farmer's cart mounted on such wheels. The writer in the paper supposes the English workman got his idea from Homer. But it is more likely the Jersey farmer got his idea thence, because ours are the only farmers who can read Homer; because, too, the Jersey practice is precisely that stated by Homer: the English practice very different. Homer's words are (comparing a young hero killed by Ajax to a poplar felled by a workman) literally thus: "He fell on the ground, like a poplar, which has grown smooth, in the west part of a great meadow; with its branches shooting from its summit. But the chariot maker, with the sharp axe, has felled it, that he may bend a wheel for a beautiful chariot. It lies drying on the banks of the river." Observe the circumstances which coincide with the Jersey practice. 1. It is a tree growing in a moist place, full of juices and easily bent. 2. It is cut while green. 3. It is bent into the circumference of a wheel. 4. It is left to dry in that form. You should write a line for the Journal to reclaim the honor of our farmers.—To M. DE CREVECOEUR. ii, 97. (P., 1787.)

4044. ———— ————. I see by the Journal that they are robbing us of another of our inventions to give it to the English. The writer, indeed, only admits them to have revived what he thinks was known to the Greeks, that is, the making the circumference of a wheel of one single piece. The farmers in New Jersey were the first who practiced it commonly. Dr. Franklin, in one of his trips to London, mentioned this practice to the man now in London, who has the patent for making those wheels. The idea struck him. The Doctor promised to go to his shop, and assist him in trying to make the wheel of one piece. The Jersey farmers do it by cutting a young sapling, and bending it, while green and juicy, into a circle; and leaving it so until it becomes perfectly seasoned. But in London there are no saplings. The difficulty was, then, to give to old wood the pliancy of young. The Doctor and the workman labored together some weeks, and succeeded: and the man obtained a patent for it, which has made his fortune. I was in his shop in London; he told me the story himself, and acknowledged, not only the origin of the idea, but how much the assistance of Dr. Franklin had contributed to perform the operation on dry wood. He spoke of him with love and gratitude.—To M. DE CREVECOEUR. ii, 97. (P., 1787.)

4045. INVENTORS, Rights of.—It has been pretended by some (and in England especially) that inventors have a natural and exclusive right to their inventions, and not merely for their own lives, but inheritable to their heirs. But while it is a moot question whether the origin of any kind of property is derived from nature at all, it would be singular to admit a natural and even an hereditary right to inventors. It is agreed by those who have seriously considered the subject, that no individual has, of natural right, a separate property in an acre of land, for instance. By an universal law, indeed, whatever, whether fixed or movable, belongs to all men equally and in common, is the property for the moment of him who occupies it; but when he relinquishes the occupation, the property goes with it. Stable ownership is the gift of social law, and is given late in the progress of society. It would be curious, then, if an idea, the fugitive fermentation of an individual brain, could, of natural right, be claimed in exclusive and stable property. If nature has made any one thing less susceptible than all others of exclusive property, it is the action of the thinking power called an idea, which an individual may exclusively possess as long as he keeps it to himself; but the moment it is divulged, it forces itself into the possession of every one, and the receiver cannot dispossess himself of it. Its peculiar character, too, is that no one possesses the less, because every other possesses the whole of it. He who receives an idea from me, receives instruction himself without lessening mine; as he who lights his taper at mine, receives light without darkening mine. That ideas should freely spread from one to another over the globe, for the moral and mutual instruction of man, and improvement of his condition, seems to have been peculiarly and benevolently designed by nature. When she made them like fire, expansible over all space, without lessening their density in any point, and like the air in which we breathe, move, and have our physical being, incapable of confinement or exclusive appropriation. Inventions then cannot, in nature, be a subject of property. Society may give an exclusive right to the profits arising from them, as an encouragement to men to pursue ideas which may produce utility, but this may or may not be done according to the will and convenience of the society, without claim or complaint from anybody. Accordingly, it is a fact, as far as I am informed, that England was, until we copied her the only country on earth which ever, by a general law, gave a legal right to the exclusive use of an idea. In some countries it is sometimes done, in a great case, and by a special and personal act, but generally speaking, other nations have thought that these monopolies produce more embarrassment than advantage to society; and it may be observed that the nations which refuse monopolies of invention, are as fruitful as England in new and useful devices.—To ISAAC MCPHERSON. vi, 180. (M., 1813.)

4046. IRELAND, America and.—You shall find me zealous in whatever may concern the interests of the two countries. [United States and Ireland.]—To W. W. SEWARD. i, 479. (P., 1785.)

4047. ———— ————. The freedom of commerce between Ireland and America is undoubtedly very interesting to both countries. If fair play be given to the natural advantages of Ireland, she must come in for a distinguished share of that commerce. She is entitled to it from the excellence of some of her manufactures, the cheapness of most of them, their correspondence with the American taste, a sameness of language, laws and manners, a reciprocal affection between the people, and the singular circumstance of her being the nearest European land to the United States.*—To W. W. Seward. i, 478. (P., 1785.)

4048. —— ——. The defeat of the Irish propositions is also in our favor.—To James Madison. i. 414. (P., 1785.)

4049. IRELAND, Commerce.—It is to be considered how far an exception in favor of Ireland in our commercial regulations might embarrass the councils of England on the one hand, and on the other how far it might give room to an evasion of the regulations.—To James Monroe. Ford ed., iv, 41. (P., 1785.)

4050. —— ——. I am sure the United States would be glad, if it should be found practicable, to make that discrimination between Great Britain and Ireland, which their commercial principles, and their affection for the latter, would dictate.—To W. W. Seward. i, 479. (P., 1785.)

4051. —— ——. I am not at present so well acquainted with the trammels of Irish commerce, as to know what they are, particularly, which obstruct the intercourse between Ireland and America; nor, therefore, what can be the object of a fleet stationed in the western ocean, to intercept that intercourse. Experience, however, has taught us to infer that the fact is probable, because it is impolite.—To W. W. Seward. i, 478. (P., 1785.)

4052. IRELAND, Great Britain and.— Bonaparte * * * seems to be looking towards the East Indies, where a most formidable cooperation has been prepared for demolishing the British power. I wish the affairs of Ireland were as hopeful.—To James Madison. iv, 280. Ford ed., vii, 341. (Pa., Jan. 1799.)

— **IRISH, The.**—See 474 and 480.

4053. IRON, Indians and.—Nothing I have ever yet heard of proves the existence of a nation here who knew the use of iron. I have never heard even of burnt bricks, though they might be made without iron. The statue you * * * send me would, because of the hardness of the stone, be a better proof of the use of iron than I ever yet saw; but as it is a solitary fact, and possible to have been made with implements of stone, and great patience, for which the Indians are remarkable, I consider it to have been so made. It is certainly the best piece of workmanship I ever saw from their hands.—To Harry Inness. iii, 217. Ford ed., v, 294. (Pa., 1791.)

4054. IRON, Swedish.—We cannot make iron in competition with Sweden, or any other

* Mr. Seward, by direction of the associated company of Irish merchants in London, had written to Jefferson on the subject.—Editor.

nation of Europe, where labor is so much cheaper.—To John Adams. i, 493. (P., 1785.)

4055. —— ——. The United States have much occasion for the productions of Sweden, particularly for its iron.—To Baron Stahe. Ford ed., iv, 242. (P., 1786.)

4056. IVERNOIS (Francois d'), Patriot. —M. d'Ivernois is a Genevan of considerable distinction for science and patriotism, and that, too, of the republican kind, though he does not carry it so far as our friends of the National Assembly of France. While I was in Paris, I knew him as an exile from his democratic principles, the aristocracy having then the upper hand in Geneva. He is now obnoxious to the democratic party.—To Wilson Nicholas. iv, 109. Ford ed., vi, 513. (M., 1794.) See Academy, Geneva.

4057. JACKSON (Andrew), Faithful.— Be assured that Tennessee, and particularly General Jackson are faithful.*—To General Wilkinson. v, 25. Ford ed., ix, 2. (W., Jan. 1807.)

4058. JACKSON (Andrew), Invitation to.—In your passages to and from Washington, should your travelling convenience ever permit a deviation to Monticello, I shall receive you with distinguished welcome. * * * I recall with pleasure the remembrance of our joint labors while in Senate together in times of great trial and of hard battling. Battles, indeed, of words, not of blood, as those you have since fought so much for your own glory, and that of your country.—To Andrew Jackson. Ford ed., x, 286. (M., 1823.)

4059. JACKSON (Andrew), Life of.—I have lately read, with great pleasure, Reid and Eaton's Life of Jackson, if "Life" may be called what is merely a history of his campaign of 1814. Reid's part is well written. Eaton's continuation is better for its matter than style. The whole, however, is valuable.— To John Adams. vii, 82. (P.F., 1817.)

4060. JACKSON (Andrew), Passionate. —I feel much alarmed at the prospect of seeing General Jackson President. He is one of the most unfit men I know of for such a place. He has had very little respect for laws or constitutions, and is, in fact, an able military chief. His passions are terrible. When I was President of the Senate he was a Senator; and he could never speak on account of the rashness of his feelings. I have seen him attempt it repeatedly, and as often choke with rage. His passions are no doubt cooler now; but he is a dangerous man.—Daniel Webster's Interview with Jefferson. Ford ed., x, 331. (1824.)

4061. JACKSON (Andrew), Presidential contest.—A threatening cloud has very suddenly darkened [General Jackson's] horizon. A letter has become public, written by him when Colonel Monroe first came into office, advising him to make up his administration *without regard to party*. (No suspicion has been entertained of any indecision in his political principles, and this evidence of it threatens a revolution of opinion respecting him.†) The solid republicanism of Pennsylvania, his principal support, is thrown into great fermentation by

* The reference is to Aaron Burr's enterprise.— Editor.
† This sentence was struck out.—Note in Ford Edition.

this apparent indifference to political principle.
—To RICHARD RUSH. FORD ED., x, 304.
(1824.)

**4062. JACKSON (Andrew), Seminole
War and.**—I observe Ritchie imputes to you
and myself opinions against Jackson's conduct
in the Seminole war. I certainly never doubted
that the military entrance into Florida, the temporary occupation of their posts, and the execution of Arbuthnot and Ambrister were all
justifiable. * * * I at first felt regret at the
execution; but I have ceased to feel [manu-
script torn] on mature reflection, and a belief
the example will save much blood.—To JAMES
MADISON. FORD ED., x, 124. (M., 1819.)

4063. JACOBINS, Battle for liberty.—
In the struggle which was necessary, many
guilty persons fell without the forms of trial,
and with them some innocent. These I deplore
as much as anybody, and shall deplore some of
them to the day of my death. But I deplore
them as I should have done had they fallen in
battle. It was necessary to use the arm of the
people, a machine not quite so blind as balls
and bombs, but blind to a certain degree. A
few of their cordial friends met at their hands
the fate of enemies. But time and truth will
rescue and embalm their memories, while their
posterity will be enjoying that very liberty for
which they would never have hesitated to offer
up their lives. The liberty of the whole earth
was depending on the issue of the contest, and
was ever such a prize won with so little innocent
blood? My own affections have been deeply
wounded by some of the martyrs to this cause,
but rather than it should have failed I would
have seen half the earth desolated; were there
but an Adam and Eve left in every country,
and left free. it would be better than as it
now is.—To WILLIAM SHORT. iii, 502. FORD
ED., vi, 153. (Pa., January 1793.)

4064. JACOBINS, Censured.—The tone
of your letters had for some time given me pain,
on account of the extreme warmth with which
they censured the proceedings of the Jacobins
of France. I considered that sect as the same
with the republican patriots, and the Feuillants
as the monarchical patriots, well known in the
early part of the Revolution, and but little distant in their views, both having in object the
establishment of a free constitution, differing
only on the question whether their chief Executive should be hereditary or not. The Jacobins (as since called) yielded to the Feuillants, and tried the experiment of retaining
their hereditary Executive. The experiment
failed completely, and would have brought on
the reestablishment of despotism had it been
pursued. The Jacobins saw this, and that the
expunging that office was of absolute necessity.
And the nation was with them in opinion, for
however they might have been formerly for
the constitution framed by the first assembly,
they were come over from their hope in it,
and were now generally Jacobins.—To WILLIAM
SHORT. iii, 501. FORD ED., vi, 153. (Pa., January 1793.)

4065. JACOBINS, Degeneration.—The
society of Jacobins was instituted on principles
and views as virtuous as ever kindled the hearts
of patriots. It was the pure patriotism of their
purposes which extended their association to
the limits of the nation, and rendered their
power within it boundless; and it was this
power which degenerated their principles and
practices to such enormities as never before
could have been imagined.—To JEDEDIAH
MORSE. vii, 235, FORD ED., x, 205. (M., 1822.)

**4066. JACOBINS, Favorable to Amer-
ica.**—The Jacobin party cannot but be favorable to America. Notwithstanding the very
general abuse of the Jacobins, I begin to consider them as representing the true revolution-
spirit of the whole nation, and as carrying the
nation with them.—To JAMES MADISON. FORD
ED., vi, 96. (Pa., June 1792.)

4067. JACOBINS, Inexperience.—The
only things wanting with the Jacobins is more
experience in business, and a little more conformity to the established style of communication with foreign powers. The latter want will,
I fear, bring enemies into the field, who would
have remained at home. The former leads them
to domineer over their executive, so as to render it unequal to its proper objects.—To JAMES
MADISON. FORD ED., vi, 96. (Pa., 1792.)

4068. JACOBINS, Republicanism.—The
reserve of President Washington had never permitted me to discover the light in which he
viewed [your censure of the Jacobins], and
as I was more anxious that you should satisfy
him than me, I had still avoided explanations
with you on the subject. But your letter induced him to break silence, and to notice the
extreme acrimony of your expressions. He
added that he had been informed the sentiments
you expressed *in your conversations* were equally offensive to our allies, and that you should
consider yourself as the representative of your
country, and that what you say might be imputed to your constituents. He desired me,
therefore, to write to you on this subject. He
added that he considered France as the sheet
anchor of this country, and its friendship as a
first object. There are in the United States
some characters of opposite principles; some of
them are high in office, others possessing great
wealth, and all of them hostile to France, and
fondly looking to England as the staff of their
hope. * * * Their prospects have certainly not
brightened. Excepting them, this country is entirely republican, friends to the Constitution,
anxious to preserve it, and to have it administered according to its own republican principles.
The little party above mentioned have espoused
it only as a stepping-stone to monarchy, and
have endeavored to approximate it to that in
its administration in order to render its final
transition more easy. The successes of republicanism in France have given the *coup de grace*
to their prospects, and I hope to their projects.
—To WILLIAM SHORT. iii, 502. FORD ED., vi, 154.
(Pa., Jan. 1793.)

4069. JAY (John), Chief Justice.—Jay
[has been] nominated Chief Justice. We were
afraid of something worse.—To JAMES MADISON.
iv, 343. FORD ED., vii, 471. (W., Dec. 1800.)

**4070. JAY (John), Monarchical princi-
ples.**—Jay, covering the same [monarchical]
principles under the veil of silence, is rising
steadily on the ruins of his friends.—To JAMES
MONROE. iii, 268. FORD ED., v, 352. (Pa., 1791.)

4071. JAY (John), Newspaper attacks.
—I observe by the public papers that Mr.
Littlepage has brought on a very disagreeable
altercation with Mr. Jay, in which he has given
to the character of the latter a coloring which
does not belong to it. * * * In truth it is
afflicting that a man who has passed his life in
serving the public, who has served them in the
highest stations with universal approbation, and
with a purity of conduct which has silenced
even party opprobrium; who, though poor, has
never permitted himself to make a shilling in
the public employ, should yet be liable to have

his peace of mind so much disturbed by any individual who shall think proper to arraign him in a newspaper. It is, however, an evil for which there is no remedy. Our liberty depends on the freedom of the press, and that cannot be limited without being lost. To the sacrifice of time, labor, fortune, a public servant must count upon adding that of peace of mind and even reputation.—To Dr. James Currie. Ford ed., iv, 131. (P., 1786.)

4072. —— ——. It is really to be lamented that after a public servant has passed a life in important and faithful services, after having given the most plenary satisfaction in every station, it should yet be in the power of every individual to disturb his quiet, by arraigning him in a gazette and by obliging him to act as if he needed a defence, an obligation imposed on him by unthinking minds which never give themselves the trouble of seeking a reflection unless it is presented to them. However it is a part of the price we pay for our liberty, which cannot be guarded but by the freedom of the press, nor that be limited without danger of losing it. To the loss of time, of labor, of money, then, must be added that of quiet, to which those must offer themselves who are capable of serving the public * * * . Your quiet may have suffered for a moment on this occasion, but you have the strongest of all supports, that of the public esteem.—To John Jay. Ford ed., iv, 186. (P., 1786.)

4073. JAY (John), Treaty-foundered.—Mr. Jay and his advocate, "Camillus", are completely treaty-foundered.—To James Monroe. iv, 149. Ford ed., vii, 90. (M., July 1796.)

4074. JAY (John), Tribute to.—I cannot take my departure without paying to yourself and your worthy colleague my homage for the good work you have completed for us, and congratulating you on the singular happiness of having borne so distinguished a part both in the earliest and latest transactions of this Revolution. * * * I am in hopes you will continue at some one of the European courts most agreeable to yourself, that we may still have the benefit of your talents.—To John Jay. i, 332. Ford ed., iii, 316. (Pa., April 1783.)

4075. JAY TREATY, Bad.—No man in the United States has had the effrontery to affirm that the treaty with England was not a very bad one except A. H. [Alexander Hamilton] under the signature of "Camillus". Its most zealous defenders only pretended that it was better than war, as if war was not invited, rather than avoided, by unfounded demands. I have never known the public pulse beat so full and in such universal union on any subject since the Declaration of Independence.—To James Monroe. Ford ed., vii, 58. (M., March 1796.)

4076. JAY TREATY, Dissatisfaction with.—So general a burst of dissatisfaction never before appeared against any transaction. Those who understand the particular articles of it, condemn these articles. Those who do not understand them minutely, condemn it generally as wearing a hostile face to France. This last is the most numerous class, comprehending the whole body of the people, who have taken a greater interest in this transaction than they were ever known to do in any other. It has, in my opinion, completely

demolished the monarchical party here.—To James Monroe. Ford ed., vii, 27. (M., Sep 1795.)

4077. —— ——. A very slight notice of [the Jay treaty] sufficed to decide my mind against it. I am not satisfied we should no be better without treaties with any nation But I am satisfied we should be better without such as this. The public dissatisfaction too, and dissension it is likely to produce are serious evils.—To H. Tazewell. iv, 120 Ford ed., vii, 30. (M., Sep. 1795.)

4078. JAY TREATY, Execrable.—I join with you in thinking the treaty an execrabl thing. But both negotiators must have understood, that, as there were articles in it which could not be carried into execution without the aid of the Legislatures on both sides, that therefore it must be referred to them, and that these Legislatures being free agents, would not give it their support if they disapproved of it. I trust the popular branch of our Legislature will disapprove of it, and thus rid us of this infamous act, which is really nothing more than a treaty of alliance between England and the Anglomen of this country, against the Legislature and people of the United States.—To Edward Rutledge. iv, 124. Ford ed., vii, 40. (M. Nov. 1795.)

4079. JAY TREATY, House of representatives and.—[John] Marshall's doctrine that the whole commercial part of the [Jay treaty (and he might have added the whole unconstitutional part of it), rests in the power of the House of Representatives, is certainly the true doctrine; and as the articles which stipulate what requires the consent of the three branches of the Legislature, must be referred to the House of Representatives for their concurrence, so they, being free agents may approve or reject them, either by a vote declaring that, or by refusing to pass acts. I should think the former mode the most safe and honorable.—To James Madison. Ford ed., vii, 38. (Nov. 1795.)

4080. —— ——. It is, indeed, surprising you [the House of Representatives] have not yet received the British treaty in form. I presume you would never receive it were not your cooperation on it necessary.—To James Madison. iv, 131. Ford ed., vii, 62 (M., March 1796.)

4081. —— ——. The British treaty has been formally, at length, laid before Congress All America is on tiptoe to see what the House of Representatives will decide on it We conceive the constitutional doctrine to be that though the President and Senate have the general power of making treaties, yet whenever, they include in a treaty matter confided by the Constitution to the three branches of the Legislature, an act of legislation will be requisite to confirm these articles, and that the House of Representatives as one branch of the Legislature, are perfectly free to pass the act or to refuse it, governing themselves by their own judgment whether it is for the good of their constituents to let the treaty go into effect or not. On the precedent now to be set will depend the future construction of our Constitution, and whether the powers of legislation shall be transferred from the President, Senate, and House of Representatives, to the President and Senate, and Piamingo or any other Indian, Algerine, or other chief. It is fortunate that the first decision is to be in a case so palpably atrocious, as to have been predetermined by all America.—To JAMES MONROE. iv, 134. FORD ED., vii, 67. (M., March 1796.)

4082. —— ——. The House of Representatives has manifested its disapprobation of the treaty. We are yet to learn whether they will exercise their constitutional right of refusing the means which depend on them for carrying it into execution. Should they be induced to lend their hand to it, it will be hard swallowing with their constituents; but will be swallowed from the habits of order and obedience to the laws which so much distinguish our countrymen.—To JAMES MONROE. FORD ED., vii, 59. (M., March 1796.)

4083. —— ——. Randolph seems to have hit upon the true theory of our Constitution; that when a treaty is made, involving matters confided by the Constitution to the three branches of the Legislature conjointly, the Representatives are as free as the President and Senate were, to consider whether the national interest requires or forbids, their giving the forms and force of law to the articles over which they have a power.—To WM. B. GILES. iv, 125. FORD ED., vii, 41. (M., Nov. 1795.)

4084. —— ——. I am well pleased with the manner in which your House have testified their sense of the treaty. While their refusal to pass the original clause of the reported answer proved their condemnation of it, the contrivance to let it disappear silently respected appearances in favor of the President, who errs as other men do, but errs with integrity.—To W. B. GILES. iv, 125. FORD ED., vii, 41. (M., Dec. 1795.)

4085. JAY TREATY, The Merchants and.—The Chamber of Commerce in New York, against the body of the town; the merchants in Philadelphia, against the body of their town, also, and our town of Alexandria have come forward in its support. Some individual champions also appear. Marshall, Carrington, Harvey, Bushrod Washington, Doctor Stewart. A more powerful one is Hamilton, under the signature of "*Camillus*". Adams holds his tongue with an address above his character.—To JAMES MONROE. FORD ED., vii, 27. (M., Sep. 1795.)

4086. —— ——. The merchants were certainly (except those of them who are English) as open mouthed at first against the treaty, as any. But the general expression of indignation has alarmed them for the strength of the Government. They have feared the shock woul1 be too great, and have chosen to tack about and support both treaty and

Government, rather than risk the Government. Thus it is, that Hamilton, Jay, &c., in the boldest act they ever ventured on to undermine the government, have the address to screen themselves, and direct the hue and cry against those who wish to drag them into light. A bolder party-stroke was never struck. For it certainly is an attempt of a party, who find they have lost their majority in one branch of the Legislature, to make a law by the aid of the other branch and of the Executive, under color of a treaty, which shall bind up the hands of the adverse branch from ever restraining the commerce of their patron nation. There appears a pause at present in the public sentiment, which may be followed by a revulsion. This is the effect of the desertion of the merchants, of the President's chiding answer to Boston and Richmond, of the writings of "*Curtius*" and "*Camillus*", and of the quietism into which the people naturally fall after first sensations are over.—To JAMES MADISON. iv, 122. FORD ED., vii, 32. (M., Sep. 1795.)

4087. JAY TREATY, A millstone.—Jay's treaty [should never] be quoted, or looked at, or even mentioned. That form will forever be a millstone round our necks unless we now rid ourselves of it once for all.—To PRESIDENT MADISON. v, 444. (M., April 1809.)

4088. JAY TREATY, Political effects of.—The British treaty produced a schism that went on widening and rankling till the years '98 and '99, when a final dissolution of all bonds, civil and social, appeared imminent. In that awful crisis, the people awakened from the frenzy into which they had been thrown, began to return to their sober and ancient principles, and have now become five-sixths of one sentiment, to wit, for peace, economy, and a government bottomed on popular election in its legislative and executive branches.—To BENJAMIN HAWKINS. iv, 465. FORD ED., viii, 212. (W., Feb. 1803.)

4089. JAY TREATY, Publication of.—The treaty is now known here by a bold act of duty in one of our Senators.—To JAMES MONROE. FORD ED., vii, 28. (M., 1795.)

4090. JAY TREATY, Ratification.—The campaign in Congress has closed. Though the Anglomen,* have in the end got their treaty through, and so have triumphed over the cause of republicanism, yet it has been to them a dear bought victory. It has given

* William Cobbett, who was then in the United States, was one of the newspaper and pamphleteering advocates of the ratification of the Jay treaty, and against Jefferson and his followers. Cobbett, after his return to England, writing to William Pitt, in 1804, said with respect to the Jay treaty: "The importance of that victory to England it would, perhaps, be difficult to render intelligible to the mind of Lord Melville, without the aid of a comparison; and, therefore, it may be necessary to observe, that it was infinitely more important than all his victories in the West Indies put together, which latter victories cost England thirty thousand men, and fifty millions of money." Mr. Windham, in the House of Commons, referring to this service of Cobbett, said that Cobbett had "rendered in America such service to his country as entitled him to a statue of gold".—EDITOR.

the most radical shock to their party which it has ever received; and there is no doubt, they would be glad to be replaced on the ground they possessed the instant before Jay's nomination extraordinary. They see that nothing can support them but the Colossus of the President's merits with the people, and the moment he retires, that his successor, if a monocrat, will be overborne by the republican sense of his constituents; if a republican, he will, of course, give fair play to that sense, and lead things into the channel of harmony between the governors and the governed. In the meantime, patience.—To JAMES MONROE. iv, 148. (July 1796.)

4091. JEALOUSY, Doubt and.—Doubts and jealousies often beget the facts they fear.—To ALBERT GALLATIN. v, 23. FORD ED., viii, 476. (W., 1806.)

4092. JEALOUSY, Government and.—Free government is founded in jealousy, and not in confidence; it is jealousy, and not confidence, which prescribes limited Constitutions, to bind down those whom we are obliged to trust with power.—KENTUCKY RESOLUTIONS. ix, 470. FORD ED., vii, 304. (1798.)

— JEFFERSON (Thomas), Ancestry.—See ANCESTRY.

— JEFFERSON (Thomas), Birthday.—See BIRTHDAY.

4093. JEFFERSON (Thomas), Education.—My father placed me at the English school at five years of age; and at the Latin at nine, where I continued until his death [in 1757]. My teacher, Mr. Douglas, a clergyman from Scotland, with the rudiments of the Latin and Greek languages, taught me the French; and on the death of my father, I went to the Reverend M. Maury, a correct classical scholar, with whom I continued two years; and then, to wit, in the spring of 1760, went to William and Mary College where I continued two years.—AUTOBIOGRAPHY. i, 2. FORD ED., i, 3. (1821.) See CONDUCT, SMALL (WILLIAM), and WYTHE (GEORGE).

— JEFFERSON (Thomas), Epitaph of.—See EPITAPH.

4094. JEFFERSON (Thomas), Family of.—In Colonel Peter Jefferson's Prayer Book, in the handwriting of Thomas Jefferson, are the following entries:

Jane Jefferson, born 1740, June 17; died 1765, Oct. 1.
Mary Jefferson, born 1741, Oct. 1; married 1760, June 24.
Thomas Jefferson, born 1743, Apr. 2; married, 1772, Jan. 1.
Elizabeth Jefferson, born 1744, Nov. 4; died 1773, Jan. 1.
Martha Jefferson, born 1746, May 29; married, 1765, July 20.
Peter Field Jefferson, born 1748, Oct. 16; died 1748, Nov. 29.
A son, born 1750, March 9; died 1750, March 9.
Lucy Jefferson, born 1752, Oct. 10; married, 1769, Sep. 12.
Anna Scott Randolph Jefferson, born 1755, Oct. 1; married, 1788, October.

—NOTE IN FORD EDITION. i, 3. (1743.) See ANCESTRY and ARMS.

4095. JEFFERSON (Thomas), Farming.—I am indeed an unskillful manager of my farms, and sensible of this from its effects, I have now committed them to better hands.*—To JOHN W. EPPES. D. L. J., 364. (1816.) See AGRICULTURE, FARMER, FARMERS and FARMING.

4096. JEFFERSON (Thomas), Father of.—My father's education had been quite neglected; but being of a strong mind, sound judgment, and eager after information, he read much and improved himself, insomuch that he was chosen, with Joshua Fry, Professor of Mathematics in William and Mary College, to continue the boundary line between Virginia and North Carolina, which had been begun by Colonel Byrd; and was afterwards employed with the same Mr. Fry, to make the first map of Virginia which had ever been made, that of Captain Smith being merely a conjectural sketch. They possessed excellent materials for so much of the country as is below the Blue Ridge; little being then known beyond that ridge. He was the third or fourth settler, about the year 1737, of the part of the country in which I live. He died, August 17, 1757, leaving my mother a widow, who lived till 1776, with six daughters and two sons, myself the elder. To my younger brother he left his estate on James River, called Snowdon, after the supposed birthplace of the family; to myself the lands on which I was born and live.—AUTOBIOGRAPHY. i, 2. FORD ED., i, 2. (1821.)

— JEFFERSON (Thomas), Habits of life.—See LIFE.

4097. JEFFERSON (Thomas), Harvard's honors.—I have been lately honored with your letter of September 24th, 1788, accompanied by a diploma for a Doctorate of Laws, which the University of Harvard has been pleased to confer on me. Conscious how little I merit it, I am the more sensible of their goodness and indulgence to a stranger, who has had no means of serving or making himself known to them. I beg you to return them my grateful thanks, and to assure them that this notice from so eminent a seat of science is very precious to me.—To DR. WILLARD. iii, 14. (P., 1789.)

4098. JEFFERSON (Thomas), History and.—Nothing is so desirable to me, as that after mankind shall have been abused by such gross falsehoods as to events while passing, their minds should at length be set to rights by genuine truth. And I can conscientiously declare that as to myself, I wish that not only no act but no thought of mine should be unknown.—To JAMES MAIN. v, 373. (W., Oct. 1808.)

4099. ——— ———. As to what is to be said of myself, I of course am not the judge. But my sincere wish is that the faithful historian, like the able surgeon, would consider me in his hands, while living, as a dead subject, that the same judgment may now be expressed

* His grandson, Thomas Jefferson Randolph.—EDITOR.

which will be rendered hereafter, so far as my small agency in human affairs may attract future notice; and I would of choice now stand as at the bar of posterity, *" cum semel occidaris, et de ultima Minos fecerit arbitria"*. The only exact testimony of a man is his actions, leaving the reader to pronounce on them his own judgment. In anticipating this, too little is safer than too much; and I sincerely assure you that you will please me most by a rigorous suppression of all friendly partialities. This candid expression of sentiments once delivered, passive silence becomes the future duty.—To L. H. GIRARDIN. vi, 455. (M., 1815.)

4100. ———. ———. Of the public transactions in which I have borne a part, I have kept no narrative with a view of history. A life of constant action leaves no time for recording. Always thinking of what is next to be done, what has been done is dismissed, and soon obliterated from the memory.—To MR. SPAFFORD. vii. 118. (M., 1819.) See HISTORY.

— JEFFERSON (Thomas), Home of.— See MONTICELLO.

4101. JEFFERSON (Thomas), Lawyer. —In 1767, Mr. [George] Wythe led me into the practice of the law at the bar of the General Court, at which I continued until the Revolution shut up the courts of justice.— AUTOBIOGRAPHY. i, 3. FORD ED., i, 4. (1821.) See WYTHE (GEORGE).

4102. JEFFERSON (Thomas), Letters of.—Selections from my letters. after my death, may come out successively as the maturity of circumstances may render their appearance seasonable.—To WILLIAM JOHNSON. vii, 277. FORD ED., x, 248. (M., 1823.)

— JEFFERSON (Thomas), Library of. —See LIBRARY.

4103. JEFFERSON (Thomas), Marriage.—On the 1st of January, 1772, I was married to Martha Skelton, widow of Bathurst Skelton, and daughter of John Wayles, then twenty-three years old. Mr. Wayles was a lawyer of much practice, to which he was introduced more by his great industry, punctuality and practical readiness than by eminence in the science of his profession. He was a most agreeable companion, full of pleasantry and good humor, and welcomed in every society. He acquired a handsome fortune, and died in May, 1773, leaving three daughters: the portion which came on that event to Mrs. Jefferson, after the debts should be paid, which were very considerable, was about equal to my own patrimony, and consequently doubled the ease of our circumstances.—AUTOBIOGRAPHY. i, 4. FORD ED., i, 5. (1821.)

4104. JEFFERSON (Thomas), Mrs. Jefferson's death.—Your letter found me a little emerging from the stupor of mind which had rendered me as dead to the world as she whose loss occasioned it. * * * Before that event my scheme of·life had been determined. I had folded myself in the arms of retirement, and rested all prospects of future happiness on domestic and literary objects. A single event wiped away all my plans and left me a blank which I had not the spirits to fill up. In this state of mind an appointment from Congress [mission to France] found me, requiring me to cross the Atlantic.—To CHEVALIER DE CHASTELLUX. i, 322. FORD ED., iii, 64. (A., Nov. 1782.)

4105. JEFFERSON (Thomas), A Nailmaker.—In our private pursuits it is a great advantage that every honest employment is deemed honorable. I am myself a nail-maker, On returning home after an absence of ten years, I found my farms so much deranged that I saw evidently they would be a burden to me instead of a support till I could regenerate them; and, consequently, that it was necessary for me to find some other resource in the meantime. I thought for a while of taking up the manufacture of potash, which requires but small advances of money. I concluded at length. however. to begin a manufacture of nails, which needs little or no capital, and I now employ a dozen little boys from ten to sixteen years of age, overlooking all the details of their business myself, and drawing from it a profit on which I can get along till I can put my farms into a course of yielding profit. My new trade of nail-making is to me in this country what an additional title of nobility or the ensigns of a new order are in Europe.—To M. DE MEUNIER. FORD ED., vii, 14. (M.. 1795.)

4106. JEFFERSON (Thomas), Offices held by.—In 1769, I became a member of the [Virginia] Legislature by the choice of the county [Albemarle] in which I live, and continued in that until it was closed by the Revolution.—AUTOBIOGRAPHY. i, 3. FORD ED., i, 5. (1821.)

4107. ———. ———. The Virginia Convention, at their * * * session of March, 1775, * * * added me * * * to the delegation [to Congress]. * * * I took my seat with them [Congress] on the 21st of June.—AUTOBIOGRAPHY. i, 9. FORD ED., i, 14. (1821.)

4108. ———. ———. Soon after my leaving Congress, in September, '76. to wit, on the last day of that month*, I had been appointed, with Dr. Franklin, to go to France, as a Commissioner, to negotiate treaties of alliance and commerce with that government. Silas Deane, then in France, acting as agent for procuring military stores, was joined with us in commission. But such was the state of my family that I could not leave it, nor could I expose it to the dangers of the sea, and of capture by the British ships, then covering the ocean. I saw, too, that the laboring oar was really at home, where much was to be done of the most permanent interest, in new modelling our governments, and much to defend our fanes and firesides

* According to a note in the FORD EDITION, the *Secret Journal of Congress* shows that Jefferson was appointed on Sept. 26.—EDITOR.

from the desolations of an invading enemy, pressing on our country in every point. I declined, therefore, and Dr. Lee was appointed in my place.—AUTOBIOGRAPHY. i, 51. FORD ED., i, 70. (1812.)

4109. —— ——. On the 1st of June, 1779, I was appointed Governor of the Commonwealth, and retired from the Legislature.— AUTOBIOGRAPHY. i, 50. FORD ED., i, 69. (1821.)

4110. —— ——. On the 15th of June,* 1781. I had been appointed, with Mr. Adams, Dr. Franklin, Mr. Jay, and Mr. Laurens, a Minister Plenipotentiary for negotiating peace, then expected to be effected through the mediation of the Empress of Russia. The same reasons obliged me still to decline; and the negotiation was in fact never entered on.—AUTOBIOGRAPHY. i, 51. FORD ED., i, 71. (1821.)

4111. —— ——. In the autumn of * * * 1782, Congress receiving assurances that a general peace would be concluded in the winter and spring, they renewed my appointment on the 13th of November of that year. I had, two months before that, lost the cherished companion of my life, in whose affections, unabated on both sides, I had lived the last ten years in unchequered happiness. With the public interests, the state of my mind concurred in recommending the change of scene proposed; and I accepted the appointment, and left Monticello on the 19th of December, 1782, for Philadelphia, where I arrived on the 27th. The Minister of France, Luzerne, offered me a passage in the Romulus frigate, which I accepted; but she was then a few miles below Baltimore, blocked up in the ice. I remained, therefore, a month in Philadelphia, looking over the papers in the office of State. in order to possess myself of the general state of our foreign relations, and then went to Baltimore, to await the liberation of the frigate from the ice. After waiting there nearly a month, we received information that a Provisional Treaty of Peace had been signed by our Commissioners on the 3d of September, 1782, to become absolute on the conclusion of peace between France and Great Britain. Considering my proceeding to Europe as now of no utility to the public, I returned immediately to Philadelphia, to take the orders of Congress, and was excused by them from further proceeding. I, therefore, returned home, where I arrived on the 15th of May, 1783.—AUTOBIOGRAPHY. i, 51. FORD ED., i, 71. (1821.)

4112. —— ——. On the 6th of June, 1783, I was appointed by the [Virginia] Legislature a Delegate to Congress, the appointment to take place on the 1st of November ensuing, when that of the existing delegation would expire. I, accordingly, left home on the 16th of October, arrived at Trenton, where Congress was sitting. on the 3d of November, and took my seat on the 4th, on which day

* The *Secret Journal of Congress* gives the date as June 14.—NOTE IN FORD EDITION.

Congress adjourned, to meet at Annapolis on the 26th.—AUTOBIOGRAPHY. i, 52. FORD ED., i, 72. (1821.)

4113. —— ——. In July, 1785, Dr. Franklin returned to America, and I was appointed his successor at Paris.—AUTOBIOGRAPHY. i, 63. FORD ED., i, 88. (1821.)

4114. —— ——. On the 14th of May, (1785) I communicated to the Count de Vergennes my appointment as Minister Plenipotentiary * * * on the 17th delivered my letter of credence to the King at a private audience, and went through the other ceremonies usual on such occasions.—To JOHN JAY. i, 344. (P., 1785.)

4115. —— ——. I had been more than a year soliciting leave to go home, with a view to place my daughters in the society and care of their friends, and to return for a short time to my station in Paris. But the metamorphosis through which our government was then passing from its chrysalid to its organic form suspended its action in a great degree; and it was not till the last of August, 1789, that I received the permission I had asked. * * * On the 26th of September, I left Paris for Havre, where I was detained by contrary winds until the 8th of October. On that day, and the 9th, I crossed o.er to Cowes, where I had engaged the Clermont, Capt. Colley, to touch for me. She did so, but here again we were detained by contrary winds, until the 22nd, when we embarked, and landed at Norfolk on the 23rd of November. On my way home, I passed some days at Eppington. in Chesterfield, the residence of my friend and connection, Mr. Eppes, and while there, I received a letter from the President, General Washington, by express, covering an appointment to be Secretary of State.—AUTOBIOGRAPHY. i, 107. FORD ED., i, 148. (1821.)

4116. —— ——. I received it [appointment as Secretary of State] with real regret. My wish had been to return to Paris, where I had left my household establishment, as if there myself, and to see the end of the Revolution, which I then thought would be certainly and happily closed in less than a year. I then meant to return home, to withdraw from political life, into which I had been impressed by the circumstances of the times, to sink into the bosom of my family and friends, and devote myself to studies more congenial to my mind. In my answer of December 15th, I expressed these dispositions candidly to the President, and my preference of a return to Paris; but assured him that if it was believed I could be more useful in the administration of the government, I would sacrifice my own inclinations, without hesitation and repair to that destination; this I left to his decision. I arrived at Monticello on the 23rd of December, where I received a second letter from the President, expressing his continued wish that I should take my station there, but leaving me still at liberty to continue in my former office, if I could not reconcile myself to that now proposed. This silenced my reluctance, and I accepted the new appointment.—AUTOBIOGRAPHY. i, 108. FORD ED., i, 149. (1821.)

4117. —— ——. The President [Washington] observed, that though I had unfixed the day on which I had intended to resign, yet I appeared fixed in doing it at no great distance of time; that in this case,* he could not but wish that I would go to Paris; that the moment was important; I possessed the confidence of both sides, and might do great good; that he wished I could do it, were it only to stay there a year or two. I told him that my mind was so bent on retirement that I could not think of launching forth again in a new business; that I could never again cross the Atlantic; and that as to the opportunity of doing good, this was likely to be the scene of action, as Genet was bringing powers to do the business here; but that I could not think of going abroad. He replied that I had pressed him to remain in the public service, and refused to do the same myself. I said the case was very different; he united the confidence of all America, and was the only person who did so; his services, therefore, were of the last importance; but for myself, my going out would not be noted or known. A thousand others could supply my place to equal advantage, therefore I felt myself free.—THE ANAS. ix, 133. FORD ED., i, 217. (Feb. 20, 1793.)

4118. —— ——. [President Washington] returned to the difficulty of naming my successor. * * * He said if I would only stay in till the end of another quarter (the last of December) it would get us through the difficulties of this year, and he was satisfied that the affairs of Europe would be settled with this campaign; for that either France would be overwhelmed by it, or the confederacy would give up the contest. By that time, too, Congress would have manifested its character and view. I told him that I had set my private affairs in motion in a line which had powerfully called for my presence the last spring, and that they had suffered immensely from my not going home; that I had now calculated them to my return in the fall, and to fail in going then, would be the loss of another year, and prejudicial beyond measure. * * * He asked me whether I could not arrange my affairs by going home. I told him I did not think the public business would admit of it; that there never was a day now in which the absence of the Secretary of State would not be inconvenient to the public. And he concluded by desiring that I would take two or three days to consider whether I could not stay in till the end of another quarter, for that like a man going to the gallows, he was willing to put it off as long as he could; but if I persisted, he must then look about him and make up his mind to do the best he could.—

* The French government was then complaining of the unfriendliness of Gouverneur Morris, and Washington deemed a change of ministers advisable.—EDITOR.

THE ANAS. ix, 167. FORD ED., i, 257. (Aug. 1793.) See ELECTIONS (PRESIDENTIAL).

4119. JEFFERSON (Thomas), Offices refused.—No circumstances will ever more tempt me to engage in anything public. I thought myself perfectly fixed in this determination when I left Philadelphia, but every day and hour since has added to its inflexibility. It is a great pleasure to me to retain the esteem and approbation of the President, and this forms the only ground of any reluctance at being unable to comply with every wish of his.*—TO EDMUND RANDOLPH. iv, 108. FORD ED., vi, 512. (M., Sep. 1794.)

4120. —— ——. President [John] Adams said he was glad to find me alone, for that he wished a free conversation with me. He entered immediately on an explanation of the situation of our affairs with France, and the danger of rupture with that nation, a rupture which would convulse the attachments of this country; that he was impressed with the necessity of an immediate mission to the Directory; that it would have been the first wish of his heart to have got me to go there, but that he supposed it was out of the question, as it did not seem justifiable for him to send away the person destined to take his place in case of accident to himself, nor decent to remove from competition one who was a rival in the public favor. * * * I told him I concurred in the opinion of the impropriety of my leaving the post assigned me, and that my inclinations, moreover, would never permit me to cross the Atlantic again.—THE ANAS. ix, 185. FORD ED., i, 272. (March 2, 1797.)

4121. —— ——. You wish to see me again in the Legislature, but this is impossible; my mind is now so dissolved in tranquillity, that it can never again encounter a contentious assembly. The habits of thinking and speaking off-hand, after a disuse of five and twenty years, have given place to the slower process of the pen.—TO JOHN TYLER. v, 525. FORD ED., ix, 277. (M., 1810.)

4122. —— ——. The assurance * * * that my aid in the councils of our government would increase the public confidence in them; because it admits an inference that they have approved of the course pursued, when I heretofore bore a part in those councils. * * * But I am past service. The hand of age is upon me. The debility of bodily faculties apprizes me that those of the mind cannot be unimpaired, had I not still better proofs.—TO WILLIAM DUANE. vi, 79. FORD ED., ix, 367. (M., Oct. 1812.)

4123. JEFFERSON (Thomas), Paine and.—A writer, under the name of "*Publicola*" [John Quincy Adams], in attacking all [Thomas] Paine's [political] principles, is very desirous of involving me in the same censure with the author. I certainly merit the same, for I profess the same principles; but it is equally certain I never meant to have

* Washington wished to send Jefferson to France·—EDITOR.

entered as a volunteer into the cause.—To JAMES MONROE. iii, 267. FORD ED., v, 351. (Pa., 1791.) See PAINE.

4124. JEFFERSON (Thomas), Portrait. —I am duly sensible of the honor proposed of giving to my portrait a place among the benefactors of our nation, and of the establishment of West Point in particular. * * * Mr. Sully, I fear, however, will consider the trouble of the journey [to Monticello], and the employment of his fine pencil, as illy bestowed on an atomy of 78.—To JARED MANSFIELD. vii, 203. (M., 1821.)

— **JEFFERSON (Thomas), Principles of.**—See PRINCIPLES.

— **JEFFERSON (Thomas), Retirement of.**—See RETIREMENT.

4125. JEFFERSON (Thomas), Scientific Societies.—Being to remove within a few months from my present residence [Washington] to one still more distant from the seat of the meetings of the American Philosophical Society [Philadelphia], I feel it a duty no longer to obstruct its service by keeping from the chair members whose position as well as qualifications, may enable them to discharge its duties with so much more effect.*—To THE VICE-PRESIDENT OF THE A. P. S. v, 392. (W., Nov. 1808.)

4126. ——— ———. I am duly sensible of the honor done me by the first class of the Royal Institute of Sciences, of Literature, and of Fine Arts [Holland], in associating me to their class, and by the approbation which his Majesty, the King of Holland, has condescended to give to their choice.—To G. VOOLIF. v, 517. (M., 1810.)

4127. ——— ———. I recieved with much gratification the diploma of the Agronomic Society of Bavaria, conferring on me the distinction of being honorary member of their society†—To BARON DE MOLL. v, 363. (M., 1814.)

4128. JEFFERSON (Thomas), Services of.—I have sometimes asked myself, whether my country is the better for my having lived at all? I do not know that it is. I have been the instrument of doing the following things; but they would have been done by others; some of them, perhaps, a little better:

The Rivanna had never been used for navigation; scarcely an empty canoe had ever passed down it. Soon after I came of age, I examined its obstructions, set on foot a subscription for removing them, got an act of Assembly passed, and the thing effected, so

* Franklin was the first President of the American Philosophical Society. He was succeeded by David Rittenhouse, who died in 1796, and after him came Jefferson. In accepting the office Jefferson said: "I feel no qualification for this distinguished post, but a sincere zeal for all the objects of our institution, and an ardent desire to see knowledge so disseminated through the mass of mankind, that it may, at length, reach even the extremes of society, beggars and kings."—EDITOR.

† Jefferson was an active or honorary member of nearly every literary and scientific society existing in his day.—EDITOR.

as to be used completely and fully for carrying down all our produce.

The Declaration of Independence.

I proposed the demolition of the Church Establishment, and the Freedom of Religion. It could only be done by degrees; to wit, the Act of 1776, c. 2, exempted dissenters from contributions to the Church, and left the Church clergy to be supported by voluntary contributions of their own sect; was continued from year to year, and made perpetual 1779, c. 36. I prepared the Act for Religious Freedom in 1777, as part of the Revisal, which was not reported to the Assembly till 1779, and that particular law not passed till 1785, and then by the efforts of Mr. Madison.

The Act putting an end to Entails.

The Act prohibiting the Importation of Slaves.

The Act concerning Citizens and establishing the natural right of man to expatriate himself, at will.

The Act changing the course of Descents, and giving the inheritance to all the children, &c., equally, I drew as part of the Revisal.

The Act for Apportioning Crimes and Punishments, part of the same work, I drew. When proposed to the Legislature, by Mr. Madison, in 1785, it failed by a single vote. G. K. Taylor afterwards, in 1796, proposed the same subject; avoiding the adoption of any part of the diction of mine, the text of which had been studiously drawn in the technical terms of the law, so as to give no occasion for new questions by new expressions. When I drew mine, public labor was thought the best punishment to be substituted for death. But, while I was in France, I heard of a society in England, who had successfully introduced solitary confinement, and saw the drawing of a prison at Lyons, in France, formed on the idea of solitary confinement. And, being applied to by the Governor of Virginia for the plan of a Capitol and Prison, I sent him the Lyons plan, accompanying it with a drawing on a smaller scale, betted adapted to our use. This was in June, 1786. Mr. Taylor very judiciously adopted this idea (which had now been acted on in Philadelphia, probably from the English model), and substituted labor in confirement, for the public labor proposed by the Committee of Revisal; which themselves would have done, had they been to act on the subject again. The public mind was ripe for this in 1796, when Mr. Taylor proposed it, and ripened chiefly by the experiment in Philadelphia; whereas, in 1785, when it had been proposed to our Assembly, they were not quite ripe for it.

In 1789 and 1790, I had a great number of olive plants, of the best kind, sent from Marseilles to Charleston, for South Carolina and Georgia. They were planted, and are flourishing; and, though not yet multiplied, they will be the germ of that cultivation in those States.

In 1790, I got a cask of heavy upland rice, from the river Denbigh, in Africa, about Latitude 9° 30′ North, which I sent to

Charleston, in hopes it might supersede the culture of the wet rice, which renders South Carolina and Georgia so pestilential through the summer. It was divided and a part sent to Georgia. I know not whether it has been attended to in South Carolina; but it has spread in the upper parts of Georgia, so as to have become almost general, and is highly prized. Perhaps it may answer in Tennessee and Kentucky. The greatest service which can be rendered any country is, to add an useful plant to its culture; especially a bread grain; next in value to bread is oil.

Whether the Act for the more General Diffusion of Knowledge will ever be carried into complete effect, I know not. It was received by the Legislature with great enthusiasm at first; and a small effort was made in 1796, by the act to establish public schools, to carry a part of it into effect, viz., that for the establishment of free English schools: but the option given to the courts has defeated the intention of the act.*—JEFFERSON PAPERS. i, 174. FORD ED., vii, 475. (1800.)

4129. ——— ———. I came of age in 1764, and was soon put into the nomination of justice of the county in which I lived, and, at the first election following. I became one of its representatives in the Legislature. I was thence sent to the old Congress. Then employed two years with Mr. Pendleton and Mr. Wythe, on the revisal and reduction to a single code of the whole body of the British Statutes, the acts of our Assembly, and certain parts of the common law. Then elected Governor. Next, to the Legislature, and to Congress again. Sent to Europe as Minister Plenipotentiary. Appointed Secretary of State to the new Government. Elected Vice-President, and President. And lastly, a Visitor and Rector of the University [of Virginia]. In these different offices, with scarcely any interval between them, I have been in the public service now sixty-one years; and during the far greater part of the time, in foreign countries or in other States. * * * If it were thought worth while to specify any particular services rendered, I would refer to the specification of them made by the [Virginia] Legislature itself in their Farewell Address,† on my retiring from the Presidency, February, 1809. There is one, however, not therein specified the most important in its consequences, of any transaction in any portion of my life; to wit, the head I personally made against the federal principles and proceedings during the Administration of Mr. Adams. Their usurpations and violations of the Constitution at that period, and their majority in both Houses of Congress, were so great, so decided, and so daring, that after combating their aggressions, inch by inch, without being able in the least to check their career, the republican leaders

thought it would be best for them to give up their useless efforts there, go home, get into their respective Legislatures, embody whatever of resistance they could be formed into. and if ineffectual, to perish there as in the last ditch. All, therefore, retired leaving Mr. Gallatin alone in the House of Representatives, and myself in the Senate. where I then presided as Vice-President. Remaining at our posts, and bidding defiance to the browbeatings and insults by which they endeavored to drive us off also, we kept the mass of republicans in phalanx together, until the Legislature could be brought up to the charge; and nothing on earth is more certain. than that if myself particularly, placed by my office of Vice-President at the head of the republicans, had given way and withdrawn from my post, the republicans throughout the Union would have given up in despair, and the cause would have been lost forever. By holding on, we obtained time for the Legislature to come up with their weight; and those of Virginia and Kentucky particularly, but more especially the former, by their celebrated resolutions. saved the Constitution at its last gasp. No person who was not a witness of the scenes of that gloomy period. can form any idea of the afflicting persecutions and personal indignities we had to brook. They saved our country, however. The spirits of the people were so much subdued and reduced to despair by the X. Y. Z. imposture, and other stratagems and machinations, that they would have sunk into apathy and monarchy, as the only form of government which could maintain itself.

If Legislative services are worth mentioning, and the stamp of liberality and equality. which was necessary to be imposed on our laws in the first crisis of our birth as a nation. was of any value, they will find that the leading and most important laws of that day were prepared by myself, and carried chiefly by my efforts; supported, indeed, by able and faithful coadjutors from the ranks of the house, very effective as seconds, but who would not have taken the field as leaders. The prohibition of the further importation of slaves was the first of these measures in time. This was followed by the abolition of entails. which broke up the hereditary and high-handed aristocracy, which, by accumulating immense masses of property in single lines of families, had divided our country into two distinct orders, of nobles and plebeians. But further to complete the equality among our citizens so essential to the maintenance of republican government, it was necessary to abolish the principle of primogeniture. I drew the law of descents, giving equal inheritance to sons and daughters, which made a part of the Revised Code. The attack on the establishment of a dominant religion was first made by myself. It could be carried at first only by a suspension of salaries for one year, by battling it again at the next session for another year. and so from year to year. until the public mind was ripened for the bill for establishing religious

* It appears from a blank space at the bottom of this paper, that a continuation had been intended. Indeed, from the loose manner in which the above notes are written, it may be inferred that they were originally intended as memoranda only, to be used in some more permanent form.—NOTE IN CONGRESS EDITION.

† Printed in the APPENDIX to this work.—EDITOR.

freedom, which I had prepared for the Revised Code also. This was at length established permanently, and by the efforts chiefly of Mr. Madison, being myself in Europe at the time that work was brought forward.

To these particular services, I think I might add the establishment of our University, as principally my work, acknowledging at the same time, as I do, the great assistance received from my able colleagues of the Visitation. But my residence in the vicinity threw, of course, on me the chief burthen of the enterprise, as well of the buildings as of the general organization and care of the whole. The effect of this institution on the future fame, fortune and prosperity of our country, can as yet be seen but at a distance. But an hundred well-educated youth, which it will turn out annually, and ere long, will fill all its offices with men of superior qualifications, and raise it from its humble state to an eminence among its associates which it has never yet known; no, not in its brightest days. That institution is now qualified to raise its youth to an order of science unequalled in any other State; and this superiority will be the greater from the free range of mind encouraged there, and the restraint imposed at other seminaries by the shackles of a domineering hierarchy, and a bigoted adhesion to ancient habits. Those now on the theatre of affairs will enjoy the ineffable happiness of seeing themselves succeeded by sons of a grade of science beyond their own ken. Our sister States will also be repairing to the same fountains of instruction, will bring hither their genius to be kindled at our fire, and will carry back the fraternal affections which, nourished by the same *Alma Mater,* will knit us to them by the indissoluble bonds of early personal friendships. The good Old Dominion, the blessed mother of us all, will then raise her head with pride among the nations, will present to them that splendor of genius which she has ever possessed, but has too long suffered to rest uncultivated and unknown, and will become a centre of ralliance to the States whose youth she has instructed, and, as it were, adopted. I claim some share in the merits of this great work of regeneration. My whole labors, now for many years, have been devoted to it, and I stand pledged to follow it up through the remnant of life remaining to me. And what remuneration do I ask? Money from the treasury? Not a cent. I ask nothing from the earnings or labors of my fellow citizens. I wish no man's comforts to be abridged for the enlargement of mine. For the services rendered on all occasions, I have been always paid to my full satisfaction. I never wished a dollar more than what the law had fixed on. My request is, only to be permitted to sell my own property freely to pay my own debts. To *sell* it, I say, and not to *sacrifice* it, not to have it gobbled up by speculators to make fortunes for themselves, leaving unpaid those who have trusted to my good faith, and myself without resource, in the last and most helpless stage of life. If permitted to sell it in a way which will bring me a fair price, all will be honestly and honorably paid, and a competence left for myself, and for those who look to me for subsistence. To sell it in a way which will offend no moral principle, and expose none to risk but the willing, and those wishing to be permitted to take the chance of gain. To give me, in short, that permission which you often allow to others for purposes not more moral.*—THOUGHTS ON LOTTERIES. ix, 506. FORD ED., x, 368. (M., 1826.)

4130. JEFFERSON (Thomas), University of Virginia and.—Against this *tedium vitæ*, I am fortunately mounted on a hobby, which, indeed, I should have better managed some thirty or forty years ago; but whose easy amble is still sufficient to give exercise and amusement to an octogenary rider. This is the establishment of a University.—To JOHN ADAMS. vii, 313. FORD ED., x, 272. (M., 1823.) See UNIVERSITY OF VIRGINIA.

— JEFFERSON (Thomas), Views on religion.—See RELIGION.

4131. JEFFERSON (Thomas), Weary of office.—The motion of my blood no longer keeps time with the tumult of the world. It leads me to seek for happiness in the lap and love of my family, in the society of my neighbors and my books, in the wholesome occupations of my farm and my affairs, in an interest or affection in every bud that opens, in every breath that blows around me, in an entire freedom of rest, of motion, of thought, owing account to myself alone of my hours and actions. What must be the principle of that calculation which should balance against these the circumstances of my present existence [Secretaryship of State], worn down with labors from morning to night, and day to day; knowing them as fruitless to others as they are vexatious to myself; committed singly in desperate and eternal contest against a host who are systematically undermining the public liberty and prosperity; even the rare hours of relaxation sacrificed to the society of persons in the same intentions, of whose hatred I am conscious even in those moments of conviviality when the heart wishes most to open itself to the effusions of friendship and confidence; cut off from my family and friends, my affairs abandoned to chaos and derangement; in short, giving everything I love in exchange for everything I hate, and all this without a single gratification in possession or prospect, in present enjoyment or future wish.—To JAMES MADISON. iii, 578. FORD ED., vi, 291. (June 1793.)

4132. JOHNSON (Joshua), Consul at London.—The President of the United States, desirous of availing his country of the talents of its best citizens, in their respective lines, has thought proper to nominate you consul for the

* Jefferson wrote the paper of which the foregoing is an extract in February, 1826, less than five months before his death. Oppressed by age and harassed by debt, he asked the Legislature of Virginia to pass a law enabling him to dispose of his property by a lottery. The act was passed.—EDITOR.

United States at the port of London. The extent of our commercial and political connections with that country marks the importance of the trust he confides to you, and the more, as we have no diplomatic character at that court.—To Joshua Johnson. iii, 176. (N.Y., 1790.)

4133. JONES (John Paul), Disinterestedness.—Captain John Paul Jones refuses to accept any indemnification for his expenses [connected with Peyrouse's expedition], which is an additional proof of his disinterested spirit, and of his devotion to the service of America.— To John Jay. i, 454. (P., 1785.)

4134. JONES (John Paul), Justice for.—Nobody can wish more that justice be done you, nor is more ready to be instrumental in doing whatever may insure it.—To Commodore Jones. i, 594. (P., 1786.)

4135. JONES (John Paul), Mission to Algiers.—The President having thought proper to appoint you commissioner for treating with the Dey and government of Algiers, on the subjects of peace and ransom of our captives, I have the honor to enclose you the commission, of which Mr. Thomas Pinckney, now on his way to London as our Minister Plenipotentiary there, will be the bearer. Supposing that there exists a disposition to thwart our negotiations with the Algerines, and that this would be very practicable, we have thought it advisable that the knowledge of this appointment should rest with the President, Mr. Pinckney and myself; for which reason you will perceive that the commissions are all in my own handwriting. For the same reason, entire secrecy is recommended to you, and that you so cover from the public your departure and destination, as that they may not be conjectured or noticed.—To John Paul Jones. iii, 431. (Pa., June 1792.)

4136. JONES (John Paul), Newspaper attacks.—What the English newspapers said of remonstrances against Paul Jones being received into the service, as far as I can learn from those who would have known it, and would have told it to me, was false, as is everything those papers say, ever did say, and ever will say.—To Mr. Cutting. ii, 437. (P., 1788.)

4137. JONES (John Paul), Prize money.—I consider Captain Jones as agent from the citizens of the United States, interested in the prizes taken in Europe under his command, and that he is properly authorized to receive the money due to them, having given good security to transmit it to the treasury office of the United States, whence it will be distributed, under the care of Congress, to the officers and crews originally entitled, or to their representatives.— To M. de Castries. i, 361. (P., 1785.)

4138. ———. I have had the honor of enclosing to Mr. Jay. Commodore Jones's receipts for one hundred and eighty-one thousand and thirty-nine livres, one sol and ten deniers, prize money, which (after deducting his own proportion) he is to remit to you, for the officers and soldiers who were under his command. I take the liberty of suggesting whether the expense and risk of double remittances might not be saved, by ordering it into the hands of Mr. Grand, immediately, for the purposes of the Treasury in Europe, while you could make provision at home for the officers and soldiers, whose demands will come in so slowly, as to leave the use of a great proportion of this money for a considerable time, and some of it

forever. We could, then, immediately quiet the French officers.—To the Treasury Commissioners. i, 522. (P., 1786.)

4139. JONES (John Paul), Russian services.—The war between the Russians and the Turks has made an opening for our Commodore Paul Jones. The Empress has invited him into her service. She insures to him the rank of rear admiral; will give him a separate command, and, it is understood, that he is never to be commanded. I think she means to oppose him to the Captain Pacha, on the Black Sea. * * * He has made it a condition, that he shall be free at all times to return to the orders of Congress, * * * and also, that he shall not in any case be expected to bear arms against France. I believe Congress had it in contemplation to give him the grade of admiral, from the date of his taking the Serapis. Such a measure would now greatly gratify him, second the efforts of fortune in his favor, and better the opportunity of improving him for our service, whenever the moment may come in which we shall want him.—To General Washington. ii, 372. (1788.)

4140. ——— ———. Paul Jones is invited into the service of the Empress [of Russia], with the rank of rear admiral, and to have a separate command. I wish it corresponded with the views of Congress to give him that rank from the taking of the Serapis. I look to this officer as our great future dependence on the sea, where alone we should think of ever having a force. He is young enough to see the day when we shall be more populous than the whole British dominions, and able to fight them ship to ship. We should procure him, then, every possible opportunity of acquiring experience.— To E. Carrington. ii, 405. Ford ed., v, 22. (P., 1788.)

4141. ——— ———. You have heard of the great victory [in the Black Sea] obtained by the Russians under command of Admiral Paul Jones, over the Turks commanded by the Captain Pacha.—To M. Limozin. ii, 443. (P., 1788.)

4142. ——— ———. I am pleased with the promotion of our countryman, Paul Jones. He commanded the right wing, in the first engagement between the Russian and Turkish galleys; his absence from the second proves his superiority over the Captain Pacha, as he did not choose to bring his ships into the shoals in which the Pacha ventured, and lost those entrusted to him. I consider this officer as the principal hope of our future efforts on the ocean.—To William Carmichael. ii, 466. (P., 1788.)

4143. ——— ———. I understand, in a general way, that some persecution on the part of his officers occasioned his being recalled to St. Petersburg, and that though protected against them by the Empress, he is not yet restored to his station.—To James Madison. iii, 101. Ford ed., v, 113. (P., 1789.)

4144. JONES (John Paul), St. Anne Decoration.—In answer to your request to obtain and transmit the proper authority of the United States for your retaining the Order of St. Anne, conferred on you by the Empress [of Russia]. The Executive are not authorized either to grant or refuse the permission you ask, and consequently cannot take on themselves to do it. Whether the Legislature would undertake to do it or not, I cannot say. In general, there is an aversion to meddle with anything of that kind here. And the event would be so doubtful that the Executive would not commit themselves by making the proposition to the Legislature.—To ADMIRAL PAUL JONES. iii, 294. (Pa., 1791.)

4145. JOSEPH II., Ambitious.—We have here under our contemplation the future miseries of human nature, like to be occasioned by the ambition of a young man, who has been taught to view his subjects as his cattle. The pretensions he sets up to the navigation of the Scheldt would have been good, if natural right had been left uncontrolled, but it is impossible for express compact to have taken away a right more effectually than it has the Emperor's.—To HORATIO GATES. FORD ED., iv, 23. (P., Dec. 1784.)

4146. ——— ———. He is a restless ambitious character, aiming at everything, persevering in nothing, taking up designs without calculating the force which will be opposed to him, and dropping them on the appearance of a firm opposition. He has some just views and much activity.—To JOHN PAGE. i, 400. (P., 1785.)

4147. JOSEPH II., Capricious.—The enterprising, unpersevering, capricious, thrasonic character of their sovereign renders it probable he will avail himself of this little condescendence in the Brabantines to recede from all his innovations.—To EDMUND RANDOLPH. ii, 212. (P., 1787.)

4148. JOSEPH II., Eccentric.—The public acts of the Emperor speak him much above the common level. Those who expect peace say that they have in view the Emperor's character which they represent as whimsical and eccentric, and that he is especially affected in the dog days.—To JAMES MONROE. FORD ED., iv, 21. (P., Dec. 1784.)

4149. JOSEPH II., Foreign complications.—The league formed by the King of Prussia against the Emperor [of Austria] is a most formidable obstacle to his ambitious designs. It certainly has defeated his views on Bavaria, and will render doubtful the election of his nephew to be King of the Romans. Matters are not yet settled between him and the Turk. In truth, he undertakes too much. At home he has made some good regulations.—To R. IZARD. i, 442. (P., 1785.)

4150. JOSEPH II., Innovations.—Weighing the fondness of the Emperor for innovation, against his want of perseverance, it is difficult to calculate what he will do with his discontented subjects in Brabant and Flanders. If those provinces alone were concerned he would probably give them back; but this would induce an opposition to his plan in all his other dominions.—JOHN JAY. ii, 158. (P., 1787.)

4151. ——— ———. The Emperor's reformations have occasioned the appearance of insurrection in Flanders, and he, according to character, will probably tread back his steps.— To J. BANNISTER, JR. ii, 150. (P., 1787.)

4152. JOSEPH II., And Holland.—The Emperor [of Austria] seems to prefer the glory of terror to that of justice; and, to satisfy this tinsel passion, plants a dagger in the heart of every Dutchman which no time will extract.— To JAMES MONROE. i, 358. FORD ED., iv, 64. (1785.)

4153. JOSEPH II., Unprincipled.—The Emperor has a head too combustible to be quiet. He is an eccentric character, all enterprise, without calculation, without principle, without

feelings. Ambitious in the extreme but too unsteady to surmount difficulties. He had in view at one time to open the Scheldt, to get Maestricht from the Dutch, to take a large district from the Turks, to exchange some of his Austrian dominions for Bavaria, to create a ninth electorate, to make his nephew King of the Romans, and to change totally the constitution of Hungary. Any one of these was as much as a wise prince would have undertaken at any one time. To JAMES MONROE. FORD ED., iv, 44. (P., 1785.)

4154. ——— ———. The Emperor [has] unmeasurable ambition, and his total want of moral principle and honor is suspected. A great share of Turkey, the recovery of Silesia, the consolidation of his dominions by the Bavarian exchange, the liberties of the Germanic body, all occupy his mind together, and his head is not well enough organized, to pursue so much only of all this as is practicable.—To GENERAL WASHINGTON. ii, 371. (P., 1788.)

4155. JUDGES, Biased.—It is better to toss up cross and pile in a cause, than to refer it to a judge whose mind is warped by any motive whatever, in that particular case.— NOTES ON VIRGINIA. viii, 372. FORD ED., iii, 236. (1782.)

4156. ——— ———. We all know that permanent judges acquire an *esprit de corps;* that being known, they are liable to be tempted by bribery; that they are misled by favor, by relationship, by a spirit of party, by a devotion to the Executive or Legislative power; that it is better to leave a cause to the decision of cross and pile, than to that of a judge biased to one side.—To M. L'ABBÉ ARNOND. iii, 81. FORD ED., v, 103. (P., 1789.)

4157. ——— ———. As, for the safety of society, we commit honest maniacs to Bedlam, so judges should be withdrawn from their bench, whose erroneous biases are leading us to dissolution. It may, indeed, injure them in fame or in fortune; but it saves the Republic, which is the first and supreme law.— AUTOBIOGRAPHY. i, 82. FORD ED., i, 114. (1821.)

4158. JUDGES, Compensation.—Their salaries [should be] ascertained and established by law.—To GEORGE WYTHE. FORD ED., ii, 60. (1776.)

4159. JUDGES, Election.—I hope to see the time when the election of judges of the Supreme Courts [of Virginia] shall be restrained to the bars of the General Court and High Court of Chancery.—To GEORGE WYTHE. i, 212. FORD ED., ii, 167. (F., 1779.)

4160. JUDGES, Executive and.—I was against writing letters to judiciary officers. I thought them independent of the Executive, not subject to its coercion, and therefore not obliged to attend to its admonitions.—ANAS. ix, 175. FORD ED., i, 265. (1793.)

4161. JUDGES, Fallibility of.—When a cause has been adjudged according to the rules and forms of the country, its justice ought to be presumed. Even error in the highest court which has been provided as the last means of correcting the errors of others, and whose decrees are, therefore, subject to no further revisal, is one of those inconveniences flowing from the imperfection of our faculties, to which every society must submit; because there must be somewhere a last resort, wherein contestations may end. Multiply bodies of revisal as you please, their number must still be finite, and they must finish in the hands of fallible men as judges.—To GEORGE HAMMOND. iii, 415. FORD ED., vi, 56. (Pa., 1792.)

4162. JUDGES, George III. and.—He has made our* judges dependent on his will alone, for the tenure of their offices, and the amount and payment of their salaries.—DECLARATION OF INDEPENDENCE AS DRAWN BY JEFFERSON.

4163. JUDGES, Impeachment of.—Our different States have differently modified their several judiciaries as to the tenure of office. Some appoint their judges for a given term of time; some continue them *during good behavior,* and that to be determined on by the concurring vote of *two-thirds* of each legislative house. In England they are removable by a *majority* only of each house. The last is a practicable remedy; the second is not. The combination of the friends and associates of the accused, the action of personal and party passions, and the sympathies of the human heart, will forever find means of influencing one-third of either the one or the other house, will thus secure their impunity, and establish them in fact for life. The first remedy is the better, that of appointing for a term of years only, with a capacity of reappointment if their conduct has been approved.—To A. CORAY. vii, 321. (M., 1823.)

4164. JUDGES, Independent.—The judges should not be dependent upon any man, or body of men.—To GEORGE WYTHE. FORD ED., ii, 60. (1776.)

4165. JUDGES, Interested.—It is not enough that honest men are appointed judges. All know the influence of interest on the mind of man, and how unconsciously his judgment is warped by that influence. To this bias add that of the *esprit de corps,* of their peculiar maxim and creed, that "it is the office of a good judge to enlarge his jurisdiction", and the absence of responsibility, and how can we expect impartial decision between the General Government, of which they are themselves so eminent a part, and an individual State, from which they have nothing to hope or fear?—AUTOBIOGRAPHY. i, 81. FORD ED., i, 112. (1821.)

4166. JUDGES, Life tenure.—The judges should hold estates for life in their offices, or, in other words, their commissions should be made during good behavior.—To GEORGE WYTHE. FORD ED., ii, 60. (1776.)

4167. JUDGES, Power of.—Whatever of the enumerated objects [in the Constitution] is to be done by a judicial sentence, the

* Congress struck out "our".—EDITOR.

judges may pass the sentence.—To WILSON C. NICHOLAS. iv, 506. FORD ED., viii, 248. (M., 1803.)

4168. —— ——. We have seen, too, that, contrary to all correct example, the judges are in the habit of going out of the question before them, to throw an anchor ahead, and grapple further hold for future advances of power.—AUTOBIOGRAPHY. i, 82. FORD ED., i, 113. (1821.)

4169. JUDGES, Prejudices of old.—Knowing that religion does not furnish grosser bigots than law, I expect little from old judges. Those now at the bar may be bold enough to follow reason further than precedent, and may bring that principle on the bench when promoted to it; but I fear this effort is not for my day.—To THOMAS COOPER. v, 532. (M., 1810.)

4170. JUDGES, Qualifications.—The judges should always be men of learning and experience in the laws, of exemplary morals, great patience, calmness and attention; their minds should not be distracted with jarring interests.—To GEORGE WYTHE. FORD ED., ii, 59. (1776.)

4171. JUDGES, Seats in State Senate.—The judges of the General Court and of the High Court of Chancery [of Virginia] shall have session and deliberative voice, but not suffrage, in the House of Senators.—PROPOSED VA. CONSTITUTION. FORD ED., ii, 16. (June 1776.)

4172. JUDGES, Superfluous.—By a fraudulent use of the Constitution, which has made judges irremovable, the [federalists] have multiplied useless judges merely to strengthen their phalanx.—To JOHN DICKINSON. iv, 425. (W., 1801.)

4173. —— ——. I should greatly prefer * * * four judges to any greater number. Great lawyers are not over abundant, and the multiplication of judges only enables the weak to out-vote the wise, and three concurrent opinions out of four give a strong presumption of right.—To WILLIAM JOHNSON. vii, 278. FORD ED., x, 249. (M., 1823.)

4174. JUDGES, Usurpation by.—One single object, if your provision [in the Louisiana Code] attains it, will entitle you to the endless gratitude of society; that of restraining judges from usurping legislation. And with no body of men is this restraint more wanting than with the judges of what is commonly called our General Government, but what I call our Foreign Department.—To EDWARD LIVINGSTON. vii, 403. (M., 1825.)

4175. JUDGES, Venality of French.—Nor should we wonder at * * * [the] pressure [for a fixed constitution in 1788-9] when we consider the monstrous abuses of power under which * * * [the French] people were ground to powder; when we pass in review * * * the venality of the judges and their partialities to the rich.—AUTOBIOGRAPHY. i, 86. FORD ED., i, 118. (1821.)

4176. JUDGMENT, Errors of.—I fear not that any motives of interest may lead me astray; I am sensible of no passion which could seduce me knowingly from the path of justice; but the weaknesses of human nature, and the limits of my own understanding, will produce errors of judgment sometimes injurious to your interests. I shall need, therefore, all the indulgence which I have heretofore experienced.—Second Inaugural Address. viii, 45. Ford ed., viii, 347. (1805.)

4177. JUDGMENT, Warped.—All know the influence of interest on the mind of man, and how unconsciously his judgment is warped by that influence.—Autobiography. i, 81. Ford ed., i, 112. (1821.)

4178. JUDICIARY (Federal), Centralization and.—We already see the power, installed for life, responsible to no authority (for impeachment is not even a scare-crow), advancing with a noiseless and steady pace to the great object of consolidation. The foundations are already deeply laid by their decisions, for the annihilation of constitutional State rights, and the removal of every check, every counterpoise to the ingulphing power of which themselves are to make a sovereign part. * * * Let the future appointments of judges be for four or six years, and removable by the President and Senate. This will bring their conduct, at regular periods, under revision and probation, and may keep them in equipoise between the general and special governments. We have erred in this point, by copying England, where certainly it is a good thing to have the judges independent of the King. But we have omitted to copy their caution also, which makes a judge removable on the address of both legislative houses. That there should be public functionaries independent of the nation, whatever may be their demerit, is a solecism in a republic, of the first order of absurdity and inconsistency.—To Wm. T. Barry. vii, 256. (M., 1822.) See Centralization.

4179. JUDICIARY (Federal), Coercion of.—In the General Government, * * * the Judiciary is independent of the nation, their coercion by impeachment being found nugatory.—To John Taylor. vi, 607. Ford ed., x, 30. (M., 1816.)

4180. JUDICIARY (Federal), Confidence in.—The Judiciary, if rendered independent, and kept strictly to their own department, merits great confidence for their learning and integrity.—To James Madison. iii, 3. Ford ed., v, 81. (P., 1789.)

4181. JUDICIARY (Federal), Control over.—The Judiciary [branch of the Government] possessing the rights of self-government from nature, cannot be controlled in the exercise of them but by a law, passed in the forms of the Constitution.—Official Opinion. vii, 499. Ford ed., v, 209. (1790.)

4182. JUDICIARY (Federal), Curbing.—You will have a * * * difficult task in curbing the Judiciary in their enterprises on the Constitution. I doubt whether the erection of the Senate into an appellate court on constitutional questions would be deemed an unexceptionable reliance; because it would enable the Judiciary, with the representatives in Senate of one-third only of our citizens, and that in a single house, to make by construction what they should please of the Constitution, and thus bind in a double knot the other two-thirds; for I believe that one-third of our citizens choose a majority of the Senate, and these, too, of the smaller States whose interests lead to lessen State influence, and strengthen that of the General Government. A better remedy I think, and indeed the best I can devise would be to give future commissions to judges for six years (the senatorial term) with a reappointability by the President with the approbation of both houses. That of the House of Representatives imports a majority of citizens, that of the Senate a majority of States, and that of both a majority of the three sovereign departments of the existing government, to wit, of its Executive and Legislative branches. If this would not be independence enough, I know not what would be such, short of the total irresponsibility under which we are acting and sinning now. The independence of the judges in England on the King alone is good; but even there they are not independent on the Parliament, being removable on the joint address of both houses, by a vote of a majority of each, but we require a majority of one house and two-thirds of the other, a concurrence which, in practice, has been and ever will be found impossible; for the judiciary perversions of the Constitution will forever be protected under the pretext of errors of judgment, which by principle are exempt from punishment. Impeachment, therefore, is a bugbear which they fear not at all. But they would be under some awe of the canvass of their conduct which would be open to both houses regularly every sixth year. It is a misnomer to call a government republican, in which a branch of the supreme power is independent of the nation. By this change of tenure a remedy would be held up to the States, which, although very distant, would probably keep them quiet. In aid of this a more immediate effect would be produced by a joint protestation of both houses of Congress, that the doctrines of the judges in the case of Cohens, adjudging a State amenable to their tribunal, and that Congress can authorize a corporation of the District of Columbia to pass any act which shall have the force of law within a State, are contrary to the provisions of the Constitution of the United States. This would be effectual; as with such an avowal of Congress, no State would permit such a sentence to be carried into execution within its limits. If, by the distribution of the sovereign powers among three branches, they were intended to be checks on one another, the present case calls loudly for the exercise of that duty, and such a counter declaration, while proper in form, would be most salutary as a precedent.—To JAMES PLEASANTS. FORD ED., x, 198. (M., Dec. 1821.)

4183. —— ——. There was another amendment [to the Federal Constitution] of which none of us thought at the time [when the Constitution was framed], and in the omission of which lurks the germ that is to destroy this happy combination of national powers in the General Government for matters of national concern, and independent powers in the States, for what concerns the States severally. In England, it was a great point gained at the Revolution, that the commissions of the judges, which had hitherto been during pleasure, should thenceforth be made during good behavior. A Judiciary, dependent on the will of the king, had proved itself the most oppressive of all tools in the hands of that magistrate. Nothing then could be more salutary than a change there to the tenure of good behavior; and the question of good behavior, left to the vote of a simple majority in the two Houses of Parliament. Before the Revolution we were all good English Whigs, cordial in their free principles, and in their jealousies of their Executive Magistrate. These jealousies are very apparent in all our State constitutions; and, in the General Government in this instance, we have gone even beyond the English caution, by requiring a vote of two-thirds in one of the houses, for removing a Judge; a vote so impossible, where* any defence is made, before men of ordinary prejudices and passions, that our judges are effectually independent of the nation. But this ought not to be. I would not, indeed, make them dependent on the Executive authority, as they formerly were in England; but I deem it indispensable to the continuance of this Government that they should be submitted to some practical and impartial control; and that this, to be impartial, must be compounded of a mixture of State and Federal authorities.—AUTOBIOGRAPHY. i, 80. FORD ED., i, 111. (1821.)

4184. JUDICIARY (Federal), Dangerous Decisions.—At the establishment of our Constitutions, the judiciary bodies were supposed to be the most helpless and harmless members of the government. Experience, however, soon showed in what way they were to become the most dangerous; that the insufficiency of the means provided for their removal gave them a freehold and irresponsibility in office; that their decisions, seeming to concern individual suitors only, pass silent and unheeded by the public at large; that these decisions, nevertheless, become law by precedent, sapping, by little and little, the foundations of the Constitution, and working its change by construction, before any one has perceived that that invisible and helpless worm has been busily employed in consuming its substance. In truth, man is

* In the impeachment of Judge Pickering of New Hampshire, a habitual and maniac drunkard, no defence was made. Had there been, the party vote of more than one-third of the Senate would have acquitted him.—NOTE BY JEFFERSON.

not made to be trusted for life, if secured against all liability to account.—To A. CORAY. vii, 322. (M., 1823.)

4185. JUDICIARY (Federal), Legislative, Executive and.—The dignity and stability of government in all its branches, the morals of the people, and every blessing of society, depend so much upon an upright and skillful administration of justice, that the judicial power ought to be distinct from both the legislative and executive, and independent upon both, that so it may be a check upon both, as both should be checks upon that.—To GEORGE WYTHE. FORD ED., ii, 59. (July 1776.)

4186. JUDICIARY (Federal), Sappers and miners.—The Judiciary of the United States is the subtle corps of sappers and miners constantly working under ground to undermine the foundations of our confederated fabric. They are construing our Constitution from a coordination of a general and special government to a general and supreme one alone. This will lay all things at their feet, and they are too well versed in English law to forget the maxim, " *boni judicis est ampliare jurisdictionem*". * * * Having found from experience, that impeachment is an impracticable thing, a mere scare-crow, they consider themselves secure for life; they skulk from responsibility to public opinion, the only remaining hold on them, under a practice first introduced into England by Lord Mansfield. An opinion is huddled up in conclave, perhaps by a majority of one, delivered as if unanimous, and with the silent acquiescence of lazy or timid associates, by a crafty chief judge, who sophisticates the law to his mind, by the turn of his own reasoning. A judiciary law was once reported by the Attorney General to Congress, requiring each judge to deliver his opinion *scriatim* and openly, and then to give it in writing to the clerk to be entered in the record. A judiciary independent of a king or executive alone, is a good thing; but independence of the will of the nation is a solecism, at least in a republican government.—To THOMAS RITCHIE. vii, 192. FORD ED., x, 170. (M., 1820.)

4187. —— ——. The judges are, in fact, the corps of sappers and miners, steadily working to undermine the independent rights of the States, and to consolidate all power in the hands of that government in which they have so important a freehold estate.—AUTOBIOGRAPHY. i, 82. FORD ED., i, 113. (1821.)

4188. —— ——. This member of the Government was at first considered as the most harmless and helpless of all its organs. But it has proved that the power of declaring what the law is, *ad libitum*, by sapping and mining, slyly, and without alarm, the foundations of the Constitution, can do what open force would not dare to attempt.—To EDWARD LIVINGSTON. vii, 404. (M., 1825.)

4189. JUDICIARY (Federal), The Senate and.—The Constitution has vested the Judiciary power in the courts of justice, with

certain exceptions in favor of the Senate.—
OPINION ON THE POWERS OF THE SENATE. vii,
465. FORD ED., v, 161. (1790.)

**4190. JUDICIARY (Federal), Suprem-
acy.**—The courts of justice exercise the sovereignty of this country, in judiciary matters,
are supreme in these, and liable neither to
control nor opposition from any other branch
of the government.—To E. C. GENET. iv, 68.
FORD ED., vi, 421. (Pa., Sep. 1793.) See
CONSTITUTION, MARSHALL and SUPREME
COURT.

4191. JUDICIARY (State), Elevate.—
Render the judiciary [of the State] respectable by every means possible, to wit, firm
tenure in office, competent salaries, and reduction of their numbers.—To ARCHIBALD
STUART. iii, 315. FORD ED., v, 410. (Pa.,
1791.)

4192. JURISDICTION, Foreign.—He
has combined with others to subject us to a
jurisdiction foreign to our constitutions and
unacknowledged by our laws; giving his assent to their acts of pretended legislation
* * * for protecting them [bodies of
armed troops], by a mock trial, from punishment, for any murders which they should
commit on the inhabitants of these States.—
DECLARATION OF INDEPENDENCE AS DRAWN BY
JEFFERSON.

4193. JURISDICTION, Unwarrantable.
—We have warned them [our British breth-
ren] from time to time of attempts by their
legislature to extend an unwarrantable jurisdiction over these our States. We have reminded them of the circumstances of our
emigration and settlement here, no one of
which could warrant so strange a pretension.*
—DECLARATION OF INDEPENDENCE AS DRAWN
BY JEFFERSON.

**4194. JURY (Grand), Federal Judges
and.**—The proceedings in the Federal court
of Virginia, to overawe the communications
between the people and their representatives,
excite great indignation. Probably a great
fermentation will be produced by it in that
State. Indeed it is the common cause of the
confederacy, as it is one of their courts
which has taken the step. The charges of the
Federal judges have for a considerable time
been inviting the grand juries to become inquisitors on the freedom of speech, of writing,
and of principle of their fellow citizens. Perhaps the grand juries in the other States, as
well as in that of Virginia, may think it incumbent in their next presentment to enter
protestations against this perversion of their
institution from a legal to a political machine,
and even to present those concerned in it.—
To PEREGRINE FITZHUGH. FORD ED., vii, 137.
(Pa., June 1797.)

**4195. JURY (Trial by), Anchor of Gov-
ernment.**—I consider trial by jury as the only

* Congress changed so as to read: "We have
warned them, from time to time, of attempts by their
legislature to extend an unwarrantable jurisdiction
over us. We have reminded them of the circumstances of our emigration and settlement here."—
EDITOR.

anchor ever yet imagined by man, by which a
government can be held to the principles of
its constitution.—To THOMAS PAINE. iii, 71.
(P., 1789.)

**— JURY (Trial by), In Chancery
Courts.**—See COURTS OF CHANCERY.

**4196. JURY (Trial by), Common sense
of Jurors.**—It is better to toss up cross and
pile in a cause than to refer it to a judge
whose mind is warped by any motive whatever, in that particular case. But the common
sense of twelve honest men gives a still better
chance of just decision, than the hazard of
cross and pile.—NOTES ON VIRGINIA. viii,
372. FORD ED., iii, 236. (1782.)

**4197. JURY (Trial by), Denied by par-
liament.**—They [Parliament] have deprived
us of the inestimable privilege of trial by a
jury of the vicinage in cases affecting both
life and property.—DECLARATION ON TAKING
UP ARMS. FORD ED., i, 468. (July 1775.)

4198. —— ——. The proposition [of Lord
North] is altogether unsatisfactory * * *
because it does not propose to repeal the
several acts of Parliament * * * taking
from us the right of a trial by jury of the
vicinage, in cases affecting both life and property.—REPLY TO LORD NORTH'S PROPOSITION.
FORD ED., i, 480. (July 1775.)

**4199. JURY (Trial by), Lack of Uni-
form Laws.**—I do not like [in the new Federal Constitution] the omission of a bill of
rights, providing clearly and without the aid
of sophisms for * * * trials by jury in all
matters of fact triable by the laws of the
land, and not by the law of nations. * * *
It was a hard conclusion to say, because
there has been no uniformity among the
States as to the cases triable by jury, because
some have been so incautious as to abandon
this mode of trial, therefore, the more prudent
States shall be reduced to the same level of
calamity. It would have been much more just
and wise to have concluded the other way
that, as most of the States had judiciously
preserved this palladium, those who had
wandered should be brought back to it, and
to have established general right instead of
general wrong.—To JAMES MADISON. ii, 329.
FORD ED., iv, 476. (P., Dec. 1787.)

**4200. JURY (Trial by), Essential prin-
ciple.**—Trial by juries impartially selected, I
deem [one of the] essential principles of
our government and, consequently, [one]
which ought to shape its administration.—
FIRST INAUGURAL ADDRESS. viii, 4. FORD ED.,
viii, 5. (1801.)

4201. JURY (Trial by), In France.—I
doubt whether France will obtain [in its proposed Constitution] the trial by jury, because
they are not sensible of its value.—To DR.
PRICE. ii, 557. (P., Jan. 1789.)

**4202. JURY (Trial by), Fundamental
right.**—There are instruments for administering the government, so peculiarly trustworthy, that we should never leave the leg-

islature at liberty to change them. The new Constitution has secured these in the executive and legislative departments; but not in the judiciary. It should have established trials by the people themselves, that is to say, by jury.—To DAVID HUMPHREYS. iii, 13. FORD ED., v, 90. (P., 1789.)

4203. JURY (Trial by), George III. and.—He [George III.] has endeavored to pervert the exercise of the kingly office in Virginia into a detestable and insupportable tyranny * * * by combining with others to subject us to a foreign jurisdiction, giving his assent to their pretended acts of legislation * * * for depriving us of the benefits of trial by jury.—PROPOSED VA. CONSTITUTION. FORD ED., ii, 11. (June 1776.)

4204. ———— ————. He has combined, with others, * * * for depriving us* of the benefits of trial by jury.—DECLARATION OF INDEPENDENCE AS DRAWN BY JEFFERSON.

4205. JURY (Trial by), Law and fact.—The people are not qualified to judge questions of law; but they are very capable of judging questions of fact. In the form of juries, therefore, they determine all matters of fact, leaving to the permanent judges to decide the law resulting from those facts. * * * It is left to the juries, if they think permanent judges are under any bias whatever in any cause, to take on themselves to judge the law as well as the fact. They never exercise this power but when they suspect partiality in the judges; and by the exercise of this power they have been the firmest bulwarks of English liberty.—To L'ABBÉ ARNOND. iii, 81. FORD ED., v, 103. (P., 1789.)

4206. ———— ————. If the question [before justices of the peace] relate to any point of public liberty, or if it be one of those in which the judges may be suspected of bias, the jury undertake to decide both law and fact.—NOTES ON VIRGINIA. viii, 372. FORD ED., iii, 236. (1782.)

4207. ———— ————. The people * * * being competent to judge of the facts occurring in ordinary life, have retained the functions of judges of facts, under the name of jurors.—To DUPONT DE NEMOURS. vi, 590. FORD ED., x, 22. (P.F., 1816.)

4208. JURY (Trial by), Medietas Linguæ.—I sincerely rejoice at the acceptance of our new Constitution by nine States. It is a good canvas, on which some strokes only want retouching. What these are, I think are sufficiently manifested by the general voice from north to south which calls for a bill of rights. It seems pretty generally understood that this should go to juries * * *. In disputes between a foreigner and a native, a trial by jury may be improper. But if this exception cannot be agreed to, the remedy will be to model the jury by giving the *medietas linguæ*, in civil as well as criminal cases.—To JAMES MADISON. ii, 445. FORD ED., v, 45. (P., July 1788.)

* Congress inserted after "us" the words "in many cases".—EDITOR.

4209. JURY (Trial by), Safeguard.—Trial by jury is the best of all safeguards for the person, the property, and the fame of every individual.—To M. CORAY. vii, 323. (M., 1823.)

4210. JURY (Trial by), Scope.—I like the declaration of rights as far as it goes, but I should have been for going further. For instance, the following alterations and additions would have pleased me. * * * Article 7. All facts put in issue before any judicature, shall be tried by jury, except: 1, in cases of admiralty jurisdiction, wherein a foreigner shall be interested; 2, in cases cognizable before a court-martial, concerning only the regular officers and soldiers of the United States, or members of the militia in actual service in time of war or insurrection; 3, in impeachments allowed by the Constitution.—To JAMES MADISON. iii, 100. FORD ED., v, 112. (P., Aug. 1789.)

4211. JURY (Trial by), Selection of Jurors.—An officer * * * who selects judges for principles which necessarily lead to condemnation, might as well lead his culprits to the scaffold at once without the mockery of trial.—To MRS. SARAH MEASE. FORD ED., viii, 35. (W., March 1801.)

4212. ———— ————. An officer who is entrusted by the law with the sacred duty of naming judges of life and death for his fellow citizens, and who selects them exclusively from among his political and party enemies, ought never to have in his power a second abuse of that tremendous magnitude.—To MRS. SARAH MEASE. FORD ED., viii, 35. (W., March 1801.)

4213. ———— ————. It will be worthy your consideration whether the protection of the inestimable institution of juries has been extended to all the cases involving the security of our persons and property. Their impartial selection also being essential to their value, we ought further to consider whether that is sufficiently secured in those States where they are named by a marshal depending on Executive will, or designated by the court or by officers dependent on them.—FIRST ANNUAL MESSAGE. viii, 14. FORD ED., viii, 123. (Dec. 1801.)

4214. ———— ————. I enclose you a petition for a reformation in the manner of appointing our juries, and a remedy against the *jury of all nations.* * * * I know it will require but little ingenuity to make objections to the details of its execution; but do not be discouraged by small difficulties; make it as perfect as you can at a first essay, and depend on amending its defects as they develop themselves in practice. * * * It is the only thing which can yield us a little present protection against the dominion of a faction, while circumstances are maturing for bringing and keeping the government in real unison with the spirit of their constituents.—To JOHN TAYLOR. iv, 260. FORD ED., vii, 311. (M., 1798.)

4215. JURY (Trial by), Powers of Jurors.—All fines, or amercements, shall be assessed, and terms of imprisonment for contempts and misdemeanors shall be fixed by the verdict of a jury.—Proposed Va. Constitution. Ford ed., ii, 24. (June 1776.)

4216. JURY (Trial by), Universal.—By a declaration of rights, I mean one which shall stipulate * * * trial by juries in all cases * * * .—To A. Donald. ii, 355. (P., 1788.)

4217. JUSTICE, Administration of.—He has suffered* the administration of justice *totally to cease in some of these States,* refusing his assent to laws for establishing judiciary powers.—Declaration of Independence as Drawn by Jefferson.

4218. —— ——. Justice is administered in all the States with a purity and integrity of which few countries can afford an example.—To Count de Vergennes. ix, 241. Ford ed., iv, 127. (P., 1785.)

4219. JUSTICE, Courts of.—Courts of justice, all over the world, are held by the laws to proceed according to certain forms, which the good of the suitors themselves requires they should not be permitted to depart from.—To Charles Hellstedt. iii, 210. (Pa., 1791.)

4220. —— ——. No nation can answer for perfect exactitude of proceedings in all their inferior courts. It suffices to provide a supreme judicature, where all error and partiality will be ultimately corrected.—To George Hammond. iii, 414. Ford ed., vi, 55. (Pa., 1792.)

4221. JUSTICE, Deaf to.—They, too [the British people], have been deaf to the voice of justice and of consanguinity.—Declaration of Independence as Drawn by Jefferson.

4222. JUSTICE, Equal and exact.—Equal and exact justice to all men, of whatever state or persuasion, religious or political, I deem [one of the] essential principles of our government and, consequently [one] which ought to shape its administration.—First Inaugural Address. viii, 4. Ford ed., viii, 4. (1801.)

4223. JUSTICE, Foundation of.—I believe that justice is instinct and innate, that the moral sense is as much a part of our constitution as that of feeling, seeing, or hearing; as a wise Creator must have seen to be necessary in an animal destined to live in society; that every human mind feels pleasure in doing good to another; that the non-existence of justice is not to be inferred from the fact that the same act is deemed virtuous and right in one society which is held vicious and wrong in another; because, as the circumstances and opinions of different societies vary, so the acts which may do them right or wrong must vary also; for virtue does not

* For "suffered", Congress substituted "obstructed"; struck out the words in italics and inserted "by".—Editor.

consist in the act we do, but in the end it is to effect. If it is to effect the happiness of him to whom it is directed, it is virtuous, while in a society under different circumstances and opinions, the same act might produce pain, and would be vicious. The essence of virtue is in doing good to others, while what is good may be one thing in one society, and its contrary in another.—To John Adams. vii, 39. (M., 1816.)

4224. JUSTICE, Fundamental Law.—Justice is the fundamental law of society.—To Dupont de Nemours. vi, 591. Ford ed., x, 24. (P.F., 1816.)

4225. JUSTICE, Government and.—The most sacred of the duties of a government is to do equal and impartial justice to all its citizens.—Note in Tracy's Political Economy. vi, 574. (1816.)

4226. JUSTICE, Impartial.—Deal out justice without partiality or favoritism.—To Hugh Williamson. Ford ed., v, 492. (Pa., 1792.)

4227. —— ——. The sword of the law should never fall but on those whose guilt is so apparent as to be pronounced by their friends as well as foes.—To Mrs. Sarah Mease. Ford ed., viii, 35. (W., March 1801.)

4228. —— ——. When one undertakes to administer justice, it must be with an even hand, and by rule; what is done for one, must be done for every one in equal degree.—To Dr. Benjamin Rush. iv, 507. Ford ed., viii, 264. (W., 1803.)

4229. JUSTICE, International.—We must make the interest of every nation stand surety for their justice, and their own loss to follow injury to us, as effect follows its cause.—To Edward Rutledge. iv, 191. Ford ed., vii, 154. (Pa., 1797.)

4230. —— ——. We think that peaceable means may be devised of keeping nations in the path of justice towards us, by making justice their interest, and injuries to react on themselves.—To Mr. Cabanis. iv, 497. (W., 1803.)

4231. —— ——. We are firmly convinced, and we act on that conviction, that with nations, as with individuals, our interests soundly calculated, will ever be found inseparable from our moral duties; and history bears witness to the fact, that a just nation is trusted on its word, when recourse is had to armaments and wars to bridle others.—Second Inaugural Address. viii, 40. Ford ed., viii, 343. (1805.)

4232. —— ——. A just nation is taken on its word, when recourse is had to armaments and wars to bridle others.—Second Inaugural Address. viii, 40. Ford ed., viii, 343. (1805.)

4233. —— ——. We ask for peace and justice from all nations.—To James Monroe. v, 12. Ford ed., viii, 450. (W., May 1806.)

4234. JUSTICE, National and individual.—A character of justice is valuable to a nation as to an individual.—To Rev. Mr. Worcester. vi, 540. (1816.)

4235. JUSTICE, Partial.—The public security against a partial dispensation of justice depends on its being dispensed by certain rules. The slightest deviation in one circumstance becomes a precedent for another, that for a third, and so on without bounds. A relaxation in a case where it is certain no fraud is intended, is laid hold of by others, afterwards, to cover fraud.—To George Joy. iii, 130. (N.Y., 1790.)

4236. JUSTICE, Peace and.—Peace and justice [should] be the polar stars of the American Societies.—To J. Correa. vii, 184. Ford ed., x, 164. (M., 1820.)

4237. JUSTICE, Pre-Revolutionary.—Before the Revolution, a judgment could not be obtained under eight years in the Supreme Court [in Virginia] where the suit was in the department of the common law, which department embraces about nine-tenths of the subject of legal contestation. In that of the Chancery, from twelve to twenty years were requisite. This did not proceed from any vice in the laws, but from the indolence of the judges appointed by the King; and these judges holding their office during his will only, he could have reformed the evil at any time. This reformation was among the first works of the Legislature after our Independence. A judgment can now be obtained in the Supreme Court in one year at the common law, and in about three years in the Chancery.*—Report to Congress. ix, 240. Ford ed., iv, 126. (P., 1785.)

4238. JUSTICE, Procurement of.—[It is my] belief that a just and friendly conduct on our part will procure justice and friendship from others.—To Earl of Buchan. iv, 494. (W., 1803.)

4239. JUSTICE, Safeguard.—The provisions we have made [for our government] are such as please ourselves; they answer the substantial purposes of government and of justice, and other purposes than these should not be answered.—Reply to Lord North's Proposition. Ford ed., i, 479. (July 1775.)

4240. JUSTICE, Sense of.—Destutt Tracy promises a work on morals, in which I lament to see that he will adopt the principles of Hobbes, or humiliation to human nature; that the sense of justice and injustice is not derived from our natural organization, but founded on convention only. * * * Assuming the fact, that the earth has been created in time, and consequently the dogma of final causes, we yield, of course, to this short syllogism: Man was created for social intercourse; but social intercourse cannot be maintained without a sense of justice; then man must have been created with a sense of justice.—To F. W. Gilmer. vii, 4. Ford ed., x, 32. (M., 1816.)

* Report of Conference with Count de Vergennes on Commerce.—Editor.

4241. JUSTICE, Universal.—Justice is to be denied to no man.—To E. C. Genet. iii, 585. Ford ed., vi, 311. (Pa., 1793.)

4242. JUSTICE, Unswerving.—I am sensible of no passion which could seduce me knowingly from the path of justice.—Second Inaugural Address. viii, 45. Ford ed., viii, 347. (1805.)

4243. JUSTICE, Views of.—All our proceedings have flowed from views of justice.—Special Message. viii, 70. Ford ed., viii, 496. (Dec. 1806.)

4244. KAMES, Writings of Lord.—Your objection to Lord Kames, that he is too metaphysical, is just, and it is the chief objection to which his writings are liable. It is to be observed, also, that though he has given us what should be the system of equity, yet it is not the one actually established, at least not in all its parts.—To Peter Carr. iii, 452. Ford ed., vi, 92. (Pa., 1792.)

4245. KENTUCKY, Asks separation.—We have transmitted a copy of a petition from the people of Kentucky to Congress praying to be separated from Virginia. Congress took no notice of it. We [delegates] sent the copy to the Governor desiring it to be laid before the Assembly. Our view was to bring on the question. It is for the interest of Virginia to cede so far immediately, because the people beyond that will separate themselves, because they will be joined by all our settlements beyond the Alleghany if they are the first movers. Whereas if we draw the line, those at Kentucky having their end, will not interest themselves for the people of Indiana, Greenbriar, &c., who will of course be left to our management, and I can with certainty almost say that Congress would approve of the meridian of the mouth of the Kanawha, and will consider it as the ultimate point to be desired from Virginia. I form this opinion from conversation with many members. Should we not be the first movers, and the Indianians and Kentuckians take themselves off and claim to the Alleghany, I am afraid Congress would secretly wish them well.—To James Madison. Ford ed., iii, 401. (A., Feb. 1784.)

4246. KENTUCKY, Danger of secession.—I fear, from an expression in your letter, that the people of Kentucky think of separating, not only from Virginia (in which they are right), but also from the confederacy. I own I should think this a most calamitous event, and such a one as every good citizen should set himself against.—To Archibald Stuart. i, 518. Ford ed., iv, 188. (P., Jan. 1786.)

4247. KENTUCKY, Independence declared.—The General Assembly of Virginia, at their session in 1785, passed an act declaring that the district, called Kentucky, shall be a separate and independent State, on these conditions. 1. That the people of that district shall consent to it. 2. That Congress shall consent to it, and shall receive them into the Federal Union. 3. That they shall take on themselves a proportionable part of the public debt of Virginia. 4. That they shall confirm all titles to lands within their district, made by the State of Virginia, before their separation.—To M. DE MEUNIER. ix, 258. FORD ED., iv, 162. (P., 1786.)

4248. —— ——. Virginia has declared Kentucky an independent State, provided its inhabitants consent to it, and Congress will receive them into a union.—To WILLIAM CARMICHAEL. FORD ED., iv, 244. (P., 1786.)

4249. KENTUCKY, Statehood.—I wish to see that country in the hands of people well disposed, who know the value of the connection between that and the maritime States, and who wish to cultivate it. I consider their happiness as bound up together, and that every measure should be taken which may draw the bands of union tighter. It will be an efficacious one to receive them into Congress, as I perceive they are about to desire. If to this be added an honest and disinterested conduct in Congress, as to everything relating to them, we may hope for a perfect harmony.—To JOHN BROWN. ii, 395. FORD ED., v. 16. (P., May 1788.)

4250. —— ——. There are now 100,000 inhabitants at Kentucky. They have accepted the offer of independence on the terms proposed by Virginia, and they have decided that their independent government shall begin on the 1st day of the next year. In the meantime, they claim admittance into Congress.—To WILLIAM CARMICHAEL. FORD ED., v, 23. (P., June 1788.)

4251. KENTUCKY, Union and.—Faithful to the Federal compact, according to the plain intent and meaning in which it was understood and acceded to by the several parties, * * * Kentucky is sincerely anxious for its preservation.—KENTUCKY RESOLUTIONS. ix, 468. FORD ED., vii, 300. (1798.)

4252. —— ——. This Commonwealth continues in the same esteem of their [the States] friendship and union which it has manifested from that moment at which a common danger first suggested a common union.—KENTUCKY RESOLUTIONS. ix, 468. FORD ED., vii, 300. (1798.)

4253. KENTUCKY, Vermont and.—Congress referred the decision as to the independence of Kentucky to the new government. Brown ascribes this to the jealousy of the northern States, who want Vermont to be received at the same time, in order to preserve a balance of interests in Congress. He was just setting out for Kentucky, disgusted, yet disposed to persuade to an acquiescence, though doubting they would immediately separate from the Union. The principal obstacle to this, he thought, would be the Indian war.—To WILLIAM SHORT. ii, 480. FORD ED., v, 50. (P., Sep. 1788.)

4254. KENTUCKY, Virginia and.—I am deeply impressed with the importance of Virginia and Kentucky pursuing the same track at the ensuing sessions of their Legislatures.—To WILSON C. NICHOLAS. iv, 304. FORD ED., vii, 389. (M., Aug. 26, 1799.)

4255. KENTUCKY RESOLUTIONS (1798), Draft of.—I enclose you a copy of the draft* of the Kentucky resolves. I think we should distinctly affirm all the important principles they contain, so as to hold to that ground in future, and leave the matter in such a train as that we may not be committed absolutely to push the matter to extremities, and yet may be free to push as far as events will render prudent.—To JAMES MADISON. iv, 258. FORD ED., vii, 288. (M., Nov. 17, 1798.)

4256. KENTUCKY RESOLUTIONS (1798), History of.—At the time when the Republicans of our country were so much alarmed at the proceedings of the Federal ascendency in Congress, in the Executive and the Judiciary departments, it became a matter of serious consideration how head could be made against their enterprises on the Constitution. The leading Republicans in Congress found themselves of no use there, browbeaten, as they were, by a bold and overwhelming majority. They concluded to retire from that field, take a stand in the State Legislatures, and endeavor there to arrest their progress. The Alien and Sedition laws furnished the particular occasion. The sympathy between Virginia and Kentucky was more cordial, and more intimately confidential, than between any other two States of Republican policy. Mr. Madison came into the Virginia Legislature. I was then in the Vice-Presidency, and could not leave my station. But your father, Colonel W. C. Nicholas, and myself happening to be together, the engaging the cooperation of Kentucky in an energetic protestation against the constitutionality of those laws, became a subject of consultation. Those gentlemen pressed me strongly to sketch resolutions for that purpose, your father undertaking to introduce them to that Legislature, with a solemn assurance, which I strictly required, that it should not be known from what quarter they came. I drew and delivered them to him, and in keeping their origin secret, he fulfilled his pledge of honor. Some years after this, Colonel Nicholas asked me if I would have any objection to its being known that I had drawn them. I pointedly enjoined that it should not. Whether he had unguardedly intimated it before to any one, I know not; but I afterwards observed in the papers repeated imputations of them to me; on which, as has been my practice on all occasions of imputation, I have observed entire silence. The question, indeed, has never before been put to me, nor should I answer it to any other than yourself; seeing no good end to be proposed by it, and the desire of tranquillity inducing with me a wish to be withdrawn from public notice.†—To —— NICHOLAS. vii, 229. (M., Dec. 1821.)

4257. KENTUCKY RESOLUTIONS (1798), Phrasing of.—The more I have reflected on the phrase in the paper you showed me, the more strongly I think it should be altered. Suppose you were instead of the invitation to cooperate in the annulment of the acts, to make it an invitation "to concur with this commonwealth in declaring, as it does hereby declare, that the said acts are, and were

---

* The Resolutions are printed in the Appendix to this volume. The principles, &c., declared in them are arranged under appropriate titles.—EDITOR.

† In the FORD EDITION, vii, 290, but addressed to John Cabel Breckenridge.—EDITOR.

ab initio, null, void, and of no force, or effect ",
I should like it better.—To W. C. NICHOLAS.
FORD ED., vii, 312. (Nov. 1798.)

4258. KENTUCKY RESOLUTIONS
(1798), Presentation of.—I entirely approve
of the confidence you have reposed in Mr.
Breckenridge, as he possesses mine entirely.
I had imagined it better these resolutions should
have originated with North Carolina. But perhaps the late changes in their representation
may indicate some doubt whether they could
have passed. In that case, it is better they
should come from Kentucky. I understand you
intend soon to go as far as Mr. Madison's. You
know of course I have no secrets from him. I
wish him, therefore, to be consulted as to these
resolutions.—To W. C. NICHOLAS. FORD ED.,
vii, 281. (M., Oct. 5. 1798.)

4259. KENTUCKY RESOLUTIONS
(1799), Outlines of.—I thought something
essentially necessary to be said, in order to
avoid the inference of acquiescence; that a resolution or declaration should be passed: 1. Answering the reasonings of such of the States
as have ventured into the field of reason, and
that of the Committee of Congress, taking some
notice, too, of those States who have either
not answered at all, or answered without reasoning. 2. Making firm protestation against the
precedent and principle, and *reserving* the right
to make this palpable violation of the Federal
Compact the ground of doing in future whatever we might now rightfully do, should repetitions of these and other violations of the compact render it expedient. 3. Expressing in
affectionate and conciliatory language our warm
attachment to union with our sister States,
and to the instrument and principles by which
we are united; that we are willing to sacrifice
to this everything but the rights of self-government in those important points which we have
never yielded, and in which alone we see liberty, safety and happiness; that not at all
disposed to make every measure of error or of
wrong a cause of scission, we are willing to look
on with indulgence, and to wait with patience
till those passions and delusions shall have
passed over, which the Federal Government
have artfully excited to cover its own abuses
and conceal its designs, fully confident that
the good sense of the American people, and their
attachment to those very rights which we are
now vindicating, will, before it shall be too late,
rally with us round the true principles of our
Federal compact. This was only meant to give
a general idea of the complexion and topics of
such an instrument. Mr. Madison * * * does
not concur in the *reservation* proposed above;
and from this I recede readily, not only in deference to his judgment, but because, as we
should never think of separation but for repeated and enormous violations, so these, when
they occur, will be cause enough of themselves. To these topics, however, should be
added animadversions on the new pretensions
to a *common law* of the United States. * * *
As to the preparing anything, I must decline it,
to avoid suspicions (which were pretty strong
in some quarters on the late occasion), and because there remains still (after their late loss)
a mass of talents in Kentucky sufficient for
every purpose. The only object of the present
communication is to procure a concert in the
general plan of action [as it is extremely desirable that Virginia and Kentucky should pursue the same track on this occasion *]. Be-

* Part in brackets not in letter-press copy.—FORD
ED. NOTE.

sides, how could you better while away the road
from hence to Kentucky, than in meditating
this very subject, and preparing something
yourself, than whom nobody will do it better.
—To WILSON C. NICHOLAS. iv, 305. FORD ED.,
vii, 390. (M., Sep. 5, 1799.)

— KENTUCKY RESOLUTIONS, Text
of.—See APPENDIX.

4260. KINGS, Abhorrence of.—Let us
turn with abhorrence from these sceptered
scelerats, and disregarding our own petty
differences of opinion about men and measures, let us cling in mass to our country and
to one another, and bid defiance, as we can if
united, to the plundering combinations of the
old world.—To DR. GEORGE LOGAN. vii, 20.
(M., 1816.)

4261. KINGS, Absolutism and.—There
is no king, who, with sufficient force, is not
always ready to make himself absolute.—To
GEORGE WYTHE. ii, 8. FORD ED., iv, 270. (P.,
1786.)

4262. KINGS, American.—It is lawful to
wish to see no emperor or king in our hemisphere.—To JAMES MONROE. FORD ED., x, 244.
(M., 1822.)

4263. KINGS, Bourbon.—France has now
a family of fools at its head, from whom,
whenever it can shake off its foreign riders,
it will extort a free constitution, or dismount
them, and establish some other on the solid
basis of national right.—To BENJAMIN AUS-
TIN. vi, 554. FORD ED., x, 11. (M., Feb.
1816.)

4264. KINGS, Breeding.—When I observed that the King of England was a
cipher, I did not mean to confine the observation to the mere individual [George III.] now
on that throne. The practice of kings marrying only in the families of kings, has been
that of Europe for some centuries. Now,
take any race of animals, confine them in idleness and inaction, whether in a sty, a stable or
a state-room, pamper them with high diet,
gratify all their sexual appetites, immerse
them in sensualities, nourish their passions, let
everything bend before them, and banish
whatever might lead them to think, and in a
few generations they become all body, and no
mind; and this, too, by a law of nature, by
that very law by which we are in the constant
practice of changing the characters and propensities of the animals we raise for our own
purposes. Such is the regimen in raising
kings, and in this way they have gone on for
centuries.—To JOHN LANGDON. v, 514. (M.,
1810.)

— KINGS, Cannibal.—See 1123.

4265. KINGS, Character of European.—
While in Europe, I often amused myself
with contemplating the characters of the then
reigning monarchs of Europe. Louis XVI.
was a fool, of my own knowledge, and in
despite of the answers made for him at his
trial. The King of Spain was a fool, and
of Naples the same. They passed their lives
in hunting, and despatched two couriers a
week, one thousand miles, to let each other

know what game they had killed the preceding days. The King of Sardinia was a fool. All these were Bourbons. The Queen of Portugal, a Braganza, was an idiot by nature. And so was the King of Denmark. Their sons, as regents, exercised the powers of government. The King of Prussia, successor to the great Frederick, was a mere hog in body as well as in mind. Gustavus of Sweden, and Joseph of Austria, were really crazy, and George of England, you know, was in a straight waistcoat. There remained, then, none but old Catherine, who had been too lately picked up to have lost her common sense. In this state Bonaparte found Europe; and it was this state of its rulers which lost it with scarce a struggle. These animals had become without mind and powerless; and so will every hereditary monarch be after a few generations. Alexander, the grandson of Catherine, is as yet an exception. He is able to hold his own. But he is only of the third generation. His race is not yet worn out. And so endeth the Book of Kings, from all of whom the Lord deliver us.—To JOHN LANGDON. v, 514. (M., 1810.)

4266. KINGS, Common sense and.—No race of kings has ever presented above one man of common sense in twenty generations. —To BENJAMIN HAWKINS. ii, 221. FORD ED., iv, 426. (P., 1787.)

4267. KINGS, Confederacy of.—I am not * * * for joining in the confederacy of kings to war against the principles of liberty. —To ELBRIDGE GERRY. iv, 268. FORD ED., vii, 328. (Pa., 1799.)

4268. KINGS, Enemies to happiness.— These descriptions of men [kings, nobles, and priests] are an abandoned confederacy against the happiness of the mass of the people.—To GEORGE WYTHE. ii, 7. FORD ED., iv, 269. (P., 1786.)

4269. KINGS, Evil passions of.—The pride, the dissipations, and the tyranny of kings, keep this hemisphere constantly embroiled in squabbles.—To MR. BELLINI. ii, 440. (P., 1788.)

4270. KINGS, Extirpation of.—Our young Republic * * * should besiege the throne of Heaven with eternal prayers, to extirpate from creation this class of human lions, tigers and mammoths called Kings; from whom, let him perish who does not say, "Good Lord deliver us".—To DAVID HUMPHREYS. ii, 253. (P., 1787.)

4271. KINGS, Lessons from.—If anybody thinks that kings, nobles, or priests are good conservators of the public happiness, send them here [France]. It is the best school in the universe to cure them of that folly. They will see with their own eyes that these descriptions of men are an abandoned confederacy against the happiness of the mass of the people.—To GEORGE WYTHE. ii, 7. FORD ED., iv, 268. (P., 1786.)

4272. KINGS, Ministers of.—No race of kings has ever presented above one man of

common sense in twenty generations. The best they can do is to leave things to their ministers; and what are their ministers but a committee badly chosen? If the king ever meddles it is to do harm.—To BENJAMIN HAWKINS. ii, 221. FORD ED., iv, 426. (P., 1787.)

4273. KINGS, Representative Government and.—Representative government is now well understood to be a necessary check on kings, whom they will probably think it more prudent to chain and tame, than to exterminate.—To JOHN ADAMS. vii, 307. FORD ED., x, 270. (M., 1823.)

4274. KINGS, Republicanism.—If all the evils which can arise among us from the republican form of our government, from this day to the day of judgment, could be put into a scale against what this country [France] suffers from its monarchical form in a week, or England in a month, the latter would predominate.—To BENJAMIN HAWKINS. ii, 221. FORD ED., iv, 426. (P., 1787.)

4275. KINGS, Scaffolds for.—Over the foreign powers I am convinced the French will triumph completely, and I cannot but hope that that triumph, and the consequent disgrace of the invading tyrants, is destined, in the order of events, to kindle the wrath of the people of Europe against those who have dared to embroil them in such wickedness, and to bring at length kings, nobles, and priests to the scaffolds which they have been so long deluging with human blood. I am still warm whenever I think of those scoundrels, though I do it as seldom as I can, preferring infinitely to contemplate the tranquil growth of my lucerne and potatoes. I have so completely withdrawn myself from these spectacles of usurpation and misrule, that I do not take a single newspaper, nor read one a month; and I feel myself infinitely the happier for it.—To TENCH COXE. iv, 104. FORD ED., vi, 507. (M., May 1794.)

— KINGS, Self-government and.—See SELF-GOVERNMENT.

4276. KINGS, Servants of the People.— Kings are the servants, not the proprietors of the people.—RIGHTS OF BRITISH AMERICA. i, 141. FORD ED., i, 446. (1774.)

4277. KINGS, Stupidity of.—There is not a crowned head in Europe, whose talents or merits would entitle him to be elected a vestryman by the people of any parish in America.—To GENERAL WASHINGTON. ii, 375. FORD ED., v, 8. (P., 1788.)

4278. KINGS, Vicious.—I am much indebted to you for the memoirs of the Margrave of Bayreuth. This singular morsel of history has given us a certain view of kings, queens and princes, disrobed of their formalities. It is a peep into the state of the Egyptian God Apis. It would not be easy to find grosser manners, coarser vices, or more meanness in the poorest huts of our peasantry. The princess shows herself the legitimate sister of

Frederick, cynical, selfish and without a heart.
—To MADAME DE TESSE. vi, 271. FORD ED.,
ix, 437. (M., 1813.)

4279. KINGS, Vulgarity.—The memoirs
of Mrs. Clarke and of her *darling* prince, and
the book. emphatically so called, because it is
the *Biblia Sacra Deorum et Diarum sub-
cælestium,* the Prince Regent, his Princess and
the minor deities of his sphere, form a worthy
sequel to the memoirs of Bayreuth; instead
of the vulgarity of the court of Berlin, giving
us the vulgarity and profusion of that of
London, and the gross stupidity and profligacy
of the latter, in lieu of the genius and mis-
anthropism of the former. The whole might
be published as a supplement to M. de Buffon,
under the title of the *"Natural History of
Kings and Princes"*, or as a separate work
and called *"Medicine for Monarchists"*.
The *"Intercepted Letters"*, a later English
publication of great wit and. humor, has put
them to their proper use by holding them up
as butts for the ridicule and contempt of
mankind. Yet by such worthless beings is a
great nation to be governed and even made to
deify their old king because he is only a fool
and a maniac, and to forgive and forget his
having lost to them a great and flourishing
empire, added nine. hundred millions sterling
to their debt, for which the fee simple of the
whole island would not sell, if offered farm
by farm at public auction, and increased
their annual taxes from eight to seventy
millions sterling, more than the whole rent-
roll of the island. What must be the dreary
prospect from the son when such a father is
deplored as a national loss? But let us drop
these odious beings and pass to those of an
higher order, the plants of the field.—To
MADAME DE TESSE. vi, 271. FORD ED., ix,
437. (M., 1813.)

4280. KINGS, Wishing for.—If any of
our countrymen wish for a king, give them
Æsop's fable of the frogs who asked a king;
if this does not cure them, send them to Europe. They will go back good republicans.—
To DAVID RAMSAY. ii, 217. (P., 1787.)

— KING'S MOUNTAIN, Battle of.—See
1085.

4281. KNOWLEDGE, Diffusion of.—
The most important bill in our whole [Vir-
ginia] code is that for the diffusion of
knowledge among the people. No other sure
foundation can be devised for the preservation of freedom and happiness.—To GEORGE
WYTHE. ii, 7. FORD ED., iv, 268. (P., 1786.)

4282. KNOWLEDGE, Honesty and.—
An honest heart being the first blessing, a
knowing head is the second.—To PETER CARR.
i, 397. (P., 1785.)

4283. KNOWLEDGE, Pursuit of.—A
patient pursuit of facts, and cautious combination and comparison of them, is the drudgery
to which man is subjected by his Maker, if
he wishes to attain sure knowledge.—NOTES
ON VIRGINIA. viii, 314. FORD ED., iii, 170.
(1782.) See EDUCATION and SCIENCE.

**4284. KNOX (Henry), Cabinet opin-
ions.**—We [the Cabinet] determined unanimously that Congress should not be called.
* * * I believe Knox's opinion was never
thought worth offering or asking for.—THE
ANAS. ix, 143. FORD ED., i, 227. (1793.)

**4285. KNOX (Henry), Financial fail-
ure.**—General Knox has become bankrupt for
$400,000, and has resigned his military com-
mission. He took in General Lincoln for $150,-
000, which breaks him. Colonel Jackson also
sunk with him.—To JAMES MADISON. iv, 262.
FORD ED., vii, 314. (Pa., Jan. 1799.)

4286. KNOX (Henry), Gossip of.—
Knox [at a Cabinet meeting] told some little
stories to aggravate the President, to wit, that
Mr. King had told him, that a lady had told
him, that she had heard a gentleman say that
the President was as great a tyrant as any of
them, and that it would soon be time to chase
him out of the city [Philadelphia].—THE
ANAS. FORD ED., i, 247. (1793.)

4287. KNOX (Henry), Hamilton and.—
Knox, for once, dared to differ from Hamilton,
and to express, very submissively, an opinion,
that a convention named by the whole body of
the [French] nation, would be competent to do
anything.—THE ANAS. ix, 126. FORD ED., i,
209. (1792.)

4288. ——— ———. Knox joined Hamilton
in everything.—THE ANAS. ix, 184. FORD ED.,
i, 271. (1793.)

4289. ——— ———. Knox subscribed at once
to Hamilton's opinion* that we ought to declare the [French] treaty void, acknowledging
at the same time, like a fool that he is, that
he knew nothing about it.—THE ANAS. ix, 143.
FORD ED., i, 227. (1793.)

4290. ——— ———. Knox, according to custom, jumped plump into all Hamilton's opinions.
—THE ANAS. ix, 169. FORD ED., i, 259.
(1793.)

4291. KNOX (Henry), Indiscreet.—
Knox [at a Cabinet meeting] said we [the Ad-
ministration] should have had fine work if
Congress had been sitting these last two months.
The fool thus let out the secret. Hamilton endeavored to patch up the indiscretion of this
blabber by saying "he did not know; he rather
thought they would have strengthened the Executive arm".—THE ANAS. ix, 165. FORD ED.,
i, 255. (Aug. 1793.)

4292. KNOX (Henry), Naval opinions.
—I think General Washington approved of
building vessels of war to the extent of a force
sufficient to keep the Barbary States in order.
General Knox, I know, did.†—To JOHN ADAMS.
vii, 264. FORD ED., x, 240. (M., 1822.)

**4293. KNOX (Henry), View of Federal
Government.**—In the course of our [the Cabi-
net] conversation [with respect to the manner
and place of swearing in the President], Knox,
stickling for parade, got into great warmth, and

* Though the question whether this treaty was not
terminated by the French Revolution was discussed
in the Cabinet, it was unanimously agreed that it
was still in force. Jefferson is, therefore, in error in
stating that Hamilton declared it void, as all he argued for was whether it "ought not to be deemed
temporarily and provisionally suspended". *Cf.* HAM-
ILTON'S *Works of Hamilton,* iii, 574, iv, 392, 394.—
NOTE IN FORD EDITION.
† Jefferson advocated this measure while he was
Minister to France, and, subsequently, when he became Secretary of State.—EDITOR.

swore that our Government must either be entirely new modeled, or it would be knocked to pieces in less than ten years; and that as it is at present, he would not give a copper for it; that it is the President's character, and not the written Constitution, which keeps it together.—THE ANAS. ix, 139. FORD ED., i, 222. (Feb. 1793.)

4294. KOSCIUSKO (General), Affection for.—For yourself, personally, I may express with safety as well as truth, my great esteem, and the interest I feel for your welfare. From the same principles of caution, I do not write to my friend Kosciusko. I know he is always doing what he thinks is right, and he knows my prayers for his success in whatever he does. Assure him of my constant affection * * * .—To JULIAN V. NIEMCEWICZ.* v, 72. (April 1807.)

4295. KOSCIUSKO (General), Disinterested patriot.—May heaven have in store for your country a restoration of the blessings of freedom and order, and you be destined as the instrument it will use for that purpose. But if this be forbidden by fate, I hope we shall be able to preserve here an asylum where your love of liberty and disinterested patriotism will be forever protected and honored, and where you will find, in the hearts of the American people, a good portion of that esteem and affection which glow in the bosom of the friend who writes this * * * .—To GENERAL KOSCIUS-KO. iv, 295. (Pa., Feb. 1799.)

4296. KOSCIUSKO (General), Emancipation for slaves.—The brave auxiliary of my country in its struggle for liberty, and from the year 1797, when our particular acquaintance began, my most intimate and much beloved friend. On his last departure from the United States in 1798, he left in my hands an instrument appropriating after his death all the property he had in our public funds, the price of his military services here, to the education and emancipation of as many of the children of bondage in this country as it should be adequate to.—To M. JULIEN. vii, 107. (M., 1818.)

4297. ——— ———. You have seen the death of General Kosciusko announced in the papers. He had in the funds of the United States a very considerable sum of money on the interest of which he depended for subsistence. On his leaving the United States, in 1798, he placed it under my direction by a power of attorney, which I executed entirely through Mr. Barnes, who regularly remitted his interest. But he left also in my hands an autograph will, disposing of his funds in a particular course of charity, and making me his executor.—To WILLIAM WIRT. vii, 98. FORD ED., x, 96. (M., 1818.)

4298. KOSCIUSKO (General), Hopes for Poland.—General Kosciusko has been disappointed by the sudden peace between France and Austria. A ray of hope seemed to gleam on his mind for a moment, that the extension of the revolutionary spirit through Italy and Germany might so have occupied the remnants of monarchy there, as that his country might have risen again.—To HORATIO GATES. iv, 213. FORD ED., vii, 205. (Pa., 1798.)

4299. KOSCIUSKO (General), Son of liberty.—He is as pure a son of liberty as I have ever known, and of that liberty which is to

* Kosciusko returned to Europe under the assumed name of Niemcewicz.—EDITOR.

go to all, and not to the few or the rich alone.—To HORATIO GATES. iv. 212. FORD ED., vii, 304. (Pa., 1798.)

4300. KOSCIUSKO (General), Tribute to.—Your principles and dispositions were made to be honored, revered and loved. True to a single object, the freedom and happiness of man, they have not veered about with the changelings and apostates of our acquaintance.—To GENERAL KOSCIUSKO. iv, 249. (1798.)

4301. LABOR, Destroying.—All the energies [of European nations] are expended in the destruction of the labor, property and lives of their people.—To PRESIDENT MONROE. vii, 288. FORD ED., x, 257. (M., 1823.)

4302. LABOR, Distribution.—In Europe, the best distribution of labor is supposed to be that which places the manufacturing hands alongside the agricultural; so that the one part shall feed both, and the other part furnish both with clothes and other comforts. Would that be best here? Egoism and first appearances say yes. Or would it be better that all our laborers should be employed in agriculture? In this case a double or treble portion of fertile lands would be brought into culture; a double or treble creation of food be produced, and its surplus go to nourish the now perishing births of Europe, who in return would manufacture and send us in exchange our clothes and other comforts.—To M. SAY. iv, 527. (W., Feb. 1804.)

4303. ——— ———. I was once a doubter whether the labor of the cultivator, aided by the creative powers of the earth itself, would not produce more value than that of the manufacturer, alone and unassisted by the dead subject on which he acted. In other words, whether the more we could bring into action of the energies of our boundless territory, in addition to the labor of our citizens, the more would not be our gain? But the inventions of later times, by labor-saving machines, do as much now for the manufacturer, as the earth for the cultivator. Experience, too, has proved that mine was but half the question. The other half is whether dollars and cents are to be weighed in the scale against real independence? The whole question then is solved; at least as far as respects our wants.—To WILLIAM SAMPSON. FORD ED., x, 73. (M. 1817.) See MANUFACTURES.

4304. LABOR, Earnings of.—Take not from the mouth of labor the bread it has earned.—FIRST INAUGURAL ADDRESS. viii, 4. FORD ED., viii, 4. (1801.)

4305. LABOR, Economy and.—Economy in the public expense, that labor may be lightly burdened, I deem [one of the] essential principles of our government and, consequently [one] which ought to shape its administration.—FIRST INAUGURAL ADDRESS. viii, 4. FORD ED., viii, 5. (1801.) See ECONOMY.

4306. LABOR, European governments and.—To constrain the brute force of the people, the European governments deem it necessary to keep them down by hard labor, poverty and ignorance, and to take from them, as from bees, so much of their earnings, as that unremitting labor shall be necessary to obtain a sufficient surplus to sustain a scanty and miserable life.—To WILLIAM JOHNSON. vii, 291. FORD ED., x, 226. (M., 1823.)

4307. LABOR, Fruits of.—The rights of the people to the exercise and fruits of their own industry can never be protected against the selfishness of rulers not subject to their control at short periods.—To ISAAC H. TIFFANY. vii, 32. (M., 1816.)

4308. LABOR, Government and.—It behooves us to avail ourselves of every occasion * * * for taking off the surcharge [of offices and expense] that it may never be seen here that, after leaving to labor the smallest portion of its earnings on which it can subsist, government shall itself consume the residue of what it was instituted to guard.— FIRST ANNUAL MESSAGE. viii, 10. FORD ED., viii, 120. (Dec. 1801.)

4309. LABOR, Land and.—Where land is cheap, and rich, and labor dear, the same labor, spread in a slighter culture over 100 acres, will produce more profit than if concentrated by the highest degree of cultivation on a small portion of the lands. When the virgin fertility of the soil becomes exhausted, it becomes better to cultivate less, and well. The only difficulty is to know at what point of deterioration in the land, the culture should be increased, and in what degree.*—NOTES ON ARTHUR YOUNG'S LETTER. FORD ED., vi, 85. (1792.)

4310. LABOR, Manufactures, Commerce and.—Too little reliance is to be had on a steady and certain course of commerce with the countries of Europe to permit us to depend more on that than we cannot avoid. Our best interest would be to employ our principal labor in agriculture, because to the profits of labor, which is dear, this adds the profits of our lands, which are cheap. But the risk of hanging our prosperity on the fluctuating counsels and caprices of others renders it wise to us to turn seriously to manufactures, and if Europe will not let us carry our provisions to their manufactures, we must endeavor to bring their manufactures to our provisions.—To DAVID HUMPHREYS. FORD ED., v, 344. (Pa., June 1791.) See COMMERCE and MANUFACTURES.

4311. LABOR, Nobility of.—My new trade of nail-making is to me in this country what an additional title of nobility is, or the ensigns of a new order are in Europe.—To M. DE MEUNIER. FORD ED., vii, 14. (M., 1795.) See JEFFERSON.

4312. LABOR, Parasites on.—I think we have more machinery of government than is necessary, too many parasites living on the

* Arthur Young, an English writer on agriculture, wrote to President Washington respecting American lands and their cultivation. Jefferson was consulted on the subject by Washington.—EDITOR.

labor of the industrious.—To WILLIAM LUDLOW. vii, 378. (M., 1824.) See ECONOMY.

4313. LABOR, Plundering.—No other depositories of power [but the people themselves] have ever yet been found, which did not end in converting to their own profit the earnings of those committed to their charge.— To SAMUEL KERCHIVAL. vii, 36. FORD ED., x, 45. (M., 1816.)

4314. LABOR, Prosperity, Agriculture and.—A prosperity built on the basis of agriculture is that which is most desirable to us, because to the efforts of labor it adds the efforts of a greater proportion of soil.— CIRCULAR TO CONSULS. iii, 431. (Pa., 1792.) See AGRICULTURE.

4315. LABOR, Protecting.—If we can prevent the government from wasting the labors of the people, under the pretence of taking care of them, they must become happy. —To THOMAS COOPER. iv, 453. FORD ED., viii, 178. (W., 1802.) See PROTECTION.

4316. LABOR, Rioting on.—I may err in my measures, but never shall deflect from the intention to fortify the public liberty by every possible means, and to put it out of the power of the few to riot on the labors of the many. —To JUDGE TYLER. iv, 548. (W., 1804.)

4317. LABOR, War and.—It is [the people's] sweat which is to earn all the expenses of the war, and their blood which is to flow in expiation of the causes of it.—To ELBRIDGE GERRY. iv, 272. FORD ED., vii, 334. (Pa., 1799.)

4318. LABORERS, America settled by. —Our ancestors who migrated hither were laborers, not lawyers.—RIGHTS OF BRITISH AMERICA. i, 139. FORD ED., i, 444. (1774.)

4319. LABORERS, American.—The great mass of our population is of laborers; our rich, who can live without labor, either manual or professional, being few, and of moderate wealth. Most of the laboring class possess property, cultivate their own lands, have families, and from the demand for their labor are enabled to exact from the rich and the competent such prices as enable them to be fed abundantly, clothed above mere decency, to labor moderately and raise their families. They are not driven to the ultimate resources of dexterity and skill, because their wares will sell although not quite so nice as those of England. The wealthy, on the other hand, and those at their ease, know nothing of what the Europeans call luxury. They have only somewhat more of the comforts and decencies of life than those who furnish them. Can any condition of life be more desirable than this?—To THOMAS COOPER. vi, 377. (M., 1814.)

4320. LABORERS, Encouraging foreign.—If foreigners come of themselves they are entitled to all the rights of citizenship; but I doubt the expediency of inviting them by extraordinary encouragements. I mean not that these doubts should be extended to the importation of useful artificers. The policy of that measure depends on very different considerations. Spare no expense in obtaining them. They will after a while go to the plow and the hoe; but, in the meantime, they will teach us something we do not know.—NOTES ON VIRGINIA. viii, 332. FORD ED., iii, 190. (1782.)

4321. LABORERS, English aristocracy and.—In the hands of the [English] aristocracy, the paupers are used as tools to maintain their own wretchedness, and to keep down the laboring portion by shooting them whenever the desperation produced by the cravings of their stomachs drives them into riots. Such is the happiness of scientific England.—To THOMAS COOPER. vi, 377. (M., 1814.)

4322. ———. The aristocracy of England, which comprehends the nobility, the wealthy commoners, the high grades of priesthood, and the officers of government, have the laws and government in their hands [and] have so managed them as to reduce the eleemosynary class, or paupers, who are about one-fifth of the whole, below the means of supporting life, even by labor. [They] have forced the laboring class, whether employed in agriculture or the arts, to the maximum of labor which the construction of the human body can endure, and to the minimum of food, and of the meanest kind, which will preserve it in life, and in strength sufficient to perform its functions. To obtain food enough, and clothing, not only their whole strength must be unremittingly exerted, but the utmost dexterity also, which they can acquire; and those of great dexterity only can keep their ground, while those of less must sink into the class of paupers. Nor is it manual dexterity alone, but the acutest resources of the mind also, which are impressed into this struggle for life; and such as have means a little above the rest, as the master-workman, for instance, must strengthen themselves by acquiring as much of the philosophy of their trade as will enable them to compete with their rivals, and keep themselves above ground. Hence, the industry and manual dexterity of their journeymen and day-laborers, and the science of their master-workmen, keep them in the foremost ranks of competition with those of other nations; and the less dexterous individuals, falling into the eleemosynary ranks, furnish materials for armies and navies to defend their country, exercise piracy on the ocean, and carry conflagration, plunder and devastation to the shores of all those who endeavor to withstand their aggressions.—To THOMAS COOPER. vi, 376. (M., 1814.)

4323. ———. No earthly consideration could induce my consent to contract such a debt as England has by her wars for commerce; to reduce our citizens by taxes to such wretchedness, as that laboring sixteen of the twenty-four hours, they are still unable to afford themselves bread, or barely to earn as much oatmeal or potatoes as will keep

soul and body together. And all this to fee the avidity of a few millionary merchant and to keep up one thousand ships of war fo the protection of their commercial specula tions.—To WILLIAM H. CRAWFORD. vii, FORD ED., x, 35. (M., 1816.)

4324. LABORERS, Federal taxes and.— The poor man in this country who uses noth ing but what is made within his own farm o family, or within the United States, pays no a farthing of tax to the General Goverr ment but on his salt; and should we go int that manufacture, as we ought to do, we wi pay not one cent.—To DUPONT DE NEMOURS v, 584. FORD ED., ix, 321. (M., 1811.)

4325. LABORERS, French.—The er croachments [in France] by the men on th offices proper for the women, is a great de rangement in the order of things. Men ar shoemakers, tailors, upholsterers, staymaker mantuamakers, cooks, housekeepers, house cleaners [and] bedmakers. The womer therefore, to live, are obliged to undertake th offices which they abandon. They becom porters, carters, reapers, sailors, lock-keeper smiters on the anvil, cultivators of the earth &c.—TRAVELS IN FRANCE. ix, 351. (1787.)

4326. ———. I set out * * * t take a view of Fontainbleau. For this pur pose I shaped my course towards the high est of the mountains in sight, to the top o which was about a league. As soon as had got clear of the town I fell in with poor woman walking at the same rate with myself, and going in the same course. Wish ing to know the condition of the laborin poor, I entered into conversation with he which I began by enquiries for the path whic would lead me into the mountain; and thenc proceeded to enquiries into her vocation, con dition and circumstances. She told me sh was a day laborer, at eight sous, or fou pence sterling the day; that she had tw children to maintain, and to pay a rent o thirty livres for her house (which would con sume the hire of seventy-five days), that ofter she could get no employment, and of cours was without bread. As we had walked to gether near a mile, and she had so far serve me as a guide, I gave her, on parting, twenty four sous. She burst into tears of a gratitud which I could perceive was unfeigned becaus she was unable to utter a word. She ha probably never before received so great a aid.—To REV. JAMES MADISON. FORD ED., vi 34. (Pa., 1785.)

4327. ———. The laboring people i France are poorer than in England. They pa about one-half their produce in rent; th English, in general, about a third.—To JOHI PAGE. i, 549. FORD ED., iv, 213. (P., 1786.)

4328. LABORERS, Importing.—Do yo not think it would be expedient to take meas ures for importing a number of Germans an Highlanders? This need not be to such a extent as to prevent the employment of eastern laborers, which is eligible for par ticular reasons. If you approve of the im

portation of Germans, and have a good
channel for it, you will use it, of course. If
you have no channel, I can help you to one.*
—To MESSRS. JOHNSON, CARROLL, AND STEW-
ART. iii, 337. (Pa., 1792.)

4329. LABORERS, Imprisoned.—Offenders, even under a course of correction,
might be rendered useful in various labors for
the public, and would be living and long-continued spectacles to deter others from committing the like offences.—CRIMES BILL. i,
148. FORD ED., ii, 204. (1779.)

**4330. ———— ————. Exhibited as a public spec-
tacle, with shaved heads and mean clothing,
working on the high roads, produced in the
criminals such a prostration of character, such
an abandonment of self-respect, as, instead of
reforming, plunged them into the most desperate and hardened depravity of morals and
character.—AUTOBIOGRAPHY. i, 45. FORD ED.,
i, 53. (1820.)

4331. LABORERS, Jefferson and.—I
made a point of paying my workmen in preference to all other claimants. I never parted
with one without settling with him, and giving him either his money or my note. Every
person that ever worked for me can attest
this, and that I always paid their notes pretty
soon.—To NICHOLAS LEWIS. FORD ED., v, 34.
(P., 1788.)

4332. LABORERS, Skilled.—While we
have land to labor, let us never wish to see
our citizens occupied at a work-bench or
twirling a distaff. Carpenters, masons,
smiths, are wanting in husbandry; but, for
the general operations of manufacture, let our
workshops remain in Europe. It is better to
carry provisions and materials to workmen
there, than bring them to the provisions and
materials, and with them their manners and
principles.—NOTES ON VIRGINIA. viii, 405.
FORD ED., iii, 269. (1782.) See ARTISANS
and MANUFACTURERS.

4333. LABORERS, Slave vs. English.—
Nor in the class of laborers do I mean to
withhold from the comparison that portion
whose color has condemned them, in certain
parts of our Union, to a subjection to the will
of others. Even these are better fed in these
States, warmer clothed, and labor less than
the journeymen or day-laborers of England.
They have the comfort, too, of numerous
families, in the midst of whom they live without want, or fear of it; a solace which few
of the laborers of England possess. They are
subject, it is true, to bodily coercion; but are
not the hundreds of thousands of British
soldiers and seamen subject to the same, without seeing, at the end of their career, when
age and accident shall have rendered them
unequal to labor, the certainty, which the
other has, that he will never want? And
has not the British seaman, as much as the
African, been reduced to this bondage by
force, in flagrant violation of his own consent, and of his natural right in his own per-

son? And with the laborers of England generally, does not the moral coercion of want
subject their will as despotically to that of
their employer, as the physical constraint does
the soldier, the seaman or the slave? But
do not mistake me. I am not advocating
slavery. I am not justifying the wrongs we
have committed on a foreign people, by the
example of another nation committing equal
wrongs on their own subjects. On the contrary, there is nothing I would not sacrifice
to a practicable plan of abolishing every vestige of this moral and political depravity. But
I am, at present, comparing the condition and
degree of suffering to which oppression has
reduced the man of one color, with the condition and degree of suffering to which oppression has reduced the man of another
color; equally condemning both.—To THOMAS
COOPER. vi. 378. (M., 1814.)

4334. LABORERS, Treatment of slave.
—My first wish is that the [colored] laborers
may be well treated; the second that they
may enable me to have that treatment continued by making as much as will admit it.—
To T. M. RANDOLPH. FORD ED., v, 508. (Pa.,
1792.)

4335. LABORERS, White vs. Black.—
The negro does not perform quite as much
work [as the white man performs] nor with
as much intelligence.—NOTES ON ARTHUR
YOUNG'S LETTER. FORD ED., vi, 84. (1792.)

**4336. LAFAYETTE (Marquis de), At-
las of Patriot Party.**—He was the head and
Atlas of the Patriot party [of the French
Revolution].—AUTOBIOGRAPHY. i, 106. FORD
ED., i, 147. (1821.)

**4337. LAFAYETTE (Marquis de), Busts
of.**—The Commonwealth of Virginia, in gratitude for the services of Major General, the
Marquis de Lafayette, have determined to erect
his bust in their Capitol. Desirous to place a
like monument of his worth, and of their sense
of it, in the country to which they are indebted
for his birth, they have hoped that the city of
Paris will consent to become the depository of
this second testimony of their gratitude. Being
charged by them with the execution of their
wishes, I have the honor to solicit of Messieurs
Le Prevot des Marchands et Echevins, on behalf of the city, their acceptance of a bust of
this gallant officer, and that they will be pleased
to place it where, doing most honor to him,
it will most gratify the feelings of an allied
nation. It is with true pleasure that I obey the
call of that Commonwealth to render just homage to a character so great in its first developments, that they would honor the close of any
other. Their country, covered by a small army
against a great one, their exhausted means supplied by his talents, their enemies finally forced
to that spot whither their allies and confederates
were collecting to receive them, and a war
which had spread its miseries into the four
quarters of the earth, thus reduced to a single
point where one blow should terminate it, and
through the whole, an implicit respect paid to
the laws of the land; these are facts which
would illustrate any character, and which fully
justify the warmth of those feelings, of which
I have the honor on this occasion to be the
organ.—To THE PREVOT DES MARCHANDS ET
ECHEVINS DE PARIS. ii, 29. (P., 1786.)

* Johnson, Carroll, and Stewart were the Commissioners of Washington City.—EDITOR.

4338. —— ——. The first of the busts of the Marquis de Lafayette will be finished next month. I shall present that one to the city of Paris, because the delay has been noticed by some.*—To Governor Henry. i, 514. Ford ed., iv, 135. (Pa., 1786.)

4339. —— ——. The inauguration of the bust of the Marquis de Lafayette has been attended with a considerable but a necessary delay. The principle that the King is the sole fountain of honor in this country opposed a barrier to our desires, which threatened to be insurmountable. No instance of a similar proposition from a foreign power had occurred in their history. The admitting it in this case, is a singular proof of the King's friendly disposition towards the States of America, and of his personal esteem for the Marquis de Lafayette.—To Governor Randolph. ii, 118. (P., 1787.)

4340. LAFAYETTE (Marquis de), Dishonored.—The Marquis de Lafayette, for signing the prayer which the deputies from Bretagne were to present, * * * has been disgraced in the old-fashioned language of the country; that is to say, the command in the South of France this summer, which [the government] had given him, is taken away. This dishonors him at Court, * * * but it will probably honor him in the eyes of the nation.—To Mrs. Cutting. ii, 439. (P., 1788.)

4341. —— ——. The disgrace of the Marquis de Lafayette, which at any other period of their history would have had the worst consequences for him, will on the contrary, mark him favorably to the nation, at present. During the present administration he can expect nothing; but perhaps it may serve him with their successors.—To James Madison. ii, 443. Ford ed., v. 43. (P., 1788.)

4342. —— ——. He is disgraced, in the ancient language of the court, but in truth honorably marked in the eyes of the nation. The ministers are so sensible of this, that they have had, separately, private conferences with him, to endeavor through him to keep things quiet. —To John Jay. ii, 452. (P., 1788.)

4343. —— ——. The Marquis de Lafayette is out of favor with the Court, but in high favor with the nation. I once feared for his personal liberty, but I hope he is on safe ground at present.—To General Washington. ii, 538. Ford ed., v, 60. (P., 1788.)

4344. —— ——. There has been a little foundation for the reports and fears relative to the Marquis de Lafayette. He has from the beginning taken openly part with those who demand a constitution; and there was a moment that we apprehended the Bastile; but they ventured on nothing more than to take from him a temporary service on which he had been ordered; and this, more to save appearances for their own authority than anything else; for at the very moment they pretended that they had put him into disgrace, they were constantly conferring and communicating

* Jefferson, in behalf of the Commonwealth of Virginia, presented a bust of Lafayette to the City of Paris in September, 1786. Carlyle, in his history of the French Revolution (Book v, chapter 8) refers to this bust as follows: " But surely, for one thing, the National Guard should have a General! Moreau de Saint-Méry, he of the 'three thousand orders', casts one of his significant glances on the Bust of Lafayette, which has stood there ever since the American War of Liberty. Whereupon, by acclamation, Lafayette is nominated."—Editor.

with him. Since this, he has stood on safe ground, and is viewed as among the foremost of the Patriots.—To James Madison. ii, 563. Ford ed., v, 64. (P., 1789.)

4345. LAFAYETTE (Marquis de), Doyen of heroes.—Among the few survivors of our Revolutionary struggles, you are as distinguished in my affections, as in the eyes of the world, and especially in those of this country. You are now, I believe, the doyen of our military heroes, and may I not say of the soldiers of liberty in the world?—To Marquis Lafayette. Ford ed., x, 228. (M., 1822.)

4346. LAFAYETTE (Marquis de), Fame.—Of him we may truly say, as was said of Germanicus, " fruitur famâ sui ".—To Edward Everett. vii, 381. (M., 1824.)

4347. LAFAYETTE (Marquis de), Foibles.—He has a great deal of sound genius, is well remarked by the King, and rising in popularity. He has nothing against him but the suspicion of republican principles. I think he will one day be of the ministry. His foible is a canine appetite for popularity and fame; but he will get above this.—To James Madison. ii, 108. Ford ed., iv, 366. (P., 1787.)

4348. LAFAYETTE (Marquis de), France and America.—Teach your children to be, as you are, a cement between our two nations.—To Marquis de Lafayette. iii, 132. Ford ed., v, 153. (N.Y., 1790.)

4349. —— ——. The Marquis de Lafayette stands in such a relation between America and France, that I should think him perfectly capable of seizing what is just [commercially] as to both. Perhaps on some occasion of free conversation, you might find an opportunity of impressing these truths [respecting commerce with the West Indies] on his mind, and that from him, they might be let out at a proper moment, as matters meriting consideration and weight, when [the National Assembly] shall be engaged in the work of forming a constitution for our neighbors.—To William Short. iii, 276. Ford ed., v, 364. (Pa., 1791.)

4350. —— ——. I think the return of Lafayette to Paris insures a reconciliation between them and us. He will so entwist himself with the envoys that they will not be able to draw off. —To T. M. Randolph. iv, 320. Ford ed., vii, 423. (Pa., Feb. 1800.)

4351. LAFAYETTE (Marquis de), And French liberty.—Behold you, then, my dear friend, at the head of a great army, establishing the liberties of your country against a foreign enemy. May heaven favor your cause, and make you the channel through which it may pour its favors.—To General Lafayette. iii, 450. Ford ed., vi, 78. (Pa., June 1792.)

4352. LAFAYETTE (Marquis de), Friendship for.—I have never ceased to cherish a sincere friendship for you, and to take a lively interest in your sufferings and losses. It would make me happy to learn that they are to have an end.—To Marquis de Lafayette. iv, 363. (W., March 1801.)

4353. —— ——. Old men do not easily contract new friendships, but neither do they forget old ones. Yours and mine, commenced in times too awful, has continued through times too trying and changeful to be forgotten at the moment when our chief solace is in our recollections.—To Marquis Lafayette. Ford ed., ix, 302. (M., 1811.)

4354. LAFAYETTE (Marquis de), Gifts of Land.—I am persuaded, that a gift of lands by the State of Virginia to the Marquis de Lafayette would give a good opinion here [France] of our character, and would reflect honor on the Marquis. Nor, am I sure that the day will not come when it might be an useful asylum to him. The time of life at which he visited America was too well adapted to receive good and lasting impressions to permit him ever to accommodate himself to the principles of monarchical government; and it will need all his own prudence, and that of his friends, to make this country a safe residence for him. How glorious, how comfortable in reflection, will it be, to have prepared a refuge for him in case of a reverse. In the meantime, he could settle it with tenants from the freest part of this country, Bretagne. I have never suggested the smallest idea of this kind to him: because the execution of it should convey the first notice. If the State has not a right to give him lands with their own officers, they could buy up at cheap prices the shares of others.—To JAMES MADISON. i, 533. FORD ED., iv, 195. (P., 1786.)

4355. —— ——. The acquisition of Louisiana * * * has enabled us to do a handsome thing for Lafayette. He had received a grant of between eleven and twelve thousand acres north of Ohio, worth, perhaps, a dollar an acre. We have obtained permission of Congress to locate it in Louisiana. Locations can be found adjacent to the city of New Orleans, in the island of New Orleans and in its vicinity, the value of which cannot be calculated.—To PHILIP MAZZEI. iv, 554. (W., 1804.)

4356. —— ——. I wrote in April to Governor Claiborne in these words: "Congress has permitted lots to be taken for M. de Lafayette as low as five hundred acres. This secures to us the parcel on the canal of Carondelet; but at the same time cuts off those similar locations proposed by M. Duplantier. Indeed, it would not be for the interest of the General to let his claim get into collision with any public interest. Were it to lose its popularity, it might excite an apparition neither agreeable to his feelings nor interest." This may already have produced some effect towards abating the expectations of M. Duplantier and the fears of the city. Still, I think it better that Mr. Madison should write explicitly to him. Indeed, I think we had better have a consultation, and determine on the proper limits of the public reservation. For, however justifiably desirous we may be to relieve a man who stands so high in the public affection as Lafayette, still, it should be only by granting to him such lands as would be granted to others if not located by him.—To ALBERT GALLATIN. FORD ED., viii, 454. (M., June 1806.)

4357. —— ——. M. Duplantier's zeal had, in one instance, led us to fear you would be injured by it. He had comprehended in his location not only the grounds vacant of all title in the vicinity of New Orleans, which had been a principal object in my eye to enable you speedily to raise a sum of money, but also grounds which had been reserved and were necessary for the range of the forts, which had been left open as a common for the citizens. Knowing this would excite reclamations dangerous to your interests, and threatening their popularity both there and here, I wrote immediately to Governor Claiborne to get him to withdraw to a certain extent (about point blank shot) from the fort, the grounds within that

being necessary for the public. But, in the meantime, an alarm was excited in the town, and they instructed their representative in Congress to claim, for the use of the town and public, the whole of the vacant lands in its vicinity. Mr. Gallatin, however, effected a compromise with him by ceding the grounds next to the fort, so as to leave your claim clear to all the lands we originally contemplated for you.—To MARQUIS DE LAFAYETTE. FORD ED., ix, 65. (W., May 1807.)

4358. —— ——. I hope Congress is prepared to go through with their compliment [to Lafayette] worthily; that they do not mean to invite him merely to dine; that provision should be made for his expenses here, which you know he cannot afford, and that they will not send him back empty-handed. This would place us under indelible disgrace in Europe. Some three or four good townships in Missouri, or Louisiana or Alabama, &c., should be in readiness for him, and may restore his family to the opulence which his virtues have lost to them.—To PRESIDENT MONROE. FORD ED., x, 294. (M., 1824.)

4359. LAFAYETTE (Marquis de), Hampered by instructions.—As it becomes more and more possible that the Noblesse will go wrong, I become uneasy for you. Your principles are decidedly with the *Tiers Etat*, and your instructions against them. A complaisance to the latter on some occasions, and an adherence to the former on others, may give an appearance of trimming between the two parties, which may lose you both. You will in the end go over wholly to the *Tiers Etat*, because it will be impossible for you to live in a constant sacrifice of your own sentiments to the prejudices of the Noblesse. But you would be received by the *Tiers Etat* at any future day, coldly, and without confidence. This appears to me the moment to take at once that honest and manly stand with them which your principles dictate. This will win their hearts forever, be approved by the world, which marks and honors you as the man of the people, and will be an eternal consolation to yourself. The Noblesse, and especially the Noblesse of Auvergne, will always prefer men who will do their dirty work for them. You are not made for that. They will, therefore, soon drop you, and the people in that case will perhaps not take you up. Suppose a scission should take place. The priests and Nobles will secede, the nation will remain in place, and, with the King, will do its own business. If violence should be attempted, where will you be? You cannot then take side with the people in opposition to your own vote, that very vote which will have helped to produce the scission. Still less can you array yourself against the people. That is impossible. Your instructions are indeed a difficulty. But to state this at its worst, it is only a single difficulty, which a single effort surmounts. Your instructions can never embarrass you a second time, whereas an acquiescence under them will reproduce greater difficulties every day, and without end. Besides, a thousand circumstances offer as many justifications of your departure from your instructions. Will it be impossible to persuade all parties that (as for good legislation two houses are necessary) the placing the privileged classes together in one house, and the unprivileged in another, would be better than a scission? I own, I think it would. People can never agree without some sacrifices; and it appears but a moderate sacrifice in each party, to meet on this middle ground. The attempt to bring this about might satisfy your instructions, and a failure in it would justify your siding with the people, even to those who think instructions are laws of conduct. Forgive me, my dear friend, if my anxiety for you makes me talk of things I know nothing about. You must not consider this as advice. I know you and myself too well to presume to offer advice.—To MARQUIS DE LAFAYETTE. iii, 20. FORD ED., v, 91. (P., May 1789.)

4360. ———. I am in great pain for the Marquis de Lafayette. His principles, you know, are clearly with the people; but having been elected for the Noblesse of Auvergne, they have laid him under express instructions to vote for the decision by orders and not persons. This would ruin him with the *Tiers Etat*, and it is not possible he could continue long to give satisfaction to the Noblesse. I have not hesitated to press on him to burn his instructions, and follow his conscience as the only sure clue, which will eternally guide a man clear of all doubts and inconsistencies. If he cannot effect a conciliatory plan, he will surely take his stand manfully at once with the *Tiers Etat*. He will in that case be what he pleases with them, and I am in hopes that base is now too solid to render it dangerous to be mounted on it.—To GENERAL WASHINGTON. iii, 31. FORD ED., v, 96. (P., 1789.)

4361. ——— ———. Forty-eight of the Nobles have joined the *Tiers Etat*. * * * The Marquis de Lafayette could not be of the number, being restrained by his instructions. He is writing to his constituents to change his instructions, or to accept his resignation.—To JOHN JAY. iii, 62. (P., June 1789.)

4362. LAFAYETTE (Marquis de), Happier in France.—Measuring happiness by the American scale, and sincerely wishing that of yourself and family, we had been anxious to see them established on this side of the great water. But I am not certain that any equivalent can be found for the loss of that species of society, to which our habits have been formed from infancy.—To MARQUIS DE LAFAYETTE. v, 129. FORD ED., ix, 113. (W., 1807.)

4363. LAFAYETTE, Imprisoned.—No one has wished with more anxiety to see him once more in the bosom of a nation, who, knowing his works and his worth, desire to make him and his family forever their own.*—To M. DE LAFAYETTE. iv, 145. (1796.)

4364. LAFAYETTE (Marquis de), Imprudent but innocent.—From what I learn from Viscount Noailles, Lafayette has been more imprudent than I expected, but certainly innocent.—To JAMES MONROE. iii, 550. FORD ED., vi, 240. (Pa., May 1793.)

4365. LAFAYETTE (Marquis de), Louisiana and.—I very much wished your presence in New Orleans during the late conspiracy of Burr. * * * It would have been of value, as a point of union and confidence, for the ancient inhabitants, American as well as Creole.—To MARQUIS DE LAFAYETTE. FORD ED., ix, 665. (W., May 1807.)

4366. ——— ———. Had you been, as I wished, at the head of the government of Orleans, Burr would never have given me one

* M. de Lafayette was the son of Marquis de Lafayette, and in the United States when Jefferson wrote to him. The Washington Administration interceded in behalf of Lafayette and secured his release.—EDITOR.

moment's uneasiness.*—To MARQUIS DE LAFAYETTE. v, 129. FORD ED., ix, 113. (W., 1807.)

4367. LAFAYETTE (Marquis de), A Notable.—Lafayette's name was placed on the list of Notables originally. Afterwards his name disappeared, but finally was reinstated. This shows that his character here is not considered as an indifferent one, and that it excites agitation. His education in our school has drawn on him a very jealous eye from a court whose principles are the most absolute despotism. * * * The King, who is a good man, is favorably disposed towards him, and he is supported by powerful family connections, and by the public good will. He is the youngest man of the Notables except one whose office placed him on the list.—To EDWARD CARRINGTON. ii, 99. FORD ED., iv, 358. (P., 1787.)

4368. LAFAYETTE (Marquis de), In peace and war.—I joy, my friends, in your joy, inspired by the visit of this our ancient and distinguished leader and benefactor. His deeds in the War of Independence you have heard and read. They are known to you and embalmed in your memories and in the pages of faithful history. His deeds in the peace which followed that war, are perhaps not known to you; but I can attest them. When I was stationed in his country, for the purpose of cementing its friendship with ours and of advancing our mutual interests, this friend of both was my most powerful auxiliary and advocate. He made our cause his own, as in truth it was that of his native country also. His influence and connections there were great. All doors of all departments were open to him at all times; to me only formally and at appointed times. In truth I only held the nail, he drove it. Honor him, then, as your benefactor in peace as well as in war.—SPEECH AT CHARLOTTESVILLE DINNER. D. L. J., 391. (1824.)

4369. LAFAYETTE (Marquis de), Promoter of commerce.—The assistance of M. de Lafayette in the whole of this business [promoting .commerce] has been so earnest and so efficacious, that I am in duty bound to place it under the eye of Congress, as worthy their notice on this occasion. Their thanks, or such other notice as they think proper, would be grateful to him without doubt. He has richly deserved and will continue to deserve it, whenever occasions shall arise of rendering services to the United States.—To JOHN JAY. ii, 47. (P., 1786.)

4370. ——— ———. The Marquis de Lafayette is a most valuable auxiliary to me. His zeal is unbounded, and his weight with those in power great. His education having been merely military, commerce was an unknown field to him. But his good sense enabling him to apprehend perfectly whatever is explained to him, his agency has been very efficacious.—To JAMES MADISON. ii, 108. FORD ED., iv, 366. (P., 1787.)

4371. ——— ———. The Marquis de Lafayette goes hand in hand with me in all these [commercial treaty] transactions, and is an invaluable auxiliary to me. I hope it will not be imputed either to partiality or affection, my naming this gentleman so often in my dispatches. Were I not to do it, it would be a suppression of truth, and the taking to myself the whole merit where he has the greatest share.—To JOHN JAY. ii, 228. (P., 1787.)

* Lafayette was Jefferson's first choice for Governor of Orleans after its acquisition. See CLAIBORNE.—EDITOR.

4372. —— ——. I was powerfully aided by all the influence and the energies of the Marquis de Lafayette [in the commercial negotiations with France], who proved himself equally zealous for the friendship and welfare of both nations.—Autobiography. i, 64. Ford ed., i, 90. (1821.)

4373. LAFAYETTE (Marquis de), Reminiscences.—What a history have we to run over from the evening that yourself, Monsieur Berman, and other patriots settled, in my house in Paris, the outlines of the constitution you wished! And to trace it through all the disastrous chapters of Robespierre, Barras, Bonaparte, and the Bourbons! These things, however, are for our meeting.—To Marquis de Lafayette. vii, 378. Ford ed., x, 320. (M., 1824.)

4374. LAFAYETTE (Marquis de), Revisiting America.—I have received * * * your letter * * * giving the welcome assurance that you will visit the neighborhood which, during the march of our enemy near it, was covered by his shield from his robberies and ravages. In passing the line of your former march you will experience pleasing recollections of the good you have done. My neighbors of our academical village have expressed to you * * * their hope that you will accept manifestations of their feelings, simple indeed, but as cordial as any you will have received. It will be an additional honor to the University of the State that you will have been its first guest.—To Marquis de Lafayette. vii, 378. Ford ed., x, 320. (M., 1824.)

4375. —— ——. You will have seen by our papers the delirium into which our citizens are thrown by a visit from General Lafayette. He is making a triumphant progress through the States, from town to town, with acclamations of welcome, such as no crowned head ever received. It will have a good effect in favor of the General with the people in Europe, but probably a different one with their sovereigns. Its effect here, too, will be salutary as to ourselves, by rallying us together and strengthening the habit of considering our country as one and indivisible, and I hope we shall close it with something more solid for him than dinners and balls. The eclat of this visit has almost merged the presidential question, on which nothing scarcely is said in our papers.—To Richard Rush. vii, 380. Ford ed., x, 322. (M., October 1824.)

4376. LAFAYETTE (Marquis de), Value to France.—Take care of yourself, * * * for though I think your nation would in any event work out her salvation, I am persuaded were she to lose you, it would cost her oceans of blood, and years of confusion and anarchy.—To Marquis de Lafayette. iii, 132. Ford ed., v, 153. (N.Y., April 1790.)

4377. LAFAYETTE (Marquis de), Washington and.—The President has seen with satisfaction that the Ministers of the United States in Europe, while they have avoided an useless commitment of their nation on the subject of the Marquis de Lafayette, have nevertheless shown themselves attentive to his situation. The interest which the President himself, and our citizens in general take in the welfare of this gentleman, is great and sincere, and will entirely justify all prudent efforts to save him. I am, therefore, to desire that you will avail yourself of every opportunity of sounding the way towards his liberation, of finding out whether those in whose power he is are very tenacious of him, of insinuating through such channels as you shall think suitable, the attentions of the government and people of the United States to this object, and the interest they take in it, and of procuring his liberation by informal solicitations, if possible. But if formal ones be necessary, and the moment should arrive when you shall find that they will be effectual, you are authorized to signify, through such channels as you shall find suitable, that our government and nation, faithful in their attachments to this gentleman for the services he has rendered them, feel a lively interest in his welfare, and will view his liberation as a mark of consideration and friendship for the United States, and as a new motive for esteem, and a reciprocation of kind offices towards the power to whom they shall be indebted for this act. A like letter being written to Mr. Pinckney, you will of course take care, that however you may act through different channels, there be still a sufficient degree of concert in your proceedings.—To Gouverneur Morris. iii, 524. Ford ed., vi, 202. (Pa., March 1793.)

4378. —— ——. For Lafayette my heart has been constantly bleeding. The influence of the United States has been put into action, as far as it could be either with decency or effect. But I fear that distance and difference of principle give little hold to General Washington on the jailers of Lafayette. However, his friends may be assured that our zeal has not been inactive.—To Mrs. Church. Ford ed., vi, 454. (G., Nov. 1793.)

4379. LAFAYETTE (Marquis de), Zeal of.—He offered his services with that zeal which commands them on every occasion respecting America.—To James Monroe. i, 567. Ford ed., iv, 224. (P., 1786.) See France, Jefferson and Revolution (French).

— LAFITAU (Joseph Francis), Views on Indians.—See Indians.

4380. LAKE GEORGE, Beauties of.—Lake George is, without comparison, the most beautiful water I ever saw; formed by a contour of mountains into a basin thirty-five miles long, and two or four miles broad, finely interspersed with islands, its waters limpid as crystal, and the mountain sides covered with rich groves of thuja, silver fir, white pine, aspen, and paper birch down to the water-edge; here and there precipices of rock to checker the scene and save it from monotony. * * * Lake Champlain, though much larger, is a far less pleasant water. It is muddy, turbulent, and yields little game.—To Martha Jefferson Randolph. Ford ed., v, 337. (1791.)

4381. LAMPS, Improvement in.—There has been a lamp called the cylinder lamp * lately invented here. It gives a light equal, as is thought, to that of six or eight candles. It requires olive oil, but its consumption is not great. The improvement is produced by forcing the wick into a hollow cylinder, so that there is a passage for the air through the hollow. The idea had occurred to Dr. Franklin a year or two before, but he tried his experiment with a rush, which not succeeding he did not prosecute it. The fact was the rush formed too small a cylinder; the one used is of an inch diameter.—To Charles Thomson. Ford ed., iv, 13. (P., 1784.)

4382. LAND, Allodial and Feudal tenures.—An error in the nature of our land

* Argand's lamp.—Editor.

holdings * * * crept in at a very early period of our settlement. The introduction of the Feudal tenures into the Kingdom of England, though ancient, is well enough understood to set this matter in a proper light. In the earlier ages of the Saxon settlement, Feudal holdings were certainly altogether unknown, and very few, if any, had been introduced at the time of the Norman Conquest. Our Saxon ancestors held their lands, as they did their personal property, in absolute dominion, disencumbered with any superior, answering nearly to the nature of those possessions which the Feudalists term Allodial. William, the Norman, first introduced that system generally. The land which had belonged to those who fell in the Battle of Hastings, and in the subsequent insurrections of his reign, formed a considerable proportion of the lands of the whole Kingdom. These he granted out, subject to Feudal duties, as did he also those of a great number of his new subjects, who, by persuasions or threats, were induced to surrender them for that purpose. But still, much was left in the hands of his Saxon subjects, held of no superior, and not subject to Feudal conditions. These, therefore, by express laws, enacted to render uniform the system of military defence, were made liable to the same military duties as if they had been Feuds; and the Norman lawyers soon found means to saddle them, also, with all the other Feudal burthens. But still they had not been surrendered to the King, they were not derived from his grant, and therefore they were not holden of him. A general principle indeed, was introduced, that " all lands in England were held either mediately or immediately of the Crown"; but this was borrowed from those holdings which were truly Feudal, and only applied to others for the purposes of illustration. Feudal holdings were therefore but exceptions out of the Saxon laws of possession, under which all lands were held in absolute right. These, therefore, still form the basis, or groundwork, of the Common law, to prevail wheresoever the exceptions have not taken place. America was not conquered by William, the Norman, nor were its lands surrendered to him or any of his successors. Possessions there are, undoubtedly, of the Allodial nature. Our ancestors, however, who emigrated hither, were laborers, not lawyers. The fictitious principle, that all lands belong originally to the King, they were early persuaded to believe real; and accordingly took grants of their own lands from the Crown. And while the Crown continued to grant for small sums, and on reasonable rents, there was no inducement to arrest the error, and lay it open to the public view. But his Majesty has lately taken on him to advance the terms of purchase, and of holding to the double of what they were, by which means the acquisition of lands being rendered difficult, the population of our country is likely to be checked. It is time, therefore to lay this matter before his Majesty, and to declare, that he has no right to grant lands of himself.—RIGHTS OF BRITISH AMERICA. i, 138. FORD ED., i, 443. (1774.)

4383. ———— ————. The opinion that our lands were Allodial possessions is one which I have very long held, and had in my eye during a pretty considerable part of my law reading which, I found, always strengthened it. * * * This opinion I have thought and still think to prove if ever I should have time to look into books again. But this is only meant with respect to the English law as transplanted here. How far our acts of Assembly, or acceptance of grants, may have converted lands

which were Allodial into Feuds, I have never considered. This matter is now become a mere speculative point; and we have it in our power to make it what it ought to be for the public good.—To ————. FORD ED., ii, 78. (Pa., 1776.)

4384. ———— ————. [The question of the public lands] may be considered in the two points of view, 1st, as bringing a revenue into the public treasury. 2d, as a tenure. * * * First, is it consistent with good policy or free government to establish a perpetual revenue? Is it not against the practice of our wise British ancestors? Have not the instances in which we have departed from this, in Virginia, been constantly condemned by the universal voice of our country? Is it safe to make the governing power, when once seated in office, independent of its revenue? Should we not have in contemplation and prepare for an event (however deprecated) which may happen in the possibility of things; I mean a reacknowledgment of the British tyrant as our King, and previously strip him of every prejudicial possession? Remember how universally the people ran into the idea of recalling Charles II., after living many years under a republican government. As to the second, was not the separation of the property from the perpetual use of lands a mere fiction? Is not its history well known, and the purposes for which it was introduced, to wit, the establishment of a military system of defence? Was it not afterwards made an engine of immense oppression? Is it wanting with us for the purpose of military defence? May not its other legal effects (such of them at least as are valuable) be performed in other more simple ways? Has it not been the practice of all other nations to hold their lands as their personal estate in absolute dominion? Are we not the better for what we have hitherto abolished of the Feudal system? Has not every restitution of the ancient Saxon laws had happy effects? Is it not better now that we return at once into that happy system of our ancestors, the wisest and most perfect ever yet devised by the wit of man, as it stood before the 8th century?—To ————. FORD ED., ii, 79. (Pa., 1776.) See COLONIES.

4385. LAND, Allotment.—From the nature and purpose of civil institutions, all the lands within the limits which any particular society has circumscribed around itself are assumed by that society, and subject to their allotment. This may be done by themselves assembled collectively, or by their legislature, to whom they may have delegated sovereign authority; and if they allotted in neither of these ways, each individual of the society, may appropriate to himself such lands as he finds vacant, and occupancy will give him title.—RIGHTS OF BRITISH AMERICA. i, 139. FORD ED., i, 444. (1774.)

4386. LAND, Appropriation.—Unappropriated, or forfeited lands, shall be appropriated by the Administrator with the consent of the Privy Council.—PROPOSED VA. CONSTITUTION. FORD ED., ii, 25. (June 1776.)

4387. ———— ————. Lands heretofore holden of the crown in fee simple, and those hereafter to be appropriated, shall be holden in full and absolute dominion, of no superior whatever.—PROPOSED VA. CONSTITUTION. FORD ED., ii, 25. (June 1776.)

4388. ———— ————. Every person, of full age, neither owning nor having owned fifty acres of land, shall be entitled to an appropriation of fifty acres, or to so much as shall make up what he owns, or has owned in full and absolute dominion. And no other person shall be capable of taking an appropriation.—Proposed Va. Constitution. Ford ed., ii, 25. (June 1776.)

4389. LAND, Colonial conquest.—America was conquered, and her settlements made and firmly established at the expense of individuals, and not of the British public. Their own blood was spilt in acquiring lands for their settlement, their own fortunes expended in making that settlement effectual.—Rights of British America. i, 126. Ford ed., i, 430. (1774.)

4390. LAND, George III. and.—He has endeavored to prevent the population of these States; for that purpose * * * raising the conditions of new appropriations of lands.—Declaration of Independence as Drawn by Jefferson.

4391. LAND, People and.—It is too soon yet in our country to say that every man, who cannot find employment, but who can find uncultivated land, shall be at liberty to cultivate it, paying a moderate rent. But it is not too soon to provide, by every possible means, that as few as possible shall be without a little portion of land.—To Rev. James Madison. Ford ed., vii, 36. (Pa., 1785.)

4392. —— ——. The small landholders are the most precious part of a State.—To Rev. James Madison. Ford ed., vii, 36. (P., 1785.)

4393. LAND, Sovereignty.—That the lands within the limits assumed by a nation belong to the nation as a body, has probably been the law of every people on earth at some period of their history. A right of property in movable things is admitted before the establishment of government. A separate property in lands not till after that establishment. The right to movables is acknowledged by all the hordes of Indians surrounding us. Yet by no one of them has a separate property in lands been yielded to individuals. He who plants a field keeps possession till he has gathered the produce, after which one has as good a right as another to occupy it. Government must be established and laws provided, before lands can be separately appropriated, and their owner protected in his possession. Till then the property is in the body of the nation, and they, or their chief as trustee, must grant them to individuals, and determine the conditions of the grant. —Batture Case. viii, 539. (1812.)

4394. LAND, Valuation.—The Confederation, in its eighth article, decides that the quota of money to be contributed by the several States shall be proportioned to the value of landed property in the State. Experience has shown it impracticable to come at that value. —Answers to M. de Meunier. ix, 286. Ford ed., iv, 141. (P., 1786.)

4395. —— ——. It seems * * * to be a principle of universal law that the lands of a country belong to its sovereign as trustee for the nation.—Batture Case. viii, 541. (1812.)

4396. LAND COMPANIES, Early western.—During the regal government, two companies, called the Loyal and the Ohio Companies, had obtained grants from the crown for 800,000 or 1,000,000 of acres of land, each, on the Ohio, on condition of settling them in a given number of years. They surveyed some, and settled them; but the war of 1755 came on, and broke up the settlements. After it was

over, they petitioned for a renewal. Four other large companies then formed themselves, called the Mississippi, the Illinois, the Wabash, and the Indiana companies, each praying for immense quantities of land, some amounting to 200 miles square; so that they proposed to cover the whole country north between the Ohio and Mississippi, and a great portion of what is south. All these petitions were depending without any answer whatever from the crown, when the Revolution war broke out. The petitioners had associated to themselves some of the nobility of England, and most of the characters in America of great influence. When Congress assumed the government, they took some of their body in as partners, to obtain their influence; and I remember to have heard, at the time, that one of them took Mr. Gerard as a partner, expecting by that to obtain the influence of the French Court, to obtain grants of those lands which they had not been able to obtain from the British government. All these lands were within the limits of Virginia and that State determined, peremptorily that they never should be granted to large companies, but left open equally to all; and when they passed their land law (which I think was in 1778), they confirmed only so much of the lands of the Loyal company, as they had actually surveyed, which was a very small proportion, and annulled every other pretension. And when that State conveyed the lands to Congress (which was not till 1784), so determined were they to prevent their being granted to these or any other large companies, that they made it an express condition of the cession, that they should be applied first towards the soldiers' bounties, and the residue sold for the payment of the national debt, and for no other purpose. This disposition has been, accordingly, rigorously made, and is still going on; and Congress considers itself as having no authority to dispose of them otherwise.—To J. M. G. de Rayneval. iv, 371. Ford ed., viii, 19. (W., March 1801.)

4397. LAND TAX, Postponed.—The affluence of the Treasury has made it possible to go on a year longer without a land tax.—To John Taylor. Ford ed., vii, 181. (Pa., 1797.)

4398. —— ——. The land tax will not be brought on. The Secretary of the Treasury says he has money enough. No doubt * * * [this] may be taken up more boldly at the next session, when most of the elections will be over.—To James Madison. iv, 205. Ford ed., vii, 189. (Pa., 1798.)

4399. LAND TAX, Proposed.—They [the federalists] already talk * * * of a land Tax. [This] will probably not be opposed. The only question will be how to modify it. On this there may be great diversity of sentiment. One party will want to make it a new course of patronage and expense.—To James Madison. iv, 234. Ford ed., vii, 237. (Pa., 1798.)

4400. —— ——. If the expenses should exceed three millions they [the federalists] will undertake a land tax. Indeed a land tax is the decided resource of many, perhaps of a majority. There is an idea of some of the Connecticut members to raise the whole money wanted by a tax on salt; so much do they dread a land tax.—To James Madison. Ford ed., vii, 243. (1798.)

4401. —— ——. The land tax is now on the carpet to raise two millions of dollars; yet I think they must at least double it. * * * I presume, therefore, the tax on lands, houses and negroes, will be a dollar a head on the population of each State.—To JAMES MONROE. IV, 242. FORD ED., vii, 256. (Pa., May 1798.)

4402. —— ——. The land tax was yesterday [May 30] debated, and a majority of six struck out the 13th section of the classification of houses, and taxing them by a different scale from the lands. Instead of this, is to be proposed a valuation of the houses and lands together.—To JAMES MADISON. iv, 244. FORD ED., vii, 261. (Pa., May 1798.)

4403. LANDS (Indian), Acquirement of title to.—The State of Georgia, having granted to certain individuals a tract of country, within their chartered limits, whereof the Indian right has never yet been acquired; with a proviso in the grants, which implies that those individuals may take measures for extinguishing the Indian rights under the authority of that Government, it becomes a question how far this grant is good? A society, taking possession of a vacant country, and declaring they mean to occupy it, does thereby appropriate to themselves as prime occupants what was before common. A practice introduced since the discovery of America, authorizes them to go further, and to fix the limits which they assume to themselves; and it seems, for the common good, to admit this right to a moderate and reasonable extent. If the country, instead of being altogether vacant, is thinly occupied by another nation, the right of the native forms an exception to that of the newcomers; that is to say, these will only have a right against all other nations except the natives. Consequently, they have the exclusive privilege of acquiring the native right by purchase or other just means. This is called the right of preemption, and is become a principle of the law of nations, fundamental with respect to America. There are but two means of acquiring the native title. First, war; for even war may, sometimes, give a just title. Second, contracts or treaty. The States of America before their present Union possessed completely, each within its own limits, the exclusive right to use these two means of acquiring the native title, and, by their act of Union, they have as completely ceded both to the General Government. Art. 2d, Section 1st, " The President shall have power, by and with the advice and consent of the Senate, to make treaties, provided two-thirds of the Senators present concur ". Art. 1st, Section 8th, " The Congress shall have power to declare war, to raise and support armies ". Section 10th, " No State shall enter into any treaty, alliance, or confederation. No State shall, without the consent of Congress, keep troops or ships of war in time of peace, enter into any agreement or compact with another State or with a foreign power, or engage in war, unless actually invaded, or in such imminent danger as will not admit of delay ". These paragraphs of the Constitution, declaring that the General Government shall have, and that the particular ones shall not have, the right of war and treaty, are so explicit that no commentary can explain them further, nor can any explain them away. Consequently, Georgia, *possessing the exclusive right to acquire the native title*, but having relinquished the *means* of doing it to the General Government, can only have put her grantee into her own condition. She could convey to them the exclusive right to acquire; but she could not convey what she had not herself, that is, the means of acquiring. For these they must come to the General Government, in whose hands they have been wisely deposited for the

purposes both of peace and justice. What is to be done? The right of the General Government is, in my opinion, to be maintained. The case is sound, and the means of doing it as practicable as can ever occur. But respect and friendship should, I think, mark the conduct of the General towards the particular government, and explanations should be asked and time and color given them to tread back their steps before coercion is held up to their view. I am told there is already a strong party in Georgia opposed to the act of their government. I should think it better, then, that the first measures, while firm, be yet so temperate as to secure their alliance and aid to the General Government. Might not the eclat of a proclamation revolt their pride and passion, and throw them hastily into the opposite scale? It will be proper, indeed, to require from the government of Georgia, in the first moment, that while the General Government shall be expecting and considering her explanations, things shall remain in *statu quo*, and not a move be made towards carrying what they have begun into execution.—OPINION ON GEORGIA LAND GRANTS. vii, 467. FORD ED., v, 165. (May 1790.)

4404. —— ——. No lands shall be appropriated until purchased of the Indian native proprietors; nor shall any purchases be made of them but on behalf of the public, by authority of acts of the General Assembly, to be passed for every purchase specially.—PROPOSED VA. CONSTITUTION. FORD ED., ii, 25. (June 1776.)

4405. LANDS (Indian), Buying.—We, indeed, are always ready to buy land; but we will never ask but when you wish to sell; and our laws, in order to protect you against imposition, have forbidden individuals to purchase lands from you; and have rendered it necessary, when you desire to sell, even to a State, that an agent from the United States should attend the sale, see that your consent is freely given, a satisfactory price paid, and report to us what has been done, for your approbation.*—To BROTHER HANDSOME LAKE. viii, 188. (1802.)

4406. LANDS (Indian), Intrusions on. —Knowing your disposition to have these people [the Cherokee Indians] protected in the possession of their unpurchased lands, I take the liberty of mentioning to you that the old Tassel, in a late message to me, complains of intrusions on their lands, and particularly of some attempts to take from them the great island. This, by the late extension of our [Virginia] boundary, falling, as I understand, within your State [North Carolina], removes the application for protection to your Excellency, whose power alone can extend to the removal of intrusions from thence. As to so much of their lands as lie within our latitudes, as well as the lands of other Indians generally, our Assembly, now sitting, has in contemplation authorized the Executive to send patrols of the military through them from time to time to destroy the habitations which shall be erected in them by intruders.—To THE GOVERNOR OF NORTH CAROLINA. FORD ED., ii, 275. (Wg., 1779.)

4407. LANDS (Indian), Surrendering.— You have it peculiarly in your power to promote among the Indians a sense of the superior value of a little land, well cultivated, over a great deal unimproved, and to encourage

* The extent of territory to which the native Indian title was extinguished under Jefferson, by purchase, embraced nearly one hundred millions of acres.—EDITOR.

them to make this estimate truly. The wisdom of the animal which amputates and abandons to the hunter the parts for which he is pursued should be theirs, with this difference, that the former sacrifices what is useful, the latter what is not.—To BENJAMIN HAWKINS. iv, 467. FORD ED., viii, 214. (W., 1803.)

4408. LANDS (Indian), Virginia and.—
That the lands of this colony [Virginia] were taken from the Indians by conquest, is not so general a truth as is supposed. I find in our histories and records, repeated proofs of purchase, which cover a considerable part of the lower country; and many more would doubtless be found on further search. The upper country, we know, has been acquired altogether by purchases made in the most unexceptionable form.—NOTES ON VIRGINIA. viii, 339. FORD ED., iii, 196. (1782.)

4409. LANDS (Public), Disposition of.—
The new plan of opening our land office, by dividing the lands among the States, and selling them at vendue, * * * separates still more the interests of the States, which ought to be made joint in every possible instance, in order to cultivate the idea of our being one nation, and to multiply the instances in which the people shall look to Congress as their head. And when the States get their portions, they will either fool them away, or make a job of it to serve individuals. Proofs of both these practices have been furnished, and by either of them that invaluable fund is lost, which ought to pay our public debt. To sell them at vendue, is to give them to the bidders of the day, be they many or few. It is ripping up the hen which lays golden eggs. If sold in lots at a fixed price, as first proposed, the best lots will be sold first; as these become occupied, it gives a value to the interjacent ones, and raises them, though of inferior quality, to the price of the first.—To JAMES MONROE. i, 347. FORD ED., iv, 52. (P., 1785.)

4410. LANDS (Public), Monopolies in.—
Vast grants of land are entirely against the policy of our government. They have ever set their faces most decidedly against such monopolies.—To T. M. RANDOLPH. FORD ED., x, 202. (M., 1821.)

— LANDS (Public), Plan of land office.
—See WESTERN TERRITORY.

4411. LANDS (Public), Sale.—I am against selling the lands at all. The people who will migrate to the westward, whether they form part of the old or of a new colony, will be subject to their proportion of the Continental debt then unpaid. They ought not to be subject to more. They will be a people little able to pay taxes. There is no equity in fixing upon them the whole burthen of this war, or any other proportion than we bear ourselves. By selling the lands to them, you will disgust them, and cause an avulsion of them from the common union. They will settle the lands in spite of everybody.—To ——. FORD ED., ii, 80. (Pa., 1776.)

4412. —— ——. The idea of Congress selling out unlocated lands has been sometimes dropped, but we have always met the hint with such determined opposition that I believe it will never be proposed.—To ——. FORD ED., ii, 80. (Pa., 1776.)

4413. —— ——. Congress have * * * passed an ordinance for disposing of their lands and, I think, a very judicious one. They pro-

pose to sell them at auction for not less than a dollar an acre, receiving their own certificates of debt as money.—To WILLIAM CARMICHAEL. i, 393. (P., 1785.)

4414. —— ——. I am much pleased with your land ordinance, and think it improved from the first, in the most important circumstances. I had mistaken the object of the division of the lands among the States. I am sanguine in my expectations of lessening our debts by this fund, and have expressed my expectations to the minister and others here.—To JAMES MONROE. i, 407. FORD ED., iv, 86. (P., 1785.)

4415. —— ——. Congress have purchased a very considerable extent of country from the Indians, and have passed an ordinance laying down rules for disposing of it. These admit only two considerations for granting lands: first, military service rendered during the late war; and secondly, money to be paid at the time of granting, for the purpose of discharging their national debt.—To MARQUIS DE PONCENS. i, 430. (P., 1785.)

4416. —— ——. A provision for the sale of the vacant lands of the United States is particularly urged by the important considerations that they are pledged as a fund for reimbursing the public debt; that, if timely and judiciously applied, they may save the necessity of burthening our citizens with new taxes for the extinguishment of the principal; and that being free to pay annually but a limited proportion of that principal, time lost in beginning the payments cannot be recovered however productive the resource may prove in event.—PARAGRAPH FOR PRESIDENT'S MESSAGE. FORD ED., v, 384. (1791.)

4417. LANDS (Public), Settlers.—It is said that wealthy foreigners will come in great numbers, and they ought to pay for the liberty we shall have provided for them. True, but make them pay in settlers. A foreigner who brings a settler for every one hundred or two hundred acres of land, to be granted him, pays a better price than if he had put into the public treasury five shillings, or five pounds. That settler will be worth to the public twenty times as much every year, as on our old plan he would have paid in one payment.—To ——. FORD ED., ii, 80. (Pa., 1776.)

4418. —— ——. I am clear that the lands should be appropriated in small quantities.—To ——. FORD ED., ii, 80. (Pa., 1776.)

4419. —— ——. I sincerely wish that your proposition to "purchase a tract of land in the Illinois on favorable terms, for introducing a colony of English farmers", may encounter no difficulties from the established rules of our land department. The general law prescribes an open sale, where all citizens may compete on an equal footing for any lot of land which attracts their choice. To dispense with this in any particular case, requires a special law of Congress, and to special legislation we are generally averse, lest a principle of favoritism should creep in and pervert that of equal rights. It has, however, been done on some occasions where a special national advantage has been expected to overweigh that of adherence to the general rule. The promised introduction of the culture of the vine procured a special law in favor of the Swiss settlement on the Ohio. That of the culture of oil, wine and other southern productions, did the same lately for the French settlement on the Tombigbee. It remains to be tried whether that of an improved system of farming, interesting to so great a proportion of our citizens, may not also be thought worth a dispensation with the general rule.—To GEORGE FLOWER. vii, 83. (P.F., 1817.)

4420. LANDS (Public), Squatting.—The Virginia Assembly finding that, in defiance of their endeavors to discourage and prevent the settling our western country, people were removing thither in great numbers, appropriating lands of their own authority, and meditating to hold them by force, after propositions, made and rejected at several sessions for legalizing those settlements, at length found it necessary to give way to the torrent, and by their act of May, 1779, to establish a land office. The irregular claims and settlements which, in the meantime, had covered that country, were become so extensive that no prudent man could venture to locate a new claim, and so numerous that, in the common administration of justice, it would have engrossed the whole time of our ordinary courts for many years to have adjusted them. So multifarious were they, at the same time, that no established principles of law or equity could be applied for their determination; many of them being built on customs and habits which had grown up in that country, being founded on modes of transmission peculiar to themselves, and which, having entered almost into every title, could not be absolutely neglected. This impressed on the minds of the Assembly the necessity of sending special commissioners to settle, on the spot, and without delay, those various claims, which being once cleared away would leave the residuary country open to the acquisition of other adventurers. The western Counties were accordingly laid off into Districts for this purpose, and the arrangement being general, included the territory on the waters of the Ohio claimed by the State of Pennsylvania. Whether the Assembly did not advert to this circumstance, or took for granted that the commissioners would never consider a law of this State as meant to be applied to those who professed themselves the citizens of another, and had been freely admitted so to profess themselves by our Government, or whether they relied that the term of one year, within which they provided that no grant should issue on any judgment of the commissioners, would give them time for the settlement of our disputed territory, or at least to provide for the peace of their citizens within it, is not within my province or power to say. This, however, I can say, that from an intimate knowledge of their cordial desire to settle this claim with them amicably, no motive inconsistent with that entered into the transaction. In fact the execution of this commission, guarded as its effects are by a twelve months' delay of the grants, appears to be as peaceable and inoffensive as the mission of so many astronomers to take the longitude or latitude of the several farms. —To THE PRESIDENT OF CONGRESS. FORD ED., ii, 293. (Wg., 1780.)

4421. ——— ———. There is indeed a clause in the act of Assembly which might, on first view, be thought to leave an opening for the introduction of force. It is that which says that judgment be rendered, if possession be *forcibly detained* by the party against whom it is, restitution may be made by the commissioners, or by any justice, in like manner as might be done in the case of lands holden by grant actually issued; a clause very necessary in our other western country, but not at all applicable to that part of it claimed by the State of Pennsylvania. By the laws of this Commonwealth

(the same in this instance with the English Law), even in the case of lands holden under actual grant, no restitution can be made after three years peaceable possession, a term much shorter than that of any *bona fide* possessions in the disputed territory. The latest of these must be of six or seven years' continuance, the present dispute having so long subsisted. The expediency and necessity, therefore, of the general measure of establishing this temporary Court, I doubt not but Congress will perceive and though it is to be wished that the disputed territory had been excerpted from this jurisdiction, in order to avoid everything which might give jealousy or uneasiness to a sister State, or which might lead them into an apprehension that we meant to do any act which should wound the amity between us; yet I hope when Congress contemplates its effects, they will be sensible that it only amounts to a settlement on paper of the rights of individuals derived from this State, and that no man's possession or quiet can be disturbed in consequence of any proceedings under it, until our Legislature * * * shall have had time to settle finally with them this unfortunate dispute, or otherwise to provide against the evils they have apprehended.—To THE PRESIDENT OF CONGRESS. FORD ED., ii, 294. (Wg., 1780.) See EARTH, GENERATIONS, WESTERN TERRITORY.

4422. LANGDON (John), Patriot.—We were fellow laborers from the beginning of the first to the accomplishment of the second revolution in our government, of the same zeal and the same sentiments, and I shall honor his memory while memory remains to me.—To MARK LANGDON HILL. vii, 154. (M., 1820.)

4423. LANGUAGE, Distorting.—When we see inspired writings made to speak whatever opposite controversialists wish them to say, we cannot ourselves expect to find language incapable of similar distortion. My expressions were general; their perversion is in their misapplication to a particular case.—To C. HAMMOND. vii, 216. (M., 1821.)

— LANGUAGE, Neology.—See NEOLOGY.

— LANGUAGE (English), Improvement of.—See NEOLOGY.

4424. LANGUAGE, Purists and.—I concur entirely with you in opposition to purists, who would destroy all strength and beauty of style, by subjecting it to a rigorous compliance with their rules. Fill up all the ellipses and syllepses of Tacitus, Sallust, Livy, &c., and the elegance and force of their sententious brevity are extinguished. "Auferre, trucidare, rapere, falsis nominibus, imperium appellant". "Deorum injurias, diis curæ". "Alieni appetens, sui profusus; ardens in cupiditatibus: satis loquentiæ, sapientiæ parum". "Annibal, peto pacem". "Per diem Sol non *uret* te, neque Luna per noctem". Wire-draw these expressions by filling up the whole syntax and sense, and they become dull paraphrases on rich sentiments. We may say then truly with Quintilian, "Aliud est Grammaticé, aliud Latiné loqui". I am no friend, therefore, to what is called purism.—To JOHN WALDO. vi, 184. (M., 1813.)

4425. ——— ———. I am not a friend to a scrupulous purism of style. I readily sacrifice the niceties of syntax to euphony and strength. It is by boldly neglecting the rigorisms of grammar that Tacitus has made himself the strongest writer in the world. The hyperesthetics call him barbarous; but I should be sorry to exchange his barbarisms for their wire-drawn purisms. Some of his sentences are as strong as language can make them. Had he scrupulously filled up the whole of their syntax, they would have been merely common. To explain my meaning by an English example, I will quote the motto of one, I believe, of the regicides of Charles I., " Rebellion *to* tyrants is obedience to God". Correct its syntax, " Rebellion *against* tyrants is obedience to God ", it has lost all the strength and beauty of the antithesis.—To EDWARD EVERETT. vii, 273. (M., 1823.)

4426. LANGUAGE, Science and.—I do not pretend that language is science. It is only an instrument for the attainment of science.—NOTES ON VIRGINIA. viii, 389. FORD ED., iii, 253. (1782.)

4427. LANGUAGE, Style.—Style, in writing or speaking, is formed very early in life, while the imagination is warm, and impressions are permanent.—To J. BANNISTER. i, 468. (P., 1785.)

4428. LANGUAGE (Anglo-Saxon), Study of.—I learn from you with great pleasure that a taste is reviving in England for the recovery of the Anglo-Saxon dialect of our language; for a mere dialect it is, as much as those of Piers Plowman, Gower, Douglas, Chaucer, Spenser, Shakspeare, Milton, for even much of Milton is already antiquated. The Anglo-Saxon is only the earliest we possess of the many shades of mutation by which the language has tapered down to its modern form. Vocabularies we need for each of these stages from Somner to Bailey, but not grammars for each or any of them. The grammar has changed so little, in the descent from the earliest to the present form, that a little observation suffices to understand its variations. We are greatly indebted to the worthies who have preserved the Anglo-Saxon form, from Dr. Hickes down to Mr. Bosworth. Had they not given to the public what we possess through the press, that dialect would by this time have been irrecoverably lost. I think it, however, a misfortune that they have endeavored to give it too much of a learned form, to mount it on all the scaffolding of the Greek and Latin, to load it with their genders, numbers, cases, declensions, conjugations, &c. Strip it of these embarrassments, vest it in the Roman type which we have adopted instead of our English black letter, reform its uncouth orthography, and assimilate its pronunciation, as much as may be, to the present English, just as we do in reading Piers Plowman or Chaucer, and with the contemporary vocabulary for the few lost words, we understand it as we do them. For example, the Anglo-Saxon text of the Lord's Prayer, as given to us 6th Matthew, ix., is spelt and written thus, in the equivalent Roman type: Faeder ure thee the eart in heafenum, si thin nama ychalgod. To becume thin rice. Gerrurthe thin willa on eartham, swa swa on heafenum. Ume doeghw amti can hlaf syle us to dœg. And forgyfus ure gyltas, swa swa we forgifath urum gyltendum. And ne ge-lœdde thu us on costmunge, ae alys us of yfele." I should spell and pronounce thus: " Father our, thou tha art in heavenum, si thine name y-hallowed. Come thin ric-y-wurth thine will on eartham, so so on heavenum. ourn daynhamlican loaf sell us to-day, and forgive us our guilts so so we forgiveth ourum guiltendum. And no y-lead thou us on costnunge, ac a-lease us of evil ". And here, it is to observed by-the-bye, that there is but the single word "temptation" in our present version of this prayer that is not Anglo-

Saxon; for the word " trespasses " taken from the French (οφειλημαια in the original), might as well have been translated by the Anglo-Saxon " guilts ".

The learned apparatus in which Dr. Hickes and his successors have muffled our Anglo-Saxon, is what has frightened us from encountering it. The simplification I propose may, on the contrary, make it a regular part of our common English education. So little reading and writing was there among our Anglo-Saxon ancestors of that day, that they had no fixed orthography. To produce a given sound, every one jumbled the letters together, according to his unlettered notion of their power, and all jumbled them differently, just as would be done at this day, were a dozen peasants, who have learnt the alphabet, but have never read, desired to write the Lord's Prayer. Hence the varied modes of spelling by which the Anglo-Saxons meant to express the same sound. The word *many*, for example, was spelt in twenty different ways; yet we cannot suppose they were twenty different words, or that they had twenty different ways of pronouncing the same word. The Anglo-Saxon orthography, then, is not an exact representation of the sounds meant to be conveyed. We must drop in pronunciation the superfluous consonants, and give to the remaining letters their present English sound; because, not knowing the true one, the present enunciation is as likely to be right as any other, and indeed more so, and facilitates the acquisition of the language.*—To J. EVELYN DENISON. vii, 415. (M., 1825.)

4429. ——— ———. [The cultivation of the Anglo-Saxon] is a hobby which too often runs away with me where I meant not to give up the rein. Our youth seem disposed to mount it with me, and to begin their course where mine is ending.—To J. EVELYN DENISON. vii, 418. (M., 1825.)

4430. ——— ———. In a letter * * * to Mr. Crofts who sent * * * me a copy of his treatise on the English and German languages, as preliminary to an etymological dictionary he meditated, I went into explanations with him of an easy process for simplifying the study of the Anglo-Saxon, and lessening the terrors and difficulties presented by its rude alphabet, and unformed orthography.—To JOHN ADAMS. vii, 173. (M., 1820.)

4431. LANGUAGE (English), Dialects.—It is much to be wished that the publication of the present county dialects of England should go on. It will restore to us our language in all its shades of variation. It will incorporate into the present one all the riches of our ancient dialects; and what a store this will be, may be seen by running the eye over the county glossaries, and observing the words we have lost by abandonment and disuse, which in sound and sense are inferior to nothing we have retained. When these local vocabularies are published and digested together into a single one, it is probable we shall find that there is not a word in Shakspeare which is not now in use in some of the counties in England, and from whence we may obtain its true sense. And what an exchange will their recovery be for the volumes of idle commentaries and conjectures with which that divine poet has been masked and metamorphosed. We shall find in him new sublimities which we had never tasted before, and find beauties in our

---

* Jefferson, first of all in America, suggested that the study of Anglo-Saxon be made a part of college education.—EDITOR.

ancient poets which are lost to us now. It is not that I am merely an enthusiast for Palæology. I set equal value on the beautiful engraftments we have borrowed from Greece and Rome, and I am equally a friend to the encouragement of a judicious neology; a language cannot be too rich.—To J. EVELYN DENISON. vii, 417. (M., 1825.)

4432. LANGUAGE (English), History of.—We want an elaborate history of the English language.—To J. EVELYN DENISON. vii, 418. (M., 1825.)

4433. LANGUAGE (French), Indispensable.—The French language is an indispensable part of education for both sexes.—To N. Burwell, vii, 102. FORD ED., x, 105. (M., 1818.)

4434. LANGUAGE (French), Learning.—You will learn to speak it [French] better from women and children in three months, than from men in a year.—To T. M. RANDOLPH, JR. ii, 176. FORD ED., iv, 404. (P., 1787.)

— LANGUAGE (Gælic), Desire to learn. —See OSSIAN.

4435. LANGUAGE (Greek), Ablative case in.—I owe you particular thanks for the copy of your translation of Buttman's Greek Grammar. * * * A cursory view of it promises me a rich mine of valuable criticism. I observe he goes with the herd of grammarians in denying an Ablative case to the Greek language. I cannot concur with him in that, but think with the Messrs. of Port Royal who admit an Ablative. And why exclude it? Is it because the Dative and Ablative in Greek are always of the same form? Then there is no Ablative to the Latin plurals, because in them, as in Greek, these cases are always in the same form. The Greeks recognized the Ablative under the appellation of the πτωσις αφαιρετιχη, which I have met with and noted from some of the scholiasts, without recollecting where. Stephens, Scapula, Hederic acknowledge it as one of the significations of the word αφαιρεμαυκος. That the Greeks used it can not be denied. For one of multiplied examples which may be produced take the following from the Hippolytus of Euripides: " ειπε τω τροπω, δικης Επαισεν αυτου ροπτρου," " dice quo modo justitiæ clava percussit eum " " Quo modo " are Ablatives, then why not τω τροπω? And translating it into English, should we use the Dative* or Ablative preposition? It is not perhaps easy to define very critically what constitutes a case in the declension of nouns. All agree as to the Nominative that it is simply the name of the thing. If we admit that a distinct case is constituted by any accident or modification which changes the relation which that bears to the actors or action of the sentence, we must agree to the six cases at least; because for example, to a thing, and from a thing are very different accidents to the thing. It may be said that if every distinct accident or change of relation constitutes a different case, then there are in every language as many cases as there are prepositions; for this is the peculiar office of the preposition. But because we do not designate by special names all the cases to which a noun is liable, is that a reason why we should throw away half of those we have, as is

* See BUTTMAN'S DATIVES, p. 230, every one of which I should consider as under the accident or relation called Ablative, having no signification of *approach* according to his definition of the Dative.—NOTE BY JEFFERSON.

done by those grammarians who reject all cases, but the Nominative, Genitive, and Accusative, and in a less degree by those also who reject the Ablative alone? As pushing the discrimination of all the possible cases to extremities leads us to nothing useful or practicable, I am contented with the old six cases, familiar to every cultivated language, ancient and modern, and well understood by all. I acknowledge myself at the same time not an adept in the metaphysical speculations of Grammar. By analyzing too minutely we often reduce our subject to atoms, of which the mind loses its hold.—To EDWARD EVERETT. vii, 272. (M., 1823.)

4436. LANGUAGE (Greek), Accent.—Against reading Greek by accent, instead of quantity, as Mr. Ciceitira, proposes, I raise both my hands. What becomes of the sublime measure of Homer, the full sounding rhythm of Demosthenes, if, abandoning quantity, you chop it up by accent? What ear can hesitate in its choice between the two following rhythms? "Τὸν, δ'απαμειβόμενος προσεφὴ πόδας ωκὺς Αχίλλευς,

and

Τον δ'απμειβομενός προςεφὴ ποδας ώχυς Αχίλλευς."

the latter noted according to prosody, the former by accent, and dislocating our teeth in its utterance; every syllable of it, except the first and last, being pronounced against quantity. And what becomes of the art of prosody? Is that perfect coincidence of its rules with the structure of their verse, merely accidental? or was it of design, and yet for no use?—To JOHN ADAMS. vii, 114. (M., 1819.)

4437. ———. Of the origin of accentuation, I have never seen satisfactory proofs. But I have generally supposed the accents were intended to direct the inflections and modulations of the voice; but not to affect the quantity of the syllables.—To JOHN ADAMS. vii, 115. (M., 1819.)

4438. LANGUAGE (Greek), Pronunciation.—Mr. Pickering's pamphlet on the pronunciation of the Greek, for which I am indebted to you, I have read with great pleasure. Early in life, the idea occurred to me that the people now inhabiting the ancient seats of the Greeks and Romans, although their languages in the intermediate ages had suffered great changes, and especially in the declension of their nouns, and in the terminations of their words generally, yet having preserved the body of the word radically the same, so they would preserve more of its pronunciation. That, at least, it was probable that a pronunciation, handed down by tradition, would retain, as the words themselves do, more of the original than that of any other people whose language has no affinity to that original. For this reason I learned, and have used the Italian pronunciation of the Latin. But that of the modern Greeks I had no opportunity of learning until I went to Paris. There I became acquainted with two learned Greeks, Count Carberri, and Mr. Paradise, and with a lady, a native Greek, the daughter of Baron de Tott, who did not understand the ancient language. Carberri and Paradise both spoke it. From these instructors I learned the modern pronunciation, and in *general* trusted to its orthodoxy. I say, in *general*, because sound being more fugitive than the written letter, we must, after such a lapse of time, presume in it some degeneracies, as we see there are in the written words. We may not, indeed, be able to put our finger on them confidently, yet neither are they entirely beyond the reach of all indication. For example, in a language so remarkable for the euphony of its sounds, if that euphony is preserved in particular combinations of its letters, by an adherence to the powers ordinarily ascribed to them, and is destroyed by a change of these powers, and the sound of the word, thereby, rendered harsh, inharmonious, and inidiomatical, here we may presume some degeneracy has taken place.

While, therefore, I gave in to the modern pronunciation generally, I have presumed, as an instance of degeneracy, their ascribing the same sound to the six letters, or combinations of letters, ε, ι, υ, $\varepsilon\iota$, $o\iota$, $\upsilon\iota$, to all of which they give the sound of our double e in the word *meet*. This useless equivalence of three vowels and three diphthongs did not probably exist among the ancient Greeks; and the less probably as, while this single sound, *ee*, is overcharged by so many different representative characters, the sounds we usually give to these characters and combinations would be left without any representative signs. This would imply either that they had not these sounds in their language, or no signs for their expression. Probability appears to me, therefore, against the practice of the modern Greeks of giving the same sound to all these different representatives, and to be in favor of that of foreign nations, who, adopting the Roman characters, have assimilated to them, in a considerable degree, the powers of the corresponding Greek letters. I' have, accordingly, excepted this in my adoption of the modern pronunciation.

I have been more doubtful in the use of the $\alpha\upsilon$, $\varepsilon\upsilon$, $\eta\upsilon$, $\omega\upsilon$, sounding the υ, upsilon, as our f or v, because I find traces of that power of υ, or of υ, in some modern languages. To go no further than our own, we have it in *laugh*, *cough*, *trough*, *enough*. The county of Louisa, adjacent to that in which I live, was, when I was a boy, universally pronounced Lovisa. That it is not the gh which gives the sound of f or v, in these words, is proved by the orthography of *plough*, *trough*, *thought*, *fraught*, *caught*. The modern Greeks themselves, too, giving up υ, upsilon, in orainary, the sound of our *ee*, strengthens the presumption that its anomalous sound of f or v, is a corruption. The same may be inferred from the cacophony of $\varepsilon\lambda\alpha\varphi\nu\varepsilon$ (elavne) for $\varepsilon\lambda\alpha\upsilon\nu\varepsilon$ (elawne.) $A\chi\iota\lambda\lambda\varepsilon\varphi\varsigma$ (Achillefs) for $A\chi\iota\lambda\lambda\varepsilon\upsilon\varsigma$ (Achilleise,) $\varepsilon\varphi\varsigma$ (eves) for $\varepsilon\ddot{\upsilon}\varsigma$ (ee-use,) $o\varphi\kappa$ (ovk) for 8κ (ouk,) $\omega\varphi\iota o\varsigma$ (ovetos) for $\omega\ddot{\upsilon}\tau o\varsigma$ (o-u-tos,) $Z\varepsilon\varphi\varsigma$ (zevs) for $Z\varepsilon\upsilon\varsigma$ (zese,) of which all nations have made their Jupiter; and the uselessness of the υ in $\varepsilon\upsilon\varphi\omega\nu\iota\alpha$, which would otherwise have been spelt $\varepsilon\varphi\omega\nu\iota\alpha$. I, therefore, excepted this also from what I consider as approvable pronunciation.—To JOHN ADAMS. vii, 112. (M., 1819.)

4439. ——— ———. Should Mr. Pickering ultimately establish the modern pronunciation of the letters without any exception, I shall think it a great step gained, and giving up my exceptions, shall willingly rally to him.—To JOHN ADAMS. vii, 115. (M., 1819.)

4440. ——— ———. If we adhere to the Erasmian pronunciation we must go to Italy for it, as we must do for the most probably correct pronunciation of the language of the Romans, because rejecting the modern, we must argue that the ancient pronunciation was prob-

ably brought from Greece, with the language itself; and, as Italy was the country to which it was brought, and from which it emanated to other nations, we must presume it better preserved there than with the nations copying from them, who would be apt to affect its pronunciation with some of their own national peculiarities. And in fact, we find that no two nations pronounce it alike, although all pretend to the Erasmian pronunciation. But the whole subject is conjectural, and allows, therefore, full and lawful scope to the vagaries of the human mind. I am glad, however, to see the question stirred here; because it may excite among our young countrymen a spirit of enquiry and criticism, and lead them to more attention to this most beautiful of all languages.—To MR. MOORE. vii, 137. (M., 1819.)

4441. ——— ———. I have little hope of the recovery of the ancient pronunciation of that finest of human languages, but still I rejoice at the attention the subject seems to excite with you, because it is an evidence that our country begins to have a taste for something more than merely as much Greek as will pass a candidate for clerical ordination.—To JOHN BRAZIER. vii, 131. (P.F., 1819.)

4442. LANGUAGE (Greek), Revival of. —The modern Greek is not yet so far departed from its ancient model, but that we might still hope to see the language of Homer and Demosthenes flow with purity from the lips of a free and ingenious people.—To JOHN PAGE. i, 400. (P., 1785.)

4443. ——— ———. I cannot help looking forward * * * to the language of Homer becoming again a living language, as among possible events.—To GEORGE WYTHE. ii, 267. FORD ED., iv, 444. (P., 1787.)

4444. ——— ———. I enjoy Homer in his own language infinitely beyond Pope's translation of him, and both beyond the dull narrative of the same events by Dares Phrygius; and it is an innocent enjoyment.*—To JOSEPH PRIESTLEY. iv, 317. FORD ED., vii, 414. (Pa., 1800.) See LANGUAGE (LATIN).

4445. LANGUAGE (Italian), French, Spanish and.—I fear the learning of Italian will confound your French and Spanish. Being all of them degenerated dialects of the Latin, they are apt to mix in conversation. I have never seen a person speaking the three languages, who did not mix them. It is a delightful language, but late events having rendered the Spanish more useful, lay it aside to prosecute that.—To PETER CARR. ii, 237. FORD ED., iv, 428. (P., 1787.)

4446. ——— ———. To a person who would make a point of reading and speaking French and Spanish, I should doubt the utility of learning Italian. These three languages, being all degeneracies from the Latin, resemble one another so much, that I doubt the probability of keeping in the head a distinct knowledge of them all. I suppose that he who learns them all, will speak a compound of the three, and neither perfectly.—To T. M. RANDOLPH, JR. ii, 177. FORD ED., iv, 405. (P., 1787.)

4447. LANGUAGE (Latin), A luxury. —To read the Latin and Greek authors in their original, is a sublime luxury; and I deem luxury in science to be at least as justifiable

* Jefferson scarcely passed a day without reading a portion of the classics.—RAYNER'S *Life of Jefferson* p. 22.

as in architecture, painting, gardening, or the other arts.—To JOSEPH PRIESTLEY. iv, 316. FORD ED., vii, 414. (Pa., 1800.)

4448. ―― ――. I thank on my knees, him who directed my early education, for having put into my possession this rich source of delight; and I would not exchange it for anything which I could then have acquired, and have not since acquired.—To JOSEPH PRIESTLEY. iv, 317. FORD ED., vii, 414. (Pa., 1800.)

4449. LANGUAGE (Latin), Models of composition.—I think the Greeks and Romans have left us the present [purest?] models which exist of fine composition, whether we examine them as works of reason, or of style and fancy; and to them we probably owe these characteristics of modern composition. I know of no composition of any other ancient people, which merits the least regard as a model for its matter or style.—To JOSEPH PRIESTLEY. iv, 316. FORD ED., vii, 414. (Pa., 1800.)

4450. ―― ――. The utilities we derive from the remains of the Greek and Latin languages are, first as models of pure taste in writing. To these we are certainly indebted for the natural and chaste style of modern composition, which so much distinguishes the nations to whom these languages are familiar. Without these models we should probably have continued the inflated style of our northern ancestors, or the hyperbolical and vague one of the East.— To JOHN BRAZIER. vii, 131. (1819.)

4451. LANGUAGE (Latin), Reading.— We [University of Virginia] must get rid of this Connecticut Latin, of this barbarous confusion of long and short syllables, which renders doubtful whether we are listening to a reader of Cherokee, Shawnee, Iroquois, or what.—To WM. B. GILES. vii, 429. FORD ED., x, 357. (M., 1825.)

4452. LANGUAGE (Latin), Study of.— The learning of Greek and Latin, I am told, is going into disuse in Europe. I know not what their manners and occupations may call for; but it would be very ill-judged in us to follow their example in this instance.—NOTES ON VIRGINIA. viii, 389. FORD ED., iii, 253. (1782.)

4453. LANGUAGE (Latin), Utility of. —To whom are they [the classical languages] useful? Certainly not to all men. There are conditions of life to which they must be forever estranged. * * * To the moralist they are valuable, because they furnish ethical writings highly and justly esteemed; although in my own opinion the moderns are far advanced beyond them in this line of science; the divine finds in the Greek language a translation of his primary code, of more importance to him than the original because better understood; and, in the same language, the newer code, with the doctrines of the earliest fathers. * * * The lawyer finds in the Latin language the system of civil law most conformable with the principles of justice of any which has ever yet been established among men, and from which much has been incorporated into our own. The physician as good a code of his art as has been given us to this day. * * * The statesman will find in these languages history, politics, mathematics, ethics, eloquence, love of country, to which he must add the sciences of his own day, for which of them should be unknown to him? And all the sciences must recur to the classical languages for the etymon, and sound understanding of their fundamental terms.

* * * To sum the whole, it may truly be said that the classical languages are a solid basis for most, and an ornament to all the sciences.—To JOHN BRAZIER. vii, 131. (P.F., 1819.)

4454. LANGUAGE (Spanish), Important to know.—Our future connection with Spain renders that the most necessary of the modern languages, after the French. When you become a public man, you may have occasion for it, and the circumstance of your possessing that language, may give you a preference over other candidates.*—To PETER CARR. i, 399. (P., 1785.)

4455. ―― ――. Bestow great attention on the Spanish language, and endeavor to acquire an accurate knowledge of it. Our future connections with Spain and Spanish America, will render that language a valuable acquisition. The ancient history of a great part of America, too, is written in that language.—To PETER CARR. ii, 238. FORD ED., iv, 428. (P., 1787.)

4456. ―― ――. Next to French, the Spanish [language] is most important to an American. Our connection with Spain is already important, and will become daily more so. Besides this, the ancient part of American history is written chiefly in Spanish.—To T. M. RANDOLPH, JR. ii, 177. FORD ED., iv, 405. (P., 1787.)

4457. ―― ――. Apply yourself to the study of the Spanish language with all the assiduity you can. It and the English covering nearly the whole face of America, they should be well known to every inhabitant, who means to look beyond the limits of his farm.—To PETER CARR. ii, 409. (P., 1788.)

4458. LANGUAGES, Filiation of.—I have long considered the filiation of languages as the best proof we can ever obtain of the filiation of nations.—To JOHN S. VATER. v, 599. (M., 1812.)

4459. LANGUAGES, Learning.—In general, I am of opinion, that till the age of about sixteen, we are best employed on languages; Latin, Greek, French, and Spanish. * * * I think Greek the least useful.—To J. W. EPPES. ii, 192. (P., 1787.)

4460. ―― ――. I suppose there is a portion of life during which our faculties are ripe enough for [learning languages], and for nothing more useful.—To JOSEPH PRIESTLEY. iv, 316. FORD ED., vii, 413. (Pa., 1800.)

4461. LANGUAGES, Perfect Knowledge of.—No instance exists of a person's writing two languages perfectly. That will always appear to be his native language, which was most familiar to him in his youth.—To J. BANNISTER. i, 468. (P., 1785.)

4462. ―― ――. I am of opinion that there never was an instance of a man's writing or speaking his native tongue with elegance, who passed from fifteen to twenty years of age out of the country where it was spoken.—To J. BANNISTER i, 468. (P., 1785.)

4463. ―― ――. Did you ever know an instance of one who could write in a foreign language with the elegance of a native? Cicero wrote Commentaries of his own Consulship in Greek; they perished unknown, while his native

* Peter Carr was Jefferson's nephew.—EDITOR.

compositions have immortalized him with themselves.—To Dupont de Nemours. vi, 509. (M., 1815.)

4464. LANGUAGES, Utility.—I omitted to say anything of the languages as part of our proposed [Virginia] University. It was not that I think, as some do, that they are useless. I am of a very different opinion. I do not think them very essential to the obtaining eminent degrees of science; but I think them very useful towards it.—To Joseph Priestly. iv, 316. Ford ed., vii, 413. (Pa., 1800.)

4465. LANGUAGES (Indian), Cherokee. —Your Cherokee grammar * * * I have gone over with attention and satisfaction. We generally learn languages for the benefit of reading the books written in them. But here our reward must be the addition made to the philosophy of language. In this point of view your analysis of the Cherokee adds valuable matter for reflection and strengthens our desire to see more of these languages as scientifically elucidated. Their grammatical devices for the modification of their words by a syllable prefixed to, or inserted in the middle, or added to its end, and by other combinations so different from ours, prove that if man came from one stock, his languages did not. A late grammarian has said that all words were originally monosyllables. The Indian languages disprove this. I should conjecture that the Cherokees, for example, have formed their language not by single words, but by phrases. I have known some children learn to speak, not by a word at a time, but by whole phrases. Thus the Cherokee has no name for "father" in the abstract, but only as combined with some one of his relations. A complex idea being a fasciculus of simple ideas bundled together, it is rare that different languages make up their bundles alike, and hence the difficulty of translating from one language to another. European nations have so long had intercourse with one another, as to have approximated their complex expressions much towards one another. But I believe we shall find it impossible to translate our language into any of the Indian, or any of theirs into ours. I hope you will pursue your undertaking, and that others will follow your example with other of their languages. It will open a wide field for reflection on the grammatical organization of languages, their structure and character. I am persuaded that among the tribes on our two continents a great number of languages, radically different, will be found. It will be curious to consider how so many, so radically different, have been preserved by such small tribes in coterminous settlements of moderate extent. I had once collected about thirty vocabularies formed of the same English words, expressive of such simple objects only as must be present and familiar to every one under these circumstances. They were unfortunately lost. But I remember that on a trial to arrange them into families or dialects, I found in one instance that about half a dozen might be so classed, in another perhaps three or four. But I am sure that a third, at least, if not more, were perfectly insulated from each other. Yet this is the only index by which we can trace their filiation.—To —— ——. vii, 399. (M., 1825.)

4466. LANGUAGES (Indian), Vocabularies of.—I had through the course of my life availed myself of every opportunity of procuring vocabularies of the languages of every [Indian] tribe which either myself or my friends could have access to. They amounted

to about forty, more or less perfect. But in their passage from Washington to Monticello the trunk in which they were was stolen and plundered, and some fragments only of the vocabularies were recovered. Still, however, they were such as would be worth incorporation with a larger work, and shall be at the service of the historical committee, if they can make any use of them.—To Mr. Duponceau. vii, 92. (M., 1817.) See Aborigines and Indians.

4467. LATITUDE AND LONGITUDE, Astronomy and.—Measures and rhombs taken on the special surface of the earth, cannot be represented on a plain surface of paper without astronomical corrections; and paradoxical as it may seem, it is nevertheless true, that we cannot know the relative position of two places on the earth, but by interrogating the sun, moon and stars.—To Governor Nicholas. vi, 587. (P.F., 1816.)

4468. LATITUDE AND LONGITUDE, Chronometers and.—Fine time-keepers have been invented, but not equal to what is requisite, all of them deriving their motion from a spring, and not from a pendulum. Indeed these pursuits have lost much of their consequence since the improvement of the lunar tables has given the motion of the moon so accurately, as to make that a foundation for estimating the longitude by her relative position at a given moment with the sun or fixed stars.—To Captain Grove. v, 374. (W., 1808.)

4469. LATITUDE AND LONGITUDE, Jupiter's Eclipses.—To get the longitude at sea by observation of the eclipses of Jupiter's satellites, two desiderata are wanting: 1st, a practicable way of keeping the planet and satellite in the field of a glass magnifying sufficiently to show the satellites; 2nd, a time-piece which will give the instant of time with sufficient accuracy to be useful. The bringing the planet and satellite to the horizon does not sensibly facilitate the observation, because the planet in his ascending and descending course is at such heights as admit the direct observation with entire convenience. On the other hand, so much light is lost by the double reflection as to dim the objects and lessen the precision with which the moment of ingress and egress may be marked. This double reflection also introduces a new source of error from the inaccuracy of the instrument; 3d, the desideratum of a time-piece which, notwithstanding the motion of the ship, shall keep time during a whole voyage with sufficient accuracy for these observations, has not yet been supplied.—To Captain Grove. v, 374. (W., 1808.)

4470. LATITUDE AND LONGITUDE, Lunar observations.—While Captain Lewis's mission was preparing, as it was understood that his reliance for his longitudes must be on the lunar observations taken, as at sea. with the aid of a time-keeper, and I knew that a thousand accidents might happen to that in such a journey as his, and thus deprive us of the principal object of the expedition, to wit, the ascertaining the geography of that river, I set myself to consider whether in making observations at land, that furnishes no resource which may dispense with the time-keeper, so necessary at sea. It occurred to me that we can always have a meridian at land that would furnish what the want of it at sea obliges us to supply by the time-keeper. Supposing Captain Lewis then furnished with a meridian, and having the requisite tables and nautical almanac with him,—first, he might find the right ascension of the moon, when on the meridian of Greenwich, on any given day; then find by observation when the moon should attain that right ascension (by the aid of a known star), and measure her distance in that moment from his meridian. This distance would be the difference of longitude between Greenwich and the place of obervation. Or secondly, observe the moon's passage over his meridian, and her right ascension at that moment. See by the tables at Greenwich when she had that right ascension. That gives her distance from the meridian of Greenwich, when she was on his meridian. Or thirdly, observe the moon's distance from his meridian at any moment, and her right ascension at that moment; and find from the tables her distance from the meridian of Greenwich, when she had that right ascension, which will give the distance of the two meridians. This last process will be simplified by taking, for the moment of observation, that of an appulse of the moon and a known star, or when the moon and a known star are in the same vertical. I suggested this to Mr. Briggs, who considered it as correct and practicable, and proposed communicating it to the Philosophical Society; but I observed that it was too obvious not to have been thought of before, and supposed it had not been adopted in practice, because of no use at sea, where a meridian cannot be had, and where alone the nations of Europe had occasion for it. Before his confirmation of the idea, however, Captain Lewis was gone. In conversation afterwards with Baron von Humboldt, he observed that the idea was correct, but not new; that I would find it in the third volume of Delalandé. I received, two days ago, the third and fourth volumes of Montucla's History of Mathematics, finished and edited by Delalandé; and find, in fact, that Morin and Vanlangren, in the Seventeenth Century, proposed observations of the moon on the meridian, but it does not appear whether they meant to dispense with the time-keeper. But a meridian at sea being too impracticable, their idea was not pursued.—To MR. DUNBAR. iv, 578. (W., 1805.)

4471. LATITUDE AND LONGITUDE, Magnetic needle.—Among other projects with which we begin to abound in America, is one for finding the latitude by the variation of the magnetic needle. The author supposes two points, one near each pole, through the northern of which pass all the magnetic meridians of the northern hemisphere, and through the southern those of the southern hemisphere. He determines their present position and periodical revolution.—To B. VAUGHAN. ii, 166. (P., 1787.)

4472. ———— ————. As far as we can conjecture your idea here [Paris], we imagine you make a table of variations of the needle, for all the different meridians. To apply this table to use, in the voyage between America and Europe. Suppose the variation to increase a degree in every one hundred and sixty miles. Two difficulties occur: 1, a ready and accurate method of finding the variation of the place; 2, an instrument so perfect as that (though the degree on it shall represent one hundred and sixty miles) it shall give the parts of the degree so minutely as to answer the purpose of the navigator. * * * I make no question you have provided against the doubts entertained here, and I shall be happy that our country may have the honor of furnishing the old world what it has so long sought in vain.—To JOHN CHURCHMAN. ii, 236. (P., 1787.)

4473. LATITUDE AND LONGITUDE, Without chronometer*.—If two persons, at different points of the same hemisphere (as Greenwich and Washington, for example), observe the same celestial phenomenon, at the same instant of time, the difference of the times marked by their respective clocks is the difference of their longitudes, or the distance of their meridians. * To catch with precision the same instant of time for these simultaneous observations, the moon's motion in her orbit is the best element; her change of place (about a half second of space in a second of time) is rapid enough to be ascertained by a good instrument with sufficient precision for the object. But suppose the observer at Washington, or in a desert, to be without a timekeeper; the equatorial is the instrument to be used in that case. Again, we have supposed a contemporaneous observer at Greenwich. But his functions may be supplied by the nautical almanac, adapted to that place, and enabling us to calculate for any instant of time the meridian distances there of the heavenly bodies necessary to be observed for this purpose. The observer at Washington, choosing the time when their position is suitable, is to adjust his equatorial to his meridian, to his latitude, and to the plane of his horizon; or if he is in a desert where neither meridian nor latitude is yet ascertained, the advantages of this noble instrument are that it enables him to find both in the course of a few hours. Thus prepared, let him ascertain by observation the right ascension of the moon from that of a known star, or their horary distance; and, at the same instant, her horary distance from his meridian. Her right ascension at the instant thus ascertained, enter with that of the nautical almanac, and calculate, by its tables, what was her horary distance from the meridian of Greenwich at the instant she had attained that point of right ascension, or that horary distance from the same star. The addition of these meridian distances, if the moon was between the two meridians, or the subtraction of the lesser from the greater, if she was on the same side of both, is the difference of their longitudes. This general theory admits different cases, of which the observer may avail himself, according to the particular position of the heavenly bodies at the moment of observation. Case 1st. When the moon is on his meridian, or on that of Greenwich. Second. When the star is on either meridian. Third. When the moon and star are on the same side of his meridian. Fourth. When they are on different sides. For instantaneousness of observation, the equatorial has great advantage over the circle or sextant; for being truly placed in the meridian beforehand, the telescope may be directed sufficiently in advance of the moon's motion, for time to note its place on the equatorial circle, before she attains that point. Then observe, until her limb touches the cross-hairs; and in that instant direct the telescope to the star; that completes the observation, and the place of the star may be read at leisure. The apparatus for correcting the effects of refraction and parallax, which is fixed on the eye-tube of the telescope, saves time by rendering the notation of altitudes unnecessary, and dispenses with the use of either a time-keeper or portable pendulum. I have observed that, if placed in a desert where neither meridian nor latitude is yet ascertained, the equatorial enables the observer to find both in a few hours. For the latitude, adjust by the cross-levels the azimuth plane of the instrument

* Jefferson called this paper "A method of finding the longitude of a place at land, without a time-keeper".—EDITOR.

to the horizon of the place. Bring down the equatorial plane to an exact parallelism with it, its pole then becoming vertical. By the nut and pinion commanding it, and by that of the semi-circle of declination, direct the telescope to the sun. Follow its path with the telescope by the combined use of these two pinions, and when it has attained its greatest altitude, calculate the latitude as when taken by a sextant. For finding the meridian, set the azimuth circle to the horizon, elevate the equatorial circle to the complement of the latitude, and fix it by the clamp and tightening screw of the two brass segments of arches below. By the declination semicircle set the telescope to the sun's declination of the moment. Turn the instrument towards the meridian by guess, and by the combined movement of the equatorial and azimuth circles direct the telescope to the sun, then by the pinion of the equatorial alone, follow the path of the sun with the telescope. If it swerves from that path, turn the azimuth circle until it shall follow the sun accurately. A distant stake or tree should mark the meridian, to guard against its loss by any accidental jostle of the instrument. The 12 o'clock line will then be in the true mèridian, and the axis of the equatorial circle will be parallel with that of the earth. The instrument is then in its true position for the observations of the night.—To —— ——. vii, 226. (M., 1821.) See LEWIS AND CLARK EXPEDITION.

4474. LATROBE (B. H.), Building of U. S. Capitol.—My memory retains no trace of the particular conversations alluded to [by you *], nor enables me to say that they are or are not correct. The only safe appeal for me is to the general impressions received at the time, and still retained with sufficient distinctness. These were that you discharged the duties of your appointment with ability, diligence and zeal, but that in the article of expense you were not sufficiently guarded. You must remember my frequent cautions to you on this head, the measures I took, by calling for frequent accounts of expenditures and contracts, to mark to you, as well as to myself, when they were getting beyond the limits of the appropriations, and the afflicting embarrassments on a particular occasion where these limits had been unguardedly and greatly transcended. These sentiments I communicated to you freely at the time, as it was my duty to do. Another principle of conduct with me was to admit no innovations on the established plans, but on the strongest grounds. When, therefore, I thought first of placing the floor of the Representative chamber on the level of the basement of the building, and of throwing into its height the cavity of the dome, in the manner of the Halle aux Bleds at Paris, I deemed it due to Dr. Thornton, author of the plan of the Capitol, to consult him on the change. He not only consented, but appeared heartily to approve of the alteration. For the same reason, as well as on motives of economy, I was anxious, in converting the Senate chamber into a Judiciary room, to preserve its original form, and to leave the same arches and columns standing. On your representation, however, that the columns were decayed and incompetent to support the incumbent weight, I acquiesced in the weight you proposed, only strikıng out the addition which would have made part of the middle building, and would involve a radical change in that which had not been sanctioned. I have

* Latrobe was the architect of the Capitol at Washington. The quotation is interesting, showing as it does the im ıress of Jefferson's taste in architecture.—EDITOR.

no reason to doubt but that in the execution of the Senate and Court rooms, you have adhered to the plan communicated to me and approved. * * * On the whole, I do not believe any one has ever done more justice to your professional abilities than myself. Besides constant commendations of your taste in architecture, and science in execution, I declared on many and all occasions that I considered you as the only person in the United States who could have executed the Representative Chamber, or who could execute the middle buildings on any of the plans proposed.—To BENJAMIN H. LATROBE. v, 578. (M., 1811.) See ARCHITECTURE.

4475. LATROBE (B. H.), Burr's Treason and.—I believe we shall send on Latrobe as a witness. He will prove that Aaron Burr endeavored to get him to engage several thousand men, chiefly Irish emigrants, whom he had been in the habit of employing in the works he directs, under pretence ot a canal opposite Louisville, or of the Washita, in which, had he succeeded, he could with that force alone have carried everything before him, and would not have been where he now is. He knows, too, of certain meetings of Burr, Bollman, Yrnjo, and one other whom we have never named yet, but have him not the less in our view.—To GEORGE HAY. v, 99. FORD ED., ix, 58. (W., June 1807.)

4476. —— ——. I have had a conversation with Latrobe. He says it was five hundred men he was desired to engage. The pretexts were, to work on the Ohio canal, and be paid in Washita lands. Your witnesses will some of them prove that Burr had no interest in the Ohio canal, and that consequently this was a mere pretext to cover the real object from the men themselves, and all others.—To GEORGE HAY. v, 100. FORD ED., ix, 59. (W., June 1807.)

4477. LAW, Administration.—Laws will be * * * honestly administered, in proportion as those who * * * administer them are wise and honest.—DIFFUSION OF KNOWLEDGE BILL. FORD ED., ii, 221. (1779.)

4478. —— ——. That people will be happiest whose laws are best, and are best administered.—DIFFUSION OF KNOWLEDGE BILL. FORD ED., ii, 221. (1779.)

4479. LAW, Agrarian.—Equal partition of inheritances [is] the best of all agrarian laws.—AUTOBIOGRAPHY. i, 49. FORD ED., i, 69. (1821.)

— **LAW, Alien and Sedition.**—See ALIEN AND SEDITION LAWS.

— **LAW, The Common.**—See COMMON LAW.

4480. LAW, Construing.—Constructions which do not result from the words of the Legislator, but lie hidden in his breast, till called forth, *ex post facto*, by subsequent occasions, are dangerous and not to be justified by ordinary emergencies.—REPORT TO CONGRESS. FORD ED., ii, 138. (1778.)

4481. —— ——. Constructions must not be favored which go to defeat instead of furthering the principal object of the law and to sacrifice the end to the means.—To W. H. CABELL. v, 159. FORD ED., ix, 94. (M., 1807.)

4482. —— ——. Ingenuity ever should be exercised [in executive cases] in devising constructions which may save to the public the benefit of the law. Its intention is the important thing; the means of attaining quite subordinate.—To W. H. Cabell. v, 159 Ford ed., ix, 94. (M., 1807.)

4483. —— ——. In the construction of a law, even in judiciary cases of *meum et tuum* where the opposite parties have a right and counter-right in the very words of the law, the judge considers the intention of the lawgiver as his true guide, and gives to all the parts and expressions of the law, that meaning which will effect, instead of defeating, its intention. But in laws merely executive, where no private right stands in the way, and the public object is the interest of all, a much freer scope of construction, in favor of the intention of the law, ought to be taken, and ingenuity ever should be exercised in devising constructions, which may save to the public the benefit of the law. Its intention is the important thing: the means of attaining it quite subordinate. It often happens that, the Legislature prescribing the details of execution, some circumstance arises unforeseen or unattended to by them, which would totally frustrate their intention, were their details scrupulously adhered to, and deemed exclusive of all others. But constructions must not be favored which go to defeat instead of furthering the principal object of the law, and to sacrifice the end to the means. It being as evidently their intention that the end shall be attained as that it should be effected by any given means, if both cannot be observed, we are equally free to deviate from the one as the other, and more rational in postponing the means to the end. * * * It is further to be considered that the Constitution gives the Executive a general power to carry the laws into execution. If the present law had enacted that the service of 30,000 volunteers should be accepted, without saying anything of the means, those means would, by the Constitution, have resulted to the discretion of the Executive. So if means specified by an act are impracticable, the constitutional power remains and supplies them. Often the means provided specially are affirmative merely, and, with the constitutional powers, stand well together; so that either may be used, or the one supplementary to the other. This aptitude of means to the end of a law is essentially necessary for those which are executive; otherwise the objection that our government is an impracticable one, would really be verified.—To W. H. Cabell. v, 158. Ford ed., ix, 94. (M., Aug. 1807.)

4484. —— ——. The true key for the construction of everything doubtful in a law, is the intention of the law givers. This is most safely gathered from the words, but may be sought also in extraneous circumstances, provided they do not contradict the express words of the law.—To Albert Gallatin. v, 291. (M., 1808.)

4485. —— ——. The omission of a caution which would have been right, does not justify the doing what is wrong. Nor ought it to be presumed that the Legislature meant to use a phrase in an unjustifiable sense, if by rules of construction it can be ever strained to what is just.—To Isaac McPherson. vi, 176. (M., 1813.)

4486. —— ——. The question whether the judges are invested with exclusive authority to decide on the constitutionality of a law, has been heretofore a subject of consideration with me in the exercise of official duties. Certainly there is not a word in the Constitution which has given that power to them more than to the Executive or Legislative branches. Questions of property, of character and of crime being ascribed to the judges, through a definite course of legal proceeding, laws involving such questions belong, of course, to them; and as they decide on them ultimately and without appeal, they of course decide *for themselves*. The constitutional validity of the law or laws again prescribing Executive action, and to be administered by that branch ultimately and without appeal, the Executive must decide for *themselves* also, whether, under the Constitution, they are valid or not. So also as to laws governing the proceedings of the Legislature, that body must judge *for itself* the constitutionality of the law, and equally without appeal or control from its co-ordinate branches. And, in general, that branch which is to act ultimately, and without appeal, on any law, is the rightful expositor of the validity of the law, uncontrolled by the opinions of the other coordinate authorities.—To W. H. Torrance. vi, 461. Ford ed., ix, 517. (M., 1815.)

4487. —— ——. It may be said that contradictory decisions may arise in such case, and produce inconvenience. This is possible, and is a necessary failing in all human proceedings. Yet the prudence of the public functionaries, and authority of public opinion, will generally produce accommodation. Such an instance of difference occurred between the judges of England (in the time of Lord Holt) and the House of Commons, but the prudence of those bodies prevented inconvenience from it. So in the cases of Duane and of William Smith, of South Carolina, whose characters of citizenship stood precisely on the same ground, the judges in a question of *meum* and *tuum* which came before them, decided that Duane was not a citizen; and in a question of membership, the House of Representatives, under the same words of the same provision, adjudged William Smith to be a citizen. This is what I believe myself to be sound.—To W. H. Torrance. vi, 462. Ford ed., ix, 518. (M., 1815.)

4488. —— ——. There is another opinion entertained by some men of such judgment and information as to lessen my confidence in my own. That is, that the Legislature alone is the exclusive expounder of the sense of the Constitution, in every part of it whatever. And they allege in its support, that this branch has authority to impeach and punish a member of either of the others acting contrary to its declaration of the sense of the Constitution. It may, indeed, be answered that an act may still be valid although the party is punished for it, right or wrong. However, this opinion which ascribes exclusive exposition to the Legislature, merits respect for its safety, there being in the body of the nation a control over them, which, if expressed by rejection on the subsequent exercise of their elective franchise, enlists public opinion against their exposition, and encourages a judge or executive on a future occasion to adhere to their former opinion. Between these two doctrines, every one has a right to choose, and I know of no third meriting any respect.—To W. H. TORRANCE. vi, 462. FORD ED., ix, 518. (M., 1815.)

4489. LAW, Cruel French.—Nor should we wonder at * * * [the] pressure [for a fixed constitution in 1788-9] when we consider the monstrous abuses of power under which they [the French] people were ground to powder; when we pass in review the * * * cruelty of the criminal code.—AUTOBIOGRAPHY. i, 86. FORD ED., i, 118. (1821.)

4490. LAW, Enacting.—Laws will be wisely formed * * * in proportion as those who form * * * them are wise and honest. —DIFFUSION OF KNOWLEDGE BILL. FORD ED., ii, 221. (1779.)

4491. LAW, Enforcing.—Laws made by common consent must not be trampled on by individuals.—To COLONEL VANNETER, FORD ED., iii, 24. (R., 1781.)

4492. ——— ———. I hope, on the first symptom of an open opposition to the [Embargo] law by force, you will fly to the scene, and aid in suppressing any commotion.—To HENRY DEARBORN. v, 334. (M., 1808.)

4493. LAW, Equality before the.—An equal application of law to every condition of man is fundamental.—To GEORGE HAY. v, 175. FORD ED., ix, 62. (M., 1807.)

4494. LAW, Execution of.—The execution of the laws is more important than the making them.—To M. L'ABBÉ ARNOND. iii, 82. FORD ED., v, 104. (P., 1789.)

4495. LAW, Executive discretion and.— There are cases in the books where the word "may" has been adjudged equivalent to "shall", but the term "is authorized" unless followed by "and required" was, I think, never so considered. On the contrary, I believe it is the very term which Congress always use towards the Executive when they mean to give a power to him, and leave the use of it to his discretion. It is the very phrase on which there is now a difference in the House of Representatives, on the bill for raising 6,000 regulars, which says,-"there shall be raised", and some desire it to say, "the President is authorized to raise", leaving him the power with a discretion to use it or not.—To ALBERT GALLATIN. v, 259. (W., March 1808.)

4496. LAW, Federal, State and Common.—Of all the doctrines which have ever been broached by the Federal Government, the novel one, of the common law being in force and cognizable as an existing law in their courts, is to me the most formidable. All their other assumptions of un-given powers have been in the detail. The bank law, the treaty doctrine, the Sedition act, Alien act, the undertaking to change the State laws of evidence in the State courts by certain parts of the Stamp act, &c., &c., have been solitary, unconsequential, timid things, in comparison with the audacious, bare-faced and sweeping pretension to a system of law for the United States, without the adoption of their Legislature, and so infinitely beyond their power to adopt. If this assumption be yielded to, the State courts may be shut up, as there will then be nothing to hinder citizens of the same State suing each other in the Federal courts in every case, as on a bond for instance, because the common law obliges payment of it, and the common law they say is their law. I am happy you have taken up the subject; and I have carefully perused and considered the notes you enclosed, and find but a single paragraph which I do not approve. It is that wherein you say, that laws being emanations from the legislative department, and, when once enacted, continuing in force from a presumption that their will so continues, that that presumption fails and the laws of course fall, on the destruction of that legislative department. I do not think this is the true bottom on which laws and the administering them rest. The whole body of the nation is the sovereign legislative, judiciary, and executive power for itself. The inconvenience of meeting to exercise these powers in person, and their inaptitude to exercise them, induce them to appoint special organs to declare their legislative will, to judge and to execute it. It is the will of the nation which makes the law obligatory; it is their will which vacates or annihilates the organ which is to declare and announce it. They may do it by a single person, as an Emperor of Russia (constituting his declarations evidence of their will), or by a few persons, as the aristocracy of Venice, or by an application of councils, as in our former regal government, or our present republican one. The law being law because it is the will of the nation, is not changed by their changing the organ through which they choose to announce their future will; no more than the acts I have done by one attorney lose their obligation by my changing or discontinuing that attorney. This doctrine has been, in a certain degree, sanctioned by the Federal Executive. For it is precisely that on which the continuance of obligation from our treaty with France was established, and the doctrine was particularly developed in a letter to Gouverneur Morris, with the approbation of President Washington and his Cabinet. Mercer once prevailed on the Virginia Assembly to declare a different doctrine in some resolutions. These met universal disapprobation in this, as well as the other

States, and if I mistake not, a subsequent Assembly did something to do away the authority of their former unguarded resolutions. In this case, as in all others, the true principle will be quite as effectual to establish the just deductions. Before the Revolution, the nation of Virginia had, by the organs they then thought proper to constitute, established a system of laws, which they divided into three denominations of 1, common law; 2, statute law; 3, chancery; or, if you please, into two only of 1, common law; 2, chancery. When, by the Declaration of Independence, they chose to abolish their former organs of declaring their will, the acts of will already formally and constitutionally declared, remained untouched. For the nation was not dissolved, was not annihilated; its will, therefore, remained in full vigor, and on the establishing the new organs, first of a convention, and afterwards a more complicated legislature, the old acts of national will continued in force, until the nation should, by its new organs, declare its will changed. The common law, therefore, which was not in force when we landed here, nor till we had formed ourselves into a nation, and had manifested by the organs we constituted that the common law was to be our law, continued to be our law, because the nation continued in being, and because though it changed the organs for the future declarations of its will, yet it did not change its former declarations that the common law was its law. Apply these principles to the present case. Before the Revolution there existed no such nation as the United States; they then first associated as a nation, but for special purposes only. They had all their laws to make, as Virginia had on her first establishment as a nation. But they did not, as Virginia had done, proceed to adopt a whole system of laws ready made to their hand. As their association as a nation was only for special purposes, to wit, for the management of their concerns with one another and with foreign nations, and the States composing the association chose to give to it powers for those purposes and no others, they could not adopt any general system, because it would have embraced objects on which this association had no right to form or declare a will. It was not the organ for declaring a national will in these cases. In the cases confided to them, they were free to declare the will of the nation, the law; but until it was declared there could be no law. So that the common law did not become, *ipso facto*, law on the new association; it could only become so by a positive adoption, and so far only as they were authorized to adopt. I think it will be of great importance when you come to the proper part, to portray at full length the consequences of this new doctrine, that the common law is the law of the United States, and that their courts have, of course, jurisdiction coextensive with that law, that is to say, general over all cases and persons. But, great heavens! Who could have conceived in 1789, that within ten years we should have to combat

such windmills?—To EDMUND RANDOLPH. iv, 301. FORD ED., vii, 383. (M., Aug. 1799.)

4497. —— ——. Though long estranged from legal reading and reasoning, and little familiar with the decisions of particular judges, I have considered that respecting the obligation of the common law in this country as a very plain one, and merely a question of document. If we are under that law, the document which made us so can surely be produced; and as far as this can be produced, so far we are subject to it, and farther we are not. Most of the States did, I believe, at an early period of their legislation, adopt the English law, common and statute, more or less in a body, as far as localities admitted of their application. In these States, then, the common law, so far as adopted, is the *lex-loci*. Then comes the law of Congress, declaring that what is law in any State, shall be the rule of decision in their courts, as to matters arising within that State, except when controlled by their own statutes. But this law of Congress has been considered as extending to civil cases only; and that no such provision has been made for criminal ones. A similar provision, then, for criminal offences, would, in like manner, be an adoption of more or less of the common law, as part of the *lex-loci*, where the offence is committed; and would cover the whole field of legislation for the General Government.—To DR. JOHN MANNERS. vii, 73. FORD ED., x, 87. (M., 1817.) See COMMON LAW.

4498. LAW, George III. vs.—His Majesty has permitted our laws to be neglected in England for years, neither confirming them by his assent, nor annulling them by his negative: so that such of them as have no suspending clause we hold on the most precarious of all tenures, his Majesty's will; and such of them as suspend themselves till his Majesty's assent be obtained, we have feared, might be called into existence at some future and distant period, when the time and change of circumstances shall have rendered them destructive to his people here. And to render this grievance still more oppressive, his Majesty by his instructions has laid his Governors under such restrictions, that they can pass no law of any moment unless it have such suspending clause: so that, however immediate may be the call for legislative interposition, the law cannot be executed till it has twice crossed the Atlantic, by which time the evil may have spent its whole force.—RIGHTS OF BRITISH AMERICA. i, 136. FORD ED., i, 440. (1774.)

4499. —— ——. He [George III.] has endeavored to pervert the exercise of the kingly office in Virginia into a detestable and insupportable tyranny * * * by denying to his governors permission to pass laws of immediate and pressing importance, unless suspended in their operations for his assent, and, when so suspended, neglecting to attend to them for many years.—PROPOSED VA. CONSTITUTION. FORD ED., i, 9. (June 1776.)

4500. —— ——. He has forbidden his governors to pass laws of immediate and pressing importance, unless suspended in their operation till his assent should be obtained; and, when so suspended, he has utterly neglected to attend to them.—DECLARATION OF INDEPENDENCE AS DRAWN BY JEFFERSON.

4501. —— ——. He has combined, with others, * * * for abolishing our most valuable laws.—DECLARATION OF INDEPENDENCE AS DRAWN BY JEFFERSON.

4502. —— ——. He has [suffered] the administration of justice [totally to cease in some of these States], refusing his assent to laws for establishing judiciary powers.*—DECLARATION OF INDEPENDENCE AS DRAWN BY JEFFERSON.

4503. —— ——. He has refused his assent to laws the most wholesome and necessary for the public good.—DECLARATION OF INDEPENDENCE AS DRAWN BY JEFFERSON.

4504. —— ——. He has refused to pass other laws for the accommodation of large districts of people, unless those people would relinquish the right of representation in the legislature * * * .—DECLARATION OF INDEPENDENCE AS DRAWN BY JEFFERSON.

4505. LAW, Ignorance.—Ignorance of the law is no excuse in any country. If it were, the laws would lose their effect, because it can be always pretended.—To M. LIMOZIN. ii, 338. (P., 1787.)

4506. LAW, Instability.—The instability of our laws is really an immense evil. I think it would be well to provide in our constitutions that there shall always be a twelvemonth between the engrossing a bill and passing it; that it should then be offered to its passage without changing a word; and that if circumstances should be thought to require a speedier passage. it should take two-thirds of both Houses, instead of a bare majority.—To JAMES MADISON. ii, 333. FORD ED., iv, 480. (P., 1787.)

4507. LAW, Intention of.—Whenever the words of a law will bear two meanings, one of which will give effect to the law, and the other will defeat it, the former must be supposed to have been intended by the Legislature, because they could not intend that meaning, which would defeat their intention, in passing that law; and in a statute, as in a will, the intention of the party is to be sought after.—To ALBERT GALLATIN. v, 328. (M., July 1808.)

4508. —— ——. Anciently before the improvement, or, perhaps, the existence of the Court of Chancery, the judges did not restrain themselves to the letter of the law. They allowed themselves greater latitude, extending the provisions of every law, not only to the cases within its letter, but to those also which came within the spirit and reason of it. This was called the equity of the law, but it is now very long since certainty

* Congress struck out the words in brackets, changed "suffered" to "obstructed" and inserted "by" before "refusing".—EDITOR.

in the law has become so highly valued by the nation, that the judges have ceased to extend the operation of laws beyond those cases which are clearly within the intention of the legislators. This intention is to be collected principally from the words of the law; only where these are ambiguous they are permitted to gather further evidence from the history of the times when the law was made, and the circumstances which produced it.—To PHILIP MAZZEI. FORD ED., iv, 109. (P., 1785.)

— **LAW, International.**—See BELLIGERENTS, CONTRABAND, ENEMY GOODS, FREE SHIPS, NEUTRALITY, PRIVATEERS, and TREATIES.

4509. LAW, Lex Talionis.—The *Lex talionis*, although a restitution of the Common Law, * * * [is] revolting to the humanized feelings of modern times. An eye for an eye, and a hand for a hand. will exhibit spectacles in execution whose moral effect would be questionable; and even the *membrum pro membro* of Bracton, or the punishment of the offending member, although long authorized by our law, for the same offence in a slave, has been not long since repealed. in conformity with public sentiment. This needs reconsideration.*—To GEORGE WYTHE. i, 146. FORD ED., ii, 204. (M., 1778.)

4510. LAW, Lynch.—It is more dangerous that even a guilty person should be punished without the forms of law, than that he should escape.—To WILLIAM CARMICHAEL. ii, 399. FORD ED., v, 26. (P., 1788.)

4511. —— ——. There is no country which is not sometimes subject to irregular interpositions of the people. There is no country able, at all times, to punish them. There is no country which has less of this to reproach itself with than the United States, nor any, where the laws have more regular course, or are more habitually and cheerfully acquiesced in.—To GEORGE HAMMOND. iii, 413. FORD ED., vi, 54. (Pa., May 1792.)

— **LAW, Moral.**—See MORALITY.

4512. LAW, Obedience to.—He is a bad citizen who can entertain a doubt whether the law will justify him in saving his country, or who will scruple to risk himself in support of the spirit of a law, where unavoidable accidents have prevented a literal compliance with it.—LETTER TO COUNTY MAGISTRATES. FORD ED., ii, 431. (R., 1781.)

4513. —— ——. While the laws shall be obeyed all will be safe.—FROM JEFFERSON'S MSS. FORD ED., viii, 1. (1801?)

4514. —— ——. That love of order and obedience to the laws, which so remarkably characterize the citizens of the United States, are sure pledges of internal tranquillity.—To BENJAMIN WARING. iv, 378. (W., March 1801.)

— **LAW, Patent.**—See PATENTS.

* From Jefferson's letter to George Wythe enclosing the draft of the bill for "Proportioning Crimes and Punishments in cases heretofore capital".—EDITOR.

4515. LAW, Protests against.—While the principles of our Constitution give just latitude to inquiry, every citizen faithful to it will deem embodied expressions of discontent, and open outrages of law and patriotism, as dishonorable as they are injurious.—R. TO A. LEESBURG CITIZENS. viii, 161. (1809.)

4516. LAW, Reason and.—Sound reason should constitute the law of every country.—BATTURE CASE. viii, 531. (1812.)

4517. LAW, Retrospective.—I agree in an almost unlimited condemnation of retrospective laws. The few instances of wrong which they redress are so overweighed by the insecurity they draw over all property and even over life itself, and by the atrocious violations of both to which they lead, that it is better to live under the evil than the remedy.—OFFICIAL OPINION. vii, 470. FORD ED., v, 176. (1790.)

4518. —— ——. The sentiment that *ex post facto* laws are against natural right, is so strong in the United States, that few, if any, of the State Constitutions have failed to proscribe them. The Federal Constitution, indeed, interdicts them in criminal cases only; but they are equally unjust in civil as in criminal cases, and the omission of a caution which would have been right, does not justify the doing what is wrong.—To ISAAC MCPHERSON. vi, 176. (M., 1813.)

4519. —— ——. Every man should be protected in his lawful acts, and be certain that no *ex post facto* law shall punish or endanger him for them.—To ISAAC MCPHERSON. vi, 175. (M., Aug. 1813.)

4520. —— ——. Nature and reason, as well as all our constitutions, condemn retrospective conditions as mere acts of power against right.—To CHARLES YANCEY. vi, 515. FORD ED., x, 2. (M., 1816.)

4521. LAW, Roman vs. Feudal.—The French code, like all those of middle and southern Europe, was originally Feudal, with some variations in the different provinces, formerly independent, of which the kingdom of France had been made up. But as circumstances changed, and civilization and commerce advanced, abundance of new cases and questions arose, for which the simple and unwritten laws of Feudalism had made no provision. At the same time, they had at hand the legal system of a nation highly civilized, a system carried to a degree of conformity with natural reason attained by no other. The study of this system, too, was become the favorite of the age, and offering ready and reasonable solutions of all the new cases presenting themselves, was recurred to by a common consent and practice; not, indeed, as laws, formally established by the legislator of the country, but as a *Ratio Scripta*, the dictate, in all cases, of that sound reason which should constitute the law of every country. Over both of these systems, however, the occasional edicts of the monarch are paramount, and amend and control their provisions whenever he deems amendment necessary; on the general principle that "*leges posteriores priores abrogant*". Subsequent laws abrogate those which are prior.—BATTURE CASE. viii, 530. (1812.)

4522. —— ——. The following instances will give some idea of the steps by which the Roman gained on the Feudal laws. A law of Burgundy provided "*Si quis post hoc barbarus vel testari voluerit, vel donare, aut Romanam consuetudinem, aut barbaricam, esse servandam, sciat*". "If any barbarian subject hereafter shall desire to dispose by legacy or donation, let him know that either the Roman or barbarian law is to be observed." And one of Lotharius II. of Germany, going still further, gives to every one an election of the system under which he chose to live, "*Volumus ut cunctus populus Romanus interrogatur quali lege vult vivere; ut tali lege, quali professi sunt vivere vivant; illisque denuntiatur, ut hoc unus-quis-que, tam judices, quam judices, vel reliquus populus sciat, quod si offensionem contra eandem legem fecerint, eidem legi, quâ profitentur vivere, subjaceant*". "We will that all the Roman people shall be asked by what law they wish to live; that they may live under such law as they profess to live by; and that it be published, that every one, judges, as well as generals, or the rest of the people, may know that if they commit offence against the said law, they shall be subject to the same law by which they profess to live." Ency. Method. Jurisprudence. Coutume. 399. Presenting the uncommon spectacle of a jurisdiction attached to persons, instead of places. Thus favored, the Roman became an acknowledged supplement to the Feudal or customary law; but still, not under any act of the legislature, but as "raison écrite", "written reason"; and the cases to which it is applicable, becoming much the most numerous, it constitutes in fact the mass of their law.—NOTE IN BATTURE CASE. viii, 531. (1812.)

4523. LAW, Sanguinary.—The experience of all ages and countries has shown that cruel and sanguinary laws defeat their own purpose, by engaging the benevolence of mankind to withhold prosecutions, to smother testimony, or to listen to it with bias, and by producing in many instances a total dispensation and impunity under the names of pardon and privilege of clergy; when, if the punishment were only proportioned to the injury, men would feel it their inclination, as well as their duty, to see the laws observed.—CRIMES BILL. i, 148. FORD ED., ii, 204. (1779.)

— LAW, The Sedition.—See ALIEN AND SEDITION LAWS, and SEDITION LAW.

4524. LAW, Simplicity.—Laws are made for men of ordinary understanding, and should therefore, be construed by the ordinary rules of common sense. Their meaning is not to be sought for in metaphysical subtleties, which may make anything mean everything or nothing, at pleasure. It should be left to the sophisms of advocates, whose trade it is, to prove that a defendant is a plaintiff, though dragged into court, *torto collo*, like Bonaparte's volunteers, into the field in chains, or that a power has been given because it ought to have been given, *et alia talia.*—To WILLIAM JOHNSON. vii, 297. FORD ED., x, 231. (M., 1823.)

— LAW, Study of.—See LAWYERS.

4525. LAW, Style of.—In its [the bill "proportioning crimes and punishments", in the Virginia Revised Code] style I have aimed at accuracy, brevity, and simplicity, preserving, however, the very words of the established law, wherever their meaning had been sanctioned by judicial decisions, or rendered technical by usage. The same matter, if couched in the modern statutory language, with all its tautologies, redundancies, and circumlocutions, would have spread itself over many pages, and been unintelligible to those whom it most concerns. Indeed, I wished to exhibit a sample of reformation in the barbarous style into which modern statutes have degenerated from their ancient simplicity.— To GEORGE WYTHE. i, 146. FORD ED., ii, 203. (M., 1778.) See 4531.

4526. —— ——. In the execution of my part [of the revision of the Virginia laws], I thought it material not to vary the diction of the ancient statutes by modernizing it, nor to give rise to new questions by new expressions. The text of these statutes had been so fully explained and defined by numerous adjudications, as scarcely ever now to produce a question in our courts.—AUTOBIOGRAPHY. i, 44. FORD ED., i, 60. (1821.)

4527. —— ——. I am pleased with the style and diction of your laws [in Louisiana Code]. Plain and intelligible as the ordinary writings of common sense, I hope it will produce imitation. Of all the countries on earth of which I have any knowledge, the style of the acts of the British parliament is the most barbarous, uncouth and unintelligible. It can be understood by those alone who are in the daily habit of studying such tautologous, involved and parenthetical jargon. Where they found their model, I know not. Neither ancient nor modern codes, nor even their own early statutes, furnish any such example. And, like faithful apes, we copy it faithfully.—To EDWARD LIVINGSTON. vii, 404. (M., 1825.)

4528. LAW, Transcending.—The question you propose, whether circumstances do not sometimes occur, which make it a duty in officers of high trust, to assume authorities beyond the law, is easy of solution in principle, but sometimes embarrassing in practice. A strict observance of the written laws is doubtless *one* of the high duties of a good citizen, but it is not the *highest.* The laws of necessity, of self-preservation, of saving our country when in danger, are of higher obligation. To lose our country by a scrupulous adherence to written law, would be to lose the law itself, with life, liberty, property, and all those who are enjoying them with us; thus absurdly sacrificing the end to the means.

When in the battle of Germantown, General Washington's army was annoyed from Chew's house, he did not hesitate to plant his cannon against it, although the property of a citizen. When he besieged Yorktown, he levelled the suburbs, feeling that the laws of property must be postponed to the safety of the nation. While the army was before York, the Governor of Virginia [Jefferson] took horses, carriages, provisions, and even men by force, to enable that army to stay together till it could master the public enemy; and he was justified. A ship at sea in distress for provisions, meets another having abundance, yet refusing a supply; the law of self-preservation authorizes the distressed to take a supply by force. In all these cases, the unwritten laws of necessity, of self-preservation, and of the public safety, control the written laws of *meum* and *tuum*. Further to exemplify the principle, I will state an hypothetical case. Suppose it had been made known to the Executive of the Union in the autumn of 1805, that we might have the Floridas for a reasonable sum, that that sum had not indeed been so appropriated by law, but that Congress were to meet within three weeks, and might appropriate it on the first or second day of their session. Ought he, for so great an advantage to his country, to have risked himself by transcending the law and making the purchase? The public advantage offered, in this supposed case, was indeed immense, but a reverence for law and the probability that the advantage might still be legally accomplished by a delay of only three weeks, were powerful reasons against hazarding the act. But suppose it foreseen that a John Randolph would find means to protract the proceeding on it by Congress, until the ensuing spring, by which time new circumstances would change the mind of the other party. Ought the Executive, in that case, and with that foreknowledge, to have secured the good to his country, and to have trusted to their justice for the transgression of the law? I think he ought, and that the act would have been approved. After the affair of the Chesapeake, we thought war a very possible result. Our magazines were illy provided with some necessary articles, nor had any appropriations been made for their purchase. We ventured, however, to provide them, and to place our country in safety; and stating the case to Congress, they sanctioned the act. To proceed to the conspiracy of Burr, and particularly to General Wilkinson's situation in New Orleans. In judging this case, we are bound to consider the state of the information, correct and incorrect, which he then possessed. He expected Burr and his band from above, a British fleet from below, and he knew there was a formidable conspiracy within the city. Under these circumstances, was he justifiable, first, in seizing notorious conspirators? On this there can be but two opinions; one, of the guilty and their accomplices; the other, that of all honest men. Secondly, in sending them to the seat of government, when the written law gave them a right to trial in the territory?

The danger of their rescue, of their continuing their machinations, the tardiness and weakness of the law, apathy of the judges, active patronage of the whole tribe of lawyers, unknown disposition of the juries, an hourly expectation of the enemy, salvation of the city, and of the Union itself, which would have been convulsed to its centre, had that conspiracy succeeded; all these constituted a law of necessity and self-preservation, and rendered the *salus populi* supreme over the written law. The officer who is called to act on this superior ground, does indeed risk himself on the justice of the controlling powers of the Constitution, and his station makes it his duty to incur that risk. But those controlling powers, and his fellow citizens generally, are bound to judge according to the circumstances under which he acted. They are not to transfer the information of this place or moment to the time and place of his action; but to put themselves into his situation. We knew here [Washington] that there never was danger of a British fleet from below, and that Burr's band was crushed before it reached the Mississippi. But General Wilkinson's information was very different, and he could act on no other. From these examples and principles you may see what I think on the question proposed. They do not go to the case of persons charged with petty duties, where consequences are trifling, and time allowed for a legal course, nor to authorize them to take such cases out of the written law. In these, the example of over-leaping the law is of greater evil than a strict adherence to its imperfect provisions. It is incumbent on those only who accept of great charges, to risk themselves on great occasions, when the safety of the nation, or some of its very high interests are at stake. An officer is bound to obey orders; yet he would be a bad one who should do it in cases for which they were not intended, and which involved the most important consequences. The line of discrimination between cases may be difficult; but the good officer is bound to draw it at his own peril, and throw himself on the justice of his country and the rectitude of his motives.—To J. B. Colvin. v, 542. Ford ed., ix, 279. (M., Sep. 1810.)

4529. ——— ———. On great occasions every good officer must be ready to risk himself in going beyond the strict line of law, when the public preservation requires it; his motives will be a justification as far as there is any discretion in his ultra-legal proceedings, and no indulgence of private feelings.—To Governor Claiborne. v, 40. (W., 1807.)

4530. ——— ———. Should we have ever gained our Revolution, if we had bound our hands by manacles of the law, not only in the beginning, but in any part of the revolutionary conflict?—To James Brown. v, 379. Ford ed., ix, 211. (W., 1808.) See 1852.

4531. LAW, Virginia's Revised Code.— The [Revision] Committee was appointed in the latter part of 1776, and reported in the spring or summer of 1779. At the first and only meeting of the whole committee (of five

persons), the question was discussed whether we would attempt to reduce the whole body of the law into a code, the text of which should become the law of the land? We decided against that, because every word and phrase in that text would become a new subject of criticism and litigation, until its sense should have been settled by numerous decisions, and that, in the meantime, the rights of property would be in the air. We concluded not to meddle with the common law, *i. e.*, the law preceding the existence of the Statutes, further than to accommodate it to our new principles and circumstances; but to take up the whole body of statutes and Virginia laws, to leave out everything obsolete or improper, insert what was wanting, and reduce the whole within as moderate a compass as it would bear, and to the plain language of common sense, divested of the verbiage, the barbarous tautologies and redundancies which render the British statutes unintelligible. From this, however, were excepted the ancient statutes, particularly those commented on by Lord Coke, the language of which is simple, and the meaning of every word so well settled by decisions, as to make it safest not to change words where the sense was to be retained. After setting our plan, Colonel Mason declined undertaking the execution of any part of it, as not being sufficiently read in the law. Mr. Lee very soon afterwards died, and the work was distributed between Mr. Wythe, Mr. Pendleton and myself. To me was assigned the common law (so far as we thought of altering it) and the statutes down to the Reformation, or the end of the reign of Elizabeth; to Mr. Wythe, the subsequent body of the statutes, and to Mr. Pendleton the Virginia laws. This distribution threw into my part the laws concerning crimes and punishments, the law of descents, and the laws concerning religion. After completing our work separately, we met (Mr. W., Mr. P., and myself) in Williamsburg, and held a long session, in which we went over the first and second parts in the order of time, weighing and correcting every word, and reducing them to the form in which they were afterwards reported. When we proceeded to the third part, we found that Mr. Pendleton had not exactly seized the intentions of the committee, which were to reform the language of the Virginia laws, and reduce the matter to a simple style and form. He had copied the acts *verbatim*, only omitting what was disapproved; and some family occurrence calling him indispensably home, he desired Mr. Wythe and myself to make it what we thought it ought to be, and authorized us to report him as concurring in the work. We accordingly divided the work, and reexecuted it entirely so as to assimilate its plan and execution to the other parts, as well as the shortness of the time would admit, and we brought the whole of the British Statutes and laws of Virginia into 127 acts, most of them short. This is the history of that work as to its execution. * * * Experience has convinced me that the change in the style of the laws was for the better, and it has sensibly reformed the style of our laws from that time downwards, insomuch that they have obtained, in that respect, the approbation of men of consideration on both sides of the Atlantic. Whether the change in the style and form of the criminal law, as introduced by Mr. Taylor, was for the better, is not for me to judge. The digest of that act employed me longer than I believe all the rest of the work, for it rendered it necessary for me to go with great care over Bracton, Britton, the Saxon statutes, and the works of authority on criminal law; and it gave me great satisfaction to find that, in general, I had only to reduce the law to its ancient Saxon condition, stripping it of all the innovations and rigorisms of subsequent times, to make it what it should be. The substitution of the penitentiary, instead of labor on the high road, and of some other punishments truly objectionable, is a just merit to be ascribed to Mr. Taylor's law. When our report was made, the idea of a penitentiary had never been suggested; the happy experiment of Pennsylvania we had not then the benefit of.—To SKELTON JONES. v, 459. (M., 1809.)

4532. ——— ———. When I left Congress in 1776, it was in the persuasion that our whole code (of Virginia) must be reviewed, adapted to our republican form of government; and now that we had no negatives of Councils, Governors, and Kings to restrain us from doing right, that it should be corrected, in all its parts, with a single eye to reason, and the good of those for whose government it was framed. Early, therefore, in the session of '76, to which I returned, I moved and presented a bill for the revision of the laws which was passed on the 24th of October; and on the 5th of November, Mr. Pendleton, Mr. Wythe, George Mason, Thomas L. Lee, and myself, were appointed a committee to execute the work. We agreed to meet at Fredericksburg to settle the plan of operation, and to distribute the work. We met there accordingly on the 13th of January, 1777. The first question was, whether we should propose to abolish the whole existing system of laws, and prepare a new and complete Institute, or preserve the general system, and only modify it to the present state of things. Mr. Pendleton, contrary to his usual disposition in favor of ancient things, was for the former proposition, in which he was joined by Mr. Lee. To this it was objected, that to abrogate our whole system would be a bold measure, and probably far beyond the views of the legislature; that they had been in the practice of revising from time to time the laws of the Colony, omitting the expired, the repealed, and the obsolete, amending only those retained, and probably meant we should now do the same, only including the British statutes as well as our own; that to compose a new Institute, like those of Justinian and Bracton, or that of Blackstone, which was the model proposed by Mr. Pendleton, would be an arduous undertaking, of vast research, of great consideration and judgment; and when reduced to a text, every word of that text, from the imperfections of human language, and its incompetence to express distinctly every shade of idea, would become a subject of question and chicanery, until settled by repeated adjudications; and this would involve us for ages in litigation, and render property uncertain until, like the statutes of old, every word had been tried and settled by numerous decisions, and by new volumes of reports and commentaries; and that no one of us, probably, would undertake such a work which, to be systematical, must be the work of one hand. This last was the opinion of Mr. Wythe, Mr. Mason, and myself. When we proceeded to the distribution of the work, Mr. Mason excused himself, as, being no lawyer, he felt himself unqualified for the work, and he resigned soon after. Mr. Lee excused himself on the same ground, and died, indeed, in a short time. The other two gentlemen, therefore, and myself divided the work among us. The common law and statutes to the 4 James I. (when our separate legislature was established) were assigned to me; the British statutes, from that period to the present day, to Mr. Wythe; and the Virginia laws to Mr. Pendleton.—AUTOBIOGRAPHY. i, 42. FORD ED., i, 57. (1821.)

4533. ——— ———. In giving this account of the laws of which I was myself the mover and draughtsman, I, by no means, mean to claim to myself the merit of obtaining their passage. I had many occasional and strenuous coadjutors in debate, and one, most steadfast, able and zealous; who was himself a host. This was George Mason.—AUTOBIOGRAPHY. i, 40. FORD ED., i, 56. (1821.)

4534. ——— ———. We were employed in this work (revising Virginia laws) from January, 1777, to February, 1779, when we met at Williamsburg, that is to say, Mr. Pendleton, Mr. Wythe and myself; and meeting day by day, we examined critically our several parts, sentence by sentence, scrutinizing and amending, until we had agreed on the whole. We then returned home, had fair copies made of our several parts, which were reported to the General Assembly, June 18, 1779, by Mr. Wythe and myself, Mr. Pendleton's residence being distant, and he having authorized us by letter to declare his approbation. We had, in this work, brought so much of the Common Law as it was thought necessary to alter, all the British statutes from *Magna Charta* to the present day, and all the laws of Virginia, from the establishment of our Legislature, in the 4th Jac. 1. to the present time, which we thought should be retained, within the compass of one hundred and twenty-six bills, making a printed folio of ninety pages only. Some bills were taken out, occasionally, from time to time, and passed: but the main body of the work was not entered on by the Legislature until after the general peace, in 1785, when, by the unwearied exertions of Mr. Madison, in opposition to the endless quibbles, chicaneries, perversions, vexations and delays of lawyers and demi-lawyers, most of the bills were passed by the Legislature, with little alteration.—AUTOBIOGRAPHY. i, 44. FORD ED., i, 61. (1821.)

4535. LAW, Voluntary support of.—The voluntary support of laws, formed by persons of their own choice, distinguishes peculiarly the minds capable of self-government. The contrary spirit is anarchy, which of necessity produces despotism.—R. TO A. PHILADELPHIA CITIZENS. viii, 145. (1809.)

4536. LAW OF WASTE, Explained.—The main objects of the law of Waste in England are: 1, to prevent any disguise of the lands which might lessen the reversioner's evidence of title, such as the change of pasture into arable, &c.; 2, to prevent any deterioration of it, as the cutting down forest, which in England is an injury. So careful is the law there against permitting a deterioration of the land, that though it will permit such improvements *in the same line,* as manuring arable lands, leading water into pasture lands, &c., yet it will not permit improvements *in a different line,* such as erecting buildings, converting pasture into arable, &c., lest these should lead to a deterioration. Hence we might argue in Virginia, that though the cutting down of forest in Virginia is, in our husbandry, rather an improvement generally, yet it is not so always, and therefore it is safer never to admit it. Consequently, there is no reason for adopting different rules of waste here from those established in England.—To Peter Carr. iii, 452. Ford ed., vi, 91. (Pa., 1792.)

4537. LAWS OF ENGLAND, History.—
The laws of England, in their progress from the earliest to the present times, may be likened to the road of a traveller, divided into distinct stages or resting places, at each of which a review is to be taken of the ground passed over so far. The first of these was Bracton's *De Legibus Angliæ;* the second Coke's *Institutes;* the third the *Abridgment of the Law* by Matthew Bacon; and the fourth, *Blackstone's Commentaries.* Doubtless there were others before Bracton which have not reached us. Alfred, in the preface to his laws, says they were compiled from those of Ina, Offa, and Æthelbert, into which, or rather preceding them, the clergy have interpolated the 20th, 21st, 22d, 23d and 24th chapters of Exodus, so as to place Alfred's preface to what was really his, awkwardly enough in the body of the work. An interpolation, the more glaring, as containing laws expressly contradicted by those of Alfred. This pious fraud seems to have been first noted by Howard, in his *Coutumes Anglo Normandes,* and the pious judges of England have had no inclination to question it. * * * This digest of Alfred of the laws of the Heptarchy into a single code, common to the whole Kingdom, by him first reduced into one, was probably the birth of what is called the Common law. He has been styled, " Magnus Juris Anglicani Conditor "; and his code, the Dom-Dec, or Doom-Book. That which was afterwards under Edward the Confessor, was but a restoration of Alfred's with some intervening alterations. And this was the code which the English so often, under the Norman princes, petitioned to have restored to them. But, all records previous to the *Magna Charta,* having been early lost, Bracton's is the first digest of the whole body of law which has come down to us entire. What materials existed for it in his time we know not, except the unauthoritative collections of Lambard and Wilkins, and the treatise of Glanville, *tempore* H. 2. Bracton's is the more valuable, because being written a very few years after the *Magna Charta,* which commences what is called the statute law, it gives us the state of the common law in its ultimate form, and exactly at the point of division between the Common and Statute law. It is a most able work, complete in its matter and luminous in its method. The statutes which introduced changes began now to be preserved; applications of the law to new cases by the courts, began soon after to be reported in the Year-Books, these to be methodized and abridged by Fitzherbert, Broke, Rolle, and others; individuals continued the business of reporting; particular treatises were written by able men, and all these, by the time of Lord Coke, had formed so large a mass of matter as to call for a new digest, to bring it within reasonable compass. This he undertook in his *Institutes,* harmonizing all the decisions and opinions which were reconcilable, and rejecting those not so. This work is executed with so much learning and judgment, that I do not recollect that a single position in it has ever been judicially denied. And although the work loses much of its value by its chaotic form it may still be considered as the fundamental code of the English law. The same processes recommencing of statutory changes, new divisions, multiplied reports, and special treatises, a new accumulation had formed, calling for new reduction, by the time of Matthew Bacon. His work, therefore, although not pretending to the textual merit of Bracton's, or Coke's, was very acceptable. His alphabetical arrangement, indeed, although better than Coke's jumble, was far inferior to Bracton's. But it was a sound digest of the materials existing on the several alphabetical heads under which he arranged them. His work was not admitted in Westminster Hall; yet it was the manual of every judge and lawyer, and, what better proves its worth, has been its daily growth in the general estimation. A succeeding interval of changes and additions of matter produced Blackstone's Commentaries, the most lucid in arrangement which had yet been written, correct in its matter, classical in style, and rightfully taking its place by the side of the Justinian Institutes. But, like them, it was only an elementary book. It did not present all the subjects of the law in all their details. It still left it necessary to recur to the original works of which it was the summary. The great mass of law books from which it was extracted, was still to be consulted on minute investigations. It wanted, therefore, a species of merit which entered deeply into the value of those of Bracton, Coke and Bacon. They had in effect swept the shelves of all the materials preceding them. To give Blackstone, therefore, a full measure of value, another work is still wanting, to wit: to incorporate with his principles a compend of the particular cases subsequent to Bacon, of which they are the essence. This might be done by printing under his text a digest like Bacon's, continued to Blackstone's time. It would * * * increase its value peculiarly to us, because just here we break off from the parent stem of the English law, unconcerned in any of its subsequent changes or decisions.—To Dr. Thomas Cooper. vi, 291. (M., 1814.)

4538. LAWS OF NATURE, Opposition to.—It is not only vain, but wicked, in a legislator to frame laws in opposition to the laws of nature, and to arm them with the terrors of death. This is truly creating crimes in order to punish them.—Note on Crimes Bill. i, 159. Ford ed., ii, 218. (1779.)

4539. LAWS OF NATURE, Writers on.—Those who write treatises of natural law, can only declare what their own moral sense and reason dictate in the several cases they state. Such of them as happen to have feelings and a reason coincident with those of the wise and honest part of mankind, are respected and quoted as witnesses of what is morally right or wrong in particular cases. Grotius, Puffendorf, Wolf, and Vattel are of this number. Where they agree their authority is strong; but where they differ (and they often differ), we must appeal to our own feelings and reason to decide between them.—OPINION ON FRENCH TREATIES. vii, 618. FORD ED., vi, 225. (1793.)

4540. LAWS OF VIRGINIA, Collection of.—The only object I had in making my collection of the laws of Virginia, was to save all those for the public which were not then already lost, in the hope that at some future day they might be republished. Whether this be by public or private enterprise, my end will be equally answered.*—To WILLIAM WALTER HENNING. v, 31. FORD ED., ix, 10. (W., 1807.)

4541. LAWYERS, Antipathies and.—No profession is open to stronger antipathies than that of the law.—To WM. WIRT. v, 233. (W., 1808.)

4542. LAWYERS, Blackstone.—I am sure you join me in lamenting the general defection of lawyers and judges from the free principles of government. I am sure they do not derive this degenerate spirit from the father of our science, Lord Coke. But it may be the reason why they cease to read him, and the source of what are now called "Blackstone Lawyers".—To DR. THOMAS COOPER. vi, 296. (M., 1814.)

4543. LAWYERS, Education of.—Carry on the study of the law with that of politics and history. Every political measure will, forever, have an intimate connection with the laws of the land; and he, who knows nothing of these, will always be perplexed and often foiled by adversaries having the advantage of that knowledge over him. Besides, it is a source of infinite comfort to reflect, that under chance of fortune, we have a resource in ourselves from which we may be able to derive an honorable subsistence.—To T. M. RANDOLPH, JR. ii, 176. FORD ED., iv, 405. (P., 1787.)

4544. ——— ———. I have long lamented the depreciation of law science. The opinion seems to be that Blackstone is to us what the Alkoran is to the Mahometans, that everything which is necessary is in him; and what is not in him is not necessary. I still lend my counsel and books to such young students as will fix themselves in the neighborhood. Coke's Institutes and reports are their first, and Blackstone their last book, after an intermediate course of two or three years. It is nothing more than an elegant digest of what they will then have acquired from the real fountains of the law. Now, men are born scholars, lawyers, doctors; in our day this was confined to poets.—To JOHN TYLER. v, 524. FORD ED., ix, 276. (M., 1810.)

4545. ——— ———. Begin with Coke's four Institutes. These give a complete body of the law as it stood in the reign of the First James, an epoch the more interesting to us, as we separated at that point from English legislation, and acknowledged no subsequent statutory alterations. Then passing over (for occasional reading as hereafter proposed) all the reports and treatises to the time of Matthew Bacon, read his abridgment, compiled about one hundred years after Coke's, in which they are all embodied. This gives numerous applications of the old principles to new cases, and gives the general state of the English law at that period. Here, too, the student should take up the Chancery branch of the law, by reading the first and second abridgments of the cases in Equity. The second is by the same Matthew Bacon, the first having been published some time before. The alphabetical order adopted by Bacon, is certainly not as satisfactory as the systematic. But the arrangement is under very general and leading heads, and these, indeed, with very little difficulty, might be systematically instead of alphabetically arranged and read. Passing now in like manner over all intervening reports and tracts, the student may take up Blackstone's Commentaries, published about twenty-five years later than Bacon's abridgment, and giving the substance of these new reports and tracts. This review is not so full as that of Bacon, by any means, but better digested. Here, too, Wooddeson should be read as supplementary to Blackstone, under heads too shortly treated by him. Fonblanque's edition of Francis's Maxims of Equity, and Bridgman's Digested Index, into which the latter cases are incorporated, are also supplementary in the Chancery branch, in which Blackstone is very short. This course comprehends about twenty-six 8vo. volumes, and reading four or five hours a day would employ about two years. After these, the best of the reporters since Blackstone should be read for the new cases which have occurred since his time. * * * By way of change and relief for another hour or two in the day, should be read the law-tracts of merit which are many, and among them all those of Baron Gilbert are of the first order. In these hours, too, may be read Bracton and Justinian's Institutes. The method of these two last works is very much the same, and their language often quite so. Justinian is very illustrative of the doctrines of Equity, and is often appealed to, and Cooper's edition is the best on account of the analogies and contrasts he has given of the Roman and English law. After Bracton, Reeves's History of the English Law may be read to advantage. During this same hour or two of lighter law reading, select and leading cases of the reporters may be successively read, which the several digests will have pointed out and referred to. I have here sketched the reading in Common Law and Chancery which I suppose necessary for a reputable practitioner in those courts. But there are other branches of law in which, although it is not expected he should be an adept, yet when it occurs to speak of them, it should be understandingly to a decent degree. These are the Admiralty law, Ecclesiastical law, and the Law of Nations. I would name as elementary books in these branches, Molloy de Jure Maritimo; Brown's Compend of

* They were published by Henning.—EDITOR.

the Civil and Admiralty Law; the *Jura Ecclesiastica*, and *Les Institutions du Droit de la Nature et des Gens de Reyneval*. Besides these six hours of law reading, light and heavy, and those necessary for the reports of the day, for exercise and sleep, which suppose to be ten or twelve, there will be six or eight hours for reading history, politics, ethics, physics, oratory, poetry, criticism, &c., as necessary as law to form an accomplished lawyer.—To DABNEY TERRELL. vii, 207. (M., 1821.)

4546. LAWYERS, Future Judges and.— I think the bar of the General Court a proper and excellent nursery for future judges, if it be so regulated that science may be encouraged and may live there. But this can never be if an inundation of insects is permitted to come from the county courts, and consume the harvest. These people, traversing the counties, seeing the clients frequently at their own courts, or, perhaps, at their own houses, must of necessity pick up all the business. The convenience of frequently seeing their counsel, without going from home, cannot be withstood by the country people. Men of science, then (if there were to be any), would only be employed as auxiliary counsel in difficult cases. But can they live by that? Certainly not. The present members of that kind therefore must turn marauders in the county courts; and in future none will have leisure to acquire science. I should, therefore, be for excluding the county court attorneys; or rather for taking the General Court lawyers from the incessant drudgery of the county courts and confining them to their studies, that they may qualify themselves as well to support their clients, as to become worthy successors to the bench.—To GEORGE WYTHE. i, 211. FORD ED., ii, 166. (F., 1779.)

4547. LAWYERS, History and.— History, especially, is necessary to form a lawyer. —To JOHN GARLAND JEFFERSON. FORD ED., v, 180. (N.Y., 1790.)

4548. LAWYERS, Monarchy and.— I join in your reprobation of our * * * lawyers, for their adherence to England and monarchy, in preference to their own country and its Constitution. * * * They have, in the mother country, been generally the firmest supporters of the free principles of their constitution. But there, too, they have changed. I ascribe much of this to the substitution of Blackstone for my Lord Coke, as an elementary work.—To HORATIO G. SPAFFORD. vi, 334. (M., 1814.)

— **LAWYERS, In office.**—See CONGRESS.

4549. LAWYERS, Opinions of.— On every question the lawyers are about equally divided, and were we to act but in cases where no contrary opinion of a lawyer can be had, we should never act.—To ALBERT GALLATIN. v, 369. (M., 1808.)

4550. LAWYERS, Politics and.— The study of the law qualifies a man to be useful to himself, to his neighbors, and to the public.

It is the most certain stepping stone to public preferment in the political line.—To T. M. RANDOLPH. iii, 144. FORD ED., v, 172. (N. Y., 1790.)

4551. LAWYERS, Prosperity of.— Never fear the want of business. A man who qualifies himself well for his calling never fails of employment in it.—To PETER CARR. iii, 452. FORD ED., vi, 92. (Pa., 1792.)

4552. LAWYERS, Success of.— It is superiority of knowledge which can alone lift you above the heads of your competitors, and insure you success.—To JOHN GARLAND JEFFERSON. FORD ED., v, 182. (N.Y., 1790.)

4553. LAWYERS, Too many.— Law is quite overdone. It is fallen to the ground, and a man must have great powers to raise himself in it to either honor or profit. The mob of the profession get as little money and less respect, than they would by digging the earth. The followers of Æsculapius are also numerous. Yet I have remarked that wherever one sets himself down in a good neighborhood, not preoccupied, he secures to himself its practice, and if prudent, is not long in acquiring whereon to retire and live in comfort. The physician is happy in the attachment of the families in which he practices. All think he has saved some one of them, and he finds himself everywhere a welcome guest, a home in every house. If, to the consciousness of having saved some lives, he can add that of having at no time, from want of caution, destroyed the boon he was called on to save, he will enjoy, in age, the happy reflection of not having lived in vain; while the lawyer has only to recollect how many, by his dexterity, have been cheated of their right and reduced to beggary.—To DAVID CAMPBELL. v, 499. (M., 1810.)

4554. LAWYERS, Trade of.— Their trade is to question everything, yield nothing and talk by the hour. That one hundred and fifty lawyers should do business together ought not to be expected.—AUTOBIOGRAPHY. i, 58. FORD ED., i, 82. (1821.)

— **LEAGUE, The marine.**—See 1335.

4555. LEANDER, Case of the.— Whereas, satisfactory information has been received that Henry Whitby, commanding a British armed vessel called the Leander, did, on the 25th day of the month of April [1806], within the waters and jurisdiction of the United States, and near to the entrance of the harbor of New York, by a cannon shot fired from the said vessel, Leander, commit a murder on the body of John Pearce, a citizen of the United States, * * * I do, hereby, especially enjoin, and require all officers, having authority, civil or military, * * * within the limits or jurisdiction of the United States * * * to apprehend * * * the said Henry Whitby, * * * and him * * * deliver to the civil authority, * * * to be proceeded against according to law.—PROCLAMATION. FORD ED., viii, 445. (May 1806.)

4556. LEAR (Tobias), Secretary of the Navy.— If General Smith does not accept [the Secretaryship of the Navy], there is no remedy but to appoint Lear permanently. He is equal to the office if he possessed equally the confidence of the public.—To JAMES MADISON. FORD ED., viii, 14. (W., March 1801.)

4557. LEARNING, Classical.—For classical learning I have ever been a zealous advocate. * * * I have not, however, carried so far as you do my ideas of the importance of a hypercritical knowledge of the Greek and Latin languages. I have believed it sufficient to possess a substantial understanding of their authors.—To THOMAS COOPER. vi, 390. (M., 1814.)

4558. —— ——. Among the values of classical learning, I estimate the luxury of reading the Greek and Roman authors in all the beauties of their originals. And why should not this innocent and elegant luxury take its preeminent stand ahead of all those addressed merely to the senses? I think myself more indebted to my father for this than for all the other luxuries his cares and affections have placed within my reach; and more now than when younger, and more susceptible of delights from other sources. When the decays of age have enfeebled the useful energies of the mind, the classic pages fill up the vacuum of *ennui*, and become sweet composers to that rest of the grave into which we are all sooner or later to descend.—To JOHN BRAZIER. vii, 131. (P.F., 1819.) See EDUCATION, LANGUAGES, SCIENCE, and UNIVERSITY.

4559. LEDYARD (John), Explorer.—In 1786, while at Paris, I became acquainted with John Ledyard, of Connecticut, a man of genius, of some science, and of fearless courage and enterprise. He had accompanied Captain Cook in his voyage to the Pacific, had distinguished himself on several occasions by an unrivalled intrepidity, and published an account of that voyage, with details unfavorable to Cook's deportment towards the savages, and lessening our regrets at his fate. Ledyard had come to Paris in the hope of forming a company to engage in the fur trade of the Western coast of America. He was disappointed in this, and, being out of business, and of a roaming, restless character, I suggested to him the enterprise of exploring the western part of our continent, by passing through St. Petersburg to Kamschatka, and procuring a passage thence in some of the Russian vessels to Nootka Sound, whence he might make his way across the continent to the United States; and I undertook to have the permission of the Empress of Russia solicited. He eagerly embraced the proposition, and M. de Sémoulin, the Russian Ambassador, and more particularly Baron Grimm, the special correspondent of the Empress, solicited her permission for him to pass through her dominions, to the western coast of America. And here I must correct a material error which I have committed in another place, to the prejudice of the Empress. In writing some notes of the life of Captain Lewis, prefixed to his " Expedition to the Pacific ", I stated that the Empress gave the permission asked, and afterwards retracted it. This idea, after a lapse of twenty-six years, had so insinuated itself into my mind, that I committed it to paper, without the least suspicion of error. Yet I find, on recurring to my letters of that date, that the Empress refused permission at once, considering the enterprise as entirely chimerical. But Ledyard would not relinquish it, persuading himself that, by proceeding to St. Petersburg, he could satisfy the Empress of its practicability, and obtain her permission. He went accordingly, but she was absent on a visit to some distant part of her dominions [the Crimea], and

he pursued his course to within two hundred miles of Kamschatka, where he was overtaken by an arrest from the Empress, brought back to Poland, and there dismissed. I must therefore, in justice, acquit the Empress of ever having for a moment countenanced, even by the indulgence of an innocent passage through her territories, this interesting enterprise.—AUTOBIOGRAPHY. i, 68. FORD ED., i, 94. (1821.)

4560. LEDYARD (John), Imaginative.—He is a person of ingenuity and information. Unfortunately, he has too much imagination.—To CHARLES THOMSON. ii, 276. FORD ED., iv. (1787.)

4561. LEDYARD (John), Poverty.—I had a letter from Ledyard lately, dated at St. Petersburg. He had but two shirts, and yet more shirts than shillings. Still he was determined to obtain the palm of the first circumambulator of the earth. He says, that having no money, they kick him from place to place, and thus he expects to be kicked round the globe.—To J. BANNISTER, JR. ii, 150. (P., 1787.)

4562. LEDYARD (John), Penetrating Africa.—A countryman of ours, a Mr. Ledyard of Connecticut, set out from Paris, some time ago, for St. Petersburg, to go thence to Kamschatka, thence to cross over to the western coast of America, and penetrate through the continent to the other side of it. He had got within a few days' journey of Kamschatka, when he was arrested by order of the Empress of Russia, sent back, and turned adrift in Poland. He went to London; engaged under the auspices of a private society, formed there for pushing discoveries into Africa; passed by Paris * * * for Marseilles, where he will embark for Alexandria and Grand Cairo; thence explore the Nile to its source, cross the head of the Niger, and descend that to its mouth. He promises me. if he escapes through his journey, he will go to Kentucky, and endeavor to penetrate westerly to the South Sea.—To REV. JAMES MADISON. ii, 433. (P., 1788.)

4563. —— ——. My last accounts of Ledyard were from Grand Cairo. He was just been plunging into the unknown regions of Africa, probably never to emerge again. If he returns, he has promised me to go to America and penetrate from Kentucky to the western side of the continent.—To WILLIAM CARMICHAEL. FORD ED., v, 75. (P., 1789.)

4564. LEE (Arthur), In the Treasury.—I am sorry to see a possibility of Arthur Lee's being put into the Treasury. He has no talents for the office, and what he has will be employed in rummaging old accounts to involve you in eternal war with Robert Morris; and he will, in a short time, introduce such dissensions into the commission as to break it up. If he goes on the other appointment to Kaskaskia. he will produce a revolt of that settlement from the United States.—To JAMES MONROE. i, 348. FORD ED., iv, 53. (P., 1785.)

4565. LEE (Richard Henry), In Convention.—I shall return to Virginia after the 11th of August. I wish my successor may be certain to come before that time; in that case I shall hope to see you and not Wythe, in convention, that the business of Government, which is of everlasting concern. may receive your aid.—To RICHARD HENRY LEE. i, 204. (1776.)

4566. LEE (Richard Henry), In the Revolution.—I presume you have received a copy of the Life of Richard H. Lee, from his grandson of the same name, author of the work. You and I know that he merited much during the Revolution. Eloquent, bold, and ever watchful at his post, of which his biographer omits no proof. I am not certain whether the friends of George Mason, of Patrick Henry, yourself,* and even of General Washington, may not reclaim some feathers of the plumage given him, noble as was his proper and original coat.—To JOHN ADAMS. vii, 422. FORD ED., x, 347. (M., 1825.)

4567. LEE (Richard Henry), As a soldier.—I am glad to see the romance of Lee removed from the shelf of history to that of fable. Some small portion of the transactions he relates were within my own knowledge; and of these I can say he has given more falsehood than fact; and I have heard many officers declare the same as to what had passed under their eyes.—To WILLIAM JOHNSON. FORD ED., x, 222. (M., 1822.)

4568. LEE (Richard Henry), As a Writer.—[John] Marshall, in the first volume of his history [of Washington], chap. 3, p. 180, ascribes the petition to the King, of 1774 (1 Journ. Cong. 67) to the pen of Richard Henry Lee. I think myself certain it was not written by him, as well from what I recollect to have heard, as from the internal evidence of style. His was loose, vague, frothy, rhetorical. He was a poorer writer than his brother Arthur; and Arthur's standing may be seen in his Monitor's letters, to insure the sale of which, they took the precaution of tacking to them a new edition of the Farmers' letters like Mezentius, who "*Mortua jungebat corpora vivis*".—To JOHN ADAMS. vi, 193. FORD ED., ix, 418. (M., 1813.)

— **LEGAL TENDER.**—See MONEY.

4569. LEGISLATION, The colonists and.—To continue their [the Colonists] connection with the friends whom they had left, they arranged themselves by charters of compact under the same common king, who thus completed their powers of full and perfect legislation and became the link of union between the several parts of the empire.—DECLARATION ON TAKING UP ARMS. FORD ED., i, 465. (July 1775.)

4570. —— ——. The proposition [of Lord North] is altogether unsatisfactory * * * because they [Parliament] do not renounce the power * * * of legislating for us themselves in all cases whatsoever.—REPLY TO LORD NORTH'S PROPOSITION. FORD ED., i, 480. (July 1775.)

4571. LEGISLATION, Dignity of.—The dignity of legislation admits not of changes backwards and forwards.—To COUNT DE MONTMORIN. ii, 531. (P., 1788.)

4572. LEGISLATION, Ex post facto.—I recollect no case where a question simply between citizens of the same State, has been transferred to the foreign department, except that of inhibiting tenders but of metallic money, and *ex post facto* legislation.—To EDWARD LIVINGSTON. vii, 342. FORD ED., x, 300. (M., 1824.)

* The address of this letter was lost.—EDITOR.
† By Johnson in his *Life of General Nathaniel Greene.*—EDITOR.

4573. LEGISLATION, Indiscriminate.—To show they [Parliament] mean no discontinuance of injury, they pass acts at the very time of holding out this proposition, for restraining the commerce and fisheries of the province of New England, and for interdicting the trade of the other colonies with all foreign nations. This proves unequivocally they mean not to relinquish the exercise of indiscriminate legislation over us.—REPLY TO LORD NORTH'S PROPOSITION. FORD ED., i, 480. (July 1775.)

4574. LEGISLATION, Powers of.—From the nature of things, every society must, at all times, possess within itself the sovereign powers of legislation. The feelings of human nature revolt against the supposition of a state so situated, as that it may not, in any emergency, provide against dangers which, perhaps, threaten immediate ruin.—RIGHTS OF BRITISH AMERICA. i, 138. FORD ED., i, 443. (1774.)

4575. LEGISLATION, Reform in.—They will not be able to undo all which the two preceding Legislatures * * * have done. Public faith and right will oppose this. But some parts of the system may be rightfully reformed; a liberation from the rest unremittingly pursued as fast as right will permit, and the door shut in future against similar commitments of the nation.—To PRESIDENT WASHINGTON. iii, 362. FORD ED., vi, 4. (Pa., May 1792.)

4576. LEGISLATION, Self-government and.—Rather than submit to the rights of legislating for us, assumed by the British Parliament, * * * I would lend my hand to sink the whole Island in the ocean.—To JOHN RANDOLPH. i, 201. FORD ED., i, 484. (M., Aug. 1775.)

4577. LEGISLATURES, Conference committees.—The House of Delegates has desired [a] conference in order to preserve that harmony and friendly correspondence with the Senate, which is necessary for the discharge of their joint duties of legislation, and to prevent, both now and in future, the delay of public business, and injury which may accrue to individuals, should the two Houses differ in opinion as to the distinct office of each.—REPORT TO CONGRESS. FORD ED., ii, 135. (1777.)

4578. LEGISLATURES, Convening.—He [George III.] has endeavored to pervert the exercise of the kingly office in Virginia into a detestable and insupportable tyranny * * * by refusing to call legislatures for a long space of time, thereby leaving the political system without any legislative head.—PROPOSED VA. CONSTITUTION. FORD ED., ii, 10. (June 1776.)

4579. —— ——. He has called together legislative bodies at places unusual, uncomfortable, and distant from the depositary of their public records, for the sole purpose of fatiguing them into compliance with his measures.—DECLARATION OF INDEPENDENCE AS DRAWN BY JEFFERSON.

4580. LEGISLATURES, Credentials.— The Legislature shall form one house only for the verification of their credentials.—Notes for a Va. Constitution. Ford ed., vi, 521. (1794.)

4581. LEGISLATURES, Despotism and. —All the powers of government, legislative, executive, and judiciary, result to the legislative body. The concentrating these in the same hands is precisely the definition of despotic government. It will be no alleviation that these powers will be exercised by a plurality of hands, and not by a single one. One hundred and seventy-three despots would surely be as oppressive as one. Let those who doubt it turn their eyes on the republic of Venice.—Notes on Virginia. viii, 361. Ford ed., iii, 223. (1782.)

4582. LEGISLATURES, Dissolution by George III.—One of the articles of impeachment against Trestlain and the other Judges of Westminster Hall, in the reign of Richard the Second, for which they suffered death, as traitors to their country, was, that they had advised the king that he might dissolve his Parliament at any time; and succeeding kings have adopted the opinion of these unjust Judges. Since the reign of the Second William, however, under which the British constitution was settled on its free and ancient principles, neither his Majesty, nor his ancestors, have exercised such a power of dissolution in the Island of Great Britain * ; and when his Majesty was petitioned, by the united voice of his people there, to dissolve the present Parliament, who had become obnoxious to them, his Ministers were heard to declare, in open Parliament, that his Majesty possessed no such power by the constitution. But how different their language, and his practice, here! To declare, as their duty required, the known rights of their country, to oppose the usurpations of every foreign judicature, to disregard the imperious mandates of a minister or governor, have been the avowed causes of dissolving Houses of Representatives in America. But if such powers be really invested in his Majesty, can he suppose they are there placed to awe the members from such purposes as these? When the representative body have lost the confidence of their constituents, when they have notoriously made sale of their most valuable rights, when they have assumed to themselves powers which the people never put into their hands, then, indeed, their continuing in office becomes dangerous to the State, and calls for an exercise of the power of dissolution. Such being the causes for which the representative body should, and should not be dissolved, will it not appear strange to an unbiased observer, that that of Great Britain was not dissolved, while those of the Colonies have repeatedly incurred that sentence?—Rights of British America. i, 137. Ford ed., i, 441. (1774.)

4583. —— ——. Your Majesty, or your governors, have carried this power [to dissolve

legislatures] beyond every limit known, or provided for, by the laws. After dissolving one House of Representatives, they have refused to call another, so that, for a great length of time, the legislature provided by the laws has been out of existence. From the nature of things, every society must at all times possess within itself the sovereign powers of legislation. The feelings of humanity revolt against the supposition of a state so situated as that it may not, in any emergency, provide against dangers which, perhaps, threaten immediate ruin. While those bodies are in existence to whom the people have delegated the powers of legislation, they alone possess and may exercise those powers. But when they are dissolved by the lopping off of one or more of their branches, the power reverts to the people, who may exercise it to unlimited extent, either assembling together in person, sending deputies, or in any other way they may think proper. * We forbear to trace consequences further; the dangers are conspicuous with which this practice is replete.—Rights of British America. i, 137. Ford ed., i, 442. (1774.)

4584. —— ——. When the representative body have lost the confidence of their constituents, when they have notoriously made sale of their most valuable rights, when they have assumed to themselves powers which the people never put into their hands, then, indeed, their continuing in office becomes dangerous to the State, and calls for an exercise of the power of dissolution.—Rights of British America. i, 137. Ford ed., i, 442. (1774.)

4585. —— ——. By one act they [Parliament] have suspended the powers of one American legislature, and by another have declared they may legislate for us themselves in all cases whatsoever. These two acts alone form a basis broad enough whereon to erect a despotism of unlimited extent.—Declaration on Taking up Arms. Ford ed., i, 469. (July 1775.)

4586. —— ——. He [George III.] has endeavored to pervert the exercise of the kingly office in Virginia into a detestable and insupportable tyranny * * * by dissolving legislative assemblies, repeatedly and continually, for opposing with manly firmness his invasions on the rights of the people.—Proposed Virginia Constitution. ii, 10. (June 1776.)

4587. —— ——. He [George III.] has dissolved Representative houses repeatedly and continually † for opposing with manly firmness his invasions on the rights of the people.— Declaration of Independence as Drawn by Jefferson.

4588. LEGISLATURES, Division of.— The Legislature shall be separated by lot into two chambers, which shall be called [a and w] ‡ on the first day of their session in every week; which separation shall be effected by presenting to the representatives from each county separately a number of lots equal to their own number, if it be an even one or to the next even number above, if their number be odd,

---

* "Since this period the King has several times dissolved the parliament a few weeks before its expiration, merely as an assertion of right."—Note by Jefferson.
"On further inquiry, I find two instances of dissolutions before the Parliament would, of itself, have been at an end : viz., the Parliament called to meet August 24, 1698, was dissolved by King William, December 19, 1700, and a new one called to meet February 6, 1701, which was also dissolved, November 11, 1701, and a new one met December 30, 1701."—Note by Jefferson.

* A note in Jefferson's pamphlet copy of the "Rights," &c., reads: "Insert 'and the frame of government, thus dissolved, should the people take upon them to lay the throne of your Majesty prostrate, or to discontinue their connection with the British empire, none will be so bold as to decide against the right or the efficacy of such avulsion'."—Editor.
† Congress struck out "and continually".—Editor.
‡ The brackets and enclosures are Jefferson's.— Editor.

one half of which lots shall be distinctively marked for the one chamber and the other half for the other, and each member shall be, for that week, of the chamber whose lot he draws. Members not present at the first drawing for the week shall draw on their first attendance after.—NOTES FOR A CONSTITUTION. FORD ED., vi, 521. (1794.)

4589. —— ——. Each chamber shall appoint a speaker for the session, and it shall be weekly decided by lot between the two speakers, of which chamber each shall be for the ensuing week; and the chamber to which he is allotted shall have one the less in the lots presented to his colleagues for that week. —NOTES FOR A CONSTITUTION. FORD ED., vi, 521. (1794.)

4590. —— ——. Our legislatures are composed of two houses, the Senate and Representatives, elected in different modes, and for different periods, and in some States, with a qualified veto in the Executive chief. But to avoid all temptation to superior pretensions of the one over the other house, and the possibility of either erecting itself into a privileged order, might it not be better to choose at the same time and in the same mode, a body sufficiently numerous to be divided by lot into two separate houses, acting as independently as the two houses in England, or in our governments, and to shuffle their names together and redistribute them by lot, once a week for a fortnight? This would equally give the benefit of time and separate deliberation, guard against an absolute passage by acclamation, derange cabals, intrigues, and the count of noses, disarm the ascendency which a popular demagogue might at any time obtain over either house, and render impossible all disputes between the two houses, which often form such obstacles to business.—To M. CORAY. vii, 321. (M., 1823.)

4591. —— ——In the structure of our legislatures, we think experience has proved the benefit of subjecting questions to two separate bodies of deliberants; but in constituting these, natural right has been mistaken, some making one of these bodies, and some both, the representatives of property instead of persons; whereas the double deliberation might be as well obtained without any violation of true principle, either by requiring a greater age in one of the bodies, or by electing a proper number of representatives of persons, dividing them by lots into two chambers, and renewing the division at frequent intervals, in order to break up all cabals.—To JOHN CARTWRIGHT. vii, 357. (M., 1824.)

4592. LEGISLATURES, Election of members.—So many [representatives] only shall be deemed elected as there are units actually v ting on that particular election, adding one for any fraction of votes exceeding the half unit. Nor shall more be deemed elected than the number last apportioned. If a county has not a half unit of votes, the Legislature shall incorporate its votes with those of some adjoining county.—NOTES FOR A VA. CONSTITUTION. FORD ED., vi, 520. (1794.)

4593. —— ——. Every elector may vote for as many representatives as were apportioned by the Legislature to his county at the last establishment of the unit.—NOTES FOR A VA. CONSTITUTION. FORD ED., vi, 520. (1794.)

4594. —— ——. There are parts of the new constitution of Spain in which you would expect, of course, that we should not concur. * * * One of these is the aristocracy, *quater sublimata*, of her legislators; for the ultimate electors of these will themselves have been three times sifted from the mass of the people, and may choose from the nation at large persons never named by any of the electoral bodies.—To CHEVALIER DE ONIS. vi, 342. (M., 1814.)

4595. —— ——. Let every man who fights or pays, exercise his just and equal right in the election of the legislature.—To SAMUEL KERCHIVAL. vii, 11. FORD ED., x, 39. (M., 1816.)

4596. LEGISLATURES, Freedom of action.—The House of Representatives, when met, shall be free to act according to their own judgment and conscience.—PROPOSED VA. CONSTITUTION. FORD ED., ii, 15. (June 1776.)

4597. LEGISLATURES, Interregnum of.—He [George III.] has refused for a long time after such dissolutions [of representative houses] to cause others to be elected, whereby the legislative powers, incapable of annihilation, have returned to the people at large for their exercise, the State remaining, in the meantime, exposed to all the dangers of invasion from without and convulsions within. —DECLARATION OF INDEPENDENCE AS DRAWN BY JEFFERSON.

4598. LEGISLATURES, Officers of.— The General Assembly shall have power to appoint the speakers of their respective houses, treasurer, auditors, attorney general, register, all general offices of the military, their own clerks and serjeants, and no other officers, except where, in other parts of this constitution, such appointment is expressly given them.—PROPOSED VA. CONSTITUTION. viii, 446. FORD ED., iii, 325. (1783.)

4599. LEGISLATURES, The people and. —The people are not qualified to legislate. With us, therefore, they only choose the legislators.—To L'ABBÉ ARNOND. iii, 89. FORD ED., v, 103. (P., 1789.)

4600. LEGISLATURES, Powers of.— Our legislators are not sufficiently apprized of the rightful limits of their power; that their true office is to declare and enforce only our natural rights and duties, and to take none of them from us.—To F. W. GILMER. vii, 3. FORD ED., x, 32. (M., 1816.)

4601. LEGISLATURES, Privileges.— The members [of the General Assembly], during the attendance on the General Assembly, and for so long a time before and after as shall be necessary for travelling to and from the same, shall be privileged from all personal restraint and assault, and shall have no other privilege whatsoever.—PROPOSED CONSTITUTION FOR VIRGINIA. viii, 444. FORD ED., iii, 324. (1783.)

4602. ———— ————. The Legislature shall form one house only for * * * what relates to their privileges.—NOTES FOR A VA. CONSTITUTION. vi, 521. (1794.)

4603. LEGISLATURES, Qualifications of Members.—Any member of the * * * Assembly accepting any office of profit under this State. or the United States, or any of them, shall thereby vacate his seat, but shall be capable of being reelected.—PROPOSED VA. CONSTITUTION. viii, 445. FORD ED., iii, 325. (1783.)

4604. ———— ————. Of this General Assembly, the treasurer, attorney general, register, ministers of the gospel, officers of the regular armies of this State, or of the United States, persons receiving salaries or emoluments from any power foreign to our confederacy, those who are not resident in the county for which they are chosen delegates, or districts for which they are chosen senators, those who are not qualified as electors, persons who shall have committed treason. felony, or such other crime as would subject them to infamous punishment, or shall have been convicted by due course of law of bribery or corruption, in endeavoring to procure an election to the said assembly, shall be incapable of being members. All others, not herein elsewhere excluded, who may elect, shall be capable of being elected thereto.—PROPOSED CONSTITUTION FOR VIRGINIA. viii, 445. FORD ED., iii, 324. (1783.)

4605. LEGISLATURES, Size of.—Is it meant to confine the legislative body to their present numbers, that they may be the cheaper bargain whenever they shall become worth a purchase?—RIGHTS OF BRITISH AMERICA. i, 136. FORD ED., i, 441. (1774.)

4606. ———— ————. Twelve hundred men in one room are too many.—TO THOMAS PAINE. iii, 71. (P., 1789.)

4607. ———— ————. The [National] Assembly [of France] proceeds slowly in the forming their constitution. The original vice of their numbers causes this. as well as a tumultuous manner of doing business.—TO JOHN JAY. iii, 115. (P., 1789.)

4608. ———— ————. Render the [Virginia] legislature a desirable station by lessening the number of representatives (say to 100) and lengthening somewhat their term, and proportion them equally among the electors.—TO ARCHIBALD STUART. iii, 315. FORD ED., v, 410. (Pa., 1791.)

4609. ———— ————. Reduce the legislature to a convenient number for full, but orderly discussion.—TO SAMUEL KERCHIVAL. vii, 11. FORD ED., x. 39. (M., 1816.)

4610. LEGISLATURES, Slothful.—The sloth of the [French National] Assembly (unavoidable from their number) has done the most sensible injury to the public cause. The patience of a people who have less of that quality than any other nation in the world,· is worn threadbare.—TO JOHN JAY. iii, 115. (P., Sep. 1789.)

4611. LEGISLATURES, Suspension of.—The act passed in the seventh year of the reign of George III., having been a peculiar attempt, must ever require peculiar mention. It is entitled, "An Act for Suspending the Legislature of New York". One free and independent legislature hereby takes upon itself to suspend the powers of another, free and independent as itself; thus exhibiting a phenomenon unknown in nature, the creator and creature of its own power.—RIGHTS OF BRITISH AMERICA. i, 131. FORD ED., i, 435. (1774.)

4612. ———— ————. The proposition [of Lord North] is altogether unsatisfactory * * * because they (Parliament) do not renounce the power of suspending our own legislatures.—REPLY TO LORD NORTH'S PROPOSITION. FORD ED., i, 480. (July 1775.)

4613. ———— ————. He [George III.] has endeavored to pervert the exercise of the kingly office in Virginia into a detestable and unsupportable tyranny * * * by combining with others to subject us to a foreign jurisdiction, giving his assent to their pretended acts of legislation * * * for suspending our own legislatures, and declaring themselves invested with power to legislate for us in all cases whatsoever.—PROPOSED VA. CONSTITUTION. FORD ED., ii, 11. (June 1776.)

4614. LEGISLATURES, Two chambers.—The purpose of establishing different houses of legislation is to introduce the influence of different interests or different principles. Thus in Great Britain, it is said. their constitution relies on the House of Commons for honesty. and the Lords for wisdom; which would be a rational reliance, if honesty were to be bought with money, and if wisdom were hereditary. In some of the American States, the delegates and senators are so chosen, as that the first represent the persons, and the second the property of the State. But with us. wealth and wisdom have equal chance for admission into both houses. We do not. therefore, derive from the separation of our legislature into two houses, those benefits which a proper complication of principles is capable of producing. and those which alone can compensate the evils which may be produced by their dissensions.—NOTES ON VIRGINIA. viii, 361. FORD ED., iii, 223. (1782.)

4615. ———— ————. For good legislation two houses are necessary.—TO MARQUIS LAFAYETTE. iii, 20. FORD ED., v. 92. (P., 1789.)

4616. ———— ————. I find my countrymen * * * thinking with the National Assembly [of France] in all points except that of a single house of legislation. They think their own experience has so decidedly proved the necessity of two Houses to prevent the tyranny of one that they fear that this single error will shipwreck your new constitution. I am myself persuaded that theory and practice are not at variance in this instance, and that you will find it necessary hereafter to add another branch.—To Duke De La Rochefoucauld. iii, 136. (N. Y., 1790.)

4617. LEGISLATURES, Tyranny of.—The executive in our governments is not the sole, it is scarcely the principal object of my jealousy. The tyranny of the Legislatures is the most formidable dread at present, and will be for many years.—To James Madison. iii, 5. Ford ed., v, 83. (P., 1789.)

4618. LEGISLATURES, Unit of representation.—The Legislature shall provide that returns be made to themselves periodically of the qualified voters in every county, by their name and qualification; and from the whole number of qualified voters * * * such an unit of representation shall be * * * taken as will keep the number of representatives within the limits of 150 and 300, allowing to every county a representative for every unit and fraction of more than half an unit it contains.—Notes for a Va. Constitution. Ford ed., vi, 520. (1794.)

4619. LEGISLATURES, Usurpation of power.—He has combined with others to subject us to a jurisdiction foreign to our constitutions and unacknowledged by our laws, giving his assent to their acts of pretended legislation for * * * suspending our own legislatures and declaring themselves invested with power to legislate for us in all cases whatsoever.—Declaration of Independence as Drawn by Jefferson.

4620. LEGISLATURES, Vacancies.—Vacancies in the House of Representatives, by death or disqualification, shall be filled by the electors, under a warrant from the Speaker of the said house.—Proposed Va. Constitution. Ford ed., ii, 14. (June 1776.)

4621. LEGISLATURES, Virginia.—Legislation shall be exercised by two separate houses, to wit, a House of Representatives, and a House of Senators, which shall be called the General Assembly of Virginia.—Proposed Va. Constitution. Ford ed., ii, 13. (June 1776.)

4622. ——— ———. The House of Representatives shall be composed of persons chosen by the people annually on the first day of October, and shall meet in General Assembly on the first day of November following, and so, from time to time, on their own adjournments, or at any time when summoned by the Administrator, and shall continue sitting so long as they shall think the public service requires.—Proposed Va. Constitution. Ford ed., ii, 14. (June 1776.)

4623. ——— ———. The Senate shall consist of not less than [15]* nor more than [50] members, who shall be appointed by the House of Representatives. One-third of them shall be removed out of office by lot at the end of the first [three] years, and their places

be supplied by a new appointment; one other third shall be removed by lot, in like manner, at the end of the second [three] years and their places be supplied by a new appointment; after which one-third shall be removed annually at the end of every [three] years according to seniority. When once removed, they shall be forever incapable of being reappointed to that House. Their qualifications shall be an oath of fidelity to the State, and of duty in their office, the being [31] years of age at the least, and the having given no bribe, directly or indirectly, to obtain their appointment. While in the senatorial office, they shall be incapable of holding any public pension, or post of profit, either themselves, or by others for their use.—Proposed Va. Constitution. Ford ed., ii, 15. (June 1776.)

4624. L'ENFANT (Major), Dismissal of.—It having been found impracticable to employ Major L'Enfant about the Federal city, in that degree of subordination which was lawful and proper, he has been notified that his services are at an end. It is now proper that he should receive the reward of his past services; and the wish that he should have no just cause of discontent, suggests that it should be liberal. The President thinks of two thousand five hundred, or three thousand dollars; but leaves the determination to you. *—To Messrs. Johnson, Carroll and Stewart. iii, 336. (Pa., 1792.)

4625. LETHARGY, Fatal to liberty.—Lethargy is the forerunner of death to the public liberty.—To W. S. Smith. ii, 318. Ford ed., iv, 467. (P., 1787.)

4626. LETTERS, Answering.—Instead of writing ten or twelve letters a day, which I have been in the habit of doing as a thing in course, I put off answering my letters now farmer-like, till a rainy day, and then find them sometimes postponed by other necessary occupations.—To John Adams. iv, 103. Ford ed., vi, 505. (M., April 1794.)

4627. LETTERS, Distorted.—Every word which goes from me, whether verbally or in writing, becomes the subject of so much malignant distortion, and perverted construction, that I am obliged to caution my friends against admitting the possibility of my letters getting into the public papers or a copy of them to be taken under any degree of confidence.—To Edward Dowse. iv, 477. (W., 1803.)

4628. LETTERS, Gleams of light.—Your letters * * * serve, like gleams of light, to cheer a dreary scene; where envy, hatred, malice, revenge, and all the worst passions of men, are marshalled to make one another as miserable as possible.—To Martha Jefferson Randolph. D. L. J. 248. (Pa., Feb. 1798.)

4629. LETTERS, Private.—I have generally great aversion to the insertion of my letters in the public papers; because of my passion for quiet retirement, and never to be exhibited in scenes on the public stage.—To John Adams. vii, 254. (M., 1822.)

4630. LETTERS, Sanctity of.—I should wish never to put pen to paper; and the more

---

* The brackets and figures within them are Jefferson's.—Editor.

* L'Enfant was a French engineer who was employed in laying out the City of Washington.—Editor

because of the treacherous practice some people have of publishing one's letters without leave. Lord Mansfield declared it a breach of trust, and punishable at law. I think it should be a penitentiary felony.—To JOHN ADAMS. vii, 244. FORD ED., x, 216. (M., 1822.)

4631. LETTERS, Unanswered.—The constant pressure of business has forced me to follow the practice of not answering letters which do not necessarily require it.—To ROBERT WILLIAMS. v, 209. FORD ED., ix, 166. (W., 1807.)

4632. LETTER-WRITING, Dangers of. —The abuse of confidence by publishing my letters has cost me more than all other pains, and makes me afraid to put pen to paper in a letter of sentiment.—To C. HAMMOND. vii, 217. (M., 1821.)

4633. ——— ———. I sometimes expressly desire that my letter may not be published; but this is so like requesting a man not to steal or cheat, that I am ashamed of it after I have done it.—To NATHANIEL MACON. vii, 223. FORD ED., x, 193. (M., 1821.)

4634. LETTER-WRITING, Drudgery of.—From sunrise to one or two o'clock, and often from dinner to dark, I am drudging at the writing table. And all this to answer letters into which neither interest nor inclination on my part enters; and often from persons whose names I have never before heard. Yet, writing civilly, it is hard to refuse them civil answers. This is the burthen of my life, a very grievous one indeed, and one which I must get rid of. Delaplaine lately requested me to give him a line on the subject of his book; meaning, as I well knew, to publish it. This I constantly refuse; but in this instance yielded, that in saying a word for him I might say two for myself. I expressed in it freely my sufferings from this source; hoping it would have the effect of an indirect appeal to the discretion of those, strangers and others, who, in the most friendly dispositions, oppress me with their concerns, their pursuits, their projects, inventions and speculations, political, moral, religious, mechanical, mathematical, historical, &c., &c. I hope the appeal will bring me relief, and that I shall be left to exercise and enjoy correspondence with the friends I love, and on subjects which they, or my own inclinations present.— To JOHN ADAMS. vii, 54. FORD ED., x, 71. (M., 1817.)

4635. LETTER-WRITING, Relief from. —It occurs then, that my condition of existence, truly stated in that letter, if better known, might check the kind indiscretions which are so heavily oppressing the departing hours of life. Such a relief [from letter-writers] would, to me, be an ineffable blessing. But yours, * * * equally interesting and affecting, should accompany that to which it is an answer. The two, taken together, would excite a joint interest, and place before our fellow-citizens the present condition of two ancient servants, who having faithfully performed their forty or fifty campaigns, *stipendiis omnibus expletus*, have a reasonable claim to repose from all disturbance in the sanctuary of invalids and superannuates. —To JOHN ADAMS. vii, 254. FORD ED., x, 218. (M., 1822.)

4636. LETTER-WRITING, Voluminous.—I do not know how far you may suffer, as I do, under the persecution of letters, of which every mail brings me a fresh load. They are letters of enquiry, for the most part, always of good will, sometimes from friends whom I

esteem, but much oftener from persons whose names are unknown to me, but written kindly and civilly, and to which, therefore, civility requires answers. * * * I happened to turn to my letter-list some time ago, and a curiosity was excited to count those received in a single year. It was the year before the last. I found the number to be one thousand two hundred and sixty-seven, many of them requiring answers of elaborate research, and all to be answered with due attention and consideration. Take an average of this number for a week or a day, and I will repeat the question * * * is this life? At best, it is but the life of a mill-horse, who sees no end to his circle but in death. To such a life, that of a cabbage is paradise.—To JOHN ADAMS. vii, 254. FORD ED., x, 218. (M., 1822.)

4637. LETTER-WRITING vs. READING.—The drudgery of letter writing often denies me the leisure of reading a single page in a week.—To EZRA STILES. vii, 127. (M., 1819.)

4638. LEWIS AND CLARK EXPEDITION, Jefferson suggests.—The river Missouri, and the Indians inhabiting it, are not as well known as is rendered desirable by their connection with the Mississippi, and consequently with us. It is, however, understood, that the country on that river is inhabited by numerous tribes, who furnish great supplies of furs and peltry to the trade of another nation, carried on in a high latitude, through an infinite number of portages and lakes, shut up by ice through a long season. The commerce on that line could bear no competition with that of the Missouri, traversing a moderate climate, offering, according to the best accounts, a continued navigation from its source, and possibly with a single portage, from the Western Ocean, and finding to the Atlantic a choice of channels through the Illinois or Wabash, the Lakes and Hudson, through the Ohio and Susquehanna, or Potomac or James rivers, and through the Tennessee and Savannah rivers. An intelligent officer, with ten or twelve chosen men, fit for the enterprise, and willing to undertake it, taken from our posts, where they may be spared without inconvenience, might explore the whole line, even to the Western Ocean; have conferences with the natives on the subject of commercial intercourse; get admission among them for our traders, as others are admitted; agree on convenient deposits for an interchange of articles; and return with the information required, in the course of two summers. Their arms and accoutrements, some instruments of observation, and light and cheap presents for the Indians, would be all the apparatus they could carry, and with an expectation of a soldier's portion of land on their return, would constitute the whole expense. Their pay would be going on, whether here or there. While other civilized nations have encountered great expense to enlarge the boundaries of knowledge, by undertaking voyages of discovery, and for other literary purposes, in various parts and directions, our nation seems to owe to the same object, as well as to its own interests, to explore this, the only line of easy communication across the continent, and so directly traversing our own part of it. The interests of commerce place the principal object within the constitutional powers and care of Congress, and that it should incidentally advance the geographical knowledge of our continent, cannot be but an additional gratification. The nation claiming the territory, regarding this as a literary pursuit, which it is in the habit of permitting within its Dominions, would not be disposed to view it with jealousy, even if the expiring state of its interests there did not render it a matter of indifference. The appropriation of two thousand five hundred dollars " for the purpose of extending the external commerce of the United States ', while understood and considered by the Executive as giving the legislative sanction, would cover the undertaking from notice, and prevent the obstructions which interested individuals might otherwise previously prepare in its way.—CONFIDENTIAL MESSAGE. viii, 243. FORD ED., viii, 201. (Jan. 1803.)

4639. LEWIS AND CLARK EXPEDITION, Preparations.—I had long deemed it incumbent on the authorities of our country to have the great western wilderness beyond the Mississippi explored, to make known its geography, its natural productions, its general character and inhabitants. Two attempts which I had myself made formerly, before the country was ours, the one from west to east, the other from east to west, had both proved abortive. When called to the administration of the general government, I made this an object of early attention, and proposed it to Congress. They voted a sum of five thousand dollars for its execution, and I placed Captain Lewis at the head of the enterprise. No man within the range of my acquaintance united so many of the qualifications necessary for its successful direction. But he had not received such an astronomical education as might enable him to give us the geography of the country with the precision desired. The Missouri and Columbia, which were to constitute the tract of his journey, were rivers which varied little in their progressive latitudes, but changed their longitudes rapidly and at every step. To qualify him for making these observations, so important to the value of the enterprise, I encouraged him to apply himself to this particular object, and gave him letters to Doctor Patterson and Mr. Ellicott, requesting them to instruct him in the necessary processes. Those for the longitude would, of course, be founded on the lunar distances. But as these require essentially the aid of a time-keeper, it occurred to me that during a journey of two, three, or four years, exposed to so many accidents as himself and the instrument would be, we might expect with certainty that it would become deranged, and in a desert country where it could not be repaired. I thought it then highly important that some means of observation should be furnished him which should be practicable and competent to ascertain his longitudes in that event. The equatorial occurred to myself as the most promising substitute. I observed only that Ramsden, in his explanation of its uses, and particularly that of finding the longitude at land, still required his observer to have the aid of a time-keeper. But this cannot be necessary, for the margin of the equatorial circle of this instrument being divided into time by hours, minutes and seconds, supplies the main functions of the time-keeper, and for measuring merely the interval of the observations, is such as not to be neglected. A portable pendulum for counting, by an assistant, would fully answer that purpose. I suggested my fears to several of our best astronomical friends, and my wishes that other processes should be furnished him, if any could be, which might guard us ultimately from disappointment. Several other methods were proposed, but all requiring the use of a time-keeper. That of the equatorial being recommended by none, and other duties refusing me time for protracted consultations, I relinquished the idea for that occasion. But, if a sound one, it should not be neglected. Those deserts are yet to be

explored, and their geography given to the world and ourselves with a correctness worthy of the science of the age. The acquisition of the country before Captain Lewis's departure facilitated our enterprise, but his time-keeper failed early in his journey. His dependence, then, was on the compass and log-line, with the correction of latitudes only; and the longitudes of the different points of the Missouri, of the Stony Mountains, the Columbia and Pacific, at its mouth, remain yet to be obtained by future enterprise.—To —— ——. vii, 224. (M., 1821.) See LATITUDE AND LONGITUDE.

4640. —— ——. In the journey you are about to undertake * * * should you reach the Pacific Ocean * * * and be * * * without money * * * your resource * * * can only be the credit of the United States; for which purpose I hereby authorize you to draw on the Secretaries of State, of the Treasury, of War, and of the Navy of the United States, according as you may find your drafts will be most negotiable, for the purpose of obtaining money or necessaries for yourself and men; and I solemnly pledge the faith of the United States that these drafts shall be paid punctually * * * And to give more entire satisfaction and confidence to those who may be disposed to aid you, I, Thomas Jefferson, President of the United States of America, have written this letter of general credit for you with my own hand, and signed it with my name.—To CAPTAIN MERIWETHER LEWIS. iv, 492. (W., July 4, 1803.)

4641. LEWIS AND CLARK EXPEDITION, Success.—The expedition of Messrs. Lewis and Clark, for exploring the river Missouri, and the best communication from that to the Pacific ocean, has had all the success which could have been expected. They have traced the Missouri nearly to its source, descended the Columbia to the Pacific ocean, ascertained with accuracy the geography of that interesting communication across our continent, learned the character of the country, of its commerce, and inhabitants; and it is but justice to say that Messrs. Lewis and Clark, and their brave companions, have by this arduous service deserved well of their country.—SIXTH ANNUAL MESSAGE. viii, 66. FORD ED., viii, 492. (Dec. 1806.)

4642. LEVEES, Presidential.—Edmund Randolph tells James Madison and myself a curious fact which he had from Lear. When the President went to New York, he resisted for three weeks the efforts to introduce levees. At length he yielded, and left it to Humphreys and some others to settle the forms. Accordingly, an antechamber and presence room were provided, and when those who were to pay their court were assembled, the President set out, preceded by Humphreys. After passing through the antechamber, the door of the inner room was thrown open, and Humphreys entered first, calling out with a loud voice, " the President of the United States". The President was so much disconcerted with it, that he did not recover from it the whole time of the levee, and when the company was gone, he said to Humphreys, " Well, you have taken me in once, but by God you shall never take me in a second time ".—THE ANAS. ix, 132. FORD ED., i, 216. (1793.)

4643. LEVEES, Washington's explanation.—President Washington [in conversation with me] went lengthily into the late attacks on him for levees, &c., and explained how he had been led into them by the persons he consulted at New York; and that if he could but know what the sense of the public was, he would most cheerfully conform to it.—THE ANAS. ix, 132. FORD ED., i, 216. (Feb. 1793.) See CEREMONY, ETIQUETTE and FORMS.

4644. LIANCOURT (Duke de), Appeal for.—I wish the present government would permit M. de Liancourt's return. He is an honest man, sincerely attached to his country, and very desirous of being permitted to live retired in the bosom of his family. My sincere affection for his connections at Rocheguyon * * * would render it a peculiar felicity to me to be any ways instrumental in having him restored to them. I have no means, however, unless you can interpose without giving offence.—To JAMES MONROE. FORD ED., vii, 88. (M., 1796.)

4645. LIANCOURT (Duke de), Patriot.—The bearer hereof is the Duke de Liancourt, one of the principal noblemen of France, and one of the richest. All this he has lost in the revolutions of his country, retaining only his virtue and good sense, which he possesses in a high degree. He was President of the National Assembly of France in its earliest stage, and forced to fly from the proscriptions of Marat.—To MR. HITE. iv, 145. (M., 1796.)

4646. LIBELS, Federal cognizance.—Libels, falsehood, and defamation, equally with heresy and false religion, are withheld from the cognizance of Federal tribunals.—KENTUCKY RESOLUTIONS. ix, 466. FORD ED., vii, 295. (1798.)

4647. LIBELS, Guarding against.—I have seen in the New York papers a calumny which I suppose will run through the Union, that I had written by Doctor Logan letters to Merlin and Talleyrand. On retiring from the Secretary of State's office, I determined to drop all correspondence with France, knowing the base calumnies which would be built on the most innocent correspondence. I have not, therefore, written a single letter to that country, within that period except to Mr. Short on his own affairs merely which are under my direction, and once or twice to Colonel Monroe. By Logan, I did not write even a letter to Mr. Short, nor to any other person whatever. I thought this notice of the matter due to my friends, though I do not go into the newspapers with a formal declaration of it.—To AARON BURR. FORD ED., vii, 259. (M., Nov. 1798.)

4648. LIBELS, Jefferson and.—At this moment my name is running through all the city [Philadelphia] as detected in a criminal correspondence with the French Directory, and fixed upon me by the documents from our Envoys, now before the two Houses. The detection of this by the publication of the papers, should they be published, will not relieve all the effects of the lie, and should they not be published, they may keep it up as long and as successfully as they did and do that of my being involved in Blount's conspiracy.—To JAMES MONROE. FORD ED., vii, 233. (Pa., April 1798.)

4649. ———. Party passions are indeed high. Nobody has more reasons to know it than myself. I receive daily bitter proofs of it from people who never saw me, nor know anything of me but through " Porcupine "

[William Cobbett] and Fenno.—To JAMES LEWIS, JR. iv, 241. FORD ED., vii, 250. (Pa., May 1798.) ·

4650. ———. Our very long intimacy as fellow laborers in the same cause, the recent expressions of mutual confidence which had preceded your mission [to France], the interesting course which that had taken, and particularly and personally as it regarded yourself, made me anxious to hear from you * * * . I was the more so, too, as I had myself, during the whole of your absence, as well as since your return, been a constant butt for every shaft of calumny which malice and falsehood could form, and the presses, public speakers, or private letters disseminate. One of these, too, was of a nature to touch yourself; as if, wanting confidence in your efforts, I had been capable of usurping powers committed to you, and authorizing negotiations private and collateral to yours. The real truth is, that though Doctor Logan, the pretended missionary, about four or five days before he sailed for Hamburg, told me he was going there, and thence to Paris, and asked and received from me a certificate of his citizenship, character, and circumstances of life, merely as a protection, should he be molested on his journey, in the present turbulent and suspicious state of Europe, yet I had been led to consider his object as relative to his private affairs; and though, from an intimacy of some standing, he knew well enough my wishes for peace and my political sentiments in general, he nevertheless received then no particular declaration of them, no authority to communicate them to any mortal, nor to speak to any one in my name, or in anybody's name, on that, or on any other subject whatever; nor did I write by him a scrip of a pen to any person whatever. This he has himself honestly and publicly declared since his return; and from his well-known character and every other circumstance, every candid man must perceive that his enterprise was dictated by his own enthusiasm. without consultation or communication with any one; that he acted in Paris on his own ground, and made his own way. Yet to give some color to his proceedings, which might implicate the republicans in general. and myself particularly, they have not been ashamed to bring forward a supposititious paper, drawn by one of their own party in the name of Logan, and falsely pretended to have been presented by him to the government of France; counting that the bare mention of my name therein, would connect that in the eye of the public with this transaction.—To ELBRIDGE GERRY. iv, 266. FORD ED., vii, 325. (Pa, Jan. 1799.)

4651. ———. It is hardly necessary for me to declare to you, on everything sacred, that the part they assigned to me was entirely a calumny. Logan called on me four or five days before his departure. and asked and received a certificate (in my private capacity) of his citizenship and circumstances of life, merely as a protection, should he be molested in the present turbulent state of Europe. I have given such to an hundred others, and they have been much more frequently asked and obtained by tories than whigs. I did not write a scrip of a pen by him to any person. From long acquaintance he knew my wishes for peace, and my political sentiments generally, but he received no particular declaration of them nor one word of authority to speak in my name, or anybody's name on that or any other subject. It was an enterprise founded in the enthusiasm of his own character. He went on his own ground, and made his own way. His object was virtuous, and the effect meritorious.—To EDMUND PENDLETON. iv, 276. FORD ED.. vii, 338. (Pa., 1799.)

4652. LIBELS, Jurisdiction over.—Nor does the [my] opinion of the unconstitutionality, and consequent nullity of that law, [Sedition] remove all restraint from the overwhelming torrent of slander, which is confounding all vice and virtue, all truth and falsehood, in the United States. The power to do that is fully possessed by the several State Legislatures. It was reserved to them, and was denied to the General Government, by the Constitution, according to our construction of it. While we deny that Congress have a right to control the freedom of the press, we have ever asserted the right of the States, and their exclusive right, to do so. They have accordingly, all of them, made provisions for punishing slander, which those who have time and inclination, resort to for the vindication of their characters.—To MRS. JOHN ADAMS. iv, 561. FORD ED., viii, 311. (M., 1804.)

4653. LIBELS, Newspaper.—Printers shall be liable to legal prosecution for printing and publishing false facts, injurious to the party prosecuting; but they shall be under no other restraint.—FRENCH CHARTER OF RIGHTS. iii, 47. FORD ED., v, 102. (P., 1789.)

4654. ——— ———. In those States where they do not admit even the truth of allegations to protect the printer, they have gone too far.—To MRS. JOHN ADAMS. iv, 561. FORD ED., viii, 311. (M., 1804.)

4655. ——— ———. No inference is here intended, that the laws, provided by the States against false and defamatory publications, should not be enforced; he who has time, renders a service to public morals and public tranquillity, in reforming these abuses by the salutary coercions of the law.—SECOND INAUGURAL ADDRESS. viii, 44. FORD ED., viii, 346. (1805.)

4656. ——— ———. We have received from your [Massachusetts] presses a very malevolent and incendiary denunciation of the administration, bottomed on absolute falsehood from beginning to end. The author would merit exemplary punishment for so flagitious a libel, were not the torment of his own abominable temper punishment sufficient for even as base a crime as this.—To LEVI LINCOLN. v, 264. (W., March 1808.)

4657. ——— ———. Mr. Wagner's malignity, like that of the rest of his tribe of brother printers, who deal out calumnies for federal readers, gives me no pain. When a printer cooks up a falsehood, it is as easy to put it into the mouth of a Mr. Fox, as of a smaller man, and safer in that of a dead than a living one.—To THOMAS LAW. v, 555. FORD ED., ix, 291. (M., 1811.)

4658. LIBELS, Prosecutions for.—While a full range is proper for actions by individuals, either private or public, for slanders affecting them, I would wish much to see the experiment tried of getting along without public prosecutions for libels. I believe we can do it. Patience and well doing, instead of punishment, if it can be found sufficiently efficacious, would be a happy change in the instruments of government.—To LEVI LINCOLN. FORD ED., viii, 139. (March 1802.)

4659. LIBELS, Punishment for.—I might have filled the courts of the United States with actions for slanders, and have ruined, perhaps many persons who are not innocent. But this would be no equivalent for the loss of character. I leave them, therefore, to the reproof of their own consciences. If these do not condemn them, there will yet come a day when the false witness will meet a Judge who has not slept over his slanders.—To URIAH M'GREGORY. iv, 333. (M., 1800.)

4660. LIBELS, Sedition law and.—Mr. Randolph has proposed an inquiry [in Congress] into certain prosecutions at common law in Connecticut, for libels on the government, and not only himself but others have stated them with such affected caution, and such hints at the same time, as to leave on every mind the impression that they had been instituted either by my direction, or with my acquiescence, at least. This has not been denied by my friends, because probably the fact is unknown to them. I shall state it for their satisfaction, and leave it to be disposed of as they think best. I had observed in a newspaper some dark hints of a prosecution in Connecticut, but so obscurely hinted that I paid little attention to it. Some considerable time after, it was again mentioned, so that I understood that some prosecution was going on in the federal court there, for calumnies uttered from the pulpit against me by a clergyman. I immediately wrote to Mr. Granger, who, I think, was in Connecticut at the time, stating that I had laid it down as a law to myself, to take no notice of the thousand calumnies issued against me, but to trust my character to my own conduct, and the good sense and candor of my fellow citizens; that I had found no reason to be dissatisfied with that course, and I was unwilling it should be broke through by others as to any matter concerning me; and I, therefore, requested him to direct the district attorney to dismiss the prosecution. Some time after this, I heard of subpœnas being served on General Lee, David M. Randolph, and others, as witnesses to attend the trial, I then for the first time conjectured the subject of the libel. I immediately wrote to Mr. Granger, to require an immediate dismission of the prosecution. The answer of Mr. Huntington, the district attorney, was that these subpœnas had been issued by the defendant without his knowledge, that it had been his intention to dismiss all the prosecutions at the first meeting of the court, and to accompany it with an avowal of his opinion, that they could not be maintained, because the federal court had no jurisdiction over libels. This was accordingly done. I did not till then know that there were other prosecutions of the same nature, nor do I now know what were their subjects. But all went off together; and I afterwards saw in the hands of Mr. Granger, a letter written by the clergyman, disavowing any personal ill will towards me, and solemnly declaring he had never uttered the words charged. I think Mr. Granger either showed me, or said there were affidavits of at least half a dozen respectable men, who were present at the sermon and swore no such expressions were uttered, and as many equally respectable men who swore the contrary. But the clergyman expressed his gratification at the dismission of the prosecution. * * * Certain it is, that the prosecutions had been instituted, and had made considerable progress, without my knowledge, that they were disapproved by me as soon as known, and directed to be discontinued. The attorney did it on the same ground on which I had acted myself in the cases of Duane, Callendar and others; to wit, that the Sedition law was unconstitutional and null, and that my obligation to execute what was law, involved that of not suffering rights secured by valid laws to be prostrated by what was no law.—To WILSON C. NICHOLAS. v, 452. FORD ED., ix, 253. (M., 1809.)

4661. LIBELS, Voltaire and.—I send you Voltaire's legacy to the King of Prussia,—a libel which will do much more injury to Voltaire than to the King. Many of the traits in the character of the latter to which the former gives a turn satirical and malicious, are real virtues.—To JAMES MONROE. FORD ED., iv, 44. (P., 1785.)

4662. LIBERTY, America and.—The last hope of human liberty in this world rests on us. We ought, for so dear a stake, to sacrifice every attachment and every enmity.—To WILLIAM DUANE. v, 577. FORD ED., ix, 313. (M., 1811.)

4663. ———— ————. When we reflect that the eyes of the virtuous all over the earth are turned with anxiety on us, as the only depositories of the sacred fire of liberty, and that our falling into anarchy would decide forever the destinies of mankind, and seal the political heresy that man is incapable of self-government, the only contest between divided friends should be who will dare farthest into the ranks of the common enemy.—To JOHN HOLLINS. v, 597. (M., 1811.) See 296.

4664. LIBERTY, Attachment to.—Our attachment to no nation on earth should supplant our attachment to liberty.—DECLARATION ON TAKING UP ARMS. FORD ED., i, 470. (1775.)

4665. LIBERTY, Blood and.—The tree of liberty must be refreshed from time to time with the blood of patriots and tyrants. It is its natural manure.—To W. S. SMITH. ii, 319. FORD ED., iv, 467. (P., 1787.)

4666. ———— ————. A warm zealot for the attainment and enjoyment by all mankind of as much liberty, as each may exercise without injury to the equal liberty of his fellow citizens. I have lamented that in France the

endeavors to obtain this should have been attended with the effusion of so much blood.—To M. DE MEUNIER. FORD ED., vii, 13. (M., April 1795.)

4667. LIBERTY, Concern for.—Affectionate concern for the liberty of my fellow citizens will cease but with life to animate my breast.—REPLY TO ADDRESS. v, 262. (1808.)

4668. LIBERTY, Contagious.—The disease of liberty is catching.—To MARQUIS LAFAYETTE. vii, 194. FORD ED., x, 179. (M., 1820.)

4669. LIBERTY, Degeneracy and.—It astonishes me to find such a change wrought in the opinions of our countrymen since I left them, as that three-fourths of them should be contented to live under a system which leaves to their governors the power of taking from them the trial by jury in civil cases, freedom of religion, freedom of the press, freedom of commerce, the *habeas corpus* laws, and of yoking them with a standing army. This is a degeneracy in the principles of liberty to which I had given four centuries instead of four years.—To WILLIAM STEPHENS SMITH. FORD ED., v, 3. (P., Feb. 1788.)

4670. LIBERTY, Degrees of.—I would rather be exposed to the inconveniences attending too much liberty than to those attending too small a degree of it.—To ARCHIBALD STUART. iii, 314. FORD ED., v, 409. (Pa., 1791.)

4671. LIBERTY, Despotism and.—The agitations of the public mind advance its powers, and at every vibration between the points of liberty and despotism, something will be gained for the former.—To THOMAS COOPER. iv, 452. FORD ED., viii, 177. (W., Nov. 1802.)

4672. LIBERTY, European.—Heaven send that the glorious example of France may be but the beginning of the history of European liberty, and that you may live many years in health and happiness to see at length that heaven did not make man in its wrath.—To LA DUCHESSE D'AUVILLE. iii, 135. FORD ED., v, 154. (N.Y., April 1790.)

4673. ———— ————. God send that all the nations who join in attacking the liberties of France may end in the attainment of their own.—To JOEL BARLOW. iii, 451. FORD ED., vi, 88. (Pa., 1792.)

4674. LIBERTY, First of all.—Postpone to the great object of Liberty every smaller motive and passion.—To THE PRESIDENT OF CONGRESS. FORD ED., ii, 298. (Wg., 1780.)

4675. LIBERTY, France and.—The atrocious proceedings of France towards this country, had well nigh destroyed its liberties. The Anglomen and monocrats had so artfully confounded the cause of France with that of freedom, that both went down in the same scale.—To T. LOMAX. iv, 301. FORD ED., vii, 374. (M., March 1799.)

4676. ———— ————. May you see France reestablished in that temperate portion of liberty which does not infer either anarchy or licentiousness, in that high degree of prosperity which would be the consequence of such a government, in that, in short, which the constitution of 1789 would have insured it, if wisdom could have stayed at that point the fervid but imprudent zeal of men, who did not know the character of their own countrymen.—To MADAME DE STAEL. vi, 120. (May 1813.)

4677. LIBERTY, Free Press and.—The functionaries of every government have propensities to command at will the liberty and property of their constituents. There is no safe deposit for these but with the people themselves; nor can they be safe with them without information. Where the press is free, and every man able to read, all is safe.—To CHARLES YANCEY. vi, 517. FORD ED., x, 4. (M., 1816.)

4678. LIBERTY, French Revolution and.—The success of the French Revolution will ensure the progress of liberty in Europe, and its preservation here.—To EDMUND PENDLETON. FORD ED., v, 358. (Pa., 1791.)

4679. ——— ———. The liberty of the whole earth was depending on the issue of the contest, and was ever such a prize won with so little innocent blood?—To WILLIAM SHORT. iii, 502. FORD ED., vi, 154. (Pa., 1793.)

4680. ——— ———. I continue eternally attached to the principles of your [French] Revolution. I hope it will end in the establishment of some firm government, friendly to liberty, and capable of maintaining it. If it does, the world will become inevitably free. —To J. P. BRISSOT DE WARVILLE. FORD ED., vi, 249. (Pa., 1793.)

4681. LIBERTY, Gift of God.—All men * * * are endowed by their Creator with inherent* and inalienable rights. Among these * * * [is] liberty.—DECLARATION OF INDEPENDENCE AS DRAWN BY JEFFERSON.

4682. ——— ———. Can the liberties of a nation be thought secure when we have removed their only firm basis, a conviction in the minds of the people that these liberties are of the gift of God?—NOTES ON VIRGINIA. viii, 404. FORD ED., iii, 267. (1782.)

4683. LIBERTY, Government and.—The natural progress of things is for liberty to yield and government to gain ground.—To EDWARD CARRINGTON. ii, 404. FORD ED., v, 20. (P., 1788.)

4684. ——— ———. The policy of the American government is to leave their citizens free, neither restraining nor aiding them in their pursuits.—To M. L'HOMMANDE. ii, 236. (P., 1787.)

4685. ——— ———. The freedom and happiness of man * * * are the sole objects of all legitimate government.—To GENERAL KOSCIUSKO. v, 50. (M., 1810.)

*Congress struck out "inherent" and inserted "certain".—EDITOR.

4686. LIBERTY, Happiness and.—It is our glory that we first put the ball of liberty into motion, and our happiness that, being foremost, we had no bad examples to follow.—To TENCH COXE. FORD ED., vii, 22. (M., 1795.)

4687. LIBERTY, Kosciusko and.—General Kosciusko is as pure a son of liberty as I have ever known, and of that liberty which is to go to all, and not to the few or the rich alone.—To HORATIO GATES. iv, 212. FORD ED., vii, 204. (Pa., 1798.)

4688. LIBERTY, Life and.—The God who gave us life, gave us liberty at the same time: the hand of force may destroy, but it cannot disjoin them.*—RIGHTS OF BRITISH AMERICA. i, 142. FORD ED., i, 447. (1774.)

4689. LIBERTY, Light and.—Light and liberty go together.—To TENCH COXE. FORD ED., vii, 22. (M., 1795.)

4690. ——— ———. I will not believe our labors are lost. I shall not die without a hope that light and liberty are on steady advance.— To JOHN ADAMS. vii, 217. (M., 1821.)

4691. LIBERTY, Love of.—The commotions in Massachusetts† are a proof that the people love liberty, and I could not wish them less than they have.—To EZRA STILES. ii, 77. (P., 1786.)

4692. LIBERTY, Napoleon and.—If the hero [Napoleon] who has saved you from a combination of enemies, shall also be the means of giving you as great a portion of liberty as the opinions, habits and character of the nation are prepared for, progressive preparation may fit you for progressive portions of that first of blessings, and you may in time attain what we erred in supposing could be hastily seized and maintained, in the present state of political information among your citizens at large.—To M. CABANIS. iv, 496. (W., 1803.)

4693. LIBERTY, Natural.—Under the law of nature, we are all born free.—LEGAL ARGUMENT. FORD ED., i, 380. (1770.)

4694. LIBERTY, No easy road to.— We are not to expect to be translated from despotism to liberty in a feather bed.—To MARQUIS DE LAFAYETTE. iii, 132. FORD ED., v, 152. (N.Y., 1790.)

4695. ——— ———. The ground of liberty is to be gained by inches and we must be contented to secure what we can get, from time to time, and eternally press forward for what is yet to get. It takes time to persuade men to do even what is for their own good.—To REV. CHARLES CLAY. iii, 126. FORD ED., v, 142. (M., 1790.)

4696. LIBERTY, Order and.—Possessing ourselves the combined blessing of liberty and order, we wish the same to other countries.—To M. CORAY. vii, 318. (M., 1823.)

* "Ab eo libertas, a quo spiritus," was the motto on one of Jefferson's seals.—EDITOR.
† Shays's Rebellion.—EDITOR.

— **LIBERTY, Personal.**—See PERSONAL
LIBERTY.

4697. LIBERTY, Preservation of.—We
do then most solemnly, before God and the
world declare that, regardless of every consequence, at the risk of every distress, the
arms we have been compelled to assume we
will use with the perseverance, exerting to
their utmost energies all those powers which
our Creator hath given us, to preserve that
liberty which He committed to us in sacred
deposit and to protect from every hostile hand
our lives and our properties.—DECLARATION
ON TAKING UP ARMS. FORD ED., i, 474. (July
1775.)

4698. —— ——. I am convinced that, on
the good sense of the people, we may rely
with the most security for the preservation
of a due degree of liberty.—To JAMES MAD-
ISON. FORD ED., iv, 480. (P., 1787.)

4699. —— ——. The people are the only
sure reliance for the preservation of our liberty.—To JAMES MADISON. ii, 332. (1787.)

4700. —— ——. The preservation of the
holy fire is confided to us by the world, and
the sparks which will emanate from it will
ever serve to rekindle it in other quarters
of the globe, *Numinibus secundis.*—To REV.
MR. KNOX. v, 503. (M., 1810.)

4701. LIBERTY, Preparation for.—A
full measure of liberty is not now perhaps
to be expected by your nation, nor am I confident they are prepared to preserve it. More
than a generation will be requisite, under the
administration of reasonable laws favoring
the progress of knowledge in the general mass
of the people, and their habituation to an
independent security of person and property,
before they will be capable of estimating the
value of freedom, and the necessity of a
sacred adherence to the principles on which
it rests for preservation. Instead of that liberty which takes root and growth in the
progress of reason, if recovered by mere
force or accident, it becomes, with an unprepared people, a tyranny still, of the many, the
few, or the one.—To MARQUIS LAFAYETTE.
vi, 421. FORD ED., ix, 505.(M., Feb. 1815.)

4702. LIBERTY, The Press and.—Our
liberty cannot be guarded but by the freedom
of the press, nor that be limited without
danger of losing it.—To JOHN JAY. FORD ED.,
iv, 186. (P., 1786.) See PRESS and NEWS-
PAPERS.

4703. LIBERTY, Progress of.—I cordially wish well to the progress of liberty in
all nations, and would forever give it the
weight of our countenance.—To T. LOMAX.
iv, 301. FORD ED., vii, 374. (M., March 1799.)

4704. LIBERTY, Resistance and.—
What country can preserve its liberties if its
rulers are not warned from time to time that
the people preserve the spirit of resistance?—
To W. S. SMITH. ii, 318. FORD ED., iv, 467.
(P., 1787.) See REBELLION.

4705. LIBERTY, Restricted.—I had
hoped that Geneva was familiarized to such a

degree of liberty, that they might without
difficulty or danger fill up the measure to its
maximum; a term, which, though in the insulated man, bounded only by his natural
powers, must, in society, be so far restricted
as to protect himself against the evil passions
of his associates, and consequently, them
against him.—To M. D'IVERNOIS. iv, 114.
FORD ED., vii, 4. (M., Feb. 1795.)

4706. LIBERTY, Royalty and.—The
public liberty may be more certainly secured
by abolishing an office [royalty] which all experience hath shown to be inveterately inimical thereto.—PROPOSED VA. CONSTITUTION.
FORD ED., ii, 12. (June 1776.)

4707. —— ——. It is impossible for you
to conceive what is passing in our conclave.
and it is evident that one or two at least,
under pretence of avoiding war on the one
side, have no great antipathy to run foul of
it on the other, and to make a part in the
confederacy of princes against human liberty.
—To JAMES MADISON. iii, 563. FORD ED., vi,
261. (Pa., May 1793.)

4708. —— ——. I am not for * * *
joining in the confederacy of kings to war
against the principles of liberty.—To ELBRIDGE
GERRY. iv, 268. FORD ED., vii, 328. (Pa.,
1799.)

4709. LIBERTY, Sacred.—For promoting
the public happiness, those persons whom nature has endowed with genius and virtue
should be rendered by liberal education
worthy to receive, and able to guard the
sacred deposit of the rights and liberties of
their fellow citizens; and they should be
called to that charge without regard to
wealth, birth, or other accidental condition or
circumstance.—DIFFUSION OF KNOWLEDGE
BILL. FORD ED., ii, 221. (1779.)

4710. —— ——. The most sacred cause
that ever man was engaged in.*—OPINION ON
THE "LITTLE SARAH". ix, 155. FORD ED., vi,
344. (1793.)

4711. LIBERTY, Safeguards of.—I disapproved from the first moment [in the new
Constitution] the want of a bill of rights, to
guard liberty against the legislative as well
as the executive branches of the government.
—To F. HOPKINSON. ii, 586. FORD ED., v,
76. (P., March 1789.)

4712. —— ——. To insure the safety of
the public liberty, its depository should be
subject to be changed with the greatest ease
possible, and without suspending or disturbing for a moment the movements of the
machine of government.—To M. DESTUTT
TRACY. v, 569. FORD ED., ix, 308. (M.,
1811.)

4713. LIBERTY, Science and virtue.—
Liberty is the great parent of science and of
virtue; and a nation will be great in both
in proportion as it is free.—To DR. WILLARD.
iii, 17. (P., 1789.)

* Jefferson. was referring to the first French Republic.—EDITOR.

4714. —— ——. The general spread of the light of science has already laid open to every view the palpable truth, that the mass of mankind has not been born with saddles on their backs, nor a favored few booted and spurred, ready to ride them legitimately, by the grace of God.—To Roger C. Weightman. vii, 451. Ford ed., x, 391. (M., 1826.)

4715. LIBERTY, Sea of.—The boisterous sea of liberty is never without a wave.—To Richard Rush. vii, 182. (M., 1820.)

4716. LIBERTY, Security for.—We agree particularly in the necessity of some * * * better security for civil liberty.—To John Taylor. iv, 259. Ford ed., vii, 309. (M., 1798.)

4717. —— ——. Since, by the choice of my constituents, I have entered on a second term of administration, I embrace the opportunity to give this public assurance, * * * that I will zealously cooperate with you in every measure which may tend to secure the liberty, property, and personal safety of our fellow citizens, and to consolidate the republican forms and principles of our government.—Fifth Annual Message. viii, 53. Ford ed., viii, 396. (Dec. 1805.)

4718. LIBERTY, Subversion of.—The moderation and virtue of a single character have probably prevented this Revolution from being closed, as most others have been, by a subversion of that liberty it was intended to establish.—To General Washington. i, 335. Ford ed., iii, 467. (A., 1784.)

4719. LIBERTY, Universal.—The ball of liberty is now so well in motion that it will roll round the globe.—To Tench Coxe. Ford ed., vii, 22. (M., 1795.)

4720. —— ——. I sincerely pray that all the members of the human family may, in the time prescribed by the Father of us all, find themselves securely established in the enjoyment of * * * liberty.—Reply to Address. viii, 119. (1807.)

4721. —— ——. That we should wish to see the people of other countries free, is as natural, and at least as justifiable, as that one king should wish to see the kings of other countries maintained in their despotism.—To Albert Gallatin. vii, 78. Ford ed., x, 90. (M., 1817.)

4722. LIBERTY vs. WEALTH.—What a cruel reflection that a rich country cannot long be a free one.—Travels in France. ix, 319. (1787.)

4723. LIBRARY, Circulating.—Nothing would do more extensive good at small expense than the establishment of a small circulating library in every county.—To John Wyche. v, 448. (M., 1809.)

4724. LIBERTY, Founding.—There shall be paid out of the treasury [of Virginia] every year the sum of two thousand pounds, to be laid out in such books and maps as may be proper to be preserved in a public library;

which library shall be established at the town of Richmond.—Public Library Bill. Ford ed., ii, 236. (1799.)

4725. LIBRARY, Free.—No person shall remove any book or map out of the library; * * * but the same [may] be made useful by indulging the researches of the learned and curious, within the said library, without fee or reward.—Public Library Bill. Ford ed., ii, 236. (1799.)

4726. LIBRARY, Jefferson's.—You know my collection, its condition and extent. I have been fifty years making it, and have spared no pains, opportunity or expense, to make it what it is. While residing in Paris, I devoted every afternoon I was disengaged, for a summer or two, in examining all the principal book stores, turning over every book with my own hand, and putting by everything which related to America, and indeed whatever was rare and valuable in every science. Besides this, I had standing orders during the whole time I was in Europe, on its principal book-marts, particularly Amsterdam, Frankfort, Madrid and London, for such works relating to America as could not be found in Paris. So that in that department particularly, such a collection was made as probably can never again be effected, because it is hardly probable that the same opportunities, the same time, industry, perseverance and expense, with some knowledge of the bibliography of the subject, would again happen to be in concurrence. During the same period, and after my return to America, I was led to procure, also, whatever related to the duties of those in the high concerns of the nation. So that the collection, which I suppose is of between nine and ten thousand volumes, while it includes what is chiefly valuable in science and literature generally, extends more particularly to whatever belongs to the American Statesman. In the diplomatic and parliamentary branches, it is particularly full.—To S. H. Smith. vi, 383. Ford ed., ix, 486. (M., Sep. 1814.)

4727. LIBRARY, Sale to Congress.—It is long since I have been sensible it ought not to continue private property, and had provided that at my death, Congress should have the refusal of it at their own price. But the loss they have now incurred, makes the present the proper moment for their accommodation, without regard to the small remnant of time and the barren use of my enjoying it. I ask of your friendship, therefore, to make for me the tender of it to the Library Committee of Congress, not knowing myself of whom the Committee consists. Nearly the whole are well bound, abundance of them elegantly, and of the choicest editions existing. They may be valued by persons named by themselves, and the payment made convenient to the public. * * * I do not know that it contains any branch of science which Congress would wish to exclude from their collection; there is, in fact, no subject to which a member of Congress may not have occasion to refer. But such a wish would not correspond with my views of preventing its dismemberment. My desire is either to place it in their hands entire, or to preserve it so here.*—To S. H. Smith. vi, 384. Ford ed., ix, 486. (M., Sep. 1814.) See 1133.

4728. —— ——. The arrangement [of the library at Monticello] is as follows: 1. Ancient

* Jefferson's library was purchased by the United States Government for the use of Congress. The price paid was $23,950.—Editor.

History. 2. Modern do. 3. Physics. 4. Nat. Hist. proper. 5. Technical Arts. 6. Ethics. 7. Jurisprudence. 8. Mathematics. 9. Gardening, architecture, sculpture, painting, music, poetry. 10. Oratory. 11. Criticism. 12. Polygraphical.—To JAMES OGILVIE. FORD ED., viii, 418. (W., 1806.)

4729. LIES, Circulating.—There is an enemy somewhere endeavoring to sow discord among us. Instead of listening first, then doubting, and lastly believing anile tales handed round without an atom of evidence, if my friends will address themselves to me directly, as you have done, they shall be informed with frankness and thankfulness.—To WILLIAM DUANE. iv, 590. FORD ED., viii, 431. (W., 1806.)

4730. LIES, Fearless of.—The man who fears no truths has nothing to fear from lies. —To DR. GEORGE LOGAN. FORD ED., x, 27. (M., 1816.)

4731. LIES, Folly of.—It is of great importance to set a resolution, not to be shaken, never to tell an untruth. There is no vice so mean, so pitiful, so contemptible; and he who permits himself to tell a lie once, finds it much easier to do it a second and third time, till at length it becomes habitual; he tells lies without attending to it, and truths without the world's believing him. This falsehood of the tongue leads to that of the heart, and in time depraves all its good dispositions.—To PETER CARR. i, 396. (P., 1785.)

4732. LIES, Newspaper.—There was an enthusiasm towards us all over Europe at the moment of the peace. The torrent of lies published unremittingly in every day's London papers first made an impression and produced a coolness. The republication of these lies in most of the papers of Europe (done probably by authority of the governments) , carried them home to the belief of every mind. They supposed everything in America was anarchy, tumult and civil war. The reception of the Marquis Lafayette gave a check to these ideas.—To JAMES MADISON. i, 413. (P., 1785.)

4733. ———. It has been so impossible to contradict all their lies, that I have determined to contradict none; for while I should be engaged with one, they would publish twenty new ones. Thirty years of public life have enabled most of those who read newspapers to judge of one for themselves.— To JAMES MONROE. FORD ED., vii, 448. (Ep., May 1800.)

4734. LIES, Political.—Were I to buy off every federal lie by a sacrifice of two or three thousand dollars, a very few such purchases would make me as bankrupt in reputation as in fortune. To buy off one lie is to give a premium for the invention of others. From the moment I was proposed for my present office, the volumes of calumny and falsehood issued to the public, rendered impracticable every idea of going into the work of finding and proving. I determined, therefore, to go

straight forward in what was right, and to rest my character with my countrymen not on depositions and affidavits, but on what they should themselves witness, the course of my life. I have had no reason to be dissatisfied with the confidence reposed in the public; on the contrary, great encouragement to persevere in it to the end.—To WILLIAM A. BURWELL. FORD ED., ix, 229. (W., 1808.)

4735. ———. Many of the [federal] lies would have required only a simple denial, but I saw that even that would have led to the infallible inference, that whatever I had not denied was to be presumed true. I have, therefore, never done even this, but to such of my friends as happen to converse on these subjects, and I have never believed that my character could hang upon every twopenny lie of our common enemies.—To WILLIAM A. BURWELL. FORD ED., ix, 230. (W., 1808.)

4736. ———. The federalists, instead of lying me down, have lied themselves down. —To WILLIAM A. BURWELL. FORD ED., ix. 230. (W., 1808.)

4737. LIES, Useless.—I consider it always useless to read lies.—To DE WITT CLINTON. iv, 520. (W., 1803.)

4738. LIFE, Art of.—The art of life is the art of avoiding pain; and he is the best pilot who steers clearest of the rocks and shoals with which it is beset.—To MRS. COSWAY. ii, 37. FORD ED., iv. 317. (P., 1786.)

4739. LIFE, Chronicles of.—Fifteen volumes of anecdotes and incidents, within the compass of my own time and cognizance. written by a man of genius, of taste, of point, an acquaintance, the measure and traverses of whose mind I know, could not fail to turn the scale in favor of life during their perusal.—To JOHN ADAMS. vii, 27. (M., 1816.)

4740. LIFE, City.—A city life offers * * * more means of dissipating time, but more frequent also and more painful objects of vice and wretchedness. New York, for example, like London seems to be a *cloacina* of all the depravities of human nature. . Philadelphia doubtless has its share. Here [Virginia], on the contrary, crime is scarcely heard of, breaches of order rare, and our societies, if not refined, are rational, moral and affectionate at least.—To WILLIAM SHORT. vii, 310. (M., 1823.)

4741. LIFE, Declining.—I endeavor to beguile the wearisomeness of declining life by the delights of classical reading and of mathematical truths, and by the consolations of a sound philosophy, equally indifferent to hope and fear.—To W. SHORT. vii, 140. FORD ED., x, 145. (M., 1819.)

4742. LIFE, Enjoyment of.—I sincerely pray that all the members of the human family may, in the time prescribed by the Father of us all, find themselves securely established in the enjoyment of life, liberty and happiness.— REPLY TO ADDRESS. viii, 119. (1807.)

4743. LIFE, Government and.—The care of human life and happiness, and not their destruction, is the first and only legitimate object of good government.—R. TO A. MARYLAND CITIZENS. viii, 165. (1809.)

4744. LIFE, Happiness and.—The Giver of life * * * gave it for happiness and not for wretchedness.—To JAMES MONROE. i, 319. FORD ED., iii, 59. (M., 1782.)

4745. LIFE, Individual.—In a government bottomed on the will of all, the life * * * of every individual citizen becomes interesting to all.—FIFTH ANNUAL MESSAGE. viii, 50. FORD ED., viii, 392. (1805.)

4746. LIFE, Jefferson's habits of.—I am retired to Monticello, where, in the bosom of my family, and surrounded by my books, I enjoy a repose to which I have been long a stranger. My mornings are devoted to correspondence. From breakfast to dinner, I am in my shops, my garden, or on horseback among my farms; from dinner to dark, I give to society and recreation with my neighbors and friends; and from candle light to early bedtime, I read. My health is perfect; and my strength considerably reinforced by the activity of the course I pursue; perhaps it is as great as usually falls to the lot of near sixty-seven years of age. I talk of ploughs and harrows, of seeding and harvesting, with my neighbors, and of politics, too, if they choose, with as little reserve as the rest of my fellow citizens, and feel, at length, the blessing of being free to say and do what I please, without being responsible for it to any mortal. A part of my occupation, and by no means the least pleasing, is the direction of the studies of such young men as ask it. They place themselves in the neighboring village, and have the use of my library and counsel, and make a part of my society.—To GENERAL KOSCIUSKO. v, 508. (M., 1810.)

4747. ——— ———. My present course of life admits less reading than I wish. From breakfast, or noon at latest, to dinner, I am mostly on horseback, attending to my farm or other concerns, which I find healthful to my body, mind and affairs; and the few hours I can pass in my cabinet, are devoured by correspondences; not those with my intimate friends, with whom I delight to interchange sentiments, but with others, who, writing to me on concerns of their own in which I have had an agency, or from motives of mere respect and approbation, are entitled to be answered with respect and a return of good will. My hope is that this obstacle to the delights of retirement, will wear away with the oblivion which follows that, and that I may at length be indulged in those studious pursuits, from which nothing but revolutionary duties would ever have called me.—To DR. BENJAMIN RUSH. v, 558. FORD ED., ix, 294. (M., 1811.)

4748. ——— ———. I am on horseback three or four hours of every day; visit three or four times a year a possession I have ninety miles distant, performing the winter journey on horseback. I walk little, however, a single mile being too much for me, and I live in the midst of my grandchildren, one of whom has lately promoted me to be a great grandfather.—To JOHN ADAMS. vi, 37. FORD ED., ix, 334. (M., 1812.)

4749. ——— ———. I have for fifty years bathed my feet in cold water every morning,

and having been remarkably exempted from colds (not having had one in every seven years of my life on an average), I have supposed it might be ascribed to that practice.—To MR. MAURY. vi, 472. (M., 1815.)

4750. ——— ———. The request of the history of my physical habits would have puzzled me not a little, had it not been for the model with which you accompanied it, of Doctor Rush's answer to a similar inquiry. I live so much like other people, that I might refer to ordinary life as the history of my own. * * * I have lived temperately, eating little animal food, and that not as an aliment, so much as a condiment for the vegetables which constitute my principal diet. I double, however, the Doctor's glass and a half of wine, and even treble it with a friend; but halve its effects by drinking the weak wines only. The ardent wines I cannot drink, nor do I use ardent spirits in any form. Malt liquors and cider are my table drinks, and my breakfast is of tea and coffee. I have been blest with organs of digestion which accept and concoct, without ever murmuring, whatever the palate chooses to consign to them, and I have not yet lost a tooth by age. I was a hard student until I entered on the business of life, the duties of which leave no idle time to those disposed to fulfil them; and now, retired, and at the age of seventy-six, I am again a hard student. Indeed, my fondness for reading and study revolts me from the drudgery of letter writing. And a stiff wrist, the consequence of an early dislocation, makes writing both slow and painful. I am not so regular in my sleep as the Doctor says he was, devoting to it from five to eight hours, according as my company or the book I am reading interests me; and I never go to bed without an hour, or half hour's previous reading of something moral, whereon to ruminate in the intervals of sleep. But whether I retire to bed early or late, I rise with the sun. I use spectacles at night, but not necessarily in the day, unless in reading small print. My hearing is distinct in particular conversation, but confused when several voices cross each other, which unfits me for the society of the table. I have been more fortunate than my friend in the article of health. So free from catarrhs that I have not had one (in the breast, I mean) on an average of eight or ten years through life. I ascribe this exemption partly to the habit of bathing my feet in cold water every morning, for sixty years past. A fever of more than twenty-four hours I have not had above two or three times in my life. A periodical headache has afflicted me occasionally, once, perhaps, in six or eight years, for two or three weeks at a time, which now seems to have left me; and except on a late occasion of indisposition, I enjoy good health; too feeble, indeed, to walk much, but riding without fatigue six or eight miles a day, and sometimes thirty or forty. I may end these egotisms, therefore, as I began, by saying that my life has been so much like that of other people, that I might say with Horace, to every one "*nomine mutato, de te fabula narratur*".—To DOCTOR VINE UTLEY. vii, 116. FORD ED., x, 125. (M., 1819.)

4751. LIFE, Liberty and.—The God who gave us life gave us liberty at the same time; the hand of force may destroy, but cannot disjoin them.*—RIGHTS OF BRITISH AMERICA. i, 142. FORD ED., i, 447. (1774.)

*"*Ab eo libertas, a quo spiritus*," was the motto on one of Jefferson's seals.—EDITOR.

4752. LIFE, Order and.—The life of a citizen is never to be endangered, but as the last melancholy effort for the maintenance of order and obedience to the laws.*—CIRCULAR LETTER TO STATE GOVERNORS. v, 414. FORD ED., ix, 238. (W., 1809.)

4753. LIFE, Outdoor.—During the pleasant season, I am always out of doors, employed, not passing more time at my writing table than will dispatch my current business. But when the weather becomes cold, I shall go out but little.—To JOEL BARLOW. v, 476. FORD ED., ix, 263. (M., 1809.)

4754. LIFE, Pledge of.—And for the support of this Declaration,† we mutually pledge to each other our lives, our fortunes, and our sacred honor.—DECLARATION OF INDEPENDENCE AS DRAWN BY JEFFERSON.

4755. —— ——. It is from the supporters of regular government only that the pledge of life, fortune and honor is worthy of confidence.—R. TO A. PHILADELPHIA CITIZENS. viii, 145. (1809.)

— LIFE, Private.—See PRIVATE LIFE.

4756. LIFE, Prolonged.—My health has been always so uniformly firm, that I have for some years dreaded nothing so much as the living too long. I think, however, that a flaw has appeared which ensures me against that, without cutting short any of the period during which I could expect to remain capable of being useful. It will probably give me as many years as I wish, and without pain or debility. Should this be the case, my most anxious prayers will have been fulfilled by Heaven. * * * My florid health is calculated to keep my friends as well as foes quiet, as they should be.—To DR. BENJAMIN RUSH. iv, 426. FORD ED., viii, 128. (W., 1801.)

4757. —— ——. The most undesirable of all things is long life; and there is nothing I have ever so much dreaded.—To DR. BENJAMIN WATERHOUSE. FORD ED., x, 336. (M., 1825.)

4758. LIFE, Reliving.—You ask, if I would agree to live my seventy or rather seventy-three years over again? To which I say, yea. I think with you, that it is a good world on the whole; that it has been framed on a principle of benevolence, and more pleasure than pain dealt out to us. There are, indeed, (who might say nay) gloomy and hypochondriac minds, inhabitants of diseased bodies, disgusted with the present, and despairing of the future; always counting that the worst will happen, because it may happen. To these I say, how much pain have cost us the evils which have never happened! My temperament is sanguine. I steer my bark with Hope in the head, leaving Fear in the stern. My hopes, indeed, sometimes fail; but not oftener than the forebodings of the gloomy. There are, I acknowledge, even in the happiest life, some terrible convulsions, heavy set-offs against the opposite page of the account.—To JOHN ADAMS. vi, 575. (M., April 1816.)

4759. —— ——. Putting to myself your question, would I agree to live my seventy-

---

* The letter was in reference to the employment of the militia to enforce the Embargo law.—EDITOR.
† Congress inserted after "Declaration" the words, "with a firm reliance on the protection of Divine Providence".—EDITOR.

---

three years over again forever? I hesitate to say. With Chew's limitations from twenty-five to sixty, I would say yes; and I might go further back, but not come lower down. For, at the latter period, with most of us, the powers of life are sensibly on the wane; sight becomes dim, hearing dull, memory constantly enlarging its frightful blank and parting with all we have ever seen or known, spirits evaporate, bodily debility creeps on palsying every limb, and so faculty after faculty quits us, and where, then, is life? If, in its full vigor, of good as well as evil, your friend Vassall could doubt its value, it must be purely a negative quantity when its evils alone remain. Yet I do not go into his opinion entirely. I do not agree that an age of pleasure is no compensation for a moment of pain. I think, with you, that life is a fair matter of account, and the balance often, nay generally, in its favor. It is not indeed easy, by calculation of intensity and time, to apply a common measure, or to fix the par between pleasure and pain; yet it exists, and is measurable.—To JOHN ADAMS. vii, 26. (M., Aug. 1816.)

4760. —— ——. You tell me my granddaughter repeated to you an expression of mine, that I should be willing to go again over the scenes of past life. I should not be unwilling, without, however wishing it; and why not? I have enjoyed a greater share of health than falls to the lot of most men; my spirits have never failed me except under those paroxysms of grief which you, as well as myself, have experienced in every form, and with good health and good spirits, the pleasures surely outweigh the pains of life. Why not, then, taste them again, fat and lean together? Were I indeed permitted to cut off from the train the last seven years, the balance would be much in favor of treading the ground over again. Being at that period in the neighborhood of our warm springs and well in health, I wished to be better, and tried them. They destroyed, in a great measure, my internal organism, and I have never since had a moment of perfect health.—To JOHN ADAMS. vii, 421. FORD ED., x, 347. (M., 1825.)

4761. LIFE, Right to.—We hold these truths to be self-evident: that all men are created equal; that they are endowed by their Creator with inherent* and inalienable rights; that among these are life, liberty and the pursuit of happiness.—DECLARATION OF INDEPENDENCE AS DRAWN BY JEFFERSON.

4762. LIFE, Security of.—In no portion of the earth were life, liberty and property ever so securely held; and it is with infinite satisfaction that withdrawing from the active scenes of life, I see the sacred design of these blessings committed to those who are sensible of their value and determined to defend them.—R. TO A. VIRGINIA ASSEMBLY. viii, 148. (1809.)

4763. LIFE, Social.—Life is of no value but as it brings us gratifications. Among the most valuable of these is rational society. It informs the mind, sweetens the temper, cheers our spirits, and promotes health.—To JAMES MADISON. FORD ED., iii, 406. (A., 1784.)

4764. LIFE, Sunshine in.—Thanks to a benevolent arrangement of things, the greater

---

* Congress struck out "inherent and" and inserted "certain".—EDITOR.

part of life is sunshine.—To Mrs. Cosway. ii, 39. Ford ed., iv, 319. (P., 1786.)

4765. LIFE, Worthy.—I cannot be insensible to the partiality which has induced several persons to think my life worthy of remembrance. And towards none more than yourself, who give me so much credit, more than I am entitled to, as to what has been effected for the safeguard of our republican Constitution. Numerous and able coadjutors have participated in these efforts, and merit equal notice. My life, in fact, has been so much like that of others, that their history is my history with a mere difference of feature.—To Mr. Spafford. vii, 118. (M., 1819.)

4766. LIFE IN PARIS.—I often wish myself among my lazy and hospitable countrymen, as I am here [Paris] burning the candle of life without present pleasure, or future object. A dozen or twenty years ago, this scene would have amused me, but I am past the age for changing habits.—To Mrs. Trist. Ford ed., iv, 330. (P., 1786.)

4767. LINCOLN (Levi), Bar.—The pure integrity, unimpeachable conduct, talents and republican firmness of Lincoln* leave him now entirely without a rival. He is not thought an able common lawyer. But there is not and never was an abler one in the New England States. Their system is *sui generis* in which the Common law is little attended to. Lincoln is one of the ablest in their system, and it is among them he is to exercise the great portion of his duties. Nothing is more material than to complete the reformation of the government by this appointment which may truly be said to be putting the keystone into the arch.—To Attorney General Rodney. v, 547. (1810.)

4768. LINCOLN (Levi), Bench.—I was overjoyed when I heard you were appointed to the Supreme Bench of national justice, and as much mortified when I heard you had declined it. You are too young to be entitled to withdraw your services from your country. You cannot yet number the *quadraginta stipendia* of the veteran.—To Levi Lincoln. vi, 8. (M., Aug. 1811.)

4769. LINCOLN (Levi), Congress.—There is good reason to believe that Levi Lincoln will be elected to Congress in Massachusetts. He will be a host in himself; being undoubtedly the ablest and most respectable man of the Eastern States.—To James Madison. Ford ed., vii, 457. (M., Sep. 1800.)

4770. LITERARY MEN, Relief of.—The efforts for the relief of literary men, made by a society of private citizens, are truly laudable; but they are * * * but a palliation of an evil, the cure of which calls for all the wisdom and the means of the nation.—To David Williams. v, 512. (W., 1803.)

4771. LITERATURE, Growth of.—Literature is not yet a distinct profession with us. Now and then a strong mind arises, and at its intervals of leisure from business, emits a flash of light. But the first object of young societies is bread and covering; science is but secondary and subsequent.—To J. Evelyn Denison. vii, 418. (M., 1825.)

* Levi Lincoln, of Massachusetts, who was Attorney General in Jefferson's first Cabinet. The extract is from a letter urging his appointment to the Supreme Court Bench to succeed Judge Cushing. Lincoln was nominated and confirmed, but declined. John Quincy Adams was then nominated, but he declined. The vacancy was then filled by the appointment of Judge Story.—Editor.

4772. LITTLEPAGE (Lewis), Polish Office-holder.—Littlepage has succeeded well in Poland. He has some office, it is said, worth five hundred guineas a year. To Dr. Currie. ii, 219. (P., 1787.)

4773. LITTLEPAGE (Lewis), Russian army officer.—Littlepage, who was in Paris as a secret agent for the King of Poland, rather overreached himself. He wanted more money. The King furnished it more than once. Still he wanted more, and thought to obtain a high bid by saying he was called for in America, and asking leave to go there. Contrary to his expectation, he received leave; but he went to Warsaw instead of America, and thence to join the Russian army.—To James Madison. ii, 444. Ford ed., v, 44. (P., 1788.)

4774. LIVINGSTON (Edward), Friendship for.—I receive Mr. Livingston's question through you with kindness, and answer it without hesitation. He may be assured I have not a spark of unfriendly feeling towards him. In all the earlier scenes of life, we thought and acted together. We differed in opinion afterwards on a single point. Each maintained his opinion, as he had a right, and acted on it as he ought. But why brood over a single difference, and forget all our previous harmonies?—To President Monroe. Ford ed., x, 298. (M., 1824.)

4775. LIVINGSTON (Edward), Louisiana Code.—Your work [Louisiana Code] will certainly arrange your name with the sages of antiquity.—To Edward Livingston. vii, 403. (M., 1825.)

4776. LIVINGSTON (Edward), Restoration.—It was with great pleasure I learned that the good people of New Orleans had restored you again to the councils of our country. I did not doubt the aid it would bring to the remains of our old school in Congress, in which your early labors had been so useful.—To Edward Livingston. vii, 342. Ford ed., x, 299. (M., 1824.)

4777. LIVINGSTON (Robert R.), Chancellor.—A part of your [letter] gave me that kind of concern which I fear I am destined often to meet. Men possessing minds of the first order, and who have had opportunities of being known, and of acquiring the general confidence, do not abound in any country beyond the wants of the country. In your case, however, it is a subject of regret rather than of complaint, as you are in fact serving the public in a very important station.*—To Robert R. Livingston. Ford ed., vii, 492. (W., Feb. 1801.)

4778. LIVINGSTON (Robert R.), French Mission.—It has occurred to me that possibly you might be willing to undertake the mission as Minister Plenipotentiary to France. If so, I shall most gladly avail the public of your services in that office. Though I am sensible of the advantages derived from your talent to your particular State, yet I cannot suppress the desire of adding them to the mass to be employed on the broader scale of the nation at large.—To Robert R. Livingston. iv, 360. Ford ed., vii, 499. (W., 1801.)

4779. ———— ————. You will find Chancellor Livingston, named to the Senate the day after I came into office as our Minister Plenipotentiary to France, * * * an able and honor-

* Chancellor of New York.

able man. He is, unfortunately, so deaf that he will have to transact all his business by writing.—To WILLIAM SHORT. iv, 415. FORD ED., viii, 99. (W., 1801.)

4780. LOANS, Corruption and.— [Among] the reasons against [a new loan] is the apprehension that the [Hamilton] head of the [Treasury] department means to provide idle money to be lodged in the banks, ready for the corruption of the next legislature, as it is believed the late ones were corrupted, by gratifying particular members with vast discounts for objects of speculation.— LOAN OPINION. vii, 636. FORD ED., vi, 506. (1793.)

4781. LOANS, Economy vs.— I learn with great satisfaction that wholesome economies have been found, sufficient to relieve us from the ruinous necessity of adding annually to our debt by new loans. The deviser of so salutary a relief deserves truly well of his country.—To SAMUEL SMITH. vii, 284. FORD ED., x, 251. (M., 1823.)

4782. LOANS, Instructions respecting. —I would take the liberty of suggesting the insertion of some such clause as the following into the instructions: " The agents to be employed shall never open a loan for more than one million of dollars at a time, nor open a new loan till the preceding one has been filled, and expressly approved by the President of the United States." A new man, alighting on the exchange of Amsterdam, with powers to borrow twelve millions of dollars, will be immediately beset with bankers and brokers, who will pour into his ear, from the most unsuspected quarters, such informations and suspicions as may lead him exactly into their snares. So wonderfully dexterous are they in wrapping up and complicating their propositions, that they will make it evident, even to a clear-headed man (not in the habit of this business), that two and two make five. The agent, therefore, should be guarded, even against himself, by putting it out of his power to extend the effect of any erroneous calculation beyond one million of dollars. Were he able, under a delusive calculation, to commit such a sum as twelve millions of dollars, what would be said of the government? Our bankers told me themselves that they would not choose, in the conduct of this great loan, to open for more than two or three millions of florins at a time, and certainly never for more than five. By contracting for only one million of dollars at a time, the agent will have frequent occasions of trying to better the terms. I dare say that this caution, though not expressed in the instructions, is intended by the Secretary of the Treasury to be carried into their execution. But, perhaps, it will be desirable for the President, that his sense of it also should be expressed in writing.—OPINION ON FOREIGN DEBT. vii, 507. FORD ED., v, 233. (1790.)

4783. LOANS, Limited.— Of the modes which are within the limits of right, that of raising within the year its whole expenses by taxation, might be beyond the abilities of our citizens to bear. It is, moreover, generally desirable that the public contribution should be as uniform as practicable from year to year, that our habits of industry and expense may become adapted to them; and that they may be duly digested and incorporated with our annual economy. There remains, then, for us but the method of limited anticipation, the laying taxes for a term of years within that of our right, which may be sold for a present sum equal to the expenses of the year; in other words, to obtain a loan equal to the expenses of the year, laying a tax adequate to its interest, and to such a surplus as will reimburse, by growing instalments, the whole principle within the term. This is, in fact, what has been called raising money on the sale of annuities for years. In this way a new loan, and of course a new tax, is requisite every year during the continuance of the war; and should that be so long as to produce an accumulation of tax beyond our ability, in time of war the resource would be an enactment of the taxes requisite to ensure good terms, by securing the lender, with a suspension of the payment of instalments of principal and perhaps of interest also, until the restoration of peace. This method of anticipating our taxes, or of borrowing on annuities for years, insures repayment to the lender, guards the rights of posterity, prevents a perpetual alienation of the public contributions, and consequent destitution of every resource even for the ordinary support of government.—To J. W. EPPES. vi, 198. FORD ED., ix, 398. (P.F., Sep. 1813.)

4784. LOANS, Negotiation of.— Dumas has been in the habit of sending his letters open to me, to be forwarded to Mr. Jay. During my absence they passed through Mr. Short's hands, who made extracts from them, by which I see he has been recommending himself and me for the money negotiations in Holland. It might be thought, perhaps, that I have encouraged him in this. Be assured that no such idea ever entered my head. On the contrary, it is a business which would be the most disagreeable to me of all others, and for which I am the most unfit person living. I do not understand bargaining, nor possess the dexterity requisite for the purpose. On the other hand, Mr. Adams, whom I expressly and sincerely recommend, stands already on ground for that business which I could not gain in years. Pray set me to rights in the minds of those who may have supposed me privy to this proposition.—To JAMES MADISON. ii, 154. FORD ED., iv, 393. (P., 1787.)

4785. LOANS, Power to negotiate.— Though much an enemy to the system of borrowing, yet I feel strongly the necessity of preserving the power to borrow. Without this we might be overwhelmed by another nation, merely by the force of its credit.—To THE TREASURY COMMISSIONERS. ii, 353. (P., 1788.)

4786. ———. I wish it were possible to obtain a single amendment to our Constitution. I would be willing to depend on that alone for the reduction of the administration of our government to the genuine principles of its Constitution; I mean an additional article, taking from the Federal Government the power of borrowing. I now deny their power of making paper money, or anything else, a legal tender. I know that to pay all proper expenses within the year, would, in case of war, be hard on us. But not so hard as ten wars instead of one. For wars could be reduced in that proportion; besides that the State governments would be free to lend *their credit* in borrowing quotas.—To JOHN TAYLOR. iv, 260. FORD ED., vii, 310. (M., Nov. 1798.)

4787. LOANS, Redeeming taxes for.— Our government has not, as yet, begun to act on the rule of loans and taxation going hand in hand. Had any loan taken place in my time, I should have strongly urged a redeeming tax. For the loan which has been made since the last session of Congress, we should now set the example of appropriating some particular tax, sufficient to pay the interest annually, and the principal within a fixed term, less than nineteen years. I hope yourself and your committee will render the immortal service of introducing this practice.— To JOHN W. EPPES. vi, 138. FORD ED., ix, 391. (M., June 1813.) See GENERATIONS.

4788. LOANS, Treasury Notes vs.—The question will be asked and ought to be looked at, what is to be the resource if loans cannot be obtained? There is but one. *"Carthago delenda est"*. Bank paper must be suppressed, and the circulating medium must be restored to the nation to whom it belongs. It is the only fund on which they can rely for loans; it is the only resource which can never fail them, and it is an abundant one for every necessary purpose. Treasury bills, bottomed on taxes, bearing or not bearing interest, as may be found necessary, thrown into circulation will take the place of so much gold and silver, which last, when crowded, will find an efflux into other countries, and thus keep the *quantum* of medium at its salutary level.—To J. W. EPPES. vi, 199. FORD ED., ix, 399. (Sep. 1813.)

4789. LOANS, Unauthorized.—The manoeuvre of opening a loan of three millions of florins, has, on the whole, been useful to the United States, and though unauthorized, I think should be confirmed.—OPINION ON FOREIGN DEBT. vii, 507. FORD ED., v, 232. (1790.)

— **LOCKE (John).**—See GOVERNMENT, WORKS ON.

4790. LOGAN (George), France and.— That your efforts did much towards preventing declared war with France, I am satisfied. Of those with England, I am not equally informed. —To DR. GEORGE LOGAN. vi, 215. FORD ED., ix, 421. (M., Oct. 1813.)

4791. ———— ————. Dr. Logan, about a fortnight ago, sailed for Hamburg. Though for a twelvemonth past he had been intending to go to Europe as soon as he could get money

enough to carry him there, yet when he had accomplished this, and fixed a time for going, he very unwisely made a mystery of it; so that his disappearance without notice excited conversation. This was seized by the war hawks, and given out as a secret mission from the Jacobins here to solicit an army from France, instruct them as to their landing, &c. This extravagance produced a real panic among the citizens; and happening just when Bache published Talleyrand's letter, Harper * * * gravely announced to the House of Representatives, that there existed a traitorous correspondence between the Jacobins here and the French Directory; that he had got hold of some threads and clews of it, and would soon be able to develop the whole. This increased the alarm; their libellists immediately set to work, directly and indirectly to implicate whom they pleased. "Porcupine" gave me a principal share in it, as I am told, for I never read his papers. —To JAMES MADISON. iv, 250. FORD ED., vii, 273. (Pa., June 1798.)

4792. LOGAN (Mingo Chief), Murder of.—In the spring of the year 1774, a robbery and murder were committed on an inhabitant of the frontier of Virginia, by two Indians of the Shawnee tribe. The neighboring whites, according to their custom, undertook to punish this outrage in a summary way. Col. [Michael] Cresap, a man infamous for the many murders he had committed on those much injured people, collected a party and proceeded down the Kanawha in quest of vengeance. Unfortunately a canoe of women and children, with one man only, was seen coming from the opposite shore, unarmed, and unsuspecting a hostile attack from the whites. Cresap and his party concealed themselves on the bank of the river, and the moment the canoe reached the shore, singled out their objects, and at one fire, killed every person in it. This happened to be the family of Logan, who had long been distinguished as a friend of the whites. This unworthy return provoked his vengeance. He accordingly signalized himself in the war which ensued. In the autumn of the same year a decisive battle was fought at the mouth of the Great Kanawha between the collected forces of the Shawnees, Mingoes and Delawares, and a detachment of the Virginia militia. The Indians were defeated and sued for peace. Logan, however, disdained to be seen among the suppliants. But lest the sincerity of a treaty should be distrusted, from which so distinguished a chief absented himself, he sent, by a messenger, the following speech * to be delivered to Lord Dunmore * * *.—NOTES ON VIRGINIA. viii, 308. FORD ED., iii, 156. (1782.)

4793. LOGAN (Mingo Chief), Speech of.—I may challenge the whole orations of Demosthenes and Cicero, and of any other eminent orator, if Europe has furnished more eminent, to produce a single passage, superior to the speech of Logan.—NOTES ON VIRGINIA. viii, 308. FORD ED., iii, 155. (1782.)

— **LOGARITHMS.**—See MOUNTAINS.

* The speech referred to is the celebrated one beginning, "I appeal to any white man to say, if he ever entered Logan's cabin hungry, and he gave him not to eat", &c. Jefferson cited it among other proofs in refutation of the theories of Count de Buffon, Raynal and others, respecting the degeneracy of animals in America, not even excepting man. Luther Martin, of Maryland, a son-in-law of Cresap, severely attacked Jefferson in defence of the memory of his relative, and questioned the authenticity of Logan's speech. Jefferson made a careful investigation of the whole case, and proved the speech to be genuine.—EDITOR.

4794. LONDON, Beauty.—The city of London, though handsomer than Paris, is not so handsome as Philadelphia.—To JOHN PAGE. i, 549. FORD ED., iv, 214. (P., 1786.)

4795. LONDON, Burning of.—She [England] may burn New York * * * by her ships and congreve rockets, in which case we must burn the city of London by hired incendiaries, of which her starving manufacturers will furnish abundance. A people in such desperation as to demand of their government *aut panem, aut furcam*, either bread or the gallows, will not reject the same alternative when offered by a foreign hand. Hunger will make them brave every risk for bread.—To GENERAL KOSCIUSKO. vi, 68. FORD ED., ix, 362. (June 1812.)

4796. LONDON, Splendor of shops.—The splendor of the shops is all that is worth looking at in London.—To MADAME DE CORNY. ii, 161. (P., 1787.)

— LONGITUDE.—See LATITUDE AND LONGITUDE.

— LOOMING.—See MIRAGE.

4797. LOTTERY, Unadvisable.—Having myself made it a rule never to engage in a lottery or any other adventure of mere chance, I can, with the less candor or effect, urge it on others, however laudable or desirable its object may be.—To HUGH L. WHITE. v, 521. (M., 1810.) See 2005.

4798. LOUISIANA, Acquisition of.—Congress witnessed, at their last session, the extraordinary agitation produced in the public mind by the suspension of our right of deposit at the port of New Orleans, no assignment of another place having been made according to treaty.* They were sensible that the continuance of that privation would be more injurious to our nation than any consequences which could flow from any mode of redress, but reposing just confidence in the good faith of the government whose officer had committed the wrong, friendly and reasonable representations were resorted to, and the right of deposit was restored. Previous, however, to this period, we had not been unaware of the danger to which our peace would be perpetually exposed while so important a key to the commerce of the western country remained under foreign power. Difficulties, too, were presenting themselves as to the navigation of other streams, which, arising within territories, pass through those adjacent. Propositions had, therefore, been authorized for obtaining, on fair conditions, the sovereignty of New Orleans, and of other possessions in that quarter interesting to our quiet,

* Spain, on October 1, 1800, ceded all Louisiana to France, but the transaction was kept so secret that it did not become known in the United States until the spring of 1802. In October of that year, the Spanish Intendant at New Orleans issued an order, in violation of treaty stipulations, depriving the United States of the right of deposit at that port. This act so inflamed the Western people that they threatened to march on New Orleans and settle the question by force of arms. The federalists clamored for war. In this perilous condition of affairs, Congress, in secret session, placed two million dollars at the disposal of the President, to be used as he saw fit, and left him free to deal with the situation. He immediately sent James Monroe as Minister Plenipotentiary to Paris, joining with him in a high Commission Robert R. Livingston, Minister to France. The purchase of Louisiana was negotiated by them.—EDITOR.

to such extent as was deemed practicable; and the provisional appropriation of two millions of dollars, to be applied and accounted for by the President of the United States, intended as part of the price, was considered as conveying the sanction of Congress to the acquisition proposed. The enlightened Government of France saw, with just discernment, the importance to both nations of such liberal arrangements as might best and permanently promote the peace, friendship, and interests of both; and the property and sovereignty of all Louisiana, which had been restored to them, have on certain conditions been transferred to the United States by instruments bearing date the 30th of April last. When these shall have received the constitutional sanction of the Senate, they will without delay be communicated to the Representatives also, for the exercise of their functions, as to those conditions which are within the powers vested by the Constitution in Congress. While the property and sovereignty of the Mississippi and its waters secure an independent outlet for the produce of the Western States, and an uncontrolled navigation through their whole course, free from collision with other powers and the dangers to our peace from that source, the fertility of the country, its climate and extent, promise in due season important aids to our treasury, an ample provision for our posterity, and a wide-spread field for the blessings of freedom and equal laws. With the wisdom of Congress it will rest to take those ulterior measures which may be necessary for the immediate occupation and temporary government of the country; for its incorporation into our Union; for rendering the change of government a blessing to our newly-adopted brethren; for securing to them the rights of conscience and of property; for confirming to the Indian inhabitants their occupancy and self-government, establishing friendly and commercial relations with them, and for ascertaining the geography of the country acquired.—THIRD ANNUAL MESSAGE. viii, 23. FORD ED., viii, 267. (October 17, 1803.)

4799. ———. The acquisition of Louisiana is a subject of mutual congratulation, as it interests every man of the nation.—To GENERAL HORATIO GATES. iv, 494. FORD ED., viii, 249. (W., 1803.)

4800. ———. This acquisition is seen by our constituents in all its importance, and they do justice to all those who have been instrumental towards it.—To JAMES MONROE. FORD ED., viii, 287. (W., Jan. 1804.)

4801. ———. On this important acquisition, so favorable to the immediate interests of our western citizens, so auspicious to the peace and security of the nation in general, which adds to our country territories so extensive and fertile, and to our citizens new brethren to partake of the blessings of freedom and self government, I offer to Congress and the country, my sincere congratulations.—SPECIAL MESSAGE. viii, 33. (Jan. 1804.)

4802. ——— ———. Whatever may be the merit or demerit of that acquisition, I divide it with my colleagues, to whose councils I was indebted for a course of administration which, notwithstanding this late coalition of clay and brass, will, I hope, continue to receive the approbation of our country.—To HENRY DEARBORN. vii, 215. FORD ED., x, 192. (M., 1821.)

4803. LOUISIANA, Area of United States doubled.—The territory acquired, as it includes all the waters of the Missouri and Mississippi, has more than doubled the area of the United States, and the new part is not inferior to the old in soil, climate, productions and important communications.—To GENERAL HORATIO GATES. iv, 494. FORD ED., viii, 249. (W., 1803.)

4804. LOUISIANA, Bonaparte and.—I very early saw that Louisiana was indeed a speck in our horizon which was to burst in a tornado; and the public are unapprized how near this catastrophe was. Nothing but a frank and friendly development of causes and effects on our part, and good sense enough in Bonaparte to see that the train was unavoidable, and would change the face of the world, saved us from that storm. I did not expect he would yield till a war took place between France and England, and my hope was to palliate and endure, if Messrs. Ross, Morris, &c. did not force a premature rupture, until that event. I believed the event not very distant, but acknowledge it came on sooner than I had expected. Whether, however, the good sense of Bonaparte might not see the course predicted to be necessary and unavoidable, even before a war should be imminent, was a chance which we thought it our duty to try; but the immediate prospect of rupture brought the case to immediate decision. The *dénouement* has been happy; and I confess I look to this duplication of area for the extending a government so free and economical as ours, as a great achievement to the mass of happiness which is to ensue.—To DR. JOSEPH PRIESTLEY. iv, 525. FORD ED., viii, 294. (W., Jan. 1804.)

4805. LOUISIANA, The Constitution and.—There is no constitutional difficulty as to the acquisition of territory, and whether, when acquired, it may be taken into the Union by the Constitution as it now stands, will become a question of expediency. I think it will be safer not to permit the enlargement of the Union but by amendment of the Constitution.—To ALBERT GALLATIN. FORD ED., viii, 241. (Jan. 1803.)

4806. ——— ———. There is a difficulty in this acquisition which presents a handle to the malcontents among us, though they have not yet discovered it. Our confederation is certainly confined to the limits established by the Revolution. The General Government has no powers but such as the Constitution has given it; and it has not given it a power of holding foreign territory, and still less of incorporating it into the Union. An amendment of the Constitution seems necessary for this. In the meantime, we must ratify and pay our money, as we have treated, for a thing beyond the Constitution, and rely on the nation to sanction an act done for its great good, without its previous authority.—To JOHN DICKINSON. FORD ED., viii, 262. (M., Aug. 1803.)

4807. ——— ———. The Constitution has made no provision for our holding foreign territory, still less for incorporating foreign nations into our Union. The Executive in seizing the fugitive occurrence [Louisiana purchase] which so much advances the good of their country, have done an act beyond the Constitution. The Legislature in casting behind them metaphysical subtleties, and risking themselves like faithful servants, must ratify and pay for it, and throw themselves on their country for doing for them unauthorized, what we know they would have done for themselves had they been in a situation to do it. It is the case of a guardian, investing the money of his ward in purchasing an important adjacent territory; and saying to him when of age, I did this for your good; I pretend to no right to bind you: you may disavow me, and I must get out of the scrape as I can: I thought it my duty to risk myself for you. But we shall not be disavowed by the nation, and their act of indemnity will confirm and not weaken the Constitution, by more strongly marking out its lines.—To JOHN C. BRECKENRIDGE. iv, 500. FORD ED., viii, 244. (M., Aug. 12, 1803.)

4808. LOUISIANA, Constitutional amendments.—

The province of Louisiana is incorporated with the United States, and made part thereof. The rights of occupancy in the soil, and of self-government are confirmed to the Indian inhabitants, as they now exist. Preemption only of the portions rightfully occupied by them, and a succession to the occupancy of such as they may abandon, with the full rights of possession as well as of property and sovereignty in whatever is not or shall cease to be so rightfully occupied by them shall belong to the United States. The Legislature of the Union shall have authority to exchange the right of occupancy in portions where the United States have full right for lands possessed by Indians within the United States on the east side

Louisiana, as ceded by France to the United States is made a part of the United States. Its white inhabitants shall be citizens, and stand, as to their rights and obligations on the same footing with other citizens of the United States in analogous situations. Save only that as to the portion thereof lying north of an east and west line drawn through the mouth of the Arkansas river, no new State shall be established, nor any grants of land made, other than to Indians in exchange for equivalent portions of land occupied by them, until authorized by further subsequent amendment to the Constitution shall be made for these purposes.

Florida, also, whenever it may be right-of the Mississippi: to exchange lands on the east side of the river for those of the white inhabitants on the west side thereof and above the latitude of 31 degrees : to maintain in any part of the province such military posts as may be requisite for peace or safety : to exercise police over all persons therein, not being Indian inhabitants: to work salt springs, or mines of coal, metals and other minerals within the possession of the United States or in any others with the consent of the possessors; to regulate trade and intercourse between the Indian inhabitants and all other persons; to explore and ascertain the geography of the province, its productions and other interesting circumstances; to open roads and navigation therein where necessary for beneficial communication; and to establish agencies and factories therein for the cultivation of commerce, peace and good understanding w i t h the Indians residing there. The Legislature shall have no authority to dispose of the lands of the province otherwise than as hereinbefore permitted, until a new amendment of the Constitution shall give that authority. Except as to that portion thereof which lies south of the latitude of 31 degrees; which whenever they deem expedient, they may erect into a territorial government, either separate or as making part with one on the eastern side of the river, vesting the inhabitants thereof with all the rights possessed by other territorial citizens of the United States.

DRAFTS OF AN AMENDMENT TO THE CONSTITUTION. iv, 503. FORD ED., viii, 241. (July 1803.)

fully obtained, shall become a part of the United States. Its white inhabitants shall thereupon be citizens, and shall stand, as to their rights and obligations, on the same footing with other citizens of the United States, in analogous situations.—

4809. —— ——. I wrote you on the 12th instant, on the subject of Louisiana, and the constitutional provision which might be necessary for it. A letter received yesterday shows that nothing must be said on that subject, which may give a pretext for retracting; but that we should do, *sub silentio*, what shall be found necessary. Be so good as to consider that part of my letter as confidential.—To JOHN C. BRECKENRIDGE. FORD ED., viii, 244. (Aug. 18 1803.)

4810. —— ——. Further reflection on the amendment to the Constitution necessary in the case of Louisiana, satisfies me it will be better to give general powers, with specified exceptions.—To JAMES MADISON. iv, 503. FORD ED., viii, 246. (M., Aug. 1803.)

4811. —— ——. On further consideration as to the amendment to our Constitution respecting Louisiana, I have thought it better, instead of enumerating the powers which Congress may exercise, to give them the same powers they have as to other portions of the Union generally, and to enumerate the special exceptions. * * * The less that is said about any constitutional difficulty, the better; and *. * * it will be desirable for Congress to do what is necessary, *in silence*.—To LEVI LINCOLN. iv, 504. FORD ED., viii, 246. (M., Aug. 1803.)

4812. —— ——. Whatever Congress shall think it necessary to do, should be done with as little debate as possible, and particularly so far as respects the constitutional difficulty. I am aware of the force of the observations you make on the power given by the Constitution to Congress, to admit new States into the Union, without restraining the subject to the territory then constituting the United States. But when I consider that the limits of the United States are precisely fixed by the treaty of 1783, that the Constitution expressly declares itself to be made for the United States, I cannot help believing that the intention was to permit Congress to admit into the Union new States, which should be formed out of the territory for which, and under whose authority alone, they were then acting. I do not believe it was meant that they might receive England, Ireland, Holland, &c., into it, which would be the case on your construction. When an instrument admits two constructions, the one safe, the other dangerous; the one precise, the other indefinite. I prefer that which is safe and precise. I had rather ask an enlargement of power from the nation, where it is found necessary, than to assume it by a construction which would make our powers boundless. Our peculiar security is in the possession of a written Constitution. Let us not make it a blank paper by construction. I say the same as to the opinion of those who consider the grant of the treaty making power as boundless. If it is, then we have no Constitution. If it has bounds, they can be no others than the definitions of the powers which that instrument gives. It specifies and delineates the operations permitted to the Federal Government, and gives all the powers necessary to carry these into execution. Whatever of these enumerated objects is proper for a law, Congress may make the law; whatever is proper to be executed by way of a treaty, the President and Senate may enter into the treaty; whatever is to be done by a judicial sentence, the judges may pass the sentence. Nothing is more likely than that their enumeration of powers is defective. This is the ordinary case of all human works. Let us go on, then, perfecting it, by adding, by way of amendment to the Constitution, those powers which time and trial show are still wanting. But it has been taken too much for granted, that by this rigorous construction the treaty power would be reduced to nothing. I had occasion once to examine its effect on the French treaty, made by the old Congress, and found that out of thirty odd articles which that contained, there were one, two or three only which could not now be stipulated under our present Constitution. I confess, then, I thought it important, in the present case, to set an example against broad construction, by appealing for new power to the people. If, however, our friends shall think differently, certainly I shall acquiesce with satisfaction; confiding, that the good sense of our country will correct the evil of construction whenever it shall produce ill effects.—To WILSON C. NICHOLAS. iv, 505. FORD ED., viii, 247. (M., Sep. 1803.)

4813. LOUISIANA, Defence of.—What would you think of raising a force for the defence of New Orleans in this manner? Give a bounty of 50 acres of land, to be delivered immediately, to every able-bodied man who will immediately settle on it, and hold himself in readiness to perform two years' military service (on the usual pay) if called on within the first seven years of his residence? The lands to be chosen by himself of any of those in the Orleans Territory, * * * each to have his choice in the order of his arrival on the spot, a proclamation to be issued to this effect to engage as many as will go on, and present themselves to the officer there; and, moreover, recruiting officers to be sent into different parts of the Union to raise and conduct settlers at the public expense? When settled there, to be well trained as militia by officers living among them?*—CIRCULAR LETTER TO CABINET OFFICERS. FORD ED., viii, 425. (Feb. 1806.)

4814. ——— ———. Satisfied that New Orleans must fall a prey to any power which shall attack it, in spite of any means we now possess, I see no security for it but in planting on the spot the force which is to defend it I therefore suggest to some members of the Senate to add to the volunteer bill now before them, as an amendment, some such section as that enclosed, which is on the principles of what we agreed on last year, except the omission of the two years' service. If, by giving one hundred miles square of that country, we can secure the rest, and at

* Jefferson framed a bill on this subject. See FORD ED., viii, 425.—EDITOR.

the same time create an American majority before Orleans becomes a State, it will be the best bargain ever made.—To ALBERT GALLATIN. v, 36. (W., Jan. 1807.)

4815. ——— ———. I propose to the members of Congress in conversation, the enlisting thirty thousand volunteers, Americans by birth, to be carried at the public expense, and settled immediately on a bounty of one hundred and sixty acres of land each, on the west side of the Mississippi, on the condition of giving two years of military service, if that country should be attacked within seven years. The defence of the country would thus be placed on the spot, and the additional number would entitle the Territory to become a State, would make the majority American, and make it an American instead of a French State. This would not sweeten the pill to the French; but in making the acquisition we had some view to our own good as well as theirs, and I believe the greatest good of both will be promoted by whatever will amalgamate us together.—To JOHN DICKINSON. v, 30. FORD ED., ix, 9. (W., 1807.)

4816. LOUISIANA, Expansion and.—I know that the acquisition of Louisiana has been disapproved by some, from a candid apprehension that the enlargement of our territory would endanger its Union. But who can limit the extent to which the federative principle may operate effectively? The larger our association, the less will it be shaken by local passions; and, in any view, is it not better that the opposite bank of the Mississippi should be settled by our own brethren and children, than by strangers of another family? With which shall we be most likely to live in harmony and friendly intercourse?—SECOND INAUGURAL ADDRESS. viii, 41. FORD ED., viii, 344. (1805.) See TERRITORY.

4817. LOUISIANA, Federalist opposition.—The opposition caught it as a plank in a shipwreck, hoping it would tack the western people to them. They raised the cry of war, were intriguing in all quarters to exasperate the western inhabitants to arm and go down on their own authority and possess themselves of New Orleans, and in the meantime were daily reiterating, in new shapes, inflammatory resolutions for the adoption of the House [of Representatives].—To ROBERT R. LIVINGSTON. iv, 460. FORD ED., viii, 209. (W., Feb. 1803.)

4818. ——— ———. These grumblers [the opposition], too, are very uneasy lest the administration should share some little credit for the acquisition, the whole of which they ascribe to the accident of war. They would be cruelly mortified could they see our files from May, 1801 [April 1801 in Ford edition], the first organization of the administration, but more especially from April, 1802. They would see, that though we could not say when war would arise, yet we said with energy what would take place when it should arise. We did not, by our intrigues, produce the war; but we availed ourselves of it when it happened. The other party saw the case now existing, on which our representations were predicted, and the wisdom of timely sacrifice. But when these people make the war give us everything, they authorize us to ask what the war gave us in their day? They had a war. What did they make it bring us? Instead of making our neutrality the ground of gain to their country, they were for plunging into the war. And if they were now in place, they would now be at war against the atheists and disorganizers of France. They were for making their country an appendage to England. We are friendly, cordially and conscientiously friendly to England. We are not hostile to France. We will be rigorously just and sincerely friendly to both. I do not believe we shall have as much to swallow from them as our predecessors had.—To GENERAL HORATIO GATES. iv, 495. FORD ED., viii, 250. (W., July 1803.)

4819. —— ——. These federalists [who are raising objections against the vast extent of our boundaries] see in this acquisition [Louisiana] the formation of a new confederacy, embracing all the waters of the Mississippi, on both sides of it, and a separation of its eastern waters from us. These combinations depend on so many circumstances which we cannot foresee, that I place little reliance on them. We have seldom seen neighborhood produce affection among nations. The reverse is almost the universal truth. Besides, if it should become the great interest of those nations to separate from this, if their happiness should depend on it so strongly as to induce them to go through that convulsion, why should the Atlantic States dread it? But especially why should we, their present inhabitants, take side in such a question? When I view the Atlantic States, procuring for those on the Eastern waters of the Mississippi friendly instead of hostile neighbors on its western waters, I do not view it as an Englishman would the procuring future blessings for the French nation, with whom he has no relations of blood or affection. The future inhabitants of the Atlantic and Mississippi States will be our sons. We leave them in distinct but bordering establishments. We think we see their happiness in their union, and we wish it. Events may prove it otherwise; and if they see their interest in separation, why should we take side with our Atlantic rather than our Mississippi descendants. It is the elder and the younger son differing. God bless them both, and keep them in union, if it be for their good, but separate them, if it be better.—To JOHN C. BRECKENRIDGE. iv, 499. FORD ED., viii, 243. (M., Aug. 1803.)

4820. —— ——. Objections are raising to the eastward against the vast extent of our boundaries, and propositions are made to exchange Louisiana, or a part of it, for the Floridas. But * * * we shall get the Floridas without, and I would not give one inch of the waters of the Mississippi to any nation, because I see in a light very impor-

tant to our peace the exclusive right to its navigation, and the admission of no nation into it, but as into the Potomac or Delaware, with our consent and under our police.—To JOHN C. BRECKENRIDGE. iv, 499. FORD ED., viii, 243. (M., Aug. 1803.)

4821. —— ——. Some inflexible federalists have still ventured to brave the public opinion. It will fix their character with the world and with posterity. who, not descending to the other points of difference between us, will judge them by this fact, so palpable as to speak for itself in all times and places. —To DUPONT DE NEMOURS. iv, 508. (W., 1803.)

4822. —— ——. The federalists spoke and voted against it, but they are now so reduced in their numbers as to be nothing.—To ROBERT R. LIVINGSTON. iv, 510. FORD ED., viii, 278. (W., Nov. 1803.)

4823. —— ——. The federal leaders have had the imprudence to oppose it pertinaciously, which has given an occasion to a great proportion of their quondam honest adherents to abandon them, and join the republican standard. They feel themselves now irretrievably lost.—To JAMES MONROE. FORD ED., viii, 287. (W., Jan. 1804.)

4824. LOUISIANA, French possession of.—The exchange, which is to give us new neighbors in Louisiana (probably the present French armies when disbanded), has opened us to a combination of enemies on that side where we are most vulnerable.—To THOMAS PINCKNEY. iv, 177. FORD ED., vii, 129. (Pa., May 1797.)

4825. —— ——. There is considerable reason to apprehend that Spain cedes Louisiana and the Floridas to France. It is a policy very unwise in both, and very ominous to us. —To JAMES MONROE. FORD ED., viii, 58. (W., May 1801.)

4826. —— ——. The cession of Louisiana and the Floridas by Spain to France, works most sorely on the United States. On this subject the Secretary of State has written to you fully, yet I cannot forbear recurring to it personally, so deep is the impression it makes on my mind. It completely reverses all the political relations of the United States, and will form a new epoch in our political course. Of all nations of any consideration, France is the one, which hitherto, has offered the fewest points on which we could have any conflict of right, and the most points of a communion of interests. From these causes, we have ever looked to her as our *natural* friend, as one with which we never could have an occasion of difference. Her growth, therefore, we viewed as our own, her misfortunes ours. There is on the globe one single spot, the possessor of which is our natural and habitual enemy. It is New Orleans, through which the produce of three-eighths of our territory must pass to market, and from its fertility it will ere long yield more than half of our whole produce, and contain more than half of our inhabitants.

France, placing herself in that door, assumes to us the attitude of defiance. Spain might have retained it quietly for years. Her pacific dispositions, her feeble state, would induce her to increase our facilities there, so that her possession of the place would be hardly felt by us, and it would not, perhaps, be very long before some circumstance might arise, which might make the cession of it to us the price of something of more worth to her. Not so can it ever be in the hands of France. The impetuosity of her temper, the energy and restlessness of her character, placed in a point of eternal friction with us, and our character, which, though quiet and loving peace and the pursuit of wealth, is high-minded, despising wealth in competition with insult or injury, enterprising and energetic as any nation on earth; these circumstances render it impossible that France and the United States can continue long friends, when they meet in so irritable a position. They, as well as we, must be blind if they do not see this; and we must be very improvident if we do not begin to make arrangements on that hypothesis. The day that France takes possession of New Orleans, fixes the sentence which is to restrain her forever within her low-water mark. It seals the union of two nations, who, in conjunction, can maintain exclusive possession of the ocean. From that moment, we must marry ourselves to the British fleet and nation. We must turn all our attention to a maritime force, for which our resources place us on very high ground; and having formed and cemented together a power which may render reinforcement of her settlements here impossible to France, make the first cannon, which shall be fired in Europe, the signal for tearing up any settlement she may have made, and for holding the two continents of America in sequestration for the common purposes of the united British and American nations. This is not a state of things we seek or desire. It is one which this measure, if adopted by France, forces on us, as necessarily as any other cause, by the laws of nature, brings on its necessary effect. It is not from a fear of France that we deprecate this measure proposed by her. For, however greater her force is than ours, compared in the abstract, it is nothing in comparison of ours, when to be exerted on our soil. But it is from a sincere love of peace, and a firm persuasion that bound to France by the interests and the strong sympathies still existing in the minds of our citizens, and holding relative positions which ensure their continuance, we are secure of a long course of peace. Whereas, the change of friends, which will be rendered necessary if France changes that position, embarks us necessarily as a belligerent power in the first war of Europe. In that case, France will have held possession of New Orleans during the interval of a peace, long or short, at the end of which it will be wrested from her. Will this short-lived possession have been an equivalent to her for the transfer of such a weight into the scale of her enemy? Will not the amalgamation of a young, thriving, nation continue to that enemy the health and force which are at present so evidently on the decline? And will a few years' possession of New Orleans add equally to the strength of France? She may say she needs Louisiana for the supply of her West Indies. She does not need it in time of peace, and in war she could not depend on them, because they would be so easily intercepted. I should suppose that all these considerations might, in some proper form, be brought into view of the government of France. Though stated by us, it ought not to give offence; because we do not bring them forward as a menace, but as consequences not controllable by us, but inevitable from the course of things. We mention them, not as things which we desire by any means, but as things we deprecate; and we beseech a friend to look forward and to prevent them for our common interests. If France considers Louisiana, however, as indispensable for her views, she might perhaps be willing to look about for arrangements which might reconcile it to our interests. If anything could do this, it would be the ceding to us the island of New Orleans and the Floridas. This would certainly, in a great degree, remove the causes of jarring and irritation between us, and perhaps for such a length of time, as might produce other means of making the measure permanently conciliatory to our interests and friendships. It would, at any rate, relieve us from the necessity of taking immediate measures for countervailing such an operation by arrangements in another quarter. But still we should consider New Orleans and the Floridas as no equivalent for the risk of a quarrel with France, produced by her vicinage.—To ROBERT R. LIVINGSTON. iv, 431. FORD ED., viii, 144. (April 1802.)

4827. ——— ———. I believe * * * that this measure will cost France, and perhaps not very long hence, a war which will annihilate her on the ocean, and place that element under the despotism of two nations, which I am not reconciled to the more because my own would be one of them. Add to this the exclusive appropriation of both continents of America as a consequence. I wish the present order of things to continue, and with a view to this I value highly a state of friendship between France and us. You know, too well how sincere I have ever been in these dispositions to doubt them. You know, too, how much I value peace, and how unwillingly I should see any event take place which would render war a necessary resource; and that all our movements should change their character and object. I am thus open with you, because I trust that you will have it in your power to impress on that government considerations, in the scale against which the possession of Louisiana is nothing. (In Europe, nothing but Europe is seen, or supposed to have any right in the affairs of nations; but this little event, of France's possessing herself of Louisiana, which is thrown in as nothing, as a mere make-weight in the general settlement of accounts,—this speck which now appears as an almost invisible point in the horizon, is the embryo of a tornado which will burst on the countries on both sides of the Atlantic, and involve in its effects their highest destinies. That it may yet be avoided is my sincere prayer; and if you can be the means of informing the wisdom of Bonaparte of all its consequences, you will have deserved well of both countries. Peace and abstinence from European interferences are our objects, and so will continue while the present order of things in America remains uninterrupted.—To DUPONT DE NEMOURS. iv, 435. (W., April 1802.)

4828. —— ——. Whatever power, other than ourselves, holds the country east of the Mississippi becomes our natural enemy. Will such a possession do France as much good, as such an enemy may do her harm? And how long would it be hers, were such an enemy, situated at its door, added to Great Britain? I confess, it appears to me as essential to France to keep at peace with us, as it is to us to keep at peace with her; and that, if this cannot be secured without some compromise as to the territory in question, it will be useful for both to make some sacrifices to effect the compromise.—To DUPONT DE NEMOURS. iv, 458. FORD ED., viii, 207. (W., Feb. 1803.)

4829. LOUISIANA, Government for.— With respect to the territory acquired, I do not think it will be a separate government, as you imagine. I presume the island of New Orleans, and the settled country on the opposite bank, will be annexed to the Mississippi territory. We shall certainly endeavor to introduce the American laws there, and that cannot be done but by amalgamating the people with such a body of Americans as may take the lead in legislation and government. Of course, they will be under the Governor of Mississippi. The rest of the territory will probably be locked up from American settlement, and under the self-government of the native occupants.—To GENERAL HORATIO GATES. FORD ED., viii, 250. (W., July 1803.)

4830. —— ——. I thought I perceived in you the other day a dread of the job of preparing a constitution for the new acquisition. With more boldness than wisdom I, therefore, determined to prepare a canvas, give it a few daubs of outline, and send it to you to fill up. * * * In communicating it to you I must do it in confidence that you will never let any person know that I have put pen to paper on the subject. * * * My time does not permit me to go into explanation of the enclosed by letter. I will only observe as to a single feature of the Legislature, that the idea of an Assembly of Notables came into my head while writing, as a thing more familiar and pleasing to the French, than a legislation of judges. True it removes their dependence from the judges to the Executive; but this is what they are used to and would prefer. Should Congress reject the nomination of judges for four years, and make them during good behavior, as is probable, then, should

the judges take a kink in their heads in favor of leaving the present laws of Louisiana unaltered, that evil will continue for their lives, unamended by us, and become so inveterate that we may never be able to introduce the uniformity of law so desirable. The making the same persons so directly judges and legislators is more against principle, than to make the same persons executive, and the elector of the legislative members. The former, too, are placed above all responsibility; the latter is under a perpetual control if he goes wrong. The judges have to act on nine out of ten of the laws which are made; the governor not on one in ten. But strike it out, and insert the judges if you think it better, as it was a sudden conceit to which I am not attached.—To JOHN BRECKENRIDGE. FORD ED., viii, 279. (W., Nov. 1803.)

4831. —— ——. Without looking at the old Territorial Ordinance, I had imagined it best to found a government for the territory or territories of *lower* Louisiana on that basis. But on examining it, I find it will not do at all; that it would turn all their laws topsy-turvy. Still, I believe it best to appoint a governor and three judges, with legislative powers; only providing that the judges shall form the laws, and the governor have a negative only, subject further to the negative of a national legislature. The existing laws of the country being now in force, the new legislature will, of course, introduce the trial by jury in *criminal* cases, first; the *habeas corpus,* the freedom of the press, freedom of religion, &c., as soon as can be, and in general draw their laws, and organizations to the mould of ours by degrees, as they find practicable, without exciting too much discontent. In proportion as we find the people there riper for receiving these first principles of freedom, Congress may from session to session, confirm their enjoyment of them.— To ALBERT GALLATIN. FORD ED., viii, 275. (Nov. 1803.)

4832. —— ——. Although it is acknowledged that our new fellow citizens are as yet as incapable of self-government as children, yet some [in Congress] cannot bring themselves to suspend its principles for a single moment. The temporary or territorial government of that country, therefore, will encounter great difficulty [in Congress].—To DE WITT CLINTON. FORD ED., viii, 283. (W., Dec. 1803.)

4833. —— ——. Our policy will be to form New Orleans, and the country on both sides of it on the Gulf of Mexico, into a State; and, as to all above that, to transplant our Indians into it, constituting them a Marechausée to prevent emigrants crossing the river, until we shall have filled up all the vacant country on this side. This will secure both Spain and us as to the mines of Mexico, for half a century, and we may safely trust the provisions for that time to the men who shall live in it.—To DUPONT DE NEMOURS. iv, 509. (W., 1803.)

4834. —— ——. The inhabited part of Louisiana, from Point Coupee to the sea, will of course be immediately a territorial government, and soon a State. But above that, the best use we can make of the country for some time, will be to give establishments in it to the Indians on the East side of the Mississippi, in exchange for their present country, and open land offices in the last, and thus make this acquisition the means of filling up the eastern side, instead of drawing off its population. When we shall be full on this side, we may lay off a range of States on the western bank from the head to the mouth, and so, range after range, advancing compactly as we multiply.—To John C. Breckenridge. iv, 500. Ford ed., viii, 244. (M., Aug. 1803.)

4835. —— ——. In order to lessen the causes of appeal to the Convention, I sincerely wish that Congress at the next session may give to the Orleans Territory a legislature to be chosen by the people, as this will be advancing them quite as fast as the rules of our government will admit; and the evils which may arise from the irregularities which such a legislature may run into, will not be so serious as leaving them the pretext of calling in a foreign umpire between them and us.—To James Madison. Ford ed., viii, 314. (M., Aug. 1804.)

4836. —— ——. We are now at work on a * * * government for Louisiana. It will probably be a small improvement of our former territorial governments, or first grade of government. The act proposes to give them an assembly of Notables, selected by the Governor from the principal characters of the territory. This will, I think, be a better legislature than the former territorial one, and will not be a greater departure from sound principle.—To Thomas McKean. Ford ed., viii, 293. (Jan. 1804.)

4837. —— ——. The Legislative Council for the Territory of New Orleans, * * * to be appointed by me, * * * ought to be composed of men of integrity, of understanding, of clear property and influence among the people, well acquainted with the laws, customs, and habits of the country, and drawn from the different parts of the Territory, whose population is considerable.*—To Governor Claiborne. iv, 551. (W., July 1804.) See Claiborne.

4838. —— ——. I am so much impressed with the expediency of putting a termination to the right of France to patronize the rights of Louisiana, which will cease with their complete adoption as citizens of the United States, that I hope to see that take place on the meeting of Congress.—To James Madison. iv, 557. Ford ed., viii, 315. (M., Aug. 1804.)

4839. —— ——. It is but too true that great discontents exist in the Territory of

* Jefferson requested Governor Claiborne to send him the names of proper persons for the council.— Editor.

Orleans. Those of the French inhabitants have for their sources, 1, the prohibition of importing slaves. This may be partly removed by Congress permitting them to receive slaves from the other States, which, by dividing that evil, would lessen its danger; 2, the administration of justice in our forms, principles, and language, with all of which they are unacquainted, and are the more abhorrent, because of the enormous expense, greatly exaggerated by the corruption of bankrupt and greedy lawyers, who have gone there from the United States and engrossed the practice; 3, the call on them by the land commissioners to produce the titles of their lands. The object of this is really to record and secure their rights. But as many of them hold on rights so ancient that the title papers are lost, they expect the land is to be taken from them whenever they cannot produce a regular deduction of title in writing. In this they will be undeceived by the final result, which will evince to them a liberal disposition of the government towards them.—To John Dickinson. v, 29. Ford ed., ix, 8. (W., 1807.)

4840. LOUISIANA, Mission to France respecting.—The urgency of the case, as well as the public spirit, induced us to make a more solemn appeal to the justice and judgment of our neighbors, by sending a Minister Extraordinary to impress them with the necessity of some arrangement. Mr. Monroe has been selected. His good dispositions cannot be doubted. Multiplied conversations with him, and views of the subject taken in all the shapes in which it can present itself, have possessed him with our estimates of everything relating to it, with a minuteness which no written communication to Mr. Livingston could ever have attained. These will prepare them to meet and decide on every form of proposition which can occur, without awaiting new instructions from hence, which might draw to an indefinite length a discussion where circumstances imperiously oblige us to a prompt decision. For the occlusion of the Mississippi is a state of things in which we cannot exist. He goes, therefore, joined with Chancellor Livingston, to aid in the issue of a crisis the most important the United States have ever met since their Independence, and which is to decide their future character and career.—To Dupont de Nemours. iv, 456. Ford ed., viii, 204. (W., Feb. 1803.) See Monroe.

4841. —— ——. The future destinies of our country hang on the event of this negotiation, and I am sure they could not be placed in more able or more zealous hands. On our parts we shall be satisfied that what you do not effect, cannot be effected.—To Robert R. Livingston. iv, 461. Ford ed., viii, 210. (W., Feb. 1803.)

4842. —— ——. It may be said, if this object be so all-important to us, why do we not offer such a sum as to ensure its purchase? The answer is simple. We are an agricultural people, poor in money, and owing great debts. These will be falling due by instalments for fifteen years to come, and require from us the practice of a rigorous economy to accomplish their payment; and it is our principle to pay to a moment whatever we have engaged, and never to engage what we cannot, and mean not faithfully to pay. We have calculated our resources, and find the sum to be moderate which they would enable us to pay, and we know from late trials that little can be added to it by borrowing.—To DUPONT DE NEMOURS. iv, 458. FORD ED., viii, 206. (W., Feb. 1803.)

4843. —— ——. The country, too, which we wish to purchase, except the portion already granted, and which must be confirmed to the private holders, is a barren sand, six hundred miles from east to west, and from thirty to forty and fifty miles from north to south, formed by deposition of the sands by the Gulf Stream in its circular course round the Mexican Gulf, and which being spent after performing a semicircle, has made from its last depositions the sand bank of East Florida. In West Florida, indeed, there are on the borders of the rivers some rich bottoms, formed by the mud brought from the upper country. These bottoms are all possessed by individuals. But the spaces between river and river are mere banks of sand; and in East Florida there are neither rivers, nor consequently any bottoms. We cannot, then, make anything by a sale of the lands to individuals. So that it is peace alone which makes it an object with us, and which ought to make the cession of it desirable to France. —To DUPONT DE NEMOURS. iv, 458. FORD ED., viii, 206. (W., Feb. 1803.)

4844. —— ——. You see with what frankness I communicate with you on this subject; that I hide nothing from you, and that I am endeavoring to turn our private friendship to the good of our respective countries. And can private friendship ever answer a nobler end than by keeping two nations at peace, who, if this new position which one of them is taking were rendered innocent, have more points of common interest, and fewer of collision, than any two on earth; who become natural friends, instead of natural enemies, which this change of position would make them.—To DUPONT DE NEMOURS. iv, 459. FORD ED., viii, 207. (W., Feb. 1803.)

4845. —— ——. The measure was moreover proposed from another cause. We must know at once whether we can acquire New Orleans or not. We are satisfied nothing else will secure us against a war at no distant period; and we cannot press this reason without beginning those arrangements which will be necessary if war is hereafter to result. For this purpose it was necessary that the negotiators should be fully possessed of every idea we have on the subject, so as to meet the propositions of the opposite party, in whatever form they may be offered; and give them a shape admissible by us without being obliged to wait new instructions hence. With this view, we have joined Mr. Monroe

with yourself at Paris, and to Mr. Pinckney at Madrid, although we believe it will be hardly necessary for him to go to this last place. Should we fail in this object of the mission, a further one will be superadded for the other side of the channel.—To ROBERT R. LIVINGSTON. iv, 461. FORD ED., viii, 209. (W., Feb. 1803.)

4846. LOUISIANA, Mississippi navigation secured.—The acquisition of New Orleans would of itself have been a great thing, as it would have ensured to our western brethren the means of exporting their produce; but that of Louisiana is inappreciable, because, giving us the sole dominion of the Mississippi, it excludes those bickerings with foreign powers, which we know of a certainty would have put us at war with France immediately; and it secures to us the course of a peaceful nation.—To JOHN DICKINSON. FORD ED., viii, 261. (M., Aug. 1803.)

4847. —— ——. The acquisition of Louisiana, although more immediately beneficial to the western States, by securing for their produce a certain market, not subject to interruptions by officers over whom we have no control, yet is also deeply interesting to the maritime portion of our country, inasmuch as by giving the exclusive navigation of the Mississippi, it avoids the burthens and sufferings of a war, which conflicting interests on that river would inevitably have produced at no distant period. It opens, too, a fertile region for the future establishments in the progress of that multiplication so rapidly taking place in all parts.—R. TO A. TENNESSEE LEGISLATURE. viii, 115. (1803.)

— **LOUISIANA, Monroe and.**—See MONROE.

— **LOUISIANA, New Orleans entrepot.** —See NEW ORLEANS.

4848. LOUISIANA, Payment for.—We shall not avail ourselves of the three months' delay after possession of the province, allowed by the treaty for the delivery of the stock, but shall deliver it the moment that possession is known here, which will be on the eighteenth day after it has taken place.— To ROBERT R. LIVINGSTON. iv, 512. FORD ED., viii, 279. (W., Nov. 1803.)

4849. —— ——. When we contemplate the ordinary annual augmentation of imposts from increasing population and wealth, the augmentation of the same revenue by its extension to the new acquisition, and the economies which may still be introduced into our public expenditures, I cannot but hope that Congress in reviewing their resources will find means to meet the intermediate interests of this additional debt without recurring to new taxes, and applying to this object only the ordinary progression of our revenue.— THIRD ANNUAL MESSAGE. viii, 27. FORD ED., viii, 271. (Oct. 1803.)

4850. —— ——. [The acquisition] was so far from being thought, by any party, a breach of neutrality, that the British minister congratulated Mr. King on the acquisition, and declared that the King had learned it with great pleasure; and when Baring, the British banker, asked leave of the minister to purchase the debt and furnish the money to France, the minister declared to him, that so far from throwing obstacles in the way, if there were any difficulty in the payment of the money, it was the interest of Great Britain to aid it.—To W. A. BURWELL. v, 20. FORD ED., viii, 469. (M., Sep. 1806.)

4851. LOUISIANA, Possession by Great Britain.—I am so deeply impressed with the magnitude of the dangers which will attend our government, if Louisiana and the Floridas be added to the British empire, that, in my opinion, we ought to make ourselves parties in the *general war* expected to take place, should this be the only means of preventing the calamity. But I think we should defer this step as long as possible; because war is so full of chances, which may relieve us from the necessity of interfering; and if necessary, still the later we interfere, the better we shall be prepared. It is often indeed more easy to prevent the capture of a place than to retake it. Should it be so in the case in question, the difference between the two operations of preventing and retaking, will not be so costly as two, three, or four years more of war. So that I am for preserving neutrality as long, and entering into the war as late, as possible.—OFFICIAL OPINION. vii, 509. FORD ED., v, 238. (August 1790.)

4852. ———— ————. It is said that Arnold is at Detroit reviewing the militia there. Other symptoms indicate a general design on all Louisiana and the two Floridas. What a tremendous position would success in these two objects place us in! Embraced from the St. Croix to the St. Mary's on one side by their possessions, on the other by their fleet, we need not hesitate to say that they would soon find means to unite to them all the territory covered by the ramifications of the Mississippi.—To JAMES MONROE. FORD ED., v, 199. (N.Y., July 1790.)

4853. LOUISIANA, Questions of boundary.—I suppose Monroe will touch on the limits of Louisiana only incidentally, inasmuch as its extension to Perdido curtails Florida, and renders it of less worth. * * * I am satisfied our right to the Perdido is substantial, and can be opposed by a quibble on form only; and our right westwardly to the bay of St. Bernard, may be strongly maintained.—To JAMES MADISON. iv, 502. FORD ED., viii, 245. (M., Aug. 1803.)

4854. ———— ————. We did not collect the sense of our brethren the other day by regular questions, but as far as I could understand from what was said, it appeared to be,—1. That an acknowledgment of our right to the Perdido, is a *sine qua non*, and no price to be given for it. 2. No absolute and perpetual relinquishment of right is to be made of the country east of the Rio Bravo del Norte, even in exchange for Florida. (I am not quite sure that this was the opinion of all.) It would be better to lengthen the term of years to any definite degree than to cede in perpetuity. 3. That a country may be laid off within which no further settlement shall be made by either party for a given time, say thirty years. This country to be from the North river eastwardly towards the Rio Colorado, or even to, but not beyond the Mexican or Sabine river. To whatever river it be extended, it might from its source run northwest, as the most eligible direction; but a due north line would produce no restraint that we should feel in twenty years. This relinquishment, and two millions of dollars, to be the price of all the Floridas east of the Perdido, or to be apportioned to whatever part they will cede. But on entering into conferences, both parties should agree that, during their continuance, neither should strengthen their situation between the Iberville, Mississippi, and Perdido, nor interrupt the navigation of the rivers therein. If they will not give such an order instantly, they should be told that we have for peace's sake only, forborne till they could have time to give such an order, but that as soon as we receive notice of their refusal to give the order, we shall enter into the exercise of our right of navigating the Mobile, and protect it, and increase our force there *pari passu* with them.—To JAMES MADISON. iv, 550. FORD ED., viii, 309. (July 1804.)

4855. ———— ————. In conversation with Mr. Gallatin as to what might be deemed the result of our conference, he seemed to have understood the former opinion as not changed, to wit, that for the Floridas east of the Perdido might be given not only the two millions of dollars and a margin to remain unsettled, but an absolute relinquishment from the North river to the Bay of St. Bernard and Colorado river. This, however, I think should be the last part of the price yielded, and only for an entire cession of the Floridas, not for a part only.—To JAMES MADISON. FORD ED., viii, 313. (1804.)

4856. LOUISIANA, Spain and acquisition.—At this moment a little cloud hovers in the horizon. The government of Spain has protested against the right of France to transfer; and it is possible she may refuse possession, and that this may bring on acts of force. But against such neighbors as France there, and the United States here, what she can expect from so gross a compound of folly and false faith, is not to be sought in the book of wisdom. She is afraid of her enemies in Mexico; but not more than we are.—To DUPONT DE NEMOURS. iv, 509. (W., Nov. 1803.)

4857. ———— ————. Spain entered with us a protestation against our ratification of the treaty, grounded, first, on the assertion that the First Consul had not executed the conditions of the treaties of cession; and, secondly, that he had broken a solemn promise not to alienate the country to any nation. We answered, that these were private questions between France and Spain, which they must settle together; that we derived our title from the First Consul, and did not doubt his guarantee of it.—To ROBERT R. LIVINGSTON. iv, 511. FORD ED., viii, 278. (W., Nov. 1803.) See SPAIN.

4858. LOUISIANA, Taking possession of.—We * * * [have] sent off orders to the Governor of the Mississippi Territory and

General Wilkinson to move down with the troops at hand to New Orleans, to receive the possession from M. Laussat. If he is heartily disposed to carry the order of the [First] Consul into execution, he can probably command a volunteer force at New Orleans, and will have the aid of ours also, if he desires it, to take the possession, and deliver it to us. If he is not so disposed, *we* shall take the possession, and it will rest with the government of France, by adopting the act as their own, and obtaining the confirmation of Spain, to supply the non-execution of their stipulation to deliver, and to entitle themselves to the complete execution of our part of the agreements.—To ROBERT R. LIVINGSTON. iv, 511. FORD ED., viii, 279. (W., Nov. 1803.)

4859. ———— ————. I think it possible that Spain, recollecting our former eagerness for the island of New Orleans, may imagine she can, by a free delivery of that, redeem the residue of Louisiana; and that she may withhold the peaceable cession of it. In that case no doubt force must be used.—To JAMES MADISON. FORD ED., viii, 263. (M., Sep. 1803.)

4860. LOUISIANA, Treaty ratified.— This treaty [Louisiana] must, of course, be laid before both Houses [of Congress], because both have important functions to exercise respecting it. They, I presume, will see their duty to their country in ratifying and paying for it, so as to secure a good which would otherwise probably be never again in their power. But, I suppose, they must then appeal to *the nation* for an additional article to the Constitution, approving and confirming an act which the nation had not previously authorized.—To JOHN C. BRECKENRIDGE. iv, 500. FORD ED., viii, 244. (M., Aug. 1803.)

4861. ———— ————. Your treaty has obtained nearly a general approbation. * * * The question on its ratification in the Senate was decided by twenty-four against seven, which was ten more than enough. The vote in the House of Representatives for making provision for its execution was carried by eighty-nine against twenty-three, which was a majority of sixty-six, and the necessary bills are going through the Houses by greater majorities.—To ROBERT R. LIVINGSTON. iv, 510. FORD ED., viii, 278. (W., Nov. 1803.)

4862. ———— ————. You will observe in the enclosed letter from Monroe a hint to do without delay what we are bound to do [regarding the treaty]. There is reason, in the opinion of our ministers, to believe, that if the thing were to do over again. it could not be obtained, and that if we give the least opening, they will declare the treaty void. A warning amounting to that has been given them, and an unusual kind of letter written by their minister to our Secretary of State, direct.—To WILSON C. NICHOLAS. iv, 505. FORD ED., viii, 247. (M., Sep. 1803.)

4863. ———— ————. M. Pichon, according to instructions from his government, proposed

to have added to the ratification a protestation against any failure in time or other circumstances of execution, on our part. He was told, that in that case we should annex a counter protestation, which would leave the thing exactly where it was; that this transaction had been conducted, from the commencement of the negotiation to this stage of it. with a frankness and sincerity honorable to both nations, and comfortable to the heart of an honest man to review; that to annex to this last chapter of the transaction such an evidence of mutual distrust, was to change its aspect dishonorably for us both, and, contrary to truth, as to us; for that we had not the smallest doubt that France would punctually execute its part; and I assured M. Pichon that I had more confidence in the word of the First Consul than in all the parchment we could sign. He saw that we had ratified the treaty; that both branches had passed, by great majorities, one of the bills for execution, and would soon pass the other two; that no circumstances remained that could leave a doubt of our punctual performance; and like an able and honest minister (which he is in the highest degree), he undertook to do what he knew his employers would do themselves, were they here spectators of all the existing circumstances, and exchanged the ratifications purely and simply; so that this instrument goes to the world as an evidence of candor and confidence of the nations in each other, which will have the best effects.—To ROBERT R. LIVINGSTON. iv, 510. FORD ED., viii, 278. (W., Nov. 1803.)

4864. ———— ————. The treaty which has so happily sealed the friendship of our two countries has been received here with general acclamation.—To DUPONT DE NEMOURS. iv, 508. (W., 1803.)

4865. ———— ————. For myself and my country, I thank you for the aids you have given in it; and I congratulate you on having lived to give those aids in a transaction replete with blessings to unborn millions of men, and which will mark the face of a portion on the globe so extensive as that which now composes the United States of America.—To DUPONT DE NEMOURS. iv, 509. (W., 1803.)

4866. ———— ————. It is not true that the Louisiana treaty was antedated, lest Great Britain should consider our supplying her enemies with money as a breach of neutrality. After the very words of the treaty were finally agreed to, it took some time, perhaps some days, to make out all the copies in the very splendid manner of Bonaparte's treaties. Whether the 30th of April. 1803, the date expressed, was the day of the actual compact, or that on which it was signed, our memories do not enable us to say. If the former, then it is strictly conformable to the day of the compact; if the latter, then it was postdated, instead of being antedated.*—To W. A. BURWELL. v, 20. FORD ED., viii, 469. (M., Sep. 1806.)

* This antedating of the treaty was one of the charges made by John Randolph against the administration of Jefferson.—EDITOR.

4867. LOUIS XVI., Character of.—He had not a wish but for the good of the nation; and for that object, no personal sacrifice would ever have cost him a moment's regret; but his mind was weakness itself, his constitution timid, his judgment null, and without sufficient firmness even to stand by the faith of his word. His Queen, too, haughty, and bearing no contradiction, had an absolute ascendency over him; and around her were rallied the King's brother, D'Artois, the court generally, and the aristocratic part of his ministers, particularly Breteuil, Broglio, Vauguyon, Foulon, Luzerne, men whose principles of government were those of the age of Louis XIV. Against this host, the good counsels of Necker, Montmorin, St. Priest, although in unison with the wishes of the King himself, were of little avail. The resolutions of the morning, formed under their advice, would be reversed in the evening, by the influence of the Queen and Court.—Autobiography. i, 88. Ford ed., i, 121. (1821.)

4868. —— ——. The King is a good man. To Edward Carrington. ii, 99. Ford ed., iv, 359. (P., 1787.)

4869. —— ——. Under a good and a young King, as the present, I think good may be made of the Assemblée des Notables.—To La Comtesse de Tesse. ii, 133. (N., March 1787.)

4870. —— ——. The model of royal excellence.—To Count de Montmorin. iii, 137. (N.Y., 1790.)

4871. —— ——. The King loves business, economy, order, and justice, and wishes sincerely the good of his people; but he is irascible. rude, very limited in his understanding, and religious, bordering on bigotry. He * * *, loves his Queen, and is too much governed by her. * * * Unhappily the King shows a propensity for the pleasures of the table. That for drink has increased lately, or, at least, it has become more known.—To James Madison. ii, 153. Ford ed., iv, 393. (P., 1787.)

4872. LOUIS XVI., Execution.—We have just received the news of the decapitation of the King of France. Should the present foment in Europe not produce republics everywhere, it will at least soften the monarchical governments by rendering monarchs amenable to punishment like other criminals, and doing away that rage of insolence and oppression, the inviolability of the King's person.—To —— ——. iii, 527. (Pa., March 1793.)

4873. —— ——. It is certain that the ladies of this city [Philadelphia], of the first circle, are open-mouthed against the murderers of a sovereign, and they generally speak those sentiments which the more cautious husband smothers.—To James Madison. iii, 520. Ford ed., vi, 193. (1793.)

4874. —— ——. The death of the King of France has not produced as open condemnations from the monocrats as I expected.—To James Madison. iii, 519. Ford ed., vi, 192. (March 1793.)

4875. —— ——. The deed which closed the mortal course of these sovereigns [Louis XVI. and Marie Antoinette], I shall neither approve nor condemn. I am not prepared to say that the first magistrate of a nation cannot commit treason against his country, or is unamenable to its punishment; nor yet, that where there is no written law, no regulated tribunal, there is not a law in our hearts, and a power in our hands, given for righteous employment in maintaining right and redressing wrong. Of those who judged the King, many thought him wilfully criminal; many that his existence would keep the nation in perpetual conflict with the horde of kings who would war against a regeneration which might come home to themselves, and that it were better that one should die than all. I should not have voted with this portion of the legislature. I should have shut up the Queen in a convent, putting harm out of her power, and placed the King in his station, investing him with limited powers, which, I verily believe, he would have honestly exercised according to the measure of his understanding. In this way no void would have been created, courting the usurpation of a military adventurer, nor occasion given for those enormities which demoralized the nations of the world, and destroyed and are yet to destroy millions and millions of its inhabitants.—Autobiography. i, 101. Ford ed., i, 141. (1821.)

4876. LOUIS XVI., Friend to America.—Our best and greatest friend.—To Marquis de la Luzerne. iii, 141. (N.Y., 1790.)

4877. LOUIS XVI., Good qualities.—The King's dispositions are solidly good. He is capable of great sacrifices. All he wants to induce him to do a thing, is to be assured it will be for the good of the nation.—To Mr. Cutting. ii, 439. (P., 1788.)

4878. LOUIS XVI., Habits.—The King, long in the habit of drowning his cares in wine, plunges deeper and deeper. The Queen cries, but sins on.—To John Adams. ii, 258. (P., 1787.)

4879. —— ——. The King goes for nothing. He hunts one half the day, is drunk the other, and signs whatever he is bid [by the Queen].—To John Jay. ii, 294. (P., 1787.)

4880. LOUIS XVI., Honesty.—The King is the honestest man in his kingdom, and the most regular and economical. He has no foible which will enlist him against the good of his people; and whatever constitution will promote this, he will befriend. But he will not befriend it obstinately: he has given repeated proofs of a readiness to sacrifice his opinion to the wish of the nation. I believe he will consider the opinion of the States General, as the best evidence of what will please and profit the nation, and will conform to it.—To Mr. Cutting. ii, 470. (P., Aug. 1788.)

4881. —— ——. He is an honest, unambitious man, who desires neither money nor power for himself.—To John Jay. iii, 28. (P., 1789.)

4882. —— ——. The King is honest, and wishes the good of his people; but the expediency of an hereditary aristocracy is too difficult a question for him. On the contrary, his prejudices, his habits and his connections, decide him in his heart to support it.—To John Jay. iii, 51. (P., 1789.)

4883. —— ——. The King has an honest heart.—To James Monroe. Ford ed., iv, 39. (P., 1785.)

4884. LOUIS XVI., Revenues.—It is urged principally against the King that his revenue is one hundred and thirty millions more than that of his predecessor was, and yet he demands one hundred and twenty millions further.—To John Adams. ii, 258. (P., 1787.)

4885. LOUIS XVI., Sincerity.—I have not a single doubt of the sincerity of the King.—To Mr. Mason. iii, 72. (P., July 1789.) See Marie Antoinette and Revolution (French).

4886. LOUIS XVIII., Restoration of.— I have received some information from an eyewitness of what passed on the occasion of the second return of Louis XVIII. The Emperor Alexander, it seems, was solidly opposed to this. In the consultation of the allied sovereigns and their representatives with the executive council at Paris, he insisted that the Bourbons were too incapable and unworthy of being placed at the head of the nation; declared he would support any other choice they should freely make, and continued to urge most strenuously that some other choice should be made. The debates ran high and warm, and broke off after midnight, every one retaining his own opinion. He lodged * * * at Talleyrand's. When they returned into council the next day, his host had overcome his firmness. Louis XVIII. was accepted, and through the management of Talleyrand, accepted without any capitulation, although the sovereigns would have consented that he should be first required to subscribe and swear to the constitution prepared, before permission to enter the kingdom. It would seem as if Talleyrand had been afraid to admit the smallest interval of time, lest a change of mind would bring back Bonaparte on them. But I observe that the friends of a limited monarchy there consider the popular representation as much improved by the late alteration, and confident it will in the end produce a fixed government in which an elective body, fairly representative of the people, will be an efficient element.—To John Adams. vii, 82. (P.F., 1817.)

4887. LUXURIES, The Republic and.— I own it to be my opinion, that good will arise from the destruction of our credit [in Europe]. I see nothing else which can restrain our disposition to luxury, and to the change of those manners which alone can preserve republican government.—To Archibald Stuart. i, 518. Ford ed., iv, 188. (1786.)

4888. LUXURIES, Taxation of.—The * * * revenue, on the consumption of foreign articles, is paid cheerfully by those who can afford to add foreign luxuries to domestic comforts.—Second Inaugural Address. viii, 41. Ford ed., viii, 343. (1805.)

4889. ——— ———. The great mass of the articles on which impost is paid is foreign luxuries, purchased by those only who are rich enough to afford themselves the use of them.—Sixth Annual Message. viii, 68. Ford ed., viii, 494. (Dec. 1806.)

4890. ——— ———. The government which steps out of the ranks of the ordinary articles of consumption to select and lay under disproportionate burthens a particular one, because it is a comfort, pleasing to the taste, or necessary to health, and will therefore be bought, is, in that particular, a tyranny.—To Samuel Smith. vii, 285. Ford ed., x, 252. (M., 1819.) See Taxation.

— **LYNCH-LAW.**—See Law.

4891. LUZERNE (Marquis de la), Disappointments.—We have, for some time, expected that the Chevalier de la Luzerne would obtain a promotion in the diplomatic line by being appointed to some of the courts where this country keeps an ambassador. But none of the vacancies taking place, I think the present disposition is to require his return to his station in America. He told me himself lately that he should return in the Spring. I have never pressed this matter on the court, though I knew it to be desirable and desired on our part; because, if the compulsion on him to return had been the work of Congress, he would have returned in such ill temper with them, as to disappoint them in the good they expected from it. He would forever have laid at their door his failure of promotion. I did not press it for another reason, which is, that I have great reason to believe that the character of the Count de Moustier, who would go, were the Chevalier to be otherwise provided for, would give the most perfect satisfaction in America.—To James Madison. ii, 106. Ford ed., iv, 364. (P., 1787.)

4892. LUZERNE (Marquis de la), Secret marriage.—The Marquis de la Luzerne had been for many years married to his brother's wife's sister, secretly. She was ugly and deformed, but sensible, amiable, and rather rich. When he was named ambassador to London, with ten thousand guineas a year, the marriage was avowed, and he relinquished his cross of Malta, from which he derived a handsome revenue for life, and which was very open to advancement. She stayed here [Paris] and not long after died. His real affection for her, which was great and unfeigned, and perhaps the loss of his order for so short-lived a satisfaction, has thrown him almost into a state of despondency.—To James Madison. ii, 445. Ford ed., v, 44. (P., 1788.)

4893. LUZERNE (Marquis de la), Tribute to.—This government is now formed, organized, and in action; and it considers among its earliest duties, and assuredly among its most cordial, to testify to you the regret which the people and government of the United States felt at your removal from among them; a very general and sincere regret, and tempered only by the consolation of your personal advancement, which accompanied it. You will receive, Sir, by order of the President of the United States, as soon as they can be prepared, a medal and chain of gold, of which he desires your acceptance in token of their esteem, and of the sensibility with which they will ever recall your recollection of their memory. But as this compliment may, hereafter, be rendered to other missions, from which yours was distinguished by eminent circumstances, the President of the United States wishes to pay you the distinct tribute of an express acknowledgment of your services, and our sense of them. You came to us, Sir, through all the perils which encompassed us on all sides. You found us struggling and suffering under difficulties, as singular and trying as our situation was new and unprecedented. Your magnanimous nation had taken side with us in the conflict, and yourself became the centre of our common councils, the link which connected our common operations. In that position you labored without ceasing, until all our labors were crowned with glory to your nation, freedom to ours, and benefit to both. During the whole, we are constant evidence of your zeal, your abilities and your good faith. We desire to convey this testimony it home to your breast, and to that of your sovereign, our best and greatest friend, and this I do, Sir, in the name, and by the express instruction of the President of the United States.—To MARQUIS DE LA LUZERNE. iii, 141. (N.Y., April 30, 1790.)

4894. LYON (Matthew), Prosecution of.—You will have seen the disgusting proceedings in the case of Lyon. It they would have accepted even of a commitment to the serjeant, it might have been had. But to get rid of his vote was the most material object. These proceedings must degrade the General Government, and lead the people to lean more on their State governments, which have been sunk under the early popularity of the former.—To JAMES MADISON. iv, 211. FORD ED., vii, 202. (Pa., Feb. 1798.)

4895. MACDONOUGH (Commodore), Victory of.—The success of Macdonough [in the battle of Lake Champlain] has been happily timed to dispel the gloom of your present meeting, and to open the present session of Congress with hope and good humor.—To JAMES MONROE. FORD ED., ix, 488. (M., 1814.)

4896. —— ——. I congratulate you on the destruction of a second hostile fleet on the Lakes by Macdonough. * * * While our enemies cannot but feel shame for their barbarous achievements at Washington, they will be stung to the soul by these repeated victories over them on that element on which they wish the world to think them invincible. We have dissipated that error. They must now feel a conviction themselves that we can beat them gun to gun, ship to ship, and fleet to fleet, and that their early successes on the land have been either purchased from traitors, or obtained from raw men entrusted of necessity with commands for which no experience had qualified them, and that every day is adding that experience to unquestioned bravery.—To PRESIDENT MADISON. vi, 386. (M., 1814.)

4897. MACE, Design for.—I send you a design for a Mace by Dr. Thornton, whose taste and inspiration are both good. But I am not satisfied with the introduction of the rattlesnake into the design. There is in man as well as brutes, an antipathy to the snake, which renders it a disgusting object wherever it is presented. I would myself rather adopt the Roman staves and axe, trite as it is; or perhaps a sword, sheathed in a roll of parchment (that is to say an imitation in metal of a roll of parchment), written over, in the raised Gothic letters of the law, with that part of the Constitution which establishes the House of Representatives, for that house, or the Senate. For the Senate, however, if you have that same disgust for the snake, I am sure you will yourself imagine some better substitute; or perhaps you will find that disgust overbalanced by stronger considerations in favor of the emblem.—To GOVERNOR HENRY LEE. FORD ED., vi, 320. (Pa., 1793.)

4898. MACON (Nathaniel) Confidence in.—Some enemy whom we know not, is sowing tares among us. Between you and myself nothing but opportunities of explanation can be necessary to defeat those endeavors. At least on my part my confidence in you is so unqualified that nothing further is necessary for my satisfaction. I must, therefore, ask a conversation with you.—To NATHANIEL MACON. FORD ED., viii, 439. (W., 1806.)

4899. —— ——. While such men as yourself and your worthy colleagues of the legislature, and such characters as compose the executive administration, are watching for us all,

I slumber without fear, and review in my dreams the visions of antiquity. *—To NATHANIEL MACON. vii, 111. FORD ED., x, 120. (M., 1819.)

— MADEIRA, Climate of.—See CLIMATE.

4900. MADISON (James), Ability of.—Mr. Madison came into the House [Legislature of Virginia] in 1776, a new member and young; which circumstances, concurring with his extreme modesty, prevented his venturing himself in debate before his removal to the Council of State, in November, '77. From thence he went to Congress, then consisting of few members. Trained in these successive schools, he acquired a habit of self-possession, which placed at ready command the rich resources of his luminous and discriminating mind, and of his extensive information, and rendered him the first of every assembly afterwards, of which he became a member. Never wandering from his subject into vain declamation, but pursuing it closely, in language pure, classical and copious, soothing always the feelings of his adversaries by civilities and softness of expression, he rose to the eminent station which he held in the great National Convention of 1787; and in that of Virginia which followed, he sustained the new Constitution in all its parts, bearing off the palm against the logic of George Mason, and the fervid declamation of Mr. [Patrick] Henry. With these consummate powers, were united a pure and spotless virtue, which no calumny has ever attempted to sully. Of the powers and polish of his pen, and of the wisdom of his administration in the highest office of the nation, I need say nothing. They have spoken, and will forever speak for themselves.—AUTOBIOGRAPHY. i, 41. FORD ED., i, 56. (1821.)

4901. MADISON (James), Administration of.—I leave everything in the hands of men so able to take care of them, that if we are destined to meet misfortunes, it will be because no human wisdom could avert them.—To DUPONT DE NEMOURS. v, 433. (W., 1809.)

4902. —— ——. If peace can be preserved, I hope and trust you will have a smooth administration. I know no government which would be so embarrassing in war as ours. This would proceed very much from the lying and licentious character of our papers; but much, also, from the wonderful credulity of the members of Congress in the floating lies of the day. And in this no experience seems to correct them. I have never seen a Congress during the last eight years, a majority of which I would not implicitly have relied on in any question, could their minds have been purged of all errors of fact. The evil, too, increases greatly with the protraction of the session, and I apprehend, in case of war, their session would have a tendency to become permanent.—To PRESIDENT MADISON. v, 437. (W., March 1809.)

4903. —— ——. Any services which I could have rendered will be more than supplied by the wisdom and virtues of my successor.—REPLY TO ADDRESS. v, 473. (M., 1809.)

* Nathaniel Macon was Speaker of the House of Representatives from 1801 to 1806, and subsequently United States Senator from North Carolina. John Randolph of Roanoke made him one of the legatees of his estate, and said of him in his will, "he is the best, the purest, and wisest man I ever knew".—EDITOR.

4904. —— ——. Mr. Madison is my successor. This ensures to us a wise and honest administration.—To BARON HUMBOLDT. v, 435. (W., 1809.)

4905. —— ——. I do not take the trouble of forming opinions on what is passing among [my successors], because I have such entire confidence in their integrity and wisdom as to be satisfied all is going right, and that every one is best in the station confided to him.—To DAVID HOWELL. v, 555. (M., 1810.)

4906. —— ——. Anxious, in my retirement, to enjoy undisturbed repose, my knowledge of my successor and late coadjutors, and my entire confidence in their wisdom and integrity, were assurances to me that I might sleep in security with such watchmen at the helm, and that whatever difficulties and dangers should assail our course, they would do what could be done to avoid or surmount them. In this confidence I envelop myself, and hope to slumber on to my last sleep. And should difficulties occur which they cannot avert, if we follow them in phalanx, we shall surmount them without danger.—To WILLIAM DUANE. v, 533. (M., 1810.)

4907. —— ——. If you will except the bringing into power and importance those who were enemies to himself as well as to the principles of republican government, I do not recollect a single measure of the President which I have not approved. Of those under him, and of some very near him, there have been many acts of which we have all disapproved, and he more than we.—To THOMAS LEIPER. vi, 465. FORD ED., ix, 521. (M., 1815.)

4908. MADISON (James), Confidence in.—In all cases I am satisfied you are doing what is for the best, as far as the means put into your hands will enable you, and this thought quiets me under every occurrence.—To PRESIDENT MADISON. vi, 114. FORD ED., ix, 384. (M., May 1813.)

— **MADISON (James), Election contest.** —See HENRY (PATRICK).

4909. MADISON (James), Federal Convention debates.—In a society of members, between whom and yourself are great mutual esteem and respect, a most anxious desire is expressed that you would publish your debates of the [Federal] Convention. That these measures of the army, navy and direct tax will bring about a revolution of public sentiment is thought certain, and that the Constitution will then receive a different explanation. Could those debates be ready to appear critically, their effect would be decisive. I beg of you to turn this subject in your mind. The arguments against it will be personal; those in favor of it moral; and something is required from you as a set off against the sin of your retirement.— To JAMES MADISON. iv, 263. FORD ED., vii, 318. (Pa., Jan. 1799.)

4910. MADISON (James), Hamilton and.—Hamilton is really a Colossus to the anti-republican party. * * * When he comes forward, there is nobody but yourself who can meet him.—To JAMES MADISON. iv, 121. FORD ED., vii, 32. (M., 1795.)

4911. —— ——. You will see in Fenno two numbers of a paper signed "Marcellus". They promise much mischief, and are ascribed, without any difference of opinion, to [Alexan-

der] Hamilton. You must take your pen against this champion. You know the ingenuity of his talents; and there is not a person but yourself who can foil him. For heaven's sake, then, take up your pen, and do not desert the public cause altogether.—To JAMES MADISON. iv, 231. FORD ED., vii, 231. (Pa., April 1798.)

4912. —— ——. Let me pray and beseech you to set apart a certain portion of every post day to write what may be proper for the public. Send it to me while here [Philadelphia], and when I go away I will let you know to whom you may send, so that your name will be sacredly secret. You can render such incalculable services in this way, as to lessen the effect of our loss of your presence here.—To JAMES MADISON. iv, 281. FORD ED., vii, 344. (Pa., Feb. 1799.)

4913. MADISON (James), Jefferson and administration of.—The unwarrantable ideas often expressed in the newspapers, and by persons who ought to know better, that I intermeddle in the Executive councils, and the indecent expressions, sometimes, of a hope that Mr. Madison will pursue the principles of my administration, expressions so disrespectful to his known abilities and dispositions, have rendered it improper in me to hazard suggestions to him, on occasions even where ideas might occur to me, that might accidentally escape him —To JAMES MONROE. vi, 123. (M., 1813.)

— **MADISON (James), Jefferson, Presidency and.**—See PRESIDENT.

4914. MADISON (James), Jefferson's bequest to.—I give to my friend, James Madison, of Montpelier, my gold-mounted walking-staff of animal horn, as a token of the cordial and affectionate friendship, which, for nearly now an half-century, has united us in the same principles and pursuits of what we have deemed for the greatest good of our country.—JEFFERSON'S WILL. ix, 514. FORD ED., x, 395. (March 1826.)

4915. MADISON (James), Jefferson's friendship for.—My friendship for Mr. Madison, my confidence in his wisdom and virtue, and my approbation of all his measures, and especially of his taking up at length the gauntlet against England, is known to all with whom I have ever conversed or corresponded on these measures.—To THOMAS LEIPER. vi, 465. FORD ED., ix, 521. (M., 1815.)

4916. —— ——. The friendship which has subsisted between us, now half a century, and the harmony of our political principles and pursuits, have been sources of constant happiness to me through that long period. And if I remove beyond the reach of attentions to the University, or beyond the bourne of life itself, as I soon must, it is a comfort to leave that institution under your care, and an assurance that it will not be wanting. It has also been a great solace to me, to believe that you are engaged in vindicating to posterity the course we have pursued for preserving to them, in all their purity, the blessings of self-government, which we had assisted, too, in acquiring for them. If ever the earth has beheld a system of administration conducted with a single and steadfast eye to the general interest and happiness of those committed to it, one which, protected by truth, can never know reproach, it is that to which our lives have been devoted. To myself you have been a pillar of support through life. Take care of me when dead, and be assured that I shall leave with you my last affections.*—To JAMES MADISON. vii, 434. FORD ED., x, 377. (M., February 1826.)

4917. MADISON (James), John Adams and.—Charles Lee consulted a member from Virginia to know whether [John] Marshall would be agreeable [as Minister to France]. He named you, as more likely to give satisfaction. The answer was, " nobody of Mr. Madison's way of thinking will be appointed ".—To JAMES MADISON. iv, 179. FORD ED., vii, 132. (Pa., June 1797.)

4918. MADISON (James), Judgment of.—There is no sounder judgment than his. To J. W. EPPES. FORD ED., ix, 484. (M., 1814.)

— MADISON (James), Marbury vs.— See MARBURY vs. MADISON.

— MADISON (James), Monroe and.— See MONROE.

4919. MADISON (James), Opinions of. —No man weighs more maturely than Mr. Madison before he takes a side on any question.—To PEREGRINE FITZHUGH. iv, 170. (M., 1797.)

4920. MADISON (James), Opposition to.—With respect to the opposition threatened, although it may give some pain, no injury of consequence is to be apprehended. Duane flying off from the government, may, for a little while, throw confusion into our ranks as John Randolph did. But, after a moment of time to reflect and rally, and to see where he is, we shall stand our ground with firmness. A few malcontents will follow him, as they did John Randolph, and perhaps he may carry off some well-meaning Anti-Snyderites of Pennsylvania. The federalists will sing hosannas, and the world will thus know of a truth what they are. This new minority will perhaps bring forward their new favorite, who seems already to have betrayed symptoms of consent. They will blast him in the bud, which will be no misfortune. They will sound the tocsin against the ancient dominion, and anti-dominionism may become their rallying point. And it is better that all this should happen two than six years hence.—To PRESIDENT MADISON. FORD ED., ix, 321. (M., April 1811.)

4921. MADISON (James), Pure principles of.—I know them both [Mr. Madison and Mr. Monroe] to be of principles as truly republican as any men living.—To THOMAS RITCHIE. vii, 191. FORD ED., x, 170. (M., 1820.)

4922. MADISON (James), Reelection as President.—I have known Mr. Madison from 1779, when he first came into the public councils, and from three and thirty years' trial, I can say conscientiously that I do not know in the world a man of purer integrity, more dispassionate, disinterested, and devoted to genuine republicanism; nor could I, in the whole scope of America and Europe, point out an abler head. He may be illy seconded by others, betrayed by the Hulls and Arnolds of our country, for such there are in every country, and with sorrow and suffering we know it. But what man can do will be done by Mr. Madison. I hope, therefore, there will be no difference among republicans as to his reelection; we shall know his

* The quotation is from the last letter written by Jefferson to Madison.—EDITOR.

value when we have to give him up, and to look at large for his successor.—To THOMAS C. FLOURNEY. vi, 82. (M., Oct. 1812.)

4923. MADISON (James), Removal of Armstrong.—If our operations have suffered or languished from any want of injury in the present head [of the War Department] which directs them, I have so much confidence in the wisdom and conscientious integrity of Mr. Madison, as to be satisfied, that however torturing to his feelings, he will fulfil his duty to the public and to his own reputation, by making the necessary change.—To WILLIAM DUANE. vi, 81. FORD ED., ix, 369. (M., Oct. 1812.)

4924. MADISON (James), Republicanism of.—Our enemies may try their cajoleries with my successor. They will find him as immovable in his republican principles as him whom they have honored with their peculiar enmity.—To DR. E. GRIFFITH. v, 451. (M., 1809.)

4925. MADISON (James), Services to Jefferson.—Mr. Madison is entitled to his full share of all the measures of my administration. Our principles were the same, and we never differed sensibly in the application of them.—To W. C. NICHOLAS. FORD ED., ix, 252. (M., 1809.)

4926. MADISON (James), Statesmanship.—Our ship is sound, the crew alert at their posts, and our ablest steersman at its helm.—To JOHN MELISH. v, 573. (M., 1811.)

4927. MADISON (James), University of Virginia and.—I do not entertain your apprehensions for the happiness of our brother Madison in a state of retirement. Such a mind as his, fraught with information and with matter for reflection, can never know ennui. Besides, there will always be work enough cut out for him to continue his active usefulness to his country. For example, he and Monroe (the President) are now here (Monticello) on the work of a collegiate institution to be established in our neighborhood, of which they and myself are three of six visitors. This, if it succeeds, will raise up children for Mr. Madison to employ his attention through life.—To JOHN ADAMS. vii, 62. (M., 1817.)

4928. MADISON (James), Wisdom of. —My successor, to the purest principles of republican patriotism, adds a wisdom and foresight second to no man on earth.—To GENERAL KOSCIUSKO. v, 508. (M., 1810.)

— MAGNETIC NEEDLE.—See LATITUDE AND LONGITUDE.

4929. MAILS, Expediting.—The President has desired me to confer with you on the proposition I made the other day, of endeavoring to move the posts at the rate of one hundred miles a day. It is believed to be practicable here, because it is practiced in every other country. * * * I am anxious that the thing should be begun by way of experiment, for a short distance, because I believe it will so increase the income of the post-office as to show we may go through with it.—To COLONEL PICKERING. iii, 344. (Pa., 1792.)

4930. MAINE, English encroachments. —The English encroachments on the province of Maine become serious. They have seized vessels, too, on our coast of Passamaquoddy, thereby displaying a pretension to the exclusive jurisdiction to the Bay of Fundy, which separates Nova Scotia and Maine, and belongs as much to us as them.—To Marquis de Lafayette. ii, 21. (P., 1786.)

4931. MAINE, Independence of.—If I do not contemplate this subject [the Missouri question] with pleasure, I do sincerely [contemplate] that of the independence of Maine, and the wise choice they have made of General King in the agency of their affairs.—To Mark Langdon Hill. vii, 155. (M., 1820.)

4932. MAJORITY, Abuses by.—The majority, oppressing an individual, is guilty of a crime; abuses its strength, and, by acting on the law of the strongest, breaks up the foundations of society.—To Dupont de Nemours. vi, 591. Ford ed., x, 24. (P.F., 1816.)

4933. MAJORITY, Dissent from.—It is true that dissentients have a right to go over to the minority, and to act with them. But I do not believe your mind has contemplated that course; that it has deliberately viewed the strange company into which it may be led, step by step, unintended and unperceived by itself. The example of John Randolph is a caution to all honest and prudent men, to sacrifice a little of self-confidence, and to go with their friends, although they may sometimes think they are going wrong. * * * As far as my good will may go (for I can no longer act), I shall adhere to my government, Executive and Legislative, and, as long as they are republican, I shall go with their measures whether I think them right or wrong; because I know they are honest, and are wiser and better informed than I am. In doing this, however, I shall not give up the friendship of those who differ from me, and who have equal right with myself to shape their own course.—To William Duane. v, 592. Ford ed., ix, 316. (M., 1811.)

4934. MAJORITY, Force vs.—Absolute acquiescence in the decisions of the majority, —the vital principle of republics, from which is no appeal but to force, the vital principle and immediate parent of despotism, I deem [one of the] essential principles of our government and, consequently, [one] which ought to shape its administration.—First Inaugural Address. viii, 4. Ford ed., viii, 4. (1801.)

4935. MAJORITY, Generations and.— This corporeal globe, and everything upon it, belong to its present corporeal inhabitants, during their generation. They alone have a right to direct what is the concern of themselves alone, and to declare the law of that direction; and this declaration can only be made by their majority.—To Samuel Kerchival. vii, 16. Ford ed., x, 44. (M., 1816.)

4936. ———. A generation may bind itself as long as its majority continues in life; when that has disappeared, another majority is in place, holds all the rights and powers

their predecessors once held, and may change their laws and institutions to suit themselves. —To John Cartwright. vii, 359. M., 1824.) See Generations.

4937. MAJORITY, Law of.—Where the law of the majority ceases to be acknowledged, there government ends; the law of the strongest takes its place, and life and property are his who can take them.—R. to A. Annapolis Citizens. viii, 150. (1809.)

4938. ———. The *lex majoris partis* [is] founded in common law as well as common right.—Notes on Virginia. viii, 367. Ford ed., iii, 229. (1782.)

4939. MAJORITY, Natural law.—The *lex majoris partis* is the natural law of every assembly of men, whose numbers are not fixed by any other law.—Notes on Virginia. viii, 367. Ford ed., iii, 230. (1782.)

4940. ———. The law of the *majority* is the natural law of every society of men.— Offical Opinion. vii, 496. Ford ed., v, 206. 1790.)

4941. ———. The *lex majoris partis* is a fundamental law of nature, by which alone self-government can be exercised by a society.—To John Breckenridge. Ford ed., vii, 417. (Pa., 1800.)

4942. MAJORITY, Oppressive.—I have seen with deep concern the afflicting oppression under which the republican citizens of Connecticut suffer from an unjust majority. The truths expressed in your letter have been long exposed to the nation through the channel of the public papers, and are the more readily believed because most of the States during the momentary ascendancy of kindred majorities in them, have seen the same spirit of oppression prevail.—To Thomas Seymour. v, 43. Ford ed., ix, 29. (W., 1807.)

4943. MAJORITY, Reasonable.—Bear in mind this sacred principle, that though the will of the majority is in all cases to prevail, that will, to be rightful, must be reasonable; that the minority possess their equal rights, which equal laws must protect, and to violate would be oppression.—First Inaugural Address. viii, 2. Ford ed., viii, 2. (March 1801.)

4944. MAJORITY, Representatives of. —Our Executive and Legislative authorities are the choice of the nation, and possess the nation's confidence. They are chosen because they possess it, and the recent elections prove it has not been abated by the attacks which have for some time been kept up against them. If the measures which have been pursued are approved by the majority, it is the duty of the minority to acquiesce and conform.—To William Duane. v, 592. Ford ed., ix, 315. (M., 1811.)

4945. MAJORITY, Respect for.—The measures of the fair majority * * * ought always to be respected.—To President Washington. iii, 461. Ford ed., vi, 103. (M., 1792.)

4946. MAJORITY, Slender.—After another election our majority will be two to one in the Senate, and it would not be for the public good to have it greater.—To JOEL BARLOW. iv, 437. FORD ED., viii, 149. (W., May 1802.)

4947. —— ——. The first principle of republicanism is that the *lex majoris partis* is the fundamental law of every society of individuals of equal rights; to consider the will of the society enounced by the majority of a single vote as sacred as if unanimous, is the first of all lessons in importance, yet the last which is thoroughly learnt. This law once disregarded, no other remains but that of force, which ends necessarily in military despotism. This has been the history of the French Revolution.—To F. H. ALEXANDER VON HUMBOLDT. vii, 75. FORD ED., x, 89. (M., 1817.)

4948. MAJORITY, Submission to.—If we are faithful to our country, if we acquiesce, with good will, in the decisions of the majority, and the nation moves in mass in the same direction, although it may not be that which every individual thinks best, we have nothing to fear from any quarter.—R. TO A. VIRGINIA BAPTISTS. viii, 139. (1808.)

4949. —— ——. I readily suppose my opinion wrong, when opposed by the majority.—To JAMES MADISON. ii, 447. FORD ED., v, 48. (P., 1788.)

4950. —— ——. The fundamental law of every society is the *lex majoris partis,* to which we are bound to submit.—To DAVID HUMPHREYS. iii, 13. FORD ED., v, 90. (P., 1789.)

4951. MAJORITY, Will of.—The will of the majority honestly expressed should give law.—ANAS. ix, 131. FORD ED., i, 215. (1793.)

4952. —— ——. It is my principle that the will of the majority should always prevail.—To JAMES MADISON. ii, 332. FORD ED., iv, 479. (P., 1787.)

4953. —— ——. It accords with our principles to acknowledge any government to be rightful which is formed by the will of the nation substantially declared.—To GOUVERNEUR MORRIS. iii, 489. (1792.)

4954. —— ——. We are sensible of the duty and expediency of submitting our opinions to the will of the majority, and can wait with patience till they get right, if they happen to be at any time wrong.—To JOHN BRECKENRIDGE. FORD ED., vii, 418. (Pa., Jan. 1800.)

4955. —— ——. The fundamental principle of the government is that the will of the majority is to prevail.—To DR. WILLIAM EUSTIS. v, 411. FORD ED., ix, 236. (W., Jan. 1809.)

4956. MALESHERBES (C. G. de la M.), Eminence.—He is unquestionably the first character in the kingdom for integrity, patriotism, knowledge and experience in business.—To JOHN JAY. ii, 157. (P., 1787.)

4957. MALESHERBES (C. G. de la M.), Integrity.—I am particularly happy at the reentry of Malesherbes into the Council. His knowledge, his integrity, render his value inappreciable, and the greater to me, because, while he had no views of office, we had established together the most unreserved intimacy.—To JAMES MADISON. ii, 153. FORD ED., iv, 392. (P., 1787.)

4958. —— ——. No man's recommendation merits more reliance than that of M. de Malesherbes.—To —— ——. v, 381. (W., 1808.)

4959. MALICE, Escape from.—If *you* meant to escape malice, you should have confined yourself within the sleepy line of regular duty.—To JAMES STEPTOE. i, 324. FORD ED., iii. 63. (1782.)

4960. MALICE, Political.—You certainly acted wisely in taking no notice of what the malice of Pickering could say of you. Were such things to be answered, our lives would be wasted in the filth of fendings and provings, instead of being employed in promoting the happiness and prosperity of our fellow citizens. The tenor of your life is the proper and sufficient answer.—To JOHN ADAMS. vii, 62. (M., 1817.)

4961. MALICE, Virtue and.—There is no act, however virtuous, for which ingenuity may not find some bad motive.—To EDWARD DOWSE. iv, 477. (W., 1803.)

4962. —— ——. Malice will always find bad motives for good actions. Shall we therefore never do good?—To PRESIDENT MADISON. v, 524. (M., 1810.)

4963. MAN, A curious animal.—Man is in all his shapes a curious animal.—To MR. VOLNEY. iv, 159. (M., 1797.)

4964. MAN, Destructive.—In the whole animal kingdom I recollect no family but man, steadily and systematically employed in the destruction of itself. Nor does what is called civilization produce any other effect, than to teach him to pursue the principle of the *bellum omnium in omnia* on a greater scale, and instead of the little contest between tribe and tribe, to comprehend all the quarters of the earth in the same work of destruction. If to this we add, that as to other animals, the lions and tigers are mere lambs compared with man as a destroyer, we must conclude that nature has been able to find in man alone a sufficient barrier against the too great multiplication of other animals and of man himself, an equilibrating power against the fecundity of generation. While in making these observations, my situation points my attention to the warfare of man in the physical world, yours may present him as equally warring in the moral one.—To JAMES MADISON. iv, 156. FORD ED., vii, 99. (1797.)

4965. —— ——. The greatest honor of a man is in doing good to his fellow men, not in destroying them.—ADDRESS TO INDIANS. viii, 208. (1807.)

4966. —— ——. The Great Spirit did not make men that they might destroy one another, but doing to each other all the good in their power, and thus filling the land with happiness instead of misery and murder.—INDIAN ADDRESS. viii, 228. (1809.)

4967. MAN, Freedom and happiness of.—The freedom and happiness of man * * * are the sole objects of all legitimate government.—To GENERAL KOSCIUSKO. v, 509. (M., 1810.)

— **MAN, Future generations and.**—See GENERATIONS.

4968. MAN, Goodness in.—I am not yet decided to drop Lownes, on account of his being a good man, and I like much to be in the hands of good men. There is great pleasure in unlimited confidence.—To JAMES MADISON. FORD ED., vii, 62. (M., 1796.)

4969. MAN, Honesty of.—Men are disposed to live honestly, if the means of doing so are open to them.—To M. DE MARBOIS. vii, 77. (M., 1817.)

4970. —— ——. In truth man is not made to be trusted for life, if secured against all liability to account.—To M. CORAY. vii, 322. (M., 1823.)

4971. MAN, Madness of.—What a Bedlamite is man!—To JOHN ADAMS. vii, 200. FORD ED., x, 186. (M., 1821.)

4972. MAN, Political equality of.—All men are created equal.—DECLARATION OF INDEPENDENCE AS DRAWN BY JEFFERSON.

4973. MAN, A rational animal.—Man is a rational animal, endowed by nature with rights, and with an innate sense of justice.—To WILLIAM JOHNSON. vii, 291. FORD ED., x, 227. (M., 1823.)

— **MAN, Rights of.**—See RIGHTS OF MAN.

4974. MAN, Schoolboy through life.—The bulk of mankind are schoolboys through life.—NOTES ON A MONEY UNIT. i, 163. (1784.)

4975. MANKIND, Government of.—Men, enjoying in ease and security, the full fruits of their own industry, enlisted by all their interests on the side of law and order, habituated to think for themselves, and to follow their reason as their guide, * * * [are] more easily and safely governed than with minds nourished in error, and vitiated and debased, as in Europe, by ignorance, indigence, and oppression.—To WILLIAM JOHNSON. vii, 292. FORD ED., x, 227. (M., 1823.)

4976. MANKIND, Improvement of.—The energies of the nation, as depends on me, shall be reserved for the improvement of the condition of man, not wasted in his destruction.—REPLY TO ADDRESS. iv, 388. (W., 1801.)

4977. —— ——. Although a soldier yourself, I am sure you contemplate the peaceable employment of man in the improvement of his condition, with more pleasure than his murders, raperies and devastations.—To GENERAL KOSCIUSKO. vi, 69. FORD ED., ix, 363. (M., June 1812.)

4978. —— ——. That every man shall be made virtuous, by any process whatever, is, indeed, no more to be expected, than that every tree shall be made to bear fruit, and every plant nourishment. The brier and bramble can never become the vine and olive; but their asperities may be softened by culture, and their properties improved to usefulness in the order and economy of the world. And I do hope that, in the present spirit of extending to the great mass of mankind the blessings of instruction, I see a prospect of great advancement in the happiness of the human race; and that this may proceed to an indefinite, although not to an infinite degree.—To C. C. BLATCHLY. vii, 263. (M., 1822.)

4979. MANKIND, Love for.—Loving mankind in my individual relations with them, I pray to be permitted to depart in their peace.—To SPENCER ROANE. vii, 136. FORD ED., x, 142. (P.F., 1819.)

4980. MANKIND, Relations with.—During a long life, as much devoted to study as a faithful transaction of the trusts committed to me would permit, no subject has occupied more of my consideration than our relations with all the beings around us, our duties to them, and our future prospects. After reading and hearing everything which probably can be suggested respecting them, I have formed the best judgment I could as to the course they prescribe, and in the due observance of that course, I have no recollections which give me uneasiness.—To WILLIAM CANBY. vi, 210. (M., 1813.)

4981. —— ——. We must endeavor to forget our former love for them, and hold them as we hold the rest of mankind, enemies in War, in Peace friends.—DECLARATION OF INDEPENDENCE AS DRAWN BY JEFFERSON.

4982. MANNERS, American vs. French.—I am much pleased with the people of this country. The roughness of the human mind is so thoroughly rubbed off with them that it seems as if one might glide through a whole life among them without a jostle. Perhaps, too, their manners may be the best calculated for happiness to a people in their situation, but I am convinced they fall far short of effecting a happiness so temperate, so uniform and so lasting as is generally enjoyed with us.—To MRS. TRIST. i, 394. (P., 1785.)

4983. —— ——. Nourish peace with their [the French] persons, but war against their manners. Every step we take towards the adoption of their manners is a step to perfect misery.—To MRS. TRIST. i, 395. (P., 1785.)

4984. MANNERS, Institutions and.—Time indeed changes manners and notions, and so far we must expect institutions to bend to them.—To SPENCER ROANE. vii, 211. FORD ED., x, 188. (M., 1821.)

4985. MANNERS, National.—The manners of every nation are the standard of orthodoxy within itself. But these standards being arbitrary, reasonable people in all allow free toleration for the manners, as for the religion of others.—To JEAN BAPTISTE SAY. vi, 433. (M., 1815.)

4986. MANSFIELD (Lord), Able and eloquent.—A man of the clearest head, and most seducing eloquence.—To PHILIP MAZZEI. FORD ED., iv, 115. (P., 1785.)

4987. MANSFIELD (Lord), Decisions of.—I hold it essential, in America, to forbid that any English decision which has happened since the accession of Lord Mansfield to the bench, should ever be cited in a court; because, though there have come many good ones from him, yet there is so much poison instilled into a great part of them, that it is better to proscribe the whole.—To MR. CUTTING. ii, 487. (P., 1788.)

4988. —— ——. The object of former judges has been to render the law more and more certain; that of this personage to render it more incertain under pretence of rendering it more reasonable.—To PHILIP MAZZEI. FORD ED., iv, 115. (P., 1785.)

4989. MANUFACTURES, Agriculture, commerce and.—I trust the good sense of our country will see that its greatest prosperity depends on a due balance between agriculture, manufactures and commerce.—To THOMAS LEIPER. v, 417. FORD ED., ix, 239. (W., 1809.)

4990. —— ——. An equilibrium of agriculture, manufactures and commerce, is certainly become essential to our independence. Manufactures sufficient for our own consumption, of what we raise the raw material (and no more). Commerce sufficient to carry the surplus produce of agriculture, beyond our own consumption, to a market for exchanging it for articles we cannot raise (and no more). These are the true limits of manufactures and commerce. To go beyond them is to increase our dependence on foreign nations, and our liability to war. These three important branches of human industry will then grow together, and be really handmaids to each other.—To JAMES JAY. v, 440. (M., April 1809.) See AGRICULTURE and COMMERCE.

4991. MANUFACTURES, British prohibition of.—By an act passed in the fifth year of the reign of his late Majesty, King George II., an American subject is forbidden to make a hat for himself, of the fur which he has taken perhaps on his own soil; an instance of despotism to which no parallel can be produced in the most arbitrary ages of British history.—RIGHTS OF BRITISH AMERICA. i, 129. FORD ED., i, 434. (1774.)

4992. —— ——. By an act passed in the twenty-third year of King George II., the iron which we make, we are forbidden to manufacture; and, heavy as that article is, and necessary in every branch of husbandry, besides commission and insurance, we are to pay freight for it to Great Britain, and freight for it back again, for the purpose of supporting, not men, but machines in the island of Great Britain.—RIGHTS OF BRITISH AMERICA. i, 129. FORD ED., i, 434. (1774.) See TRADE.

—— MANUFACTURES, Centralization and.—See 1159.

4993. MANUFACTURES, The Colonies and.—I think nothing can bring the security of our continent and its cause into danger, if we can support the credit of our paper. To do that, I apprehend, one of two steps must be taken. Either to procure free trade by alliance with some naval power able to protect it; or, if we find there is no prospect of that, to shut our ports totally, to all the world, and turn our Colonies into manufactories. The former would be most eligible, because most conformable to the habits and wishes of our people.—To BENJAMIN FRANKLIN. i, 205. FORD ED., ii, 132. (1777.)

4994. —— ——. During the present contest we have manufactured within our families the most necessary articles of clothing. Those of cotton will bear some comparison with the same kinds of manufacture in Europe; but those of wool, flax and hemp are very coarse, unsightly, and unpleasant; and such is our attachment to agriculture, and such our preference for foreign manufactures, that be it wise or unwise, our people will certainly return as soon as they can, to the raising raw materials, and exchanging them for finer manufactures than they are able to execute themselves.—NOTES ON VIRGINIA. viii. 404. FORD ED., iii, 268. (1782.)

4995. MANUFACTURES, Cotton.—Great advances are making in the establishment of manufactures. Those of cotton will. I think, be so far proceeded on, that we shall never again have to recur to the importation of cotton goods for our own use.—To WILLIAM LYMAN. v, 280. (W., 1808.)

4996. —— ——. I am much pleased to find our progress in manufactures to be so great. That of cotton is peculiarly interesting, because we raise the raw material in such abundance, and because it may, to a great degree, supply our deficiencies both in wool and linen.—To J. DORSEY. v, 235. (W., 1808.)

4997. MANUFACTURES, The Embargo and.—The Embargo * * * promises lasting good by promoting among ourselves the establishment of manufactures hitherto sought abroad, at the risk of collisions no longer regulated by the laws of reason or morality.—R. TO A. PHILADELPHIA DEMOCRATIC-REPUBLICANS. viii, 128. (1808.)

4998. —— ——. The suspension of our foreign commerce, produced by the injustice of the belligerent powers, and the consequent losses and sacrifices of our citizens, are subjects of just concern. The situation into which we have thus been forced, has impelled us to apply a portion of our industry and capital to internal manufactures and improvements. The extent of this conversion is daily increasing, and little doubt remains that the establishments formed and forming will, under the auspices of cheaper materials and subsistence, the freedom of labor from taxation with us, and of protecting duties and prohibitions, become permanent.—EIGHTH ANNUAL MESSAGE. viii, 109. FORD ED., ix, 223. (1808.)

4999. —— ——. As a countervail to our short-lived sacrifices [by the Embargo], when these shall no longer be felt, we shall permanently retain the benefit they have prompted, of fabricating for our own use the materials of our own growth, heretofore carried to the work-houses of Europe, to be wrought and returned to us.—R. TO A. BALTIMORE TAMMANY SOCIETY. viii, 170. (1809.)

5000. —— ——. It is true that the Embargo laws have not had all the effect in bringing the powers of Europe to a sense of justice which a more faithful observance of them might have produced. Yet they have had the important effects of saving our seamen and property, of giving time to prepare for defence; and they will produce the further inestimable advantage of turning the attention and enterprise of our fellow citizens, and the patronage of our State Legislatures to the establishment of useful manufactures in our country. They will have hastened the day when an equilibrium between the occupations of agriculture, manufactures, and commerce, shall simplify our foreign concerns to the exchange only of that surplus which we cannot consume for those articles of reasonable comfort or convenience which we cannot produce.— R. TO A. PENNA. DEMOCRATIC-REPUBLICANS. viii, 163. (1809.)

5001. —— ——. Amidst the pressure of evils with which the belligerent edicts [Berlin decrees, Orders of Council, &c.], have afflicted us, some permanent good will arise; the spring given to manufactures will have durable effects. Knowing most of my own State, I can affirm with confidence that were free intercourse opened again to-morrow, she would never again import one-half of the coarse goods which she has done down to the date of the edicts. These will be made in our families. For finer goods we must resort to the larger manufactories established in the towns.—To DAVID HUMPHREYS. v, 415. FORD ED., ix, 226. (W., 1809.)

5002. —— ——. The interruption of our commerce with England, produced by our Embargo and Non-Intercourse law, and the general indignation excited by her bare-faced attempts to make us accessories and tributaries to her usurpation on the high seas, have generated in this country an universal spirit for manufacturing for ourselves, and of reducing to a minimum the number of articles for which we are dependent on her. The advantages, too, of lessening the occasions of risking our peace on the ocean, and of planting the consumer in our own soil by the side of the grower of produce, are so palpable, that no temporary suspension of injuries on

her part, or agreements founded on that, will now prevent our continuing in what we have begun. The spirit of manufacturing has taken deep root among us, and its foundations are laid in too great expense to be abandoned.— To DUPONT DE NEMOURS. v, 456. (M., June 1809.)

5003. —— ——. Nothing more salutary for us has ever happened than the British obstructions to our demands for their manufactures. Restore free intercourse when they will, their commerce with us will have totally changed its form, and the articles we shall in future want from them will not exceed their own consumption of our produce.—To JOHN ADAMS. vi, 36. FORD ED., ix, 333. (M., Jan. 1812.)

5004. MANUFACTURES, Encouragement of.—The present aspect of our foreign relations has encouraged here a general spirit of encouragement to domestic manufactures. The Merino breed of sheep is well established with us, and fine samples of cloth are sent to us from the North. Considerable manufactures of cotton are also commencing. Philadelphia, particularly, is becoming more manufacturing than commercial.—To MR. MAURY. v, 214. (W., Nov. 1807.)

5005. —— ——. My idea is that we should encourage home manufactures to the extent of our own consumption of everything of which we raise the raw material.—To DAVID HUMPHREYS. v, 416. FORD ED., ix, 226. (W., 1809.)

5006. —— ——. Every syllable uttered in my name becomes a text for the federalists to torment the public mind on by their paraphrases and perversions. I have lately inculcated the encouragement of manufactures to the extent of our own consumption at least, in all articles of which we raise the raw material. On this the federal papers and meetings have sounded the alarm of Chinese policy, destruction of commerce, &c.; that is to say, the iron which we make must not be wrought here into plows, axes, hoes, &c., in order that the ship-owner may have the profit of carrying it to Europe, and bringing it back in a manufactured form, as if after manufacturing our own raw materials for our own use, there would not be a surplus produce sufficient to employ a due proportion of navigation in carrying it to market and exchanging it for those articles of which we have not the raw material. Yet this absurd hue and cry has contributed much to federalize New England. Their doctrine goes to the sacrificing agriculture and manufactures to commerce; to the calling off our people from the interior country to the sea shore to turn merchants, and to convert this great agricultural country into a city of Amsterdam. But I trust the good sense of our country will see that its greatest prosperity depends on a due balance between agriculture, manufactures and commerce, and not in this protuberant navigation which has kept us in hot water from the commencement of our government, and is now engaging us in war. —To Thomas Leiper. v, 417. Ford ed., ix, 239. (W., Jan. 1809.)

5007. —— ——. The government of the United States, at a very early period, when establishing its tariff on foreign importations, were very much guided in their selection of objects by a desire to encourage manufactures within themselves.—To —— ——. vii, 220. (M., 1821.)

5008. MANUFACTURES, Fear of British competition.—I much fear the effect on our infant establishments of the policy avowed by Mr. Brougham. Individual British merchants may lose by their late immense importations; but British commerce and manufactures, in the mass, will gain by beating down the competition of ours, in our own markets. Against this policy, our protecting duties are as nothing, our patriotism less.—To William Sampson. Ford ed., x, 74. (M., 1817.)

5009. MANUFACTURES, Fostering.— Enough of the non-importation law should be reserved * * * to support those manufacturing establishments which the British Orders [of Council] and our interests forced us to make.—To President Madison. v, 442. Ford ed., ix, 251. (M., April 1809.)

5010. MANUFACTURES, Great Britain and American.—Radically hostile to our navigation and commerce, and fearing its rivalry, Great Britain will completely crush it, and force us to resort to agriculture, not aware that we shall resort to manufactures also, and render her conquests over our navigation and commerce useless, at least, if not injurious, to herself in the end, and perhaps salutary to us, as removing out of our way the chief causes and provocations to war.—To Henry Dearborn. v, 530. Ford ed., ix, 278. (M., 1810.)

5011. MANUFACTURES, Home.— There can be no question, in a mind truly American, whether it is best to send our citizens and property into certain captivity, and then wage war for their recovery, or to keep them at home, and to turn seriously to that policy which plants the manufacturer and the husbandman side by side, and establishes at the door of every one that exchange of mutual labors and comforts, which we have hitherto sought in distant regions, and under perpetual risk of broils with them.—R. to A. of New York Tammany Society. viii, 127. (Feb. 1808.)

5012. —— ——. I see with satisfaction * * * that our citizens * * * are preparing to provide for themselves those comforts and conveniences of life, for which it would be unwise evermore to recur to distant countries.—R. to A. New Hampshire Legislature. viii, 131. (1808.)

5013. —— ——. I have not formerly been an advocate for great manufactories. I doubted whether our labor, employed in agriculture, and aided by the spontaneous energies of the earth, would not procure us more than we could make ourselves of other necessaries. But other considerations entering into the question, have settled my doubts.—To John Melish. vi, 94. Ford ed., ix, 373. (M., Jan. 1813.)

5014. —— ——. If the piracies of France and England are to be adopted as the law of nations, or should become their practice, it will oblige us to manufacture at home all the material comforts. This may furnish a reason to check imports until necessary manufactures are established among us. This offers the advantage, too, of placing the consumer of our produce near the producer.—To William Short. vi, 128. (M., 1813.)

5015. —— ——. We are become manufacturers to a degree incredible to those who do not see it, and who only consider the short period of time during which we have been driven to them by the suicidal policy of England.—To Jean Baptiste Say. vi, 431. (M., March 1815.)

5016. —— ——. The prohibiting duties we lay on all articles of foreign manufacture which prudence requires us to establish at home, with the patriotic determination of every good citizen to use no foreign article which can be made within ourselves, without regard to difference of price, secures us against a relapse into foreign dependency.—To Jean Baptiste Say. vi, 431. (M., March 1815.)

5017. —— ——. It is our business to manufacture for ourselves whatever we can, to keep our markets open for what we can spare or want.—To Thomas Leiper. vi, 465. Ford ed., ix, 520. (M., 1815.) See Markets.

5018. —— ——. No one has been more sensible than myself of the advantages of placing the consumer by the side of the producer, nor more disposed to promote it by example.—To Mrs. K. D. Morgan. Ford ed., viii, 473. (M., 1822.) See Protection and Tariff.

5019. MANUFACTURES, Homespun.— Homespun is become the spirit of the times. I think it an useful one, and, therefore, that it is a duty to encourage it by example. The best fine cloth made in the United States is, I am told, at the manufacture of Colonel Humphreys in your neighborhood [New Haven]. Could I get the favor of you to procure me there as much of his best as would make me a coat? I should prefer a deep blue, but, if not to be had, then a black.—To Abraham Bishop. Ford ed., ix, 225. (W., 1808.)

5020. MANUFACTURES, Household.— There is no manufacture of wire or of cotton cards, or if any, it is not worth notice. No manufacture of stocking-weaving, consequently none for making the machine; none of cotton cloths of any kind for sale; though in almost every family some is manufactured for the use of the family, which is always good in quality, and often tolerably fine. In the same way, they make excellent stockings of cotton, weaving it in like manner, carried on principally in the family way. Among the poor, the wife weaves generally, and the rich either have a weaver among their servants, or employ their poor neighbors.—To Thomas Digges. ii, 412. Ford ed., v, 28. (P., 1788.)

5021. —— ——. The checks which the commercial regulations of Europe have given to the sale of our produce, has produced a very considerable degree of domestic manufacture, which, so far as it is in the household way, will doubtless continue; and so far as it is more public, will depend on the continuance or discontinuance of this policy of Europe.—To C. W. F. Dumas. Ford ed., vi, 70. (Pa., 1792.)

5022. —— ——. I shall be glad to hear * * * any improvements in the arts applicable to * * * household manufacture. —To Tench Coxe. iv, 105. Ford ed., vi, 509. (M., May 1794.)

5023. —— ——. The mass of *household* manufacture, unseen by the public eye, and so much greater than what is seen, is such at present, that let our intercourse with England be opened when it may, not one-half the amount of what we have heretofore taken from her will ever again be demanded. The great call from the country has hitherto been of coarse goods. These are now made in our families, and the advantage is too sensible ever to be relinquished. It is one of those obvious improvements in our condition which needed only to be forced on our attention, never again to be abandoned.—To Dupont de Nemours. v, 456. (M., June 1809.)

5024. —— ——. We are going greatly into manufactures; but the mass of them are household manufactures of the coarse articles worn by the laborers and farmers of the family. These I verily believe we shall succeed in making to the whole extent of our necessities. But the attempts at fine goods will probably be abortive. They are undertaken by company establishments, and chiefly in the towns; will have but little success and short continuance in a country where the charms of agriculture attract every being who can engage in it. Our revenue will be less than it would be were we to continue to import instead of manufacturing our coarse goods. But the increase of population and production will keep pace with that of manufactures, and maintain the quantum of exports at the present level at least; and the imports need be equivalent to them, and consequently the revenue on them be undiminished.—To Dupont de Nemours. v, 583. Ford ed., ix, 317. (M., 1811.)

5025. —— ——. The economy and thriftiness resulting from our household manufactures are such that they will never again be laid aside.—To John Adams. vi, 36. Ford ed., ix, 333. (M., Jan. 1812.)

5026. —— ——. Our manufacturers are now very nearly on a footing with those of England. She has not a single improvement which we do not possess, and many of them better adapted by ourselves to our ordinary use. We have reduced the large and expensive machinery for most things to the compass of a private family, and every family of any size is now getting machines on a small scale for their household purposes. Quoting myself as an example, and I am much behind many others in this business, my household manufactures are just getting into operation on the scale of a carding machine costing $60 only, which may be worked by a girl of twelve years old, a spinning machine, which may be had for $10. carrying six spindles for wool, to be worked by a girl also, another which can be made for $25, carrying twelve spindles for cotton, and a loom, with a flying shuttle, weaving its twenty yards a day. I need 2,000 yards of linen. cotton, and woollen yearly, to clothe my family, which this machinery, costing $150 only, and worked by two women and two girls, will make more than furnish.—To General Kosciusko. vi, 68. Ford ed., ix, 362. (M., June 1812.)

5027. —— ——. I have hitherto myself depended entirely on foreign manufactures; but I have now thirty-five spindles agoing, a hand carding machine, and looms with the flying shuttle, for the supply of my own farms, which will never be relinquished in my time. The continuance of the war will fix the habit generally, and out of the evils of impressment and of the Orders of Council, a great blessing for us will grow.—To John Melish. vi, 94. Ford ed., ix, 373. (M., Jan. 1813.)

5028. —— ——. Small spinning jennies of from half a dozen to twenty spindles, will soon make their way into the humblest cottages, as well as the richest houses [in the South]; and nothing is more certain, than that the coarse and middling clothing for our families, will forever hereafter continue to be made within ourselves.—To John Melish. vi, 94. Ford ed., ix, 373. (M., Jan. 1813.)

5029. —— ——. Household manufacture is taking deep root with us. I have a carding machine, two spinning machines, and looms with the flying shuttle in full operation for clothing my own family; and I verily believe that by the next winter this State will not need a yard of imported coarse or middling cloth. I think we have already a sheep for every inhabitant, which will suffice for clothing; and one-third more, which a single year will add, will furnish blanketing.—To James Ronaldson. vi, 92. Ford ed., ix, 371. (M., Jan. 1813.)

5030. —— ——. The specimens of Mrs. Mason's skill in manufactures excite the admiration of all. They prove she is really a more dangerous adversary to our British foes than all our generals. These attack the hostile armies only; she the source of their subsistence. What these do counts nothing, because they take one day and lose another: what she does counts double, because what she takes from the enemy is added to us. I hope, too, she will have more followers than our generals, but few rivals, I fear. These specimens exceed anything I saw during the Revolutionary war: although our ladies of that day turned their whole efforts to these objects, and with great praise and success.—To John T. Mason. Ford ed., ix, 473. (M., 1814.)

5031. —— ——. I presume, like the rest of us in the country, you are in the habit of household manufacture, and that you will not, like too many, abandon it on the return of peace, to enrich our late enemy, and to nourish foreign agents in our bosom, whose baneful influence and intrigues cost us so much embarrassment and dissension.—To George Fleming. vi, 506. (M., Dec. 1815.)

5032. —— ——. The interruption of our intercourse with England has rendered us one essential service in planting, radically and firmly, coarse manufactures among us. I make in my family two thousand yards of cloth a year, which I formerly bought from England, and it only employs a few women, children and invalids, who could do little on the farm. The State generally does the same, and allowing ten yards to a person, this amounts to ten millions of yards; and if we are about the medium degree of manufacturers in the whole Union, as I believe we are, the whole will amount to one hundred millions of yards a year, which will soon reimburse us the expenses of the war.—To Mr. Maury. vi, 471. (M., 1815.)

5033. MANUFACTURES, Independence, prosperity and.—The risk of hanging our prosperity on the fluctuating counsels and caprices of others renders it wise in us to turn seriously to manufactures, and if Europe will not let us carry our provisions to their manufactures, we must endeavor to bring their manufactures to our provisions.—To David Humphreys. Ford ed., v, 344. (Pa., 1791.)

5034. MANUFACTURES, Jefferson's views in 1782.—The political economists of Europe have established it as a principle, that every State should endeavor to manufacture for itself; and this principle, like many others, we transfer to America, without calculating the difference of circumstance which should often produce a difference of result. In Europe, the lands are either cultivated, or locked up against the cultivator. Manufacture must, therefore, be resorted to of necessity, not of choice, to support the surplus of their people. But we have an immensity of land courting the industry of the husbandman. Is it best then that all our citizens should be employed in its improvement, or that one half of them should be called off from that to exercise manufactures and handicrafts for the other? Those who labor in the earth are the chosen people of God, if ever He had a chosen people, whose breasts He has made His peculiar deposit for substantial and genuine virtue. It is the focus in which He keeps alive that sacred fire, which otherwise might escape

from the face of the earth. Corruption of morals in the mass of cultivators is a phenomenon of which no age nor nation has furnished an example. It is the mark set on those, who, not looking up to heaven, to their own soil and industry, as does the husbandman, for their subsistence, depend for it on casualities and caprice of customers. Dependence begets subservience and venality, suffocates the germ of virtue, and prepares fit tools for the designs of ambition. This, the natural progress and consequence of the arts, has sometimes perhaps been retarded by accidental circumstances; but, generally speaking, the proportion which the aggregate of the other classes of citizens bears in any State to that of its husbandmen, is the proportion of its unsound to its healthy parts, and is a good barometer whereby to measure its degree of corruption. While we have land to labor, then, let us never wish to see our citizens occupied at a work bench, or twirling a distaff. Carpenters, masons, smiths, are wanting in husbandry; but, for the general operations of manufacture, let our workshops remain in Europe. It is better to carry provisions and materials to workmen there, than bring them to the provisions and materials, and with them their manners and principles. The loss by the transportation of commodities across the Atlantic will be made up in happiness and permanence of government. The mobs of great cities add just so much to the support of pure government, as sores do to the strength of the human body. It is the manners and spirit of a people which preserve a republic in vigor. A degeneracy in these is a canker which soon eats to the heart of its laws and constitution.—Notes on Virginia. viii, 405. Ford ed., iii, 268. (1782.)

5035. MANUFACTURES, Jefferson's views in 1816.—You tell me I am quoted by those who wish to continue our dependence on England for manufactures. There was a time when I might have been so quoted with more candor, but within the thirty years which have since elapsed, how are circumstances changed! We were then in peace. Our independent place among nations was acknowledged. A commerce which offered the raw material in exchange for the same material after receiving the last touch of industry, was worthy of welcome to all nations. It was expected that those especially to whom manufacturing industry was important, would cherish the friendship of such customers by every favor, by every inducement, and, particularly, cultivate their peace by every act of justice and friendship. Under this prospect the question seemed legitimate, whether, with such an immensity of unimproved land, courting the hand of husbandry, the industry of agriculture, or that of manufactures, would add most to the national wealth? And the doubt was entertained on this consideration chiefly, that to the labor of the husbandman a vast addition is made by the spontaneous energies of the earth on which it is employed; for one grain of wheat committed to the earth, she renders twenty, thirty, and even fifty-fold, whereas to the labor of the manufacturer nothing is added. Pounds of flax, in his hands, yield, on the contrary, but pennyweights of lace. This exchange, too, laborious as it might seem, what a field did it promise for the occupations of the ocean; what a nursery for that class of citizens who were to exercise and maintain our equal rights on that element? This was the state of things in 1785, when the "Notes on Virginia" were first printed; when, the ocean being open to all nations, and their common right in it acknowledged and exercised under regulations sanctioned by the assent and usage of all, it was thought that the doubt might claim some consideration. But who, in 1785, could foresee the rapid depravity which was to render the close of that century the disgrace of the history of man? Who could have imagined that the two most distinguished in the rank of nations, for science and civilization, would have suddenly descended from that honorable eminence, and setting at defiance all those moral laws established by the Author of nature between nation and nation, as between man and man, would cover earth and sea with robberies and piracies, merely because strong enough to do it with temporal impunity; and that under this disbandment of nations from social order, we should have been despoiled of a thousand ships, and have thousands of our citizens reduced to Algerine slavery? Yet all this has taken place. One of these nations [Great Britain] interdicted to our vessels all harbors of the globe without having first proceeded to some one of hers, there paid a tribute proportioned to the cargo, and obtained her license to proceed to the port of destination. The other [France] declared them to be lawful prize if they had touched at the port, or been visited by a ship of the enemy nation. Thus were we completely excluded from the ocean. Compare this state of things with that of 1785, and say whether an opinion founded in the circumstances of that day can be fairly applied to those of the present? We have experienced what we did not then believe, that there exists both profligacy and power enough to exclude us from the field of interchange with other nations; that to be independent for the comforts of life we must fabricate them ourselves. We must now place the manufacturer by the side of the agriculturist. The former question is suppressed, or rather assumes a new form. Shall we make our own comforts, or go without them, at the will of a foreign nation? He, therefore, who is now against domestic manufacture, must be for reducing us either to dependence on that foreign nation, or to be clothed in skins, and to live, like wild beasts, in dens and caverns. I am not one of these; experience has taught me that manufactures are now as necessary to our independence as to our comfort; and if those who quote me as of a different opinion, will keep pace with me in purchasing nothing foreign where an equivalent of domestic fabric can be obtained, with-

out regard to difference of price, it will not be our fault if we do not soon have a supply at home equal to our demand, and wrest that weapon of distress from the hand which has wielded it. If it shall be proposed to go beyond our own supply, the question of 1785 will then recur, Will our *surplus* labor be then most beneficially employed in the culture of the earth, or in the fabrications of art? We have time yet for consideration, before that question will press upon us; and the maxim to be applied will depend on the circumstances which shall then exist; for in so complicated a science as political economy, no one axiom can be laid down as wise and expedient for all times and circumstances, and for their contraries. Inattention to this is what has called for this explanation, which reflection would have rendered unnecessary with the candid, while nothing will do with those who use the former opinion only as a stalking horse to cover their disloyal propensities to keep us in eternal vassalage to a foreign and unfriendly people.*—To BENJAMIN AUSTIN. vi, 521. FORD ED., x, 8. (M., Jan. 1816.)

5036. MANUFACTURES, Labor and.— In general, it is impossible that manufactures should succeed in America from the high price of labor. This is occasioned by the great demand of labor for agriculture. A manufacturer, going from Europe, will turn to labor of other kinds if he finds more to be got by it, and he finds some employment so profitable that he can soon lay up money enough to buy fifty acres of land, to the culture of which he is irresistibly tempted by the independence in which that places him, and the desire of having a wife and family around him. If any manufactures can succeed there, it will be that of cotton.—To THOMAS DIGGES. ii, 412. FORD ED., v, 27. (P., 1788.)

5037. MANUFACTURES, Machinery and.— The endeavors which Dr. Wallace informed you we were making in the line of manufactures are very humble indeed. We have not as yet got beyond the clothing of our laborers. We hope, indeed, soon to begin finer fabrics, and for higher uses. But these will probably be confined to cotton and wool. * * * I have lately seen the improvement of the loom by Janes, the most beautiful machine I have ever seen. * * * I am endeavoring to procure this improvement. These cares are certainly more pleasant than those of the state.—To JOHN T. MASON. FORD ED., ix, 475. (M., 1814.)

5038. MANUFACTURES, National defence and.— The endeavors of five years, aided with some internal manufacturers, have

* Mr. Austin asked Jefferson's permission to publish the letter containing the foregoing extract. Jefferson wrote in reply: "I am, in general, extremely unwilling to be carried into the newspapers, no matter what the subject; the whole pack of the Essex [Junto] Kennel would open upon me. With respect, however, to so much of my letter * * * as relates to manufactures, I have less repugnance, because there is, perhaps, a degree of duty to avow a change of opinion called for by a change of circumstance, and especially on a point now becoming peculiarly interesting."—EDITOR.

not yet found a tolerable supply of arms. To make these within ourselves, then, as well as the other implements of war, is as necessary as to make our bread within ourselves.—To SPEAKER HOUSE OF DELEGATES. FORD ED., ii, 267. (Wg., 1779.)

5039. —— ——. I suppose that the establishing a manufacture of arms [in Virginia] to go hand in hand with the purchase of them from hence [France] is at present opposed by good reasons. This alone would make us independent for an article essential to our preservation, and workmen could probably be either got here, or drawn from England to be embarked hence.—To GOVERNOR HENRY. FORD ED., iv, 48. (P., 1785.)

5040. MANUFACTURES, Navigation vs.—Some jealousy of this spirit of manufacture seems excited among commercial men. It would have been as just when we first began to make our own plows and hoes. They have certainly lost the profit of bringing these from a foreign country. * * * I do not think it fair in the shipowners to say we ought not to make our own axes, nails, &c., here, that they may have the benefit of carrying the iron to Europe, and bringing back the axes, nails, &c. Our agriculture will still afford surplus produce enough to employ a due proportion of navigation.—To DAVID HUMPHREYS. v, 415. FORD ED., ix, 226. (W., 1809.)

5041. MANUFACTURES, Protection of.—To protect the manufactures adapted to our circumstances * * * [is one of] the landmarks by which we are to guide ourselves in all our proceedings.—SECOND ANNUAL MESSAGE. viii, 21. FORD ED., viii, 187. (1802.) See PROTECTION and TARIFF.

5042. MANUFACTURES, Rivalry in foreign markets.—We hope to remove the British fully and finally from our continent. And what they will feel more, for they value their colonies only for the bales of cloth they take from them, we have established manufactures, not only sufficient to supersede our demand from them, but to rivalize them in foreign markets.—To MADAME DE TESSE. vi, 273. FORD ED., ix, 440. (Dec. 1813.)

5043. MANUFACTURES, Rooted.—Our domestic manufactures * * * have taken such deep root * * * [that they] never again can be shaken.—To MARQUIS LAFAYETTE. vi, 427. FORD ED., ix, 511. (M., 1815.)

5044. —— ——. We owe to the past follies and wrongs of the British the incalculable advantage of being made independent of them for every material manufacture. These have taken such root in our private families especially, that nothing now can ever extirpate them.—To W. H. CRAWFORD. vi, 420. FORD ED., ix, 504. (M., Feb. 1815.)

5045. MANUFACTURES, State aid to.—The House of Delegates of Virginia seemed disposed to adventure £2,500 for the establishing a woollen manufactory in Virginia, but the Senate did not concur. By their returning to the subject, however, at a subsequent session, and wishing more specific propositions, it is probable they might be induced to concur, if they saw a certain provision that their money would not be paid for nothing. Some unsuccessful experiments heretofore may have suggested this caution. Suppose the propositions brought into some such shape as this: The undertaker is to contribute £1,000, the State £2,500, viz.: the undertaker having laid out his £1,000 in the necessary implements to be brought from Europe, and these being landed in Virginia as a security that he will proceed, let the State pay for the first necessary purpose then to occur £1,000.

Let it pay him a stipend of £100 a year for the first three years.......................... £300
Let it give him a bounty (suppose one-third) on every yard of woollen cloth equal to good plains, which he shall weave for five years, not exceeding £250 a year (20,000 yards) the four first years, and £200 the fifth............ 1,200

£2,500

To every workman whom he shall import, let them give, after he shall have worked in the manufactory five years, warrants for — acres of land, and pay the expenses of survey, patents, &c. (This last article is to meet the proposition of the undertaker. I do not like it, because it tends to draw off the manufacturer from his trade. I should better like a premium to him on his continuance in it; as, for instance, that he should be free from State taxes as long as he should carry on his trade.)

The President's intervention seems necessary till the contracts shall be concluded. It is presumed he would not like to be embarrassed afterwards with the details of superintendence. Suppose, in his answer to the Governor of Virginia, he should say that the undertaker being in Europe, more specific propositions cannot be obtained from him in time to be laid before this assembly; that in order to secure to the State the benefits of the establishment, and yet guard them against an unproductive grant of money, he thinks some plan like the preceding one might be proposed to the undertaker. That as it is not known whether he would accept it exactly in that form, it might disappoint the views of the State were they to prescribe that or any other form rigorously, consequently that a discretionary power must be given to a certain extent. That he would willingly cooperate with their Executive in effecting the contract, and certainly would not conclude it on any terms worse for the State than those before explained, and that the contracts being once concluded, his distance and other occupations would oblige him to leave the execution open to the Executive of the State.—OFFICIAL OPINION. vii, 460. (1790.)

5046. MANUFACTURES, Tariff on foreign.—Where a nation imposes high duties on our productions, or prohibits them altogether, it may be proper for us to do the same by theirs; first burdening or excluding those productions which they bring here, in competition with our own of the same kind; selecting next, such manufactures as we take from them in greatest quantity, and which, at the same time, we could the soonest furnish to ourselves, or obtain from other countries; imposing on them duties lighter at first, but heavier and heavier, afterwards, as other channels of supply open. Such duties, having the effect of indirect encouragement to domestic manufactures of the same kind, may induce the manufacturer to come himself into these States, where cheaper subsistence, equal laws, and a vent of his wares, free of duty, may ensure him the highest profits from his skill and industry. And here, it would be in the power of the State governments to cooperate essentially, by opening the resources of encouragement which are under their control, extending them liberally to artists in those particular branches of manufacture for which their soil, climate, population and other circumstances have matured them, and fostering the precious efforts and progress of *household* manufacture, by some patronage suited to the nature of its objects, guided by the local informations they possess, and guarded against abuse by their presence and attentions. The oppressions on our agriculture, in foreign ports, would thus be made the occasion of relieving it from a dependence on the councils and conduct of others, and of promoting arts, manufactures and population at home.—FOREIGN COMMERCE REPORT. vii. 648. FORD ED., vi, 481. (Dec. 1793.) See DUTIES, PROTECTION and TARIFF.

5047. MANUFACTURES, Virginia.— In Virginia we do little in the fine way, but in coarse and middling goods a great deal. Every family in the country is a manufactory within itself, and is very generally able to make within itself all the stouter and middling stuffs for its own clothing and household use. We consider a sheep for every person in the family as sufficient to clothe it, in addition to the cotton, hemp and flax which we raise ourselves. For fine stuff we shall depend on your northern manufactories. Of these, that is to say, of company establishments we have none. We use little machinery. The spinning jenny, and loom with the flying shuttle, can be managed in a family; but nothing more complicated.—To JOHN ADAMS. vi, 36. FORD ED., ix, 332. (M., Jan. 1812.)

5048. —— ——. For fine goods there are numerous establishments at work in the large cities, and many more daily growing up: and of merinos we have some thousands, and these multiplying fast. We consider a sheep for every person as sufficient for their woollen clothing, and this State and all to the north have fully that, and those to the south and west will soon be up to it. In other articles we are equally advanced, so that nothing is more certain than that, come peace when it will, we shall never again go to England for a shilling where we have gone for a dollar's worth. Instead of applying to her manufacturers there, they must starve or come here to be employed.—To GENERAL KOSCIUSKO. vi, 69. FORD ED., ix, 363. (M., June 1812.)

— MAPLE SUGAR.—See SUGAR.

5049. MARBURY vs. MADISON, Case of.—I observe that the case of *Marbury vs. Madison* has been cited [in the trial of Aaron Burr], and I think it material to stop at the threshold the citing that case as authority and to have it denied to be law. 1. Because the

judges in the outset, disclaimed all cognizance of the case, although they then went on to say what would have been their opinion, had they had cognizance of it. This, then, was confessedly an extra-judicial opinion, and, as such of no authority. 2. Because, had it been judicially pronounced, it would have been against law; for to a commission, a deed, a bond, *delivery* is essential to give validity. Until, therefore, the commission is delivered out of the hands of the Executive and his agents, it is not his deed. He may withhold or cancel it at pleasure, as he might his private deed in the same situation. The Constitution intended that the three great branches of the government should be coordinate, and independent of each other. As to acts, therefore, which are to be done by either, it has given no control to another branch. A judge, I presume, cannot sit on a bench without a commission, or a record of a commission; and the Constitution having given to the Judiciary branch no means of compelling the Executive either to *deliver* a commission, or to make a record of it, shows that it did not intend to give the Judiciary that control over the Executive, but that it should remain in the power of the latter to do it or not. Where different branches have to act in their respective lines, finally and without appeal, under any law, they may give to it different and opposite constructions. Thus, in the case of William Smith, the House of Representatives determined he was a citizen; and in the case of William Duane (precisely the same in every material circumstance), the judges determined he was no citizen. In the cases of Callender and some others, the judges determined the Sedition Act was valid under the Constitution, and exercised their regular powers of sentencing them to fine and imprisonment. But the Executive determined that the Sedition Act was a nullity under the Constitution, and exercised his regular power of prohibiting the execution of the sentence, or rather of executing the real law, which protected the acts of the defendants. From these different constructions of the same act by different branches, less mischief arises than from giving to any one of them a control over the others. The Executive and Senate act on the construction, that until delivery from the Executive department, a commission is in their possession, and within their rightful power; and in cases of commissions not revocable at will, where, after the Senate's approbation and the President's signing and sealing, new information of the unfitness of the person has come to hand before the *delivery* of the commission, new nominations have been made and approved, and new commissions have issued. On this construction I have hitherto acted; on this I shall ever act, and maintain it with the powers of the government, against any control which may be attempted by the judges, in subversion of the independence of the Executive and Senate within their peculiar department. I presume, therefore, that in a case where our decision is by the Constitution the supreme one, and that which can be carried into effect, it is the constitutionally authoritative one, and that that by the judges was *coram non judice,* and unauthoritative, because it cannot be carried into effect. I have long wished for a proper occasion to have the gratuitous opinion in *Marbury vs. Madison* brought before the public, and denounced as not law; and I think the present a fortunate one, because it occupies such a place in the public attention. I should be glad, therefore, if, in noticing that case, you could take occasion to express the determination of the Executive, that the doctrines of that case were given extra-judicially and against law. and that their reverse will be the rule of action with the Executive.—To GEORGE HAY. v, 84. FORD ED., ix, 53. (W., June 1807.)

5050. MARIE ANTOINETTE, Character.—This angel, as gaudily painted in the rhapsodies of the Rhetor Burke, with some smartness of fancy, but no good sense, was proud, disdainful of restraint, indignant at all obstacles to her will, eager in the pursuit of pleasure, and firm enough to hold to her desires, or perish in their wreck.—AUTOBIOGRAPHY. i, 101. FORD ED., i, 140. (1821.)

5051. —— ——. She is capricious like her brother, and governed by him; devoted to pleasure and expense; and not remarkable for any other vices or virtues.—To JAMES MADISON. ii, 154. FORD ED., iv, 393. (P., 1787.)

5052. —— ——. It may be asked what is the Queen disposed to do in the present situation of things? Whatever rage, pride and fear can dictate in a breast which never knew the presence of one moral restraint.—To JOHN JAY. iii, 118. (P., Sep. 1789.)

5053. MARIE ANTOINETTE, Extravagance.—Nor should we wonder at * * * [the] pressure [for a fixed constitution in 1788-9] when we consider the monstrous abuses of power under which * * * [the French] people were ground to powder; when we pass in review * * * the enormous expenses of the Queen, the princes and the Court.—AUTOBIOGRAPHY. i, 86. FORD ED., i, 118. (1821.)

5054. MARIE ANTOINETTE, Gambling.—Her inordinate gambling and dissipations, with those of the Count d'Artois and others of her clique, had been a sensible item in the exhaustion of the treasury.—AUTOBIOGRAPHY. i, 101. FORD ED., i, 140. (1821.)

5055. MARIE ANTOINETTE, Reform.—The exhaustion of the treasury called into action the reforming hand of the nation; and her opposition to it, her inflexible perverseness and dauntless spirit, led herself to the guillotine, drew the King on. with her, and plunged the world into crimes and calamities which will forever stain the pages of modern history.—AUTOBIOGRAPHY. i, 101. FORD ED., i, 140. (1821.)

5056. MARIE ANTOINETTE, The Revolution and.—I have ever believed, that had there been no Queen, there would have been no Revolution. No force would have been provoked, nor exercised. The King would have gone hand in hand with the wisdom of his sounder counsellors, who, guided by the increased lights of the age, wished only, with the

same pace, to advance the principles of their social constitution.—AUTOBIOGRAPHY. i, 101. FORD ED., i, 140. (1821.)

5057. MARINE HOSPITALS, Establishment of.—With respect to marine hospitals, I presume you know that such establishments have been made by the General Government in the several States, that a portion of seamen's wages is drawn for their support, and the Government furnishes what is deficient. Mr. Gallatin is attentive to them, and they will grow with our growth.—To JAMES RONALDSON. vi, 92. FORD ED., ix, 371. (M., Jan. 1813.)

— MARINE LEAGUE.—See 1335.

5058. MARITIME LAW, Violation of.—A statement of the conduct of Great Britain towards this country, so far as respects the violations of the Maritime Law of nations [must be laid before Congress]. Here it would be necessary to state each distinct principle violated, and to quote the cases of violation, and to conclude with a view of her vice-admiralty courts, their venality and rascality, in order to show that however for conveniences (and not of right) the court of the captor is admitted to exercise the jurisdiction, yet that in so palpable an abuse of that trust, some remedy must be applied.—To CAESAR A. RODNEY. v, 200. FORD ED., ix, 144. (W., Oct. 1807.)

5059. MARKETS, Access to.—It is not to the moderation and justice of others we are to trust for fair and equal access to market with our productions, or for our due share in the transportation of them; but to our own means of independence, and the firm will to use them.—FOREIGN COMMERCE REPORT. vii, 650. FORD ED., vi, 483. (Dec. 1793.)

5060. MARKETS, British.—It is but too true. that Great Britain furnishes markets for three-fourths of the exports of the eight northernmost States,—a truth not proper to be spoken of, but which should influence our proceedings with them.—To JAMES MONROE. i. 406. FORD ED., iv, 85. (P., 1785.)

5061. MARKETS, Exclusion from.—Let them [the British] not think to exclude us from going to other markets to dispose of those commodities which they cannot use, nor to supply those wants which they cannot supply.—RIGHTS OF BRITISH AMERICA. i, 142. FORD ED., i, 446. (1774.)

5062. —— ——. Besides the duties * * * [the acts of Parliament] impose on our articles of export and import they prohibit our going to any markets northward of Cape Finisterre, in the Kingdom of Spain, for the sale of commodities which great Britain will not take from us, and for the purchase of others, with which she cannot supply us; and that, for no other than the arbitrary purpose of purchasing for themselves, by a sacrifice of our rights and interests, certain privileges in their commerce with an allied State, who, in confidence, that their exclusive trade with America will be continued, while the principles and power of the British Parliament be the same, have indulged themselves in every exorbitance which their avarice could dictate or our necessity extort; have raised their commodities called for in America, to the double and treble of what they sold for, before such exclusive privileges were given them, and of what better commodities of the same kind would cost us elsewhere; and, at the same time, give us much less for what we carry thither, than might be had at more convenient ports.—RIGHTS OF BRITISH AMERICA. i, 128. FORD ED., i, 433. (1774.)

5063. —— ——. These acts [of Parliament] prohibit us from carrying, in quest of other purchasers, the surplus of our tobaccos, remaining after the consumption of Great Britain is supplied; so that we must leave them with the British merchant for whatever he will please to allow us, to be by him reshipped to foreign markets, where he will reap the benefits of making sale of them for full value.—RIGHTS OF BRITISH AMERICA. i, 129. FORD ED., i, 433. (1774.)

5064. MARKETS, Extension of.—The mass of our countrymen being interested in agriculture, I hope I do not err in supposing that in a time of profound peace, as the present, to enable them to adopt their productions to the market, to point out markets for them, and endeavor to obtain favorable terms of reception, is within the line of my duty.—To JOHN JAY. ii, 139. FORD ED., iv, 378. (1787.)

5065. MARKETS, Fish oil.—The duty on whale oil [in the British markets] amounts to a prohibition. This duty was originally laid on all foreign fish oil with a view to favor the British and American fisheries. When we became independent, and of course foreign to Great Britain, we became subject to the foreign duty. No duty, therefore, which France may think proper to lay on this article, can drive it to the English market. It could only oblige the inhabitants of Nantucket to abandon their fishery. But the poverty of their soil, offering them no other resource, they must quit their country, and either establish themselves in Nova Scotia, where, as British fishermen, they may participate of the British premium in addition to the ordinary price of their whale oil, or they must accept the conditions which this government offers for the establishment they have proposed at Dunkirk. Your Excellency will judge what conditions may counterbalance in their minds the circumstances of the vicinity of Nova Scotia, sameness of language, laws, religion, customs and kindred. Remaining in their native country, to which they are most singularly attached, excluded from commerce with England, taught to look to France as the only country from which they can derive sustenance, they will in case of war become useful rovers against its enemies. Their position, their poverty, their courage, their address, and their hatred will render them formidable scourges on the British commerce.—To COUNT DE MONTMORIN. ii, 312. (P., 1787.)

5066. —— ——. You have heard of the *Arret* of September 28th [1788] excluding foreign whale oils from the ports of this country [France]. I have obtained the promise of an explanatory *Arret* to declare that that of September 28th was not meant to extend to us. Orders are accordingly given in the ports to receive ours, and the *Arret* will soon be published. This places us on a better footing than ever, as it gives us a monopoly of this market in conjunction with the French fishermen.—To THOMAS PAINE. ii, 549. (P., 1788.)

5067. —— ——. You recollect well the *Arret* of December 29th, 1787, in favor of our commerce, and which, among other things, gave free admission to our whale oil, under a duty of about two louis a ton. In consequence of the English treaty, their oils flowed in and overstocked the market. The light duty they were liable to under the treaty, still lessened by false estimates and aided by the high premiums of the British government, enabled them to undersell the French and American oils. This produced an outcry of the Dunkirk fishery. It was proposed to exclude all European oils, which would not infringe the British treaty. I could not but encourage this idea, because it would give to the French and American fisheries a monopoly of the French market. The *Arret* was so drawn up; but, in the very moment of passing it, they struck out the word *European*, so that our oils became involved. * * * As soon as it was known to me I wrote to Monsieur de Montmorin, and had conferences with him and the other ministers. * * * An immediate order was given for the present admission of our oils. * * * It was observed that if our States would prohibit all foreign oils from being imported into them, it would be a great safeguard, and an encouragement to them to continue the admission.—To JOHN ADAMS. ii, 538. (P., 1788.)

5068. —— ——. The *Arret* of September 28th [1788], to comprehend us with the English, in the exclusion of whale oil from their ports * * * would be a sentence of banishment to the inhabitants of Nantucket, and there is no doubt they would have removed to Nova Scotia or England, in preference to any other part of the world.—To WILLIAM CARMICHAEL. ii, 551. (P., 1788.)

5069. —— ——. This branch of commerce [whale oils] * * * will be on a better footing than ever as enjoying jointly with the French oil, a monopoly of the French markets.—To JOHN JAY. ii, 513. (P., 1788.)

5070. —— ——. The English began [in 1787] to deluge the markets of France with their whale oils; and they were enabled, by the great premiums given by their government, to undersell the French fisherman, aided by feebler premiums, and the American, aided by his poverty alone. Nor is it certain that these speculations were not made at the risk of the British government, to suppress the French and American fishermen in their only market. Some remedy seemed necessary. Perhaps it would not have been a bad one to subject, by a general law, the merchandise of every nation, and of every nature, to pay additional duties in the ports of France, exactly equal to the premiums and drawbacks given on the same merchandise by their own government. This might not only counteract the effect of premiums in the instance of whale oils, but attack the whole British system of bounties and drawbacks, five-eighths of our whale oil, and two-thirds of our salted fish, they take from us one-fourth of our tobacco, three-fourths of our live stock, * * * a considerable and growing portion of our rice, great supplies, occasionally, of other grain; in 1789, which, indeed, was extraordinary, four millions of bushels of wheat, and upwards of a million of bushels of rye and barley * * * and nearly the whole carried in our own vessels. They are a free market now, and will, in time, be a valuable one for ships and ship timber, potash and peltry.—REPORT ON THE FISHERIES. vii, 551. (1791.)

5071. —— ——. France is the only country which can take our surplus, and they take principally of the common oil; as the habit is but commencing with them of a just value to spermaceti whale. Some of this, however, finds its vent there. There was, indeed, a particular interest perpetually soliciting the exclusion of our oils from their markets. The late government there saw well that what we should lose thereby would be gained by others, not by themselves. And we are to hope that the present government, as wise and friendly, will also view us, not as rivals, but as cooperators against a common rival (England). Friendly arrangements with them, and accommodation to mutual interest, rendered easier by friendly dispositions existing on both sides, may long secure to us this important resource for our seamen. Nor is it the interest of the fisherman alone which calls for the cultivation of friendly arrangements with that nation; besides by the aid of which they make London the centre of commerce for the earth. A less general remedy, but an effectual one, was to prohibit the oils of all *European* nations; the treaty with England requiring only that she should be treated as well as the most favored *European* nation. But the remedy adopted was to prohibit all oils, without exception.—To COUNT DE MONTMORIN. ii, 520. (P., 1788.)

5072. —— ——. England is the market for the greatest part of our spermaceti oil. They impose on all our oils a duty of eighteen pounds five shillings sterling the ton, which, as to the common kind, is a prohibition, * * * and as to the spermaceti, gives a preference of theirs over ours to that amount, so as to leave, in the end, but a scanty benefit to the fishermen; and, not long since, by a change of construction, without any change of law, it was made to exclude our oils from their ports, when carried in our vessels. On some change of circumstance, it was construed back again to the reception of our oils,

on paying always, however, the same duty of eighteen pounds five shillings. This serves to show that the tenure by which we hold the admission of this commodity in their markets, is as precarious as it is hard. Nor can it be announced that there is any disposition on their part to arrange this or any other commercial matter to mutual convenience.—REPORT ON THE FISHERIES. vii, 552. (1791.)

5073. MARKETS, Fisheries.—Agriculture has too many markets to be allowed to take away those of the fisheries.—REPORT ON THE FISHERIES. vii, 544. (1791.)

5074. MARKETS, Foreign.—We have hitherto respected the indecision of Spain [with respect to the navigation of the Mississippi], * * * because our western citizens have had vent at home for their productions. A surplus of production begins now to demand foreign markets. Whenever they shall say, "We cannot, we will not, be longer shut up", the United States will be reduced to the following dilemma: 1. To force them to acquiescence. 2. To separate from them rather than take part in a war against Spain. 3. Or to preserve them in our Union, by joining them in the war. * * * The third is the alternative we must adopt.—INSTRUCTIONS TO WILLIAM CARMICHAEL. ix, 412. FORD ED., v, 226. (1790.)

5075. —— ——. Our commerce is certainly of a character to entitle it to favor in most countries. The commodities we offer are either necessaries of life, or materials for manufacture, or convenient subjects of revenue; and we take in exchange, either manufactures, when they have received the last finish of art and industry, or mere luxuries. Such customers may reasonably expect welcome and friendly treatment at every market. Customers, too, whose demands, increasing with their wealth and population, must very shortly give full employment to the whole industry of any nation whatever, in any line of supply they may get into the habit of calling for from it.—FOREIGN COMMERCE REPORT. vii, 646. FORD ED., vi, 479. (Dec. 1793.)

5076. MARKETS, Fostering.—The way to encourage purchasers is to multiply their means of payment.—To COUNT DE MONTMORIN. ii, 529. (P., 1788.)

5077. MARKETS, French.—No two countries are better calculated for the exchanges of commerce. France wants rice, tobacco, potash, furs, and ship-timber. We want wines, brandies, oils, and manufactures.—To COUNT DE VERGENNES. i, 390. (P., 1785.)

5078. —— ——. If American produce can be brought into the ports of France, the articles of exchange for it will be taken in those ports; and the only means of drawing it hither is to let the merchant see that he can dispose of it on better terms here than anywhere else. If the market price of this country does not in itself offer this superiority, it may be worthy of consideration, whether it should be obtained by such abatements of duties, and even by such other encouragements as the importance of the article may justify. Should some loss attend this in the beginning, it can be discontinued when the trade shall be well established in this channel.—To MARQUIS LAFAYETTE. i, 597. FORD ED., iv, 256. (P., 1786.)

5079. —— ——. I have laid my shoulder to the opening the markets of France to our produce, and rendering its transportation a nursery for our seamen.—To GENERAL WASHINGTON. ii, 536. FORD ED., v, 58. (P., 1788.)

5080. —— ——. I very much fear that France will experience a famine this summer. The effects of this admit of no calculation. Grain is the thing for us now to cultivate. The demand will be immense, and the price high. I think cases were shown us that to sell it before the spring is an immense sacrifice. I fear we shall experience a want of vessels to carry our produce to Europe. In this case the tobacco will be left, because bread is more essential to them.—To T. M. RANDOLPH. FORD ED., vi, 241. (Pa., May 1793.)

5081. MARKETS, French Asiatic.—Article 13 of the *Arret* gives us the privileges and advantages of native subjects in all the French possessions in Asia, and in the *scales leading thereto.* This expression means at present the Isles of France and Bourbon, and will include the Cape of Good Hope, should any future event put it into the hands of France. It was with a view to this that I proposed the expression, because we were then in hourly expectation of a war, and it was suspected that France would take possession of that place. It will, in no case, be considered as including anything westward of the Cape of Good Hope. I must observe further, on this article, that it will only become valuable on the suppression of their East India Company; because as long as their monopoly continues, even native subjects cannot enter their Asiatic ports for the purposes of commerce. It is considered, however, as certain that this company will be immediately suppressed.—To JOHN JAY. ii, 343. (P., 1787.)

5082. MARKETS, Fur.—The fur trade is an object of desire in this country [France]. London is at present their market for furs. They pay for them there in ready money. Could they draw their furs into their own ports from the United States they would pay us for them in productions. Nor should we lose by the change of market, since, though the French pay the London merchants in cash, those merchants pay us with manufactures. A very wealthy and well connected company is proposing here to associate themselves with an American company, each to possess half the interest, and to carry on the fur trade between the two countries. The company here expect to make the principal part of the advances; they also are soliciting considerable indulgences from this government from which the part of the company

on our side of the water will reap half the advantage. As no exclusive idea enters into this scheme, it appears to me worthy of encouragement. It is hoped the government here will interest themselves for its success. If they do, one of two things may happen: either the English will be afraid to stop the vessels of a company consisting partly of French subjects, and patronized by the Court; in which case the commerce will be laid open generally; or if they stop the vessels, the French company, which is strongly connected with men in power, will complain in form to their government, who may thus be interested as principals in the rectification of this abuse. As yet, however, the proposition has not taken such a form as to assure us that it will be prosecuted to this length.— To JOHN JAY. FORD ED., iv, 231. (P., 1786.)

5083. MARKETS, Home.—There can be no question, in a mind truly American, whether it is best to send our citizens and property into certain captivity, and then wage war for their recovery, or to keep them at home, and to turn seriously to that policy which plants the manufacturer and the husbandman side by side, and establishes at the door of every one that exchange of mutual labors and comforts, which we have hitherto sought in distant regions, and under perpetual risk of broils with them.—R. TO A. N. Y. TAMMANY SOCIETY. viii, 127. (Feb. 1808.)

5084. —— ——. The advantages * * * of planting the consumer in our own soil by the side of the grower of produce, are so palpable, that no temporary suspension of injuries on England's part, or agreements founded on that, will now prevent our continuing in what we have begun [manufacturing].—To DUPONT DE NEMOURS. v, 456. (M., June 1809.)

5085. —— ——. The bringing our countrymen to a sound comparative estimate of the vast value of internal commerce, and the disproportionate importance of what is foreign, is the most salutary effort which can be made for the prosperity of these States, which are entirely misled from their true interests by the infection of English prejudices, and illicit attachments to English interests and connections.—To DR. THOMAS COOPER. vi, 294. (M., 1814.)

5086. MARKETS, Land.—The long succession of years of stunted crops, of reduced prices, the general prostration of the farming business, under levies for the support of manufacturers, &c., with the calamitous fluctuations of value in our proper medium, have kept agriculture in a state of abject depression, which has peopled the Western States by silently breaking up those on the Atlantic, and glutted the land market, while it drew off its bidders. In such a state of things, property has lost its character of being a resource for debts. Highland in Bedford, which, in the days of our plethory, sold readily for from fifty to one hundred dollars the acre (and such sales were many then), would not now sell for more than from ten to twenty dollars, or one-quarter or one-fifth of its former price.—To JAMES MADISON. vii, 434. FORD ED., x, 377. (M., February 1826.)

5087. MARKETS, Monopolized.—It is contrary to the spirit of trade, and to the dispositions of merchants, to carry a commodity to any market where but one person is allowed to buy it, and where. of course, that person fixes its price, which the seller must receive, or reexport his commodity, at the loss of his voyage thither. Experience accordingly shows, that they carry it to other markets, and that they take in exchange the merchandise of the place where they deliver it.—To COUNT DE VERGENNES. i, 386. (P., 1785.)

5088. MARKETS, Necessity and.—We must accept bread from our enemies if our friends cannot furnish it.—To COUNT DE MONTMORIN. ii, 523. (P., 1788.)

5089. MARKETS, Neutrality and.—If the new government wears the front which I hope it will. I see no impossibility in the availing ourselves of the wars of others to open up the other parts [West India Islands] of America to our commerce as the price of our neutrality.—To GENERAL WASHINGTON. ii, 533. FORD ED., v, 57. (P., 1788.)

5090. MARKETS, Reciprocity and.—It were to be wished that some positively favorable stipulations respecting our grain, flour and fish, could be obtained, even on our giving reciprocal advantages to some other commodities of Spain, say her wines and brandies. But if we quit the ground of the *most favored* nation, as to certain articles for our convenience, Spain may insist on doing the same for other articles for her convenience. * * * If we grant favor to the wines and brandies of Spain, then Portugal and France will demand the same; and in order to create an equivalent, Portugal may lay a duty on our fish and grain, and France, a prohibition on our whale oils. the removal of which will be proposed as an equivalent. This much, however, as to grain and flour, may be attempted. There has, not long since, been a considerable duty laid on them in Spain. This was while a treaty on the subject of commerce was pending between us and Spain, as that Court considers the matter. It is not generally thought right to change the state of things .pending a treaty concerning them. On this consideration, and on the motive of cultivating our friendship, perhaps the Commissioners may induce them to restore this commodity to the footing on which it was on opening the conferences with Mr. Gardoqui, on the 26th day of July, 1785. If Spain says, "do the same by your tonnage on our vessels", the answer may be, that our tonnage affects Spain very little, and other nations very much; whereas the duty on flour in Spain affects us very much, and other na-

tions very little. Consequently, there would be no equality in reciprocal relinquishment, as there had been none in the reciprocal innovation; and Spain, by insisting on this, would, in fact, only be aiding the interests of her rival nations, to whom we should be forced to extend the same indulgence. At the time of opening the conferences, too, we had as yet not erected any system; our government itself being not yet erected. Innovation then was unavoidable on our part, if it be innovation to establish a system. We did it on fair and general ground, on ground favorable to Spain. But they had a system and, therefore, innovation was avoidable on their part.—MISSISSIPPI RIVER INSTRUCTIONS. vii, 590. FORD ED., v, 479. (March 1792.)

5091. MARKETS, Salted provisions.—I wish that you could obtain the free introduction of our salted provisions into France. Nothing would be so generally pleasing from the Chesapeake to New Hampshire.—To WILLIAM SHORT. FORD ED., v, 168. (N.Y., 1790.)

5092. ———— ————. It gives great satisfaction that the *Arret du Conseil* of December, 1787, stands a chance of being saved. It is, in truth, the sheet-anchor of our connection with France, which will be much loosened when that is lost. This *Arret* saved, a free importation of salted meats into France. and of provisions of all kinds into her colonies. will bind our interests to that country more than to all the world besides.—To WILLIAM SHORT. iii, 225. (Pa., 1791.)

5093. MARKETS, Speculation and.—I think the best rule is, never to sell on a rising market. Wait till it begins to fall. Then, indeed, one will lose a penny or two, but with a rising market you never know what you are to lose.—To FRANCIS EPPES. FORD ED., vi, 163. (Pa., 1793.)

5094. MARKETS, Steady.—Sudden vicissitudes of opening and shutting ports do little injury to merchants settled on the opposite [British] coast, watching for the opening, like the return of a tide, and ready to enter with it. But they ruin the adventurer whose distance requires six months' notice.—To COUNT DE MONTMORIN. ii, 525. (P., 1788.)

5095. ———— ————. A regular course of trade is not quitted in an instant, nor constant customers deserted for accidental ones.—To MARQUIS DE LAFAYETTE. iii, 68. (P., 1789.)

5096. MARKETS, Sugar.—Evidence grows upon us that the United States may not only supply themselves with sugar for their own consumption, but be great exporters.—To T. M. RANDOLPH. FORD ED., v, 325. (Pa., 1791.)

5097. MARKETS, Tobacco.—While the navigating and provision States. who are the majority, can keep open all the markets, or at least sufficient ones for their objects, the cries of the tobacco makers, who are the minority, and not at all in favor, will hardly be listened to. It is truly the fable of the monkey pulling the nuts out of the fire with the cat's paw; and it shows that George Mason's proposition in the [Federal] Convention was wise, that on laws regulating commerce, two-thirds of the votes should be required to pass them.—To JAMES MADISON. iv, 323. FORD ED., vii, 432. (Pa., March 1800.) See TOBACCO.

5098. MARKETS, Wheat and flour.— We can sell them [the Portuguese] the flour ready manufactured for much less than the wheat of which it is made. In carrying to them wheat, we carry also the bran, which does not pay its own freight. In attempting to save and transport wheat to them, much is lost by the weavil, and much spoiled by heat in the hold of the vessel. This loss must be laid on the wheat which gets safe to market, where it is paid for by the consumer. Now, this is much more than the cost of manufacturing it with us, which would prevent that loss. * * * Let them buy of us as much wheat as will make a hundred weight of flour. They will find that they have paid more for the wheat than we should have asked for the flour, besides having lost the labor of their mills in grinding it. The obliging us, therefore, to carry it to them in the form of wheat, is a useless loss to both parties.—To JOHN ADAMS. i, 492. (P., 1785.)

5099. ―― ――. It seems that so far from giving new liberties to our corn trade, Portugal contemplates the prohibition of it, by giving that trade exclusively to Naples. What would she say should we give her wine trade exclusive to France and Spain? * * * Can a wise statesman seriously think of risking such a prospect as this?—To DAVID HUMPHREYS. iii, 488. (Pa., 1792.)

5100. ―― ――. I must forever repeat that, instead of excluding our wheat, Portugal will open her ports to our flour.—To DAVID HUMPHREYS. FORD ED., vi, 205. (Pa., 1793.)

5101. MARQUE, Letters of.— The Administrator shall not possess the prerogative * * * of issuing letters of marque, or reprisal.—PROPOSED VA. CONSTITUTION. FORD ED., ii. 19. (June 1776.)

5102. ―― ――. Our delegates [to Congress] inform us that we might now obtain letters of marque for want of which our people [in Virginia] have long and exceedingly suffered. I have taken the liberty of desiring them to apply for fifty.—To THE PRESIDENT OF CONGRESS. FORD ED., ii, 241. (1799.)

5103. ―― ――. I have to-day consulted the other gentlemen [of the Cabinet] on the question whether letters of marque were to be considered as written within our interdict. We are unanimously of opinion they are not. We consider them as essentially *merchant vessels;* that commerce is their main object, and arms merely incidental and defensive.—To ALBERT GALLATIN. v, 123. FORD ED., ix, 104. (W., July 1807.)

5104. MARRIAGE, Congratulations on. —It is customary in America to "wish joy" to a new married couple, and this is generally done by those present in the moment after the ceremony. A friend of mine, however, always delayed the wish of joy till one year after the ceremony, because he observed they had *by that time* need *of it.* I am entitled fully then to express the wish to you as you must now have been married at least three years. I have no doubt, however, that you have found real joy in the possession of a good wife, and the endearments of a child. —To PHILIP MAZZEI. FORD ED., viii, 15. (W., 1801.)

5105. MARRIAGE, Happiness in.— I * * * give you my sincere congratulations on your marriage. Your own dispositions, and the inherent comforts of that state, will insure you a great addition of happiness.— To JAMES MONROE. i, 590. FORD ED., iv, 250. (P., 1786.)

5106. ―― ――. The happiness of your life now depends on the continuing to please a single person. To this all other objects must be secondary, even your love for me, were it possible that could ever be an obstacle. But this it never can be. Neither of you can ever have a more faithful friend than myself, nor one on whom you can count for more sacrifices. My own is become a secondary object to the happiness of you both. Cherish, then, for me, my dear child, the affection of your husband, and continue to love me as you have done, and to render my life a blessing by the prospect it may hold up to me of seeing you happy.—To MARTHA JEFFERSON RANDOLPH. D. L. J., 180. (N. Y., 1790.)

5107. ―― ――. I have one daughter married to a man of science, sense, virtue, and competence; in whom indeed I have nothing more to wish. * * * If the other shall be as fortunate, * * * I shall imagine myself as blessed as the most blessed of the patriarchs.—To MRS. CHURCH. FORD ED., vi, 455. (G., 1793.)

5108. MARRIAGE, Harmony in.— Harmony in the married state is the very first object to be aimed at. Nothing can preserve affections uninterrupted but a firm resolution never to differ in will, and a determination in each to consider the love of the other as of more value than any object whatever on which a wish had been fixed. How light in fact is the sacrifice of any other wish when weighed against the affections of one with whom we are to pass our whole life! And though opposition in a single instance will hardly of itself produce alienation, yet every one has their pouch into which all these little oppositions are put; while that is filling the alienation is insensibly going on, and when filled it is complete.—To MARY JEFFERSON EPPES. D. L. J., 246. (Pa., 1798.)

5109. MARRIAGE, Motherhood and.— It [motherhood] is undoubtedly the key-

stone of the arch of matrimonial happiness.—
To MARTHA JEFFERSON RANDOLPH. D. L. J.,
192. (Pa., 1791.)

5110. MARRIAGE, Youthful.—I sincerely sympathize with you on the step which
your brother has taken without consulting
you, and wonder indeed how it could be done,
with any attention in the agents, to the laws
of the land. I fear he will hardly persevere
in the second plan of life adopted for him,
as matrimony illy agrees with study, especially in the first stages of both. However,
you will readily perceive that, the thing being done, there is now but one question, that
is what is to be done to make the best of it,
in respect both to his and your happiness?
A step of this kind indicates no vice, nor
other foible than of following too hastily the
movements of a warm heart. It admits,
therefore, of the continuance of cordial affection, and calls perhaps more indispensably
for your care and protection. To conciliate
the affection of all parties, and to banish all
suspicion of discontent, will conduce most to
your own happiness also.—To JAMES MONROE. FORD ED., v, 317. (Pa., 1791.)

5111. MARRIAGE WITH ROYALTY.
—Our young Republic * * * should prevent its citizens from becoming so established
in wealth and power, as to be thought worthy
of alliance by marriage with the nieces, sisters, &c., of kings.—To COLONEL HUMPHREYS.
ii, 253. (P., 1787.)

5112. MARSHALL (John), Crafty.—A
crafty chief judge, who sophisticates the law to
his mind, by the turn of his own reasoning.—To
THOMAS RITCHIE. vii, 192. FORD ED., x, 171.
(M., 1820.)

**5113. MARSHALL (John), Hamilton
and.**—I learn that [Alexander] Hamilton has
expressed the strongest desire that Marshall
shall come into Congress from Richmond, declaring that there is no man in Virginia whom
he wishes so much to see there; and I am told
that Marshall has expressed half a mind to
come. Hence I conclude that Hamilton has
plied him well with flattery and solicitation, and
I think nothing better could be done than to
make him a judge.—To JAMES MADISON. FORD
ED., vi, 95. (Pa., 1792.)

**5114. MARSHALL (John), Marbury
vs. Madison Case.**—His twistifications in the
case of Marbury, in that of Burr, and the Yazoo
case show how dexterously he can reconci'e law
to his personal biases.—To PRESIDENT MADISON. FORD ED., ix, 276. (M., 1810.)

5115. MARSHALL (John), Mischiefmaker.—Though Marshall will be able to
embarrass the republican party in the Assembly
a good deal, yet upon the whole. his having
gone into it will be of service. He has been
hitherto able to do more mischief acting under
the mask of republicanism than he will be able
to do throwing it plainly off. His lax lounging
manners have made him popular with the bulk
of the people of Richmond. and a profound
hypocrisy with many thinking men of our
country. But having come forth in the full
plenitude of his English principles. the latter
will see that it is high time to make him known.
—To JAMES MADISON. FORD ED., vii, 37. (Nov.
1795.)

**5116. MARSHALL (John), Moot cases
and.**—The practice of Judge Marshall, of
travelling out of his case to prescribe what the
law would be in a moot case not before the
court, is very irregular and very censurable.—
To WILLIAM JOHNSON. vii, 295. FORD ED., x,
230. (M., 1823.)

**5117. MARSHALL (John), Sophistry
of.**—The rancorous hatred which Marshall
bears to the government of his country, and
* * * the cunning and sophistry within which
he is able to enshroud himself.—To PRESIDENT
MADISON. FORD ED., ix, 275. (M., 1810.) See
HISTORY, JUDICIARY, MAZZEI, and SUPREME
COURT.

5118. MARTIAL LAW, Recourse to.—
There are extreme cases where the laws become inadequate even to their own preservation, and where the universal resource is a
dictator, or martial law.—To DR. JAMES
BROWN. v, 379. FORD ED., ix, 211. (W.,
1808.)

5119. MARTIN (Luther), Burr and.—
Shall we move to commit Luther Martin as
particeps criminis with Burr? Graybell will fix
upon him misprision of treason at least. And
at any rate, his evidence will put down this
unprincipled and impudent federal bull-dog, and
add another proof that the most clamorous defenders of Burr are all his accomplices. It will
explain why Luther Martin flew so hastily to
the " aid of his honorable friend ", abandoning
his clients and their property during a session of
a principal court in Maryland, now filled, as I
am told, with the clamors and ruin of his
clients.—To GEORGE HAY. v, 99. FORD ED., ix,
58. (W., June 1807.) See LOGAN.

5120. MASON (George), Ability of.—
George Mason [was] a man of the first order
of wisdom among those who acted on the theatre of the Revolution, of expansive mind, profound judgment, cogent in argument, learned in
the lore of our former constitution, and earnest
for the republican change on democratic principles.* His elocution was neither flowing or
smooth; but his language was strong, his manner most impressive, and strengthened by a
dash of biting cynicism when provocation made
it seasonable.—AUTOBIOGRAPHY. i, 40. FORD
ED., i, 56. (1821.)

5121. MASON (George), Virginia Constitution and.—What are George Mason's
sentiments as to the amendment of our Constitution? What amendment would he approve?
Is he determined to sleep on, or will he rouse
and be active?—To JAMES MADISON. FORD ED.,
iii, 347. (A., Dec. 1783.)

5122. ———— ————. That George Mason was
the author of the Bill of Rights and of the
Constitution founded on it, the evidence of the
day established fully in my mind.—To HENRY
LEE. vii, 407. FORD ED., x, 342. (M., 1825.)

5123. ———— ————. The fact is unquestionable, that the Bill of Rights and the Constitution
of Virginia were drawn originally by George
Mason, one of our really great men, and of the
first order of greatness.—To A. B. WOODWARD.
vii, 405. FORD ED., x, 341. (M., 1825.)

5124. MASON (J. M.), Red-hot Federalist.—I do not know Dr. [John M.] Mason

* George Mason was one of the signers of the Declaration. " Mason," said James Madison, " possessed
the greatest talents for debate of any man I have ever
seen or heard speak."—EDITOR.

personally, but by character well. He is the
most red-hot federalist, famous, or rather infamous for the lying and slandering which he
vomited from the pulpit in the political ha-
rangues with which he polluted the place.
I was honored with much of it. He is a man
who can prove everything if you will take his
word for proof. Such evidence of Hamilton's
being a republican he may bring; but Mr.
Adams, Edmund Randolph, and myself, could
repeat an explicit declaration of Hamilton's
against which Dr. Mason's proofs would weigh
nothing.—To JOEL BARLOW. v, 495. FORD ED.,
ix, 269. (M., 1810.)

5125. MASON (J. T.), Meteoric.—John
Thompson Mason is a meteor whose path cannot
be calculated. All the powers of his mind seem
at present to be concentrated in one single object, the producing a convention to new model
the [State] Constitution.—To JAMES MADISON.
FORD ED., iii, 318. (T., May 1783.)

5126. MASSACHUSETTS, Apostasy.—
Oh Massachusetts! how have I lamented the
degradation of your apostasy! Massachusetts,
with whom I went in pride in 1776, whose vote
was my vote on every public question, and
whose principles were then the standard of
whatever was free or fearless. But she was
then under the counsels of the two Adamses;
while Strong, her present leader, was promoting
petitions for submission to British power and
British usurpation. While under her present
counsels, she must be contented to be nothing;
as having a vote, indeed, to be counted, but
not respected. But should the State, once more,
buckle on her republican harness, we shall receive her again as a sister, and recollect her
wanderings among the crimes only of the parricide party, which would have basely sold what
their fathers so bravely won from the same
enemy. Let us look forward, then, to the act
of repentance, which, by dismissing her venal
traitors, shall be the signal of return to the
bosom, and to the principles of her brethren;
and, if her late humiliation can just give her
modesty enough to suppose that her southern
brethren are somewhat on a par with her in
wisdom, in information, in patriotism, in
bravery, and even in honesty, although not in
psalm-singing, she will more justly estimate her
own relative *momentum* in the Union. With
her ancient principles, she would really be
great, if she did not think herself the whole.—
To GENERAL DEARBORN. vi, 451. (M., March
1815.)

5127. MASSACHUSETTS, Defection of.
—Some apprehend danger from the defection
of Massachusetts. It is a disagreeable circumstance but not a dangerous one. If they become neutral, we are sufficient for one enemy
without them, and in fact we get no aid from
them now. If their administration determines
to join the enemy, their force will be annihilated
by equality of division among themselves. Their
federalists will then call in the English army,
the republicans ours, and it will only be a transfer of the scene of war from Canada to Massachusetts; and we can get ten men to go to Massachusetts for one who will go to Canada.
Every one, too, must know that we can at any
moment make peace with England at the expense of the navigation and fisheries of Massachusetts. But it will not come to this. Their
own people will put down these factionists as
soon as they see the real object of their opposition; and of this Vermont, New Hampshire,
and even Connecticut itself, furnish proofs.—To
WILLIAM SHORT. vi, 402. (M., Nov. 1814.)

— MASSACHUSETTS, Federal Constitution and.—See CONSTITUTION (FEDERAL).

5128. MASSACHUSETTS, Federalism
in.—Massachusetts still lags; because most
deeply involved in the parricide crimes and
treasons of the war. But her gangrene is
contracting, the sound flesh advancing on it,
and all there will be well.—To MARQUIS DE
LAFAYETTE. vii, 66. FORD ED., x, 83. (M.,
1817.)

5129. MASSACHUSETTS, Justice to.—
So far as either facts or opinions have been
truly quoted from me, they have never been
meant to intercept the just fame of Massachusetts for the promptitude and perseverance of
her early resistance. We willingly cede to her
the laud of having been (although not exclusively) "the cradle of sound principles", and,
if some of us believe she has deflected from
them in her course, we retain full confidence in
her ultimate return to them.—To SAMUEL A.
WELLS. i, 117. FORD ED., x, 129. (M., 1819.)

5130. MASSACHUSETTS, Patriotism
of People.—The progression of sentiment in
the great body of our fellow citizens of Massachusetts, and the increasing support of their
opinion, I have seen with satisfaction, and was
ever confident I should see; persuaded that an
enlightened people, whenever they should view
impartially the course we have pursued, could
never wish that our measures should have been
reversed; could never desire that the expenses
of the government should have been increased,
taxes multiplied, debt accumulated, wars undertaken, and the tomahawk and scalping knife
left in the hands of our neighbors, rather than
the hoe and plough. In whatever tended to
strengthen the republican features of our Constitution, we could not fail to expect from
Massachusetts, the cradle of our Revolutionary
principles, an ultimate concurrence; and cultivating the peace of nations, with justice and
prudence, we yet were always confident that,
whenever our rights would have to be vindicated against the aggression of foreign foes, or
the machinations of internal conspirators, the
people of Massachusetts, so prominent in the
military achievements which placed our country
in the right of self-government, would never be
found wanting in their duty to the calls of their
country, or the requisitions of their government.
—R. TO A. MASSACHUSETTS LEGISLATURE. viii,
116. (Feb. 1807.)

5131. MASSACHUSETTS, Republican-
ism in.—I sincerely congratulate you on the
triumph of republicanism in Massachusetts.
The hydra of federalism has now lost all its
heads but two [Connecticut and Delaware].—
To MR. BIDWELL. v, 14. (W., 1806.)

5132. ———. I tender to yourself, to
Mr. Lincoln, and to your State, my sincere congratulations on the happy event of the election
of a republican Executive to preside over its
councils. The * * * just respect with which all
the States have ever looked to Massachusetts,
could leave none of them without anxiety, while
she was in a state of alienation from her family
and friends.—To JAMES SULLIVAN. v, 100. FORD
ED., ix, 75. (W., June 1807.)

5133. ———. Of the return of Massachusetts to sound principles I never had a
doubt. The body of her citizens has never
been otherwise than republican. Her would-be
dukes and lords, indeed, have been itching for
coronets; her lawyers for robes of ermine, her

priests for lawn sleeves, and for a religious establishment which might give them wealth, power, and independence of personal merit. But her citizens, who were to supply with the sweat of their brow the treasures on which these drones were to riot, could never have seen anything to long for in the oppressions and pauperism of England. After the shackles of aristocracy of the bar and priesthood have been burst by Connecticut, we cannot doubt the return of Massachusetts to the bosom of the republican family.—To SAMUEL A. WELLS. FORD ED., x, 133. (M., 1819.)

5134. MASSACHUSETTS, Saddled by. —We are completely under the saddle of Massachusetts and Connecticut, and they ride us very hard, cruelly insulting our feelings, as well as exhausting our strength and subsistence. Their natural friends, the three other eastern States, join them from a sort of family pride, and they have the art to divide certain other parts of the Union, so as to make use of them to govern the whole.—To JOHN TAYLOR. iv, 245. FORD ED., vii, 263. (Pa., June 1798.)

5135. MASSACHUSETTS, Selfishness of.—Could the people of Massachusetts emerge from the deceptions under which they are kept by their clergy, lawyers, and English presses, our salvation would be sure and easy. Without that, I believe it will be effected; but it will be uphill work. Nor can we expect ever their cordial cooperation, because they will not be satisfied longer than while we are sacrificing everything to navigation and a navy.— To EDMUND PENDLETON. FORD ED., vii, 376. (M., 1799.)

5136. MASSACHUSETTS, The Union and.—The conduct of Massachusetts, which is the subject of your address to Mr. Quincy is serious, as embarrassing the operations of the war, and jeopardizing its issue; and is still more so, as an example of contumacy against the Constitution. One method of proving their purpose would be to call a convention of their State, and to require them to declare themselves members of the Union, and obedient to its determinations, or not members, and let them go. Put this question solemnly to their people, and their answer cannot be doubtful. One half of them are republicans, and would cling to the Union from principle. Of the other half, the dispassionate part would consider, first, that they do not raise bread sufficient for their own subsistence, and must look to Europe for the deficiency if excluded from our ports, which vital interests would force us to do. Secondly, that they are navigating people without a stick of timber for the hull of a ship, nor a pound of anything to export in it, which would be admitted at any market. Thirdly, that they are also a manufacturing people, and left by the exclusive system of Europe without a market but ours. Fourthly, that as rivals of England in manufactures, in commerce, in navigation, and fisheries, they would meet her competition in every point. Fifthly, that England would feel no scruples in making the abandonment and ruin of such a rival the price of a treaty with the producing States; whose interest too it would be to nourish a navigation beyond the Atlantic, rather than a hostile one at our own door. And sixthly, that in case of war with the Union, which occurrences between coterminous nations frequently produce, it would be a contest of one against fifteen. The remaining portion of the federal moiety of the State would, I believe, brave all these obstacles, because they are monarchists in principle, bear-

ing deadly hatred to their republican fellow citizens, impatient under the ascendency of republican principles, devoted in their attachment to England, and preferring to be placed under her despotism, if they cannot hold the helm of government here. I see, in their separation, no evil but the example, and I believe that the effect of that would be corrected by an early and humiliating return to the Union, after losing much of the population of their country, insufficient in its own resources to feed her numerous inhabitants, and inferior in all its allurements to the more inviting soils, climates, and governments of the other States. Whether a dispassionate discussion before the public, of the advantages and disadvantages of separation to both parties, would be the best medicine of this dialytic fever, or to consider it as a sacrilege ever to touch the question, may be doubted. I am, myself, generally disposed to indulge, and to follow reason; and believe that in no case would it be safer than in the present. Their refractory course, however, will not be unpunished by the indignation of their co-States, their loss of influence with them, the censures of history, and the stain on the character of their State.—To JAMES MARTIN. vi. 213. FORD ED., ix, 420. (M., Sep. 1813.) See FEDERALISTS, HARTFORD CONVENTION, and PARTIES.

5137. MASTODON, Bones of.—Of the bones you sent me, I reserved a very few for myself. I got Dr. Wistar to select from the rest every piece which could be interesting to the Philosophical Society [of Philadelphia], and sent the residue to the National Institute of France. These have enabled them to decide that the animal was neither a mammoth nor an elephant, but of a distinct kind, to which they have given the name of Mastodont, from the protuberance of its teeth. These, from their forms, and the immense mass of their jaws, satisfy me this animal must have been arboriverous. Nature seems not to have provided other food sufficient for him, and the limb of a tree would be no more to him than a bough of a cotton tree to a horse.—To GENERAL WILLIAM CLARKE. v, 467. (M., 1809.) See PALEONTOLOGY.

5138. MATCHES, Phosphoric.—I should have sent you a specimen of the phosphoric matches, but that I am told Mr. Rittenhouse has had some of them. They are a beautiful discovery and very useful, especially to heads which, like yours and mine, cannot at all times be got to sleep. The convenience of lighting a candle without getting out of bed, of sealing letters without calling a servant, of kindling a fire without flint, steel, punk, &c., is of value. —To CHARLES THOMSON. FORD ED., iv, 14. (1784.)

5139. MATERIALISM, Views on.—I consider [Dugald] Stewart and [Destutt] Tracy as the ablest metaphysicians living; by which I mean investigators of the thinking faculty of man. Stewart seems to have given its natural history from facts and observations; Tracy its modes of action and deduction, which he calls Logic, and Ideology; and Cabanis, in his *Physique et Morale de l'Homme*, has investigated anatomically, and most ingeniously, the particular organs in the human structure which may most probably exercise that faculty. And they ask, why may not the mode of action called thought, have been given to a material organ of peculiar structure, as that of magnetism is to the needle, or of elasticity to the spring by a particular manipulation of the steel. They observe that on ignition of the needle or spring, their magnetism and elasticity cease. So on dissolution of the material organ by death, its action of thought may cease a.so, and that nobody supposes that the magnetism or elasticity retires to hold a substantive and distinct existence. These were qualities only of particular conformations of matter; change the conformation, and its qualities change also. Mr. Locke and other materialists have charged with blasphemy the spiritualists who have denied the Creator the power of endowing certain forms of matter with the faculty of thought. These, however, are speculations and subtleties in which, for my own part, I have little indulged myself. When I meet with a proposition beyond finite comprehension, I abandon it as I do a weight which human strength cannot lift, and I think ignorance in these cases is truly the softest pillow on which I can lay my head. Were it necessary, however, to form an opinion, I confess I should, with Mr. Locke, prefer swallowing one incomprehensibility rather than two. It requires one effort only to admit the single incomprehensibility of matter endowed with thought, and two to believe, first that of an existence called spirit, of which we have neither evidence nor idea, and then, secondly, how that spirit, which has neither extension nor solidity, can put material organs into motion. These are things which you and I may perhaps know ere long. We have so lived as to fear neither horn of the dilemma.—To JOHN ADAMS. vii, 153. (M., 1820.)

5140. ——. The crowd of scepticisms in your puzzling letter on matter, spirit, motion, &c., kept me from sleep. I read it and laid it down; read it, and laid it down, again and again; and to give rest to my mind, I was obliged to recur ultimately to my habitual anodyne, "I feel, therefore I exist". I feel bodies which are not myself: there are other existences then. I call them *matter*. I feel them changing place. This gives me *motion*. Where there is an absence of matter, I call it *void*, or *nothing*, or *immaterial space*. On the basis of sensation, of matter, and motion, we may erect the fabric of all the certainties we can have or need. I can conceive *thought* to be an action of a particular organization of matter, formed for that purpose by its creator, as well as that *attraction* is an action of matter, or *magnetism* of loadstone. When he who denies to the Creator the power of endowing matter with the mode of action called *thinking*, shall show how He could endow the sun with the mode of action called *attraction*, which reins the planets in the track of their orbits, or how an absence of matter can have a will, and by that will put matter into motion, then the materialist may be lawfully required to explain the process by which matter exercises the faculty of thinking. When once we quit the basis of sensation, all is in the wind. To talk of *immaterial* existences, is to talk of *nothings*. To say that the human soul, angels, God, are immaterial, is to say, they are nothings, or that there is no God, no angels, no soul. I cannot reason otherwise; but I believe I am supported in my creed of materialism by the Lockes, the Tracys, and the Stewarts.—To JOHN ADAMS. vii, 175. (M., 1820.)

5141. MATHEMATICS, Favorite study.
—Having to conduct my grandson through his course of mathematics, I have resumed that study with great avidity. It was ever my favorite one. We have no theories there, no uncertainties remain on the mind: all is demonstration and satisfaction. I have forgotten much, and recover it with more difficulty than when in the vigor of my mind I originally acquired it.—To BENJAMIN RUSH. vi, 3. FORD ED., ix, 328. (P.F., 1811.)

5142. MAZZEI (Philip), Book by.—Mazzei will print soon two or three volumes 8vo., of *Recherches Historiques* and *Politiques sur les Etats d'Amerique*, which are sensible.—To M. OTTO. ii, 95. (P., 1787.)

5143. MAZZEI (Philip), Consulship and.—An alarming paragraph in your letter says Mazzei is coming to Annapolis. I tremble at the idea. I know he will be worse to me than a return of my double quotidian headache. There is a resolution, reported to Congress by a committee, that they will never appoint to the office of minister, chargé des affaires, consul, agent, &c., any but natives. To this I think there will not be a dissenting voice; and it will be taken up among the first things. Could you not, by making him acquainted with this, divert him from coming here? A consulate is his object, in which he will assuredly fail. But his coming will be attended with evil. He is the violent enemy of Franklin, having been some time at Paris, and, from my knowledge of the man, I am sure he will have employed himself in collecting on the spot facts true or false to impeach him. You know there are people here who, on the first idea of this, will take him to their bosom, and turn all Congress topsy-turvy. For God's sake, then, save us from this confusion if you can.—To JAMES MADISON. FORD ED., iii, 425. (A., 1784.)

5144. MAZZEI (Philip), Jefferson's letter to.—[Respecting] the letter to Mazzei imputed to me in the papers, the general substance is mine, though the diction has been considerably varied in the course of its translations from English into Italian, from Italian into French, and from French into English. I first met with it at Bladensburg, and for a moment conceived I must take the field of the public papers. I could not disavow it wholly, because the greatest part of it was mine, in substance though not in form. I could not avow it as it stood, because the form was not mine, and, in one place, the substance very materially falsified. This, then, would render explanations necessary; nay, it would render proofs of the whole necessary, and draw me at length into a publication of all (even the secret) transactions of the administration [of Washington] while I was of it; and embroil me personally with every member of the Executive, with the Judiciary, and with others still. I soon decided in my own mind, to be entirely silent. I consulted with several friends at Philadelphia, who, every one of them, were clearly against my avowing or disavowing, and some of them conjured me most earnestly to let nothing provoke me to it. I corrected, in conversation with them, a substantial misrepresentation in the copy published. The original has a sentiment *like* this (for I have it not before me), "they are endeavoring to submit us to the substance, as they already have to the *forms* of the British government"; meaning by *forms*, the birth-days, levees, processions to parliament, inauguration pomposities, &c. But the copy published says, "as they have already submitted us to the *form* of the British", &c., making me express hostility to the form of our government, that is to say, to the Constitution itself. For this is really the difference of the word *form*, used in the singular or plural, in that phrase, in the English language. Now, it would be impossible for me to explain this publicly, without bringing on a personal difference between General Washington and myself, which nothing before the publication of this letter has ever done. It would embroil me also with all those with whom his character is still popular, that is to say, nine-tenths of the people of the United States; and what good would be obtained by avowing the letter with the necessary explanations? Very little indeed, in my opinion, to counterbalance a good deal of harm. From my silence in this instance, it can never be inferred that I am afraid to own the general sentiments of the letter. If I am subject to either imputation, it is to that of avowing such sentiments too frankly both in private and public, often when there is no necessity for it, merely because I disdain everything like duplicity. Still, however, I am open to conviction. Think for me, * * * advise me what to do, and confer with Colonel Monroe.—To JAMES MADISON. iv, 193. FORD ED., vii 164. (M., Aug. 1797.)

5145. ———— ————. The letter to Mazzei has been a precious theme of crimination for federal malice. It was a long letter of business in which was inserted a single paragraph only of political information as to the state of our country. In this information there was not one word which would not then have been, or would not now be approved by every republican in the United States, looking back to those times, as you will see by a faithful copy now enclosed of the whole of what that letter said on the subject of the United States, or of its government. This paragraph, extracted and translated, got into a Paris paper at a time when the persons in power there were laboring under very general disfavor, and their friends were eager to catch even at straws to buoy them up. To them, therefore, I have always imputed the interpolation of an entire paragraph additional to mine, which makes me charge my own country with ingratitude and injustice to France. There was not a word in my letter respecting France, or any of the proceedings or relations between this country and that. Yet this interpolated paragraph has been the burden of federal calumny, has been constantly quoted by them, made the subject of unceasing and virulent abuse, and is still quoted, * * * as if it were genuine, and really written by me. And even Judge Marshall makes history descend from its dignity, and the ermine from its sanctity, to exaggerate, to record and to sanction this forgery. In the very last note of his book [*Life of Washington*] he says, "a letter from Mr. Jefferson to Mr. Mazzei, an Italian, was published in Florence, and republished in the *Moniteur*, with very severe strictures on the conduct of the United States". And instead of the letter itself, he copies what he says are the remarks of the editor, which are an exaggerated commentary on the fabricated paragraph itself, and silently leaves to his reader to make the ready inference that these were the sentiments of the letter. Proof is the duty of the affirmative side. A negative cannot be positively proved. But, in defect of impossible proof of what was not in the original letter, I have its press-copy still in my possession. It has been shown to several and is open to anyone who wishes to see it. I have presumed only that the interpolation was done in Paris. But I never saw the letter in either its Italian or French dress, and it may have been done here, with the commentary handed down to posterity by the Judge. The genuine paragraph, retranslated through Italian and French into English, as it appeared here in a federal paper, besides the mutilated hue which these translations and retranslations of it produced generally, gave a mistranslation of a single word, which entirely perverted its meaning, and made it a pliant and fertile text of misrepresentation of my political principles. The original, speaking of an Anglican, monarchical and aristocratical party, which had sprung up since he had left us, states their object to be "to draw over us the substance, as they had already done the *forms* of the British Government". Now the "forms" here meant, were the levees, birthdays, the pompous cavalcade to the State house on the meeting of Congress, the formal speech from the throne, the procession of Congress in a body to reecho the speech in an answer, &c., &c. But the translator here, by substituting *form*, in the singular number, for *forms* in the plural, made it mean the frame or organization of our government, or its form of legislative, executive and judiciary authorities, coordinate and independent; to which *form* it was to be inferred that I was an enemy. In this sense they always quoted it, and in this sense Mr. Pickering still quotes it and countenances the inference.—To MARTIN VAN BUREN. vii, 365. FORD ED., x, 308. (1824.)

5146. **MAZZEI (Philip), King of Poland and.**—The King of Poland sent an ancient Secretary here [Paris], * * * to look out for a correspondent, a mere letter writer for him. A happy hazard threw Mazzei in his way, * * * and he is appointed. He has no diplomatic character whatever, but is to receive eight thousand livres a year, as an intelligencer. I hope this employment may have some permanence. The danger is that he will overact his part.—To JAMES MADISON. ii, 444. FORD ED., v, 44. (P., 1788.)

5147. **MAZZEI (Philip), Worth of.**—An intimacy of forty years had proved to me his great worth, and a friendship which had begun in personal acquaintance, was maintained after separation, without abatement by a constant interchange of letters. His esteem, too, in this country was very general; his early and zealous cooperation in the establishment of our Independence having acquired for him here a great degree of favor.—To GIOVANNI CARMIGIANI. FORD ED., x, 49. (M., 1816.)

5148. ———— ————. Your letter brought me the first information of the death of my ancient friend Mazzei, which I learn with sincere regret. He had some peculiarities (and who of us has not?), but he was of solid worth; honest, able, zealous in sound principles, moral and political, constant in friendship, and punctual in all his undertakings. He was greatly esteemed in this country, and some one has inserted in our papers an account of his death, with a handsome and just eulogy of him, and a proposition to publish his life.—To THOMAS APPLETON. FORD ED., x, 46. (M., 1816.)

—— **MEASURES, Standard of.**—See STANDARD OF MEASURES.

—— **MECKLENBURG DECLARATION.** —See DECLARATION OF INDEPENDENCE.

5149. **MEDICINAL SPRINGS, France.** —I stayed at Aix [France] long enough to prove the inefficiency of the waters.—To JOHN JAY. ii, 138. FORD ED., iv, 376. (1787.)

5150. **MEDICINAL SPRINGS, Virginian.**—We [in Virginia] have taken too little pains to ascertain the properties of our different mineral waters, the cases in which they are respectively remedial, the proper process in their use, and other circumstances necessary to give us their full value.—To Miss Wright. vii, 408. (M., 1825.)

5151. MEDICINE, Molière and.—Medical science was demolished here [France] by the blows of Molière, and in a nation so addicted to ridicule, I question if ever it rises under the weight while his comedies continue to be acted. It furnished the most striking proof I have ever seen in my life of the injury which ridicule is capable of doing.—To Dr. James Currie. Ford ed., iv, 132. (P., 1786.)

5152. MEDICINE, Surgery vs.—While surgery is seated in the temple of the exact sciences, medicine has scarcely entered its threshold. Her theories have passed in such rapid succession as to prove the insufficiency of all, and their fatal errors are recorded in the necrology of man.—To Dr. Crawford. vi, 32. (M., 1812.)

5153. MEDICINE, Theories of.—Theories and systems of medicine have been in perpetual change from the days of the good Hippocrates to the days of the good Rush, but which of them is the true one? The present, to be sure, as long as it is the present, but to yield its place in turn to the next novelty, which is then to become the true system, and is to mark the vast advance of medicine since the days of Hippocrates. Our situation is certainly benefited by the discovery of some new and very valuable medicines; and substituting those for some of his with the treasure of facts, and of sound observations recorded by him (mixed to be sure with anilities of his day), we shall have nearly the present sum of the healing art.—To John Brazier. vii, 132. (P. F., 1819.)

5154. ――― ―――. In his theory of bleeding and mercury I was ever opposed to my friend Rush, whom I greatly loved. He did much harm, in the sincerest persuasion that he was preserving life and happiness to all around him.—To Thomas Cooper. vi, 390. (M., 1814.)

5155. MEDICINE, Views on Science of. —We know from what we see and feel, that the animal body is, in its organs and functions, subject to derangement, inducing pain, and tending to its destruction. In this disordered state, we observe nature providing for the reestablishment of order, by exciting some salutary evacuation of the morbific matter, or by some other operation which escapes our imperfect senses and researches. She brings on a crisis, by stools, vomiting, sweat, urine, expectoration, bleeding, &c., which, for the most part, ends in the restoration of healthy action. Experience has taught us, also, that there are certain substances, by which, applied to the living body, internally or externally, we can at will produce these small evacuations, and thus do, in a short time, what nature would do but slowly, and do effectually, what perhaps she would not have strength to accomplish. * * * So far, I bow to the utility of medicine. It goes to the well-defined forms of disease, and happily, to those the most frequent. But the disorders of the animal body, and the symptoms indicating them, are as various as the elements of which the body is composed. The combinations, too, of these symptoms are so infinitely diversified, that many associations of them appear too rarely to establish a definite disease: and to an unknown disease, there cannot be a known remedy. Here, then, the

judicious, the moral, the humane physician should stop. Having been so often a witness to the salutary efforts which nature makes to reestablish the disordered functions, he should rather trust to their action, than hazard the interruption of that, and a greater derangement of the system, by conjectural experiments on a machine so complicated and so unknown as the human body, and a subject so sacred as human life. Or, if the appearance of doing something be necessary to keep alive the hope and spirits of the patient, it should be of the most innocent character. One of the most successful physicians I have ever known, has assured me, that he used more bread pills, drops of colored water, and powders of hickory ashes, than of all other medicines put together. It was certainly a pious fraud. But the adventurous physician goes on, and substitutes presumption for knowledge. From the scanty field of what is known, he launches into the boundless region of what is unknown. He establishes for his guide some fanciful theory of corpuscular attraction, of chemical agency, of mechanical powers, of stimuli, of irritability accumulated or exhausted, of depletion by the lancet and repletion by mercury, or some other ingenious dream, which lets him into all nature's secrets at short hand. On the principle which he thus assumes, he forms his table of nosology, arrays his diseases into families, and extends his curative treatment, by analogy, to all the cases he has thus arbitrarily marshalled together. I have lived myself to see the disciples of Hoffman, Boerhaave, Stahl, Cullen, Brown, succeed one another like the shifting figures of a magic lantern, and their fancies, like the dresses of the annual doll-babies from Paris, becoming from their novelty, the vogue of the day, and yielding to the next novelty their ephemeral favor. The patient, treated on the fashionable theory, sometimes gets well in spite of the medicine. The medicine, therefore, restored him, and the young doctor receives new courage to proceed in his bold experiments on the lives of his fellow creatures. I believe we may safely affirm, that the inexperienced and presumptuous band of medical tyros let loose upon the world, destroys more of human life in one year, than all the Robinhoods, Cartouches, and Macheaths do in a century. It is in this part of medicine that I wish to see a reform, an abandonment of hypothesis for sober facts, the first degree of value set on clinical observation, and the lowest on visionary theories. I would wish the young practitioner, especially, to have deeply impressed on his mind, the real limits of his art, and that when the state of his patient gets beyond these, his office is to be a watchful, but quiet spectator of the operations of nature, giving them fair play by a well-regulated regimen, and by all the aid they can derive from the excitement of good spirits and hope in the patient. I have no doubt, that some diseases not yet understood may in time be transferred to the table of those known. But, were I a physician, I would rather leave the transfer to the slow hand of accident, than hasten it by guilty experiments on those who put their lives into my hands. The only sure foundations of medicine are, an intimate knowledge of the human body, and observation on the effects of medicinal substances on that. The anatomical and clinical schools, therefore, are those in which the young physician should be formed. If he enters with innocence that of the theory of medicine, it is scarcely possible he should come out untainted with error. His mind must be strong indeed, if, rising above juvenile credulity, it can maintain a wise infidelity against the authority of his instructors, and the bewitching delusions of their theories. You see that I estimate justly that portion of instruction which our medical students derive from your labors; and, associating with it one of the chairs which my old and able friend, Dr. Rush, so honorably fills, I consider them as the two fundamental pillars of the edifice. Indeed, I have such an opinion of the talents of the professors in the other branches which constitute the school of medicine with you, as to hope and believe, that it is from this side of the Atlantic, that Europe, which has taught us so many other things, will at length be led into sound principles in this branch of science, the most important of all others, being that to which we commit the care of health and life.

I dare say, that by this time, you are sufficiently sensible that old heads as well as young, may sometimes be charged with ignorance and presumption. The natural course of the human mind is certainly from credulity to skepticism; and this is perhaps the most favorable apology I can make for venturing so far out of my depth, and to one, too, to whom the strong as well as the weak points of this science are so familiar. But having stumbled on the subject in my way, I wished to give a confession of my faith to a friend; and the rather, as I had perhaps, at times, to him as well as others, expressed my skepticism in medicine, without defining its extent or foundation. At any rate, it has permitted me, for a moment, to abstract myself from the dry and dreary waste of politics, into which I have been impressed by the times on which I happened, and to indulge in the rich fields of nature, where alone I should have served as a volunteer, if left to my natural inclinations and partialities.—To DR. CASPAR WISTAR. v, 105. FORD ED., ix, 81. (W., June 1807.)

5156. MEDITERRANEAN TRADE, Reestablishment of.—It rests with Congress to decide between war, tribute, and ransom, as the means of reestablishing our Mediterranean commerce. If war, they will consider how far our own resources shall be called forth, and how far they will enable the Executive to engage in the forms of the Constitution, the coöperation of other powers. If tribute or ransom, it will rest with them to limit and provide the amount; and with the Executive, observing the same constitutional forms, to take arrangements for employing it to the best advantage.—REPORT ON MEDITERRANEAN TRADE. vii, 526. (1790.)

— **MEDIUM, Circulating.**—See MONEY.

5157. MEMORY, Decay of.—Of all the faculties of the human mind, that of memory is the first which suffers decay from age. * * * It was my earliest monition to retire from public business.—To MR. LATROBE. vi, 74. (M., 1812.)

5158. MERCER (John Francis), Politics of.—Our old friend, Mercer, broke off from us some time ago; at first professing to disdain joining the federalists, yet, from the habit of voting together, becoming soon identified with them. Without carrying over with him one single person, he is now in a state of as perfect obscurity as if his name had never been known. Mr. J. Randolph is in the same track, and will end in the same way.—To JAMES MONROE. v, 9. FORD ED., viii, 447. (W., May 1806.)

5159. MERCHANTS, Anglomaniac.—I join in your reprobation of our merchants, priests and lawyers, for their adherence to

England and monarchy, in preference to their own country and its Constitution. But merchants have no country. The mere spot they stand on does not constitute so strong an attachment as that from which they draw their gains.—To HORATIO G. SPAFFORD. vi, 334. (M., 1814.)

5160. MERCHANTS, Education of.—For the merchant I should not say that the [classical] Languages are a necessary. Ethics, mathematics, geography, political economy, history, seem to constitute the immediate foundations of his calling.—To JOHN BRAZIER. vii, 133. (P.F., 1819.)

5161. MERCHANTS, Freedom of Commerce and.—The merchants will manage commerce the better, the more they are left free to manage for themselves.—To GIDEON GRANGER. iv, 331. FORD ED., vii, 452. (M., 1800.)

5162. MERCHANTS, Natural Republicans.—A merchant is naturally a republican, and can be otherwise only from a vitiated state of things.—To ALBERT GALLATIN. FORD ED., viii, 252. (1803.)

5163. MERCHANTS, Patriotism of.—Merchants are the least virtuous citizens and possess the least of the *amor patriæ*.—To M. DE MEUNIER. ix, 288. FORD ED., iv, 143. (P., 1786.)

5164. MERCHANTS, Peace and.—Some of our merchants have been milking the cow; yet the great mass of them have become deranged. They are daily falling down by bankruptcies, and on the whole, the condition of our commerce is far less firm and really prosperous, than it would have been by the regular operations and steady advances which a state of peace would have occasioned. Were a war to take place, and throw our agriculture into equal convulsions with our commerce, our business would be done at both ends.—To HORATIO GATES. iv, 213. FORD ED., vii, 204. (Pa., 1798.)

5165. MERCHANTS, Protection of.—Where a nation refuses permission to our merchants and factors to reside within certain parts of their dominions, we may, if it should be thought expedient, refuse residence to theirs in any and every part of ours, or modify their transactions.—FOREIGN COMMERCE REPORT. vii, 649. FORD ED., vi, 482. (Dec. 1793.)

5166. MERCHANTS, Selfish.—Ministers and merchants love nobody.—To JOHN LANGDON. i, 429. (P., 1785.)

5167. ———. The merchants here [France] are endeavoring to exclude us from their islands. [West Indies].—To JOHN LANGDON. i, 429. (P., 1785.)

5168. MERCIER (James), Rescued from slavery.—In Mr. Barclay's letter (from Morocco) is this paragraph: "There is a young man now under my care who has been a slave some time with the Arabs in the desert." His name is James Mercier, born at the town of

Suffolk, Nansemond County, Virginia. The King sent him after the first audience, and I shall take him to Spain. On Mr. Barclay's return to Spain, he shall find there a letter from me to forward this young man to his own country, for the expenses of which I will make myself responsible.—To GOVERNOR HENRY. i, 601. (P., 1786.)

5169. MERIT, Relief of distressed.—I do not know that I can proffer you any reward for this favor [to my friend], other than the sublime pleasure of relieving distressed merit, a pleasure which can be properly felt by the virtuous alone.—To THOMAS ADAMS. FORD ED., i, 382. (1770.)

5170. MERRY (A.), Character.—With respect to Merry [British Minister] he appears so reasonable and good a man, that I should be sorry to lose him as long as there remains a possibility of reclaiming him to the exercise of his own dispositions. If his wife perseveres, she must eat her soup at home, and we shall endeavor to draw him into society as if she did not exist. It is unfortunate that the good understanding of nations should hang on the caprice of an individual, who ostensibly has nothing to do with them.—To JAMES MONROE. FORD ED., viii, 292. (W., Jan. 1804.)

5171. MERRY (A.), Social claims of.—Mr. Merry is with us, and we believe him to be personally as desirable a character as could have been sent us. But he is unluckily associated with one of an opposite in every point. She has already disturbed our harmony extremely. He began by claiming the first visit from the national ministers. He corrected himself in this. But a pretension to take precedence at dinners, &c., over all others is persevered in. We have told him that the principle of society, as well as of government, with us, is the equality of the individuals composing it; that no man here would come to a dinner, where he was to be marked with inferiority to any other; that we might as well attempt to force our principle of equality at St. James's as he his principle of precedence here. I had been in the habit, when I invited female company (having no lady in my family) to ask one of the ladies of the four Secretaries to come and take care of my company; and as she was to do the honors of the table I handed her to dinner myself. That Mr. Merry might not construe this as giving them a precedence over Mrs. Merry, I have discontinued it. And here, as well as in private houses, the pele-mele practice is adhered to. They have got Yrujo to take a zealous part in the question of precedence. It has excited generally emotions of great contempt and indignation (in which the members of the Legislature participate sensibly), that the agents of foreign nations should assume to dictate to us what shall be the laws of our society. The consequence will be that Mr. and Mrs. Merry will put themselves into Coventry, and that he will lose the best half of his usefulness to his nation, that derived from a perfectly familiar and private intercourse with the Secretaries and myself. The latter, be assured, is a virago, and in the short course of a few weeks has established a degree of dislike among all classes which one would have thought impossible in so short a time. Thornton has entered into their ideas. At this we wonder, because he is a plain man, a sensible one, and too candid to be suspected of wishing to bring on their recall, and his own substitution. To counterwork their misrepresentations, it would be as well their government should understand as much of these things as can be communicated with decency, that they may know the spirit in which their letters are written.—To JAMES MONROE. FORD ED., viii, 290. (W., Jan. 1804.)

— MESMERISM.—See FRANKLIN (BENJAMIN).

— MESSAGES TO CONGRESS.—See CONGRESS.

5172. METAPHYSICS, Views on.—The relations between the physical and moral faculties of man have ever been a subject of great interest to the inquisitive mind * * *. That thought may be a faculty of our material organization has been believed in the gross; and though the *modus operandi* of nature, in this, as in most other cases, can never be developed and demonstrated to beings limited as we are, yet I feel confident you will have conducted us as far on the road as we can go, and have lodged us within reconnoitering distance of the citadel itself.—To M. CABANIS. iv, 496. (W., 1803.)

5173. ———. The science of the human mind is curious, but is one on which I have not indulged myself in much speculation. The times in which I have lived, and the scenes in which I have been engaged, have required me to keep the mind too much in action to have leisure to study minutely its laws of action.—To EZRA STILES. vii, 127. (M., 1819.)

5174. METEORIC STONES, Origin.—[With respect] to the stone in your possession, supposed meteoric, its descent from the atmosphere presents so much difficulty as to require careful examination. But I do not know that the most effectual examination could be made by the members of the national Legislature, to whom you have thought of exhibiting it. * * * I should think that an inquiry by some of our scientific societies, * * * would be likely to be directed * * * with such knowledge of the subject, as would inspire a general confidence. We certainly are not to deny whatever we cannot account for. A thousand phenomena present themselves daily which we cannot explain, but where facts are suggested, bearing no analogy with the laws of nature as yet known to us, their verity needs proofs proportioned to their difficulty. A cautious mind will weigh well the opposition of the phenomenon to everything hitherto observed, the strength of the testimony by which it is supported, and the errors and misconceptions to which even our senses are liable. It may be very difficult to explain how the stone you possess came into the position in which it was found, but is it easier to explain how it got into the clouds from whence it is supposed to have fallen? The actual fact, however, is the thing to be established, and this I hope will be done by those whose situations and qualifications enable them to do it.—To DANIEL SALMON. v, 245. (W., 1808.)

5175. METEOROLOGY, Slow progress in.—Of all the departments of science no one seems to have been less advanced for the last hundred years than that of meteorology. The new chemistry, indeed, has given us a new principle of the generation of rain, by proving water to be a composition of different gases, and has aided our theory of meteoric lights. Electricy stands where Dr. Franklin's early discoveries placed it, except with its new modification of galvanism. But the phenomena of snow, hail, halo, aurora borealis, haze, looming,

&c., are as yet very imperfectly understood. I am myself an empiric in natural philosophy, suffering my faith to go no further than my facts. I am pleased, however, to see the efforts of hypothetical speculation, because by the collisions of different hypotheses, truth may be elicited and science advanced in the end. This skeptical disposition does not permit me to say whether your hypothesis for looming and floating volumes of warm air occasionally perceived, may or may not be confirmed by future observations. More facts are yet wanting to furnish a solution on which we may rest with confidence. I even doubt as yet whether the looming at sea and on land is governed by the same laws.—To GEORGE F. HOPKINS. vii, 259. (M., 1822.) See CLIMATE.

— **METROPOTAMIA, Proposed State of.**—See WESTERN TERRITORY.

5176. MEXICO, Interesting.—Mexico is one of the most interesting countries of ur hemisphere, and merits every attention.—To DR. BARTON. v, 470. (M., 1809.)

— **MICHIGANIA, Proposed State of.**— See WESTERN TERRITORY.

5177. MILITIA, Bravery.—Ill armed and untried militia, who never before saw the face of an enemy, have, at times during the course of this war [of the Revolution] given occasions of exultation to our enemies, but they afforded us, while at Warwick, a little satisfaction in the same way. Six or eight hundred of their picked men of light infantry, with General Arnold at their head, having crossed the [James] river from Warwick, fled from a patrol of sixteen horse, every man into his boat as he could, some pushing North, some South as their fears drove them.—To GENERAL WASHINGTON. i, 306. FORD ED., iii, 33. (R., 1781.)

5178. ——— ———. Our militia are heroes when they have heroes to lead them on.—To W. H. CRAWFORD. vi, 420. FORD ED., ix, 504. (M., 1815.)

5179. MILITIA, Classification.—You will consider whether it would not be expedient, for a state of peace as well as of war, so to organize or class the militia, as would enable us, on any sudden emergency, to call for the services of the younger portions, unencumbered with the old and those having families. Upwards of three hundred thousand able bodied men, between the ages of eighteen and twenty-six years, which the last census shows we may now count within our limits, will furnish a competent number for offence or defence in any point where they may be wanted, and give time for raising regular forces after the necessity of them shall become certain; and the reducing to the early period of life all its active service, cannot but be desirable to our younger citizens, of the present as well as future times, inasmuch as it engages to them in more advanced age a quiet and undisturbed repose in the bosom of their families. I cannot, then, but earnestly recommend to your early consideration the expediency of so modifying our militia system as, by a separation of the more active part from that which is less so, we

may draw from it, when necessary, an efficient corps, fit for real and active service, and to be called to it in regular rotation.— FIFTH ANNUAL MESSAGE. viii, 49. FORD ED., viii, 392. (Dec. 1805.)

5180. ——— ———. A militia of young men will hold on until regulars can be raised, and will be the nursery which will furnish them. —To WILLIAM A. BURWELL. FORD ED., viii, 416. (W., 1806.)

5181. ——— ———. A militia can never be used for distant service on any other plan; and Bonaparte will conquer the world, if they do not learn his secret of composing armies of young men only, whose enthusiasm and health enable them to surmount all obstacles. —To MR. BIDWELL. v, 16. (W., 1806.)

5182. ——— ———. Convinced that a militia of all ages promiscuously are entirely useless for distant service, and that we never shall be safe until we have a selected corps for a year's distant service at least, the classification of our militia is now the most essential thing the United States have to do. Whether, on Bonaparte's plan of making a class for every year between certain periods, or that recommended in my message, I do not know, but I rather incline to his. The idea is not new, as you may remember we adopted it once in Virginia during the Revolution, but abandoned it too soon. It is the real secret of Bonaparte's success.—To JAMES MADISON. v, 76. FORD ED., ix, 49. (M., May 1807.)

5183. ——— ———. The session before the last I proposed to the Legislature the classification of the militia, so that those in the prime of life only, and unburthened with families, should ever be called into distant service; and that every man should receive a stand of arms the first year he entered the militia. * * * It will prevail in time.— To MR. COXE. v, 58. (W., 1807.)

5184. ——— ———. Against great land armies we cannot attempt defence but by equal armies. For these we must depend on a classified militia, which will give us the service of the class from twenty to twenty-six, in the nature of conscripts, comprising a body of about 250,000, to be specially trained. This measure, attempted at a former session, was pressed at the last, and might, I think, have been carried by a small majority. But considering that great innovations should not be forced on a slender majority, and seeing that the general opinion is sensibly rallying to it, it was thought better to let it lie over to the next session, when, I trust, it will be passed.—To GENERAL ARMSTRONG. v, 281. FORD ED., ix, 194. (W., May 1808.)

5185. ——— ———. In the beginning of our government we were willing to introduce the least coercion possible on the will of the citizen. Hence a system of military duty was established too indulgent to his indolence. This [war] is the first opportunity we have had of trying it, and it has completely failed; an issue foreseen by many, and for which remedies have been proposed. That of classing the militia according to age, and allotting each age to the particular kind of service to which it was competent, was proposed to Congress in 1805, and subsequently; and, on the last trial, was lost, I believe, by a single vote. Had it prevailed, what has now happened would not have happened. Instead of burning our Capitol, we should have possessed theirs in Montreal and Quebec. We must now adopt it, and all will be safe.—To THOMAS COOPER. vi, 379. (M., 1814.)

5186. MILITIA, Comfort of.—The soldiers themselves will thank you, when separated from domestic accommodation. they find themselves, through your attention to their comfort, provided with conveniences which will administer to their first wants.—LETTER TO COUNTY LIEUTENANTS. FORD ED., ii, 428. (R., 1781.)

5187. MILITIA, Commissions in.—The Executive, apprehending they have no authority to grant brevet commissions, refer to the General Assembly the expedience of authorizing them to give to this gentleman* a Lieutenant Colonel's commission by way of brevet.—To SPEAKER OF HOUSE OF DELEGATES. FORD ED., ii, 266. (Wg., 1779.)

5188. MILITIA, Compulsory service in.—We must train and classify the whole of our male citizens, and make military instruction a regular part of collegiate education. We can never be safe till this is done.—To JAMES MONROE. vi, 131. (M., 1813.)

5189. ———. I think the truth must now be obvious that our people are too happy at home to enter into regular service, and that we cannot be defended but by making every citizen a soldier, as the Greeks and Romans who had no standing armies; and that in doing this all must be marshalled, classed by their ages, and every service ascribed to its competent class.—To J. W. EPPES. FORD ED., ix, 484. (M., 1814.)

5190. MILITIA, Crimes and punishments.—Any officer or soldier, guilty of mutiny, desertion, disobedience of command, absence from duty or quarters, neglect of guard, or cowardice, shall be punished at the discretion of a courtmartial by degrading, cashiering, drumming out of the army, whipping not exceeding twenty lashes, fine not exceeding two months, or imprisonment not exceeding one month.—INVASION BILL. FORD ED., ii, 127. (1777.)

5191. MILITIA, Defects in organization.—Congress have had too much experience of the radical defects and inconveniences of militia service to need my enumerating them.—To THE PRESIDENT OF CONGRESS. FORD ED., ii, 277. (Wg., 1779.)

5192. MILITIA, Distant service.—Militia do well for hasty enterprises, but cannot

be relied on for lengthy service, and out of their own country.—To NORTH CAROLINA ASSEMBLY. FORD ED., ii, 480. (R., 1781.)

5193. ———. We hope it will be the last time we shall have occasion to require our militia to go out of their own country, as we think it most advisable to put that distant, disagreeable service on our regulars, * * * and to employ our militia on service in our own country.—To COLONEL ABRAHAM PENN. FORD ED., iii, 29. (R., 1781.)

5194. ———. I am sensible it is much more practicable to carry on a war with militia within our own country [State] than out of it.—To MAJOR GENERAL GREENE. FORD ED., iii, 2. (R., 1781.)

5195. ———. The law of a former session of Congress, for keeping a body of 100,000 militia in readiness for service at a moment's warning, is still in force. * * * When called into action, it will not be for a lounging, but for an active, and perhaps distant, service.*—To THE GOVERNOR OF OHIO. v, 51. FORD ED., ix, 34. (W., March 1807.)

5196. ———. If the marching of the militia into an enemy's country be once ceded as unconstitutional (which I hope it never will be), then will [the British] force [in Canada], as now strengthened, bid us permanent defiance.—To JAMES MONROE. vi, 131. (M., June 1813.)

5197. ———. Abolish, by a declaratory law, the doubts which abstract scruples in some, and cowardice and treachery in others, have conjured up about passing imaginary lines, and limiting, at the same time, the services of the militia to the *contiguous* provinces of the enemy.—To PRESIDENT MADISON. vi, 391. FORD ED., ix, 489. (M., Oct. 1814.)

— MILITIA, Draft law.—See DRAFT.

5198. MILITIA, Employment of.—I must desire that, so far as the agency of the militia be employed, it may be with the utmost discretion, and with no act of force beyond what shall be necessary to maintain obedience to the laws, using neither deeds nor words unnecessarily offensive.—To CHARLES SIMMS. v, 418. (W., Jan. 1809.)

5199. MILITIA, Enrolment.—For making provision against invasions and insurrections, and laying the burthen equally upon all * * * the commanding officer of every county * * * shall enroll under some captain such persons * * * as ought to make a part of the militia, who together with those before enrolled, and not yet formed into tenths * * * shall by such captain * * * be divided into equal parts. as nearly as may be. each part to be distinguished by fair and equal lot by numbers from one to ten, and when so distinguished, to be added to and make part of the militia of the county. Where any person * * * shall not attend,

* M. Le Mair, a Frenchman, who had purchased arms in Europe for Virginia and requested a brevet-commission as a reward for his services. Jefferson was then Governor of Virginia.—EDITOR.

* The Governors of Kentucky, Tennessee and Mississippi Territory were also urged to furnish volunteers.—EDITOR.

or shall refuse to draw for himself, the captain shall cause his lot to be drawn for him.—INVASION BILL. FORD ED., ii, 123. (1777.)

5200. MILITIA, Equalization of duty.—As militia duty becomes heavy, it becomes our duty to divide it equally.—To GENERAL NELSON. FORD ED., ii. 464. (R., 1781.)

5201. —— ——. Where any county shall have sent but half the quota called for, they have performed but half their tour, and ought to be called on again. Where any county has furnished their full complement, they have performed their full tour, and it would be unjust to call on them again till we have gone through the counties. Militia becoming burthensome, it is our duty to divide it as equally as we can.—To COLONEL JAMES INNES. FORD ED., ii, 465. (R., 1781.)

5202. —— ——. The spirit of disobedience * * * in your county must be subdued. Laws made by common consent must not be trampled on by individuals. It is very much [to] the [public] good to force the unworthy into their due share of contributions to the public support, otherwise the burthen on [the worthy] will become oppressive indeed.—To COLONEL VANMETER. FORD ED., iii, 24. (R., 1781.)

5203. MILITIA, Expensive.—Whether it be practicable to raise and maintain a sufficient number of regulars to carry on the war, is a question. That it would be burthensome is undoubted, yet perhaps it is as certain that no possible mode of carrying it on can be so expensive to the public, so distressing and disgusting to individuals, as the militia.—To THE HOUSE OF DELEGATES. FORD ED., ii, 474. (R., 1781.)

5204. MILITIA, Improving.—We should at every session [of Congress] continue to amend the defects * * * in the laws for regulating the militia, until they are sufficiently perfect. Nor should we now or at any time separate, until we can say we have done everything for the militia which we could do were an enemy at our door.—FIRST ANNUAL MESSAGE. viii, 12. FORD ED., viii, 121. (Dec. 1801.)

5205. —— ——. Uncertain as we must ever be of the particular point in our circumference where an enemy may choose to invade us, the only force which can be ready at every point and competent to oppose them, is the body of neighboring citizens as formed into a militia. On these, collected from the parts most convenient, in numbers proportioned to the invading foe, it is best to rely, not only to meet the first attack, but if it threatens to be permanent, to maintain the defence until regulars may be engaged to relieve them.—FIRST ANNUAL MESSAGE. viii, 11. FORD ED., viii, 121. (Dec. 1801.)

5206. —— ——. Considering that our regular troops are employed for local purposes, and that the militia is our general reliance for great and sudden emergencies, you will doubtless think this institution worthy of a review, and give it those improvements of which you find it susceptible.—SECOND ANNUAL MESSAGE. viii, 19. FORD ED., viii, 185. (Dec. 1802.)

5207. —— ——. In compliance with a request of the House of Representatives, as well as with a sense of what is necessary, I take the liberty of urging on you the importance and indispensable necessity of vigorous exertions, on the part of the State governments, to carry into effect the militia system adopted by the national Legislature, agreeable to the powers reserved to the States respectively, by the Constitution of the United States, and in a manner the best calculated to ensure such a degree of military discipline, and knowledge of tactics, as will under the auspices of a benign Providence, render the militia a sure and permanent bulwark of national defence.—To ——. iv, 469. (W., Feb. 1803.)

5208. —— ——. It is incumbent on us at every meeting, to revise the condition of the militia, and to ask ourselves if it is prepared to repel a powerful enemy at every point of our territories exposed to invasion. Some of the States have paid a laudable attention to this object; but every degree of neglect is to be found among others. Congress alone have power to produce a uniform state of preparation in this great organ of defence; the interests which they so deeply feel in their own and their country's security will present this as among the most important objects of their deliberation.—ANNUAL MESSAGE. viii, 108. FORD ED., ix, 223. (1808.)

5209. MILITIA, Maintenance of.—[The maintenance of] a well-disciplined militia, our best reliance in peace and for the first moments of war, till regulars may relieve them, I deem [one of the] essential principles of our government and, consequently [one] which ought to shape its administration.—FIRST INAUGURAL ADDRESS. viii, 4. FORD ED., viii, 4. (1803.)

5210. MILITIA, Menial labor.—A militia of freemen cannot easily be induced to labor in works of that kind [building forts].—To THE HOUSE OF DELEGATES. FORD ED., iii, 36. (R., 1781.)

5211. MILITIA, Mutiny.—The precedent of a * * * mutiny would be so mischievous as to induce us to believe that an accommodation to their present temper [would be] most prudent.—To MAJOR-GENERAL STEUBEN. FORD ED., ii. 466. (R., Feb. 1781.)

5212. —— ——. The best way, perhaps, is not to go against the mutineers [militiamen] when embodied, which would bring on, perhaps, an open rebellion, or bloodshed most certainly; but, when they shall have dispersed, to go and take them out of their beds, singly and without noise; or, if they be not found, the first time, to go again and again, so that they may never be able to remain in quiet at home. This is what I must recommend to you and, therefore, furnish the bearers with the commissions as you desire.—To COLONEL VANMETER. FORD ED., iii, 25. (R., 1781.)

5213. MILITIA, Naval.—I send you a copy of the marine regulations of France. There are things in it which may become interesting to us; particularly, what relates to the establishment of a marine militia, and their classification.—To JOHN JAY. ii, 91. (P., 1787.)

5214. —— ——. I wish to consult you on a plan of a regular naval militia, to be composed of all our sea-faring citizens, to enable us to man a fleet speedily by supplying voluntary enlistments by calls on that militia.—To ROBERT SMITH. FORD ED., viii, 381. (W., Oct. 1805.)

5215. —— ——. I think it will be necessary to erect our sea-faring men into a naval militia, and subject them to tours of duty in whatever port they may be.—To GENERAL SMITH. v, 147. (W., July 1807.)

5216. —— ——. It is * * * material that the seaport towns should have artillery-militia duly trained * * * .—To W. H. CABELL. v, 191. (M., 1807.)

5217. —— ——. I think our *naval militia* plan, both as to name and structure, better for us than the English plan of Sea-fencibles. —To ROBERT SMITH. v, 234. (1808.)

5218. MILITIA, Officers.—Any officer resigning his commission on being called into duty by the Governor, or his commanding officer, shall be ordered into the ranks, and shall moreover suffer punishment as for disobedience of command.—INVASION BILL. FORD ED., ii, 125. (1777.)

5219. —— ——. Much will depend on the proper choice of officers.—INVASION CIRCULAR-LETTER. FORD ED., ii, 398. (R., 1781.)

5220. —— ——. The good of the service requires that the field officers at least be experienced in the service. For this reason, these will be provided for at the rendezvous. I beg that this may not be considered by the militia field officers [as arising] from want of respect to them. We know and confide in their zeal; but it cannot be disreputable to them to be less knowing in the art of war than those who have greater experience in it; and being less knowing. I am quite sure the spirit of patriotism, with which they are animated, will lead them to wish that measure to be adopted which will most promote the public safety, however it may tend to keep them from the post in which they would wish to appear in defence of their country.*—To COUNTY LIEUTENANTS. FORD ED., ii, 398. (R., 1781.)

5221. —— ——. I enclose you a charge against * * * [three militia officers], as having become members of an organized company, calling themselves the Tar Com-

* From a letter calling out the militia of several counties of Virginia when the State was invaded by the British forces.—EDITOR.

pany, avowing their object to be the tarring and feathering citizens of some description. Although in some cases the animadversions of the law may be properly relied on to prevent what is unlawful, yet with those clothed with authority from the Executive, and being a part of the Executive, other preventives are expedient. These officers should be warned that the Executive cannot tamely look on and see its officers threaten to become the violators instead of the protectors of the rights of our citizens.—To HENRY DEARBORN. v, 383. (1808.)

5222. MILITIA, Payment of Ohio.—If we suffer the question of paying the [Ohio] militia embodied to be thrown on their Legislature, it will excite acrimonious debate in that body, and they will spread the same dissatisfaction among their constituents, and finally it will be forced back on us through Congress. Would it not, therefore, be better to say to Mr. Kirker, that the General Government is fully aware that emergencies which appertain to them will sometimes arise so suddenly as not to give time for consulting them, before the State must get into action; that the expenses in such cases, incurred on reasonable grounds, will be met by the General Government; and that in the present case [Burr's Conspiracy], although it appears there was no real ground for embodying the militia, and that more certain measures for ascertaining the truth should have been taken before embodying them, yet an unwillingness to damp the public spirit of our countrymen, and the justice due to the individuals who came forward in defence of their country, and could not know the grounds on which they were called, have determined us to consider the call as justifiable, and to defray the expenses.—To GENERAL DEARBORN. v, 206. FORD ED., ix, 22. (W., Oct. 1807.)

5223. MILITIA, Public property and. —Be pleased to give the same notice to the militia as formerly, that no man will be ever discharged till he shall have returned whatever public arms or accoutrements he shall have received.—To BRIGADIER-GENERAL NELSON. FORD ED., ii, 396. (R., 1781.)

5224. MILITIA, Regular army and.—I am for relying for internal defence on our militia solely, till actual invasion.—To ELBRIDGE GERRY. iv, 268. FORD ED., vii, 328. (Pa., 1799.)

5225. —— ——. None but an armed nation can dispense with a standing army. To keep ours armed and disciplined, is therefore at all times important.—To ——. iv, 469. (W., 1803.)

5226. MILITIA, Security in.—For a people who are free. and who mean to remain so, a well organized and armed militia is their best security.—EIGHTH ANNUAL MESSAGE. viii, 108. FORD ED., ix, 223. (Nov. 1808.)

5227. MILITIA, Slaves and.—Slaves are by the law excluded from the militia, and wisely as to that part of a soldier's duty which consists in exercise of arms. But whether male slaves might not under proper regulations be subjected to the routine of duty as pioneers, and to other military labors, can only be determined by the wisdom of the Legislature.—To THE VA. HOUSE OF DELEGATES. FORD ED., iii, 36. (R., 1781.)

5228. MILITIA, Standing fire.—The scene of military operations has been hitherto so distant from these States that their militia are strangers to the actual presence of danger. Habit alone will enable them to view this with familiarity, to face it without dismay; a habit which must be purchased by calamity, but cannot be purchased too dear.—To THE PRESIDENT OF CONGRESS. FORD ED., ii, 335. (R., 1780.)

5229. MILITIA, Subsistence of.—The present [British] invasion [of Virginia] having rendered it necessary to call into the field a large body of militia, the providing them with subsistence, and the means of transportation becomes an arduous task in the unorganized state of our military system. To effect this we are obliged to vest the heads of the Commissary's and Quartermaster's departments with such powers as, if abused, will be most afflicting to the people. Major General Steuben, taught by experience on similar occasions, has pressed on us the necessity of calling to the superintendence of these officers some gentleman of distinguished character and abilities, who, while he prescribes to them such rules as will effectually produce the object of their appointment, will yet stand between them and the people as a guard from oppression. * * * Under the exigency we have taken the liberty of casting our eyes on yourself as most likely to fulfill our wishes and, therefore, solicit your undertaking this charge.—To COLONEL RICHARD MEADE. FORD ED., ii, 400. (R., 1781.)

5230. MILITIA, Washington on use of.—In conversation with the President, and speaking about General [Nathaniel] Greene, he said that he and General Greene had always differed in opinion about the manner of using militia. Greene always placed them in his front; himself was of opinion they should always be used as a reserve to improve any advantage, for which purpose they were the *finest fellows* in the world. He said he was on the ground of the battle of Guilford, with a person who was in the action, and who explained the whole of it to him. That General Greene's front was behind a fence at the edge of a large field, through which the enemy were obliged to pass to get at them; and that in their passage through this, they must have been torn all to pieces, if troops had been posted there who would have stood their ground; and that the retreat from that position was through a thicket, perfectly secure. Instead of this, he posted the North Carolina militia there, who only gave one fire and fell back, so that the whole benefit of their position was lost. He thinks that the regulars, with their field pieces,

would have hardly let a single man get through that field.—THE ANAS. ix, 146. FORD ED., i, 232. (1793.) See ARMY and WAR.

5231. MILITIA FOR LOUISIANA.—The spirit of this country is totally adverse to a large military force. I have tried for two sessions to prevail on the Legislature to let me plant thirty thousand well chosen volunteers on donation lands on the west side of the Mississippi, as a militia always at hand for the defence of New Orleans; but I have not yet succeeded.—To MR. CHANDLER PRICE. v, 47. (W., 1807.)

5232. ——— ———. The defence of Orleans against a land army can never be provided for, according to the principles of the Constitution, till we can get a sufficient militia there—To ALBERT GALLATIN. v, 215. FORD ED., ix, 167. (Nov. 1807.)

5233. ——— ———. A measure has now twice failed, which I have warmly urged, the immediate settlement by donation lands, of such a body of militia in the Territories of Orleans and Mississippi, as will be adequate to the defence of New Orleans.—To GENERAL ARMSTRONG. v, 281. (W., May 1808.)

5234. MIND, Body and.—If this period [youth] be suffered to pass in idleness, the mind becomes lethargic and impotent, as would the body it inhabits if unexercised during the same time. The sympathy between body and mind during their rise, progress and decline, is too strict and obvious to endanger our being misled while we reason from the one to the other.—NOTES ON VIRGINIA. viii, 390. FORD ED., iii, 253. (1782.)

5235. MIND, Freedom of.—Almighty God hath created the mind free, and manifested His supreme will that free it shall remain by making it altogether insusceptible of restraint.—STATUTE OF RELIGIOUS FREEDOM. viii, 454. FORD ED., ii, 227. (1779.)

5236. MIND, Influencing.—All attempts to influence [the mind] by temporal punishments, or burthens, or by civil incapacitations, tend only to beget habits of hypocrisy and meanness, and are a departure from the plan of the Holy Author of our religion, who being Lord both of body and mind, yet choose not to propagate it by coercions on either, as was in his Almighty power to do, but to exalt it by its influence on reason alone.—STATUTE OF RELIGIOUS FREEDOM. viii, 454. FORD ED., ii, 238. (1779.)

5237. MIND, Qualities of.—I estimate the qualities of the mind; 1, good humor; 2, integrity; 3, industry; 4, science. The preference of the first to the second quality may not at first be acquiesced in; but certainly we had all rather associate with a good-humored, light-principled man, than with an ill-tempered rigorist in morality.—To DR. BENJAMIN RUSH. v, 225. (W., 1808.)

5238. MINERALOGISTS IN AMERICA.—I have never known in the United

States but one eminent mineralogist, who could have been engaged on hire. This was a Mr. Goudon from France, who came over to Philadelphia six or seven years ago.—To GOVERNOR NICHOLAS. vi, 588. (P.F., 1816.)

5239. MINERALOGY, Utility.—To learn * * * the ordinary arrangement of the different strata of minerals in the earth, to know from their habitual collocations and proximities, where we find one mineral; whether another, for which we are seeking, may be expected to be in its neighborhood, is useful. But the dreams about the modes of creation, enquiries whether our globe has been formed by the agency of fire or water, how many millions of years it has cost Vulcan or Neptune to produce what the fiat of the Creator would effect by a single act of will, is too idle to be worth a single hour of any man's life.—To DR. JOHN P. EMMETT. vii, 443. (M., 1826.)

5240. MINES, Federal Government and.—I am afraid we know too little as yet of the lead mines to establish a permanent system. I verily believe that of leasing will be far the best for the United States. But it will take time to find out what rent may be reserved, so as to enable the lessee to compete with those who work mines in their own right, and yet have an encouraging profit for themselves. Having on the spot two such men as Lewis and Bates, in whose integrity and prudence unlimited confidence may be placed, would it not be best to confide to them the whole business of leasing and regulating the management of our interests, recommending to them short leases, at first, till themselves shall become thoroughly acquainted with the subject, and shall be able to reduce the management to a system, which the government may then approve and adhere to? I think one article of it should be that the rent shall be paid in metal, not in mineral, so that we may have nothing to do with works which will always be mismanaged, and reduce our concern to a simple rent. We shall lose more by ill-managed smelting works than the digging the ore is worth. Then, it would be better that our ore remained in the earth than in a storehouse, and consequently we give nine-tenths of the ore for nothing. These thoughts are merely for your consideration.—To ALBERT GALLATIN. v, 210. (Nov. 1807.)

5241. —— ——. It is not merely a question about the terms we have to consider, but the expediency of working them.—To ALBERT GALLATIN. v, 290. (M., 1808.)

5242. —— ——. I received your favor covering an offer * * * of an iron mine to the public, and I thank you for * * * making the communication * * * . But having always observed that public works are much less advantageously managed than they are by private hands, I have thought it better for the public to go to market for whatever it wants which is to be found there; for there competition brings it down to the minimum of value. I have no doubt we can buy brass cannon at market cheaper than we could make iron ones. I think it material, too, not to abstract the high executive officers from those functions which nobody else is charged to carry on, and to employ them in superintending works which are going on abundantly in private hands. Our predecessors went on different principles; they bought iron mines, and sought for copper ones. We own a mine at Harper's Ferry of the finest iron ever put into a cannon, which we are afraid to attempt to work. We have rented it

heretofore, but it is now without a tenant.—To MR. BIBB. v, 326. (M., July 1808.)

5243. MINES, Silver.—I enclose for your information the account of a silver mine to fill your treasury.—To ALBERT GALLATIN. v, 245. (1808.)

5244. —— ——. With respect to the silver mine on the Platte, 1700 miles from St. Louis, I will observe that in the present state of things between us and Spain, we could not propose to make an establishment at that distance from all support. It is interesting, however, that the knowledge of its position should be preserved, which can be done either by confiding it to the government, who will certainly never make use of it without an honorable compensation for the discovery to yourself or your representatives, or by placing it wherever you think safest.—To ANTHONY G. BETTAY. v, 246. (W., 1808.)

5245. MINES, Virginia lead.—We take the liberty of recommending the lead mines to you as an object of vast importance. We think it impossible they can be worked to too great an extent. Considered as, perhaps, the sole means of supporting the American cause, they are inestimable. As an article of commerce to our Colony, too, they will be valuable; and even the wagonage, if done either by the Colony or individuals belonging to it, will carry to it no trifling sum of money.*—To GOVERNOR PATRICK HENRY. FORD ED., ii, 67. (July 1776.)

5246. MINISTERS (Foreign), Appointment and grade.—The Constitution having declared that the President shall *nominate* and, by and with the advice and consent of the Senate, shall *appoint*, ambassadors, other public ministers, and consuls, the President desired my opinion whether the Senate has a right to negative the *grade* he may think it expedient to use in a foreign mission as well as the *person* to be appointed. I think the Senate has no right to negative the *grade*. The Constitution has divided the powers of government into three branches, Legislative, Executive and Judiciary, lodging each with a distinct magistracy. The Legislative it has given completely to the Senate and House of Representatives. It has declared that the Executive powers shall be vested in the President, submitting only special articles of it to a negative by the Senate, and it has vested the Judiciary power in the courts of justice, with certain exceptions also in favor of the Senate. The transaction of business with foreign nations is Executive altogether. It belongs, then, to the head of that department, except as to such portions of it as are specially submitted to the Senate. Exceptions are to be construed strictly. The Constitution itself indeed has taken care to circumscribe this one within very strict limits: for it gives the *nomination* of the foreign agents to the President, the *appointments* to him and the Senate jointly, and the *commissioning* to the President. This analysis calls our attention to the strict import of each term. To *nominate* must be to *propose*. Appointment seems that act of the will which constitutes or makes the agent, and the *commission* is the public evidence of it. But there are still other acts previous to these not specially enumerated in the Constitution, to wit: 1st. The destination of a mission to the particular country where the public service calls for it, and 2nd,

* A note in the FORD EDITION says this paper was evidently intended to be signed by the whole Virginia delegation.—EDITOR.

the character or grade to be employed in it. The natural order of all these is first, destination; second, grade; third, nomination; fourth, appointment; fifth, commission. If *appointment* does not comprehend the neighbor ng acts *nomination* or *commission* (and the Con titution says it shall not, by giving them exclusively to the President), still less can it pretend to comprehend those previous and more remote, of *destination* and *grade.* The Constitut on, analyzing the three last, shows they do not comprehend the two first. The fourth is the only one it submits to the Senate. Shaping it into a right to say that " A or B is unfit to be appointed ". Now, this cannot comprehend a right to say that A or B is indeed fit to be appointed, but the grade fixed on is not the fit one to emp!oy, or, " our connections with the country of his destination are not such as to call for any mission ". The Senate is not supposed by the Constitution to be acquainted with the concerns of the Executive Department. It was not* intended that these should be communicated to them, nor can they, therefore, be qualified to judge of the necessity which calls for a mission to any particular place. or of the particular grade, more or less marked, which special and secret circumstances may call for. All this is left to the President. They are only to see that no unfit person be employed. It may be objected that the Senate may by continual negatives on the *person*, do what amounts to a negative on the *grade*, and so, indirectly, defeat this right of the President. But this would be a breach of tru t; an abuse of the power confided to the Senate, of which that body cannot be supposed capable. So the President has power to convoke the Legislature, and the Senate might defeat that power by refusing to come. This equally amounts to a negative on the power of convoking. Yet nobody will say they possess such a negative, or would be capable of usuming it by such oblique means. If the Constitution had meant to give the Senate a negative on the grade, or destination, as well as on the person, it would have said so in direct terms, and not left it to be effected by a sidewind. It could never mean to give them the use of one power through the abuse of another.—OPINION ON POWERS OF THE SENATE. vii, 465. FORD ED., v, 161. (1790.)

5247. —— ——. The Secretary of State recapitulated [to a committee of the Senate] the circumstances which justified the President's having continued the grade of Minister Plenipotentiary [at The Hague]; but added, that whenever the biennial bill should come on. each House would have a constitutional right to review the establishment again, and whenever it should appear that either House thought any part of it might be reduced, on giving to the Executive time to avail themselves of the first convenient occasion to reduce it, the Executive could not but do it; but that it would be extremely injurious * * * to do it so abruptly as to occasion the recall of ministers, or unfriendly sensations in any of those countries with which our commerce is interesting.—THE ANAS. ix, 422. FORD ED., i, 172. (January 1792.)

5248. —— ——. After mature consideration and consultation, I am of opinion that the

* In one of the two editions of JEFFERSON'S WRITINGS, quoted in this work, "not" is omitted. The MS. copy of the opinion which, with the other papers of Jefferson, is preserved in the Department of State, was examined in order to verify the text. Jefferson wrote " it was *not* intended".—EDITOR.

Constitution has made the President the sole competent judge to what places circumstances render it expedient that ambassadors, or other public ministers, should be sent, and of what grade they should be; and that it has ascribed to the Senate no executive act but the single one of giving or withholding their consent to the person nominated. I think it my duty, therefore, to protest, and do protest against the validity of any resolutions of the Senate asserting or implying any right in that House to exercise any executive authority, but the single one before mentioned.—PARAGRAPH FOR PRESIDENT'S MESSAGE. FORD ED., v, 415. (1792.)

5249. MINISTERS (Foreign), Exchange of.—I doubt whether it be honorable for us to keep anybody at London unless they keep some person at New York.—To W. S. SMITH. ii, 284. (P., 1787.)

5250. —— ——. The President * * * authorized Mr. Gouverneur Morris to enter into conference with the British ministers in order to discover their sentiments on the exchange of a minister. The letters of Mr. Morris * * * [to the President] state the communications, oral and written, which have passed between him and the ministers; and from these the Secretary of State draws the following inference: That * * * their Secretary for Foreign Affairs is disposed to exchange a minister, but meets with opposition in h's Cabinet, so as to render the issue uncertain. The Secretary of State is of opinion that Mr. Morris's letters remove any doubts which might have been entertained as to the intentions and dispositions of the British Cabinet; that it would be dishonorable to the United States, useless and even injurious, to renew the propositions for * * * the exchange of a minister, and that this subject should now remain dormant, till it shall be brought forward earnestly by them.—OFFICIAL REPORT. vii, 517. FORD ED., v, 261. (December 1790.)

5251. —— ——. You have placed the British proposition of exchanging a minister on proper ground. It must certainly come from them, and come in unequivocal form. With those who respect their own dignity so much. ours must not be counted at naught. On their own proposal formally, to exchange a minister we sent them one. They have taken no notice of that, and talk of agreeing to exchange one now, as if the idea were new. Besides, what they are saying to you, they are talking to us through Quebec; but so informally, that they may disavow it when they please.—To GOUVERNEUR MORRIS. iii, 182. FORD ED., v, 224. (N. Y., Aug. 1790.)

5252. MINISTERS (Foreign). Extraordinary expenses.—With respect to the extraordinary expenses which you may be under the necessity of incurring at the coronation, I am not authorized to give any advice. * * * I should certainly suppose that the representative of the United States at Madrid, was to do as the representatives of other sovere gnties do, and that it would be viewed as the compliment of our nation and not of its minister. If this be the true point of view, it proves at whose expense it should be.—To WILLIAM CARMICHAEL. FORD ED., v, 125. (P., 1789.)

5253. MINISTERS (Foreign), Outfit of.—When Congress made their first appointments of ministers to be resident in Europe, I have understood (for I was not then in Congress) that they allowed them all their expenses, and a fixed sum over and above for their time. Among their expenses was necessarily understood their outfit. Afterwards they thought proper to give them fixed salaries of eleven thousand one hundred and eleven dollars and one-ninth a year; and again by a resolution of May the 6th and 8th, 1784, the " salaries " of their ministers at foreign courts were reduced to nine thousand dollars, to take place on the 1st of August ensuing. On the 7th of May, I was appointed in addition to Mr. Adams and Dr. Franklin, for the negotiation of treaties of commerce; but this appointment being temporary, for two years only, and not as of a resident minister, the article of outfit did not come into question. I asked an advance of six months' salary, that I might be in cash to meet the first expenses, which was ordered. The year following I was appointed to succeed Dr. Franklin at this court [France]. This was the first appointment of a minister resident, since the original ones, under which all expenses were to be paid. So much of the ancient regulation as respected annual expenses had been altered to a sum certain; so much of it as respected first expenses, or outfit, remained unaltered; and I might, therefore, expect that the actual expenses for outfit were to be paid. When I prepared my account for settlement with Mr. Barclay, I began a detail of the articles of clothing, carriage, horses, and household furniture. I found they were numerous, minute, and incapable from their nature of being vouched; and often entered in my memorandum book under a general head only, so that I could not specify them. I found they would exceed a year's salary. Supposing, therefore, that mine being the first case, Congress would make a precedent of it, and prefer a sum fixed for the outfit as well as the salary, I have charged it in my account at a year's salary; presuming that there can be no question that an outfit is a reasonable charge. It is the usage here (and I suppose at all courts), that a minister resident shall establish his house in the first instant. If this is to be done out of his salary, he will be a twelvemonth, at least, without a copper to live on. It is the universal practice, therefore, of all nations to allow the outfit as a separate article from the salary. I have enquired here into the usual amount of it. I find that sometimes the sovereign pays the actual cost. This is particularly the case of the Sardinian ambassador now coming here, who is to provide a service of plate, and every article of furniture and other matters of first expense, to be paid for by his court. In other instances, they give a service of plate, and a fixed sum for all other articles, which fixed sum is in no case lower than a year's salary. I desire no service of plate, having no ambition for splendor. My furniture, carriage and apparel are all plain, yet they have cost me more than a year's salary. I suppose that in every country, and in every condition of life, a year's expense would be found a moderate measure for the furniture of a man's house. It is not more certain to me that the sun will rise tomorrow, than that our government must allow the outfit on their future appointment of foreign ministers; and it would be hard on me so to stand between the discontinuance of a former rule, and institution of a future one, as to have the benefit of neither.—To JOHN JAY. ii, 401. (P., 1788.)

5254. —— ——. The outfit given to ministers resident to enable them to furnish their house, but given by no nation to a temporary minister, who is never expected to take a

house or to entertain, but considered on the footing of a *voyageur*, our predecessors gave to their extraordinary ministers by the wholesale. In the beginning of our administration, among other articles of reformation in expense, it was determined not to give an outfit to ministers extraordinary, and not to incur the expense with any minister of sending a frigate to carry or bring him. The Boston happened to be going to the Mediterranean, and was permitted, therefore, to take up Mr. Livingston, and touch in a port of France. A frigate was denied to Charles Pinckney, and has been refused to Mr. King for his return. Mr. Madison's friendship and mine to you being so well known, the public will have eagle eyes to watch if we grant you any indulgences out of the general rule; and on the other hand, the example set in your case [as Minister Extraordinary to France] will be more cogent on future ones, and produce greater approbation to our conduct. The allowance, therefore, will be in this, and all similar cases, all the expenses of your journey and voyage, taking a ship's cabin to yourself, nine thousand dollars a year from your leaving home till the proceedings of your mission are terminated, and then the quarter's salary for the expenses of your return, as prescribed by law.—To JAMES MONROE. iv, 455. FORD ED., viii, 191. (W., 1803.)

5255. MINISTERS (Foreign), Privileges.—Legal provision should be made for protecting and vindicating those privileges and immunities to which foreign ministers, and others attending on Congress are entitled by the law of nations.—CONGRESS RESOLUTION. FORD ED., iii, 463. (April 1784.)

5256. —— ——. Foreign ministers are not bound to an acquaintance with the laws of the land. They are privileged by their ignorance of them. They are bound by the laws of natural justice only.—To WILLIAM SHORT. FORD ED., v, 246. (M., 1790.)

5257. —— ——. Every person, diplomatic *in his own right*, is entitled to the privileges of the law of nations, in his own right. Among these is the receipt of all packages unopened and unexamined by the country which receives him. The usage of nations has established that this shall liberate whatever is imported *bonâ fide* for his own use, from paying duty. A government may control the number of diplomatic characters it will receive; but if it receives them it cannot control their rights while *bonâ fide* exercised. Thus Dr. Franklin, Mr. Adams, Colonel Humphreys and myself, all residing at Paris at the same time, had all of us our importation duty free. Great Britain had an ambassador and a minister plenipotentiary there, and an ambassador extra for several years; all three had their entries free. In most countries this privilege is permanent. Great Britain is niggardly, and allows it only on the first arrival. But in this, as she treats us only as *she does* the most favored nations, so we should treat her as *we do* the most favored nations. If these principles are correct, Mr. Foster is duty free.—To ALBERT GALLATIN. iv, 588. (W., 1805.)

5258. MINISTERS (Foreign), Reception of.—The Secretary of State has the honor to inform the Minister of France that the President will receive his letters of credence to-day at half after two: that this will be done in a room of private audience, without any ceremony whatever, or other person present than the Secretary of State, this being the usage which will be observed. As the Secretary of State will be with the President before that hour on business, the Minister will find him there.—To JEAN BAPTISTE TERNANT. FORD ED., v, 370. (Pa., 1791.)

5259. —— ——. The reception of the minister at all * * * (in favor of which Colonel Hamilton has given his opinion, though reluctantly, as he confessed), is an acknowledgment of the legitimacy of their [the French] government.—OPINION ON FRENCH TREATIES. vii. 616. FORD ED., vi, 223. (1793.)

5260. —— ——. It has been said without contradiction, and the people have been made to believe, that the refusal of the French to receive our Envoys was contrary to the law of nations, and a sufficient cause of war; whereas, every one who has ever read a book on the law of nations knows, that it is an unquestionable right in every power to refuse any minister who is personally disagreeable.—To EDMUND PENDLETON. iv, 289. FORD ED., vii, 359. (Pa., 1799.)

5261. —— ——. The Constitution has made the Executive the organ for managing our intercourse with foreign nations. It authorizes him to appoint and receive ambassadors, other public ministers, and consuls. The term minister being applicable to other agents as well as diplomatic, the constant practice of the government, considered as a commentary, established this broad meaning; and the public interest approves it; because it would be extravagant to employ a diplomatic minister for a business which a mere rider would execute. The Executive being thus charged with the foreign intercourse, no law has undertaken to prescribe its secific duties.—To ALBERT GALLATIN. iv, 520. (1804.)

5262. MINISTERS (Foreign), Rejection.—The public interest certainly made the rejection of Chevalier de Onis expedient, and as that is a motive which it is not pleasant always to avow, I think it fortunate that the contending claims of Charles and Ferdinand. furnished such plausible embarrassment to the question of right; for, on our principles, I presume, the right of the Junta to send a minister could not be denied.—To PRESIDENT MADISON. v, 480. (M., Nov. 1809.)

5263. MINISTERS (Foreign), Revolutions and.—Whenever the scene [Paris during Revolution] became personally dangerous to you, it was proper you should leave it, as well from personal as public motives. But what degree of danger should be awaited, to what distance or place you should retire, are circumstances which must rest with your own discretion, it being impossible to prescribe them from hence.—To GOUVERNEUR MORRIS. iii, 489. FORD ED., vi, 131. (Pa., Nov. 1792.)

5264. MINISTERS (Foreign), Rotation in.—I think it possible that it will be established into a maxim of the new government to discontinue its foreign servants after a certain time of absence from their own country, because they lose in time that sufficient degree of intimacy with its circumstances which alone can enable them to know and pursue its interests. Seven years have been talked of.—To WILLIAM SHORT. FORD ED., v, 244. (M., 1790.)

5265. MINISTERS (Foreign), Salaries.—You have doubtless heard of the complaints of our foreign ministers as to the incompetency of their salaries. I believe it would be better

were they somewhat enlarged. Yet a moment's reflection will satisfy you that a man may live in any country on any scale he pleases, and more easily in that [France] than this, because there the grades are more distinctly marked. From the ambassador there a certain degree of representation is expected. But the lower grades of Envoy, Minister, Resident, Chargé, have been introduced to accommodate both the sovereign and missionary as to the scale of expense. I can assure you from my own knowledge of the ground, that these latter grades are left free in the opinion of the place to adopt any style they please, and that it does not lessen their estimation or their usefulness. When I was at Paris, two-thirds of the diplomatic men of the second and third orders entertained nobody. Yet they were as much invited out and honored as those of the same grades who entertained. * * * This procures one some sunshine friends who like to eat of your good things, but has no effect on the men of real business, the only men of real use to you, in a place where every man is estimated at what he really is.—To GENERAL JOHN ARMSTRONG. FORD ED., viii, 302. (W., 1804.)

—— MINISTERS (Foreign), Secretaries of Legation and.—See SUMTER.

5266. MINISTERS (Foreign), Verbal communications.—Verbal communications are very insecure; for it is only necessary to deny them or to change their terms, in order to do away their effect at any time. Those in writing have many and obvious advantages, and ought to be preferred.—To THOMAS PINCKNEY. iv, 63. FORD ED., vi, 416. (Pa., 1793.) See DIPLOMATIC ESTABLISHMENT.

5267. MINISTERS (Imperial).—What are their [Kings] ministers but a committee, badly chosen?—To BENJAMIN HAWKINS. ii, 221. FORD ED., iv, 426. (P., 1787.)

5268. MINISTERS (Imperial), Politic.—Ministers and merchants love nobody. The merchants here [France] are endeavoring to exclude us from their [West India] islands. The ministers will be governed in it by political motives, and will do it, or not do it, as these shall appear to dictate, without love or hatred to anybody.—To JOHN LANGDON. i, 429. (P., 1785.)

5269. MINISTERS (Religious), Fearless of.—You judge truly that I am not afraid of the priests. They have tried upon me all their various batteries, of pious whining, hypocritical canting, lying and slandering, without being able to give me one moment of pain.—To HORATIO GATES SPAFFORD. FORD ED., x, 13. (M., 1816.)

5270. MINISTERS (Religious), French.—The Curés throughout the [French] Kingdom form the mass of the clergy. They are the only part favorably known to the people, because solely charged with the duties of baptism, burial, confession, visitation of the sick, instruction of the children, and aiding the poor. They are themselves of the people, and united with them. The carriages and equipage only of the higher clergy, not their persons, are known to the people, and are in detestation with them.—To JAMES MADISON. iii, 58. (P., 1789.)

5271. —— ——. Nor should we wonder at * * * [the] pressure [for a fixed constitution in 1788-9] when we consider the monstrous abuses of power under which * * * the

[French] people were ground to powder; when we pass in review * * * the riches, luxury, indolence and immorality of the clergy.—Auto-biography. i, 86. Ford ed., i, 118. (1821.)

5272. MINISTERS (Religious), Hostility to Jefferson.—The delusion into which the X. Y. Z. plot shows it possible to push the people; the successful experiment made under the prevalence of that delusion on the clause of the Constitution, which, while it secured the freedom of the press, covered also the freedom of religion, had given to the clergy a very favorite hope of obtaining an establishment of a particular form of Christianity through the United States; and as every sect believes its own form the true one, every one, perhaps hoped for his own, but especially the Episcopalians and Congregationalists. The returning good sense of our country threatens abortion to their hopes, and they believe that any portion of power confided to me, will be exercised in opposition to their schemes. And they believe rightly; for I have sworn upon the altar of God eternal hostility against every form of tyranny over the mind of man. But this is all they have to fear from me; and enough, too, in their opinion. And this is the cause of their printing lying pamphlets against me, forging conversations for me with Mazzei, Bishop Madison, &c., which are absolute falsehoods without a circumstance of truth to rest on; falsehoods, too, of which I acquiet Mazzei and Bishop Madison for they are men of truth. But enough of this. It is more than I have before committed to paper on the subject of all the lies that have been preached and printed against me.—To Dr. Benjamin Rush. iv, 336. Ford ed., vii, 460. (M., Sep. 1800.)

5273. MINISTERS (Religious), Liberty and.—In every country and in every age, the priest has been hostile to liberty. He is always in alliance with the despot, abetting his abuses in return for protection to his own.—To Horatio G. Spafford. vi, 334. (M., 1814.)

5274. MINISTERS (Religious), New England.—The sway of the clergy in New England is indeed formidable. No mind beyond mediocrity dares there to develop itself. If it does, they excite against it the public opinion which they command, and by little, but incessant and tearing persecutions, drive it from among them. Their present emigrations to the Western country are real flights from persecution, religious and political, but the abandonment of the country by those who wish to enjoy freedom of opinion leaves the despotism over the residue more intense, more oppressive.— To Horatio Gates Spafford. Ford ed., x, 13. (M., 1816.)

5275. —— ——. The advocate of religious freedom is to expect neither peace nor forgiveness from the New England clergy.—To Levi Lincoln. iv, 427. Ford ed., viii, 129. (1802.) See Church, Church and State, Clergy, and Religion.

5276. MINORITY, Censorship by.—A respectable minority [in Congress] is useful as censors. The present one is not respectable, being the bitterest remains of the cup of federalism, rendered desperate and furious by despair.—To Joel Barlow. iv, 437. Ford ed., viii, 149. (W., May 1802.)

5277. MINORITY, Equal rights of.— Bear in mind this sacred principle that * * * the minority possess their equal rights, which

equal laws must protect, and to violate which would be oppression.—First Inaugural Address. viii, 2. Ford ed., viii, 2. (1801.)

5278. MINORITY, Sacrifices to.—The minorities [against the new Constitution] in most of the accepting States have been very respectable; so much so as to render it prudent, were it not otherwise reasonable, to make some sacrifice to them.—To General Washington. ii, 533. Ford ed., v, 56. (P., 1788.)

5279. —— ——. The minorities [against the new Constitution] are too respectable, not to be entitled to some sacrifice of opinion; especially when a great proportion of them would be contented with a bill of rights.—To James Madison. ii, 506. Ford ed., v, 53. (P., Nov. 1788.)

5280. MINT, Establishment of.—The propositions* under consideration [by Congress] suppose that the coinage is to be carried on in a foreign country, and that the implements are to remain the property of the undertaker; which conditions, in the opinion [of the Secretary of State] render them inadmissible, for these reasons: Coinage is peculiarly an attribute of sovereignty. To transfer its exercise into another country, is to submit it to another sovereign. Its transportation across the sea, besides the ordinary dangers of the sea, would expose it to acts of piracy, by the crews to whom it would be confided, as well as by others apprized of its passage. In time of war, it would offer to the enterprises of an enemy what have been emphatically called the sinews of war. If the war were with the nation within whose territory the coinage is, the first act of war, or reprisal, might be to arrest this operation, with the implements and materials coined and uncoined, to be used at their discretion. The reputation and principles of the present undertaker are safeguards against the abuses of a coinage, carried on in a foreign country, where no checks could be provided by the proper sovereign, no regulations established, no police, no guard exercised; in short, none of the numerous cautions hitherto thought essential at every mint; but in hands less entitled to confidence, these will become dangers. We may be secured, indeed, by proper experiments as to the purity of the coin delivered us according to contract, but we cannot be secured against that which, though less pure, shall be struck in the general die, and protected against the vigilance of Government, till it shall have entered into circulation. We lose the opportunity of calling in and recoining the clipped money in circulation, or we double our risk by a double transportation. We lose, in like manner, the resource of coining up our household plate in the instant of great distress. We lose the means of forming artists to continue the works, when the common accidents of mortality shall have deprived us of those who began them. In fine, the carrying on a coin-

* The question was referred to Jefferson by the House of Representatives.—Editor.

age in a foreign country, as far as the Secretary knows, is without example; and general example is weighty authority. He is, therefore, of opinion, on the whole, that a mint, whenever established, should be established at home.—COINAGE REPORT. vii, 463. (April 1790.)

5281. MIRAGE AT MONTICELLO.—The elevation and particular situation at Monticello afford an opportunity of seeing a phenomenon which is rare at land, though frequent at sea. The seamen call it *looming*. Philosophy is as yet in the rear of the seamen, for so far from having accounted for it, she has not given it a name. Its principal effect is to make distant objects appear larger, in opposition to the general law of vision, by which they are diminished. I know an instance, at Yorktown, from whence the water prospect eastwardly is without termination, wherein a canoe with three men, at a great distance was taken for a ship with its three masts. I am little acquainted with the phenomenon as it shows itself at sea; but at Monticello it is familiar. There is a solitary mountain about forty miles off in the South, whose natural shape, as presented to view there, is a regular cone; but by the effect of looming, it sometimes subsides almost totally in the horizon: sometimes it rises more acute and more elevated; sometimes it is hemispherical; and sometimes its sides are perpendicular, its top flat, and as broad as its base. In short, it assumes at times the most whimsical shapes, and all these perhaps successively in the same morning. The Blue Ridge of mountains comes into view, in the north-east, at about one hundred miles distance. and approaching in a direct line, passes by within twenty miles, and goes off to the south-west. This phenomenon begins to show itself on these mountains at about fifty miles distance, and continues beyond that as far as they are seen. I remark no particular state, either in the weight, moisture, or heat of the atmosphere, necessary to produce this. The only constant circumstances are its appearance in the morning only, and on objects at least forty or fifty miles distant. In this latter circumstance, if not in both, it differs from the looming on the water. Refraction will not account for the metamorphosis. That only changes the proportions of length and breadth, base and altitude, preserving the general outlines. Thus it may make a circle appear elliptical, raise or depress a cone, but by none of its laws, as yet developed, will it make a circle appear a square, or a cone a sphere.—NOTES ON VIRGINIA. viii, 327. FORD ED., iii, 186. (1782.)

5282. MIRANDA EXPEDITION, Jefferson's knowledge of.—That the expedition of Miranda was countenanced by me, is an absolute falsehood, let it have gone from whom it might; and I am satisfied it is equally so as to Mr. Madison. To know as much of it as we could was our duty, but not to encourage it.—To WILLIAM DUANE. iv, 592. FORD ED., viii, 433. (W., 1806.)

5283. ——— ———. Your predecessor, soured on a question of etiquette against the administration of this country, wished to impute wrong to them in all their actions, even where he did not believe it himself. In this spirit, he wished it to be believed that we were in unjustifiable cooperation in Miranda's expedition. I solemnly, and on my personal truth and honor, declare to you. that this was entirely without foundation, and that there was neither cooperation, nor connivance on our part. He informed

us he was about to attempt the liberation of his native country from bondage, and intimated a hope of our aid, or connivance at least. He was at once informed, that although we had great cause of complaint against Spain, and even of war, yet whenever we should think proper to act as her enemy, it should be openly and above board, and that our hostility should never be exercised by such petty means. We had no suspicion that he expected to engage men here, but merely to purchase military stores. Against this there was no law, nor consequently any authority for us to interpose obstacles. On the other hand, we deemed it improper to betray his voluntary communication to the agents of Spain. Although his measures were many days in preparation at New York, we never had the least intimation or suspicion of his engaging men in his enterprise, until he was gone; and. I presume, the secrecy of his proceeding kept them equally unknown to the Marquis Yrujo at Philadelphia, and the Spanish consul at New York, since neither of them gave us any information of the enlistment of men, until it was too late for any measures taken at Washington to prevent their departure. The officer in the customs, who participated in the transaction with Miranda, we immediately removed. and should have had him and others further punished, had it not been for the protection given them by private citizens at New York, in opposition to the government, who, by their impudent falsehoods and calumnies, were able to overbear the minds of the jurors.—To DON VALENTINE DE FORONDA. v, 474. FORD ED., ix, 25c. (M., Oct. 1809.)

5284. MIRANDA EXPEDITION, Prosecutions.—On the prosecution of Ogden and Smith for participation in Miranda's expedition, the defendants and their friends have contrived to make it a government question, in which they mean to have the Administration and the judge tried as the culprits instead of themselves. Swartwout. the marshal to whom, in his duel with Clinton. Smith was second. and his bosom friend. summoned a panel of jurors, the greater part of which were of the bitterest federalists. His letter, too. covering to a friend a copy of Aristides,* and affirming that every fact in it was true as Holy Writ [was considered in Cabinet]. Determined unanimously that he be removed.—THE ANAS. FORD ED., i, 316. (May 1806.)

5285. MISFORTUNE, Pleasure and.—Pleasure is always before us; but misfortune is at our side; while running after that, this arrests us.—To MRS. COSWAY. ii, 37. FORD ED., iv, 317. (P., 1786.)

5286. MISFORTUNE, Solace in.—I most cordially sympathize in your losses. It is a situation in which a man needs the aid of all his wisdom and philosophy. But as it is better to turn from the contemplation of our misfortunes to the resources we possess of extricating ourselves, you will, of course, have found solace in your vigor of mind, health of body. talents, habits of business, in the consideration that you have time yet to retrieve everything, and a knowledge that the very activity necessary for this, is a state of greater happiness than the unoccupied one to which you had a thought of retiring.—To DR. CURRIE. ii, 218. (P., 1787.)

5287. MISSIONARIES, Foreign.—I do not know that it is a duty to disturb by missionaries the religion and peace of other

* W. P. Van Ness, who wrote a pamphlet in favor of Burr.—EDITOR.

countries, who may think themselves bound to extinguish by fire and fagot the heresies to which we give the name of conversions, and quote our own example for it.—To Mr. Megear. vii, 287. (M., 1823.)

5288. MISSISSIPPI RIVER NAVIGATION, Absolute cession.—The navigation of the Mississippi we must have. This is all we are as yet ready to receive.—To Archibald Stuart. i, 518. Ford ed., iv, 189. (P., Jan. 1786.)

5289. ——— ———. A cession of the navigation of the Mississippi, with such privileges as to make it useful, and free from future chicane, can be no longer dispensed with on our part.—To William Short. iii, 223. Ford ed., v, 299. (Pa., 1791.)

5290. MISSISSIPPI RIVER NAVIGATION, Congress and.—The affair of the Mississippi, by showing that Congress is capable of hesitating on a question, which proposes a clear sacrifice of the western to the maritime States, will with difficulty be obliterated. The proposition of my going to Madrid to try to recover there the ground which has been lost at New York, by the concession of the vote of seven States, I should think desperate.—To James Madison. ii, 153. Ford ed., iv, 392. (P., 1787.)

5291. ——— ———. I was pleased to see the vote of Congress, of September the 16th, on the subject of the Mississippi, as I had before seen, with great uneasiness, the pursuits of other principles, which I could never reconcile to my own ideas of probity or wisdom, and from which, and my knowledge of the character of our western settlers, I saw that the loss of that country was a necessary consequence. I wish this return to true policy may be in time to prevent evil.—To James Madison. ii, 563. Ford ed., v, 63. (P., 1789.)

5292. MISSISSIPPI RIVER NAVIGATION, Law of nature and.—But our right is built on ground still broader and more unquestionable, to wit: On the law of nature and nations. If we appeal to this, as we feel it written in the heart of man, what sentiment is written in deeper characters than that the ocean is free to all men, and their rivers to all their inhabitants? Is there a man, savage or civilized, unbiased by habit, who does not feel and attest this truth? Accordingly, in all tracts of country united under the same political society, we find this natural right universally acknowledged and protected by laying the navigable rivers open to all their inhabitants. When their rivers enter the limits of another society, if the right of the upper inhabitants to descend the stream is in any case obstructed, it is an act of force by a stronger society against a weaker, condemned by the judgment of mankind. The late case of Antwerp and the Scheldt was a striking proof of a general union of sentiment on this point; as it is believed that Amsterdam had scarcely an advocate out of Holland, and even there its pretensions were advocated on the ground of treaties, and not of natural right. * * * The Commissioners will be able perhaps to find, either in the practice or the pretensions of Spain as to the Douro, Tagus, and Guadiana, some acknowledgments of this principle on the part of that nation. This sentiment of right in favor of the upper inhabitants must become stronger in the proportion which their extent of country bears to the lower. The United States hold 600,000

square miles of habitable territory on the Mississippi and its branches, and this river and its branches afford many thousands of miles of navigable waters penetrating this territory in all its parts. The inhabitable grounds of Spain below our boundary, and bordering on the river, which alone can pretend any fear of being incommoded by our use of the river, are not the thousandth part of that extent. This vast portion of the territory of the United States has no other outlet for its productions, and these productions are of the bulkiest kind. And in truth, their passage down the river may not only be innocent as to the Spanish subjects on the river, but cannot fail to enrich them far beyond their present condition. The real interests then of all the inhabitants, upper and lower, concur in fact with their rights. If we appeal to the law of nature and nations, as expressed by writers on the subject, it is agreed by them, that, were the river, where it passes between Florida and Louisiana, the exclusive right of Spain, still an innocent passage along it is a natural right in those inhabiting its borders above. It would indeed be what those writers call an imperfect right, because the modification of its exercise depends in a considerable degree on the conveniency of the nation through which they are to pass. But it is still a right as real as any other right, however well-defined; and were it to be refused, or to be so shackled by regulations, not necessary for the peace or safety of its inhabitants, as to render its use impracticable to us, it would then be an injury, of which we should be entitled to demand redress. The right of the upper inhabitants to use this navigation is the counterpart to that of those possessing the shore below, and founded in the same natural relations with the soil and water. And the line at which their rights meet is to be advanced or withdrawn, so as to equalize the inconveniences resulting to each party from the exercise of the right by the other. This estimate is to be fairly made, with a mutual disposition to make equal sacrifices, and the numbers on each side are to have their due weight in the estimate. Spain holds so very small a tract of habitable land on either side below our boundary, that it may in fact be considered as a strait of the sea; for though it is eighty leagues from our boundary to the mouth of the river, yet it is only here and there, in spots and slips, that the land rises above the level of the water in times of inundation. There are, then, and ever must be, so few inhabitants on her part of the river, that the freest use of its navigation may be admitted to us without their annoyance.—Mississippi River Instructions. vii, 577. Ford ed., v, 467. (1792.)

5293. MISSISSIPPI RIVER NAVIGATION, Sectional opposition.—It is true, there were characters whose stations entitled them to credit, and who, from geographical prejudices, did not themselves wish the navigation of the Mississippi to be restored to us, and who believe, perhaps, as is common with mankind, that their opinion was the general opinion. But the sentiments of the great mass of the Union were decidedly otherwise then, and the very persons to whom M. Gardoqui alluded, have now come over to the opinion heartily, that the navigation of the Mississippi, in full and unrestrained freedom, is indispensably necessary, and must be obtained by any means it may call for.—To William Carmichael. iii, 246. (Pa., 1791.)

5294. MISSISSIPPI RIVER NAVIGATION, Spain and.—In the course of the

Revolutionary War, in which the thirteen colonies, Spain and France, were opposed to Great Britain, Spain took possess on of several posts held by the British in Florida. It is unnecessary to inquire whether the possession of half a dozen posts scattered through a country of seven or eight hundred miles extent, could be considered as the possession and conquest of that country. If it was, it gave still but an inchoate right, as was before explained, which could not be perfected but by the relinquishment of the former possession at the close of the war; but certainly it could not be cons dered as a conquest *of the river*, even against Great Britain, since the possession of the shores, to wit, of the island of New Orleans on the one side, and Louisiana on the other, having undergone no change, the right in the water would remain the same, if considered in its relation to them; and if considered as a distinct right, independent of the shores, then no naval victories obtained by Spain over Great Britain, in the course of the war, gave her the color of conquest over any water which the British fleet could enter. Still less can she be considered as having conquered the river, as against the United States, with whom she was not at war. We had a common right of navigation in the part of the river between Florida, the island of New Orleans, and the western bank, and nothing which passed between Spain and Great Britain, either during the war or at its conclusion, could lessen that right. Accordingly, at the treaty of November, 1782, Great Britain confirmed the rights of the United States to the navigation of the river, from its source to its mouth, and in January, 1783, completed the right of Spain to the territory of Florida, by an absolute relinquishment of all her rights in it. This relinquishment could not include the navigation held by the United States in their own right, because this right existed in themselves only, and was not in Great Britain. If it added anything to the rights of Spain respecting the river between the eastern and western banks, it could only be that portion of right which Great Britain had retained to herself in the treaty with the United States, held seven weeks before, to wit, a right of using it in common with the United States. So that as by the treaty of 1763, the United States had obtained a common right of navigating the whole river from its source to its mouth, so by the treaty of 1782, that common right was confirmed to them by the only power who could pretend claims against them, founded on the state of war; nor has that common right been transferred to Spain by either conquest or cession.—MISSISSIPPI RIVER INSTRUCTIONS. vii, 576. FORD ED., v, 466. (1792.)

5295. MISSISSIPPI RIVER NAVIGATION, Treaty of Paris and.—The war of 1755-1763, was carried on jointly by Great Britain and the Thirteen Colonies, now the United States of America, against France and Spain. At the peace which was negotiated by our common magistrate, a right was secured to the subjects of Great Britain (the common designation of all those under his government) to navigate the Mississippi in its whole breadth and length, from its source to the sea, and expressly that part which is between the Island of New Orleans and the right bank of the river, as well as the passage both in and out of its mouth; and that the vessels should not be stopped, visited, or subjected to the payment of any duty whatsoever. These are the words of the treaty, article VII. Florida was at the same time ceded by Spain, and its extent westwardly

was fixed to the Lakes Pontchartrain and Maurepas, and the River Mississippi; and Spain received soon after from France a cession of the island of New Orleans, and all the country she held westward of the Mississippi, subject, of course, to our right of navigating between that country and the island previously granted to us by France. This right was not parcelled out to us in severalty, that is to say, to each the exclusive navigation of so much of the river as was adjacent to our several shores, in which way it would have been useless to all; but it was placed on that footing, on which alone it could be worth anything, to wit: as a right to all to navigate the whole length of the river in common. The import of the terms, and the reason of the thing, prove it was a right of common in the whole, and not a several right to each of a particular part. To which may be added the evidence of the stipulation itself, that we should navigate between New Orleans and the western bank, which, being adjacent to none of our States, could be held by us only as a right of common. Such was the nature of our right to navigate the Mississippi, as far as established by the Treaty of Paris.—MISSISSIPPI RIVER INSTRUCTIONS. vii, 575. FORD ED., v, 466. (1792.)

5296. MISSISSIPPI RIVER NAVIGATION, Western people and.—The difficulty on which the negotiation with Spain hangs is a *sine qua non* with us. It would be to deceive them and ourselves, to suppose that an amity can be preserved while this right is withheld. Such a supposition would argue not only an ignorance of the people to whom this is most interesting, but an ignorance of the nature of man, or an inattention to it. Those who see but half way into our true interest will think that that concurs with the views of the other party. But those who see it in all its extent, will be sensible that our true interest will be best promoted, by making all the just claims of our fellow citizens, wherever situated, our own, by urging and enforcing them with the weight of our whole influence, and by exercising in this, as in every other instance, a just government in their concerns, and making common cause even where our separate interest would seem opposed to theirs. No other conduct can attach us together; and on this attachment depends our happiness.—To JAMES MONROE. i, 605. FORD ED., iv, 262. (P., 1786.)

5297. ————. ————. If they declare themselves a separate people, we are incapab'e of a single effort to retain them. Our citizens can never be induced, either as militia or as soldiers, to go there to cut the throats of their own brothers and sons, or rather, to be themselves the subjects, instead of the perpetrators of the parricide. Nor would that country requite the cost of being retained against the will of its inhabitants, could it be done. But it cannot be done. They are able already to rescue the navigation of the Mississippi out of the hands of Spain, and to add New Orleans to their own territory. They will be joined by the inhabitants of Louisiana. This will bring on a war between them and Spain; and that will produce the question with us, whether it will not be worth our while to become parties with them in the war, in order to reunite them with us, and thus correct our error? And were I to permit my forebodings to go one step further, I should predict that the inhabitants of the United States would force their rulers to take the affirmative of that question.—To JAMES MADISON. ii, 106. FORD ED., iv, 363. (P., 1787.)

5298. —— ——. I never had any interest westward of the Alleghany; and I never will have any. But I have had great opportunities of knowing the character of the people who inhabit that country; and I will venture to say, that the act which abandons the navigation of the Mississippi is an act of separation between the eastern and western country. It is a relinquishment of five parts out of eight of the territory of the United States; an abandonment of the fairest subject for the payment of our public debts, and the chaining those debts on our necks, *in perpetuum*.—To JAMES MADISON. ii, 105. FORD ED., iv, 363. (P., 1787.)

5299. —— ——. The navigation of the Mississippi was perhaps the strongest trial to which the justice of the Federal Government could be put. If ever they thought wrong about it, I trust they have got to rights. I should think it proper for the Western country to defer pushing their right to that navigation to extremity as long as they can do without it tolerab.y; but that the moment it becomes absolutely necessary for them, it will become the duty of the maritime States to push it to every extremity to which they would their own right of navigating the Chesapeake, the Delaware, the Hudson, or any other water.—To JOHN BROWN. ii, 395. FORD ED., v, 17. (P., May 1788.)

5300. —— ——. It is impossible to answer for the forbearance of our western citizens. We endeavor to quiet them with the expectation of an attainment of their rights by peaceable means. But should they, in a moment of impatience, hazard others, there is no saying how far we may be led; for neither themselves nor their rights will be ever abandoned by us.—To WILLIAM CARMICHAEL. iii, 173. FORD ED., v, 217. (N.Y., 1790.)

5301. —— ——. The navigation of the Mississippi is necessary to us. More than half the territory of the United States is on the waters of that river. Two hundred thousand of our citizens are settled on them, of whom forty thousand bear arms. These have no other outlet for their tobacco, rice, corn, hemp, lumber, house timber, ship timber. We have hitherto respected the indecision of Spain, because we wish peace;—because our western citizens have had vent at home for their productions. A surplus of production begins now to demand foreign markets. Whenever they shall say, "We cannot, we will not, be longer shut up", the United States will be reduced to the following dilemma: 1. To force them to acquiescence. 2. To separate from them, rather than take part in a war against Spain. 3. Or to preserve them in our Union, by joining them in the war. The 1st is neither in our principles, nor in our power. 2. A multitude of reasons decide against the second. It may suffice to speak but one: were we to give up half our territory rather than engage in a just war to preserve it, we should not keep the other half long. The third is the alternative we must adopt.—INSTRUCTIONS TO WILLIAM CARMICHAEL. ix, 412. FORD ED., v, 225. (1790.) See LOUISIANA and NEW ORLEANS.

5302. MISSISSIPPI TERRITORY, Government of.—As to the people you are to govern, we are apprised that they are divided into two adverse parties, the one composed of the richer and better informed, attached to the first grade of government, the other of the body of the people, not a very homogeneous mass, advocates for the second grade which they possess in fact. Our love of freedom, and the value we set on self-government dispose us to prefer the principles of the second grade, and they are strengthened by knowing they are [faded in MS.] by the will of the majority. While cooperation with that plan, therefore, is essentially to be observed, your best endeavors should be exerted to bring over those opposed to it by every means soothing and conciliatory. The happiness of society depends so much on preventing party spirit from infecting the common intercourse of life, that nothing should be spared to harmonize and amalgamate the two parties in social circles.—To WILLIAM C. CLAIBORNE. FORD ED., viii, 71. (W., July 1801.) See LOUISIANA.

5303. MISSOURI, Admission of.—I rejoice that * * * Missouri is at length a member of our Union. Whether the question it excited is dead, or only sleepeth, I do not know. I see only that it has given resurrection to the Hartford Convention men. They have had the address, by playing on the honest feelings of our former friends, to seduce them from their kindred spirits, and to borrow their weight into the Federal scale. Desperate of regaining power under political distinctions, they have adroitly wriggled into its seat under the auspices of morality, and are again in the ascendency from which their sins had hurled them. * * * I still believe that the Western extension of our Confederacy will insure its duration, by overruling local factions, which might shake a smaller association.—To HENRY DEARBORN. vii, 215. FORD ED., x, 191. (M., 1821.)

5304. MISSOURI QUESTION, A breaker.—The banks, bankrupt law, manufactures, Spanish treaty, are nothing. These are occurrences which, like waves in a storm, will pass under the ship. But the Missouri question is a breaker on which we lose the Missouri country by revolt, and what more, God only knows. From the battle of Bunker's Hill to the treaty of Paris, we never had so ominous a question. * * * I thank God that I shall not live to witness its issue.*—To JOHN ADAMS. vii, 148. FORD ED., x, 151. (M., December 1819.)

5305. MISSOURI QUESTION, Federalists and.—Nothing has ever presented so threatening an aspect as what is called the Missouri question. The federalists, completely put down and despairing of ever rising again under the old divisions of Whig and Tory, devised a new one of slave-holding and non-slave-holding States, which, while it had a semblance of being moral, was at the same time geographical, and calculated to give them ascendency by debauching their old opponents to a coalition with them. Moral the question certainly is not, because the re-

* Mr. Adams replied as follows: "The Missouri question, I hope, will follow the other waves under the ship, and do no harm. I know it is high treason to express a doubt of the perpetual duration of our vast American empire, and our free institution; and I say as devoutly as father Paul, *esto perpetua*, but I am sometimes Cassandra enough to dream, that another Hamilton, and another Burr, might rend this mighty fabric in twain, or perhaps into a leash; and a few more choice spirits of the same stamp, might produce as many nations in North America as there are in Europe."—EDITOR.

moval of slaves from one State to another, no more than their removal from one country to another, would never make a slave of one human being who would not be so without it. Indeed, if there were any morality in the question it is on the other side; because by spreading them over a larger surface their happiness would be increased, and the burden for their future liberation lightened by bringing a greater number of shoulders under it. However, it served to throw dust into the eyes of the people and to fanaticize them, while to the knowing ones it gave a geographical and preponderant line of the Potomac and Ohio, throwing fourteen States to the North and East, and ten to the South and West. With these, therefore, it is merely a question of power; but with this geographical minority it is a question of existence. For if Congress once goes out of the Constitution to arrogate a right of regulating the condition of the inhabitants of the States, its majority may, and probably will, next declare that the condition of all men within the United States shall be that of freedom; in which case all the whites south of the Potomac and Ohio must evacuate their States, and most fortunate those who can do it first. And so far this crisis seems to be advancing.—To ALBERT GALLATIN. FORD ED., x, 177. (M., Dec. 1820.)

5306. MISSOURI QUESTION, Geographical line.—I am so completely withdrawn from all attention to public matters, that nothing less could arouse me than the definition of a geographical line, which on an abstract principle is to become the line of separation of these States, and to render desperate the hope that man ever enjoys the two blessings of peace and self-government. The question sleeps for the present, but is not dead.—To H. NELSON. vii, 151. FORD ED., x, 156. (M., March 1820.)

5307. ——. I congratulate you on the sleep of the Missouri question. I wish I could say in its death, but of this I despair. The idea of a geographical line once suggested will brood in the minds of all those who prefer the gratification of their ungovernable passions to the peace and union of their country.—To MARK LANGDON HILL. vii, 155. (M., April 1820.)

5308. ——. This momentous question, like a fire bell in the night, awakened and filled me with terror. I considered it at once as the knell of the Union. It is hushed, indeed, for the moment. But this is a reprieve only, not a final sentence. A geographical line, coinciding with a marked principle, moral and political, once conceived and held up to the angry passions of men, will never be obliterated; and every new irritation will mark it deeper and deeper.—To JOHN HOLMES. vii, 159. FORD ED., x, 157. (M., April 1820.)

5309. MISSOURI QUESTION, A Party trick.—The Missouri question is a mere party trick. The leaders of federalism, defeated in their schemes of obtaining power by rallying partisans to the principle of monarchism, a principle of personal not of local division, have changed their tack, and thrown out another barrel to the whale. They are taking advantage of the virtuous feelings of the people to effect a division of parties by a geographical line; they expect that this will insure them, on local principles, the majority they could never obtain on principles of federalism; but they are still putting their shoulder to the wrong wheel; they are wasting Jeremiads on the miseries of slavery, as if we were advocates for it. Sincerity in their declamations should direct their efforts to the true point of difficulty, and unite their counsels with ours in devising some reasonable and practicable plan of getting rid of it. Some of these leaders, if they could attain the power, their ambition would rather use it to keep the Union together, but others have ever had in view its separation. If they push it to that, they will find the line of separation very different from their 36° of latitude, and as manufacturing and navigating States, they will have quarreled with their bread and butter, and I fear not that after a little trial they will think better of it and return to the embraces of their natural and best friends. But this scheme of party I leave to those who are to live under its consequences. We who have gone before have performed an honest duty, by putting in the power of successors a state of happiness which no nation ever before had within their choice. If that choice is to throw it away, the dead will have neither the power nor the right to control them.—To CHARLES PINCKNEY. vii, 180. FORD ED., x, 162. (M., 1820.)

5310. MISSOURI QUESTION, Portentous.—The Missouri question is the most portentous one which ever yet threatened our Union. In the gloomiest moment of the Revolutionary war I never had any apprehensions equal to what I feel from this source.—To HUGH NELSON. FORD ED., x, 156. (M., Feb. 1820.)

5311. ——. Last and most portentous of all is the Missouri question. It is smeared over for the present; but its geographical demarcation is indelible. What it is to become I see not.—To SPENCER ROANE. vii, 212. FORD ED., x, 189. (M., 1821.)

5312. MISSOURI QUESTION, Presidential politics.—The boisterous sea of liberty is never without a wave, and that from Missouri is now rolling towards us, but we shall ride over it as we have over all others. It is not a moral question, but one merely of power. Its object is to raise a geographical principle for the choice of a President, and the noise will be kept up till that is effected.—To MARQUIS LAFAYETTE. vii, 194. FORD ED., x, 180. (M., 1820.)

5313. ——. Nothing disturbs us so much as the dissension lately produced by what is called the Missouri question; a question having just enough of the semblance of morality to throw dust into the eyes of the people and to fanaticize; while with the knowing ones it is simply a question of power.—To D. B. WARDEN. FORD ED., x, 172. (M., Dec. 1820.)

5314. MISSOURI QUESTION, Separation.—The Missouri question aroused and filled me with alarm. The old schism of federal and republican threatened nothing, because it existed in every State, and united them together by the fraternism of party. But the coincidence of a marked principle, moral and political, with a geographical line, once conceived, I feared would never more be obliterated from the mind; that it would be recurring on every occasion and renewing irritations, until it would kindle such mutual and mortal hatred, as to render separation preferable to eternal discord. I have been among the most sanguine in believing that our Union would be of long duration. I now doubt it much, and see the event at no great distance, and the direct consequence of this question; not by the line which has been so confidently counted on; the laws of nature control this; but by the Potomac, Ohio and Missouri, or more probably, the Mississippi upwards to our northern boundary. My only comfort and confidence is, that I shall not live to see this; and I envy not the present generation the glory of throwing away the fruits of their fathers' sacrifices of life and fortune, and of rendering desperate the experiment which was to decide ultimately whether man is capable of self-government. This treason against human hope, will signalize their epoch in future history, as the counterpart of the medal of their predecessors.—To WILLIAM SHORT. vii, 158. (M., April 1820.)

5315. —— ——. Should the schism [on the Missouri question] be pushed to separation it will be for a short term only; two or three years' trial will bring them back, like quarrelling lovers to renewed embraces, and increased affections. The experiment of separation would soon prove to both that they had mutually miscalculated their best interests. And even were the parties in Congress to secede in a passion, the soberer people would call a convention and cement again the severance attempted by the insanity of their functionaries. With this consoling view, my greatest grief would be for the fatal effect of such an event on the hopes and happiness of the world. We exist, and are quoted, as standing proofs that a government, so modelled as to rest continually on the will of the whole society, is a practicable government. Were we to break to pieces, it would damp the hopes and the efforts of the good, and give triumph to those of the bad through the whole enslaved world. As members, therefore, of the universal society of mankind, and standing in high and responsible relation with them, it is our sacred duty to suppress passion among ourselves, and not to blast the confidence we have inspired of proof that a government of reason is better than one of force.—To RICHARD RUSH. vii, 182. (M., 1820.)

5316. MISSOURI QUESTION, Slavery extension.—All know that permitting the slaves of the south to spread into the west will not add one being to that unfortunate condition, that it will increase the happiness of those existing, and by spreading them over a larger surface, will dilute the evil everywhere, and facilitate the means of getting finally rid of it, an event more anxiously wished by those on whom it presses than by the noisy pretenders to exclusive humanity. In the meantime, it is a ladder for rivals climbing to power.—To M. DE LAFAYETTE. vii, 194. FORD ED., x, 180. (M., 1820.)

5317. —— ——. A hideous evil, the magnitude of which is seen, and at a distance only, by the one party, and more sorely felt and sincerely deplored by the other, from the difficulty of the cure, divides us at this moment too angrily. The attempt by one party to prohibit willing States from sharing the evil, is thought by the other to render desperate, by accumulation, the hope of its final eradication. If a little time, however, is given to both parties to cool, and to dispel their visionary fears, they will see that concurring in sentiment as to the evil, moral and political, the duty and interest of both is to concur also in devising a practicable process of cure. Should time not be given, and the schism be pushed to separation, it will be for a short term only; two or three years' trial will bring them back, like quarrelling lovers to renewed embraces, and increased affections. The experiment of separation would soon prove to both that they had mutually miscalculated their best interests.—To RICHARD RUSH. vii, 182. (M., October 1820.)

5318. —— ——. Our anxieties in this quarter [the South] are all concentrated in the question, what does the Holy Alliance in and out of Congress mean to do with us on the Missouri question? And this, by-the-bye, is but the name of the case, it is only the John Doe or Richard Roe of the ejectment. The real question, as seen in the States afflicted with this unfortunate population, is, are our slaves to be presented with freedom and a dagger? For if Congress has the power to regulate the conditions of the inhabitants of the States, within the States, it will be but another exercise of that power, to declare that all shall be free. Are we then to see again Athenian and Lacedemonian confederacies? To wage another Peloponnesian war to settle the ascendency between them? Or is this the tocsin of merely a servile war? That remains to be seen; but not, I hope, by you or me.—To JOHN ADAMS. vii, 200. FORD ED., x, 186. (M., January 1821.)

5319. MOBS, Government and.—The mobs of great cities add just so much to the support of pure government, as sores do to the strength of the human body.—NOTES ON VIRGINIA. viii, 406. FORD ED., iii, 269. (1782.)

5320. MOBS, Imaginary.—It is in the London newspapers only that exist those mobs and riots, which are fabricated to deter strangers from going to America. Your person will be sacredly safe and free from insult.—To MRS. SPROWLE. FORD ED., iv, 66. (P., 1785.)

5321. MOBS, Revolutionary.—For sometime mobs of ten, twenty and thirty thousand people collected daily, surrounded the Parliament House [in Paris], huzzaed the members, even entered the doors and examined into their conduct, took the horses out of the carriages of those who did well, and drew them home. The government thought it prudent to prevent these, drew some regiments into the neighborhood, multiplied the guards, had the streets constantly patrolled by strong parties, suspended privileged places, forbade all clubs, &c. The mobs have ceased; perhaps this may be partly owing to the absence of parliament.—To JOHN ADAMS. ii, 258. (P., Aug. 1787.) See BASTILE.

5322. MODERATION, Political.—A moderate conduct throughout, which may not revolt our new friends [the federalists], and which may give them tenets with us, must be observed.—To JOHN PAGE. iv, 378. (W., March 1801.)

5323. MODESTY, American.—There is modesty often which does itself injury. Our countrymen possess this. They do not know their own superiority.—To WILLIAM RUTLEDGE. ii, 350. FORD ED., v, 5. (P., 1788.)

5324. MONARCHY, Advocates for.—I know there are some among us who would now establish a monarchy. But they are inconsiderable in number and weight of character.—To JAMES MADISON. iii, 5. FORD ED., v, 83. (P., 1789.)

5325. ———. It cannot be denied that we have among us a sect who believe that the English constitution contains whatever is perfect in human institutions; that the members of this sect have, many of them, names and offices which stand high in the estimation of our countrymen. I still rely that the great mass of our community is untainted with these heresies, as its head. On this I build my hope that we have not labored in vain, and that our experiment will still prove that men can be governed by reason.—To GEORGE MASON. iii, 209. FORD ED., v, 275. (Pa., 1791.)

5326. ———. We have some names of note here who have apostatized from the true faith: but they are few indeed, and the body of our citizens pure and insusceptible of taint in their republicanism. Mr. Paine's answer to Burke will be a refreshing shower to their minds.—To BENJAMIN VAUGHAN. FORD ED., v, 334. (Pa., 1791.)

5327. ———. There are high names* here in favor of [monarchy], but the publications in Bache's paper have drawn forth pretty generally expressions of the public sentiment on the subject, and I thank God to find they are, to a man, firm as a rock in their republicanism. I much fear that the honestest man of the party will fall a victim to his imprudence on this occasion, while another of them, from the mere caution of holding his tongue, and buttoning

* At this point a series of cipher figures is written on the margin, which, when translated, reads: "Adams, Jay, Hamilton, Knox. Many of the Cincinnati. The second says nothing. The third is open. Both are dangerous. They pant after union with England as the power which is to support their projects, and are most determined Anti-gallicans. It is prognosticated that our republic is to end with the president's life. But I believe they will find themselves all head and no body."—NOTE IN FORD EDITION.

himself up, will gain what the other loses.—To WILLIAM SHORT. FORD ED., v, 361. (Pa., 1791.)

5328. ———. The ultimate object of all this increase of public debt, establishment of a paper money system, corruption of Congress, etc., is, it is charged, to prepare the way for a change from the present republican form of government to that of a monarchy, of which the English constitution is to be the model. That this was contemplated in the [Federal] Convention is no secret, because its partisans have made none of it. To effect it then was impracticable, but they are still eager after their object, and are predisposing everything for its ultimate attainment. So many of them have got into the Legislature, that, aided by the corrupt squadron of paper dealers, who are at their devotion, they make a majority in both houses. The republican party, who wish to preserve the government in its present form, are fewer in number. They are fewer even when joined by the two, three, or half dozen anti-federalists, who, though they dare not avow it, are still opposed to any General Government; but, being less so to a republican than a monarchical one, they natural y join those whom they think pursuing the lesser evil.—To PRESIDENT WASHINGTON. iii, 361. FORD ED., vi, 3. (Pa., May 1792.)

5329. ———. While you [in France] are exterminating the monster aristocracy, and pulling out the teeth and fangs of its associate, monarchy, a contrary tendency is discovered in some here. A sect has shown itself among us, who declare they espoused our new Constitution not as a good and sufficient thing in itself, but only as a step to an English constitution, the only thing good and sufficient in itself, in their eyes. It is happy for us that these are preachers without followers, and that our people are firm and constant in their republican purity. You will wonder to be told that it is from the Eastward chiefly that these champions for a King, lords and commons, come. They get some important associates from New York, and are puffed up by a tribe of Agioteurs which have been hatched in a bed of corruption made up after the model of their beloved England. Too many of these stock-jobbers and king-jobbers have come into our Legislature, or rather too many of our Legislature have become stock-jobbers and king-jobbers. However, the voice of the people is beginning to make itself heard, and will probably cleanse their seats at the ensuing election. —To GENERAL LAFAYETTE. iii, 450. FORD ED., vi, 78. (Pa., 1792.)

5330. ———. He [President Washington] said that as to the idea of transforming this government into a monarchy he did not believe there were ten men in the United States whose opinions were worth attention, who entertained such a thought. I told him there were many more than he imagined. I recalled to his memory a dispute at his own table * * * between General Schuyler, on one side, and Pinckney and myself on the other, wherein the former maintained the position, that hereditary descent was as likely to produce good magistrates as election. I told him, that though the people were sound, there was a numerous sect who had monarchy in contemplation; that the Secretary of the Treasury was one of these; that I had heard him say that this Constitution was a shilly-shally thing of mere milk and water, which could not last, and was only good as a step to something better. That when we reflected, that he had endeavored in the convention, to make an English constitution out of it, and when failing in that, we saw all his measures tending to bring it to the same thing, it was natural for us to be jealous; and particularly, when we saw that these measures had established corruption in the Legislature, where there was a squadron devoted to the nod of the Treasury, doing whatever he had directed, and ready to do what he should direct. That if the equilibrium of the three great bodies, Legislative, Executive, and Judiciary, could be preserved, if the Legislature could be kept independent, I should never fear the result of such a government; but that I could not but be uneasy when I saw that the Executive had swallowed up the Legislative branch. He said, that as to that interested spirit in the Legislature, it was what could not be avoided in any government, unless we were to exclude particular descriptions of men, such as the holders of the funds from all office. I told him, there was great difference between the little accidental schemes of self-interest, which would take place in every body of men, and influence their votes, and a regular system for forming a corps of interested persons who should be steadily at the orders of the Treasury.—THE ANAS. ix, 121. FORD ED., i, 204. (Oct. 1792.)

5331. —— ——. In the course of our [members of the Cabinet] conversation Knox, stickling for parade, got into great warmth and swore that our government must either be entirely new modeled or it would be knocked to pieces in less than ten years, and that, as it is at present, he would not give a copper for it; that it is the President's character, and not the written Constitution, which keeps it together.— THE ANAS. ix, 139. FORD ED., i, 222. (Feb. 1793.)

5332. —— ——. The aspect of our politics has wonderfully changed since you left us. In place of that noble love of liberty, and republican government which carried us triumphantly through the war, an Anglican, monarchical, aristocratical party has sprung up, whose avowed object is to draw over us the substance, as they have already done the forms of the British government. The mass of our citizens, however, remain true to their republican principles; the whole landed interest is republican, and so is a great mass of talents. Against us are the Executive, the Judiciary, two out of three branches of the Legislature, all the officers of the Government, all who want to be officers, all timid men who prefer the calm of despotism to the boisterous sea of liberty. British merchants and Americans trading on British capitals, speculators and holders in the banks and public funds, a contrivance invented for the purposes of corruption, and for assimilating us in all things to the rotten as well as the sound parts of the British model. It would give you a fever were I to name to you the apostates who have gone over to these heresies, men who were Samsons in the field and Solomons in the council, but who have had their heads shorn by * * * England. In short, we are likely to preserve the liberty we have obtained only by unremitting labors and perils. But we shall preserve it; and our mass of weight and wealth on the good side is so great, as to leave no danger that force will ever be attempted against us. We have only to awake and snap the Lilliputian cords with which they have been entangling us during the first sleep which succeeded our labors.—To PHILIP MAZZEI. iv, 139. FORD ED., vii, 75. (M., April 1796.) See MAZZEI.

5333. —— ——. It would seem that changes in the principles of our government are to be pushed till they accomplish a monarchy peaceably, or force a resistance which, with the aid of an army, may end in monarchy. Still, I hope that this will be peaceably prevented by the eyes of the people being opened, and the consequent effect of the elective principle.—To CHARLES PINCKNEY. FORD ED., vii, 398. (M., Oct. 1799.)

5334. —— ——. I know, indeed, that there are monarchists among us. One character of these is in theory only, and perfectly acquiescent in our form of government as it is, and not entertaining a thought of destroying it merely on their theoretic opinions. A second class, at the head of which is our quondam colleague [in the cabinet, Hamilton], are ardent for introduction of monarchy, eager for armies, making more noise for a great naval establishment than better patriots, who wish it on a rational scale only, commensurate to our wants and our means. This last class ought to be tolerated but not trusted.—To GENERAL HENRY KNOX. iv, 386. FORD ED., viii, 36. (W., March 1801.)

5335. MONARCHY, Colonists and.—I believe you may be assured, that an idea or desire of returning to anything like their [the Colonists'] ancient government, never entered into their heads.*—To DAVID HARTLEY. ii, 165. (P., 1787.)

5336. —— ——. I am satisfied that the King of England believes the mass of our people to be tired of their independence, and desirous of returning under his government, and that the same opinion prevails in the ministry and nation. They have hired their newswriters to repeat this lie in their gazettes so long, that they have become the dupes of it themselves.—To JOHN JAY. ii, 305. (P., 1787.)

5337. MONARCHY, Evils of.—If anybody thinks that kings, nobles or priests are good conservators of the public happiness, send him here [France]. It is the best school in the universe to cure him of that folly. He will see here, with his own eyes, that these descriptions of men are an abandoned confederacy against the happiness of the mass of the people. The omnipotence of their effect cannot be better proved than in this country particularly, where, notwithstanding the finest soil upon earth, the finest climate under heaven, and a people of the most benevolent, the most gay and amiable character of which the human form is susceptible; where such a people, I say, surrounded by so many blessings from nature, are loaded with misery, by kings, nobles and priests, and by them alone.—To GEORGE WYTHE. ii, 7. FORD ED., iv, 268. (P., 1786.)

5338. —— ——. I am astonished at some people's considering a kingly government as a refuge [from the evils of the Confederation]. Advise such to read the fable of the frogs who solicited Jupiter for a king. If that does not put them to rights send them to Europe to see something of the trappings of monarchy, and I will undertake that every man shall go back thoroughly cured. If all the evils which can arise among us from the republican form of government from this day to the day of judgment could be put into a scale against what this country [France] suffers from its monarchical form in a week, or England in a month, the latter would predominate. Consider the

* David Hartley was the British agent in Paris.— EDITOR.

contents of the Red Book in England, or the Almanac Royale of France, and say what a people gain by monarchy. No race of kings has ever presented above one man of common sense in twenty generations. The best they can do is to leave things to their ministers, and what are their ministers but a committee, badly chosen? If the king ever meddles it is to do harm.—To BENJAMIN HAWKINS. ii, 220. FORD ED., iv, 426. (P., Aug. 1787.)

5339. ——— ———. I hear there are people among you who think the experience of our governments has already proved that republican government will not answer. Send those gentry here to count the blessings of monarchy. A king's sister, for instance, stopped on the road, and on a hostile journey, is sufficient cause for him to march immediately twenty thousand men to revenge this insult.—To JOSEPH JONES. ii, 249. FORD ED., iv, 438. (P., 1787.)

5340. ——— ———. There is scarcely an evil known in the European countries which may not be traced to their king, as its source, nor a good which is not derived from the small fibres of republicanism existing among them.—To GENERAL WASHINGTON. ii, 375. FORD ED., v, 8. (P., 1788.)

5341. MONARCHY, The Federal Convention and.—The want of some authority which should procure justice to the public creditors, and an observance of treaties with foreign nations, produced * * * the call of a convention of the States at Annapolis. Although, at this meeting, a difference of opinion was evident on the question of a republican or kingly government, yet, so generally through the States was the sentiment in favor of the former, that the friends of the latter confined themselves to a course of obstruction only, and delay, to everything proposed. They hoped, that nothing being done, and all things going from bad to worse, a kingly government might be usurped, and submitted to by the people, as better than anarchy and wars, internal and external, the certain consequences of the present want of a general government. The effect of their manœuvres, with the defective attendance of deputies from the States, resulted in the measure of calling a more general convention, to be held at Philadelphia. At this, the same party exhibited the same practices, and with the same views of preventing a government of concord, which they foresaw would be republican, and of forcing through anarchy their way to monarchy. But the mass of that convention was too honest, too wise, and too steady, to be baffled or misled by their manœuvres. One of these was a form of government proposed by Colonel Hamilton, which would have been in fact a compromise between the two parties of royalism and republicanism. According to this, the Executive and one branch of the Legislature were to be during good behavior, i. e. for life, and the governors of the States were to be named by these two prominent organs. This, however, was rejected; on which Hamilton left the Convention, as desperate, and never returned again, until near its conclusion. These opinions and efforts, secret or avowed, of the advocates for monarchy, had begotten great jealousy through the States generally; and this jealousy it was which excited the strong opposition to the conventional Constitution; a jealousy which yielded at last only to a general determination to establish certain amendments as barriers against a government either monarchical

or consolidated.*—THE ANAS. ix, 89. FORD ED., i, 158. (1818.)

5342. MONARCHY, French Revolution and.—The failure of the French Revolution would have been a powerful argument with those who wish to introduce a king, lords, and commons here, a sect which is all head and no body.—To EDMUND PENDLETON. FORD ED., v, 358. (Pa., 1791.)

5343. ——— ———. President Washington added that he considered France as the sheet anchor of this country and its friendship as a first object. There are in the United States some characters of opposite principles; some of them are high in office, others possessing great wealth, and all of them hostile to France, and fondly looking to England as the staff of their hope. * * * They * * * have espoused [the Constitution] only as a stepping-stone to monarchy, and have endeavored to approximate it to that in its administration in order to render its final transition more easy. The successes of republicanism in France have given the *coup de grace* to their prospects, and I hope to their projects.—To WILLIAM SHORT. iii, 503. FORD ED., vi, 155. (Pa., 1793.)

5344. MONARCHY, Hamilton and.—[Alexander] Hamilton's financial system had then [1790] passed. It had two objects. First, as a puzzle, to exclude popular understanding and inquiry. Secondly, as a machine for the corruption of the Legislature; for he avowed the opinion, that man could be governed by one of two motives only, force or interest.† Force, he observed, in this country was out of the question; and the interests, therefore, of the members must be laid hold of, to keep the Legislature in unison with the Executive. And with grief and shame it must be acknowledged that his machine was not without effect; that even in this, the birth of our government, some members were found sordid enough to bend their duty to their interests, and to look after personal, rather than public good. * * * [The measures of Hamilton's financial system, —the Funding and United States Bank Acts,

---

* Jefferson added: "In what passed through the whole period of these conventions, I have gone on the information of those who were members of them, being myself absent on my mission to France." A note in the FORD EDITION reads: "No evidence whatever has been found to confirm Jefferson's account of this Convention * * *."—EDITOR.

† The subjoined extracts from *Hamilton's Works* set forth his principles of government in this respect:

"A vast majority of mankind is naturally biased by the motives of self-interest."—*Hamilton's Works*, ii, 10.

"The safest reliance of every government is on men's interests. This is a principle of human nature on which all political speculation, to be just, must be founded."—*Hamilton's Works*. ii, 298.

"We may preach until we are tired of the theme the necessity of disinterestedness in republics, without making a single proselyte."—*Hamilton's Works*. ii, 197.

"A small knowledge of human nature will convince us that with far the greatest part of mankind interest is the governing principle, and that almost every man is more or less under its influence. Motives of public virtue may for a time, or in particular instances, actuate men to the observance of a conduct purely disinterested, but they are not sufficient of themselves to produce a conformity to the refined dictates of social duty. Few men are capable of making a continual sacrifice of all views of profit, interest, or advantage, to the common good. It is in vain to exclaim against the depravity of human nature on this account; the fact is so, and we must in a great measure change the constitution of man before we can make it otherwise. No institution not built on the presumptive truth of these maxims can succeed."—*Hamilton's Works*. ii, 140.—EDITOR.

&c.,] added to the number of votaries to the Treasury, and made its Chief the master of every vote in the Legislature, which might give to the government the direction suited to his political views. I know well, and so must be understood, that nothing like a majority in Congress had yielded to this corruption. Far from it. But a division, not very unequal, had already taken place in the honest part of that body, between the parties styled republican and federal. The latter being monarchists in principle, adhered to Hamilton of course, as their leader in that principle, and this mercenary phalanx added to them, ensured him always a majority in both Houses; so that the whole action of the Legislature was now under the direction of the Treasury. * * * By this combination, legislative expositions were given to the Constitution, and all the administrative laws were shaped on the model of England, and so passed. * * * Here then was the real ground of the opposition which was made to the course of administration. Its object was to preserve the Legislature pure and independent of the Executive, to restrain the administration to republican forms and principles, and not permit the Constitution to be construed into a monarchy, and to be warped in practice into all the principles and pollutions of their favorite English model. Nor was this an opposition to General Washington. He was true to the republican charge confided to him; and has solemnly and repeatedly protested to me, in our conversations that he would lose the last drop of his blood in support of it; and he did this the oftener, and with the more earnestness, because he knew my suspicions of Hamilton's designs against it, and wished to quiet them. For he was not aware of the drift, or of the effect of Hamilton's schemes. Unversed in financial projects, and calculations and budgets, his approbation of them was bottomed on his confidence in the man.—The Anas. ix, 91. Ford ed., i, 160, 164, 165. (1818.)

5345. —— ——. Hamilton was not only a monarchist, but for a monarchy bottomed on corruption. In proof of this, I will relate an anecdote, for the truth of which I attest the God who made me. Before the President [Washington] set out on his southern tour in April, 1791, he addressed a letter of the fourth of that month, from Mount Vernon, to the Secretaries of State, Treasury, and War, desiring that if any serious and important cases should arise during his absence, they would consult and act on them. And he requested that the Vice-President should also be consulted. This was the only occasion on which that officer was ever requested to take part in a cabinet question. Some occasion for consultation arising, I invited those gentlemen (and the Attorney General as well as I remember), to dine with me, in order to confer on the subject. After the cloth was removed, and our question agreed and dismissed, conversation began on other matters, and, by some circumstance, was led to the British Constitution, on which Mr. Adams observed, " Purge that constitution of its corruption, and give to its popular branch equality of representation, and it would be the most perfect constitution ever devised by the wit of man ", Hamilton paused and said, " purge it of its corruption, and give to its popular branch equality of representation, and it would become an *impracticable* government: as it stands at present, with all its supposed defects, it is the most perfect government which ever existed ". And this was assuredly the exact line which separated the political creeds of these two gentlemen. The one was for two hereditary branches and an honest elective one; the other for an hereditary King, with a House of Lords and Commons corrupted to his will, and standing between him and the people. The Anas. ix, 96. Ford ed., i, 165. (1818.)

5346. —— ——. Hamilton frankly avowed that he considered the British constitution, with all the corruptions of its administration, as the most perfect model of government which had ever been devised by the wit of man; professing however, at the same time, that the spirit of this country was so fundamentally republican that it would be visionary to think of introducing monarchy here, and that, therefore, it was the duty of its administrators to conduct it on the principles their constituents had elected.—To Martin Van Buren. vii, 371. Ford ed., x, 314. (M., 1824.)

5347. —— ——. Harper takes great pains to prove that Hamilton was no monarchist, by exaggerating his own intimacy with him, and the impossibility, if he was so, that he should not at some time have betrayed it to him. This may pass with uninformed readers, but not with those who have had it from Hamilton's own mouth. I am one of those, and but one of many. At my own table, in presence of Mr. Adams, Knox, Randolph and myself, in a dispute between Mr. Adams and himself, he avowed his preference of monarchy over every other government, and his opinion that the English was the most perfect model of government ever devised by the wit of man, Mr. Adams agreeing, " if its corruptions were done away "; while Hamilton insisted that "with these corruptions it was perfect, and without them it would be an impracticable government'. —To William Short. vii, 389. Ford ed., x, 330. (M., 1825.)

5348. MONARCHY, Imitation of.— When on my return from Europe, I joined the government in March, 1790, at New York, I was much astonished, indeed, at the mimicry I found established of royal forms and ceremonies, and more alarmed at the unexpected phenomenon, by the monarchical sentiments I heard expressed and openly maintained in every company, executive and judiciary (General Washington alone excepted), and by a great part of the Legislature, save only some members who had been of the old Congress, and a very few of recent introduction. I took occasion, at various times, of expressing to General Washington my disappointment at these symptoms of a change of principle, and that I thought them encouraged by the forms and ceremonies which I found prevailing, not at all in character with the simplicity of republican government, and looking as if wishfully to those of European courts. His general explanations to me were, that when he arrived at New York to enter on the executive administration of the new government, he observed to those who were to assist him, that placed as he was in an office entirely new to him, unacquainted with the forms and ceremonies of other governments, still less apprised of those which might be properly established here, and himself perfectly indifferent to all forms, he wished them to consider and prescribe what they should be; and the task was assigned particularly to General Knox, a man of parade, and to Colonel Humphreys, who had resided sometime at a foreign court. They, he said, were the authors of the present regulations, and that others were proposed so highly strained that he absolutely rejected them. Attentive to the difference of opinion prevailing on this subject, when the term of his second election arrived, he called the heads of Departments together, observed to them the situation in which he had been at the commencement of the government, the advice he had taken and the course he had observed in compliance with it; that a proper occasion had now arrived of revising that course, of correcting it in any particulars not approved in experience; and he desired us to consult together, agree on any changes we should think for the better, and that he should willingly conform to what we should advise. We met at my office. Hamilton and myself agreed at once that there was too much ceremony for the character of our government, and particularly that the parade of the installation at New York ought not to be copied on the present occasion, that the President should desire the Chief Justice to attend him at his chambers, that he should administer the oath of office to him in the presence of the higher officers of the government, and that the certificate of the fact should be delivered to the Secretary of State to be recorded. Randolph and Knox differed from us, the latter vehemently; they thought it not advisable to change any of the established forms, and we authorized Randolph to report our opinions to the President. As these opinions were divided, and no positive advice given as to any change, no change was made.—To Martin Van Buren. vii, 367. Ford ed., x, 310. (M., 1824.)

5349. —— ——. The forms which I had censured in my letter to Mazzei were perfectly understood by General Washington, and were those which he himself but barely tolerated. He had furnished me a proper occasion for proposing their reformation, and my opinion not prevailing, he knew I could not have meant any part of the censure for him.—To Martin Van Buren. vii, 368. Ford ed., x, 311. (M., 1824.)

5350. MONARCHY, Inimical to.—I was much an enemy to monarchies before I came to Europe. I am ten thousand times more so, since I have seen what they are.—To General Washington. ii, 375. Ford ed., v, 8. (P., 1788.)

5351. MONARCHY, Preference for.—I returned from the mission [to France] in the first year of the new government * * * and proceeded to New York to enter on the office of Secretary of State. Here, certainly, I found a state of things which, of all I had ever contemplated, I the least expected. I had left France in the first year of her Revolution, in the fervor of natural rights, and zeal for reformation. My conscientious devotion to these rights could not be heightened, but it had been aroused and excited by daily exercise. The President received me cordially, and my colleagues and the circle of principal citizens, apparently, with welcome. The courtesies of dinner parties given me, as a stranger newly arrived among them, placed me at once in their familiar society. But I cannot describe the wonder and mortification with which the table conversations filled me. Politics was the chief topic, and a preference of kingly, over republican, government was evidently the favorite sentiment. An apostate I could not be, nor yet a hypocrite; and I found myself, for the most part the only advocate on the republican side of the question, unless among the guests there chanced to be some member of that party

from the Legislative Houses.—The Anas. ix, 91. Ford ed., i, 159. (1818.)

5352. —— ——. When I arrived at New York in 1790, to take a part in the administration, being fresh from the French Revolution, while in its first and pure stage, and consequently somewhat whetted up in my own republican principles, I found a state of things, in the general society of the place, which I could not have supposed possible. Being a stranger there, I was feasted from table to table, at large set dinners, the parties generally from twenty to thirty. The revolution I had left, and that we had just gone through in the recent change of our own government, being the common topics of conversation, I was astonished to find the general prevalence of monarchical sentiments, insomuch that in maintaining those of republicanism, I had always the whole company on my hands, never scarcely finding among them a single coadvocate in that argument, unless some old member of Congress happened to be present. The furthest that any one would go, in support of the republican features of our new government, would be to say, "the present Constitution is well as a beginning and may be allowed a fair trial; but it is, in fact, only a stepping stone to something better". Among their writers, [Joseph] Dennie, the editor of the "Portfolio", who was a kind of oracle with them, and styled "the Addison of America", openly avowed his preference of monarchy over all other forms of government, prided himself on the avowal, and maintained it by argument freely and without reserve in his publications. I do not myself know that the Essex Junta, of Boston, were monarchists, but I have always heard it so said, and never doubted. These are but detached items from a great mass of proofs then fully before the public. * * * They are now disavowed by the party. But, had it not been for the firm and determined stand then made by a counter party, no man can say what our government would have been at this day. Monarchy, to be sure, is now defeated, and they wish it should be forgotten that it was ever advocated. They see that it is desperate, and treat its imputation to them as a calumny; and I verily believe that none of them have it now in direct aim. Yet the spirit is not done away. The same party takes now what they deem the next best ground, the consolidation of the government; the giving to the Federal member of the Government, by unlimited constructions of the Constitution, a control over all the functions of the States, and the concentration of all power ultimately at Washington.—To William Short. vii, 390. Ford ed., x, 332. (M., 1825.)

5353. MONARCHY, Throwing off.—With respect to the State of Virginia in particular, the people seem to have laid aside the monarchical, and taken up the republican form of government with as much ease as would have attended their throwing off an old and putting on a new suit of clothes. Not a single throe has attended this important transformation. A half-dozen aristocratical gentlemen, agonizing under the loss of preeminence, have sometimes ventured their sarcasms on our political metamorphosis. They have been thought fitter objects of pity than of punishment.—To Benjamin Franklin. i, 204. Ford ed., ii, 131. (August 1777.)

5354. MONARCHY, Washington and.—I am satisfied that General Washington had not a wish to perpetuate his authority; but he who supposes it was practicable, had he wished it, knows nothing of the spirit of America, either of the people or of those who possessed their confidence. There was, indeed, a cabal of the officers of the army who proposed to establish a monarchy and to propose it to General Washington. He frowned indignantly at the proposit on (according to the information which got abroad), and Rufus King and some few civil characters, chiefly (indeed, I believe, to a man) north of Maryland, who joined in this intrigue. But they never dared openly to avow it, knowing that the spirit which had produced a change in the form of government was alive to the preservation of it.—NOTES ON MARSHALL'S LIFE OF WASHINGTON. ix, 478. FORD ED., ix, 262.

5355. —— ——. The next effort was (on suggestion of the same individuals, in the moment of their separation), the establishment of an hereditary order, under the name of the Cincinnati, ready prepared, by that distinction, to be engrafted into the future form of government, and placing General Washington still at their head. The General wrote to me on this subject, while I was in Congress at Annapolis. * * ‖* He afterwards called on me at that place, on his way to a meeting of the society, and after a whole evening of consultation, he left that place fully determined to use all his endeavors for its total suppression. But he found it so firmly riveted in the affections of the members that, strengthened as they happened to be by an adventitious occurrence of the moment [the arrival of the badges of the Order from France], he could effect no more than the abolition of its hereditary principle.* He called again on his return,† and explained to me fully the opposition which had been made, the effect of the occurrence from France, and the difficulty with which its duration had been limited to the lives of the present members.—THE ANAS. ix, 89. FORD ED., i, 157. (1818.) See CINCINNATI SOCIETY.

5356. MONARCHY vs. REPUBLIC, —With all the defects of our Constitution, whether general or particular, the comparison of our governments with those of Europe, is like a comparison of heaven and hell. England, like the earth, may be allowed to take the intermediate station.—To J. JONES. ii, 249. (P., 1787.)

5357. —— ——. We were educated in royalism; no wonder if some of us retain that idolatry still. Our young people are educated in republican'sm; an apostasy from that to royalism, is unprecedented and impossible.— To JAMES MADISON. iii, 5. FORD ED., v, 83. (P., 1789.)

5358. MONEY, Circulating Medium.— The increase of circulating medium * * * according to my ideas of paper money, is clearly a demerit [in the bill providing for the establishment of a national bank.]—NATIONAL BANK OPINION. vii, 558. FORD ED., v, 287. (1791.)

5359. —— ——. The adequate price of a thing depends on the capital and labor nec-

* This is an error. The abolition of the hereditary principle was proposed, but never adopted.—NOTE IN FORD EDITION.

† This cannot be so, as Washington did not leave Philadelphia till after May 16th, and Jefferson left Annapolis for France on May 11th.—NOTE IN FORD EDITION.

essary to produce it. In the term *capital,* I mean to include science, because capital as well as labor has been employed to acquire it. Two things requiring the same capital and labor, should be of the same price. If a gallon of wine requires for its production the same capital and labor with a bushel of wheat, they should be expressed by the same price, derived from the application of a common measure to them. The comparative prices of things being thus to be estimated and expressed by a common measure, we may proceed to observe that were a country so insulated as to have no commercial intercourse with any other, to confine the interchange of all its wants and supplies within itself, the amount of circulating medium, as a common measure for adjusting these exchanges, would be quite immaterial. If their circulation, for instance, were a million of dollars, and the annual produce of their industry equivalent to ten millions of bushels of wheat, the price of a bushel of wheat might be one dollar. If, then, by a progressive coinage, their medium should be doubled, the price of a bushel of wheat might become progressively two dollars. and without inconvenience. Whatever be the proportion of the circulating medium to the value of the annual produce of industry, it may be considered as the representative of that industry. In the first case, a bushel of wheat will be represented by one dollar; in the second, by two dollars. This is well explained by Hume, and seems to be admitted by Adam Smith. But where a nation is in a full course of interchange of wants and supplies with all others, the proportion of its medium to its produce is no longer indifferent.—To J. W. EPPES. vi, 233. FORD ED., ix, 406. (M., 1813.)

5360. —— ——. One of the great advantages of specie as a medium is, that being of universal value. it will keep itself at a general level, flowing out from where it is too high into parts where it is lower. Whereas, if the medium be of local value only, as paper money, if too little, indeed, gold and silver will flow in to supply the deficiency; but if too much, it accumulates, banishes the gold and silver not locked up in vaults and hoards, and depreciates itself; that is to say, its proportion to the annual produce of industry being raised, more of it is required to represent any particular article of produce than in the other countries. This is agreed to by [Adam] Smith, the principal advocate for a paper circulation; but advocating it on the sole condition that it be strictly regulated. He admits, nevertheless, that " the commerce and industry of a country cannot be so secure when suspended on the Dædalian wings of paper money, as on the solid ground of gold and silver; and that in time of war, the insecurity is greatly increased, and great confusion possible where the circulation is for the greater part in paper ". But in a country where loans are uncertain. and a specie circulation the only sure resource for them, the preference of that circulation assumes a far different degree of importance.—To J. W. Eppes. vi, 233. Ford ed., ix, 407. (M., Nov. 1813.)

5361. —— ——. The only advantage which [Adam] Smith proposes by substituting paper in the room of gold and silver money, B. 2. c. 2. 434, is "to replace an expensive instrument with one much less costly, and *sometimes* equally convenient"; that is to say, page 437, "to allow the gold and silver to be sent abroad and converted into foreign goods", and to substitute paper as being a cheaper measure. But this makes no addition to the stock or capital of the nation. The coin sent was worth as much, while in the country, as the goods imported and taking its place. It is only, then, a change of form in a part of the national capital, from that of gold and silver to other goods. He admits, too, that while a part of the goods received in exchange for the coin exported may be materials, tools and provisions for the employment of an additional industry, a part, also, may be taken back in foreign wines, silks, &c., to be consumed by idle people who produce nothing; and so far the substitution promotes prodigality, increases expense and corruption, without increasing production. So far also, then, it lessens the capital of the nation. What may be the amount which the conversion of the part exchanged for productive goods may add to the former productive mass, it is not easy to ascertain, because, as he says, page 441. "it is impossible to determine what is the proportion which the circulating money of any country bears to the whole value of the annual produce. It has been computed by different authors, from a fifth to a thirtieth of that value". In the United States it must be less than in any other part of the commercial world; because the great mass of their inhabitants being in responsible circumstances, the great mass of their exchanges in the country is effected on credit, in their merchants' ledger, who supplies all their wants through the year, and at the end of it receives the produce of their farms, or other articles of their industry. It is a fact that a farmer with a revenue of ten thousand dollars a year, may obtain all his supplies from his merchant, and liquidate them at the end of the year by the sale of his produce to him, without the intervention of a single dollar of cash. This, then, is merely barter, and in this way of barter a great portion of the annual produce of the United States is exchanged without the intermediation of cash. We might safely, then, state our medium at the minimum of one-thirtieth. —To J. W. Eppes. vi, 234. Ford ed., ix, 407. (M., Nov. 1813.)

5362. —— ——. But what is one-thirtieth of the value of the annual produce of the industry of the United States? Or what is the whole value of the annual produce of the United States? An able writer and competent judge of the subject, in 1799, on as good grounds as probably could be taken, estimated it, on the then population of four and a half millions of inhabitants, to be thirty-seven and a half millions sterling, or one hundred and sixty-eight and three-fourths millions of dollars. According to the same estimate for our present population, it will be three hundred millions of dollars, one-thirtieth of which, Smith's minimum, would be ten millions, and one-fifth, his maximum, would be sixty millions for the quantum of circulation. But suppose that instead of our needing the least circulating medium of any nation, from the circumstance before mentioned, we should place ourselves in the middle term of the calculation, to wit: at thirty-five millions. One-fifth of this, at the least, Smith thinks, should be retained in specie, which would leave twenty-eight millions of specie to be exported in exchange for other commodities; and if fifteen millions of that should be returned in productive goods, and not in articles of prodigality, that would be the amount of capital which this operation would add to the existing mass. But to what mass? Not that of the three hundred millions, which is only its gross annual produce, but to that capital of which the three hundred millions are but the annual produce. But this being gross, we may infer from it the value of the capital by considering that the rent of lands is generally fixed at one-third of the gross produce, and is deemed its net profit, and twenty times that its fee simple value. The profits on landed capital may, with accuracy enough for our purpose, be supposed to be on a par with those of other capital. This would give us, then, for the United States, a capital of two thousand millions, all in active employment, and exclusive of unimproved lands lying in a great degree dormant. Of this, fifteen millions would be the hundred and thirty-third part. And it is for this petty addition to the capital of the nation, this minimum of one dollar, added to one hundred and thirty-three and a third or three-fourths per cent., that we are to give up our gold and silver medium, its intrinsic solidity, its universal value, and its saving powers in time of war, and to substitute for it paper, with all its train of evils, moral, political, and physical, which I will not pretend to enumerate. There is another authority to which we may appeal for the proper quantity of circulating medium for the United States. The old Congress, when we were estimated at about two millions of people, on a long and able discussion, June 22, 1775, decided the sufficient quantity to be two millions of dollars, which sum they then emitted,[*] According to this, it should be eight millions, now that we are eight millions of people. This differs little from Smith's minimum of ten millions, and strengthens our respect for that estimate.—To J. W. Eppes. vi, 234. Ford ed., ix, 408. (M., Nov. 1813.) See Banks and Debt.

5363. —— ——. Specie is the most perfect medium because it will preserve its own level;

---

[*] Within five months after this, they were compelled by the necessities of the war, to abandon the idea of emitting only an adequate circulation, and to make their necessities the sole measure of their emissions.—Note by Jefferson.

because, having intrinsic and universal value, it can never die in our hands, and it is the surest resource of reliance in time of war.—To J. W. EPPES. vi, 246. FORD ED., ix, 416. (M., Nov. 1813.)

5364. —— ——. It would be best that our medium should be so proportioned to our produce, as to be on a par with that of the countries with which we trade, and whose medium is in a sound state.—To J. W. EPPES. vi, 246. FORD ED., ix, 416. (M., Nov. 1813.)

5365. —— ——. Instead of yielding to the cries of scarcity of medium set up by speculators, projectors and commercial gamblers, no endeavors should be spared to begin the work of reducing it by such gradual means as may give time to private fortunes to preserve their poise, and settle down with the subsiding medium.—To J. W. EPPES. vi, 246. FORD ED., ix, 417. (M., Nov. 1813.)

5366. —— ——.We are already at ten or twenty times the due quantity of medium; insomuch, that no man knows what his property is now worth, because it is bloating while he is calculating; and still less what it will be worth when the medium shall be relieved from its present dropsical state.—To J. W. EPPES. vi, 246. FORD ED., ix, 417. (M., Nov. 1813.)

5367. —— ——. This State [Virginia] is in a condition of unparalleled distress. The sudden reduction of the circulating medium from a plethory to all but annihilation is producing an entire revolution of fortune. In other places I have known lands sold by the sheriff for one year's rent; beyond the mountains we hear of good slaves selling for one hundred dollars, good horses for five dollars, and the sheriffs generally the purchasers. Our produce is now selling at market for one-third of its price before this commercial catastrophe, say flour at three and a quarter and three and a half dollars the barrel. We should have less right to expect relief from our legislators if they had been the establishers of the unwise system of banks. A remedy to a certain degree was practicable, that of reducing the quantum of circulation gradually to a level with that of the countries with which we have commerce, and an eternal abjuration of paper. * * * I fear local insurrections against these horrible sacrifices of property.—To H. NELSON. vii, 151. FORD ED., x, 156. (M., 1820.) See NATIONAL CURRENCY and PAPER MONEY.

5368. MONEY, Clipped.—The Legislatures should cooperate with Congress in providing that no money be received or paid at their treasuries, or by any of their officers, or any bank, but on actual weight; in making it criminal, in a high degree, to diminish their own coins and, in some smaller degree, to offer them in payment when diminished.—NOTES ON A MONEY UNIT. i, 169. FORD ED., iii, 453. (1784.)

5369. MONEY, Coinage.—The Administrator [Governor] shall not possess the pre-

rogative * * * of coining moneys, or regulating their values.—PROPOSED VA. CONSTITUTION. FORD ED., ii, 19. (June 1776.)

5370. —— ——. For rendering the half penny pieces of copper coin of this Commonwealth of more convenient value, and by that means introducing them into more general circulation; Be it enacted by the General Assembly of the Commonwealth of Virginia that * * * the said pieces of copper coin shall pass in all payments for one penny each of current money of Virginia. Provided * * * that no person shall be obliged to take above one shilling of * * * copper coin in any one payment of twenty shillings, or under, nor more than two shillings and six pence * * * in any one payment of a greater sum than twenty shillings.—COPPER COINAGE BILL. FORD ED., ii, 118. (1776.)

5371. —— ——. It is difficult to familiarize a new coin to the people; it is more difficult to familiarize them to a new coin with an old name.—NOTES ON A MONEY UNIT. i, 165. FORD ED., iii, 449. (1784.) See DOLLAR.

5372. —— ——. A great deal of small change is useful in a State, and tends to reduce the price of small articles.—NOTES ON A MONEY UNIT. i, 166. FORD ED., iii, 450. (1784.)

5373. —— ——. I think it my duty to inform Congress that a Swiss, of the name of Drost, established in Paris, has invented a method of striking the two faces and the edge of a coin, at one stroke. By this, and other simplifications of the process of coinage, he is enabled to coin from twenty-five to thirty thousand pieces a day, with the assistance of only two persons, the pieces of metal being first prepared. I send you by Colonel Franks three coins of gold, silver and copper, which you will perceive to be perfect medals; and I can assure you, from having seen him coin many, that every piece is as perfect as these. There has certainly never yet been seen any coin, in any country, comparable to this. The best workmen in this way, acknowledge that his is like a new art. Coin should always be made in the highest perfection possible, because it is a great guard against the danger of false coinage. This man would be willing to furnish his implements to Congress, and if they please, he will go over and instruct a person to carry on the work; nor do I believe he would ask anything unreasonable. It would be very desirable, that in the institution of a new coinage, we could set out on so perfect a plan as this, and the more so as while the work is so exquisitely done, it is done cheaper.—To JOHN JAY. ii, 89. (P., Jan. 1787.)

5374. —— ——. Coinage is peculiarly an attribute of sovereignty. To transfer its exercise into another country, is to submit it to another sovereign.—COINAGE REPORT. vii, 463. (April 1790.)

5375. —— ——. The carrying on a coinage in a foreign country, as far as the Secretary [of State] knows, is without example; and general experience is weighty authority. —COINAGE REPORT. vii, 464. (April 1790.)

5376. —— ——. Perfection in the engraving is among the greatest safeguards against counterfeits, because engravers of the first class are few, and elevated by their rank in their art, and far above the base and dangerous business of counterfeiting.—COINAGE REPORT. vii, 463. (April 1790.)

5377. —— ——. As to the question on whom the expense of coinage is to fall, I have been so little able to make up an opinion satisfactory to myself, as to be ready to concur in either decision.—To ALEXANDER HAMILTON. iii, 330. (1792.)

5378. MONEY, Foreign.—The quantity of fine silver which shall constitute the Unit being settled, and the proportion of the value of gold to that of silver; a table should be formed * * * classing the several foreign coins according to their fineness, declaring the worth of a pennyweight or grain in each class, and that they shall be lawful tenders at those rates, if not clipped or otherwise diminished; and, where diminished, offering their value for them at the mint, deducting the expense of recoinage.—NOTES ON A MONEY UNIT. i, 169. FORD ED., iii, 453. (1784.) See GOLD and SILVER.

5379. —— ——. Most of the gold and silver coins of Europe pass in the several States of America according to the quantity of pure metal they contain.—M. DU RIVAL. ii, 52. (P., 1786.)

5380. —— ——. A bill has passed the Representatives giving three years longer currency to foreign coins. * * * The effect of stopping the currency of gold and silver is to force bank paper through all the States. However, I presume the State Legislatures will exercise their acknowledged right of regulating the value of foreign coins, when not regulated by Congress, and their exclusive right of declaring them a tender.—To JAMES MONROE. FORD ED., vii, 183. (Pa., Dec. 1797.)

5381. —— ——. By the Constitution Congress may regulate the value of foreign coin; but if they do not do it, the old power revives to the State, the Constitution only forbidding them to make anything but gold and silver a tender in payment of debts.—To JOHN TAYLOR. FORD ED., vii, 182. (Pa., 1797.)

5382. —— ——. A bill has passed the Representatives to suspend for three years the law arresting the currency of foreign coins. The Senate proposed an amendment, continuing the currency of the foreign gold only. * * * The object of opposing the bill is to make the French crowns a subject of speculation (for it seems they fell on the President's proclamation to a dollar in most of the States), and to force bank paper (for want of other medium) through all the States generally.—To JAMES MADISON. iv, 205. FORD ED., vii, 189. (Pa., 1798.)

5383. MONEY, Legal tender.—I deny the power of the General Government of making paper money, or anything else, a legal tender.—To JOHN TAYLOR. iv, 260. FORD ED., vii, 310. (M., 1798.)

— **MONEY, Loaning.**—See TRADE.

5384. MONEY, Morality and.—Money, and not morality, is the principle of commercial nations.—To JOHN LANGDON. v, 513. (1810.)

5385. MONEY, National rights and.—Money is the agent by which modern nations will recover their rights.—To COMTE DE MOUSTIER. ii, 389. FORD ED., v, 12. (P., 1788.)

— **MONEY, Prices and.**—See PAPER MONEY.

5386. MONEY, Scarcity of.—An unparalleled want of money here, and stoppage of discount at all the banks, oblige the merchants to slacken the price of wheat and flour; but it is only temporary.—To GEORGE GILMER. FORD ED., vi, 202. (Pa., 1793.)

5387. MONEY, Standard.—I believe all the countries in Europe determine their standard of money in gold as well as silver. Thus, the laws of England direct that a pound Troy of gold, of twenty-two carats fine, shall be cut into forty-four and a half guineas, each of which shall be worth twenty-one and a half shillings. that is, into 956 3-4 shillings. This establishes the shilling at 5.518 grains of *pure* gold. They direct that a pound of silver, consisting of 11 1-10 ounces of pure silver and 9-10 of an ounce alloy, shall be cut into sixty-two shillings. This establishes the shilling at 85.93 grains of pure silver, and, consequently, the proportion of gold to silver as 85.93 to 5.518, or as 15.57 to 1. If this be the true proportion between the value of gold and silver at the general market of Europe, then the value of the shilling, depending on two standards, is the same, whether a payment be made in gold or in silver. But if the proportion of the general market at Europe be as fifteen to one, then the Englishman who owes a pound weight of gold at Amsterdam, if he sends the pound of gold to pay it, sends 1043.72 shillings; if he sends fifteen pounds of silver, he sends only 1030.5 shillings; if he pays half in gold and half in silver. he pays only 1037.11 shillings. And this medium between the two standards of gold and silver, we must consider as furnishing the true medium value of the shilling. If the parliament should now order the pound of gold (of one-twelfth alloy as before) to be put into a thousand shillings instead of nine hundred and fifty-six and three-fourths, leaving the silver as it is, the medium or true value of the shilling would suffer a change of half the difference; and in the case before stated, to pay a debt of a pound weight of gold. at Amsterdam, if he sent the pound weight of gold, he would send 1090.9 shillings; if he sent fifteen pounds of silver, he would send 1030.5 shillings; if half in gold and half in silver, he would send 1060.7 shillings; which shows that this parliamentary operation would reduce the value of the shilling in the proportion of 1060.7 to 1037.11.—To J. SARSFIELD. iii, 18. (P., April 1789.)

5388. —— ——. Now this is exactly the effect of the late change in the quantity of gold contained in your louis. Your *marc d'argent fin* is cut into 53.45 livres (fifty-three livres and nine sous), the *marc de l'or fin* was cut, heretofore, by law, into 784.6 livres (seven hundred and eighty-four livres and twelve sous); gold was to silver then as 14.63 to 1. And if this was different from the proportion at the markets of Europe, the true value of your livre stood half way between the two standards. By the ordinance of October the 30th, 1785, the *marc* of pure gold has been cut into 828.6 livres. If your standard had been in gold alone, this would have reduced the value of your livre in the proportion of 828.6 to 784.6. But as you had a standard of silver as well as gold, the true standard is the medium between the two; consequently the value of the livre is reduced only one-half the difference, that is as 806.6 to 784.6, which is very nearly three per cent. Commerce, however, has made a difference of four per cent., the average value of the pound sterling, formerly twenty-four livres, being now twenty-five livres. Perhaps some other circumstance has occasioned an addition of one per cent. to the change of your standard.—To J. SARSFIELD. iii, 19. (P., April 1789.)

5389. —— ——. To trade on equal terms, the common measure of values should be as nearly as possible on a par with that of its corresponding nations, whose medium is in a sound state; that is to say, not in an accidental state of excess or deficiency. Now, one of the great advantages of specie as a medium is, that being of universal value, it will keep itself at a general level, flowing out from where it is too high into parts where it is lower. Whereas, if the medium be of local value only, as paper money, if too little, indeed, gold and silver will flow in to supply the deficiency; but if too much, it accumulates, banishes the gold and silver not locked up in vaults and hoards, and depreciates itself; that is to say, its proportion to the annual produce of industry being raised, more of it is required to represent any particular article of produce than in the other countries. This is agreed by [Adam] Smith, (B. 2. c. 2. 437.) the principal advocate for a paper circulation; but advocating it on the sole condition that it be strictly regulated. He admits, nevertheless, that "the commerce and industry of a country cannot be so secure when suspended on the Dædalian wings of paper money, as on the solid ground of gold and silver; and that in time of war, the insecurity is greatly increased, and great confusion possible where the circulation is for the greater part in paper". (B. 2. c. 2. 484.) But in a country where loans are uncertain, and a specie circulation the only sure resource for them, the preference of that circulation assumes a far different degree of importance.—To J. W. EPPES. vi, 233. FORD ED., ix, 407. (M., Nov. 1813.)

5390. —— ——. Our dropsical medium is long since divested of the quality of a medium of value; nor can I find any other. In most countries a fixed quantity of wheat is perhaps the best permanent standard. But here the blockade of our whole coast, preventing all access to a market, has depressed the price of that, and exalted that of other things, in opposite directions, and, combined with the effects of the paper deluge, leaves really no common measure of values to be resorted to.—To M. CORREA. vi, 406. (M., 1814.)

5391. —— ——. We have no metallic measure of values at present, while we are overwhelmed with bank paper. The depreciation of this swells nominal prices, without furnishing any stable index of real value.—To JEAN BAPTISTE SAY. vi, 434. (M., March 1815.)

5392. —— ——. We are now without any common measure of the value of property, and private fortunes are up or down at the will of the worst of our citizens. Yet there is no hope of relief from the Legislatures who have immediate control over this subject. As little seems to be known of the principles of political economy as if nothing had ever been written or practiced on the subject, or as was known in old times, when the Jews had their rulers under the hammer. It is an evil, therefore, which we must make up our minds to meet and to endure as those of hurricanes, earthquakes and other casualties.—To ALBERT GALLATIN. vi, 499. (M., Oct. 1815.)

5393. —— ——. The flood with which the banks are deluging us of nominal money has placed us completely without any certain measure of value, and, by interpolating a false measure, is deceiving and ruining multitudes of our citizens.—To ALBERT GALLATIN. FORD ED., x, 116. (M., 1818.)

5394. —— ——. There is one evil which awakens me at times, because it jostles me at every turn. It is that we have now no measure of value. I am asked eighteen dollars for a yard of broadcloth, which, when we had dollars, I used to get for eighteen shillings; from this I can only understand that a dollar is now worth but two inches of broadcloth, but broadcloth is no standard of measure or value. I do not know, therefore, whereabouts I stand in the scale of property, nor what to ask, or what to give for it. I saw, indeed, the like machinery in action in the years '80 and '81, and without dissatisfaction; because in wearing out, it was working out our salvation. But I see nothing in this renewal of the game of "*Robin's Alive*" but a general demoralization of the nation, a filching from industry its honest earnings, wherewith to build up palaces, and raise gambling stock for swindlers and shavers, who are to close, too, their career of piracies by fraudulent bankruptcies.—To NATHANIEL MACON. vii, 111. FORD ED., x, 121. (M., 1819.)

5395. —— ——. The evils of this deluge of paper money are not to be removed, until our citizens are generally and radically instructed in their cause and consequences, and silence by their authority the interested clamors and sophistry of speculating, shaving, and banking institutions. Till then we must be content to return, *quoad hoc*, to the savage state, to recur to barter in the exchange of our property, for want of a stable, common measure of value, that now in use being less fixed than the beads and wampum of the Indian, and to deliver up our citizens, their property and their labor, passive victims to the swindling tricks of bankers and mountebankers.—To JOHN ADAMS. vii, 115. (M., 1819.) See BANKS, DOLLAR, NATIONAL CURRENCY, and PAPER MONEY.

5396. MONEY, Unit of.—The plan reported by the Financier [Robert Morris] is worthy of his sound judgment. It admits, however, of objection in the size of the Unit. He proposes that this shall be the 1440th part of a dollar; so that it will require 1440 of his units to make the one before proposed. He was led to adopt this by a mathematical attention to our old currencies, all of which this Unit will measure without leaving a fraction. But as our object is to get rid of those currencies, the advantage derived from this coincidence will soon be past, whereas the inconveniences of this Unit will forever remain, if they do not altogether prevent its introduction. It is defective in two of the three requisites of a Money Unit. 1. It is inconvenient in its application to the ordinary money transactions. Ten thousand dollars will require eight figures to express them, to wit, 14,400,000 units. A horse or bullock of eighty dollars' value, will require a notation of six figures, to wit, 115,200 units. As a money of account, this will be laborious, even when facilitated by the aid of decimal arithmetic: as a common measure of the value of property, it will be too minute to be comprehended by the people. The French are subjected to very laborious calculations, the livre being their ordinary money of account, and this but between 1-5th and 1-6th of a dollar; but what will be our labors, should our money of account be 1-1440th of a dollar? 2. It is neither equal, nor near to any of the known coins in value.—NOTES ON A MONEY UNIT. i, 166. FORD ED., iii, 450. (1784.) See DOLLAR.

5397. —— ——. I concur with you in thinking that the Unit must stand on both metals.—To ALEXANDER HAMILTON. iii, 330. (Feb. 1792.)

5398. MONEY, War and.—Money is the nerve of war.—To ALBERT GALLATIN. vi, 498. (M., 1815.)

5399. MONEY BILLS, Origination.— Bills for levying money shall be originated

and amended by the Representatives only.— PROPOSED VA. CONSTITUTION. FORD ED., ii, 17. (June 1776.)

5400. —— ——. The Senate and the House of Representatives [of Virginia] shall each * * * have power to originate and amend bills; save only that bills for levying money shall be originated and amended by the representatives only: the assent of both houses shall be requisite to pass a law.— PROPOSED VA. CONSTITUTION. FORD ED., ii, 17. (June 1776.)

5401. MONEY BILLS, Parliament and. —By the law and usage of the British parliament, all those are understood to be money bills which raise money in any way, or which dispose of it, and which regulate those circumstances of matter, method and time, which attend as of consequence on the right of giving and disposing. Again, the law and customs of their Parliament, which include the usage as to "money bills", are a part of the law of their land; our ancestors adopted their system of law in the general, making from time to time such alterations as local diversities required; but that part of their law, which relates to the matter now in question, was never altered by our Legislature, in any period of its history; but on the contrary, the two Houses of Assembly, both under our regal and republican governments, have ever done business on the constant admission that the law of Parliament was their law.— CONGRESS REPORT. FORD ED., ii, 136. (1777.)

5402. —— ——. The right of levying money, in whatever way, being * * * exercised by the Commons, as their exclusive office, it follows, as a necessary consequence, that they may also exclusively direct its application. *"Cujus est dare, ejus est disponere"*, is an elementary principle both of law and of reason. That he who gives, may direct the application of the gift: or, in other words, may dispose of it; that if he may give absolutely, he may also carve out the conditions, limitations, purposes, and measure of the gift, seems as evidently true as that the greater power contains the lesser.—CONGRESS REPORT. FORD ED., ii, 139. (1778.)

5403. —— ——. In 1701, the Lords having amended a bill, "for stating and examining the public accounts", by inserting a clause for allowing a particular debt, the Commons disagreed to the amendment; and declared for a reason, "that the disposition, as well as granting of money by act of Parliament, hath ever been in the House of Commons; and, that the amendment relating to the disposal of money does entrench upon that right". And, to a bill of the same nature the year following, the Lords having proposed an amendment, and declared, "that their right in gaming, limiting, and disposing of public aids, being the main hinge of the controversy, they thought it of the highest concern that it should be cleared and settled". They then go on to prove the usage by precedents, and declarations, and from these conclude," that the limitation, disposition, and manner of account belong only to them ". —CONGRESS REPORT. FORD ED., ii, 140. (1778.)

5404. MONEY BILLS, Virginia Constitution and.—Had those who framed the [Virginia] Constitution, as soon as they had completed that work, been asked, man by man, what a money bill was, it is supposed that, man by man, they would have referred for answer to the well known laws and usages of Parliament, or would have formed their answer on the Parliamentary idea of that term. Its import, at this day, must be the same as it was then. And it would be as unreasonable, now, to send us to seek its definition in the subsequent proceedings of that body, as it would have been for them, at that day, to have referred us to such proceedings before they had come into existence. The meaning of the term must be supposed complete at the time they use it; and to be sought for in those resources only which existed at the time. Constructions, which do not result from the words of the legislator, but lie hidden in his breast, till called forth, *ex post facto*, by subsequent occasions, are dangerous, and not to be justified by ordinary emergencies.—CONGRESS REPORT. FORD ED., ii, 138. (1778.)

5405. MONEY (Continental), Depreciation of.—Previous to the Revolution, most of the States were in the habit, whenever they had occasion for more money than could be raised immediately by taxes, to issue paper notes or bills, in the name of the State, wherein they promised to pay to the bearer the sum named in the note or bill. In some of the States no time of payment was fixed, nor tax laid to enable payment. In these, the bills depreciated. But others of the States named in the bill the day when it should be paid, laid taxes to bring in money for that purpose, and paid the bills punctually, on or before the day named. In these States, paper money was in as high estimation as gold and silver. On the commencement of the late Revolution, Congress had no money. The external commerce of the States being suppressed, the farmer could not sell his produce, and, of course, could not pay a tax. Congress had no resource then but in paper money. Not being able to lay a tax for its redemption, they could only promise that taxes should be laid for that purpose, so as to redeem the bills by a certain day. They did not foresee the long continuance of the war, the almost total suppression of their exports, and other events, which rendered the performance of their engagement impossible. The paper money continued for a twelve-month equal to gold and silver. But the quantities which they were obliged to emit for the purpose of the war, exceeded what had been the usual quantity of the circulating medium. It began, therefore, to become cheaper, or, as we expressed it, it depreciated, as gold and silver would have done, had they been thrown into circulation in equal quantities. But not having, like them, an intrinsic value, its depreciation was more rapid and greater than could ever have happened with them. In two years, it had fallen to two dollars of paper money for one of silver; in three years, to four for one; in nine months more, it fell to ten for one; and in the six months following, that is to say, by September, 1779, it had fallen to twenty for one. Congress, alarmed at the consequences which were to be apprehended should they lose this resource altogether, thought it necessary to make a vigorous effort to stop its further depreciation. They, therefore, determined, in the first place, that their emissions should not exceed two hundred millions of dollars, to which term they were then nearly arrived; and though they knew that twenty dollars of what they were then issuing would buy no more for their army than one silver dollar would buy, yet they thought it would be worth while to submit to the sacrifice of nineteen out of twenty dollars, if they could thereby stop further depreciation. They, therefore published an address to their constituents, in which they renewed their original declarations, that this paper money should be redeemed at dollar for dollar. They proved the ability of the States to do this, and that their liberty would be cheaply bought at that price. The declaration was ineffectual. No man received the money at a better rate; on the contrary, in six months more, that is, by March, 1780, it had fallen to forty for one. Congress then tried an experiment of a different kind. Considering their former offers to redeem this money at par, as relinquished by the general refusal to take it but in progressive depreciation, they required the whole to be brought in, declared it should be redeemed at its present value, of forty for one, and that they would give to the holders new bills, reduced in their denomination to the sum of gold or silver, which was actually to be paid for them. This would reduce the nominal sum of the mass in circulation to the present worth of that mass, which was five millions; a sum not too great for the circulation of the States, and which, they therefore hoped, would not depreciate further, as they continued firm in their purpose of emitting no more. This effort was as unavailing as the former. Very little of the money was brought in. It continued to circulate and to depreciate till the end of 1780, when it had fallen to seventy-five for one, and the money circulated from the French army, being, by that time, sensible in all the States north of the Potomac, the paper ceased its circulation altogether in those States. In Virginia and North Carolina it continued a year longer, within which time it fell to one thousand for one, and then expired, as it had done in the other States, without a single groan. Not a murmur was heard on this occasion among the people. On the contrary, universal congratulations took place on their seeing this gigantic mass, whose dissolution had threatened convulsions which should shake their infant confederacy to its centre, quietly interred in its grave. Foreigners, indeed, who do not, like the natives, feel indulgence for its memory, as of a being which vindicated their liberties, and fallen in the moment of victory, have been loud, and still are loud in their complaints. A few of them have reason; but the most noisy are not the best of them. They are persons who have become bankrupt by unskilful attempts at commerce with America. That they may have some pretext to offer to their creditors, they have bought up great masses of this dead money in America, where it is to be had at five thousand for one. and they show the certificates of their paper possessions, as if they had all died in their hands, and had been the cause of their bankruptcy. Justice will be done to all, by paying to all persons what this money actually cost them, with an interest of six per cent. from the time they received it. If difficulties present themselves in the ascertaining the epoch of the receipt, it has been thought better that the State should lose. by admitting easy proofs, than that individuals. and especially foreigners, should, by being held to such as would be difficult, perhaps impossible.—To M. DE MEUNIER. ix, 248. FORD ED., iv, 153. (P., 1786.)

5406. MONEY (Continental), Redemption of.—It will be asked, how will the two masses of Continental and State money have cost the people of the United States seventy-two millions of dollars, when they are to be redeemed. now, with about six millions? I answer, that the difference, being sixty-six millions. has been lost on the paper bills, separately, by the successive holders of them. Every one, through whose hands a bill passed, lost on that bill what it lost in value, during the time it was in his hands. This was a real tax on him; and, in this way, the people of the United States actually contributed those sixty-six millions of dollars, during the war, and by a mode of taxation the most oppressive of all, because the most unequal of all.—To M. DE MEUNIER. ix, 260. FORD ED., iv, 165. (P., 1786.)

5407. —— ——. The soldier, victualer, or other person who received forty dollars for a service. at the close of the year 1779, received in fact, no more than he who received one dollar for the same service, in the year 1775, or 1776; because, in those years, the paper money was at par with silver; whereas, by the close of 1799, forty paper dollars were worth but one of silver, and would buy no more of the necessaries of life. —To M. DE MEUNIER. ix, 259. FORD ED., iv, 163. (P., 1786.)

5408. —— ——. As to the paper money in your hands. the States have not yet been able to take final arrangements for its redemption. But, as soon as they get their finances into some order, they will assuredly pay for what it was worth in silver at the time you received it, with interest.—To M. DULER. ii, 64. (P., 1786.) See ASSUMPTION OF STATE DEBTS.

— MONEY (Metallic) Alloy in.—See DOLLAR.

5409. MONEY (Metallic) Gold and silver ratio.—The proportion between the values of gold and silver is a mercantile problem altogether. It would be inaccurate to fix it by the popular exchanges of a half Joe for eight dollars, a Louis for four French crowns, or five Louis for twenty-three dollars. The first of these, would be to adopt* the Spanish proportion between gold and silver; the second, the French; the third, a mere popular barter, wherein convenience is consulted more than accuracy. The legal proportion in Spain is 16 for 1; in England 15 1-2 for 1; in France, 15 for 1. * * * Just principles will lead us to disregard legal proportions altogether; to enquire into the market price of gold, in the several countries with which we shall principally be connected in commerce, and to take an average from them. Perhaps we might, with safety, lean to a proportion somewhat above par for gold, considering our neighborhood, and commerce with the sources of the coins, and the tendency which the high price of gold in Spain has, to draw thither all that of their mines, leaving silver principally for our and other markets. It is not impossible that 15 for 1, may be found an eligible proportion. I state it, however, as a conjecture only.—NOTES ON A MONEY UNIT. i, 168. FORD ED., iii, 452. (1784.)

5410. —— ——. I observed * * * that the true proportion or value between gold and silver was a mercantile problem altogether and that, perhaps, fifteen for one might be found an eligible proportion. The Financier [Robert Morris] is so good as to inform me that this would be higher than the market would justify. Confident of his better information on this subject, I recede from that idea.†—SUPPLEMENTARY EXPLANATIONS. i, 171. FORD ED., iii, 454. (1784.)

5411. —— ——. There are particular public papers here [Paris] which collect and publish with a good deal of accuracy the facts connected with political arithmetic. In one of these I have just read the following table of the proportion between the value of gold and silver in several countries: Germany I. to 14 11-71. Spain I. to 14 3-10. Holland I. to 14 3-4. England I. to 15 1-2. France I. to 14 42-100. Savoy I. to 14 3-5. Russia I. to 15. The average is 1. to 14 5-8.—To JAMES MONROE. FORD ED., iv, 45. (P., 1785.)

5412. —— ——. I concur with you * * * in the proportion you establish between the value of the two metals.—To ALEXANDER HAMILTON. iii, 330. (Feb. 1792.) See DOLLAR.

* In the FORD EDITION the text reads, "would be *about* the Spanish proportion".—EDITOR.
† Jefferson appends this note: "In a newspaper, which frequently gives good details in political economy, I find under the Hamburg head, that the present market price of gold and silver is, in England, 15.5 for 1; in Russia, 15; in Holland, 14.75; in Savoy, 14.6; in France, 14.42; in Spain, 14.3; in Germany, 14.155; the average of which is 14.675 or 14 5-8. I would still incline to give a little more than the market price for gold, because of its superior convenience in transportation."—EDITOR.

5413. MONEY (Metallic), Payments in.
—As the laws authorize the payment of a given number of dollars to you, and as your duties place you in London, I suppose we are to pay you *the dollars* there, or other money of equal value, estimated by the par of the metals. Such has, accordingly, been the practice ever since the close of the war.—To Thomas Pinckney. iii, 526. (Pa., 1793.) See Banks, Dollar, Money, National Currency, and Paper Money.

5414. MONEY (Metallic) vs. PAPER MONEY.—Sober thinkers cannot prefer a paper medium at 13 per cent. interest to gold and silver for nothing.—To James Madison. Ford ed., v, 350. (Pa., 1791.)

5415. —— ——. Experience has proved to us that a dollar of silver disappears for every dollar of paper emitted.—To James Monroe. iii, 268. Ford ed., v, 353. (Pa., July, 1791.)

5416. —— ——. Admit none but a *metallic circulation* that will take its proper level with the like circulation in other countries.—To Charles Pinckney. vii, 180. Ford ed., x, 162. (M., 1820.) See Money.

5417. MONOPOLY, Abolish.—It is better to abolish monopolies in all cases, than not to do it in any.—To James Madison. ii, 446. Ford ed., v, 46. (P., 1788.)

5418. MONOPOLY, Banking.—The bill for establishing a National Bank undertakes * * * , to form the subscribers into a corporation [and] * * * to give them the sole and exclusive right of banking under the national authority; and so far is against the laws of *Monopoly*.—National Bank Opinion. vii, 555. Ford ed., v, 285. (1791.) See Banks, National Currency and Paper Money.

5419. —— ——. These foreign and false citizens * * * are advancing fast to a monopoly of our banks and public funds, thereby placing our finances under their control.—To Elbridge Gerry. iv, 172. Ford ed., vii, 121. (Pa., 1797.)

5420. MONOPOLY, Colonies and.—The monopoly of our [the Colonies] trade * * * brings greater loss to us and benefit to them than the amount of our proportional contributions to the common defence [of the empire].—Address to Governor Dunmore. Ford ed., i, 457. (1775.)

5421. —— ——. The Congress stated the lowest terms they thought possible to be accepted, in order to convince the world they were not unreasonable. They gave up the monopoly and regulation of trade, and all acts of Parliament prior to 1764, leaving to British generosity to render these, at some future time, as easy to America as the interest of Britain would admit.—To John Randolph. i, 201. Ford ed., i, 483. (M., 1775.)

5422. —— ——. It is not just that the Colonies should be required to oblige them-selves to other contributions while Great Britain possesses a monopoly of their trade. This does of itself lay them under heavy contribution. To demand, therefore, an additional contribution in the form of a tax, is to demand the double of their equal proportion. If we are to contribute equally with the other parts of the empire, let us equally with them enjoy free commerce with the whole world. But while the restrictions on our trade shut to us the resources of wealth, is it just we should bear all other burthens equally with those to whom every resource is open?—Reply to Lord North's Proposition. Ford ed., i, 479. (July 1775.) See Colonies.

5423. MONOPOLY, Commerce and.—By a declaration of rights, I mean one which shall stipulate * * * freedom of commerce against monopolies.—To A. Donald. ii, 355. (P., 1788.)

5424. —— ——. The British have wished a monopoly of commerce * * * with us, and they have in fact obtained it.—To Elbridge Gerry. iv, 172. Ford ed., vii, 121. (Pa., 1797.) See Commerce and Free Trade.

5425. —— ——. Nor should we wonder at * * * [the] pressure [for a fixed constitution in 1788-9] when we consider the monstrous abuses of power under which * * * [the French] people were ground to powder; when we pass in review the * * * shackles on commerce by monopolies.—Autobiography. i, 86. Ford ed., i, 118. (1821.)

5426. MONOPOLY, Corporations.—Nor should we wonder at the pressure [for a fixed constitution in France in 1788-9], when we consider the monstrous abuses of power under which this people were ground to powder, * * * the shackles * * * ; on industry by guilds and corporations * * * .—Autobiography. i, 86. Ford ed., i, 118. (1821.) See Incorporation.

5427. MONOPOLY, Farmers General.—The true obstacle to this proposition has penetrated, in various ways, through the veil which covers it. The influence of the Farmers General has been heretofore found sufficient to shake a minister in his office. Monsieur de Calonne's continuance or dismission has been thought, for some time, to be on a poise. Were he to shift this great weight, therefore, out of his own scale into that of his adversaries, it would decide their preponderance. The joint interests of France and America would be insufficient counterpoise in his favor.—Report to Congress. ix, 242. Ford ed., iv, 129. (P., 1785.)

5428. —— ——. As to the article of tobacco, which had become an important branch of remittance to almost all the States, I had the honor of communicating to you my proposition to the Court to abolish the monopoly of it in their farm; that the Count de Vergennes was, I thought, thoroughly sensible of the expediency of this proposition, and disposed to befriend it; that the renewal of the lease of the farms had been consequently suspended six months and was still in suspense, but that so powerful were the Farmers General and so tottering the tenure of the Minister of Finance in his office, that I despaired of preventing the renewal of the farm at that time. Things were in this state when the Marquis de Lafayette * * * proposed to me a conference with some persons well acquainted with the commercial system of this country. We met. They proposed the endeavoring to have a committee appointed to inquire into the subject. The proposition was made to the Count de Vergennes, who befriended it, and had the Marquis de Lafayette named a member of the committee. He became, of course, the active and truly zealous member for the liberty of commerce; others, though well-disposed, not choosing to oppose the farm openly. * * * The committee showed an early and decisive conviction that the measure taken by the farm to put the purchase of their tobaccos into monopoly on that side of the water, as the sale of them was on this, tended to the annihilation of commerce between the two countries. Various palliatives were proposed from time to time. I confess that I met them all with indifference; my object being a radical cure of the evils by discontinuing the farm, and not a mere assuagement of it for the present moment, which, rendering it more bearable, might lessen the necessity of removing it totally, and perhaps prevent that removal.—To JOHN JAY. FORD ED., iv, 232. (P., 1786.)

5429. —— ——. The Count de Vergennes said that the difficulty of changing so ancient an institution [Farmers General] was immense; that the King draws from it a revenue of 29 millions of livres; that an interruption of this revenue at least, if not a diminution, would attend a change; that their finances were not in a condition to bear even an interruption, and in short that no minister could venture to take upon himself so hazardous an operation. This was only saying explicitly what I had long been sensible of, that the Comptroller General's continuance in office was too much on a poise to permit him to shift this weight out of his own scale into that of his adversaries; and that we must be contented to await the completion of the public expectation that there will be a change in this office, which change may give us another chance for effecting this desirable reformation.—To JOHN JAY. FORD ED., iv, 234. (P., 1786.)

5430. —— ——. The only question agitated [at the next meeting of the committee] was how best to relieve the trade under its double monopoly. The committee found themselves supported by the presence and sentiments of the Count de Vergennes. They, therefore, resolved that the contract with Mr. Morris, if executed on his part, ought not to be annulled here, but that no similar one should ever be made hereafter; that, so long as it continued, the Farmers should be obliged to purchase from twelve to fifteen thousand hhds. of tobacco a year, over and above what they should receive from Mr. Morris, from such merchants as should bring it in French or American vessels, on the same conditions contracted with Mr. Morris; providing, however, that where the cargo shall not be assorted, the prices shall be $38, $36 and $34 for the 1st, 2d and 3d qualities of whichsoever the cargo may consist. In case of dispute about the quality, specimens are to be sent to the council, who will appoint persons to examine and decide on it. This is indeed the least bad of all the palliatives which have been proposed; but it contains the seeds of perpetual trouble. It is easy to foresee that the Farmers will multiply the difficulties and vexations on those who shall propose to sell to them by force, and that these will be making perpetual complaints, so that both parties will be kept on the fret. If, without fatiguing the friendly dispositions of the ministry, this should give them just so much trouble as may induce them to look to the demolition of the monopoly as a desirable point of rest, it may produce permanent as well as temporary good.—To JOHN JAY. FORD ED., iv, 235. (P., 1786.)

5431. —— ——. The body [Farmers General] to which this monopoly [tobacco] was given, was not mercantile. Their object is to simplify as much as possible the administration of their affairs. They sell for cash; they purchase, therefore, with cash. Their interest, their principles and their practice, seem opposed to the general interest of the kingdom, which would require that this capital article should be laid open to a free exchange for the productions of this country. So far does the spirit of simplifying their operations govern this body, that relinquishing the advantages to be derived from a competition of sellers, they contracted some time ago with a single person (Mr. Morris), for three years' supplies of American tobacco, to be paid for in cash. They obliged themselves too, expressly, to employ no other person to purchase in America, during that term. In consequence of this, the mercantile houses of France, concerned in sending her productions to be exchanged for tobacco, cut off, for three years, from the hope of selling these tobaccos in France, were of necessity to abandon that commerce. In consequence of this, too, a single individual, constituted sole purchaser of so great a proportion of the tobaccos made, had the price in his own power. A great reduction in it took place, and that, not only on the quantity he bought, but on the whole quantity made. The loss to the States producing the article did not go to cheapening it for their friends here. Their price was fixed. What was gained on their consumption was to enrich the person purchasing it; the rest, the monopolists and merchants of other countries.—To COUNT DE MONTMORIN. ii, 186. (P., 1787.)

5432. MONOPOLY, Indian trade.— Colonel McGillivray, with a company of British merchants, having hitherto enjoyed a monopoly of the commerce of the Creek nation, with a right of importing their goods duty free, and considering these privileges as the principal sources of his power over that nation, is unwilling to enter into treaty with us, unless they can be continued to him. And the question is how this may be done consistently with our laws, and so as to avoid just complaints from those of our citizens who would wish to participate of the trade? Our citizens, at this time, are not permitted to trade in that nation. The nation has a right to give us their peace, and to withhold their commerce, to place it under whatever monopolies or regulations they please. If they insist that only Colonel McGillivray and his company shall be permitted to trade among them, we have no right to say the contrary. We shall even gain some advantage in substituting citizens of the United States instead of British subjects, as associates of Colonel McGillivray, and excluding both British subjects and Spaniards from the country. Suppose, then, it be expressly stipulated by treaty, that no person be permitted to trade in the Creek country, without a license from the President, but that a fixed number shall be permitted to trade there at all, and that the goods imported for and sent to the Creek nation, shall be duty free. It may further be either expressed that the person licensed shall be approved by the leader or leaders of the nation, or without this, it may be understood between the President and McGillivray that the stipulated number of licenses shall be sent to him blank, to fill up.—OPINION ON INDIAN TRADE. vii, 504. FORD ED., v, 215. (1790.)

5433. ——— ———. The enclosed reclamations of Girod and Choate against the claims of Bapstropp to a monopoly of the Indian commerce, supposed to be under the protection of the 3rd article of the Louisiana Convention, as well as some other claims to abusive grants, will probably force us to meet that question. * * * Congress has [extended] about twenty particular laws * * * to Louisiana. Among these is the act concerning intercourse with the Indians, which establishes a system of intercourse with them admitting no monopoly. That class of rights, therefore, is now taken from under the treaty, and placed under the principles of our laws. —To JAMES MADISON. FORD ED., viii, 313. (July 1804.)

5434. MONOPOLY, Of influence.—The British have wished a monopoly of influence with us, and they have, in fact, obtained it.—To ELBRIDGE GERRY. iv, 172. FORD ED., vii, 121. (Pa., 1797.)

5435. MONOPOLY, Inventions and.—I like the declaration of rights as far as it goes, but I should have been for going further. For instance, the following alterations and additions would have pleased me. * * * . Article. 9. Monopolies may be allowed to persons for their own productions in literature, and their own inventions in the arts, for a term not exceeding — years, but for no

longer term, and for no other purpose.—To JAMES MADISON. iii, 101. FORD ED., v, 113. (P., Aug. 1789.)

5436. ——— ———. To embarrass society with monopolies for every utensil existing, and in all the details of life, would be more injurious to them than had the supposed inventors never existed; because the natural understanding of its members would have suggested the same things or others as good. —To OLIVER EVANS. v, 75. (M., 1807.) See INVENTIONS and PATENTS.

5437. MONOPOLY, Of the judiciary.— It is the self-appointment [of the county courts] I wish to correct; to find some means of breaking up a cabal, when such a one gets possession of the bench. When this takes place, it becomes the most afflicting of tyrannies, because its powers are so various, and exercised on everything most immediately around us. And how many instances have you and I known of these monopolies of county administration? I know a county in which a particular family (a numerous one) got possession of the bench, and for a whole generation never admitted a man on it who was not of its clan or connection. I know a county now of one thousand and five hundred militia, of which sixty are federalists. Its court is of thirty members, of whom twenty are federalists (every third man of the sect). There are large and populous districts in it without a justice, because without a federalist for appointment; the militia are as disproportionably under federal officers. * * * The remaining one thousand four hundred and forty, free, fighting and paying citizens, are governed by men neither of their choice or confidence, and without a hope of relief. They are certainly excluded from the blessings of a free government for life, and indefinitely, for aught the Constitution has provided. This solecism may be called anything but republican.—To JOHN TAYLOR. vii, 18. FORD ED., x, 52. (M., 1816.)

5438. MONOPOLY, Land.—The property of France is absolutely concentrated in a very few hands, having revenues of from half a million of guineas a year downwards. These employ the flower of the country as servants, some of them having as many as two hundred domestics, not laboring. They employ also a great number of manufacturers, and tradesmen, and lastly the class of laboring husbandmen. But after all, there comes the most numerous of all the classes, that is, the poor who cannot find work. I asked myself what could be the reason that so many should be permitted to beg who are willing to work, in a country where there is a very considerable proportion of uncultivated lands? Those lands are undisturbed only for the sake of game. It should seem then that it must be because of the enormous wealth of the proprietors which places them above attention to the increase of their revenues by permitting these lands to be labored.—To REV. JAMES MADISON. FORD ED., vii, 35. (P., 1785.)

5439. MONOPOLY, Limited.—I sincerely rejoice at the acceptance of the new Constitution by nine States. It is a good canvas, on which some strokes only want retouching. What these are, I think are sufficiently manifested by the general voice from north to south, which calls for a bill of rights. It seems pretty generally understood that this should go to * * * monopolies. * * * The saying there shall be no monopolies, lessens the incitements to ingenuity, which is spurred on by the hope of a monopoly for a limited time, as of fourteen years; but the benefit of even limited monopolies is too doubtful to be opposed to that of their general suppression.—To JAMES MADISON. ii, 445. FORD ED., v, 45. (P., July 1788.)

5440. MONOPOLY, Military.—Nor should we wonder at the pressure [for a fixed constitution in 1788-9], when we consider the monstrous abuses of power under which * * * the [French] people were ground to powder, when we pass in review the * * * monopoly of military honors by the noblesse * * * .—AUTOBIOGRAPHY. i, 86. FORD ED., i, 118. (1821.)

5441. MONOPOLY, Of office.—When it is considered that during the late administration, those who were not of a particular sect of politics were excluded from all office; when, by a steady pursuit of this measure, nearly the whole offices of the United States were monopolized by that sect; when the public sentiment at length declared itself, and burst open the doors of honor and confidence to those whose opinions they more approved, was it to be imagined that this monopoly of office was still to be continued in the hands of the minority? Does it violate their *equal rights* to assert some rights in the majority also? Is it *political intolerance* to claim a proportionate share in the direction of the public affairs? Can they not *harmonize* in society unless they have everything in their own hands? —To THE NEW HAVEN COMMITTEE. iv, 404. FORD ED., viii, 69. (W., July 1801.)

5442. MONOPOLY, Restrict.—I do not like [in the new Federal Constitution] the omission of a bill of rights, providing clearly and without the aid of sophisms for * * * restriction of monopolies.—To JAMES MADISON. ii, 329. FORD ED., iv, 476. (P., December 1787.)

5443. MONOPOLY, Special privileges. —Monopolizing compensations are among the most fatal abuses which some governments practice from false economy.—OPINION ON STEVENS CASE. ix, 474. (1804.)

5444. MONOPOLY, Suppress.—A company had silently and by unfair means obtained a monopoly for the making and selling spermaceti candles [in France]. As soon as we* discovered it, we solicited its suppression which is effected by a clause in the *Arret.*—To JOHN JAY. ii, 342. (P., 1787.).

* An acknowledgment of Lafayette's assistance.— EDITOR.

5445. MONOPOLY, Tobacco.—The abolition of the monopoly of our tobacco in the hands of the Farmers General will be pushed by us with all our force. But it is so interwoven with the very foundations of their system of finance that it is of doubtful event.— To JAMES MONROE. FORD ED., iv, 20. (P., Dec. 1784.)

5446. ——— ———. The monopoly of the purchase of tobacco in France discourages both the French and American merchant from bringing it here, and from taking in exchange the manufactures and productions of France. It is contrary to the spirit of trade, and to the dispositions of merchants, to carry a commodity to any market where but one person is allowed to buy it, and where, of course, that person fixes its price which the seller must receive, or reexport his commodity, at the loss of his voyage thither. Experience accordingly shows that they carry it to other markets, and that they take in exchange the merchandise of the place where they deliver it. I am misinformed, if France has not been furnished from a neighboring nation with considerable quantities of tobacco since the peace, and been obliged to pay there in coin, what might have been paid here (France) in manufactures, had the French and American merchants brought the tobacco originally here. I suppose, too, that the purchases made by the Farmers General in America are paid for chiefly in coin, which coin is also remitted directly hence to England, and makes an important part of the balance supposed to be in favor of that nation against this. Should the Farmers General, by themselves, or by the company to whom they may commit the procuring these tobaccos from America, require, for the satisfaction of government on this head, the exportation of a proportion of merchandise in exchange for them, it would be an unpromising expedient. It would only commit the exports, as well as imports, between France and America, to a monopoly which, being secure against rivals in the sale of the merchandise of France, would not be likely to sell at such moderate prices as might encourage its consumption there, and enable it to bear a competition with similar articles from other countries. I am persuaded this exportation of coin may be prevented, and that of commodities effected, by leaving both operations to the French and American merchants, instead of the Farmers General. They will import a sufficient quantity of tobacco, if they are allowed a perfect freedom in the sale; and they will receive in payment, wines, oils, brandies, and manufactures, instead of coin; forcing each other, by their competition, to bring tobaccos of the best quality; to give to the French manufacturer the full worth of his merchandise, and to sell to the American consumer at the lowest price they can afford; thus encouraging him to use, in preference, the merchandise of this country.—To COUNT DE VERGENNES. i, 386. (P., 1785.)

5447. —— ——. If, by a simplification of the collection of the King's duty on tobacco, the cost of that collection can be reduced even to five per cent., or a million and a half, instead of twenty-five millions; the price to the consumer will be reduced from three to two livres the pound. * * * The price, being thus reduced one-third, would be brought within the reach of a new and numerous circle of the people, who cannot, at present, afford themselves this luxury. The consumption, then, would probably increase, and perhaps, in the same if not a greater proportion with the reduction of the price; that is to say, from twenty-four to thirty-six millions of pounds; and the King, continuing to receive twenty-five sous on the pound, as at present, would receive forty-five instead of thirty millions of livres, while his subjects would pay but two livres for an object which has heretofore cost them three. Or if, in event, the consumption were not to be increased, he would levy only forty-eight millions on his people, where seventy-two millions are now levied, and would leave twenty-four millions in their pockets, either to remain there, or to be levied in some other form, should the state of revenue require it. It will enable his subjects, also, to dispose of between nine and ten millions worth of their produce and manufactures, instead of sending nearly that sum annually, in coin, to enrich a neighboring nation.—To COUNT DE VERGENNES. i, 388. (P., 1785.)

5448. —— ——. I have heard two objections made to the suppression of this monopoly. 1. That it might increase the importation of tobacco in contraband. 2. That it would lessen the abilities of the Farmers General to make occasional loans of money to the public treasury. * * * With respect to the first * * * I may observe that contraband does not increase on lessening the temptations to it. It is now encouraged by those who engage in it being able to sell for sixty sous what cost but fourteen, leaving a gain of forty-six sous. When the price shall be reduced from sixty to forty sous, the gain will be but twenty-six, that is to say, a little more than one-half of what it is at present. It does not seem a natural consequence then, that contraband should be increased by reducing its gain nearly one-half. As to the second objection, if we suppose (for elucidation and without presuming to fix) the proportion of the farm on tobacco, at one-eighth of the whole mass farmed, the abilities of the Farmers General to lend will be reduced one-eighth, that is, they can hereafter lend only seven millions, where heretofore they have lent eight. It is to be considered, then, whether this eighth (or other proportion, whatever it be) is worth the annual sacrifice of twenty-four millions, or if a much smaller sacrifice to other moneyed men, will not produce the same loans of money in the ordinary way.—To COUNT DE VERGENNES. i, 389. (P., 1785.)

5449. —— ——. While the advantages of an increase of revenue to the crown, a diminution of impost on the people, and a payment in merchandise, instead of money, are conjectured as likely to result to France from a suppression of the monopoly on tobacco, we have also reason to hope some advantages on our part * * * . I do not expect this advantage will be by any augmentation of price. The other markets of Europe have too much influence on this article to admit any sensible augmentation of price to take place. But the advantage I principally expect is an increase of consumption. This will give us a vent for so much more, and, of consequence, find employment for so many more cultivators of the earth; and, in whatever proportion it increases this production for us, in the same proportion will it procure additional vent for the merchandise of France, and employment for the hands that produce it. I expect, too, that by bringing our merchants here, they would procure a number of commodities in exchange, better in kind and cheaper in price.—To THE COUNT DE VERGENNES. i, 390. (P., 1785.)

5450. —— ——. I observed [to the Count de Vergennes] that France paid us two millions of livres for tobacco; that for such portions of it as were bought in London, they sent the money directly there, and for what they bought in the United States, the money was still remitted to London by bills of exchange; whereas, if they would permit our merchants to sell this article freely, they would bring it here, and take the returns on the spot in merchandise, not money. The Count observed that my proposition contained what was doubtless useful, but that the king received on this article, at present, a revenue of twenty-eight millions, which was so considerable as to render them fearful of tampering with it; that the collection of this revenue by way of Farm was of very ancient date, and that it was always hazardous to alter arrangements of long standing, and of such infinite combinations with the fiscal system. I answered, that the simplicity of the mode of collection proposed for this article, withdrew it from all fear of deranging other parts of their system; that I supposed they would confine the importation to some of their principal ports, probably not more than five or six; that a single collector in each of these was the only new officer requisite; that he could get rich himself on six livres a hogshead, and would receive the whole revenue, and pay it into the treasury, at short hand.—CONFERENCE WITH COUNT DE VERGENNES. ix, 232. FORD ED., iv, 119. (1785.)

5451. —— ——. I have received the propositions of Messrs. Ross, Pleasants, &c., for furnishing tobacco to the Farmers General; but Mr. Morris had, in the meantime, obtained the contract. I have been fully sensible of the baneful influence on the commerce of France and America, which this double monopoly will have. I have struck at its root here, and spared no pains to have the farm itself demolished, but it has been in vain. The persons interested in it are too powerful to be opposed, even by the interest of the whole country.—To GOVERNOR PATRICK HENRY. i, 515. FORD ED., iv, 137. (P., 1786.)

5452. —— ——. Till I see all hope of removing the evil [the tobacco monopoly in France] by the roots desperate, I cannot propose to prune its branches.—To JOHN PAGE. i, 549. FORD ED., iv, 213. (P., 1786.)

5453. —— ——. Morris's contract for sixty thousand hogsheads of tobacco has been concluded with the Farmers General. I have been for some time occupied in endeavoring to destroy the root of the evils which the tobacco trade encounters in this country, by making the ministers sensible that merchants will not bring a commodity to a market, where but one person is allowed to buy it; and that so long as that single purchaser is obliged to go to foreign markets for it, he must pay for it in coin, and not in commodities. These truths have made their way to the minds of the ministry, insomuch as to have delayed the execution of the new lease of the Farms six months. It is renewed, however, for three years, but so as not to render impossible a reformation of this great evil. They are sensible of the evil, but it is so interwoven with their fiscal system, that they find it hazardous to disentangle. The temporary distress, too, of the revenue, they are not prepared to meet. My hopes, therefore, are weak, though not quite desperate. When they become so, it will remain to look about for the best palliative this monopoly can bear. My present idea is that it will be found in a prohibition to the Farmers General to purchase tobacco anywhere but in France.—To JAMES ROSS. i, 560. FORD ED., iv, 216. (P., 1786.)

5454. —— ——. I consider [the suppression of the tobacco monopoly in France] as the most effectual means of procuring the full value of our produce, of diverting our demands for manufactures from Great Britain to this country to a certain amount, and of thus producing some equilibrium in our commerce which, at present, lies all in the British scale. It would cement an union with our friends, and lessen the torrent of wealth we are pouring into the laps of our enemies.—To T. PLEASANTS. i, 563. (P., 1786.)

5455. —— ——. I think that so long as the monopoly in the sale [of tobacco] is kept up, it is of no consequence to us how they modify the pill for their own internal relief; but, on the contrary, the worse it remains, the more necessary it will render a reformation. Any palliative would take from us all those arguments and friends that would be satisfied with accommodation. The Marquis de Lafayette, though differing from me in opinion on this point, has, however, adhered to my principle of absolute liberty or nothing.—To COL. MONROE. i, 568. FORD ED., iv, 225. (P., 1786.)

5456. —— ——. Some symptoms make me suspect that my proceedings to reduce the abusive administration of tobacco by the Farmers General have indisposed towards me a powerful person in Philadelphia, who was profiting from that abuse. An expression in the enclosed letter of M. de Calonnes would seem to imply that I had asked the abolition of Mr. Morris's contract. I never did. On the contrary, I always observed to them that it would be unjust to annul that contract. I was led to this by principles both of justice and interest. Of interest, because that contract would keep up the price of tobacco here to thirty-four, thirty-six and thirty-eight livres, from which it will fall when it shall no longer have that support. However, I have done what was right, and I will not so far wound my privilege of doing that, without regard to any man's interest, as to enter into any explanation of this paragraph with him. Yet I esteem him highly, and suppose that hitherto he had esteemed me.—To JAMES MONROE. ii, 70. (P., 1786.)

5457. —— ——. I shall certainly press for something to be done by way of antidote to the monopoly under which tobacco is placed in France.—To JOSEPH FENWICK. ii, 182. (P., 1787.)

5458. —— ——. Of these eighty millions [of American exports to Europe], thirty are constituted by the single article of tobacco. Could the whole of this be brought into the ports of France, to satisfy its own demands, and the residue be revended to other nations, it would be a powerful link of commercial connection. But we are far from this.

Even her own consumption, supposed to be nine millions, under the administration of the monopoly to which it is farmed, enters little, as an article of exchange, into the commerce of the two nations. When this article was first put into Farm, perhaps it did not injure the commercial interests of the kingdom; because nothing but British manufactures were then allowed to be given in return for American tobaccos. The laying the trade open, then, to all the subjects of France, would not have relieved her from a payment in money. Circumstances are changed; yet the old institution remains.—To COUNT DE MONTMORIN. ii, 186. (P., 1787.)

5459. —— ——. The effect of this operation was vitally felt by every farmer in America, concerned in the culture of this plant. At the end of the year, he found he had lost a fourth or a third of his revenue; the State, the same proportion of its subjects of exchange with other nations. The manufacturers of this country [France], too, were either not to go there at all, or go through the channel of a new monopoly, which, freed from the control of competition in prices and qualities, was not likely to extend their consumption. It became necessary to relieve the two countries from the fatal effects of this double monopoly.—To COUNT DE MONTMORIN. ii, 187. (P., 1787.)

5460. —— ——. The governments have nothing to do, but not to hinder their merchants from making the exchange.—To COUNT DE MONTMORIN. ii, 189. (P., 1787.)

5461. MONOPOLY, Western trade.— The Ohio and its branches, which head up against the Potomac, afford the shortest water communication by five hundred miles of any which can ever be got between the western waters and Atlantic; and, of course, promise us almost a monopoly of the Western and Indian trade.—To JAMES MADISON. FORD ED., iii, 402. (A., Feb. 1784.)

5462. MONOPOLY, Whale oil.—My endeavors for emancipating the tobacco trade have been less successful [than have been those with respect to whale oil]. I still continue to stir, however, this and all other articles.—To MR. OTTO. i, 559. (P., 1786.)

5463. —— ——. On the subject of the whale fishery, I enclose you some observations I drew up for the ministry here, in order to obtain a correction of their *Arret* of September last, whereby they had involved our oils with the English, in a general exclusion from their ports. They will accordingly correct this, so that our oils will participate with theirs, in the monopoly of their markets.—To GENERAL WASHINGTON. ii, 538. FORD ED., v, 60. (P., 1788.)

5464. —— ——. I have obtained the promise of an explanatory *Arret* to declare that that of September 28 [1788], was not meant to extend to us. Orders are accordingly given in the ports to receive our [oils]. This places us on a better footing than ever, as it gives us a monopoly of this market in conjunction with the French fishermen.—To THOMAS PAINE. ii, 549. (P., 1788.)

5465. MONROE DOCTRINE, Jefferson and.—The question presented by the letters*

* The letters were those of Mr. Rush, our minister at the Court of St. James's, in which he communi-

you have sent me, is the most momentous which has been offered to my contemplation since that of Independence. That made us a nation, this sets our compass and points the course which we are to steer through the ocean of time opening on us. And never could we embark on it under circumstances more auspicious. Our first and fundamental maxim should be, never to entangle ourselves in the broils of Europe. Our second, never to suffer Europe to intermeddle with cis-Atlantic affairs. America, North and South, has a set of interests distinct from those of Europe, and peculiarly her own. She should therefore have a system of her own, separate and apart from that of Europe. While the last is laboring to become the domicile of despotism, our endeavor should surely be, to make our hemisphere that of freedom. One nation, most of all, could disturb us in this pursuit: she now offers to lead, aid, and accompany us in it. By acceding to her proposition, we detach her from the bands, bring her mighty weight into the scale of free government, and emancipate a continent at one stroke, which might otherwise linger long in doubt and difficulty. Great Britain is the nation which can do us the most harm of any one, or all on earth; and with her on our side we need not fear the whole world. With her, then, we should most sedulously cherish a cordial friendship; and nothing would tend more to knit our affections than to be fighting once more, side by side in the same cause. Not that I would purchase even her amity at the price of taking part in her wars. But the war in which the present proposition might engage us, should that be its consequence, is not her war, but ours. Its object is to introduce and establish the American system, of keeping out of our land all foreign powers, of never permitting those of Europe to intermeddle with the affairs of our nations. It is to maintain our own principle, not to depart from it. And if, to facilitate this, we can effect a division in the body of the European powers, and draw over to our side its most powerful member, surely we should do it. But I am clearly of Mr. Canning's opinion, that, it will prevent instead of provoke war. With Great Britain withdrawn from their scale and shifted into that of our two continents, all Europe combined would not undertake such a war. For how would they propose to get at either enemy without superior fleets? Nor is the occasion to be slighted which this proposition offers, of declaring our protest against the atrocious violations of the rights of nations, by the interference of any one in the internal affairs of another, so flagitiously begun by Bonaparte, and now continued by the equally

cated to President Monroe the proposition of Mr. Canning that the United States and England should issue a joint declaration announcing that, while the two governments desired for themselves no portion of the Spanish-American colonies, then in revolt against Spain, they would not view with indifference any foreign intervention in their affairs, or their acquisition by a third power. The declaration was intended to be a warning to the allied powers, Russia, Prussia and Austria, the members of the Holy Alliance.—EDITOR.

lawless Alliance, calling itself Holy. But we have first to ask ourselves a question. Do we wish to acquire to our own confederacy any one or more of the Spanish provinces? I candidly confess, that I have ever looked on Cuba as the most interesting addition which could ever be made to our system of States. The control which, with Florida Point, this island would give us over the Gulf of Mexico, and the countries and isthmus bordering on it, as well as all those whose waters flow into it, would fill up the measure of our political well-being. Yet, as I am sensible that this can never be obtained, even with her own consent, but by war; and its independence, which is our second interest (and especially its independence of England), can be secured without it. I have no hesitation in abandoning my first wish to future chances, and accepting its independence, with peace and the friendship of England, rather than its association, at the expense of war and her enmity. I could honestly, therefore, join in the declaration proposed, that we aim not at the acquisition of any of those possessions, that we will not stand in the way of any amicable arrangement between them and the mother country; but that we will oppose, with all our means, the forcible interposition of any other power, as auxiliary, stipendiary, or under any other form or pretext, and most especially, their transfer to any power by conquest, cession, or acquisition in any other way.* I should

* The subjoined extract from President Monroe's Message to Congress on Dec. 2d, 1823, embodies the Monroe Doctrine:

"In the wars of European powers, in matters relating to themselves, we have never taken any part, nor does it comport with our policy so to do. It is only when our rights are invaded or seriously menaced that we resent injuries or make preparations for our defence. With the movements on this hemisphere we are, of necessity, more immediately connected, and by causes which must be obvious to all enlightened and impartial observers. The political system of the allied powers [the Holy Alliance] is essentially different in this respect from that of America. This difference proceeds from that which exists in their respective governments. And to the defence of our own, which has been achieved by the loss of so much blood and treasure, and matured by the wisdom of their most enlightened citizens, and under which we have enjoyed unexampled felicity, this whole Nation is devoted. We owe it, therefore, to candor and to the amicable relations existing between the United States and those powers to declare that we should consider any attempt on their part to extend their system to any portion of this hemisphere as dangerous to our peace and safety. With the existing colonies or dependencies of any European power we have not interfered, and shall not interfere. But with the Governments who have declared their independence and maintained it we have, on great consideration and on just principles, acknowledged, we could not view any interposition for the purpose of oppressing them, or controlling in any other manner their destiny, by any European power, in any other light than as the manifestation of an unfriendly disposition towards the United States. Our policy in regard to Europe, which was adopted at an early stage of the wars which have so long agitated that quarter of the globe, nevertheless remains the same, which is not to interfere in the internal concerns of any of its powers; to consider the Government de facto as the legitimate Government for us; to cultivate friendly relations with it, and to preserve those relations by a frank, firm, and manly policy; meeting in all instances the just claims of every power, submitting to injuries from none. But in regard to these continents, circumstances are eminently and conspicuously different. It is impossible that the allied powers should extend think it, therefore, advisable, that the Executive should encourage the British government to a continuance in the dispositions expressed in these letters, by an assurance of his concurrence with them as far as his authority goes; and that as it may lead to war, the declaration of which requires an act of Congress, the case shall be laid before them for consideration at their first meeting, and under the reasonable aspect in which it is seen by himself. I have been so long weaned from political subjects, and have so long ceased to take any interest in them, that I am sensible I am not qualified to offer opinions on them worthy of any attention. But the question now proposed involves consequences so lasting, and effects so decisive of our future destinies, as to rekindle all the interest I have heretofore felt on such occasions, and to induce me to the hazard of opinions, which will prove only my wish to contribute still my mite towards anything which may be useful to our country.*—To PRESIDENT MONROE. vii, 315. FORD ED., x, 277. (M., October 1823.) See POLICY.

5466. MONROE (James), Ability.— Many points in Monroe's character would render him the most valuable acquisition the republican interest in this Legislature [Congress] could make.—To JOHN TAYLOR. FORD ED., vii, 322. (Pa., Jan. 1799.)

**5467. ————. ** I clearly think with you on the competence of Monroe to embrace great views of action. The decision of his character, his enterprise, firmness, industry, and unceasing vigilance, would, I believe, secure, as I am sure they would merit, the public confidence, and give us all the success which our means can accomplish.—To WILLIAM DUANE. vi, 81. FORD ED., ix, 368. (M., Oct. 1812.)

5468. MONROE (James), Book by.— Your book * * * works irresistibly. It would be very gratifying to you to hear the unqualified eulogies both on the matter and manner by all who are not hostile to it from principle.—To JAMES MONROE. FORD ED., vii, 183. (Pa., Dec. 1797.)

5469. ————. Monroe's book is considered as masterly by all those who are not opposed in principle, and it is deemed unanswerable. An answer, however, is commenced in Fenno's paper, under the signature of "Scipio" [Uriah Tracy]. The real author is not yet

their political system to any portion of either continent without endangering our peace and happiness; nor can any one believe that our Southern brethren, if left to themselves, would adopt it of their own accord. It is equally impossible, therefore, that we should behold such interposition, in any form, with indifference."—EDITOR.
* Morse, in his *Life of Jefferson* (p. 235), says: "It is curious to note that in the course of this business (navigation of Mississippi), there was already a faint foreshadowing of that principle, which many years afterwards was christened with the name of Monroe. For a brief time it was thought, not without reason, that so soon as hostilities should break out between England and Spain, the former power would seize upon the North American possessions of the latter. Jefferson wrote to Gouverneur Morris: 'We wish you, therefore, to intimate to them (the British ministry) that we cannot be indifferent to enterprises of this kind. That we should contemplate a change of neighbors with extreme uneasiness. That a due balance on our borders is not less desirable to us than a balance of power in Europe has always appeared to them'."—EDITOR.

conjectured.—To JAMES MADISON. iv, 206. FORD ED., vii, 190. (Pa., Jan. 1798.)

5470. MONROE (James), British treaty and.— You complain of the manner in which the [British] treaty was received. But what was that manner? I cannot suppose you to have given a moment's credit to the stuff which was crowded in all sorts of forms into the public papers, or to the thousand speeches they put into my mouth, not a word of which I had ever uttered. I was not insensible at the time of the views to mischief, with which these lies were fabricated. But my confidence was firm, that neither yourself nor the British government, equally outraged by them, would believe me capable of making the editors of newspapers the confidants of my speeches or opinions. The fact was this. The treaty was communicated to us by Mr. Erskine on the day Congress was to rise. Two of the senators enquired of me in the evening, whether it was my purpose to detain them on account of the treaty. My answer was, "that it was not; that the treaty containing no provision against the impressment of our seamen, and being accompanied by a kind of protestation of the British ministers, which would leave that government free to consider it as a treaty or no treaty, according to their own convenience, I should not give them the trouble of deliberating on it". This was substantially, and almost verbally, what I said whenever spoken to about it, and I never failed when the occasion would admit of it, to justify yourself and Mr. Pinckney, by expressing my conviction, that it was all that could be obtained from the British government; that you had told their commissioners that your government could not be pledged to ratify, because it was contrary to their instructions; of course, that it should be considered but as a *projet;* and in this light I stated it publicly in my message to Congress on the opening of the session. Not a single article of the treaty was ever made known beyond the members of the administration, nor would an article of it be known at this day, but for its publication in the newspapers, as communicated by somebody from beyond the water, as we have always understood. But as to myself, I can solemnly protest, as the most sacred of truths, that I never, one instant, lost sight of your reputation and favorable standing with your country, and never omitted to justify your failure to attain our wish, as one which was probably unattainable. Reviewing, therefore, this whole subject, I cannot doubt you will become sensible, that your impressions have been without just ground.—To JAMES MONROE. v, 254. FORD ED., ix, 179. (W., March 1808.) See IMPRESSMENT.

5471. MONROE (James), Confidence in.— I have had, and still have, such entire confidence in the late and present Presidents, that I willingly put both soul and body into their pockets.—To NATHANIEL MACON. vii, 111. FORD ED., x, 120. (M., 1819.)

5472. MONROE (James), Defence of.— I should be glad to see the defence of Monroe's conduct which you possess, though no paper of that title is necessary to me. He was appointed to an office during pleasure merely to get him out of the Senate, and with an intention to seize the first pretext for exercising the pleasure of recalling him. * * * I think with you it will be best to publish nothing concerning Colonel Monroe till his return, that he may accommodate the complexion of his publication to times and circumstances.—To JOHN EDWARDS. iv, 164. FORD ED., vii, 112. (M., Jan. 1797.)

5473. —— ——. I understand that the opposite party admit that there is nothing in your conduct which can be blamed, except the divulging secrets; and this, I think, might be answered by a few sentences, discussing the question whether an ambassador is the representative of his country or of the President.—To JAMES MONROE. FORD ED., vii, 197. (Pa., Feb. 1798.)

5474. MONROE (James), Diplomatic expenses.—Although it is not pleasant to fall short in returning civilities, yet necessity has rendered this so familiar in Europe as not to lessen respect for the person whose circumstances do not permit a return of hospitalities. I see by your letters the pain which this situation gives you, and I can estimate its acuteness from the generosity of your nature. But, my dear friend, calculate with mathematical rigor the pain annexed to each branch of the dilemma, and pursue that which brings the least. To give up entertainment, and to live with the most rigorous economy till you have cleared yourself of every demand is a pain for a definite time only; but to return here with accumulated encumbrances on you, will fill your life with torture. We wish to do everything for you which law and rule will permit. But more than this would injure you as much as us. Believing that the mission to Spain will enable you to suspend expense greatly in London, and to apply your salary during your absence to the clearing off your debt, you will be instructed to proceed there as soon as you shall have regulated certain points of neutral right for us with England, or as soon as you find nothing in that way can be done.—To JAMES MONROE. FORD ED., viii, 288. (W., Jan. 1804.)

5475. MONROE (James), Distaste for law.—You wish not to engage in the drudgery of the bar. You have two asylums from that. Either to accept a seat in the Council, or in the Judiciary department. The latter, however, would require a little previous drudgery at the bar to qualify you to discharge your duty with satisfaction to yourself. Neither of these would be inconsistent with a continued residence at Albemarle. It is but twelve hours' drive in a sulky from Charlottesville to Richmond, keeping a fresh horse always at the half-way, which would be a small annual expense.—To JAMES MONROE. ii, 71. (P., 1786.)

5476. MONROE (James), English mission.—I perceive that painful impressions have been made on your mind during your late mission, of which I had never entertained a suspicion. I must, therefore, examine the grounds, because explanations between reasonable men can never but do good. 1. You consider the mission of Mr. Pinkney as an associate, to have been in some way injurious to you. Were I to take that measure on myself, I might say in its justification, that it has been the regular and habitual practice of the United States to do this, under every form in which their government has existed. I need not recapitulate the multiplied instances, because you will readily recollect them. I went as an adjunct to Dr. Franklin, and Mr. Adams, yourself as an adjunct first to Mr. Livingston, and then to Mr. Pinkney, and I really believe there has scarcely been a great occasion which has not produced an extraordinary mission. Still, however, it is well known that I was strongly opposed to it in the case of which you complain. A committee of the Senate called on

me with two resolutions of that body, on the subject of impressment and spoliations by Great Britain, and requesting that I would demand satisfaction. After delivering the resolutions, the committee entered into free conversation, and observed that although the Senate could not, in form, recommend any extraordinary mission, yet that as individuals, there was but one sentiment among them on the measure, and they pressed it. I was so much averse to it, and gave them so hard an answer, that they felt it, and spoke of it. But it did not end here. The members of the other House took up the subject, and set upon me individually, and these the best friends to you, as well as myself, and represented the responsibility which a failure to obtain redress would throw on us both, pursuing a conduct in opposition to the opinion of nearly every member of the Legislature. I found it necessary, at length, to yield my own opinion to the general sense of the national council, and it really seemed to produce a jubilee among them; not from any want of confidence in you, but from a belief in the effect which an extraordinary mission would have on the British mind, by demonstrating the degree of importance which this country attached to the rights which we considered as infracted.—To JAMES MONROE. v, 253. FORD ED., ix, 178. (W., March 1808.)

5477. MONROE (James), Friendship for.—I have ever viewed Mr. Madison and yourself as two principal pillars of my happiness. Were either to be withdrawn, I should consider it as among the greatest calamities which could assail my future peace of mind. I have great confidence that the candor and high understanding of both will guard me against this misfortune, the bare possibility of which has so far weighed on my mind, that I could not be easy without unburthening it.*—To JAMES MONROE. v, 248. FORD ED., ix, 178. (W., Feb. 1808.)

5478. MONROE (James), Leaves Congress.—I look forward with anxiety to the approaching moment of your departure from Congress. Besides the interest of the Confederacy and of the State, I have a personal interest in it. I know not to whom I may venture confidential communications after you are gone.—To JAMES MONROE. i, 607. FORD ED., iv, 265. (P., 1786.)

5479. —— ——. I regret your departure [from Congress]. I feel, too, the want of a person there to whose discretion I can trust confidential communications, and on whose friendship I can rely against the designs of malevolence.—To JAMES MONROE. ii, 70. (P., 1786.)

5480. MONROE (James), Louisiana purchase.—I find our opposition is very willing to pluck feathers from Monroe [on the acquisition of Louisiana], although not fond of sticking them into Livingston's coat. The truth is, both have a just portion of merit; and were it necessary or proper, it could be shown that each has rendered peculiar services, and of important value.—To GENERAL HORATIO GATES. iv, 495. FORD ED., viii, 249. (W., July 1803.) See LOUISIANA.

5481. MONROE (James), Madison and. —I had * * * a frank conversation with Colonel Monroe. * * * I reminded him that in the letter I wrote to him while in Eu-

* From a letter concerning the Presidential contest and his neutrality in the struggle for the nomination.—EDITOR.

rope, proposing the government of Orleans, I also suggested that of Louisiana, if fears for health should be opposed to the other. I said something on the importance of the post, its advantages, &c.—expressed my regret at the curtain which seemed to be drawn between him and his best friends, and my wish to see his talents and integrity engaged in the service of his country again, and that his going into any post would be a signal of reconciliation, on which the body of republicans, who lamented his absence from the public service, would again rally to him. * * * The sum of his answers was, that to accept of that office was incompatible with the respect he owed himself; that he never would act in any office where he should be subordinate to anybody but the President himself, or which did not place his responsibility substantially with the President and the nation; that at your accession to the chair, he would have accepted a place in the cabinet, and would have exerted his endeavors most faithfully in support of your fame and measures; that he is not unready to serve the public, and especially in the case of any difficult crisis in our affairs; that he is satisfied that such is the deadly hatred of both France and England, and such their self-reproach and dread at the spectacle of such a government as ours, that they will spare nothing to destroy it; that nothing but a firm union among the whole body of republicans can save it, and, therefore, that no schism should be indulged on any ground; that in his present situation, he is sincere in his anxieties for the success of the Administration, and in his support of it as far as the limited sphere of his action or influence extends; that his influence to this end had been used with those with whom the world had ascribed to him an interest he did not possess, until, whatever it was, it was lost (he particularly named J. Randolph, who, he said, had plans of his own, on which he took no advice); and that he was now pursuing what he believed his properest occupation, devoting his whole time and faculties to the liberation of his pecuniary embarrassments, which, three years of close attention, he hoped, would effect. In order to know more exactly what were the kinds of employ he would accept, I adverted to the information of the papers, * * * that General Hampton was dead, but observed that the military life in our present state, offered nothing which could operate on the principle of patriotism; he said he would sooner be shot than take a command under Wilkinson. * * * On the whole, I conclude he would accept a place in the cabinet, or a military command dependent on the Executive alone, and I rather suppose a diplomatic mission, because it would fall within the scope of his views, and not because he said so, for no allusion was made to anything of that kind in our conversation. Everything from him breathed the purest patriotism, involving, however, a close attention to his own honor and grade. He expressed himself with the utmost devotion to the interests of our own country, and I am satisfied he will pursue them with honor and zeal in any character in which he shall be willing to act.—To PRESIDENT MADISON. v, 481. FORD ED., ix, 265. (M., Nov. 1809.)

5482. MONROE (James), Mission to France.—The fever into which the western mind is thrown by the affair at New Orleans [suspension of right of deposit], stimulated by the mercantile and generally the federal interests, threatens to overbear our peace. In this situation we are obliged to call on you for a temporary sacrifice of yourself, to prevent this greatest of evils in the present prosperous tide of our affairs. I shall to-morrow nominate you to the Senate for an extraordinary mission to France, and the circumstances are such as to render it impossible to decline; because the whole public hope will be vested on you.—To JAMES MONROE. FORD ED., viii, 188. (W., Jan. 10, 1803.)

5483. ——— ———. You possess the unlimited confidence of the Administration, and of the western people; and generally of the republicans everywhere; and were you to refuse to go, no other man can be found who does this. * * * All eyes, all hopes, are now fixed on you; and were you to decline, the chagrin would be universal, and would shake under your feet the high ground on which you stand with the public. Indeed, I know nothing which would produce such a shock, for on the event of this mission depend the future destinies of this republic. If we cannot, by a purchase of the country, ensure to ourselves a course of perpetual peace and friendship with all nations, then, as war cannot be distant, it behooves us immediately to be preparing for that course, without, however, hastening it; and it may be necessary (on your failure on the continent) to cross the channel. We shall get entangled in European politics, and figuring more, be much less happy and prosperous. This can only be prevented by a successful issue to your present mission. I am sensible after the measures you have taken for getting into a different line of business, that it will be a great sacrifice on your part, and presents from the season and other circumstances serious difficulties. But some men are born for the public. Nature by fitting them for the service of the human race on a broad scale, has stamped them with the evidences of her destination and their duty.—To JAMES MONROE. vi, 454. FORD ED., iv, 190. (W., Jan. 1803.) See LOUISIANA.

5484. MONROE (James), Orleans governorship.—When mentioning your going to New Orleans [as Governor], and that the salary there would not increase the ease of your situation, I meant to have added that the only considerations which might make it eligible to you were the facility of getting there the richest land in the world, the extraordinary profitableness of its culture, and that the removal of your slaves there might immediately put you under way.—To JAMES MONROE. FORD ED., viii, 290. (W., Jan. 1804.)

5485. ——— ———. I wish you were here at present, to take your choice of the two governments of Orleans and Louisiana, in either of which I could now place you; and I verily believe it would be to your advantage to be just that much withdrawn from the focus of the ensuing contest, until its event should be known. —To JAMES MONROE. v, 11. FORD ED., viii, 448. (W., May 1806.)

5486. ——— ———. The government of New Orleans is still without such a head as I wish. The salary of five thousand dollars is too small; but I am assured the Orleans Legislature would make it adequate, would you accept it. It is the second office in the United States in importance, and I am still in hopes you will accept it. It is impossible to let you stay at home while the public has so much need of talents.—To JAMES MONROE. v, 54. FORD ED., ix, 37. (W., March 1807.)

5487. MONROE (James), President.— Nor is the election of Monroe an inefficient circumstance in our felicities. Four and twenty years, which he will accomplish, of administration in republican forms and principles, will so consecrate them in the eyes of the people as to secure them against the danger of change.—To MARQUIS LAFAYETTE. vii, 67. FORD ED., x, 84. (M., 1817.)

5488. —— ——. I had had great hopes that while in your present office you would break up the degrading practice of considering the President's house as a general tavern, and economize sufficiently to come out of it clear of difficulties. I learn the contrary with great regret.—To JAMES MONROE. FORD ED., x, 246. (M., 1823.)

5489. MONROE (James), Presidential contest.—I had intended to have written ycu to counteract the wicked efforts which the federal papers are making to sow tares between you and me, as if I were lending a hand to measures unfriendly to any views which our country might entertain respecting you. But I have not done it, because I have before assured you that a sense of duty, as well as of delicacy, would prevent me from ever expressing a sentiment on the subject, and that I think you know me well enough to be assured I shall conscientiously observe the line of conduct I profess.—To JAMES MONROE. v, 82. (W., May 1807.)

5490. —— ——. I cannot, indeed, judge what falsehoods may have been written or told you; and that, under such forms as to command belief. But you will soon find that so inveterate is the rancor of party spirit among us, that nothing ought to be credited but what we hear with our own ears. If you are less on your guard than we are here, at this moment, the designs of the mischief-makers will not fail to be accomplished, and brethren and friends will be made strangers and enemies to each other, without ever having said or thought a thing amiss of each other. I presume that the most insidious falsehoods are daily carried to you, as they are brought to me, to engage us in the passions of our informers, and stated so positively and plausibly as to make even *doubt* a rudeness to the narrator; who, imposed on himself, has no other than the friendly view of putting us on our guard. My answer is, invariably, that my knowledge of your character is better testimony to me of a negative, than an affirmative which my informant did not hear *from yourself*, with his own ears. In fact, when you shall have been a little longer among us,* you will find that little is to be believed which interests the prevailing passions, and happens beyond the limits of our own senses. Let us not, then, my dear friend, embark our happiness and our affections on the ocean of slander, of falsehood and of malice, on which our credulous friends are floating. If you have been made to believe that I ever did, said, or thought a thing unfriendly to your fame and feelings, you do me injury as causeless as it is afflicting to me.—To JAMES MONROE. v, 255. FORD ED., ix, 180. (W., March 1808.)

5491. —— ——. In the present contest in which you are concerned, I feel no passion, I take no part, I express no sentiment. Whichever of my friends is called to the supreme cares of the nation, I know that they will be wisely and faithfully administered, and as far as my individual conduct can influence, they shall be cordially supported. For myself I have nothing further to ask of the world, than

* Monroe had just returned from Europe.—EDITOR.

to preserve in retirement so much of their esteem as I may have fairly earned, and to be permitted to pass in tranquillity, in the bosom of my family and friends, the days which yet remain for me. Having reached the harbor myself, I shall view with anxiety (but certainly not with a wish to be in their place) those who are still buffeting the storm, uncertain of their fate.—To JAMES MONROE. v, 255. FORD ED., ix, 181. (W., March 1808.) See MADISON.

5492. MONROE (James), Purity of.—He is a man whose soul might be turned wrong side outwards, without discovering a blemish to the world.—To W. T. FRANKLIN. i, 555. (P., 1786.)

5493. MONROE (James), Randolph and.—One popular paper is endeavoring to maintain equivocal ground; approving the administration in all its proceedings, and Mr. [John] Randolph in all those which have heretofore merited approbation, carefully avoiding to mention his late aberration. The ultimate view of this paper is friendly to you; and the editor, with more judgment than him who assumes to be at the head of your friends, sees that the ground of opposition to the administration is not that on which it would be advantageous to you to be planted. The great body of your friends are among the firmest adherents to the administration; and in their support of you, will suffer Mr. Randolph to have no communications with them. * * * But it is unfortunate for you to be embarrassed with such a *soi-disant* friend. You must not commit yourself to him.—To JAMES MONROE. v, 10. FORD ED., viii, 448. (W., May 1806.)

5494. MONROE (James), Recall from France.—I should not wonder if Monroe were * * * recalled [from France], under the idea of his being of the partisans of France, whom the President [Washington] considers as the partisans of *war and confusion,* * * * and as disposed to excite them to hostile measures, or at least to unfriendly sentiments; a most infatuated blindness to the true character of the sentiments entertained in favor of France.—To W. B. GILES. iv, 127. FORD ED., vii, 44. (M., Dec. 1795.)

5495. MONROE (James), Republicanism of.—I know them both [Mr. Madison and Mr. Monroe] to be of principles as truly republican as any men living.—To THOMAS RITCHIE. vii, 191. FORD ED., x, 170. (M., 1820.)

5496. MONROE (James), Secretary of State.—Although I may not have been among the first, I am certainly with the sincerest, who congratulate you on your entrance into the national councils. Your value there has never been unduly estimated by those whom personal feelings did not misguide.—To JAMES MONROE. v, 597. FORD ED., ix, 323. (M., May 1811.)

5497. MONROE (James), Selection of a home.—On my return from the South of France, I shall send you * * * a plan of your house. I wish to heaven you may continue in the disposition to fix it in Albemarle. Short will establish himself there, and perhaps Madison may be tempted to do so. This will be society enough, and it will be the great sweetener of our lives. Without society, and a society to our taste, men are never contented. The one here supposed, we can regulate to our minds, and we may extend our regulations to the sumptuary department so as to set a good example to a country which needs it, and to preserve our own happiness clear of embarrassment. * * * I am in hopes that Mrs. Monroe will have, in her domestic cares, occupation and pleasure sufficient to fill her time and insure her against the *tedium vitæ;* that she will find that the distractions of a town and the waste of life under these can bear no comparison with the tranquil happiness of domestic life. If her own experience has not yet taught her this truth, she has in its favor the testimony of one who has gone through the various scenes of business, of bustle, of office, of rambling and of quiet retirement and who can assure her that the latter is the one point upon which the mind can settle at rest. Though not clear of inquietudes, because no earthly situation is so, they are fewer in number and mixed with more objects of contentment than in any other mode of life.—To JAMES MONROE. ii, 71. (P., 1786.)

5498. —— ——. I had entertained hopes of your settling in my neighborhood; but these were determined by your desiring a plan of a house for Richmond. However reluctantly I relinquish this prospect, I shall not the less readily obey your commands by sending you a plan.—To JAMES MONROE. i, 564. FORD ED., iv, 220. (P., 1786.)

5499. MONROE (James), Slanderous attack on.—I have reason to believe they are preparing a batch of small stuff, such as refusing to drink General Washington's health, speaking ill of him, and the government, withdrawing civilities from those attached to him, countenancing Paine, to which they add connivance at the equipment of privateers by Americans. * * * We are of opinion here that Dr. Edward's certificate * * * should be reserved to repel these slanders—To JAMES MONROE. FORD ED., vii, 232. (Pa., April 1798.)

5500. —— ——. I have had a consultation with Mr. Dawson on the matter respecting Skipwith. We have neither of us the least hesitation, on a view of the ground, to pronounce against your coming forward in it at all. Your name would be the watchword of party at this moment, and the question would give opportunities of slander, personal hatred, and injustice, the effect of which on the justice of the case cannot be calculated. Let it, therefore, come forward in Skipwith's name, without your appearing even to know of it. * * * I do not think "Scipio" worth your notice. * * * Your narrative and letters, wherever they are read, produce irresistible conviction, and cannot be attacked but by a contradiction of facts, on which they do not venture.—To JAMES MONROE. FORD ED., vii, 232. (Pa., April 1798.)

5501. —— ——. You will have seen, among numerous addresses [to the President] and answers, one from Lancaster in Pennsylvania, and its answer; the latter travelling out of the topics of the address altogether, to mention you in a most injurious manner. Your feelings have no doubt been much irritated by it, as in truth it had all the characters necessary to produce irritation. What notice you should take of it, is difficult to say. But there is one step in which two or three with whom I have spoken concur with me, that feeble as the hand is from which this shaft is thrown, yet with a great mass of our citizens, strangers to the leading traits of the character from which it came, it will have considerable effect; and that in order to replace yourself on the high ground you are entitled to, it is absolutely necessary

that you should reappear on the public theatre, and take an independent stand, from which you can be seen and known to your fellow citizens. The House of Representatives appears the only place which can answer this end, as the proceedings of the other House are too obscure. Cabell has said he would give way to you, should you choose to come in, and I really think it would be expedient for yourself as well as the public, that you should not wait until another election, but come to the next session. No interval should be admitted between this last attack of enmity and your reappearance with the approving voice of your constituents, and your taking a commanding attitude. * * * If this be done, I should think it best that you take no notice at all of the answer.—To JAMES MONROE. iv, 242. FORD ED., vii, 257. (Pa., May 1798.)

5502. MONTESQUIEU (Baron), Author.—The history of Montesquieu's " Spirit of Laws ' is well known. He had been a great reader, and had commonplaced everything he read. At length he wished to undertake some work into which he could bring his whole commonplace book in a digested form. He fixed on the subject of his " Spirit of Laws ", and wrote the book. He consulted his friend Helvetius about publishing it, who strongly dissuaded it. He published it, however, and the world did not confirm Helvetius's opinion.— To WILLIAM DUANE. v, 535. (M., 1810.)

5503. —— ——. Every man who reflects as he reads, has considered it as a book of paradoxes; having, indeed, much of truth and sound principle. but abounding also with inconsistencies, apocryphal facts and false inferences.—To WILLIAM DUANE. v, 535. (M., 1810.)

5504. —— ——. I had, with the world, deemed Montesquieu's work of much merit; but saw in it, with every thinking man, so much of paradox, of false principle and misapplied fact, as to render its value equivocal on the whole. Williams and others had nibbled only at its errors. A radical correction of them, therefore, was a great desideratum. This want is now supplied, and with a depth of thought. precision of idea, of language and of logic, which will force conviction into every mind. I declare to you, in the spirit of truth and sincerity, that I consider it the most precious gift the present age has received. But what would it have been, had the author, or would the author, take up the whole scheme of Montesquieu's work, and following the correct analysis he has here developed, fill up all its parts according to his sound views of them. Montesquieu's celebrity would be but a small portion of that which would immortalize the author.—To M. DESTUTT TRACY. v, 566. FORD ED., ix, 305. (M., 1811.)

5505. MONTESQUIEU (Baron), Monarchist.—I am glad to hear of everything which reduces Montesquieu to his just level, as his predilection for monarchy, and the English monarchy in particular, has done mischief everywhere.—To WILLIAM DUANE. v, 539. (M., 1810.)

5506. MONTICELLO, Beauties of.—And our own dear Monticello: where has nature spread so rich a mantle under the eye? Mountains, forests, rocks. rivers! With what majesty do we there ride above the storms! How sublime to look down into the workhouse of nature, to see her clouds, hail, snow, rain, thunder, all fabricated at our feet! And the

glorious sun when rising, as if out of a distant water, just gilding the tops of the mountains, and giving life to all nature!*—To Mrs. Cosway. ii, 35. Ford ed., iv, 315. (P., 1786.) See Mirage.

5507. MONTICELLO, Guests at.—You know our practice of placing our guests at their ease, by showing them we are so ourselves and that we follow our necessary vocations, instead of fatiguing them by hanging unremittingly on their shoulders.—To Francis W. Gilmer. vii, 5. (1816.)

5508. MONTICELLO, Recollections of.—All my wishes end, where I hope my days will end, at Monticello. Too many scenes of happiness mingle themselves with all the recollections of my native woods and fields, to suffer them to be supplanted in my affection by any other.—To Dr. George Gilmer. ii, 243. Ford ed., iv, 436. (P., 1787.)

5509. MONTMORIN (Count), Honest.—I am pleased with Montmorin. His honesty proceeds from the heart as well as the head, and therefore there may be more securely counted on.—To James Madison. ii, 153. Ford ed., iv, 393. (P., 1787.)

5510. MONTMORIN (Count), Modest.—I am extremely pleased with his modesty, the simplicity of his manners, and his dispositions towards us. I promise myself a great deal of satisfaction in doing business with him.—To Marquis de Lafayette. ii, 131. (P., 1787.)

5511. MONTMORIN (Count), Weak but worthy.—Montmorin is weak, though a most worthy character. He is indolent and inattentive, too, in the extreme.—To James Madison. ii, 444. Ford ed., v, 43. (P., 1788.)

— **MOON.**—See Latitude and Longitude.

5512. MORAL LAW, Evidence of.—Man has been subjected by his Creator to the moral law, of which his feelings, or conscience as it is sometimes called, are the evidence with which his Creator has furnished him.—Opinion on French Treaties. vii, 613. Ford ed., vi, 220. (1793.)

5513. MORAL LAW, Nations and.—The moral duties which exist between individual and individual in a state of nature, accompany them into a state of society, and the aggregate of the duties of all the individuals composing the society constitutes the duties of that society towards any other; so that between society and society the same moral duties exist as did between the individuals composing them while in an unassociated state, their Maker not having released them from those duties on

* With the cares and delights of his family, his books and his farm, he mingled the gratification of his devotion to the Fine Arts, particularly architecture. He superintended [in 1781-2] the construction of his elegant mansion, which had been commenced some years before, and was already in a habitable condition. The plan of the building was entirely original in this country. He had drawn it himself from books, with a view to improve the architecture of his countrymen, by introducing an example of the tastes and arts of Europe. The original design of the structure, which was executed before his travels in Europe had supplied him with any models, is allowed by European travelers to have been infinitely superior, in taste and convenience, to that of any other house in America. The fame of the Monticellean philosopher having already spread over Europe, his hospitable seat was made the resort of scientific adventurers, and of dignified travelers from many parts of that continent. — Rayner s *Life of Jefferson*, p. 221.

their forming themselves into a nation.—Opinion on French Treaties. vii, 613. Ford ed., vi, 220. (1793.)

5514. MORAL SENSE, Innate.—I think it is lost time to attend lectures on moral philosophy. He who made us would have been a pitiful bungler, if He had made the rules of our moral conduct a matter of science. For one man of science, there are thousands who are not. What would have become of them? Man was destined for society. His morality, therefore, was to be formed to this object. He was endowed with a sense of right and wrong, merely relative to this. This sense is as much a part of his nature, as the sense of hearing, seeing, feeling; it is the true foundation of morality, and not the τo καλον, truth, &c., as fanciful writers have imagined. The moral sense, or conscience, is as much a part of man as his leg or arm. It is given to all human beings in a stronger or weaker degree, as force of members is given them in a greater or less degree. It may be strengthened by exercise, as may any particular limb of the body. This sense is submitted, indeed, in some degree, to the guidance of reason; but it is a small stock which is required for this; even a less one than what we call common sense. State a moral case to a plowman and a professor. The former will decide it as well and often better than the latter, because he has not been led astray by artificial rules. In this branch, therefore, read good books, because they will encourage as well as direct your feelings. The writings of Sterne, particularly, form the best course of morality that ever was written. Lose no occasion of exercising your dispositions to be grateful, to be generous, to be charitable, to be humane, to be true, just, firm, orderly, courageous, &c. Consider every act of this kind as an exercise which will strengthen your moral faculties, and increase your worth.—To Peter Carr. ii, 238. Ford ed., iv, 428. (P., 1787.)

5515. —— ——. I sincerely believe in the general existence of a moral instinct. I think it the brightest gem with which the human character is studded, and the want of it as more degrading than the most hideous of the bodily deformities.—To Thomas Law. vi, 351. (M., 1814.)

5516. —— ——. I believe * * * that the moral sense is as much a part of our constitution as that of feeling, seeing, or hearing; as a wise Creator must have seen to be necessary in an animal destined to live in society.—To John Adams. vii, 39. (M., 1816.)

5517. —— ——. The moral sense [is] the first excellence of well-organized man.—To John Adams. vii, 275. (M., 1823.)

5518. MORAL SENSE, Utility and.—Some have argued against the existence of a moral sense, by saying that if nature had given us such a sense, impelling us to virtuous actions, and warning us against those which are vicious, then nature would also have designated, by some particular earmarks, the two sets of actions which are, in themselves, the one virtuous and the other vicious. Whereas, we find, in fact, that the same actions are deemed virtuous in one country and vicious in another. The answer is that nature has constituted *utility* to man the standard and test of virtue. Men living in different countries, under different circumstances, different habits and regimens, may have different utilities; the same act, therefore, may be useful, and consequently virtuous in one country which is injurious and vicious in another differently circumstanced.—To THOMAS LAW. vi, 351. (M., 1814.)

5519. MORAL SENSE, Want of.—The Creator would, indeed, have been a bungling artist, had He intended man for a social animal, without planting in him social dispositions. It is true that they are not planted in every man, because there is no rule without exceptions; but it is false reasoning which converts exceptions into the general rule. Some men are born without the organs of sight, or of hearing. or without hands. Yet it would be wrong to say that man is born without these faculties, and sight, hearing, and hands may with truth enter into the general definition of man. The want or imperfection of the moral sense in some men, like the want or imperfection of the senses of sight and hearing in others, is no proof that it is a general characteristic of the species.—To THOMAS LAW. vi, 350. (M., 1814.)

5520. —— ——. When the moral sense is wanting, we endeavor to supply the defect by education, by appeals to reason and calculation, by presenting to the being so unhappily conformed, other motives to do good and to eschew evil, such as the love, or the hatred, or the rejection of those among whom he lives, and whose society is necessary to his happiness and even existence; demonstrations by sound calculation that honesty promotes interest in the long run; the rewards and penalties established by the laws; and ultimately the prospects of a future state of retribution for the evil as well as the good done while here. These are the correctives which are supplied by education, and which exercise the functions of the moralist, the preacher, and legislator; and they lead into a course of correct action all those whose depravity is not too profound to be eradicated.— To THOMAS LAW. vi, 350. (M., 1814.)

5521. MORALITY, Code of.—I know but one code of morality for men, whether acting singly or collectively. He who says I will be a rogue when I act in company with a hundred others, but an honest man when I act alone, will be believed in the former assertion, but not in the latter. I would say with the poet, " *hic niger est, hunc tu Romane cavato* ". If the morality of one man produces a just line of conduct in him, acting individually, why should not the morality of one hundred men produce a just line of conduct in them, acting together?—To JAMES MADISON. iii, 99. FORD ED., v, 111. (P., 1789.)

5522. —— ——. I never did, or countenanced, in public life, a single act inconsistent with the strictest good faith; having never believed there was one code of morality for a public, and another for a private man.—To DON VALENTINE DE FERONDA. v, 475. FORD ED., ix, 260. (M., 1809.)

5523. MORALITY, Foundations of.—It is really curious that on a question so fundamental, such a variety of opinions should have prevailed among men, and those, too, of the most exemplary virtue and first order of understanding. It shows how necessary was the care of the Creator in making the moral principle so much a part of our constitution as that no errors of reasoning or of speculation might lead us astray from its observance in practice. Of all the theories on this question, the most whimsical seems to have been that of Wollaston, who considers *truth* as the foundation of morality. The thief who steals your guinea does wrong only inasmuch as he acts a lie in using your guinea as if it were his own. Truth is certainly a branch of morality, and a very important one to society. But presented as its foundation, it is as if a tree taken up by the roots, had its stem reversed in the air, and one of its branches planted in the ground.—To THOMAS LAW. vi, 348. (M., 1814.)

5524. —— ——. Some have made the *love of God* the foundation of morality. This, too, is but a branch of our moral duties, which are generally divided into duties to God and duties to man. If we did a good act merely from the love of God and a belief that it is pleasing to Him, whence arises the morality of the atheist? It is idle to say, as some do, that no such Being exists. We have the same evidence of the fact as of most of those we act on, to wit their own affirmations, and their reasonings in support of them. I have observed, indeed, generally that while in Protestant countries the defections from the Platonic Christianity of the priests is to Deism, in Catholic countries they are to Atheism. Diderot, D'Alembert, D'Holbach, Condorcet, are known to have been among the most virtuous of men. Their virtue, then, must have had some other foundation than the love of God.—To THOMAS LAW. vi, 348. (M., 1814.)

5525. —— ——. The *To καλον* of others is founded in a different faculty, that of taste, which is not even a branch of morality. We have. indeed, an innate sense of what we call *the beautiful*, but that is exercised chiefly on subjects addressed to the fancy, whether through the eye in visible forms, as landscape, animal figure, dress, drapery, architecture, the composition of colors, &c., or to the imagination directly, as imagery, style, or measure in prose or poetry, or whatever constitutes the domain of criticism or taste, a faculty entirely distinct from the moral one.—To THOMAS LAW. vi, 349. (M., 1814.)

5526. —— ——. Self-interest, or rather self-love, or *egoism*, has been more plausibly substituted as the basis of morality. But I consider our relations with others as constituting the boundaries of morality. With ourselves we stand on the ground of identity, not of relation, which last. requiring two subjects, excludes self-love confined to a single one. To ourselves, in strict language, we can owe no duties, obligation requiring also two parties. Self-love, therefore, is no part of morality. Indeed it is exactly its counterpart. It is the sole antagonist of virtue, leading us constantly by our propensities to self-gratification in violation of our moral duties to others. Accordingly, it is against this enemy that are erected the batteries of moralists and religionists, as the only obstacle to the practice of morality. Take from man his selfish propensities, and he can have nothing to seduce him from the practice of virtue. Or subdue those propensities by education, instruction, or restraint, and virtue remains without a competitor.—To THOMAS LAW. vi, 349. (M., 1814.)

5527. —— ——. Egoism in a broader sense, has been thus presented as the source of moral action. It has been said that we feed the hungry, clothe the naked. bind up the wounds of the man beaten by thieves, pour oil and wine into them, set him on our own beast and bring him to the inn, because we receive ourselves pleasure from these acts. So Helvetius, one of the best men on earth, and the most ingenious advocate of this principle, after defining " interest " to mean not merely that which is pecuniary, but whatever may procure us pleasure, or withdraw us from pain (*De l'Esprit 2, 1*), says (ib. 2, 2), "the humane man is he to whom the sight of misfortune is insupportable, and who to rescue himself from this spectacle, is forced to succor the unfortunate object". This, indeed, is true. But it is one step short of the ultimate question. These good acts give us pleasure, but how happens it that they give us pleasure? Because nature hath implanted in our breasts a love of others, a sense of duty to them, a moral instinct, in short, which prompts us irresistibly to feel and to succor their distresses, and protests against the language of Helvetius (ib. 2, 5), "what other motive than self-interest could determine a man to generous actions? It is as impossible for him to love what is good for the sake of good, as to love evil for the sake of evil".—To THOMAS LAW. vi, 349. (M., 1814.)

5528. ——. God has formed us moral agents. Not that, in the perfection of His state, He can feel pain or pleasure in anything we may do; He is far above our power; but that we may promote the happiness of those with whom He has placed us in society, by acting honestly towards all, benevolently to those who fall within our way, respecting sacredly their rights, bodily and mental, and cherishing especially their freedom of conscience, as we value our own.—To MILES KING. vi, 388. (M., 1814.)

5529. MORALITY, Religion and.— Reading, reflection and time have convinced me that the interests of society require the observation of those moral precepts only in which all religions agree (for all forbid us to steal, murder, plunder, or bear false witness), and that we should not intermeddle with the particular dogmas in which all religions differ, and which are totally unconnected with morality. In all of them we see good men, and as many in one as another. The varieties in the structure and action of the human mind as in those of the body, are the work of our Creator, against which it cannot be a religious duty to erect the standard of uniformity. The practice of morality being necessary for the well-being of society, he has taken care to impress its precepts so indelibly on our hearts that they shall not be effaced by the subtleties of our brain. We all agree in the obligation of the moral precepts of Jesus, and nowhere will they be found delivered in greater purity than in His discourses. It is, then, a matter of principle with me to avoid disturbing the tranquillity of others by the expression of any opinion on the innocent questions on which we schismatize.— To JAMES FISHBACK. v, 471. (M., 1809.)

5530. ——. In that branch of religion which regards the moralities of life, and the duties of a social being, which teaches us to love our neighbors as ourselves, and to do good to all men, I am sure that you and I do not differ.—To EZRA STILES. vii, 127. (M., 1819.)

5531. MORALITY, Sublimest system of.—There never was a more pure and sublime system of morality delivered to man than is to be found in the four Evangelists.—To SAMUEL GREENHOW. vi, 309. (M., 1814.)

5532. ——. I know nothing more moral, more sublime, more worthy of your preservation than David's description of the good man, in 15th Psalm.—To ISAAC ENGLEBRECHT. vii, 337. (M., 1824.)

5533. MORALITY (National), Abandonment of.—It was not expected in this age, that nations so honorably distinguished by their advances in science and civilization, would suddenly cast away the esteem they had merited from the world, and, revolting from the empire of morality, assume a character in history, which all the tears of their posterity will never wash from its pages.—REPLY TO ADDRESS. viii, 128. (1808.)

5534. ——. It has been peculiarly unfortunate for us, personally, that the portion in the history of mankind, at which we were called to take a share in the direction of their affairs, was such an one as history has never before presented. At any other period, the even-handed justice we have observed towards all nations, the efforts we have made to merit their esteem by every act which candor or liberality could exercise, would have preserved our peace, and secured the unqualified confidence of all other nations in our faith and probity. But the hurricane which is now blasting the world, physical and moral, has prostrated all the mounds of reason as well as right. All those calculations which, at any other period, would have been deemed honorable, of the existence of a moral sense in man, individually or associated, of the connection which the laws of nature have established between his duties and his interests, of a regard for honest fame and the esteem of our fellow men, have been a matter of reproach on us, as evidences of imbecility. As if it could be a folly for an honest man to suppose that another could be honest also, when it is their interest to be so. And when is this state of things to end? The death of Bonaparte would, to be sure, remove the first and chiefest apostle of the desolation of men and morals, and might withdraw the scourge of the land. But what is to restore order and safety on the ocean? The death of George III.? Not at all. He is only stupid: and his ministers, however weak and profligate in morals, are ephemeral. But his nation is permanent, and it is that which is the tyrant of the ocean. The principle that force is right, is become the principle of the nation itself. They would not permit an honest minister, were accident to bring such an one into power, to relax their system of lawless piracy. These were the difficulties when I was with you. I know they are not lessened, and I pity you.— To CAESAR A. RODNEY. v, 500. FORD ED., ix, 271. (M., Feb. 1810.)

5535. MORALITY (National), Extinction of.—There are three epochs in history, signalized by the total extinction of national morality. The first was of the successors of Alexander, not omitting himself. The next, the successors of the first Cæsar. The third, our own age. This was begun by the partition of Poland, followed by that of the treaty of Pilnitz; next the conflagration of Copenhagen; then the enormities of Bonaparte, partitioning the earth at his will, and devastating it with fire and sword; now the conspiracy of Kings the successors of Bonaparte, blasphemously calling themselves the Holy Alliance, and treading in the footsteps of their incarcerated leader: not yet indeed usurping the government of other nations, avowedly and in detail, but controlling by their armies the forms in which they will permit them to be governed; and reserving, *in petto*, the order and extent of the usurpations further meditated.—AUTOBIOGRAPHY. i, 102. FORD ED., i, 141. (1821.)

5536. MORALITY (National), Governments and.—Your ideas of the moral obligations of governments are perfectly correct. The man who is dishonest as a statesman would be a dishonest man in any station. It is strangely absurd to suppose that a million of human beings, collected together, are not under the same moral laws which bind each of them separately.—To GEORGE LOGAN. FORD ED., x, 68. (P.F., Nov. 1816.)

5537. —— ——. Moral duties are as obligatory on nations as on individuals.*—THE ANAS. FORD ED., i, 332. (1808.)

5538. MORALITY (National), Progress in.—The eighteenth century certainly witnessed the sciences and arts, manners and morals, advanced to a higher degree than the world had ever before seen. And might we not go back to the era of the Borgias, by which time the barbarous ages had reduced national morality to its lowest point of depravity, and observe that the arts and sciences, rising from that point, advanced gradually through all the sixteenth, seventeenth and eighteenth centuries, softening and correcting the manners and morals of man?—To JOHN ADAMS. vi, 523. (M., 1816.)

5539. —— ——. With some exceptions only, through the seventeenth and eighteenth centuries, morality occupied an honorable chapter in the political code of nations. You must have observed while in Europe, as I thought I did, that those who administered the governments of the greater powers at least, had a respect to faith, and considered the dignity of their government as involved in its integrity. A wound indeed was inflicted on this character of honor in the eighteenth century by the partition of Poland. But this was the atrocity of a barbarous government chiefly, in conjunction with a smaller one still scrambling to become great, while one only of those already great, and having character to lose, descended to the baseness of an accomplice in the crime. France, England, Spain, shared in it only inasmuch as they stood aloof and permitted its perpetration. How, then, has it happened that these nations, France especially, and England, so great, so dignified, so distinguished by science and the arts, plunged all at once into all the depths of human enormity, threw off suddenly and openly all the restraints of morality, all sensation to character, and unblushingly avowed and acted on the principle that power was right? Can this sudden apostasy from national rectitude be accounted for? The treaty of Pilnitz seems to have begun it, suggested perhaps by the baneful precedent of Poland. Was it from the terror of monarchs, alarmed at the light returning on them from the west, and kindling a volcano under their thrones? Was it a combination to extinguish that light, and to bring back, as their best auxiliaries, those enumerated by you, the Sorbonne, the Inquisition, the *Index Expurgatorius*, and the knights of Loyola? Whatever it was, the close of the new century saw the moral world thrown back again to the age of the Borgias, to the point from which it had departed three hundred years before. France, after crushing and punishing the conspiracy of Pilnitz, went deeper herself and deeper into the crimes she had been chastising. I say France and not Bonaparte; for, although he was the head and mouth, the nation furnished the hands which executed his enormities. England, although in opposition, kept full pace with France, not indeed by the manly force of her own arms, but by oppressing the weak and bribing the strong. At

* Reply, rejecting the proposal of a person entrusted with the British minister's dispatches, to turn them over to the United States government for a reward.—EDITOR.

length the whole choir joined and divided the weaker nations among them.—To JOHN ADAMS. vi, 524. (M., Jan. 1816.)

5540. MORALITY (National), United States and.—Let us hope that our new [Federal] government will * * * show that they mean to proscribe no virtue from the canons of their conduct with other nations.—To JAMES MADISON. iii, 100. FORD ED., v, 112. (P., 1789.)

5541. —— ——. We are firmly convinced, and we act on that conviction, that with nations, as with individuals, our interests soundly calculated, will ever be found inseparable from our moral duties; and history bears witness to the fact, that a just nation is taken on its word, when recourse is had to armaments and wars to bridle others.—SECOND INAUGURAL ADDRESS. viii, 40. FORD ED., viii, 343. (1805.)

5542. —— ——. It is a great consolation to me that our government, as it cherishes most its duties to its own citizens, so is it the most exact in its moral conduct towards other nations. I do not believe that in the four Administrations which have taken place, there has been a single instance of departure from good faith towards other nations. We may sometimes have mistaken our rights, or made an erroneous estimate of the actions of others, but no voluntary wrong can be imputed to us.—To GEORGE LOGAN. FORD ED., x, 68. (P.F., Nov. 1816.)

5543. —— ——. It is of great consequence to us, and merits every possible endeavor, to maintain in Europe a correct opinion of our political morality.—To PRESIDENT MONROE. FORD ED., x, 123. (M., 1819.)

5544. MORALS, Preservation of.—The pursuits of agriculture are * * * the best preservative of morals.—To J. BLAIR. ii, 248. (P., 1787.)

5545. —— ——. We wish to preserve the morals of our citizens from being vitiated by courses of lawless plunder and murder.—To GEORGE HAMMOND. iii, 559. FORD ED., vi, 253. (Pa., 1793.)

5546. MORALS, Science and.—I fear, from the experience of the last twenty-five years, that morals do not of necessity advance hand in hand with the sciences.—To M. CORREA. vi, 480. (M., 1815.)

5547. MOREAU (General J. Victor), Esteem for.—No one entertains a more cordial esteem for General Moreau's character than I do, and although our relations with France have rendered it a duty in me not to seek any public manifestation of it, yet were accident to bring us together, I could not be so much wanting to my sentiments and those of my constituents individually, as to omit a cordial manifestation of it.—To WILLIAM SHORT. v, 212. (W., Nov. 1807.)

5548. MOREAU (General J. Victor), Reception of.—I confess that the enclosed letter from General Turreau excites in me both jealousy and offence in undertaking, and without apology, to say in what manner to receive and treat Moreau within our own country. Had Turreau been here longer he would have known that the national authority pays honors to no foreigners. That the State authorities, municipalities and individuals, are free to render whatever they please, voluntarily, and free from restraint by us; and he ought to know that no part of the criminal sentence of another country can have any effect here. The style of that government in the Spanish business, was calculated to excite indignation; but it was a case in which that might have done injury. But the present is a case which would justify some notice in order to let them understand we are not of those powers who will receive and execute mandates. I think the answer should show independence as well as friendship.—To James Madison. iv, 584. Ford ed., viii, 376. (M., Aug. 1805.)

5549. MORGAN (George), Exposure of Burr.—Your situation and the knowledge you already possess would probably put it in your power to trace the footsteps of this enterprise [Burr's conspiracy] on the public peace with more effect than any other with whom I could communicate. Whatever zeal you might think proper to use in this pursuit, would be used in fulfilment of the duties of a good citizen, and any communications you may be so good as to make to me on the subject shall be thankfully received, and so made use of as not to commit you any further than yourself may think proper to express. A knowledge of the persons who may reject, as well as of those who may accept parricide propositions will be peculiarly useful.—To George Morgan. Ford ed., viii, 473. (M., Sep. 1806.)

5550. ———.———. Yours was the very first intimation I had of Burr's plot, for which it is but justice to say you have deserved well of your country.—To Colonel George Morgan. v, 57. (W., 1807.)

5551. ———.———. Colonel Morgan first gave us notice of the mad project of that day, which if suffered to proceed, might have brought afflicting consequences on persons whose subsequent lives have proved their integrity and loyalty to their country.—To Mrs. K. D. Morgan. Ford ed., viii, 473. (M., 1822.)

5552. MORGAN (George), Land grant.—Spain has granted to Colonel Morgan, of New Jersey, a vast tract of land on the western side of the Mississippi with the monopoly of the navigation of that river. He is inviting settlers and they swarm to him. Even the settlement of Kentucky is likely to be much weakened by emigrations to Morgan's grant.—To William Short. ii, 574. Ford ed., v, 71. (P., 1789.)

5553. MOROCCO, Brig Betsey.—The Court of Madrid has obtained the delivery of the crew of the brig Betsey, taken by the Emperor of Morocco. The Emperor had treated them kindly, new clothed them, and delivered them to the Spanish minister, who sent them to Cadiz. This is the only American vessel ever taken by the Barbary States.—To James Madison. i, 413. (P., 1785.)

5554. MOROCCO, Proofs of friendship.—The Emperor [of Morocco] continues to give proofs of his desire to be in friendship with us, or, in other words, of receiving us into the number of his tributaries. Nothing further need be feared from him.—To James Madison. i, 413. (P., 1785.)

5555. MOROCCO, Treaty.—The treaty with Morocco * * * is signed before this time: for which we are much indebted to Spain.—To David Humphreys. ii, 10. (P., 1786.)

5556. MOROCCO, Tribute or war.—The Emperor of Morocco * * * is ready to receive us into the number of his tributaries. What will be the amount of tribute remains yet to be known, * * * but it will surely be more than a free people ought to pay to a power owning only four or five frigates, under twenty-two guns. He has not a port into which a larger vessel can enter. The Algerines possess fifteen or twenty frigates, from that size up to fifty guns. Disinclination on their part has lately broken off a treaty between Spain and them, whereon they were to have received a million of dollars, besides great presents in naval stores. What sum they intend we shall pay, I cannot say. Then follow Tunis and Tripoli. You will probably find the tribute to all these powers make such a proportion of the Federal taxes, as that every man will feel them sensibly when he pays those taxes. The question is whether their peace or war will be cheaper? But it is a question which should be addressed to our honor, as well as our avarice. Nor does it respect us as to these pirates only, but as to the nations of Europe. If we wish our commerce to be free and uninsulted, we must let these nations see that we have an energy which at present they disbelieve. The low opinion they entertain of our powers cannot fail to involve us soon in a naval war.—To John Page. i, 401. (P., 1785.)

5557. MORRIS (Gouverneur), Monarchist.—Gouverneur Morris, a high flying monarchy man, shutting his eyes and his faith to every fact against his wishes, and believing everything he desires to be true, has kept the President's [Washington's] mind constantly poisoned with his forebodings [respecting the French Revolution].—The Anas. ix, 111. Ford ed., i, 188. (1792.)

5558. MORRIS (Gouverneur), Opposition to.—The opposition to Gouverneur Morris was upon the following principles: 1. His general character, being such that we would not confide in it. 2. His known attachment to monarchy, and contempt of republican government; and 3, his present employment abroad being a news vender of back-lands and certificates. We took the yeas and nays on his appointment and eleven voted against it.—To Archibald Stuart. Ford ed., v, 454. (Pa., 1792.)

5559. ———.———. The nomination of Mr. Morris was so extremely unpopular, and so little relished by several of the Senate, that every effort was used to negative it. Those whose personal objections to Mr. Morris overruled their deference to the President, finding themselves in a minority, joined with another small party who were against all foreign appointments, and endeavored with them to put down the whole system rather than let this article pass. This plan was defeated, and Mr. Morris passed by a vote of 16 against 11.—To William Short. iii, 329. Ford ed., v, 434. (Pa., 1792.)

5560. MORRIS (Gouverneur), Services in England.—President Washington's letter of January 22d [1790], authorized Mr. Morris to enter into conference with the British ministers in order to discover their sentiments on [certain] subjects. * * * The Secretary of State is of opinion that Mr. Morris's letters [to the President] remove any doubts which might have been entertained as to the intentions and dispositions of the British cabinet; * * * that Mr. Morris should be informed that he has fulfilled the object of his agency to the satisfaction of the President.—Official Report. vii, 517. Ford ed., v, 261. (December 1790.)

5561. MORTMAIN, Laws of.—The bill for establishing a National Bank undertakes * * * to form the subscribers into a corporation and enables them in their corporate capacities to receive grants of land, and, so far, is against the laws of Mortmain. Though the Constitution controls the laws of Mortmain so far as to permit Congress itself to hold land for certain purposes, yet not so far as to permit them to communicate a similar right to other corporate bodies.—NATIONAL BANK OPINION. vii, 555. FORD ED., v, 284. (1791.)

5562. MOTTOES, Beauty of.—I shall omit the word *agisos*, according to the license you allow me, because I think the beauty of a motto is to condense much matter in as .few words as possible.*—To GEORGE WYTHE. ii, 6. FORD ED., iv, 267. (P., 1786.)

5563. MOUNTAINS, Altitude of.—I examined, with great satisfaction, your barometrical estimate of the heights of our mountains; and with the more, as they corroborated conjectures on this subject which I had made before. My estimates had made them a little higher than yours (I speak of the Blue Ridge). Measuring with a very nice instrument the angle subtended vertically by the highest mountain of the Blue Ridge opposite to my own house, a distance of about eighteen miles southwestward, I made the highest about two thousand feet, as well as I remember. * * * I do not remember from what principles I estimated the Peaks of Otter at four thousand feet; but some late observations of Judge Tucker's coincided very nearly with my estimate. Your measures confirm another opinion of mine, that the Blue Ridge, on its south side, is the highest ridge in our country compared with its base.— To JONATHAN WILLIAMS. iv, 146. FORD ED., vii, 85. (M., 1796.)

5564. MOUNTAINS, Barometrical **measurement.**—The method of estimating heights [of mountains] by the barometer, is convenient and useful, as being ready, and furnishing an approximation to truth. Of what degree of accuracy it is susceptible we know not as yet; no certain theory being established for ascertaining the density and weight of that portion of the column of atmosphere contiguous to the mountain; from the weight of which, nevertheless, we are to infer the height of the mountain. The most plausible seems to be that which supposes the mercury of barometer divided into horizontal lamina of equal *thickness*; and a similar column of the atmosphere into lamina of equal *weights*. The former divisions give a set of arithmetical, the latter of geometrical progressionals, which being the character of logarithms and their numbers, the tables of these furnish ready computations, needing, however, the corrections which the state of the thermometer calls for. It is probable that in taking heights in the vicinity of each other in this way, there may be no considerable error, because the passage between them may be quick and repeated. The height of a mountain from its base, thus taken, merits, therefore, a very different degree of credit from that of its height above the level of the sea, where that is distant. According, for example, to the theory above mentioned, the height of Monticello from its base is 580 feet, and its base 610 feet 8 inches, above the level of the ocean; the former, from

* Jefferson proposed this motto for the Coat of Arms of Virginia: " Rex est qui regem non habet. " The mottoes on his own seals were: "Ab eo libertas, a quo spiritus", and " Rebellion to tyrants is obedience to God".—EDITOR.

other facts, I believe to be near the truth; but a knowledge of the different falls of water from hence to the tide-water at Richmond, a distance of seventy-five miles, enables us to say that the whole descent to that place is but 170 or 180 feet. From thence to the ocean may be a distance of one hundred miles; it is all tide-water, and through a level country. I know not what to conjecture as the amount of descent, but certainly not 435 feet, as that theory would suppose, nor the quarter part of it. I do not know by what rule General Williams made his computations. He reckons the foot of the Blue Ridge, twenty miles from here, but 100 feet above the tide-water at Richmond. We know the descent, as before observed, to be at least 170 feet from hence, to which is to be added that from the Blue Ridge to this place, a very hilly country, with constant and great waterfalls. His estimate, therefore, must be much below truth. Results so different prove that for distant comparisons of height, the barometer is not to be relied on according to any theory yet known. While, therefore, we give a good degree of credit to the results of operations between the summit of a mountain and its base, we must give less to those between its summit and the level of the ocean.—To CAPT. A. PARTRIDGE. vi, 495. (M., 1815.)

5565. MOUNTAINS, Trigonometrical measurement.—I thank you for * * * the corrections of Colonel Williams's altitudes of the mountains of Virginia, * * * and especially for the very able extract on barometrical measures. The precision of the calculations, and soundness of the principles on which they are founded, furnish, I am satisfied, a great approximation towards truth, and raise that method of estimating heights to a considerable degree of rivalship with the trigonometrical. The last is not without some sources of inaccuracy. The admeasurement of the base is liable to errors which can be rendered insensible only by such degrees of care as have been exhibited by the mathematicians who have been employed in measuring degrees on the surface of the earth. * * * No two men can differ on a principle of trigonometry. Not so on the theories of barometrical mensuration. On these have been great differences of opinion, and among characters of just celebrity. * * * In 1776, I observed the height of the mercury at the base and summit of the mountain I live on, and by Nettleton's tables, estimated the height at 512.17 feet, and called it about 500 feet in the *Notes on Virginia.* But calculating it since on the same observations, according to Bongour's method with De Luc's improvements, the result was 579.5 feet; and lately I measured the same height trigonometrically, with the aid of a base line of 1,175 feet in a vertical plane with the summit, and at the distance of about 1500 yards from the axis of the mountain, and made it 599.35 feet. I consider this as testing the advance of the barometrical process towards truth by the adoption of the logarithmic ratio of heights and densities; and continued observations and experiments will continue to advance it still more. But the first character of a common measure of things being that of invariability, I can never suppose that a substance so heterogeneous and variable as the atmospheric fluid, changing daily and hourly its weight and dimensions to the amount, sometimes, of one-tenth of the whole, can be applied as a standard of measure to anything, with as much mathematical exactness, as a trigonometrical process. It is still, however, a resource of great value for these purposes, because its use is so easy, in comparison with the other, and especially where the grounds are unfavorable for a base; and its results are so near the truth as to answer all the common purposes of information. Indeed, I should in all cases, prefer the use of both, to warn us against gross error, and to put us, when that is suspected on a repetition of our process.*— To CAPT. A. PARTRIDGE. vi, 510. (M., 1816.)

5566. MOURNING, Official.—No one would more willingly than myself pay the just tribute due to the services of Captain [John] Barry, by writing a letter of condolence to his widow, as you suggest. But when one undertakes to administer justice, it must be with an even hand, and by rule; what is done for one, must be done for every one in equal degree. To what a train of attentions would this draw a President. How difficult it would be to draw the line between that degree of merit entitled to such a testimonial of it, and that not so entitled? If drawn in a particular case differently from what the friends of the deceased would judge right, what offence would it give, and of the most tender kind? How much offence would be given by accidental inattentions, or want of information? The first step into such an undertaking ought to be well weighed. On the death of Dr. Franklin, the King and Convention of France went into mourning. So did the House of Representatives of the United States. The Senate refused. I proposed to General Washington that the Executive department should wear mourning. He declined it, because he said he should not know where to draw the line, if he once began that ceremony. Mr. Adams was then Vice-President, and I thought General Washington had his eye on him, whom he certainly did not love. I told him the world had drawn so broad a line between himself and Dr. Franklin, on the one side, and the residue of mankind, on the other, that we might wear mourning for them, and the question still remain new and undecided as to all others. He thought it best, however, to avoid it. On these considerations alone, however well affected to the merit of Commodore Barry, I think it prudent not to engage myself in a practice which may become embarrassing.—To DR. BENJAMIN RUSH. iv, 507. FORD ED., viii, 264. (W., 1803.)

5567. MOUSTIER (Count), Attachment for.—Fortune seems to have arranged among her destinies that I should never continue for any time with a person whose manners and principles had excited my warm attachment. While I resided in France, you resided in America. While I was crossing over to America, you were crossing back to France; when I am come to reside with our government, your residence is transferred to Berlin. Of all this, Fortune is the mistress, but she cannot change my affections, nor lessen the regrets I feel at their perpetual disappointment.—To COUNT MOUSTIER. iii, 199. (Pa., 1790.)

5568. MOUSTIER (Count), Character of.—You will find him open, communicative, candid, simple in his manners, and a declared enemy to ostentation and luxury. He goes with a resolution to add no aliment to it by his example, unless he finds that the dispositions of our countrymen require it indispensably.—To JOHN JAY. ii, 293. (P., 1787.)

5569. ———— ————. De Moustier is remarkably communicative. With adroitness he may

be pumped of anything. His openness is from character, not from affectation. An intimacy with him may, on this account, be politically valuable.—To JAMES MADISON. FORD ED., iv, 461. (P., 1787.)

5570. MOUSTIER (Count), Medal for.—The President, in a letter to the King, has expressed his sense of your merit, and his entire approbation of your conduct while here, and has charged me to convey to yourself the same sentiments on his part. Had you returned to your station with us, you would have received new and continued marks of the esteem inspired by the general worth of your character, as well as by the particular dispositions you manifested towards this country. * * * As a testimony of these sentiments, we ask your acceptance of a medal and chain of gold.*—To COUNT MOUSTIER. iii, 216. (Pa., 1791.)

5571. MOUSTIER (Count), Minister to America.—The count Moustier is nominated Minister Plenipotentiary to America, and a frigate is ordered to Cherbourg to carry him over.—To JOHN JAY. ii, 274. (P., Sept. 1787.)

5572. MOUSTIER (Count), Recall.—We had before understood * * * that the conduct of the Count Moustier was politically and morally offensive. It was delicate for me to speak on the subject to the Count de Montmorin. The invaluable mediation of * * * the Marquis de Lafayette was, therefore, resorted to, and the subject explained, though not pressed. Later intelligence showing the necessity of pressing it, it has been represented through the same medium to the Count de Montmorin, that recent information proved to us, that his minister's conduct had rendered him personally odious in America, and might even influence the dispositions of the two nations; that his recall was become a matter of mutual concern; that we had understood he was instructed to remind the new government of their debt to this country, and that he was in the purpose of doing it in very harsh terms; that this could not increase their desire of hastening payment, and might wound their affections; that, therefore, it was much to be desired that his discretion should not be trusted to, as to the form in which the demand should be made, but that the letter should be written here, and he instructed to add nothing but his signature; nor was his private conduct omitted. The Count de Montmorin was sensibly impressed. * * * It had been decided, on the request of the Marquis de la Luzerne, that Otto should go to London; that they would send a person [Colonel Ternant] to America as Chargé des Affaires in place of Otto, and that if the President (General Washington) approved of him, he should be afterwards made minister. * * * Ternant will see that his predecessor is recalled for unconciliatory deportment, and that he will owe his own promotion to the approbation of the President.—To JOHN JAY. ii, 571. (P., 1789.)

5573. MOUSTIER (Count), Unostentatious.—He is a great enemy to formality, etiquette, ostentation and luxury. He goes with the best dispositions to cultivate society, without poisoning it by ill example. He is sensible, disposed to view things favorably, and being well acquainted with the constitution of England, her manners and language, is the

---

* Captain Partridge was an Engineer officer at West Point.—EDITOR.

* De Moustier was appointed minister to Berlin. —EDITOR.

better prepared for his station with us.—To JAMES MADISON. ii, 292. FORD ED., iv, 460. (P., 1787.) See ETIQUETTE.

5574. MURDER, Child.—By the stat. 21. Jac. 1. c. 27. and Act. Ass. 1170. c. 12. concealment by the mother of the death of a bastard child is made murder. In justification of this, it is said, that shame is a feeling which operates so strongly on the mind, as frequently to induce the mother of such a child to murder it, in order to conceal her disgrace. The act of concealment, therefore, proves she was influenced by shame, and that influence produces a presumption that she murdered the child. The effect of this law, then is, to make what, in its nature, is only presumptive evidence of a murder conclusive of that fact. To this I answer, 1. So many children die before or soon after birth, that to presume all those murdered who are found dead, is a presumption which will lead us oftener wrong than right, and consequently would shed more blood than it would save. 2. If the child were born dead, the mother would naturally choose rather to conceal it, in hopes of still keeping a good character in the neighborhood. So that the act of concealment is far from proving the guilt of murder on the mother. 3. If shame be a powerful affection of the mind. is not parental love also? Is it not the strongest affection known? Is it not greater even than that of self-preservation? While we draw presumptions from shame, one affection of the mind, against the life of the prisoner, should we not give some weight to presumptions from parental love, an affection at least as strong, in favor of life? If concealment of the fact is a presumptive evidence of murder, so strong as to overbalance all other evidence that may possibly be produced to take away the presumption, why not trust the force of this incontestable presumption to the jury, who are, in a regular course, to hear presumptive, as well as positive testimony? If the presumption arising from the act of concealment, may be destroyed by proof, positive or circumstantial, to the contrary, why should the legislature preclude that contrary proof? Objection. The crime is difficult to prove, being usually committed in secret. Answer. But circumstantial proof will do; for example. marks of violence, the behavior, countenance, &c., of the prisoner, &c. And if conclusive proof be difficult to be obtained, shall we, therefore, fasten irremovably upon equivocal proof? Can we change the nature of what is contestable, and make it incontestable? Can we make that conclusive which God and nature have made inconclusive? Solon made no law against parricide, supposing it impossible that any one could be guilty of it; and the Persians from the same opinion, adjudged all who killed their reputed parents to be bastards; and although parental be yet stronger than filial affection. we admit saticide proved on the most equivocal testimony, whilst they rejected all proof of an act certainly not more repugnant to nature, as of a thing impossible, unprovable.—NOTE TO CRIMES BILL. i, 149. FORD ED., ii, 206. (1778.)

5575. MURDER, Of colonists.—The proposition [of Lord North] is altogether unsatisfactory * * * because it does not propose to repeal the several acts of Parliament * * * exempting, by mock trial, the murderers of colonists from punishment.—REPLY TO LORD NORTH'S PROPOSITION. FORD ED., i, 480. (July 1775.)

5576. ———— ————. He has combined with others to subject us to a jurisdiction foreign to our constitutions and unacknowledged by our laws, giving his assent to their acts of pretended legislation, for quartering large bodies of armed troops among us; for protecting them by a mock trial from punishment for any murders which they should commit on the inhabitants of these States.—DECLARATION OF INDEPENDENCE AS DRAWN BY JEFFERSON.

5577. MURDER, Degrees of.—Manslaughter is the killing a man with design, but in a sudden gust of passion, and where the killer has not had time to cool. The first offence is not punished capitally, but the second is. This is the law of England and of all the American States; and is not now a new proposition. Those laws have supposed that a man, whose passions have so much dominion over him, as to lead him to repeated acts of murder, is unsafe to society; that it is better he should be put to death by the law, than others more innocent than himself, on the movements of his impetuous passions.—To M. DE MEUNIER. ix, 263. FORD ED., iv, 169. (P., 1786.)

5578. ———— ————. In 1796, our Legislature passed the law for amending the penal laws of the Commonwealth. [Virginia.] * * * Instead of the settled distinctions of murder and manslaughter, preserved in my bill, they introduced the new terms of murder in the first and second degrees. *—AUTOBIOGRAPHY. i, 47. FORD ED., i, 65. (1821.)

5579. MURDER, Excusable.—Excusable homicides are in some cases not quite unblamable. These should subject the party to marks of contrition; viz., the killing of a man in defence of property; so also in defence of one's person, which is a species of excusable homicide; because, although cases may happen where these are also commendable, yet most frequently they are done on too slight appearance of danger; as in return for a blow, kick, fillip, &c., or on a person's getting into a house. not *animo furandi*, but perhaps *veneris causa*, &c. Excusable homicides are by misadventure, or in self-defence.—NOTE TO CRIMES BILL. i, 152. FORD ED., ii, 209. (1779.)

5580. MURDER, Indian.—I wish Governor Harrison may be able to have the murder of the Kaskaskian by the Kickapoo settled in the Indian way. * * * Both the Indians and our own people need some example of punishment for the murder of an Indian.—To HENRY DEARBORN. v, 162. (M., 1807.)

5581. ———— ————. When a murder has been committed on one of our stragglers, the murderer should be demanded. If not delivered, give time, and still press the demand. We find it difficult, with our regular government, to take and punish a murderer of an Indian. Indeed, I believe we have never been able to do it in a single instance. They have their difficulties also, and require time. In fact, it is a case where indulgence on both sides is just and necessary, to prevent the two nations from being perpetually committed in war, by the acts of the most vagabond and ungovernable of their members. When the refusal to deliver

* The clause of Jefferson's bill read as follows: "And where persons, meaning to commit a trespass only, or larceny, or other unlawful deed, and doing an act from which involuntary homicide hath ensued, have heretofore been adjudged guilty of manslaughter, or of murder, by transferring such their unlawful intention to an act, much more penal than they could have in probable contemplation; no such case shall hereafter be deemed manslaughter, unless manslaughter was intended, nor murder, unless murder was intended."—EDITOR.

the murderer is permanent, and proceeds from the want of will, and not of ability we should then interdict all trade and intercourse with them till they give us complete satisfaction.—To Meriwether Lewis. v, 350. (M., 1808.)

5582. —— ——. If we had to go to war [with the Indians] for every hunter or trader killed, and murderer refused, we should have had general and constant war. The process to be followed, in my opinion, when a murder has been committed, is first to demand the murderer, and not regarding a first refusal to deliver, give time and press it. If perseveringly refused, recall all traders, and interdict commerce with them, until he be delivered.—To Henry Dearborn. v, 348. (M., Aug. 1808.)

5583. MURDER, Punishment for.—As there was but one white man murdered by the Indians, I should be averse to the execution of more than one of them, selecting the most guilty and worst character. Nothing but extreme criminality should induce the execution of a second, and nothing beyond that. Their idea is that justice allows only man for man, that all beyond that is new aggression, which must be expiated by a new sacrifice of an equivalent number of our people.—To Meriwether Lewis. v, 354. (M., 1808.)

5584. —— ——. There is the more reason for moderation, as we know we cannot punish any murder which shall be committed by us on them. Even if the murderer can be taken, our juries have never yet convicted the murderer of an Indian.—To Meriwether Lewis. v, 354. (M., 1808.)

5585. MURDER, Self.—Suicide is by law punishable by forfeiture of chattels. This bill (revising the Virginia Code) exempts it from forfeiture. The suicide injures the State less than he who leaves it with his effects. If the latter then be not punished, the former should not. As to the example, we need not fear its influence. Men are too much attached to life, to exhibit frequent instances of depriving themselves of it. At any rate, the quasi-punishment of confiscation will not prevent it. For if one be found who can calmly determine to renounce life, who is so weary of his existence here, as rather to make experiment of what is beyond the grave, can we suppose him, in such a state of mind, susceptible of influence from the losses to his family from confiscation? That men in general, too, disapprove of this severity, is apparent from the constant practice of juries finding the suicide in a state of insanity; because they have no other way of saving the forfeiture. Let it then be done away.—Note to Crimes Bill. i, 152. Ford ed., ii, 210. (1779.)

5586. MUSEUMS, Maintenance of.—Nobody can desire more ardently than myself, to concur in whatever may promote useful science, and I view no science with more partiality than Natural History. But I have ever believed that in this, as in most other cases, abortive attempts retard rather than promote this object. To be really useful we must keep pace with the state of society, and not dishearten it by attempts at what its population, means, or occupations will fail in attempting. In the particular enterprises for museums, we have seen the populous and wealthy cities of Boston and New York unable to found or maintain such an institution. The feeble condition of that in each of these places sufficiently proves this. In Philadelphia alone, has this attempt succeeded to a good degree. It has

been owing there to a measure of zeal and perseverance in an individual rarely equalled; to a population, crowded, wealthy, and more than usually addicted to the pursuit of knowledge. And, with all this, the institution does not maintain itself.—To Mr. De La Coste. v, 79. (W., 1807.)

5587. MUSIC, Domestic bands.—The bounds of an American fortune will not admit the indulgence of a domestic band of musicians, yet I have thought that a passion for music might be reconciled with that economy which we are obliged to observe. I retain, for instance, among my domestic servants a gardener, a weaver, a cabinet-maker, and a stone-cutter, to which I would add a *vigneron*. In a country where, like yours [France], music is cultivated and practiced by every class of men, I suppose there might be found persons of these trades who could perform on the French horn, clarionet, or hautboy, and bassoon, so that one might have a band of two French horns, two clarionets, two hautboys, and a bassoon, without enlarging his domestic expenses. A certainty of employment for a half dozen years, and at the end of that time, to find them, if they chose, a conveyance to their own country, might induce them to come here on reasonable wages. Without meaning to give you trouble, perhaps it might be practicable for you * * * to find out such men disposed to come to America. Sobriety and good nature would be desirable parts of their characters. If you think such a plan practicable, and will be so kind as to inform me what will be necessary to be done on my part, I will take care that it shall be done. To —— ——. i, 209. Ford ed., ii, 159. (Wg., 1778.)

5588. MUSIC, Ear for.—Music is invaluable where a person has an ear. Where they have not, it should not be attempted.—To N. Burwell. vii, 103. Ford ed., x, 105. (M., 1818.)

5589. MUSIC, Enjoyment of.—Music is an enjoyment [in France] the deprivation of which with us, cannot be calculated. I am almost ready to say, it is the only thing which from my heart I envy them, and which, in spite of all the authority of the Decalogue, I do covet.—To Mr. Bellini. i, 445. (P., 1785.)

5590. MUSIC, Foot-bass.—I have lately examined a foot-bass, newly invented by the celebrated Krumfoltz. It is precisely a pianoforte, about ten feet long, eighteen inches broad, and nine inches deep. It is of one octave only, from fa to fa. The part where the keys are projects at the side in order to lengthen the levers of the keys. It is placed on the floor, on the harpsichord or other pianoforte, is set over it, the foot acting in concert on that, while the fingers play on this. There are three unison chords to every note, of strong brass wire, and the lowest have wire wrapped on them as the lowest in the pianoforte. The chords give a fine, clear, deep tone almost like the pipe of an organ.—To Francis Hopkinson. ii, 75. (P., 1786.)

5591. MUSIC, Harmonica.—I am very much pleased with your project on the harmonica, and the prospect of your succeeding in the application of keys to it. It will be the greatest present which has been made to the musical world this century, not excepting the piano-forte. If its tone approaches that given by the finger as nearly only as the harpsichord does that of the harp, it will be very valuable. —To Francis Hopkinson. ii, 75. (P., 1786.)

5592. MUSIC, Harpsichord.—I applaud much your perseverance in improving this instrument [harpsichord], and benefiting mankind almost in spite of their teeth.—To Francis Hopkinson. i, 440. (P., 1785.)

5593. MUSIC, Keeping time.—Monsieur Renaudin's invention for determining the true time of the musical movements, Largo, Adagio, &c. * * * has been examined by the [Paris] Academy of Music, who are so well satisfied of its utility, that they have ordered all music which shall be printed here, in future, to have the movements numbered in correspondence with this plexi-chronometer. * * * The instrument is useful, but still it may be greatly simplified. I got him to make me one, and having fixed a pendulum vibrating seconds, I tried by that the vibrations of his pendulum, according to the several movements. I find the pendulum regulated to

Largo			5	
Adagio			60	times
Andante	vibrates		70	in a
Allegro			95	minute
Presto			135	

Every one, therefore, may make a chronometer adapted to his instrument. For a harpsichord, the following occurs to me: In the wall of your chamber, over the instrument, drive five little brads, as 1, 2, 3, 4, 5, in the following manner. Take a string with a bob to it, of such length, as that hung on No. 1, it shall vibrate fifty-two times in a minute. Then proceed by trial to drive number No. 2, at such a distance, that drawing the loop of the string to that, the part remaining between 1 and the bob, shall vibrate sixty times in a minute. Fix the third for seventy vibrations, &c.; the chord always hanging over No. 1, as the centre of vibration. A person, playing on the violin, may fix this on his music stand. A pendulum, thrown into vibration, will continue in motion long enough to give you the time of your piece.—To Francis Hopkinson. i, 504. (P., 1786.)

5594. MUSIC, Negroes and.—In music the blacks are more generally gifted than the whites, with accurate ears for tune and time, and they have been found capable of imagining a small catch.* Whether they will be equal to the composition of a more extensive run of melody, or of complicated harmony, is yet to be proved.—Notes on Virginia. viii, 383. Ford ed., iii, 246. (1782.)

5595. MUSIC, Passion for.—If there is a gratification which I envy any people in this world, it is to your country [France] its music. This is the favorite passion of my soul, and fortune has cast my lot in a country where it is in a state of deplorable barbarism.—To ——. i, 209. Ford ed., ii, 158. (Wg., 1778.)

5596. MUSIC, Piano.—I wrote [you] for a Clavichord. I have since seen a Forte-piano and am charmed with it. Send me this instrument then instead of the Clavichord: let the case be of fine mahogany, solid, not veneered, the compass from Double G. to F. in alt, a plenty of spare strings; and the workmanship

* The instrument proper to them is the banjer (corrupted by the negroes into "banjo") which they brought hither from Africa, which is the original of the guitar, its chords being precisely the four lower chords of the guitar.—Note by Jefferson.

of the whole very handsome and worthy the acceptance of a lady for whom I intend it.—To Thomas Adams. Ford ed., i, 395. (M., 1771.)

5597. —— ——. I had almost decided, on Piccini's advice, to get a piano-forte for my daughter; but your last letter may pause me, till I see its effect.—To Francis Hopkinson. i, 440. (P., 1785.)

5598. MUSIC, Quilling.—I do not altogether despair of making something of your method of quilling, though, as yet, the prospect is not favorable.—To Francis Hopkinson. i, 440. (P., 1785.)

5599. —— ——. I mentioned to Piccini the improvement [quilling] with which I am entrusted. He plays on the piano-forte, and therefore did not feel himself personally interested.—To Francis Hopkinson. i, 440. (P., 1785.)

5600. MUSKETS, Improved.—An improvement is made here [France] in the construction of muskets, which it may be interesting to Congress to know, should they at any time propose to procure any. It consists in the making every part of them so exactly alike, that what belongs to any one, may be used for every other musket in the magazine. * * * As yet, the inventor has only completed the lock of the musket, on this plan. * * * He presented me the parts of fifty locks taken to pieces, and arranged in compartments. I put several together myself, taking pieces at hazard as they came to hand, and they fitted in the most perfect manner.—To John Jay. i, 411. (P., 1785.)

— NAIL-MAKING.—See Jefferson (Thomas.)

5601. NAMES, Authority of great.—It is surely time for men to think for themselves, and to throw off the authority of names so artificially magnified.—To William Short. vii, 165. (M., 1820.)

5602. NAMES, Bestowal of.—I agree with you entirely in condemning the mania of giving names to objects of any kind after persons still living. Death alone can seal the title of any man to this honor, by putting it out of his power to forfeit it.—To Dr. Benjamin Rush. iv, 335. Ford ed., vii, 459. (M., 1800.)

5603. —— ——. There is one * * * mode of recording merit, which I have often thought might be introduced, so as to gratify the living by praising the dead. In giving, for instance, a commission of Chief Justice to Bushrod Washington, it should be in consideration of his integrity, and science in the laws, and of the services rendered to our country by his illustrious relation, &c. A commission to a descendant of Dr. Franklin, besides being in consideration of the proper qualifications of the person, should add that of the great services rendered by his illustrious ancestor, Benjamin Franklin, by the advancement of science, by inventions useful to man, &c.—To Dr. Benjamin Rush. iv, 335. Ford ed., vii, 459. (M., 1800.)

5604. —— ——. I am sensible of the mark of esteem manifested by the name you have given to your son. Tell him from me, that he must consider as essentially belonging to it, to love his friends and wish no ill to his enemies.—To David Campbell. v, 499. (M., 1810.)

5605. NAMES, Opinions and.—If * * * opinions are sound - * * they will prevail by their own weight without the aid of names.—To SAMUEL KERCHIVAL. vii, 35. FORD ED., x, 45. (M., 1816.)

5606. NAMES, Political party.—The appellation of aristocrats and democrats is the true one expressing the essence of all [parties].—To H. LEE. vii, 376. FORD ED., x, 318. (M., 1824.)

5607. NAMES, Property in.—I am not sure that we ought to change all our names. During the regal government, sometimes, indeed, they were given through adulation; but often also as the reward of the merit of the times, sometimes for services rendered the colony. Perhaps, too, a name when given, should be deemed a sacred property.—To DR. BENJAMIN RUSH. iv, 335. FORD ED., vii, 459. (M., 1800.)

5608. NASSAU, Fame of.—Nassau is a village the whole rents of which would not amount to more than a hundred or two guineas. Yet it gives the title of Prince to the house of Orange to which it belongs.—TRAVELS IN HOLLAND. ix, 383. (1787.)

5609. NATION (United States), Building the.—The interests of the States ought to be made joint in every possible instance, in order to cultivate the idea of our being one nation, and to multiply the instances in which the people shall look up to Congress as their head.—To JAMES MONROE. i, 347. FORD ED., iv, 52. (P., 1785.)

5610. ——— ———. It is, indeed, an animating thought that, while we are securing the rights of ourselves and posterity, we are pointing out the way to struggling nations who wish, like us, to emerge from their tyrannies also.—REPLY TO ADDRESS. iii, 128. FORD ED., v, 147. (1790.)

5611. NATION (United States), Conscience of.—It is true that nations are to be judges for themselves since no one nation has a right to sit in judgment over another. But the tribunal of our consciences remains, and that also of the opinion of the world. These will revise the sentence we pass in our own case, and as we respect these, we must see that in judging ourselves we have honestly done the part of impartial and rigorous judges.—OPINION ON FRENCH TREATIES. vii, 614. FORD ED., vi, 221. (1793.)

5612. NATION (United States), Foreign policy.—Unmeddling with the affairs of other nations, we presume not to prescribe or censure their course.—To MADAME DE STAEL. v, 133. (W., 1807.)

5613. ——— ———. We wish the happiness and prosperity of every nation.—To MADAME DE STAEL. vi, 482. (M., 1815.)

5614. NATION (United States), Liberality.—I am in all cases for a liberal conduct towards other nations, believing that the practice of the same friendly feelings and generous dispositions, which attach individuals in private life, will attach societies on the larger scale, which are composed of individuals.—To ALBERT GALLATIN. FORD ED., viii, 222. (M., 1803.)

5615. NATION (United States), Objects of.—Peace with all nations, and the right which that gives us with respect to all nations, are our object.—To C. W. F. DUMAS. iii, 535. (Pa., 1793.)

5616. ——— ———. I hope the United States will ever place themselves among [the number of] peaceable nations.—To ROBERT R. LIVINGSTON. iv, 411. FORD ED., viii, 91. (M., Sep. 1801.)

5617. NATION (United States), Supremacy.—Not in our day, but at no distant one, we may shake a rod over the heads of all, which may make the stoutest of them tremble. But I hope our wisdom will grow with our power, and teach us, that the less we use our power the greater it will be.—To THOMAS LEIPER. vi, 465. FORD ED., ix, 520. (M., 1815.) See POLICY.

5618. ——— ———. The day is not distant, when we may formally require a meridian of partition through the ocean which separates the two hemispheres, on the hither side of which no European gun shall ever be heard, nor an American on the other; and when, during the rage of the eternal wars of Europe, the lion and the lamb, within our regions, shall lie down together in peace.—To WILLIAM SHORT. vii, 168. (M., 1820.)

— NATIONAL CAPITAL.—See WASHINGTON CITY.

5619. NATIONAL CURRENCY, Bank paper and.—The question will be asked and ought to be looked at, what is to be the resource if loans cannot be obtained? There is but one, "*Carthago delenda est*". Bank paper must be suppressed, and the circulating medium must be restored to the nation to whom it belongs. It is the only fund on which they can rely for loans; it is the only resource which can never fail them and it is an abundant one for every necessary purpose. Treasury bills, bottomed on taxes, bearing or not bearing interest, as may be found necessary, thrown into circulation will take the place of so much gold and silver, which last, when crowded, will find an efflux into other countries, and thus keep the quantum of medium at its salutary level. Let banks continue if they please, but let them discount for cash alone or for treasury notes. They discount for cash alone in every other country on earth except Great Britain, and her too often unfortunate copyist, the United States. If taken in time, they may be rectified by degrees, and without injustice, but if let alone till the alternative forces itself on us, of submitting to the enemy for want of funds, or the suppression of bank paper, either by law or by convulsion, we cannot foresee how it will end.—To J. W. EPPES. vi, 199. FORD ED., ix, 399. (P.F., Sep. 1813.)

5620. ——— ———. Put down the banks, and if this country could not be carried through the longest war against her most powerful enemy, without ever knowing the want of a dollar, without dependence on the traitorous classes of her citizens, without bearing hard on the resources of the people, or loading the public with an indefinite burthen of debt, I know nothing of my countrymen. Not by any novel project, not by any charlatanerie, but by ordinary and well-experienced means; by the total prohibition of all private paper at all times, by reasonable taxes in war aided by the necessary emissions of public paper of circulating size, this bottomed on special taxes, redeemable annually as this special tax comes in, and finally within a moderate period.—To ALBERT GALLATIN. vi, 498. (M., Oct. 1815.)

5621. NATIONAL CURRENCY, Bank suspensions and.—The failure of our banks * * * restores to us a fund which ought never to have been surrendered by the nation, and which now, prudently used, will carry us through all the fiscal difficulties of the war.—To PRESIDENT MADISON. vi, 386. (M., Sep. 1814.)

5622. NATIONAL CURRENCY, Borrowing fund.—I am sorry to see our loans begin at so exorbitant an interest. And yet, even at that you will soon be at the bottom of the loan-bag. We are an agricultural nation. Such an one employs its sparings in the purchase or improvement of land or stocks. The lendable money among them is chiefly that of orphans and wards in the hands of executors and guardians, and that which the former lays by till he has enough for the purchase in view. In such a nation there is one, and only one, resource for loans, sufficient to carry them through the expense of a war; and that will always be sufficient, and in the power of an honest government, punctual in the preservation of its faith. The fund I mean, is *the mass of circulating coin.* Every one knows, that although not literally, it is nearly true, that every paper dollar emitted banishes a silver one from the circulation. A nation, therefore, making its purchases and payments with bills fitted for circulation, thrusts an equal sum of coin out of circulation. This is equivalent to borrowing that sum, and yet the vendor, receiving in payment a medium as effectual as coin for his purchases or payments, has no claim to interest. And so the nation may continue to issue its bills as far as its wants require, and the limits of the circulation will admit. Those limits are understood to extend with us at present, to two hundred millions of dollars, a greater sum than would be necessary for any war. But this, the only resource which the government could command with certainty, the States have unfortunately fooled away, nay corruptly alienated to swindlers and shavers, under the cover of private banks. Say, too, as an additional evil, that the disposal funds of individuals, to this great amount, have thus been withdrawn from improvement and useful enterprise, and employed in the useless, usu-

rious and demoralizing practices of bank directors and their accomplices. In the year 1775, our State [Virginia] availed itself of this fund by issuing a paper money, bottomed on a specific tax for its redemption, and, to insure its credit, bearing an interest of five per cent. Within a very short time, not a bill of this emission was to be found in circulation. It was locked up in the chests of executors, guardians, widows, farmers, &c. We then issued bills bottomed on a redeeming tax, but bearing no interest. These were readily received, and never depreciated a single farthing. In the Revolutionary war, the old Congress and the States issued bills without interest, and without a tax. They occupied the channels of circulation very freely, till those channels were overflowed by an excess beyond all the calls of circulation. But, although we have so improvidently suffered the field of circulating medium to be filched from us by private individuals, yet I think we may recover it in part, and even in the whole, if the States will cooperate with us. If Treasury bills are emitted on a tax appropriated for their redemption in fifteen years, and (to ensure preference in the first moments of competition) bearing an interest of six per cent. there is no one who would not take them in preference to the bank paper now afloat, on a principle of patriotism as well as interest; and they would be withdrawn from circulation into private hoards to a considerable amount. Their credit once established, others might be emitted, bottomed also on a tax, but not bearing interest, and if even their credit faltered, open public loans, on which these bills alone should be received as specie. These, operating as a sinking fund, would reduce the quantity in circulation, so as to maintain that in an equilibrium with specie. It is not easy to estimate the obstacles which, in the beginning, we should encounter in ousting the banks from their possession of the circulation; but a steady and judicious alternation of emissions and loans, would reduce them in time. But while this is going on, another measure should be pressed, to recover ultimately our right to the circulation. The States should be applied to, to transfer the right of issuing circulating paper to Congress exclusively, *in perpetuum,* if possible, but during the war at least, with a saving of charter rights. I believe that every State west and south of the Connecticut River, except Delaware, would immediately do it; and the others would follow in time. Congress would, of course, begin by obliging unchartered banks to wind up their affairs within a short time, and the others as their charters expired, forbidding the subsequent circulation of their paper. This, they would supply with their own, bottomed, every emission, on an adequate tax, and bearing or not bearing interest, as the state of the public pulse should indicate. Even in the non-complying States, these bills would make their way, and supplant the unfunded paper of their banks, by their solidity, by the universality of their currency, and by their receivability for customs and taxes. It would be in their power, too, to curtail those banks to the amount of their actual specie, by gathering up their paper, and running it constantly on them. The national paper might thus take place even in the non-complying States. In this way, I am not without a hope, that this great, this sole resource for loans in an agricultural country, might yet be recovered for the use of the nation during war; and, if obtained *in perpetuum*, it would always be sufficient to carry us through any war; provided, that in the interval between war and war, all the outstanding paper should be called in, coin be permitted to flow in again, and to hold the field of circulation until another war should require its yielding place again to the national medium.—To John Wayles Eppes. vi, 139. Ford ed., ix, 391. (M., June 1813.)

5623. ———. I like well your idea of issuing treasury notes bearing interest, because I am persuaded they would soon be withdrawn from circulation and locked up in vaults in private hoards. It would put it in the power of every man to lend his $100 or $1000, though not able to go forward on the great scale, and be the most advantageous way of obtaining a loan.—To Thomas Law. Ford ed., ix, 433. (M., Nov. 1813.)

5624. ——— ———. The circulating fund is the only one we can ever command with certainty. It is sufficient for all our wants; and the impossibility of even defending the country without its aid as a borrowing fund, renders it indispensable that the nation should take and keep it in their own hands, as their exclusive resource.— To President Madison. vi, 393. Ford ed., ix, 491. (M., Oct. 1814.)

5625. ——— ———. Although a century of British experience has proved to what a wonderful extent the funding on specific redeeming taxes enables a nation to anticipate in war the resources of peace, and although the other nations of Europe have tried and trodden every path of force or folly in fruitless quest of the same object, yet *we* still expect to find in juggling tricks and banking dreams, that money can be made out of nothing, and in sufficient quantities to meet the expenses of a heavy war by sea and land. It is said, indeed, that money cannot be borrowed from our merchants as from those of England. But it can be borrowed from our people. They will give you all the necessaries of war they produce, if, instead of the bankrupt trash they are now obliged to receive for want of any other, you will give them a paper promise funded on a specific pledge, and of a size for common circulation. But you say the merchants will not take this paper. What the people take the merchants must take, or sell nothing. All these doubts and fears prove only the extent of the dominion which the banking institutions have obtained over the minds of our citizens, and especially of those inhabiting cities or other banking places; and this

dominion must be broken, or it will break us. But * * * we must make up our minds to suffer yet longer before we can get right. The misfortune is, that in the meantime, we shall plunge ourselves in unextinguishable debt, and entail on our posterity an inheritance of eternal taxes, which will bring our government and people into the condition of those of England, a nation of pikes and gudgeons, the latter bred merely as food for the former.—To James Monroe. vi, 409. Ford ed., ix, 497. (M., Jan. 1815.)

5626. NATIONAL CURRENCY, Circulating medium.—If I have used any expression restraining the emissions of treasury notes to a *sufficient* medium, * * * I have done it inadvertently, and under the impression then possessing me, that the war would be very short. A *sufficient* medium would not, on the principles of any writer, exceed thirty millions of dollars, and of those of some not ten millions. Our experience has proved it may be run up to two or three hundred millions, without more than doubling what would be the prices of things under a *sufficient* medium, or say a metallic one, which would always keep itself at the *sufficient* point; and, if they rise to this term, and the descent from it be gradual, it would not produce sensible revolutions in private fortunes. I shall be able to explain my views more definitely by the use of numbers. Suppose we require, to carry on the war, an annual loan of twenty millions, then I propose that, in the first year, you shall lay a tax of two millions, and emit twenty millions of treasury notes, of a size proper for circulation, and bearing no interest, to the redemption of which the proceeds of that tax shall be inviolably pledged and applied, by recalling annually their amount of the identical bills funded on them. The second year, lay another tax of two millions, and emit twenty millions more. The third year the same, and so on, until you have reached the maximum of taxes which ought to be imposed. Let me suppose this maximum to be one dollar a head, or ten millions of dollars, merely as an exemplification more familiar than would be the algebraical symbols x or y. You would reach this in five years. The sixth year, then, still emit twenty millions of treasury notes, and continue all the taxes two years longer. The seventh year, twenty millions more, and continue the whole taxes another two years; and so on. Observe, that although you emit twenty millions of dollars a year. you call in ten millions, and, consequently, add but ten millions annually to the circulation. It would be in thirty years, then, *primâ facie*, that you would reach the present circulation of three hundred millions, or the ultimate term to which we might venture. But observe, also, that in that time we shall have become thirty millions of people, to whom three hundred millions of dollars would be no more than one hundred millions to us now; which sum would probably not have raised prices more than fifty per cent. on what may be deemed the standard, or metallic prices. This increased population and consumption, while it would be increasing the proceeds of the redemption tax, and lessening the balance annually thrown into circulation, would also absorb, without saturation, more of the surplus medium, and enable us to push the same process to a much higher term, to one which we might safely call indefinite, because extending so far beyond the limits, either in time or expense, of any supposable war. All we should have to do would be, when the war should be ended, to leave the gradual extinction of these notes to the operation of the taxes pledged for their redemption; not to suffer a dollar of paper to be emitted either by public or private authority, but let the metallic medium flow back into the channels of circulation, and occupy them until another war should oblige us to recur, for its support, to the same resource, and the same process, on the circulating medium.—To PRESIDENT MADISON. vi, 392. FORD ED., ix, 489. (M., Oct. 1814.)

5627. ———— ————. The government is now issuing Treasury notes for circulation, bottomed on solid funds and bearing interest. The banking confederacy (and the merchants bound to them by their debts) will endeavor to crush the credit of these notes; but the country is eager for them, as something they can trust to, and as soon as a convenient quantity of them can get into circulation the bank notes die.—To JEAN BAPTISTE SAY. vi, 434. (M., 1815.)

5628. ———— ————. The war, had it proceeded, would have upset our government; and a new one, whenever tried, will do it. And so it must be while our money, the nerve of war, is much or little, real or imaginary, as our bitterest enemies choose to make it.— To ALBERT GALLATIN. vi, 498. (M., Oct. 1815.)

5629. NATIONAL CURRENCY, Congressional control.—From the establishment of the United States Bank, to this day, I have preached against this system, and have been sensible no cure could be hoped but in the catastrophe now happening. The remedy was to let banks drop gradually at the expiration of their charters, and for the State governments to relinquish the power of establishing others. This would not, as it should not, have given the power of establishing them to Congress. But Congress could then have issued treasury notes payable within a fixed period, and founded on a specific tax, the proceeds of which, as they came in, should be exchangeable for the notes of that particular emission only. This depended, it is true, on the will of the State Legislatures, and would have brought on us the phalanx of paper interest. But that interest is now defunct.—To THOMAS COOPER. vi, 381. (M., Sep. 1814.)

5630. ———— ————. To give readier credit to their bills, without obliging themselves to give cash for them on demand, let their collectors be instructed to do so, when they have cash; thus, in some measure, performing the functions of a bank, as to their own notes.— To THOMAS COOPER. vi, 382. (M., Sep. 1814.)

5631. NATIONAL CURRENCY, Redemption.—Treasury notes of small as well as high denomination, bottomed on a tax which would redeem them in ten years, would place at our disposal the whole circulating medium of the United States; a fund of credit sufficient to carry us through any probable length of war. A small issue of such paper is now commencing. It will immediately supersede the bank paper; nobody receiving that now but for the purposes of the day, and never in payments which are to lie by for any time. In fact, all the banks having declared they will not give cash in exchange for their own notes, these circulate merely because there is no other medium of exchange. As soon as the treasury notes get into circulation, the others will cease to hold any competition with them. I trust that another year will confirm this experiment, and restore this fund to the public, who ought never more to permit its being filched from them by private speculators and disorganizers of the circulation.—To W. H. CRAWFORD. vi, 419. FORD ED., ix, 503. (M., Feb. 1815.)

5632. ———— ————. The third great measure necessary to ensure us permanent prosperity, should ensure resources of money by the suppression of all paper circulation during peace, and licensing that of the nation alone during war. The metallic medium of which we should be possessed at the commencement of a war, would be a sufficient fund for all the loans we should need through its continuance; and if the national bills issued, be bottomed (as is indispensable) on pledges of specific taxes for their redemption within certain and moderate epochs, and be of proper denominations for circulation, no interest on them would be necessary or just, because they would answer to every one the purposes of the metallic money withdrawn and replaced by them.—To WILLIAM H. CRAWFORD. vii, 8. FORD ED., x, 36. (M., 1816.) See BANKS, DOLLAR, MONEY, and PAPER MONEY.

— NATIONAL UNIVERSITY.—See UNIVERSITY.

5633. NATIONS, Constitutions for.— Such indeed are the different circumstances, prejudices, and habits of different nations, that the constitution of no one would be reconcilable to any other in every point.—To M. CORAY. vii, 320. (M., 1823.)

5634. NATIONS, Dictation to.—The presumption of dictating to an independent nation the form of its government, is so arrogant, so atrocious, that indignation, as well as moral sentiment, enlists all our partialities and prayers in favor of one, and our equal execrations against the other.—To JAMES MONROE. vii, 287. FORD ED., x, 257. (M., 1823.)

5635. NATIONS, European.—The European societies * * * under pretence of governing, have divided their nations into two classes, wolves and sheep.—To EDWARD CARRINGTON. ii, 100. FORD ED., iv, 360. (P., 1787.)

5636. —— ——. The European are nations of eternal war. All their energies are expended in the destruction of the labor, property, and lives of their people.—To PRESIDENT MONROE. vii, 288. FORD ED., x, 257. (M., 1823.)

5637. NATIONS, Extinction of.—I shall not wonder to see the scenes of ancient Rome and Carthage renewed in our day; and if not pursued to the same issue, it may be because the republic of modern powers will not permit the extinction of any one of its members.—To C. W. F. DUMAS. i, 553. (P., 1786.)

5638. NATIONS, Good faith.—A character of good faith is of as much value to a nation as to an individual.—THE ANAS. FORD ED., i, 332. (1808.)

5639. NATIONS, Government of.—I think, with others, that nations are to be governed according to their own interest, but I am convinced that it is their interest, in the long run to be grateful, faithful to their engagements, even in the worst of circumstances, and honorable and generous always. —To M. DE LAFAYETTE. iii, 132. FORD ED., v, 152. (N.Y., 1790.)

5640. NATIONS, History and.—Wars and contentions, indeed, fill the pages of history with more matter. But more blest is that nation whose silent course of happiness furnishes nothing for history to say. This is what I ambition for my own country.—To COUNT DIODATI. v, 62. (W., 1807.)

5641. NATIONS, Ignorant.—If a nation expects to be ignorant and free, in a state of civilization, it expects what never was and never will be.—To CHARLES YANCEY. vi, 517. FORD ED., x, 4. (M., 1816.)

5642. NATIONS, Interest of.—The interests of a nation, when well understood, will be found to coincide with their moral duties.—PARAGRAPH FOR PRESIDENT'S MESSAGE. FORD ED., vi, 119. (1792.)

5643. NATIONS, Jefferson's prayer for all.—I wish that all nations may recover and retain their independence; that those which are overgrown may not advance beyond safe measures of power, that a salutary balance may be ever maintained among nations, and that our peace, commerce and friendship, may be sought and cultivated by all.—To THOMAS LEIPER. vi, 464. FORD ED., ix, 520. (M., 1815.)

5644. —— ——. Notwithstanding all the French and British atrocities, which will forever disgrace the present era of history, their shameless prostration of all the laws of morality which constitute the security, the peace and comfort of man—notwithstanding the waste of human life, and measure of human suffering which they have inflicted on the world—nations hitherto in slavery have desired through all this bloody mist a glimmering of their own rights. have dared to open their eyes, and to see that their own power will suffice for their emancipation. Their tyrants must now give them more moderate forms of government, and they seem now to be sensible of this themselves. Instead of the parricide treason of Bonaparte in employing the means confided to him as a republican magistrate to the overthrow of that republic, and establishment of a military despotism in himself and his descendants, to the subversion of the neighboring governments, and erection of thrones for his brothers, his sisters and sycophants, had he honestly employed that power in the establishment and support of the freedom of his own country, there is not a nation in Europe which would not at this day have had a more rational government, one in which the will of the people should have had a moderating and salutary influence. The work will now be longer, will swell more rivers with blood, produce more sufferings and more crimes. But it will be consummated; and that it may be will be the theme of my constant prayers while I shall remain on the earth beneath, or in the heavens above.—To WILLIAM BENTLEY. vi, 503. (M., 1815.)

5645. NATIONS, Just and unjust.—A just nation is taken on its word, when recourse is had to armaments and wars to bridle others.—SECOND INAUGURAL ADDRESS. viii, 40. FORD ED., viii, 343. (1805.)

5646. —— ——. No nation, however powerful, any more than an individual, can be unjust with impunity. Sooner or later public opinion, an instrument merely moral in the beginning, will find occasion physically to inflict its sentences on the unjust.—To JAMES MADISON. FORD ED., viii, 300. (M., 1804.)

5647. NATIONS, Justice and.—No nation can answer for perfect exactitude of proceedings in all their inferior courts. It suffices to provide a supreme judicature, where all error and partiality will be ultimately corrected.—To GEORGE HAMMOND. iii, 414. FORD ED., vi, 55. (Pa., 1792.)

5648. NATIONS, Liberal.—A nation, by establishing a character of liberality and magnanimity, gains in the friendship and respect of others more than the worth of mere money.—SPECIAL MESSAGE. viii, 56. (1806.)

5649. NATIONS, Manners of.—It is difficult to determine on the standard by which the manners of a nation may be tried. whether *catholic* or *particular*. It is more difficult for a native to bring to that standard the manners of his own nation, familiarized to him by habit.—NOTES ON VIRGINIA. viii, 403. FORD ED., iii, 266. (1782.)

5650. NATIONS, Money and rights of. —Money is the agent by which modern nations will recover their rights.—To COMTE DE MOUSTIER. ii, 389. FORD ED., v, 12. (P., 1788.)

5651. NATIONS, Morality.—A nation, as a society, forms a moral person, and every member of it is personally responsible for his society.—To George Hammond. iii, 419. Ford ed., vi, 59. (Pa., 1792.) See Morality (National).

5652. ——— ———. The moral obligations constitute a law for nations as well as individuals.—R. to A. N. Y. Tammany Society. viii, 127. (1808.)

5653. NATIONS, Natural rights of.— In no case are the laws of a nation changed, of natural right. by their passage from one to another domination. The soil, the inhabitants, their property, and the laws by which they are protected go together. Their laws are subject to be changed only in the ease. and extent which their new legislature shall will.—Batture Case. viii, 528. (1812.)

5654. NATIONS, Neighboring.—We have seldom seen neighborhood produce affection among nations. The reverse is almost the universal truth.—To John C. Breckenridge. iv, 499. Ford ed., viii, 243. (M., 1803.)

5655. NATIONS, Oppressed.—That we should wish to see the people of other countries free, is as natural, and at least as justifiable, as that one King should wish to see the Kings of other countries maintained in their despotism.—To Albert Gallatin. vii, 78. Ford ed., x, 90. (M., 1817.)

5656. NATIONS, Peculiarities of.—In reading the travels of a Frenchman through the United States what he remarks as peculiarities in us, prove to us the contrary peculiarities of the French. We have the accounts of Barbary from European and American travellers. It would be more amusing if Melli Melli would give us his observations on the United States. If, with the fables and follies of the Hindoos, so justly pointed out to us by yourself and other travellers. we could compare the contrast of those which an Hindoo traveller would imagine he found among us, it might enlarge our instruction. It would be curious to see what parallel among us he would select for his Veeshni.—To Nathaniel Greene. vi, 72. (M., 1812.)

5657. NATIONS, Political conditions in.—The condition of different descriptions of inhabitants in any country is a matter of municipal arrangement, of which no foreign country has a right to take notice. All its inhabitants are as men to them.—To Samuel Kerchival. vii, 37. Ford ed., x, 46. (M., 1816.)

5658. NATIONS, Representation and. —The [representative principle] has taken deep root in the European mind, and will have its growth; their despots,* sensible of this, are already offering this modification of their governments, as if of their own accord. In

* In consenting to the newspaper publication of this extract, Jefferson directed that "despots" be changed to "rulers".—Editor.

stead of the parricide treason of Bonaparte, in perverting the means confided to him as a republican magistrate, to the subversion of that republic and erection of a military despotism for himself and his family, had he used it honestly for the establishment and support of a free government in his own country, France would now have been in freedom and rest: and her example operating in a contrary direction, every nation in Europe would have had a government over which the will of the people would have had some control. His atrocious egotism has checked the salutary progress of principle, and deluged it with rivers of blood which are not yet run out. To the vast sum of devastation and of human misery, of which he has been the guilty cause, much is still to be added. But the object is fixed in the eye of nations, and they will press on to its accomplishment and to the general amelioration of the condition of man. What a germ have we planted, and how faithfully should we cherish the parent tree at home!—To Benjamin Austin. vi, 520. Ford ed., x, 8. (M., 1816.)

5659. NATIONS, Revolution.—When subjects are able to maintain themselves in the field, they are then an independent power as to all neutral nations, are entitled to their commerce, and to protection within their limits.—To James Monroe. vi, 550. Ford ed., x, 19. (M., 1816.)

5660. NATIONS, Standing of.—The just standing of all nations is the health and security of all.—To James Maury. vi, 52. Ford ed., ix, 349. (M., 1812.)

5661. NATIONS, Unity of large.—The laws of nature render a large country unconquerable if they adhere firmly together, and to their purpose.—To H. Innes. Ford ed., vi, 266. (Pa., 1793.)

5662. ——— ———. Without union of action and effort in all its parts, no nation can be happy or safe.—To James Sullivan. v, 100. Ford ed., ix, 75. (W., 1807.)

5663. ——— ———. A nation united can never be conquered. We have seen what the ignorant, bigoted and unarmed Spaniards could do against the disciplined veterans of their invaders. * * * The oppressors may cut off heads after heads, but like those of the Hydra they multiply at every stroke. The recruits within a nation's own limits are prompt and without number; while those of their invaders from a distance are slow, limited, and must come to an end.—To John Adams. vi, 525. (M., 1816.)

5664. NATIONS, Young.—The first object of young societies is bread and covering; science is but secondary and subsequent.—To J. Evelyn Denison. vii, 418. (M., 1825.)

5665. NATIONS (American), Coalition of.—Nothing is so important as that America shall separate herself from the systems of Europe, and establish one of her own. Our circumstances, our pursuits, our interests, are distinct, the principles of our policy should be so also. All entanglements with that quarter of the globe should be avoided if we mean that peace and justice shall be the polar stars of the American societies. * * * [This] would be a leading principle with me, had I longer to live.—To J. CORREA DE SERRA. vii, 184. FORD ED., x, 162. (M., Oct. 1820.)

5666. NATURAL BRIDGE, Description.—The Natural Bridge, the most sublime of Nature's works, * * * is on the ascent of a hill which seems to have been cloven through its length by some great convulsion. The fissure, just at the Bridge, is, by some admeasurements, 270 feet deep, by others only 205. It is about 45 feet wide at the bottom and 90 feet at the top; this of course determines the length of the bridge, and its height from the water. Its breadth in the middle is about 60 feet, but more at the ends, and the thickness of the mass, at the summit of the arch, about forty feet. A part of this thickness is constituted by a coat of earth, which gives growth to many large trees. The residue, with the hill on both sides, is one solid rock of limestone. The arch approaches the semi-elliptical form; but the larger axis of the ellipsis, which would be the chord of the arch, is many times longer than the semi-axis which gives its height. Looking down from this height about a minute, gave me a violent headache. If the view from the top be painful and intolerable, that from below is delightful in an equal extreme. It is impossible for the emotions arising from the sublime to be felt beyond what they are here; so beautiful an arch, so elevated, so light, and springing as it were up to heaven, the rapture of the spectator is really indescribable! The fissure continuing narrow, deep and straight, for a considerable distance above and below the Bridge, opens a short but very pleasing view of the North Mountain on one side and the Blue Ridge on the other, at the distance each of them of about five miles.—NOTES ON VIRGINIA. viii, 269. FORD ED., iii, 109. (1782.)

5667. NATURAL BRIDGE, Greatest curiosity.—The greatest of our curiosities, the Natural Bridge.—To REV. CHAS. CLAY. iii, 125. FORD ED., v, 142. (M., 1790.)

5668. NATURAL BRIDGE, Hermitage near.—I sometimes think of building a little hermitage at the Natural Bridge (for it is my property) and of passing there a part of the year at least.—To WILLIAM CARMICHAEL. ii, 80. FORD ED., iv, 345. (P., 1786.)

5669. NATURAL HISTORY, American animals.—I really doubt whether the flat-horned elk exists in America. * * * I have seen the daim, the cerf, the chevreuil of Europe. But the animal we call elk, and which may be distinguished as the round-horned elk, is very different from them. * * * I suspect that you will find that the moose, the round-horned elk, and the American deer are species not existing in Europe. The moose is perhaps of a new class.—To COMTE DE BUFFON. ii, 286. FORD ED., iv, 458. (P., 1787.)

5670. NATURAL HISTORY, Anatomy and.—The systems of Cuvier and Blumenbach, and especially that of Blumenbach, are liable to the objection of going too much into the province of anatomy. It may be said, indeed, that anatomy is a part of natural his-

tory. In the broad sense of the word, it certainly is. In that sense, however, it would comprehend all the natural sciences, every created thing being a subject of natural history in extenso. * * * As soon as the structure of any natural production is destroyed by art, it ceases to be a subject of natural history, and enters into the domain ascribed to chemistry, to pharmacy, to anatomy, &c. Linnæus's method was liable to this objection so far as it required the aid of anatomical dissection, as of the heart, for instance, to ascertain the place of any animal, or of a chemical process for that of a mineral substance. It would certainly be better to adopt as much as possible such exterior and visible characteristics as every traveler is competent to observe, to ascertain and to relate.—To DR. JOHN MANNERS. vi, 321. (M., 1814.) See ANATOMY.

5671. NATURAL HISTORY, Buffon and.—You must not presume too strongly that your comb-footed bird is known to M. de Buffon. He did not know our panther. I gave him the striped skin of one I bought in Philadelphia, and it presents him a new species which will appear in his next volume.—To FRANCIS HOPKINSON. ii, 74. (P., 1786.)

5672. ——— ———. I have convinced M. de Buffon that our deer is not a chevreuil, and would you believe that many letters to different acquaintances in Virginia, where this animal is so common, have never enabled me to present him with a large pair of their horns, a blue and a red skin stuffed, to show him their colors at different seasons. He has never seen the horns of what we call the elk. This would decide whether it be an elk or a deer.*—To FRANCIS HOPKINSON. ii, 74. (P., 1786.)

5673. ——— ———. I have made a particular acquaintance with Monsieur de Buffon, and have a great desire to give him the best idea I can of our elk. You could not oblige me more than by sending me the horns, skeleton and skin of an elk, were it possible to procure them. * * * Everything of this kind is precious here [France].—To ARCHIBALD STUART. i, 518. FORD ED., iv, 189. (P., 1786.) See BUFFON.

5674. NATURAL HISTORY, Costly specimens.—You ask if you shall say anything to Sullivan about the bill. No; only that it is paid. I have received letters from him explaining the matter. It was really for the skin and bones of the moose, as I had conjectured. It was my fault that I had not given him a rough idea of the expense I would be willing to incur for them. He made the acquisition an object of a regular campaign, and that, too, of a winter one. The troops he employed sallied forth, as he writes me, in the month of March—much snow—a herd attacked —one killed—in the wilderness—a road to cut twenty miles—to be drawn by hand from the frontiers to his house—bones to be cleaned, &c., &c. In fine, he puts himself to an infinitude of trouble, more than I meant. He did it cheerfully, and I feel myself really under obligations to him. That the tragedy might not want a proper catastrophe, the box, bones, and all are lost; so that this chapter of natural history will still remain a blank. But I have

* "The venerable Buffon was indebted to Jefferson for torrents of information concerning nature in America, as well as for many valuable specimens. Buffon wrote to Jefferson, ' I should have consulted you, sir, before publishing my natural history, and then I should have been sure of my facts '."—PARTON'S *Life of Jefferson.*

written to him not to send me another.—To
W. S. SMITH. ii, 284. (P., 1787.)

**5675. NATURAL HISTORY, Elk and
deer.**—In my conversations with the Count
de Buffon on the subjects of natural history,
I find him absolutely unacquainted with our
elk and our deer. He has hitherto believed
that our deer never had horns more than a
foot long; and has, therefore, classed them
with the roe buck which, I am sure, you know
them to be different from. * * * Will you
take the trouble to procure for me the largest
pair of buck's horns you can, and a large skin
of each color, that is to say, a red and a blue?
If it were possible to take these from a buck
just killed, to leave all the bones of the head
in the skin, with the horns on, to leave the
bones of the legs in the skin also, and the hoofs
to it, so that, having only made an incision
all along the belly and neck, to take the animal
out at, we could, by sewing up that incision,
and stuffing the skin, present the true size and
form of the animal; it would be a most precious
present.—To A. CARY. i, 507. (P., 1786.)

5676. ——— ———. You give me hopes of
being able to procure for me some of the big
bones. * * * A specimen of each of the
several species of bones now to be found, is
to me the most desirable object in natural history. And there is no expense of package or
of safe transportation which I will not gladly
reimburse to procure them safely. Elk horns
of very extraordinary size, or anything else
uncommon, would be very acceptable.—To
JAMES STEPTOE. i, 323. FORD ED., iii, 62.
(1782.)

**5677. NATURAL HISTORY, Export-
ing deer.**—Our deer have been often sent to
England and Scotland. Do you know (with
certainty) whether they have ever bred with
the red deer of those countries?—To A. CARY.
i, 508. (P., 1786.)

**5678. NATURAL HISTORY, Far
West.**—Any observations of your own on
the subject of the big bones or their history,
or anything else in the western country, will
come acceptably to me, because I know you
see the works of nature in the great, and not
merely in detail. Descriptions of animals,
vegetables, minerals or other curious things;
notes as to the Indians' information of the
country between the Mississippi and the waters
of the South Sea, &c., &c., will strike your mind
as worthy being communicated.—To JAMES
STEPTOE. i, 323. FORD ED., iii, 63. (1782.)

**5679. NATURAL HISTORY, French
deer.**—I have examined some of the red deer
of this country [France] at the distance of
about sixty yards, and I find no other difference
between them and ours than a shade or two in
the color.—To A. CARY. i, 507. (P., 1786.)

**5680. NATURAL HISTORY, Grouse
and pheasant.**—In the King's cabinet of
Natural History, of which Monsieur de Buffon
has the superintendence, I observed that they
had neither our grouse nor our pheasant.
* * * Pray buy the male and female of
each, employ some apothecary's boy to prepare
them, and send them to me.—To F. HOPKIN-
SON. i, 506. (P., 1786.) See BIRDS.

**5681. NATURAL HISTORY, Import-
ing Useful Animals.**—A fellow passenger
with me from Boston to England, promised to
send to you, in my name, some hares, rabbits,
pheasants, and partridges, by the return of the
ship, which was to go to Virginia, and the

captain promised to take great care of them.
My friend procured the animals, and the ship
changing her destination, he kept them in
hopes of finding some other conveyance, till
they all perished. I do not despair, however,
of finding some opportunity still of sending a
colony of useful animals.—To A. CARY. i,
508. (P., 1786.)

**5682. NATURAL HISTORY, Nomen-
clature.**—The uniting all nations under one
language in natural history had been happily
effected by Linnæus, and can scarcely be
hoped for a second time. Nothing, indeed,
is so desperate as to make all mankind agree
in giving up a language they possess, for one
which they have to learn. * * * Disciples
of Linnæus, of Blumenbach, and of Cuvier,
exclusively possessing their own nomenclatures,
can no longer communicate intelligibly with one
another.—To DR. JOHN MANNERS. vi, 321.
(M., 1814.)

5683. ——— ———. To disturb Linnæus's
system was unfortunate. The new system attempted in botany, by Jussieu, in mineralogy,
by Haüiy, are subjects of the same regret, and
so also the no-system of Buffon, the great advocate of individualism in opposition to classification. He would carry us back to the days
and to the confusion of Aristotle and Pliny,
give up the improvements of twenty centuries,
and cooperate with the neologists in rendering
the science of one generation useless to the
next by perpetual changes of its language.—
To DR. JOHN MANNERS. vi, 322. (M., 1814.)

**5684. NATURAL HISTORY, A pas-
sion.**—Natural History is my passion.—To
HARRY INNES. iii, 217. FORD ED., v, 294.
(Pa., 1791.)

**5685. NATURAL HISTORY, Weevil
fly.**—I do not think the natural history of the
weevil fly of Virginia has been yet sufficiently
detailed. What do you think of beginning to
turn your attention to this insect, in order to
give its history to the Philosophical Society?
It would require some Summers' observations.
* * * I long to be free for pursuits of this
kind instead of the detestable ones in which I
am now laboring without pleasure to myself,
or profit to others. In short, I long to be with
you at Monticello.—To T. M. RANDOLPH. FORD
ED., v, 325. (Pa., 1791.)

**5686. NATURAL HISTORY, Wild
sheep.**—I have never known to what family
you ascribed the Wild Sheep, or Fleecy Goat,
as Governor Lewis called it, or the *Potio-
trajos*, if its name must be Greek. He gave
me a skin, but I know he carried a more perfect one, with the horns on, to Mr. Peale;
and if I recollect well those horns, they, with
the fleece, would induce one to suspect it to
be the Lama, or at least a *Lamæ affinis*. I
will thank you to inform me what you determine it to be.—To DR. WISTAR. v, 218. (W.,
1807.)

— **NATURAL LAW.**—See MAJORITY.

5687. NATURAL RIGHTS, Abridging.
—All natural rights may be abridged or modi-
fied in their exercise by law.—OFFICIAL OPIN-
ION. vii, 498. FORD ED., v, 206. (1790.)

5688. ——— ———. Laws abridging the natural right of the citizen, should be restrained
by rigorous constructions within their narrowest limits.—To ISAAC MCPHERSON. vi,
176. (M., 1813.) See DUTY (NATURAL).

5689. NATURAL RIGHTS, Authority over.—Our rulers can have * * * authority over such natural rights only as we have submitted to them.—Notes on Virginia. viii, 400. Ford ed., iii, 263. (1782.)

5690. NATURAL RIGHTS, Choice of vocation.—Everyone has a natural right to choose that vocation in life which he thinks most likely to give him comfortable subsistence.—Thoughts on Lotteries. ix, 505. Ford ed., x, 366. (M., Feb. 1826.)

5691. NATURAL RIGHTS, Equal Rights vs.—No man has a natural right to commit aggression on the equal rights of another; and this is all from which the laws ought to restrain him.—To F. W. Gilmer. vii, 3. Ford ed., x, 32. (M., 1816.)

5692. NATURAL RIGHTS, Kings and.—These are our grievances, which we have thus laid before his Majesty, with that freedom of language and sentiment which becomes a free people, claiming their rights as derived from the laws of nature, and not as the gift of their Chief Magistrate.—Rights of British America. i, 141. Ford ed., i, 445. (1774.)

5693. NATURAL RIGHTS, Moral sense and.—Questions of natural right are triable by their conformity with the moral sense and reason of man.—Opinion on French Treaties. vii, 618. Ford ed., vi, 225. (1793.) See Moral Sense.

5694. NATURAL RIGHTS, Restoring.—I shall see with sincere satisfaction the progress of those sentiments which tend to restore to man all his natural rights.—R. to A. Danbury Baptists. viii, 113. (1802.)

5695. NATURAL RIGHTS, Retention of.—The idea is quite unfounded that on entering into society we give up any natural rights.—To F. W. Gilmer. vii, 3. Ford ed., x, 32. (M., 1816.)

5696. NATURAL RIGHTS, Self-government and.—Every man, and every body of men on earth, possesses the right of self-government. They receive it with their being from the hand of nature. Individuals exercise it by their single will; collections of men by that of their majority; for the law of the *majority* is the natural law of every society of men. When a certain description of men are to transact together a particular business, the times and places of their meeting and separating, depend on their own will; they make a part of the natural right of self-government. This, like all other natural rights, may be abridged or modified in its exercise by their own consent, or by the law of those who depute them, if they meet in the right of others; but as far as it is not abridged or modified, they retain it as a natural right, and may exercise them in what form they please, either exclusively by themselves, or in association with others, or by others altogether, as they shall agree.—Official Opinion. vii, 496. Ford ed., v, 205. (1790.)

5797. NATURAL RIGHTS, Social duties and.—I am convinced man has no natural right in opposition to his social duties.—R. to A. Danbury Baptists. viii, 113. (1802.) See Rights.

— NATURAL SELECTION, Application to mankind.—See Race.

5698. NATURALIZATION, Eligibility.—All persons who, by their own oath or affirmation, or by other testimony, shall give satisfactory proof to any court of record in this Colony that they propose to reside in the same seven years, at the least, and who shall subscribe the fundamental laws, shall be considered as residents, and entitled to all the rights of persons natural born.—Proposed Va. Constitution. Ford ed., ii, 26. (June 1776.)

5699. NATURALIZATION, Laws.—I cannot omit recommending a revisal of the laws on the subject of naturalization. Considering the ordinary chances of human life, a denial of citizenship under a residence of fourteen years is a denial to a great proportion of those who ask it, and controls a policy pursued from their first settlement by many of these States, and still believed of consequence to their prosperity. And shall we refuse the unhappy fugitives from distress that hospitality which the savages of the wilderness extended to our fathers arriving in this land? Shall oppressed humanity find no asylum on this globe? The Constitution, indeed, has wisely provided that, for admission to certain offices of important trust, a residence shall be required sufficient to develop character and design. But might not the general character and capabilities of a citizen be safely communicated to every one manifesting a *bonâ fide* purpose of embarking his life and fortunes permanently with us? with restrictions, perhaps, to guard against the fraudulent usurpation of our flag; an abuse which brings so much embarrassment and loss on the genuine citizen, and so much danger to the nation of being involved in war, that no endeavor should be spared to detect and suppress it.—First Annual Message. viii, 124. Ford ed., viii, 124. (Dec. 1801.) See Citizens and Expatriation.

5700. NATURALIZATION, Non-recognition of.—The decrees of the British courts that British subjects adopted here since the peace, and carrying on commerce from hence, are still British subjects, and their cargoes British property, have shaken these quasi-citizens in their condition. The French adopt the same principle as to their cargoes when captured. * * * Is it worth our while to go to war to support the contrary doctrine? The British principle is clearly against the law of nations, but which way our interest lies is also worthy of consideration.—To James Monroe. Ford ed., vii, 214. (Pa., March 1798.)

5701. NATURALIZATION, Obstructing.—He [George III.] has endeavored to pervert the exercise of the kingly office in

Virginia into a detestable and insupportable tyranny * * * by endeavoring to prevent the population of our country, and for that purpose obstructing the laws for naturalization of foreigners.—Proposed Va. Constitution. Ford ed., ii, 10. (June 1776.)

5702. NATURALIZATION, Power of. —The Administrator [of Virginia] shall not possess the prerogative * * * of making denizens.—Proposed Va. Constitution. Ford ed., ii, 19. (June 1776.)

5703. NATURE, Classifications.—Ray formed one classification on such lines of division as struck him most favorably; Klein adopted another; Brisson a third, and other naturalists other designations, till Linnæus appeared. Fortunately for science, he conceived in the three kingdoms of nature, modes of classification which obtained the approbation of the learned of all nations. This system was accordingly adopted by all, and united all in a general language. It offered the three great desiderata; First, of aiding the memory to retain a knowledge of the productions of nature. Secondly, of rallying all to the same names for the same objects, so that they could communicate understandingly on them. And, thirdly, of enabling them, when a subject was first presented, to trace it by its character up to the conventional name by which it was agreed to be called. This classification was indeed liable to the imperfection of bringing into the same group individuals which, though resembling in the characteristics adopted by the author for his classification, yet have strong marks of dissimilitude in other respects. But to this objection every mode of classification must be liable, because the plan of creation is inscrutable to our limited faculties. Nature has not arranged her productions on a single and direct line. They branch at every step, and in every direction, and he who attempts to reduce them into departments, is left to do it by the lines of his own fancy. The objection of bringing together what are disparata in nature, lies against the classifications of Blumenbach and of Cuvier, as well as that of Linnæus, and must forever lie against all.—To Dr. John Manners. vi, 320. (M., 1814.)

5704. NATURE, Love of.—There is not a sprig of grass that shoots uninteresting to me.—To Martha Jefferson Randolph. D. L. J., 192. (Pa., 1790.)

5705. NATURE, Units in.—Nature has, in truth, produced units only through all her works. Classes, orders, genera, species, are not of her work. Her creation is of individuals. No two animals are exactly alike; no two plants, nor even two leaves or blades of grass; no two crystallizations. And if we may venture from what is within the cognizance of such organs as ours, to conclude on that beyond their powers, we must believe that no two particles of matter are of exact resemblance. This infinitude of units or individuals being far beyond the capacity of our memory, we are obliged, in aid of that, to distribute them into masses, throwing into each of these all the individuals which have a certain degree of resemblance; to subdivide these again into smaller groups, according to certain points of dissimilitude observable in them, and so on until we have formed what we call a system of classes, orders, genera, and species. In doing this, we fix arbitrarily on such characteristic resemblances and differences as seem to us

most prominent and invariable in the several subjects, and most likely to take a strong hold in our memories.—To Dr. John Manners. vi, 319. (M., 1814.)

5706. NATURE AND FREEDOM.— Under the law of nature we are all born free. —Legal Argument. Ford ed., i, 380. (1770.)

5707. NAVIES, Equalization of.—I have read with great satisfaction your observations on the principles for equalizing the power of the different nations on the sea, and think them perfectly sound. Certainly it will be better to produce a balance on that element, by reducing the means of its great monopolizer [England], than by endeavoring to raise our own to an equality with theirs.— To Tench Coxe. v, 199. Ford ed., ix, 142. (M., Sep. 1807.) See Navy.

5708. NAVIGATION, Coasting and carrying trade.—I like your convoy bill, because although it does not assume the maintenance of all our maritime rights, it assumes as much as it is our interest to maintain. Our coasting trade is the first and most important branch, never to be yielded but with our existence. Next to that is the carriage of our own productions in our own vessels, and bringing back the returns for our own consumption; so far I would protect it and force every part of the Union to join in the protection at the point of the bayonet. But though we have a right to the remaining branch of carrying for other nations, its advantages do not compensate its risks. Your bill first rallies us to the ground the Constitution ought to have taken, and to which we ought to return without delay; the moment is the most favorable possible, because the Eastern States, by declaring they will not protect that cabotage by war, and forcing us to abandon it, have released us from every future claim for its protection on that part. Your bill is excellent in another view: It presents still one other ground to which we can retire before we resort to war; it says to the belligerents, rather than go to war, we will retire from the brokerage of other nations, and will confine ourselves to the carriage and exchange of our own productions; but we will vindicate that in all its rights—if you touch it, it is war.—To Mr. Burwell. v, 505. (M., Feb. 1810.)

5709. NAVIGATION, Defensive value of.—Our navigation * * * as a resource of defence, [is] essential, [and] will admit neither neglect nor forbearance. The position and circumstances of the United States leave them nothing to fear on their landboard, and nothing to desire beyond their present rights. But on their seaboard, they are open to injury, and they have there, too, a commerce which must be protected. This can only be done by possessing a respectable body of citizen-seamen, and of artists and establishments in readiness for ship-building. * * * If we lose the seamen and artists whom [our navigation] now occupies, we lose the present means of marine defence, and time will be requisite to raise up others, when disgrace or losses shall bring home to our feelings the error of having abandoned them. —FOREIGN COMMERCE REPORT. vii, 647-8. FORD ED., vi, 480. (Dec. 1793.)

5710. NAVIGATION,   Develop.—Our people are decided in the opinion that it is necessary for us to take a share in the occupation of the ocean, and their established habits induce them to require that the sea be kept open to them, and that that line of policy be pursued which will render the use of that element to them as great as possible. I think it a duty in those intrusted with the administration of their affairs to conform themselves to the decided choice of their constituents; and that therefore, we should, in every instance, preserve an equality of right to them in the transportation of commodities, in the right of fishing and in the other uses of the sea.—To JOHN JAY. i, 404. FORD ED., iv, 88. (P.. 1785.)

5711. NAVIGATION, Encourage.—Our people have a decided taste for navigation and commerce. They take this from their mother country; and their servants are in duty bound to calculate all their measures on this datum. We wish to do it by throwing open all the doors of commerce, and knocking off its shackles. But as this cannot be done for others, unless they will do it for us, and there is no great probability that Europe will do this, I suppose we shall be obliged to adopt a system which may shackle them in our ports, as they do us in theirs.—To COUNT VAN HOGENDORP. i, 465. FORD ED., iv, 105. (P., 1785.)

5712. NAVIGATION, English monopoly of.—The British say they will pocket our carrying trade as well as their own.—To JOHN PAGE. i, 550. FORD ED., iv, 215. (P., 1786.)

5713. NAVIGATION, Freedom of.—I think, whatever sums we are obliged to pay for freedom of navigation in the European seas, should be levied on the European commerce with us by a separate impost. that these powers may see that they protect these enormities [Barbary piracies] for their own loss.—To GENERAL GREENE. i, 509. (P., 1786.)

5714. ——— ———. What sentiment is written in deeper characters on the heart of man than that the ocean is free to all men, and their rivers to all their inhabitants? Is there a man, savage or civilized, unbiased by habit, who does not feel and attest this truth? Accordingly. in all tracts of country united under the same political society, we find this natural right universally acknowledged and protected by laying the navigable rivers open to all their inhabitants. When their rivers enter the limits of another society, if the right of the upper inhabitants to descend the stream is in any case obstructed, it is an act of force by a stronger society against a weaker, condemned by the judgment of mankind. The late case of Antwerp and the Scheldt was a striking proof of a general

union of sentiment on this point; as it is believed that Amsterdam had scarcely an advocate out of Holland, and even there its pretensions were advocated on the ground of treaties, and not of natural right.—MISSISSIPPI RIVER INSTRUCTIONS. vii, 577. FORD ED., v, 468. (March 1792.)

5715. NAVIGATION, French and English hostility.—The difference of sixty-two livres ten sols the hogshead established by the National Assembly [of France] on tobacco brought in their and our ships, is such an act of hostility against our navigation, as was not to have been expected from the friendship of that nation. It is as new in its nature as extravagant in its degree; since it is unexampled that any nation has endeavored to wrest from another the carriage of its own produce, except in the case of their colonies.—To WILLIAM SHORT. iii, 274. FORD ED., v, 362. (Pa., 1791.)

5716. ——— ———. I apprehend that these two great nations [France and England] will think it their interest not to permit us to be navigators.—To HORATIO GATES. iv, 213. FORD ED., vii, 205. (Pa., Feb. 1798.)

5717. ——— ———. Every appearance and consideration render it probable that, on the restoration of peace, both France and Britain will consider it their interest to exclude us from the ocean, by such peaceable means as are in their power. Should this take place, perhaps it may be thought just and politic to give to our *native capitalists* the monopoly of our internal commerce.—To JAMES MADISON. iv, 214. FORD ED., vii, 206. (Pa., Feb. 1798.)

5718. ——— ———. The countervailing acts of Great Britain, now laid before Congress, threaten, in the opinion of merchants, the entire loss of our navigation to England. It makes a difference, from the present state of things, of five hundred guineas on a vessel of three hundred and fifty tons.—To HORATIO GATES. iv, 213. FORD ED., vii, 205. (Pa., Feb. 1798.)

5719. ——— ———. The [British] countervailing act ' * * * will, confessedly, put American bottoms out of employ in our trade with Great Britain.—To JAMES MADISON. iv, 214. FORD ED., vii, 206. (Pa., Feb. 1798.)

5720. ——— ———. I hope we shall rub through the war [between France and England], without engaging in it ourselves, and that when in a state of peace our Legislature and Executive will endeavor to provide peaceable means of obliging foreign nations to be just to us, and of making their injustice recoil on themselves.—To PEREGRINE FITZHUGH. iv, 216. FORD ED., vii, 209. (Pa., Feb. 1798.)

5721. NAVIGATION, Industrial value. —Our navigation * * * as a branch of industry * * * is valuable * * * . Its value, as a branch of industry, is enhanced by the dependence of so many other branches on it. In times of general peace it multiplies competitors for employment in transportation, and so keeps that at its proper level; and in times of war, that is to say, when those nations who may be our principal carriers, shall be at war with each other, if we have not within ourselves the means of transportation, our produce must be exported in belligerent vessels, at the increased expense of war-freight and insurance, and the articles which will not bear that, must perish on our hands.—FOREIGN COMMERCE REPORT. vii, 647. FORD ED., vi, 480. (Dec. 1793.)

5722. NAVIGATION, Jefferson's report on.—You may recollect that a report which I gave into Congress in 1793, and Mr. Madison's propositions of 1794, went directly to establish a navigation act on the British principle. On the last vote given on this (which was in Feb. 1794), from the three States of Massachusetts, Connecticut, and Rhode Island there were two votes for it, and twenty against it; and from the three States of Virginia, Kentucky, and North Carolina, wherein not a single top-mast vessel is, I believe, owned by a native citizen, there were twenty-five votes for and four against the measure. I very much suspect that were the same proposition now brought forward, the northern vote would be nearly the same, while the southern one, I am afraid, would be radically varied. The suggestion of their disinterested endeavors for placing our navigation on an independent footing, and forcing on them the British treaty, have not had a tendency to invite new offers of sacrifice, and especially under the prospect of a new rejection. You observe that the rejection would change the politics of New England. But it would afford no evidence which they have not already in the records of January and February, 1794. However, I will * * * sound the dispositions [of members of Congress] on that subject. If the proposition should be likely to obtain a reputable vote, it may do good. As to myself, I sincerely wish that the whole Union may accommodate their interests to each other, and play into their hands mutually as members of the same family, that the wealth and strength of any one part should be viewed as the wealth and strength of the whole.—To HUGH WILLIAMSON. FORD ED., vii, 200. (Pa., Feb. 1798.)

5723. NAVIGATION, Madness for.—We are running navigation mad.—To JOSEPH PRIESTLEY. iv, 311. FORD ED., vii, 406. (Pa., Jan. 1800.)

5724. NAVIGATION, Maintain.—To maintain commerce and navigation in all their lawful enterprises * * * [is one of] the landmarks by which we are to guide ourselves in all our proceedings.—SECOND ANNUAL MESSAGE. viii, 21. FORD ED., viii, 186. (Dec. 1802.)

5725. NAVIGATION, Mediterranean.—We must consider the Mediterranean as absolutely shut to us until we can open it with money. Whether this will be best expended in buying or forcing a peace is for Congress to determine.—To MR. HAWKINS. ii, 4. (P., 1786.)

5726. NAVIGATION, Nurseries of.—We have three nurseries for forming seamen: 1. Our coasting trade, already on a safe footing. 2. Our fisheries, which in spite of natural advantages, give just cause of anxiety. 3. Our carrying trade, our only resource of indemnification for what we lose in the other. The produce of the United States, which is carried to foreign markets, is extremely bulky. That part of it which is now in the hands of foreigners, and which we may resume into our own, without touching the rights of those nations who have met us in fair arrangements by treaty, or the interests of those who, by their voluntary regulations, have paid so just and liberal a respect to our interests, as being measured back to them again, places both parties on as good ground, perhaps, as treaties could place them—the proportion, I say, of our carrying trade, which may be resumed without affecting either of these descriptions of nations, will find constant employment for ten thousand seamen, be worth two millions of dollars, annually, will go on augmenting with the population of the United States, secure to us a full indemnification for the seamen we lose, and be taken wholly from those who force us to this act of self-protection in navigation. * * * If regulations exactly the counterpart of those established against us, would be ineffectual, from a difference of circumstances, other regulations equivalent can give no reasonable ground of complaint to any nation. Admitting their right of keeping their markets to themselves, ours cannot be denied of keeping our carrying trade to ourselves. And if there be anything unfriendly in this, it was in the first example.—REPORT ON THE FISHERIES. vii, 553. (1791.)

5727. ———.—The loss of seamen, unnoticed, would be followed by other losses in a long train. If we have no seamen, our ships will be useless, consequently our shiptimber, iron and hemp; our shipbuilding will be at an end, ship carpenters go over to other nations, our young men have no call to the sea, our produce, carried in foreign bottoms, be saddled with war freight and insurance in times of war; and the history of the last hundred years shows, that the nation which is our carrier has three years of war for every four years of peace. We lose, during the same periods, the carriage for belligerent powers, which the neutrality of our flag would render an incalculable source of profit; we lose at this moment the carriage of our own produce to the annual amount of two millions of dollars, which, in the possible progress of the encroachment, may extend to five or six millions, the worth of the whole, with an increase in the proportion of the increase of our members. It is easier, as well as better, to stop this train at its entrance, than when it shall have ruined or banished whole classes of useful and industrious citizens. It will doubtless be thought expedient that the resumption suggested should take effect so gradually, as not to endanger the loss of produce for the want of transportation; but that, in order to create transportation, the whole plan should be developed, and made known at once, that the individuals who may be disposed to lay themselves out for the carrying business, may make their calculations on a full view of all the circumstances.—REPORT ON THE FISHERIES. vii, 554. (1791.)

5728. NAVIGATION, Protection of.— The British attempt, without disguise, to possess themselves of the carriage of our produce, and to prohibit our own vessels from participating of it. This has raised a general indignation in America. The States see, however, that their constitutions have provided no means of counteracting it. They are, therefore, beginning to invest Congress with the absolute power of regulating their commerce, only reserving all revenue arising from it to the State in which it is levied. This will consolidate our federal building very much, and for this we shall be indebted to the British.—To COUNT VAN HOGENDORP. i. 465. FORD ED., iv, 104. (P., 1785.)

5729. ——— ———. I think it essential to exclude the British from the carriage of American produce.—To JAMES MONROE. FORD ED., iv, 41. (P., 1785.)

5730. ——— ———. The determination of the British cabinet to make no equal treaty with us, confirms me in the opinion expressed in your letter that the United States must pass a navigation act against Great Britain, and load her manufactures with duties so as to give a preference to those of other countries; and I hope our Assemblies will wait no longer, but transfer such a power to Congress, at the sessions of this fall.—To JOHN ADAMS. i, 486. (P., 1785.)

5731. ——— ———. I hope we shall show [the British] we have sense and spirit enough * * * to exclude them from any share in the carriage of our commodities.—To DAVID HUMPHREYS. i, 560. (P., 1786.)

5732. ——— ———. A bill which may be called the true navigation act for the United States, is before Congress, and will probably pass. I hope it will lay the foundation of a due share of navigation for us.—To JOHN COFFIN JONES. iii, 155. (N.Y., 1790.)

5733. ——— ———. I participate fully of your indignation at the trammels imposed on our commerce with Great Britain. Some attempts have been made in Congress, and others are still making to meet their restrictions by effectual restrictions on our part. It was proposed to double the foreign tonnage for a certain time, and after that to prohibit the exportation of our commodities in the vessels of nations not in treaty with us. This has been rejected. It is now proposed to prohibit any nation from bringing or carrying in their vessels what may not be brought or carried in ours from or to the same ports; also to prohibit those from bringing to us anything not of their own produce, who prohibit us from carrying to them anything but our own produce. It is thought, however, that this cannot be carried. The fear is that it would irritate Great Britain were we to feel any irritation ourselves.—To EDWARD RUTLEDGE. iii, 164. FORD ED., v, 196. (N.Y., 1790.)

5734. ——— ———. Were the ocean, which is the common property of all, open to the industry of all, so that every person and vessel should be free to take employment wherever it could be found, the United States would certainly not set the example of appropriating to themselves, exclusively, any portion of the common stock of occupation. They would rely on the enterprise and activity of their citizens for a due participation of the benefits of the seafaring business, and for keeping the marine class of citizens equal to their object. But if particular nations grasp at undue shares, and, more especially, if they seize on the means of the United States, to convert them into aliment for their own strength, and withdraw them entirely from the support of those to whom they belong, defensive and protecting measures become necessary on the part of the nation whose marine resources are thus invaded; or it will be disarmed of its defence; its productions will lie at the mercy of the nation which has possessed itself exclusively of the means of carrying them, and its politics may be influenced by those who command its commerce. The carriage of our own commodities, if once established in another channel, cannot be resumed in the moment we may desire. If we lose the seamen and artists whom it now occupies, we lose the present means of marine defence, and time will be requisite to raise up others, when disgrace or losses shall bring home to our feelings the error of having abandoned them. The materials for maintaining our due share of navigation, are ours in abundance. And, as to the mode of using them, we have only to adopt the principles of those who put us on the defensive, or others equivalent and better fitted to our circumstances.—FOREIGN COMMERCE REPORT. vii, 647. FORD ED., vi, 481. (Dec. 1793.)

5735. ——— ———. I have ever wished that all nations would adopt a navigation law against those who have one, which perhaps would be better than against all indiscriminately, and while in France I proposed it there.—To TENCH COXE. v, 199. FORD ED., ix, 142. (M., 1807.)

5736. ——— ———. Among the laws of the late Congress, some were of note; a navigation act, particularly, applicable to those nations only who have navigation acts; pinching one of them especially, not only in the general way, but in the intercourse with her foreign possessions. This part may react on us, and it remains for trial which may bear longest. —To ALBERT GALLATIN. vii, 78. FORD ED., x, 90. (M., 1817.)

5737. NAVIGATION, Protuberant.—I trust the good sense of our country will see that its greatest prosperity depends on a due balance between agriculture, manufactures and commerce, and not in this protuberant navigation which has kept us in hot water from the commencement of our government, and is now engaging us in war.—To THOMAS LEIPER. v, 417. FORD ED., ix, 239. (W., 1809.)

5738. NAVIGATION, Reciprocity and.—The following principles, being founded in reciprocity, appear perfectly just, and to offer no cause of complaint to any nation: Where a nation refuses to receive in our vessels any productions but our own, we may refuse to receive, in theirs, any but their own productions. Where a nation refuses to consider any vessel as ours which has not been built within our territories, we should refuse to consider as theirs, any vessel not built within their territories. Where a nation refuses to our vessels the carriage even of our own productions, to certain countries under their domination, we might refuse to theirs of every description, the carriage of the same productions to the same countries. But as justice and good neighborhood would dictate that those who have no part in imposing the restriction on us, should not be the victims of measures adopted to defeat its effect, it may be proper to confine the restriction to vessels owned or navigated by any subjects of the same dominant power, other than the inhabitants of the country to which the said productions are to be carried. And to prevent all inconvenience to the said inhabitants, and to our own, by too sudden a check on the means of transportation, we may continue to admit the vessels marked for future exclusion, on an advanced tonnage, and for such length of time only, as may be supposed necessary to provide against that inconvenience. The establishment of some of these principles by Great Britain, alone, has already lost us in our commerce with that country and its possessions, between eight and nine hundred vessels of near 40,000 tons burden, according to statements from official materials, in which they have confidence. This involves a proportional loss of seamen, shipwrights, and ship-building, and is too serious a loss to admit forbearance of some effectual remedy.—REPORT ON COMMERCE AND NAVIGATION. vii, 648. FORD ED., vi, 481. (Dec. 1793.)

5739. NAVIGATION, Reduction of British.—It has been proposed in Congress to pass a navigation act which will deeply strike at that of Great Britain. * * * Would it not be worth while to have the bill now enclosed, translated, printed and circulated among the members of the [French] National Assembly? If you think so, have it done at the public expense, with any little comment you may think necessary, concealing the quarter from whence it is distributed; or take any other method you think better, to see whether that Assembly will not pass a similar act? I shall send copies of it to Mr. Carmichael, at Madrid, and to Colonel Humphreys, appointed resident at Lisbon, with a desire for them to suggest similar acts there. The measure is just, perfectly innocent as to all other nations, and will effectually defeat the navigation act of Great Britain, and reduce her power on the ocean within safer limits.—To WILLIAM SHORT. iii, 225. (Pa., 1791.)

5740. —— ——. The navigation act, if it can be effected, will form a remarkable and memorable epoch in the history and freedom of the ocean. Mr. Short will press it at Paris, and Colonel Humphreys at Lisbon.—To WILLIAM CARMICHAEL. iii, 245. (Pa., 1791.)

5741. —— ——. The Navigation Act proposed in the late Congress, but which lies over to the next, * * * is perfectly innocent as to other nations, is strictly just as to the English, cannot be parried by them, and if adopted by other nations would inevitably defeat their navigation act, and reduce their power on the sea within safer limits. It is indeed extremely to be desired that other nations would adopt it. * * * Could France, Spain and Portugal agree to concur in such a measure, it would soon be fatally felt by the navy of England.—To DAVID HUMPHREYS. FORD ED., v, 302. (Pa., March 1791.)

5742. NAVIGATION, Retaliatory duties.—Where a nation refuses to our vessels the carriage even of our own productions, to certain countries under their domination, we might refuse to theirs of every description, the carriage of the same productions to the same countries. But as justice and good neighborhood would dictate that those who have no part in imposing the restriction on us, should not be the victims of measures adopted to defeat its effect, it may be proper to confine the restriction to vessels owned or navigated by any subjects of the same dominant power, other than the inhabitants of the country to which the said productions are to be carried. And to prevent all inconvenience to the said inhabitants, and to our own, by too sudden a check on the means of transportation, we may continue to admit the vessels marked for future exclusion, on an advanced tonnage, and for such length of time only, as may be supposed necessary to provide against that inconvenience.—FOREIGN COMMERCE REPORT. vii, 649. FORD ED., vi, 482. (Dec. 1793.)

— NAVIGATION, Subsidies.—See BOUNTIES.

5743. NAVIGATION, Sufficient.—It is essentially interesting to us to have shipping and seamen enough to carry our surplus produce to market; but beyond that I do not think we are bound to give it encouragement by drawbacks or other premiums.—To BENJAMIN STODDERT. v, 426. FORD ED., ix, 245. (W., 1809.) See COMMERCE, DUTIES, EMBARGO, FREE TRADE, PROTECTION and SHIPS.

5744. NAVY, Bravery of.—Our public ships have done wonders. They have saved our military reputation sacrificed on the shores of Canada.—To GENERAL BAILEY. vi, 101. (M., Feb. 1813.)

5745. —— ——. No one has been more gratified than myself by the brilliant achievements of our little navy. They have deeply wounded the pride of our enemy, and been balm to ours, humiliated on the land where our real strength was felt to lie.—To PRESIDENT MADISON. vi, 112. FORD ED., ix, 383. (M., May 1813.)

5746. —— ——. I sincerely congratulate you on the successes of our little navy; which must be more gratifying to you than to most men, as having been the early and constant advocate of wooden walls. If I have differed with you on this ground, it was not on the principle, but the time; supposing that we cannot build or maintain a navy, which will not immediately fall into the gulf which has swallowed not only the minor navies, but even those of the great second-rate powers of the sea. Whenever these can be resuscitated, and brought so near to a balance with England that we can turn the scale, then is my epoch for aiming at a navy. In the meantime, one competent to keep the Barbary States in order, is necessary; these being the only smaller powers disposed to quarrel with us.—To JOHN ADAMS. vi, 122. (M., May 1813.)

5747. —— ——. At sea we have rescued our character; but the chief fruit of our victories there is to prove to those who have fleets, that the English are not invincible at sea, as Alexander has proved that Bonaparte is not invincible by land.—To SAMUEL BROWN. vi, 165. (M., July 1813.)

5748. —— ——. I congratulate you on the brilliant affair of the Enterprise and Boxer. No heart is more rejoiced than mine at these mortifications of English pride, and lessons to Europe that the English are not invincible at sea. If these successes do not lead us too far into the navy mania, all will be well.—To WILLIAM DUANE. vi, 211. (M., Sep. 1813.)

5749. —— ——. Strange reverse of expectations that our land force should be under the wing of our little navy.—To WILLIAM DUANE. vi, 212. (M., Sep. 1813.)

5750. —— ——. On the water we have proved to the world the error of British invincibility, and shown that with equal force and well-trained officers, they can be beaten by other nations as brave as themselves.—To DON V. TORONDA CORUNA. vi, 275. (M., Dec. 1813.)

5751. —— ——. I * * * congratulate you on the destruction of a second hostile fleet on the Lakes by Macdonough. While our enemies cannot but feel shame for their barbarous achievements at Washington [burning of Capitol], they will be stung to the soul by these repeated victories over them on that element on which they wish the world to think them invincible. We have dissipated that error. They must now feel a conviction themselves that we can beat them gun to gun, ship to ship, and fleet to fleet, and that their early successes on the land have been either purchased from traitors, or obtained from raw men entrusted of necessity with commands for which no experience had qualified them, and that every day is adding that experience to unquestioned bravery.—To PRESIDENT MADISON. vi, 386. (M., Sep. 1814.) See CAPITOL.

5752. —— ——. Frigates and seventy-fours are a sacrifice we must make, heavy as it is, to the prejudices of a part of our citizens. They have, indeed, rendered a great moral service, which has delighted me as much as any one in the United States. But they have had no physical effect sensible to the enemy; and now, while we must fortify them in our harbors, and keep armies to defend them, our *privateers* are bearding and blockading the enemy in their own seaports. —To JAMES MONROE. vi, 409. FORD ED., ix, 498. (M., Jan. 1815.)

5753. —— ——. Through the whole period of the war, we have beaten them [the British] single-handed at sea, and so thoroughly established our superiority over them with equal force, that they retire from that kind of contest, and never suffer their frigates to cruise singly. The Endymion would never have engaged the frigate President, but knowing herself blocked by three frigates and a razee, who, though somewhat slower sailers, would get up before she could be taken.—To MARQUIS DE LAFAYETTE. vi, 424. FORD ED., ix, 508. (M., 1815.)

5754. NAVY, Build a.—We ought to begin a naval power, if we mean to carry on our own commerce.—To JAMES MONROE. FORD ED., iv, 10. (P., Nov. 1784.)

5755. —— ——. Tribute or war is the usual alternative of these [Barbary] pirates. * * * Why not begin a navy then and decide on war? We cannot begin in a better cause nor against a weaker foe.—To HORATIO GATES. FORD ED., iv, 24. (P., Dec. 1784.)

5756. —— ——. It is proper and necessary that we should establish a small marine force.—To JOHN ADAMS. i, 592. (P., 1786.)

— NAVY, Censure of officers.—See PORTER.

— NAVY, Chesapeake.—See CHESAPEAKE.

5757. NAVY, Coercion by a.—[A naval force] will arm the federal head with the safest of all the instruments of coercion over its delinquent members, and prevent it from using what would be less safe.—To JOHN ADAMS. i, 592. (P., 1786.)

5758. —— ——. Every rational citizen must wish to see an effective instrument of coercion, and should fear to see it on any other element than the water.—To JAMES MONROE. i. 606. FORD ED., iv, 265. (P., 1786.)

5759. NAVY, Dockyards for.—Presuming it will be deemed expedient to expend annually a sum towards providing the naval defence which our situation may require, I cannot but recommend that the first appropriations for that purpose may go to the saving what we already possess. No cares, no attentions, can preserve vessels from rapid decay which lie in water and exposed to the sun. These decays require great and constant repairs, and will consume, if continued, a great portion of the money destined to naval purposes. To avoid this waste of our resources, it is proposed to add to our navy yard here [Washington] a dock, within which our vessels may be laid up dry and under cover from the sun. Under these circumstances experience proves that works of wood will remain scarcely at all affected by time. The great abundance of running water which this situation possesses, at heights far above the level of the tide, if employed as is practiced for lock navigation, furnishes the means of raising and laying up our vessels on a dry and sheltered bed.—SECOND ANNUAL MESSAGE. viii, 20. FORD ED., viii, 186. (Dec. 1802.)

5760. ———. The proposition for building lock-docks for the preservation of our navy, has local rivalries to contend against. Till these can be overruled or compromised, the measure can never be adopted. Yet there ought never to be another ship built until we can provide some method of preserving them through the long intervals of peace which I hope are to be the lot of our country.—To MR. COXE. v, 58. (W., 1807.)

5761. ———. While I was at Washington, in the administration of the government, Congress was much divided in opinion on the subject of a navy, a part of them wishing to go extensively into the preparation of a fleet, another part opposed to it, on the objection that the repairs and preservation of a ship, even idle in harbor, in ten or twelve years, amount to her original cost. It has been estimated in England, that if they could be sure of peace a dozen years it would be cheaper for them to burn their fleet, and build a new one when wanting, than to keep the old one in repair during that term. I learnt that, in Venice, there were then ships, lying on their original stocks, ready for launching at any moment, which had been so for eighty years, and were still in a state of perfect preservation; and that this was effected by disposing of them in docks pumped dry, and kept so by constant pumping. It occurred to me that this expense of constant pumping might be saved by combining a lock with the common wet dock, wherever there was a running stream of water, the bed of which, within a reasonable distance, was of sufficient height above the high-water level of the harbor. This was the case at the navy yard, on the Eastern Branch at Washington, the high-water line of which was seventy-eight feet lower than the ground on which the Capitol stands, and to which it was found that the water of the Tiber Creek could be brought for watering the city. My proposition then was as follows: Let *a b* be the high-water level of the harbor, and the vessel to be laid up draw eighteen feet of water. Make a chamber A twenty feet deep below

high-water and twenty feet high above it as *c d e f*, and at the upper end make another chamber, B,

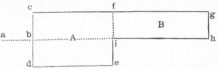

the bottom of which should be in the high-water level, and the tops twenty feet above that. *g h* is the water of the Tiber. When the vessel is to be introduced, open the gate at *c b a*. The tide water rises in tne chamber A to the level *b i*, and floats the vessel in with it. Shut the gate *c b d* and open that of *f i*. The water of the Tiber fills both chambers to the level *c f g*, and the vessel floats into the chamber B; then opening both gates *c b d* and *f i*, the water flows out, and the vessel settles down on the stays previously prepared at the bottom *i h* to receive her. The gate at *g h* must of course be closed, and the water of the feeding stream be diverted elsewhere. The chamber B is to have a roof over it of the construction of that over the meal market at Paris, except that that is hemispherical, this semi-cylindrical. For this construction see Delenne's Architecture, whose invention it was. The diameter of the dome of the meal market is considerably over one hundred feet. It will be seen at once that instead of making the chamber B of sufficient width and length for a single vessel only, it may be widened to whatever span the semi-circular framing of the roof can be trusted, and to whatever length you please, so as to admit two or more vessels in breadth, and as many in length as the localities render expedient. I had a model of this lock-dock made and exhibited in the President's house during the session of Congress at which it was proposed. But the advocates for a navy did not fancy it, and those opposed to the building of ships altogether, were equally indisposed to provide protection for them. Ridicule was also resorted to, the ordinary substitute for reason, when that fails, and the proposition was passed over. I then thought and still think the measure wise, to have a proper number of vessels always ready to be launched, with nothing unfinished about them except the planting their masts, which must of necessity be omitted, to be brought under a roof. Having no view in this proposition but to combine for the public a provision for defence, with economy in its preservation. I have thought no more of it since. And if any of my ideas anticipated yours, you are welcome to appropriate them to yourself, without objection on my part.—To LEWIS M. WISS. vii, 419. (M., 1825.)

5762. NAVY, Early history of.—I have racked my memory and ransacked my papers, to enable myself to answer the inquiries of your favor of Oct. the 15th; but to little purpose. My papers furnish me nothing, my memory, generalities only. I know that while I was in Europe, and anxious about the fate of our sea-faring men, for some of whom, then in captivity in Algiers, we were treating, and all were in like danger, I formed, undoubtedly, the opinion that our government, as soon as practicable, should provide a naval force sufficient to keep the Barbary States in order; and on this subject we communicated together, as you observe. When I returned to the United States and took part in the administration under General Washington, I constantly maintained that opinion; and in December, 1790, took advantage of a reference to me from the first Congress which met after I was in office, to report in favor of a force sufficient for the protection of our Mediterranean commerce; and I laid before them an accurate statement of the whole Barbary force, public and private. I think General Washington approved of building vessels of war to that extent. General Knox, I know, did. But what was Colonel Hamilton's opinion, I do not in the least remember. Your recollections on that subject are certainly corroborated by his known anxieties for a close connection with Great Britain, to which he might apprehend danger from collisions between their vessels and ours. Randolph was then Attorney-General; but his opinion on the question I also entirely forget. Some vessels of war were accordingly built and sent into the Mediterranean. The additions to these in your time, I need not note to you, who are well known to have ever been an advocate for the wooden walls of Themistocles. Some of those you added, were sold under an act of Congress passed while you were in office. I thought, afterwards, that the public safety might require some additional vessels of strength, to be prepared and in readiness for the first moment of a war, provided they could be preserved against the decay which is unavoidable if kept in the water, and clear of the expense of officers and men. With this view I proposed that they should be built in dry docks, above the level of the tide waters, and covered with roofs. I further advised that places for these docks should be selected where there was a command of water on a high level, as that of the Tiber at Washington, by which the vessels might be floated out, on the principle of a lock. But the majority of the Legislature was against any addition to the Navy, and the minority, although for it in judgment, voted against it on a principle of opposition. We are now, I understand, building vessels to remain on the stocks, under shelter, until wanted, when they will be launched and finished. On my plan they could be in service at an hour's notice. On this, the finishing, after launching, will be a work of time. This is all I recollect about the origin and progress of our navy. That of the late war, certainly raised our rank and character among nations. Yet a navy is a very expensive engine. It is admitted, that in ten or twelve years a vessel goes to entire decay; or, if kept in repair, costs as much as would build a new one: and that a nation who could count on twelve or fifteen years of peace, would gain by burning its navy and building a new one in time. Its extent, therefore, must be governed by circumstances. Since my proposition for a force adequate to the piracies of the Mediterranean, a similar necessity has arisen in our own seas for considerable addition to that force. Indeed, I wish we could have a convention with the naval powers of Europe, for them to keep down the pirates of the Mediterranean, and the slave ships on the coast of Africa, and for us to perform the same duties for the society of nations in our seas. In this way, those collisions would be avoided between the vessels of war of different nations, which beget wars and constitute the weightiest objection to navies.*—To JOHN ADAMS. vii, 264. FORD ED., x, 238. (M., 1822.)

— **NAVY, Equalization of sea-power.**— See NAVIES.

* Mr. Adams in the letter to which the quotation is a reply said that he "always believed the navy to be Jefferson's child".—EDITOR.

5763. NAVY, Europe and.—A maritime force is the only one by which we can act on Europe.—To GENERAL WASHINGTON. ii, 536. FORD ED., v, 58. (P., 1788.)

5764. NAVY, Expansion and.—Nothing should ever be accepted which would require a navy to defend it.—To PRESIDENT MADISON. v, 445. (M., April 1809.)

5765. NAVY, Future of.—Paul Jones is young enough to see the day * * * when we shall be able to fight the British ship to ship.—To E. CARRINGTON. ii, 405. FORD ED., v, 22. (P., 1788.)

5766. NAVY, Gunboats.—The obstacle to naval enterprise which vessels of this construction offer for our seaport towns; their utility toward supporting within our waters the authority of the laws; the promptness with which they will be manned by the seamen and militia of the place the moment they are wanted; the facility of their assembling from different parts of the coast to any point where they are required in greater force than ordinary; the economy of their maintenance and preservation from decay when not in actual service; and the competence of our finances to this defensive provision, without any new burden, are considerations which will have due weight with Congress in deciding on the expediency of adding to their number from year to year, as experience shall test their ability, until all our important harbors, by these and auxiliary means, shall be ensured against insult and opposition to the laws.—FOURTH ANNUAL MESSAGE. viii, 38. FORD ED., viii, 331. (Nov. 1804.)

5767. ———. The efficacy of gunboats for the defence of harbors, and of other smooth and enclosed waters, may be estimated in part from that of galleys, formerly much used, but less powerful, more costly in their construction and maintenance, and requiring more men. But the gunboat itself is believed to be in use with every modern maritime nation for the purpose of defence. In the Mediterranean, on which are several small powers, whose system like ours is peace and defence, few harbors are without this article of protection. Our own experience there of the effect of gunboats for harbor service is recent. Algiers is particularly known to have owed to a great provision of these vessels the safety of its city, since the epoch of their construction. Before that it had been repeatedly insulted and injured. The effect of gunboats at present in the neighborhood of Gibraltar, is well known, and how much they were used both in the attack and defence of that place during a former war. The extensive resort to them by the two greatest naval powers in the world, on an enterprise of invasion not long since in prospect, shows their confidence in their efficacy for the purpose for which they are suited. By the northern powers of Europe, whose seas are particularly adapted to them, they are still more used. The remarkable action between the Russian flotilla of gunboats and galleys, and a Turkish fleet of ships-of-the-line and frigates in the Liman Sea, 1788, will be readily recollected. The latter, commanded by their most celebrated admiral, were completely defeated, and several of their ships-of-the-line destroyed.—SPECIAL MESSAGE. viii, 80. FORD ED., ix, 24. (Feb. 1807.)

5768. ———. Of these boats a proper proportion would be of the larger size, such as those heretofore built, capable of navigating any seas, and of reinforcing occasionally the strength of even the most distant port when menaced with danger. The residue would be confined to their own or the neighboring harbors, would be smaller, less furnished for accommodation, and consequently less costly. Of the number supposed necessary, seventy-three are built or building, and the hundred and twenty-seven still to be provided, would cost from five to six hundred thousand dollars. * * * At times when Europe as well as the United States shall be at peace, it would not be proposed that more than six or eight of these vessels should be kept afloat. When Europe is in war, treble that number might be necessary to be distributed among those particular harbors which foreign vessels of war are in the habit of frequenting, for the purpose of preserving order therein. But they would be manned, in ordinary, with only their complement for navigation, relying on the seamen and militia of the port if called into action on sudden emergency. It would be only when the United States should themselves be at war, that the whole number would be brought into actual service, and would be ready in the first moments of the war to cooperate with other means for covering at once the line of our seaports. At all times, those unemployed would be withdrawn into places not exposed to sudden enterprise, hauled up under sheds from the sun and weather, and kept in preservation with little expense for repairs or maintenance. It must be superfluous to observe, that this species of naval armament is proposed merely for defensive operation; that it can have but little effect toward protecting our commerce in the open seas even on our coast; and still less can it become an excitement to engage in offensive maritime war, toward which it would furnish no means.—SPECIAL MESSAGE. viii, 81. FORD ED., ix, 26. (Feb. 1807.)

5769. —— ——. I believe that gunboats are the only *water* defence which can be useful to us, and protect us from the ruinous folly of a navy.—To THOMAS PAINE. v, 189. FORD ED., ix, 137. (M., Sep. 1807.) See GUNBOATS.

5770. NAVY, Increase of.—The building some ships of the line instead of our most indifferent frigates is not to be lost sight of. That we should have a squadron properly composed to prevent the blockading our ports is indispensable. The Atlantic frontier from numbers, wealth, and exposure to potent enemies, have a proportionate right to be defended with the Western frontier, for whom we keep up 3,000 men. Bringing forward the measure, therefore, in a moderate form, placing it on the ground of comparative right, our nation which is a just one, will come into it, notwithstanding the repugnance of some on the subject being first presented.— To JACOB CROWNINSHIELD. FORD ED., viii, 453. (M., May 1806.)

5771. NAVY, Liberty and a.—A naval force can never endanger our liberties, nor occasion bloodshed; a land force would do both.—To JAMES MONROE. i, 606. FORD ED., iv, 265. (P., 1786.)

5772. —— ——. A public force on that element [the ocean] * * * can never be dangerous.—To COLONEL HUMPHREYS. ii, 10. (P., 1786.)

5773. —— ——. It is on the sea alone [that] we should think of ever having a force. —To E. CARRINGTON. ii, 405. FORD ED., v, 22. (P., 1788.)

5774. NAVY, Madness for.—We are running navigation mad, and commerce mad, and navy mad, which is worst of all.—To JOSEPH PRIESTLEY. iv, 311. FORD ED., vii, 406. (Pa., Jan. 1800.)

5775. NAVY, Mediterranean pirates and.—The promptitude and energy of Commodore Preble, the efficacious cooperation of Captains Rodgers and Campbell of the returning squadron, the proper decision of Captain Bainbridge that a vessel which had committed an open hostility was of right to be detained for inquiry and consideration, and the general zeal of the other officers and men, are honorable facts which I make known with pleasure. And to these I add what was indeed transacted in another quarter—the gallant enterprise of Captain Rodgers in destroying, on the coast of Tripoli, a corvette of that power, of twenty-two guns.—SPECIAL MESSAGE. viii, 32. (Dec. 1803.)

5776. —— ——. Reflecting with high satisfaction on the distinguished bravery displayed whenever occasion permitted in the late Mediterranean service, I think it would be an useful encouragement to make an opening for some present promotion, by enlarging our peace establishment of captains and lieutenants.—FIFTH ANNUAL MESSAGE. viii, 50. FORD ED., viii, 393. (1805.)

5777. NAVY, Midshipmen.—The places of midshipman are so much sought that (being limited) there is never a vacancy. Your son shall be set down for the second which shall happen; the first being anticipated. We are not long generally without vacancies happening. As soon as he can be appointed, you shall know it.—To THOMAS COOPER. iv, 453. FORD ED., viii, 178. (W., 1802.)

5778. NAVY, Militia and.—For the purpose of manning the gunboats in sudden attacks on our harbors, it is a matter for consideration, whether the seamen of the United States may not justly be formed into a special militia, to be called on for tours of duty in defence of the harbors where they shall happen to be; the ordinary militia furnishing that portion which may consist of landsmen.—SEVENTH ANNUAL MESSAGE. viii, 86. FORD ED., ix, 161. (Oct. 1807.) See MILITIA.

5779. NAVY, National respect and.— Were we possessed even of a small naval force what a bridle would it be in the mouths of the West Indian powers, and how respectfully would they demean themselves towards us. Be assured that the present disrespect of the nations of Europe for us will inevitably bring on insults which must involve us in war.—To JAMES MONROE. FORD ED., iv, 34. (P., 1785.)

5780. NAVY, Navigation and.—[Our navigation] will require a protecting force on the sea. Otherwise the smallest power in Europe, every one which possesses a single ship of the line, may dictate to us, and enforce their demands by captures on our commerce. Some naval force then is necessary if we mean to be commercial. Can we have a better occasion of beginning one? or find a foe* more certainly within our dimensions? The motives pleading for war rather than tribute are numerous and honorable, those opposing them are mean and short-sighted.— To JAMES MONROE. FORD ED., iv, 32. (P., 1785.)

5781. —— ——. A naval force alone can countenance our people as carriers on the water.—To JOHN JAY. i, 405. FORD ED., iv, 90. (P., 1785.) See NAVIGATION.

5782. NAVY, Necessary.—A land army would be useless for offence, and not the best nor safest instrument of defence. For either of the sea purposes, the sea is the field on which we should meet an European enemy. On that element we should possess some power.—NOTES ON VIRGINIA. viii, 413. FORD ED., iii, 279. (1782.)

5783. —— ——. A small naval force is sufficient for us, and a small one is necessary. —NOTES ON VIRGINIA. viii, 414. FORD ED., iii, 280. (1782.)

5784. —— ——. The justest dispositions possible in ourselves, will not secure us against war. It would be necessary that all other nations were just also. Justice indeed, on our part, will save us from those wars which would have been produced by a contrary disposition. But how can we prevent those produced by the wrongs of other nations? By putting ourselves in a condition to punish them. Weakness provokes insult and injury, while a condition to punish, often prevents them. This reasoning leads to the necessity of some naval force; that being the only weapon by which we can reach an enemy. I think it to our interest to punish the first insult; because an insult unpunished is the parent of many others. We are not, at this moment, in a condition to do it, but we should put ourselves into it, as soon as possible. If a war with England should take place, it seems to me that the first thing necessary would be a resolution to abandon the carrying trade, because we cannot protect it. Foreign nations must, in that case, be invited to bring us what we want, and to take our productions in their own bottoms. This alone could prevent the loss of those productions to us, and the acquisition of them to our enemy. Our seamen might be employed in depredations on their trade. But how dreadfully we shall suffer on our coasts, if we have no force on the water, former experience has taught us. Indeed, I look forward with horror to the very possible case of war with an European power, and think there is no protection against them, but from the possession of some force on the sea. Our vicinity to their West India possessions, and to the fisheries, is a bridle which a small naval force, on our part, would hold in the mouths of the most powerful of these countries. I hope our land office will rid us of

* The Barbary powers.—EDITOR.

our debts, and that our first attention then, will be to the beginning a naval force of some sort. This alone can countenance our people as carriers on the water, and I suppose them to be determined to continue such.—To JOHN JAY. i, 404. FORD ED., iv, 89. (P., 1785.)

5785. —— ——. A little navy [is] the only kind of force we ought to possess.—To RICHARD HENRY LEE. FORD ED., iv, 70. (P., July 1785.)

5786. NAVY, Peace establishment.— The law providing for a naval peace establishment fixes the number of frigates which shall be kept in constant service in time of peace, and prescribes that they shall be manned by not more than two-thirds of their complement of seamen and ordinary seamen. Whether a frigate may be trusted to two-thirds only of her proper complement of men must depend on the nature of the service on which she is ordered. She may sometimes, for her safety, so as to ensure her object, require her fullest complement. * * * Congress will perhaps consider whether the best limitation on the Executive discretion * * * would not be by the number of seamen which may be employed in the whole service, rather than the number of vessels.—FIFTH ANNUAL MESSAGE. viii, 51. FORD ED., viii, 393. (Dec. 1805.)

5787. NAVY, Reduction.—The navy will be reduced to the legal establishment by the last of this month.—To NATHANIEL MACON. iv, 397. (W., May 1801.)

5788. —— ——. The session of the first Congress, convened since republicanism has recovered its ascendency, * * * will pretty completely fulfil all the desires of the people. They have reduced the * * * navy to what is barely necessary.—To GENERAL KOSCIUSKO. iv, 430. (W., April 1802.)

5789. NAVY, Secretary of.—I believe I shall have to advertise for a Secretary of the Navy. General Smith is performing the duties gratis, as he refuses both commission and salary, even his expenses, lest it should affect his seat in the House of Representatives.—To GOUVERNEUR MORRIS. FORD ED., viii, 49. (W., May 1801.) See LEAR.

5790. NAVY, Size of.—The actual habits of our countrymen attach them to commerce. They will exercise it for themselves. Wars, then, must sometimes be our lot; and all the wise can do, will be to avoid that half of them which would be produced by our own follies and our own acts of injustice; and to make for the other half the best preparations we can. Of what nature should these be? A land army would be useless for offence, and not the best nor safest instrument of defence. For either of these purposes, the sea is the field on which we should meet an European enemy. On that element it is necessary we should possess some power. To aim at such a navy as the greater nations of Europe possess, would be a foolish and wicked waste of the energies of our countrymen. It would be to pull on our own heads that load of military expense which makes the European laborer go supperless to bed, and moistens his bread with the sweat of his brows. It will be enough if we enable ourselves to prevent insults from those nations of Europe which are weak on the sea, because circumstances exist, which render even the stronger ones weak as to us. Providence has placed their richest and most defenceless possessions at our door; has obliged their most precious commerce to pass, as it were, in review before us. To protect this, or to assail, a small part only of their naval force will ever be risked across the Atlantic. The dangers to which the elements expose them here are too well known, and the greater dangers to which they would be exposed at home were any general calamity to involve their whole fleet. They can attack us by detachment only; and it will suffice to make ourselves equal to what they may detach. Even a smaller force than they may detach will be rendered equal or superior by the quickness with which any check may be repaired with us, while losses with them will be irreparable till too late. A small naval force, then, is sufficient for us, and a small one is necessary. * * * It should by no means be so great as we are able to make it.—NOTES ON VIRGINIA. viii, 413. FORD ED., iii, 279. (1782.)

5791. —— ——. I am for such a naval force only as may protect our coasts and harbors from such depredations as we have experienced; * * * not for a navy, which by its own expenses and the eternal wars in which it will implicate us, will grind us with public burthens, and sink us under them.—To ELBRIDGE GERRY. iv, 268. FORD ED., vii, 328. (Pa., 1799.)

5792. —— ——. With respect to the extent to which our naval preparations should be carried, some difference of opinion may be expected to appear; but just attention to the circumstances of every part of the Union will doubtless reconcile all. A small force will probably continue to be wanted for actual service in the Mediterranean. Whatever annual sum beyond that you may think proper to apportionate to naval preparations, would perhaps be better employed in providing those articles which may be kept without waste or consumption, and be in readiness when any exigence calls them into use.—FIRST INAUGURAL MESSAGE. viii, 12. FORD ED., viii, 122. (Dec. 1801.)

5793. NAVY, Submarine boats.—I have ever looked to the submarine boat as most to be depended on for attaching the torpedoes, and * * * I am in hopes it is not abandoned as impracticable. I should wish to see a corps of young men trained to this service. It would belong to the engineers if at hand, but being nautical, I suppose we must have a corps of naval engineers, to practice and use them. I do not know whether we have authority to put any part of our existing naval establishment in a course of training, but it shall be the subject

of a consultation with the Secretary of the Navy.—To ROBERT FULTON. v, 165. FORD ED., ix, 125. (M., Aug. 1807.)

5794. —— ——. I wait [Colonel Fulton's] answer as to the submarine boat, before I make you the proposition in form. The very name of a corps of submarine engineers would be a defence.—To ROBERT SMITH. v, 172. (M., Aug. 1807.)

5795. NAVY DEPARTMENT, Bill to establish.—The bill for establishing a Department of Secretary of the Navy was tried yesterday [April 25th] on its passage to the third reading, and prevailed by 47 against 41.—To JAMES MADISON. iv, 237. FORD ED., vii, 244. (Pa., 1798.)

5796. NAVY YARDS, Location of.— From the federalists [in Virginia] I expect nothing on any principle of duty or patriotism; but I did suppose they would pay some attentions to the interests of Norfolk. Is it the interest of that place to strengthen the hue and cry against the policy of making the Eastern Branch [Washington] our great naval deposit? Is it their interest that this should be removed to New York or Boston, to one of which it must go if it leaves this? Is it their interest to scout a defence by gunboats in which they would share amply, in hopes of a navy which will not be built in our day, and would be no defence if built, or of forts which will never be built or maintained, and would be no defence if built? Yet such are the objects which they patronize in their papers. This is worthy of more consideration than they seem to have given it.—To WILSON C. NICHOLAS. FORD ED., viii, 338. (W., Dec. 1804.)

5797. NECESSITY, Law of.—A strict observance of the written law is * * * one of the high duties of a good citizen, but it is not the *highest*. The laws of necessity, of self-preservation, of saving our country when in danger, are of higher obligation. To lose our country by a scrupulous adherence to written law, would be to lose the law itself, with life, liberty, property, and all those who are enjoying them with us; thus absurdly sacrificing the end to the means.— To J. B. COLVIN. v, 542. FORD ED., ix, 279. (M., 1810.)

5798. NECKER (Jacques), Ambition of. —It is a tremendous cloud, indeed, which hovers over this nation, and he at the helm has neither the courage nor the skill necessary to weather it. Eloquence in a high degree, knowledge in matters of account and order, are distinguishing traits in his character. Ambition is his first passion, virtue his second. He has not discovered that sublime truth, that a bold, unequivocal virtue is the best handmaid even to ambition, and would carry him further, in the end, than the temporizing, wavering policy he pursues. His judgment is not of the first order, scarcely even of the second; his resolution frail; and upon the whole, it is rare to meet an instance of a person so much below the reputation he has obtained.—To JOHN JAY. iii, 52. (P., 1789.)

5799. NECKER (Jacques), Friend of liberty.—Though he has appeared to trim a little, he is still, in the main, a friend to public liberty.—To JOHN JAY. iii, 28. (P., 1789.)

5800. NECKER (Jacques), Praise of.— The grandson of M. Necker cannot fail of a hearty welcome in a country which so much respected him. To myself, who loved the virtues and honored the talents of the grandfather, the attentions I received in his natal house, and particular esteem for yourself, are additional titles to whatever service I can render him.— To MADAME DE STAEL. v, 133. (W., 1807.)

5801. NECKER (Jacques), Unfriendly to America.— Necker never set any store by us, or the connection with us.—To JOHN JAY. ii, 342. (P., 1787.)

5802. NEGROES, Amalgamation.— Their amalgamation with the other color produces a degradation to which no lover of his country, no lover of excellence in the human character can innocently consent.—To EDWARD COLES. FORD ED., ix, 478. (M., 1814.)

5803. NEGROES, Bravery.— They are at least as brave, and more adventuresome. But this may proceed from a want of forethought, which prevents their seeing a danger till it be present. When present, they do not go through it with more coolness or steadiness than the whites.—NOTES ON VIRGINIA. viii, 381. FORD ED., iii, 245. (1782.)

5804. NEGROES, Colonization.— The bill reported by the revisors* of the whole [Virginia] code does not itself contain the proposition to emancipate all slaves born after the passing the act; but an amendment containing it was prepared, to be offered to the Legislature whenever the bill should be taken up, and further directing, that they should continue with their parents to a certain age, then to be brought up, at the public expense, to tillage, arts or sciences, according to their geniuses, till the females should be eighteen, and the males twenty-one years of age, when they should be colonized to such place as the circumstances of the time should render most proper, sending them out with arms, implements of household and of the handicraft arts, seeds, pairs of the useful domestic animals, &c., to declare them a free and independent people, and extend to them our alliance and protection, till they shall have acquired strength; and to send vessels at the same time to other parts of the world for an equal number of white inhabitants; to induce them to migrate hither, proper encouragements were to be proposed.—NOTES ON VIRGINIA. viii, 380. FORD ED., iii, 243. (1782.)

5805. ——— ———. This unfortunate difference of color, and perhaps of faculty, is a powerful obstacle to the emancipation of these people. Many of their advocates, while they wish to vindicate the liberty of human nature, are anxious also to preserve its dignity and beauty. Some of these, embarrassed by the question, " What further is to be done with them "? join themselves in opposition with those who are actuated by sordid avarice only. Among the Romans emancipation required but one effort. The slave, when made free, might mix with, without straining the blood of his master. But with us a second is necessary, unknown to history. When freed, he is to be removed beyond the reach of mixture.—NOTES ON VIRGINIA. viii, 386. FORD ED., iii, 250. (1782.)

5806. ——— ———. You ask my opinion on the proposition of Mrs. Mifflin, to take measures for procuring, on the coast of Africa, an establishment to which the people of color of these States might, from time to time, be colonized,

*Jefferson prepared the report and bill.—EDITOR.

under the auspices of different governments. Having long ago made up my mind on this subject, I have no hesitation in saying that I have ever thought it the most desirable measure which could be adopted, for gradually drawing off this part of our population, most advantageously for themselves as well as for us. Going from a country possessing all the useful arts, they might be the means of transplanting them among the inhabitants of Africa, and would thus carry back to the country of their origin, the seeds of civilization which might render their sojournment and sufferings here a blessing in the end to that country.—To JOHN LYNCH. v, 563. FORD ED., ix, 303. (M., 1811.)

5507. ——— ———. Nothing is more to be wished than that the United States would themselves undertake to make such an establishment on the coast of Africa. Exclusive of motives of humanity, the commercial advantages to be derived from it might repay all its expenses. But for this, the national mind is not yet prepared. It may perhaps be doubted whether many of these people would voluntarily consent to such an exchange of situation, and very certain that few of those advanced to a certain age in habits of slavery, would be capable of self-government. This should not, however, discourage the experiment, nor the early trial of it.—To JOHN LYNCH. v, 565. FORD ED., ix, 304. (M., 1811.)

5808. ——— ———. I received in the first year of my coming into the administration of the General Government, a letter from the Governor of Virginia (Colonel Monroe), consulting me, at the request of the Legislature of the State, on the means of procuring some such asylum, to which these people might be occasionally sent. I proposed to him the establishment of Sierra Leone, to which a private company in England had already colonized a number of negroes and particularly the fugitives from these States during the Revolutionary War; and at the same time suggested, if this could not be obtained, some of the Portuguese possessions in South America, as next most desirable. The subsequent Legislature approving these ideas, I wrote, the ensuing year, 1802, to Mr. King, our Minister in London, to endeavor to negotiate with the Sierra Leone company a reception of such of these people as might be colonized thither. He opened a correspondence with Mr. Wedderburne and Mr. Thornton, secretaries of the company, on the subject, and, in 1803, I received through Mr. King the result, which was that the colony was going on, but in a languishing condition; that the funds of the company were likely to fail, as they received no returns of profit to keep them up; that they were, therefore, in treaty with their government to take the establishment off their hands; but that in no event should they be willing to receive more of these people from the United States, as it was exactly that portion of their settlers which had gone from hence, which, by their idleness and turbulence, had kept the settlement in constant danger of dissolution, which could not have been prevented but for the aid of the maroon negroes from the West Indies, who were more industrious and orderly than the others, and supported the authority of the government and its laws. * * * The effort which I made with Portugal, to obtain an establishment for them within their claims in South America, proved also abortive.—To JOHN LYNCH. v, 564. FORD ED., ix, 303. (M., 1811.) See COLONIZATION.

5809. NEGROES, Elevating.— Nobody wishes more ardently than I do to see a good system commenced for raising the condition both of their body and mind to what it ought to be, as fast as the imbecility of their present existence, and other circumstances which cannot be neglected, will admit.—To Benjamin Banneker. iii, 291. Ford ed., v, 377. (Pa., 1791.)

— NEGROES,   Emancipation.—See Slavery.

5810. NEGROES, Future of.—I have supposed the black man, in his present state, might not be in body and mind equal to the white man; but it would be hazardous to affirm, that, equally cultivated for a few generations, he would not become so.—To General Chastellux. i, 341. Ford ed., iii, 138. (P., 1785.)

5811. NEGROES, Griefs.—Their griefs are transient. Those numberless afflictions, which render it doubtful whether Heaven has given life to us in mercy or in wrath, are less felt, and sooner forgotten with them.—Notes on Virginia. viii, 382. Ford ed., iii, 245. (1782.)

5812. NEGROES, Improvement.—The improvement of the blacks in body and mind. in the first instance of their mixture with the whites, has been observed by every one, and proves that their inferiority is not the effect merely of their condition in life.—Notes on Virginia. viii, 384. Ford ed., iii, 247. (1782.)

5813. —— ——. Bishop Grégoire wrote to me on the doubts I had expressed five or six and twenty years ago, in the Notes on Virginia, as to the grade of understanding of the negroes, and he sent me his book on the literature of the negroes. His credulity has made him gather up every story he could find of men of color (without distinguishing whether black, or of what degree of mixture), however slight the mention, or light the authority on which they are quoted. The whole do not amount, in point of evidence, to what we know ourselves of Banneker. We know he had spherical trigonometry enough to make almanacs, but not without the suspicion of aid from Ellicot, who was his neighbor and friend, and never missed an opportunity of puffing him. I have a long letter from Banneker, which show: him to have had a mind of very common stature indeed. As to Bishop Grégoire, I wrote him a very soft answer. It was impossible for doubt to have been more tenderly or hesitatingly expressed than that was in the Notes on Virginia, and nothing was or is farther from my intentions, than to enlist myself as the champion of a fixed opinion, where I have only expressed a doubt. St. Domingo will, in time, throw light on the question.—To Joel Barlow. v, 475. Ford ed., ix, 261. (M., 1809.)

5814. NEGROES, Indians vs.—Comparing them by their faculties of memory, reason, and imagination, it appears to me that in memory they are equal to the whites; in reason much inferior, as I think one could scarcely be found capable of tracing and comprehending the investigations of Euclid; and that in imagination they are dull, tasteless, and anomalous. It would be unfair to follow them to Africa for this investigation. We will consider them here, on the same stage with the whites, and where the facts are not apocryphal on which a judgment is to be formed. It will be right to make great allowances for the difference of condition, of education, of conversation, of the sphere in which they move. Many millions of them have been brought to, and born in Amer-

ica. Most of them, indeed, have been confined to tillage, to their own homes, and their own society; yet many of them have been so situated that they might have availed themselves of the conversation of their masters; many of them have been brought up to the handicraft arts, and from that circumstance have always been associated with the whites. Some have been liberally educated, and all have lived in countries where the arts and sciences are cultivated to a considerable degree, and have had before their eyes samples of the best works from abroad. The Indians, with no advantages of this kind, will often carve figures on their pipes not destitute of design and merit. They will crayon out an animal, a plant, or a country, so as to prove the existence of a germ in their minds which only wants cultivation. They astonish you with strokes of the most sublime oratory; such as prove their reason and sentiment strong, their imagination glowing and elevated. But never yet could I find that a black had uttered a thought above the level of plain narration; never saw even an elementary trait of painting or sculpture.—Notes on Virginia. viii, 382. Ford ed., iii, 245. (1782.)

5815. NEGROES, Industry.—An opinion is hazarded by some, but proved by none, that moral urgencies are not sufficient to induce the negro to labor; that nothing can do this but physical coercion. But this is a problem which the present age alone is prepared to solve by experiment. It would be a solecism to suppose a race of animals created, without sufficient foresight and energy to preserve their own existence. It is disproved, too, by the fact that they exist, and have existed through all the ages of history. We are not sufficiently acquainted with all the nations of Africa, to say that there may not be some in which habits of industry are established, and the arts practiced which are necessary to render life comfortable. The experiment now in progress in St. Domingo, those of Sierra Leone and Cape Mesurado, are but beginning. Your proposition has its aspects of promise also; and should it not fully answer to calculations in figures, it may yet, in its developments, lead to happy results.—To Miss Fanny Wright. vii, 408. Ford ed., x, 344. (M., 1825.)

5816. NEGROES, Integrity.—Notwithstanding these considerations which must weaken their respect for the laws of property, we find among them numerous instances of the most rigid integrity, and as many as among their better instructed masters, of benevolence, gratitude, and unshaken fidelity.—Notes on Virginia. viii, 386. Ford ed., iii, 249. (1782.) See Slavery.

5817. NEGROES, Literary.—Misery is often the parent of the most affecting touches in poetry. Among the blacks is misery enough, God knows, but no poetry. Love is the peculiar œstrum of the poet. Their love is ardent, but it kindles the senses only, not the imagination. Religion, indeed, has produced a Phyllis Wheatley;* but it could not produce a poet. The compositions published under her name are below the dignity of criticism. The heroes of the Dunciad are to her, as Hercules to the author of that poem.—Notes on Virginia. viii, 383. Ford ed., iii, 246. (1782.)

5818. —— ——. Ignatius Sancho has approached nearer to merit in composition [than Phyllis Wheatley]: yet his letters do more honor to the heart than the head. They breathe the

* A collection of poems by Phyllis Wheatley was printed in London in 1773.—Editor.

purest effusions of friendship and general philanthropy, and show how great a degree of the latter may be compounded with strong religious zeal. He is often happy in the turn of his compliments, and his style is easy and familiar, except when he affects a Shandean fabrication of words. But his imagination is wild and extravagant, escapes incessantly from every restraint of reason and taste, and, in the course of its vagaries, leaves a tract of thought as incoherent and eccentric, as is the course of a meteor through the sky. His subjects should often have led him to a process of sober reasoning; yet we find him always substituting sentiment for demonstration. Upon the whole, though we admit him to the first place among those of his own color who have presented themselves to the public judgment, yet when we compare him with the writers of the race among whom he lived and particularly with the epistolary class in which he has taken his own stand, we are compelled to enroll him at the bottom of the column. This criticism supposes the letters published under his name to be genuine, and to have received amendment from no other hand; points which would not be of easy investigation.—NOTES ON VIRGINIA. viii, 383. FORD ED., iii, 247. (1782.)

5819. NEGROES, Music.—In music they are more generally gifted than the whites, with accurate ears for tune and time, and they have been found capable of imagining a small catch.* Whether they will be equal to the composition of a more extensive run of melody, or of complicated harmony, is yet to be proved.—NOTES ON VIRGINIA. viii, 383. FORD ED., iii, 246. (1782.)

5820. NEGROES, Natural History and. —The opinion that they are inferior in the faculties of reason and imagination, must be hazarded with great diffidence. To justify a general conclusion, requires many observations, even where the subject may be submitted to the anatomical knife, to optical glasses, to analysis by fire or by solvents. How much more then where it is a faculty, not a substance, we are examining; where it eludes the research of all the senses; where the conditions of its existence are various and variously combined; where the effects of those which are present or absent bid defiance to calculation; let me add, too, as a circumstance of great tenderness, where our conclusion would degrade a whole race of men from the rank in the scale of beings which their Creator may perhaps have given them. To our reproach it must be said, that though for a century and a half we have had under our eyes the races of black and of red men, they have never yet been viewed by us as subjects of natural history. I advance it, therefore, as a suspicion only, that the blacks, whether originally a distinct race, or made distinct by time and circumstances, are inferior to the whites in the endowments both of body and mind. It is not against experience to suppose that different species of the same genus, or varieties of the same species, may possess different qualifications. Will not a lover of natural history, then, one who views the gradations in all the races of animals with the eye of philosophy, excuse an effort to keep those in the department of man as distinct as nature has formed them?—NOTES ON VIRGINIA. viii, 386. FORD ED., iii, 249. (1782.)

* The instrument proper to them is the Banjer [corrupted by the negroes into "banjo"] which they brought hither from Africa, and which is the original of the guitar, its chords being precisely the four lower chords of the guitar.—NOTE BY JEFFERSON.

5821. NEGROES, Peculiarities.—To these objections, which are political, may be added others, which are physical and moral. Whether the black of the negro resides in the reticular membrane between the skin and scarfskin, or in the scarf-skin itself; whether it proceeds from the color of the blood, the color of the bile, or from that of some other secretion, the difference is fixed in nature, and is as real as if its seat and cause were better known to us. And is this difference of no importance? Is it not the foundation of a greater or less share of beauty in the two races? Are not the fine mixtures of red and white, the expressions of every passion by greater or less suffusions of color in the one, preferable to that eternal monotony, which reigns in the countenances, that immovable veil of black which covers all the emotions of the other race? Add to these, flowing hair, a more elegant symmetry of form, their own judgment in favor of the whites, declared by their preference of them, as uniformly as is the preference of the Oranootan for the black woman over those of his own species. The circumstance of superior beauty, is thought worthy attention in the propagation of our horses, dogs, and other domestic animals; why not in that of man? Besides those of color, figure, and hair, there are other physical distinctions proving a difference of race. They have less hair on the face and body. They secrete less by the kidneys, and more by the glands of the skin, which gives them a very strong and disagreeable odor. This greater degree of transpiration renders them more tolerant of heat, and less of cold than the whites. Perhaps, too, a difference of structure in the pulmonary apparatus, which a late ingenious experimentalist (Crawford) has discovered to be the principal regulator of animal heat, may have disabled them from extricating, in the act of inspiration, so much of that fluid from the outer air, or obliged them in expiration, to part with more of it.—NOTES ON VIRGINIA. viii, 381. FORD ED., iii, 244. (1782.)

— NEGROES, Penal Colony for.—See COLONY, PENAL.

5822. NEGROES, Racial differences.—It will probably be asked, why not retain and incorporate the blacks into the State, and thus save the expense of supplying by importation of white settlers, the vacancies they will leave? Deep-rooted prejudices entertained by the whites; ten thousand recollections, by the blacks, of the injuries they have sustained; new provocations; the real distinctions which nature has made; and many other circumstances will divide us into parties, and produce convulsions, which will probably never end but in the extermination of the one or the other race.—NOTES ON VIRGINIA. viii, 380. FORD ED., iii, 244. (1782.)

5823. NEGROES, Rights of.—Be assured that no person living wishes more sincerely than I do, to see a complete refutation of the doubts I have myself entertained and expressed on the grade of understanding allotted to the negroes by nature, and to find that in this respect they are on a par with ourselves. My doubts were the result of personal observation on the limited sphere of my own State, where the opportunities for the development of their genius were not favorable, and those of exercising it still less so. I expressed them, therefore, with great hesitation; but whatever be their degree of talent it is no measure of their rights. Because Sir Isaac Newton was superior to others in understanding, he was not therefore lord of the person or property of others. On this subject they are gaining daily in the opinions of nations, and hopeful advances are making towards their reestablishment on an equal footing with the other colors of the human family. I pray you, therefore, to accept my thanks for the many instances you have enabled me to observe of respectable intelligence in that race of men, which cannot fail to have effect in hastening the day of their relief.—To HENRI GREGOIRE. v, 429. FORD ED., ix, 246. (W., 1809.)

5824. NEGROES, Sleep and amusements.—They seem to require less sleep. A black, after hard labor through the day, will be induced by the slightest amusements to sit up till midnight, or later, though knowing he must be out with the first dawn of the morning.—NOTES ON VIRGINIA. viii, 381. FORD ED., iii, 245. (1782.)

5825. ———— ————. In general, their existence appears to participate more of sensation than reflection. To this must be ascribed their disposition to sleep when abstracted from their diversions, and unemployed in labor. An animal whose body is at rest, and who does not reflect, must be disposed to sleep of course.—NOTES ON VIRGINIA. viii, 382. FORD ED., iii, 245. (1782.)

5826. NEGROES, Talents.—Nobody wishes more than I do to see such proofs as you exhibit, that nature has given to our black brethren talents equal to those of the other colors of men, and that the appearance of a want of them is owing merely to the degraded condition of their existence, both in Africa and America. * * * I have taken the liberty of sending your Almanac to Monsieur de Condorcet. Secretary of the Academy of Sciences at Paris, and member of the Philanthropic Society, because I considered it as a document to which your color had a right for their justification against the doubts which have been entertained of them.—To BENJAMIN BANNEKER. iii, 291. FORD ED., v, 377. (Pa., 1791.) See BANNEKER.

5827. NELSON (Thomas), Governor of Virginia.—[Governor Jefferson's] office was now [June, 1781,] near expiring, the country [Virginia] under invasion by a powerful army, no services but military of any avail, unprepared by his line of life and education for the command of armies, he believed it right not to stand in the way of talents better fitted than his own to the circumstances under which the country was placed. He, therefore, himself proposed to his friends in the Legislature that General Nelson, who commanded the militia of the State, should be appointed Governor, as he was sensible that the union of the civil and military power in the same hands at this time, would greatly facilitate military measures. This appointment accordingly took place on the 12th of June, 1781.—INVASION OF VA. MEMORANDUM. ix, 223. (M., 1781.)

5828. NEOLOGY, American.—I am no friend to what is called *Purism*, but a zealous one to the *Neology* which has introduced these two words without the authority of any dictionary. I consider the one as destroying the nerve and beauty of language, while the other improves both, and adds to its copiousness. I have been not a little disappointed, and made suspicious of my own judgment, on seeing the Edinburgh Reviewers, the ablest critics of the age, set their faces against the introduction of new words into the English language; they are particularly apprehensive that the writers of the United States will adulterate it. Certainly so great growing a population, spread over such an extent of country, with such a variety of climates, of productions, of arts, must enlarge their language, to make it answer its purpose of expressing all ideas, the new as well as the old. The new circumstances under which we are placed, call for new words, new phrases, and for the transfer of old words to new objects. An American dialect will, therefore, be formed; so will a West-Indian and Asiatic, as a Scotch and an Irish are already formed. But whether will these adulterate, or enrich the English language? Has the beautiful poetry of Burns, or his Scottish dialect, disfigured it? Did the Athenians consider the Doric, the Ionian, the Aeolic, and other dialects as disfiguring or as beautifying their language? Did they fastidiously disavow Herodotus, Pindar, Theocritus, Sappho, Alcæus, as Grecian writers? On the contrary, they were sensible that the variety of dialects, still infinitely varied by poetical license, constituted the riches of their language, and made the Grecian Homer the first of poets, as he must ever remain, until a language equally ductile and copious shall again be spoken.—To JOHN WALDO. vi, 184. (M., 1813.)

5829. NEUTRALITY, Carrying trade and.—If war in Europe take place, I hope the new world will fatten on the follies of the old. If we can but establish the principles of the armed neutrality for ourselves, we must become carriers for all parties as far as we can raise vessels.—To E. RUTLEDGE. iii, 165. FORD ED., v, 197. (N.Y., 1790.)

5830. ———— ————. A stoppage by some of the belligerent powers of one of our vessels going with grain to an unblockaded port, would be so unequivocal an infringement of the neutral rights, that we cannot conceive it will be attempted.—To THOMAS PINCKNEY. iii, 551. FORD ED., vi, 243. (Pa., May 1793.)

5831. ———— ————. The rights of a neutral to carry on a commercial intercourse with every part of the dominions of a belligerent, permitted by the laws of the country (with the exception of blockaded ports and contraband of war), was believed to have been decided between Great Britain and the United States by the sentence of the commissioners mutually appointed to decide on that and other questions of difference between the two nations, and by the actual payment of damages awarded by them against Great Britain for the infraction of that right. When, therefore, it was perceived that the same principle was revived with others more novel, and extending the injury, instructions were given to the Minister Plenipotentiary of the United States at the court of London, and remonstrances duly made by him on the subject. These were followed by a partial and temporary suspension only, without the disavowal of the principle. He has, therefore, been instructed to urge this subject anew, to bring it more fully to the bar of reason, and to insist on the rights too evident and too important to be surrendered. SPECIAL MESSAGE. viii, 57. FORD ED., viii, 417. (Jan. 1806.)

5832. ———— ————. To former violations of maritime rights, another is now added of very extensive effect. The government of that nation [Great Britain] has issued an order interdicting all trade by neutrals between ports not in amity with them; and being now at war with nearly every nation on the Atlantic and Mediterranean seas, our vessels are required to sacrifice their cargoes at the first port they touch, or to return home without the benefit of going to any other market. Under this new law of the ocean, our trade on the Mediterranean has been swept away by seizures and condemnations, and that in other seas is threatened with the same fate.— SEVENTH ANNUAL MESSAGE. viii, 84. FORD ED., ix, 156. (1807.) See NAVIGATION.

5833. NEUTRALITY, Contraband of war.—In our treaty with Prussia, we have gone ahead of other nations in doing away with restraints on the commerce of peaceful nations, by declaring that nothing shall be contraband. For, in truth, in the present improved state of the arts, when every country has such ample means of procuring arms within and without itself, the regulations of contraband answer no other end than to draw other nations into the war. However, as other nations have not given sanction to this improvement, we claim it, at present, with Prussia alone.—To THOMAS PINCKNEY. iii, 551. FORD ED., vi, 243. (Pa., May 1793.) See BELLIGERENTS and CONTRABAND OF WAR.

5834. NEUTRALITY, Duties.—We have seen with sincere concern the flames of war lighted up again in Europe, and nations with which we have the most friendly and useful relations engaged in mutual destruction. While we regret the miseries in which we see others involved, let us bow with gratitude to that kind Providence which, inspiring with wisdom and moderation our late legislative councils while placed under the urgency of the greatest wrongs, guarded us from hastily entering into the sanguinary contest, and left us only to look on and to pity its ravages. These will be heaviest on those immediately engaged. Yet the nations pursuing peace will not be exempt from all evil. In the course of this conflict [France and England], let it be our endeavor, as it is our interest and desire, to cultivate the friendship of the belligerent nations by every act of justice and of incessant kindness; to receive their armed vessels with hospitality from distresses of the sea, but to administer the means of annoyance to none; to establish in our harbors such a police as may maintain law and order; to restrain our citizens from embarking individually in a war in which their country takes no part; to punish severely those persons, citizen or alien, who shall usurp the cover of our flag for vessels not entitled to it, infecting thereby with suspicion those of real Americans, and committing us into controversies for the redress of wrongs not our own; to exact from every nation the observance, toward our vessels and citizens, of those principles and practices which all civilized people acknowledge; to merit the character of a just nation, and maintain that of an independent one, preferring every consequence to insult and habitual wrong. Congress will consider whether the existing laws enable us efficaciously to maintain this course with our citizens in all places, and with others while within the limits of our jurisdiction, and will give them the new modifications necessary for these objects. Some contraventions of right have already taken place, both within our jurisdictional limits and on the high seas. The friendly disposition of the governments from whose agents they have proceeded, as well as their wisdom and regard for justice, leave us in reasonable expectation that they will be rectified and prevented in future; and that no act will be countenanced by them which threatens to disturb our friendly intercourse. Separated by a wide ocean from the nations of Europe, and from the political interests which entangle them together, with productions and wants which render our commerce and friendship useful to them and theirs to us, it cannot be the interest of any to assail us, nor ours to disturb them.

We should be most unwise, indeed, were we to cast away the singular blessings of the position in which nature has placed us, the opportunity she has endowed us with of pursuing, at a distance from foreign contentions, the paths of industry, peace and happiness; of cultivating general friendship, and of bringing collisions of interest to the umpirage of reason rather than of force. How desirable, then, must it be, in a government like ours, to see its citizens adopt individually the views, the interests, and the conduct which their country should pursue, divesting themselves of those passions and partialities which tend to lessen useful friendships, and to embarrass and embroil us in the calamitous scenes of Europe. Confident that you will duly estimate the importance of neutral dispositions toward the observance of neutral conduct, that you will be sensible how much it is our duty to look on the bloody arena spread before us with commiseration indeed, but with no other wish than to see it closed, I am persuaded you will cordially cherish these dispositions in all discussions among yourselves, and in all communications with your constituents; and I anticipate with satisfaction the measures of wisdom which the great interests now committed to *you* will give you an opportunity of providing, and *myself* that of approving and carrying into execution with the fidelity I owe to my country.—THIRD ANNUAL MESSAGE. viii, 27. FORD ED., viii, 272. (Oct. 1803.)

5835. NEUTRALITY, Enemy goods.— Another source of complaint with Mr. Genet has been that the English take French goods out of American vessels, which he says is against the law of nations and ought to be prevented by us. On the contrary, we suppose it to have been long an established principle of the law of nations, that the goods of a friend are free in an enemy's vessel, and an enemy's goods lawful prize in the vessel of a friend. The inconvenience of this principle which subjects merchant vessels to be stopped at sea, searched, ransacked, led out of their course, has induced several nations latterly to stipulate against it by treaty, and to substitute another in its stead, that free bottoms shall make free goods, and enemy bottoms enemy goods; a rule equal to the other in point of loss and gain, but less oppressive to commerce. As far as it has been introduced, it depends on the treaties stipulating it, and forms exceptions, in special cases, to the general operation of the law of nations. We have introduced it into our treaties with France, Holland and Prussia; and French goods found by the two latter nations in American bottoms are not made prize of. It is our wish to establish it with other nations. But this requires their consent also, is a work of time, and in the meanwhile, they have a right to act on the general principle, without giving to us or to France cause of complaint. Nor do I see that France can lose by it on the whole. For though she loses *her* goods when found in our vessels by the nations with whom we have no treaties, yet she gains *our* goods, when found in the vessels of the same and all other nations; and we believe the latter mass to be greater than the former.—To GOUVERNEUR MORRIS. iv, 43. FORD ED., vi, 387. (Pa., Aug. 1793.)

5836. ———— ————. It is to be lamented, indeed, that the general principle has operated so cruelly in the dreadful calamity which has lately happened in St. Domingo. The miserable fugitives, who, to save their lives, had taken asylum in our vessels, with such valuable and portable things as could be gathered in the moment out of the ashes of their houses and wrecks of their fortunes, have been plundered of these remains by the licensed sea rovers of their enemies. This has swelled, on this occasion, the disadvantages of the general principle, that "an enemy's goods are free prize in the vessels of a friend". But it is one of those deplorable and unforeseen calamities to which they expose themselves who enter into a state of war, furnishing to us an awful lesson to avoid it by justice and moderation, and not a cause of encouragement to expose our own towns to the same burning and butcheries, nor of complaint because we do not.—To GOUVERNEUR MORRIS. iv, 44. FORD ED., vi, 387. (Pa., Aug. 1793.) See ENEMY GOODS.

5837. NEUTRALITY, Fraudulent use of flag.—As there appears * * * a probability of a very general war in Europe, you will be pleased to be particularly attentive to preserve for our vessels all the rights of neutrality, and to endeavor that our flag be not usurped by others to procure to themselves the benefits of our neutrality. This usurpation tends to commit us with foreign nations, to subject those vessels truly ours to rigorous scrutinies and delays, to distinguish them from counterfeits, and to take the business of transportation out of our hands.—To DAVID HUMPHREYS. iii, 533. FORD ED., vi, 205. (Pa., 1793.)

5838. —— ——. It will be necessary for all our public agents to exert themselves with vigilance for securing to our vessels all the rights of neutrality.—To C. W. F. DUMAS. iii, 535. (Pa., 1793.) See FLAG.

5839. NEUTRALITY, The Grange capture.—The capture of the British ship Grange, by the French frigate L'Embuscade, has been found to have taken place within the * * * jurisdiction of the United States * * * . The government, is, therefore, taking measures for the liberation of the crew and restitution of the ship and cargo.—To GEORGE HAMMOND. iii, 559. FORD ED., vi, 253. (Pa., May 1793.)

5840. —— ——. The government deems the capture [of the Grange] to have been unquestionably within its jurisdiction, and that according to the rules of neutrality and the protection it owes to all persons while within its limits, it is bound to see that the crew be liberated, and the vessel and cargo restored to their former owners. * * * I am, in consequence, charged by the President of the United States to express to you his expectation, and at the same time his confidence, that you will be pleased to take immediate and effectual measures for having the ship Grange and her cargo restored to the British owners, and the persons taken on board her set at liberty.—To JEAN BAPTISTE TERNANT. iii, 561. FORD ED., vi, 256. (Pa., May 15, 1793.)

5841. —— ——. In forming these determinations [respecting Grange, &c.,] the government of the United States has listened to nothing but the dictates of immutable justice; they consider the rigorous exercise of that virtue as the surest means of preserving perfect harmony between the United States and the powers at war.—To JEAN BAPTISTE TERNANT. iii, 562. FORD ED., vi, 257. (Pa., May 1793.)

5842. NEUTRALITY, Impartial.—Our conduct as a neutral nation is marked out in our treaties with France and Holland, two of the belligerent powers; and as the duties of neutrality require an *equal* conduct to both parties, we should, on that ground, act on the same principles towards Great Britain.—To THOMAS PINCKNEY. iii, 551. FORD ED., vi, 243. (Pa., May 1793.)

5843. —— ——. A manly neutrality, claiming the liberal rights ascribed to that condition by the very powers at war, was the part we should have taken, and would, I believe, have given satisfaction to our allies. If anything prevents its being a mere English neutrality, it will be that the penchant of the President is not that way, and above all, the ardent spirit of our constituents.—To JAMES MADISON. iii, 557. FORD ED., vi, 251. (May 1793.)

5844. —— ——. The line is now drawn so clearly as to show on one side, 1. The fashionable circles of Philadelphia, New York. Boston and Charleston (natural aristocrats). 2. Merchants trading on British capital. 3. Paper men (all the old tories are found in some one of the three descriptions). On the other side are, 1. Merchants trading on their own capital. 2. Irish merchants. 3. Tradesmen, mechanics, farmers, and every other possible description of our citizens.—To JAMES MADISON. iii, 557. FORD ED., vi, 251. (May 1793.)

5845. —— ——. I trust that in the readiness with which the United States have attended to the redress of such wrongs as are committed by their citizens, or within their jurisdiction, you will see proofs of their justice and impartiality to all parties, and that it will ensure to their citizens pursuing their lawful business by sea or by land, in all parts of the world, a like efficacious interposition of the governing powers to protect them from injury, and redress it, where it has taken place. With such dispositions on both sides, vigilantly and faithfully carried into effect, we may hope that the blessings of peace, on the one part, will be as little impaired, and the evils of war on the other, as little aggravated, as the nature of things will permit; and that this should be so, is, we trust, the prayer of all.—To GEORGE HAMMOND. iii, 559. FORD ED., vi, 254. (Pa., 1793.)

5846. —— ——. The course intended to be pursued being that of a strict and impartial neutrality, decisions, rendered by the President on that principle, dissatisfy both parties, and draw complaints from both.—To GOUVERNEUR MORRIS. iii, 580. FORD ED., vi, 299. (Pa., June 1793.)

5847. —— ——. It will never be easy to convince me that by a firm yet just conduct in 1793. we might not have obtained such a respect for our neutral rights from Great Britain, as that her violations of them and use of our means to wage her wars, would not have furnished any pretence to the other party to do the same. War with both would have been avoided, commerce and navigation protected and enlarged. We shall now either be forced into a war, or have our commerce and navigation at least totally annihilated, and the produce of our farms for some years left to rot on our hands. A little time will unfold these things, and show which class of opinions would have been most friendly to the firmness of our government, and to the interests of those for whom it was made.—To DR. JOHN EDWARDS. iv, 165. FORD ED., vii, 113. (M., Jan. 1797.)

5848. —— ——. It is to be deplored that distant as we are from the storms and convulsions which agitate the European world, the pursuit of an honest neutrality, beyond the reach of reproach, has been insufficient to secure to us the certain enjoyments of peace with those whose interests as well as ours would be promoted by it.—R. to A. New Jersey Legislature. viii, 122. (1807.)

5849. —— ——. I verily believe that it will ever be in our power to keep so even a stand between England and France, as to inspire a wish in neither to throw us into the scale of his adversary. If we can do this for a dozen years only, we shall have little to fear from them.—To Mr. Coxe. v, 58. (W., 1807.)

5850. —— ——. Neither belligerent pretends to have been injured by us, or can say that we have in any instance departed from the most faithful neutrality.—R. to A. Virginia Assembly. viii, 148. (1809.)

5851. —— ——. A law respecting our conduct as a neutral between Spain and her contending colonies was passed [by the late Congress] by a majority of one only, I believe, and against the very general sentiment of our country. It is thought to strain our complaisance to Spain beyond her right or merit, and almost against the right of the other party, and certainly against the claims they have to our good wishes and neighborly relations. That we should wish to see the people of other countries free, is as natural, and, at least as justifiable, as that one king should wish to see the kings of other countries maintained in their despotism. Right to both parties, innocent favor to the juster cause, is our proper sentiment.—To Albert Gallatin. vii, 78. Ford ed., x, 90. (M., 1817.)

5852. NEUTRALITY, Markets and.— If the new government wears the front which I hope it will, I see no impossibility in the availing ourselves of the wars of others to open the other parts of America [West Indies] to our commerce, as the price of our neutrality.—To General Washington. ii, 533. Ford ed., v, 57. (P., 1788.)

5853. —— ——. With England, I think we shall cut off the resource of impressing our seamen to fight her battles, and establish the inviolability of our flag in its commerce with her enemies. We shall thus become what we sincerely wish to be, honestly neutral, and truly useful to both belligerents. To the one, by keeping open market for the consumption of her manufactures, while they are excluded from all the other countries under the power of her enemy; to the other, by securing for her a safe carriage of all her productions, metropolitan or colonial, while her own means are restrained by her enemy, and may, therefore, be employed in other useful pursuits. We are certainly more useful friends to France and Spain as neutrals, than as allies.—To James Bowdoin. v, 18. (W., 1806.) See Commerce, Markets, and Navigation.

5854. NEUTRALITY, Obligations of. —Where [treaties] are silent, the general principles of the law of nations must give the rule [of neutral obligation]. I mean the principles of that law as they have been liberalized in latter times by the refinement of manners and morals, and evidenced by the declarations, stipulations, and practice of every civilized nation.— To Thomas Pinckney. iii, 551. Ford ed., vi, 243. (Pa., May 1793.)

5855. NEUTRALITY, Passage of troops.— It is well enough agreed in the laws of nations, that for a neutral power to give or

refuse permission to the troops of either belligerent party to pass through their territory, is no breach of neutrality, provided the same refusal or permission be extended to the other party. If we give leave of passage then to the British troops, Spain will have no just cause of complaint against us, provided we extend the same leave to her when demanded. If we refuse (as indeed we have a right to do), and the troops should pass notwithstanding, of which there can be little doubt, we shall stand committed. For either we must enter immediately into the war, or pocket an acknowledged insult in the face of the world; and one insult pocketed soon produces another. There is, indeed, a middle course which I should be inclined to prefer; that is to avoid giving any answer. They will proceed notwithstanding, but to do this under our silence, will admit of palliation, and produce apologies, from military necessity; and will leave us free to pass it over without dishonor, or to make it a handle of quarrel hereafter, if we should have use for it as such. But, if we are obliged to give an answer, I think the occasion not such as should induce us to hazard that answer which might commit us to the war at so early a stage of it; and, therefore, that the passage should be permitted. If they should pass without having asked leave, I should be for expressing our dissatisfaction to the British court, and keeping alive an altercation on the subject, till events should decide whether it is most expedient to accept their apologies, or to profit of the aggression as a cause of war.— Official Opinion. vii, 509. Ford ed., v, 239. (1790.)

5856. NEUTRALITY, Passports for vessels.— The proposition to permit all our vessels destined for any port in the French West India Islands to be stopped, unless furnished with passports from yourself, is so far beyond the powers of the Executive, that it will be unnecessary to enumerate the objections to which it would be liable.—To E. C. Genet. iv, 88. Ford ed., vi, 460. (Pa., Nov. 1793.)

5857. NEUTRALITY, Preserving.— Amidst the confusion of a general war which seems to be threatening that quarter of the globe [Europe], we hope to be permitted to preserve the line of neutrality.—To C. W. F. Dumas. iii, 535. (Pa., March 1793.)

5858. —— ——. I wish we may be able to repress the spirit of the people within the limits of a fair neutrality.—To James Monroe. iii, 548. Ford ed., vi, 238. (Pa., 1793.)

5859. —— ——. You may, on every occasion, give assurances [to the British government] which cannot go beyond the real desires of this country, to preserve a fair neutrality in the present war, on condition that the rights of neutral nations are respected in us, as they have been settled in *modern* times, either by the express declarations of the powers of Europe, or their adoption of them on particular occasions.—To Thomas Pinckney. iii, 542. (Pa., April 1793.)

5860. —— ——. We shall be a little embarrassed occasionally till we feel ourselves firmly seated in the saddle of neutrality.—To George Wythe. Ford ed., vi, 218. (Pa., April 1793.)

5861. —— ——. I fear that a fair neutrality will prove a disagreeable pill to our friends [the French], though necessary to keep out of the calamities of a war.—To James Madison. Ford ed., vi, 232. (Pa., April 1793.)

5862. —— ——. No country, perhaps, was ever so thoroughly against war as ours. These dispositions pervade every description of its citizens, whether in or out of office. They cannot, perhaps, suppress their affections, nor their wishes. But they will suppress the effects of them so as to preserve a fair neutrality. Indeed we shall be more useful as neutrals than as parties, by the protection which our flag will give to supplies of provisions. In this spirit let all your assurances be given to the government [of France].—To GOUVERNEUR MORRIS. FORD ED., vi, 217. (Pa., April 1793.)

5863. —— ——. If we preserve even a sneaking neutrality, we shall be indebted for it to the President, and not to his counsellors.—To COLONEL MONROE. iii, 548. FORD ED., vi, 239. (Pa., May 1793.)

5864. NEUTRALITY, Profitable.—The great harvest for [the profits of navigation] is when other nations are at war and our flag neutral.—OPINION ON SHIP PASSPORTS. vii, 625. (1793.)

5865. —— ——. Let us milk the cow while the Russian holds her by the horns and the Turk holds her by the tail.—To JOHN ADAMS. vii, 245. FORD ED., x, 217. (M., 1822.)

5866. NEUTRALITY, Provisions not contraband.—This article* is so manifestly contrary to the law of nations, that nothing more would seem necessary than to observe that it is so. Reason and usage have established that when two nations go to war, those who choose to live in peace retain their natural right to pursue their agriculture, manufactures, and other ordinary vocations, to carry the produce of their industry for exchange to all nations, belligerent or neutral, as usual, to go and come freely, without injury or molestation, and, in short, that the war among others shall be, for them, as if it did not exist. One restriction on their natural rights has been submitted to by nations at peace; that is to say, that of not furnishing to either party implements merely of war, for the annoyance of the other, nor anything whatever to a place blockaded by its enemy. What these implements of war are, has been so often agreed and is so well understood, as to leave little question about them at this day. There does not exist, perhaps, a nation in our common hemisphere which has not made a particular enumeration of them, in some or all of their treaties, under the name of contraband. It suffices for the present occasion, to say, that corn flour and meal, are not of the class of contraband, and consequently remain articles of free commerce. A culture, which, like that of the soil, gives employment to such a proposition of mankind, could never be suspended by the whole earth, or interrupted for them, whenever any two nations should think proper to go to war.—To THOMAS PINCKNEY. iv, 59. FORD ED., vi, 413. (Pa., Sept. 1793.)

5867. —— ——. The state of war existing between Great Britain and France, furnishes no legitimate right either to interrupt the agriculture of the United States, or the peaceable exchange of its produce with all nations; and

* Instructions to commanders of British war ships directing them to stop vessels carrying provisions to French ports, and send them to English ports where their cargoes may be purchased by that government, or released on security that they will be taken to the ports of some country in amity with Great Britain.—EDITOR.

consequently, the assumption of it will be as lawful hereafter as now, in peace as in war. No ground, acknowledged by the common reason of mankind, authorizes this act now, and unacknowledged ground may be taken at any time and all times. We see, then, a practice begun, to which no time, no circumstances prescribe any limits, and which strikes at the root of our agriculture, that branch of industry which gives food, clothing and comfort to the great mass of the inhabitants of these States. If any nation whatever has a right to shut up to our produce all the ports of the earth except her own, and those of her friends, she may shut up these also, and so confine us within our own limits. No nation can subscribe to such pretensions; no nation can agree, at the mere will or interest of another, to have its peaceable industry suspended, and its citizens reduced to idleness and want. The loss of our produce, destined for foreign markets, or that loss which would result from an arbitrary restraint of our markets, is a tax too serious for us to acquiesce in. It is not enough for a nation to say, we and our friends will buy your produce. We have a right to answer, that it suits us better to sell to their enemies as well as their friends. Our ships do not go to France to return empty. They go to exchange the surplus of our produce, which we can spare, for surpluses of other kinds, which they can spare, and we want; which they can furnish on better terms, and more to our mind, than Great Britain or her friends. We have a right to judge for ourselves what market best suits us, and they have none to forbid to us the enjoyment of the necessaries and comforts which we may obtain from any other independent country.—To THOMAS PINCKNEY. iv, 60. FORD ED., vi, 413. (Pa., Sep. 1793.)

5868. —— ——. This act, too, tends directly to draw us from that state of peace in which we are wishing to remain. It is an essential character of neutrality to furnish no aids (not stipulated by treaty) to one party, which we are not equally ready to furnish to the other. If we permit corn to be sent to Great Britain and her friends, we are equally bound to permit it to France. To restrain it, would be a partiality which might lead to war with France; and, between restraining it ourselves, and permitting her enemies to restrain it unrightfully, is no difference. She would consider this as a mere pretext, of which she would not be the dupe; and on what honorable ground could we otherwise explain it? Thus we should see ourselves plunged, by this unauthorized act of Great Britain, into a war with which we meddle not, and which we wish to avoid, if justice to all parties, and from all parties, will enable us to avoid it. In the case where we found ourselves obliged, by treaty, to withhold from the enemies of France the right of arming in our ports, we thought ourselves in justice bound to withhold the same right from France also, and we did it. Were we to withhold from her supplies of provisions, we should, in like manner, be bound to withhold them from her enemies also; and thus shut to ourselves all the ports of Europe, where corn is in demand, or make ourselves parties in the war. This is a dilemma, which Great Britain has no right to force upon us, and for which no pretext can be found in any part of our conduct. She may, indeed, feel the desire of starving an enemy nation; but she can have no right of doing it at our loss, nor of making us the instruments of it.—To THOMAS PINCKNEY. iv, 61. FORD ED., vi, 414. (Pa., Sep. 1793.)

5869. NEUTRALITY, Public vessels.— The public ships of war of both nations [France and England] enjoy a perfect equality in our ports; first, in cases of urgent necessity; secondly, in cases of comfort or convenience; and thirdly, in the time they choose to continue; and all a friendly power can ask from another is, to extend to her the same indulgences which she extends to other friendly powers.—To George Hammond. iv, 66. Ford ed., vi, 423. (Pa., 1793.) See Asylum.

5870. ——— ———. The bringing vessels to, of whatever nation, while within the limits of the protection of the United States, will be pointedly forbidden; the government being firmly determined to enforce a peaceable demeanor among all the parties within those limits, and to deal to all the same impartial measure.—To the Governor of Virginia. iii, 564. (Pa., May 1793.)

5871. ——— ———. Mr. Thornton's attempt to justify his nation in using our ports as cruising stations on our friends and ourselves, renders the matter so serious as to call, I think, for answer. That we ought, in courtesy and friendship, to extend to them all the rights of hospitality is certain; that they should not use our hospitality to injure our friends or ourselves is equally enjoined by morality and honor. After the rigorous exertions we made in Genet's time to prevent this abuse on his part, and the indulgences extended by Mr. Adams to the British cruisers even after our pacification with France, by ourselves also from an unwillingness to change the course of things as the war was near its close, I did not expect to hear from that quarter charges of partiality.—To James Madison. iv, 501. (M., Aug. 1803.)

5872. ——— ———. I do not think the loan of our navy yard any more contrary to neutrality than that of our ports. It is merely admitting a ship to a proper station in our waters.—To James Madison. Ford ed., viii, 475. (M., Sep. 1806.)

5873. ——— ———. Several French vessels of war, disabled from keeping the sea, * * * put into the harbors of the United States to avoid the danger of shipwreck. The minister of their nation states that their crews are without resources for subsistence, and other necessaries, for the reimbursement of which he offers bills on his government, the faith of which he pledges for their punctual payment. The laws of humanity make it a duty for nations, as well as individuals, to succor those whom accident and distress have thrown upon them. By doing this in the present case, to the extent of mere *subsistence and necessaries*, and so as to aid no military equipment, we shall keep within the duties of rigorous neutrality, which never can be in opposition to those of humanity. We furnished, on a former occasion, to a distressed crew of the other belligerent party, similar accommodations, and we have ourselves received from both those powers, friendly and free supplies to the necessities of our vessels of war in their Mediterranean ports. In fact, the governments of civilized nations generally are in the practice of exercising these offices of humanity towards each other. Our government having as yet made no regular provision for the exchange of these offices of courtesy and humanity between nations, the honor, the interest, and the duty of our country require that we should adopt any other mode by which it may legally be done on the present occasion. It is expected that we shall want a large sum of money in Europe, for the purposes of the present negotiation with Spain, and besides this we want annually large sums there, for the discharge of our installments of debt. Under these circumstances, supported by the unanimous opinion of the heads of Departments, * * * and firmly trusting that the government of France will feel itself peculiarly interested in the punctual discharge of the bills drawn by their Minister, * * * I approve of the Secretary of the treasury's taking the bills of the Minister of France, to an amount not exceeding sixty thousand dollars.—To Albert Gallatin. v, 35. (W., Jan. 1807.)

5874. ——— ———. Armed vessels remaining within our jurisdiction in defiance of the authority of the laws, must be viewed either as rebels, or public enemies. The latter character' it is most expedient to ascribe to them; the laws of intercourse with persons of that description are fixed and known. If we relinquish them we shall have a new code to settle with those individual offenders, with whom self-respect forbids any intercourse but merely for purposes of humanity.—To Governor W. H. Cabell. v, 170. (M., 1807.)

5875. NEUTRALITY, Rights.—The doctrine that the rights of nations remaining quietly under the exercise of moral and social duties, are to give way to the convenience of those who prefer plundering and murdering one another, is a monstrous doctrine; and ought to yield to the more rational law, that "the wrongs which two nations endeavor to inflict on each other, must not infringe on the rights or conveniences of those remaining at peace".—To Robert R. Livingston. iv, 410. Ford ed., viii, 90. (M., 1801.)

5876. ——— ———. It would indeed be advantageous to us to have neutral rights established on a broad ground; but no dependence can be placed in any European coalition for that. They have so many other bye-interests of greater weight, that some one or other will always be bought off. To be entangled with them would be a much greater evil than a temporary acquiescence in the false principles which have prevailed.—To William Short. iv, 414. Ford ed., viii, 98. (W., 1801.)

5877. ——— ———. With respect to the rights of neutrality, we have certainly a great interest in their settlement. But this depends exclusively on the will of two characters, Bonaparte and Alexander. The dispositions of the former to have them placed on liberal grounds are known. The interest of the latter should insure the same disposition. The only thing to be done is to bring the two characters together to treat on the subject. All the minor maritime powers of Europe will of course concur with them. We have not failed to use such means as we possess to induce these two sovereigns to avail the world of its present situation to declare and enforce the laws of nature and convenience on the seas. But the organization of the treaty-making power by our Constitution is too particular for us to commit the nation in so great an operation with all the European powers. With such a federal phalanx in the Senate, compact and vigilant for opportunities to do mischief, the addition of a very few other votes, misled by accidental or imperfect views of the subject, would suffice to commit us most dangerously. All we can do, therefore, is to encourage others to declare and guarantee neutral rights, by excluding all intercourse with any nation which infringes them, and so leave a niche in their compact for us, if our treaty-making power shall choose to occupy it.—To THOMAS PAINE. FORD ED., viii, 437. (W., March 1806.)

5878. ———— ————. The license to four British vessels to sail to Lima proves that belligerents may, either by compact or force, conduct themselves towards one another as they please; but not that a neutral may, unless by some express permission of the belligerent.—To ALBERT GALLATIN. FORD ED., viii, 466. (M., Aug. 1806.)

5879. ———— ————. It is all important that we should stand in terms of the strictest cordiality with France. In fact, we are to depend on her and Russia for the establishment of neutral rights by the treaty of peace, among which should be that of taking no persons by a belligerent out of a neutral ship, unless they be the *soldiers* of an enemy.—To JAMES BOWDOIN. v, 64. FORD ED., ix, 40. (W., April 1807.)

5880. ———— ————. The instructions given to our ministers [to England] were framed in the sincerest spirit of amity and moderation. They accordingly proceeded, in conformity therewith, to propose arrangements which might embrace and settle all the points in difference between us, which might bring us to a mutual understanding on our neutral and national rights, and provide for a commercial intercourse on conditions of some equality. After long and fruitless endeavors to effect the purposes of their mission, and to obtain arrangements within the limits of their instructions, they concluded to sign such as could be obtained, and to send them for consideration, candidly declaring to the other negotiators, at the same time, that they were acting against their instructions, and that their government, therefore, could not be pledged for ratification. Some of the articles proposed might have been admitted on a principle of compromise, but others were too highly disadvantageous, and no sufficient provision was made against the principal source of the irritations and collisions which were constantly endangering the peace of the two nations. The question, therefore, whether a treaty should be accepted in that form could have admitted but of one decision, even had no declarations or the other party impaired our confidence in it. Still anxious not to close the door against friendly adjustment, new modifications were framed, and further concessions authorized than could before have been supposed necessary; and our ministers were instructed to resume their negotiations on these grounds. On this new reference to amicable discussion, we were reposing in confidence, when on the 22nd day of June last, by a formal order from the British admiral, the frigate Chesapeake, leaving her port for distant service, was attacked by one of those vessels which had been lying in our harbors under the indulgences of hospitality, was disabled from proceeding, had several of her crew killed, and four taken away.—SEVENTH ANNUAL MESSAGE. viii, 83. FORD ED., ix, 150. (Oct. 27, 1807.) See CHESAPEAKE.

5881. ———— ————. The nations of the earth prostrated at the foot of power, the ocean submitted to the despotism of a single nation, the laws of nature and the usages which have hitherto regulated the intercourse of nations and interposed some restraint between power and right, now totally disregarded. Such is the state of things when the United States are left single-handed to maintain the rights of neutrals, and the principles of public right against a warring world.—R. TO A. NIAGARA REPUBLICANS. viii, 155. (1809.)

5882. ———— ————. When two nations go to war, it does not abridge the rights of neutral nations but in the two articles of blockade and contraband of war.—To BENJAMIN STODDERT. v, 425. FORD ED., ix, 245. (W., 1809.) See ALEXANDER OF RUSSIA and EMBARGO.

5883. NEUTRALITY, Sale of arms.— The manufacture of arms is the occupation and livelihood of some of our citizens; and * * * it ought not to be expected that a war among other nations should produce such an internal derangement of the occupations of a nation at peace, as the suppression of a manufacture which is the support of some of its citizens; but * * * if they should export these arms to nations at war, they would be abandoned to the seizure and confiscation which the law of nations authorized to be made of them on the high seas.—To E. C. GENET. iv, 87. FORD ED., vi, 460. (Pa., Nov. 1793.) See BELLIGERENTS.

— NEUTRALITY, Sale of ships.—See BELLIGERENTS.

5884. NEUTRALITY, Treasury Department and.—Hamilton produced [at a cabinet meeting] the draft of a letter by himself to the collectors of the customs, giving them in charge to watch over all proceedings in their districts, contrary to the laws of neutrality, or tending to infract our peace with the belligerent powers, and particularly to observe if vessels pierced for guns should be built, and to inform *him* of it. This was objected to. 1. As setting up a system of espionage, destructive of the peace of society. 2. Transferring to the Treasury Department the conservation of the laws of neutrality and peace with foreign nations. 3. It was rather proposed to intimate to the judges that the laws respecting neutrality being now come into activity, they should charge the grand juries with the observance of them; these being constitutional and public informers, and the persons accused knowing of what they should do, and having an opportunity of justifying themselves. E. R. [Edmund Randolph] found a hair to split, which, as always happens, became the decision. Hamilton is to write to the collectors of the customs, who are to convey their information to the attorneys of the district to whom E. R. is to write to receive their information and proceed by indictment. The clause respecting the building vessels pierced for guns was omitted, for though three against one thought it would be a breach of neutrality, yet they thought we might defer giving a public opinion on it as yet.—To JAMES MADISON. iii, 556. FORD ED., vi, 250. (May 1793.)

5885. ———— ————. I have been still reflecting on the draft of the letter from the Secretary of the Treasury to the custom house officers, instructing them to be on the watch as to all infractions or tendencies to infraction of the laws of neutrality by our citizens, and to communicate the same to him. When this paper was first communicated to me, though the whole of it struck me disagreeably, I did not in the first moment see clearly the improprieties but of the last clause. The more I have reflected, the more objectionable the whole appears. By this proposal the collectors of the customs are to be made an established corps of spies or informers against their fellow citizens, whose actions they are to watch in secret, inform against in secret to the Secretary of the Treasury, who is to communicate it to the President. If the action and evidence appear to justify a prosecution, a prosecution is to be set on foot on the *secret information* of a collector. If it will not justify it, then the only consequence is that the mind of government has been poisoned against a citizen, neither known nor suspecting it, and perhaps too distant to bring forward his justification. This will at least furnish the collector with a convenient weapon to keep down a rival, draw a cloud over an inconvenient censor, or satisfy mere malice and private enmity. The object of this new institution is to be to prevent infractions of the laws of neutrality, and preserve our peace with foreign nations; but I cannot possibly conceive how the superintendence of the laws of neutrality, or the preservation of our peace with foreign nations can be ascribed to the department of the Treasury, which I suppose to comprehend merely matters of revenue. It would be to add a new and a large field to a department already amply provided with business, patronage, and influence. It was urged as a reason that the collectors of the customs are in convenient positions for this espionage. They are in convenient positions, too, for building ships of war; but will that business be transplanted from its department, merely because it can be conveniently done in another? It seemed the desire that if this means was disapproved, some other equivalent might be adopted. Though we consider the acts of a foreigner making a captive within our limits, as an act of public hostility, and therefore to be turned over to the military rather than the civil power; yet the acts of our citizens infringing the laws of neutrality, or contemplating that, are offences against the ordinary laws and cognizable by them. Grand juries are the constitutional inquisitors and informers of the country; they are scattered everywhere, see everything, see it while they suppose themselves mere private persons, and not with the prejudiced eye of a permanent and systematic spy. Their information is on *oath*, is public, it is in the vicinage of the party charged, and can be at once refuted. These officers taken only occasionally from among the people, are familiar to them, the office respected, and the experience of centuries has shown that it is safely entrusted with our character, property and liberty. A grand juror cannot carry on systematic persecution against a neighbor whom he hates, because he is not permanent in the office. The judges generally, by a charge, instruct the grand jurors in the infractions of law which are to be noticed by them; and our judges are in the habit of printing their charges in the newspapers. The judges, having notice of the proclamation, will perceive that the occurrence of a foreign war has brought into activity the laws of neutrality, as a part of the law of the land. This new branch of the law they will know needs explanation to the grand juries more than any other. They will study and define the subjects to them and to the public. The public mind will by this be warned against the acts which may endanger our peace, foreign nations will see a much more respectable evidence of our *bonâ fide* intentions to preserve neutrality, and society will be relieved from the inquietude which must forever be excited by the knowledge of the existence of such a poison in it as secret accusation. It will be easy to suggest this matter to the attention of the judges, and that alone puts the whole machine into motion. The one is a familiar, impartial and precious instrument; the other, not popular in its present functions, will be odious in the new ones. and

the odium will reach the Executive, who will be considered as having planted a germ of private inquisition absolutely unknown to our laws.—To EDMUND RANDOLPH. iii, 553. FORD ED., vi, 245. (May 1793.)

5886. NEUTRALITY, Usurpation of jurisdiction.—The United States being at peace with both parties, will certainly not see with indifference its territory or jurisdiction violated by [France or England] either. and will proceed immediately to enquire into the facts and to do what these shall show ought to be done with exact impartiality.—To GEORGE HAMMOND. FORD ED., vi, 236. (Pa., May 1793.)

5887. ——. It is the *right* of every nation to prohibit acts of sovereignty from being exercised by any other within its limits; and the *duty* of a neutral nation to prohibit such as would injure one of the warring powers.—To E. C. GENET. iii. 572. FORD ED., vi, 283. (Pa., June 1793.) See CONSULS, GENET, and PRIVATEERS.

5888. NEUTRALITY, Violations of.—Since our last meeting the aspect of our foreign relations has considerably changed. Our coasts have been infested and our harbors watched by private armed vessels, some of them without commissions, some with illegal commissions, others with those of legal form but committing piratical acts beyond the authority of their commissions. They have captured in the very entrance of our harbors, as well as on the high seas, not only the vessels of our friends coming to trade with us, but our own also. They have carried them off under pretence of legal adjudication, but not daring to approach a court of justice, they have plundered and sunk them by the way, or in obscure places where no evidence could arise against them; maltreated the crews, and abandoned them in boats in the open sea, or on desert shores without food or covering. These enormities appearing to be unreached by any control of their sovereigns, I found it necessary to equip a force to cruise within our own seas, to arrest all vessels of these descriptions found hovering on our coast within the limits of the Gulf Stream, and to bring the offenders in for trial as pirates. The same system of hovering on our coasts, and harbors under color of seeking enemies, has been also carried on by public armed ships, to the great annoyance and oppression of our commerce. New principles, too, have been interpolated into the law of nations, founded neither in justice, nor the usage, or acknowledgment of nations. According to those, a belligerent takes to itself a commerce with its own enemy, which it denies to a neutral on the ground of its aiding that enemy in the war. But reason revolts at such an inconsistency; and the neutral having equal right with the belligerent to decide the question, the interest of our constituents and the duty of maintaining the authority of reason, the only umpire between just nations, impose on us the obligation of providing an effectual and determined opposition to a doctrine so injurious to the rights of peaceable nations. Indeed, the confidence we ought to have in the justice of others, still countenances the hope that a sounder view of those rights will of itself induce from every belligerent a more correct observance of them.—FIFTH ANNUAL MESSAGE. viii, 47. FORD ED., viii, 389. (Dec. 1805.)

5889. NEUTRALITY PROCLAMATION, History of.—The public papers giving us reason to believe that the war is becoming nearly general in Europe, and that it has already involved nations with which we are in daily habits of commerce and friendship, the President has thought it proper to issue the Proclamation of which I enclose you a copy, in order to mark out to our citizens the line of conduct they are to pursue. That this intimation, however, might not work to their prejudice, by being produced against them as conclusive evidence of their knowledge of the existence of war and of the nations engaged in it, in any case where they might be drawn into courts of justice for acts done without that knowledge, it has been thought necessary to write to the representatives of the belligerent powers here, * * * reserving to our citizens those immunities to which they are entitled, till authentic information shall be given to our government by the parties at war, and be thus communicated, with due certainty, to our citizens. You will be pleased to present to the government where you reside this proceeding of the President, as a proof of the earnest desire of the United States to preserve peace and friendship with all the belligerent powers, and to express his expectation that they will in return extend a scrupulous and effectual protection to all our citizens, wheresoever they may need it, in pursuing their lawful and peaceable concerns with their subjects, or within their jurisdiction. You will, at the same time, assure them that the most exact reciprocation of this benefit shall be practiced by us towards their subjects, in the like cases.—To MESSRS. MORRIS, PINCKNEY and SHORT. iii, 543. (Pa., April 26, 1793.)

5890. —— ——. I dare say you will have judged from the pusillanimity of the proclamation, from whose pen it came. A fear lest any affection [to France] should be discovered is distinguishable enough. This base fear will produce the very evil they wish to avoid. For our constituents, seeing that the government does not express their mind, perhaps rather leans the other way, are coming forward to express it themselves.—To JAMES MADISON. iii, 562. FORD ED., vi, 259. (Pa., May 1793.)

5891. —— ——. The proclamation as first proposed was to have been a declaration of neutrality. It was opposed on these grounds. 1. That a declaration of neutrality was a declaration there should be no war, to which the Executive was not competent. 2. That it would be better to hold back the declaration of neutrality, as a thing worth something to the powers at war; that they would bid for it, and we might reasonably ask a price, the *broadest privileges* of neutral nations. The first objection was so far respected as to avoid inserting the term *neutrality*, and the drawing the instrument was left to E. R. [Edmund Randolph]. —To JAMES MADISON. iii, 591. FORD ED., vi, 315. (1793.)

5892. —— ——. That there should be a proclamation was passed unanimously with the approbation or the acquiescence of all parties. Indeed, it was not expedient to oppose it altogether, lest it should prejudice what was the next question, the boldest and greatest that ever was hazarded, and which would have called for extremities had it prevailed.—To JAMES MADISON. iii, 591. FORD ED., vi, 316. (June 1793.)

5893. —— ——. You have most perfectly seized the *original* idea of the proclamation. When first proposed as a declaration of neutrality, it was opposed, first, because the Execu-

tive had no power to declare neutrality. Secondly, as such a declaration would be premature, and would lose us the benefit for which it might be bartered. It was urged that there was a strong impression in the minds of many that they were free to join in the hostilities on the side of France. Others were unapprised of the danger they would be exposed to in carrying contraband goods. It was, therefore, agreed that a proclamation should issue, declaring that we were in a state of peace with all the parties, admonishing the people to do nothing contravening it, and putting them on their guard as to contraband. On this ground it was accepted or acquiesced in by all [the cabinet], and E. R. [Edmund Randolph] who drew it, brought to me the draft, to let me see there was no such word as *neutrality* in it. Circumstances forbid other criticism. The public, however, soon took it up as a declaration of neutrality, and it came to be considered at length as such.—To JAMES MONROE. iv, 17. FORD ED., vi, 346. (Pa., 1793.)

5894. —— ——. "On the declaration of war between France and England, the United States being at peace with both, their situation was so new and unexperienced by themselves, that their citizens were not, in the first instant, sensible of the new duties resulting therefrom, and of the laws it would impose *even on their dispositions* towards the belligerent powers. Some of them imagined (and chiefly their transient sea-faring citizens) that they were free to indulge those dispositions, to take side with either party, and enrich themselves by depredations on the commerce of the other, and were meditating enterprises of this nature, as was said. In this state of the public mind, and before it should take an erroneous direction difficult to be set right, and dangerous to themselves and their country, the President thought it expedient, by way of Proclamation, * to remind our fellow-citizens that we were in a state of peace with all the belligerent powers; that in that state it was our duty neither to aid nor injure any; to exhort and warn them against acts which might contravene this duty, and particularly those of positive hostility, for the punishment of which the laws would be appealed to, and to put them on their guard also as to the risks they would run if they should attempt to carry articles of contraband to any. Very soon afterwards we learnt that Genet was undertaking the fitting and arming vessels in that port [Charleston], enlisting men, foreigners and citizens, and giving them commissions to commit hostilities against nations at peace with us; that these vessels were taking and bringing prizes into our ports; that the consuls of France were assuming to hold courts of admiralty on them, to try, condemn and authorize their sale as legal prizes, and all this before Mr. Genet had presented himself or his credentials to the President, before he was received by him, without his consent or consultation, and directly in contravention of the state of peace existing and declared to exist in the President's proclamation, and which it was incumbent on him to preserve till the constitutional au-

* In sending this explanation of the intention of the proclamation to Madison, Jefferson wrote: " Having occasion to state it (the intention, &c.) in a paper which I am preparing, I have done it in the following [above quoted] terms. Edmund Randolph called on me just as I had finished so far [within the quotation marks], and he said it presented fairly his view of the matter. He recalled to my mind that I had, at the time, opposed its being made a declaration of neutrality, on the ground that the Executive was not the competent authority for that, and, therefore, that it was agreed the instrument should be drawn with great care."—EDITOR.

thority should otherwise declare. These proceedings became immediately, as was naturally to be expected, the subject of complaint by the representative here of that power against whom they would chiefly operate." This was the true sense of the proclamation in the view of the draftsman and of the two signers; but H. [Hamilton] had other views. The instrument was badly drawn, and made the President go out of his line to declare things which, though true, it was not his province to declare. The instrument was communicated to me after it was drawn, but I was busy, and only ran an eye over it to see that it was not made a declaration of neutrality, and gave it back again, without, I believe, changing a tittle.—To JAMES MADISON. iv, 29. FORD ED., vi, 368. (Aug. 1793.)

5895. ——— ———. You will see a piece signed "Pacificus" [Alexander Hamilton] in defence of the proclamation. You will readily know the pen. I know it the more readily because it is an amplification only of the topics urged in discussing the question [in cabinet] when first proposed. The right of the *Executive* to declare that we are *not bound to execute the guarantee* [to France] was then advanced by him and denied by me. No other opinion was expressed on it. In this paper he repeats it, and even considers the proclamation as such a declaration; but if anybody intended it as such (except himself) they did not then say so. The passage beginning with the words, "the answer to this is," &c., is precisely the answer he gave at the time to my objection, that the Executive had no authority to issue a declaration of neutrality, nor to do more than declare the actual state of things to be that of peace. "For until the new government is acknowledged the treaties, &c., are, of course, suspended." This, also, is the sum of his arguments the same day on the great question which followed that of the proclamation, to wit, whether the Executive might not, and ought not to declare the [French] treaties suspended. * * * Upon the whole, my objections to the competence of the Executive to declare neutrality (that being understood to respect the future) were supposed to be got over by avoiding the use of that term. The declaration of the disposition of the United States can hardly be called illegal, though it was certainly officious and improper. The truth of the fact lent it some cover. My objections to the impolicy of a premature declaration were answered by such arguments as timidity would reasonably suggest. I now think it extremely possible that Hammond might have been instructed to have asked it, and to offer the *broadest neutral privileges*, as the price, which was exactly the price I wanted that we should contend for. But is it not a miserable thing that the three heresies I have quoted from this paper, should pass unnoticed and unanswered, as these certainly will, for none but mere bunglers and brawlers have for some time past taken the trouble to answer anything?—To JAMES MADISON. FORD ED., vi, 327. (June 1793.)

5896. ——— ———. The real milk and water views of the proclamation appeared to me to have been truly given in a piece published in the papers soon after [it was issued], and which I knew to be E. R.'s [Edmund Randolph's] from its exact coincidence with what he has expressed.—To JAMES MADISON. FORD ED., vi, 328. (1793.)

— NEW ENGLAND, Secession of.—See SECESSION.

5897. NEW HAMPSHIRE, Opinion in. —The public sentiment in New Hampshire is no longer progressive in any direction; * * * it is dead water.—To JAMES MADISON. FORD ED., vii, 343. (Pa., Feb. 1799.)

5898. NEW HAMPSHIRE, Republicanism in.—Although we have not yet got a majority into the fold of republicanism in your State, yet one long pull more will effect it, * * * unless it be true, as is sometimes said, that New Hampshire is but a satellite of Massachusetts. In this last State, the public sentiment seems to be under some influence additional to that of the clergy and lawyers. I suspect there must be a leaven of State pride at seeing itself deserted by the public opinion, and that their late popular song of "Rule New England" betrays one principle of their present variance from the Union. But I am in hopes they will in time discover that the shortest road to rule is to join the majority.—To JOHN LANGDON. FORD ED., viii, 161. (W., June 1802.)

— NEW HAVEN, Remonstrance.—See BISHOP.

5899. NEW JERSEY, Republicanism in.—Jersey is coming majestically round to the true principles.—To T. LOMAX. iv, 300. FORD ED., vii, 374. (M., March 1799.)

5900. NEW ORLEANS, Battle of.—I am glad we closed our war with the eclat of the action at New Orleans.—To MARQUIS LAFAYETTE. vi, 427. FORD ED., ix, 510. (M., 1815.)

5901. ——— ———. Peace was indeed desirable; yet it would not have been as welcome without the successes of New Orleans. These last have established truths too important not to be valued; that the people of Louisiana are sincerely attached to the Union; that their city can be defended; that the Western States make its defence their peculiar concern; that the militia are brave; that their deadly aim countervails the manœuvring skill of the enemy; that we have officers of natural genius now starting forward from the mass; and that putting together all our conflicts, we can beat the British by sea and by land, with equal numbers.—To GENERAL DEARBORN. vi, 450. (M., 1815.)

5902. ——— ———. The affair of New Orleans was fraught with useful lessons to ourselves, our enemies, and our friends, and will powerfully influence our future relations with the nations of Europe. It will show them we mean to take no part in their wars, and count no odds when engaged in our own.—To PRESIDENT MADISON. vi, 453. FORD ED., ix, 512. (M., 1815.)

5903. ——— ———. It may be thought that useless blood was spilt at New Orleans, after the treaty of peace had been actually signed. I think it had many valuable uses. It proved the fidelity of the Orleanese to the United States. It proved that New Orleans can be defended both by land and water; that the Western country will fly to its relief (of which ourselves had doubted before); that our militia are heroes when they have heroes to lead them on; and that, when unembarrassed by field evolutions, which they do not understand, their skill in the fire-arm, and deadly aim, give them advantage over regulars.—To W. H. CRAWFORD. vi, 420. FORD ED., ix, 504. (M., 1815.) See FEDERALISTS.

__ NEW ORLEANS, Batture Case.—See BATTURE.

5904. NEW ORLEANS, Right of deposit.—We state in general the necessity, not only of our having a port near the mouth of the river (without which we could make no use of the navigation at all) but of its being so well separated from the territories of Spain and her jurisdiction, as not to engender daily disputes and broils between us. It is certain, that if Spain were to retain any jurisdiction over our *entrepôt*, her officers would abuse that jurisdiction, and our people would abuse their privileges in it. Both parties must foresee this, and that it will end in war. Hence the necessity of a well-defined separation. Nature has decided what shall be the geography of that in the end, whatever it might be in the beginning, by cutting off from the adjacent countries of Florida and Louisiana, and enclosing between two of its channels, a long and narrow strip of land, called the Island of New Orleans. The idea of ceding this could not be hazarded to Spain, in the first step; it would be too disagreeable at first view; because this island, with its town, constitutes at present, their principal settlement in that part of their dominions, containing about ten thousand white inhabitants of every age and sex. Reason and events, however, may by little and little, familiarize them to it. That we have a right to some spot as an *entrepôt* for our commerce, may be at once affirmed. The expediency, too, may be expressed of so locating it as to cut off the source of future quarrels and wars. A disinterested eye, looking on a map, will remark how conveniently this tongue of land is formed for the purpose.— To WILLIAM SHORT. iii, 178. FORD ED., v, 219. (N.Y., 1790.)

5905. —— ——. Observe always, that to accept the navigation of the river without an *entrepôt* would be perfectly useless, and that an *entrepôt*, if trammelled, would be a certain instrument for bringing on war instead of preventing it.—To WILLIAM SHORT. iii, 228. FORD ED., v, 305. (Pa., 1791.)

5906. —— ——. To conclude the subject of navigation, each of the following conditions is to be considered by the Commissioners [to Spain] as a *sine quâ non*. 1. That our right be acknowledged of navigating the Mississippi in its whole breadth and length, from its source to the sea, as established by the treaty of 1763. 2. That neither the vessels, cargoes, or the persons on board, be stopped, visited, or subjected to the payment of any duty whatsoever; or, if a visit must be permitted, that it be under such restrictions as to produce the least possible inconvenience. But it should be altogether avoided, if possible, as the parent of perpetual broils. 3. That such conveniences be allowed us ashore, as may render our right of navigation practicable and under such regulations as may *bonâ fide* respect the preservation of peace and order alone, and may not have in object to embarrass our navigation, or raise a revenue on it. *—MISSISSIPPI RIVER INSTRUCTIONS. vii, 585. FORD ED., v, 475. (1792.)

* " The right of navigation (of the Mississippi) was conceded by the treaty of 1795, and with it a right to the free use of the port of New Orleans upon reasonably satisfactory terms for a period of three years, and thereafterward until some equally convenient harbor should be allotted. The credit of this ultimate achievement was Mr. Jefferson's, none the less because the treaty was not signed until he had retired from office. It was really his statesmanship which had secured it, not only in spite of the natural repugnance of Spain, but also in spite of the obstacles in-

5907. NEW ORLEANS, Suspension of right.—The suspension of the right of deposit at New Orleans, ceded to us by our treaty with Spain, threw our whole country into such a ferment as imminently threatened its peace. This, however, was believed to be the act of the Intendant, unauthorized by his government. But it showed the necessity of making effectual arrangements to secure the peace of the two countries against the indiscreet acts of subordinate agents.—To DUPONT DE NEMOURS. iv, 456. FORD ED., viii, 204. (W., Feb. 1803.)

5908. —— ——. The government of Spain has instantly redressed the infraction of treaty by her Intendant at New Orleans. * * * By a reasonable and peaceable process we have obtained in four months, what would have cost us seven years of war, 100,000 human lives, 100 millions of additional debt, besides ten hundred millions lost by the want of market for our produce, or depredations on it in seeking markets, and the general demoralizing of our citizens which war occasions.—To JOHN BACON. FORD ED., viii, 229. (W., April 1803.) See LOUISIANA and MISSISSIPPI RIVER NAVIGATION.

5909. NEW YORK, Politics of.—I have been much pleased to see a dawn of change in the spirit of your State [New York]. The late elections have indicated something, which, at a distance, we do not understand. However, what with the English influence in the lower, and the Patroon influence in the upper part of your State, I presume little is to be hoped.—To AARON BURR. iv, 186. FORD ED., vii, 147. (Pa., June 1797.)

5910. —— ——. New York is coming majestically round to the true principles.—To T. LOMAX. iv, 300. FORD ED., vii, 374. (M., March 1799.)

5911. NEW YORK CITY, Depravity in.—New York, like London. seems to be a cloacina of all the depravities of human nature. —To WILLIAM SHORT. vii, 310. (M., 1823.)

5912. NEW YORK CITY, Washington's defence.—The maxim laid down by Congress to their generals was that not a foot of territory was to be ceded to their enemies where there was a possibility of defending it. In consequence of these views, and against his own judgment, General Washington was obliged to fortify and attempt to defend the city of New York. But that could not be defended without occupying the heights on Long Island which commanded the city of New York. He was, therefore, obliged to establish a strong detachment in Long Island to defend those heights. The moment that detachment was routed, which he had much expected, his first object was to withdraw them, and his second to evacuate New York. He did this, therefore, immediately, and without waiting any movement of the enemy. He brought off his whole baggage, stores, and other implements, without leaving a single article except the very heaviest of his cannon, and things of little value. I well remember his letter to Congress, wherein he expressed his wonder that the enemy had given him this leisure, as, from the heights they had got possession of, they might have compelled him to a very precipitate retreat. This was one of the instances where our commanding officers

directly thrown in his way in the earlier stages by many persons in the United States, who privately gave the Spanish minister to understand that the country cared little about the Mississippi, and would not support the Secretary in his demands."— MORSE'S *Life of Jefferson.*

were obliged to conform to popular views, though they foresaw certain loss from it. Had he proposed at first to abandon New York, he might have been abandoned himself. An obedience to popular will cost us an army in Charleston in the year 1779.—NOTES ON M. SOULES'S WORK. ix, 298. FORD ED.. iv, 305. (P., 1786.)

5913. NEWS, Home.—But why has nobody else written to me? Is it that one is forgotten as soon as his back is turned? I have a better opinion of men. It must be either that they think that the details known to themselves are known to everybody, and so come to us through a thousand channels, or that we should set no value on them. Nothing can be more erroneous than both those opinions. We value those details, little and great, public and private, in proportion to our distance from our own country; and so far are they from getting to us through a thousand channels, that we hear no more of them or of our country here [Paris] than if we were among the dead.—To JAMES MONROE. FORD ED., iv, 45. (P., 1785.)

5914. ——— ———. It is unfortunate that most people think the occurrences passing daily under their eyes, are either known to all the world, or not worth being known. * * * I hope you will be so good as to continue your friendly information. The proceedings of our public bodies, the progress of the public mind on interesting questions, the casualities which happen among our private friends, and whatever is interesting to yourself and family, will always be anxiously received by me.—To JOHN PAGE. i, 549. FORD ED., iv, 212. (P., 1786.)

5915. ——— ———. I give you thanks for the details of small news contained in your letter. You know how precious that kind of information is to a person absent from his country, and how difficult it is to be procured. —To DAVID HUMPHREYS. iii, 13. FORD ED., v, 91. (P., 1789.)

5916. ——— ———. If there is any news stirring in town or country, such as deaths, courtships, or marriages, in the circle of my acquaintance, let me know it.—To JOHN PAGE. i. 183. FORD ED., i, 344. (F., 1762.)

5917. NEWS, Minor.—Details, political and literary, and even of the small history of our country, are the most pleasing communications possible.—To JOHN PAGE. i, 402. (P., 1785.)

5918. ——— ———. I pray you to write to me often. Do not turn politician too; but write me all the small news—the news about persons and about States; tell me who dies, that I may meet these disagreeable events in detail, and not all at once when I return (from France); who marry, who hang themselves because they cannot marry, &c.—To MRS. TRIST. i, 395. (P., 1785.)

5919. ——— ———. It is more difficult here [Paris] to get small than great news, because most of our correspondents in writing letters to cross the Atlantic, think they must always tread in buskins, so that half one's friends might be dead without its being ever spoken of here.—To DR. JAMES CURRIE. FORD ED., iv, 131. (P., 1786.)

5920. ——— ———. Nothing is so grateful to me, at this distance [Paris], as details, both great and small, of what is passing in my own country. * * * When one has been long absent from his neighborhood, the small news

of that is the most pleasing, and occupies his first attention.—To ARCHIBALD STUART. i, 517. FORD ED., iv, 187. (P., 1786.)

5921. NEWS, Useful.—The details from my own country of the proceedings of the legislative, executive and judiciary bodies, and even those which respect individuals only, are the most pleasing treat we can receive at this distance [Paris], and the most useful, also.—To JOSEPH JONES. i, 354. (P., 1785.)

5922. NEWSPAPERS, Abuses by.—The abuses of the freedom of the press here have been carried to a length never before known or borne by any civilized nation.—To M. PICTET. iv, 463. (W., 1803.)

5923. NEWSPAPERS, Advertisements.—We have been trying to get another weekly or half weekly paper set up [in Philadelphia], excluding advertisements, so that it might go through the States, and furnish a whig vehicle of intelligence. We hoped at one time to have persuaded Freneau to set up here. but failed. In the meantime, Bache's paper [The Advertiser] the principles of which were always republican, improves in its matter. If we can persuade him to throw all his advertisements on one leaf, by tearing that off, the leaf containing intelligence may be sent without overcharging the post, and generally taken instead of Fenno's.—To T. M. RANDOLPH. FORD ED., v, 336. (Pa., 1791.)

5924. NEWSPAPERS, Agitation by.—In the first moments of quietude which have succeeded the [Presidential] election, the printers seem to have aroused their lying faculties beyond their ordinary state, to reagitate the public mind. What appointments to office have they detailed which had never been thought of, merely to found a text for their calumniating commentaries.—To ELBRIDGE GERRY. iv, 392. FORD ED., viii, 43. (W., March 1801.)

5925. NEWSPAPERS, Attacks by.—I have been for some time used as the property of the newspapers, a fair mark for every man's dirt. Some, too. have indulged themselves in this exercise who would not have done it, had they known me otherwise than through these impure and injurious channels. It is hard treatment, and for a singular kind of offence, that of having obtained by the labors of a life the indulgent opinions of a part of one's fellow citizens. However, these moral evils must be submitted to, like the physical scourges of tempest, fire. &c.—To PEREGRINE FITZHUGH. iv, 216. FORD ED., vii, 208. (Pa., 1798.)

5926. ——— ———. Were I to undertake to answer the calumnies of the newspapers. it would be more than all my own time and that of twenty aids could effect. For while I should be answering one, twenty new ones would be invented. * * * But this is an injury to which duty requires every one to submit whom the public think proper to call into its councils.—To SAMUEL SMITH. iv, 255. FORD ED., vii, 279. (M., 1798.)

5927. —— ——. [I said to Colonel Burr] that as to the attack excited against him in the newspapers. I had noticed it but as the passing wind; that I had seen complaints that Cheetham, employed in publishing the laws, should be permitted to eat the public bread and abuse its second officer; * * * that these federal printers did not in the least intermit their abuse of me, though receiving emoluments from the government and that I have never thought it proper to interfere for myself, and consequently not in the case of the Vice-President.—THE ANAS. ix, 206. FORD ED., i, 302. (Jan. 1804.)

5928. —— ——. That tory printers should think it advantageous to identify me with that paper [The National Intelligencer], the Aurora, &c., in order to obtain ground for abusing me, is perhaps fair warfare. But that anyone who knows me should listen one moment to such an insinuation, is what I did not expect. I neither have, nor ever had, any more connection with those papers than our antipodes have; nor know what is to be in them until I see it in them, except proclamations and other documents sent for publication.—To THOMAS PAINE. iv, 582. FORD ED., viii, 361. (W., June 1805.)

5929. —— ——. I met the scurrilities of the newswriters without concern, while in pursuit of the great interests with which I was charged. But in my present retirement, no duty forbids my wish for quiet.—To J. B. COLVIN. v, 544. FORD ED., ix, 282. (M., 1810.)

5930. NEWSPAPERS, Banks and.— Notwithstanding the magnitude of this calamity [bank failures], every newspaper almost is silent on it, Frenau's excepted, in which you will see it mentioned.—To THOMAS MANN RANDOLPH. FORD ED., v, 510. (April 1792.)

5931. NEWSPAPERS, Caricatures.— Our newspapers for the most part, present only the caricatures of disaffected minds.— To M. PICTET. iv, 463. (W., 1803.)

5932. NEWSPAPERS, Classics vs.—I read one or two newspapers a week, but with reluctance give even that time from Tacitus and Horace, and so much other more agreeable reading.—To DAVID HOWELL. v, 555. (M., 1810.)

5933. —— ——. I have given up newspapers in exchange for Tacitus, and Thucydides, for Newton and Euclid, and I find myself much the happier.—To JOHN ADAMS. vi, 37. FORD ED., ix, 334. (M., 1812.)

5934. —— ——. I read but a single paper, and that hastily. I find Horace and Tacitus so much better writers than the champions of the gazettes, that I lay those down to take up these with great reluctance. —To JAMES MONROE. vii, 287. FORD ED., x, 256. (M., 1823.)

5935. NEWSPAPERS, Defamation.— Defamation is becoming a necessary of life; insomuch, that a dish of tea in morning or evening cannot be digested without this stimulant. Even those who do not believe these abominations, still read them with complacence to their auditors, and instead of the abhorrence and indignation which should fill a virtuous mind, betray a secret pleasure in the possibility that some may believe them, though they do not themselves.—To JOHN NORVELL. v. 93. FORD ED., ix, 74. (W., 1807.) See CALUMNY.

— NEWSPAPERS, Editors of.—See EDITORS.

5936. NEWSPAPERS, English.—The English papers are so incessantly repeating their lies about the tumults, the anarchy, the bankruptcies, and distresses of America, that these ideas prevail very generally in Europe. —To JAMES MONROE. i, 407. FORD ED., iv, 87. (P., 1785.)

5937. —— ——. The English papers— those infamous fountains of falsehood.—To F. HOPKINSON. ii, 204. (P., 1787.)

5938. NEWSPAPERS, Falsehoods.— The press is impotent when it abandons itself to falsehood.—To THOMAS SEYMOUR. v, 44. FORD ED., ix, 30. (W., 1807.)

5939. —— ——. Nothing can now be believed which is seen in a newspaper.—To JOHN NORVELL. v, 92. FORD ED., ix, 73. (W., 1807.)

5940. —— ——. Truth itself becomes suspicious by being put into that polluted vehicle.—To JOHN NORVELL. v, 92. FORD ED., ix, 73. (W., 1807.)

5941. —— ——. The real extent of the misinformation [in the newspapers] is known only to those who are in situations to confront facts within their knowledge with the lies of the day.—To JOHN NORVELL. v, 92. FORD ED., ix, 73. (W., 1807.)

5942. —— ——. The man who never looks into a newspaper is better informed than he who reads them; inasmuch as he who knows nothing is nearer to truth than he whose mind is filled with falsehoods and errors. He who reads nothing will still learn the great facts, and the details are all false. —To JOHN NORVELL. v, 92. FORD ED., ix, 73. (W., 1807.)

5943. —— ——. These texts of truth relieve me from the floating falsehoods of the public papers.—To PRESIDENT MONROE. vii, 160. FORD ED., x, 158. (M., 1820.) See LIES.

5944. NEWSPAPERS, Freedom of.— Considering the great importance to the public liberty of the freedom of the press, and the difficulty of submitting it to very precise rules, the laws have thought it less mischievous to give greater scope to its freedom than to the restraint of it. The President has, therefore, no authority to prevent publications of the nature of those you complain of.* —To THE SPANISH COMMISSIONERS. iv, 21 FORD ED., vi, 350. (Pa., 1793.)

* Attacks on the King of Spain—EDITOR.

5945. —— ——. No experiment can be more interesting than that we are now trying, and which we trust will end in establishing the fact, that man may be governed by reason and truth. Our first object should therefore be, to leave open to him all the avenues to truth. The most effectual hitherto found, is the freedom of the press. It is, therefore, the first shut up by those who fear the investigation of their actions.—To JUDGE TYLER. iv, 548. (W., 1804.)

5946. —— ——. The liberty of speaking and writing guards our other liberties.—REPLY TO ADDRESS. viii, 129. (1808.)

5947. —— ——. Where the press is free, and every man able to read, all is safe.—To CHARLES YANCEY. vi, 517. FORD ED., x, 4. (M., 1816.)

5948. —— ——. The only security of all is in a free press. The force of public opinion cannot be resisted, when permitted freely to be expressed. The agitation it produces must be submitted to. It is necessary to keep the waters pure.—To MARQUIS DE LAFAYETTE. vii, 325. FORD ED., x, 280. (M., 1823.) See PRESS, FREEDOM OF.

5949. NEWSPAPERS, Friends of Liberty.—Within the pale of truth, the press is a noble institution, equally the friend of science and of civil liberty.—To THOMAS SEYMOUR. v, 44. FORD ED., ix, 30. (W., 1807.)

5950. NEWSPAPERS, Government and.—The basis of our governments being the opinion of the people, the very first object should be to keep that right; and were it left to me to decide whether we should have a government without newspapers or newspapers without a government, I should not hesitate a moment to prefer the latter.—To EDWARD CARRINGTON. ii, 100. FORD ED., iv, 359. (P., 1787.)

5951. NEWSPAPERS, And history.—I really look with commiseration over the great body of my fellow citizens, who, reading newspapers, live and die in the belief, that they have known something of what has been passing in the world in their time; whereas the accounts they have read in newspapers are just as true a history of any other period of the world as of the present, except that the real names of the day are affixed to their fables.—To JOHN NORVELL. v, 92. FORD ED., ix, 73. (W., 1807.)

5952. NEWSPAPERS, Indifference to.—A truth now and then projecting into the ocean of newspaper lies, serves like headlands to correct our course. Indeed, my scepticism as to everything I see in a newspaper, makes me indifferent whether I ever see one.—To JAMES MONROE. vi, 407. FORD ED., ix, 496. (M., 1815.)

5953. —— ——. I have almost ceased to read newspapers. Mine remain in our post office a week or ten days, sometimes, unasked for. I find more amusement in studies to which I was always attached, and from which I was dragged by the events of the times in which I have happened to live.—To THOMAS LEIPER. vi, 466. FORD ED., ix, 521. (M., 1815.)

5954. NEWSPAPERS, Licentiousness of.—During this course of administration [first term] and in order to disturb it, the artillery of the press has been levelled against us, charged with whatsoever its licentiousness could devise or dare. These abuses of an institution so important to freedom and science, are deeply to be regretted, inasmuch as they tend to lessen its usefulness, and to sap its safety; they might, indeed, have been corrected by the wholesome punishments reserved and provided by the laws of the several States against falsehood and defamation; but public duties more urgent press on the time of public servants, and the offenders have therefore been left to find their punishment in the public indignation. Nor was it uninteresting to the world, that an experiment should be fairly and fully made, whether freedom of discussion, unaided by power, is not sufficient for the propagation and protection of truth—whether a government, conducting itself in the true spirit of its Constitution, with zeal and purity, and doing no act which it would be unwilling the world should witness, can be written down by falsehood and defamation. The experiment has been tried; you have witnessed the scene; our fellow-citizens looked on, cool and collected; they saw the latent source from which these outrages proceeded; they gathered around their public functionaries, and when the Constitution called them to the decision by suffrage, they pronounced their verdict, honorable to those who had served them, and consolatory to the friend of man, who believes he may be intrusted with his own affairs. No inference is here intended, that the laws, provided by the States against false and defamatory publications, should not be enforced; he who has time, renders a service to public morals and public tranquillity, in reforming these abuses by the salutary coercions of the law; but the experiment is noted, to prove that, since truth and reason have maintained their ground against false opinions in league with false facts, the press, confined to truth, needs no other legal restraint; the public judgment will correct false reasonings and opinions, on a full hearing of all parties; and no other definite line can be drawn between the inestimable liberty of the press and its demoralizing licentiousness. If there be still improprieties which this rule would not restrain, its supplement must be sought in the censorship of public opinion.*—SECOND INAUGURAL ADDRESS. viii, 43. FORD ED., viii, 346. (1805.)

5955. NEWSPAPERS, And light.—Our citizens may be deceived for awhile, and have been deceived; but as long as the presses can be protected, we may trust to them for light.—To ARCHIBALD STUART. FORD ED., vii, 378. (M., 1789.)

* This was Jefferson's reply to the severe attacks made on his first administration.—EDITOR.

5956. NEWSPAPERS, Mischief-makers.—The federal papers appear desirous of making mischief between us and England, by putting speeches into my mouth which I never uttered.—To ROBERT R. LIVINGSTON. v, 54. FORD ED., ix, 37. (W., 1807.)

5957. —— ——. That first of all human contrivances for generating war.—To MR. MAURY. vi, 469. (M., 1815.)

5958. NEWSPAPERS, Monarchical.—Fenno's [The United States Gazette] is a paper of pure toryism, disseminating the doctrines of monarchy, aristocracy, and the exclusion of the influence of the people. —To T. M. RANDOLPH. FORD ED., v, 336. (Pa., 1791.)

5959. NEWSPAPERS, Official.—You have seen too much of the conduct of the press in countries where it is free, to consider the gazettes as evidence of the sentiments of any part of the government; you have seen them bestow on the government itself, in all its parts, its full share of inculpation.—To GEORGE HAMMOND. iii, 331. FORD ED., v, 436. (Pa., 1792.)

5960. NEWSPAPERS, Political bulldogs.—The malignity with which political enemies torture every sentence from me into meanings imagined by their own wickedness only, justify my expressing a solicitude, that this * * * communication may in nowise be permitted to find its way into the public papers. Not fearing these political bulldogs, I yet avoid putting myself in the way of being baited by them, and do not wish to volunteer away that portion of tranquillity, which a firm execution of my duties will permit me to enjoy.—To JOHN NORVELL. v, 93. FORD ED., ix, 75. (W., 1807.)

5961. NEWSPAPERS, Postoffice and. —The expense of French postage is so enormous, that I have been obliged to desire that my newspapers, from the different States, may be sent to the office for Foreign Affairs at New York; and I have requested of Mr. Jay to have them always packed in a box and sent as merchandise.—To R. IZARD. i, 443. (P., 1785.)

5962. NEWSPAPERS, Power of.—Freneau's paper has saved our Constitution, which was galloping fast into monarchy, and has been checked by no means so powerfully as by that paper. It is well and universally known, that it has been that paper which has checked the career of the Monocrats.—THE ANAS. ix, 145. FORD ED., i, 231. (1793.)

5963. —— ——. These foreign and false citizens * * * possess our printing presses, a powerful engine in their government of us. —To ELBRIDGE GERRY. iv, 173. FORD ED., vii, 122. (Pa., 1797.)

5964. —— ——. This paper [The Aurora] has unquestionably rendered incalculable services to republicanism through all its struggles with the federalists, and has been the rallying point for the orthodoxy of the whole Union. It was our comfort in the gloomiest days, and is still performing the office of a watchful sentinel.—To DABNEY CARR. FORD ED., ix, 316. (M., 1811.)

5965. NEWSPAPERS, President and. —The Chief Magistrate cannot enter the arena of the newspapers.—To PRESIDENT MADISON. v, 601. FORD ED., ix, 326. (M., July 1811.)

5966. NEWSPAPERS, Principles of.—A paper which shall be governed by the spirit of Mr. Madison's celebrated report [on the Virginia Resolutions] cannot be false to the rights of all classes.—To H. LEE. vii, 376. FORD ED., x, 318. (M., 1824.)

5967. NEWSPAPERS, Prosecution of. —The federalists having failed in destroying the freedom of the press by their gag-law, seem to have attacked it in an opposite direction; that is by pushing its licentiousness and its lying to such a degree of prostitution as to deprive it of all credit. And the fact is that so abandoned are the tory presses in this particular, that even the least informed of the people have learned that nothing in a newspaper is to be believed. This is a dangerous state of things, and the press ought to be restored to its credibility if possible. The restraints provided by the laws of the States are sufficient for this, if applied. And I have, therefore, long thought that a few prosecutions of the most prominent offenders would have a wholesome effect in restoring the integrity of the presses. Not a general prosecution, for that would look like persecution; but a selected one.—To THOMAS McKEAN. FORD ED., viii, 218. (W., Feb. 1803.)

5968. NEWSPAPERS, Purifiers.—Newspapers serve to carry off noxious vapors and smoke.—To GENERAL KOSCIUSKO. iv, 431. (W., April 1802.)

5969. NEWSPAPERS, Reading of.—Reading the newspapers but little and that little but as the romance of the day, a word of truth now and then comes like the drop of water on the tongue of Dives.—To PRESIDENT MADISON. v, 442. FORD ED., ix, 251. (M., April 1809.)

5970. NEWSPAPERS, Reform by.—This formidable censor of the public functionaries, by arraigning them at the tribunal of public opinion, produces reform peaceably, which must otherwise be done by revolution. It is also the best instrument for enlightening the mind of man, and improving him as a rational, moral, and social being.—To M. CORAY. vii, 324. (M., 1823.)

5971. NEWSPAPERS, Reformation of. —Perhaps an editor might begin a reformation [of his newspaper] in some such way as this: Divide his paper into four chapters, heading the first "Truths"; the second, "Probabilities"; third, "Possibilities"; fourth, "Lies". The first chapter would be very short, as it would contain little more than authentic papers, and information from such sources, as the editor would be willing to risk his own reputation for their truth. The second would contain what, from a mature consideration of all circumstances, his judgment should conclude to be probably true. This, however, should rather contain too little than too much. The third and fourth should be professedly for those readers who would rather have lies for their money than the blank paper they would occupy.—To JOHN NORVELL. v, 92. FORD ED., ix, 74. (W., 1807.)

5972. NEWSPAPERS, Regulation of.— It is so difficult to draw a clear line of separation between the abuse and the wholesome use of the press, that as yet we have found it better to trust the public judgment, than the magistrate, with the discrimination between truth and falsehood.—To M. PICTET. iv, 463. (W., 1803.)

5973. NEWSPAPERS, Reliability of.— General facts may indeed be collected from the newspapers, such as that Europe is now at war, that Bonaparte has been a successful warrior, that he has subjugated a great portion of Europe to his will, &c., but no details can be relied on.—To JOHN NORVELL. v, 92. FORD ED., ix, 73. (W., 1807.)

5974. NEWSPAPERS, Responsibility for.— It is not he who prints, but he who pays for printing a slander, who is its real author. —To JOHN NORVELL. v, 93. FORD ED., ix, 74. (W., 1807.)

5975. NEWSPAPERS, Restraint on.— To your request of my opinion of the manner in which a newspaper should be conducted, so as to be most useful, I should answer: "By restraining it to true facts and sound principles only." Yet I fear such a paper would find few subscribers.—To JOHN NORVELL. v, 91. FORD ED., ix, 73. (W., 1807.)

5976. ———. The papers have lately advanced in boldness and flagitiousness beyond even themselves. Such daring and atrocious lies as fill the third and fourth columns of the third page of the United States Gazette of August 31st were never before, I believe, published with impunity in any country. However, I have from the beginning determined to submit myself as the subject on whom may be proved the impotency of a free press in a country like ours, against those who conduct themselves honestly and enter into no intrigue. I admit at the same time that restraining the press *to truth,* as the present laws do, is the only way of making it useful. But I have thought necessary first to prove it can never be dangerous.—To WILLIAM SHORT. v, 362. (M., Sep. 1808.)

5977. NEWSPAPERS, Rulers and.— It is the office of the rulers on both sides [United States and England] to rise above these vulgar vehicles of passion.—To MR. MAURY. vi, 469. (M., 1815.)

5978. NEWSPAPERS, Slanders in.— An editor [should] set his face against the

demoralizing practice of feeding the public mind habitually on slander, and the depravity of taste which this nauseous aliment induces. —To JOHN NORVELL. v, 93. FORD ED., ix, 74. (W., 1807.) See LIBELS and SLANDER.

5979. NEWSPAPERS, Support of.— Bache's paper and also Carey's totter for want of subscriptions. We should really exert ourselves to procure them, for if these papers fall, republicanism will be entirely browbeaten.*—To JAMES MADISON. iv, 237. FORD ED., vii, 245. (Pa., 1798.) See CALLENDER and DUANE.

5980. ———. The engine is the press. Every man must lay his purse and his pen under contribution.—To JAMES MADISON. iv, 281. FORD ED., vii, 344. (Pa., 1799.)

5981. NEWSPAPERS, Suppression of. —It is a melancholy truth, that a suppression of the press could not more completely deprive the nation of its benefits, than is done by its abandoned prostitution to falsehood.— To JOHN NORVELL. v, 92. FORD ED., ix, 73. (W., 1807.)

5982. NEWSPAPERS, Torture by.— I confide them [opinions on government] to your honor, so to use them as to preserve me from the gridiron of the public papers.— To SAMUEL KERCHIVAL. vii, 17. FORD ED., x, 44. (M., 1816.)

5983. NEWSPAPERS, Uncertain.— Newspaper information is too uncertain ground for the government to act on.—To JAMES MADISON. FORD ED., viii, 81. (M., 1801.)

5984. NEWSPAPERS, Vulgar.— I deplore with you the putrid state into which our newspapers have passed, and the malignity, the vulgarity, and mendacious spirit of those who write for them. * * * These ordures are rapidly depraving the public taste, and lessening its relish for sound food. As vehicles of information, and a curb on our functionaries, they have rendered themselves useless, by forfeiting all title to belief. This has in a great degree been produced by the violence and malignity of party spirit.—To DR. WALTER JONES. vi, 284. FORD ED., ix, 446. (M., Jan. 1814.)

5985. NEWSPAPERS, Weaned from.— I have never seen a Philadelphia paper since I left it, till those you enclosed me; and I feel myself so thoroughly weaned from the interest I took in the proceedings there, while there, that I have never had a wish to see one, and believe that I never shall take another newspaper of any sort. I find my mind totally absorbed in my rural occupations.—To JAMES MADISON. iv, 103. FORD ED., vi, 503. (M., April 1794.)

5986. NEWSPAPERS, Writing for.— I have preserved through life a resolution, set

* Of the two hundred newspapers then (1800) in the United States all but about twenty were enlisted by preference or patronage on the Federal side.—ALEXANDER H. STEPHENS *History of the United States,* p. 386.

in a very early part of it, never to write in a public paper without subscribing my name.—To EDMUND RANDOLPH. iii, 470. FORD ED., vi, 112. (M., 1792.)

5987. ———. From a very early period of my life, I had laid it down as a rule of conduct, never to write a word for the public papers. From this, I have never departed in a single instance; and on a late occasion, when all the world seemed to be writing, besides a rigid adherence to my own rule, I can say with truth, that not a line for the press was ever communicated to me, by any other, except a single petition referred for my correction; which I did not correct, however, though the contrary, as I have heard, was said in a public place, by one person through error, through malice by another [General Henry Lee].—To PRESIDENT WASHINGTON. iv, 142. FORD ED., vii, 82. (M., June 1796.)

5988. ———. At a very early period of my life, I determined never to put a sentence into any newspaper. I have religiously adhered to the resolution through my life, and have great reason to be contented with it.—To SAMUEL SMITH. iv, 255. FORD ED., vii, 279. (M., 1798.)

5989. ———. I pray that my letter may not go out of your own hands, lest it should get into the newspapers, a bear-garden scene into which I have made it a point to enter on no provocation.—To URIAH M'GREGORY. iv, 334. (M., 1800.)

5990. ———. I never in my life, directly or indirectly, wrote one sentence for a newspaper.—THE ANAS. ix, 199. FORD ED., i, 285. (1800.)

5991. NICE, Climate.—I find the climate of Nice quite as delightful as it has been represented. Hieres is the only place in France, which may be compared with it. The climates are equal.—To WILLIAM SHORT. ii, 137. (Ne., 1787.)

5992. NICHOLAS (W. C.), Character.—I have ascertained that on Mr. Nicholas no impression unfavorable to you was made by * * * [the removal of Secretary Robert Smith], and that his friendship for you has never felt a moment's abatement. Indeed we might have been sure of this from his integrity, his good sense, and his sound judgment of men and things.—To PRESIDENT MADISON. FORD ED., ix, 378. (M., Feb. 1813.)

5993. NICHOLAS (W. C.), French mission.—A last effort at friendly settlement with Spain is proposed to be made at Paris, and under the auspices of France. For this purpose, General Armstrong and Mr. Bowdoin (both now at Paris) have been appointed joint commissioners; but such a cloud of dissatisfaction rests on General Armstrong in the minds of many persons, * * * that we have in contemplation to add a third commissioner, in order to give the necessary measure of public confidence to the commission. Of these two gentlemen, one being of Massachusetts and one of New York, it is thought the third should be a southern man; and the rather, as the interests to be negotiated are almost entirely southern and western. * * * My wish is

that you may be willing to undertake it.*—To WILSON C. NICHOLAS. v, 3. FORD ED., viii, 434. (W., March 1806.)

— NICHOLAS (W. C.), Leadership in Congress.—See CONGRESS.

— NIGHTINGALES, Jefferson's delight in.—See BIRDS.

5994. NON-IMPORTATION, Efficacy of.—The most eligible means of effecting * * * the reestablishment of the constitutional rights of our fellow-subjects, will be to put an immediate stop to all imports from Great Britain * * * and to all exports thereto. * * * and immediately to discontinue all commercial intercourse with every part of the British Empire which shall not, in like manner, break off their commerce with Great Britain.†—RESOLUTION OF ALBEMARLE COUNTY. FORD ED., i, 419. (July 26, 1774.)

5995. ———. These measures [non-intercourse] should be pursued until a repeal be obtained of the act for blocking up the harbor of Boston; of the acts prohibiting or restraining internal manufactures in America; of the acts imposing on any commodities duties to be paid in America; and of the act laying restrictions on the American trade; and, on such repeal, it will be reasonable to grant to our brethren of Great Britain such privileges in commerce as may amply compensate their fraternal assistance, past and future.—RESOLUTION OF ALBEMARLE COUNTY. FORD ED., i, 419. (July 26, 1774.)

5996. ———. The idea seems to gain credit that the naval powers, combined against France, will prohibit supplies even of provisions to that country. Should this be formally notified, I should suppose Congress would be called, because it is a justifiable cause of war, and as the Executive cannot decide the question of war on the affirmative side, neither ought it to do so on the negative side, by preventing the competent body from deliberating on the question. But I should hope that war would not be their choice. I think it will furnish us a happy opportunity of setting another example to the world, by showing that nations may be brought to justice by appeals to their interests as well as by appeals to arms. I should hope that Congress, instead of a denunciation of war, would instantly exclude from our ports all the manufactures, produce, vessels, and subjects of the nations committing this aggression, during the continuance of the aggression, and till full satisfaction is made for it. This would work well in many ways, safely in all, and introduce between nations another umpire than arms. It would relieve us, too, from the risks and the horrors of cutting throats.—To JAMES MADISON. iii, 519. FORD ED., vi, 192. (March 1793.)

5997. NON-IMPORTATION, Popular.—I have never known a measure more universally desired by the people than the passage of the non-importation bill.—To JAMES MADISON. iv, 107. FORD ED., vi, 511. (M., May 1794.)

5998. ———. I love Mr. Clarke's proposition of cutting off all communication with the nation [Great Britain] which has con-

* Mr. Nicholas was prevented from accepting by business considerations.—EDITOR.
† Albemarle was Jefferson's native county. The date of putting the regulations into effect was October 1, 1775.—EDITOR.

ducted itself so atrociously. This may bring on war. If it does we will meet it like men; but it may not bring on war, and then the experiment will have been a happy one.—To TENCH COXE. iv, 105. FORD ED., vi, 508. (M., May 1794.)

5999. NON-IMPORTATION, Principle of.—To yield the principle of the non-importation act would be yielding the only peaceable instrument for coercing all our rights.— THE ANAS. FORD ED., i, 322. (Feb. 1807.)

6000. NON-IMPORTATION vs. IMPRESSMENTS.—If [the British] keep up impressments, we must adhere to non-intercourse, manufacturer's and a navigation act.— To JAMES MADISON. v, 362. FORD ED., ix, 208. (M., Sep. 1808.)

6001. NON-INTERCOURSE, Unpopular.—Our affairs are certainly now at their ultimate point of crisis. I understand the Eastern republicans will agree to nothing which shall render non-intercourse effectual, and that in any question of that kind, the federalists will have a majority. There remains, then, only war or submission, and if we adopt the former, they will desert us.—To W. C. NICHOLAS. v, 488. (M., Dec. 1809.)

— **NORFOLK.**—See ALEXANDRIA.

6002. NORTH CAROLINA, Political conditions in.—North Carolina is at present in the most dangerous state. The lawyers all tories, the people substantially republican, but uninformed and deceived by the lawyers, who are elected of necessity because few other candidates. The medicine for that State must be very mild and secretly administered. But nothing should be spared to give them true information.—To P. N. NICHOLAS. iv, 328. FORD ED., vii, 440. (Pa., April 1800.)

— **NORTH (Lord), Ability of.**—See GEORGE III., CONTROL OF.

6003. NORTH (Lord), Hostile to America.—Lord North's hostility to us is notorious.—To BENJAMIN HARRISON. FORD ED., iii, 414. (A., March 1784.)

6004. NORTH (Lord), Proposition of.— I was under appointment to attend the General Congress; but knowing the importance of the answer to be given to the Conciliatory Proposition, and that our leading whig characters were then in Congress, I determined to attend on the Assembly, and, though a young member, to take on myself the carrying through an answer to the Proposition. The Assembly met the 1st of June. I drew and proposed the answer, and carried it through the House with very little alteration, against the opposition of our timid members who wished to speak a different language. This was finished before the 11th of June, because on that day, I set out from Williamsburg to Philadelphia, and was the bearer of an authenticated copy of this instrument to Congress. The effect it had in fortifying their minds, and in deciding their measures, renders its true date important; because only Pennsylvania had as yet answered the Proposition. Virginia was the second. It was known how Massachusetts would answer it; and the example of these three principal Colonies would determine the measures of all the others, and of course the fate of the Proposition. Congress received it, therefore, with much satisfaction. The Assembly of Virginia did not deliver the answer to Lord Dunmore

till late in the session. They supposed it would bring on a dissolution of their body whenever they should deliver it to him; and they wished previously to get some important acts passed. For this reason they kept it up. I think Lord Dunmore did not quit the metropolis till he knew that the answer framed by the House was a rejection of the Proposition, though that answer was not yet communicated to him regularly.—NOTES ON M. SOULES'S WORK. ix, 302. FORD ED., iv, 309. (P., 1786.)

6005. ————. ————. On the receipt of Lord North's Proposition, in May or June, 1775, Lord Dunmore called the Assembly. Peyton Randolph, the President of Congress, and Speaker of the House of Burgesses, left the former body and came home to hold the Assembly, leaving in Congress the other delegates who were the ancient leaders of our House. He, therefore, asked me to prepare the answer to Lord North's Proposition, which I did. Mr. Nicholas, whose mind had as yet acquired no tone for that contest, combatted the answer from *alpha* to *omega*, and succeeded in diluting it in one or two small instances. It was firmly supported, however, in Committee of the Whole, by Peyton Randolph, who had brought with him the spirit of the body over which he had presided, and it was carried, with very little alteration, by strong majorities. I was the bearer of it myself to Congress, by whom, as it was the first answer given to the Proposition by any Legislature, it was received with peculiar satisfaction.— To WILLIAM WIRT. vi, 487. FORD ED., ix 475. (M., 1815.)

— **NORTHWEST BOUNDARY.**—See BOUNDARIES.

6006. NOTES ON VIRGINIA, History of.—Before I had left America, that is to say, in the year 1781, I had received a letter from M. de Marbois, of the French legation in Philadelphia, informing me that he had been instructed by his government to obtain such statistical accounts of the different States of our Union, as might be useful for their information; and addressing to me a number of queries relative to the State of Virginia. I had always made it a practice, whenever an opportunity occurred, of obtaining any information of our country which might be of use to me in any station, public or private, to commit it to writing. These memoranda were on loose papers, bundled up without order, and difficult of recurrence, when I had occasion for a particular one. I thought this a good occasion to embody their substance, which I did in the order of M. Marbois's queries, so as to answer his wish, and to arrange them for my own use. Some friends, to whom they were occasionally communicated, wished for copies; but their volume rendering this too laborious by hand, I proposed to get a few printed for their gratification. I was asked such a price, however, as exceeded the importance of the object. On my arrival at Paris, I found it could be done for a fourth of what I had been asked here. I, therefore, corrected and enlarged them, and had two hundred copies printed, under the title of "Notes on Virginia". I gave a very few copies to some particular persons in Europe, and sent the rest to my friends in America. An European copy, by the death of the owner, got into the hands of a bookseller, who engaged its translation, and, when ready for the press, communicated his intentions and manuscript to me, suggesting that I should correct it without asking any other permission for the publication. I never had seen so wretched an attempt at translation. Interverted, abridged, mutilated, and often reversing the sense of the original, I found it a blotch of errors from beginning to end. I corrected some of the most material, and, in that form, it was printed in French. A London bookseller, on seeing the translation, requested me to permit him to print the English original. I thought it best to do so, to let the world see that it was not really so bad as the French translation had made it appear. And this is the true history of that publication.—AUTOBIOGRAPHY. i, 61. FORD ED., i, 85. (1821.)

6007. NOTES ON VIRGINIA, Principles in.—The experience of nearly forty years additional in the affairs of mankind has not altered a single principle [in the " Notes on Virginia "].—To JOHN MELISH. vi, 404. FORD ED., iii, 79. (M., 1814.)

6008. NOTES ON VIRGINIA, Slavery and.—I had two hundred copies [of my " Notes on Virginia "] printed, but do not put them out of my own hands, except two or three copies here and two which I shall send to America, to yourself and Colonel Monroe. * * * I beg you to peruse it carefully, because I ask your advice on it, and ask nobody's else. I wish to put it into the hands of the young men at the College [William and Mary,] as well on account of the political as the physical parts. But there are sentiments on some subjects which I apprehend might be displeasing to the country, perhaps to the Assembly, or to some who lead it. I do not wish to be exposed to their censure; nor do I know how far their influence, if exerted, might effect a misapplication of law to such a publication were it made. Communicate it, then, in confidence to those whose judgments and information you would pay respect to; and if you think it will give no offense, I will send a copy to each of the students of William and Mary College, and some others to my friends and to your disposal; otherwise I shall send over only a very few copies to particular friends in confidence and burn the rest. Answer me soon and without reserve. Do not view me as an author, and attached to what he has written. I am neither. They were at first intended only for Marbois. When I had enlarged them, I thought first of giving copies to three or four friends. I have since supposed they might set our young students into a useful train of thought, and in no event do I propose to admit them to go to the public at large.—To JAMES MADISON. FORD ED., iv, 46. (P., May 1785.)

6009. ———— ————. I send you a copy of the " Notes on Virginia ". * * * I have taken measures to prevent its publication. My reason is that I fear the terms in which I speak of slavery and of our [State] Constitution may produce an irritation, which will revolt the minds of our countrymen against reformation in these two articles, and thus do more harm than good.—To JAMES MONROE. i, 347. FORD ED., iv, 53. (P., 1785.)

6010. NOVA SCOTIA, Conciliation of.—Is it impossible to persuade our countrymen to make peace with the Nova Scotians? I am persuaded nothing is wanting but advances on our part; and that it is in our power to draw off the greatest proportion of that settlement, and thus to free ourselves from rivals [in the fisheries] who may become of consequence. We are at present cooperating with Great Britain, whose policy it is to give aliment to that bitter enmity between her States and ours, which may secure her against their ever joining us. But would not the existence of a cordial friendship between us and them, be the best bridle we could possibly put into the mouth of England?—To JOHN ADAMS. i, 488. (P., 1785.)

—— NOVELS, Good and bad.—See FICTION.

6011. NULLIFICATION, British statutes.—We do not point out to his Majesty the injustice of these acts [of Parliament], with intent to rest on that principle the cause of their nullity; but to show that experience confirms the propriety of those political principles which exempt us from the jurisdiction of the British Parliament. The true ground on which we declare these acts void is, that the British Parliament has no right to exercise authority over us.—RIGHTS OF BRITISH AMERICA. i, 129. FORD ED., i, 434. (P.F., 1774.)

6012. NULLIFICATION, States and.—Every State has a natural right in cases not within the compact (*casus non foederis*), to nullify of their own authority all assumptions of power by others within their limits. Without this right they would be under the dominion, absolute and unlimited, of whosoever might exercise this right of judgment for them.—KENTUCKY RESOLUTIONS. ix, 469. FORD ED., vii, 301. (1798.)

6013. ———— ————. Where powers are assumed which have not been delegated, a nullification of the act is the rightful remedy.—KENTUCKY RESOLUTIONS. ix, 469. FORD ED., vii, 301. (1798.)

6014. OATH, Against tyranny.—I have sworn upon the altar of God eternal hostility against every form of tyranny over the mind of man.—To DR. BENJAMIN RUSH. iv, 336. FORD ED., vii, 460. (M., 1800.)

6015. OATH OF OFFICE, Presidential.—I propose to take the oath or oaths of office as President of the United States, on Wednesday the 4th inst., at 12 o'clock, in the Senate chamber. May I hope the favor of your attendance to administer the oath? As the two Houses have notice of the hour, I presume a precise punctuality to it will be expected from me. I would pray you, in the meantime, to consider whether the oath prescribed in the Constitution be not the only one necessary to take? It seems to comprehend the substance of that prescribed by the act of Congress to all officers, and it may be questionable whether the Legislature can require any new oath from the President. I do not know what has been done in this heretofore; but I presume the oaths administered to my predecessors are recorded in the Secretary of State's office.—To JOHN MARSHALL. iv, 364. (W., March 2, 1801.)

6016. OBSCURITY, Happiness in.—He is happiest of whom the world says least, good or bad.—To JOHN ADAMS. FORD ED., iv, 297. (P., 1786.)

6017. OCCUPATIONS, Agricultural.—The class principally defective is that of Agriculture. It is the first in utility, and ought to be the first in respect. The same artificial means which have been used to produce a competition in learning, may be equally successful in restoring agriculture to its primary dignity in the eyes of men. It is a science of the very first order. It counts among its handmaids the most respectable sciences, such as Chemistry, Natural Philosophy, Mechanics,

Mathematics, generally, Natural History, Botany. In every college and university, a professorship of agriculture, and the class of its students, might be honored as the first. Young men closing their academical education with this, as the crown of all other sciences, fascinated with its solid charms, and at a time when they are to choose an occupation, instead of crowding the other classes, would return to the farms of their fathers, their own, or those of others, and replenish and invigorate a calling now languishing under contempt and oppression. The charitable schools, instead of storing their pupils with a love which the present state of society does not call for, converted into schools of agriculture, might restore them to that branch qualified to enrich and honor themselves, and to increase the productions of the nation instead of consuming them. An abolition of the useless offices, so much accumulated in all governments, might close this drain also from the labors of the field, and lessen the burthens imposed on them. By these, and the better means which will occur to others, the surcharge of the learned, might in time be drawn off to recruit the laboring class of citizens, the sum of industry be increased, and that of misery diminished.—To DAVID WILLIAMS. iv, 513. (W., 1803.)

6018. OCCUPATIONS, Choice of.— Every one has a natural right to choose that vocation in life which he thinks most likely to give him comfortable subsistence.—THOUGHTS ON LOTTERIES. ix, 505. FORD ED., x, 366. (M., Feb. 1826.)

6019. OCCUPATIONS, Governmental regulation.—The greatest evils of populous society have ever appeared to me to spring from the vicious distribution of its members among the occupations called for. I have no doubt that those nations are essentially right, which leave this to individual choice, as a better guide to an advantageous distribution than any other which could be devised. But when, by a blind concourse, particular occupations are ruinously overcharged, and others left in want of hands, the national authorities can do much towards restoring the equilibrium.—To DAVID WILLIAMS. iv, 512. (W., 1803.)

6020. OCCUPATIONS OF IMMIGRANTS.—Among the ancients, the redundance of population was sometimes checked by exposing infants. To the moderns, America has offered a more humane resource. Many, who cannot find employment in Europe, accordingly come here. Those who can labor, do well for the most part. Of the learned class of emigrants, a small proportion find employments analogous to their talents. But many fail, and return to complete their course of misery in the scenes where it began.—To DAVID WILLIAMS. iv, 514. (W., 1803.)

6021. OCEAN, American supremacy.— The day is within my time as well as yours, when we may say by what laws other nations shall treat us on the sea. And we will say it. —To WILLIAM SHORT. iv, 415. FORD ED., viii, 98. (W., 1801.) See NAVY.

6022. ——— ———. The possession of Louisiana will cost France * * * a war which will annihilate her on the ocean, and place that element under the despotism of two nations, which I am not reconciled to the more because my own would be one of them. —To M. DUPONT DE NEMOURS. iv, 435. (W., April 1802.)

6023. OCEAN, Barrier of liberty.—I am happy in contemplating the peace, prosperity, liberty and safety of my country, and especially the wide ocean, the barrier of all these.—To MARQUIS LAFAYETTE. FORD ED., ix, 302. (M., 1811.)

6024. OCEAN, Claimed by England.—I despair of accommodation with [the British government], because I believe they are weak enough to intend seriously to claim the ocean as their conquest, and think to amuse us with embassies and negotiations, until the claim shall have been strengthened by time and exercise, and the moment arrive when they may boldly avow what hitherto they have only squinted at.—To PRESIDENT MADISON. v, 468. (M., Sep. 1809.)

6025. ——— ———. It has now been some years that I am perfectly satisfied that Great Britain's intentions have been to claim the ocean as her conquest, and prohibit any vessel from navigating it but on such a tribute as may enable her to keep up such a standing navy as will maintain her dominion over it. She has hauled in, or let herself out, been bold or hesitating, according to occurrences, but has in no situation done anything which might amount to a relinquishment of her intentions.—To HENRY DEARBORN. v, 529. FORD ED., ix, 278. (M., 1810.)

6026. ——— ———. It can no longer be doubted that Great Britain means to claim the ocean as her conquest, and to suffer not even a cock-boat, as they express it, to traverse it but on paying them a transit duty to support the very fleet which is to keep the nations under tribute, and to rivet the yoke around their necks. Although their government has never openly avowed this, yet their orders of council, in their original form, were founded on this principle, and I have observed for years past, that however ill success may at times have induced them to amuse by negotiation, they have never on any occasion dropped a word disclaiming this pretension, nor one which they would have to retract when they shall judge the times ripe for openly asserting it. * * * They do not wish war with us, but will meet it rather than relinquish their purpose.—To JOHN HOLLINS. v, 597. (M., May 1811.)

6027. ——— ———. The intention which the British now formally avow of taking possession of the ocean as their exclusive domain, and of suffering no commerce on it but through their ports, makes it the interest of all mankind to contribute their efforts to bring such usurpations to an end.—To CLEMENT CAINE. vi, 14. FORD ED., ix, 330. (M., Sep. 1811.)

6028. ——— ———. Ever since the rupture of the treaty of Amiens, the object of Great Britain has visibly been the permanent conquest of the ocean, and levying a tribute on every vessel she permits to sail on it, as the Barbary powers do on the Mediterranean, which they call their sea.—To WILLIAM SHORT. vi, 128. (M., June 1813.) See EMBARGO and IMPRESSMENT.

6029. OCEAN, Common birthright.— The ocean, like the air, is the common birthright of mankind.—R. TO A. N. Y. TAMMANY SOCIETY. viii, 127. (1808.)

6030. OCEAN, Common property.— The ocean is the common property of all.—FOREIGN COMMERCE REPORT. vii, 647. FORD ED., vi, 481. (1793.)

6031. —— ——. Nature has not subjected the ocean to the jurisdiction of any particular nation, but has made it common to all for the purposes to which it is fitted.—To ROBERT R. LIVINGSTON. iv, 409. FORD ED., viii, 89. (M., Sep. 1801.)

6032. OCEAN, Dominion of.— I fear the dominion of the sea is the insanity of the nation itself.—To HENRY DEARBORN. v, 608. (P.F., Aug. 1811.)

6033. OCEAN, England's policy.— If the British ministry are changing their policy towards us, it is because their nation, or rather the city of London, which is the nation to them, is shaking as usual, by the late reverses in Spain. I have for some time been persuaded that the government of England was systematically decided to claim a dominion of the sea, and to levy contributions on all nations, by their licenses to navigate, in order to maintain that dominion to which their own resources are inadequate. The mobs of their cities are unprincipled enough to support this policy in prosperous times, but change with the tide of fortune, and the ministers to keep their places, change with them.—To PRESIDENT MADISON. v, 442. FORD ED., ix, 251. (M., April 1809.) See ENGLAND.

6034. OCEAN, English ascendency.— An English ascendency on the ocean is safer for us than that of France.—To JAMES MONROE. v, 12. FORD ED., viii, 450. (W., 1806.)

6035. OCEAN, Freedom of.— I join you * * * in a sense of the necessity of restoring freedom to the ocean. But I doubt, with you, whether the United States ought to join in an armed confederacy for that purpose; or rather I am satisfied they ought not. It ought to be the very first object of our pursuits to have nothing to do with the European interests and politics. Let them be free or slaves at will, navigators or agriculturists, swallowed into one government or divided into a thousand, we have nothing to fear from them in any form. * * * To take part in their conflicts would be to divert our energies from creation to destruction. Our commerce is so valuable to them that they will be glad to purchase it when the only price we ask is to do us justice. I believe we have in our own hands the means of peaceable coercion; and that the moment they see our government so united as that they can make use of it, they will for their own interest be disposed to do us justice. In this way you shall not be obliged by any

treaty of confederation to go to war for injuries done to others.—To DR. GEORGE LOGAN. FORD ED., viii, 23. (W., March 1801.) See NAVIGATION and SHIPS.

6036. OCEAN, Lawlessness on.— The sea has become a field of lawless and indiscriminate rapine and violence.—To ——. iv, 223. (Pa., 1798.)

6037. OCEAN, Piracy.— I sincerely wish the British orders may be repealed. If they are it will be because the nation will not otherwise let the ministers keep their places. Their object has unquestionably been fixed to establish the Algerine system, and to maintain their possession of the ocean by a system of piracy against all nations.—To COLONEL LARKIN SMITH. v, 441. (M., April 1809.) See BARBARY STATES, MOROCCO and PIRACY.

6038. OCEAN, Usurpation of.— The usurpation of the sea has become a national disease.—To W. A. BURWELL. v, 5. (P.F., Aug. 1811.)

6039. OFFICE, Appointment to.— I like as little as you do to have the gift of appointments. I hope Congress will not transfer the appointment of their consuls to their ministers.—To JOHN ADAMS. i, 502. (P., 1785.)

6040. —— ——. Every office becoming vacant, every appointment made. *me donne un ingrat, et cent ennemis.*—To JOHN DICKINSON. v, 31. FORD ED., ix, 10. (W., 1807.)

6041. —— ——. I know none but public motives in making appointments.—To JOSEPH B. VARNUM. v, 223. (W., 1807.)

6042. —— ——. I am thankful at all times for information on the subject of appointments, even when it comes too late to be used. It is more difficult and more painful than all the other duties of my office, and one in which I am sufficiently conscious that involuntary error must often be committed.—To JOSEPH B. VARNUM. v, 223. (W., 1807.)

6043. —— ——. My usage is to make the best appointment my information and judgment enable me to do, and then fold myself up in the mantle of conscience, and abide unmoved the peltings of the storm. And oh! for the day when I shall be withdrawn from it; when I shall have leisure to enjoy my family, my friends, my farm and books.—To DR. BENJAMIN RUSH. v, 225. (W., 1808.)

6044. —— ——. I shall make no new appointments which can be deferred until the 4th of March, thinking it fair to leave to my successor to select the agents for his own administration.—To DR. LOGAN. v, 404. (W., Dec. 1808.) See OFFICE-HOLDERS.

6045. OFFICE, Choice of.— It is not for an individual to choose his post. You are to marshal us as may be best for the public good.—To PRESIDENT WASHINGTON. iii, 125. FORD ED., v, 141. (Dec. 1789.)

6046. ——. A good citizen should take his stand where the public authority marshals him.—To LA DUCHESSE D'AUVILLE. iii, 135. FORD ED., v, 153. (N.Y., 1790.)

6047. ——. I never thought of questioning the free exercise of the right of my fellow citizens, to marshal those whom they call into their service according to their fitness, nor ever presumed that they were not the best judges of that.—To JAMES SULLIVAN. iv, 168. FORD ED., vii, 116. (M., 1797.)

6048. ——. I profess so much of the Roman principle, as to deem it honorable for the general of yesterday to act as a corporal to-day, if his services can be useful to his country; holding that to be false pride, which postpones the public good to any private or personal considerations.—To WILLIAM DUANE. vi, 80. FORD ED., ix, 367. (M., Oct. 1812.)

6049. OFFICE, Claims to.—In appointments to public offices of mere profit, I have ever considered faithful service in either our first or second* revolution as giving preference of claim, and that appointments on that principle would gratify the public, and strengthen confidence so necessary to enable the Executive to direct the whole public force to the best advantage of the nation.— To JOHN PAGE. v, 135. FORD ED., ix, 117. (W., July 1807.)

6050. OFFICE, Declination of.—Whether the State may command the political services of all its members to an indefinite extent, or, if these be among the rights never wholly ceded to the public power, is a question which I do not find expressly decided in England. Obiter dictums on the subject I have indeed met with, but the complexion of the times in which these have dropped would generally answer them; besides that, this species of authority is not acknowledged in our profession. In this country, however, since the present government has been established, the point has been settled by uniform, pointed and multiplied precedents. Offices of every kind, and given by every power, have been daily and hourly declined and resigned from the Declaration of Independence to this moment. The General Assembly has accepted these without discrimination of office, and without ever questioning them in point of right. If the difference between the office of a delegate and any other could ever have been supposed, yet in the case of Mr. Thompson Mason, who declined the office of delegate, and was permitted so to do by the House, that supposition has been proved to be groundless. But, indeed, no such distinction of offices can be admitted. Reason, and the opinions of the lawyers, putting all on a footing as to this question, and so giving to the delegate the aid of all the precedents of the refusal of other offices. The law then does not warrant the assumption of such a power by the State

* The political revolution of 1800.—EDITOR.

over its members. For if it does, where is that law? nor yet does reason. For though I will admit that this does subject every individual, if called on, to an equal tour of political duty, yet it never can go so far as to submit to it his whole existence. If we are made in some degree for others, yet in a greater, are we made for ourselves. It were contrary to feeling and, indeed, ridiculous to suppose that a man had less right in himself than one of his neighbors, or indeed, all of them put together. This would be slavery, and not that liberty which the bill of rights [of Virginia] has made inviolable, and for the preservation of which our government has been charged. Nothing could so completely divest us of that liberty as the establishment of the opinion, that the State has a *perpetual* right to the services of all its members. This, to men of certain ways of thinking, would be to annihilate the blessing of existence, and to contradict the Giver of life, who gave it for happiness and not for wretchedness. And certainly, to such it were better that they had never been born.—To JAMES MONROE. i, 318. FORD ED., iii, 57. (M., 1782.)

6051. ——. Though I will admit that * * * reason does subject every individual, if called on, to an equal tour of political duty, yet it never can go so far as to submit to it his whole existence.—To JAMES MONROE. i, 319. FORD ED., iii, 58. (M., 1782.)

6052. OFFICE, Desire for.—No man ever had less desire of entering into public offices than myself.—THE ANAS. ix, 102. FORD ED., i, 175. (1792.)

6053. OFFICE, Distribution.—Should distributive justice give preference to a successor of the same State with the deceased. I take the liberty of suggesting to you Mr. Hayward.—To PRESIDENT WASHINGTON. iii, 249. FORD ED., v, 322. (Pa., 1791.)

6054. OFFICE, A duty.—To my fellow-citizens the debt of service has been fully and faithfully paid. I acknowledge that such a debt exists, that a tour of duty, in whatever line he can be most useful to his country, is due from every individual. It is not easy perhaps to say of what length exactly this tour should be, but we may safely say of what length it should not be. Not of our whole life, for instance, for that would be to be born a slave,—not even of a very large portion of it. I have now been in the public service four and twenty years; one half of which has been spent in total occupation with their affairs, and absence from my own. I have served my tour then.—To JAMES MADISON. iii, 577. FORD ED., vi, 290. (June 1793.)

6055. ——. The duties of office are a corvée which must be undertaken on far other considerations than those of personal happiness.—To GENERAL ARMSTRONG. vi, 103. (M., 1813.)

6056. OFFICE, Exclusion from.—The republicans have been excluded from all offices from the first origin of the division into republican and federalist. They have a reasonable claim to vacancies till they occupy their due share.—To DR. B. S. BARTON. iv, 353. FORD ED., vii, 489. (W., Feb. 1801.)

6057. ——— ———. Exercising that discretion which the Constitution has confided to me in the choice of public agents, I have been sensible, on the one hand, of the justice due to those who have been systematically excluded from the service of their country, and attentive, on the other, to restore justice in such a way as might least affect the sympathies and the tranquillity of the public mind. —To WILLIAM JUDD. viii, 114. (Nov. 1802.)

6058. OFFICE, Good behavior.—In the office to which I have been called [Secretaryship of State] all was full, and I could not in any case think it just to turn out those in possession who have behaved well, merely to put others in.—To FRANCIS WILLIS. FORD ED., v, 157. (N.Y., 1790.)

6059. ——— ———. There are no offices in my gift [as Secretary of State] but of mere scribes in the office room at $800 and $500 a year. These I found all filled, and of long possession in the hands of those who held them, and I thought it would not be just to remove persons in possession, who had behaved well, to make places for others.—To COLONEL HENRY LEE. FORD ED., v, 163. (N. Y., 1790.)

6060. OFFICE, Happiness and.—Were happiness the only legitimate object, the public councils would be deserted. That corvée once performed, however, the independent happiness of domestic life may rightfully be sought and enjoyed.—To JOHN T. MASON. FORD ED., ix, 476. (M., 1814.)

6061. OFFICE, Life appointments to. —Appointments in the nature of freehold render it difficult to undo what is done.—To JAMES MADISON. iv, 344. FORD ED., vii, 474. (W., Dec. 1800.)

6062. OFFICE, Motives for holding.—I have no motive to public service but the public satisfaction.—To PRESIDENT WASHINGTON. iii, 124. FORD ED., v, 140. (Dec. 1789.)

6063. OFFICE, Poisonous.—We have put down the great mass of offices which gave such patronage to the President. These had been so numerous, that presenting themselves to the public eye at all times and places, office began to be looked to as a resource for every man whose affairs were getting into derangement, or who was too indolent to pursue his profession, and for young men just entering into life. In short, it was poisoning the very source of industry, by presenting an easier resource for a livelihood, and was corrupting the principles of the great mass of those who passed a wishful eye on office. —To THOMAS McKEAN. FORD ED., viii, 217. (W., Feb. 1803.)

6064. OFFICE, Poverty and.—There is not, and has not been, a single vacant office

at my disposal. Nor would I, as your friend, ever think of putting you into the petty clerkships in the several offices, where you would have to drudge through life for a miserable pittance, without a hope of bettering your situation.—To JOHN GARLAND JEFFERSON. FORD ED., v, 180. (N.Y., 1790.)

6065. OFFICE, Private advantage.— Public employment contributes neither to advantage nor happiness. It is but honorable exile from one's family and affairs.—To FRANCIS WILLIS. FORD ED., v, 157. (N.Y., 1790.)

6066. OFFICE, Profits in.—I love to see honest and honorable men at the helm, men who will not bend their politics to their purses, nor pursue measures by which they may profit, and then profit by their measures. —To EDWARD RUTLEDGE. iv, 153. FORD ED., vii, 95. (M., 1796.)

6067. OFFICE, Refusing.—We find it of advantage to the public to ask of those to whom appointments are proposed, if they are not accepted, to say nothing of the offer, at least for a convenient time. The refusal cheapens the estimation of the public appointments, and renders them less acceptable to those to whom they are secondarily proposed. —To GENERAL JOHN ARMSTRONG. FORD ED., viii, 302. (W., 1804.)

6068. OFFICE, Sale of.—These exercises [by Parliament] of usurped power* have not been confined to instances alone in which themselves were interested, but they have also intermeddled with the regulation of the internal affairs of the Colonies. The act of the 9th of June for establishing a Post Office in America seems to have had little connection with British convenience, except that of accommodating his Majesty's ministers and favorites with the sale of an easy and lucrative office.—RIGHTS OF BRITISH AMERICA. i, 130. FORD ED., i, 434. (1774.)

6069. OFFICE, Seekers of.—Whenever a man has cast a longing eye on offices, a rottenness begins in his conduct.—To TENCH COXE. FORD ED., vii, 381. (M., 1799.)

6070. OFFICE, Solicitation.—With respect to the young gentlemen in the office of foreign affairs, their possession and your recommendation are the strongest titles. But I suppose the ordinance establishing my office allows but one assistant; and I should be wanting in candor to you and them, were I not to tell you that another candidate has been proposed to me, on ground that cannot but command respect.—To CHIEF JUSTICE JAY. iii, 127. FORD ED., v, 144. (M., 1790.)

6071. OFFICE, Talents and.—Talents and science are sufficient motives with me in appointments to which they are fitted.—To PRESIDENT WASHINGTON. iii, 466. FORD ED., vi, 107. (M., 1792.)

6072. OFFICE, Training for.—For promoting the public happiness, those persons,

* Over manufactures, exports and imports, &c.—EDITOR.

whom nature has endowed with genius and virtue, should be rendered by liberal education worthy to receive, and able to guard the sacred deposit of the rights and liberties of their fellow citizens; and they should be called to that charge without regard to wealth, birth, or other accidental condition or circumstance.—DIFFUSION OF KNOWLEDGE BILL. FORD ED., ii, 221. (1779.)

6073. OFFICE, Unprincipled men and.—An unprincipled man, let his other fitnesses be what they will, ought never to be employed.—To DR. GILMER. iv, 5. FORD ED., vi, 325. (Pa., 1793.)

6074. OFFICE, Weariness of.—I must yet a little while bear up against my weariness of public office.—To T. M. RANDOLPH. FORD ED., v, 417. (Pa., Jan. 1792.)

6075. OFFICES, Administration of.—Nothing presents such difficulties of administration as offices.—To GIDEON GRANGER. FORD ED., viii, 44. (W., March 1801.)

6076. —— ——. To you I need not make the observation that of all the duties imposed on the executive head of a government, appointment to office is the most difficult and irksome.—To GEORGE CLINTON. FORD ED., viii, 52. (W., May 1801.)

6077. —— ——. The transaction of the great interests of our country costs us little trouble or difficulty. There the line is plain to men of some experience. But the task of appointment is a heavy one indeed. He on whom it falls may envy the lot of a Sisyphus or Ixion. Their agonies were of the body: this of the mind. Yet, like the office of hangman, it must be executed by some one. It has been assigned to me and made my duty. I make up my mind to it, therefore, and abandon all regard to consequences.—To LARKIN SMITH. FORD ED., viii, 336. (W., Nov. 1804.)

6078. OFFICES, Bestowal.—I have firmly refused to follow the counsels of those who have desired the giving offices to some of the [federal] leaders, in order to reconcile. I have given, and will give only to republicans, under existing circumstances.—To JAMES MONROE. iv, 368. FORD ED., viii, 10. (W., March 1801.)

6079. —— ——. The consolidation of our fellow citizens in general is the great object we ought to keep in view, and that being once obtained, while we associate with us in affairs, to a certain degree, the federal sect of republicans, we must strip of all the means of influence the Essex Junto, and their associate monocrats in every part of the Union. —To LEVI LINCOLN. iv, 398. FORD ED., viii, 66. (W., July 1801.)

6080. OFFICES, Burthens.—In a virtuous government, and more especially in times like these, public offices are, what they should be, burthens to those appointed to them, which it would be wrong to decline, though foreseen to bring with them intense labor,

and great private loss.—To RICHARD HENRY LEE. FORD ED., ii, 192. (Wg., 1779.)

6081. OFFICES, Charity and.—I did not think the public offices confided to me to give away as charities.—To JAMES MONROE. iv, 446. FORD ED., viii, 166. (W., 1802.)

6082. OFFICES, Confirming power.—I have always considered the control of the Senate as meant to prevent any bias or favoritism in the President towards his own relations, his own religion, towards particular States, &c., and perhaps to keep very obnoxious persons out of offices of the first grade. But in all subordinate cases, I have ever thought that the selection made by the President ought to inspire a general confidence that it has been made on due enquiry and investigation of character, and that the Senate should interpose their negative only in those particular cases where something happens to be within their knowledge, against the character of the person, and unfitting him for the appointment.—To ALBERT GALLATIN. FORD ED., viii, 211. (1803.)

6083. OFFICES, Creation of.—The Administrator [of Virginia] shall not possess the prerogative * * * of erecting offices.— PROPOSED VA. CONSTITUTION. FORD ED., ii, 19. (June 1776.)

6084. —— ——. He has erected a multitude of new offices by a self-assumed power.*—DECLARATION OF INDEPENDENCE AS DRAWN BY JEFFERSON.

6085. —— ——. He has sent hither swarms of new officers to harass our people, and eat out their substance.—DECLARATION OF INDEPENDENCE AS DRAWN BY JEFFERSON.

6086. OFFICES, Difficult to fill.—The present situation of the President, unable to get the offices filled, really calls with uncommon obligation on those whom nature has fitted for them.—To EDWARD RUTLEDGE. iv, 124. FORD ED., vii, 40. (M., Nov. 1795.)

6087. —— ——. Should the [federalists] yield the election, I have reason to expect, in the outset, the greatest difficulties as to nominations. The late incumbents, running away from their offices and leaving them vacant, will prevent my filling them without the *previous* advice of the Senate. How this difficulty is to be got over I know not.—To JAMES MONROE. iv, 355. FORD ED., vii, 491. (W., Feb. 1801.)

6088. OFFICES, Factions and.—In appointments to office, the government refuses to know any difference between descriptions of republicans, all of whom are in principle, and cooperate with the government.—To WILLIAM SHORT. v, 362. (M., Sep. 1808.)

6089. OFFICES, Favoritism.—Mr. Nicholas's being a Virginian is a bar. It is essential that I be on my guard in appointing persons from that State.—To SAMUEL SMITH. FORD ED., viii, 29. (W., March 1801.)

* Congress struck out " by a self-assumed power ". —EDITOR.

6090. OFFICES, Federal monarchists and.—Amiable monarchists are not safe subjects of republican confidence.—To LEVI LINCOLN. iv, 399. FORD ED., viii, 67. (W., 1801.)

6091. —— ——. I do not know that [the introducing republicans to some share in the offices] will be pushed further * * * except as to Essex [Junto] men. I must ask you to make out a list of those in office in your own State and the neighboring ones, and to furnish me with it. There is little of this spirit south of the Hudson. I understood that Jackson is a very determined one, though in private life amiable and honorable. * * * What will be the effect of his removal? How should it be timed? Who his successor? What place can General Lyman properly occupy?—To LEVI LINCOLN. iv, 399. FORD ED., viii, 67. (W., July 1801.)

6092. —— ——. I have spoken of the federalists as if they were a homogeneous body, but this is not the truth. Under that name lurks the heretical sect of monarchists. Afraid to wear their own name, they creep under the mantle of federalism, and the federalists, like sheep, permit the fox to take shelter among them, when pursued by the dogs. These men have no right to office. If a monarchist be in office anywhere, and it be known to the President, the oath he has taken to support the Constitution imperiously requires the instantaneous dismission of such officer; and I should hold the President criminal if he permitted such to remain. To appoint a monarchist to conduct the affairs of a republic, is like appointing an atheist to the priesthood. As to the real federalists, I take them to my bosom as brothers. I view them as honest men, friends to the present Constitution.*—FROM A NEWSPAPER LETTER. FORD ED., viii, 237. (June 1803.)

6093. OFFICES, Geographical equilibrium.—In our country, you know, talents alone are not to be the determining circumstance, but a geographical equilibrium is to a certain degree expected. The different parts in the Union expect to share the public appointments.—To HORATIO GATES. FORD ED., viii, 11. (W., March 1801.)

6094. —— ——. Virginia is greatly over her due proportion of appointments in the General Government; and though this has not been done by me, it would be imputed as blamed to me to add to her proportion. So that for all general offices persons to fill them must, for some time, be sought from other States, and only offices which are to be exercised within the State can be given to its own citizens.—To JOHN PAGE. FORD ED., viii, 133. (W., Feb. 1802.)

6095. —— ——. Mr. R[obert] S. S[mith, Attorney-General], has had a commission given to Eli Williams as commissioner of the

* An article in the New York Evening Post led Jefferson to write a letter, signed "Fair Play", with a view to publication in New England. It was the second instance of Jefferson's departure from his rule of not writing for newpapers. The object was to provoke discussion.—EDITOR.

Western road. I am sorry he has gone out of Baltimore for the appointment, and also out of the ranks of Republicanism. It will furnish new matter for clamor.—To ALBERT GALLATIN. FORD ED., viii, 464. (M., Aug. 1806.)

6096. OFFICES, Gift of.— I dare say you have found that the solicitations for office are the most painful incidents to which an executive magistrate is exposed. The ordinary affairs of a nation offer little difficulty to a person of any experience; but the gift of office is the dreadful burthen which oppresses him.—To JAMES SULLIVAN. v, 252. (W., 1808.)

6097. —— ——. A person who wishes to make [the gift of office] an engine of self-elevation, may do wonders with it; but to one who wishes to use it conscientiously for the public good, without regard to the ties of blood or friendship, it creates enmities without number, many open, but more secret, and saps the happiness and peace of his life.—To JAMES SULLIVAN. v, 252. (W., 1808.)

6098. OFFICES, Importunity for.—When I retired from the government four years ago, it was extremely my wish to withdraw myself from all concern with public affairs, and to enjoy with my fellow citizens the protection of government, under the auspices and direction of those to whom it was so worthily committed. Solicitations from my friends, however, to aid them in their applications for office, drew from me an unwary compliance, till at length these became so numerous as to occupy a great portion of my time in writing letters to the President and heads of departments, and although these were attended to by them with great indulgence, yet I was sensible they could not fail of being very embarrassing. They kept me, at the same time, standing forever in the attitude of a suppliant before them, daily asking favors as humiliating and afflicting to my own mind, as they were unreasonable from their multitude. I was long sensible of putting an end to these unceasing importunities, when a change in the heads of the two departments to which they were chiefly addressed, presented me an opportunity. I come to a resolution, therefore, on that change, never to make another application. I have adhered to it strictly, and find that on its rigid observance, my own happiness and the friendship of the government too much depend, for me to swerve from it in future.—To THOMAS PAINE M'MATRON. vi, 108. (M., 1813.)

6099. OFFICES, Intolerance and.—Our gradual reformations seem to produce good effects everywhere except in Connecticut. Their late session of Legislature has been more intolerant than all others. We must meet them with equal intolerance. When they will give a share in the State offices, they shall be replaced in a share of the general offices. Till then, we must follow their example.—To LEVI LINCOLN. iv, 399. FORD ED., viii, 67. (W., July 1801.)

6100. —— ——. When I entered on office, after giving a very small participation in office to republicans by removal of a very few federalists, selected on the principle of their own intolerance while in office, I never meant to have touched another, but to leave to the ordinary accidents to make openings for republicans, but the vindictive, indecent and active opposition of some individuals has obliged me from time to time to disarm them of the influence of office.—To ANDREW ELLICOTT. FORD ED., viii, 479. (W., Nov. 1806.)

6101. OFFICES, Jefferson and.—I have solicited none, intrigued for none. Those which my country has thought proper to confide to me have been of their own mere motion, unasked by me.—To JAMES LYON. vi, 10. (M., 1811.)

6102. OFFICES, Labor and.—Considering the general tendency to multiply offices and dependencies, and to increase expense to the ultimate term of burden which the citizen can bear, it behooves us to avail ourselves of every occasion which presents itself for taking off the surcharge; that it may never be seen here that, after leaving to labor the smallest portion of its earnings on which it can subsist, government shall itself consume the residue of what it was instituted to guard.—FIRST ANNUAL MESSAGE. viii, 10. FORD ED., viii, 120. (Dec. 1801.)

6103. OFFICES, Local.—Where an office is local we never go out of the limits for the officer.—To CÆSAR A. RODNEY. FORD ED., viii, 498. (W., 1806.)

6104. OFFICES, Lopping off.—I had foreseen, years ago, that the first republican President who should come into office after all the places in the government had become exclusively occupied by federalists, would have a dreadful operation to perform. That the republicans would consent to a continuation of everything in federal hands, was not to be expected, because neither just nor politic. On him, then, was to devolve the office of an executioner, that of lopping off. I cannot say that it has worked harder than I expected.—To LEVI LINCOLN. iv, 406. FORD ED., viii, 83. (M., Aug. 1801.)

6105. OFFICES, Midnight appointments.—The nominations crowded in by Mr. Adams, after he knew he was not appointing for himself, I treat as mere nullities. His best friends do not disapprove of this.—To WILLIAM FINDLEY. FORD ED., viii, 28. (W., March 1801.)

6106. —— ——. In the class of removals, I do not rank the new appointments which Mr. Adams crowded in with whip and spur from the 12th of December, when the event of the election was known (and, consequently, that he was making appointments, not for himself, but his successor), until 9 o'clock of the night, at 12 o'clock of which he was to go out of office. This outrage on decency should not have its effect, except in the life appointments which are irremovable; but as to the others, I consider the nomina-

tions as nullities, and will not view the persons as even candidates for *their* office, much less as possessing it by any title meriting respect.—To GENERAL HENRY KNOX. iv, 386. FORD ED., vi , 36. (W., March 1801.)

6107. —— ——. Mr. Adams's last appointments, when he knew he was naming counsellors and aids for me and not for himself, I set aside as far as depends on me.—To ELBRIDGE GERRY. iv, 391. FORD ED., viii, 42. (W., March 1801.)

6108. —— ——. I consider as nullities all the appointments (of a removable character) crowded in by Mr. Adams, when he knew he was appointing counsellors and agents for his successor and not for himself.—To GIDEON GRANGER. FORD ED., viii, 44. (W., March 1801.)

6109. —— ——. I have not considered as candid, or even decorous, the crowding of appointments by Mr. Adams after he knew he was making them for his successor and not himself even to nine o'clock of the night at twelve of which he was to go out of office. I do not think I ought to permit that conduct to have any effect as to the offices removable in their nature.—To PIERREPONT EDWARDS. FORD ED., viii, 44. (W., March 1801.)

6110. —— ——. The last Congress established a Western Judiciary district in Virginia, comprehending chiefly the Western countries. Mr. Adams, who continued filling all the offices till nine o'clock of the night, at twelve of which he was to go out of office himself, took care to appoint for this district also. The judge, of course, stands till the laws shall be repealed, which we trust will be at the next Congress. But as to all others I made it immediately known that I should consider them as nullities, and appoint others.—To A. STUART. iv, 393. FORD ED., viii, 46. (M., April 1801.)

6111. —— ——. If the will of the nation, manifested by their various elections, calls for an administration of government according with the opinions of those elected; if, for the fulfillment of that will, displacements are necessary, with whom can they so justly begin as with persons appointed in the last moments of an administration, not for its own aid, but to begin a career at the same time with their successors, by whom they had never been approved, and who could scarcely expect from them a cordial cooperation?—To THE NEW HAVEN COMMITTEE. iv, 404. FORD ED., viii. 69. (W., July 1801.)

6112. OFFICES, Multiplication of.—The multiplication of public offices, increase of expense beyond income, growth and entailment of a public debt, are indications soliciting the employment of the pruning knife.—To SPENCER ROANE. vii, 212. FORD ED., x, 188. (M., 1821.)

6113. OFFICES, Newspaper cajolery and.—I was not deluded by the eulogiums of the public papers in the first moments of change. If they could have continued to get all the loaves and fishes, that is, if I would have gone over to them, they would continue to eulogize. But I well knew that the moment that such removals should take place, as the justice of the preceding administration ought to have executed, their hue and cry would be set up, and they would take their old stand. I shall disregard that also.—To ELBRIDGE GERRY. iv, 391. FORD ED., viii, 41. (W., March 1801.)

6114. OFFICES, Nominations.—There is nothing I am so anxious about as good nominations, conscious that the merit as well as reputation of an administration depends as much on that as on its measures.—To A. STUART. iv, 394. FORD ED., viii, 47. (M., April 1801.)

6115. —— ——. My nominations are sometimes made on my own knowledge of the persons; sometimes on the information of others given either voluntarily, or at my request and in personal confidence. This I could not communicate without a breach of confidence, not I am sure, under the contemplation of the committee.* They are sensible the Constitution has made it my duty to nominate; and has not made it my duty to lay before them the evidences or reasons whereon my nominations are founded; and of the correctness of this opinion the established usage in the intercourse between the Senate and President is a proof. During nearly the whole of the time this Constitution has been in operation, I have been in situations of intimacy with this part of it, and may observe, from my knowledge, that it has not been the usage of the President to lay before the Senate, or a committee, the information on which he makes his nominations. In a single instance lately, I did make a communication of papers, but there were circumstances so peculiar in that case as to distinguish it from all others.—To URIAH TRACY. FORD ED., viii, 412. (1806.)

6116. —— ——. Nomination to office is an executive function. To give it to the Legislature, as we [in Virginia] do, is a violation of the principle of the separation of powers. It swerves the members from correctness, by temptations to intrigue for office themselves, and to a corrupt barter of votes; and destroys responsibility by dividing it among a multitude. By leaving nomination in its proper place, among executive functions, the principle of the distribution of power is preserved, and responsibility weighs with its force on a single head.—To SAMUEL KERCHIVAL. vii, 12. FORD ED., x, 40. (M., 1816.)

6117. OFFICES, Participation in.—It would have been to me a circumstance of great relief, had I found a moderate participation of office in the hands of the majority. I would gladly have left to time and accident to raise them to their just share. But their

* A committee of the Senate which had asked Jefferson concerning the characters and qualifications of certain persons nominated by him. This paper was not sent.—EDITOR.

total exclusion calls for prompter correctives.—To THE NEW HAVEN COMMITTEE. iv, 405. FORD ED., viii, 70. (W., July 1801.)

6118. —— ——. After so long and complete an exclusion from office as republicans have suffered, insomuch that every place is filled with their opponents, justice as well as principle requires that they should have some participation. I believe they will be contented with less than their just share for the sake of peace and conciliation.—To PIERCE BUTLER. FORD ED., viii, 82. (M., Aug. 1801.)

6119. —— ——. If a due participation of office is a matter of right, how are vacancies to be obtained? Those by death are few; by resignation, none. Can any other mode than that of removal be proposed?—To THE NEW HAVEN COMMITTEE. iv, 404. FORD ED., viii, 70. (W., July 1801.)

6120. —— ——. I still think our original idea as to office is best; that is, to depend, for the obtaining a just participation, on deaths, resignations, and delinquencies. This will least affect the tranquillity of the people, and prevent their giving in to the suggestion of our enemies, that ours has been a contest for office, not for principle. This is rather a slow operation, but it is sure if we pursue it steadily, which, however, has not been done with the undeviating resolution I could have wished.—To LEVI LINCOLN. iv, 451. FORD ED., viii, 176. (W., Oct. 1802.)

6121. —— ——. The present administration had a task imposed on it which was unavoidable, and could not fail to exert the bitterest hostility in those who opposed it. The preceding administration left ninety-nine out of every hundred in public office of the federal sect. Republicanism had been the mark on Cain which had rendered those who bore it exiles from all portion in the trusts and authorities of their country. This description of citizens called imperiously and justly for a restoration of right. It was intended, however, to have yielded to this in so moderate a degree as might conciliate those who had obtained exclusive possession; but as soon as they were touched, they endeavored to set fire to the four corners of the public fabric, and obliged us to deprive of the influence of office several who were using it with activity and vigilance to destroy the confidence of the people in their government, and thus to proceed in the drudgery of removal farther than would have been, had not their own hostile enterprises rendered it necessary in self-defence.—To BENJAMIN HAWKINS. iv, 466. FORD ED., viii, 212. (W., 1803.)

6122. —— ——. Whether a participation of office in proportion to numbers should be effected in each State separately, or in the whole States taken together, is difficult to decide, and has not yet been settled in my own mind. It is a question of vast complications.—To WILLIAM DUANE. FORD ED., viii, 258. (W., July 1803.)

6123. OFFICES, Perplexity over.—My position is painful enough between federalists who cry out on the first touch of their monopoly, and republicans who clamor for universal removal. A subdivision of the latter will increase the perplexity. I am proceeding with deliberation and enquiry to do what I think just to both descriptions and conciliatory to both.—To John Dickinson. Ford ed., viii, 76. (W., July 1801.)

6124. OFFICES, Policy respecting.—You know the moderation of our views in this business, and that we all concurred in them. We determined to proceed with deliberation. This produced impatience in the republicans, and a belief we meant to do nothing.—To Levi Lincoln. iv, 406. Ford ed., viii, 83. (M., Aug. 1801.)

6125. ——— ———. All offices were in the hands of the federalists. The injustice of having totally excluded republicans was acknowledged by every man. To have removed one half, and to have placed good republicans in their stead, would have been rigorously just, when it was known that these composed a very great majority of the nation. Yet such was their moderation in most of the States, that they did not desire it. In these, therefore, no removals took place but for malversation. In the middle States, the contention had been higher, spirits were more sharpened and less accommodating. It was necessary in these to practice a different treatment, and to make a few changes to tranquilize the injured party.—To William Short. iv, 414. Ford ed., viii, 97. (W., 1801.)

6126. OFFICES, Public opinion and.—Some States require a different regimen from others. What is done in one State very often shocks another, though where it is done it is wholesome. South of the Potomac, not a single removal has been asked. On the contrary, they are urgent that none shall be made. Accordingly, only one has been made, which was for malversation. They censure much the removals north of this. You see, therefore, what various tempers we have to harmonize.—To Thomas McKean. Ford ed., viii, 78. (W., July 1801.)

6127. OFFICES, Qualifications.—I shall * * * return with joy to that state of things when the only questions concerning a candidate shall be: Is he honest? Is he capable? Is he faithful to the Constitution?—To the New Haven Committee. iv, 405. Ford ed., viii, 70. (W., 1801.)

6128. OFFICES, Refusal.—For God's sake get us relieved from this dreadful drudgery of refusal.—To Albert Gallatin. v, 398. (Dec. 1808.)

6129. OFFICES, Regeneration of.—We are proceeding gradually in the regeneration of offices, and introducing republicans to some share in them.—To Levi Lincoln. iv, 399. Ford ed., viii, 67. (W., July 1801.)

6130. OFFICES, Unconstitutional nominations.—The President cannot, before the 4th of March, make nominations [of Vermont officers] which will be good in law; because till that day, Vermont will not be a separate and integral member of the U. S., and it is only to integral members of the Union that his right of nomination is given by the Constitution.—Report on Admission of Vermont. Ford ed., v. 290. (1791.)

6131. OFFICES, Vacancies.—I think I have a preferable right to name agents for my own administration, at least to the vacancies falling after it was known that Mr. Adams was not naming for himself.—To A. Stuart. iv, 393. Ford ed., viii, 46. (M., April 1801.)

6132. ——— ———. The phrase in the Constitution is, "to fill up all vacancies that may happen during the recess of the Senate". This may mean "vacancies that may happen to be", or "may happen to fall"; it is, certainly, susceptible of both constructions, and we took the practice of our predecessors as the commentary established. This was done without deliberation; and we have not before taken an exact view of the precedents. They more than cover our cases, but I think some of them are not justifiable. We propose to take the subject into consideration, and to fix on such a rule of conduct, within the words of the Constitution, as may save the government from serious injury, and yet restrain the Executive within limits which might admit mischief. You will observe the cases of Reade and Putnam, where the persons nominated declining to accept, the vacancy remained unfilled, and had happened before the recess. It will be said these vacancies did not remain unfilled by the intention of the Executive, who had, by nomination, endeavored to fill them. So in our cases, they were not unfilled by the intention of the successor, but by the omission of the predecessor. Charles Lee informed me that wherever an office became vacant so short a time before Congress rose, as not to give an opportunity of enquiring for a proper character, they let it lie always till recess. * * * We must establish a correct and well digested rule of practice, to bind up our successors as well as ourselves. If we find that any of our cases go beyond the limits of such a rule, we must consider what will be the best way of preventing their being considered authoritative examples.—To Wilson C. Nicholas. Ford ed., viii, 131. (W., Jan. 1802.)

6133. ——— ———. The mischievous law vacating, every four years, nearly all the executive offices of the government, saps the constitutional and salutary functions of the President, and introduces a principle of intrigue and corruption, which will soon leaven the mass, not only of senators, but of citizens. It is more baneful than the attempt which failed in the beginning of the government, to make all officers irremovable but with the consent of the Senate. This places, every four years, all appointments under their power, and even obliges them to act on every one nomination. It will keep in constant excitement all the hungry cormorants for office, render them, as well as those in place, sycophants to their Senators, engage these in eternal intrigue to turn out one and put in another, in cabals to swap work; and make of them what all executive directories become, mere sinks of corruption and faction. This must have been one of the midnight signatures of the President when he had not time to consider, or even to read the law; and the more fatal as being irrepealable but with the consent of the Senate, which will never be obtained.—To JAMES MADISON. vii, 190. FORD ED., x, 168. (P.F., 1820.)

6134. OFFICES, Women and.—The appointment of a woman to office is an innovation for which the public is not prepared, nor am I.—To ALBERT GALLATIN. FORD ED., ix, 7. (W., Jan. 1807.)

6135. OFFICE-HOLDERS, Appointments.—With regard to appointments, I have so much confidence in the justice and good sense of the federalists, that I have no doubt they will concur in the fairness of the position, that after they have been in the exclusive possession of all offices from the very first origin of party among us, to the 3d of March, at 9 o'clock in the night, no republican ever admitted, and this doctrine newly avowed, it is now perfectly just that the republicans should come in for the vacancies which may fall in, until something like an equilibrium in office be restored; after which "*Tros Tyriusque mihi nullo discrimine agetur.*"*—To DR. BENJAMIN RUSH. iv, 382. FORD ED., viii, 31. (W., March 1801.)

6136. —— ——. About appointments to offices the rule is simple enough. The federalists having been in exclusive possession of them from the first origin of the party among us, to the 3d of March, nine o'clock p. m. of the evening, at twelve of which Mr. Adams was to go out of office, their reason will acknowledge the justice of giving vacancies, as they happen, to those who have been so long excluded, till the same general proportion prevails in office which exists out of it.—To GIDEON GRANGER. FORD ED., viii. 44. (W., March 1801.)

6137. —— ——. Which appointment would be most respected by the public, for that circumstance is not only generally the best criterion of what is best, but the public respect can alone give strength to the government.—To ARCHIBALD STUART. FORD ED., viii, 47. (M., April 1801.)

6138. —— ——. There is nothing I am so anxious about as making the best possible appointments, and no case in which the best men are more liable to mislead us, by yielding to the solicitations of applicants.—To NATHANIEL MACON. iv, 396. FORD ED., viii, 52. (W., May 1801.)

* The Congress edition omits the Latin quotation. In the Ford edition, "habetur", not "agetur".—EDITOR.

6139. —— ——. The grounds on which one of the competitors stood, set aside of necessity all hesitation. Mr. Hall's having been a member of the Legislature, a Speaker of the Representatives, and a member of the Executive Council, were evidences of the respect of the State towards him, which our respect for the State could not neglect.—To J. F. MERCER. iv, 562. (W., 1804.)

6140. OFFICE-HOLDERS, Caucuses and.—The allegations against Pope, of New Bedford, are insufficient. Although meddling in political caucuses is no part of that freedom of personal suffrage which ought to be allowed him, yet his mere presence at a caucus does not necessarily involve an active and official influence in opposition to the government which employs him.—To ALBERT GALLATIN. FORD ED., viii, 499. (W., 1806.)

6141. OFFICE-HOLDERS, Charges against.—I have made it a rule not to give up letters of accusation, or copies of them, in any case.—To ALBERT GALLATIN. FORD ED., viii, 500. (W., 1806.)

6142. OFFICE-HOLDERS, Elections and.—Interferences with elections, whether of the State or General Government, by officers of the latter, should be deemed cause of removal; because the constitutional remedy by the elective principle becomes nothing, if it may be smothered by the enormous patronage of the General Government.—To THOMAS McKEAN. iv, 350. FORD ED., vii, 487. (W., 1801.)

6143. —— ——. To these means [deaths, resignations, and delinquencies] of obtaining a just share in the transaction of the public business, shall be added one other, to wit, removal for electioneering activity, or open and industrious opposition to the principles of the present government, Legislative and Executive. Every officer of the government may vote at elections according to his conscience; but we should betray the cause committed to our care, were we to permit the influence of official patronage to be used to overthrow that cause.—To LEVI LINCOLN. iv, 451. FORD ED., viii, 176. (W., Oct. 1802.)

6144. —— ——. I think it not amiss that it should be known that we are determined to remove officers who are active or open mouthed against the government, by which I mean the Legislature as well as the Executive.—To LEVI LINCOLN. iv, 452. FORD ED., viii, 176. (W., Oct. 1802.)

6145. —— ——. I have received two addresses from meetings of democratic republicans at Dover. praying the removal of Allen McLane. * * * If he has been active in electioneering in favor of those who wish to subvert the present order of things, it would be a serious circumstance. I do not mean as to giving his personal vote, in which he ought not to be controlled; but as to using his influence (which necessarily includes his official influence) to sway the votes of others.—To CÆSAR A. RODNEY. FORD ED., viii, 154. (W., 1802.)

6146. —— ——. I think the officers of the Federal Government are meddling too much with the public elections. Will it be best to admonish them privately or by proclamation?—To ALBERT GALLATIN. iv, 559. FORD ED., viii, 320. (M., Sep. 1804.)

6147. OFFICE-HOLDERS, Executive explanations and.—It has not been the custom, nor would it be expedient, for the Executive to enter into details for the rejection of candidates for offices or removal of those who possess them.—To MRS. SARAH MEASE. FORD ED., viii, 35. (W., March 1801.)

6148. —— ——. These letters [from you] all relating to office, fall within the general rule which even the very first week of my being engaged in the administration obliged me to establish, to wit, that of not answering letters on office specifically, but leaving the answer to be found in what is done or not done on them. You will readily conceive into what scrapes one would get by saying *no*, either with or without reason, by using a softer language which might excite false hope, or by saying *yes* prematurely. And to take away all offence from this silent answer, it is necessary to adhere to it in every case rigidly, as well with bosom friends as strangers.—To AARON BURR. FORD ED., viii, 102. (W., Nov. 1801.)

6149. —— ——. The circumstance of exhibiting our recommendations even to our friends, requires great consideration. Recommendations, when honestly written, should detail the bad as well as the good qualities of the person recommended. That gentlemen may do freely, if they know their letter is to be confined to the President or the head of a department; but if communicated further, it may bring on them troublesome quarrels. In General Washington's time, he resisted every effort to bring forth his recommendations. In Mr. Adams's time, I only know that the republicans knew nothing of them. * * * To Mr. Tracy, at any rate, no exhibition or information of recommendations ought to be communicated. He may be told that the President does not think it regular to communicate the grounds or reasons of his decision.—To ALBERT GALLATIN. FORD ED., viii, 210. (Feb. 1803.)

6150. —— ——. The address of the Ward Committee of Philadelphia on the subject of removals from office was received. I cannot answer it, because I have given no answers to the many others I have received from other quarters. * * * Although no person wishes more than I do to learn the opinions of respected *individuals*, because they enable me to examine, and often to correct my own, yet I am not satisfied that I ought to admit the addresses even of those bodies of men which are organized by the Constitution (the Houses of Legislature for instance) to influence the appointment to office for which the Constitution has chosen to rely on the independence and integrity of the Executive, controlled by the Senate, chosen both of them by the whole Union. Still less of those bodies whose organization is unknown to the Constitution. As revolutionary instruments (when nothing but revolution will cure the evils of the State) they are necessary and indispensable, and the right to use them is inalienable by the people; but to admit them as ordinary and habitual instruments as a part of the machinery of the Constitution, would be to change that machinery by introducing moving powers foreign to it, and to an extent depending solely on local views, and therefore incalculable. The opinions offered by *individuals*, and of right, are on a different ground; they are sanctioned by the Constitution; which has also prescribed, when they choose to act in bodies, the organization, objects and rights of those bodies. * * * This view of the subject forbids me, in my judgment, to give answers to addresses of this kind.*—To WILLIAM DUANE. FORD ED., viii, 255. (M., 1803.)

6151. —— ——. You complain that I did not answer your letters applying for office. But if you will reflect a moment you may judge whether this ought to be expected. To the successful applicant for an office the commission is the answer. To the unsuccessful multitude am I to go with every one into the reasons for not appointing him? Besides that this correspondence would literally engross my whole time, into what controversies would it lead me? Sensible of this dilemma, from the moment of coming into office I laid it down as a rule to leave the applicants to collect their answer from the facts. To entitle myself to the benefit of the rule in any case it must be observed in every one; and I never have departed from it in a single case, not even for my bosom friends. You observe that you are, or probably will be appointed an elector. I have no doubt you will do your duty with a conscientious regard to the public good, and to that only. Your decision in favor of another would not excite in my mind the slightest dissatisfaction towards you. On the contrary, I should honor the integrity of your choice. In the nominations I have to make, do the same justice to my motives. Had you hundreds to nominate, instead of one, be assured they would not compose for you a bed of roses. You would find yourself in most cases with one loaf and ten wanting bread. Nine must be disappointed, perhaps become secret. if not open enemies.—To LARKIN SMITH. FORD ED., viii, 336. (W., Nov. 1804.)

6152. OFFICE-HOLDERS, Freedom of opinion and.—Opinion, and the just maintenance of it, shall never be a crime in my view; nor bring injury on the individual.—To SAMUEL ADAMS. iv, 389. FORD ED., viii, 39. (W., March 1801.)

6153. —— ——. The right of opinion shall suffer no invasion from me. Those who have acted well have nothing to fear, however they may have differed from me in opinion;

* The letter containing this extract was not sent to Mr. Duane.—EDITOR.

those who have done ill, however, have nothing to hope; nor shall I fail to do justice lest it should be ascribed to that difference of opinion.—To ELBRIDGE GERRY. iv, 391. FORD ED., viii, 42. (W., March 1801.)

6154. OFFICE-HOLDERS, Half-breeds.
—I never did the federalists an act of injustice, nor failed in any duty to them imposed by my office. Out of about six hundred officers, named by the President, there were six republicans only when I came into office, and these were chiefly half-breeds. Out of upwards of three hundred holding during pleasure, I removed about fifteen, or those who had signalized themselves by their own intolerance in office, because the public voice called for it imperiously, and it was just that the republicans should at length have some participation in the government. There never was another removal but for such delinquencies as removed the republicans equally. In this horrid drudgery I always felt myself as a public executioner, an office which no one who knows me, I hope, supposes very grateful to my feelings. It was considerably alleviated, however, by the industry of their newspapers in endeavoring to excite resentment enough to enable me to meet the operation. However, I hail the day which is to relieve me from being viewed as an official enemy. In private life, I never had above one or two; to the friendship of that situation I look with delight.—To WILLIAM SHORT. FORD ED., ix, 51. (W., May 1807.)

6155. OFFICE-HOLDERS, Malignant opposition.—Deaths, resignations, delinquencies, malignant and active opposition to the order of things established by the will of the nation, will, it is believed, within a moderate space of time, make room for a just participation in the management of the public affairs; and that being once effected, future changes at the helm will be viewed with tranquillity by those in subordinate station.—To WILLIAM JUDD. viii, 114. (1802.)

6156. OFFICE-HOLDERS, Matrimony and.—Mr. Remsen having decided definitely to resign his office of Chief clerk, I have considered with all the impartiality in my power the different grounds on which yourself and Mr. Taylor stand in competition for the succession. I understand that he was appointed a month before you, and that you came into actual service about a month before he did. These circumstances place you so equally, that I cannot derive from them any ground of preference. Yet obliged to decide one way or the other, I find in a comparison of your conditions a circumstance of considerable equity in his favor. He is a married man, with a family; yourself single. There can be no doubt but that $500 place a single man as much at his ease as $800 do a married one. On this single circumstance, then, I have thought myself bound to appoint Mr. Taylor chief clerk.—To JACOB BLACKWELL. FORD ED., v, 490. (Pa., 1792.)

6157. OFFICE-HOLDERS, Multiplication of.—I am not for a multiplication of

officers * * * merely to make partizans.—To ELBRIDGE GERRY. iv, 268. FORD ED., vii, 327. (Pa., 1799.)

6158. OFFICE-HOLDERS, Partizan.—
A few examples of justice on officers who have perverted their functions to the oppression of their fellow citizens, must, in justice to those citizens, be made.—To SAMUEL ADAMS. iv, 389. FORD ED., viii, 39. (W., March 1801.)

6159. —— ——. Those whose misconduct in office ought to have produced their removal even by my predecessor, must not be protected by the delicacy due only to honest men.—To SAMUEL ADAMS. iv, 389. FORD ED., viii, 39. (W., March 1801.)

6160. —— ——. Officers who have been guilty of gross abuses of office, such as marshals packing juries, &c., I shall now remove, as my predecessor ought in justice to have done. The instances will be few, and governed by strict rule, and not party passion.—To ELBRIDGE GERRY. iv, 391. FORD ED., viii, 42. (W., March 1801.)

6161. —— ——. I have never removed a man merely because he was a federalist. I have never wished them to give a vote at an election, but according to their own wishes. But as no government could discharge its duties to the best advantage of its citizens, if its agents were in a regular course of thwarting instead of executing all its measures, and were employing the patronage and influence of their offices against the government and its measures, I have only requested they would be quiet, and they should be safe; that if their conscience urges them to take an active and zealous part in opposition, it ought also to urge them to retire from a post which they could not conscientiously conduct with fidelity to the trust reposed in them; and on failure to retire, I have removed them; that is to say, those who maintained an active and zealous opposition to the government.—To JOHN PAGE. v, 136. FORD ED., ix, 118. (W., July 1807.)

6162. —— ——. Our principles render federalists in office safe, if they do not employ their influence in opposing the government, and only give their own vote according to their conscience. And this principle we act on as well with those put in office by others, as by ourselves.—To LEVI LINCOLN. v, 264. (W., March 1808.)

6163. OFFICE-HOLDERS, Recommendations.—Should I be placed in office, nothing would be more desirable to me than the recommendations of those in whom I have confidence, of persons fit for office; for if the good withhold their testimony, we shall be at the mercy of the bad.—To DR. B. S. BARTON. iv, 353. FORD ED., vii, 489. (W., Feb. 1801.)

6164. —— ——. It is so far from being improper to receive the communications you had in contemplation as to arrangements [respecting the offices] in your State, that I have been in the constant expectation you would find time to do me the favor of calling and making them, when we could in conversation explain them better than by writing, and I should with frankness and thankfulness enter into the explanations. The most valuable source of information we have is that of the members of the Legislature, and it is one to which I have resorted and shall resort with great freedom.—To CHARLES PINCKNEY. FORD ED., viii, 6. (W., March 1801.)

6165. —— ——. We want an attorney and marshal for the Western [Virginia] district. * * * Pray recommend [persons] to me; and let them be the most respectable and unexceptionable possible, and especially let them be republicans.—To A. STUART. iv, 393. FORD ED., viii, 46. (M., April 1801.)

6166. —— ——. In all cases, when an office becomes vacant in your State [North Carolina], as the distance would occasion a great delay were you to wait to be regularly consulted, I shall be much obliged to you to recommend the best characters.—To NATHANIEL MACON. iv, 396. FORD ED., viii, 52. (W., May 1801.)

6167. —— ——. Disposed myself to make as few changes in office as possible, to endeavor to restore harmony by avoiding everything harsh, and to remove only for malconduct, I have, nevertheless, been persuaded that circumstances in New York, and still more in the neighboring States on both sides, require something more. It is represented that the Collector, Naval Officer, and Supervisor ought all to be removed for the violence of their characters and conduct. The following arrangement was agreed on by Colonel Burr and some of your Senators and Representatives: David Gelston, Collector, Theodorus Bailey, Naval Officer, and M. L. Davis, Supervisor. Yet all did not agree in all the particulars, and I have since received letters expressly stating that Mr. Bailey has not readiness and habit enough of business for the office of Naval Officer, and some suggestions that Mr. Davis's standing in society, and other circumstances will render his not a respectable appointment to the important office of Supervisor. Unacquainted myself with these and the other characters in the State which might be proper for these offices, and forced to decide on the opinions of others, there is no one whose opinion would command with me greater respect than yours, if you would be so good as to advise me, which of these characters and what others would be fittest for these offices. Not only competent talents, but respectability in the public estimation are to be considered.—To GEORGE CLINTON. FORD ED., viii, 53. (W., May 1801.)

6168. —— ——. To exhibit recommendations would be to turn the Senate into a court of honor, or a court of slander, and to expose the character of every man nominated to an ordeal, without his own consent, subjecting the Senate to heats and waste of time.—To ALBERT GALLATIN. FORD ED., viii, 211. (1803.)

6169. —— ——. The friendship which has long subsisted between the President of the United States and myself gave me reason to expect, on my retirement from office, that I might often receive applications to interpose with him on behalf of persons desiring appointments. Such an abuse of his dispositions towards me would necessarily lead to the loss of them, and to the transforming me from the character of a friend to that of an unreasonable and troublesome solicitor. It, therefore, became necessary for me to lay down as a law for my future conduct never to interpose in any case, either with him or the heads of departments, in any application whatever for office.—CIRCULAR LETTER. FORD ED., ix, 248. (March 1809.)

6170. OFFICE-HOLDERS, Reduction.—Among those [officers] who are dependent on Executive discretion, I have begun the reduction of what was deemed necessary. The expense of diplomatic agency have been considerably diminished. The inspectors of internal revenue, who were found to obstruct the accountability of the institution, have been discontinued. Several agencies created by Executive authority, on salaries fixed by that also, have been suppressed, and should suggest the expediency of regulating that power by law, so as to subject its exercises to legislative inspection and sanction. Other reformations of the same kind will be pursued with that caution which is requisite in removing useless things, not to injure what is retained. But the great mass of public offices is established by law, and, therefore, by law alone can be abolished.—FIRST ANNUAL MESSAGE. viii, 10. FORD ED., viii, 120. (Dec. 1801.)

6171. —— ——. When we consider that this government is charged with the eternal and mutual relations only of these States; that the States themselves have principal care of our persons, our property, and our reputation, constituting the great field of human concerns, we may well doubt whether our organization is not too complicated, too expensive; whether offices and officers have not been multiplied unnecessarily, and sometimes injuriously to the service they were meant to promote. I will cause to be laid before you an essay towards a statement of those who, under public employment of various kinds, draw money from the treasury or from our citizens.—FIRST ANNUAL MESSAGE. viii, 9. FORD ED., viii, 120. (Dec. 1801.)

6172. —— ——. The session of the first Congress, convened since republicanism has recovered its ascendancy, * * * will pretty completely fulfil all the desires of the people. * * * They are disarming executive patronage and preponderance, by putting down one half the offices of the United States, which are no longer necessary.—To GENERAL KOSCIUSKO. iv, 430. (W., April 1802.)

6173. OFFICE-HOLDERS, Removals.—
Some [removals] I know must be made.
They must be as few as possible, done gradually, and bottomed on some malversation or
inherent disqualification.—To JAMES MONROE.
iv, 368. (W., March 1801.)

6174. —— ——. I believe with others,
that deprivations of office, if made on the
ground of political principles alone, would revolt our new converts, and give a body to
leaders who now stand alone. Some, I
know, must be made. They must be as few
as possible, done gradually, and bottomed on
some malversation or inherent disqualification. Where we shall draw the line between
retaining all and none, is not yet settled, and
it will not be till we get our administration
together; and perhaps even then, we shall
proceed à tâtons, balancing our measures according to the impression we perceive them
to make.—To JAMES MONROE. iv, 368. FORD
ED., viii, 10. (W., March 1801.)

6175. —— ——. That some ought to be
removed from office, and that all ought not,
all mankind will agree. But where to draw
the line, perhaps no two will agree. Consequently, nothing like a general approbation on
this subject can be looked for. Some principles have been the subject of conversation
[in cabinet] but not of determination, c. g.,
1. All appointments to *civil* offices *during
pleasure*, made after the event of the election
was certainly known to Mr. Adams, are considered as nullities. I do not view the persons appointed as even candidates for the
office, but make others without noticing or
notifying them. Mr. Adams's best friends
have agreed this is right. 2. Officers who
have been guilty of *official* malconduct are
proper subjects of removal. 3. Good men,
to whom there is no objection but a difference
of political principle, practiced on only as
far as the right of a private citizen will justify, are not proper subjects of removal except in the case of attorneys and marshals.
The courts being so decidedly federal and irremovable, it is believed that republican attorneys and marshals, being the doors of entrance into the courts, are indispensably
necessary as a shield to the republican part
of our fellow citizens, which, I believe, is
the main body of the people.—To WILLIAM
B. GILES. iv, 380. FORD ED., viii, 25. (W.,
March 1801.)

6176. —— ——. As to removals from
office, great differences of opinion exist.
That some ought to be removed, all will
agree. That all should, nobody will say.
And no two will probably draw the same
line between these two extremes; consequently nothing like general approbation can
be expected. Malconduct is a just ground of
removal: mere difference of political opinion
is not. The temper of some States requires
a stronger procedure; that of others would
be more alienated even by a milder course.
Taking into consideration all circumstances,
we can only do in every case what to us seems
best, and trust to the indulgence of our fellow
citizens who may see the same matter in a
different point of view. * * * Time, prudence, and patience will, perhaps, get us over
this whole difficulty.—To WILLIAM FINDLEY.
FORD ED., viii, 27. (W., March 1801.)

6177. —— ——. The great stumbling
block will be removals, which, though made
on those just principles only on which my
predecessor ought to have removed the same
persons, will nevertheless be ascribed to removal on party principles. 1st. I will expunge the effects of Mr. Adams's indecent
conduct, in crowding nominations after he
knew they were not for himself, till 9 o'clock
of the night, at 12 o'clock of which he was
to go out of office. So far as they are during
pleasure, I shall not consider the persons
named, as even candidates for the office, nor
pay the respect of notifying them that I consider what was done as a nullity. 2d. Some
removals must be made for misconduct. One
of these is of the marshal in your city, who
being an officer of justice, intrusted with the
function of choosing impartial judges for the
trial of his fellow citizens, placed at the awful
tribunal of God and their country, selected
judges who either avowed, or were known
to him to be predetermined to condemn;
and if the lives of the unfortunate persons were not cut short by the sword of
the law, it was not for want of *his* good
will. In another State, I have to perform the same act of justice on the dearest connection of my dearest friend, for
similar conduct, in a case not capital. The
same practice of packing juries, and prosecuting their fellow citizens with the bitterness
of party hatred, will probably involve several
other marshals and attorneys. Out of this
line, I see but very few instances where past
misconduct has been in a degree to call for
notice. Of the thousands of officers, therefore,
in the United States, a very few individuals
only, probably not twenty, will be removed;
and these only for doing what they ought not
to have done. Two or three instances, indeed, where Mr. Adams removed men because
they would not sign addresses, &c., to him,
will be rectified—the persons restored. The
whole world will say this is just. I know that
in stopping thus short in the career of removal, I shall give great offence to many of
my friends. That torrent has been pressing
me heavily, and will require all my force to
bear up against; but my maxim is, *"fiat
justitia, ruat cœlum."*—To DR. BENJAMIN
RUSH. iv, 383. FORD ED., viii, 31. (W.,
March 1801.)

6178. —— ——. I am aware that the
necessity of a few removals for legal oppressions, delinquencies, and other official
malversations, may be misconstrued as done
for political opinions, and produce hesitation
in the coalition so much to be desired; but
the extent of these will be too limited to
make permanent impressions.—To GENERAL
HENRY KNOX. iv, 386. FORD ED., viii, 36.
(W., March 1801.)

6179. —— ——. No one will say that all should be removed, or that none should. Yet no two scarcely draw the same lines. * * * Persons who have perverted their offices to the oppression of their fellow citizens, as marshals packing juries, attorneys grinding their legal victims, intolerants removing those under them for opinion's sake, substitutes for honest men removed for their republican principles, will probably find few advocates even among their quondam party. But the freedom of opinion, and the reasonable maintenance of it, is not a crime, and ought not to occasion injury.—To GIDEON GRANGER. FORD ED., viii, 44. (W., March 1801.)

6180. —— ——. In Connecticut alone, a general sweep seems to be called for on principles of justice and policy. Their Legislature are removing every republican even from the commissions of the peace and the lowest offices. There, then, we will retaliate. Whilst the federalists are taking possession of all the State offices, exclusively, they ought not to expect we will leave them the exclusive possession of those at our disposal. The republicans have some rights and must be protected.—To WILSON C. NICHOLAS. FORD ED., viii, 64. (W., June 1801.)

6181. —— ——. I am satisfied that the heaping of abuse on me, personally, has been with the design and hope of provoking me to make a general sweep of all federalists out of office. But as I have carried no passion into the execution of this disagreeable duty, I shall suffer none to be excited. The clamor which has been raised will not provoke me to remove one more, nor deter me from removing one less, than if not a word had been said on the subject.—To LEVI LINCOLN. iv, 407. FORD ED., viii, 84. (M., Aug. 1801.)

6182. —— ——. The removal of excrescences from the judiciary is the universal demand.—To LEVI LINCOLN. iv, 407. FORD ED., viii, 85. (M., Aug. 1801.)

6183. —— ——. Rigorous justice required that as the federalists had filled every office with their friends to the avowed exclusion of republicans, that the latter should be admitted to a participation of office, by the removal of some of the former. This was done to the extent of about twenty only out of some thousands, and no more was intended. But instead of their acknowledging its moderation, it has been a ground for their more active enmity. After a twelve months' trial I have at length been induced to remove three or four more of those most marked for their bitterness, and active zeal in slandering, and in electioneering. Whether we shall proceed any further, will depend on themselves. Those who are quiet, and take no part against that order of things which the public will has established, will be safe. Those who continue to clamor against it, to slander and oppose it, shall not be armed with its wealth and power for its own destruction. The late re-

movals have been intended merely as monitory, but such officers, as shall afterwards continue to bid us defiance, shall as certainly be removed, if the case shall become known. A neutral conduct is all I ever desired, and this the public have a right to expect.—To ELBRIDGE GERRY. FORD ED., viii, 169. (W., Aug. 1802.)

6184. —— ——. We laid down our line of proceedings on mature inquiry and consideration in 1801, and have not departed from it. Some removals, to wit, sixteen to the end of our first session of Congress were made on political principles alone, in very urgent cases; and we determined to make no more but for delinquency, or active and bitter opposition to the order of things which the public will had established. On this last ground nine were removed from the end of the first to the end of the second session of Congress; and one since that. So that sixteen only have been removed on the whole for political principles, that is to say, to make room for some participation for the republicans. * * * Pursuing our object of harmonizing all good people of every description, we shall steadily adhere to our rule, and it is with sincere pleasure I learn that it is approved by the more moderate part of our friends.—To MR. NICHOLSON. iv, 485. (W., May 1803.)

6185. —— ——. Many vacancies have been made by death and resignation, many by removal for malversation in office, and for open, active, and virulent abuse of official influence in opposition to the order of things established by the will of the nation. Such removals continue to be made on sufficient proof. The places have been steadily filled with republican characters until out of 316 officers in all the United States, subject to appointment and removal by me, 130 only are held by federalists. I do not include in this estimate the judiciary and military, because not removable but by established process, nor the officers of the internal revenue, because discontinued by law, nor postmasters, or any others not named by me. And this has been effected in little more than two years by means so moderate and just as cannot fail to be approved in future.*—To WILLIAM DUANE. FORD ED., viii, 258. (W., July 1803.)

6186. —— ——. I give full credit to the wisdom of the measures pursued by the Governor of Pennsylvania in removals from office. I have no doubt he followed the wish of the State; and *he* had no other to consult. But in the General Government each State is to be administered, not on its local principles, but on the principles of all the States formed into a general result. That I should administer the affairs of Massachusetts and Connecticut, for example, on federal principles, could not be approved. I dare say, too, that the extensive removals from office in Pennsylvania may have contributed to the great conversion which has been manifested among

* The letter containing this extract was not sent to Mr. Duane.—EDITOR.

its citizens. But I respect them too much to believe it has been the exclusive or even the principal motive. I presume the sound measures of their government, and of the General one, have weighed more in their estimation and conversation, than the consideration of the particular agents employed.—To WILLIAM DUANE. FORD ED., viii, 259. (M., July 1803.)

6187. ———. Although I know that it is best generally to assign no reason for a removal from office, yet there are also times when the declaration of a principle is advantageous. Such was the moment at which the New Haven letter appeared. It explained our principles to our friends, and they rallied to them. The public sentiment has taken a considerable stride since that, and seems to require that they should know again where we stand. I suggest, therefore, for your consideration, instead of the following passage in your letter to Bowen, " I think it due to candor at the same time to inform you, that I had for some time been determined to remove you from office, although a successor has not yet been appointed by the President, nor the precise time fixed for that purpose communicated to him ", to substitute this, " I think it due to candor at the same time to inform you, that the President, considering that the patronage of public office should no longer be confided to one who uses it for active opposition to the national will, had, some time since, determined to place your office in other hands. But a successor not being yet fixed on, I am not able to name the precise time when it will take place ". My own opinion is, that the declaration of this principle will meet the entire approbation of all moderate republicans, and will extort indulgence from the warmer ones. Seeing that we do not mean to leave arms in the hands of active enemies, they will care the less at our tolerance of the inactive.—To ALBERT GALLATIN. iv, 543. FORD ED., viii, 303. (May 1804.)

6188. ———. In the case of the removal proposed by the collector of Baltimore, I consider it as entirely out of my sphere, and resting solely with yourself. Were I to give an opinion on the subject, it would only be by observing that in the cases under my immediate care, I have never considered the length of time a person has continued in office, nor the money he has made in it, as entering at all into the reasons for a removal.— To ALBERT GALLATIN. FORD ED., viii, 499. (W., 1806.)

6189. OFFICE-HOLDERS, Tenure of.— Should I be placed in office * * * no man who has conducted himself according to his duties would have anything to fear from me, as those who have done ill, would have nothing to hope, be their political principles what they might.—To DR. B. S. BARTON. iv, 353. FORD ED., vii, 489. (W., Feb. 1801.)

6190. OFFICE-HOLDERS, Useless.— The suppression of useless offices * * * will probably produce some disagreeable al-

tercations [in Congress].—To DR. BENJAMIN RUSH. iv, 426. FORD ED., viii, 128. (W., 1801.)

— OIL OF BENI.—See OLIVE, SUBSTITUTE FOR.

— OLD AGE.—See AGE.

6191. OLIVE, Adapted to America.— The olive tree * * * would surely succeed in your country, and would be an infinite blessing after some fifteen or twenty years. The caper would also probably succeed, and would offer a very great and immediate profit.—To E. RUTLEDGE. ii, 180. FORD ED., iv, 410. (P., 1787.)

6192. OLIVE, Blessing to the poor.— After bread, I know no blessing to the poor, in this world, equal to that of oil.—To RALPH IZARD. FORD ED., v, 128. (P., 1789.)

6193. OLIVE, Cultivation of.—The olive is a tree the least known in America, and yet the most worthy of being known. Of all the gifts of heaven to man, it is next to the most precious, if it be not the most precious. Perhaps it may claim a preference even to bread, because there is such an infinitude of vegetables, which it renders a proper and comfortable nourishment. In passing the Alps at the Col de Tende, where they are mere masses of rock, wherever there happens to be a little soil, there are a number of olive trees, and a village supported by them. Take away these trees, and the same ground in corn would not support a single family. A pound of oil which can be bought for three or four pence sterling, is equivalent to many pounds of flesh, by the quantity of vegetables it will prepare, and render fit and comfortable food. Without this tree, the country of Provence and territory of Genoa would not support one-half, perhaps not one-third, their present inhabitants. The nature of the soil is of little consequence if it be dry. The trees are planted from fifteen to twenty feet apart, and when tolerably good, will yield fifteen or twenty pounds of oil yearly, one with another. There are trees which yield much more. They begin to render good crops at twenty years old, and last till killed by cold, which happens at some time or other, even in their best positions in France. But they put out again from their roots. In Italy, I am told they have trees two hundred years old.—To WILLIAM DRAYTON. ii, 199. (P., 1787.)

6194. OLIVE, Heaven's gift.—The olive tree is assuredly the richest gift of heaven. I can scarcely except bread.—To GEORGE WYTHE. ii, 266. FORD ED., iv, 443. (P., 1787.)

6195. OLIVE, Importing trees.—I wish the cargo of olive plants * * * may arrive to you in good order. This is the object for the patriots of your country [South Carolina] ; for that tree once established there will be the source of the greatest wealth and happiness. But to insure success, perseverance may be necessary. An essay or two may fail. I think, therefore, that an annual sum should be subscribed, and it need not be a great one.—To E. RUTLEDGE. iii, 110. (P., 1789.)

6196. ———. I have arrived at Baltimore from Marseilles forty olive trees of the best kind, and a box of seed, the 'atter to raise stocks, and the former, cuttings to enfraft on the stocks. I am ordering them on instantly to Charleston. * * * Another cargo is on its way from Bordeaux, so that I hope to secure the commencement of this culture, and from the best species. Sugar and oil will be no mean addition to the articles of our culture.—To PRESIDENT WASHINGTON. iii, 255. FORD ED., v, 327. (Pa., 1791.)

6197. —— ——. I have one hundred olive trees, and some caper plants from Marseilles, which I am sending on to Charleston where * * * they have already that number living of those I had before sent them.—To PRESIDENT WASHINGTON. iii, 357. FORD ED., v, 514. (Pa., 1792.)

6198. —— ——. It is now twenty-five years since I sent my southern fellow citizens two shipments (about 500 plants) of the olive tree of Aix, the finest olives in the world. If any of them still exist, it is merely as a curiosity in their gardens; not a single orchard of them has been planted.—To JAMES RONALDSON. vi, 92. FORD ED., ix, 371. (M., Jan. 1813.)

6199. OLIVE, Oil.—The oil of the olive is an article the consumption of which will always keep pace with its production. Raise it, and it begets its own demand. Little is carried to America because Europe has it not to spare. We, therefore, have not learned the use of it. But cover the Southern States with it, and every man will become a consumer of oil. within whose reach it can be brought in point of price.—To WILLIAM DRAYTON. ii, 200. (P., 1787.)

6200. OLIVE, Planting trees.—Were the owner of slaves to view it only as the means of bettering their condition, how much would he better that by planting one of those trees for every slave he possessed! Having been myself an eye-witness to the blessings which this tree sheds on the poor, I never had my wishes so kindled for the introduction of any article of new culture into our own country. —To WILLIAM DRAYTON. ii, 201. (P., 1787.)

6201. OLIVE, South Carolina and.—If the memory of those persons is held in great respect in South Carolina who introduced there the culture of rice, a plant which sows life and death with almost equal hand, what obligations would be due to him who should introduce the olive tree, and set the example of its culture!—To WILLIAM DRAYTON. ii, 200. (P., 1787.)

6202. —— ——. I am gratified by letters from South Carolina, which inform me that in consequence of the information I had given them on the subject of the olive tree, and the probability of its succeeding with them, several rich individuals propose to begin its culture there.—To M. DE BERTROUS. ii, 359. (P., 1788.)

6203. —— ——. This is the most interesting plant in the world for South Carolina and Georgia. You will see in various places [on your tour] that it gives being to whole villages in places where there is not soil enough to subsist a family by the means of any other culture. But consider it as the means of bettering the condition of your slaves in South Carolina. See in the poorer parts of France and Italy what a number of vegetables are rendered eatable by the aid of a little oil, which would otherwise be useless.—To WILLIAM RUTLEDGE. ii, 414. (P., 1788.)

6204. OLIVE, Substitute for.—I lately received from Colonel Few in New York, a bottle of the oil of Beni, believed to be a sesamum. I did not believe there existed so perfect a substitute for olive oil. Like that of

Florence, it has no taste, and is perhaps rather more limpid. A bushel of seed yields three gallons of oil; and Governor Milledge, of Georgia, says the plant will grow wherever the Palmi Christi will.—To ROBERT R. LIVINGSTON. v, 225. (W., 1808.)

6205. OPINION, Avowal of.—I never had an opinion in politics or religion which I was afraid to own.—To F. HOPKINSON. ii. 587. FORD ED., v, 78. (P., 1789.)

6206. —— ——. There is, perhaps, a degree of duty to avow a change of opinion called for by a change of circumstances.—To BENJAMIN AUSTIN. vi, 553. FORD ED., x, 11. (M., 1816.)

6207. OPINION, Coercion.—Subject opinion to coercion: whom will you make your inquisitors? Fallible men; governed by bad passions, by private as well as public reasons. And why subject it to coercion? To produce uniformity? But is uniformity of opinion desirable? No more than of face and stature.—NOTES ON VIRGINIA. viii, 401. FORD ED., iii, 264. (1782.)

6208. OPINION, Collisions of.—I wish to avoid all collisions of opinion with all mankind.—To CHARLES YANCEY. vi, 517. FORD ED., x, 4. (M., 1816.)

6209. OPINION, Compromise of.—Some [members of Congress] think that independence requires them to follow always their own opinion, without respect for that of others. This has never been my opinion, nor my practice, when I have been of that or any other body. Differing, on a particular question, from those whom I knew to be of the same political principles with myself, and with whom I generally thought and acted, a consciousness of the fallibility of the human mind, and of my own in particular, with a respect for the accumulated judgment of my friends, has induced me to suspect erroneous impressions in myself, to suppose my own opinion wrong, and to act with them on theirs. The want of this spirit of compromise, or of self-distrust, proudly, but falsely called independence, is what gives the federalists victories which they could never obtain, if these brethren could learn to respect the opinions of their friends more than of their enemies, and prevents many able and honest men from doing all the good they otherwise might do. These considerations * * * have often quieted my own conscience in voting and acting on the judgment of others against my own.—To WILLIAM DUANE. v, 591. FORD ED., ix, 315. (M., 1811.)

6210. OPINION, Differences of.—Even if we differ in principle more than I believe we do, you and I know too well the texture of the human mind, and the slipperiness of human reason, to consider differences of opinion otherwise than differences of form or feature.—To ELBRIDGE GERRY. iv, 273. FORD ED., vii, 335. (Pa., 1799.)

6211. —— ——. In every country where man is free to think and to speak, differences of opinion will arise from difference of perception, and the imperfection of reason; but these differences when permitted, as in this happy country, to purify themselves by free discussion, are but as passing clouds overspreading our land transiently, and leaving our horizon more bright and serene.—To BENJAMIN WARING. iv, 378. (W., March 1801.)

6212. —— ——. Every difference of opinion is not a difference of principle. We have called by different names brethren of the same principle. We are all republicans: we are all federalists.—FIRST INAUGURAL ADDRESS. viii, 2. FORD ED., viii, 3. (1801.)

6213. —— ——. I lament sincerely that unessential differences of opinion should ever have been deemed sufficient to interdict half the society from the rights and the blessings of self-government, to proscribe them as characters unworthy of every trust.—TO THE NEW HAVEN COMMITTEE. iv, 405. FORD ED., viii, 70. (W., July 1801.)

6214. —— ——. I tolerate with the utmost latitude the right of others to differ from me in opinion without imputing to them criminality. I know too well the weakness and uncertainty of human reason to wonder at its different results.—To MRS. JOHN ADAMS. iv, 562. FORD ED., viii, 312. (M., 1804.)

6215. —— ——. That in a free government there should be differences of opinion as to public measures and the conduct of those who direct them, is to be expected. It is much, however, to be lamented, that these differences should be indulged at a crisis which calls for the undivided counsels and energies of our country, and in a form calculated to encourage our enemies in the refusal of justice, and to force their country into war as the only resource for obtaining it.—R. TO A. NEW LONDON REPUBLICANS. viii, 151. (1809.)

6216. —— ——. That differences of opinion should arise among men, on politics, on religion, and on every other topic of human inquiry, and that these should be freely expressed in a country where all our faculties are free, is to be expected. But these valuable privileges are much perverted when permitted to disturb the harmony of social intercourse, and to lessen the tolerance of opinion.—R. TO A. CITIZENS OF WASHINGTON. viii, 158. (1809.)

6217. —— ——. Some friends have left me by the way, seeking by a different political path, the same object, their country's good, which I pursued with the crowd along the common highway. It is a satisfaction to me that I was not the first to leave them.—To DAVID CAMPBELL. v, 499. (M., 1810.)

6218. —— ——. I have never thought that a difference in political, any more than in religious opinions, should disturb the friendly intercourse of society.—To DAVID CAMPBELL. v, 499. (M., 1810.)

6219. —— ——. With respect to impressions from any differences of political opinion, whether major or minor, * * * I have none. I left them·all behind me on quitting Washington, where alone the state of things had, till then, required some attention to them. Nor was that the lightest part of the load I was there disburthened of; and could I permit myself to believe that with the change of circumstances a corresponding change had taken place in the minds of those who differed from me, and that I now stand in the peace and good will of my fellow-citizens generally, it would, indeed, be a sweetening ingredient in the last dregs of my life.—To JOHN NICHOLAS. vii, 143. FORD ED., x. 148. (M., 1819.)

6220. —— ——. Difference of opinion was never, with me, a motive of separation from a friend.—To PRESIDENT MONROE. FORD ED., x, 298. (M., 1824.)

6221. —— ——. Men, according to their constitutions and the circumstances in which they are placed, differ honestly in opinion. Some are whigs, liberals, democrats, call them what you please. Others are tories, serviles, aristocrats, &c.—To WILLIAM SHORT. vii, 391. FORD ED., x, 334. (M., 1825.)

6222. OPINION, Freedom of.—The will of the people is the only legitimate foundation of any government, and to protect its free expression should be our first object.—To BENJAMIN WARING. iv, 379. (W., March 1801.)

6223. —— ——. Opinion, and the just maintenance of it, shall never be a crime in my view; nor bring injury on the individual.—To SAMUEL ADAMS. iv, 389. FORD ED., viii, 39. (W., March 1801.)

6224. —— ——. The freedom of opinion, and the reasonable maintenance of it, is not a crime, and ought not to occasion injury.—To GIDEON GRANGER. FORD ED., viii, 44. (W., March 1801.)

6225. —— ——. The right of opinion shall suffer no invasion from me. Those [office-holders] who have acted well have nothing to fear, however they may have differed from me in opinion: those who have done ill, however, have nothing to hope; nor shall I fail to do justice lest it should be ascribed to that difference of opinion.—To ELBRIDGE GERRY. iv, 391. FORD ED., viii, 42. (W., March 1801.)

6226. —— ——. The legislative powers of government reach actions only and not opinions.—REPLY TO BAPTIST ADDRESS. viii, 113. (1802.)

6227. —— ——. Where thought is free in its range, we need never fear to hazard what is good in itself.—To MR. OGILVIE. v, 604. (M., 1811.)

6228. —— ——. Difference of opinion leads to enquiry, and enquiry to truth; and I am sure * * * we both value too much the freedom of opinion sanctioned by our Constitution, not to cherish its exercise even where in opposition to ourselves.—To Mr. WENDOVER. vi, 447. (M., 1815.)

6229. —— ——. The amendments [to the constitution of Massachusetts] of which we have as yet heard, prove the advance of liberalism * * * and encourage the hope that the human mind will some day get back to the freedom it enjoyed two thousand years ago.—To JOHN ADAMS. vii, 199. FORD ED., x, 185. (M., 1821.)

6230. —— ——. I respect the right of free opinion too much to urge an uneasy pressure of [my own] opinion on [others]. Time and advancing science will ripen us all in its course, and reconcile all to wholesome and necessary changes.—To SAMUEL KERCHIVAL. FORD ED., x, 320. (M., 1824.)

6231. OPINION, Government and.— Government is founded in opinion and confidence.—THE ANAS. ix, 121. FORD ED., i, 204. (1792.)

6232. OPINION, Individual.—I never submitted the whole system of my opinions to the creed of any party of men whatever, in religion, in philosophy, in politics, or in anything else, where I was capable of thinking for myself. Such an addiction is the last degradation of a free and moral agent. If I could not go to heaven but with a party, I would not go there at all.—To FRANCIS HOPKINSON. ii, 585. FORD ED., v, 76. (P., 1789.)

6233. OPINION, Legal.—On every question the lawyers are about equally divided, and were we to act but in cases where no contrary opinion of a lawyer can be had, we should never act.—To ALBERT GALLATIN. v, 369. (M., 1808.)

6234. OPINION, Majority and.—I readily suppose my opinion wrong, when opposed by the majority.—To JAMES MADISON. ii, 447. FORD ED., v, 48. (P., 1788.)

6235. OPINION, Power of.—Opinion is power.—To JOHN ADAMS. vi, 525. (M., 1816.)

6236. OPINION, Right of.—I may sometimes differ in opinion from some of my friends, from those whose views are as pure and sound as my own. I censure none, but do homage to every one's right of opinion.— To WILLIAM DUANE. v, 577. FORD ED., ix, 314. (M., 1811.)

6237. OPINION, Sacrifices of.—If we do not learn to sacrifice small differences of opinion, we can never act together. Every man cannot have his way in all things. If his own opinion prevails at some times, he should acquiesce on seeing that of others preponderate at other times. Without this mutual disposition we are disjointed individuals, but not a society.—To JOHN DICKINSON. FORD ED., viii, 76. (W., July 1801.)

6238. —— ——. I see too many proofs of the imperfection of human reason, to entertain wonder or intolerance at any difference

of opinion on any subject; and acquiesce in that difference as easily as on a difference of feature or form; experience having long taught me the reasonableness of mutual sacrifices of opinion among those who are to act together for any common object, and the expediency of doing what good we can, when we cannot do all we would wish.—To JOHN RANDOLPH. iv, 518. FORD ED., viii, 282. (W., Dec. 1803.)

6239. —— ——. To the principles of union I sacrifice all minor differences of opinion. These, like differences of face, are a law of our nature, and should be viewed with the same tolerance.—To WILLIAM DUANE. v, 603. (M., 1811.)

6240. OPINION, Uniformity.—Suppose the State should take into head that there should be an uniformity of countenance. Men would be obliged to put an artificial bump or swelling here, a patch there, &c., but this would be merely hypocritical, or if the alternative was given of wearing a mask, ninety-nine one-hundredths must immediately mask. Would this add to the beauty of nature? Why otherwise in opinions?—NOTES ON RELIGION. FORD ED., ii, 95. (1776?)

6241. —— ——. Is uniformity of opinion desirable? No more than that of face and stature.—NOTES ON VIRGINIA. viii, 401. FORD ED., iii, 264. (1782.)

6242. OPINION, War an —If we are forced into war [with France] we must give up differences of opinion, and unite as one man to defend our country.—To GENERAL KOSCIUSKO. iv, 295. (Pa., 1799.)

6243. OPINION (Public), Administration and.—Ministers * * * cannot in any country be uninfluenced by the voice of the people.—To JOHN JAY. ii, 46. (P., 1786.)

6244. OPINION (Public), Advantageous.—The advantage of public opinion is like that of the weather-gauge in a naval action.—To JAMES MONROE. vi, 408. FORD ED., ix, 496. (M., 1815.)

6245. OPINION (Public), Attention to.—More attention should be paid to the general opinion.—To GEORGE MASON. iii, 209. FORD ED., v, 275. (Pa., 1791.)

6246. OPINION (Public), Censorship by.—Public opinion is a censor before which the most exalted tremble for their future as well as present fame.—To JOHN ADAMS. vi, 524. (M., 1816.)

6247. —— ——. The public judgment will correct false reasonings and opinions, on a full hearing of all parties; and no other definite line can be drawn between the inestimable liberty of the press and its demoralizing licentiousness. If there be still improprieties which this rule would not restrain, its supplement must be sought in the censorship of public opinion.—SECOND INAUGURAL ADDRESS. viii, 44. FORD ED., viii, 346. (1805.)

6248. OPINION (Public), Changes in.— When public opinion changes, it is with the rapidity of thought.—To CHARLES YANCEY. vi, 516. FORD ED., x, 3. (M., 1816.)

6249. OPINION (Public), Conforming to.— I think it a duty in those intrusted with the administration of their affairs to conform themselves to the decided choice of their constituents.—To JOHN JAY. i, 404. FORD ED., iv, 89. (P., 1785.)

6250. OPINION (Public), Degeneracy.— It is the manners and spirit of a people which preserve a republic in vigor. A degeneracy in these is a canker which soon eats to the heart of its laws and constitution.—NOTES ON VIRGINIA. viii, 406. FORD ED., iii, 269. (1782.)

6251. OPINION (Public), Force of.— The public mind [in France] is manifestly advancing on the abusive prerogatives of their governors, and bearing them down. No force in the government can withstand this in the long run.—To COMTE DE MOUSTIER. ii, 389. FORD ED., v, 12. (P., 1788.)

6252. ———. A King [Louis XVI.] with two hundred thousand men at his orders, is disarmed by force of public opinion and want of money.—To MADAME DE BRÉHAN. ii, 591. FORD ED., v, 79. (P., 1789.)

6253. ———. The good opinion of mankind, like the lever of Archimedes, with the given fulcrum, moves the world.—To M. CORRÊA. vi, 405. (M., 1814.)

6254. ———. The spirit of our people would oblige even a despot to govern us republicanly.—To SAMUEL KERCHIVAL. vii, 11. FORD ED., x, 39. (M., 1816.)

6255. ———. The force of public opinion cannot be resisted, when permitted freely to be expressed. The agitation it produces must be submitted to. It is necessary, to keep the waters pure.—To THE MARQUIS DE LAFAYETTE. vii, 325. FORD ED., x, 280. (M., 1823.)

6256. OPINION (Public), Indian.— I am convinced that those societies (as the Indians) which live without government, enjoy in their general mass an infinitely greater degree of happiness, than those who live under the European governments. Among the former, public opinion is in the place of law, and restrains morals as powerfully as laws ever did anywhere.—To EDWARD CARRINGTON. ii, 100. FORD ED., iv, 360. (P., 1787.)

6257. OPINION (Public), Inquisition of.— This country, which has given to the world the example of physical liberty, owes to it that of moral emancipation also, for as yet it is but nominal with us. The inquisition of public opinion overwhelms in practice the freedom asserted by the laws in theory.—To JOHN ADAMS. vii, 200. FORD ED., x, 185. (M., 1821.)

6258. OPINION (Public), Nourish.— Secure self-government by the republicanism of our constitution, as well as by the spirit of the people; and nourish and perpetuate that spirit.—To SAMUEL KERCHIVAL. vii, 13. FORD ED., x, 41. (M., 1816.)

6259. OPINION (Public), Preserving.— The basis of our governments being the opinion of the people, the very first object should be to keep that right.—To EDWARD CARRINGTON. ii, 100. FORD ED., iv, 359. (P., 1787.)

6260. OPINION (Public), Respect for.— When, in the course of human events, it becomes necessary for one people to dissolve the political bands which have connected them with another, and to assume among the powers of the earth the separate and equal station to which the laws of nature and of nature's God entitle them, a decent respect to the opinions of mankind requires that they should declare the causes which impel them to the separation.—DECLARATION OF INDEPENDENCE AS DRAWN BY JEFFERSON.

6261. ———. There are certainly persons in all the departments who are driving too fast. Government being founded on opinion, the opinion of the public, even when it is wrong, ought to be respected to a certain degree.—To NICHOLAS LEWIS. FORD ED., v, 282. (Pa., 1791.)

6262. ———. We have believed we should afford England an opportunity of making reparation, as well from justice and the usage of nations, as a respect to the opinion of an impartial world, whose approbation and esteem are always of value.—To W. H. CABELL. v, 142. FORD ED., ix, 90. (W., July 1807.)

6263. ———. A regard for reputation, and the judgment of the world, may sometimes be felt where conscience is dormant.—To EDWARD LIVINGSTON. vii, 404. (M., 1825.)

6264. OPINION (Public), Revolution by.— A complete revolution in the French government has, within the space of two years, been effected by the mere force of public opinion, aided, indeed, by the want of money which the dissipations of the Court had brought on.—To DAVID HUMPHREYS. iii, 10. FORD ED., v, 86. (P., 1789.)

6265. OPINION (Public), Supremacy.— Public opinion, that lord of the universe.—To WILLIAM SHORT. vii, 157. (M., 1820.)

6266. OPINION (Public), Wisdom of.— It is rare that the public sentiment decides immorally or unwisely, and the individual who differs from it ought to distrust and examine well his own opinion.—To WILLIAM FINDLEY. FORD ED., viii, 27. (W., March 1801.)

6267. OPINIONS, Canvassing.— In canvassing my opinions you have done what every man has a right to do, and it is for the good of society that that right should be freely exercised.—To NOAH WEBSTER. iii, 201. FORD ED., v, 254. (Pa., 1790.)

6268. OPINIONS, Exchange of.—I shall be happy, at all times, in an intercommunication of sentiments with you, believing that the dispositions of the different parts of our country have been considerably misrepresented and misunderstood in each part, as to the other, and that nothing but good can result from an exchange of information and opinions between those whose circumstances and morals admit no doubt of the integrity of their views.—To ELBRIDGE GERRY. iv, 174. FORD ED., vii, 123. (Pa., 1797.)

6269. OPINIONS, Formation.—The opinions and belief of men depend not on their own will, but follow involuntarily the evidence proposed to their minds.—STATUTE OF RELIGIOUS FREEDOM. FORD ED., ii, 237. (1779.)

6270. OPINIONS, Government and.—The opinions of men are not the object of civil government, nor under its jurisdiction.—STATUTE OF RELIGIOUS FREEDOM. FORD ED., ii. 238. (1779.)

6271. OPINIONS, Moral facts.—Opinions constitute moral facts, as important as physical ones to the attention of the public functionary.—To RICHARD RUSH. vii, 183. (M., 1820.)

6272. OPINIONS, Propagation of.—To compel a man to furnish contributions of money for the propagation of opinions which he disbelieves and abhors, is sinful and tyrannical.—STATUTE OF RELIGIOUS FREEDOM. FORD ED., ii, 238. (1779.)

6273. OPINIONS, Revealing.—The sentiments of men are known not only by what they receive, but what they reject.—AUTOBIOGRAPHY. i, 19. FORD ED., i, 28. (1821.)

6274. OPINIONS, Social intercourse and.—Opinions, which are equally honest on both sides, should not affect personal esteem or social intercourse.—To JOHN ADAMS. vi, 146. (M., 1813.)

6275. OPINIONS, Strength of sound.—If * * * opinions are sound * * * they will prevail by their own weight, without the aid of names.—To SAMUEL KERCHIVAL. vii, 35. FORD ED., x, 45. (M., 1816.)

6276. OPINIONS, Vindication of.—My occupations do not permit me to undertake to vindicate all my opinions, nor have they importance enough to merit it.—To NOAH WEBSTER. iii, 203. FORD ED., v, 257. (Pa., 1790.)

6277. OPPOSITION, To Administrations.—A quondam colleague of yours, who had acquired some distinction and favor in the public eye, is throwing it away by endeavoring to obtain his end by rallying an opposition to the administration. This error has already ruined some among us, and will ruin others who do not perceive that it is the steady abuse of power in other governments which renders that of opposition always the popular party.—To ALBERT GALLATIN. FORD ED., x, 106. (M., 1818.)

6278. OPPOSITION, Continual.—In the Middle and Southern States, as great an union of sentiment has now taken place as is perhaps desirable. For as there will always be an opposition, I believe it had better be from avowed monarchists than republicans.—To ELDRIDGE GERRY. iv, 536. FORD ED:, viii, 297. (W., March 1804.)

6279. OPPOSITION, Crushing.—I have removed those [officeholders] who maintained an active and zealous opposition to the government.—To JOHN PAGE. v, 136. FORD ED., ix, 119. (W., 1807.)

6280. OPPOSITION, Of enemies.—The clouds which have appeared for some time to be gathering around us, have given me anxiety lest an enemy, always on the watch, always prompt and firm, and acting in well-disciplined phalanx, should find an opening to dissipate hopes, with the loss of which I would wish that of life itself.—To WILLIAM DUANE. v, 603. (M., 1811.)

6281. OPPOSITION, Federal elements.—I have never dreamed that all opposition was to cease. The clergy who have missed their union with the State, the Anglomen, who have missed their union with England, and the political adventurers, who have lost the chance of swindling and plunder in the waste of public money, will never cease to bawl, on the breaking up of their sanctuary. But among the people, the schism is healed, and with tender treatment the wound will not reopen. Their quondam leaders have been astounded with the suddenness of the desertion; and their silence and appearance of acquiescence have proceeded not from a thought of joining us, but the uncertainty what ground to take.—To GIDEON GRANGER. iv, 395. FORD ED., viii, 48. (W., May 1801.)

6282. OPPOSITION, Federalist.—The federalists meant by crippling my rigging to leave me an unwieldy hulk at the mercy of the elements.—To THEODORE FOSTER. FORD ED., viii, 51. (W., May 1801.)

6283. —— ——. Their rallying point is "war with France and Spain, and alliance with Great Britain"; and everything is wrong with them which checks their new ardor to be fighting for the liberties of mankind; on the sea always excepted. There, one nation is to monopolize all the liberties of the others.—To MR. BIDWELL. v, 15. (W., 1806.)

6284. —— ——. I should suspect error where the federalists found no fault.—To MR. BIDWELL. v, 15. (W., 1806.)

6285. OPPOSITION, Fighting.—While duty required it, I met opposition with a firm and fearless step.—To SPENCER ROANE. vii, 136. FORD ED., x, 142. (P.F., 1819.)

6286. OPPOSITION, Malicious.—There is nothing against which human ingenuity will not be able to find something to say.—To GIDEON GRANGER. iv, 396. FORD ED., viii 48. (W., 1801.)

6287. OPPRESSION, Colonies and.—A series of oppressions, begun at a distinguished period, and pursued unalterably through every change of ministers, too plainly prove a deliberate, systematical plan of reducing us to slavery.—Rights of British America. i, 130. Ford ed., i. 435. (1774.)

6288. OPPRESSION, Nations and.—It is, indeed, an animating thought that, while we are securing the rights of ourselves and our posterity, we are pointing out the way to struggling nations who wish, like us, to emerge from their tyrannies also. Heaven help their struggles, and lead them, as it has done us, triumphantly through them.—Reply to Address. iii, 128. Ford ed., v, 147. (1790.)

6289. OPTICS, Laws of.—To distinct vision it is necessary not only that the visual angle should be sufficient for the powers of the human eye, but that there should be sufficient light also on the object of observation. In microscopic observations, the enlargement of the angle of vision may be more indulged, because auxiliary light may be concentrated on the object by concave mirrors. But in the case of the heavenly bodies we can have no such aid. The moon, for example, receives from the sun but a fixed quantity of light. In proportion as you magnify her surface, you spread that fixed quantity over a greater space, dilute it more, and render the object more dim. If you increase her magnitude infinitely, you dim her face infinitely also, and she becomes invisible. When under total eclipse, all the direct rays of the sun being intercepted, she is seen but faintly, and would not be seen at all but for the refraction of the solar rays in their passage through our atmosphere. In a night of extreme darkness, a house or a mountain is not seen, as not having light enough to impress the limited sensibility of our eye. I do suppose in fact that Herschel has availed himself of the properties of the parabolic mirror to the point beyond which its effect would be countervailed by the diminution of light on the object. I barely suggest this element, not presented to view in your letter, as one which must enter into the estimate of the improved telescope you propose.—To Thomas Skidman. vii, 259. (M., 1822.)

6290. ORATORY, Art in.—In a republican nation, whose citizens are to be led by reason and persuasion, and not by force, the art of reasoning becomes of first importance. In this line antiquity has left us the finest models for imitation; and he who studies and imitates them most nearly, will nearest approach the perfection of the art. Among these I should consider the speeches of Livy, Sallust and Tacitus as preeminent specimens of logic, taste, and that sententious brevity which, using not a word to spare, leave not a moment for inattention to the hearer. Amplification is the vice of modern oratory. It is an insult to an assembly of reasonable men, disgusting and revolting instead of persuading. Speeches measured by the hour die with the hour.—To David Harding. vii, 347. (M., 1824.)

6291. ORATORY, Models for.—The models for that oratory which is to produce the greatest effect by securing the attention of hearers and readers, are to be found in Livy, Tacitus, Sallust, and most assuredly not in Cicero. I doubt if there is a man in the world

who can now read one of his orations through but as a piece of task work.—To J. W. Eppes. v, 490. Ford ed., ix, 267. (M., 1810.)

6292. ORATORY, Modern and Ancient.—The short, the nervous, the unanswerable speech of Carnot, in 1803, on the proposition to declare Bonaparte consul for life,—this creed of republicanism should be well translated, and placed in the hands and heart of every friend to the rights of self-government.—To Abraham Small. vi, 347. (M., 1814.)

6293. ——— ———. The finest thing, in my opinion, which the English language has produced, is the defence of Eugene Aram, spoken by himself at the bar of the York assizes, in 1759.—To Abraham Small. vi, 347. (M., 1814.)

6294. ——— ———. I consider the speeches of Aram and Carnot, and that of Logan, as worthily standing in a line with those of Scipio and Hannibal in Livy, and of Cato and Cæsar in Sallust.—To Abraham Small. vi, 347. (M., 1814.)

6295. ORATORY, Scathing.—Lord Chatham's reply to Horace Walpole, on the Seamen's bill, in the House of Commons, in 1740, is one of the severest which history has recorded.—To Abraham Small. vi, 346. (M., 1814.)

6296. ORDER, Liberty and.—Possessing ourselves the combined blessing of liberty and order, we wish the same to other countries. —To M. Coray. vii, 318. (M., 1823.)

6297. ORDER, Maintenance of.—The life of the citizen is never to be endangered, but as the last melancholy effort for the maintenance of order and obedience to the laws.*—To the Governors of the States. v, 414. Ford ed., ix, 238. (W., 1809.)

6298. ORDER, Preservation of.—Every man being at his ease, feels an interest in the preservation of order, and comes forth to preserve it at the first call of the magistrate. —To M. Pictet. iv, 463. (W., 1803.)

6299. ORDERS IN COUNCIL, Repeal of.—The British ministry has been driven from its Algerine system, not by any remaining morality in the people, but by their unsteadiness under severe trial. But whencesoever it comes, I rejoice in it as the triumph of our forbearing and yet persevering system. It will lighten your anxieties, take from cabal its most fertile ground of war, will give us peace during your time, and by the complete extinguishment of our public debt, open upon us the noblest application of revenue that has ever been exhibited by any nation.—To President Madison. v, 443. (M., April 1809.) See Berlin Decrees and Embargo.

— OREGON.—See Lewis and Clark Expedition.

6300. ORLEANS (Duke of), Unprincipled.—The Duke d'Orleans is as unprincipled as his followers; sunk in debaucheries of the lowest kind, and incapable of quitting them for business; not a fool, yet not head enough to conduct anything.—To John Jay. iii, 95. (P., 1789.)

* From a letter in regard to the employment of the militia.—Editor.

6301. ORLEANS (Duke of), Vicious.— He is a man of moderate understanding, of no principle, absorbed in low vice, and incapable of extracting himself from the filth of that, to direct anything else. His name and his money, therefore, are mere tools in the hands of those who are duping him. Mirabeau is their chief.—To JAMES MADISON. iii, 98. FORD ED., v, 109. (P., 1789.)

6302. OSSIAN, Poems of.— These pieces have been and will, I think, during my life, continue to be to me the sources of daily and exalted pleasures. The tender and the sublime emotions of the mind were never before so wrought up by the human hand. I am not ashamed to own that I think this rude bard of the North the greatest poet that has ever existed. Merely for the pleasure of reading his works, I am become desirous of learning the language in which he sung, and of possessing his songs in their original form.—To CHARLES MCPHERSON. i, 195. FORD ED., i, 413. (A., 1773.)

6303. ——— ———. If not ancient, it is equal to the best morsels of antiquity.—To MARQUIS LAFAYETTE. vii, 326. FORD ED., x, 282. (M., 1823.)

6304. OSTENTATION, Good deeds and. —What is proposed, though but an act of duty, may be perverted into one of ostentation, but malice will always find bad motives for good actions. Shall we therefore never do good?—To PRESIDENT MADISON. v, 524. (M., 1810.)

— OUTACITE, Indian Chief.—See INDIANS.

— PACIFIC, Exploration of the.—See LEWIS AND CLARK EXPEDITION.

6305. PAGE (John), Jefferson and.—It had given me much pain, that the zeal of our respective friends should ever have placed you and me in the situation of competitors.* I was comforted, however, with the reflection, that it was their competition, not ours, and that the difference of the numbers which decided between us, was too insignificant to give to you a pain, or me a pleasure, had our dispositions towards each other been such as to admit those sensations.—To JOHN PAGE. i, 210. FORD ED., ii, 187. (1779.)

6306. PAGE (John), Tribute to.—I have known Mr. Page from the time we were boys and classmates together, and love him as a brother, but I have always known him the worst judge of men existing. He has fallen a sacrifice to the ease with which he gives his confidence to those who deserve it not. * * * I am very anxious to do something useful for him; and so universally is he esteemed in this country [Virginia], that no man's promotion would be more generally approved. He has not an enemy in the world.—To ALBERT GALLATIN. FORD ED., viii, 85. (M., 1801.)

6307. PAIN, Pleasure vs.—We have no rose without its thorn; no pleasure without alloy. It is the law of our existence; and we must acquiesce. It is the condition annexed to all our pleasures, not by us who receive, but by Him who gives them.—To MRS. COSWAY. ii, 41. FORD ED., iv, 321. (P., 1786.)

6308. ——— ———. I do not agree that an age of pleasure is no compensation for a mo-

*For the governorship of Virginia. On the first vote, the figures were: Jefferson, 55; Nelson, 32; and Page, 38. The second vote resulted: Jefferson, 67, Page 61.—EDITOR.

ment of pain.—To JOHN ADAMS. vii, 26. (M., 1816.)

6309. PAIN, Security against.—The most effectual means of being secure against pain is to retire within ourselves and to suffice for our own happiness. Those which depend on ourselves are the only pleasures a wise man will count on; for nothing is ours which another may deprive us of. Hence the inestimable value of intellectual pleasures. Ever in our power, always leading us to something new, never cloying, we ride serene and sublime above the concerns of this mortal world, contemplating truth and nature, matter and motion, the laws which bind up their existence, and that Eternal Being who made and bound them up by those laws.—To MRS. COSWAY. ii, 37. FORD ED., iv, 317. (P., 1786.)

6310. PAINE (Thomas), Common Sense.—Paine's Common Sense electrified us. —AUTOBIOGRAPHY. i, 91. FORD ED., i, 127. (1821.)

6311. PAINE (Thomas), Correspondence.—I have been in daily intention of answering your letters, fully and confidentially; but you know, such a correspondence between you and me cannot pass through the post, nor even by the couriers of ambassadors.—To THOMAS PAINE. ii, 545. (P., 1788.)

6312. PAINE (Thomas), Gunboats.—The model of a contrivance for making one gunboat do nearly double execution has all the ingenuity and simplicity which generally mark your inventions. I am not nautical enough to judge whether two guns may be too heavy for the bow of a gunboat, or whether any other objection will countervail the advantage it offers, and which I see visibly enough. I send it to the Secretary of the Navy, within whose department it lies to try and to judge it.— To THOMAS PAINE. v, 189. FORD ED., ix, 136. (M., 1807.)

6313. PAINE (Thomas), Honors to.—You expressed a wish to get a passage to this country in a public vessel. Mr. Dawson is charged with orders to the captain of the Maryland, a sloop of war, to receive and accommodate you.—To THOMAS PAINE. iv, 371. FORD ED., viii, 18. (W., March 1801.)

6314. ——— ———. I am in hopes you will [on your return from France] find us returned generally to sentiments worthy of former times. In these it will be your glory to have steadily labored, and with as much effect as any man living.—To THOMAS PAINE. iv, 371. FORD ED., viii, 19. (W., March 1801.)

6315. PAINE (Thomas), Iron bridge.—Mr. Paine (Common Sense) is in Paris on his way to England. He has brought the model of an iron bridge, with which he supposes a single arch of four hundred feet, may be made.— To B. VAUGHAN. ii, 166. (P., 1787.)

6316. ——— ———. I feel myself interested in your bridge, and it is with great pleasure that I learn that the execution of the arch of experiment exceeds your expectation. In your former letter, you mention that instead of arranging your tubes and bolts as ordinates to the chord of the arch, you had reverted to your first idea, of arranging them in the direction of the radii. I am sure it will gain both in beauty and strength. It is true that the divergence of those radii recurs as a difficulty, in getting the rails upon the bolts; but I thought this removed by the answer you first gave me, when I suggested that difficulty, to wit, that you should place the rails first, and drive the bolts through them, and not, as I had imagined, place the bolts first, and put the rails on them. I must doubt whether what you now suggest, will be as good as your first idea; to wit, to have every rail split into two pieces longitudinally, so that there shall be but the halves of the holes in each, and then to clamp the two halves together. The solidity of this method cannot be equal to that of the solid rail, and it increases the suspicious part of the whole machine, which, in a first experiment, ought to be rendered as few as possible. But of all this, the practical iron men are much better judges than we theorists. You hesitate between the catenary and portion of a circle. I have lately received from Italy, a treatise on the equilibrium of arches by the Abbé Mascheroni. * * * I find that the conclusions of his demonstrations are that every part of the catenary is in perfect equilibrium. It is a great point, then, in a new experiment, to adopt the sole arch, where the pressure will be equally borne by every point of it. If any one point is pushed with accumulated pressure, it will introduce a danger foreign to the essential part of the plan. The difficulty you suggest is, that the rails being all in catenaries, the tubes must be of different lengths, as these approach nearer, or recede farther from each other, and therefore, you recur to the portions of concentric circles, which are equi-distant in all their parts. But I would rather propose that you make your middle rail an exact catenary, and the interior and exterior rails parallels to that. It is true they will not be exact catenaries, but they will depart very little from it; much less than portions of circles will.—To THOMAS PAINE, ii, 546. (P., 1788.)

6317. ———— ————. To say another word about the catenary arch, without caring about mathematical demonstrations, its nature proves it to be in equilibrio in every point. It is the arch formed by a string fixed at both ends, and swaying loose in all the intermediate points. Thus at liberty, they must finally take that position, wherein every one will be equally pressed; for if any one was more pressed than the neighboring point, it would give way, from the flexibility of the matter of the string.—To THOMAS PAINE, ii, 547. (P., 1788.)

6318. ———— ————. Mr. Paine, the author of "Common Sense", has invented an iron bridge, which promises to be cheaper by a great deal than stone, and to admit of a much greater arch. He supposes it may be ventured for an arch of five hundred feet. He has obtained a patent for it in England, and is now executing the first experiment with an arch of between ninety and one hundred feet.—To DR. WILLARD, iii, 16. (P., 1789.)

6319. ———— ————. I congratulate you sincerely on the success of your bridge. I was sure of it before from theory; yet one likes to be assured from practice also.—To THOMAS PAINE, iii, 40. (P., 1789.)

6320. PAINE (Thomas), Planing Machine.—How has your planing machine answered? Has it been tried and persevered in by any workmen?—To THOMAS PAINE, iv, 582. FORD ED., viii, 360. (W., 1805.)

6321. PAINE (Thomas), Republicanism.—A host of writers have risen in favor of Paine, and prove that in this quarter [Philadelphia], at least, the spirit of republicanism is sound. The contrary spirit of the high officers

of government is more understood than I expected.—To JAMES MONROE, iii, 268. FORD ED., v, 352. (Pa., 1791.)

6322. ———— ————. Would you believe it possible that, in this country, there should be high and important characters who need your lessons in republicanism, and who do not heed them? It is but too true that we have a sect preaching up and panting after an English constitution of king, lords, and commons, and whose heads are itching for crowns, coronets, and mitres. But our people * * * are firm and unanimous in their principles of republicanism, and there is no better proof of it than that they love what you write and read it with delight. The printers season every newspaper with extracts from your last, as they did before from your first part of the Rights of Man.—To THOMAS PAINE. FORD ED., vi, 87. (Pa., June 1792.)

6323. PAINE (Thomas), Respect for.—You have certainly misconceived what you deem shyness. Of that I have not had a thought towards you, but on the contrary have openly maintained in conversation the duty of showing our respect to you, and of defying federal calumny in this as in other cases, by doing what is right. As to fearing it, if I ever could have been weak enough for that, they have taken care to cure me of it thoroughly.—To THOMAS PAINE. FORD ED., viii, 189. (W., 1803.)

6324. PAINE (Thomas), Rewards to.—The Assembly of New York have made Paine, the author of "Common Sense", a present of a farm. Could you prevail on our Assembly to do something for him? I think their quota of what ought to be given him would be 2000 guineas, or an inheritance within 100 guineas a year. It would be peculiarly magnanimous in them to do it; because it would show that no particular and smaller passion has suppressed the grateful impressions which his services have made on our minds.—To JAMES MADISON. FORD ED., iii, 499. (Pa., May 1784.)

6325. ———— ————. I still hope something will be done for Paine. He richly deserves it; and it will give a character of littleness to our State if they suffer themselves to be restrained from the compensation due for his services by the paltry consideration that he opposed our right to the Western country. Who was there out of Virginia who did not oppose it? Place this circumstance in one scale, and the effect of his writings produced in uniting us in independence in the other, and say which preponderates. Have we gained more by his advocacy of independence than we lost by his opposition to our territorial right? Pay him the balance only.—To JAMES MADISON. FORD ED., iv, 17. (P., Dec. 1784.)

6326. PAINE (Thomas), Rights of Man.—The "Rights of Man" would bring England itself to reason and revolution, if it was permitted to be read there. However, the same things will be said in milder forms, will make their way among the people, and you must reform at last.—To BENJAMIN VAUGHAN. FORD ED., v, 334. (Pa., 1791.)

6327. ———— ————. The "Rights of Man" has been much read in America with avidity and pleasure. A writer under the signature of "Publicola" has attacked it. A host of champions entered the arena immediately in our defence. The discussion excited the public attention, recalled it to the "Defence of the American Constitutions", and the "Discourses on Davila", which it had kindly passed over without censure in the moment, and very general expressions of their sense have been now drawn forth; and I thank God that they appear him in their republicanism, notwithstanding the contrary hopes and assertions of a sect here, high in names, but small in numbers. These had flattered themselves that the silence of the people under the "Defence" and "Davila" was a symptom of their conversion to the doctrine of king, lords, and commons. They are checked at least by your pamphlet, and the people confirmed in their good old faith.—To THOMAS PAINE. iii, 278. FORD ED., v, 367. (Pa., 1791.)

6328. PAINE (Thomas), Thinker.—
Paine thought more than he read.—To JOHN CARTWRIGHT. vii, 355. (M., 1824.)

6329. PALEONTOLOGY, Bones.—General Clark has employed ten laborers several weeks at the Big-bone Lick, and has shipped the result * * * for this place [Washington]. He has sent, 1st, of the Mammoth, as he calls it, frontals, jaw-bones, tusks, teeth, ribs, a thigh, and a leg, and some bones of the paw; 2d, of what he calls the Elephant, a jaw-bone, tusks, teeth, ribs; 3d, of something of the Buffalo species, a head and some other bones unknown. My intention, in having this research thoroughly made, was to procure for the [Philosophical] Society as complete a supplement to what is already possessed as that lick can furnish at this day, and to serve them first with whatever they wish to possess of it. There are a tusk and a femur which General Clark procured particularly at my request, for a special kind of Cabinet I have at Monticello. But the great mass of the collection are mere duplicates of what you possess at Philadelphia, of which I would wish to make a donation to the National Institute of France, which I believe has scarcely any specimens of the remains of these animals. But how make the selection without the danger of sending away something which might be useful to our own Society? Indeed, my friend, you must give a week to this object, * * * examine these bones, and set apart what you would wish for the Society.— To DR. WISTAR. v, 219. (W., 1807.)

6330. PALEONTOLOGY, Mammoth.—
It is well known, that on the Ohio, and in many parts of America further north, tusks, grinders, and skeletons of unparalleled magnitude, are found in great numbers, some lying on the surface of the earth, and some a little below it. A Mr. Stanley, taken prisoner near the mouth of the Tennessee, relates, that after being transferred through several tribes, from one to another, he was at length carried over the mountains west of the Missouri to a river which runs westwardly; that these bones abounded there, and that the natives described to him the animal to which they belonged as still existing in the northern parts of their country; from which description he judged it to be an elephant. Bones of the same kind have been lately found, some feet below the surface of the earth, in salines opened on the North Holston, a branch of the Tennessee, about the latitude of 36½° north. From the accounts published in Europe, I suppose it to be decided that these are of the same kind with those found in Siberia. * * * It is remarkable that the tusks and skeletons have been ascribed by the naturalists of Europe to the elephant, while the grinders have been given to the hippopotamus, or river horse. Yet it is acknowledged, that the tusks and skeletons are much larger than those of the elephant, and

the grinders many times greater than those of the hippopotamus, and essentially different in form. * * * We must agree, then, that these remains belong to each other, that they are of one and the same animal, that this was not a hippopotamus, because the hippopotamus had no tusks, nor such a frame, and because the grinders differ in their size as well as in the number and form of their points. That this was not an elephant, I think ascertained by proofs equally decisive. * * * I have never heard an instance, and suppose there has been none, of the grinder of an elephant being found in America. From the known temperature and constitution of the elephant, he could never have existed in those regions where the remains of the mammoth have been found. The elephant is a native only of the torrid zone and its vicinities. * * * No bones of the mammoth, have ever been found farther south than the salines of Holston, and they have been found as far north as the Arctic circle. * * * For my own part, I find it easier to believe that an animal may have existed, resembling the elephant in his tusks, and general anatomy, while his nature was in other respects extremely different. From the 30th degree of south latitude to the 30th degree of north, are nearly the limits which nature has fixed for the existence and multiplication of the elephant known to us. Proceeding thence northwardly to 36½° degrees, we enter those assigned to the mammoth. The farther we advance north, the more their vestiges multiply as far as the earth has been explored in that direction; and it is as probable as otherwise, that this progression continues to the pole itself, if land extends so far. The centre of the frozen zone, then, may be the acme of their vigor, as that of the torrid is of the elephant. Thus nature seems to have drawn a belt of separation between these two tremendous animals, whose breadth, indeed, is not precisely known, though at present we may suppose it about 6½ degrees of latitude; to have assigned to the elephant the regions south of these confines, and those north to the mammoth, founding the constitution of the one in the extreme of heat, and that of the other in the extreme of cold. * * * But to whatever animal we ascribe these remains, it is certain that such a one has existed in America, and that it has been the largest of all terrestrial beings.—NOTES ON VIRGINIA. viii, 286. FORD ED., iii, 134. (1782.)

6331. ———— ————. I have heard of the discovery of some large bones, supposed to be of the mammoth, at about thirty or forty miles distant from you; and among the bones found, are said to be some which we have never been able to procure. The first interesting question is, whether they are the bones of the mammoth? The second, what are the particular bones, and could I possibly procure them? * * * If they are to be bought I will gladly pay for them whatever you shall agree to as reasonable.—To ROBERT R. LIVINGSTON. iv, 337. FORD ED. vii, 463. (W., 1800.)

— PANAMA CANAL.—See CANAL.

6332. PANICS, Evils of.—Buildings and other improvements are suspended. Workmen turned adrift. Country produce is not to be sold at any price; because even substantial merchants, who never meddled with paper, cannot tell how many of their debtors have meddled and may fail; consequently they are afraid to make any new money arrangements till they shall know how they stand.—To T. M. RANDOLPH. FORD ED., v, 509. (Pa., April 1792.)

6333. PANICS, Financial.—I learn with real concern the calamities which are fallen on New York, and which must fall on Philadelphia also. No man of reflection who had ever attended to the South Sea bubble, in England, or that of Law in France, and who applied the lessons of the past to the present time, could fail to foresee the issue though he might not calculate the moment at which it would happen. The evidences of the public debt are solid and sacred. I presume there is not a man in the United States who would not part with his last shilling to pay them. But all that stuff called scrip, of whatever description, was folly or roguery, and under a resemblance to genuine public paper, it buoyed itself up to a par with that. It has given a severe lesson; yet such is the public gullibility in the hands of cunning and unprincipled men, that it is doomed by nature to receive these lessons once in an age at least. Happy if they now come about and get back into the tract of plain unsophisticated common sense which they ought never to have been decoyed from.—To Francis Eppes. Ford ed., v, 507. (Pa., April 1792.) See Banks.

6334. PANICS, Losses by.—It is computed there is a dead loss at New York of about five millions of dollars, which is reckoned the value of all the buildings of the city: so that if the whole town had been burned to the ground it would have been just the measure of the present calamity, supposing goods to have been saved. In Boston, the dead loss is about a million of dollars. * * * It is conjectured that the loss in Philadelphia will be about equal to that of Boston.—To T. M. Randolph. Ford ed., v, 509. (1792.)

6335. —— ——. The losses on this occasion would support a war such as we now have on hand, five or six years. Thus you will see that the calamity has been greater in proportion than that of the South Sea in England, or Law in France.—To William Short. Ford ed., v, 510. (Pa., April 1792.)

6336. PANICS, Paper money and.—At length our paper bubble is burst. The failure of Duer, in New York, soon brought on others, and these still more, like nine pins knocking one another down, till at that place the bankruptcy is become general. Every man concerned in paper being broke, and most of the tradesmen and farmers, who had been laying down money, having been tempted by these speculators to lend it to them at an interest of from 3 to 6 per cent. a month, have lost the whole.—To T. M. Randolph. Ford ed., v, 509. (Pa., 1792.) See Paper Money.

6337. —— ——. The paper debt of the United States is scarcely at par. Bank stock is at 25 per cent. It was once upwards of 300 per cent.—To William Short. Ford ed., v, 510. (Pa., April 1792.)

6338. PANICS, Stocks and.—What a loss you would have suffered if we had laid out your paper for bank stock? * * * Though it would have been improper for me to have given at any time, an opinion on the subject of stocks to Mr. Brown, or any man dealing in them, yet I have been unable to refrain from interposing for you on the present occasion. I found that your stock stood so as not to charge Donald & Co. I know Brown to be a good man, but to have dealt in paper, I did not know how far he was engaged. I knew that good men might sometimes avail themselves of the property of others in their power, to help themselves out of a present difficulty in

an honest but delusive confidence that they will be able to repay; that the best men and those whose transactions stand all in an advantageous form, may fail by the failure of others. Under the impulse, therefore, of the general panic, I ventured to enter a caveat in the treasury office against permitting the transfer of any stock standing in your name, or in any other for your use. This was on the 19th of April. I knew your stock had not been transferred before March 31, and that from that time to this, Mr. Brown had not been in Virginia, so as to give me a reasonable confidence that it had not been transferred between the 1st and 19th inst. If so, it is safe. But it would be still safer invested in Ned Carter's lands at five dollars the acre.—To William Short. Ford ed., v, 510. (Pa., April 1792.) See Speculation.

6339. PAPER AND CIVILIZATION.—This article, the creature of art, and but latterly so comparatively, is now interwoven so much into the conveniences and occupations of men, as to have become one of the necessaries of civilized life.—To Robert R. Livingston. Ford ed., vii, 445. (Pa., 1800.)

6340. PAPER MONEY, Abuses.—Paper is liable to be abused, has been, is, and forever will be abused, in every country in which it is permitted.—To J. W. Eppes. vi, 246. Ford ed., ix, 416. (M., Nov. 1813.)

6341. —— ——. Paper is already at a term of abuse in these States, which has never been reached by any other nation, France excepted, whose dreadful catastrophe should be a warning against the instrument which produced it.—To J. W. Eppes. vi, 246. Ford ed., ix, 416. (M., Nov. 1813.)

6342. PAPER MONEY, A cheat.—Paper money was a cheat. Tobacco was the counter-cheat. Everyone is justifiable in rejecting both except so far as his contracts bind him.—To Francis Eppes. Ford ed., v, 212. (N.Y., 1790.)

6343. PAPER MONEY, Continental.—When I speak comparatively of the paper emission of the old Congress and the present banks, let it not be imagined that I cover them under the same mantle. The object of the former was a holy one; for if ever there was a holy war it was that which saved our liberties and gave us independence. The object of the latter is to enrich swindlers at the expense of the honest and industrious part of the nation.—To J. W. Eppes. vi, 246. Ford ed., ix, 416. (M., Nov. 1813.)

6344. —— ——. The errors of that day* cannot be recalled. The evils they have engendered are now upon us, and the question is how we are to get out of them? Shall we build an altar to the old money of the Revolution. which ruined individuals but saved the Republic, and burn on that all the bank charters, present and future, and their notes with them? For these are to ruin both Republic and individuals. This cannot be done. The mania is too strong. It has seized, by its delusions and corruptions, all

* When the United States Bank was founded.—Editor.

the members of our governments, general, special and individual.—To JOHN ADAMS. vi, 305. (M., Jan. 1814.)

6345. PAPER MONEY, Contraction.—I have been endeavoring to persuade a friend in our Legislature to try and save this State [Virginia] from the general ruin by timely interference. I propose to him, first, to prohibit instantly, all foreign paper. Secondly, to give our banks six months to call in all their five-dollar bills (the lowest we allow); another six months to call in their ten-dollar notes, and six months more to call in all below fifty dollars. This would produce so gradual a diminution of medium, as not to shock contracts already made—would leave finally, bills of such size as would be called for only in transactions between merchant and merchant, and ensure a metallic circulation for those of the mass of citizens. But it will not be done. You might as well, with the sailors, whistle to the wind, as suggest precautions against having too much money. We must bend, then, before the gale, and try to hold fast ourselves by some plank of the wreck. God send us all a safe deliverance.— To JOHN ADAMS. vi, 306. (M., Jan. 1814.)

6346. ——— ———. I had been in hopes that good old Virginia, not yet so far embarked as her northern sisters, would have set the example this winter, of beginning the process of cure, by passing a law that, after a certain time, suppose of six months, no bank bill of less than ten dollars should be permitted. That after some reasonable term, there should be none less than twenty dollars, and so on, until those only should be left in circulation whose size would be above the common transactions of any but merchants. This would ensure us an ordinary circulation of metallic money, and would reduce the quantum of paper within the bounds of moderate mischief. And it is the only way in which the reduction can be made without a shock to private fortunes. A sudden stop to this trash, either by law or its own worthlessness, would produce confusion and ruin. Yet this will happen by its own extinction if left to itself. Whereas, by a salutary interposition of the Legislature, it may be withdrawn insensibly and safely. Such a mode of doing it, too, would give less alarm to the bankholders, the discreet part of whom must wish to see themselves secured by circumscription. It might be asked what we should do for change? The banks must provide it, first to pay off their five-dollar bills, next their ten-dollar bills and so on, and they ought to provide it to lessen the evils of their institution. But I now give up all hope. After producing the same revolutions in private fortunes as the old Continental paper did, it will die like that, adding a total incapacity to raise resources for the war.—To JOSEPH C. CABELL. vi, 300. (M., Jan. 1814.)

6347. ——— ———. Let us be allured by no projects of banks, public or private, or ephemeral expedients, which, enabling us to gasp and flounder a little longer, only increase, by protracting the agonies of death.— To JAMES MONROE. vi, 395. FORD ED., ix, 492. (M., 1814.)

6348. ——— ———. Different persons, doubtless, will devise different schemes of relief. One would be to suppress instantly the currency of all paper not issued under the authority of our own State or of the General Government; to interdict after a few months the circulation of all bills of five dollars and under; after a few months more, all of ten dollars and under; after other terms, those of twenty, fifty, and so on to one hundred dollars, which last, if any must be left in circulation, should be the lowest denomination. These might be a convenience in mercantile transactions and transmissions, and would be excluded by their size from ordinary circulation. But the disease may be too pressing to await such a remedy. With the Legislature I cheerfully leave it to apply this medicine, or no medicine at all. I am sure their intentions are faithful; and embarked in the same bottom, I am willing to swim or sink with my fellow citizens. If the latter is their choice, I will go down with them without a murmur. But my exhortation would rather be " not to give up the ship ".—To CHARLES YANCEY. vi, 516. FORD ED., x, 3. (M., Jan. 1816.)

6349. ——— ———. That in the present state of the circulation the banks should resume payments in specie, would require their vaults to be like the widow's cruse. The thing to be aimed at is, that the excesses of their emissions should be withdrawn gradually, but as speedily, too, as is practicable, without so much alarm as to bring on the crisis dreaded.—To CHARLES YANCEY. vi, 516. FORD ED., x, 3. (M., Jan. 1816.)

6350. PAPER MONEY, Convenience of. —There is, indeed, a convenience in paper; its easy transmission from one place to another. But this may be mainly supplied by bills of exchange, so as to prevent any great displacement of actual coin. Two places trading together balance their dealings, for the most part, by their mutual supplies, and the debtor individuals of either may, instead of cash, remit the bills of those who are creditor in the same dealings; or may obtain them through some third place with which both have dealings. The cases would be rare where such bills could not be obtained, either directly or circuitously, and too unimportant to the nation to overweigh the train of evils flowing from paper circulation.—To J. W. EPPES. vi, 237. FORD ED., ix, 409. (M., Nov. 1813.)

6351. PAPER MONEY, A deluge of.—I told the President [Washington] that a system had there [the Treasury Department] been contrived, for deluging the States with paper money instead of gold and silver, for withdrawing our citizens from the pursuits of commerce, manufactures, buildings, and other branches of useful industry, to occupy themselves and their capitals in a species of gambling, destructive of morality, and which had introduced its poison into the government itself.—THE ANAS. ix, 104. FORD ED., i, 177. (Feb. 1792.)

6352. PAPER MONEY, Depreciation.— The first symptom of the depreciation of our present paper money, was that of silver dollars selling at six shillings, which had before been worth but five shillings and nine pence. The Assembly thereupon raised them by law to six shillings.—NOTES ON VIRGINIA. viii, 410. FORD ED., iii, 275. (1782.)

6353. ———. The acknowledged depreciation of the paper circulation of England, with the known laws of its rapid progression to bankruptcy, will leave that nation shortly without revenue.—To CLEMENT CAINE. vi, 14. FORD ED., ix, 330. (M., Sep. 1811.)

6354. ———. The rapid rise in the nominal price of land and labor (while war and blockade should produce a fall) proves the progressive state of the depreciation of our medium.—To THOMAS LAW. FORD ED., ix, 433. (M., 1813.)

6355. PAPER MONEY, Economy of.— The trifling economy of paper, as a cheaper medium, or its convenience for transmission, weighs nothing in opposition to the advantages of the precious metals.—To J. W. EPPES. vi, 246. FORD ED., ix, 416. (M., Nov. 1813.)

6356. PAPER MONEY, English assignats.— England is emitting assignats also, that is to say exchequer bills, to the amount of five millions English, or one hundred and twenty-five millions French; and these are not founded on land as the French assignats are, but on pins, thread, buckles, hops, and whatever else you will pawn in the exchequer of double the estimated value. But we all know that five millions of such stuff forced for sale on the market of London, where there will be neither cash nor credit, will not pay storage. This paper must rest, then, ultimately on the credit of the nation as the rest of their public paper does, and will sink with that.—To JAMES MONROE. iv, 7. FORD ED., vi, 322. (Pa., June 1793.)

6357. ———. England, too, is issuing her paper, not founded, like the assignats, on land, but on pawns of thread, ribbons, buckles, &c. They will soon learn the science of depreciation, and their whole paper system vanish into nothing, on which it is bottomed. —To DR. GILMER. iv, 6. FORD ED., vi, 325. (Pa., 1793.)

6358. ———. The English are trying to stop the torrent of bankruptcies by an emission of five millions of exchequer bills, loaned on the pawn-broking plan, consequently much inferior to the assignats in value. But the paper will sink to an immediate level with their other public paper, and consequently can only complete the ruin of those who take it from the government at par, and on a pledge of pins, buckles, &c., of double value, which will not sell so as to

pay storage in a country where there is no specie, and we may say no paper of confidence. Every letter which comes expresses a firm belief that the whole paper system will now vanish into that nothing on which it is bottomed. For even the public faith is nothing, as the mass of paper bottomed on it is known to be beyond its possible redemption. I hope this will be a wholesome lesson to our future Legislature.—To JAMES MADISON. iv, 8. FORD ED., vi, 326. (June 1793.)

6359. PAPER MONEY, Evils of.— Stock dealers and banking companies, by the aid of a paper system, are enriching themselves to the ruin of our country, and swaying the government by their possession of the printing presses, which their wealth commands, and by other means, not always honorable to the character of our countrymen.—To ARTHUR CAMPBELL. iv, 197. FORD ED., vii, 170. (M., 1797.)

6360. PAPER MONEY, Farmers and.— The redundancy of paper in the cities is palpably a tax on the distant farmer.—To JAMES MADISON. FORD ED., vi, 404. (Pa., 1793.)

6361. PAPER MONEY, Fluctuations in.— The long succession of years of stunted crops, of reduced prices, the general prostration of the farming business, under levies for the support of manufactures, &c., with the calamitous fluctuations of value in our paper medium, have kept agriculture in a state of abject depression, which has peopled the Western States by silently breaking up those on the Atlantic, and glutted the land market, while it drew off its bidders. In such a state of things, property has lost its character of being a resource for debts. Highland, in Bedford, which, in the days of our plethory, sold readily for from fifty to one hundred dollars the acre (and such sales were many then), would not now sell for more than from ten to twenty dollars, or one-quarter to one-fifth of its former price.—To JAMES MADISON. vii, 434. FORD ED., x, 377. (M., February 1826.)

6362. PAPER MONEY, Gambling in.— What do you think of this scrippomany? Ships are lying idle at the wharves, buildings are stopped, capital withdrawn from commerce, manufactures, arts and agriculture, to be employed in gambling, and the tide of prosperity almost unparalleled in any country, is arrested in its course, and suppressed by the rage of getting rich in a day. No mortal can tell where this will stop; for the spirit of gaming, when once it has seized a subject, is incurable. The tailor who has made thousands in one day, though he has lost them the next, can never again be content with the slow and moderate earnings of his needle. Nothing can exceed the public felicity, if our papers are to be believed, because our papers are under the orders of the scripmen. I imagine, however, we shall hear that all our cash has quitted the extremities of the nation, and accumulated here [Philadelphia]; that produce and property fall to half price there, and the same things rise to double price here; that the cash accumulated and stagnated here, as soon as the bank paper gets out, will find its vent into foreign countries; and instead of this solid medium, which we might have kept for nothing, we shall have a paper one, for the use of which we are to pay these gamesters fifteen per cent. per annum, as they say.—To E. RUTLEDGE. iii, 285. FORD ED.. v, 375. (Pa., 1791.)

6363. ————. Our public credit is good, but the abundance of paper has produced a spirit of gambling in the funds, which has laid up our ships at the wharves, as too slow instruments of profit, and has even disarmed the hand of the tailor of his needle and thimble. They say the evil will cure itself. I wish it may; but I have rarely seen a gamester cured, even by the disasters of his vocation.—To GOUVERNEUR MORRIS. iii, 290. (Pa., 1791.) See SPECULATION.

6364. PAPER MONEY, Manufactures. —New schemes are on foot for bringing more paper to market by encouraging great manufacturing companies to form, and their actions, or paper-shares, to be transferable as bank stock.—To JAMES MONROE. FORD ED., v, 320. (Pa., 1791.)

6365. PAPER MONEY, Mississippi scheme.—The Mississippi scheme, it is well known, ended in France in the bankruptcy of the public treasury, the crash of thousands and thousands of private fortunes, and scenes of desolation and distress equal to those of an invading army, burning and laying waste all before it.—To J. W. EPPES. vi. 239. FORD ED., ix, 411. (M., Nov. 1813.)

6366. PAPER MONEY, Perilous.—Paper money would be perilous even to the paper men.—To JOHN TAYLOR. iv, 259. FORD ED., vii, 310. (M., 1798.)

6367. PAPER MONEY, Plan to reduce. —The plethory of circulating medium which raised the prices of everything to several times their ordinary and standard value, in which state of things many and heavy debts were contracted; and the sudden withdrawing too great a proportion of that medium, and reduction of prices far below that standard, constitute the disease under which we are now laboring, and which must end in a general revolution of property, if some remedy is not applied. That remedy is clearly a gradual reduction of the medium to its standard level, that is to say, to the level which a metallic medium will always find for itself, so as to be in *equilibrio* with that of the nations with which we have commerce. To effect this: Let the whole of the present paper medium be suspended in its circulation after a certain and not distant day. Ascertain by proper inquiry the greatest sum of it which has at any one time been in actual circulation. Take a certain term of years for its gradual reduction. Suppose it to be five years; then let the solvent banks issue 5-6 of that amount in new notes. to be attested by a public officer. as a security that neither more nor less is issued, and to be given out in exchange

for the suspended notes, and the surplus in discount. Let 1-5 of these notes bear on their face that the bank will discharge them with specie at the end of one year: another 5th at the end of two years: a third 5th at the end of three years; and so of the 4th and 5th. They will be sure to be brought in at their respective periods of redemption. Make it a high offense to receive or pass within this State a note of any other. There is little doubt that our banks will agree readily to this operation; if they refuse, declare their charters forfeited by their former irregularities, and give summary process against them for the suspended notes. The Bank of the United States will probably concur also; if not, shut their doors and join the other States in respectful, but firm applications to Congress, to concur in constituting a tribunal (a special convention, *e. g.*) for settling amicably the question of their right to institute a bank, and that also of the States to do the same. A stay-law for the suspension of executions, and their discharge at five annual instalments, should be accommodated to these measures. Interdict forever, to both the State and National Governments, the power of establishing any paper bank; for without this interdiction. we shall have the same ebbs and flows of medium, and the same revolutions of property to go through every twenty or thirty years. In this way the value of property, keeping pace nearly with the sum of circulating medium, will descend gradually to its proper level, at the rate of about 1-5 every year, the sacrifices of what shall be sold for payment of the first instalments of debts will be moderate, and time will be given for economy and industry to come in aid of those subsequent. Certainly no nation ever before abandoned to the avarice and jugglings of private individuals to regulate. according to their own interests, the quantum of circulating medium for the nation; to inflate, by deluges of paper, the nominal prices of property, and then to buy up that property at 1s. in the pound, having first withdrawn the floating medium which might endanger a competition in purchase. Yet this is what has been done, and will be done, unless stayed by the protecting hand of the Legislature. The evil has been produced by the error of their sanction of this ruinous machinery of banks; and justice, wisdom, duty, all require that they should interpose and arrest it before the schemes of plunder and spoliation desolate the country. It is believed that Harpies are already hoarding their money to commence these scenes on the separation of the Legislature; and we know that lands have been already sold under the hammer for less than a year's rent.—To W. C. RIVES. vii, 145. FORD ED., x, 150. (M., Nov. 1819.)

6368. PAPER MONEY, Poverty.—Paper is poverty. It is only the ghost of money, and not money itself.—To E. CARRINGTON. ii, 405. FORD ED., v, 21. (P., 1788.)

6369. PAPER MONEY, Prices and.— All the imported commodities are raised about fifty per cent. by the depreciation of the money. Tobacco shares the rise, because it has no competition abroad. Wheat has been extravagantly high from other causes. When these cease, it must fall to its ancient nominal price, notwithstanding the depreciation of that, because it must contend at market with foreign wheats. Lands have risen within the notice of the papers, and as far out as that can influence. They have not risen at all here [Virginiia]. On the contrary, they are

lower than they were twenty years ago.—
To JAMES MONROE. iv, 141. FORD ED., vii,
80. (M., June 1796.) See PRICE.

6370. PAPER MONEY, Private property and.—Money is leaving the remoter
parts of the Union, and flowing to this place
[Philadelphia] to purchase paper; and here,
a paper medium supplying its place, it is
shipped off in exchange for luxuries. The
value of property is necessarily falling in the
places left bare of money. In Virginia, for
instance, property has fallen 25 per cent. in
the last twelve months.—To WILLIAM SHORT.
iii. 343. FORD ED., v, 459. (Pa., March
1792.)

6371. —— ——. That paper money has
some advantages, is admitted. But that its
abuses also are inevitable, and, by breaking
up the measure of value, makes a lottery of
all private property, cannot be denied. Shall
we ever be able to put a constitutional veto
on it?—To DR. JOSEPHUS B. STUART. vii,
65. (M., May 1817.)

**6372. PAPER MONEY, Redeeming
taxes.**—M. Say will be surprised to find, that
forty years after the development of sound
financial principles by Adam Smith and the
Economists, and a dozen years after he has
given them to us in a corrected, terse, and
lucid form, there should be so much ignorance
of them in our country; that instead of funding
issues of paper on the hypothecation of
specific redeeming taxes (the only method of
anticipating, in a time of war, the resources
of times of peace, tested by the experience of
nations), we are trusting to the tricks of
jugglers on the cards, to the illusions of banking
schemes for the resources of the war, and
for the cure of colic to inflations of more
wind.—To M. CORREA. vi, 406. (M., 1814.)

6373. PAPER MONEY, Ruin by.—Not
Quixotic enough to attempt to reason Bedlam
to rights, my anxieties are turned to the most
practicable means of withdrawing us from the
ruin into which we have run. Two hundred
millions of paper in the hands of the people
(and less cannot be from the employment of
a banking capital known to exceed one hundred
millions), is a fearful tax to fall at haphazard
on their heads. The debt which
purchased our Independence was but of
eighty millions, of which twenty years of taxation
had, in 1889, paid but the one-half.
And what have we purchased with this tax
of two hundred millions which we are to
pay, by wholesale, but usury, swindling, and
new forms of demoralization?—To CHARLES
YANCEY. vi, 515. FORD ED., x, 2. (M., Jan.
1816.)

6374. PAPER MONEY, Silver for.—It
is said that our paper is as good as silver, because
we may have silver for it at the bank
where it issues. This is not true. One, two,
or three persons might have it; but a general
application would soon exhaust their vaults,
and leave a ruinous proportion of their paper
in its intrinsic worthless form. It is a fallacious
pretence, for another reason. The inhabitants

of the banking cities might obtain cash for
their paper, as far as the cash of the vaults
would hold out, but distance puts it out of
the power of the country to do this. A
farmer having a note of a Boston or Charleston
bank, distant hundreds of miles, has no
means of calling for the cash. And while
these calls are impracticable for the country,
the banks have no fear of their being made
from the towns; because their inhabitants are
mostly on their books, and there on sufferance
only, and during good behavior.—To J. W.
EPPES. vi, 243. FORD ED., ix, 414. (M.,
Nov. 1813.)

6375. PAPER MONEY, Specie and.—
The unlimited emission of bank paper has
banished all Great Britain's specie, and is
now, by a depreciation acknowledged by her
own statesmen, carrying her rapidly to bankruptcy,
as it did France, as it did us, and will
do us again, and every country permitting
paper money to be circulated, other than that
by public authority, rigorously limited to the
just measure for circulation.—To JOHN W.
EPPES. vi, 142. FORD ED., ix, 394. (M., June
1813.)

6376. —— ——. Revolutionary history
has warned us of the probable moment when
this baseless trash is to receive its fiat.
Whenever so much of the precious metals
shall have returned into the circulation as
that every one can get some in exchange for
his produce, paper, as in the Revolutionary
war, will experience at once an universal rejection.
When public opinion changes, it is
with the rapidity of thought. Confidence in
already on the totter, and every one now
handles this paper as if playing at "Robin's
Alive".—To CHARLES YANCEY. vi, 516.
FORD ED., x, 3. (M., Jan. 1816.)

**6377. PAPER MONEY, Treasury notes
vs.**—Even with the flood of private paper by
which we were deluged, would the treasury
have ventured its credit in bills of circulating
size, as of fives or ten dollars, &c., they
would have been greedily received by the
people in preference to bank paper. But unhappily
the towns of America were considered
as the nation of America, the dispositions
of the inhabitants of the former as
those of the latter, and the treasury, for want
of confidence in the country, delivered itself
bound hand and foot to bold and bankrupt
adventurers and pretenders to be moneyholders,
whom it could have crushed at any
moment. Even the last half-bold, half-timid
threat of the Treasury showed at once that
these jugglers were at the feet of the government.
For it never was, and is not, any confidence
in their frothy bubbles, but the want
of all other medium, which induced, or now
induces, the *country* people to take their
paper; and at this moment, when nothing
else is to be had, no man will receive it but
to pass it away instantly, none for distant
purposes.—To ALBERT GALLATIN. vi, 498.
(M., Oct. 1815.) See NATIONAL CURRENCY.

6378. PAPER MONEY, Tricks with.—
We are now taught to believe that legerde-

main tricks upon paper can produce as solid wealth as hard labor in the earth. It is vain for common sense to urge that *nothing* can produce but *nothing;* that it is an idle dream to believe in a philosopher's stone which is to turn everything into gold, and to redeem man from the original sentence of his Maker, "in the sweat of his brow shall he eat his bread".—To Charles Yancey. vi, 515. Ford ed., x, 2. (M., Jan. 1816.)

6379. PAPER MONEY, War and.—If this war continues, bank circulation must be suppressed, or the government shaken to its foundation by the weight of taxes, and impracticability to raise funds on them.—To J. W. Eppes. vi, 204. Ford ed., ix, 402. (P.F., Sep. 1813.) See Banks, Dollar, Money, and National Currency.

6380. PAPERS, Communication of.—With respect to [Executive] papers, there is certainly a public and a private side to our offices. To the former belong grants of land, patents for inventions, certain commissions, proclamations, and other papers patent in their nature. To the other belong mere executive proceedings. All nations have found it necessary, that for the advantageous conduct of their affairs, some of these proceedings, at least, should remain known to their executive functionary only. He, of course, from the nature of the case, must be the sole judge of which of them the public interests will permit publication. Hence, under our Constitution, in requests of papers, from the Legislative to the Executive branch, an exception is carefully expressed, as to those which he may deem the public welfare may require not to be disclosed. —To George Hay. v, 97. Ford ed., ix, 57. (W., 1807.)

6381. PAPERS, Confidential.—Understanding that it is thought important that a letter of Nov. 12, 1806, from General Wilkinson to myself, should be produced in evidence on the charges against Burr, * * * I send you a copy of it, omitting only certain passages, * * * entirely confidential, given for my information in the discharge of my executive functions, and which my duties and the public interest forbid me to make public.—To George Hay. v, 190. Ford ed., ix, 63. (M., Sep. 1807.)

6382. ———— ————. You are certainly free to make use of any of the papers we put into Mr. Hay's hands, with a single reservation: to wit, some of them are expressed to be confidential, and others are of that kind which I always consider as confidential, conveying censure on particular individuals, and therefore never communicate them beyond the immediate executive circle.—To General Wilkinson. v, 198. Ford ed., ix, 141. (M., 1807.)

6383. ———— ————. Papers containing censures on particular individuals, * * * I always deem confidential, and therefore cannot communicate, but for regularly official purposes, without a breach of trust.—To George Hay. v, 198. Ford ed., ix, 141. (M., 1807.)

6384. PAPERS, Executive.—Reserving the necessary right of the President of the United States to decide, independently of all other authority, what papers, coming to him as President, the public interests permit to be communicated, and to whom, I assure you of my readiness, under that restriction, voluntarily to furnish on all occasions, whatever the purposes of justice may require.—To George Hay. v, 94. Ford ed., ix, 55. (W., June 1807.)

6385. ———— ————. When the request goes to "copies of the orders issued in relation to Colonel Burr, to the officers at Orleans, Natchez, &c., by the Secretaries of the War and Navy Departments", it seems to cover a correspondence of many months, with such a variety of officers, civil and military, all over the United States, as would amount to laying open the whole executive books. I have desired the Secretary of War to examine his official communications; and on a view of these, we may be able to judge, what can and ought to be done, towards a compliance with the request. If the defendant alleges that there was any particular order, which, as a cause, produced any particular act on his part, then he must know what this order was, can specify it, and a prompt answer can be given.—To George Hay. v, 95. Ford ed., ix, 55. (W., June 1807.)

6386. PAPERS, Retention of.—I enclose you a copy of [General] Armstrong's letter, covering the papers sent to Congress. The date was blank, as in the copy; the letter was so immaterial that I had really forgotten it altogether when I spoke with you. I feel myself much indebted to you for having given me this private opportunity of showing that I have kept back nothing material. That the federalists and a few others should by their vote make such a charge on me, is never unexpected. But how can any join in it who call themselves friends? The President sends papers to the House, which he thinks the public interest requires they should see. They immediately pass a vote, implying irresistibly their belief that he is capable of having kept back other papers which the same interest requires they should see. They pretend to no direct proof of this. It must, then, be founded in presumption; and on what act of my life or of my administration is such a presumption founded? What interest can I have in leading the Legislature to act on false grounds? My wish is certainly to take that course with the public affairs which the body of the Legislature would prefer. It is said, indeed, that such a vote is to satisfy the federalists and their partisans. But were I to send twenty letters, they would say, "You have kept back the twenty-first; send us that". If I sent one hundred, they would say, "There were one hundred and one"; and how could I prove the negative? Their malice can be cured by no conduct; it ought, therefore, to be disregarded, instead of countenancing their imputations by the sanction of a vote. Indeed I should consider such a vote as a charge, in the face of the nation calling for a serious and public defence of myself.*—To Joseph B. Varnum. v, 249. (W., Feb. 1808.)

6387. PARASITES, Government and.—I think we have more machinery of government than is necessary, too many parasites living on the labor of the industrious.—To William Ludlow. vii, 378. (M., 1824.)

6388. PARDONS, Abolition of.—Nor shall there be power anywhere to pardon crimes or to remit fines or punishments.—Proposed Va. Constitution. Ford ed., ii, 17. (June 1776.)

6389. PARDONS, Conditions of.—I have made it a rule to grant no pardon in any criminal case but on the recommendation of the

* Mr. Varnum was then Speaker of the House of Representatives.— Editor.

judges who sat on the trial, and the district attorney, or two of them. I believe it a sound rule, and not to be departed from but in extraordinary cases.—To ALBERT GALLATIN. FORD ED., viii, 465. (M., 1806.)

6390. —— ——. In all cases I have referred petitions [for pardons] to the judges and prosecuting attorney, who having heard all the circumstances of the case, are the best judges whether any of them were of such a nature as ought to obtain for the criminal a remission or abridgment of the punishment.— To GEORGE BLAKE. v, 113. (W., 1807.)

6391. —— ——. The Legislature having made stripes a regular part of the punishment [for robbing the mails], the pardoning them cannot be a thing of course, as that would be to repeal the law. Extraordinary and singular considerations are necessary to entitle the criminal to that remission.—To E. RANDOLPH. v, 406. (W., 1808.)

6392. PARDONS, Imprudent.—It would be against every rule of prudence for me to undertake to revise the verdict of a jury on *ex parte* affidavits and recommendations.—To GEORGE BLAKE. v, 371. (W., 1808.)

6393. PARDONS, Proper.—The power of pardon, committed to Executive discretion, [can] never be more properly exercised than where citizens [are] suffering without the authority of law, or, which [is] equivalent, under a law unauthorized by the Constitution, and therefore null.—To SPENCER ROANE. vii, 135. FORD ED., x, 141. (P.F., 1819.)

6394. PARDONS FOR COUNTERFEIT-ERS.—Pardons for counterfeiting bank paper are yielded with much less facility than others. —To GEORGE BLAKE. v, 113. (W., 1807.)

6395. PARDONS OF INDIANS.—As the case of the five Alabamas, under prosecution for the murder of a white man, may not admit delay, if a conviction takes place, I have thought it necessary to recommend to you in that case to select the leader, or most guilty, for execution, and to reprieve the others; * * * letting them return to their friends, with whom you will of course take just merit for this clemency. Our wish * * * [is] merely to make them sensible by the just punishment of one, that our citizens are not to be murdered or robbed with impunity.—To GOVERNOR CLAIBORNE. v, 345. (M., 1808.)

6396. PARDONS BY LAW.—The " privilege of clergy ", originally allowed to the clergy, is now extended to every man, and even to women. It is a right of exemption from capital punishment, for the first offence in most cases. It is, then, a pardon by the law. In other cases, the Executive gives the pardon. But when laws are made as mild as they should be, both those pardons are absurd. The principle of Beccaria is sound. Let the legislators be merciful, but the executors of the law inexorable.—To M. DE MEUNIER. ix, 263. FORD ED., iv, 168. (P., 1786.)

6397. PARIS, Bois de Boulogne.—The Bois de Boulogne invites you earnestly to come and survey its beautiful verdure, to retire to its umbrage from the heats of the season. I was through it to-day, as I am every day.—To MADAME DE CORNY. ii, 161. (P., 1787.)

6398. PARIS, Evils of.—From what I have seen in Paris, I know not one good purpose on earth which can be effected by a young

gentleman coming here. He may learn indeed to speak the language, but put this in the scale amongst other things he will learn and evils he is sure to acquire, and it will be found too light. I have always disapproved of a European education for our youth from theory; I now do it from inspection.—To CHARLES THOMSON. FORD ED., iv, 15. (P., 1784.)

6399. PARK (Mungo), Work on Africa. —I fear Park's work on Africa will throw cold water on the hopes of the friends of freedom.—To DR. BENJAMIN RUSH. iv, 336. FORD ED., vii, 461. (M., 1800.)

6400. PARLIAMENT, Dignity of.—The dignity of Parliament, it seems, can brook no opposition to its power. Strange, that a set of men, who have made sale of their virtue to the Minister, should yet talk of retaining dignity.—To DR. WILLIAM SMALL. i, 199. FORD ED., i, 454. (1775.)

6401. PARLIAMENT, Executive Power of.—A new executive power, unheard of till then [the date of the Boston Port bill, 14. G. 3.], that of a British Parliament.—RIGHTS OF BRITISH AMERICA. i, 133. FORD ED., i, 438. (1774.)

6402. PARLIAMENT, Injuries by.— [During] the reigns which preceded his Majesty's [George III.] the violations of our rights were less alarming, because repeated at more distant intervals, than that rapid and bold succession of injuries, which is likely to distinguish the present from all other periods of American history. Scarcely have our minds been able to emerge from the astonishment into which one stroke of Parliamentary thunder has involved us, before another more heavy and more alarming is fallen on us.—RIGHTS OF BRITISH AMERICA. i, 130. FORD ED., i, 435. (1774.)

6403. PARLIAMENT, Jurisdiction of. —The British Parliament has no right to exercise authority over us.—RIGHTS OF BRITISH AMERICA. i, 130. FORD ED., i, 434. (1774.)

6404. —— ——. He [George III.] has endeavored to pervert the exercise of the kingly office in Virginia into a detestable and insupportable tyranny * * * by combining with others to subject us to a foreign jurisdiction, giving his assent to their pretended acts of legislation.—PROPOSED VA. CONSTITUTION. FORD ED., ii, 10. (June 1776.)

6405. —— ——. He has combined with others to subject us to a jurisdiction foreign to our constitutions and unacknowledged by our laws, giving his assent to their acts of pretended legislation, * * * declaring themselves invested with power to legislate for us in all cases whatsoever.—DECLARATION OF INDEPENDENCE AS DRAWN BY JEFFERSON.

6406. PARLIAMENT, Misgovernment by.—Not only the principles of common sense, but the feelings of human nature, must be surrendered up before his Majesty's subjects here, can be persuaded to believe that they hold their political existence at the will of a British Parliament. Shall these governments be dissolved, their property annihilated, and their people reduced to a state of nature, at the imperious breath of a body of men whom they never saw, in whom they never confided, and over whom they have no powers of punishment or removal, let their crimes against the American public be ever so great? Can any one reason be assigned why one hundred and sixty thousand electors in the Island of Great Britain should give law to four millions in the States of America, every individual of whom is equal to every individual of them, in virtue, in understanding, and in bodily strength? Were this to be admitted, instead of being a free people, as we have hitherto supposed, and mean to continue ourselves, we should suddenly be found the slaves, not of one, but of one hundred and sixty thousand tyrants, distinguished, too, from all others by this singular circumstance, that they are removed from the reach of fear, the only restraining motive which may hold the hand of a tyrant.—RIGHTS OF BRITISH AMERICA. i, 131. FORD ED., i, 436. (1774.)

6407. PARLIAMENT, Purchase of favor.—Congress are of opinion that the proposition * * * [of Lord North] is unreasonable and insidious: unreasonable because, if we declare we accede to it, we declare without reservation we will purchase the favor of parliament not knowing at the same time at what price they will please to estimate their favor. It is insidious because any individual Colonies, having bid and bidden again till they find the avidity of the seller unattainable by all their powers, are then to return into opposition, divided from their sister Colonies whom the minister will have previously detached by a grant of easier terms, or by an artful procrastination of a definitive answer.—REPLY TO LORD NORTH'S PROPOSITION. FORD ED., i, 478. (July 1775.)

6408. PARLIAMENT, Repudiation of. —A body of men foreign to our constitutions, and unacknowledged by our laws.—RIGHTS OF BRITISH AMERICA. i, 134. FORD ED., i, 439. (1774.)

6409. —— ——. Rather than submit to the rights of legislating for us, assumed by the British Parliament, * * * I would lend my hand to sink the whole Island in the ocean.— To JOHN RANDOLPH. i, 201. FORD ED., i, 484. (M., 1775.)

6410. —— ——. We utterly dissolve all political connection which may heretofore have subsisted between us and the people or parliament of Great Britain.*—DECLARATION OF INDEPENDENCE AS DRAWN BY JEFFERSON.

6411. PARLIAMENT, Submission to.— In constituting indeed our several forms of government, we had adopted one common king, thereby laying a foundation for perpetual league and amity with them; but that submission to their parliament was no part of our constitution, nor ever in idea, if history may be credited. † —DECLARATION OF INDEPENDENCE AS DRAWN BY JEFFERSON.

6412. PARLIAMENT, Tyranny of.— History has informed us that bodies of men as well as individuals are susceptible of the spirit of tyranny. A view of these acts of Parliament for regulation, as it has been affectedly called, of the American trade, if all other evidences were removed out of the case, would undeniably evince the truth of this observation.— RIGHTS OF BRITISH AMERICA. i, 128. FORD ED., i, 433. (1774.)

6413. PARLIAMENTARY LAW, Compilation of.—I do not mention the Parliamentary Manual published for the use of the Senate of the United States because it was a mere compilation into which nothing entered of my own but the arrangement and a few observations necessary to explain that and some of the cases. —To JOHN W. CAMPBELL. v, 466. FORD ED., ix, 258. (M., 1809.)

6414. PARLIAMENTARY LAW, Study of.—It seems probable that I will be called on to preside in a legislative chamber. It is now so long since I have acted in the legislative line, that I am entirely rusty in the Parliamentary rules of procedure. I know they have been more studied and are better known by you than by any man in America, perhaps by any man living. I am in hopes that while inquiring into the subject you made notes on it. If any such remain in your hands, however informal, in books or in scraps of paper, and you will be so good as to trust me with them a little while, they shall be most faithfully returned.—To GEORGE WYTHE. iv, 163. FORD ED., vii, 110. (M., 1797.)

6415. PARTIES, Amalgamation of.— What do you think of the state of parties at this time [1822]? An opinion prevails that there is no longer any distinction, that the republicans and federalists are completely amalgamated, but it is not so. The amalgamation is of name only, not of principle. All, indeed, call themselves by the name of republicans, because that of the federalists was extinguished in the battle of New Orleans. But the truth is that finding that monarchy is a desperate wish in this country, they rally to the point which they think next best, a consolidated government. Their aim is now, therefore, to break down the rights reserved by the Constitution to the States as a bulwark against that consolidation, the fear of which produced the whole of the opposition to the Constitution at its birth. Hence new republicans in Congress, preaching the doctrines of the old federalists, and the new nicknames of "Ultras" and "Radicals". But, I trust, they will fail under the new, as the old name, and that the friends of the real Constitution and Union will prevail against consolidation, as they have done against monarchism. I scarcely know myself which is most to be deprecated, a consolidation, or dissolution of the States. The horrors of both are beyond the reach of human foresight.—To WILLIAM JOHNSON. FORD ED., x, 225. (M., Oct. 1822.)

6416. —— ——. You are told, indeed, that there are no longer parties among us; that they are all now amalgamated; the lion and the lamb lie down together in peace. Do not believe a word of it. The same parties exist now as ever did. No longer, indeed, under the name of republicans and federalists. The latter name was extinguished in the battle of Orleans. Those who wore it, finding monarchism a desperate wish in this country, are rallying to what they deem the next best point, a consolidated government. Although this is not yet avowed (as that of monarchy, you know, never was), it exists decidedly, and is the true key to the debates in Congress, wherein you see many calling themselves republicans, and preaching the rankest doctrines of the old federalists.*—To ALBERT GALLATIN. FORD ED., x, 235. (M., Oct. 1822.)

6417. —— ——. You will be told that parties are now all amalgamated; the wolf now dwells with the lamb, and the leopard lies down with the kid. It is true that federalism has changed its name and hidden itself among us. Since the Hartford convention it is deemed even by themselves a name of reproach. In some degree, too, they have varied their object. To monarchize this nation they see is impossible; the next best thing in their view is to consolidate it into one government as a *premier pas* to monarchy. The party is now as strong

* Struck out by the Congress.—EDITOR.
† Congress struck out this passage.—EDITOR.

* Gallatin was then in Europe.—EDITOR.

as it ever has been since 1800; and though mixed with us are to be known by their rallying together on every question of power in a general government. The judges, as before, are at their head, and are their entering wedge. Young men are more easily seduced into this principle than the old one of monarchy.—To ALBERT GALLATIN. FORD ED., x, 262. (M., Aug. 1823.)

6418. ——— ———. [It is] an amalgamation of name but not of principle. Tories are tories still, by whatever name they may be called.— To MARTIN VAN BUREN. vii, 373. FORD ED., x. 316. (M., 1824.)

6419. ——— ———. I am no believer in the amalgamation of parties, nor do I consider it as either desirable or useful for the public; but only that, like religious differences, a difference in politics should never be permitted to enter into social intercourse, or to disturb its friendships, its charities, or justice. In that form, they are censors of the conduct of each other, and useful watchmen for the public.—To H. LEE. vii, 376. FORD ED., x, 317. (M., 1824.)

6420. ——— ———. There is really no amalgamation [of parties]. The parties exist now as heretofore. The one, indeed, has thrown off its old name, and has not yet assumed a new one, although obviously consolidationists. And among those in the offices of every denomination I believe it to be a bare minority.—To WILLIAM SHORT. vii, 392. FORD ED., x, 335. (M., January 1825.)

6421. PARTIES, Birth of.—At the formation of our government, many had formed their political opinions on European writings and practices, believing the experience of old countries, and especially of England, abusive as it was, to be a safer guide than mere theory. The doctrines of Europe were, that men in numerous associations cannot be restrained within the limits of order and justice, but by forces physical and moral, wielded over them by authorities independent of their will. Hence their organization of kings, hereditary nobles, and priests. Still further to constrain the brute force of the people, they deem it necessary to keep them down by hard labor, poverty and ignorance, and to take from them, as from bees, so much of their earnings, as that unremitting labor shall be necessary to obtain a sufficient surplus barely to sustain a scanty and miserable life. And these earnings they apply to maintain their privileged orders in splendor and idleness, to fascinate the eyes of the people, and excite in them an humble adoration and submission, as to an order of superior beings. Although few among us had gone all these lengths of opinion, yet many had advanced, some more, some less, on the way. And in the convention which formed our government, they endeavored to draw the cords of power as tight as they could obtain them, to lessen the dependence of the general functionaries on their constituents, to subject to them those of the States, and to weaken their means of maintaining the steady equilibrium which the majority of the convention had deemed salutary for both branches, general and local. To recover, therefore, in practice the powers which the nation had refused, and to warp to their own wishes those actually given, was the steady object of the Federal party. Ours, on the contrary, was to maintain the will of the majority of the convention, and of the people themselves. We believed, with them, that man was a rational animal, endowed by nature with rights, and with an innate sense of justice; and that he could be restrained from wrong and protected in right, by moderate powers, confided to persons of his own choice, and held to their duties by dependence on his own will. We believed that the complicated organization of kings, nobles, and priests, was not the wisest nor best to effect the happiness of associated man; that wisdom and virtue were not hereditary; that the trappings of such a machinery, consumed by their expense, those earnings of industry. they were meant to protect, and, by the inequalities they produced, exposed liberty to sufferance. We believed that men, enjoying in ease and security the full fruits of their own industry, enlisted by all their interests on the side of law and order, habituated to think for themselves, and to follow their reason as their guide, would be more easily and safely governed, than with minds nourished in error, and vitiated and debased, as in Europe, by ignorance, indigence and oppression. The cherishment of the people then was our principle, the fear and distrust of them, that of the other party. Composed, as we were, of the landed and laboring interests of the country, we could not be less anxious for a government of law and order than were the inhabitants of the cities, the strongholds of federalism. And whether our efforts to save the principles and form of our Constitution have not been salutary, let the present republican freedom, order and prosperity of our country determine.—To WILLIAM JOHNSON. vii, 290. FORD ED., x, 226. (M., June, 1823.)

6422. PARTIES, History.—Let me implore you to finish your history of parties, leaving the time of publication to the state of things you may deem proper, but taking especial care that we do not lose it altogether. We have been too careless of our future reputation, while our tories will omit nothing to place us in the wrong. Besides the five-volumed libel which represents us as struggling for office, and not at all to prevent our government from being administered into a monarchy, the Life of Hamilton is in the hands of a man who, to the bitterness of the priest, adds the rancor of the fiercest federalism. Mr. Adams's papers, too, and his biography will descend, of course, to his son whose pen, you know, is pointed, and his prejudices not in our favor. And, doubtless, other things are in preparation, unknown to us. On our part, we are depending on truth to make itself known, while history is taking a contrary set which may become too inveterate for correction. Mr. Madison will probably leave something, but, I believe, only particular passages of our history, and these chiefly confined to the period between the dissolution of the old and commencement of the new government, which is peculiarly within his knowledge. After he joined us in the administration, he had no leisure to write. This, too, was my case. But although I had not time to prepare anything express, my letters (all preserved) will furnish the daily occurrences and views from my return from Europe in 1790, till I retired finally from office. These will command more conviction than anything I could have written after my retirement; no day having ever passed during that period without a letter to somebody. Written, too, in the moment, and in the warmth and freshness of fact and feeling. they will carry internal evidence that what they breathe is genuine. Selections from these, after my death, may come out successively as the maturity of circumstances may render their appearance seasonable. But multiplied testimony, multiplied views will be necessary to give solid establishment to truth. Much is known to one which is not known to another, and no one knows everything. It is the sum of individual knowledge which is to make up the whole truth, and to give its correct current through future time. Then, do not * * * withhold your stock of information; and I would moreover recommend that you trust it not to a single copy, nor to a single depositary. Leave it not in the power of any one person, under the distempered view of an unlucky moment, to deprive us of the weight of your testimony, and to purchase, by its destruction, the favor of any party or person.—To WILLIAM JOHNSON. vii, 277. FORD ED., x, 247. (M., 1823.)

6423. ———— ————. Our opponents are far ahead of us in preparations for placing their cause favorably before posterity. Yet I hope even from some of them the escape of precious truths, in angry explosions or effusions of vanity, which will betray the genuine monarchism of their principles. They do not themselves believe what they endeavor to inculcate, that we were an opposition party, not on principle, but merely seeking for office.—To WILLIAM JOHNSON. vii, 290. FORD ED., x, 226. (M., 1823.)

6424. PARTIES, Independent of.—If I could not go to heaven but with a party, I would not go there at all.—To FRANCIS HOPKINSON. ii, 585. FORD ED., v, 76. (P., 1789.)

6425. PARTIES, Jay's Treaty and.— You well know how strong a character of division had been impressed on the Senate by the British treaty. Common error, common censure, and common efforts of defence had formed the treaty majority into a common band, which feared to separate even on other subjects. Towards the close of the last Congress, however, it had been hoped that their ties began to loosen, and their phalanx to separate a little. This hope was blasted at the very opening of the present session, by the nature of the appeal which the President made to the nation; the occasion for which had confessedly sprung from the fatal British treaty. This circumstance rallied them again to their standard, and hitherto we have had pretty regular treaty votes on all questions of principle. And, indeed, I fear, that as long as the same individuals remain, so long we shall see traces of the same division.—To AARON BURR. iv, 184. FORD ED., vii, 145. (Pa., June 1797.)

6426. PARTIES, Motives.—That each party endeavors to get into the administration of the government, and exclude the other from power, is true, and may be stated as a motive of action; but this is only secondary; the primary motive being a real and radical difference of political principle. I sincerely wish our differences were but personally who should govern, and that the principles of our Constitution were those of both parties. Unfortunately, it is otherwise; and the question of preference between monarchy and republicanism, which has so long divided mankind elsewhere, threatens a permanent division here.—To JOHN MELISH. vi, 95. FORD ED., ix, 374. (M., Jan. 1813.)

6427. PARTIES, Names.—The appellation of aristocrats and democrats is the true one expressing the essence of all [political parties].—To H. LEE. vii, 376. FORD ED., x, 318. (M., 1824.)

6428. PARTIES, Natural division.— The division into whig and tory is founded in the nature of men; the weakly and nerveless,

the rich and the corrupt, seeing more safety and accessibility in a strong executive; the healthy, firm, and virtuous, feeling confidence in their physical and moral resources, and willing to part with only so much power as is necessary for their good government; and, therefore, to retain the rest in the hands of the many, the division will substantially be into whig and tory, as in England formerly.—To JOEL BARLOW. iv, 438. FORD ED., viii, 150. (W., May 1802.)

6429. ———— ————. I consider the party division of whig and tory the most wholesome which can exist in any government, and well worthy of being nourished, to keep out those of a more dangerous character.—To WILLIAM T. BARRY. vii, 255. (M., 1822.)

6430. ———— ————. The parties of whig and tory are those of nature. They exist in all countries, whether called by these names, or by those of aristocrats and democrats, *coté droite* and *coté gauche*, ultras and radicals, serviles and liberals. The sickly, weakly, timid man fears the people, and is a tory by nature. The healthy, strong and bold, cherishes them, and is formed a whig by nature.—To MARQUIS LAFAYETTE. vii, 325. FORD ED., x, 281. (M., 1823.)

6431. ———— ————. Men by their constitutions are naturally divided into two parties: 1. Those who fear and distrust the people, and wish to draw all powers from them into the hands of the higher classes. 2. Those who identify themselves with the people, have confidence in them, cherish and consider them as the most honest and safe, although not the most wise depositary of the public interests. In every country these two parties exist, and in every one where they are free to think, speak and write, they will declare themselves. Call them, therefore, liberals and serviles, Jacobins and ultras, whigs and tories, republicans and federalists, aristocrats and democrats, or by whatever name you please, they are the same parties still, and pursue the same object. The last appellation of aristocrats and democrats is the true one expressing the essence of all.— To H. LEE. vii, 376. FORD ED., x, 317. (M., 1824.)

6432. ———— ————. The division of whig and tory, or, according to our denominations, of republican and federal, is the most salutary of all divisions, and ought, therefore, to be fostered, instead of being amalgamated; for, take away this, and some more dangerous principle of division will take its place.—To WILLIAM SHORT. vii, 392. FORD ED., x, 335. (M., 1825.)

6433. PARTIES, Opposite.—In every free and deliberating society, there must, from the nature of man, be opposite parties, and violent dissensions and discords; and one of these, for the most part, must prevail over the other for a longer or shorter time.—To JOHN TAYLOR. iv, 246. FORD ED., vii, 264. (Pa., 1798.)

6434. ———— ————. Wherever there are men, there will be parties; and wherever there are free men they will make themselves heard. Those of firm health and spirits are unwilling to cede more of their liberty than is necessary to preserve order; those of feeble constitutions will wish to see one strong arm able to protect them from the many. These are the whigs and tories of nature. These mutual jealousies produce mutual security; and while the laws shall be obeyed, all will be safe. He alone is your enemy who disobeys them.—JEFFERSON'S MSS. FORD ED., viii, 1. (1801?)

6435. —— ——. Men have differed in opinion, and been divided into parties by these opinions, from the first origin of societies, and in all governments where they have been permitted freely to think and to speak. The same political parties which now agitate the United States, have existed through all time. Whether the power of the people or that of the αριςτοι should prevail, were questions which kept the States of Greece and Rome in eternal convulsions, as they now schismatize every people whose minds and mouths are not shut up by the gag of a despot. And in fact, the terms of whig and tory belong to natural as well as to civil history. They denote the temper and constitution of mind of different individuals.— To JOHN ADAMS. vi, 143. (M., 1813.)

6436. —— ——. To me it appears that there have been differences of opinion and party differences, from the first establishment of government to the present day, and on the same question which now divides our own country; that these will continue through all future time; that every one takes his side in favor of the many, or of the few, according to his constitution, and the circumstances in which he is placed; that opinions which are equally honest on both sides, should not affect personal esteem or social intercourse; that as we judge between the Claudii and the Gracchi, the Wentworths and the Hampdens of past ages, so of those among us whose names may happen to be remembered for awhile, the next generations will judge favorably or unfavorably, according to the complexion of individual minds, and the side they shall themselves have taken; that nothing new can be added by you or me in support of the conflicting opinions on government; and that wisdom and duty dictate an humble resignation to the verdict of our future peers. —To JOHN ADAMS. vi, 145. (M., 1813.)

6437. —— ——. To come to our own country, and to the times when you and I became first acquainted, we well remember the violent parties which agitated the old Congress, and their bitter contests. There you and I were together, and the Jays, and the Dickinsons, and other anti-independents, were arrayed against us. They cherished the monarchy of England, and we the rights of our countrymen. When our present government was in the mew, passing from Confederation to Union, how bitter was the schism between the "Feds" and the "Antis". Here you and I were together again. For although, for a moment, separated by the Atlantic from the scene of action, I favored the opinion that nine States should confirm the Constitution, in order to secure it, and the others hold off until certain amendments, deemed favorable to freedom, should be made. I rallied in the first instant to the wiser proposition of Massachusetts, that all should confirm, and then all instruct their delegates to urge those amendments. The amendments were made, and all were reconciled to the government. But as soon as it was put into motion, the line of division was again drawn. We broke into two parties, each wishing to give the government a different direction; the one to strengthen the most popular branch, the other the more permanent branches, and to extend their permanence.—To JOHN ADAMS. vi, 143. (M., 1813.)

6438. —— ——. Here you and I separated for the first time, and as we had been longer than most others on the public theatre, and our names were more familiar to our countrymen, the party which considered you as thinking with them, placed your name at their head; the other, for the same reason, selected mine. But neither decency nor inclination permitted us to become the advocates of ourselves, or to take part personally in the violent contests which followed. We suffered ourselves, as you so well expressed it, to be passive subjects of public discussion. And these discussions, whether relating to men, measures or opinions, were conducted by the parties with an animosity, a bitterness and an indecency which had never been exceeded. All the resources of reason and of wrath were exhausted by each party in support of its own, and to prostrate the adversary opinions; one was upbraided with receiving the anti-federalists, the other the old tories and refugees, into their bosom. Of this acrimony, the public papers of the day exhibit ample testimony, in the debates of Congress, of State Legislatures, of stump-orators, in addresses, answers, and newspaper essays; and to these, without question, may be added the private correspondences of individuals; and the less guarded in these, because not meant for the public eye, not restrained by the respect due to that, but poured forth from the overflowings of the heart into the bosom of a friend, as a momentary easement of our feelings.—To JOHN ADAMS. vi, 144. (1813.)

6439. PARTIES, Principles and.—Were parties here divided merely by a greediness for office, as in England, to take a part with either would be unworthy of a reasonable or moral man. But where the principle of difference is as substantial, and as strongly pronounced as between the republicans and the monocrats of our country, I hold it as honorable to take a firm and decided part, and as immoral to pursue a middle line, as between the parties of honest men and rogues, into which every country is divided.—To WILLIAM B. GILES. iv, 126. FORD ED., vii, 43. (M., Dec. 1795.)

6440. —— ——. What in fact is the difference of principle between the two parties? The one desires to preserve an entire independence of the Executive and Legislative on each other, and the dependence of both on the same source—the free election of the people. The other party wishes to lessen the dependence of the Executive, and of one branch of the Legislature on the people, some by making them hold for life, some hereditary, and some even for giving the Executive an influence by patronage or corruption over the remaining popular branch, so as to reduce the elective franchise to its minimum.—To J. F. MERCER. iv, 563. (W., 1804.)

6441. —— ——. It is indeed of little consequence who governs us, if they sincerely and zealously cherish the principles of union and republicanism.—To HENRY DEARBORN. vii, 215. FORD ED., x, 192. (M., 1821.)

6442. PARTIES, Public welfare and.—Both of our political parties, at least the honest part of them, agree conscientiously in the same object—the public good; but they differ essentially in what they deem the means of promoting that good. One side believes it best done by one composition of the governing powers; the other, by a different one. One fears most the ignorance of the people; the other, the selfishness of rulers independent of them. Which is right, time and experience will prove. We think that one side of this experiment has been long enough tried, and proved not to promote the good of the many; and that the other has not been fairly and sufficiently tried. Our opponents think the reverse. With whichever opinion the body of the nation concurs, that must prevail.—To Mrs. John Adams. iv, 562. Ford ed., viii, 312. (M., 1804.)

6443. PARTIES, Republican vs. Monarchical.—Where a Constitution, like ours, wears a mixed aspect of monarchy and republicanism, its citizens will naturally divide into two classes of sentiment according to their tone of body or mind. Their habits, connections and callings induce them to wish to strengthen either the monarchical or the republican features of the Constitution. Some will consider it as an elective monarchy, which had better be made hereditary, and, therefore, endeavor to lead towards that all the forms and principles of its administration. Others will view it as an energetic republic, turning in all its points on the pivot of free and frequent elections. The great body of our native citizens are unquestionably of the republican sentiment. Foreign education, and foreign conventions of interest, have produced some exceptions in every part of the Union, North and South, and perhaps other circumstances in your quarter, better known to you, may have thrown into the scale of exceptions a greater number of the rich. Still there, I believe, and here [the South] I am sure, the great mass is republican. Nor do any of the forms in which the public disposition has been pronounced in the last half dozen years, evince the contrary. All of them, when traced to their true source, have only been evidences of the preponderant popularity of a particular great character. That influence once withdrawn, and our countrymen left to the operation of their own unbiased good sense, I have no doubt we shall see a pretty rapid return of general harmony, and our citizens moving in phalanx in the paths of regular liberty, order, and a sacrosanct adherence to the Constitution. Thus I think it will be, if war with France can be avoided. But if that untoward event comes athwart us in our present point of deviation, nobody, I believe, can foresee into what port it will drive us.—To James Sullivan. iv, 168. Ford ed., vii, 117. (M., Feb. 1797.)

6444. ———. The toryism with which we struggled in 1777 differed but in name from the federalism of 1799, with which we struggled also; and the Anglicism of 1808, against which we are now struggling, is but the same thing still in another form. It is a longing for a king and an English king rather than any other. This is the true source of their sorrows and wailings.—To John Langdon. v, 512. (M., 1810.)

6445. PARTIES, Washington's relations to.—You expected to discover the difference of our party principles in General Washington's valedictory, and my inaugural address. Not at all. General Washington did not harbor one principle of federalism. He was neither an Angloman, a monarchist, nor a separatist. He sincerely wished the people to have as much self-government as they were competent to exercise themselves. The only point on which he and I ever differed in opinion, was, that I had more confidence than he had in the natural integrity and discretion of the people, and in the safety and extent to which they might trust themselves with a control of their government. He has asseverated to me a thousand times his determination that the existing government should have a fair trial, and that in support of it he would spend the last drop of his blood. He did this the more repeatedly, because he knew General Hamilton's political bias, and my apprehensions from it. It is a mere calumny, therefore, in the monarchists, to associate General Washington with their principles. But that may have happened in this case which has been often seen in ordinary cases, that, by oft repeating an untruth, men come to believe it themselves. It is a mere artifice in this party to bolster themselves up on the revered name of that first of our worthies.—To John Melish. vi, 97. Ford ed., ix, 376. (M., Jan. 1813.) See Federalists, Hartford Convention, Monarchists, Republicanism and Republicans.

6446. PASSIONS, Control.—We must keep the passions of men on our side, even when we are persuading them to do what they ought to do.—To M. de Meunier. ix, 272. Ford ed., iv, 177. (P., 1786.)

6447. PASSIONS, Suppress.—It is our sacred duty to suppress passion among ourselves, and not to blast the confidence we have inspired of proof that a government of reason is better than one of force.—To Richard Rush. vii, 183. (M., 1820.)

6448. PATENTS, Benefits of.—In the arts, and especially in the mechanical arts, many ingenious improvements are made in consequence of the patent-right giving exclusive use of them for fourteen years.—To M. Pictet. iv, 462. (W., 1803.)

6449. PATENTS, Combinations in.—If we have a right to use three things separately, I see nothing in reason, or in the patent law, which forbids our using them all together. A man has a right to use a saw, an axe, a plane separately; may he not combine their uses on the same piece of wood? He has a right to use his knife to cut his meat, a fork to hold it; may a patentee take from him the right to continue their use on the same subject? Such a law, instead of enlarging our conveniences, as was intended, would most fearfully abridge them, and crowd us by monopolies out of the use of the things we have.—To Oliver Evans. vi, 298. (M., 1814.)

6450. PATENTS, Duration of.—Certainly an inventor ought to be allowed a right to the benefit of his invention for some certain time. It is equally certain it ought not to be perpetual; for to embarrass society with monopolies for every utensil existing, and in all the details of life, would be more injurious to them than had the supposed inventors never existed; because the natural understanding of its members would have suggested the same things or others as good. How long the term should be, is the difficult question. Our legislators have copied the English estimate of the term, perhaps without sufficiently considering how much longer, in a country so much more sparsely settled, it takes for an invention to become known, and used to an extent profitable to the inventor. Nobody wishes more than I do that ingenuity should receive a liberal encouragement.—To Oliver Evans. v, 75. (M., 1807.)

6451. PATENTS, Frivolous.—The abuse of frivolous patents is likely to cause more inconvenience than is countervailed by those really useful. We know not to what uses we may apply implements which were in our hands before the birth of our government, and even the discovery of America.—To Dr. Thomas Cooper. vi, 295. (M., 1814.)

6452. PATENTS, Granting of.—Considering the exclusive right to invention as given not of natural right, but for the benefit of society, I know well the difficulty of drawing a line between the things which are worth to the public the embarrassment of an exclusive patent, and those which are not. As a member of the patent board for several years, while the law authorized a board to grant or refuse patents, I saw with what slow progress a system of general rules could be matured. Some, however, were established by that board. One of these was, that a machine of which we were possessed, might be applied to every man to any use of which it is susceptible, and that this right ought not to be taken from him and given to a monopolist, because the first perhaps had occasion to apply it. Thus a screw for crushing plaster might be employed for crushing corncobs. And a chain-pump for raising water might be used for raising wheat; this being merely a change of application. Another rule was that a change of material should not give title to a patent. * * * A third was that a mere change of form should give no right to a patent. * * * But there were still abundance of cases which could not be brought under rule, until they should have presented themselves under all their aspects; and these investigations occupying more time of the members of the board than they could spare from higher duties, the whole was turned over to the judiciary, to be matured into a system, under which every one might know when his actions were safe and lawful. Instead of refusing a patent in the first instance, as the board was authorized to do, the patent now issues of course, subject to be declared void on such principles as should be established by the courts of law. This business, however, is but little analogous to their course of reading, since we might in vain turn over all the lubberly volumes of the law to find a single ray which would lighten the path of the mechanic or the mathematician. It is more within the information of a board of academical professors, and a previous refusal of patent would better guard our citizens against harassment by lawsuits. But England had given it to her judges, and the usual predominancy of her examples carried it to ours.—To Isaac McPherson. vi, 181. (M., 1813.)

— **PATENTS, Inventors and.**—See Inventions and Inventors, Rights of.

6453. PATENTS, Law of.—I found it more difficult than I had on first view imagined, to draw the clause you wish to have introduced in the inclosed bill. * Will you make the first trial against the patentee conclusive against all others who might be interested to contest his patent? If you do he will always have a conclusive suit brought against himself at once. Or will you give every one a right to bring actions separately. If you do, besides running him down with the expenses and vexations of lawsuits, you will be sure to find some jury in the long run, who from motives of partiality or ignorance, will find a verdict against him, though a hundred should have been before found in his favor. I really believe that less evil will follow from leaving him to bring suits against those who invade his right.—To Hugh Williamson. Ford ed., v, 392. (1791.)

* Jefferson's bill "to Promote the Progress of the Useful Arts" was introduced into the House of Representatives by Mr. White on Feb. 7, 1791. No action was taken upon it, however; but in the next Congress it was passed after many minor alterations had been made.—Editor.

6454. PATENTS, Monopoly and.—If a new application of our old machines be a ground of monopoly, the patent law will take from us much more good than it will give.—To Oliver Evans. vi, 298. (M., 1814.)

6455. PATENTS, Regulation of.—A rule has occurred to me, which I think, would * * * go far towards securing the citizen against the vexation of frivolous patents. It is to consider the invention of any new mechanical power, or of any new combination of the mechanical powers already known, as entitled to an exclusive grant; but that the purchaser of the right to use the invention should be free to apply it to every purpose of which it is susceptible.—To Thomas Cooper. vi, 372. (M., 1814.)

6456. PATENTS, Scope of.—[You say] that your patent is for your improvement in the manufacture of flour by the application of certain principles, and of such machinery as will carry those principles into operation, whether of the improved elevator, improved hopper-boy, or (without being confined to them) of any machinery known and free to the public. I can conceive how a machine may improve the manufacture of flour; but not how a *principle* abstracted from any machine can do it. It must then be the machine, and the principle of that machine, which is secured to you by your patent. Recurring now to the words of your definition, do they mean that, while all are free to use the old string of buckets, and Archimedes's screw for the purposes to which they have been formerly applied, you alone have the exclusive right to apply them to the manufacture of flour? that no one has a right to apply his old machines to all the purposes of which they are susceptible? that every one, for instance, who can apply the hoe, the spade, or the axe, to any purpose to which they have not been before applied, may have a patent for the exclusive right to that application? and may exclude all others, under penalties, from using their hoe, spade, or axe? If this be the meaning, [it is] my opinion that the Legislature never meant by the patent law to sweep away so extensively the rights of their constituents [and thus] to environ everything they touch with snares.—To Oliver Evans. vi, 297. (M., 1814.)

6457. PATERNALISM, Condemned.—Having always observed that public works are much less advantageously managed than the same are by private hands, I have thought it better for the public to go to market for whatever it wants which is to be found there; for there competition brings it down to the minimum of value. * * * I think it material, too, not to abstract the high executive officers from those functions which nobody else is charged to carry on, and to employ them in superintending works which are going on abundantly in private hands. Our predecessors went on different principles; they bought iron mines, and sought for copper ones. We own a mine at Harper's Ferry of the finest iron ever put into a cannon, which we are afraid to attempt to work. We have rented it heretofore, but it is now without a tenant.—To Mr. Bibb. v. 326. (M., 1808.)

6458. PATERNALISM, Private enterprise vs.—Private enterprise manages * * * much better [than the government] all the concerns to which it is equal.—Sixth Annual Message. viii, 68. Ford ed., viii, 494. (1806.)

6459. PATIENCE, Abuse of.—When patience has begotten false estimates of its motives, when wrongs are pressed because it is believed they will be borne, resistance becomes morality.—To Madame de Stael. v, 133. (W., 1807.)

6460. PATRIOTISM, Cherish.—Let the love of our country soar above all minor passions.—To John Hollins. v, 597. (M., 1811.)

6461. ——— ———. The first object of my heart is my country. In that is embarked my family, my fortune, and my own existence. I have not one farthing of interest, nor one fibre of attachment out of it, nor a single motive of preference of any one nation to another, but in proportion as they are more or less friendly to us.—To Elbridge Gerry. iv, 269. Ford ed., vii, 329. (Pa., 1799.)

⨯**6462. PATRIOTISM, Disinterested.**—The man who loves his country on its own account, and not merely for its trappings of interest or power, can never be divorced from it, can never refuse to come forward when he finds that she is engaged in dangers which he has the means of warding off.—To Elbridge Gerry. iv, 188. Ford ed., vii, 151. (Pa., June 1797.)

6463. ——— ———. Let us deserve well of our country by making her interests the end of all our plans, and not our own pomp, patronage, and irresponsiblity.—To Albert Gallatin. iv, 429. Ford ed., viii, 141. (W., 1802.)

⨯**6464. PATRIOTISM, Inspirations to.**—I sincerely wish you may find it convenient to come to Europe. * * * It will make you adore your own country, its soil, its climate, its equality, liberty, laws, people and manners. * * * While we shall see multiplied instances of Europeans going to live in America, I will venture to say, no man now living will ever see an instance of an American removing to settle in Europe, and continuing there. Come, then, and see the proofs of this, and on your return add your testimony to that of every thinking American, in order to satisfy our countrymen how much it is their interest to preserve, uninfected by contagion, those peculiarities in their government and manners, to which they are indebted for those blessings.—To James Monroe. i, 352. Ford ed., iv, 59. (P., 1785.)

6465. PATRIOTISM, Sacrifices for.—To preserve the peace of our fellow citizens, promote their prosperity and happiness, reunite opinion, cultivate a spirit of candor, moderation, charity and forbearance toward one another, are objects calling for the efforts and sacrifices of every good man and patriot. Our religion enjoins it; our happiness demands it; and no sacrifice is requisite but of passions hostile to both.—To Rhode Island Assembly. iv, 397. (W., 1801.)

6466. PATRONAGE, Advantages of.—Those who have once got an ascendancy, and possessed themselves of all the resources of the nation, their revenues and offices, have immense means for retaining their advantage.—To John Taylor. iv, 246. Ford ed., vii, 263. (Pa., June 1798.)

6467. PATRONAGE, Corruption and.—Bad men will sometimes get in [the Presidency], and with such an immense patronage, may make great progress in corrupting the public mind and principles. This is a subject with which wisdom and patriotism should be occupied.—To Moses Robinson. iv, 380. (W., 1801.)

6468. PATRONAGE, Curtailing.—They [first republican Congress] * * * are disarming executive patronage and preponderance, by putting down one-half the offices of the United States, which are no longer necessary.—To General Kosciusko. iv, 430. (W., April 1802.) See Offices and Officeholders.

6469. PATRONAGE, Distribution of.—I am sensible of the necessity as well as justice of dispersing employments over the whole of the United States. But this is difficult as to the smaller offices, which require to be filled immediately as they become vacant and are not worth coming for from the distant States. Hence they will unavoidably get into the sole occupation of the vicinities of the seat of government,—a reason the more for removing that seat to the true centre.—To Colonel Henry Lee. Ford ed., v, 163. (N.Y., 1790.)

6470. PATRONAGE, Elections and.—The elective principle becomes nothing, if it may be smothered by the enormous patronage of the General Government.—To Governor Thomas M'Kean. iv, 350. Ford ed., vii, 487. (W., 1801.)

6471. PATRONAGE, Necessity for.—The safety of the government absolutely required that its direction in its higher departments should be taken into friendly hands. Its safety did not even admit that the whole of its immense patronage should be left at the command of its enemies to be exercised secretly or openly to reestablish the tyrannical and dilapidating system of the preceding administration, and their deleterious principles of government.—To Elbridge Gerry. Ford ed., viii, 169. (W., 1802.)

6472. PATRONAGE, Partizans and.—Every officer of the government may vote at elections according to his conscience; but we should betray the cause committed to our care, were we to permit the influence of official patronage to be used to overthrow that cause.—To Levi Lincoln. iv, 451. Ford ed., viii, 176. (W., 1802.)

6473. PATRONAGE, For personal ends.—A person who wishes to make [the bestowal of office] an engine of self-elevation, may do wonders with it; but to one who wishes to use it conscientiously for the public good, without regard to the ties of blood or friendship, it creates enmities without number, many open, but more secret, and saps the happiness and peace of his life.—To JAMES SULLIVAN. v, 252. (W., 1808.)

6474. PATRONAGE, Use of.—The patronage of public office should no longer be confided to one who uses it for active opposition to the national will.—To ALBERT GALLATIN. iv, 544. FORD ED., viii, 304. (1804.)

6475. —— ——. No government [can] discharge its duties to the best advantage of its citizens, if its agents [are] in a regular course of thwarting instead of executing all its measures, and [are] employing the patronage and influence of their offices against the government and its measures.—To JOHN PAGE. v, 136. FORD ED., ix, 118. (W., July 1807.)

6476. PATRONAGE vs. PATRIOTISM. —Let us deserve well of our country by making her interests the end of all our pains, and not our own pomp, patronage, and irresponsibility.—To ALBERT GALLATIN. iv, 429. FORD ED., viii, 141. (W., 1802.)

6477. PAUPERS, No American.—We have no paupers, the old and crippled among us, who possess nothing and have no families to take care of them, being too few to merit notice as a separate section of society, or to affect a general estimate. The great mass of our population is of laborers; our rich who can live without labor, either manual or professional, being few, and of moderate wealth. Most of the laboring class possess property, cultivate their own lands, have families, and from the demand for their labor are enabled to exact from the rich and the competent such prices as enable them to be fed abundantly, clothed above mere decency, to labor moderately and raise their families.—To THOMAS COOPER. vi, 377. (M., 1814.)

6478. PEACE, America and.—Twenty years of peace, and the prosperity so visibly flowing from it, have but strengthened our attachment to it, and the blessings it brings, and we do not despair of being always a peaceable nation.—To M. CABANIS. iv, 497. (W., 1803.)

6479. PEACE, Blessings of.—Wars and contentions, indeed, fill the pages of history with more matter. But more blessed is that nation whose silent course of happiness furnishes nothing for history to say. This is what I ambition for my own country.—To COMTE DIODATI. v, 62. (W., 1807.)

6480. PEACE, Bread and.—Were I in Europe, *pax et panis* [peace and a loaf] would certainly be my motto.—To COMTE DIODATI. v, 62. (W., 1807.)

6481. PEACE, Cherishing.—I believe that through all America there has been but a single sentiment on the subject of peace and war, which was in favor of the former. The Executive here has cherished it with equal and unanimous desire. We have differed, perhaps, as to the tone of conduct exactly adapted to the securing it.—To JAMES MONROE. iv, 6. FORD ED., vi, 321. (Pa., June 1793.)

6482. —— ——. Having seen the people of all other nations bowed down to the earth under the wars and prodigalities of their rulers, I have cherished their opposites, peace, economy, and riddance of public debt, believing that these were the high road to public as well as private prosperity and happiness.— To HENRY MIDDLETON. vi, 90. (M., Jan. 1813.)

6483. PEACE, Cultivate.—Young as we are, and with such a country before us to fill with people and with happiness, we should point in that direction the whole generative force of nature, wasting none of it in efforts of * * * destruction.—NOTES ON VIRGINIA. viii, 412. FORD ED., iii, 278. (1782.)

6484. —— ——. It should be our endeavor to cultivate the peace and friendship of every nation, even of that which has injured us most, when we shall have carried our point against her.—NOTES ON VIRGINIA. viii, 412. FORD ED., iii, 279. (1782.)

6485. —— ——. I am decidedly of opinion we should take no part in European quarrels, but cultivate peace and commerce with all.—To GENERAL WASHINGTON. ii, 533. FORD ED., v, 57. (P., 1788.)

6486. —— ——. We wish to cultivate peace and friendship with all nations, believing that course most conducive to the welfare of our own.—To SIR JOHN SINCLAIR. vii, 24. (M., 1816.)

6487. PEACE, The Deity and.—I bless the Almighty Being, Who, in gathering together the waters under the heavens into one place, divided the dry land of your hemisphere from the dry lands of ours, and said, at least be there peace.—To EARL OF BUCHAN. iv, 493. (W., 1803.)

6488. PEACE, Desire for.—The power of making war often prevents it, and in our case would give efficacy to our desire of peace.— To GENERAL WASHINGTON. ii, 533. FORD ED., v, 57. (P., Dec. 1788.)

6489. —— ——. The bravery exhibited by our citizens on that element [the ocean] will, I trust, be a testimony to the world that it is not the want of that virtue which makes us seek their peace, but a conscientious desire to direct the energies of our nation to the multiplication of the human race, and not to its destruction.—FIRST ANNUAL MESSAGE. viii, 8. FORD ED., viii, 118. (1801.)

6490. PEACE, With England.—I am glad of the pacification of Ghent, and shall still be more so, if, by a reasonable arrangement against impressment, they will make it truly a treaty of peace, and not a mere truce, as we must all consider it, until the principle of the war is settled.—To GENERAL DEARBORN. vi, 450. (M., March 1815.)

6491. —— ——. The United States and Great Britain ought to wish for peace and cordial friendship; we, because you can do us more harm than any other nation; and you, because we can do you more good than any other nation.—To SIR JOHN SINCLAIR. vii, 22. (M., 1816.)

6492. —— ——. I reciprocate congratulations with you sincerely on the restoration of peace between our two nations. * * * Let both parties now count soberly the value of mutual friendship.—To SIR JOHN SINCLAIR. vii, 22. (M., 1816.)

6493. **PEACE, European wars and.**— Till our treaty with England be fully executed, it is desirable to us that all the world should be in peace. That done, their wars would do us little harm.—To SAMUEL OSGOOD. i, 450. (P., 1785.)

6494. **PEACE, Faith, honor and.**—I hope some means will turn up of reconciling our faith and honor with peace.—To JOHN ADAMS. iv, 104. FORD ED., vi, 505. (M., April 1794.)

6495. —— ——. I wish for peace, if it can be preserved, *salvê fide et honore.*—To JAMES MONROE. FORD ED., vi, 504. (M., 1794.)

6496. **PEACE, With France.**—The agents of the two people[United States and France] are either great bunglers or great rascals, when they cannot preserve that peace which is the universal wish of both.—To JAMES MONROE. iv, 20. FORD ED., vi, 349. (Pa., 1793.)

6497. —— ——. [My assailant] says I am " for peace; but it is only with France ". He has told half the truth. He would have told the whole, if he had added England. I am for peace with both countries.—To SAMUEL SMITH. iv, 254. FORD ED., vii, 277. (M., 1798.)

6498. **PEACE, Happiness and prosperity.**—Always a friend to peace, and believing it to promote eminently the happiness and prosperity of nations, I am ever unwilling that it should be disturbed, until greater and more important interests call for an appeal to force.—To GENERAL SHEE. v, 33. (W., 1807.)

6499. —— ——. All the energies of the European nations are expended in the destruction of the labor, property and lives of their people. On our part, never had a people so favorable a chance of trying the opposite system, of peace and fraternity with mankind, and the direction of all our means and faculties to the purposes of improvement instead of destruction.—To PRESIDENT MONROE. vii, 288. FORD ED., x, 257. (M., 1823.)

6500. **PEACE, Importance of.**—Peace is our most important interest, and a recovery from debt.—To WILLIAM SHORT. iv, 414. FORD ED., viii, 98. (W., 1801.)

6501. **PEACE, Independence and.**— Peace is the most important of all things for

us, except the preserving an erect and independent attitude.—To ROBERT R. LIVINGSTON. iv, 448. FORD ED., viii, 173. (W., Oct. 1802.)

6502. **PEACE, A landmark.**—To cultivate peace * * * [is one of] the landmarks by which we are to guide ourselves in all our proceedings.—SECOND ANNUAL MESSAGE. viii, 21. FORD ED., viii, 186. (Dec. 1802.)

6503. **PEACE, Love of.**—I love peace, and am anxious that we should give the world still another useful lesson, by showing to them other modes of punishing injuries than by war, which is as much a punishment to the punisher as to the sufferer.—To TENCH COXE. iv, 105. FORD ED., vi, 508. (M., May 1794.)

6504. **PEACE, With mankind.**—I do not recall these recollections [of conflicts with the federal monarchists] with pleasure, but rather wish to forget them, nor did I ever permit them to affect social intercourse. And now, least of all, am I disposed to do so. Peace and good will with all mankind is my sincere wish.—To WILLIAM SHORT. vii, 392. FORD ED., x, 335. (M., 1825.)

6505. **PEACE, Markets and.**—I hope France, England and Spain will all see it their interest to let us make bread for them in peace, and to give us a good price for it.— To COLONEL M. LEWIS. iii, 163. (N.Y., 1790.)

6506. **PEACE, National reputation and.** —I am so far from believing that our reputation will be tarnished by our not having mixed in the mad contests of the rest of the world that, setting aside the ravings of pepper-pot politicians, of whom there are enough in every age and country, I believe it will place us high in the scale of wisdom, to have preserved our country tranquil and prosperous during a contest which prostrated the honor, power, independence, laws and property of every country on the other side of the Atlantic. Which of them have better preserved their honor? Has Spain, has Portugal, Italy, Switzerland, Holland, Prussia, Austria, the other German powers, Sweden, Denmark, or even Russia? And would we accept of the infamy of France or England in exchange for our honest reputation, or of the result of their enormities, despotism to the one, and bankruptcy and prostration to the other, in exchange for the prosperity, the freedom and independence, which we have preserved safely through the wreck?—To J. W. EPPES. vi, 15. (M., Sep. 1811.)

6507. **PEACE, Our object.**—Peace with all nations, and the right which that gives us with respect to all nations, are our object.— To C. W. F. DUMAS. iii, 535. (Pa., 1793.)

6508. **PEACE, Passion for.**—Peace is our passion.—To SIR JOHN SINCLAIR. iv, 491. (W., 1803.)

6509. **PEACE, Pipe of.**—I have joined with you sincerely in smoking the pipe of peace; it is a good old custom handed down by your ancestors, and as such I respect and join in it with reverence. I hope we shall long continue to smoke in friendship together.—To Brother John Baptist de Coigne. viii, 172. (1781.)

6510. PEACE, A Polar star.—Peace and justice [should] be the polar stars of the American Societies.—To J. Correa. vii, 184. Ford ed., x, 164. (M., 1820.)

6511. PEACE, A policy of.—Determined as we are to avoid, if possible, wasting the energies of our people in war and destruction, we shall avoid implicating ourselves with the powers of Europe, even in support of principles which we mean to pursue. They have so many other interests different from ours, that we must avoid being entangled in them. We believe we can enforce those principles, as to ourselves, by peaceable means, now that we are likely to have our public councils detached from foreign views.—To Thomas Paine. iv, 370. Ford ed., viii, 18. (W., March 1801.)

6512. —— ——. I hope that peace and amity with all nations will long be the character of our land, and that its prosperity under the Charter will react on the mind of Europe, and profit her by the example.—To Earl of Buchan. iv, 494. (W., 1803.)

6513. —— ——. We ask for peace and justice from all nations.—To James Monroe. v, 12. Ford ed., viii, 450. (W., May 1806.)

6514. —— ——. The desire to preserve our country from the calamities and ravages of war, by cultivating a disposition, and pursuing a conduct, conciliatory and friendly to all nations, has been sincerely entertained and faithfully followed. It was dictated by the principles of humanity, the precepts of the gospel, and the general wish of our country.—Reply to Address. viii, 118. (1807.)

6515. PEACE, Politics and.—We have great need of peace in Europe, that foreign affairs may no longer bear so heavily on ours. We have great need for the ensuing twelve months to be left to ourselves. The enemies of our Constitution are preparing a fearful operation, and the dissensions in this State [Pennsylvania] are too likely to bring things to the situation they wish, when our Bonaparte, surrounded by his comrades in arms, may step in to give us political salvation in his way. It behooves our citizens to be on their guard, to be firm in their principles, and full of confidence in themselves. We are able to preserve our self-government if we will but think so.—To T. M. Randolph. iv, 319. Ford ed., vii, 422. (Pa., Feb. 1800.)

6516. PEACE, Prayers for.—I pray for peace, as best for all the world, best for us, and best for me, who have already lived to see three wars, and now pant for nothing more than to be permitted to depart in peace.—To Thomas Leiper. vi, 466. Ford ed., ix, 522. (M., 1815.)

6517. PEACE, Preserving.—My hope of preserving peace for our country is not founded in the greater principles of non-resistance under every wrong, but in the belief that a just and friendly conduct on our part will produce justice and friendship from others.—To Earl of Buchan. iv, 494. (W., 1803.)

6518. —— ——. If nations go to war for every degree of injury, there would never be peace on earth.—To Madame de Stael. v, 133. (W., 1807.)

6519. —— ——. To preserve and secure peace has been the constant aim of my administration.—R. to A. Baltimore Baptists. viii, 137. (1808.)

6520. PEACE, A principle of government.—Peace, commerce and honest friendship with all nations, entangling alliances with none, * * * I deem [one of the] essential principles of our government and, consequently, [one] which ought to shape its administration.—First Inaugural Address. viii, 4. Ford ed., viii, 4. (1801.)

6521. —— ——. Peace has been our principle, peace is our interest, and peace has saved to the world this only plant of free and rational government now existing in it. * * * However, therefore, we may have been reproached for pursuing our Quaker system, time will affix the stamp of wisdom on it, and the happiness and prosperity of our citizens will attest its merit. And this, I believe, is the only legitimate object of government, and the first duty of governors, and not the slaughter of men and devastation of the countries placed under their care, in pursuit of a fantastic honor, unallied to virtue or happiness; or in gratification of the angry passions, or the pride of administrators, excited by personal incidents, in which their citizens have no concern.—To General Kosciusko. v, 585. (M., 1811.)

6522. PEACE, And profit.—Peace and profit will, I hope, be our lot.—To Benjamin Vaughan. iii, 159. (N.Y., 1790.)

6523. PEACE, Prosperity and.—Our desire is to pursue ourselves the path of peace as the only one leading surely to prosperity.—To George Hammond. iii, 559. Ford ed., vi, 253. (Pa., 1793.)

6524. —— ——. I have ever cherished the same spirit with all nations, from a consciousness that peace, prosperity, liberty and morals, have an intimate connection.—To Dr. George Logan. vi, 215. Ford ed., ix, 421. (M., 1813.)

6525. PEACE, Public welfare and.—We wish to cultivate peace and friendship with all nations, believing that course most conducive to the welfare of our own.—To Rufus King. iv, 444. Ford ed., viii, 164. (W., 1802.)

6526. PEACE, Pursuit of.—From the moment which sealed our peace and independence, our nation has wisely pursued the paths of peace and justice. During the period in which I have been charged with its concerns, no effort has been spared to exempt us from the wrongs and the rapacity of foreign nations, and * * * I feel assured that no American will hesitate to rally round the standard of his insulted country, in defence of that freedom and independence achieved by the wisdom of sages, and consecrated by the blood of heroes.—R. TO A. GEORGETOWN REPUBLICANS. viii, 159. (1809.)

6527. —— ——. Do what is right, leaving the people of Europe to act their follies and crimes among themselves, while we pursue in good faith the paths of peace and prosperity.—To PRESIDENT MONROE. vii, 290. FORD ED., x, 259. (M., 1823.)

6528. PEACE, Securing.—Whatever enables us to go to war, secures our peace.—To JAMES MONROE. FORD ED., v, 198. (N.Y., 1790.)

6529. PEACE, Wisdom of.—Peace and friendship with all mankind is our wisest policy; and I wish we may be permitted to pursue it.—To C. W. F. DUMAS. i, 553. (P., 1786.)

6530. PEACE, Wishes for.—That peace, safety, and concord may be the portion of our native land, and be long enjoyed by our fellow-citizens, is the most ardent wish of my heart, and if I can be instrumental in procuring or preserving them, I shall think I have not lived in vain.—To BENJAMIN WARING. iv, 378. (W., March 1801.)

6531. —— ——. It is impossible that any other man should wish peace as much as I do; although duty may control that wish.— To JOEL BARLOW. v, 216. FORD ED., ix, 168. (W., Dec. 1807.) See ALLIANCES.

6532. PEACE vs. WAR.—I value peace, and I should unwillingly see any event take place which would render war a necessary resource.—To M. DUPONT DE NEMOURS. iv, 435. (W., April 1802.)

6533. —— ——. I hope we shall prove how much happier for man the Quaker policy is, and that the life of the feeder, is better than that of the fighter; and it is some consolation that the desolation by these maniacs [European kings] of one part of the earth is the means of improving it in other parts.—To JOHN ADAMS. vii, 245. FORD ED., x, 217. (M., 1822.)

— **PELISIPIA, Proposed State of.**—See WESTERN TERRITORY.

6534. PENDLETON (Edmund), Address of.—Your patriarchal address to your country is running through all the republican papers, and has a very great effect on the people. It is short, simple, and presents things in a view they readily comprehend. The character and circumstances, too, of the writer leave them without doubts of his motives.—To EDMUND PENDLETON. iv, 274. FORD ED., vii, 336. (Pa., 1799.)

6535. PENDLETON (Edmund), Perseverance.—Mr. Pendleton * * * was the ablest man in debate I have ever met with. He had not, indeed, the poetical fancy of Mr. Henry, his sublime imagination, his lofty and overwhelming diction; but he was cool, smooth and persuasive; his language flowing, chaste and embellished; his conceptions quick, acute and full of resource; never vanquished: for if he lost the main battle, he returned upon you, and regained so much of it as to make it a drawn one, by dexterous manœuvres, skirmishes in detail, and the recovery of small advantages which, little singly, were important altogether. You never knew when you were clear of him, but were harassed by his perseverance, until the patience was worn down of all who had less of it than himself. Add to this, that he was one of the most virtuous and benevolent of men, the kindest friend, the most amiable and pleasant of companions, which insured a favorable reception to whatever came from him.—AUTOBIOGRAPHY. i, 37. FORD ED., i, 50. (1821.)

6536. PENDULUM, Advantages of.—The great and decisive superiority of the pendulum, as a standard of measure, is its accessibility to all men, at all times, and in all places. —To DR. ROBERT PATTERSON. vi, 20. (M., 1811.)

6537. PENDULUM, Construction of.—I have a curiosity to try the length of a pendulum vibrating seconds here. * * * The bob should be spherical, of lead, and its radius, I presume, about one inch. * * * The suspending rod should be such as not to be affected by heat or cold, nor yet so heavy as to affect too sensibly the centre of oscillation. Would not a rod of wood not larger than a large wire answer this double view? * * * Iron has been found but about six times as strong as wood while its specific gravity is eight times as great. * * * A rod of white oak not larger than a seine twine, would probably support a spherical bob of lead of one inch radius.—To DR. ROBERT PATTERSON. vi, 26. (M., 1811.)

6538. PENDULUM, Experiments with. —I had taken no notice of the precaution of making the experiment of the pendulum on the sea-shore, because the highest mountain in the United States would not add 1-5000 part to the length of the earth's radius, nor 1-128 of an inch to the length of the pendulum. The highest part of the Andes, indeed, might add about 1-1000 to the earth's radius, and 1-25 of an inch to the pendulum. As it has been thought worth mention, I will insert it also.—To DAVID RITTENHOUSE. iii, 149. (N.Y., 1790.)

— **PENNSYLVANIA, Boundary line.**— See BOUNDARIES.

6539. PENNSYLVANIA, Electoral influence.—In Pennsylvania, the election has been triumphantly carried by the republicans; their antagonists having got but two out of eleven members [of Congress], and the vote of this State can generally turn the balance.—To T. M. RANDOLPH. iii, 491. FORD ED., vi, 134. (Pa., 1792.)

6540. PENNSYLVANIA, Patriotism.— I shall always be thankful for any information * * * which may enable me to understand the differences of opinion and interest which seem to be springing up in Pennsylvania, and to be subjects of uneasiness. If that State splits it will let us down into the abyss. I hope so much from the patriotism of all, that they will make all smaller interests give way to the greater importance of the general welfare.—To WILLIAM DUANE. FORD ED., viii, 54. (W., May 1801.)

6541. PENNSYLVANIA, Religious freedom.—The laws of Pennsylvania set us the first example of the wholesome and happy effects of religious freedom.—To M. DUFIEF. vi, 341. (M., 1814.)

6542. ——— ———. The cradle of toleration and freedom of religion.—To DR. THOMAS COOPER. vii, 266. FORD ED., x, 242. (M., 1822.)

6543. PENNSYLVANIA, Republicanism.—Pennsylvania is coming majestically round to the true principles.—To T. LOMAX. iv, 300. FORD ED., vii, 374. (M., March 1799.)

6544. ——— ———. In the electoral election [1808] Pennsylvania really spoke in a voice of thunder to the monarchists of our country, and while that State continues so firm, with the solid mass of republicanism to the South and West, such efforts as we have lately seen in the anti-republican portion of our country cannot ultimately affect our security.—To DR. E. GRIFFITH. v, 450. (M., 1809.)

6545. PENNSYLVANIA, Virginia and.—With respect to your State particularly, we shall take very great pleasure in cultivating every disposition to harmony and mutual aid. That policy would be very unsound which should build our interest or happiness on anything inconsistent with yours.—To THE PRESIDENT OF PENNSYLVANIA. FORD ED., iii, 17. (R., 1781.)

6546. ——— ———. The permanence of our Union hanging on the harmony of Pennsylvania and Virginia, I hope that will continue as long as our government continues to be a blessing to mankind.—To THOMAS LEIPER. FORD ED., x, 299. (M., 1824.)

6547. PENSACOLA, Capture of.—The capture of Pensacola, which furnished so much speculation for European news-writers (who imagine that our political code, like theirs, had no chapter of morality), was nothing here. In the first moment, indeed there was a general outcry of condemnation of what appeared to be a wrongful aggression. But this was quieted at once by information that it had been taken without orders, and would be instantly restored. * * * This manifestation of the will of our citizens to countenance no injustice towards a foreign nation filled me with comfort as to our future course.—To ALBERT GALLATIN. FORD ED., x, 115. (M., Nov. 1818.)

6548. PENSIONS, Prodigalities of.—Nor should we wonder at * * * [the] pressure [for a fixed constitution in 1788-9] when we consider the monstrous abuses of power under which * * * [the French] people were ground to powder; when we pass in review * * * the prodigalities of pensions.—AUTOBIOGRAPHY. i, 86. FORD ED., i, 118. (1821.)

6549. PENSIONS, Public.—Every person * *.* qualified to elect [to the House of Representatives of Virginia] shall be capable of being elected [to the House of Representatives]. * * * During his continuance in the said office, he shall hold no public pension * * *'.—PROPOSED VA. CONSTITUTION. FORD ED., ii, 15. (June 1776.)

6550. ——— ———. While in the senatorial office they [the members] shall be incapable of holding any public pension.—PROPOSED VA. CONSTITUTION. FORD ED., ii, 16. (June 1776.)

6551. PENSIONS, Taxes and.—We do not mean that our people shall be burthened with oppressive taxes to provide sinecures for the idle or the wicked, under color of providing for a civil list.—REPLY TO LORD NORTH'S PROPOSITION. FORD ED., i, 480. (July 1775.)

6552. PEOPLE, Administration of law and.—That people will be happiest whose laws are best, and are best administered.—DIFFUSION OF KNOWLEDGE BILL. FORD ED., ii, 221. (1779.)

6553. PEOPLE, American vs. British.—Our country is getting into a ferment against yours, or rather has caught it from yours. God knows how this will end; but assuredly in one extreme or the other. There can be no medium between those who have loved so much.—To DR. PRICE. i, 378. FORD ED., iv, 84. (P., 1785.)

6554. PEOPLE, American and European.—If all the sovereigns of Europe were to set themselves to work to emancipate the minds of their subjects from their present ignorance and prejudices, and that, as zealously as they now endeavor the contrary, a thousand years would not place them on that high ground on which our common people are now setting out. Ours could not have been so fairly put into the hands of their own common sense, had they not been separated from their parent stock, and kept from contamination, either from them, or the other people of the old world, by the intervention of so wide an ocean.—To GEORGE WYTHE. ii, 7. FORD ED., iv, 268. (P., 1786.)

6555. PEOPLE, American and French.—There is an affection between the two peoples [the Americans and French] which disposes them to favor one another.—To COUNT DE VERGENNES. i, 390. (P., 1785.)

6556. PEOPLE, Animosities.—The animosities of sovereigns are temporary and may be allayed; but those which seize the whole body of a people, and of a people, too, who dictate their own measures, produce calamities of long duration.—To C. W. F. DUMAS. i, 553. (P., 1786.)

6557. PEOPLE, Ascendency of.—Lay down true principles and adhere to them inflexibly. Do not be frightened into their surrender by the alarms of the timid, or the croakings of wealth against the ascendency of the people. If experience be called for, appeal to that of our fifteen or twenty governments for forty years, and show me where the people have done half the mischief in these forty years, that a single despot would have done in a single year; or show half the riots and rebellions, the crimes and the punishments, which have taken place in any single nation, under kingly government, during the same period.—To SAMUEL KERCHIVAL. vii, 11. FORD ED., x, 39. (M., 1816.)

6558. PEOPLE, Authority of.—I consider the people who constitute a society or nation as the source of all authority in that nation; as free to transact their common concerns by any agents they think proper; to change these agents individually, or the organization of them in form or function whenever they please; that all the acts done by these agents under the authority of the nation, are the acts of the nation, are obligatory on them, and enure to their use, and can in no wise be annulled or affected by any change in the form of the government, or of the persons administering it.—OPINION ON FRENCH TREATIES. vii, 612. FORD ED., vi, 220. (April 1793.)

6559. ——. Leave no authority existing not responsible to the people.—To ISAAC H. TIFFANY. vii, 32. (M., 1816.)

6560. ——. All authority belongs to the people.—To SPENCER ROANE. vii, 213. FORD ED., x, 190. (M., 1821.)

6561. PEOPLE, Blood of.—On this side of the Atlantic [Europe] the blood of the people is become an inheritance, and those who fatten on it will not relinquish it easily.—To E. RUTLEDGE. ii, 435. FORD ED., v, 42. (P., 1788.)

6562. PEOPLE, Cities and.—When the people get piled upon one another in large cities, as in Europe, they will become corrupt as in Europe.*—To JAMES MADISON. ii, 332. FORD ED., iv, 479. (P., 1787.)

6563. PEOPLE, City and country.—The inhabitants of the commercial cities are as different in sentiment and character from the country people as any two distinct nations, and are clamorous against the order of things [republicanism] established by the agricultural interest.—To M. PICTET. iv, 463. (W., 1803.)

6564. PEOPLE, Confidence in.—My confidence * * * in my countrymen generally leaves me without much fear for the future.—To JAMES FISHBACK. v, 470. (M., 1809.)

6565. PEOPLE, Control by.—Unless the mass retains sufficient control over those intrusted with the powers of their government, these will be perverted to their own oppression, and to the perpetuation of wealth and power in the individuals and their families selected for the trust. Whether our Constitution has hit on the exact degree of control necessary, is yet under experiment; and it is a most encouraging reflection that distance and other difficulties securing us against the brigand governments of Europe, in the safe enjoyment of our farms and firesides, the experiment stands a better chance of being satisfactorily made here than on any occasion yet presented by history.—To MR. VANDER KEMP. vi, 45. (M., 1812.)

6566. ——. I know no safe depositary of the ultimate powers of the society but the people themselves; and if we think them not enlightened enough to exercise their control with a wholesome discretion, the

* In the Congress edition "When we get piled upon one another in large cities, as in Europe, we shall become as corrupt as in Europe, and go to eating one another as they do there."—EDITOR.

remedy is not to take it from them, but to inform their discretion by education. This is the true corrective of abuses of constitutional power.—To WILLIAM C. JARVIS. vii, 179. FORD ED., x, 161. (M., 1820.)

6567. PEOPLE, Corruption and.—A germ of corruption indeed has been transferred from our dear mother country, and has already borne fruit, but its blight is begun from the breath of the people.—To J. P. BRISSOT DE WARVILLE. FORD ED., vi, 249. (Pa., 1793.)

6568. PEOPLE, Deception of.—The spirit of 1776 is not dead. It has only been slumbering. The body of the American people is substantially republican. But their virtuous feelings have been played on by some fact with more fiction; they have been the dupes of artful manœuvres, and made for a moment to be willing instruments in forging chains for themselves. But time and truth have dissipated the delusion, and opened their eyes.—To T. LOMAX. iv, 300. FORD ED., vii, 373. (M., March 1799.)

6569. ——. Our citizens may be deceived for awhile, and have been deceived; but as long as the presses can be protected, we may trust to them for light.—To ARCHIBALD STUART. FORD ED., vii, 378. (M., 1799.)

6570. ——. The lesson we have had will probably be useful to the people at large, by showing to them how capable they are of being made the instruments of their own bondage.—To JOHN DICKINSON. iv, 424. (W., 1801.)

6571. PEOPLE, Duty of rulers.—To inform the minds of the people, and to follow their will, is the chief duty of those placed at their head.—To M. DUMAS. ii, 297. (P., 1787.)

6572. PEOPLE, Enforcement of rights.—The spirit of the times may alter, will alter. Our rulers will become corrupt, our people careless. * * * They will be forgotten, and their rights disregarded. They will forget themselves, but in the sole faculty of making money, and will never think of uniting to effect a due respect for their rights.—NOTES ON VIRGINIA. viii, 402. FORD ED., iii, 266. (1782.)

6573. PEOPLE, English.—For the achievement of this happy event [peace] we call for and confide in the good offices of our fellow-subjects beyond the Atlantic. Of their friendly dispositions we do not cease to hope; aware, as they must be, that they have nothing more to expect from the same common enemy, than the humble favor of being last devoured.—DECLARATION ON TAKING UP ARMS. FORD ED., i, 475. (July 1775.)

6574. ——. Nor have we been wanting in attentions to our British brethren. We have warned them from time to time of attempts by their legislature to extend an unwarrantable jurisdiction over these our States. We have reminded them of the circumstances of our emigration and settlement here, no one of which could warrant so strange a pretension; that these were effected at the expense of our own blood and treasure, unassisted by the wealth or strength of Great Britain; that in constituting, indeed, our several forms of government, we had adopted one common king, thereby laying a foundation for perpetual league and amity with them; but that submission to their parliament was no part of our constitution, nor ever in idea, if history may be credited; and we have appealed to their native justice and magnanimity as well as to the ties of our common kindred to disavow these usurpations which were likely to interrupt our connection and correspondence. They, too, have been deaf to the voice of justice and of consanguinity, and when occasions have been given them, by the regular course of their laws, of removing from their councils the disturbers of our harmony, they have, by their free elections, reestablished them in power. At this very time, too, they are permitting their chief Magistrate to send over not only soldiers of our common blood, but Scotch and foreign mercenaries, to invade and destroy us. These facts have given the last stab to agonizing affection, and manly spirit bids us to renounce forever these unfeeling brethren. We must endeavor to forget our former love for them, to hold them as we hold the rest of mankind, enemies in war, in peace, friends. We might have been a free and a great people together; but a communication of grandeur and of freedom, it seems, is below their dignity. Be it so, since they will have it. The road to happiness and to glory is open to us, too. We will tread it apart from them, and acquiesce in the necessity which denounces our eternal separation.*—DECLARATION OF INDEPENDENCE AS DRAWN BY JEFFERSON.

6575. —— ——. The spirit of hostility to us has always existed in the mind of the King, but it has now extended itself through the whole mass of the people, and the majority of the public councils. In a country, where the voice of the people influences so much the measures of administration, and where it coincides with the private temper of the King, there is no pronouncing on future events. It is true they have nothing to gain, and much to lose by a war with us; but interest is not the strongest passion in the human breast.—To JAMES ROSS. i, 561. FORD ED., iv, 217. (P., 1786.)

6576. —— ——. The people of England, I think, are less oppressed than the people in France. But it needs but half an eye to see, when among them, that the foundation is laid in their

* Congress changed the passage as follows. "Nor have we been wanting in attentions to our British brethren. We have warned them, from time to time, of attempts by their legislature to extend an unwarrantable jurisdiction over us. We have reminded them of the circumstances of our emigration and settlement here. We have appealed to their native justice and magnanimity, and we have conjured them, by the ties of our common kindred, to disavow these usurpations, which would inevitably interrupt our connection and correspondence. They, too, have been deaf to the voice of justice and of consanguinity. We must, therefore, acquiesce in the necessity, which denounces our separation, and hold them, as we hold the rest of mankind, Enemies in War, in Peace, Friends."—EDITOR.

dispositions for the establishment of a despotism. Nobility, wealth and pomp are the objects of their admiration. They are by no means the free-minded people we suppose them in America. Their learned men, too, are few in number, and are less learned, and infinitely less emancipated from prejudices than are those of this country [France].—To GEORGE WYTHE. ii, 8. FORD ED., iv, 269. (P., 1786.)

6577. —— ——. England presents the singular phenomenon of a nation, the individuals of which are as faithful to their private engagements and duties, as honorable, as worthy, as those of any nation on earth, and whose government is yet the most unprincipled at this day known.—To JOHN LANGDON. v, 514. (M., 1810.)

6578. —— ——. The English people are individually as respectable as those of other nations,—it is her government which is so corrupt, and which has destroyed the nation.— To WILLIAM DUANE. v, 552. FORD ED., ix, 287. (M., 1810.)

6579. —— ——. I should be glad to see their farmers and mechanics come here, but I hope their nobles, priests and merchants will be kept at home to be moralized by the discipline of the new government.—To WILLIAM DUANE. v, 552. FORD ED., ix, 287. (M., 1810.)

6580. —— ——. The English have been a wise, a virtuous and truly estimable people. But commerce and a corrupt government have rotted them to the core. Every generous, nay, every just sentiment, is absorbed in the thirst for gold. I speak of their cities, which we may certainly pronounce to be ripe for despotism, and fitted for no other government. Whether the leaven of the agricultural body is sufficient to regenerate the residuary mass, and maintain it in a sound state, under any reformation of government, may still be doubted.—To MR. OGILVIE. v, 604. (M., 1811.)

6581. —— ——. The individuals of the [British] nation I have ever honored and esteemed, the basis of their character being essentially worthy; but I consider their government as the most flagitious which has existed since the days of Philip of Macedon, whom they make their model.—To JOHN ADAMS. vii, 46. (P.F., 1816.)

6582. PEOPLE, Errors of.—The people are the only censors of their governors; and even their errors will tend to keep these to the true principles of their institution. To punish these errors too severely would be to suppress the only safeguard of the public liberty.—To EDWARD CARRINGTON. ii, 99. FORD ED., iv, 359. (P., 1787.)

6583. PEOPLE, European.—Behold me at length on the vaunted scene of Europe! * * * You are, perhaps, curious to know how this new scene has struck a savage of the mountains of America. Not advantageously, I assure you. I find the general fate of humanity here most deplorable. The truth of Voltaire's observation offers itself perpetually, that every man here must be either the hammer or the anvil. It is a true picture of that country to which they say we shall pass hereafter, and where we are to see God and His angels in splendor, and crowds of the damned trampled under their feet. While the great mass of the people are thus suffering under physical and moral oppression, I have endeavored to examine more nearly the condition of the great, to appreciate the true value of the circumstances in their situation which dazzle the bulk of spectators, and, especially, to compare it with that degree of happiness which is enjoyed in America, by every class of people. Intrigues of love occupy the younger, and those of ambition, the elder part of the great. Conjugal love having no existence among them, domestic happiness, of which that is the basis, is utterly unknown. In lieu of this, are substituted pursuits which nourish and invigorate all our bad passions, and which offer only moments of ecstacy amidst days and months of restlessness and torment. Much, very much inferior, this, to the tranquil, permanent felicity with which domestic society in America blesses most of its inhabitants: leaving them to follow steadily those pursuits which health and reason approve, and rendering truly delicious the intervals of those pursuits.—To Mr. Bellini. i, 444. (P., 1785.)

6584. PEOPLE, Freedom and.—I am not among those who fear the people. They, and not the rich, are our dependence for continued freedom.—To Samuel Kerchival. vii, 14. Ford ed., x, 41. (M., 1816.)

6585. PEOPLE, French.—I do love this people with all my heart, and think that with a better religion, a better form of government and their present governors, their condition and country would be most enviable.—To Mrs. John Adams. Ford ed., iv, 61. (P., 1785.)

6586. ———— ————. It is difficult to conceive how so good a people, with so good a King, so well-disposed rulers in general, so genial a climate, so fertile a soil, should be rendered so ineffectual for producing human happiness by one single curse,—that of a bad form of government. But it is a fact. In spite of the mildness of their governors, the people are ground to powder by the vices of the form of government. Of twenty millions of people supposed to be in France, I am of opinion there are nineteen millions more wretched, more accursed in every circumstance of human existence than the most conspicuously wretched individual of the whole United States.—To Mrs. Trist. i, 394. (P., 1785.)

6587. ———— ————. Two peoples whose interests, whose principles, whose habits of attachment, founded on fellowship in war and mutual kindnesses, have so many points of union, cannot but be easily kept together.—To M. Odit. iv, 123. (M., Oct. 1795.)

6588. ———— ————. The body of the people of * * * [France] love us cordially.—To John Langdon. i, 429. (P., 1785.)

6589. ———— ————. In science the mass of the people [of France] are two centuries behind ours; their literati a dozen years before us. Books, really good, acquire just reputation in that time, and so become known to us, and communicate to us all their advances in knowledge. Is not this delay compensated by our being placed out of the reach of that swarm of nonsensical publications which issues daily from a thousand presses, and perishes in the issuing?—To Mr. Bellini. i, 444. (P., 1785.)

6590. ———— ————. Certain it is that they [the farming classes in South of France] are less happy and less virtuous in villages, than they would be insulated with their families on the grounds they cultivate.—Travels in France. ix, 313. (1787.)

6591. ———— ————. I cannot leave this great and good country without expressing my sense of its preeminence of character among the nations of the earth. A more benevolent people I have never known, nor greater warmth and devotedness in their select friendships. Their kindness and accommodation to strangers is unparalleled, and the hospitality of Paris is beyond anything I had conceived to be practicable in a large city. Their eminence, too, in science, the communicative dispositions of their scientific men, the politeness of the general manners, the ease and vivacity of their conversation, give a charm to their society, to be found nowhere else. In a comparison of this with other countries, we have the proof of primacy, which was given to Themistocles after the battle of Salamis. Every general voted to himself the first reward of valor, and the second to Themistocles. So, ask the travelled inhabitant of any nation, in what country on earth would you rather live? Certainly, in my own, where are all my friends, my relations, and the earliest and sweetest affections and recollections of my life. Which would be your second choice? France.—Autobiography. i, 107. Ford ed., i, 148. (1821.)

6592. PEOPLE, Frugality and happiness.—Kindly separated by nature and a wide ocean from the exterminating havoc of one quarter of the globe; too high-minded to endure the degradations of the others; possessing a chosen country, with room enough for our descendants to the hundredth and thousandth generation; entertaining a due sense of our equal right to the use of our own faculties, to the acquisitions of our own industry, to honor and confidence from our fellow-citizens, resulting, not from birth, but from our actions, and their sense of them; enlightened by a benign religion, professed, indeed, and practiced in various forms, yet all of them inculcating honesty, truth, temperance, gratitude and the love of man; acknowledging and adoring an overruling Providence, which, by all its dispensations, proves that it delights in the happiness of man here and his greater happiness hereafter,—with all these blessings, what more is necessary to make us a happy and prosperous people? Still one thing more, fellow-citizens—a wise and frugal government, which shall restrain men from injuring one another, which shall leave them otherwise free to regulate their own pursuits of industry and improvement, and shall not take from the mouth of labor the bread it has earned. This is the sum of good government, and this is necessary to close the circle of our felicities.—First Inaugural Address. viii, 3. Ford ed., viii, 3. (1801.)

6593. PEOPLE, Government and.—Every government degenerates when trusted to the rulers of the people alone. The people themselves, therefore, are its only safe depositaries. And to render even them safe, their minds must be improved to a certain degree.—Notes on Virginia. viii, 390. Ford ed., iii, 254. (1782.)

6594. ———— ————. A tractable people may be governed in large bodies; but, in proportion as they depart from this character, the extent of their government must be less.—To JAMES MADISON. ii, 66. FORD ED., iv, 333. (P., 1786.)

6595. ———— ————. The government which can wield the arm of the people must be the strongest possible.—To MR. WEAVER. v, 89. (W., 1807.)

6596. ———— ————. No government can continue good, but under the control of the people.—To JOHN ADAMS. vii, 149. FORD ED., x, 153. (M., 1819.)

6597. PEOPLE, Imposing upon.—As little [as to shut up the press] is it necessary to impose on the people's senses, or dazzle their minds by pomp, splendor, or forms. Instead of this artificial, how much surer is that real respect, which results from the use of their reason, and the habit of bringing everything to the test of common sense.—To JUDGE TYLER. iv, 548. (W., 1804.)

6598. PEOPLE, Independent of all.—Independence can be trusted nowhere but with the people in mass. They are inherently independent of all but moral law.—To SPENCER ROANE. vii, 134. FORD ED., x, 141. (P. F., 1819.)

6599. PEOPLE, Industry.—The rights [of the people] to the exercise and fruits of their own industry can never be protected against the selfishness of rulers not subject to their control at short periods.—To ISAAC H. TIFFANY. vii, 32. (M., 1816.)

6600. ———— ————. No other depositaries of power [than the people themselves] have ever yet been found, which did not end in converting to their own profit the earnings of those committed to their charge.—To SAMUEL KERCHIVAL. vii, 36. FORD ED., x, 45. (M., 1816.) See INDUSTRY.

6601. PEOPLE, Judgment of.—The firmness with which the people have withstood the late abuses of the press, the discernment they have manifested between truth and falsehood, show that they may safely be trusted to hear everything true and false, and to form a correct judgment between them.—To JUDGE TYLER. iv, 549. (W., 1804.) See NEWSPAPERS.

6602. PEOPLE, Legislative powers.—While those bodies are in existence to whom the people have delegated the powers of legislation, they alone possess, and may exercise, those powers. But when they are dissolved by the lopping off of one or more of their branches, the power reverts to the people, who may exercise it to unlimited extent, either assembling together in person, sending deputies, or in any other way they may think proper.—RIGHTS OF BRITISH AMERICA. i, 138. FORD ED., i, 443. (1774.)

6603. PEOPLE, Liberty and the.—The people are the only sure reliance for the preservation of our liberty.—To JAMES MADISON. ii, 332. (P., 1787.)

6604. PEOPLE, New England.—The adventurous genius and intrepidity of those peo-

ple [New Englanders] is amazing. They are now intent on burning Boston as a hive which gives cover to [British] regulars; and none are more bent upon it than the very people who come out of it, and whose prosperity lies there.—To FRANCIS EPPES. FORD ED., i, 461. (Pa., July 4, 1775.)

6605. PEOPLE, Oppressed.—To constrain the brute force of the people, the European governments deem it necessary to keep them down by hard labor, poverty and ignorance, and to take from them, as from bees, so much of their earnings, as that unremitting labor shall be necessary to obtain a sufficient surplus barely to sustain a scanty and miserable life. And these earnings they apply to maintain their privileged orders in splendor and idleness, to fascinate the eyes of the people, and excite in them an humble adoration and submission, as to an order of superior beings.—To WILLIAM JOHNSON. vii, 291. FORD ED., x, 226. (M., 1823.)

6606. PEOPLE, Participation in government.—We think in America that it is necessary to introduce the people into every department of government, as far as they are capable of exercising it; and that this is the only way to ensure a long-continued and honest administration of its powers.—To M. L'ABBÉ ARNOND. iii, 81. FORD ED., v, 103. (P., 1789.)

6607. ———— ————. The people are not qualified to exercise themselves the executive department, but they are qualified to name the person who shall exercise it. With us, therefore, they choose this officer every four years.—To L'ABBÉ ARNOND. iii, 81. FORD ED., v, 103. (P., 1789.)

6608. ———— ————. The people are not qualified to legislate. With us, therefore, they only choose the legislators.—To M. L'ABBÉ ARNOND. iii, 81. FORD ED., v, 103. (P., 1789.)

6609. ———— ————. Were I called upon to decide whether the people had best be omitted in the Legislative or Judiciary department, I would say it is better to leave them out of the Legislative. The execution of the laws is more important than the making them. However, it is best to have the people in all the three departments where that is possible. —To M. L'ABBÉ ARNOND. iii, 82. FORD ED., v, 104. (P., 1789.)

6610. ———— ————. The people, being the only safe depositary of power, should exercise in person every function which their qualifications enable them to exercise, consistently with the order and security of society.—To DR. WALTER JONES. vi, 285. FORD ED., ix, 447. (M., 1814.)

6611. PEOPLE, Prussian.—The transition from ease and opulence to extreme poverty is remarkable on crossing the line between the Dutch and Prussian territories. The soil and climate are the same; the governments alone differ. With the poverty, the fear also of slaves is visible in the faces of the Prussian subjects. —TRAVELS IN PRUSSIA. ix, 378. (1787.)

6612. PEOPLE, Reasonable.—It is a blessing that our people are reasonable; that they are kept so well informed of the state of things as to judge for themselves, to see the true sources of their difficulties, and to maintain their confidence undiminished in the wisdom and integrity of their functionaries.—To Cæsar A. Rodney. v, 501. Ford ed., ix. 272.   (M., 1810.)

6613. PEOPLE, Representation.—I look for our safety to the broad representation of the people [in Congress]. It will be more difficult for corrupt views to lay hold of so large a mass.—To T. M. Randolph. Ford ed., v, 455.   (Pa., 1792.)

6614. PEOPLE, Representation and taxation.—Preserve inviolate the fundamental principle, that the people are not to be taxed but by representatives chosen immediately by themselves.—To James Madison. ii, 328. Ford ed., iv, 475.   (P., 1787.)

6615. PEOPLE, Republic.—It is the manners and spirit of a people which preserve a republic in vigor. A degeneracy in these is a canker which soon eats to the heart of its laws and constitution.—Notes on Virginia.   viii, 406.   Ford ed., iii, 269.   (1782.)

6616. PEOPLE, Respect for.—My visit to Philadelphia will be merely out of respect to the public, and to the new President.—To Mr. Volney. iv, 159.   (M., Jan. 1797.)

6617. PEOPLE, Rights of.—Their rights * * * [are] derived from the laws of nature, and [are] not the gift of their Chief Magistrate.—Rights of British America. i, 141. Ford ed., i, 446.   (1774.)

6618. ——— ———. The people of every country are the only safe guardians of their own rights, and are the only instruments which can be used for their destruction. And certainly they would never consent to be so used were they not deceived. To avoid this they should be instructed to a certain degree.—To John Wyche. v, 448. (M., 1809.)

6619. ——— ———. The people, especially when moderately instructed, are the only safe, because the only honest, depositaries of the public rights, and should, therefore, be introduced into the administration of them in every function to which they are sufficient. They will err sometimes and accidentally, but never designedly, and with a systematic and persevering purpose of overthrowing the free principles of the government.—To M. Coray. vii, 319.   (M., 1823.)

6620. PEOPLE, Roman.—The letters of Cicero breathe the purest effusions of an exalted patriot, while the parricide Cæsar is lost in odious contrast. When the enthusiasm, however, kindled by Cicero's pen and principles, subsides into cool reflection, I ask myself, what was that government, which the virtues of Cicero were so zealous to restore, and the ambition of Cæsar to subvert? And if Cæsar had been as virtuous as he was daring and sagacious, what could he, even in the plenitude of his usurped power, have done to lead his fellow citizens into good government? I do not say to *restore* it, because they never had it, from the rape of the Sabines to the ravages of the Cæsars. If their people, indeed, had been, like ourselves, enlightened, peaceable and really free, the answer would be obvious. " Restore independence to all your foreign conquests, relieve Italy from the government of the rabble of Rome, consult it as a nation entitled to self-government, and do its will ". But steeped in corruption, vice and venality, as the whole nation was (and nobody had done more than Cæsar to corrupt it), what could even Cicero, Cato, Brutus have done, had it been referred to them to establish a good government for their country? They had no ideas of government themselves, but of their degenerate Senate, nor the people of liberty, but of the factious opposition of their Tribunes. They had afterwards their Tituses, their Trajans and Antoninuses, who had the will to make them happy, and the power to mould their government into a good and permanent form. But it would seem as if they could not see their way clearly to do it. No government can continue good, but under the control of the people; and their people were so demoralized and depraved, as to be incapable of exercising a wholesome control. Their reformation then was to be taken up *ab incunabulis*. Their minds were to be informed by education what is right and what wrong; to be encouraged in habits of virtue and deterred from those of vice by the dread of punishments proportioned, indeed, but irremissible; in all cases, to follow truth as the only safe guide, and to eschew error, which bewilders us in one false consequence after another, in endless succession. These are the incu'cations necessary to render the people a sure basis for the structure of order and good government. But this would have been an operation of a generation or two, at least, within wh'ch period would have succeeded many Neros and Commoduses, who would have quashed the whole process. I confess, then, I can neither see what Cicero, Cato and Brutus, united and uncontrolled, could have devised to lead their people into good government, nor how this enigma can be solved, nor how further shown why it has been the fate of that delightful country never to have known, to this day, and through a course of five and twenty hundred years, the history of which we possess, one single day of free and rational government. Your intimacy with their history, ancient, middle and modern, your familiarity with the improvements in the science of government at this time, will enable you, if anybody, to go back with our principles and opinions to the times of Cicero, Cato and Brutus, and tell us by what process these great and virtuous men could have led so unenlightened and vitiated a people into freedom and good government.*—To John Adams. vii, 148. Ford ed., x, 152.   (M., 1819.)

6621. PEOPLE, Self-government.—The panic into which the people were artfully thrown in 1798, the frenzy which was excited in them by their enemies against their apparent readiness to abandon all the principles established for their own protection, seemed for awhile to countenance the opinions of those who say they cannot be trusted

* "I never could discover," wrote Mr. Adams in reply, "that they possessed much virtue, or real liberty. Their Patricians were in general griping usurers, and tyrannical creditors in all ages. Pride, strength, and courage, were all the virtues that composed their national characters."—Editor.

with their own government. But I never doubted their rallying; and they did rally much sooner than I expected. On the whole, that experiment on their credulity has confirmed my confidence in their ultimate good sense and virtue.—To JUDGE TYLER. iv, 549. (W., 1804.)

6622. ———— ————. To open the doors of truth, and to fortify the habit of testing everything by reason, are the most effectual manacles we can rivet on the hands of our successors to prevent their manacling the people with their own consent.—To JUDGE TYLER. iv, 549. (W., 1804.)

6623. PEOPLE, Spirit of.—Cherish the spirit of our people and keep alive their attention. Do not be too severe upon their errors, but reclaim them by enlightening them. If once they become inattentive to the public affairs, you and I and Congress and assemblies, judges and governors shall all become wolves.—To EDWARD CARRINGTON. ii, 100. FORD ED., iv, 360. (P., 1787.)

6624. PEOPLE, Supreme.—He [George III.] is no more than the chief officer of the people, appointed by the laws, and circumscribed with definite powers, to assist in working the great machine of government, erected for their use, and, consequently, subject to their superintendence.—RIGHTS OF BRITISH AMERICA. i, 125. FORD ED., i, 429. (1774.)

6625. PEOPLE, A united.—Spain, under all her disadvantages, physical and mental, is an encouraging example of the impossibility of subduing a people acting with an undivided will. She proves, too, another truth not less valuable, that a people having no king to sell them for a mess of pottage for himself, no shackles to restrain their powers of self-defence, find resources within themselves equal to every trial. This we did during the Revolutionary war, and this we can do again, let who will attack us, if we act heartily with one another. This is my creed. To the principles of union I sacrifice all minor differences of opinion. These, like differences of face, are a law of our nature, and should be viewed with the same tolerance.—To WILLIAM DUANE. v, 603. (M., July 1811.)

6626. PEOPLE, A well-informed.—Whenever the people are well-informed they can be trusted with their own government.—To DR. PRICE. ii, 553. (P., 1789.)

6627. ———— ————. Whenever the people are well-informed * * * and things get so far wrong as to attract their notice, they may be relied on to set them to rights.—To DR. PRICE. ii, 553. (P., 1789.)

6628. PEOPLE, The western.—That our fellow citizens of the West would need only to be informed of criminal machinations [by Aaron Burr] against the public safety to crush them at once, I never entertained a doubt.—To GOVERNOR H. D. TIFFIN. v, 37. FORD ED., ix, 21. (W., 1807.)

6629. ———— ————. They are freer from prejudices than we are, and bolder in grasping at truth. The time is not distant, though neither you nor I shall see it, when we shall be but a secondary people to them. Our greediness for wealth, and fantastical expense, have degraded, and will degrade, the minds of our maritime citizens. These are the peculiar vices of commerce.—To JOHN ADAMS. vii, 103. FORD ED., x, 107. (M., 1818.)

6630. ———— ————. The bait of local interests, artfully prepared for their palate, has decoyed them [the Western people] from their kindred attachments to alliances alien to them.—To C. W. GOOCH. vii, 430. (M., 1826.)

6631. PEOPLE, Will of.—It accords with our principles to acknowledge any government to be rightful, which is formed by the will of the people· substantially declared. —To GOUVERNEUR MORRIS. iii, 489. FORD ED., vi, 131. (Pa., Nov. 1792.)

6632. ———— ————. The will of the people is the only legitimate foundation of any government, and to protect its free expression should be our first object.—To BENJAMIN WARING. iv, 379. (W., March 1801.)

6633. PEOPLE, Wisdom of.—Our people in a body are wise, because they are under the unrestrained and unperverted operation of their own understandings.—To DR. JOSEPH PRIESTLEY. iv, 440. FORD ED., viii, 158. (W., 1802.)

6634. PERCEVAL (Spencer), Ministry. —I am glad of the reestablishment of a Perceval ministry. * The opposition would have recruited our minority by half-way offers.—To PRESIDENT MADISON. vi, 77. (M., Aug. 1812.)

6635. PERPETUAL MOTION, Delusion of.—I am very thankful to you for the description of Redhefer's machine. I had never been able to form an idea of what his principle of deception was. He is the first of the inventors of perpetual motion within my knowledge, who has had the cunning to put his visitors on a false pursuit, by amusing them with a sham machinery whose loose and vibratory motion might impose on them the belief that it is the real source of the motion they see. To this device he is indebted for a more extensive delusion than I have before witnessed on this point. We are full of it as far as this State, and I know not how much farther. In Richmond, they have done me the honor to quote me as having said that it was a possible thing. A poor Frenchman who called on me the other day, with another invention of perpetual motion, assured me that Dr. Franklin, many years ago, expressed his opinion to him that it was not impossible. Without entering into contest on this abuse of the Doctor's name, I gave him the answer I had given to others be-

* Spencer Perceval, who succeeded the Duke of Portland as Premier, was assassinated in the lobby of the House of Commons on May 11, 1812, three months before this letter was written, by John Bellingham, an English merchant, who was engaged in business at Archangel, and who had been unable to obtain redress from the Russian Government for some alleged injury. The murderer was hanged.— EDITOR.

fore, that the Almighty himself could not construct a machine of perpetual motion while the laws exist which he has prescribed for the government of matter in our system; that the equilibrium established by him between cause and effect must be suspended to effect that purpose.—To DR. ROBERT PATTERSON. vi, 83. (M., 1812.)

6636. PERPETUAL MOTION, Friction and.—The diminution of friction is certainly one of the most desirable reformations in mechanics. Could we get rid of it altogether we should have perpetual motion. I was afraid that using a fluid for a fulcrum, the pivot (for so we may call them) must be of such a diameter as to lose what had been gained. I shall be glad to hear the event of any other experiments you may make on this subject.— To ROBERT R. LIVINGSTON. FORD ED., v, 277. (Pa., 1791.)

6637. PERSONAL LIBERTY, Children of slaves.—The reducing the mother to servitude was a violation of the law of nature, surely, then, the same law cannot prescribe a continuance of the violation to her issue, and that, too, without end, for if it extends to any, it must to every degree of descendants.—LEGAL ARGUMENT. FORD ED., i, 376. (1770.)

6638. ——— ———. That the bondage of the mother does not under the law of nature, infer that of her issue, as included in her, is further obvious from this consideration, that by the same reason, the bondage of the father would infer that of his issue; for he may with equal, and some anatomists say with greater reason, be said to include all his posterity.—LEGAL ARGUMENT. FORD ED., i, 377. (1770.)

6639. PERSONAL LIBERTY, Inconsistent laws.—If it be a law of nature that the child shall follow the condition of the parent, it would introduce a very perplexing dilemma; as where the one parent is free and the other a slave. Here the child is to be a slave, says this law, by inheritance of the father's bondage; but it is also to be free, says the same law, by inheritance of its mother's freedom. This contradiction proves it to be no law of nature.—LEGAL ARGUMENT. FORD ED., i, 377. (1770.)

6640. PERSONAL LIBERTY, Invasion of.—There are rights which it is useless to surrender to the government, and which governments have yet always been found to invade. [Among] these is * * * the right of personal freedom.—To DAVID HUMPHREYS. iii, 13. FORD ED., v, 89. (P., 1789.)

6641. PERSONAL LIBERTY, Lettres de cachet.—Nor should we wonder at * * * [the] pressure [for a fixed constitution in 1788-9] when we consider the monstrous abuses of power under which * * * [the French] people were ground to powder; when we pass in review the shackles * * * on the freedom * * * of the person by Lettres de Cachet.—AUTOBIOGRAPHY. i, 86. FORD ED., i, 118. (1821.)

6642. PERSONAL LIBERTY, Natural. —Under the law of nature, all men are born free, every one comes into the world with a right to his own person, which includes the liberty of moving and using it at his own will. This is what is called personal liberty, and is given him by the Author of nature, because necessary for his own sustenance.— LEGAL ARGUMENT. FORD ED., i, 376. (1770.)

6643. PERSONAL LIBERTY, Preservation of.—If we are made in some degree for others, yet in a greater are we made for ourselves. It were contrary to feeling, and indeed ridiculous to suppose that a man had less rights in himself than one of his neighbors, or indeed all of them put together. This would be slavery, and not that liberty which the bill of rights has made inviolable, and for the preservation of which our government has been charged.—To JAMES MONROE. i, 319. FORD ED., iii, 58. (M., 1782.)

6644. PERSONAL LIBERTY, In private life.—I feel at length [in my retirement from public life] the blessing of being free to say and do what I please, without being responsible for it to any mortal.—To GEN. KOSCIUSKO. v, 50. (M., 1810.)

6645. PERSONAL LIBERTY, Universal.—In a government bottomed on the will of all, the * * * liberty of every individual citizen becomes interesting to all.— FIFTH ANNUAL MESSAGE. viii, 50. FORD ED., viii, 392. (1805.)

— PERSONAL RIGHTS.—See RIGHTS.

6646. PETITION, Right of.—The people have a right to petition, but not to use that right to cover calumniating insinuations. —To JAMES MADISON. v, 367. FORD ED., ix. 209. (M., 1808.)

6647. PETITIONS, The Executive and. —In my report on How's case, where I state that it should go to the President, it will become a question with the House [of Representatives] whether they shall refer it to the President themselves, or give it back to the petitioner, and let him so address it, as he ought to have done at first. I think the latter proper. 1. because it is a case belonging purely to the Executive; 2. because the Legislature should never show itself in a matter with a foreign nation, but where the case is very serious and they mean to commit the nation on its issue; 3. because if they indulge individuals in handing through the Legislature their applications to the Executive, all applicants will be glad to avail themselves of the weight of so powerful a solicitor. Similar attempts have been repeatedly made by individuals to get the President to hand in their petitions to the Legislature, which he has constantly refused. It seems proper that every person should address himself directly to the department to which the Constitution has allotted his case; and that the proper answer to such from any other department is, " that it is not to us that the Constitution has assigned the transaction of this business ".—To JAMES MADISON. iii, 296. FORD ED., v, 391. (Pa., 1791.)

6648. —— ——. The Executive of the Union is, by the Constitution, made the channel of communication between *foreign* powers and the United States. But citizens, whether individually, or in bodies corporate, or associated, have a right to apply directly to any department of their government, whether Legislative, Executive, or Judiciary, the exercise of whose powers they have a right to claim; and neither of these can regularly offer its intervention in a case belonging to the other. The communication and recommendation by me to Congress of the memorial you * * * enclose me, would be an innovation, not authorized by the practice of our government, and, therefore, the less likely to add to its weight or effect.—To JAMES SULLIVAN. v, 203. (W., 1807.)

6649. —— ——. I cannot lay petitions before Congress consistently with my own opinion of propriety, because where the petitioners have a right to petition their immediate representatives in Congress directly, I have deemed it neither necessary nor proper for them to pass their petition through the intermediate channel of the Executive.—To JOSEPH B. VARNUM. v, 388. (W., 1808.)

6650. —— ——. I have never presumed to place myself between the Legislative Houses and those who have a constitutional right to address them directly.—To ANDREW GREGG. v, 431. (W., 1809.)

6651. PETITIONS, Punishment for.— He [George III.] has endeavored to pervert the exercise of the kingly office of Virginia into a detestable and insupportable tyranny * * * by answering our repeated petitions for redress with a repetition of injuries.—PROPOSED VA. CONSTITUTION. FORD ED., ii, 12. (June 1776.)

6652. PETITIONS, Rejected.—We [Virginia] have exhausted every mode of application which our invention could suggest as proper and promising. We have decently remonstrated with Parliament: they have added new injuries to the old. We have wearied our King with applications; he has not deigned to answer us. We have appealed to the native honour and justice of the British Nation: their efforts in our favor have been hitherto ineffectual. What, then, remains to be done? That we commit our injuries to the even-handed justice of the Being who doth no wrong, earnestly beseeching Him to illuminate the councils, and prosper the endeavors of those to whom America hath confided her hopes, that through their wise direction we may again see reunited the blessings of liberty, property, and harmony with Great Britain.—ADDRESS OF HOUSE OF BURGESSES TO LORD DUNMORE. FORD ED., i, 458. (1775.)

6653. PETITIONS, Repetition of injury and.—In every stage of these oppressions we have petitioned for redress, in the most humble terms; Our repeated petitions have been answered only by repeated injuries.—DECLARATION OF INDEPENDENCE AS DRAWN BY JEFFERSON.

6654. PETITIONS, Unanswered.—Our complaints were either not heard at all, or were answered with new and accumulated injuries.—REPLY TO LORD NORTH'S PROPOSITION. FORD ED., i, 481. (July 1775.)

6655. PETITIONS, Vain.—We have supplicated our king at various times in terms almost disgraceful to freedom; we have reasoned, we have remonstrated with parliament in the most mild and decent language; we have even proceeded to break off our commercial intercourse with our fellow-subjects, as the last peaceful admonition that our attachment to no nation on earth should supplant our attachment to liberty. And here we had well hoped was the ultimate step of the controversy. But subsequent events have shown how vain was even this last remain of confidence in the moderation of the British ministry.—DECLARATION ON TAKING UP ARMS. FORD ED., i, 470. (July 1775.)

6656. PEYROUSE EXPEDITION, Objects of.—You have, doubtless, seen in the papers, that this court [France] was sending two vessels into the South Sea, under the conduct of a Captain Peyrouse. They give out that the object is merely for the improvement of our knowledge of the geography of that part of the globe. And certain it is, that they carry men of eminence in different branches of science. Their loading, however, as detailed in conversations, and some other circumstances, appeared to me to indicate some other design; perhaps that of colonizing on the Western coast of America; or, it may be, only to establish one or more factories there, for the fur trade. Perhaps we may be little interested in either of these objects. But we are interested in another, that is, to know whether they are perfectly weaned from the desire of possessing continental colonies in America. Events might arise, which would render it very desirable for Congress to be satisfied they have no such wish. If they would desire a colony on the western side of America, I should not be quite satisfied that they would refuse one which should offer itself on the eastern side. Captain Paul Jones being at L'Orient, within a day's journey of Brest, where Captain Peyrouse's vessels lay, I desired him, if he could not satisfy himself at L'Orient of the nature of this equipment, to go to Brest for that purpose; conducting himsef so as to excite no suspicion that we attended at all to this expedition. His discretion can be relied on.—To JOHN JAY. i, 382. (P., 1785.)

6657. —— ——. The circumstances are obvious which indicate an intention to settle factories and not colonies, at least for the present.—To JOHN JAY. i, 454. (P., 1785.)

6658. —— ——. The Gazette of France announces the arrival of Peyrouse at Brazil, that he was to touch at Otaheite, and proceed to California, and still further northwardly. * * * The presumption is, that they will make an establishment of some sort, on the northwest coast of America.—To JOHN JAY. i, 602. (P., 1786.)

6659. PHILADELPHIA, Injuries by war.—I sincerely congratulate you on the recovery of Philadelphia and wish it may be found uninjured by the enemy. How far the interests of literature may have suffered by the injury, or removal of the Orrery (as it is miscalled), the public libraries, your papers and implements, are doubts which still excite anxiety.—To DAVID RITTENHOUSE. i, 210. FORD ED., ii, 162. (M., July 1778.)

6660. PHILOSOPHY, Ancient.—The moral principles inculcated by the most esteemed of the sects of ancient philosophy, or of their individuals; particularly, Pythagoras, Socrates, Epicurus, Cicero, Epictetus, Seneca and Antoninus, related chiefly to ourselves, and the government of those passions which, unrestrained, would disturb our tranquillity of mind. In this branch of philosophy they were really great. In developing our duties to others, they were short and defective. They embraced, indeed, the circles of kindred and friends, and inculcated patriotism, or the love of our country in the aggregate, as a primary obligation; towards our neighbors and countrymen they taught justice, but scarcely viewed them as within the circle of benevolence. Still less have they inculcated peace, charity, and love to our fellow men, or embraced with benevolence the whole family of mankind.—SYLLABUS OF THE DOCTRINES OF JESUS. iv, 480. FORD ED., viii, 224. (1803.)

6661. PHILOSOPHY, Epicureanism.—I am Epicurean. I consider the genuine (not the imputed) doctrines of Epicurus as containing everything rational in moral philosophy which Greece and Rome have left us. Epictetus, indeed, has given us what was good of the Stoics; all beyond, of their dogmas being hypocrisy and grimace. Their great crime was in their calumnies of Epicurus and misrepresentations of his doctrines; in which we lament to see the candid character of Cicero engaging as an accomplice.—To WILLIAM SHORT. vii, 138. FORD ED., x, 143. (M., 1819.)

— PHILOSOPHY, Platonic.—See PLATO.

6662. PHILOSOPHY, Seneca.—Seneca is, indeed, a fine moralist, disfiguring his work at times with some Stoicisms, and affecting too much of antithesis and point, yet giving us on the whole a great deal of sound and practical morality.—To WILLIAM SHORT. vii, 139. FORD ED., x, 144. (M., 1819.)

6663. PHILOSOPHY, Socratic.—Of Socrates we have nothing genuine but in the Memorabilia of Xenophon; for Plato makes him one of his collocutors, merely to cover his own whimsies under the mantle of his name: a liberty of which we are told Socrates himself complained.—To WILLIAM SHORT. vii, 139. FORD ED., x, 144. (M., 1819.)

6664. PHILOSOPHY, War against.—I still dare to use the word philosophy, notwithstanding the war waged against it by bigotry and despotism.—To DR. HUGH WILLIAMSON. iv, 347. FORD ED., vii, 481. (W., Jan. 1801.)

6665. PICKERING (Timothy), Jefferson and.—I could not have believed that for so many years, and to such a period of advanced age. Mr. Pickering could have nourished passions so vehement and viperous. It appears that for thirty years past, he has been industriously collecting materials for vituperating the characters he had marked for his hatred; some of whom, certainly, if enmities towards him had ever existed, had forgotten them all, or buried them in the grave with themselves. As to myself, there never had been anything personal between us, nothing but the general opposition of party sentiment; and our personal intercourse

had been that of urbanity, as himself says. But it seems he has been all this time brooding over an enmity which I had never felt, and that with respect to myself, as well as others, he has been writing far and near, and in every direction, to get hold of original letters, where he could, copies, where he could not, certificates and journals, catching at every gossiping story he could hear of in any quarter, supplying by suspicions what he could find nowhere else, and then arguing on this motley farrago as if established on gospel evidence. * * * He arraigns me on two grounds, my actions and my motives. The very actions, however, which he arraigns, have been such as the great majority of my fellow citizens have approved. The approbation of Mr. Pickering and of those who thought with him, I had no right to expect. My motives he chooses to ascribe to hypocrisy, to ambition, and a passion for popularity. Of these the world must judge between us. It is no office of his or mine. To that tribunal I have ever submitted my actions and motives, without ransacking the Union for certificates, letters, journals and gossiping tales to justify myself and weary them. * * * If no action is to be deemed virtuous for which malice can imagine a sinister motive, then there never was a virtuous action; no, not even in the life of our Saviour himself. But He has taught us to judge the tree by its fruit and to leave motives to Him who can alone see into them. * * * I leave to its fate the libel of Mr. Pickering, with the thousands of others like it, to which I have given no other answer than a steady course of similar action * * * .—To MARTIN VAN BUREN. vii, 362. FORD ED., x, 305. (M., 1824.) See DECLARATION OF INDEPENDENCE.

6666. PICKERING (Timothy), Josiah Quincy and.—The termination of Mr. Rose's mission, re infecta, put it in my power to communicate to Congress yesterday, everything respecting our relations with England and France, which will effectually put down Mr. Pickering, and his worthy coadjutor Mr. [Josiah] Quincy. Their tempers are so much alike, and really their persons, as to induce a supposition that they are related.—To LEVI LINCOLN. v, 264. (W., March 1808.)

6667. PIERS, Power to build.—You know my doubts, or rather convictions, about the unconstitutionality of the act for building piers in the Delaware, and the fears that it will lead to a bottomless expense, and to the greatest abuses. There is, however, one intention of which the act is susceptible, and which will bring it within the Constitution; and we ought always to presume that the real intention which is alone consistent with the Constitution. Although the power to regulate commerce does not give a power to build piers, wharves, open ports, clear the beds of rivers, dig canals, build warehouses, build manufacturing machines, set up manufactories, cultivate the earth, to all of which the power would go if it went to the first, yet a power to provide and maintain a navy is a power to provide receptacles for it, and places to cover and preserve it. In choosing the places where this money should be laid out, I should be much disposed, as far as contracts will permit, to confine it to such place or places as the ships of war may lie at, and be protected from ice; and I should be for stating this in a message to Congress, in order to prevent the effect of the present example. This act has been built on the exercise of the power of building light houses, as a regulation of commerce. But I well remember the opposition, on this very ground, to the first act for building a lighthouse. The utility of the thing has sanctioned the infraction. But if, on that infraction, we build a second, and on that second a third, &c., any one of the powers in the Constitution may be made to comprehend every power of government.—To ALBERT GALLATIN. iv, 449. FORD ED., viii, 174. (Oct. 1802.)

6668. ———— ————. The act of Congress of 1789, c. 9, assumes on the General Government the maintenance and repair of all lighthouses, beacons, buoys, and public piers then existing, and provides for the building a new lighthouse. This was done under the authority given by the Constitution " to regulate commerce ", and was contested at the time as not within the meaning of its terms, and yielded to only on the urgent necessity of the case. The act of 1802, c. 20, f. 8, for repairing and erecting public piers in the Delaware, does not take any new ground—it is in strict conformity with the act of 1789. While we pursue, then, the construction of the Legislature, that the repairing and erecting lighthouses, beacons, buoys, and piers, is authorized as belonging to the regulation of commerce, we must take care not to go ahead of them, and strain the meaning of the terms still further to the clearing out the channels of all the rivers, &c., of the United States. The removing a sunken vessel is not the repairing of a pier. How far the authority " to levy taxes to provide for the common defence ", and that " for providing and maintaining a navy ", may authorize the removing obstructions in a river or harbor, is a question not involved in the present case.—To ALBERT GALLATIN. iv, 478. (April 1803.)

6669. PIKE (General Z. M.), Death of.—He died in the arms of victory gained over the enemies of his country. * * * [He was] an honest and zealous patriot who lived and died for his country.—To BARON VON HUMBOLDT. vi, 270. FORD ED., ix, 432. (1813.)

6670. PIKE (General Z. M.), Expedition.—On the transfer of Louisiana by France to the United States, according to its boundaries when possessed by France, the government of the United States considered itself as entitled as far west as the Rio Norte; but understanding soon afterwards that Spain, on the contrary, claimed eastwardly to the river Sabine, it has carefully abstained from doing any act in the intermediate country, which might disturb the existing state of things, until these opposing claims should be explained and accommodated amicably. But that the Red River and all its waters belonged to France, that she made several settlements on that river, and held them as a part of Louisiana until she delivered that country to Spain, and that Spain, on the contrary, had never made a single settlement on the river are circumstances so well known, and so susceptible of proof, that it was not supposed that Spain would seriously contest the facts; or the right established by them. Hence our government took measures for exploring that river, as it did that of the Missouri, by sending Mr. Freeman to proceed from the mouth upwards, and Lieutenant Pike from the source downwards merely to acquire its geography, and so far enlarge the boundaries of science. For the day must be very distant when it will be either the interest or the wish of the United States to extend settlements into the interior of that country. Lieutenant Pike's orders were accordingly strictly confined to the waters of the Red river, and from his known observance of orders, I am persuaded that it must have been, as he himself declares, by miss-

ing his way that he got on the waters of the Rio Norte, instead of those of the Red river. That your Excellency should excuse this involuntary error, and indeed misfortune, was expected from the liberality of your character; and the kindnesses you have shown him are an honorable example of those offices of good neighborhood on your part, which it will be so agreeable to us to cultivate. * * * To the same liberal sentiment Lieutenant Pike must appeal for the restoration of his papers. You must have seen in them no trace of unfriendly views towards your nation, no symptoms of any other design than that of extending geographical knowledge; and it is not in the nineteenth century, nor through the agency of your Excellency, that science expects to encounter obstacles.*—To GENERAL HENRY DEARBORN. v, 110. FORD ED., ix, 85. (W., 1807.)

6671. PIKE (General Z. M.), Mission.—I think that the truth as to Pike's mission might be so simply stated as to need no argument to show that (even during the suspension of our claims to the eastern border of the Rio Norte) his getting on it was a mere error, which ought to have called for the setting him right, instead of forcing him through the interior country.—To JAMES MADISON. v, 294. FORD ED., x, 195. (M., May 1808.)

6672. PINCKNEY (Charles), Political ambition.—There is here a great sense of the inadequacy of C. Pinckney to the office he is in. His continuance is made a subject of standing reproach to myself personally, by whom the appointment was made before I had collected the administration. He declared at the time that nothing would induce him to continue so as not to be here at the ensuing Presidential election. I am persuaded he expected to be proposed at it as V. P. After he got to Europe his letters asked only a continuance of two years; but he now does not drop the least hint of a voluntary return. Pray, avail yourself of his vanity, his expectations, his fears, and whatever will weigh with him to induce him to ask leave to return, and obtain from him to be the bearer of the letter yourself. You will render us in this the most acceptable service possible. His enemies here are perpetually dragging his character in the dirt, and charging it on the administration. He does, or ought to know this, and to feel the necessity of coming home to vindicate himself, if he looks to anything further in the career of honor.—To JAMES MONROE. FORD ED., viii, 289. (W., Jan. 1804.)

6673. PINCKNEY (Thomas), Character.—An honest, sensible man, and good republican.—To JOEL BARLOW. iii, 451. FORD ED., vi, 88. (Pa., 1792.)

6674. PINCKNEY (Thomas), Minister.—Your nomination as Minister to London gave general satisfaction.—To THOMAS PINCKNEY. iii, 321. FORD ED., v, 423. (Pa., Jan. 1792.)

6675. PINCKNEY (Thomas), Vice-Presidency.—The federalists will run Mr. Pinckney for the Vice-Presidency. They regard his southern position rather than his principles.—To JAMES MONROE. iv, 149. FORD ED., vii, 89. (M., July 1796.)

6676. PITT (William), Friend of America.—Pitt is rather well disposed to us.—To GOVERNOR BENJ. HARRISON. FORD ED., iii, 414. (A., March 1784.)

* Draft of letter to be sent to Spanish governor.—EDITOR.

6677. PLANTS, Useful.—The greatest service which can be rendered any country is to add an useful plant to its culture; especially, a bread grain; next in value to bread is oil.—JEFFERSON'S MSS. i, 176. (M., 1821.)

6678. PLATO, Teachings of.—No writer, ancient or modern, has bewildered the world with more *ignes fatui*, than this renowned philosopher, in ethics, in politics, and physics.— To WILLIAM SHORT. vii, 165. (M., 1820.)

6679. PLATO, Whimsies.—Plato * * * used the name of Socrates to cover the whimsies of his own brain.—SYLLABUS OF THE DOCTRINES OF JESUS. iv, 481. (1803.)

6680. PLATO'S REPUBLIC.—I amused myself [recently] with reading Plato's Republic. I am wrong, however, in calling it amusement, for it was the heaviest task-work I ever went through. I had occasionally before taken up some of his other works, but scarcely ever had patience to get through a whole dialogue. While wading through the whimsies, the puerilities, and unintelligible jargon of this work, I laid it down often to ask myself how it could have been that the world should have so long consented to give reputation to such nonsense as this? How the soi-disant Christian world, indeed, should have done it, is a piece of historical curiosity. But how could the Roman good sense do it? And particularly, how could Cicero bestow such eulogies on Plato? Although Cicero did not wield the dense logic of Demosthenes, yet he was able, learned, laborious, practiced in the business of the world, and honest. He could not be the dupe of mere style, of which he was himself the first master in the world. With the moderns, I think, it is rather a matter of fashion and authority. Education is chiefly in the hands of persons who, from their profession, have an interest in the reputation and the dreams of Plato. They give the tone while at school, and few in after years have occasion to revise their college opinions. But fashion and authority apart, and bringing Plato to the test of reason, take from him his sophisms, futilities and incomprehensibilities, and what remains? In truth, he is one of the race of genuine Sophists, who has escaped the oblivion of his brethren, first, by the eloquence of his diction, but chiefly, by the adoption and incorporation of his whimsies into the body of artificial Christianity. His foggy mind is forever presenting the semblances of objects which, half seen through a mist, can be defined neither in form nor dimensions. * * * Socrates had reason, indeed, to complain of the misrepresentations of Plato; for in truth, his dialogues are libels on Socrates.—To JOHN ADAMS. vi, 354. FORD ED., ix, 462. (M., 1814.)

6681. —— ——. It is fortunate for us, that Platonic republicanism has not obtained the same favor as Platonic Christianity; or we should now have been all living men, women and children pell mell together, like beasts of the field or forest.—To JOHN ADAMS. vi, 355. (1814.)

6682. PLEASURE, Bait of.—Do not bite at the bait of pleasure till you know there is no hook beneath it.—To MRS. COSWAY. ii, 37. FORD ED., iv, 317. (P., 1786.)

6683. PLEASURE AND PAIN.—We have no rose without its thorn; no pleasure without alloy. It is the law of Existence; and we must acquiesce. It is the condition annexed to all our pleasures, not by us who receive, but by Him who gives them.—To MRS. COSWAY. ii, 41. FORD ED., iv, 321. (P., 1786.)

6684. —— ——. I do not agree that an age of pleasure is no compensation for a moment of pain.—To JOHN ADAMS. vii, 26. (M., 1816.)

6685. POETRY, Judging.—It is not for a stranger to decide on the merits of poetry in a language foreign to him.—To M. HILLIARD D'AUBERTEUIL. ii, 103. (P., 1787.)

6686. —— ——. To my own mortification, * * * of all men living, I am the last who should undertake to decide as to the merits of poetry. In earlier life I was fond of it, and easily pleased. But as age and cares advanced, the powers of fancy have declined. Every year seems to have plucked a feather from her wings, till she can no longer waft one to those sublime heights to which it is necessary to accompany the poet. So much has my relish for poetry deserted me that, at present, I cannot read even Virgil with pleasure. I am consequently utterly incapable to decide on the merits of poetry. The very feelings to which it is addressed are among those I have lost. So that the blind man might as well undertake to [faded in MS.] a painting, or the deaf a musical composition. *—To JOHN D. BURKE. FORD ED., viii, 65. (W., 1801.)

6687. POLAND, Partition of.—The history of Poland gives a lesson which all our countrymen should study; the example of a country erased from the map of the world by the dissensions of its own citizens. The papers of every day read them the counter lesson of the impossibility of subduing a people acting with an undivided will. Spain, under all her disadvantages, physical and mental, is an encouraging example of this.—To WILLIAM DUANE. v, 603. (M., July 1811.)

6688. —— ——. The partition of Poland * * * was the atrocity of a barbarous government chiefly, in conjunction with a smaller one still scrambling to become great, while one only of those already great, and having character to lose, descended to the baseness of an accomplice in the crime.—To JOHN ADAMS. vi, 524. (M., 1816.)

6689. POLICY (American), Balance of power.—We especially ought to pray that the powers of Europe may be so poised and counterpoised among themselves, that their own safety may require the presence of all their force at home, leaving the other quarters of the globe in undisturbed tranquillity. —To DR. CRAWFORD. vi, 33. (1812.)

6690. POLICY (American), Coalition of American nations.—From many conversations with him [M. Correa] I hope he sees, and will promote in his new situation [in Brazil] the advantages of a cordial fraternization among all the American nations, and the importance of their coalescing in an American system of policy, totally independent of and unconnected with that of Europe. The day is not distant, when we may formally require a meridian of partition through the ocean which separates the two hemispheres, on the hither side of which no European gun shall ever be heard, nor an American on the other; and when, during the rage of the eternal wars of Europe, the lion

* Mr. Burke had sent Jefferson a copy of the Columbiad.—EDITOR.
† Portuguese Minister at Washington.—EDITOR.

and the lamb, within our regions, shall lie down together in peace. * * * I wish to see this coalition begun.—To WILLIAM SHORT. vii, 168. (1820.)

6691. —— ——. I wish to see this coalition begun. I am earnest for an agreement with the maritime powers of Europe, assigning them the task of keeping down the piracies of their seas and the cannibalism of the African coasts, and to us, the suppression of the same enormities within our seas; and for this purpose, I should rejoice to see the fleets of Brazil and the United States riding together as brethren of the same family, and pursuing the same object. And indeed it would be of happy augury to begin at once this concert of action here, on the invitation of either to the other government, while the way might be preparing for withdrawing our cruisers from Europe, and preventing naval collisions there which daily endanger our peace.—To WILLIAM SHORT. vii, 169. (M., 1820.)

6692. POLICY (American), Coercion of Europe.—We think that peaceable means may be devised of keeping nations in the path of justice towards us, by making justice their interest and injuries to react on themselves. Our distance enables us to pursue a course which the crowded situation of Europe renders, perhaps, impracticable there. —To M. CABANIS. iv, 497. (W., 1803.)

6693. POLICY (American), Detachment from Europe.—We cannot too distinctly detach ourselves from the European system, which is essentially belligerent, nor too sedulously cultivate an American system, essentially pacific.—To PRESIDENT MADISON. vi, 453. FORD ED., ix, 513. (M., March 1815.)

6694. POLICY (American), European politics and.—The politics of Europe render it indispensably necessary that, with respect to everything external, we be one nation only, firmly hooped together.—To JAMES MADISON. i, 531. FORD ED., iv, 192. (P., February 1786.)

6695. POLICY (American), European quarrels.—I am decidedly of opinion we should take no part in European quarrels, but cultivate peace and commerce with all. —To GENERAL WASHINGTON. ii, 533. FORD ED., v, 57. (P., 1788.)

6696. —— ——. At such a distance from Europe, and with such a distance between us, we hope to meddle little in its quarrels or combinations. Its peace and its commerce are what we shall court.—To M. DE PINTO. iii. 174. (N.Y., 1790.)

6697. POLICY (American), European system and.—The European nations constitute a separate division of the globe; their localities make them part of a distinct system; they have a set of interests of their own in which it is our business never to engage ourselves.—To BARON VON HUMBOLDT. vi, 268. FORD ED., ix, 431. (Dec. 1813.)

6698. POLICY (American), France and England.—We owe gratitude to France, justice to England, good will to all, and subservience to none.—To ARTHUR CAMPBELL. iv, 198. FORD ED., vii, 170. (M., 1797.)

6699. —— ——. It is our unquestionable interest and duty to conduct ourselves with such sincere friendship and impartiality towards both France and England, as that each may see unequivocally, what is unquestionably true, that we may be very possibly driven into her scale by unjust conduct in the other.—To JAMES MADISON. iv, 557. FORD ED., viii, 315. (M., Aug. 1804.)

6700. POLICY (American), Freedom of the ocean.—That the persons of our citizens shall be safe in freely traversing the ocean, that the transportation of our own produce, in our own vessels, to the markets of our choice, and the return to us of the articles we want for our own use, shall be unmolested. I hold to be fundamental, and the gauntlet that must be forever hurled at him who questions it.—To JOHN ADAMS. vi, 459. (M., June 1815.)

6701. POLICY (American), Great Britain and.—With respect to the English government, or policy, as concerning themselves or other nations, we wish not to intermeddle in word or deed, and that it be not understood that our government permits itself to entertain either a will or opinion on the subject.—To THOMAS PINCKNEY. iii, 442. FORD ED., vi, 75. (Pa., 1792.)

6702. POLICY (American), Gulf of Mexico.—We begin to broach the idea that we consider the Gulf Stream as of our waters, in which hostilities and cruising are to be frowned on for the present, and prohibited so soon as either consent or force will permit us. We shall never permit another privateer to cruise within it, and shall forbid our harbors to national cruisers. This is essential for our tranquillity and commerce.—To JAMES MONROE. v, 12. FORD ED., viii, 450. (W., May 1806.)

6703. POLICY (American), Internal resources.—The promotion of the arts and sciences * * * becomes peculiarly interesting to us, at this time, when the total demoralization of the governments of Europe, has rendered it safest, by cherishing internal resources, to lessen the occasions of intercourse with them.—To DR. JOHN L. E. W. SHECUT. vi, 153. (M., 1813.)

6704. POLICY (American), A just.—Let it be our endeavor * * * to merit the character of a just nation.—THIRD ANNUAL MESSAGE. viii, 28. FORD ED., viii, 272. (1803.)

6705. POLICY (American), Markets.—Our object is to feed and theirs to fight. —To JAMES MONROE. FORD ED., v, 198. (N. Y., 1790.)

6706. POLICY (American), Mid-Atlantic meridian.—When our strength will permit us to give the law of our hemisphere, it should be that the meridian of the mid-Atlantic should be the line of demarcation between war and peace, on this side of which no act of hostility should be committed, and the lion and the lamb lie down in peace together.—To Dr. Crawford. vi, 33. (M., Jan. 1812.)

6707. POLICY (American), Peace and friendship.—Peace and friendship with all mankind is our wisest policy. and I wish we may be permitted to pursue it.—To C. W. F. Dumas. i, 553. (1786.)

6708. —— ——. Peace with all nations, and the right which that gives us with respect to all nations, are our object.—To C. W. F. Dumas. iii, 535. (Pa., 1793.)

6709. —— ——. Peace, justice, and liberal intercourse with all the nations of the world, will, I hope, characterize this commonwealth.—Reply to Address. iv, 388. (W., 1801.)

6710. —— ——. Separated by a wide ocean from the nations of Europe, and from the political interests which entangle them together, with productions and wants which render our commerce and friendship useful to them and theirs to us, it cannot be the interest of any to assail us, nor ours to disturb them. We should be most unwise, indeed were we to cast away the singular blessings of the position in which nature has placed us, the opportunity she has endowed us with of pursuing at a distance from foreign contentions, the paths of industry, peace and happiness; of cultivating general friendship, and of bringing collisions of interest to the umpirage of reason rather than of force.—Third Annual Message. viii, 29. Ford ed., viii, 273. (Oct. 1803.)

6711. POLICY (American), Peace and justice.—We ask for peace and justice from all nations.—To James Monroe. ii, 12. Ford ed., viii, 450. (W., May 1806.)

6712. POLICY (American), Peopling the continent.—Our Confederacy must be viewed as the nest from which all America, North and South, is to be peopled.—To Archibald Stuart. i, 518. Ford ed., iv, 188. (P., Jan. 1786.)

6713. POLICY (American), Principles.—On the question you propose [James Monroe], whether we can, in any form, take a bolder attitude than formerly in favor of liberty, I can give you but commonplace ideas. They will be but the widow's mite, and offered only because requested. The matter which now embroils Europe, the presumption of dictating to an independent nation the form of its government, is so arrogant, so atrocious, that indignation, as well as moral sentiment, enlists all our partialities and prayers in favor of one, and our equal execrations against the other. I do not know. indeed, whether all nations do not owe to one another a bold and open declaration of their sympathies with the one party, and their

detestation of the conduct of the other. But farther than this we are bound to go; and indeed, for the sake of the world, we ought not to increase the jealousies, or draw on ourselves the power of this formidable confederacy [The Holy Alliance], I have ever deemed it fundamental for the United States never to take active part in the quarrels of Europe. Their political interests are entirely distinct from ours. Their mutual jealousies, their balance of power, their complicated alliances, their forms and principles of government, are all foreign to us. They are nations of eternal war. All their energies are expended in the destruction of the labor, property and lives of their people. On our part, never had a people so favorable a chance of trying the opposite system, of peace and fraternity with mankind, and the direction of all our means and faculties to the purposes of improvement instead of destruction. With Europe we have few occasions of collision, and these, with a little prudence and forbearance, may be generally accommodated. Of the brethren of our own hemisphere, none is yet, or for an age to come will be, in a shape, condition, or disposition to war against us. And the foothold which the nations of Europe had in either America, is slipping from under them. so that we shall soon be rid of their neighborhood. Cuba alone seems at present to hold up a speck of war to us. Its possession by Great Britain would indeed be a great calamity to us. Could we induce her to join us in guaranteeing its independence against all the world, *except* Spain. it would be nearly as valuable to us as if it. were our own.[*] But should she take it, I would not immediately go to war for it; because the first war on other accounts will give it to us; or the island will give itself to us, when able to do so. While no duty, therefore, calls on us to take part in the present war of Europe, and a golden harvest offers itself in reward for doing nothing. peace and neutrality seem to be our duty and interest. We may gratify ourselves, indeed, with a neutrality as partial to Spain as would be justifiable without giving cause of war to her adversary; we might and ought to avail ourselves of the happy occasion of procuring and cementing a cordial reconciliation with her, by giving assurance of every friendly office which neutrality admits, and especially, against all apprehension of our intermeddling in the quarrel with her colonies. And I expect daily and confidently to hear of a spark kindled in France. which will employ her at home, and relieve Spain from all further apprehension of danger. That England is playing false with Spain cannot be doubted. Her government is looking one way and rowing another. * * * You will do what is right, leaving the people of Europe to act their follies and crimes among themselves, while we pursue in good faith the paths of peace and prosperity.—To President Monroe. vii, 287. Ford ed., x, 257. (M., June 1823.)

[*] See note under Cuba.—Editor..

6714. POLICY (American), Resistance to wrong.—We believe that the just standing of all nations is the health and security of all. We consider the overwhelming power of England on the ocean, and of France on the land, as destructive of the prosperity and happiness of the world, and wish both to be reduced only to the necessity of observing moral duties. We believe no more in Bonaparte's fighting for the liberty of the seas, than in Great Britain fighting for the liberties of mankind. The object of both is the same. to draw to themselves the power, the wealth and the resources of other nations. We resist the enterprises of England first, because they first come vitally home to us. And our feelings repel the logic of bearing the lash of George III. for fear of that of Bonaparte at some future day. When the wrongs of France shall reach us with equal effect, we shall resist them also. But one at a time is enough; and having offered a choice to the champions, England first takes up the gauntlet.—To James Maury. vi, 52. Ford ed., ix, 349. (M., April 1812.)

6715. POLICY (American), A system of.—America has a hemisphere to itself. It must have its separate system of interests, which must not be subordinated to those of Europe.—To Baron von Humboldt. vi, 268. Ford ed., ix, 431. (Dec. 1813.)

6716. ——— ———. Distance, and difference of pursuits, of interests, of connections and other circumstances, prescribe to us a different system, having no object in common with Europe, but a peaceful interchange of mutual comforts for mutual wants.—To Madame de Stael. vi, 481. (M., 1815.)

6717. ——— ———. Nothing is so important as that America shall separate herself from the systems of Europe, and establish one of her own. Our circumstances, our pursuits, our interests, are distinct; the principles of our policy should be so also. All entanglements with that quarter of the globe should be avoided if we mean that peace and justice shall be the polar stars of the American Societies. * * * This would be a leading principle with me, had I longer to live. * * * —To J. Correa. vii, 184. Ford ed., x, 164. (M., 1820.)

6718. ——— ———. Our first and fundamental maxim should be never to entangle ourselves in the broils of Europe. Our second, never to suffer Europe to intermeddle with cis-Atlantic affairs. America, North and South, has a set of interests distinct from those of Europe, and peculiarly her own. She should therefore have a system of her own, separate and apart from that of Europe. While the last is laboring to become the domicil of despotism, our endeavor should surely be, to make our hemisphere that of freedom.—To President Monroe. vii, 315. Ford ed., x, 277. (M., 1823.)

6719. POLICY (American), Wars of Europe.—The insulated state in which nature has placed the American continent, should so far avail it that no spark of war kindled in the other quarters of the globe should be wafted across the wide oceans which separate us from them. And it will be so. In fifty years more the United States alone will contain fifty millions of inhabitants, and fifty years are soon gone over. The peace of 1763 is within that period. I was then twenty years old, and of course remember well all the transactions of the war preceding it. And you will live to see the period equally ahead of us; and the numbers which will then be spread over the other parts of the American hemisphere, catching long before that the principles of our portion of it, and concurring with us in the maintenance of the same system. * * * I am anticipating events of which you will be the bearer to me in the Elysian fields fifty years hence.—To Baron von Humboldt. vi, 268. Ford ed., ix, 431. (Dec. 1813.)

6720. ——— ———. Your exhortations to avoid taking any part in the war * * * in Europe were a confirmation of the policy I had myself pursued, and which I thought and still think should be the governing canon of our republic.—To Madame de Stael. vi, 481. (M., July 1815.)

6721. ——— ———. I hope no American patriot will ever lose sight of the essential policy of interdicting in the seas and territories of both Americas, the ferocious and sanguinary contests of Europe.—To William Short. vii, 168. (M., 1820.)

6722. POLITENESS, European.—With repect to what are termed polite manners, without sacrificing too much the sincerity of language, I would wish my countrymen to adopt just so much of European politeness, as to be ready to make all those little sacrifices of self, which really render European manners amiable, and relieve society from the disagreeable scenes to which rudeness often subjects it. Here (France), it seems that a man might pass a life without encountering a single rudeness.—To Mr. Bellini. i, 445. (P., 1785.)

6723. POLITENESS, Good humor and.—I have mentioned good humor as one of the preservatives of our peace and tranquillity. It is among the most effectual, and its effect is so well imitated and aided, artificially, by politeness, that this also becomes an acquisition of first rate value. In truth, politeness is artificial good humor; it covers the natural want of it, and ends by rendering habitual a substitute nearly equivalent to the real virtue. It is the practice of sacrificing to those whom we meet in society, all the little conveniences and preferences which will gratify them, and deprive us of nothing worth a moment's consideration; it is the giving a pleasing and flattering turn to our expressions, which will conciliate others, and make them pleased with us as well as themselves. How cheap a price for the good will of another! When this is in return for a rude thing said by another, it brings him to his senses, it mortifies and corrects him in the most salutary way, and places him at the feet of your good nature, in the eyes of the company.—To Thomas Jefferson Randolph. v, 389. Ford ed., ix, 231. (W., 1808.)

— POLITICAL ECONOMY.—See Economy (Political).

6724. POLITICS, Bigotry in.—What an effort of bigotry in politics * * * have we gone through! The barbarians really flattered themselves they should be able to bring back the times of Vandalism, when ignorance put everything into the hands of power and priestcraft. All advances in science were proscribed as innovations. They pretended to praise and encourage education, but it was to be the education of our ancestors. We were to look backwards, not forwards, for improvement; the President himself [John Adams] declaring in one of his answers to addresses, that we were never to expect to go beyond them in real science.—To Dr. Joseph Priestley. iv, 373. Ford ed., viii, 21. (W., 1801.)

6725. POLITICS, Commercial influence.—The system of alarm and jealousy which has been so powerfully played off in England, has been mimicked here, not entirely without success. The most long-sighted politician could not, seven years ago, have imagined that the people of this wide-extended country could have been enveloped in such delusion, and made so much afraid of themselves and their own power, as to surrender it spontaneously to those who are manœuvring them into a form of government, the principal branches of which may be beyond their control. The commerce of England, however, has spread its roots over the whole face of our country. This is the real source of all the obliquities of the public mind.—To A. H. Rowan. iv, 256. Ford ed., vii, 280. (M., 1798.)

6726. POLITICS, Conversations on.—Political conversations I really dislike, and therefore avoid where I can without affectation. But when urged by others, I have never conceived that having been in public life requires me to belie my sentiments, or even to conceal them. When I am led by conversation to express them, I do it with the same independence here which I have practiced everywhere, and which is inseparable from my nature.—To President Washington. iv, 142. Ford ed., vii, 83. (M., 1796.)

6727. POLITICS, Destructive of happiness.—Politics and party hatreds destroy the happiness of every being here. They seem, like salamanders, to consider fire as their element.—To Martha Jefferson Randolph. D. L. J., 249. (Pa., May 1798.)

6728. POLITICS, Differences in.—I never suffered a political to become a personal difference.—To Timothy Pickering. vii, 210. (M., 1821.)

6729. POLITICS, Dislike of.—It is a relief to be withdrawn from the torment of the scenes amidst which we are. Spectators of the heats and tumults of conflicting parties, we cannot help participating of their feelings. * * *.—To Martha Jefferson Randolph. Ford ed., v, 487. (Pa., March 1792.)

6730. POLITICS, Divorce from.—In my retirement I shall certainly divorce myself from all part in political affairs. To get rid of them is the principal object of my retirement, and the first thing necessary to the happiness which it is in vain to look for in any other situation.—To Benjamin Stoddert. v, 427. Ford ed., ix, 246. (W., 1809.)

6731. POLITICS, A duty.—Politics is my duty.—To Harry Innes. Ford ed., v, 294. (Pa., 1791.)

6732. POLITICS, Estrangement from.—I think it is Montaigne who has said that ignorance is the softest pillow on which a man can rest his head. I am sure it is true as to everything political, and shall endeavor to estrange myself to everything of that character.—To Edmund Randolph. iv, 101. Ford ed., vi, 498. (M., Feb. 1794.)

6733. POLITICS, French furnace of.—The gay and thoughtless Paris is now become a furnace of politics. All the world is now politically mad. Men, women, children talk nothing else, and you know that naturally they talk much, loud and warm. Society is spoiled by it, at least for those who, like myself, are but lookers on.—To Mrs. William Bingham. Ford ed., v, 9. (P., 1788.)

6734. POLITICS, Hateful.—The ensuing year will be the longest of my life, and the last of such hateful labors. The next we will sow our cabbages together.—To Martha Jefferson Randolph. Ford ed., v, 488. (March 1792.)

6735. ———— ————. I am to thank you for forwarding M. d'Ivernois's book on the French Revolution. But it is on politics, a subject I never loved, and now hate.—To John Adams. Ford ed., vii, 56. (M., Feb. 1796.)

6736. POLITICS, Influencing.—I have made great progress into the MS., and still with the same pleasure. I have no doubt it must produce great effect. But that this may be the greatest possible, its coming out should be timed to the best advantage. It should come out just so many days before the meeting of Congress as will prevent suspicions of its coming with them, yet so as to be a new thing when they arrive, ready to get into their hands while yet unoccupied. * * * I will direct it to appear a fortnight before their meeting unless you order otherwise. It might as well be thrown into a churchyard, as come out now.—To James Madison. Ford ed., vi, 404. (Pa., 1793.)

6737. POLITICS, Knowledge of European.—I often doubt whether I should trouble Congress or my friends with * * * details of European politics. I know they do not excite that interest in America of which it is impossible for one to divest himself here. I know, too, that it is a maxim with us, and I think it a wise one, not to entangle ourselves with the affairs of Europe. Still, I think we should know them. The Turks have practiced the same maxim of not meddling in the complicated wrangles of this continent. But they have unwisely chosen to be ignorant of them also, and it is this total ignorance of Europe, its combinations, and its movements which exposes them to that annihilation possibly about taking place. While there are powers in Europe which fear our views, or have views on us, we should keep an eye on them, their connections and oppositions, that in a moment of need we may avail ourselves of their weakness with respect to others as well as ourselves, and calculate their designs and movements on all the circumstances under which they exist. Though I am persuaded, therefore, that these details are read by many with great indifference, yet I think it my duty to enter into them, and to run the risk of giving too much, rather than too little information.—To E. Carrington. ii, 334. Ford ed., iv, 482. (P., 1787.)

6738. POLITICS, Liberation from.—I shall be liberated from the hated occupations of politics, and remain in the bosom of my family, my farm, and my books.—To Mrs. Church. Ford ed., vi, 455. (G., 1793.)

6739. POLITICS, A maxim in.—The maxim of your lettter " slow and sure " is not less a good one in agriculture than in politics. I sincerely wish it may extricate us from the event of a war, if this can be done saving our faith and our rights.—To President Washington. iv, 106. Ford ed., vi, 510. (M., May 1794.)

6740. POLITICS, Moral right and.—Political interest can never be separated in the long run from moral right.—To James Monroe. Ford ed., viii, 477. (W., 1806.)

6741. POLITICS, Neutrality in factional.—We must be neutral between the discordant republicans, but not between them and their common enemies.—To Robert Smith. Ford ed., viii, 318. (M., 1804.)

6742. POLITICS, Pamphlets on.—You will receive some pamphlets * * * on the acts of the last session. These I would wish you to distribute, not to sound men who have no occasion for them, but to such as have been misled, are candid, and will be open to the conviction of truth, and are of influence among their neighbors. It is the sick who need medicine, and not the well. —To Archibald Stuart. iv, 286. Ford ed., vii, 354. (Pa., 1799.)

6743. POLITICS, Partizan.—You have found on your return [from Europe] a higher style of political difference than you had left here. I fear this is inseparable from the different constitutions of the human mind, and that degree of freedom which permits unrestrained expression.—To Thomas Pinckney. iv, 176. Ford ed., vii, 128. (Pa., 1797.)

6744. POLITICS, Passions and.—You and I have formerly seen warm debates and high political passions. But gentlemen of different politics would then speak to each other, and separate the business of the Senate

from that of society. It is not so now. Men who have been intimate all their lives, cross the streets to avoid meeting, and turn their heads another way, lest they should be obliged to touch their hats. This may do for young men with whom passion is enjoyment; but it is afflicting to peaceable minds.—To Edward Rutledge. iv, 191. Ford ed., vii, 154. (Pa., June 1797.)

6745. POLITICS, Price of wheat and.—Wherever there was any considerable portion of federalism, it has been so much reinforced by those of whose politics the price of wheat is the sole principle, that federalists will be retained from many districts of Virginia.—To President Madison. v, 443. (M., April 1809.)

6746. POLITICS, Propriety and.—I have had a proposition to meet Mr. [Patrick] Henry this month, to confer on the subject of a convention, to the calling of which he is now become a convert; * * * but the impropriety of my entering into consultation on a measure in which I would take no part, is a permanent one.—To James Madison. iv, 118. Ford ed., vii, 11. (M., April 1795.)

6747. ———— ————. The question of a [constitutional] convention is become a party one with which I shall not intermeddle.—To Samuel Kerchival. Ford ed., x, 47. (M., 1816.)

6748. POLITICS, Pursuit of.—I am glad to find that among the various branches of science presenting themselves to your mind, you have fixed on that of politics as your principal pursuit. Your country will derive from this a more immediate and sensible benefit. She has much for you to do. For, though we may say with confidence, that the worst of the American constitutions is better than the best which ever existed before in any other country, and that they are wonderfully perfect for a first essay, yet every human essay must have defects. It will remain, therefore, to those now coming on the stage of public affairs, to perfect what has been so well begun by those going off it.—To T. M. Randolph, Jr. ii, 175. Ford ed., iv, 403. (P., 1787.)

6749. ———— ————. Having pursued your main studies [in France] about two years, and acquired a facility in speaking French, take a tour of four or five months through this country and Italy, return then to Virginia, and pass a year in Williamsburg under the care of Mr. Wythe; and you will be ready to enter on the public stage, with superior advantages.—To T. M. Randolph, Jr. ii, 176. Ford ed., iv, 405. (P., 1787.)

6750. POLITICS, Reformation of.—Politics, like religion, holds up the torches of martyrdom to the reformers of error.—To Mr. Ogilvie. v, 605. (M., 1811.)

6751. POLITICS, Retirement from.—I ought not to quit the port in which I am quietly moored to commit myself again to the stormy ocean of political or party contest.

to kindle new enmities, and lose old friends. No, tranquillity is the *summum bonum* of old age, and there is a time when it is a duty to leave the government of the world to the existing generation, and to repose one's self under their protecting hand. That time is come with me, and I welcome it.—To SAMUEL H. SMITH. FORD ED., x, 263. (M., Aug. 1823.) See RETIREMENT.

6752. POLITICS, Revolution in.— Things have so much changed their aspect, it is like a new world. Those who know us only from 1775 to 1793, can form no better idea of us now than of the inhabitants of the moon; I mean as to political matters.— To COLONEL HAWKINS. iv, 326. FORD ED., vii, 435. (Pa., March 1800.)

6753. POLITICS, Taxation and.—The purse of the people is the real seat of sensibility. It is to be drawn upon largely, and they will then listen to truths which could not excite them through any other organ.— To A. H. ROWAN. iv, 257. FORD ED., vii, 281. (M., 1798.)

6754. ———. Excessive taxation * * * will carry reason and reflection to every man's door, and particularly in the hour of election.—To JOHN TAYLOR. iv, 259. FORD ED., vii, 310. (M., 1798.)

6755. POLITICS, Torment of.—It is a relief to be withdrawn from the torment of the scenes amidst which we are. Spectators of the heats and tumults of conflicting parties, we cannot help participating of their feelings.—To MARTHA JEFFERSON RANDOLPH. FORD ED., v, 487. (Pa., March 1792.)

6756. ———. Politics is such a torment that I would advise every one I love not to mix with it.—To MARTHA JEFFERSON RANDOLPH. D. L. J., 262. (Pa., 1800.)

— POLYGRAPH.—See INVENTIONS.

— POLYPOTAMIA, Proposed State of. —See WESTERN TERRITORY.

6757. POOR, Care of.—The poor who have neither property, friends, nor strength to labor, are boarded in the houses of good farmers, to whom a stipulated sum is annually paid. To those who are able to help themselves a little, or have friends from whom they derive some succor, inadequate however to their full maintenance, supplementary aids are given which enable them to live comfortably in their own houses, or in the houses of their friends. * * * From Savannah to Portsmouth, you will seldom meet a beggar. In the larger towns, indeed, they sometimes present themselves. These are usually foreigners, who have never obtained a settlement in any parish. I never yet saw a native American begging in the streets or highways.—NOTES ON VIRGINIA. viii, 375. FORD ED., iii, 234. (1782.)

6758. POPE PIUS VI., Influence of.— A dispute has arisen between the Papal See and the King of Naples, which may in its progress enable us to estimate what degree of influence that See retains at the present day. The Kingdom of Naples, at an early period of its history, became feudatory to the See of Rome, and in acknowledgment thereof, has annually paid a hackney to the Pope in Rome, to which place it has always been sent by a splendid embassy. The hackney has been refused by the King this year, and the Pope, giving him three months to return to obedience, threatens, if he does not, to proceed seriously against him.—To JOHN JAY. ii, 454. (P., 1788.)

6759. POPULATION, America's capacity for.—The territory of the United States contains about a million of square miles, English. There is, in them, a greater proportion of fertile lands than in the British dominions in Europe. Suppose the territory of the United States, then, to attain an equal degree of population with the British European dominions, they will have an hundred millions of inhabitants. Let us extend our views to what may be the population of North and South America, supposing them divided at the narrowest part of the Isthmus of Panama. Between this line and that of 50° of north latitude, the northern continent contains about five millions of square miles, and south of this line of division the southern continent contains about seven millions of square miles. * * * Here are twelve millions of square miles which, at the rate of population before assumed, will nourish twelve hundred millions of inhabitants, a greater number than the present population of the whole globe is supposed to amount to. If those who propose medals for the resolution of questions, about which nobody makes any question, those who have invited discussion on the pretended problem, "whether the discovery of America was for the good of mankind"? if they, I say, would have viewed it only as doubling the numbers of mankind, and, of course, the quantum of existence and happiness, they might have saved the money and the reputation which their proposition has cost them.—To M. DE MEUNIER. ix, 275. FORD ED., iv, 179. (P., 1786.)

6760. POPULATION, Extension of.— The present population of the inhabited parts of the United States is of about ten to the square mile; and experience has shown us, that wherever we reach that, the inhabitants become uneasy, as too much compressed, and so go off in great numbers to search for vacant country. Within forty years their whole territory will be peopled at that rate. We may fix that, then, as the term beyond which the people of those States will not be restricted within their present limits; we may fix that population, too, as the limit which they will not exceed till the whole of those two continents are filled up to that mark, that is to say, till they shall contain one hundred and twenty millions of inhabitants.—To M. DE MEUNIER. ix, 275. FORD ED., iv, 180. (P., 1786.)

6761. ———. The soil of the country on the western side of the Mississippi, its climate and its vicinity to the United States, point it out as the first which will receive population from that nest. The present occupiers will just have force enough to repress and restrain the emigrations to a certain degree of consistence. —To M. DE MEUNIER. ix, 276. FORD ED., iv, 180. (P., 1786.)

6762. ———. We have lately seen a single person go and decide on a settlement in Kentucky, many hundred miles from any white inhabitant, remove thither with his family and a few neighbors; and though perpetually harassed by the Indians, that settlement in the course of ten years has acquired thirty thousand inhabitants.—To M. DE MEUNIER. ix, 276. FORD ED., iv, 181. (P., 1786.)

6763. POPULATION, Growth of.—The census just now concluded, shows we have added to our population a third of what it was ten years ago. This will be a duplication in twenty-three or twenty-four years. If we can delay but for a few years the necessity of vindicating the laws of nature on the ocean, we shall be the more sure of doing it with effect.—To WILLIAM SHORT. iv, 415. FORD ED., viii, 98. (W., Oct. 1801.)

6764. ———— ————. Our growth is now so well established by regular enumerations through a course of forty years, and the same grounds of continuance so likely to endure for a much longer period, that, speaking in round numbers, we may safely call ourselves twenty millions in twenty years, and forty millions in forty years.—To SIR JOHN SINCLAIR. vii, 22. (M., 1816.) See EMIGRATION.

6765. POPULATION, Happiness and.—The increase of numbers during the last ten years, proceeding in a geometrical ratio, promises a duplication in a little more than twenty-two years. We contemplate this rapid growth, and the prospect it holds up to us, not with a view to the injuries it may enable us to do to others in some future day, but to the settlement of the extensive country still remaining vacant within our limits, to the multiplications of men susceptible of happiness, educated in the love of order, habituated to self-government, and valuing its blessings above all price.—FIRST ANNUAL MESSAGE. viii, 8. FORD ED., viii, 119. (1801.)

6766. POPULATION, Malefactors and.—The malefactors sent to America were not sufficient in number to merit enumeration as one class out of three which peopled America. It was at a late period of their history that this practice began. * * * I do not think the whole number sent would amount to two thousand, and being principally men, eaten up with disease, they married seldom and propagated little. I do not suppose that themselves and their descendants are at present four thousand, which is little more than one thousandth part of the whole inhabitants.—To M. DE MEUNIER. ix, 254. FORD ED., iv, 158. (P., 1786.)

6767. POPULATION, Preventing.—He has endeavored to prevent the population of these States; for that purpose, obstructing the laws for naturalization of foreigners; refusing to pass other laws to encourage their migrations hither, and raising the conditions of new appropriations of lands.—DECLARATION OF INDEPENDENCE AS DRAWN BY JEFFERSON.

6768. POPULATION, Theories of Malthus.—Malthus's work on Population is a work of sound logic, in which some of the opinions of Adam Smith, as well as of the Economists, are ably examined. * * * The differences of circumstances between this and the old countries of Europe, furnish differences of fact whereon to reason in questions of political economy, and will consequently produce sometimes a difference of result. There, for example, the quantity of food is fixed, or increasing in a slow and only arithmetical ratio, and the proportion is limited by the same ratio. Supernumerary births consequently add only to our mortality. Here the immense extent of uncultivated and fertile lands enables every one who will labor to marry young, and to raise a family of any size. Our food, then, may increase geometrically with our laborers, and our births, however multiplied, become effective. Again, there the best distribution of labor is supposed to be that which places the manufacturing hands alongside of the agricultural; so that the one part shall feed both, and the other part furnish both with clothes and other comforts. Would that be best here? Egoism and first appearances say "yes". Or would it be better that all our laborers should be employed in agriculture? In this case a double or treble portion of fertile lands would be brought into culture; a double or treble creation of food be produced, and its surplus go to nourish the now perishing births of Europe, who in return would manufacture and send us in exchange our clothes and other comforts. Morality listens to this, and so invariably do the laws of nature create our duties and interests, that when they seem to be at variance, we ought to suspect some fallacy in our reasonings. In solving this question, too, we should allow just weight to the moral and physical preference of the agricultural, over the manufacturing, man.—To M. SAY. iv, 526. (W., Feb. 1804.) See MALTHUS.

6769. PORTER (David), Complaint against.—Mr. Madison * * * suggests the expediency of immediately taking up the case of Captain Porter, against whom Mr. Erskine [British minister] lodged a very serious complaint, for an act of violence committed on a British seaman in the Mediterranean. While Mr. Erskine was reminded of the mass of complaints we had against his government for similar violences, he was assured that contending against such irregularities ourselves, and requiring satisfaction for them, we did not mean to follow the example, and that on Captain Porter's return, it should be properly inquired into. The sooner this is done the better; because if Great Britain settles with us satisfactorily all our subsisting differences, and should require in return (to have an appearance of reciprocity of wrong as well as redress), a marked condemnation of Captain Porter, it would be embarrassing were that the only obstacle to a peaceable settlement, and the more so as we cannot but disavow his act. On the contrary, if we immediately look into it, we shall be more at liberty to be moderate in the censure of it, on the very ground of British example; and the case being once passed upon, we can more easily avoid the passing on it a second time, as against a settled principle. It is, therefore, to put it in our power to let Captain Porter off as easily as possible, as a valuable officer whom we all wish to favor, that I suggest to you the earliest attention to the inquiry, and the promptest settlement of it.—To ROBERT SMITH. v, 192. FORD ED., ix, 138. (M., Sep. 1807.)

6770. PORTUGAL, Commerce with.—I am in hopes Congress will send a minister to Lisbon. I know no country with which we are likely to cultivate a more useful commerce. I have pressed this in my private letters.—To JOHN ADAMS. i, 530. (P., 1786.)

6771. ———— ————. [In arranging the treaty of commerce] we wished much to have had some privileges in their American possessions; but this was not to be effected. The right to import flour into Portugal, though not conceded by the treaty, we are not without hopes of obtaining.—To WILLIAM CARMICHAEL. i, 551. (P., 1786.)

6772. ———— ————. While in London we entered into negotiations with the Chevalier Pinto, Ambassador of Portugal at that place. The only article of difficulty between us was a stipulation that our bread stuff should be received in Portugal in the form of flour as well as of grain. He approved of it himself, but observed that several Nobles, of great influence at their court, were the owners of wind-mills in the neighborhood of Lisbon which depended much for their profits on manufacturing our wheat, and that this stipulation would endanger the whole treaty. He signed it, however, and its fate was what he had candidly portended.— AUTOBIOGRAPHY. i, 64. FORD ED., i, 90. (1821.)

6773. PORTUGAL, Government of.— The government of Portugal is so peaceable and inoffensive that it has never any altercations with its friends. If their minister abroad writes them once a quarter that all is well, they desire no more.—To F. W. GILMER. vii, 5. FORD ED., x, 33. (M., 1816.)

6774. ————. During six and thirty years that I have been in situations to attend to the conduct and characters of foreign nations, I have found the government of Portugal the most just, inoffensive, and unambitious of any one with which we had concern, without a single exception. I am sure that this is the character of ours also. Two such nations can never wish to quarrel with each other.—To J. CORREA. vii, 184. FORD ED., x. 164. (M., 1820.)

6775. POSTERITY, Judgment of.—It is fortunate for those in public trust, that posterity will judge them by their works, and not by the malignant vituperations and invectives of the Pickerings and Gardiners of their age.— To JOHN ADAMS. vii, 62. (M., 1817.)

6776. POSTERITY, Sacrifices for.—It is from posterity we are to expect remuneration for the sacrifices we are making for their service, of time, quiet and good will.—To JOSEPH C. CABELL. vii, 394. (M., 1825.)

6777. ————. It has been a great solace to me to believe that you are engaged in vindicating to posterity the course we have pursued for preserving to them, in all their purity, the blessings of self-government, which we had assisted, too, in acquiring for them.— To JAMES MADISON. vii, 435. FORD ED., x, 378. (M., 1826.)

6778. POST OFFICE, Appointments.— A very early recommendation * * * [was] given to the Postmaster General to employ no printer, foreigner, or revolutionary tory in any of his offices.—To NATHANIEL MACON. iv, 397. (W., May 1801.)

6779. ————. The true remedy for putting those [Post office] appointments into a wholesome state would be a law vesting them in the President, but without the intervention of the Senate. That intervention would make the matter worse. Every Senator would expect to dispose of all the post offices in his vicinage, or perhaps in his State. At present the President has some control over those appointments by his authority over the postmaster himself.— To PRESIDENT MADISON. FORD ED., ix, 460. (M., 1814.)

6780. POST OFFICE, Benefits of.—I wish the regulation of the post office, adopted by Congress * * * , could be put in practice. It was for the travel night and day, and to go their several stages three times a week. The speedy and frequent communication of intelligence is really of great consequence. So many falsehoods have been propagated that nothing now is believed unless coming from Congress or camp. Our people, merely for want of intelligence which they may rely on, are becoming lethargic and insensible of the state they are in.—To JOHN ADAMS. FORD ED., ii, 130. (May 1777.)

6781. POST OFFICE, The Colonial.— [The] exercises of usurped power [by Parliament] have not been confined to instances alone in which themselves were interested; but they have also intermeddled with the regulation of the internal affairs of the Colonies. —RIGHTS OF BRITISH AMERICA. i, 130. FORD ED., i, 434. (1774.)

6782. ————. The act of the 9th [year] of [Queen] Anne for establishing a post office in America, seems to have had little connection with British convenience, except that of accommodating his Majesty s ministers and favorites with the sa'e of a lucrative and easy office.— RIGHTS OF BRITISH AMERICA. i, 130. FORD ED., i, 434. (1774.)

6783. POST OFFICE, Expediting mails. —Congress have adopted the late improvement in the British post office, of sending their mails by the stages.—To WM. CARMICHAEL. i, 475. (P., 1785.)

6784. ————. I opened to the President a proposition for doubling the velocity of the post riders, who now travel about fifty miles a day, and might, without difficulty, go one hundred, and for taking measures (by way-bills) to know where the delay is, when there is any. —THE ANAS. ix, 101. FORD ED., i, 174. (1792.)

6785. ————. I am now on a plan with the Postmaster General to make the posts go from Philadelphia to Richmond in two days and a half instead of six, which I hope to persuade him is practicable.—To T. M. RANDOLPH. FORD ED., v, 456. (Pa., 1792.)

6786. POST OFFICE, Foreign mails.— The person at the head of the post office here says he proposed to Dr. Franklin a convention to facilitate the passage of letters through their office and ours, and that he delivered a draft of the convention proposed, that it might be sent to Congress. I think it possible he may be mistaken in this, as, on my mentioning it to Dr. Franklin, he did not recollect any such draft having been put into his hands. An answer, however, is expected by them. I mention it, that Congress may decide whether they will make any convention on the subject, and on what principle. The one proposed here was, that, for letters passing hence into America, the French postage should be collected by our post officers, and paid every six months, and for letters coming from America here, the American postage should be collected by the post officers here, and paid to us in like manner. A second plan, however, presents itself; that is, to suppose the sums to be thus collected, on each side, will be equal, or so nearly equal, that the balance will not pay for the trouble of keeping accounts, and for the little bickerings that the settlement of accounts and demands of the balances may occasion; and therefore, to make an exchange of postage. This would better secure our harmony; but I do not know that it would be agreed to here. If not, the other might then be agreed to.—To JOHN JAY. i, 410. (P., 1785.)

6787. POST OFFICE, Infidelities in foreign.—The infidelities of the post offices, both of England and France, are not unknown to you. The former are the most rascally, because they retain one's letters, not choosing to take the trouble of copying them. The latter, when they have taken copies, are so civil as to send the originals, resealed clumsily with a composition, on which they have previously taken the impression of the seal.—To R. Izard. i, 442. (P., 1785.)

6788. —— ——. Send your letters by the French packet. They come by that conveyance with certainty, having first undergone the ceremony of being opened and read in the post office, which I am told is done in every country in Europe.—To James Monroe. Ford ed., iv, 33. (P., 1785.)

6789. —— ——. All letters [are] opened which come either through the French or English channel, unless trusted to a messenger. I think I never received one through the post office which had not been. It is generally discoverable by the smokiness of the wax and faintness of the reimpression. Once they sent me a letter open, having forgotten to reseal it. —To Richard H. Lee. Ford ed., iv, 69. (P., 1785.)

6790. —— ——. [I wrote] on such things only as both the French and English post offices were welcome to see.—To James Monroe. i, 590. Ford ed., iv, 250. (P., 1786.)

6791. POST OFFICE, Newspaper postage.—I desired you * * * to send the newspapers notwithstanding the expense. I had then no idea of it. Some late instances have made me perfectly acquainted with it. I have, therefore been obliged * * * to have my newspapers from the different States, enclosed to the office for Foreign Affairs, and to desire Mr. Jay to pack the who'e in a box, and send it * * * as merchandise. * * * In this way, they will cost me livres where they now cost me guineas.—To F. Hopkinson. i, 441. (P., 1785.)

6792. POST OFFICE, Patronage of.—[I said to President Washington] that I thought it would be advantageous to declare [that the Post office is included in the Department of State] for another reason, to wit, that the Department of Treasury possessed already such an influence as to swallow up the whole Executive powers, and that even the future Presidents (not supported by the weight of character which himself possessed) would not be able to make head against this Department. That in urging this measure I had certainly no personal interest, since, if I was supposed to have any appetite for power, yet as my career would certainly be exactly as short as his own, the intervening time was too short to be an object. My real wish was to avail the public of every occasion during the residue of the President's period, to place things on a safe footing.—The Anas. ix, 101. Ford ed., i, 174. (Feb. 1792.)

6793. POST OFFICE, Political spies in. —The interruption of letters is becoming so notorious, that I am forming a resolution of declining correspondence with my friends through the channels of the Post Office altogether.—To E. Randolph. iv, 192. Ford ed., vii, 156. (Pa., June 1797.)

6794. —— ——. The impression of my seal on wax (which shall be constant hereafter) will discover whether my letters are opened by the way. The nature of some of my communications furnishes ground of inquietude for their safe conveyance.—To James Madison. iv, 231. Ford ed., vii, 230. (Pa., April 1798.)

6795. —— ——. To avoid the suspicions and curiosity of the post office, which would

have been excited by seeing your name* and mine on the back of a letter, I have delayed acknowledging the receipt of your favor * * * till an occasion to write to an inhabitant of Wilmington gives me an opportunity of putting my letter under cover to him.—To Archibald Hamilton Rowan. iv, 256. Ford ed., vii, 280. (M., 1798.)

6796. —— ——. The infidelities of the post office and the circumstances of the times are against my writing fully and freely.—To John Taylor. iv, 259. Ford ed., vii, 309. (M., 1798.)

6797. —— ——. I shall follow your direction in conveying this [letter] by a private hand, though I know not as yet when one worthy of confidence will occur. * * * Did we ever expect to see the day, when, breathing nothing but sentiments of love, to our country and its freedom and happiness, our correspondence must be as secret as if we were hatching its destruction!—To Elbridge Gerry. iv, 273. Ford ed., vii, 335. (Pa., 1799.)

6798. —— ——. A want of confidence in the post office deters me from writing to my friends on the subject of politics.—To Robert R. Livingston. iv, 297. Ford ed., vii, 368. (Pa., 1799.)

6799. —— ——. From the commencement of the ensuing session [of Congress], I shall trust the post offices with nothing confidential, persuaded that during the ensuing twelve months they will lend their inquisitorial aid to furnish matter for newspapers.—To James Madison. iv, 307. Ford ed., vii, 400. (M., Nov. 1799.)

6800. —— ——. One of your electors * * * offers me a safe conveyance at a moment when the post offices will be peculiarly suspicious and prying. Your answer may come by post without danger, if directed in some other handwriting than your own.—To Robert R. Livingston. iv, 339. Ford ed., vii, 466. (W., Dec. 1800.)

6801. —— ——. Mr. Brown's departure for Virginia enables me to write confidentially what I could not have ventured by the post at this prying season.—To James Madison. iv, 342. Ford ed., vii, 470. (W., Dec. 1800.)

6802. —— ——. I shall neither frank nor subscribe my letter, because I do not choose to commit myself to the fidelity of the post office. For the same reason, I have avoided putting pen to paper through the whole summer, except on mere business, because I knew it was a prying season.—To Tench Coxe. iv, 345. Ford ed., vii, 474. (W., Dec. 1800.)

6803. —— ——. I dare not through the channel of the post hazard a word to you on the subject of the [Presidential] election. Indeed the interception and publication of my letters expose the republican cause, as well as myself personally, to such obloquy that I have come to a resolution never to write another sentence of politics in a letter.—To James Madison. Ford ed., vii, 484. (W., Feb. 1801.)

6804. —— ——. Several letters from you have not been acknowledged. By the post I dare not, * * * .—To James Monroe. iv, 354. Ford ed., vii, 490. (W., Feb. 1801.)

* Rowan was one of the leaders in the Irish Rebellion of 1798.—Editor.

6805. POST OFFICE, Reformed.—Your letters through the post will now come safely.—To ELBRIDGE GERRY. iv, 393. FORD ED., viii, 43. (W., March 1801.)

6806. —— ——. I trust that the post is become a safe channel to and from me. I have heard, indeed, of some extraordinary licences practiced in the post offices of your State, and there is nothing I desire so much as information of facts on that subject, to rectify the office.—To GIDEON GRANGER. FORD ED., viii, 44. (W., March 1801.)

6807. POST ROADS, Building.—Have you considered all the consequences of your proposition respecting post roads? I view it as a source of boundless patronage to the Executive, jobbing to members of Congress and their friends, and a bottomless abyss of public money. You will begin by appropriating only the surplus of the Post Office revenues; but the other revenues will soon be called into their aid, and it will be the source of eternal scramble among the members, who can get the most money wasted in their State; and they will always get most who are meanest. We have thought, hitherto, that the roads of a State could not be so well administered even by the State Legislature, as by the magistracy of the county, on the spot. How will it be when a member of New Hampshire is to mark out a road for Georgia? Does the power to *establish* post roads, given you by the Constitution, mean that you shall *make* the roads, or only *select* from those already made, those on which there shall be a post? If the term be equivocal (and I really do not think it so,) which is the safer construction? That which permits a majority of Congress to go cutting down mountains and bridging of rivers, or the other, which, if too restricted, may be referred to the States for amendment, securing still due measure and proportion among us, and providing some means of information to the members of Congress tantamount to that ocular inspection, which, even in our county determinations, the magistrate finds cannot be supplied by any other evidence? The fortification of harbors was liable to great objection. But national circumstances furnished some color. In this case there is none. The roads of America are the best in the world except those of France and England. But does the state of our population, the extent of our internal commerce, the want of sea and river navigation, call for such expense on roads here, or are our means adequate to it?—To JAMES MADISON. iv, 131. FORD ED., vii, 63. (M., March 1796.)

6808. POST ROADS, Expense.—I very much fear the road system will be urged. The mines of Peru would not supply the moneys which would be wasted on this object, nor the patience of any people stand the abuses which would be incontrollably committed under it.—To JAMES MADISON. iv, 344. FORD ED., vii. 472. (W., Dec. 1800.)

6809. POST ROADS, Jobbery.—The Roads bill will be a bottomless abyss for money, the most fruitful field for ——* and the richest provision for jobs to favorites that has ever yet been proposed.—To CÆSAR RODNEY. FORD ED., vii, 473. (W., Dec. 1800.)

6810. POSTS (Western), England's detention of.—England shows no dispositions to enter into friendly connections with us. On the contrary, her detention of our posts seems to be the speck which is to produce a storm.—To R. IZARD. i, 442. (P., 1785.)

6811. —— ——. The British garrisons were not withdrawn with all convenient speed, nor have ever yet been withdrawn from Machilimackinac, on Lake Michigan; Detroit, on the straits of Lake Erie and Huron; Fort Erie, on Lake Erie; Niagara, Oswego, on Lake Ontario; Oswegatchie, on the River St. Lawrence; Point Au-Fer, and Dutchman's Point, on Lake Champlain.—To GEORGE HAMMOND. FORD ED., vi, 468. (P., Dec. 1793.)

6812. POSTS (Western), France and.—The question * * * proposed [by you], "How far France considers herself as bound to insist on the delivery of the posts", would infallibly produce another, "How far we consider ourselves as guarantees of their American possessions, and bound to enter into any future war in which these may be attacked"? The words of the treaty of alliance seem to be without ambiguity on either head, yet I should be afraid to commit Congress by answering without authority. I will endeavor on my return [from London to Paris] to sound the opinion of the minister, if possible without exposing myself to the other question. Should anything forcible be meditated on these posts, it would possibly be thought prudent, previously, to ask the good offices of France to obtain their delivery. In this case, they would probably say, we must first execute the treaty on our part by repealing all acts which have contravened it. Now this measure, if there be any candor in the court of London, would suffice to obtain a delivery of the posts from them without the mediation of any third power. However, if this mediation should be finally needed, I see no reason to doubt our obtaining it, and still less to question its omnipotent influence on the British court.—To JOHN JAY. i, 539. FORD ED., iv, 200. (L., March 1786.)

6813. POSTS (Western), Indian murders.—Were the western posts in our possession, it cannot be doubted but there would be an end to the murders daily committed by the Indians on our Northwestern frontier, and to a great part of the expense of our armaments in that quarter.—To GEORGE HAMMOND. FORD ED., vi, 321. (1793.)

6814. POTATO, Nativity of.—You say in your "General Geography" the potato is a native of the United States. I presume you speak of the Irish potato. I have inquired much into the question, and think I can assure you that the plant is not a native of North America. Zimmerman, in his "Geographical Zoology", says it is a native of Guiana; and Clavigers, that the Mexicans got it from South America, *its native country*. The most probable account I have been able to collect is, that a vessel of Sir Walter Raleigh's, returning from Guiana, put into the west of Ireland in distress, having on board some potatoes which they called earth apples. That the season of the year, and circumstance of their being already sprouted, induced them to give them all out

* Illegible in MS.

there, and they were no more heard or thought of, till they had spread considerably into that island, whence they were carried over into England, and, therefore, called the Irish potato. From England they came to the United States bringing their name with them.—To Mr. Spafford. v, 445. (M., 1809.)

— POTOMAC AND OHIO CANAL.—
See Canal.

6815. POWER, Abridgment of.—The functionaries of public power rarely strengthen in their dispositions to abridge it.— To John Taylor. vi, 608. Ford ed., x, 31. (M., 1816.)

6816. POWER, Abuses.—Education is the true corrective of abuses of constitutional power.—To William C. Jarvis. vii, 179. Ford ed., x. 161. (M., 1820.)

6817. POWER, Depositaries of.—No other depositaries of power [than the people themselves] have ever yet been found, which did not end in converting to their own profit the earnings of those committed to their charge.—To Samuel Kerchival. vii, 36. Ford ed., x, 45. (M., 1816.)

6818. ———— ————. I know no safe depository of the ultimate powers of the society but the people themselves; and if we think them not enlightened enough to exercise their control with a wholesome discretion, the remedy is not to take it from them, but to inform their discretion by education.— To William C. Jarvis. vii, 179. Ford ed., x, 161. (M., 1820.)

6819. POWER, Exercise of.—I have never been able to conceive how any rational being could propose happiness to himself from the exercise of power over others.—To M. Destutt Tracy. v, 569. Ford ed., ix, 308. (M., 1811.)

6820. ———— ————. An honest man can feel no pleasure in the exercise of power over his fellow citizens. And considering as the only offices of power those conferred by the people directly, that is to say, the Executive and Legislative functions of the General and State Governments, the common refusal of these, and multiplied resignations, are proofs sufficient that power is not alluring to pure minds, and is not with them, the primary principle of contest. This is my belief of it; it is that on which I have acted; and had it been a mere contest who should be permitted to administer the Government according to its genuine republican principles, there has never been a moment of my life in which I should have relinquished for it the enjoyments of my family, my farm, my friends and books.—To John Melish. vi, 96. Ford ed., ix, 376. (M., 1813.)

6821. ———— ————. In one sentiment of [your] speech I particularly concur,—" if we have a doubt relative to any power, we ought not to exercise it ".—To Edward Livingston. vii, 343. Ford ed., x, 300. (M., 1824.)

6822. POWER, Independent.—It should be remembered, as an axiom of eternal truth in politics. that whatever power in any government is independent, is absolute also; in theory only, at first, while the spirit of the people is up. but in practice, as fast as that relaxes. Independence can be trusted nowhere but with the people in mass. They are inherently independent of all but moral law.—To Spencer Roane. vii, 134. Ford ed., x, 141. (P.F., 1819.)

6823. POWER, Limitation.—In a free country every power is dangerous which is not bound up by general rules.—To Philip Mazzei. Ford ed., iv, 116. (P., 1785.)

6824. POWER, Origin of.—Hume. the great apostle of toryism. says [in his History of England, c. 159] " the Commons established a principle, which is noble in itself, and seems specious, but is belied by all history and experience, that the people are the origin of all just power". And where else will this degenerate son of science, this traitor to his fellow men, find the origin of just power, if not in the majority of the society? Will it be in the minority? Or in an individual of that minority?—To John Cartwright. vii, 356. (M., 1824.)

6825. ———— ————. All power is inherent in the people.—To John Cartwright. vii, 357. (M., 1824.)

6826. POWER, Perpetuation of.—The principles of our Constitution are wisely opposed to all perpetuations of power, and to every practice which may lead to hereditary establishments.—Reply to Address. v, 473. (M., 1809.)

6827. POWER, Perversion of.—Even under the best forms [of government] those entrusted with power have perverted it into tyranny.—Diffusion of Knowledge Bill. Ford ed., ii, 221. (1779.)

6828. POWER, Shifting.—I have never been so well pleased as when I could shift power from my own, on the shoulders of others.—To M. Destutt Tracy. v, 569. Ford ed., ix, 308. (M., 1811.)

6829. POWER, Use of.—I hope our wisdom will grow with our power, and teach us. that the less we use our power, the greater will it be.—To Thomas Leiper. vi, 465. Ford ed., ix, 520. (M., 1815.) See Authority.

6830. POWERS, Assumed.—I had rather ask an enlargement of power from the nation, where it is found necessary, than to assume it by a construction [of the Constitution] which would make our powers boundless.— To Wilson C. Nicholas. iv, 506. Ford ed., viii, 247. (M., 1803.)

6831. ———— ————. If, wherever the Constitution assumes a single power out of many which belong to the same subject, we should consider it as assuming the whole, it would vest the General Government with a mass of powers never contemplated. On the contrary, the assumption of particular powers seems an exclusion of all not assumed.—To JOSEPH C. CABELL. vi, 310. FORD ED., ix, 452. (M., 1814.)

6832. —— ——. If the three powers maintain their mutual independence on each other our Government may last long, but not so if either can assume the authorities of the other.—To WILLIAM C. JARVIS. vii, 179. FORD ED., x, 161. (M., 1820.)

6833. POWERS, Civil.—Civil powers alone have been given to the President of the United States, and no authority to direct the religious exercises of his constituents.—To REV. SAMUEL MILLAR. v, 237. FORD ED., ix, 175. (W., 1808.) See RELIGION.

6834. POWERS, Conflicting.—The peculiar happiness of our blessed system is, that in differences of opinion between these different sets of servants [in the three departments of the Federal Government], the appeal is to neither, but to their employers, peaceably assembled by their representatives in convention.—To SPENCER ROANE. vii, 214. FORD ED., x, 190. (M., 1821.)

6835. POWERS, Constitutional.—To keep in all things within the pale of our constitutional powers. * * * [is one of] the landmarks by which we are to guide ourselves in all our proceedings.—SECOND ANNUAL MESSAGE. viii, 21. FORD ED., viii, 187. (Dec. 1802.)

6836. POWERS, Constructive.—The States supposed that by their Tenth Amendment, they had secured themselves against constructive powers. They were not lessoned yet by Cohen's Case, nor aware of the slipperiness the eels of the law. I ask for no straining of words against the General Government, nor yet against the States. I believe the States can best govern our home concerns, and the General Government our foreign ones. I wish, therefore, to see maintained that wholesome distribution of powers established by the Constitution for the limitation of both; and never to see all offices transferred to Washington, where, further withdrawn from the eyes of the people, they may more secretly be bought and sold as at market.—To WILLIAM JOHNSON. vii, 297. FORD ED., x, 232. (M., 1823.)

6837. POWERS, Control by the people.—Unless the mass retains sufficient control over those intrusted with the powers of their government, these will be perverted to their own oppression, and to the perpetuation of wealth and power in the individuals and their families selected for the trust.—To MR. VAN DER KEMP. vi, 45. (M., 1812.)

6838. POWERS, Delegated.—The Constitution of the United States * * * [has] delegated to Congress a power to punish treason, counterfeiting the securities and current coin of the United States, piracies, and felonies committed on the high seas, and offences against the law of nations, and no other crimes whatsoever; and it being true, as a general principle, and one of the amend-

ments to the Constitution having also declared, that " the powers not delegated to the United States by the Constitution, nor prohibited by it to the States, are reserved to the States respectively, or to the people ", * * * the power to create, define, and punish * * * other crimes is reserved, and of right, appertains solely and exclusively to the respective States, each within its own territory.—KENTUCKY RESOLUTIONS. ix, 465. FORD ED., vii, 292. (1798.)

6839. —— ——. In case of an abuse of the delegated powers, the members of the General Government, being chosen by the people, a change by the people would be the constitutional remedy.—KENTUCKY RESOLUTIONS. ix, 469. FORD ED., vii, 301. (1798.)

6840. POWERS, Distribution of.—To preserve the republican form and principles of our Constitution, and cleave to the salutary distribution of powers, which that has established, * * * are the two sheet anchors of our Union. If driven from either, we shall be in danger of foundering.—To WILLIAM JOHNSON. vii, 298. FORD ED., x, 232. (M., 1823.)

6841. POWERS, Enlarging.—It [is] inconsistent with the principles of civil liberty, and contrary to the natural rights of the other members of the society, that any body of men therein should have authority to enlarge their own powers * * * without restraint.*—ALLOWANCE BILL. FORD ED., ii, 165. (1778.)

6842. —— ——. Nothing is more likely than that their [the framers of the Constitution] enumeration of powers is defective. This is the ordinary case of all human works. Let us go on, then, perfecting it by adding, by way of amendment, to the Constitution those forms which time and trial show are still wanting.—To WILSON C. NICHOLAS. iv, 506. FORD ED., viii, 248. (M., 1803.)

6843. POWERS, The enumerated.—To take a single step beyond the boundaries specifically drawn around the powers of Congress [in the enumerated powers] is to take possession of a boundless field of power, no longer susceptible of any definition.—NATIONAL BANK OPINION. vii, 556. FORD ED., v, 285. (1791.)

6844. —— ——. A little *difference* in the degree of *convenience* cannot constitute the necessity which the Constitution makes the ground for assuming any non-enumerated power.—NATIONAL BANK OPINION. vii, 559. FORD ED., v, 288. (1791.)

6845. —— ——. [By] the general phrase " to make all laws *necessary* and proper for carrying into execution the enumerated powers " * * * the Constitution allows only the means which are " *necessary* ", not those which are merely " convenient " for effecting the enumerated powers. If such a latitude of construction be allowed to this phrase as to

* A Bill in the Virginia Legislature providing for increased pay and allowances to members.—EDITOR.

give any non-enumerated power, it will go to every one, for there is not one which ingenuity may not torture into a *convenience* in some instance *or other*, to *some one* of so long a list of enumerated powers. It would swallow up all the delegated powers, and reduce the whole to one power. Therefore it was that the Constitution restrained them to the *necessary* means, that is to say, to those means without which the grant of power would be nugatory.—NATIONAL BANK OPINION. vii, 558. FORD ED., v, 287. (1791.) See MANUFACTURES.

6846. POWERS, Indestructible.—Legislative powers [are] incapable of annihilation.—DECLARATION OF INDEPENDENCE AS DRAWN BY JEFFERSON.

6847. POWERS, Nullification.—Where powers are assumed which have not been delegated, a nullification of the act is the rightful remedy.—KENTUCKY RESOLUTIONS. ix, 469. FORD ED., vii, 301. (1798.)

6848. POWERS, Organization.—Whenever any form of government becomes destructive of these ends [life, liberty and the pursuit of happiness], it is the right of the people to alter or to abolish it, and to institute new government, laying its foundation on such principles, and organizing its powers in such form, as to them shall seem most likely to effect their safety and happiness.—DECLARATION OF INDEPENDENCE AS DRAWN BY JEFFERSON.

6849. POWERS, Self-constituted.—I shall not undertake to draw the line of demarcation between private associations of laudable views and unimposing numbers, and those whose magnitude may rivalize and jeopardize the march of regular government. Yet such a line does exist. I have seen the days,—they were those which preceded the Revolution,—when even this last and perilous engine became necessary; but they were days which no man would wish to see a second time. That was the case where the regular authorities of the government had combined against the rights of the people, and no means of correction remained to them but to organize a collateral power, which, with their support, might rescue and secure their violated rights. But such is not the case with our government. We need hazard no collateral power, which, by a change of its original views, and assumption of others we know not how virtuous or how mischievous, would be ready organized and in force sufficient to shake the established foundations of society, and endanger its peace and the principles on which it is based. Is not the machine* now proposed of this gigantic stature?—To JEDEDIAH MORSE. vii, 234. FORD ED., x, 204. (M., 1822.)

---

* The "machine" was a society for the civilization of the Indians, to be composed of nearly all the officers of the Federal and State Governments, the clergy of all denominations, and as many citizens as would pay for membership. Jefferson commended the object, but condemned so vast an organization as unnecessary, dangerous and bad as a precedent.—EDITOR.

6850. ——— ———. Might we not as well appoint a committee for each department of the Government, to counsel and direct its head separately, as volunteer ourselves to counsel and direct the whole, in mass? And might we not do it as well for their foreign, their fiscal, and their military, as for their Indian affairs? And how many societies, auxiliary to the Government, may we expect to see spring up, in imitation of this, offering to associate themselves in this and that of its functions? In a word, why not take the Government out of its constitutional hands, associate them indeed with us, to preserve a semblance that the acts are theirs, but ensuring them to be our own by allowing them a minor vote only?—To JEDEDIAH MORSE. vii, 236. FORD ED., x, 206. (M., 1822.)

6851. POWERS, Separation of.—The principle of the Constitution is that of a separation of Legislative, Executive and Judiciary functions, except in cases specified. If this principle be not expressed in direct terms, it is clearly the spirit of the Constitution, and it ought to be so commented and acted on by every friend of free government.—To JAMES MADISON. iv, 161. FORD ED., vii, 108. (M., Jan. 1797.)

6852. POWERS, Undelegated.—Whenever the General Government assumes undelegated powers, its acts are unauthoritative, void, and of no force.—KENTUCKY RESOLUTIONS. ix, 464. FORD ED., vii, 291. (1798.)

6853. ——— ———. This Commonwealth [Kentucky] is determined, as it doubts not its co-States are, to submit to undelegated, and consequently unlimited powers in no man, or body of men on earth.—KENTUCKY RESOLUTIONS. ix, 469. FORD ED., vii, 301. (1798.)

6854. ——— ———. The power to regulate commerce does not give a power to build piers, wharves, open ports, clear the beds of rivers, dig canals, build warehouses, build manufacturing machines, set up manufactories, cultivate the earth, to all of which the power would go if it went to the first.—To ALBERT GALLATIN. iv, 449. FORD ED., viii, 174. (1802.)

6855. POWERS, Unlimited.—I have no idea of entering into the contest, whether it be expedient to delegate unlimited powers to our ordinary governors? My opinion is against that expediency; but my occupations do not permit me to undertake to vindicate all my opinions, nor have they importance enough to merit it.—To NOAH WEBSTER. iii, 203. FORD ED., v, 257. (Pa., 1790.) See BANK (U. S.), CONSTITUTIONALITY.

6856. PRADT (Abbe de), Writings of.—Of the character of M. de Pradt his political writings furnish a tolerable estimate, but not so full as you have favored me with. He is eloquent, and his pamphlet on colonies shows him ingenious. I was gratified by his *Recit Historique*, because, pretending, as all men do, to some character, and he to one of some distinction, I supposed he would not place before the world facts of glaring falsehood, on which so many living and distinguished witnesses could convict him.—To JOHN QUINCY ADAMS. vii, 87. (M., 1817.)

6857. PRAISE, Undeserved.—To give praise where it is not due might be well from the venal, but it would ill beseem those who are asserting the rights of human nature.—RIGHTS OF BRITISH AMERICA. i, 141. FORD ED., i, 446. (1774.)

6858. PRECEDENT, Oppression and.—For what oppression may not a precedent be found in this world of the *bellum omnium in omnia?*—NOTES ON VIRGINIA. viii, 371. FORD ED., iii, 235. (1782.)

6859. PRECEDENT, Power and.—One precedent in favor of power is stronger than an hundred against it.—NOTES ON VIRGINIA. viii, 367. FORD ED., iii, 230. (1782.)

6860. PREEMPTION, Right of.—If the country, instead of being altogether vacant, is thinly occupied by another nation, the right of the native forms an exception to that of the new comers; that is to say, these will only have a right against all other nations except the natives. Consequently, they have the exclusive privilege of acquiring the native right by purchase or other just means. This is called the right of preemption, and is become a principle of the law of nations, fundamental with respect to America. There are but two means of acquiring the native title. First, war; for even war may, sometimes, give a just title. Second, contracts, or treaty.—OPINION ON GEORGIAN LAND GRANTS. vii, 467. FORD ED., v, 166. (1790.)

6861. PREROGATIVE, Barriers against.—The privilege of giving or withholding our moneys is an important barrier against the undue exertion of prerogative, which if left altogether without control may be exercised to our great oppression.—REPLY TO LORD NORTH'S PROPOSITION. FORD ED., i, 477. (July 1775.)

6862. PRESBYTERIAN SPIRIT, Liberty and.—The Presbyterian spirit is known to be so congenial with friendly liberty, that the patriots, after the Restoration, finding that the humor of the people was running too strongly to exalt the prerogative of the crown, promoted the dissenting interest as a check and balance, and thus was produced the Toleration Act.—NOTES ON RELIGION. FORD ED., ii, 98. (1776?)

6863. PRESENTS, Declination of.—I return you my thanks for a bust of the Emperor Alexander [of Russia]. These are the more cordial, because of the value the bust derives from the great estimation in which its original is held by the world, and by none more than myself. It will constitute one of the most valued ornaments of the retreat I am preparing for myself at my native home. * * * I had laid it down as a law for my conduct while in office, and hitherto scrupulously observed, to accept of no present beyond a book, a pamphlet or other curiosity of minor value; as well to avoid imputation on my motives of action, as to shut out a practice susceptible to such abuse. But my particular esteem for the character of the Emperor, places his image in my mind above the scope of law. I receive it, therefore, and shall cherish it with affection. It nourishes the contemplation of all the good placed in his

power, and of his disposition to do it.—To MR. HARRIS. v, 6. (W., 1806.)

6864. ———. Mr. Granger has sent me the very elegant ivory staff of which you wished my acceptance. The motives of your wish are honorable to me, and gratifying, as they evidence the approbation of my public conduct by a stranger who has not viewed it through the partialities of personal acquaintance. Be assured, Sir, that I am as grateful for the testimony, as if I could have accepted the token of it which you have so kindly offered. On coming into public office, I laid it down as a law of my conduct, while I should continue in it, to accept no present of any sensible pecuniary value. A pamphlet, a new book, or an article of new curiosity, have produced no hesitation, because below suspicion. But things of sensible value, however innocently offered in the first examples, may grow at length into abuse, for which I wish not to furnish a precedent. The kindness of the motives which led to this manifestation of your esteem, sufficiently assures me that you will approve of my desire, by a perseverance in the rule, to retain that consciousness of a disinterested administration of the public trusts, which is essential to perfect tranquillity of mind.—To SAMUEL HAWKINS. v, 393. (W., Nov. 1808.)

6865. PRESENTS, Diplomatic.—As custom may have rendered some presents necessary in the beginning or progress of this business [negotiation of a treaty with the Emperor of Morocco] and before it is concluded, or even in a way to be concluded, we authorize you to conform to the custom, confiding in your discretion to hazard as little as possible before a certainty of the event. We trust to you also to procure the best information as to what persons, and in what form, these presents should be made, and to make them accordingly.—To THOMAS BARCLAY. i, 421. (P., 1785.)

6866. PRESENTS, To Foreign Ministers.—It was proposed that the medal [to be given to recalled foreign ministers] should always contain 150 dollars' worth of gold; it was presumed the gentleman would always keep this. The chain was to contain 365 links always, but these were to be proportioned in value to the time the person had been here, making each link worth 3 dimes for every year of residence. No expense was to be bestowed on the making because it was expected they would turn the chain into money.—NOTE BY JEFFERSON. FORD ED., vi, 263. (1793.)

6867. ———. It has become necessary to determine on a present proper to be given to diplomatic characters on their taking leave of us; and it is concluded that a medal and chain of gold will be the most convenient. I have, therefore, to ask the favor of you to order the dies to be engraved with all the dispatch practicable. The medal must be of thirty lines diameter with a loop on the edge to receive the chain. On one side, must be the arms of the United States, of which I send you a written description; * * * round them as a legend must be " The United States of America ". The device of the other side we do not decide on. One suggestion has been a Columbia (a fine female figure) delivering the emblems of peace and commerce to a Mercury, and the date of our republic, to wit, 4th July, MDCCLXXVI.—To WILLIAM SHORT. iii. 142. (N.Y., 1790.)

6868. PRESENTS, To Indians.—I hope we shall give the Indians a thorough drubbing this summer, and I should think it better perhaps afterwards to take up the plan of liberal and repeated presents to them. This would be much the cheapest in the end and would save all the blood which is now being spilt; in time, too, it would produce a spirit of peace and friendship between us. The expense of a single expedition would last very long for presents.—To President Washington. iii, 248. Ford ed., v, 321. (Pa., 1791.)

6869. ———— ————. The giving medals and marks of distinction to the Indian chiefs * * * has been an ancient custom from time immemorial. The medals are considered as complimentary things, as marks of friendship to those who come to see us, or who do us good offices, conciliatory of their good will towards us, and not designed to produce a contrary disposition towards others. They confer no power, and seem to have taken their origin in the European practice, of giving medals or other marks of friendship to the negotiators of treaties and other diplomatic characters, or visitors of distinction. The British government, while it prevailed here, practiced the giving medals, gorgets, and bracelets to the savages, invariable.—To Carmichael and Short. iv, 15. Ford ed., vi, 336. (Pa., 1793.)

6870. PRESENTS, Public.—The bounties from one's country, expressions of its approbation, are honors which it would be arrogance to refuse, especially where flowing from the willing only.—To Thomas Ritchie. Ford ed., x, 382. (M., 1826.)

6871. PRESENTS, Tribute and.—We rely that you will be able to obtain an acknowledgment of our treaty with Morocco, giving very moderate presents. As the amount of these will be drawn into precedent, on future similar repetitions of them, it becomes important. Our distance, our seclusion from the ancient world, its politics and usages, our agricultural occupations and habits, our poverty, and lastly, our determination to prefer war in all cases, to tribute under any form, and to any people whatever, will furnish you with topics for opposing and refusing high or dishonorable pretensions.—To Thomas Barclay. i i, 262. (Pa., 1791.)

— PRESIDENT, Administration and Cabinet.—See Administration and Cabinet.

6872. PRESIDENT, Depositions by.—If the defendant supposes there are any facts within the knowledge of the heads of departments, or of myself, which can be useful for his defence, from a desire of doing anything our situation will permit in furtherance of justice, we shall be ready to give him the benefit of it, by way of deposition through any persons whom the Court shall authorize to take our testimony at this place [Washington].—To George Hay. v, 97. Ford ed., ix, 57. (W., June 1807.)

6873. PRESIDENT, Direct vote for.—One part of the subject of one of your letters is of a nature which forbids my interference altogether. The amendment to the Constitution of which you speak. would be a remedy to a certain degree. So will a different amendment which I know will be proposed, to wit, to have no electors, but let the people vote directly, and the ticket which has a plurality of the votes of any State to be considered as receiving thereby the vote of the State.—To Albert Gallatin. Ford ed., viii, 94. (M., Sep. 1801.)

6874. ———— ————. The President is chosen by ourselves, directly in *practice,* for we vote for A as elector only on the condition he will vote for B.—To Dupont de Nemours. vi, 590. Ford ed., x, 23. (P.F., 1816.)

6875. PRESIDENT, Election of.—The bill for the election of the President and Vice-President has undergone much revolution. Marshall made a dexterous maneuver. He declares against the constitutionality of the Senate's bill, and proposed that the right of decision of their grand committee should be controllable by the *concurrent* vote of the two houses of Congress; but to stand good if not rejected by a concurrent vote. You will readily estimate the amount of this sort of control. The committee of the House of Representatives, however, took from the committee the right of giving any opinion, requiring them to report the facts only, and that the votes returned by the States should be counted, unless reported by a concurrent vote of both houses.—To E. Livingston. iv, 328. Ford ed., vii, 443. (Pa., April 1800.)

6876. ———— ————. That great opposition is and will be made by federalists to this amendment [to the Constitution], is certain. They know that if it prevails, neither a President nor Vice-President can ever be made but by the fair vote of the majority of the nation, of which they are not. That either their opposition to the principle of discrimination now, or their advocation of it formerly was on party, not moral motives, they cannot deny. Consequently, they fix for themselves the place in the scale of moral rectitude to which they are entitled. I am a friend to the discriminating principle; and for a reason more than others have, inasmuch as the discriminated vote of my constituents will express unequivocally the verdict they wish to cast on my conduct.—To Thomas McKean. Ford ed., viii, 292. (W., Jan. 1804.)

6877. PRESIDENT, The judiciary and.—The interference of the Executive can rarely be proper where that of the Judiciary is so.—To George Hammond. Ford ed., vi. 298. (Pa., 1793.)

— PRESIDENT, Oath of office.—See Washington.

6878. PRESIDENT, Petitions to.—The right of our fellow citizens to represent to the public functionaries their opinion on proceedings interesting to them. is unquestionably a constitutional right, often useful. sometimes necessary, and will always be respectfully acknowledged by me.—To the New Haven Committee. iv, 402. Ford ed., viii, 68. (W., 1801.)

6879. PRESIDENT, Polish Kings and.—The President seems a bad edition of a Polish King.—To John Adams. ii, 316. (P., Nov. 1787.)

6880. ———— ————. What we have lately read in the history of Holland, in the chapter on the Stadtholder,* would have sufficed to

* See " Holland " in this volume.—Editor.

set me against a chief magistrate eligible for a long duration, if I had ever been disposed towards one; and what we have always read of the elections of Polish Kings should have forever excluded the idea of one continuable for life.—To W. S. SMITH. ii, 318. FORD ED., iv, 466. (P., 1787.) See CONSTITUTION (FEDERAL).

6881. PRESIDENT, Reelection.—I fear much the effects of the perpetual reeligibility of the President. But it is not thought of in America, and I have, therefore, no prospect of a change of that article [in the Constitution].—To WILLIAM STEPHENS SMITH. FORD ED., v, 3. (P., 1788.)

6882. —— ——. There is a strong feature in the new Constitution which I strongly dislike. That is the perpetual reeligibility of the President. Of this I expect no amendment at present because I do not see that anybody has objected to it on your side of the water. But it will be productive of cruel distress to our country, even in your day and mine. The importance to France and England, to have our government in the hands of a friend or a foe, will occasion their interference by money, and even by arms. Our President will be of much more consequence to them than a King of Poland. We must take care, however, that neither this, nor any other objection to the new form produces a schism in our Union.—To A. DONALD. ii, 355. (P., 1788.)

6883. —— ——. I dislike strongly [in the new Constitution] the perpetual reeligibility of the President. This, I fear, will make that an office for life, first, and then hereditary. * * * However, I shall hope that before there is danger of this change taking place in the office of President, the good sense and free spirit of our countrymen will make the changes necessary to prevent it.—To GENERAL WASHINGTON. ii, 375. FORD ED., v, 8. (P., 1788.)

6884. —— ——. Reeligibility makes the President an officer for life, and the disasters inseparable from an elective monarchy, render it preferable, if we cannot tread back that step, that we should go forward and take refuge in an hereditary one. Of the correction of this article [in the new Constitution], I entertain no present hope, because I find it has scarcely excited an objection in America. And if it does not take place ere long, it assuredly never will. The natural progress of things is for liberty to yield and government to gain ground. As yet our spirits are free. Our jealousy is only put to sleep by the unlimited confidence we all repose in the person to whom we all look as our President. After him inferior characters may perhaps succeed, and awaken us to the danger which his merit has led us into.—To E. CARRINGTON. ii, 404. FORD ED., v, 20. (P., 1788.)

6885. —— ——. The perpetual reeligibility of the same President will probably not be cured during the life of General Washington. His merit has blinded our country-

men to the danger of making so important an officer reeligible.—To WILLIAM CARMICHAEL. ii, 465. (P., Aug. 1788.)

6886. —— ——. The convention of Virginia annexed to their ratification of the new Constitution * * * propositions for specific alterations of the Constitution. Among these was one for rendering the President incapable of serving more than eight years in any term of sixteen. New York has followed the example of Virginia, * * * proposing amendments, * * * which concur as to the President, only proposing that he shall be incapable of being elected more than twice. But I own I should like better than either of these, what Luther Martin tells us was repeatedly voted and adhered to by the Federal Convention, and only altered about twelve days before their rising, when some members had gone off; to wit, that he should be elected for seven years, and incapable forever after.—To WILLIAM SHORT. ii, 480. FORD ED., v, 48. (P., 1788.)

6887. —— ——. I am glad to see that three States have at length considered the perpetual reeligibility of the President, as an article [of the new Constitution] which should be amended.—To JAMES MADISON. ii, 506. FORD ED., v, 53. (P., Nov. 1788.)

6888. —— ——. The general voice * * * has not authorized me to consider as a real defect [in the new Constitution] what I thought and still think one, the perpetual reeligibility of the President. But three States out of eleven, having declared against this, we must suppose we are wrong, according to the fundamental law of every society, the *lex majoris partis*, to which we are bound to submit. And should the majority change their opinion, and become sensible that this trait in their Constitution is wrong, I would wish it to remain uncorrected, as long as we can avail ourselves of the services of our great leader, whose talents and whose weight of character, I consider as peculiarly necessary to get the government so under way, as that it may afterwards be carried on by subordinate characters.—To DAVID HUMPHREYS. iii, 13. FORD ED., v, 90. (P., 1789.) See CONSTITUTION (FEDERAL).

6889. PRESIDENT, The senate and.— The transaction of business with foreign nations is Executive altogether. It belongs, then, to the head of that department, except as to such portions of it as are specially submitted to the Senate. Exceptions are to be construed strictly.—OPINION ON THE POWERS OF THE SENATE. vii, 465. FORD ED., v, 161. (1790.)

6890. —— ——. The Senate is not supposed by the Constitution to be acquainted with the concerns of the Executive department. It was not* intended that these should be communicated to them.—OPINION ON THE POWERS OF THE SENATE. vii, 466. FORD ED., v, 162. (1790.)

* " Not " is omitted in the FORD EDITION. It is in the original MS.—EDITOR.

6891. PRESIDENT, State executives and.—I have the honor to enclose you the draft of a letter to Governor Pinckney, and to observe, that I suppose it to be proper that there should, on fit occasions, be a direct correspondence between the President of the United States and the Governors of the States; and that it will probably be grateful to them to receive from the President, answers to the letters they address to him. The correspondence with them on ordinary business, may still be kept up by the Secretary of State, in his own name.—To PRESIDENT WASHINGTON. iii, 297. (1791.)

6892. PRESIDENT, State powers and. —As to the portions of power within each State assigned to the General Government, the President is as much the Executive of the State, as their particular governor is in relation to State powers.—To MR. GOODENOW. vii, 251. (M., 1822.)

6893. PRESIDENT, Subpœnas for.—As to our personal attendance at Richmond, I am persuaded the Court is sensible, that paramount duties to the nation at large control the obligation of compliance with their summons in [Burr's] case; as they would, should we receive a similar one, to attend the trials of Blennerhassett and others in the Mississippi Territory, those instituted at St. Louis and other places on the western waters, or at any place, other than the seat of government. To comply with such calls would leave the nation without an Executive branch, whose agency, nevertheless, is understood to be so constantly necessary, that it is the sole branch which the Constitution requires to be always in function. It could not then mean that it should be withdrawn from its station by any coordinate authority.—To GEORGE HAY. v, 97. FORD ED., ix, 57. (W., June 1807.)

6894. ——— ———. I did not see till last night the opinion of the Judge [Marshall] on the *subpœna duces tecum* against the President. Considering the question there as *coram non judice*, I did not read his argument with much attention. Yet I saw readily enough that, as is usual where an opinion is to be supported, right or wrong, he dwells much on smaller objections, and passes over those which are solid. Laying down the position generally, that all persons owe obedience to *subpœnas* he admits no exception unless it can be produced in his law books. But if the Constitution enjoins on a particular officer to be always engaged in a particular set of duties imposed on him, does not this supersede the general law, subjecting him to minor duties inconsistent with these? The Constitution enjoins his constant agency in the concerns of six millions of people. Is the law paramount to this, which calls on him on behalf of a single one? Let us apply the Judge's own doctrine to the case of himself and his brethren. The sheriff of Henrico summons him from the bench, to quell a riot somewhere in his county. The Federal judge is, by the general law, a part of the *posse* of the State sheriff. Would the judge abandon major duties to perform lesser ones? Again: the court of Orleans or Maine commands, by subpœnas, the attendance of all the judges of the Supreme Court. Would they abandon their posts as judges, and the interests of millions committed to them, to serve the purposes of a single individual? The leading principle of our Constitution is the independence of the Legislature, Executive, and Judiciary of each other, and none are more jealous of this than the Judiciary. But would the Executive be independent of the Judiciary, if he were subject to the *commands* of the latter, and to imprisonment for disobedience; if the several courts could bandy him from pillar to post, keep him constantly trudging from north to south and east to west, and withdraw him entirely from his constitutional duties? The intention of the Constitution, that each branch should be independent of the others, is further manifested by the means it has furnished to each, to protect itself from enterprises of force attempted on them by the others, and to none has it given more effectual or diversified means than to the Executive. Again, because ministers can go into a court in London as witnesses, without interruption to their executive duties, it is inferred that they would go to a court one thousand or one thousand five hundred miles off, and that ours are to be dragged from Maine to Orleans by every criminal who will swear that their testimony " may be of use to him ". The Judge says, " *it is apparent* that the President's duties as Chief Magistrate do not demand his whole time, and are not unremitting ". If he alludes to our annual retirement from the seat of government, during the sickly season, he should be told that such arrangements are made for carrying on the public business, at and between the several stations we take, that it goes on as unremittingly there, as if we were at the seat of government. I pass more hours in public business at Monticello than I do here, every day; and it is much more laborious, because all must be done in writing.—To GEORGE HAY. v, 103. FORD ED., ix, 59. (W., June 1807.)

6895. ——— ———. As I do not believe that the District Courts have a power of *commanding* the Executive government to abandon superior duties and attend on them, at whatever distance, I am unwilling, by any notice of the subpœna, to set a precedent which might sanction a proceeding so preposterous. I enclose you, therefore, a letter, public and for the court, covering substantially all they ought to desire.—To GEORGE HAY. v, 191. (M., Sep. 1807.)

6896. ——— ———. The enclosed letter is written in a spirit of conciliation and with the desire to avoid conflicts of authority between the high branches of the government, which would discredit it equally at home and abroad. That Burr and his counsel should wish to [struck out " divert the public attention from him to this battle of giants was to be "] convert his trial into a contest between the Judiciary and Executive authorities, was to be expected. But that the Chief Justice should lend himself to it, and take the first step to bring it on, was not expected. Nor can it be now believed that his prudence or good sense will permit him to press it. But should he, contrary to expectation, proceed to issue any process which should involve any act of force to be committed on the persons of the Executive or heads of departments, I must desire you to give me instant notice, and by express if you find that can be quicker done than by post; and that, moreover, you will advise the marshal on his conduct, as he will be critically placed between us. His safest way will be to take no part in the exercise of any act of force ordered in this case. The powers given to the Executive by the Constitu-

tion are sufficient to protect the other branches from Judiciary usurpation of preeminence, and every individual also from Judiciary vengeance. and the marshal may be assured of its effective exercise to cover him. I hope, however, that the discretion of the Chief Justice will suffer this question to lie over for the present, and at the ensuing session of the Legislature he may have means provided for giving to individuals the benefit of the testimony of the Executive functionaries in proper cases, without breaking up the Government. Will not the associate judge assume to divide his court and procure a truce at least in so critical a conjuncture? *—DRAFT OF A LETTER TO GEORGE HAY. FORD ED., ix, 62. (1807.)

6897. PRESIDENCY, Burden.—I part with the powers entrusted to me by my country, as with a burden of heavy bearing.—R. TO A. CITIZENS OF WASHINGTON. viii, 158. (March 4, 1809.)

6898. PRESIDENCY, Corruption and.—I sincerely wish we could see our government so secured as to depend less on the character of the person in whose hands it is trusted. Bad men will sometimes get in, and with such an immense patronage, may make great progress in corrupting the public mind and principles. This is a subject with which wisdom and patriotism should be occupied.—To MOSES ROBINSON. iv, 380. (W., March 1801.)

6899. PRESIDENCY, Electoral college.—The contrivance in the Constitution for marking the votes works badly, because it does not enounce precisely the true expression of the public will.—To TENCH COXE. iv, 345. FORD ED., vii, 474. (W., Dec. 1800.)

6900. ———. I have ever considered the constitutional mode of election ultimately by the Legislature, voting by States, as the most dangerous blot in our Constitution, and one which some unlucky chance will some day hit, and give us a pope and anti-pope. I looked, therefore, with anxiety to the amendment proposed by Colonel Taylor at the last session of Congress, which I thought would be a good substitute, if on an equal division of the electors, after a second appeal to them, the ultimate decision between the two highest had been given by it to the Legislature, voting per capita. But the States are now so numerous that I despair of ever seeing another amendment to the Constitution, although the innovations of time will certainly call, and now already call, for some, and especially the smaller States are so numerous as to render desperate every hope of obtaining a sufficient number of them in favor of "Phocion's" proposition. Another general convention can alone relieve us. What, then, is the best palliative of the evil in the meantime? Another short question points to the answer. Would we rather the choice should be made by the Legislature voting in Congress by States, or in caucus per capita? The remedy is indeed bad, but the disease

* A note in the FORD EDITION says this letter may have never been sent.—EDITOR.

worse.—To GEORGE HAY. FORD ED., x, 264. (M., Aug. 1823.)

6901. PRESIDENCY, Expenses of.—I had hoped to keep the expenses of my office within the limits of its salary. so as to apply my private income entirely to the improvement and enlargement of my estate; but I have not been able to do it.—To REV. CHARLES CLAY. v, 27. FORD ED., ix, 6. (W., 1807.)

6902. PRESIDENCY, Jefferson, Adams and.—My letters inform me that Mr. Adams speaks of me with * * * satisfaction in the prospect of administering the government in concurrence with me. * * * If by that he meant the Executive Cabinet, both *duty* and *inclination* will shut that door to me. I cannot have a wish to see the scenes of 1793 revived as to myself, and to descend daily into the arena. like a gladiator, to suffer martyrdom in every conflict. As to duty, the Constitution will know me only as the member of a legislative body; and its principle is, that of a separation of Legislative, Executive, and Judiciary functions, except in cases specified. If this principle be not expressed in direct terms, yet it is clearly the spirit of the Constitution, and it ought to be so commented and acted on by every friend to free government.—To MR. MADISON. iv, 161. FORD ED., vii. 107. (January 1797.)

6903. ———. No arguments were wanting to reconcile me to a relinquishment of the first office, or *acquiescence under* the second. As to the first it was impossible that a more solid unwillingness, settled on full calculation, could have existed in any man's mind, short of the degree of absolute refusal. The only view on which I would have gone into it for awhile was to put our vessel on her republican tack, before she should be thrown too much to leeward of her true principles. As to the second, it is the only office in the world which I cannot decide in my own mind, whether I had rather have it or not have it. Pride does not enter into the estimate. For I think with the Romans of old, that the general of to-day should be a common soldier to-morrow if necessary.—To JAMES MADISON. iv, 155. FORD ED., vii, 98. (Jan. 1797.)

6904. ———. If Mr. Adams could be induced to administer the government on its true principles, quitting his bias for an English constitution. it would be worthy consideration whether it would not be for the public good. to come to a good understanding with him as to his future elections. He is the only sure barrier against Hamilton's getting in.—To JAMES MADISON. iv, 155. FORD ED., vii, 99. (Jan. 1797.)

6905. ———. As to Mr. Adams. particularly, I could have no feelings which would revolt at being placed in a secondary station to him. I am his junior in life, was his junior in Congress, his junior in the diplomatic line, his junior lately in the civil government.—To JAMES MADISON. iv, 155. FORD ED., vii, 99. (Jan. 1797.) See ADAMS, JOHN.

6906. PRESIDENCY, Jefferson, Madison and.—I do not see in the minds of those with whom I converse, a greater affliction than the fear of your retirement; but this must not be, unless to a more splendid and a more efficacious post. There I should rejoice to see you; I hope I may say, I shall rejoice to see you. I have long had much in my mind to say to you on that subject. But double delicacies have kept me silent. I ought perhaps to say, while I would not give up my own retirement for the empire of the universe, how I can justify wishing one whose happiness I have so much at heart as yours, to take the front of the battle which is fighting for my security. This would be easy enough to be done, but not at the heel of a lengthy epistle.—To JAMES MADISON. iv, 112. FORD ED., vi, 519. (M., Dec. 1794.)

6907. ———. In my letter * * * I expressed my hope of the only change of position I ever wished to see you make, and I expressed it with entire sincerity, because there is not another person in the United States, who being placed at the helm of our affairs, my mind would be so completely at rest for the fortune of our political bark. The wish, too, was pure, and unmixed with anything respecting myself personally. For as to myself, the subject had been thoroughly weighed and decided on, and my retirement from office had been meant from all office high or low, without exception. I can say, too, with truth, that the subject had not been presented to my mind by any vanity of my own. I know myself and my fellow citizens too well to have ever thought of it. But the idea was forced upon me by continual insinuations in the public papers, while I was in office. As all these came from a hostile quarter, I knew that their object was to poison the public mind as to my motives, when they were not able to charge me with facts. But the idea being once presented to me, my own quiet required that I should face it and examine it. I did so thoroughly, and had no difficulty to see that every reason which had determined me to retire from the office I then held, operated more strongly against that which was insinuated to be my object. I decided then on those general grounds which could alone be present to my mind at the time, that is to say, reputation, tranquility, labor; for as to public duty, it could not be a topic of consideration in my case. If these general considerations were sufficient to ground a firm resolution never to permit myself to think of the office, or to be thought of for it, the special ones which have supervened on my retirement, still more insuperably bar the door to it. My health is entirely broken down within the last eight months; my age requires that I should place my affairs in a clear state; these are sound if taken care of but capable of considerable dangers if longer neglected; and above all things, the delights I feel in the society of

my family, and the agricultural pursuits in which I am so eagerly engaged. The little spice of ambition which I had in my younger days has long since evaporated, and I set still less store by a posthumous than present name. In stating to you the heads of reasons which have produced my determination, I do not mean an opening for future discussion, or that I may be reasoned out of it. The question is forever closed with me; my sole object is to avail myself of the first opening ever given me from a friendly quarter (and I could not with decency do it before), of preventing any division or loss of votes, which might be fatal to the republican interest. If that has any chance of prevailing, it must be by avoiding the loss of a single vote, and by concentrating all its strength on one object. Who this should be, is a question I can more freely discuss with anybody than yourself. In this I feel painfully the loss of Monroe. Had he been here, I should have been at no loss for a channel through which to make myself understood, if I have been misunderstood by anybody through the instrumentality of Mr. Fenno and his abettors.—To JAMES MADISON. iv, 116. FORD ED., vii, 8. (M., April 1795.)

6908. ——— ———. I think our foreign affairs never wore so gloomy an aspect since the year 1783. Let those come to the helm who think they can steer clear of the difficulties. I have no confidence in myself for the undertaking.—To JAMES MADISON. iv, 150. FORD ED., vii, 92. (M., Dec. 1796.)

6909. ——— ———. The honeymoon would be as short in that case [election to the Presidency] as in any other, and its moments of ecstacy would be ransomed by years of torment and hatred.—To EDWARD RUTLEDGE. iv, 152. FORD ED., vii, 93. (M., Dec. 1796.)

6910. ——— ———. You, who know me, know that my private gratifications would be most indulged by that issue, which should leave me most at home. If anything supersedes this propensity, it is merely the desire to see this government brought back to its republican principles.—To JAMES MONROE. iv, 309. FORD ED., vii, 402. (Pa., Jan. 1800.)

6911. PRESIDENCY, Misery in.—The second office of the* government is honorable and easy; the first is but a splendid misery.—To ELBRIDGE GERRY. iv, 171. FORD ED., vii, 120. (Pa., 1797.)

6912. PRESIDENCY, Reelection to.—I sincerely regret that the unbounded calumnies of the federal party have obliged me to throw myself on the verdict of my country for trial, my great desire having been to retire, at the end of the present term, to a life of tranquillity; and it was my decided purpose when I entered into office. They force my continuance. If we can keep the vessel of State as steadily in her course for another four years, my earthly purposes will be accomplished, and I shall be free to enjoy

* "This" government in FORD EDITION.—EDITOR.

* * * my family, my farm, and my books. —To ELBRIDGE GERRY. iv, 536. FORD ED., viii, 297. (W., March 1804.)

6913. PRESIDENCY, Reputation and. —No man will ever bring out of the presidency the reputation which carries him into it.—To EDWARD RUTLEDGE. iv, 152. FORD ED., vii, 93. (M., 1796.)

6914. —— ——. I have learned to expect that it will rarely fall to the lot of imperfect man to retire from this station with the reputation and the favor which bring him into it.—FIRST INAUGURAL ADDRESS. viii, 5. FORD ED., viii, 5. (1801.)

6915. PRESIDENCY, Tired of the.—I am tired of an office where I can do no more good than many others, who would be glad to be employed in it. To myself, personally, it brings nothing but unceasing drudgery and daily loss of friends. Every office becoming vacant, every appointment made, *me donne un ingrat, et cent ennemis.* My only consolation is in the belief that my fellow citizens at large will give me credit for good intentions.—To JOHN DICKINSON. v. 31. FORD ED., ix, 10. (W., Jan. 1807.)

6916. PRESIDENCY, Unattractive.—Neither the splendor, nor the power, nor the difficulties, nor the fame or defamation, as may happen, attached to the First Magistracy, have any attractions for me.—To JAMES SULLIVAN. iv, 168. FORD ED., vii, 117. (M., 1797.)

— **PRESS (Copying).**—See COPYING PRESS and INVENTIONS.

6917. PRESS (Freedom of the), Abolished.—The press, the only tocsin of a nation, is completely silenced in France.—To THOMAS COOPER. iv, 452. FORD ED., viii, 177. (W., Nov. 1802.)

6918. PRESS (Freedom of the), Abused. —The firmness with which the people have withstood the late abuses of the press, the discernment they have manifested between truth and falsehood, show that they may safely be trusted to hear everything true and false, and to form a correct judgment between them.—To JUDGE TYLER. iv, 549. (W., 1804.)

— **PRESS (Freedom of the), Bill of Rights and.**—See BILL OF RIGHTS.

6919. PRESS (Freedom of the), Control of.—While we deny that Congress have a right to control the freedom of the press, we have ever asserted the right of the States, and their exclusive right, to do so. They have accordingly, all of them, made provisions for punishing slander. * * * In general, the State laws appear to have made the presses responsible for slander as far as is consistent with its useful freedom. In those States where they do not admit even the truth of allegations to protect the printer, they have gone too far.—To MRS. JOHN ADAMS. iv, 561. FORD ED., viii, 311. (M., 1804.)

6920. PRESS (Freedom of the), The Constitution and.—It is true as a general principle, and is also expressly declared by one of the amendments to the Constitution, that "the powers not delegated to the United States by the Constitution, nor prohibited by it to the States, are reserved to the States respectively, or to the people; and * * * no power over the freedom of religion, freedom of speech, or freedom of the press being delegated to the United States by the Constitution, nor prohibited by it to the States, all lawful powers respecting the same did of right remain, and were reserved to the States or the people. * * * Thus was manifested their determination to retain to themselves the right of judging how far the licentiousness of speech, and of the press, may be abridged without lessening their useful freedom, and how far those abuses which cannot be separated from their use should be tolerated, rather than the use be destroyed. And thus also they guarded against all abridgment by the United States of the freedom of religious opinions and exercises, and retained to themselves the right of protecting the same, as this State [Kentucky], by a law passed on the general demand of its citizens, had already protected them from all human restraint or interference. * * * In addition to this general principle and express declaration, another and more special provision has been made by one of the amendments to the Constitution, which expressly declares, that "Congress shall make no law respecting an establishment of religion, or prohibiting the free exercise thereof, or abridging the freedom of speech, or of the press", thereby guarding in the same sentence, and under the same words, the freedom of religion, of speech and of the press; insomuch, that whatever violates either, throws down the sanctuary which covers the others, and that libels, falsehood, and defamation, equally with heresy and false religion, are withheld from the cognizance of Federal tribunals. * * * Therefore, the act of Congress of the United States passed on the 14th day of July, 1798, intituled, "An Act in addition to the act intituled 'An Act for the punishment of certain crimes against the United States'", which does abridge the freedom of the press, is not law, but is altogether void, and of no force.—KENTUCKY RESOLUTIONS. ix, 465. FORD ED., vii, 294. (1798.)

6921. —— ——. I am for freedom of the press, and against all violations of the Constitution to silence by force and not by reason the complaints or criticisms, just or unjust, of our citizens against the conduct of their agents.—To ELBRIDGE GERRY. iv, 269. FORD ED., vii, 328. (Pa., 1799.)

6922. PRESS (Freedom of the), Government and.—No government ought to be without censors; and where the press is free, no one ever will.—To PRESIDENT WASHINGTON. iii, 467. FORD ED., vi, 108. (M., 1792.)

6923. —— ——. Conscious that there was not a *truth* on earth which I feared should be known, I have lent myself willingly as the subject of a great experiment, which was to prove that an administration, conducting itself with integrity and common understanding, cannot be battered down, even by the falsehoods of a licentious press, and consequently still less by the press, as restrained within the legal and wholesome limits of truth. This experiment was wanting for the world to demonstrate the falsehood of the pretext that freedom of the press is incompatible with orderly government. I have never, therefore, even contradicted the thousands of calumnies so industriously propagated against myself. But the fact being once established, that the press is impotent when it abandons itself to falsehood. I leave to others to restore it to its strength, by recalling it within the pale of truth. Within that, it is a noble institution, equally the friend of science and of civil liberty.—To THOMAS SEYMOUR. v, 43. FORD ED., ix, 30. (W., Feb. 1807.)

6924. PRESS (Freedom of the), Invasions of.—There are rights which it is useless to surrender to the government, and which governments have yet always been found to invade. [Among] are the rights of thinking and publishing our thoughts by * * * writing.—To DAVID HUMPHREYS. iii, 13. FORD ED., v, 89. (P., 1789.)

6925. PRESS (Freedom of the), Libels.—Printing presses shall be subject to no other restraint than liableness to legal prosecution for false facts printed and published.—PROPOSED CONSTITUTION FOR VIRGINIA. viii, 452. FORD ED., iii, 332. (1783.)

6926. ——— ———. Printing presses shall be free except as to false facts published maliciously, either to injure the reputation of another, whether followed by pecuniary damages or not, or to expose him to the punishment of the law.—NOTES FOR A CONSTITUTION. FORD ED., vi, 521. (1794.)

6927. PRESS (Freedom of the), Liberty and.—Our liberty depends on the freedom of the press, and that cannot be limited without being lost.—To DR. JAMES CURRIE. FORD ED., iv, 132. (P., 1786.)

6928. ——— ———. The liberty of speaking and writing guards our other liberties.—REPLY TO ADDRESS. viii, 129. (1808.)

6929. PRESS (Freedom of the), Mankind and.—The press is the best instrument for enlightening the mind of man, and improving him as a rational, moral, and social being.—To M. CORAY. vii, 324. (M., 1823.)

6930. PRESS (Freedom of the), Principle of government.—Freedom of the press I deem [one of the] essential principles of our government and, consequently, [one] which ought to shape its administration.—FIRST INAUGURAL ADDRESS. viii, 4. FORD ED., viii, 5. (1801.)

6931. ——— ———. There are certain principles in which the constitutions of our several States all agree, and which all cherish

as vitally essential to the protection of the life, liberty, property and safety of the citizen. [One is] Freedom of the Press, subject only to liability for personal injuries.—To M. CORAY. vii, 323. (M., 1823.)

6932. PRESS (Freedom of the), Private injury.—Printing presses shall be free, except so far as, by commission of private injury, cause may be given of private action.—PROPOSED VA. CONSTITUTION. FORD ED., ii, 27. (June 1776.)

6933. PRESS (Freedom of the), Reform through.—This formidable censor of the public functionaries, by arraigning them at the tribunal of public opinion, produces reform peaceably, which must otherwise be done by revolution.—To M. CORAY. vii, 324. (M., 1823.)

6934. PRESS (Freedom of the), Safety in.—Where the press is free, and every man able to read, all is safe.—To CHARLES YANCEY. vi, 517. FORD ED., x, 4. (M., 1816.)

6935. PRESS (Freedom of the), Security in.—The only security of all is in a free press. The force of public opinion cannot be resisted, when permitted freely to be expressed. The agitation it produces must be submitted to. It is necessary to keep the waters pure.—To MARQUIS LAFAYETTE. vii, 325. FORD ED., x, 280. (M., 1823.)

6936. PRESS (Freedom of the), Shackled.—Nor should we wonder at * * * [the] pressure [for a fixed constitution in 1788-9] when we consider the monstrous abuses of power under which * * * [the French] people were ground to powder; when we pass in review the shackles * * * on the freedom of the press by the Censure.—AUTOBIOGRAPHY. i, 86. FORD ED., i, 118. (1821.) See EDITORS, NEWSPAPERS, and PUBLICITY.

6937. PRICE, Basis of.—The adequate price of a thing depends on the capital and labor necessary to produce it. In the term *capital,* I mean to include science, because capital as well as labor has been employed to acquire it. Two things requiring the same capital and labor, should be of the same price. If a gallon of wine requires for its production the same capital and labor with a bushel of wheat, they should be expressed by the same price, derived from the application of a common measure to them.—To J. W. EPPES. vi, 233. FORD ED., ix, 406. (M., 1813.)

6938. PRICE OF WHEAT.—The average price of wheat on the continent of Europe, at the commencement of its present war with England, was about a French crown, of one hundred and ten cents, the bushel. With us it was one hundred cents, and consequently we could send it there in competition with their own. That ordinary price has now doubled with us, and more than doubled in England; and although a part of this augmentation may proceed from the war demand, yet from the extraordinary nominal rise in the prices of land and labor here, both of which have nearly doubled in that period, and are still rising with every new bank, it is evident that were a general peace to take place to-morrow, and time allowed for the reestablishment of commerce, justice and order, we could not raise wheat for much less than two dollars, while the continent of Europe, having no paper circulation, and that of its specie not being augmented, would raise it at their former price of one hundred and ten cents. It follows, then, that with our redundancy of paper, we cannot, after peace, send a bushel of wheat to Europe, unless extraordinary circumstances double its price in particular places. and that then the exporting countries of Europe could undersell us.—To J. W. Eppes. vi, 242. Ford ed., ix, 414. (M., Nov. 1813.)

6939. PRIESTLEY (Joseph), Author.— The papers of political arithmetic in your pamphlets * * * are the most precious gifts that can be made us; for we are running navigation mad, and commerce mad, and navy mad, which is worst of all. * * * From the "*Porcupines*" of our country you will receive no thanks; but the great mass of our nation will edify and thank you.—To Joseph Priestley. iv, 311. Ford ed., vii, 406. (Pa., Jan. 1800.) See Government, Works on.

6940. PRIESTLEY (Joseph), Dupont and.— I have a letter from Mr. Dupont [de Nemours], since his arrival at New York. * * * How much it would delight me if a visit from you at the same time, were to show us two such illustrious foreigners embracing each other in my country, as the asylum for whatever is great and good.—To Joseph Priestley. iv, 317. Ford ed., vii, 415. (Pa., 1800.)

6941. PRIESTLEY (Joseph), Persecuted.— How deeply have I been chagrined and mortified at the persecutions which fanaticism and monarchy have excited against you, even here. At first I believed it was merely a continuance of the English persecution. But I observe that on the demise of "*Porcupine*", and division of his inheritance between Fenno and Brown, the latter (though succeeding only to the *federal* portion of Porcupinism, not the *Anglican*, which is Fenno's part) serves up for the palate of his sect, dishes of abuse against you as high seasoned as "*Porcupine's*" were. You have sinned against church and king, and can, therefore, never be forgiven.—To Joseph Priestley. iv, 311. Ford ed., vii, 406. (Pa., Jan. 1800.)

6942. PRIESTLEY (Joseph), Revered. — I revered the character of no man living more than his.—To Thomas Cooper. v, 182. (M., 1807.)

6943. PRIESTLEY (Joseph), Services. — No man living had a more affectionate respect for Dr. Priestley. In religion, in politics in physics, no man has rendered more service.—To Thomas Cooper. v, 121. Ford ed., ix, 102. (W., 1807.)

6944. PRIESTLEY (Joseph), Welcome to.— Yours is one of the few lives precious to mankind, and for the continuance of which every thinking man is solicitous. Bigots may be an exception. What an effort, my dear sir, of bigotry in politics and religion have we gone through. The barbarians really flattered themselves they should be able to bring back the times of Vandalism. when ignorance put everything into the hands of power and priestcraft. All advances in science were proscribed as innovations. They pretended to praise and encourage education, but it was to be the education of our ancestors. We were to look backwards, not forwards, for improvement: the President himself [John Adams] declaring, in one of his answers to addresses, that we were

never to expect to go beyond them in real science. This was the real ground of all the attacks on you. * * * Our countrymen have recovered from the alarm into which art and industry had thrown them; science and honesty are replaced on their high ground; and you, as their great apostle, are on its pinnacle. It is with heartfelt satisfaction that, in the first moments of my public action, I can hail you with welcome to our land, tender to you the homage of its respect and esteem, cover you under the protection of those laws which were made for the wise and good like you, and disclaim the legitimacy of that libel on legislation, which under the form of a law was for some time placed among them.*—To Joseph Priestley. iv, 373. Ford ed., viii, 21. (W., March 1801.)

6945. PRIMOGENITURE, Abolition of law.— As the law of Descents, and the Criminal law fell, of course, within my portion [in the revision of the Virginia Code], I wished the Committee to settle the leading principles of these, as a guide for me in framing them; and, with respect to the first, I proposed to abolish the law of primogeniture, and to make real estate descendible in parcenary to the next of kin, as personal property is, by the statute of distribution. Mr. Pendleton wished to preserve the right of primogeniture, but seeing at once that that could not prevail, he proposed we should adopt the Hebrew principle, and give a double portion to the elder son. I observed that if the eldest son could eat twice as much, or do double work, it might be a natural evidence of his right to a double portion; but. being on a par in his powers and wants with his brothers and sisters, he should be on a par also in the partition of the patrimony; and such was the decision of the other members. †—Autobiography. i. 43. Ford ed., i, 59. (1821.)

6946. PRIMOGENITURE, Feudal and unnatural.— The abolition of primogeniture, and equal partition of inheritances, removed the feudal and unnatural distinctions which made one member of every family rich, and all the rest poor, substituting equal partition, the best of all Agrarian laws. ‡—Autobiography. i. 49. Ford ed., i, 69. (M., 1821.) See Entails.

* Jefferson wrote on the margin "Alien Law".— Editor.
† The preamble to this great law is as follows: " Whereas, the perpetuation of property in certain families, by means of gifts made to them in fee taille, is contrary to good policy, tends to deceive fair traders, who give credit on the visible possession of such estates, discourages the holders thereof from taking care and improving the same, and sometimes does injury to the morals of youth, by rendering them independent of, and disobedient to their parents; and whereas, the former method of docking such estates taille, by special act of Assembly, formed for every particular case, employed very much of the time of the Legislature, and the same, as well as the method of defeating such estates, when of small value, was burthensome to the public, and also to individuals. Be it therefore enacted."—Editor.
‡ It was an audacious move. From generation to generation lands and slaves—almost the only valuable kind of property in Virginia—had been handed down protected against creditors, even against the very extravagance of spendthrift owners; and it was largely by this means that the quasi-nobility of the colony had succeeded in establishing and maintaining itself. A great groan seemed to go up from all respectable society at the terrible suggestion of Jefferson, a suggestion daringly cast before an Assembly thickly sprinkled with influential delegates strongly bound by family ties and self-interest to defend the present system. * * * Thus was a great social revolution wrought in a few months by one man. * * * But his brilliant triumph cost him a price. That distinguished class, whose existence as

6947. PRINCIPLE, Departure from.—A departure from principle in one instance becomes a precedent for a second; that second for a third; and so on, till the bulk of the society is reduced to be mere automatons of misery, to have no sensibilities left but for sin and suffering. Then begins, indeed, the *bellum omnium in omnia*, which some philosophers observing to be so general in this world, have mistaken it for the natural, instead of the abusive state of man. And the forehorse of this frightful team is public debt. Taxation follows that, and in its train wretchedness and oppression.—To SAMUEL KERCHIVAL. vii, 14. FORD ED., x, 42. (M., 1816.)

6948. PRINCIPLE, Doubt and.—If doubtful, we should follow principle.—To SAMUEL KERCHIVAL. vii, 12. FORD ED., x, 40. (M., 1816.)

6949. PRINCIPLE, A guide.—Principle will in * * * most * * * cases open the way for us to correct conclusion.—To SAMUEL KERCHIVAL. vii, 36. FORD ED., x, 45. (M., 1816.)

6950. PRINCIPLE, Opinion and.—Every difference of opinion is not a difference of principle. We have called by different names brethren of the same principle. We are all republicans: we are all federalists.—FIRST INAUGURAL ADDRESS. viii, 2. FORD ED., viii, 3. (1801.)

6951. PRINCIPLE, Republican vs. Monarchical.—The contests of that day [1793-1800] were contests of principle, between the advocates of republican and those of kingly government, and had not the former made the efforts they did, our government would have been, even at this early day (1818) a very different thing from what the successful issue of those efforts have made it.—THE ANAS. ix, 88. FORD ED., i, 156. (1818.)

6952. PRINCIPLES, Adherence to.—An adherence to fundamental principles is the most likely way to save both time and disagreement [between legislative bodies]; and [as] a departure from them may at some time or other be drawn into precedent for dangerous innovations. * * * it is better for both Houses, and for those by whom they are entrusted, to correct error while new, and before it becomes inveterate by habit and custom.—CONFERENCE REPORT. FORD ED., ii, 135. (1777.)

6953. ——— ———. I am happy in your approbation of the principles I avowed on entering on the government. Ingenious minds, availing themselves of the imperfections of language, have tortured the expressions out of their plain meaning in order to infer departures from them in practice. If revealed

language has not been able to guard itself against misinterpretations I could not expect it. But if an administration, "quadrating with the obvious import of my language, can conciliate the affections of my opposers", I will merit that conciliation.—To THE REV. ISAAC STORY. iv, 423. FORD ED., viii, 107. (W., 1802.)

6954. ——— ———. On taking this station [Presidency] on a former occasion, I declared the principles on which I believed it my duty to administer the affairs of our commonwealth. My conscience tells me that I have, on every occasion, acted up to that declaration, according to its obvious import, and to the understanding of every candid mind.—SECOND INAUGURAL ADDRESS. viii, 40. FORD ED., viii, 342. (1805.)

6955. ——— ———. Continue to go straight forward, pursuing always that which is right, as the only clue which can lead us out of the labyrinth.—To CÆSAR A. RODNEY. v, 501. FORD ED., ix, 272. (M., 1810.)

6956. ——— ———. Lay down true principles, and adhere to them inflexibly. Do not be frightened into their surrender by the alarms of the timid, or the croakings of wealth against the ascendency of the people.—To SAMUEL KERCHIVAL. vii, 11. FORD ED., x, 39. (M., 1816.)

6957. PRINCIPLES, Application of.—When principles are well understood their application is less embarrassing.—To GOUVERNEUR MORRIS. FORD ED., vi, 149. (Pa., 1792.)

6958. PRINCIPLES, Avowal of.—I know my own principles to be pure, and therefore am not ashamed of them. On the contrary, I wish them known, and therefore willingly express them to every one. They are the same I have acted on from the year 1775 to this day, and are the same, I am sure, with those of the great body of the American people. I only wish the real principles of those who censure mine were also known.—To SAMUEL SMITH. iv, 254. FORD ED., vii, 277. (M., 1798.)

6959. ——— ———. I make no secret of my principles; on the contrary, I wish them known to avoid the imputation of those which are not mine.—To JEREMIAH MOOR. FORD ED., vii, 454. (M., Aug. 1800.)

6960. PRINCIPLES, Constitutional.—A part of the Union having held on to the principles of the Constitution, time has been given to the States to recover from the temporary frenzy into which they had been decoyed, to rally round the Constitution, and to rescue it from the destruction with which it had been threatened even at their own hands.—To GIDEON GRANGER. iv, 332. FORD ED., vii, 452. (M., 1800.)

6961. PRINCIPLES, Independence and.—The contest which began with us, which ushered in the dawn of our national existence and led us through various and trying scenes, was for everything dear to free-born man.

The principles on which we engaged, of which the charter of our independence is the record, were sanctioned by the laws of our being, and we but obeyed them in pursuing undeviatingly the course they called for. It issued finally in that inestimable state of freedom which alone can ensure to man the enjoyment of his equal rights.—R. TO A. GEORGETOWN REPUBLICANS. viii, 159. (1809.)

6962. PRINCIPLES, Jefferson's in 1799.—In confutation of * * * all future calumnies, by way of anticipation, I shall make to you a profession of my political faith: in confidence that you will consider every future imputation on me of a contrary complexion as bearing on its front the mark of falsity and calumny. I do then, with sincere zeal, wish an inviolable preservation of our Federal Constitution, according to the true sense in which it was adopted by the States: that in which it was advocated by its friends, and not that which its enemies apprehended, who therefore became its enemies; and I am opposed to the monarchizing its features by the forms of its administration, with a view to conciliate a first transition to a President and Senate for life, and from that to an hereditary tenure of these offices, and thus to worm out the elective principle. I am for preserving to the States the powers not yielded by them to the Union, and to the Legislature of the Union its constitutional share in the division of powers; and I am not for transferring all the powers of the States to the General Government, and all those of that Government to the Executive branch. I am for a government rigorously frugal and simple, applying all the possible savings of the public revenue to the discharge of the national debt; and not for a multiplication of officers and salaries merely to make partizans, and for increasing, by every device, the public debt, on the principle of its being a public blessing. I am for relying for internal defence on our militia solely, till actual invasion, and for such a naval force only as may protect our coasts and harbors from such depredations as we have experienced; and not for a standing army in time of peace, which may overawe the public sentiment; nor for a navy, which, by its own expenses and the eternal wars in which it will implicate us, will grind us with public burdens and sink us under them. I am for free commerce with all nations; political connection with none; and little or no diplomatic establishment. And I am not for linking ourselves by new treaties with the quarrels of Europe; entering that field of slaughter to preserve their balance, or joining in the confederacy of kings to war against the principles of liberty. I am for freedom of religion, and against all manœuvres to bring about a legal ascendency of one sect over another; for freedom of the press, and against all violations of the Constitution to silence by force and not by reason the complaints or criticisms, just or unjust, of our citizens against the conduct of their agents. And I am for encouraging the progress of

science in all its branches; and not for raising a hue and cry against the sacred name of philosophy; for awing the human mind by stories of raw-head and bloody bones to a distrust of its own vision, and to repose implicitly on that of others; to go backwards instead of forwards to look for improvement; to believe that government, religion, morality, and every other science were in the highest perfection in the ages of the darkest ignorance, and that nothing can ever be devised more perfect than what was established by our forefathers. To these I will add, that I was a sincere well-wisher to the success of the French Revolution, and still wish it may end in the establishment of a free and well-ordered republic; but I have not been insensible under the atrocious depredations they have committed on our commerce. The first object of my heart is my country. In that is embarked my family, my fortune, and my own existence. I have not one farthing of interest, nor one fibre of attachment out of it, nor a single motive of preference of any one nation to another, but in proportion as they are more or less friendly to us. * * * These are my principles. They are unquestionably the principles of the great body of our fellow-citizens, and I know there is not one of them which is not yours also. In truth, we never differed but on one ground, the Funding System; and as, from the moment of its being adopted by the constituted authorities, I became religiously principled in the sacred discharge of it to the uttermost farthing, we are united now even on that single ground of difference.*—To ELBRIDGE GERRY. iv, 267. FORD ED., vii, 327. (Pa., January 1799.) See ADMINISTRATION; also INAUGURAL ADDRESSES, in APPENDIX.

6963. —— ——. In the maintenance of * * * [our] principles * * * I verily believe the future happiness of our country essentially depends.—To SPENCER ROANE. vii, 136. FORD ED., x, 143. (P.F., 1819.)

6964. PRINCIPLES, Not men.—Two facts are certainly as true as irreconcilable. The people of Massachusetts love economy and freedom, civil and religious. The present legislative and executive functionaries endeavor to practice economy, and to strengthen civil and religious freedom. Yet they are disapproved by the people of Massachusetts. It cannot be that these had rather give up principles than men. However the riddle is to be solved, our duty is plain, to administer their interests faithfully, and to overcome evil with good.—To JOHN BACON. FORD ED., viii, 228. (W., April 1803.)

6965. —— ——. If our fellow citizens * * * will sacrifice favoritism towards men for the preservation of principle, we

---

* Jefferson differed from the time-serving politician, because he staked his individual success upon the success of what he deemed intrinsically right principles. He differed even from the statesman who acts conscientiously upon every measure, inasmuch as, beyond devising specific measures, he set forth a broad faith or religion in statesmanship, making special measures only single blocks in the wide pavement of his road.—MORSE'S *Life of Jefferson.*

may hope that no divisions will again endanger a degeneracy in our government.—To RICHARD M. JOHNSON. v, 526. (1808.)

6966. PRINCIPLES, Political schism and.—We ought not to schismatize on either men or measures. Principles alone can justify that.—To WILLIAM DUANE. v, 577. FORD ED., ix, 313. (M., 1811.)

6967. PRINCIPLES, Practice and.—True wisdom does not lie in mere practice without principle.—To JOHN ADAMS. vii, 39. (M., 1816.)

6968. PRINCIPLES, Toleration of.—It is time enough, for the rightful purposes of civil government, for its officers to interfere when principles break out into overt acts against peace and good order.—STATUTE OF RELIGIOUS FREEDOM. FORD ED., ii, 239. (1779.)

6969. PRINTING, Preservative.—The art of printing secures us against the retrogradation of reason and information; the examples of its safe and wholesome guidance in government, which will be exhibited through the wide-spread regions of the American continent, will obliterate, in time, the impressions left by the abortive experiment of France.— To M. PAGANEL. v, 582. (M., 1811.)

6970. PRINTING, Progress in.—Among the arts which have made great progress among us is that of printing. Heretofore, we imported our books, and with them much political principle from England. We now print a great deal, and shall soon supply ourselves with most of the books of considerable demand. But the foundation of printing, you know, is the type-foundry, and a material essential to that is antimony. Unfortunately that mineral is not among those as yet found in the United States, and the difficulty and dearness of getting it from England, will force us to discontinue our type-founderies, and resort to her again for our books, unless some new source of supply can be found.—To DUPONT DE NEMOURS. v, 457. (M., June 1809.) See EDITORS, NEWSPAPERS and PRESS.

6971. PRINTING vs. BARBARISM.—We have seen, indeed, once within the records of history, a complete eclipse of the human mind continuing for centuries. And this, too, by swarms of the same northern barbarians, conquering and taking possession of the countries and governments of the civilized world. Should this be again attempted, should the same northern hordes, allured again by the corn, wine, and oil of the south, be able again to settle their swarms in the countries of their growth, the art of printing alone, and the vast dissemination of books, will maintain the mind where it is, and raise the conquering ruffians to the level of the conquered, instead of degrading these to that of their conquerors. And even should the cloud of barbarism and despotism again obscure the science and liberties of Europe, this country remains to preserve and restore light and liberty to them.—To JOHN ADAMS. vii 218. (M., 1821.)

6972. PRISON, Breaking.—It is not only vain, but wicked, in a legislator to frame laws in opposition to the laws of nature, and to arm them with the terrors of death. This is truly creating crimes in order to punish them. The law of nature impels every one to escape from confinement; it should not, therefore, be subjected to punishment. Let the legislator restrain his criminal by walls, not by parchment. As to strangers breaking prison to enlarge an offender, they should, and may be fairly considered as accessories after the fact.—NOTE ON CRIMES BILL. i, 159. FORD ED., ii, 218. (1779.)

— **PRISON, Plan of.**—See ARCHITECTURE.

— **PRISONERS OF WAR.**—See WAR.

6973. PRIVACY, Indispensable.—A room to myself, if it be but a barrack, is indispensable. *—To JAMES MADISON. FORD ED., iii, 339. (M., 1783.)

6974. PRIVATE LIFE, Contentment.—I thank you * * * for your felicitations on my present quiet. The difference of my present and past situation is such as to leave me nothing to regret, but that my retirement has been postponed four years too long. The principles on which I calculated the value of life, are entirely in favor of my present course.—To JOHN ADAMS. iv, 103. FORD ED., vi, 504. (M., April 1794.)

6975. ——. As to the concerns of my own country, I leave them willingly and safely to those who will have a longer interest in cherishing them. My books, my family, my friends, and my farm, furnish more than enough to occupy me the remainder of my life, and of that tranquil occupation most analogous to my physical and moral constitution.—To M. ODIT. iv, 123. (M., Oct. 1795.)

6976. ——. My farm, my family, my books and my building, give me more pleasure than any public office would, and, especially, one which would keep me constantly from them.—To MR. VOLNEY. iv, 158. (M., 1797.)

6977. PRIVATE LIFE, Freedom of.—I am now a private man, free to express my feelings, and their expression will be estimated at neither more nor less than they weigh, to wit, the expressions of a private man. Your struggles for liberty keep alive the only sparks of sensation which public affairs now excite in me.—To M. ODIT. iv, 123. (M., Oct. 1795.)

6978. PRIVATE LIFE, Happiness.—The happiness of the domestic fireside is the first boon of heaven; and it is well it is so, since it is that which is the lot of the mass of mankind.—To GENERAL ARMSTRONG. vi, 103. (M., Feb. 1813.)

6979. PRIVATE LIFE, Independence of.—The independence of private life, under the protection of republican laws, will I hope yield me the happiness from which no slave is so remote as the minister of a commonwealth.—To MARQUIS LAFAYETTE. i, 312. FORD ED., iii, 49. (M., 1781.)

* From a letter requesting Madison to select a lodging for him.—EDITOR.

6980. PRIVATE LIFE, Public duty and.—You hope I have not abandoned entirely the service of our country. After five and twenty years' continual employment in it, I trust it will be thought I have fulfilled my tour, like a punctual soldier, and may claim my discharge. But I am glad of the sentiment from you, because it gives a hope you will practice what you preach, and come forward in aid of the public vessel. I will not admit your old excuse that you are in public service though at home. The campaigns which are fought in a man's own house are not to be counted. The present situation of the President, unable to get the offices filled, really calls with uncommon obligation on those whom nature has fitted for them.—To EDWARD RUTLEDGE. iv, 124. FORD ED., vii, 39. (M., Nov. 1795.)

6981. PRIVATE LIFE, Retirement to.—My first wish is a restoration of our just rights; my second, a return of the happy period, when, consistently with duty, I may withdraw myself totally from the public stage and pass the rest of my days in domestic ease and tranquillity, banishing every desire of ever hearing what passes in the world.—To JOHN RANDOLPH. i, 200. FORD ED., i, 482. (M., 1775.)

6982. ——. I have laid up my Rosinante in his stall, before his unfitness for the road shall expose him faultering to the world.—To MANN PAGE. iv, 119. FORD ED., vii, 24. (M., 1795.) See RETIREMENT.

6983. PRIVATE LIFE, Rural.—I am savage enough to prefer the woods, the wilds, and the independence of Monticello, to all the brilliant pleasures of this gay capital.—To BARON GEISMER. i, 427. (P., 1785.) See LIFE and MONTICELLO.

6984. PRIVATE LIFE vs. PUBLIC LIFE.—I had rather be shut up in a very modest cottage, with my books, my family and a few old friends, dining on simple bacon, and letting the world roll on as it liked, than to occupy the most splendid post which any human power can give.—To A. DONALD. ii, 356. (P., 1788.)

6985. ——. I ever preferred the pursuits of private life to those of public life.—ANAS. ix, 121. FORD ED., i, 203. (1792.)

6986. ——. The pomp, the turmoil, the bustle and splendor of office, have drawn but deeper sighs for the tranquil and irresponsible occupations of private life.—To THE INHABITANTS OF ALBEMARLE COUNTY, VA. v, 439. FORD ED., ix, 250. (M., April 1809.)

6987. PRIVATEERING, Abolition of.—If war should hereafter arise between the two contracting parties, * * * all merchants and traders, exchanging the products of different places, and thereby rendering the necessaries, conveniences, and comforts of human life more easy to obtain and more general, shall be allowed to pass free and unmolested; and neither of the contracting powers shall grant or issue any commission to any private armed vessels, empowering them to take or destroy such trading ships, or interrupt such commerce. *—TREATY INSTRUCTIONS. FORD ED., iii, 490. (May 1784.)

6988. ——. I am to acknowledge the receipt of your letter, proposing a stipulation for the abolition of the practice of privateering in times of war. The benevolence of this proposition is worthy of the nation [France] from which it comes, and our sentiments on it have been declared in the treaty to which you are pleased to refer, as well as in some others which have been proposed. There are in those treaties some other principles which would probably meet the approbation of your government, as flowing from the same desire to lessen the occasions and the calamities of war. On all these * * * we are ready to enter into negotiation with you, only proposing to take the whole into consideration at once.—To JEAN BAPTISTE TERNANT. iii, 477. FORD ED., vi, 122. (Pa., 1792.)

6989. ——. During the negotiations for peace [in 1783] with the British Commissioner David Hartley, our Commissioners had proposed, on the suggestion of Dr. Franklin, to insert an article exempting from capture by the public or private armed ships of either belligerent, when at war, all merchant vessels and their cargoes, employed merely in carrying on the commerce between nations. It was refused by England, and unwisely in my opinion. For, in the case of a war with us, their superior commerce places infinitely more at hazard on the ocean than ours; and, as hawks abound in proportion to game, so our privateers would swarm in proportion to the wealth exposed to their prize, while theirs would be few for want of subjects of capture. We [Adams, Franklin and Jefferson] inserted this article in our form, with a provision against the molestation of fishermen, husbandmen, citizens unarmed and following their occupations in unfortified places, for the humane treatment of prisoners of war, the abolition of contraband of war, which exposes merchant vessels to such vexations and ruinous detentions and abuses; and for the principle of free bottoms, free goods.—AUTOBIOGRAPHY. i, 62. FORD ED., i, 86. (1821.)

6990. PRIVATEERS, Advantages of.—Our ships of force will undoubtedly be blockaded by the enemy, and we shall have no means of annoying them at sea but by small, swift-sailing vessels; these will be better managed and more multiplied in the hands of individuals than of the government. In short, they are our true and only weapon in a war against Great Britain, when once Canada and Nova Scotia shall have been rescued from them. The opposition to them in Congress is merely partial. It is a part of the navy fever, and proceeds from the desire of securing men for the public ships by suppressing all other employments from them. But I do not apprehend that this ill-judged principle is that of a majority of Congress. I hope, on the contrary, they will spare no encouragement to that kind of enterprise. Our public ships, to be sure, have done wonders. They have saved our military reputation sacrificed on the shores of Canada; but in point of real injury and depredation on the enemy, our privateers without question have been most effectual. Both species of force have their peculiar value.—To GENERAL BAILEY. vi, 100. (M., Feb. 1813.)

* Instructions respecting the negotiation of commercial treaties with European nations.—EDITOR.

6991. PRIVATEERS, Commerce destroyers.—I hope we shall confine ourselves to the conquest of their possessions, and defence of our harbors, leaving the war on the ocean to our privateers. These will immediately swarm in every sea, and do more injury to British commerce than the regular fleets of all Europe would do.—To GENERAL KOSCIUSKO. vi, 68. FORD ED., ix, 362. (M., June 1812.)

6992. —— ——. Our privateers will eat out the vitals of British commerce.—To WILLIAM DUANE. vi, 76. FORD ED., ix, 366. (M., Aug. 1812.)

6993. —— ——. Every sea on the globe where England has any commerce, and where any port can be found to sell prizes, will be filled with our privateers.—To GENERAL KOSCIUSKO. vi, 77. (M., Aug. 1812.)

6994. PRIVATEERS, Encouragement of.—Privateers will find their own men and money. Let nothing be spared to encourage them. They are the dagger which strikes at the heart of the enemy, their commerce.—To JAMES MONROE. vi, 409. FORD ED., ix, 498. (M., 1815.)

6995. PRIVATEERS, Exclusion of.—Measures are taking for excluding, from all further asylum in our ports, vessels armed in them to cruise on nations with which we are at peace.—To GEORGE HAMMOND. iv, 56. FORD ED., vi, 408. (Pa., Sep. 1793.)

6996. PRIVATEERS, Fitting out foreign.—By our treaties with several of the belligerent powers, which are a part of the laws of our land, we have established a state of peace with them. But, without appealing to treaties, we are at peace with them all by the law of nature. For by nature's law, man is at peace with man, till some aggression is committed, which, by the same law, authorizes one to destroy another as his enemy. For our citizens, then, to commit murders and depredations on the members of nations at peace with us, or combine to do it, appeared to the Executive, and to those with whom they consulted, as much against the laws of the land, as to murder or rob, or combine to murder or rob its own citizens; and as much to require punishment, if done within their limits, where they have a territorial jurisdiction, or on the high seas, where they have a personal jurisdiction, that is to say, one which reaches their own citizens only, this being an appropriate part of each nation, on an element where all have a common jurisdiction. So say our laws, as we understand them ourselves. To them the appeal is made; and whether we have construed them well or ill, the constitutional judges will decide. Till that decision shall be obtained, the government of the United States must pursue what they think right with firmness, as is their duty.—To E. C. GENET. iii, 589. FORD ED., vi, 310. (Pa., June 1793.)

6997. —— ——. Besides taking efficacious measures to prevent the future fitting out of privateers in the ports of the United States, they will not give asylum therein to any which shall have been at any time so fitted out, and will cause restitution of all such prizes as shall be hereafter brought within their ports by any of the said privateers.—To E. C. GENET. iv, 27. FORD ED., vi, 366. (Pa., Aug. 1793.)

6998. PRIVATEERS, French.—Some privateers have been fitted out in Charleston by French citizens, with their own money, manned by themselves, and regularly commissioned by their nation. They have taken several prizes, and brought them into our ports. Some native citizens had joined them. These are arrested and under prosecution, and orders are sent to all the ports to prevent the equipping privateers by any persons foreign or native. So far is right. But the vessels so equipped at Charleston are ordered to leave the ports of the United States. This, I think, was not right. Hammond [British Minister] demanded further a surrender of the prizes they had taken. This is refused, on the principle that by the laws of war the property is transferred to the captors.—To JAMES MADISON. iii, 568. FORD ED., vi, 277. (June 1793.)

6999. —— ——. The arming and equipping vessels in the ports of the United States to cruise against nations with whom they are at peace, is incompatible with the territorial sovereignty of the United States. It makes them instrumental to the annoyance of those nations and thereby tends to compromit their peace.—To EDMOND CHARLES GENET. iii, 571. FORD ED., vi, 282. (Pa., June 1793.)

7000. PRIVATEERS, Gulf of Mexico and.—Our [the Cabinet's] general opinion is that as soundings on our coast cease at the beginning of the Gulf Stream, we ought to endeavor to assume all the waters within the Gulf Stream as our waters, so far as to exclude privateers from hovering within them.—THE ANAS. FORD ED., i, 308. (July 1805.)

7001. PRIVATEERS, Merchant vessels and.—Can it be necessary to say that a merchant vessel is not a privateer? That though she has arms to defend herself in time of war, in the course of her regular commerce, this no more makes her a privateer, than a husbandman following his plow, in time of war, with a knife or pistol in his pocket, is, thereby, made a soldier? The occupation of a privateer is attack and plunder, that of a merchant vessel is commerce and self-preservation.—To GOUVERNEUR MORRIS. iv, 41. FORD ED., vi, 385. (Pa., Aug. 1793.)

7002. PRIVATEERS, Prizes.—Encourage the privateers to burn all their prizes, and let the public pay for them. They will cheat us enormously. No matter; they will make the merchants of England feel, and squeal, and cry out for peace.—To JAMES MONROE. vi, 410. FORD ED., ix, 498. (M., 1815.)

7003. PRIVILEGES, Abolition of.—All pecuniary privileges and exemptions, enjoyed by any description of persons, are abolished.—FRENCH CHARTER OF RIGHTS. iii, 47. FORD ED., v, 102. (P., 1789.)

7004. PRIVILEGES, Unequal.—To unequal privileges among members of the same society the spirit of our nation is, with one accord, adverse.—REPLY TO ADDRESS. iv, 394. (W., 1801.) See EQUALITY, EQUAL RIGHTS, FAVORITISM and RIGHTS.

7005. PRIZES, Condemnation of.—The condemnation by the consul of France at Charleston, as legal prize, of a British vessel captured by a French frigate, is not, as you justly [observe], a judicial act warranted by the law of nations, nor by the stipulations existing between the United States and France. I observe further that it is not warranted by any law of the land. It is consequently a mere nullity; as such it can be respected in no court, can make no part in the title to the vessel, nor give to the purchaser any other security than what he would have had without it. In short, it is so absolutely nothing as to give no foundation of just concern to any person interested in the fate of the vessel. * * * The proceeding, indeed, * * * [if the information be correct], has been an act of disrespect towards the United States, to which its government cannot be inattentive. A just sense of our own rights and duties, and the obviousness of the principle are a security that no inconveniences will be permitted to arise from repetitions of it.—To George Hammond. iii, 558. Ford ed., vi, 252. (Pa., May 1793.)

7006. PRIZES, Consular jurisdiction.— No particular rules have been established by the President for the conduct of consuls with respect to prizes. In one particular case where a prize is brought into our ports by any of the *belligerent* parties, and is reclaimed of the Executive, the President has hitherto permitted the consul of the captor to hold the prize until his determination is known. But in all cases respecting a neutral nation, their vessels are placed exactly on the same footing with our own, entitled to the same remedy from our courts of justice, and the same protection from the Executive, as our own vessels in the same situation. The remedy in the courts of justice, the only one which they or our own can have access to, is slower than where it lies with the Executive, but it is more complete, as damages can be given by the Court but not by the Executive.—To Mr. Soderstrom. iv, 83. (G., Nov. 1793.)

7007. PRIZES, Restitution.— The restitution of the prizes [which French privateers might bring into the ports of the United States]. is understood to be inconsistent with the rules which govern such cases, and would, therefore, be unjustifiable towards the other party.—To George Hammond. iii, 573. Ford ed., vi, 286. (Pa., June 1793.)

7008. ——— ———. Restitution of prizes has been made by the Executive of the United States only in the two cases: 1, of capture within their jurisdiction, by armed vessels, originally constituted such without the limits of the United States; or, 2, of capture, either within or without their jurisdiction, by armed vessels, originally constituted such within the limits of the United States. Such last have been called proscribed vessels.—To George Hammond. iv, 78. Ford ed., vi, 444. (G., Nov. 1793.)

7009. ——— ———. Can prizes and the proceeds of them, taken after the date of the treaty [of peace] with France be restored by the Executive, or need an act of the Legislature? The Constitution has authorized the ordinary Legislature alone to declare war against any foreign nation. If they may enact a perfect, they may a qualified war, and appropriate the proceeds of it. In this state of things, they may modify the acts of war, and appropriate the proceeds of it. The act authorizing the capture of French armed vessels, and dividing and appropriating their proceeds, was of this kind. The Constitution has given to the President and Senate alone the power (with the consent of the foreign nation) of enacting peace. Their treaty for this purpose is an absolute repeal of the declaration of war, and of all laws authorizing or modifying war measures. The treaty with France had this effect. From the moment it was signed all the acts legalizing war measures ceased *ipso facto*; and all subsequent captures became unlawful.

Property wrongfully taken from a friend on the high sea is not thereby transferred to the captor. In whatever hands it is found, it remains the property of those from whom it was taken; and any person possessed of it, private or public, has a right to restore it. If it comes to the hands of the Executive, they may restore it. If into those of the Legislature (as by formal payment into the Treasury), they may restore it. Whoever, private or public, undertakes to restore it, takes on themselves the risk of proving that the goods were taken without authority of law, and consequently that the captor had no right to them. The Executive, charged with our exterior relations, seems bound, if satisfied of the fact, to do right to the foreign nation, and take on itself the risk of justification.—To James Madison. Ford ed., viii, 73. (W., July 1801.)

7010. PRIZES, Rules governing.— The doctrine as to the admission of prizes, maintained by the government from the commencement of the war between England and France, &c., to this day, has been this: The treaties give a right to armed vessels, with their prizes, to go where they please (consequently into our ports), and that these prizes shall not be detained, seized, nor adjudicated; but that the armed vessel may depart as *speedily as may be, with her prize,* to the place of her commission; and we are not to suffer their enemies to sell in our ports the prizes taken by their privateers. Before the British treaty, no stipulation stood in the way of permitting France to sell her prizes here; and we did permit it, but expressly as a favor, not a right. * * * These stipulations admit the prizes to put into our ports in cases of necessity, or perhaps of convenience, but no right to remain if disagreeable to us; and absolutely not to be sold.—To Albert Gallatin. Ford ed., viii, 86. (M., Aug. 1801.) See Privateers and Neutrality.

7011. PROCRASTINATION, Indolence and.— My acknowledgments have been delayed by a blamable spirit of procrastination, forever suggesting to our indolence that we need not do to-day what may be done to-morrow.—To Thomas Pinckney. iv, 176. Ford ed., vii, 127. (Pa., 1797.)

7012. PRODUCTION, National.— In general, it is a truth that if every nation will employ itself in what it is fittest to produce, a greater quantity will be raised of the things contributing to human happiness, than if every nation attempts to raise everything it wants within itself.—To M. Lasteyrie. v, 315. (W., 1808.)

7013. PROGRESS, Constant.— When I contemplate the immense advances in science and discoveries in the arts which have been made within the period of my life, I look forward with confidence to equal advances by the present generation, and have no doubt they will consequently be as much wiser than we have been as we than our fathers were, and they than the burners of witches.—To Dr. Benjamin Waterhouse. vii. 101. Ford ed., x, 103. (M., 1818.)

7014. PROGRESS, Gothic idea of.— The Gothic idea that we were to look backwards instead of forwards for the improvement of the human mind, and to recur to the annals of our ancestors for what is most perfect in government, in religion and in learning, is worthy of those bigots in religion and government, by whom it has been recommended, and whose purposes it would answer. But it is not an idea which this country will endure.—To JOSEPH PRIESTLEY. iv, 318. FORD ED., vii, 415. (Pa., 1800.)

7015. PROGRESS, In government.—Laws and institutions must go hand in hand with the progress of the human mind. As that becomes more developed, more enlightened, as new discoveries are made, new truths disclosed, and manners and opinions change with the change of circumstances, institutions must advance also, and keep pace with the times. We might as well require a man to wear still the coat which fitted him when a boy, as civilized society to remain ever under the regimen of their barbarous ancestors. It is this preposterous idea which has lately deluged Europe in blood. Their monarchs, instead of wisely yielding to the general change of circumstances, of favoring progressive accommodation to progressive improvement, have clung to old abuses, entrenched themselves behind steady habits, and obliged their subjects to seek through blood and violence rash and ruinous innovations, which, had they been referred to the peaceful deliberations and collected wisdom of the nation, would have been put into acceptable and salutary forms. Let us follow no such examples, nor weakly believe that one generation is not as capable as another of taking care of itself, and of ordering its own affairs.—To SAMUEL KERCHIVAL. vii, 15. FORD ED., x, 42. (M., 1816.) See GENERATIONS.

7016. PROGRESS, Perseverance and.—In endeavors to improve our situation, we should never despair.—To JOHN QUINCY ADAMS. vii, 89. (M., 1817.)

7017. PROGRESS, In Science.—One of the questions, you know, on which our parties took different sides, was on the improvability of the human mind in science, in ethics, in government, &c. Those who advocated reformation of institutions, *pari passu* with the progress of science, maintained that no definite limits could be assigned to that progress. The enemies of reform, on the other hand, denied improvement, and advocated steady adherence to the principles, practices and institutions of our fathers, which they represented as the consummation of wisdom, and acme of excellence, beyond which the human mind could never advance. Although in the passage of your answer alluded to, you expressly disclaim the wish to influence the freedom of inquiry, you predict that that will produce nothing more worthy of transmission to posterity than the principles, institutions and systems of education received from their ancestors. I do not consider this as your deliberate opinion. You possess, yourself, too much science, not to see how much is still ahead of you, unexplained and unexplored. Your own consciousness must place you as far before our ancestors as in the rear of posterity.—To JOHN ADAMS. vi, 126. FORD ED., ix, 387. (M., 1813.)

7018. PROGRESS, Sluggish.—There is a snail-paced gait for the advance of new ideas on the general mind, under which we must acquiesce. A forty years' experience of popular assemblies has taught me, that you must give them time for every step you take. If too hard pushed, they balk, and the machine retrogrades.—To JOEL BARLOW. v, 217. FORD ED., ix, 169. (W., Dec. 1807.)

7019. PROGRESS, Time and.—Time indeed changes manners and notions, and so far we must expect institutions to bend to them.—To SPENCER ROANE. vii, 211. FORD ED., x, 188. (M., 1821.)

— PROHIBITION.—See WHISKY.

7020. PROPERTY, Acquisition of.—The political institutions of America, its various soils and climates opened a certain resource to the unfortunate and to the enterprising of every country, and insured to them the acquisition and free possession of property.—DECLARATION ON TAKING UP ARMS. FORD ED., i, 465. (July 1775.)

7021. PROPERTY, Of aliens.—Resolved, that no right be stipulated for aliens to hold real property within these States, this being utterly inadmissible by their several laws and policy; but when on the death of any person holding real estate within the territories of one of the contracting parties, such real estate would by their laws descend on a subject or citizen of the other, were he not disqualified by alienage, then he shall be allowed reasonable time to dispose of the same, and withdraw the proceeds without molestation.—COMMERCIAL TREATIES INSTRUCTIONS. FORD ED., iii, 492. (1784.)

7022. ———. It is reasonable that every one who asks justice should do justice; and it is usual to consider the property of a foreigner, in any country, as a fund appropriated to the payment of what he owes in that country exclusively. It is a care which most nations take of their own citizens, not to let the property, which is to answer their demands, be withdrawn from its jurisdiction, and send them to seek it in foreign countries, and before foreign tribunals.—To GEORGE HAMMOND. iii, 395. FORD ED., vi, 37. (Pa., May 1792.)

7023. PROPERTY, Annihilation of.—They [Parliament] have interdicted all commerce to one of our principal towns, thereby annihilating its property in the hands of the holders.—DECLARATION ON TAKING UP ARMS. FORD ED., i, 468. (July 1775.)

7024. PROPERTY, Confiscation of.—[In Lord North's proposition] our adversaries still claim a right of demanding *ad libitum*, and of taxing us themselves to the full amount of their demand, if we do not comply with it. This leaves us without anything we can call property.—REPLY TO LORD NORTH'S PROPOSITION. FORD ED., i, 481. (July 1775.)

7025. ——— ———. He has incited treasonable insurrections of our fellow citizens, with the allurements of forfeiture and confiscation of our property.*—DECLARATION OF INDEPENDENCE AS DRAWN BY JEFFERSON.

7026. PROPERTY, Defence of.—In defence of our persons and properties under actual violation, we took up arms. When that violence shall be removed, when hostilities shall cease on the part of the aggressors, hostilities shall cease on our part also.—DECLARATION ON TAKING UP ARMS. FORD ED., i, 475. (July 1775.)

7027. PROPERTY, Depreciation.—Money is leaving the remoter parts of the Union, and flowing to this place [Philadelphia] to purchase paper; and here. a paper medium supplying its place, it is shipped off in exchange for luxuries. The value of property is necessarily falling in the places left bare of money. In Virginia, for instance, property has fallen 25 per cent. in the last twelve months.—To WILLIAM SHORT. iii, 343. FORD ED., v, 459. (Pa., March 1792.)

7028. ———— ————. The long succession of years of stunted crops. of reduced prices, the general prostration of the farming business, under levies for the support of manufacturers, &c., with the calamitous fluctuations of value in our paper medium, have kept agriculture in a state of abject depression, which has peopled the western States by silently breaking up those on the Atlantic. and glutted the land market. while it drew off its bidders. In such a state of things, property has lost its character of being a resource for debts. Highland in Bedford, which, in the days of our plethory, sold readily for from fifty to one hundred dollars the acre (and such sales were many then), would not now sell for more than from ten to twenty dollars. or one quarter to one-fifth of its former price.—To JAMES MADISON. vii, 434. FORD ED., x, 377. (M., February 1826.) See BANKS, MONEY and PAPER MONEY.

7029. PROPERTY, Descent of.—The descent of property of every kind to all the children, or to all the brothers and sisters, or other relations, in equal degree, is a politic measure, and a practicable one.—To REV. JAMES MADISON. FORD ED., vii, 35. (P., 1785.) See DESCENTS, ENTAIL and PRIMOGENITURE.

7030. PROPERTY, Division of.—I am conscious that an equal division of property is impracticable. But the consequences of this enormous inequality [in France] producing so much misery to the bulk of mankind, legislators cannot invent too many devices for subdividing property, only taking care to let their subdivisions go hand in hand with the natural affections of the human mind.—To REV. JAMES MADISON. FORD ED., vii, 35. (P., 1785.) See DESCENTS, ENTAIL and PRIMOGENITURE.

7031. PROPERTY, Equal rights and.—The true foundation of republican government is the equal right of every citizen, in his person and property, and in their management.—To SAMUEL KERCHIVAL. vii, 11. FORD ED., x, 39. (M., 1816.)

7032. PROPERTY, Federal.—The property of the United States can never be questioned in any court, but in special cases in which, by some particular law, they delegate a special power, as to the boards of commissioners, and in some small fiscal cases. But a general jurisdiction over the national demesnes, being more than half the territory of the United States, has never been by them, and never ought to be. subjected to any tribunal.—BATTURE CASE. viii, 521. (1812.)

7033. PROPERTY, Forfeited.—All forfeitures heretofore going to the king, shall go to the State; save only such as the legislature may hereafter abolish.—PROPOSED VA. CONSTITUTION. FORD ED., i, 27. (June 1776.)

7034. ———— ————. In all cases of petty treason and murder, one-half of the lands and goods of the offender shall be forfeited to the next of kin to the person killed, and the other half descend and go to his representatives. Save only, where one shall slay the challenger in a duel, in which case, no part of his lands or goods shall be forfeited to the kindred of the party slain, but instead thereof. a moiety shall go to the Commonwealth.*—CRIMES BILL. i, 150. FORD ED., ii, 207. (1779.)

7035. PROPERTY, Free Press and.—The functionaries of every government have propensities to command at will the liberty and property of their constituents. There is no safe deposit for these but with the people themselves; nor can they be safe with them without information. Where the press is free, and every man able to read. all is safe.—To CHARLES YANCEY. vi, 517. FORD ED., x, 4. (M., 1816.)

7036. PROPERTY, Impressing.—In a country where means of payment are neither prompt, nor of the most desirable kind, impressing property for the public use has been found indispensable. We have no fears of complaint under your exercise of those powers.—To MAJOR-GENERAL LAFAYETTE. FORD ED., ii, 502. (R., 1781.)

7037. PROPERTY, Industry and.—Our wish is that * * * [there be] maintained that state of property, equal or unequal, which results to every man from his own industry, or that of his fathers.—SECOND INAUGURAL ADDRESS. viii, 44. FORD ED., viii, 347. (1805.)

7038. PROPERTY, Inequality of.—Another means of silently lessening the inequality of property [in France] is to exempt all from taxation below a certain point, and to tax the higher portions of property in geometrical progression as they rise.—To REV. JAMES MADISON. FORD ED., vii, 36. (P., 1785.)

* Struck out by Congress.—EDITOR.

* Quære, if the estates of both parties in a duel, should not be forfeited? The deceased is equally guilty with a suicide.—NOTE BY JEFFERSON.

7039. PROPERTY, Inventions as.—Inventions cannot in nature be a subject of property.—To Isaac McPherson. vi, 181. (M., 1813.) See Inventions and Patents.

7040. PROPERTY, Jurisdiction over.—The functions of the Executive are not competent to the decision of questions of property between individuals. They are ascribed to the Judiciary alone, and when either persons or property are taken into their custody, there is no power in this country that can take them out.—To Edmond Charles Genet. iii, 586. Ford ed., vi, 312. (Pa., 1793.)

7041. PROPERTY, Laws of.—Whenever there is in any country, uncultivated lands and unemployed poor, it is clear that the laws of property have been so far extended as to violate natural right.—To Rev. James Madison. Ford ed., vii, 36. (P., 1785.)

7042. PROPERTY, Life and.—They [Parliament] have deprived us of the inestimable privilege of trial by a jury of the vicinage in cases affecting both life and property.—Declaration on Taking up Arms. Ford ed., i, 468. (July 1775.)

7043. PROPERTY, Paper money and.—That paper money has some advantages, is admitted. But that its abuses also are inevitable, and, by breaking up the measure of value, makes a lottery of all private property, cannot be denied.—To Dr. Josephus B. Stuart. vii, 65. (M., May 1817.) See Banks and Paper Money.

7044. PROPERTY, Protection of.—The persons and property of our citizens are entitled to the protection of our government in all places where they may lawfully go.—Opinion on Ship Passports. vii, 624. (May 1793.)

7045. ———. We give you [Choctaws] a copy of the law, made by our great Council, for punishing our people, who may encroach on your lands, or injure you otherwise. Carry it with you to your homes, and preserve it, as the shield which we spread over you, to protect your land, your property, and persons.—Address to the Choctaws. viii, 192. (1803.)

7046. ———. When once you [the Indians] have property, you will want laws and magistrates to protect your property and persons, and to punish those among you who commit crimes. You will find that our laws are good for this purpose.—Address to Delawares. viii, 226. (1808.)

7047. ———. We wish to see you [the Indians] possessed of property, and protecting it by regular laws.—Indian Address. viii, 234. (1809.)

7048. ———. The first foundations of the social compact would be broken up, were we definitely to refuse to its members the protection of their persons and property, while in their lawful pursuits.—To James Maury. vi, 52. Ford ed., ix, 348. (M., 1812.)

7049. PROPERTY, Public office as.—The field of public office will not be perverted by me into a family property.—To Dr. Horatio Turpin. v, 90. (W., 1807.) See Relations.

7050. PROPERTY, Recovery of.—By nature's law, every man has a right to seize and retake by force. his own property taken from him by another, by force or fraud. Nor is this natural right among the first which is taken into the hands of regular government, after it is instituted. It was long retained by our ancestors. It was a part of their common law, laid down in their books, recognized by all the authorities, and regulated as to circumstances of practice.—Batture Case. viii, 584. (1812.)

7051. PROPERTY, Representation of.—In some of the American States, the delegates and Senators are so chosen as that the first represent the persons. and the second the property of the State. But with us [Virginia] wealth and wisdom have equal chance for admission into both houses.—Notes on Virginia. viii, 361. Ford ed., iii, 223. (1782.)

7052. PROPERTY, Rescue of.—Nature has given to all men, individual or associated, the right of rescuing their own property wrongfully taken. In cases of forcible entry on individual possessions, special provisions, both of the common and civil law, have restrained the right of rescue by private force, and substituted the aid of the civil power. But no law has restrained the right of the nation itself from removing by its own arm, intruders on its possessions.—To Governor Claiborne. v, 518. (M., 1810.)

7053. PROPERTY, Restitution.—Congress should immediately and earnestly recommend to the legislatures of the respective States to provide for the restitution of all estates, rights and properties which have been confiscated, belonging to British subjects; and also of the estates, rights and properties of persons resident in districts which were in the possession of his Britannic Majesty's arms at any time between the 30th day of November, 1782, and the 14th day of January, 1784, and who have not borne arms against the United States, and that persons of any other description shall have free liberty to go to any part or parts of any of the thirteen United States, and therein to remain twelve months unmolested in their endeavors to obtain the restitution of such of their estates, rights and properties as may have been confiscated.—Report on Peace Treaty. Ford ed., iii, 349. (Dec. 1783.)

7054. PROPERTY, Restoration.—I am not fond of encouraging an intercourse with the enemy for the recovery of property; however, I shall not forbid it while conducted on principles which are fair and general. If the British commander chooses to discriminate between the several species of property taken from the people; if he chooses to say he will restore all of one kind, and retain all of another, I am contented that individuals shall avail themselves of this discrimination; but no distinctions of persons must be admitted. The moment it is proposed that the same species of property shall be restored to one which is refused to another, let every application to him for restitution be prohibited. The principles by which his discrimination would be governed are but too obvious, and they are the reverse of what we should approve.—To COLONEL JOHN NICHOLAS. FORD ED., ii, 409. (1781.)

7055. ———— ————. A right to take the side, which every man's conscience approves in a civil contest, is too precious a right, and too favorable to the preservation of liberty not to be protected by all its well informed friends. The Assembly of Virginia have given sanction to this right in several of their laws, discriminating honorably those who took side against us before the Declaration of Independence, from those who remained among us and strove to injure us by their treacheries. I sincerely wish that you, and every other to whom this distinction applies favorably, may find, in the Assembly of Virginia, the good effects of that justice and generosity which have dictated to them this discrimination. It is a sentiment which will gain strength in their breasts in proportion as they can forget the savage cruelties committed on them, and will, I hope, in the end induce them to restore the property itself wherever it is unsold, and the price received for it, where it has been actually sold.—To MRS. SPROWLE. FORD ED., iv, 66. (P., 1785.)

7056. PROPERTY, Right to.—A right to property is founded in our natural wants, in the means with which we are endowed to satisfy these wants, and the right to what we acquire by those means without violating the similar rights of other sensible beings. —To DUPONT DE NEMOURS. vi, 591. FORD ED., x, 24. (P.F., 1816.)

7057. PROPERTY, Sale under execution.—The immensity of this [Virginia] debt [to British creditors] was another reason for forbidding such a mass of property to be offered for sale under execution at once, as, from the small quantity of circulating money, it must have sold for little or nothing, whereby the creditor would have failed to receive his money, and the debtor would have lost his whole estate without being discharged of his debt.*—REPORT TO CONGRESS. ix, 241. FORD ED., iv, 127. (F., 1785.) See DEBTS DUE BRITISH.

— PROPERTY, At sea.—See TREATIES.

7058. PROPERTY, Seizure in war.—It cannot be denied that a state of war directly permits a nation to seize the property of its enemies found within its own limits or taken in war and in whatever form it exists whether in action or possession.—To GEORGE HAMMOND. iii, 369. FORD ED., vi, 15. (Pa., 1792.)

* Report of Conference with Count de Vergennes, Foreign Minister of France, respecting commerce.— EDITOR.

7059. PROPERTY, Sequestration.—For securing to the citizens of the Commonwealth [of Virginia] an indemnification out of the property of British subjects here, * * * in case the sovereign of the latter should confiscate the property of the former in his dominions, as well as to prevent that accession of strength which the enemy might derive by withdrawing their property * * * hence * * * the lands, slaves, flocks, implements of industry * * * of British subjects, shall be sequestered.—BRITISH PROPERTY BILL. FORD ED., ii, 199. (1779.)

7060. PROPERTY, Slaves as.—The cession of that kind of property [Slaves], for so it is misnamed, is a bagatelle which would not cost me a second thought, if, in that way, a general emancipation and expatriation could be effected.—To JOHN HOLMES. vii, 159. FORD ED., x, 157. (M., 1820.)

7061. ———— ————. Actual property has been lawfully vested in [negroes] and who can lawfully take it from the possessors?—To JARED SPARKS. vii, 333. FORD ED., x, 290. (M., 1824.)

7062. PROPERTY, Stable ownership.— By an universal law, indeed, whatever [property], whether fixed or movable, belongs to all men equally and in common, is the property for the moment of him who occupies it; but when he relinquishes the occupation, the property goes with it. Stable ownership is the gift of social law, and is given late in the progress of society.—To ISAAC McPHERSON. vi, 180. (M., 1813.)

7063. PROPERTY, Taxation.—I am principally afraid that commerce will be overloaded by the assumption [of the State debts], believing it would be better that property should be duly taxed.—To MR. RANDOLPH. iii, 185. (N.Y., 1790.) See TAXATION.

7064. PROPERTY, Unequal division.— The unequal division of property [in France] * * * occasions numberless instances of wretchedness and is to be observed all over Europe.—To REV. JAMES MADISON. FORD ED., vii, 35. (P., 1785.)

7065. PROPERTY, Untaxed.—The clergy and nobles [in France], by their privileges and influence, have kept their property in a great measure untaxed.—To DR. PRICE. ii, 556. (P., Jan. 1789.)

7066. PROPHECY, Conditional.—Who can withhold looking into futurity on events which are to change the face of the world, and the condition of man throughout it, without indulging himself in the effusions of the holy spirit of Delphos? I may do it the more safely, as to my vaticinations I always subjoin the proviso "that nothing unexpected happen to change the predicted course of events".—To WILLIAM SHORT. FORD ED., x, 249. (M., 1823.)

7067. PROPHECY, Fallacious.—Perhaps in that super-mundane region, we may be amused with seeing the fallacy of our own guesses.—To JOHN ADAMS. vii, 105. FORD ED., x, 109. (M., 1818.)

7068. PROPHET, Wabash.—With respect to the [Wabash] prophet, if those who are in danger from him would settle it in their own way, it would be their affair. But we should do nothing towards it. That kind of policy is not in the character of our government, and still less of the paternal spirit we wish to show towards that people. But could not [General] Harrison gain over the Prophet, who no doubt is a scoundrel, and only needs his price?—To GENERAL DEARBORN. v, 163. (M., Aug. 1807.)

7069. PROSCRIPTION vs. JUST TRIAL.—To fill up the measure of irritation, a proscription of individuals has been substituted in the room of just trial. Can it be believed that a grateful people will suffer those to be consigned to execution whose sole crime has been the developing and asserting their rights? Had the Parliament possessed the power of reflection, they would have avoided a measure as impotent, as it was inflammatory.—To DR. WILLIAM SMALL. i, 199. FORD ED., i, 454. (May 1775.)

7070. PROSPERITY, American.—There is not a nation under the sun enjoying more present prosperity, nor with more in prospect.—To C. W. F. DUMAS. iii, 260. (Pa., 1791.)

7071. PROSPERITY, Basis.—A prosperity built on the basis of agriculture is that which is most desirable to us, because to the efforts of labor it adds the efforts of a greater proportion of soil.—CIRCULAR TO CONSULS. iii, 431. (Pa., 1792.)

7072. PROSPERITY, Concern for.—Affectionate concerns for the prosperity of my fellow citizens will cease but with life to animate my breast.—REPLY TO ADDRESS. v, 262. (W., 1808.)

7073. PROSPERITY, Conditions of.—I trust the good sense of our country will see that its greatest prosperity depends on a due balance between agriculture, manufactures and commerce.—To THOMAS LEIPER. v, 417. FORD ED., ix, 239. (W., 1809.)

7074. PROSPERITY, Pillars of.—Agriculture, manufactures, commerce, and navigation, the four pillars of our prosperity, are the most thriving when left most free to individual enterprise.—FIRST ANNUAL MESSAGE. viii, 13. FORD ED., viii, 123. (Dec. 1801.)

7075. PROSPERITY, Stability of.—On the useful pursuits of peace alone, a stable prosperity can be founded.—R. TO A. PITTSBURG REPUBLICANS. viii, 142. (1808.)

7076. PROTECTION, Commerce and navigation.—We wish [to encourage navigation and commerce] by throwing open all the doors of commerce, and knocking off its shackles. But as this cannot be done for others, unless they will do it for us, and there is no probability that Europe will do this, I suppose we shall be obliged to adopt a system which may shackle them in our ports, as they do us in theirs.—To COUNT VAN HOGENDORP. i, 465. FORD ED., iv, 105. (P., 1785.) See COMMERCE and NAVIGATION.

7077. ——— ———. Should any nation, contrary to our wishes, suppose it may better find its advantage by continuing its system of prohibitions, duties and regulations, it behooves us to protect our citizens, their commerce and navigation, by counter prohibitions, duties and regulations, also. Free commerce and navigation are not to be given in exchange for restrictions and vexations; nor are they likely to produce a relaxation of them.—FOREIGN COMMERCE REPORT. vii, 647. FORD ED., vi, 480. (Dec. 1793.) See DUTIES and FREE TRADE.

7078. PROTECTION, Manufactures and.—To protect the manufactures adapted to our circumstances * * * [is one of] the landmarks by which we are to guide ourselves in all our proceedings.—SECOND ANNUAL MESSAGE. viii, 21. FORD ED., viii, 187. (Dec. 1802.)

7079. ——— ———. Little doubt remains that the [manufacturing] establishments formed and forming will, under the auspices of cheaper materials and subsistence, the freedom of labor from taxation with us, and of protecting duties and prohibitions, become permanent.—EIGHTH ANNUAL MESSAGE. viii, 109. FORD ED., ix, 224. (Nov. 1808.) See MANUFACTURES and TARIFF.

7080. PROTECTION, Oppressive.—I do not mean to say that it may not be for the general interest to foster for awhile certain infant manufactures, until they are strong enough to stand against foreign rivals; but when evident that they will never be so, it is against right to make the other branches of industry support them.—To SAMUEL SMITH. vii, 285. FORD ED., x, 252. (M., 1823.)

7081. PROTECTION, Petitions for.—I observe you [Congress] are loaded with petitions from the manufacturing, commercial and agricultural interests, each praying you to sacrifice the others to them. This proves the egoism of the whole and happily balances their cannibal appetites to eat one another. * * * I do not know whether it is any part of the petitions of the farmers that our citizens shall be restrained to eat nothing but bread, because that can be made here. But this is the common spirit of all their petitions.—To HUGH NELSON. FORD ED., x, 156. (M., 1820.)

7082. PROTECTION, Printing and.—None of these [books in foreign living languages] are printed here, and the duty on them becomes consequently not a protecting, but really a prohibitory one.—To ———. vii, 220. (M., 1821.) See BOOKS.

7083. PROTESTANTS, French edict respecting.—The long expected edict for the Protestants at length appears here [Paris]. Its analysis is this: It is an acknowledgment (hitherto withheld by the laws,) that Protestants can beget children, and that they can die, and be offensive unless buried. It does not give them permission to think, to speak, or to worship. It enumerates the humiliations to which they shall remain subject, and the burthens to which they shall continue to be unjustly exposed. What are we to think of the condition of the human mind in a country where such a wretched thing as this has thrown the State into convulsions, and how must we bless our own situation in a country where the most illiterate peasant of which is a Solon compared with the authors of this law?—To WILLIAM RUTLEDGE. ii, 350. FORD ED., v, 4. (P., Feb. 1788.)

7084. PROVIDENCE, An approving.—
We remark with special satisfaction those circumstances which, under the smiles of Providence, result from the skill, industry and order of our citizens. managing their own affairs in their own way and for their own use, unembarrassed by too much regulations, unoppressed by fiscal exactions.— SECOND ANNUAL MESSAGE. viii, 15. FORD ED., viii, 182. (Dec. 1802.)

7085. PROVIDENCE, Goodness of.—
Providence in His goodness gave it [the yellow fever] an early termination * * * and lessened the number of victims which have usually fallen before it.—FIFTH ANNUAL MESSAGE. viii, 461. FORD ED., viii, 386. (Dec. 1805.)

7086. PROVIDENCE, Gratitude to.—
Let us bow with gratitude to that kind Providence which * * * guarded us from hastily entering into the sanguinary contest [between France and England].—THIRD ANNUAL MESSAGE. viii, 28. FORD ED., viii, 272. (Oct. 1803.)

7087. PROVIDENCE, Human happiness and.—An overruling Providence * * * by all its dispensations proves that it delights in the happiness of man here and his greater happiness hereafter.—FIRST INAUGURAL ADDRESS. viii, 3. FORD ED., viii, 4. (1801.)

7088. PROVIDENCE, A just.—You [General Washington] have persevered till these United States, aided by a magnanimous king and nation, have been enabled, under a just Providence, to close the war in freedom, safety, and independence. * * * We join you in commending the interests of our dearest country to the protection of Almighty God, beseeching Him to dispose the hearts and minds of its citizens to improve the opportunity afforded them of becoming a happy and respectable nation.*—CONGRESS TO WASHINGTON ON SURRENDERING HIS COMMISSION. (Dec. 23, 1783.)

7089. PROVIDENCE, Prayers to.—I pray that Providence in whose hands are the nations of the earth, may continue towards ours His fostering care, and bestow on yourselves the blessings of His protection and favor.—R. TO A. MASSACHUSETTS LEGISLATURE. viii, 117. (1807.)

* Thomas Mifflin, the President of Congress, read the reply of Congress to Washington's address on surrendering his commission. It was written by Jefferson. but is not included in the editions of his works.—EDITOR.

7090. PROVIDENCE, Slavery and.—
We must await with patience the workings of an overruling Providence, and hope that that is preparing the deliverance of these, our suffering brethren [Slaves].—To M. DE MEUNIER. ix, 279. FORD ED., iv, 185. (P., 1786.) See DEITY and GOD.

7091. PROVIDENCE, Supplicating.—I supplicate a protecting Providence to watch over your own and our country's freedom and welfare.—R. TO A. N. Y. TAMMANY SOCIETY. viii, 127. (Feb. 1808.)

7092. ——— ———. I sincerely supplicate that overruling Providence which governs the destinies of men and nations, to dispense His choicest blessings on yourselves and our beloved country.—R. TO A. MASSACHUSETTS CITIZENS. viii, 161. (1809.)

— PRUSSIA.—See FREDERICK THE GREAT.

7093. PSALMS, Estimate of the.—I acknowledge all the merit of the hymn of Cleanthes to Jupiter, which you ascribe to it. It is as highly sublime as a chaste and correct imagination can permit itself to go. Yet in the contemplation of a Being so superlative, the hyperbolic flights of the Psalmist may often be followed. with approbation, even with rapture; and I have no hesitation in giving him the palm over all the hymnists of every language and of every time. Turn to the 148th psalm. in Brady and Tate's version. Have such conceptions been ever before expressed? Their version of the 15th psalm is more to be esteemed for its pithiness than its poetry. Even Sternhold, the leaden Sternhold, kindles, in a single instance, with the sublimity of his original, and expresses the majesty of God descending on the earth, in terms not unworthy of the subject:

> "The Lord descended from above,
> And bowed the heav'ns most high,
> And underneath His feet He cast,
> The darkness of the sky.
> On Cherubim and Seraphim
> Full royally He rode;
> And on the wings of mighty winds
> Came flying all abroad."—PSALM XVIII.

* * * The best collection of these psalms is that of the Octagonian dissenters of Liverpool. * * * Indeed. bad is the best of the English versions; not a ray of poetical genius having ever been employed on them. And how much depends on this, may be seen by comparing Brady and Tate's 15th psalm with Blacklock's *Justum et tenacem propositi virum* of Horace. A translation of David in this style. or in that of Pompei's Cleanthes, might give us some idea of the merit of the original. The character, too, of the poetry of these hymns is singular to us; written in monostichs, each divided into strophe and anti-strophe, the sentiment of the first member responded with amplification or antithesis in the second.—To JOHN ADAMS. vi, 220. (M., 1813.)

7094. PUBLIC CONFIDENCE, Abuse of.—In questions of power * * * let no more be heard of confidence in man, but bind him down from mischief by the chains of the Constitution.—KENTUCKY RESOLUTIONS. ix. 471. FORD ED., vii, 305. (1798.)

7095. PUBLIC CONFIDENCE, Acquirement of.—The energy of the government depending mainly on the confidence of the people in the Chief Magistrate, makes it his duty to spare nothing which can strengthen him with that confidence.—To DR. HORATIO TURPIN. v, 90. (W., 1807.)

7096. ——— ———. In a government like ours, it is the duty of the Chief Magistrate, in order to enable himself to do all the good which his station requires, to endeavor, by all honorable means, to unite in himself the confidence of the whole people. This alone, in any case where the energy of the nation is required, can produce a union of the powers of the whole, and point them in a single direction, as if all constituted but one body and one mind; and this alone can render a weaker nation unconquerable by a stronger one. Towards acquiring the confidence of the people, the very first measure is to satisfy them of his disinterestedness, and that he is directing their affairs with a single eye to their good, and not to build up fortunes for himself and family.—To J. GARLAND JEFFERSON. v, 498. FORD ED., ix, 270. (M., 1810.)

7097. PUBLIC CONFIDENCE, Asked for.—Without pretensions to that high confidence you reposed in our first and greatest revolutionary character, * * * I ask so much confidence only as may give firmness and effect to the legal administration of your affairs.—FIRST INAUGURAL ADDRESS. viii, 5. FORD ED., viii, 5. (1801.)

7098. PUBLIC CONFIDENCE, Dangerous.—It would be a dangerous delusion were a confidence in the men of our choice to silence our fears for the safety of our rights.—KENTUCKY RESOLUTIONS. ix, 470. FORD ED., vii, 303. (1798.)

7099. PUBLIC CONFIDENCE, Despotism and.—Confidence is everywhere the parent of depotism—free government is founded in jealousy, and not in confidence.—KENTUCKY RESOLUTIONS. ix, 470. FORD ED., vii, 304. (1798.)

7100. PUBLIC CONFIDENCE, Lack of.—We do not find it easy to make commercial arrangements in Europe. There is a want of confidence in us.—To NATHANIEL GREENE. FORD ED., iv, 25. (P., 1785.)

7101. PUBLIC CONFIDENCE, Limits to.—Our Constitution has * * * fixed the limits to which, and no further, our confidence may go; and let the honest advocate of confidence read the Alien and Sedition Acts, and say if the Constitution has not been wise in fixing limits to the government it created, and whether we should be wise in destroying those limits.—KENTUCKY RESOLUTIONS. ix, 470. FORD ED., vii, 304. (1798.)

7102. ——— ———. Is confidence or discretion, or is strict limit, the principle of our Constitution?—To JEDEDIAH MORSE. vii, 235. FORD ED., x, 205. (M., 1822.)

7103. PUBLIC CONFIDENCE, Perversion of.—What person, who remembers the times and tempers we have seen, would have believed that within so short a period, not only the jealous spirit of liberty which shaped every operation of our Revolution, but even

the common principles of English whigism would be scouted, and the tory principle of passive obedience under the new-fangled names of confidence and responsibility, become entirely triumphant? That the tories, whom in mercy we did not crumble to dust and ashes, could so have entwined us in their scorpion toils, that we cannot now move hand or foot?—To ROBERT R. LIVINGSTON. iv, 297. FORD ED., vii, 369. (Pa., Feb. 1799.)

7104. PUBLIC CONFIDENCE, Preserve.—Let nothing be spared of either reason or passion, to preserve the public confidence entire, as the only rock of our safety.—To CÆSAR A. RODNEY. v, 501. FORD ED., ix, 272. (M., 1810.)

7105. PUBLIC CONFIDENCE, Sacrifices and.—Bringing into office no desires of making it subservient to the advancement of my own private interests, it has been no sacrifice, by postponing them, to strengthen the confidence of my fellow citizens.—To HORATIO TURPIN. v, 90. (W., 1807.)

7106. PUBLIC CONFIDENCE, Wisdom and.—It is not wisdom alone, but public confidence in that wisdom, which can support an administration.—To PRESIDENT MONROE. FORD ED., x, 316. (M., 1824.)

— PUBLIC IMPROVEMENTS.—See INTERNAL IMPROVEMENTS.

— PUBLIC OFFICE.—See OFFICE and OFFICES.

7107. PUBLIC WORKS, Government and.—The New Orleans Canal Company ask specifically that we should loan them $50,000, or take the remaining fourth of their shares now on hand. This last measure is too much out of our policy of not embarking the public in enterprises better managed by individuals, and which might occupy as much of our time as those political duties for which the public functionaries are particularly instituted. Some money could be lent them, but only on an assurance that it would be employed so as to secure the public objects.—To GOVERNOR CLAIBORNE. v, 319. (W., July 1808.)

7108. PUBLICITY, Adams's administration and.—Reserve as to all their proceedings is the fundamental maxim of the Executive department.—To BENJAMIN HAWKINS. iv, 326. FORD ED., vii, 435. (Pa., March 1800.)

7109. PUBLICITY, Complete.—There is not a truth existing which I fear, or would wish unknown to the whole world.—To HENRY LEE. vii, 448. FORD ED., x, 389. (M., 1826.)

7110. PUBLICITY, Darkness and.—Ours, as you know, is a government which will not tolerate the being kept entirely in the dark.—To JAMES MONROE. v, 52. FORD ED., ix, 36. (W., 1807.) See CONVENTION (FEDERAL).

7111. PUBLICITY, Demanded.—The journals of Congress not being printed earlier, gives more uneasiness than I would wish ever to see produced by any act of that body, from whom alone, I know, our salvation can proceed. In our [Virginia] Assembly, even the best affected think it an indignity to freemen to be voted away, life and fortune, in the dark.—To JOHN ADAMS. FORD ED., ii, 130. (Wg., 1777.)

7112. PUBLICITY, Executive, Congress and.—I remember Mr. Gallatin expressed an opinion that our negotiations with England should not be laid before Congress at their meeting, but reserved to be communicated all together with the answer they should send us, whenever received. I am not of this opinion. I think, on the meeting of Congress, we should lay before them everything that has passed to that day, and place them on the same ground of information we are on ourselves.—To JAMES MADISON. v, 174. FORD ED., ix, 131. (M., 1807.)

7113. ——— ———. I am desirous that nothing shall be omitted on my part which may add to your information on this subject [relations with France], or contribute to the correctness of the views which should be formed.—SPECIAL MESSAGE. viii, 102. FORD ED., ix. 187. (1808.)

7114. PUBLICITY, Executive support. —No ground of support for the Executive will ever be so sure as a complete knowledge of their proceedings by the people; and it is only in cases where the public good would be injured, and *because* it would be injured, that proceedings should be secret. In such cases it is the duty of the Executive to sacrifice their personal interests (which would be promoted by publicity) to the public interest.—To PRESIDENT WASHINGTON. iv, 89. FORD ED., vi, 461. (1793.)

7115. PUBLICITY, Expediency of.—If the negotiations with England are at an end, if not given to the public now, when are they to be given? and what moment can be so interesting? If anything amiss should happen from the concealment, where will the blame originate at least? It may be said, indeed, that the President *puts it in the power* of the Legislature to communicate these proceedings to *their constituents;* but is it more their duty to communicate them to their constituents, than it is the President's to communicate them to *his constituents?* And if they were desirous of communicating them, ought the President to restrain them by making the communication confidential? I think no harm can be done by the publication, because it is impossible England, after doing us an injury, should *declare war* against us, merely because we tell our constituents of it; and I think good may be done, because while it puts it in the power of the Legislature to adopt peaceable measures of doing ourselves justice, it prepares the minds of our constituents to go cheerfully into an acquiescence under these measures, by impressing them with a thorough and enlightened conviction that they are founded in right.—To PRESIDENT WASHINGTON. iv, 89. FORD ED., vi, 461. (Dec. 1793.)

7116. ——— ———. On a severe review of the question, whether the British communication should carry any such mark of being confidential as to prevent the Legislature from publishing them, he is clearly of opinion they ought not. Will they be kept secret if secrecy be enjoined? Certainly not, and all the offence will be given (if it be possible any should be given) which would follow their complete publication. If they would be kept secret, from whom would it be? From our own constituents only, for Great Britain is possessed of every tittle. Why, then, keep it secret from them?—To PRESIDENT WASHINGTON. iv, 89. FORD ED., vi, 461. (Dec. 1793.)

7117. PUBLICITY, Full.—I hope that to preserve this weather-gauge of public opinion, and to counteract the slanders and falsehoods disseminated by the English papers, the government will make it a standing instruction to their ministers at foreign courts, to keep Europe truly informed of occurrences here, by publishing in their papers the naked truth always, whether favorable or unfavorable. For they will believe the good, if we candidly tell them the bad also.—To JAMES MONROE. vi, 408. FORD ED., ix, 497. (M., 1815.)

7118. PUBLICITY, The people and.—I have not been in the habit of mysterious reserve on any subject, nor of buttoning up my opinions within my own doublet. On the contrary, while in public service especially, I thought the public entitled to frankness, and intimately to know whom they employed.— To SAMUEL KERCHIVAL. vii, 9. FORD ED., x, 37. (M., 1816.)

7119. PUBLICITY, Preservation of order and.—The way to prevent these* irregular interpositions of the people is to give them full information of their affairs through the channel of the public papers, and to contrive that those papers should penetrate the whole mass of the people.—To EDWARD CARRINGTON. ii, 99. FORD ED., iv, 359. (P., 1787.)

7120. PUBLICITY, War intelligence.— When our constituents are called on for considerable exertions to relieve a part of their fellow-citizens, suffering from the hand of an enemy, it is desirable for those entrusted with the administration of their affairs to communicate without reserve what they have done to ward off the evil.†—To PRESIDENT WASHINGTON. FORD ED., v, 431. (1792.)

* Jefferson was discussing Shays's rebellion.—EDITOR.

† The extract is from the draft of a letter written by Jefferson for President Washington, to be sent by him to the Secretary of War, as an introduction to a report on Indian affairs. Hamilton doubted " whether ' our constituents ' was a proper phrase to be used by the President in addressing a subordinate officer ", and suggested instead of it, " the community ". Washington adopted it. Hamilton also suggested that the close of the sentence after " desirable " be made to read, " to manifest that due pains have been taken by those entrusted with the administration of their affairs to avoid the evil ". Washington made the change.—EDITOR.

7121. —— ——. A fair and honest narrative of the bad, is a voucher for the truth of the good. In this way the old Congress set an example to the world, for which the world amply repaid them, by giving unlimited credit to whatever was stamped with the name of Charles Thomson. It is known that this was never put to an untruth but once, and that where Congress was misled by the credulity of their General (Sullivan). The first misfortune of the Revolutionary war, induced a motion to suppress or garble the account of it. It was rejected with indignation. The whole truth was given in all its details, and there never was another attempt in that body to disguise it.—To MATTHEW CARR. vi, 133. (M., 1813.)

7122. PUNISHMENT, Excessive.—All excess of punishment is a crime.—REPORT ON SPANISH CONVENTION. iii, 354. FORD ED., v, 484. (1792.)

7123. QUAKERS, English attachments of.—An attempt has been made to get the Quakers to come forward with a petition [against war with France], to aid with the weight of their body the feeble band of peace. They have, with some effort, got a petition signed by a few of their society; the main body of their society refuse it. M'Lay's peace motion in the Assembly of Pennsylvania was rejected with an unanimity of the Quaker vote, and it seems to be well understood, that their attachment to England is stronger than to their principles or their country. The Revolutionary war was a proof of this.—To JAMES MADISON. iv, 227. FORD ED., vii, 226. (Pa., 1798.)

7124. —— ——. I sincerely wish the circulation of the letters of "Cerus and Amicus" among the Society of Friends may have the effect you expect, of abating their prejudices against the government of their country. But I apprehend their disease is too deeply seated; that identifying themselves with the mother Society in England, and taking from them implicitly their politics, their principles and passions, it will be long before they cease to be Englishmen in everything but the place of their birth, and to consider that, and not America, as their real country.—To MR. BALDWIN. v, 494. (M., 1810.)

7125. QUAKERS, Indian civilization and.—In this important work [Indian civilization,] I owe to your Society an acknowledgment that we have felt the benefits of their zealous cooperation, and approved its judicious direction towards producing among those people habits of industry, comfortable subsistence, and civilized usages, as preparatory to religious instruction and the cultivation of letters.—REPLY TO ADDRESS. viii, 118. (1807.)

7126. QUAKERS, Jefferson's administration and.—Conscious that the present administration has been essentially pacific, and that in all questions of importance it has been governed by the identical principles professed by the Society of Friends, it has been quite at a loss to conjecture the unknown cause of the opposition of the greater part, and bare neutrality of the rest. The hope, however, that prejudices would at length give way to facts, has never been entirely extinguished, and still may be realized in favor of another administration.—To MR. FRANKLIN. v, 303. (W., 1808.)

7127. —— ——. You observe very truly, that both the late and the present administration conducted the government on principles professed by the Friends. Our efforts to preserve peace, our measures as to the Indians, as to slavery, as to religious freedom, were all in consonance with their profession. Yet I never expected we should get a vote from them, and in this I was neither deceived nor disappointed. There is no riddle in this to those who do not suffer themselves to be duped by the professions of religious sectaries. The theory of American Quakerism is a very obvious one. The mother Society is in England. Its members are English by birth and residence, devoted to their own country, as good citizens ought to be. The Quakers of these States are colonies or filiations from the mother Society, to whom that Society sends its yearly lessons. On these, the filiated Societies model their opinions, their conduct, their passions and attachments. A Quaker is essentially an Englishman, in every part of the earth he is born or lives. The outrages of Great Britain on our navigation and commerce have kept us in perpetual bickerings with her. The Quakers have taken side against their own government, not on their profession of peace, for they saw that peace was our object also; but from devotion to the views of the mother Society. In 1797-'98, when an administration sought war with France, the Quakers were the most clamorous for war. Their principle of peace, as a secondary one, yielded to the primary one of adherence to the Friends in England, and what was patriotism in the original, became treason in the copy. On that occasion, they obliged their good old leader, Mr. Pemberton, to erase his name from a petition to Congress against war, which had been delivered to a representative of Pennsylvania, a member of the late and present administration; he accordingly permitted the old gentleman to erase his name. * * * I apply this to the Friends in general, not universally. I know individuals among them as good patriots as we have.—To SAMUEL KERCHIVAL. v, 492. (M., 1810.)

7128. QUAKERS, Oppression of.—The first settlers in this country [Virginia] were emigrants from England, of the English Church, just at a point of time when it was flushed with complete victory over the religions of all other persuasions. Possessed, as they became, of the powers of making, administering, and executing the laws, they showed equal intolerance in this country with their Presbyterian brethren, who had emigrated to the northern government. The poor Quakers were flying from persecution in England. They cast their eyes on these new countries as asylums of civil and religious freedom; but they found them free only for the reigning sect. Several acts of the Virginia Assembly of 1659, 1662, and 1693, had made it penal in parents to refuse to have their children baptized; had prohibited the unlawful assembling of Quakers; had made it penal for any master of a vessel to bring a Quaker into the State; had ordered those already here, and such as should come thereafter, to be imprisoned till they should abjure the country; provided a milder punishment for their first and second return, but death for the third; had inhibited all persons from suffering their meetings in or near their houses, entertaining them individually, or disposing of books which supported their tenets. If no capital execution took place here, as did in New England, it was not owing to the moderation of the church, or spirit of the legislature, as may be inferred from the law itself; but to historical circumstances which have not been handed down to us. The Anglicans retained full possession of the country about a century. Other opinions began then to creep in, and the great care of the government to support their own church, having begotten an equal degree of indolence in its clergy, two-thirds of the people had become dissenters at the commencement of the present Revolution. The laws, indeed, were still oppressive on them, but the spirit of the one party had subsided into moderation, and of the other had risen to a degree of determination which commanded respect.—Notes on Virginia. viii, 398. Ford ed., iii, 261. (1786.)

7129. QUARANTINE, Uniform laws.— Many are the exercises of power preserved to the States, wherein a uniformity of proceeding would be advantageous to all. Such are quarantines, health laws, &c.—To James Sullivan. v, 101. Ford ed., ix, 76. (W., 1807.)

7130. QUARRELS, Among friends. —The way to make friends quarrel is to put them in disputation under the public eye. An experience of near twenty years has taught me that few friendships stand this test; and that public assemblies, where every one is free to act and speak, are the most powerful looseners of the bands of private friendship.—To General Washington. i, 334. Ford ed., iii, 466. (A., 1784.)

7131. QUARRELS, Cowards and.—A coward is much more exposed to quarrels than a man of spirit.—To James Monroe. Ford ed., iv, 34. (P., 1785.)

7132. QUARRELS, European.—I am decidedly of opinion we should take no part in European quarrels.—To General Washington. ii, 533. Ford ed., v, 57. (P., 1788.) See Alliances.

7133. QUARRELS, Human nature and. —An association of men who will not quarrel with one another is a thing which never yet existed, from the greatest confederacy of nations down to a town meeting or a vestry.—To John Taylor. iv, 247. Ford ed., vii, 265. (Pa., 1798.)

— QUEBEC, Expedition against.—See Arnold.

7134. QUIET, Love of.—I want to be quiet; and although some circumstances, now and then, excite me to notice them, I feel safe, and happier in leaving events to those whose turn it is to take care of them; and, in general, to let it be understood, that I meddle little or not at all with public affairs.—To Joseph C. Cabell. vi, 310. Ford ed., ix, 452. (M., 1814.)

— QUILLING.—See Music.

7135. QUORUM, Constitution of.—Two-thirds of the members of either house shall be a quorum.—Proposed Va. Constitution. Ford ed., ii, 17. (June 1776.)

7136. ———— ————. Two-thirds of the members of the General Court, High Court of Chancery, or Court of Appeals, shall be a quorum * * * .—Proposed Va. Constitution. Ford ed., ii, 24. (June 1776.)

7137. ———— ————. A majority of either house shall be a quorum, * * * but any smaller proportion which from time to time shall be thought expedient by the respective houses, shall be sufficient to call for, and to punish, their non-attending members, and to adjourn themselves for any time not exceeding one week.—Proposed Constitution for Virginia. viii, 444. Ford ed., iii, 324. (1783.)

7138. QUORUM, Size of.—The Assembly exercises a power of determining the quorum of their own body which may legislate for us.* After the establishment of the new form they adhered to the *Lex majoris partis*, founded in common law as well as common right (Bro. abr. Corporations, 31, 34. Hakewell, 93.) It is the natural law of every assembly of men, whose numbers are not fixed by any other law. (Puff. Off. hom. 1, 2, c. 6, § 12.) They continued for some time to require the presence of a majority of their whole number to pass an act. But the British parliament fixes its own quorum; our former assemblies fixed their own quorum; and one precedent in favor of power is stronger than an hundred against it. The House of Delegates, therefore, have lately voted (June 4, 1781), that, during the present dangerous invasion, forty members shall be a house to proceed to business. They have been moved to this by the fear of not being able to collect a house. But this danger could not authorize them to call that a house which was none; and if they may fix it at one number, they may at another, till it loses its fundamental character of being a representative body. As this vote expires with the present invasion, it is probable the former rule will be permitted to revive; because at present no ill is meant. The power, however, of fixing their own quorum has been avowed, and a precedent set. From forty it may be reduced to four, and from four to one; from a house to a committee, from a committee to a chairman or speaker, and thus an oligarchy or monarchy be substituted under forms supposed to be regular. "*Omnia mala exempla ex bonis orta sunt; sed ubi imperium ad ignaros aut minus bonos pervenit, novum illud exemplum ab dignis et idoneis ad indignos et non indoneos fertur*". When, therefore, it is considered that there is no legal obstacle to the assumption by the Assembly of all the powers legislative, executive and judiciary, and that these may come to the hands of the smallest rag of delegation, surely the people will say, and their representatives, while yet they have honest representatives, will advise them to say, that they will not acknowledge as laws any acts not considered and assented to by the major part of their delegates.—Notes on Virginia. viii, 367. Ford ed., iii, 229. (1782.)

7139. RACE, Improvement of human. —The passage you quote from Theognis, I think has an ethical rather than a political object. The whole piece is a moral *exhortation*, * * * and this passage particularly seems to be a reproof to man, who, while with his domestic animals he is curious to improve the race, by employing always the finest male, pays no attention to the improvement of his own race, but intermarries with the vicious, the ugly or the old, for considerations of wealth or ambition. It is in conformity with the principle adopted afterwards by the Pythagoreans, and expressed by Ocellus in another form * * * which, as literally as intelligibility will admit, may be thus translated, "concerning the interprocreation of men, how, and of whom it sha'l be, in a perfect manner, and according to the laws of modesty and sanctity, conjointly, this is what I think right. First, to lay it down that we do not commix for the sake of pleasure, but of the procreation of children. For the powers, the organs and desires for coition have not been given by God to man for the sake of pleasure, but for the procreation of the race. For as it were incongruous, for a mortal born to partake of divine life, the immortality of the race being

* Jefferson characterized this power as one of the defects of the first Virginia constitution.—Editor.

taken away. God fulfilled the purpose by making the generations uninterrupted and continuous. This, therefore, we are especially to lay down as a principle, that coition is not for the sake oi p.easure". But nature, not trusting to this moral and abstract motive, seems to have provided more securely for the perpetuation of the species, by making it the effect of the *oestrum* implanted in the constitution of both sexes. And not only has the commerce of love been indulged on this unhallowed impulse, but made subservient also to wealth and ambition by marriage, without regard to the beauty, the healthiness, the understanding, or virtue of the subject from which we are to breed. The selecting the best male for a harem of well chosen females also, which Theognis seems to recommend from the example of our sheep and asses, would doubtless improve the human. as it does the brute animal, and produce a race of veritable αριστοι. For experience proves that the moral and physical qualities of man, whether good or evil, are transmissible in a certain degree from father to son. But I suspect that the equal rights of man will rise up against this privileged Solomon and his harem, and oblige us to continue acquiescence under the "Αμαμρωσις γενεος αστων" which Theognis complains of, and to content ourselves with the accidental aristoi produced by the fortuitous concourse of breeders.—To JOHN ADAMS. vi, 222. FORD ED., ix, 424. (M., 1813.)

7140. RACES, Mingling of.—In time, you [Indians] will be as we are; you will become one people with us. Your blood will mix with ours; and will spread with ours, over this great Island.—INDIAN ADDRESS. viii, 234. (1809.)

7141. RAINBOWS, Formation of.—An Abbé here [Paris] has shaken, if not destroyed, the theory of Dominis, Descartes and Newton, for explaining the phenomenon of the rainbow. According to that theory, you know, a cone of rays issuing from the sun, and falling on a cloud in the opposite part of the heavens, is reflected back in the form of a smaller cone. the apex of which is the eye of the observer; so that the eye of the observer must be in the axis of both cones, and equally distant from every part of the bow. But he observes that he has repeatedly seen bows, the one end of which has been very near to him, and the other at a very great distance. I have often seen the same thing myself. I recollect well to have seen the end of a rainbow between myself and a house, or between myself and a bank, not twenty yards distant; and this repeatedly. But I never saw, what he says he has seen, different rainbows at the same time intersecting each other. I never saw coexistent bows, which were not concentric also. Again, according to the theory, if the sun is in the horizon, the horizon intercepts the lower half of the bow; if above the horizon, that intercepts more than half, in proportion. So that, generally, the bow is less than a semi-circle, and never more. He says he has seen it more than a semi-circle. I have often seen the leg of the bow below my level. My situation at Monticello admits this, because there is a mountain there in the opposite direction of the afternoon's sun, the valley between which and Monticello, is five hundred feet deep. I have seen a leg of a rainbow plunge down on the river running through the valley. But I do not recollect to have remarked at any time that the bow was more than half a circle. It appears to me that these facts demolish the Newtonian hypothesis, but they do not support that in its

stead by the Abbé. He supposes a cloud between the sun and the observer, and that through some opening in that cloud, the rays pass, and form an iris on the opposite part of the heavens, just as a ray passing through a hole in the shutter of a darkened room, and falling on a prism there, forms the prismatic colors on the opposite wall. According to this, we might see bows of more than the half circle, as often as of less. A thousand other objections occur to this hypothesis. * * * The result is that we were wiser than we were, by having an error the less in our catalogue.—To REV. JAMES MADISON. ii, 430. (P., 1788.)

7142. RAINBOWS, Lunar.—I have twice seen bows formed by the moon. They were of the color of the common circle round the moon, and were very near, being within a few paces of me in both instances.—To WILLIAM DUNBAR. iv, 348. FORD ED., vii, 482. (W., Jan. 1801.)

7143. RAINBOWS AT MONTICELLO. —I remark a rainbow of a great portion of the circle observed by you when on the line of demarcation. I live in a situation which has given me an opportunity of seeing more than the semicircle often. I am on a hill five hundred feet perpendicularly high. On the east side it breaks down abruptly to the base, where a river passes through. A rainbow, therefore, about sunset, plunges one of its legs down to the river, five hundred feet below the level of the eye on the top of the hill.—To WILLIAM DUNBAR. iv, 348. FORD ED., vii, 482. (W., Jan. 1801.)

7144. RANDOLPH (Edmund), Indecisiveness.—Everything [in the cabinet] hangs upon the opinion of a single person [Edmund Randolph] and that the most indecisive one I ever had to do business with. He will always contrive to agree in principle with one but in conclusion with the other.—To JAMES MADISON. iii, 556. (1793.)

7145. RANDOLPH (Edmund), Principles and practice.—Though he mistakes his own political character in the aggregate, yet he gives it * * * in the detail [in his pamphlet entitled "Vindication"]. Thus, he supposes himself a man of no party (page 97); that his opinions not containing any systematic adherence to party, fall sometimes on one side and sometimes on the other (page 58). Yet he gives you these facts, which show that they fall generally on both sides, and are complete inconsistencies. 1. He never gave an opinion in the cabinet against the rights of the people (page 97); yet he advised the denunciation of the popular [Democratic] societies (page 67). 2. He would not neglect the overtures of a commercial treaty with France (page 70); yet he always opposed it while Attorney General, and never seems to have proposed it while Secretary of State. 3. He concurs in resorting to the militia to quell the pretended insurrections in the west (page 81). and proposes an augmentation from twelve thousand five hundred to fifteen thousand, to march against men at their ploughs (page 80); yet on the 5th of August he is against their marching (pages 83, 101), and on the 25th of August he is for it (page 84). 4. He concurs in the measure of a mission extraordinary to London (as inferred from page 58), but objects to the men, to wit, Hamilton and Jay (page 58). 5. He was against granting commercial powers to Mr. Jay (page 58); yet he besieged the doors of the Senate to procure their advice to ratify. 6. He advises the President to a ratification on the merits of the [Jay] treaty (page 97), but to a suspension till the provision order is repealed (page 98). The fact is, that he has generally given his principles to the one party, and his practice to the other, the oyster to one, the shell to the other. Unfortunately, the shell was generally the lot of his friends, the French and republicans, and the oyster of their antagonists. Had he been firm to the principles he professes in the year 1793, the President would have been kept from an habitual concert with the British and anti-republican party. But at that time I do not know which Randolph feared most, a British fleet, or French disorganizers. Whether his conduct is to be ascribed to a superior view of things, an adherence to right without regard to party, as he pretends, or to an anxiety to trim between both, those who know his character and capacity will decide.—To WILLIAM B. GILES. iv, 125. FORD ED., vii, 40. (M., Dec. 1795.)

7146. —— ——. [Edmund Randolph's] narrative [in his pamphlet] is so straight and plain, that even those who did not know him will acquit him of the charge of bribery. Those who knew him had done it from the first.—To WILLIAM B. GILES. iv, 125. FORD ED., vii, 41. (M., Dec. 1795.)

7147. RANDOLPH (Edmund), Resignation.—The resignation, or rather the removal, of Randolph, you will have learned. His vindication bears hard on the Executive in the opinions of this quarter, and though it clears him in their judgment of the charge of bribery, it does not give them high ideas of his wisdom or steadiness.—To JAMES MONROE. FORD ED., vii, 59. (M., 1796.)

7148. RANDOLPH (John), Attacks on Jefferson.—That Mr. Randolph has openly attacked the Administration is sufficiently known. We were not disposed to join in league with Britain, under any belief that she is fighting for the liberties of mankind, and to enter into war with Spain, and consequently France. The House of Representatives were in the same sentiment when they rejected Mr. Randolph's resolutions for raising a body of regular troops for the western service. We are for a peaceable accommodation with all those nations, if it can be effected honorably. This, perhaps, is not the only ground of his alienation; but which side retains its orthodoxy, the vote of eighty-seven to eleven republicans may satisfy you.— To WILLIAM DUANE. iv, 591. FORD ED., viii, 432. (W., March 1806.)

7149. RANDOLPH (John), Defection.— The separation of a member of great talents and weight from the present course of things, scattered dismay for a time among those who had been used to see him with them. A little time, however, enabled them to rally to their own principles, and to resume their track under the guidance of their own good sense. As long as we pursue without deviation the principles we have always professed, I have no fear of deviation from them in the main body of republicans.— To CAESAR A. RODNEY. FORD ED., viii, 436. (W., March 1806.)

7150. —— ——. Unexpected and strange phenomena in the early part of the session, produced a momentary dismay within the walls of the House of Representatives. However the body of republicans soon discovered their true situation, rallied to their own principles, and moved on towards their object in a solid phalanx; insomuch that the session did most of the good which was in their power, and did it well. Republicanism may perhaps have lost a

few of its anomalous members, but the steadiness of its great mass has considerably increased on the whole my confidence in the solidity and permanence of our government.—To JOHN TYLER. FORD ED., viii, 442. (W., April 1806.)

7151. —— ——. His course [in opposition to the administration] has excited considerable alarm. Timid men consider it as a proof of the weakness of our government, and that it is to be rent into pieces by demagogues, and to end in anarchy. I survey the scene with a different eye and draw a different augury from it. In a House of Representatives of a great mass of good sense, Mr. Randolph's popular eloquence gave him such advantages as to place him unrivalled as a leader of the House; and although not conciliatory to those whom he led, principles of duty and patriotism induced many of them to swallow humiliations he subjected them to, and to vote as was right, as long as he kept the path of right himself. The sudden defection of such a man could not but produce a momentary astonishment, and even dismay; but for a moment only. The good sense of the House rallied around its principles, and without any leader pursued steadily the business of the session, did it well, and by a strength of vote which has never before been seen. Upon all trying questions, exclusive of the federalists, the minority of republicans voting with him has been from four to six or eight, against from ninety to one hundred; and although he treats the federalists with ineffable contempt, yet, having declared eternal opposition to this administration, and consequently associated with them, in his votes, he will * * * end with them. The augury I draw from this is, that there is a steady, good sense in the Legislature, and in the body of the nation, joined with good intentions, which will lead them to discern and to pursue the public good under all circumstances which can arise, and that no ignis fatuus will be able to lead them long astray.— To JAMES MONROE. v, 9. FORD ED., viii, 447. (W., May 1806.)

7152. RANDOLPH (John), Florida purchase.—He speaks of secret communications between the Executive and members [of Congress], of backstairs' influence, &c. But he never spoke of this while he and Mr. Nicholson enjoyed it almost solely. But when he differed from the Executive in a leading measure, and the Executive, not submitting to him, expressed their sentiments to others, the very sentiments (to wit, the purchase of Florida) which he acknowledges they expressed to him, then he roars out upon the backstairs' influence.—To W. A. BURWELL. v, 21. FORD ED., viii, 470. (M., Sep. 1806.) See CONGRESS, LEADERSHIP.

7153. RANDOLPH (Peyton), Estimate of.—He was indeed a most excellent man; and none was ever more beloved and respected by his friends. Somewhat cold and coy towards strangers, but of the sweetest affability when ripened into acquaintance. Of Attic pleasantry in conversation, always good humored and conciliatory. With a sound and logical head, he was well read in the law; and his opinions, when consulted, were highly regarded, presenting always a learned and sound view of the subject, but generally, too, a listlessness to go into its thorough development; for being heavy and inert in body, he was rather too indolent and careless for business, which occasioned him to get a smaller proportion of it at the bar than his abilities would otherwise have commanded. Indeed, after his appointment as Attorney-General [of the King], he did not seem to court, nor scarcely to welcome business. In that office, he considered himself equally charged with the rights of the Colony as with those of the crown; and in criminal prosecutions, exaggerating nothing. he aimed at a candid and just state of the transaction, believing it more a duty to save an innocent than to convict a guilty man. Although not eloquent, his matter was so substantial that no man commanded more attention. which, joined with a sense of his great worth. gave him a weight in the House of Burgesses which few ever attained.—To JOSEPH DELAPLAINE. FORD ED., x, 59. (M., 1816.)

7154. RANDOLPH (Thomas Mann), Independence.—I am aware that in parts of the Union, and even with persons to whom Mr. Eppes and Mr. [T. M.] Randolph are unknown, and myself little known, it will be presumed, from their connection,* that what comes from them comes from me. No men on earth are more independent in their sentiments than they are, nor any one less disposed than I am to influence the opinions of others. We rarely speak of politics, or of the proceedings of the House, but merely historically, and I carefully avoid expressing an opinion on them in their presence, that we may all be at our ease. With other members [of Congress], I have believed that more unreserved communications would be advantageous to the public.—To JOHN RANDOLPH. D. L. J., 293. (W., Dec. 1803.)

7155. RANDOLPH (Thomas Mann), Tribute to.—A gentleman of genius, science, and honorable mind.† He filled a dignified station in the General Government, and the most dignified in his own State.—AUTOBIOGRAPHY. i, 108. FORD ED., i, 150. (1821.)

— RATIO OF APPORTIONMENT.— See APPORTIONMENT.

7156. READING, Passion for.—My repugnance to the writing table becomes daily and hourly more deadly and insurmountable. In place of this has come on a canine appetite for reading. And I indulge in it, because I see in it a relief against the *tædium senectutis;* a lamp to lighten my path through the dreary wilderness of time before me, whose bourne I see not. Losing daily all interest in the things around us, something else is necessary to fill the void. With me it is reading, which occupies the mind without the labor of producing ideas from my own stock.—To JOHN ADAMS. vii, 104. FORD ED., x, 108. (M., 1818.)

7157. REASON, Action and.—Every one must act according to the dictates of his own reason.—To REV. SAMUEL MILLER. v, 237. FORD ED., ix, 175. (W., 1808.)

7158. REASON, Diverting.—Is reason to be forever amused with the crochets of physical sciences, in which she is indulged merely to divert her from solid speculations on the rights of man, and wrongs of his oppressors? It is impossible. The day of deliverance will come, although I shall not live to see it.—To M. PAGANEL. v, 582. (M., 1811.)

7159. REASON, Fallible.—I have learned to be less confident in the conclusions of human reason, and give more credit to the

honesty of contrary opinions.—To EDWARD LIVINGSTON. vii, 342. FORD ED., x, 300. (M., 1824.)

7160. REASON, Government and.—I hope that we have not labored in vain and that our experiment will still prove that men can be governed by reason.—To GEORGE MASON. iii, 209. FORD ED., v, 275. (Pa., 1791.)

7161. REASON, Oracle.—Every man's own reason must be his oracle.—To DR. BENJAMIN RUSH. vi, 106. (M., 1813.)

7162. REASON, Power of.—Truth and reason are eternal. They have prevailed. And they will eternally prevail. however, in times and places they may be overborne for a while by violence. military, civil, or ecclesiastical.—To REV. MR. KNOX. v, 503. (M., 1810.)

7163. REASON, Seeking.—The public say from all quarters that they wish to hear *reason* and not *disgusting blackguardism.*— To JAMES MADISON. iv, 281. FORD ED., vii, 344. (Pa., 1799.)

7164. REASON, Surrender of.—Man once surrendering his reason, has no remaining guard against absurdities the most monstrous, and like a ship without rudder, is the sport of every wind.—To JAMES SMITH. vii, 270. (M., 1822.)

7165. REASON, Umpirage of.—We should be most unwise, indeed, were we to cast away the singular blessings of the position in which nature has placed us, the opportunity she has endowed us with * * * of cultivating general friendship, and of bringing collisions of interest to the umpirage of reason rather than of force.—THIRD ANNUAL MESSAGE. viii, 29. FORD ED., viii, 273. (1803.)

7166. ——— ———. Every man's reason is his own rightful umpire. This principle, with that of acquiescence in the will of the majority. will preserve us free and prosperous as long as they are sacredly observed.— To JOHN F. WATSON. vi, 346. (M., 1814.)

7167. REASON vs. ERROR.—Reason and experiment have been indulged, and error has fled before them.—NOTES ON VIRGINIA. viii, 401. FORD ED., iii, 264. (1782.)

7168. ——— ———. Reason and free inquiry are the only effectual agents against error.—NOTES ON VIRGINIA. viii, 400. FORD ED., iii, 263. (1782.)

7169. REASON vs. FORCE.—A government of reason is better than one of force.— To RICHARD RUSH. vii, 183. (M., 1820.)

7170. REBELLION, Bacon's.—I return you the manuscript history of Bacon's rebellion. * * * It is really a valuable morsel in the history of Virginia. That transaction is the more marked, as it was the only rebellion or insurrection * * * in the colony before the American Revolution.—To RUFUS KING. iv, 528. (W., 1804.)

7171. REBELLION, Freedom from.— We have had thirteen States independent eleven

---

* Sons-in-law of Jefferson.—EDITOR.
† He married Jefferson's eldest daughter.—EDITOR.

years. There has been one rebellion. That comes to one rebellion in a century and a half for each State. What country before ever existed a century and a half without a rebellion?—To W. S. SMITH. ii, 318. FORD ED., iv, 467. (P., 1787.) See GOVERNMENT.

7172. REBELLION, Necessary.—I hold it that a little rebellion, now and then, is a good thing, and as necessary in the political world as storms are in the physical.—To JAMES MADISON. ii, 105. FORD ED., iv, 362. (P., 1787.)

7173. ———. A little rebellion now and then * * * is a medicine necessary for the sound health of government.—To JAMES MADISON. ii, 105. FORD ED., iv, 363. (P., 1787.)

— REBELLION, Shays's.—See SHAYS'S REBELLION.

7174. REBELLION, Spirit of.—The spirit of resistance to government is so valuable on certain occasions, that I wish it to be always kept alive. It will often be exercised when wrong, but better so than not to be exercised at all.—To MRS. JOHN ADAMS. FORD ED., iv, 370. (P., 1787.)

7175. REBELLION, Remedy for.—What country can preserve its liberties if its rulers are not warned, from time to time, that the people preserve the spirit of resistance? Let them take arms. The remedy is to set them right as to facts, pardon and pacify them.—To W. S. SMITH. ii, 318. FORD ED., iv, 467. (P., 1787.) See PUBLICITY.

7176. REBELLION, Unsuccessful.—Unsuccessful rebellions generally establish the encroachments on the rights of the people which have produced them. An observation of this truth should render honest republican governors so mild in their punishment of rebellions, as not to discourage them too much.—To JAMES MADISON. ii, 105. FORD ED., iv, 362. (P., 1787.)

7177. REBELLION, Useful.—I like a little rebellion now and then. It is like a storm in the atmosphere.—To MRS. JOHN ADAMS. FORD ED., iv, 370. (P., 1787.)

— RECEPTIONS, Presidential.—See CEREMONY, ETIQUETTE, FORMALITIES and LEVEES.

7178. RECIPROCITY, British.—It is with satisfaction I lay before you an act of the British Parliament anticipating this subject so far as to authorize a mutual abolition of the duties and countervailing duties permitted under the treaty of 1794. It shows on their part a spirit of justice and friendly accommodation which it is our duty and our interest to cultivate with all nations. Whether this would produce a due equality in the navigation between the two countries, is a subject for your consideration.—SECOND ANNUAL MESSAGE. viii, 16. FORD ED., viii, 182. (Dec. 1802.)

7179. RECIPROCITY, Commerce and.—Free commerce and navigation are not to be given in exchange for restrictions and vexations; nor are they likely to produce any relaxation of them.—FOREIGN COMMERCE REPORT. vii, 647. FORD ED., vi. 480. (1793.)

7180. RECIPROCITY, French.—I have been laboring with the ministry to get the trade between France and the United States put on a better footing, by admitting a free importation and sale of our produce, assuring them that we should take their manufactures at whatever extent they would enable us to pay for them.—To MR. OTTO. i, 558. (P., 1786.)

7181. RECIPROCITY, Justice and.—On the restoration of peace in Europe, that portion of the general carrying trade which had fallen to our share during the war. was abridged by the returning competition of the belligerent powers. This was to be expected, and was just. But in addition we find in some parts of Europe monopolizing discriminations, which, in the form of duties, tend effectually to prohibit the carrying thither our own produce in our own vessels. From existing amities, and a spirit of justice, it is hoped that friendly discussion will produce a fair and adequate reciprocity. But should false calculations of interest defeat our hope, it rests with the Legislature to decide whether they will not meet inequalities abroad with countervailing inequalities at home, or provide for the evil in any other way.—SECOND ANNUAL MESSAGE. viii, 16. FORD ED., viii, 182. (Dec. 1802.)

7182. RECIPROCITY, Modification of.—Where the circumstances of either party render it expedient to levy a revenue, by way of impost, on commerce, its freedom might be modified, in that particular, by mutual and equivalent measures, preserving it entire in all others.—FOREIGN COMMERCE REPORT. vii, 646. FORD ED., vi, 479. (Dec. 1793.)

— RECORDS, Preservation of.—See HISTORY, RECORDS OF.

7183. RECTITUDE, Contentment and.—Crooked schemes will end by overwhelming their authors and coadjutors in disgrace, and he alone who walks strict and upright, and who, in matters of opinion, will be contented that others should be as free as himself, and acquiesce when his opinion is fairly overruled, will attain his object in the end.—To GIDEON GRANGER. iv, 543. FORD ED., viii, 300. (M., 1804.)

7184. RECTITUDE, Fame and.—Give up money, give up fame, give up science, give the earth itself and all it contains, rather than do an immoral act. And never suppose, that in any possible situation, or under any circumstances, it is best for you to do a dishonorable thing, however slightly so it may appear to you.*—To PETER CARR. i, 396. (P., 1785.)

— REDEMPTIONERS.—See POPULATION.

7185. REFORM, Adequate.—The hole and the patch should be commensurate.—To JAMES MADISON. ii, 152. FORD ED., iv, 390. (P., 1787.)

7186. REFORM, Congress and.—The representatives of the people in Congress are alone competent to judge of the general disposition of the people and to what precise point of reformation they are ready to go.—To MR. RUTHERFORD. iii, 499. (Pa., 1792.)

---

* Peter Carr was the young nephew of Jefferson.—EDITOR.

7187. REFORM, Constitutional.—Happily for us that when we find our constitutions defective and insufficient to secure the happiness of our people, we can assemble with all the coolness of philosophers, and set them to rights, while every other nation on earth must have recourse to arms to amend, or to restore their constitutions.—To M. DUMAS. ii, 264. (P., 1787.)

7188. REFORM, In France.—Surely under such a mass of misrule and oppression [as existed in France in 1788] a people might justly press for a thorough reformation, and might even dismount their rough-shod riders and leave them to walk on their own legs.—AUTOBIOGRAPHY. i, 86. FORD ED., i, 119. (1821.)

7189. REFORM, Generations and.—The idea that institutions established for the use of the nation cannot be touched nor modified, even to make them answer their end, because of rights gratuitously supposed in those employed to manage them in trust for the public, may perhaps be a salutary provision against the abuses of a monarch, but is most absurd against the nation itself. Yet our lawyers and priests generally inculcate this doctrine, and suppose that preceding generations held the earth more freely than we do; had a right to impose laws on us, unalterable by ourselves, and that we, in like manner, can make laws and impose burthens on future generations, which they will have no right to alter; in fine, that the earth belongs to the dead and not to the living.—To GOVERNOR PLUMER. vii, 19. (M., 1816.) See GENERATIONS.

7190. REFORM, Government and.—Our citizens may be deceived for awhile, and have been deceived; but as long as the presses can be protected, we may trust to them for light; still more perhaps to the taxgatherers; for it is not worth the while of our anti-republicans to risk themselves on any change of government, but a very *expensive* one. Reduce every department to economy, and there will be no temptation to them to betray their constituents.—To ARCHIBALD STUART. FORD ED., vii, 378. (M., 1799.)

7191. REFORM, Gradual.—A forty years' experience of popular assemblies has taught me, that you must give them time for every step you take. If too hard pushed, they balk, and the machine retrogrades.—To JOEL BARLOW. v, 217. FORD ED., ix, 169. (W., 1807.)

7192. ——— ———. Truth advances, and error recedes step by step only; and to do our fellow-men the most good in our power, we must lead where we can, follow where we cannot, and still go with them, watching always the favorable moment for helping them to another step.—To THOMAS COOPER. vi, 390. (M., 1814.)

7193. REFORM, Moderation in.—Things even salutary should not be crammed down the throats of dissenting brethren, especially when they may be put into a form to be willingly swallowed.*—To EDWARD LIVINGSTON. vii, 343. FORD ED., x, 301. (M., 1824.)

7194. REFORM, Necessity for.—I think moderate imperfections [in constitutions and laws] had better be borne with; because, when once known, we accommodate ourselves to them, and find practical means of correcting their ill effects. But I know also, that laws and institutions must go hand in hand with the progress of the human mind. As that becomes more developed, more enlightened, as new discoveries are made, new truths disclosed, and manners and opinions change with the change of circumstances, institutions must advance also, and keep pace with the times.—To SAMUEL KERCHIVAL. vii, 15. FORD ED., x, 42. (M., 1816.)

7195. REFORM, Peaceable.—Go on doing with your pen what in other times was done with the sword: show that reformation is more practicable by operation on the mind than on the body of man.—To THOMAS PAINE. FORD ED., vi, 88. (Pa., 1792.)

7196. ——— ———. All [reforms] can be * * * [achieved] peaceably, by the people confining their choice of Representatives and Senators to persons attached to republican government and the principles of 1776, not office-hunters, but farmers, whose interests are entirely agricultural. Such men are the true representatives of the great American interest, and are alone to be relied on for expressing the proper American sentiments.—To ARTHUR CAMPBELL. iv, 198. FORD ED., vii, 170. (M., 1797.)

7197. REFORM, People and.—Whenever things get so far wrong as to attract their notice, the people, if well informed, may be relied on to set them to rights.—To DR. PRICE. ii, 553. (P., 1789.)

7198. ——— ———. [Reformation] must be brought about by the people, using their elective rights with prudence and self-possession, and not suffering themselves to be duped by treacherous emissaries.—To ARTHUR CAMPBELL. iv, 198. FORD ED., vii, 170. (M., 1797.)

7199. REFORM, Persistent.—No good measure was ever proposed which, if duly pursued, failed to prevail in the end.—To EDWARD COLES. FORD ED., ix, 479. (M., 1814.)

7200. ——— ———. In endeavors to improve our situation, we should never despair.—To JOHN QUINCY ADAMS. vii, 89. (M., 1817.)

7201. REFORM, Public money and.—I am sensible how far I should fall short of effecting all the reformation which reason would

* From the time when Jefferson began his great reforms in the Virginia House of Burgesses, the general tendency and large lines of his purposes and policy held with much steadiness in the noble direction of a perfect humanitarianism. To this day [1886] the multitude cherish and revere his memory, and in so doing pay a just debt of gratitude to a friend who not only served them, as many have done, but who honored and respected them, as very few have done.—MORSE'S *Life of Jefferson.*

suggest, and experience approve, were I free to do whatever I thought best; but when we reflect how difficult it is to move or inflect the great machine of society, how impossible to advance the notions of a whole people suddenly to ideal right, we see the wisdom of Solon's remark, that no more good must be attempted than the nation can bear, and that all will be chiefly to reform the waste of public money, and thus drive away the vultures who prey upon it and improve some little upon old routines. Some new fences for securing constitutional rights may, with the aid of a good Legislature, perhaps be attainable. —To DR. WALTER JONES. iv, 392. (W., March 1801.)

7202. REFORM, Quixotic.—Don Quixote undertook to redress the bodily wrongs of the world, but the redressment of mental vagaries would be an enterprise more than Quixotic.— To DR. WATERHOUSE. vii, 257. FORD ED., x, 220. (M., 1822.)

7203. REFORM, Retrenchment and.— Levees are done away. The first communication to the next Congress will be, like all subsequent ones, by message, to which no answer will be expected. The diplomatic establishment in Europe will be reduced to three ministers. The compensations to collectors depend on you [Congress], and not on me. The army is undergoing a chaste reformation. The navy will be reduced to the legal establishment by the last of this month. Agencies in every department will be revised. We shall push you to the uttermost in economizing. A very early recommendation * * * [was] to the Postmaster General to employ no printer. foreigner, or revolutionary tory in any of his offices.—To NATHANIEL MACON. iv, 396. FORD ED., viii, 52. (W., May 1801.)

7204. —— ——. The multiplication of public offices, increase of expense beyond income, growth and entailment of a public debt, are indications soliciting the employment of the pruning knife.—To SPENCER ROANE. vii, 212. FORD ED., x, 188. (M., 1821.)

7205. REFORM, Suffrage and.—The revolution of 1800 was as real a revolution in the principles of our government as that of 1776 was in its form; not effected, indeed, by the sword. as that, but by the rational and peaceable instrument of reform, the suffrage of the people. To SPENCER ROANE. vii, 133. FORD ED., x. 140. (P.F., 1819.)

7206. REFORM, Timely.—It can never be too often repeated that the time for fixing every essential right, on a legal basis, is while our rulers are honest and ourselves united.— NOTES ON VIRGINIA. viii, 402. FORD ED., iii, 266. (1782.)

7207. REFORMERS, Dangerous.—The office of reformer of the superstitions of a nation is ever dangerous.—To WILLIAM SHORT. vii, 167. (M., 1820.)

7208. REGENCIES, Peaceable.—Regencies are generally peaceable.—To DR. CURRIE. ii, 544. (P., 1788.)

7209. RELATIONS, Appointment to office.—The public will never be made to believe that an appointment of a relative is made on the ground of merit alone, uninfluenced by family views; nor can they ever see with approbation offices the disposal of which they entrust to their Presidents for public purposes, divided out as family property. Mr. Adams degraded himself infinitely by his conduct on this subject, as General Washington had done himself the greatest honor. With two such examples to proceed by, I should be doubly inexcusable to err. It is true that this places the relations of the President in a worse situation than if he were a stranger, but the public good, which cannot be affected if its confidence be lost, requires this sacrifice. Perhaps, too, it is compensated by sharing in the public esteem.—To GEORGE JEFFERSON. iv, 388. FORD ED., viii, 38. (W., March 1801.)

7210. —— ——. I am much concerned to learn that any disagreeable impression was made on your mind, by the circumstances which are the subject of your letter. Permit me first to explain the principles which I had laid down for my own observance. In a government like ours, it is the duty of the Chief Magistrate, in order to enable himself to do all the good which his station requires, to endeavor, by all honorable means, to unite in himself the confidence of the whole people. This alone, in any case where the energy of the nation is required, can produce a union of the powers of the whole, and point them in a single direction, as if all constituted but one body and one mind. and this alone can render a weaker nation unconquerable by a stronger one. Towards acquiring the confidence of the people, the very first measure is to satisfy them of his disinterestedness, and that he is directing their affairs with a single eye to their good, and not to build up fortunes for himself and family, and especially, that the officers appointed to transact their business, are appointed because they are the fittest men, and not because they are his relations. So prone are they to suspicion, that where a President appoints a relation of his own, however worthy, they will believe that favor and not merit, was the motive. I, therefore. laid it down as a law of conduct for myself, never to give an appointment to a relation. Had I felt any hesitation in adopting this rule, examples were not wanting to admonish me what to do and what to avoid. Still, the expression of your willingness to act in any office for which you were qualified. could not be imputed to you as blame. It would not readily occur that a person qualified for office ought to be rejected merely because he was related to the President, and the then more recent examples favored the other opinion. In this light I considered the case as presenting itself to your mind, and that the application might be perfectly justifiable on your part, while, for reasons occurring to none perhaps, but the person in my situation, the public interest might render it unadvisable. Of this, however, be assured that I considered the proposition as innocent on your part, and that it never lessened my esteem for you, or the interest I felt in your welfare.—To J. GARLAND JEFFERSON. v, 497. FORD ED., ix, 270. (M., 1810.)

7211. —— ——. I have never enquired what number of sons, relations and friends of Senators, Representatives, printers, or other useful partisans Colonel Hamilton has provided for among the hundred clerks of his department, the thousand excisemen, custom house officers, loan officers, &c., &c., &c., appointed by him, or at his nod, and spread over the Union; nor could I ever have imagined that the man who has the shuffling of millions backwards and forwards from paper into money and money into paper, from Europe to America, and America to Europe, the dealing out of Treasury-secrets among his friends in what 'time and measure he pleases, and who never slips an occasion of making friends with his means, that such an one, I say, would have brought forward a charge against me for having appointed the poet, Freneau, translating clerk to my office, with a salary of 250 dollars a year.—To PRESIDENT WASHINGTON. iii, 464. FORD ED., vi, 105. (M., 1792.)

7212. RELATIONS, Recommending.— Does Mr. Lee go back to Bordeaux? If he does, I have not a wish to the contrary. If he does not, permit me to place my friend and kinsman G. J. [George Jefferson] on the list of candidates. No appointment can fall on an honester man, and his talents though not of the first order, are fully adequate to the station. His judgment is very sound, and his prudence consummate.—To PRESIDENT MADISON. FORD ED., ix, 284. (M., 1810.)

7213. RELIGION, Compulsion.—Compulsion in religion is distinguished peculiarly from compulsion in every other thing. I may grow rich by art I am compelled to follow; I may recover health by medicines I am compelled to take against my own judgment; but I cannot be saved by a worship I disbelieve and abhor.—NOTES ON RELIGION. FORD ED., ii, 102. (1776?)

7214. RELIGION, Differences.—If thinking men would have the courage to think for themselves, and to speak what they think, it would be found they do not differ in religious opinions as much as is supposed.—To JOHN ADAMS. vi, 191. FORD ED., ix, 410. (M., 1813.)

7215. RELIGION, Discussions concerning.—I not only write nothing on religion, but rarely permit myself to speak on it, and never but in a reasonable society.—To CHARLES CLAS. vi, 412. (M., 1815.)

7216. RELIGION, Essence of.—The life and essence of religion consist in the internal persuasion or belief of the mind.—NOTES ON RELIGION. FORD ED., ii, 101. (1776?)

7217. RELIGION, Faith and.—No man has power to let another prescribe his faith. Faith is not faith without believing.—NOTES ON RELIGION. FORD ED., ii, 101. (1776?)

7218. RELIGION, Federal government and.—In matters of religion, I have considered that its free exercise is placed by the Constitution independent of the powers of the General Government. I have, therefore, undertaken, on no occasion, to prescribe the religious exercises suited to it; but have left them, as the Constitution found them, under the direction and discipline of State or church authorities acknowledged by the several religious societies.—SECOND INAUGURAL ADDRESS. viii, 42. FORD ED., viii, 344. (1805.)

7219. ————. I consider the government of the United States as interdicted by the Constitution from intermeddling with religious institutions, their doctrines, discipline, or exercises. This results not only from the provision that no law shall be made respecting the establishment or free exercise of religion, but from that also which reserves to the States the powers not delegated to the United States. Certainly, no power to prescribe any religious exercise, or to assume any authority in religious discipline, has been delegated to the General Government. It must then rest with the States, as far as it can be in any human authority.—To REV. SAMUEL MILLER. v, 236. FORD ED., ix, 174. (W., 1808.)

7220. ————. I do not believe it is for the interest of religion to invite the civil magistrate to direct its exercises, its discipline, or its doctrines; nor of the religious societies, that the General Government should be invested with the power of effecting any uniformity of time or matter among them.—To REV. SAMUEL MILLER. v, 237. FORD ED., ix, 175. (W., 1808.)

7221. RELIGION, Freedom of.—All persons shall have full and free liberty of religious opinion.—PROPOSED VA. CONSTITUTION. FORD ED., ii, 27. (June 1776.)

7222. ————. From the dissensions among Sects themselves arise, necessarily, a right of choosing and necessity of deliberating to which we will conform. But if we choose for ourselves, we must allow others to choose also. This establishes religious liberty. —NOTES ON RELIGION. FORD ED., ii, 98. (1776?)

7223. ————. If I be marching on with my utmost vigor in that way which according to the sacred geography leads to Jerusalem straight, why am I beaten and ill used by others because my hair is not of the right cut; because I have not been dressed right; because I eat flesh on the road; because I avoid certain by-ways which seem to lead into briars; because among several paths I take that which seems shortest and cleanest; because I avoid travellers less grave and keep company with others who are more sour and austere; or because I follow a guide crowned with a mitre and clothed in white? Yet these are the frivolous things which keep Christians at war.—NOTES ON RELIGION. FORD ED., ii, 100. (1776?)

7224. ————. We [the Assembly of Virginia] * * * declare that the rights hereby asserted [in the Statute of Religious Freedom] are of the natural rights of mankind, and that if any act shall be hereafter passed to repeal the present [act], or to narrow its operations, such act will be an infringement of natural right.—STATUTE OF RELIGIOUS FREEDOM. viii, 456. FORD ED., ii, 239. (1779.)

7225. ————. I do not like [in the Federal Constitution] the omission of a bill of rights, providing clearly and without the aid of sophisms for freedom of religion.—To JAMES MADISON. ii, 329. FORD ED., iv, 476. (P., Dec. 1787.)

7226. —— ——. Almighty God hath created the mind free, and manifested His supreme will that free it shall remain by making it altogether insusceptible of restraint. * * * All attempts to influence it by temporal punishments or burthens, or by civil incapacitations, tend only to beget habits of hypocrisy and meanness, and are a departure from the plan of the Holy Author of our religion, who, being Lord both of body and mind, yet chose not to propagate it by coercions on either, as was in his Almighty power to do, but to exalt it by its influence on reason alone.—STATUTE OF RELIGIOUS FREEDOM. viii, 454. FORD ED., ii, 237. (1779.)

7227. —— ——. By a declaration of rights I mean one which shall stipulate freedom of religion.—To A. DONALD. ii, 355. (P., 1788.)

7228. —— ——. I sincerely rejoice at the acceptance of our new Constitution by nine States. It is a good canvas, on which some strokes only want retouching. What these are, I think are sufficiently manifested by the general voice from north to south, which calls for a bill of rights. It seems pretty generally understood that this should go to * * * religion. * * * The declaration, that religious faith shall be unpunished, does not give impunity to criminal acts, dictated by religious error.—To JAMES MADISON. ii, 445. FORD ED., v, 45. (P., July 1788.)

7229. —— ——. One of the amendments to the Constitution * * * expressly declares, that " Congress shall make no law respecting an establishment of religion, or prohibiting the free exercise thereof, or abridging the freedom of speech, or of the press "; thereby guarding in the same sentence, and under the same words, the freedom of religion, of speech and of the press; insomuch, that whatever violates either, throws down the sanctuary which covers the others.—KENTUCKY RESOLUTIONS. ix, 466. FORD ED., vii, 295. (1798.)

7230. —— ——. I am for freedom of religion, and against all manœuvres to bring about a legal ascendancy of one sect over another.—To ELBRIDGE GERRY. iv, 268. FORD ED., vii, 328. (Pa., 1799.)

7231. —— ——. Freedom of religion I deem [one of the] essential principles of our government and, consequently, [one] which ought to shape its administration.—FIRST INAUGURAL ADDRESS. viii, 4. FORD ED., viii, 5. (1801.)

7232. —— ——. Among the most inestimable of our blessings is that * * * of liberty to worship our Creator in the way we think most agreeable to His will; a liberty deemed in other countries incompatible with good government and yet proved by our experience to be its best support.—R. TO A. OF BAPTISTS. viii, 119. (1807.)

7233. —— ——. We have solved * * * the great and interesting question whether freedom of religion is compatible with order in government, and obedience to the laws. And we have experienced the quiet as well as the comfort which results from leaving every one to profess freely and openly those principles of religion which are the inductions of his own reason, and the serious convictions of his own inquiries.—R. TO A. VIRGINIA BAPTISTS. viii, 139. (1808.)

7234. —— ——. Having ever been an advocate for the freedom of religious opinion and exercise, from no person, certainly, was an abridgment of these sacred rights to be apprehended less than from myself.—R. TO A. PITTSBURG METHODISTS. viii, 142. (1808.)

7235. —— ——. The Constitution has not placed our religious rights under the power of any public functionary.—R. TO A. PITTSBURG METHODISTS. viii, 142. (1808.)

7236. —— ——. There are certain principles in which the constitutions of our several States all agree, and which all cherish as vitally essential to the protection of the life, liberty, property and safety of the citizen. [One is] Freedom of Religion, restricted only from *acts* of trespass on that of others.—To M. CORAY. vii, 323. (M., 1823.) See VIRGINIA STATUTE OF RELIGIOUS FREEDOM, in APPENDIX.

7237. RELIGION, Government and.— Whatsoever is lawful in the Commonwealth, or permitted to the subject in the ordinary way, cannot be forbidden to him for religious uses; and whatsoever is prejudicial to the Commonwealth in their ordinary uses and, therefore, prohibited by the laws, ought not to be permitted to churches in their sacred rites. For instance, it is unlawful in the ordinary course of things, or in a private house, to murder a child. It should not be permitted any sect then to sacrifice children: it is ordinarily lawful (or temporarily lawful) to kill calves or lambs. They may, therefore, be religiously sacrificed, but if the good of the State required a temporary suspension of killing lambs, as during a siege, sacrifices of them may then be rightfully suspended also. This is the true extent of toleration.—NOTES ON RELIGION. FORD ED., ii, 102. (1776?)

7238. RELIGION, Growth of.—To me no information could be more welcome than that the minutes of the several religious societies should prove, of late, larger additions than have been usual, to their several associations.—R. TO A. NEW LONDON METHODISTS. viii, 147. (1809.)

7239. RELIGION, Honesty of life and. —I must ever believe that religion substantially good which produces an honest life. —To MILES KING. vi, 388. (M., 1814.)

7240. RELIGION, Interference with.— No man complains of his neighbor for ill management of his affairs, for an error in sowing his land, or marrying his daughter, for consuming his substance in taverns, pulling down, building, &c. In all these he has his liberty; but if he do not frequent the church, or there conform to ceremonies, there is an immediate uproar. The care of every man's soul belongs to himself. But what if he neglect the care of it? Well, what if he neglect the care of his health or estate, which more nearly relate to the State? Will the magistrate make a law that he shall not be poor or sick? Laws provide against injury from others, but not from ourselves. God Himself will not save men against their wills.—Notes on Religion. Ford ed., ii, 99. (1776?)

7241. RELIGION, Intermeddling with. —With the religion of other countries my own forbids intermeddling.—To Samuel Greenhow. vi, 308. (M., 1814.)

7242. RELIGION, And law.—I consider * * * religion a supplement to law in the government of men.—To Mr. Woodward. vii, 339. (M., 1824.)

7243. RELIGION, Opinions respecting. —It is a matter of principle with me to avoid disturbing the tranquillity of others by the expression of any opinion on the innocent questions on which we schismatize.—To James Fishback. v, 471. (M., 1809.)

7244. RELIGION, Personal.—Neither of us knows the religious opinions of the other; that is a matter between our Maker and ourselves.—To Thomas Leiper. v, 417. Ford ed., ix, 238. (W., 1809.)

7245. —— ——. I have considered religion as a matter between every man and his Maker, in which no other, and far less the public had a right to intermeddle.—To Richard Rush. Ford ed., ix, 385. (M., 1813.)

7246. —— ——. Religion is a subject on which I have ever been most scrupulously reserved. I have considered it as a matter between every man and his Maker, in which no other, and far less the public had a right to intermeddle.—To Richard Rush. Ford ed., ix, 385. (M., 1813.)

7247. —— ——. I inquire after no man's religion, and trouble none with mine; nor is it given us in this life to know whether yours or mine, our friends' or our foes', is exactly the right.—To Miles King. vi, 388. (M., 1814.)

7248. —— ——. Our particular principles of religion are a subject of accountability to our God alone.—To Miles King. vi, 388. (M., 1814.)

7249. —— ——. I have ever thought religion a concern purely between our God and our consciences, for which we were accountable to Him, and not to the priests. I never told my own religion, nor scrutinized that of another. I never attempted to make a convert nor wished to change another's creed. I have ever judged of the religion of others by their lives * * * for it is in our lives,

and not from our words, that our religion must be read.—To Mrs. M. Harrison Smith. vii, 28. (M., 1816.)

7250. —— ——. I do not wish to trouble the world with my creed, nor to be troubled for them. These accounts are to be settled only with Him who made us; and to Him we leave it, with charity for all others, of whom, also, He is the only rightful and competent judge.—To Timothy Pickering. vii, 211. (M., 1821.)

7251. —— ——. I am of a sect by myself, as far as I know.—To Ezra Stiles. vii, 127. (M., 1819.)

7252. —— ——. One of our fan-coloring biographers, who paints small men as very great, enquired of me lately, with real affection, too, whether he might consider as authentic, the change in my religion much spoken of in some circles. Now this supposed that they knew what had been my religion before, taking for it the word of their priests, whom I certainly never made the confidants of my creed. My answer was, "say nothing of my religion. It is known to my God and myself alone. Its evidence before the world is to be sought in my life; if that has been *honest and dutiful* to society, the religion which has regulated it cannot be a bad one".—To John Adams. vii, 55. Ford ed., x, 73. (M., 1817.)

7253. RELIGION, Political sermons.— On one question I differ, * * * the right of discussing public affairs in the pulpit. * * * The mass of human concerns, moral and physical, is so vast, the field of knowledge requisite for man to conduct them to the best advantage is so extensive, that no human being can acquire the whole himself, and much less in that degree necessary for the instruction of others. It has of necessity, then, been distributed into different departments, each of which singly, may give occupation enough to the whole time and attention of a single individual. Thus we have teachers of languages, teachers of mathematics, of natural philosophy, of chemistry, of medicine, of law, of history, of government, &c. Religion, too, is a separate department, and happens to be the only one deemed requisite for all men, however high or low. Collections of men associate under the name of congregations, and employ a religious teacher of the particular set of opinions of which they happen to be, and contribute to make up a stipend as a compensation for the trouble of delivering them, at such periods as they agree on, lessons in the religion they profess. If they want instruction in other sciences or arts, they apply to other instructors; and this is generally the business of early life. But, I suppose, there is not a single instance of a single congregation which has employed their preacher for the mixed purposes of lecturing them *from the pulpit* in chemistry in medicine, in law, in the science and principles of government, or in anything but religion exclusively. Whenever, therefore, preachers, instead of a lesson in religion, put them off with a discourse on the Copernican system, on chemical affinities, on the construction of government, or the characters or conduct of those administering it, it is a breach of contract, depriving their audience of the kind of service for which they are salaried. and giving them, instead of it, what they did not want, or, if wanted, would rather seek from better sources in that particular art or science. In choosing our pastor, we look to his religious qualifications, without enquiring into his physical or political dogmas, with which we mean to have nothing to do. I am aware that arguments may be found, which may twist a thread of politics into the cord of religious duties. So may they for every other branch of human art or science. Thus, for example, it is a religions duty to obey the laws of our country; the teacher of religion, therefore, must instruct us in those laws, that we may know how to obey them. It is a religious duty to assist our sick neighbors; the preacher must, therefore. teach us medicine, that we may do it understandingly. It is a religious duty to preserve our health; our religious teacher, then, must tell us what dishes are wholesome, and give us recipes in cookery, that we may learn how to prepare them. And so, ingenuity, by generalizing more and more, may amalgamate all the branches of science into every one of them, and the physician who is paid to visit the sick, may give a sermon instead of medicine; and the merchant to whom money is sent for a hat, may send a handkerchief instead of it. But notwithstanding this possible confusion of all sciences into one, common sense draws the lines between them sufficiently distinct for the general purposes of life, and no one is at a loss to understand that a recipe in medicine or cookery, or a demonstration in geometry, is not a lesson in religion. I do not deny that a congregation may if they please, agree with their preacher that he shall instruct them in medicine also, or law, or politics. Then, lectures in these, from the pulpit, become not only a matter of right, but of duty also. But this must be with the consent of every individual; because the association being voluntary, the majority has no right to apply the contributions of the minority to purposes unspecified in the agreement of the congregation.—To MR. WENDOVER. vi, 445. (M., 1815.)

7254. —— ——. I agree, too, that on all other occasions. the preacher has the right, equally with every other citizen, to express his sentiments. in speaking or writing, on the subjects of medicine, law, politics, &c., his leisure time being his own, and his congregation not obliged to listen to his conversation or to read his writings.—To MR. WENDOVER. vi, 446. (M., 1815.)

7255. RELIGION, Public office and.— The proscribing any citizen as unworthy the public confidence, by laying upon him an incapacity of being called to offices of trust or emolument. unless he profess or renounce this

or that religious opinion, * * * tends to corrupt the principles of that very religion it is meant to encourage, by bribing with a monopoly of worldly honors and emoluments, those who will externally profess and conform to it.—STATUTE OF RELIGIOUS FREEDOM. viii, 455. FORD ED., ii, 238. (1779.)

7256. RELIGION, Public opinion and. —We ought with one heart and one hand to hew down the daring and dangerous efforts of those who would seduce the public opinion to substitute itself into that tyranny over religious faith which the laws have so justly abdicated. For this reason, were my opinions up to the standard of those who arrogate the right of questioning them, I would not countenance that arrogance by descending to an explanation.—To EDWARD DOWSE. iv, 478. (W., 1803.)

7257. RELIGION, Reason and.—Dispute as long as we will on religious tenets, our reason at last must ultimately decide, as it is the only oracle which God has given us to determine between what really comes from Him and the phantasms of a disordered or deluded imagination. When He means to make a personal revelation, He carries conviction of its authenticity to the reason He has bestowed as the umpire of truth. You believe you have been favored with such a special communication. Your reason. not mine, is to judge of this; and if it shall be His pleasure to favor me with a like admonition, I shall obey it with the same fidelity with which I would obey His known will in all cases.—To MILES KING. vi, 387. (M., 1814.)

7258. —— ——. Hitherto I have been under the guidance of that portion of reason which God has thought proper to deal out to me. I have followed it faithfully in all important cases. to such a degree at least as leaves me without uneasiness; and if on minor occasions I have erred from its dictates. I have trust in Him who made us what we are. and I know it was not His plan to make us always unerring.—To MILES KING. vi, 388. (M., 1814.)

7259. RELIGION, Schismatics.—It was the misfortune of mankind that during the darker centuries the Christian priests, following their ambition and avarice, combining with the magistrate to divide the spoils of the people, could establish the notion that schismatics might be ousted of their possessions and destroyed. This notion we have not yet cleared ourselves from. In this case no wonder the oppressed should rebel, and they will continue to rebel. and raise disturbance, until their civil rights are fully restored to them, and all partial distinctions, exclusions and incapacitations are removed.—NOTES ON RELIGION. FORD ED., ii, 103. (1776?)

7260. RELIGION, Toleration.—How far does the duty of toleration extend? 1. No church is bound by the duty of toleration to retain within her bosom obstinate offenders against her laws. 2. We have no right to prejudice another in his *civil* enjoyments because he is of another church. If any man err from the right way, it is his own misfortune, no injury to thee; nor therefore art thou to punish him in the things of this life because thou supposeth he will be miserable in that which is to come—on the contrary, according to the spirit of the gospel, charity, bounty, liberality are due him.—NOTES ON RELIGION. FORD ED., ii, 99. (1776?) See PRESBYTERIAN SPIRIT.

7261. —— ——. Why have Christians been distinguished above all people who have ever lived, for persecutions? Is it because it is the genius of their religion? No, its genius is the reverse. It is the refusing *toleration* to those of a different opinion which has produced all the bustles and wars on account of religion.—NOTES ON RELIGION. FORD ED., ii. 103. (1776?)

7262. —— ——. Three of our papers have presented us the copy of an act of the Legislature of New York, which if it has really passed, will carry us back to the times of the darkest bigotry and barbarism, to find a parallel. Its purport is, that all those who shall *hereafter* join in communion with the religious sect of Shaking Quakers, shall be deemed civilly dead, their marriages dissolved, and all their children and property taken out of their hands. This act being published nakedly in the papers, without the usual signatures, or any history of the circumstances of its passage, I am not without a hope it may have been a mere abortive attempt. It contrasts singularly with a cotemporary vote of the Pennsylvania Legislature, who, on a proposition to make the belief in God a necessary qualification for office, rejected it by a great majority, although assuredly there was not a single atheist in their body. And you may remember to have heard that when the act for Religious Freedom was before the Virginia Assembly, a motion to insert the name of Jesus Christ before the phrase, "the author of our holy religion", which stood in the bill, was rejected, although that was the creed of a great majority of them.—To ALBERT GALLATIN. vii, 79. FORD ED., x, 91. (M., 1817.)

7263. RELIGION, Virginia laws respecting.—The present [1782] state of our [Virginia] laws on the subject of religion is this. The convention of May, 1776, in their declaration of rights, declared it to be a truth, and a natural right. that the exercise of religion should be free; but when they proceeded to form on that declaration the ordinance of government, instead of taking up every principle declared in the bill of rights, and guarding it by legislative sanction, they passed over that which asserted our religious rights, leaving them as they found them. The same convention, however, when they met as a member of the General Assembly in October, 1776, repealed all *acts of Parliament* which had rendered criminal the maintaining any opinions in matters of religion, the forbearing to repair to church, and the exercising any mode of worship; and suspended the laws giving salaries to the clergy, which suspension was made perpetual in October, 1779. Statutory oppressions in religion being thus wiped away, we remain at present under those only imposed by the common law, or by our own acts of Assembly. At the common law. *heresy* was a capital offence, punishable by burning. Its definition was left to the ecclesiastical judges, before whom the conviction was, till the statute of the 1 El. c. 1. circumscribed it, by declaring, that nothing should be deemed heresy, but what had been so determined by authority of the canonical Scriptures, or by one of the four first general councils, or by some other council, having for the grounds of their declaration the express and plain words of the Scriptures. Heresy, thus circumscribed, being an offence against the common law, our act of Assembly of October, 1777. c. 17, gives cognizance of it to the General Court. by declaring that the jurisdiction of that Court shall be general in all matters at the common law. The execution is by the writ *De hæretico comburendo*. By our act of Assembly of 1705, c. 30, if a person brought up in the Christian religion denies the being of a God, or the Trinity, or asserts that there are more gods than one, or denies the Christian religion to be true, or the Scriptures to be of divine authority, he is punishable on the first offence by incapacity to hold any office or employment, ecclesiastical, civil, or military; on the second, by disability to sue. to take any gift or legacy, to be guardian, executor, or administrator, and by three years' imprisonment, without bail. A father s right to the custody of his own children being founded in law on his right of guardianship, this being taken away, they may, of course, be severed from him, and put by the authority of a court, into more orthodox hands. This is a summary view of that religious slavery under which a people have been willing to remain, who have lavished their lives and fortunes for the establishment of their civil freedom. The error seems not sufficiently eradicated, that the operations of the mind, as well as the acts of the body, are subject to the coercion of the laws. But our rulers can have no authority over such natural rights. only as we have submitted to them. The r ghts of conscience we never submitted, we could not submit. We are answerable for them to our God. The legitimate powers of government extend to such acts only as are injurious to others. * But it does me no injury for my neighbor to say there are twenty gods, or no god. It neither picks my pocket nor breaks my legs. If it be said, his testimony in a court cannot be relied on, reject it then, and be the stigma on him. Constraint may make him worse by making him a hypocrite, but it will never make him a truer man. It may fix him obstinately in his errors, but will not cure them.—NOTES ON VIRGINIA. viii, 398. FORD ED., iii, 262. (1782.)

7264. REPARATION, Demand for.—It will be very difficult to answer Mr. Erskine's demand respecting the water casks in the tone proper for such a demand. I have heard of one who, having broken his cane over the head of another, demanded payment for his cane. This demand might well enough have made part of an offer to pay the damages

---

* Jefferson makes the following note from "Tertullianus ad Scapulam, cap. ii."
" Tamen humani juris et naturalis postestatis est, unicuique quod putaverit, colere; *nec alii obest, aut prodest, alterius religio.* Sed nec religionis est cogere religionem, quæ sponte suscipi debeat, non vi."—EDITOR. See CHURCH and CHURCH AND STATE.

done to the Chesapeake, and to deliver up the authors of the murders committed on board her.—To JAMES MADISON. v, 169. FORD ED., ix. 127. (M., Aug. 1807.) See CHESAPEAKE.

7265. REPARATION, War and.—Congress could not declare war without a demand of satisfaction.—To GENERAL SMITH. v, 146. (W., July 1807.) See INDEMNIFICATION.

7266. REPOSE, Evils of.—Your love of repose will lead, in its progress, to a suspension of healthy exercise, a relaxation of mind, an indifference to everything around you, and finally to a debility of body, and hebetude of mind, the farthest of all things from the happiness which the well-regulated indulgences of Epicurus ensure.—To WILLIAM SHORT. vii, 140. FORD ED., x, 145. (M., 1819.)

7267. REPRESENTATION, Apportionment and.—No invasions of the Constitution are fundamentally so dangerous as the tricks played on their own numbers, apportionment, and other circumstances respecting themselves, and affecting their legal qualifications to legislate for the Union.—OPINION ON APPORTIONMENT BILL. vii, 601. FORD ED., v, 500. (1792.) See APPORTIONMENT.

7268. REPRESENTATION, Aristocracy and.—It will be forever seen that of bodies of men even elected by the people, there will always be a greater proportion aristocratic than among their constituents.—To BENJAMIN HAWKINS. iv, 466. FORD ED., viii, 212. (W., 1803.)

7269. REPRESENTATION, Broad.—I look for our safety to the broad representation of the people [in Congress]. It will be more difficult for corrupt views to lay hold of so large a mass.—To T. M. RANDOLPH. FORD ED., v, 455. (Pa., 1792.)

— REPRESENTATION, In Congress.— See CONGRESS.

7270. REPRESENTATION, Democratic.—The full experiment of a government democratical, but representative, was and is still reserved for us. The idea (taken, indeed, from the little specimen formerly existing in the English constitution, but now lost) has been carried by us, more or less, into all our legislative and executive departments; but it has not yet, by any of us, been pushed into all the ramifications of the system, so far as to leave no authority existing not responsible to the people; whose rights, however, to the exercise and fruits of their own industry, can never be protected against the selfishness of rulers not subject to their control at short periods. The introduction of this new principle of representative democracy has rendered useless almost everything written before on the structure of government; and, in a great measure, relieves our regret, if the political writings of Aristotle, or of any other ancient, have been lost, or are unfaithfully rendered or explained to us.—To ISAAC H. TIFFANY. vii, 32. (M., 1816.)

7271. ———. My most earnest wish is to see the republican element of popular

control pushed to the maximum of its practicable exercise. I shall then believe that our Government may be pure and perpetual.—To ISAAC H. TIFFANY. vii, 32. (M., 1816.)

7272. REPRESENTATION, Deprivation of.—George III. in execution of the trust confided to him, has, within his own day, loaded the inhabitants of Great Britain with debts equal to the whole fee-simple value of their island, and, under pretext of governing it, has alienated its whole soil to creditors who could lend money to be lavished on priests, pensions, plunder and perpetual war. This would not have been so, had the people retained organized means of acting on their agents. In this example, then, let us read a lesson for ourselves, and not "go and do likewise".—To SAMUEL KERCHIVAL. vii, 36. FORD ED., x, 45. (M., 1816.) See DEBT, OPPRESSIVE ENGLISH.

7273. REPRESENTATION, Equal.—The French flatter themselves they shall form a better constitution than the English one. I think it will be better in some points—worse in others. It will be better in the article of representation, which will be more equal.—To DR. PRICE. ii. 557. (P., Jan. 1789.)

7274. ———. At the birth of our republic I committed my opinion [an equal representation] to the world in the draft of a constitution annexed to the "Notes on Virginia", in which a provision was inserted for a representation permanently equal. The infancy of the subject at that moment, and our inexperience of self-government, occasioned gross departures in that draft from genuine republican canons. In truth, the abuses of monarchy had so much filled all the space of political contemplation, that we imagined everything republican which was not monarchy. We had not yet penetrated to the mother principle, that "governments are republican only in proportion as they embody the will of their people, and execute it". Hence, our first constitutions had really no leading principles in them. But experience and reflection have but more and more confirmed me in the particular importance of the equal representation then proposed.—To SAMUEL KERCHIVAL. vii, 9. FORD ED., x, 37. (M., 1816.)

7275. ———. A government is republican in proportion as every member composing it has his equal voice in the direction of its concerns (not indeed in person, which would be impracticable beyond the limits of a city, or small township, but) by representatives chosen by himself, and responsible to him at short periods.—To SAMUEL KERCHIVAL. vii, 10. FORD ED., x, 38. (M., 1816.)

7276. ———. Let every man who fights or pays, exercise his just and equal right in the election of [members of the Legislature].—To SAMUEL KERCHIVAL. vii, 11. FORD ED., x, 39. (M., 1816.)

7277. REPRESENTATION, Freedom and.—To us is committed [by the Constitution] the important task of proving by example that a government, if organized in all its parts on the representative principle, unadulterated by the infusion of spurious elements. if founded, not in the fears and follies of man. but on his reason, on his sense of right, on the predominance of the social over his dissocial passions, may be so free as to restrain him in no moral right, and so firm as to protect him from every moral wrong. —REPLY TO VERMONT ADDRESS. iv, 418. (W., 1801.)

7278. REPRESENTATION, Government by.—Modern times have * * * discovered the only device by which the [equal] rights [of man] can be secured, to wit: government by the people, acting not in person, but by representatives chosen by themselves, that is to say, by every man of ripe years and sane mind, who either contributes by his purse or person to the support of his country. —To M. CORAY. vii, 319. (M., 1823.)

7279. REPRESENTATION, Government without.—Shall these governments be dissolved, their property annihilated, and their people reduced to a state of nature. at the imperious breath of a body of men whom they never saw, in whom they never confided, and over whom they have no powers of punishment or removal, let their crimes against the American public be ever so great?— RIGHTS OF BRITISH AMERICA. i, 131. FORD ED., i, 436. (1774.)

7280. ———. Can any one reason be assigned why one hundred and sixty thousand electors in the Island of Great Britain should give law to four millions in the States of America, every individual of whom is equal to every individual of them, in virtue, in understanding, and in bodily strength? Were this to be admitted, instead of being a free people, as we have hitherto supposed, and mean to continue ourselves, we should suddenly be found the slaves not of one but of one hundred and sixty thousand tyrants, distinguished, too, from all others by the singular circumstances, that they are removed from the reach of fear, the only restraining motive which may hold the hand of a tyrant.— RIGHTS OF BRITISH AMERICA. i, 131. FORD ED., i, 436. (1774.)

7281. REPRESENTATION, Human happiness and.—A representative government, responsible at short intervals of election. * * * produces the greatest sum of happiness to mankind.—R. TO A. VERMONT LEGISLATURE. viii, 121. (1807.)

7282. REPRESENTATION, Imperfect. —The small and imperfect mixture of representative government in England, impeded as it is by other branches, aristocratical and hereditary, shows yet the power of the representative principle towards improving the condition of man.—To M. CORAY. vii, 319. (M., 1823.)

7283. REPRESENTATION, Principles of.—In the structure of our Legislatures, we think experience has proved the benefit of

subjecting questions to two separate bodies of deliberants; but in constituting these, natural right has been mistaken, some making one of these bodies, and some both, the representatives of property instead of persons; whereas the double deliberation might be as well obtained without any violation of true principle. either by requiring a greater age in one of the bodies, or by electing a proper number of representatives of persons, dividing them by lot into two chambers, and renewing the division at frequent intervals, in order to break up all cabals.—To JOHN CARTWRIGHT. vii, 357. (M., 1824.)

7284. REPRESENTATION, Qualified. —Were our State a pure democracy. in which all its inhabitants should meet together to transact all their business. there would yet be excluded from their deliberations: 1. Infants. until arrived at age of discretion. 2. Women, who, to prevent depravation of morals and ambiguity of issue, could not mix promiscuously in the public meetings of men. 3. Slaves, from whom the unfortunate state of things with us takes away the rights of will and of property. Those, then, who have no will could be permitted to exercise none in the popular assembly; and. of course, could delegate none to an agent in a representative assembly. The business. in the first case, would be done by qualified citizens only.— To SAMUEL KERCHIVAL. vii, 36. FORD ED., x. 46. (M., 1816.)

7285. REPRESENTATION, Right of.— Does his Majesty seriously wish. and publish it to the world. that his subjects should give up the glorious right of representation, with all the benefits derived from that, and submit themselves the absolute slaves of his sovereign will?—RIGHTS OF BRITISH AMERICA. i, 136. FORD ED., i, 441. (1774.)

7286. ———. He [George III.] has endeavored to pervert the exercise of the kingly office in Virginia into a detestable and insupportable tyranny * * * by refusing to pass certain laws unless the persons to be benefited by them would relinquish the inestimable right of representation in the Legislature.—PROPOSED VA. CONSTITUTION. FORD ED., ii, 10. (June 1776.)

7287. ———. He has refused to pass * * * laws for the accommodation of large districts of people, unless those people would relinquish the right of representation in the legislature, a right inestimable to them, and formidable to tyrants only.—DECLARATION OF INDEPENDENCE AS DRAWN BY JEFFERSON.

7288. REPRESENTATION, For slaves. —I have been told, that on the question of equal representation. our fellow-citizens in some sections of the State [Virginia] claim peremptorily a right of representation for their slaves. Principle will, in this, as in most other cases, open the way for us to correct conclusion. * * * It is true, that in the general Constitution, our State is allowed a larger representation on account of its slaves. But every one knows, that that Consitutíon was a matter of compromise; a capitulation between conflicting interests and opinion. In truth; the condition of different descriptions of inhabitants in any country is a matter of municipal arrangement, of which no foreign country has a right to take notice. All its inhabitants are men as to them. Thus, in the New England States, none have the powers of citizens but those whom they call *freemen;* and none are *freemen* until admitted by a vote of the freemen of the town. Yet, in the General Government, these non-freemen are counted in their quantum of representation and of taxation. So, slaves with us have no powers as citizens; yet, in representation in the General Government, they count in the proportion of three to five; and so also in taxation. Whether this is equal, is not here the question. It is a capitulation of discordant sentiments and circumstances, and is obligatory on that ground. But this view shows there is no inconsistency in claiming representation for them for the other States, and refusing it within our own.—To SAMUEL KERCHIVAL. vii. 36. FORD ED., x, 45. (M., 1816.)

7289. REPRESENTATION, Taxation and.—Preserve inviolate the fundamental principle that the people are not to be taxed but by representatives chosen immediately by themselves.—To JAMES MADISON. ii, 328. FORD ED., iv, 475. (P., 1787.)

7290. REPRISAL, Act of war.—Remonstrance and refusal of satisfaction ought to precede reprisal, and when reprisal follows it is considered as an act of war, and never yet failed to produce it in the case of a nation able to make war.—OPINION ON THE "LITTLE SARAH". vii. 628. FORD ED., vi, 259. (1793.)

7291. REPRISAL, Congress and.—If the case were important enough to require reprisal, and ripe for that step, Congress must be called on to take it; the right of reprisal being expressly lodged with them by the Constitution, and not with the Executive.—OPINION ON THE "LITTLE SARAH". vii, 628. FORD ED., vi, 259. (1793.)

7292. REPRISAL, Retaliation by.—The determination to take all our vessels bound to any other than her ports, amounting to all the war she can make (for we fear no invasion), it would be folly in us to let that war be all on one side only, and to make no effort towards indemnification and retaliation by reprisal.—To CLEMENT CAINE. vi, 14. FORD ED., ix, 330. (M., Sep. 1811.)

7293. REPUBLIC, Definition of.—It must be acknowledged that the term *republic* is of very vague application in every language. Witness the self-styled republics of Holland, Switzerland, Genoa, Venice, Poland. Were I to assign to this term a precise and definite idea, I would say, purely and simply, it means a government by its citizens in mass, acting directly and personally, according to rules established by the majority; and that every other government is more or less republican, in proportion as it has in its compo-

sition more or less of this ingredient of the direct action of the citizens. Such a government is evidently restrained to very narrow limits of space and population. I doubt if it would be practicable beyond the extent of a New England township.—To JOHN TAYLOR. vi, 605. FORD ED., x, 28. (M., 1816.)

7294. ——— ———. The first shade from this pure element, which, like that of pure vital air, cannot sustain life of itself, would be where the powers of the government, being divided, should be exercised each by representatives chosen either *pro hoc vice,* or for such short terms as should render secure the duty of expressing the will of their constituents. This I should consider as the nearest approach to a pure republic, which is practicable on a large scale of country or population. And we have examples of it in some of our State constitutions, which, if not poisoned by priestcraft, would prove its excellence over all mixtures with other elements; and, with only equal doses of poison, would still be the best. —To JOHN TAYLOR. vi, 605. FORD ED., x, 29. (M., 1816.)

7295. ——— ———. Other shades of republicanism may be found in other forms of government, where the executive, legislative and judiciary functions, and the different branches of the latter, are chosen by the people more or less directly, for longer terms of years, or for life, or made hereditary; or where there are mixtures of authorities, some dependent on, and others independent of the people. The further the departure from direct and constant control by the citizens, the less has the government the ingredient of republicanism; evidently none where the authorities are hereditary, as in France, Venice, &c., or self-chosen, as in Holland; and little, where for life, in proportion as the life continues in being after the act of election.—To JOHN TAYLOR. vi, 606. FORD ED., x, 29. (M., 1816.)

7296. ——— ———. The purest republican feature in the government of our own State, is the House of Representatives. The Senate is equally so the first year, less the second, and so on. The Executive still less, because not chosen by the people directly. The judiciary seriously anti-republican, because for life; and the national arm wielded * * * by military leaders, irresponsible but to themselves. Add to this the vicious constitution of our county courts (to whom the justice, the executive administration, the taxation, police, the military appointments of the county, and nearly all our daily concerns are confided), self-appointed, self-continued, holding their authorities for life, and with an impossibility of breaking in on the perpetual succession of any faction once possessed of the bench. They are in truth, the executive, the judiciary, and the military of their respective counties, and the sum of the counties makes the State. And add, also, that one-half of our brethren who fight and pay taxes, are excluded, like helots, from the rights of representation, as if society were instituted for the soil, and not for the men inhabiting it; or one-half of these could dispose of the rights and the will of the other half, without their consent.*—To John Taylor. vi, 606. Ford ed., x, 29. (M., 1816.)

7297. —— ——. If, then, the control of the people over the organs of their government be the measure of its republicanism, and I confess I know no other measure, it must be agreed that our governments have much less of republicanism than ought to have been expected; in other words, that the people have less regular control over their agents than their rights and their interests require. And this I ascribe, not to any want of republican dispositions in those who formed these constitutions, but to a submission of true principle to European authorities, to speculators on government, whose fears of the people have been inspired by the populace of their own great cities, and were unjustly entertained against the independent, the happy, and, therefore, orderly citizens of the United States. Much I apprehend that the golden moment is past for reforming these heresies. The functionaries of public power rarely strengthen in their dispositions to abridge it, and an unorganized call for timely amendment is likely to prevail against an organized opposition to it. We are told that things are going on well; why change them? "*Chi sta bene, non si muova,*" said the Italian, "let him who stands well, stand still". This is true; and I verily believe they would go on well with us under an absolute monarch, while our present character remains, of order, industry and love of peace, and restrained, as he would be, by the proper spirit of the people. But it is while it remains such, we should provide against the consequences of its deterioration. And let us rest in the hope that it will yet be done, and spare ourselves the pain of evils which may never happen.—To John Taylor. vi, 607. Ford ed., x, 30. (M., 1816.)

7298. —— ——. In the General Government, the House of Representatives is mainly republican; the Senate scarcely so at all, as not elected by the people directly, and so long secured even against those who do elect them; the Executive more republican than the Senate, from its shorter term, its election by the people, in *practice* (for they vote for A only on an assurance that he will vote for B) and because, in practice also, a principle of rotation seems to be in a course of establishment; the judiciary independent of the nation, their coercion by impeachment being found nugatory.—To John Taylor. vi, 607. Ford ed., x, 30. (M., 1816.)

7299. —— ——. On this view of the import of the term *republic*, instead of saying, as has been said, " that it may mean anything or nothing ", we may say with truth and meaning, that governments are more or less republican, as they have more or less of the element of popular election and control in

---

their composition; and believing, as I do, that the mass of the citizens is the safest depositary of their own rights, and especially, that the evils flowing from the duperies of the people are less injurious than those from the egoism of their agents, I am a friend to that composition of government which has in it the most of this ingredient. And I sincerely believe * * * that banking establishments are more dangerous than standing armies; and that the principle of spending money to be paid by posterity, under the name of funding, is but swindling futurity on a large scale.—To John Taylor. vi, 608. Ford ed., x, 31. (M., 1816.)

7300. REPUBLIC, Essence of.—Action by the citizens in person, in affairs within their reach and competence, and in all others by representatives, chosen immediately, and removable by themselves, constitutes the essence of a republic.—To Dupont de Nemours. vi, 591. Ford ed., x, 24. (P.F., 1816.)

7301. REPUBLIC, First principle of.— The first principle of republicanism in that the *lex majoris partis* is the fundamental law of every society of individuals of equal right; to consider the will of the society enounced by the majority of a single vote, as sacred as if unanimous, is the first of all lessons of importance, yet the last which is thoroughly learnt. This law once disregarded, no other remains but that of force, which ends necessarily in military despotism.—To Baron Humboldt. vii, 75. Ford ed., x, 89. (M., 1817.)

7302. REPUBLIC (American), Establishment of.—In the great work which has been effected in America, no individual has a right to take any great share to himself. Our people in a body are wise, because they are under the unrestrained and unperverted operation of their own understanding. Those whom they have assigned to the direction of their affairs, have stood with a pretty even front. If any one of them was withdrawn, many others entirely equal, have been ready to fill his place with as good abilities. A nation, composed of such materials, and free in all its members from distressing wants, furnishes hopeful implements for the interesting experiment of self-government; and we feel that we are acting under obligations not confined to the limits of our own society. It is impossible not to be sensible that we are acting for all mankind; that circumstances denied to others, but indulged to us, have imposed on us the duty of proving what is the degree of freedom and self-government in which a society may venture to leave its individual members.—To Dr. Joseph Priestley. iv, 440. Ford ed., viii, 158. (W., 1802.)

7303. REPUBLIC (American), Maintenance of.—Whatever may be the fate of republicanism in France, we are able to preserve it inviolate here.—To John Breckenridge. Ford ed., vii, 418. (Pa., Jan. 1800.)

---

* Jefferson here quotes from Sir William Jones's ode the lines beginning: "What constitutes a State?"—Editor.

7304. REPUBLIC (American), A model.
—The spirit of our citizens * * * will make this government in practice, what it is in principle, a model for the protection of man in a state of *freedom* and *order.*—To General Kosciusko. iv, 295. (Pa., Feb. 1799.)

7305. REPUBLIC (American), Perils of.—I had sent to the President yesterday [May 22] drafts of a letter from him to the Provisory Executive Council of France, and one from myself to Mr. Ternant, both on the occasion of his recall. I called on him to-day [May 23]. He said there was an expression in one of them, which he had never before seen in any of our public communications, to wit, " our republic ". The letter prepared for him to the Council, began thus : " The Citizen Ternant has delivered to me the letter wherein you inform me, that yielding, &c., you had determined to recall him from his mission, as your Minister Plenipotentiary to *our republic.*" He had underscored the words, *our republic.* He said that certainly ours was a republican government, but yet we had not used that style in this way ; that if anybody wanted to change its form into a monarchy, he was sure it was only a few individuals, and that no man in the United States would set his face against it more than himself; but that this was not what he was afraid of; his fears were from another quarter; that there was more danger of anarchy being introduced. He adverted to a piece in Freneau's paper of yesterday, said he despised all their attacks on him personally, but that there never had been an act of the government, not meaning in the Executive line only, but in any line, which that paper had not abused. He had also marked the word republic thus ∨ where it was applied to the French republic. He was evidently sore and warm, and I took his intention to be, that I should interpose in some way with Freneau, perhaps withdraw his appointment of translating clerk to my office. But I will not do it. His paper has saved the Constitution, which was galloping fast into monarchy, and has been checked by no means so powerfully as by that paper. It is well and universally known, that it has been that paper which has checked the career of the monocrats; and the President, not sensible of the designs of the party, has not with his usual good sense and *sang froid,* looked on the efforts and effects of this free press, and seen that, though some bad things have passed through it to the public, yet the good have preponderated immensely.— The Anas. ix, 144. Ford ed., i, 230. (May 1793.)

7306. REPUBLIC (American), Salvation of.—To save the Republic * * * is the first and supreme law.—Autobiography. i, 82. Ford ed., i, 114. (1821.)

7307. REPUBLIC (American), Stability of.—We can no longer say there is nothing new under the sun. For this whole chapter in the history of man is new. The great extent of our Republic is new. Its sparse habi-

tation is new. The mighty wave of public opinion which has rolled over it is new. But the most pleasing novelty is, its so quietly subsiding over such an extent of surface to its true level again. The order and good sense displayed in this recovery from delusion, and in the momentous crisis which lately arose [election of President], really bespeak a strength of character in our nation which augurs well for the duration of our Republic; and I am much better satisfied now of its stability than I was before it was tried.—To Dr. Joseph Priestley. iv, 374. Ford ed., viii, 22. (W., March 1801.)

7308. ——— ———. We may still believe with security that the great body of the American people must for ages yet be substantially republican.—To Robert R. Livingston. iv, 297. Ford ed., vii, 369. (Pa., 1799.)

7309. ——— ———. The resistance which our Republic has opposed to a course of operation, for which it was not destined, shows a strength of body which affords the most flattering presage of duration. I hope we shall now be permitted to steer her in her natural course, and to show by the smoothness of her motion the skill with which she has been formed for it.—To General Warren. iv, 375. (W., March 1801.)

7310. ——— ———. We are never permitted to despair of the Commonwealth.—To James Madison. ii, 331. (P., 1787.)

7311. ——— ———. The good citizen must never despair of the Commonwealth.—To Nathaniel Niles. iv, 376. Ford ed., viii, 24. (W., 1801.)

7312. REPUBLIC (American), Triumphant.—The cause of republicanism, triumphing in Europe, can never fail to do so here in the long run.—To Archibald Stuart. Ford ed., vii, 378. (M., May 1799.)

7313. REPUBLIC (American), Washington and.—I was happy to see that Randolph had, by accident, used the expression " our republic ", in the [President's] speech. The President, however, made no objection to it, and so, as much as it had disconcerted him on a former occasion with me, it was now put into his own mouth to be pronounced to the two Houses of Legislature.*—The Anas. ix, 183. Ford ed., i, 270. (Nov. 1793.)

7314. REPUBLIC (English), France and.—Nothing can establish firmly the republican principles of our government but an establishment of them in England. France will be the apostle for this.—To E. Randolph. iv, 192. Ford ed., vii, 156. (Pa., June 1797.)

7315. REPUBLIC (English), Prospective.—If I could but see the French and Dutch at peace with the rest of their continent, I should have little doubt of dining with Piche-

* Edmund Randolph, Attorney General, had been selected to write the speech, or message, to Congress.—Editor.

gru in London, next autumn; for I believe I should be tempted to leave my clover for awhile, to go and hail the dawn of liberty and republicanism in that island.—To WILLIAM B. GILES. iv. 118. FORD ED., vii, 11. (M., April 1795.)

7316. REPUBLIC (French), America and.—I look with great anxiety for the firm establishment of the new government in France, being perfectly convinced that if it takes place there, it will spread sooner or later all over Europe. On the contrary, a check there would retard the revival of liberty in other countries. I consider the establishment and success of their government as necessary to stay up our own, and to prevent it from falling back to that kind of halfway house, the English constitution.—To GEORGE MASON. iii, 209. FORD ED., v, 274. (Pa., Feb. 1791.)

7317. REPUBLIC (French), Bonaparte and.—I fear our friends on the other side of the water, laboring in the same cause, have a great deal of crime and misery to wade through. My confidence has been placed in the head, not in the heart of Bonaparte. I hoped he would calculate truly the difference between the fame of a Washington and a Cromwell. Whatever his views may be, he has transferred the destinies of the republic from the civil to the military arm. Some will use this as a lesson against the practicability of republican government. I read it as a lesson against the danger of standing armies.—To SAMUEL ADAMS. iv, 321. FORD ED., vii, 425. (Pa., Feb. 1800.)

7318. REPUBLIC (French), Future.—France will yet attain representative government. You observe it makes the basis of every constitution which has been demanded or offered.—of that demanded by their Senate; of that offered by Bonaparte; and of that granted by Louis XVIII. The idea, then, is rooted, and will be established, although rivers of blood may yet flow between them and their object.—To JOHN ADAMS. vi, 525. (M., 1816.)

7319. REPUBLIC (French), Gratitude to.—I hope you have been sensible of the general interest which my countrymen take in all the successes of your republic. In this no one joins with more enthusiasm than myself, an enthusiasm kindled by our love of liberty, by my gratitude to your nation who helped us to acquire it, by my wishes to see it extended to all men, and first to those whom we love most.—To M. ODIT. iv, 123. (M., May 1795.)

7320. REPUBLIC (French), Sympathy with.—Be assured that the government and the citizens of the United States view with the most sincere pleasure every advance of France towards its happiness, an object essentially connected with its liberty, and they consider the union of principles and pursuits between our two countries as a link which binds still closer their interests and affections. The genuine and general effusions of joy which

you saw overspread our country, on their seeing the liberties of yours rise superior to foreign invasion and domestic trouble, have proved to you that our sympathies are great and sincere, and we earnestly wish on our part that these our natural* dispositions may be improved to mutual good, by establishing our commercial intercourse on principles as friendly to natural right and freedom, as are those of our government.—To JEAN BAPTISTE TERNANT. iii, 517. FORD ED., vi, 189. (Pa., Feb. 1793.)

7321. REPUBLIC (French), Washington and.—I have laid before the President of the United States your notification, * * * in the name of the Provisory Executive Council charged with the administration of your government, that the French nation has constituted itself into a Republic. The President receives with great satisfaction this attention of the Executive Council, and the desire they have manifested of making known to us the resolution entered into by the National Convention, even before a definitive regulation of their new establishment could take place.—To JEAN BAPTISTE TERNANT. iii, 516. FORD ED., vi, 189. (Pa., Feb. 1793.)

7322. REPUBLIC (French), Washington's cabinet and.—We met at the President's to examine by paragraphs the draft of a letter I had prepared to Gouverneur Morris on the conduct of Mr. Genet. There was no difference of opinion on any part of it, except on this expression. "An attempt to embroil both, to add still another nation to the enemies of his country, and to draw on both a reproach which, it is hoped, will never stain the history of either, that of *liberty warring on herself*". Hamilton moved to strike out these words, "that of liberty warring on herself". He urged generally that it would give offence to the combined powers; that it amounted to a declaration that they were warring on liberty; that we were not called on to declare that the cause of France was that of liberty; that he had at first been with them with all his heart, but that he had long since left them, and was not for encouraging the idea here, that the cause of France was the cause of liberty in general, or could have either connection or influence in our affairs. Knox, according to custom, jumped plump into all his opinions. The President, with a good deal of positiveness, declared in favor of the expression; that he considered the pursuit of France to be that of liberty, however they might sometimes fail of the best means of obtaining it; that he had never at any time entertained a doubt of their ultimate success, if they hung well together; and that as to their dissensions, there were such contradictory accounts given, that no one could tell what to believe. I observed that it had been supposed among us all along that the present letter might become public; that we had, therefore, three parties to attend to,—1st, France; 2d, her enemies; 3d, the people of

* Mutual in FORD EDITION.—EDITOR.

the United States; that as to the enemies of France, it ought not to offend them, because the passage objected to, only spoke of an attempt to make the United States, a *free nation*, war on France, a *free nation*, which would be liberty warring on herself, and, therefore, a true fact; that as to France, we were taking so harsh a measure (desiring her to recall her minister) that a precedent for it could scarcely be found; that we knew that minister would represent to his government that our Executive was hostile to liberty, leaning to monarchy, and would endeavor to parry the charges on himself, by rendering suspicious the source from which they flowed; that, therefore, it was essential to satisfy France, not only of our friendship to her, but our attachment to the general cause of liberty, and to hers in particular; that as to the people of the United States, we knew there were suspicions abroad that the Executive, in some of its parts, was tainted with a hankering after monarchy, an indisposition towards liberty, and towards the French cause; and that it was important, by an explicit declaration, to remove these suspicions, and restore the confidence of the people in their government. Randolph opposed the passage on nearly the same ground with Hamilton. He added, that he thought it had been agreed that this correspondence should contain no expressions which could give offence to either party. I replied that it had been my opinion in the beginning of the correspondence, that while we were censuring the conduct of the French minister, we should make the most cordial declarations of friendship to them; that in the first letter or two of the correspondence, I had inserted expressions of that kind, but that himself and the other two gentlemen had struck them out; that I thereupon conformed to their opinion in my subsequent letters, and had carefully avoided the insertion of a single term of friendship to the French nation, and the letters were as dry and husky as if written between the generals of two enemy nations; that on the present occasion, however, it had been agreed that such expressions ought to be inserted in the letter now under consideration, and I had accordingly charged it pretty well with them; that I had further thought it essential to satisfy the French and our own citizens of the light in which we viewed their cause, and of our fellow feeling for the general cause of liberty, and had ventured only four words on the subject; that there was not from beginning to end of the letter one other expression or word in favor of liberty, and I should think it singular, at least, if the single passage of that character should be struck out. The President again spoke. He came into the idea that attention was due to the parties who had been mentioned. France and the United States; that as to the former, thinking it certain their affairs would issue in a government of some sort—of considerable freedom—it was the only nation with whom our relations could be counted on; that as to the United

States, there could be no doubt of their universal attachment to the cause of France, and of the solidity of their republicanism. He declared his strong attachment to the expression, but finally left it to us to accommodate. It was struck out, of course, and the expressions of affection in the context were a good deal taken down.—THE ANAS. ix, 169. FORD ED., i, 259. (Aug. 1793.)

7323. REPUBLIC OF LETTERS, Dictatorship.—No republic is more real than that of letters, and I am the last in principles, as I am the least in pretensions to any dictatorship in it.—To NOAH WEBSTER. iii, 201. FORD ED., v, 254. (Pa., 1790.)

7324. REPUBLIC OF LETTERS, Wars and.—The republic of letters is unaffected by the wars of geographical divisions of the earth.—To DR. PATTERSON. vi, 11. (M., 1811.)

7325. REPUBLICANISM (Governmental), American.—The light from our West seems to have spread and illuminated the very engines employed to extinguish it. It has given them a glimmering of their rights and their power. The idea of representative government has taken root and growth among them. Their masters feel it, and are saving themselves by timely offers of this modification of their powers. Belgium, Prussia, Poland, Lombardy, &c., are now offered a representative organization; illusive, probably, at first, but it will grow into power in the end. Opinion is power, and that opinion will come. —To JOHN ADAMS. vi, 525. (M., 1816.)

7326. REPUBLICANISM (Governmental) Apostasy from.—An apostasy from republicanism to royalism is unprecedented and impossible.—To JAMES MADISON. iii, 5. FORD ED., v, 83. (P., 1789.)

7327. REPUBLICANISM (Governmental), Catholic principle of.—The catholic principle of republicanism is that every people may establish what form of government they please, and change it as they please, the will of the nation being the only thing essential.*—THE ANAS. ix, 129. FORD ED., i, 214. (1792.)

7328. REPUBLICANISM (Governmental), Extension of.—It is hoped that by a due poise and partition of powers between the General and particular governments, we have found the secret of extending the benign blessings of republicanism over still greater tracts of country than we possess, and that a subdivision may be avoided for ages, if not for ever.—To JAMES SULLIVAN. FORD ED., v, 369. (Pa., 1791.)

7329. REPUBLICANISM (Governmental), Happiness and.—I conscientiously believe that governments founded in republican principles are more friendly to the happiness of the people at large, and especially

* " I took the occasion," says Jefferson, "furnished by Pinckney's letter of Sep. 19, asking instructions how to conduct himself with respect to the French Revolution to lay down this principle."—EDITOR.

of a people so capable of self-government as ours.—To DAVID HOWELL. v, 554. (M., 1810.)

7330. REPUBLICANISM (Governmental), Majority rule.—A nation ceases to be republican * * * when the will of the majority ceases to be the law.—REPLY TO ADDRESS. v, 262. (W., 1808.)

7331. REPUBLICANISM (Governmental), Rights of man and.—The republican is the only form of government which is not eternally at open or secret war with the rights of mankind.—REPLY TO ADDRESS. iii, 128. FORD ED., v, 147. (1790.)

7332. REPUBLICANISM (Governmental), Schools of.—The best schools for republicanism are London, Versailles, Madrid, Vienna, Berlin, &c.—TO GOVERNOR RUTLEDGE. ii, 234. (P., 1787.)

7333. REPUBLICANISM (Governmental), Union and.—It is, indeed, of little consequence who govern us, if they sincerely and zealously cherish the principles of Union and republicanism.—TO GENERAL DEARBORN. vii, 215. FORD ED., x, 192. (M., 1821.)

7334. REPUBLICANISM (Partisan), Ardent and moderate.—I had always expected that when the republicans should have put down all things under their feet, they would schismatize among themselves. I always expected, too, that whatever names the parties might bear, the real division would be into moderate and ardent republicanism. In this division there is no great evil,—not even if the minority obtain the ascendency by the accession of federal votes to their candidate; because this gives us one shade only, instead of another, of republicanism. It is to be considered as apostasy only when they purchase the votes of federalists with a participation in honor and power.—TO THOMAS COOPER. v, 121. FORD ED., ix, 102. (W., July 1807.)

7335. REPUBLICANISM (Partisan), Benefits of.—If we are left in peace, I have no doubt the wonderful turn in the public opinion now manifestly taking place and rapidly increasing, will * * * become so universal and so weighty, that friendship abroad and freedom at home will be firmly established by the influence and constitutional powers of the people at large.—TO GENERAL KOSCIUSKO. iv, 295. (Pa., Feb. 1799.)

7336. REPUBLICANISM (Partisan), Corruption.—How long we can hold our ground I do not know. We are not incorruptible; on the contrary, corruption is making sensible though silent progress. Offices are as acceptable in Virginia as elsewhere, and whenever a man has cast a longing eye on them, a rottonness begins in his conduct.—TO TENCH COXE. FORD ED., vii, 380. (M., May, 1799.)

7337. REPUBLICANISM (Partisan), Faith in.—The tide against our Constitution is unquestionably strong, but it will turn.

Everything tells me so, and everything verifies the prediction.—To WILLIAM BRANCH GILES. FORD ED., vi, 516. (M., Dec. 1797.)

7338. REPUBLICANISM (Partisan), Fidelity to.—I have taken the liberty of referring him [Brissot de Warville] to you for a true state of republicanism here, as for the characters, objects, numbers and force of our parties. It is really interesting that these should be well understood in France, and particularly by their government. Particular circumstances have generated suspicions among them that we are swerving from our republicanism.—To DR. ENOCH EDWARDS. FORD ED., vi, 248. (Pa., 1793.)

7339. REPUBLICANISM (Partisan), Fortifying.—My great anxiety at present is, to avail ourselves of our ascendency to establish good principles and good practices: to fortify republicanism behind as many barriers as possible, that the outworks may give time to rally and save the citadel, should that be again in danger.—To JOHN DICKINSON. iv, 424. (W., 1801.)

7340. REPUBLICANISM (Partisan), The Judiciary and.—The revolution of 1800 was as real a revolution in the principles of our government as that of 1776 was in its form; not effected, indeed, by the sword, as that, but by the rational and peaceable instrument of reform, the suffrage of the people. The nation declared its will by dismissing functionaries of one principle, and electing those of another, in the two branches, Executive and Legislative, submitted to their election. Over the Judiciary department, the Constitution had deprived them of their control. That, therefore, has continued the reprobated system, and although new matter has been occasionally incorporated into the old, yet the leaven of the old mass seems to assimilate to itself the new, and after twenty years' confirmation of the federal system by the voice of the nation, declared through the medium of elections, we find the Judiciary on every occasion, still driving us into consolidation.—To SPENCER ROANE. vii, 133. FORD ED., x, 140. (P.F., 1819.) See CENTRALIZATION, JUDICIARY and SUPREME COURT.

7341. REPUBLICANISM (Partisan), Liberty and.—Under republicanism, our citizens generally are enjoying a very great degree of liberty and security in the most temperate manner.—To M. PICTET. iv, 463. (W., 1803.)

7342. REPUBLICANISM (Partisan), Missouri question and.—[The Missouri question] has given resurrection to the Hartford Convention men. They have had the address, by playing on the honest feelings of our former friends, to seduce them from their kindred spirits, and to borrow their weight into the federal scale. Desperate of regaining power under political distinctions, they have adroitly wriggled into its seat under the auspices of morality, and are again in the ascendency from which their sins had hurled them. It is, indeed, of little consequence who govern us if they sincerely and zealously cherish the principles of union and republicanism.—To HENRY DEARBORN. vii, 215. FORD ED., x, 191. (M., 1821.) See MISSOURI QUESTION and PARTIES.

7343. REPUBLICANISM (Partisan), Outlawed.—Republicanism had been the mark on Cain, which had rendered those who bore it exiles from all portion in the trusts and authorities of their country.—To BENJAMIN HAWKINS. iv, 466. FORD ED., viii, 212. (W., 1803.) See OFFICE and OFFICES.

7344. REPUBLICANISM (Partisan), The people and.—The people are essentially republican. They retain unadulterated the principles of '75, and those who are conscious of no change in themselves have nothing to fear in the long run.—To JAMES LEWIS, JR. iv, 241. FORD ED., vii, 250. (Pa., May 1798.)

7345. ——— ———. The people through all the States are for republican forms, republican principles, simplicity. economy, religious and civil freedom.—To E. LIVINGSTON. iv, 328. FORD ED., vii, 443. (Pa., 1800.)

7346. REPUBLICANISM (Partisan), Preservation of.—Whether the surrender of our opponents, their reception into our camp, their assumption of our name, and apparent accession to our objects, may strengthen or weaken the genuine principles of republicanism, may be a good or an evil, is yet to be seen.—To WILLIAM T. BARRY. vii, 255. (M., 1822.)

7347. REPUBLICANISM (Partisan), Safety in.—So long as the pure principles of our revolution [of 1800] prevail, we are safe from everything which can assail us from without or within.—To MR. LAMBERT. v, 528. (M., 1810.)

7348. REPUBLICANISM (Partisan), Seceders from.—My opinion is that two or three years more will bring back to the fold of republicanism all our wandering brethren whom the cry of "wolf" scattered in 1798. Till that is done, let every man stand to his post, and hazard nothing by change. And when that is done, you and I may retire to that tranquillity which our years begin to call for, and review with satisfaction the efforts of the age we happened to be born in, crowned with complete success. In the hour of death, we shall have the consolation to see established in the land of our fathers the most wonderful work of wisdom and disinterested patriotism that has ever yet appeared on the globe.—To DE WITT CLINTON. iv, 521. (W., 1803.)

7349. REPUBLICANISM (Partisan), Ship of State and.—The time is coming when we shall fetch up the lee-way of our vessel. The changes in your House [of Representatives] I see, are going on for the better, and even the Augean herd over your heads are slowly purging off their impurities. Hold on, then, that we may not shipwreck in the meanwhile.—To JAMES MADISON. iv, 112. FORD ED., vi, 519. (M., Dec. 1794.)

7350. ——— ———. The storm through which we have passed has been tremendous indeed. The tough sides of our Argosy have been thoroughly tried. Her strength has stood the waves into which she was steered, with a view to sink her. We shall put her on her republican tack, and she will now show by the beauty of her motion the skill of her builders.—To JOHN DICKINSON. iv, 365. FORD ED., viii, 7. (W., March 1801.)

7351. ——— ———. The storm is over, and we are in port. The ship was not rigged for the service she was put on. We will show the smoothness of her motions on her republican tack.—To SAMUEL ADAMS. iv, 389. FORD ED., viii, 39. (W., March 1801.)

7352. REPUBLICANISM (Partisan), Sincerity in.—That I have acted through life on principles of sincere republicanism, I feel in every fibre of my constitution. And when men, who feel like myself, bear witness in my favor, my satisfaction is complete.—To REV. MR. KNOX. v, 502. (M., 1810.)

7353. REPUBLICANS, Aims of.—Surely we had in view to obtain the theory and practice of good government; and how any, who seemed so ardent in this pursuit, could as shamelessly have apostatized, and supposed we meant only to put our government into other hands, but not other forms, is indeed wonderful.—To JOHN DICKINSON. iv, 424. (W., 1801.)

7354. ——— ———. The federalists wished for everything which would approach our new government to a monarchy. The republicans to preserve it essentially republican. This was the true origin of the division, and remains still the essential principle of difference between the two parties.—NOTES ON MARSHALL'S LIFE OF WASHINGTON. ix, 480. FORD ED., ix, 263. (M., 1809.) See FEDERALISTS and PARTIES.

7355. REPUBLICANS, Antagonistic to England.—The war between France and England has brought forward the republicans and monocrats in every State so openly, that their relative numbers are perfectly visible. It appears that the latter are as nothing.—To JAMES MADISON. iv, 9. FORD ED., vi, 326. (June 1793.) See FEDERALISTS.

7356. REPUBLICANS, Belief of.—[The Republicans] believed that men, enjoying in ease and security the full fruits of their own industry, enlisted by all their interests on the side of law and order, habituated to think for themselves, and to follow their reason as their guide, would be more easily and safely governed than with minds nourished in error, and vitiated and debased, as in Europe, by ignorance, indigence and oppression.—To WILLIAM JOHNSON. vii, 292. FORD ED., x, 227. (M., 1823.)

7357. REPUBLICANS, Defeated.—I had always hoped, that the popularity of the active President being once withdrawn from active effect, the natural feelings of the people towards liberty would restore the equilibrium between the Executive and Legislative departments, which had been destroyed by the superior weight and effect of that popularity; and that their natural feelings of moral obligation would discountenance the ungrateful predilection of the Executive in favor of Great Britain. But, unfortunately, the preceding measures had already alienated the nation which was the object of them, had excited reaction from them and this reaction has on the minds of our citizens an effect which supplies that of the Washington popularity. This effect was sensible on some of the late congressional elections, and this it is which has lessened the republican majority in Congress. When it will be reinforced, must depend on events, and these are so incalculable, that I consider the future character of our republic as in the air; indeed its future fortune will be in the air, if war is made on us by France, and if Louisiana becomes a Gallo-American colony.—To AARON BURR. iv, 185. FORD ED., vii, 147. (Pa., June 1797.) See FEDERALISTS.

7358. REPUBLICANS, Dividing.—Little squibs in certain papers had long ago apprised me of a design to sow tares between particular republican characters, but to divide those by lying tales whom truths cannot divide, is the hackneyed policy of the gossips of every society. Our business is to march straight forward to the object which has occupied us for eight and twenty years, without turning either to the right or left.—To DE WITT CLINTON. iv, 520. (W., 1803.)

7359. REPUBLICANS, Divisions among.—The operations of this session of Congress, when known among the people at large, will consolidate them. We shall now be so strong that we shall certainly split again; for freemen, thinking differently and speaking and acting as they think, will form into classes of sentiment, but it must be under another name. That of federalism is become so odious that no party can rise under it.—To JOEL BARLOW. iv, 437. FORD ED., viii, 150. (W., May 1802.)

7360. —— ——. I have for some time been satisfied a schism was taking place in Pennsylvania between the moderates and highflyers. The same will take place in Congress whenever a proper head for the latter shall start up, and we must expect division of the same kind in other States as soon as the republicans shall be so strong as to fear no other enemy.— To ALBERT GALLATIN. FORD ED., viii, 222. (M., March 1803.)

7361. —— ——. I think it possibly may happen that we shall divide among ourselves whenever federalism is completely eradicated, yet I think it the duty of every republican to make great sacrifices of opinion to put off the evil day.—To JOSEPH SCOTT. FORD ED., viii, 305. (W., March 1804.)

7362. —— ——. The divisions among the republicans * * * are distressing, but they are not unexpected to me. From the moment I foresaw the entire prostration of federalism, I knew that at that epoch more distressing divisions would take its place. The opinions of men are as various as their faces, and they will always find some rallying principle or point at which those nearest to it will unite, reducing

themselves to two stations, under a common name for each. These stations, or camps, will be formed of very heterogeneous materials, combining from very different motives, and with very different views.—To WILSON C. NICHOLAS. FORD ED., viii, 348. (M., March 1805.)

7363. —— ——. I did believe my station in March, 1801, as painful as could be undertaken, having to meet in front all the terrible passions of federalism in the first moment of its defeat and mortification, and to grapple with it until completely subdued. But I consider that as less painful than to be placed between conflicting friends. There my way was clear and my mind made up. I never for a moment had to balance between two opinions. In the new divisions which are to arise the case will be very different. Even those who seem to coalesce will be like the image of clay and brass. However, under difficulties of this kind, I have ever found one, and only one rule, *to do what is right*, and generally we shall disentangle ourselves without almost perceiving how it happens.—To WILSON C. NICHOLAS. FORD ED., viii, 349. (M., March 1805.)

7364. —— ——. The duty of an upright Administration is to pursue its course steadily, to know nothing of these family dissensions, and to cherish the good principles of both parties. The war *ad internecionem* which we have waged against federalism, has filled our later times with strife and unhappiness. We have met it, with pain indeed, but with firmness, because we believed it the last convulsive effort of that hydra, which in earlier times we had conquered in the field. But if any degeneracy of principle should ever render it necessary to give ascendancy to one of the rising sections over the other, I thank my God it will fall to some other to perform that operation. The only cordial I wish to carry into my retirement, is the undivided good will of all those with whom I have acted.—To DR. GEORGE LOGAN. iv, 575. FORD ED., viii, 353. (W., May 1805.)

7365. —— ——. I see with infinite pain the bloody schism which has taken place among our friends in Pennsylvania and New York, and will probably take place in other States. The main body of both sections mean well, but their good intentions will produce great public evil. The minority, whichever section shall be the minority, will end in coalition with the federalists, and some compromise of principle; because these will not sell their aid for nothing. Republicanism will thus lose, and royalism gain, some portion of that ground which we thought we had rescued to good government. I do not express my sense of our misfortunes from any idea that they are remediable. I know that the passions of men will take their course, that they are not to be controlled but by despotism, and that this melancholy truth is the pretext for despotism.—To DR. GEORGE LOGAN. iv, 575. FORD ED., viii, 352. (W., May 1805.)

7366. —— ——. I see with extreme concern the acrimonious dissensions into which our friends in Pennsylvania have fallen, but have long since made up my mind on the propriety of the General Government's taking no side in State quarrels. And with respect to myself particularly, after eight and thirty years of uniform action in harmony with those now constituting the republican party, without one single instant of alienation from them, it cannot be but my most earnest desire to carry into retirement with me their undivided approbation and esteem. I retain, therefore, a cordial friendship for both the sections now so unhappily dividing your State.—To THOMAS LEIB. FORD ED., viii, 353. (M., Aug. 1805.)

7367. —— ——. Of the unhappy effects of the schisms in Pennsylvania and New York, you see the fruit in the State lying between them, where the federalists have recovered a majority in one branch of the legislature, are very near it in the other, and as soon as they shall reach it, they place the executive and every office under it in federal hands. If the two sections of republicans were irreconcilable, still the minor one should not have coalesced with, and voted for federalists. If, on the contrary, they would keep themselves independent, and set up their own ticket, their whole body would come forward and vote, which would give them the benefit of that part of their force which kept back because it could not support federalists, and the federalists themselves, having no hope of bringing in men of their own, would have to choose between the two republican tickets that least disagreeable to themselves. This would only bring into the public councils the different shades of republicans so that the whole body should be represented.— To ANDREW ELLIOTT. FORD ED., viii, 479. (W., Nov. 1806.)

7368. —— ——. I determined from the first dawn of the first schism, never to take part in any schism of republicans, nor in distributing the public trusts ever to ask of which section a party was.—To ANDREW ELLICOTT. FORD ED., viii, 480. (W., Nov. 1806.)

7369. —— ——. I have long seen, and with very great regret, the schisms which have taken place among the republicans, and principally those of Pennsylvania and New York. As far as I have been able to judge, they have not been produced by any difference of political principle,—at least, any important difference, but by a difference of opinion as to persons. I determined from the first moment to take no part in them, and that the Government should know nothing of any such differences. Accordingly, it has never been attended to in any appointment, or refusal of appointment.—To JAMES GAMBLE. v, 204. FORD ED., ix, 129. (W., 1807.)

7370. —— ——. If we schismatize on either men or measures, if we do not act in phalanx, as when we rescued the country from the satellites of monarchism, I will not say our *party* (the term is false and degrading), but our *nation* will be undone. For the republicans are the *nation*. Their opponents are but a faction, weak in numbers, but powerful and profuse in the command of money, and backed by a nation [England], powerful also and profuse in the use of the same means; and the more profuse, in both cases, as the money they thus employ is not their own but their creditors, to be paid off by a bankruptcy, which whether it pays a dollar or a shilling in the pound, is of little concern with them. The last hope of human liberty in this world rests on us. We ought, for so dear a stake, to sacrifice every attachment and every enmity. Leave the President free to choose his own coadjutors, to pursue his own measures, and support him and them, even if we think we are wiser than they, honester than they, or possessing more enlarged information of the state of things. If we move in mass, be it ever so circuitously, we shall attain our object; but if we break into squads, every one pursuing the path he thinks

most direct, we become an easy conquest to those who can now barely hold us in check. I repeat again, that we ought not to schismatize on either men or measures. Principles alone can justify that. If we find our government in all its branches rushing headlong, like our predecessors, into the arms of monarchy, if we find them violating our dearest rights, the trial by jury, the freedom of the press, the freedom of opinion, civil or religious, or opening on our peace of mind or personal safety the sluices of terrorism; if we see them raising standing armies, when the absence of all other danger points to these as the sole objects on which they are to be employed, then, indeed, let us withdraw and call the nation to its tents. But, while our functionaries are wise, and honest, and vigilant, let us move compactly under their guidance, and we have nothing to fear. Things may here and there go a little wrong. It is not in our power to prevent it. But all will be right in the end, though not, perhaps, by the shortest means. You know that this union of republicans has been the constant theme of my exhortations, that I have ever refused to know any sub-divisions among them, to take part in any personal differences; and, therefore, you will not give to the present observations any other than general application. I may sometimes differ in opinion from some of my friends, from those whose views are as pure and sound as my own. I censure none, but do homage to everyone's right of opinion.— To WILLIAM DUANE. v, 576. FORD ED., ix, 313. (M., March 1811.)

7371. —— ——. The only contest between divided [political] friends should be who will dare farthest into the ranks of the common enemy.—To JOHN HOLLINS. v, 597. (M., 1811.)

7372. —— ——. The schism in Massachusetts, when brought to the crisis of principle, will be found to be exactly the same as in the Revolutionary war. The monarchists will be left alone, and will appear to be exactly the tories of the last war.—To THOMAS LETRE. vi, 79. (M., Aug. 1812.)

7373. REPUBLICANS, Early contests of.—The inconveniences of an inefficient government, driving the people as is usual, into the opposite extreme, the elections to the first Congress ran very much in favor of those who were known to favor a very strong government. Hence the anti-republicans appeared a considerable majority in both houses of Congress. They pressed forward the plan, therefore, of strengthening all the features of the government which gave it resemblance to an English constitution, of adopting the English forms and principles of administration, and of forming like them a moneyed interest, by means of a funding system, not calculated to pay the public debt, but to render it perpetual, and to make it an engine in the hands of the executive branch of government which, added to the great patronage it possessed in the disposal of public offices, might enable it to assume by degrees a kingly authority. The biennial period of Congress being too short to betray to the people, spread over this great continent, this train of things during the first Congress, little change was made in members to the second. But, in the meantime, two very distinct parties had formed in Congress; and before the third election, the people in general became apprised of the game which was playing for drawing over them a kind of government which they never had in contemplation. At the third election, therefore, a decided majority of republicans were sent to the lower House of Congress; and, as information spread still farther among the people, after the fourth election the anti-republican members have become a weak minority.—To C. D. EBELING. FORD ED., vii, 46. (1795.)

7374. —— ——. When Congress first met, the assemblage of facts presented in the President's [Adams's] speech [message], with the multiplied accounts of spoliations by the French West Indians, appeared by sundry votes on the address, to incline a majority to put themselves in a posture of war. Under this influence the address was formed, and its spirit would probably have been pursued by corresponding measures, had the events of Europe been of an ordinary train. But this has been so extraordinary, that numbers have gone over to those, who, from the first, feeling with sensibility the French insults, as they had felt those of England before, thought now as they thought then, that war measures should be avoided, and those of peace pursued. Their favorite engine, on the former occasion, was *commercial regulations* in preference to negotiations, to war preparations, and increase of debt. On the latter, as we have no commerce with France, the restriction of which could press on them, they wished for negotiation. Those of the opposite sentiment had, on the former occasion, preferred negotiation, but at the same time voted for great war preparations, and increase of debt; now also they were for negotiation, war preparations and debt. The parties have in debate mutually charged each other with inconsistency, and with being governed by an attachment to this or that of the belligerent nations, rather than the dictates of reason and pure Americanism. But, in truth, both have been consistent; the same men having voted for war measures who did before, and the same against them now who did before.—To EDWARD RUTLEDGE. iv, 190. FORD ED., vii, 152. (Pa., June 1797.)

7375. —— ——. The spirit of both the speech [message of the President] and the address [of Congress] has been so whittled down by Bonaparte's victories, victories on the Rhine, the Austrian peace, Irish insurgency, English bankruptcy, insubordination of the [British] fleet, &c., that Congress is rejecting, one by one, the measures brought in on the principles of their own address. But nothing less than such miraculous events, as have been pouring in on us from the first of our convening, could have assuaged the fermentation produced in men's minds. In consequence of these events, what was the majority at first, is by degrees become the minority, so that we may say that, in the Representatives, moderation will govern.—To E. RANDOLPH. iv, 192. FORD ED., vii, 155. (Pa., June 1797.) See FEDERALISTS.

7376. REPUBLICANS, Federalists vs. —Two parties * * * exist within the United States. They embrace respectively the following descriptions of persons. The anti-republicans consist of: 1. The old refugees and tories. 2. British merchants residing among us, and composing the main body of our merchants. 3. American merchants trading on British capital, another great portion. 4. Speculators and holders in the banks and public funds. 5. Officers of the Federal Government with some exceptions. 6. Office-hunters, willing to give up principles for places,—a numerous and noisy tribe. 7. Nervous persons, whose languid fibres have more analogy with a passive than active state of things. The republican part of our Union comprehends: 1. The entire body of landholders throughout the United States. 2. The body of laborers, not being landholders, whether in husbanding or the arts. The latter is to the aggregate of the former party probably as 500 to 1; but their wealth is not as disproportionate, though it is also greatly superior, and is in truth the foundation of that of their antagonists. Trifling as are the numbers of the anti-republican party, there are circumstances which give them an appearance of strength and numbers. They all live in cities, together, and can act in a body readily at all times; they give chief employment to the newspapers, and, therefore, have most of them under their command. The agricultural interest is dispersed over a great extent of country, have little means of intercommunication with each other, and feeling their own strength and will, are conscious that a single exertion of these will, at any time, crush the machinations against their government.—To C. D. EBELING. FORD ED., vii, 47. (1795.)

7377. —— ——. I trust that no section of republicans will countenance the suggestions of the federalists that there has ever been any difference at all in our political principles, or any sensible one in our views of the public interest.—To JAMES MADISON. FORD ED., ix, 242. (M., 1809.)

7378. —— ——. [It was] a contest* which was to change the condition of man over the civilized globe.—THE ANAS. FORD ED., i, 156. (1818.) See MONARCHY.

7379. REPUBLICANS, Federalist coalition with.—The gross [Chesapeake] insult lately received from the English has forced the federalists into a momentary coalition with the mass of republicans; but the moment we begin to act in the very line they have joined in approving, all will be wrong, and every act the reverse of what it should have been. Still, it is better to admit their coalescence, and leave to themselves their short-lived existence.—To THOMAS COOPER. v, 121. FORD ED., ix, 102. (W., July 1807.) See CHESAPEAKE and FEDERALISTS.

7380. REPUBLICANS, French victories and.—I think we may safely rely that the

* The contest between the Republicans and Federalists.—EDITOR.

Duke of Brunswick has retreated; and it is certainly possible enough that between famine, disease, and a country abounding with defiles, he may suffer some considerable catastrophe. The monocrats here [Philadelphia] still affect to disbelieve all this, while the republicans are rejoicing and taking to themselves the name of Jacobins, which two months ago was fixed on them by way of stigma.—To JOHN FRANCIS MERCER. iii, 495. FORD ED., vi, 147. (Pa., Dec. 1792.)

7381. REPUBLICANS, Historical misrepresentation of.—Were a reader of this period [immediately following the establishment of the Constitution] to form his idea of it from this history alone [Marshall's *Life of Washington*] he would suppose the republican party (who were in truth endeavoring to keep the government within the line of the Constitution, and prevent its being monarchised in practice) were a mere set of grumblers, and disorganizers, satisfied with no government, without fixed principles of any, and, like a British parliamentary opposition, gaping after loaves and fishes, and ready to change principles, as well as position, at any time, with their adversaries. But * * * the contests of that day were contests of principle, between the advocates of republican and those of kingly government, and had not the former made the efforts they did, our government would have been, even at this early day [1818], a very different thing from what the successful issue of those efforts have made it.—THE ANAS. FORD ED., i, 156. (1818.)

7382. —— ——. We [the republicans] have been too careless of our own future reputation, while our tories will omit nothing to place us in the wrong.—To WILLIAM JOHNSON. vii, 277. FORD ED., x. 247. (M., 1823.)

7383. REPUBLICANS, Leadership of.—The monocrats [in Pennsylvania] have kept up the ball with respect to myself till they begin to be tired of it themselves. Their chief object was to influence the election of this State, by persuading [the people] there was a league against the government, and as it was necessary to designate a head to the league, they did me that honor.—To T. M. RANDOLPH. FORD ED., vi, 128. (Pa., 1792.)

7384. REPUBLICANS, Loyalty of.—Without knowing the views of what is called the republican party here [Philadelphia], or having any communication with them, I could undertake to assure him [President Washington] from my intimacy with that party in the late Congress, that there was not a view in the republican party as spread over the United States, which went to the frame of the government; that I believed the next Congress would attempt nothing material, but to render their own body independent; that that party were firm in their dispositions to support the government; that the maneuvers of Mr. Genet might produce some little embarrassment, but that he would be abandoned by the republicans the moment they

knew the nature of his conduct.—THE ANAS. ix, 166. FORD ED., i, 257. (Aug. 1793.)

7385. —— ——. He [President Washington] said he believed the views of the republican party were perfectly pure, but when men put a machine into motion, it is impossible for them to stop it exactly where they would choose, or to say where it will stop. That the Constitution we have is an excellent one, if we can keep it where it is; that it was, indeed, supposed there was a party disposed to change it into a monarchical form, but that he could conscientiously declare there was not a man in the United States who would set his face more decidedly against it than himself. Here, I interrupted him, by saying: "No rational man in the United States suspects you of any other disposition; but there does not pass a week, in which we cannot prove declarations dropping from the monarchical party that our government is good for nothing, is a milk and water thing which cannot support itself, we must knock it down, and set up something of more energy." He said if that was the case, he thought it a proof of their insanity, for that the republican spirit of the Union was so manifest and so solid, that it was astonishing how any one could expect to move it.—THE ANAS. ix, 166. FORD ED., i, 257. (Aug. 1793.)

7386. REPUBLICANS, New England and.—If a prospect could be once opened upon us of the penetration of truth into the Eastern States; if the people there, who are unquestionably republicans, could discover that they have been duped into the support of measures calculated to sap the very foundations of republicanism, we might still hope for salvation, and that it would come, as of old, from the East. But will that region ever awake to the true state of things? Can the Middle, Southern and Western States hold on till they awake? These are painful and doubtful questions; and if, * * * you can give me a comfortable solution of them, it will relieve a mind devoted to the preservation of our republican government in the true form and spirit in which it was established, but almost oppressed with apprehension that fraud will at length effect what force could not, and that what with currents and counter-currents, we shall, in the end, be driven back to the land from which we launched twenty years ago. Indeed, we have been but a sturdy fish on the hook of a dexterous angler, who, letting us flounce till we have spent our force, brings us up at last.—TO AARON BURR. iv, 186. FORD ED., vii, 147. (Pa., June 1797.)

7387. —— ——. The Eastern States will be the last to come over, on account of the dominion of the clergy, who had got a smell of union between Church and State, and began to indulge reveries which can never be realized in the present state of science. If, indeed, they could have prevailed on us, to view all advances in science as dangerous innovations, and to look back to the opinions and practices of our forefathers, instead of looking forward for improvement, a promising groundwork would have been laid. But I am in hopes their good sense will dictate to them, that since the mountain will not come to them, they had better go to the mountain; that they will find their interest in acquiescing in the liberty and science of their country, and that the Christian religion, when divested of the rags in which they have enveloped it, and brought to the original purity and simplicity of its benevolent institutor is a religion of all others the most friendly to liberty, science, and the freest expansion of the human mind.—To Moses Robinson. iv, 379. (March 1801.)

7388. REPUBLICANS, Patronage and. —We do not mean to leave arms in the hands of active enemies.—To Albert Gallatin. iv, 544. Ford ed., viii, 304. (May 1804.)

7389. ———. That I have denounced republicans by the epithet of Jacobins, and declared I would appoint none but those called moderates of both parties, and that I have avowed or entertain any predilection for those called the third party, or "Quids", is in every tittle of it false.—To William Duane. iv, 592. Ford ed., viii, 433. (W., 1806.) See Office, Offices and Parties.

7390. REPUBLICANS, Platform of. — Divide the Treasury Department. Abolish the Bank. Repeal the Excise Law and let States raise the money. Lower impost. Treasurer to pay and receive cash not bills. Repeal irredeemable quality and borrow at 4 per cent. Exclude paper holders. Condemn report of.*—Jefferson MSS. Ford ed., vi, 171. (Feb. ? 1793.)

7391. REPUBLICANS, Relations to Genet.—We [the Administration] have decided unanimously to require the recall of Genet. He will sink the republican interest if they do not abandon him.—To James Madison. Ford ed., vi, 361. (Aug. 1793.) See Genet.

7392. REPUBLICANS, Rights of man and.—Whether the principles of the majority of our fellow citizens, or of the little minority still opposing them, be most friendly to the rights of man, posterity will judge; and to that arbiter I submit my own conduct with cheerfulness.—To C. F. Welles. v, 484. (M., 1809.) See Rights of Man.

7393. REPUBLICANS, Slandered.— They endeavored [in the elections] to conjure up the ghost of anti-federalism, and to have it believed that this and republicanism

* Paul Leicester Ford, in his edition of *Jefferson's Writings*, makes the following note: "This paper is undated, but is apparently an outline of the reforms in the government desired by Jefferson. In the absence of a definite platform of the newly formed democratic party, it is therefore of considerable importance, and is of especial interest as showing Jefferson's plans to break up the 'Treasury Junto', by dividing the treasury, and by excluding from Congress all holders of Bank Stock. The report referred to is probably 'Hamilton's Report on the Foreign Loans of Jan. 3, 1793', which was an especially obnoxious one to Jefferson."—Editor.

were the same, and that both were Jacobinism. But those who felt themselves republicans and federalists, too, were little moved by this artifice.—To Thomas Pinckney. iii, 494. Ford ed., vi, 143. (Pa., Dec. 1792.)

7394. REPUBLICANS, States rights and.—On the eclipse of federalism, although not its extinction, its leaders got up the Missouri question, under the false front of lessening the measure of slavery, but with the real view of producing a geographical division of parties, which might ensure them the next President. The people of the north went blindfolded into the snare, followed their leaders for awhile with a zeal truly moral and laudable, until they became sensible that they were injuring instead of aiding the real interests of the slaves, that they had been used merely as tools for electioneering purposes; and that trick of hypocrisy then fell as quickly as it had been got up. To that is now succeeded a distinction, which, like that of republican and federal, or whig and tory, being equally intermixed through every State, threatens none of those geographical schisms which go immediately to a separation. The line of division now is the preservation of State rights as reserved in the Constitution, or by strained constructions of that instrument, to merge all into a consolidated government. The tories are for strengthening the Executive and General Government; the whigs cherish the representative branch, and the rights reserved by the States, as the bulwark against consolidation, which must immediately generate monarchy. And although this division excites, as yet, no warmth, yet it exists, is well understood, and will be a principle of voting at the ensuing election, with the reflecting men of both parties.—To Marquis Lafayette. vii, 326. Ford ed., x, 281. (M., November 1823.) See Centralization, Judiciary, Missouri Question and Supreme Court.

7395. REPUBLICANS, Sympathy with France.—Parties seem to have taken a very well defined form in this quarter The old tories, joined by our merchants who trade on British capital, paper dealers, and the idle rich of the great commercial towns, are with the kings. All other descriptions with the French. The war has kindled and brought forward the two parties with an ardor which our interests merely, could never excite.—To James Monroe. Ford ed., vi, 281. (Pa., June 1793.) See Federalists and Monarchy.

7396. REPUBLICANS, Unfaltering.— As long as we pursue without deviation the principles we have always professed. I have no fear of deviation from them in the main body of republicans.—To Cæsar A. Rodney. Ford ed., viii, 436. (W., March 1806.)

7397. REPUBLICANS, The Union and. —Our lot has been cast by the favor of heaven in a country and under circumstances highly auspicious to our peace and prosperity, and where no pretence can arise for the degrading and oppressive establishments of Europe. It is our happiness that honorable distinctions flow only from public approbation; and that finds no object in titled dignitaries and pageants. Let us then endeavor carefully to guard this happy state of things, by keeping a watchful eye over the disaffection of wealth and ambition to the republican principles of our Constitution, and by sacrificing all our local and personal interests to the cultivation of the Union, and maintenance of the authority of the laws.—R. TO A. PENNA. DEMOCRATIC REPUBLICANS. viii, 163. (1809.) See UNION.

7398. REPUBLICANS, Washington's administration and.—The object of the opposition which was made to the course of administration was to preserve the Legislature pure and independent of the Executive. to restrain the administration to republican forms and principles, and not permit the Constitution to be construed into a monarchy, and to be warped in practice into all the principles and pollutions of their favorite English model. Nor was this an opposition to General Washington. He was true to the republican charge confided to him; and has solemnly and repeatedly protested to me, in our private conversations, that he would lose the last drop of his blood in support of it, and he did this the oftener, and with the more earnestness, because he knew my suspicions of [Alexander] Hamilton's designs against it; and wished to quiet them.—THE ANAS. ix, 95. FORD ED., i, 165. (1818.) See FEDERALISTS, MONARCHY and WASHINGTON.

7399. REPUBLICS, Contending.—I would not gratify the combination of kings with the spectacle of the only two republics on earth destroying each other for two cannon; nor would I, for infinitely greater cause, add this country to that combination, turn the scale of contest, and let it be from our hands that the hopes of man receive their last stab. —OPINION ON "THE LITTLE SARAH". ix, 155. FORD ED., vi, 343. (July 1793.)

7400. REPUBLICS, Irresistible.—A republican government is slow to move, yet when once in motion, its momentum becomes irresistible.—To F. C. GRAY. vi, 438. (M., 1815.)

7401. REPUBLICS, Size of.—I suspect that the doctrine, that small States alone are fitted to be republics. will be exploded by experience. with some other brilliant fallacies accredited by Montesquieu and other political writers. Perhaps it will be found, that to obtain a just republic (and it is to secure our just rights that we resort to government at all) it must be so extensive as that local egoisms may never reach its greater part; that on every particular question, a majority may be found in its councils free from particular interests, and giving. therefore, an uniform prevalence to the principles of justice. The smaller the societies, the more violent and convulsive their schisms.—To M. D'IVERNOIS. iv, 114. FORD ED., vii, 4. (M., Feb. 1795.)

7402. ——— ———. The extent [of the Republic] has saved us. While some parts were laboring under the paroxysm of delusion, others retained their senses, and time was thus given to the affected parts to recover their health. Your part of the Union [New England] is longest recovering, because the deceivers there wear a more imposing form; but a little more time and they too will recover.—To GENERAL WARREN. iv, 376. (W., 1801.)

7403. ——— ———. The late chapter of our history furnishes * * * a new proof of the falsehood of Montesquieu's doctrine, that a republic can be preserved only in a small territory. The reverse is the truth. Had our territory been even a third only of what it is, we were gone.—To NATHANIEL NILES. iv, 376. FORD ED., viii, 24. (W., March 1801.)

7404. REPUTATION, Regard for.—A regard for reputation and the judgment of the world may sometimes be felt where conscience is dormant, or indolence inexcitable. —To EDWARD LIVINGSTON. vii, 404. (M., 1825.)

7405. RESIGNATION, To Divine will. —The most fortunate of us, in our journey through life, frequently meet with calamities and misfortunes which may greatly afflict us; and, to fortify our minds against the attacks of these calamities and misfortunes, should be one of the principal studies and endeavors of our lives. The only method of doing this is to assume a perfect resignation to the Divine will. to consider that whatever does happen, must happen; and that, by our uneasiness, we cannot prevent the blow before it does fall, but we may add to its force after it has fallen. These considerations. and others such as these. may enable us in some measure to surmount the difficulties thrown in our way; to bear up with a tolerable degree of patience under this burden of life; and to proceed with a pious and unshaken resignation, till we arrive at our journey's end, when we may deliver up our trust into the hands of Him who gave it, and receive such reward as to Him shall seem proportioned to our merit. Such will be the language of the man who considers his situation in this life, and such should be the language of every man who would wish to render that situation as easy as the nature of it will admit. Few things will disturb him at all: nothing will disturb him much.—To JOHN PAGE. i, 187. FORD ED., i, 349. (S., 1763.)

7406. RESISTANCE, Morality and.— When wrongs are pressed because it is believed they will be borne, resistance becomes morality.—To MADAME DE STAEL. v, 133. (W., 1807.)

7407. RESISTANCE, Spirit of.—What country can preserve its liberties if its rulers are not warned from time to time that its people preserve the spirit of resistance?—To W. S. SMITH. ii, 318. FORD ED., iv, 467. (P., 1787.)

7408. RESOLUTION, Power of.—I do not like your saying that you are unable to read the ancient print of your Livy but with the aid of your master. We are always equal to what we undertake with resolution. A little degree of this will enable you to decipher your

Livy. If you always lean on your master, you will never be able to proceed without him. It is part of the American character to consider nothing as desperate, to surmount every difficulty by resolution and contrivance. In Europe there are shops for every want; its inhabitants, therefore, have no idea that their wants can be supplied otherwise. Remote from all other aid, we are obliged to invent and to execute; to find means within ourselves, and not to lean on others. Consider, therefore, the conquering your Livy as an exercise in the habit of surmounting difficulties; a habit which will be necessary to you in the country where you are to live, and without which you will be thought a very helpless animal, and less esteemed.—To MARTHA JEFFERSON. FORD ED., iv, 373. (1787.)

7409. RESPECT, A safeguard.—Respect is a safeguard to interest.—To JOHN ADAMS. i, 592. (P., 1786.)

7410. RESPECT, Strengthening.—Our national respect certainly needs strengthening in Europe.—To JAMES MONROE. FORD ED., iv, 223. (P., 1786.)

7411. RESPECTABILITY, National.—It should ever be held in mind, that insult and war are the consequences of a want of respectability in the national character.—To JAMES MADISON. i, 531. FORD ED., iv, 192. (P., 1786.)

7412. —— ——. An alliance* with the Emperor of Austria will give us respectability in Europe, which we have occasion for.—To ELBRIDGE GERRY. i, 557. (P., 1786.) See JOSEPH II.

7413. RESPONSIBILITY, Essential principle.—In truth, man is not made to be trusted for life, if secured against all liability to account.—To M. CORAY. vii, 322. (M., 1823.)

7414. RESPONSIBILITY, Free Government and.—Responsibility is a tremendous engine in a free government.—To ARCHIBALD STUART. iii, 315. FORD ED., v, 410. (Pa., 1791.)

7415. RESPONSIBILITY, Individual.—Responsibility weighs with its heaviest force on a single head.—To SAMUEL KERCHIVAL. vii, 12. FORD ED., x, 40. (M., 1816.)

7416. RESPONSIBILITY, Official.—I am for responsibilities at short periods, seeing neither reason nor safety in making public functionaries independent of the nation for life, or even for long terms of years.—To JAMES MARTIN. vi, 213. FORD ED., ix, 420. (M., Sep. 1813.)

7417. —— ——. That there should be public functionaries independent of the nation, whatever may be their demerit, is a solecism in a republic, of the first order of absurdity and inconsistency.—To WILLIAM T. BARRY. vii, 256. (M., 1822.)

7418. RESPONSIBILITY, People and.—It should be remembered, as an axiom of

* By alliance Jefferson meant a commercial treaty.—EDITOR.

eternal truth in politics, that whatever power in any government is independent, is absolute also; in theory only, at first, while the spirit of the people is up, but in practice, as fast as that relaxes. Independence can be trusted nowhere but with the people in mass. They are inherently independent of all but moral law.—To SPENCER ROANE. vii, 134. FORD ED., x, 141. (P.F., 1819.)

7419. RESPONSIBILITY, Shirking.—Leave no screen of a Council behind which to skulk from responsibility.—To SAMUEL KERCHIVAL. vii, 12. FORD ED., x, 39. (M., 1816.)

7420. RETALIATION, Barbarous.—The English have burned our Capitol and President's House by means of their force. We can burn their St. James's and St. Paul's by means of our money, offered to their own incendiaries, of whom there are thousands in London who would do it rather than starve. But it is against the laws of civilized warfare to employ secret incendiaries. Is it not equally so to destroy the works of art by armed incendiaries? Bonaparte, possessed at times of almost every capital of Europe, with all his despotism and power, injured no monument of art. If a nation, breaking through all the restraints of civilized character, uses its means of destruction (power, for example) without distinction of objects, may we not use our means (our money and their pauperism) to retaliate their barbarous ravages? Are we obliged to use for resistance exactly the weapons chosen by them for aggression? When they destroyed Copenhagen by superior force, against all the laws of God and man, would it have been unjustifiable for the Danes to have destroyed their ships by torpedoes? Clearly not; and they and we should now be justifiable in the conflagration of St. James's and St. Paul's. And if we do not carry it into execution, it is because we think it more moral and more honorable to set a good example, than follow a bad one.—To THOMAS COOPER. vi, 380. (M., 1814.)

7421. RETALIATION, Burning cities.—Perhaps the British fleet will burn New York or Boston. If they do, we must burn the city of London, not by expensive fleets or Congreve rockets, but by employing an hundred or two Jack-the-painters, whom nakedness, famine, desperation, and hardened vice, will abundantly furnish from among themselves.—To WILLIAM DUANE. vi, 76. FORD ED., ix, 366. (M., Aug. 1812.)

7422. RETALIATION, Deplorable.—We deplore the event which shall oblige us to shed blood for blood, and shall resort to retaliation but as the means of stopping the progress of butchery.—REPORT TO CONGRESS. FORD ED., i, 495. (1775.)

7423. RETALIATION, Destructive.—Humane conduct on our part was found to produce no effect; the contrary therefore was to be tried. If it produces a proper lenity to our prisoners in captivity, it will have the effect we meant: if it does not, we shall return a severity as terrible as universal. * * * If, declining the tribunal of truth and reason, they choose to pervert this into a contest of cruelty and destruction, we will contend with them in that line, and measure out misery to those in our power in that multiplied proportion which the advantage of superior numbers enables us to do. * * * Iron will be retaliated by iron * * * ; prison ships by prison ships, and like for like in general.*—To COL. MATHEWS. i, 234. FORD ED., ii, 262. (1779.)

7424. RETALIATION, A duty.—Retaliation is a duty we owe to those engaged in the cause of their country, to assure them that if any unlucky circumstance, baffling the efforts of their bravery, shall put them in the power of their enemies, we will use the pledges in our hands to warrant their lives from sacrifice.—REPORT TO CONGRESS. FORD ED., i, 495. (1775.)

7425. RETALIATION, Effective.—The numbers of our countrymen betrayed into the hands of the enemy by the treachery, cowardice or incompetence of our high officers, reduce us to the humiliating necessity of acquiescing in the brutal conduct observed towards them. When, during the last war, I put Governor Hamilton and Major Hay into a dungeon and in irons for having themselves personally done the same to the American prisoners who had fallen into their hands, and was threatened with retaliation by Phillips, then returned to New York, I declared to him I would load ten of their Saratoga prisoners (then under my care and within half a dozen miles of my house) with double irons for every American they should misuse under pretence of retaliation, and it put an end to the practice. But the ten for one are now with them.—To WILLIAM DUANE. vi, 211. (M., Sep. 1813.)

7426. RETALIATION, France and.—A recent fact, proving the anxiety of France for a reconciliation with us is the following. You know that one of the armed vessels which we took from her was refitted by us, sent to cruise on them, recaptured, and carried into Guadaloupe under the name of the Retaliation. On the arrival there of Desfourneaux, the new commissioner, he sent Victor Hughes home in irons; called up our captain; told him that he found he had a regular commission as an officer of the United States; that his vessel was then lying in harbor; that he should enquire into no fact preceding his own arrival (by this he avoided noticing that the vessel was really French property) and that therefore, himself and crew were free to depart with their vessel; that as to the differences between France and the United States, commissioners were coming to settle them, and in the meantime, no injury should be done on their part. The captain insisted on being a prisoner; the other disclaimed; and so he arrived here [Philadelphia] the day before yesterday. Within an hour after this was known to the Senate, they passed a retaliation bill. This was the more remarkable, as the bill was founded expressly on the *Arret* of Oct. 29, which had been communicated by the President as soon as received, and he remarked, " that it could not be too soon communicated to the two Houses and the public ". Yet he almost in the same instant received, through the same channel, Mr. King, information that the *Arret* was suspended, and though he knew we were making it the foundation of a retaliation bill, he has never yet communicated it. But the Senate knew the fact informally from the Sec-

> * The practical inculcation of such a lesson produced a sensible humiliation in the conduct of the enemy, through the subsequent stages of the war. The door of British magnanimity, which was barred to the dictates of reason, justice, and national honor, was compelled, reluctantly, to yield to the cries of their own countrymen, and the fatal admonitions of experience.—RAYNER's *Life of Jefferson*. New York edition, p. 194.

retary of State, and knowing it, passed the bill. —To EDMUND PENDLETON. iv, 288. FORD ED., vii, 357. (Pa., Feb. 14, 1799.)

7427. ————. ————. Our government contemplate restoring the Frenchmen taken originally in the same vessel, and kept at Lancaster [Penna.] as prisoners. This has furnished the idea of calling her a *cartel* vessel, and pretending that she came as such for an exchange of prisoners, which is false. She was delivered free and without condition, but it does not suit to let any new evidence appear of the desire of conciliation in France.—To EDMUND PENDLETON. iv, 290. FORD ED., vii, 360. (Pa., Feb. 1799.)

7428. ————. ————. Leblanc, an agent from Desfourneaux of Guadaloupe, came in the Retaliation. You will see in the papers Desfourneaux's letter to the President. * * * The vessel and crew were liberated without condition. Notwithstanding this, they have obliged Leblanc to receive the French prisoners, and to admit, in the papers, the terms, " in *exchange* for *prisoners* taken from us ", he denying at the same time that they consider them as *prisoners*, or had any idea of *exchange*. The object of his mission was not at all relative to that; but they choose to keep up the idea of a cartel, to prevent the transaction from being used as evidence of the sincerity of the French towards a reconciliation. He came to assure us of a discontinuance of all irregularities in French privateers from Guadaloupe. He has been received very cavalierly.—To JAMES MADISON. iv, 291. FORD ED., vii, 361. (Pa., Feb. 19, 1799.)

7429. RETALIATION, Governor Hamilton's case.—I hope you will ascribe the advice of the [Governor's] Council [confining Governor Hamilton], not to want of attention to the sacred nature of public conventions, of which I hope we shall never, in any circumstances, lose sight, but to a desire of stopping the effusion of the unoffending blood of women and children, and the unjustifiable severities exercised on our captive officers and soldiers in general, by proper severities on our part.— To SIR GUY CARLETON. FORD ED., ii, 256. (1779.) See WAR, PRISONERS OF.

7430. ————. ————. On receipt of your letter of August 6th, during my absence, the Council had the irons taken off the prisoners of war. When your advice was asked, we meant it should decide with us; and upon my return to Williamsburg, the matter was taken up and the enclosed advice* given.—To GENERAL WASHINGTON. i, 230. FORD ED., ii, 258. (1779.)

> * The advice was in the form of an Order of Council which was written by Governor Jefferson as follows: " The Board having been at no time unmindful of the circumstances attending the confinement of Lieutenant Governor Hamilton, Captain Lamothe and Philip Dejean, which the personal cruelties of those men, as well as the general conduct of the enemy had constrained them to advise; wishing, and willing to expect, that their sufferings may lead them to the practice of humanity, should any future turn of fortune, in their favor, submit to their discretion the fate of their fellow-creatures; that it may prove an admonition to others, meditating like cruelties, not to rely for impunity in any circumstances of distance or present security; and that it may induce the enemy to reflect what must be the painful consequences should a continuation of the same conduct on their part impel us again to severities, while such multiplied subjects of retaliation are within our power; sensible that no impression can be made on the event of the war by wreaking vengeance on miserable captives; that the great

7431. —— ——. Governor Hamilton and his companions were imprisoned and ironed, 1st. In retaliation for cruel treatment of our captive citizens by the enemy in general. 2d. For the barbarous species of warfare which himself and his savage allies carried on in our western frontier. 3d. For particular acts of barbarity, of which he himself was personally guilty, to some of our citizens in his power. Any one of these charges was sufficient to justify the measures we took.—To COLONEL MATHEWS. i, 233. FORD ED., ii, 262. (Wg., 1779.)

7432. RETALIATION, Humanity and. —A uniform exercise of kindness to prisoners on our part has been returned by as uniform severity on the part of our enemies. * * * It is high time * * * to teach respect to the dictates of humanity; in such a case retaliation becomes an act of humanity.— To SIR GUY CARLETON. FORD ED., ii, 251. (1779.)

7433. RETALIATION, Legislative.— Legislative warfare was begun by the British parliament. * * * The stat. 12 G. 3, c. 24 for carrying our citizens *charged* with the offences it describes, to be tried in a foreign country; by foreign judges instead of a jury of their vicinage, by laws not their own, without witnesses, without friends, or the means of making them; that of the 14 G. 3, c. 39, for protecting from punishment those who should murder an American in the execution of a British law, were previous to our acts of exile, and even to the commencement of the war. Their act of 14 G. 3, c. 19, for shutting up the harbor of Boston, and thereby annihilating, with the commerce of that city, the value of its property; that of 15 G. 3, c. 10, forbidding us to export to foreign markets the produce we have hitherto raised and sold at those markets, and thereby leaving that produce useless on our hands; that of 10 G. 3, c. 5, prohibiting all exports even to British markets, and making them legal prize when taken on the high seas, was dealing out confiscation, by wholesale, on the property of entire nations, which our acts, cited by you, retaliated but on the small scale of individual confiscation. But we never retaliated the 4th section of the last mentioned act, under which multitudes of our citizens taken on board our vessels were forced by starving, by periodical whippings, and by constant chains to become the murderers of their countrymen, perhaps of their fathers and brothers. If from this legislative warfare we turn to those scenes of active hostility which wrapped our houses in flame, our families in slaughter, our property in universal devastation, is the wonder that our Legislature did so much, or so little? Compare their situation with that of the British Parliament enjoying in ease and safety all the comforts and blessings of the earth, and hearing of these distant events as of the wars of cause which has animated the two nations against each other is not to be decided by unmanly cruelties on wretches, who have bowed their necks to the power of the victor, but by the exercise of honorable valor in the field; earnestly hoping that the enemy, viewing the subject in the same light, will be content to abide the event of that mode of decision, and spare us the pain of a second departure from kindness to our captives; confident that commiseration to our prisoners is the only possible motive to which can be candidly ascribed, in the present actual circumstances of the war, the advice we are now about to give; the Board does advise the Governor to send Lieutenant Governor Hamilton, Captain Lamothe and Philip Dejean, to Hanover Court House, there to remain at large, within reasonable limits, taking the parole in the usual manner. The Governor orders accordingly."—EDITOR.

Benaris, or the extermination of the Rohillas, and say with candor whether the difference of scene and situation would not have justified a contrary difference of conduct towards each other? *—To GEORGE HAMMOND. FORD ED., vi, 12. (Pa., 1792.)

7434. RETALIATION, Life for life.— If the [British] enemy shall put to death, torture, or otherwise ill-treat any of the hostages in their hands, or of the Canadian, or other prisoners captivated by them in the service of the United Colonies,† recourse must be had to retaliation as the sole means of stopping the progress of human butchery, and for that purpose punishments of the same kind and degree shall be inflicted on an equal number of their subjects taken by us, till they shall be taught due respect to the violated rights of nations.—REPORT TO CONGRESS. FORD ED., ii, 34. (June 1776.)

7435. RETALIATION, Necessary.—I shall give immediate orders for having in readiness every engine which the enemy have contrived for the destruction of our unhappy citizens, captured by them. The presentiment of these operations is shocking beyond expression. I pray heaven to avert them; but nothing in this world will do it, but a proper conduct in the enemy. In every event, I shall resign myself to the hard necessity under which I shall act.— To GEN. WASHINGTON. i, 232. FORD ED., ii, 261. (Wg., 1779.)

7436. RETALIATION, Opportunity for. —It is impossible [that the British] can be serious in attempting to bully us * * *. We have too many of their subjects in our power and too much iron to clothe them with and, I will add, too much resolution to avail ourselves of both, to fear their pretended retaliation.‡—To GENERAL WASHINGTON. i, 231. FORD ED., ii, 259. (Wg., 1779.)

7437. RETALIATION, On prisoners of war.—This question [contest with Great Britain] will not be decided by wreaking vengeance on a few helpless captives but by achieving success in the fields of war, and gathering there those laurels which grow for the warrior brave. In this light we view the object between us, in this line we have hitherto conducted ourselves for its attainment.§—REPORT TO CONGRESS. FORD ED., i, 494. (1775.)

7438. —— ——. Should you think proper in these days to revive ancient barbarism and again disgrace our nature with the sacrifice, the fortune of war has put into our power subjects for multiplied retaliation. To them, to you, and to the world we declare they shall not be wretched unless their imprudence or your example shall oblige us to make them so; but we declare that their lives shall teach our enemies to respect the rights of nations. REPORT TO CONGRESS. FORD ED., i, 494. (Dec. 1775.)

* From Jefferson's letter to George Hammond, British Minister, on the infractions of the peace treaty. The extract was in reply to a charge made by Hammond. Alexander Hamilton thought "it may involve irritating discussion", and Jefferson struck it out.—EDITOR.

† Here Jefferson had written "States of America ", which has been stricken out by another hand and "Colonies" written in its place.—NOTE IN FORD EDITION.

‡ Jefferson was then Governor of Virginia, and a controversy had arisen respecting the treatment of prisoners of war.—EDITOR.

§ Ethan Allen and others were at that time prisoners in the hands of the British army. The report was not accepted by Congress.—EDITOR.

7439. ———— ————. It is my duty, as well as it was my promise to the Virginia captives, to take measures for discovering any change which may be made in their situation. For this purpose, I must apply for your Excellency s interposition. I doubt not but you have an established mode of knowing. at all times, through your commissary of prisoners, the precise state of those in the power of the enemy. I must, therefore, pray you to put into mot'on, any such means you have, for obtaining knowledge of the situation of the Virginia officers in captivity. If you should think, proper, as I could wish, to take upon yourself to retaliate any new sufferings which may be imposed on them, it will be more likely to have due weight, and to restore the unhappy on both sides, to that benevolent treatment for which all should wish.—To GENERAL WASHINGTON. i, 237. FORD ED., ii, 280. (Wg., Nov. 1779.)

7440. RETALIATION, On Savages.— To do wrong is a melancholy resource, even where retaliation renders it indispensably necessary. It is better to suffer much from the scalpings, the conflagrations, the rapes and rapine of savages, than to countenance and strengthen such barbarisms by retortion. I have ever deemed it more honorable and more profitable, too. to set a good example than to follow a bad one.—To M. CORREA. vi, 405. (M., 1814.)

7441. RETIREMENT, Called from.—I had folded myself in the arms of retirement, and rested all prospects of future happiness on domestic and literary objects. A single event [Mrs. Jefferson's death] wiped away all my plans, and left me a blank which I had not the spirits to fill up. In this state of mind an appointment [Minister to France] from Congress found me, requiring me to cross the Atlantic.—To M. DE CHASTELLUX. i, 322. FORD ED., iii, 65. (Am., 1782.)

7442. ———— ————. I had retired after five and twenty years of constant occupation in public affairs, and total abandonment of my own. I retired much poorer than when I entered the public service, and desired nothing but rest and oblivion. My name, however, was again brought forward [for the Presidency], without concert or expectation on my part. On my salvation I declare it.—To EDWARD RUTLEDGE. iv, 151. FORD ED., vii, 93. (M., Dec. 1796.)

7443. RETIREMENT, Desire for.— However ardently my retirement to my own home and my own affairs, may be wished for by others, * * * there is no one of them who feels the wish once where I do a thousand times.—To FRANCIS EPPES. FORD ED., v, 507. (Pa., April 1792.)

7444. RETIREMENT, Happiness in.— If I can carry into retirement the good will of my fellow citizens, nothing else will be wanting to my happiness.—To JAMES SULLIVAN. v, 252. (1808.)

7445. RETIREMENT, Longing for.— Oh for the day when I shall be withdrawn from [office] ; when I shall have leisure to enjoy my family, my friends, my farm and books !—To DR. BENJAMIN RUSH. v, 225. (W., January 1808.)

7446. ———— ————. It is now among my most fervent longings to be on my farm, which, with a garden and fruitery. will constitute my principal occupation in retirement.—To ROBERT R. LIVINGSTON. v, 224. (W., 1808.)

7447. ———— ————. My longings for retirement are so strong, that I with difficulty encounter the daily drudgeries of my duty.—To JAMES MONROE. v, 248. FORD ED., ix, 178. (W., Feb. 1808.)

7448. ———— ————. As the moment of my retirement approaches, I become more anxious for its arrival, and to begin at length to pass what yet remains to me of life and health in the bosom of my family and neighbors, and in communication with my friends, undisturbed by political concerns or passions.—To DR. LOGAN. v, 405. (W., Dec. 1808.)

7449. ———— ————. Five weeks more will relieve me from a drudgery to which I am no longer equal, and restore me to a scene of tranquillity, amidst my family and friends, more congenial to my age and natural inclinations.—To JAMES MONROE. v, 420. FORD ED., ix, 244. (W., Jan. 1809.)

7450. RETIREMENT, Newspaper attacks and.—I have for some time past been under an agitation of mind which I scarcely ever experienced before, produced by a check on my purpose of returning home at the close of this session of Congress. My operations at Monticello had been all made to bear upon that point of time, my mind was fixed on it with a fondness which was extreme, the purpose firmly declared to the President, when I became assailed from all quarters with a variety of objections. Among these it was urged that my return just when I had been attacked in the public papers, would injure me in the eyes of the public, who would suppose I either withdrew from investigation, or because I had not tone of mind sufficient to meet slander. The only reward I ever wished on my retirement was to carry with me nothing like a disapprobation of the public. These representations have, for some weeks past, shaken a determination which I had thought the whole world could not have shaken. I have not yet finally made up my mind on the subject, nor changed my declaration to the President. But having perfect reliance in the disinterested friendship of some of those who have counselled and urged it strongly; believing that they can see and judge better a question between the public and myself than I can, I feel a possibility that I may be detained here [Philadelphia] into the summer.—To MARTHA JEFFERSON RANDOLPH. iii, 506. FORD ED., vi, 163. (Pa., Jan. 1793.)

7451. ———— ————. It happened unfortunately that the attack made on me in the newspapers came out soon after I began to speak freely and publicly of my purpose to retire this Spring. * * * I find that as well those who are my friends as those who are not, putting the two things together as cause and effect, conceived I was driven from office either from want of firmness or perhaps fear of investigation. Desirous that my retirement may be clouded by no imputations of this kind, I see not only a possibility, but rather a probability, that I shall postpone it for some time.—To T. M. RANDOLPH. D. L. J., 215. (Pa., Feb. 1793.)

7452. RETIREMENT, Occupations in. —In [retirement] I shall devote myself to occupations much more congenial with my inclinations, than those to which I have been called by the character of the times into which my lot was cast. About to be relieved from this *corvée* by age and the fulfillment of the *quadragena stipendia*, what remains to me of physical activity will chiefly be employed in the amusements of agriculture. Having little practical skill, I count more on the pleasures than the profits of that occupation.—To M. LASTEYRIE. v, 315. (W., 1808.)

7453. —— ——. Within a few days I retire to my family, my books and farms.; and having gained the harbor myself, I shall look on my friends still buffeting the storm with anxiety indeed, but not with envy.—To DUPONT DE NEMOURS. v, 432. (W., March 1809.)

7454. —— ——. I retire from scenes of d.fficulty, anxiety, and of contending passions, to the elysium of domestic affections, and the irresponsible direction of my own affairs. Safe in port myself, I shall look anxiously at my friends still buffeting the storm, and wish you all safe in port also.—To GENERAL ARMSTRONG. v, 434. (W., 1809.)

7455. —— ——. I shall now bury myself in the groves of Monticello, and become a mere spectator of the passing events.—To BARON HUMBOLDT. v, 435. (W., 1809.)

7456. —— ——. I am now retired: I resign myself, as a passenger, with confidence to those at present at the helm, and ask but for rest, peace and good will.—To SAMUEL KERCHIVAL. vii, 9. FORD ED., x, 37. (M., 1816.)

7457. RETIREMENT, Old age.—I am too desirous of quiet to place myself in the way of contention. Against this I am admonished by bodily decay, which cannot be unaccompanied by corresponding wane of the mind. Of this I am as yet sensible, sufficiently to be unwilling to trust myself before the public, and when I cease to be so, I hope that my friends will be too careful of me to draw me forth and present me, like a Priam in armor, as a spectacle for public compassion. I hope our political bark will ride through all its dangers; but I can in future be but an inert passenger. —To THOMAS RITCHIE. vii, 193. FORD ED., x, 171. (M., 1820.)

7458. RETIREMENT, Power and.— Never did a prisoner, released from his chains, feel such relief as I shall on shaking off the shackles of power. Nature intended me for the tranquil pursuits of science, by rendering them my supreme delight. But the enormities of the times in which I have lived, have forced me to take a part in resisting them, and to commit myself on the boisterous ocean of political passions. I thank God for the opportunity of retiring from them without censure, and carrying with me the most consoling proofs of public approbation.—To DUPONT DE NEMOURS. v, 432. (W., March 2, 1809.)

7459. RETIREMENT, Principle and.— At the end of the next four years I shall certainly retire. Age, inclination and principle all dictate this.—To PHILIP MAZZEI. iv, 554. (W., July 1804.)

7460. RETIREMENT, Reasons for.— The President [Washington] said, in an affectionate tone, that he had felt much concern at an expression which dropped from me yesterday [Feb. 28, 1792], and which marked my intention of retiring [from the Secretaryship of State] when he should; that as to himself, many motives obliged him to it, * * * yet he should consider it as unfortunate, if that should bring on the retirement of the great officers of the government, and that this might produce a shock on the public mind of dangerous consequence. I told him that no man had ever had less desire of entering into public of-

fices than myself; that the circumstance of a perilous war, which had brought everything into danger, and called for all the services which every citizen could render, had induced me to undertake the administration of the government of Virginia; that I had both before and after refused repeated appointments of Congress to go abroad in that sort of office, which, if I had consulted my own gratification, would almost have been the most agreeable to me; that at the end of two years, I resigned the government of Virginia, and retired with a firm resolution never more to appear in public life; that a domestic loss, however, happened, and made me fancy that absence and a change of scene for a time might be expedient for me; that I, therefore, accepted a foreign appointment, limited to two years; that at the close of that, Dr. Franklin having left France, I was appointed to supply his place, which I had occupied, and though I continued in it three or four years, it was under the constant idea of remaining only a year or two longer; that the Revolution in France coming on, I had so interested myself in the event of that, that when obliged to bring my family home, I had still an idea of returning and awaiting the close of that, to fix the era of my final retirement; that on my arrival here I found he had appointed me to my present office [Secretary of State]; that he knew I had not come into it without some reluctance; that it was, on my part, a sacrifice of inclination to the opinion that I might be more serviceable here than in France, and with a firm resolution in my mind, to indulge my constant wish for retirement at no very distant day; that when, therefore, I had received his letter, written from Mount Vernon, on his way to Carolina and Georgia (April 1, 1791), and discovered from an expression in that, that he meant to retire from the government ere long, and as to the precise epoch there could be no doubt, my mind was immediately made up, to make that the epoch of my own retirement from those labors of which I was heartily tired. That, however, I did not believe there was any idea in any of my brethren in the administration of retiring; that, on the contrary, I had perceived at a late meeting of the trustees of the sinking fund, that the Secretary of the Treasury had developed the plan he intended to pursue, and that it embraced years in its view. He said that he considered the Treasury Department as a much more limited one, going only to the single object of revenue, while that of the Secretary of State, embracing nearly all the objects of administration, was much more important, and the retirement of the officer, therefore, would be more noticed; that though the government had set out with a pretty general good will of the public, yet that symptoms of dissatisfaction had lately shown themselves far beyond what he could have expected, and to what height these might arise in case of too great a change in the administration, could not be foreseen.—THE ANAS. ix, 102. FORD ED., i, 175. (Feb. 29, 1792.)

7461. —— ——. I expressed to him [Washington] my excessive repugnance to public life, the particular uneasiness of my situation in this place [Philadelphia], where the laws of society oblige me always to move exactly in the circle which I know to bear me peculiar hatred; that is to say, the wealthy aristocrats, the merchants connected closely with England, the new created paper fortunes; that thus surrounded, my words were caught, multiplied, misconstrued, and even fabricated and spread abroad to my injury; that he saw also, that there was such an opposition of views between myself and another part of the Administration, as to render it peculiarly unpleasing, and to destroy the necessary harmony.—THE ANAS. ix, 166. FORD ED., i, 256. (Aug. 1793.)

7462. RETIREMENT, Washington opposed to Jefferson's.—The President calls on me [to-day, August 6], at my house in the country, and introduces my letter of July 31, announcing that I should resign at the close of the next month. He again expressed his repentance at not having resigned himself, and how much it was increased by seeing that he was to be deserted by those on whose aid he had counted; that he did not know where he should look to find characters to fill up the offices; that mere talents did not suffice for the Department of State, but it required a person conversant in foreign affairs, perhaps acquainted with foreign courts; that without this, the best talents would be awkward and at a loss. He told me that Colonel Hamilton had three or four weeks ago written to him, informing him that private as well as public reasons had brought him to the determination to retire, and that he should do it towards the close of the next session. He said he had often before intimated dispositions to resign, but never as decisively before; that he supposed he had fixed on the latter part of next session, to give an opportunity to Congress to examine into his conduct; that our going out at times so different increased his difficulty; for if he had both places to fill at once, he might consult both the particular talents and geographical situation of our successors. He expressed great apprehension at the fermentation which seemed to be working in the mind of the public; that many descriptions of persons, actuated by different causes, appeared to be uniting; what it would end in he knew not; a new Congress was to assemble, more numerous, perhaps of a different spirit; the first expressions of their sentiments would be important; if I would only stay to the end of that, it would relieve him considerably. —THE ANAS. ix, 165. FORD ED., i, 256. (Aug. 1793.)

7463. RETIREMENT, Welcome.—The moment of my retiring [from the Secretaryship of State] is now approaching, and is to me as land was to Columbus in his first American voyage.—To DAVID HUMPHREYS. iii, 490. (Nov. 1792.)

7464. ——— ———. I now contemplate the approach of the moment of my retirement with the fondness of a sailor who has land in view. —To THOMAS PINCKNEY. FORD ED., vi, 132. (Pa., Nov. 1792.)

7465. ——— ———. When I came into office, it was with a resolution to retire from it as soon as I could with decency. It pretty early appeared to me that the proper moment would be the first of those epochs at which the Constitution seems to have contemplated a periodical change or renewal of the public servants. * * * I look to that period with the longing of a wave-worn mariner, who has at length the land in view, and shall count the days and hours which still lie between me and it.—To PRESIDENT WASHINGTON. iii, 467. FORD ED., vi, 108. (M., Sep. 1792.) See APPROBATION.

7466. RETRENCHMENT, Salutary.— These views of reducing our burdens are formed on the expectation that a sensible, and at the same time a salutary reduction may take place in our habitual expenditures. For this purpose,

those of the civil government, the army and navy, will need revisal.—FIRST ANNUAL MESSAGE. viii, 9. FORD ED., viii, 119. (Dec. 1801.)

7467. REVENGE, For abuse.—I shall take no other revenge [for the slanders heaped upon me] than, by a steady pursuit of economy and peace, and by the establishment of republican principles in substance and in form, to sink federalism into an abyss from which there shall be no resurrection for it.—To LEVI LINCOLN. iv, 451. FORD ED., viii, 175. (W., Oct. 1802.)

7468. REVENUE, Imports and.—Our revenue will be less than it would be were we to continue to import instead of manufacturing our coarse goods. But the increase of population and production will keep pace with that of manufactures, and maintain the quantum of exports at the present level at least; and the imports need be equivalent to them, and consequently the revenue on them be undiminished. —To DUPONT DE NEMOURS. v, 583. FORD ED., ix, 319. (M., 1811.) See DEBT (UNITED STATES), INTERNAL IMPROVEMENTS, SURPLUS and TAXATION.

7469. REVOLUTION, Completion of.— The generation which commences a revolution rarely completes it. Habituated from their infancy to passive submission of body and mind to their kings and priests, they are not qualified when called on to think and provide for themselves; and their inexperience, their ignorance and bigotry make them instruments often, in the hands of the Bonapartes and Iturbides, to defeat their own rights and purposes. This is the present situation of Europe and Spanish America.—To JOHN ADAMS. vii, 307. FORD ED., x, 269. (M., 1823.)

7470. REVOLUTION, Right of.—Prudence, indeed, will dictate that governments long established should not be changed for light and transient causes; and accordingly all experience hath shown that mankind are more disposed to suffer, while evils are sufferable, than to right themselves by abolishing the forms to which they are accustomed. But, when a long train of abuses and usurpations [begun at a distinguished period and], pursuing invariably the same object, evinces a design to reduce them under absolute despotism, it is their right, it is their duty, to throw off such government, and to provide new guards for their future security. Such has been the patient sufferance of these Colonies; and such is now the necessity which constrains them to expunge * their former systems of government. —DECLARATION OF INDEPENDENCE AS DRAWN BY JEFFERSON.

7471. REVOLUTION (American), Appeal to British people.—In defence of our persons and properties under actual violation, we took up arms. When that violence shall be removed, when hostilities shall cease on the part of the aggressors, hostilities shall cease on our part also. For the achievement of this happy event, we call for and confide in the good offices of our fellow-subjects beyond the Atlantic. Of their friendly dispositions we do not cease to hope; aware, as they must be, that they have nothing more to expect from the same common enemy, than the

* Congress struck out the words in brackets and substituted "alter" for "expunge".—EDITOR.

humble favor of being last devoured.—DEC-LARATION ON TAKING UP ARMS. FORD ED., i. 475. (July 1775.)

7472. REVOLUTION (American), Battle of Lexington.—Within this week we have received the unhappy news of an action of considerable magnitude, between the King's troops and our brethren of Boston, in which it is said five hundred of the former, with the Earl of Percy, are slain. * * * This accident * has cut off our last hope of reconciliation, and a frenzy of revenge seems to have seized all ranks of people.—To DR. WILLIAM SMALL. i, 198. FORD ED., i, 453. (May 1775.)

7473. REVOLUTION (American), Beginning of.—The question who commenced the Revolution? is as difficult as that of the first inventors of a thousand good things. For example, who first discovered the principle of gravity? Not Newton; for Galileo, who died the year that Newton was born, had measured its force in the descent of gravid bodies. Who invented the Lavoiserian chemistry? The English say Dr. Black, by the preparatory discovery of latent heat. Who invented the steamboat? Was it Gerbert, the Marquis of Worcester, Newcommen, Savary, Papin, Fitch, Fulton? The fact is, that one new idea leads to another, that to a third, and so on through a course of time until some one, with whom no one of these ideas was original, combines all together, and produces what is justly called a new invention. I suppose it would be as difficult to trace our Revolution to its first embryo. We do not know how long it was hatching in the British cabinet before they ventured to make the first of the experiments which were to develop it in the end and to produce complete parliamentary supremacy. Those you mention in Massachusetts as preceding the Stamp Act, might be the first visible symptoms of that design. The proposition of that Act in 1764, was the first here. Your opposition, therefore, preceded ours, as occasion was sooner given there than here, and the truth, I suppose, is, that the opposition in every colony began whenever the encroachment was presented to it. This question of priority is as the inquiry would be who first, of the three hundred Spartans, offered his name to Leonidas?—To DR. BENJAMIN WATERHOUSE. vii, 99. FORD ED., x, 102. (M., 1818.)

7474. ———— ————. It would * * * be as difficult to say at what moment the Revolution began, and what incident set it in motion, as to fix the moment that the embryo becomes an animal, or the act which gives him a beginning. —To JOHN ADAMS. vii, 104. FORD ED., x, 107. (M., 1818.)

7475. ———— ————. A * * * misapprehension of * * * a passage in Mr. [William] Wirt's book, for which I am quoted, has produced a * * * reclamation of the part of Massachusetts, by some of her most distinguished and estimable citizens. I had been applied to by Mr. Wirt for such facts respecting Mr. [Patrick] Henry, as my intimacy with him and participation in the transactions of the day,

* Commenting on this passage, PARTON, in his *Life of Jefferson*, says: "We may judge of the strength of the tie between the mother country and the Colonies, by the fact that so un-English a mind as Jefferson's clung with sentimental fondness to the union long after there was any reasonable hope of their preserving it." Dr. Small, Jefferson's professor and friend at William and Mary College, was then living in England.—EDITOR.

might have placed within my knowledge. I accordingly committed them to paper; and Virginia being the theatre of his action, was the only subject within my contemplation, while speaking of him. Of the resolutions and measures here, in which he had the acknowledged lead, I used the expression that "Mr. Henry certainly gave the first impulse to the ball of revolution". (Wirt, page 41.) The expression is, indeed, general, and in all its extension, would comprehend all the sister States; but indulgent construction would restrain it, as was really meant, to the subject matter under contemplation, which was Virginia alone; according to the rule of the lawyers and a fair canon of general criticism, that every expression should be construed *secundum subjectam materiem*. Where the first attack was made, there must have been, of course, the first act of resistance, and that was in Massachusetts. Our [Virginia's] first overt act of war was Mr. Henry's embodying a force of militia from several counties, regularly armed and organized, marching them in military array and making reprisal on the King's treasury at the seat of government, for the public powder taken away by his Governor. This was in the last days of April, 1775. Your formal battle of Lexington was ten or twelve days before that, which greatly overshadowed in importance, as it preceded in time, our little affray, which merely amounted to a levying of arms against the King; and, very possibly, you had had military affrays before the regular battle of Lexington.—To SAMUEL A. WELLS. i, 116. vii, 120. FORD ED., x, 128. (M., 1819.)

—— REVOLUTION (American), British cruelty in.—See CRUELTY.

7476. REVOLUTION (American), Canada and.—In a short time, we have reason to hope, the delegates of Canada will join us in Congress, and complete the American union, as far as we wish to have it completed.—To JOHN RANDOLPH. i, 202. FORD ED., i, 492. (Pa., Nov. 1775.)

7477. REVOLUTION (American), Change of government.—With respect to the State of Virginia in particular, the people seem to have laid aside the monarchical, and taken up the republican government, with as much ease as would have attended their throwing off an old, and putting on a new suit of clothes. Not a single throe has attended this important transformation. A half-dozen aristocratical gentlemen, agonizing under the loss of preeminence, have sometimes ventured their sarcasms on our political metamorphosis. They have been thought fitter objects of pity, than of punishment.—To BENJAMIN FRANKLIN. i, 204. FORD ED., ii, 131. (1777.)

7478. REVOLUTION (American), Confident of victory.—We have long been out of all fear for the event of the war.—To JOHN ADAMS. i, 207. FORD ED., ii, 157. (Wg., June 1778.)

7479. REVOLUTION (American), Consequences of.—The enquiry which has been excited among the mass of mankind by our Revolution and its consequences, will ameliorate the condition of men over a great portion of the globe.—To JOHN DICKINSON. iv, 366. FORD ED., viii, 8. (W., March 1801.)

7480. REVOLUTION (American), French alliance and.—If there could have been a doubt before as to the event of the war, it is now totally removed by the interposition of France, and the generous alliance she has entered into with us.—To ————. i, 208. Ford ed., ii, 157. (Wg., 1778.)

7481. REVOLUTION (American), Gage's perfidy.—Hostilities thus commenced [at Lexington, &c.], on the part of the ministerial army have been since by them pursued without regard to faith or fame. The inhabitants of the town of Boston, in order to procure their enlargement, having entered into treaty with General Gage, their Governor, it was stipulated that the said inhabitants, having first deposited their arms with their own magistrates, should have liberty to depart from out of the said town taking with them their other effects. Their arms they accordingly delivered in, and claimed the stipulated license of departing with their effects. But in open violation of plighted faith and honor, in defiance of the sacred obligation of treaty which even savage nations observe, their arms, deposited with their own magistrates to be preserved as their property, were immediately seized by a body of armed men under orders from the said General; the greater part of the inhabitants were detained in the town, and the few permitted to depart were compelled to leave their most valuable effects behind. We leave the world to its own reflections on this atrocious perfidy.—Declaration on Taking up Arms. Ford ed., i, 471. (July 1775.)

7482. REVOLUTION (American), Hopes of reconciliation.—When I saw Lord Chatham's bill, I entertained high hope that a reconciliation could have been brought about. The difference between his terms and those offered by our Congress might have been accommodated, if entered by both parties with a disposition to accommodate. But the dignity of Parliament, it seems, can brook no opposition to its power.—To Dr. William Small. i, 190. Ford ed., i, 454. (May 1775.)

7483. ————. Looking with fondness towards a reconciliation with Great Britain, I cannot help hoping that you * may be able to contribute towards expediting this good work. I think it must be evident to yourself, that the Ministry have been deceived by their officers on this side of the water, who (for what purpose I cannot tell) have constantly represented the American opposition as that of a small faction, in which the body of the people took little part. This, you can inform them, of your own knowledge, is untrue. They have taken it into their heads, too, that we are cowards, and shall surrender at discretion to an armed force. * * * I wish they were thoroughly and minutely acquainted with every circumstance relative to America, as it exists in truth. I am persuaded, this would go far towards disposing them to reconciliation.—To John Randolph. i, 200. Ford ed., i, 482. (M., August 1775.)

7484. ————. If undeceiving the Minister, as to matters of fact, may change his disposition, it will, perhaps, be in your power, by assisting to do this, to render service to the whole empire, at the most critical time, certainly, that it has ever seen. Whether Britain shall continue the head of the greatest empire on earth, or shall return to her original station in the political scale of Europe, depends, perhaps, on the resolutions of the succeeding win-

* This John Randolph was the King's Attorney General, and a son of Sir John Randolph. He sided with the Crown and went to England. Peyton Randolph was his brother.—Editor.

ter. God send they may be wise and salutary for us all.—To John Randolph. i, 201. Ford ed., i, 484. (M., August 1775.)

7485. ————. One bloody campaign will probably decide, everlastingly, our future course; and I am sorry to find a bloody campaign is decided on. If our winds and waters should not combine to rescue their shores from slavery, and General Howe's reinforcements should arrive in safety, we have hopes he will be inspirited to come out of Boston and take another drubbing; and we must drub him soundly, before the sceptred tyrant will know we are not mere brutes, to crouch under his hand, and kiss the rod with which he designs to scourge us.—To John Randolph. i, 203. Ford ed., i, 493. (M., Nov. 1775.)

7486. REVOLUTION (American), Influence on France.—The American Revolution seems first to have awakened the thinking part of the French nation in general from the sleep of despotism in which they were sunk.—Autobiography. i, 69. Ford ed., i, 96. (1821.) See Revolution, French.

7487. REVOLUTION (American), Losses in.—I think that upon the whole [our loss * in the war] has been about one-half the number lost by the British. * * * This difference is ascribed to our superiority in taking aim when we fire; every soldier in our army having been intimate with his gun from his infancy.—To ————. i, 208. Ford ed., ii, 157. (Wg., 1778.)

7488. REVOLUTION (American), Memory of.—The memory of the American Revolution will be immortal, and will immortalize those who record it. The reward is encouraging, and will justify all those pains which a rigorous investigation of facts will render necessary.—To Hilliard D'Auberteuil. i, 535. (P., 1786.)

7489. REVOLUTION (American), Mythical British victories.—From the kind anxiety expressed in your letter, as well as from other sources of information, we discover that our enemies have filled Europe with Thrasonic accounts of victories they had never won and conquests they were fated never to make. While these accounts alarmed our friends in Europe, they afforded us diversion.—To ————. i, 207. Ford ed., ii, 156. (Wg., 1778.)

7490. REVOLUTION (American), New England and Virginia.—Throughout the whole of the Revolution, Virginia and the four New England States acted together; indeed they made the Revolution. Their five votes were always to be counted on; but they had to pick up the remaining two for a majority, when and where they could.—Daniel Webster's Conversation with Jefferson. Ford ed., x, 329.

7491. REVOLUTION (American), Peace propositions.—Though this Congress, during the dependence of these States on the British crown with unwearied supplications sued for peace and just redress, and though they still retain a sincere disposition to peace; yet as his Britannic majesty by an obstinate perseverance in injury and a callous indifference to the sufferings and the complaints of these States, has driven them to the necessity of declaring themselves independent, this Congress bound by the voice of their constituents, which coincides with their own sentiments, have no power to enter into conference or to receive any

* From Lexington to the end of 1777.—Editor.

propositions on the subject of peace which do not, as a preliminary, acknowledge these States to be sovereign and independent; and that whenever this shall have been authoritatively admitted on the part of Great Britain, they shall at all times and with that earnestness which the love of peace and justice inspires, be ready to enter into conference or treaty for the purpose of stopping the effusion of so much kindred blood.—RESOLUTIONS ON PEACE PROPOSITIONS. FORD ED., ii, 90. (Aug. 1776.)

7492. REVOLUTION (American), Resources of.—The main confidence of the Colonies was in their own resources. They considered foreign aid as probable and desirable, but not essential. I believe myself, from the whole of what I have seen of our resources and perseverance, 1, that had we never received any foreign aid, we should not have obtained our independence; but that we should have made a peace with Great Britain on any terms we pleased, short of that, which would have been a subjection to the same king, a union of force in war, &c. 2. That had France supplied us plentifully with money, suppose about four millions of guineas a year, without entering into the war herself at all, we should have established our Independence; but it would have cost more time, and blood, but less money. 3. That France, aiding us as she did, with money and forces, shortened much the time, lessened the expense of blood, but at a greater expense of money to her than would have otherwise been requisite.—NOTES ON M. SOULES'S WORK. ix, 297. FORD ED., iv, 305. (P., 1786.)

7493. —— ——. The submission of the States would not have been effected but by a long course of disasters, and such, too, as were irreparable in their nature. Their resources were great, and their determination so rooted, that they would have tried the last of them.—NOTES ON M. SOULES'S WORK. ix, 297. FORD ED., iv, 305. (P., 1786.)

7494. REVOLUTION (American), Royal incendiarism.—It is a lamentable circumstance, that the only mediatory power, acknowledged by both parties, instead of leading to a reconciliation his divided people, should pursue the incendiary purpose of still blowing up the flames, as we find him constantly doing, in every speech and public declaration.—To DR. WILLIAM SMALL. i, 199. FORD ED., i, 454. (May 1775.) See GEORGE III.

7495. REVOLUTION (American), Separation.—There is not in the British empire a man who more cordially loves a union with Great Britain, than I do. But by the God that made me, I will cease to exist before I yield to a connection on such terms as the British Parliament propose; and in this, I think I speak the sentiments of America. We want neither inducement nor power, to declare and assert a separation. It is will, alone, which is wanting, and that is growing apace under the fostering hand of our King.—To JOHN RANDOLPH. i, 203. FORD ED., i, 493. (Pa., November 1775.)

7496. REVOLUTION (American), Spirit of.—Even those in Parliament who are called friends to America seem to know nothing of our real determinations. I observe, they pronounced in the last Parliament that the Congress of 1774 did not mean to insist rigorously on the terms they held out, but kept something in reserve to give up; and, in fact, that they would give up everything but the article of taxation. Now, the truth is far from this, as I

can affirm, and put my honor to the assertion. Their continuance in this error may, perhaps, produce very ill consequences. The Congress stated the lowest terms they thought possible to be accepted, in order to convince the world they were not unreasonable. They gave up the monopoly and regulation of trade and all acts of Parliament prior to 1764, leaving to British generosity to render these, at some time, as easy to America as the interest of Britain would admit. But this was before blood was spilt. I cannot affirm, but have reason to think these terms would not now be accepted.—To JOHN RANDOLPH. i, 200. FORD ED., i, 483. (M., 1775.)

7497. REVOLUTION (American), Treaty of peace.—The terms obtained for us are indeed great, and are so deemed by your country, a few ill-designing debtors excepted.—To JOHN JAY. i, 332. FORD ED., iii, 316. (Pa., 1783.)

—— REVOLUTION (American), Underlying causes of.—See COLONIES (AMERICAN).

7498. REVOLUTION (American), Unnatural contest.—I hope the returning wisdom of Great Britain will, ere long, put an end to this unnatural contest.—To JOHN RANDOLPH. i, 200. FORD ED., i, 482. (M., August 1775.)

7499. REVOLUTION (American), Washington and.—The moderation and virtue of a single character have probably prevented this Revolution from being closed, as most others have been, by a subversion of that liberty it was intended to establish.—To GENERAL WASHINGTON. i, 335. FORD ED., iii, 467. (A., 1784.) See COLONIES, CORNWALLIS, DECLARATION OF INDEPENDENCE, GEORGE III., PARLIAMENT, RIGHTS OF BRITISH AMERICA, WAR and WASHINGTON.

7500. REVOLUTION (French), American revolution and.—Celebrated writers of France and England had already sketched good principles on the subject of government; yet the American Revolution seems first to have awakened the thinking part of the French nation in general from the sleep of despotism in which they were sunk. The officers, too, who had been to America, were mostly young men, less shackled by habit and prejudice, and more ready to assent to the suggestions of common sense, and feeling of common rights, than others. They came back with new ideas and impressions. The press, notwithstanding its shackles, began to disseminate them; conversation assumed new freedoms. Politics became the theme of all societies, male and female, and a very extensive and zealous party was formed, which acquired the appellation of the Patriotic Party, who, sensible of the abusive government under which they lived, sighed for occasions of reforming it. This party comprehended all the honesty of the kingdom, sufficiently at leisure to think, the men of letters, the easy Bourgeois, the young nobility, partly from reflection, partly from mode; for these sentiments became matter of mode, and as such, united most of the young women to the party.—AUTOBIOGRAPHY. i, 69. FORD ED., i, 96. (1821.)

7501. —— ——. The French nation has been awakened by our Revolution, they feel their strength, they are enlightened, their lights are spreading, and they will not retrograde.—To GENERAL WASHINGTON. ii, 535. (P., Dec. 1788.)

— **REVOLUTION (French), Bill of rights.**—See BILL OF RIGHTS.

7502. REVOLUTION (French), Clergy and nobles.—It was imagined the ecclesiastical elections would have been generally in favor of the higher clergy; on the contrary, the lower clergy have obtained five-sixths of these deputations. These are the sons of peasants, who have done all the drudgery of the service for ten, twenty, and thirty guineas a year, and whose oppressions and penury, contrasted with the pride and luxury of the higher clergy, have rendered them perfectly disposed to humble the latter. They have done it, in many instances, with a boldness they were thought insusceptible of. Great hopes have been formed that these would concur with the *Tiers Etat* in voting by persons. In fact, about half of them seem as yet so disposed; but the bishops are intriguing, and drawing them over with the address which has ever marked ecclesiastical intrigue.—To JOHN JAY. iii, 27. (P., May 1789.)

7503. —— ——. The clergy and the nobles, by their privileges and their influence, have hitherto screened their property in a great degree, from public contribution. That half of the orange, then, remains yet to be squeezed, and for this operation there is no agent powerful enough but the people. They are, therefore, brought forward as the favorites of the Court, and will be supported by them.— To JOHN JAY. ii, 561. (P., 1789.)

7504. —— ——. The Clergy will leave nothing unattempted to secure [the voting by orders in the States General]; for they see that the spirit of reformation will not confine itself to the political, but will extend to the ecclesiastical establishment also.—To JOHN JAY. ii, 561. (P., 1789.)

— **REVOLUTION (French), Constitutional reforms.**—See CONSTITUTION, FRENCH.

— **REVOLUTION (French), Execution of Louis XVI.**—See LOUIS XVI.

— **REVOLUTION (French), Fall of Bastile.**—See BASTILE.

7505. REVOLUTION (French), Famine and.—We have had such a winter here as is not on record. The mercury was 18½° below freezing on Reaumur's scale, and I think it was nearly two months varying between that and zero. It gave occasion for a display of the benevolent character of this nation, which, great as I had thought it, went beyond my expectations. There seems to be a very general apprehension of the want of bread this spring. Supplies are hoped from our country, and indeed they have already reduced the price of flour at Bordeaux from 36l. to 33l. the barrel. —To COUNT DE MOUSTIER. ii, 590. (P., March 1789.)

7506. —— ——. We have had such a winter as makes me shiver yet whenever I think of it. All communications, almost, were cut off. Dinners and suppers were suppressed, and the money laid out in feeding and warming the poor, whose labors were suspended by the rigor of the season.—To MADAME DE BREHAN. ii, 591. FORD ED., v, 79. (P., 1789.)

7507. —— ——. The want of bread is very seriously dreaded through the whole kingdom. Between twenty and thirty shiploads of wheat and flour have already arrived from the United States, and there will be about the same quantity of rice sent from Charleston to this country directly. * * * Paris consumes about a shipload a day (say two hundred and fifty tons).—To WILLIAM CARMICHAEL. iii, 22. (P., May 1789.)

7508. —— ——. There have been some mobs, occasioned by the want of bread, in different parts of the kingdom, in which there may have been some lives lost, perhaps a dozen or twenty. These had no professed connection, generally, with the constitutional revolution. A more serious riot happened lately in Paris, in which about one hundred of the mob were killed. This execution has been universally approved, as they seemed to have no view but mischief and plunder.—To JAMES MADISON. iii, 34. (P., May 1789.)

7509. —— ——. The want of bread had been foreseen for some time past, and M. de Montmorin had desired me to notify it in America, and that, in addition to the market price, a premium should be given on what should be brought from the United States. Notice was accordingly given, and produced considerable supplies. Subsequent information made the importations from America, during the months of March, April and May, into the Atlantic ports of France, amount to about twenty-one thousand barrels of flour, besides what went to other ports, and in other months; while our supplies to their West Indian islands relieved them also from that drain. This distress for bread continued till July.—AUTOBIOGRAPHY. i, 89. FORD ED., i, 123. (1821.)

7510. REVOLUTION (French), Financial abuses.—The discovery of the abominable abuses of public money by the late Comptroller General, some new expenses of the Court, not of a piece with the projects of reformation, and the imposition of new taxes, have, in the course of a few weeks, raised a spirit of discontent in the nation, so great and so general, as to threaten serious consequences. The parliaments in general, and particularly that of Paris, put themselves at the head of this effervescence, and direct its object to the calling of the States General, who have not been assembled since 1614. The object is to fix a constitution, and to limit expenses. The King has been obliged to hold a bed of justice, to enforce the registering the new taxes; the parliament on their side, propose to issue a prohibition against their execution. Very possibly this may bring on their exile.—To GENERAL WASHINGTON. ii, 251. (P., 1787.)

7511. REVOLUTION (French), Flight of the King.—We are now under the first impression of the news of the King's flight from Paris, and his recapture. It would be unfortunate were it in the power of any one man to defeat the issue of so beautiful a revolution. I hope and trust it is not, and that, for the good of suffering humanity all over the earth, that revolution will be established and spread through the whole world.—To SIR JOHN SINCLAIR. iii, 284. (Pa., 1791.)

7512. —— ——. You have heard of the peril into which the French Revolution is brought by the flight of their King. Such are the fruits of that form of government which heaps importance on idiots, and of which the tories of the present day are trying to preach into our favor.—To EDWARD RUTLEDGE. iii, 285. FORD ED., v, 376. (Pa., 1791.)

7513. REVOLUTION (French), History of.—As yet, we are but in the first chapter of its history.—Autobiography. i, 106. Ford ed., i, 147. (1821.)

7514. REVOLUTION (French), Imperial imbecility.—The government has published an *Arret*, suspending all reimbursements of capital, and reducing the payments of the principal mass of demands for interest to twelve sous in the livre; the remaining eight sous to be paid with certificates. * * * The consternation is as yet too great to let us judge of the issue. It will probably ripen the public mind to the necessity of a change in their constitution, and to the substituting the collected wisdom of the whole in place of a single will, by which they have been hitherto governed. It is a remarkable proof of the total incompetency of a single head to govern a nation well, when, with a revenue of six hundred millions, they are led to a declared bankruptcy, and to stop the wheels of government, even in its most essential movements, for want of money.—To John Jay. ii, 468. (P., August 1788.)

7515. REVOLUTION (French), Influence of women.—In my opinion, a kind of influence which none of their plans of reform take into account, will elude them all; I mean the influence of women in the government. The manners of the nation allow them to visit, alone, all persons in office, to solicit the affairs of the husband, family, or friends, and their solicitations bid defiance to laws and regulations. This obstacle may seem less to those who, like our countrymen, are in the precious habit of considering right as a barrier against all solicitation. Nor can such an one, without the evidence of his own eyes, believe in the desperate state to which things are reduced in this country from the omnipotence of an influence which, fortunately for the happiness of the sex itself, does not endeavor to extend itself in our country beyond the domestic line.—To General Washington. ii, 536. (P., Dec. 1788.)

7516. REVOLUTION (French), Jefferson's relations to.—I considered a successful reformation of government in France, as insuring a general reformation through Europe, and the resurrection, to a new life, of their people, now ground to dust by the abuses of the governing powers. I was much acquainted with the leading patriots of the Assembleé. Being from a country which had successfully passed through a similar reformation, they were disposed to my acquaintance, and had some confidence in me. I urged, most strenuously, an immediate compromise; to secure what the government was now ready to yield, and trust to future occasions for what might still be wanting. It was well understood that the King would grant, at this time, 1. Freedom of the person by *habeas corpus;* 2. Freedom of conscience: 3. Freedom of the press: 4. Trial by jury: 5. A representative legislature: 6. Annual meetings: 7. The origination of laws: 8. The exclusive right of taxation and appropriation: and 9. The responsibility of ministers; and with the exercise of these powers they could obtain, in future, whatever might be further necessary to improve and preserve their constitution. They thought otherwise, however, and events have proved their lamentable error. For, after thirty years of war, foreign and domestic, the loss of millions of lives, the prostration of private happiness, and foreign subjugation of their own country for a time, they have obtained no more,

nor even that securely. They were unconscious of (for who could foresee?) the melancholy sequel of their well-meant perseverance; that their physical force would be usurped by a first tyrant to trample on the independence, and even the existence, of other nations; that this would afford a fatal example for the atrocious conspiracy of kings against their people: would generate their unholy and homicide alliance to make common cause among themselves, and to crush, by the power of the whole, the efforts of any part, to moderate their abuses and oppressions.—Autobiography. i, 93. Ford ed., i, 129. (1821.) See Holy Alliance.

7517. ——— ———. Possibly you may remember, at the date of the *jeu de paume*, how earnestly I urged yourself and the patriots of my acquaintance, to enter then into a compact with the King, securing freedom of religion, freedom of the press, trial by jury, *habeas corpus*, and a national legislature, all of which it was known he would then yield, to go home, and let these work on the amelioration of the condition of the people, until they should have rendered them capable of more, when occasions would not fail to arise for communicating to them more. This was as much as I then thought them able to bear soberly and usefully for themselves. You thought otherwise, and that the dose might still be larger. And I found you were right; for subsequent events proved they were equal to the constitution of 1791. Unfortunately, some of the most honest and enlightened of our patriotic friends (but closet politicians merely, unpracticed in the knowledge of man), thought more could still be obtained and borne. They did not weigh the hazards of a transition from one form of government to another, the value of what they had already rescued from those hazards, and might hold in security if they pleased, nor the imprudence of giving up the certainty of such a degree of liberty, under a limited monarchy, for the uncertainty of a little more under the form of a republic. You differed from them. You were for stopping there and for securing the constitution which the National Assembly had obtained. Here, too, you were right; and from this fatal error of the republicans, from their separation from yourself and the constitutionalists, in their councils, flowed all the subsequent sufferings and crimes of the French nation. The hazards of a second change fell upon them by the way. The foreigner gained time to anarchise by gold the government he could not overthrow by arms, to crush in their own councils the genuine republicans, by the fraternal embraces of exaggerated and hired pretenders, and to turn the machine of Jacobinism from the change to the destruction of order; and, in the end, the limited monarchy they had secured was exchanged for the unprincipled and bloody tyranny of Robespierre, and the equally unprincipled and maniac tyranny of Bonaparte. You are now rid of him, and I sincerely wish you may continue so. But this may depend on the wisdom and moderation of the restored dynasty. It is for them now to read a lesson in the fatal errors of the republicans; to be contented with a certain portion of power, secured by a formal compact with the nation, rather than, grasping at more, hazard all upon uncertainty, and risk meeting the fate of their predecessor, or a renewal of their own exile.—To Marquis Lafayette. vi, 421. Ford ed., ix, 505. (M., Feb. 1815.)

7518. ——— ———. I had no apprehension that the tempest, of which I saw the beginning was to spread over such an extent of space and time.—To Comte Diodati. v, 62. (W., 1807.)

7519. REVOLUTION (French), Leaders in.—I was intimate with the leading characters of the year 1789. So I was with those of the Brissotine party who succeeded them; and have always been persuaded that their views were upright. Those who have followed them have been less known to me.—To M. DE MEUNIER. FORD ED., vii, 13. (M., 1795.)

7520. —— ——. When I left France at the close of '89, your revolution was, as I thought, under the direction of able and honest men. But the madness of some of their successors, the vices of others, the malicious intrigues of an envious and corrupting neighbor, the *tracasserie* of the Directory, the usurpations, the havoc, and devastations of your Attila, and the equal usurpations, depredations and oppressions of your hypocritical deliverers, will form a mournful period in the history of man, a period of which the last chapter will not be seen in your day or mine, and one which I still fear is to be written in characters of blood. Had Bonaparte reflected that such is the moral construction of the world, that no national crime passes unpunished in the long run, he would not now be in the cage of St. Helena; and were your oppressors to reflect on the same truth, they would spare to their own countries the penalties on their present wrongs which will be inflicted on them in future times. The seeds of hatred and revenge which they are now sowing with a large hand, will not fail to produce their fruits in time. Like their brother robbers on the highway, they suppose the escape of the moment a final escape, and deem infamy and future risk countervailed by present gain.—To M. DE MARBOIS. vii, 76. (M., 1817.)

7521. REVOLUTION (French), Lettres de cachet.—Though they see the evil of *lettres de cachet*, they believe they do more good on the whole. They will think better in time.—To DR. CURRIE. ii, 544. (P., 1788.)

7522. REVOLUTION (French), Liberty and.—The liberty of the whole earth was depending on the issue of the contest, and was ever such a prize won with so little innocent blood?—To WILLIAM SHORT. iii, 502. FORD ED., vi, 154. (Pa., 1793.)

—— REVOLUTION (French), Marie Antoinette.—See MARIE ANTOINETTE.

7523. REVOLUTION (French), Ministerial reforms.—I hope the internal affairs of this country will be finally arranged without having cost a drop of blood. Looking on as a bystander, no otherwise interested, than as entertaining a sincere love for the nation in general, and a wish to see their happiness promoted, keeping myself clear of the particular views and passions of individuals, I applaud extremely the patriotic proceedings of the present ministry. Provincial Assemblies established, the States General called, the right of taxing the nation without their consent abandoned, *corvées* abolished, torture abolished, the criminal code reformed, are facts which will do eternal honor to their administration, in history.—To WILLIAM CARMICHAEL. ii, 466. (P., Aug. 1788.)

7524. —— ——. The internal good they are doing to their country makes me completely their friend.—To WILLIAM CARMICHAEL. ii, 467. (P., 1788.)

7525. REVOLUTION (French), Monarchy and parliaments.—The struggle in France is as yet * * * between the monarchy and the parliaments. The nation is no otherwise concerned, but as both parties may be induced to let go some of its abuses, to court the public favor. The danger is that the people, deceived by a false cry of liberty, may be led to take side with one party, and thus give the other a pretext for crushing them still more.—To E. RUTLEDGE. ii, 435. FORD ED., v, 42. (P., July 1788.)

7526. —— ——. This nation is * * * under great internal agitation. The authority of the crown on one part, and that of the parliaments on the other, are fairly at issue. Good men take part with neither, but have raised an opposition, the object of which is to obtain a fixed and temperate constitution. There was a moment when this opposition ran so high as to endanger an appeal to arms, in which case, perhaps, it would have been crushed. The moderation of government has avoided this, and they are yielding daily one right after another. They have given them Provincial Assemblies, which will be very perfect representatives of the nation, and stand somewhat in the place of our State Assemblies. They have reformed the criminal laws; acknowledged the King cannot lay a new tax, without the consent of the States General; and they will call the States General the next year. —To COLONEL MONROE. ii, 457. (P., 1788.)

7527. —— ——. The contest here is ex- actly what it was in Holland: a contest between the monarchical and aristocratical parts of the government, for a monopoly of despotism over the people. The aristocracy in Holland, seeing that their common prey was likely to escape out of their clutches, chose rather to retain its former portion, and therefore coalesced with the single head. The people remained victims. Here, I think, it will take a happier turn. The parliamentary part of the aristocracy is alone firmly united. The Noblesse and Clergy, but especially the former, are divided partly between the parliamentary and the despotic party, and partly united with the real patriots, who are endeavoring to gain for the nation what they can, both from the parliamentary and the single despotism. I think I am not mistaken in believing that the King and some of his ministers are well affected to this band; and surely, that they make great concessions to the people, rather than small ones to the parliament. They are, accordingly, yielding daily to the national reclamations, and will probably end in according a well-tempered constitution. —To M. DE CREVECOEUR. ii, 457. (P., 1788.)

7528. REVOLUTION (French), Monarchy waning.—In the course of three months, the royal authority has lost, and the rights of the nation gained as much ground by a revolution of public opinion only, as England gained in all her civil wars under the Stuarts. I rather believe, too, they will retain the ground gained because it is defended by the young and the middle aged in opposition to the old only. The first party increases, and the latter diminishes daily from the course of nature.—To JOHN ADAMS. ii, 259. (P., 1787.)

7529. REVOLUTION (French), National Assembly.—The National Assembly (for that is the name they take), having shown through every stage of these transactions a coolness, wisdom, and resolution to set fire to the four corners of the kingdom and to perish with it themselves, rather than to relinquish an iota from their plan of a total change of government, are now in complete and undisputed possession of the sovereignty. The executive and aristocracy are at their feet; the mass of the nation, the mass of the clergy, and the army are with them. They have prostrated the old government, and are now beginning to build one from the foundation.—To THOMAS PAINE. iii, 69. (P., July 1789.)

7530. ————. It is impossible to desire better dispositions towards us than prevail in the National Assembly. Our proceedings have been viewed as a model for them on every occasion; and though in the heat of debate men are generally disposed to contradict every authority urged by their opponents, ours has been treated like that of the Bible, open to explanation but not to question. I am sorry that in the moment of such a disposition, anything should come from us to check it. The placing them on a mere footing with the English will have this effect.—To JAMES MADISON. iii, 99. FORD ED., v, 110. (P., Aug. 1789.)

7531. ————. The difficulties which now appear threatening to my mind are those which will result from the size of the Assembly. Twelve hundred persons of any rank and of any nation assembled together would with difficulty be prevented from tumult and confusion. But when they are to compose an assembly for which no rules of debate or proceeding have been yet formed, in whom no habits of order have been yet established, and to consist moreover of Frenchmen, among whom there are always more speakers than listeners, I confess to you I apprehend some danger.—To MR. SHIPPEN. ii, 580. (P., March 1789.)

7532. REVOLUTION (French), National debt.—Calonné stated to * * * [the Assembly of Notables] that the annual excess of expenses beyond the revenue, when Louis XVI. came to the throne, was thirty-seven millions of livres; that four hundred and forty millions had been borrowed to reestablish the navy; that the American war had cost them fourteen hundred and forty millions (two hundred and fifty-six millions of dollars), and that the interest of these sums, with other increased expenses had added forty millions more to the annual deficit. (But a subsequent and more candid estimate made it fifty-six millions.)—AUTOBIOGRAPHY. i, 70. FORD ED., i, 97. (1821.)

7533. REVOLUTION (French), Necker recalled.—The Archbishop [of Toulouse] has been removed * * * and M. Necker called in as Director General of finance. To soften the Archbishop's dismission, a cardinal's hat is asked for him from Rome, and his nephew promised the succession to the archbishopric of Sens. The public joy, on this change of administration, was very great indeed. The people of Paris were amusing themselves with trying and burning the Archbishop in effigy, and rejoicing on the appointment of M. Necker. The commanding officer of the city guards undertook to forbid this, and not being obeyed, he charged the mob with fixed bayonets, killed two or three, and wounded many. This stopped their rejoicings for that day; but enraged at being thus obstructed in amusements wherein they had committed no disorder whatever, they collected in great numbers the next day, attacked the guards in various places, burned ten or twelve guard houses, killed two or three of the guards, and had about six or eight of their own number killed. The city was, hereupon, put under martial law, and after a while, the tumult subsided, and peace was restored.—To JOHN JAY. ii, 471. (P., Sep. 1788.)

7534. REVOLUTION (French), Nobles and people.—With respect to the nobles, the younger members are generally for the people, and the middle-aged are daily coming over to the same side.—To JOHN JAY. ii, 561. (P Jan. 1789.)

7535. REVOLUTION (French), Notables called.—The King has called an Assemblée des Notables. This has not been done for one hundred and sixty years past. Of course it calls up all the attention of the people. The objects of this Assembly are not named. Several are conjectured. T. e tolerating the Protestant re.igion; removing all the internal custom houses to the frontier; equalizing the gabelles on salt through the kingdom; the sale of the King's domains to raise money; or, finally, the effecting this necessary end by some other means are talked of. But in truth, nothing is known about it. This government practices secrecy so systematically, that it never publishes its purposes or its proceedings sooner or more extensively than is necessary.—To JOHN JAY. ii, 91. (P., 1787.)

7536. ————. The Assemblée des Notables met yesterday [Feb. 22]. The King, in a short but affectionate speech, informed them of his wish to consult with them on the plans he had digested, and on the general good of his people, and his desire to imitate the head of his family, Henry IV., whose memory is so dear to the nation. The Gardé des Sceaux then spoke about twenty minutes, chiefly in compliment to the orders present. The Comptroller General, in a speech of about an hour, opened the budget, and enlarged on the several subjects which will be under their deliberation, * * * and the institution of Provincial Assemblies. The Assemblée was then divided into committees, with a prince of the blood at the head of each.—To JOHN JAY. ii, 129. (P., 1787.)

7537. ————. The first step of the deputies to the Assemblée des Notables should be to get themselves divided into two chambers instead of seven; the noblesse and the commons separately. The second, to persuade the King, instead of choosing the deputies of the Commons himself, to summon those chosen by the people for the Provincial administrations. The third, as the noblesse is too numerous to be of the Assemblée, to obtain permission for that body to choose its own deputies. Two houses, so elected, would contain a mass of wisdom which would make the people happy, and the King great; would place him in history where no other act can possibly place him. They would thus put themselves in the track of the best guide they can follow; they would soon overtake it, become its guide in turn and lead to the wholesome modifications wanting in that model and necessary to constitute a rational government. Should they attempt more than the established habits of the people are ripe for, they may lose all, and retard indefinitely the ultimate object of their aim.—To MADAME LA COMTESSE DE TESSE. ii, 133. (N., 1787.)

7538. ————. The Assemblée des Notables has been productive of much good. The reformation of some of the most oppressive laws has taken place, and is taking place. The allotment of the State into subordinate governments, the administration of which is committed to persons chosen by the people, will work in time a very beneficial change in their constitution. The expense of the trappings of monarchy, too, is lightening. Many of the useless officers, high and low, of the King, Queen, and Princes, are struck off.—To GENERAL WASHINGTON. ii, 251. (P., 1787.)

7539. REVOLUTION (French), Principles of.—I continue eternally attached to the principles of your [the French] Revolution. I hope it will end in the establishment of some firm government, friendly to liberty, and capable of maintaining it. If it does, the world will become inevitably free. If it does not, I feel that the zealous apostles of English despotism here, will increase the number of its disciples. However, we shall still remain free. Though they may harass our spirits, they cannot make impression on our centre.—To J. P. BRISSOT DE WARVILLE. FORD ED., vi, 249. (Pa., May 1793.)

7540. REVOLUTION (French), Provincial Assemblies.—The establishment of the Provincial Assemblies was, in itself, a fundamental improvement. They would be of the choice of the people, one-third renewed every year, in those provinces where there are no States, that is to say, over about three-fourths of the kingdom. They would be partly an Executive themselves, and partly an executive council to the Intendant, to whom the executive power, in his province, had been, heretofore, entirely delegated. Chosen by the people, they would soften the execution of hard laws and, having a right of representation to the King, they would censure bad laws, suggest good ones, expose abuses, and their representations, when united, would command respect. To the other advantages might be added the precedent itself of calling the *Assemblée des Notables*, which would perhaps grow into habit. The hope was that the improvements thus promised would be carried into effect; that they would be maintained during the present [Louis XVI.] reign, and that that would be long enough for them to take some root in the constitution, so that they might come to be considered as a part of that, and be protected by time, and the attachment of the nation.—AUTOBIOGRAPHY. i, 71. FORD ED., i, 98. (1821.)

7541. REVOLUTION (French), Reform and.—If the people do not obtain now so much as they have a right to, they will in the long run. The misfortune is that they are not yet ripe for receiving the blessings to which they are entitled. I doubt, for instance, whether the body of the nation, if they could be consulted, would accept of a *habeas corpus* law, if offered them by the King.—To JAMES MADISON. ii, 506. FORD ED., v, 53. (P., Nov. 1788.)

7542. REVOLUTION (French), Riots.—We have had in Paris a very considerable riot, in which about one hundred people have been probably killed. It was the most unprovoked, and is therefore, justly, the most unpitied catastrophe of that kind I ever knew. Nor did the wretches know what they wanted, except to do mischief. It seems to have had no particular connection with the great national question now in agitation.—To WILLIAM CARMICHAEL. iii, 22. (P., May 1789.)

7543. ———. ———. Hitherto no acts of popular violence had been produced by the struggle for political reformation. Little riots, on ordinary incidents, had taken place, as at other times, in different parts of the kingdom, in which some lives, perhaps a dozen or twenty, had been lost; but in the month of April, 1788, a more serious one occurred in Paris, unconnected, indeed, with the revolutionary principle,

but making part of the history of the day. The Faubourg St. Antoiné is a quarter of the city inhabited entirely by the class of day laborers and journeymen in every line. A rumor was spread among them, that a great paper manufacturer, of the name of Reveillon, had proposed, on some occasion, that their wages should be lowered to fifteen sous a day. Inflamed at once into rage, and without inquiring into its truth, they flew to his house in vast numbers, destroyed everything in it, and in his magazines and workshops, without secreting, however, a pin's worth to themselves, and were continuing this work of devastation, when the regular troops were called in. Admonitions being disregarded, they were of necessity fired on, and a regular action ensued, in which about one hundred and twenty of them were killed, before the rest would disperse. There had rarely passed a year without such a riot, in some part or other of the Kingdom; and this is distinguished only as contemporary with the Revolution, although not produced by it.—AUTOBIOGRAPHY. i, 89. FORD ED., i, 124. (1821.)

7544. ———. ———. They were the most abandoned banditti of Paris, and never was a riot more unprovoked and unpitied. They began, under a pretence that a paper manufacturer had proposed in an assembly to reduce their wages to fifteen sous a day. They rifled his house, destroyed everything in his magazines and shops, and were only stopped in their career of mischief by the troops engaging in regular action with them and killing probably one hundred of them. Neither this nor any of the other riots has had a professed connection with the great national reformation now going on. They are such as have happened every year since I have been here, and as will continue to be produced by common incidents. —To JOHN JAY. iii, 26. (P., May 1789.)

7545. REVOLUTION (French), States General.—The States General were opened on the 5th of May, 1789, by speeches from the King, the *Gardé des Sceaux*, Lamoignon, and M. Necker. The last was thought to trip too lightly over the constitutional reformations which were expected. His notices of them in this speech were not as full as in his previous "*Rapport au Roi*". This was observed to his disadvantage; but much allowance should have been made for the situation in which he was placed, between his own counsels, and those of the ministers and party of the Court. Overruled in his own opinions, compelled to deliver, and to gloss over those of his opponents, and even to keep their secrets, he could not come forward in his own attitude. The composition of the *Assemblée*, although equivalent on the whole to what had been expected, was something different in its elements. It had been supposed, that a superior education would carry into the scale of the Commons a respectable portion of the *Noblesse*. It did so as to those of Paris, of its vicinity and of the other considerable cities, whose greater intercourse with enlightened society had liberalized their minds, and prepared them to advance up to the measure of the times. But the Noblesse of the country, which constituted two-thirds of that body, were far in their rear. Residing constantly on their patrimonial feuds, and familiarized, by daily habit, with seigneurial powers and practices, they had not yet learned to suspect their inconsistence with reason and right. They were willing to submit to equality of taxation, but not to descend from their rank and prerogatives to be incorporated in session with the *Tiers Etat*. Among the Clergy, on the other hand, it had been apprehended that the higher orders of the hierarchy, by their wealth and connections, would have carried the elections generally; but it proved that in most cases the lower clergy had obtained the popular majorities. These consisted of the curés, sons of the peasantry, who had been employed to do all the drudgery of parochial services for ten, twenty, or thirty Louis a year; while their superiors were consuming their princely revenues in palaces of luxury and indolence. The objects for which this body was convened, being of the first order of importance, I felt it very interesting to understand the views of the parties of which it was composed, and especially the ideas prevalent as to the organization contemplated for their government. I went, therefore, daily from Paris to Versailles, and attended their debates, generally till the hour of adjournment. Those of the *Noblesse* were impassioned and tempestuous. They had some able men on both sides, and actuated by equal zeal. The debates of The Commons were temperate, rational, and inflexibly firm. As preliminary to all other business, the awful questions came on, Shall the States sit in one, or in distinct apartments? And shall they vote by heads or houses? The opposition was soon found to consist of the Episcopal order among the clergy, and two-thirds of the *Noblesse;* while the *Tiers Etat* were to a man united and determined. After various propositions of compromise had failed, the Commons undertook to cut the Gordian Knot. The Abbé Sieyés, the most logical head of the nation (author of the pamphlet "*Qu'est ce que le Tiers Etat*"? which had electrified that country, as Paine's "Common Sense" did us), after an impressive speech on the 10th of June, moved that a last invitation should be sent to the *Noblesse* and Clergy, to attend in the hall of the States, collectively or individually, for the verification of powers, to which the Commons would proceed immediately, either in their presence or absence. This verification being finished, a motion was made, on the 15th, that they should constitute themselves a National Assembly; which was decided on the 17th, by a majority of four-fifths. During the debates on this question, about twenty of the curés had joined them, and a proposition was made in the chamber of the Clergy that their whole body should join them. This was rejected at first by a small majority only; but, being afterwards somewhat modified, it was decided affirmatively, by a majority of eleven. While this was under debate and unknown to the court, to wit, on the 10th, a council was held in the afternoon at Marly, wherein it was proposed that the King should interpose by a declaration of his sentiments, in a *seance royale*. A form of declaration was proposed by Necker, which, while it censured in general the proceedings both of the Nobles and Commons, announced the King's views, such as substantially to coincide with the Commons. It was agreed to in Council, the *seance* was fixed for the 22d, the meetings of the States were till then to be suspended, and everything, in the meantime, kept secret. The members, the next morning (20th), repairing to their house, as usual, found the doors shut and guarded, a proclamation posted up for a *seance royale* on the 22d, and a suspension of their meetings in the meantime. Concluding that their dissolution was now to take place, they repaired to a building called the "Jeu de paume" (or Tennis, court) and there bound themselves by oath to each other, never to separate of their own accord, till they had settled a constitution for the nation, on a solid basis, and, if separated by force, that they would reassemble in some other

place. The next day they met in the church of St. Louis, and were joined by a majority of the clergy.—AUTOBIOGRAPHY. i, 90. FORD ED., i, 125. (1821.)

7546. —— ——. Viewing it as an opera, it was imposing.—To WILLIAM CARMICHAEL. iii, 22. (P., May 1789.)

7547. —— ——. I was present at that august ceremony. Had it been enlightened with lamps and chandeliers, it would have been almost as brilliant as the opera.—To M. DE CREVECOEUR. iii, 43. (P., 1789.)

7548. —— ——. The States General are too numerous. I see great difficulty in preventing twelve hundred people from becoming a mob.—To WILLIAM CARMICHAEL. FORD ED., v, 73. (P., Mar. 1789.)

7549. —— ——. Should confusion * * * be prevented, I suppose the States General, with the consent of the King, will establish some of the leading features of a good constitution.—To WILLIAM CARMICHAEL. FORD ED., v, 73. (P., Mar. 1789.)

7550. REVOLUTION (French), Sympathy with.—I still hope the French Revolution will issue happily. I feel that the permanence of our own leans in some degree on that, and that a failure there would be a powerful argument to prove that there must be a failure here.—To EDWARD RUTLEDGE. iii, 285. FORD ED., v, 377. (Pa., 1791.)

7551. —— ——. The success of the French Revolution will ensure the progress of liberty in Europe, and its preservation here. The failure of that would have been a powerful argument with those who wish to introduce a king, lords, and commons here, a sect which is all head and no body.—To EDMUND PENDLETON. FORD ED., v, 358. (Pa., 1791.)

7552. —— ——. I am looking ardently to the completion of the glorious work in which France is engaged. I view the general condition of Europe as hanging on the success or failure of France. Having set such an example of philosophical arrangement within, I hope it will be extended without your limits also, to your dependents and to your friends in every part of the earth.—To MARQUIS DE CONDORCET. FORD ED., v, 379. (Pa., 1791.)

7553. —— ——. I was a sincere wellwisher to the success of the French Revolution, and still wish it may end in the establishment of a free and well-ordered republic.—To ELBRIDGE GERRY. iv, 269. FORD ED., vii, 329. (Pa., 1799.)

7554. —— ——. I have expressed to you my sentiments, because they are really those of ninety-nine in an hundred of our citizens. The universal feasts and rejoicings, which have lately been had on account of the successes of the French, showed the genuine effusions of their hearts.—To WILLIAM SHORT. iii, 502. FORD ED., vi, 154. (Pa., Jan. 1793.)

7555. —— ——. The event of the French Revolution is now little doubted of, even by its enemies. The sensations it has produced here, and the indications of them in the public papers, have shown that the form our own government was to take depended much more on the events of France than anybody had before imagined. The tide which, after our former relaxed government, took a violent course towards the opposite extreme, and seemed ready to hang everything round with the tassels and baubles of monarchy, is now getting back as we hope to a just mean, a government of laws addressed to the reason of the people, and not to their weaknesses.—To T. M. RANDOLPH. iii, 504. FORD ED., vi, 157. (Pa., Jan. 1793.)

7556. RHODE ISLAND, Adoption of Constitution.—What do you propose to do with Rhode Island [on the question of the new Federal Constitution]? As long as there is hope, we should give her time. I cannot conceive but that she will come to rights in the long run. Force, in whatever form, would be a dangerous precedent.—To E. CARRINGTON. ii. 405. FORD ED., v, 21. (P., 1788.)

7557. ———. The little *vautrien*, Rhode Island, will come over [to the new Constitution] with a little time.—To M. DE LA-FAYETTE. iii, 132. FORD ED., v, 152. (N.Y., 1790.)

7558. ——— ———. Rhode Island has at length acceded to the Union by a majority of two voices only in their convention.—To WILLIAM SHORT. FORD ED., v, 178. (N.Y., June 1790.)

7559. RHODE ISLAND, Characteristics of.—How happens it that Rhode Island is opposed to every useful proposition? Her geography accounts for it, with the aid of one or two observations. The cultivators of the earth are the most virtuous citizens, and possess most of the *amor patriæ*. Merchants are the least virtuous, and possess the least of the *amor patriæ*. The latter reside principally in the seaboard towns, the former in the interior country. Now, it happened that of the territory constituting Rhode Island and Connecticut, the part containing the seaports was erected into a State by itself, called Rhode Island, and that containing the interior country was erected into another State called Connecticut. For though it has a little seacoast, there are no good ports in it. Hence it happens that there is scarcely one merchant in the whole State of Connecticut, while there is not a single man in Rhode Island who is not a merchant of some sort. Their whole territory is but a thousand square miles, and what of that is in use is laid out in grass farms almost entirely. Hence they have scarcely anybody employed in agriculture. All exercise some species of commerce. This circumstance has decided the character of these two States. The remedies to this evil are hazardous. One would be to consolidate the two States into one. Another would be to banish Rhode Island from the Union. A third. to compel her submission to the will of the other twelve. A fourth, for the other twelve to govern themselves according to the new propositions, and to let Rhode Island go on by herself according to the ancient articles. But the dangers and difficulties attending all these remedies are obvious.—ANSWERS TO M. DE MEUNIER. ix, 288. FORD ED., iv, 143. (P., 1786.)

7560. RHODE ISLAND, College of.—I was honored in the month of January last with a letter * * * from the corporation of Rhode Island College to his most Christian Majesty [Louis XVI.] * * *. I turned my attention to that object which was the establishment of a professorship of the French language in the college, and the obtaining a collection of the best French authors with the aid of the king. That neither the college nor myself might be compromitted uselessly. I thought it necessary to sound previously those who were able to inform me what would be the success

of the application. I was assured so as to leave no doubt, that it would not be complied with; that there had never been an instance of the king's granting such a demand in a foreign country, and that they would be cautious of setting the precedent; that in this moment, too, they were embarrassed with the difficult operation of putting down all establishments of their own, which could possibly be dispensed with, in order to bring their expenditures down to the level of their receipts. Upon such information I was satisfied that it was most prudent not to deliver the letter. * * * The king did give two colleges in America copies of the works printed in the public press, * * * of no consequence. * * * No endeavors of mine should have been spared, could they have effected their wish.—To RHODE ISLAND DELEGATES. ii, 184. (P., 1787.)

7561. RHODE ISLAND, Regeneration of.—A new subject of congratulation has arisen. I mean the regeneration of Rhode Island. I hope it is the beginning of that resurrection of the genuine spirit of New England which arises for life eternal. According to natural order, Vermont will emerge next, because least, after Rhode Island, under the yoke of hierocracy.—To GIDEON GRANGER. iv, 395. FORD ED., viii, 48. (W., 1801.)

7562. RICE, African.—I was fortunate in receiving from the coast of Africa last fall a cask of mountain rice. This I have dispersed into many hands, having sent the mass of it to South Carolina.—To BENJAMIN VAUGHAN. FORD ED., v, 332. (Pa., 1791.)

7563. ——— ———. In 1790, I got a cask of heavy upland rice, from the river Denbigh, in Africa, about lat. 9° 30′ North, which I sent to Charleston, in hopes it might supersede the culture of the wet rice, which renders South Carolina and Georgia so pestilential through the summer.—JEFFERSON'S MSS. i, 176. (M., 1821.)

7564. RICE, Chinese.—In Asia they have several distinct species of this grain. Monsieur Poivre, a former governor of the Isle of France, in travelling through several countries of Asia, observed with particular attention the objects of their agriculture, and tells us that in Cochin-China they cultivate six several kinds of rice. which he describes, three of them requiring water, and three growing on highlands. The rice of Carolina is said to come from Madagascar, and De Poivre tells us, it is the white rice which is cultivated there. This favors the probability of its being of a different species originally, from that of Piedmont; and time, culture, and climate may have made it still more different. Under this idea I thought it would be well to furnish you with some of the Piedmont rice. unhusked, but was told it was contrary to the laws to export it in that form. I took such measures as I could, however. to have a quantity brought out, and lest these should fail, I brought myself a few pounds. A part of this I have addressed to you by way of London; a part comes with this letter; and I shall send another parcel by some other conveyance to prevent the danger of miscarriage. Any one of them arriving safe may serve to put in seed. should the society think it an object.—To WILLIAM DRAYTON. ii, 196. (P., 1787.)

7565. ——— ———. The dry rice of Cochin-China has the reputation of being the whitest to the eye, best flavored to the taste. and most productive. It seems, then. to unite the good qualities of both the others known to us. Could it supplant them, it would be a great happiness, as it would enable us to get rid of those ponds of stagnant water, so fatal to human health and life. But such is the force of habit, and caprice of taste, that we could not be sure beforehand it would produce this effect. The experiment, however, is worth trying, should it only end in producing a third quality, and increasing the demand. I will endeavor to procure some to be brought from Cochin-China.—To WILLIAM DRAYTON. ii, 197. (P., 1787.)

7566. ——— ———. I have considerable hopes of receiving some dry rice from Cochin-China, the young prince of that country lately gone hence [Paris], having undertaken that it shall come to me. * * * These are all but experiments. The precept, however, is wise which directs us to try all things, and hold fast that which is good.—To WILLIAM DRAYTON. ii, 347. (F., 1788.)

7567. RICE, Egyptian.—I have forwarded to you two couffes of rough rice, which I had brought from Egypt. I wish both may arrive in time for the approaching seed time, and that the trials with this and the Piedmont rice may furnish new advantages to your agriculture.—To WILLIAM DRAYTON. ii, 347. (P., 1788.)

7568. RICE, Italian.—I wished particularly to know whether it was the use of a different machine for cleaning, which brought European rice to market less broken than ours, as had been represented to me by those who deal in that article in Paris. I found several persons who had passed through the rice country of Italy, but not one who could explain to me the nature of the machine. But I was given to believe that I might see it myself immediately on entering Piedmont. I determined to go and ascertain this point, as the chance only of placing our rice above all rivalship in quality, as it is in color, by the introduction of a better machine, if a better existed * * *. I found the rice country to be in truth Lombardy, * * * and that though called Piedmont rice, not a grain is made in the country of Piedmont. I passed through the rice fields of the Venellese and Milanese, about sixty miles, * * * and found that the machine is absolutely the same as ours. * * * It is a difference in the species of grain, of which the government of Turin is so sensible, that, as I was informed, they prohibit the exportation of rough rice on pain of death. I have taken measures, however, which I think will not fail for obtaining a quantity of it, and I bought on the spot a small parcel. * * * I propose * * * to send the rice to the society at Charleston for promoting agriculture, supposing that they will be best able to try the experiment of cultivating the rice of this quality, and to communicate the species to South Carolina and Georgia, if they find it answer.—To JOHN JAY. ii, 138. FORD ED., iv, 377. (Mar. 1787.)

7569. ——— ———. I had expected to satisfy myself at Marseilles, of the cause of the differences of quality between the rice of Carolina, and that of Piedmont, which is brought in quantities to Marseilles. Not being able to do it, I made an excursion of three weeks into the rice country beyond the Alps, going through it from Vercelli to Pavia about sixty miles. I found the difference to be not in the management, as had been supposed both here and in Carolina, but in the species of rice; and I hope to enable them in Carolina to begin the cultivation of the Piedmont rice, and carry it on. hand in hand, with their own, that they may supply

both qualities; which is absolutely necessary at this market.—To JOHN ADAMS. ii, 162. FORD ED., iv, 396. (P., 1787.)

7570. ——— ———. At Marseilles I hoped to know what the Piedmont machine was, but I could find nobody who knew anything of it. I determined, therefore, to sift the matter to the bottom, by crossing t.e Alps into the rice country. I found their machine exactly such a one as you had described to me in Congress in the year 1775. There was but one conclusion, then, to be drawn, to wit, that the rice was of a different species, and I determined to take enough to put you in seed. They informed me, however, that its exportation in the husk was prohibited, so I could only bring off as much as my coat and surtout pockets would hold. I took measures with a muleteer to run a couple of sacks across the Apennines to Genoa, but have not great dependence on its success. The little, therefore, which I brought myself, must be relied on for fear we should get no more; and because, also, it is genuine from Vercelli, where the best is made of all the Sardinian Lombardy, the whole of which is considered as producing a better rice than the Milanese. This is assigned as the reason for the strict prohibition.—To E. RUTLEDGE. ii, 178. FORD ED., iv, 407. (P., 1787.)

7571. ——— ———. Having observed that the consumption of rice in this country [France], and particularly in this capital [Paris], was very great, I thought it my duty to inform myself from what markets they draw their supplies. * * * [I found] that the dealers in Paris were in the habit of selling two qualities of rice, that of Carolina, with which they were supplied chiefly from England, and that of Piedmont; that the Carolina rice was long, slender, white and transparent, answers well when prepared with milk, sugar, &c., but not so well when prepared au gras; that that of Piedmont was shorter, thicker, and less white; but that it presented its form better when dressed au gras, was better tasted, and, therefore, preferred by good judges for those purposes. * * * [The dealers] supposed this difference of quality to proceed from a difference of management: that the Carolina rice was husked with an instrument that broke it more, and that less pains were taken to separate the broken from the unbroken grains, imagining that it was the broken grains which dissolved in oily preparations. * * * The objection to the Carolina rice, then, being that it crumbles in certain forms of preparation, and this supposed to be the effect of a less perfect machine for husking, I flattered myself I should be able to learn what might be the machine of Piedmont, when I should arrive at Marseilles. * * * At Marseilles, however, they differed as much in account of the machines, as at Paris they had differed about other circumstances. Some said it was husked between mill-stones, others between rubbers of wood in the form of mill-stones, others of cork. They concurred in one fact, however, that the machine might be seen by me immediately on crossing the Alps. This would be an affair of three weeks. I crossed them and went through the rice country from Vercelli to Pavia, about sixty miles. I found the machine to be absolutely the same with that used in Carolina. * * * In some of them, indeed, they arm each pestle with an iron tooth, consisting of nine spikes hooked together, which I do not remember in the description [of the machine] of Mr. Rutledge. I, therefore, had a tooth made, which I forward you: observing, at the same time, that as many of their machines are without teeth as with them, and of course, that the advantage is not very palpable. It seems to follow, then, that the rice of Lombardy (for though called Piedmont rice, it does not grow in that country, but in Lombardy) is of a different species from that of Carolina; different in form, in color and in quality.—To WILLIAM DRAYTON. ii, 194. (P., 1787.)

7572. RICE, Smuggling.—Poggio, a muleteer who passes every week between Vercelli and Genoa, will smuggle a sack of rough rice for me to Genoa; it being death to export it in that form.—TRAVELS IN ITALY. ix, 338. (1787.)

7573. RICE, Southern cultivation.— The upland rice which I procured fresh from Africa and sent them [the South], has been preserved and spread in the upper parts of Georgia, and I believe in Kentucky.—To JAMES RONALDSON. vi, 92. FORD ED., ix, 371. (M., Jan. 1813.)

7574. RICE, Upland vs. Swamp.—I first became informed of the existence of a rice which would grow in uplands without any more water than the common rains, by reading a book of M. de Poivre, who had been Governor of the Isle of France, who mentions it as growing there and all along the coast of Africa successfully, and as having been introduced from Cochin-China. I was at that time (1784-89) in France, and there happening to be there a Prince of Cochin-China, on his travels, and then returning home, I obtained his promise to send me some. I never received it, however, and mention it only as it may have been sent, and furnished the ground for the inquiries of Dr. De Carro, respecting my receiving it from China. When at Havre on my return from France, I found there Captain Nathaniel Cutting, who was the ensuing spring to go on a voyage along the coast of Africa. I engaged him to enquire for this. * * * He procured and sent me a thirty gallon cask of it. * * * I divided it between the Agricultural Society of Charleston and some private gentlemen of Georgia, recommending it to their care, in the hope which had induced me to endeavor to obtain it, that if it answered as well as the swamp rice, it might rid them of that source of their summer diseases. Nothing came of the trials in South Carolina, but being carried into the upper hilly parts of Georgia, it succeeded there perfectly, has spread over the country, and is now commonly cultivated; still, however, for family use chiefly, as they cannot made it for sale in competition with the rice of the swamps.—To DR. BENJAMIN WATERHOUSE. v, 393. (W., 1808.)

7575. RICHMOND (Va.), Capture of.— Is the surprise of an open and unarmed place, although called a city, and even a capital, so unprecedented as to be a matter of indelible reproach? Which of our own capitals, during the same war, was not in possession of the same enemy, not merely by surprise and for a day only, but permanently? That of Georgia? Of South Carolina? North Carolina? Pennsylvania? New York? Connecticut? Rhode Island? Massachusetts? And if others were not, it was because the enemy saw no object in taking possession of them. Add to the list in the late war (1812) Washington, the metropolis of the Union, covered by a fort, with troops and a dense population. And what capital on the continent of Europe (St. Petersburg and its regions of ice excepted), did not Bonaparte take and hold at his pleasure? Is it then just that Richmond and its authorities alone should be placed under the reproach of history, because, in a moment of peculiar denudation of resources, by the *coup de main* of an enemy, led on by the hand of fortune directing the winds and weather to their wishes, it was surprised and held for twenty-four hours? Or strange that that enemy with such advantages, should be enabled, then, to get off, without risking the honors he had achieved by burnings and destructions of property peculiar to his principles of warfare? We, at least, may leave these glories to their own trumpet.—To HENRY LEE. vii, 447. FORD ED., x, 388. (M., 1826.)

7576. RICHMOND (Va.), Street architecture.—There is one street in Richmond (from the bridge straight on towards Curries) which would be considered as handsomely built in any city of Europe.—To WILLIAM SHORT. FORD ED., v, 137. (1789.)

7577. RIDICULE, Reason and.—Resort is had to ridicule only when reason is against us.—To PRESIDENT MADISON. vi, 112. FORD ED., ix, 382. (M., 1813.)

7578. RIDICULE, Reformation and.— The most remarkable effect as yet of the convention of the Notables is the number of puns and *bon mots* it has generated. I think, were they all collected, it would make a more voluminous work than the Encyclopédie. This occasion, more than anything I have seen, convinces me that this nation is incapable of any serious effort but under the word of command. The people at large view every object only as it may furnish puns and *bon mots*; and I pronounce that a good punster would disarm the whole nation were they ever so seriously disposed to revolt. Indeed, they are gone, when a measure so capable of doing good, as the calling the Notables, is treated with so much ridicule; we may conclude the nation desperate, and in charity pray that heaven may send them good kings.—To MRS. JOHN ADAMS. FORD ED., iv, 370. (P., 1787.)

7579. RIEDESEL (Baron), Jefferson and.—I thank you for your kind congratulations; though condolations would be better suited to the occasion, not only on account of the labors of the office [Governorship] to which I am called, and its withdrawing me from retirement, but also the loss of the agreeable society I have left of which Madame Riedesel and yourself were an important part.*—To BARON DE RIEDESEL. FORD ED., ii, 245. (1779.)

7580. RIENZI (Nicolo Gabrini) Estimate of.—This poor counterfeit of the Gracchi seems to have had enthusiasm and eloquence, without either wisdom or firmness.— To F. VAN DER KEMP. FORD ED., x, 78. (M., 1817.)

7581. RIGHT, Administer.—Deal out to all equal and impartial right.—RIGHTS OF BRITISH AMERICA. i, 141. FORD ED., i, 446. (1774.)

7582. RIGHT, Doing.—I shall pursue in silence the path of right.—To GENERAL WASHINGTON. i, 337. (A., 1784.)

7583. —— ——. My principle is to do whatever is right, and leave the consequences to Him who has the disposal of them.—To DR. GEORGE LOGAN. vi, 217. FORD ED., ix, 423. (M., 1813.)

* Baron Riedesel was then a prisoner near Charlottesville. He commanded the Hessian troops in Burgoyne's army.—EDITOR.

7584. RIGHT, Moral.—It has a great effect on the opinion of our people and the world to have the moral right on our side.—To President Madison. v, 442. Ford ed., ix, 251. (M., April 1809.)

7585. RIGHT AND WRONG.—The great principles of right and wrong are legible to every reader; to preserve them, requires not the aid of many counsellors.—Rights of British America. i, 141. Ford ed., i, 446. (1774.)

— RIGHT OF ASYLUM.—See Asylum.

7586. RIGHT OF EXPATRIATION.—Nature has given to all men the right of departing from the country in which chance * * * has placed them.—Rights of British America. i, 125. Ford ed., i, 429. (1774.) See Expatriation.

7587. RIGHT OF REPRESENTATION.—He has refused to pass * * * laws for the accommodation of large districts of people, unless those people would relinquish the right of representation in the legislature, a right inestimable to them and formidable to tyrants only.—Declaration of Independence as Drawn by Jefferson

7588. RIGHT OF SUFFRAGE.—Let every man who fights and pays exercise his just and equal right in the election of the Legislature.—To Samuel Kerchival. vii, 11. Ford ed., x, 39. (M., 1816.) See Suffrage.

7589. RIGHTS, Advancing.—Circumstances sometimes require, that rights the most unquestionable should be advanced with delicacy.—To William Short. iii, 275. Ford ed., v, 364. (Pa., 1791.)

7590. RIGHTS, Aggression on.—No man has a natural right to commit aggression on the equal rights of another; and this is all from which the laws ought to restrain him.—To F. W. Gilmer. vii, 3. Ford ed., x, 32. (M., 1816.)

7591. RIGHTS, Aristocratic encroachments on.—Hereditary bodies * * * always existing, always on the watch for their own aggrandizement, profit of every opportunity of advancing the privileges of their order, and encroaching on the rights of the people.—To M. Coray. vii, 319. (M., 1823.)

7592. RIGHTS, Attainment of.—If we cannot secure all our rights, let us secure what we can.—To James Madison. iii, 4. Ford ed., v, 82. (P., March 1789.)

7593. RIGHTS, Availability of.—It is a principle that the right to a thing gives a right to the means without which it could not be used, that is to say, that the means follow their end.—Mississippi River Instructions. vii, 579. (1791.)

— RIGHTS, Bill of.—See Bill of Rights.

7594. RIGHTS, Defence of.—We will ever be ready to join with our fellow-subjects in every part of the British empire, in executing all those rightful powers which God has given us, for the reestablishment and guaranteeing their constitutional rights, when, where, and by whomsoever invaded.*—Resolutions of Albemarle County. Ford ed., i, 419. (July 26, 1774.)

7595. RIGHTS, Deprivation of.—The proscribing any citizen as unworthy the public confidence, by laying upon him an incapacity of being called to offices of trust or emolument, unless he profess or renounce this or that religious opinion, is depriving him injudiciously of those privileges and advantages to which, in common with his fellow citizens, he has a natural right.—Statute of Religious Freedom. Ford ed., ii, 238. (1779.)

7596. RIGHTS, Education and.—For promoting the public happiness, those persons, whom nature has endowed with genius and virtue, should be rendered by liberal education worthy to receive, and able to guard the sacred deposit of the rights and liberties of their fellow citizens; and they should be called to that charge without regard to wealth, birth or other accidental condition or circumstance.—Diffusion of Knowledge Bill. Ford ed., ii, 221. (1779.)

— RIGHTS, Equal.—See Equality and Equal Rights.

7597. RIGHTS, Establishing.—It can never be too often repeated, that the time for fixing every essential right on a legal basis is while our rulers are honest, and ourselves united.—Notes on Virginia. viii, 402. Ford ed., iii, 266. (1782.)

7598. RIGHTS, Fortifying popular.—I am particularly happy to perceive that you still manfully maintain our good old principle of cherishing and fortifying the rights and authorities of the people in opposition to those who fear them, who wish to take all power from them, and to transfer all to Washington.—To Nathaniel Macon. Ford ed., x, 378. (M., 1826.)

7599. RIGHTS, Inalienable.—We hold these truths to be self-evident that all men are created equal; that they are endowed by their Creator with inherent† and inalienable rights; that among these, are life, liberty, and the pursuit of happiness. That, to secure these rights, governments are instituted among men, deriving their just powers from the consent of the governed; that, whenever any form of government becomes destructive of these ends, it is the right of the people to alter or to abolish it, and to institute new government, laying its foundation on such principles, and organizing its powers in such form, as to them shall seem most likely to effect their safety and happiness.—Declaration of Independence as Drawn by Jefferson.

7600. RIGHTS, Infringements on.—Let no act be passed by any one legislature

---

* Jefferson's own county.—Editor.
† Congress struck out "inherent and" and inserted "certain".—Editor.

[Parliament] which may infringe on the rights and liberties of another.—RIGHTS OF BRITISH AMERICA. i, 141. FORD ED., i, 446. (1774.)

7601. RIGHTS, Invasions of.—He has dissolved Representative houses repeatedly [and continually]* for opposing, with manly firmness, his invasions on the rights of the people.—DECLARATION OF INDEPENDENCE AS DRAWN BY JEFFERSON.

7602. —— ——. There are rights which it is useless to surrender to the government, and which governments have yet always been found to invade. [Among] these * * * is the right of free commerce.—To DAVID HUMPHREYS. iii, 13. FORD ED., v, 89. (P., 1789.)

7603. RIGHTS, Money and.—Courtiers had rather give up power than pleasure. They will barter, therefore, the usurped prerogatives of the King for the money of the people. This is the agent by which modern nations will recover their rights.—To COMTE DE MOUSTIER. ii, 389. FORD ED., v, 12. (P., 1788.)

— RIGHTS, Natural.—See NATURAL RIGHTS.

7604. RIGHTS, The people and.—The people, especially when moderately instructed, are the only safe, because the only honest, depositaries of the public rights, and should therefore, be introduced into the administration of them in every function to which they are sufficient; they will err sometimes and accidentally, but never designedly, and with a systematic and persevering purpose of overthrowing the free principles of the government.—To M. CORAY. vii, 319. (M., 1823.)

7605. RIGHTS, Personal.—It were contrary to feeling, and indeed, ridiculous to suppose that a man had less right in himself than one of his neighbors, or indeed, than all of them put together. This would be slavery, and not that liberty which the bill of rights has made inviolable, and for the preservation of which our government has been charged. Nothing could so completely divest us of that liberty as the establishment of the opinion, that the State has a *perpetual* right to the services of all its members. This, to men of certain ways of thinking, would be to annihilate the blessing of existence, and to contradict the Giver of life, who gave it for happiness and not for wretchedness.—To JAMES MONROE. i, 319. FORD ED., iii, 58. (M., 1782.)

7606. —— ——. Every man should be protected in his lawful acts.—To ISAAC McPHERSON. vi, 175. (M., 1813.)

7607. RIGHTS, Persons and.—Rights and powers can only belong to persons, not to things, not to mere matter, unendowed with will.—To JOHN CARTWRIGHT. vii, 359. (M., 1824.)

* Congress struck out the words in brackets.—EDITOR.

7608. RIGHTS, Religion and civil.—Our civil rights have no dependence upon our religious opinions, more than our opinions in physics or geometry.—STATUTE OF RELIGIOUS FREEDOM. viii, 455. FORD ED., ii, 238. (1779.)

7609. RIGHTS, Reserved.—It had become an universal and almost uncontroverted position in the several States, that the purposes of society do not require a surrender of all our rights to our ordinary governors; that there are certain portions of right not necessary to enable them to carry on an effective government, and which experience has nevertheless proved they will be constantly encroaching on, if submitted to them; that there are also certain fences which experience has proved peculiarly efficacious against wrong, and rarely obstructive of right. which yet the governing powers have ever shown a disposition to weaken and remove. Of the first kind, for instance, is freedom of religion; of the second, trial by jury, *habeas corpus* laws, free presses. These were the settled opinions of all the States,—of that of Virginia, of which I was writing [in the Notes on Virginia], as well as of the others. The others had, in consequence, delineated these unceded portions of right, and these fences against wrong, which they meant to exempt from the power of their governors, in instruments called declarations of rights and constitutions; and as they did this by conventions, which they appointed for the express purpose of reserving those rights. and of delegating others to their ordinary legislative, executive and judiciary bodies. none of the reserved rights can be touched without resorting to the people to appoint another convention for the express purpose of permitting it. Where the constitutions, then. have been so formed by conventions, named for this express purpose, they are fixed and unalterable but by a convention or other body to be specially authorized; and they have been so formed by, I believe, all the States, except Virginia. That State concurs in all these opinions, but has run into the wonderful error that her constitution, though made by the ordinary legislature. cannot yet be altered by the ordinary legislature.—To NOAH WEBSTER. iii, 201. FORD ED., v, 254. (Pa., 1790.)

7610. RIGHTS, Safest depository of.—The mass of the citizens is the safest depositary of their own rights.—To JOHN TAYLOR. vi, 608. FORD ED., x, 31. (M., 1816.)

7611. RIGHTS, Safety of.—It would be a dangerous delusion were a confidence in the men of our choice to silence our fears fo. the safety of our rights.—KENTUCKY RESOLUTIONS. ix, 470. FORD ED., vii, 303. (1798.)

7612. RIGHTS, Securing.—It is to secure our rights that we resort to government at all.—To M. D'IVERNOIS. iv, 114. FORD ED., vii, 4. (M., Feb. 1795.)

— RIGHTS, State.—See STATE RIGHTS.

7613. RIGHTS, Suppression of.—It is impossible the world should continue long insensible to so evident a truth as that the right to have commerce and intercourse with our neighbors is a natural right. To suppress this neighborly intercourse is an exercise of force, which we shall have a just right to remove when the superior force.—To T. M. RANDOLPH. iii, 146. FORD ED., v, 174. (N. Y., 1790.)

7614. RIGHTS, Surrendering.—The justifiable rights of our country ought not to be given up by those * * * appointed and trusted to defend them where they may be justly defended.—To ALEXANDER HAMILTON. FORD ED., vi, 9. (1792.)

7615. RIGHTS, Swallowing up.—Did his Majesty possess such a right as this [sending troops], it might swallow up all our other rights, whenever he should think proper.—RIGHTS OF BRITISH AMERICA. i, 140. FORD ED., i, 445. (1774.)

7616. RIGHTS, Unmerited praise and.—To give praise where it is not due might be well from the venal, but it would ill become those who are asserting the rights of human nature.—RIGHTS OF BRITISH AMERICA. i, 141. FORD ED., i, 446. (1774.)

7617. RIGHTS, Usurpation of.—The royal claim to wrecks, waifs, strays, treasure-trove, royal mines, royal fish, royal birds, are declared to have been usurpations on common right.—PROPOSED VA. CONSTITUTION. FORD ED., ii, 28. (June 1776.)

— RIGHTS OF BRITISH AMERICA, A summary view of the.—See APPENDIX.

— RIGHTS OF CONSCIENCE.—See CONSCIENCE.

7618. RIGHTS OF MAN, Appeal to.—The appeal to the rights of man, which had been made in the United States, was taken up by France, first of the European nations. From her, the spirit has spread over those of the South. The tyrants of the North have allied indeed against it; but it is irresistible. Their opposition will only multiply its millions of human victims; their own satellites will catch it, and the condition of man through the civilized world will be finally and greatly ameliorated. This is a wonderful instance of great events from small causes. So inscrutable is the arrangement of causes and consequences in this world, that a two-penny duty on tea, unjustly imposed in a sequestered part of it, changes the condition of all its inhabitants.—AUTOBIOGRAPHY. i, 106. FORD ED., i, 147. (1821.)

7619. RIGHTS OF MAN, Assertion of.—I hope and firmly believe that the whole world will, sooner or later, feel benefit from the issue of our assertion of the rights of man.—To BENJAMIN GALLOWAY. vi, 41. (M., 1812.)

7620. RIGHTS OF MAN, Charter of.—The Declaration of Independence, the Declaratory Charter of our rights, and of the rights of man.—To SAMUEL A. WELLS. i, 121. FORD ED., x, 131. (M., 1819.)

7621. RIGHTS OF MAN, Equal.—The equal rights of man, and the happiness of every individual, are now acknowledged to be the only legitimate objects of government. Modern times * * * have discovered the only device by which these rights can be secured, to wit: government by the people, acting not in person, but by representatives chosen by themselves, that is to say, by every man of ripe years and sound mind, who contributes either by his purse or person to the support of his country.—To M. CORAY. vii, 319. (M., 1823.)

7622. RIGHTS OF MAN, Government and.—No interests are dearer to men than those which ought to be secured to them by their form of government, and none deserve better of them than those who contribute to the amelioration of that form.—To M. RUELLE. v, 430. (W., 1809.)

7623. RIGHTS OF MAN, Immortal.—Although the horrors of the French Revolution have damped for awhile the ardor of the patriots in every country, yet it is not extinguished—it will never die. The sense of right has been excited in every breast, and the spark will be rekindled by the very oppressions of that detestable tyranny employed to quench it. The errors of the honest patriots of France, and the crimes of her Dantons and Robespierres, will be forgotten in the more encouraging contemplation of our sober example, and steady march to our object.—To BENJAMIN GALLOWAY. vi, 41. (M., 1812.)

7624. RIGHTS OF MAN, Immutable.—Nothing is unchangeable but the inherent and inalienable rights of man.—To JOHN CARTWRIGHT. vii, 359. (M., 1824.)

7625. RIGHTS OF MAN, Legal.—The laws of the land are the inheritance and the right of every man before whatever tribunal he is brought.—NOTES ON STEVENS CASE. ix, 475. (1804.)

7626. RIGHTS OF MAN, Legislators and.—Our legislators are not sufficiently apprized of the rightful limits of their power; that their true office is to declare and enforce only our natural rights and duties, and to take none of them from us.—To F. W. GILMER. vii, 3. FORD ED., x, 32. (M., 1816.)

7627. RIGHTS OF MAN, Moral and political.—That man may at length find favor with Heaven, and his present struggles issue in the recovery and establishment of his moral and political rights will be the prayer of my latest breath.—To HARRY INNES. FORD ED., vii, 383. (M., 1799.)

7628. RIGHTS OF MAN, Recognition of.—All eyes are opened, or opening, to the rights of man. The general spread of the light of science has already laid open to every view the palpable truth, that the mass of mankind has not been born with saddles on their backs, nor a favored few booted and spurred, ready to ride them legitimately, by the grace of God.*—To ROGER C. WEIGHT-MAN. vii, 450. FORD ED., x, 391. (M., June 24, 1826.)

7629. RIGHTS OF MAN, Securing.—Modern times * * * have discovered the only device by which the rights of man can be secured, to wit, government by the people, acting not in person, but by representatives chosen by themselves; that is to say, by every man of ripe years and sane mind, who contributes either by his purse or person to the support of his country.—To M. CORAY. vii, 319. (M., 1823.) See PAINE.

7630. RITTENHOUSE (David), Astronomer.—That this Commonwealth [of Virginia] may not be without so great an ornament, nor its youth such an help towards attaining astronomical science, as the mechanical representation, or model of the solar system, conceived and executed by that greatest of astronomers, David Rittenhouse, * * * the visitors [of William and Mary College] * * * shall be author zed [to purchase] one of the models.—WILLIAM AND MARY COLLEGE BILL. FORD ED., ii, 235. (1779.)

7631. —— ——. We have supposed Mr. Rittenhouse second to no astronomer living, that in genius he must be first, because he is self-taught. As an artist, he has exhibited as great a proof of mechanical genius as the world has ever produced. He has not indeed made a world; but he has by imitation approached nearer its Maker, than has any man who has lived from the creation to this day.—NOTES ON VIRGINIA. viii, 313. FORD ED., iii, 169. (1782.)

7632. RITTENHOUSE (David), Genius of.—The amazing mechanical representation of the solar system, which you conceived and executed, has never been surpassed by any but the work of which it is a copy. Are these powers, then, which being intended for the condition of the world are like air and light, the world's common property, to be taken from their proper pursuit to do the commonplace drudgery of governing a single State, a work which may be executed by men of an ordinary stature, such as are always and everywhere to be found?—To DAVID RITTENHOUSE. FORD ED., ii, 163. (M., 1778.)

7633. —— ——. I doubt not there are in your country many persons equal to the task of conducting government; but you should consider that the world has but one Rittenhouse, and that it never had one before.—To DAVID RITTENHOUSE. FORD ED., ii, 163. (1778.)

7634. —— ——. I have been much pleased to hear you had it in contemplation to endeavor to establish Rittenhouse in our College. This would be an immense acquisition, and would draw youth to it from every part of the continent.—To JOHN PAGE. i, 400. (P., 1785.)

7635. RITTENHOUSE (David), Invaluable friend.—Our late invaluable friend, Rittenhouse.—To DR. BENJAMIN RUSH. iv, 165. FORD ED., vii, 113. (M., 1797.)

7636. RITTENHOUSE (David), Mechanician.—Rittenhouse, as an astronomer, would stand on a line with any of his time;

*From the last letter written by Jefferson. Mr. Weightman was Mayor of Washington City, and the letter was in reply to an invitation to be present at a Fourth of July celebration at the capital. Jefferson and Adams both died on that day.—EDITOR.

and as a mechanician, he certainly has not been equaled. In this view he was truly great; but, placed alongside of Newton, every human character must appear diminutive, and none would have shrunk more feelingly from the painful parallel than the modest and amiable Rittenhouse, whose gen us and merit are not the less for this exaggerated comparison of his over zealous biographer.—To JOHN ADAMS. vi, 307. (M., 1814.)

7637. RIVER, Illinois.—The Illinois is a fine river, clear, gentle, and without rapids; insomuch that it is navigable for bateaux to its source. From thence is a portage of two miles only to the Chicago, which affords a bateau navigation of sixteen miles to its entrance into Lake Michigan.—NOTES ON VIRGINIA. viii, 255. FORD ED., iii, 93. (1782.)

7638. RIVER, James.—James River itself affords a harbor for vessels of any size in Hampton Road, but not in safety through the whole winter. * * * In some future state of population, I think it possible, that its navigation may also be made to interlock with that of the Potomac, and through that to communicate by a short portage with the Ohio.—NOTES ON VIRGINIA. viii, 251. FORD ED., iii, 89. (1782.)

7639. RIVER, Kanawha.—The Great Kanawha is a river of considerable note for the fertility of its lands, and still more, as leading towards the head waters of James river. Nevertheless it is doubtful whether its great and numerous rapids will admit a navigation, but at an expense to which it will require ages to render its inhabitants equal. The great obstacles begin at what are called the great falls, ninety miles above the mouth, below which are only five or six rapids, and these passable, with some difficulty, even at low water. * * * It is said, however, that at a very moderate expense the whole current of the upper part of the Kanawha may be turned into the South Fork of Roanoke, the Alleghany there subsiding, and the two rivers approaching so near, that a canal nine miles long, and thirty feet deep, at the deepest part would draw the water of the Kanawha into this branch of the Roanoke; this canal would be in Montgomery County, the court-house of which is on the top of the Alleghanies.—NOTES ON VIRGINIA. vii, 259. FORD ED., iii, 96. (1782.)

7640. —— ——. The Little Kanawha * * * yields a navigation of ten miles only. Perhaps its northern branch, called Junius's Creek, wh:ch interlocks with the western of Monongahela, may one day admit a shorter passage from the latter into the Ohio.—NOTES ON VIRGINIA. viii, 259. FORD ED., iii, 97. (1782.)

7641. RIVER, Mississippi.—The Mississippi will be one of the principal channels of future commerce for the country westward of the Alleghany.—NOTES ON VIRGINIA. viii, 253. FORD ED., iii, 91. (1782.)

7642. —— ——. The country watered by the Mississippi and its eastern branches constitutes five-eighths of the United States, two of which five-eighths are occupied by the Ohio and its waters; the residuary streams which run into the Gulf of Mexico, the Atlantic, and the St. Lawrence, water the remaining three-eighths.—NOTES ON VIRGINIA. viii, 261. FORD ED., iii, 98. (1782.)

7643. RIVER, Missouri.—The Missouri is, in fact, the principal river, contributing more to the common stream than does the Mississippi, even after its junction with the Illinois. It is remarkably cold, muddy and rapid.—NOTES ON VIRGINIA. viii, 254. FORD ED., iii, 92. (1782.)

7644. RIVER, Ohio.—The Ohio is the most beautiful river on earth. Its current gentle, waters clear, and bosom smooth and unbroken by rocks and rapids, a single instance only excepted.—NOTES ON VIRGINIA. viii, 256. FORD ED., iii, 93. (1782.)

7645. RIVER, Potomac.—The passage of the Potomac through the Blue Ridge is, perhaps, one of the most stupendous scenes in nature. You stand on a very high point of land. On your right comes up the Shenandoah, having ranged along the foot of the mountain an hundred miles to seek a vent. On your left approaches the Potomac, in quest of a passage also. In the moment of their junction, they rush together against the mountain, rend it asunder, and pass off to the sea. The first glance of this scene nurries our senses into the opinion, that this earth has been created in time, that the mountains were formed first, that the rivers began to flow afterwards, that in this place, particularly, they have been dammed up by the Blue Ridge of mountains, and have formed an ocean which filled the whole valley; that continuing to rise they have at length broken over at this spot, and have torn the mountain down from its summit to its base. The piles of rock on each hand, but particularly on the Shenandoah, the evident marks of their disruptive and avulsion from their beds by the most powerful agents of nature, corroborate the impression. But the distant finishing which nature has given to the picture, is of a very different character. It is a true contrast to the foreground. It is as placid and delightful as that is wild and tremendous. For the mountain being cloven asunder, she presents to your eye, through the cleft, a small catch of smooth blue horizon, at an infinite distance in the plain country, inviting you as it were, from the riot and tumult roaring around, to pass through the breach and participate of the calm below. Here the eye ultimately composes itself; and that way, too, the road happens actually to lead. You cross the Potomac above the junction, pass along its side through the base of the mountain for three miles, its terrible precipices hanging in fragments over you, and within about twenty miles reach Fredericktown, and the fine country round that. This scene is worth a voyage across the Atlantic. Yet here, as in the neighborhood of the Natural Bridge, are people who have passed their lives within half a dozen miles, and have never been to survey these monuments of a war between rivers and mountains, which must have shaken the earth itself to its centre.—NOTES ON VIRGINIA. viii, 264. FORD ED., iii, 102. (1782.)

7646. RIVER, Red.—Your observations * * * have determined me to confine the ensuing mission to the ascent of the Red river to its source, and to descend the same river again, which will give an opportunity of better ascertaining that which, in truth, next to the Missouri, is the most interesting water of the Mississippi. You will accordingly receive instructions to this effect from the Secretary of War.—To MR. DUNBAR. iv, 577. (W., May 1805.)

7647. ——— ———. The work we are now doing is, I trust, done for posterity, in such a way that they need not repeat it. For this we are much indebted to you, not only for the labor and time you have devoted to it, but for the excellent method of which you have set the example, and which I hope will be the model to be followed by others. We shall delineate with correctness the great arteries of this great country. Those who come after us will extend the ramifications as they become acquainted with them, and fill up the canvas we begin.—To MR. DUNBAR. iv, 580. (W., 1805.)

7648. RIVER, Rhone.—Nature never formed a country of more savage aspect, than that on both sides the Rhone. A huge torrent rushes like an arrow between high precipices, often of massive rock, at other times of loose stone, with but little earth. Yet has the hand of man subdued this savage scene, by planting corn where there is little fertility, trees where there is still less, and vines where there is none. On the whole, it assumes a romantic, picturesque, and pleasing air.—TRAVELS IN FRANCE. ix, 320. (1787.)

7649. RIVER, St. Croix.—A difference of opinion having arisen as to the river intended by the Plenipotentiaries [in the treaty of peace] to be the boundary between us and the dominions of Great Britain, and by them called the St. Croix, which name, it seems, is given to two different rivers, the ascertaining of this point becomes a matter of present urgency. It has heretofore been the subject of application from us to the Government of Great Britain.—To GEORGE HAMMOND. FORD ED., vi, 469. (Pa., Dec. 1793.)

7650. RIVER, Wabash.—The Wabash is a very beautiful river.—NOTES ON VIRGINIA. viii, 258. FORD ED., iii, 95. (1782.)

7651. RIVERS, Exploration of.—I should be glad of a copy of any sketch or account you may have made of the river Platte of the passage from its head across the mountains, and of the river Cashecatungo, which you suppose to run into the Pacific. This would probably be among the first exploring journeys we undertake after a settlement with Spain, as we wish to become acquainted with all the advantageous water connections across our continent.—To ANTHONY G. BETTAY. v, 246. (W., 1808.)

7652. RIVERS, Highways of commerce.—The principal connections of the western waters with the Atlantic are three: the Hudson River, the Potomac, and the Mississippi itself. Down the last will pass all heavy commodities. But the navigation through the Gulf of Mexico is so dangerous, and that up the Mississippi so difficult and tedious, that it is thought probable that European merchandise will not return through that channel. It is most likely that flour, timber, and other heavy articles will be floated on rafts, which will themselves be an article for sale as well as their loading, the navigators returning by land, or in light bateaux. There will, therefore, be a competition between the Hudson and Potomac rivers for the residue of the commerce of all the country westward of Lake Erie, on the waters of the Lakes, of the Ohio, and upper parts of the Mississippi.—NOTES ON VIRGINIA. viii, 261. FORD ED., iii, 98. (1782.)

7653. RIVERS, Increments of.—In granting appropriations [of lands], some sovereigns have given away the increments of rivers to a greater, some to a lesser extent, and some not at all. Rome, which was not feudal, and Spain and England which were, have granted them largely; France, a feudal country, has not granted them at all on navigable rivers. Louis XIV., therefore, was strictly correct when in his edict of 1693, he declared that the increments of rivers were incontestably his, *as a necessary consequence of the sovereignty.* That is to say, that where no special grant of them to an individual could be produced, they remained in him, as a portion of the original lands of the nation, or as new created lands, never yet granted to any individual. They are unquestionably a regalian, or national right, paramount, and pre-existent to the establishment of the feudal system. That system has no fixed principle on the subject, as is evident from the opposite practices of different feudal nations. The position, therefore, is entirely unfounded, that the right to them is derived from the feudal law.—BATTURE CASE. viii, 541. (1812.)

7654. RIVERS, Obstructions in.—I think the State should reserve a right to the use of the [river] waters for navigation, and that where an individual landholder impedes that use, he shall remove that impediment, and leave the subject in as good a state as nature formed it.—To JOSEPH C. CABELL. vi, 541. (M., 1816.)

7655. ———. I think the power of permitting dams to be erected across our river [Fluviana], ought to be taken from the courts, so far as the stream has water enough for navigation.—To CHARLES YANCEY. vi, 514. FORD ED., x. 1. (M., 1816.)

7656. RIVERS, Right of navigation.— The movements of the King of Prussia to emancipate the navigation of the Vistula, and of the Emperor [of Germany] to free that of the Scheld do not, I believe, threaten the peace of Europe. * * * This assertion, then, of the natural right of the inhabitants of the upper part of a river to an innocent passage through the country below is pleasing to us. It tends to establish a principle favorable to our right of navigating the Mississippi.—To GOVERNOR BENJ. HARRISON. FORD ED., iii, 414. (A., March 1784.)

7657. RIVERS, Velocity of.—I shall forward your ingenious paper on the subject of the Mississippi to the Philosophical Society. To prove the value I set on it, and my wish that it may go to the public without any imperfection about it, I will take the liberty of submitting to your consideration the only passage which I think may require it. You say, " the velocity of rivers is greatest at the surface, and generally diminishes downwards ". And this principle enters into some subsequent parts of the paper, and has too much effect on the phenomena of that river not to merit mature consideration. I can but suppose it at variance with the law of motion in rivers. In strict theory, the velocity of water at any given depth in a river is (in addition to its velocity at its surface) whatever a body would have acquired by falling through a space equal to that depth.—To WILLIAM DUNBAR. iv, 537. (W., 1804.)

7658. ROANE (Spencer), Courage of.— Against this [consolidation] I know no one who, equally with Judge Roane himself, possesses the power and the courage to make resistance; and to him I look, and have long looked, as our strongest bulwark.—To ARCHIBALD THWEAT. vii, 199. FORD ED., x. 184. (M., 1821.)

7659. ROANE (Spencer), Judge Marshall and.—On the decision of the case of

Cohens *vs.* the State of Virginia, in the Supreme Court of the United States, in March, 1821, Judge Roane, under the signature of " Algernon Sidney ", wrote for the Enquirer [Richmond] a series of papers on the law of that case. I considered these papers maturely as they came out, and confess that they appeared to me to pulverize every word which had been delivered by Judge Marshall, of the extra-judicial part of his opinion.—To WILLIAM JOHNSON. vii, 294. FORD ED., x, 229. (M., 1823.)

7660. ROBESPIERRE, Atrocities of.— What a tremendous obstacle to the future attempts at liberty will be the atrocities of Robespierre!—To TENCH COXE. FORD ED., vii, 22. (M., 1795.)

7661. ROBESPIERRE, Condemned.— Robespierre met the fate, and his memory the execration, he so justly merited. The rich were his victims, and perished by thousands.—To MADAME DE STAEL. vi, 114. (M., May 1813.)

7662. ROCHAMBEAU (Count), Proposed bust.—Count Rochambeau has really deserved more attention than he has received. Why not set up his bust, that of Gates, Greene, Franklin, in your new capitol?—To JAMES MADISON. i, 534. FORD ED., iv, 196. (P., 1786.)

7663. RODNEY (Cæsar A.), Affection for.—I avail myself of this occasion * * * to express all the depth of my affection for you; the sense I entertain of your faithful cooperation in my late labors, and the debt I owe for the valuable aid I received from you [in the cabinet].—To CAESAR A. RODNEY. v. 502. FORD ED., ix, 272. (M., 1810.)

7664. RODNEY (Cæsar A.), Appeal to. —I am told you are the only person who can unite the greatest portion of the republican votes [in Delaware], and the only one, perhaps, who can procure the dismission of your present representative [in Congress] to that obscurity of situation where his temper and principles may be disarmed of all effect. You are, then, bound to do this good office to the rest of America. You owe to your State to make her useful to her friends, instead of being an embarrassment and a burden. Her long speeches and wicked workings at this session have added at least thirty days to its length, cost us $30,000, and filled the Union with falsehoods and misrepresentations.—To CAESAR A. RODNEY. FORD ED., viii, 148. (W., 1802.)

7665. RODNEY (Cæsar A.), Retirement. —I lament the necessity which calls for your retirement, if that necessity really exists. I had looked to you as one of those calculated to give cohesion to our rope of sand.—To CAESAR A. RODNEY. FORD ED., viii, 296. (W., Feb. 1804.)

7666. ROGUES, Diplomacy and.—Our part of the country [Virginia] is in considerable fermentation on what they suspect to be a recent roguery of this kind. They say that while all hands were below deck mending sails, splicing ropes, and every one at his own business, and the captain in his cabin attending to his log-book and chart, a rogue of a pilot has run them into an enemy's port. But metaphor apart, there is much dissatisfaction with Mr. Jay and his treaty.—To MANN PAGE. iv, 120. FORD ED., vii, 25. (M., Aug. 1795.) See JAY TREATY.

7667. ROGUES, Proportion of.—I do not believe with the Rochefoucaulds and Montaignes, that fourteen out of fifteen men are rogues; I believe a great abatement from that proportion may be made in favor of general honesty. But I have always found that rogues would be uppermost, and I do not know that the proportion is too strong for the higher orders, and for those who, rising above the swinish multitude, always contrive to nestle themselves into the places of power and profit. These rogues set out with stealing the people's good opinion, and then steal from them the right of withdrawing it, by contriving laws and associations against the power of the people themselves.—To MANN PAGE. iv, 119. FORD ED., vi², 24. (M., 1795.)

7668. ROGUES, Railing.—The rogues may rail without intermission.—To DR. BENJAMIN RUSH. iv, 426. FORD ED., viii, 128. (W., 1801.)

7669. ROHAN (Cardinal de), Imprisonment.—The Cardinal de Rohan and Cagliostro remain * * * in the Bastile; nor do their affairs seem as yet to draw towards a conclusion. It has been a curious matter, in which the circumstances of intrigue and detail have busied all the tongues, the public liberty none.—To MR. OTTO. i, 558. (P., 1786.)

7670. ROTATION IN OFFICE, Abandonment of.—I dislike, and greatly dislike [in the new Federal Constitution] the abandonment in every instance of the principle* of rotation in office, and most particularly in the case of the President.—To JAMES MADISON. ii, 330. FORD ED., iv, 477. (P., Dec. 1787.) See PRESIDENT.

7671. —— ——. I apprehend that the total abandonment of the principle of rotation in the offices of President and Senator [in the Federal Constitution] will end in abuse.—To E. RUTLEDGE. ii, 435. FORD ED., v, 42. (P., 1788.)

7672. —— ——. The abandoning the principle of necessary rotation in the Senate has, I see, been disapproved by many; in the case of the President, by none. I readily, therefore, suppose my opinion wrong, when opposed by the majority, as in the former instance, and the totality, as in the latter. In this, however, I should have done it with more complete satisfaction, had we all judged from the same position.—To JAMES MADISON. ii, 447. FORD ED., v, 48. (P., July 1788.)

7673. ROTATION IN OFFICE, Approval of.—I am for responsibilities at short periods, seeing neither reason nor safety in making the public functionaries independent of the nation for life, or even for a long term of years. On this principle I prefer the Presidential term of four years to that of seven years which I myself had at first suggested, annexing to it, however, ineligibility to it forever after; and I wish it were now annexed to the second quadrennial election of President.—To JAMES MARTIN. vi, 213. FORD ED., ix, 420. (M., 1813.) See THIRD TERM.

7674. ROTATION IN OFFICE, Definition of.—Rotation is the change of officers

* " Necessity " of rotation in FORD EDITION.—EDITOR.

required by the laws at certain epochs, and in a certain order. Thus, in Virginia, our justices of the peace are made sheriffs, one after the other, each remaining in office two years, and then yielding it to his next brother in order of seniority. This is the just and classical meaning of the word. But in America, we have extended it (for want of a proper word), to all cases of officers who must be necessarily changed at a fixed epoch, though the successor be not pointed out in any particular order, but comes in by free election. By the term rotation in office, then, we mean an obligation on the holder of that office to go out at a certain period. In our first confederation, the principle of rotation was established in the office of President of Congress, who could serve but one year in three; and in that of a member of Congress, who could serve but three years in six.—To J. SARSFIELD. iii, 17. (P., 1789.)

7675. ROTATION IN OFFICE, Restoration of.—The second amendment [to the new Federal Constitution], which appears to me to be essential, is the restoring the principle of necessary rotation, particularly to the Senate and Presidency, but most of all to the last.—To E. CARRINGTON. ii, 404. FORD ED., v, 20. (P., 1788.)

7676. ROWAN (A. H.), Asylum for.—Should you choose Virginia for your asylum, the laws of the land, administered by upright judges, would protect you from an exercise of power unauthorized by the Constitution of the United States. The *Habeas Corpus* secures every man here, alien or citizen, against everything which is not law, whatever shape it may assume. Should this, or any other circumstance, draw your footsteps this way, I shall be happy to be among those who may have an opportunity of testifying, by every attention in our power, the sentiments of esteem and respect which the circumstances of your history have inspired.*—To A. H. ROWAN. iv, 257. FORD ED., vii, 281. (1798.)

7677. RULES, Forming.—The forming a general rule requires great caution.—To PRESIDENT WASHINGTON. FORD ED., vi, 408. (Pa., 1793.)

— RULES, Jefferson's ten.—See ADVICE.

7678. RUSH (Benjamin), Tribute to.—A better man than Rush could not have left us; more benevolent, more learned, of finer genius, or more honest.—To JOHN ADAMS. vi, 120. (M., 1813.)

7679. RUSH (Benjamin), Virtues.—His virtues rendered him dear to all who knew him, and his benevolence led him to do all men every good in his power. Much he was able to do, and much, therefore, will be missed.—To RICHARD RUSH. FORD ED., ix, 385. (M., 1813.)

7680. RUSSIA, Empress Catherine.—The Empress endeavored to bully the Turk, who laughed at her, and she is going back.—To J. BANNISTER, JR. ii, 150. (P., 1787.) See ALEXANDER OF RUSSIA and DASHKOFF.

* Archibald Hamilton Rowan was one of the leaders in the rebellion in Ireland in 1798. He was a refugee in Wilmington, Delaware, when Jefferson wrote to him.—EDITOR.

7681. RUSSIA, United States and.— Russia and the United States being in character and practice essentially pacific, a common interest in the rights of peaceable nations gives us a common cause in their maintenance. —To M. Dashkoff. v, 463. (M., 1809.)

7682. RUTLEDGE (Edward), Appeal to,— Would to God yourself, General Pinckney and Major Pinckney, would come forward and aid us with your efforts. You are all known, respected, wished for; but you refuse yourselves to everything. What is to become of us if the vine and the fig tree withdraw, and leave us to the bramble and the thorn?—To Edward Rutledge. iii, 285. Ford ed., v, 376. (Pa., 1791.)

7683. RUTLEDGE (Edward), Politics.— I have often doubted whether most to praise or to blame your line of conduct. If you had lent to your country the excellent talents you possess, on you would have fallen those torrents of abuse which have lately been poured forth on me. So far, I praise the wisdom which has descried and steered clear of a waterspout ahead. But now for the blame. There is a debt of service due from every man to his country, proportioned to the bounties which nature and fortune have measured to him. Counters will pay this from the poor of sp'rit; but from you coin was due. There is no bankrupt law in heaven, by which you may get off with shillings in the pound; with rendering to a single State what you owed to the whole confederacy. I think it was by the Roman law that a father was denied sepulture, unless his son would pay his debts. Happy for you and us, that you have a son whom genius and education have qualified to pay yours. But as you have been a good father in everything else, be so in this also. Come forward and pay your own debts. Your friends, the Pinckneys, have at length undertaken their tour. My joy at this would be complete if you were in gear with them.—To Edward Rutledge. iv, 152. Ford ed., vii. 94. (M., 1796.)

7684. RUTLEDGE (John), Chief Justice.— The rejection of Mr. Rutledge [to be Chief Justice] by the Senate is a bold thing: because they cannot pretend any objection to him but his disapprobation of the [Jay] treaty. It is, of course, a declaration that they will receive none but tories hereafter into any department of the government.—To W. B. Giles. iv, 127. Ford ed., vii, 44. (M., Dec. 1795.)

7685. ———. The appointment of J. Rutledge to be Chief Justice seems to have been intended merely to establish a precedent against the descent of that office by seniority, and to keep five mouths always gaping for one sugar plum; for it was immed:ately negatived by the very votes which so implicitly concur with the will of the Executive.—To James Monroe. Ford ed., vi², 59. (M., 1796.)

7686. SACRIFICES, Necessary.— Temporary sacrifices are necessary to save permanent rights.—To Dr. William Eustis. v, 411. Ford ed., ix, 236. (W., 1809.)

7687. SACRIFICES, Rewarding.— It is for the public interest to encourage sacrifices and services, by rewarding them, and they should weigh to a certain point, in the decision between candidates.—To John Adams. i, 503. (P., 1785.)

7688. SAFETY, Rights and.— It would be a dangerous delusion were a confidence in

the men of our choice to silence our fears for the safety of our rights.—Kentucky Resolutions. ix, 470. Ford ed., vii, 303. (1798.)

7689. SAFETY, Union and.— Our safety rests on the preservation of our Union.— To the Rhode Island Assembly. iv, 397. (W., May 1801.)

7690. SALARIES, Adequate.— Congress were pleased to order me an advance of two quarters' salary. At that time, I supposed that I might refund it, or spare so much from my expenses, by the time the third quarter became due. Probably they might expect the same. But it has been impossible. The expense of my outfit, though I have taken it up, on a scale as small as could be admitted, has been very far beyond what I had conceived. I have, therefore, not only been unable to refund the advance ordered, but been obliged to go beyond it. I wished to have avoided so much as was occasioned by the purchase of furniture. But those who hire furniture asked me forty per cent. a year for the use of it. It was better to buy, therefore; and this article, clothes, carriage, &c., have amounted to considerably more than the advance ordered. Perhaps, it may be thought reasonable to allow me an outfit. The usage of every other nation has established this, and reason really pleads for it. I do not wish to make a shilling: but only my expenses to be defrayed, and in a moderate style. On the most moderate, which the reputation or interest of those I serve would admit, it will take me several years to liquidate the advances for my outfit. I mention this to enable you to understand the necessities which have obliged me to call for more money than was probably expected, and, understanding them, to explain them to others.*—To Samuel Osgood. i, 452. (P., 1785.)

7691. SALARIES, Competent.— Render the [State] judiciary respectable by every means possible. to wit firm tenure in office. [and] competent salaries.—To Archibald Stuart. iii, 315. Ford ed., v, 410. (Pa., 1791.)

7692. SALARIES, Foreign Ministers.— The bill on the intercourse with foreign nations restrains the President from allowing to Ministers Plenipotentiaries, or to Congress, more than $9,000, and $4,500 for their "personal services, and other expenses". This definition of the object for which the allowance is provided appearing vague, the Secretary of State thought it his duty to confer with the gentlemen heretofore employed as ministers in Europe, to obtain from them, in aid of his own information, an enumeration of the expenses incident to these offices, and their opinion which of them would be included within the fixed salary, and which would be entitled to be charged separately. He, therefore, asked a conference with the

---

* During his public life Jefferson sometimes lived on his salary, sometimes exceeded it, and only while he was Vice-President saved anything from it.— Morse's *Life of Jefferson*, 335.

Vice-President, who was acquainted with the residences of London and the Hague, and the Chief Justice, who was acquainted with that of Madrid. The Vice-President, Chief Justice, and Secretary of State concurred in the opinion that the salaries named by the act are much below those of the same grade at the courts of Europe, and less than the public good requires they should be. Consequently, that the expenses not included within the definition of the law, should be allowed as an additional charge.*—OPINION ON SALARIES. vii, 501. (1790.)

7693. SALARIES, Increasing.—It * * * [is] inconsistent with the principles of civil liberty, and contrary to the natural rights of the other members of the society, that any body of men therein should have authority to enlarge their own powers, prerogatives, or emoluments without restraint, the General Assembly cannot at their own will increase the allowance which their members are to draw from the public treasury for their expenses while in assembly: but to enable them to do so on application to the body of the people * * * is necesssary.—ADEQUATE ALLOWANCE BILL. FORD ED., ii, 165. (1778.)

7694. SALARIES, Legislators'.—It is just that members of General Assembly, delegated by the people to transact for them the legislative business, should, while attending that business, have their reasonable sustenance defrayed, dedicating to the public service their time and labors freely and without account: and it is also expedient that the public councils should not be deprived of the aid of good and able men, who might be deterred from entering into them by the insufficiency of their private fortunes to [meet] the extraordinary expenses they must necessarily incur.—ADEQUATE ALLOWANCE BILL. FORD ED., ii, 165. (1778.)

7695. SALARIES, Multiplication of.—I am not for a multiplication of * * * salaries merely to make partisans.—To ELBRIDGE GERRY. iv, 268. FORD ED., vii, 327. (Pa., 1799.)

7696. SALARIES, Official.—No salaries, or perquisites, shall be given to any officer but by some future act of the Legislature.—PROPOSED VA. CONSTITUTION. FORD ED., ii, 28. (June 1776.)

7697. ——— ———. No salaries shall be given to the Administrator, members of the legislative houses, judges of the Court of Appeals, judges of the County Courts, or other inferior jurisdictions, privy counsellors, or delegates to the American Congress; but the reasonable expenses of the Administrator, members of the House of Representatives,

judges of the Court of Appeals, privy counsellors, and delegates for subsistence, while acting in the duties of their office, may be borne by the public, if the Legislature shall so direct.—PROPOSED VA. CONSTITUTION. FORD ED., ii, 28. (June 1776.)

7698. SALARIES, Reduction of.—I remark [in your address to the Legislature] the phenomenon of a chief magistrate recommending the reduction of his own compensation. This is a solecism of which the wisdom of our late Congress cannot be accused.—To GOVERNOR PLUMER. vii, 19. (M., 1816.)

7699. SALT WATER, Distillation.—The obtaining fresh from salt water was for ages considered as an important desideratum for the use of navigators. The process for doing this by simple distillation is so efficacious, the erecting an extempore still with such utensils as are found on board of every ship, is so practicable, as to authorize the assertion that this desideratum is satisfied to a very useful degree. * But though this has been done for upwards of thirty years, though its reality has been established by the actual experience of several vessels which have had recourse to it, yet neither the fact nor the process is known to the mass of seamen, to whom it would be the most useful, and for whom it was principally wanted. The Secretary of State is, therefore, of opinion that since the subject has now been brought under observation, t should be made the occasion of disseminating its knowledge generally and effectually among the seafaring citizens of the United States.—REPORT TO CONGRESS. vii, 459. (1790.)

——— SANCHO (Ignatius).—See NEGROES, LITERARY.

7700. SAN DOMINGO, Commerce with. —A clause in a bill now under debate for opening commerce with Toussaint and his black subjects, now in open rebellion against France will be a circumstance of high aggravation to that country, and in addition to our cruising around their islands will put their patience to a great proof.—To JAMES MONROE. iv, 265. FORD ED., vii, 321. (Pa., Jan. 1799.)

7701. ——— ———. As it is acknowledged * * * that it is impossible the French should invade us since the annihilation of their power on the sea, our constituents will see in the [army and navy] preparations the utmost anxiety to guard them against even impossibilities. The Southern States do not discover the same care, however, in the bill author'zing Toussaint's subjects to a free commerce with them, and free ingress and intercourse with their black brethren in these States. However, if they are guarded against the cannibals of the terrible republic, they ought not to object to being eaten by a more civilized enemy.—To AARON BURR. FORD ED., vii, 348. (Pa., Feb. 1799.)

7702. ——— ———. Toussaint's clause was retained.† Even South Carolinians in the House of Representatives voted for it. We may expect, therefore, black crews, and supercargoes.

---

* There is an impression that we owe to Jefferson the system of paying extravagantly low salaries to high men. Not so. He was far too good a republican to favor an idea so aristocratic. Make offices desirable, he says, if you wish to get superior men to fill them, * * * There is nothing in the writings of Jefferson which gives any show of support to temptation salaries or to ignorant suffrage.—JAMES PARTON'S *Life of Jefferson*, 378.

* The House of Representatives had referred to Jefferson the petition of Jacob Isaacs of Rhode Island, who claimed to have discovered a method of converting salt water into fresh. Isaacs desired the government to buy his secret.—EDITOR.

† Jefferson referred to the exemption of San Domingo in the French non-intercourse bill.—EDITOR.

and missionaries thence into the Southern States; and when that leaven begins to work. I would gladly compound with a great part of our northern country, if they would honestly stand neuter. If this combustion can be introduced among us under any veil whatever, we have to fear it.—To JAMES MADISON. FORD ED., vii, 349. (Pa., Feb. 1799.)

7703. SAN DOMINGO, England and.— Rigaud, at the head of the people of color, maintains his allegiance [to France]. But they are only twenty-five thousand souls, against five hundred thousand, the number of the blacks. The [British] treaty made with them by Maitland is (if they are to be separated from France) the best thing for us. They must get their provisions from us. It will, indeed, be in English bottoms, so that we shall lose the carriage. But the English w'll probably forbid them the ocean, confine them to their island, and thus prevent their becoming an American Algiers. It must be admitted, too, that they may play them off on us when they please. Against this there is no remedy but time'y measures on our part, to clear ourselves, by degrees, of the matter on which that lever can work.—To JAMES MADISON. iv, 281. FORD ED., vii, 343. (Pa., Feb. 1799.)

7704. SAN DOMINGO, Exile of aristocrats.— Genet tells me that the Patriotic party in St. Domingo had taken possession of s'x hundred aristocrats and monocrats, had sent two hundred of them to France, and were sending four hundred here. * * * I wish we could distribute our four hundred among the Indians, who would teach them lessons of liberty and equality.—To MARTHA JEFFERSON RANDOLPH. FORD ED., vi, 268. (Pa., 1793.)

7705. SAN DOMINGO, Fugitives from. —The situation of the St. Domingo fugitives (aristocrats as they are) calls aloud for pity and charity. Never was so deep a tragedy presented to the feelings of man. I deny the power of the General Government to apply money to such a purpose, but I deny it with a bleeding heart. It belongs to the State governments. Pray urge ours to be liberal. The Executive should hazard themselves here on such an occasion, and the Legislature when it meets ought to approve and extend it. It will have a great effect in doing away the impression of other disobligations towards France. —To JAMES MONROE. iv, 20. FORD ED., vi, 349. (Pa., July 1793.)

7706. SAN DOMINGO, Military expeditions to.— It is not permitted by the law to prohibit the departure of the emigrants to St. Domingo, according to the wish you express, any more than it is to force them away, according to that expressed by you in a former letter. Our country is open to all men, to come and go peaceably, when they choose; and your letter does not mention that these emigrants meant to depart armed, and equipped for war. Lest, however, this should be attempted, the Governors of * * * Pennsylvania and Maryland are requested * * * to see that no military expedition be covered or permitted under color of the right which the passengers have to depart from these States.—To E. C. GENET. iv, 87. FORD ED., vi, 459. (Pa., Nov. 1793.)

7707. SAN DOMINGO, Supplies to.— When the distresses in St. Domingo first broke forth, we thought we could not better evidence our friendship to that, and to the Mother country also, than to step into its relief, on your application, without wa'ting a formal au-

thorization from the National Assembly. As the case was unforeseen, so it was unprovided for on their part, and we did what we doubted not they would have desired us to do, had there been time to make the application, and what we presumed they would sanction as soon as known to them. We have now been going on more than a twelve-month, in making advances for the relief of the Colony, without having, as yet, received any such sanction; for the decree of four millions of livres in aid of the Colony, besides the circuitous and informal manner by wh'ch we became acquainted with it, describes and applies to operations very different from those which have actually taken place. The wants of the Colony appear likely to continue, and their reliance on our supplies to become habitual. We feel every disposition to continue our efforts for administering to those wants; but that cautious attention to forms wh'ch would have been unfriendly in the first moment, becomes a duty to ourselves; when the business assumes the appearance of long continuance, and respectful also to the National Assembly itself, who have a right to prescribe the line of an interference so materially interesting to the Mother country and the Colony. By the estimate you were pleased to deliver me, we perceive that there will be wanting, to carry the Colony through the month of December, between thirty and forty thousand dollars, in addition to the sums before engaged to you. I am authorized to inform you, that the sum of forty thousand dollars shall be paid to your orders at the Treasury of the United States, and to assure you, that we feel no abatement in our dispositions to contr'bute these aids from time to time, as they shall be wanting, for the necessary subsistence of the Colony; but the want of express approbation from the National Legislature, must ere long produce a presumption that they contemplate perhaps other modes of relieving the Colony and dictate to us the propriety of doing only what they shall have regularly and previously sanctioned. —To JEAN BAPTISTE TERNANT. iii, 491. FORD ED., vi, 136. (Pa., Nov. 1792.)

7708. ——— ———. We are continuing our supplies to the island of St. Domingo, at the request of the minister of France here. We would wish, however, to receive a more formal sanction from the government of France than has yet been given. Indeed, we know of none but a vote of the late National Assembly for four millions of livres of our debt, sent to the government of St. Domingo, communicated by them to the minister here, and by him to us. And this was 'n terms not properly applicable to the form of our advances. We wish, therefore, for a full sanction of the past, and a complete expression of the desires of the'r government as to future supplies to their colonies. —To GOUVERNEUR MORRIS. FORD ED., vi, 151. (Pa., 1792.)

— **SAN JUAN (Porto Rico).—** See FREE PORTS.

— **SARATOGA, Proposed State of.—** See WESTERN TERRITORY.

7709. SARDINIA, Commerce with.— A desire of seeing a commerce commenced between the dominions of his Majesty, the King of Sardinia, and the United States of America, and a direct exchange of their respective productions, without passing through a third nation, led me into the conversation which I had the honor of having with you on that subject, and afterwards with Monsieur Tallon at Turin. * * * The articles of your produce wanted with us are brandies, wines, oils, fruits, and manufactured silks. Those wh'ch we can furnish you are ind go, potash, tobacco, flour, salt fish, furs and peltries, ships and materials for building them.—To M. GUIDE. ii, 146. (Ms., 1787.)

7710. SAUSSURE (Horace B.), Philosopher.—M. Saussure is one of the best philosophers of the present age. Cautious in not letting his assent run before his evidence, he possesses the wisdom which so few possess, of preferring ignorance to error. The contrary disposition in those who call themselves philosophers in this country classes them, in fact, with the writers of romance.—To WILLIAM RUTLEDGE. ii, 475. (P., 1788.)

— **SAY (Jean Baptiste).**—See GOVERNMENT, WORKS ON.

7711. SCENERY, American.—The Falling Spring, the Cascade of Niagara, the passage of the Potomac through the Blue Mountains, the Natural Bridge,—it is worth a voyage across the Atlantic to see those objects, much more to paint and make them, and thereby ourselves, known to all ages.—To MRS. COSWAY. i', 35. FORD ED., iv, 315. (P., 1786.)

7712. SCHISM, Dangers of.—Strong in our numbers, our position and resources, we can never be endangered but by schisms at home.—R. TO A. WILMINGTON CITIZENS. viii, 149. (1809.)

7713. SCHISM, Governmental.—Government, as well as religion, has furnished its schisms, its persecutions, and its devices for fattening idleness on the earnings of the people. It has its hierarchy of emperors, kings, princes, and nobles, as that has of popes, cardinals, archbishops, bishops and priests.—To CHARLES CLAS. vi, 413. (M., 1815.)

7714. SCHISM, Self-government and.—All these schisms, small or great, only accumulate truths of the solid qualifications of our citizens for self-government.—To THOMAS LEIPER. FORD ED., viii, 503. (W., 1806.)

7715. SCHISM, Silence.—Frown into silence all disorganizing movements.—R. TO A. WILMINGTON CITIZENS. viii 149. (1809.)

7716. SCHOOLS, Abortive.—The annual reports show that our plan of primary schools [in Virginia] is becoming completely abortive, and must be abandoned very shortly, after costing us to this day one hundred and eighty thousand dollars, and yet to cost us forty-five thousand dollars a year more until it shall be discontinued; and if a single boy has received the elements of common education, it must be in some part of the country not known to me. Experience has but too fully confirmed the early predictions of its fate.—To WILLIAM T. BARRY. vii, 256. (M., 1822)

7717. SCHOOLS, European.—Why send an American youth to Europe for education? What are the objects of an useful American education? Classical knowledge, modern languages, chiefly French, Spanish and Italian; mathematics, natural philosophy, natural history, civil history and ethics. In natural philosophy, I mean to include chemistry and agriculture; and in natural history to include botany, as well as the other branches of those departments. It is true that the habit of speaking the modern languages cannot be so well acquired in America; but every other article can be as well acquired at William and Mary College, as at any place in Europe. When college education is done with,

and a young man is to prepare h'mself for public life, he must cast his eyes (for America) either on law or physics. For the former, where can he apply so advantageously as to Mr. Wythe? For the latter, he must come to Europe; the medical class of students, therefore, is the only one which need come to Europe.—To J. BANNISTER. i, 467. (P., 1785.)

7718. ———. Let us view the disadvantages of sending a youth to Europe. To enumerate them all would require a volume. I will select a few. If he goes to England, he learns drinking, horse racing and boxing. These are the peculiarities of English education. The following circumstances are common to education in that and the other countries of Europe. He acquires a fondness for European luxury and dissipation, and a contempt for the simplicity of his own country; he is fascinated with the privileges of the European aristocrats, and sees, with abhorrence, the lovely equality which the poor enjoy with the rich in his own country; he contracts a partiality for aristocracy or monarchy; he forms foreign friendships which will never be useful to him, and loses the seasons of life for forming, in his own country, those friendships which, of all others, are the most faithful and permanent; * * * and * * * he returns to his own country unacquainted w'th the practices of domestic economy, necessary to preserve him from ruin, speaking and writing his native tongue as a foreigner, and, therefore, unqualified to obtain those distinctions, which eloquence of the pen and tongue ensures in a free country; for I would observe to you, that what is called style in writing or speaking, is formed very early in life, while the imagination is warm, and impressions are permanent.—To J. BANNISTER. i, 467. (P., 1785.)

7719. ———. An American, coming to Europe for education, loses in his knowledge, in his morals, in his health, in his habits, and in his happiness. I had entertained only doubts on this head before I came to Europe; what I see and hear, since I came here, proves more than I had even suspected.—To J. BANNISTER. i, 468. (P., 1785.)

7720. ———. Cast your eye over America: who are the men of most learning, of most eloquence, most beloved by their countrymen and most trusted and promoted by them? They are those who have been educated among them, and whose manners, morals, and habits, are perfectly homogeneous with those of the country. * * * The consequences of foreign education are alarming to me as an American.—To J. BANNISTER. i, 468. (P., 1785.)

7721. ———. With respect to the schools of Europe, my mind is perfectly made up, and on full enquiry. The best in the world is Edinburgh. Latterly, too, the spirit of republicanism has become that of the students in general, and of the younger professors; so on that account it is eligible for an American. On the continent of Europe, no place is comparable to Geneva. The sciences are there more modernized than anywhere else. There, too, the spirit of republicanism is strong with the body of the inhabitants; but that of the aristocracy is strong also with a particular class; so that it is of some consequence to attend to the class of society in which a youth is made to move.—To MR. M'ALISTER. iii, 313. (Pa., 1791.)

7722. SCHOOLS, Fostering genius in.—By that part of our plan [of education in Virginia] wh'ch prescribes the selection of the youths of genius from among the classes of the poor, we hope to avail the State of those talents which nature has sown as liberally among the poor as the rich, but which perish without use, if not sought for and cultivated.—NOTES ON VIRGINIA. viii, 390. FORD ED., iii, 254. (1782.) See GENIUS.

7723. SCHOOLS, Government of.—If it is believed that the elementary schools will be better managed by the Governor and Council, the Commissioners of the Literary Fund, or any other general authority of the government, than by the parents within each ward, it is a belief against all experience.—To JOSEPH C. CABELL. vi, 543. (1816.)

7724. SCHOOLS, History in.—At these [Virginia public] schools shall be taught reading, wr'ting, and common arithmetic, and the books which shall be used therein for instructing the children to read shall be such as will, at the same time, make them acquainted with Græcian, Roman, English, and American history.—DIFFUSION OF KNOWLEDGE BILL. FORD ED., ii, 223. (1779.)

7725. SCHOOLS, Trustees.—I have received your favor, informing me that the Board of Trustees for the public school in Washington had unanimously reappointed me their President. I pray you to present to them my thanks for the mark of their confidence, with assurances that I shall at all times be ready to render to the institution any services which shall be in my power.—To ROBERT BRENT. v, 196. (M., Sep. 1807.)

7726. SCHOOLS, Visitors.—I had formerly thought that visitors of the school might be chosen by the county, and charged to provide teachers for every ward, and to superintend them. I now think it would be better for every ward to choose 'ts own resident visitor, whose business it would be to keep a teacher in the ward, to superintend the school, and to call meetings of the ward for all purposes relating to it; their accounts to be settled, and wards laid off by the courts. I think ward elections better for many reasons, one of which is sufficient, that it will keep elementary education out of the hands of fanatic'sing preachers, who, 'n county elections, would be universally chosen, and the predominant sect of the county would possess itself of all its schools.—To JOSEPH C. CABELL. vii, 189. FORD ED., x, 167. (P.F., 1820.)

7727. SCHOOLS, Wealth and.—In the elementary bill they [the Legislature] inserted a provision which completely defeated it; for they left it to the court of each county to determine for itself when this act should be carried into execution within their county. One provision of the bill was that the expenses of these schools should be borne by the inhabitants of the county, every one in proportion to his general tax rate. This would throw on wealth the education of the poor; and the justices, being generally of the more wealthy class, were unwilling to incur that burden, and I believe 't was not suffered to commence in a single county.—AUTOBIOGRAPHY. i, 48. FORD ED., i, 67. (1821.) See ACADEMY, EDUCATION, LANGUAGES, and UNIVERSITY.

7728. SCIENCE, Acquirement of.—The possession of science is, what (next to an honest heart) will above all things render you dear to your friends, and give you fame and promotion in your own country.—To PETER CARR. i, 395. (P., 1785.)

7729. SCIENCE, American field of.—What a field have we at our doors to signalize ourselves in. The Botany of America is far from being exhausted, its Mineralogy 's untouched, and its Natural History or Zoology, totally mistaken and misrepresented. As far as I have seen, there is not one single species of terrestrial birds common to Europe and America, and I question if there be a single species of quadrupeds. (Domestic animals are to be excepted.) It is for such institutions as that [Harvard] over which you preside so worthily to do justice to our country, its productions and its genius. It is the work to which the young men whom you are forming should lay their hands. We have spent the prime of our lives in procuring them the precious blessing of liberty. Let them spend theirs in showing that it is the great parent of science and of virtue; and that a nation will be great in both, always in proportion as it is free.—To DR. WILLARD. iii, 16. (P., 1789.)

7730. SCIENCE, Common property.—The field of knowledge is the common property of mankind, and any discoveries we can make in 't will be for the benefit of yours and of every other nation, as well as our own.—To HENRY DEARBORN. v, 111. FORD ED., ix, 86. (W., 1807.)

7731. SCIENCE, Delight in.—Nature intended me for the tranquil pursuits of science, by rendering them my supreme delight.—To DUPONT DE NEMOURS. v, 432. (W., March 2, 1809.)

7732. SCIENCE, Elementary works.—I have received a copy of your mathematical principles of natural philosophy, which I have looked into with all the attention which the rust of age and long continued avocations of a very different character permit me to exercise. I think them entirely worthy of approbation, both as to matter and method, and for their brevity as a text book; and I remark particularly the clearness and precision with which the propositions are enounced and, in the demonstrations, the easy form in which ideas are presented to the mind, so as to be almost intuitive and self-evident. Of Cavallo's book, which you say you are enjoined to teach [in William and Mary College], I have no knowledge, having never seen it; but its character is, I think, that of mere mediocrity; and, from my personal acquaintance with the man, I should expect no more. He was heavy, capable enough of understanding what he had read, and with memory to retain it, but without the talent of digestion or 'improvement. But, indeed, the English generally have been very stationary in latter times, and the French, on the contrary, so active and successful, particularly in preparing elementary books, in the mathematical and natural sciences, that those who wish for instruction, without caring from what nation they get 't. resort universally to the latter language. Besides the earlier and invaluable works of Euler and Bezont, we have latterly that of Lacroix in mathematics. of Legendre in geometry, Lavoisier in chemistry, the elementary works of Haüy in physics, Biot in experimental physics and physical astronomy, Dumeril in natural history, to say nothing of many detached essays of Monge and others, and the transcendent labors of Laplace. I am informed by a highly instructed person recently from Cambridge. that the mathematic'ans of that institution, sensible of being in the rear of those of the continent, and ascribing the cause much to their too long-continued preference of the geometrical over the analytical methods, which the French have so much cultivated and improved, have now adopted the latter; and that they have also g ven up the fluxionary, for the differential calculus. To confine a school, therefore, to the obsolete work of Cavallo, is to shut out all advances in the physical sciences which have been so great in latter times.—To PATRICK K. RODGERS. vii, 327. (M., 1824.)

7733. SCIENCE, Encouragement of.—I am for the encouraging the progress of science in all its branches; and not for raising a hue ·and cry against the sacred name of philosophy; for awing the human mind by stories of raw-head and bloody bones to a distrust of its own vision, and to repose implicitly on that of others; to go backward instead of forward to look for improvement: to believe that government, religion, morality, and every other science were in the highest perfection in the ages of the darkest ignorance, and that nothing can ever be devised more perfect than what was established by our forefathers.—To ELBRIDGE GERRY. iv, 269. FORD ED., vii, 328. (Pa., 1799.)

7734. SCIENCE, Mother of freedom.— Freedom, the first-born daughter of science.— To M. D'IVERNOIS. iv, 113. FORD ED., vii, 3. (M., Feb. 1795.)

7735. SCIENCE, Objects of.—The main objects of all science are the freedom and happiness of man.—To GENERAL KOSCIUSKO. v, 509. (M., 1810.)

7736. SCIENCE, Pursuit of.—On the revival of letters, learning became the universal favorite [pursuit]. And with reason, because there was not enough of it ex'sting to manage the affairs of a nation to the best advantage, nor to advance its 'ndividuals to the happiness of which they were susceptible, by improvements in their minds, their morals, their health, and in those conveniences which contribute to the comfort and embellishment of life. All the efforts of the soc'ety, therefore, were directed to the increase of learning, and the inducements of respect, ease, and profit were held up for its encouragement. Even the charities of the nation forgot that misery was their object, and spent themselves in founding schools to transfer to science the hardy sons of the plow. To these incitements were added the powerful fascinations of great cities. These circumstances have long s nce produced an overcharge in the class of competitors for learned occupation, and great distress among the supernumerary candidates; and the more, as the r habits of life have disqualified them for reentering into the laborious class. The evil cannot be suddenly, nor perhaps ever entirely cured: nor should I presume to say by what means it may be cured. Doubtless th re are many engines which the nation might bring to bear on this object. Public opinion, and publ c encouragement are among these.—To DAVID WILLIAMS. iv, 513. (W., 1803.)

7737. SCIENCE, Republican government and.—Science is more important in a republican than in any other government.—To ———. vii, 221. (M., 1821.)

7738. ———. ———. Science is important to the preservation of our republican government and it is also essential to its protection against foreign power.—To ———. vii, 222. (M., 1821.)

7739. SCIENCES, Distribution of the.— I have received the copy of your System of Universal Science. * * * It will be a monument of the learning of the author and of the

analyzing powers of his mind. * * * These analytical views indeed must always be ram fied according to their object. Yours is on the great scale of a methodical encyclopedia of all human sciences, taking for the basis of their distribution, matter, mind, and the union of both. Lord Bacon founded his first great division on the faculties of the mind wh'ch have cognizance of these sciences. It does not seem to have been observed by any one that the origination of this division was not with him. It had been proposed by Charron, more than twenty years before, in his book de la Sagesse. B. i, c. 14, and an imperfect ascription of the sciences to these respective faculties was there attempted. This excellent moral work was published in 1600. Lord Bacon is said not to have entered on his great work until his retirement from public office in 1621. Where sciences are to be arranged in accommodation to the schools of an university, they will be grouped to coincide with the kindred qualifications of professors in ordinary. For a library, which was my object, their divisions and subdivisions will be made such as to throw convenient masses of books under each separate head. Thus, in the library of a physician, the books of that science, of which he has many, will be subdivided under many heads; and those of law, of which he has few, will be placed under a single one. The lawyer, again, will distribute his law books under many subdivisions, his medical under a single one. Your idea of making the subject matter of the sciences the basis of their distribution, is certainly more reasonable than that of the faculties to which they are addressed. * * * Were I to re-compose my tabular view of the sciences, I should certainly transpose a certain branch. The naturalists, you know, distribute the history of nature into three kingdoms or departments: zoology, botany, mineralogy. Ideology, or mind, however, occupies so much space in the field of science, that we might perhaps erect it into a fourth kingdom or department. But, inasmuch as 't makes a part of the animal construction only, it would be more proper to subdivide zoology into physical and moral. The latter includ'ng ideology, ethics, and mental science generally, in my catalogue, considering ethics, as well as religion, as supplements to law in the government of man. I had them in that sequence. But certainly the faculty of thought belongs to animal history, is an important portion of it, and should there find its place.—To MR. WOODWARD. vii, 338. (M., 1824.)

— SCIENTIFIC SOCIETIES.—See SOCIETIES, SCIENTIFIC.

— SCIPIO.—See ORATORY.

— SCREW PROPELLER.—See INVENTIONS.

7740. SCULPTURE, Style.—As to the style or costume [for a statue of General Washington], I am sure the artist, and every person of taste in Europe, would be for the Roman. * * * Our boots and regimentals have a very puny effect.—To NATHANIEL MACON. vi, 535. (M., 1816.)

7741. SEAMEN, American.—The seamen which our navigation raises had better be of our own. It is neither our wish nor our interest ever to employ [those of England].—To WILLIAM SHORT. vi, 128. (M., June 1813.)

7742. SEAMEN, Distressed.—Another circumstance which claims attention, as directly affect ng the very source of our navigation, is the defect or the evasion of the law providing for the return of seamen, and particularly of those belonging to vessels sold abroad. Numbers of them, discharged in foreign ports, have been thrown on the hands of our consuls, who, to rescue them from the dangers into which their distresses might plunge them, and save them to their country, have found it necessary in some cases to return them at the public charge.—SECOND ANNUAL MESSAGE. viii, 16. FORD ED., v ii, 182. (Dec. 1802.)

7743. SEAMEN, Foreign.—Your estimate of the number of foreign seamen in our employ, renders it prudent, in my opinion, to drop the idea of any proposition not to employ them.—To ALBERT GALLATIN. v, 71. (M., April 1807.)

— **SEARCH, Right of.**—See IMPRESSMENT.

7744. SECESSION, Baleful.—Mr. New showed me your letter * * * which gave me an opportunity of observing what you said as to the effect, with you, of public proceedings, and that it was not unwise* now to estimate the separate mass of Virginia and North Carolina, with a view to their separate existence. It is true that we are completely under the saddle of Massachusetts and Connecticut, and that they ride us very hard, cruelly insulting our feelings, as well as exhausting our strength and subsistence. Their natural friends, the three other Eastern States, join them from a sort of family pride, and they have the art to divide certain other parts of the Union, so as to make use of them to govern the whole. This is not new, it is the old practice of despots; to use a part of the people to keep the rest in order. And those who have once got an ascendency, and possessed themselves of all the resources of the nation, their revenues and offices, have immense means of retaining their advantage. But our present situation is not a natural one. The republicans, through every part of the Union, say that it was the irresistible influence and popularity of General Washington played off by the cunning of Hamilton, which turned the government over to anti-republican hands, or turned the republicans chosen by the people into anti-republicans. He delivered it over to his successor in this state, and very untoward events since, improved with great artifice, have produced on the public mind the impressions we see. But, still, I repeat it, this is not the natural state. Time alone would bring round an order of things more correspondent to the sentiments of our constituents. But, are there no events impending, which will do it within a few months? The crisis with England, the public and authentic avowal of sentiments hostile to the leading principles of our Constitution, the prospect of a war, in which we shall stand alone, land tax, stamp tax, increase of public debt, &c. Be this as it may, in every free and deliberating society, there must, from the nature of man, be opposite parties, and violent dissensions and discords;

and one of these, for the most part, must prevail over the other for a longer or shorter time. Perhaps this party division is necessary to induce each to watch and debate to the people the proceedings of the other. But if on a temporary superiority of the one party, the other is to resort to a scission of the Union, no federal government can ever exist. If to rid ourselves of the present rule of Massachusetts and Connecticut, we break the Union, will the evil stop there? Suppose the New England States alone cut off, will our nature be changed? Are we not men still to the south of that, and with all the passions of men? Immediately, we shall see a Pennsylvania and a Virginia party arise in the residuary confederacy, and the public mind will be distracted with the same party spirit. What a game, too, will the one party have in their hands, by eternally threatening the other that unless they do so and so, they will join their northern neighbors. If we reduce our Union to Virginia and North Carolina, immediately the conflict will be established between the representatives of these two States, and they will end by breaking into their simple units. Seeing, therefore, that an association of men who will not quarrel with one another is a thing which never existed, from the greatest confederacy of nations down to a town meeting or a vestry; seeing that we must have somebody to quarrel with, I had rather keep our New England associates for that purpose, than to see our bickerings transferred to others. They are circumscribed within such narrow limits, and their population so full, that their numbers will ever be the minority, and they are marked, like the Jews, with such a perversity of character, as to constitute, from that circumstance, the natural division of our parties. A little patience, and we shall see the reign of witches pass over, their spells dissolved, and the people recovering their true sight, restoring their government to its true principles. It is true that, in the meantime, we are suffering deeply in spirit, and incurring the horrors of a war, and long oppressions of enormous public debt. But who can say what would be the evils of a scission, and when and where they would end? Better keep together as we are, haul off from Europe as soon as we can, and from all attachments to any portions of it; and if they show their power just sufficiently to hoop us together, it will be the happiest situation in which we can exist. If the game runs sometimes against us at home, we must have patience till luck turns, and then we shall have an opportunity of winning back the *principles* we have lost. For this is a game where principles are the stake.—To JOHN TAYLOR. iv, 245. FORD ED., vii, 263. (Pa., June 1798.)

— **SECESSION, Kentucky and.**—See KENTUCKY.

7745. SECESSION, Local discontentedness and.—Dangers of another kind [than usurpation] might more reasonably be apprehended from this perfect and distinct or-

* A descendant of Mr. Taylor claimed that he wrote "it is not *usual* now", &c. See FORD EDITION.—EDITOR.

ganization, civil and military, of the States; to wit, that certain States from local and occasional discontents, might attempt to secede from the Union. This is certainly possible and would be befriended by this regular [civil and military] organization. But it is not probable that local discontents can spread to such an extent as to be able to faze the sound parts of so extensive a Union; and if ever they should reach the majority, they would then become the regular government, acquire the ascendency in Congress, and be able to redress their own grievances by laws peaceably and constitutionally passed. And even the States in which local discontents might engender a commencement of fermentation, would be paralyzed and self-checked by that very division into parties into which we have fallen, into which all States must fall wherein men are at liberty to think, speak, and act freely, according to the diversities of their individual conformations, and which are, perhaps, essential to preserve the purity of the government, by the censorship which these parties habitually exercise over each other.—To DESTUTT TRACY. v, 571. FORD ED., ix, 309. (M., 1811.)

7746. SECESSION, Louisiana purchase and.—Whether we remain in one confederacy, or form into Atlantic and Mississippi confederacies, I believe not very important to the happiness of either part.* Those of the Western confederacy will be as much our children and descendants as those of the Eastern, and I feel myself as much identified what that country, in future time, as with this: and did I now foresee a separation at some future day, yet I should feel the duty and the desire to promote the Western interests as zealously as the Eastern, doing all the good for both portions of our future family which should fall within my power.—To DR. JOSEPH PRIESTLEY. iv, 525. FORD ED., viii, 295. (W., Jan. 1804.)

7747. SECESSION, Missouri question and.—Should time not be given, and the schism [Missouri] be pushed to separation, it will be for a short term only; two or three years' trial will bring them back, like quarrelling lovers to renewed embraces, and increased affections. The experiment of separation would soon prove to both that they had mutually miscalculated their best interests. And even were the parties in Congress to secede in a passion, the soberer people would call a convention and cement again the severance attempted by the insanity of their functionaries.—To RICHARD RUSH. vii, 182. (M., 1820.)

7748. SECESSION, New England and.—I am glad of an occasion of congratulating you [William Eustis] as well as my country, on your accession to a share in the direction of our Executive councils. [Secretaryship of War.] Besides the general advantages we may promise ourselves from the employment

* The opponents of the Louisiana purchase were, at this period, predicting dire disaster to the Union because of its acquisition.—EDITOR.

of your talents and integrity in so important a station, we may hope peculiar effect from it towards restoring deeply wounded amity between your native State [Massachusetts] and her sisters. The design of the leading federalists then having direction of the State, to take advantage of the first war with England to separate the New England States from the Union, has distressingly impaired our future confidence in them. In this, as in all other cases, we must do them full justice, and make the fault all their own, should the last hope of human liberty be destined to receive its final stab from them.—To WILLIAM EUSTIS. FORD ED., ix, 236. (M., Oct. 1809.) See EUSTIS.

7749. ———, ———. Should the determination of England, now formally expressed, to take possession of the ocean, and to suffer no commerce on it but through her ports, force a war upon us, I foresee a possibility of a separate treaty between her and your Essex men, on the principles of neutrality and commerce. Pickering here, and his nephew Williams there, can easily negotiate this. Such a lure to the quietists in our ranks with you, might recruit theirs to a majority. Yet, excluded as they would be from intercourse with the rest of the Union and of Europe, I scarcely see the gain they would propose to themselves, even for the moment. The defection would certainly disconcert the other States, but it could not ultimately endanger their safety. They are adequate, in all points, to a defensive war. However, I hope your majority, with the aid it is entitled to, will save us from this trial, to which I think it possible we are advancing.—To HENRY DEARBORN. v, 607. (P.F., Aug. 1811.) See EMBARGO, FEDERALISTS, HARTFORD CONVENTION and MONARCHY.

7750. SECESSION, Suppression of.—What does this English faction with you [in New England] mean? Their newspapers say rebellion, and that they will not remain united with us unless we will permit them to govern the majority. If this be their purpose, their anti-republican spirit, it ought to be met at once. But a government like ours should be slow in believing this, should put forth its whole might, when necessary, to suppress it, and promptly return to the paths of reconciliation. The extent of our country secures it, I hope, from the vindictive passions of the petty incorporations of Greece. I rather suspect that the principal office of the other seventeen States will be to moderate and restrain the excitement of our friends with you, when they (with the aid of their brothers of the other States, if they need it), shall have brought the rebellious to their feet. They count on British aid. But what can that avail them by land? They would separate from their friends, who alone furnish employment for their navigation, to unite with their only rival for that employment. When interdicted the harbors of their quondam brethren, they will go, I suppose, to ask and share in the carrying trade of their rivals, and a dispensation with their navigation act. They think they will be happier in an association under the rulers of Ireland, the East and West Indies, than in an independent government, where they are obliged to put up with their proportional share only in the direction of affairs. But, I trust, that such perverseness will not be that of the honest and well-meaning mass of the federalists of Massachusetts; and that when the questions of separation and rebellion shall be nakedly proposed to them, the Gores and the Pickerings will find their levees crowded with silk stocking gentry, but no yeomanry; an army of officers without soldiers.—To ELBRIDGE GERRY. vi, 63. FORD ED., ix, 359. (M., 1812.)

7751. SECESSION, War with France and.—It is quite impossible when we consider all the existing circumstances, to find any reason in its favor [war against France] resulting from views either of interest or honor, and plausible enough to impose even on the weakest mind; and especially, when it would be undertaken by a majority of one or two only. Whatever, then, be our stock of charity or liberality, we must resort to other views. And those so well known to have been entertained at Annapolis, and afterwards at the grand [Philadelphia] convention, by a particular set of men, present themselves as those alone which can account for so extraordinary a degree of impetuosity. Perhaps, instead of what was then in contemplation, a separation of the Union, which has been so much the topic to the eastward of late, may be the thing aimed at.—To JAMES MADISON. iv, 222. FORD ED., vii, 220. (Pa., March 1798.)

7752. SECRECY, Government and.— All nations have found it necessary, that for the advantageous conduct of their affairs, some of their proceedings, at least, should remain known to their executive functionary only.— To GEORGE HAY. v, 97. FORD ED., ix, 57. (W., 1807.)

7753. SECRET SERVICE MONEY, Necessary.—That in cases of military operations some occasions for secret service money must arise, is certain. But I think that they should be more fully explained to the government than General Wilkinson has done, seems also proper.—To HENRY DEARBORN. v, 322. (W., July 1808.)

— SECRET SOCIETIES.—See SOCIETIES (SECRET).

7754. SECRETARIES OF LEGATION, Training.—I explained to you in my former letter the principles on which [the appointment of Mr. Sumter to be Secretary of Legation] was made, to wit, * * * to teach for public service in future such subjects as from their standing in society, talents, principles and fortune, may probably come into the public councils.—To ROBERT R. LIVINGSTON. FORD ED., vii, 30. (1801.)

7755. SECTIONALISM, Dangers of.— The idea of a geographical line, once suggested, will brood in the minds of all those who prefer the gratification of their ungovernable passions to the peace and union of their country.—To M. L. HILL. vii, 155. (M., 1820.)

7756. ——— ———. All, I fear, do not see the speck in our horizon which is to burst on us as a tornado, sooner or later. The line

of division lately marked out between different portions of our confederacy, is such as will never, I fear, be obliterated, and we are now trusting to those who are against us in position and principle, to fashion to their own form the minds and affections of our youth. —To GENERAL BRECKENRIDGE. vii, 204. (M., 1821.)

7757. SECTIONALISM, Moral and political.—A geographical line, coinciding with a marked principle, moral and political, once conceived and held up to the angry passions of men, will never be obliterated; and every new irritation will mark it deeper and deeper. —To JOHN HOLMES. vii, 159. FORD ED., x, 157. (M., 1820.)

7758. SECTIONALISM, Peace and.—I am so completely withdrawn from all attention to public matters, that nothing less could arouse me than the definition of a geographical line which, as an abstract principle, is to become the line of separation of these States, and to render desperate the hope that man can ever enjoy the two blessings of peace and self-government.—To H. NELSON. vii, 151. FORD ED., x, 156. (M., 1820.) See APPORTIONMENT and SECESSION.

7759. SEDITION LAW, Connecticut cases.—With respect to the dismission of the prosecutions for sedition in Connecticut, it is well known to have been a tenet of the republican portion of our fellow citizens, that the Sedition law was contrary to the Constitution and therefore void. On this ground I considered it as a nullity wherever I met it in the course of my duties; and on this ground I directed *nolle prosequis* in all the prosecutions which had been instituted under it, and as far as the public sentiment can be inferred from the occurrences of the day, we may say that this opinion had the sanction of the nation. The prosecutions, therefore, which were afterwards instituted in Connecticut, of which two were against printers, two against preachers, and one against a judge, were too inconsistent with this principle to be permitted to go on. We were bound to administer to others the same measure of law, not which they had meted out to us, but we to ourselves, and to extend to all equally the protection of the same constitutional principles. Those prosecutions too were chiefly for charges against myself, and I had from the beginning laid it down as a rule to notice nothing of the kind. I believed that the long course of services in which I had acted on the public stage, and under the eye of my fellow citizens, furnished better evidence to them of my character and principles, than the angry invectives of adverse partisans in whose eyes the very acts most approved by the majority were subjects of the greatest demerit and censure. These prosecutions against them, therefore, were to be dismissed as a matter of duty.—To GIDEON GRANGER. vi, 332. FORD ED., ix, 456. (M., 1814.) See LIBELS.

7760. SEDITION LAW, England and.— I enclose you a column, cut out of a London paper, to show you that the English, though charmed with our making their enemies our enemies, yet blush and weep over our Sedition law.—To JOHN TAYLOR. iv, 260. FORD ED., vii, 311. (M., 1798.)

7761. SEDITION LAW, Executive vs. Judiciary.—You seem to think it devolved on the judges to decide on the validity of the Sedition law. But nothing in the Constitution has given them a right to decide for the Executive, more than the Executive to decide for them. Both magistrates are equally independent in the sphere of action assigned to them. The judges, believing the law constitutional, had a right to pass a sentence of fine and imprisonment; because the power was placed in their hands by the Constitution. But the Executive, believing the law to be unconstitutional, were bound to remit the execution of it; because that power has been confided to them by the Constitution. That instrument meant that its coordinate branches should be checks on each other. But the opinion which gives to the judges the right to decide what laws are constitutional, and what not, not only for themselves in their own sphere of action, but for the Legislature and Executive also, in their spheres, would make the judiciary a despotic branch. Nor does the opinion of the unconstitutionality, and consequent nullity of that law, remove all restraint from the overwhelming torrent of slander, which is confounding all vice and virtue, all truth and falsehood, in the United States. The power to do that is fully possessed by the several State Legislatures. It was reserved to them, and was denied to the General Government, by the Constitution, according to our construction of it. While we deny that Congress have a right to control the freedom of the press, we have ever asserted the right of the States, and their exclusive right, to do so.—To MRS. JOHN ADAMS. iv, 561. FORD ED., viii, 311. (M., Sep. 1804.)

7762. SEDITION LAW, Unconstitutional.—I found a prosecution going on against Duane for an offence against the Senate, founded on the Sedition act. I affirm that act to be no law, because in opposition to the Constitution; and I shall treat 't as a nullity, wherever it comes in the way of my functions. —To EDWARD LIVINGSTON. FORD ED., viii, 58. (W., Nov. 1801.)

7763. ———. The ground on which I acted in the cases of Duane, Callender, and others [was] that the Sedition law was unconstitutional and null, and that my obligation to execute what was law, involved that of not suffering rights secured by valid laws to be prostrated by what was no law.—To WILSON C. NICHOLAS. v, 453. FORD ED., ix, 254. (M., 1809.) See ALIEN AND SEDITION LAWS.

7764. SELF-GOVERNMENT, America and.—Before the establishment of the American States, nothing was known to history but the man of the old world, crowded within limits either small or overcharged, and steeped in the vices which that situation generates. A government adapted to such men would be one thing; but a very different one, that for the man of these States. Here every man may have land to labor for himself, if he chooses; or, preferring the exercise of any other industry, may exact for it such compensation as not only to afford a comfortable subsistence, but wherewith to provide for a cessation from labor in old age. Every one, by his property, or by his satisfactory situation, is interested in the support of law and order. And such men may safely and advantageously reserve to themselves a wholesome control over their public affairs, and a degree of freedom, which, in the hands of the *canaille* of the cities of Europe, would be instantly per-

verted to the demolition and destruction of everything public and private. The history of the last twenty-five years of France, and of the last forty years in America, nay of its last two hundred years, proves the truth of both parts of this observation.—To JOHN ADAMS. vi, 226. FORD ED., ix, 428. (M., 1813.)

7765. SELF-GOVERNMENT, British parliament and.—The British Parliament has no right to intermeddle with our provisions for the support of civil government, or administration of justice. * * * While Parliament pursue their plan of civil government, within their own jurisdiction, we, also, hope to pursue ours without molestation.— REPLY TO LORD NORTH'S PROPOSITION. FORD ED., i, 479. (July 1775.)

7766. ———. While Parliament pursue their plan of civil government within their own jurisdiction we hope also to pursue ours without molestation.—REPLY TO LORD NORTH'S PROPOSITION. FORD ED., i, 480. (July 1775.)

7767. ———. The proposition [of Lord North] is altogether unsatisfactory * * * because they [Parliament] do not renounce the power of * * * legislating for us themselves in all cases whatsoever.—REPLY TO LORD NORTH'S PROPOSITION. FORD ED., i, 480. (July 1775.)

7768. SELF-GOVERNMENT, Classes vs. Masses.—The general spread of the light of science has already laid open to every view the palpable truth, that the mass of mankind has not been born with saddles on their backs, nor a favored few booted and spurred, ready to ride them legitimately, by the grace of God.—To ROGER C. WEIGHTMAN. vii, 450. FORD ED., x, 391. (M., June 1826.)

7769. SELF-GOVERNMENT, Connecticut and.—It would seem impossible that an intelligent people [of Connecticut] with the faculty of reading and right of thinking, should continue much longer to slumber under the pupilage of an interested aristocracy of priests and lawyers, persuading them to distrust themselves, and to let them think for them. I sincerely wish that your efforts may awaken them from this voluntary degradation of mind, restore them to a due estimate of themselves and their fellow citizens, and a just abhorrence of the falsehoods and artifices which have seduced them.—To THOMAS SEYMOUR. v, 44. FORD ED., ix, 31. (W., 1807.) See CONNECTICUT.

7770. SELF-GOVERNMENT, Education and.—Whenever the people are well informed, they can be trusted with their own government.—To DR. PRICE. ii, 553. (P., 1789.)

7771. SELF-GOVERNMENT, Europe and.—A first attempt to recover the right of self-government may fail, so may a second, a third, etc. But as a younger and more instructed race comes on, the sentiment becomes more and more intuitive, and a fourth, a fifth, or some subsequent one of the ever renewed attempts will ultimately succeed. In France, the first effort was defeated by Robespierre, the second by Bonaparte, the third by Louis XVIII. and his holy allies; another is yet to come, and all Europe, Russia excepted, has caught the spirit; and all will attain representative government, more or less perfect. * * * To attain all this, however, rivers of blood must yet flow, and years of desolation pass over; yet the object is worth rivers of blood, and years of desolation. For what inheritance so valuable, can man leave to his posterity? You and I shall look down from another world on these glorious achievements to man, which will add to the joys even of heaven.—To JOHN ADAMS. vii. 307. FORD ED., x, 270. (M., 1823.)

7772. SELF-GOVERNMENT, Experiments in.—We have no interests nor passions different from those of our fellow citizens. We have the same object, the success of representative government. Nor are we acting for ourselves alone, but for the whole human race. The event of our experiment is to show whether man can be trusted with self-government. The eyes of suffering humanity are fixed on us with anxiety as their only hope, and on such a theatre, for such a cause, we must suppress all smaller passions and local considerations.—To GOVERNOR HALL. FORD ED., viii, 156. (W., July 1802.)

7773. SELF-GOVERNMENT, French people and.—The people of France have never been in the habit of self-government, are not yet in the habit of acknowledging that fundamental law of nature, by which alone self-government can be exercised by a society, I mean the *lex majoris partis*. Of the sacredness of this law, our countrymen are impressed from their cradle, so that with them it is almost innate.—To JOHN BRECKENRIDGE. FORD ED., vii, 417. (Pa., 1800.)

7774. ———. Who could have thought the French nation incapable of self-government?—To DR. JOSEPH PRIESTLEY. FORD ED., viii, 179. (W., 1802.)

7775. SELF-GOVERNMENT, Generations and.—The present generation has the same right of self-government which the past one has exercised for itself.—To JOHN H. PLEASANTS. vii, 346. FORD ED., x, 303. (M., 1824.)

7776. SELF-GOVERNMENT, Growth of.—When forced to assume self-government, we were novices in its science. Its principles and forms had entered little into our former education. We established however some, although not all its important principles.—To JOHN CARTWRIGHT. vii, 356. (M., 1824.)

7777. SELF-GOVERNMENT, Interference with.—We [the Virginia House of Burgesses] cannot, my Lord, close with the terms of that resolution [Lord North's Conciliatory Propositions] * * * because the British Parliament has no right to intermeddle with the support of civil government in the Colonies. For us, not for them, has govern-

ment been instituted here. Agreeable to our ideas, provision has been made for such officers as we think necessary for the administration of public affairs; and we cannot conceive that any other legislature has a right to prescribe either the number or pecuniary appointments of our offices. As a proof that the claim of Parliament to interfere in the necessary provisions for the support of civil government is novel, and of a late date, we take leave to refer to an Act of our Assembly, passed so long since as the thirty-second year of the reign of King Charles the Second, intituled, "An Act for Raising a Publick Revenue, and for the Better Support of the Government of His Majesty's Colony of Virginia". This act was brought over by Lord Culpepper, then Governor, under the great seal of England, and was enacted in the name of the "King's most Excellent Majesty, by and with the consent of the General Assembly".—ADDRESS TO GOVERNOR DUNMORE. FORD ED., i, 456. (1775.)

7778. SELF-GOVERNMENT, Irresistible.—Alliances, holy or hellish, may be formed, and retard the epoch of deliverance, may swell the rivers of blood which are yet to flow, but their own will close the scene, and leave to mankind the right of self-government.—To MARQUIS LAFAYETTE. vii, 324. FORD ED., x, 280. (M., 1823.)

7779. SELF-GOVERNMENT, Limitations of.—The right of self-government does not comprehend the government of others.—OFFICIAL OPINION. vii, 499. FORD ED., v, 208. (1790.)

7780. SELF-GOVERNMENT, Local.— ✓ My bill for the more general diffusion of learning had for a further object to impart to these wards those portions of self-government for which they are best qualified, by confiding to them the care of their poor, their roads, police, elections, the nomination of jurors, administration of justice in small cases, elementary exercises of militia; in short, to have made them little republics, with a warden at the head of each, for all those concerns which, being under their eye, they would better manage than the larger republics of the county or State. A general call of ward meetings by their wardens on the same day through the State, would at any time produce the genuine sense of the people on any required point, and would enable the State to act in mass, as [the New England] people have so often done, and with so much effect by their town meetings.—To JOHN ADAMS. vi, 225. FORD ED., ix, 427. (M., 1813.) See WARDS.

7781. SELF-GOVERNMENT, Louisiana and.—Although it is acknowledged that our new fellow citizens [in Louisiana] are as yet as incapable of self-government as children, yet some [in Congress] cannot bring themselves to suspend its principles for a single moment. The temporary or territorial government of that country, therefore, will encounter great difficulty.—To DE WITT CLINTON. FORD ED., viii, 283. (W., Dec. 1803.)

7782. SELF-GOVERNMENT, Maximum.—My most earnest wish is to see the republican element of popular control pushed to the maximum of its practicable exercise. I shall then believe that our government may be pure and perpetual.—To Isaac H. Tiffany. vii, 32. (M., 1816.)

7783. SELF-GOVERNMENT, Men capable of.—I have no fear but that the result of our experiment will be, that men may be trusted to govern themselves without a master. Could the contrary of this be proved, I should conclude, either that there is no God, or that he is a malevolent being.—To David Hartley. ii, 165. (P., 1787.)

7784. ――― ―――. I have not any doubt that the result of our experiment will be that men are capable of governing themselves without a master.—To T. B. Hollis. ii, 168. (P., 1787.)

7785. ――― ―――. Sometimes it is said that man cannot be trusted with the government of himself. Can he then be trusted with the government of others? Or have we found angels, in the form of kings, to govern him? Let history answer this question.—First Inaugural Address. viii, 3. Ford ed., viii, 3. (1801.)

7786. ――― ―――. It is a happy truth that man is capable of self-government, and only rendered otherwise by the moral degradation designedly superinduced on him by the wicked acts of his tyrant.—To M. de Marbois. vii, 77. (M., 1817.)

7787. SELF-GOVERNMENT, Natural.—From the nature of things, every society must at all times possess within itself the sovereign powers of legislation.—Rights of British America. i, 138. Ford ed., i, 443. (1774.)

7788. SELF-GOVERNMENT, Preservation of.—It behooves our citizens to be on their guard, to be firm in their principles, and full of confidence in themselves. We are able to preserve our self-government if we will but think so.—To T. M. Randolph. iv, 320. Ford ed., vii, 423. (Pa., Feb. 1800.)

7789. SELF-GOVERNMENT, Purposes of.—The provisions we have made [for our government] are such as please ourselves; they answer the substantial purposes of government and of justice, and other purposes than these should not be answered.—Reply to Lord North's Proposition. Ford ed., i, 479. (July 1775.)

7790. SELF-GOVERNMENT, Qualifications for.—Some preparation seems necessary to qualify the body of a nation for self-government.—To Dr. Joseph Priestley. Ford ed., viii, 179. (W., 1802.)

7791. SELF-GOVERNMENT, Reason and.—It is honorable for us to have produced the first legislature who had the courage to declare that the reason of man may be trusted with the formation of his own action.—To James Madison. ii, 67. Ford ed., iv, 334. (P., 1786.)

7792. SELF-GOVERNMENT, Right to.—The inhabitants of the several States of *British America* are subject to the laws which they adopted at their first settlement, and to such others as have since been made by their respective Legislatures, duly constituted and appointed with their own consent. No other Legislature whatever can rightly exercise authority over them; and these privileges they hold as the common rights of mankind, confirmed by the political constitutions they have respectively assumed, and also by several charters of compact from the Crown.—Resolution of Albemarle* County. Ford ed., i, 418. (July 26, 1774.)

7793. ――― ―――. Every man, and every body of men on earth, possesses the right of self-government. They receive it with their being from the hand of nature. Individuals exercise it by their single will, collections of men by that of their majority; for the law of the *majority* is the natural law of every society of men.—Official Opinion. vii, 496. Ford ed., v, 205. (1790.)

7794. SELF-GOVERNMENT, Rightful limits.—We owe every other sacrifice† to ourselves, to our federal brethren, and to the world at large, to pursue with temper and perseverance the great experiment which shall prove that man is capable of living in society, governing itself by laws self-imposed, and securing to its members the enjoyment of life, liberty, property and peace; and further to show, that even when the government of its choice shall manifest a tendency to degeneracy, we are not at once to despair but that the will and the watchfulness of its sounder parts will reform its aberrations, recall it to original and legitimate principles and restrain it within the rightful limits of self-government.—Virginia Protest. ix. 498. Ford ed., x. 351. (M., 1825.)

7795. SELF-GOVERNMENT, Spaniards and.—I fear the Spaniards are too heavily oppressed by ignorance and superstition for self-government, and whether a change from foreign to domestic despotism will be to their advantage remains to be seen.—To Dr. Samuel Brown. vi, 165. (M., 1813.)

7796. SELF-GOVERNMENT, Study of.—I sincerely think that the prominent characters of the country where you are could not better prepare their sons for the duties they will have to perform in their new government than by sending them here [the University of Virginia] where they might become familiarized with the habits and practice of self-government. This lesson is scarcely to be acquired but in this country, and yet without it, the political vessel is all sail and no ballast.‡—To Henry Dearborn. Ford ed., x, 237. (M., 1822.)

7797. SELF-GOVERNMENT, Training for.—The qualifications for self-government

* Jefferson's own county.—Editor..
† "Except that of living under a government of unlimited powers."—Editor.
‡ General Dearborn was then Minister to Portugal. —Editor.

in society are not innate. They are the result of habit and long training.*—To EDWARD EVERETT. vii, 341. (M., 1824.)

7798. SELF-GOVERNMENT, Universal.—I wish to see all mankind exercising self-government, and capable of exercising it.—To MARQUIS LAFAYETTE. vii, 67. FORD ED., x, 85. (M., 1817.)

7799. SELF-GOVERNMENT, Usurpation and.—[The] exercises of usurped power [by Parliament] have not been confined to instances alone in which themselves were interested, but they have also intermeddled with the regulation of the internal affairs of the Colonies.—RIGHTS OF BRITISH AMERICA. i, 130. FORD ED., i, 434. (1774.)

7800. SELF-GOVERNMENT, Voluntary associations and.—If [the society] is merely a voluntary association, the submission of its members will be merely voluntary also, as no act of coercion would be permitted by the general law.—To WILLIAM LEE. vii. 57. (M., 1817.)

7801. SELF-PRESERVATION, Law of.—The law of self-preservation overrules the laws of obligation to others.—OPINION ON FRENCH TREATIES. vii, 613. FORD ED., vi, 221. (1793.)

7802. SENATE (French), Plan of.—They [the French] propose a Senate, chosen on the plan of our Federal Senate by the Provincial Assemblies, but to be for life, of a certain age (they talk of forty years), and certain wealth (four or five hundred guineas a year), but to have no other power as to laws but to remonstrate against them to the representatives, who will then determine their fate by a simple majority. This * * * is a mere council of revision like that of New York, which, in order to be something, must form an alliance with the King, to avail themselves of his veto. The alliance will be useful to both, and to the nation.—To JAMES MADISON. iii, 97. FORD ED., v, 108. (P., Aug. 1789.)

7803. SENATE (United States), Advice and consent.—When the British treaty of —— arrived, without any provision against the impressment of our seamen, I determined not to ratify it. The Senate thought I should ask their advice. I thought that would be a mockery of them, when I was predetermined against following it, should they advise ratification.—To SPENCER ROANE. vii, 135. FORD ED., x, 142. (P.F., Sep. 1819.)

7804. ——— ———. The Constitution has made the advice of the Senate necessary to confirm a treaty, but not to reject it. This has been blamed by some; but I have never doubted its soundness.—To SPENCER ROANE. vii, 135. FORD ED., x, 142. (P.F., 1819.)

7805. SENATE (United States), Cabal in.—Mischief may be done negatively as well

as positively. Of this a cabal in the Senate of the United States has furnished many proofs.—To JOHN ADAMS. vi, 224. FORD ED., ix, 426. (M., 1813.)

7806. SENATE (United States), Check on House of Representatives.—The Senate was intended as a check on the will of the Representatives when too hasty. They are not only that, but completely so on the will of the people also; and in my opinion are heaping coals of fire, not only on their persons, but on their body, as a branch of the Legislature. * * * It seems that the opinion is fairly launched into public that they should be placed under the control of a more frequent recurrence to the will of their constituents.* This seems requisite to complete the experiment, whether they do more harm or good.—To JAMES MADISON. iv, 107. FORD ED., vi, 511. (M., May 1794.)

7807. SENATE (United States), Executive and.—The President desired my opinion whether the Senate has a right to negative the *grade* he may think it expedient to use in a foreign mission as well as the *person* to be appointed. I think the Senate has no right to negative the *grade*.—OPINION ON THE POWERS OF THE SENATE. vii, 465. FORD ED., v, 161. (1790.)

7808. ——— ———. The Senate is not supposed by the Constitution to be acquainted with the concerns of the Executive Department. It was not† intended that these should be communicated to them.—OPINION ON POWERS OF SENATE. vii, 466. FORD ED., v, 162. (1790.)

7809. ——— ———. It may be objected that the Senate may by continual negatives on the *person*, do what amounts to a negative on the *grade*, and so, indirectly, defeat this right of the President. But this would be a breach of trust; an abuse of the power confided to the Senate, of which that body cannot be supposed capable.—OPINION ON THE POWERS OF THE SENATE. vii, 466. FORD ED., v, 162. (1790.) See APPOINTMENT.

7810. SENATE (United States), Executive information and.—The Secretary of State, having received a note from Mr. Strong, as chairman of a Committee of Senate, asking a conference with him on the subject of the late diplomatic nominations to Paris, London and the Hague, he met them in the Senate chamber in the evening of the same day, and stated to them in substance * * * that he should on all occasions be ready to give to the Senate, or to any other branch of the government, whatever information might properly be communicated, and might be necessary to enable them to proceed in the line of their respective offices: that on the present occasion particularly, *as the Senate had to decide on the fitness of certain persons to act for the United States at certain*

---

* Jefferson was considering the condition of affairs in South America, and he added, " for these (habit and training), they will require time and probably much suffering ".—EDITOR.

* Jefferson was condemning the failure to pass the Non-Importation bill.—EDITOR.

† " Not " is omitted in the FORD EDITION. " It was not intended " is the reading in the original MS. —EDITOR.

courts, they would be the better enabled to decide, if they were informed of the state of our affairs at those courts, and what we had to do there. [Jefferson then explained the situation of affairs.]—THE ANAS. ix, 420. FORD ED., i, 170. (W., January 1792.)

7811. SENATE (United States), Firmness.—The Senate alone remained undismayed to the last. Firm to their purposes, regardless of public opinion, and more disposed to coerce than to court it, not a man of their majority gave way in the least.—To JAMES MADISON. iv, 330. FORD ED., vii, 447. (Pa., May 1800.)

7812. SENATE (United States), Honorable.—The Senate is the most honorable and independent station in our government, one where you can peculiarly raise yourself in the public estimation.—To WILLIAM SHORT. FORD ED., v, 244. (M., 1790.)

7813. SENATE (United States), Jefferson's address to.—To give the usual opportunity of appointing a President *pro tempore*, I now propose to retire from the chair of the Senate; and, as the time is near at hand when the relations will cease which have for some time subsisted between this honorable house and myself, I beg leave, before I withdraw, to return them my grateful thanks for all the instances of attention and respect with which they have been pleased to honor me. In the discharge of my functions here, it has been my conscientious endeavor to observe impartial justice, without regard to persons or subjects; and if I have failed in impressing this on the mind of the Senate, it will be to me a circumstance of the deepest regret. I may have erred at times. No doubt I have erred. This is the law of human nature. For honest errors, however, indulgence may be hoped. I owe to truth and justice at the same time to declare that the habits of order and decorum, which so strongly characterize the proceedings of the Senate, have rendered the umpirage of their president an office of little difficulty; that in times and on questions which have severely tried the sensibilities of the house, calm and temperate discussion has rarely been disturbed by departures from order. Should the support which I received from the Senate, in the performance of my duties here, attend me into the new station to which the public will has transferred me, I shall consider it as commencing under the happiest auspices. With these expressions of my dutiful regard to the Senate, as a body, I ask leave to mingle my particular wishes for the health and happiness of the individuals who compose it, and to tender them my cordial and respectful adieu. —SPEECH TO THE U. S. SENATE. iv, 362. FORD ED., vii, 501. (Feb. 28, 1801.)

7814. SENATE (United States), John Adams's opinions.—The system of the Senate may be inferred from their transactions heretofore, and from the following declaration made to me personally by their oracle [President Adams]: " No republic can ever

be of any duration without a Senate, and a Senate deeply and strongly rooted; strong enough to bear up against all popular storms and passions. The only fault in the constitution of our Senate is, that their term of office is not durable enough. Hitherto they have done well, but probably they will be forced to give way in time." I suppose " their having done well hitherto ", alluded to the stand they made on the British treaty. This declaration may be considered as their text; that they consider themselves as the bulwarks of the government, and will be rendering that the more secure, in proportion as they can assume greater powers.—To JAMES MADISON. iv, 215. FORD ED., vii, 207. (Pa., Feb. 1798.)

7815. —— ——. President Adams and I got on the Constitution; and in the course of our conversation he said, that no republic could ever last which had not a Senate, and a Senate deeply and strongly rooted, strong enough to bear up against all popular storms and passions; that he thought our Senate as well constituted as it could have been, being chosen by the Legislatures; for if these could not support them, he did not know what could do it; that perhaps it might have been as well for them to be chosen by the State at large, as that would insure a choice of distinguished men, since none but such could be known to a whole people; that the only fault in our Senate was that it was not durable enough, that, hitherto, it had behaved very well; however, he was afraid they would give way in the end. That as to trusting to a popular assembly for the preservation of our liberties, it was the merest chimera imaginable; they never had any rule of decision but their own will, that he would as lieve be again in the hands of our old committees of safety, who made the law and executed it at the same time; that it had been observed by some writer * * * that anarchy did more mischief in one night than tyranny in an age; and that in modern times we might say with truth, that in France, anarchy had done more harm in one night, than all the despotism of their kings had ever done in twenty or thirty years. The point in which he views our Senate, as the Colossus of the Constitution, serves as a key to the politics of the Senate, who are two-thirds of them in his sentiments, and accounts for the bold line of conduct they pursue.—THE ANAS. ix, 189. FORD ED., i, 277. (Nov. 1798.)

7816. SENATE (United States), Nominations.—Should the [federalists] yield the election, I have reason to expect, in the outset, the greatest difficulties as to nominations. The late incumbents, running away from their offices and leaving them vacant, will prevent my filling them without the *previous* advice of the Senate. How this difficulty is to be got over I know not.—To JAMES MONROE. iv, 355. FORD ED., vii, 491. (W., Feb. 1801.)

7817. SENATE (United States), People and.—In the General Government, the Senate is scarcely republican at all, as not

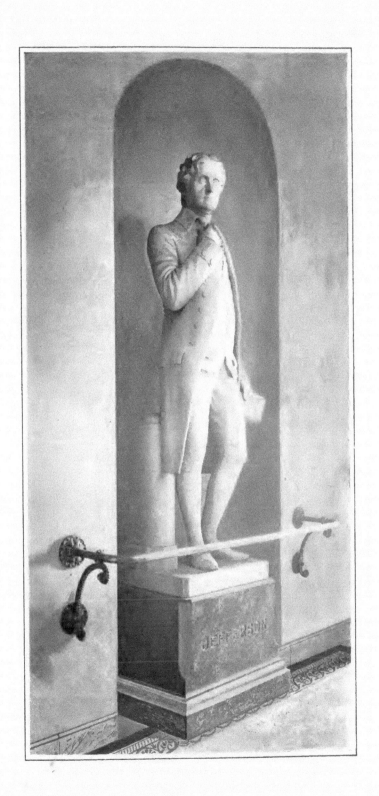

elected by the people directly, and so long secured even against those who do elect them.—To JOHN TAYLOR. vi, 607. FORD ED., x, 30. (M., 1816.)

7818. SENATE (United States), Rules of.—The rules of the [British]Parliament are probably as wisely constructed for governing the debates of a considerable body, and obtaining its true sense, as any which can become known to us; and the acquiescence of the Senate hitherto under the references to them, has given them the sanction of their approbation.—PARLIAMENTARY MANUAL. ix, 3. (1797.)

7819. —— ——. I have begun a sketch which those who come after me will successively correct and fill up, till a code of rules shall be formed for the use of the Senate, the effects of which may be accuracy in business, economy of time, order, uniformity, and impartiality.—PARLIAMENTARY MANUAL. ix, 4. (1797.)

7820. —— ——. In the old Congress [of the confederation] the mode of managing the business of the House was not only unparliamentary, but the forms were so awkward and inconvenient that it was impossible sometimes to get at the true sense of the majority. The House of Representatives of the United States are now pretty much in the same situation. In the Senate it is in our power to get into a better way. Our ground is this: The Senate have established a few rules for their government, and have subjected the decisions on these and on *all other points of order* without debate, and without appeal, to the judgment of their President. He, for his own sake, as well as theirs, must prefer recurring to some system of rules ready formed; and there can be no question that the parliamentary rules are the best known to us for managing the debates, and obtaining the sense of a deliberative body. I have, therefore, made them my rule of decision, rejecting those of the old Congress altogether, and it gives entire satisfaction to the Senate; insomuch that we shall not only have a good system there, but probably, by the example of its effects, produce a conformity in the other branch. But in the course of this business I find perplexities, * * * and so little has the parliamentary branch of the law been attended to, that I not only find no person here [Philadelphia], but not even a book to aid me. * * * You will see by the enclosed paper what they are. I know with what pain you write; therefore, I have left a margin in which you can write a simple negative or affirmative opposite every position. This is what I earnestly solicit from you, and I would not give you the trouble if I had any other resource. But you are, in fact, the only spark of parliamentary science now remaining to us. I am the more anxious, because I have been forming a Manual of Parliamentary Law, which I mean to deposit with the Senate as the standard by which I judge, and am willing to be judged.—To GEORGE WYTHE. ix, 5. FORD ED., vii, 426. (Pa., Feb. 1800.) See PARLIAMENTARY LAW.

7821. SENATE (United States), Wisdom.—The Senate * * * must from its constitution be a wise and steady body.—To C. W. F. DUMAS. ii, 367. (A., 1788.) See CONGRESS and JUDICIARY.

7822. SENATE (Virginia), Defects in.—The Senate [of Virginia] is, by its constitution, too homogeneous with the House of Delegates. Being chosen by the same electors, at the same time, and out of the same subjects, the choice falls of course on men of the same description. The purpose of establishing different houses of legislation is to introduce the influence of different interests or different principles. Thus in Great Britain it is said their constitution relies on the House of Commons for honesty, and the Lords for wisdom; which would be a rational reliance, if honesty were to be bought with money, and if wisdom were hereditary. In some of the American States, the delegates and Senators are so chosen, as that the first represent the persons, and the second the property of the State. But with us, wealth and wisdom have equal chance for admission into both houses. We do not, therefore, derive from the separation of our Legislature into two houses, those benefits which a proper complication of principles is capable of producing, and those which alone can compensate the evils which may be produced by their dissensions.—NOTES ON VIRGINIA. viii, 361. FORD ED., iii, 223. (1782.)

7823. SENATE (Virginia), Election of members.—For the election of Senators, let the several counties be allotted by the Senate, from time to time, into such and so many districts as they shall find best; and let each county at the time of electing its delegates, choose senatorial electors, qualified as themselves are, and four in number for each delegate their county is entitled to send, who shall convene, and conduct themselves in such manner as the legislature shall direct, with the senatorial electors from the other counties of their district, and then choose, by ballot, one senator for every six delegates which their district is entitled to choose.—PROPOSED CONSTITUTION FOR VIRGINIA. viii, 443. FORD ED., iii, 323. (1783.)

— **SENATORS (United States), Election of.**—See CONSTITUTION (FEDERAL).

7824. SENATORS (United States), Term of office.—The term of office to our Senate, like that of the judges, is too long for my approbation.—To JAMES MARTIN. vi, 213. FORD ED., ix, 420. (M., Sep. 1813.)

7825. SENECA, Moral system of.—Seneca is a fine moralist, disfiguring his work at times with some Stoicisms and affecting too much antithesis and point, yet giving us on the whole a great deal of sound and practical morality.—To WILLIAM SHORT. vii, 139. FORD ED., x, 144. (M., 1819.)

7826. SENILITY, Abhorrent.—Bodily decay is gloomy in prospect, but of all human contemplations the most abhorrent is body without mind.—To JOHN ADAMS. vii, 27. (M., 1816.)

7827. SENILITY, Unconscious.—The misfortune of a weakened mind is an insensibility of its weakness.—To EDWARD LIVINGSTON. vii, 405. (M., 1825.)

7828. SENSE, Directed by.—The good sense of our people w ll direct the boat ultimately to ts proper point.—To MARQUIS LAFAYETTE. FORD ED., x, 234. (M., 1822.)

7829. SENSE, National.—My chief object is to let the good sense of the nation have fair play, believing it will best take care of itself.—To DR. JOSEPH PRIESTLEY. FORD ED., viii, 181. (W., 1802.)

7830. SENSE, People and.—I am persuaded myself that the good sense of the people will always be found to be the best army.—To EDWARD CARRINGTON. ii, 99. FORD ED., iv, 359. (P., 1787.)

7831. ——— ———. I have such reliance on the good sense of the body of the people, and the honesty of their leaders, that I am not afraid of their letting things go wrong to any length in any cause.—To M. DUMAS. ii, 358. (P., 1788.)

7832. ——— ———. The operations which have lately taken place in America [adoption of Constitution] fill me with pleasure. They realize the confidence I had, that whenever our affairs go obviously wrong, the good sense of the people will interpose, and set them to rights. —To DAVID HUMPHREYS. iii, 12. FORD ED., v, 89. (P., 1789.)

7833. SENSE, Republicanism and.—It was by the sober sense of our citizens that we were safely and steadily conducted from monarchy to republicanism, and it is by the same agency alone we can be kept from falling back. —To ARTHUR CAMPBELL. iv, 198. FORD ED., vii, 170. (M., 1797.) See COMMON SENSE.

7834. SERVICE, Civic.—Every man is under the natural duty of contributing to the necessities of the society; and this is all the laws should enforce on him.—To F. W. GILMER. vii, 3. FORD ED., x, 32. (M., 1816.) See DUTY.

7835. SERVICE, Credit for.—The inquiries in your printed letter * * * would lead to the writing the history of my whole life, than which nothing could be more repugnant to my feelings. I have been connected, as many fellow laborers were, with the great events which happened to mark the ej och of our lives. But these belong to no one in particular, all of us did our parts, and no one can claim the transactions to himself.—To SKELTON JONES. v, 462. (M., 1809.)

7836. ——— ———. I was only of a band devoted to the cause of Independence, all of whom exerted equally their best endeavors for its success, and have a common right to the merits of its acquisition. So also is the civil revolution of 1801. Very many and very meritorious were the worthy patriots who assisted in bringing back our government to its republican tack.—To WILLIAM T. BARRY. vii, 255. (M., 1822.)

7837. SERVICE, Old age and.—Had it been my good fortune to preserve at the age of seventy, all the activity of body and mind which I enjoyed in earlier life, I should have employed it now, as then, in incessant labors to serve those to whom I could be useful.— To M. DE LOMERIE. vi, 107. (M., 1813.)

7838. SERVICE, Rendering.—Nothing makes me more happy than to render any service in my power, of whatever descript on.—To SAMUEL OSGOOD. i, 451. (P., 1785.)

7839. SERVICE, Reward of.—If, in the course of my life, it has been in any degree useful to the cause of humanity, the fact itself bears its full reward.—To DAVID BARROW. vi, 456. FORD ED., ix, 515. (M., 1815.)

7840. SERVICE, Tours of.—You say I " must not make my final exit from public life till it will be marked with just fying circumstances which all good citizens will respect. and to which my friends can appeal ". To my fellow-citizens the debt of service has been fully and faithfully paid. I acknowledge that such a debt exists, that a tour of duty, in whatever line he can be most useful to his country, is due from every individual. It is not easy, perhaps, to say of what length exactly this tour should be, but we may safely say of what length it should not be. Not of our whole life, for instance, for that would be to be born a slave— not even of a very large portion of it. I have now been in the public service four and twenty years; one-half of which has been spent in total occupation with their affairs, and absence from my own. I have served my tour then. No positive engagement, by word or deed, binds me to the r further service. No commitment of their interests in any enterprise by me requires that I should see them through it. I am pledged by no act which gives any tribunal a call upon me before I withdraw. Even my enemies do not pretend this. I stand clear, then, of public right on all points. My friends I have not committed. No circumstances have attended my passage from office to office, which could lead them, and others through them, into deception as to the time I might remain, into particularly they and all have known with what reluctance I engaged and have continued in the present one [Secretary of State], and of my uniform determination to retire from it at an early day. If the public, then, has no claim on me, and my friends nothing to justify, the decision will rest on my own feelings alone. There has been a time when these were very different from what they are now; when perhaps the esteem of the world was of higher value in my eye than everything in it. But age, experience and reflection preserving to that only its due value, have set a higher on tranquillity.—To JAMES MADISON. iii, 577. FORD ED., vi, 290. (June 1793.) See JEFFERSON.

7841. SHAYS'S REBELLION, Conduct and motives of.—Can history produce an instance of rebellion so honorably conducted? I say nothing of its motives. They were founded in ignorance, not wickedness. God forbid we should ever be twenty years without such a rebellion. The people cannot be all, and always, well informed. The part which is wrong will be discontented in proportion to the importance of the facts they misconce ve. If they remain quiet under such misconceptions, it is a lethargy, the forerunner of death to the public liberty.—To W. S. SMITH. ii, 318. FORD ED., iv, 467. (P., 1787.)

7842. SHAYS'S REBELLION, European opinion of.—The tumults in America, I expected, would have produced in Europe an unfavorable opinion of our political state. But it has not. On the contrary, the small effect of these tumults seems to have given more confidence in the firmness of our governments. The interposition of the people themselves on the side of government has had a great effect on the opinion here.—To Edward Carrington. ii, 99. Ford ed., iv, 359. (1787.)

7843. SHAYS'S REBELLION, Excuse for.—Those people are not entirely without excuse. Before the war, those States depended on their whale oil and fish. The former was consumed 'n England, and much of the latter in the Mediterranean. The heavy duties on American whale oil, now required in England, exclude it from that market; and the Algerines exclude them from bringing their fish into the Mediterranean. France is opening her ports for their oil, but in the meanwhile, their ancient debts are pressing them, and they have nothing to pay with. The Massachusetts Assembly, too, in their zeal for paying their public debt had laid a tax too heavy to be paid in the circumstances of their State. The Indians seem disposed, too, to make war on us. These compl cated causes determined Congress to increase their forces to 2000 men. The latter was the sole object avowed, yet the former entered for something into the measure.—To William Carmichael. ii, 81. Ford ed., iv, 345. (P., 1786.)

7844. SHAYS'S REBELLION, Government and.—I am not discouraged by this; for thus I calculate: An insurrection in one of thirteen States in the course of eleven years that they have subsisted, amounts to one in any particular State, in one hundred and forty-three years, say a century and a half. This would not be near as many as have happened in every other government that has ever existed. So that we shall have the difference between a light and a heavy government as clear gain.—To David Hartley. ii, 165. (P., 1787.)

7845. ——— ———. This insurrection will not weigh against the inconveniences of a government of force, such as are monarchies and aristocracies.—To T. B. Hollis. ii, 168. (P., 1787.)

7846. SHAYS'S REBELLION, Lessons of.—The commotions that have taken place in America, as far as they are yet known to me, offer nothing threatening. They are a proof that the people have liberty enough, and I could not wish them less than they have. If the happiness of the mass of the people can be secured at the expense of a little tempest now and then, or even of a l'ttle blood, it will be a precious purchase. *Malo libertatem periculosam quam quietem servitutem.* Let common sense and honesty have fair play, and they will soon set things to rights.—To Ezra Stiles. ii, 77. (P., 1786.)

7847. SHAYS'S REBELLION, The people and.—The interposition of the people themselves on the side of the government has had a great effect on the opinion here [Europe]. I am persuaded myself that the good sense of the people will always be found to be the best army. They may be led astray for a moment, but will soon correct themselves. The people are the only censors of their governors; and even their errors will tend to keep these to the true principles of their institution. To punish these errors too severely would be to suppress the only safeguard of the public liberty. The way to prevent these irregular interpositions of the people is to give them full information of their affairs through the channels of the public papers, and to contrive that those papers should penetrate the whole mass of the people. The basis of our government being the opinion of the people, the very first ob-

ject should be to keep that right; and were it left to me to decide whether we should have a government without newspapers, or newspapers without a government, I should not hesitate a moment to prefer the latter. But I should mean that every man should receive those papers, and be capable of reading them.—To Edward Carrington. ii, 99. Ford ed., iv, 359. (P., 1787.)

7848. SHAYS'S REBELLION, Unalarmed by.—I had seen without alarm accounts of the disturbances in the East. * * * I can never fear that things will go far wrong where common sense has fair play.—To John Adams. ii, 73. (P., 1786.)

7849. ——— ———. The late rebellion in Massachusetts has given more alarm than I think it should have done. Calculate that one rebellion in thirteen States 'n the course of eleven years, is but one for each State in a century and a half. No country should be so long without one. Nor will any degree of power in the hands of government prevent insurrections. France, with all its despotism, and two or three hundred thousand men always in arms, has had three insurrections in the three years I have been here, in every one of which greater numbers were engaged than in Massachusetts, and a great deal more blood was spilt. In Turkey, which Montesquieu supposes more despotic, insurrections are the events of every day. In England, where the hand of power is lighter than here, but heavier than with us, they happen every half dozen years. Compare again the ferocious depredations of their insurgents with the order, the moderation, and the almost self-extinguishment of ours.—To James Madison. ii, 331. Ford ed., iv, 479. (P., 1787.)

7850. SHAYS'S REBELLION, Unjustifiable.—I am impatient to learn your sentiments on the late troubles in the Eastern States. So far as I have yet seen, they do not appear to threaten serious consequences. Those States have suffered by the stoppage of the channels of their commerce, which have not yet found other issues. This must render money scarce, and make the people uneasy. This uneasiness has produced acts absolutely unjustifiable; but I hope they will provoke no severities from their governments. A consciousness of those in power that their administration of the public affairs has been honest may, perhaps, produce too great a degree of indignation; and those characters, wherein fear predominates over hope, may apprehend too much from these instances of irregularity. They may conclude too hastily that nature has formed man insusceptible of any other government than that of force, a conclusion not founded in truth nor experience.—To James Madison. ii, 104. Ford ed., iv, 361. (P., 1787.)

7851. SHEEP, Profits from.—I had never before considered, with due attention, the profit from sheep. I shall not be able to put the farm into that form exactly the ensuing autumn, but against another I hope I shall. —To President Washington. iv, 5. Ford ed., vi, 83. (Pa., 1793.)

7852. SHEEP, Protection of.—If you return to us, bring a couple of pair of true-bred shepherd's dogs. You will add a valuable possession to a country now beginning to pay great attention to the raising of sheep.—To Dupont de Nemours. v, 433. (W., 1809.)

7853. SHEEP, Wolves and.—Sheep are subject to many diseases which carry them off in great numbers. In the middle and upper parts of Virginia they are subject to the wolf, and in all parts of it to dogs. These are great obstacles to their multiplication.—NOTES ON ARTHUR YOUNG'S LETTER. FORD ED., vi, 85. (1792.)

7854. SHEEP (Merinos), Importing.— The necessity we are under, and the determination we have formed of emancipating ourselves from a dependence on foreign countries for manufactures which may be advantageously established among ourselves, has produced a very general desire to improve the quality of our wool by the introduction of the Merino race of sheep. Your sense of the duties you owe to your station will not permit me to ask, nor yourself to do any act which might compromit you with the government [Spain] with which you reside, or forfeit that confidence on their part which can alone enable you to be useful to your country. But, as far as that will permit you to give aid to the procuring and bringing away some of the valuable race, I take the liberty of soliciting you to do so. It will be an important service rendered to your country; to which you will be further encouraged by the assurance that the enterprise is solely on the behalf of agricultural gentlemen of distinguished character in Washington and its neighborhood, with a view of disseminating the benefits of their success as widely as they can. Without any interest in it myself, other than the general one. I cannot help wishing a favorable result * * * .—To GEORGE W. IRVING. v, 479. (M., Nov. 1809.)

7855. SHEEP (Merinos), Present of.— I send you a Merino ram of full blood, born of my imported ewe of the race called Agueirres, by the imported ram of the Paular race which belonged to the Prince of Peace, was sold by order of the Junto of Estremadura, was purchased and sent to me, 1810, by Mr. Jarvis, our consul at Lisbon. The Paulars are deemed the finest race in Spain for size and wool taken together, the Agueirres superior to all in wool, but small.—To ARCHIBALD STUART. FORD ED., x, 109. (M., 1818.)

7856. SHEEP (Merinos), Raising.— I thank you [President Madison] for your promised attention to my portion of the Merinos. * * * What shall we do with them? I have been so disgusted with the scandalous extortions lately practiced in the sale of these animals, and with the ascription of patriotism and praise to the sellers, as if the thousands of dollars apiece they have not been ashamed to receive were not rewards enough, that I am disposed to consider as right, whatever is the reverse of what they have done. Since fortune has put the occasion upon us, is it not incumbent upon us so to dispose this benefit to the farmers of our country, as to put to shame those who, forgetting their own wealth, and the honest simplicity of the farmers, have thought them fit objects of the shaving art, and to excite, by a better example, the condemnation due to theirs? No sentiment is more acknowledged in the family of agriculturists than that the few who can afford it should incur the risk and expense of all new improvements, and give the benefit freely to the many of more restricted circumstances. The question then recurs, what are we to do with them? I shall be willing to concur with you in any plan you shall approve, and in order that we may have some proposition to begin upon, I will throw out a first idea, to be modified or postponed to whatever you shall think better.

Give all the full-blooded males we can raise to the different counties of our State, one to each, as fast as we can furnish them. And as there must be some rule of priority for the distribution, let us begin with our own counties, which are contiguous and nearly central to the State, and proceed, circle after circle, till we have given a ram to every county. This will take about seven years, if we add to the full descendants those which will have passed to the fourth generation from common ewes. To make the benefit of a single male as general as practicable to the county, we may ask some known character in each county to have a small society formed which shall receive the animal and prescribe rules for his care and government. We should retain ourselves all the full-blooded ewes, that they may enable us the sooner to furnish a male to every county. When all shall have been provided with rams, we may in a year or two more, be in a condition to give a ewe also to every county, if it be thought necessary. * * * In the meantime, we shall not be without a profit indemnifying our trouble and expense. For if of our present stock of common ewes, we place with the ram as many as he may be competent to, suppose fifty, we may sell the male lambs of every year for such reasonable price as, in addition to the wool, will pay for the maintenance of the flock. The first year they will be half-bloods, the second three-quarters, the third seven-eighths, and the fourth full-blooded. If we take care in selling annually half the ewes also, to keep those of the highest blood, this will be a fund for kindnesses to our friends, as well as for indemnification to ourselves; and our whole State may thus, from this small stock, so dispersed, be filled in a very few years with this valuable race, and more satisfaction result to ourselves than money ever administered to the bosom of a shaver. There will be danger that what is here proposed, though but an act of ordinary duty, may be perverted into one of ostentation, but malice will always find bad motives for good actions. Shall we therefore never do good?—To PRESIDENT MADISON. v, 522. (M. 1810.)

7857. SHELLS, Growth of.— It will not be difficult to induce me to give up the theory of the growth of shells, without their being the nidus of animals. It is only an idea, and not an opinion, with me. In the Notes [on Virginia] * * * I had observed that there were three opinions as to the origin of these shells. 1. That they have been deposited, even in the highest mountains, by an universal deluge. 2. That they, with the calcareous stones and earths, are animal remains. 3. That they grow or shoot as crystals do. I find that I could swallow the last opinion, sooner than either of the others; but I have not yet swallowed it. Another opinion might have been added, that some throe of nature has forced up parts which had been the bed of the ocean. But have we any better proof of such an effort of nature, than of her shooting a lapidific juice into the form of a shell? No such convulsion has taken place in our time, nor within the annals of history: nor is the distance greater between the shooting of the lapidific juice into the form of a crystal or a diamond, which we see, and into the form of a shell, which we do not see, than between the forcing volcanic matter a little above the surface, where it is in fusion, which we see, and the forcing the bed of the sea fifteen thousand feet above the ordinary surface of the earth, which we do not see. It is not possible to believe any of these hypotheses; and, if we lean towards any of them, it should be only till some other is produced, more analagous to the known operations of nature.—To MR. RITTENHOUSE. i, 515. (P., 1786.)

7858. SHELLS, Voltaire's errors.—I have lately become acquainted with a memoir on a petrifaction mixed with shells by a Monsieur de La Sauvagere, giving an exact account of what Voltaire had erroneously stated in his questions Encyclopediques, article coquilles, from whence I had transferred it into my Notes. Having been lately at Tours, I had an opportunity of enquiring into de La Sauvagere's character and the facts he states. The result was entirely in his and their favor. This fact is so curious, so circumstantially detailed, and yet so little like any known operation of nature, that it throws the mind under absolute suspense.—To REV. JAMES MADISON. ii, 247. (P., 1787.) See DELUGE.

7859. SHERIFF, Election in Virginia.—High sheriffs * * * of Counties shall be annually elected by those qualified to vote for Representatives; and no person who shall have served as high sheriff one year shall be capable of being reelected to the said office, in the same county, till he shall have been out of office five years.—PROPOSED CONSTITUTION FOR VIRGINIA. FORD ED., ii, 20. (June 1776.)

7860. SHERIFF, Important office.—The office of sheriff is the most important of all the executive offices of the county.—To SAMUEL KERCHIVAL. vii, 11. FORD ED., x, 38. (M., 1816.)

7861. SHIPPING (American), British hostility.—The British Parliament have a bill before them for allowing wheat, imported in British bottoms, to be warehoused free. In order further to circumscribe the carrying business of the United States, they now refuse to consider as an American bottom any vessel not built here. By this construction, they take from us the right of defining, by our own laws, what vessels shall be deemed ours, and naturalized here; and in the event of a war, in which we should be neutral, they put it out of our power to benefit ourselves of our neutrality, by increasing suddenly, by purchase and naturalization, our means of carriage. If we are permitted to do this by building only, the war will be over before we can be prepared to take advantage of it.—To PRESIDENT WASHINGTON. iii, 249. FORD ED., v, 322. (Pa., 1791.)

7862. —— ——. Great Britain is still endeavoring to plunder us of our carrying business. The Parliament have a bill before them to. admit wheat brought in British bottoms to be warehoused rent free, so that the merchants are already giving a preference to British bottoms for that commodity. Should we lose the transportation of our own wheat, it will put down a great proportion of our shipping, already pushed by British vessels out of some of the best branches of business. In order further to circumscribe our carrying, the Commissioners of the Treasury have lately determined to admit no vessel as American, unless built here. This takes from us the right of prescribing by our own laws the conditions of naturalizing vessels in our own country, and in the event of a war in which we should be neutral, prevents our increasing. by purchase. the quantity of our shipping, so as to avail ourselves of the full benefit of the neutrality of our flag. If we are to add to our own stock of shipping only as much as we can build, a war will be over before we shall be the better of it.—To JAMES MONROE. FORD ED., v, 318. (Pa., 1791.)

7863. —— ——. Our ships, though purchased and navigatated by their own [British] subjects, are not permitted to be used even in their trade with us. While the vessels of other nations are secured by standing laws, which cannot be altered but by the concurrent will of the three branches of the British legislature, in carrying thither any produce or manufacture of the country to which they belong, which may be lawfully carried in any vessels, ours, with the same prohibition of what is foreign, are further prohibited by a standing law (12 Car. 2, 18, sect. 3,) [the Navigation Act] from carrying thither all and any of our own domestic productions and manufactures. A subsequent act, indeed, has authorized their executive to permit the carriage of our own productions in our own bottoms, at its sole discretion; and the permission has been given from year to year by proclamation, but subject every moment to be withdrawn on that single will; in which event, our vessels having anything on board, stand interdicted from the entry of all British ports. The disadvantage of a tenure which may be so suddenly discontinued, was experienced by our merchants on a late occasion (April 12, 1792), when an official notification that this law would be strictly enforced, gave them just apprehensions for the fate of their vessels and cargoes despatched or destined for the ports of Great Britain. The minister of that court, indeed, frankly expressed his personal conviction that the words of the order went farther than was intended, and so he afterwards officially informed us; but the embarrassments of the moment were real and great, and the possibility of their renewal lays our commerce to that country under the same species of discouragement as to other countries, where it is regulated by a single legislator; and the distinction is too remarkable not to be noticed, that our navigation is excluded from the security of fixed laws, while that security is given to the navigation of others.—FOREIGN COMMERCE REPORT. vii, 641. FORD ED., vi, 474. (Dec. 1793.)

7864. SHIPPING (American), French decree against.—The French decree making the vessel, friendly or enemy, according to the hands by which the cargo was manufactured, has produced a great sensation among the merchants of Philadelphia. Its operation is not yet perhaps well understood; but it probably will put our shipping out of competition, because British bottoms, which can come under convoy, will alone be trusted with return cargoes. Ours, losing this benefit, would need a higher freight out, in which, therefore, they will be underbid by the British. They must then retire from the competition.—To JAMES MADISON. iv, 220. FORD ED., vii, 216. (Pa., March 1798.)

7865. SHIPPING (American), Navigation act.—Our navigation law (if it be wise to have any) should be the reverse of that of England. Instead of confining *importations* to home-bottoms, or those of the *producing* nation, I think we should confine *exportations* to home-bottoms, or to those of nations *having treaties* with us. Our exportations are heavy, and would nourish a great force of our own, or be a tempting price to the nation to whom we should offer a participation of it, in exchange for free access to all their possessions. This is an object to which our government alone is adequate, in the gross; but I have ventured to pursue it here [France], so far as the consumption of our productions by this country extends. Thus, in our arrangements relative to tobacco, none can be received here, but in French or American bottoms. This is employment for near two thousand seamen, and puts nearly that number of British out of employ.—To General Washington. ii, 536. Ford ed., v, 58. (P., 1788.)

7866. SHIPPING (American), Peculiarities of.—It is doubted whether it will be expedient to regulate the duty, payable by an American vessel entering a French port, either by her draught or the number of her masts. If by the draught of water, it will fall unequally on us as a nation; because we build our vessels sharp-bottomed, for swift sailing, so that they draw more water than those of other nations, of the same burthen. If by the number of masts, it will fall unequally on individuals; because we often see ships of one hundred and eighty tons, and brigs of three hundred and sixty. This, then, would produce an inequality among individuals of six to one. The present principle is the most just, to regulate by the burthen.—To Count de Montmorin. ii, 172. Ford ed., iv, 399. (P., 1787.)

7867. SHIPPING (American), Protection of.—When a nation refuses to consider any vessel as ours which has not been built within our territories, we should refuse to consider as theirs, any vessel not built within their territories.—Foreign Commerce Report. vi, 649. Ford ed., vi, 482. (Dec. 1793.)

7868. SHIPPING (American), Simplification of duties.—It is certainly desirable that these duties should be reduced to a single one. Their names and numbers perplex and harass the merchant more than their amount; subject him to imposition, and to the suspicion of it when there is none.—To Count de Montmorin. ii, 173. Ford ed., iv, 400. (P., 1787.)

7869. SHIPPING (American), West Indian trade.—The British allow our commodities to be taken from our own ports to the West Indies in their vessels only. Let us allow their vessels to take them to no port. The transportation of our own produce is worth seven hundred and fifty thousand pounds sterling annually, will employ 200,000 tonnage of ships, and 12,000 seamen constantly. It will be no misfortune that Great Britain obliges us to exclude her from a participation in this business. Our own shipping will grow fast under the exclusion, and till it is equal to the object the Dutch will supply us.—To James Madison. Ford ed., iv, 37. (P., 1785.) See Commerce. Duties. Discriminating, Flag Protection and Navigation.

7870. SHIPS, Passports.—It has been stated in our treaties with the French, Dutch and Prussians, that when it happens that either party is at war, and the other neutral, the neutral shall give passports of a certain tenor to the *vessels belonging to their subjects*, in order to avoid dissension; and it has been thought that passports of such high import to the persons and property of our citizens should have the highest sanction; that of the signature of the President, and seal of the United States. The authority of Congress also, in the case of sea letters to East India vessels, was in favor of this sanction. It is now become a question whether these passports shall be given only to ships *owned and built* in the United States, or may be given also to those *owned* in the United States, though *built* in foreign countries. The persons and property of our citizens are entitled to the protection of our government in all places where they may lawfully go. No

laws forbid a merchant to buy, own, and use a *foreign-built* vessel. She is, then, his lawful property, and entitled to the protection of his nation wherever he is lawfully using her. The laws, indeed, for the encouragement of ship-building, have given to home-built vessels the exclusive privilege of being registered and paying lighter duties. To this privilege, therefore, the foreign-built vessel, though owned at home, does not pretend. But the laws have not said that they withdraw their protection from the foreign-built vessel. To this protection, then, she retains her title, notwithstanding the preference given to the home-built vessel as to duties. It would be hard, indeed, because the law has given one valuable right to home-bu lt vessels, to infer that it had taken away all rights from those foreign-built. In conformity with the idea that all the vessels of a State are entitled to its protection, the treaties before menioned have settled that passports shall be given, not merely to vessels *built* in the United States, but to the vessels belonging to them; and when one of these nations shall take a vessel, if she has not such a passport, they are to conclude she does not *belong* to the United States, and is, therefore, lawful prize; so that to refuse these passports to foreign-built vessels *belonging* to our merchants, is to give them up to capture with their cargoes. * * * France and Holland permit our vessels to be neutralized with them; not even to suffer theirs to be purchased here might give them just cause to revoke the privilege of naturalization given to ours, and would inflict on the ship-building States and artizans a severe injury. *Objection.* To protect foreign-built vessels will lessen the demand for ship-building here. *Answer.* Not all; because as long as we can build cheaper than other nations, we shall be employed in preference to others; besides, shall we permit the greatest part of the produce of our fields to rot on our hands, or lose half its value by subjecting it to high insurance, merely that our ship-builders may have brisker employ? Shall the whole mass of our farmers be sacrificed to the class of ship wrights? *Objection.* There will be collusive transfers of foreign ships to our merchants, merely to obtain for them the cover of our passports. *Answer.* The same objection lies to giving passports to home-built vessels. They may be owned, and are owned by foreigners, and may be collusively re-transferred to our merchants to obtain our passports. To lessen the danger of collusion, however, I should be for delivering passports in our own ports only. If they were to be sent blank to foreign ports, to be delivered there. the power of checking collusion would be small, and they might be employed to cover purposes of no benefit to us (which we ought not to countenance). and to throw our vessels out of business; but if issued only to vessels in our own ports, we can generally be certain that the vessel is our property; and always that the *cargo* is of our produce. State the case that it shall be found that all our shipping, home-built and foreign-built, is inadequate to the transportation of our produce to market; so that after all these are loaded. there shall yet remain produce on hand. This must be put into vessels owned by foreigners. Should these obtain collusively the protection of our passport, it will cover their *vessel*, indeed, but it will cover also our *cargo*. I repeat it, then, that if the issuing passports be continued to our ports, it will be our own *vessels* for the most part, and always our *cargoes* which will be covered by them. I am, therefore, of opinion. that passports ought to be issued to all vessels *belonging* to citizens of the United States, but only on their clearing out from our own ports, and for that voyage only.—Opinion on Ship Passports. vii, 624. (May 1793.)

7871. —— ——. The most important interests of the United States hang upon this quest on. [Giving passports to foreign-built ships.] The produce of the earth is their principal source of wealth. Our home-built vessels would suffice for the transportation of a very small part of this produce to market, and even a part of these vessels will be withdrawn by high premiums to other lines of business. All the rest of our produce, then, must remain on our hands, or have its price reduced by a war insurance. Many descriptions of our produce will not bear this reduction and would, therefore, remain on hand. We shall lose, also, a great proportion of the profits of navigation. The great harvest for these is when other nations are at war, and our flag neutral. But if we can augment our stock of shipping only by the slow process of building, the harvest will be over while we are only preparing instruments to reap it. The moment of breeding seamen will be lost for want of bottoms to embark them in.—Opinion on Ship Passports. vii, 625. (May 1793.)

7872. —— ——. It has been stated in our treaties with the French, Dutch, and Prussians, that when it happens that either party is at war, and the other neutral, the neutral shall give passports of a certain tenor to the *vessels belonging to their subjects*, in order to avoid dissension; and it has been thought that passports of such high import to the persons and property of our citizens should have the highest sanction; that of the signature of the President, and seal of the United States. The authority of Congress also, in the case of sea letters to East India vessels, was in favor of this sanction. It is now become a question whether these passports shall be given only to ships *owned and built* in the United States, or may be given also to those *owned* in the United States, though *built* in foreign countries. * * * I am of opinion that passports ought to be issued to all vessels *belonging* to citizens of the United States, but only on their clearing out from our own ports, and for that voyage only.—Opinion on Ship Passports. vii, 624-6. (Dec. 1793.)

7873. —— ——. As our citizens are free to purchase and use *foreign-built* vessels, and these, like all their other lawful property, are entitled to the protection of their government, passports will be issued to them as freely as to *home-built* vessels. This is strictly within our treaties, the letter of which, as well as their spirit, authorizes passports to all vessels *belonging* to citizens of the United States.—To Thomas Pinckney. iii, 550. Ford ed., vi, 242. (Pa., 1793.)

7874. —— ——. Before the receipt of * * * the form of your passports, it had been determined here, that passports should be issued in *our own ports* only, as well to secure us against those collusions which would be fraudulent towards our friends, and would introduce a competition injurious to our own vessels, as to induce these to remain in our own service, and thereby give to the productions of our own soil the protection of its own flag in its passage to foreign markets.—To Thomas Pinckney. iii, 550. Ford ed., vi, 242. (Pa., May 1793.)

7875. —— ——. It is determined that passports shall be given in our own ports only,

and to serve but for one voyage. It has also been determined that they shall be g ven to all vessels *bonâ fide* owned by American citizens *wholly*, whether built here or not. Our property, whether in the form of vessels, cargoes, or anything else, has a right to pass the seas untouched by any nation, by the law of nations; and no one has a right to ask where a vessel was built, but where she is owned.—To Gouverneur Morris. iii, 581. Ford ed., vi, 301. (Pa., June 1793.)

7876. —— ——. The most rigorous measures will be taken to prevent any vessel, not wholly and *bonâ fide* owned by American citizens, from obtaining our passports. It is much our interest to prevent the competition of other nations from taking from us the benefits we have a right to expect from the neutrality of our flag.—To Gouverneur Morris. iii, 582. Ford ed., vi, 301. (Pa., June 1793.)

7877. SHIPS, Purchase of foreign.—As our home-built vessels are adequate to but a small proportion of our transportation, if we could not suddenly augment the stock of our shipping, our produce would be subject to war insurance in the vessels of the belligerent powers, though we remain at peace ourselves.—To Thomas Pinckney. iii, 550. Ford ed., vi, 242. (Pa., May 1793.)

7878. —— ——. Had it not been in our power to enlarge our national stock of shipping suddenly in the present exigency, a great proportion of our produce must have remained on our hands for want of the means of transportation to market.—To Gouverneur Morris. iii, 581. Ford ed., vi, 301. (Pa., June 1793.)

7879. —— ——. With respect to the increase of our shipping, our merchants have no need * * * of a permission to buy up foreign bottoms. There is no law prohibit ng it, and when bought they are American property, and as such entitled to pass freely by our treaties with some nations, and by the law of nations, with all. Such accordingly, by a determination of the Executive, will receive American passports. They will not be entitled, indeed, to import goods on the low duties of *home-built* vessels, the laws having confined that privilege to these only.—To James Monroe. iv, 7. Ford ed., vi, 323. (Pa., 1793.)

7880. SHIPS, Registers.—Our laws, indeed, indulge home-built vessels with the payment of a lower tonnage, and to evidence their right to this, permit them alone to take out registers from our own offices; but they do not exclude foreign-built vessels owned by our citizens from any other right.—To Thomas Pinckney. iii, 550. Ford ed., vi, 242. (Pa., 1793.)

7881. —— ——. The laws of the United States confine registers to *home-built* vessels belonging to citizens: but they do not make it unlawful for citizens to own foreign-built vessels; and the treaties give the right of sea-letters to all vessels belonging to citizens. But who are citizens? The laws of registry consider a citizenship obtained by a foreigner who comes merely for that purpose, and returns to reside in his own country, as fraudulent, and deny a register to such an one, even owning home-built vessels. I consider the distinction as sound and safe, and that we ought not to give sea-letters to a vessel belonging to such a pseudo-citizen. It compromises our peace, by lending our flag to cover the goods of one of the belligerents to the injury of the other. It produces vexatious searches on the vessels of our real citizens, and gives to others the participation of our neutral advantages, which belong to the real citizen only.—To ALBERT GALLATIN. iv, 566. (1805.)

— SHIPS, Screw-propeller.—See INVENTIONS.

7882. SHIPS, Sea-letters.—Sea-letters are the creatures of treaties. No act of the ordinary Legislature requires them. The only treaties now existing with us, and calling for them, are those with Holland, Spain, Prussia, and France. In the two former, we have stipulated that when the other party shall be at war, the vessels belonging to our people shall be furnished with sea-letters; in the two latter, that the *vessels of the neutral* party shall be so furnished. France being now at war, the sea-letter is made necessary for our vessels; and consequently it is our duty to furnish them.—To ALBERT GALLATIN. iv, 566. (1805.)

7883. ———. I would propose as a rule that sea-letters be given to all vessels *belonging* to citizens under whose ownership of a registered vessel such vessel would be entitled to the benefits of her register.—To ALBERT GALLATIN. iv, 567. (1805.)

7884. SHIPS, Subsidies for.—I should be happy to hear that Congress thought of establishing packets of their own between New York and Havre. * * * Could not the surplus of the Post Office revenue be applied to this? This establishment would look like the commencement of a little Navy, the only kind of force we ought to possess.—To RICHARD HENRY LEE. FORD ED., iv, 69. (P., 1785.)

7885. SHIPS, Tonnage duties.—The French complain of our tonnage duty; but it is because it is not understood. In the ports of France, we pay fees for anchorage, buoys and beacons, fees to measurers, weighers and gaugers, and in some countries for light-houses. We have thought it better that the public here should pay all these, and reimburse itself by a consolidation of them into one fee, proportioned to the tonnage of the vessel, and therefore called by that name. They complain that the foreign tonnage is higher than the domestic. If this complaint had come from the English, it would not have been wonderful, because the foreign tonnage operates really as a tax on their commerce, which, under this name, is found to pay 16½ dollars for every dollar paid by France.—To WILLIAM SHORT. iii, 275. FORD ED., v, 363. (Pa., 1791.)

7886. ———. I like your idea of proportioning the tonnage of the vessel to the value (in some degree) of the property, but its bulk must also be taken into consideration.—To ALBERT GALLATIN. v, 260. (W., 1808.)

7887. SHIPS, Voyage to China.—I have the honor of enclosing to your Excellency [Count de Vergennes] a report of the voyage of an American ship, the first which has gone to China. The circumstances which induce Congress to direct this communication is the very friendly conduct of the consul of his Majesty at Macao, and of the commanders and other officers of the French vessels in those seas. It has been with singular satisfaction that Congress have seen these added to the many other proofs of the cordiality of this nation towards our citizens. It is the more pleasing, when it appears in the officers of government, because it is then viewed as an emanation of the spirit of the government. It would be an additional gratification to Congress, in this particular instance, should any occasion arise of notifying

those officers, that their conduct has been justly represented to your Excellency on the part of the United States, and has met your approbation.—To COUNT DE VERGENNES. i, 456. (P., 1785.)

— SHIPS, Water for.—See SALT-WATER.

7888. SHORT (William), Attachment to.—I see with extreme concern that you have received an impression that my attachment to you has become lessened, and that you have drawn this inference from circumstances taking place while you were in Washington. What these circumstances could be is to me incomprehensible, but one thing I certainly know, that they have been misconstrued. That this change could not be previous to my retirement from the government in 1794, your appointments to France, to Holland, to Spain are proofs. And if, during my present place in the government, I have not met your desires, the public motives which have been frankly declared have given the real grounds. You think them not founded in fact; but if the testimony we receive is of different complexions, neither should wonder at the difference of conclusion drawn by the other, and I do trust that you will become sensible that there is no necessity, at least, for supposing a change in affections, which are the same now as they have ever been. Certainly I shall not, on my part, permit a difference of view on a single subject to efface the recollections and attachments of a whole life.—To WILLIAM SHORT. FORD ED., ix, 70. (W., 1807.)

7889. SHORT (William), Diplomatic services.—Mr. Short has desired me to suggest his name as that of a person willing to become a legatine secretary, should these offices be continued. I have apprised him of the possibility that they may not. You know my high opinion of his abilities and merits; I will, therefore, only add that a peculiar talent for prying into facts seems to mark his character as proper for such a business. He is young, and little experienced in business, though well prepared for it. These defects will lessen daily. Should persons be proposed less proper on the whole, you would on motives of public good, knowing his willingness to serve, give him a nomination and do justice to his character.—To JAMES MADISON. FORD ED., iii, 318. (T., May 1783.)

7890. ———. A treaty of commerce between the United States of America and his Majesty the King of Prussia having been arranged with the Baron de Thulemeyer, his Majesty's envoy extraordinary at the Hague, specially empowered for this purpose, and it being inconsistent with our other duties to repair to that place ourselves for the purpose of executing and exchanging the instruments of treaty, we hereby appoint you special secretary for that purpose.—To WILLIAM SHORT. i, 372. (P., 1785.)

7891. ———. The President has appointed you Minister Resident * * * at the Hague which was approved by the Senate on January 16.—To WILLIAM SHORT. iii, 322. FORD ED., v, 425. (Pa., Jan. 1792.)

7892. ———. The President has joined you in a special and temporary commission with Mr. Carmichael to repair to Madrid, and there negotiate certain matters respecting the navigation of the Mississippi, and other points of common interest between Spain and us.—To WILLIAM SHORT. iii, 324. FORD ED., v, 427. (Pa., Jan. 1792.)

7893. SHORT (William), Private secretary.—I shall, on Mr. Short's return from the Hague, appoint him my private secretary, till Congress shall think proper to signify their pleasure.—To JAMES MONROE. i, 407. FORD ED., iv, 86. (P., 1785.)

7894. —— ——. His talents and character allow me to say, with confidence, [are such] that nothing will suffer in his hands [during my absence from Paris at home]. The friendly dispositions of Monsieur de Montmorin would induce him readily to communicate with Mr. Short in his present character [private secretary to Jefferson]; but should any of his applications be necessary to be laid before the Council, they might suffer difficulty; nor could he attend the diplomatic societies, which are the most certain sources of good intelligence. Would Congress think it expedient to remove the difficulties by naming him Secretary of Legation, so that he would act, of course, as Chargé des Affaires during my absence?—To JOHN JAY. ii, 514. (P., 1788.)

7895. SHORT (William), Rejected by Senate.—It is with much concern I inform you that the Senate has negatived your appointment. We thought it best to keep back the nomination to the close of the session, that the mission might remain secret as long as possible, which you know was our purpose from the beginning. It was then sent in with an explanation of its object and motives. We took for granted, if any hesitation should arise, that the Senate would take time, and that our friends in that body would make inquiries of us, and give us the opportunity of explaining and removing objections. But to our great surprise, and with an unexampled precipitancy, they rejected it at once. This reception of the last of my official communications to them could not be unfelt, nor were the causes of it spoken out by them. Under this uncertainty, Mr. Madison, on his entering into office, proposed another person (John Quincy Adams). He also was negatived, and they adjourned *sine dic.* Our subsequent information was that, on your nomination, your long absence from this country, and their idea that you do not intend to return to it, had very sensible weight; but that all other motives were superseded by an unwillingness to extend our diplomatic connections, and a desire even to recall the foreign ministers we already have. All were sensible of the great virtues, the high character, the powerful influence, and valuable friendship of the Emperor. But riveted to the system of unentanglement with Europe, they declined the proposition. * * * I pray you to place me *rectus in curiâ* in this business with the Emperor, and to assure him that I carry into my retirement the highest veneration for his virtues, and fondly cherish the belief that his dispositions and power are destined by heaven to better, in some degree at least, the condition of oppressed man—To WILLIAM SHORT v, 435. FORD ED., ix, 249. (W., March 1809.) See 261.

7896. SHORT (William), Republicanism.—I know your republicanism to be pure, and that it is no decay ot that which has embittered you against its votaries in France, but too great a sensibility at the partial evil [with] which its object has been accomplished there —To WILLIAM SHORT. iii, 503. FORD ED., vi, 155. (Pa., 1793.)

7897. SHORT (William), Talents.—I wish in the next election of delegates for Congress, Short could be sent. His talents are great, and his weight in our State must ere

long become principal.—To JAMES MADISON. FORD ED., iii, 403. (A., Feb. 1784.)

7898. —— ——. His talents and merits are such as to have placed him, young as he is, in the Supreme Executive Council of Virginia, an office which he relinquished to visit Europe. —To BARON THULEMEYER. i, 369. (P., 1785.)

7899. SIEYES (Abbe), Logical.—The Abbé Sieyes was the most logical head of the [French] nation. His pamphlet "*Qu'est ce que le Tiers Etat*"? electrified that country, as Paine's *Common Sense* did us.—AUTOBIOGRAPHY. i, 91. FORD ED., i, 127. (1821.)

7900. SILENCE, Golden.—We often repent of what we have said, but never of that which we have not.—To GIDEON GRANGER. vi, 333. FORD ED., ix, 458. (M., 1814.)

— SILVER, Intrinsic value of.—See DOLLAR and MONEY.

7901. SIMPLICITY, Government and.—I am for a government rigorously frugal and simple.—To ELBRIDGE GERRY. iv, 268. FORD ED., vii, 327. (1799.)

7902. —— ——. We have suppressed all those public forms and ceremonies which tended to familiarize the public eye to the harbingers of another form of government.— To GENERAL KOSCIUSKO. iv, 430. (W., April 1802.)

7903. —— ——. Levees are done away.— To NATHANIEL MACON. iv, 396. FORD ED., viii, 52. (W., May 1801.)

7904. SIMPLICITY, Individual.—Let us deserve well of our country by making her interests the end of all our plans, and not our own pomp, patronage and irresponsibility.—To ALBERT GALLATIN. iv, 429. FORD ED., viii, 141. (W., 1802.) See CEREMONY.

7905. SINCERITY, Language and.— Such is become the prostitution of language that sincerity has no longer distinct terms in which to express her own truths.—To GEORGE WASHINGTON. i, 325. FORD ED., iii, 298. (Pa., 1783.)

7906. SINCERITY, Valued.—Sincerity I value above all things; as between those who practice it, falsehood and malice work their efforts in vain.—To WILLIAM DUANE. iv, 590. FORD ED., viii, 431. (W., 1806.)

7907. SINCLAIR (Sir John), Benefactor.—Like our good old Franklin, your labors and science go all to the utilities of human life. —To SIR JOHN SINCLAIR. vii, 22. (M., 1816.)

7908. SINECURES, Taxation and.—We do not mean that our people shall be burdened with oppressive taxes to provide sinecures for the idle or the wicked, under color of providing for a civil list.—REPLY TO LORD NORTH'S PROPOSITION. FORD ED., i, 480. (July 1775.)

7909. SLANDER, Anonymous.—Your favor has been received * * * with the tribute of respect due to a person, who, unurged by motives of personal friendship or acquaintance, and unaided by particular information, will so far exercise his justice as to advert to the proofs of approbation given to a public character by his own State and the United States, and weigh them in the scale against the fatherless calumnies he hears uttered against him. These public acts are known even to those who know nothing of my private life, and surely are better evidence to a mind disposed to truth, than slanders which no man will affirm on his own knowledge, or ever saw one who would.—To Uriah M'Gregory. iv, 333. (M., 1800.)

7910. SLANDER, Answer to.—As to federal slanders, I never wished them to be answered but by the tenor of my life, half a century of which has been on a theatre at which the public have been spectators, and competent judges of its merit. Their approbation has taught a lesson, useful to the world, that the man who fears no truths has nothing to fear from lies. I should have fancied myself half guilty had I condescended to put pen to paper in refutation of their falsehoods, or drawn to them respect by any notice from myself.—To Dr. George Logan. Ford ed., x, 27. (M., 1816.)

7911. ——— ———. I ascribe these hard expressions to the ardor of his zeal for the public good, and as they contain neither argument nor proof, I pass them over without observation. Indeed, I have not been in the habit of noticing these morbid ejections of spleen either with or without the names of those venting them. But I have thought it a duty on the present occasion to relieve my fellow citizens and my country from the degradation in the eyes of the world to which this informer is endeavoring to reduce it by representing it as governed hitherto by a succession of swindlers and speculators. Nor shall I notice any further endeavors to prove or to palliate this palpable misinformation. I am too old and inert to undertake minute investigations of intricate transactions of the last century; and I am not afraid to trust to the justice and good sense of my fellow-citizens on future as on former attempts to lessen me in their esteem.—To Ritchie and Gooch. vii, 242. Ford ed., x, 211. (M., 1822.)

7912. SLANDER, Brutal.—I certainly have known, and still know, characters eminently qualified for the most exalted trusts, who could not bear up against the brutal hackings and hewings of these heroes of Billingsgate. I may say, from intimate knowledge, that we should have lost the services of the greatest character of our country, had he been assailed with the degree of abandoned licentiousness now practiced. The torture he felt under rare and slight attacks, proves that under those of which the federal bands have shown themselves capable, he would have thrown up the helm in a burst of indignation.—To James Sullivan. iv, 576. Ford ed., viii, 355. (W., 1805.)

7913. SLANDER, Character vs.—For myself, when placed under the necessity of deciding in a case where on the one hand is a young and worthy person, all the circumstances of whose education and position in life pronounce her virtuous and innocent, and on the other the proneness of the world to sow and spread slander, there is no hesitation in my mind.—To St. George Tucker. Ford ed., vi, 425. (Pa., 1793.)

7914. SLANDER, Chrism of.—You have indeed received the federal unction of lying and slandering. But who has not? Who will ever again come into eminent office, unanointed with this chrism? It seems to be fixed that falsehood and calumny are to be their ordinary engines of opposition; engines which will not be entirely without effect. The circle of characters equal to the first stations is not too large, and

will be lessened by the voluntary retreat of those whose sensibilities are stronger than their confidence in the justice of public opinion. * * * Yet this effect of sensibility must not be yielded to. If we suffer ourselves to be frightened from our post by mere lying, surely the enemy will use that weapon; for what one so cheap to those of whose system of politics morality makes no part?—To James Sullivan. iv, 576. Ford ed., viii, 355. (W., 1805.)

7915. SLANDER, Disregard of.—My rule of life has been never to harass the public with fendings and provings of personal slanders. —To Martin Van Buren. vii, 372. Ford ed., x, 315. (M., 1824.)

7916. SLANDER, Hamilton and.—To a thorough disregard of the honors and emoluments of office, I join as great a value for the esteem of my countrymen, and conscious of having merited it by an integrity which cannot be reproached, and by an enthusiastic devotion to their rights and liberty, I will not suffer my retirement to be clouded by the slanders of a man [Alexander Hamilton] whose history, from the moment at which history can stoop to notice him, is a tissue of machinations against the liberty of the country which has not only received and given him bread, but heaped its honors on his head.—To President Washington. iii, 468. Ford ed., vi, 109. (M., 1792.)

7917. SLANDER, Irritating.—I am fond of quiet, willing to do my duty, but irritable by slander, and apt to be forced by it to abandon my post.—To Mrs. John Adams. Ford ed., iv, 100. (P., 1785.)

7918. SLANDER, Newspapers and.—An editor * * * [should] set his face against the demoralizing practice of feeding the public mind habitually on slander, and the depravity of taste which this nauseous aliment induces.— To John Norvell. v, 93. Ford ed., ix, 74. (W., 1807.)

7919. SLANDER, Of patriots.—The patriot, like the Christian, must learn that to bear revilings and persecutions is a part of his duty; and in proportion as the trial is severe, firmness under it becomes more requisite and praiseworthy. It requires, indeed, self-command. But that will be fortified in proportion as the calls for its exercise are repeated.— To James Sullivan. iv, 576. Ford ed., viii, 355. (W., 1805.)

7920. SLANDER, Political.—The federal leaders have gone too far ever to change. Their bitterness increases with their desperation. They are trying slanders now which nothing could prompt but a gall which blinds their judgments as well as their consciences. I shall take no other revenge, than, by a steady pursuit of economy and peace, and by the establishment of republican principles in substance and in form, to sink federalism into an abyss from which there shall be no resurrection for it.—To Levi Lincoln. iv, 451. Ford ed., viii, 175. (W., Oct. 1802.)

7921. SLANDER, Prevalent.—Defamation is becoming a necessary of life; insomuch, that a dish of tea in the morning or evening cannot be digested without this stimulant.—To John Norvell. v, 93. Ford ed., ix, 74. (W., 1807.)

7922. SLANDER, Public office and.—It is really a most afflicting consideration, that it is impossible for a man to act in any office for the public without encountering a persecution which even his retirement will not withdraw him from.—To JAMES MONROE. FORD ED., vii, 233. (Pa., 1798.)

7923. SLANDER, Punishment for.— Slanderers I have thought it best to leave to the scourge of public opinion.—To DE WITT CLINTON. v, 80. FORD ED., ix, 63. (W., 1807.)

7924. SLANDER, Secret.— Secret slanders cannot be disarmed because they are secret.—To WILLIAM DUANE. iv, 591. FORD ED., vii, 431. (W., 1806.)

7925. SLANDER, Voluminous.— As to the volume of slanders supposed to have been cut out of newspapers and preserved [by me] it would not, indeed, have been a single volume, but an encyclopedia in bulk. But I never had such a volume; indeed, I rarely thought those libels worth reading, much less preserving and remembering.—To JOHN ADAMS. vii, 274. (M., 1823.) See ABUSE, CALUMNY, LIBELS and NEWSPAPERS.

7926. SLAVE TRADE, Abolition of.— I congratulate you [Congress] on the approach of the period at which you may interpose your authority constitutionally, to withdraw the citizens of the United States from all further participation in those violations of human rights have been so long continued on the unoffending inhabitants of Africa, and which the morality, the reputation, and the best interests of our country, have long been eager to proscribe. Although no law you may pass can take prohibitory effect till the first day of the year one thousand eight hundred and eight, yet the intervening period is not too long to prevent, by timely notice, expeditions which cannot be completed before that day.—SIXTH ANNUAL MESSAGE. viii, 67. FORD ED., viii, 492. (Dec. 1806.)

7927. ——— ———. I am very sensible of the honor you propose to me of becoming a member of the society for the abolition of the slave trade. You know that nobody wishes more ardently to see an abolition, not only of the trade, but of the condition of slavery; and certainly nobody will be more willing to encounter every sacrifice for that object. But the influence and information of the friends to this proposition in France will be far above the need of my association. I am here as a public servant, and those whom I serve, having never yet been able to give their voice against this practice, it is decent for me to avoid too public a demonstration of my wishes to see it abolished. Without serving the cause here, it might render me less able to serve it beyond the water. I trust you will be sensible of the prudence of those motives, therefore, which govern my conduct on this occasion.—To J. P. BRISSOT DE WARVILLE. ii, 357. FORD ED., v, 6. (P., Feb. 1788.)

7928. SLAVERY, Abolition of.— After the year 1800 of the Christian era, there shall be neither slavery nor involuntary servitude in any of the said States, * otherwise than in punishment of crimes, whereof the party shall have been duly convicted to have been personally guilty.—WESTERN TERRITORY REPORT. FORD ED., iii, 409. (March 1. 1784.)

* In 1784, Jefferson was chairman of a committee of Congress, appointed to devise a plan of government for the western country above the parallel of 31° north latitude The measure was defeated by one vote. In addition to the Northwestern Territory, the region embraced what afterwards became the States of Alabama, Mississippi, Tennessee and Kentucky.—EDITOR.

7929. ——— ———. The clause respecting slavery was lost by an individual vote only. Ten States were present. The four Eastern States, New York and Pennsylvania, were for the clause. Jersey would have been for it, but there were but two members, one of whom was sick in his chambers. South Carolina, Maryland, and! Virginia! voted against it. North Carolina was divided, as would have been Virginia, had not one of its delegates been sick in bed.—To JAMES MADISON. FORD ED., iii, 471. (A., April 25, 1784.)

7930. ——— ———. There were ten States present; six voted unanimously for it, three against it, and one was divided; and seven votes being requisite to decide the proposition affirmatively. it was lost. The voice of a single individual of the State which was divided, or of one of those which were of the negative, would have prevented this abominable crime from spreading itself over the new country. Thus we see the fate of millions unborn hanging on the tongue of one man, and heaven was silent in that awful moment! But it is to be hoped it will not always be silent, and that the friends to the rights of human nature will in the end prevail.—To M. DE MEUNIER. ix, 276. FORD ED., iv, 181. (P., 1786.)

7931. ——— ———. What a stupendous, what an incomprehensible machine is man! who can endure toil, famine, stripes, imprisonment, and death itself, in vindication of his own liberty, and, the next moment, be deaf to all those motives whose power supported him through his trial, and inflict on his fellow men a bondage, one hour of which is fraught with more misery than ages of that which he rose in rebellion to oppose. *—To M. DE MEUNIER. ix, 279. FORD ED., iv, 185. (P., 1786.)

7932. ——— ———. I have long since given up the expectation of any early provision for the extinguishment of slavery among us There are many virtuous men who would make any sacrifices to effect it, many equally virtuous who persuade themselves either that the thing is not wrong, or that it cannot be remedied. and very many with whom interest is morality. The older we grow, the larger we are disposed to believe the last party to be. But interest is really going over to the side of morality. The value of the slave is every day lessening; his burden on his master daily increasing. Interest is, therefore. preparing the disposition to be just; and this will be goaded from time to time by the insurrectionary spirit of the slaves. This is easily quelled in its first efforts; but from being local it will become general, and whenever it does, it will rise more formidable after every defeat, until we shall be forced, after dreadful scenes and sufferings, to release them in their own way, which, without such sufferings we might now model after our own convenience.—To WILLIAM A. BURWELL. FORD ED., viii, 340. (W., Jan. 1805.)

7933. ——— ———. I can say with conscious truth that there is not a man on earth who would sacrifice more than I would to relieve us from this heavy reproach in any practicable way. The cession of that kind of property. for so it is misnamed, is a bagatelle which would not cost me a second thought, if, in that way, a general emancipation and expatriation could be effected; and, gradually. and with due sacrifices, I think it might be. But, as it is, we have the wolf by the ears, and we can

* The reference is to the passage of the slave bill by the Virginia Legislature without the emancipation amendment.—EDITOR.

neither hold h'm, nor safely let him go. Justice is in one scale and self-preservation in the other.—To JOHN HOLMES. vii, 159. FORD ED., x, 157. (M., 1820.)

7934. ————. The abolition of the evil is not impossible; it ought never, therefore, to be despaired of. Every plan should be adopted. every experiment tried, wh ch may do something towards the ultimate object. That which you propose is well worthy of trial. It has succeeded with certain portions of our white brethren, under the care of a Rapp and an Owen; and why may it not succeed with the man of color?—To MISS FANNY WRIGHT. vii, 408. FORD ED., x, 344. (M., 1825.)

7935. SLAVERY, Abomination.—This abomination must have an end. And there is a superior bench reserved in heaven for those who hasten it.—To E. RUTLEDGE. ii, 180. FORD ED., iv, 410. (P., 1787.)

7936. SLAVERY, Colonial condemnation.—The abolition of domestic slavery is the great object of desire 'n those Colonies, where it was, unhappily, introduced in their infant state. But previous to the enfranchisement of the slaves we have, it is necessary to exclude all further importations from Africa. Yet our repeated attempts to effect this by prohibitions, and by imposing duties which might amount to a prohibition, have been hitherto defeated by his Majesty's negative: Thus preferring the immed'ate advantages of a few British corsairs to the lasting interests of the Amer'can States, and to the rights of human nature, deeply wounded by this infamous practice.*—RIGHTS OF BRITISH AMERICA. i, 135. FORD ED., i, 440. (1774.)

7937. SLAVERY, Constitutional inhibition.—No person hereafter coming into this country shall be held within the same in slavery under any pretext whatever.—PROPOSED VA. CONSTITUTION. FORD ED., ii, 26. (June 1776.)

7938. ————. The General Assembly [of Virginia] shall not have power to * * * permit the introduction of any more slaves to reside in this State, or the continuance of slavery beyond the generation which shall be living on the 31st day of December, 1800; all persons born after that day being hereby declared free.—PROPOSED CONSTITUTION FOR VIRGINIA. viii, 446. FORD ED., iii, 325. (1783.)

7939. SLAVERY, Deplorable results of.—The whole commerce between master and slave is a perpetual exercise of the most boisterous passions. the most unremitting despotism on the one part, and degrading submissions on the other. Our children see this, and learn to imitate it; for man is an 'mitative animal. This quality is the germ of all education in him. From his cradle to his grave he is learning to do what he sees others do. If a parent could find no motive either in his philanthropy or his self-love, for restraining the intemperance of passion towards his slave. it should always be a sufficient one that his child is present. But, generally, it is not sufficient. The parent storms, the child looks on, catches the lineaments of wrath. puts on the same airs in the circle of smaller slaves. gives a loose to the worst of pass'ons, and thus nursed, educated, and daily exercised in tyranny, cannot but be stamped by it with odious peculiarities. The man must be a prodigy who can retain his manners and morals undepraved by such circumstances. And with what execrations should the statesman be loaded. who, permitting one-

* See note under Veto.—EDITOR.

half the citizens thus to trample on the rights of the other, transforms those into despots, and these into enemies, destroys the morals of the one part, and the *amor patriæ* of the other. For if a slave can have a country in this world, it must be any other in preference to that in which he 's born to live and labor for another; in which he must lock up the faculties of his nature, contribute as far as depends on his individual endeavors to the evanishment of the human race, or entail his own miserable condition on the endless generations proceeding from him.—NOTES ON VIRGINIA. viii, 403. FORD ED., iii, 266. (1782.)

7940. SLAVERY, Destructive of industry.—With the morals of the people, their industry also is destroyed. For in a warm climate, no man will labor for himself who can make another labor for him. This is so true, that of the proprietors of slaves a very small proportion indeed are ever seen to labor.—NOTES ON VIRGINIA. viii, 403. FORD ED., iii, 267. (1782.)

7941. SLAVERY, Divine justice and.—Can the liberties of a nation be thought secure when we have removed their only firm basis, a conviction in the minds of the people that these liberties are of the gift of God? That they are not to be violated but with his wrath? Indeed, I tremble for my country when I reflect that God is just; that his justice cannot sleep forever; that considering numbers, nature and natural means only, a revolution of the wheel of fortune, an exchange of situation is among possible events; that it may become probable by supernatural interference! The Almighty has no attribute which can take side with us in such a contest.—NOTES ON VIRGINIA. viii, 404. FORD ED., i'i, 267. (1782.)

7942. SLAVERY, Establishment in Virginia.—The first establishment [of slavery] in Virginia which became permanent, was made in 1607. I have found no mention of negroes in the Colony until about 1650. The first brought here as slaves were by a Dutch ship; after which the English commenced the trade, and continued it until the Revolutionary war. That suspended, *ipso facto*, their further importation for the present, and the business of the war pressing constantly on the legislature, this subject was not acted on finally until the year '78, when I brought in a bill to prevent their further importation. This passed without opposition, and stopped the increase of the evil by importation, leaving to future efforts its final eradication.—AUTOBIOGRAPHY. i, 38. FORD ED., i, 51. (1821.)

7943. SLAVERY, Extension of.—Of one thing I am certain, that as the passage of slaves from one State to another, would not make a slave of a single human being who would not be so without it. so their diffusion over a greater surface would make them individually happier, and proportionally facilitate the accomplishment of their emancipation. by dividing the burden on a greater number of coadjutors. An abstinence. too, from this act of power would remove the jealousy excited by the undertak'ng of Congress to regulate the condition of the different descriptions of men composing a State. This certainly is the exclusive right of every State, wh'ch nothing in the Constitution has taken from them and given to the General Government. Could Congress, for example, say that the non-freemen of Connecticut shall be freemen, or that they shall not emigrate into any other State?—To JOHN HOLMES. vii, 159. FORD ED., x, 158. (M., 1820.)

7944. SLAVERY, George III. and.—He [George III.] has waged cruel war against human nature itself, v olating its most sacred rights of life and liberty in the persons of a distant people who never offended him, captivating and carrying them into slavery in another hemisphere, or to incur miserable death in their transportation thither. This piratical warfare, the opprobrium of INFIDEL powers, is the warfare of the CHRISTIAN King of Great Britain. Determined to ..eep open a market where MEN should be bought and sold, he has prostituted his negative for suppressing every leg'slative attempt to prohibit or to restrain th's execrable commerce. And that this assemblage of horrors might want no fact of distinguished dye, he is now excit'ng those very people to rise in arms among us. and to purchase that liberty of which he has deprived them, by murdering the people upon whom he has obtruded them: thus paying off former crimes committed against the LIBERTIES of one people, with crimes which he urges them to commit against the LIVES of another.*—DECLARATION OF INDEPENDENCE AS DRAWN BY JEFFERSON.

7945. SLAVERY, Indians and.—An inhuman practice once prevailed in this country, of·making slaves of the Inuians. This practice commenced with the Spaniards with the first discovery of America.—NOTES ON VIRGINIA. viii, 306. FORD ED., iii, 154. (1782.)

7946. SLAVERY, Lawfulness.—On the question of the .awfulness of slavery, that is of the right of one man to appropriate to himself the faculties of another without his consent, I certainly retain my early opinions. On that, however, of third persons to interfere between the parties, and the effect of conventional modificat:ons of that pretension, we are probably nearer together.—To EDWARD EVERETT. vii, 437. FORD ED., x, 385. (M., 1826.)

7947. SLAVERY, Moral reproach of.—My sentiments on the subject of slavery of negroes have long since been in possession of the public, and time has only served to give them stronger root. The love of justice and the love of country plead equally the cause of these people, and it is a moral reproach to us that they should have pleaded it so long in vain, and should have produced not a single effort, nay I fear not much serious willingness to relieve them and ourselves from our present condition of moral and political reprobation. * * * I had always hoped that the younger generation rece'ving their early impressions after the flame of liberty had been kindled in every breast, and had become, as it were, the vital spirit of every American, that the generous temperament of youth, analogous to the motion of the blood, and above the suggestions of avarice, would have sympathized with oppression wherever found, and proved their love of liberty beyond their own share of it. But my intercourse with them since my return [from Europe] has not been sufficient to ascertain that they had made towards this point the progress I had hoped.—To EDWARD COLES. FORD ED., ix, 477. (M., 1814.)

* "This clause," says Jefferson, in his Autobiography (i, 19), "was struck out in complaisance to South Carolina and Georgia, who had never attempted to restrain the importation of slaves, and who, on the contrary, still wished to continue it. Our northern brethren, also, I believe, felt a little tender under those censures; for though their people had very few slaves themselves, yet they had been pretty considerable carriers of them to others."—EDITOR.

7948. SLAVERY, Poem against.—I have received a letter from Mr. Thomas Brannagan, * * * Philadelphia, asking my subscription to the work announced in the enclosed paper.* The cause in which he embarks is so holy, the sentiments he expresses in his letter so friendly, that it is highly painful to me to hesitate on a compliance which appears so smail. But that is not its true character, and it would be injurious even to his views, for me to commit myself on paper by answering his letter. I have most carefully avoided every public act or manifestation on that subject. Should an occasion ever occur in which I can interpose with decisive effect, I shall certainly know and do my duty with promptitude and zeal. But, in the meantime, it would only be disarming myself of influence to be taking smail means. The subscr.ption to a book on this subject is one of those little irritating measures, which, without advancing its end at all, would, by lessening the confidence and good will of a description of friends composing a large body. only lessen my powers of doing them good in the other great relations in which I stand to the public. Yet, I cannot be easy in not answering Mr. Brannagan's letter, unless he can be made sensible that it is better I should not answer it; and I do not know how to effect this, unless you would have the goodness * * * to enter into an explanation with him. —To DR. GEORGE LOGAN. FORD ED., viii, 351. (W., May 1805.)

7949. SLAVERY, Political error of.—Whatever may have been the circumstances which influenced our forefathers to permit the introduction of personal bondage into any part of these States, and to participate in the wrongs committed on an unoffending quarter of the globe, we may rejoice that such circumstances, and such a sense of them, exist no longer. It is honorable to the nation at large that their Legislature availed themselves of the first practicable moment for arresting the progress of this great moral and political error.—R. TO A. OF QUAKERS. viii, 119. (Nov. 1807.)

7950. SLAVERY, Roman.—We know that among the Romans, about the Augustan age especially, the condition of their slaves was much more deplorable than that of the blacks on the continent of America. The two sexes were confined in separate apartments, because to ra'se a child cost the master more than to buy one. Cato, for a very restricted indulgence to his slaves in this particular, took from them a certain price. But in this country the slaves multiply as fast as the free inhab'tants. * * * The same Cato, on a principle of economy, always sold his sick and superannuated slaves. He gives it as a standing precept to a master visiting his farm, to sell his old oxen, old wagons, old tools, old and diseased servants, and everything else become useless. * * * The American slaves cannot erumerate this among the injuries and 'nsults they receive. It was the common practice to expose in the island Æsculapius, in the Tiber, diseased slaves whose cure was likely to become tedious. The Emperor Claudius, by an edict, gave freedom to such of them as should recover, and first declared that if any person chose to kill rather than to expose them, it should be deemed homicide. The exposing them is a cr'me of which no instance has existed with us; and were it to be followed by death, it would be punished cap-

* This refers to "Avenia; or, A Tragical Poem on the Oppression of the Human Species", an anti-slavery work printed in Philadelphia in 1805.—NOTE IN THE FORD EDITION.

itally. We are told of a certain Vedius Pollio, who, in the presence of Augustus, would have given a slave as food to his fish for having broken a glass. With the Romans, the regular method of taking the evidence of their slaves was under torture. Here it has been thought better never to resort to their evidence. When a master was murdered, all his slaves, in the same house, or within hearing, were condemned to death. Here punishment falls on the guilty only, and as precise proof is required against him as against a freeman. Yet notwithstanding these and other discouraging circumstances among the Romans, their slaves were often their rarest artists. They excelled, too, in science, insomuch as to be usually employed as tutors to their master's children. Epictetus, Terence, and Phœdrus, were slaves. But they were of the race of whites. It is not their condition then, but nature which has produced the distinction. Whether further observation w'll or will not verify the conjecture, that nature has been less bountiful to them in the endowments of the head, I believe that in those of the heart she will be found to have done them justice.—NOTES ON VIRGINIA. viii, 384. FORD ED., iii, 247. (1782.) See NEGROES.

7951. SLAVERY, Sectional views in 1785.—Southward of the Chesapeake, your pamphlet [against slavery] will find but few readers concurring with it in sentiment on the subject of slavery. From the mouth to the head of the Chesapeake, the bulk of the people will approve it in theory, and it will find a respectable minority ready to adopt it in practice; a minority which for weight and worth of character preponderates against the greater number, who have not the courage to divest their families of a property which, however, keeps their conscience unquiet. Northward of the Chesapeake, you may find here and there an opponent to your doctrine, as you may find here and there a robber and murderer; but in no greater number. In that part of America, there being but few slaves, they can easily disencumber themselves of them; and emancipation is put into such a train that in a few years there will be no slaves northward of Maryland. In Maryland, I do not find such a disposition to begin the redress of this enormity as in Virginia. This is the next State to which we may turn our eyes for the interesting spectacle of justice in conflict with avarice and oppression; a conflict wherein the sacred side is gaining daily recruits from the influx into office of young men grown, and growing up. These have sucked in the principles of liberty, as it were, with their mother's milk; and it is to them I look with anxiety to turn the fate of this question. Be not therefore discouraged. What you have written will do a great deal of good.—To DR. PRICE. i, 377. FORD ED., iv, 82. (P., 1785.)

7952. SLAVERY, Strictures on.—The strictures on slavery [in the Notes on Virginia] * * * I do not wish to have made public, at least till I know whether their publication would do most harm or good. It is possible, that in my own country, these strictures might produce an irritation, which would indispose the people towards [one of] the two great objects I have in view; that is, the emancipation of their slaves.*—To GENERAL CHASTELLUX. i, 339. FORD ED., iii, 71. (P., 1785.) See COLONIZATION, COLONY and MISSOURI QUESTION.

* General Chastellux had proposed to print extracts from a private copy in a French scientific paper.—EDITOR.

7953. SLAVES, Abuse of.—The check on the tenants against abusing my slaves was, by the former lease, that I might discontinue it on a reference to arbitrators. Would it not be well to retain an optional right to sue them for ill-usage of the slaves or to discontinue it by arbitration, whichever you should choose at the time?—To NICHOLAS LEWIS. FORD ED., v, 31. (P., 1788.)

7954. SLAVES, British seizure of.—The British army, after ravaging the State of Virginia, had sent off a very great number of slaves to New York. By the seventh article of the treaty of peace, they stipulated not to carry away any of these. Notwithstanding this, 't was known, when they were evacuating New York, that they were carrying away the slaves, General Washington made an official demand of Sir Guy Carleton, that he should cease to send them away. He answered, that these people had come to them under promise of the King's protection, and that that promise should be fulfilled in preference to the stipulation in the treaty. The State of Virginia, to which nearly the whole of these slaves belonged, passed a law to forbid the recovery of debts due to British subjects. They declared, at the same time, they would repeal the law, if Congress were of opinion they ought to do it. But, desirous that their citizens should be discharging their debts, they afterwards permitted British creditors to prosecute their suits, and to receive their debts in seven equal and annual payments; relying that the demand for the slaves would be either admitted or denied in time to lay their hands on some of the latter payments for reimbursement.*—REPORT TO CONGRESS. ix, 240. FORD ED., iv, 127. (P., 1785.)

7955. SLAVES, Comfort of.—I am miserable till I shall owe not a shilling. The moment that shall be the case, I shall feel myself at liberty to do something for the comfort of my slaves.—To NICHOLAS LEWIS. FORD ED., iv, 343. (P., 1786.)

7956. SLAVES, Duty to.—My opinion has ever been that, until more can be done for them, we should endeavor, with those whom fortune has thrown on our hands, to feed and clothe them well, protect them from ill usage, require such reasonable labor only as is performed voluntarily by freemen, and be led by no repugnances to abdicate them, and our duties to them. The laws do not permit us to turn them loose, if that were for their good; and to commute them for other property is to commit them to those whose usage of them we cannot control.—To EDWARD COLES. FORD ED., ix, 479. (M., 1814.)

7957. SLAVES, European laborers and.—Our only blot is becoming less offensive by the great improvement in the condition and civilization of that race, who can now more advantageously compare their situation with that of the laborers of Europe. Still it is a hideous blot, as well from the heteromorph peculiarities of the race, as that, with them, physical compulsion to action must be substituted for the moral necess'ty which constrains the free laborers to work equally hard. We feel and deplore it morally and politically, and we look without entire despair to some redeeming means not yet specifically foreseen. I am happy in believing that the conviction of

* The extract is from a report to Congress of a conference with Count de Vergennes, Foreign Minister of France, on the subject of commerce.—EDITOR.

the necessity of removing this evil gains ground with time. Their emigration to the westward lightens the difficulty by dividing it, and renders it more practicable on the whole. And the neighborhood of a government of their color promises a more accessible asylum than that from whence they came.—To WILLIAM SHORT. vii, 310. (M., 1823.)

7958. SLAVES, Hiring out.—I observe in your letter * * * that the profits of the whole estate [of Monticello] would be no more than the hire of the few negroes hired out would amount to. Would 't be better to hire more where good masters could be got? Would it be better to hire plantations and all, if proper assurance can be provided for the good usage of everything?—To NICHOLAS LEWIS. FORD ED., iv, 342. (P., 1786.)

7959. SLAVES, Importation of.—During the regal government we had, at one time, obtained a law which imposed such a duty on the importation of slaves as amounted nearly to a prohibition, when one inconsiderate assembly, placed under a peculiarity of circumstance, repealed the law. This repeal met a joyful sanction from the then reigning sovereign, and no devices, no expedients which could ever be attempted by subsequent assemblies (and they seldom met without attempting them) could succeed in getting the royal assent to a renewal of the duty. In the very first session held under the republican government, the assembly passed a law for the perpetual prohibition of the importation of slaves. This will, in some measure, stop the increase of this great political and moral evil, while the minds of our citizens may be ripening for a complete emancipation of human nature.—NOTES ON VIRGINIA. vii, 334. FORD ED., iii, 192. (1782.)

7960. ——— ———. I congratulate you on the law of your State [South Carolina] for suspending the importation of slaves, and for the glory you have justly acquired by endeavoring to prevent it forever.—To E. RUTLEDGE. ii, 180. FORD ED., iv, 410. (P., 1787.)

7961. SLAVES, Increase of.—Under the mild treatment our slaves experience, and their wholesome, though coarse food, this blot in our country increases as fast, or faster than the whites.—NOTES ON VIRGINIA. viii, 334. FORD ED., iii, 192. (1782.)

7962. SLAVES, Labor and.—An opinion is hazarded by some, but proved by none, that moral urgencies are not sufficient to induce [the negro] to labor; th t nothing can do this but physical coercion. But this is a problem which the present age alone is prepared to solve by experiment. It would be a solecism to suppose a race of animals created without sufficient foresight and energy to preserve their own existence. It is disproved, too, by the fact that they exist and have existed through all the ages of history. We are not sufficiently acquainted with all the nations of Africa to say that there may not be some in which habits of industry are established, and the arts practiced which are necessary to render life comfortable. The experiment now in progress in Santo Domingo, those of Sierra Leone and Cape Mesurado, are but beginning. Your proposition has its aspects of promise also; and should it not answer fully to calculations in figures, it may yet, in its developments, lead to happy results. —To MISS FANNY WRIGHT. vii, 408. FORD ED., x, 344. (M., 1825.)

7963. SLAVES, Manumission of.—As far as I can judge from the experiments which have been made to g've liberty to, or rather, to abandon persons whose habits have been formed in slavery is like abandoning children. —To DR. EDWARD BANCROFT. FORD ED., v, 66. (P., 1789.)

7964. SLAVES, Masters and.—The inculcation [in your book] on the master of the slave, in return for the benefits of his service, that is to say, of food, clothing, care in sickness, and maintenance under age and disability, so as to make him in fact as comfortable and more secure than the laboring man in most parts of the world, * * * gives great merit to the work, and will, I have no doubt, produce wholesome impressions.—To CLEMENT CAINE. vi, 13. FORD ED., ix, 329. (M., 1811.)

7965. SLAVES, Metayers and.—I am decided on my final return to America to try this experiment. I shall endeavor to import as many Germans as I have grown slaves. I will settle them and my slaves, on farms of fifty acres each, intermingled, and place all on the footing of the Metayers (Medietani) of Europe. Their children shall be brought up, as others are, in habits of property and foresight, and I have no doubt but that they will be good citizens. Some of their fathers will be so; others I suppose will need government. With these all that can be done is to oblige them to labor as the laboring poor of Europe do, and to apply to their comfortable subsistence the produce of their labor, retaining such a moderate portion of it as may be a just equivalent for the use of the lands they labor, and the stocks and other necessary advances.—To DR. EDWARD BANCROFT. FORD ED., v, 67. (P., 1789.)

7966. SLAVES, Property in.—Actual property has been lawfully vested in that form [negroes] and who can lawfully take it from the possessors?—To JARED SPARKS. vii, 333. FORD ED., x, 290. (M., 1824.)

7967. SLAVES, Protection of.—In the first or second session of the Legislature after I became a member, I drew to this subject the attention of Colonel Bland, one of the oldest, ablest, and most respected members, and he undertook to move for certain moderate extensions of the protection of the laws to these people. I seconded his motion and, as a younger member, was more spared in the debate; but he was denounced as an enemy of his country, and was treated with the grossest indecorum.—To EDWARD COLES. FORD ED., ix, 477. (M., 1814.)

7968. SLAVES, Recovery of fugitive.—We have received with great satisfaction notification of the orders of his Catholic Majesty, not to permit that persons, held in slavery within the United States, introduce themselves as free persons into the Province of Florida. * * * As a consequence of the same principles of justice and friendship, we trust that your Excellency will permit, and aid the recovery of persons of the same description, who have heretofore taken refuge within your government.—To GOVERNOR QUESADA. iii, 219. FORD ED., v, 296. (Pa., 1791.)

7969. ——— ———. The governor of East Florida informs me that he has received the King's orders, not to permit, under any pretext, that persons held in slavery in the United States introduce themselves as free, into the province of East Florida. I am happy that this grievance, which had been a subject of great complaint from the citizens of Georgia, s to be removed.—To Mr. Viar. iii, 195. (M., 1790.)

7970. SLAVES, San Domingo insurrection.—If something is not done, and soon done, we shall be the murderers of our own children. The *"murmura venturos nautis prudentia ventos"* has already reached us [from San Domingo]; the revolutionary storm, now sweeping the globe. will be upon us, and happy if we make timely provision to give it an easy passage over our land. From the present state of things in Europe and America, the day which begins our combustion must be near at hand; and only a single spark is wanting to make that day to-morrow. If we had begun sooner, we might probably have been allowed a lengthier operation to clear ourselves, but every day's delay lessens the time we may take for emancipation. Some people derive hope from the aid of the confederated States. But this is a delusion. There is but one State in the Union which will aid us sincerely. if an insurrection begins, and that one may. perhaps, have its own fire to quench at the same time.— To St. George Tucker. iv, 196. Ford ed., vii, 168. (M., 1797.)

7971. ———— ————. As to the mode of emancipation, I am satisfied that that must be a matter of compromise between the passions, the prejudices, and the real difficulties which will each have its weight in that operation. Perhaps the first chapter of th's history, which has begun in St. Domingo, and the next succeeding ones, will recount how all the whites were driven from all the other islands, may prepare our minds for a peaceable accommodation between justice, policy and necessity; and furnish an answer to the difficult question, whither shall the colored emigrants go? and the sooner we put some plan under way, the greater hope there is that 't may be permitted to proceed peaceably to its ultimate effect.—To St. George Tucker. iv, 196. Ford ed., vii, 167. (M., 1797.)

7972. SLAVES, Thievery and.—That disposition to theft with which they have been branded, must be ascribed to their situation, and not to any depravity of the moral sense. The man in whose favor no laws of property exist, probably feels himself less bound to respect those made in favor of others. When arguing for ourselves, we lay it down as a fundamental, that laws, to be just, must give a reciprocation of right; that, without this, they are mere arbitrary rules of conduct, founded in force, and not in conscience; and it is a problem which I give to the master to solve. whether the religious precepts against the violation of property were not framed for him as well as his slave? And whether the slave may not as justifiably take a little from one who has taken all from him, as he may slay one who would slay him? That a change in the relations in which a man is placed should change h's ideas of moral right or wrong, is neither new, nor peculiar to the color of the blacks. Homer tells us it was so two thousand six hundred years ago.—Notes on Virginia. viii, 385. Ford ed., iii, 249. (1782.)

7973. SLAVES (Emancipation), Bill for.—The bill to emancipate all slaves born after the passing of the act, reported by the revisers [of the Virginia Code] did not contain this proposition; but an amendment containing it was prepared, to be offered to the Legislature

whenever the bi'l should be taken up, and further directing that they should continue with their parents to a certain age, then to be brought up, at the public expense, to tillage, arts, or sciences, according to their geniuses, till the females should be eighteen, and the males twenty-one years of age, when they should be colonized to such place as the circumstances of the time should render most proper, sending them out with arms, implements of household and of the handicraft arts, seeds, pairs of the useful domestic animals, &c., to declare them a free and independent people. and extend to them our alliance and protection, till they have acqu'red strength; and to send vessels, at the same time. to other parts of the world for an equal number of white inhabitants; to induce them to migrate hither, proper encouragements were to be proposed.—Notes on Virginia. viii, 380. Ford ed., iii, 243. (1782.)

7974. ———— ————. The separation of infants from their mothers would produce some scruples of humanity. But this would be straining at a gnat, and swallowing a camel.— To Jared Sparks. vii, 335. Ford ed., x, 293. (M., 1824.)

7975. SLAVES (Emancipation), Blessings of.—Who could estimate its blessed effects? I leave this to those who will live to see their accomplishment, and to enjoy a beatitude forbidden to my age. But I leave it with this admonition,—to rise and be doing. A million and a half are within our control; but six m:llions (which a majority of those now living will see them attain), and one million of these fighting men, will say, " we will not go ".—To Jared Sparks. vi, 335. Ford ed., x, 292. (M., 1824.)

7976. SLAVES (Emancipation), Certain.—The hour of emancipation is advancing, in the march of time. It will come; and whether brought on by the generous energy of our own minds; or by the bloody process of St. Domingo, excited and conducted by the power of our present enemy [England], if once stationed permanently within our country, and offering asylum and arms to the oppressed, is a leaf of our history not yet turned over.—To Edward Coles. Ford ed., ix, 478. (M., 1814.)

7977. ———— ————. It was found that the public mind would not bear the proposition [gradual emanc'pation], nor will it bear it even at this day (1821). Yet the day is not distant, when it must bear and adopt it, or worse will follow. Noth:ng is more certainly written in the book of fate, than that these people are to be free; nor is it less certain, that the two races, equally free, cannot live in the same government. Nature, habit. opinion have drawn indelible lines of distinction between them. It is still in our power to direct the process of emancipation and deportat'on, peaceably, and in such slow degree, as that the evil will wear off insensibly, and their place be, *pari passu,* filled up by free white laborers. If, on the contrary, it is left to force itself on. human nature must shudder at the prospect held up. We should in vain look for an example in the Spanish deportation, or deletion of the Moors. This precedent would fall far short of our case. —Jefferson MSS. Rayner, 164.

7978. SLAVES (Emancipation), Defeated.—In 1769, I became a member of the leg'slature by the choice of the county in which I live [Albemarle], and so continued until it was closed by the Revolution. I made one effort in that body for the permission of the emancipation of slaves, which was rejected: and indeed, during the regal government, nothing liberal could expect success. Our minds were circumscribed within narrow limits, by an habitual belief that it was our duty to be subordinate to the mother country in all matters of government, to direct all our labors in subservience to her interests, and even to observe a bigoted intolerance for all religions but hers. The difficulties w th our representatives were of habit and despair, not of reflection and conviction. Experience soon proved that they could bring their m nds to rights on the first summons of their attention. But the King's Council. which acted as another house of legislature, held the r places at will, and were in most humble obedience to that will; the Governor, too, who had a negative on our laws, held by the same tenure, and with still greater devotedness to it; and, last of all, the royal negative closed the last door to every hope of amel oration.*—AUTOBIOGRAPHY. i, 3. FORD ED., i, 5. (1821.)

7979. SLAVES (Emancipation), Gradual.—I concur entirely in your leading principles of gradual emancipation, of establishment on the coast of Africa, and the patronage of our nation until the emigrants shall be able to protect themselves.—To DR. THOMAS HUMPHREYS. vii, 57. FORD ED., x, 76. (M., 1817.)

7980. SLAVES (Emancipation), Methods of.—As to the method by which this difficult work is to be effected, if permitted to be done by ourselves. I have seen no proposition so expedient on the whole, as that of emancipation of those born after a given day, and of their education and expatriation after a given age.—To EDWARD COLES. FORD ED., ix, 478. (M., 1814.)

7981. SLAVES (Emancipation), Prayers for.—It shall have all my prayers, and these are the only weapons of an old man.—To EDWARD COLES. FORD ED., ix, 479. (M., 1814.)

7982. SLAVES (Emancipation), Preparations for.—Unhappily it is a case for which both parties require long and difficult preparation. The mind of the master is to be apprized by reflection, and strengthened by the energies of conscience, against the obstacles of self interest to an acquiescence in the rights of others; that of the slave is to be prepared by instruction and habit for self-government, and for the honest pursuits of industry and social duty. Both of these courses of preparation require time, and the former must precede the latter. Some progress is sensibly made in it; yet not so much as I had hoped and expected. But it will yield in time to temperate and steady pursuit, to the enlargement of the human mind, and its advancement in science. We are not in a world ungoverned by the laws and the power of a Superior Agent. Our efforts are in His hand, and directed by it; and He will give them their effect in his own time. Where the disease is most deeply seated, there it will be slowest in eradication. In the Northern States it was merely superficial, and easily corrected. In the Southern it is incorporated with the whole system, and requires time, patience and perseverance in the curative process. That it may finally be effected, and its process hastened, will be my last and fondest prayer.—To DAVID BARROW. vi, 456. FORD ED., ix, 515. (M., May 1815.)

* This was Jefferson's first public measure.—EDITOR.

7983. SLAVES (Emancipation), Principle and.—From those of the former generation who were in the fulness of age when I came into public life, which was while our controversy with England was on paper only, I soon saw that nothing was to be hoped. Nursed and educated in the daily habit of seeing the degraded condition, both bodily and mental, of those unfortunate beings, not reflecting that that degradation was very much the work of themselves and their fathers, few minds have yet doubted but that they were as legitimate subjects of property as their horses and cattle. The quiet and monotonous course of colonial life had been disturbed by no alarm, and little reflection on the value of liberty. And when alarm was taken at an enterprise on their own, it was not easy to carry them to the whole length of the principles which they invoked for themselves.—To EDWARD COLES. FORD ED., ix, 477. (M., 1814.)

7984. SLAVES (Emancipation), Propaganda for.—I hope you will reconcile yourself to your country and its unfortunate condition; that you will not lessen its stock of sound disposition by withdrawing your portion from the mass; that, on the contrary, you will come forward in the public councils, become the missionary of this doctrine truly Christian, insinuate and inculcate it softly but steadily, through the medium of writing and conversation; associate others in your labors, and when the phalanx is formed, bring on and press the proposition perseveringly until its accomplishment. —To EDWARD COLES. FORD ED., ix, 479. (M., 1814.)

7985. SLAVES (Emancipation), Providence and.—We must await with patience the workings of an overruling Providence, and hope that that is preparing the deliverance of these, our suffering brethren. When the measure of their tears shall be full, when their groans shall have involved heaven itself in darkness, doubtless a God of justice will awaken to their distress, and by diffusing light and liberality among their oppressors, or, at length, by His exterminating thunder, manifest His attention to the things of this world, and that they are not left to the guidance of a blind fatality.—To M. DE MEUNIER. ix, 279. FORD ED., iv, 185. (P., 1786.)

7986. SLAVES (Emancipation), Time and.—I have not perceived the growth of this disposition [to emancipate the slaves and settle them elsewhere] in the rising generation, of which I once had sanguine hopes. No symptoms inform me that it will take place in my day. I leave it, therefore, to time, and not at all without hope that the day w ll come, equally desirable and welcome to us as to them. Perhaps the proposition now on the carpet at Washington to provide an establishment on the coast of Africa for voluntary emigrations of people of color may be the corner stone of this future edifice.—To THOMAS HUMPHREYS. vii, 58. FORD ED., x, 77. (M., 1817.)

7987. ——— ———. At the age of eighty-two, with one foot in the grave and the other uplifted to follow it, I do not permit myself to take part in any new enterprises, even for bettering the condition of man, not even in the great one which is the subject of your letter, and which has been through life that of my greatest anxieties. The march of events has not been such as to render its completion practicable within the limits of time allotted to me; and I leave its accomplishment as the work

of another generation.—To Miss Fanny
Wright. vii, 408. Ford ed., x, 344. (M.,
1825.)

7988. SLAVES (Emancipation), Total.
—It is impossible to be temperate and to
pursue this subject through the various considerations of policy, of morals, of history, natural
and civ'l. We must be contented to hope they
will force their way into every one's mind.
* * * The way, I hope, is preparing, under
the auspices of heaven, for a total emancipa-
t'on, and that this is disposed, in the order of
events, to be with the consent of the masters,
rather than by their extirpation.—Notes on
Virginia. vii·, 404. Ford ed., iii, 267.
(1782.)

**7989. SLAVES (Emancipation), United
States purchase of.**—The bare proposition
of purchase [of the slaves] by the United
States generally would excite infinite indignation in all the States north of Maryland. The
sacrifice must fall on the States alone which
hold them; and the difficult question will be
how to lessen this so as to reconcile our fellow
citizens to it. Personally, I am ready and desirous to make any sacrifice which shall ensure
their gradual but complete retirement from the
State, and effectually, at the same time, establish them elsewhere in freedom and safety.—To
Dr. Thomas Humphreys. vii, 58. Ford ed.,
x, 76. (M., 1817.)

**7990. SLAVES (Emancipation), West
Indies and.**—I become daily more convinced
that all the West India Islands will remain in
the hands of the people of color, and a total
expulsion of the wh'tes sooner or later take
place. It is high time we should foresee the
bloody scenes which our children certainly, and
possibly ourselves (south of the Potomac), have
to wade through and try to avert them.—To
James Monroe. iv, 20. Ford ed., vi, 349.
(Pa., July 1793.)

7991. ———— ————. On the subject of emancipation I have ceased to think because not to
be a work of my day. The plan of converting
the blacks into serfs would certainly be better
than keeping them in their present pos'tion, but
I consider that of expatriation to the governments of the West Indies of their own color as
entirely practicable, and greatly preferable to
the mixture of color here. To this I have great
aversion.—To William Short. Ford ed., x,
362. (M., 1826.) See Colonization.

7992. SLEEP, Habits of.—I am not so
regular in my sleep as the doctor [Dr. Rush]
says he was, devoting to it from five to eight
hours, according as my company or the book I
am reading interests me; and I never go to bed
without an hour, or half hour's, previous reading of something moral whereon to ruminate in
the intervals of sleep. But whether I retire to
bed early or late I am up with the sun.—To
Doctor Vine Utley. vii, 117. Ford ed., x, 126.
(M., 1819.)

**7993. SMALL (William), Guide and
friend.**—Dr. Small was * * * to me as a
father. To his enlightened and affectionate
guidance of my studies while at college, I am
indebted for everything. He was Professor of
Mathematics at William and Mary, and, for
some time, was in the philosophical chair. · He
first introduced into both schools rational and
elevated courses of study, and, from an extraordinary conjunction of eloquence and logic,
was enabled to communicate them to the students with great effect. He procured for me

the patronage of Mr. Wythe, and both of them,
the attentions of Governor Fauquier, the ablest
man who ever filled the chair of government
here. They were inseparable friends, and at
their frequent dinners with the Governor
(after his family had returned to England), he
admitted me always, to make it a *partie
quarree*. At these dinners I have heard more
good sense, more rational and philosophical
conversation, than in a'l my life besides. They
were truly Attic societ'es. The Governor was
musical, also, and a good performer, and associated me with two or three other amateurs in
his weekly concerts. He merits honorable
mention in your history if any proper occasion
offers.—To Mr. Girardin. vi, 411. (M.,
1815.)

**7994. SMALL (William), Jefferson's
early companion.**—It was my great good
fortune, and what probably fixed the destinies
of my life, that Dr. William Small of Scotland,
was then (1760) professor of mathematics [in
William and Mary College], a man profound in
most of the useful branches of science, with a
happy ta'ent of communication, correct and
gentlemanly manners, and an enlarged and liberal mind. He, most happily for me, became
soon attached to me, and made me his daily companion when not engaged in the school; and
from his conversation, I got my first views of
the expansion of science, and of the system of
things in which we are placed.—Autobiography. i, 2. Ford ed., i, 4. (1821.)

—— SMITH (Adam).—See Government,
Works on.

**7995. SMITH (John), Services to Vir-
ginia.**—Captain Smith, who next to Sir Walter Rale'gh may be considered as the founder of
our Colony, has written its history. He was
a member of the council, and afterwards president of the Colony; and to his efforts principally may be ascribed its support against the
opposition of the natives. He was honest, sensible, and well informed; but his style is barbarous and uncouth. His history, however, is
a'most the only source from which we derive
any knowledge of the infancy of our State.—
Notes on Virginia. vii·, 415. Ford ed., iii,
281. (1782.)

7996. SMITH (Robert), Estimate of.—I
have seen with very great concern the late address of Mr. [Robert] Smith to the public.
He has been very ill-advised, both personally
and publicly. As far as I can judge from what
I hear, the impression made is entirely unfavorable to him.—To President Madison.
v, 600. Ford ed., ix, 325. (M., 1811.)

**7997. SMITH (Samuel), Tender of
office.**—If you can be added to the Administration I am forming it will constitute a magistracy entirely possessed of the public confidence.
* * * You will bring us the benefit of adding in a considerable degree the acqu'escence,
at least, of the leaders who have hitherto opposed. Your geographical situation [Mary-
land], too, is peculiarly advantageous, and will
favor the policy of drawing our naval resources
towards the States from which their benefits
and production may be extended equally to all
parts. * * * If you refuse, I must abandon
from necessity, what I have been so falsely
charged with doing from cho'ce, the expectation
of procuring to our country such benefits as
may compensate the expenses of their navy.—
To General Samuel Smith. Ford ed., viii,
13. (W., March 1801.)

7998. SMITH (William S.), Character of.—I learn that Mr. Adams desires to be recalled, and that Smith should be appo nted Chargé des Affaires there. * * * You can judge of Smith's abilities by his letters. They are not of the first order, but they are good. For his honesty, he is like our friend Monroe; turn his soul wrong side outwards, and there is not a speck on it. He has one foible, an excessive inflammability of temper, but he feels it when it comes on, and has resolution enough to suppress it, and to remain silent till it passes over.—To JAMES MADISON. ii, 110. FORD ED., iv, 368. (P., 1787.)

7999. SMUGGLING, Temptations to.—Contraband does not increase on lessening the temptations to it.—To COUNT DE VERGENNES. i, 389. (P., 1785.)

8000. SNAKES, Antipathy to.—There 's in man as well as in brutes an antipathy to the snake, which makes it a disgusting object wherever it is presented.—To GOVERNOR HENRY LEE. FORD ED., vi, 320. (Pa., 1793.)

8001. SOCIAL INTERCOURSE, Contentment and.—Without society, and a society to our taste, men are never contented.—To JAMES MONROE. ii, 71. (P., 1786.) See SOCIETY.

8002. SOCIAL INTERCOURSE, Harmony and.—If we can once more get social intercourse restored to its pristine harmony, I shall believe we have not lived in vain.—To THOMAS LOMAX. iv, 361. FORD ED., vii, 500. (W., Feb. 1801.)

8003. SOCIAL INTERCOURSE, Opinions and.—Opinions, which are equally honest on both sides, should not affect personal esteem or social intercourse.—To JOHN ADAMS. vi, 146. (M., 1813.)

8004. SOCIAL INTERCOURSE, Politics and.—A difference in politics should never be permitted to enter into social intercourse, or to disturb its friendships, its charities or justice.—To H. LEE. vii, 376. FORD ED., x, 317. (M., 1824.)

8005. SOCIETIES (Communal), Experiments.—A society of seventy families, the number you name, may very possibly be governed as a single family, subsisting on their common industry, and holding all things in common. Some regulators of the family you still must have, and it remains to be seen at what period of your increasing population your simple regulations will cease to be sufficient to preserve order, peace, and justice. The experiment is interesting: I shall not live to see its issue, but I wish it success equal to your hopes.—To WILLIAM LUDLOW. vii, 378. (M., 1824.)

8006. SOCIETIES (Communal), Practicability.—That, on the principle of a communion of property, small societies may exist in habits of virtue, order, industry, and peace, and consequently in a state of as much happiness as heaven has been pleased to deal out to imperfect humanity, I can readily conceive, and, indeed, have seen its proofs in various small societies which have been constituted on that principle. But I do not feel authorized to conclude from these that an extended society like that of the United States, or of an individual State, could be governed happily on the same principle. I look to the diffusion of light and education as the resource most to be

relied on for ameliorating the condition, promoting the v rtue, and advancing the happiness of man.—To C. C. BLATCHLY. vii, 263. (M., 1822.)

— SOCIETIES (Democratic).—See DEMOCRATIC SOCIETIES.

8007. SOCIETIES (Scientific), Peaceful.—These [scientific] societies are always in peace, however their nations may be at war. Like the republic of letters, they form a great fraternity spreading over the whole earth, and their correspondence is never interrupted by any civilized nation.—To JOHN HOLLINS. v, 428. (W., 1809.)

8008. SOCIETIES (Secret), Dangerous.—I acknowledge the right of voluntary associations for laudable purposes and in moderate numbers. I acknowledge, too, the expediency, for revolutionary purposes, of general associations, coextensive with the nation. But where, as in our case, no abuses call for revolution, voluntary associations so extensive as to grapple with and control the government, should such be or become their purpose, are dangerous machines, and should be frowned down in every well regulated government.—To JAMES MADISON. FORD ED., x, 207. (M., 1822.)

8009. SOCIETIES (Secret), Government and.—As revolutionary instruments (when nothing but revolution will cure the evils of the State) they [secret societies] are necessary and indispensable, and the right to use them is inalienable by the people; but to admit them as ordinary and habitual instruments as a part of the machinery of the Constitution, would be to change that machinery by introducing moving powers foreign to it, and to an extent depending solely on local views. and, therefore, incalculable. *—To WILLIAM DUANE. FORD ED., viii, 256. (M., 1803.) See DEMOCRATIC SOCIETIES.

8010. SOCIETY, American.—In America * * * the society of your husband, the fond cares of the children, the arrangements of the house, the improvements of the grounds, fill every moment with a healthy and an useful activity. Every exertion is encouraging, because, to present amusement, it joins the promise of some future good. The intervals of leisure are filled by the society of real friends, whose affections are not th nned to cob-web by being spread over a thousand objects. This is the picture, in the light it 's presented to my mind.—To MRS. BINGHAM. ii, 117. (P., 1787.)

8011. SOCIETY, Jefferson's choice.—I have changed my circle here [Philadelphia] according to my wish, abandoning the rich and declining their dinners and parties, and associating entirely with the class of science, of whom there is a valuable society here.—To MARTHA JEFFERSON RANDOLPH. D. L. J. 262. (Pa., 1800.)

8012. SOCIETY, Majority rule.—The fundamental law of every society [is] the *lex majoris partis*, to which we are bound to submit.—To DAVID HUMPHREYS. iii, 13. FORD ED., v, 90. (P., 1789.)

8013. SOCIETY, Necessity for.—I am convinced our own happiness requires that we should continue to m x with the world, and to keep pace with it as it goes; and that every

* A political committee of Philadelphia had sent a communication to Jefferson on the subject of removals from office.—EDITOR.

person who retires from free communication with it is severely punished afterwards by the state of mind into which he gets, and which can only be prevented by feeding our sociable principles. I can speak from experience on this subject. From 1793 to 1797, I remained closely at home, saw none but those who came there, and at length became very sensible of the ill effect it had on my own mind, and of its direct and irresistible tendency to render me unfit for society and uneasy when necessarily engaged in it. I felt enough of the effect of withdrawing from the world then to see that it led to an anti-social and misanthropic state of mind, which severely punishes him who gives into it; and it will be a lesson I never shall forget as to myself.—To MARY JEFFERSON EPPES, D. L. J. 284. (W., March 1802.) See SOCIAL INTERCOURSE.

8014. SOCIETY, Parisian.—To what does the bustle of Paris tend? At eleven o'clock, it is day, *chez madame*. The curtains are drawn. Propped on bolsters and pillows, and her head scratched into a little order, the bulletins of the sick are read, and the billets of the well. She writes to some of her acquaintance, and receives the visits of others. If the morning is not very thronged, she is able to get out and hobble round the cage of the Palais Royal; but she must hobble quickly, for the *coiffeur's* turn is come; and a tremendous turn it is! Happy, if he does not make her arrive when dinner is half over! The torpitude of digestion a little passed, she flutters half an hour through the streets, by way of paying visits, and then to the spectacles. These finished, another half hour is devoted to dodging in and out of the doors of her very sincere friends, and away to supper. After supper, cards; and after cards, bed; to rise at noon the next day, and to tread, like a mill horse, the same trodden circle over again. Thus the days of life are consumed, one by one, without an object beyond the present moment; ever flying from the ennui of that, yet carrying it with us; eternally in pursuit of happiness, which keeps eternally before us. If death or bankruptcy happen to trip us out of the circle, it is matter for the buzz of the evening, and is completely forgotten by the next morning.—To MRS. BINGHAM. ii, 116. (P., 1787.)

— SOCIETY OF THE CINCINNATI.— See CINCINNATI SOCIETY.

8015. SOCRATES, Dæmon of.—An expression in your letter * * * that "the human understanding is a revelation from its Maker", gives the best solution that I believe can be given of the question, "what did Socrates mean by his Dæmon"? He was too wise to believe, and too honest to pretend that he had real and familiar converse with a superior and invisible being. He probably considered the suggestions of his conscience, or reason, as revelations, or inspirations from the Supreme Mind, bestowed, on important occasions, by a special superintending Providence.—To JOHN ADAMS. vi, 220. (M., 1813.)

8016. SOCRATES, Plato and.—The superlative wisdom of Socrates is testified by all antiquity, and placed on ground not to be questioned. When, therefore, Plato puts into his mouth such paralogisms, such quibbles on words, and sophisms as a schoolboy would be ashamed of, we conclude they were the whimsies of Plato's own foggy brain, and acquit Socrates of puerilities so unlike his character.—To WILLIAM SHORT. vii, 165. (M., 1820.) See PHILOSOPHY.

8017. SOLITUDE, Philosophy and.—Let the gloomy monk, sequestered from the world, seek unsocial pleasures in the bottom of his cell! Let the sublimated philosopher grasp visionary happiness, while pursuing phantoms dressed in the garb of truth! Their supreme wisdom is supreme folly; and they mistake for happiness the mere absence of pain. Had they ever felt the solid pleasure of one generous spasm of the heart, they would exchange for it all the frigid speculations of their lives.—To MRS. COSWAY. ii, 39. FORD ED., iv. 319. (P., 1786.)

8018. SOULS, Transmigration of.—It is not for me to pronounce on the hypothesis you present of a transmigration of souls from one body to another in certain cases. The laws of nature have withheld from us the means of physical knowledge of the country of spirits, and revelation has, for reasons unknown to us, chosen to leave us in the dark as we were. When I was young I was fond of the speculations which seemed to promise some insight into that hidden country, but observing at length that they left me in the same ignorance in which they had found me, I have for very many years ceased to read or to think concerning them, and have reposed my head on that pillow of ignorance which a benevolent Creator has made so soft for us, knowing how much we should be forced to use it. I have thought it better, by nourishing the good passions and controlling the bad, to merit an inheritance in a state of being of which I can know so little, and to trust for the future to Him who has been so good for the past.—To REV. ISAAC STORY. iv, 422. FORD ED., viii, 107. (W., 1801.) See IMMORTALITY.

8019. SOUTH AMERICA, Revolt in.—I enter into all your doubts as to the event of the revolution of South America. They will succeed against Spain. But the dangerous enemy is within their own breasts. Ignorance and superstition will chain their minds and bodies under religious and military despotism. I do believe it would be better for them to obtain freedom by degrees only: because that would by degrees bring on light and information, and qualify them to take charge of themselves understandingly; with more certainty, if in the meantime, under so much control as may keep them at peace with one another. Surely, it is our duty to wish them independence and self-government, because they wish it themselves, and they have the right, and we none, to choose for themselves; and I wish, moreover, that our ideas may be erroneous and theirs prove well-founded. But these are speculations which we may as well deliver over to those who are to see their development.—To JOHN ADAMS. vii, 104. FORD ED., x, 108. (M., 1818.) See SPANISH AMERICA.

8020. SOUTH CAROLINA, Fidelity.—The steady union of our fellow citizens of South Carolina is entirely in their character. They have never failed in fidelity to their country and the republican spirit of its Constitution.—To MR. LETUE. v, 384. (W., 1808.)

8021. SOUTH CAROLINA, Free government and.—I see with pleasure another proof that South Carolina is ever true to the principles of free government.—To HENRY MIDDLETON. vi, 91. (M., Jan. 1813.)

8022. SOVEREIGNTY, Infringement.—The granting military commissions within the United States by any other authority than their own, is an infringement on their sovereignty, and particularly so when granted to their own citizens to lead them to acts contrary to the duties they owe their own country.—To EDMOND CHARLES GENET. iii, 572. FORD ED., vi, 283. (Pa., June 1793.)

8023. ———— ————. Mr. Hammond says the issuing the commission [to the Citoyen Genet] by M. Genet, within our territory, was an infringement of our sovereignty; therefore, the proceeds of it should be given up to Great Britain. The infringement was a matter between France and us. Had we insisted on any penalty or forfeiture by way of satisfaction to our insulted rights. it would have belonged to us, not to a third party. As between Great Britain and us, * * * we deemed we did enough to satisfy her.— To THOMAS PINCKNEY. iii. 583. FORD ED., vi, 302. (Pa., June 1793.)

8024. SOVEREIGNTY, Justice and.— The administration of justice is a branch of the sovereignty over a country, and belongs exclusively to the nation inhabiting it. No foreign power can pretend to participate in their jurisdiction, or that their citizens received there are not subject to it.—To GEORGE HAMMOND. iii, 415. FORD ED., vi, 56. (Pa., 1792.)

8025. SOVEREIGNTY, Partition of.—I see with great pleasure every testimony to the principles of pure republicanism; and every effort to preserve untouched that partition of the sovereignty which our excellent Constitution has made between the general and particular governments.—To JAMES SULLIVAN. FORD ED., v, 369. (Pa., 1791.)

8026. SPAIN, Bonaparte and.—I suppose Napoleon will get possession of Spain; but her colonies will deliver themselves to any member of the Bourbon family. Perhaps Mexico will choose its sovereign within itself. He will find them much more difficult to subdue than Austria or Prussia; because an enemy (even in peace an enemy) possesses the element over which he is to pass to get at them: and a more powerful enemy (climate) will soon mow down his armies after arrival. This will be, without any doubt, the most difficult enterprise the Emperor has ever undertaken. He may subdue the small colonies; he never can the old and strong; and the former will break off from him the first war he has again with a naval power.—To GENERAL ARMSTRONG. v. 434. (W., March 1809.)

8027. SPAIN, Common interests.—It may happen * * * that the interests of Spain and America may call for a concert of proceedings against that State (Algiers). * * * May not the affairs of the Mosquito coast, and our western posts, produce another instance of a common interest? Indeed, I meet this correspondence of interest in so many quarters, that I look with anxiety to the issue of Mr. Gardoqui's mission, hoping it will be a removal of the only difficulty at present subsisting between the two nations, or which is likely to arise.—To WILLIAM CARMICHAEL. i, 393. (P., 1785.)

8028. SPAIN, Conciliation of.—We consider Spain's possession of the adjacent country as most favorable to our interests, and should see with extreme pain any other nation substituted for them. In all communications, therefore, with their officers, conciliation and mutual accommodation are to be mainly attended to. Everything irritating to be avoided, everything friendly to be done for them.—To WILLIAM C. CLAIBORNE. FORD ED., viii, 71. (W., July 1801.)

8029. SPAIN, English alliance against. —I think you have misconceived the nature of the treaty I thought we should propose to England. I have no idea of committing ourselves immediately or independently of our further will to the war. The treaty should be provisional only, to come into force on the event of our being engaged in war with either France or Spain during the present war in Europe. In that event we should make common cause, and England should stipulate not to make peace without our obtaining the objects for which we go to war, to wit, the acknowledgment by Spain of the rightful boundaries of Louisiana (which we should reduce to our minimum by a second article) and 2, indemnification for spoliations, for which purpose we should be allowed to make reprisal on the Floridas and retain them as an indemnification. Our cooperation in the war (if we should really enter into it) would be sufficient consideration for Great Britain to engage for its object; and it being generally known to France and Spain that we had entered into treaty with England, would probably ensure us a peaceable and immediate settlement of both points. But another motive much more powerful would indubitably induce England to go much further. Whatever ill-humor may at times have been expressed against us by individuals of that country, the first wish of every Englishman's heart is to see us once more fighting by their sides against France; nor could the King or his ministers do an act so popular as to enter into an alliance with us. The nation would not weigh the consideration by grains and scruples. They would consider it as the price and pledge of an indissoluble friendship. I think it possible that for such a provisional treaty they would give us their general guarantee of Louisiana and the Floridas. At any rate we might try them. A failure would not make our situation worse. If such a one could be obtained, we might await our convenience for calling up the casus fœderis. I think it important that England should receive an overture as early as possible. as it might prevent her listening to terms of peace. If I recollect rightly. we had instructed Monroe, when he went to Paris, to settle the deposit; if he failed in that object to propose a treaty to England immediately. We could not be more engaged to secure the deposit than we are the country now, after paying fifteen millions for it. I do expect, therefore, that. considering the present state of things as analagous to that, and virtually within his instructions, he will very likely make the proposition to England.—To JAMES MADISON. iv, 585. FORD ED., viii, 377. (M., Aug. 1805.)

8030. ———— ————. A letter from Charles Pinckney of May 22 [1805], informs me that Spain refuses to settle a limit, and perseveres in withholding the ratification of the convention. He says not a word of the status quo, from which I conclude it has not been proposed. * * * I think the status quo, if not already proposed, should be immediately offered through Bowdoin. Should it even be refused, the refusal to settle a limit is not of itself a sufficient cause of war, nor is the withholding a ratification worthy of such a redress. Yet these acts show a purpose both in Spain and France which we ought to provide before the conclusion of a peace. I think, therefore, we should take into consideration whether we ought not immediately to propose to England an eventual treaty of alliance, to come into force whenever (within — years) a war shall take place with Spain or France. It may be proper for the ensuing Congress to make some preparations for such an event, and it should be in our power to show we have done the same.—To JAMES MADISON. FORD ED., viii, 374. (M., Aug. 1805.)

8031. —— ——. On a view of our affairs with Spain, * * * I wrote you * * * that I thought we should offer them the *status quo*, but immediately propose provisional alliance with England. I have not yet received the whole correspondence. But the portion of the papers now enclosed to you, confirm me in the expediency of a treaty with England, but make the offer of the *status quo* more doubtful. * * * From the papers already received I infer a confident reliance on the part of Spain on the omnipotence of Bonaparte, but a desire of procrastination till peace in Europe shall leave us without an ally.—To JAMES MADISON. iv, 583. FORD ED., viii, 375. (M., Aug. 1805.)

8032. SPAIN, Friendship with.—Under an intimate conviction of long standing in my mind, of the importance of an honest friendship with Spain, and one which shall identify her American interests with our own, I see in a strong point of view the necessity that the organ of communication which we establish near the King should possess the favor and confidence of that government. I have, therefore, destined for that mission a person whose accommodating and reasonable conduct, which will be still more fortified by instructions, will render him agreeable there, and an useful channel of communication between us. I have no doubt the new appointment by that government to this, in the room of the Chevalier d'Yrujo, has been made under the influence of the same motives.—To DON JOSEPH YZNARDI. iv, 385. FORD ED., viii, 33. (W., March 1801.)

8033. —— ——. The Chevalier d'Yrujo being intimately known to us, the integrity, sincerity, and reasonableness of his conduct having established in us a perfect confidence, in nowise diminished by the bickerings which took place between him and a former Secretary of State [Pickering], whose irritable temper drew on more than one affair of the same kind, it will be a subject of great regret if we lose him. However, if the interests of Spain require that his services should be employed elsewhere, it is the duty of a friend to acquiesce; and we shall certainly receive any successor the King may choose to send, with every possible degree of favor and friendship.—To DON JOSEPH YZNARDI. iv, 385. FORD ED., viii, 33. (W., March 1801.)

8034. SPAIN, Good faith towards.—No better proof of the good faith of the United States could have been given, than the vigor with which we have acted, and the expense incurred, in suppressing the enterprise meditated lately by Burr against Mexico. Although at first he proposed a separation of the Western country, and on that ground received encouragement and aid from Yrujo, according to the usual spirit of his government towards us, yet he very early saw that the fidelity of the Western country was not to be shaken, and turned himself wholly towards Mexico. And so popular is an enterprise on that country in this, that we had only to be still, and he would

have had followers enough to have been in the city of Mexico in six weeks.—To JAMES BOWDOIN. v, 64. FORD ED., ix, 41. (W., April 1807.)

8035. SPAIN, Good offices of.—I see with extreme satisfaction and gratitude the friendly interposition of the court of Spain with the Emperor of Morocco on the subject of the brig Betsey, and I am persuaded it will produce the happiest effects in America. Those, who are intrusted with the public affairs there, are sufficiently sensible how essential it is for our interest to cultivate peace with Spain, and they will be pleased to see a corresponding disposition in that court. The late good office of emancipating a number of our countrymen from slavery is peculiarly calculated to produce a sensation among our people, and to dispose them to relish and adopt the pacific and friendly views of their leaders towards Spain.—To W. CARMICHAEL. i. 392. (P., 1785.)

8036. SPAIN, Government of.—If anything thrasonic and foolish from Spain could add to my contempt of that government, it would be the demand of satisfaction now made by Foronda. However, respect to ourselves requires that the answer should be decent, and I think it fortunate that this opportunity is given to make a strong declaration of facts, to wit, how far our knowledge of Miranda's objects went, what measures we took to prevent anything further, the negligence of the Spanish agents to give us earlier notice, the measures we took for punishing those guilty, and our quiet abandonment of those taken by the Spaniards.—To JAMES MADISON. v, 164. FORD ED., ix. 124. (M., Aug. 1807.) See MIRANDA EXPEDITION.

8037. SPAIN, Honest, but unwise.—Spain is honest if it is not wise.—To JOHN ADAMS. FORD ED., iv, 295. (P., 1786.)

8038. SPAIN, Hostility of.—Our relations with Spain are vitally interesting. That they should be of a peaceable and friendly character has been our most earnest desire. Had Spain met us with the same dispositions, our idea was that her existence in this hemisphere and ours should have rested on the same bottom; should have swam or sunk together. We want nothing of hers, and we want no other nation to possess what is hers. But she has met our advances with jealousy, secret malice and ill-faith. Our patience under this unworthy return of disposition is now on its last trial. And the issue of what is now depending between us will decide whether our relations with her are to be sincerely friendly, or permanently hostile. I still wish and would cherish the former, but have ceased to expect it.—To JAMES BOWDOIN. FORD ED., viii, 351. (W., April 1805.)

8039. SPAIN, Incitement of Indians.—With respect to the treaties, the speech and the letter, you will see that they undertake to espouse the concerns of Indians within our limits; to be mediators of boundary between them and us; to guarantee that boundary to them; to support them with their whole power; and hazard to us intimations of acquiescence to avoid disagreeable results. They even propose to extend their intermedddlings to the northern Indians. These are pretensions so totally inconsistent with the usages established among the white nations, with respect to Indians living within their several limits, that it is believed no example of them can be produced, in times of peace; and they are presented to us in

a manner wh'ch we cannot deem friendly.—
To CARMICHAEL AND SHORT. iii, 366. FORD ED.,
vi, 272. (Pa., May 1793.)

8040. —— ——. The papers communicated you [in October and November, 1792]
made it evident that the Baron de Carondelet,
the Governor of New Orleans, had industriously excited the southern Indians to war
against us, and furnished them with arms and
ammunition in abundance, for that express purpose. We placed this under the view of the
commissioners of Spain here, who undertook to
communicate it to their court, and also to write
on the subject to the Baron de Carondelet.
They have lately made us communications from
both these quarters; the aspect of which, however, is by no means such as to remove the
causes of our dissatisfaction. I send you these
communications, consisting of treaties between
Spain, the Creeks, Choctaws, Chickasaws, and
Cherokees, handed us by express order from
their court, a speech of Baron de Carondelet
to the Cherokees, and a letter from Messrs. de
Viar and Jaudenes, covering that speech, and
containing in itself very serious matter. I will
first observe to you, that the question stated
in that letter, to have been proposed to the
Cherokees, what part they would take, in the
event of a war between the United States and
Spain? was never proposed by authority from
this government. Its instructions to its agents
have, on the contrary, been explicitly to cultivate, with good faith, the peace between Spain
and the Indians; and from the known prudence
and good conduct of Governor Blount, to whom
it is imputed, it is not believed to have been
proposed by him. This proposition, then, you
are authorized to disavow to the court of
Madrid, in the most unequivocal terms.—To
CARMICHAEL AND SHORT. iii, 566. FORD ED.,
vi, 271. (Pa., May 1793.)

8041. —— ——. The consequence is that
the Indians, and particularly the Creeks, finding themselves so encouraged, have passed,
without the least provocation on our part, from
a state of peace, which appeared to be well settled, to that of serious hostility. Their murders and depredations, which, for some months
we were willing to hope were only individual
aggressions, now assume the appearance of unequivocal war. Yet, such is our desire of
courting and cultivating the peace of all our
Indian neighbors, that instead of marching at
once into their country, and taking satisfaction
ourselves, we are peaceably requiring punishment of the individual aggressors; and, in the
meantime, are holding ourselves entirely on
the defensive. But this state of things cannot
continue. Our citizens are entitled to effectual
protection, and defensive measures are, at the
same time, the most expensive and least effectual. If we find, then, that peace cannot be obtained by the temperate means we are still pursuing, we must proceed to those which are extreme, and meet all the consequences, of whatever nature, or from whatever quarter they may
be.—To CARMICHAEL AND SHORT. iii, 567.
FORD ED., vi, 272. (Pa., May 1793.)

8042. —— ——. We have certainly been
always desirous to avoid whatever might disturb our harmony w'th Spa'n. We should be
st'll more so, at a moment when we see that
nation making part of so powerful a confederacy as is formed in Europe, and under particular
good understanding with England, our other
neighbor. In so delicate a position, therefore,
instead of expressing our sense of these things,
by way of answer to Messrs. Viar and Jaudenes, the President has thought it better that

it should be done to you, and to trust to your
discretion the moment, the measure, and the
form of communicating it to the Court of Madrid. The actual state of Europe at the time
you will receive this, the solidity of the confederacy, and especially, as between Spain and
England, the temper and views of the former,
or of both, towards us, the state of your negotiation, are circumstances which will enable you
better to decide how far it may be necessary to
soften, or even, perhaps, to suppress, the expressions of our sentiments on this subject.
To your discretion, therefore, it is committed
by the President, to let the Court of Spain see
how impossible it is for us to submit with folded
arms, to be butchered by these savages, and to
prepare them to view, with a just eye, the more
vigorous measures we must pursue to put an
end to their atrocities, if the moderate ones we
are now taking, should fail of that effect.—To
CARMICHAEL AND SHORT. iii, 567. FORD ED.,
vi, 272. (Pa., May 1793.)

8043. SPAIN, Invasion of.—The invasion of Spain has been the most unprecedented
and unprincipled of the transactions of modern
times. The crimes of its enemies, the licentiousness of its associates in defence, the exertions and sufferings of its inhabitants under
slaughter and famine, and its consequent de-
population, will mark indelibly the baneful ascendency of the tyrants of the sea and continent, and characterize with blood and wretchedness the age in which they have lived.—To LE
CHEVALIER DE ONIS. vi, 341. (M., 1814.)

8044. SPAIN, Loss of colonies.—I hail
your country as now likely to resume and sur-
pass its ancient splendor among nations. This
might perhaps have been better secured by a
just confidence in the self-sufficient strength
of the peninsula itself; everything without its
limits being its weakness, not its force.—To
CHEVALIER DE ONIS. vi, 342. (M., April
1814.)

8045. SPAIN, Peace with.—Spain is so
evidently *picking a quarrel* with us, that we
see a war absolutely inevitable with her. We
are making a last effort to avoid it.—To JAMES
MONROE. iv, 6. FORD ED., vi, 322. (June
1793.)

8046. —— ——. We are sending a cou-
rier to Madrid to make a last effort for the preservation of honorable peace.—To JAMES MADI-
SON. iv, 8. FORD ED., vi, 325. (June 1793.)

8047. SPAIN, Perfidy of.—Never did a
nation act towards another with more perfidy
and injustice than Spain has constantly practiced against us; and if we have kept
our hands off her till now, it has been purely
out of respect to France, and from the value
we set on the friendship of France. We expect, therefore, from the friendship of the Emperor, that he will either compel Spain to do
us justice, or abandon her to us. We ask but
one month to be in possession of the c'ty of
Mexico.—To JAMES BOWDOIN. v, 64. FORD
ED., ix, 40. (W., April 1807.)

8048. SPAIN, Reprisal on.—While war
with England is probable, everything leading to
it with every other nation should be avoided,
except Spain. As to her, I think it the precise
moment when we should declare to the French
government that we will instantly seize on the
Floridas as reprisal for the spoliations denied
us, and, that if by a given day they are paid to
us, we will restore all east of the Perdido, and
hold the rest subject to amicable decision.

Otherwise, we will hold them forever as a compensation for the spoliations.—To JAMES MADISON. v, 181. FORD ED., ix, 134. (M., Sep. 1807.)

8049. SPAIN, Republicanism in.— The spirit of the Spaniard, and his deadly and eternal hatred to a Frenchman, give me much confidence that he will never submit, but finally defeat this atrocious violation of the laws of God and man, under which he is suffering; and the wisdom and firmness of the Cortes afford reasonable hope that that nation will settle down in a temperate representative government, with an executive properly subordinated to that.—To JOHN ADAMS. vii, 308. FORD ED., x, 270. (M., 1823.)

8050. SPAIN, Spanish America and.— The most advantageous relation in wh'ch Spain can stand with her American colonies is that of independent friendship, secured by the ties of consanguinity, sameness of language, religion, manners, and habits, and certain from the influence of these, of a preference in her commerce, if, instead of the eternal irritations, thwartings, machinations against their new governments, the insults and aggressions which Great Britain has so unwisely practiced towards us, to force us to hate her against our natural inclinations, Spain yields, like a genuine parent, to the forisfamiliation of her colonies, now at maturity, if she extends to them her affections, her aid, her patronage in every court and country, it will weave a bond of union indissoluble by t'me.—To DON V. DE TORONDA CORUNA. vi, 274. (M., Dec. 1813.)

8051. ——— ———. That Spain's divorce from its American colonies, which is now unavoidable, will be a great blessing, 't is impossible not to pronounce on a review of what she was when she acquired them, and of her gradual descent from that proud eminence to the condition in which her present war found her. Nature has formed that peninsula to be the second, and why not the first nation in Europe? Give equal habits of energy to the bodies, and of science to the minds of her citizens, and where could her superior be found?—To DON V. DE TORONDA CORUNA. vi, 274. (M., Dec. 1813.)

8052. SPAIN, Spoliations and boundaries.— With Spain our negotiations for a settlement of differences have not had a satisfactory issue. Spoliations during the former war, for which she had formally acknowledged herself responsible, have been refused to be compensated, but on conditions affecting other claims in nowise connected with them. Yet the same practices are renewed in the present war, and are already of great amount. On the Mobile, our commerce passing through that river continues to be obstructed by arbitrary duties and vexatious searches. Propositions for adjusting amicably the boundaries of Louisiana have not been acceded to. While, however, the right is unsettled, we have avoided changing the state of things, by taking new posts, or strengthening ourselves in the disputed territories, in the hope that the other power would not, by a contrary conduct, oblige us to meet the'r example, and endanger conflicts of authority, the issue of which may not be entirely controlled. But in this hope we have now reason to lessen our confidence. Inroads have been recently made into the territories of Orleans and the M'ssissippi, our citizens have been seized and their property plundered in the very parts of the former which had been actually delivered up by Spain, and this by the regular

officers and soldiers of that government. I have, therefore, found it necessary at length to give orders to our troops on that frontier to be in readiness to protect our citizens, and to repel by arms any similar aggressions in future.—FIFTH ANNUAL MESSAGE. viii, 48. FORD ED., viii, 390. (Dec. 3, 1805.)

8053. ——— ———. The depredations which had been committed on the commerce of the United States during a preceding war, by persons under the authority of Spain * * * made it a duty to require from that government indemnifications for our injured citizens. A convention was accordingly entered 'nto * * * by which it was agreed that spoliations committed by Spanish subjects and carr'ed into ports of Spain should be paid for by that nation; and that those committed by French subjects, and carried into Spanish ports should remain for further discussion. Before this convention was returned to Spain with our ratification, the transfer of Louisiana by France to the United States took place, an event as unexpected as disagreeable to Spain. From that moment she seemed to change her conduct and dispositions towards us. It was first manifested by her protest against the right of France to alienate Lou'siana to us, which however was soon retracted, and the right confirmed. Then, high offence was manifested at the act of Congress establishing a collection disfrict on the Mobile, although by an authentic declaration immediately made, it was expressly confined to our acknowledged limits. And she now refused to ratify the convention s'gned by her own minister under the eye of his sovereign, unless we would relinquish all consent to alterations of its terms which would have affected our claims against her for the spoliations by French subjects carried into Spanish ports. To obtain justice, as well as to restore friendship, I thought a special mission advisable, and accordingly appointed James Monroe, Minister Extraordinary and Plenipotentiary, to repair to Madrid, and in conjunction with our Minister Resident there, to endeavor to procure a ratification of the former convention and to come to an understanding with Spain as to the boundaries of Louisiana. It appeared at once that her policy was to reserve herself for events, and in the meantime to keep our differences in an undetermined state. This will be evident from the papers now communicated to you. After nearly five months of fruitless endeavor to bring them to some definite and satisfactory result our ministers ended the conferences without having been able to obtain indemnity for spoliations of any description, or any satisfaction as to the boundaries of Louisiana, other than a declaration that we had no rights eastward of the Iberville, and that our line to the west was one which would have left us but a string of land on that bank of the river Mississippi. Our injured c'tizens were thus left without any prospect of retribution from the wrongdoer; and as to the boundary each party was to take its own course. That which they have chosen to pursue will appear from the documents now communicated. They authorize the inference that it 's their intention to advance on our possessions until they shall be repressed by an opposing force. Considering that Congress alone is constitutionally invested with the power of changing our condition from peace to war, I have thought it my duty to await their authority for using force in any degree which could be avoided. I have barely instructed the officers stationed in the neighborhood of the aggressions to protect our citizens from violence, to patrol within the borders actually delivered to us, and not to go out of them but when necessary to repel an inroad, or to rescue a citizen or his property.—CONFIDENTIAL MESSAGE. FORD ED., viii, 397. (Dec. 6, 1805.)

8054. ———— ————. With Spain we are making a last effort at peaceable accommodation. The subject is merely a settlement of the limits of Louisiana, and our right of passing down the rivers of Florida. This negotiation is to be held at Paris, where we may have the benefit of the good offices of France, but she will be no party to the contract.—To THOMAS PAINE. FORD ED., viii, 436. (W., March 1806.)

8055. ———— ————. Notwithstanding the efforts made here, and made professedly to assassinate the negotiation in embryo, if the good sense of Bonaparte should prevail over his temper, the present state of things in Europe may induce him to require of Spain that she should do us justice at least. That he should require her to sell us East Florida, we have no right to insist; yet there are not wanting considerations which may induce him to wish a permanent foundation for peace laid between us.—To MR. BIDWELL. v, 15. (W., July 1806.)

8056. ———— ————. It is grossly false that our ministers * * * had proposed to surrender our claims to compensation for Spanish spoliations, or even for French. Their instructions were to make no treaty in which Spanish spoliations were not provided for; and although they were permitted to be silent as to French spoliations carried into Spanish ports, they were not expressly to abandon even them.—To W. A. BURWELL. v, 20. FORD ED., viii, 469. (M., Sep. 1806.)

8057. ———— ————. Our affairs with Spain laid dormant during the absence of Bonaparte from Paris, because we know Spain would do nothing towards settling them, but by compulsion. Immediately on his return, our terms were stated to him, and his interposition obtained. If it was with good faith, its effect will be instantaneous; if not with good faith, we shall discover it by affected delays, and must decide accordingly.—To WILLIAM SHORT. v, 211. (W., Nov. 1807.)

8058. SPAIN, Treaty with.—Some fear our envelopment in the wars engendering from the unsettled state of our affairs with Spain, and therefore are anxious for a ratification of our treaty with her. I fear no such thing, and hope that if ratified by Spain, it will be rejected here. We may justly say to Spain, "When this negotiation commenced, twenty years ago, your authority was acknowledged by those you are selling to us. That authority is now renounced, and their right of self-disposal asserted. In buying them from you, then, we buy but a war-title, a right to subdue them, which you can neither convey nor we acquire. This is a family quarrel, in which we have no right to meddle. Settle it between yourselves, and we will then treat with the party whose right is acknowledged". With whom that will be, no doubt can be entertained. And why should we revolt them by purchasing them as cattle, rather than receiving them as fellow-men? Spain has held off until she sees they are lost to her, and now thinks it better to get something than nothing for them. When she shall see South America equally desperate, she will be wise to sell that also.—To M. DE LAFAYETTE. vii, 194. FORD ED., x, 179. (M., Dec. 1820.)

8059. SPAIN, War against.—I had rather have war against Spain than not, if we go to war against England. Our southern defensive force can take the Floridas, volunteers for a Mexican army will flock to our standard, and rich pabulum will be offered to our privateers in the plunder of their commerce and coasts. Probably Cuba would add itself to our confederation.—To JAMES MADISON. v, 164. FORD ED., ix, 124. (M., Aug. 1807.) See FLORIDA, LOUISIANA, MISSISSIPPI RIVER NAVIGATION, NEW ORLEANS and SPANISH AMERICA.

8060. SPANISH AMERICA, Aid to.—Every kindness which can be shown the South Americans, every friendly office and aid within the limits of the law of nations, I would extend to them, without fearing Spain or her Swiss auxiliaries. For this is but an asserton of our own independence. But to join in their war, as General Scott proposes, and to which even some members of Congress seem to squint, is what we ought not to do as yet.—To JAMES MONROE. vi, 550. FORD ED., x, 19. (M., Feb. 1816.)

8061. ———— ————. That a war is brewing between us and Spain cannot be doubted. When that disposition is matured on both sides, and open rupture can no longer be deferred, then will be the time for our joining the South Americans, and entering into treaties of alliance with them. There will then be but one opinion, at home or abroad, that we shall be justifiable in choosing to have them with us, rather than against us. In the meantime, they will have organized regular governments, and perhaps have formed themselves into one or more confederacies; more than one, I hope, as in single mass they would be a very formidable neighbor.—To JAMES MONROE. vi, 551. FORD ED., x, 19. (M., Feb. 1816.)

8062. ———— ————. The Spanish Colonies cannot reasonably expect us to sink ourselves uselessly and even injuriously for them by a quixotic encounter of the whole world in arms. Were it Spain alone I should have no fear. But Russia is said to have seventy ships of the line; France approaching that number, and what should we be in fronting such a force? It is not for the interest of Spanish America that our Republic should be blotted out of the map, and to the rest of the world it would be an act of treason.—To PRESIDENT MONROE. FORD ED., x, 316. (M., July 1824.)

8063. SPANISH AMERICA, Constitution for.—For such a condition of society, the constitution you [Dupont de Nemours] have devised is probably the best imaginable. It is certainly calculated to elicit the best talents; although perhaps not well guarded against the egoism of its functionaries. But that egoism will be light in comparison with the pressure of a military despot and his army of Janizaries. Like Solon to the Athenians, you have given to your Columbians, not the best possible government, but the best they can bear.—To DUPONT DE NEMOURS. vi, 592. FORD ED., x, 25. (P.F., 1816.)

8064. SPANISH AMERICA, Ignorance in.—Another great field of political experiment is opening in our neighborhood, in Spanish America. I fear the degrading ignorance into which their priests and kings have sunk them, has disqualified them from the maintenance or even knowledge of their rights, and that much blood may be shed for little improvement in their condition. Should their new rulers honestly lay their shoulders to remove the great obstacles of ignorance, and press the remed es of education and information, they will still be in jeopardy until another generation comes into place, and what may happen in the interval cannot be predicted.—To DUPONT DE NEMOURS. v, 584. FORD ED., ix, 322. (M., 1811.)

8065. —— ——. No mortal wishes them more success than I do. But if what I have heard of the ignorance and bigotry of the mass be true, I doubt their capacity to understand and to support a free government; and fear that their emancipation from the foreign tyranny of Spain, will result in a military despotism at home. Palacios may be great; others may be great; but it is the multitude which possess force; and wisdom must yield to that.—To DUPONT DE NEMOURS. vi, 592. FORD ED., x, 25. (P.F., 1816.)

8066. SPANISH AMERICA, Independence of.—It is intimated to us, in such a way as to attract our attention, that France means to send a strong force early this spring to offer independence to the Spanish American colonies, beginning with those on the Mississippi and that she will not object to the receiving those on the East side into our confederation. Interesting considerations require that we should keep ourselves free to act in this case according to circumstances, and consequently that you should not, by any clause of treaty, bind us to guarantee any of the Spanish colonies against their own independence; nor indeed against any other nation. For, when we thought we might guarantee Louisiana on their ceding the Floridas to us, we apprehended it would be seized by Great Britain, who would thus completely encircle us with her colonies and fleets. This danger is now removed by the concert between Great Britain and Spain. And the times will soon enough give independence, and consequently free commerce to our neighbors, without our risking the involving ourselves in a war for them.*—To CARMICHAEL AND SHORT. iii, 534. FORD ED., vi, 206. (Pa., March 1793.)

8067. —— ——. On the question of our interest in their independence, were that alone a sufficient motive of action, much may be said on both sides. When they are free, they will drive every article of our produce from every market, by underselling it, and change the condition of our existence, forcing us into other habits and pursuits. We shall indeed, have n exchange some commerce with them, but in what I know not, for we shall have nothing to offer which they cannot raise cheaper; and their separation from Spain seals our everlasting peace with her. On the other hand, so long as they are dependent, Spain, from her jealousy, is our natural enemy, and always in either open or secret hostility with us. These countries, too, in war will be a powerful weight in her scale, and, in peace, totally shut to us. Interest, then, on the whole, would wish their independence, and justice makes the wish a duty. They have a right to be free, and we a right to aid them, as a strong man has a right to assist a weak one assailed by a robber or murderer.—To JAMES MONROE. vi, 550. FORD ED., x, 19. (M., Feb. 1816.)

8068. —— ——. We go with you all lengths in friendly affections to the independ-

* Short and Carmichael were commissioners to negotiate a treaty with Spain. Appended to the extract are the words in President Washington's handwriting: " The above meets the approval of George Washington."—EDITOR.

ence of South America. But an immediate acknowledgment of it calls up other considerations. We view Europe as covering at present a smothered fire, which may shortly burst forth and produce general conflagration. From this it is our duty to keep aloof. A formal acknowledgment of the independence ot her Colonies would involve us with Spa n certainly, and perhaps, too, with England, if she thinks that a war would divert her internal troubles. Such a war would hurt us more than it would help our brethren of the South; and our right may be doubted of mortgaging posterity for the expenses of a war in which they will have a right to say their interests were not concerned. —To DESTUTT TRACY. FORD ED., x, 174. (M., 1820.)

8069. SPANISH AMERICA, Interest in.—However distant we may be, both in condition and dispositions, from taking an active part in any commotions in that country [South America], nature has placed it too near us, to make its movements altogether indifferent to our interests, or to our curiosity.—To JOHN JAY. ii, 145. FORD ED., iv, 385. (Mar. 1787.)

8070. SPANISH AMERICA, Name for. —I wish you had called them the Columbian republics, to distinguish them from our American republics. Theirs would be the more honorable name, and they best entitled to it; for Columbus discovered their continent, but never saw ours.—To DUPONT DE NEMOURS. vi, 593. FORD ED., x, 25. (P.F., 1816.)

8071. SPANISH AMERICA, Natural divisions of.—The geography of the [Spanish-American] country seems to indicate three confederacies. 1. What is north of the Isthmus. 2. What is south of it on the Atlantic; and 3. the southern part on the Pacific. In this form, we might be the balancing power.— To JAMES MONROE. vi, 551. FORD ED., x, 20. (M., Feb. 1816.)

8072. SPANISH AMERICA, Relations with Spain.—If the mother country [Spain] has not the magnanimity to part with the colonies in friendship, thereby making them what they would certainly be, her natural and firmest allies, these will emancipate themselves, after exhausting her strength and resources in ineffectual efforts to hold them in subjection. They will be rendered enemies of the mother country, as England has rendered us by an unremitting course of insulting injuries and silly provocations. I do not say this from the impulse of national interest, for I do not know that the United States would find an interest in the independence of neighbor nations, whose produce and commerce would rivalize ours. It could only be that kind of interest which every human being has in the happiness and prosperity of every other. But putting right and reason out of the question, I have no doubt that on calculations of interest alone, it is that of Spain to anticipate voluntarily, and as a matter of grace, the independence of her colonies, which otherwise necessity will force.—To CHEVALIER DE ONIS. vi, 342. (M., April 1814.)

8073. SPANISH AMERICA, Revolt of. —Behold another example of man rising in his might and bursting the chains of his oppressor, and in the same hemisphere. Spanish America is all in revolt. The insurgents are triumphant in many of the States, and will be so in all. But there the danger is that the cruel arts of their oppressors have enchained their minds, have kept them in the ignorance of children, and as incapable of self-government as children. If the obstacles of bigotry and priestcraft can be surmounted, we may hope that common sense will suffice to do everything else. God send them a safe deliverance.—To GENERAL KOSCIUSKO. v, 586. (M., 1811.)

8074. —— ——. That they will throw off their European dependence I have no doubt; but in what kind of government their revolution will end I am not so certain. History, I believe, furnishes no example of a priest-ridden people maintaining a free civil government. This marks the lowest grade of ignorance, of which their civil as well as religious leaders will always avail themselves for their own purposes. The vicinity of New Spain to the United States, and their consequent intercourse, may furnish schools for the higher, and example for the lower classes of their citizens. And Mexico, where we learn from you that men of science are not wanting, may revolutionize itself under better auspices than the Southern provinces. These last, I fear, must end in military despotisms. The different castes of their inhabitants, their mutual hatreds and jealousies, their profound ignorance and bigotry, will be played off by cunning leaders, and each be made the instrument of enslaving others. * * * But in whatever governments they end they will be *American* governments, no longer to be involved in the never-ceasing broils of Europe.—To BARON VON HUMBOLDT. vi, 267. FORD ED., ix, 430. (Dec. 1813.)

8075. SPANISH AMERICA, Self-government and.—The Spanish-American countries are beginning to be interesting to the whole world. They are now becoming the scenes of political revolution, to take their stations as integral members of the great family of nations. All are now in insurrection. In several, the Independents are already triumphant, and they will undoubtedly be so in all. What kind of government will they establish? How much liberty can they bear without intoxication? Are their chiefs sufficiently enlightened to form a well-guarded government, and their people to watch their chiefs? Have they mind enough to place their domesticated Indians on a footing with the whites? All these questions you [Baron Humboldt] can answer better than any other. I imagine they will copy our outlines of confederation and elective government, abolish distinction of ranks, bow the neck to their priests, and persevere in intolerantism. Their greatest difficulty will be in the construction of their executive. I suspect that, regardless of the experiment of France, and of that of the United States in 1784, they will begin with a directory, and when the unavoidable schisms in that kind of executive shall drive them to something else, their great question will come on whether to substitute an executive elective for years, for life, or an hereditary one. But unless instruction can be spread among them more rapidly than experience promises, despotism may come upon them before they are qualified to save the ground they will have gained.—To BARON VON HUMBOLDT. v, 580. (M., April 1811.)

8076. —— ——. The achievement [by the Spanish Colonies] of their independence of Spain is no longer a question. But it is a very serious one, what will then become of them? Ignorance and bigotry, like other insanities, are incapable of self-government. They will fall under military despotism, and become the murderous tools of the ambition of their respective Bonapartes; and whether this will be for their greater happiness, the rule of one only has taught you to judge. No one, I hope, can doubt my wish to see them and all mankind exercising self-government, and capable of exercising it. But the question is not what we wish, but what is practicable? As their sincere friend and brother, then, I do believe the best thing for them, would be for themselves to come to an accord with Spain, under the guarantee of France, Russia, Holland, and the United States, allowing, to Spain a nominal supremacy, with authority only to keep the peace among them, leaving them otherwise all the powers of self-government, until their experience in them, their emancipation from their priests, and advancement in information, shall prepare them for complete independence. I exclude England from this confederacy, because her selfish principles render her incapable of honorable patronage or disinterested co-operation.—To MARQUIS LAFAYETTE. vii, 67. FORD ED., x, 84. (M., 1817.)

8077. —— ——. The issue of [Spanish America's] struggles, as they respect Spain, is no longer matter of doubt. As it respects their own liberty, peace and happiness, we cannot be quite so certain. Whether the blinds of bigotry, the shackles of the priesthood, and the fascinating glare of rank and wealth, give fair play to the common sense of the mass of their people, so far as to qualify them for self-government, is what we do not know. Perhaps our wishes may be stronger than our hopes.—To F. H. ALEXANDER VON HUMBOLDT. vii, 74. FORD ED., x, 88. (M., 1817.)

8078. —— ——. I feared from the beginning that these people were not yet sufficiently enlightened for self-government; and that after wading through blood and slaughter, they would end in military tyrannies, more or less numerous. Yet, as they wished to try the experiment, I wished them success in it; they have now tried it, and will possibly find that their safest road will be an accommodation with the mother country, which shall hold them together by the single link of the same chief magistrate, leaving to him power enough to keep them in peace with one another, and to themselves the essential power of self-government and self-improvement, until they shall be sufficiently trained by education and habits of freedom, to walk safely by themselves. Representative government, native functionaries, a qualified negative on their laws, with a previous security by compact for freedom of commerce, freedom of the press, *habeas corpus* and trial by jury, would make a good beginning. This last would be the school in which their people might begin to learn the exercise of civic duties as well as rights. For freedom of religion they are not yet prepared. The scales of bigotry have not sufficiently fallen from their eyes, to accept it for themselves individually, much less to trust others with it. But that will come in time, as well as a general ripeness to break entirely from the parent stem.—To JOHN ADAMS. vii, 200. FORD ED., x, 186. (M., Jan. 1821.)

8079. SPANISH AMERICA, United States and.—I cannot help suspecting the Spanish squadron to be gone to South America, and that some disturbances have been excited there by the British. The Court of Madrid may suppose we would not see this with an unwilling eye. This may be true as to the uninformed part of our people; but those who look into futurity farther than the present moment or age, and who combine well what is, with what is to be, must see that our interests, well understood, and our wishes are, that Spain shall (not forever, but) very long retain her possessions in that quarter; and that her views and ours must, in a good degree, and for a long time, concur.—To WILLIAM CARMICHAEL. ii, 398. FORD ED., v, 23. (P., 1788.)

8080. SPECIAL LEGISLATION, Favoritism and.—To special legislation we are generally averse, lest a principle of favoritism should creep in and pervert that of equal rights. It has, however, been done on some occasions where a special national advantage has been expected to overweigh that of adherence to the general rule.—To GEORGE FLOWER. vii, 83. (P.F., 1817.)

— SPECIE.—See MONEY, METALLIC.

8081. SPECULATION, Agriculture vs.—A war wherein France, Holland, and England should be parties, seems, *primâ facie*, to promise much advantage to us. But, in the first place, no war can be safe for us which threatens France with an unfavorable issue; and in the next, it will probably embark us again into the ocean of speculation, engage us to overtrade ourselves, convert us into sea-rovers, under French and Dutch colors, divert us from agriculture, which is our wisest pursuit, because it will in the end contribute most to real wealth, good morals and happiness.—To GENERAL WASHINGTON. ii, 251. (P., Aug. 1787.)

8082. SPECULATION, A crime.—Wilson Nicholas is attacked in his election. The ground on which the attack is made is that he is a speculator. The explanations which this has produced prove it a serious crime in the eyes of the people.—To JAMES MADISON. FORD ED., vii, 1. (M., Feb. 1795.)

8083. SPECULATION, Excessive.—It is impossible to say where the appetite for gambling will stop. The land office, the Federal town, certain schemes of manufacture, are all likely to be converted into aliment for that rage.—To JAMES MONROE. iii, 268. FORD ED., v, 353. (Pa., 1791.)

8084. ———. The *unmoneyed* farmer, as he is termed, his cattle and crops are no more thought of here [Philadelphia*] than if they did not feed us. Scrip and stock are food and raiment here.—To T. M. RANDOLPH. FORD ED., v, 455. (Pa., 1792.)

8085. SPECULATION, In France.—All the money men [in France] are playing deeply in the stocks of the country. The spirit of "*agiotage*" (as they call it) was never so high in any country before. It will probably produce as total deprivation of morals as the system of [John] Law did. All the money of France is now employed in this, none being free even for the purposes of commerce, which suffers immensely from this cause.—To R. IZARD. ii, 206. (P., 1787.)

8086. SPECULATION, Gambling and.—The wealth acquired by speculation and

* Philadelphia was then the capital.—EDITOR.

plunder, is fugacious in its nature, and fills society with the spirit of gambling.—To GENERAL WASHINGTON. ii, 252. (P., 1787.)

8087. ———. A spirit of gambling in the public paper has lately seized too many of our citizens. Commerce, manufactures, the arts and agriculture will suffer from it, if not checked. Many are ruined by it; but I fear that ruin will be no more a correction in this case than in common gaming.—To DAVID HUMPHREYS. FORD ED., v, 372. (Pa., 1791.)

8088. ———. The credit and fate of the nation seem to hang on the desperate throws and plunges of gambling scoundrels.—To T. M. RANDOLPH. FORD ED., v, 455. (Pa., 1792.)

8089. SPECULATION, Land.—You mention that my name is used by some speculators in Western land jobbing, as if they were acting for me as well as for themselves. About the years 1776 or 1777, I consented to join Mr. Harvey and some others in an application for lands there; which scheme, however, I believe he dropped on the threshold, for I never after heard one syllable on the subject. In 1782, I joined some gentlemen in a project to obtain some lands in the western part of North Carolina. But in the winter of 1782 and 1783, while I was in expectation of going to Europe, and that the title to western lands might possibly come under the discussion of the ministers, I withdrew myself from this company. I am further assured that the members never prosecuted their views. These were the only occasions in which I ever took a single step for the acquisition of western lands, and in these I retracted at the threshold. I can with truth, therefore, declare to you, and wish you to repeat it on every proper occasion, that no person on earth is authorized to place my name in any adventure for lands on the western waters, that I am not engaged in any but the two before mentioned. I am one of eight children to whom my father left his share in the loyal company, whose interests, however, I never espoused, and they have long since received their quietus. Excepting these, I never was, nor am I now, interested in one foot of land on earth off the waters of James River.—To JAMES MADISON. FORD ED., iv, 2. (P. 1784.)

8090. SPECULATION, Morality and.—Though we shall be neutrals, and as such shall derive considerable pecuniary advantages, yet I think we shall lose in happiness and morals by being launched again into the ocean of speculation, led to overtrade ourselves, tempted to become sea-robbers, under French colors, and to quit the pursuits of agriculture, the surest road to affluence, and best preservative of morals.—To J. BLAIR. ii, 248. (P., 1787.)

8091. SPECULATION, Stocks.—I wish to God you had some person who could dispose of your paper at a judicious moment for you, and invest it in good lands. I would do anything my duty [as Secretary of State] would permit, but were I to advise your agent (who is himself a stock dealer) to sell out yours at this or that moment, it would be used as a signal to guide speculations.—To WILLIAM SHORT. iii, 343. FORD ED., v, 459. (Pa., March 1792.) See CAPITAL.

8092. SPELLING, Correct.—Take care that you never spell a word wrong. Always before you write a word, consider how it is spelled, and, if you do not remember it, turn to a dict ionary. It produces great praise to a lady to spell well.—To MARTHA JEFFERSON. FORD ED., iii, 346. (A., 1783.)

8093. SPELLING, Reform of English.—A change has been long desired in English orthography, such as might render it an easy and true index of the pronunciation of words. The want of conformity between the combinations of letters, and the sounds they should represent, increases to foreigners the difficulty of acquiring the language, occasions great loss of time to children in learning to read, and renders correct spelling rare but in those who read much. In England a variety of plans and propositions has been made for the reformation of their orthography. Passing over these, two of our countrymen, Dr. Franklin and Dr. Thornton, have also engaged in the enterprise; the former proposing an addition of two or three new characters only, the latter a reformation of the whole alphabet nearly. But these attempts in England, as well as here, have been without effect. About the middle of the last century an attempt was made to banish the letter *d* from the words bridge, judge, hedge, knowledge, &c., others of that termination, and to write them as we write age, cage, sacrilege, privilege; but with little success. The attempt was also made, which you mention, * * * to drop the letter *u* in words of Latin derivation ending in o*ur*, and to write honor, candor, rigor, &c., instead of honour, candour, rigour. But the *u* having been picked up in the passage of these words from the Latin, through the French, to us, is still preserved by those who consider it as a memorial of our title to the words. Other partial attempts have been made by individual writers, but with as little success. Pluralizing nouns in *y* and *ey*, by adding *s* only, as you propose, would certainly simplify the spelling, and be analogous to the general idiom of the language. It would be a step gained in the progress of general reformation, if it could prevail. But my opinion being requested I must give it candidly, that judging **of** the future by the past, I expect no better fortune to this than similar preceding propositions have experienced. It is very difficult to persuade the great body of mankind to give up what they have once learned, and are now masters of, for something to be learned anew. Time alone insensibly wears down old habits, and produces small changes at long intervals, and to this process we must all accommodate ourselves, and be content to follow those who will not follow us. Our Anglo-Saxon ancestors had twenty ways of spelling the word "many". Ten centuries have dropped all of them and substituted that which we now use. I now return your MS.* without being able, with the gentlemen whose letters are cited, to encourage hope as to its effect. I am bound, however, to acknowledge that this is a subject to which I have not paid much attention; and that my

* It is proposed that the plurals of words ending in *y* and *ey* be formed by adding *s* only.—EDITOR.

doubts, therefore, should weigh nothing against their more favorable expectations. That these may be fulfilled, and mine prove unfounded, I sincerely wish, because I am a friend to the reformation generally of whatever can be made better.—To JOHN WILSON. vi, 190. FORD ED., ix, 396. (M., 1813.)

8094. SPIES, Congress and.—As in time of war the enemies of these States might employ emissaries and spies to discover the views and proceedings of Congress, that body should have authority, within a certain distance of the place of their session, to arrest and deal with as they shall think proper, all persons, not being citizens of any of these States nor entitled to their protection, whom they shall have cause to suspect to be spies.—RESOLVE ON CONTINENTAL CONGRESS. FORD ED., ii', 464. (1784.)

8095. SPIES, Employment of.—Will it not be proper to rebut Foronda's charge [with respect to Lieutenant Pike's expedition] of this government sending a spy to Santa Fé, by saying that this government has never employed a spy in any case?—To JAMES MADISON. v, 178. (Aug. 1807.)

8096. SPIES, Jefferson and.—All my motions at Philadelphia, here [Monticello], and everywhere, are watched and recorded.—To SAMUEL SMITH. iv, 253. FORD ED., vii, 276. (M., 1798.)

—— SPIES, Treasury.—See NEUTRALITY.

8097. SPIRIT, Party.—The happiness of society depends so much on preventing party spirit from infecting the common intercourse of life, that nothing should be spared to harmonize and amalgamate the two parties in social circles.—To WILLIAM C. CLAIBORNE. FORD ED., viii, 70. (W., 1801.)

8098. SPIRIT, Of the people.—It is the manners and spirit of the people which preserve a republic in vigor.—NOTES ON VIRGINIA. viii, 406. FORD ED., iii, 269. (1782.)

8099. SPRINGS, Medicinal.—There are several medicinal springs [in Virginia], some of which are indubitably efficacious, while others seem to owe their reputation as much to fancy and change of air and regimen, as to their real virtues.—NOTES ON VIRGINIA. viii, 279. FORD ED., iii, 121. (1782.) See MEDICINAL SPRINGS.

8100. SQUATTERS, Prohibition of.—I do not recollect the instructions to Governor [Meriwether] Lewis respecting squatters. But if he had any they were unquestionably to prohibit them rigorously. I have no doubt, if he had not written instructions, that he was verbally so instructed.—To ALBERT GALLATIN. v, 408. (W., Jan. 1809.)

8101. SQUATTERS, Removal.—The General Government have never hesitated to remove by force the squatters and intruders on the public lands. Indeed, if the nation were put to action against every squatter, for the recovery of their lands, we should have only lawsuits, not lands for sale.—BATTURE CASE. viii, 588. (1812.)

8102. STABILITY, Laudable.—Perseverance in object, though not by the most direct way, is often more laudable than perpetual changes, as often as the object shifts light.—To GOVERNOR HENRY. i, 220. FORD ED., ii, 178. (Alb., 1779.)

8103. STABILITY, Of the Republic.— The order and good sense displayed in this recovery from delusion, and in the momentous crisis which lately arose [Presidential election], really bespeak a strength of character in our nation which augurs well for the duration of our Republic; and I am much better satisfied now of its stability than I was before it was tried.—To DR. JOSEPH PRIESTLEY. iv, 374. FORD ED., viii, 22. (W., March 1801.)

8104. STAEL (Madame de), Sympathy. —[I assure you] of my sincere sympathies for the share which you bear in the afflictions of your country, and the deprivation to which a lawless will has subjected you. In return, you enjoy the dignified satisfaction of having met them, rather than be yoked with the abject, to his car; and that, in withdrawing from oppression, you have followed the virtuous example of a father whose name will ever be dear to your country and to mankind.—To MADAME DE STAEL. vi, 119. (May 1813.)

8105. STANDARD, Arbitrary.—The first question to be decided is between those who are for units of measures, weights, and coins, having a known relation to something in nature of fixed dimension, and those who are for an arbitrary standard. On this *" dice vexata quaestio"* it is useless to say a word, every one having made up his mind on a view of all that can be said. Mr. Dorsey was so kind as to send me his pamphlet, by which I found he was for the arbitrary standard of one-third of the standard yard of H. G. of England, supposed to be in the Exchequer of that nation, a fac simile of which was to be procured and lodged in Philadelphia. I confess myself to be of the other sect, and to prefer an unit bearing a given relation to some fixed subject of nature, and of preference to the pendulum, because it may be in the possession of every man, so that he may verify his measures for himself. I proposed alternative plans to Congress, that they might take the one or the other, according to the degree of courage they felt. Were I now to decide, it would be in favor of the first, with this single addition, that each of the denominations there adopted, should be divisible decimally at the will of every individual. The iron-founder deals in tons; let him take the ton for his unit, and divide it into 10ths, 100ths, and 1000ths. The dry-goods merchant deals in pounds and yards; let him divide them decimally. The land-measurer deals in miles and poles; divide them decimally, only noting over his figures what the unit is, thus:

Tons.	Lbs.	Yds.	Miles.
18.943,	18.943,	18.943,	18.943, etc.

—To THOMAS COOPER. v, 377. (W., 1808.)

8106. STANDARD, Decimal system.— Is it in contemplation with the House of Representatives to * * * arrange * * * our measures and weights [the same as the coinage] in a decimal ratio? The facility which this would introduce into the vulgar arithmetic would, unquestionably, be soon and sensibly felt by the whole mass of the people, who would thereby be enabled to compute for themselves whatever they should have occasion to buy, to sell, or to measure, which the present complicated and dif-

ficult ratios place beyond their computation for the most part.—COINAGE, WEIGHTS AND MEASURES REPORT. vii, 477. (July 1790.)

8107. ——— ———. It will give me real pleasure to see some good system of measures and weights introduced and combined with the decimal arithmetic. It is a great and difficult question whether to venture only on a half reformation, * * * or, as the French have tried with success, make a radical reform.—To J. DORSEY. v, 236. (W., 1808.)

— STANDARD, Money.—See DOLLAR and MONEY.

8108. STANDARD, Regulating.—The Administrator shall not possess the prerogative * * * of regulating weights and measures. —PROPOSED VA. CONSTITUTION. FORD ED., ii, 19. (June 1776.)

8109. STANDARD (Measures), English.—The cogent reason which will decide the fate of whatever you report is, that England has lately adopted the reference of its measures to the pendulum. It is the mercantile part of our community which will have most to do in this innovation; it is that which having command of all the presses can make the loudest outcry, and you know their identification with English regulations, practices, and prejudices. It is from this identification alone you can hope to be permitted to adopt even the English reference to a pendulum. But the English proposition goes only to say what proportion their measures bear to the second pendulum of their own latitude, and not at all to change their unit, or to reduce into any simple order the chaos of their weights and measures. That would be innovation, and innovation there is heresy and treason.—To JOHN QUINCY ADAMS. vii, 89. (M., 1817.)

8110. STANDARD (Measures), French.—Candor obliges me to confess that the element of measure, adopted by France, is not what I would have approved. It is liable to the inexactitude of mensuration as to that part of the quadrant of the earth which is to be measured, that is to say as to one-tenth of the quadrant, and as to the remaining nine-tenths they are to be calculated on conjectural data, presuming the figure of the earth which has not yet been proved. It is liable, too, to the objection that no nation but your own can come at it; because yours is the only nation within which a meridian can be found of such extent crossing the 45th degree, and terminating at both ends in a level. We may certainly say, then, that this measure is uncatholic, and I would rather have seen you depart from catholicism in your religion than in your philosophy.—To THE MARQUIS DE CONDORCET. FORD ED., v, 378. (Pa., 1791.)

8111. STANDARD (Measures), Invariable.—On the subject of weights and measures, you will have, at its threshold, to encounter the question on which Solon and Lycurgus acted differently. Shall we mould our citizens to the law, or the law to our citizens? And in solving this question their peculiar character is an element not to be neglected. Of the two only things in nature which can furnish an invariable standard, to wit, the dimensions of the globe itself, and the time of its diurnal revolution on its axis, it is not perhaps of much importance which we adopt. * * * I sincerely wish you may be able to rally us to either standard, and to give us an unit, the aliquot part of something invariable which may be applied simply and conveniently to our measures, weights and coins, and most especially that the decimal divisions may pervade the whole. The convenience of this in our moneyed system has been approved by all, and France has followed the example.—To John Quincy Adams. vii, 87. (M., 1817.)

8112. STANDARD (Measures), Method of obtaining.—To obtain uniformity in measures, weights and coins. it is necessary to find some measure of invariable length, with which, as a standard, they may be compared. There exists not in nature, as far as has been hitherto observed, a single subject or species of subject, accessible to man, which presents one constant and uniform dimension. The globe of the earth itself, indeed, might be considered as invariable in all its dimensions, and that its circumference would furnish an invariable measure: but no one of its circles, great or small, is accessible to admeasurement through all its parts, and the various trials to measure definite portions of them, have been of such various result as to show there is no dependence on that operation for certainty. Matter, then, by its mere extension, furnishing nothing invariable, its motion is the only remaining resource. The motion of the earth round its axis, though not absolutely uniform and invariable, may be considered as such for every human purpose. It is measured obviously, but unequally, by the departure of a given meridian from the sun, and its returning to it, constituting a solar day. Throwing together the inequalities of solar days, a mean interval, or day, has been found, and divided, by very general consent, into 86,400 equal parts. A pendulum, vibrating freely, in small and equal arcs, may be so adjusted in its length, as, by its vibrations, to make this division of the earth's motion into 86,400 equal parts, called seconds of mean time. Such a pendulum, then, becomes itself a measure of determinate length, to which all others may be referred to as to a standard. But even a pendulum is not without its uncertainties.—Coinage, Weights and Measures Report. vii, 473. (July 1790.)

8113. STANDARD (Measures), Odometer.—I have lately had a proof how familiar this division into dimes, cents, and mills, is to the people when transferred from their money to anything else. I have an odometer fixed to my carriage, which gives the distances in miles, dimes, and cents. The people on the road inquire with curiosity what exact distance I have found from such a place to such a place. I answer so many miles, so many cents. I find they universally and at once form a perfect idea of the relation of the cent to the mile as an unit. They would do the same as to yards of cloth, pounds of shot, ounces of silver, or of medicine. I believe, therefore, they are susceptible to this degree of approximation to a standard rigorously philosophical; beyond this I might doubt.—To Thomas Cooper. v, 378. (W., 1808.)

8114. STANDARD (Measures), Pendulum.—But why leave this adoption to the tardy will of governments who are always, in their stock of information, a century or two behind the intelligent part of mankind, and who have interests against touching ancient institutions? Why should not the college of the literary societies of the world adopt the second pendulum as the unit of measure on the authorities of reason, convenience and common consent? And why should not our Society [American Philosophical] open the proposition by a circular letter to the other learned institu-

tions of the earth? If men of science, in their publications, would express measures always in multiples and decimals of the pendulum, annexing their value in municipal measures as botanists add the popular to the botanical names of plants, they would soon become familiar to all men of instruction, and prepare the way for legal adoptions. At any rate, it would render the writers of every nation intelligible to the readers of every other, when expressing the measures of things.—To Dr. Patterson. vi, 12. (M., 1811.)

8115. ———— ————. In favor of the standard to be taken from the time employed in a revolution of the earth on its axis, it may be urged that this revolution is a matter of fact present to all the world, that its division into seconds of time is known and received by all the world, that the length of a pendulum vibrating seconds in the different circles of latitude is already known to all, and can at any time and in any place be ascertained by any nation or individual, and inferred by known laws from their own to the medium latitude of 45°, whenever any doubt may make this desirable; and that this is the particular standard which has at different times been contemplated and desired * by the philosophers of every nation, and even by those of France, except at the particular moment when this change was suddenly proposed and adopted, and under circumstances peculiar to the history of the moment.—To John Quincy Adams. vii, 88. (M., 1817.)

8116. ———— ————. [The standard based on] the dimensions of the globe, preferred ultimately by the French, after first adopting the other [that founded on the time of the diurnal revolution of the earth on its axis], has been objected to from the difficulty, not to say impracticability, of the verification of their admeasurement by other nations. Except the portion of a meridian which they adopted for their operation, there is not another on the globe which fulfills the requisite condition. to wit, of so considerable length, that length too divided, not very unequally, by the 45th degree of latitude, and terminating at each end in the ocean. Now, this singular line lies wholly in France and Spain. Besides the immensity of expense and time which a verification would always require, it cannot be undertaken by any nation without the joint consent of these two powers. France having once performed the work, and refusing, as she may. to let any other nation reexamine it, she makes herself the sole depository of the original standard for all nations; and all must send to her to obtain, and from time to time to prove their standards. To this, indeed, it may be answered, that there can be no reason to doubt that the mensuration has been as accurately performed as the intervention of numerous waters and of high ridges of craggy mountains would admit; that all the calculations have been free of error, their coincidences faithfully reported, and that, whether in peace or war. to foes as well as friends, free access to the original will at all times be admitted.—To John Quincy Adams. vii, 88. (M., 1817.) See Pendulum.

8117. STANDARD (Measures), Rod.—Congress having referred to me to propose a plan of invariable measures, I have considered maturely your proposition, and am abundantly

* If, conforming to this desire of other nations, we adopt the second pendulum, 3-10 of that for our foot will be the same as 1-5 or 2-10 of the second rod, because that rod is to the pendulum, as 3 to 2. This would make our foot 1-4 inch less than the present one.—Note by Jefferson.

satisfied of its utility; so that if I can have your leave, I mean to propose in my report to adopt the rod in preference to the pendulum, mentioning expressly that we are indebted to you for the idea.—To MR. LESLIE. iii, 156. (N.Y., 1790.)

8118. STANDARD (Measures), Universal.—The pendulum is equally [with the meridian] fixed by the laws of nature, is in the possession of every nation, may be verified everywhere and by every person, and at an expense within every one's means. I am not, therefore, without a hope that the other nations of the world will still concur, some day, in making the pendulum the basis of a common system of measures, weights and coins, which applied to the present metrical systems of France and of other countries, will render them all intelligible to one another. England and this country may give it a beginning, notwithstanding the war they are entering into. The republic of letters is unaffected by the wars of geographical divisions of the earth.—To DR. PATTERSON. vi, 11. (M., 1811.)

8119. —— ——. I do not like the new system of French measures, because not the best, and adapted to a standard accessible to themselves exclusively, and to be obtained by other nations only from them. For, on examining the map of the earth, you will find no meridian on it but the one passing through their country, offering the extent of land on both sides of the 45th degree, and terminating at both ends in a portion of the ocean which the conditions of the problem for an universal standard of measures require. Were all nations to agree, therefore, to adopt this standard, they must go to Paris to ask it; and they might as well long ago have all agreed to adopt the French foot, the standard of which they could equally have obtained from Paris.—To DR. PATTERSON. vi, 11. (M., 1811.)

8120. STANDARD (Weights), Avoirdupois and Troy.—It would be for their [the people's] convenience to suppress the pound and ounce troy, and the drachm and quarter avoirdupois; and to form into one series the avoirdupois pound and ounce, and the troy pennyweight and grain.—C O I N A G E, WEIGHTS AND MEASURES REPORT. vii, 486. (1790.)

8121. STANDARD (Weights), Basis.—Let it be established that an ounce is of the weight of a cube of rain water of one-tenth of a foot; or, rather, that it is the thousandth part of the weight of a cubic foot of rain water, weighed in the standard temperature; that the series of weights of the United States shall consist of pounds, ounces, pennyweights and grains; whereof 24 grains shall be one pennyweight; 18 pennyweights one ounce; 16 ounces one pound.—COINAGE, WEIGHTS AND MEASURES REPORT. vii, 487. (1790.)

8122. STANDARD (Weights), Ratios.—The weight of the pound troy is to that of the pound avoirdupois as 144 to 175. It is remarkable that this is exactly the proportion of the ancient liquid gallon of Guildhall of 224 cubic inches to the corn gallon of 272. It is further remarkable still that this is also the exact proportion between the specific weight of any measure of wheat and of the same measure of water. * * * This seems to have been so combined as to render it indifferent whether a thing were dealt out by weight or measure.—COINAGE, WEIGHTS AND MEASURES REPORT. vii, 484. (1790.)

8123. —— ——. Another remarkable correspondence is that between weights and measures. For 1,000 ounces avoirdupois of pure water fills a cubic foot, with mathematical exactness. What circumstances of the times, or purpose of barter or commerce, called for this combination of weights and measures, with the subjects to be exchanged or purchased, are not now to be ascertained. But a triple set of exact proportionals representing weights, measures and the things to be weighed or measured, and a relation so integral between weights and solid measures, must have been the result of design and scientific calculation and not a mere coincidence of hazard.—COINAGE, WEIGHTS AND MEASURES REPORT. vii, 485. (1790.)

8124. STATE RIGHTS, Coercion.—Respect and friendship should, I think, mark the conduct of the General towards the particular government, and explanations should be asked and time and color given them to tread back their steps before coercion is held up to their view.—OPINION ON GEORGIAN LAND GRANTS. vii, 468. FORD ED., v, 167. (1790.) See COERCION OF A STATE.

8125. STATE RIGHTS, Congress and.—Can it be thought that the Constitution intended that for a shade or two of *convenience*, more or less, Congress should be authorized to break down the most ancient and fundmental laws of the several States; such as those against Mortmain, the laws of Alienage, the rules of Descent, the acts of Distribution, the laws of Escheat and Forfeiture, the laws of Monopoly? Nothing but a necessity invincible by any other means, can justify such a prostitution of laws, which constitute the pillars of our whole system of jurisprudence. Will Congress be too straightlaced to carry the Constitution into honest effect, unless they may pass over the foundation-laws of the State government for the slightest convenience of theirs?—NATIONAL BANK OPINION. vii, 560. FORD ED., v, 289. (1791.) See BANK (U. S.), CONSTITUTIONALITY OF.

8126. —— ——. [The States] alone being parties to the [Federal] compact, * * * [are] solely authorized to judge in the last resort of the powers exercised under it. Congress being not a party, but merely the creature of the compact, and subject as to its assumptions of power to the final judgment of those by whom, and for whose use itself and its powers were all created and modified.—KENTUCKY RESOLUTIONS. ix, 469. FORD ED., vii, 301. (1798.) See KENTUCKY RESOLUTIONS.

8127. STATE RIGHTS, Constitution and.—I am firmly persuaded that it is by giving due tone to the particular governments that the general one will be preserved in vigor also, the Constitution having foreseen its incompetency to all the objects of government, and, therefore, confined it to those specially described.—To JAMES SULLIVAN. FORD ED., v, 369. (Pa., 1791.)

8128. STATE RIGHTS, Encroachments on.—Whilst the General Assembly [of Virginia] thus declares the rights retained by the States, rights which they have never yielded, and which this State will never voluntarily yield, they do not mean to raise the banner of disaffection, or of separation from their sister States, coparties with themselves to this compact. They know and value too highly the blessings of their Union as to foreign nations and questions arising among themselves, to consider every infraction of it as to be met by actual resistance. They respect too affectionately the opinions of those possessing the same rights under the same instrument, to make that difference of construction a ground of immediate rupture. They would, indeed, consider such a rupture as among the greatest calamities which could befall them; but not the greatest. There is yet one greater, submission to a government of unlimited powers. It is only when the hope of avoiding this shall have become absolutely desperate, that further forbearance could not be indulged. Should a majority of the coparties, therefore, contrary to the expectation and hope of this Assembly, prefer, at this time acquiescence in these assumptions of power by the Federal member of the government, we will be patient and suffer much under the confidence that time, ere it be too late, will prove to them also the bitter consequences in which that usurpation will involve us all. In the meantime we will breast with them, rather than separate from them, every misfortune, save that only of living under a government of unlimited powers. We owe every other sacrifice to ourselves, to our Federal brethren, and to the world at large, to pursue with temper and with perseverance the great experiment which shall prove that man is capable of living in society, governing itself by laws self-imposed, and securing to its members the enjoyment of life, liberty, property, and peace; and further to show, that even when the government of its choice shall manifest a tendency to degeneracy we are not at once to despair, but that the will and the watchfulness of its sounder parts will reform its aberrations, recall it to original and legitimate principles, and restrain it within the rightful limits of self-government.—VIRGINIA PROTEST. ix, 498. FORD ED., x, 351. (1825.)

8129. STATE RIGHTS, Freedom and. —The States should be left to do whatever acts they can do as well as the General Government.—To JOHN HARVIE. FORD ED., v. 214. (N.Y., 1790.)

8130. STATE RIGHTS, General welfare.—This Assembly [of Virginia] does disavow and declare to be most false and unfounded, the doctrine that the compact, in authorizing its Federal branch to lay and collect taxes, duties, imposts, and excises, to pay the debts and provide for the common defence and general welfare of the United States, has given them thereby a power to do whatever *they* may *think*, or pretend, would promote the general welfare. which construction would make that of itself, a complete government,

without limitation of powers; but that the plain sense and obvious meaning were, that they might levy the taxes necessary to provide for the general welfare, by the various acts of power therein specified and delegated to them, and by no others.—VIRGINIA PROTEST. ix, 497. FORD ED., x, 350. (1825.) See GENERAL WELFARE CLAUSE.

8131. STATE RIGHTS, Home rule.—I believe the States can best govern our home concerns.—To WILLIAM JOHNSON. vii, 297. FORD ED., x, 232. (M., 1823.)

8132. ——— ———. To the State governments are reserved all legislation and administration, in affairs which concern their own citizens only.—To JOHN CARTWRIGHT. vii, 358. (M., 1824.)

8133. STATE RIGHTS, Interior Government.—Interior government is what each State should keep to itself.—To JAMES MADISON. i, 531. FORD ED., iv, 192. (P., 1786.)

8134. STATE RIGHTS, Lines of demarcation.—I have always thought that where the line of demarcation between the powers of the General and the State governments was doubtfully or indistinctly drawn, it would be prudent and praiseworthy in both parties never to approach it but under the most urgent necessity.—To J. C. CABELL. vi, 310. FORD ED., ix, 452. (M., 1814.)

8135. STATE RIGHTS, Metallic money and.—I recollect but one instance of control vested in the Federal over the State authorities, in a matter purely domestic, which is that of metallic tenders.—To ROBERT J. GARNETT. vii, 336. FORD ED., x, 295. (M., 1824.)

8136. STATE RIGHTS, National bank and.—The bill for establishing a National Bank undertakes * * * to form the subscribers into a corporation [and] * * * communicates to them, in their corporate capacities, a power to make laws paramount to the laws of the States; for so they must be construed, to protect the institution from the control of the State legislatures; and so, probably, they will be construed.—NATIONAL BANK OPINION. vii, 555-6. FORD ED., v, 285. (1791.) See BANK (U. S.), CONSTITUTIONALITY OF.

8137. STATE RIGHTS, Nullification. —Every State has a natural right in cases not within the compact (*casus non fœderis*) to nullify of their own authority all assumptions of power by others within their limits: without this right, they would be under the dominion, absolute and unlimited, of whosoever might exercise this right of judgment for them.—KENTUCKY RESOLUTIONS. ix, 469. FORD ED., vii, 301. (1798.)

8138. STATE RIGHTS, Preservation of.—I am for preserving to the States the powers not yielded by them to the Union and to the Legislature of the Union its constitutional share in the division of powers; and I am not for transferring all the powers of the States to the General Government, and all those of that government to the Executive branch.—To ELBRIDGE GERRY. iv, 268. FORD ED., vii, 327. (1799.) See CENTRALIZATION.

8139. —— ——. I wish to preserve [in a new constitution for Virginia] the line drawn by the Federal Constitution between the General and particular governments as it stands at present, and to take every prudent means of preventing either from stepping over it.—To ARCHIBALD STUART. iii, 314. FORD ED., v, 409. (Pa., 1791.) See CONSTITUTION (FEDERAL).

8140. STATE RIGHTS, Judiciary and. —It is of immense consequence that the States retain as complete authority as possible over their own citizens. The withdrawing themselves under the shelter of a foreign jurisdiction, is so subversive of order and so pregnant of abuse, that it may not be amiss to consider how far a law of *præmunire* should be revised and modified, against all citizens who attempt to carry their causes before any other than the State courts, in cases where those other courts have no right to their cognizance. A plea to the jurisdiction of the courts of their State, or a reclamation of a foreign jurisdiction, if adjudged valid, would be safe; but if adjudged invalid, would be followed by the punishment of *præmunire* for the attempt.—To JAMES MONROE. iv, 200. FORD ED., vii, 173. (M., 1797.) See JUDICIARY and SUPREME COURT.

8141. STATE RIGHTS, Reserved.—Nor is it admitted * * * that the people of these States, by not investing their Federal branch with all the means of bettering their condition, have denied to themselves any which may effect that purpose; since in the distribution of those means they have given to that branch those which belong to its department, and to the States have reserved separately the residue which belong to them separately. And thus by the organization of the two branches taken together, they have completely secured the first object of human association, the full improvement of their condition, and reserved to themselves all the faculties of multiplying their own blessings. —VIRGINIA PROTEST. ix, 497. FORD ED., x, 351. (1825.)

8142. STATE RIGHTS, Slavery and.— An abstinence from this act of power [prohibition of slavery in Missouri], would remove the jealousy excited by the undertaking of Congress to regulate the condition of the different descriptions of men composing a State. This certainly is the exclusive right of every State, which nothing in the Constitution has taken from them and given to the General Government. Could Congress, for example, say, that the non-freemen of Connecticut shall be freemen, or that they shall not emigrate into any other State?—To JOHN HOLMES. vii, 159. FORD ED., x, 158. (M., 1820.)

8143. STATE RIGHTS, Sovereignty.— The States should severally preserve their sovereignty in whatever concerns themselves alone, and whatever may concern another State, or any foreign nation, should be made a part of the Federal sovereignty.—To GEORGE WYTHE. ii, 267. FORD ED., IV, 445. (P., Sep. 1787.)

8144. STATE RIGHTS, Support of.— The support of the State governments in all their rights, as the most competent administrations for our domestic concerns and the surest bulwarks against anti-republican tendencies, I deem [one of the] essential principles of our government and, consequently [one] which ought to shape its administration.—FIRST INAUGURAL ADDRESS. viii, 4. FORD ED., viii, 4. (1801.)

8145. STATE RIGHTS, Surrender of.— Can it be believed, that under the jealousies prevailing against the General Government, at the adoption of the Constitution, the States meant to surrender the authority of preserving order, of enforcing moral duties and restraining vice within their own territory?—To WILLIAM JOHNSON. vii, 297. FORD ED., x. 231. (M., 1823.) See FEDERAL GOVERNMENT AND UNION (FEDERAL).

8146. STATES, Admission of new.— The 11th Article of Confederation admits Canada to accede to the Confederation at its own will, but adds that, " no other Colony shall be admitted to the same, unless such admission be agreed to by nine States". When the plan of April, 1784. for establishing new States was on the carpet, the committee who framed the report of that plan, had inserted this clause, " provided nine States agree to such admission, according to the reservation of the 11th of the Articles of Confederation". It was objected, 1. That the words of the Confederation, " no other Colony", could only refer to the residuary possessions of Great Britain, as the two Floridas, Nova Scotia, &c., not being already parts of the Union; that the law for " admitting " a new member into the Union, could not be applied to a territory which was already in the Union, as making part of a State which was a member of it. 2. That it would be improper to allow " nine " States to receive a new member, because the same reasons which rendered that number proper now, would render a greater one proper when the number composing the Union should be increased. They, therefore, struck out this paragraph, and inserted a proviso. that " the consent of so many States, in Congress, shall be first obtained, as may, at the time be competent "; thus leaving the question. whether the 11th Article applies to the admission of new States? to be decided when that admission shall be asked. (See the Journal of Congress of April 20, 1784.) Another doubt was started in this debate, viz.: whether the agreement of the nine States, required by the Confederation, was to be made by their legislatures, or by their delegates in Congress? The expression adopted. viz.: " so many States in Congress is first obtained", shows what was their sense in this matter. If it be agreed that the 11th

Article of the Confederation is not to be applied to the admission of these new States, then it is contended that their admission comes within the 13th Article, which forbids " any alteration, unless agreed to in a Congress of the United States, and afterwards confirmed by the legislatures of every State ".—ANSWERS TO M. DE MEUNIER. ix, 251. FORD ED., iv, 156. (P., 1786.) See CONFEDERATION, DEFECTS.

8147. STATES, Barriers of liberty.— The true barriers of our liberty are our State governments; and the wisest conservative power ever contrived by man, is that of which our Revolution and present government found us possessed. Seventeen distinct States, amalgamated into one as to their foreign concerns, but single and independent as to their internal administration, regularly organized with legislature and governor resting on the choice of the people, and enlightened by a free press, can never be so fascinated by the arts of one man, as to submit voluntarily to his usurpation. Nor can they be constrained to it by any force he can possess. While that may paralyze the single State in which it happens to be encamped, sixteen others, spread over a country of two thousand miles diameter, rise up on every side, ready organized for deliberation by a constitutional legislature, and for action by their governor, constitutionally the commander of the militia of the State, that is to say, of every man in it able to bear arms; and that militia, too, regularly formed into regiments and battalions, into infantry, cavalry and artillery, trained under officers general and subordinate, legally appointed, always in readiness, and to whom they are already in habits of obedience. The republican government of France was lost without a struggle, because the party of *" un et indivisible "* had prevailed; no provisional organizations existed to which the people might rally under authority of the laws, the seats of the directory were virtually vacant, and a small force sufficed to turn the legislature out of their chamber, and to salute its leader chief of the nation. But with us, sixteen out of seventeen States rising in mass, under regular organization, and legal commanders, united in object and action by their Congress, or, if that be in *duresse*, by a special convention, present such obstacles to an usurper as forever to stifle ambition in the first conception of that object.—To M. DESTUTT TRACY. v, 570. FORD ED., ix, 308. (M., 1811.)

8148. STATES, Confederation of.— The alliance between the States under the old Articles of Confederation, for the purpose of joint defence against the aggression of Great Britain, was found insufficient, as treaties of alliance generally are, to enforce compliance with their mutual stipulations; and these, once fulfilled, that bond was to expire of itself, and each State to become sovereign and independent in all things.—THE ANAS. lx, 88. FORD ED., i, 157. (1818.) See CONFEDERATION, DEFECTS.

8149. STATES, Cooperation of.— Your opinion of the propriety and advantage of a more intimate correspondence between the Executives of the several States, and that of the Union, as a central point, is precisely that which I have ever entertained; and on coming into office I felt the advantages which would result from that harmony. I had it even in contemplation, after the annual recommendation to Congress of those measures called for by the times, which the Constitution had placed within their power, to make communications in like manner to the Executives of the several States, as to any parts of them to which the legislatures might be alone competent. For many are the exercises of power reserved to the States, wherein an uniformity of proceeding would be advantageous to all. Such are quarantines, health laws, regulations of the press, banking institutions, training militia, &c., &c. But you know what was the state of the several governments when I came into office. That a great proportion of them were federal, and would have been delighted with such opportunities of proclaiming their contempt, and of opposing republican men and measures. Opportunities so furnished and used by some of the State governments, would have produced an ill effect, and would have insured the failure of the object of uniform proceeding. If it could be ventured even now (Connecticut and Delaware being still hostile) it must be on some greater occasion than is likely to arise within my time. I look to it, therefore, as a course which will probably be left to the consideration of my successor.—To JAMES SULLIVAN. v, 100. FORD ED., ix, 76. (W., 1807.)

8150. STATES, Commerce between.— Experience shows that the States never bought foreign goods of one another. The reasons are, that they would, in so doing, pay double freight and charges; and again, that they would have to pay mostly in cash, what they could obtain for commodities in Europe.—To JOHN ADAMS. i, 493. (P., 1785.)

8151. ——— ———. What a glorious exchange would it be could we persuade our navigating fellow citizens to embark their capital in the internal commerce of our country, exclude foreigners from that, and let them take the carrying trade in exchange; abolish the diplomatic establishments, and never suffer any armed vessel of any nation to enter our ports. [Faded] things can be thought of only in times of wisdom, not of party and folly.—To EDMUND PENDLETON. FORD ED., vii, 376. (M., April 1799.)

8152. STATES, Common interests.— The interests of the States ought to be made joint in every possible instance, in order to cultivate the idea of our being one nation, and to multiply the instances in which the people shall look up to Congress as their head.—To JAMES MONROE. i, 347. FORD ED., iv, 52. (P., 1785.)

8153. STATES, Correspondence between Executives.— As to the mode of correspondence between the general and particular executives, I do not think myself a good judge. Not because my position gives me any prejudice on the occasion; for if it be possible to be certainly conscious of anything, I am conscious of feeling no difference between writing to the highest or lowest being on earth; but because I have ever thought that forms should yield to whatever should facilitate business. Comparing the two governments together, it is observable that in all those cases where the independent or reserved rights of the States are in question, the two Executives, if they are to act together, must be exactly coordinate; they are, in those cases, each the supreme head of an independent government. Such is the case in the beginning of this letter where the two Executives were to treat *de pair en pair*. In other cases, to wit, those transferred by the Constitution to the General Government, the general Executive is certainly preordinate: *e. g.*, in a question respecting the militia, and others easily to be recollected. Were these, therefore, to be a stiff adherence to etiquette, I should say that in the former cases the correspondence should be between the two heads, and that in the latter, the Governor must be subject to receive orders from the War Department as any other subordinate officer would. And were it observed that either party set up unjustifiable pretensions, perhaps the other might be right in opposing them by a tenaciousness of his own rigorous right. But I think the practice in General Washington's administration was most friendly to business, and was absolutely equal. Sometimes he wrote to the Governors, and sometimes the heads of departments wrote. If a letter is to be on a general subject, I see no reason why the President should not write; but if it is to go into details, these being known only to the head of the department, it is better he should write directly. Otherwise, the correspondence must involve circuities. If this be practiced promiscuously in both classes of cases, each party setting examples of neglecting etiquette, both will stand on equal ground, and convenience alone will dictate through whom any particular communication is to be made. All the governors have freely corresponded with the heads of departments, except Hancock, who refused it. But his Legislature took advantage of a particular case which justified them in interfering, and they obliged him to correspond with the head of a department. General Washington sometimes wrote to them. I presume Mr. Adams did, as you mention his having written to you. On the whole, I think a free correspondence best, and shall never hesitate to write myself to the Governors even in a federal case, where the occasion presents itself to me particularly.—To GOVERNOR MONROE. iv, 401. FORD ED., viii, 59. (W., May 1801.)

8154. STATES, Counties and.—A county of a State cannot be governed by its own laws, but must be subject to those of the State of which it is a part.—To WILLIAM LEE. vii, 57. (M., 1817.) See COUNTIES.

8155. STATES, Division of authority. —The way to have good and safe government, is not to trust it all to one, but to divide it among the many, distributing to every one exactly the functions he is competent to. Let the National Government be entrusted with the defence of the nation, and its foreign and federal relations; the State governments with the civil rights, laws, police, and administration of what concerns the State generally; the counties with the local concerns of the counties, and each ward direct the interests within itself. It is by dividing and subdividing these republics from the great national one down through all its subordinations, until it ends in the administration of every man's farm by himself; by placing under every one what his own eye may superintend, that all will be done for the best.—To JOSEPH C. CABELL. vi, 543. (M., 1816.) See CENTRALIZATION.

8156. STATES, Equality in size.—In establishing new States regard is had to a certain degree of equality in size.—To WILLIAM LEE. vii, 57. (M., 1817.)

8157. STATES, Federal government and.—I [shall] consider the most perfect harmony and interchange of accommodations and good offices with the State governments, as among the first objects [of my administration].—To GOVERNOR THOMAS M'KEAN. iv, 350. FORD ED., vii, 487. (W., 1801.)

8158. —— ——. Considering the General and State governments as cooperators in the same holy concerns, the interest and happiness of our country, the interchange of mutual aid is among the most pleasing of the exercises of our duty.—To W. H. CABELL. v, 114. FORD ED., ix, 87. (W., 1807.)

8159. —— ——. The States can best govern our home concerns, and the General Government our foreign ones.—To WILLIAM JOHNSON. vii, 297. FORD ED., x, 232. (M., 1823.)

8160. —— ——. The extent of our country was so great, and its former division into distinct States so established, that we thought it better to confederate as to foreign affairs only. Every State retained its self-government in domestic matters, as better qualified to direct them to the good and satisfaction of their citizens, than a general government so distant from its remoter citizens, and so little familiar with the local peculiarities of the different parts.—To M. CORAY. vii, 320. (M., 1823.)

8161. —— ——. If the Federal and State governments should claim each the same subject of power, where is the common umpire to decide ultimately between them? In cases of little importance or urgency, the prudence of both parties will keep them aloof from the questionable ground; but if it can neither be avoided nor compromised, a convention of the States must be called, to ascribe the doubtful power to that department which they may think best.—To JOHN CARTWRIGHT. vii, 358. (M., 1824.) See FEDERAL GOVERNMENT.

8162. STATES, Fundamental principles of new.—The temporary and permanent governments* [shall] be established on these principles as their basis. 1. They shall forever remain a part of the United States of America. 2. In their persons, property and territory, they shall be subject to the Government of the United States in Congress assembled, and to the Articles of Confederation in all those cases in which the original States shall be so subject. 3. They shall be subject to pay a part of the Federal debts, contracted or to be contracted, to be apportioned on them by Congress, according to the same common rule and measure by which apportionments thereof shall be made on the other States. 4. Their respective governments shall be in republican forms, and shall admit no person to be a citizen, who holds any hereditary title. 5. After the year 1800 of the Christian era, there shall be neither slavery nor involuntary servitude in any of the said States, otherwise than in punishment of crimes, whereof the party shall have been duly convicted to have been personally guilty.†— WESTERN TERRITORY REPORT. FORD ED., iii, 409. (Mar. 1784.) See SLAVERY, ABOLITION.

8163. ———— ————. Whenever any of the said States shall have, of free inhabitants as many as shall then be in any one of the least numerous of the thirteen original States, such State shall be admitted by its delegates into the Congress of the United States, on an

* Of the States to be formed out of the Western Territory.—EDITOR.

† Next to the Declaration of Independence (if indeed standing second to that), this document ranks in historical importance of all those drawn by Jefferson; and, but for its being superseded by the "Ordinance of 1787", would rank among all American State papers immediately after the National Constitution. * * * That it contains practically every provision which has made the latter ordinance famous, has been carefully overlooked by those who have desired to give the credit of them to Northerners. Still more have these special pleaders suppressed the fact that Jefferson proposed to interdict slavery in all the Western Territory and not merely in the Northwest Territory, as the ordinance of 1787 did. Had it been adopted as Jefferson reported it, slavery would have died a natural death, and secession would have been impossible. There is another reason, however, for the little reputation this paper has brought to Jefferson, aside from the studious suppression of its importance by the special pleaders of New England. This plan, with its limitations of slavery, though failing by only one vote of adoption in 1784, was unpopular at the South and increasingly so as slavery became more and more profitable and more and more a southern institution. As early as 1790, Jefferson's partisans were already his apologists for this document, and from that time Jefferson carefully avoided any public utterance on slavery. This change of attitude is alone sufficient explanation why Southerners acquiesced with the Northerners in the suppression of this paper, and of Jefferson's drafting of it. In Jefferson's memoranda of the services which he took pride in having rendered his country, written in 1800, he carefully omitted all mention, as also in his autobiography written in 1821. And thus it has been left to the Massachusetts orators to glorify King, Dane, and Cutler for clauses in the Ordinance of 1787, which the latter had in truth taken from the Ordinance of 1784, and which they made sectional, where Jefferson had made them national.—NOTE IN FORD EDITION, iii, 430.

equal footing with the said original States.— WESTERN TERRITORY REPORT. FORD ED., iii, 409. (1784.)

8164. STATES, Government of.—Though the experiment has not yet had a long enough course to show us from which quarter encroachments are most to be feared, yet it is easy to foresee, from the nature of things, that the encroachments of the State governments will tend to an excess of liberty which will correct itself (as in the late instance), while those of the General Government will tend to monarchy, which will fortify itself from day to day, instead of working its own cure, as all experience shows. I would rather be exposed to the inconveniences attending too much liberty, than those attending too small a degree of it. Then it is important to strengthen the State governments; and as this cannot be done by any change in the Federal Constitution (for the preservation of that is all we need contend for), it must be done by the States themselves, erecting such barriers at the constitutional line as cannot be surmounted either by themselves or by the General Government. The only barrier in their power is a wise government. A weak one will lose ground in every contest. To obtain a wise and a safe government, I consider the following changes as important: Render the legislature a desirable station by lessening the number of representatives (say to 100) and lengthening somewhat their term, and proportion them equally among the electors. Adopt also a better mode of appointing senators. Render the Executive a more desirable post to men of abilities by making it more independent of the legislature. To wit, let him be chosen by other electors, for a longer time, and ineligible forever after. Responsibility is a tremendous engine in a free government. Let him feel the whole weight of it then, by taking away the shelter of his Executive Council. Experience both ways has already established the superiority of this measure. Render the judiciary respectable by every means possible, to wit, firm tenure in office, competent salaries, and reduction of their numbers. Men of high learning and abilities are few in every country; and by taking in those who are not so, the able part of the body have their hands tied by the unable. This branch of the government will have the weight of the conflict on their hands because they will be the last appeal of reason. These are my general ideas of amendments; but, preserving the ends, I should be flexible and conciliatory as to the means.—To ARCHIBALD STUART. iii, 314. FORD ED., v, 409. (Pa., 1791.)

8165. STATES, Kentucky's appeal to.— * * * This Commonwealth * * * calls on its co-States for an expression of their sentiments on the acts concerning aliens, and for the punishment of certain crimes hereinbefore specified, plainly declaring whether these acts are or are not authorized by the Federal compact. And it doubts not that their sense will be so announced as to prove their attachment unaltered to limited government, whether general or particular. And that the rights and liberties of their co-States will be exposed to no dangers by remaining embarked in a common bottom with their own. That they will concur with this Commonwealth in considering the said acts as so palpably against the Constitution as to amount to an undisguised declaration that that compact is not meant to be the measure of the powers of the General Government, but that it will proceed in the exercise over these States, of all powers whatsoever: that they will view this as seizing the rights of the States, and consolidating them in the hands of the General Government, with a power assumed to bind the States (not merely in the cases made Federal (*casus fœderis*), but, in all cases whatsoever, by laws made, not with their consent, but by others against their consent: that this would be to surrender the form of government we have chosen, and live under one deriving its powers from its own will, and not from our authority; and that the co-States recurring to their natural right in cases not made federal, will concur in declaring these acts void, and of no force, and will each take measures of its own for providing that neither these acts, nor any others of the General Government, not plainly and intentionally authorized by the Constitution, shall be exercised within their respective territories.—KENTUCKY RESOLUTIONS. ix, 471. FORD ED., vii, 305. (1798.) See KENTUCKY RESOLUTIONS.

8166. STATES, Power of.—As long as the States exercise, separately, those acts of power which respect foreign nations, so long will there continue to be irregularities committed by some one or other of them, which will constantly keep us on an ill-footing with foreign nations.—TO JAMES MADISON. i, 531. FORD ED., iv, 192. (P., February 1786.)

8167. STATES, Respect for.—I do not think it for the interest of the General Government itself, and still less of the Union at large, that the State governments should be so little respected as they have been. However, I dare say that in time all these as well as their central government, like the planets revolving round their common sun, acting and acted upon according to their respective weights and distances, will produce that beautiful equilibrium on which our Constitution is founded, and which, I believe, it will exhibit to the world in a degree of perfection, unexampled but in the planetary system itself. The enlightened statesman, therefore, will endeavor to preserve the weight and influence of every part, as too much given to any member of it would destroy the general equilibrium.—TO PEREGRINE FITZHUGH. iv, 217. FORD ED., vii, 210. (Pa., 1798.)

8168. STATES, Safety of citizens.—For the ordinary safety of the citizens of the several States, whether against dangers within or without, their reliance must be on the means to be provided by their respective States.—TO GOVERNOR TOMPKINS. v, 239. (W., 1808.)

8169. STATES, Sovereignty of.—The several States, now comprising the United States of America, were, from their first establishment, separate and distinct societies, dependent on no other society of men whatever. They continued at the head of their respective governments the executive Magistrate who presided over the one they had left. * * * The part which our chief magistrate took in a war waged against us by the nation among whom he resided, obliged us to discontinue him, and to name one within every State.—MISSISSIPPI RIVER INSTRUCTIONS. vii, 570. FORD ED., v, 461. (1792.)

8170. STATES, Union of.—We are so * * * sincerely disposed to render the union of the States more perfect that we shall, on all occasions, endeavor to render to our neighbors every friendly office which circumstances shall bring within the compass of our powers.—TO THE PRESIDENT OF PENNSYLVANIA. iii, 17. (R., 1781.)

8171. ——— ———. Our citizens have wisely formed themselves into one nation as to others, and several States as among themselves. To the united nation belong our external and mutual relations; to each State, severally, the care of our persons, our property, our reputation, and religious freedom. This wise distribution, if carefully preserved, will prove, I trust from example, that while smaller governments are better adapted to the ordinary objects of society, larger confederations more effectually secure independence, and the preservation of republican government.—TO THE RHODE ISLAND ASSEMBLY. iv, 397. (W., May 1801.) See STATE RIGHTS and UNION (FEDERAL).

8172. STATES, Vermont and Franklin. —I am anxious to hear what is done with the States of Vermont and Franklin. I think that the former is the only innovation on the system of April 23, 1784, which ought ever possibly be admitted. If Congress are not firm on that head, our several States will crumble to atoms by the spirit of establishing every little canton into a separate State. I hope Virginia will concur in that plan as to her territory South of the Ohio, and not leave to the Western country to withdraw themselves by force, and become our worst enemies instead of our best friends.—TO RICHARD HENRY LEE. FORD ED., iv, 71. (P., 1785.)

8173. STATESMEN, Honesty and.— The man who is dishonest as a statesman, would be a dishonest man in any station.— TO GEORGE LOGAN. FORD ED., x, 68. (P.F., 1816.)

8174. STEAM, Application of.—You asked me * * * whether the steam mill in London was turned by the steam immediately, or by the intermediate agency of water raised by the steam. When I was in London, Boulton made a secret of his mill. Therefore I was permitted to see it only superficially. I saw no water wheels, and therefore supposed none. I answered you accordingly that there were none. But when I was at Nismes, I went to see the steam mill there, and they showed 't to me in all its parts. I saw that their steam raised water, and that this water turned a wheel. I expressed my doubts of the necessity of the inter-agency of water, and that the London mill was without it. But they supposed me mistaken. Perhaps I was so. I have had no opportunity since of clearing up the doubt.—To CHARLES THOMSON. ii, 277. FORD ED., iv, 449. (P., 1787.)

8175. STEAM, Domestic use.—A smaller agent, applicable to our daily concerns, is infinitely more valuable than the greatest which can be used only for great objects. For these interest the few alone, the former the many. I once had an idea that it might perhaps be possible to economize the steam of a common pot, kept boiling on the kitchen fire until its accumulation should be sufficient to give a stroke, and although the strokes might not be rapid, there would be enough of them in the day to raise from an adjacent well the water necessary for daily use; to wash the linen, knead the bread, beat the hom'ny, churn the butter, turn the spit, and do all other household offices which require only a regular mechanical motion. The unproductive hands now necessarily employed in these, might then increase the produce of our fields. I proposed it to Mr. Rumsey, one of our greatest mechanics, who believed in its possibility. * * * but his death disappointed this hope.—To GEORGE FLEMING. vi, 505. (M., 1815.)

8176. STEAM, Engines.—It happens that of all the machines which have been employed to aid human labor, I have made myself the least acquainted with (that which is certainly the most powerful of all) the steam engine. In its original and simple form indeed, as first constructed by Newcommen and Savary, it had been a subject of my early studies; but once possessed of the principle, I ceased to follow up the numerous modifications of the machinery for employing it, of which I do not know whether England or our own country has produced the greater number.—To GEORGE FLEMING. vi, 504. (M., 1815.)

8177. STEAM, Fire engine.—You speak of a new method of raising water by steam, which, you suppose, will come into general use. I know of no new method of that kind, and suppose (as you say the account you have received of it is very imperfect) that some person has represented to you, as new, a fire engine erected at Paris, and which supplies the greater part of the town with water. But this is nothing more than the fire engine you have seen described in the books of hydraulics, and particularly in the Dictionary of Arts and Sciences, published by Owen, the idea of which was first taken from Papin's Digester. It would have been better called the steam engine. The force of the steam of water, you know, is immense. In this engine, it is made to exert itself towards the working of pumps. That of Paris is, I believe, the largest known, raising four hundred thousand cubic feet (French) of water in twenty-four hours; or, rather, I should have said, those of Paris, for there are two under one roof, each raising that quantity.—To PROFESSOR JAMES MADISON.* i, 446. (P., 1785.)

8178. STEAM, Grist mills.—I could write you volumes on the improvements which I find made, and making here [England], in the arts. One deserves particular notice, be-

* Professor in William and Mary College; a cousin of the President.—EDITOR.

cause it is simple, great, and likely to have extensive consequences. It 's the application of steam, as an agent for working grist mills. I have visited the one lately made here. It was, at that time, turning eight pair of stones. It consumes one hundred bushels of coal a day. It is proposed to put up thirty pair of stones. I do not know whether the quantity of fuel is to be increased.—To CHARLES THOMSON. i, 542. (L., 1786.)

8179. ———— ————. In the arts, the most striking thing I saw in England, new, was the application of the principle of the steam-engine to grist mills. I saw eight pairs of stones which are worked by steam, and there are to be set up thirty pair in the same house. A hundred bushels of coal a day, are consumed at present. I do not know in what proportion the consumption will be increased by the additional gear.—To JOHN PAGE. i, 550. FORD ED., iv, 215. (P., 1786.)

8180. STEAM, Horse power vs.—You say you have not been able to learn whether, in the new mills in London, steam is the immediate mover of the machinery, or raises water to move it. It is the immediate mover. The power of this agent, though long known, is but now, beginning to be applied to the various purposes of which it is susceptible. * * * I have had a conversation on the subject * * * with the famous Boulton to whom those mills belong. * * * He compares the effect of steam with that of horses in the following manner: Six horses, aided with the most advantageous combination of the mechanical powers hitherto tried will grind six bushels of flour in an hour; at the end of which time they are all in a foam, and must rest. They can work thus six hours in the twenty-four, grinding thirty-six bushels of flour, which is six to each horse, for the twenty-four hours. His steam mill in London consumes one hundred and twenty bushels of coal in twenty-four hours, turns ten pair of stones, which grind eight bushels of flour an hour each, which is nineteen hundred and twenty bushels in the twenty-four hours. This makes a peck and a half of coal perform exactly as much as a horse in one day can perform.*—To CHARLES THOMSON. ii, 67. FORD ED., iv, 337. (P., 1786)

8181. STEAM, Livingston's experiments.—I have received with great pleasure your favor on the subject of the steam engine. Though deterred by the complexity of that hitherto known, from making myself minutely acquainted with it, yet I am sufficiently acquainted with it to be sensible of the superior simplicity of yours, and its superior economy. I particularly thank you for the permission to communicate it to the Philosophical Society.—To ROBERT R. LIVINGSTON. iv, 295. FORD ED., vii. 367. (Pa., 1799.)

8182. STEAM, Navigation.—I hear you are applying steam in America to navigate boats, and I have little doubt, but that it will be applied generally to machines, so as to super-

* Parton, in his *Life of Jefferson*, p. 303, says: " It was Jefferson who first sent to America the most important piece of mechanical intelligence that pen ever recorded,—the success of the Watt steam engine, by means of which 'a peck and a half of coal performs as much work as a horse in a day'. He conversed at Paris with Boulton, who was Watts's partner in the manufacture of the engines, and learned from his lips this astounding fact. But it did not astound him in the least. He mentions it quietly in the postscript of a long letter; for no man yet foresaw the revolution in all human affairs which that invention was to effect."—EDITOR.

sede the use of water ponds, and, of course, to lay open all the streams for navigation. We know that steam is one of the most powerful engines we can employ; and in America, fuel is abundant.—To CHARLES THOMSON. i, 543. (L., 1786.)

8183. ———— ————. Internal navigation by steamboats is rapidly spreading through all our States, and that by sails and oars will ere long be looked back to as among the curiosities of antiquity. We count much, too, on its efficacy for harbor defence; and it will soon be tried for navigation by sea.—To BARON HUMBOLDT. vii, 75. FORD ED., x, 89. (M., 1817.)

8184. STEAM, Rumsey's ship.—Mr. Rumsey has obtained a patent in England for his navigation by the force of steam, and is soliciting a similar one here [France]. His principal merit is in the improvement of the boiler, and instead of the complicated machinery of oars and paddles, proposed by others, the substitution of so simple a thing as the reaction of a stream of water on his vessel. He is building a sea vessel at this time in England. He has suggested a great number of mechanical improvements in a variety of branches; and, upon the whole, is the most original and the greatest mechanical genius I have ever seen.—To DOCTOR WILLARD. iii, 16. (P., 1789.)

8185. STEAM, Water supply.—There is one object to which I have often wished a steam engine could be adapted. You know how desirable it is both in town and country to be able to have large reservoirs of water on the top of our houses, not only for use (by pipes) in the apartments, but as a resource against fire. * * * Could any agent be employed which would be little or no additional expense or trouble except the first purchase, it would be done. Every family has such an agent, its kitchen fire. It is small, indeed, but if its small but constant action could be accumulated so as to give a stroke from time to time which might throw ever so small a quantity of water from the bottom of a well to the top of the house (say one hundred feet), it would furnish more than would waste by evaporation, or be used by the family. I know nobody who must better know the value of such a machine than yourself, nor more equal to the invention of it.—To ROBERT R. LIVINGSTON. iv, 296. FORD ED., vii, 367. (Pa., 1799.)

—— STERNE (Laurence), Writings of.—See MORAL SENSE.

8186. STEUBEN (Baron), Services of. —Baron Steuben, a zealous friend, has descended from the dignity of his proper command to direct our [Virginia] smallest movements. His vigilance has, in a great measure, supplied the want of force in preventing the enemy from crossing the [James] river, which might have been * * * fatal. He has been assiduously employed in preparing equipments for the militia as they should assemble, pointing them to a proper object, and other offices of a good commander.—To GENERAL WASHINGTON. i, 284. FORD ED., ii, 408. (R., 1781.)

8187. STEWART (Dugald), Metaphysician.—Stewart is a great man, and among the most honest living. After you left Europe he * * * came to Paris. He brought me a letter from Lord Wycombe, whom you knew. I became immediately intimate with him, calling mutually on each other and almost daily during his stay at Paris, which was of some months.

I consider him and Tracy as the ablest metaphysicians living.—To JOHN ADAMS. vii, 152. (M., 1820.)

—— STRAWBERRY.—See AGRICULTURE.

8188. STRENGTH, National.—Weakness provokes insult and injury while a condition to punish often prevents them.—To JOHN JAY. i, 404. FORD ED., iv, 89. (P., 1785.)

8189. ———— ————. We confide in our strength, without boasting of it; we respect that of others, without fearing it.—To CARMICHAEL AND SHORT. iv, 17. FORD ED., vi, 338. (Pa., 1793.)

8190. STUART (Archibald), Talented. —A young man of good talents from the westward.—To JAMES MADISON. FORD ED., iii, 318. (T., May 1783.)

8191. STUART (House of), America and.—This country [American Colonies] which had been acquired by the lives, the labors, and fortunes of individual adventurers, was, by these Princes [the Stuarts], several times, parted out and distributed among the favorites and followers of their fortunes; and, by an assumed right of the Crown alone, were erected into distinct and independent governments; a measure, which, it is believed, his Majesty's prudence and understanding would prevent him from imitating at this day; as no exercise of such power, of dividing and dismembering a country, has ever occurred in his Majesty's realm of England, though now of very ancient standing; nor could it be justified or acquiesced under there, or in any part of his Majesty's empire.—RIGHTS OF BRITISH AMERICA. i, 127. FORD ED., i, 431. (1774.)

8192. STUART (House of), Crimes.— The treasonable crimes [of the Stuarts] against their people brought on them the exertion of those sacred and sovereign rights of punishment, reserved in the hands of the people for cases of extreme necessity, and judged by the constitution unsafe to be delegated to any other judicature.—RIGHTS OF BRITISH AMERICA. i, 127. FORD ED., i, 431. (1774.)

8193. STUART (House of), Evil influence.—It is not in the history of modern England or among the advocates of the principles or practices of her government, that the friend of freedom, or of political morality, is to seek instruction. There has, indeed, been a period, during which both were to be found, not in her government, but in the band of worthies who so boldly and ably reclaimed the rights of the people, and wrested from their government theoretic acknowledgments of them. This period began with the Stuarts, and continued but one reign after them. Since that, the vital principle of the English constitution is *corruption*, its practices the natural results of that principle, and their consequences a pampered aristocracy, annihilation of the substantial middle class, a degraded populace, oppressive taxes, general pauperism, and national bankruptcy.—To JOHN F. WATSON. vi, 346. (M., 1814.)

8194. STUART (House of), Hume and. —Hume spared nothing to wash the Stuarts white, and to palliate their misgovernment. For this purpose he suppressed truths, advanced falsehoods, forged authorities, and falsified records.—To ———— ————. vii, 412. (M., 1825.)

8195. STUDY, In old age.—I was a hard student until I entered on the business of life, the duties of which leave no idle time to those disposed to fulfil them; and now, retired, and at the age of seventy-six, I am again a hard student.—To DR. VINE UTLEY. vii, 116. FORD ED., x, 126. (M., 1819.)

8196. STUDY, Young men and.—A part of my occupation, and by no means the least pleasing, is the direction of the studies of such young men as ask it. They place themselves in the neighboring village and have the use of my library and counsel. and make a part of my society. In advising the course of their reading, I endeavor to keep their attention fixed on the main objects of all science, the freedom and happiness of man. So that coming to bear a share in the councils and government of their country, they will keep ever in view the sole objects of all legitimate government.—To GENERAL KOSCIUSKO. v, 509. (M., 1810.)

— STYLOGRAPH.—See INVENTIONS.

8197. SUBMISSION, To parliament.—Submission to their parliament was no part of our Constitution, nor ever in idea. if history may be credited.*—DECLARATION OF INDEPENDENCE AS DRAWN BY JEFFERSON.

8198. SUBSERVIENCE, Americans and.—We owe gratitude to France, justice to England, good-will to all, and subservience to none.—To ARTHUR CAMPBELL. iv, 198. FORD ED., vii, 170. (M., 1797.)

— SUBSIDIES.—See BOUNTIES.

8199. SUBSISTENCE, Discoveries and.—Every discovery which multiplies the subsistence of man must be a matter of joy to every friend of humanity.—To MONSIEUR L HOMMANDE. ii, 236. (P., 1787.)

8200. SUFFRAGE, Ark of safety.—The elective franchise, if guarded as the ark of our safety, will peaceably dissipate all combinations to subvert a Constitution, dictated by the wisdom, and resting on the will of the people.—To BENJAMIN WARING. iv, 378. (W., March 1801.)

8201. SUFFRAGE, Bribery and.—I believe we may lessen the danger of buying and selling votes. by making the number of voters too great for any means of purchase; I may further say that I have not observed men's honesty to increase with their riches.—To JEREMIAH MOOR. FORD ED., vii, 454. (M., Aug. 1800.)

8202. SUFFRAGE, Education and.—There is one provision [in the new constitution of Spain] which will immortalize its inventors. It is that which, after a certain epoch, disfranchises every citizen who cannot read and write. This is new, and is the fruitful germ of the improvement of everything good, and the correction of everything imperfect in the present constitution.—To CHEVALIER DE ONIS. vi, 342. (M., 1814.)

8203. —— ——. In the constitution of Spain, as proposed by the late Cortes, there was a principle entirely new to me, * * * that no person, born after that day, should ever acquire the rights of citizenship until he

* Struck out by Congress.—EDITOR.

could read and write. It is impossible sufficiently to estimate the wisdom of this provision. Of all those which have been thought of for securing fidelity in the administration of the government, constant ralliance to the principles of the Constitution, and progressive amendments with the progressive advances of the human mind, or changes in human affairs, it is the most effectual. Enlighten the people generally, and tyranny and oppressions of body and mind will vanish like evil spirits at the dawn of day. * * * The constitution of the Cortes had defects enough; but when I saw in it this amendatory provision, I was satisfied all would come right in time, under its salutary operation.—To DUPONT DE NEMOURS. vi, 592. FORD ED., x, 24. (P.F., 1816.) See CONSTITUTION, SPANISH.

8204. —— ——. By the bill [in the revision of the Virginia Code] for a general education, the people would be qualified to understand their rights, to maintain them, and to exercise with intelligence their parts in self-government.—AUTOBIOGRAPHY. i, 49. FORD ED., i, 69. (1821.)

8205. SUFFRAGE, Exercise of.—Should things go wrong at any time, the people will set them to rights by the peaceable exercise of their elective rights.—To WILSON C. NICHOLAS. v, 5. FORD ED., viii, 435. (W., 1806.)

8206. SUFFRAGE, General.—When the Constitution of Virginia was formed I was in attendance at Congress. Had I been here, I should probably have proposed a general suffrage; because my opinion has always been in favor of it. Still, I find some very honest men who, thinking the possession of some property necessary to give due independence of mind, are for restraining the elective franchise to property.—To JEREMIAH MOOR. FORD ED., vii, 454. (M., Aug. 1800.)

8207. SUFFRAGE, Instrument of reform.—The rational and peaceable instrument of reform. the suffrage of the people.—To SPENCER ROANE. vii, 133. FORD ED., x, 140. (P.F., 1819.)

8208. SUFFRAGE, Property qualification.—All male persons of full age and sane mind, having a freehold estate in one-fourth of an acre of land in any town, or in twenty-five acres of land in the country, and all persons resident in the colony, who shall have paid, scot and lot, to government the last two years. shall have right to give their vote in the election of their respective representatives.—PROPOSED VA. CONSTITUTION. FORD ED., ii, 14. (June 1776.)

8209. —— ——. All free male citizens, of full age and sane mind, who for one year before shall have been resident in the county. or shall through the whole of that time have possessed therein real property to the value of ——, or shall for the same time have been enrolled in the militia, and no others, shall have a right to vote for delegates for the * * * county, and for senatorial electors for the district. They shall give their votes personally, and *vivâ voce.*—Proposed Va. Constitution. viii, 444. Ford ed., iii, 323. (1783.)

8210. ——— ———. In the scheme of constitution for Virginia which I prepared in 1783, * * * I found [the suffrage] on a year's residence in the country, or the possession of property in it, or a year's enrollment in its militia.—To Jeremiah Moor. Ford ed., vii, 454. (M., Aug. 1800.)

8211. SUFFRAGE, Restricted.—It has been thought that corruption is restrained by confining the right of suffrage to a few of the wealthier of the people; but it would be more effectually restrained by an extension of that right to such numbers as would bid defiance to the means of corruption.—Notes on Virginia. viii, 391. Ford ed., iii, 255. (1782.)

8212. SUFFRAGE, Taxes and militia duty.—Every male citizen of the commonwealth, liable to taxes or to militia duty in any county, shall have a right to vote for representatives for that county to the legislature.—Notes for a Constitution. Ford ed., vi, 520. (1794.) See Voting.

8213. SUGAR, Maple.—What a blessing to substitute a sugar [maple] which requires only the labor of children for that which is said to render the slavery of the blacks necessary.—To Benjamin Vaughan. iii, 158. (N.Y., 1790.)

8214. ——— ———. I am sorry to hear my sugar maples have failed. I shall be able, however, to get here [Philadelphia] any number I may desire. * * * It is too hopeful an object to be abandoned.—To T. M. Randolph. Ford ed., v, 508. (Pa., 1792.)

8215. ——— ———. I should think the sugar-maple more worthy of experiment [in France than the sugar cane]. There is no part of France of which the climate would not admit this tree. I have never seen a reason why every farmer should not have a sugar orchard, as well as an apple orchard. The supply of sugar for his family would require as little ground, and the process of making it is as easy as that of cider. Mr. Micheaux, your botanist here, could send you plants as well as seeds, in any quantity from the United States.—To M. Lasteyrie. v, 314. (W., July 1808.)

8216. SUGAR, The poor and.—Sugar and coffee being articles of food for the poorer class, a small increase of price places them above the reach of this class.—To Marquis Lafayette. i, 597. Ford ed., iv, 257. (P., 1786.)

— SUICIDE.—See Murder, Self.

8217. SUMTER (Thomas), Description of.—I think I have selected a governor for Louisiana, as perfect in all points as we can expect. Sound judgment, standing in society, knowledge of the world, wealth, liberality, familiarity with the French language, and having a French wife. You will perceive I am describing Sumter. I do not know a more proper character for the place.—To James Madison. Ford ed., viii, 260. (M., July 1803.)

8218. SUN, Almighty physician.—The sun,—my almighty physician.—To James Monroe. Ford ed., iv, 41. (P., 1785.)

8219. SUN-DIAL, Calculations for a.—While much confined to the house by my rheumatism, I have amused myself w th calculating the hour lines of an horizontal d al for the latitude of this place [Poplar Forest]. * * * As I do not know that anybody here has taken this trouble before, I have supposed a copy would be acceptable to you.—To Mr. Clay. vi, 7. (P.F., 1811.)

8220. SUPREME COURT, Appointments to.—The appointment of a successor to Judge Patterson was bound up by rule. The last judiciary system requiring a judge for each district, rendered it proper that he should be of the district. This has been observed in both the appointments to the Supreme Bench made by me. Where an office is local we never go out of the limits for the officer.—To Cæsar A. Rodney. Ford ed., viii, 497. (W., Dec. 1806.)

8221. SUPREME COURT, Centralization and.—The great object of my fear is the Federal Judiciary. That body, like gravity, ever acting, with noiseless foot, and unalarming advance, gaining ground step by step, and holding what it gains, is engulfing insidiously the special governments into the jaws of that which feeds them.—To Spencer Roane. vii, 212. Ford ed., x, 189. (M., 1821.)

8222. ——— ———. There is no danger I apprehend so much as the consolidation of our Government by the noiseless, and therefore unalarming, instrumentality of the Supreme Court. This is the form in which federalism now arrays itself, and consolidation is the present principle of distinction between republicans and the pseudo-republicans but real federalists.—To William Johnson. vii, 278. Ford ed., x, 248. (M., 1823.)

8223. SUPREME COURT, Individual opinions.—A most condemnable practice of the Supreme Court to be corrected is that of cooking up a decision in caucus and delivering it by one of their members as the opinion of the Court, without the possibility of our knowing how many, who, and for what reasons each member concurred. This completely defeats the possibility of impeachment by smothering evidence. A regard for character in each being now the only hold we can have of them, we should hold·fast to it. They would, were they to give their opinions *seriatim* and publicly, endeavor to justify themselves to the world by explaining the reasons which led to their opinion.—To James Pleasants. Ford ed., x, 199. (M., Dec. 1821.)

8224. ——— ———. There is a subject respecting the practice of the Court of which you are a member which has long weighed on my mind. * * * It is the habitual mode of making up and delivering the opinions. You know that from the earliest ages of the English law, from the date of the Year-Books, at least, to the end of the Second George, the judges of England, in all but self-evident cases, delivered their opinions *seriatim*, with the reasons and authorities which governed their decisions. If they sometimes consulted together, and gave a general opinion, it was so rarely as not to excite either alarm or notice. Besides the light which their separate arguments threw on the subject, and the instruction communicated by their several modes of reasoning, it showed whether the judges were unanimous or divided, and gave accordingly more or less weight to the judgment as a precedent. It sometimes happened, too, that when there were three opinions against one, the reasoning of the one was so much the most cogent as to become afterwards the law of the land. When Lord Mansfield came to the bench he introduced the habit of caucusing opinions. The judges met at their chambers, or elsewhere, secluded from the presence of the public, and made up what was to be delivered as the opinion of the court. On the retirement of Mansfield, Lord Kenyon put an end to the practice, and the judges returned to that of *seriatim* opinions, and practice it habitually to this day I believe. I am not acquainted with the late Reporters, do not possess them, and state the fact from the information of others. To come now to ourselves, I know nothing of what is done in other States, but in this [Virginia] our great and good Mr. Pendleton was, after the Revolution, placed at the head of the Court of Appeals. He adored Lord Mansfield, and considered him as the greatest luminary of law that any age had ever produced, and he introduced into the court over which he presided, Mansfield's practice of making up opinions in secret, and delivering them as the oracle of the court, in mass. Judge Roane, when he came to that bench, broke up the practice, refused to hatch judgments, in conclave, or to let others deliver opinions for him. At what time the *seriatim* opinions ceased in the Supreme Court of the United States, I am not informed. They continued I know to the end of the 3d Dallas in 1800, later than which I have no Reporter of that court. About that time the present Chief-Justice [Marshall] came to the bench. Whether he carried the practice of Mr. Pendleton to it, or who, or when I do not know; but I understand from others it is now the habit of the Court, and I suppose it is true from the cases sometimes reported in the newspapers, and others which I casually see, wherein I observed that the opinions were uniformly prepared in private. Some of these cases, too, have been of such importance, of such difficulty, and the decisions so grating to a portion of the public as to have merited the fullest explanation from every judge, *seriatim*, of the reasons which had produced such convictions on his mind. It was interesting to the public to know whether these decisions were really unanimous, or might not perhaps be of four against three, and, consequently, prevailing by the preponderance of one voice only. The Judges, holding their offices for life, are under two responsibilities only. 1. Impeachment. 2. Individual reputation. But this practice completely withdraws them from both. For no-

body knows what opinion any individual member gave in any case, nor even that he who delivers the opinion, concurred in it himself. Be the opinion, therefore, ever so impeachable, having been done in the dark, it can be proved on no one. As to the second guarantee, personal reputation, it is shielded completely. The practice is certainly convenient for the lazy, the modest and the incompetent. It saves them the trouble of developing their opinion methodically and even of making up an opinion at all. That of *seriatim* argument shows whether every judge has taken the trouble of understanding the case, of investigating it minutely, and of forming an opinion for himself, instead of pinning it on another's sleeve. It would certainly be right to abandon this practice in order to give to our citizens one and all, that confidence in their judges which must be so desirable to the judges themselves, and so important to the cement of the Union. During the administration of General Washington, and while E. Randolph was Attorney General, he was required by Congress to digest the judiciary laws into a single one, with such amendments as might be thought proper. He prepared a section requiring the judges to give their opinions *seriatim*, in writing to be recorded in a distinct volume. Other business prevented this bill from being taken up, and it passed off; but such a volume would have been the best possible book of reports, and the better as unincumbered with the hired sophisms and perversions of counsel.—To WILLIAM JOHNSON. FORD ED., x, 223. (M., Oct. 1822.)

8225. ——— ———. I rejoice in the example you set of *seriatim* opinions. Some of your brethren will be encouraged to follow it occasionally, and in time, it may be felt by all as a duty, and the sound practice of the primitive court be again restored. Why should not every judge be asked his opinion, and give it from the bench, if only by yea or nay? Besides ascertaining the fact of his opinion, which the public have a right to know, in order to judge whether it is impeachable or not, it would show whether the opinions were unanimous or not, and thus settle more exactly the weight of their authority.—To WILLIAM JOHNSON. vii. 298. FORD ED., x, 232. (M., 1823.)

8226. ——— ———. I must comfort myself with the hope that the judges will see the importance and the duty of giving their country the only evidence they can give of fidelity to its Constitution and integrity in the administration of its laws; that is to say, by every one's giving his opinion *seriatim* and publicly on the cases he decides. Let him prove by his reasoning that he has read the papers, that he has considered the case, that in the application of the law to it, he uses his own judgment independently and unbiased by party views and personal favor or disfavor. Throw himself in every case on God and his country; both will excuse him for error and value him for his honesty. The very idea of cooking up opinions in conclave, begets suspicions that something passes which fears the public ear, and this, spreading by degrees, must produce at some time abridgment of tenure, facility of removal, or some other modification which may promise a remedy. For, in truth, there is at this time more hostility to the Federal Judiciary than to any other organ of the government.— To WILLIAM JOHNSON. vii, 278. FORD ED., x, 248. (M., 1823.)

8227. SUPREME COURT, Marshall's opinions.—This practice of Judge Marshall, of travelling out of his case to prescribe what the law would be in a moot case not before the court, is very irregular and very censurable. I recollect another instance, and the more particularly, perhaps, because it in some measure bore on myself. Among the midnight appointments of Mr. Adams, were commissions to some Federal justices of the peace for Alexandria. These were signed and sealed by him, but not delivered. I found them on the table of the Department of State, on my entrance into office, and I forbade their delivery. Marbury, named in one of them, applied to the Supreme Court for a mandamus to the Secretary of State (Mr. Madison) to deliver the commission intended for him. The Court determined at once, that being an original process, they had no cognizance of it; and, therefore, the question before them was ended. But the Chief Justice went on to lay down what the law would be, had they jurisdiction of the case, to wit: that they should command the delivery. The object was clearly to instruct any other court having the jurisdiction, what they should do if Marbury should apply to them. Besides the impropriety of this gratuitous interference, could anything exceed the perversion of law? For, if there is any principle of law never yet contradicted, it is that delivery is one of the essentials to the validity of a deed. Although signed and sealed, yet as long as it remains in the hands of the party himself, it is in *fieri* only, it is not a deed, and can be made so only by its delivery. In the hands of a third person it may be made an escrow. But whatever is in the Executive officers is certainly deemed to be in the hands of the President; and in this case, was actually in my hands, because, when I countermanded them, there was as yet no Secretary of State. Yet this case of "Marbury *vs.* Madison" is continually cited by bench and bar, as if it were settled law, without any animadversion on its being an *obiter* dissertation of the Chief Justice. It may be impracticable to lay down any general formula of words which shall decide at once, and with precision, in every case, this limit of jurisdiction. But there are two canons which will guide us safely in most of the cases. First. The capital and leading object of the Constitution was to leave with the States all authorities which respected their own citizens only, and to transfer to the United States those which respected citizens of foreign or other States; to make us several as to our-

selves, but one as to all others. In the latter case, then, constructions should lean to the general jurisdiction, if the words will bear it; and in favor of the States in the former, if possible to be so construed. And indeed, between citizens and citizens of the same State, and under their own laws, I know but a single case in which a jurisdiction is given to the General Government. That is, where anything but gold or silver is made a lawful tender, or the obligation of contracts is any otherwise impaired. The separate legislatures had so often abused that power, that the citizens themselves chose to trust it to the General, rather than to their own special authorities. Secondly. On every question of construction, carry ourselves back to the time when the Constitution was adopted, recollect the spirit manifested in the debates, and instead of trying what meaning may be squeezed out of the text, or invented against it, conform to the probable one in which it was passed. Let us try Cohen's case by these canons only, referring always, however, for full argument, to the essays before cited. 1. It was between a citizen and his own State, and under a law of his State. It was a domestic case, therefore, and not a foreign one. 2. Can it be believed, that under the jealousies prevailing against the General Government, at the adoption of the Constitution, the States meant to surrender the authority of preserving order, of enforcing moral duties and restraining vice, within their own territory? And this is the present case, that of Cohen being under the ancient and general law of gaming. Can any good be effected by taking from the States the moral rule of their citizens, and subordinating it to the General authority, or to one of their corporations, which may justify forcing the meaning of words, hunting after possible constructions, and hanging inference on inference, from heaven to earth, like Jacob's ladder? Such an intention was impossible, and such a licentiousness of construction and inference, if exercised by both governments, as may be done with equal right, would equally authorize both to claim all power, general and particular, and break up the foundations of the Union. Laws are made for men of ordinary understanding, and should, therefore, be construed by the ordinary rules of common sense. Their meaning is not to be sought for in metaphysical subtleties, which may make anything mean anything or nothing, at pleasure. It should be left to the sophisms of advocates, whose trade it is, to prove that a defendant is a plaintiff, though dragged into court, *torto collo*, like Bonaparte's volunteers, into the field in chains, or that a power has been given, because it ought to have been given, *et alia talia*. The States supposed that by their Tenth Amendment, they had secured themselves against constructive powers. They were not lessened yet by Cohen's case, nor aware of the slipperiness of the eels of the law. I ask for no straining of words against the General Government nor yet against the States. I believe the

States can best govern our home concerns, and the General Government our foreign ones. I wish, therefore, to see maintained that wholesome distribution of powers established by the Constitution for the limitation of both; and never to see all offices transferred to Washington, where, further withdrawn from the eyes of the people, they may more secretly be bought and sold as at market. But the Chief Justice says, "there must be an ultimate arbiter somewhere". True, there must; but does that prove it is either party? The ultimate arbiter is the people of the Union, assembled by their deputies in convention, at the call of Congress, or of two-thirds of the States. Let them decide to which they mean to give an authority claimed by two of their organs. And it has been the peculiar wisdom and felicity of our Constitution, to have provided this peaceable appeal, where that of other nations is at once to force.—To WILLIAM JOHNSON.* vii, 293. FORD ED., x, 230. (M., 1823.) See MARSHALL.

8228. SUPREME COURT, Questions of constitutionality.—It is a very dangerous doctrine to consider the judges as the ultimate arbiters of all constitutional questions. It is one which would place us under the despotism of an oligarchy. * * * The Constitution has erected no such single tribunal, knowing that to whatever hands confided, with the corruptions of time and party, its members would become despots. It has more wisely made all the departments coequal and cosovereign within themselves.—To WILLIAM C. JARVIS. vii, 178. FORD ED., x, 160. (M., 1820.)

8229. —— ——. If the Legislature fails to pass laws for a census, for paying the Judges and other officers of government, for establishing a militia, for naturalization as prescribed by the Constitution, or if they fail to meet in Congress, the Judges cannot issue their mandamus to them; if the President fails to supply the place of a judge, to appoint other civil or military officers, to issue requisite commissions, the Judges cannot force him. They can issue their mandamus or distringas to no executive or legislative officer to enforce the fulfilment of their official duties any more than the President or Legislature may issue orders to the Judges or their officers. Betrayed by English example, and unaware, as it should seem, of the control of our Constitution in this particular, they have at times overstepped their limit by undertaking to command executive officers in the discharge of their executive duties; but the Constitution, in keeping the three departments distinct and independent, restrains the authority of the Judges to judiciary organs, as it does the Executive and Legislative to executive and legislative organs. The Judges certainly have more frequent occasion to act on constitutional questions, because the law, of *meum* and *tuum* and of criminal action,

* Associate Justice William Johnson, of South Carolina, appointed by Jefferson to the Supreme Court bench, March, 1804.—EDITOR.

forming the great mass of the system of law, constitute their particular department. When the legislative or executive functionaries act unconstitutionally, they are responsible to the people in their elective capacity. The exemption of the Judges from that is quite dangerous enough.—To WILLIAM C. JARVIS. vii, 178. FORD ED., x, 160. (M., 1820.)

8230. SUPREME COURT, Republicanism and.—At length, we have a chance of getting a republican majority in the Supreme Judiciary. For ten years has that branch braved the spirit and will of the nation, after the nation had manifested its will by a complete reform in every branch depending on them. The event is a fortunate one, and so timed as to be a God-send to me. I am sure its importance to the nation will be felt, and the occasion employed to complete the great operation they have so long been executing, by the appointment of a decided republican, with nothing equivalent about him.—To ALBERT GALLATIN. v, 549. FORD ED., ix, 284. (M., 1810.)

8231. —— ——. The misfortune of Bidwell removes an able man from the competition. Can any other bring equal qualifications to those of [Levi] Lincoln? I know he was not deemed a profound common lawyer; but was there ever a profound common lawyer known in one of the Eastern States? There never was, nor never can be, one from those States. The basis of their law is neither common nor civil; it is an original, if any compound can be so called. Its foundation seems to have been laid in the spirit and principles of Jewish law, incorporated with some words and phrases of common law, and an abundance of notions of their own. This makes an *amalgam sui generis*, and it is well known that a man, first and thoroughly initiated into the principles of one system of law, can never become pure and sound in any other. Lord Mansfield was a splendid proof of this. Therefore, I say, there never was, nor can be a profound common lawyer from those States. Sullivan had the reputation of preeminence there as a common lawyer, but we have his History of Land Titles, which gives us his measure. Mr. Lincoln is, I believe, considered as learned in their laws as any one they have. Federalists say that Parsons is better. But the criticalness of the present nomination puts him out of the question. As the great mass of the functions of the new judge are to be performed in his own district, Lincoln will be most unexceptionable and acceptable there; and on the Supreme bench equal to any who can be brought thence. Add to this his integrity, political firmness, and unimpeachable character, and I believe no one can be found to whom there will not be more serious objections.—To ALBERT GALLATIN. v, 550. FORD ED., ix, 285. (M., Sep. 1810.)

3232. —— ——. Bidwell's disgrace withdraws the ablest man of the section in which Cushing's successor must be named. The pure integrity, unimpeachable conduct, talents and republican firmness of [Levi] Lincoln, leave him now, I think, without a rival. He is thought not an able *common* lawyer. But there is not and never was an able one in the New England States. Their system is *sui generis,* in which the common law is little attended to. Lincoln is one of the ablest in their system, and it is among them he is to execute the great portion of his duties.—To CÆSAR A. RODNEY. v, 547. (M., Sep. 1810.)

8233. —— ——. The death of [Associate Justice] Cushing is opportune, as it gives an opening for at length getting a republican majority on the Supreme Bench. Ten years has the anti-civism of that body been bidding defiance to the spirit of the whole nation, after they had manifested their will by reforming every other branch of government. I trust the occasion will not be lost. * * * Nothing is more material than to complete the reformation of the government by this appointment, which may truly be said to be putting the keystone into the arch.—To CÆSAR A. RODNEY. v, 547. (M., Sep. 1810.)

8234. —— ——. A circumstance of congratulation is the death of Cushing. The nation ten years ago declared its will for a change in the principles of the administration of their affairs. They have changed the two branches depending on their will, and have steadily maintained the reformation in those branches. The third, not dependent on them, has so long bid defiance to their will, erecting themselves into a political body, to correct what they deem the errors of the nation. The death of Cushing gives an opportunity of closing the reformation by a successor of unquestionable republican principles. Our friend, Lincoln, has, of course, presented himself to your recollection. I know you think lightly of him as a lawyer; and I do not consider him as a correct common lawyer, yet as much so as any one which ever came, or ever can come from one of the Eastern States. Their system of jurisprudence made up from the Jewish law, a little dash of common law, and a great mass of original notions of their own, is a thing *sui generis,* and one educated in that system can never so far eradicate early impressions as to imbibe thoroughly the principles of another system. It is so in the case of other systems of which Lord Mansfield is a splendid example. Lincoln's firm republicanism, and known integrity, will give complete confidence to the public in the long desired reformation of their judiciary. Were he out of the way, I should think Granger prominent for the place. His abilities are great; I have entire confidence in his integrity, though I am sensible that J.[ohn] R.[andolph] has been able to lessen the confidence of many in him. But that I believe he would soon reconcile to him, if placed in a situation to show himself to the public, as he is, and not as an enemy has represented him. As the choice must be of a New Englander, to exercise his functions for New England men, I confess I know of none but these two characters. Morton is really a republican, but inferior to both the others

in every point of view. Blake calls himself republican, but never was one at heart. His treachery to us under the Embargo should put him by forever. Story and Bacon are exactly the men who deserted us on that measure, and carried off the majority. The former, unquestionably a tory, and both are too young. I say nothing of professing federalists. Granger and Morton have both been interested in Yazooism. The former, however, has long been clear of it. I have said thus much because I know you must wish to learn the sentiments of others, to hear all, and then do what on the whole you perceive to be best.—To PRESIDENT MADISON. FORD ED., ix, 282. (M., Oct. 1810.)

8235. —— ——. I consider the substituting, in the place of Cushing, a firm, unequivocating republican, whose principles are born with him, and not an occasional ingraftment, as necessary to complete that great reformation in our government to which the nation gave its fiat ten years ago. They have completed and maintained it steadily in the two branches dependent on them, but the third, unfortunately and unwisely, made independent not only of the nation, but even of their own conduct, have hitherto bid defiance to the public will. and erected themselves into a political body with the assumed functions of correcting what they deem the errors of the nation.—To GIDEON GRANGER. FORD ED., ix, 286. (M., Oct. 1810.)

8236. SUPREME COURT, State rights and.—There are two measures which if not taken, we are undone. First,* to check these unconstitutional invasions of State rights by the Federal judiciary. How? Not by impeachment, in the first instance, but by a strong protestation of both houses of Congress that such and such doctrines, advanced by the Supreme Court, are contrary to the Constitution; and if afterwards they relapse into the same heresies, impeach and set the whole adrift. For what was the government divided into three branches, but that each should watch over the others and oppose their usurpations?—To NATHANIEL MACON. FORD ED., x, 192. (M., Aug. 1821.)

8237. —— ——. The Legislative and Executive branches may sometimes err, but elections and dependence will bring them to rights. The Judiciary branch is the instrument which, working like gravity, without intermission, is to press us at last into one consolidated mass. * * * If Congress fails to shield the States from dangers so palpable and so imminent, the States must shield themselves, and meet the invader foot to foot.—To ARCHIBALD THWEAT. vii, 199. FORD ED., x, 184. (M., 1821.)

8238. —— ——. You request me confidentially, to examine the question, whether the Supreme Court has advanced beyond its constitutional limits, and trespassed on those of the State authorities? I do not undertake it, because I am unable. Age and the

* For the " second " one, see No. 2066. —EDITOR.

wane of mind consequent on it, have disqualified me from investigations so severe, and researches so laborious. And it is the less necessary in this case, as having been already done by others with a logic and learning to which I could add nothing. On the decision of the case of *Cohen* vs. *The State of Virginia*, in the Supreme Court of the United States, in March, 1821, Judge Roane, under the signature of "Algernon Sidney", wrote for the [Richmond] *Enquirer* a series of papers on the law of that case. I considered these papers maturely as they came out, and confess that they appeared to me to pulverize every word which had been delivered by Judge Marshall, of the extra-judicial part of his opinion; and all was extra-judicial, except the decision that the act of Congress had not purported to give to the Corporation of Washington the authority claimed by their lottery law, of controlling the laws of the States within the States themselves. But, unable to claim that case, he could not let it go entirely, but went on gratuitously to prove, that notwithstanding the Eleventh Amendment of the Constitution, a State *could* be brought as a defendant, to the bar of his court; and again, that Congress might authorize a corporation of its territory to exercise legislation within a State, and paramount to the laws of that State. I cite the sum and result only of his doctrines, according to the impression made on my mind at the time, and still remaining. If not strictly accurate in circumstance, it is so in substance. This doctrine was so completely refuted by Roane, that if he can be answered, I surrender human reason as a vain and useless faculty, given to bewilder, and not to guide us. And I mention this particular case as one only of several, because it gave occasion to that thorough examination of the constitutional limits between the General and State jurisdictions, which you have asked for. There were two other writers in the same paper, under the signatures of "Fletcher of Saltoun", and "Somers", who, in a few essays, presented some very luminous and striking views of the question. And there was a particular paper which recapitulated all the cases in which it was thought the Federal Court had usurped on the State jurisdictions. * * * The subject was taken up by our [Virginia] Legislature of 1821-'22, and two drafts of remonstrances were prepared and discussed. As well as I remember, there was no difference of opinion as to the matter of right; but there was as to the expediency of a remonstrance at that time, the general mind of the States being then under extraordinary excitement by the Missouri question; and it was dropped on that consideration. But this case is not dead, it only sleepeth. The Indian chief said he did not go to war for every petty injury by itself, but put it into his pouch, and when that was full, he then made war. Thank heaven, we have provided a more peaceable and rational mode of redress.—To Judge William Johnson. vii, 293. Ford ed., x, 229. (M., June 1823.)

— SURGERY.—See Medicine.

8239. SURPLUS, Accumulation of.—[We] have left us in the treasury eight millions and a half of dollars. A portion of this sum may be considered as a commencement of accumulation of the surpluses of revenue, which, after paying the instalments of debts as they shall become payable, will remain without any specific object. It may partly, indeed, be applied toward completing the defence of the exposed points of our country, on such a scale as shall be adapted to our principles and circumstances. This object is doubtless among the first entitled to attention, in such a state of our finances, and it is one which, whether we have peace or war, will provide security where it is due. Whether what shall remain of this, with the future surpluses, may be usefully applied to purposes already authorized, or more usefully to others requiring new authorities, or how otherwise they shall be disposed of, are questions calling for the notice of Congress, unless indeed they shall be superseded by a change in our public relations now awaiting the determinations of others.—Seventh Annual Message. viii, 88. Ford ed., ix, 165. (Oct. 1807.)

8240. SURPLUS, Congress and.—The probable accumulation of the surpluses of revenue * * * merits the consideration of Congress. Shall it lie unproductive in the public vaults? Shall the revenue be reduced? Or shall it rather be appropriated to the improvements of roads, canals, rivers, education, and other great foundations of prosperity and union, under the powers which Congress may already possess, or such amendments of the Constitution as may be approved by the States?—Eighth Annual Message. viii, 110. Ford ed., ix, 224. (Nov. 1808.)

8241. SURPLUS, Disposition of.—When both of these branches of revenue [Mediterranean fund and Salt tax] shall * * * be relinquished, there will still ere long be an accumulation of moneys in the treasury beyond the instalments of public debt which we are permitted by contract to pay. They cannot, then, without a modification assented to by the public creditors, be applied to the extinguishment of this debt, and the complete liberation of our revenues—the most desirable of all objects; nor, if our peace continues, will they be wanting for any other existing purpose. The question, therefore, now comes forward,—to what other objects shall these surpluses be appropriated, and the whole surplus of impost, after the entire discharge of the public debt, and during those intervals when the purposes of war shall not call for them? Shall we suppress the impost and give that advantage to foreign over domestic manufactures? On a few articles of more general and necessary use, the suppression in due season will doubtless be right, but the great mass of the articles on which impost is paid is foreign luxuries, purchased by those only who are rich enough to afford themselves the use of them. Their patriotism would certainly prefer its continuance and application to the great purposes of the public education, roads, rivers, canals, and such other objects of public improvement as it may be thought proper to add to the constitutional enumeration of federal powers. By these operations new channels of communication will be opened between the States; the lines of separation will disappear, their interests will be identified, and their Union cemented by new and indissoluble ties.—SIXTH ANNUAL MESSAGE. viii, 68. FORD ED., viii, 493. (Dec. 1806.)

8242. SURPLUS, Taxation and.—Sound principles will not justify our taxing the industry of our fellow citizens to accumulate treasure for wars to happen we know not when, and which might not perhaps happen but from the temptations offered by that treasure.—FIRST ANNUAL MESSAGE. viii, 9. FORD ED., viii, 119. (1801.)

8243. SURVEYING, Method of platting.—You requested for the use of your school, an explanation of a method of platting the courses of a survey, which I mentioned to you as of my own practice. This is so obvious and simple, that as it occurred to myself, so I presume it has to others, although I have not seen it stated in any of the books. For drawing parallel lines, I use the triangular rule, the hypothenusal side of which being applied to the side of a common straight rule, the triangle slides on that, as thus, always parallel to itself. Instead of drawing meridians on his paper, let the pupil draw a parallel of latitude, or east and west line, and note in that a point for his first station, then applying to it his protractor, lay off the first course, and distance in the usual way to ascertain his second station. For the second course, lay the triangular rule to the east and west line, or first parallel, holding the straight or guide rule firmly against its hypothenusal side. Then slide up the triangle (for a northerly course) to the point of his second station, and pressing it firmly there, lay the protractor to that, and mark off the second course, and distance as before, for the third station. Then lay the triangle to the first parallel again, and sliding it as before to the point of the third station, then apply to it the protractor for the third course and distance, which gives the fourth station; and so on. When a course is southwardly, lay the protractor, as before, to the northern edge of the triangle, but prick its reversed course, which reversed again in drawing, gives the true course. When the station has got so far from the first parallel, as to be out of the reach of the parallel rule sliding on its hypothenuse, another parallel must be drawn by laying the edge, or longer leg of the triangle to the first parallel as before, applying the guide-rule to the end, or short leg (instead of the hypothenuse), as in the margin, and sliding the triangle up to the point for the new parallel. I have found this, in practice, the quickest and most correct method of platting which I have ever tried, and the neatest also, because it

disfigures the paper with the fewest unnecessary lines.—To MR. GIRARDIN. vi, 338. (M., 1814.)

8244. SWARTWOUT (Samuel), Character of.—The distribution of so atrocious a libel as the pamphlet "Aristides", and still more the affirming its contents to be true as Holy Writ, presents a snade in the morality of Mr. Swartwout, of which his character had not before been understood to be susceptible. Such a rejection of all regard to truth, would have been sufficient cause against receiving him into the corps of executive officers at first; but whether it is expedient after a person is appointed, to be as nice on a question of removal requires great consideration.—To DE WITT CLINTON. FORD ED., viii, 322. (W., Oct. 1804.)

— SYLVANIA, Proposed state of.— See WESTERN TERRITORY.

8245. SYMPATHY, For the afflicted.— What more sublime delight than to mingle tears with one whom the hand of heaven hath smitten! To watch over the bed of sickness, and to beguile its tedious and its painful moments! To share our bread with one whom misfortune has left none! This world abounds indeed with misery; to lighten its burthen, we must divide it with one another.—To MRS. COSWAY. ii, 38. FORD ED., iv, 318. (P., 1786.)

8246. SYMPATHY, Of friends.—When languishing under disease, how grateful is the solace of our friends! How are we penetrated with their assiduities and attentions! How much are we supported by their encouragement and kind offices! When heaven has taken from us some object of our love, how sweet is it to have a bosom whereon to recline our heads, and into which we may pour the torrent of our tears! Grief, with such a comfort, is almost a luxury!—To MRS. COSWAY. ii, 38. FORD ED., iv, 318. (P., 1786.)

8247. TALENTS, Hidden.—The object [of my educational bill] is to bring into action that mass of talents which lies buried in poverty in every country, for want of the means of development, and thus give activity to a mass of mind, which, in proportion to our population, shall be the double or treble of what it is in most countries.—To M. CORREA. vii, 94. (P.F., 1817.)

8248. TALENTS, Public councils and. —Talents in our public councils are at all times important.—To CÆSAR A. RODNEY. FORD ED., viii, 296. (W., 1804.)

8249. TALENTS, Republics and.—I hold it to be one of the distinguishing excellences of elective over hereditary successions, that the talents which nature has provided in sufficient proportion, should be selected by the society for the government of their affairs, rather than that this should be transmitted through the loins of knaves and fools, passing from the debauches of the table to those of the bed.—To PRESIDENT WASHINGTON. iii, 466. FORD ED., vi, 107. (M., 1792.)

8250. TALENTS, Science and.—Talents and science are sufficient motives with me in appointments to which they are fitted.—To PRESIDENT WASHINGTON. iii, 466. FORD ED., vi, 107. (M., 1792.)

8251. TALENTS, Useful.—The times do not admit of the inactivity of such talents as yours.—To JAMES MADISON. FORD ED., vii, 244. (Pa., 1798.) See ABILITY, EDUCATION, GENIUS and SCHOOLS.

8252. TALLEYRAND, Connection with X. Y. Z. plot.—There were interwoven with these overtures* some base propositions on the part of Talleyrand, through one of his agents, to sell his interest and influence with the Directory towards smoothing difficulties with them, in consideration of a large sum (fifty thousand pounds sterling); and the arguments to which his agent resorted to induce compliance with this demand, were very unworthy of a great nation (could they be imputed to them), and calculated to excite disgust and indignation in Americans generally, and alienation in the republicans particularly, whom they so far mistake, as to presume an attachment to France and hatred to the federal party, and not the love of their country, to be their first passion. —To JAMES MADISON. iv, 232. FORD ED., vii, 235. (Pa., April 1798.)

8253. TALLEYRAND, Corrupt.—The Envoys have been assailed by swindlers, whether with or without the participation of Talleyrand is not very apparent. The known corruption of his character renders it very possible he may have intended to share largely in the £50,000 demanded. But that the Directory knew anything of it, is neither proved nor probable. On the contrary, when the Portuguese ambassador yielded to like attempts of swindlers, the conduct of the Directory in imprisoning him for an attempt at corruption, as well as their general conduct, really magnanimous, places them above suspicion.—To PETER CARR. iv, 235. FORD ED., vii, 238. (Pa., April 1798.)

8254. TALLEYRAND, Hostility of.—I am told that Talleyrand is personally hostile to us. This, I suppose, has been occasioned by the X. Y. Z. history. He should consider that that was the artifice of a party, willing to sacrifice him to the consolidation of their power. This nation has done him justice by dismissing them; * * * those in power are precisely those who disbelieved that story; saw in it nothing but an attempt to deceive our country; that we entertain towards him personally the most friendly dispositions.+—To M. DUPONT DE NEMOURS. iv, 436. (April 1802.)

8255. TARIFF, Burdens of.—I wish it were possible to increase the impost on any articles affecting the rich chiefly, to the amount of the sugar tax, so that we might relinquish that at the next session. But this must depend on our receipts keeping up. As to the tea and coffee tax, the people do not regard it. The next tax which an increase of revenue should enable us to suppress, should be the salt tax, perhaps; indeed, the production of that article at home is already undermining that tax.—To ALBERT GALLATIN. FORD ED., viii, 171. (M., Sep. 1802.)

8256. ——. The revenue on the consumption of foreign articles, is paid cheerfully by those who can afford to add foreign luxuries to domestic comforts, being collected on our seaboards and frontiers only, and incorporated with the transactions of our mercantile citizens, it may be the pleasure and pride of an American to ask, what farmer, what mechanic, what laborer, ever sees a tax-gatherer of the United States?—SECOND INAUGURAL ADDRESS. viii, 41. FORD ED., viii, 343. (1805.)

8257. ——. These revenues will be levied entirely on the rich, the business of household manufacture being now so established that the farmer and laborer clothe themselves entirely. The rich alone use imported articles, and on these alone the whole taxes of the General Government are levied. The poor man, who uses nothing but what is made in his own farm or family, or within his own country, pays not a farthing of tax to the General Government, but on his salt; and should we go into that manufacture also, as is probable, he will pay nothing. Our revenues liberated by the discharge of the public debt, and its surplus applied to canals, roads, schools, &c., the farmer will see his government supported, his children educated, and the face of his country made a paradise by the contributions of the rich alone, without his being called on to spend a cent from his earnings.*—To GENERAL KOSCIUSKO. v, 586. (M., 1811.)

8258. TARIFF, Confederation and.—Congress, on the 18th of April, 1783, recommended to the States to invest them with a power, for twenty-five years, to levy an impost of five per cent. on all articles imported from abroad.—To M. DE MEUNIER. ix, 256. FORD ED., iv, 161. (P., 1786.)

8259. TARIFF, Debts and.—The principal objection [to assumption] now is that all the debts, general and State, will have to be raised by tax on imposts, which will thus be overburdened; whereas had the States been left to pay the debts themselves, they could have done it by taxes on land and other property, which would thus have lightened the burden on commerce.—To DR. GILMER. iii, 167. (N.Y., 1790.)

8260. TARIFF, Direct taxation and.—Would it not have been better [in the new Federal Constitution] to assign to Congress exclusively the articles of imposts for Federal purposes, and to have left direct taxation exclusively to the States? I should suppose the former fund sufficient for all probable events, aided by the land office.—To E. CARRINGTON. ii, 334. FORD ED., iv, 482. (P., 1787.)

8261. TARIFF, Discriminating.—Between nations who favor our productions and navigation and those who do not favor them, one distinction alone will suffice: one set of moderate duties for the first, and a fixed advance on these as to some articles, and prohibitions as to others, for the last.—FOREIGN COMMERCE REPORT. vii, 650. FORD ED., vi, 483. (Dec. 1793.)

8262. TARIFF, Excessive.—It is really an extraordinary proposition that the agri-

---

* See X. Y. Z. PLOT.—EDITOR.
+ Jefferson requested that these representations be made to Talleyrand.—EDITOR.

* Jefferson wrote a similar letter to Dupont de Nemours.—EDITOR.

cultural, mercantile, and navigating classes shall be taxed to maintain that of manufactures.—To THOMAS COOPER. FORD ED., x, 285. (M., 1823.)

8263. —— ——. Congress has done nothing remarkable except the passing a tariff bill by squeezing majorities, very revolting to a great portion of the people of the States, among whom it is believed it would not have received a vote but of the manufacturers themselves. It is considered as a levy on the labors and efforts of the other classes of industry to support that of manufactures, and I wish it may not draw on our surplus, and produce retaliatory impositions from other nations.— To RICHARD RUSH. FORD ED., x, 304. (M., 1824.)

8264. TARIFF, Incidental protection.— As to the tariff, I should say put down all banks, admit none but *a metallic circulation,* that will take its proper level with the like circulation in other countries, and then our manufacturers may work in fair competition with those of other countries, and the import duties which the government may lay for the purposes of revenue will so far place them above equal competition.—To CHARLES PINCKNEY. vii, 180. FORD ED., x, 162. (M., 1820.)

8265. TARIFF, Paper money.—The long succession of years of stunted crops, of reduced prices, the general prostration of the farming business, under levies for the support of manufacturers, &c., with the calamitous fluctuations of value in our paper medium, have kept agriculture in a state of abject depression, which has peopled the Western States by silently breaking up those on the Atlantic, and glutted the land market, while it drew off its bidders. In such a state of things, property has lost its character of being a resource for debts. Highland in Bedford, which, in the days of our plethory, sold readily for from fifty to one hundred dollars the acre (and such sales were many then), would not now sell for more than from ten to twenty dollars, or one-quarter or one-fifth of its former price.—To JAMES MADISON. vii, 434. FORD ED., x, 377. (M., February 1826.)

8266. TARIFF, Patriotism and.—Shall we suppress the impost and give that advantage to foreign over domestic manufactures? On a few articles of more general and necessary use, the suppression in due season will doubtless be right, but the great mass of the articles on which impost is paid is foreign luxuries, purchased by those only who are rich enough to afford themselves the use of them. Their patriotism would certainly prefer its continuance and application to the great purposes of the public education, roads, rivers, canals, and such other objects of public improvement as it may be thought proper to add to the constitutional enumeration of Federal powers.—SIXTH ANNUAL MESSAGE. viii, 68. FORD ED., viii, 493. (1806.)

8267. TARIFF, Prohibitory.—Duties of from ten to twenty per cent. on articles of heavy carriage, prevent their importation. They eat up all the profits of the merchant, and often subject him to loss. This has been much the case with respect to turpentine, tar and pitch, which are principal articles of remittance from the State of North Carolina. It is hoped that it will coincide with the views of the government * * * to suppress the duties on these articles, which of all others can bear them least.—To COUNT DE MONTMORIN. ii, 175. FORD ED., iv, 402. (P., 1787.)

8268. TARIFF, Protective.—Where a nation imposes high duties on our productions, or prohibits them altogether, it may be proper for us to do the same by theirs; first burdening or excluding those productions which they bring here in competition with our own of the same kind; selecting next, such manufactures as we take from them in greatest quantity, and which, at the same time, we could the soonest furnish to ourselves, or obtain from other countries; imposing on them duties lighter at first, but heavier and heavier, afterwards, as other channels of supply open. Such duties, having the effect of indirect encouragement to domestic manufactures of the same kind, may induce the manufacturer to come himself into these States, where cheaper subsistence, equal laws, and a vent of his wares, free of duty, may ensure him the highest profits from his skill and industry. And here, it would be in the power of the State governments to co-operate essentially, by opening the resources of encouragement which are under their control, extending them liberally to artists in those particular branches of manufacture for which their soil, climate, population and other circumstances have matured them, and fostering the precious efforts and progress of *household* manufacture, by some patronage suited to the nature of its objects, guided by the local informations they possess, and guarded against abuse by their presence and attentions. The oppressions on our agriculture, in foreign ports, would thus be made the occasion of relieving it from a dependence on the councils and conduct of others, and of promoting arts, manufactures and population at home.—FOREIGN COMMERCE REPORT. vii, 648. FORD ED., vi, 481. (Dec. 1793.)

8269. TARIFF, Public improvements and.—Of the two questions of the tariff and public improvements, the former, perhaps, is not yet at rest, and the latter will excite boisterous discussions. It happens that both these measures fall in with the western interests, and it is their secession from the agricultural States which gives such strength to the manufacturing and consolidating parties, on these two questions. The latter is the most dreaded, because thought to amount to a determination in the Federal Government to assume all powers non-enumerated as well as enumerated in the Constitution, and by giving a loose to construction, make the text say whatever will relieve them from the bridle of the States. These are all difficulties for your day; I shall give them the slip.—To RICHARD RUSH. · vii, 380. FORD ED., x, 322. (M., 1824.)

8270. TARIFF, Reciprocal.—There might have been mentioned a third* species of arrangement, that of making special agreements on every special subject of commerce, and of settling a tariff of duty to be paid on each side, on every particular article; but this would require in our Commissioners [to Spain] a very minute knowledge of our commerce; as it is impossible to foresee every proposition, of this kind, which might be brought into discussion, and to prepare them for it by information and instruction from hence. Our commerce, too, is, as yet, rather in a course of experiment, and the channels in which it will ultimately flow are not sufficiently known to enable us to provide for it by special agreement. Nor have the exigencies of our new government, as yet, so far developed themselves, as that we can know to what degree we may, or must have recourse to commerce, for the purpose of revenue. No common consideration, therefore, ought to induce us, as yet, to arrangements of this kind. Perhaps nothing should do it, with any nation, short of the privileges of natives, in all their possessions, foreign and domestic.—MISSISSIPPI RIVER INSTRUCTIONS. vii, 589. FORD ED., v, 479. (March 1792.)

8271. TARIFF, Revenue and.—The powers of the government for the collection of taxes are found to be perfect, so far as they have been tried. This has been as yet only by duties on consumption. As these fall principally on the rich, it is a general desire to make them contribute the whole money we want, if possible. And we have a hope that they will furnish enough for the expenses of Government and the interest of our whole public debt, foreign and domestic.—To COMTE DE MOUSTIER. iii, 200. (Pa., 1790.)

8272. ———— ————. The imports are not a proper object to bear all the taxes of a State. —To JOHN HARVIE. FORD ED., v, 214. (N.Y., 1790.)

8273. TARIFF, Salt and.—The duties composing the Mediterranean fund will cease by law at the end of the present season. Considering, however, that they are levied chiefly on luxuries, and that we have an impost on salt, a necessary of life, the free use of which otherwise is so important, I recommend to your consideration the suppression of the duties on salt, and the continuance of the Mediterranean fund, instead thereof, for a short time, after which that also will become unnecessary for any purpose now within contemplation. SIXTH ANNUAL MESSAGE. viii, 67. FORD ED., viii, 493. (1806.)

8274. TARIFF, Specific and ad valorem duties.—There must be something more in this increase of revenue than the *natural and war* increase; *depreciation* to a small de-

* The first was that of exchanging the privileges of *native citizens ;* and the second, those of the *most favored nation.*—EDITOR.

gree in other countries, a sensible one in this, and a great one in England, must make a part of it, and is a lesson to us to prefer ad valorem to fixed duties. The latter require often retouching, or they become delusive.— To ALBERT GALLATIN. FORD ED., viii, 357. (May 1805.)

8275. TARIFF, States and.—Several States have passed acts for vesting Congress with the whole regulation of their commerce, reserving the revenue arising from these regulations to the disposal of the State in which it is levied; * * * but the Assembly of Virginia, apprehensive that this disjointed method of proceeding may fail in its effect, or be much retarded, passed a resolution on the 21st of January, 1786, appointing commissioners to meet others from the other States, whom they invite into the same measure, to digest the form of an act for investing Congress with such powers over their commerce as shall be thought expedient, which act is to be reported to their several Assemblies for their adoption.—To M. DE MEUNIER. ix, 257. FORD ED., iv, 162. (P., 1786.) See DEBT, DRAWBACKS, DUTIES, EXCISE LAW, FREE TRADE, GENERAL WELFARE CLAUSE, INTERNAL IMPROVEMENTS, MANUFACTURES, PROTECTION, SURPLUS, and TAXATION.

8276. TARLETON (Colonel Bannastre), Raid on Monticello.—Colonel Tarleton, with his regiment of horse, was detached by Lord Cornwallis to surprise Mr. Jefferson (whom they thought still in office) [as Governor] and the Legislature now sitting in Charlottesville. The Speakers of the two houses, and some other members of the Legislature, were lodging with Mr. Jefferson at Monticello. Tarleton, early in the morning, when within ten miles of that place, detached a company of horse to secure him and his guests, and proceeded himself rapidly with his main body to Charlottesville, where he hoped to find the Legislature unapprized of his movement. Notice of it, however, had been brought, both to Monticello and Charlottesville, about sunrise. The Speakers, with their colleagues returned to Charlottesville, and with the other members of the Legislature, had barely time to get out of his way. Mr. Jefferson sent off his family to secure them from danger, and was himself still at Monticello making arrangements for his own departure, when a Lieutenant Hudson arrived there at half speed, and informed him that the enemy were then ascending the hill at Monticello. He departed immediately, and knowing that he would be pursued if he took the high road, he plunged into the woods of the adjoining mountain, where, being at once safe, he proceeded to overtake his family. This is the famous adventure of Carter's Mountain, which has been so often resounded through the slanderous chronicles of federalism. But they have taken care never to detail the facts, lest these should show that this favorite charge amounted to nothing more than that he did not remain in his house, and there singly fight a whole troop of horse, or suffer himself to be taken prisoner. Having accompanied his family one day's journey, he returned to Monticello. Tarleton had retired after eighteen hours' stay in Charlottesville. Mr. Jefferson then rejoined his family, and proceeded with them to an estate he had in Bedford, about eighty miles southwest, where, riding on his farm sometime after, he was thrown from his horse, and disabled from riding on horseback for a considerable time. But Mr. Turner finds it more convenient to give him this fall in his retreat from Tarleton, which had happened some weeks before, as a proof that he withdrew from a troop of horse with a precipitancy which Don Quixote would not have practiced.—INVASION OF VA. MEMORANDUM. ix, 223. (M., 1781.)

8277. ——— ———. I did not suffer by Colonel Tarleton. On the contrary, he behaved very genteelly with me. On his approach to Charlottesville, which is within three miles of my house at Monticello, he dispatched a troop of his horse, under Captain McLeod, with the double object of taking me prisoner, with the two Speakers of the Senate and Delegates, who then lodged with me, and of remaining in *vidette*, my house command'ng a view of ten or twelve counties round about. He gave strict orders to Captain McLeod to suffer nothing to be injured. The troop failed in one of their objects, as we had notice of their coming, so that the two Speakers had gone off about two hours before their arrival at Monticello, and myself with my family, about five m'nutes. Captain McLeod preserved everything with sacred care.—To DR. WILLIAM GORDON. ii. 425. FORD ED., v, 38. (P., 1788.) See CORNWALLIS.

8278. TASTE, Control of.—Taste cannot be controlled by law.—NOTES ON A MONEY UNIT. i, 168. FORD ED., iii, 451. (1784.)

8279. TAXATION, Basis of.—The taxes with which we are familiar, class themselves readily according to the basis on which they rest. 1. Capital. 2. Income. 3. Consumption. These may be considered as commensurate; Consumption being generally equal to Income, and Income the annual profit of Capital. A government may select any one of these bases for the establishment of its system of taxation, and so frame it as to reach the faculties of every member of the society, and to draw from him his equal proportion of the public contributions; and, if this be correctly obtained, it is the perfection of the function of taxation. But, when once a government has assumed its basis, to select and tax special articles from either of the other classes, is double taxation. For example, if the system be established on the basis of Income, and his just proportion on that scale has been already drawn from every one, to step into the field of Consumption, and tax special articles in that, as broadcloth or homespun, wine or whiskey, a coach or a wagon, is doubly taxing the same article. For that portion of Income with which these articles are purchased, having already paid its tax as Income, to pay another tax on the thing it purchased, is paying twice for the same thing, it is an aggrievance on the citizens who use these articles in exoneration of those who do not, contrary to the most sacred of the duties of a government, to do equal and impartial justice to all its citizens. How far it may be the interest and the duty of all to submit to this sacrifice on other grounds; for instance, to pay for a time an impost on the importation of certain articles, in order to encourage their manufac-

ture at home, or an excise on others injurious to the morals or health of the citizens, will depend on a series of considerations of another order, and beyond the proper limits of this note. * * * To this a single observation shall yet be added. Whether property alone, and the whole of what each citizen possesses, shall be subject to contribution, or only its surplus after satisfying his first wants, or whether the faculties of body and mind shall contribute also from their annual earnings, is a question to be decided. But, when decided, and the principle settled, it is to be equally and fairly applied to all. To take from one, because it is thought that his own industry and that of his fathers' has acquired too much, in order to spare to others, who, or whose fathers have not exercised equal industry and skill, is to violate arbitrarily the first principle of association, " the guarantee to every one of a free exercise of his industry, and the fruits acquired by it ". If the overgrown wealth of an individual be deemed dangerous to the State, the best corrective is the law of equal inheritance to all in equal degree; and the better, as this enforces a law of nature, while extra-taxation violates it.—NOTE IN DESTUTT TRACY'S POLITICAL ECONOMY. vi, 573. (1816.)

8280. TAXATION, Commerce, property and.—I am principally afraid that commerce will be overloaded by the assumption [of the State debts], believing that it would be better that property should be duly taxed.—To MR. RANDOLPH. iii, 185. (N.Y., 1790.)

8281. TAXATION, Control over.—The Congress * * * are of opinion that the Colonies of America possess the exclusive privilege of giving and granting their own money; that this involves the right of deliberating whether they will make any gift, for what purpose it shall be made, and what shall be the amount of the gift, and that it is a high breach of this privilege, for any body of men, extraneous to their constitutions to prescribe the purposes for which money shall be levied on them; to take to themselves the authority of judging of their conditions, circumstances and situation, of determining the amount of the contributions to be levied. As they possess a right of appropriating their gifts, so are they entitled, at all times, to inquire into their application, to see that they be not wasted among the venal and corrupt, for the purpose of undermining the civil rights of the givers, nor yet be diverted to the support of standing armies, inconsistent with their freedom and subversive of their quiet.—REPLY TO LORD NORTH'S CONCILIATORY PROPOSITION. FORD ED., i, 477. (July 1775.)

8282. TAXATION, Debt and.—Taxation follows public debt, and in its train wretchedness and oppression.—To SAMUEL KERCHIVAL. vii, 14. FORD ED., x, 42. (M., 1816.)

8283. TAXATION, Direct.—Would it not have been better [in the new Federal Constitution] * * * to have left direct taxation exclusively to the States?—To E. CAR-RINGTON. ii, 334. FORD ED., iv, 482. (P., 1787.)

8284. —— ——. I will add one question to what I have said there [letter to Mr. Madison]. Would it not have been better to assign to Congress exclusively the article of imposts for Federal purposes, and to have left direct taxation exclusively to the States? I should suppose the former fund sufficient for all probable events, aided by the land office.—To EDWARD CARRINGTON. ii, 334. FORD ED., iv, 482. (P., Dec. 1787.)

8285. —— ——. I have no doubts that the States * * * could have availed themselves of resources for this government [Assumption] which are cut off from the General Government by the prejudices existing against direct taxation in their hands.—To JOHN HARVIE. FORD ED., v, 214. (N.Y., 1790.)

8286. —— ——. The disgusting particularities of the direct tax.—To EDMUND PENDLETON. iv, 275. FORD ED., vii, 338. (Pa., 1799.)

8287. TAXATION, Direct and indirect.—It is uncertain what will be the fate of the proposed tax on horses. Besides its partiality, it is infinitely objectionable as foisting in a *direct* tax under the name of an indirect one.—To T. M. RANDOLPH. FORD ED., vi, 149. (Pa., 1792.)

8288. —— ——. A proposition has been made to Congress to begin sinking the public debt by a tax on pleasure horses; that is to say, on all horses not employed for the draught or farm. It is said there is not a horse of that description eastward of New York. And as to call this a *direct tax* would oblige them to proportionate it among the States according to the census, they choose to class it among the *indirect* taxes.—To DR. GEORGE GILMER. iii, 494. FORD ED., vi, 146. (Pa., 1792.)

8289. TAXATION, Equalization of.—To equalize and moderate the public contributions, that while the requisite services are invited by due remuneration, nothing beyond this may exist to attract the attention of our citizens from the pursuits of useful industry, nor unjustly to burthen those who continue in those pursuits— * * * [is one of the] functions of the General Government on which you have a right to call.—REPLY TO VERMONT ADDRESS. iv, 418. (W., 1801.)

8290. TAXATION, Exports and.—I have read with attention and satisfaction the pamphlet you have sent me. It is replete with sound views, some of which will doubtless be adopted. Some may be checked by difficulties. None more likely to be so than the proposition to amend the Constitution, so as to authorize Congress to tax exports. The provision against this in the framing of that instrument, was a *sine quâ non* with the States of peculiar productions, such as rice, indigo, cotton and tobacco, to which may now be added sugar. A jealousy prevailing that to the few States producing these articles, the justice of the others might not be a sufficient protection in opposition to their interest, they moored themselves to this anchor. Since the hostile dispositions lately manifested by the Eastern States, they would be less willing than before to place themselves at their mercy; and the rather as the Eastern States have no exports which can be taxed equivalently. It is possible, however, that this difficulty might be got over; but the subject looking forward beyond my time, I leave it to those to whom its burthens and benefits will belong.—To A. C. MITCHELL. vi, 483. (M., 1815.)

8291. TAXATION, Extravagant.—If anything could revolt our citizens against the war, it would be the extravagance with which they are about to be taxed. It is strange indeed that at this day, and in a country where English proceedings are so familiar, the principles and advantages of funding should be neglected, and expedients resorted to. Their new bank, if not abortive at its birth, will not last through one campaign; and the taxes proposed cannot be paid. How can a people who cannot get fifty cents a bushel for their wheat, while they pay twelve dollars a bushel for their salt, pay five times the amount of taxes they ever paid before? Yet that will be the case in all the States south of the Potomac. Our resources are competent to the maintenance of the war if duly economized and skillfully employed in the way of anticipation. However, we must suffer, I suppose, * * * and consider now, as in the Revolutionary war, that although the evils of resistance are great, those of submission would be greater. We must meet, therefore, the former as the casualties of tempests and earthquakes, and like them necessarily resulting from the constitution of the world.—To WILLIAM SHORT. vi, 400. (M., Nov. 1814.)

8292. TAXATION, Federal Government and.—I thought at first that the power of taxation [given in the new Federal Constitution] might have been limited. A little reflection soon convinced me it ought not to be.—To F. HOPKINSON. ii, 586. FORD ED., v, 76. (P., March 1789.)

8293. TAXATION, French.—It is confidently believed * * * that the stamp tax and land tax will be repealed, and other means devised of accommodating their receipts and expenditures. Those supposed to be in contemplation are a rigorous levy of the old tax of the *deux vingtièmes* on the rich, who had in a great measure withdrawn their property from it, as well as on the poor, on whom it had principally fallen.—To JOHN JAY. ii, 272. (P., 1787.)

8294. —— ——. The right of taxation includes the idea of * * * equalizing the taxes on the clergy and nobility as well as the commons. The two former orders do not pay one-third of the proportion *ad valorem*, which the last pay.—To DR. CURRIE. ii, 544. (P., 1788.)

8295. —— ——. The clergy and nobles [in France], by their privileges and influence, have kept their property in a great measure untaxed.—To Dr. Price. ii, 556. (P., Jan. 1789.)

8296. —— ——. Nor should we wonder at * * * [the] pressure [for a fixed constitution in 1788-9] when we consider the monstrous abuses of power under which * * * [the French] people were ground to powder; when we pass in review * * * the oppressions of the tithes, the tailles, the corvées, the gabelles, the farms and the barriers.—Autobiography. i, 86. Ford ed., i, 118. (1821.)

8297. —— ——. [We] should not wonder at * * * [the] pressure [for a fixed constitution in 1788-9] when we consider the monstrous abuses of power under which * * * [the French] people were ground to powder; when we pass in review the weight of their taxes and the inequality of their distribution.—Autobiography. i, 86. Ford ed., i, 118. (1821.)

8298. TAXATION, Internal.—Many of the opposition [to the new Federal Constitution] wish to take from Congress the power of internal taxation. Calculation has convinced me that this would be very mischievous.—To William Carmichael. ii, 550. (P., Dec. 1788.)

8299. —— ——. All are willing to add a bill of rights [to the Federal Constitution] but they fear the power of internal taxation will be abridged.—To William Short. ii, 542. (P., 1788.)

8300. TAXATION, Luxuries.—The government which steps out of the ranks of the ordinary articles of consumption to select and lay under disproportionate burdens a particular one, because it is a comfort, pleasing to the taste, or necessary to the health, and will, therefore, be bought, is, in that particular, a tyranny.—To Samuel Smith. vii, 285. Ford ed., x, 252. (M., 1823.)

8301. TAXATION, Oppressive English.—No earthly consideration could induce my consent to contract such a debt as England has by her wars for commerce, to reduce our citizens by taxes to such wretchedness, as that laboring sixteen of the twenty-four hours, they are still unable to afford themselves bread, or barely to earn as much oatmeal or potatoes as will keep soul and body together. And all this to feed the avidity of a few millionary merchants, and to keep up one thousand ships of war for the protection of their commercial speculations.—To William Crawford. vii, 7. Ford ed., x, 35. (M., 1816.)

8302. —— ——. If we run into such debts, as that we must be taxed in our meat and in our drink, in our necessaries and our comforts, in our labors and our amusements, for our callings and our creeds, as the people of England are, our people, like them, must come to labor sixteen hours in the twenty-four, give the earnings of fifteen of these to the government for their debts and daily expenses; and the sixteenth being insufficient to afford us bread, we must live, as they now do, on oatmeal and potatoes; have no time to think, no means of calling the mismanagers to account; but be glad to obtain subsistence by hiring ourselves to rivet their chains on the necks of our fellow-sufferers. * * * And this is the tendency of all human governments. A departure from principle in one instance becomes a precedent for a second; that second for a third; and so on, till the bulk of the society is reduced to be mere automatons of misery, to have no sensibilities left but for sinning and suffering. Then begins, indeed, the *bellum omnium in omnia*, which some philosophers observing to be so general in this world, have mistaken it for the natural instead of the abusive state of man. And the fore horse of this frightful team is public debt. Taxation follows that, and in its train wretchedness and oppression.—To Samuel Kerchival. vii, 14. Ford ed., x, 41. (M., 1816.)

8303. TAXATION, Parliamentary.—We [Virginia House of Burgesses] cannot, my Lord, close with the terms of that Resolution [Lord North's Conciliatory Proposition]. * * * because to render perpetual our exemption from an unjust taxation, we must saddle ourselves with a perpetual tax, adequate to the expectations, and subject to the disposal of Parliament alone; Whereas, we have a right to give our money, as the Parliament do theirs, without coercion, from time to time, as public exigencies may require. We conceive that we alone are the judges of the condition, circumstances, and situation of our people, as the Parliament are of theirs. It is not merely the mode of raising, but the freedom of granting our money, for which we have contended. Without this, we possess no check on the royal prerogative; and what must be lamented by dutiful and loyal subjects, we should be stripped of the only means, as well of recommending this country to the favors of our most gracious Sovereign, as of strengthening those bonds of amity with our fellow-subjects, while we would wish to remain indissoluble.—Address to Governor Dunmore. Ford ed., i, 456. (1775.)

8304. —— ——. By several acts of Parliament * * * they [the Ministers] have undertaken to give and grant our money without our consent—a right of which we have ever had the exclusive exercise.—Declaration on Taking up Arms. Ford ed., i, 467. (July 1775.)

8305. —— ——. Congress are of opinion * * * that the suspension of the exercise of their [Parliament's] pretended power of taxation being expressly made commensurate with the continuing of our gifts, these must be perpetual to make that so: whereas no experience has shown that a gift of perpetual revenues secures a perpetual return of duty or of kind dispositions. On the contrary, the parliament itself, wisely attentive to this observation, are in the established practice of granting their own money from year to year only.—REPLY TO LORD NORTH'S PROPOSITION. FORD ED., i, 478. (July 1775.)

8306. ———— ————. A proposition to give our money, when accompanied with large fleets and armies, seems addressed to our fears rather than to our freedom.—REPLY TO LORD NORTH'S PROPOSITION. FORD ED., i, 479. (July 1775.)

8307. ———— ————. We think the attempt unnecessary and unwarrantable to raise upon us, by force or by threats, our proportional contributions to the common defence, when all know and themselves acknowledge, we have fully contributed whenever called to contribute, in the character of freemen.—REPLY TO LORD NORTH'S PROPOSITION. FORD ED., i, 479. (July 1775.)

8308. ———— ————. The proposition [of Lord North] is altogether unsatisfactory because it imports only a suspension of the mode, not a renunciation of the pretended right to tax us. —REPLY TO LORD NORTH'S PROPOSITION. FORD ED., i, 480. (July 1775.)

8309. ———— ————. We had been so long in the habit of seeing the British consider us merely as objects for the extension of their *commerce*, and of submitting to every duty or regulation imposed with that view, that we had ceased to complain of them. But when they proposed to consider us as objects of *taxation*, all the States took the alarm.— NOTES ON M. SOULÉS'S WORK. ix, 295. FORD ED., iv, 302. (P., 1786.)

8310. TAXATION, Politics and.—The principle of the present [federalist] majority is *excessive expense*, money enough to fill all their maws, or it will not be worth the risk of their supporting. * * * Paper money would be perilous even to the paper men. Nothing then but excessive taxation can get us along; and this will carry reason and reflection to every man's door, and particularly in the hour of election.—To JOHN TAYLOR. iv, 259. FORD ED., vii, 310. (M., 1798.)

8311. TAXATION, Problem of.—Taxation is the most difficult function of government, and that against which their citizens are most apt to be refractory. The general aim is, therefore, to adopt the mode most consonant with the circumstances and sentiments of the country.—PREFACE TO TRACY'S POLITICAL ECONOMY. vi, 570. (1816.)

8312. TAXATION, Public opinion and. —The purse of the people is the real seat of sensibility. It is to be drawn upon largely, and they will then listen to truths which could not excite them through any other organ.—To A. H. ROWAN. iv, 257. FORD ED., vii, 281. (M., 1798.)

8313. ———— ————. All the [party] passions are boiling over, and one who keeps himself cool and clear of the contagion, is so far below the point of ordinary conversation, that he finds himself isolated in every society.

However, the fever will not last. War, land tax and stamp tax, are sedatives which must cool its ardor. They will bring on reflection, and that, with information, is all which our countrymen need, to bring themselves and their affairs to rights.—To JAMES LEWIS, JR. iv, 241. FORD ED., vii, 250. (Pa., May 1798.)

8314. TAXATION, Redress of grievances and.—The privilege of giving or withholding our moneys is an important barrier against the undue exertion of prerogative, * * * and all history shows how efficacious its intercession [is] for redress of grievances and reestablishment of rights, and how improvident would be the surrender of so powerful a mediator.—REPLY TO LORD NORTH'S PROPOSITION. FORD ED., i, 477. (July 1775.)

8315. TAXATION, Regulation of.—Our properties, within our own territories, shall [not] be taxed or regulated by any power on earth, but our own.—RIGHTS OF BRITISH AMERICA. i, 142. FORD ED., i, 447. (1774.)

8316. TAXATION, Religion and.—The restoration of the rights of conscience [in Virginia by the Revised Code] relieved the people from taxation for the support of a religion not theirs; for the [Church of England] Establishment was truly of the religion of the rich, the dissenting sects being entirely composed of the less wealthy people.—AUTOBIOGRAPHY. i, 49. FORD ED., i, 69. (1821.)

8317. TAXATION, Representation and. —Preserve inviolate the fundamental principle, that the people are not to be taxed but by representatives chosen immediately by themselves.—To JAMES MADISON. ii, 328. FORD ED., iv, 475. (P., 1787.)

8318. ———— ————. There are certain principles in which the constitutions of our several States all agree, and which all cherish as vitally essential to the protection of the life, liberty, property and safety of the citizen. [One is] the exclusive right of legislation and taxation in the representatives of the people. —To M. CORAY. vii, 323. (M., 1823.)

8319. TAXATION, Revolution from unjust.—So inscrutable is the arrangement of causes and consequences in this world, that a two-penny duty on tea, unjustly imposed in a sequestered part of it, changes the condition of all its inhabitants.—AUTOBIOGRAPHY. i, 106. FORD ED., i, 147. (1821.)

8320. TAXATION, Simplest system.— The simplest system of taxation yet adopted is that of levying on the land and the laborer. But it would be better to levy the same sums on the produce of that labor when collected in the barn of the farmer; because then if through the badness of the year he made little, he would pay little. It would be better yet to levy only on the surplus of this product above his own wants. It would be better, too, to levy it not in his hands, but in those of the merchant purchaser; because though the farmer would in fact pay it, as the merchant purchaser would deduct it from the original price of his produce, yet the farmer would not be sensible that he paid it. This idea would no doubt meet its difficulties and objections when it should come to be reduced to practice; yet I suspect it would be practical and expedient. * * * What a comfort to the farmer to be allowed to supply his own wants before he should be liable to pay anything, and then only pay on his surplus.—To JAMES MADISON. FORD ED., iv, 16. (P., Dec. 1784.)

8321. TAXATION, Uniformity of.—The public contributions should be as uniform as practicable from year to year, that our habits of industry and of expense may become adapted to them; and that they may be duly digested and incorporated with our annual economy.—To J. W. EPPES. vi, 198. FORD ED., ix, 398. (P.F., Sep. 1813.)

8322. TAXATION, War and.—War requires every resource of taxation and credit. —To GENERAL WASHINGTON. ii, 533. FORD ED., v, 57. (P., 1788.)

8323. ———— ————. Calculation has convinced me that circumstances may arise, and probably will arise, wherein all the resources of taxation will be necessary for the safety of the State.—To GENERAL WASHINGTON. ii, 533. FORD ED., v, 56. (P., Dec. 1788.)

8324. ———— ————. Sound principles will not justify our taxing the industry of our fellow citizens for wars to happen we know not when, and which might not perhaps happen but from temptations offered by that treasure.—FIRST ANNUAL MESSAGE. viii, 9. FORD ED., viii, 119. (1801.)

8325. TAXES, Abolition of internal.—Other circumstances, combined with the increase of numbers, have produced an augmentation of revenue arising from consumption, in a ratio far beyond that of population alone; and though the changes of foreign relations now taking place so desirable for the world, may for a season affect this branch of revenue, yet, weighing all probabilities of expense, as well as of income, there is reasonable ground of confidence that we may now safely dispense with all the internal taxes—comprehending excises, stamps, auctions, licenses, carriages, and refined sugars, to which the postage on newspapers may be added, to facilitate the progress of information; and that the remaining sources of revenue will be sufficient to provide for the support of the government, to pay the interest of the public debts, and to discharge the principals in shorter periods than the laws or the general expectation, had contemplated. War, indeed, and untoward events, may change this prospect of things, and call for expenses which the imposts could not meet; but sound principles will not justify our taxing the industry of our fellow-citizens to accumulate treasure for wars to happen we know not when, and which might not perhaps happen but from the temptations offered by that treasure.—FIRST ANNUAL MESSAGE. viii, 9. FORD ED., viii, 119. (1801.)

8326. ———— ————. You will perhaps have been alarmed, as some have been, at the proposition to abolish the whole of the internal taxes. But it is perfectly safe. They are under a million of dollars, and we can economize the government two or three millions a year. The impost alone gives us ten or eleven millions annually, increasing at a compound ratio of six and two-thirds per cent. per annum, and consequently doubling in ten years. But leaving that increase for contingencies, the present amount will support the government, pay the interest of the public debt, and discharge the principal in fifteen years. If the increase proceeds, and no contingencies demand it, it will pay off the principal in a shorter time. Exactly one half of the public debt, to wit, thirty-seven millions of dollars, is owned in the United States. That capital, then, will be set afloat, to be employed in rescuing our commerce from the hands of foreigners, or in agriculture, canals, bridges, or other useful enterprises. By suppressing at once the whole internal taxes, we abolish three-fourths of the offices now existing, and spread over the land.—To JOHN DICKINSON. iv, 425. (W., Dec. 1801.)

8327. ———— ————. The economies of the [first] session of the first Congress, convened since republicanism has recovered its ascendency, * * * have enabled them to suppress all the internal taxes, and still to make such provision for the payment of their public debt as to discharge that in eighteen years.—To GENERAL KOSCIUSKO. iv, 430. (W., April 1802.)

8328. ———— ————. The suppression of unnecessary offices, of useless establishments and expenses, enabled us to discontinue our internal taxes. These, covering our land with officers, and opening our doors to their intrusions, had already begun that process of domiciliary vexation which, once entered, is scarcely to be restrained from reaching successively every article of produce and property. If among these taxes some minor ones fell which had not been inconvenient, it was because their amount would not have paid the officers who collected them, and because, if they had any merit, the State authorities might adopt them, instead of others less approved. The remaining revenue on the consumption of foreign articles, is paid cheerfully by those who can afford to add foreign luxuries to domestic comforts, being collected on our seaboards and frontiers only, and incorporated with the transactions of our mercantile citizens, it may be the pleasure and pride of an American to ask, what farmer, what mechanic, what laborer, ever sees a tax-gatherer of the United States? These contributions enable us to support the current expenses of the government, to fulfill contracts with foreign nations, to extinguish the native right of soil within our limits, to extend those limits, and to apply such a surplus to our public debts, as places at a short day their final redemption; and that redemption once effected, the revenue thereby liberated may, by a just repartition among the States, and a corresponding amendment of the Constitution, be applied, *in time of peace,* to rivers, canals, roads, arts, manufactures, education, and other great objects within each State. *In time of war,* if injustice, by ourselves or others, must sometimes produce war, increased as the same revenue will be increased by population and consumption, and aided by other resources reserved for that crisis, it may meet within the year all the expenses of the year, without encroaching on the rights of future generations, by burdening them with the debts of the past. War will then be but a suspension of useful works, and a return to a state of peace, a return to the progress of improvement.—SECOND INAUGURAL ADDRESS. viii. 40. FORD ED., viii, 343. (1805.)

8329. TAXES, Consent and.—He [George III.] has endeavored to pervert the exercise of the kingly office in Virginia into a detestable and unsupportable tyranny * * * by combining with others to subject us to a foreign jurisdiction, giving his assent to their pretended acts of legislation * * * for imposing taxes on us without our consent.—PROPOSED VA. CONSTITUTION. FORD ED., ii, 10. (June 1776.)

8330. —— ——. He has combined with others * * * for imposing taxes on us without our consent.—DECLARATION OF INDEPENDENCE AS DRAWN BY JEFFERSON.

8331. —— ——. From the * * * origin [of the controversy with Great Britain] to this day, there never was a time when these States intimated a disposition to give away *in perpetuum* their essential right of judging whether they should give or withhold their money, for what purposes they should make the gift, and what should be its continuance.—RESOLUTIONS ON PEACE PROPOSITIONS. FORD ED., ii, 91. (Aug. 28, 1776.)

8332. TAXES, Consumption and.—The objects of finance in the United States have hitherto been very simple; merely to provide for the support of the government on its peace establishment, and to pay the debt contracted in the Revolutionary war. The means provided for these objects were ample, and resting on a consumption which little affected the poor, may be said to have been felt by none.—To J. W. EPPES. vi, 194. FORD ED., ix, 395. (P.F., Sep. 1813.)

8333. TAXES, Exact division of.—It will be said that, though, for taxes, there may always be found a divisor which will apportion them among the States according to numbers exactly, without leaving any remainder, yet, for representatives, there can be no such common ratio, or divisor, which, applied to the several numbers, will divide them exactly, without a remainder or fraction. I answer, then, that taxes must be divided *exactly,* and representatives *as nearly as the nearest ratio* will admit.—OPINION ON APPORTIONMENT BILL. vii, 596. FORD ED., v, 495. (1792.)

8334. TAXES, Excessive.—Our taxes are now a third and will soon be half of our whole exports; and when you add the expenses of the State Governments we shall be found to have got to the plenum of taxation in ten short years of peace. Great Britain, after centuries of wars and revolutions, had at the commencement of the present war taxed only to the amount of two-thirds of her exports.—To ARCHIBALD STUART. iv, 284. FORD ED., vii, 351. (Pa., Feb. 1799.)

8335. TAXES, Excise.—The excessive unpopularity of the excise and bank bills in the South, I apprehend, will produce a stand against the Federal Government.—To WILLIAM SHORT. FORD ED., v, 296. (Pa., March 1791.)

8336. —— ——. I hope the death blow to that most vexatious and unproductive of all taxes [excise] was given at the commencement of my administration, and believe its revival would give the deathblow to any administration whatever.—To DUPONT DE NEMOURS. v, 583. FORD ED., ix, 320. (M., 1811.)

8337. —— ——. If the excise tax could be collected from those who buy to sell again, so as to prevent domiciliary visits by the officers, I think it would be acceptable, and, I am sure, a wholesome tax.—To MR. NELSON. vi, 47. (M., April 1812.)

8338. TAXES, Imposition of.—No tax should ever be yielded for a longer term than that of the Congress wanting it, except when pledged for the reimbursement of a loan.—To J. W. EPPES. vi, 195. FORD ED., ix, 395. (P.F., Sep. 1813.)

8339. TAXES, Income.—Taxes on consumption like those on capital or income, to be just, must be uniform.—To SAMUEL SMITH. vii, 285. FORD ED., x, 252. (M., 1823.) See TAXATION, BASIS OF.

8340. TAXES, Land.—I am suggesting an idea on the subject of taxation which might, perhaps, facilitate much that business, and reconcile all parties. That is * * * to lay a land tax, leviable in 1798, &c. But if by the last day of 1798, any State shall bring its *whole* quota into the Federal Treasury, the tax shall be suspended one year for that State. If by the end of the next year they bring another year's tax, it shall be suspended a second year as to them, and so *toties quoties* forever. If they fail, the Federal collectors will go on, of course, to make their collection. In this way, those who prefer excises may raise their quota by excises, and those who prefer land taxes may raise by land taxes, either on the Federal plan, or on any other of their own which they like better. This would tend, I think, to make the General Government popular, and to render the State Legislatures useful allies and associates instead of rivals, and to mollify the harsh tone of government which has been asserted. I find the idea pleasing to most of those to whom I have suggested it. It will be objected to by those who are for consolidation.—To PEREGRINE FITZHUGH. FORD ED., vii, 136. (Pa., June 1797.)

8341. —— ——. I think that the matter of finances, which has set the people of Europe to thinking, is now advanced to that point with us, that the next step (and it is an unavoidable one), a land tax, will awaken our constituents, and call for inspection into past proceedings.—To St. George Tucker. iv, 197. Ford ed., vii, 169. (M., 1797.)

8342. —— ——. It had been expected that we must have laid a land tax this session [of Congress]. However, it is thought we can get along another year without it.—To Peregrine Fitzhugh. iv, 217. Ford ed., vii, 210. (Pa., Feb. 1798.)

8343. —— ——. A land tax is the decided resource of many [of the federalists], perhaps of a majority.—To James Madison. Ford ed., vii, 243. (Pa., April 1798.)

8344. —— ——. The federalists talk * * * of a land tax. This will probably not be opposed. The only question will be, how to modify it. On this there may be a great diversity of sentiment. One party will want to make it a new source of patronage and expense.—To James Madison. iv, 234. Ford ed., vii, 237. (Pa., April 1798.)

8345. —— ——. The land tax is now on the carpet to raise two millions of dollars; yet I think they must at least double it, as the expenses of the provisional army were not provided for in it, and will require of itself four millions a year.—To James Monroe. iv, 242. Ford ed., vii, 156. (Pa., May 1798.)

8346. —— ——. In most of the middle and southern States some land tax is now paid into the State treasury, and for this purpose the lands have been classed and valued, and the tax assessed according to that valuation. In these an excise is most odious. In the eastern States land taxes are odious, excises less unpopular.—To Dupont de Nemours. v, 583. Ford ed., ix, 321. (M., April 1811.)

8347. TAXES, Legislation and.—Taxes should be continued by annual or biennial reenactments.—To J. W. Eppes. vi, 195. Ford ed., ix, 395. (P.F., Sep. 1813.)

8348. —— ——. Taxes should be continued by annual or biennial reenactments, because a constant hold, by the nation, of the strings of the public purse, is a salutary restraint from which an honest government ought not to wish, nor a corrupt one to be permitted to be free.—To J. W. Eppes. vi, 195. Ford ed., ix, 395. (P.F., Sep. 1813.)

8349. TAXES, Necessary wants and.— Taxes should be proportioned to what may be annually spared by the individual.—To James Madison. Ford ed., iv, 15. (P., Dec. 1784.)

8350. TAXES, Paper money and.— Every one, through whose hands a bill passed, lost on that bill what it lost in value, during the time it was in his hands. This was a real tax on him; and * * * the most op-

pressive of all, because the most unequal of all, —To M. de Meunier. ix, 260. Ford ed., iv, 165. (P., 1786.)

8351. TAXES, Politics and suppression of.—Bitter men are not pleased with the suppression of taxes. Not daring to condemn the measure, they attack the motive; and too disingenuous to ascribe it to the honest one of freeing our citizens from unnecessary burthens and unnecessary systems of office, they ascribe it to a desire of popularity. But every honest man will suppose honest acts to flow from honest principles, and the rogues may rail without intermission.—To Dr. Benjamin Rush. iv, 426. Ford ed., viii, 128. (W., 1801.)

8352. TAXES, Resources of internal.— Whenever we are destined to meet events which shall call forth all the energies of our countrymen, we have * * * the comfort of leaving for calls like these the extraordinary resources of loans and internal taxes.— Second Annual Message. viii, 19. Ford ed., viii, 185. (Dec. 1802.)

8353. TAXES, Sinecures and.—We do not mean that our people shall be burdened with oppressive taxes to provide sinecures for the idle or the wicked, under color of providing for a civil list.—Reply to Lord North's Proposition. Ford ed., i, 480. (July 1775.)

8354. TAXES, Stamp.—To the stamp tax I have not seen a man who is not totally irreconcilable. * * * Yet, although a very disgusting pill, I think there can be no question the people will swallow it, if their representatives determine on it.—To Mr. Nelson. vi, 47. (M., April 1812.)

8355. TAXES, Unnecessary.—To impose on our citizens no unnecessary burden, * * * [is one of] the landmarks by which we are to guide ourselves in all our proceedings.—Second Annual Message. viii, 21. Ford ed., viii, 187. (Dec. 1802.)

8356. TAXES, War and.—The report of the Committee of Finance proposes taxes to the amount of twenty millions. This is a dashing proposition. But, if Congress pass it, I shall consider it sufficient evidence that their constituents generally can pay the tax. No man has greater confidence than I have in the spirit of the people, to a rational extent. Whatever they can, they will. But, without either market or medium, I know not how it is to be done. All markets abroad, and all at home are shut, to us; so that we have been feeding our horses on wheat. Before the day of collection, bank notes will be but as oak leaves; and of specie, there is not within all the United States, one half of the proposed amount of the taxes. I had thought myself as bold as was safe in contemplating, as possible, an annual taxation of ten millions, as fund for emissions of treasury notes; and when further emissions should be necessary, that it would be better to enlarge the time, than the tax for redemption. Our position, with respect to our enemy, and our markets, distinguish us from all other nations; inasmuch, as a state of war, with us annihilates in an instant all our surplus produce, that on which we depended for many comforts of life. This renders particularly expedient the throwing a part of the burdens of war on times of peace and commerce.—To JAMES MONROE. vi, 395. FORD ED., ix, 493. (M., Oct. 1814.)

8357. —— ——. Instead of taxes for the whole year's expenses, which the people cannot pay, a tax to the amount of the interest and a reasonable portion of the principal will command the whole sum, and throw a part of the burdens of war on times of peace and prosperity.—To WILLIAM SHORT. vi, 401. (M., 1814.)

8358. TAXES, Wasted.—If there be anything amiss in the present state of our affairs, as the formidable deficit lately unfolded to us indicates, I ascribe it to the inattention of Congress to their duties, to their unwise dissipation and waste of the public contributions. They seemed, some little while ago, to be at a loss for objects whereon to throw away the supposed fathomless funds of the treasury. * * * I am aware that in one of their most ruinous vagaries the people were themselves betrayed into the same phrenzy with their representatives. The deficit produced, and a heavy tax to supply it, will, I trust, bring both to their sober senses.—To THOMAS RITCHIE. vii, 191. FORD ED., x, 170. (M., 1820.)

8359. TAX-GATHERERS, Cost of.— Our tax-gatherers in Virginia cost as much as the whole civil list besides.—To JAMES MADISON. FORD ED., iv, 16. (P., 1784.)

8360. TAX-GATHERERS, Discontent and.—The tax-gatherer has already excited discontent.—To JAMES MADISON. iv, 261. FORD ED., vii, 313. (Pa., Jan. 1799.)

8361. TAYLOR (John), Political principles.—Colonel Taylor and myself have rarely, if ever, differed in any political principle of importance. Every act of his life, and every word he ever wrote, satisfies me of this.— To THOMAS RITCHIE. vii, 191. FORD ED., x, 170. (M., 1820.)

8362. —— ——. Colonel Taylor's book of "Constructions Construed" * * * is the most logical retraction of our governments to the original and true principles of the Constitution creating them, whi h has appeared since the adoption of that instrument. I may not perhaps concur in all its opinions, great and small, for no two men ever thought alike on so many points. But on all important questions, it contains the true political faith, to which every catholic republican should steadfastly hold. It should be put into the hands of all our functionaries, authoritatively, as a standing instruction and true exposition of our Constitution, as understood at the time we agreed to it.—To SPENCER ROANE. vii, 213. FORD ED., x, 189. (M., 1821.)

8363. TEA, Duty on.— So inscrutable is the arrangement of causes and consequences in this world, that a two-penny duty on tea, unjustly imposed in a sequestered part of it, changes the condition of all its inhabitants.— AUTOBIOGRAPHY. i, 106. FORD ED., i, 147. (1821.) See BOSTON PORT BILL.

8364. TEACHERS, Appreciation of.— Respect and gratitude [are] due to those who devote their time and efforts to render the youths of every successive age fit governors for the next.—To HUGH L. WHITE. v, 522. (M., 1810.)

8365. TEMPER, Southern.—Our Southern sun has been accused of sometimes sublimating the temper too highly.—To E. RUTLEDGE. iii, 166. FORD ED., v, 197. (N.Y., 1790.)

8366. TEMPER, Smooth.—Nothing enables a man to get along in business so well as a smooth temper.—ANAS. FORD ED., i, 337. (1808.)

8367. TEMPERANCE, At table.—In the pleasures of the table [the French] are far before us, because, with good taste they unite temperance. They do not terminate the most sociable meals by transforming themselves into brutes.—To MR. BELLINI. i, 445. (P., 1785.)

8368. TEMPERANCE, France and.—I have never yet seen a man drunk in France, even among the lowest of the people.—To MR. BELLINI. ', 445. (P., 1785.)

8369. TEMPERANCE, Principles of.—I have received and read with thankfulness and pleasure your denunciation of the abuses of tobacco and wine. Yet, however sound in its principles, I expect it will be but a sermon to the wind. You will find it * * * difficult to inculcate these sanative precepts on the sensualities of the present day.—To DR. BENJAMIN WATERHOUSE. vii, 252. FORD ED., x, 219. (M., 1822.)

— TEMPERATURE.—See CLIMATE.

8370. TENANTS, For Monticello.—The subject [obtaining tenants] is one I have very much at heart, for I find I am not fit to be a farmer with the kind of labor we have, and also subject to such long avocation.—To S. T. MASON. FORD ED., vii, 396. (M., Oct. 1799.)

8371. TENANTS, Seeking.—You promised to endeavor to send me some tenants. I am waiting for them. * * * Tenants of any size may be accommodated with the number of fields suited to their force. Only send me good people.—To S. T. MASON. FORD ED., vii, 283. (M., 1798.)

8372. TERNANT (J. B.), Hamilton and.—Ternant has at length openly hoisted the flag of monarchy by going into deep mourning for his prince [Louis XVI.]. I suspect he thinks a cessation of his visits to me a necessary accompaniment to this pious duty. A connection between him and Hamilton seems to be springing up.—To JAMES MADISON. iii, 520. FORD ED., vi, 193. (Pa., 1793.)

8373. TERNANT (J. B.), Medal for.— The President of the United States, in a letter addressed to the Primary Executive Council of the French Republic, has expressed his sense of your merit, and his entire approbation of your conduct while here. He has also charged me to convey to yourself the same sentiments on his part. It is with pleasure I obey this charge, in bearing witness to the candor and integrity of your conduct with us, and to the share you may justly claim in the cultivation of harmony and good understanding between the two nations * * *. As testimony of the regard of the United States, we shall take an early occasion to ask your acceptance of a medal and chain of gold on their part.—To JEAN BAPTISTE TERNANT. FORD ED., vi, 263. (Pa., 1793.)

8374. TERNANT (J. B.), Shifting affiliations.—When Ternant received certain account of his appointment, thinking he had nothing further to hope from the Jacobins, he that very day found out something to be offended at in me (in which I had been made *ex officio* the ostensible agent in what came from another quarter, and he has never been undeceived), attached himself intimately to Hamilton, put on mourning for the King, and became a perfect counter-revolutioner. A few days ago, he received a letter from Genet, giving him a hope they will employ him in the army. On this, he tacked about again, became a Jacobin, and refused to present the Viscount Noailles, and some other French aristocrats arrived here. However, he will hardly have the impudence to speak to me again.—To JAMES MONROE. iii, 549. FORD ED., vi, 240. (Pa., May 1793.)

8375. TERNANT (J. B.), Soldier.—Ternant established a solid reputation in Europe by his conduct when Generalissimo of one of the United Provinces, during their late disturbances; and it is generally thought that if he had been put at the head of the principal province, instead of the Rhingrave de Salm, he would have saved that cause.—To JOHN JAY. ii, 572. (P., 1789.)

8376. TERRITORY, Acquisition of.—I know that the acquisition of Louisiana has been disapproved by some, from a candid apprehension that the enlargement of our territory would endanger its Union. But who can limit the extent to which the federative principle may operate effectively?—SECOND INAUGURAL ADDRESS. viii, 41. FORD ED., viii, 344. (1805.) See LOUISIANA.

— TERRITORY, Acquisition of Canada. —See CANADA.

8377. TERRITORY, Admission of new States.—I am aware of the force of the observations you make on the power given by the Constitution to Congress, to admit new States into the Union, without restraining the subject to the territory then constituting the United States. But when I consider that the limits of the United States are precisely fixed by the treaty of 1783, that the Constitution expressly declares itself to be made for the United States, I cannot help believing the intention was to permit Congress to admit into the Union new States, which should be formed out of the territory for which, and under whose authority alone, they were then acting. I do not believe it was meant that they might receive England, Ireland, Holland, &c., into it, which would be the case on your construction.—To WILSON C. NICHOLAS. iv, 505. FORD ED., viii, 247. (M., Sep. 1803.)

8378. TERRITORY, Alienation of.—The power to alienate the *unpeopled* territories of any State, is not among the enumerated powers given by the Constitution to the General Government, and if we may go out of that instrument, and *accommodate to exigencies which may arise* by alienating the *unpeopled* territory of a State, we may accommodate ourselves a little more by alienating that which is *peopled*, and still a little more by selling the *people* themselves. A shade or two more in the degree of exigency is all that will be requisite, and of that degree we shall ourselves be the judges. However, may it not be hoped that these questions are forever laid to rest by the * * * amendment * * * to the Constitution, declaring expressly that "the powers not delegated to the United States by the Constitution are reserved to the States respectively"? And if the General Government has no power to alienate the territory of a State, it is too irresistible an argument to deny ourselves the use of it on the present occasion.*—To ALEXANDER HAMILTON. FORD ED., v, 443. (1792.)

8379. ——— ———. A disastrous war might, by necessity, supersede this stipulation [the provision of the Constitution guaranteeing every State against the invasion of its territory] (as necessity is above all law), and oblige them to abandon a part of a State; but nothing short of this can justify or obtain such an abandonment.—MISSISSIPPI RIVER INSTRUCTIONS. vii, 573. FORD ED., v, 464. (1792.)

8380. ——— ———. We have neither the right nor the disposition to alienate an inch of what belongs to any member of our Union. —MISSISSIPPI RIVER INSTRUCTIONS. vii, 586. FORD ED., v, 476. (1792.)

8381. ——— ———. [President Washington, at a Cabinet meeting, submitted the question]: "Will it be expedient to relinquish to the Indians the right of soil of any part of the land north of the Ohio, if essential to peace?" The Secretaries of the Treasury and War, and the Attorney General are of opinion it will be expedient to make such relinquishment if essential to peace, provided it do not include any lands sold or reserved for special purposes (the reservations for trading places excepted). The Secretary of State is of opinion that the Executive and Senate have authority to stipulate with the Indians, and that if essential to peace, it will be expedient to stipulate that we will not settle any lands between those already sold or reserved for special purposes, and the lines heretofore validly established with the Indians.—OPINION ON INDIAN WAR. FORD ED., vi, 191. (Feb. 1793.)

8382. ——— ———. I considered [at a Cabinet meeting] that the Executive, with either or both branches of the Legislature, could not alien any part of our territory; that by the law of nations it was settled, that the unity and indivisibility of the society was so fundamental, that it could not be dismembered by the constituted authorities, except, 1, where *all power* was delegated to them (as in the case of despotic governments), or, 2, where it was expressly delegated; that neither of these delegations had been made to our General Government and, therefore, that it had no right to dismember or alienate any portion of territory once ultimately consolidated with us; and that we could no more cede to the Indians

* The navigation of the Mississippi River was the subject under consideration.—EDITOR.

than to the English or Spaniards, as it might, according to acknowledged principles, remain as irrevocably and eternally with the one as the other. But I thought, that as we had a right to sell and settle lands once comprehended within our lines, so we might forbear to exercise that right, retaining the property till circumstances should be more favorable to the settlement, and this I agreed to do in the present instance, if necessary for peace.—THE ANAS. ix, 137. FORD ED., i, 219. (Feb. 1793.)

8383. —— ——. The Cabinet met * * * on the subject of your [President Washington's] circular letter, and agreed on all points, except as to the power of ceding territory, on which point there remained the same difference of opinion as when the subject was discussed in your presence.—To PRESIDENT WASHINGTON. FORD ED., vi, 212. (Pa., April 1793.)

8384. ————. The negotiators at Ghent are agreed in everything except as to a rag of Maine, which we cannot yield nor they seriously care about.—To MRS. TRIST. D. L. J. 359. (M., Dec. 1814.)

8385. TERRITORY, Annexation of Canada.—That Bonaparte would give us the Floridas to withhold intercourse with the residue of the [Spanish] colonies cannot be doubted. But that is no price; because they are ours in the first moment of the first war; and until a war they are of no particular necessity to us. But, although with difficulty, he will consent to our receiving Cuba into our Union, to prevent our aid to Mexico and the other provinces. That would be a price, and I would immediately erect a column on the southernmost limit of Cuba and inscribe on it a *ne plus ultra* as to us in that direction. We should then have only to include the north in our Confederacy, which would be, of course, in the first war, and we should have such an empire for liberty as she has never surveyed since the creation; and I am persuaded no Constitution was ever before so well calculated as ours for extensive empire and self-government.—To PRESIDENT MADISON. v, 444. (M., April 1809.) See CANADA.

8386. TERRITORY, British acquisition of American.—The consequences of their [the British] acquiring all the country on our frontier, from the St. Croix to the St. Mary's, are too obvious to you to need development. You will readily see the dangers which would then environ us. We wish you, therefore, to intimate to them that we cannot be indifferent to enterprises of this kind; that we should contemplate a change of neighbors with extreme uneasiness; and that a due balance on our borders is not less desirable to us, than a balance of power in Europe has always appeared to them. We wish to be neutral, and we will be so, *if they will execute the treaty* [of peace] *fairly, and attempt no conquests adjoining us.* The first condition is just; the second imposes no hardship on them. They cannot complain that the other dominions of

Spain would be so narrow as not to leave them room enough for conquest.*—To GOUVERNEUR MORRIS. iii, 182. FORD ED., v, 224. (N.Y., 1790.)

8387. —— ——. It was evident to me that the British had it in view to claim a slice on our north-western quarter, that they may get into the Mississippi; indeed, I thought it presented as a sort of make-weight with the posts to compensate the great losses their citizens had sustained by the infractions [of the treaty of peace] charged on us.—THE ANAS. ix, 428. FORD ED., i, 196. (June 1792.)

8388. TERRITORY, Cession of Northwest.—The territories contained within the charters erecting the Colonies of Maryland, Pennsylvania, North and South Carolina, are hereby ceded, released, and forever confirmed to the people of those Colonies respectively, with all the rights of property, jurisdiction and government, and all other rights whatsoever which might at any time, heretofore, have been claimed by this colony [Virginia]. The western and northern extent of this country shall in all other respects stand as fixed by the charter of —— until, by act of the Legislature, one or more Territories shall be laid off westward of the Alleghany mountains for new colonies, which colonies shall be established on the same fundamental laws contained in this instrument, and shall be free and independent of this Colony and of all the world.—PROPOSED VA. CONSTITUTION. FORD ED., ii. 25. (June 1776.) See WESTERN TERRITORY.

8389. —— ——. The General Assembly shall have power to sever from this State all or any parts of its territory westward of the Ohio, or of the meridian of the mouth of the Great Kanawha.—PROPOSED CONSTITUTION FOR VIRGINIA. viii, 446. FORD ED., iii, 325. (1783.)

8390. —— ——. I do myself the honor of transmitting to your Excellency a resolution of the General Assembly of this Commonwealth, entered into in consequence of the resolution of Congress of September 6th, 1780, on the subject of confederation. I shall be rendered very happy if the other States of the Union, equally impressed with the necessity of that important convention, shall be willing to sacrifice equally to its completion. This single event, could it take place shortly, would overweigh every success which the enemy [England] have hitherto obtained, and render desperate the hopes to which those successes have given birth.—To THE PRESIDENT OF CONGRESS. i, 287. FORD ED., ii, 423. (R., January 17, 1781.)

8391. TERRITORY, Constitution and. —No constitution was ever before so well calculated as ours for extensive empire and self-government.—To PRESIDENT MADISON. v, 444. (M., April 1809.)

* Morris was then informal agent of the United States in London. It was feared that England would wrest Louisiana from Spain.—EDITOR.

— **TERRITORY, Constitution and acquisition of foreign.**—See LOUISIANA.

8392. TERRITORY, Cuba.—I candidly confess that I have ever looked on Cuba as the most interesting addition which could ever be made to our system of States.—To PRESIDENT MONROE. vii, 316. FORD ED., x, 278. (M., 1823.) See CUBA.

8393. TERRITORY, Disputed.—The Colony of Virginia does not entertain a wish that one inch should be added to theirs from the territory of a sister Colony * * *. The decision, whatever it be, will not annihilate the lands. They will remain to be occupied by Americans, and whether these be counted in the members of this or that of the United States will be thought a matter of little moment.—LETTER TO PENNSYLVANIA CONVENTION. FORD ED., ii, 65. (July 1776.)

8394. TERRITORY, Dissensions and.— The larger our association, the less will it be shaken by local passions.—SECOND INAUGURAL ADDRESS. viii, 41. FORD ED., viii, 344. (1805.)

8395. —— ——. It seems that the smaller the society the bitterer the dissensions into which it breaks. Perhaps this observation answers all the objections drawn by Mr. [John] Adams from the small republics of Italy. I believe ours is to owe its permanence to its great extent, and the smaller portion comparatively, which can ever be convulsed at one time by local passions.—To GOVERNOR ROBERT WILLIAMS. v, 209. FORD ED., ix, 167. (W., 1807.)

8396. —— ——. The extent of our territory secures it, I hope, from the vindictive passions of the petty incorporations of Greece. —To ELBRIDGE GERRY. vi, 63. FORD ED., ix, 360. (M., 1812.)

8397. —— ——. I see our safety in the extent of our confederacy, and in the probability that in the proportion of that the sound parts will always be sufficient to crush out local poison.—To HORATIO G. SPAFFORD. vi, 335. (M., 1814.)

8398. —— ——. I still believe that the western extension of our territory will ensure its duration, by overruling local factions, which might shake a smaller association.—To HENRY DEARBORN. vii, 215. FORD ED., x, 192. (M., 1821.)

8399. TERRITORY, European influence in American.—We consider their interests [Cuba and Mexico] and ours as the same, and that the object of both must be to exclude all European influence from this hemisphere. —To GOVERNOR CLAIBORNE. v, 381. FORD ED., ix, 213. (W., Oct. 1808.)

8400. TERRITORY, Expansion of.— Our confederacy must be viewed as the nest from which all America, North and South, is to be peopled. We should take care, too, not to think it for the interest of that great Continent to press too soon on the Spaniards. Those countries cannot be in better hands. My fear is that they are too feeble to hold

them till our population can be sufficiently advanced to gain it from them piece by piece. —To ARCHIBALD STUART. i, 518. FORD ED., iv, 188. (P., 1786.)

8401. —— ——. However our present interests may restrain us within our own limits, it is impossible not to look forward to distant times, when our rapid multiplication will expand itself beyond those limits, and cover the whole northern, if not the southern continent, with a people speaking the same language, governed in similar forms, and by similar laws * * * .—To JAMES MONROE. iv, 420. FORD ED., viii, 105. (W., Nov. 1801.)

8402. TERRITORY, Good government and.—Our present federal limits are not too large for good government, nor will the increase of votes in Congress produce any ill effect. On the contrary, it will drown the little divisions at present existing there.—To ARCHIBALD STUART. i, 518. FORD ED., iv, 188. (P., Jan. 1786.)

8403. TERRITORY, Holding foreign.— The Constitution has made no provision for our holding foreign territory, still less for incorporating foreign nations into our Union. The Executive in seizing the fugitive occurrence [Louisiana purchase] which so much advances the good of their country, have done an act beyond the Constitution. The Legislature in casting behind them metaphysical subtleties, and risking themselves like faithful servants, must ratify and pay for it, and throw themselves on their country for doing for them unauthorized, what we know they would have done for themselves had they been in a situation to do it. It is the case of a guardian, investing the money of his ward in purchasing an important adjacent territory; and saying to him when of age, I did this for your good; I pretend to no right to bind you: you may disavow me, and I must get out of the scrape as I can. I thought it my duty to risk myself for you. But we shall not be disavowed by the nation, and their act of indemnity will confirm and not weaken the Constitution, by more strongly marking out its lines.—To JOHN C. BRECKENRIDGE. iv, 500. FORD ED., viii, 244. (M., Aug. 1803.)

8404. TERRITORY, Naval defence and. —Nothing should ever be accepted which would require a navy to defend it.—To PRESIDENT MADISON. v, 445. (M., April 1809.)

8405. TERRITORY, Pacific.—On the waters of the Pacific, we can found no claim in right of Louisiana. If we claim that country at all, it must be on Astor's settlement near the mouth of the Columbia, and the principle of the *jus gentium* of America, that when a civilized nation takes possession of the mouth of a river in a new country, that possession is considered as including all its waters.—To JOHN MELISH. vii, 51. (M., 1816.)

8406. TERRITORY, Preservation of.— Were we to give up half our territory [Mississippi region] rather than engage in a just war to preserve it, we should not keep the other half long.—INSTRUCTIONS TO WILLIAM CARMICHAEL. ix, 412. FORD ED., v, 226. (1790.)

— **TERRITORY, Purchase of Florida.**— See FLORIDA.

8407. TERRITORY, Purchases of Indian.—To be prepared against the occupation of Louisiana by a powerful and enterprising people [the French], it is important that. setting less value on interior extens·on of purchases from the Indians, we bend our whole views to the purchase and settlement of the country on the Mississippi, from its mouth to its northern regions, that we may be able to present as strong a front on our western as on our eastern border, and plant on the Mississippi itself the means of its own defence. We now own from 31° to the Yazoo, and hope this summer to purchase what belongs to the Choctaws from the Yazoo up to the·r boundary, supposed to be about opposite the mouth of Arkansas. We wish at the same time to begin in your quarter, for which there is at present a favorable opening. The Cahokias extinct, we are entitled to their country by our paramount sovereignty. The Peorias, we understand, have all been driven off from their country, and we might claim it in the same way; but as we understand there is one chief remain·ng, who would, as the survivor of the tribe, sell the right, it is better to give him such terms as will make him easy for life, and take a conveyance from him. The Kaskaskias being reduced to a few families, I presume we may purchase their whole country for what would place every individual of them at his ease, and be a small pr·ce to us,—say by laying off for each family, wherever they would choose it, as much land as they could cultivate, adjacent to each other, enclosing the whole in a s·ngle fence, and giving them such an annuity in money or goods forever as would place them in happiness; and we might take them also under the protection of the United States. Thus possessed of the rights of these tribes, we should proceed to the settling of their boundaries with the Pottawatamies and Kickapoos, claiming all doubtful territory, but paying them a pr·ce for the relinquishment of their concurrent claim, and even prevailing on them, if possible, to cede, for a price, such of their own unquestioned territory as would give us a convenient northern boundary. Before broaching this, and whi·e we are bargaining with the Kaskaskias, the minds of the Pottawatamies and K·ckapoos should be soothed and conciliated by liberalities and sincere assurances of friendship. Perhaps by sending a well-qualified character to stay some time in Duquoin·s village, as if on other business, and to sound him and ·ntroduce the subject by degrees to his mind and that of the other heads of families, inculcating in the way of conversation, all those considerations which prove the advantages they would receive by a cession on these terms, the object might be more easily and effectually obtained than by abruptly proposing it to them at a formal treaty. Of the means, however, of obtaining what we wish, you will be the best judge; and I have given you this view of the system which we suppose will best promote the interests of the Indians and ourselves, and finally consolidate our whole country into one nation only; that you may be enabled the better to adapt your means to the object, for this purpose we have given you a general commission for treating.—To GOVERNOR HARRISON. iv, 473. (W., Feb. 1803.)

8408. —— ——. The crisis is pressing: whatever can now be obta·ned must be obtained quickly. The occupation of New Orleans, hourly expected, by the French, is already felt like a light breeze by the Indians. You know the sentiments they entertain of that nation; under the hope of their protection they will ·mmediately stiffen against cessions of lands to us. We had better, therefore, do at once what can now be done. This letter is to be considered as private. * * * You will perceive how sacredly it must be kept within your own breast, and especially how improper to be understood by the Indians. For their interests and their tranquillity, it is best they should see only the present age of their history.—To GOVERNOR HARRISON. iv, 474. (W., Feb. 1803.)

8409. —— ——. As a means of increasing the security, and providing a protection for our lower possessions on the Mississippi, I think it also all important to press on the Indians, as steadily and strenuously as they can bear, the extension of our purchases on the Mississippi from the Yazoo upwards; and to encourage a settlement along the whole length of that river, that ·t may possess on its own banks the means of defending itself, and presenting as strong a frontier on our western as we have on our eastern border. We have, therefore, recommended to Governor Dickinson taking. on the Tombigbee, only as much as will cover our actual settlements, to transfer the purchase from the Choctaws to their lands westward of the Big Black, rather than the fork of Tombigbee and Alabama, which has been offered by them in order to pay their debt to Ponton and Leslie. I have confident expectations of purchasing this summer a good breadth on the Mississippi, from the mouth of the Illinois down to the mouth of the Ohio, which would settle immediately and thickly; and we should then have between that settlement and the lower one, only the uninhabited lands of the Chickasaws on the Mississippi; on which we could be working at both ends. You w·ll be sensible that the preced·ng views, as well those which respect the European powers as the Indians, are such as should not be formally declared, but be held as a rule of action to govern the conduct of those within whose agency they lie; and it is for this reason that instead of having it said to you in an official letter, committed to records wh·ch are open to many, I have thought it better that you should learn my views from a private and confidential letter, and be enabled to act upon them yourself, and guide others into them.— To GOVERNOR CLAIBORNE. iv, 487. (W., May 1803.)

8410. —— ——. Another important acquisition of territory has also been made since the last session of Congress. The friendly tribe of Kaskaskia Indians, with which we have never had a difference. reduced by the wars and wants of savage life to a few individuals unable to defend themselves against the neighboring tribes, has transferred its country to the United States, reserving only for its members what is sufficient to maintain them in an agricultural way. The considerations stipulated are that we shall extend to them our patronage and protection, and give them certain annual aids in money, in implements of agriculture, and other articles of their choice. This country, among the most fertile within our limits, extending along the Mississippi from the mouth of the Illinois to and up the Ohio, though not so necessary as a barrier since the acquisition of the other bank, may yet be well worthy of being laid open to immediate settlement, as its inhabitants may descend with rapidity in support of the lower country should future circumstances expose that to foreign enterprise.—THIRD ANNUAL MESSAGE. viii, 25. FORD ED., viii, 269. (Oct. 1803.)

8411. —— ——. On this side the Mississippi, an important relinquishment of native title has been received from the Delawares. That tribe, desiring to extinguish in their people the spirit of hunting, and to convert superfluous lands into the means of improving what they retain, have ceded to us all the country between the Wabash and the Ohio, south of, and including the road from the rapids towards Vincennes, for which they are to receive annuities in animals and implements for agriculture, and in other necessaries. This acquisition is important, not only for its extent and fertility, but as fronting three hundred miles on the Ohio, and near half that on the Wabash. The produce of the settled countries descending those rivers will no longer pass in review of the Indian frontier but in a small portion, and with the cession heretofore made with the Kaskaskias, nearly consolidates our possessions north of the Ohio, in a very respectable breadth, from Lake Erie to the Mississippi. The Piankeshaws having some claim to the country ceded by the Delawares, t has been thought best to quiet that by fair purchase also.—FOURTH ANNUAL MESSAGE. viii, 37. FORD ED., viii, 330. (Nov. 1804.)

8412. —— ——. The northern [Indian] tribes have sold to us: the lands between the Connecticut Reserve, and the former Indian boundary; and those on the Ohio, from the same boundary to the Rapids, and for a considerable depth inland. The Chickasaws and Cherokees have sold us their country between the two districts of and adjacent to the two districts of Tennessee, and the Creeks, the residue of their lands in the fork of Ocmulgee, up to the river which we expect is by this time ceded by are important, inasmuch as they consolidate disjointed parts of our settled country, and render their intercourse secure; and the second particularly so, as with the small point on the river which we expect is by this time ceded by the Piankeshaws, it completes our possession of the whole of both banks of the Ohio, from its source to near its mouth, and the navigation of that river is thereby rendered forever safe to our citizens settled and settling on its extensive waters.—FIFTH ANNUAL MESSAGE. viii, 52. FORD ED., viii, 394. (Dec. 1805.)

8413. TERRITORY, Republicanism and.—The late chapter* of our history * * * furnishes a new proof of the falsehood of Montesquieu's doctrine, that a republic can be preserved only in a small territory. The reverse is the truth. Had our territory been even a third only of what it is, we were gone. But while frenzy and delusion, like an epidemic, gained certain parts the residue remained sound and untouched, and held on till their brethren could recover from the temporary delusion.—To NATHANIEL NILES. iv, 376. FORD ED., viii, 24. (W., March 1801.)

8414. —— ——. While smaller governments are better adapted to the ordinary objects of society, larger confederations more effectually secure independence, and the pres-

* The Presidential contest in the House of Representatives.—EDITOR.

ervation of republican government.—To THE RHODE ISLAND ASSEMBLY. iv, 397. (W., May 1801.)

8415. —— ——. I have much confidence that we shall proceed successfully for ages to come, and that, contrary to the principle of Montesquieu, it will be seen that the larger the extent of country, the more firm its republican structure, if founded, not on conquest, but in principles of compact and equality. My hope of its duration is built much on the enlargement of the resources of life going hand in hand with the enlargement of territory, and the belief that men are disposed to live honestly, if the means of doing so are open to them.—To M. DE MARBOIS. vii, 77. (M., 1817.)

8416. TERRITORY, Seizure.—I consider war between France and England as unavoidable. * * * In this conflict, our neutrality will be cheaply purchased by a cession of the island of New Orleans and the Floridas; because taking part in the war, we could so certainly seize and securely hold them and more. And although it would be unwise in us to let such an opportunity pass of obtaining the necessary accession to our territory even by force, if not obtainable otherwise, yet it is infinitely more desirable to obtain it with the blessing of neutrality rather than the curse of war.—To GOVERNOR CLAIBORNE. iv, 487. (W., May 1803.)

8417. —— ——. You have thought it advisable sooner to take possession of adjacent territories. But we know that they are ours the first moment that any war is forced upon us for other causes, that we are at hand to anticipate their possession, if attempted by any other power, and, in the meantime, we are lengthening the term of our prosperity, liberating our revenues, and increasing our power.—To GENERAL ARMSTRONG. v, 433. (W., March 1809.)

8418. TERRITORY, Spanish pretensions.—I say nothing of the claims of Spain to our territory north of the thirty-first degree, and east of the Mississippi. They never merited the respect of an answer [to Spain]; and * * * it has been admitted at Madrid that they were not to be maintained.—To WILLIAM CARMICHAEL. iii, 173. FORD ED., v, 217. (N.Y., 1790.)

8419. TESTS, Religious.—The proscribing any citizen as unworthy the public confidence, by laying upon him an incapacity of being called to offices of trust or emolument, unless he profess or renounce this or that religious opinion, is depriving him injudiciously of those privileges and advantages, to which in common with his fellow citizens, he has a natural right.—STATUTE OF RELIGIOUS FREEDOM. FORD ED., ii, 238. (1779.)

8420. —— ——. All men shall be free to profess, and by argument to maintain, their opinion in matters of religion; and * * * the same shall in no wise diminish, enlarge, or affect their civil capacities.—STATUTE OF RELIGIOUS FREEDOM. FORD ED., ii, 239. (1799.)

— **THANKSGIVING.**—See FAST DAYS.

8421. THEATRES, Utility of.—I have never expressed an objection to the part of your plan relative to the theatre. The utility of this in America is a great question on which I may be allowed to have an opinion; but it is not for me to decide on it, nor to object to the proposal of establishing one at Richmond. The only objection to your plan which I have ever made, is that * * * I feared it was too extensive for the poverty of the country. You remove the objection by observing it is to extend to several States. Whether professors itinerant from one State to another may succeed, I am unable to say, having never known an experiment of it. The fear that these professors may be disappointed in their expectations, has determined me not to meddle in the business at all.—To M. DE QUESNAY. ii, 346. (P., 1788.)

8422. THEORY, Demolishing.—Theories are more easily demolished than rebuilt.—To REV. JAMES MADISON. ii, 430. (P., 1788.)

8423. THEORY, Imagination and.—The moment a person forms a theory, his imagination sees, in every object, only the traits which favor that theory.—To CHARLES THOMSON. ii, 276. FORD ED., iv, 447. (P., 1787.)

8424. THEORY, Victims of.—Men come into business at first with visionary principles. It is practice alone which can correct and conform them to the actual current of affairs. In the meantime, those to whom their errors were first applied have been their victims.—To JAMES MADISON. ii, 408. FORD ED., v, 16. (P., 1788.)

8425. THIRD TERM, Age and.—I owe you much thankfulness for the favorable opinion you entertain of my services, and the assurance expressed that they would again be acceptable in the Executive chair. But I was sincere in stating age as one of the reasons of my retirement from office, beginning then to be conscious of its effects, and now much more sensible of them. Senile inertness is not what is to save our country; the conduct of a war requires the vigor and enterprise of younger heads. All such undertakings, therefore, are out of the question with me, and I say so with the greater satisfaction when I contemplate the person to whom the Executive powers were handed over.—To THOMAS C. FLOURNOY. vi, 82. (M., Oct. 1812.)

8426. THIRD TERM, Constitution and. —Your approbation of the reasons which induced me to retire from the honorable station in which my countrymen had placed me, is the proof of your devotion to the principles of our Constitution. These are wisely opposed to all perpetuations of power, and to every practice which may lead to hereditary establishments.—REPLY TO ADDRESS. v, 473. (M., 1809.)

8427. THIRD TERM, Dangers of.—My opinion originally was that the President of the United States should have been elected for seven years, and forever ineligible afterwards. I have since become sensible that seven years is too long to be irremovable, and that there should be a peaceable way of withdrawing a man in midway who is doing wrong. The service for eight years, with a power to remove at the end of the first four, comes nearly to my principle as corrected by experience; and it is in adherence to that, that I determine to withdraw at the end of my second term. The danger is that the indulgence and attachments of the people will keep a man in the chair after he becomes a dotard, that reelection through life shall become habitual, and election for life follow that. General Washington set the example of voluntary retirement after eight years. I shall follow it. And a few more precedents will oppose the obstacle of habit to any one after awhile who shall endeavor to extend his term. Perhaps it may beget a disposition to establish it by an amendment of the Constitution. I believe I am doing right, therefore, in pursuing my principle. I had determined to declare my intention, but I have consented to be silent on the opinion of friends, who think it best not to put a continuance out of my power in defiance of all circumstances. There is, however, but one circumstance which could engage my acquiescence in another election; to wit, such a division about a successor, as might bring in a monarchist. But that circumstance is impossible.—To JOHN TAYLOR. iv, 565. FORD ED., viii, 339. (W., Jan. 1805.)

8428. ————. If some period be not fixed, either by the Constitution or by practice, to the services of the First Magistrate, his office, though nominally elective, will, in fact, be for life; and that will soon degenerate into an inheritance.—To MR. WEAVER. v, 89. (W., June 1807.)

8429. ————. That there are in our country a great number of characters entirely equal to the management of its affairs, cannot be doubted. Many of them, indeed, have not had opportunities of making themselves known to their fellow citizens; but many have had, and the only difficulty will be to choose among them. These changes are necessary, too, for the security of republican government. —To MR. WEAVER. v, 89. (W., June 1807.)

8430. THIRD TERM, Determination to refuse.—Believing that a definite period of retiring from this station will tend materially to secure our elective form of government; and sensible, too, of that decline which advancing years bring on, I have felt it a duty to withdraw at the close of my present term of office; and to strengthen by practice a principle which I deem salutary.—To ABNER WATKINS. viii, 125. (W., Dec. 1807.)

8431. THIRD TERM, Duty and.—That I should lay down my charge at a proper season, is as much a duty as to have borne it faithfully.—To MR. WEAVER. v, 88. (W., June 1807.)

8432. ————. Having myself highly approved the example of an illustrious predecessor, in voluntarily retiring from a trust, which, if too long continued in the same hands, might become a subject of reasonable uneasiness and apprehension, I could not mistake my own duty when placed in a similar situation.—R. TO A. CONNECTICUT REPUBLICANS. viii, 140. (1808.)

8433. THIRD TERM, Irksome.—At the end of my present term, of which two years are yet to come, I propose to retire from public life, and to close my days on my patrimony of Monticello, in the bosom of my family. I have hitherto enjoyed uniform health; but the weight of public service begins to be too heavy for me, and I long for the enjoyment of rural life, among my books, my farms and my family. Having performed my *quadragena stipendia*, I am entitled to my discharge, and should be sorry, indeed, that others should be sooner sensible than myself when I ought to ask it. I have, therefore, requested my fellow citizens to think of a successor for me, to whom I shall deliver the public concerns with greater joy than I received them. I have the consolation, too, of having added nothing to my private fortune, during my public service, and of retiring with hands as clean as they are empty.—To COMTE DIODATI. v, 62. (W., March 1807.)

8434. THIRD TERM, Jefferson urged to accept.—I am panting for retirement, but am as yet nearly two years from that goal. The general solicitations I have received to continue another term give me great consolation, but considerations public as well as private determine me inflexibly on that measure.—To MARQUIS DE LAFAYETTE. FORD ED., ix, 67. (W., May 1807.)

8435. THIRD TERM, Massachusetts and.—I derive great personal consolation from the assurances in your friendly letter, that the electors of Massachusetts would still have viewed me with favor as a candidate for a third Presidential term. But the duty of retirement is so strongly impressed on my mind, that it is impossible for me to think of that.—To JAMES SULLIVAN. v, 252. (W., March 1808.)

8436. THIRD TERM, Opposed to.—I am for responsibilities at short periods, seeing neither reason nor safety in making public functionaries independent of the nation for life, or even for long terms of years. On this principle I prefer the Presidential term of four years, to that of seven years, which I myself had at first suggested, annexing to it, however, ineligibility forever after; and I wish it were now annexed to the second quadrennial election of President.—To JAMES MARTIN. vi, 213. FORD ED., ix, 420. (M., Sep. 1813.)

8437. THIRD TERM, Physical decline and.—My determination to retire is the result of mature reflections, and on various considerations. Not the least weighty of these is that a consciousness that a decline of physical faculties cannot leave those mental en-

tirely unimpaired; and it will be happy for me if I am the first who shall become sensible of it. As to a successor, there never will be a time when it will not produce some difficulty, and never less, I believe, than at present. That some of the federalists should prefer my continuance to the uncertainty of a successor, I can readily believe. There are among them men of candor, who do not join in the clamor and condemnation of everything, nor pretend that even chance never throws us on a right measure. There are some who know me personally, and who give a credit to my intentions, which they deny to my understanding; some who may fear a successor, preferring a military glory of a nation to the prosperity and happiness of its individuals. But to the mass of that political sect, it is not the less true, the 4th of March, 1809, will be a day of jubilee, but it will be a day of greater joy to me. I never did them an act of injustice, nor failed in any duty to them imposed by my office.—To WILLIAM SHORT. FORD ED., ix, 50. (W., May 1807.)

8438. THIRD TERM, Precedent against.—The reeligibility of the President for life [in the new Constitution], I quite disapproved.* * * My fears of that feature were founded on the importance of the office, on the fierce contentions it might excite among ourselves, if continuable for life, and the dangers of interference, either with money or arms, by foreign nations, to whom the choice of an American President might become interesting. Examples of this abounded in history; in the case of the Roman Emperors, for instance; of the Popes, while of any significance; of the German Emperors; the Kings of Poland and the Deys of Barbary. I had observed, too, in the Feudal history, and in the recent instance, particularly, of the Stadtholder of Holland, how easily offices, or tenures for life, slide into inheritances. My wish, therefore, was, that the President should be elected for seven years, and be incligible afterwards. This term I thought sufficient to enable him, with the concurrence of the Legislature, to carry through and establish any system of improvement he should propose for the general good. But the practice adopted, I think is better, allowing his continuance for eight years, with a liability to be dropped at half way of the term, making that a period of probation. That his continuance should be restrained to seven years, was the opinion of the Convention at an earlier stage of its session, when it voted that term, by a majority of eight against two, and by a simple majority that he should be ineligible a second time. This opinion was confirmed by the House so late as July 26, referred to the Committee of Detail, reported favorably by them, and changed to the present form by final vote, on the last day but one only of their session.* Of this

* This is an evident error. On September 4th, the committee of eleven reported a clause making the term four years, which was adopted by the convention on the 6th, and not altered thereafter.—NOTE IN FORD EDITION.

change, three States expressed their disapprobation; New York, by recommending on amendment, that the President should not be eligible a third time, and Virginia and North Carolina that he should not be capable of serving more than eight, in any term of sixteen years; and although this amendment has not been made in form, yet practice seems to have established it. The example of four Presidents voluntarily retiring at the end of their eighth year, and the progress of public opinion, that the principle is salutary, have given it in practice the force of precedent and usage; insomuch, that, should a President consent to be a candidate for a third election, I trust he would be rejected, on this demonstration of ambitious views.—AUTOBIOGRAPHY. i, 79. FORD ED., i, 109. (1821.)

8439. THIRD TERM, Retirement and.—A retirement from the exercise of my present charge is equally for your good and my own happiness.—R. TO A. PENNSYLVANIA CITIZENS. v, 262. (W., 1808.)

8440. THIRD TERM, Rotation in office and.—I am sensible of the kindness of your rebuke on my determination to retire from office at a time when our country is laboring under difficulties truly great. But if the principle of rotation be a sound one, as I conscientiously believe it to be with respect to this office. no pretext should ever be permitted to dispense with it, because there never will be a time when real difficulties will not exist, and furnish a plausible pretext for dispensation. You suppose I am " in the prime of life for rule ". I am sensible I am not; and before I am so far declined as to become insensible of it, I think it right to put it out of my own power. I have the comfort, too, of knowing that the person whom the public choice has designated to receive the charge from me, is so eminently qualified as a safe depository by the endowments of integrity, understanding. and experience. On a review, therefore, of my reasons for retirement, I think you cannot fail to approve them.—To HENRY GUEST. v, 407. (W., January 1809.)

8441. ——— ———. In no office can rotation be more expedient; and none less admits the indulgence of age.—R. TO A. PHILADELPHIA CITIZENS. viii, 145. (1809.)

8442. THIRD TERM, Vermont and.—I received the *address* of the Legislature of Vermont, bearing date the 5th of November, 1806, in which, with their approbation of the general course of my administration, they were so good as to express their desire that I would consent to be proposed again, to the public voice, on the expiration of my present term of office. Entertaining, as I do, for the Legislature of Vermont those sentiments of high respect which would have prompted an immediate answer, I was certain, nevertheless, they would approve a delay which had for its object to avoid a premature agitation of the public mind, on a subject so interesting as the election of the Chief Magistrate. That I should lay down my charge at a proper period, is as much a duty as to have borne it faithfully. If some termination to the services of the Chief Magistrate be not fixed by the Constitution, or supplied by practice, his office, nominally for years, will, in fact, become for life; and history shows how easily that degenerates into an inheritance. Believing that a representative government, responsible at short intervals of election, is that which produces the greatest sum of happiness to mankind, I feel it a duty to do no act which shall essentially impair that principle; and I should unwillingly be the person who, disregarding the sound precedent set by an illustrious predecessor, should furnish the first example of prolongation beyond the second term of office. Truth, also, requires me to add, that I am sensible of that decline which advancing years bring on; and feeling their physical, I ought not to doubt their mental effect. Happy if I am the first to perceive and to obey this admonition of nature, and to solicit a retreat from cares too great for the wearied faculties of age.—R. TO A. VERMONT LEGISLATURE. viii, 121. (Dec. 1807.)

— THRESHING MACHINE.—See INVENTIONS.

8443. TIFFIN (H. D.), Fidelity.—I have seen with the greatest satisfaction that among those who have distinguished themselves by their fidelity to their country, on the occasion of the enterprise of Mr. Burr, yourself and the Leg'slature of Ohio have been the most eminent. The promptitude and energy displayed by your State have been as honorable to itself as salutary to its sister States; and in declaring that you have deserved well of your country. I do but express the grateful sentiment of every faithful citizen in it. The hand of the people has given the mortal blow to a conspiracy which. in other countries, would have called for an appeal to armies, and has proved that government to be the strongest of which every man feels himself a part. It is a happy illustration, too. of the importance of preserving to the State authorities all that vigor which the Constitution foresaw would be necessary. not only for their own safety. but for that of the whole.—To GOVERNOR H. D. TIFFIN. v, 37. FORD ED., ix, 21. (W., 1807.)

8444. TIME, Waste of.—Determine never to be idle. No person will have occasion to complain of the want of time who never loses any. It is wonderful how much may be done, if we are always doing.—To MARTHA JEFFERSON. FORD ED., iv, 387. (Mar. 1787.)

8445. TITLE, President's.—The Senate and Representatives differed about the title of the President. The former wanted to style him, " His Highness, George Washington. President of the United States, and Protector of Their Liberties ". The latter insisted, and prevailed, to give no title but that of office, to wit, " George Washington, President of the United States ". I hope the terms of Excellency, Honor, Worship, Esquire, forever disappear from among us, from that moment. I wish that of Mr. would follow them.—To WILLIAM CARMICHAEL. iii, 88. (P., 1789.)

8446. —— ——. The President's title, as proposed by the Senate, was the most superlatively ridiculous thing I ever heard of.—To JAMES MADISON. FORD ED., v, 104. (P., 1789.)

8447. —— ——. I will presume to suggest to Mr. [John Quincy] Adams the question whether he should not send back Onis's letters in which he has the impudence to qualify you by the term " His Excellency "? An American gentleman in Europe can rank with the first nobility because we have no titles which stick him at any particular place in their line. So the President of the United States, under that designation ranks with the emperors and kings; but add Mr. Onis's courtesy of " His Excellency " and he is then on a level with Mr. Onis himself, with the governors of provinces, and even of every petty fort in Europe, or the colonies.—To PRESIDENT MONROE. FORD ED., x, 123. (M., 1819.)

8448. TITLES, Adulatory.—The new government has shown genuine dignity, in my opinion, in exploding adulatory titles. They are the offerings of abject baseness, and nourish that degrading vice in the people.— To JAMES MADISON. iii, 100. FORD ED., v, 112. (P., 1789.)

8449. TITLES, Granting.—The Administrator [of Virginia] shall not possess the prerogative * * * of creating dignities or granting rights of precedence.—PROPOSED VA. CONSTITUTION. FORD ED., ii, 19. (June 1776.)

8450. TITLES, Hereditary.—[The proposed new States] shall admit no person to be a citizen, who holds any hereditary title.— WESTERN TERRITORY REPORT. FORD ED., iii, 409. (1784.)

8451. —— ——. The clause respecting hereditary honors was struck out, not from an approbation of such honors, but because it was thought an improper place to encounter them.—To JAMES MADISON. FORD ED., iii, 471. (A., April 1784.)

8452. TOBACCO, Culture of.—It is a culture productive of infinite wretchedness. Those employed in it are in a continual state of exertion beyond the power of human nature to support. Little food of any kind is raised by them; so that the men and animals on these farms are badly fed, and the earth is rapidly impoverished.—NOTES ON VIRGINIA. viii, 407. FORD ED., iii, 271. (1782.)

8453. TOBACCO, Differential duties.— The difference of duty on tobacco carried to France in French and American bottoms, has excited great uneasiness. We presume the National Assembly must have been hurried into the measure without being allowed time to reflect on its consequences. A moment's consideration must convince anybody, that no nation upon earth ever submitted to so enormous an assault on the transportation of their own produce. Retaliation, to be equal, will have the air of extreme severity and hostility.—To M. LA MOTTE. iii, 289. (Pa., 1791.)

8454. —— ——. I take for granted the National Assembly were surprised into the measure by persons whose avarice blinded them to the consequences, and hope it will be repealed before our legislature shall be obliged to act on it. Such an attack on our carriage of our own productions, and such a retaliation would illy prepare the minds of the two nations for a liberal treaty as wished for by the real friends of both.—To JOSEPH FENWICK. FORD ED., v, 380. (Pa., 1791.)

8455. TOBACCO, European use of.—The European nations can do well without all our commodities except tobacco.—To JOHN ADAMS. i. 488. (P., 1785.)

8456. TOBACCO, Monopoly in France.— I take the liberty of offering to your attention some papers * * * written by * * * merchants of L'Orient, and others, some of whom are citizens of the United States, and all of them concerned in the trade between the two countries. This has been carried on by an exchange of the manufactures and produce of France for the produce of the United States, and principally for tobacco, which, though on its arrival here, confined to a single purchaser, has been received equally from all sellers. In confidence of a continuance of this practice, the merchants of both countries were carrying on their commerce of exchange. A late contract by the Farm has, in a great measure, fixed in a single mercantile house the supplies of tobacco wanted for this country. This arrangement found the established merchants with some tobacco on hand, some on the seas coming to them, and more still due. By the papers now enclosed, it seems that there are six thousand four hundred and eight hogsheads in the single port of L'Orient. Whether the government may interfere, as to articles furnished by the merchants after they had notice of the contract before mentioned, must depend on principles of policy. But those of justice seem to urge that, for commodities furnished before such notice, they should be so far protected, as that they may wind up without loss, the transactions in which the new arrangement found them actually engaged.—To COUNT DE VERGENNES. i, 547. (P., 1786.)

8457. —— ——. My hopes on that subject (suppression of the monopoly in the purchase of tobacco in France), are not desperate, but neither are they flattering.—To T. PLEASANTS. i, 563. (P., 1786.)

8458. —— ——. My letters from New York inform me that * * * the monopoly of the purchase of tobacco for France, which had been obtained by Robert Morris, had thrown the commerce of that article in agonies. He had been able to reduce the price in America from 40| to 22|6, lawful the hundred weight, and all other merchants being deprived of that medium of remittance, the commerce between America and that country, so far as it depended on that article, which was very capitally too, was absolutely ceasing. An order has been obtained, obliging the Farmers General to purchase from such other merchants as shall offer fifteen thousand hogsheads of tobacco at thirty-four, thirty-six and thirty-eight livres the hundred, according to the quality, and to grant to the sellers in other respects the same terms as they had granted to Robert Morris. As this agreement with Morris is the basis of this order, I send you some copies of it, which I will thank you to give to any American (not British) merchants in London who may be in that line. During the year this contract has subsisted, Virginia and Maryland have lost £400,000 by the

reduction of the price of their tobacco.—To
JOHN ADAMS. i, 586. FORD ED., iv, 252. (P.,
1786.)

8459. —— ——. During the former government of France (the monarchy), our tobacco was under a monopoly, but paid no duties.
* * * The first National Assembly * * *
emancipated tobacco from its monopoly, but
subjected it to duties of eighteen livres, fifteen
sous the quintal, carried in their own vessels,
and five livres carried in ours—a difference
more than equal to the freight of the article.—
FOREIGN COMMERCE REPORT. vii, 640. FORD
ED., vi, 474. (Dec. 1793.) See MONOPOLY.

8460. TOBACCO, Oppressions by merchants.—Long experience has proved to us
that there never was an instance of a man's
getting out of debt, who was once in the hands
of a tobacco merchant, and bound to consign his
tobacco to him. It is the most delusive of all
snares. The merchant feeds the inclination
of his customer to be credited till he gets the
burthen of debt so increased that he cannot
throw it off at once; he then begins to give
him less for his tobacco, and ends with giving
him what he pleases for it.—To MRS. PARADISE.
FORD ED., iv, 288. (P., 1786.)

8461. TOBACCO, Price of.—I am offered
at Monticello four shillings above the present
market price. * * * You know I have an
established privilege of being considerably above
the market. * * * The quality of last year's
crop is inferior, but still mine preserving its
comparative superiority, stands on its usual
ground with respect to others.—To JAMES
BROWN. FORD ED., vii, 6. (M., 1795.)

8462. TOLERATION, Political.—I feel
extraordinary gratification in addressing this
letter to you, with whom shades of difference
in political sentiment have not prevented the
interchange of good opinion, nor cut off the
friendly offices of society and good correspondence. This political tolerance is the more
valued by me, who consider social harmony
as the first of human felicities, and the happiest moments, those which are given to the
effusions of the heart.—To GOVERNOR JOHN
HENRY. FORD ED., iii, 159. (P., 1797.)

8463. —— ——. During the contest of
opinion [Presidential election] through which
we have passed, the animation of discussion
and of exertions has sometimes worn an aspect which might impose on strangers, unused to think freely, and to speak and to write
what they think; but, this being now decided
by the voice of the nation, announced, according to the rules of the Constitution, all will,
of course, arrange themselves under the will
of the law, and unite in common efforts for
the common good. All, too, will bear in mind
this sacred principle, that, though the will
of the majority is in all cases to prevail, that
will, to be rightful, must be reasonable; that
the minority possess their equal rights, which
equal laws must protect, and to violate which
would be oppression. Let us, then, fellow-citizens, unite with one heart and one mind;
let us restore to social intercourse that harmony and affection without which liberty and
even life itself are but dreary things. And let
us reflect, that, having banished from our land
that religious intolerance under which mankind so long bled and suffered, we have yet
gained little, if we countenance a political intolerance as despotic, as wicked, and capable
of as bitter and bloody persecutions. During
the throes and convulsions of the ancient
world; during the agonizing spasms of infuriated man, seeking, through blood and
slaughter, his long-lost liberty, it was not
wonderful that the agitation of the billows
should reach even this distant and peaceful
shore; that this should be more felt and
feared by some, and less by others; that this
should divide opinions as to measures of
safety. But every difference of opinion is not
a difference of principle. We have called by
different names brethren of the same principle. We are all republicans; we are all federalists. If there be any among us who
would wish to dissolve this Union, or to
change its republican form, let them stand,
undisturbed, as monuments of the safety with
which error of opinion may be tolerated
where reason is left free to combat it. * * *
Let us, then, with courage and confidence,
pursue our own federal and republican principles—our attachment to our Union and
representative government.—FIRST INAUGURAL ADDRESS. viii, 2. FORD ED., viii, 2.
(1801.)

8464. TONTINE, Raising money by.—
The raising money by Tontine, more practiced
on the continent of Europe than in England, is
liable to the same objection [as funding], of
encroachment on the independent rights of
posterity; because the annuities not expiring
gradually, with the lives on which they rest,
but all on the death of the last survivor only,
they will, of course, overpass the term of a
generation, and the more probably as the subjects on whose lives the annuities depend, are
generally chosen of the ages, constitutions, and
occupations most favorable to long life.—To
J. W. EPPES. vi, 197. FORD ED., ix, 397.
(P.F., 1813.)

8465. TORIES, Confederacy and.—The
tories would, at all times, have been glad to
see the confederacy dissolved, even by particles at a time, in hopes of their attaching
themselves again to Great Britain.—ANSWERS
TO M. DE MEUNIER. ix, 251. FORD ED., iv,
156. (P., 1786.)

8466. TORIES, Definition of.—A tory
has been properly defined to be a traitor in
thought, but not in deed. The only description by which the laws have endeavored to
come at them, was that of non-jurors, or persons refusing to take the oath of fidelity to
the State.—NOTES ON VIRGINIA. viii, 396.
FORD ED., iii, 260. (1782.)

8467. TORIES, Nature and.—Nature has
made some men monarchists and tories by
their constitution, and some, of course, there
always will be.—To ALBERT GALLATIN. vii,
80. FORD ED., x, 92. (M., 1817.)

8468. TORIES, Taxation of.—Persons of
this description were at one time subjected
to double taxation, at another to treble, and
lastly were allowed retribution, and placed on
a level with good citizens.—NOTES ON VIRGINIA. viii, 396. FORD ED., iii, 260. (1782.)

8469. TORIES, Whigs and.—It has ever appeared to me, that the difference between the whig and the tory of England is, that the whig deduces his rights from the Anglo-Saxon source, and the tory from the Norman.—To JOHN CARTWRIGHT. vii, 356. (M., 1824.)

8470. TORPEDOES, Defensive value.—I consider your torpedoes as very valuable means of the defence of harbors, and have no doubt that we should adopt them to a considerable degree. Not that I go the whole length (as I believe you do) of considering them as solely to be relied on. Neither a nation nor those entrusted with its affairs, could be justifiable, however sanguine its expectations, in trusting solely to an engine not yet sufficiently tried, under all the circumstances which may occur, and against which we know not as yet what means of parrying may be devised. If, indeed, the mode of attaching them to the cable of a ship be the only one proposed, modes of prevention cannot be difficult. But I have ever looked to the submarine boat as most to be depended on for attaching them, and though I see no mention of it in your letter, or your publications, I am in hopes it is not abandoned as impracticable. I should wish to see a corps of young men trained to this service. It would belong to the engineers if at hand, but being naut cal, I suppose we must have a corps of naval engineers, to practice and use them.—To ROBERT FULTON. v, 165. FORD ED., ix, 125. (M., Aug. 1807.)

8471. ———. Although no public servant could justify the risking the safety of an important seaport, solely on untried means of defence, yet I have great confidence in those proposed by you as additional to the ordinary means.—To ROBERT FULTON. v, 341. (M., Aug. 1808.)

8472. TORPEDOES, Experiments with.—Mr. Fulton writes to me under a great desire to prepare a decisive experiment of his torpedo at Washington, for the meeting of Congress. This means of harbor-defence has acquired such respectability, from its apparent merit, from the attention shown it by other nations, and from our own experiments at New York, as to entitle it to a full experiment from us. He asks only two workmen for one month from us, which he estimates at $130 only. But should it cost considerably more I should really be for granting it, and would accordingly recommend it to you. This sum is a mere trifle as an encroachment on our appropriation.—To ROBERT SMITH. v, 337. (M., Aug. 1808.)

8473. TORPEDOES, Success of.—Your torpedoes will be to cities what vaccination has been to mankind. It extinguishes their greatest danger.—To ROBERT FULTON. v, 517. (M., 1810.)

8474. TORTURE, Forbidden.—The General Assembly shall not have power to * * * prescribe torture in any case whatever.*—PROPOSED VA. CONSTITUTION. viii, 445. FORD ED., iii, 325. (1783.)

8475. TORTURE, In France.—Nor should we wonder at * * * [the] pressure [for a fixed constitution in 1788-9] when we consider the monstrous abuses of power under which * * * [the French] people were

* Heresy was then punishable by burning in Virginia.—EDITOR.

ground to powder; when we pass in review * * * * the atrocities of the rack.—AUTOBIOGRAPHY. i, 86. FORD ED., i, 118. (1821.)

8476. TOULOUSE (Archbishop of), Character of.—The Archbishop of Toulouse is made minister principal, a virtuous, patriotic, and able character.—To JOHN ADAMS. ii, 258. (P., 1787.)

8477. TOULOUSE (Archbishop of), Garde des sceaux and.—The *Garde des sceaux* is considered as the Archbishop of Toulouse's bull dog, braving danger like that animal. His talents do not pass mediocrity.—To JAMES MADISON. ii, 444. FORD ED., v, 43. (P., 1788.)

8478. TOULOUSE (Archbishop of), Influence with Queen.—It may not be uninstructive to give you the origin and nature of his influence with the Queen [Marie Antoinette]. When the Duke de Choiseul proposed the marriage of the Dauphin with this lady, he thought it proper to send a person to Vienna to perfect her in the language. He asked his friend, the Archbishop of Toulouse, to recommend to him a proper person. He recommended a certain abbé. The abbé, from his first arrival in Vienna, either tutored by his patron, or prompted by gratitude, impressed on the Queen's mind the exalted talents and merit of the Archbishop, and continually represented him as the only man fit to be placed at the helm of affairs. On his return to Paris, being retained near the person of the Queen, he kept him constantly in her view. The Archbishop was named of the Assemblee des Notables, had occasion enough there to prove his talents, and Count de Vergennes, his great enemy, dying opportunely, the Queen got him into place. He uses the abbé even yet for instilling all his notions into her mind.—To JOHN JAY. ii, 310. FORD ED., iv, 463. (P., 1787.)

8479. ———. The Archbishop continues well with his patroness [Marie Antoinette]. Her object is a close connection with her brother. I suppose he convinces her that peace will furnish the best occasion of cementing that connection.—To JOHN JAY. ii, 310. FORD ED., iv, 463. (P., 1787.)

8480. TOULOUSE (Archbishop of), Minister.—The Archbishop of Toulouse * * * is a good and patriotic minister for peace, and very capable in the department of finance. At least he is so in theory. I have heard his talents for execution censured.—To JOHN JAY. ii, 294. (P., 1787.)

8481. TOULOUSE (Archbishop of), Talents.—That he has imposing talents and patriotic dispositions, I think is certain. Good judges think him a theorist only, little acquainted with the details of business, and spoiling all his plans by a bungled execution.—To JOHN JAY. ii, 310. FORD ED., iv, 464. (P., 1787.)

— TOWNS.—See WARD GOVERNMENT.

8482. TRACY (Comte de), Books of.—Destutt Tracy is, in my judgment, the ablest living writer on intellectual subjects, or the operations of the understanding. His three octavo volumes on Ideology, which constitute the foundation of what he has since written, I have not entirely read; because I am not fond of reading what is merely abstract, and unapplied immediately to some useful science. Bonaparte, with his repeated derisions of Ideologists (squinting at this author), has by this time felt that true wisdom does not lie in mere practice without principle. The next work Tracy wrote was the "Commentary on Montesquieu", never published in the original, because not safe; but translated and published in Philadelphia, yet without the author's name. He has since permitted his name to be mentioned. Although called a commentary, it is, in truth, an elementary work on the principles of government, comprised in about three hundred pages octavo. He has lately published a third work, on "Political Economy", comprising the whole subject within about the same compass; in which all its principles are demonstrated with the severity of Euclid, and, like him, without ever using a superfluous word. I have procured this to be translated, and have been four years endeavoring to get it printed; but as yet, without success. In the meantime, the author has published the original in France, which he thought unsafe while Bonaparte was in power. * * * He has his fourth and last work now in the press at Paris, closing as he conceives, the circle of metaphysical sciences. This work, which is on ethics, I have not seen, but suspect I shall differ from it in its foundation, although not in its deductions. I gather from his other works that he adopts the principle of Hobbes, that justice is founded in contract solely, and does not result from the construction of man.— To John Adams. vii, 38. (M., 1816.)

8483. ————. Tracy comprehends under the word "Ideology" all the subjects which the French term *Morale*, as the correlation to *Physique*. His works on Logic, Government, Political Economy and Morality, he considers as making up the circle of ideological subjects, or of those which are within the scope of the understanding, and not of the senses. His Logic occupies exactly the ground of Locke's work on the Understanding. The translation of that on Political Economy is now printing; but it is no translation of mine. I have only had the correction of it, which was, indeed, very laborious. *Le premier jet* having been by some one who understood neither French nor English, it was impossible to make it more than faithful. But it is a valuable work.—To John Adams. vii, 55. Ford ed., x, 72. (M., 1817.)

8484. TRACY (Comte de), Infirmity of.—The Tracy I mentioned to you is the one connected by marriage with Lafayette's family. * * * He writes me that he is become blind, and so infirm that he is no longer able to compose anything; so that we are to consider his works as now closed.—To John Adams. vii, 43. (M., 1816.)

8485. TRADE, Carrying.—I think it essential to exclude the English from the carriage of American produce.—To James Monroe. Ford ed., iv, 41. (P., 1785.) See Carrying Trade, Commerce, Markets, Navigation and Ships.

8486. TRADE, Destroying.—He [George III.] has endeavored to pervert the exercise of the kingly office in Virginia into a detestable and insupportable tyranny * * * by combining with others to subject us to a foreign jurisdiction, giving his assent to their pretended acts of legislation * * * for cutting off our trade with all parts of the world.—Proposed Va. Constitution. Ford ed. ii, 10. (June 1776.)

8487. ————. He has combined, with others, * * * for cutting off our trade with all parts of the world.—Declaration of Independence as Drawn by Jefferson.

8488. TRADE, Monopolizing.—It is not just that the colonies should be required to oblige themselves to other contributions while Great Britain possesses a monopoly of their trade. This of itself lays them under heavy contribution. To demand, therefore, an additional contribution in the form of a tax is to demand the double of their equal proportion. If we contribute equally with other parts of the empire, let us, equally with them, enjoy free commerce with the whole world; but while the restrictions on our trade shut to us the resources of wealth, is it just, we should bear all other burdens equally with those to whom every resource is open?—Reply to Lord North's Proposition. Ford ed., i, 479. (July 1775.)

8489. TRADE, Restraining.—The proposition [of Lord North] is altogether unsatisfactory * * * because it does not propose to repeal the several acts of Parliament, passed for the purposes of restraining the trade * * * of the Eastern colonies.—Reply to Lord North's Proposition. Ford ed., i, 480. (July 1775.)

8490. TRADE, Restrictions on.—Some of the colonies having thought proper to continue the administration of their government in the name and under the authority of his Majesty, King Charles I. whom, notwithstanding his late deposition by the Commonwealth of England, they continued in the sovereignty of their State, the Parliament for the Commonwealth, took the same in high offence, and assumed upon themselves the power of prohibiting their trade with all other parts of the world, except the Island of Great Britain. This arbitrary act, however, they soon recalled, and by solemn treaty entered into on the 12th day of March, 1651, between the said Commonwealth, by their Commissioners, and the Colony of Virginia by their House of Burgesses, it was expressly stipulated by the eighth article of the said treaty, that they should have "free trade as the people of England do enjoy to all places and with all nations, according to the laws of that Commonwealth". But * * * upon the restoration of his Majesty, King Charles II., their rights of free commerce fell once more a victim to arbitrary power; and by several acts of his reign, as well as of some of his successors. the trade of the Colonies was laid under such restrictions, as show what hopes they might form from the justice of a British Parliament, were its uncontrolled power admitted over these States.—Rights of British America. i, 127. Ford ed., i, 432. (1774.)

8491. ————. We cannot, my lord. close with the terms of that resolution [Lord North's conciliatory Proposition] because on our agreeing to contribute our proportion towards the common defence. they do not propose to lay open to us a free trade with all the world: whereas, to us it appears just that those who bear equally the burdens of government should equally participate of its benefits; either be contented with the monopoly of our trade, which brings greater loss to us and benefit to them than the amount of our proportional contributions to the common defence; or, if the latter be preferred, relinquish the former, and not propose, by holding both, to exact from us double contributions.—Address to Lord Dunmore. Ford ed., i, 457. (R., 1775.)

8492. TRADE, Right to.—No man has a natural right to the trade of a money lender but he who has the money to lend.—To J. W. Eppes. vi, 141. Ford ed., ix, 394. (M., 1813.)

8493. TRADE MARKS, Recommended. —The Secretary of State, to whom was referred by the House of Representatives the petition of Samuel Breck and others, proprietors of a sail-cloth manufactory in Boston, praying that they may have the exclusive privilege of using particular marks for designating the sailcloth of their manufactory, has had the same under consideration, and thereupon reports: That it would, in h.s opinion, contribute to fidelity in the execution of manufactures, to secure to every manufactory an exclusive right to some mark on its wares, proper to itself. This should be done by general laws, extending equal right to every case to which the authority of the Legislature should be competent. These cases are of divided jurisdiction: Manufactures made and consumed within a State being subject to State legislation, while those which are exported to foreign nations, or to another State, or into the Indian Territory, are alone within the legislation of the General Government. That it will, therefore, be reasonable for the General Government to provide in this behalf by law for those cases of manufacture generally, and those only which relate to commerce w'th foreign nations, and among the several States, and with the Indian tribes. This may be done by permitting the owner of every manufactory, to enter in the records of the court of the district wherein his manufactory is, the name with which he chooses to mark or designate his wares, and rendering it penal in others to put the same mark to any other wares.— Report on Trade Marks. vii, 563. (December 1791.)

8494. TRANQUILLITY, Basis of.— Tranquillity of mind depends much on ourselves, and greatly on due reflection "how much pain have cost us the evils which have never happened".—To William Short. vi, 402. (M., 1814.)

8495. TRANQUILLITY, Love of.—I cherish tranquillity too much to suffer political th ngs to enter my m'nd at all.—To President Washington. iv, 106. Ford ed., v:, 510. (M., May 1794.)

8496. TRANQUILLITY, National.— That love of order and obedience to the laws, which so remarkably characterize the c'tizens of the United States, are sure pledges of internal tranquillity.—To Benjamin Waring. iv, 378. (W., 1801.)

8497. TRANQUILLITY, Old age and.— Tranquillity is the old man's milk. I go to enjoy it in a few days, and to exchange the roar and tumult of bulls and bears, for the prattle of my grandchildren and senile rest.—To Edward Rutledge. iv, 191. Ford ed., vii, 155. (Pa., 1797.)

8498. ———. My object at present is peace and tranquillity, neither doing nor saying anything to be quoted, or to make me the subject of newspaper disqu sitions.—To David Howell. v, 554. (M., 1810.)

8499. ———. The *summum bonum* w'th me is now truly epicurean, ease of body and tranquillity of mind.—To John Adams. vi, 143. (M., 1813.)

8500. ———. Tranquillity is the *summum bonum* of age. I wish, therefore, to offend no man's opinion, nor to draw disquieting animadversions on my own. While duty required it, I met opposition with a firm and fearless step. But loving mankind in my individual relations with them, I pray to be permitted to depart in their peace; and like the superannuated soldier, "*quadragenis stipendiis emeritis*", to hang my arms on the post.—To Spencer Roane. vii, 136. Ford ed., x, 142. (P.F., 1819.)

8501. ———. There is a time for things: for advancing and for retiring; for a Sabbath of rest as well as for days of labor, and surely that Sabbath has arrived for one near entering on his 80th year. Tranquillity is the *summum bonum* of that age. I wish now for quiet, to withdraw from the broils of the world, to soothe the enmities, and to die in the peace and good will of all mankind.—To Archibald Thweat. Ford ed., x, 185. (M., 1821.)

8502. ———. Tranquillity is the last and sweetest asylum of age.—To Spencer Roane. vii, 211. Ford ed., x, 188. (M., 1821.)

8503. ———. At the age of eighty, tranquillity is the greatest good of life, and the strongest of our desires that of dying in the good will of a'l mankind.—To James Smith. vii, 270. (M., 1822.)

— TRANSMIGRATION OF SOULS.— See Souls, Transmigration of.

8504. TRAVEL, Advice as to.—The people you will naturally see the most of will be tavern keepers, *valets de place*, and postillions. These are the hackneyed rascals of every country. Of course they must never be considered when we calculate the national character.— Travelling Hints. x, 404. (1788.)

8505. ———. To pass once along a public road through a country, and in one direction only, to put up at its tavern, and get into conversation with the idle. drunken individuals who pass their time lounging in these taverns, is not the way to know a country, its inhabitants, or manners.—To Professor Ebeling. Ford ed., vi, 45. (1795.)

8506. TRAVEL, Philanthropy and.— From the first olive fields of Pierrelatte to the orangeries of Hières, has been continued rapture to me. I have often wished for you [Lafayette]. I think you have not made this journey. It is a pleasure you have to come, and an improvement to be added to the many you have already made. It will be a great comfort to you to know, from your own inspection, the condition of all the provinces of your own country, and it will be interesting to them, at some future day, to be known to you. Th's is, perhaps, the only moment of your life in wh'ch you can acquire that knowledge. And to do it most effectually, you must be absolutely *incognito;* you must ferret the people out of their hovels as I have done, look into their kettles, eat their bread, loll on their beds under pretense of resting yourself, but in fact to find if they are soft. You will feel a sublime pleasure in the course of this investigation, and a sublimer one hereafter, when you shall be able to apply your knowledge to the softening of their beds, or the throwing a morsel of meat into their kettle of vegetables.—To Marquis de Lafayette. ii, 136. (Ne., 1787.)

8507. —— ——. I am never satiated with rambling through the fields and farms [in France], examining the culture and cultivators, with a degree of curiosity which makes some take me to be a fool, and others to be much wiser than I am.—To Marquis de Lafayette. ii, 135. (Ne., 1787.)

8508. —— ——. The politics of each country [is] well worth studying so far as respects internal affairs. Examine its influence on the happiness of the people. Take every possible occasion for entering into the houses of the laborers, and especially at the moments of the r repast; see what they eat, how they are clothed, whether they are obliged to work too hard; whether the government or their landlord takes from them an unjust proportion of their labor; on what footing stands the property they call their own, their personal liberty, &c., &c.—Travelling Hints. ix, 405. (1788.)

8509. TRAVEL, Reflection during.—I think one travels more usefully when alone, because he reflects more.—To J. Bannister, Jr. ii, 151. (P., 1787.)

8510. TRAVEL, Tours of political.— With respect to the tour my friends to the north have proposed that I should make in that quarter, I have not made up a final opinion. The course of life which General Washington had run, civil and military, the services he had rendered, and the space he therefore occupied in the affections of his fellow citizens, take from his examples the weight of precedents for others; because no others can arrogate to themselves the claims which he had on the public homage. To myself, therefore, it comes as a new question, to be viewed under all the phases it may present. I confess that I am not reconciled to the idea of a Chief Magistrate parading himself through the several States, as an object of public gaze, and in quest of applause which, to be valuable, should be purely voluntary. I had rather acquire silent good will by a faithful discharge of my duties, than owe expressions of it to my putting myself in the way of receiving them.—To James Sullivan. v. 101. Ford ed., ix, 77. (W., June 1807.)

8511. —— ——. A journey to Boston or Portsmouth, after I shall be a private citizen, would much better harmonize with my feelings, as well as duties; and, founded in curiosity, would give no claims to an extension of it. I should see my friends, too, more at our mutual ease, and be left more exclusively to their society.—To James Sullivan. v, 102. Ford ed., ix. 78. (W., June 1807.)

8512. TRAVEL, Wisdom, happiness and.—Travelling makes men wiser, but less happy. When men of sober age travel, they gather knowledge, which they may apply usefully for their country; but they are subject ever after to recollections mixed with regret: their affections are weakened by being extended over more objects; and they learn new habits which cannot be gratified when they return home.—To Peter Carr. ii, 241. Ford ed., iv, 432. (P., 1787.)·

8513. TRAVEL, Young men and.— Young men, who travel, * * * do not acquire that wisdom for which a previous foundation is requisite, by repeated and just observations at home. The glare of pomp and pleasure is analogous to the motion of the blood; it absorbs all their affection and attention, and they are torn from it as from the only good in this world, and return to their home as to a place of exile and condemnation. Their eyes are forever turned back to the object they have lost, and its recollection poisons the residue of their lives. * * * A habit of idleness, an inability to apply themselves to business s acquired, and renders them useless to themselves and their country. These observations are founded in experience. There is no place where your pursuit of knowledge will be so little obstructed by foreign objects as in your own country, nor any, wherein the virtues of the heart will be less exposed to be weakened. Be good, be learned, and be industrious, and you will not want the aid of travelling to render you precious to your country, dear to your friends, happy within yourself.—To Peter Carr. ii, 241. Ford ed., iv, 433. (P., 1787.)

8514. TRAVELERS, Entertaining.—It is the general interest of our country that strangers of distinction passing through it should be made acquainted with its best citizens, and those most qualified to give favorable impressions of it.—To Mr. Hite. iv, 146. (M., 1796.)

8515. TREASON, Executions for.—It may be mentioned as a proof, both of the lenity of our government, and unanimity of its inhabitants, that though this [Revolutionary] war has now raged near seven years, not a single execution for treason has taken place. —Notes on Virginia. viii, 396. Ford ed., iii, 260. (1782.)

8516. TREASON, Patriotism vs.—Treason, when real, merits the highest punishment. But most codes extend their definitions of treason to acts not really against one's country. They do not distinguish between acts against the government, and acts against the oppressions of the government. The latter are virtues; yet have furnished more victims to the executioner than the former. Real treasons are rare; oppressions frequent. The unsuccessful strugglers against tyranny have been the chief martyrs of treason laws in all countries. Reformation of government with our neighbors* [being] as much wanting now as reformation of religion is, or ever was anywhere, we should not wish then to give up to the executioner the patriot who fails, and flees to us.—Report on Spanish Convention. iii, 353. Ford ed., v, 483. (1792.)

8517. TREASON, Punishment for.— Treasons, taking the simulated with the real, are sufficiently punished by exile.—Report on Spanish Convention. iii, 353. Ford ed., v, 483. (1792.)

8518. TREASON, Security against.— The framers of our Constitution certainly supposed they had guarded, as well their government against destruction by treason, as their citizens against oppression, under pre-

* The Spanish provinces.—Editor.

tence of it; and if these ends are not attained, it is of importance to enquire by what means, more effectual, they may be secured.—Seventh Annual Message. viii, 88. Ford ed., ix, 164. (1807.)

8519. TREASON, Suspected.—Having received information that divers citizens of this Commonwealth [Virginia], in the counties of James and York, have lately committed acts some of which amount to high treason and others to misprision of treason; and that some, though they may have been able to disguise and conceal their transactions as that legal evidence cannot be obtained by which they may be subjected to prosecution, * * * yet have so conducted themselves as to furnish the most pregnant circumstances of suspicion that they have been guilty of those offences, or are disaffected to the Independence of the United States, and will, whenever they shall have opportunity, aid or advise the measures of the public enemy, which persons, in the critical situation of this Commonwealth, it is indispensably necessary to punish for their crimes by way of example to others and to disable from doing mischief; I must, therefore, * * * desire and authorize you to make enquiry into the premises, and where you shall have probable cause to believe that any persons have been guilty of treason, or misprision of treason; that there is legal evidence to commit them thereof; and that an examining court can be had on them in the county where the offence was committed before there shall be any danger of rescue by the enemy, you have them delivered to the warrant of a justice of the peace, in order that they may be prosecuted in the usual forms of law; and that you aid in their safe conveyance to the public jail in Richmond, if they be ordered to be conveyed. But where you shall be of opinion that legal evidence cannot be obtained, that an examining court cannot be procured in the county before there will be danger of a rescue by the enemy, and that there are pregnant circumstances of suspicion that they have been guilty of the offences of treason or misprision of treason, or where there shall be pregnant causes of suspicion that persons in these counties are disaffected to the Independence of the United States; and when occasion serves, aid or advise the operations of the enemy; that in those cases, you apprehend such persons, and send them in safe custody to the jail of Richmond county. * * * They shall be treated by those into whose hands they shall be committed with no insult or rudeness unnecessary for their safe custody.—To Colonel James Innes. Ford ed., iii, 27. (R., May 1781.)

8520. TREASURY, Conduct of.—There is a point * * * on which I should wish to keep my eye, and to which I should aim to approach by every tack which previous arrangements force upon us. That is, to form into one consolidated mass all the moneys received into the treasury, and to the several expenditures, giving them a preference of payment according to the order in which they should be arranged. As for example. 1. The interest of the public debt. 2. Such portions of the principal as are exigible. 3. The expenses of government. 4. Such other portions of principal as, though not exigible, we are still free to pay when we please. The last object might be made to take up the residuum of money remaining in the treasury at the end of every year, after the three first

objects were complied with, and would be the barometer whereby to test the economy of the administration. It would furnish a simple measure by which every one could mete their merit, and by which every one could decide when taxes were deficient or superabundant.—To Albert Gallatin. iv, 428. Ford ed., viii, 140. (W., 1802.)

8521. TREASURY, Hamilton and.—This constellation of great men in the Treasury department was of a piece with the rest of Hamilton's plans. He took his own stand as a lieutenant general, surrounded by his major generals, and stationed his brigadiers and colonels under the name of supervisors, inspectors, &c., in the different States. Let us deserve well of our country by making her interests the end of all our plans, and not our own pomp, patronage, and irresponsibility.—To Albert Gallatin. iv, 429. Ford ed., viii, 141. (W., 1802.)

8522. TREASURY, Necessity for.—Every circumstance we hear induces us to believe that it is the want of will, rather than of ability, to furnish contributions which keeps the public treasury so poor. The Algerines will probably do us the favor to produce a sense of the necessity of a public treasury and a public force on that element where it can never be dangerous.—To David Humphreys. ii, 10. (P., 1786.)

8523. TREASURY, Organization of.—We shall now get rid of the commissioner of the internal revenue, and superintendent of stamps. It remains to amalgamate the comptroller and auditor into one, and reduce the register to a clerk of accounts; and then the organization will consist, as it should at first, of a keeper of money, a keeper of accounts, and the head of the department.—To Albert Gallatin. iv, 429. Ford ed., viii, 141. (W., 1802.)

— TREASURY, Patronage.—See Post-office.

8524. TREASURY, Separate department.—The act of September 2d, 1789, establishing a Department of Treasury, should be so amended as to constitute the office of the Treasurer of the United States a separate department, independent of the Secretary of the Treasury.—Giles Treasury Resolutions. Ford ed., vi, 171. (1793.)

— TREASURY NOTES.—See National Currency.

8525. TREATIES, Binding force of.—The moral duties which exist between individual and individual in a state of nature, accompany them into a state of society, and the aggregate of the duties of all the individuals composing the society constitutes the duties of that society towards any other; so that between society and society the same moral duties exist as did between the individuals composing them, while in an unassociated state, and their Maker not having released them from those duties on their forming themselves into a nation.—OPINION ON FRENCH TREATIES. vii, 613. FORD ED., vi, 220. (1793.)

8526. —— ——. Compacts between nation and nation are obligatory on them by the same moral law which obliges individuals to observe their compacts. There are circumstances, however, which sometimes excuse the non-performance of contracts between man and man; so are there also between nation and nation. When performance, for instance, becomes impossible, non-performance is not immoral. So if performance becomes *self-destructive* to the party, the law of self-preservation overrules the laws of obligation in others. For the reality of these principles I appeal to the true fountains of evidence, the head and heart of every rational and honest man. It is there nature has written her moral laws, and where every man may read them for himself. He will never read there the permission to annul his obligations for a time, or forever, whenever they become "dangerous, useless, or disagreeable", certainly not when merely *useless* or *disagreeable*, as seems to be said in an authority which has been quoted,* Vattel. 2. 197, and though he may, under certain degrees of *danger*, yet the danger must be imminent, and the degree great. Of these, it 's true, that nations are to be judges for themselves; since no nation has a right to sit in judgment over another. But the tribunal of our consciences remains, and that also of the opinion of the world. These will revise the sentence we pass in our own case, and as we respect these, we must see that in judging ourselves we have honestly done the part of impartial and rigorous judges.—OPINION ON FRENCH TREATIES. vii, 613. FORD ED., vi, 220. (1793.)

8527. —— ——. It is not the *possibility of danger* which absolves a party from his contract, for that possibility always exists, and in every case. * * * If possibilities would void contracts, there never could be a valid contract, for possibilities hang over everything. Obligation is not suspended till the danger is become real, and the moment of it so imminent, that we can no longer avoid decision without forever losing the opportunity to do it.—OPINION ON FRENCH TREATIES. vii, 614. FORD ED., vi, 222. (1793.)

8528. —— ——. I deny that the most explicit declaration made at this moment, that we acknowledge the obligation of the [French] treaties, could take from us the right of non-compliance at any future time, when compliance would involve us in great and inevitable danger.—OPINION ON FRENCH TREATIES. vii, 617. FORD ED., vi, 224. (1793.)

8529. —— ——. The doctrine of Grotius, Puffendorf and Wolf is that "treaties remain obligatory, notwithstanding any change in the form of government, except in the single case, where the preservation of that form was the object of the treaty". There, the treaty ex-

* By Alexander Hamilton.—EDITOR.

tinguishes, not by the election or declaration of the party remaining in *statu quo*, but independently of that, by the evanishment of the object. Vattel lays down, in fact, the same doctrine, that treaties continue obligatory, notwithstanding a change of government by the will of the other party; that to oppose that will would be a wrong; and that the ally remains an ally, notwithstanding the change. So far he concurs with all the previous writers:—but he then adds what they had not said, nor would say,—"but if this change renders the alliance *useless*, dangerous or *disagreeable* to it, it is free to renounce it". (Vattel. 2. 197.) It was unnecessary for him to have specified the exception of *danger* in this particular case, because that exception exists in all cases, and its extent has been considered; but when he adds that, because a contract is become merely *useless* or *disagreeable* we are free to renounce it,—he is in opposition to Grotius, Puffendorf and Wolf, who admit no such license against the obligation of treaties, and he is in opposition to the morality of every honest man, to whom we may safely appeal to decide whether he feels himself free to renounce a contract the moment it becomes merely *useless* or *disagreeable* to him.—OPINION ON FRENCH TREATIES. vii, 619. FORD ED., vi, 227. (1793.)

8530. TREATIES, Construction of.— Where the missionary of one government construes differently from that to which he is sent, the treaties and laws which are to form a common rule of action for both, it would be unjust in either to claim an exclusive right of construction. Each nation has an equal right to expound the meaning of their common rule; and reason and usage have established, in such cases, a convenient and well-understood train of proceeding. It is the right and duty of the foreign missionary to urge his own constructions, to support them with reasons, which may convince, and in terms of decency and respect which may reconcile the government of the country to a concurrence. It is the duty of that government to listen to his reasonings with attention and candor, and to yield to them when just. But if it shall still appear to them that reason and right are on their side, it follows of necessity, that exercising the sovereign powers of the country, they have a right to proceed on their own constructions and conclusions as to whatever is to be done within their limits. The minister then refers the case to his own government, asks new instructions, and, in the meantime, acquiesces in the authority of the country. His government examines his constructions, abandons them if wrong, insists on them if right, and the case then becomes a matter of negotiation between the two nations.—TO GOUVERNEUR MORRIS. iv, 44. FORD ED., vi, 388. (Aug. 1793.)

8531. TREATIES, Embarrassing.—It is against our system to embarrass ourselves with treaties, or to entangle ourselves at all with the affairs of Europe.—To PHILIP MAZ-ZEI. iv, 553. (W., July 1804.)

8532. —— ——. Our system is to have no treaties with any nation. as far as can be avoided. The treaty with England has, there-fore, not been renewed, and all overtures for treaty with other nations have been declined. We believe, that with nations as with individ-uals, dealings may be carried on as advan-tageously, perhaps more so, while their con-tinuance depends on a voluntary good treat-ment, as if fixed by a contract. which, when it becomes injurious to either, is made, by forced constructions, to mean what suits them, and becomes a cause of war instead of a bond of peace.—To PHILIP MAZZEI. iv, 552. (W., 1804.)

8533. —— ——. We are infinitely better off without treaties of commerce with any na-tion.—To PRESIDENT MADISON. vi, 453. FORD ED., ix, 513. (M., March 1815.)

8534. TREATIES, Infractions of.—On the breach of any article of a treaty by the one party, the other has its election to declare it dissolved in all its articles, or to compen-sate itself by withholding execution of equiv-alent articles; or to waive notice of the breach altogether.—To GEORGE HAMMOND. iii, 391. FORD ED., vi, 33. (1792.)

8535. —— ——. When one party breaks any stipulation of a treaty, the other is free to break it also, either in the whole, or in equivalent parts at its pleasure.—To GEORGE HAMMOND. iii, 424. FORD ED., vi, 64. (1792.)

8536. —— ——. If, in withholding a compliance with any part of the treaties, we do it without just cause or compensation, we give to France a cause of war, and so become associated in it on the other side.—OPINION ON FRENCH TREATIES. vii, 618. FORD ED., vi, 225. (1793.)

8537. TREATIES, Laws of the land.—Treaties are legislative acts. A treaty is a law of the land. It differs from other laws only as it must have the consent of a foreign nation, being but a contract with respect to that nation. In all countries, I believe, except England, treaties are made by the legislative power; and there, also. if they touch the laws of the land, they must be ap-proved by Parliament. * * * An act of Parliament was necessary to validate the American treaty of 1783.—PARLIAMENTARY MANUAL. ix, 80.

8538. TREATIES, Nations and.—I con-sider the people who constitute a society or nation as the source of all authority in that nation; as free to transact their common con-cerns by any agents they think proper; to change these agents individually, or the or-ganization of them in form or function when-ever they please; that all the acts done by those agents under the authority of the nation, are the acts of the nation, are obligatory on them and enure to their use, and can in no wise be annulled or affected by any change

in the form of the government, or of the persons administering it.—OPINION ON FRENCH TREATIES. vii, 612. FORD ED., vi, 220. (April 1793.)

8539. —— ——. The treaties between the United States and France were not treaties between the United States and Louis Capet, but between the two nations of America and France; and the nations remaining in ex-istence, though both of them have since changed their forms of government, the treat-ies are not annulled by these changes.—OPIN-ION ON FRENCH TREATIES. vii, 613. FORD ED., vi, 220. (April 1793.)

8540. TREATIES, Opposition to Euro-pean.—I am not for linking ourselves by new treaties with the quarrels of Europe; entering that field of slaughter to preserve their bal-ance, or joining in the confederacy of kings to war against the principles of liberty.—To ELBRIDGE GERRY. iv, 268. FORD ED., vii, 328. (Pa., 1799.)

8541. —— ——. We wish to let every treaty we have drop off without renewal. * * * The interest which European nations feel, as well as ourselves, in the mutual pat-ronage of commercial intercourse, is a suf-ficient stimulus on both sides to ensure that patronage. A treaty, contrary to that interest. renders war necessary to get rid of it.—To WILLIAM SHORT. iv, 415. FORD ED., viii, 98. (W., 1801.)

8542. TREATIES, Power to make.—The States of America before their present Union possessed completely. each within its own limits, the exclusive right to * * * [make treaties and] by their act of Union, they have as completely ceded [it] to the General Gov-ernment. Art. 2d. Section 1st. " The Presi-dent shall have power, by and with the ad-vice and consent of the Senate, to make treat-ies, provided two-thirds of the Senators pres-ent concur." Section 10th, " No State shall enter into any treaty. alliance, or confeder-ation. No State shall. without the consent of Congress, * * * enter into any agree-ment of compact with another State, or with a foreign power * * * ." These para-graphs of the Constitution, declaring that the General Government shall have, and that the particular ones shall not have, the right of * * * treaty, are so explicit that no com-mentary can explain them further, nor can any explain them away.—OPINION ON GEOR-GIAN LAND GRANTS. vii, 468. FORD ED., v, 166. (1790.)

8543. —— ——. Consulted verbally by the President [Washington] on whom a com-mittee of the Senate are to wait * * * to know whether he will think it proper to re-deem our Algerine captives, and make a treaty with the Algerines, on the single vote of the Senate. without taking that of the Rep-resentatives. * * * The subsequent ap-probation of the Senate being necessary to validate a treaty, they expect to be consulted beforehand, if the case admits. So the sub-sequent act of the Representatives being necessary where money is given, why should not they expect to be consulted in like manner, when the case admits? A treaty is a law of the land. But prudence will point out this difference to be attended to in making them; viz., where a treaty contains such articles only as will go into execution of themselves, or be carried into execution by the judges, they may be safely made; but where there are articles which require a law to be passed afterwards by the legislature, great caution is requisite. Therefore [I am] against hazarding this transaction without the sanction of both houses. The President concurred.—THE ANAS. ix, 106. FORD ED., i, 183. (March 1792.)

8544. —— ——. The subsequent approbation of the Senate being necessary to validate a treaty, [the Senate] expect to be consulted beforehand, if the case admits. So the subsequent act of the Representatives being necessary where money is given, why should not they expect to be consulted in like manner, when the case admits? A treaty is a law of the land. But prudence will point out this difference to be attended to in making them; viz., where a treaty contains such articles only as will go into execution of themselves, or be carried into execution by the judges, they may be safely made; but where there are articles which require a law to be passed afterwards by the Legislature, great caution is requisite. For example, the consular convention with France required a very small legislative regulation. This convention was unanimously ratified by the Senate. Yet the same identical men threw by the law to enforce it at the last session, and the Representatives at this session have placed it among the laws which they may take up or not, at their own convenience, as if that was a higher motive than the public faith. I am, therefore, against hazarding this transaction without the sanction of both Houses.*—THE ANAS. ix, 106. FORD ED., i, 184. (March 1792.)

8545. —— ——. President Washington wished to redeem our captives at Algiers and to make peace with them on paying an annual tribute. The Senate were willing to approve this, but unwilling to have the lower house applied to previously to furnish the money; they wished the President to take the money from the treasury, or open a loan for it. They thought that to consult the Representatives on one occasion would give them a handle always to claim it, and would let them into a participation of the power of making treaties, which the Constitution had given exclusively to the President and Senate. They said, too, that if the particular sum was voted by the Representatives, it would not be a secret. The President had no confidence in the secrecy of the Senate, and did not choose to take money from the treasury or to borrow. But he agreed he

* The transaction was the making a treaty with the Algerines, and providing for the redemption of the Algerine prisoners, which involved the raising of a loan.—EDITOR.

would enter into the provisional treaties with the Algerines, not to be binding on us till ratified here. I prepared questions for consultation with the Senate, and added, that on the return of the provisional treaty, and after they should advise the ratification, he would not have the seal put to it till the *two* Houses should vote the money. He asked me, if the treaty stipulating a sum and ratified by him, with the advice of the Senate, would not be good under the Constitution, and obligatory on the Representatives to furnish the money? I answered it certainly would, and that it would be the duty of the Representatives to raise the money; but that they might decline to do what was their duty, and I thought it might be incautious to commit himself by a ratification with a foreign nation, where he might be left in the lurch in the execution; it was possible, too, to conceive a treaty, which it would not be their duty to provide for. He said he did not like throwing too much into democratic hands, that if they would not do what the Constitution called them to do, the government would be at an end, and must *then assume another form.*—THE ANAS. ix, 114. FORD ED., i, 190. (April 1792.)

8546. —— ——. I had observed, that wherever the agency of either or both Houses would be requisite subsequent to a treaty, to carry it into effect, it would be prudent to consult them previously, if the occasion admitted: that thus it was, we were in the habit of consulting the Senate previously, when the occasion permitted, because their subsequent ratification would be necessary; that there was the same reason for consulting the lower House previously, where they were to be called on afterwards, and especially in a case of money, as they held the purse strings, and would be jealous of them.—THE ANAS. ix, 115. FORD ED., i, 191. (April 1792.)

8547. —— ——. [Alexander] Hamilton laid down this position* with great positiveness: That the Constitution having given power to the President and Senate to make treaties, they might make a treaty of neutrality which should take from Congress the right to declare war in that particular case, and that under the form of a treaty they might exercise any powers whatever, even those exclusively given by the Constitution to the House of Representatives. Randolph opposed this position, and seemed to think that where they undertook to do acts by treaty (as to settle a tariff of duties), which were exclusively given to the Legislature, that an act of the Legislature would be necessary to confirm them, as happens in England, when a treaty interferes with duties established by law. I insisted that in giving to the President and Senate a power to make treaties, the Constitution meant only to authorize them to carry into effect, by way of treaty, any powers they might constitutionally exercise. I was sensible of the weak points in this po-

* At a Cabinet meeting to consider the Neutrality Proclamation.—EDITOR.

sition, but there were still weaker in the other hypothesis; and if it be impossible to discover a rational measure of authority to have been given by this clause, I would rather suppose that the cases which my hypothesis would leave unprovided, were not thought of by the convention, or if thought of, could not be agreed on, or were thought on and deemed unnecessary to be invested in the government. Of this last description, were treaties of neutrality, treaties offensive and defensive, &c. In every event, I would rather construe so narrowly as to oblige the nation to amend, and thus declare what powers they would agree to yield, than too broadly, and indeed, so broadly as to enable the Executive and Senate to do things which the Constitution forbids.—THE ANAS. ix, 181. FORD ED., i, 268. (Nov. 1793.)

8548. ——— ———. According to the rule established by usage and common sense, of construing one part of the instrument by another, the objects on which the President and Senate may exclusively act by treaty are much reduced, but the field on which they may act with the sanction of the Legislature, is large enough; and I see no harm in rendering their sanction necessary, and not much harm in annihilating the whole treaty-making power, except as to making peace.—To JAMES MADISON. iv, 135. FORD ED., vii, 69. (M., March 1796.)

8549. ——— ———. If you [House of Representatives] decide in favor of your right to refuse cooperation in any case of treaty, I should wonder on what occasion it is to be used, if not on one where the rights, the interests, the honor and faith of our nation are so grossly sacrificed; where a faction has entered into a conspiracy with the enemies of their country to chain down the Legislature at the feet of both; where the whole mass of your constituents have condemned this work in the most unequivocal manner, and are looking to you as their last hope to save them from the effects of the avarice and corruption of the first agent, the revolutionary machinations of others, and the incomprehensible acquiescence of the only honest man who has assented to it. I wish that his honesty and his political errors may not furnish a second occasion to exclaim, " curse on his virtues, they have undone his country ".—To JAMES MADISON. iv, 135. FORD ED., vii, 69. (M., March 1796.)

8550. ——— ———. I was glad to hear it admitted on all hands in discussion [in the Senate], that laws of the United States, subsequent to a treaty, control its operation, and that the Legislature is the only power which can control a treaty. Both points are sound beyond doubt.—To JAMES MADISON. iv, 244. FORD ED., vii, 261. (Pa., May 1798.)

8551. ——— ———. To what subject the treaty-making power extends, has not been defined in detail by the Constitution; nor are we entirely agreed among ourselves. 1. It is admitted that it must concern the foreign na-

tion, party to the contract, or it would be a mere nullity res inter alia acta. 2. By the general power to make treaties, the Constitution must have intended to comprehend only those objects which are usually regulated by treaty, and cannot be otherwise regulated. 3. It must have meant to except out of these the rights reserved to the States; for surely the President and Senate cannot do by treaty what the whole government is interdicted from doing in any way. 4. And also to except those subjects of legislation in which it gave a participation to the House of Representatives. This last exception is denied by some, on the ground that it would leave very little matter for the treaty power to work on. The less the better say others. The Constitution thought it wise to restrain the Executive and Senate from entangling and embroiling our affairs with those of Europe. Besides, as the negotiations are carried on by the Executive alone, the subjecting to the ratification of the Representatives such articles as are within their participation, is no more inconvenient than to ..e Senate. But the ground of this exemption is denied as unfounded. For examine, e. g., the treaty of commerce with France, and it will be found that out of thirty-one articles, there are not more than small portions of two or three of them which would not still remain as subjects of treaties, untouched by these exceptions.—PARLIAMENTARY MANUAL. ix, 80.

8552. ——— ———. The property and sovereignty of all Louisiana * * * have on certain conditions been transferred to the United States by instruments bearing date the 30th of April last. When these shall have received the constitutional sanction of the Senate, they will without delay be communicated to the Representatives also, for the exercises of their functions, as to those conditions which are within the powers vested by the Constitution in Congress.—THIRD ANNUAL MESSAGE. viii, 24. FORD ED., viii, 268. (Oct. 1803.)

8553. ——— ———. Whatever of the enumerated objects is proper to be executed by way of a treaty, the President and Senate may enter into the treaty.—To WILSON C. NICHOLAS. iv, 506. FORD ED., viii, 248. (M., 1803.)

8554. ——— ———. A writer in the National Intelligencer of Feb. 24, 1816, who signs himself " B.", is endeavoring to shelter under the cloak of General Washington, the present enterprise of the Senate to wrest from the House of Representatives the power, given them by the Constitution, of participating with the Senate in the establishment and continuance of laws on specified subjects. Their aim is, by associating an Indian chief, or foreign government, in form of a treaty, to possess themselves of the power of repealing laws become obnoxious to them, without the assent of the third branch, although that assent was necessary to make it a law. We are then to depend for the secure possession of our laws, not on our immediate representatives chosen by ourselves, and amenable to ourselves every other year, but on Senators chosen by the Legislatures, amenable to them only, and that but at intervals of six years, which is nearly the common estimate for a term for life. But no act of that sainted worthy, no thought of General Washington, ever countenanced a change of our Constitution so vital as would be the rendering insignificant the popular, and giving to the aristocratical branch of our government, the power of depriving us of our laws. The case for which General Washington is quoted is that of his treaty with the Creeks, wherein was a stipulation that their supplies of goods should continue to be imported duty free. * * * General Washington's stipulation in that treaty was nothing more than that our laws should not levy duties where we have no right to levy them, that is, in foreign ports, or foreign countries. * * * The same writer quotes from a note in Marshall's *History,* an opinion of Mr. Jefferson, given to General Washington on the same occasion of the Creek treaty. Two or three little lines only of that opinion are given us, which do indeed express the doctrine in broad and general terms. Yet we know how often a few words withdrawn from their place may seem to bear a general meaning, when their context would show that their meaning must have been limited to the subject with respect to which they were used. If we could see the whole opinion, it might probably appear that its foundation was the peculiar circumstances of the Creek nation. We may say, too, on this opinion, as on that of a judge whose positions beyond the limits of the case before him are considered as *obiter* sayings, never to be relied on as authority. In July '90, moreover, the Government was but just getting under way. The duty law was not passed until the succeeding month of August. This question of the effect of a treaty was then of the first impression; and none of us, I suppose, will pretend that on our first reading of the Constitution we saw at once all its intentions, all the bearings of every word of it, as fully and as correctly as we have since understood them, after they have become subjects of public investigation and discussion; and I well remember the fact that, although Mr. Jefferson had retired from office before Mr. Jay's mission, and the question on the British treaty, yet during its discussion we were well assured of his entire concurrence in opinion with Mr. Madison and others who maintained the rights of the House of Representatives, so that, if on a *primâ facie* view of the question, his opinion had been too general, on stricter investigation, and more mature consideration, his ultimate opinion was with those who thought that the subjects which were confided to the House of Representatives in conjunction with the President and Senate, were exceptions to the general treaty power given to the President and Senate alone (according to the general rule that an instrument is to be so construed as to

reconcile and give meaning and effect to all its parts); that whenever a treaty stipulation interferes with a law of the three branches, the consent of the third branch is necessary to give it effect; and that there is to this but the single exception of the question of war and peace. There the Constitution expressly requires the concurrence of the three branches to commit us to the state of war, but permits two of them, the President and Senate, to change it to that of peace, for reasons as obvious as they are wise. I think, then, I may affirm in contradiction to B., that the present attempt of the Senate is not sanctioned by the opinion either of General Washington or of Mr. Jefferson.—JEFFERSON MSS. vi, 557. (March 1816.)

8555. —— ——. When the British treaty of 18— arrived, without any provision against the impressment of our seamen, I determined not to ratify it. The Senate thought I should ask their advice. I thought that would be a mockery of them, when I was predetermined against following it, should they advise its ratification. The Constitution had made their advice necessary to confirm a treaty, but not to reject it. This has been blamed by some; but I have never doubted its soundness.—To SPENCER ROANE. vii, 135. FORD ED., x, 142. (P.F., 1819.)

8556. TREATIES, Preliminary.—I consider a preliminary treaty as establishing certain heads of agreement, and a truce till these and others can be definitely arranged; as suspending acts of hostility, and as not changing the legal character of the *enemy* into that of a *friend.*—To ALEXANDER HAMILTON. FORD ED., vi, 10. (Pa., 1792.)

8557. TREATIES, Ratification of.—It has been the usage of the Executive, when it communicates a treaty to the Senate for their ratification, to communicate also the correspondence of the negotiations. This, having been omitted in the case of the Prussian treaty, was asked by a vote of the House of February 12, 1800, and was obtained. And in December, 1800, the Convention of that year, between the United States and France, with the report of the negotiations by the envoys, but not their instructions, being laid before the Senate, the instructions were asked for, and communicated by the President.—PARLIAMENTARY MANUAL. ix, 81.

8558. TREATIES, Regulation of commerce by.—Treaties are very imperfect machines for regulating commerce in detail.—To M. DE MEUNIER. ix, 287. FORD ED., iv, 142. (P., 1786.)

8559. —— ——. It is desirable, in many instances, to exchange mutual advantages by legislative acts rather than by treaty; because the former, though understood to be in consideration of each other, and therefore greatly respected, yet when they become too inconvenient, can be dropped at the will of either party; whereas stipulations by treaty are forever irrevocable but by joint consent let a change of circumstances render them ever so bothersome.— REPORT ON TONNAGE LAW. FORD ED., v, 273. (1791.)

8560. TREATIES, Repeal of.—A treaty made by the President, with the concurrence of two-thirds of the Senate, is a law of the land, and a law of superior order, because it not only repeals past laws, but cannot itself be repealed by future ones.*—OFFICIAL OPINION. vii, 505. FORD ED., v, 216. (1790.)

8561. TREATIES, Rescinding.—Treaties being declared, equally with the laws of the United States, to be the supreme law of the land, it is understood that an act of the Legislature alone can declare them infringed and rescinded. This was accordingly the process adopted in the case of France, 1798.— PARLIAMENTARY MANUAL. ix, 81.

8562. TREATIES, Self-liberation from. —Reason which gives * * * [the] right of self-liberation from a contract in certain cases, has subjected it to certain just limitations. 1. The danger which absolves us must be great, inevitable and imminent. * * * 2. A second limitation on our right of releasing ourselves is that we are to do it from so much of the treaties only as is bringing great and inevitable danger on us, and not from the residue, allowing the other party a right at the same time, to determine whether on our non-compliance with that part, they will declare the whole void. This right they would have, but we should not. * * * 3. A third limitation is that when a party, from necessity or danger, withholds compliance with that part of a treaty, it is bound to make compensation where the nature of the case admits and does not dispense with it.†—OPINION ON FRENCH TREATIES. vii, 614. FORD ED., vi, 221. (1793.)

8563. TREATIES, Short.—Your observations on the expediency of making short treaties are most sound. Our situation is too changing and too improving, to render an unchangeable treaty expedient for us.—To E. RUTLEDGE. iii, 165. FORD ED., v, 196. (N.Y., 1790.)

8564. TREATIES OF COMMERCE, British.—In February, 1786. Mr. Adams wrote to me [at Paris], pressingly to join him

---

* Jefferson, at a later period, modified this opinion in the following note: "Unless with the consent or default of the other contracting party. It may well be doubted, too, and perhaps denied, that the treaty power can control a law. The question here proposed was then of the first impression. Subsequent investigations have proved that the contrary position is the more general truth."—EDITOR.

† The question under consideration, when this opinion was given, was "whether the United States had the right to renounce their treaties with France, or to hold them suspended till the government of that country shall be established". Alexander Hamilton took the ground that as France was a monarchy when the United States entered into an alliance with it, and had since declared itself to be a republic, which might issue in a military despotism and thereby render the alliance "dangerous", to the United States, we had the right either to renounce the treaty or to declare it suspended until a settled government had been formed. Jefferson opposed this view, maintaining that the danger to be apprehended was not sufficient in sound morality to justify the United States in declaring the treaty null.—EDITOR.

---

in London immediately, as he thought he discovered there some symptoms of better disposition towards us. Colonel [William Stephens] Smith, his Secretary of Legation, was the bearer of his urgencies for my immediate attendance. I, accordingly, left Paris on the 1st of March and, on my arrival in London, we agreed on a very summary form of treaty, proposing an exchange of citizenship for our citizens, our ships, and our productions generally, except as to office.—AUTOBIOGRAPHY. i, 63. FORD ED., i, 88. (1821.)

8565. ——— ———. On my presentation as usual to the King and Queen, at their levées, it was impossible for anything to be more ungracious than their notice of Mr. Adams and myself. I saw at once that the ulcerations in the narrow mind of that mulish being left nothing to be expected on the subject of my attendance; and on the first conference with the Marquis of Carmarthen, his Minister of Foreign Affairs, the distance and disinclination which he betrayed in his conversation, the vagueness and evasions of his answers to us. confirmed me in the belief of their aversion to have anything to do with us. We delivered him, however, our projét. Mr. Adams not despairing as much as I did of its effect. We afterwards, by one or more notes, requested his appointment of an interview and conference. which, without directly declining, he evaded by pretences of other pressing occupations for the moment. After staying there seven weeks, till within a few days of the expiration of our commission, I informed the minister by note that my duties at Paris required my return to that place, and that I should with pleasure be the bearer of any commands to his Ambassador there. He answered that he had none, and wishing me a pleasant journey, I left London the 26th. and arrived at Paris the 30th of April. —AUTOBIOGRAPHY. i, 64. FORD ED., i, 89. (1821.)

8566. ——— ———. There is no doubt what the determination [of the British Court with respect to a treaty] will be; but it will be useful to have it; as it may put an end to all further expectations on our side the water, and show that the time is come for doing whatever is to be done by us for counteracting the unjust and greedy designs of this country [England]. —To JOHN JAY. i, 539. FORD ED., iv, 200. (L., March 1786.)

8567. ——— ———. I am quite at a loss what you will do with England. To leave her in possession of our posts, seems inadmissible; and yet to take them, brings on a state of things for which we seem not to be in readiness. Perhaps a total suppression of her trade, or an exclusion of her vessels from the carriage of our produce, may have some effect; but I believe not very great. Their passions are too deeply and too universally engaged in opposition to us. The ministry have found means to persuade the nation that they are richer than they were while we participated of their commercial privileges. We should try to turn our trade into other channels. I am in hopes this country [France] will endeavor to give it more encouragement.—To ELBRIDGE GERRY. i, 557. (P., 1786.)

8568. ——— ———. I am sorry the British are sending a minister to attempt a treaty. They never made an equal commercial treaty with any nation, and we have no right to expect to be the first. It will place you between the injunctions of true patriotism and the clamors of a faction devoted to a foreign interest, in preference to that of their own country. It will confirm the English, too, in their practice of whipping us into a treaty. They did it in Jay's case, were near doing it in Monroe's, and on failure of that, have applied the scourge with tenfold vigor, and now come on to try its effect. But it is the moment when we should prove our consistency, by recurring to the principles we dictated to Monroe, the departure from which occasioned our rejection of his treaty, and by protesting against Jay's treaty being ever quoted or looked at, or even mentioned. That form will forever be a mill-stone round our necks unless we now rid ourselves of it once for all. The occasion is highly favorable, as we never can have them more in o power.—To PRESIDENT MADISON. v, 443. (M., April 1809.)

— **TREATIES OF COMMERCE, Confederation and.**—See CONFEDERATION.

8569. TREATIES OF COMMERCE, Efforts to negotiate.—Without urging, we [Franklin, Adams and Jefferson] sounded the ministers of the several European nations at the Court of Versailles, on their dispositions towards mutual commerce, and the expediency of encouraging it by the protection of a treaty. Old Frederick of Prussia met us cordially and w'thout hesitation, and appointing the Baron de Thulemeyer, his Minister at The Hague, to negotiate with us, we communicated to him our projet, which, with little alteration by the King, was soon concluded. Denmark and Tuscany entered also into negotiations with us. Other powers appearing indifferent we did not think it proper to press them. * * * The negotiations, therefore, begun with Denmark and Tuscan we protracted designedly until our powers had expired; and abstained from making new propositions to others having no colonies; because our commerce being an exchange of raw for wrought materials, is a competent price for admission into the colonies of those possessing them: but were we to give it, without price, to others, all would claim it without price on the ordinary ground of *gentis amicissimæ*.—AUTOBIOGRAPHY. i, 62. FORD ED., i, 87. (1821.)

8570. —— ——. The European powers seemed in fact to know little about us but as rebels, who had been successful in throwing off the yoke of the mother country. They were ignorant of our commerce, which had been always monopolized by England, and of the exchange of articles it might offer advantageously to both parties. They were inclined, therefore, to stand aloof until they could see better what relations might be usefully instituted with us.—AUTOBIOGRAPHY. i, 62. FORD ED., i, 88. (1821.)

8571. —— ——. On the conclusion of peace [w'th Great Britain], Congress, sensib'e of their right to assume independence, would not condescend to ask its acknowledgment from other nations, yet were willing, by some of the ordinary international transactions, to receive what would imply that acknowledgment. They appointed commissioners, therefore, to propose treaties of commerce to the principal nations of Europe. I was then a member of Congress, was of the committee appo'nted to prepare instructions for the commissioners, was, as you suppose, the draughtsman of those actually agreed to, and was joined with your father and Dr. Franklin, to carry them into execution. But the stipulations making part of these instructions, which respected privateering, blockades, contraband, and freedom of the fisheries, were not original conceptions of mine. They

had before been suggested by Dr. Franklin, in some of his papers in possession of the public, and had, I think, been recommended in some letter of his to Congress. I happen only to have been the inserter of them in the first public act which gave the formal sanction of a public authority. We accordingly proposed our treaties, containing these stipulations, to the principal governments of Europe. But we were then just emerged from a subordinate condition; the nations had as yet known nothing of us, and had not yet reflected on the relations which it might be their interest to establish with us. Most of them, therefore, listened to our propositions with coyness and reserve; old Frederick [the Great] alone closing with us without hesitation. The negotiator of Portugal, indeed, signed a treaty with us, which his government did not ratify, and Tuscany was near a final agreement. Becoming sensible, however, ourselves, that we should do nothing with the greater powers, we thought it better not to hamper our country with engagements to those of less significance, and suffered our powers to expire without closing any other negotiations. Austria soon after became desirous of a treaty with us, and her ambassador pressed it often on me; but our commerce with her being no object, I evaded her repeated invitations. Had these governments been then apprized of the station we should so soon occupy among nations, all, I believe, would have met us promptly and with frankness. These principles would then have been established with all, and from being the conventional law with us alone, would have slid into their engagements with one another, and become general.

These are the facts within my recollection. They have not yet got into written history; but their adoption by our southern brethren will bring them into observance, and make them what they should be, a part of the law of the world, and of the reformation of principles for which they will be indebted to us.—To JOHN QUINCY ADAMS. vii, 436. FORD ED., x, 383. (M., March 1826.)

8572. TREATIES OF COMMERCE, Favored nation principle.—I know of no investigation, at the instance of any nation, of the extent of the clause giving the rights of the most favored nation but from the import of the words themselves, and from the clause that a privilege granted to any other nation shall immediately become common, freely where freely granted, or *yielding the compensation* where a compensation is given, I have no doubt that if any one nation will admit our goods free in consideration of our doing the same by them, no other nation can claim an exception from duties in our ports without y'elding us the same in theirs.—To JAMES MONROE. FORD ED., iv, 19. (P., Dec. 1784.)

8573. —— ——. When the first article of our instructions of May 7th, 1784, was under debate in Congress, it was proposed that neither party should make the other pay, in their ports, greater duties, than they paid n the ports of the other. One objection to this was its impracticability; another, that it would put it out of our power to lay such duties on alien importation as might encourage importation by natives. Some members, much attached to Engl'sh policy, thought such a distinction should actually be established. Some thought the power to do it should be reserved, in case any peculiar circumstances should call for it, though under the present, or, perhaps, any probable circumstances, they did not think it would be good policy ever to exercise it. The footing *gentis amicissimæ* was, therefore, adopted, as you see in the instruction. As far as my enquiries enable me to judge, France and Holland make no distinction of duties between aliens and natives. I also rather believe that the other States of Europe make none, England excepted, to whom this policy, as that of her navigation act, seems peculiar. The question then is, should we disarm ourselves of the power to make this distinction aga'nst all nat'ons, in order to purchase an exception from the alien duties in England only; for if we put her importations on the footing of native, all other nations with whom we treat w'll have a right to claim the same. I think we should, because against other nations, who make no d'stinction in their ports between us and their own subjects, we ought not to make a distinction in ours. And if the English will agree, in like manner, to make none, we should, w'th equal reason, abandon the right as against them. I think a'l the world would gain, by setting commerce at perfect liberty. I remember this proposition to put foreigners and natives on the same footing was considered; and we were all three, Dr. Franklin as well as you and myself, in favor of it. We finally, however, did not admit it, partly from the objection you mention, but more still on account of our instructions. But though the English proclamation had appeared in America at the time of framing these instructions, i think its effect, as to alien duties, had not yet been experienced, and therefore was not attended to. If it had been noted in the debate, I am sure that the annihilation of our whole trade would have been thought too great a price to pay for the reservation of a barren power, which a majority of the members did not propose ever to exercise, though they were willing to retain 't. Stipulating for equal rights for foreigners and natives, we obtain more in foreign ports' than our instruct'ons required, and we only part with, in our own ports, a power of which sound policy would probably forever forbid the exercise. Add to this, that our treaty will be for a very short term, and if any evil be experienced under it, a reformation will soon be in our power. I am, therefore, for putting th's among our original propositions to the court of London. If it should prove an insuperable obstacle with them, or if it should stand in the way of a greater advantage, we can but abandon 't in the course of the negotiation.—To JOHN ADAMS. i, 370. FORD ED., iv, 79. (P., July 1785.)

8574. —— ——. Though treaties, which merely exchange the rights of the most favored nations, are not without all inconven'ence, yet they have their conveniences also. It is an important one that they leave each party free to make what internal regulations they please, and to give what preferences they find expedient to native merchants, vesse's, and productions.—MISSISSIPPI RIVER INSTRUCTIONS. vii, 587. FORD ED., v, 477. (1792.)

8575. —— ——. It will probably be urged, because it was urged on a former occasion, that, if Spain *grants** to us the right of navigating the Mississippi, other nat'ons will become entitled to it by virtue of treaties giving them the rights to the *most favored nation.* * * * When those treaties were made, no nations could be under

* This extract is from Jefferson's Ins'ructions to the Commissioners with respect to the navigation of the Mississippi river. It should not be inferred from the use of the word "grants" that Jefferson admitted the Spanish pretension to the control of the lower part of the river. He maintained, on the contrary, that we had an inherent right and also treaty rights to the navigation.—EDITOR.

contemplation but those then existing, or those, at most, who might exist under similar circumstances. America did not then exist as a nation; and the circumstances of her pos'tion and commerce, are so totally dissimilar to everything then known, that the treaties of that day were not adapted to any such being. They would better fit even China than America; because, as a manufacturing nation, China resembles Europe more. When we solicited France to adm't our whale oils into her ports, though she had excluded all foreign whale oils, her Minister made the objection now under consideration, and the foregoing answer was given. It was found to be solid; and whale oils of the United States are in consequence admitted, though those of Portugal and the Hanse towns and of all other nations, are excluded. Again, when France and England were negotiating their late treaty of commerce, the great dissimilitude of our commerce (which furnishes raw materials to employ the industry of others, in exchange for articles whereon industry has been exhausted) from the commerce of the European nations (which furnishes things ready wrought only) was suggested to the attention of both negotiators, and that they should keep their nations free to make particular arrangements with ours, by commun'cating to each other only the rights of the most favored *European* nation. Each was separately sensible of the importance of the distinction; and as soon as it was proposed by the one, it was acceded to by the other, and the word *European* was inserted in their treaty. It may fairly be considered, then, as the rational and received interpretation of the diplomatic term, "*gentis amicissima*", that it has not in view a nation, unknown in many cases at the time of using the term, and so dissimilar in all cases, as to furnish no ground of just reclamation to any other nation.—MISSISSIPPI RIVER INSTRUCTIONS. vii, 583. FORD ED., v, 473. (1792.)

8576. TREATIES OF COMMERCE, Instructions respecting.—Whereas, instructions bearing date the 29th day of October, 1783, were sent to the Ministers Plenipotentiary of the United States of America at the Court of Versailles, empowered to negotiate a peace, or to any one or more of them, for concerting drafts or propositions for treat'es of amity and commerce with the commercial powers of Europe: Resolved, That it will be advantageous to these United States to conclude such treaties with Russia, the Court of Vienna, Prussia, Denmark, Saxony, Hamburg, Great Britain, Spain, Portugal, Genoa, Tuscany, Rome, Naples, Venice, Sardinia, and the Ottoman Porte. Resolved, That in the formation of these treaties the following points be carefully stipulated: 1st. That each party shall have a right to carry the'r own produce, manufactures, and merchandise in their own bottoms to the ports of the other, and thence the produce and merchandise of the other, paying, in both cases, such duties only as are paid by the most favored nation, freely, where 't is freely granted to such nation, or paying the compensation where such nation does the same. 2. That with the nations hold-ing territorial possessions in America, a direct and similar intercourse be admitted between the United States and such possessions; or if this cannot be obta'ned, then a direct and similar intercourse between the United States and certain free ports within such possessions; that if this neither can be obtained, permission be stipulated to bring from such possessions, in their own bottoms, the produce and merchandise thereof to their States directly; and for these States to carry in their own bottoms the 1 produce and merchandise to such possessions directly. 3. That these United States be considered in all such treaties, and in every case arising under them, as one nation, upon the principles of the Federal constitution. 4. That it be proposed, though not indispensably required, that if war should hereafter arise between the two contracting parties, the merchants of either country, then residing in the other. shall be allowed to remain nine months to collect their debts and settle their affairs, and may depart freely, carrying off all their effects, without molestation or hinderance. and all fishermen, all cultivators of the earth, and all artisans or manufacturers, unarmed and inhabiting unfortified towns, villages or places, who labor for the common subsistence and benefit of mankind, and peaceably following their respective employments. shall be allowed to continue the same, and shall not be molested by the armed force of the enemy, in whose power. by the events of war, they may happen to fall ; but if anything is necessary to be taken from them, for the use of such armed force, the same shall be paid for at a reasonable price ; and all merchants and traders, exchanging the products of different places, and thereby rendering the necessaries, conveniences, and comforts of human life more easy to obtain and more general, shall be allowed to pass free and unmolested ; and neither of the contracting powers shall grant or issue any commission to any private armed vessels empowering them to take or destroy such trading ships. or interrupt such commerce. 5. And in case either of the contracting parties shall happen to be engaged in war with any other nation, it be further agreed. in order to prevent all the difficulties and misunderstandings that usually arise respecting the merchandise heretofore called contraband, such as arms. ammunition and military stores of all kinds, that no such articles. carrying by the ships or subjects of one of the parties to the enemies of the other, shall, on any account, be deemed contraband, so as to induce confiscation, and a loss of property to individuals. Nevertheless, it shall be lawful to stop such ships and detain them for such length of time as the captors may think necessary, to prevent the inconvenience or damage that might ensue, from their proceeding on their voyage, paying. however, a reasonable compensation for the loss such arms shall occasion to the proprietors ; and it shall be further allowed to use in the service of the captors, the whole or any part of the military stores so detained, paying the owners the full value of the same, to be ascertained by the current price at the place of its destination. But if the other contracting party will not consent to discontinue the confiscation of contraband goods, then that it be stipulated, that if the master of the vessel stopped, will deliver out the goods charged to be contraband, he shall be admitted to do it, and the vessel shall not in that case be carried into any port ; but shall be allowed to proceed on her voyage. 6. That in the same case, when either of the contracting parties shall happen to be engaged in war with any other power, all goods. not contraband, belonging to the subjects of that other power, and shipped in the bottoms of the party hereto, who is not engaged in the war. shall be entirely free. And that to ascertain what shall constitute the blockade of any place or port, it shall be understood to be in such predicament, when the assailing power shall have taken such a station as to expose to imminent danger any ship or ships. that would attempt to sail in or out of the said port ; and that no vessel of the party, who is not engaged in the said war, shall be stopped without a material and well grounded

cause ; and in such cases justice shall be done, and an indemnification given, without loss of time to the persons aggrieved, and thus stopped without sufficient cause. 7. That no right be stipulated for aliens to hold real property within these States, this being utterly inadmissible by their several laws and policy ; but when on the death of any person holding real estate within the territories of one of the contracting parties, such real estate would by their laws descend on a subject or citizen of the other, were he not disqualified by alienage, then he shall be allowed reasonable time to dispose of the same, and withdraw the proceeds without molestation. 8. That such treaties be made for a term not exceeding ten years from the exchange of ratification. 9. That these instructions be considered as supplementary to those of October 29th, 1783 ; and not as revoking, except when they contradict them. That where in treaty with a particular nation they can procure particular advantages. to the specification of which we have been unable to descend, our object in these instructions having been to form out'ines only and general principles of treaty with many nations. it is our expectation they will procure them, though not pointed out in these instructions ; and where they may be able to form treaties on principles which, in their judgment. will be more beneficial to the United States than those herein directed to be made their basis, they are permitted to adopt such principles. That as to the duration of treaties, though we have proposed to restrain them to the term of ten years, yet they are at liberty to extend the same as far as fifteen years with any nation which may pertinaciously insist thereon. And that it will be agreeable to us to have supplementary treaties with France, the United Netherlands and Sweden, which may bring the treaties we have entered into with them as nearly as may be to the principles of those now directed ; but that this be not pressed. if the proposal should be found disagreeable. *Resolved.* That treaties of amity, or of amity and commerce, be entered into with Morocco, and the Regencies of Algiers, Tunis and Tripoli, to continue for the same term of ten years, or for a term as much longer as can be procured. That our Ministers, to be commissioned for treating with foreign nations, make known to the Emperor of Morocco the great satisfaction which Congress feel from the amicable disposition he has shown towards these States, and his readiness to enter into alliance with them. That the occupations of the war, and distance of our situation have prevented our meeting his friendship so early as we wished. But the powers are now delegated to them for entering into treaty with him, in the execution of which they are ready to proceed, and that as to the expenses of his Minister, they do therein what is for the honor and interest of the United States. Resolved, That a commission be issued to Mr. J. Adams, Mr. B. Frank'in, and Mr. T. Jefferson, giving powers to them, or the greater part of them, to make and receive propositions for such treaties of amity and commerce, and to negotiate and sign the same. transmitting them to Congress for their final ratification ; and that such commission be in force for a term not exceeding two years.— TREATY INSTRUCTIONS OF CONGRESS. ix, 226. FORD ED., iii, 489. (May 7, 1784.)

8577. TREATIES OF COMMERCE, Objects of.—My wish to enter treaties with the other powers of Europe arises more from a desire of bringing all our commerce under the jurisdiction of Congress. than from any other views. Because, according to my idea, the commerce of the United States with those countries, not under treaty with us, is under the jurisdiction of each State separately; but that of the countries, which have treated with us, is under the jurisdiction of Congress with the two fundamental restraints only which I have before noted.—To JOHN ADAMS. i, 360. (P., 1785.)

8578. TREATIES OF COMMERCE, Portugal.—Considering the treaty with Portugal among the most interesting to the United States, I some time ago took occasion * * * to ask of the Portuguese Ambassador if he had yet received from his Court an answer to our letter. He told me he had not; but that he would make it the subject of another letter. Two days ago, his Secretaire d'Ambassade called on me with a letter from his Minister to the Ambassador. * * * By this [extract from the letter], it would seem that this power is more disposed to pursue a track of negotiation similar to that which Spain has done. I consider this answer as definitive of all further measures under our commission to Portugal.—To JOHN JAY. i, 458. (P., 1785.)

— **TREATY, Jay.**—See JAY TREATY.

8579. TREATY (British peace), Ratification of.—The definitive treaty of peace which had been signed at Paris on the 3rd of September, 1783, and received here, could not be ratified without a House of nine States. On the 23d of December, therefore, we [the Congress sitting at Annapolis] addressed letters to the several Governors, stating the receipt of the definitive treaty; that seven States only were in attendance, while nine were necessary to its ratification; and urging them to press on their delegates the necessity of their immediate attendance. And on the 26th, to save time, I moved that the Agent of Marine (Robert Morris) should be instructed to have ready a vessel at this place, at New York, and at some Eastern port, to carry over the ratification of the treaty when agreed to. It met the general sense of the House, but was opposed by Dr. [Arthur] Lee, on the ground of expense, which it would authorize the Agent to incur for us; and, he said, it would be better to ratify at once, and send on the ratification. Some members had before suggested that seven States were competent to the ratification. My motion was therefore postponed, and another brought forward by Mr. Read, of South Carolina, for an immediate ratification. This was debated the 26th and 27th. [Jacob] Read [of South Carolina], Lee, [Hugh] Williamson and Jeremiah Chase, urged that the ratification was a mere matter of form, that the treaty was conclusive from the moment it was signed by the ministers; that, although the Confederation requires the assent of *nine States* to *enter into a* treaty, yet, that its conclusion could not be called *entrance into it;* that supposing nine States requisite, it would be in the power of five States to keep us always at war; that nine States had virtually authorized the ratification, having ratified the provisional treaty, and instructed their ministers to agree to a definitive one in the same terms, and the present one was, in fact, substantially, and almost verbatim, the same: that there now remain but sixty-seven days for the ratification, for its passage across the Atlantic, and its exchange: that there was no hope of our soon having nine States present; in fact, that this was the ultimate point of time to which we could venture to wait; that if the ratification was not in Paris by the time stipulated, the treaty would become void; that if ratified by seven States, it would go under our

seal, without its being known to Great Britain that only seven had concurred; that it was a question of which they had no right to take cognizance, and we were only answerable for it to our constituents; that it was like the ratification which Great Britain had received from the Dutch, by the negotiations of Sir William Temple. On the contrary, it was argued by Monroe, Gerry, Howel, Ellery and myself, that by the modern usage of Europe, the ratification was considered as the act which gave validity to a treaty, until which, it was not obligatory. * That the commission to the ministers reserved the ratification to Congress; that the treaty itself stipulated that it should be ratified; that it became a second question, who were competent to the ratification? That the confederation expressly required nine States to enter into any treaty; that, by this, that instrument must have intended, that the assent of nine States should be necessary, as well to the *completion* as to the *commencement* of the treaty, its object having been to guard the rights of the Union in all those important cases where nine States are called for; that, by the contrary construction, seven States, containing less than one-third of our whole citizens, might rivet on us a treaty, commenced indeed under commission and instructions from nine States, but formed by the minister in express contradiction to such instructions, and in direct sacrifice of the interests of so great a majority; that the definitive treaty was admitted not to be a verbal copy of the provisional one, and whether the departures from it were of substance or not, was a question on which nine States alone were competent to decide; that the circumstances of the ratification of the provisional articles by nine States, the instructions of our ministers to form a definitive one by them, and their actual agreement in substance, do not render us competent to ratify in the present instance; if these circumstances are in themselves a ratification, nothing further is requisite than to give attested copies of them in exchange for the British ratification; if they are not, we remain where we were, without a ratification by nine States, and incompetent ourselves to ratify; that it was but four days since the seven States, now present, unanimously concurred in a resolution, to be forwarded to the Governors of the absent States, in which they stated as a cause for urging on their delegates, that nine States were necessary to ratify the treaty; that in the case of the Dutch ratification, Great Britain had courted it, and therefore was glad to accept it as it was; that they knew our Constitution, and would object to a ratification by seven; that, if that circumstance was kept back, it would be known hereafter, and would give them ground to deny the validity of a ratification into which they should have been surprised and cheated, and it would be a dishonorable prostitution of our seal; that there is a hope of nine States: that if the treaty would become null, if not ratified in time, it would not be saved by an imperfect ratification: but that, in fact, it would not be null, and would be placed on better ground, going in unexceptional form, though a few days too late, and rested on the small importance of this circumstance, and the physical impossibilities which had prevented a punctual compliance in point of time: that this would be approved by all nations, and by Great Britain herself, if not determined to renew the war, and if so determined, she would never want excuses, were this out of the way. Mr. Read gave notice, he should call for the yeas and nays; whereon

* Vattel L. 2 § 156. L. 4. § 77. 1. Mably Droi D'Europe, 86.—NOTE BY JEFFERSON.

those in opposition, prepared a resolution, expressing pointedly the reasons of their dissent from his motion. It appearing, however, that his proposition could not be carried, it was thought better to make no entry at all. Massachusetts alone would have been for it; Rhode Island, Pennsylvania and Virginia against it, Delaware, Maryland and North Carolina would have been divided. * * * Those who thought seven States competent to the ratification, being very restless under the loss of their motion, I proposed on the 3rd of January, to meet them on middle ground, and therefore moved a resolution, which premised that there were but seven States present, who were unanimous for the ratification, but that they differed in opinion on the question of competency; that those, however, in the negative were unwilling that any powers which it might be supposed they possessed, should remain unexercised for the restoration of peace, provided it could be done, saving their good faith, and without importing any opinion of Congress, that seven States were competent, and resolving that the treaty be ratified so far as they had power; that it should be transmitted to our ministers, with instructions to keep it uncommunicated; to endeavor to obtain three months longer for exchange of ratifications; that they should be informed that so soon as nine States shall be present, a ratification by nine shall be sent them: if this should get to them before the ultimate point of time for exchange, they were to use it, and not the other; if not, they were to offer the act of the seven States in exchange, informing them the treaty had come to hand while Congress was not in session; that but seven States were as yet assembled, and these had unanimously concurred in the ratification. This was debated on the 3rd and 4th *; and on the 5th, a vessel being to sail for England, from Annapolis, the House directed the President to write to our ministers accordingly. January 14. Delegates from Connecticut having attended yesterday, and another from South Carolina coming in this day, the treaty was ratified without a dissenting voice; and three instruments of ratification were ordered to be made out, one of which was sent by Colonel Harmer, another by Colonel Franks, and the third transmitted to the Agent of Marine, to be forwarded by any good opportunity.—AUTOBIOGRAPHY. i, 55. FORD ED., i, 77. (1821.)

8580. TREATY (British peace), Violations of.—In the 7th article [of the treaty of peace], it was stipulated, that his Britannic majesty should withdraw his armies, garrisons, and fleets, without carrying away any negroes, or other property of the American inhabitants. This stipulation was known to the British commanding officers, before the 19th of March, 1783, as *provisionally* agreed; and on the 5th of April they received official notice from their court of the conclusion and ratification of the preliminary articles between France, Spain, and Great Britain, which gave activity to ours, as appears by the letter of Sir Guy Carleton to General Washington, dated April 6, 1783. From this time, then, surely no negroes could be carried away without a violation of the treaty. Yet we find that so early as May 6, a *large* number of them had already been embarked for Nova Scotia, of which, as contrary to an express stipulation in the treaty, General Washington declared to him his sense and his surprise. In the letter of Sir Guy Carleton of May 12, he admits the fact; palliates it by saying he had no

* A note in the FORD EDITION says Jan. 4th was a Sunday, and that Congress was not in session.—EDITOR.

right " to deprive the negroes of that liberty he found them *possessed* of; that it was unfriendly to suppose that the King's minister could stipulate to be guilty of a notorious breach of the public faith towards the negroes; and that, *if it was his intention, it must be adjusted by compensation*, restoration being utterly impracticable, where inseparable from a breach of public faith ". But surely, Sir, an officer of the King is not to question the validity of the King's engagements, nor violate his solemn treaties, on his own scruples about the public faith. Under this pretext, however, General Carleton went on in daily infractions, embarking, from time to time, between his notice of the treaty and the 5th of April, and the evacuation of New York, November 25, 3,000 negroes, of whom our commissioners had inspection, and a very large number more, in public and private vessels, of whom they were not permitted to have inspection. Here, then, was a direct, unequivocal, and avowed violation of this part of the 7th article, in the first moments of its being known; an article which had been of extreme solicitude on our part; on the fulfilment of which depended the means of paying debts, in proportion to the number of laborers withdrawn; and when in the very act of violation we warn, and put the commanding officer on his guard, he says directly he will go through with the act, and leave it to his court to adjust it by compensation.—To GEORGE HAMMOND. iii, 387. FORD ED., vi, 30. (Pa., May 1792.)

8581. ———— ————. By the 7th article [of the treaty of peace], his Britannic majesty stipulates that he will, *with all convenient speed*, withdraw his garrisons from every *post* within the United States. " When no precise term ", says a writer on the Law of Nations (Vattel, L. 4. c. 26), " has been marked for the accomplishment of a treaty, and for the execution of each of its articles, good sense determines that every point should be executed *as soon as possible*. This is, without doubt, what was understood. The term in the treaty, *with all convenient speed*, amounts to the same thing, and clearly excludes all unnecessary delay. The general pacification being signed on the 20th of January, some time would be requisite for the orders for evacuation to come over to America, for the removal of stores, property and persons, and finally for the act of evacuation. The larger the post, the longer the time necessary to remove all its contents; the smaller, the sooner done. Hence, though General Carleton received his orders to evacuate New York in the month of April, the evacuation was not completed till late in November. It had been the principal place of arms and stores; the seat, as it were, of their general government, and the asylum of those who had fled to them. A great quantity of shipping was necessary, therefore, for the removal, and the General was obliged to call for a part from foreign countries. These causes of delay were duly respected on our part. But the posts of Michillimackinac, Detroit, Niagara, Oswego, Oswegatchie, Point-au-Fer, Dutchman's Point, were not of this magnitude. The orders for evacuation, which reached General Carleton, in New York, early in April, might have gone, in one month more, to the most remote of these posts. Some of them might have been evacuated in a few days after, and the largest in a few weeks. Certainly they might all have been delivered, without any *inconvenient* speed in the operations, by the end of May, from the known facility furnished by the lakes, and the water connecting them; or by crossing immediately over into their own territory, and availing themselves of the season for making new establishments there, if that was intended. Or whatever time might, in event, have been necessary for their evacuation, certainly the order for it should have been given from England, and might have been given as early as that from New York. Was any order ever given? Would not an *unnecessary delay* of the order, producing an equal delay in the evacuation, be an infraction of the treaty? Let us investigate this matter *. * * * Now is it not fair to conclude, if the order was not arrived on the 13th of August, 1783, if it was not arrived on the 10th of May, 1784, nor yet on the 13th of July, in the same year, that, in truth, the order had never been given? and if it had never been given, may we not conclude that it never had been intended to be given? From what moment is it we are to date this infraction? From that, at which, with convenient speed, the order to evacuate the upper posts might have been given. No legitimate reason can be assigned, why that order might not have been given as early, and at the same time, as the order to evacuate New York; and *all delay, after this, was in contravention of the treaty.*—To GEORGE HAMMOND. iii, 388. FORD ED., vi, 31. (Pa., 1792.)

8582. ———— ————. Was this delay merely innocent and unimportant as to us, setting aside all considerations but of interest and safety? 1. It cut us off from the fur-trade, which before the war had been always of great importance as a branch of commerce, and as a source of remittance for the payment of our debts to Great Britain; for the injury of withholding our posts, they added the obstruction of all passage along the lakes and their communications. 2. It secluded us from connection with the Northwestern Indians, from all apportunity of keeping up with them friendly and neighborly intercourse, brought on us consequently, from their known dispositions, constant and expensive war, in which numbers of men, women, and children, have been, and still are, daily falling victims to the scalping knife, and to which there will be no period, but in our possession of the posts which command their country.—To GEORGE HAMMOND. iii, 391. FORD ED., vi, 33. (Pa., 1792.)

8583. ———— ————. It may safely be said that the treaty was violated in England before it was known in America, and in America, as soon as it was known, and that, too, in points so essential, as that, without them, it would never have been concluded.—To GEORGE HAMMOND. iii, 391. FORD ED., vi, 33. (Pa., 1792.)

8584. TREES, Birds and.—What would I not give that the trees planted nearest round the house at Monticello were full-grown!—To MARTHA JEFFERSON RANDOLPH. D. L. J. 222. (Pa., 1793.) See MOCKING BIRD.

8585. TREES, Cork.—I have been long endeavoring to procure the cork tree from Europe but without success. A plant which I brought with me from Paris died after languishing some time.—To JAMES RONALDSON. vi, 92. FORD ED., ix, 370. (M., 1813.)

8586. TREES, Fig and mulberry.—The culture of the fig and mulberry is by women and children, and therefore earnestly to be desired in countries where there are slaves. In these. the women and children are often employed in labors disproportioned to their sex and age.

* Jefferson here quotes the official replies of the British officers commanding different posts to the request for their surrender that they had not received the evacuation order.—EDITOR.

By presenting to the master objects of culture, easier and equally beneficial, all temptation to misemploy them would be removed, and the lot of this tender part of our species be much softened.—To WILLIAM DRAYTON. ii, 199. (P., 1787.)

8587. TREES, Peach.—I thank you for your experiment on the peach tree. It proves my speculation practicable, as it shows that five acres of peach trees at twenty-one feet apart will furnish dead wood enough to supply a fireplace through the winter, and may be kept up at the trouble of only planting about seventy peach stones a year. Suppose this extended to ten fire-places, it comes to fifty acres of ground. five thousand trees, and the replacing about seven hundred of them annually by planting so many stones. If it be disposed at some little distance, say in a circular annulus from one hundred to three hundred yards from the house, it would render a cart almost useless.—To T. M. RANDOLPH. FORD ED., v, 416. (Pa., 1792.)

— TRIAL BY JURY.—See JURY.

8588. TRIBUTE, War and.—We prefer war in all cases to tribute under any form, and to any people whatever.—To THOMAS BARCLAY. iii, 262. (Pa., 1791.)

8589. TRIPOLI, European powers and. —There is reason to believe the example we have set, begins already to work on the dispositions of the powers of Europe to emancipate themselves from that degrading yoke. Should we produce such a revolution there. we shall be amply rewarded for all that we have done.—To JUDGE TYLER. iv, 574. (M., March 1805.)

8590. TRIPOLI, Expedition against.—I have never been so mortified as at the conduct of our foreign functionaries on the loss of the Philadelphia. They appear to have supposed that we were all lost now, and without resource; and they have hawked us in *forma pauperis* begging alms at every court in Europe. This self-degradation is the more unpardonable as, uninstructed and unauthorized, they have taken measures which commit us by moral obligations which cannot be disavowed. The most serious of these is with the First Consul of France, the Emperor of Russia and Grand Seigneur. The interposition of the two first has been so prompt, so cordial, so energetic, that it is impossible for us to decline the good offices they have done us. From the virtuous and warm-hearted character of the Emperor, and the energy he is using with the Ottoman Porte, I am really apprehensive that our squadron will, on its arrival, find our prisoners all restored. If this should be the case, it would be ungrateful and insulting to these three great powers. to chastise the friend (Tripoli) whom they had induced to do us voluntary justice. Our expedition will in that case be disarmed, and our just desires of vengeance disappointed, and our honor prostrated. To anticipate these measures, and to strike our blow before they shall have had their effect, are additional and cogent motives for getting off our squadron without a moment's avoidable delay.—To ROBERT SMITH. FORD ED., viii, 301. (M., April 1804.)

8591. ———— ————. Five fine frigates have left the Chesapeake * * * for Tripoli, which. in addition to the force now there, will, I trust, recover the credit which Commodore Morris's two years' sleep lost us. and for which he has been broke. I think they will make Tripoli sensible, that they mistake their interest in choosing war with us; and Tunis also, should she have declared war as we expect, and almost wish.—To PHILIP MAZZEI. iv, 553. (W., July 1804.)

8592. TRIPOLI, Grounds for war.—The war with Tripoli stands on two grounds of fact. 1st. It is made known to us by our agents with the three other Barbary States, that they only wait to see the event of this, to shape their conduct accordingly. If the war is ended by additional tribute, they mean to offer us the same alternative. 2dly. If peace was made, we should still, and shall ever, be obliged to keep a fr'gate in the Mediterranean to overawe rupture, or we must abandon that market. Our intention in sending Morris with a respectable force, was to try whether peace could be forced by a coercive enterprise on their town. His inexecution of orders baffled that effort. Having broke him, we try the same experiment under a better commander. If, in the course of the summer, they cannot produce peace, we shall recall our force, except one frigate and two small vessels, which will keep up a perpetual blockade. Such a blockade will cost us no more than a state of peace, and will save us from increased tributes, and the disgrace attached to them.—To JUDGE TYLER. iv, 574. (M., March 1805.)

8593. TRIPOLI, War with.—Tripoli * * * had come forward with demands unfounded either in right or in compact, and had perm'tted itself to denounce war, on our failure to comply before a given day. The style of the demand admitted but one answer. I sent a small squadron of frigates into the Mediterranean with assurances to that power of our sincere desire to remain in peace, but with orders to protect our commerce against the threatened attack. The measure was seasonable and salutary. The Bey had already declared war in form. His cruisers were out. Two had arrived at Gibraltar. Our commerce in the Mediterranean was blockaded, and that of the Atlantic 'n peril. The arrival of our squadron dispelled the danger. One of the Tripolitan cruisers * * * engaged the small schooner Enterprise, commanded by Lieutenant Sterret. * * * was captured after a heavy slaughter of her men, without the loss of a single one on our part. * * * Unauthorized by the Constitution, without the sanction of Congress, to go beyond the line of defence, the vessel being disabled from comm'tting further hostilities, was liberated with its crew.—FIRST ANNUAL MESSAGE. viii, 7. FORD ED., viii, 116. (Dec. 1801.)

8594. TROUBLE, Borrowing.—Are there so few inquietudes tacked to this momentary life of ours, that we must need be loading ourselves with a thousand more?—To JOHN PAGE. i, 183. FORD ED., i, 343. (F., 1762.)

8595. TRUMBULL (John), Artist.—Our countryman Trumbull is here [Paris], a young painter of the most promis'ng talents. He brought with him his Battle of Bunker Hill and Death of Montgomery to have them engraved here, and we may add, to have them sold; for like Dr. Ramsey's history, they are too true to suit the English palate.—To F. HOPKINSON. FORD ED., iv, 272. (P., 1786.) See CORNWALLIS.

8596. TRUST, Public.—When a man assumes a public trust, he should consider himself as public property.—To BARON VON HUMBOLDT. RAYNER, BOSTON EDITION, 356. (W., 1807.)

8597. TRUTH, Error vs.—Truth is the proper and sufficient antagonist to error, and has nothing to fear from the conflict, unless by human interposition disarmed of her natural weapons, free argument and debate; errors ceasing to be dangerous when it is permitted freely to contradict them.—STATUTE OF RELIGIOUS FREEDOM. FORD ED., ii, 239. (1779.)

8598. ———— ————. Truth being as cheap as error, it is as well to rectify it for our own satisfaction.—To JOHN ADAMS. vii, 309. FORD ED., x, 272. (M., 1823.)

8599. TRUTH, Eternal.—Truth and reason are eternal. They have prevailed. And they will eternally prevail, however, in times and places they may be overborne for a while by violence—military, civil, or ecclesiastical.—To REV. MR. KNOX. v, 503. (M., 1810.)

8600. TRUTH, Falsehood and.—The firmness with which the people have withstood the late abuses of the press, the discernment they have manifested between truth and falsehood, show that they may safely be trusted to hear everything true and false, and to form a correct judgment between them.—To JUDGE TYLER. iv, 549. (W., 1804.)

8601. TRUTH, Following.—Here [the University of Virginia] we are not afraid to follow truth wherever it may lead, nor to tolerate any error so long as reason is left free to combat it.—To MR. ROSCOE. vii, 196. (M., 1820.)

8602. TRUTH, Greatness of.—Truth is great and will prevail if left to herself.—STATUTE OF RELIGIOUS FREEDOM. viii, 455. FORD ED., ii, 239. (1779.)

8603. TRUTH, Harmless.—Truth between candid minds can never do harm.—To JOHN ADAMS. iii, 270. FORD ED., v, 354. (Pa., 1791.)

8604. TRUTH, Importance of.—It is of great importance to set a resolution, not to be shaken, never to tell an untruth. There is no vice so mean, so pitiful, so contemptible; and he who permits himself to tell a lie once, finds it much easier to do it a second and a third time, till at length it becomes habitual; he tells lies without attending to it, and truths without the world's believing him. This falsehood of the tongue leads to that of the heart, and in time depraves all its good dispositions.—To PETER CARR. i, 396. (P., 1785.)

8605. TRUTH, Lies and.—The man who fears no truths has nothing to fear from lies.—To DR. GEORGE LOGAN. FORD ED., x, 27. (M., 1816.)

8606. TRUTH, Newspapers and.—The restraining the press *to truth*, as the present laws do, is the only way of making it useful.—To WILLIAM SHORT. v, 362. (M., 1808.)

8607. TRUTH, Only safe guide.—In all cases, follow truth as the only safe guide, and eschew error, which bewilders us in one false consequence after another, in endless succession.—To JOHN ADAMS. vii, 149. FORD ED., x, 153. (M., 1819.)

8608. TRUTH, Primary object.—Truth is the first object.—To DR. MAESE. v, 413. (W., 1809.)

8609. TRUTH, Propagation of.—Nor was it less uninteresting to the world. that an experiment should be fairly and fully made, whether freedom of discussion, unaided by power, is not sufficient for the propagation and protection of truth.—SECOND INAUGURAL ADDRESS. viii, 43. FORD ED., viii, 346. (1805.)

8610. TRUTH, Reason and.—No experiment can be more interesting than that we are now trying, and which we trust will end in establishing the fact, that man may be governed by reason and truth. Our first object should therefore be, to leave open to him all the avenues to truth. The most effectual hitherto found, is the freedom of the press. It is, therefore, the first shut up by those who fear the investigation of their actions.—To JUDGE TYLER. iv, 548. (W., 1804.)

8611. TRUTH, Refreshing.—We, who are retired from the business of the world, are glad to catch a glimpse of truth. here and there as we can, to guide our path through the boundless field of fable in which we are bewildered by public prints, and even by those calling themselves histories. A word of truth to us is like the drop of water supplicated from the tip of Lazarus's finger. It is as an observation of latitude and longitude to the mariner long enveloped in clouds, for correcting the ship's way.—To JOHN QUINCY ADAMS. vii, 87. (M., 1817.)

8612. TRUTH, Self-evident.—We hold these truths to be self-evident: that all men are created equal; that they are endowed by their Creator with inherent* and inalienable rights; that among these, are life, liberty, and the pursuit of happiness.—DECLARATION OF INDEPENDENCE AS DRAWN BY JEFFERSON.

8613. TRUTH, Self-reliant.—It is error alone which needs the support of government. Truth can stand by itself.—NOTES ON VIRGINIA. viii, 401. FORD ED., iii, 264. (1782.)

8614. TRUTH, Strength of.—Truth will do well enough if left to shift for herself. She seldom has received much aid from the power of great men to whom she is rarely known and seldom welcome. She has no need of force to procure entrance into the minds of men.—NOTES ON RELIGION. FORD ED., ii, 102. (1776?)

8615. TRUTH, Suppression of.—Truths necessary for our own character, must not be suppressed out of tenderness to its calumniators.—To PRESIDENT MADISON. vi, 452. FORD ED., ix, 512. · (M., 1815.)

8616. TRUTH, Unfeared.—There is not a truth on earth which I fear or would dis-

* Congress struck out "inherent and" and inserted "certain".—EDITOR.

guise.—To WILLIAM DUANE. iv, 591. FORD ED., viii, 431. (W., 1806.)

8617. ——— ———. There is not a truth on earth which I fear should be known.—To THOMAS SEYMOUR. v, 43. FORD ED., ix, 30. (W., 1807.)

8618. ——— ———. I feel no falsehood and fear no truth.—To ISAAC HILLARD. v, 551. (M., 1810.)

8619. ——— ———. There is not a truth existing which I fear, or would wish unknown to the whole world.—To HENRY LEE. vii, 448. FORD ED., x, 389. (M., May 15. 1826.)

8620. TRUXTUN (Thomas), Medal for. —I have considered the letter of the director of the mint stating the ease with which the errors of Commodore Truxtun's medal may be corrected on the medal itself and the unpracticability of doing it on the die. * * * A second law would be required to make a second die or medal. * * * It certainly may be as well or better done by the graver, and with more delicate traits. I remember it was the opinion of Doctor Franklin that where only one or a few medals were to be made it was better to have them engraved. The medal being corrected, the die becomes immaterial, that has never been delivered to the party, the medal itself being the only thing voted to him. I say this on certain grounds, because I think this and Preble's are the only medals given by the United States which have not been made under my immediate direction. The dies of all those given by the old Congress, and made at Paris, remain to this day deposited with our bankers at Paris. That of General Lee, made in Philadelphia, was retained in the mint.—To JACOB CROWNINSHIELD. v, 300. (1808.)

8621. TUDE (M. A. de la), Imprisonment.—De la Tude comes sometimes to take family soup with me, and entertains me with anecdotes of his five and thirty years' imprisonment. How fertile is the mind of man, which can make The Bastile and dungeon of Vincennes yield interesting anecdotes! You know this [imprisonment] was for making four verses on Madame du Pompadour. *—To MRS. COSWAY. ii, 42. FORD ED., iv, 322. (P., 1786.)

8622. TURKEY, Decline of army.—The Turks have lost their warlike spirit, and their troops cannot be induced to adopt the European arms.—To JAMES MONROE. i, 358. FORD ED., iv, 65. (P., 1785.)

8623. TURKEY, Greeks and.—It has been thought that the two imperial courts [Austria and Russia] have a plan of expelling the Turks from Europe. It is really a pity so charming a country should remain in the hands of a people, whose religion forbids the admission of science and the arts among them. We should wish success to the object of the two empires, if they meant to leave the country in possession of the Greek inhabitants. We might then expect, once more. to see the language of Homer and Demosthenes a living language. For I am persuaded the modern Greek would easily get back to its classical models. But this is not intended. They only propose to put the Greeks under other masters: to substitute one set of barbarians for another.—To DR. STILES. i, 365. (P.. 1785.)

* Jefferson gives the verses as follows: "Sans esprit, sans sentiment. "Sans etre belle. ni neuve, "En France on peut avoir le premier amant "Pompadour en est l'epreuve". —EDITOR.

8624. TURKEY, Humanity and.—A lover of humanity would wish to see that charming country from which the Turks exclude science and freedom, in any hands rather than theirs, and in those of the native Greeks rather than any others. The recovery of the r ancient language would not be desperate, could they recover their ancient liberty. But those who wish to remove the Turks, wish to put themselves in their places. This would be exchanging one set of barbarians for another only.—To RICHARD HENRY LEE. FORD ED., iv, 72. (P., 1785.)

8625. TURKEY, Russia, Austria and.—It is believed that the Emperor [of Austria] and the Empress [of Russia] have schemes in contemplation for driving the Turks out of Europe. Were this with a view to reestablish the native Greeks in the sovereignty of their own country, I could wish them success, and to see driven from that delightful country a set of barbarians with whom an opposition to all science is an article of religion. * * * But these powers have in object to divide the country between themselves. This is only to substitute one set of barbarians for another, breaking, at the same time, the balance among the European powers.—To JOHN PAGE. i, 400. (P., 1785.)

8626. TURKEY, Terra incognita.—I cannot think but that it would be desirable to all commercial nations to have Turkey and all its dependencies driven from the seacoast into the interior parts of Asia and Africa. What a field would thus be restored to commerce! The finest parts of the old world are now dead in a great degree to commerce, to arts, to sciences, and to society. Greece, Syria, Egypt, and the northern coast of Africa, constituted the whole world almost for the Romans, and to us they are scarcely known, scarcely accessible at all.— To JOHN BROWN. ii, 396. FORD ED., v, 18. (P., 1788.) See CONSTANTINOPLE.

8627. TYLER (John), Judge.—Judge John Tyler is an able and well read lawyer, about 59 years of age. He was popular as a judge, and is remarkably so as a governor, for his incorruptible integrity, which no circumstances have ever been able to turn from its course. It will be difficult to find a character of firmness enough to preserve his independence on the same bench with Marshall. Tyler, I am certain, would do it. * * * and be a counterpoint to the rancorous hatred which Marshall bears to the government of his country, and * * * the cunning and sophistry within which he is able to enshroud himself.—To PRESIDENT MADISON. FORD ED., ix, 275. (1810.)

8628. TYLER (John), Patriot.—The concurrence of a veteran patriot, who from the first dawn of the Revolution to this day has pursued unchangeably the same honest course, cannot but be flattering to his fellow laborers.— To GOVERNOR TYLER. v, 425. (W., Feb. 1809.)

8629. TYPHUS FEVER, Treatment of. —While I was in Paris, both my daughters were taken with what we formerly called a nervous fever, now a typhus. * * * Dr. Gem, * * * never gave them a single dose of physic. He told me it was a disease which tended with certainty to wear itself off, but so slowly that the strength of the patient might first fail if not kept up; that this alone was the object to be attended to by nourishment and stimulus. He forced them to eat a cup of rice, or panada, or gruel, or of some of the farinaceous substances of easy digestion every two hours, and to drink a glass of Madeira.

The youngest took a pint of Madeira a day without feeling it, and that for many weeks. For costiveness, injections were used; and he observed that a single dose of medicine taken into the stomach and consuming any of the strength of the patient was often fatal. * * * I have had this fever in my family three or four times since, * * * and have carried between twenty and thirty patients through without losing a single one, by a rigorous observance of Dr. Gem's plan and principle. Instead of Madeira I have used toddy or French brandy.—To JAMES MADISON. FORD ED., x, 181. (M., 1821.)

8630. TYRANNY, Absolute.—The history of the present King of Great Britain is a history of *unremitting* injuries and usurpations, *among which appears no solitary fact to contradict the uniform tenor of the rest, but all have* in direct object the establishment of an absolute tyranny over these States.*— DECLARATION OF INDEPENDENCE AS DRAWN BY JEFFERSON.

8631. TYRANNY, British.—That rapid and bold succession of injuries which is likely to distinguish the present from all other periods of American history.—RIGHTS OF BRITISH AMERICA. i, 130. FORD ED., i, 435. (1774.)

8632. TYRANNY, Despotism and.— But why should we enumerate their injuries in detail? By one act they have suspended the powers of one American legislature, and by another have declared they may legislate for us themselves in all cases whatsoever. These two acts alone form a basis broad enough whereon to erect a despotism of unlimited extent.—DECLARATION ON TAKING UP ARMS. FORD ED., i, 469. (July 1775.)

8633. TYRANNY, Eternal hostility to. —I have sworn upon the altar of God eternal hostility against every form of tyranny over the mind of man.—To DR. BENJAMIN RUSH. iv, 336. FORD ED., vii, 460. (M., 1800.)

8634. TYRANNY, Fear and.—Fear is the only restraining motive which may hold the hand of a tyrant.—RIGHTS OF BRITISH AMERICA. i, 131. FORD ED., i, 436. (1774.)

8635. TYRANNY, Foundation for.— Future ages will scarcely believe that the hardiness of one man adventured, within the short compass of twelve years only, to lay a foundation so broad and so undisguised for tyranny over a people fostered and fixed in the principles of freedom.†—DECLARATION OF INDEPENDENCE AS DRAWN BY JEFFERSON.

8636. TYRANNY, George III.—A prince whose character is thus marked by every act which may define a tyrant is unfit to be the ruler of a people *who mean to be free.*‡— DECLARATION OF INDEPENDENCE AS DRAWN BY JEFFERSON.

8637. TYRANNY, Guarding against.— The time to guard against corruption and tyranny is before they shall have gotten hold

* Congress struck out the words in italics.—EDITOR.
† Struck out by Congress.—EDITOR.
‡ Congress struck the words in italics and inserted "free" before "people".—EDITOR.

of us. It is better to keep the wolf out of the fold, than to trust to drawing his teeth and talons after he shall have entered.—NOTES ON VIRGINIA. viii, 363. FORD ED., iii, 225. (1782.)

8638. TYRANNY, Insurrection against.—The general insurrection of the world against its tyrants will ultimately prevail by pointing the object of government to the happiness of the people, and not merely to that of their self-constituted governors.— To MARQUIS LAFAYETTE. FORD ED., x, 233. (M., 1822.)

8639. TYRANNY, Political.—If there be a God, and He is just, His day will come. He will never abandon the whole race of man to be eaten up by the leviathans and mammoths of a day.—To MARQUIS LAFAYETTE. FORD ED., x, 302. (M., 1811.)

8640. TYRANNY, Rebellion against.— Rebellion to tyrants is obedience to God.— MOTTO ON JEFFERSON'S SEAL, *Domestic Life of Jefferson*, title page. See LANGUAGES, PURISM.

8641. TYRANNY, Spirit of.—Bodies of men, as well as individuals, are susceptible of the spirit of tyranny.—RIGHTS OF BRITISH AMERICA. i, 128. FORD ED., i, 433. (1774.)

8642. TYRANNY, Systematic.—Single acts of tyranny may be ascribed to the accidental opinion of a day; but a series of oppressions, begun at a distinguished period, and pursued unalterably through every change of ministers, too plainly prove a deliberate, systematical plan of reducing us to slavery.—RIGHTS OF BRITISH AMERICA. i, 130. FORD ED., i, 435. (1774.)

8643. UMPIRE, Impartial.—No man having a natural right to be the judge between himself and another, it is his natural duty to submit to the umpirage of an impartial third.—To F. W. GILMER. vii, 3. FORD ED., x, 32. (M., 1816.)

8644. UNEARNED INCREMENT, Definition.—If [the public lands are] sold in lots at a fixed price, as first proposed, the best lots will be sold first; as these become occupied, it gives a value to the interjacent ones, and raises them, though of inferior quality, to the price of the first.—To JAMES MONROE. i, 347. FORD ED., iv, 53. (P., 1785.)

8645. UNGER (John Louis de), Courtesies to.—The very small amusements which it has been in my power to furnish, in order, to lighten some of your heavy hours, by no means merited the acknowledgment you make. Their impression must be ascribed to your extreme sensibility rather than to their own weight.—To LIEUTENANT DE UNGER.* ii, 278. FORD ED., ii, 373. (R., 1780.)

8646. UNGER (John Louis de), Invited to America.—Should your fondness for philosophy resume its merited ascendency, is it impossible to hope that this unexplored country may tempt your residence by holding out ma-

* One of the Saratoga prisoners in Virginia.—EDITOR.

terials wherewith to bu'ld a fame, founded on the happiness and not the calamities of human nature?—To LIEUTENANT DE UNGER. i, 278. FORD ED., ii, 374. (R., 1780.)

8647. UNIFORMITY, Mental.—The varieties in the structure and action of the human mind, as in those of the body, are the work of our Creator, against which it cannot be a religious duty to erect the standard of uniformity.—To JAMES FISHBACK. v, 471. (M., 1809.)

8648. UNIFORMITY, Physical and moral.—It is a singular anxiety which some people have that we should all think alike. Would the world be more beautiful were all our faces alike? were our tempers, our talents, our tastes, our forms, our wishes, aversions and pursuits cast exactly in the same mould? If no varieties existed in the animal, vegetable or mineral creation, but all moved strictly uniform, catholic and orthodox, what a world of physical and moral monotony would it be. These are the absurdities into which those run who usurp the throne of God, and dictate to Him what He should have done. May they with all their metaphysical riddles appear before that tribunal with as clean hands and hearts as you and I shall. There, suspended in the scales of eternal justice, faith and works will show their worth by their weight. —To CHARLES THOMSON. FORD ED., x, 76. (M., 1817.)

8649. UNIFORMITY, Religious.—Is uniformity attainable? Millions of innocent men, women and children, since the introduction of Christianity, have been burnt, tortured, fined and imprisoned; yet we have not advanced one inch towards uniformity.— NOTES ON VIRGINIA. viii, 401. FORD ED., iii, 265. (1782.)

8650. UNION (The Federal), Anchor of hope.—I have been happy in believing * * * that whatever follies we may be led into as to foreign nations, we shall never give up our Union, the last anchor of our hope, and that alone which is to prevent this heavenly country from becoming an arena of gladiators.—To ELBRIDGE GERRY. iv, 173. FORD ED., vii, 122. (Pa., May 1797.)

8651. UNION (The Federal), Attempts to disrupt.—Not less worthy of your indignation have been the machinations of parricides who have endeavored to bring into danger the Union of these States, and to subvert, for the purposes of inordinate ambition, a government founded in the will of its citizens, and directed to no object but their happiness.—R. TO A. NORTH CAROLINA LEGISLATURE. viii, 125. (1808.)

8652. ——— ———. Surrounded by such difficulties and dangers, it is really deplorable that any should be found among ourselves vindicating the conduct of the aggressors; cooperating with them in multiplying embarrassments to their own country, and encouraging disobedience to the laws provided for its safety. But a spirit which should go further, and countenance the advocates for a dissolution of the Union, and for setting in hostile array one portion of our citizens against another, would require to be viewed under a more serious aspect. It would prove indeed that it is high time for every friend to his country, in a firm and decided manner, to express his sentiments of the measures which government has adopted to avert the impending evils, unhesitatingly to pledge himself for the support of the laws, liberties and independence of his country; and with the * * * republicans of Connecticut, to resolve that, for the preservation of the Union, the support and enforcement of the laws, and for the resistance and repulsion of every enemy, they will hold themselves in readiness and put at stake, if necessary, their lives and fortunes, on the pledge of their sacred honor.—R. TO A. CONNECTICUT REPUBLICANS. viii, 169. (1809.)

8653. ——— ———. The times do certainly render it incumbent on all good citizens, attached to the rights and honor of their country, to bury in oblivion all internal differences, and rally around the standard of their country in opposition to the outrages of foreign nations. All attempts to enfeeble and destroy the exertions of the General Government, in vindication of our national rights, or to loosen the bands of union by alienating the affections of the people, or opposing the authority of the laws at so eventful a period, merit the discountenance of all.—To GOVERNOR TOMPKINS. viii, 153. (1809.)

8654. UNION (The Federal), Benefits of.—Union for specified national purposes, and particularly * * * [for] those specified in * * * [the] * * * Federal compact * * * [is] friendly to the peace, happiness and prosperity of all the States.—KENTUCKY RESOLUTIONS. ix, 468. FORD ED., vii, 300. (1798.)

8655. UNION (The Federal), Bond of.— The sacred bond which unites these States together.—R. TO A. PHILADELPHIA CITIZENS. viii, 144. (1809.)

8656. UNION (The Federal), Cement of the.—The cement of this Union is in the heart-blood of every American. I do not believe there is on earth a government established on so immovable a basis.—To MARQUIS DE LAFAYETTE. vi, 425. FORD ED., ix, 509. (M., 1815.)

8657. UNION (The Federal), Cherish.— [Our] Union cannot be too much cherished.— REPLY TO ADDRESS. viii, 114. (1802.)

8658. ——— ———. Cherish every measure which may foster our brotherly Union and perpetuate a constitution of government, destined to be the primitive and precious model of what is to change the condition of man over the globe.—To EDWARD LIVINGSTON. vii, 344. FORD ED., x, 301. (M., 1824.)

8659. UNION (The Federal), Constitution and.—We must take care that * * * no objection to the new form [Constitution] produces a schism in our Union. This would

be an incurable evil, because near friends falling out, never reunite cordially; whereas, all of us going together, we shall be sure to cure the evils of our new Constitution before they do great harm.—To A. DONALD. ii, 356. (P., 1788.)

8660. UNION (The Federal), Constitutional encroachments and.—When obvious encroachments are made on the plain meaning of the Constitution, the bond of Union ceases to be the equal measure of justice to all its parts.—To ARCHIBALD STUART. FORD ED., v, 454. (Pa., 1792.)

8661. UNION (The Federal), Cultivate. —Our lot has been cast by the favor of heaven in a country and under circumstances highly auspicious to our peace and prosperity, and where no pretence can arise for the degrading and oppressive establishments of Europe. It is our happiness that honorable distinctions flow only from public approbation; and that finds no object in titled dignitaries and pageants. Let us, then, endeavor carefully to guard this happy state of things, by keeping a watchful eye over the disaffection of wealth and ambition to the republican principles of our Constitution, and by sacrificing all our local and personal interests to the cultivation of the Union, and maintenance of the authority of the laws.—R. TO A. PENNA. DEMOCRATIC-REPUBLICANS. viii, 163. (1809.)

8662. UNION (The Federal), Dissolution of.—I can scarcely contemplate a more incalculable evil than the breaking of the Union into two or more parts.—To PRESIDENT WASHINGTON. iii, 363. FORD ED., vi, 4. (1792.)

8663. ——— ———. I have been among the most sanguine in believing that our Union would be of long duration. I now doubt it much, and see the event at no great distance, and the direct consequence of this question; [Missouri] not by the line which has been so confidently counted on,—the laws of nature control this,—but by the Potomac, Ohio and Missouri, or, more probably, the Mississippi upwards to our northern boundary. My only comfort and confidence is, that I shall not live to see this; and I envy not the present generation the glory of throwing away the fruits of their fathers' sacrifices of life and fortune, and of rendering desperate the experiment which was to decide ultimately whether man is capable of self-government. This treason against human hope will signalize their epoch in future history as the counterpart of the medal of their predecessors.—To WILLIAM SHORT. vii, 158. (M., 1820.)

8664. ——— ———. Were we to break to pieces, it would damp the hopes and the efforts of the good, and give triumph to those of the bad through the whole enslaved world. As members, therefore, of the universal society of mankind, and standing in high and responsible relation with them, it is our sacred duty to suppress passion among ourselves, and not to blast the confidence we have inspired of proof that a government of reason is better than one of force.—To RICHARD RUSH. vii, 183. (M., 1820.)

8665. UNION (The Federal), Europe and.—Let us cling in mass to our country and to one another, and bid defiance, as we can if united, to the plundering combinations of the old world.—To DR. GEORGE LOGAN. vii, 20. (M., 1816.)

8666. UNION (The Federal), Expansion and.—Our present federal limits are not too large for good government, nor will the increase of votes in Congress produce any ill effect. On the contrary, it will drown the little divisions at present existing there. Our confederacy must be viewed as the nest, from which all America, North and South, is to be peopled. We should take care, too, not to think it for the interest of that great Continent to press too soon on the Spaniards. Those countries cannot be in better hands. My fear is, that they are too feeble to hold them till our population can be sufficiently advanced to gain it from them, piece by piece. The navigation of the Mississippi we must have. This is all we are as yet ready to receive.—To ARCHIBALD STUART. i, 578. FORD ED., iv, 188. (P., Jan. 1786.)

8667. UNION (The Federal), Family of States.—I sincerely wish that the whole Union may accommodate their interests to each other, and play into their hands mutually as members of the same family, that the wealth and strength of any one part should be viewed as the wealth and strength of the whole.—To HUGH WILLIAMSON. FORD ED., vii, 201. (Pa., Feb. 1798.)

8668. UNION (The Federal), Foreign plots against.—The request of a communication of any information, which may have been received at any time since the establishment of the present [Federal] Government, touching combinations with foreign nations for dismembering the Union, or the corrupt receipt of money by any officer of the United States, from the agents of foreign governments, can be complied with but in a partial degree. It is well understood that, in the first or second year of the presidency of General Washington, information was given to him relating to certain combinations with the agents of a foreign government for the dismemberment of the Union; which combinations had taken place before the establishment of the present Federal Government. This information, however, is believed never to have been deposited in any public office, or left in that of the President's secretary, these having been duly examined, but to have been considered as personally confidential, and therefore, retained among his private papers. A communication from the Governor of Virginia to General Washington, is found in the office of the President's secretary, which, though not strictly within the terms of the request of the House of Representatives, is communicated, inasmuch as it may throw some light on the subjects of the correspond-

ence of that time, between certain foreign agents and citizens of the United States. In the first or second year of the administration of President Adams, Andrew Ellicott, then employed in designating, in conjunction with the Spanish authorities the boundaries between the territories of the United States and Spain, under the treaty with that nation, communicated to the Executive of the United States papers and information respecting the subjects of the present inquiry, which were deposited in the office of State. Copies of these are now transmitted to the House of Representatives, except of a single letter and a reference from the said Andrew Ellicott, which being expressly desired to be kept secret, is, therefore, not communicated, but its contents can be obtained from him in a more legal form, and directions have been given to summon him to appear as a witness before the court of inquiry. [Wilkinson court of inquiry.] A paper " on the commerce of Louisiana ", bearing date of the 18th of April, 1798, is found in the office of State, supposed to have been communicated by Mr. Daniel Clark, of New Orleans, then a subject of Spain, and now of the House of Representatives of the United States, stating certain commercial transactions of General Wilkinson, in New Orleans; an extract from this is now communicated, because it contains facts which may have some bearing on the questions relating to him. The destruction of the War Office, by fire, in the close of 1800, involved all information it contained at that date. The papers already described, therefore, constitute the whole information on the subjects, deposited in the public offices, during the preceding administrations, as far as has yet been found; but it cannot be affirmed that there may be no others, because the papers of the office being filed, for the most part, alphabetically, unless aided by the suggestion of any particular name which may have given such information, nothing short of a careful examination of the papers in the offices generally, could authorize such affirmation. About a twelvemonth after I came to the administration of the government, Mr. Clark gave some verbal information to myself, as well as to the Secretary of State, relating to the same combination for the dismemberment of the Union. He was listened to freely, and he then delivered the letter of Governor Gayoso, addressed to himself, of which a copy is now communicated. After his return to New Orleans, he forwarded to the Secretary of State other papers, with a request, that, after perusal, they should be burned. This, however, was not done, and he was so informed by the Secretary of State, and that they would be held subject to his order. These papers have not yet been found in the office. A letter, therefore, has been addressed to the former chief clerk, who may, perhaps, give information respecting them. As far as our memories enable us to say, they related only to the combinations before spoken of, and not at all to the corrupt receipt of money by any officer of the United States; consequently, they respected what was considered as a dead matter, known to the preceding administrations, and offering nothing new to call for investigations, which those nearest the dates of the transactions had not thought proper to institute. In the course of the communications made to me on the subject of the conspiracy of Aaron Burr, I sometimes received letters, some of them anonymous, some under names true or false, expressing suspicions and insinuations against General Wilkinson. But only one of them and that anonymous, specified any particular fact, and that fact was one of those which had already been communicated to a former administration. No other information within the purview of the request of the House is known to have been received by any department of the Government from the establishment of the present Federal Government. That which has recently been communicated to the House of Representatives, and by them to me, is the first direct testimony ever made known to me, charging General Wilkinson with the corrupt receipt of money; and the House of Representatives may be assured that the duties which this information devolves on me shall be exercised with rigorous impartiality. Should any want of power in the court to compel the rendering of testimony, obstruct that full and impartial inquiry, which alone can establish guilt or innocence, and satisfy justice, the legislative authority only will be competent to the remedy.*—SPECIAL MESSAGE. viii, 90. (Jan. 1808.)

8669. UNION (The Federal), Love for. —Sincere love I shall forever strive to cultivate with all our sister States.—To THE PRESIDENT OF CONGRESS. FORD ED., ii, 298. (Wg., 1780.)

8670. UNION (The Federal), Massachusetts federalists and.—The design of the leading federalists, then having direction of the State [Massachusetts], to take advantage of the first war with England to separate the Northeast States from the Union has distressingly impaired our future confidence in them. In this, as in all other cases, we must do them full justice, and make the fault all their own, should the last hope of human liberty be destined to receive its final stab from them.—To DR. WILLIAM EUSTIS. FORD ED., ix, 237. (M., Oct. 1809.)

8671. UNION (The Federal), Miseries of secession.—What would you think of a discourse on the benefit of the Union and miseries which would follow a separation of the States, to be exemplified in the eternal and wasting wars of Europe, in the pillage and profligacy to which these lead, and the abject oppression and degradation to which they reduce its inhabitants? Painted by your vivid pencil, what could make deeper impres-

* In a subsequent message Jefferson informed Congress that the Clark letters had been found, and transmitted some extracts from them. As to combinations with foreign agents for the dismemberment of the Union they contained nothing new, "nor have we found any intimation of the corrupt receipt of money by any officer of the United States from any foreign nation".—EDITOR.

sions, and what impressions could come more home to our concerns, or kindle a livelier sense of our present blessings?—To MR. OGILVIE. v, 605. (M., 1811.)

8672. UNION (The Federal), Nourish.— Possessed of the blessing of self-government, and of such a portion of civil liberty as no other civilized nation enjoys, it now behooves us to guard and preserve them by a continuance of the sacrifices and exertions by which they were acquired, and especially to nourish that Union which is their sole guarantee.— R. TO A. NEW LONDON PLYMOUTH SOCIETY. viii, 166. (1809.)

8673. UNION (The Federal), Pennsylvania, Virginia and.—I wish and hope you may consent to be added to our [Virginia] Assembly itself. There is no post where you can render greater services, without going out of your State. Let but this block stand firm on its basis, and Pennsylvania do the same, our Union will be perpetual, and our General Government kept within the bounds and form of the Constitution.—To JAMES MADISON. iv, 162. FORD ED., vii, 110. (M., Jan. 1797.)

8674. UNION (The Federal), Rock of safety.—A solid Union is the best rock of our safety.—To C. W. F. DUMAS. iii, 260. (Pa., 1791.)

8675. ——— ———. To cherish the Federal Union as the only rock of our safety, * * * [is one of] the landmarks by which we are to guide ourselves in all our proceedings.— SECOND ANNUAL MESSAGE. viii, 21. FORD ED., viii, 187. (Dec. 1802.)

8676. UNION (The Federal), Safety in. —It is a momentous truth, and happily of universal impression on the public mind, that our safety rests on the preservation of our Union.—To THE RHODE ISLAND ASSEMBLY. iv, 397. (W., May 1801.)

8677. ——— ———. I trust the Union of these States will ever be considered as the palladium of their safety, their prosperity and glory, and all attempts to sever it, will be frowned on with reprobation and abhorrence. —To GOVERNOR TOMPKINS. viii, 153. (1809.)

8678. UNION (The Federal), Sectional ascendency.—If on a temporary superiority of one party, the other is to resort to a scission of the Union, no federal government can ever exist.—To JOHN TAYLOR. iv, 246. FORD ED., vii, 264. (Pa., 1798.)

8679. UNION (The Federal), Self-government and.—I regret that I am now to die in the belief, that the useless sacrifice of themselves by the generation of 1776, to acquire self-government and happiness to their country, is to be thrown away by the unwise and unworthy passions of their sons, and that my only consolation is to be, that I live not to weep over it. If they would but dispassionately weigh the blessings they will throw away, against an abstract principle more likely to be effected by union than by scission, they would pause before they would perpetrate this act of suicide on themselves, and of treason against the hopes of the world.—To JOHN HOLMES. vii, 160. FORD ED., x, 158. (M., 1820.)

8680. UNION (The Federal), Sheet anchor.—The sheet anchor of our peace at home and safety abroad.—FIRST INAUGURAL ADDRESS. viii, 4. FORD ED., viii, 4. (1801.)

8681. ——— ———. To preserve the republican form and principles of our Constitution, and cleave to the salutary distribution of powers which that has established, are the two sheet anchors of our Union. If driven from either, we shall be in danger of foundering.—To WILLIAM JOHNSON. vii, 298. FORD ED., x, 232. (M., 1823.)

8682. UNION (The Federal), State rights and.—I am for preserving to the States the powers not yielded by them to the Union, and to the Legislature of the Union its constitutional share in the division of powers; and I am not for transferring all the powers of the States to the General Government, and all those of that Government to the Executive branch.—To ELBRIDGE GERRY. iv, 268. FORD ED., vii, 327. (Pa., 1799.)

8683. UNION (The Federal), Strength.—If there be any among us who would wish to dissolve this Union, or to change its republican form, let them stand undisturbed as monuments of the safety with which error of opinion may be tolerated where reason is left free to combat it. I know, indeed, that some honest men fear that a republican government cannot be strong; that this Government is not strong enough. But would the honest patriot, in full tide of successful experiment, abandon a Government which has so far kept us free and firm, on the theoretic and visionary fear that this Government, the world's best hope, may by possibility want energy to preserve itself? I trust not. I believe this, on the contrary, the strongest government on earth. I believe it is the only one where every man, at the call of the laws, would fly to the standard of the law, and would meet invasions of the public order as his own personal concern. Sometimes it is said that man cannot be trusted with the government of himself. Can he, then, be trusted with the government of others? Or have we found angels, in the forms of kings, to govern him? Let history answer this question.—FIRST INAUGURAL ADDRESS. viii, 2. FORD ED., viii, 3. (1801.)

8684. UNION (The Federal), War and.—If we engage in a war during our present passions, and our present weakness in some quarters, our Union runs the greatest risk of not coming out of that war in the shape in which it enters it.—To ELBRIDGE GERRY. iv, 188. FORD ED., vii, 150. (M., June 1797.)

8685. UNION (The Federal), Washington and.—I can scarcely contemplate a more incalculable evil than the breaking of the Union into two or more parts. Yet when we review the mass which opposed the original coalescence, when we consider that it lay chiefly in the Southern quarter, that the Legislature have availed themselves of no occasion of allaying it, but on the contrary whenever the Northern and Southern prejudices have come into conflict, the latter have been sacrificed and the former soothed; that the owers of the [public] debt are in the Southern and the holders of it in the Northern division; that the anti-federal champions are now strengthened in argument by the fulfilment of their predictions; that this has been brought about by the monarchical federalists themselves, who, having been for the new government merely as a stepping stone to monarchy, have themselves adopted the very constructions of the Constitution, of which, when advocating its acceptance before the tribunal of the people, they declared it insusceptible; that the republican federalists, who espoused the same government for its intrinsic merits, are disarmed of their weapons; that which they denied as prophecy, having now become true history, who can be sure that these things may not proselyte the small number which was wanting to place the majority on the other side? And this is the event at which I tremble, and to prevent which I consider your [President Washington] continuing at the head of affairs as of the last importance. The confidence of the whole Union is centred in you. Your being at the helm, will be more than answer to every argument which can be used to alarm and lead the people in any quarter into violence and secession. North and South will hang together, if they have you to hang on; and, if the first correction of a numerous representation [in Congress] should fail in its effect, your presence will give time for trying others not inconsistent with the Union and peace of the States.—To PRESIDENT WASHINGTON. iii, 363. FORD ED., vi, 4. (Pa., May 1792.)

8686. UNION (The Federal), Western interests and.—Our true interest will be best promoted by making all the just claims of our fellow citizens, wherever situated, our own; by urging and enforcing them with the weight of our whole influence; and by exercising in * * *, every * * * instance, a just government in their concerns, and making common cause even where our separate interest would seem opposed to theirs. No other conduct can attach us together; and on this attachment depends our happiness.—To JAMES MONROE. i, 605. FORD ED., iv, 263. (P., 1786.)

8687. ——— ———. This measure [dividing the Western country into fewer and smaller States] with the disposition to shut up the Mississippi, gives me serious apprehensions of the severance of the Eastern and Western parts of our confederacy. It might have been made the interest of the Western States to remain united with us, by managing their interests honestly, and for their own good. But, the moment we sacrifice their interests to our own, they will see it is better to govern themselves. The moment they resolve to do this, the point is settled. A forced connection is

neither our interest, nor within our power.—
To JAMES MADISON. ii, 66. FORD ED., iv, 333.
(P., Dec. 1786.)

8688. —— ——. I fear, from an expression in your letter, that the people of Kentucky
think of separating, not only from Virginia
(in which they are right), but also from the
Confederacy. I own, I should think this a
most calamitous event, and such an one as
every good citizen on both sides should set
himself against.—To ARCHIBALD STUART. i,
518. FORD ED., iv, 188. (P., Jan. 1786.)

8689. —— ——. Whether we remain in
one confederacy, or break into Atlantic and
Mississippi confederacies, I believe not very
important to the happiness of either part.
Those of the western confederacy will be as
much our children and descendants as those
of the eastern, and I feel myself as much
identified with that country, in future time,
as with this; and did I now foresee a separation at some future day, yet I should feel the
duty and the desire to promote the western
interests as zealously as the eastern, doing all
the good for both portions of our future
family which should fall within my power.—
To DR. JOSEPH PRIESTLEY. iv, 525. FORD
ED., viii, 295. (W., Jan. 1804.) See CEN-
TRALIZATION, COLONIES, CONFEDERATION, CON-
STITUTION, FEDERAL GOVERNMENT and UNITED
STATES.

**8690. UNITED STATES, Assumption
of title.**—We, therefore, the representatives
of the United States of America, in General Congress assembled, do in the name,
and by the authority of the good people of these States reject and renounce
all allegiance and subjection to the kings
of Great Britain and all others who may
hereafter claim by, through, or under them;
we utterly dissolve all political connection
which may heretofore have subsisted between us and the people or parliament of
Great Britain: and finally we do assert and
declare these Colonies to be free and independent States; and that as free and independent States, they have full power to levy
war, conclude peace, contract alliances, establish commerce, and to do all other acts and
things which independent States may of right
do. And for the support of this declaration,
we mutually pledge to each other our lives,
our fortunes, and our sacred honor.*—
DECLARATION OF INDEPENDENCE AS DRAWN BY
JEFFERSON.

* Congress changed the above so as to make it read
"We, therefore, the representatives of the UNITED
STATES OF AMERICA in GENERAL CONGRESS assembled, appealing to the Supreme Judge of the World
for the rectitude of our intentions, do in the name,
and by the authority of the good people of these
Colonies, solemnly publish and declare, that these
united Colonies are, and of right ought to be, FREE
AND INDEPENDENT STATES; that they are absolved
from all allegiance to the British crown, and that all
political connection between them and the state of
Great Britain is, and ought to be, totally dissolved:
and that as FREE AND INDEPENDENT STATES, they
have full power to levy war, conclude peace, contract
alliances, establish commerce, and to do all other
acts and things which INDEPENDENT STATES may of
right do. And for the support of this Declaration,

**8691. UNITED STATES, Benign influ-
ence.**—The station which we occupy among
the nations of the earth is honorable, but
awful. Trusted with the destinies of this
solitary republic of the world the only monument of human rights, and the sole depositary
of the sacred fire of freedom and self-government, whence it is to be lighted up in
other regions of the earth, if other regions of
the earth shall ever become susceptible of its
benign influence. All mankind ought then,
with us, to rejoice in its prosperous, and
sympathize in its adverse fortunes, as involving everything dear to man. And to what
sacrifices of interest, or convenience, ought
not these considerations to animate us? To
what compromises of opinion and inclination,
to maintain harmony and union among ourselves, and to preserve from all danger this
hallowed ark of human hope and happiness.
—R. TO A. CITIZENS OF WASHINGTON. viii,
157. (1809.)

**8692. UNITED STATES, Continental
influence.**—When our strength shall permit
us to give the law of our hemisphere it
should be that the meridian of the mid-Atlantic should be the line of demarcation between peace and war, on this side of which
no act of hostility should be committed, and
the lion and the lamb lie down in peace together.—To DR. CRAWFORD. vi, 33. (1812.)

8693. UNITED STATES, Destinies of.—
A rising nation, spread over a wide and
fruitful land, traversing all the seas with the
rich productions of their industry, engaged in
commerce with nations who feel power and
forget right, advancing rapidly to destinies
beyond the reach of mortal eye,—when I contemplate these transcendent objects, and see
the honor, the happiness, and the hopes of
this beloved country committed to the issue
and the auspices of this day, I shrink from
the contemplation, and humble myself before
the magnitude of the undertaking.—FIRST IN-
AUGURAL ADDRESS. viii, 1. FORD ED., viii, 2.
(1801.)

**8694. UNITED STATES, Disputed ter-
ritory.**—Spain sets up a claim to possessions
within the State of Georgia. founded on her
having rescued them by force from the British. during the late war. The following view
of the subject seems to admit no reply: The
several States, now comprising the United
States of America, were, from their first establishment, separate and distinct societies,
dependent on no other society of men whatever. They continued at the head of their respective governments the executive magistrate who presided over the one they had left,
and thereby secured, in effect, a constant
amity with that nation. In this stage of their
government, their several boundaries were
fixed; and particularly the southern boundary
of Georgia, the only one now in question, was
established at the 31st degree of latitude from
the Apalachicola westwardly; and the west-
with a firm reliance on the protection of DIVINE
PROVIDENCE, we mutually pledge to each other our
lives, our fortunes, and our sacred honor."—EDITOR

ern boundary, originally the Pacific Ocean, was, by the Treaty of Paris, reduced to the middle of the Mississippi. The part which our chief magistrate took in a war waged against us by the nation among whom he resided, obliged us to discontinue him, and to name one within every State. In the course of this war, we were joined by France as an ally, and by Spain and Holland as associates having a common enemy. Each sought that common enemy wherever they could find him. France, on our invitation, landed a large army within our territories, continued it with us two years, and aided us in recovering sundry places from the possession of the enemy. But she did not pretend to keep possession of the places rescued. Spain entered into the remote western part of our territory, dislodged the common enemy from several of the posts they held therein, to the annoyance of Spain; and perhaps thought it necessary to remain in some of them, as the only means of preventing their return. We, in like manner, dislodged them from several posts in the same western territory, to wit: Vincennes, Cahokia, Kaskaskia, &c., rescued the inhabitants, and retained constantly afterwards both them and the territory under our possession and government. At the conclusion of the war, Great Britain, on the 30th of November, 1782, by treaty acknowledged our Independence, and our boundary, to wit, the Mississippi to the West, and the completion of the 31st degree, &c., to the South. In her treaty with Spain, concluded seven weeks afterwards, to wit, January 20th, 1783, she ceded to her the two Floridas (which had been defined in the proclamation of 1763), and Minorca; and by the eighth article of the treaty, Spain agreed to *restore without compensation*, all the territories conquered by her, and not included in the treaty either under the head of cessions or restitutions, that is to say, all except Minorca and the Floridas. According to this stipulation, Spain was expressly bound to have delivered up the possessions she had taken within the limits of Georgia, to Great Britain, if they were conquests on Great Britain, who was to deliver them over to the United States; or rather she should have delivered them over to the United States themselves, as standing, *quoad hoc*, in the place of Great Britain. And she was bound by natural right to deliver them to the same United States on a much stronger ground, as the real and only proprietors of those places which she had taken possession of, in a moment of danger, without having had any cause of war with the United States, to whom they belonged, and without having declared any; but on the contrary, conducting herself in other respects as a friend and associate.—(*Vattel*, L. 3, 122.)—MISSISSIPPI RIVER INSTRUCTIONS. vii, 570. FORD ED., v, 461. (1792.)

8695. ——— ———. Should Spain pretend * * * that there was a secret article of treaty between the United States and Great Britain, agreeing if, at the close of the [Revolutionary] war, the latter should retain the Floridas, that then the southern boundary of

Georgia should be the completion of the 32d degree of North latitude, the commissioners [appointed to negotiate with Spain to secure the free navigation of the Mississippi], may safely deny all knowledge of the fact, and refuse conference on any such postulatum. Or, should they find it necessary to enter into any argument on the subject, they will, of course, do it hypothetically; and in that way may justly say, on the part of the United States: "Suppose that the United States, exhausted by a bloody and expensive war with Great Britain, might have been willing to have purchased peace by relinquishing, under a particular contingency, a small part of their territory, it does not follow that the same United States, recruited and better organized, must relinquish the same territory to Spain without striking a blow. The United States, too, have irrevocably put it out of their power to do it, by a new Constitution, which guarantees every State against the invasion of its territory. A disastrous war, indeed, might, by necessity, supersede this stipulation (as necessity is above all law), and oblige them to abandon a part of a State; but nothing short of this can justify, or obtain such an abandonment.—MISSISSIPPI RIVER INSTRUCTIONS. vii, 572. FORD ED., v, 463. (1792.)

8696. ——— ———. It is an established principle, that conquest gives only an inchoate right, which does not become perfect till confirmed by the treaty of peace, and by a renunciation or abandonment by the former proprietor. Had Great Britain been that former proprietor, she was so far from confirming to Spain the right to the territory of Georgia, invaded by Spain, that she expressly relinquished to the United States any right that might remain in her; and afterwards completed that relinquishment by procuring and consolidating with it the agreement of Spain herself to restore such territory without compensation. It is still more palpable that a war existing between two nations, as Spain and Great Britain, could give to neither the right to seize and appropriate the territory of a third, which is even neutral, much less which is an associate in the war, as the United States were with Spain. See, on this subject, *Grotius*, L. 3, c. 6 § 26. *Puffendorf*, L. 8, c. 6. § 17, 23. *Vattel*, L. 3 § 197, 198.—MISSISSIPPI RIVER INSTRUCTIONS. vii, 572. FORD ED., v, 463. (1792.)

8697. ——— ———. A disastrous war might, by necessity, supersede this stipulation [the provision of the Constitution guaranteeing every State against the invasion of its territory] (as necessity is above all law), and oblige them to abandon a part of a State; but nothing short of this can justify, or obtain such an abandonment.—MISSISSIPPI RIVER INSTRUCTIONS. vii, 573. FORD ED., v, 464. (1792.)

8698. UNITED STATES, Enduring.— When the General Government shall become incompetent [to the objects of government specially assigned to it] instead of flying to monarchy or that tranquillity which it is the

nature of slavery to hold forth, the true remedy would be a subdivision, as you observe. But it is to be hoped that by a due poise and partition of powers between the General and particular governments we have found the secret of extending the benign blessing of Republicanism over still greater tracts of country than we possess, and that a subdivision may be avoided for ages, if not forever.—To JAMES SULLIVAN. FORD ED., v, 369. (Pa., 1791.)

8699. ——— ———. I have much confidence that we shall proceed successfully for ages to come, and that, contrary to the principle of Montesquieu, it will be seen that the larger the extent of country, the more firm its republican structure, if founded, not on conquest. but in principles of compact and equality. My hope of its duration is built much on the enlargement of the resources of life going hand in hand with the enlargement of territory, and the belief that men are disposed to live honestly, if the means of doing so are open to them.—To M. DE MARBOIS. vii, 77. (M., 1817.)

8700. UNITED STATES, England and. —These two nations [the United States and England], holding cordially together, have nothing to fear from the united world. They will be the models for regenerating the condition of man, the sources from which representative government is to flow over the whole earth.—To J. EVELYN DENISON. vii, 415. (M., 1825.)

8701. UNITED STATES, Esteemed.—I shall rejoin myself to my native country, with new attachments, and with exaggerated esteem for its advantages; for though there is less wealth there, there is more freedom, more ease, and less misery.—To BARON GEISMER. i, 427. (P., 1785.)

8702. UNITED STATES, European powers and.—While there are powers in Europe which fear our views, or have views on us, we should keep an eye on them, their connections and oppositions, that in a moment of need we may avail ourselves of their weakness with respect to others as well as ourselves, and calculate their designs and movements on all the circumstances under which they exist.—To E. CARRINGTON. ii, 335. FORD ED., iv, 483. (P., 1787.)

8703. UNITED STATES, Foreign policy.—We must make the interest of every nation stand surety for their justice, and their own loss to follow injury to us, as effect follows its cause. As to everything except commerce, we ought to divorce ourselves from them all.—To EDWARD RUTLEDGE. iv, 191. FORD ED., vii, 154. (Pa., 1797.)

8704. ——— ———. The less we have to do with the amities or enmities of Europe the better.—To THOMAS LEIPER. vi, 465. FORD ED., ix, 520. (M., 1815.) See ALLIANCE and POLICY.

8705. UNITED STATES, Freedom from turmoil.—How happy is it for us that we are beyond the reach of those storms which

are eternally desolating Europe. We have indeed a neighbor with whom misunderstandings are possible; but they must be the effect of interests ill calculated. Nothing is more demonstrable than is the unity of their and our interest for ages to come.—To WILLIAM CARMICHAEL. FORD ED., v, 74. (P., 1789.)

8706. ——— ———. Our difficulties are indeed great, if we consider ourselves alone. But when viewed in comparison to those of Europe, they are the joys of Paradise. In the eternal revolution of ages, the destinies have placed our portion of existence amidst such scenes of tumult and outrage, as no other period, within our knowledge, had presented. Every government but one on the continent of Europe, demolished, a conqueror roaming over the earth with havoc and destruction, a pirate spreading misery and ruin over the face of the ocean. Indeed, ours is a bed of roses. And the system of government which shall keep us afloat amidst the wreck of the world, will be immortalized in history. We have, to be sure, our petty squabbles and heart burnings, and we have something of the blue devils at times, as to these Rawheads and Bloodybones who are eating up other nations. But happily for us, the Mammoth cannot swim, nor the Leviathan move on dry land; and if we will keep out of their way, they cannot get at us. If, indeed, we choose to place ourselves within the scope of their tether, a gripe of the paw, or flounce of the tail, may be our fortune. But a part of our nation chose to declare against this, in such a way as to control the wisdom of the government. I yielded with others to avoid a greater evil. But from that moment, I have seen no system which could keep us entirely aloof from these agents of destruction.—To DR. WALTER JONES. v, 510. FORD ED., ix, 274. (M., March 1810.)

8707. UNITED STATES, Future greatness.—I do believe we shall continue to grow, to multiply and prosper until we exhibit an association, powerful, wise and happy beyond what has yet been seen by men.—To JOHN ADAMS. vi, 37. FORD ED., ix, 333. (M., 1812.)

8708. ——— ———. Not in our day, but at no distant one, we may shake a rod over the heads of all [the European nations], which may make the stoutest of them tremble. But I hope our wisdom will grow with our power, and teach us, that the less we use our power, the greater will it be.—To THOMAS LEIPER. vi, 465. FORD ED., ix, 520. (M., 1815.)

8709. ——— ———. We are destined to be a barrier against the returns of ignorance and barbarism. Old Europe will have to lean on our shoulders, and to hobble along by our side, under the monkish trammels of priests and kings, as she can. What a Colossus shall we be when the southern continent comes up to our mark! What a stand will it secure as a ralliance for the reason and freedom of the globe!—To JOHN ADAMS. vii, 27. (M., 1816.)

8710. UNITED STATES, Guardian of liberty.—The eyes of the virtuous all over the earth are turned with anxiety on us as the only depositaries of the sacred fire of liberty.—To JOHN HOLLINS. v, 597. (M., 1811.)

8711. UNITED STATES, Independence of.—The several States, now comprising the United States of America, were, from their first establishment, separate and distinct societies, dependent on no other society of men whatever. They continued at the head of their respective governments the executive magistrate who presided over the one they had left, and thereby secured in effect a constant amity with that nation. * * * The part which our chief magistrate took in a war, waged against us by the nation among whom he resided, obliged us to discontinue him, and to name one within every State.—MISSISSIPPI RIVER INSTRUCTIONS. vii, 571. FORD ED., v, 461. (March 1792.)

— UNITED STATES, Inviolability of territory.—See TERRITORY, ALIENATION OF.

8712. UNITED STATES, Manufacturing nation.—Our enemy [Great Britain] has indeed the consolation of Satan on removing our first parents from Paradise; from a peaceable and agricultural nation, he makes us a military and maufacturing one.—To WILLIAM SHORT. vi, 400. (M., 1814.) See MANUFACTURES and PROTECTION.

— UNITED STATES, National capital.—See WASHINGTON CITY.

8713. UNITED STATES, Natural interests.—The American hemisphere * * * is endowed by nature with a system of interests and connections of its own.—R. TO A. PITTSBURG REPUBLICANS. viii, 142. (1808.) See MONROE DOCTRINE and POLICY,

8714. UNITED STATES, Permanence. —Looking forward with anxiety to the future destinies [of my countrymen] I trust that, in their steady character unshaken by difficulties, in their love of liberty, obedience to law, and support of the public authorities, I see a sure guarantee of the permanence of our Republic; and retiring from the charge of their affairs, I carry with me the consolation of a firm persuasion that heaven has in store for our beloved country long ages to come of prosperity and happiness.—EIGHTH ANNUAL MESSAGE. viii, 110. FORD ED., ix, 225. (Nov. 1808.)

8715. UNITED STATES, Praise for.— There is not a country on earth where there is greater tranquillity; where the laws are milder, or better obeyed; where every one is more attentive to his own business or meddles less with that of others; where strangers are better received, more hospitably treated, and with a more sacred respect.—To MRS. COSWAY. ii, 36. FORD ED., iv, 316. (P., 1786.)

8716. UNITED STATES, Prosperity.— When you witnessed our first struggles in the War of Independence, you little calculated, more than we did, on the rapid growth and prosperity of this country; on the practical demonstration it was about to exhibit, of the happy truth that man is capable of self-government, and only rendered otherwise by the moral degradation designedly superinduced on him by the wicked acts of his tyrants.—To M. DE MARBOIS. vii, 77. (M., 1817.)

8717. UNITED STATES, Safety of.— Our safety rests in the preservation of our Union.—To THE RHODE ISLAND ASSEMBLY. iv, 397. (W., May 1801.) See UNION.

8718. UNITED STATES, Slanders on.— Nations, like individuals, wish to enjoy a fair reputation. It is, therefore, desirable for us that the slanders on our country, disseminated by hired or prejudiced travellers, should be corrected; but politics, like religion, holds up the torches of martyrdom to the reformers of error. Nor is it in the theatre of Ephesus alone that tumults have been excited when the crafts were in danger. You must be cautious. therefore, in telling unacceptable truths beyond the water.—To MR. OGILVIE. v, 605. (M., 1811.)

8719. UNITED STATES, Superiority over Europe.—I sincerely wish you may find it convenient to come here [Europe]; the pleasure of the trip will be less than you expect, but the utility greater. It will make you adore your own country, its soil, its climate, its equality, liberty, laws, people, and manners. My God! how little do my countrymen know what precious blessings they are in possession of, and which no other people on earth enjoy. I confess I had no idea of it myself. While we shall see multiplied instances of Europeans going to live in America, I will venture to say, no man now living will ever see an instance of an American removing to settle in Europe. and continuing there. Come, then, and see the proofs of this, and on your return add your testimony to that of every thinking American, in order to satisfy our countrymen how much it is to their interest to preserve, uninfected by contagion, those peculiarities in their government and manners, to which they are indebted for those blessings.—To JAMES MONROE. i, 352. FORD ED., iv, 59. (P., 1785.)

8720. UNITED STATES, Supremacy.— To the overwhelming power of England, I see but two chances of limit. The first is her bankruptcy, which will deprive her of the *golden* instrument of all her successes. The other is that ascendency which nature destines for us by immutable laws. But to hasten this consummation, we must exercise patience and forbearance. For twenty years to come we should consider peace as the *summum bonum* of our country. At the end of that period we shall be twenty millions in number. and forty in energy, when encountering the starved and rickety paupers and dwarfs of English workshops.—To M. DUPONT DE NEMOURS. vi, 508. (M., Dec. 1815.)

8721. UNITED STATES, Title of inhabitants.—You have properly observed (in your book on the commerce of France and the United States) that we can no longer be called Anglo-Americans. That appellation now describes only the inhabitants of Nova Scotia, Canada, &c. I had applied that of Federo-Americans to our citizens, as it would not be so decent for us to assume to ourselves the flattering appellation of free Americans.—To M. DE WARVILLE. ii, 12. FORD ED., iv, 281. (P., 1786.)

8722. UNITED STATES, Troubles and triumphs.—A letter from you calls up recollections very dear to my mind. It carries me back to the times when, beset with difficulties and dangers, we were fellow-laborers in the same cause, struggling for what is most valuable to man, his right of self-government. Laboring always at the same oar, with some wave ever ahead, threatening to overwhelm us, and yet passing harmless under our bark, we knew not how we rode through the storm with heart and hand, and made a happy port. Still we did not expect to be without rubs and difficulties; and we have had them. First, the detention of the Western posts, then the coalition of Pilnitz, outlawing our commerce with France, and the British enforcement of the outlawry. In your day, French depredations; in mine, English, and the Berlin and Milan decrees: now the English orders of Council, and the piracies they authorize. When these shall be over, it will be the impressment of our seamen or something else: and so we have gone on, and so we shall go on, puzzled and prospering beyond example in the history of man.—To JOHN ADAMS. vi, 36. FORD ED., ix, 333. (M., Jan. 1812.)

8723. UNITED STATES, Western territory.—[The proposed new States of the Western territory] shall forever remain a part of the United States of America.—WESTERN TERRITORY REPORT. FORD ED., iii, 409. (1784.) See CENTRALIZATION, CONFEDERATION, COLONIES, CONSTITUTION, FEDERAL GOVERNMENT and UNION.

8724. UNITY, Duty of.—Sole depositaries of the remains of human liberty, our duty to ourselves, to posterity, and to mankind, calls on us by every motive which is sacred or honorable, to watch over the safety of our beloved country during the troubles which agitate and convulse the residue of the world, and to sacrifice to that all personal and local considerations.—R. TO A. NEW YORK LEGISLATURE. viii, 167. (1809.)

8725. UNITY, National.—If we are forced into a war we mus give up differences of opinion and unite as one man to defend our country.—To GENERAL KOSCIUSKO. iv, 295. (Pa., 1799.)

8726. ———.—The times do certainly render it incumbent on all good citizens, attached to the rights and honor of their country, to bury in oblivion all internal differences, and rally around the standard of their

country in opposition to the outrages of foreign nations. All attempts to enfeeble and destroy the exertions of the General Government, in vindication of our national rights, or to loosen the bands of Union by alienating the affections of the people, or opposing the authority of the laws at so eventful a period, merit the discountenance of all.—To GOVERNOR TOMPKINS. viii, 153. (Feb. 1809.)

8727. UNITY, Strength in.—If the well-known energies and enterprise of our countrymen * * * are embodied by an union of will, and by a confidence in those who direct it, our nation, so favored in its situation, has nothing to fear from any quarter.—REPLY TO ADDRESS. v, 262. (W., 1808.)

8728. UNIVERSITY (National), Proposed establishment.—Education is here placed among the articles of public care, not that it would be proposed to take its ordinary branches out of the hands of private enterprise, which manages so much better all the concerns to which it is equal: but a public institution can alone supply those sciences which, though rarely called for, are yet necessary to complete the circle, all the parts of which contribute to the improvement of the country, and some of them to its preservation. The subject is now proposed for the consideration of Congress, because, if approved by the time the State Legislatures shall have deliberated on this extension of the Federal trusts, and the laws shall be passed, and other arrangements made for their execution, the necessary funds will be on hand and without employment. I suppose an amendment to the Constitution, by consent of the States, necessary, because the objects now recommended are not among those enumerated in the Constitution, and to which it permits the public moneys to be applied. The present consideration of a national establishment for education, particularly, is rendered proper by the circumstance, also, that if Congress, approving the proposition, shall yet think it more eligible to found it on a donation of lands, they have it now in their power to endow it with those which will be among the earliest to produce the necessary income. This foundation would have the advantage of being independent on war, which may suspend other improvements by requiring for its own purposes the resources destined for them.—SIXTH ANNUAL MESSAGE. viii, 68. FORD ED., viii, 494. (Dec. 1806.)

8729. ———.—The desire of peace is very much strengthened in me by that which I feel in favor of the great subjects of your and Mr. Fulton's letters. I had fondly hoped to set those enterprises into motion with the last Legislature I shall meet. But the chance of war is an unfortunate check. I do not, however, despair that the proposition of amendment may be sent down this session to the [State] Legislatures. But it is not certain. There is a snail paced gait for the advance of new ideas on the general mind, un-

der which we must acquiesce. A forty years'
experience of popular assemblies has taught
me that you must give them time for every
step you take. If too hard pushed, they
balk, and the machine retrogrades.—To JOEL
BARLOW. v, 216. FORD ED., ix, 168. (W.,
Dec. 1807.)

**8730. UNIVERSITY OF VIRGINIA,
Aim of.**—Our aim [is] the securing to our
country a full and perpetual institution for all
the useful sciences; one which will restore us
to our former station in the confederacy. * * *
Patience and perseverance on our part will secure the blessed end. If we shrink, it is gone
forever.—To GENERAL BRECKENRIDGE. vii, 239.
(M., 1822.)

**8731. UNIVERSITY OF VIRGINIA,
Basis of.**—This institution of my native
State, the hobby of my old age, will be based
on the illimitable freedom of the human mind,
to explore and to expose every subject susceptible of its contemplation.—To DESTUTT TRACY.
FORD ED., x, 174. (M., 1820.)

8732. —— ——. This institution (University of Virginia) will be based on the illimitable freedom of the human mind. For here we
are not afraid to follow truth wherever it may
lead, nor to tolerate any error so long as reason
is left free to combat it.—To MR. ROSCOE. vii,
196. (M., 1820.)

**8733. UNIVERSITY OF VIRGINIA,
Discipline.**—The rock which I most dread is
the discipline of the institution, and it is that
on which most of our public schools labor. The
insubordination of our youth is now the greatest obstacle to their education. We may lessen
the difficulty, perhaps, by avoiding too much
government, by requiring no useless observances, none which shall merely multiply occasions for dissatisfaction, disobedience and revolt by referring to the more discreet of themselves the minor discipline, the graver to the
civil magistrate, as in Edinburgh.—To GEORGE
TICKNOR. vii, 301. (M., 1823.)

**8734. UNIVERSITY OF VIRGINIA,
Elective studies.**—I am not fully informed
of the practices at Harvard, but there is one
from which we shall certainly vary, although
it has been copied, I believe, by nearly every
college and academy in the United States. That
is, the holding the students all to one prescribed
course of reading, and disallowing exclusive
application to those branches only which are
to qualify them for the particular vocations
to which they are destined. We shall, on the
contrary, allow them uncontrolled choice in
the lectures they shall choose to attend, and
require elementary qualification only, and sufficient age. Our institution will proceed on
the principle of doing all the good it can without consulting its own pride or ambition; of
letting every one come and listen to whatever
he thinks may improve the condition of his
mind.—To GEORGE TICKNOR. vii, 300. (M.,
1823.)

**8735. UNIVERSITY OF VIRGINIA,
Future of.**—I contemplate the University of
Virginia as the future bulwark of the human
mind in this hemisphere.—To DR. THOMAS
COOPER. vii, 172. (M., 1820.)

8736. —— ——. I had hoped that we
should open with the next year an institution
on which the fortunes of our country may de-

pend more than may meet the general eye.—
To GENERAL BRECKENRIDGE. vii, 204. (M.,
1821.)

8737. —— ——. I hope the University of
Virginia will prove a blessing to my own State,
and not unuseful perhaps to some others.—To
EDWARD LIVINGSTON. vii, 405. (M., 1825.)

**8738. UNIVERSITY OF VIRGINIA,
Government and.**—I fear not to say that
within twelve or fifteen years from this time, a
majority of the rulers of our State will have
been educated here. They shall carry hence
the correct principles of our day, and you may
count assuredly that they will exhibit their country in a degree of sound respectability it has
never known, either in our days, or those of
our forefathers.—To W. B. GILES. vii, 429.
FORD ED., x, 357. (M., 1825.)

**8739. UNIVERSITY OF VIRGINIA,
Historical course.**—In modern history, there
are but two nations with whose course it is interesting to us to be intimately acquainted, to
wit: France and England. For the former,
Millot's General History of France may be sufficient to the period when 1 Davila commences.
He should be followed by Perefixe, Sully, Voltaire's Louis XIV. and XV., Lacretelles
XVIIIme. Siècle, Marmontel's Regence, Fou-
longion's French Revolution, and Madame de
Stael's, making up by a succession of particular
history, the general one which they want.—To
—— ——. vii, 412. (M., 1825.)

8740. —— ——. Hume, with Brodie,
should be the last histories of England to be
read [in the University of Virginia course].
If first read, Hume makes [his reader] an English tory, whence it is an easy step to American
toryism. But there is a history by Baxter, in
which, abridging somewhat by leaving out some
entire incidents as less interesting now than
when Hume wrote, he has given the rest in
the identical words of Hume, except that when
he comes to a fact falsified, he states it truly,
and when to a suppression of truth, he supplies
it, never otherwise changing a word. It is,
in fact, an editic expurgation of Hume. Those
who shrink from the volume of Rapin, may read
this first, and from this lay a first foundation in
a basis of truth.—To —— ——. vii, 414. (M.,
1825.)

**8741. UNIVERSITY OF VIRGINIA,
Jefferson's last service.**—Our University is
the last of my mortal cares, and the last service
I can render my country.—To J. CORREA. vii,
183. FORD ED., x, 163. (M., 1820.)

8742. —— ——. It is the last act of use-
fulness I can render, and could I see it open
I would not ask an hour more of life.—To
SPENCER ROANE. vii, 212. FORD ED., x, 189.
(M., 1821.)

8743. —— ——. The University of Virginia is the last object for which I shall obtrude
myself on the public observation.—To EDWARD
LIVINGSTON. vii, 405. (M., 1825.)

8744. —— ——. I am closing the last
scenes of my life by fashioning and fostering
an establishment for the instruction of those
who are to come after us. I hope its influence
on their virtue, freedom, fame, and happiness
will be salutary and permanent.—To A. B.
WOODWARD. vii, 406. FORD ED., x, 342. (M.,
1825.)

**8745. UNIVERSITY OF VIRGINIA,
Necessity for.**—I have wondered at the

change of political principles wh'ch has taken place in many in this State [Virginia], however much less than in others. I am still more alarmed to see, in the other States, the general political dispositions of those to whom is confided the education of the rising generation. Nor are all the academies of this State free from grounds of uneasiness. I have great confidence in the common sense of mankind in general; but it requires a great deal to get the better of notions which our tutors have instilled into our minds while incapable of questioning them, and to rise superior to antipathies strongly rooted. However, I suppose when the evil rises to a certain height, a remedy will be found, if the case admits any other than the prudence of parents and guardians.—To JEREMIAH MOOR. FORD ED., vii, 455. (M., Aug. 1800.)

8746. —— ——. How many of our youths Harvard now has, learning the lessons of anti-Missourianism, I know not; but a gentleman lately from Princeton, told me he saw there the list of the students at that place, and that more than half were Virginians. These will return home, no doubt, deeply impressed with the sacred principles of our Holy Alliance of restrictionists.—To JOSEPH C. CABELL. vii, 202. (M., 1821.)

8747. —— ——. The reflections that the boys of this age are to be the men of the next; that they should be prepared to receive the holy charge which we are cherishing to deliver over to them; that in establishing an institution of wisdom for them, we secure it to all our future generations; that in fulfilling this duty, we bring home to our own bosoms the sweet consolation of seeing our sons rising under a luminous tuition, to destinies of high promise; these are considerations which will occur to all; but all, I fear, do not see the speck 'n our horizon which is to burst on us as a tornado, sooner or later. The line of division lately marked out between different portions of our confederacy is such as will never, I fear, be obliterated, and we are now trusting to those who are against us in position and principle, to fashion to their own form the minds and affections of our youth. If, as has been estimated, we send three hundred thousand dollars a year to the northern seminaries, for the instruction of our own sons, then we must have there five hundred of our sons, imbibing opinions and principles in discord with those of their own country. This canker is eating on the vitals of our existence, and if not arrested at once, will be beyond remedy. We are now certainly furnishing recruits to their school.—To GENERAL BRECKENRIDGE. vii, 204. (M., 1821.)

8748. **UNIVERSITY OF VIRGINIA, Novelties in.**—There are some novelties in [the University of Virginia]. Of that of a professorship of the principles of government, you express your approbation. They will be founded in the rights of man. That of agriculture, I am sure, you will approve; and that also of Anglo-Saxon. As the histories and laws left us in that type and dialect, must be the text books of the reading of the learners, they will imbibe with the language their free principles of government.—To JOHN CARTWRIGHT. vii, 361. (M., 1824.)

8749. **UNIVERSITY OF VIRGINIA, Opposition to.**—An opposition [to the University] has been got up. That of our *alma mater*, William and Mary, is not of much weight. She must descend into the secondary rank of academies of preparation for the University. The serious enemies are the priests of the different religious sects, to whose spells on the human mind its improvement is ominous. Their pulpits are now resounding with denunciations against the appointment of Dr. Cooper whom they charge as a monetheist in opposition to their tritheism.—To WILLIAM SHORT. vii, 157. (M., 1820.) See COOPER.

8750. —— ——. You say my "handwriting and my letters have great effect at Richmond". I am sensible of the kindness with which this encouragement is held up to me. But my views of their effect are very different. When I retired from the administration of public affairs, I thought I saw some evidence that I retired with a good degree of public favor, and that my conduct in office had been considered by one party at least with approbation and with acquiescence by the other. But the attempt [University of Virginia], in which I have embarked so earnestly to procure an improvement in the moral condition of my native State, although, perhaps, in other States it may have strengthened good dispositions, it has assuredly weakened them within our own. The attempt ran foul of so many local interests, of so many personal views, and so much ignorance, and I have been considered as so particularly its promoter, that I see evidently a great change of sentiment towards myself. I cannot doubt its having dissatisfied with myself a respectable minority, if not a majority of the House of Delegates. I feel it deeply and very discouragingly. Yet I shall not give way. I have ever found in my progress through life that, acting for the public, if we do always what is right, the approbation denied in the beginning will surely follow us in the end. It is from posterity we are to expect remuneration for the sacrifices we are making for their service, of time, quiet and good will. And I fear not the appeal. The multitude of fine young men whom we shall redeem from ignorance, who will feel that they owe to us the elevation of mind, of character and station they will be able to attain from the result of our efforts, w'll insure their remembering us with gratitude.—To JOSEPH C. CABELL. vii, 394. (M., 1825.)

8751. **UNIVERSITY OF VIRGINIA, Personal sacrifices for.**—I know well your devotion to your country, and your foresight of the awful scenes coming on her, sooner or later. With this foresight, what service can we ever render her equal to this? [Support of the University of Virginia.] What object of our lives can we propose so important? What interest of our own which ought not to be postponed to this? Health, time, labor, on what in the single life which nature has given us, can these be better bestowed than on this immortal boon to our country? The exertions and the mortifications are temporary: the benefit eternal. If any member of our college of visitors could justifiably withdraw from this sacred duty, it would be myself, * * * but I will die in the last ditch, and so, I hope, you will, my friend, as well as our firm-breasted brothers and colleagues, Mr. Johnson and General Breckenridge. Nature will not give you a second life wherein to atone for the omissions of this. Pray then, dear and very dear Sir, do not think of deserting us, but view the sacrifices which seem to stand in your way, as the lesser duties, and such as ought to be postponed to this, the greatest of all. Continue with us in these holy labors, until having seen their accomplishment, we may say with old Simeon, "*nunc dimittas, Domine*".—To JOSEPH C. CABELL. vii, 202. (M., 1821.)

8752. UNIVERSITY OF VIRGINIA, Political principles.—In the selection of our law professor [for the University of Virginia], we must be rigorously attentive to his political principles. You will recollect that before the Revolution Coke-Littleton was the universal elementary book of law students, and a sounder whig never wrote, nor of profounder learning in the orthodox doctrines of the British constitution, or in what were called English liberties. You remember, also, that our lawyers were then all whigs. But when his black-letter text, and uncouth but cunning learning got out of fashion, and the honied Mansfieldism of Blackstone became the student's hornbook, from that moment, that profession (the nursery of our Congress), began to slide into toryism, and nearly all the young brood of lawyers now are of that hue. They suppose themselves, indeed, to be whigs because they no longer know what whiggism or republicanism means. It is in our seminary that that vestal flame is to be kept alive; it is thence it is to spread anew over our own and the sister States. If we are true and vigilant in our trust, within a dozen or twenty years a majority of our own Legislature will be from one school, and many disciples will have carried its doctrines home with them to their several States, and will have leavened thus the whole mass.—To JAMES MADISON. vii, 433. FORD ED., x, 376. (M., 1826.)

8753. UNIVERSITY OF VIRGINIA, Proctorship.—The establishment of a proctor is taken from the practice of Europe, where an equivalent officer is made a part, and is a very essential one, of every such institution; and as the nature of his functions requires that he should always be a man of discretion, understanding, and integrity, above the common level, it was thought that he would never be less worthy of being trusted with the powers of a justice, within the limits of institution here, than the neighboring justices generally are; and the vesting him with the conservation of the peace within that limit, was intended, while it should equally secure its object, to shield the young and unguarded student from the disgrace of the common prison, except where the case was an aggravated one. A confinement to his own room was meant as an act of tenderness to him, his parents and friends; in fine, it was to give them a complete police of their own, tempered by the paternal attentions of their tutors. And, certainly, in no country is such a provision more called for than in this, as has been proved from times of old, from the regular annual riots and battles between the students of William and Mary with the town boys, before the Revolution, *quorum pars fui*, and the many and more serious affrays of later times. Observe, too, that our bill proposes no exclusion of the ordinary magistrate, if the one attached to the institution is thought to execute his power either partially or remissly.—To JOSEPH C. CABELL. vi, 537. (M., 1816.)

8754. UNIVERSITY OF VIRGINIA, Professors.—Our wish is to procure natives [for professorships] where they can be found * * * of the first order of requirement in their respective lines; but, preferring foreigners of the first order to natives of the second, we shall certainly have to go for several of our professors to countries more advanced in science than we are.—To JOHN ADAMS. vii, 130. FORD ED., x, 139. (M., 1819.)

8755. ——— ———. No secondary character will be received among them. Either the ablest which America or Europe can furnish, or none

at all. They will give us the selected society of a great city separated from the dissipations and levities of its ephemeral insects.—To WILLIAM SHORT. vii, 141. FORD ED., x, 145. (M., 1819.)

8756. ——— ———. Our intention is that its professors shall be of the first order in their respective lines which can be procured on either side of the Atlantic.—To ALBERT GALLATIN. FORD ED., x, 236. (M., 1822.)

8757. ——— ———. A man is not qualified for a professor, knowing nothing but merely his own profession. He should be otherwise well educated as to the sciences generally; able to converse understandingly with the scientific men with whom he is associated, and to assist in the councils of the faculty on any subject of science on which they may have occasion to deliberate. Without this, he will incur their contempt, and bring disreputation on the institution.—To JOSEPH C. CABELL. vii, 331. (M., 1824.)

8758. ——— ———. I have the most unlimited confidence that in the appointment of professors to our nursling institution, every individual of my associates will look with a single eye to the sublimation of its character, and adopt, as our sacred motto, "*detur digniori*". In this way it will honor us, and bless our country.—To JOSEPH C. CABELL. vii, 331. (M., 1824.)

8759. ——— ———. In some departments of science we believe Europe to be in advance before us, and that it would advance ourselves were we to draw from thence instructors in these branches, and thus to improve our science, as we have done our manufactures, by borrowed skill. I have been much squibbed for this, perhaps by disappointed applicants for professorships, to which they were deemed incompetent.—To JOHN ADAMS. vii, 388. (M., 1825.)

8760. ——— ———. I have no reason to regret the measure taken of procuring professors from abroad where science is so much ahead of us. You witnessed some of the puny squibs of which I was the butt on that account. They were probably from disappointed candidates, whose unworthiness had occasioned their applications to be passed over. The measure has been generally approved in the South and West; and by all liberal minds in the North. It has been peculiarly fortunate, too, that the professors brought from abroad were as happy selections as could have been hoped, as well for their qualifications in science as correctness and amiableness of character. I think the example will be followed, and that it cannot fail to be one of the efficacious means of promoting that cordial good will, which it is so much the interest of both nations to cherish. These teachers can never utter an unfriendly sentiment towards their native country; and those into whom their instructions will be infused, are not of ordinary significance only; they are exactly the persons who are to succeed to the government of our country, and to rule its future enmities, its friendships and fortunes. As it is our interest to receive instruction through this channel, so I think it is yours to furnish it; for these two nations holding cordially together, have nothing to fear from the united world. They will be the models for regenerating the condition of man, the sources from which representative government is to flow over the whole earth.—To J. EVELYN DENISON. vii, 415. (M., 1825.)

8761. UNIVERSITY OF VIRGINIA, Scope.—Our views are catholic for the improvement of our country by science.—To GEORGE TICKNOR. vii, 301. (M., 1823.)

8762. UNIVERSITY OF VIRGINIA, Studies.—A material question is what is the whole term of time which the students can give to the whole course of instruction? I should say that three years should be allowed to general education, and two, or rather three, to the particular profession for which they are destined. We [University of Virginia] receive our students at the age of sixteen, expected to be previously so far qualified in the languages, ancient and modern, as that one year in our schools shall suffice for their last polish. A student then with us may give his first year here to languages and mathematics; h's second to mathematics and physics; his third to physics and chemistry, with the other objects of that school. I particularize this distribution merely for illustration, and not as that which e'ther is, or perhaps ought to be established. This would ascribe one year to languages, two to mathematics, two to physics, and one to chemistry and its associates.—To DR. JOHN P. EMMETT. vii, 442. (M., 1826.)

8763. UNIVERSITY OF VIRGINIA, Text books.—In most public seminaries textbooks are prescribed to each of the several schools, as the *norma docendi* in that school; and this is generally done by authority of the trustees. I should not propose this generally in our University, because I believe none of us are so much at the heights of science in the several branches, as to undertake this, and therefore that it will be better left to the professors until occasion of interference shall be given. But there is one branch in which we are the best judges, in which heresies may be taught, of so 'nteresting a character to our own State and to the United States, as to make it a duty in us to lay down the principles which are to be taught. It is that of government. Mr. Gilmer being withdrawn, we know not who his successor may be. He may be a Richmond lawyer, or one of that school of quondam federalism, now consolidation. It is our duty to guard against such principles being disseminated among our youth, and the diffusion of that poison, by a previous prescription of the texts to be followed in their discourses.—To ——. vii, 397. (M., 1825.)

8764. UNIVERSITY OF VIRGINIA, Theology.—I agree with you that a professorship of theology should have no place in our institution.—To THOMAS COOPER. vi, 389. (M., 1814.)

8765. —— ——. In our University there is no professorship of divinity. A handle has been made of this to disseminate an idea that this is an nstitution, not merely of no religion, but against all religion. Occasion was taken at the last meeting of the Visitors, to bring forward an idea that might silence this calumny, which weighed on the minds of some honest friends to the institution. In our annual report to the Legislature, after stating the constitutional reasons against a public establishment of any religious instruction, we suggest the expediency of encouraging the different religious sects to establish, each for itself, a professorship of their own tenets, on the confines of the University, so near as that their students may attend the lectures there, and have the free use of our library, and every other accommodation we can give them; preserving, however, their independence of us and of each other. This fills the chasm objected to ours, as a defect in an institution professing to give instruction in *all* useful sciences. I think the invitation will be accepted, by some sects from candid intentions, and by others from jealousy and rivalship. And by bringing the sects together, and mixing them with the mass of other students, we shall soften their asperities, liberalize and neutralize their prejudices, and make the general religion a religion of peace, reason and morality.—To DR. THOMAS COOPER. vii, 267. FORD ED., x, 243. (M., 1822.) See EDUCATION, LANGUAGES and SCHOOLS.

8766. USURPATION, Appeal against.—We have appealed to their [British people] native justice and magnanimity, as well as to the ties of our common kindred, to disavow these usurpations which were likely to interrupt our connection and correspondence. They, too, have been deaf to the voice of justice and of consanguinity.*—DECLARATION OF INDEPENDENCE AS DRAWN BY JEFFERSON.

8767. USURPATION, Parliamentary.—The act passed in the 4th year of his Majesty's reign [George III.], entitled "An Act for granting certain duties in the British Colonies and Plantations in America, &c."; one other act passed in the 5th year of his reign, entitled, "An Act for granting and applying certain stamp duties and other duties in the British Colonies and Plantations in America, &c."; one other act passed in the 6th year of his reign, entitled, "An Act for the better securing the dependency of his Majesty's dominions in America upon the Crown and Parliament of Great Britain"; and one other act, passed in the 7th year of his reign, entitled, "An Act for granting duties on paper, tea, &c.", form that connected chain of parliamentary usurpation, which has been the subject of frequent applications to his Majesty, and the Houses of Lords and Commons of Great Britain * * *.—RIGHTS OF BRITISH AMERICA. i, 130. FORD ED., i, 435. (1774.)

8768. VACATIONS, Health and.—The diseases of the season incident to most situations on the tide waters, now begin to show themselves here [Washington], and to threaten some of our members [of the cabinet] together with the probability of a uniform course of things in the Chesapeake [affair], induce us to prepare for leaving this place during the two sickly months, as well for the purposes of health as to bestow some little attention to our private affairs, which is necessary at some time of every year. Our respective stations will be fixed and known, so that everything will find us at them, with the same certainty as if they were here; and such measures of intercourse will be established as that the public business will be carried on at them, with all the regularity and dispatch necessary.—To W. H. CABELL. v, 144. FORD ED., ix, 91. (W., July 1807.)

8769. —— ——. In consideration of the unhealthy season now approaching at this as

*Congress changed so as to read: "We have appealed to their native justice and magnanimity, and we have conjured them, by the ties of our common kindred, to disavow these usurpations, which would inevitably interrupt our connection and correspondence. They, too, have been deaf to the voice of justice and of consanguinity."—EDITOR.

other places on the tide-waters, and which we have always retired from about this time, the members of the Administration, as well as myself, shall leave this place [Washington] in three or four days, not to return till the sickly term is over, unless something extraordinary should reassemble us.—To COLONEL TATHAM. v. 145. (W., July 1807.)

8770. VACATIONS, Presidential.—I consider it as a trying experiment for a person from the mountains to pass the two bilious months on the tide-water. I have not done it these forty years, and nothing should induce me to do it. As it is not possible but that the Administration must take some portion of time for their own affairs, I think it best they should select that season for absence. General Washington set the example of those two months; Mr. Adams extended them to eight months. I should not suppose our bringing it back to two months a ground for grumbling, but, grumble who will, I will never pass those two months on tide-water.—To ALBERT GALLATIN. FORD ED., viii, 95. (M., Sep. 1801.)

8771. VACATIONS, Public officials and.—One reason for suggesting the discontinuance of the daily post was, that it was not kept up by contract, but at the expense of the United States. But the principal reason was to avoid giving ground for clamor. The general idea is, that those who receive annual compensations should be constantly at their posts. Our constituents might not in the first moment consider 1st, that we have property to take care of, which we cannot abandon for temporary salaries; 2nd, that we have health to take care of, which at this season cannot be preserved at Washington; 3d, that while at our separate homes our public duties are fully executed, and at much greater personal labor than while we are together when a short conference saves a long letter.—To JAMES MADISON. v, 181. FORD ED., ix, 134. (M., Sep. 1807.)

8772. VACCINATION, Utility of.—I am happy to see that vaccination is introduced, and likely to be kept up, in Philadelphia; but I shall not think it exhibits all its utility until experience shall have hit upon some mark or rule by which the popular eye may distinguish genuine from spurious virus. It was with this view that I wished to discover whether time could not be made the standard, and supposed, from the little experience I had, that matter, taken at eight times twenty-four hours from the time of insertion, could always be in the proper state. As far as I went I found it so; but I shall be happy to learn what the immense field of experience in Philadelphia will teach us on that subject.—To DR. BENJAMIN RUSH. iv, 425. FORD ED., viii, 126. (W., Dec. 1801.)

— **VALUE, Intrinsic.**—See DOLLAR and MONEY.

8773. VANITY, Personal.—I have not the vanity to count myself among those whom the State would think worth oppressing with perpetual service.—To JAMES MONROE. i, 320. FORD ED., iii, 59. (M., 1782.)

8774. VAN RENSSELAER (General S.), Failure of.—Will not Van Rensselaer be broke for cowardice and incapacity? To advance such a body of men across a river without securing boats to bring them off in case of disaster, has cost us seven hundred men; and to have taken no part himself in such an action, and against such a general could be nothing but cowardice.—To PRESIDENT MADISON. FORD ED., ix, 370. (M., Nov. 1812.)

8775. VATTEL (Emmerich von), Character of.—Let us appeal to enlightened and disinterested judges. No one is more so than Vattel.—To E. C. GENET. iii, 588. FORD ED., vi, 309. (Pa., 1793.)

8776. ——. Vattel is one of the most zealous and constant advocates for the preservation of good faith in all our dealings.—OPINION ON FRENCH TREATIES. vii, 620. FORD ED., vi, 228. (1793.)

8777. VEGETABLES, Cultivating.—The wealthy people [in Virginia] are attentive to the raising of vegetables, but very little so to fruits. The poorer people attend to neither, living principally on milk and animal diet. This is the more inexcusable, as the climate requires indispensably a free use of vegetable food, for health as well as comfort.—NOTES ON VIRGINIA. viii, 393. FORD ED., iii, 257. (1782.)

8778. VEGETABLES, Jefferson's diet.—I live so much like other people, that I might refer to ordinary life as the history of my own. I have lived temperately, eating little animal food, and that not as an aliment, so much as a condiment for the vegetables, which constitute my principal diet. I double, however, the Doctor's [Rush's] glass and a half of wine, and even treble it with a friend; but halve its effects by drinking the weak wines only. The ardent wines I cannot drink, nor do I use ardent spirits in any form. Malt liquors and cider are my table drinks, and my breakfast is of tea and coffee. I have been blest with organs of digestion which accept and concoct, without ever murmuring, whatever the palate chooses to consign to them, and I have not yet lost a tooth by age.—To DR. VINE UTLEY. vii, 116. FORD ED., x, 125. (M., 1819.)

8779. VEGETATION, Electricity, light and.—Dr. Ingenhouse, you know, discovered as he supposed, from experiment, that vegetation might be promoted by occasional streams of the electrical fluid to pass through a plant, and that other physicians had received and confirmed this theory. He now, however, retracts it, and finds by more decisive experiments that the electrical fluid can neither forward nor retard vegetation. Uncorrected still of the rage of drawing general conclusions from partial and equivocal observations, he hazards the opinion that light promotes vegetation. I have heretofore supposed from observation, that light affects the color of living bodies, whether vegetable or animal; but that either the one or the other receives nutriment from that fluid, must be permitted to be doubted of, till better confirmed by observation. It is always better to have no ideas than false ones: to believe nothing than to believe what is wrong. In my mind, theories are more easily demolished than rebuilt.—To REV. JAMES MADISON. ii, 430. (P., 1788.)

8780. VENISON, Philosophy and.—You have sent me a noble animal, legitimated by superior force as a monarch of the forest; and he has incurred the death which his brother legitimates have so much more merited; like them, in death, he becomes food for a nobler race, he for man, they for worms that will revel on them: but he dies innocent, and with death all his fears and pains are at an end; they die loaded with maledictions, and liable to a sentence and sufferings which we will leave to the justice of heaven to award. In plain English, we shall heartily feast on him, and thank you heartily as the giver of the feast.—To JOHN FRY. FORD ED., x, 284. (M., 1823.)

8781. VERGENNES (Count de), Assistants.—Reyneval and Hennin are the two eyes of Count de Vergennes. The former is the more important character, because possessing the most of the confidence of the Count. He is rather cunning than wise, his views of things being neither great nor liberal. He governs himself by principles which he has learned by rote, and is fit only for the details of execution. His heart is susceptible of little passions, but not of good ones. He is brother-in-law to M. Gerard, from whom he received disadvantageous impressions of us, which cannot be effaced. He has much duplicity. Hennin is a philosopher, sincere, friendly, liberal, learned, beloved by everybody; the other by nobody. I think it a great misfortune that the United States are in the department of the former.—To James Madison. ii, 109. Ford ed., iv, 368. (P., 1787.)

8782. VERGENNES (Count de), Great and good.—He is a great and good minister, and an accident to him might endanger the peace of Europe.—To Edward Carrington. i, 99. Ford ed., iv, 359. (P., 1787.)

8783. ——. His loss would at all times have been great; but it would be immense during the critical poise of European affairs existing at this moment.—To John Jay. ii, 113. (P., 1787.)

8784. VERGENNES (Count de), Monarchist.—Vergennes is a great minister in European affairs, but has very imperfect ideas of our institutions, and no confidence in them. His devotion to the principles of pure despotism renders him unaffectionate to our governments. But his fear of England makes him value us as a make-weight. He is cool, reserved in political conversations, but free and familiar on other subjects, and a very attentive, agreeable person to do business with. It is impossible to have a clearer, better organized head, but age has chilled his heart.—To James Madison. ii, 108. Ford ed., iv, 366. (P., 1787.)

8785. VERGENNES (Count de), Reputation.—The Count de Vergennes had the reputation with the diplomatic corps of being wary and slippery in his diplomatic intercourse; and so he might be with those whom he knew to be slippery and double-faced themselves. As he saw that I had no indirect views, practiced no subtleties, meddled in no intrigues, pursued no concealed object, I found him as frank, as honorable, as easy of access to reason, as any man with whom I had ever done business; and I must say the same for his successor, Montmorin, one of the most honest and worthy of human beings.—Autobiography. i, 64. Ford ed., i, 90. (M., 1821.)

8786. VERMONT, Separation from New York.—The four northernmost States wish Vermont to be received into the Union. The middle and southernmost States are rather opposed to it. But the great difficulty arises with New York which claims that territory. In the beginning every individual of that State revolted at the idea of giving them up. Congress, therefore, only interfered from time to time to prevent the two parties from coming to an open rupture. In the meanwhile the minds of the New Yorkers have been familiarizing to the idea of a separation, and I think it will not be long before they will consent to it.—Answers to M. de Meunier. ix, 284. Ford ed., iv, 140. (P., 1786.) See Offices, Unconstitutional.

8787. VETERINARY COLLEGES, Advantages.—The advantages of the veterinary institution proposed, may perhaps be doubted. If it be problematical whether physicians prevent death where the disease, una ded, would have terminated fatally,—oftener than they produce it, where order would have been restored to the system by the process, if uninterrupted, provided by nature, and in the case of a man who can describe the seat of his disease, its character, progress, and often its cause, what might we expect in the case of the horse, mule. &c., yielding no sensible and certain indications of his disease? They have long had these institutions in Europe; has the world received as yet one iota of valuable information from them? If it has, it is unknown to me. At any rate, it may be doubted whether, where so many institutions of obvious utility are yet wanting, we should select this one to take the lead.—To Joel Barlow. v, 402. (W., 1808.)

8788. VETERINARY COLLEGES, Utility.—I know nothing of the veterinary institution of London * * *. I know well the Veterinary school of Paris, of long standing, and saw many of its publications during my residence there. They were classically written, announced a want of nothing but certainty as to their facts, which granted, the hypotheses were learned and plausible. The coach-horses of the rich of Paris were availed of the institution; but the farmers even of the neighborhood could not afford to call a veterinary doctor to their plough horses in the country, or to send them to a livery stable to be attended in the city. On the whole, I was not a convert to the utility of the Institution.—To Dr. Benjamin Rush. vi, 105. (M., 1813.)

8789. ——. That there are certain diseases of the human body, so distinctly pronounced by well-articulated symptoms, and recurring so often, as not to be mistaken, wherein experience has proved that certain substances applied, will restore order, I cannot doubt. * * * But there are also a great mass of indistinct diseases, presenting themselves under no form clearly characterized, nor exactly recognized as having occurred before, and to which of course, the application of no particular substance can be known to have been made, nor its effect on the case experienced. These may be called unknown cases, and they may in time be lessened by the progress of observation and experiment. Observing that there are in the construction of the animal system some means provided unknown to us, which have a tendency to restore order, when disturbed by accident, called by physicians the *vis medicatrix naturæ*. I think it safer to trust to this power in the unknown cases, than to uncertain conjectures built on the ever-changing hypothetical systems of medicine. Now in the Veterinary department all are unknown cases. Man can tell his physician the seat of his pain, its nature, history, and sometimes its cause, and can follow his directions for the curative process; but the poor dumb horse cannot signify where his pain is, what it is, or when or whence it came, and resists all process for its cure. If in the case of man, then, the benefit of medical interference in such cases admits of question, what must it be in that of the horse? And to what narrow limits is the real importance of the veterinary art reduced?—To Dr. Benjamin Rush. vi, 105. (M., 1813.)

8790. VETO, Abuse of.—He (George III.) has endeavored to pervert the exercise of the kingly office in Virginia into a detestable and insupportable tyranny, by putting his negative on laws the most wholesome and necessary for the public good.—PROPOSED VA. CONSTITUTION. FORD ED., ii, 8. (June 1776.)

8791. VETO, By council.—The governor, two councillors of State, and a judge from each of the superior courts of chancery, common law, and admiralty, shall be a council to revise all bills which shall have passed both houses of Assembly, in which council the governor, when present, shall preside. Every bill, before it becomes a law, shall be represented to this council, who shall have a right to advise its rejection, returning the bill, with their advice and reasons in writing, to the house in which it originated, who shall proceed to reconsider the said bill. But if after such reconsideration, two-thirds of the house shall be of opinion that the bill should pass finally, they shall pass it and send it, with the advice and written reasons of the said Council of Revision, to the other house, wherein if two-thirds also shall be of opinion it should pass finally, it shall thereupon become law; otherwise it shall not.—PROPOSED VA. CONSTITUTION. viii, 451. FORD ED., iii, 330. (1783.)

8792. VETO, Congressional.—The negative, proposed to be given to Congress on all the acts of the several legislatures, is now, for the first time, suggested to my mind. *Primâ facie* I do not like it. It fails in an essential character, that the hole and the patch should be commensurate. But this proposes to mend a small hole by covering the whole government. Not more than one out of one hundred State acts concerns the Confederacy. This proposition, then, in order to give them one degree of power, which they ought to have, gives them ninety-nine more which they ought not to have, upon a presumption that they will not exercise the ninety-nine. But upon every act, there will be a preliminary question, does this concern the Confederacy? And was there ever a proposition so plain as to pass Congress without a debate? Their decisions are almost always wise; they are like pure metal. But you know of how much dross this is the result.—TO JAMES MADISON. ii, 152. FORD ED., iv, 390. (P., June 1787.)

8793. VETO, Denial of.—.The Administrator shall have no negative on the bills of the Legislature.—PROPOSED VA. CONSTITUTION. FORD ED., ii, 18. (June 1776.)

8794. VETO, Discretion in use of.—If the pro and con for and against a bill hang so even as to balance the President's judgment, a just respect for the wisdom of the Legislature would naturally decide the balance in favor of their opinion. It is chiefly for cases where they are clearly misled by error, ambition, or interest, that the Constitution has placed a check in the negative of the President.—NATIONAL BANK OPINION. vii, 560. FORD ED., v, 289. (1791.)

8795. VETO, Effects of non-use.—The non-user of his negative begins already to excite a belief that no President will ever

venture to use it; and has, consequently, begotten a desire to raise up barriers in the State legislatures against Congress, throwing off the control of the Constitution.—OPINION ON APPORTIONMENT BILL. vii, 601. FORD ED., v, 500. (1792.)

8796. VETO, Executive.—I like the negative given [in the Federal Constitution] to the Executive, with a third of either house; though I should have liked it better had the Judiciary been associated for that purpose, or invested with a similar and separate power.*—To JAMES MADISON. ii, 329. FORD ED., iv, 475. (P., 1787.)

8797. VETO, First Presidential.—He [President Washington] sent it [veto of the Apportionment bill] to the House of Representatives. A few of the hottest friends of the bill expressed passion but the majority were satisfied and both in and out of doors it gave pleasure to have at length an instance of the negative being exercised.†—THE ANAS. ix, 115. (1792.)

8798. VETO, Inhuman.—He [George III.] has endeavored to pervert the exercise of the kingly office in Virginia into a detestable and insupportable tyranny * * * by prompting our negroes to rise in arms among us; those very negroes whom, by an inhuman use of his negative, he had refused us permission to exclude by law.—PROPOSED VA. CONSTITUTION. FORD ED., ii, 11. (June 1776.)

8799. VETO, King's.—By the Constitution of Great Britain, as well as of the several American States, his Majesty possesses the power of refusing to pass into a law, any bill which has already passed the other two branches of the legislature. His Majesty, however, and his ancestors, conscious of the impropriety of opposing their single opinion to the united wisdom of two houses of Parliament, while their proceedings were unbiased by interested principles, for several ages past have modestly declined the exercise of this power, in that part of his empire called Great Britain. But by change of circumstances, other principles than those of justice simply, have obtained an influence on their determinations. The addition of new States to the British Empire has produced an addition of new, and, sometimes, opposite interests. It is now, therefore, the great office of his Majesty, to resume the exercise of his negative power, and to prevent the passage of laws by any one legislature of the Empire, which might bear injuriously on the rights and interests of another. Yet this will not excuse the wanton exercise of this power, which we have seen his Majesty practice on the laws of the American legislatures. For the most trifling reasons, and, sometimes for

---

* This extract from the Ford edition is in Jefferson's own words. In the Congress edition, they are as follows: "I like the negative given to the Executive, conjointly with a third of either house; though I should have liked it better had the judiciary been associated for that purpose, or invested separately with a similar power."—EDITOR.

† This was the first instance of the exercise of the veto power under the Constitution.—EDITOR.

no conceivable reason at all, his Majesty has rejected laws of the most salutary tendency. The abolition of domestic slavery is the great object of desire* in those Colonies, where it was, unhappily, introduced in their infant state. But previous to the enfranchisement of the slaves we have, it is necessary to exclude all further importations from Africa. Yet our repeated attempts to effect this. by prohibitions, and by imposing duties which might amount to a prohibition, have been hitherto defeated by his Majesty's negative: Thus preferring the immediate advantages of a few British corsairs to the lasting interests of the American States, and to the rights of human nature, deeply wounded by this infamous practice. Nay, the single interposition of an interested individual against a law was scarcely ever known to fail of success. though, in the opposite scale were placed the interests of a whole country. This is so shameful an abuse of a power, trusted with his Majesty for other purposes, as if not reformed, would call for some legal restrictions. —RIGHTS OF BRITISH AMERICA. i, 134. FORD ED., i, 439. (1774.)

8800. —— ——. The royal negative closed the last door [in the Virginia House of Burgesses] to every hope of amelioration. [Regarding Slavery.]—AUTOBIOGRAPHY. i, 3. FORD ED., i, 5. (1821.)

8801. VETO, Prostituted.—Determined to keep open a market where MEN should be bought and sold, he has prostituted his negative for suppressing every legislative attempt to prohibit or to restrain this execrable commerce.†—DECLARATION OF INDEPENDENCE AS DRAWN BY JEFFERSON.

8802. VETO, Protection by.—The negative of the President is the shield provided by the Constitution to protect against the invasions of the Legislature: 1. The right of the Executive. 2. Of the Judiciary. 3. Of the States and State Legislatures.—NATIONAL BANK OPINION. vii, 560. FORD ED., v, 289. (1791.)

8803. VETO, Qualified.—I approved, from the first moment. of the great mass of what is in the new Constitution; * * * the qualified negative on laws given to the Executive, which, however, I should have liked better if associated with the judiciary also, as in New York.—To F. HOPKINSON. ii, 586. FORD ED., v, 76. (P., March 1789.)

8804. VETO, Satisfactory use.—The negative of the President can never be used more pleasingly to the public than in the protection of the Constitution.—OPINION ON APPORTIONMENT BILL. vii, 601. FORD ED., v, 500. (1792.)

* " In asserting," says Parton in his *Life of Jefferson,* "that the great object of desire in the Colonies was the abolition of slavery, he expressed rather the feeling of his own set,—the educated and high-minded young Whigs of the Southern Colonies, than the sentiments of the great body of the slaveholders. He could boast that the first act of his own life had been an attempt in that direction."—EDITOR.
† Struck out by Congress.—EDITOR.

8805. VETO, Suspensive.—The National Assembly [of France] have determined that the King shall have a *suspensive and iterative* veto; that is, after negativing a law, it cannot be presented again till after a new election. If he negatives it then, it cannot be presented a third time till after another new election. If it be then presented, he is obliged to pass it. This is perhaps justly considered as a more useful negative than an absolute one, which a King would be afraid to use.—To JOHN JAY. iii, 115. (P., 1789.)

8806. VICE, Knowledge and.—Although I do not, with some enthusiasts, believe that the human condition will ever advance to such a state of perfection as that there shall no longer be pain or vice in the world, yet I believe it susceptible of much improvement, and most of all, in matters of government and religion; and that the diffusion of knowledge among the people is to be the instrument by which it is to be effected.—To DUPONT DE NEMOURS. vi, 592. FORD ED., x, 25. (P.F. 1816.)

8807. VICE-PRESIDENCY, Acceptance of.—The idea that I would accept the office of President, but not that of Vice-President of the United States, had not its origin with me. I never thought of questioning the free exercise of the right of my fellow citizens to marshal those whom they call into their service according to their fitness, nor ever presumed that they were not the best judges of that. Had I indulged a wish in what manner they should dispose of me, it would precisely have coincided with what they have done.—To JAMES SULLIVAN. iv, 168. FORD ED., vii, 116. (M., Feb. 9, 1797.)

8808. VICE-PRESIDENCY, Candidates for.—I presume there will not be a vote against General Washington [for President] in the United States. It is more doubtful who will be Vice-President. The age of Dr. Franklin, and the doubt whether he would accept it. are the only circumstances that admit a question, but that he would be the man. After these two characters of first magnitude, there are so many which present themselves equally, on the second line, that we cannot see which of them will be singled out. John Adams, Hancock, Jay, Madison, Rutledge, will all be voted for.—To WILLIAM CARMICHAEL. ii, 465. (P., Aug. 1788.)

8809. VICE-PRESIDENCY, Ceremony and.—I hope I shall be made a part of no ceremony whatever. I shall escape into the city as covertly as possible. If Governor Mifflin should show any symptoms of ceremony, pray contrive to parry them.—To JAMES MADISON. iv, 167. FORD ED., vii, 116. (M., Jan. 1797.)

8810. VICE-PRESIDENCY, Duties of. —As to duty. the Constitution will know me only as the member of the Legislative body; and its principle is. that of a separation of Legislative. Executive and Judiciary functions, except in cases specified. If this principle be not expressed in direct terms, it is clearly the spirit of the Constitution and it ought to be so commented and acted on by every friend of free government.—To JAMES MADISON. iv, 161. FORD ED., vii, 108. (M., Jan. 1797.)

8811. VICE-PRESIDENCY, Easy and honorable.—The second office of the* government is honorable and easy; the first is but a splendid misery.—To ELBRIDGE GERRY. iv, 171. FORD ED., vii, 120. (Pa., 1797.)

8812. VICE-PRESIDENCY, Jefferson and.—I was not aware of any necessity of going on to Philadelphia immediately, yet I had determined to do it, as a mark of respect to the public, and to do away the doubts which have spread, that I should consider the second office as beneath my acceptance.—To JAMES MADISON. iv, 161. FORD ED., vii, 107. (M., Jan. 1797.)

8813. ———— ————. I know not from what source an idea has spread itself * * * that I would accept the office of President of the United States, but not of Vice-President. When I retired from the office I last held, no man in the Union less expected than I did ever to have come forward again; and, whatever has been insinuated to the contrary, to no man in the Union was the share which my name bore in the late contest more unexpected than it was to me. If I had contemplated the thing beforehand, and suffered my will to enter into action at all on it, it would have been in a direction exactly the reverse of what has been imputed to me; but I had no right to a will on the subject, much less to control that of the people of the United States in arranging us according to our capacities. Least of all could I have any feelings which would revolt at taking a station secondary to Mr. Adams. I have been secondary to him in every situation in which we ever acted together in public life for twenty years past. A contrary position would have been the novelty, and his the right of revolting at it. Be assured, then, that if I had had a fibre in my composition still looking after public office, it would have been gratified precisely by the very call you are pleased to announce to me, and no other.—To JOHN LANGDON. iv, 163. FORD ED., vii, 111. (M., Jan. 1797.)

8814. ———— ————. Since I am called out, an object of great anxiety to me is that those with whom I am to act, shutting their minds to the unfounded abuse of which I have been the subject, will view me with the same candor with which I shall certainly act.—To JOHN LANGDON. iv, 164. FORD ED., vii, 112. (M., Jan. 1797.)

8815. VICE-PRESIDENCY, Notification of election.—I suppose that the choice of Vice-President has fallen on me * * * I believe it belongs to the Senate to notify the Vice-President of his election. I recollect to have heard, that on the first election of President and Vice-President, gentlemen of considerable office were sent to notify the parties chosen. But this was the inauguration

of our new government, and ought not to be drawn into example. At the second election, both gentlemen were on the spot and needed no messengers. On the present occasion, the President will be on the spot, so that what is now to be done respects myself alone; and considering that the season of notification will always present one difficulty, that the distance in the present case adds a second, not inconsiderable, and which may in future happen to be sometimes much more considerable, I hope the Senate will adopt that method of notification, which will always be least troublesome and most certain. The channel of the post is certainly the least troublesome. is the most rapid, and, considering also that it may be sent by duplicates and triplicates, is unquestionably the most certain. Enclosed to the postmaster at Charlottesville, with an order to send it by express, no hazard can endanger the notification. Apprehending, that should there be a difference of opinion on this subject in the Senate, my ideas of self-respect might be supposed by some to require something more formal and inconvenient, I beg leave to avail myself of your friendship to declare, if a different proposition should make it necessary, that I consider the channel of the post-office as the most eligible in every respect, and that it is to me the most desirable; which I take the liberty of expressing, not with a view of encroaching on the respect due to that discretion which the Senate have a right to exercise on the occasion, but to render them the more free in the exercise of it, by taking off whatsoever weight the supposition of a contrary desire in me might have on the mind of any member. —To HENRY TAZEWELL. iv, 160. FORD ED., vii, 106. (M., Jan. 1797.)

8816. VICE-PRESIDENCY, Oath of office.—I have turned to the Constitution and laws, and find nothing to warrant the opinion that I might not have been qualified here [Monticello] or wherever else I could meet with a Senator; any member of that body being authorized to administer the oath, without being confined to time or place, and consequently to make a record of it, and to deposit it with the records of the Senate. However, I shall come on, on the principle which had first determined me—respect to the public.—To JAMES MADISON. iv, 167. FORD ED., vii, 116. (M., 1797.)

8817. VICE-PRESIDENCY, Preference for.—It seems possible * * * that you may see me in Philadelphia about the beginning of March, exactly in that character which. if I were to reappear at Philadelphia, I would prefer to all others; for I change the sentiment of Clorinda to "L'alte temo, l'humile non sdegno".—To MR. VOLNEY. iv, 158. (M., Jan. 1797.)

8818. VICE-PRESIDENCY, Pride and. —As to the second [office], it is the only office in the world about which I am unable to decide in my own mind whether I had rather have it, or not have it. Pride does not enter into the estimate; for I think with the

Romans that the general of to-day should be a soldier to-morrow if necessary. I can particularly have no feelings which would revolt at a secondary position to Mr. Adams. I am his junior in life, was his junior in Congress, his junior in the diplomatic line, his junior lately in the civil government.—To JAMES MADISON. iv, 155. FORD ED., vii, 98. (M., Jan. 1797.)

8819. VICE-PRESIDENCY, Tranquil and unoffending.—I thank you for your congratulations on the public call on me to undertake the second office in the United States, but still more for the justice you do me in viewing as I do the *escape* from the first. I have no wish again to meddle in public affairs, being happier at home than I can be anywhere else. Still less do I wish to engage in an office where it would be impossible to satisfy either friends or foes, and least of all at a moment when the storm is about to burst, which has been conjuring up for four years past. If I am to act, however, a more tranquil and unoffending station could not have been found for me, nor one so analogous to the dispositions of my mind. It will give me philosophical evenings in the winter, and rural days in summer.—To DR. BENJAMIN RUSH. iv, 165. FORD ED., vii, 113. (M., Jan. 1797.)

8820. —— ——. I am so much attached to my domestic situation, that I would not have wished to leave it at all. However, if I am to be called from it, the shortest absences and most tranquil station suit me best. —To JAMES SULLIVAN. iv, 168. FORD ED., vii, 117. (M., 1797.)

8821. VIGILANCE, Eye of.—Be not weary of well doing. Let the eye of vigilance never be closed.—To SPENCER ROANE. vii, 212. FORD ED., x, 189. (M., 1821.)

8822. VINCENNES, Danger from Indians.—I have the pleasure to enclose you the particulars of Colonel Clark's success against Vincennes. * * * I fear it will be impossible for Colonel Clark to be so strengthened as to enable him to do what he desires. Indeed, the express who brought this letter, gives us reason to fear Vincennes is in danger from a large body of Indians collected to attack it, and said, when he came from Kaskaskias, to be within thirty leagues of the place.—To GENERAL WASHINGTON. i, 221. FORD ED., ii, 240. (Wg., 1779.)

8823. VINCENNES, Loyalty of.—I have ever considered them as sober, honest, and orderly citizens, submissive to the laws, and faithful to the nation of which they are a part. And should occasion arise of proving their fidelity in the cause of their country, I count on their aid with as perfect assurance as on that of any other part of the United States.—To WILLIAM M'INTOSH. v, 242. (W., 1808.)

8824. VINDICATION, Appeal for.—I should have retired at the end of the first four years, but that the immense load of tory calumnies which have been manufactured respecting me, and have filled the European market, have obliged me to appeal once more to my country for justification. I have no

fear but that I shall receive honorable testimony by their verdict on these calumnies. At the end of the next four years I shall certainly retire. Age, inclination, and principle all dictate this.—To PHILIP MAZZEI. iv, 553. D. L. J., 310. (July 1804.)

8825. VINDICATION, Seeking.—A desire to leave public office, with a reputation not more blotted than it has deserved, will oblige me to emerge at the next session of our Assembly and, perhaps, to accept of a seat in it. But as I go with a single object, I shall withdraw when that shall be accomplished.— To EDMUND RANDOLPH. i, 313. FORD ED., iii, 50. (M., 1781.)

8826. VINE, Cultivation of.—The vine is the parent of misery. Those who cultivate it are always poor, and he who would employ himself with us in the culture of corn, cotton, &c., can procure, in exchange for them, much more wine, and better, than he could raise by its direct culture.—To GEORGE WYTHE. ii, 266. FORD ED., iv, 443. (P., 1787.) See WINES.

8827. VIRGINIA, American Revolution and.—An inquiry into the exertions of Virginia in the common cause during the period of her exemption from military invasion would be proper for the patriotic historian, because her character has been very unjustly impeached by the writers of other States, as having used no equal exertions at that time. I know it to be false; because having all that time been a member of the Legislature, I know that our whole occupation was in straining the resources of the State to the utmost, to furnish men. money, provisions and other necessaries to the common cause. The proofs of this will be found in the journals and acts of the Legislature, in executive proceedings and papers, and in the auditor's accounts. Not that Virginia furnished her quota of *requisitions* of either men or money; but that she was always above par, in what was *actually* furnished by the other States.—To SKELTON JONES. v, 461. (M., 1809.)

8828. VIRGINIA, British invasion.—On the 31st of December, a letter from a private gentleman to General Nelson came to my hands, notifying, that in the morning of the preceding day, twenty-seven sail of vessels had entered the capes; and from the tenor of the letter we had reason to expect, within a few hours, further intelligence; whether they were friends or foes, their force and other circumstances. We immediately dispatched General Nelson to the lower country, with powers to call on the militia in that quarter, or to act otherwise as exigencies should require; but waited further intell'gence before we would call for militia from the middle or upper country. No further intelligence came unt'l the 2d instant, when the former was confirmed; it was ascertained they had advanced up James River in Warrasqueak bay. All arrangements were immediately taken for calling in a sufficient body of militia for opposition. In the night of the 3d, we received advice that they were at anchor opposite Jamestown. We then supposed Williamsburg to be their object. The wind, however, which had hitherto been unfavorable, shifted fair, and the tide being also in their favor, they ascended the river to Kennon's that evening and, with the next tide, came up to Westover, having on their way taken possession of some works we had at Hood's by which two or three of their vessels received some damage but which were of necessity abandoned by the small garrison of fifty men placed there, on the enemy's landing to invest the works. Intelligence of their having quitted the station at Jamestown, from which we supposed they meant to land for Williamsburg, and of their having got in the evening to Kennon's, reached us the next morning at five o'clock, and was the first indication of their meaning to penetrate towards this place (Richmond) or Petersburg. As the orders for drawing militia here had been given but two days, no opposition was in readiness. Every effort was therefore necessary, to withdraw the arms and other military stores, records, &c., from this place. Every effort was, accordingly, exerted to convey them to the foundry five miles, and to a laboratory six miles, above this place, till about sunset of that day, when we learned the enemy had come to an anchor at Westover that morning. We then knew that this, and not Petersburg was their object, and began to carry across the river everything remaining here, and to remove what had been transported to the foundry and laboratory to Westham, the nearest crossing, seven miles above this place, which operation was continued till they had approached very near. They marched from Westover at two o'clock in the afternoon of the 4th, and entered Richmond at one o'clock in the afternoon of the 5th. A regiment of infantry and about thirty horse continued on, without halting, to the foundry. They burned that, the boring mill, the magazine and two other houses, and proceeded to Westham: but nothing being in their power there, they retired to Richmond. The next morning, they burned some buildings of public and private property, with what stores remained in them, destroyed a great quantity of private stores and, about twelve o'clock, retired towards Westover, where they encamped within the neck the next day. The loss sustained is not yet accurately known. As far as I have been able to discover, it consisted, at this place, of about three hundred muskets, some soldiers' clothing to a small amount, some quartermaster's stores, of which one hundred and twenty sides of leather was the principal article, part of the artificer's tools, and three wagons. Besides which, five brass four pounders which we had sunk in the river, were discovered to them, raised and carried off. At the foundry we lost the greater part of the papers belonging to the Auditor's office, and of the books and papers of the Council office. About five or six tons of powder, as we conjecture, was thrown into the canal, of which there will be a considerable saving by remanufacturing it. The roof of the foundry was burned, but the stacks of chimneys and furnaces not at all injured. The boring mill was consumed. Within less than forty-eight hours from the time of their landing, and nineteen from our knowing their destination, they had penetrated thirty-three miles, done the whole injury, and retired.—To GENERAL WASHINGTON. i, 282. FORD ED., ii, 405. (M., 1809.)

8829. ——— ———. Their numbers, from the best intelligence I have had, are about fifteen hundred infantry; and, as to their cavalry, accounts vary from fifty to one hundred and twenty; the whole commanded by the parricide Arnold. Our militia, dispersed over a large tract of country, can be called in but slowly. On the day the enemy advanced to this place, two hundred only were embodied. They were of this town and its neighborhood and were too few to do anything. At this time they are assembled in pretty considerable numbers on the south side of James River, but are not yet brought to a point. On the north side are two or three small bodies, amounting in the whole, to about nine hundred men. The enemy were, at four o'clock yesterday evening, still remaining in their encampment at Westover and Berkeley Neck. In the meanwhile, Baron Steuben, a zealous friend, has descended from the dignity of his proper command to direct our smallest movements. His vigilance has in a great measure supplied the want of force in preventing the enemy from crossing the river, which might have been very fatal. He has been assiduously employed in preparing equipments for the militia as they should assemble, pointing them to a proper object, and other offices of a good commander. Should they loiter a little longer, and he be able to have a sufficient force, I still flatter myself they will not escape with total impunity. To what place they will point their next exertions, we cannot even conjecture. The whole country on the tide waters and some distance from them is equally open to similar insult.—To GENERAL WASHINGTON. i, 284. FORD ED., ii, 408. (January 1781.)

8830. VIRGINIA, Conventions in.—These were at first chosen anew for every particular session. But in March, 1775, they recommended to the people to choose a convention which should continue in office a year. This was done, accordingly, in April, 1775, and in July following that convention passed an ordinance for the election of delegates in the month of April annually. It is well known, that in July, 1775, a separation from Great Britain and establishment of republican government, had never yet entered into any person's mind. A convention, therefore, chosen under that ordinance, cannot be said to have been chosen for the purposes which certainly did not exist in the minds of those who passed it. Under this ordinance, at the annual election in April, 1776, a convention for the year was chosen. Independence, and the establishment of a new form of government, were not even the objects of the people at large. One extract from the pamphlet called *Common Sense* had appeared in the Virginia papers in February, and copies of the pamphlet itself had got in a few hands. But the idea had not been opened to the mass of the people in April, much less can it be said that they had made up their minds in its favor. So that the electors of April, 1776, no more than the legislators of July, 1775, not thinking of independence and a permanent republic, could not mean to vest in these delegates powers of establishing them, or any authorities other than those of the ordinary legislature. So far as a temporary organization of government was necessary to render our opposition energetic, so far their organization was valid. But they received in their creation no powers but what were given to every legislature before and since. They could not, therefore, pass an act transcendent to the powers of other legislatures.—NOTES ON VIRGINIA. viii, 363. FORD ED., iii, 225. (1782.) See VIRGINIA CONSTITUTION, REPEALABILITY.

8831. VIRGINIA, Division of counties.—In what terms reconcilable to Majesty, and at the same time to truth, shall we speak of a late instruction to the Governor of the Colony of Virginia, by which he is forbidden to assent to any law for the division of a county, unless the new county will consent to have no representative in Assembly? That Colony has as yet affixed no boundary to the westward. Their western counties, therefore, are of an indefinite extent. Some of them are actually seated many hundred miles from their eastern limits. Is it possible, then, that his Majesty can have bestowed a single thought on the situation of those people, who, in order to obtain justice for injuries, however great or small, must, by the laws of that Colony, attend their county court. at such a distance, with all their witnesses, monthly, till their litigation be determined?—RIGHTS OF BRITISH AMERICA. i, 136. FORD ED., i, 441. (1774.)

8832. VIRGINIA, Love for.—My native State is endeared to me by every tie which can attach the human heart.—R. TO A. VIRGINIA ASSEMBLY. vii, 148. (1809.)

8833. VIRGINIA, Political opposition in.—Better that any one [of the other States] take the lead [against consolidation] than Virginia, where opposition is considered as commonplace, and a mere matter of form and habit. —To C. W. GOOCH. vii, 430. (M., 1826.)

8834. VIRGINIA CONSTITUTION, Amendments to.—That it is really important to provide a constitution for our State cannot be doubted; as little can it be doubted that the ordinance called by that name has important defects. But before we attempt it, we should endeavor to be as certain as is practicable that in the attempt we should not make bad worse. I have understood that Mr. Henry has always been opposed to this undertaking; and I confess that I consider his talents and influence such as that, were it decided that we should call a convention for the purpose of amending, I should fear he might induce that convention either to fix the thing as at present, or change it for the worse. Would it not, therefore, be well that means should be adopted for coming at his ideas of the changes he would agree to, and for communicating to him those which we should propose? Perhaps he might find ours not so distant from his, but that some mutual sacrifices might bring them together. I shall hazard my own ideas to you as hastily as my business obliges me. I wish to preserve the line drawn by the Federal Constitution between the General and particular governments as it stands at present, and to take every prudent means of preventing either from stepping over it. Though the experiment has not yet had a long enough course to show us from which quarter encroachments are most to be feared, yet it is easy to foresee, from the nature of things, that the encroachments of the State governments will tend to an excess of liberty which will correct itself (as in the late instance), while those of the General Government will tend to monarchy, which will fortify itself from day to day, instead of working its own cure, as all experience shows. I would rather be exposed to the inconveniences attending too much liberty than those attending too small a degree of it. Then it is important to strengthen the State governments; and as this cannot be done by any change in the Federal Constitution (for the preservation of that is all we need contend for), it must be done by the States themselves, erecting such barriers at the constitutional line as cannot be surmounted either by themselves or by the General Government. The only barrier in their power is a wise government. A weak one will lose ground in every contest. To obtain a wise and an able

government, I consider the following changes as important. Render the Legislature a desirable station by lessening the number of representatives (say to 100) and lengthening somewhat their term, and proportion them equally among the electors; adopt, also, a better mode of appointing senators. Render the Executive a more desirable post to men of abilities by making it more independent of the Legislature; to wit, let him be chosen by other electors, for a longer time, and ineligible forever after. Responsibility is a tremendous engine in a free government. Let him feel the whole weight of it then, by taking away the shelter of his executive council. Experience both ways has already established the superiority of this measure. Render the Judiciary respectable by every possible means, to wit, firm tenure in office, competent salaries, and reduction of their numbers. Men of high learning and abilities are few in every country; and by taking in those who are not so, the able part of the body have their hands tied by the unable. This branch of the government will have the weight of the conflict on their hands, because they will be the last appeal of reason. These are my general ideas of amendments; but, preserving the ends, I should be flexible and conciliatory as to the means.—To ARCHIBALD STUART. iii, 314. FORD ED., v, 408. (Pa., Dec. 1791.)

8835. VIRGINIA CONSTITUTION, Bill of rights.—The fact is unquestionable that the Bill of Rights, and the Constitution of Virginia, were originally drawn by George Mason, one of our really great men, and of the first order of greatness.—To AUGUSTUS B. WOODWARD. vii, 405. FORD ED., x, 341. (M., 1825.)

8836. VIRGINIA CONSTITUTION, Equal rights and.—The basis of our [Virginia] Constitution is in opposition to the principle of equal political rights, refusing to all but freeholders any participation in the natural right of self-government. It is believed, for example, that a very great majority of the militia, on whom the burthen of military duty was imposed in the late war, were unrepresented in the legislature, which imposed this burthen on them. However nature may by mental or physical disqualifications have marked infants and the weaker sex for the protection, rather than the direction of government, yet among the men who either pay or fight for their country, no line of right can be drawn. The exclusion of a majority of our freemen from the right of representation is merely arbitrary, and an usurpation of the minority over the majority; for it is believed that the non-freeholders compose the majority of our free and adult male citizens. And even among our citizens who participate in the representative privilege, the equality of political right is entirely prostrated by our constitution. Upon which principle of right or reason can any one justify the giving to every citizen of Warwick as much weight in the government as to twenty-two equal citizens in Loudon and similar inequalities among the other counties? If these fundamental principles are of no importance in actual government, then no principles are important.—To John Hambden Pleasants. vii, 345. Ford ed., x, 303. (M., 1824.)

8837. VIRGINIA CONSTITUTION, Improvements on.—The other States, who successively formed constitutions for themselves also, had the benefit of our (Virginia's) outline, and have made on it, doubtless, successive improvements. One in the very outset, and which has been adopted in every subsequent constitution, was to lay its foundation in the authority of the nation. To our convention no special authority had been delegated by the people to form a permanent Constitution, over which their successors in legislation should have no powers of alteration. They had been elected for the ordinary purposes of legislation only, and at a time when the establishment of a new government had not been proposed or contemplated. Although, therefore, they gave to this act the title of a Constitution, yet it could be no more than an act of legislation subject, as their other acts were, to alteration by their successors. It has been said, indeed, that the acquiescence of the people supplied the want of original power. But it is a dangerous lesson to say to them, "whenever your functionaries exercise unlawful authority over you, if you do not go into actual resistance, it will be deemed acquiescence and confirmation". How long had we acquiesced under usurpations of the British parliament? Had that confirmed them in right, and made our revolution a wrong? Besides, no authority has yet decided whether this resistance must be instantaneous; when the right to resist ceases, or whether it has yet ceased? Of the twenty-four States now organized, twenty-three have disapproved our doctrine and example, and have deemed the authority of their people a necessary foundation for a constitution.—To John Hambden Pleasants. vii, 344. Ford ed., x. 302. (M., April 1824.)

8838. VIRGINIA CONSTITUTION, Preamble to.—The history of the Preamble to the [first] Constitution of Virginia is this: I was then at Philadelphia with Congress; and knowing that the convention of Virginia was engaged in forming a plan of government, I turned my mind to the same subject, and drew a sketch or outline of a Constitution, with a preamble, which I sent to Mr. Pendleton, president of the convention. on the mere possibility that it might suggest something worth incorporation into that before the convention. He informed me afterwards by letter, that he received it on the day on which the committee of the whole had reported to the house the plan they had agreed to; that that had been so long in hand, so disputed inch by inch, and the subject of so much altercation and debate; that they were worried with the contention it had produced, and could not from mere lassitude, have been induced to open the instrument again; but that, being pleased with the preamble to mine, they adopted it in the house, by way of amendment to the report of the committee; and thus my preamble became tacked to the work of George Mason. The Constitution, with the preamble, was passed on the 29th of June, and the Committee of Congress had only the day before that reported to that body the draught of the Declaration of Independence. The fact is, that that preamble was prior in composition to the Declaration; and both having the same object, of justifying our separation from Great Britain, they used necessarily the same materials of justification, and hence their similitude.—To A. B. Woodward. vii, 405. Ford ed., x, 341. (M., 1825.)

8839. VIRGINIA CONSTITUTION, Repealability of.—If the present Assembly pass an act, and declare it shall be irrevocable by subsequent assemblies, the declaration is merely void, and the act repealable, as other acts are. So far, and no farther authorized, they [the first Virginia convention] organized the government by the ordinance entitled a Constitution or form of government. It pretends to no higher authority than the other ordinances of the same session; it does not say that it shall be perpetual; that it shall be unalterable by other legislatures; that it shall be transcendent above the powers of those who they knew would have equal power with themselves. Not only the silence of the instrument is a proof they thought it would be alterable, but their own practice also; for this very convention, meeting as a House of Delegates in General Assembly with the Senate in the autumn of that year, passed acts of assembly in contradiction to their ordinance of government; and every assembly from that time to this has done the same. I am safe, therefore, in the position that the Constitution itself is alterable by the ordinary legislature. Though this opinion seems founded on the first elements of common sense, yet is the contrary maintained by some persons. First, because, say they, the conventions were vested with every power necessary to make effectual opposition to Great Britain. But to complete this argument, they must go on, and say further, that effectual opposition could not be made to Great Britain without establishing a form of government perpetual and unalterable by the Legislature; which is not true. An opposition which at some time or other was to come to an end, could not need a perpetual constitution to carry it on; and a government amendable as its defects should be discovered, was as likely to make effectual resistance, as one that should be unalterably wrong. Besides, the assemblies were as much vested with all powers requisite for resistance as the Conventions were. If, therefore, these powers included that of modelling the form of government in the one case, they did so in the other. The assemblies then as well as the conventions may model the government; that is, they may alter the ordinance of government. Second, they urge, that if the convention had meant that this instrument should be alterable, as their other ordinances were, they would have called it an ordinance; but they have called it a *constitution*, which, *ex vi termini*, means "an act above the power of the ordinary legislature." I answer that *constitutio, constitutum, statutum, lex*, are convertible terms. * * * Thirdly. But, say they, the people have acquiesced, and this has given it an authority superior to the laws. It is true that the people did not rebel against it; and was that a time for the people to rise in rebellion? Should a prudent acquiescence, at a critical time, be construed into a confirmation of every illegal thing done during that period? Besides, why should they rebel? At an annual election they had chosen delegates for the year, to exercise the ordinary powers of legislation, and to manage the great contest in which they were engaged. These delegates thought the contest would be best managed by an organized government. They, therefore, among others, passed an ordinance of government. They did not presume to call it perpetual and unalterable. They well knew they had no power to make it so; that our choice of them had been for no such purpose, and at a time when we could have no such purpose in contemplation. Had an unalterable form of government been meditated, perhaps we should have chosen a different set of people. There was no cause, then, for the people to rise in rebellion. But to what dangerous lengths will this argument lead? Did the acquiescence of the Colonies under the various acts of power exercised by Great Britain in our infant state, confirm these acts, and so far invest them with the authority of the people as to render them unalterable, and our present resistance wrong? On every unauthoritative exercise of power by the legislature must the people rise in rebellion, or their silence be construed into a surrender of that power to them? If so, how many rebellions should we have had already? One certainly for every session of assembly. The other States in the Union have been of opinion that to render a form of government unalterable by ordinary acts of Assembly, the people must delegate persons with special powers. They have accordingly chosen special conventions to form and fix their governments. The individuals then who maintain the contrary opinion in this country, should have the modesty to suppose it possible that they may be wrong, and the rest of America right. But if there be only a possibility of their being wrong, if only a plausible doubt remains of the validity of the ordinance of government, is it not better to remove that doubt by placing it on a bottom which none will dispute? If they be right we shall only have the unnecessary trouble of meeting once in convention. If they be wrong, they expose us to the hazard of having no fundamental rights at all. True it is, this is no time for deliberating on forms of government. While an enemy is within our bowels, the first object is to expel him. But when this shall be done, when peace shall be established, and leisure given us for intrenching

within good forms the rights for which we have bled, let no man be found indolent enough to decline a little more trouble for placing them beyond the reach of question.—NOTES ON VIRGINIA. viii, 364. FORD ED., iii, 226. (1782.) See VIRGINIA, CONVENTIONS.

8840. VIRGINIA CONSTITUTION, Representation under.—The first Constitution [of Virginia] was formed when we were new and inexperienced in the science of government. It was the first, too, which was formed in the whole United States. No wonder, then, that time and trial have discovered very capital defects in it. The majority of the men in the State, who pay and fight for its support, are unrepresented in the Legislature, the roll of freeholders entitled to vote, not including generally the half of those on the roll of the militia, or of the taxgatherers. Among those who share the representation, the shares are very unequal. Thus the county of Warwick, with only one hundred fighting men, has an equal representation with the county of Loudon, which has one thousand seven hundred and forty-six. So that every man in Warwick has as much influence as seventeen men in Loudon.—NOTES ON VIRGINIA. viii, 359. FORD ED., iii, 222. (1782.)

8841. VIRGINIA CONSTITUTION, Republican heresies in.—Inequality of representation in both houses of our Legislature, is not the only republican heresy in this first essay of our revolutionary patriots at forming a constitution. For let it be agreed that a government is republican in proportion as every member composing it has his equal voice in the direction of its concerns (not indeed in person, which would be impracticable beyond the limits of a city, or a small township, but) by representatives chosen by himself, and responsible to him at short periods, and let us bring to the test of this canon every branch of our Constitution. In the Legislature, the House of Representatives is chosen by less than half the people, and not at all in proportion to those who do choose. The Senate are still more disproportionate, and for long terms of irresponsibility. In the Executive, the Governor is entirely independent of the choice of the people, and of their control; his Council equally so, and at best but a fifth wheel to a wagon. In the Judiciary, the judges of the highest courts are dependent on none but themselves. In England, where judges were named and removable at the will of an hereditary executive, from which branch most misrule was feared, and has flowed, it was a great point gained, by fixing them for life, to make them independent of that executive. But in a government founded on the public will, this principle operates in an opposite direction, and against that will. There, too, they are still removable on a concurrence of the executive and legislative branches. But we have made them independent of the nation itself. They are irremovable, but by their own body, for any depravities of conduct, and even by their own body for the imbecilities of dotage. The justices of the inferior courts are self-chosen, are for life, and perpetuate their own body in succession forever, so that a faction once possessing themselves of the bench of a county, can never be broken up, but hold their county in chains, forever indissoluble. Yet these justices are the real executive as well as judiciary, in all our minor and most ordinary concerns. They tax us at will; fill the office of sheriff, the most important of all the executive officers of the county; name nearly all our military leaders, which leaders, once named, are removable but by themselves. The juries, our judges of all fact, and of law when they choose it, are not selected by the people, nor amenable to them. They are chosen by an officer named by the court and executive. Chosen, did I say? Picked up by the sheriff from the loungers of the court yard, after everything respectable has retired from it. Where, then, is our republicanism to be found? Not in our Constitution certainly, but merely in the spirit of our people. That would obĭ ge even a despot to govern us republicanly. Owing to this spirit, and to nothing in the form of our Constitution, all things have gone well. But this fact, so triumphantly misquoted by the enemies of reformation, is not the fruit of our Constitution, but has prevailed in spite of it. Our functionaries have done well, because generally honest men. If any were not so, they feared to show it.—To SAMUEL KERCHIVAL. vii, 10. FORD ED., x, 38. (M., 1816.)

8842. VIRGINIA CONSTITUTION, Revision of.—Let us [Virginia] provide in our Constitution for its revision at stated periods. What these periods should be, nature herself indicates. By the European tables of mortality, of the adults living at any one moment of time, a majority will be dead in about nineteen years. At the end of that period, then, a new majority is come into place; or, in other words, a new generation. Each generation is as independent of the one preceding, as that was of all which had gone before. It has, then, like them, a right to choose for itself the form of government it believes most promotive of its own happiness; consequently, to accommodate to the circumstances in which it finds itself, that received from its predecessors; and it is for the peace and good of mankind, that a solemn opportunity of doing this every nineteen or twenty years, should be provided by the constitution; so that it may be handed on, with periodical repairs, from generation to generation, to the end of time, if anything human can so long endure.—To SAMUEL KERCHIVAL. vii, 15. FORD ED., x, 42. (M., 1816.)

8843. VIRGINIA CONSTITUTION, War power.—The power of declaring war and concluding peace, of contracting alliances, of issuing letters of marque and reprisal, of raising and introducing armed forces, of building armed vessels, forts, or strongholds, of coining money or regulating its value, of regulating weights and measures, we leave to be exercised under the authority of the Confederation; but in all cases respecting them which are out of the said Confederation, they shall be exercised by the Governor, under the regulation of such laws as the Legislature may think it expedient to pass.—PROPOSED CONSTITUTION FOR VIRGINIA. viii, 446. FORD ED., iii, 326. (1783.)

8844. VIRTUE, Agriculture and.—I think our governments will remain virtuous for many centuries; as long as they are chiefly agricultural; and this will be as long as there shall be vacant lands in any part of America.*—To JAMES MADISON. FORD ED., iv, 479 (P., Dec. 1787.)

8845. ———— ————. That there is much vice and misery in the world, I know; but more virtue and happiness I believe, at least in our part of it; the latter being the lot of those employed in agriculture in a greater degree than of other callings.—To ABBE SALIMANKIS. v, 516. (M., 1810.)

8846. VIRTUE, Ambition and.—It is a sublime truth that a bold, unequivocal virtue is the best handmaid even to ambition.—To JOHN JAY. iii, 52. (P., 1789.)

8847. VIRTUE, Aristocracy of.—Nature has wisely provided an aristocracy of virtue and talent for the direction of the interests of society, and scattered it with equal hand through all its conditions.—AUTOBIOGRAPHY. i, 36. FORD ED., i, 49. (1821.)

8848. VIRTUE, Essence of.—Virtue does not consist in the act we do, but in the end it is to effect. If it is to effect the happiness of him to whom it is directed, it is virtuous, while in a society under different circumstances and opinions, the same act might produce pain, and would be vicious. The essence of virtue is in doing good to others, while what is good may be one thing in one society, and its contrary in another.—To JOHN ADAMS. vii, 40. (M., 1816.)

8849. VIRTUE, Happiness and.—Without virtue, happiness cannot be.—To AMOS J. COOK. vi, 532. (M., 1816.)

8850. VIRTUE, Interest and.—Virtue and interest are inseparable.—To GEORGE LOGAN. FORD ED., x, 69. (P.F., 1816.)

8851. VIRTUE, Not hereditary.—Virtue is not hereditary.—To WILLIAM JOHNSON. vii, 291. FORD ED., x, 227. (M., 1823.)

8852. VIRTUE, Practice of.—Encourage all your virtuous dispositions, and exercise them whenever an opportunity arises; being assured that they will gain in strength by exercise, as a limb of the body does, and that exercise will make them habitual. From the practice of the purest virtue, you may be assured you will derive the most sublime com-

* In the Congress edition, Vol. 2, p. 332, this extract has been " edited " so as to read: " I think we shall be so [virtuous] as long as agriculture is our principal object, which will be the case, while there remain vacant lands in any part of America." —EDITOR.

forts in every moment of life, and in the moment of death.—To PETER CARR. i, 396. (P., 1785.)

✕ **8853. VIRTUE, Principles of.**—Everything is useful which contributes to fix in the principles and practices of virtue. When any original act of charity or of gratitude, for instance, is presented either to our sight or imagination, we are deeply impressed with its beauty, and feel a strong desire in ourselves of doing charitable and grateful acts also.—To ROBERT SKIPWITH. FORD ED., i, 396. (M., 1771.)

8854. VIRTUE, Public office and.—For promoting the public happiness, those persons, whom nature has endowed with genius and virtue, should be rendered by liberal education worthy to receive, and able to guard the sacred deposit of the rights and liberties of their fellow citizens; and they should be called to that charge without regard to wealth, birth or other accidental condition or circumstance.—DIFFUSION OF KNOWLEDGE BILL. FORD ED., ii, 221. (1779.)

— **VISION.**—See OPTICS.

8855. VOLNEY (Comte de), Alien law and.—Volney has in truth been the principal object aimed at by the [Alien] law.—To JAMES MADISON. iv, 239. FORD ED., vii, 248. (Pa., May 1798.) See ALIEN AND SEDITION LAWS.

8856. VOLNEY (Comte de), Opposed to war.—Volney and a shipload of French sail [soon]. * * * It is natural to expect they go under irritations calculated to fan the flame. Not so Volney. He is most thoroughly impressed with the importance of preventing war, whether considered with reference to the interests of the two countries, of the cause of republicanism, or of man on the broad scale.—To JAMES MADISON. iv, 245. FORD ED., vii, 262. (Pa., May 1798.)

8857. VOLUNTEERS, Organizing.—I have encouraged the acceptance of volunteers, * * * [who] have offered themselves with great alacrity in every part of the Union.* They are ordered to be organized * * *.—SEVENTH ANNUAL MESSAGE. viii, 87. FORD ED., ix, 162. (Oct. 1807.) See ARMY and MILITIA.

8858. VOTES, Traffic in.—I believe we may lessen the danger of buying and selling votes, by making the number of voters too great for any means of purchase.—To JEREMIAH MOOR. FORD ED., vii, 454. (M., Aug. 1800.)

8859. VOTING, Courtesy to age.—Older electors presenting themselves should be received to vote before the younger ones, and the Legislature shall provide for the secure and convenient claim and exercise of this privilege of age.—NOTES FOR A CONSTITUTION FOR VIRGINIA. FORD ED., vi, 521. (1794.)

8860. VOTING, Viva voce.—All free male citizens of full age and sane mind * * * shall have a right to vote for delegates. * * * They shall give their votes personally, and *viva voce*.—PROPOSED VIRGINIA CONSTITUTION. viii, 444. FORD ED., iii, 323. (1783.)

* To oppose Burr's treason.—EDITOR.

8861. WABASH PROPHET, Pretensions of.—The Wabash Prophet is more rogue than fool, if to be a rogue is not the greatest of all follies. He arose to notice while I was in the administration, and became, of course, a proper subject of inquiry for me. * * * His declared object was the reformation of his red brethren, and their return to their pristine manner of living. He pretended to be in constant communication with the Great Spirit; that he was instructed by Him to make known to the Indians that they were created by Him distinct from the whites, of different natures, for different purposes, and placed under different circumstances, adapted to their nature and destinies; that they must return from all the ways of the whites to the habits and opinions of their forefathers; they must not eat the flesh of hogs, of bullocks, of sheep, &c., the deer and buffalo having been created for their food; they must not make bread of wheat but of Indian corn; they must not wear linen nor woollen, but dress like their fathers in the skins and furs of animals; they must not drink ardent spirits, and I do not remember whether he extended his inhibitions to the gun and gunpowder, in favor of the bow and arrow. I concluded from all this ' at he was a visionary, enveloped in the clo. is of their antiquities, and vainly endeavoring to lead back his brethren to the fancied beatitudes of their golden age. I thought there was little danger of his making many proselytes from the habits and comfort they had learned from the whites, to the habits and privations of savageism, and no great harm if he did. We let him go on, therefore, unmolested. But his followers increased till the English thought him worth corruption and found him corruptible. I suppose his views were then changed; but his proceedings in consequence of them were after I left the administration, and are, therefore, unknown to me.—To JOHN ADAMS. vi, 49. FORD ED., ix, 346. (M., 1812.)

8862. WALSH (Robert), English critics and.—The malevolence and impertinence of Great Britain's critics and writers really called for the rod, and I rejoiced when I heard it was in hands so able to wield it with strength and correctness. Your work will furnish the first volume of every future American history; the Anti-Revolutionary part especially.—To ROBERT WALSH. FORD ED., x, 155. (M., 1820.)

**8863. ———— ————. After the severe chastisement given by Mr. Walsh in his American Register to English Scribblers, which they well deserved and I was delighted to see, I hoped there would be an end of this inter-crimination, and that both parties would prefer the course of courtesy and conciliation, and I think these considerate writers have since shown that disposition, and that it would prevail if equally cultivated by us.—To C. J. INGERSOLL. FORD ED., x, 325. (M., 1824.)

8864. WAR, Abhorrent.—I abhor war and view it as the greatest scourge of mankind.—To ELBRIDGE GERRY. iv, 173. FORD ED., vii, 122. (Pa., 1797.)

8865. WAR, America and.—The insulated state in which nature has placed the American continent should so far avail it that no spark of war kindled in the other quarters of the globe should be wafted across the wide oceans which separate us from them.—To BARON HUMBOLDT. vi, 268. FORD ED., ix, 431. (M., 1813.)

8866. WAR, Americans in.—Whenever an appeal to force shall take place, I feel a perfect confidence that the energy and enterprise displayed by my fellow citizens in the pursuits of peace, will be equally eminent in those of war.—To GENERAL SHEE. v, 33. (W., 1807.)

8867. WAR, Avoidance of.—To remove as much as possible the occasions of making war, it might be better for us to abandon the ocean altogether, that being the element whereon we shall be principally exposed to jostle with other nations; to leave to others to bring what we shall want, and to carry what we can spare. This would make us invulnerable to Europe, by offering none of our property to their prize, and would turn all our citizens to the cultivation of the earth. It might be time enough to seek employment for them at sea, when the land no longer offers it.—NOTES ON VIRGINIA. viii, 413. FORD ED., iii, 279. (1782.)

8868. ———. How much better is it for neighbors to help than to hurt one another; how much happier must it make them. If you will cease to make war on one another, if you will live in friendship with all mankind, you can employ all your time in providing food and clothing for yourselves and your families. Your men will not be destroyed in war, your women and children will lie down to sleep in their cabins without fear of being surprised by their enemies and killed or carried away. Your numbers will be increased instead of diminished, and you will live in plenty and in quiet.—ADDRESS TO MANDAR NATION. viii, 201. (1806.)

8869. ———. To cherish and maintain the rights and liberties of our citizens, and to ward from them the burthens, the miseries, and the crimes of war, by a just and friendly conduct towards all nations * * * [are] among the most obvious and important duties of·those to whom the management of their public interests * * * [are] confided.— REPLY TO BAPTIST ADDRESS. viii, 119. (1807.)

8870. ———. It is much to be desired that war may be avoided, if circumstances will admit. Nor in the present maniac state of Europe, should I estimate the point of honor by the ordinary scale. I believe we shall on the contrary, have credit with the world, for having made the avoidance of being engaged in the present unexampled war, our first object.—To PRESIDENT MADISON. v, 438. (M., March 1809.)

8871. WAR, Bankruptcy and.—Bankruptcy is a terrible foundation to begin a war on against the conquerors of the universe. —To JAMES MONROE. FORD ED., vii, 241. (Pa., 1798.)

8872. WAR, Bribery vs.—I hope we shall drub the Indians well this summer, and then change our plan from war to bribery. We must do as the Spaniards and English do, keep them in peace by liberal and constant presents. They find it the cheapest plan, and

so shall we. The expense of this summer's expedition would have served for presents for half a century. In this way, hostilities being suspended for some length of time, a real affection may succeed on our frontiers to that hatred now existing there. Another powerful motive is that in this way we may leave no pretext for raising or continuing an army. Every rag of an Indian depredation will, otherwise, serve as a ground to raise troops with those who think a standing army and a public debt necessary for the happiness of the United States, and we shall never be permitted to get rid of either.—To JAMES MONROE. FORD ED., v, 319. (Pa., 1791.)

8873. ———. I hope we shall give the Indians a good drubbing this summer, and then change our tomahawk into a golden chain of friendship. The most economical as well as the most humane conduct towards them is to bribe them into peace, and to retain them in peace by eternal bribes. The expedition this year would have served for presents on the most liberal scale for one hundred years; nor shall we otherwise ever get rid of an army, or of our debt. The least rag of Indian depredation will be an excuse to raise troops for those who love to have troops, and for those who think that a public debt is a good thing.—To CHARLES CARROLL. iii, 246. (Pa., 1791.)

8874. WAR, Commerce and.—This exuberant commerce * * * brings us into collision with other powers in every sea, and will force us into every war of the European powers.—To BENJAMIN STODDERT. v, 426. FORD ED., ix, 245. (W., 1809.)

8875. WAR, Commerce vs.—War is not the best engine for us to resort to; nature has given us one *in our commerce*, which, if properly managed, will be a better instrument for obliging the interested nations of Europe to treat us with justice.—To THOMAS PINCKNEY. iv, 177. FORD ED., vii, 129. (Pa., May 1797.)

8876. WAR, Contracts in.—I have the highest idea of the sacredness of those contracts which take place between nation and nation at war, and would be the last on earth to do anything in violation of them.—To GENERAL WASHINGTON. i, 228. FORD ED., ii, 247. (1779.)

8877. WAR, Debt and.—We wish to avoid the necessity of going to war, till our revenue shall be entirely liberated from debt. Then it will suffice for war, without creating new debt or taxes.—To GOVERNOR CLAIBORNE. v, 381. FORD ED., ix, 213. (W., Oct. 1808.)

8878. WAR, Deprecated.—Wars with any European powers are devoutly to be deprecated.—NOTES ON VIRGINIA. viii, 412. FORD ED., iii, 278. (1782.)

8879. WAR, Distresses of.—I desire to see the necessary distresses of war alleviated in every possible instance.—To BARON DE RIEDESEL. i, 240. FORD ED., ii, 302. (R., 1780.)

8880. WAR, Embargo vs.—I have ever been anxious to avoid a war with England, unless forced by a situation more losing than war itself. But I did believe we could coerce her to justice by peaceable means, and the Embargo, evaded as it was, proved it would have coerced her had it been honestly executed.—To HENRY DEARBORN. v, 529. FORD ED., ix, 278. (M.. July 1810.)

8881. WAR, Evils of.—The evils of war are great in their endurance, and have a long reckoning for ages to come.—R. TO A. PITTSBURG REPUBLICANS. viii, 142. (1808.)

8882. WAR, Executives and.—We have received a report that the French Directory has proposed a declaration of war against the United States to the Council of Ancients, who have rejected it. Thus we see two nations, who love one another affectionately, brought by the ill temper of their executive administrations, to the very brink of a necessity to imbrue their hands in the blood of each other. —To AARON BURR. iv, 187. FORD ED., vii, 148. (Pa., June 1797.)

8883. WAR, Genius for.—I see the difficulties and defects we have to encounter in war, and should expect disasters if we had an enemy on land capable of inflicting them. But the weakness of our enemy there will make our first errors innocuous, and the seeds of genius which nature sows with even hand through every age and country, and which need only soil and season to germinate, will develop themselves among our military men. Some of them will become prominent, and seconded by the native energy of our citizens, will soon, I hope, to our force add the benefits of skill.—To WILLIAM DUANE. vi, 75. FORD ED., ix, 365. (M., Aug. 1812.)

8884. WAR, Holy.—If ever there was a holy war, it was that which saved our liberties and gave us independence.—To J. W. EPPES. vi, 246. FORD ED., ix, 416. (M., 1813.)

8885. ———. The war of the Revolution will be sanctioned by the approbation of posterity through all future ages.—To J. W. EPPES. vi, 194. FORD ED., ix, 395. (P.F., Sep. 1813.)

8886. WAR, Honor and.—We are alarmed here [Virginia] with the apprehensions of war, and sincerely anxious that it may be avoided; but not at the expense either of our faith or honor.—To TENCH COXE. iv, 105. FORD ED., vi, 508. (M., May 1794.)

8887. WAR, Indian allies in.—[I argued in cabinet] against employing Indians in war. [It was] a dishonorable policy.—THE ANAS. FORD ED., i, 183. (1792.)

8888. WAR, Injury.—If nations go to war for every degree of injury, there would never be peace on earth.—To MADAME DE STAEL. v, 133. (W., 1807.)

8889. WAR, Insult and.—I think it to our interest to punish the first insult; because an insult unpunished is the parent of many others.—To JOHN JAY. i, 405. FORD ED., iv, 89. (P., 1785.)

8890. ———. It is an eternal truth that acquiescence under insult is not the way to escape war.—To H. TAZEWELL. iv, 121. FORD ED., vii, 31. (M., 1795.)

8891. WAR, Interest and.—Never was so much false arithmetic employed on any subject, as that which has been employed to persuade nations that it is their interest to go to war. Were the money which it has cost to gain, at the close of a long war, a little town, or a little territory, the right to cut wood here, or to catch fish there, expended in improving what they already possess, in making roads, opening rivers, building ports, improving the arts, and finding employment for their idle poor, it would render them much stronger, much wealthier and happier. This I hope will be our wisdom.—NOTES ON VIRGINIA. viii, 413. FORD ED., iii, 279. (1782.)

8892. WAR, Justifiable.—On the final and formal declarations of England, that she never would repeal her Orders of Council as to us, until those of France should be repealed as to other nations as well as us, and that no practicable arrangement against her impressment of our seamen could be proposed or devised, war was justly declared, and ought to have been declared.—To J. W. EPPES. vi, 196. FORD ED., ix, 396. (P.F., Sep. 1813.)

8893. WAR, Losses in Revolutionary.—I think that upon the whole [our loss during the war] has been about one-half the number lost by the British; in some instances more, but in others less. This difference is ascribed to our superiority in taking aim when we fire; every soldier in our army having been intimate with his gun from his infancy.—To ——— ———. i, 208. FORD ED., ii, 157. (Wg.. 1778.)

8894. WAR, Markets and.—To keep open sufficient markets is the very first object towards maintaining the popularity of the war. —To PRESIDENT MADISON. vi, 78. (M., Aug. 1812.)

8895. WAR, Monarchies and.—War is not the most favorable moment for divesting the monarchy of power. On the contrary, it is the moment when the energy of a single hand shows itself in the most seducing form. —To H. S. CREVECŒUR. ii, 458. (P., 1788.)

8896. WAR, Moral duty.—When wrongs are pressed because it is believed they will be borne, resistance becomes morality.—To MADAME DE STAEL. v, 133. (W., 1807.)

8897. WAR, One enough.—I have seen enough of one war never to wish to see another.—To JOHN ADAMS. iv, 104. FORD ED., vi, 505. (M., 1794.)

8898. ———. I think one war enough for the life of one man; and you and I have gone through one which at least may lessen our impatience to embark in another. Still, if it becomes necessary, we must meet it like men, old men indeed, but yet good for something.—To JOHN LANGDON. FORD ED., ix, 201. (M., 1808.)

8899. —— ——. One war, such as that of our Revolution, is enough for one life.—To M. CORREA. vi, 407. (M., 1814.)

8900. WAR, Opposition to.—No country, perhaps, was ever so thoroughly against war as ours. These dispositions pervade every description of its citizens, whether in or out of office.—To GOUVERNEUR MORRIS. FORD ED., vi, 217. (Pa., April 1793.)

8901. WAR, Paroles.—By the law of nations, a breach of parole can only be punished by strict confinement. No usage has permitted the putting to death a prisoner for this cause. I would willingly suppose that no British officer had ever expressed a contrary purpose. It has, however, become my duty to declare that should such a threat be carried into execution, it will be deemed as putting prisoners to death in cold blood, and shall be followed by the execution of so many British prisoners in our possession. I trust, however, that this horrid necessity will not be introduced by you, and that you will, on the contrary, concur with us in endeavoring, as far as possible, to alleviate the inevitable miseries of war by treating captives as humanity and natural honor require. The event of this contest will hardly be affected by the fate of a few miserable captives in war.*—FORD ED., ii, 511. (R., March 1781.)

8902. WAR, Peace vs.—The evils which of necessity encompass the life of man are sufficiently numerous. Why should we add to them by voluntarily distressing and destroying one another? Peace, brothers, is better than war. In a long and bloody war, we lose many friends and gain nothing.—ADDRESS TO INDIANS. viii, 185. (1802.)

8903. —— ——. The cannibals of Europe are going to eating one another again. A war between Russia and Turkey is like the battle of the kite and snake. Whichever destroys the other, leaves a destroyer the less for the world. This pugnacious humor of mankind seems to be the law of his nature, one of the obstacles to too great multiplication provided in the mechanism of the Universe. The cocks of the henyard kill one another up. Bears, bulls, rams, do the same. And the horse, in his wild state, kills all the young males, until worn down with age and war, some vigorous youth kills him, and takes to himself the harem of females. I hope we shall prove how much happier for man the Quaker policy is, and that the life of the feeder is better than that of the fighter; and it is some consolation that the desolation by these maniacs of one part of the earth is the means of improving it in other parts. Let the latter be our office, and let us milk the cow, while the Russian holds her by the horns, and the Turk by the tail.—To JOHN ADAMS. vii, 244. FORD ED., x, 217. (M., 1822.)

8904. WAR, Power to declare.—The Administrator [of Virginia] shall not possess

* Addressed "To the Commanding Officer of the British Force at Portsmouth". That officer was Major-General Benedict Arnold.—EDITOR.

the prerogative * * * of declaring war or concluding peace.—PROPOSED VA. CONSTITUTION. FORD ED., ii, 19. (June 1776.)

8905. —— ——. We have already given, in example, one effectual check to the dog of war, by transferring the power of declaring war from the Executive to the legislative body, from those who are to spend to those who are to pay. I should be pleased to see this second obstacle [that no generation shall contract debts greater than may be paid during the course of its own existence], held out by us also, in the first instance.—To JAMES MADISON. iii, 108. FORD ED., v, 123. (P., 1789.) See GENERATIONS.

8906. —— ——. The States of America before their present Union possessed completely, each within its own limits, the exclusive right to * * * [make war and] by their act of Union, they have as completely ceded [it] to the General Government. Art. 1st. Section 8th, "The Congress shall have power to declare war, to raise and support armies". Section 10th, * * * "No State shall without the consent of Congress, keep troops or ships of war in time of peace, enter into any agreement or compact with another State or with a foreign power, or engage in war, unless actually invaded or in such danger as will not admit of delay". These paragraphs of the Constitution, declaring that the General Government shall have, and that the particular ones shall not have, the right of war * * * are so explicit that no commentary can explain them further, nor can any explain them away.—OPINION ON GEORGIAN LAND GRANTS. vii, 468. FORD ED., v, 166. (1790.)

8907. —— ——. The question of declaring war is the function equally of both Houses.—THE ANAS. ix, 123. FORD ED., i, 206. (1792.)

8908. —— ——. I thought [the paper] should be laid before both houses [of Congress], because it concerned the question of declaring war, which was the function equally of both houses.—THE ANAS. ix, 123. FORD ED., i, 206. (1792.)

8909. —— ——. The question of war, being placed by the Constitution with the Legislature alone, respect to that made it my duty to restrain the operations of our militia to those merely defensive; and considerations involving the public satisfaction, and peculiarly my own, require that the decision of that question, whichever way it be, should be pronounced definitely by the Legislature themselves.*—PARAGRAPH FOR PRESIDENT'S MESSAGE. FORD ED., vi, 144. (1792.)

8910. —— ——. I opposed the right of the President to declare anything future on the question, Shall there or shall there not be war?—THE ANAS. ix, 178. FORD ED., i, 266. (1793.)

* This is not dated, but was probably written in December, 1792. The message was entirely different.—NOTE IN FORD EDITION.

8911. —— ——. As the Executive cannot decide the question of war on the affirmative side, neither ought it to do so on the negative side, by preventing the competent body from deliberating on the question.*—To James Madison. iii, 519. Ford ed., vi, 192. (1793.)

8912. —— ——. If Congress are to act on the question of war, they have a right to information [from the Executive].—To James Monroe. Ford ed., vii, 221. (Pa., March 1798.)

8913. —— ——. We had reposed great confidence in that provision of the Constitution which requires two-thirds of the Legislature to declare war. Yet it can be entirely eluded by a majority's taking such measures as will bring on war.—To James Monroe. Ford ed., vii, 222. (Pa., March 1798.)

8914. —— ——. We see a new instance of the inefficiency of constitutional guards. We had relied with great security on that provision which requires two-thirds of the Legislature to declare war. But this is completely eluded by a majority's taking such measures as will be sure to produce war.—To James Madison. iv, 222. Ford ed., vii, 220. (Pa., 1798.)

8915. —— ——. The power of declaring war being with the Legislature, the Executive should do nothing necessarily committing them to decide for war.†—To Vice-President Clinton. v, 116. Ford ed., ix, 100. (W., 1807.)

8916. WAR, Preferable.—War may become a less losing business than unresisted depredation.—To President Madison. v, 438. (M., March 1809.)

8917. WAR, Premeditated.—That war with us had been predetermined may be fairly inferred from the diction of Berkley's order, the Jesuitism of which proves it ministerial from its being so timed as to find us in the midst of Burr's rebellion as they expected, from the contemporaneousness of the Indian excitements, and of the wide and sudden spread of their maritime spoliations.—To Thomas Paine. v, 189. Ford ed., ix, 137. (M., Sep. 1807.)

8918. WAR, Preparations for.—Considering war as one of the alternatives which Congress may adopt on the failure of proper satisfaction for the outrages committed on us by Great Britain, I have thought it my duty to put into train every preparation for that which the executive powers * * * will admit of.—To John Nicholas. v, 168. (M., 1807.)

8919. WAR, Prevention of.—The power of making war often prevents it, and in our case would give efficacy to our desire of peace.—To General Washington. ii, 533. Ford ed., v, 57. (P., 1788.)

* Not to convene Congress in special session would be, in Jefferson's opinion, to "prevent" deliberation.—Editor.

† This extract, Jefferson explained to Clinton, defined one of the principles that controlled his action in the issuance of his proclamation after the attack on the Chesapeake.—Editor.

8920. WAR, Principles and.—I do not believe war the most certain means of enforcing principles. Those peaceable coercions which are in the power of every nation, if undertaken in concert and in time of peace, are more likely to produce the desired effect.—To Robert R. Livingston. iv, 411. Ford ed., viii, 91. (M., 1801.)

— WAR, Prisoners of.—See 8966.

8921. WAR, Punishment by.—War is as much a punishment to the punisher as to the sufferer.—To Tench Coxe. iv, 105. Ford ed., vi, 508. (M., May 1794.)

8922. WAR, Quixotic.—War against Bedlam would be just as rational as against Europe, in its present condition of total demoralization. When peace becomes more losing than war, we may prefer the latter on principles of pecuniary calculation. But for us to attempt, by war, to reform all Europe, and bring them back to principles of morality, and a respect for the equal rights of nations, would show us to be only maniacs of another character. We should, indeed, have the merit of the good intentions as well as of the folly of the hero of La Mancha.—To William Wirt. v, 595. Ford ed., ix, 319. (M., May 1811.)

8923. WAR, Readiness for.—Whatever enables us to go to war, secures our peace.—To James Monroe. Ford ed., v, 198. (N.Y., 1790.)

8924. WAR, Reason and.—The large strides of late taken by the legislature of Great Britain towards establishing over these Colonies their absolute rule, and the hardiness of the present attempt to effect by force of arms what by law or right they could never effect, render it necessary for us also to change the ground of opposition, and to close with their last appeal from reason to arms.—Declaration on Taking up Arms. Ford ed., i, 462. (July 1775.)

8925. WAR, Redress of wrongs by.—The answer to the question: "Is it common for a nation to obtain a redress of wrongs by war"? you will, of course, draw from history. In the meantime, reason will answer it on grounds of probability, that where the wrong has been done by a weaker nation, the stronger one has generally been able to enforce redress; but where by a stronger nation, redress by war has been neither obtained nor expected by the weaker. On the contrary, the loss has been increased by the expenses of the war in blood and treasure. Yet it may have obtained another object equally securing itself from future wrong. It may have retaliated on the aggressor losses of blood and treasure far beyond the value to him of the wrong he has committed, and thus have made the advantage of that too dear a purchase to leave him in a disposition to renew the wrong in future.—To Rev. Mr. Worcester. vi, 539. (M., 1816.)

8926. WAR, Resort to.—The lamentable resource of war is not authorized for evils of imagination, but for those actual injuries only, which would be more destructive of our well-being than war itself.—REPLY TO ADDRESS. iv, 388. (W., 1801.)

8927. WAR, Retaliation in.—England may burn New York by her ships and congreve rockets, in which case we must burn the city of London by hired incendiaries, of which her starving manufacturers will furnish abundance. A people in such desperation as to demand of their government *aut panem, aut furcam,* either bread or the gallows, will not reject the same alternative when offered by a foreign hand. Hunger will make them brave every risk for bread.—To GENERAL KOSCIUSKO. vi, 68. FORD ED., ix, 362. (M., June 1812.)

8928. WAR, Revolutionary.—The circumstances of our [Revolutionary] war were without example. Excluded from all commerce, even with neutral nations, without arms, money or the means of getting them abroad, we were obliged to avail ourselves of such resources as we found at home. Great Britain, too, did not consider it as an ordinary war, but a rebellion; she did not conduct it according to the rules of war, established by the law of nations, but according to her acts of parliament, made from time to time, to suit circumstances. She would not admit our title even to the *strict rights* of ordinary war. —To GEORGE HAMMOND. iii, 369. FORD ED., vi, 16. (Pa., May 1792.) See REVOLUTION (AMERICAN).

8929. WAR, Secretaryship of.—I much regretted your acceptance of the War Department. Not that I know a person who I think would better conduct it. But conduct it ever so wisely, it will be a sacrifice of yourself. Were an angel from heaven to undertake that office, all our miscarriages would be ascribed to him. Raw troops, no troops, insubordinate militia, want of arms, want of money, want of provisions all will be charged to want of management in you. * * * Not that I have seen the least disposition to censure you. On the contrary, your conduct on the attack of Washington has met the praises of every one, and your plan for regulars and militia, their approbation. But no campaign is as yet opened. No generals have yet an interest in shifting their own incompetence on you, no army agents their rogueries.—To JAMES MONROE. vi, 410. FORD ED., ix, 498. (M., 1815.)

8930. WAR, Security against.—The justest dispositions possible in ourselves, will not secure us against war. It would be necessary that all other nations were just also. Justice, indeed, on our part, will save us from those wars which would have been produced by a contrary disposition. But how can we prevent those produced by the wrongs of other nations? By putting ourselves in a position to punish them. Weakness provokes insult and injury, while a condition to punish often prevents them. This reasoning leads to the necessity of some naval force; that being the

only weapon by which we can reach an enemy. —To JOHN JAY. i, 404. FORD ED., iv, 89. (P., 1785.)

8931. WAR, Taxation and.—War requires every resource of taxation and credit. —To GENERAL WASHINGTON. ii, 533. FORD ED., v, 57. (P., 1788.)

8932. WAR, Taxation for.—Sound principles will not justify our taxing the industry of our fellow citizens to accumulate treasure for wars to happen we know not when, and which might not perhaps happen but from the temptations offered by that treasure.— FIRST ANNUAL MESSAGE. viii, 9. FORD ED., viii, 119. (1801.)

8933. WAR, Unfeared.—We love and we value peace; we know its blessings from experience. We abhor the follies of war, and are not untried in its distresses and calamities. Unmeddling with the affairs of other nations, we had hoped that our distance and our dispositions would have left us free, in the example and indulgence of peace with all the world. We had, with sincere and particular dispositions, courted and cultivated the friendship of Spain. We have made to it great sacrifices of time and interest, and were disposed to believe she would see her interests also in a perfect coalition and good understanding with us. Cherishing still the same sentiments, we have chosen, in the present instance, to ascribe the intimations in this letter [of the Spanish Commissioners] to the particular character of the writers, displayed in the peculiarity of the style of their communications, and therefore, we have removed the cause from them to their sovereign, in whose justice and love of peace we have confidence. If we are disappointed in this appeal, if we are to be forced into a contrary order of things, our mind is made up. We shall meet it with firmness. The necessity of our position will supersede all appeal to calculation now, as it has done heretofore. We confide in our strength, without boasting of it, we respect that of others without fearing it. If we cannot otherwise prevail on the Creeks to discontinue their depredations, we will attack them in force. If Spain chooses to consider our defence against savage butchery as a cause of war to her, we must meet her also in war, with regret, but without fear; and we shall be happier to the last moment, to repair with her to the tribunal of peace and reason. The President charges you to communicate the contents of this letter to the Court at Madrid, with all the temperance and delicacy which the dignity and character of that Court render proper; but with all the firmness and self-respect which befit a nation conscious of its rectitude, and settled in its purpose.—To CARMICHAEL AND SHORT. iv, 16. FORD ED., vi, 337. (Pa., June 1793.)

8934. ———— ————. Should the lawless violences of the belligerent powers render it necessary to return their hostilities, no nation has less to fear from a foreign enemy.— R. TO A. VIRGINIA REPUBLICANS. viii, 168. (1809.)

8935. WAR, Unity in.—It is our duty still to endeavor to avoid war; but if it shall actually take place, no matter by whom brought on, we must defend ourselves. If our house be on fire, without inquiring whether it was fired from within or without, we must try to extinguish it. In that, I have no doubt, we shall act as one man.—To JAMES LEWIS, JR. iv, 241. FORD ED., vii, 250. (Pa., May 1798.)

8936. ————. If we are forced into war [with France], we must give up political differences of opinion, and unite as one man to defend our country. But whether at the close of such a war, we should be as free as we are now, God knows.—To GEN. KOSCIUSKO. iv, 295. (Pa., 1799.)

8937. WAR, Unprepared for.—We are now at the close of our second campaign with England. During the first we suffered several checks, from the want of capable and tried officers; all the higher ones of the Revolution having died off during an interval of thirty years of peace. But this second campaign has been more successful, having given us all the Lakes and country of Upper Canada, except the single post of Kingston, at its lower extremity.—To DON V. TORONDA CORUNA. vi, 275. (M., Dec. 1813.)

8938. WAR, Unprofitable.—The most successful war seldom pays for its losses.—To EDMUND RANDOLPH. i, 435. (P., 1785.)

8939. WAR, Weakness provokes.—It should ever be held in mind that insult and war are the consequences of a want of respectability in the national character.—To JAMES MADISON. i, 531. FORD ED., iv, 192. (P., 1786.) See ARMY, GENERALS and REVOLUTION.

8940. WARDS, Advantages of.—My partiality for the division of counties into wards is not founded in views of education solely, but infinitely more as the means of a better administration of our government, and the eternal preservation of its republican principles. The example of this most admirable of all human contrivances in government, is to be seen in our Eastern States; and its powerful effect in the order and economy of their internal affairs, and the momentum it gives them as a nation, is the single circumstance which distinguishes them so remarkably from every other national association.—To GOVERNOR NICHOLAS. vi, 566. (M., 1816.)

8941. WARDS, Good government and.—I have long contemplated a division of our own State into hundreds or wards, as the most fundamental measure for securing good government, and for instilling the principles and exercise of good government into every fibre of every member of our commonweal.h.—To JOSEPH C. CABELL. vi, 301. (M., 1814.)

8942. WARDS, Primary schools and.—One of the principal objects in my endeavors to get our counties divided into wards, is the establishment of a primary school in each [of them].—To JOHN TAYLOR. vii, 17. FORD ED., x, 51. (M., 1816.)

8943. WARDS, Size of.—I hope [the convention to amend the Virginia Constitution] will adopt the subdivision of our counties into wards. The former may be estimated at an average of twenty-four miles square; the latter should be about six miles square each, and would answer to the hundreds of your Saxon Alfred. * * * The wit of men cannot devise a more solid basis for a free, durable, and well-administered republic.—To JOHN CARTWRIGHT. vii, 357. (M., 1824.)

8944. WARDS, Vital principle.—These wards, called townships in New England, are the vital principles of their governments, and have proved themselves the wisest invention ever devised by the wit of man for the perfect exercise of self-government, and for its preservation.—To SAMUEL KERCHIVAL. vii, 13. FORD ED., x, 41. (M., 1816.) See COUNTIES.

8945. WAR OF 1812, Acrimonious.—The exasperation produced * * * by the late war * * * is great with you [Great Britain], as I judge from your newspapers; and greater with us, as I see myself. The reason lies in the different degrees in which the war has acted on us. To your people it has been a matter of distant history only, a mere war in the carnatic; with us it has reached the bosom of every man, woman and child. The maritime ports have felt it in the conflagration of their houses and towns, and desolation of their farms; the borderers in the massacres and scalpings of their husbands, wives and children; and the middle parts in their personal labors and losses in defence of both frontiers, and the revolting scenes they have there witnessed. It is not wonderful, then, if their irritations are extreme. Yet time and prudence on the part of the two governments may get over these.—To SIR JOHN SINCLAIR. vii, 23. (M., 1816.)

8946. WAR OF 1812, Benefits of.—The British war has left us in debt; but that is a cheap price for the good it has done us. The establishment of the necessary manufactures among ourselves, the proof that our government is solid and can stand the shock of war, and is superior even to civil schism, are precious facts for us; and of these the strongest proofs were furnished, when, with four Eastern States tied to us, as dead to living bodies, all doubt was removed as to the achievements of the war, had it continued. But its best effect has been the complete suppression of party. The federalists who were truly American, and their great mass was so, have separated from their brethren who were mere Anglomen, and are received with cordiality into the republican ranks.—To MARQUIS DE LAFAYETTE. vii, 66. FORD ED., x, 83. (M., 1817.)

8947. ————. The war [of 1812] has done us * * * the further [good] of assuring the world, that although attached to peace from a sense of its blessings, we will meet war when it is made necessary.—To MARQUIS DE LAFAYETTE. vii, 67. FORD ED., x, 84. (M., 1817.)

8948. WAR OF 1812, British expectations in.—Earl Bathhurst [in his speech in Parliament] shuffles together chaotic ideas merely to darken and cover the views of the ministers in protracting the war; the truth being, that they expected to give us an exemplary scourging, to separate us from the States east of the Hudson, take for their Indian allies those west of the Ohio, placing three hundred thousand American citizens under the government of the savages, and to leave the residuum a powerless enemy, if not submissive subjects. I cannot conceive what is the use of your Bedlam when such men are out of it. And yet that such were their views we have in evidence, under the hand of their Secretary of State in Henry's case, and of their Commissioners at Ghent.—To MR. MAURY. vi, 471. (M., June 1815.)

8949. WAR OF 1812, Causes of.—It is incomprehensible to me that the Marquis of Wellesley * * * [should] say that "the aggression which led to the war, was from the United States, not from England". Is there a person in the world who, knowing the circumstances, thinks this? The acts which produced the war were, 1st, the impressment of our citizens by their ships of war, and, 2d, the Orders of Council forbidding our vessels to trade with any country but England, without going to England to obtain a special license. On the first subject the British minister declared to our Charge, Mr. Russel, that this practice of their ships of war would not be discontinued, and that no admissible arrangement could be proposed; and as to the second, the Prince Regent, by his proclamation of April 21st, 1812, declared in effect solemnly that he would not revoke the Orders of Council *as to us*, on the ground that Bonaparte had revoked his decrees *as to us:* that, on the contrary, we should continue under them until Bonaparte should revoke *as to all the world*. These categorical and definite answers put an end to negotiation, and were a declaration of a continuance of the war in which they had already taken from us one thousand ships and six thousand seamen. We determined then to defend ourselves, and to oppose further hostilities by war on our side also. Now, had we taken one thousand British ships and six thousand of her seamen without any declaration of war, would the Marquis of Wellesley have considered a declaration of war by Great Britain as an aggression on her part? They say we denied their maritime rights. We never denied a single one. It was their taking our citizens, native as well as naturalized, for which we went into war, and because they forbade us to trade with any nation without entering and paying duties in their ports on both the outward and inward cargo. Thus, to carry a cargo of cotton from Savannah to St. Mary's, and take returns in fruits, for example, our vessel was to go to England, enter and pay a duty on her cottons there, return to St. Mary's, then go back to England to enter and pay a duty on her fruits, and then return to Savannah, after crossing the Atlantic four times, and paying tributes on both cargoes to England, instead of the direct passage of a few hours. And the taking ships for not doing this, the Marquis says, is no aggression.—To MR. MAURY. vi, 470. (M., June 1815.)

8950. WAR OF 1812, Conquest and.—The war, undertaken, on both sides, to settle the questions of impressment, and the Orders of Council, now that these are done away by events, is declared by Great Britain to have changed its object, and to have become a war of conquest, to be waged until she conquers from us our fisheries, the province of Maine, the Lakes, States and territories north of the Ohio, and the navigation of the Mississippi; in other words, till she reduces us to unconditional submission. On our part, then, we ought to propose, as a counterchange of object, the establishment of the meridian of the mouth of the

Sorel northwardly, as the western boundary of all her possessions.—To PRESIDENT MADISON. vi, 391. FORD ED., ix, 489. (M., Oct. 1814.)

8951. WAR OF 1812, Declaration of.—War was declared on June 18th, thirty years after the signature of our peace in 1782. * * * It is not ten years since Great Britain began a series of insults and injuries which would have been met with war in the threshold by any European power. This course has been unremittingly followed up by increased wrongs, with glimmerings, indeed, of peaceable redress, just sufficient to keep us in quiet, till she has had the impudence at length to extinguish even these glimmerings by open avowal. This would not have been borne so long, but that France has kept pace with England in iniquity of principle, although not in the power of inflicting wrongs on us. The difficulty of selecting a foe between them has spared us many years of war, and enabled us to enter into it with less debt, more strength and preparation.—To GENERAL KOSCIUSKO. vi, 67. FORD ED., ix, 361. (M., June 1812.)

8952. ———— ————. [The declaration of war was] accompanied with immediate offers of peace on simply doing us justice. These offers were made through Russel, through Admiral Warren, through the government of Canada, and the mediation proposed by her best friend Alexander, was accepted without hesitation.—To DR. GEORGE LOGAN. vi, 216. FORD ED., ix, 422. (M., Oct. 1813.)

8953. WAR OF 1812, Grounds of.—The essential grounds of the war were, first, the Orders of Council; and, secondly, the impressment of our citizens (for I put out of sight from the love of peace the multiplied insults on our government and aggressions on our commerce, with which our pouch, like the Indian's, had long been filled to the mouth). What immediately produced the declaration was, 1st, the proclamation of the Prince Regent that he would never repeal the Orders of Council as to us, until Bonaparte should have revoked his decrees as to all other nations as well as ours; and 2d, the declaration of his minister to ours that no arrangement whatever could be devised, admissible in lieu of impressment. It was certainly a misfortune that *they* did not know themselves at the date of this silly and insolent proclamation, that within one month they would repeal the Orders, and that *we*, at the date of our declaration, could not know of the repeal which was then going on one thousand leagues distant. Their determinations, as declared by themselves, could alone guide us, and they shut the door on all further negotiation, throwing down to us the gauntlet of war or submission as the only alternatives. We cannot blame the government for choosing that of war, because certainly the great majority of the nation thought it ought to be chosen.—To WILLIAM SHORT. vi, 398. (M., Nov. 1814.)

8954. WAR OF 1812, Hartford convention and.—The negotiators at Ghent are agreed now on every point save one, the demand and cession of a portion of Maine. This, it is well known, cannot be yielded by us, nor deemed by them an object for continuing a war so expensive, so injurious to their commerce and manufactures, and so odious in the eyes of the world. But it is a thread to hold by until they can hear the result, not of the Congress of Vienna, but of Hartford. When they shall know as they will know, that nothing will be done there, they will let go their hold, and complete the peace of the world, by agreeing to the *status ante bellum*. Indemnity for the past, and security for the future, which was our motto at the beginning of this war, must be adjourned to another, when, disarmed and bankrupt, our enemy shall be less able to insult and plunder the world with impunity.—To M. CORREA. vi, 407. (M., 1814.) See HARTFORD CONVENTION.

8955. WAR OF 1812, Justifiable.— [Great Britain threw] down to us the gauntlet of war or submission as the only alternatives. We cannot blame the government for choosing that of war, because certainly the great majority of the nation thought it ought to be chosen, not that they were to gain by it in dollars and cents; all men know that war is a losing game to both parties. But they know, also, that if they did not resist encroachment at some point, all will be taken from them, and that more would then be lost even in dollars and cents by submission than resistance. It is the case of giving a part to save the whole, a limb to save life. It is the melancholy law of human societies to be compelled sometimes to choose a great evil in order to ward off a greater; to deter their neighbors from rapine by making it cost them more than honest gains. * * * Had we adopted the other alternative of submission, no mortal can tell what the cost would have been. I consider the war then as entirely justifiable on our part, although I am still sensible it is a deplorable misfortune to us.—To WILLIAM SHORT. vi, 399. (M., Nov. 1814.)

8956. WAR OF 1812, Lessons of.—I consider the war as made * * * for just causes, and its dispensation as providential, inasmuch as it has exercised our patriotism and submission to order, has planted and invigorated among us arts of urgent necessity, has manifested the strong and the weak parts of our republican institutions, and the excellence of a representative democracy compared with the misrule of kings, has rallied the opinions of mankind to the natural rights of expatriation, and of a common property in the ocean, and raised us to that grade in the scale of nations which the bravery and liberality of our citizen soldiers, by land and by sea, the wisdom of our institutions and their observance of justice, entitled us to in the eyes of the world.—To MR. WENDOVER. vi, 444. (M., 1815.)

8957. WAR OF 1812, Markets and.— To keep the war popular, we must keep open the markets. As long as good prices can be had, the people will support the war cheerfully.—To JAMES RONALDSON. vi, 93. FORD ED., ix, 372. (M., Jan. 1813.)

8958. WAR OF 1812, Misrepresented.— England has misrepresented to all Europe this ground of the war [of 1812]. She has called it a new pretension, set up since the repeal of her Orders of Council. She knows there has never been a moment of suspension of our reclamation against it, from General Washington's time inclusive, to the present day; and that it is distinctly stated in our declaration of war, as one of its principal causes.—To MADAME DE STAEL. vi, 118. (M., May 1813.)

8959. ——— ———. She has pretended we have entered into the war to establish the principle of " free bottoms, free goods ", or to protect her seamen against her own rights over them. We contend for neither of these.— To MADAME DE STAEL. vi, 118. (May 1813.)

8960. ——— ———. She pretends we are partial to France; that we have observed a

fraudulent and unfaithful neutrality between her and her enemy. She knows this to be false, and that if there has been any inequality in our proceedings towards the belligerents, it has been in her favor. Her ministers are in possession of full proofs of this. Our accepting at once, and sincerely, the mediation of the virtuous Alexander, their greatest friend, and the most aggravated enemy of Bonaparte, sufficiently proves whether we have partialities on the side of her enemy. I sincerely pray that this mediation may produce a just peace.—To MADAME DE STAEL. vi, 119. (May 1813.)

8961. WAR OF 1812, Prolongation of. —As soon as we heard of her partial repeal of her Orders of Council, we offered instantly to suspend hostilities by an armistice, if she would suspend her impressments, and meet us in arrangements for securing our citizens against them. She refused to do it, because impracticable by any arrangement, as she pretends; but, in truth, because a body of sixty to eighty thousand of the finest seamen in the world, which we possess, is too great a resource for manning her exaggerated navy, to be relinquished, as long as she can keep it open. Peace is in her hand, whenever she will renounce the practice of aggression on the persons of our citizens. If she thinks it worth eternal war, eternal war we must have. She alleges that the sameness of language, of manners, of appearance, renders it impossible to distinguish us from her subjects. But because we speak English, and look like them, are we to be punished? Are free and independent men to be submitted to their bondage?—To MADAME DE STAEL. vi, 118. (May 1813.)

8962. WAR OF 1812, Provocation.— Nothing but the total prostration of all moral principle could have produced the enormities which have forced us at length into the war. On one hand, a ruthless tyrant, drenching Europe in blood to obtain through future time the character of the destroyer of mankind; on the other, a nation of buccaneers, urged by sordid avarice, and embarked in the flagitious enterprise of seizing to itself the maritime resources and rights of all other nations, have left no means of peace to reason and moderation. And yet there are beings among us who think we ought still to have acquiesced. As if while full war was waging on one side, we could lose by making some reprisal on the other.—To HENRY MIDDLETON. vi, 91. (M., Jan. 1813.)

8963. WAR OF 1812, Reparation and. —The sword once drawn, full justice must be done. " Indemnification for the past and security for the future " should be painted on our banners. For one thousand ships taken, and six thousand seamen impressed, give us Canada for indemnification, and the only security they can give us against their Henrys, and the savages, and agree that the American flag shall protect the persons of those sailing under it, both parties exchanging engagements that neither will receive the seamen of the other on board their vessels. This done, I should be for peace with England, and then war with France. One at a time is enough, and in fighting the one we need the harbors of the other for our prizes.—To MR. WRIGHT. vi, 78. (M., Aug. 1812.)

8964. WAR OF 1812, Victory and defeat.—Perhaps this Russian mediation may cut short the history of the present war, and leave to us the laurels of the sea, while our enemies are bedecked with those of the land.

This would be the reverse of what has been expected, and perhaps of what was to be wished.—To WILLIAM DUANE. vi, 110. (M., April 1813.)

8965. ———— ————. I rejoice exceedingly that our war with England was single-handed. In that of the Revolution, we had France, Spain, and Holland on our side, and the credit of its success was given to them. On the late occasion, unprepared, and unexpecting war, we were compelled to declare it, and to receive the attack of England, just issuing from a general war, fully armed, and freed from all other enemies, and have not only made her sick of it, but glad to prevent by peace, the capture of her adjacent possessions, which one or two campaigns more would infallibly have made ours. She has found that we can do her more injury than any other enemy on earth, and henceforward will better estimate the value of our peace.—To THOMAS LEIPER. vi. 466. FORD ED., ix, 521. (M. 1815.) See IMPRESSMENT.

8966. WAR (Prisoners of), Comfort of.—Is an enemy so execrable, that, though in captivity, his wishes and comforts are to be disregarded and even crossed? I think not. It is for the benefit of mankind to mitigate the horrors of war as much as possible. The practice, therefore, of modern nations, of treating captive enemies with politeness and generosity, is not only delightful in contemplation, but really interesting to all the world, friends, foes and neutrals.—To GOVERNOR HENRY. i, 218. FORD ED., ii, 176. (Alb., 1779.)

8967. WAR (Prisoners of), Exchange of.—I am sorry to learn that the negotiations for the exchange of prisoners have proved abortive, as well from a desire to see the necessary distresses of war alleviated in every possible instance, as that I am sensible how far yourself and family are interested in it. Against this, however, is to be weighed the possibility that we may again have a pleasure we should otherwise, perhaps, never have had—that of seeing you again.*—To GENERAL DE RIEDESEL. i, 241. FORD ED., ii, 303. (R., 1780.)

8968. WAR (Prisoners of), Health of.—The health [of the British prisoners] is also of importance. I would not endeavor to show that their lives are valuable to us, because it would suppose a possibility, that humanity was kicked out of doors in America, and interest only 'attended to.—To GOVERNOR HENRY. i, 218. FORD ED., ii, 175. (Alb., 1779.)

8969. WAR (Prisoners of), Relief of.—Be assured there is nothing consistent with the honor of your country which we shall not, at all times, be ready to do for the relief of yourself and companions in captivity. We know that ardent spirit and hatred for tyranny, which brought you into your present situation, will enable you to bear up against it with the firmness which has distinguished you as a soldier, and to look forward with pleasure to the day when events shall take place against which the wounded spirits of your enemies will find no comfort, even from reflections on the most refined of the cruelties with which they have

* General Riedesel, commander of the Hessian troops, captured at Saratoga, was among the prisoners sent to Albemarle, in 1770, and, with many of his fellow officers, was a frequent guest at Monticello. They all expressed their deep obligations to Jefferson for the courtesies extended to them and the efforts made by him to lighten the hardships of their captivity.—EDITOR.

glutted themselves.*—To COLONEL GEORGE MATTHEWS. i, 235. FORD ED., ii, 264. (Wg., 1779.)

8970. WAR (Prisoners of), Treatment of.—We think ourselves justified in Governor Hamilton's strict confinement on the general principle of national retaliation. * * * Governor Hamilton's conduct has been such as to call for exemplary punishment on him personally. In saying this I have not so much in view his particular cruelties to our citizens, prisoners with him, * * * as the general nature of the service he undertook at Detroit, and the extensive exercise of cruelties which it involved. Those who act together in war are answerable for each other. No distinction can be made between principal and ally by those against whom the war is waged. He who employs another to do a deed makes the deed his own. If he calls in the hand of the assassin or murderer, himself becomes the assassin or murderer. The known rule of warfare of the Indian savages is an indiscriminate butchery of men, women and children. These savages, under this well known character, are employed by the British nation as allies in the war against the Americans. Governor Hamilton undertakes to be the conductor of the war. In the execution of that undertaking, he associates small parties of the whites under his immediate command with large parties of the savages, and sends them to act, sometimes jointly, and sometimes separately, not against our forts or armies in the field, but the farming settlements on our frontiers. Governor Hamilton is himself the butcher of men, women and children. I will not say to what length the fair rules of war would extend the right of punishment against him; but I am sure that confinement under its strictest circumstances, for Indian devastation and massacre must be deemed lenity.—To SIR GUY CARLETON. FORD ED., ii, 249. (1779.)

8971. WASHINGTON (City), Appropriations.—We cannot suppose Congress intended to tax the people of the United States at large, for all the avenues in Washington and roads in Columbia.—To ROBERT BRENT. v, 50. FORD ED., ix, 33. (W., 1807.)

8972. WASHINGTON (City), Attachment to.—It is with sincere regret that I part with the society in which I have lived here. It has been the source of much happiness to me during my residence at the seat of government, and I owe it much for its kind dispositions. I shall ever feel a high interest in the prosperity of the city, and an affectionate attachment to its inhabitants.—R. TO A. CITIZENS OF WASHINGTON. viii, 158. (March 4, 1809.)

8973. WASHINGTON (City), British capture of.—In the late events at Washington I have felt so much for you that I cannot withhold the expression of my sympathies. For although every reasonable man must be sensible that all you can do is to order, that execution must depend on others, and failures be imputed to them alone; yet I know that when such failures happen they afflict even those who have done everything they could to prevent them. Had General Washington himself been now at the head of our affairs, the same event would probably have happened. We all remember the disgraces which befell us in his time in a trifling war with one or two petty tribes of Indians, in which two armies

* Colonel Matthews was an American officer in the hands of the British. Jefferson was Governor of Virginia.—EDITOR.

were cut off by not half their numbers. Every one knew, and I personally knew, because I was then of his council, that no blame was imputable to him, and that his officers alone were the cause of the disasters. They must now do the same justice.—To PRESIDENT MADISON. vi, 385. (M., Sep. 1814.)

8974. —— ——. [The incendiarism at Washington] enlists the feelings of the world on our side; and the advantage of public opinion is like that of the weather-gauge in a naval action. In Europe, the transient possession of our capital can be no disgrace. Nearly every capital there was in possession of its enemy; some often and long. But diabolical as they paint that enemy, he burned neither public edifices nor private dwellings. It was reserved for England to show that Bonaparte, in atrocity, was an infant to their ministers and their generals. They are taking his place in the eyes of Europe, and have turned into our channel all its good will. This will be worth the million of dollars their conflagration will cost us.—To JAMES MONROE. vi, 408. FORD ED., ix, 496. (M., Jan. 1815.)

8975. —— ——. The embarrassments at Washington in August last, I expected would be great in any state of things; but they proved greater than expected. I never doubted that the plans of the President were wise and sufficient. Their failure we all impute, 1, to the insubordinate temper of Armstrong; and 2, to the indecision of Winder. However, it ends well. It mortifies ourselves and so may check, perhaps, the silly boasting spirit of our newspapers.—To JAMES MONROE. vi, 408. FORD ED., ix, 496. (M., Jan. 1815.)

8976. —— ——. I set down the *coup de main* at Washington as more disgraceful to England than to us.—To W. H. CRAWFORD. vi, 418. FORD ED., ix, 502. (M., 1815.)

8977. —— ——. The transaction has helped rather than hurt us, by arousing the general indignation of our country, and by marking to the world of Europe, the Vandalism and brutal character of the English government. It has merely served to immortalize their infamy.—To MARQUIS LAFAYETTE. vi, 424. FORD ED., ix, 508. (M., 1815.) See CAPITOL.

8978. WASHINGTON (City), Building line.—I doubt much whether the obligation to build the houses at a given distance from the street, contributes to its beauty. It produces a disgusting monotony; all persons make this complaint against Philadelphia. The contrary practice varies the appearance, and is much more convenient to the inhabitants.—FEDERAL CAPITAL OPINION. vii, 513. FORD ED., v, 253. (1790.)

8979. WASHINGTON (City), Foundation of.—As to the future residence of Congress, I can give you an account only from the information of others, all this having taken place before my arrival [in Philadelphia]. Congress, it seems, thought it best to generalize their first determination by putting questions on the several rivers on which it had been proposed that they should fix their residence. The Hudson river, the Delaware, and the Potomac, were accordingly offered to the vote. The first obtained scarcely any votes; the Delaware obtained seven. This, of course, put the Potomac out of the way; and the Delaware being once determined on, there was scarcely any difference of opinion as to the particular spot. The Falls met the approbation of all the States pres-

ent, except Pennsylvania, which was for Germantown, and Delaware, which was for Wilmington. As to the latter, it appeared that she had been induced to vote for the Delaware on the single idea of getting Congress to Wilmington, and that being disappointed in this, they would not wish them on that river at all, but would prefer Georgetown to any other place. This being discovered, the Southern delegates, at a subsequent day, brought on a reconsideration of the question, and obtained a determination that Congress should sit one-half of their time at Georgetown, and that till all accommodations should be provided there, Annapolis should be substituted in its place. This was considered by some as a compromise; by others as only unhinging the first determination and leaving the whole matter open for discussion at some future day. It was in fact a rally, of making a drawn battle of what had at first appeared to be decided against us.—To GOVERNOR BENJAMIN HARRISON. FORD ED., iii, 340. (Pa., Nov. 1783.)

8980. —— ——. I take the following to be the disposition of the several States: The four Eastern States are for any place in preference to Philadelphia, the more northern it is, however, the more agreeable to them. New York and New Hampshire are for the Falls of Delaware. Pennsylvania is for Germantown first, and next for the Falls of Delaware. It is to be noted that Philadelphia had no attention as a permanent seat. Delaware is for Wilmington; but for Georgetown in preference to the Falls of Delaware, or any other situation which [may] attract the trade of their river. Maryland is for Annapolis, and the smallest hope for this will sacrifice a certainty for Georgetown. Virginia, every place southward of Potomac being disregarded by the States as every place north of the Delaware, saw it would be useless to consider her interests as to more southern positions. The Falls of Potomac will probably, therefore, unite the wishes of the whole State. If this fails, Annapolis and the Falls of Delaware are then the candidates. Were the convenience of the delegates alone to be considered, or the general convenience to government in their transaction of business with Congress, Annapolis would be preferred without hesitation. But those who respect commercial advantages more than the convenience of individuals, will probably think that every position on the bay of Chesapeake, or any of its waters, is to be dreaded by Virginia, as it may attract the trade of that bay and make us, with respect to Maryland, what Delaware State is to Pennsylvania. Considering the residence of Congress, therefore, as it may influence trade, if we cannot obtain it on the Potomac, it seems to be our interest to bring it past all the waters of the Chesapeake bay. The three Southern States are for the most southern situation. It should be noted that New Hampshire and Georgia were absent on the decisions of these questions, but considering their interests would be directly opposite, it was thought their joint presence or absence would not change the result. From the preceding state of the views of the several members of our Union, your Excellency will be enabled to judge what will be the probable determination on any future revision of the present plan. The establishment of new States will be friendly or adverse to Georgetown according to their situation. If a State be first laid off on the Lakes, it will add a vote to the northern scale; if on the Ohio, it will add one to the southern.—To GOVERNOR BENJAMIN HARRISON. FORD ED., iii, 342. (Pa., Nov. 1783.)

8981. —— ——. The General Assembly shall have power * * * to cede to Congress one hundred square miles of territory in any other part of this State, exempted from the jurisdiction and government of this State, so long as Congress shall hold their sessions therein, or in any territory adjacent thereto, which may be tendered to them by any other State.—PROPOSED CONSTITUTION FOR VIRGINIA. viii, 446. FORD ED., iii, 325. (1783.)

8982. —— ——. Georgetown languishes. The smile is hardly covered now when the federal towns are spoken of. I fear that our chance is at this time desperate. Our object, therefore, must be, if we fail in an effort to remove to Georgetown, to endeavor then to get to some place off the waters of the Chesapeake where we may be ensured against Congress considering themselves as fixed.—To JAMES MADISON. FORD ED., iii, 400. (A., Feb. 1784.)

8983. —— ——. The remoteness of the Falls of Potomac from the influence of any overgrown commercial city recommends [that place for the] permanent seat of Congress.—NOTES ON PERMANENT SEAT OF CONGRESS. FORD ED., iii, 458. (April 1784.)

8984. —— ——. Philadelphia. In favor of it. 1. Its unrivalled conveniency for transacting the public business, and accommodating Congress. 2. Its being the only place where all the public offices, particularly that of Finance could be kept under the inspection and control of, and proper intercourse with Congress. 3. Its conveniency for foreign ministers, to which, ceteris paribus, some regard would be expected. 4. The circumstances which produced a removal from Philadelphia; which rendered a return, as soon as the insult had been expiated, expedient for supporting in the eyes of foreign nations the appearance of internal harmony, and preventing an appearance of resentment in Congress against the State of Pennsylvania, or city of Philadelphia, an appearance which was very much strengthened by some of their proceedings at Princeton—particularly by an unneccessary and irregular declaration not to return to Philadelphia. In addition to these overt reasons, it was concluded by sundry of the members, who were most anxious to fix Congress permanently at the Falls of the Potomac, that a temporary residence in Philadelphia would be most likely to prepare a sufficient number of votes for that place in preference to the Falls of Delaware, and to produce a reconsideration of the vote in favor of the latter. Against Philadelphia were alleged. 1. The difficulty and uncertainty of getting away from it at the time limited. 2. The influence of a large commercial and wealthy city on the public councils. In addition to these objections, the hatred against Mr. Morris, and the hope of accelerating his final resignation were latent motives with some, as perhaps envy of the prosperity of Philadelphia, and dislike of the support of Pennsylvania to obnoxious recommendations of Congress were with others.—NOTES ON PERMANENT SEAT OF CONGRESS. FORD ED., iii, 459. (April 1784.)

8985. —— ——. I like your removal to New York, and hope Congress will continue there, and never execute the idea of building their Federal town. Before it could be finished, a change in members of Congress, or the admission of new States, would remove them somewhere else. It is evident that when a sufficient number of the Western States come in, they will remove it to Georgetown. In the meantime, it is our interest that it should re-

main where it is, and give no new pretensions to any other place.—To JAMES MONROE. i, 347. FORD ED., iv, 52. (P., 1785.)

8986. —— ——. Philadelphia was first proposed, and had six and a half votes. The half vote was Delaware, one of whose members wanted to take a vote on Wilmington. Then Baltimore was proposed and carried, and afterwards rescinded, so that the matter stood open as ever on the 10th of August; but it was allowed the dispute lay only between New York and Philadelphia, and rather thought in favor of the last.—To WILLIAM SHORT. ii, 480. FORD ED., v, 49. (P., Sep. 1788.)

8987. —— ——. On the question of residence, the compromise proposed is to give it to Philadelphia for fifteen years, and then permanently to Georgetown by the same act. This is the best arrangement we have now any prospect of, and therefore the one to which all our wishes are at present pointed. If this does not take place, something much worse will; to wit, an unqualified assumption [of the State debts], and the permanent seat on the Delaware.—To T. M. RANDOLPH. FORD ED., v, 186. (N.Y., 1790.)

8988. WASHINGTON (City), Future of.—That the improvement of this city must proceed with sure and steady steps, follows from its many obvious advantages, and from the enterprising spirit of its inhabitants, which promises to render it the fairest seat of wealth and science.—R. TO A. CITIZENS OF WASHINGTON. viii, 158. (1809.)

8989. WASHINGTON (City), Houses.—In Paris it is forbidden to build a house beyond a given height, and it is admitted to be a good restriction. It keeps down the price of ground, keeps the houses low and convenient, and the streets light and airy. Fires are much more manageable where houses are low.—FEDERAL CAPITOL OPINION. vii, 513. FORD ED., v, 253. (1790.)

8990. —— ——. I cannot help again suggesting one regulation formerly suggested, to wit: To provide for the extinguishment of fires, and the openness and convenience of the town, by prohibiting houses of excessive height; and making it unlawful to build on any one's purchase any house with more than two floors between the common level of the earth and the eaves.—FEDERAL CAPITAL OPINION. vii, 561. (March 1791.)

8991. WASHINGTON (City), Lots.—The lots [should] be sold in breadths of fifty feet; their depths to extend to the diagonal of the square.—FEDERAL CAPITAL OPINION. vii, 513. FORD ED., v, 253. (1790.)

8992. WASHINGTON (City), Plans of.—I shall send you * * * two dozen plans of the city of Washington, which you are desired to display, not for sale, but for public inspection, wherever they may be most seen by those descriptions of people worthy and likely to be attracted to it, dividing the plans among the cities of London and Edinburgh chiefly, but sending them also to Glasgow, Bristol, and Dublin.—To THOMAS PINCKNEY. iii, 500. (Pa., 1792.)

8993. —— ——. I sent you * * * a dozen plans of the city of Washington in the Federal territory, hoping you would have them displayed to public view where they would be most seen by those descriptions of men worthy and likely to be attracted to it. Paris, Lyons, Rouen, and the seaport towns of Havre, Nantes, Bourdeaux and Marseilles would be proper places to send some of them.—To GOUVERNEUR MORRIS. iii, 523. FORD ED., vi, 201. (Pa., 1793.)

8994. WASHINGTON (City), Residence in.—On the subject of your location for the winter, it is impossible in my view of it, to doubt on the preference which should be given to this place. Under any circumstances it could not but be satisfactory to you to acquire an intimate knowledge of our political machine, not merely of its organization, but the individuals and characters composing it, their general mode of thinking, and of acting openly and secretly. Of all this you can learn no more at Philadelphia than of a diet of the empire. None but an eyewitness can really understand it, and it is quite as important to be known to them, and to obtain a certain degree of their confidence in your own right. In a government like ours, the standing of a man well with this portion of the public must weigh against a considerable difference of other qualifications. —To WILLIAM SHORT. v, 210. (W., Nov. 1807.)

8995. WASHINGTON (City), Streets.— I should propose the streets [of the Federal capital] to be at right angles, as in Philadelphia, and that no street be narrower than one hundred feet with footways of fifteen feet. Where a street is long and level, it might be one hundred and twenty feet wide. I should prefer squares of at least two hundred yards every way.— FEDERAL CAPITAL OPINION. vii, 512. FORD ED., v, 253. (1790.)

8996. WASHINGTON (George), Advice and.—His mind has been so long used to unlimited applause that it could not brook contradiction, or even advice offered unasked. To advice, when asked, he is very open.—To ARCHIBALD STUART. FORD ED., vii, 101. (M., Jan. 1797.)

8997. WASHINGTON (George), Attacks on.—The President is extremely affected by the attacks made and kept up on him in the public papers. I think he feels those things more than any person I ever yet met with. I am sincerely sorry to see them.—To JAMES MADISON. iii, 579. FORD ED., vi, 293. (June 1793.)

8998. ——— ———. [At a cabinet meeting] [Secretary] Knox in a foolish, incoherent sort of a speech, introduced the pasquinade lately printed, called the funeral of George Washington and James Wilson [Associate Justice of the Supreme Court]; King and Judge, &c., where the President was placed on a guillotine. The President was much inflamed; got into one of those passions when he cannot command himself: ran on much on the personal abuse which had been bestowed on him; defied any man on earth to produce one single act of his since he had been in the government, which was not done on the purest motives; that he had never repented but once the having slipped the moment of resigning his office, and that was every moment since, that *by God* he had rather be in his grave than in his present situation; that he had rather be on his farm than to be made *Emperor of the world*, and yet they were charging him with wanting to be a King. That that *rascal Freneau* sent him three of his papers every day, as if he thought he would become the distributor of his papers: that he could see in this, nothing but an impudent design to in-

sult him: he ended in this high tone.*—THE ANAS. ix, 164. FORD ED., i, 254. (Aug. 1793.)

8999. WASHINGTON (George), Ceremony and.—I remember an observation of yours, made when I first went to New York, that the satellites and sycophants that surrounded him [Washington] had wound up the ceremonials of the government to a pitch of stateliness which nothing but his personal character could have supported, and which no character after him could ever maintain. It appears now that even his will be insufficient to justify them in the appeal of the times to common sense as the arbiter of everything. Naked, he would have been sanctimoniously reverenced; but enveloped in the rags of royalty, they can hardly be torn off without laceration. It is the more unfortunate that this attack is planted on popular ground, on the love of the people to France and its cause, which is universal.—To JAMES MADISON. iii, 579. FORD ED., vi, 293. (June 1793.)

9000. WASHINGTON (George), Cincinnati and.—I have wished to see you standing on ground separated from it [the Society of the Cincinnati]; and that the character which will be handed to future ages at the head of our Revolution, may, in no instance, be compromitted in subordinate altercations.—To GENERAL WASHINGTON. i, 333. FORD ED., iii, 465. (1784.) See CINCINNATI SOCIETY.

9001. WASHINGTON (George), Confidence in.—Without pretensions to that high confidence you reposed in our first and greatest revolutionary character, whose preeminent services had entitled him to the first place in his country's love, and destined for him the fairest page in the volume of faithful history, I ask so much confidence only as may give firmness and effect to the legal administration of your affairs.—FIRST INAUGURAL ADDRESS. viii, 5. FORD ED., viii, 5. (1801.)

9002. WASHINGTON (George), Crown refused.—The alliance between the States under the old Articles of Confederation, for the purpose of joint defence against the aggressions of Great Britain, was found insufficient, as treaties of alliance generally are, to enforce compliance with their mutual stipulations; and these, once fulfilled, that bond was to expire of itself, and each State to become sovereign and independent in all things. Yet it could not but occur to every one, that these separate independencies, like the petty States of Greece, would be eternally at war with each other, and would become at length the mere partisans and satellites of the leading powers of Europe. All then must have looked to some further bond of union, which would insure internal peace, and a political system of our own, independent of that of Europe. Whether all should be consolidated into a single government, or each remain independent as to internal matters, and the whole form a single nation as to what was foreign only, and whether that national government should be a monarchy or a republic, would of course divide opinions according to the constitutions, the habits, and the circumstances of each individual. Some officers of the army, as it has always been said and believed (and Steuben and Knox have ever been named as the leading agents), trained to monarchy by military habits, are understood to have proposed to General Washington to decide this great question by the army before its disbandment, and

* Genet's case was under consideration at the meeting of the cabinet.—EDITOR.

to assume himself the crown, on the assurance of their support. The indignation with which he is said to have scouted this parricide proposition was equally worthy of his virtue and his wisdom.—THE ANAS. ix, 88. FORD ED., i, 157. (1818.)

9003. WASHINGTON (George), Errors of.—He errs as other men do, but errs with integrity.—To W. B. GILES. iv, 125. FORD ED., vii, 41. (M., 1795.)

9004. ——— ———. I wish that his honesty and his political errors may not furnish a second occasion to exclaim " curse on his virtues, they have undone his country ".—To JAMES MADISON. iv, 136. FORD ED., vii, 69. (M., 1796.)

9005. ——— ———. The President [Washington] is fortunate to get off just as the [bank and paper] bubble is bursting, leaving others to hold the bag. Yet, as his departure will mark the moment when the difficulties begin to work, you will see that they will be ascribed to the new administration, and that he will have his usual good fortune of reaping credit from the good acts of others, and leaving to them that of his errors.—To JAMES MADISON. FORD ED., vii, 104. (M., Jan. 1797.)

9006. WASHINGTON (George), Estimate of.—His mind was great and powerful, without being of the very first order; his penetration strong, though not so acute as that of a Newton, Bacon, or Locke; and as far as he saw, no judgment was ever sounder. It was slow in operation, being little aided by invention or imagination, but sure in conclusion. Hence the common remark of his officers, of the advantage he derived from councils of war, where, hearing all suggestions, he selected whatever was best; and certainly no general ever planned his battles more judiciously. But if deranged during the course of the action, if any member of his plan was dislocated by sudden circumstances, he was slow in readjustment. The consequence was that he often failed in the field, and rarely against an enemy in station, as at Boston and York. He was incapable of fear, meeting personal dangers with the calmest unconcern. Perhaps the strongest feature in his character was prudence, never acting until every circumstance, every consideration, was maturely weighed; refraining if he saw a doubt, but, when once decided, going through with his purpose, whatever obstacles opposed. His integrity was most pure, his justice the most inflexible I have ever known, no motives of interest or consanguinity, of friendship or hatred, being able to bias his decision. He was, indeed, in every sense of the words, a wise, a good, and a great man. His temper was naturally irritable and high toned; but reflection and resolution had obtained a firm and habitual ascendency over it. If ever, however, it broke its bonds, he was most tremendous in his wrath. In his expenses he was honorable, but exact; liberal in contributions to whatever promised utility; but frowning and unyielding on all visionary projects, and all unworthy calls on his charity. His heart was not warm in its affections; but he exactly calculated every man's value, and gave him a solid esteem proportioned to it. His person was fine, his stature exactly what one would wish, his deportment easy, erect and noble; the best horseman of his age, and the most graceful figure that could be seen on horseback. Although in the circle of his friends, where he might be unreserved with safety, he took a free share in conversation, his colloquial talents were not above mediocrity, possessing

neither copiousness of ideas, nor fluency of words. In public, when called on for a sudden opinion, he was unready, short and embarrassed. Yet he wrote readily, rather diffusely, in an easy and correct style. This he had acquired by conversation with the world, for his education was merely reading, writing, and common arithmetic, to which he added surveying at a later day. His time was employed in action chiefly, reading little, and that only in agriculture and English history. His correspondence became necessarily extensive, and, with journalizing his agricultural proceedings, occupied most of his leisure hours within doors. On the whole, his character was, in its mass, perfect, in nothing bad, in few points indifferent; and it may truly be said, that never did nature and fortune combine more perfectly to make a man great, and to place him in the same constellation with whatever worthies have merited from man an everlasting remembrance. For his was the singular destiny and merit, of leading the armies of his country successfully through an arduous war for the establishment of its independence; of conducting its councils through the birth of a government, new in its forms and principles, until it had settled down into a quiet and orderly train; and of scrupulously obeying the laws through the whole of his career, civil and military, of which the history of the world furnishes no other example. How, then, can it be perilous for you to take such a man on your shoulders? I am satisfied the great body of republicans think of him as I do. We were, indeed, dissatisfied with him on his ratification of the British treaty. But this was short-lived. We knew his honesty, the wiles with which he was encompassed, and that age had already begun to relax the firmness of his purposes; and I am convinced he is more deeply seated in the love and gratitude of the republicans, than in the Pharisaical homage of the federal monarchists. For he was no monarchist from preference of his judgment. The soundness of that gave him correct views of the rights of man, and his severe justice devoted him to them. He has often declared to me that he considered our new Constitution as an experiment on the practicability of republican government, and with what dose of liberty man could be trusted for his own good; that he was determined the experiment should have a fair trial, and would lose the last drop of his blood in support of it. * * * I felt on his death with my countrymen, that verily a great man hath fallen this day in Israel.—To DR. WALTER JONES. vi, 286. FORD ED., ix, 448. (M., Jan. 1814.)

9007. WASHINGTON (George), Fame of.—Washington's fame will go on increasing until the brightest constellation in yonder heavens shall be called by his name.—DOMESTIC LIFE OF JEFFERSON. 358.

9008. ——— ———. Our first and greatest revolutionary character, whose preeminent services have entitled him to the first place in his country's love, and destined for him the fairest page in the volume of faithful history.—FIRST INAUGURAL ADDRESS. viii, 5. FORD ED., viii, 5. (1801.)

9009. ——— ———. The moderation of his desires, and the strength of his judgment, enabled him to calculate correctly, that the right to that glory which never dies is to use power for the support of the laws and liberties of our country, not for its destruction; and his will accordingly survive the wreck of everything now living.—To EARL OF BUCHAN. iv, 494. (W., 1803.)

9010. WASHINGTON (George), Farewell address of.—With respect to his [President Washington's] Farewell Address, to the authorship of which, it seems, there are conflicting claims, I can state to you some facts. He had determined to decline reelection at the end of his first term, and so far determined, that he had requested Mr. Madison to prepare for him something valedictory, to be addressed to his constituents on his retirement. This was done, but he was finally persuaded to acquiesce in a second election, to which no one more strenuously pressed him than myself, from a conviction of the importance of strengthening, by longer habit, the respect necessary for that office, which the weight of his character only could effect. When, at the end of this second term, his Valedictory came out, Mr. Madison recognized in it several passages of his draft; several others, we were both satisfied, were from the pen of Hamilton, and others from that of the President himself. These he probably put into the hands of Hamilton to form into a whole, and hence it may all appear in Hamilton's handwriting, as if it were all of his composition.—To WILLIAM JOHNSON. vii, 292. FORD ED., x, 228. (M., 1823.)

9011. WASHINGTON (George), Federalists and.—General Washington, after the retirement of his first cabinet, and the composition of his second, entirely federal. * * * had no opportunity of hearing both sides of any question. His measures, consequently, took the hue of the party in whose hands he was. These measures were certainly not approved by the republicans; yet they were not imputed to him but to the counsellors around him; and his prudence so far restrained their impassioned course and bias, that no act of strong mark, during the remainder of his administration, excited much dissatisfaction. He lived too short a time after, and too much withdrawn from information, to correct the views into which he had been deluded; and the continued assiduities of the party drew him into the vortex of their intemperate career: separated him still farther from his real friends, and excited him to actions and expressions of dissatisfaction, which grieved them, but could not loosen their affections from him. They would not suffer the temporary aberration to weigh against the immeasurable merits of his life; and although they tumbled his seducers from their places, they preserved his memory embalmed in their hearts with undiminished love and devotion; and there it will forever remain embalmed, in entire oblivion of every temporary thing which might cloud the glories of his splendid life. It is vain, then, for Mr. Pickering and his friends to endeavor to falsify his character, by representing him as an enemy to republicans and republican principles, and as exclusively the friend of those who were so; and had he lived longer, he would have returned to his ancient and unbiased opinions, would have replaced his confidence in those whom the people approved and supported, and would have seen that they were only restoring and acting on the principles of his own first administration.—To MARTIN VAN BUREN. vii, 371. FORD ED., x, 314. (M., 1824.)

9012. ——— ———. The federalists, pretending to be the exclusive friends of General Washington, have ever done what they could to sink his character, by hanging theirs on it, and by representing as the enemy of republicans him, who, of all men, is best entitled to the appellation of the father of that republic which they were endeavoring to subvert, and the repub-

licans to maintain. They cannot deny, because the elections proclaimed the truth, that the great body of the nation approved the republican measures.—To MARTIN VAN BUREN. vii, 371. FORD ED., x, 314. (M., 1824.)

9013. ——— ———. From the moment * * * of my retiring from the administration, the federalists got unchecked hold of General Washington. His memory was already sensibly impaired by age, the firm tone of mind for which he had been remarkable, was beginning to relax, its energy was abated; a listlessness of labor, a desire for tranquillity had crept on him, and a willingness to let others act, and even think for him. Like the rest of mankind, he was disgusted with the atrocities of the French Revolution, and was not sufficiently aware of the difference between the rabble who were used as instruments of their perpetration, and the steady and rational character of the American people, in which he had not sufficient confidence. The opposition too of the republicans to the British treaty, and zealous support of the federalists in that unpopular, but favorite measure of theirs, had made him all their own. Understanding, moreover, that I disapproved of that treaty, and copiously nourished with falsehoods by a malignant neighbor of mine [Henry Lee, " Light-Horse Harry "], who ambitioned to be his correspondent, he had become alienated from myself personally, as from the republican body generally of his fellow citizens; and he wrote the letters to Mr. Adams and Mr. Carroll, over which, in devotion to his imperishable fame, we must forever weep as monuments of mortal decay.—THE ANAS. ix, 99. FORD ED., i, 168. (1818.)

9014. WASHINGTON (George), Influence of.—You will have seen by the proceedings of Congress the truth of what I always observed to you, that one man outweighs them all in influence over the people, who have supported his judgment against their own and that of their representatives. Republicanism must lie on its oars, resign the vessel to its pilot, and themselves to the course he thinks best for them.—To JAMES MONROE. iv, 140. FORD ED., vii, 80 (M., June 1796.)

9015. WASHINGTON (George), Jefferson and.—I learn that he [General H. Lee] has thought it worth his while to try to sow tares between you and me, by representing me as still engaged in the bustle of politics, and in turbulence and intrigue against the government. I never believed for a moment that this could make any impression on you, or that your knowledge of me would not overweigh the slander of an intriguer, dirtily employed in sifting the conversations of my table, where alone he could hear of me; and seeking to atone for his sins against you by sins against another, who had never done him any other injury than that of declining his confidences. Political conversations I really dislike, and therefore avoid where I can without affectation. But when urged by others, I have never conceived that having been in public life requires me to belie my sentiments, or even to conceal them. When I am led by conversation to express them, I do it with the same independence here which I have practiced everywhere, and which is inseparable from my nature. But enough of this miserable tergiversator, who ought, indeed, either to have been of more truth, or less trusted by his country.—To PRESIDENT WASHINGTON. iv, 142. FORD ED., vii, 82. (M., 1796.)

9016. WASHINGTON (George), Just.—General Washington was always just in ascribing to every officer the merit of his own works.—NOTES ON M. SOULES'S WORK. ix, 301. FORD ED., iv, 309. (P., 1786.)

9017. WASHINGTON (George), Loved and venerated.—He possessed the love, the veneration, and confidence of all.—THE ANAS. FORD ED., i, 155. (1818.)

9018. WASHINGTON (George), Marshall's life of.—The party feelings of General Washington's biographer [Marshall] to whom after his death the collection of [Washington's papers] was confided, have culled from it a composition as different from what General Washington would have offered, as was the candor of the two characters during the period of the war. The partiality of this pen is displayed in lavishments of praise on certain military characters, who had done nothing military, but who afterwards, and before he wrote, had become heroes in party, although not in war; and in his reserve on the merits of others, who rendered signal services indeed, but did not earn his praise by apostatizing in peace from the republican principles for which they had fought in war. It shows itself too in the cold indifference with which a struggle for the most animating of human objects is narrated. No act of heroism ever kindles in the mind of this writer a single aspiration in favor of the holy cause which inspired the bosom, and nerved the arm of the patriot warrior. No gloom of events, no lowering of prospects ever excites a fear for the issue of a contest which was to change the condition of man over the civilized globe. The sufferings inflicted on endeavors to vindicate the rights of humanity are related with all the frigid insensibility with which a monk would have contemplated the victims of an auto da fé. Let no man believe that General Washington ever intended that his papers should be used for the suicide of the cause for which he had lived, and for which there never was a moment in which he would not have died. The abuse of these materials is chiefly, however, manifested in the history of the period immediately following the establishment of the present Constitution. * * * Were a reader of this period to form his idea of it from this history alone, he would suppose the republican party (who were, in truth, endeavoring to keep the government within the line of the Constitution, and prevent its being monarchized in practice) were a mere set of grumblers, and disorganizers, satisfied with no government, without fixed principles of any, and, like a British parliamentary opposition, gaping after loaves and fishes, and ready to change principles, as well as position, at any time, with their adversaries. But a short review of facts omitted, or uncandidly stated in this history will show that the contests of that day were contests of principle between the advocates of republican and those of kingly government, and that had not the former made the efforts they did, our government would have been, even at this early day, a very different thing from what the successful issue of those efforts have made it.*—THE ANAS. FORD ED., i, 155. (1818.)

9019. WASHINGTON (George), Medallion of.—That our own nation should entertain sentiments of gratitude and reverence for the great character who is the subject of your medallion, is a matter of duty. His disinterested and valuable services to them have rendered it so; but such a monument to his memory by the member of another community, proves a zeal

* In the Congressional edition this extract is omitted except the last sentence.—EDITOR.

for virtue in the abstract, honorable to him who inscribes it, as to him whom it commemorates. * * * This testimonial in favor of the first worthy of our country will be grateful to the feelings of our citizens generally.—To DANIEL ECCLESTON. v, 213. (W., 1807.)

9020. WASHINGTON (George), Memory of.—His memory will be adored while liberty shall have votaries, his name will triumph over time and will in future ages assume its just station among the most celebrated worthies of the world.—NOTES ON VIRGINIA. viii, 312. FORD ED., iii, 168. (1782.)

9021. WASHINGTON (George), National monument to.—In a former letter I enclosed you an idea of Mr. Lee's for an immediate appropriation of a number of lots to raise a sum of money for erecting a national monument in the city of Washington. It was scarcely to be doubted but that you would avoid appropriations for matters of ornament till a sufficient sum should be secured out of the proceeds of your sales to accomplish the public buildings, bridges and such other objects as are essential. Mr. Caracchi, the artist, who had proposed to execute the monument, has had hopes that a subscription set on foot for that purpose, would have sufficed to effect it. That hope is now over, and he is about to return to Europe. He is unquestionably an artist of the first class. He has had the advantage of taking the President's person in plaster, equal to every wish in resemblance and spirit. It is pretty certain that the equestrian statue of the President can never be executed by an equal workman, who has had equal advantages, and the question is whether a prudent caution will permit you to enter into any engagement now, taking time enough before the term of payment to have accomplished the more material objects of the public buildings, &c. He says to execute the equestrian statue, with the cost of the materials, in marble, will be worth twenty thousand guineas; that he would begin it on his return, if four or five years hence you can engage to pay him twenty thousand dollars, and the same sum annually afterwards, till the whole is paid, before which time the statue will be ready. It is rather probable that within some time Congress would take it off your hands, in compliance with an ancient vote of that body. The questions for your consideration are, whether, supposing no difficulty as to the means, you think such a work might be undertaken by you? Whether you can have so much confidence in the productiveness of your funds as to engage for a residuum of this amount, all the more necessary objects being first secured, and that this may be within the time first proposed? And, in fine, which will preponderate in your minds, the hazard of undertaking this now, or that of losing the aid of the artist? The nature of this proposition will satisfy you that it has not been communicated to the President, and of course would not be, unless a previous acceptance on your part, should render it necessary to obtain his sanction. Your answer is necessary for the satisfaction of Mr. Caracchi, at whose instance I submit the proposal to you, and who, I believe, will only wait here the return of that answer.—To THE COMMISSIONERS OF WASHINGTON. iii, 346. (1792.)

9022. WASHINGTON (George), Oath of office.—Knox, Randolph and myself met at Knox's where Hamilton was also to have met, to consider the time, manner and place of the President's swearing in.* Hamilton had been

* On the occasion of Washington's second inauguration.—EDITOR.

there before [us] and had left his opinion with Knox, to wit, that the President should ask a judge to attend him in his own house to administer the oath, in the presence of the heads of Departments, which oath should be deposited in the Secretary of State's office. I concurred in this opinion. E. Randolph was for the President's going to the Senate chamber to take the oath, attended by the Marshal of the United States who should then make proclamation, &c. Knox was for this and for adding the House of Representatives to the presence, as they would not yet be departed. Our individual opinions were written to be communicated to the President out of which he might form one.—THE ANAS. ix, 139. FORD ED., i, 221. (Feb. 1793.)

9023. WASHINGTON (George), Opinions of.—His opinions merit veneration and respect; for few men have lived whose opinions were more unbiased and correct. Not that it is pretended he never felt bias. His passions were naturally strong; but his reason, generally stronger.—THE ANAS. FORD ED., i, 155. (1818.)

9024. WASHINGTON (George), Opposition to administration.—I told the President [Washington] that in my opinion there was only a single source of the discontents [with the administration]. Though they had indeed appeared to spread themselves over the War Department also, yet I considered that as an overflowing only from their real channel, which would never have taken place, if they had not first been generated in another Department, to wit, that of the Treasury. That a system had there been contrived, for deluging the States with paper money instead of gold and silver, for withdrawing our citizens from the pursuits of commerce, manufactures, buildings, and other branches of useful industry, to occupy themselves and their capitals in a species of gambling destructive of morality, and which had introduced its poison into the government itself. That it was a fact, as certainly known as that he and I were then conversing, that particular members of the Legislature, while those laws were on the carpet, had feathered their nests with paper, had then voted for the laws, and constantly since lent all the energy of their talents, and instrumentality of their offices to the establishment and enlargement of this system; that they had chained it about our necks for a great length of time, and in order to keep the game in their hands had, from time to time, aided in making such legislative constructions of the Constitution, as made it a very different thing from what the people thought they had submitted to; that they had now brought forward a proposition. far beyond every one yet advanced, and to which the eyes of many were turned, as the decision which was to let us know, whether we live under a limited or an unlimited government. He asked me to what proposition I alluded? I answered to that in the Report on Manufactures, which, under color of giving *bounties* for the encouragement of particular manufactures. meant to establish the doctrine, that the power given by the Constitution to collect taxes to provide for the *general welfare* of the United States, permitted Congress to take everything under their management which *they* should deem for the *public welfare*, and which is susceptible of the application of money; consequently, that the subsequent enumeration of their powers was not the description to which resort must be had, and did not at all constitute the limits of their authority; that this was a very different question from that of the bank, which was thought an

incident to an enumerated power; that, therefore, this decision was expected with great anxiety; that, indeed, I hoped the proposition would be rejected, believing there was a majority in both Houses against it, and that if it should be, it would be considered as a proof that things were returning into their true channel; and that, at any rate, I looked forward to the broad representation which would shortly take place, for keeping the general Constitution on its true ground; and that this would remove a great deal of the discontent which had shown itself.—THE ANAS. ix, 104. FORD ED., i, 176. (Feb. 29, 1792.)

9025. ———— ————. The President said Governor Lee had that day informed him of the general discontent prevailing in Virginia, of which he never had had any conception, much less sound information; that it appeared to him very alarming. * * * I confirmed him in the fact of the great discontents in the South; that they were grounded on seeing that their judgments and interests were sacrificed to those of the Eastern States on every occasion, and their belief that it was the effect of a corrupt squadron of voters in Congress, at the command of the Treasury; and they see that if the votes of those members who had an interest distinct from, and contrary to the general interest of their constituents, had been withdrawn, as in decency and honesty they should have been, the laws would have been the reverse of what they are on all the great questions. I instanced the new Assumption carried in the House of Representatives by the Speaker's vote. On this subject he made no reply.—THE ANAS. ix, 130. FORD ED., i, 215. (Feb. 7, 1793.)

9026. ———— ————. The object of the opposition which was made to the course of administration was to preserve the Legislature pure and independent of the Executive, to restrain the Administration to republican forms and principles, and not permit the Constitution to be construed into a monarchy, and to be warped, in practice, into all the principles and pollutions of their favorite English model. Nor was this an opposition to General Washington. He was true to the republican charge confided to him; and has solemnly and repeatedly protested to me, in our conversations that he would lose the last drop of his blood in support of it; and he did this the oftener and with the more earnestness, because he knew my suspicions of Hamilton's designs against it, and wished to quiet them. For he was not aware of the drift or of the effect of Hamilton's schemes. Unversed in financial projects and calculations and budgets, his approbation of them was bottomed on his confidence in the man.—THE ANAS. ix, 95. FORD ED., i, 165. (1818.)

9027. WASHINGTON (George), Popularity of.—Such is the popularity of President Washington that the people will support him in whatever he will do or will not do, without appealing to their own reason, or to anything but their feelings towards him.—To ARCHIBALD STUART. FORD ED., vii, 101. (M., Jan. 1797.)

9028. WASHINGTON (George), President.—Though we [in Paris] have not heard of the actual opening of the new Congress, and consequently have not official information of your election as President of the United States, yet, as there never could be a doubt entertained of it, permit me to express here my felicitations, not to yourself, but to my country. Nobody who has tried both public and private life, can doubt that you were much happier on the banks of the Potomac than you will be at New York. But there was nobody so well qualified as yourself to put our new machine into a regular course of action; nobody, the authority of whose name could have so effectually crushed opposition at home, and produced respect abroad. I am sensible of the immensity of the sacrifice on your part. Your measure of fame was full to the brim; and, therefore, you have nothing to gain. But there are cases where it is a duty to risk all against nothing, and I believe this was exactly the case. We may presume, too, according to every rule of probability, that after doing a great deal of good, you will be found to have lost nothing but private repose.—To GENERAL WASHINGTON. iii, 30. FORD ED., v, 94. (P., May 1789.)

9029. WASHINGTON (George), Presidential reeligibility and.—The perpetual reeligibility of the same President will probably not be cured during the life of General Washington. His merit has blinded our countrymen to the danger of making so important an officer reeligible. I presume there will not be a vote against him in the United States.—To WILLIAM CARMICHAEL. ii, 465. (P., Aug. 1788.)

9030. WASHINGTON (George), Prudent.—The prudence of the President is an anchor of safety to us.—To NICHOLAS LEWIS. FORD ED., v, 282. (Pa., 1791.)

9031. WASHINGTON (George), Republicanism of.—It is fortunate that our first Executive Magistrate is purely and zealously republican. We cannot expect all his successors to be so, and therefore, should avail ourselves the present day to establish principles and examples which may fence us against future heresies preached now, to be practiced hereafter.—To HARRY INNES. iii, 224. FORD ED., v, 300. (Pa., 1791.)

9032. —— ——. General Washington was himself sincerely a friend to the republican principles of our Constitution. His faith perhaps in its duration, might not have been as confident as mine; but he repeatedly declared to me, that he was determined it should have a fair chance for success, and that he would lose the last drop of his blood in its support, against any attempt which might be made to change it from its republican form. He made these declarations the oftener, because he knew my suspicions that Hamilton had other views, and he wished to quiet my jealousies on this subject.—To MARTIN VAN BUREN. vii, 371. FORD ED., x, 314. (M., 1824.)

9033. WASHINGTON (George), Republicans and.—I have long thought it was best for the republican interest to soothe him by flattering where they could approve his measures, and to be silent where they disapprove, that they may not render him desperate as to their affections, and entirely indifferent to their wishes, in short to lie on their oars while he remains at the helm, and let the bark drift as his will and a superintending Providence shall direct.—To ARCHIBALD STUART. FORD ED., vii, 102. (M., Jan. 1797.)

9034. WASHINGTON (George), Second term.—When you first mentioned to me your purpose of retiring from the government, though I felt all the magnitude of the event, I was in a considerable degree silent. I knew that, to such a mind as yours, persuasion was idle and impertinent; that before forming your decision

you had weighed all the reasons for and against the measure, had made up your mind on full view of them, and that there could be little hope of changing the result. Pursuing my reflections, too, I knew we were some day to try to walk alone, and if the essay should be made while you should be alive and looking on, we should derive confidence from that circumstance, and resource, if it failed. The public mind, too, was calm and confident, and therefore in a favorable state for making the experiment. Had no change of circumstances intervened, I should not, with any hopes of success, have now ventured to propose to you a change of purpose. But the public mind is no longer confident and serene; and that from causes in which you are no ways personally mixed. Though these causes have been hackneyed in the public papers in detail, it may not be amiss, in order to calculate the effect they are capable of producing, to take a view of them in the mass, giving to each the form, real or imaginary, under which they have been presented. It has been urged, then, that the public debt, greater than we can possibly pay before other causes of adding new debt to it will occur, has been artificially created by adding together the whole amount of the debtor and creditor sides of accounts, instead of only taking their balances, which could have been paid off in a short time; that this accumulation of debt has taken forever out of our power those easy sources of revenue which, applied to the ordinary necessities and exigencies of government, would have answered them habitually, and covered us from habitual murmurings against taxes and taxgatherers, reserving extraordinary calls for those extraordinary occasions which would animate the people to meet them; that though the calls for money have been no greater than we must expect generally, for the same or equivalent exigencies, yet we are already obliged to strain the impost till it produces clamor, and will produce evasion and war on our own citizens to collect it, and even to resort to an *excise* law of most odious character, partial in its operation, unproductive unless enforced by arbitrary and vexatious means, and committing the authority of the government in parts where resistance is most probable and coercion least practicable. They cite propositions in Congress, and suspect other projects on foot still to increase the mass of debt. They say, that by borrowing at two-thirds of the interest, we might have paid off the principal in two-thirds of the time; but that from this we are precluded by its being made irredeemable but in small portions and long terms; that this irredeemable quality was given it for the avowed purpose of inviting its transfer to foreign countries. They predict that this transfer of the principal, when completed, will occasion an exportation of three millions of dollars annually for the interest, a drain of coin, of which as there have been no examples, no calculation can be made of its consequences: that the banishment of our coin will be complicated by the creation of ten millions of paper money, in the form of bank bills now issuing into circulation. They think that the ten or twelve per cent. annual profit paid to the lenders of this paper medium taken out of the pockets of the people, who would have had without interest the coin it is banishing; that all the capital employed in paper speculation is barren and useless, producing, like that on a gaming table, no accession to itself, and is withdrawn from commerce and agriculture, where it would have produced addition to the common mass: that it nourishes in our citizens habits of vice and idleness, instead of industry and morality; that it has furnished effectual means of corrupting such a portion of the Legislature as turns the balance between the honest voters, whichever way it is directed: that this corrupt squadron, deciding the voice of the Legislature, have manifested their dispositions to get rid of the limitations imposed by the Constitution on the general Legislature, limitations, on the faith of which, the States acceded to that instrument: that the ultimate object of all this is to prepare the way for a change from the present republican form of government to that of a monarchy, of which the English constitution is to be the model: that this was contemplated by the convention is no secret, because its partisans have made none of it. To effect it then was impracticable, but they are still eager after their object, and are predisposing everything for its ultimate attainment. So many of them have got into the Legislature, that, aided by the corrupt squadron of paper dealers, who are at their devotion, they make a majority in both houses. The republican party, who wish to preserve the government in its present form, are fewer in number; they are fewer even when joined by the two, three, or half dozen anti-federalists, who, though they dare not avow it, are still opposed to any general government; but, being less so to a republican than a monarchical one, they naturally join those whom they think pursuing the lesser evil. Of all the mischiefs objected to the system of measures before mentioned, none is so afflicting and fatal to every honest hope, as the corruption of the Legislature. As it was the earliest of these measures, it became the instrument for producing the rest, and will be the instrument for producing in future a king, lords and commons, or whatever else those who direct it may choose. Withdrawn such a distance from the eye of their constituents, and these so disposed as to be inaccessible to public information, and particularly to that of the conduct of their own representatives, they will form the most corrupt government on earth, if the means of their corruption be not prevented. The only hope of safety now hangs on the numerous representation which is to come forward the ensuing year. Some of the new members will be, probably, either in principle or interest, with the present majority; but it is expected that the great mass will form an accession to the republican party. They will not be able to undo all which the two preceding Legislatures, and especially the first, have done. Public faith and right will oppose this. But some parts of the system may be rightfully reformed, a liberation from the rest unremittingly pursued as fast as right will permit, and the door shut against similar commitments of the nation. Should the next Legislature take this course, it will draw upon them the whole monarchical and paper interest; but the latter, I think, will not go all lengths with the former, because creditors will never, of their own accord, fly off entirely from their debtors; therefore, this is the alternative least likely to produce convulsion. But should the majority of the new members be still in the same principles with the present, and show that we have nothing to expect but a continuance of the same practices, it is not easy to conjecture what would be the result, nor what means would be resorted to for correction of the evil. True wisdom would direct that they should be temperate and peaceable; but the division of sentiment and interest happens unfortunately to be so geographical, that no mortal man can say that what is most wise and temperate would prevail against what is most easy and obvious? I can scarcely contemplate a more incalculable evil than the breaking of the Union into two or more parts. Yet when we consider the mass which opposed the original coalescence; when we consider that it lay chiefly in the Southern quarter; that the Legislature have availed themselves of no occasion of allaying it, but on the contrary whenever Northern and Southern prejudices have come into conflict, the latter have been sacrificed and the former soothed; that the owers of the debt are in the Southern, and the holders of it in the Northern division: that the anti-federal champions are now strengthened in argument by the fulfillment of their predictions; that this has been brought about by the monarchical federalists themselves, who, having been for the new government merely as a stepping stone to monarchy, have themselves adopted the very constructions of the Constitution, of which, when advocating its acceptance before the tribunal of the people, they declared it unsusceptible; that the republican federalists who espoused the same government for its intrinsic merits, are disarmed of their weapons; that which they denied as prophecy, having now become true history, who can be sure that these things may not proselyte the small number which was wanting to place the majority on the other side? And this is the event at which I tremble, and to prevent which I consider your continuance at the head of affairs as of the last importance. [The confidence of the whole Union is centered in you. Your being at the helm will be more than an answer to every argument which can be used to alarm and lead the people in any quarter, into violence and secession. North and South will hang together if they have you to hang on; and if the first correction of a numerous representation should fail in its effect, your presence will give time for trying others, not inconsistent with the Union and peace of the States. I am perfectly aware of the oppression under which your present office lays your mind, and of the ardor with which you pant for domestic life. But there is sometimes an eminence of character on which society have such peculiar claims as to control the predilections of the individual for a particular walk of happiness, and restrain him to that alone arising from the present and future benedictions of mankind. This seems to be your condition, and the law imposed on you by Providence in forming your character, and fashioning the events on which it was to operate; and it is to motives like these, and not to personal anxieties of mine or others who have no right to call on you for sacrifices, that I appeal, and urge a revisal of it, on the ground of change in the aspect of things. Should an honest majority result from the new and enlarged representation; should those acquiesce whose principles or interest they may control, your wishes for retirement would be gratified with less danger, as soon as that shall be manifest, without awaiting the completion of the second period of four years. One or two sessions will determine the crisis; and I cannot but hope that you can resolve to add more to the many years you have already sacrificed to the good of mankind. The fear of suspicion that any selfish motive of continuance in office may enter into this solicitation on my part, obliges me to declare that no such motive exists. It is a thing of mere indifference to the public whether I retain or relinquish my purpose of closing my tour with the first political renovation of the government. I know my own measure too well to suppose that my services contribute anything to the public confidence, or the public utility. Multitudes can fill the office in which you have been pleased to place me, as much to their advantage and satisfaction. I have, therefore, no motive to consult but my own inclination, which is bent irresistibly on the tranquil enjoyment of my family, my farm and my books. I should repose among them, it is true, in far greater security, if I were to know that you remained at the watch; and I hope it will be so. To the inducements urged from a view of our domestic affairs, I will add a bare mention, of what indeed need only to be mentioned, that weighty motives for your consideration are to be found in our foreign affairs. I think it probable that both the Spanish and English negotiations, if not completed before your purpose is known, will be suspended from the moment it is known, and that the latter nation will then use double diligence in fomenting the Indian war.—To PRESIDENT WASHINGTON. iii, 360. FORD ED., vi, 1. (Pa., May 1792.)

9035. ———— ————. My letter to the President [May 23, 1792], directed to him at Mount Vernon, came to him here [Philadelphia]. He told me of this, and that he would take occasion of speaking with me on the subject. He did so this day [July 10]. He began by observing that he had put it off from day to day, because the subject was painful, to wit, his remaining in office, which that letter solicited. He said that the declaration he had made when he quitted his military command, of never again acting in public life, was sincere. That, however, when he was called on to come forward to set the present government in motion, it appeared to him that circumstances were so changed, as to justify a change in his resolution; he was made to believe that in two years all would be well in motion, and he might retire. At the end of two years he found some things still to be done. At the end of the third year, he thought it was not worth while to disturb the course of things, as in one year more his office would expire, and he was decided then to retire. Now he was told there would still be danger in it. Certainly, if he thought so, he would conquer his longing for retirement. But he feared it would be said his former professions of retirement had been mere affectation, and that he was like other men, when once in office he could not quit it. He was sensible, too, of a decay of his hearing; perhaps his other faculties might fall off, and he not be sensible of it. That with respect to the existing causes of uneasiness, he thought there were suspicions against a particular party, which had been carried a great deal too far; there might be *desires*, but he did not believe there were *designs* to change the form of government into a monarchy; that there might be a few who wished it in the higher walks of life, particularly in the great cities, but that the main body of the people in the eastern States were as steadily for republicanism as in the southern. That the pieces lately published, and particularly in Freneau's paper, seemed to have in view the exciting opposition to the government. That this had taken place in Pennsylvania as to the Excise law, according to information he had received from General Hand. That they tended to produce a separation of the Union, the most dreadful of all calamities, and that whatever tended to produce anarchy, tended. of course, to produce a resort to monarchical government. He considered those papers as attacking him directly, for he must be a fool indeed to swallow the little sugar plums here and there thrown out to him. That in condemning the administration of the government, they condemned him, for if they thought there were measures pursued contrary to his sentiment, they must conceive him too careless to attend to them, or too stupid to understand them. That though, indeed, he had signed many acts which he did not approve in all their

parts, yet he had never put his name to one which he did not think, on the whole, was eligible. That as to the Bank, which had been an act of so much complaint, until there was some infallible criterion of reason, a difference of opinion must be tolerated. He did not believe the discontents extended far from the seat of government. He had seen and spoken with many people in Maryland and Virginia in his late journey. He found the people contented and happy. He wished, however, to be better informed on this head. If the discontent were more extensive than he supposed, it might be that the desire that he should remain in the government was not general.—THE ANAS. ix, 116. FORD ED., i, 198. (July 1792.)

9036. ———— ————. President Washington said [in conversation with me] that as yet he was quite undecided whether to retire in March or not. His inclinations led him strongly to do it. Nobody disliked more the ceremonies of his office, and he had not the least taste or gratification in the execution of its functions. That he was happy at home alone, and that his presence there was now peculiarly called for by the situation of Major Washington, whom he thought irrecoverable, and should he get well, he would remove into another part of the country, which might better agree with him. That he did not believe his presence necessary; that there were other characters who would do the business as well or better. Still, however, if his aid was thought necessary to save the cause to which he had devoted his life principally, he would make the sacrifice of a longer continuance. That he, therefore, reserved himself for future decision, as his declaration would be in time if made a month before the day of election. He had desired Mr. Lear to find out from conversation. without appearing to make the inquiry, whether any other person would be desired by anybody. He had informed him, he judged from conversations that it was the universal desire he should continue, and he believed that those who expressed a doubt of his continuance, did it in the language of apprehension, and not of desire. But this, says he, is only from the north; it may be very different in the south. I thought this meant as an opening to me to say what was the sentiment in the south, from which quarter I come. I told him, that as far as I knew, there was but one voice there, which was for his continuance.—THE ANAS. ix, 120. FORD ED., i, 202. (Oct. 1792.)

9037. WASHINGTON (George), Statue of.—There could be no question raised as to the sculptor who should be employed [to execute Washington's statue]; the reputation of Monsieur Houdon of this city [Paris] being unrivalled in Europe. He is resorted to for the statues of most of the sovereigns in Europe. On conversing with him, Doctor Franklin and myself became satisfied that no statue could be executed so as to obtain the approbation of those to whom the figure of the original is known, but on an actual view by the artist. Of course no statue of General Washington, which might be a true evidence of his figure to posterity, could be made from his picture. Statues are made every day from portraits; but if the person be living, they are always condemned by those who know him for a want of resemblance, and this furnishes a conclusive presumption that similar representations of the dead are equally unfaithful. Monsr. Houdon, whose reputation is such as to make it his principal object, was so anxious to be the person who should hand down the figure of the General to future ages, that without hesitating a moment, he offered to abandon his business here, to leave the statues of Kings unfinished, and to go to America to take the true figure by actual inspection and mensuration. We believe, from his character, that he will not propose any very considerable sum for making this journey; probably two or three hundred guineas, as he must necessarily be absent three or four months, and his expenses will make at least a hundred guineas of the money. When the whole merit of the piece was to depend on this previous expenditure, we could not doubt your approbation of the measure; and that you would think with us that things which are just or handsome should never be done by halves. We shall regulate the article of expense as economically as we can with justice to the wishes of the world. This article, together with the habit, attitude, devices, &c., are now under consideration, and till they be decided on, we cannot ultimately contract with Monsr. Houdon. We are agreed in one circumstance, that the size shall be precisely that of life. Were we to have executed a statue in any other case, we should have preferred making it somewhat larger than life; because as they are generally a little elevated they appear smaller, but we think it important that some one monument should be preserved of the true size as well as figure, from which all other countries (and our own at any future day when they shall desire it), may take copies, varying them in their dimensions as may suit the particular situation in which they wish to place them. The duty as well as the glory of this presentation we think belongs peculiarly to Virginia. We are sensible that the eye alone considered will not be quite as well satisfied; but connecting the consideration that the whole, and every part of it presents the true size of the life, we suppose the beholders will receive a greater pleasure on the whole.—To THE GOVERNOR OF VIRGINIA. FORD ED., iv, 26. (P., 1785.)

9038. ——— ———. I am happy to find * * * that the modern dress for your statue would meet your approbation. I found it strongly the sentiment of West, Copley, Trumbull, and Brown, in London; after which, it would be ridiculous to add, that it was my own. I think a modern in an antique dress as just an object of ridicule as a Hercules or Marius with a periwig and a chapeau bras.—To GENERAL WASHINGTON. ii, 250. (P., 1787.)

9039. ——— ———. The marble statue of General Washington in the Capitol at Richmond, with its pedestal, cost in Paris 24,000 livres or 1,000 Louis d'ors. It is of the size of life, and made by Houdon, reckoned one of the first statuaries in Europe. Besides this, we paid Houdon's expenses coming to and returning from Virginia to take the General's likeness, which, as well as I recollect, were about 500 guineas, and the transportation of the statue to Virginia with a workman to put it up, the amount of which I never heard.—To MR. PARKER. iv, 309. (Pa., 1800.) See HOUDON.

9040. **WATERHOUSE (Dr.), Marine hospital appointment.**—When the appointment of Dr. Waterhouse to the care of the marine hospital was decided on, no other candidate had been named to me as desiring the place. The respectable recommendations I had received, and his station as professor of medicine in a college of high reputation, sufficiently warranted his abilities as a physician, and to these was added a fact well known, that to his zeal, the United States were indebted for the introduction of a great blessing,—vaccination, which has extirpated one of the most loathsome

and mortal diseases which has afflicted humanity some years, probably, sooner than would otherwise have taken place. It was a pleasure, therefore, as well as a duty, in dispensing the public favors, to make this small return for the great service rendered our country by Dr. Waterhouse.—To JOSEPH B. VARNUM. v, 222. (W., 1807.)

9041. ——— ———. Dr. Waterhouse has been appointed to the Marine Hospital of Boston, as you wished. It was a just though small return for his merit, in introducing the vaccination earlier than we should have had it. His appointment makes some noise there and here, being unacceptable to some; but I believe that schismatic divisions in the medical fraternity are at the bottom of it.—To DR. BENJAMIN RUSH. v, 225. (W., 1808.)

9042. ——— ———. You have the blessings of all the friends of human happiness for the great peril from which they are rescued.—To DR. BENJAMIN WATERHOUSE. FORD ED., ix, 532. (M., 1815.)

9043. **WEAKNESS, National.**—Weakness provokes insult and injury, while a condition to punish often prevents them.—To JOHN JAY. i, 404. FORD ED., iv, 89. (P., 1785.)

9044. **WEALTH, Acquirement of.**—Wealth acquired by speculation and plunder is fugacious in its nature, and fills society with the spirit of gambling.—To GENERAL WASHINGTON. ii, 252. (P., 1787.)

9045. **WEALTH, Aristocracy of.**—An aristocracy of wealth [is] of more harm and danger than benefit to society.—AUTOBIOGRAPHY. i, 36. FORD ED., i, 49. (1821.)

9046. **WEALTH, Checks on.**—Our young Republic * * * should prevent its citizens from becoming so established in wealth and power, as to be thought worthy of alliance by marriage with the nieces, sisters, &c., of Kings.—To DAVID HUMPHREYS. ii, 253. (P., 1787.)

9047. **WEALTH, Croakings of.**—Do not be frightened into the surrender of [true principles] by the alarms of the timid, or the croakings of wealth against the ascendency of the people.—To SAMUEL KERCHIVAL. vii, 11. FORD ED., x, 39. (M., 1816.)

9048. **WEALTH, Dominion of.**—Our experience so far, has satisfactorily manifested the competence of a republican government to maintain and promote the best interests of its citizens; and every future year, I doubt not, will contribute to settle a question on which reason, and a knowledge of the character and circumstances of our fellow citizens, could never admit a doubt, and much less condemn them as fit subjects to be consigned to the dominion of wealth and force.—R. TO A. CONNECTICUT REPUBLICANS. viii, 140. (1808.)

9049. **WEALTH, Freedom vs.**—Though there is less wealth in America [than there is in Europe], there is more freedom, more ease, and less misery.—To BARON GEISMER. i, 427. (P., 1785.)

9050. ——— ———. There is no such thing in this country as what would be called wealth in Europe. The richest are but a little at ease, and obliged to pay the most rigorous attention to their affairs to keep them together. I do not mean to speak here of the Beaujons of America; for we have some of those though happily they are but ephemeral. —To M. DE MEUNIER. FORD ED., vii, 13. (M., 1795.)

9051. WEALTH, Greediness for.—Our greediness for wealth, and fantastical expense, have degraded, and will degrade, the minds of our maritime citizens. These are the peculiar vices of commerce.—To JOHN ADAMS. vii, 104. FORD ED., x, 107. (M., 1818.)

9052. WEALTH, Liberty and.—What a cruel reflection that a rich country cannot long be a free one.—TRAVELS IN FRANCE. ix, 319. (1787.)

9053. WEALTH, Overgrown.—If the overgrown wealth of an individual be deemed dangerous to the State, the best corrective is the law of equal inheritance to all in equal degree; and the better, as this enforces a law of nature, while extra-taxation violates it.— NOTE IN TRACY'S POLITICAL ECONOMY. vi, 575. (1816.)

9054. WEALTH, Protection of.—Enough wealthy men will find their way into every branch of the legislature to protect themselves.—To JOHN ADAMS. vi, 224. FORD ED., ix, 426. (M., 1813.)

9055. WEALTH, Public office and.— For promoting the public happiness those persons, whom nature has endowed with genius and virtue, should be rendered by liberal education worthy to receive, and able to guard the sacred deposit of the rights and liberties of their fellow citizens; and they should be called to that charge without regard to wealth * * * or other accidental condition or circumstance.—DIFFUSION OF KNOWLEDGE BILL. FORD ED., ii, 221. (1779.)

9056. WEATHER, Contemporary observations.—As soon as I get into the house [in New York] I have hired, * * * I will propose to you to keep a diary of the weather here. and wherever you shall be, exchanging observations from time to time. I should like to compare the two climates by cotemporary observations. My method is to make two observations a day, the one as early as possible in the morning, the other from 3 to 4 o'clock, because I have found 4 o'clock the hottest and daylight the coldest point of the 24 hours. I state them in an ivory pocket book in the following form, and copy them out once a week. * * * The first column is the day of the month, and the second the thermometer in the morning. The fourth do. in the evening. The third the weather in the morning. The fifth do. in the afternoon. The sixth is for miscellanies, such as the appearance of birds, leafing and flowering of trees, frosts remarkably late or early, Aurora Borealis, &c. * * * I distinguish weather into fair or cloudy, according as the sky is more or less than half covered with clouds.—To T. M. RANDOLPH. FORD ED., v, 159. (N.Y., 1790.)

9057. WEATHER, Daily observations. —I make my daily observations as early as possible in the morning, and again about four o'clock in the afternoon, these generally showing the maxima of cold and heat in the course of 24 hours.—To —— ——. i, 208. FORD ED., ii, 158. (Wg., 1778.)

9058. WEATHER, Extreme cold.—It is so cold that the ink freezes in my pen, so that my letter will scarcely be legible. * * * In the winter of 1779-80, the mercury in Fahrenheit's thermometer fell at Williamsburg once to six degrees above zero. In 1783-84, I was at Annapolis without a thermometer, and I do not know that there was one in that State; I heard from Virginia, that the mercury was again down to six degrees. In 1789-90, I was at Paris. The mercury here was as low as eighteen degrees below zero, of Fahrenheit. These have been the most remarkable cold winters ever known in America. We are told, however, that in 1762, at Philadelphia, it was twenty-two degrees below zero; in December, 1793, it was three degrees below zero there by my thermometer. On the 31st of January, 1796, it was one and three-fourth degrees above zero at Monticello. I shall, therefore, have to change the maximum of our cold, if ever I revise the Notes on Virginia; as six degrees above zero was the greatest which had ever been observed.—To MR. VOLNEY. iv, 157. (M., Jan. 1797.)

9059. WEATHER, Moon and.—I do not know that the coincidence has ever been remarked between the new moon and the greater degrees of cold, or the full moon and the lesser degrees; or that the reflected beams of the moon attemper the weather at all. On the contrary, I think I have understood that the most powerful concave mirror presented to the moon, and throwing its focus on the bulb of a thermometer, does not in the least affect it.—To DR. HUGH WILLIAMSON. iv, 346. FORD ED., vii, 479. (W., 1801.)

9060. WEATHER, Parisian.—From my observations (I guess, because I have not calculated their result carefully) the sun does not shine here [Paris] more than five hours of the twenty-four through the whole year.—To JAMES MADISON. FORD ED., v, 105. (P., 1789.)

9061. WEBSTER (Daniel), Future of.— I am much gratified by the acquaintance made with Mr. Webster. He is likely to become of great weight in our government.—To JAMES MONROE. FORD ED., x, 327. (M., 1824.)

9062. WEBSTER (Noah), Estimate of. —Though I view Webster as a mere pedagogue, of very limited understanding and very strong prejudices and party passions, yet as editor of a paper and as of the New Haven association, he may be worth striking.—To JAMES MADISON. FORD ED., viii, 80. (M., Aug. 1801.)

— WEIGHTS, Standard of.—See STANDARD (WEIGHTS).

9063. WELFARE, Public.—To preserve the peace of our fellow citizens, promote their prosperity and happiness, reunite opinion, cultivate a spirit of candor, moderation, charity and forbearance toward one another, are objects calling for the efforts and sacrifices of every good man and patriot. Our religion enjoins it; our happiness demands it; and no sacrifice is requisite but of passions hostile to both.—To THE RHODE ISLAND ASSEMBLY. iv, 397. (W., 1801.)

— WELFARE CLAUSE, General.—See GENERAL WELFARE CLAUSE.

9064. WEST AND SOUTH, Free government in.—It seems to me that in proportion as commercial avarice and corruption advance on us from the north and east, the principles of free government are to retire to the agricultural States of the south and west, as their last asylum and bulwark. With honesty and self-government for her portion, agriculture may abandon contentedly to others the fruits of commerce and corruption.—To HENRY MIDDLETON. vi, 91. (M., Jan. 1813.)

9065. —— ——. I fear, with you, all the evils which the present lowering aspect of our political horizon so ominously portends. That at some future day, which I hoped to be very distant, the free principles of our government might change with the change of circumstances was to be expected. But I certainly did not expect that they would not over-live the generation which established them. And what I still less expected was, that my favorite Western country was to be made the instrument of change. I had ever and fondly cherished the interests of that country, relying on it as a barrier against the degeneracy of public opinion from our original and free principles. But the bait of local interests, artfully prepared for their palate, has decoyed them from their kindred attachments, to alliances alien to them.—To CLAIBORNE W. GOOCH. vii, 430. (M., January 1826.)

9066. WEST INDIES, British.—I think that the trade with Great Britain is a ruinous one to ourselves; and that nothing would be an inducement to tolerate it, but a free commerce with their West Indies; and that this being denied to us, we should put a stop to the losing branch. The question is, whether they are right in their prognostications that we have neither resolution nor union enough for this.—To T. PLEASANTS. i, 563. (P., 1786.)

9067. WEST INDIES, Coalition with French.—In policy, if not in justice, the National Assembly [of France] should be disposed to avoid oppression, which, falling on us, as well as on their colonies, might tempt us to act together.—To WILLIAM SHORT. iii, 276. FORD ED., v, 364. (Pa., 1791.)

9068. WEST INDIES, Commerce with.—The commerce with the English West Indies is valuable and would be worth a sacrifice to us. But the commerce with the British dominion in Europe is a losing one and deserves no sacrifice. Our tobacco they must have from whatever place we make its deposit, because they can get no other whose quality so well suits the habits of their people. It is not a commodity like wheat which will not bear a double voyage. Were it so, the privilege of carrying it directly to England might be worth something.—To JAMES MADISON. FORD ED., iv, 37. (P., 1785.)

9069. —— ——. Our commerce is in agonies at present, and these would be relieved by opening the British ports in the West Indies.—To JOHN ADAMS. i, 436. (P., 1785.)

9070. —— ——. The merchants of this country [France] are very clamorous against our admission into the West Indies, and ministers are afraid for their places.—To JAMES MONROE. FORD ED., iv, 31. (P., 1785.)

9071. —— ——. The effecting treaties with the powers holding positions in the West Indies, I consider as the important part of our business. It is not of great consequence whether the others treat or not. Perhaps trade may go on with them well enough without.—To JAMES MONROE. FORD ED., iv, 31. (1785.)

9072. —— ——. Access to the West Indies is indispensably necessary to us. Yet how gain it, when it is the established system of these nations [France and England] to exclude all foreigners from their colonies? The only chance seems to be this: our commerce to the mother countries is valuable to them. We must endeavor, then, to make this the price of an admission into their West Indies, and to those who refuse the admission, we must refuse our commerce, or load theirs by odious discriminations in our ports.—To JAMES MONROE. i, 351. FORD ED., iv, 58. (P., 1785.)

9073. —— ——. To nations with which we have not yet treated, and who have possessions in America, we may offer a free vent of their manufactures in the United States, for a full or modified admittance into those possessions. But to France, we are obliged to give that freedom for a different compensation: to wit, for her aid in effecting our independence. It is difficult, therefore, to say what we have now to offer her, for an admission into her West Indies. Doubtless, it has its price; but the question is what this would be, and whether worth our while to give it. Were we to propose to give to each other's citizens all the rights of natives, they would of course count what they should gain by this enlargement of right, and examine whether it would be worth to them as much as their monopoly of their West India commerce. If not, that commercial freedom which we wish to preserve, and which indeed is so valuable, leaves us little to offer. An expression in my letter to the Count de Vergennes * * * wherein I hinted that both nations might, perhaps, come into the opinion that the condition of *natives* might be a better ground of intercourse for their citizens, than that of the *most favored* nation, was intended to furnish an opportunity to the minister of parleying on that subject, if he was so disposed, and to myself, of seeing whereabouts they would begin, that I might communicate it to Congress, and leave them to judge of the expediency of pursuing the subject. But no overtures have followed.*—REPORT TO CONGRESS. ix, 243. FORD ED., iv, 129. (P., 1785.)

9074. —— ——. Our commerce with the West Indies had never admitted amelioration during my stay in France. The temper of that period did not allow even the essay, and it was as much as we could do to hold the ground given us by the Marshal de Castries' *Arret*, admitting us to their colonies with salted provisions, &c.—To GOUVERNEUR MORRIS. iii, 448. FORD ED., vi, 80. (Pa., 1792.)

9075. WEST INDIES, Confederation of.—Could Napoleon obtain, at the close of the present war, the independence of all the West India islands, and their establishment in a separate confederacy, our quarter of the globe would exhibit an enrapturing prospect into futurity. You will live to see much of this. I shall follow, however, cheerfully my fellow laborers, contented with having borne a part in beginning this beatific reformation.—To BARON HUMBOLDT. v, 581. (M., April 1811.)

* Report of a Conference with Count de Vergennes, Foreign Minister of France, on the question of Commerce.—EDITOR.

9076. WEST INDIES, Dominion of.—Whenever jealousies are expressed as to any supposed views of ours on the dominion of the West Indies, you cannot go farther than the truth in asserting we have none. If there be one principle more deeply rooted than any other in the mind of every American, it is that we should have nothing to do with conquest. As to commerce, indeed, we have strong sensations. In casting our eyes over the earth, we see no instance of a nation forbidden, as we are, by foreign powers, to deal with our neighbors, and obliged with them to carry into another hemisphere, the mutual supplies necessary to relieve mutual wants. * * * An exchange of surpluses and wants between neighbor nations, is both a right and a duty under the moral law, and measures against right should be mollified in their exercise, if it be wished to lengthen them to the greatest term possible.—To WILLIAM SHORT. iii, 275. FORD ED., v, 363. (Pa., 1791.)

9077. WEST INDIES, French.—A jealousy of our taking away the French carrying trade is the principal reason which obstructs our admission into their West India Islands.—To M. LIMOZIN. ii. 339. (P., 1787.)

9078. WEST INDIES, French concession.—France gives us an access to her West Indies, which, though not all we wish, is yet extremely valuable to us.—To JOHN ADAMS. i, 487. (P., 1785.)

9079. —— ——. France has explained herself generously. She does not mean to interrupt our prosperity by calling for our guarantee. On the contrary, she wishes to promote it by giving us, in all her possessions, all the rights of her native citizens, and to receive our vessels as her vessels.—To JAMES MONROE. FORD ED., vi, 281. (Pa., 1793.)

9080. WEST INDIES, Interposition in.—As to the guarantee of the French Islands, whatever doubts may be entertained of the moment at which we ought to interpose, yet I have no doubt but that we ought to interpose at a proper time, and declare both to England and France, that these Islands are to rest with France, and that we will make a common cause with the latter for that object.—To JAMES MADISON. iv, 103. FORD ED., vi, 502. (M., April 1794.)

9081. WEST INDIES, Liberty in French.—The emancipation of their islands is an idea prevailing in the minds of several members of the National Assembly, particularly those most enlightened and most liberal in their views. Such a step by this country would lead to other emancipations or revolutions in the same quarter.—To JOHN JAY. iii, 96. (P., 1789.)

9082. WEST INDIES, Monopoly of.—I observed [to the Count de Montmorin] that it would be much against our interest that any one power should monopolize all the West India islands.—To JOHN JAY. iii, 96. (P., 1789.)

9083. WEST INDIES, Negroes in.—What are you doing for your colonies? They will be lost if not more effectually succored. Indeed, no future efforts you can make will ever be able to reduce the blacks. All that can be done, in my opinion, will be to compound with them, as has been done formerly in Jamaica. We have been less zealous in aiding them, lest your government should feel any jealousy on our account. But, in truth, we as sincerely wish their restoration and their connection with you, as you do yourselves. We

are satisfied that neither your justice nor their distresses will ever again permit their being forced to seek at dear and distant markets those first necessaries of life which they may have at cheaper markets, placed by nature at their door, and formed by her for their support.—To GENERAL LAFAYETTE. iii, 450. FORD ED., vi, 78. (Pa., 1792.)

9084. —— ——. I become daily more convinced that all the West India Islands will remain in the hands of the people of color, and a total expulsion of the whites sooner or later take place. It is high time we should foresee the bloody scenes which our children certainly, and possibly ourselves (south of the Potomac), have to wade through, and try to avert them.—To JAMES MONROE. iv, 20. FORD ED., vi, 349. (P., July 1793.)

9085. —— ——. Inhabited already by a people of their own race and color; climates congenial with their natural constitution; insulated from the other descriptions of men; nature seems to have formed these islands to become the receptacle of the blacks transplanted into this hemisphere.—To JAMES MONROE. iv, 421. FORD ED., viii, 105. (W., 1801.)

9086. WEST INDIES, Opening the.—Your communications to the Count de Moustier, whatever they may have been, cannot have done injury to my endeavors here [Paris], to open the West Indies to us. On this head, the ministers are invincibly mute, though I have often tried to draw them into the subject. I have, therefore, found it necessary to let it lie, till war, or other circumstance, may force it on. Whenever they are at war with England, they must open the Islands to us, and perhaps during that war they may see some price which might make them agree to keep them always open.—To GENERAL WASHINGTON. ii, 536. FORD ED., v, 57. (P., 1788.)

9087. WEST INDIES, Portuguese.—Portugal [in making a commercial treaty with us] will probably restrain us to their dominions in Europe. We must expressly include the Azores, Madeiras and Cape de Verde islands, some of which are deemed to be in Africa. We should also contend for an access to their possessions in America * * * .—To JOHN ADAMS. i, 495. (P., 1785.)

9088. WEST INDIES, Prosperity of.—Our wishes are cordial for the reestablishment of peace and commerce in those colonies, and to give such proofs of our good faith both to them and the mother country [France] as to suppress all that jealousy which might oppose itself to the free exchange of our *mutual productions,* so essential to the prosperity of those colonies, and to the preservation of our agricultural interest. This is our true interest and our true object, and we have no reason to conceal our views so justifiable, though the expression of them may require that the occasions be proper, and the terms chosen with delicacy.—To GOUVERNEUR MORRIS. iii, 339. FORD ED., v, 450. (Pa., 1792.)

9089. WEST INDIES, Proximity.—Our vicinity to their West India possessions, and to the fisheries is a bridle which a small naval force, on our part, would hold in the mouths of the most powerful of * * * the [European] countries.—To JOHN JAY. i, 405. FORD ED., iv, 90. (P., 1785.)

9090. WEST INDIES, San Domingo.—I expressed to [the San Domingo deputies] freely my opinion * * * that as to ourselves there was one case which would be peculiarly alarming to us, to wit, were there a danger of their falling under any other power [than France].—To WILLIAM SHORT. iii, 304. FORD ED., v, 395. (Pa., Nov. 1791.)

— **WEST POINT, Academy.**—See ACADEMY (MILITARY).

9091. WESTERN EXPLORATION, Michaux expedition.—The chief objects of your journey are to find the shortest and most convenient route of communication between the United States and the Pacific ocean, within the temperate latitudes, and to learn such particulars as can be obtained of the country through which the Missouri passes, its productions, inhabitants, and other interesting circumstances. As a channel of communication between these States and the Pacific ocean, the Missouri, so far as it extends, presents itself under circumstances of unquestioned preference. * * * It would seem by the latest maps as if a, river called the Oregon interlocked with the Missouri for a considerable distance, and entered the Pacific ocean not far southward from Nootka Sound. But the [Philosophical] Society are aware that these maps are not to be trusted, so far as to be the ground of any positive instruction to you. * * * You will in the course of your journey, take notice of the country you pass through, its general face, soil, rivers, mountains, its productions—animal, vegetable, and mineral—so far as they may be new to us, and may also be useful or very curious.*—To ANDRE MICHAUX. ix, 434. FORD ED., vi, 159. (Jan. 1793.)

9092. WESTERN POSTS, British retention of.—I had a good deal of conversation with the Count de Vergennes on the situation of affairs between England and the United States, and particularly on their refusal to deliver up our posts. I observed to him that the obstructions thrown in the way of the recovery of their debts were the effect and not the cause, as they pretended, of their refusal to deliver up the posts; that the merchants interested in these debts showed a great disposition to make arrangements with us; that the article of time we could certainly have settled, and probably that of the interest during the war, but that the minister, showing no disposition to have these matters arranged, I thought it a sufficient proof that this was not the true cause of their retaining the posts. He concurred as to the justice of our requiring time for the payment of our debts; said nothing which showed a difference of opinion as to the article of interest, and seemed to believe fully that their object was to divert the channel of the fur trade before they delivered up the posts, and expressed a strong sense of the importance of that commerce to us. I told him I really could not foresee what would be the event of this detention; that the situation of the British funds, and desire of their minister to begin to reduce the national debt, seemed to indicate that they could not wish a war. He thought so, but that neither were we in a condition to go to war. I told him I was yet uninformed what Congress proposed to do on this subject but that we should certainly always count on the good offices of France, and I was sure that the offer of them would suffice to induce Great Britain to do us justice. He said that surely we might always count on the friendship of

* This expedition was started by private subscriptions under the patronage of the American Philosophical Society. Jefferson was a large subscriber to the fund.—EDITOR.

France. I added that, by the treaty of alliance, she was bound to guarantee our limits to us as they should be established at the moment of peace. He said they were so, " *mais qu'il nous etoit necessaire de les constater* ". I told him there was no question what our boundaries were; that the English themselves admitted they were clear beyond all question. I feared, however, to press this any further, lest a reciprocal question should be put to me.—To JOHN JAY. i, 575. FORD ED., iv, 228. (P., 1786.)

9093. WESTERN POSTS, Demand for surrender.—The President * * * authorized Mr. Gouverneur Morris to enter into conference with the British ministers in order to discover their sentiments on their * * * retention of the western posts contrary to the treaty of peace. * * * The letters of Mr. Morris * * * [to the President] state the communications, oral and written, which have passed between him and the ministers; and from these the Secretary of State draws the following inference: That the British court is decided not to surrender the posts in any event: and that they will urge as a pretext that though our courts of justice are now open to British subjects, they were so long shut after the peace as to have defeated irremediably the recovery of debts in many cases. They suggest, indeed, the idea of an indemnification on our part. But, probably, were we disposed to admit their right to indemnification, they would take care to set it so high as to insure a disagreement. * * * The Secretary of State is of opinion * * * that the demands of the posts * * * should n t be again made till we are in readiness to do ourselves the justice which may be refused.—OFFICIAL REPORT. vii, 517. FORD ED., v, 261. (December 1790.)

9094. WESTERN TERRITORY, Acceptance of cession.—On receiving the act of Assembly for the Western cession, our delegation agreed on the form of a deed; we then delivered to Congress a copy of the act, and the form of the deed we were ready to execute whenever they should think proper to declare they would accept it. They referred the act and deed to a committee, who reported the act of Assembly to comport perfectly with the propositions of Congress, and that the deed was proper in its form, and that Congress ought to accept the same. On the question to agree to the report of the Committee, eight States being present, Jersey was in the negative, and South Carolina and Pennsylvania divided (being represented each by two members). Of course there were five ayes only and the report fell. We determined on consultation that our proper duty was to be still, having declared we were ready to execute, we would leave it to them to come forward and tell us they were ready to accept. We meddled not at all, therefore, and showed a perfect indifference. New Hampshire came to town which made us nine States. A member proposed that we should execute the deed and lay it on the table, which after what had been done by Congress would be final, urging the example of New York which had executed their deed, laid it on the table. where it remained eighteen months before Congress accepted it. We replied, " No", if the lands are not offered for sale the ensuing spring, they will be taken from us all by adventurers; we will, therefore, put it out of our power, by the execution of a deed, to sell them ourselves, if Congress will not. A member from Rhode Island then moved that Congress should accept. Another from Jersey proposed as an amendment a proviso that it should not amount to an acknowledgment of our right. We told them we were not authorized to admit any conditions or provisions; that their acceptance must be simple, absolute and unqualified, or we could not execute. On the question there were six ayes; Jersey, " No "; South Carolina and Pennsylvania divided. The motion dropped, and the House proceeded to other business. About an hour after, the dissenting Pennsylvanian asked and obtained leave to change his " no " into " aye "; the vote then passed and we executed the deed. We have desired an exemplification of it under the Seal of the States. * * * This shows the wisdom of the Assembly in not taking any new conditions, which would certainly have defeated their accommodating intentions.—To GOVERNOR BENJ. HARRISON. FORD ED., iii, 411. (A., March 1784.)

9095. WESTERN TERRITORY, Deed of cession.—To all who shall see these presents we [here name the delegates] the underwritten delegates for the Commonwealth of Virginia in the Congress of the United States of America send greeting:

Whereas the General Assembly of the Commonwealth of Virginia at their sessions begun on the 20th day of October, 1783, passed an " Act entituled ' An Act to authorize the delegates, &c.'—in these words following to wit, ' Whereas the Congress, &c.' [reciting the act verbatim].

And whereas the said General Assembly by their Resolution of June 6th, 1783, had constituted and appointed us the said A. B. C. &c., delegates to represent the said Commonwealth in Congress for one year from the first Monday in November then next following, which resolution remains in full force.

Now, therefore, know ye that we the said A. B. C. &c., by virtue of the power and authority, committed to us by the act of the said General Assembly of Virginia before recited, and in the name and for and on behalf of the said Commonwealth, do by these presents convey, transfer, assign, and make over unto the United States in Congress assembled, for the benefit of the said States, Virginia inclusive, all right, title and claim as well of soil as of jurisdiction which the said Commonwealth hath to the territory or tract of country within the limits of the Virginia charter, situate, lying, and being to the Northwest of the river Ohio, to and for the uses and purposes and on the conditions of the said recited act. In testimony whereof we have hereunto subscribed our names and affixed our seals in Congress the ——— day of ——— in the year of our Lord 1784, and of the Independence of the United States the eighth.—DEED OF CESSION. FORD ED., iii, 406. (March 1, 1784.)

9096. WESTERN TERRITORY, Division into States.—With respect to the new States, were the question to stand simply in this form: How may the ultramontane territory be disposed of, so as to produce the greatest and most immediate benefit to the inhabitants of the maritime States of the Union? The plan would be more plausible, of laying it off into two or more States only. Even on this view, however, there would still be something to be said against it, which might render it at least doubtful. But that is a question which good faith forbids us to receive into discussion. This requires us to state the question in its just form: How may the territories of the Union be disposed of, so as to produce the greatest degree of happiness to their inhabitants? With respect to the maritime States, little or nothing remains to be done. With respect, then, to the

ultramontane States, will their inhabitants be happiest, divided into States of thirty thousand square miles, not quite as large as Pennsylvania, or into States of one hundred and sixty thousand square miles, each, that is to say, three times as large as Virginia within the Alleghany? They will not only be happier in States of a moderate size, but it is the only way in which they can exist as a regular Society. Considering the American character in general, that of those people particularly, and the energetic nature of our governments, a State of such extent as one hundred and sixty thousand square miles, would soon crumble into little ones. These are the circumstances which reduce the Indians to such small societies. They would produce an effect on our people, similar to this. They would not be broken into such small pieces, because they are more habituated to subordination, and value more a government of regular law. But you would surely reverse the nature of things, in making small States on the ocean, and large ones beyond the mountains. If we could, in our consciences, say, that great States beyond the mountains will make the people happiest, we must still ask, whether they will be contented to be laid off into large States? They certainly will not: and, if they decide to divide themselves, we are not able to restrain them. They will end by separating from our confederacy, and becoming its enemies. We had better, then, look forward, and see what will be the probable course of things. This will surely be a division of that country into States of a small, or, at most, of a moderate size. If we lay them off into such, they will acquiesce; and we shall have the advantage of arranging them so as to produce the best combinations of interest. What Congress has already done in this matter is an argument the more in favor of the revolt of those States against a different arrangement, and of their acquiescence under a continuance of that. Upon this plan, we treat them as fellow citizens; they will have a just share in their own government; they will love us, and pride themselves in an union with us. Upon the other, we treat them as subjects; we govern them, and not they themselves; they will abhor us as masters, and break off from us in defiance. I confess to you, that I can see no other turn that these two plans would take. But I respect your opinion, and your knowledge of the country too much, to be ever confident in my own.—To JAMES MONROE. i, 587. FORD ED., iv, 246. (P., 1786.)

9097. ———. I find Congress have reversed their division of the Western States and proposed to make them fewer and larger. This is reversing the natural order of things. A tractable people may be governed in large bodies; but, in proportion as they depart from this character, the extent of their government must be less. We see into what small divisions the Indians are obliged to reduce their societies.—To JAMES MADISON. ii, 66. FORD ED., iv, 333. (P., 1786.)

9098. WESTERN TERRITORY, Government for.—The Committee appointed to prepare a plan for the temporary Government of the Western Territory have agreed to the following resolutions: Resolved, that the territory ceded or to be ceded by individual States to the United States whensoever the same shall have been purchased of the Indian inhabitants and offered for sale by the United States shall be formed into distinct States bounded in the following manner as nearly as such cessions will admit, that is to say: Northwardly and

Southwardly by parallels of latitude so that each State shall comprehend from South to North two degrees of latitude beginning to count from the completion of thirty-one degrees North of the equator, but any territory Northwardly of the 47th degree shall make part of the State next below, and Eastwardly and Westwardly they shall be bounded, those on the Mississippi by that river on one side and the meridian of the lowest point of the rapids of Ohio on the other; and those adjoining on the East by the same meridian on their Western side, and on their Eastern by the meridian of the Western cape of the mouth of the Great Kanawha. And the territory eastward of this last meridian between the Ohio, Lake Erie and Pennsylvania shall be one State. That the settlers within the territory so to be purchased and offered for sale shall, either on their own petition or on the order of Congress, receive authority from them, with appointments of time and place for their free males of full age to meet together for the purpose of establishing a temporary government, to adopt the constitution and laws of any one of these States, so that such laws nevertheless shall be subject to alteration by their ordinary legislature, and to erect, subject to a like alteration counties or townships for the election of members for their legislature. That such temporary government shall only continue in force in any State until it shall have acquired 20,000 free inhabitants, when, giving due proof thereof to Congress, they shall receive from them authority with appointments of time and place to call a convention of representatives to establish a permanent Constitution and Government for themselves. Provided, that both the temporary and permanent Governments be established on these principles as their basis. 1. That they shall forever remain a part of the United States of America. 2. That in their persons, property and territory, they shall be subject to the Government of the United States in Congress assembled, and to the Articles of Confederation in all those cases in which the original States shall be so subject. 3. That they shall be subject to pay a part of the federal debts contracted or to be contracted, to be apportioned on them by Congress, according to the same common rule and measure by which apportionments thereof shall be made on the other States. 4. That their respective Governments shall be in republican forms, and shall admit no person to be a citizen, who holds any hereditary title. 5. That after the year 1800 of the Christian era, there shall be neither slavery nor involuntary servitude in any of the said States, otherwise than in punishment of crimes, whereof the party shall have been duly convicted to have been personally guilty. That whenever any of the said States shall have, of free inhabitants as many as shall then be in any one the least numerous of the thirteen original States, such State shall be admitted by its delegates into the Congress of the United States, on an equal footing with the said original States: After which the assent of two-thirds of the United States in Congress assembled shall be requisite in all those cases, wherein by the Confederation the assent of nine States is now required. Provided the consent of nine States to such admission may be obtained according to the eleventh of the Articles of Confederation. Until such admission by their delegates into Congress, any of the said States, after the establishment of their temporary Government, shall have authority to keep a sitting Member in Congress, with a right of debating, but not of voting. That the territory Northward of the 45th degree, that is to say of the completion of 45°

from the Equator and extending to the Lake of the Woods, shall be called SYLVANIA. That of the territory under the 45th and 44th degrees, that which lies Westward of Lake Michigan shall be called MICHIGANIA, and that which is Eastward thereof, within the peninsula formed by the lakes and waters of Michigan, Huron, St. Clair and Erie, shall be called CHERRONESUS, and shall include any part of the peninsula which may extend above the 45th degree. Of the territory under the 43d and 42d degrees, that to the Westward through which the Assenisipi or Rock river runs shall be called ASSENISIPIA, and that to the Eastward in which are the fountains of the Muskingum, the two Miamis of Ohio, the Wabash, the Illinois, the Miami of the lake and Sandusky rivers, shall be called METROPOTAMIA. Of the territory which lies under the 41st and 40th degrees the Western, through which the river Illinois runs, shall be called ILLINOIA; that the next adjoining to the Eastward SARATOGA, and that between this last and Pennsylvania and extending from the Ohio to Lake Erie shall be called WASHINGTON. Of the territory which lies under the 39th and 38th degrees to which shall be added so much of the point of land within the fork of the Ohio and Mississippi as lies under the 37th degree, that to the Westward within and adjacent to which are the confluences of the rivers Wabash, Shawanee, Tennessee, Ohio, Illinois, Mississippi and Missouri, shall be called POLYPOTAMIA, and that to the Eastward, farther up the Ohio, otherwise called the Pelisipi, shall be called PELISIPIA. That the preceding articles shall be formed into a charter of Compact, shall be duly executed by the President of the United States in Congress assembled, under his hand and the seal of the United States, shall be promulgated, and shall stand as fundamental constitutions between the thirteen original States, and those now newly described, unalterable but by the joint consent of the United States in Congress assembled, and of the particular State within which such alteration is proposed to be made.—REPORT ON GOVERNMENT FOR WESTERN TERRITORY. FORD ED., iii, 407. (March 1, 1784.)

9099. ——— ———. The committee to whom was recommitted the report of a plan for a temporary government of the Western Territory have agreed to the following resolutions: Resolved. That so much of the territory ceded or to be ceded by individual States to the United States as is already purchased or shall be purchased of the Indian inhabitants and offered for sale by Congress, shall be divided into distinct States, in the following manner, as nearly as such cessions will admit; that is to say, by parallels of latitude, so that each State shall comprehend from South to North two degrees of latitude beginning to count from the completion of thirty-one degrees North of the Equator; and the meridian of longitude, one of which shall pass through the lowest point of the rapids of Ohio, and the other through the Western Cape of the mouth of the Great Kanawha, but the territory Eastward of this last meridian, between the Ohio, Lake Erie, and Pennsylvania shall be one State, whatsoever may be its comprehension of latitude. That which may lie beyond the completion of the 45th degree between the sd. meridians shall make part of the State adjoining it on the South, and that part of the Ohio which is between the same meridians coinciding nearly with the parallel of 39° shall be substituted so far in lieu of that parallel as a boundary line. That the settlers on any territory so purchased and offered for sale, either on their own petition, or on the order of Congress, receive authority from them, with appointments of time and place for their free males of full age, within the limits of their State to meet together for the purpose of establishing a temporary government, to adopt the constitution and laws of any one of the original States, so that such laws nevertheless shall be subject to alteration by their ordinary legislature; and to erect, subject to a like alteration, counties or townships for the election of members for their legislature. That such temporary government shall only continue in force in any State until it shall have acquired 20,000 free inhabitants, when giving due proof thereof to Congress, they shall receive from them authority with appointment of time and place to call a convention of representatives to establish a permanent Constitution and Government for themselves. Provided that both the temporary and permanent governments be established on these principles as their basis. 1. They shall forever remain a part of this confederacy of the United States of America. 2. That in their persons, property, and territory, they shall be subject to the Government of the United States in Congress assembled, and to the articles of Confederation in all those cases in which the original States shall be so subject. 3. That they shall be subject to pay a part of the federal debts contracted or to be contracted, to be apportioned on them by Congress, according to the same common rule and measure, by which apportionments thereof shall be made on the other States. 4. That their respective Governments shall be in republican forms and shall admit no person to be a citizen who holds any hereditary title. 5. That after the year 1800 of the Christian era, there shall be neither slavery nor involuntary servitude in any of the sd States, otherwise than in punishment of crimes whereof the party shall have been convicted to have been personally guilty. That whensoever any of the sd States shall have, of free inhabitants, as many as shall be in any one the least numerous, of the thirteen original States, such State shall be admitted by its delegates into the Congress of the United States on an equal footing with the said original States: provided nine States agree to such admission according to the reservation of the 11th of the Articles of Confederation, and in order to adapt the sd Articles of Confederation to the State of Congress when its numbers shall be thus increased, it shall be proposed to the Legislatures of the States originally parties thereto, to require the assent of two-thirds of the United States in Congress assembled in all those cases wherein by the said Articles the assent of nine States is now required; which being agreed to by them shall be binding on the new States. Until such admission by their delegates into Congress, any of the said States after the establishment of their temporary government shall have authority to keep a sitting member in Congress, with a right of debating, but not of voting. That the preceding articles shall be duly executed by the President of the United States in Congress assembled, under his hand and the seal of the United States, shall be promulgated and shall stand as fundamental constitutions between the thirteen original States and each of the several States now newly described, unalterable but by the joint consent of the United States in Congress assembled, and of the particular State within which such alteration is proposed to be made. That measures not inconsistent with the principles of the Confederation, and necessary for the preservation of peace and good order among the settlers in any of the said new States until they shall assume a temporary government as aforesaid, may from time to time be taken by the United States in Congress as-

sembled.—WESTERN TERRITORY REPORT. FORD ED., iii, 429. (March 22, 1784.)

9100. WESTERN TERRITORY, Inhabitants.—I wish to see the Western country in the hands of people well disposed, who know the value of the connection between that and the maritime States and who wish to cultivate it. I consider their hanpiness as bound up together, and that every measure should be taken which may draw the bands of union tighter. It will be an efficacious one to receive them into Congress, as I perceive they are about to desire. If to this be added an honest and disinterested conduct in Congress, as to everything relating to them, we may hope for a perfect harmony.—To JOHN BROWN. ii, 395. FORD ED., v, 16. (P., 1788.)

9101. ——. In availing our western brethren of those circumstances which occur for promoting their interests, we only perform that duty which we owe to every portion of our Union, under circumstances equally favorable; and, impressed with the inconveniences to which the citizens of Tennessee are subjected by a want of contiguity in the portions composing their State, I shall be ready to do for their relief, whatever the general Legislature may authorize, and justice to our neighbors permit.—R. TO A. TENNESSEE LEGISLATURE. viii, 115. (1803.)

9102. WESTERN TERRITORY, Separation from Virginia.—I suppose some people on the western waters who are ambitious to be governors, &c., will urge a separation by authority of Congress. But the bulk of the people westward are already thrown into great ferment by the report of what is proposed, to which I think they will not submit. This separation is unacceptable to us in form only, and not in substance. On the contrary, I may safely say it is desired by the eastern part of our country whenever their western brethren shall think themselves able to stand alone. In the meantime, on the petition of the western counties, a plan is digesting for rendering their access to government more easy.—To JAMES MADISON. i, 316. FORD ED., iii, 53. (M., 1782.)

9103. ——. I hope our country will of herself determine to cede still further to the meridian of the mouth of the Great Kanawha. Further she cannot govern; so far is necessary for her own well being.—To GEORGE WASHINGTON. FORD ED., iii, 421. (A., 1784.)

9104. WESTERN TERRITORY, Slavery in.—I am glad to find we have 4,000,000 acres west of Chafalaya. How much better to have every 160 acres settled by an able-bodied militiaman, than by purchasers with their hordes of negroes, to add weakness instead of strength.—To ALBERT GALLATIN. v, 222. (Dec. 1807.)

— WESTERN TERRITORY, Trade of. —See MONOPOLY.

9105. WHALE OIL, Candles.—A Mr. Barrett has arrived here [Paris] from Boston with letters of recommendation from Governor Bowdoin, Cushing and others, * * * to get the whale business put on a general bottom, instead of the particular one which had been settled, the last year, for a special company. * * * I propose to Mr. Barrett that he should induce either his State, or individuals, to send a sufficient number of boxes of the spermaceti candle to give one to every leading house in Paris; I mean to those who lead the *ton;* and, at the same time to deposit a quantity for sale here and advertise them in the *petites affiches.*—To John Adams. i, 498. (P., 1785.)

9106. WHALE OIL, Duties on.—The result [of applications to the French government] was to put us on the footing of the Hanseatic towns, as to whale oil, and to reduce the duties to * * * about a guinea and a half the ton. But the oil must be brought in American or French ships, and the indulgence is limited to one year. However, as to this, I expressed to Count de Vergennes my hopes that it would be continued; and should a doubt arise, I should propose at the proper time, to claim it under the treaty on the footing *gentis amicissimæ.*—To John Adams. i, 498. (P., 1785.)

9107. —— ——. It being material that the reduction of the duties on whale oil, which would expire with the close of this year, should be revised in time for the whalemen to take measures in consequence, we have applied for a continuance of the reduction, and even for an abolition of all duties.—To John Jay. i, 584. (P., 1786.)

9108. WHALE OIL, England and.—I hope that England will, within a year or two, be obliged to come here [France] to buy whale oil for her lamps.—To John Adams. i, 502. (P., 1785.)

9109. WHALE OIL, Lafayette and.—The importation of our whale oil is, by the successful endeavors of M. de Lafayette, put on a good footing for this year.—To Mr. Otto. i, 559. (P., 1786.)

9110. WHALE OIL, Markets for.—I am trying here [Paris] to get contracts for the supplying the cities of France with whale oil by the Boston merchants. It would be the greatest relief possible to that State, whose commerce is in agonies, in consequence of being subjected to alien duties on their oil, in Great Britain, which has, heretofore, been their only market. Can anything be done in this way in Spain? Or do they light their streets there in the night?—To William Carmichael. i, 475. (P., 1785.)

9111. WHALING, Encouragement of.—To obtain leave for our whaling vessels to refit and refresh on the coast of the Brazils [is] an object of immense importance to that class of our vessels. We must acquiesce under such modifications as they [Portugal] may think necessary for regulating this indulgence, in hopes to lessen them in time, and to get a *pied a terre* in that country.—To John Adams. i, 495. (P., 1785.)

9112. WHEAT, British prohibition of.—The prohibition of our wheat in England would, of itself, be of no great moment, because I do not know that it is much sent there. But it is the publishing a libel on our wheat, sanctioned with the name of Parliament, and which can have no object but to do us injury, by spreading a groundless alarm in those countries of Europe where our wheat is constantly and kindly received. It is a mere assassination. If the insect they pretend to fear be the Hessian fly, it never existed in the grain. If it be the weevil, our grain always had that: and the experience of a century has proved that either the climate of England is not warm enough to hatch the egg and continue the race, or that some other unknown cause prevents any evil from it. —To Mr. Vaughan. iii, 38. (P., 1789.)

9113. WHEAT, Cultivation of.—The cultivation of wheat is the reverse in every circumstance of that of tobacco. Besides clothing the earth with herbage, and preserving its fertility, it feeds the laborers plentifully. requires from them only a moderate toil, except in the season of harvest, raises great numbers of animals for food and service, and diffuses plenty and happiness among the whole. We find it easier to make a hundred bushels of wheat than a thousand weight of tobacco, and they are worth more when made.—Notes on Virginia. viii, 407. Ford ed., iii, 271. (1782.)

9114. WHEAT, Weevils and.—The weevil is a formidable obstacle to the cultivation of wheat with us. But principles are already known which must lead to a remedy. Thus a certain degree of heat, to wit, that of the common air in summer, is necessary to hatch the eggs. If subterranean granaries, or others, therefore, can be contrived below that temperature, the evil will be cured by cold. A degree of heat beyond that which hatches the egg we know will kill it. But in aiming at this we easily run into that which produced putrefaction. To produce putrefaction, however, three agents are requisite, heat, moisture, and the external air. If the absence of any one of these be secured, the other two may safely be admitted. Heat is the one we want. Moisture then, or external air, must be excluded. The former has been done by exposing the grain in kilns to the action of fire, which produces heat, and extracts moisture at the same time; the latter, by putting the grain into hogsheads, covering it with a coating of lime, and heading it up. In this situation its bulk produced a heat sufficient to kill the egg; the moisture is suffered to remain indeed, but the external air is excluded. A nicer operation yet has been attempted; that is, to produce an intermediate temperature of heat between that which kills the egg, and that which produces putrefaction. The threshing the grain as soon as it is cut, and laying it in its chaff in large heaps, has been found very nearly to hit this temperature, though not perfectly, nor always. The heap generates heat sufficient to kill most of the eggs, whilst the chaff commonly restrains it from rising into putrefaction. But all these methods abridge too much the quantity which the farmer can manage, and enable other countries to undersell him, which are not infested with this insect.—Notes on Virginia. viii, 407. Ford ed., iii, 271. (1782.)

— WHEATLEY (Phyllis).—See Negroes, Literary.

— WHEELS (Wooden).—See Inventions.

9115. WHIGS, Loyalty of.—I do not believe there has ever been a moment, when a single whig in any one State, would not have shuddered at the very idea of a separation of their State from the Confederacy.—Answers to M. de Meunier. ix, 251. Ford ed., iv, 155. (P., 1786.)

9116. WHIGS, Principles of.—Before the Revolution we were all good English Whigs, cordial in their free principles, and in their jealousies of their executive magistrate. These jealousies are very apparent in all our State constitutions.—Autobiography. i, 81. Ford ed., i, 112. (1821.)

9117. WHIGS, Tories and.—It has ever appeared to me, that the difference between the whig and tory of England is, that the whig deduces his rights from the Anglo-Saxon source, and the tory from the Norman.—To JOHN CARTWRIGHT. vii, 355. (M., 1824.)

9118. WHISKY, Commutation.—Rum and other spirits we [Virginia] can furnish to a greater amount than you require * * * and shall be glad to commute into that article some others which we have not, particularly sugar, coffee and salt.—To GENERAL GATES. i, 260. (R., 1780.)

9119. —— ——. [As to] your application for spirits, there is not a hogshead belonging to the State, but very great quantities are in the hands of the Continental commissaries. I have special returns of upwards of twenty thousand gallons delivered them by the Commissioners * * * and [there are] no doubt great quantities of which there is no return. * * * I would observe to you that Baron Steuben informed me in conversation that spirit would be allowed as a part of the daily ration, but only on particular occasions.—To GENERAL NELSON. FORD ED., ii, 436. (R., 1781.)

9120. WHISKY, Indians and.—I am happy to hear that you have been so favored by the Divine Spirit as to be made sensible of those things which are for your good and that of your people, and of those which are hurtful to you; and particularly that you and they see the ruinous effects which the abuse of spirituous liquors has produced upon them. It has weakened their bodies, enervated their minds, exposed them to hunger, cold, nakedness, and poverty, kept them in perpetual broils, and reduced their population. I do not wonder, then, brother, at your censures, not only on your own people, who have voluntarily gone into these fatal habits, but on all the nations of white people who have supplied their calls for this article. But these nations have done to you only what they do among themselves. They have sold what individuals wish to buy, leaving to every one to be the guardian of his own health and happiness. Spirituous liquors are not in themselves bad; they are often found to be an excellent medicine for the sick; it is the improper and intemperate use of them, by those in health, which makes them injurious. But as you find that your people cannot refrain from an ill use of them, I greatly applaud your resolution not to use them at all. We have too affectionate a concern for your happiness to place the paltry gain on the sale of these articles in competition with the injury they do you. And as it is the desire of your nation, that no spirits should be sent among them, I am authorized by the great council of the United States to prohibit them. I will sincerely cooperate with your wise men in any proper measures for this purpose, which shall be agreeable to them.—To BROTHER HANDSOME LAKE. viii, 187. (1802.)

9121. WHISKY, Loathsome effects.—The loathsome and fatal effects of whisky, destroying the fortunes, the bodies, the minds, and morals of our citizens.—To WILLIAM H. CRAWFORD. FORD ED., x, 113. (M., 1818.)

9122. WHISKY, Military supplies.—We approve of your accommodating * * * the Maryland troops with spirits. They really deserve the whole, and I wish we had means of transportation for much greater quantities which we have on hand and cannot convey. This article we could furnish plentifully to you and them.—To GENERAL EDWARD. STEVENS. i, 253. FORD ED., ii, 339. (R., 1780.)

9123. WHISKY, Sale to Indians.—The Indians are becoming very sensible of the baneful effects produced on their morals, their health and existence, by the abuse of ardent spirits, and some of them earnestly desire a prohibition of that article from being carried among them. The Legislature will consider whether the effectuating that desire would not be in the spirit of benevolence and liberality which they have hitherto practiced toward these our neighbors, and which has had so happy an effect toward conciliating their friendship.—SPECIAL MESSAGE. viii, 22. (Jan. 1802.)

9124. —— ——. We have taken measures to prevent spirituous liquors being carried into your country, and we sincerely rejoice at this proof of your wisdom. Instead of spending the produce of your hunting in purchasing this pernicious drink, which produces poverty, broils and murders, it will be now employed in procuring food and clothing for your families, and increasing instead of diminishing your numbers.—ADDRESS TO MIAMIS AND DELAWARES. viii, 191. (1803.)

9125. —— ——. Perceiving the injurious effects produced by the Indians' inordinate use of spirituous liquors, Congress passed laws authorizing measures against the vending or distributing such liquors among them. Their introduction by traders was accordingly prohibited, and for some time was attended with the best effects. I am informed, however, that latterly the Indians have got into the practice of purchasing such liquors themselves in the neighboring settlements of whites, and of carrying them into their towns, and that in this way our regulations so salutary to them, are now defeated. I must, therefore, request your Excellency to submit this matter to the consideration of your Legislature. I persuade myself that in addition to the moral inducements which will readily occur, they will find it not indifferent to their own interests to give us their aid in removing, for their neighbors, this great obstacle to their acquiring industrious habits, and attaching themselves to the regular and useful pursuits of life; for this purpose it is much desired that they should pass effectual laws to restrain their citizens from vending, and distributing liquors to the Indians.—To —— ——. v. 407. (W., Dec. 1808.)

9126. —— ——. The French and afterwards the English kept the hatchet always in your hand, exposing you to be killed in their quarrels, and then gave you whisky that you might quarrel and kill one another.—INDIAN ADDRESS. viii, 235. (1809.)

9127. —— ——. I have not filled you with whisky, as the English do, to make you promise, or give up what is against your interest, when out of your senses.—INDIAN ADDRESS. viii, 240. (1809.)

9128. —— ——. What do the English for you? They furnish you with plenty of whisky, to keep you in idleness, drunkenness and poverty.—INDIAN ADDRESS. viii, 233. (1809.)

9129. —— ——. If we feared you, if we were your enemies, we should have furnished you plentifully with whisky.—INDIAN ADDRESS. viii, 233. (1809.)

9130. WHISKY, Tax on.—I shall be glad if an additional tax of one-fourth of a dollar a gallon on whisky shall enable us to meet all our engagements with punctuality. Viewing that tax as an article in a system of excise, I was once glad to see it fall with the rest of the system, which I considered as prematurely and unnecessarily introduced. It was evident that our existing taxes were *then* equal to our existing debts. It was clearly foreseen, also, that the surplus from excise would only become aliment for useless offices, and would be swallowed in idleness by those whom it would withdraw from useful industry. Considering it only as a fiscal measure, this was right. But the prostration of body and mind which the cheapness of this liquor is spreading through the mass of our citizens, now calls the attention of the legislator on a very different principle. One of his important duties is as guardian of those who, from causes susceptible of precise definition, cannot take care of themselves. Such are infants, maniacs, gamblers, drunkards. The last, as much as the maniac, requires restrictive measures to save him from the fatal infatuation under which he is destroying his health, his morals, his family, and his usefulness to society. One powerful obstacle to his ruinous self-indulgence would be a price beyond his competence. As a sanitary measure, therefore, it becomes one of duty in the public guardians. Yet I do not think it follows necessarily that imported spirits should be subjected to similar enhancement, until they become as cheap as those made at home. A tax on whisky is to discourage its consumption; a tax on foreign spirits encourages whisky by removing its rival from competition. The price and present duty throw foreign spirits already out of competition with whisky, and accordingly they are used but to a salutary extent. You see no persons besotting themselves with imported spirits, wines, liquors, cordials, &c. Whisky claims to itself alone the exclusive office of sot-making. Foreign spirits, wines, teas, coffee, cigars, salt, are articles of as innocent consumption as broadcloths and silks; and ought, like them, to pay but the average *ad valorem* duty of other imported comforts. All of them are ingredients in our happiness, and the government which steps out of the ranks of the ordinary articles of consumption to select and lay under disproportionate burdens a particular one, because it is a comfort, pleasing to the taste, or necessary to health, and will therefore, be bought, is, in that particular, a tyranny.—To SAMUEL SMITH. vii, 284. FORD ED., x, 251. (M., 1823.)

9131. WHISKY INSURRECTION, Commencement.—The people in the western parts of Pennsylvania have been to the excise officer, and threatened to burn his house, &c. They were blackened and otherwise disguised, so as to be unknown. He has resigned, and Hamilton says there is no possibility of getting the law executed, and that probably the evil will spread. A proclamation is to be issued, and another instance of my being forced to appear to approve what I have condemned uniformly from its first conception.—To JAMES MADISON. iii, 563. FORD ED., vi, 261. (Pa., May 1793.)

9132. WHISKY INSURRECTION, Hamilton and.—The servile copyist of Mr. Pitt [Alexander Hamilton] thought he, too, must have his alarms, his insurrections and plots against the Constitution. * * * Hence the example of employing military force for civil purposes, when it has been impossible to produce a single fact of insurrection, unless that term be entirely confounded with occasional riots, and when ordinary process of law had been resisted indeed in a few special cases but by no means generally, nor had its effect been duly tried. But it answered the favorite purposes of strengthening government and increasing public debt; and, therefore, an insurrection was announced and proclaimed, and armed against, but could never be found. And all this under the sanction of a name which has done too much good not to be sufficient to cover harm also. What is equally astonishing is that by the pomp of reports, proclamations, armies, &c., the mind of the Legislature itself was so fascinated as never to have asked where, when, and by whom this insurrection has been produced? The original of this scene in another country was calculated to excite the indignation of those whom it could not impose on; the mimicry of it here is too humiliating to excite any feeling but shame.—To JAMES MONROE. FORD ED., vii, 16. (M., May 1795.)

9133. WHISKY INSURRECTION, Military and.—The information of our [Virginia's] militia, returned from the westward. is uniform, that though the people there let them pass quietly, they were objects of their laughter, not of their fear: that one thousand men could have cut off their whole force in a thousand places of the Alleghany; that their detestation of the excise law is universal, and has now associated to it a detestation of the government; and that a separation which was perhaps a very distant and problematical event, is now near, and certain, and determined in the mind of every man.—To JAMES MADISON. iv, 112. FORD ED., vi, 518. (M., Dec. 1794.)

9134. WHISKY INSURRECTION, Proclamation against.—The proclamation on the proceedings against the laws for raising a revenue on distilled spirits, I return with my signature. I think if, instead of the words. " to render laws dictated by weighty reasons of public exigency and policy as acceptable as possible ", it stood, " to render the laws as acceptable as possible ", it would be better. I see no other particular expressions which need alteration.—To PRESIDENT WASHINGTON. iii, 471. FORD ED., vi, 113. (M., Sep. 1792.)

9135. ———— ————. I am sincerely sorry to learn that such proceedings have taken place; and I hope the proclamation will lead the persons concerned into a regular line of application which may end either in an amendment of the law, if it needs it, or in their conviction that it is right.—To PRESIDENT WASHINGTON. iii, 471. FORD ED., vi, 114. (M., Sep. 1792.)

9136. WILKINSON (James), Burr's conspiracy.—I have ever and carefully restrained myself from the expression of any opinion respecting General Wilkinson, except in the case of Burr's conspiracy, wherein, after he had got over his first agitations, we believed his decision firm, and his conduct zealous for the defeat of the conspiracy, and although injudicious, yet meriting, from sound intentions, the support of the nation. As to the rest of his life, I have left it to his friends and his enemies, to whom it furnishes matter enough for disputation. I classed myself with neither.—To JAMES MONROE. vi, 35. FORD ED., ix, 332. (M., Jan. 1812.)

9137. WILKINSON (James), Commended.—I sincerely congratulate you on your safe arrival at Richmond, against the impudent surmises and hopes of the band of conspirators, who, because they are as yet permitted to walk abroad, and even to be in the character of witnesses until such a measure of evidence shall be collected as will place them securely at the bar of justice, attempt to cover their crimes under noise and insolence. You have indeed had a fiery trial at New Orleans, but it was soon apparent that the clamorous were only the criminal, endeavoring to turn the public attention from themselves and their leader upon any other object.—To GENERAL WILKINSON. v, 109. FORD ED., ix, 5. (W., June 1807.)

9138. WILKINSON (James), Confidence in.—I am thoroughly sensible of the painful difficulties of your situation, expecting an attack from an overwhelming force, unversed in law, surrounded by suspected persons, and in a nation tender as to everything infringing liberty, and especially trom the military. You have doubtless seen a good deal of malicious insinuation in the papers against you. This, of course, begot suspicion and distrust in those unacquainted with the line of your conduct. We, who knew it, have not failed to strengthen the public confidence in you; and I can assure you that your conduct, as now known, has placed you on ground extremely favorable with the public. Burr and his emissaries found it convenient to sow a distrust in your mind of our dispositions towards you; but be assured that vou will be cordially supported in the line of your duties.—To GENERAL WILKINSON. v, 39. FORD ED., ix, 4. (W., Feb. 1807.)

9139. WILKINSON (James), Injustice for.—Your enemies have filled the public ear with slanders, and your mind with trouble on that account. The establishment of their guilt will let the world see what they ought to think of their clamors; it will dissipate the doubts of those who doubted for want of knowledge, and will place you on higher ground in the public estimate and public confidence. No one is more sensible than myself of the injustice which has been aimed at you.—To GENERAL WILKINSON. v, 110. FORD ED., ix, 6. (W., June 1807.)

9140. WILKINSON (James), Plans against Burr.—Although we at no time believed Burr could carry any formidable force out of the Ohio, yet we thought it safest that you should be prepared to receive him with all the force which could be assembled, and with that view our orders were given; and we were pleased to see that without waiting for them, you adopted nearly the same plan yourself, and acted on it with promptitude; the difference between yours and ours proceeding from your expecting an attack by sea, which we knew was impossible, either by England or by a fleet under Truxtun, who was at home; or by our own navy, which was under our eye. Your belief that Burr would really descend with six or seven thousand men, was no doubt founded on what you knew of the numbers which could be raised in the western country for an expedition to Mexico, *under the authority of the government;* but you probably did not calculate that the want of that authority would take from him every honest man, and leave him only the desperadoes of his party, which in no part of the United States can ever be a numerous body.—To GENERAL WILKINSON. v, 39. FORD ED., ix, 4. (W.. Feb. 1807.)

9141. WILKINSON (James), Suspicions.—General Wilkinson, being expressly declared by Burr to General Eaton, to be engaged with him in his design as his Lieutenant, or first in command, and suspicions of infidelity in Wilkinson being now become very general, a question is proposed [in cabinet] what is proper to be done as to him on this account, as well as for his disobedience of orders received by him June 11, at St. Louis, to descend with all practicable dispatch to New Orleans, to mark out the site of certain defensive works there, and then repair to take command at Natchitoches, on which business he did not leave St. Louis till September.—THE ANAS. FORD ED., i, 319. (Oct. 1806.)

9142. WILLIAM AND MARY COLLEGE, Aid for.—The late change in the form of our government, as well as the contest of arms in which we are at present engaged, calling for extraordinary abilities both in council and field, it becomes the peculiar duty of the Legislature, at this time, to aid and improve [William and Mary] Seminary, in which those who are to be the future guardians of the rights and liberties of their country may be endowed with science and virtue, to watch and preserve the sacred deposit.—WILLIAM AND MARY COLLEGE BILL. FORD ED., ii, 233. (1779.)

9143. WILLIAM AND MARY COLLEGE, Attachment for.—To William and Mary, as my *alma mater,* my attachment has been ever sincere, although not exclusive.—To PATRICK K. RODGERS. vii, 328. (M., 1824.)

9144. WILLIAM AND MARY COLLEGE, Changes.—Being elected, in 1779, one of the Visitors of William and Mary College, a self-electing body, I effected, during my residence in Williamsburg [as Governor of the State] that year, a change in the organization of that institution, by abolishing the Grammar school, and the two professorships of Divinity and Oriental languages, and substituting a professorship of Law and Police, one of Anatomy, Medicine and Chemistry, and one of Modern Languages; and the charter confining us to six professorships, we added the Law of Nature and Nations, and the Fine Arts to the duties of the Moral professor, and Natural History to those of the professor of Mathematics and Natural Philosophy.—AUTOBIOGRAPHY. i, 50. FORD ED., i, 69. (1821.)

9145. WILLIAM AND MARY COLLEGE, Church establishment.—The College of William and Mary was an establishment purely of the Church of England; the Visitors were required to be all of that Church; the professors to subscribe its Thirty-nine Articles; its students to learn its catechism; and one of its fundamental objects was declared to be to raise up ministers for that Church. The religious jealousies, therefore, of all the dissenters took alarm lest this might give an ascendancy to the Anglican sect, and refused acting on that bill. Its local eccentricity, too, and unhealthy autumnal climate, lessened the general inclination towards it.—AUTOBIOGRAPHY. i, 48. FORD ED., i, 67. (M., 1821.)

9146. WILLIAM AND MARY COLLEGE, Rivalry.—When the college [of William and Mary] was located at the middle plantation in 1693, Charles City was a frontier county, and there were no inhabitants above the falls of the rivers, sixty miles only higher up. It was, therefore, a position nearly central to the population, as it then was; but when the frontier became extended to the Sandy river, three hundred miles west of Williamsburg, the public convenience called, first for a removal of the seat of government, and latterly, not for a removal of the college, but for the establishment of a new one in a more central and healthy location; not disturbing the old one in its possessions or functions, but leaving them unimpaired for the benefit of those to whom it is convenient. And indeed, I do not foresee that the number of its students is likely to be much affected; because I presume that, at present, its distance and autumnal climate prevent its receiving many students from above the tidewaters, and especially from above the mountains. This is, therefore, one of the cases where the lawyers say there is *damnum absque injuriâ;* and they instance, as in point, the settlement of a new schoolmaster in the neighborhood of an old one. At any rate, it is one of those cases wherein the public interest rightfully prevails, and the justice of which will be yielded by none, I am sure, with more dutiful and candid acquiescence than the enlightened friends of our ancient and venerable institution. The only rivalship, I hope, between the old and the new (the University of Virginia) will be in doing the most good possible in their respective sections of country.—To PATRICK K. RODGERS. vii, 328. (M., 1824.)

9147. WILLIAM AND MARY COLLEGE, Unfavorable location.—We have in Virginia a college (William and Mary) just well enough endowed to draw out the miserable existence to which a miserable constitution has doomed it. It is moreover eccentric in its position, exposed to all bilious diseases as all the lower country is, and therefore, abandoned by the public care, as that part of the country itself is in a considerable degree by its inhabitants.—To JOSEPH PRIESTLEY. iv, 312. FORD ED., vii, 407. (Pa., 1800.) See UNIVERSITY OF VIRGINIA.

9148. WINDS, Systematic observations on.—I am sorry you have received so little information on the subject of our winds. I had once (before our Revolution-war) a project on the same subject. As I had then an extensive acquaintance over this State [Virginia], I meant to have engaged some person in every county of it, giving them each a thermometer, to observe that and the winds twice a day, for one year, to wit, at sunrise and at four p. m. (the coldest and the warmest point of the twenty-four hours), and to communicate their observations to me at the end of the year. I should then have selected the days in which it appeared that the winds blew to a centre within the State, and have made a map of them, and seen how far they had analogy with the temperature of the air. I meant this to be merely a specimen to be communicated to the Philosophical Society at Philadelphia, in order to engage them, by means of their correspondents, to have the same thing done in every State, and through a series of years. By seizing the days when the winds centred in any part of the United States, we might, in time, have come to some of the causes which determine the direction of the winds, which I suspect to be very various. But this long-winded project was prevented by the war * * * and since that I have been far otherwise engaged. I am sure you will have viewed the subject from much higher ground, and I shall be glad to learn your views in some of the hours of *delassement,* which I hope we are yet to pass together.—To MR. VOLNEY. iv, 159. (M., 1797.)

9149. WINES, Making.—The culture of the vine is not desirable in lands capable of producing anything else. It is a species of gambling, and desperate gambling, too, wherein, whether you make much or nothing, you are equally ruined. The middling crop alone is the saving point, and that the seasons seldom hit. Accordingly, we see much wretchedness among this class of cultivators. Wine, too, is so cheap in these countries [of Europe], that a laborer with us, employed in the culture of any other article, may exchange it for wine, more and better than he could raise himself. It is a resource for a country the whole of whose good soil is otherwise employed, and which still has some barren spots, and surplus of population to employ on them. There the vine is good, because it is something in the place of nothing. It may become a resource to us at a still later period; when the increase of population shall increase our productions beyond the demand for them, both at home and abroad. Instead of going on to make an useless surplus of them, we may employ our supernumerary hands on the vine.—To WILLIAM DRAYTON. ii, 198. (P., 1787.)

9150. ——— ———. An experiment was made in Virginia by a Mr. Mazzei, for the raising vines and making wines. He was an Italian, and brought over with him about a dozen laborers of his own country, bound to serve him four or five years. We had made up a subscription for him of £2,000 sterling, and he began his experiment on a piece of land adjoining mine. His intention was, before the time of his people should expire, to import more from Italy. He planted a considerable vineyard, and attended to it with great diligence for three years. The war then came on, the time of his people soon expired, some of them enlisted, others chose to settle on other lands and labor for themselves; some were taken away by the gentlemen of the country for gardeners, so that there did not remain a single one with him, and the interruption of navigation prevented his importing others. In this state of things he was himself employed by the State of Virginia to go to Europe as their agent to do some particular business. He rented his place to General Riedesel, whose horses in one week destroyed the whole labor of three or four years; and thus ended an experiment which, from every appearance, would in a year or two more have established the practicability of that branch of culture in America.—To ALBERT GALLATIN. iii, 505. (Pa., 1793.)

9151. ——— ———. We could, in the United States, make as great a variety of wines as are made in Europe, not exactly of the same kinds, but doubtless as good. Yet I have ever observed to my countrymen, who think its introduction important, that a laborer cultivating wheat, rice, tobacco, or cotton here, will be able with the proceeds, to purchase double the quantity of the wine he could make.—To M. LASTEYRIE. v, 314. (W., 1808.)

9152. WINES, Sobriety and.—I am persuaded that were the duty on cheap wines put on the same ratio with the dear, it would wonderfully enlarge the field of those who use wine, to the expulsion of whisky. The introduction of a very cheap wine into my neighborhood, within two years past, has quadrupled in that time the number of those who keep wine, and will ere long increase them tenfold. This would be a great gain to the treasury, and to the sobriety of our country.—To ALBERT GALLATIN. v, 86. FORD ED., ix, 69. (W., June 1807.)

9153. WINES, Tax on.—I rejoice, as a moralist, at the prospect of a reduction of the duties on wine, by our national Legislature. It is an error to view a tax on that liquor as merely a tax on the rich. It is a prohibition of its use to the middling class of our citizens, and a condemnation of them to the poison of whisky, which is desolating their houses. No nation is drunken where wine is cheap: and none sober, where the dearness of wine substitutes ardent spirits as the common beverage. It is, in truth, the only antidote to the bane of whisky. Fix but the duty at the rate of other merchandise, and we can drink wine here as cheap as we do grog; and who will not prefer it? Its extended use will carry health and comfort to a much enlarged circle. Every one in easy circumstances (as the bulk of our citizens are) will prefer it to the poison to which they are now driven by their government. And the treasury itself will find that a penny apiece from a dozen, is more than a groat from a single one. This reformation, however, will require time.—To M. DE NEUVILLE. vii, 110. (M., 1818.)

9154. ——— ———. I think it a great error to consider a heavy tax on wines, as a tax on luxury. On the contrary, it is a tax on the health of our citizens. It is a legislative declaration that none but the richest of them shall be permitted to drink wine, and, in effect, a condemnation of all the middling and lower conditions of society to the poison of whisky. * * * Surely it is not from the necessities of our treasury that we thus undertake to debar the mass of our citizens the use of not only an innocent gratification, but a healthy substitute instead of a bewitching poison. This aggression on the public taste and comfort has been ever deemed among the most arbitrary and oppressive abuses of the English government. It is one which, I hope, we shall never copy.—To WILLIAM H. CRAWFORD. FORD ED., x, 112. (M., 1818.) See LIFE, JEFFERSON'S HABITS OF.

9155. WIRT (William), Seat in Congress.—I pray you that this letter may be sacredly secret, because it meddles in a line wherein I should myself think it wrong to intermeddle, were it not that it looks to a period when I shall be out of office, but others might think it wrong notwithstanding that circumstance. I suspected, from your desire to go into the army, that you disliked your profession, notwithstanding that your prospects in it were inferior to none in the State. Still, I know that no profession is open to stronger antipathies than that of the law. The object of this letter, then, is to propose to you to come into Congress. Th t is the great commanding theatre of this nation, and the threshold to whatever department of office a man is qualified to enter. With your reputation, talents, and correct views, used with the necessary prudence, you will at once be placed at the head of the republican body in the House of Representatives; and after obtaining the standing which a little time will ensure you, you may look, at your own will, into the military, the judiciary, diplomatic, or other civil departments, with a certainty of being in either whatever you please. And in the present state of what may be called the eminent talents of our country, you may be assured of being engaged through life in the most honorable employments. If you come in at the next election, you will begin your course with a new administration. That administration will be opposed by a faction, small in numbers, but governed by no principle but the most envenomed malignity. They will endeavor to batter down the Executive before it will have time, by its purity

and correctness, to build up a confidence with the people, founded on experiment. By supporting them you will lay for yourself a broad foundation in the public confidence, and indeed you will become the Colossus of the republican government of your country. * * * Perhaps I ought to apologize for the frankness of this communication. It proceeds from an ardent zeal to see this government (the idol of my soul) continue in good hands, and from a sincere desire to see you whatever you wish to be.—To WILLIAM WIRT. v, 233. (W., Jan. 1808.)

9156. WISDOM, Hereditary.—Wisdom is not hereditary.—To WILLIAM JOHNSON. vii, 291. FORD ED., x, 227. (M., 1823.)

9157. WISDOM, Honesty and.—A wise man, if nature has not formed him honest, will yet act as if he were honest; because he will find it the most advantageous and wise part in the long run.—To JAMES MONROE. FORD ED., iv, 40. (P., 1785.)

9158. WISTAR (Caspar), Philosophical society and.—I rejoice in the election of Dr. Wistar [to the presidency of the Philosophical Society], and trust that his senior standing in the Society will have been considered as a fair motive of preference of those whose merits, standing alone, would have justly entitled them to the honor, and who, as juniors, according to the course of nature, may still expect their turn.—To JOHN VAUGHAN. vi, 417. (M., 1815.)

— WOMEN, Appointment to office.— See OFFICES.

9159. WOMEN, Barbarism and.—The [Indian] women are submitted to unjust drudgery. This, I believe, is the case with every barbarous people. With such, force is law. The stronger sex, therefore, imposes on the weaker. * * * Were we in equal barbarism, our females would be equal drudges. —NOTES ON VIRGINIA. viii, 305. FORD ED., iii, 153. (1782.)

9160. WOMEN, Civilization and.—It is an honorable circumstance for man, that the first moment he is at his ease, he allots the internal employments to his female partner, and takes the external on himself. And this circumstance, or its reverse, is a pretty good indication that a people are, or are not at their ease. Among the Indians, this indication fails from a particular cause; every Indian man is a soldier or warrior, and the whole body of warriors constitute a standing army, always employed in war or hunting. To support that army, there remain no laborers but the women. Here, then, is so heavy a military establishment, that the civil part of the nation is reduced to women only. But this is a barbarous perversion of the natural destination of the two sexes—TRAVELS IN LORRAINE. ix, 396. (1787.)

9161. WOMEN, Domestic life.—You think that the pleasures of Paris more than supply its want of domestic happiness; in other words, that a Parisian is happier than an American. You will change your opinion, and come over to mine in the end. Recollect the women of this capital [Paris], some on foot, some on horses, and some in carriages, hunting pleasure in the streets, in routs and assemblies, and forgetting that they have left it behind them in their nurseries; compare them with our own countrywomen occupied in the tender and tranquil amusements of domestic life, and confess that it is a comparison of Americans and angels.—To Mrs. William Bingham. Ford ed., v, 9. (P., 1788.)

9162. ———— ————. American women have the good sense to value domestic happiness above all other, and the art to cultivate it beyond all other. There is no part of the earth where so much of this is enjoyed as in America.—To Mrs. William Bingham. Ford ed., v, 9. (P., 1788.)

— **WOMEN, Education.**—See Education, Female.

9163. WOMEN, Government and.— However nature may by mental or physical disqualifications have marked infants and the weaker sex for the protection, rather than the direction of government, yet among the men who either pay or fight for their country, no line of right can be drawn.—To John H. Pleasants. vii, 345. Ford ed., x, 303. (M., 1824.)

9164. WOMEN, Horseback riding.—A lady should never ride a horse which she might not safely ride without a bridle.—To Mary Jefferson. Ford ed., v, 328. (Pa., 1791.)

9165. WOMEN, Labor and.—I observe women and children carrying heavy burdens, and laboring with the hoe. This is an unequivocal indication of extreme poverty. Men, in a civilized country, never expose their wives and children to labor above their force and sex, as long as their own labor can protect them from it.—Travels in France. ix, 313. (1787.)

9166. ———— ————. The women here [Lorraine] as in Germany, do all sorts of work. While one considers them as useful and rational companions, one cannot forget that they are also objects of our pleasures; nor can they ever forget it. While employed in dirt and drudgery, some tag of a ribbon, some ring, or bit of bracelet, earbob or necklace, or something of that kind, will show that the desire of pleasing is never suspended in them.— Travels in Lorraine. ix, 396. (1787.)

9167. WOMEN, Natural equality of.— It is civilization alone which replaces women in the enjoyment of their natural equality. That first teaches us to subdue the selfish passions, and to respect those rights in others which we value in ourselves.—Notes on Virginia. viii, 305. Ford ed., iii, 153. (1782.)

9168. WOMEN, Needlework.—In the country life of America, there are many moments when a woman can have recourse to nothing but her needle for employment. In a dull company, and in dull weather, for instance, it is ill-mannered to read, ill manners to leave them; no card-playing there among genteel people—that is abandoned to black-

guards. The needle is, then, a valuable resource. Besides, without knowing how to use it herself, how can the mistress of a family direct the work of her servants?—To Martha Jefferson. Ford ed., iv, 373. (1787.)

9169. WOMEN, Politics and.—All the world is now politically mad. Men, women, children talk nothing else, and you know that naturally they talk much, loud and warm. Society is spoiled by it, at least for those who, like myself, are but lookers on. You, too, [in America] have had your political fever. But our good ladies, I trust, have been too wise to wrinkle their foreheads with politics. They are contented to soothe and calm the minds of their husbands returning ruffled from political debate.—To Mrs. William Bingham. Ford ed., v, 9. (P., 1788.)

9170. WOMEN, Tenderness for.— Women are formed by nature for attentions, not for hard labor. A woman never forgets one of the numerous train of little offices which belong to her. A man forgets often.— Travels in France. ix, 397. (1787.)

9171. WORDS, Use of.—I am not scrupulous about words when they are once explained. —To George Hammond. iii, 515. Ford ed., vi, 187. (Pa., 1793.)

9172. WORLD, End of.—I hope you will have good sense enough to disregard those foolish predictions that the world is to be at an end soon. The Almighty has never made known to anybody at what time He created it; nor will He tell anybody when He will put an end to it, if He ever means to do it. As to preparations for that event, the best way for you is to be always prepared for it. The only way to be so is, never to say or do a bad thing. If ever you are about to say anything amiss, or to do anything wrong, consider beforehand you will feel something within you which will tell you it is wrong, and ought not to be said or done. This is your conscience, and be sure and obey it. Our Maker has given us all this faithful internal monitor, and if you always obey it you will always be prepared for the end of the world; or for a much more certain event, which is death. This must happen to all; it puts an end to the world as to us; and the way to be ready for it is never to do a wrong act.—To Martha Jefferson. D. L. J. 70. (1783.)

9173. WORTH, American appreciation of.—I know no country where * * * public esteem is so attached to worth, regardless of wealth [as it is in America].—To Mrs. Church. Ford ed., vi, 455. (G., 1793.)

9174. WORTH, Esteem for moral.—My anxieties on this subject will never carry me beyond the use of fair and honorable means, of truth and reason; nor have they ever lessened my esteem for moral worth, nor alienated my affections from a single friend, who did not first withdraw himself. Whenever this happened, I confess I have not been insensible to it; yet have ever kept myself open to a return of their justice.—To Mrs. John Adams. iv, 562. Ford ed., viii, 312. (M., 1804.)

9175. WRETCHEDNESS, Life and.— The Giver of life gave it for happiness and not for wretchedness.—To JAMES MONROE. i, 319. FORD ED., iii, 59. (M., 1782.)

9176. WRIGHT (Frances), Works of.— Miss Wright had before favored me with the first edition of her American work; but her "Few Days in Athens", was entirely new, and has been a treat to me of the highest order. The matter and manner of the dialogue is strictly ancient; and the principles of the sects are beautifully and candidly explained and contrasted; and the scenery and portraiture of the interlocutors are of higher finish than anything in that line left us by the ancients; and like Ossian, if not ancient, it is equal to the best morsels of antiquity. I augur, from this instance, that Herculaneum is likely to furnish better specimens of modern than of ancient genius; and may we not hope more from the same pen?—To MARQUIS LAFAYETTE. vii, 326. FORD ED., x, 282. (M., 1823.)

9177. WRITING, For newspapers.— I have preserved through life a resolution, set in a very early part of it, never to write in a public paper without subscribing my name to it, and to engage openly an adversary who does not let himself be seen, is staking all against nothing.—To EDWARD RANDOLPH. iii, 470. (1792.)

9178. WRITING, Illegible.— I return you Mr. Coxe's letter which has cost me much time at two or three different attempts to decipher it. Had I such a correspondent, I should certainly admonish him that, if he would not so far respect my time as to write to me legibly, I should so far respect it myself as not to waste it in decomposing and recomposing his hieroglyphics.—To JAMES MADISON. FORD ED., x, 275. (M., 1823.)

9179. WRONG, Correction of.— A conviction that we are right accomplishes half the difficulty of correcting wrong.—To ARCHIBALD THWEAT. vii, 199. FORD ED., x, 184. (M., 1821.)

9180. WRONG, Opposition to foreign.— I doubt not your aid * * * towards carrying into effect the measures of your country, and enforcing the sacred principle, that in opposing foreign wrong there must be but one mind.—R. TO A. N. Y. TAMMANY SOCIETY. viii, 127. (Feb. 1808.)

9181. WRONG, Resistance to.— We have borne patiently a great deal of wrong, on the consideration that if nations go to war for every degree of injury, there would never be peace on earth. But when patience has begotten false estimates of its motives, when wrongs are pressed because it is believed they will be borne, resistance becomes morality. —To MADAME DE STAEL. v, 133. (W., 1807.)

9182. WRONG, Restrain.— We * * * owe it to mankind, as well as to ourselves, to restrain wrong by resistance, and to defeat those calculations of which justice is not the basis.—SEVENTH ANNUAL MESSAGE. viii. FORD ED., ix, 146.

9183. WRONG, Submission to.— We love peace, yet spurn a tame submission to wrong.—R. TO A. N. Y. TAMMANY SOCIETY. viii, 127. (1808.)

9184. WRONGS, Republican vs. Monarchical.— Compare the number of wrongs

committed with impunity by citizens among us, with those committed by the sovereigns in other countries, and the last will be found most numerous, most oppressive on the mind, and most degrading to the dignity of man.— ANSWERS TO M. DE MEUNIER. ix, 292. FORD ED., iv, 147. (P., 1786.)

9185. WYTHE (George), Ability of.— The pride of William and Mary College is Mr. Wythe, one of the Chancellors of the State, and Professor of Law. He is one of the greatest men of the age, having held without competition the first place at the bar of our General Court for twenty-five years, and always distinguished by the most spotless virtue.—To RALPH IZARD. ii, 428. (P., 1788.)

9186. WYTHE (George), American Revolution and.— George Wythe was one of the very few (for I can barely speak of them in the plural number) * * * who, from the commencement of the [Revolutionary] contest, hung our connection with Great Britain on its true hook, that of a common king. His unassuming character, however, made him appear as a follower, while his sound judgment kept him in a line with the freest spirit.—To WILLIAM WIRT. vi, 368. FORD ED., ix, 469. (M., 1814.)

9187. ——— ———. On the dawn of the Revolution, instead of higgling on half-way principles, as others did who feared to follow their reason, he took his stand on the solid ground that the only link of political union between us and Great Britain, was the identity of our Executive; that that nation and its Parliament had no more authority over us than we had over them, and that we were coordinate nations with Great Britain and Hanover.—To JOHN SAUNDERSON. i, 113. (M., 1820.)

9188. WYTHE (George), Cato of America.— No man ever left behind him a character more venerated than George Wythe. His virtue was of the purest tint; his integrity inflexible and his justice exact; of warm patriotism, and, devoted as he was to liberty and the natural and equal rights of man, he might truly be called the Cato of his country, without the avarice of the Roman, for a more disinterested person never lived.*—To JOHN SAUNDERSON. i, 114. (M., 1820.)

9189. WYTHE (George), Honor of his age.— The honor of his own, and the model of future times.—To JOHN SAUNDERSON. i, 114. (M., 1820.)

9190. WYTHE (George), Lectures of.— Your favor gave me the first information that the lectures of my late master and friend exist in MS. * * * His mind was too accurate, his reasoning powers too strong, to have committed anything to paper materially incorrect. It is unfortunate that there should be *lacunæ* in them. But you are mistaken in supposing I could supply them. It is now thirty-seven years since I left the bar, and have ceased to think on subjects of law; and the constant occupation of my mind by other concerns has obliterated from it all but the strongest traces of the science. Others, I am sure, can be found equal to it, and none more so than Judge Roane. It is not my time or trouble which I wish to spare on this occasion. They are due, in any extent, to the memory of one who was

* George Wythe was one of the signers of the Declaration, Jefferson, Chief Justice Marshall and Henry Clay were among his law pupils.—EDITOR.

my second father. My incompetence is the real obstacle; and in any other circumstance connected with the publication, in which I can be useful to his fame, and the public instruction, I shall be most ready to do my duty.—To JOHN TYLER. FORD ED., ix, 288. (M., 1810.)

9191. WYTHE (George), Mentor and friend.—Mr. Wythe continued to be my faithful and beloved mentor in youth, and my most affectionate friend through life. In 1767, he led me into the practice of the law at the bar of the General Court, at which I continued until the Revolution shut up the courts of justice.—AUTOBIOGRAPHY. i, 3. FORD ED., i, 4. (1821.)

9192. WYTHE (George), Supporter of Jefferson.—Mr. Wythe, while speaker [of the Virginia Legislature] in the two sessions of 1777, * * * was an able and constant associate [ot mine] in whatever was before a committee of the whole. His pure integrity, judgment and reasoning powers, gave him great weight.—AUTOBIOGRAPHY. i, 41. FORD ED., i, 56. (1821.)

9193. WYTHE (George), Virtuous.— One of the most virtuous of characters, and whose sentiments on the subject of slavery are unequivocal.—To DR. PRICE. i, 377. FORD ED., iv, 83. (P., 1785.)

9194. —— ——. The exalted virtue of the man will be a polar star to guide you in all matters which may touch that element of his character. But on that you will receive imputation from no man; for, as far as I know, he never had an enemy.—To JOHN SAUNDERSON. i, 112. (M., 1820.)

— XENOPHON.—See PHILOSOPHY.

9195. X. Y. Z. PLOT, Artful misrepresentation of.—The most artful misrepresentations of the contents of these papers have been published, and have produced such a shock in the republican mind, as has never been seen since our independence. We are to dread the effects of this dismay till their fuller information.*—To JAMES MADISON. iv, 233. FORD ED., vii, 236. (Pa., April 1798.)

9196. X. Y. Z. PLOT, Astonishment over.—The public mind appears still in a state of astonishment. There never was a moment in which the aid of an able pen was so important to place things in their just attitude. On this depend the inchoate movement in the eastern mind, and the fate of the elections in that quarter. * * * I would not propose to you such a task on any ordinary occasion. But be assured that a well-digested analysis of these papers would now decide the future turn of things, which are at this moment on the creen.—To JAMES MADISON. iv, 234. FORD ED., vii, 237. (Pa., April 1798.)

9197. X. Y. Z. PLOT, Delusion through. —There is a most respectable part of our State [Virginia] who have been enveloped in the X. Y. Z. delusion, and who destroy our

* In 1797, Charles Cotesworth Pinckney, Elbridge Gerry and John Marshall were sent on an extraordinary mission to the French Republic, the Directory being then in power. Shortly after their arrival in Paris, they received letters from unofficial persons signed X. Y. and Z, intimating that, as a preliminary to the negotiation, it would be necessary to expend a large sum of money in the way of bribes to the members of the Government. These demands were not acceded to, and the federalists made skilful political use of the incident in their warfare against the republicans.—EDITOR.

unanimity for the present moment. This disease of the imagination will pass over, because the patients are essentially republican. Indeed, the doctor is now on his way to cure it, in the guise of a tax gatherer. But give time for the medicine to work, and for the repetition of stronger doses, which must be administered. —To JOHN TAYLOR. iv, 259. FORD ED., vii, 309. (M., 1798.)

9198. —— ——. There is real reason to believe that the X. Y. Z. delusion is wearing off, and the public mind beginning to take the same direction it was getting into before that measure. Gerry's dispatches will tend strongly to open the eyes of the people. Besides this several other impressive circumstances will be bearing on the public mind. The Alien and Sedition laws as before, the direct tax, the additional army and navy, an usurious loan to set these follies on foot, a prospect of heavy additional taxes as soon as they are completed, still heavier taxes if the government forces on the war recruiting officers lounging at every court-house and decoying the laborer from his plow.—To JAMES MONROE. iv, 265. FORD ED., vii, 320. (Pa., Jan. 1799.)

9199. —— ——. The violations of the Constitution, propensities to war, to expense, and to a particular foreign connection [Great Britain], which we have lately seen, are becoming evident to the people, and are dispelling that mist which X. Y. Z. had spread before their eyes.—To EDMUND PENDLETON. iv, 287. FORD ED., vii, 356. (Pa., Feb. 1799.)

9200. X. Y. Z. PLOT, Federalists and.— When Pinckney, Marshall, and Dana were nominated to settle our differences with France, it was suspected by many, from what was understood of their dispositions, that their mission would not result in a settlement of differences, but would produce circumstances tending to widen the breach, and to provoke our citizens to consent to a war with that nation, and union with England. Dana's resignation and your appointment gave the first gleam of hope of a peaceable issue to the mission. For it was believed that you were sincerely disposed to accommodation; and it was not long after your arrival there, before symptoms were observed of that difference of views which had been suspected to exist. In the meantime, however, the aspect of our government towards the French Republic had become so ardent, that the people of America generally took the alarm. To the southward, their apprehensions were early excited. In the eastern States also, they at length began to break out. Meetings were held in many of your towns, and addresses to the government agreed on in opposition to war. The example was spreading like a wildfire. Other meetings were called in other places, and a general concurrence of sentiment against the apparent inclinations of the government was imminent; when, most critically for the government, the [X. Y. Z.] despatches of October 22d, prepared by your colleague Marshall, with a view to their being made public, dropped into their laps. It was truly a godsend to them, and they made the most of it. Many thousands of copies were printed and dispersed gratis, at the public expense; and the zealots for war cooperated so heartily, that there were instances of single individuals who printed and dispersed ten or twelve thousand copies at their own expense. The odiousness of the corruption supposed in those papers excited a general and high indignation among the people. Unexperienced in such maneuvres, they did not permit themselves even to suspect that the turpitude of private swindlers might mingle itself unobserved, and give its own hue to the communications of the French government, of whose participation there was neither proof nor probability. It served, nowever, for a time, the purpose intended. The people, in many places, gave a loose to the expressions of their warm indignation, and of their honest preference of war to dishonor The fever was long and successfully kept up, and in the meantime, war measures as ardently crowded. Still, however, as it was known that your colleagues were coming away, and vourself to stay. though disclaiming a senarate power to conclude a treaty, it was hoped by the lovers of peace, that a project of treaty wouid have been prepared, *ad referendum*, on principles which would have satisfied our citizens, and overawed any bias of the government towards a different policy. But the expedition of the Sophia, and, as was supposed, the suggestions of the person charged with your dispatches, and his probable misrepresentations of the real wishes of the American people, prevented these hopes. They had then only to look forward to your return for such information, either through the Executive, qr from yourself, as might present to our view the other side of the medal. The despatches of October 22d, 1797, had presented one face. That information, to a certain degree, is now received, and the public will see from your correspondence with Talleyrand, that France, as you testify, "was sincere and anxious to obtain a reconciliation, not wishing us to break the British treaty. but only to give her equivalent stipulations; and in general was disposed to a liberal treaty". And they will judge whether Mr. Pickering's report shows an inflexible determination to believe no declarations the French government can make, nor any opinion which you, judging on the spot and from actual view, can give of their sincerity, and to meet their designs of peace with operations of war.—To ELBRIDGE GERRY. iv, 270. FORD ED., vii, 330. (Pa., Jan. 1799.)

9201. X. Y. Z. PLOT, French government and.—You know what a wicked use has been made of the French negotiation; and particularly the X. Y. Z. dish cooked up by Marshall, where the swindlers are made to appear as the French government. Art and industry combined have certainly wrought out of this business a wonderful effect on the people. Yet they have been astonished more than they have understood it, and now that Gerry's correspondence comes out, clearing the French government of that turpitude, and showing them "sincere in their dispositions for peace. not wishing us to break the British treaty, and willing to arrange a liberal one with us", the people will be disposed to suspect they have been duped. But these communications are too voluminous for them, and beyond their reach. A recapitulation is now wanting * * * . Nobody in America can do it so well as vourself * * * . If the understanding of the people could be rallied to the truth on this subject, by exposing the dupery practiced on them, there are so many other things about to bear on them favorably for the resurrection of their republican spirit, that a reduction of the administration to constitutional principles cannot fail to be the effect.—To EDMUND PENDLETON. iv, 274. FORD ED., vii, 337. (Pa., 1799.)

9202. X. Y. Z. PLOT, War and.—Young E. Gerry informed me some time ago that he had engaged a person to write the life of his father, and asked for any materials I could furnish. I sent him some letters, but in searching for them I found two, too precious to be trusted by mail, of the date of 1801, January 15 and 20, in answer to one I had written him January 26, 1799, two years before. It furnishes authentic proof that in the X. Y. Z. mission to France, it was the wish of Pickering, Marshall, Pinckney and the Federalists of that stamp, to avoid a treaty with France and to bring on war, a fact we charged on them at the time and this lette proves, and that their X. Y. Z. report was cooked up to dispose the people to war. Gerry, tneir colleague, was not of their sentiment, and this is his statement of that transaction. During the two years between my letter and his answer, he was wavering between Mr. Adams and myself, between his attachment to Mr. Adams personally on the one hand, and to republicanism on the other; for he was republican, but timid and indecisive. The event of the election of 1800-1, put an end to his hesitations.—To JAMES MADISON. FORD ED., x, 245. (M., Jan. 1823.)

9203. YAZOO LANDS, Speculation in.—Arthur Campbell * * * says the Yazoo bargain is likely to drop with the consent of the purchasers. He explains it thus: They expected to pay for the lands in public paper at par, which they had bought at half a crown a pound. Since the rise in the value of the public paper, they have gained as much on that as they would have done by investing it in the Yazoo lands; perhaps more, as it puts a large sum of specie at their command, which they can turn to better account. They are, therefore, likely to acquiesce under the determination of the government of Georgia to consider the contract as forfeited by non-payment.—To PRESIDENT WASHINGTON. iii, 251. FORD ED., v, 324. (Pa., 1791.)

9204. YAZOO LANDS, Title to.—I * * * return the petition of Mr. Moultrie on behalf of the South Carolina Yazoo Company. Without noticing that some of the highest functions of sovereignty are assumed in the very papers which he annexes as his justification, I am of opinion that the government should formally maintain this ground; that the Indians have a right to the occupation of their lands, independent of the States within whose chartered lines they happen to be; that until they cede them by treaty or other transaction equivalent to a treaty, no act of a State can give a right to such lands; that neither under the present Constitution, nor the ancient confederation, had any State or person a right to treat with the Indians, without the consent of the General Government; that that consent has never been given to any treaty for the cession of the lands in question: that the government is determined to exert all its energy for the patronage and protection of the rights of the Indians, and the preservation of peace between the United States and them; and that if any settlements are made on lands not ceded by them, without the previous consent of the United States, the government will think itself bound, not only to declare to the Indians that such settlements are without the authority or protection of the United States, but to remove them also by the public force.—To HENRY KNOX. iii, 280. FORD ED., v, 370. (Pa., 1791.)

9205. YELLOW FEVER, Cities and.—[As to] the town which you have done me the honor to name after me. and to lay out according to an idea I had formerly expressed to you, I am thoroughly persuaded that it will be found handsome and pleasant, and I do believe it to be the best means of preserving the cities of America from the scourge of the yellow fever, which being peculiar to our country, must be derived from some peculiarity in it. That peculiarity I take to be our cloudless skies. In Europe, where the sun does not shine more than half the number of days in the year which it does in America, they can build their town in a solid block with impunity; but here a constant sun produces too great an accumulation of heat to admit that. Ventilation is indispensably necessary. Experience has taught us that in the open air of the country the yellow fever is not only not generated, but ceases to be infectious.—To GOVERNOR HARRISON. iv, 471. (W., 1803.)

9206. —— ——. I have supposed it practicable to prevent its generation by building our cities on a more open plan. Take, for instance, the checker board for a plan. Let the black squares only be building squares, and the white ones be left open, in turf and trees. Every square of houses will be surrounded by four open squares, and .every house will front an open square. The atmosphere of such a town would be like that of the country, insusceptible of the miasmata which produce yellow fever. I have proposed that the enlargements of the city of New Orleans * * * shall be on this plan.—To C. F. VOLNEY. iv, 572. (W., 1805.)

9207. —— ——. I really wish effect to the hints in my letter to you for so laying off the additions to the city of New Orleans, as to shield it from yellow fever. My confidence in the idea is founded in the acknowledged experience that we have never seen the *genuine* yellow fever extend itself into the country, or even to the outskirts or open parts of a close-built city. In the plan I propose, every square would be surrounded, on every side, by open and pure air, in fact, be a separate town with fields or open suburbs around it.—To GOVERNOR CLAIBORNE. v, 520. (M., 1810.)

9208. YELLOW FEVER, Infectious.— On the question whether the yellow fever is infectious or endemic, the medical faculty is divided into two parties, and it certainly is not the office of the public functionary to denounce either party as Dr. Rush proposes. Yet, so far as they are called on to act, they must form for themselves an opinion to act on. In the early history of the disease, I did suppose it to be infectious. Not reading any of the party papers on either side, I continued in this supposition until the fever at Alexandria brought facts under my own eye, as it were, proving it could not be communicated but *in a local atmosphere*, pretty exactly circumscribed. With the composition of this atmosphere we are unacquainted. We know only that it is generated *near the water side, in close built cities, under warm climates.* According to the rules of philosophizing when one sufficient cause for an effect is known, it is not within the economy of nature to employ two. If local atmosphere suffices to produce the fever, miasmata from a human subject are not necessary and probably do not enter into the cause. Still, it is not within my province to decide the question; but as it may be within yours to require the performance of quarantine or not, I execute a private duty in submitting Dr. Rush's letter to your consideration.—To GOVERNOR PAGE. FORD ED., viii, 316. (M., 1804.)

9209. YELLOW FEVER, Origin.—Facts appear to have established that it is originated here by a local atmosphere, which is never generated but in the lower, closer, and dirtier parts of our large cities, and in the neighborhood of the water; and that, to catch the disease, you must enter the local atmosphere. Persons having taken the disease in the infected quarter, and going into the country, are nursed and buried by their friends, without an example of communicating it. * * * It is certainly an epidemic, not a contagious disease.—To C. F. VOLNEY. iv, 570. (W., 1805.)

9210. YELLOW FEVER, Quarantine and.—In the course of the several visitations by this disease [yellow fever], it has appeared that it is strictly local, incident to the cities and on the tide waters only; incommunicable in the country, either by persons under· the disease or by goods carried from diseased places; that its access is with the autumn, and that it disappears with the early frost·. These restrictions, within narrow limits of time and space, give security even to our maritime cities, during three-fourths of the year, and to the country always. Although from these facts it appears unnecessary, yet to satisfy the fears of foreign nations, and cautions on their part not to be complained of in a danger whose limits are yet unknown to them, I have strictly enjoined on the officers at the head of the customs to certify with exact truth for every vessel sailing for a foreign port, the state of health respecting this fever which prevailed at the place from which she sailed. Under every motive from character and duty to certify the truth, I have no doubt they have faithfully executed this injunction. Much real injury has, however, been sustained from a propensity to identify with this endemic, and to call by the same name, fevers of very different kinds, which have always been known at all times and in almost all countries, and never have been placed among those deemed contagious. As we advance in our knowledge of this disease, as facts develop the source from which individuals receive it, the State authorities charged with the care of the public health, and Congress with that of the general commerce, will become able to regulate with effect their respective functions in these departments. The burden of quarantines is at home as well as abroad: their efficacy merits examination. Although the health laws of the States should be found to need no present revisal by Congress, yet commerce claims that their attention be ever awake to them.—FIFTH ANNUAL MESSAGE. viii, 46. FORD ED., viii, 387. (Dec. 1805.)

— YEOMANRY, Beggared.—See EMBARGO, 2589.

9211. YORKTOWN, Gratitude to France.—If in the minds of any, the motives of gratitude to our good allies were not sufficiently apparent, the part they have borne in this action [Yorktown] must amply evince them.—To GENERAL WASHINGTON. i, 314. FORD ED., iii, 51. (M., 1781.)

9212. YOUNG MEN, Education.—I am not a friend to placing young men in populous cities [for their education] because they acquire there habits and partialities which do not contribute to the happiness of their after life.—To DR. WISTAR. v, 104. FORD ED., ix, 79. (W., 1807.)

9213. —— ——. A part of my occupation, and by no means the least pleasing, is the direction of the studies of such young men as ask it. They place themselves in the neighboring village and have the use of my library and counsel, and make a part of my society. In advising the course of their reading, I endeavor to keep their attention fixed on the main objects of all science, the freedom and happiness of man. So that coming to bear a share in the councils and government of their country, they will keep ever in view the sole objects of all legitimate government.—To GENERAL KOSCIUSKO. v, 509. (M., 1810.)

9214. YOUNG MEN, Enthusiasm of.— Bonaparte will conquer the world if they [the European powers] do not learn his secret of composing armies of young men only, whose enthusiasm and health enable them to surmount all obstacles.—To MR. BIDWELL. v, 16. (W., 1806.)

9215. YOUNG MEN, Future rulers.— They [the students of the University of Virginia] are exactly the persons who are to succeed to the government of our country, and to rule its future enmities, its friendships and fortunes.—To J. EVELYN DENISON. vii. 415. (M., 1825.)

9216. YOUNG MEN, Patronizing.—I have written to you in the style to which I have been always accustomed with you, and which perhaps it is time I should lay aside. But while old men are sensible enough of their own advance in years, they do not sufficiently recollect it in those whom they have seen young.—To WILLIAM SHORT. iii, 503. FORD ED., vi, 156. (Pa., 1793.)

9217. YOUNG MEN, Public life and.— Wythe's school is numerous. They hold weekly courts and assemblies in the Capitol. The professors join in it, and the young men dispute with elegance, method and learning. This single school, by throwing from time to time new hands well principled, and well-informed into the Legislature, will be of infinite value.—To JAMES MADISON. FORD ED., ii, 322. (R., 1780.)

9218. YOUNG MEN, Reform and.—The [French] officers, who had been to America, were mostly young men, less shackled by habit and prejudice, and more ready to assent to the suggestions of common sense and feeling of common rights, than others. They come back [to France] with new ideas and impressions.—AUTOBIOGRAPHY. i, 69. FORD ED., i, 96. (1821.)

9219. YOUNG MEN, Self-government and.—Three sons, and hopeful ones too, are a rich treasure. I rejoice when I hear of young men of virtue and talents, worthy to receive, and likely to preserve the splendid inheritance of self-government, which we have acquired and shaped for them.—To JUDGE TYLER. iv, 549. (W., 1804.)

9220. —— ——. The sentiments you express * * * are particularly solacing to those who, having labored faithfully in establishing the right of self-government, see in the rising generation, into whose hands it is passing, that purity of principle, and energy of character, which will protect and preserve it through their day, and deliver it over to their sons as they receive it from their fathers. —R. TO A. PITTSBURG YOUNG REPUBLICANS. viii, 141. (1808.)

9221. YOUNG MEN, Slavery and.—I look to the rising generation, and not to the one now in power, for these great reformations. [Respecting slavery.]—To GENERAL CHASTELLUX. i, 340. FORD ED., iii, 71. (P., 1785.)

9222. —— ——. The college of William and Mary * * * is the place where are collected together all the young men of Virginia under preparation for public life. * * * I am satisfied if you could resolve to address an exhortation to those young men, with all that eloquence of which you are master, that its influence on the future decision of this important question [slavery] would be great, perhaps decisive.—To DR. PRICE. i, 377. FORD ED., iv, 83. (P., 1785.)

9223. —— ——. [In Virginia] * * * the sacred side [in the conflict with slavery] is gaining daily recruits from the influx into office of young men grown and growing up. These have sucked in the principles of liberty, as it were, with their mothers' milk; and it is to them I look with anxiety to turn the fate of this question.—To DR. PRICE. i, 377. FORD ED., iv, 83. (P., 1785.)

9224. YOUNG MEN, Surrender to.—I leave the world and its affairs to the young and energetic, and resign myself to their care, of whom I have endeavored to take care when young.—To CHARLES PINCKNEY. vii, 180. FORD ED., x, 162. (M., 1820.)

9225. YOUNG WOMEN, Power of.—All the handsome young women [of Paris] are for the *Tiers État*, and this is an army more powerful in France than the 200,000 men of the King.—To DAVID HUMPHREYS. iii, 11. FORD ED., v, 87. (P., 1789.)

9226. ZEAL, Fervent.—Fervent zeal is all which I can be sure of carrying into their [Congress] service.—To JOHN JAY. i, 339. (P., 1785.)

9227. ZEAL, Resources of.—Utterly indeed, should I despair, did not the presence of many whom I here see remind me, that in the high authorities provided by our Constitution, I shall find resources of wisdom, of virtue, and of zeal, on which to rely under all difficulties.—FIRST INAUGURAL ADDRESS. viii, 1. FORD ED., viii, 2. (1801.)

9228. ZEAL, Ridicule and.—I fear that my zeal will make me expose myself to ridicule * * * but this risk becomes a duty by the bare possibility of doing good.—To DR. RAMSAY. ii, 216. (P., 1787.)

APPENDIX

CONTENTS

	PAGE
Reply to Lord North's Conciliatory Proposition	959
Committees of Correspondence	961
A Summary View of the Rights of British America	963
Declaration of Independence	969
Preamble to the Virginia Constitution	972
Debates on the Articles of Confederation	973
A Bill for Establishing Religious Freedom	976
Kentucky Resolutions	977
First Inaugural Address	980
Second Inaugural Address	982
Address to the General Assembly of Virginia	984
Address to the Inhabitants of Albemarle Co., in Virginia	985
Declaration and Protest of the Commonwealth of Virginia	986
Estrangement and Reconciliation of Jefferson and Adams	988

APPENDIX

REPLY TO LORD NORTH'S CONCILIATORY PROPOSITION

The Congress proceeding to take into their consideration a resolution of the House of Commons of Great Britain, referred to them by the several Assemblies of New Jersey, Pennsylvania, and Virginia, which resolution is in these words: " That it is the opinion, &c.," are of opinion:

That the Colonies of America possess the exclusive privilege of giving and granting their own money; that this involves the right of deliberating whether they will make any gift, for what purposes it shall be made, and what shall be the amount of the gift; and that it is a high breach of this privilege for any body of men, extraneous to their constitutions, to prescribe the purposes for which money shall be levied on them; to take to themselves the authority of judging of their conditions, circumstances, and situation, of determining the amount of the contribution to be levied:

That, as they possess a right of appropriating their gifts, so are they entitled at all times to inquire into their application, to see that they be not wasted among the venal and corrupt for the purpose of undermining the civil rights of the givers, nor yet be diverted to the support of standing armies, inconsistent with their freedom, and subversive of their quiet. To propose, therefore, as this resolution does, that the moneys, given by the Colonies, shall be subject to the disposal of Parliament alone, is to propose, that they shall relinquish this right of inquiry, and put it in the power of others, to render their gifts ruinous, in proportion as they are liberal:

That this privilege of giving, or withholding our moneys, is an important barrier against the undue exertion of prerogative, which, if left altogether without control, may be exercised to our great oppression; and all history shows how efficacious its intercession for redress of grievances, and reestablishment of rights, and how improvident would be the surrender of so powerful a mediator.

We are of opinion:

That the proposition contained in this resolution is unreasonable and insidious; unreasonable, because if we declare we accede to it, we declare without reservation we will purchase the favor of Parliament, not knowing, at the same time, at what price they will please to estimate their favor. It is insidious, because individual colonies, having bid and bidden again, till they find the avidity of the seller unattainable by all their powers, are then to return into opposition, divided from their sister Colonies, whom the minister will have previously detached by a grant of easier terms, or by an artful procrastination of a definitive answer:

That the suspension of the exercise of their pretended power of taxation being expressly made commensurate with the continuing of our gifts, these must be perpetual to make that so; whereas no experience has shown that a gift of perpetual revenue secures a perpetual return of duty, or of kind dispositions. On the contrary, the Parliament itself, wisely attentive to this observation, are in the established practice of granting their own money from year to year only.

Though desirous and determined to consider, in the most dispassionate view every advance towards reconciliation, made by the British Parliament, let our brethren of Britain reflect what could have been the sacrifice to men of free spirits, had even fair terms been proffered by freemen when attended as these were, with circumstances of insult and defiance. A proposition to give our money, when accompanied with large fleets and armies, seems addressed to our fears, rather than to our freedom. With what patience, would they have received articles of treaty, from any power on earth, when borne on the point of the bayonet, by military plenipotentiaries?

We think the attempt unnecessary and unwarrantable to raise upon us, by force or by threats, our proportional contributions to the common defence, when all know, and themselves acknowledge, we have fully contributed, whenever called to contribute, in the character of freemen.

We are of opinion it is not just that the Colonies should be required to oblige themselves to other contributions, while Great Britain possesses a monopoly of their trade. This does of itself lay them under heavy contribution. To demand, therefore, an additional contribution in the form of a tax, is to demand the double of their equal proportion. If we are to contribute equally with the other parts of the empire, let us equally with them enjoy free commerce with the whole world. But while the restrictions on our trade shut to us the resources of wealth, is it just we should bear all other burthens, equally with those to whom every resource is open?

We conceive, that the British Parliament has no right to intermeddle with our provisions for the support of civil government, or administration of justice; that the provisions we have made are such as please ourselves. They answer the substantial purposes of government, and of justice, and other purposes than these should not be answered. We do not mean that our people shall be burthened with oppressive taxes to provide sinecures for the idle or wicked, under color of providing for a civil list. While Parliament pursue their plan of civil government within their own jurisdiction, we hope, also, to pursue ours without molestation.

We are of opinion the proposition is altogether unsatisfactory because it imports only a suspension, not a renunciation of the right to tax us; because, too, it does not propose to repeal the several acts of Parliament, passed for the purposes of restraining the trade, and altering the form of government of one of the Eastern Colonies; extending the boundaries, and changing the government and religion of Quebec; enlarging the jurisdiction of the Courts of Admiralty and Vice-admiralty; taking from us the rights of trial by jury of the vicinage in cases affecting both life and prosperity; transporting us into other countries to be tried for criminal offences; exempting, by mock trial, the murderers of Colonists from punishment; and for quartering soldiers upon us, in times of profound peace. Nor do they renounce the power of suspending our own legislatures, and of legislating for us themselves in all cases whatsoever. On the contrary, to show they mean no discontinuance of injury, they pass acts, at the very time of holding out this proposition, for restraining the commerce and fisheries of the Province of New England; and for interdicting the trade of the other Colonies, with all foreign nations. This proves unequivocally, they mean not to relinquish the exercise of indiscriminate legislation over us.

Upon the whole, this proposition seems to have been held up to the whole world to deceive it into a belief that there is no matter in dispute between us but the single circumstance of the mode of levying taxes, which mode they are so good as to give up to us, of course that the Colonies are unreasonable if they are not. thereby, perfectly satisfied; whereas, in truth, our adversaries not only still claim a right of demanding *ad libitum*, and of taxing us themselves to the full amount of their demands if we do not fulfil their pleasure, which leaves us without anything we can call property, but, what is of more importance, and what they keep in this proposal out of sight, as if no such point was in contest, they claim a right of altering our charters, and established laws which leave us without the least security for our lives or liberties.

The proposition seems, also, calculated more particularly to lull into fatal security our well-affected fellow subjects on that other side of the water, till time should be given for the operation of those arms which a British minister pronounced would instantaneously reduce the "*cowardly*" sons of America to unreserved submission. But, when the world reflects how inadequate to justice are the vaunted terms, when it attends to the rapid and bold succession of injuries, which, during a course of eleven years, have been aimed at these Colonies, when it reviews the pacific and respectful expostulations, which, during that whole time, have been made the sole arms we oppose to them, when it observes, that our complaints were either not heard at all, or were answered with new and accumulated injuries; when it recollects, that the minister himself declared on an early occasion, "that he would never treat with America, till he had brought her to his feet"; and that an avowed partisan of ministry has, more lately, denounced against America the dreadful sentence "*Delenda est Carthago*"; and that this was done in the presence of a British senate, and being unreproved by them, must be taken to be their own sentiments, when it considers the great armaments with which they have invaded us and the circumstances of cruelty, with which these have commenced and prosecuted hostilities; when these things, we say, are laid together, and attentively considered, can the world be deceived into an opinion that we are unreasonable, or can it hesitate to believe with us, that nothing but our own exertions, may defeat the ministerial sentence of death, or submission? *—Ford ed., i, 476. (July 25, 1775.)

* This is Jefferson's draft. Congress made several verbal alterations.—Editor.

COMMITTEES OF CORRESPONDENCE

A court of inquiry held in Rhode Island in 1762, with a power to send persons to England to be tried for offences committed here,* was considered at our session [Virginia House of Burgesses] of the spring of 1773, as demanding attention. Not thinking our old and leading members up to the point of forwardness and zeal which the times required, Mr. [Patrick] Henry. Richard Henry Lee, Francis L. Lee, Mr. [Dabney] Carr and myself agreed to meet in the evening, in a private room of the Raleigh [tavern], to consult on the state of things. * * * We were all sensible that the most urgent of all measures was that of coming to an understanding with all the other Colonies to consider the British claims as a common cause to all, and to produce a unity of action; and, for this purpose, that a Committee of Correspondence in each Colony would be the best instrument for intercommunication; and that their first measure would probably be, to propose a meeting of deputies from every Colony, at some central place, who should be charged with the direction of the measures which should be taken by all. * * * The consulting members proposed to me to move * * * [the resolutions agreed upon], but I urged that it should be done by Mr. [Dabney] Carr, my friend and brother-in-law, then a new member, to whom I wished an opportunity should be given of making known to the house his great worth and talents. It was so agreed; he moved them, they were agreed to *nem. con.*, and a Committee of Correspondence appointed, of whom Peyton Randolph, the Speaker, was chairman. The Governor (then Lord Dunmore) dissolved us, but the Committee met the next day, prepared a circular letter to the Speakers of the other Colonies, enclosing to each a copy of the resolutions, and left it in charge with their chairman to forward them by expresses.—AUTOBIOGRAPHY. i, 5. FORD ED., 7. (1821.)

The next event which excited our sympathies for Massachusetts, was the Boston port bill. by which that port was to be shut up on the 1st of June, 1774. This arrived while we [Virginia House of Burgesses] were in session in the spring of that year. The lead in the House, on these subjects, being no longer left to the old members, Mr. Henry, R. H. Lee, Francis L. Lee, three or four other members, whom I do not recollect, and myself, agreeing that we must boldly take an unequivocal stand in the line with Massachusetts, determined to meet and consult on the proper measures in the council chamber, for the benefit of the library in that room. We were under conviction of the necessity of arousing our people from the lethargy into which they had fallen, as to passing events; and thought that the appointment of a day of general fasting and prayer would be most likely to call up and alarm their attention. No example of such a solemnity had existed since the days of our distresses in the war of '55. since which a new generation had grown up. With the help, therefore, of Rushworth, whom we rummaged over for the revolutionary precedents and forms of the Puritans of that day, preserved by him, we cooked up a resolution, somewhat modernizing their phrases, for appointing the 1st day of June, on which the port bill was to commence, for a day of fasting, humiliation. and prayer, to implore Heaven to avert from us the evils of civil war, to inspire us with firmness in support of our rights, and to turn the hearts of the King and Parliament to moderation and justice. To give greater emphasis to our proposition, we agreed to wait the next morning on Mr. [Robert Carter] Nicholas, whose grave and religious character was more in unison with the tone of our resolution, and to solicit him to move it. We accordingly went to him in the morning. He moved it the same day; the 1st of June was proposed; and it passed without opposition. The Governor dissolved us as usual. * * * We returned home, and in our several counties invited the clergy to meet assemblies of the people on the 1st of June.† to perform the ceremonies of the day, and to address to them discourses suited to the occasion. The people met generally, with anxiety and alarm in their countenances, and the effect of the day, through the whole colony, was like a shock of electricity, arousing every man, and placing him erect and solidly on his centre.—AUTOBIOGRAPHY. i, 6. FORD ED., i. 9. (1821.)

The Governor dissolved us as usual. We retired to the Apollo. agreed to an association. and instructed the Committee of Correspondence to propose to the corresponding committees of the other Colonies. to appoint deputies to meet in Congress at such place, *annually*, as should be convenient, to direct, from time to time, the measures required by the general interest: and we declared that an attack on any one Colony, should be considered as an attack on the whole. This was in May [27, 1774]. We further recommended to the several counties to elect deputies to meet at Williamsburg, the 1st of August, ensuing, to consider the state of the Colony, and particularly to appoint delegates to a general Congress, should that measure be acceded to by the committees of correspondence generally. It was acceded to; Philadelphia was appointed for the place, and the 5th of September for the time of meeting.—AUTOBIOGRAPHY. i, 7. FORD ED., i. 11. (1821.)

Respecting the question, whether Committees of Correspondence originated in Virginia or Massachusetts? * * * You suppose me to have claimed it for Virginia; but certainly I have never made such a claim. The idea, I suppose, has been taken up from what is said in WIRT'S *Life of Patrick Henry*, page 87, and from an inexact attention to its precise terms. It is there said. "this House (of Burgesses, of Virginia) had the merit of originating that powerful engine of resistance, Corresponding Committees *between the Legislatures and the different Colonies*". That the fact, as here expressed is true, your letter bears witness, when it says, that the resolutions of Virginia, for this purpose, were transmitted to the speakers of the different assemblies, and by that of Massachusetts. was laid, at the next session, before that body, who appointed a committee for the specified object: adding, "thus. in Massachusetts, there were two Committees of Correspondence, one chosen by the people, the other appointed by the House of Assembly; in the former, Massachusetts preceded Virginia; in the latter, Virginia preceded Massachusetts". To the origination of committees for the interior correspondence between the counties and towns of a State, I know of no claim on the part of Virginia; and

---

* This was the famous "Gaspee" inquiry, the date being a slip for 1772.—NOTE IN FORD EDITION.
† The invitation read June 23d.
‡ The name of a public room in the Raleigh tavern.

certainly none was ever made by myself. I perceive, however, one error, into which memory had led me. Our Committee for national correspondence, was appointed in March, '73, and I well remember, that going to Williamsburg, in the month of June following, Peyton Randolph, our chairman, told me that messengers bearing dispatches between the two States, had crossed each other by the way, that of Virginia carrying our propositions for a committee of national correspondence, and that of Massachusetts, bringing, as my memory suggested, a similar proposition. But here I must have misremembered; and the resolutions brought us from Massachusetts, were probably those you mention of the town-meeting of Boston, on the motion of Mr. Samuel Adams, appointing a committee " to state the rights of the colonists, and of that province in particular, and the infringements of them; to communicate them to the several towns, as the sense of the town of Boston, and to request, of each town, a free communication of its sentiments on the subject." I suppose, therefore, that these resolutions were not received, as you think, while the House of Burgesses was in session in March, 1773, but a few days after we rose, and were probably what was sent by the messenger, who crossed ours by the way. They may, however, have been still different. I must, therefore, have been mistaken in supposing, and stating to Mr. Wirt, that the proposition of a committee for national correspondence was nearly simultaneous in Virginia and Massachusetts.—To SAMUEL A. WELLS. i, 115. FORD ED., X, 127. (M., 1819.)

A SUMMARY VIEW OF THE RIGHTS OF BRITISH AMERICA*

Resolved, That it be an instruction to the said deputies, when assembled in General Congress, with the deputies from the other States of British America, to propose to the said Congress, that an humble and dutiful address be presented to his Majesty, begging leave to lay before him, as Chief Magistrate of the British Empire, the united complaints of his Majesty's subjects in America: complaints which are excited by many unwarrantable encroachments and usurpations, attempted to be made by the legislature of one part of the empire, upon the rights which God, and the laws have given equally and independently to all. To represent to his Majesty that these, his States, have often individually made humble application to his imperial throne, to obtain, through its intervention, some redress of their injured rights; to none of which was ever even an answer condescended. Humbly to hope that this, their joint address, penned in the language of truth, and divested of those expressions of servility, which would persuade his Majesty that we are asking favors, and not rights, shall obtain from his Majesty a more respectful acceptance: and this his Majesty will think we have reason to expect, when he reflects that he is no more than the chief officer of the people, appointed by the laws, and circumscribed with definite powers, to assist in working the great machine of government, erected for their use, and, consequently, subject to their superintendence; and, in order that these, our rights, as well as the invasions of them, may be laid more fully before his Majesty, to take a view of them, from the origin and first settlement of these countries.

To remind him that our ancestors, before their emigration to America, were the free inhabitants of the British dominions in Europe, and possessed a right, which nature has given to all men, of departing from the country in which chance, not choice, has placed them of going in quest of new habitations, and of there establishing new societies, under such laws and regulations as, to them, shall seem most likely to promote public happiness. That their Saxon ancestors had, under this universal law, in like manner, left their native wilds and woods in the North of Europe, had possessed themselves of the Island of Britain, then less charged with inhabitants, and had established there that system of laws which has so long been the glory and protection of that country. Nor was ever any claim of superiority or dependence asserted over them, by that mother country from which they had migrated; and were such a claim made, it is believed his Majesty's subjects in Great Britain have too firm a feeling of the rights derived to them from their ancestors, to bow down the sovereignty of their State before such visionary pretensions.

And it is thought that no circumstance has occurred to distinguish, materially, the British from the Saxon emigration. America was conquered, and her settlements made and firmly established, at the expense of individuals, and not of the British public. Their own blood was spilt in acquiring lands for their settlement, their own fortunes expended in making that settlement effectual. For themselves they fought, for themselves they conquered, and for themselves alone they have right to hold. No shilling was ever issued from the public treasures of his Majesty, or his ancestors, for their assistance, till of very late times, after the Colonies had become established on a firm and permanent footing. That then, indeed, having become valuable to Great Britain for her commercial purposes, his Parliament was pleased to lend them assistance against an enemy who would fain have drawn to herself the benefits of their commerce, to the great aggrandizement of herself, and danger of Great Britain. Such assistance, and in such circumstances, they had often before given to Portugal and other allied States, with whom they carry on a commercial intercourse. Yet these States never supposed, that by calling in her aid, they thereby submitted themselves to her sovereignty. Had such terms been proposed, they would have rejected them with disdain, and trusted for better, to the moderation of their enemies, or to a vigorous exertion of their own force. We do not, however, mean to underrate those aids, which, to us, were doubtless valuable, on whatever principles granted; but we would show that they cannot give a title to that authority which the British Parliament would arrogate over us; and that they may amply be repaid by our giving to the inhabitants of Great Britain such exclusive privileges in trade as may be advantageous to them, and, at the same time, not too restrictive to ourselves. That settlement having been thus effected in the wilds of America, the emigrants thought proper to adopt that system of laws, under which they had hitherto lived in the mother country, and to continue their union with her, by submitting themselves to the same common sovereign, who was thereby made the central link, connecting the several parts of the empire thus newly multiplied.

But that not long were they permitted, however far they thought themselves removed from the hand of oppression, to hold undisturbed the rights thus acquired at the hazard of their lives and loss of their fortunes. A family of princes was then on the British throne, whose treasonable crimes against their people, brought on them, afterwards, the exertion of those sacred and sovereign rights of punishment, reserved in the hands of the people for cases of extreme necessity, and judged by the constitution unsafe to be delegated to any other judicature. While every day brought forth some new and unjustifiable exertion of power over their subjects on that side of the water, it was not to be expected that those here, much less able at that time to oppose the designs of despotism, should be exempted from injury. Accordingly, this country which had been acquired by the lives, the labors, and fortunes of individual adventurers, was by these Princes, several times, parted out and distributed among the favorites and followers of their fortunes; and, by an assumed right of the Crown alone, were erected into distinct and independent governments; a measure which, it is believed, his Majesty's prudence and understanding would prevent him from imitating at this day; as no exercise of such power, of dividing

* The SUMMARY VIEW was not written for publication. It was a draft I had prepared for a petition to the King, which I meant to propose in my place as a member of the convention of 1774. Being stopped on the road by sickness, I sent it on to the Speaker, who laid it on the table for the perusal of the members. It was thought too strong for the times, and to become the act of the convention, but was printed by subscription of the members, with a short preface written by one of them. If it had any merit, it was that of first taking our true ground, and that which was afterwards assumed and maintained.—TO JOHN W. CAMPBELL. v, 465. FORD ED., ix, 258. (M., Aug. 1809.)

and dismembering a country, has ever occurred in his Majesty's realm of England, though now of very ancient standing; nor could it be justified or acquiesced under there, or in any part of his Majesty's empire.

That the exercise of a free trade with all parts of the world, possessed by the American colonists, as of natural right, and which no law of their own had taken away or abridged, was next the object of unjust encroachment. Some of the colonies having thought proper to continue the administration of their government in the name and under the authority of his Majesty, King Charles the First, whom, notwithstanding his late deposition by the Commonwealth of England, they continued in the sovereignty of their State, the Parliament, for the Commonwealth, took the same in high offence, and assumed upon themselves the power of prohibiting their trade with all other parts of the world except the Island of Great Britain. This arbitrary act, however, they soon recalled, and by solemn treaty entered into on the 12th day of March, 1651, between the said Commonwealth, by their Commissioners, and the colony of Virginia by their House of Burgesses, it was expressly stipulated by the eighth article of the said treaty, that they should have "free trade as the people of England do enjoy to all places and with all nations, according to the laws of that Commonwealth"? But that, upon the restoration of his Majesty, King Charles the Second, their rights of free commerce fell once more a victim to arbitrary power; and by several acts of his reign, as well as of some of his successors, the trade of the colonies was laid under such restrictions, as show what hopes they might form from the justice of a British Parliament, were its uncontrolled power admitted over these States.* History has informed us, that bodies of men as well as individuals, are susceptible of the spirit of tyranny. A view of these acts of Parliament for regulation, as it has been affectedly cal'ed, of the American trade, if all other evidences were removed out of the case, would undeniably evince the truth of this observation. Besides the duties they impose on our articles of export and import, they prohibit our going to any markets Northward of Cape Finisterre, in the kingdom of Spain, for the sale of commodities which Great Britain will not take from us, and for the purchase of others, with which she cannot supply us; and that, for no other than the arbitrary purpose of purchasing for themselves, by a sacrifice of our rights and interests, certain privileges in their commerce with an allied State, who, in confidence, that their exclusive trade with America will be continued, while the principles and power of the British Parliament be the same, have indulged themselves in every exorbitance which their avarice could dictate or our necessity extort; have raised their commodities called for in America, to the double and treble of what they sold for, before such exclusive privileges were given them, and of what better commodities of the same kind would cost us elsewhere; and, at the same time, given us much less for what we carry thither, than might be had at more convenient ports. That these acts prohibit us from carrying, in quest of other purchasers, the surplus of our tobaccos, remaining after the consumption of Great Britain is supplied; so that we must leave them with the British merchant, for whatever he will please to allow us, to be by him re-shipped to foreign markets, where he will reap the benefits of making sale of them for full value.

That, to heighten still the idea of Parliamentary justice, and to show with what moderation they are like to exercise power, where themselves are to feel no part of its weight, we take leave to mention to his Majesty, certain other acts of the British Parliament, by which they would prohibit us from manufacturing, for our own use, the articles we raise on our own lands, with our own labor. By an act passed in the fifth year of the reign of his late Majesty, King George the Second, an American subject is forbidden to make a hat for himself, of the fur which he has taken, perhaps, on his own soil; an instance of despotism, to which no parallel can be produced in the most arbitrary ages of British history. By one other act, passed in the twenty-third year of the same reign, the iron which we make, we are forbidden to manufacture; and, heavy as that article is, and necessary in every branch of husbandry, besides commission and insurance, we are to pay freight for it to Great Britain, and freight for it back again, for the purpose of supporting, not men, but machines, in the island of Great Britain. In the same spirit of equal and impartial legislation, is to be viewed the act of Parliament, passed in the fifth year of the same reign, by which American lands are made subject to the demands of British creditors, while their own lands were still continued unanswerable for their debts; from which, one of these conclusions must necessarily follow, either that justice is not the same thing in America as in Britain, or else, that the British Parliament pay less regard to it here than there. But, that we do not point out to his Majesty the injustice of these acts, with intent to rest on that principle the cause of their nullity; but to show that experience confirms the propriety of those political principles, which exempt us from the jurisdiction of the British Parliament. The true ground on which we declare these acts void, is, that the British Parliament has no right to exercise authority over us.

That these exercises of usurped power have not been confined to instances alone, in which themselves were interested; but they have also intermeddled with the regulation of the internal affairs of the Colonies. The act of the 9th of Anne for establishing a post office in America, seems to have had little connection with British convenience, except that of accommodating his Majesty's ministers and favourites with the sale of a lucrative and easy office.

That thus have we hastened through the reigns which preceded his Majesty's, during which the violations of our rights were less alarming, because repeated at more distant intervals, than that rapid and bold succession of injuries, which is likely to distinguish the present from all other periods of American story. Scarcely have our minds been able to emerge from the astonishment into which one stroke of Parliamentary thunder has involved us, before another more heavy and more alarming is fallen on us. Single acts of tyranny may be ascribed to the accidental opinion of a day; but a series of oppressions, begun at a distinguished period, and pursued unalterably through every change of ministers, too plainly prove a deliberate, systematical plan of reducing us to slavery.

* 12 C. 2 c. 18.   15 C. 2 c. 11.   25 C. 2 c. 7.   7. 8 W M. c. 22.   11 W. 34 Anne   6 C 2 c. 13.—NOTE BY JEFFERSON.

Act for granting certain duties.
Stamp act.
Act declaring right of Parliament over the Colonies.
Act for granting duties on paper, tea, &c.
Act suspending legislature of New York.

That the act passed in the fourth year of his Majesty's reign, entitled " An Act
One other act passed in the fifth year of his reign entitled " An Act
One other act passed in the sixth year of his reign, entitled " An Act
And one other act, passed in the seventh year of his reign, entitled " An Act
From that connected chain of Parliamentary usurpation, which has already been the subject of frequent application to his Majesty, and the Houses of Lords and Commons of Great Britain; and, no answers having yet been condescended to any of these, we shall not trouble his Majesty with a repetition of the matters they contained.

But that one other act passed in the same seventh year of his reign, having been a peculiar attempt, must ever require peculiar mention. It is entitled "An Act

One free and independent Legislature, hereby takes upon itself to suspend the powers of another, free and independent as itself; thus exhibiting a phenomenon unknown in nature, the creator and creature of its own power. Not only the principles of common sense, but the common feelings of human nature must be surrendered up, before his Majesty's subjects here, can be persuaded to believe that they hold their political existence at the will of a British Parliament. Shall these governments be dissolved, their property annihilated, and their people reduced to a state of nature, at the imperious breath of a body of men whom they never saw, in whom they never confided, and over whom they have no powers of punishment or removal, let their crimes against the American public be ever so great? Can any one reason be assigned, why one hundred and sixty thousand electors in the island of Great Britain, should give law to four millions in the States of America, every individual of whom is equal to every individual of them in virtue, in understanding, and in bodily strength? Were this to be admitted, instead of being a free people, as we have hitherto supposed, and mean to continue ourselves, we should suddenly be found the slaves, not of one, but of one hundred and sixty thousand tyrants; distinguished, too, from all others, by this singular circumstance, that they are removed from the reach of fear, the only restraining motive which may hold the hand of a tyrant.

That, by " An Act [14 G. 3.] to discontinue in such manner, and for such time as are therein mentioned, the landing and discharging, lading or shipping of goods, wares and merchandise, at the town and within the harbor of Boston, in the province of Massachusetts Bay, in North America', which was passed at the last session of the British Parliament, a large and populous town, whose trade was their sole subsistence, was deprived of that trade, and involved in utter ruin. Let us for a while, suppose the question of right suspended, in order to examine this act on principles of justice. An act of Parliament had been passed, imposing duties on teas, to be paid in America, against which act the Americans had protested, as inauthoritative. The East India Company, who, till that time, had never sent a pound of tea to America on their own account, step forth on that occasion, the asserters of Parliamentary right, and send hither many shiploads of that obnoxious commodity. The masters of their several vessels, however, on their arrival in America, wisely attended to admonition, and returned with their cargoes. In the province of New England alone, the remonstrances of the people were disregarded, and a compliance, after being many days waited for, was flatly refused. Whether in this, the master of the vessel was governed by his obstinacy, or his instructions, let those who know, say. There are extraordinary situations which require extraordinary interposition. An exasperated people, who feel that they possess power, are not easily restrained within limits strictly regular. A number of them assembled in the town of Boston, threw the tea into the ocean, and dispersed without doing any other act of violence. If in this they did wrong, they were known, and were amenable to the laws of the land; against which, it could not be objected, that they had ever, in any instance, been obstructed or diverted from the regular course, in favor of popular offenders. They should, therefore, not have been distrusted on this occasion. But that ill-fated colony had formerly been bold in their enmities against the house of Stuart, and were now devoted to ruin, by that unseen hand which governs the momentous affairs of this great empire. On the partial representations of a few worthless ministerial dependants, whose constant office it had been to keep that government embroiled, and who, by their treacheries, hope to obtain the dignity of British knighthood, without calling for a party accused, without asking a proof, without attempting a distinction between the guilty and the innocent, the whole of that ancient and wealthy town, is in a moment reduced from opulence to beggary. Men who had spent their lives in extending the British commerce, who had invested, in that place, the wealth their honest endeavors had merited, found themselves and their families, thrown at once on the world for subsistence by its charities. Not the hundredth part of the inhabitants of that town, had been concerned in the act complained of; many of them were in Great Britain, and in other parts beyond sea; yet all were involved in one indiscriminate ruin, by a new executive power, unheard of till then, that of a British Parliament. A property of the value of many millions of money, was sacrificed to revenge, not repay, the loss of a few thousands. This is administering justice with a heavy hand indeed! And when is this tempest to be arrested in its course? Two wharves are to be opened again when his Majesty shall think proper; the residue, which lined the extensive shores of the bay of Boston, are forever interdicted the exercise of commerce. This little exception seems to have been thrown in for no other purpose, than that of setting a precedent for investing his Majesty with legislative powers. If the pulse of his people shall beat calmly under this experiment, another and another will be tried, till the measure of despotism be filled up. It would be an insult on common sense, to pretend that this exception was made, in order to restore its commerce to that great town. The trade, which cannot be received at two wharves alone, must of necessity be transferred to some other place; to which it will soon be followed by that of the two wharves. Considered in this light, it would be an insolent and cruel mockery at the annihilation of the town of Boston.

By the act for the suppression of riots and tumults in the town of Boston [14 G. 3.], passed also in the last session of Parliament, a murder committed there, is, if the Governor pleases, to be tried in the court of King's Bench, in the island of Great Britain, by a jury of Middlesex. The witnesses, too, on receipt of such a sum as the Governor shall think it reasonable for them to expend, are to enter into recognizance to appear at the trial. This is, in other words, taxing them to the amount of their recognizance; and that amount may be whatever a governor pleases. For who, does his Majesty think, can be prevailed on to cross the Atlantic for the sole purpose of bearing evidence to a fact? His expenses are to be borne, indeed, as they shall be estimated by a governor; but who are to feed the wife and children whom he leaves behind, and who have had no other subsistence but his daily labor? Those epidemical disorders, too, so terrible in a foreign climate, is the cure of them to be estimated among the articles of expense, and their danger to be warded off by the almighty power of a Parliament? And the wretched criminal, if he happen to have offended on the American side, stripped of his privilege of trial by peers of his vicinage, removed from the place where alone full evidence could be obtained, without money, without counsel, without friends, without exculpatory proof, is tried before judges predetermined to condemn. The cowards who would suffer a countryman to be torn from the bowels of their society, in order to be thus offered a sacrifice to Parliamentary tyranny, would merit that everlasting infamy now fixed on the authors of the act! A clause, for a similar purpose, had been introduced into an act passed in the twelfth year of his Majesty's reign, entitled, "An Act for the better securing and preserving his Majesty's dockyards, magazines, ships, ammunition and stores"; against which, as meriting the same censures, the several Colonies have already protested.

That these are the acts of power, assumed by a body of men foreign to our constitutions, and unacknowledged by our laws; against which we do, on behalf of the inhabitants of British America, enter this, our solemn and determined protest. And we do earnestly entreat his Majesty, as yet the only mediatory power between the several States of the British empire, to recommend to his Parliament of Great Britain, the total revocation of these acts, which, however nugatory they may be, may yet prove the cause of further discontents and jealousies among us.

That we next proceed to consider the conduct of his Majesty, as holding the executive powers of the laws of these States, and mark out his deviations from the line of duty. By the Constitution of Great Britain, as well as of the several American States, his Majesty possesses the power of refusing to pass into a law, any bill which has already passed the other two branches of the Legislature. His Majesty, however, and his ancestors, conscious of the impropriety of opposing their single opinion to the united wisdom of two Houses of Parliament, while their proceedings were unbiased by interested principles, for several ages past, have modestly declined the exercise of this power, in that part of his empire called Great Britain. But, by change of circumstances, other principles than those of justice simply, have obtained an influence on their determinations. The addition of new States to the British empire has produced an addition of new, and, sometimes, opposite interests. It is now, therefore, the great office of his Majesty to resume the exercise of his negative power, and to prevent the passage of laws by any one legislature of the empire, which might bear injuriously on the rights and interests of another. Yet this will not excuse the wanton exercise of this power, which we have seen his Majesty practice on the laws of the American Legislature. For the most trifling reasons, and, sometimes for no conceivable reason at all, his Majesty has rejected laws of the most salutary tendency. The abolition of domestic slavery is the great object of desire in those Colonies, where it was, unhappily, introduced in their infant state. But previous to the enfranchisement of the slaves we have, it is necessary to exclude all further importations from Africa. Yet our repeated attempts to effect this, by prohibitions, and by imposing duties which might amount to a prohibition, having been hitherto defeated by his Majesty's negative; thus preferring the immediate advantages of a few British corsairs, to the lasting interests of the American States, and to the rights of human nature, deeply wounded by this infamous practice. Nay, the single interposition of an interested individual against a law was scarcely ever known to fail of success, though, in the opposite scale, were placed the interests of a whole country. That this is so shameful an abuse of a power, trusted with his Majesty for other purposes, as if, not reformed, would call for some legal restrictions.

While equal inattention to the necessities of his people here, has his Majesty permitted our laws to lie neglected, in England, for years, neither confirming them by his assent, nor annulling them by his negative; so that, such of them as have no suspending clause, we hold on the most precarious of all tenures, his Majesty's will; and such of them as suspend themselves till his Majesty's assent be obtained, we have feared might be called into existence at some future and distant period, when time and change of circumstances shall have rendered them destructive to his people here. And, to render this grievance still more oppressive, his Majesty, by his instructions, has laid his Governors under such restrictions, that they can pass no law, of any moment, unless it have such suspending clause; so that, however immediate may be the call for legislative interposition, the law cannot be executed, till it has twice crossed the Atlantic, by which time the evil may have spent its whole force.

But in what terms reconcilable to Majesty, and at the same time to truth, shall we speak of a late instruction to his Majesty's Governor of the Colony of Virginia, by which he is forbidden to assent to any law for the division of a county, unless the new county will consent to have no representative in Assembly? That Colony has as yet affixed no boundary to the westward. Their western counties, therefore, are of an indefinite extent. Some of them are actually seated many hundred miles from their eastern limits. Is it possible, then, that his Majesty can have bestowed a single thought on the situation of those people, who, in order to obtain justice for injuries, however great or small, must, by the laws of that Colony, attend their county court at such a distance, with all their witnesses, monthly, till their litigation be determined? Or does his Majesty seriously wish, and publish it to the world, that his subjects should give up the glorious right of representation, with all the benefits derived from that, and submit themselves the absolute slaves of his sovereign will? Or is it rather meant to confine the legislative body to their present numbers, that they may be the cheaper bargain, whenever they shall become worth a purchase?

One of the articles of impeachment against Tresilian, and the other Judges of Westminster Hall, in the reign of Richard the Second, for which they suffered death, as traitors to their country, was, that they had advised the King, that he might dissolve his Parliament at any time;

and succeeding kings have adopted the opinion of these unjust judges. Since the establishment, however, of the British constitution, at the glorious Revolution, on its free and ancient principles, neither his Majesty, nor his ancestors, have exercised such a power of dissolution in the island of Great Britain; * and when his Majesty was petitioned by the united voice of his people there, to dissolve the present Parliament, who had become obnoxious to them, his ministers were heard to declare, in open Parliament, that his Majesty possessed no such power by the constitution. But how different their language, and his practice, here! To declare, as their duty required, the known rights of their country, to oppose the usurpation of every foreign judicature, to disregard the imperious mandates of a minister or governor, have been the avowed causes of dissolving Houses of Representatives in America. But if such powers be really vested in his Majesty, can he suppose they are there placed to awe the members from such purposes as these? When the representative body have lost the confidence of their constituents, when they have notoriously made sale of their most valuable rights, when they have assumed to themselves powers which the people never put into their hands, then, indeed, their continuing in office becomes dangerous to the State, and calls for an exercise of the power of dissolution. Such being the cause for which the representative body should, and should not, be dissolved, will it not appear strange, to an unbiased observer, that that of Great Britain was not dissolved, while those of the Colonies have repeatedly incurred that sentence?

But your Majesty, or your Governors, have carried this power beyond every limit known or provided for by the laws. After dissolving one House of Representatives, they have refused to call another, so that, for a great length of time, the Legislature provided by the laws, has been out of existence. From the nature of things, every society must, at all times, possess within itself the sovereign powers of legislation. The feelings of human nature revolt against the supposition of a State so situated, as that it may not, in any emergency, provide against dangers which, perhaps, threaten immediate ruin. While those bodies are in existence to whom the people have delegated the powers of legislation, they alone possess, and may exercise, those powers. But when they are dissolved, by the lopping off of one or more of their branches, the power reverts to the people, who may use it to unlimited extent, either assembling together in person, sending deputies, or in any other way they may think proper. We forbear to trace consequences further; the dangers are conspicuous with which this practice is replete.

That we shall, at this time also, take notice of an error in the nature of our land holdings, which crept in at a very early period of our settlement. The introduction of the Feudal tenures into the kingdom of England, though ancient, is well enough understood to set this matter in a proper light. In the earlier ages of the Saxon settlement, feudal holdings were certainly altogether unknown, and very few, if any, had been introduced at the time of the Norman Conquest. Our Saxon ancestors held their lands, as they did their personal property, in absolute dominion, disencumbered with any superior, answering nearly to the nature of those possessions which the feudalist termed allodial. William the Norman, first introduced that system generally. The lands which had belonged to those who fell in the battle of Hastings, and in the subsequent insurrections of his reign, formed a considerable proportion of the lands of the whole kingdom. These he granted out, subject to feudal duties, as did he also those of a great number of his new subjects, who, by persuasions or threats, were induced to surrender them for that purpose. But still, much was left in the hands of his Saxon subjects, held of no superior, and not subject to feudal conditions. These, therefore, by express laws, enacted to render uniform the system of military defence, were made liable to the same military duties as if they had been feuds; and the Norman lawyers soon found means to saddle them, also, with the other feudal burthens. But still they had not been surrendered to the king, they were not derived from his grant, and therefore they were not holden of him. A general principle was introduced, that "all lands in England were held either mediately or immediately of the Crown"; but this was borrowed from those holdings which were truly feudal, and only applied to others for the purposes of illustration. Feudal holdings were, therefore, but exceptions out of the Saxon laws of possession, under which all lands were held in absolute right. These, therefore, still form the basis or groundwork of the Common law, to prevail wheresoever the exceptions have not taken place. America was not conquered by William the Norman, nor its lands surrendered to him or any of his successors. Possessions there are, undoubtedly, of the allodial nature. Our ancestors, however, who migrated hither, were laborers, not lawyers. The fictitious principle, that all lands, belong originally to the king, they were early persuaded to believe real, and accordingly took grants of their own lands from the Crown. And while the Crown continued to grant for small sums and on reasonable rents, there was no inducement to arrest the error, and lay it open to public view. But his Majesty has lately taken on him to advance the terms of purchase and of holding, to the double of what they were; by which means, the acquisition of lands being rendered difficult, the population of our country is likely to be checked. It is time, therefore, for us to lay this matter before his Majesty, and to declare, that he has no right to grant lands of himself. From the nature and purpose of civil institutions, all the lands within the limits, which any particular party has circumscribed around itself, are assumed by that society, and subject to their allotment; this may be done by themselves assembled collectively, or by their legislature, to whom they may have delegated sovereign authority; and, if they are allotted in neither of these ways, each individual of the society, may appropriate to himself such lands as he finds vacant, and occupancy will give him title.

That, in order to enforce the arbitrary measures before complained of, his Majesty has, from time to time, sent among us large bodies of armed forces, not made up of the people here, nor raised by the authority of our laws. Did his Majesty possess such a right as this, it might swallow up all our other rights, whenever he should think proper. But his Majesty has no right to land a single armed man on our shores; and those whom he sends here are

---

* On further inquiry, I find two instances of dissolutions before the Parliament would, of itself, have been at an end, viz.: the Parliament called to meet August 24, 1698, was dissolved by King William, December 19, 1700, and a new one was called to meet February 6, 1701, which was also dissolved, November 11, 1701, and a new one met December 30, 1701.—NOTE BY JEFFERSON.

liable to our laws, for the suppression and punishment of riots, routs, and unlawful assemblies, or are hostile bodies invading us in defiance of law. When, in the course of the late war, it became expedient that a body of Hanoverian troops should be brought over for the defence of Great Britain, his Majesty's grandfather, our late sovereign, did not pretend to introduce them under any authority he possessed. Such a measure would have given just alarm to his subjects of Great Britain, whose liberties would not be safe if armed men of another country, and of another spirit, might be brought into the realm at any time, without the consent of their legislature. He, therefore, applied to Parliament, who passed an act for that purpose, limiting the number to be brought in, and the time they were to continue. In like manner is his Majesty restrained in every part of the empire. He possesses indeed the executive power of the laws in every State; but they are the laws of the particular State, which he is to administer within that State, and not those of any one within the limits of another. Every State must judge for itself, the number of armed men which they may safely trust among them, of whom they are to consist, and under what restrictions they are to be laid. To render these proceedings still more criminal against our laws, instead of subjecting the military to the civil power, his Majesty has expressly made the civil subordinate to the military. But can his Majesty thus put down all law under his feet? Can he erect a power superior to that which erected himself? He has done it indeed by force; but let him remember that force cannot give right.

That these are our grievances, which we have thus laid before his Majesty, with that freedom of language and sentiment which becomes a free people, claiming their rights as derived from the laws of nature, and not as the gift of their Chief Magistrate. Let those flatter, who fear; it is not an American art. To give praise where it is not due might be well from the venal, but it would ill beseem those who are asserting the rights of human nature. They know, and will, therefore, say, that kings are the servants, not the proprietors of the people. Open your breast, Sire, to liberal and expanded thought. Let not the name of George the Third, be a blot on the page of history. You are surrounded by British counsellors, but remember that they are parties. You have no ministers for American affairs, because you have none taken from among us, nor amenable to the laws on which they are to give you advice. It behooves you, therefore, to think and to act for yourself and your people. The great principles of right and wrong are legible to every reader; to pursue them, requires not the aid of many counsellors. The whole art of government consists in the art of being honest. Only aim to do your duty, and mankind will give you credit where you fail. No longer persevere in sacrificing the rights of one part of the empire to the inordinate desires of another; but deal out to all equal and impartial right. Let no act be passed by any one legislature which may infringe on the rights and liberties of another. This is the important post in which fortune has placed you, holding the balance of a great, if a well-poised empire. This, Sire, is the advice of your great American council, on the observance of which may perhaps depend your felicity and future fame, and the preservation of that harmony which alone can continue, both to Great Britain and America, the reciprocal advantages of their connection. It is neither our wish nor our interest to separate from her. We are willing, on our part, to sacrifice everything which reason can ask, to the restoration of that tranquillity for which all must wish. On their part, let them be ready to establish union on a generous plan. Let them name their terms, but let them be just. Accept of every commercial preference it is in our power to give, for such things as we can raise for their use, or they make for ours. But let them not think to exclude us from going to other markets to dispose of those commodities which they cannot use, nor to supply those wants which they cannot supply. Still less, let it be proposed, that our properties, within our territories, shall be taxed or regulated by any power on earth, but our own. The God who gave us life, gave us liberty at the same time; the hand of force may destroy, but cannot disjoin them.

This, Sire, is our last, our determined resolution. And that you will be pleased to interpose, with that efficacy which your earnest endeavors may insure, to procure redress of these our great grievances, to quiet the minds of your subjects in British America against any apprehensions of future encroachment, to establish fraternal love and harmony through the whole empire, and that that may continue to the latest ages of time, is the fervent prayer of all British America.—i, 124. FORD ED., i, 426. (1774.)

DECLARATION OF INDEPENDENCE*

A Declaration by the Representatives of the United States of America, in General Congress assembled.

When, in the course of human events, it becomes necessary for one people to dissolve the political bands which have connected them with another, and to assume among the powers of the earth the separate and equal station to which the laws of nature and of nature's God entitle them, a decent respect to the opinions of mankind requires that they should declare the causes which impel them to the separation.

We hold these truths to be self evident: that all men are created equal; that they are endowed by their creator with [*inherent and*] inalienable rights; that among these are life, liberty, and the pursuit of happiness; that to secure these rights, governments are instituted among men, deriving their just powers from the consent of the governed; that whenever any form of government becomes destructive of these ends, it is the right of the people to alter or to abolish it, and to institute new government, laying its foundation on such principles, and organizing its powers in such form, as to them shall seem most likely to effect their safety and happiness. Prudence, indeed, will dictate that governments long established should not be changed for light and transient causes; and accordingly all experience hath shown that mankind are more disposed to suffer while evils are sufferable, than to right themselves by abolishing the forms to which they are accustomed. But when a long train of abuses and usurpations, [*begun at a distinguished period and*] pursuing invariably the same object, evinces a design to reduce them under absolute despotism, it is their right, it is their duty to throw off such government, and to provide new guards for their future security. Such has been the patient sufferance of these colonies; and such is now the necessity which constrains them to [*expunge*] their former systems of government. The history of the present king of Great Britain is a history of [*unremitting*] injuries and usurpations [*among which appears no solitary fact to contradict the uniform tenor of the rest, but all have*] in direct object the establishment of an absolute tyranny over these states. To prove this, let facts be submitted to a candid world [*for the truth of which we pledge a faith yet unsullied by falsehood.*]

certain

alter

repeated

all having

He has refused his assent to laws the most wholesome and necessary for the public good.

He has forbidden his governors to pass laws of immediate and pressing importance, unless suspended in their operation till his assent should be obtained; and, when so suspended, he has utterly neglected to attend to them.

He has refused to pass other laws for the accommodation of large districts of people, unless those people would relinquish the right of representation in the legislature, a right inestimable to them, and formidable to tyrants only.

He has called together legislative bodies at places unusual, uncomfortable, and distant from the depository of their public records, for the sole purpose of fatiguing them into compliance with his measures.

He has dissolved representative houses repeatedly [*and continually*] for opposing with manly firmness his invasions on the rights of the people.

He has refused for a long time after such dissolutions to cause others to be elected, whereby the legislative powers, incapable of annihilation, have returned to the people at large for their exercise, the state remaining, in the meantime, exposed to all the dangers of invasion from without and convulsions within.

He has endeavored to prevent the population of these states; for that purpose obstructing the laws for naturalization of foreigners, refusing to pass others to encourage their migrations hither, and raising the conditions of new appropriations of lands.

obstructed by

He has [*suffered*] the administration of justice [*totally to cease in some of these states*] refusing his assent to laws for establishing judiciary powers.

He has made [*our*] judges dependent on his will alone for the tenure of their offices, and the amount and payment of their salaries.

He has erected a multitude of new offices [*by a self-assumed power*], and sent hither swarms of officers to harass our people and eat out their substance.

He has kept among us in times of peace standing armies [*and ships of war*] without the consent of our legislatures.

He has affected to render the military independent of, and superior to, the civil power.

He has combined with others to subject us to a jurisdiction foreign to our constitutions and unacknowledged by our laws, giving his assent to their acts of pretended legislation for quartering large bodies of armed troops among us; for protecting them by a mock trial from punishment for any murders which they should commit on the inhabitants of these States; for cutting off our trade with all parts of the world; for imposing taxes on us without our consent; for depriving us [   ] of the benefits of trial by jury; for transporting us beyond seas to be tried for pretended offences; for abolishing the free system of English laws in a neighboring province, establishing therein an arbitrary government, and enlarging its boundaries, so as to render it at once an example and fit instrument for introducing the same absolute rule into these [*states*]; for taking away our charters, abolishing our most valuable laws, and altering fundamentally the forms of our governments; for suspending our own legislatures, and declaring themselves invested with power to legislate for us in all cases whatsoever.

in many cases

colonies

by declaring us out of his protection, and waging war against us

He has abdicated government here [*withdrawing his governors, and declaring us out of his allegiance and protection*].

He has plundered our seas, ravaged our coasts, burnt our towns, and destroyed the lives of our people.

He is at this time transporting large armies of foreign mercenaries to complete the works of death, desolation and tyranny already begun with circumstances of cruelty and perfidy [   ] unworthy the head of a civilized nation.

scarcely paralleled in the most barbarous ages, and totally

He has constrained our fellow citizens taken captive on the high seas, to bear arms against their country, to become the executioners of their friends and brethren, or to fall themselves by their hands.

He has [   ] endeavored to bring on the inhabitants of our frontiers, the merciless Indian savages, whose known rule of warfare is an undistinguished destruction of all ages, sexes and conditions [*of existence*].

excited domestic insurrection among us, and has

[*He has incited treasonable insurrections of our fellow citizens, with the allurements of forfeiture and confiscation of our property.*

He has waged cruel war against human nature itself, violating its most sacred rights of life and liberty in the persons of a distant people who never offended him, captivating and carrying them into slavery in another hemisphere, or to incur miserable death in their transportation thither. This piratical warfare, the opprobrium of INFIDEL *powers, is the warfare of the* CHRISTIAN *king of Great Britain. Determined to keep open a market where* MEN *should be bought and sold, he has prostituted his negative for suppressing every legislative attempt to prohibit or to restrain this execrable commerce. And that this assemblage of horrors might want no fact of distinguished dye, he is now exciting those very people to rise in arms among us, and to purchase that liberty of which he has deprived them, by murdering the people upon whom he also obtruded them: thus paying off former crimes committed against the* LIBERTIES *of one people, with crimes which he urges them to commit against the* LIVES *of another*].

In every stage of these oppressions we have petitioned for redress in the most humble terms: our repeated petitions have been answered only by repeated injuries.

A prince whose character is thus marked by every act which may define a tyrant is unfit to be the ruler of a [   ] people [*who mean to be free. Future ages will scarcely believe that the hardiness of one man adventured, within the short compass of twelve years only, to lay a foundation so broad and undisguised for tyranny over a people fostered and fixed in principles of freedom*].

free

Nor have we been wanting in attentions to our British brethren. We have warned them from time to time of attempts by their legislature to extend [*a*] jurisdiction over [*these our states*]. We have reminded them of the circumstances of our emigration and settlement here [*no one of which could warrant so strange a pretension: that these were effected at the expense of our own blood and treasure, unassisted by the wealth or the strength of Great Britain; that in constituting indeed our several forms of government, we had adopted one com-*

an unwarantable us

mon king, thereby laying a foundation for perpetual league and amity with **have**
them; but that submission to their parliament was no part of our constitution,
nor ever in idea, if history may be credited: and], we [ ] appealed to their **have**
native justice and magnanimity [*as well as to*] the ties of our common kindred **and we have**
to disavow these usurpations which [*were likely to*] interrupt our connection **conjured them**
and correspondence.   They too have been deaf to the voice of justice and of **by**
consanguinity [*and when occasions have been given them, by the regular* **would inevit-**
course of their laws, of removing from their councils the disturbers of our **ably**
harmony, they have, by their free election, re-established them in power. At
this very time too, they are permitting their chief magistrate to send over not
only soldiers of our common blood, but Scotch and foreign mercenaries to
invade and destroy us. These facts have given the last stab to agonizing
affection, and manly spirit bids us to renounce forever these unfeeling breth-
ren. We must endeavor to forget our former love for them, and hold them
as we hold the rest of mankind, enemies in war, in peace friends. We might
have been a free and a great people together; but a communication of grandeur
and of freedom, it seems, is below their dignity. Be it so, since they will have
it. The road to happiness and to glory is open to us too. We will tread it **we must**
apart from them, and], acquiesce in the necessity which denounces our [*eter-* **therefore**
nal] separation [ ]!

and hold them
as we hold the
rest of man-
kind, enemies
in war, in
peace friends.

We, therefore, the representatives of the United States of America in General Congress assembled, do in the name, and by the authority of the good people of these [*states reject and renounce all allegiance and subjection to the kings of Great Britain and all others who may hereafter claim by, through or under them; we utterly dissolve all political connection which may heretofore have subsisted between us and the people or parliament of Great Britain: and finally we do assert and declare these colonies to be free and independent states*], and that as free and independent states, they have full power to levy war, conclude peace, contract alliances, establish commerce, and to do all other acts and things which independent states may of right do.

And for the support of this declaration, we mutually pledge to each other our lives, our fortunes, and our sacred honor

We, therefore, the representatives of the United States of America in General Congress assembled, appealing to the Supreme Judge of the world for the rectitude of our intentions, do in the name, and by the authority of the good people of these colonies, solemnly publish and declare, that these united colonies are, and of right ought to be free and independent states; that they are absolved from all allegiance to the British crown, and that all political connection between them and the state of Great Britain is, and ought to be, totally dissolved; and that as free and independent states, they have full power to levy war, conclude peace, contract alliances, establish commerce, and to do all other acts and things which independent states may of right do.

And for the support of this declaration, with a firm reliance on the protection of Divine Providence, we mutually pledge to each other our lives, our fortunes, and our sacred honor.—i, 19. FORD ED., ii, 42.

PREAMBLE TO THE VIRGINIA CONSTITUTION

Whereas, the delegates and representatives of the good people of Virginia, in convention assembled, on the twenty-ninth day of June, in the year of our Lord one thousand seven hundred and seventy-six, reciting and declaring, that whereas George the Third, King of Great Britain and Ireland, and Elector of Hanover, before that time intrusted with the exercise of the kingly office in the government of Virginia, had endeavored to pervert the same into a detestable and insupportable tyranny, by putting his negative on laws the most wholesome and necessary for the public good; by denying his governors permission to pass laws of immediate and pressing importance, unless suspended in their operation for his assent, and when so suspended, neglecting to attend to them for many years; by refusing to pass certain other laws unless the persons to be benefited by them would relinquish the inalienable right of representation in the legislature; by dissolving legislative assemblies, repeatedly and continually, for opposing with manly firmness his invasions of the rights of the people; when dissolved by refusing to call others for a long space of time, thereby leaving the political system without any legislative head; by endeavoring to prevent the population of our country, and for that purpose obstructing the laws for naturalization of foreigners; by keeping among us, in time of peace, standing armies and ships of war; by affecting to render the military independent of and superior to the civil power; by combining with others to subject us to a foreign jurisdiction, giving his assent to their pretended acts of legislation for quartering large bodies of armed troops among us; for cutting off our trade with all parts of the world; for imposing taxes on us without our consent; for depriving us of the benefit of trial by jury; for transporting us beyond the seas for trial for pretended offences; for suspending our own legislatures, and declaring themselves invested with power to legislate for us in all cases whatsoever; by plundering our seas, ravaging our coasts, burning our towns, and destroying the lives of our people; by inciting insurrection of our fellow-subjects with the allurements of forfeiture and confiscation; by prompting our negroes to rise in arms among us—those very negroes whom, by an inhuman use of his negative, he had refused us permission to exclude by law; by endeavoring to bring on the inhabitants of our frontiers the merciless Indian savages, whose known rule of warfare is an undistinguished destruction of all ages, sexes and conditions of existence; by transporting hither a large army of foreign mercenaries to complete the work of death, desolation and tyranny, then already begun, with circumstances of cruelty and perfidy unworthy the head of a civilized nation; by answering our repeated petitions for redress with a repetition of our injuries; and finally, by abandoning the helm of government and declaring us out of his allegiance and protection—by which several acts of misrule, the government of this country, as before exercised under the crown of Great Britain, was totally dissolved—did, therefore, having maturely considered the premises, and viewing with great concern the deplorable condition to which this once happy country would be reduced unless some regular, adequate mode of civil policy should be speedily adopted, and in compliance with the recommendation of the general Congress, ordain and declare a form of government of Virginia.—POORE'S FEDERAL AND STATE CONSTITUTIONS.

DEBATES ON THE ARTICLES OF CONFEDERATION

On Friday, July 12 [1776], the committee appointed to draw the Articles of Confederation reported them, and, on the 22d, the House resolved themselves into a committee to take them into consideration. On the 30th and 31st of that month, and 1st of the ensuing, those articles were debated which determined the proportion, or quota, of money which each state should furnish to the common treasury, and the manner of voting in Congress. The first of these articles was expressed in the original draught in these words. " Art. XI. All charges of war and all other expenses that shall be incurred for the common defence, or general welfare, and allowed by the United States assembled, shall be defrayed out of a common treasury, which shall be supplied by the several colonies in proportion to the number of inhabitants of every age, sex, and quality, except Indians not paying taxes, in each colony, a true account of which, distinguishing the white inhabitants, shall be triennially taken and transmitted to the Assembly of the United States."

Mr. Chase moved that the quotas should be fixed, not by the number of inhabitants of every condition, but by that of the " white inhabitants." He admitted that taxation should be always in proportion to property, that this was, in theory, the true rule; but that, from a variety of difficulties, it was a rule which could never be adopted in practice. The value of the property in every State, could never be estimated justly and equally. Some other measure for the wealth of the State must therefore be devised, some standard referred to, which would be more simple. He considered the number of inhabitants as a tolerably good criterion of property, and that this might always be obtained. He therefore thought it the best mode which we could adopt, with one exception only: he observed that negroes are property, and as such, cannot be distinguished from the lands or personalties held in those States where there are few slaves; that the surplus of profit which a Northern farmer is able to lay by, he invests in cattle, horses, &c., whereas a Southern farmer lays out the same surplus in slaves. There is no more reason, therefore, for taxing the Southern States on the farmer's head, and on his slave's head, than the Northern ones on their farmer's heads and the heads of their cattle; that the method proposed would, therefore, tax the Southern States according to their numbers and their wealth conjunctly, while the Northern would be taxed on numbers only; that negroes, in fact, should not be considered as members of the State, more than cattle, and that they have no more interest in it.

Mr. John Adams observed, that the numbers of people were taken by this article, as an index of the wealth of the State, and not as subjects of taxation; that, as to this matter, it was of no consequence by what name you called your people, whether by that of freemen or of slaves; that in some countries the laboring poor were called freemen, in others they were called slaves; but that the difference as to the state was imaginary only. What matters it whether a landlord, employing ten laborers on his farm, gives them annually as much money as will buy them the necessaries of life, or gives them those necessaries at short hand? The ten laborers add as much wealth annually to the State, increase its exports as much in the one case as the other. Certainly five hundred freemen produce no more profits, no greater surplus for the payment of taxes, than five hundred slaves. Therefore, the State in which are the laborers called freemen, should be taxed no more than that in which are those called slaves. Suppose by an extraordinary operation of nature or of law, one-half the laborers of a State could in the course of one night be transformed into slaves; would the State be made the poorer or the less able to pay taxes? That the condition of the laboring poor in most countries, that of the fishermen particularly of the Northern States, is as abject as that of slaves. It is the number of laborers which produces the surplus for taxation, and numbers, therefore, indiscriminately, are the fair index of wealth; that it is the use of the word " property " here, and its application to some of the people of the State, which produces the fallacy. How does the Southern farmer procure slaves? Either by importation or by purchase from his neighbor. If he imports a slave, he adds one to the number of laborers in his country, and proportionably to its profits and abilities to pay taxes; if he buys from his neighbor, it is only a transfer of a laborer from one farm to another, which does not change the annual produce of the State, and therefore, should not change its tax: that if a Northern farmer works ten laborers on his farm, he can, it is true, invest the surplus of ten men's labor in cattle; but so may the Southern farmer, working ten slaves: that a State of one hundred thousand freemen can maintain no more cattle, than one of one hundred thousand slaves. Therefore, they have no more of that kind of property; that a slave may indeed, from the custom of speech, be more properly called the wealth of his master, than the free laborer might be called the wealth of his employer; but as to the State, both were equally its wealth, and should, therefore, equally add to the quota of its tax.

Mr. Harrison proposed, as a compromise, that two slaves should be counted as one freeman. He affirmed that slaves did not do as much work as freemen, and doubted if two effected more than one; that this was proved by the price of labor; the hire of a laborer in the Southern colonies being from 8 to £ 12, while in the Northern it was generally £ 24.

Mr. Wilson said, that if this amendment should take place, the Southern colonies would have all the benefit of slaves, whilst the Northern ones would bear the burthen: that slaves increase the profits of a State, which the Southern States mean to take to themselves; that they also increase the burthen of defence, which would of course fall so much the heavier on the Northern: that slaves occupy the places of freemen, and eat their food. Dismiss your slaves, and freemen will take their places. It is our duty to lay every discouragement on the importation of slaves; but this amendment would give the *jus trium liberorum* to him who would import slaves; that other kinds of property were pretty equally distributed through all the colonies: there were as many cattle, horses and sheep, in the North as the South, and South as the North; but not so as to slaves: that experience has shown that those colonies have been always able to pay most, which have the most inhabitants, whether they be black or white; and the practice of the Southern colonies has always been to make every farmer pay poll taxes upon all his laborers, whether they be black or white. He acknowledges, indeed, that freemen work the most; but they consume the most also. They do not produce a greater surplus for taxation. The slave is neither fed nor clothed so expensively as a freeman. Again, white women are exempted from labor generally, but negro women are not. In this, then, the Southern States have an advantage as the article now stands. It has sometimes been said, that slavery is necessary, because the commodities they raise would be too dear for market if cultivated by freemen; but now it is said that the labor of the slave is the dearest.

Mr. Payne urged the original resolution of Congress, to proportion the quotas of the States to the number of souls.

Dr. Witherspoon was of opinion, that the value of lands and houses was the best estimate of the wealth of a nation, and that it was practicable to obtain such a valuation. This is the true barometer of wealth. The one now proposed is imperfect in itself, and unequal between the States. It has been objected that negroes eat the food of freemen, and, therefore, should be taxed; horses also eat the food of freemen; therefore they also should be taxed. It has been said too, that in carrying slaves into the estimate of the taxes the State is to pay, we do no more than those States themselves do, who always take slaves into the estimate of the taxes the individual is to pay. But the cases are not parallel. In the Southern colonies slaves pervade the whole colony; but they do not pervade the whole continent. That as to the original resolution of Congress, to proportion the quotas according to the souls, it was temporary only, and related to the moneys heretofore emitted: whereas we are now entering into a new compact, and therefore stand on original ground.

August 1. The question being put, the amendment proposed was rejected by the votes of New Hampshire, Massachusetts, Rhode Island, Connecticut, New York, New Jersey, and Pennsylvania, against those of Delaware, Maryland, Virginia, North and South Carolina. Georgia was divided.

The other article was in these words. "Art. XVII. In determining questions, each colony shall have one vote."

July 30, 31, August 1. Present forty-one members. Mr. Chase observed this article was the most likely to divide us, of any one proposed in the draught then under consideration: that the larger colonies had threatened they would not confederate at all, if their weight in Congress should not be equal to the numbers of people they added to the confederacy; while the smaller ones declared against a union, if they did not retain an equal vote for the protection of their rights. That it was of the utmost consequence to bring the parties together, as, should we sever from each other, either no foreign power will ally with us at all, or the different States will form different alliances, and thus increase the horrors of those scenes of civil war and bloodshed, which in such a state of separation and independence, would render us a miserable people. That our importance, our interests, our peace required that we should confederate, and that mutual sacrifices should be made to effect a compromise of this difficult question. He was of opinion, the smaller colonies would lose their rights, if they were not in some instances allowed an equal vote; and, therefore, that a discrimination should take place among the questions which would come before Congress. That the smaller States should be secured in all questions concerning life or liberty, and the greater ones, in all respecting property. He therefore, proposed, that in votes relating to money, the voice of each colony should be proportioned to the number of its inhabitants.

* Dr. Franklin thought, that the votes should be so proportioned in all cases. He took notice that the Delaware counties had bound up their delegates to disagree to this article. He thought it a very extraordinary language to be held by any State, that they would not confederate with us, unless we would let them dispose of our money. Certainly, if we vote equally, we ought to pay equally; but the smaller States will hardly purchase the privilege at this price. That had he lived in a State where the representation, originally equal, had become unequal by time and accident, he might have submitted rather than disturb government; but that we should be very wrong to set out in this practice, when it is in our power to establish what is right. That at the time of the Union between England and Scotland, the latter had made the objection which the smaller States now do; but experience had proved that no unfairness had ever been shown them: that their advocates had prognosticated that it would again happen, as in times of old, that the whale would swallow Jonas, but he thought the prediction reversed in event, and that Jonas had swallowed the whale; for the Scotch had in fact got possession of the government, and gave laws to the English. He reprobated the original agreement of Congress to vote by colonies, and, therefore, was for their voting, in all cases, according to the number of taxables.

Dr. Witherspoon opposed every alteration of the article. All men admit that a confederacy is necessary. Should the idea get abroad that there is likely to be no union among us, it will damp the minds of the people, diminish the glory of our struggle, and lessen its importance; because it will open to our view future prospects of war and dissension among ourselves. If an equal vote be refused, the smaller States will become vassals to the larger; and all experience has shown that the vassals and subjects of free States are the most enslaved. He instanced the Helots of Sparta, and the provinces of Rome. He observed that foreign powers, discovering this blemish, would make it a handle for disengaging the smaller States from so unequal a confederacy. That the colonies should in fact be considered as individuals; and that, as such, in all disputes, they should have an equal vote; that they are now collected as individuals making a bargain with each other, and, of course, had a right to vote as individuals. That in the East India Company they voted by persons, and not by their proportion of stock. That the Belgic confederacy voted by provinces. That in questions of war the smaller States were as much interested as the larger, and therefore, should vote equally; and indeed, that the larger States were more likely to bring war on the confederacy, in proportion as their frontier was more extensive. He admitted that equality of representation was an excellent principle, but then it must be of things which are co-ordinate: that is, of things similar, and of the same nature: that nothing relating to individuals could ever come before Congress; nothing but what would respect colonies. He distinguished between an incorporating and a federal union. The union of England was an incorporating one; yet Scotland had suffered by that union; for that its inhabitants were drawn from it by the hopes of places and employments: nor was it an instance of equality of representation; because, while Scotland was allowed nearly a thirteenth of representation, they were to pay only one-fortieth of the land tax. He expressed his hopes, that in the present enlightened state of men's minds, we might expect a lasting confederacy, if it was founded on fair principles.

John Adams advocated the voting in proportion to numbers. He said that we stand here as the representatives of the people: that in some States the people are many, in others they are few; that therefore, their vote here should be proportioned to the numbers from whom it comes. Reason, justice and equity never had weight enough on the face of the earth, to govern the councils of men. It is interest alone which does it, and it is interest alone which can be trusted: that therefore the interests within doors, should be the mathematical representatives of the interests without doors: that the individuality of the colonies is a mere sound. Does the individuality of a colony increase its wealth or numbers? If it does, pay equally. If it does not add weight in the scale of the confederacy, it cannot add to their rights, nor weigh in argument. A. has £50, B. £500, C. £1000 in partnership. Is it just they should equally dispose of the moneys of the partnership? It has been said, we are independent individuals making a bargain together. The question is not what we are now, but what we ought to be when our bargain shall be made. The confederacy is to make us one individual only; it is to form us like separate parcels of metal, into one common mass. We shall no longer retain our separate individuality, but become a single individual as to all questions submitted to the confederacy. Therefore, all those reasons, which prove the justice and expediency of equal representation in other assemblies, hold good here. It has been objected that a proportional vote will endanger the smaller States. We answer that an equal vote will endanger the larger. Virginia, Pennsylvania, and Massachusetts, are the three greater colonies. Consider their distance, their difference of produce, of interests, and of manners, and it is apparent they can never have an interest or inclination to combine for the oppression of the smaller: that the smaller will naturally divide on all questions with the larger. Rhode Island, from its relation, similarity and intercourse, will generally pursue the same objects with Massachusetts; Jersey, Delaware, and Maryland, with Pennsylvania.

Dr. Rush took notice, that the decay of the liberties of the Dutch republic proceeded from three causes. 1. The perfect unanimity requisite on all occasions. 2. Their obligation to consult their constituents. 3. Their voting by provinces. This last destroyed the equality of representation, and the liberties of Great Britain also are sinking from the same defect. That a part of our rights is deposited in the hands of our legislatures. There, it was admitted, there should be an equality of representation. Another part of our rights is deposited in the hands of Congress: why is it not equally necessary there should be an equal representation there? Were it possible to collect the whole body of the people together, they would determine the questions submitted to them by their majority. Why should not the same majority decide when voting here, by their representatives? The larger colonies are so providentially divided in situation, as to render every fear of their combining visionary. Their interests are different, and their circumstances dissimilar. It is more probable they will become rivals, and leave it in the power of the smaller States to give preponderance to any scale they please. The voting by the number of free inhabitants, will have one excellent effect, that of inducing the colonies to discourage slavery, and to encourage the increase of their free inhabitants.

Mr. Hopkins observed, there were four larger, four smaller, and four middle-sized colonies. That the four largest would contain more than half the inhabitants of the confederated States, and therefore, would govern the others as they should please. That history affords no instance of such a thing as equal representation. The Germanic body votes by States. The Helvetic body does the same; and so does the Belgic confederacy. That too little is known of the ancient confederations, to say what was their practice.

Mr. Wilson thought, that taxation should be in proportion to wealth, but that representation should accord with the number of freemen. That government is a collection or result of the wills of all: that if any government could speak the will of all, it would be perfect; and that, so far as it departs from this, it becomes imperfect. It has been said that Congress is a representation of States, not of individuals. I say, that the objects of its care are all the individuals of the States. It is strange that annexing the name of "State" to ten thousand men, should give them an equal right with forty thousand. This must be the effect of magic, not of reason. As to those matters which are referred to Congress, we are not so many States; we are one large State. We lay aside our individuality, whenever we come here. The Germanic body is a burlesque on government; and their practice, on any point, is a sufficient authority and proof that it is wrong. The greatest imperfection in the constitution of the Belgic confederacy is their voting by provinces. The interest of the whole is constantly sacrificed to that of the small States. The history of the war in the reign of Queen Anne sufficiently proves this. It is asked, shall nine colonies put it into the power of four to govern them as they please? I invert the question, and ask, sha'l two millions of people put it in the power of one million to govern them as they please? It is pretended, too, that the smaller colonies will be in danger from the greater. Speak in honest language and say, the minority will be in danger from the majority. And is there an assembly on earth, where this danger may not be equally pretended? The truth is, that our proceedings will then be consentaneous with the interests of the majority, and so they ought to be. The probability is much greater, that the larger States will disagree, than that they will combine. I defy the wit of man to invent a possible case, or to suggest any one thing on earth, which shall be for the interests of Virginia, Pennsylvania and Massachusetts, and which will not also be for the interest of the other States.

These articles, reported July 12, '76, were debated from day to day, and time to time, for two years, were ratified July 9, '78, by ten States, by New Jersey on the 26th of November of the same year, and by Delaware on the 23d of February following. Maryland alone held off two years more, acceding to them March 1, '81, and thus closing the obligation.—i, 26. FORD ED., i, 38.

A BILL FOR ESTABLISHING RELIGIOUS FREEDOM

SECTION I. Well aware that the opinions and belief of men depend not on their own will, but follow involuntarily the evidence proposed to their minds; that Almighty God hath created the mind free, and manifested His supreme will that free it shall remain by making it altogether insusceptible of restraint: that all attempts to influence it by temporal punishments or burthens, or by civil incapacitations, tend only to beget habits of hypocrisy and meanness, and are a departure from the plan of the Holy Author of our religion, who being Lord both of body and mind, yet chose not to propagate it by coercions on either, as was in his Almighty power to do, but to exalt it by its influence on reason alone: that the impious presumption of legislature and ruler, civil as well as ecclesiastical, who, being themselves but fallible and uninspired men, have assumed dominion over the faith of others, setting up their own opinions and modes of thinking as the only true and infallible, and as such endeavoring to impose them on others, hath established and maintained false religions over the greatest part of the world, and through all time: That to compel a man to furnish contributions of money for the propagation of opinions which he disbelieves and abhors is sinful and tyrannical; that even the forcing him to support this or that teacher of his own religious persuasion, is depriving him of the comfortable liberty of giving his contributions to the particular pastor whose morals he would make his pattern, and whose powers he feels most persuasive to righteousness; and is withdrawing from the ministry those temporary rewards, which, proceeding from an approbation of their personal conduct, are an additional incitement to earnest and unremitting labors for the instruction of mankind, that our civil rights have no dependence on our religious opinions, any more than our opinions in physics or geometry; and therefore the proscribing any citizen as unworthy the public confidence by laying upon him an incapacity of being called to office of trust or emolument, unless he profess or renounce this or that religious opinion, is depriving him injudiciously of those privileges and advantages to which, in common with his fellow citizens, he has a natural right; that it tends also to corrupt the principles of that very religion it is meant to encourage, by bribing with a monopoly of worldly honors and emoluments, those who will externally profess and conform to it; that though indeed these are criminals who do not withstand such temptation, yet neither are those innocent who lay the bait in their way; that the opinions of men are not the object of civil government, nor under its jurisdiction; that to suffer the civil magistrate to intrude his powers into the field of opinion, and to restrain the profession or propagation of principles on supposition of their ill tendency is a dangerous fallacy which at once destroys all religious liberty, because, he being of course judge of that tendency, will make his opinions the rule of judgment, and approve or condemn the sentiments of others only as they shall square with or differ from his own; that it is time enough for the rightful purposes of civil government for its officers to interfere when principles break out into overt acts against peace and good order; and finally, that truth is great and will prevail if left to herself; that she is the proper and sufficient antagonist to error, and has nothing to fear from the conflict unless, by human interposition, disarmed of her natural weapons, free argument and debate; errors ceasing to be dangerous when it is permitted freely to contradict them:

SECT. II. We, the General Assembly of Virginia, do enact that no man shall be compelled to frequent or support any religious worship, place, or ministry whatsoever, nor shall be enforced, restrained, molested, or burthened in his body or goods, or shall otherwise suffer on account of his religious opinions or belief; but that all men shall be free to profess, and by argument to maintain, their opinions in matters of religion, and that the same shall in no wise diminish, enlarge, or affect their civil capacities.

SECT. III. And though we well know that this Assembly, elected by the people for the ordinary purposes of legislation only, have no power to restrain the acts of succeeding Assemblies, constituted with powers equal to our own, and that, therefore, to declare this act to be irrevocable would be of no effect in law; yet we are free to declare, and do declare, that the rights hereby asserted are of the natural rights of mankind, and that if any act shall be hereafter passed to repeal the present or to narrow its operations, such act will be an infringement of natural right.—viii, 454. FORD ED., ii, 237. (1786.)

KENTUCKY RESOLUTIONS

1. *Resolved,* That the several States composing the United States of America, are not united on the principle of unlimited submission to their General Government; but that, by a compact under the style and title of a Constitution for the United States, and of Amendments thereto, they constituted a General Government for special purposes,—delegated to that government certain definite powers, reserving, each State to itself, the residuary mass of right to their own self-government; and that whensoever the General Government assumes undelegated powers, its acts are unauthoritative, void, and of no force: that to this compact each State acceded as a State, and is an integral party, its co-States forming, as to itself, the other party: that the Government created by this compact was not made the exclusive or final judge of the extent of the powers delegated to itself; since that would have made its discretion, and not the Constitution, the measure of its powers: but that, as in all other cases of compact among powers having no common judge, each party has an equal right to judge for itself, as well of infractions as of the mode and measure of redress.

2. *Resolved,* That the Constitution of the United States, having delegated to Congress a power to punish treason, counterfeiting the securities and current coin of the United States, piracies, and felonies committed on the high seas, and offences against the law of nations, and no other crimes whatsoever; and it being true as a general principle, and one of the amendments to the Constitution having also declared, that "the powers not delegated to the United States by the Constitution, nor prohibited by it to the States, are reserved to the States respectively, or to the people", therefore the act of Congress, passed on the 14th day of July, 1798, and intituled "An Act in addition to the act intituled 'An Act for the punishment of certain crimes against the United States'", as also the act passed by them on the —— day of June, 1789, intituled "An Act to punish frauds committed on the Bank of the United States" (and all their other acts which assume to create, define, or punish crimes, other than those so enumerated in the Constitution), are altogether void, and of no force: and that the power to create, define, and punish such other crimes is reserved, and, of right, appertains solely and exclusively to the respective States, each within its own territory.

3. *Resolved,* That it is true as a general principle, and is also expressly declared by one of the amendments to the Constitution, that "the powers not delegated to the United States by the Constitution, nor prohibited by it to the States, are reserved to the States respectively, or to the people"; and that no power over the freedom of religion, freedom of speech, or freedom of the press being delegated to the United States by the Constitution, nor prohibited by it to the States, all lawful powers respecting the same did of right remain, and were reserved to the States or the people; that thus was manifested their determination to retain to themselves the right of judging how far the licentiousness of speech and of the press may be abridged without lessening their useful freedom, and how far those abuses which cannot be separated from their use should be tolerated, rather than the use be destroyed. And thus also they guarded against all abridgment by the United States of the freedom of religious opinions and exercises, and retained to themselves the right of protecting the same, as this State, by a law passed on the general demand of its citizens, had already protected them from all human restraint or interference. And that in addition to this general principle and express declaration, another and more special provision has been made by one of the amendments to the Constitution, which expressly declares, that "Congress shall make no law respecting an establishment of religion, or prohibiting the free exercise thereof, or abridging the freedom of speech, or of the press"; thereby guarding in the same sentence, and under the same words, the freedom of religion, of speech, and of the press: insomuch, that whatever violated either, throws down the sanctuary which covers the others, and that libels, falsehoods, and defamation, equally with heresy and false religion, are withheld from the cognizance of Federal tribunals. That, therefore, the act of Congress of the United States, passed on the 14th day of July, 1798, intituled "An Act in addition to the act intituled 'An Act for the punishment of certain crimes against the United States'" which does abridge the freedom of the press, is not law, but is altogether void, and of no force.

4. *Resolved,* That alien friends are under the jurisdiction and protection of the laws of the State wherein they are; that no power over them has been delegated to the United States, nor prohibited to the individual States, distinct from their power over citizens. And it being true as a general principle, and one of the amendments to the Constitution having also declared, that "the powers not delegated to the United States by the Constitution, nor prohibited by it to the States, are reserved to the States respectively, or to the people", the act of the Congress of the United States, passed on the —— day of July, 1798, intituled "An Act concerning aliens", which assumes powers over alien friends, not delegated by the Constitution, is not law, but is altogether void, and of no force.

5. *Resolved,* That in addition to the general principle, as well as the express declaration, that powers not delegated are reserved, another and more special provision, inserted in the Constitution from abundant caution, has declared that "the migration or importation of such persons as any of the States now existing shall think proper to admit, shall not be prohibited by the Congress prior to the year 1808": that this Commonwealth does admit the migration of alien friends, described as the subject of the said act concerning aliens: that a provision against prohibiting their migration, is a provision against all acts equivalent thereto, or it would be nugatory: that to remove them when migrated, is equivalent to a prohibition of their migration, and is, therefore, contrary to the said provision of the Constitution, and void.

6. *Resolved,* That the imprisonment of a person under the laws of this Commonwealth, on his failure to obey the simple *order* of the President to depart out of the United States, as is undertaken by said act intituled "An Act concerning aliens" is contrary to the Constitution, one amendment to which has provided that "no person shall be deprived of liberty without due process of law"; and that another having provided that "in all criminal prosecutions the accused shall enjoy the right to public trial by an impartial jury, to be informed of the nature and cause of the accusation, to be confronted with the witnesses against him, to have compulsory process for obtaining witnesses in his favor, and to have the assistance of counsel for his

defence ", the same act, undertaking to authorize the President to remove a person out of the United States, who is under the protection of the law, on his own suspicion, without accusation, without jury, without public trial, without confrontation of the witnesses against him, without hearing witnesses in his favor, without defence, without counsel, is contrary to the provision also of the Constitution, is therefore not law, but utterly void, and of no force: that transferring the power of judging any person, who is under the protection of the laws, from the courts to the President of the United States, as is undertaken by the same act concerning aliens, is against the article of the Constitution which provides that " the judicial power of the United States shall be vested in courts, the judges of which shall hold their offices during good behavior "; and that the said act is void for that reason also. And it is further to be noted, that this transfer of judiciary power is to that magistrate of the General Government who already possesses all the Executive and a negative on all Legislative powers.

7. *Resolved*, That the construction applied by the General Government (as is evidenced by sundry of their proceedings) to those parts of the Constitution of the United States which delegate to Congress a power " to lay and collect taxes, duties, imposts and excises, to pay the debts, and provide for the common defence and general welfare of the United States ", and " to make all laws which shall be necessary and proper for carrying into execution the powers vested by the Constitution in the government of the United States, or in any department or officer thereof ", goes to the destruction of all limits prescribed to their power by the Constitution: that words meant by the instrument to be subsidiary only to the execution of limited powers, ought not to be so construed as themselves to give unlimited powers, nor a part to be so taken as to destroy the whole residue of that instrument: that the proceedings of the General Government under color of these articles, will be a fit and necessary subject of revisal and correction, at a time of greater tranquillity, while those specified in the preceding resolution call for immediate redress.

8. *Resolved*, That a committee of conference and correspondence be appointed, who shall have in charge to communicate the preceding resolutions to the Legislatures of the several States: to assure them that this Commonwealth continues in the same esteem of their friendship and union which it has manifested from that moment at which a common danger first suggested a common union: that it considers union, for specified national purposes, and particularly to those specified in their late Federal compact, to be friendly to the peace, happiness and prosperity of all the States: that faithful to that compact, according to the plain intent and meaning in which it was understood and acceded to by the several parties, it is sincerely anxious for its preservation: that it does also believe, that to take from the States all the powers of self-government and transfer them to a general and consolidated government, without regard to the special delegations and reservations solemnly agreed to in that compact, is not for the peace, happiness or prosperity of these States; and that, therefore, this Commonwealth is determined, as it doubts not its co-States are, to submit to undelegated, and consequently unlimited powers in no man, or body of men on earth: that in cases of an abuse of the delegated powers, the members of the General Government, being chosen by the people, a change by the people would be the constitutional remedy; but, where powers are assumed which have not been delegated, a nullification of the act is the rightful remedy; that every State has a natural right in cases not within the compact (*casus non fœderis*), to nullify of their own authority all assumptions of power by others within their limits: that without this right, they would be under the dominion, absolute and unlimited, of whosoever might exercise this right of judgment for them: that nevertheless, this Commonwealth, from motives of regard and respect for its co-States, has wished to communicate with them on the subject: that with them alone it is proper to communicate, they alone being parties to the compact, and solely authorized to judge in the last resort of the powers exercised under it, Congress being not a party, but merely the creature of the compact, and subject as to its assumptions of power to the final judgment of those by whom, and for whose use itself and its powers were all created and modified: that if the acts before specified should stand, these conclusions would flow from them; that the General Government may place any act they think proper on the list of crimes, and punish it themselves whether enumerated or not enumerated by the Constitution as cognizable by them; that they may transfer its cognizance to the President, or any other person, who may himself be the accuser, counsel, judge, and jury, whose *suspicions* may be the evidence, his *order* the sentence, his *officer* the executioner, and his breast the sole record of the transaction: that a very numerous and valuable description of the inhabitants of these States being, by this precedent, reduced, as outlaws, to the absolute dominion of one man, and the barrier of the Constitution thus swept away from us all, no rampart now remains against the passions and the powers of a majority in Congress to protect from a like exportation, or other more grievous punishment, the minority of the same body, the legislatures, judges, governors, and councillors of the States, nor their other peaceable inhabitants, who may venture to reclaim the constitutional rights and liberties of the States and people, or who for other causes, good or bad, may be obnoxious to the views, or marked by the suspicions of the President, or be thought dangerous to his or their election, or other interests, public or personal: that the friendless alien has indeed been selected as the safest subject of a first experiment; but the citizen will soon follow, or rather, has already followed, for already has a Sedition Act marked him as its prey; that these and successive acts of the same character, unless arrested at the threshold, necessarily drive these States into revolution and blood, and will furnish new calumnies against republican government, and new pretexts for those who wish it to be believed that man cannot be governed but by a rod of iron; that it would be a dangerous delusion were a confidence in the men of our choice to silence our fears for the safety of our rights: that confidence is everywhere the parent of despotism—free government is founded in jealousy, and not in confidence: it is jealousy and not confidence which prescribes limited constitutions, to bind down those whom we are obliged to trust with power: that our Constitution has accordingly fixed the limits to which, and no further, our confidence may go; and let the honest advocate of confidence read the Alien and Sedition Acts, and say if the Constitution has not been wise in fixing limits to the government it created, and whether we should be wise in destroying those limits. Let him say what the government is, if it be not a tyranny, which the men of our choice have conferred on our President, and the President of our choice has assented to, and accepted over the friendly strangers to whom the

mild spirit of our country and its laws have pledged hospitality and protection: that the men of our choice have more respected the bare *suspicions* of the President, than the solid right of innocence, the claims of justification, the sacred force of truth, and the forms and substance of law and justice. In questions of power, then, let no more be heard of confidence in man, but bind him down from mischief by the chains of the Constitution. That this Commonwealth does, therefore, call on its co-States for an expression of their sentiments on the acts concerning aliens, and for the punishment of certain crimes herein before specified, plainly declaring whether these acts are or are not authorized by the Federal compact. And it doubts not that their sense will be so announced as to prove their attachment unaltered to limited government, whether general or particular. And that the rights and liberties of their co-States will be exposed to no dangers by remaining embarked in a common bottom with their own. That they will concur with this Commonwealth in considering the said acts as so palpably against the Constitution as to amount to an undisguised declaration that that compact is not meant to be the measure of the powers of the General Government, but that it will proceed in the exercise over these States, of all powers whatsoever: that they will view this as seizing the rights of the States, and consolidating them in the hands of the General Government, with a power assumed to bind the States (not merely in the cases made Federal (*casus fœderis*) but) in all cases whatsoever, by laws made, not with their consent, but by others against their consent; that this would be to surrender the form of government we have chosen, and live under one deriving its powers from its own will, and not from our authority; and that the co-States, recurring to their natural right in cases not made Federal, will concur in declaring these acts void, and of no force, and will each take measures of its own for providing that neither these acts, nor any others of the General Government not plainly and intentionally authorized by the Constitution, shall be exercised within their respective territories.

9. *Resolved,* That the said committee be authorized to communicate by writing or personal conferences, at any times or places whatever, with any person or persons who may be appointed by any one or more co-States to correspond or confer with them; and that they lay their proceeding before the next session of Assembly.—ix, 464. FORD ED., vii, 289. (1798.)

FIRST INAUGURAL ADDRESS

March 4, 1801

Friends and fellow-citizens:

Called upon to undertake the duties of the first executive office of our country, I avail myself of the presence of that portion of my fellow-citizens which is here assembled, to express my grateful thanks for the favor with which they have been pleased to look toward me, to declare a sincere consciousness that the task is above my talents, and that I approach it with those anxious and awful presentiments which the greatness of the charge and the weakness of my powers so justly inspire. A rising nation, spread over a wide and fruitful land; traversing all the seas with the rich productions of their industry; engaged in commerce with nations who feel power and forget right; advancing rapidly to destinies beyond the reach of mortal eye,—when I contemplate these transcendent objects, and see the honor, the happiness, and the hopes of this beloved country committed to the issue and the auspices of this day, I shrink from the contemplation, and humble myself before the magnitude of the undertaking. Utterly, indeed, should I despair, did not the presence of many whom I here see remind me that in the other high authorities provided by our Constitution I shall find resources of wisdom, of virtue, and of zeal, on which to rely under all difficulties. To you, then, gentlemen, who are charged with the sovereign functions of legislation, and to those associated with you, I look with encouragement for that guidance and support which may enable us to steer with safety the vessel in which we are all embarked, amid the conflicting elements of a troubled world.

During the contest of opinion through which we have passed, the animation of discussion and of exertions has sometimes worn an aspect which might impose on strangers, unused to think freely, and to speak and to write what they think; but, this being now decided by the voice of the nation, announced according to the rules of the Constitution, all will, of course, arrange themselves under the will of the law, and unite in common efforts for the common good. All, too, will bear in mind this sacred principle, that, though the will of the majority is in all cases to prevail, that will, to be rightful, must be reasonable; that the minority possess their equal rights, which equal laws must protect, and to violate which would be oppression. Let us, then, fellow-citizens, unite with one heart and one mind; let us restore to social intercourse that harmony and affection without which liberty and even life itself are but dreary things. And let us reflect that having banished from our land that religious intolerance under which mankind so long bled and suffered, we have yet gained little if we countenance a political intolerance as despotic, as wicked, and capable of as bitter and bloody persecutions. During the throes and convulsions of the ancient world, during the agonizing spasms of infuriated man, seeking through blood and slaughter his long-lost liberty, it was not wonderful that the agitation of the billows should reach even this distant and peaceful shore; that this should be more felt and feared by some and less by others; that this should divide opinions as to measures of safety. But every difference of opinion is not a difference of principle. We have called by different names brethren of the same principle. We are all republicans; we are all federalists. If there be any among us who would wish to dissolve this Union, or to change its republican form, let them stand, undisturbed, as monuments of the safety with which error of opinion may be tolerated where reason is left free to combat it. I know, indeed, that some honest men fear that a republican government cannot be strong; that this Government is not strong enough. But would the honest patriot, in the full tide of successful experiment, abandon a Government which has so far kept us free and firm, on the theoretic and visionary fear that this Government, the world's best hope, may, by possibility, want energy to preserve itself? I trust not. I believe this, on the contrary, the strongest Government on earth. I believe it is the only one where every man, at the call of the law, would fly to the standard of the law, and would meet invasions of the public order as his own personal concern. Sometimes it is said that man cannot be trusted with the government of himself. Can he, then, be trusted with the government of others? Or have we found angels in the form of kings to govern him? Let history answer this question.

Let us, then, with a courage and confidence, pursue our own federal and republican principles, our attachment to our Union and representative government. Kindly separated by nature and a wide ocean from the exterminating havoc of one quarter of the globe; too high-minded to endure the degradations of the others; possessing a chosen country, with room enough for our descendants to the hundredth and thousandth generation; entertaining a due sense of our equal right to the use of our own faculties, to the acquisitions of our industry, to honor and confidence from our fellow-citizens, resulting not from birth but from our actions, and their sense of them; enlightened by a benign religion, professed, indeed, and practiced in various forms, yet all of them inculcating honesty, truth, temperance, gratitude, and the love of man; acknowledging and adoring an overruling Providence, which, by all its dispensations, proves that it delights in the happiness of man here, and his greater happiness hereafter; with all these blessings, what more is necessary to make us a happy and prosperous people? Still one thing more, fellow-citizens,— a wise and frugal Government, which shall restrain men from injuring one another, which shall leave them otherwise free to regulate their own pursuits of industry and improvement, and shall not take from the mouth of labor the bread it has earned. This is the sum of good government, and this is necessary to close the circle of our felicities.

About to enter, fellow-citizens, on the exercise of duties which comprehend every thing dear and valuable to you, it is proper that you should understand what I deem the essential principles of our Government, and, consequently, those which ought to shape its administration. I will compress them within the narrowest compass they will bear, stating the general principle, but not all its limitations. Equal and exact justice to all men, of whatever state or persuasion, religious or political; peace, commerce, and honest friendship with all nations, entangling alliances with none: the support of the State governments in all their rights, as the most competent administrations for our domestic concerns, and the surest bulwarks against anti-republican tendencies; the preservation of the General Government in its whole constitutional vigor, as the sheet-anchor of our peace at home and safety abroad; a jealous care of the right of election by the people,—

a mild and safe corrective of abuses which are lopped by the sword of revolution, where peaceable remedies are unprovided; absolute acquiescence in the decisions of the majority,— the vital principle of republics, from which is no appeal but to force, the vital principle and immediate parent of despotism; a well-disciplined militia,—our best reliance in peace and for the first moments of war, till regulars may relieve them; the supremacy of the civil over the military authority; economy in the public expense, that labor may be lightly burdened; the honest payment of our debts and sacred preservation of the public faith; encouragement of agriculture, and of commerce as its handmaid; the diffusion of information and arraignment of all abuses at the bar of public reason; freedom of religion; freedom of the press; freedom of person under the protection of the *habeas corpus;* and trial by juries impartially selected. These principles form the bright constellation which has gone before us, and guided our steps through an age of revolution and reformation. The wisdom of our sages and the blood of our heroes have been devoted to their attainment. They should be the creed of our political faith, the text of civic instruction, the touch-stone by which to try the services of those we trust; and should we wander from them in moments of error or of alarm, let us hasten to retrace our steps, and to regain the road which alone leads to peace, liberty, and safety.

I repair, then, fellow-citizens, to the post you have assigned me. With experience enough in subordinate offices to have seen the difficulties of this, the greatest of all, I have learned to expect that it will rarely fall to the lot of imperfect man to retire from this station with the reputation and the favor which bring him into it. Without pretensions to that high confidence reposed in our first and greatest revolutionary character, whose pre-eminent services had entitled him to the first place in his country's love, and destined for him the fairest page in the volume of faithful history, I ask so much confidence only as may give firmness and effect to the legal administration of your affairs. I shall often go wrong, through defect of judgment. When right, I shall often be thought wrong by those whose positions will not command a view of the whole ground. I ask your indulgence for my own errors, which will never be intentional; and your support against the errors of others, who may condemn what they would not if seen in all its parts. The approbation implied by your suffrage is a consolation to me for the past; and my future solicitude will be to retain the good opinion of those who have bestowed it in advance, to conciliate that of others by doing them all the good in my power, and to be instrumental to the happiness and freedom of all.

Relying, then, on the patronage of your good will, I advance with obedience to the work, ready to retire from it whenever you become sensible how much better choice it is in your power to make. And may that Infinite Power which rules the destinies of the universe, lead our councils to what is best, and give them a favorable issue for your peace and prosperity.— viii, 1. FORD ED., viii, 1. (March 4, 1801.)

SECOND INAUGURAL ADDRESS

March 4, 1805

Proceeding, fellow-citizens, to that qualification which the Constitution requires before my entrance on the charge again conferred upon me, it is my duty to express the deep sense I entertain of this new proof of confidence from my fellow-citizens at large, and the zeal with which it inspires me so to conduct myself as may best satisfy their just expectations.

On taking this station, on a former occasion, I declared the principles on which I believed it my duty to administer the affairs of our commonwealth. My conscience tells me that I have, on every occasion, acted up to that declaration, according to its obvious import, and to the understanding of every candid mind.

In the transaction of your foreign affairs, we have endeavored to cultivate the friendship of all nations, and especially of those with which we have the most important relations. We have done them justice on all occasions, favor where favor was lawful, and cherished mutual interests and intercourse on fair and equal terms. We are firmly convinced, and we act on that conviction, that with nations, as with individuals, our interests soundly calculated, will ever be found inseparable from our moral duties; and history bears witness to the fact, that a just nation is taken on its word, when recourse is had to armaments and wars to bridle others.

At home, fellow-citizens, you best know whether we have done well or ill. The suppression of unnecessary offices, of useless establishments and expenses, enabled us to discontinue our internal taxes. These, covering our land with officers, and opening our doors to their intrusions, had already begun that process of domiciliary vexation, which, once entered, is scarcely to be restrained from reaching, successively, every article of produce and property. If, among these taxes some minor ones fell which had not been inconvenient, it was because their amount would not have paid the officers who collected them, and because, if they had any merit, the State authorities might adopt them instead of others less approved.

The remaining revenue, on the consumption of foreign articles, is paid cheerfully by those who can afford to add foreign luxuries to domestic comforts. Being collected on our seaboard and frontiers only, and incorporated with the transactions of our mercantile citizens, it may be the pleasure and pride of an American to ask, what farmer, what mechanic, what laborer, ever sees a tax-gatherer of the United States? These contributions enable us to support the current expenses of the Government; to fulfil contracts with foreign nations; to extinguish the native right of soil within our limits; to extend those limits; and to apply such a surplus to our public debts as places at a short day their final redemption; and, that redemption once effected, the revenue thereby liberated may, by a just repartition among the States, and a corresponding amendment of the Constitution, be applied, *in time of peace*, to rivers, canals, roads, arts, manufactures, education, and other great objects, within each State. *In time of war*, if injustice by ourselves or others must sometimes produce war, increased, as the same revenue will be increased by population and consumption, and aided by other resources reserved for that crisis, it may meet, within the year all the expenses of the year, without encroaching on the rights of future generations, by burdening them with the debts of the past. War will then be but a suspension of useful works; and a return to a state of peace, a return to the progress of improvement.

I have said, fellow-citizens, that the income reserved had enabled us to extend our limits; but that extension may possibly pay for itself before we are called on, and, in the mean time, may keep down the accruing interest; in all events, it will repay the advances we have made. I know that the acquisition of Louisiana has been disapproved by some, from a candid apprehension that the enlargement of our territory may endanger its union. But who can limit the extent to which the federative principle may operate effectively? The larger our association, the less will it be shaken by local passions; and, in any view, is it not better that the opposite bank of the Mississippi should be settled by our own brethren and children, than by strangers of another family? With which shall we be most likely to live in harmony and friendly intercourse?

In matters of religion, I have considered that its free exercise is placed by the Constitution independent of the powers of the General Government. I have therefore undertaken, on no occasion, to prescribe the religious exercises suited to it, but have left them as the Constitution found them, under the direction and discipline of State and Church authorities acknowledged by the several religious societies.

The aboriginal inhabitants of these countries I have regarded with the commiseration their history inspires. Endowed with the faculties and the rights of men, breathing an ardent love of liberty and independence, and occupying a country which left them no desire but to be undisturbed, the stream of overflowing population from other regions directed itself on these shores. Without power to divert, or habits to contend against, they have been overwhelmed by the current, or driven before it. Now reduced within limits too narrow for the hunter state, humanity enjoins us to teach them agriculture and the domestic arts, to encourage them to that industry which alone can enable them to maintain their place in existence, and to prepare them, in time, for that state of society which to bodily comforts adds the improvement of the mind and morals. We have, therefore, liberally furnished them with the implements of husbandry and household use; we have placed among them instructors in the arts of first necessity; and they are covered with the ægis of the law against aggressors from among ourselves.

But the endeavors to enlighten them on the fate which awaits their present course of life, to induce them to exercise their reason, follow its dictates, and change their pursuits with the change of circumstances, have powerful obstacles to encounter. They are combated by the habits of their bodies, prejudice of their minds, ignorance, pride, and the influence of interested and crafty individuals among them, who feel themselves something in the present order of things, and fear to become nothing in any other. These persons inculcate a sancti-monious reverence for the customs of their ancestors; that whatsoever they did must be done through all time; that reason is a false guide, and to advance under its counsel in their physical, moral, or political conditions, is perilous innovation; that their duty is to remain as their Creator made them—ignorance being safety, and knowledge full of danger. In short, my friends, among them is seen the action and counteraction of good sense and bigotry. They, too, have their anti-philosophers, who find an interest in keeping things in their present state, who dread reformation, and exert all their faculties to maintain the ascendency of habit over the duty of improving our reason and obeying its mandates.

In giving these outlines, I do not mean, fellow-citizens, to arrogate to myself the merit of the measures; that is due, in the first place, to the reflecting character of our citizens at large, who, by the weight of public opinion, influence and strengthen the public measures. It is due to the sound discretion with which they select from among themselves those to whom they confide the legislative duties. It is due to the zeal and wisdom of the characters thus selected, who lay the foundations of public happiness in wholesome laws, the execution of which alone remains for others. And it is due to the able and faithful auxiliaries whose patriotism has associated with me in the executive functions.

During this course of administration, and in order to disturb it, the artillery of the press has been levelled against us, charged with whatsoever its licentiousness could devise or dare. These abuses of an institution so important to freedom and science are deeply to be regretted, inasmuch as they tend to lessen its usefulness and to sap its safety. They might, indeed, have been corrected by the wholesome punishments reserved and provided by the laws of the several States against falsehood and defamation; but public duties more urgent press on the time of public servants, and the offenders have therefore been left to find their punishment in the public indignation.

Nor was it uninteresting to the world, that an experiment should be fairly and fully made, whether freedom of discussion, unaided by power, is not sufficient for the propagation and protection of truth? Whether a government, conducting itself in the true spirit of its constitution, with zeal and purity, and doing no act which it would be unwilling the whole world should witness, can be written down by falsehood and defamation? The experiment has been tried. You have witnessed the scene. Our fellow-citizens have looked on cool and collected. They saw the latent source from which these outrages proceeded. They gathered around their public functionaries; and, when the Constitution called them to the decision by suffrage, they pronounced their verdict, honorable to those who had served them, and consolatory to the friend of man, who believes he may be intrusted with his own affairs.

No inference is here intended that the laws provided by the State against false and defamatory publications should not be enforced. He who has time, renders a service to public morals and public tranquillity in reforming these abuses by the salutary coercions of the law. But the experiment is noted to prove that, since truth and reason have maintained their ground against false opinions, in league with false facts, the press, confined to truth, needs no other legal restraint. The public judgment will correct false reasonings and opinions, on a full hearing of all parties; and no other definite line can be drawn between the inestimable liberty of the press and its demoralizing licentiousness. If there be still improprieties which this rule would not restrain, its supplement must be sought in the censorship of public opinion.

Contemplating the union of sentiment now manifested so generally, as auguring harmony and happiness to our future course, I offer to our country sincere congratulations. With those, too, not yet rallied to the same point, the disposition to do so is gaining strength. Facts are piercing through the veil drawn over them; and our doubting brethren will at length see that the mass of their fellow-citizens, with whom they cannot yet resolve to act, as to principles and measures, think as they think, and desire what they desire; that our wish, as well as theirs, is, that the public efforts may be directed honestly to the public good, that peace be cultivated, civil and religious liberty unassailed, law and order preserved, equality of rights maintained, and that state of property, equal or unequal, which results to every man from his own industry, or that of his father's. When satisfied of these views, it is not in human nature that they should not approve and support them. In the meantime, let us cherish them with patient affection; let us do them justice, and more than justice, in all competitions of interest,—and we need not doubt that truth, reason, and their own interests, will at length prevail—will gather them into the fold of their country, and will complete their entire union of opinion which gives to a nation the blessing of harmony, and the benefit of all its strength.

I shall now enter on the duties to which my fellow-citizens have again called me, and shall proceed in the spirit of those principles which they have approved. I fear not that any motives of interest may lead me astray. I am sensible of no passion which could seduce me, knowingly, from the path of justice; but the weaknesses of human nature, and the limits of my own understanding, will produce errors of judgment sometimes injurious to your interests. I shall need, therefore, all the indulgence I have heretofore experienced, the want of it will certainly not lessen with increasing years. I shall need, too, the favor of that Being in whose hands we are: who led our forefathers, as Israel of old, from their native land, and planted them in a country flowing with all the necessaries and comforts of life; who has covered our infancy with His providence, and our riper years with His wisdom and power; and to whose goodness I ask you to join with me in supplications, that He will so enlighten the minds of your servants, guide their councils, and prosper their measures, that whatsoever they do shall result in your good, and shall secure to you the peace, friendship, and approbation of all nations.—viii, 40. FORD ED., viii, 341. (March 4, 1805.)

ADDRESS OF THE GENERAL ASSEMBLY OF VIRGINIA

The "Valedictory Address of the General Assembly of Virginia", which was agreed to on the 7th of February, 1809, gives a good idea of the high estimation in which Jefferson was held by his party, and the great majority of his countrymen, when he retired from the Presidency. It is as follows:—

"Sir.—The General Assembly of your native State cannot close their session, without acknowledging your services in the office which you are just about to lay down, and bidding you a respectful and affectionate farewell.

"We have to thank you for the model of an administration conducted on the purest principles of republicanism; for pomp and state laid aside; patronage discarded; internal taxes abolished; a host of superfluous officers disbanded; the monarchic maxim that 'a national debt is a national blessing', renounced, and more than thirty-three millions of our debt discharged; the native right to nearly one hundred millions of acres of our national domain extinguished; and, without the guilt or calamities of conquest, a vast and fertile region added to our country, far more extensive than her original possessions, bringing along with it the Mississippi and the port of Orleans, the trade of the West to the Pacific ocean, and in the intrinsic value of the land itself, a source of permanent and almost inexhaustible revenue. These are points in your administration which the historian will not fail to seize, to expand, and teach posterity to dwell upon with delight. Nor will he forget our peace with the civilized world, preserved through a season of uncommon difficulty and trial; the good will cultivated with the unfortunate aborigines of our country, and the civilization humanely extended among them; the lesson taught the inhabitants of the coast of Barbary, that we have the means of chastising their piratical encroachments, and awing them into justice; and that theme, on which, above all others, the historic genius will hang with rapture, the liberty of speech and of the press, preserved inviolate, without which genius and science are given to man in vain.

"In the principles on which you have administered the government, we see only the continuation and maturity of the same virtues and abilities, which drew upon you in your youth the resentment of Dunmore. From the first brilliant and happy moment of your resistance to foreign tyranny, until the present day, we mark with pleasure and with gratitude the same uniform, consistent character, the same warm and devoted attachment to liberty and the Republic, the same Roman love of your country, her rights, her peace, her honor, her prosperity.

"How blessed will be the retirement into which you are about to go! How deservedly blessed will it be! For you carry with you the richest of all rewards, the recollection of a life well spent in the service of your country, and proofs the most decisive, of the love, the gratitude, the veneration of your countrymen.

"That your retirement may be as happy as your life has been virtuous and useful; that our youth may see, in the blissful close of your days, an additional inducement to form themselves on your model, is the devout and earnest prayer of your fellow-citizens who compose the General Assembly of Virginia."—RAYNER'S *Life of Jefferson*, p. 494.

ADDRESS TO THE INHABITANTS OF ALBEMARLE CO., IN VIRGINIA

Returning to the scenes of my birth and early life, to the society of those with whom I was raised, and who have been ever dear to me, I receive, fellow-citizens and neighbors, with inexpressible pleasure, the cordial welcome you were so good as to give me. Long absent on duties which the history of a wonderful era made incumbent on those called to them, the pomp, the turmoil, the bustle and splendor of office; have drawn but deeper sighs for the tranquil and irresponsible occupations of private life, for the enjoyment of an affectionate intercourse with you, my neighbors and friends, and the endearments of family love, which nature has given us all, as the sweetner of every hour. For these I gladly lay down the distressing burthen of power, and seek, with my fellow-citizens, repose and safety under the watchful cares, the labors and perplexities of younger and abler minds. The anxieties you express to administer to my happiness, do, of themselves, confer that happiness; and the measure will be complete, if any endeavors to fulfil my duties in the several public stations to which I have been called, have obtained for me the approbation of my country. The part which I have acted on the theatre of public life, has been before them; and to their sentence I submit it; but the testimony of my native county, of the individuals who have known me in private life, to my conduct in its various duties and relations, is the more grateful, as proceeding from eye-witnesses and observers, from triers of the vicinage. Of you, then, my neighbors, I may ask, in the face of the world, "whose ox have I taken, or whom have I defrauded? Whom have I oppressed, or of whose hand have I received a bribe to blind mine eyes therewith"? On your verdict I rest with conscious security. Your wishes for my happiness are received with just sensibility, and I offer sincere prayers for your own welfare and prosperity.—To THE INHABITANTS OF ALBEMARLE COUNTY, VA. v, 439. FORD ED., ix, 250. (M., April 3, 1809.)

DECLARATION AND PROTEST OF THE COMMONWEALTH OF VIRGINIA*

We, the General Assembly of Virginia, on behalf, and in the name of the people thereof, do declare as follows:

The States of North America which confederated to establish their independence of the government of Great Britain, of which Virginia was one, became, on that acquisition free and independent States, and as such, authorized to constitute governments, each for itself, in such form as it thought best.

They entered into a compact (which is called the Constitution of the United States of America), by which they agreed to unite in a single government as to their relations with each other, and with foreign nations, and as to certain other articles particularly specified. They retained at the same time, each to itself, the other rights of independent government, comprehending mainly their domestic interests.

For the administration of their Federal branch, they agreed to appoint, in conjunction, a distinct set of functionaries, legislative, executive and judiciary, in the manner settled in that compact; while to each, severally, and of course remained its original right of appointing, each for itself, a separate set of functionaries, legislative, executive and judiciary, also, for administering the domestic branch of their respective governments.

These two sets of officers, each independent of the other, constitute thus a *whole* of government, for each State separately; the powers ascribed to the one, as specifically made federal, exercised over the whole, the residuary powers, retained to the other, exercisable exclusively over its particular State, foreign herein, each to the others, as they were before the original compact.

To this construction of government and distribution of its powers, the Commonwealth of Virginia does religiously and affectionately adhere, opposing, with equal fidelity and firmness, the usurpation of either set of functionaries of the rightful powers of the other.

But the Federal branch has assumed in some cases, and claimed in others, a right of enlarging its own powers by constructions, inferences, and indefinite deductions from those directly given, which this Assembly does declare to be usurpations of the powers retained to the independent branches, mere interpolations into the compact, and direct infractions of it.

They claim, for example, and have commenced the exercise of a right to construct roads, open canals, and effect other internal improvements within the territories and jurisdictions exclusively belonging to the several States, which this Assembly does declare has not been given to that branch by the constitutional compact, but remains to each State among its domestic and unalienated powers, exercisable within itself and by its domestic authorities alone.

This Assembly does further disavow and declare to be most false and unfounded, the doctrine that the compact, in authorizing its Federal branch to lay and collect taxes, duties, imposts and excises, to pay the debts and provide for the common defence and general welfare of the United States, has given them thereby a power to do whatever *they* may think, or pretend, would promote the general welfare, which construction would make that, of itself, a complete government, without limitation of powers; but that the plain sense and obvious meaning were, that they might levy the taxes necessary to provide for the general welfare, by the various acts of power therein specified and delegated to them, and by no others.

Nor is it admitted, as has been said, that the people of these States, by not investing their Federal branch with all the means of bettering their condition, have denied to themselves any which may effect that purpose; since, in the distribution of these means they have given to that branch those which belong to its department, and to the States have reserved separately the residue which belong to them separately. And thus by the organization of the two branches taken together, have completely secured the first object of human association, the full improvement of their condition, and reserved to themselves all the faculties of multiplying their own blessings.

Whilst the General Assembly thus declares the rights retained by the States, rights which they have never yielded, and which this State will never voluntarily yield, they do not mean to raise the banner of dissatisfaction, or of separation from their sister States, co-parties with themselves to this compact. They know and value too highly the blessings of their Union as to foreign nations and questions arising among themselves, to consider every infraction as to be met by actual resistance. They respect too affectionately the opinions of those possessing the same rights under the same instrument, to make every difference of construction a ground of immediate rupture. They would, indeed, consider such a rupture as among the greatest calamities which could befall them; but not the greatest. There is yet one greater, submission to a government of unlimited powers. It is only when the hope of avoiding this shall have become absolutely desperate, that further forbearance could not be indulged. Should a majority of the co-parties, therefore, contrary to the expectation and hope of this Assembly, prefer, at this time, acquiescence in these assumptions of power by the Federal member of the government, we will be patient and suffer much, under the confidence that time, ere it be too late, will prove to them also the bitter consequences in which that usurpation will involve us all. In the meanwhile, we will breast with them, rather than separate from them, every misfortune, save that only of living under a government of unlimited powers. We owe every other sacrifice to ourselves, to our federal brethren, and to the world at large, to pursue with temper and with perseverance the great experiment which shall prove that man is capable of living in society, governing itself by laws self-imposed, and securing to its members the enjoyment of life, liberty, property, and peace; and further to show, that even when the govern-

---

* This paper was entitled by Jefferson, "The Solemn Declaration and Protest of the Commonwealth of Virginia, on the Principles of the Constitution of the United States of America, and on the violations of them". Jefferson sent it to Madison in December, 1825, with an explanatory letter (vii, 422. Ford Ed., x, 348) in which he said: "It may intimidate the wavering. It may break the western coalition, by offering the same thing in a different form. It will be viewed with favor in contrast with the Georgia opposition, and fear of strengthening that. It will be an example of a temperate mode of opposition in future and similar cases."—Editor.

ment of its choice shall manifest a tendency to degeneracy, we are not at once to despair but that the will and the watchfulness of its sounder parts will reform its aberrations, recall it to original and legitimate principles, and restrain it within the rightful limits of self-government. And these are the objects of this Declaration and Protest.

Supposing, then, that it might be for the good of the whole, as some of its co-States seem to think, that the power of making roads and canals should be added to those directly given to the Federal branch, as more likely to be systematically and beneficially directed, than by the independent action of the several States, this Commonwealth, from respect to these opinions, and a desire of conciliation with its co-States, will consent, in concurrence with them, to make this addition, provided it be done regularly by an amendment of the compact, in the way established by that instrument, and provided also, it be sufficiently guarded against abuses, compromises, and corrupt practices, not only of possible, but of probable occurrence.

And as a further pledge of the sincere and cordial attachment of this Commonwealth to the Union of the whole, so far as has been consented to by the compact called " The Constitution of the United States of America ' (constructed according to the plain and ordinary meaning of its language, to the common intendment of the time, and of those who framed it) ; to give also to all parties and authorities, time for reflection and consideration, whether, under a temperate view of the possible consequences, and especially of the constant obstructions which an equivocal majority must ever expect to meet, they will still prefer the assumption of this power rather than its acceptance from the free will of their constituents; and to preserve peace in the meanwhile, we proceed to make it the duty of our citizens, until the Legislature shall otherwise and ultimately decide, to acquiesce under those acts of the Federal branch of our government which we have declared to be usurpations, and against which, in point of right, we do protest as null and void, and never to be quoted as precedents of right.

We, therefore, do enact, and Be It Enacted by the General Assembly of Virginia, That all citizens of this Commonwealth, and persons and authorities within the same, shall pay full obedience at all times to the acts which may be passed by the Congress of the United States, the object of which shall be the construction of post roads, making canals of navigation, and maintaining the same in any part of the United States, in like manner as if said acts were *totidem verbis,* passed by the Legislature of this Commonwealth.—ix, 496. FORD ED., x, 349. (Dec. 24, 1825.)

ESTRANGEMENT AND RECONCILIATION OF JEFFERSON AND ADAMS

[To Mrs. John Adams.]

Dear Madam,—The affectionate sentiments which you have had the goodness to express in your letter of May 20, towards my dear departed daughter, have awakened in me sensibilities natural to the occasion, and recalled your kindness to her, which I shall ever remember with gratitude and friendship. I can assure you with truth, they had made an indelible impression on her mind, and that to the last, on our meetings after long separations, whether I had heard lately of you, and how you did, were among the earliest of her enquiries. In giving you this assurance I perform a sacred duty for her, and, at the same time, am thankful for the occasion furnished me, of expressing my regret that circumstances should have arisen, which have seemed to draw a line of separation between us. The friendship with which you honored me has ever been valued, and fully reciprocated; and although events have been passing which might be trying to some minds, I never believed yours to be of that kind, nor felt that my own was. Neither my estimate of your character, nor the esteem founded in that, has ever been lessened for a single moment, although doubts whether it would be acceptable may have forbidden manifestations of it.

Mr. Adams's friendship and mine began at an earlier date. It accompanied us through long and important scenes. The different conclusions we had drawn from our political reading and reflections, were not permitted to lessen personal esteem; each party being conscious they were the result of an honest conviction in the other. Like differences of opinion existing among our fellow citizens, attached them to one or the other of us, and produced a rivalship in their minds which did not exist in ours. We never stood in one another's way; for if either had been withdrawn at any time, his favorers would not have gone over to the other, but would have sought for some one of homogeneous opinions. This consideration was sufficient to keep down all jealousy between us, and to guard our friendship from any disturbance by sentiments of rivalship; and I can say with truth, that one act of Mr. Adams's life, and one only, ever gave me a moment's personal displeasure. I did consider his last appointments to office as personally unkind. They were from among my most ardent political enemies, from whom no faithful cooperation could ever be expected; and laid me under the embarrassment of acting through men whose views were to defeat mine, or to encounter the odium of putting others in their places. It seemed but common justice to leave a successor free to act by instruments of his own choice. If my respect for him did not permit me to ascribe the whole blame to the influence of others, it left something for friendship to forgive, and after brooding over it for some little time, and not always resisting the expressing of it, I forgave it cordially, and returned to the same state of esteem and respect for him which had so long subsisted. Having come into life a little later than Mr. Adams, his career has preceded mine, as mine is followed by some other; and it will probably be closed at the same distance after him which time originally placed between us. I maintain for him, and shall carry into private life, an uniform and high measure of respect and good will, and for yourself a sincere attachment. * * *—To Mrs. John Adams. iv, 545. Ford ed., viii, 306. (W., June 1804.)

[To Mrs. John Adams.]

Dear Madam,—Your favor of the 1st inst. was duly received, and I would not have again intruded on you, but to rectify certain facts which seem not to have been presented to you under their true aspects.* My charities to Callender are considered as rewards for his calumnies. As early, I think, as 1796, I was told in Philadelphia that Callender, the author of the " Political Progress of Britain ", was in that city, a fugitive from persecution for having written that book, and in distress. I had read and approved the book ; I considered him as a man of genius, unjustly persecuted. I knew nothing of his private character, and immediately expressed my readiness to contribute to his relief, and to serve him. It was a considerable time after, that, on application from a person who thought of him as I did, I contributed to his relief, and afterwards repeated the contribution. Himself I did not see till long after, nor ever more than two or three times. When he first began to write, he told some useful truths in his coarse way; but nobody sooner disapproved of his writing than I did, or wished more that he would be silent. My charities to him were no more meant as encouragements to his scurrilities, than those I give to the beggar at my door are meant as rewards for the vices of his life, and to make them chargeable to myself. In truth, they would have been greater to him, had he never written a word after the work for which he fled from Britain . * * *

But another fact is, that " I liberated a wretch who was suffering for a libel against Mr. Adams ". I do not know who was the particular wretch alluded to; but I discharged every person under punishment or prosecution under the Sedition law, because I considered, and now consider, that law to be a nullity, as absolute and as palpable as if Congress had ordered us to fall down and worship a golden image; and that it was as much my duty to arrest its execution in every stage, as it would have been to have rescued from the fiery furnace those who should have been cast into it for refusing to worship the image. It was accordingly done in every instance, without asking what the offenders had done, or against whom they had offended, but whether the pains they were suffering were inflicted under the pretended Sedition law. It was certainly possible that my motives for contributing to the relief of Callender, and liberating sufferers under the Sedition law, might have been to protect, encourage, and reward slander; but they may also have been those which inspire ordinary charities to objects of distress, meritorious or not, or the obligation of an oath to protect the Constitution, violated by an unauthorized act of Congress. Which of these were my motives, must be decided by a

* Mrs. Adams, in replying to the preceding letter, put forward Jefferson's patronage of Editor Callender as an offset to the midnight appointments. See CALLENDER.—EDITOR.
+ Quotation 59 gives the part of the letter omitted at this point.—EDITOR.

regard to the general tenor of my life. On this I am not afraid to appeal to the nation at large, to posterity, and still less to that Being who sees Himself our motives, who will judge us from His own knowledge of them, and not on the testimony of " *Porcupine* " or Fenno.
  You observe, there has been one other act of my administration personally unkind, and suppose it will readily suggest itself to me. I declare on my honor, Madam, I have not the least conception what act is alluded to. I never did a single one with an unkind intention. * * *—To Mrs. JOHN ADAMS. iv, 555. FORD ED., viii, 308. (July 1804.)

[To Mrs. John Adams.]

  Your letter, Madam, of the 18th of August, has been some days received, but a press of business has prevented the acknowledgment of it; perhaps, indeed, I may have already trespassed too far on your attention. With those who wish to think amiss of me, I have learned to be perfectly indifferent; but where I know a mind to be ingenuous, and to need only truth to set it to rights, I cannot be as passive. The act of personal unkindness alluded to in your former letter, is said in your last to have been the removal of your eldest son from some office to which the judges had appointed him. I conclude, then, he must have been a commissioner of bankruptcy. But I declare to you, on my honor, that this is the first knowledge I have ever had that he was so. It may be thought, perhaps, that I ought to have enquired who were such, before I appointed others. But it is to be observed, that the former law permitted the judges to name commissioners occasionally only, for every case as it arose, and not to make them permanent officers. Nobody, therefore, being in office, there could be no removal. The judges, you well know, have been considered as highly federal; and it was noted that they confined their nominations exclusively to federalists. The Legislature, dissatisfied with this, transferred the nomination to the President, and made the offices permanent. The very object in passing the law was, that he should correct, not confirm, what was deemed the partiality of the judges. I thought it, therefore, proper to inquire, not whom they had employed, but whom I ought to appoint to fulfil the intentions of the law. In making these appointments, I put in a proportion of federalists, equal, I believe, to the proportion they bear in numbers through the Union generally. Had I known that your son had acted, it would have been a real pleasure to me to have preferred him to some who were named in Boston, in what was deemed the same line of politics. To this I should have been led by my knowledge of his integrity, as well as my sincere dispositions towards yourself and Mr. Adams*. * * * The candor manifested in your letter, and which I ever believed you to possess, has alone inspired the desire of calling your attention, once more, to those circumstances of fact and motive by which I claim to be judged. I hope you will see these intrusions on your time to be, what they really are, proofs of my great respect for you. I tolerate with the utmost latitude the right of others to differ from me in opinion without imputing to them criminality. I know too well the weakness and uncertainty of human reason to wonder at its different results. Both of our political parties, at least the honest part of them, agree conscientiously in the same object—the public good; but they differ essentially in what they deem the means of promoting that good. One side believes it best done by one composition of the governing powers; the other, by a different one. One fears most the ignorance of the people: the other, the selfishness of rulers independent of them. Which is right, time and experience will prove. We think that one side of this experiment has been long enough tried, and proved not to promote the good of the many; and that the other has not been fairly and sufficiently tried. Our opponents think the reverse. With whichever opinion the body of the nation concurs, that must prevail. My anxieties on this subject will never carry me beyond the use of fair and honorable means, of truth and reason; nor have they ever lessened my esteem for moral worth, nor alienated my affections from a single friend, who did not first withdraw himself. Whenever this has happened, I confess I have not been insensible to it; yet have ever kept myself open to a return of their justice. I conclude with sincere prayers for your health and happiness, that yourself and Mr. Adams may long enjoy the tranquillity you desire and merit, and see in the prosperity of your family what is the consummation of the last and warmest of human wishes.—To Mrs. JOHN ADAMS. iv, 560. FORD ED., viii, 310. (M., Sep. 11, 1804.)

[To Dr. Benjamin Rush.]

  I receive with sensibility your observations on the discontinuance of friendly correspondence between Mr. Adams and myself, and the concern you take in its restoration. This discontinuance has not proceeded from me, nor from the want of sincere desire and of effort on my part, to renew our intercourse. You know the perfect coincidence of principle and of action, in the early part of the Revolution, which produced a high degree of mutual respect and esteem between Mr. Adams and myself. Certainly no man was ever truer than he was, in that day, to those principles of rational republicanism which, after the necessity of throwing off our monarchy, dictated all our efforts in the establishment of a new government. And although he swerved, afterwards, towards the principles of the English constitution, our friendship did not abate on that account†. * * *
  You remember the machinery which the federalists played off, about that time, to beat down the friends to the real principles of our Constitution, to silence by terror every expression in their favor, to bring us into war with France and alliance with England, and finally to homologate our Constitution with that of England. Mr. Adams, you know, was overwhelmed with feverish addresses, dictated by the fear, and often by the pen, of the *bloody buoy*, and was seduced by them into some open indications of his new principles of

---

* The part of the letter omitted here is printed in this volume under the title, SEDITION LAW. EXECUTIVE VS. JUDICIARY.—EDITOR.
† For omitted clause, see quotation 89.—EDITOR.

government, and in fact, was so elated as to mix with his kindness a little superciliousness towards me. Even Mrs. Adams, with all her good sense and prudence, was sensibly flushed. And you recollect the short suspension of our intercourse, and the circumstance which gave rise to it which you were so good as to bring to an early explanation, and have set to rights, to the cordial satisfaction of us all *. * * *

Two or three years after, having had the misfortune to lose a daughter, between whom and Mrs. Adams there had been a considerable attachment, she made it the occasion of writing me a letter, in which, with the tenderest expression of concern at this event, she carefully avoided a single one of friendship towards myself, and even concluded it with the wishes " of her who *once* took pleasure in subscribing herself your friend, Abigail Adams ". Unpromising as was the complexion of this letter, I determined to make an effort towards removing the cloud from between us. This brought on a correspondence which I now enclose for your perusal, after which be so good as to return it to me, as I have never communicated it to any mortal breathing, before. I send it to you, to convince you I have not been wanting either in the desire, or the endeavor to remove this misunderstanding. Indeed, I thought it highly disgraceful to us both, as indicating minds not sufficiently elevated to prevent a public competition from affecting our personal friendship. I soon found from the correspondence that conciliation was desperate, and yielding to an intimation in her last letter, I ceased from further explanation+. * * *

I have gone into these details, that you might know everything which had passed between us, might be fully possessed of the state of facts and dispositions, and judge for yourself whether they admit a revival of that friendly intercourse for which you are so kindly solicitous. I shall certainly not be wanting in anything on my part which may second your efforts, which will be the easier with me, inasmuch as I do not entertain a sentiment of Mr. Adams, the expression of which could give him reasonable offence.—To Dr. BENJAMIN RUSH. v, 558. FORD ED., ix, 299. (M., Jan. 1811.)

[To Dr. Benjamin Rush.]

I communicated to you the correspondence which had parted Mrs. Adams and myself, in proof that I could not give friendship in exchange for such sentiments as she had recently taken up towards myself, and avowed and maintained in her letters to me. Nothing but a total renunciation of these could admit a reconciliation, and that could be cordial only in proportion as the return to ancient opinions was believed sincere. In these jaundiced sentiments of hers I had associated Mr. Adams, knowing the weight which her opinions had with him, and notwithstanding she declared in her letters that they were not communicated to him. A late incident has satisfied me that I wronged him as well as her, in not yielding entire confidence to this assurance on her part. Two of the Mr. —— ——, my neighbors and friends, took a tour to the northward during the last summer. In Boston they fell into company with Mr. Adams, and * * * passed a day with him at Braintree. He spoke out to them everything which came uppermost, * * * and seemed most disposed to dwell on those things which happened during his own administration. He spoke of his *masters*, as he called his Heads of departments, as acting above his control, and often against his opinions. Among many other topics, he adverted to the unprincipled licentiousness of the press against myself, adding, " I always loved Jefferson, and still love him ".

This is enough for me. I only needed this knowledge to revive towards him all the affections of the most cordial moments of our lives. Changing a single word only in Dr. Franklin's character of him, I knew him to be always an honest man, often a great one, but sometimes incorrect and precipitate in his judgments; and it is known to those who have ever heard me speak of Mr. Adams, that I have ever done him justice myself, and defended him when, assailed by others, with the single exception as to political opinions. But with a man possessing so many other estimable qualities, why should we be dissocialized by mere differences of opinion in politics, in religion, in philosophy, or anything else? His opinions are as honestly formed as my own. Our different views of the same subject are the result of a difference in our organization and experience. I never withdrew from the society of any man on this account, although many have done it from me; much less should I do it from one with whom I had gone through, with hand and heart, so many trying scenes. I wish, therefore, but for an apposite occasion to express to Mr. Adams my unchanged affections for him. There is an awkwardness which hangs over the resuming a correspondence so long discontinued, unless something could arise which should call for a letter. Time and chance may perhaps generate such an occasion, of which I shall not be wanting in promptitude to avail myself. From this fusion of mutual affections, Mrs. Adams is, of course, separated. It will only be necessary that I never name her. In your letters to Mr. Adams, you can, perhaps suggest my continued cordiality towards him, and knowing this, should an occasion of writing first present itself to him, he will, perhaps, avail himself of it, as I certainly will, should it first occur to me. No ground for jealousy now existing, he will certainly give fair play to the natural **warmth of his** heart.—To DR. BENJAMIN RUSH. vi, 30. FORD ED., ix, 299. (P.F., Dec. 1811.)

* Quotations 77, 78, 83 and 88 give the continuation of the text.—EDITOR.
+ Quotations 72 and 60, read consecutively, supply the omission in the text.—EDITOR.

TOPICAL INDEX

WITH CROSS-REFERENCES

Abilities, 1
  Character, 133
  Genius, 381
  Talents, 848
Aborigines, 1
  Cherokees, 136
  Indians, 420, 944, 948, 952
Abuse, 2
  Abuses, 2
  Calumny, 122
  ——Libels, 497
  Ministers, 558
  Newspapers, 635
  —— Slander, 809
Academy, 3
  Academies, 4
  Education, 273
  Schools, 790
  University (National), 899
  University of Va., 900
Accounts, 5
  Finances, 336
Acquisition of Territory, 860
  Canada, 121
  Conquest, 185
  Cuba, 222
  Expansion, 319, 468, 512, 617, 862
  Florida, 339
  Louisiana, 509
  Nova Scotia, 642
  Policy (American), C97
Actions, 5
  Conduct, 167
  Disinterestedness, 258
  Labor, 458
Adair (James), 421
  Indians, 421
Adams (John), 6, 13, 18, 678, 715, 763, 800
  Adams (John Quincy), 12
  Adams (Mrs. John), 988
  Adams (Samuel), 13
Address, Washington's Farewell, 929
  Addresses, 13
  Addresses (Jefferson's Inaugural), 980, 982
Adjournment, 14
  Congress, 172
Administration, 16
  Cabinet, 117
Admiralty Courts, 19
  Courts, 214
Admission of States, 941, 942
  States, 834
Advertisements, 20
  Newspapers, 635
Advice, 20
  Council, 211
  Instructions, 426
Aeronautics, 66
  Balloons, 66
Affection, 21
  Family, 321
  Friends, 363
  Friendship, 363
  Happiness, 397
  Home, 409
  Sympathy, 848

Affliction, 21
  Despair, 254
  Grief, 395
  Misfortune, 560
Age, Old, 21
  Antiquities, 39
  Time, 867
Agents, 342
  Foreign Agents, 342
Aggression, 23
  Filibusterism, 335
Agitation, 23
  Lethargy, 419
Agrarianism, 23
  Descents, 253
  Entail, 307
  Inheritances, 426
  Primogeniture, 719
  Monopoly, 579
  Mortmain, 596
Agriculture, 23
  Farmer, 322
  Farmers, 322
  Farming, 323
  Horticulture, 411
  Olive, 658
  Potato, 707
  Rice, 777
  Sugar, 842
  Tobacco, 868
  Vegetables, 904
  Wheat, 943
Alexander of Russsa, 27, 809
  Catherine of Russia, 421, 786
  Dashkoff (M.), 223
  Russia, 786, 888
Alexandria, Va., 30
  Cities, 143
Algiers, 80
  Captives, 128
Alienage, 30
  Land, 465
Alienation of Territory, 860
  Territory, 860
  Western Territory, 939
Alien and Sedition Laws, 30
  Aliens, 32
  Sedition, Law, 795
Aliens, 32
  Alien and Sedition Laws, 30——
  Citizens, 144
  Deportation Act, 252
  Deportation of Aliens, 253
  Expatriation 319, 780
  Naturalization, 609
  Sedition Law, 795
Allegiance, 32
  Expatriation, 319, 780
Allen, Ethan, 32
  Retaliation, 762
Alliance, 32
  Alliance, Holy, 408
  Alliances, 34
  Policy (American), 697
Allodial Tenures, 465
  Feudal Tenures, 465
  Land, 465

Alloy in Money, 262
  Coinage, 261, 573
  Mint, 559
Allston, Washington, 34
  Burr (Aaron), 111
Almanacs, 35
  Astronomy, 61
Almighty, The, 248
  Bible, 88
  Church and State, 141
  Deity, 248
  God, 384
  Providence, 731
  Religion, 742
Alms, 134
  Charity, 134
Altercations, 35
  Aggression, 23
Amalgamation of Parties, 675
  Politics, 701
Ambassadors, 555
  Diplomacy, 258
  Diplomatic Establishment, 258
Ambition, 35, 363
  Applause, 39
  Approbation, 42
  Reputation, 761
Amendments to Constitution, 35
  Bill of Rights, 88
  Constitution (The Federal), 188
  Internal Improvements, 429
  Judiciary (Federal), 449
  Louisiana, 510
  President, 712
  Virginia Protest, 986
America, 35
  America (British), Rights of, 963
  American Independence, 420
  American Policy, 697
Americus Vespucius, 36
  History (American), 406
Anarchy, 36
  Law, 479, 481
  Law (Lynch), 481
  Order, 864
Anatomy, 36
  Medicine, 547
Ancestors, 36
  Ancestry, 36
  Aristocracy, 48
  Aristocrats, 51
  Birth, 92
  Birthday, 92
  Posterity, 705
  Primogeniture, 719
Angels, 37
  Self-government, 796
Anger, 37
  Passions, 679
  Revenge, 767
  Temper, 859
Anglomania, 37
  Anglophobia, 37
Anglo-Saxon Language, 471
  Language, 470
  Neology, 624

Animals, 110
  Horses, 411, 504, 949
  Natural History, 607
  Paleontology, 667
  Sheep, 803
Animosities, 37
  Peace, 682
Annexation, 861
  Canada, 124
  Louisiana, 509
  Territory, 860
Annuities, 38
  Tontine, 869
Anonymous Writing, 38
  Letters, 494
  Letter-writing, 495
Anti-Federalists, 38
  Democratic Societies, 251
  Democrats, 252
  Federalism, 328
  Federalists, 329
  Hartford Convention, 400
  Jacobins, 435
  Missouri Question, 563
  Monarchy, 566
  Parties, 675
  Politics, 701
  Republicanism (Partisan), 754
  Republicans, 755
Antiquities, 39
  Age, Old, 21
Apostasy, 39
  Principle, 720
Applause, 39
  Approbation, 42
  Honor, 410
  Honors, 411
  Praise, 711
  Reputation, 761
Appointment, 39
  Office, 644
  Offices, 647
  Office-holders, 652
  Relations, 741
Apportionment, 39
  Apportionment Bill, 41
  Representation, 747
Approbation, 42
  Ambition, 35
  Applause, 39
  Reputation, 761
Appropriations, 43
  Finances, 336
  Funding, 369
  Treasury, 874
Arbitration, 44
  Umpire, 890
Arboriculture, 45
  Trees, 886
Architecture, 45
  Arts, 58
Aristocracy, 48
  Aristocrats, 51
  Birth, 92
  Birthday, 92
Aristocrats, 51
  Aristocracy, 48
  Birth, 92
Aristotle, 51
  Philosophy, 695
Arms, 51, 631
  Arms, American, 51
  Arms of Jefferson Family, 52
  Arms of Virginia, 52
Armstrong (John), 52
  War of 1812, 921

Army, 52
  Army Officers, 56
  Deserters, 254
  Discipline, 258
  Draft, 263
  Generals, 372
  Martial Law, 542
  Militia, 550
  Volunteers, 915
  War, 915
  War of 1812, 921
  War (Prisoners of), 924
Arnold, Benedict, 56
  Treason, 873
Art, 57
  Architecture, 45
  Artisans, 57
  Artists, 58
  Arts, 58
  Music, 599
  Sculpture, 792
Artisans, 57
  Labor, 458
  Laborers, 459
Artists, 58
  Arts, 58
Assassination, 58
  Murder, 598
Assennisipia, Proposed State of, 941
  Western Territory, 939
Assignats, 58
  Paper Money, 668
Assumption of State Debts, 58
  Funding, 369
Astor's Settlement, 61
  Fur Trade, 369, 939
Astronomy, 61
  East and West Line, 271
  Latitude and Longitude, 475
Asylum, 62
  Neutrality, 624
Atheism, 62
  Atheist, 62
  Deity, 248
Athens, 62, 950
  Greeks, 394
Atmosphere, 23
  Climate, 147
  Cold, 148
Attachments, Foreign, 343
  Alliance, 32
  Alliances, 34
Attainder, 63
  Law, 477
Attire, 264
  Dress, 264
  Fashion, 323
  Foppery, 342
Attorney-General, 63
  Attorneys, 63
  Lawyers, 487
Aubaine, Droit d', 63
  Law, 477
Austria, 446
  Treaties of Commerce, 882
Authority, 63
  Government, 384
  Power, 708
Avarice, 65
  Economy, 271
  Generosity, 378

B

Bacon's Rebellion, 738
  Rebellion, 738
  Shays's Rebellion, 802
Badges, 65
  Cockades, 150
Bainbridge (William), 66
  Navy, 618
Balloons, 66
  Inventions, 431
Ballot, 841
  Suffrage, 841
  Votes, 915
  Voting, 915
Banishment, 319
  Exile, 3.9
Bank (National), 66
  Bank of North America, 68
  Bank (U. S.), 68
  Banks, 73
  Dollar, 260
  Money, 571
  Money Bills, 576
  Money (Continental), 577
  Money (Metallic), 578
  Paper Money, 668
Bankruptcy, 72
  Bubbles, 109
  Panics, 667
  Speculation, 828
Banneker (Benjamin), 80
  Negroes, 622
Barbarism, 80
  Civilization, 145
Barbary States, 80
  Algiers, 80
  Morocco, 595
  Tripoli, 886
Barclay (Thomas), 83
  Barbary States, 80
Barlow (Joel), 84
  Poetry, 697
Barruel (Abbé), 412
  Illuminati, 413
Barry (Commodore J.), 597
  Mourning, 597
Bastile, 84
  French Revolution, 770
Bastrop's Case, 84
  Yazoo Lands, 952
Batture, New Orleans, 85
  Supreme Court, 845
Bayard (James A.), 86
  Elections (Presidential), 282
Beaumarchais (M.), 86
Bee, 86
  Natural History, 607
Beer, 86
  Intemperance, 427
  Whisky, 944
  Wines, 947
Belligerents, 86
  Blockades, 95
  Neutrality, 624
  Privateers, 723
Beneficence, 87
  Charity, 134
  Generosity, 378
Berlin Decrees, 87
  Bonaparte, 96
  Embargo, 286
  Orders in Council, 664

Bible, 88
  Deity, 248
  Providence, 731
  Religion, 742
Bigotry, 88
  Bigotries, 88
  Intolerance, 431
Bill of Rights, 88
  Bill of Rights (French), 91
  Constitution, 35, 186
  Goverment, 384
Bimetalism, 574
  Dollar, 260
  Money, 571
Bingham (William), 92
Birds, 92
  Natural History, 607
Birth, 92
  Aristocracy, 48
  Aristocrats, 51
  Birthday, 92
Birthday, 92
  Birth, 92
  Aristocracy, 48
  Aristocrats, 51
Bishop (Samuel), 93
  Office, 644
  Offices, 647
  Office-holders, 652
Blackstone (Sir William), 94, 482
  Lawyers, 487
Bland (Richard), 94
Blockades, 95
  Belligerents, 86
  Neutrality, 624
  Privateers, 723
Blount (William) 95
  Impeachment, 416
Bolingbroke (Lord), 95
  Language, 470
  Paine (Thomas), 665
Bollman (Eric), 95
  Burr's (A.) Treason, 113
Bonaparte (Joseph), 96
Bonaparte (N.), 96
  Berlin Decrees, 87
  France, 347
  Louisiana, 509
  Spain, 821
Books, 102
  Copyright, 102, 377, 384
  Education, 273
  History, 404
  Knowledge, 457
  Language, 470
  Learning, 489
  Library, 502
  Literary Men, 506
  Literature, 506
  Printing, 722
  Reading, 738
  Study, 811
Boston Port Bill, 104, 769
  Faneuil Hall, 322
  Tea, 859
Botany, 105, 791
  Horticulture, 411
  Plants, 697
  Trees, 886
Botta (C.), 105
  History (American), 405, 406
Bottetourt (Lord), 105
  Colonies (The American), 151

Boundaries, 106
  Louisiana, 106
  Massachusetts and New York, 106
  Northwest, 106
  Pennsylvania and Virginia, 107
  United States and Great Britain, 107
  Virginia and Maryland, 108
Bounties, 108, 348, 931
  Fisheries, 337
  France, Commerce with, 348
  Free Trade, 361
  General Welfare Clause, 374
  Manufactures, 534
  Subsidies, 808
Bourbons, 108
  France, 347
  Kings, 455
Bowles (W. A.), 108
  Indians, 420
Boys, 108, 901
  Children, 138
  Discipline, 258
  Young Men, 953
Brazil, 108
  Correa de Serra (J.), 208
  Portugal, 704
Bribery, 109,
  Corruption, 209
  Crime, 219
Briggs (Isaac), 109
  Office (Talents), 646
Broglio (Marshal de), 109
  Revolution (French), 770
Brown (James), 109
  Union (Federal), 890
Bubbles, 109
  Speculation, 828
Buchan (Earl of), 110
Buchanan (George), 110
Buffon (Count de), 110
  Chemistry (Utility), 135
  Natural History, 607
Bunker Hill, 110
  Revolution (American), 767
Burke (Edmund), 111
  Marie Antoinette (Character), 536
Business, 111
  Occupations, 642
  Trade, 871
Burr (Aaron), 111
  Burr's (A.) Treason, 113
  Burr's (A.) Trial, 115
  Morgan (George), 595
  Tiffin (H. D.), 867
  Wilkinson (James), 945, 946

C

Cabell (J. C.), 117
  University of Virginia, 900
Cabinet, 117
  Administration, 16
  Cabinet Officers, 120
  Cabinet Officers in Congress, 173
Cabot Family, 92
  Birds, 92
Cæsar (Julius), 142
  People (Roman), 691
Callender (J. T.), 120
  Estrangement of Jefferson and Adams, 988
Calonne (C. A. de), 122
  Revolution (French), 770

Calumny, 122
  Abuse, 2
  Libels, 497
  Lies, 503
  Ministers, 558
  Newspapers, 635
  Slander, 809
Camden, Battle of, 123
  Gates (General Horatio), 372
Campbell (David), 123
Canada, 124
  Arnold (Benedict), 56
  Colonies (The American), 151
Canal, 125
  River, 783
  Rivers, 784
Candor, 126
  Frankness, 357
  Honesty, 410
  Sincerity, 809
  Truth, 887
Cannibals, 126
  Kings, 455
Canning (George), 126
  England (Jefferson and), 301
Canova (A.), 126
  Sculpture, 792
Capital, 126
  Labor, 458
  Laborers, 459
  Wealth, 935
Capital (National), 924
  Capitals (State), 127
Capitol (United States), 48, 127
  Capitol (Va.), 47
Captives, 128
  Prisoners of War, 924
Carmichael (William), 128
  Mississippi River Navigation, 561
Carondelet (Baron), 129
  Louisiana, 509
Carr (Dabney), 129
  Committees of Correspondence, 961
Carriages, 129
  Exercise, 318
  Horses, 411
Carrying Trade, 129, 624, 871
  Drawbacks, 263
  Free Ports, 358
  Navigation, 610
  Shipping, 805
  Ships, 806
Carter (Landon), 129
Carthage, 129
  Creek Indians, 219
  People, Roman, 69
Catherine of Russia, 421, 786
  Alexander of Russia, 27, 809
  Russia, 786, 888
Censors, 130
  Censure, 130
  Criticism, 221
Censure, 130
  Censors, 130
  Criticism, 221
Census, 130
  Population, 703
Centralization, 130
  General Welfare Clause, 374
  Judiciary, 448
  State Rights, 832
  Supreme Court, 842

Ceremony, 133
  Etiquette, 311
  Formalities, 344
  Levees, 496
Chancellors, English, 133
  Chancery Courts, 214
Chaplains, 133
  Clergy, 146
  Ministers, 558
Character, 133
  Abilities, 1
  Genius, 381
  Reputation, 761
  Talents, 848
Charity, 134
  Beneficence, 87
  Friendship, 363
Charters, 134
  Compacts, 166
Chase (Samuel), 135
  Impeachment, 416
Chatham (Lord), 135
  Colonies (The American), 151
  Oratory, 664
Chemistry, 135
  Buffon (Count de), 110
  Science, 791
  Sciences, 792
Cherbourg, 135
  France, 347
Cherokees, 136
  Aborigines, 1
  Indians, 420, 944, 948, 952
Cherronesus, Proposed State of, 941
  Western Territory, 939
Chesapeake Frigate, 136
  Indemnification, 419
Children, 138
  Boys, 108
  Young Men, 953
  Young Women, 954
China, 139
  Ships, 808
Chocolate, 139
  Tea, 104, 859
Christianity, 162
  Church, 139
  Church (Anglican), 140
  Church and State, 141
  Religion, 742
Church, 139
  Church (Anglican), 140
  Church and State, 141
  Religion, 742
Cicero, 142
  Eloquence, 286
  Oratory, 664
  People (Roman), 691
  Plato's Republic, 698
Cincinnati Society, 142
  Democratic Societies, 251
Cipher, 143
  Writing, 950
Ciracchi, 143
  Sculpture, 792
Cities, 143
  Alexandria, 30
  Baltimore, 30
  Boston, 104, 110
  Carthage, 129
  Cherbourg, 135
  Constantinople, 186
  London, 509
  New Orleans, 634

Cities, 143 — (Continued)
  New York, 634
  Nice, 640
  Norfolk, Va., 30
  Paris, 674
  Pensacola, 686
  Philadelphia, 694
  Richmond, Va., 779
  San Juan, 359
  Washington City, 924
Citizens, 144
  Citizenship, 145
  Expatriation, 319
  Naturalization, 609
Civilization, 145
  Barbarism, 80
Claiborne (W. C. C.), 146
Claimants, 146
  Claims, 146
Clark (Geo. R.), 146
  Lewis and Clark Expedition, 495
Clarke (Daniel), 146
  Union (The Federal), 692
Classical Learning, 489
  Education, 273
  Language, 470
  Science, 791
  University of Virginia, 900
Clay (Henry), 146
Clergy, 146
  Chaplains, 133
  Clergy (French), 771, 775
  Ministers, 558
Climate, 147
  Atmosphere, 23
  Cold, 148, 771
  Weather, 936
  Winds, 947
Clinton (De Witt), 149
Clinton (George), 149
Coast Line, 149
Cockades, 150
  Badges, 65
Coercion (State), 150
  State Rights, 832
Coinage, 261, 573
  Decimal System, 240
  Dollars, 260
  Mint, 559
Coke (Lord), 150
Coles (Edward), 150
College (Electoral), 715
  Elections (Presidential), 280
Colleges, Buildings, 4
  Colleges, Veterinary, 905
Colonies (American), 151
Colonies (Ancient), 154
Colonization (Negro), 154
Colony (Penal), 155
Columbia River, 61
  River, 783
  Rivers, 784
Cold, 148, 771
  Atmosphere, 23
  Climate, 147
  Weather, 936
  Winds, 947
Columbus (Christopher), 36, 156
  History (American), 406
Commerce, 156
  Commerce, Treaties of, 880
Commissions, 161
  Commissioners, 161

Committee of the States, 169
  Confederation, 167
Common Law, 162
  Law, 477
Common Sense, 166
  Judgment, 448
  Moral Sense, 591
  Senility, 801
  Sense, 802
Compact, 166
  Compacts, 166
  Treaties, 874
Compromise, 167
  Conciliation, 167
  Harmony, 399
Conciliation, 167
  Compromise, 167
  Harmony, 399
Conchology, 804
  Shells, 804
Condorcet (M.), 167
Conduct, 167
  Actions, 5
Confederation, The, 167, 973
  Colonies (The American), 151
Confidence (Public), 731
  Credit, 217
  Credulity, 219
  Faith, 321
  Jealousy, 438
  Public Confidence, 731
Confiscation, 171
  Property, 726
Congress, 172
  Continental Congress, 174
  Senate, U. S., 799, 876, 877, 878
  Senators, U. S., 188
Continental Congress, 174
  Congress, 172
  Senate, U. S., 799, 876, 877, 878
  Senators, U. S., 188
Connecticut, 184, 777
Conquest, 185
  Glory, 384
  Tyranny, 889
  War, 915
Conscience, 185, 949
  Actions, 5
  Character, 133
  Conduct, 167
Consent of Governed, 385
  Authority, 63
  Government, 384
  Rights, 780
  Rights of Man, 782
  Self-government, 796
Constantinople, 186
  Turkey, 888
Constitution, 35, 186
  Bill of Rights, 88
  Constitution (The Federal), 186
  Constitution (French), 195
  Constitution (Great Britain), 197
  Constitution (Spanish), 197
  Constitutions (American), 198
Construction of the Constitution, 190, 200
  Centralization, 130
  Construction of Instruments, 200
  General Welfare Clause, 374
  Judiciary, 448
  Supreme Court, 842
Consular Convention, 200
  Consuls, 200

Contention, 203
  Controversy, 205
  Disputation, 259
  Disputes, 259
  Dissension, 259
  Duel, 265
  Quarrels, 735
Contentment, 204
  Happiness, 398
  Peace, 682
  Repose, 747
  Retirement, 765
  Tranquillity, 872
Contraband of War, 204, 625, 628
  Belligerents, 86
  Enemy Goods, 296
  Free Ships, Free Goods, 359
  Neutrality, 625
  War, 915
Contracts, 204
  Compacts, 166
  Treaties, 874
Controversy, 205
  Contention, 203
  Dissension, 259
Convent, 205
  Religion, 742
Convention (Federal), 205
  Convention, National, 205
  Convention (Virginia), 206
  Conventions (Constitutional), 206
Convicts, 206
  Crime, 219
  Criminals, 221
  Prison, 46, 722
Cookery, 372
  Gastronomy, 372
Cooper (Thomas), 206
  Priestley (Joseph), 719
  University of Virginia, 900
Copying Press, 207
  Engraving, 307
  Polygraph, 432
Copyright, 102, 377, 381
  Books, 102
  Library, 489
  Printing, 722
Coray (A.), 207
  Athens, 62
  Greeks, 394
Cornwallis (Lord), 207
  Cruelty, 221
Coroners, 208
  Counties, 212
Corporations, 418
  Bank, 66
  Banks, 73
  Monopoly, 579
Correa de Serra (J.), 208
  Brazil, 108
  Portugal, 704
Correspondence, 208
  Correspondence, Committees of, 961
  Letters, 494
  Letters of Introduction, 481
  Letter-writing, 495
Corruption, 209
  Bribery, 109
  Crime, 219
Cotton, 211
  Cotton Gin, 211
  Manufactures, 528
Council, 211
  Advice, 20
  Instructions, 426

Counties, 212
  Wards, 921
Courtesy, 213
  Courtiers, 213
  Politeness, 700
Courtiers, 213
  Courtesy, 213
  Politeness, 700
Courts, 214
  Courts (Admiralty), 19
  Courts (Appeals), 214
  Courts (Chancery), 214
  Courts (County), 216
  Courts (Federal), 448, 842
  Courts (French Plenary), 217
  Courts (Monarchical), 217
  Courts (State), 450
  Judiciary (Federal), 448
  U. S. Supreme Court, 842
Crawford (W. H.), 217
  Elections (Presidential, 1824), 286
Creation, 270
  Deluge, 250
  Earth, 269
  World, 949
Credit, 217
  Credulity, 219
  Faith, 321
  Public Confidence, 731
Credulity, 219
  Credit, 217
  Faith, 321
  Public Confidence, 731
Creek Indians, 219
  Aborigines, 1
  Cherokees, 136
  Indians, 420, 944, 948, 952
Cresap (Captain), 508
  Logan (Mingo Chief), 508
Crime, 219
  Convicts, 206
  Criminals, 221
  Murder, 598
  Prison, 46, 722
Criminals, 221
  Crime, 219
  Pardons, 673
Criticism, 221
  Censors, 130
  Censure, 130
Cruelty, 221
  Cornwallis (Lord), 207
  Retaliation, 762
  Revenge, 767
  Tyranny, 889
Cuba, 222
  Monroe Doctrine, 584
  Territory, 860
Currency, National, 601
  Money, 571
  Paper Money, 668
"Curtius," 223
  Webster (Noah), 936
Cushing (W.), 845, 846

D

Dalrymple (-), 223
Dana (Francis), 951
  X. Y. Z. Plot, 951
Dancing, 223
  Music, 599
  Theatres, 865
Dashkoff (M.), 223
  Russia, 786

David (J. L.), 223
  Arts, 58
Dayton (J.), 223
  Burr's (A.) Treason, 113
  Burr's (A.) Trial, 115
Dead, 223
  Death, 224
  Death Penalty, 225
  Epitaph, 308
Deane (S.), 223
Dearborn (H.), 224
Death, 224
  Death Penalty, 225
  Dead, 223
  Epitaph, 308
Debate, 225
  Congress (Previous Question), 180
  Eloquence, 286
  Language, 470
  Oratory, 664
  Speech, 358
  Words, 949
Debt, 226
  Debt (French), 230
  Debt (Revolutionary), 233
  Debt (United States), 234, 932
Debtors (Fugitive), 367
  Debt, 226
Debts Due British, 237
  Treaty (British Peace), 884
Decimal System, 240, 830
  Coinage, 261, 573
  Dollar, 260
  Mint, 559
"Decius," 737
  Randolph (John), 737
Declaration of Independence, 241, 969
  Declaration, Mecklenburg, 247
  Independence, 420
  Fourth of July, 346
  Liberty, 499
Defence, 247
  Fortifications, 345
  Gunboats, 395, 617
  Navy, 615
  Torpedoes, 870
Deity, 248
  Bible, 88
  God, 384
  Providence, 731
  Religion, 742
Delaware, 250
Delay, 250
  Idleness, 412
  Procrastination, 725
Deluge, 250
  Creation, 270
  Earth, 269
  World, 949
Delusion, 251
  X. Y. Z. Plot, 951
Democratic Societies, 251
  Anti-Federalists, 38
  Democrats, 252
  Federalism, 328
  Federalists, 329
  Hartford Convention, 400
  Jacobins, 435
  Missouri Question, 563
  Monarchy, 566
  Parties, 675
  Politics, 701
  Republicanism, Partisan, 754
  Republicans, 755

Democrats, 252
  Aristocrats, 51
  Anti-Federalists, 38
  Democratic Societies, 251
  Federalism, 328
  Federalists, 329
  Hartford Convention. 400
  Jacobins, 435
  Missouri Question, 563
  Monarchy, 566
  Parties, 675
  Politics, 701
  Republicanism (Partisan), 754
  Republicans, 755

Denmark, 252
  Free Ports, 359
  Jones (John Paul), 445

Dennie (Joseph), 252
  Monarchy, 566

Dependence, 252
  Submission. 841
  Subservience, 841
  Tribute, 886

Deportation Act, 252
  Deportation of Aliens, 253

Descents, 253
  Entail, 307
  Primogeniture, 719

Deserters, 254
  Fugitives, 367

Despair, 254
  Affliction, 21
  Grief, 395

Despotism, 254
  Despots, 254
  Oppression, 664
  Tyranny, 889

Detail, 254
  Labor, 458

Detroit, 254

Dickinson (John), 256
  Declaration of Independence. 241, 969

Dictator, 256
  Despots, 254
  Kings, 455
  Tyranny, 889

Dictionary, 257
  Dictionaries, 257
  Language, 470, 471
  Languages, 474
  Neology, 624

Difficulties, 257
  Trouble, 887

Dignity, 258
  Honor, 410
  Pride, 20

Diplomacy, 258
  Diplomatic Establishment, 258
  Ministers, 555, 558

Direct Tax, 39, 852
  Taxation, 852

Directory, 314
  Executive, 314

Discipline, 258
  University of Virginia, 900

Discretion, 258
  Judgment, 448
  Wisdom, 948

Discriminating Duties, 267
  Duties, 267
  Protection, 730
  Tariff. 849

Disinterestedness, 258
  Fortune, 346

Disputation, 259
  Disputes, 259
  Dissension, 259

Dissension, 259
  Contention, 203
  Disputation, 259
  Disputes, 259
  Duel, 265
  Quarrels, 735

Distribution, 260
  Inheritances, 426

Disunion, 260
  Rebellion, 738
  Secession, 793
  Union (The Federal), 890

Doctors, 547
  Medicine, 547
  Sun, 842

Dollar, 260
  Bank, 66
  Banks, 73
  Money, 571
  Money Bills, 576
  Money (Continental), 577
  Money (Metallic), 578
  Paper Money, 668

Domestic Economy, 271
  Political Economy, 271, 272

Double Standard, 574

Doubt, 263
  Principle, 720

Draft, 263
  Impressment, 417

Drawbacks, 263
  Duties, 267
  Tariff, 849

Dreams, 264
  Repose, 747
  Sleep, 818

Dress, 264
  Attire, 264
  Fashion, 323
  Foppery, 342

Drunkards, 427
  Intemperance, 427
  Whisky. 944
  Wines, 947

Duane (W.), 264

Duel, 265
  Contention, 203

Duer (W.), 265

Dumas (C. W. F.), 265

Dumouriez (C. F.), 266

Dunbar (W.), 266

Dunmore (Lord), 266

Duplicity, 266
  Falsehood, 321
  Lies, 503

Dupont de Nemours, 266

Dupuis (C. F.), 267

Duties (Discriminating), 267
  Drawbacks. 263
  Duties (Natural), 269, 608
  Free Trade, 361
  Tariff, 849

E

Earth, 269
  Atmosphere, 23
  Climate, 147
  Creation, 270
  Deluge, 250
  Geology, 383
  Meteorology, 549
  Mineralogy, 555

Earth, 269 — (Continued)
  Mountains, 596
  Shells, 804
  Weather, 936
  Winds, 947
  World, 949

East Indies, 270
  Commerce, 156
  Markets, 536
  West Indies, 936

East and West Line, 271
  Astronomy, 61
  Latitude and Longitude, 475
  Mirage, 560
  Rainbows, 736

Economy, 271
  Avarice, 65
  Economy (Domestic). 271
  Economy (Political), 271, 272
  Extravagance, 320
  Frugality, 367

Eden (W.), 273

Editors, 273
  News, 635
  Newspapers, 635
  Press, 89, 717

Education, 273
  Academics, 4
  Academy, 3
  Genius, 381
  Knowledge, 457
  Learning, 489
  Schools. 790
  Talents, 848
  Teachers, 859
  University, 899

Election, 279
  Elections, 279
  Elections (Presidential), 280
  Electoral College, 715

Electricity, 904
  Vegetation, 904

Ellsworth (O.), 286

Eloquence, 286
  Debate, 225
  Oratory, 664
  Speech, 358
  Words, 949

Emancipation of Slaves, 154, 816

Embargo, 286
  Berlin Decrees, 87
  Bonaparte, 96
  Orders in Council, 664
  War of 1812, 721

Emigration, 296
  Immigrants, 413
  Immigration, 414
  Population, 703

Enemies, 296
  Contention, 203
  Dissension, 259
  Revenge, 767

Enemy Goods, 296
  Free Ships, Free Goods, 359
  Neutrality, 624

England, 297
  Embargo, 286
  Friendship with England, 365
  George III.. 381
  Parliament, 674
  Treaties of Commerce, 880
  Treaty (British Peace), 884

Engraving, 307
  Copying Press, 207

Entail, 307
  Agrarianism, 23
  Descents, 253
  Mortmain, 596
  Primogeniture, 719
  Monopoly, 579

Enthusiasm, 307
  Ambition, 35
  Character, 133
  Zeal, 954

Epicurus, 307, 695
  Philosophy, 695

Epitaph, 308
  Dead, 223
  Death, 224

Equality, 308
  Equal Rights, 308
  Favoritism, 324
  Privileges, 724
  Special Legislation, 828

Equity, 133
  Justice, 452

Erie Canal, 125
  Canal, 125
  Rivers, 784

Error, 309
  Evils, 313
  Reason, 738

Erskine (William), 310

Escheat, 311
  Bank, 66

Estaing (Count d'), 311

Esteem, 311
  Friendship, 363

Ethics, 311
  Moral Law, 591
  Moral Sense, 591
  Morality, 592
  Morality, National, 593
  Morals, 594
  Virtue, 914

Ethnology, 1, 421
  Race (Human), 735

Etiquette, 311
  Ceremony, 133
  Formalities, 344
  Levees, 496

Europe, 312
  Alliance, 32
  America, 35
  Monroe Doctrine, 584
  Policy (American), 697

Eustis (W.), 313

Evils, 313
  Bribery, 109
  Crime, 219
  Error, 309
  Misfortune, 560

Example, 313
  Duty, 268
  Experience, 320
  Experiment, 320

Excise, 313
  Excise Law, 313, 945
  Whisky Insurrection, 945

Executive, 314
  President, 712
  Presidency, 715

Exercise, 318
  Health, 402

Exile, 319
  Fugitives, 367

Expansion, 319, 512, 617, 862, 892
  Lands (Indian), 468
  Policy (American), 697
  Territory, 860

Expatriation, 319, 780
  Citizens, 144
  Citizenship, 145
  Naturalization, 609

Experience, 320
  Experiment, 320

Exploration, 495
  Ledyard (John), 489
  Lewis and Clark Expedition, 495
  Pike Expedition, 696
  Western Exploration, 939

Exports, 320
  Free Ports, 358
  Markets, 536

Extravagance, 320
  Economy, 271
  Frugality, 367

F

Faction, 320
  Parties, 675
  Passions, 679
  Politics, 701
  Social Intercourse, 819

Faith (Good), 321
  Faith (Public), 321
  Confidence, 731
  Credit, 217
  Credulity, 219
  Public Confidence, 731

Falsehood, 321
  Calumny, 122
  Duplicity, 266
  Libels, 497
  Lies, 503
  Slander, 809

Family, 321
  Affection, 21
  Friends, 363
  Friendship, 363
  Happiness, 397
  Home, 409
  Sympathy, 848

Famine, 322
  Paupers, 682
  Poor, 703

Fanaticism, 322
  Enthusiasm, 307

Faneuil Hall, 322
  Boston Port Bill, 104, 769
  Tea, 859

Farmer, 322
  Agriculture, 23
  Farmers, 295, 322
  Farmers-General, 579
  Farming, 323

Fashion, 323
  Attire, 264
  Foppery, 342

Fast-days, 323
  Church and State, 141

Fauquier (Francis), 324
  Small (William), 818

Favoritism, 324
  Equality, 308
  Equal Rights, 308
  Favors, 324
  Privileges, 724
  Special Legislation, 828

Federal City, 924
  Capitals (State), 127
  Capitol (U. S.), 48, 127

Federal Courts, 448
  Judiciary, U. S., 448
  Supreme Court, U. S., 842

Federal Government, 325
  Centralization, 130
  Congress, 172
  Constitution (The Federal), 186
  Judiciary (Federal), 448
  U. S. Supreme Court, 842

Federalism, 328
  Anti-Federalism, 38
  Democratic Societies, 251
  Democrats, 252
  Federalists, 329
  Hartford Convention, 400
  Jacobins, 435
  Missouri Question, 563
  Monarchy, 566
  Parties, 675
  Politics, 701
  Republicanism (Partisan), 754
  Republicans, 755

Federalists, 329, 760
  Anti-Federalists, 38
  Democratic Societies, 251
  Democrats, 252
  Federalism, 328
  Hartford Convention, 400
  Jacobins, 435
  Missouri Question, 563
  Monarchy, 566
  Parties, 675
  Politics, 701
  Republicanism, Partisan, 754
  Republicans, 755

Fenner (James), 335

Fenno (J.), 335

Feudal Tenures, 465
  Allodial Tenures, 465

Fever, Typhus, 889
  Yellow Fever, 952

Fiction, 335
  Books, 102
  Literary Men, 506
  Literature, 506

Filibusterism, 335
  Aggression, 23
  Miranda Expedition, 560

Finances, 336
  Appropriations, 43
  Debt, 226
  Funding, 369
  Hamilton (A.), 396, 397

Fisheries, 337
  Impressment, 417
  Navigation, 610
  Seamen, 792

Flag, U. S., 339
  Neutrality, 626

Flattery, 339
  Approbation, 42
  Praise, 711

Fletcher of Saltoun, 339

Florida, 339
  Louisiana, 509
  Spain, 821
  Spanish America, 825

Folly, 341
  Foppery, 342
  Vanity, 904

Fontainbleu, 341
  Louis XVI., 520
  Marie Antoinette, 536

Foppery, 342
  Attire, 264
  Fashion, 323

Force, 342
  Power, 708
  Strength, National, 840
Foreign Agents, 342
  Ministers, 555
Foreign Influence, 343
  Alliance, 32
  England, 301
  War, 915
Foreign Intervention, 344
  Alliance, 32
  War, 915
Formalities, 344
  Ceremony, 133
  Etiquette, 311
  Levees, 496
Fortifications, 345
  Defence, 247
  Gunboats, 395, 617
  Navy, 615
  Torpedoes, 870
Fortitude, 346
  Character, 133
  Duty, 268
Fortune, 346
  Disinterestedness, 258
  Fortunes, 346
Fourth of July, 346
  Declaration of Independence, 241
Fox (C. J.), 347
France, 347
  Bonaparte (N.), 96
  Executive, 315
  French Revolution, 770
  Genet (E. C.), 378
  San Domingo, 788
  West Indies, 937
  X. Y. Z. Plot, 951
Franking Privilege, 355
  Letters, 491
  Letter-writing, 495
Franklin (B.), 355
  Franklin (W. T.), 357
Frankness, 357
  Candor, 126
  Honesty, 410
  Sincerity, 809
  Truth, 887
Franks (D.), 357
Frederick, The Great, 357
  Frederick William II., 357
Freedom, 357
  Freedom of Opinion, 660
  Freedom of Person, 357
  Freedom of the Press, 89, 717
  Freedom of Religion, 742
  Freedom of Speech, 358
  Liberty, 499
  Rights, 780
  Rights of Man, 782
  Slavery, 811
Free Ports, 358
  Free Trade, 361
Free Ships, Free Goods, 359
  Belligerents, 86
  Contraband of War, 204, 625, 628
  Enemy Goods, 296
  Free Ships, Free Goods, 359
  Neutrality, 625
  War, 915
Free Trade, 361
  Production, 725
  Protection, 730
  Tariff, 849

French Revolution, 770
  Bastile, 84
  Louis XVI., 520
  Marie Antoinette, 536
Freneau (P.), 362
  Newspapers, 638
Friends, 363, 949
  Affection, 21
  Family, 221
  Friendship, 363
  Happiness, 397
  Home, 409
  Sympathy, 848
Friendship, 363
  Affection, 21
  Family, 321
  Friends, 363, 949
  Friendship with England, 365
  Happiness, 397
  Home, 409
  Sympathy, 848
Friendship With England, 365
  England, 297
Frugality, 367, 689
  Economy, 271
  Paupers, 682
  Poor, 703
Fugitives, 367
  Deserters, 254
Funding, 369
  Assumption of State Debts, 58
  Hamilton (A.), 396
Fur Trade, 369
  Astor's Settlement, 61
Future, 370
  Future Life, 370
  Immortality, 416

G

Gage (T.), 370, 769
  Boston Port Bill, 104, 769
Gallatin (A.), 371
  Publicity, 733
Gambling, 372
  Bubbles, 109
  Speculation, 828
Gardening, 411
  Agriculture, 23
  Arboriculture, 45
  Botany, 105, 791
  Plants, 697
  Trees, 886
  Vegetables, 904
Gastronomy, 372
  Vegetables, 904
Gates (Horatio), 372
  Camden, Battle of, 123
Geismer (Baron), 372
Gem (Dr.), 372
Generals, 372
  Army, 52
  Army Officers, 56
General Welfare Clause, 374
  Centralization, 130
  State Rights, 832
Generations, 375
  Posterity, 705
Generosity, 378
  Avarice, 65
  Beneficence, 87
  Charity, 134
Genet (E. C.), 378
Genius, 381
  Abilities, 1
  Character, 133
  Talents, 848

Geographical Lines, 381
  Missouri Question, 563
  Sectionalism, 795
  Union, 890
George III., 381, 769
  George IV., 383
Geology, 383
  Creation, 270
  Earth, 269
  Mountains, 596
  Shells, 804
Gerry (E.), 383
  X. Y. Z. Plot, 951
Giles (W. B.), 384
  Hamilton (Alexander), 396
Glory, 384
  Conquest, 185
  Tyranny, 889
  War, 915
God, 384
  Deity, 248
  Providence, 731
Gold and Silver Ratio, 578
Goodrich (Elizur), 93, 384
  Bishop (Samuel), 93
Government, 384
  Authority, 63
  Centralization, 130
  Detail, 254
  Federal Government, 325
  Governments (American), 392
  Governments (European), 394
  Power, 708
  Republicanism (Governmental), 753
  Self-government, 796
Grammar, 394
  Language, 470
  Languages, 474
Granger (G.), 394
Gratitude, 394
  Morality (National), 593
Great Britain, 297
Greek Language, 472
  Athens, 62
  Greeks, 394, 888
Greene (N.), 394
Grief, 395
  Affliction, 21
Grimm (Baron), 395
Gulf Stream, 126
  Canal, Panama, 126
Gunboats, 395, 617
  Navy, 615

H

Habeas Corpus, 395
  Jury, 450
Hamilton (Alexander), 5, 395
  Assumption of State Debts, 58
  Bank, 66
  Monarchy, 568, 569
  Retirement, 767
  Treasury, 874
  Treaties, 875, 877
  Washington (George), 931
  Whisky Insurrection, 945
Hamilton (Henry), 398
  Prisoners of War, 924
  Retaliation, 762
Happiness, 398
  Affection, 21
  Contentment, 204
  Family, 321

Happiness, 398 — (Continued)
  Friends, 363
  Friendship, 363
  Home, 409
  Sympathy, 848
Harmony, 399
  Conciliation, 167
Hartford Convention, 400
  Federalism, 328
  Federalists, 329
  Monarchy, 566
  Secession, 793
Hastings (Warren), 401
  Impeachment, 416
Hawkins (B.), 402
Health, 402
  Life, 503
  Medicinal Springs, 546
  Medicine, 547
  Sun, 842
Heaven, 402
  Deity, 248
  Future Life, 370
  Immortality, 416
Henry (Patrick), 402
  Committees of Correspondence, 961
  History (Panegyric), 405
  Yazoo Lands, 952
Hereditary Officers, 387
  Aristocracy, 48
  Birth, 92
  Elections, 279
  Governments, 384
  Rotation in Office, 786
Heresy, 404
  Religion, 742
Hessians, 404
Herschel (Sir W.), 404
  Astronomy, 611
History, 404, 791, 900
  History (American), 405
  History (English), 406
  History (Natural), 607
  Reading, 738
  Study, 841
Hogendorp (Count van), 407
Holland, 407
  Nassau, 601
  Orange (Prince of), 407
Holy Alliance, 408
  Alliance, 32
  Alliances, 34
Home, 409
  Affection, 21
  Family, 321
  Friends, 363
  Friendship, 363
  Happiness, 397
  Monticello, 590
  Retirement, 765
  Sympathy, 848
  Tranquillity, 872
Honesty, 410
  Candor, 126
  Honor, 410
  Rogues, 785
  Sincerity, 809
Honor, 410
  Character, 133
  Dignity, 258
  Glory, 384
  Honors, 411
  Honesty, 410
Hope, 411
  Despair, 254

Hopkinson (F.), 411
  Music, 599
Horses, 411, 504, 949
  Veterinary Colleges, 905
Horticulture, 411
  Agriculture, 23
  Arboriculture, 45
  Botany, 105, 791
  Plants, 697
  Trees, 886
  Vegetables, 904
Hospitality, 411
  Friends, 363, 949
Hospitals (Marine), 536
Houdon (J. A.), 412
  Sculpture, 792
Howe (Lord W.), 412
Hull (W.), 412
Humboldt (Baron), 412
Humphreys (D.), 412
  Levees, 496

I

Ideas, 412
  Inventions, 431
  Inventors, 433
  Theory, 865
Idleness, 412
  Delay, 250
  Procrastination, 725
Ignorance, 413
  Education, 273
  Folly, 341
  Learning, 489
  Study, 841
  Wisdom, 948
Illinoia, Proposed State of, 941
  Western Territory, 939
Illinois River, 783
  River, 783
  Rivers, 784
Illuminati, Order of, 413
Imbecility, 413
  Dependence, 252
  Insult, 426
  Strength (National), 840
  Tribute, 886
Immigrants, 413
  Emigration, 296
  Immigration, 414
  Population, 703
Immortality, 416
  Deity, 248
  Future Life, 370
  Heaven, 402
  Religion, 742
Impeachment, 416
  Judges, 446
  Judiciary, 448
Impost, 313
  Excise, 313
Impressment, 417
  Draft, 263
Improvements (Internal), 429
  General Welfare Clause, 374
  Piers, 695
  Post Roads, 707
  Virginia Protest, 986
Inaugural Addresses, 980, 982
Income Tax, 852
  Taxation, 852
Incorporation, 418
  Bank 66
  Monopoly, 579

Indemnification, 419
  Reparation, 746
  Reprisal, 749
Independence, 420
  Declaration of Independence, 241
  Fourth of July, 346
  Freedom, 357
  Liberty, 499
  Rights, 780
Indians, 420, 944, 948, 952
  Aborigines, 1
  Cherokees, 136
  Greeks, 219
Industry, 424
  Capital, 126
  Labor, 458
  Wealth, 935
Influence, Foreign, 343
  Alliance, 32
  England, Influence in U. S., 301
  War, 915
Information, 425
  Publicity, 732
Injury, 425
  Insult, 426
  Wrong, 950
Inheritances, 426
  Distribution, 260
  Entail, 307
Inness (H.), 426
Institutions, 426
  Government, 384
  Reform, 739
Innovation, 426
  Reform, 739
Instructions, 426
  Advice, 20
  Council, 211
  Lafayette, Hampered, 463
Insult, 426
  Injury, 425
  Wrong, 950
Insurrection, 427
  Disunion, 260
  Insurrection (Whisky), 945
  Rebellion, 738
  Secession, 793
  Treason, 873
Intemperance, 427
  Drunkards, 427
  Temperance, 859
  Whisky, 944
Interest, 428
  Banks, 73
  Interest, Money, 428
  Money, 571
Internal Improvements, 429
  General Welfare Clause, 374
  Piers, 695
  Post Roads, 707
  Virginia Protest, 986
International Law, 62
  Asylum, 62
  Belligerents, 86
  Consular Convention, 200
  Consuls, 200
  Contraband of War, 204
  Enemy Goods, 296
  Free Ships, 359
  Genet (E. C.), 378
  Ministers (Foreign), 555
  Neutrality, 625
  Privateering, 723
  Privateers, 723
  Treaties, 874

Intervention Foreign, 344
  Alliance, 32
  War, 915
Intolerance, 431
  Bigotry, 88
Intrigue, 431
  Duplicity, 266
  Frankness, 357
Introduction, Letters of, 431
  Friends, 363
  Friendship, 363
Invasion, 431
  Defence, 247
  Fortifications, 345
Inventions, 431
  Inventors, 433
  Genius, 381
  Science, 791
Ireland, 433
  Aristocracy, 50
  Aristocracy in Virginia, 50
Iron, 434
Ivernois (F.), 434
  Academy, Geneva, 4

J

Jackson (Andrew), 434
  New Orleans, 633
Jacobins, 435
  French Revolution, 770
James River, 783
  James River Canal, 125
  River, 783
  Rivers, 784
Jay (John), 435
  Jay Treaty, 436, 785
Jealousy, 438
  Confidence (Public), 731
Jefferson (Thomas), 7, 438
  Adams (John), Friendship of
    Jefferson for, 7, 988
  Adams (John), Jefferson and
    Election of, 8
  Adams (John), Jefferson's Election and, 9
  Adams (John), Jefferson, Paine, and, 10
  Adams (Mrs. John), Jefferson and, 988
  Address, Jefferson to Inhabitants of Albemarle Co., 985
  Addresses, Jefferson's Inaugural, 980, 982
  Administration, Summary of Jefferson's First, 18
  Advice, Jefferson's Ten Precepts, 20
  Agriculture, Model Plow, 25
  Ancestry, Thomas Jefferson's, 36
  Anti-Federalists, Jefferson and, 38
  Arms of Jefferson Family, 52
  Assumption of State Debts, Jefferson's Agency in, 60
  Barbary States, Jefferson's Views on, 81
  Batture, Jefferson's Action in, 85
  Birthday, Jefferson's, 92
  Burr (Aaron), Relations with Jefferson, 111
  Burr (Aaron), Threatens Jefferson, 112
  Burr's Trial, Jefferson Subpœnaed, 914
  Cabinet, Rules of Jefferson's, 118
  Callender (J. T.), Relations with Jefferson, 121

Jefferson (Thomas), 7, 438—(Continued)
  Captives, Jefferson and, 128
  Cipher, Jefferson's, 143
  Clay (Henry), Opposition to Jefferson, 146
  Clinton (George), Estrangement from Jefferson, 149
  Congress, Messages to, 178
  Constitution (French), Advice of Jefferson, 195
  Constitution (French), Cooperation of Jefferson Invited, 196
  Constitution (French), Jefferson, Patriots, and, 196
  Copying Press, Jefferson's Portable, 207
  Creation, Jefferson's Views on, 270
  Debt, Jefferson's Personal, 227, 238
  Declaration of Independence, 241
  Editors, Jefferson's Relations with, 273
  Education, Jefferson's, 438
  Education, Jefferson's Bills on, 275, 276
  Election (Presidential, 1796), Candidature of Jefferson, 280
  Election (Presidential, 1800), Balloting in House, 281
  Election (Presidential, 1800), Demanding Terms, 282
  Election (Presidential, 1808), Neutrality of Jefferson, 285
  Election (Presidential, 1824), Passiveness of Jefferson, 286
  England, Jefferson and, 301, 302
  Epitaph, Jefferson's, 308
  Family of Jefferson, 438
  Farmer, Jefferson as a, 322, 438
  Father of Jefferson, 438
  Formalities, Jefferson and, 344
  Franking Privilege, Jefferson and, 355
  Franklin (Benjamin), Greatness of, 356
  Freneau (Philip), Jefferson's Relations with, 362
  Harvard's Honors to Jefferson, 438
  History, Jefferson and, 438
  Home of Jefferson, 590
  Lawyer, Jefferson Becomes a, 439
  Letters of Jefferson, 439
  Lewis and Clark Expedition, Jefferson Suggests, 495
  Libels, Jefferson and, 497
  Library of Jefferson, 502
  Madison, Jefferson and, 523
  Manufactures, Jefferson and, 532, 533
  Marriage of Jefferson, 439
  Mazzei, Jefferson's Letter to, 545
  Ministers, Hostility to Jefferson, 559
  Monticello, 590
  Monroe (James), 587
  Mrs. Jefferson's Death, 439
  Nailmaker, Jefferson as a, 439
  Navigation, Jefferson's Report, 612
  Office, Weary of, 444
  Offices Held by Jefferson, 439
  Offices Refused by Jefferson, 441
  Paine (Thomas), Jefferson and, 441
  Portrait of Jefferson, 442
  Principles of Jefferson in 1799, 721

Jefferson (Thomas), 7, 438—(Continued)
  Relations, Appointment to Office, 741
  Religion, 744
  Retirement of Jefferson, 765
  Revolution (French), Jefferson's Relations to, 772
  Scientific Societies, Membership in, 442
  Services of Jefferson, 442
  University of Virginia, Jefferson and, 444, 900
  Washington (George), Jefferson and, 927
Johnson (Joshua), 444
Jones (John Paul), 445
Joseph II., 446
Journalism, 273, 635
  Editors, 273
  Newspapers, 635
  Press, 89, 717
Judges, 446
  Judiciary (Federal), 448
  Judiciary (State), 450
  Supreme Court (U. S.), 842
Judiciary (Federal), 448
  Judiciary (State), 450
  Supreme Court (U. S.), 842
Judgment, 448
  Common Sense, 166
  Discretion, 258
  Moral Sense, 591
  Senility, 801
  Sense, 802
Jurisdiction, 450
  Sovereignty, 820
Jury (Grand), 450
  Jury (Trial by), 450
  Neutrality, Treasury Department, 630
Justice, 452
  Equity, 133

K

Kames (Lord), 453
Kanawha, River, 783
  River, 783
  Rivers, 784
Kentucky, 453
  Kentucky Resolutions, 454, 977
Kings, 455
  Cannibals, 126
  Despots, 254
  Monarchy, 566
  Self-government, 796
King's Mountain, Battle, 123
  Campbell (Col.), 123
Knowledge, 457
  Education, 273
  Learning, 489
  Science, 791
  Sciences, 792
  Scientific Societies, 819
  Study, 841
Knox (Henry), 457
Kosciusko (General), 458
  Poland, 697

L

Labor, 458
  Artisans, 57
  Laborers, 459
  Industry, 424
  Offices (Labor and), 649
  Property, 726

Lafayette (Marquis de), 461
  France, 347
  Instructions, 426
  Revolution (American), 767
  Revolution (French), 770
Lafitau (J. F.), 423, 424
Lake George, 465
  Scenery, 790
Lamps, 465
  Franklin (B.), Argand's Lamp, 355
  Matches. 544
Land, 465
  Allodial Tenures, 465
  Earth, 269
  Feudal Tenures, 465
  Land Companies, 467
  Land Tax, 467
  Lands (Indian), 468
  Lands (Public), 469
  Territory, 860
  Unearned Increment, 890
  Western Territory, 939
Langdon (J.), 470
Language, 470
  Language (Anglo-Saxon), 471
  Language (English), 471
  Language (French), 472
  Language (Gaelic), 665
  Language (Greek), 472
  Language (Italian), 473
  Language (Latin), 473
  Language (Spanish), 474
  Languages, 474
  Languages (Indian), 475
  Neology, 624
  Speech, Freedom of, 358
  Words, 949
Languedoc Canal, 125
  Canal, 125
  River, 783
  Rivers, 784
Latitude and Longitude, 475
  Astronomy, 61
  East and West Line, 271
Latrobe (B. H.), 477
  Architecture, 48
Law, 477
  Law (Common), 162
  Law (Excise), 313
  Law (International), 296, 359. 624
  Law (Lynch), 481
  Law (Maritime), 536
  Law (Martial), 542
  Law (Moral), 591
  Law (Natural), 525
  Law of Necessity, 620
  Law (Patent), 680
  Law (Parliamentary), 675
  Law (Study), 487
  Law of Waste, 485
  Laws (Alien and Sedition), 30
  Laws of England, 486
  Laws of Nature, 486
  Laws of Virginia, 487
Lawyers, 176, 487
  Attorney-General, 63
  Attorneys, 63
  Judges, 446
League, Marine, 150
Leander, Case of, 488
  Chesapeake, 136
Lear (Tobias), 488
Learning (Classical), 489
  Books, 102
  Education, 273
  Knowledge, 457

Learning (Classical), 489—(Continued)
  Language, 470, 472, 473
  Literary Men, 506
  Literature, 506
  Science, 791
  Scientific Societies. 819
  Study, 841
Ledyard (John), 489
Lee (A.), 489
  Lee (R. H.), 489
Legal Tender, 574
  Money, 571
Legislation, 490
  Congress. 172
  Legislatures, 490
  Parliament, 674
  Revolution (French), 773, 774, 775
L'Enfant (Major), 494
  Washington (City). 924
Lethargy, 494
  Agitation. 23
Letters, 494
  Correspondence, 208
  Letters of Introduction. 431
  Letters, Republic of, 753
  Letter-writing, 495
  Post-office, 705
  Mails, 524
Letters of Marque, 541
  Privateering. 723
  Privateers, 723
  Prizes, 724
Lewis and Clark Expedition. 495
  Clark (George Rogers), 146
Levees, Presidential, 496
  Ceremony, 133
  Etiquette, 311
  Formalities, 344
Liancourt (Duke of), 497
Libels, 497
  Abuse, 2
  Calumny, 122
  Ministers, 558
  Newspapers, 635
  Slander, 809
Liberty, 499
  Declaration of Independence. 241
  Freedom, 357
  Independence, 420
  Patriotism, 681
  Personal Liberty, 693
  Rights, 780
Library, 502
  Books, 102
  Reading, 738
Lies, 503
  Duplicity, 266
  Falsehood, 321
Life, 503
  Death, 224
  Future Life, 370
  Generations, 375
  Happiness, 398
  Health, 402
  Immortality, 416
  Liberty, 499
  Life (Private), 723
  Souls (Transmigration), 820
Lincoln (Levi), 506
  Supreme Court, 845
Literary Men, 506
  Literature, 506
  Books, 102
  Editors, 273
  Fiction, 335

Literary Men, 506—(Continued)
  History, 404
  Learning, 489
  Library, 502
  Newspapers, 635
  Poetry, 697
  Press, 89
Literature, 506
  Books, 102
  Editors, 273
  Fiction, 335
  Generations, 377
  History, 404
  Learning, 489
  Library, 502
  Monopoly (Inventions), 581
  Newspapers. 635
  Poetry, 697
  Press, 89
Littlepage (L.), 506
  Jay (John), 435
Livingston (E.), 506
  Livingston (R. R.), 506
Loans, 507
  Funding, 369
  Taxation, 852
Locke (John), 392
Logan (George), 508
  Logan, Mingo Chief, 508
London, 509
Longitude, 475
  Astronomy, 61
  East and West Line. 271
Looming, 560
  Rainbows, 736
Lottery, 509
  Gambling, 372
  Speculation, 828
Louisiana, 509
  Bonaparte (N.), 587
  Dupont De Nemours, 267
  Monroe (James), 587, 588
  New Orleans, Right of Deposit, 634
  Pike (Gen. Z. M.), 696
  Territory, 860
Louis XVI., 520
  Bastile, 84
  Fontainbleau, 341
  French Revolution, 770
  Louis XVIII., 521
  Marie Antoinette, 536
Luxuries, 521
  Wines, 947
Lynch Law, 481
  Jury (Trial by), 450
Luzerne (Marquis de la), 521
Lyon (Matthew), 522

M

Macdonough (Commodore), 522
Mace, 522
  Arms, American, 51
  Arms of Jefferson Family, 52
  Arms of Virginia, 52
  Mottoes, 596
Macon (Nathaniel), 522
Madeira, 148
Madison (James), 522
  England, 302
  Presidency, 716
Magnetic Needle, 476
Mails, 524
  Letters, 494
  Post Office, 705
  Post Roads, 707

Maine, 524
Majority, 525
  Minority, 559
Malesherbes (C. G. de la M.), 526
Malice, 526
  Slander, 809
Malthus (T. R.), 704
  Population, 703
Mammoth, 667
  Mastodon, 544
  Natural History, 607
  Paleontology, 667
Man, 526
  Man, Rights of, 782
  Mankind, 527
Manners, American, 527
  Manners, National, 528
Mansfield (Lord), 528
  Supreme Court, 843
Manufactures, 528
  Duties, 267
  General Welfare Clause, 374
  Protection, 730
  Tariff, 849
Marbury vs. Madison, 535
  Constitution (Federal), 190, 200
  Marshall (John), 542
Marie Antoinette, 536
  Bastile, 84
  French Revolution, 770
  Louis XVI., 520
  Toulouse, Archbishop of, 870
Marine Hospitals, 536
Marine League, 150
Maritime Law, 536
  Neutrality, 625
Markets, 536
  Exports, 320
  Prosperity, 730
Marque, Letters of, 541
  Privateering, 723
  Privateers, 723
  Prizes, 724
Marriage, 541
  Children, 138
  Family, 321
  Happiness, 398
  Home, 409
  Office-holders, 654
Marshall (John), 542
  Batture, 85
  History, 404
  Judiciary (Federal), 448
  Marbury vs. Madison, 535
  Mazzei (Philip), 546
  Supreme Court, 844
  Washington (Geo.), Life of, 930
  X. Y. Z. Plot, 951
Martial Law, 542
  War, 915
Martin (Luther), 542
Mason (George), 543
  Mason (J. M.), 542
  Mason (J. T.), 543
Massachusetts, 543
  Boston Port Bill, 104, 769
  Constitution (Federal), 187
  Revolution (American), 768
Mastodon, 544
  Mammoth, 667
  Paleontology, 667
Matches, Phosphoric, 544
  Lamps, 465

Materialism, 544
  Metaphysics, 549
  Souls, 820
Mathematics, 545
  Science, 791
Mazzei (Philip), 545
Measures, Standard, 830
  Weights, Standard, 832
Mecklenburg Declaration, 247
  Declaration of Independence, 241
Medicinal Springs, 546
  Medicine, 547
Medicine, 547
  Doctors, 547
  Sun, 842
Mediterranean Trade, 548
  Barbary States, 80
  Trade, 871
Medium, Circulating, 571
Memory, 548
  Mind, 554
Mercer (J. F.), 548
Merchants, 159, 548
  England, Influence in U. S., 301
  Jay Treaty, 437
Mercier (J.), 548
Merit, 549
  Character, 133
  Worth, 949
Merry (A.), 549
  Etiquette, 311
Messages to Congress, 178
  Simplicity, 809
Metaphysics, 549
  Materialism, 544
  Mind, 554
  Souls, 820
Meteoric Stones, 549
  Meteorology, 549
  Weather, 936
  Winds, 947
Metropotamia, Proposed State of, 941
  Western Territory, 939
Mexico, 550
  Spanish America, 825
Michaux (André), 939
Michigania, Proposed State of, 941
  Western Territory, 939
Midnight Commissions (Adams'), 161
Militia, 550
  Army, 52
  Draft, 263
  Militia, Naval, 618
Mind, 554
  Error, 309
  Opinion, 659
  Philosophy, 695
  Reason, 738
  Souls, 820
Mineralogists, 554
  Geology, 383
  Mineralogy, 555
  Mines, 555
Ministers (Foreign), 555
  Diplomacy, 258
  Diplomatic Establishment, 258
  Ministers (Imperial), 558
  Ministers (Religious), 558
  Chaplains, 133
  Clergy, 146

Minority, 559
  Majority, 525
Mint, 559
  Coinage, 261, 573
Mirage, 560
  Rainbows, 736
Miranda Expedition, 560
  Filibusterism, 335
Misfortune, 560
  Affliction, 21
  Despair, 254
  Grief, 395
Missionaries, 560
  Religion, 742
Mississippi River, 783
  Mississippi River Navigation, 562
  Mississippi Territory, 563
Missouri, 563
  Geographical Lines, 381
  Missouri Question, 563
  Missouri River, 783
  Sectionalism, 795
Mobs, 565
  Insurrection, 427
  Revolution (French), 771, 774, 775
Moderation, 566
  Contentment, 204
  Happiness, 398
Modesty, 566
  Obscurity, 642
Monarchy, 566
  Federalism, 328
  Federalists, 329
  Kings, 455
  Prerogative, 71
  Washington (Geo.), 931, 932, 93
Money, 571
  Bank, 66
  Banks, 73
  Dollar, 260
  Money Bills, 576
  Money (Continental), 577
  Money (Metallic), 578
  National Currency, 601
  Paper Money, 668
Monopoly, 579
  Agrarianism, 23
  Bank, 66
  Entail, 307
  Incorporation, 418
  Lands (Public), 469
  Primogeniture, 719
Monroe Doctrine, 584
  Monroe (James), 586
  Policy (American), 697
Montesquieu (Baron), 590
  Republics, Size of, 761
Monticello, 590
  Home, 409
Montmorin (Count), 591
Moral Law, 591
  Government, 388
  Moral Sense, 591
  Morality, 592
  Morality, National, 593
  Morals, 594
  Virtue, 914
Moreau (J. V.), 594
Morgan (G.), 595
Morocco, 595
  Barbary States, 80
  Tripoli, 886
Morris (Commodore), 406
  History (American) Naval, 406

Morris (Gouverneur), 595
Mortmain, 596
  Entail, 307
  Primogeniture, 719
Mottoes, 596
  Arms, American, 51
  Arms of Jefferson Family, 52
  Arms of Virginia, 52
  Mace, 522
Mountains, 596
  Earth, 269
  Geology, 383
  Mineralogy, 555
Mourning, 597
  Grief, 395
Moustier (Count), 597
Murder, 598
  Crime, 219
  Duel, 265
  Pardons, 673
Museums, 599
  Theatres, 865
Music, 599
  Arts, 58
Muskets, 600
  Arms, 51

N

Nailmaker, Jefferson a, 439
Names, 600
  Character, 133
  Reputation, 761
Nassau, 601
  Holland, 407
Nation (United States), 601
  Nations, 604
National capital, 924
National currency, 601
  Bank, 66
  Banks, 73
  Dollar, 260
  Money, 571
  Money Bills, 576
  Money (Continental), 577
  Money (Metallic), 578
  Paper Money, 668
National University, 899
  University of Virginia, 900
Natural Bridge, 607, 790
Natural History, 607, 791
  Animals, 110
  Horses, 411, 504, 949
  Paleontology, 667
  Sheep, 803
Natural Law, 525
  Law, 477
  Moral Law, 591
Natural Rights, 608
  Duties, Natural, 269, 608
  Rights, 780
  Rights of Man, 782
Natural Selection, 735
  Man, 526
  Mankind, 527
Naturalization, 609
  Citizens, 144
  Citizenship, 145
  Expatriation, 319
Nature, 610
  Creation, 270
  Deluge, 250
  Earth, 269
  Natural History, 607
  World, 949

Navies, Equalization of, 610
  Navy, 615
Naval Academy, 4
  Military Academy, 3
Navigation, 610
  Carrying Trade, 129
  Ocean, 643
  Shipping (American), 805
  Ships, 806
Navy, 615
  Navy Department, 620
  Navy yards, 620
  Privateers, 723
Necessity, Law of, 620
  Self-preservation, 799
Necker (Jacques), 620
  French Revolution, 774, 775
  Stael (Madame de), 830
Negroes, 621
  Colonization (Negro), 154
  Slavery, 811
  Slaves, 814
Nelson (T.), 624
Neology, 624
  Dictionary, 257
  Language, 470, 471
  Languages, 474
Neutrality, 624
  Alexander of Russia, 28
  Arms, 87
  Asylum, 62
  Belligerents, 86
  Contraband of war, 204
  Embargo, 286
  Enemy's Goods, 296
  Flag, 339
  Free ships, Free goods, 360
  Genet (E. C.), 378
  Privateers, 723
New England Secession, 794
  Embargo, 286
  Hartford Convention, 400
New Hampshire, 633
New Haven Remonstrance, 93
  Office, 644
  Offices, 647
  Office-holders, 652
New Jersey, 633
New Orleans, 633
  New Orleans Batture, 85
  New Orleans Canal, 125
  New Orleans, Right of Deposit, 634
  New Orleans, Yellow Fever, 953
New York, 634
  New York City, 634
News, 635
  Newspapers, 635
Newspapers, 635
  Editors, 273
  Press, 80, 717
  Publicity, 732
Nice, city of, 640
Nicholas (W. C.), 640
Nightingales, 92
  Birds, 92
Non-importation, 640
  Embargo, 286
  Non-intercourse, 641
Norfolk, Va., 30
  Cities, 143
North Carolina, 641
North (Lord), 641
  Reply to Lord North's Concilia-
    tory Proposition, 959

Northwest boundary, 106
  Boundaries, 106
Notes on Virginia, 641
  Virginia, 909
Nova Scotia, 642
Nullification, 642
  Secession, 793
  State Rights, 832
  Union (The Federal), 890

O

Oath, 642
  Oath of Office, 642
Obscurity, 642
  Modesty, 566
Occupations, 642
  Natural Rights, 609
  Trade, 871
Ocean, 643
  Carrying Trade, 129
  Navigation, 610
  Shipping (American), 805
  Ships, 806
Office, 644
  Appointment, 39
  Offices, 647
  Office-holders, 652
Ohio River, 784
  River, 783
Old age, 21
  Time, 867
Olive, 658
  Plants, 698
Opinion, 659
  Error, 309
  Opinion (Public), 661
  Opinions, 662
  Reason, 738
Opposition, 663
  Parties, 675
Oppression, 664
  Despotism, 254
  Despots, 254
  Tyranny, 889
Optics, 664
Orange, Prince of, 407
  Nassau, 601
Oratory, 664
  Debate, 225
  Eloquence, 286
  Speech, 358
  Words, 949
Order, 664
  Berlin Decrees, 87
  Embargo, 286
  Orders in Council, 664
Oregon, 495
Orleans (Duke of), 664
  French Revolution, 767
  Marie Antoinette, 536
Ossian, 665
Ostentation, 665
  Modesty, 566
Outacite, 423

P

Page (John), 665
Pain, 665
  Affliction, 21
  Grief, 395
Paine (Thomas), 665
  Bolingbroke (Lord), 95
Paleontology, 667
  Mammoth, 667
  Mastodon, 544
  Natural History, 607

Panama Canal, 126
  Canal, 125
Panics, 667
  Banks, 80
  Bubbles, 109
  Paper Money, 668
  Speculation, 828
Paper and Civilization, 668
  Papers (Executive), 179, 673
Paper Money, 668
  Bank, 66
  Banks, 73
  Dollar, 260
  Money, 571
  Money Bills, 576
  Money (Continental), 577
  Money (Metallic), 578
Parasites, 673
  Office, 644
  Office-holders, 652
  Parties, 675
Pardons, 673
  Crime, 219
  Murder, 598
Paris, 674
  Cities, 143
Park (Mungo), 674
Parliament, 674
  Colonies (American), 151
  Parliamentary Law, 675, 801
Parties, 675
  Anti-Federalists, 38
  Democratic Societies, 251
  Democrats, 252
  Federalism, 328
  Federalists, 329
  Hartford Convention, 400
  Jacobins, 435
  Missouri Question, 563
  Monarchy, 566
  Politics, 701
  Republicanism (Partisan), 754
  Republicans, 755
Passions, 679
  Politics, 701
  Temper, 859
Patents, 679
  Inventions, 431
  Trade Marks, 872
Paternalism, 680
  Mines, 555
  Canal, New Orleans, 125
  Public Works, 732
Patience, 681
  Stability, 820
Patriotism, 681
  Declaration of Independence, 241
  Fourth of July, 346
  Freedom, 357
  Liberty, 490
  Union (The Federal), 890
  Unity, 899
  United States, 895
Patronage, 681
  Office, 644
  Offices, 647
  Office-holders, 652
Paupers, 682
  Labor, 458
  Poor, 703
  Wealth, 935
Peace, 682
  Contentment, 204
  Repose, 747
  Tranquillity, 872
Pedometer, 432
  Inventions, 431

Pelisipia, Proposed State of, 941
  Western Territory, 939
Pendleton (Edmund), 685
  Law, 484
Pendulum, 685
  Music, 600
  Standard (Measures), 830
Pennsylvania, 107, 685
  Boundaries, 107
Pensacola, 686
  Florida, 339
  Jackson (Andrew), 434
Pensions, 686
  Taxation, 852
  Taxes, 856
People, 686
  People, English, 687
  People, European, 688
  People, French, 689
  People, Prussian, 690
  People, Roman, 691
Perceval (Spencer), 692
Perpetual Motion, 692
  Inventions, 431
Personal Liberty, 693
  Rights, 780
  Rights, Personal, 781
Petition, 693
  Petitions, 693
Peyrouse Expedition, 694
Philadelphia, 694
  Cities, 143
Philosophy, 695
  Epicurus, 308
  Plato, 697
Pickering (Timothy), 695
  Declaration of Independence, 244
  X. Y. Z. Plot, 951
Piers, 695
  General Welfare Clause, 374
  Internal Improvements, 429
  Post Roads, 707
Pike (Z. M.), 696
  Lewis and Clark Expedition, 495
Pinckney (Charles), 696, 951
  Pinckney (Thomas), 696
Pitt (William), 696
  Chatham (Lord), 135
Plants, 697
  Arboriculture, 45
  Botany, 105
  Horticulture, 411
  Trees, 886
Plato, 697
  Plato's Republic, 697
  Philosophy, 695
Pleasure, 697
  Dancing, 223
  Music, 599
  Pain, 665
  Theatres, 865
Poetry, 697
  Fiction, 335
  Literature, 506
Poland, 697
  Kosciusko, 458
Policy (American), 697
  Alliance, 32
  Alliances, 34
Politeness, 700
  Courtesy, 213
  Courtiers, 213
Political Economy, 272
  Domestic Economy, 271

Politics, 701
  Anti-Federalists, 38
  Democratic Societies, 251
  Democrats, 252
  Federalism, 328
  Federalists, 329
  Hartford Convention, 400
  Missouri Question, 563
  Monarchy, 566
  Parties, 675
  Republicanism (Partisan), 754
  Republicans, 755
Polygraph, 432
  Copying Press, 207
  Engraving, 307
Polypotamia, Proposed State of, 941
  Western Territory, 939
Poor, 703
  Economy, 271
  Frugality, 367
  Paupers, 682
Pope Pius VI., 703
Population, 703
  Census, 130
  Emigration, 296
  Immigrants, 413
  Immigration, 414
Porter (David), 704
Porto Rico, 359
  West Indies, 937
Portugal, 704
  Brazil, 108
  Correa de Serra (J.), 208
  Treaties of Commerce, 884
Posterity, 705
  Generations, 375
Post Office, 705
  Mails, 524
  Post Roads, 707
Post Roads, 707
  General Welfare Clause, 374
  Internal Improvements, 429
  Virginia, Protest, 986
Posts, Western, 707, 939
  Treaty (British Peace), 885
Potato, 707
  Horticulture, 411
  Vegetables, 904
Potomac and Ohio Canal, 126
  Canal, 125
  Potomac River, 784
Power, 708
  Authority, 63
  Government, 384
  Powers, 708
Powers (Assumed), 708
  Centralization, 130
Pradt (Abbé de), 710
Praise, 711
  Applause, 39
  Approbation, 42
  Honor, 410
  Honors, 411
Precedent, 711
  Abuses, 2
  Example, 313
Preemption, Right of, 711
  Land, 465
  Lands, 468
Prerogative, 711
  Privileges, 724
Presbyterian Spirit, 711
  Liberty, 499

Presents, 711
  Bribery, 109
President, The, 712
  Constitution (Federal), 188, 191
  Elections (Presidential), 289
  Electoral College, 715
  Presidency, 715
  Third Term, 865
  Vice-Presidency, 907
Press (Freedom of the), 89, 717
  Editors, 273
  Libels, 497
  Newspapers, 635
Price, Basis of, 718
  Price of Wheat, 718
Priestley (Joseph), 719
Primogeniture, 719
  Agrarianism, 23
  Descents, 253
  Entail, 307
  Monopoly, 579
Principle, 720
  Principles, 720
  Truth, 887
Printing, 722
  Books, 102
  Newspapers, 635
  Press, 89, 717
Prison, 46, 722
  Crime, 219
  Pardons, 673
Prisoners of War, 764, 765, 924
  Captives, 128
  Retaliation, 762
Privacy, 722
  Private Life, 722
Privateering, 723
  Letters of Marque, 541
  Privateers, 723
  Prizes, 724
Privilege (Franking), 355
Privileges, 724
  Equality, 308
  Equal Rights, 308
  Favoritism, 324
  Special Legislation, 828
Prizes, 724
  Privateers, 723
Procrastination, 725
  Delay, 250
  Idleness, 412
Production, 725
  Free Trade, 361
  Protection, 730
  Tariff, 849
Progress, 725
  Innovation, 426
  Reform, 739
  Reformers, 741
Prohibition, 944
  Intemperance, 427
  Temperance, 859
Property, 726
  Taxation, 852
Prophecy, 729
  Prophet, Wabash, 730
Proscription, 730
  Tyranny, 889
Prosperity, 730
  Markets, 536
  Peace, 682
Protection, 730
  Duties, 267
  Free Trade, 361
  Tariff, 849

Protestants, 730
  Bible, 88
Providence, 731
  Bible, 88
  Deity, 248
  Religion, 742
Provisions, 628
  Contraband of War, 204
Prussia, 357
  Frederick the Great, 357
  Frederick William II., 357
Psalms, 731
  Bible, 88
  Religion, 742
Public Confidence, 731
  Credit, 217
  Credulity, 219
  Faith, 321
Public Works, 732
  Paternalism, 680
Publicity, 732
  Information, 425
  Newspapers, 635
Punishment, 734
  Crime, 219
  Pardons, 673

Q

Quakers, 734
Quarantine, 735, 953
Quarrels, 735
  Contention, 203
  Dissension, 259
  Rebellion, 738
Quebec, 56
  Canada, 124
Quiet, 735
  Repose, 747
Quorum, 735
  Dictator, 256

R

Race (Human), 735
  Man, 526
  Mankind, 527
  Races, Mingling of, 736
Rainbows, 736
  Meteorology, 549
  Mirage, 560
  Weather, 936
Randolph (Edmund), 736
  Randolph (John), 176, 180, 737
  Randolph (Peyton), 737
  Randolph (Thomas Mann), 738
Ratio of Apportionment, 39
Reading, 738
  Books, 102
  Education, 273
  Learning, 489
  Library, 502
  Study, 841
Reason, 738
  Error, 309
  Mind, 554
  Opinion, 659
  Philosophy, 695
  Souls, 820
Rebellion, 738
  Disunion, 260
  Rebellion, Bacon's, 738
  Rebellion, Shays's, 802
  Secession, 793
Reciprocity, 739
  Duties, 267
  Free Trade, 361
  Markets, 540
  Protection, 730
  Tariff, 849

Rectitude, 739
  Honor, 410
  Virtue, 914
Red River, 784
  River, 783
Reform, 739
  Innovation, 426
  Progress, 725
  Reformers, 741
Regencies, 741
  Kings, 455
Relations, 741
  Apppointment, 39
  Office, 644
  Offices, 647
  Office-holders, 652
  Parasites, 673
  Patronage, 681
Religion, 742
  Bible, 88
  Deity, 248
  Providence, 731
Reparation, 746
  Indemnification, 419
Repose, 747
  Contentment, 204
  Peace, 682
  Retirement, 765
  Sleep, 818
  Tranquillity, 872
Representation, 747
  Elections, 279
  Republicanism, 753
  Suffrage, 841
  Votes, 915
  Voting, 915
Reprisal, 749
  Indemnification, 419
  Reparation, 746
Republic, 749
  Republic (American), 750
  Republic (English), 751
  Republic (French), 752
  Republic of Letters, 753
  Republic (Plato's), 697
  Republicanism (Governmental), 753
  Republicanism (Partisan), 754
  Republicans, 755
  Republics, 761
Republicanism (Governmental), 753
  Republicanism (Partisan), 754
  Republicans, 755
Republicanism (Partisan), 754
  Republicans, 755
  Democratic Societies, 251
  Democrats, 252
  Missouri Question, 563
  Parties, 675
  Politics, 701
Reputation, 761
  Ambition, 35
  Applause, 39
  Approbation, 42
Resignation, 761
  Patience, 681
Resistance, 761
  Force, 342
  Rebellion, 738
  Strength, 840
  War, 915
Resolution, 761
  Character, 133
Respect, 762
  Insult, 426
  Respectability, 762
  Wrong, 950

Respectability, 762
Responsibility, 762
  Duty, 268
  Honor, 410
Retaliation, 762
  Captives, 128
  Cruelty, 221
  Prisoners of War, 924
Retirement, 765
  Repose, 747
  Tranquillity, 872
Retrenchment, 767
  Economy, 271
  Frugality, 367
  Surplus, 847
Revenge, 767
  Anger, 37
  Enemies, 296
  Passions, 679
  Punishment, 734
  Retaliation, 762
Revenue, 767
  Debt (United States), 234
  Internal Improvements, 429
  Surplus, 847
  Tariff, 849
  Taxation, 852
Revolution, 767
  Revolution (American), 767
  Revolution (French), 770
  War, 915
Rhode Island, 777
Rhone River, 784
  River, 783
Rice, 777
  Agriculture, 23
  Farming, 323
Richmond, Va., 779
  Cities, 143
Ridicule, 779
  Abuse, 2
  Medicine, Molière and, 547
Riedesel (Baron), 779
Rienzi (Nicolo Gabrini), 779
Right, 779
  Right of Asylum, 62
  Right of Expatriation, 319, 780
  Right of Representation, 780
  Right of Search, 417
  Right of Suffrage, 780
  Rights, 780
  Rights, Bill of, 88
  Rights, Equal, 308
  Rights, Natural, 608
  Rights, State, 832
  Rights of British America, 963
  Rights of Conscience, 185
  Rights of Man, 782
Rittenhouse (David), 783
River, Columbia, 61
  Illinois, 783
  James, 783
  Kanawha, 783
  Mississippi, 783
  Missouri, 783
  Ohio, 784
  Potomac, 784
  Red, 784
  Rhone, 784
  St. Croix, 784
  Wabash, 784
Rivers, 784
Roane (Spencer), 785
Roads, Post, 707
  Internal Improvements, 429
  Virginia Protest, 986

Robespierre, 785
  Jacobins, 435
  Revolution (French), 770
Rochambeau (Count), 785
Rodney (Cæsar A.), 785
Rogues, 785
  Honesty, 410
Rohan (Cardinal de), 786
Rotation in Office, 786
  Elections, 279
  Hereditary Officers, 387
  Third Term, 865
Rowan (A. H.), 786
  Ireland, 433
Rules, 786
  Rules (Jefferson's Ten), 20
Rush (Benjamin), 786
Russia, 786, 888
  Alexander of Russia, 27
  Bonaparte (N.), 101
  Catherine of Russia, 421, 786
  Dashkoff (M.), 223
Rutledge (Edward), 787
  Rutledge (John), 787

S

Sacrifices, 787
  Duty, 268
  Service, 802
Safety, 787
  Confidence (Public), 731
  Rights, 780
St. Croix River, 784
  River, 783
  Rivers, 784
Salaries, 787
  Congress (Compensation), 174
  Judges, 446
Salt Water (Distillation), 788
Sancho (Ignatius), 622
San Domingo, 788
  West Indies, 937
San Juan (Porto Rico), 359
  West Indies, 937
Santee Canal, 126
  Canal, 125
  River, 783
  Rivers, 784
Saratoga, Proposed State of, 941
  Western Territory, 939
Sardinia, 789
Saussure (Horace B.), 790
Say (Jean Baptiste), 392
Scenery, American, 790
  Lake George, 465
  Monticello, 590
  Natural Bridge, 607
  Niagara, 790
  Potomac, 784, 790
Schism, 790
  Union, 890
  Unity, 899
Schools, 790
  Academies, 4
  Academy, 3
  Education, 273
  University, National, 899
  University of Virginia, 900
Science, 791
  Education, 273
  Sciences, 792
  Scientific Societies, 819
Scipio, 664
  People, Roman, 691

Screw Propeller, 431
  Balloons, 66
  Inventions, 431
  Steam, 838
Sculpture, 792
  Art, 57
  Arts, 58
  Houdon (J. A.), 412, 934
Seamen, 792
  Fisheries, 337
  Impressment, 417
  Navigation, 610
  Ships, 806
Search, Right of, 417
  Impressment, 417
Secession, 793
  Disunion, 260
  Kentucky, 453
  Kentucky Resolutions, 454, 977
  Rebellion, 738
  Union (The Federal), 890
Secrecy, 795
  Secret Societies, 819
Secret Service Money, 795
Secretaries of Legation, 795
  Diplomacy, 258
  Ministers (Foreign), 555
Sectionalism, 795
  Geographical Lines, 381
  Missouri Question, 563
  Union, 890
Sedition Law, 795
  Alien and Sedition Laws, 30
  Aliens, 32
Self-government, 796
  Authority, 63
  Consent of Governed, 385
  Government, 384
  Rights, 780
  Rights of Man, 782
Self-preservation, 799
  Necessity, Law of, 620
Senate (French), 799
  Revolution (French), 770
Senate (Virginia), 801
  Virginia Constitution, 911
Senate (United States), 799
  Congress, 172
  Constitution (The Federal), 188, 194
  Impeachment, 417
  Treaties, 876
Senators (United States), 188, 192
  Congress, 172
  Senate (United States), 799
Seneca, 801
  Philosophy, 695
Senility, 801
  Common Sense, 166
  Moral Sense, 591
  Sense, 802
Sense, 802
  Common Sense, 166
  Moral Sense, 591
  Senility, 801
Sermons, Political, 744
  Ministers (Religious), 558
Service, 802
  Duty, 268
  Jefferson, Services of, 442
  Sacrifices, 787
Shays's Rebellion, 802
  Bacon's Rebellion, 738
  Rebellion, 738
  Whisky Insurrection, 945

Shakespeare, 471
  Duty, 268
Sheep, 803
  Sheep (Merinos), 804
  Manufactures, 528
Shells, 804
  Deluge, 250
  Geology, 383
  Mineralogy, 555
  Mountains, 596
Sheriff, 805
  Counties, 212
Shipping (American), 805
  Carrying Trade, 129
  Drawbacks, 263
  Navigation, 610
  Ocean, 643
  Ships, 806
Short (William), 808
Sierra Leone, 155
  Colonization (Negro), 154
Sieyes (Abbé), 809
  Revolution (French), 770
Silence, 809
  Debate, 225
  Lawyers, 487
Silver, 262
  Bank, 66
  Banks, 73
  Dollar, 260
  Mint, 559
  Money, 571
  Money (Continental), 577
  Money (Metallic), 578
  Paper Money, 668
Simplicity, 809
  Ceremony, 133
  Etiquette, 311
  Formalities, 344
  Levees, 496
Sincerity, 809
  Candor, 126
  Frankness, 357
  Honesty, 410
  Truth, 887
Sinclair (Sir John), 809
Sinecures, 809
  Patronage, 681
Slander, 809
  Abuse, 2
  Calumny, 122
  Libels, 497
  Malice, 526
  Ministers, 558
  Newspapers, 635
Slave Trade, 811
  Colonization (Negro), 154
  Negroes, 621
  Slavery, 811
  Slaves, 814
  Slaves (Emancipation), 816
Sleep, 818
  Dreams, 264
  Repose, 747
Small (William), 818
Smith (Adam), 392
  Smith (John), 818
  Smith (Robert), 818
  Smith (Samuel), 818
  Smith (William S.), 819
Smuggling, 819
  Commerce, 156
  Free Ports, 358
  Free Trade, 361
  Tariff, 849

Snakes, 819
  Natural History, 607
Social Intercourse, 819
  Conciliation, 167
  Harmony, 399
  Spirit (Party), 829
Societies (Communal), 819
  Societies (Democratic), 251
  Societies (Scientific), 819
  Societies (Secret), 819
  Society, 819
  Society of the Cincinnati, 142
Socrates, 820
  Epicurus, 307, 695
  Philosophy, 695
  Plato, 697
Solitude, 820
  Silence, 809
  Tranquillity, 872
Souls, Transmigration of, 820
  Metaphysics, 549
  Materialism, 544
  Mind, 554
South America, 820
  Spain, 821
  Spanish America, 825
South and West, 937
South Carolina, 820
Sovereignty, 820
  Jurisdiction, 450
  Land, 467
Spain, 821
  Spanish America, 825
Special Legislation, 828
  Equality, 308
  Equal Rights, 308
  Favoritism, 324
  Privileges, 724
Specie, 578
Speculation, 828
  Bubbles, 109
  Banks, 80
  Gambling, 372
  Panics, 667
  Paper Money, 668
Speech, Freedom of, 358
  Debate, 225
  Eloquence, 286
  Language, 470
  Oratory, 664
Spelling, 829
  Grammar, 394
  Language, 470
  Languages, 474
Spies, Treasury, 630, 706, 829
  Spies, Post Office, 706
Spirit (Party), 829
  Conciliation, 167
  Harmony, 399
  Social Intercourse, 819
Springs, Medicinal, 829
  Medicinal Springs, 546
  Medicine, 547
Squatters, 470, 829
  Lands, 470
  Preemption, 711
Stability, 829
  Union (The Federal), 890
  United States, 895
Stael (Madame de), 830
  Necker (Jacques), 620
Standard, 830
  Pendulum, 685
  Standard (Money), 574
  Standard (Measures), 830
  Standard (Weights), 832

State Rights, 832
  Coercion, State, 150
  Centralization, 130
  General Welfare Clause, 374
  Judiciary, 448
  Supreme Court, 842
States, 834
  Union (The Federal), 890
  United States, 895
Statesmen, 838
  Abilities, 1
  Genius, 381
Steam, 838
  Inventions, 431
  Screw Propeller, 431
Sterne (Laurence), 591
Steuben (Baron), 840
  Washington (George), 927
Stewart (Dugald), 840
  Metaphysics, 549
  Tracy (Comte de), 870
Strength, National, 840
  Force, 342
  Power, 708
Strickland (William), 92
Stuart (Archibald), 840
Stuart (House of), 840
  History (English), 406
Study, 841
  Education, 273
  Learning, 489
Submarine Boats, 620
  Torpedoes, 870
Submission, 841
  Dependence, 252
  Subservience, 841
  Tribute, 886
Subservience, 841
  Dependence, 252
  Submission, 841
  Tribute, 886
Subsidies, 108
  Fisheries, 337
  France (Commerce with), 348
  General Welfare Clause, 374
  Manufactures, 534
  Ships, 808
Subsistence, 841
  Olive, 658
  Plants, 697
Suffrage, 841
  Votes, 915
  Voting, 915
Sugar, 842
  Agriculture, 23
Suicide, 599
  Crime, 219
Sumter (Thomas), 842
Sun, 842
  Astronomy, 61
  Sun-dial, 842
Supreme Court, 842
  Constitution (Federal), 190
  Impeachment, 416
  Judges, 446
  Judiciary, 448
  Law, 477
Surgery, 547
Surplus, 847
  Economy, 271
  Frugality, 367
  Retrenchment, 767
Surveying, 848
  Land, 465
  Lands, 468

Swartwout (Samuel), 848
Sylvania, Proposed State of, 941
  Western Territory, 939
Sympathy, 848
  Affection, 21
  Family, 321
  Friends, 363
  Friendship, 363
  Happiness, 397
  Home, 409

T

Talents, 848
  Abilities, 1
  Character, 133
  Genius, 381
  Power, 708
Talleyrand, 849
  X. Y. Z. Plot, 951
Tariff, 849
  Duties, 267
  Free Trade, 361
  Protection, 730
  Reciprocity, 160
Tarleton (Col. B.), 851
Taste, 852
  Manners, 527
Taxation, 852
  Taxes, 39, 856
  Tax-gatherers, 859
Taylor (John), 859
Tea, 859
  Boston Port Bill, 104, 769
Teachers, 859
  Academies, 4
  Academy, 3
  Knowledge, 457
  Learning, 489
  Schools, 790
  University of Virginia, 900
Temper, 859
  Passions, 679
Temperance, 859
  Beer, 86
  Intemperance, 427
  Whisky, 944
  Wines, 947
Tenants, 859
  Immigration, 414
Tender, Legal, 574
  Money, 571
Ternant (J. B.), 859
Territory, 860
  Canada, 124
  Conquest, 185
  Consent of Governed, 385
  Cuba, 222
  Expansion, 319, 468, 617, 802
  Florida, 339
  Louisiana, 509
  Western Territory, 939
Tests, Religious, 864
  Equality, 308
Thanksgiving, 323
  Fast-day, 323
Theatres, 865
  Dancing, 223
  Music, 599
  Pain, 665
  Pleasure, 697
Theory, 865
  Ideas, 412
  Knowledge, 457

Third Term, 865
  Elections, 279
  Hereditary officers, 387
  President, 712
  Presidency, 715
  Rotation in Office, 786
Tiffin (H. D.), 867
Time, 867
  Age, old, 21
  Antiquities, 39
Title, 867
  Simplicity, 809
  Titles, 868
Tobacco, 868
  Agriculture, 23
Toleration, 869
  Conciliation, 167
  Harmony, 399
Tontine, 869
  Annuities, 38
Tories, 869
  Parties, 676
  Whigs, 943
Torpedoes, 870
  Defence, 247
  Fortifications, 345
  Gunboats, 395, 617
  Navy, 615
Torture, 870
  Cruelty, 221
  Retaliation, 762
Toulouse, Archbishop of, 870
  Marie Antoinette, 536
  French Revolution, 770
Tracy (Comte de), 870
  Metaphysics, 549
  Stewart (Dugald), 840
Trade, 871
  Carrying Trade, 129, 871
  Free Trade, 361
  Free Ports, 358
  Mediterranean Trade, 548
  Slave Trade, 811
  Trade Marks, 872
Tranquillity, 872
  Happiness, 398
  Repose, 747
  Retirement, 765
Transmigration of Souls, 872
  Metaphysics, 549
  Mind, 554
Travel, 872
  Europe, 312
  Travelers, 873
Treason, 873
  Burr's Treason, 113
  Hartford Convention, 400
  Rebellion, 738
  Whisky Insurrection, 945
Treasury, 874
  Assumption, 58
  Finances, 336
  Funding, 369
  Hamilton (Alexander), 395
  Loans, 507
Treasury spies, 630
  Post-office spies, 706
Treaties, 874
  Alliance, 32, 34
  Alliances, 33, 34
  Compact, 166
  Compacts, 166
  Treaties of Commerce, 880
Treaty (British Peace), 884
  Jay Treaty, 436

Trees, 886
  Arboriculture, 45
Tribute, 886
  Dependence, 252
  Insult, 426
Tripoli, 886
  Barbary States, 80
  Captives, 128
  Morocco, 595
Trouble, 887
  Difficulties, 257
Trumbull (John), 887
  Cornwallis (Lord), 208
Trust, 887
  Duty, 268
  Office, 644
Truth, 887
  Candor, 126
  Frankness, 357
  Honor, 410
  Sincerity, 809
Truxtun (Thomas), 888
Tude (M. A. de la), 888
  Bastile, 84
Turkey, 888
  Constantinople, 186
  Greeks, 394
Tyler (John), 889
Typhus Fever, 889
  Yellow Fever, 952
Tyranny, 889
  Conquest, 185
  Cruelty, 221
  Despotism, 254
  Glory, 384
  War, 915

U

Umpire, 890
  Arbitration, 44
Unearned Increment, 890
  Earth, 269
  Labor, 458
  Land, 465
Unger (John Louis de), 890
Uniformity, 890
  Opinion, 660
Union (The Federal), 890
  Embargo, 294
  Schism, 790
  United States, 895
Unit, Money, 576
United States, 895
  Colonies, 151
  Confederation, 167
  Union (The Federal), 890
Unity, 899
  Schism, 790
  Secession, 793
  Union (The Federal), 890
University (National), 899
  Academies, 4
  Academy, 3
  University of Virginia, 900
  William and Mary College, 946
Usurpation, 903
  Tyranny, 889

V

Vacations, 903
  Repose, 747
  Retirement, 765
Vaccination, 904
  Medicine, 547
  Waterhouse (Dr.), 935

Vanity, 904
　Flattery, 339
　Folly, 341
　Foppery, 342
Van Rensselaer (Gen. S.), 904
　Generals, 372
Vattel (Emmerich von), 904
Vegetables, 904
　Agriculture, 23
　Plants, 697
　Vegetation, 904
Venison, 904
　Kings, 455
　Natural History, 607
Vergennes (Count de), 905
Vermont, 838, 905
Vespucius (Americus), 36, 156
　History (American), 406
Veterinary Colleges, 905
　Horses, 411, 949
Veto, 41, 905
Vice, 907
　Crime, 219
Vice-Presidency, 907
　Elections (Presidential), 280
　Presidency, 715
Vigilance, 909
　Wisdom, 948
Vincennes, 909
Vindication, 909
　Reputation, 761
Vine, 909
　Wines, 947
Virginia, 909
　Virginia Constitution, 911
Virtue, 914
　Vice, 907
Volney (Comte de), 915
Voltaire (F. M. A. de), 250, 499, 805
Volunteers, 915
　Army, 52
　Militia, 550
Votes, 915
　Voting, 915
　Suffrage, 841

W

Wabash Prophet, 730, 915
　Prophecy, 729
Wabash River, 784
　River, 783
　Rivers, 784
Walsh (Robert), 915
War, 915
　Conquest, 185
　Contraband of War, 204, 625, 626
　War of 1812, 921
　War (Prisoners of), 924
Wards, 921
　Cities, 143
　Counties, 212
Washington City, 924
　Capitol, U. S., 48, 127
　Cities, 143

Washington (George), 570, 679, 759, 761, 766, 810, 927
　Washington, Proposed State of, 941
Waterhouse (Dr.), 935
　Vaccination, 904
Weakness, National, 935
　Injury, 425
　Insult, 426
　Strength, 840
　Tribute, 886
　Wrong, 950
Wealth, 935
　Capital, 126
　Labor, 458
　Laborers, 459
Weather, 936
　Meteorology, 549
　Winds, 936
Webster (Daniel), 936
　Webster (Noah), 223, 936
Weights (Standard), 832
　Decimal System, 241
　Pendulum, 685
　Measures (Standard), 830
Welfare, 936
　Welfare Clause (General), 374
West and South, 937
　Sectionalism, 795
West Indies, 937
　Cuba, 222
　Free Ports, 358
　San Domingo, 788
West Point Academy, 3
　Naval Academy, 4
Western Exploration, 939
　Lewis and Clark Expedition, 495
Western Posts, 939
　Treaty (British Peace), 884
Western Territory, 939
　Louisiana, 509
　Territory, 860
　United States, 895
Whale oil, 942
　Fisheries, 337
　Whaling, 943
Wheat, 718, 943
　Agriculture, 23
Wheatley (Phyllis), 622
Wheels, Wooden, 433
　Inventions, 431
Whigs, 943
　Parties, 676
　Tories, 869
Whisky, 944
　Beer, 86
　Intemperance, 427
　Whisky Insurrection, 945
　Wines, 947
Wilkinson (James), 945
　Burr's (A.) Treason, 113
William and Mary College, 946
　University of Virginia, 900
Winds, 947
　Meteorology, 549
　Weather, 936

Wines, 947
　Beer, 86
　Intemperance, 427
　Whisky, 944
Wirt (William), 948
Wisdom, 948
　Discretion, 258
Wistar (Caspar), 948
Women, 772, 948
　Children, 138
　Dress, 364
　Economy, 271
　Education, Female, 274
　Fashion, 323
　Home, 409
　Marriage, 541
　Office-holders, Matrimony and, 654
　Offices, Women and, 652
　Representation, Qualified, 748
　Young Women, 954
Words, 949
　Language, 470
　Languages, 474
Works, Public, 732
　Paternalism, 680
World, 949
　Creation, 270
　Deluge, 250
　Earth, 269
Worth, 949
　Character, 133
　Merit, 549
Wretchedness, 949
　Happiness, 398
Wright (Frances), 950
Writing, 950
　Cipher, 143
　Writing, Anonymous, 38
Wrong, 950
　Wrongs, 950
Wythe (George), 950

X

Xenophon, 695
X. Y. Z. Plot, 951
　France, Peace with, 351
　Gerry (Elbridge), 383
　Talleyrand, 849

Y

Yazoo Lands, 952
　Henry (Patrick), 404
　Marshall (John), 542
Yellow Fever, 952
　Typhus Fever, 889
Yeomanry, Beggared, 295
Yorktown, 953
Young Men, 953
Young Women, 954

Z

Zeal, 954
　Ambition, 35
　Enthusiasm, 307
　Resolution, 761